5 New and Enhanced Material in Each Chapter

Added and revised material reflects major changes and discoveries in the field. This edition includes over 1,400 new reference citations. (A list of new material can be found in the Preface for Instructors.)

6 Beautiful Artwork, Graphics, and Photographs

Visually stunning, the art, graphics, and photos effectively illustrate major points and enhance student interest and understanding.

7 Outstanding Pedagogical Features

Outstanding pedagogical features support students' mastery of the material.

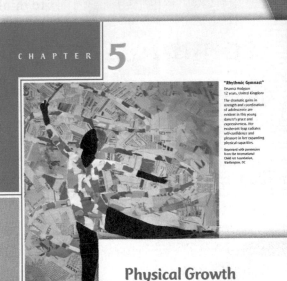

Chapter Introductions

Chapter openers begin with an outline and an engaging real-life story.

Learning Objectives

NEW! Learning objectives appear at the start of their corresponding sections to guide students in their reading.

End-of-Chapter Summaries

Chapter summaries are organized by learning objectives, encouraging active study. They also include bolded key terms, which help students acquire and master the vocabulary of the field.

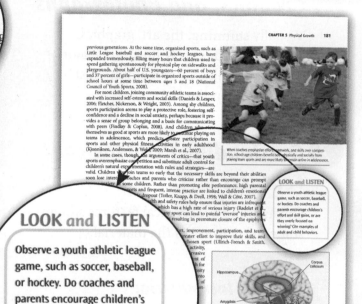

Take a Moment...

Built into the text narrative, this feature engages students by asking them to "take a moment" to think about an important point, integrate information on children's development, or engage in an exercise or an application to clarify a challenging concept.

Look and Listen

This **NEW** active-learning feature asks students to observe what real children say and do, speak with or observe parents and teachers, and inquire into community programs and practices that influence children.

LOOK and LISTEN

Observe a youth athletic league game, such as soccer, baseball, or hockey. Do coaches and parents encourage children's effort and skill gains, or are they overly focused on winning? Cite examples of adult and child behaviors.

Ask Yourself Questions

Review questions help students recall and comprehend information they have just read.

Connect questions help students build an image of the whole child by integrating what they have learned across age periods and domains of development.

Apply questions encourage the application of knowledge to controversial issues and problems faced by children, parents, and professionals who work with them.

Reflect questions help make the study of child development personally meaningful by asking students to reflect on their own development and life experiences.

See page v for a complete listing of feature boxes.

Feature Boxes

See page v for a complete listing of feature boxes.

Social Issues boxes discuss the impact of social conditions on children and emphasize the need for sensitive social policies to ensure their well-being:

NEW! **Social Issues: Education** boxes focus on home, school, and community influences on children's learning. Examples include *Baby Learning from TV and Video: The Video Deficit Effect*; *Media Multitasking Disrupts Learning*; *The Head Start REDI Program: Strengthening School Readiness in Economically Disadvantaged Preschoolers*; and *Magnet Schools: Equal Access to High-Quality Education.*

NEW! **Social Issues: Health** boxes address values and practices relevant to children's physical and mental health. Examples include *Family Chaos Undermines Children's Well-Being*; *A Cross-National Perspective on Health Care and Other Policies for Parents and Newborn Babies*; *Does Child Care Threaten Infant Attachment Security and Later Adjustment?*; and *Adolescent Substance Use and Abuse.*

Biology and Environment boxes highlight the growing attention to the complex, bidirectional relationship between biology and environment. Examples include *A Case of Epigenesis: Smoking During Pregnancy Alters Gene Expression*; *Prenatal Iron Deficiency and Memory Impairments in Infants of Diabetic Mothers: Findings of ERP Research*; *Children with Attention-Deficit Hyperactivity Disorder*; and *"Mindblindness" and Autism.*

Cultural Influences boxes deepen the attention to culture threaded throughout the text and accentuate both cross-cultural and multicultural variations in child development—for example, *Immigrant Youths: Adapting to a New Land*; *Cultural Variation in Infant Sleeping Arrangements*; *Identity Development among Ethnic Minority Adolescents*; and *Impact of Ethnic and Political Violence on Children.*

Applying What We Know Tables

This feature summarizes research-based applications, speaking directly to students as parents or future parents and to those pursuing different careers or areas of study, such as teaching, health care, counseling, or social work.

See page v for a complete listing of Applying What We Know tables.

Milestones Tables

These beautifully illustrated tables summarize major developments within each topical area, providing a convenient overview of the chronology of development.

In-Text Highlighted Key Terms with Definitions

Mastery of terms is promoted through in-text highlighting of key-term and concept definitions.

End-of-Chapter Term List, and End-of-Book Glossary

Key terms also appear in an end-of-chapter page-referenced term list and an end-of-book page-referenced glossary.

❽ *Valuable Teaching Resources*

Instructor's Resource Manual (IRM). Each chapter includes a Chapter-at-a-Glance grid, Brief Chapter Summary, Learning Objectives, detailed Lecture Outlines, Lecture Enhancements, Learning Activities, "Ask Yourself" questions with answers, Suggested Student Readings, and Media Materials list.

Test Bank. The Test Bank contains over 2,000 multiple-choice and essay questions, each page-referenced to chapter content and classified by type.

PowerPoint™ Presentation. The PowerPoint presentation provides illustrations and outlines of key topics for each chapter of the text. **A NEW video-enhanced version is also available to instructors.**

Child Development

NINTH EDITION

Laura E. Berk

Illinois State University

In loving memory of my parents, Sofie and Philip Eisenberg

Original edition, entitled *Child Development*, 9th Edition, by Berk, Laura E., published by Pearson Education, Inc, Copyright © 2013 by Pearson Education, Inc.

Indian edition

Copyright © 2017 Pearson India Education Services Pvt. Ltd.

ISBN: 978-93-325-8520-1

First Impression, 2017
Second Impression, 2018

This edition is manufactured in India and is authorized for sale only in India, Bangladesh, Bhutan, Pakistan, Nepal, Sri Lanka and the Maldives. Circulation of this edition outside of these territories is UNAUTHORIZED.

Published by Pearson India Education Services Pvt. Ltd, CIN: U72200TN2005PTC057128.

Head Office: 15th Floor, Tower-B, World Trade Tower, Plot No. 1, Block-C, Sector 16, Noida 201301, Uttar Pradesh, India.
Registered Office: 4th Floor, Software Block, Elnet Software City, TS-140, Block 2 & 9 Rajiv Gandhi Salai, Taramani, Chennai, Tamil Nadu 600113.

Fax: 080-30461003, Phone: 080-30461060,
Website: www.pearson.co.in
Email: companysecetary.india@pearson.com

Printed in India by Sai Printo Pack Pvt. Ltd.

About the Author

Laura E. Berk is a distinguished professor of psychology at Illinois State University, where she has taught child and human development to both undergraduate and graduate students for more than three decades. She received her bachelor's degree in psychology from the University of California, Berkeley, and her master's and doctoral degrees in child development and educational psychology from the University of Chicago. She has been a visiting scholar at Cornell University, UCLA, Stanford University, and the University of South Australia.

Berk has published widely on the effects of school environments on children's development, the development of private speech, and recently, the role of make-believe play in development. Her research has been funded by the U.S. Office of Education and the National Institute of Child Health and Human Development. It has appeared in many prominent journals, including *Child Development, Developmental Psychology, Merrill-Palmer Quarterly, Journal of Abnormal Child Psychology, Development and Psychopathology,* and *Early Childhood Research Quarterly.* Her empirical studies have attracted the attention of the general public, leading to contributions to *Psychology Today* and *Scientific American.* She has also been featured on National Public Radio's *Morning Edition* and in *Parents Magazine, Wondertime,* and *Reader's Digest.*

Berk has served as research editor of *Young Children* and consulting editor of *Early Childhood Research Quarterly.* Currently, she is associate editor of the *Journal of Cognitive Education and Psychology.* She is a frequent contributor to edited volumes on early childhood development, having recently authored chapters on the importance of parenting, on make-believe play and self-regulation, and on the kindergarten child. She has also written the chapter on development for *The Many Faces of Psychological Research in the Twenty-First Century* (Society for the Teaching of Psychology); the article on social development for *The Child: An Encyclopedic Companion;* the article on Vygotsky for the *Encyclopedia of Cognitive Science;* and the chapter on storytelling as a teaching strategy for *Voices of Experience: Memorable Talks from the National Institute on the Teaching of Psychology* (Association for Psychological Science).

Berk's books include *Private Speech: From Social Interaction to Self-Regulation; Scaffolding Children's Learning: Vygotsky and Early Childhood Education; Landscapes of Development: An Anthology of Readings;* and *A Mandate for Playful Learning in Preschool: Presenting the Evidence.* In addition to *Child Development,* she is author of the best-selling texts *Infants, Children, and Adolescents; Development Through the Lifespan;* and *Exploring Lifespan Development,* published by Pearson. Her book for parents and teachers is *Awakening Children's Minds: How Parents and Teachers Can Make a Difference.*

Berk is active in work for children's causes. In addition to service in her home community, she is a member of the national board of directors and chair of the Chicago advisory board of Jumpstart, a nonprofit organization that provides intensive literacy intervention to thousands of low-income preschoolers across the United States, using college and university students as interveners. Berk is a fellow of the American Psychological Association, Division 7: Developmental Psychology.

Brief Contents

I THEORY AND RESEARCH IN CHILD DEVELOPMENT

1 History, Theory, and Applied Directions   2

2 Research Strategies   40

II FOUNDATIONS OF DEVELOPMENT

3 Biological Foundations, Prenatal Development, and Birth   72

4 Infancy: Early Learning, Motor Skills, and Perceptual Capacities   128

5 Physical Growth   174

III COGNITIVE AND LANGUAGE DEVELOPMENT

6 Cognitive Development: Piagetian, Core Knowledge, and Vygotskian Perspectives   224

7 Cognitive Development: An Information-Processing Perspective   276

8 Intelligence   318

9 Language Development   358

IV PERSONALITY AND SOCIAL DEVELOPMENT

10 Emotional Development   400

11 Self and Social Understanding   446

12 Moral Development   484

13 Development of Sex Differences and Gender Roles   528

V CONTEXTS FOR DEVELOPMENT

14 The Family   566

15 Peers, Media, and Schooling   606

Features at a Glance

BIOLOGY AND ENVIRONMENT

Resilient Children 10

Prenatal Iron Deficiency and Memory Impairments in Infants of Diabetic Mothers: Findings of ERP Research 49

A Case of Epigenesis: Smoking During Pregnancy Alters Gene Expression 125

"Tuning In" to Familiar Speech, Faces, and Music: A Sensitive Period for Culture-Specific Learning 156

Brain Plasticity: Insights from Research on Brain-Damaged Children and Adults 188

Low-Level Lead Exposure and Children's Development 193

Children with Attention-Deficit Hyperactivity Disorder 290

Infantile Amnesia 301

Deaf Children Invent Language 362

Language Development in Children with Williams Syndrome 366

Parental Depression and Child Development 404

Development of Shyness and Sociability 422

"Mindblindness" and Autism 457

Two Routes to Adolescent Delinquency 520

Sex Differences in Spatial Abilities 556

Does Parenting Really Matter? 578

Bullies and Their Victims 621

CULTURAL INFLUENCES

!Kung Infancy: Acquiring Culture 26

Immigrant Youths: Adapting to a New Land 53

Cultural Variation in Infant Sleeping Arrangements 134

Social Origins of Make-Believe Play 270

Children in Village and Tribal Cultures Observe and Participate in Adult Work 273

The Powerful Role of Paternal Warmth in Development 439

Cultural Variations in Personal Storytelling: Implications for Early Self-Concept 451

Identity Development among Ethnic Minority Adolescents 475

Ethnic Differences in the Consequences of Physical Punishment 493

Impact of Ethnic and Political Violence on Children 524

Sweden's Commitment to Gender Equality 536

The African-American Extended Family 583

SOCIAL ISSUES: HEALTH

Family Chaos Undermines Children's Well-Being 29

Welfare Reform, Poverty, and Child Development 36

Children's Research Risks: Developmental and Individual Differences 68

The Pros and Cons of Reproductive Technologies 86

A Cross-National Perspective on Health Care and Other Policies for Parents and Newborn Babies 118

The Mysterious Tragedy of Sudden Infant Death Syndrome 136

Lesbian, Gay, and Bisexual Youth: Coming Out to Oneself and Others 216

Does Child Care Threaten Infant Attachment Security and Later Adjustment? 442

Adolescent Suicide: Annihilation of the Self 472

The Transition to Parenthood 570

Child Sexual Abuse 601

Adolescent Substance Use and Abuse 626

SOCIAL ISSUES: EDUCATION

Can Musical Experiences Enhance Intelligence? 59

Development of Infants with Severe Visual Impairments 162

Sex Differences in Gross-Motor Development 180

Baby Learning from TV and Video: The Video Deficit Effect 237

Speech–Gesture Mismatches: Using the Hand to Read the Mind 285

Media Multitasking Disrupts Learning 293

Emotional Intelligence 327

High-Stakes Testing 343

The Head Start REDI Program: Strengthening School Readiness in Economically Disadvantaged Preschoolers 351

Parent–Child Interaction: Impact on Language and Cognitive Development of Deaf Children 372

Two Approaches to Bilingual Education: Canada and the United States 397

Development of Civic Responsibility 508

Children Learn About Gender Through Mother–Child Conversations 540

Teaching Children to Challenge Peers' Sexist Remarks 545

School Recess—A Time to Play, a Time to Learn 639

Magnet Schools: Equal Access to High-Quality Education 645

APPLYING WHAT WE KNOW

Do's and Don'ts for a Healthy Pregnancy 107

Soothing a Crying Baby 137

Reasons to Breastfeed 195

Communicating with Adolescents About Sexual Issues 213

Enhancing Make-Believe Play in Early Childhood 241

Handling Consequences of Teenagers' New Cognitive Capacities 255

Promoting Children's Cognitive Self-Regulation 305

Supporting Emergent Literacy in Early Childhood 309

Features of a High-Quality Home Life in Infancy and Toddlerhood, Early Childhood, and Middle Childhood: The HOME Subscales 344

Promoting Children's Creativity 355

Supporting Early Language Learning 373

Helping Children Manage Common Fears of Early Childhood 411

Signs of Developmentally Appropriate Infant and Toddler Child Care 443

Fostering a Mastery-Oriented Approach to Learning 468

Supporting Healthy Identity Development 474

Positive Parenting 495

Reducing Children's Gender Stereotyping and Gender-Role Conformity 563

Helping Children Adjust to Their Parents' Divorce 594

Signs of Developmentally Appropriate Early Childhood Programs 598

Regulating TV, Computer, and Cell Phone Use 636

Contents

A Personal Note to Students   xiii
Preface for Instructors   xiv

PART I
Theory and Research in Child Development

CHAPTER 1

History, Theory, and Applied Directions   2

The Field of Child Development   4
Domains of Development   4
Periods of Development   5

Basic Issues   6
Continuous or Discontinuous Development?   7
One Course of Development or Many?   8
Relative Influence of Nature and Nurture?   8
A Balanced Point of View   9

BIOLOGY AND ENVIRONMENT *Resilient Children*   10

Historical Foundations   10
Medieval Times   10
The Reformation   11
Philosophies of the Enlightenment   12
Scientific Beginnings   13

Mid-Twentieth-Century Theories   14
The Psychoanalytic Perspective   15
Behaviorism and Social Learning Theory   17
Piaget's Cognitive-Developmental Theory   19

Recent Theoretical Perspectives   21
Information Processing   21
Developmental Cognitive Neuroscience   23
Ethology and Evolutionary Developmental Psychology   23
Vygotsky's Sociocultural Theory   24

CULTURAL INFLUENCES *!Kung Infancy: Acquiring Culture*   26
Ecological Systems Theory   26

SOCIAL ISSUES: HEALTH *Family Chaos Undermines Children's Well-Being*   29
New Directions: Development as a Dynamic System   30

Comparing Child Development Theories   31

Applied Directions: Child Development and Social Policy   32
Culture and Public Policies   34
Contributions of Child Development Research   35

SOCIAL ISSUES: HEALTH *Welfare Reform, Poverty, and Child Development*   36
Looking Toward the Future   37

Summary   38

Important Terms and Concepts   39

CHAPTER 2

Research Strategies   40

From Theory to Hypothesis   41

Common Research Methods   42
Systematic Observation   42
Self-Reports: Interviews and Questionnaires   46
Neurobiological Methods   47

BIOLOGY AND ENVIRONMENT *Prenatal Iron Deficiency and Memory Impairments in Infants of Diabetic Mothers: Findings of ERP Research*   49
The Clinical, or Case Study, Method   50
Methods for Studying Culture   51

CULTURAL INFLUENCES *Immigrant Youths: Adapting to a New Land*   53

Reliability and Validity: Keys to Scientifically Sound Research   54
Reliability   54
Validity   54

General Research Designs   55
Correlational Design   55
Experimental Design   56
Modified Experimental Designs   58

SOCIAL ISSUES: EDUCATION *Can Musical Experiences Enhance Intelligence?*   59

Designs for Studying Development   60
The Longitudinal Design   60
The Cross-Sectional Design   62
Improving Developmental Designs   63

Ethics in Research on Children   66

SOCIAL ISSUES: HEALTH *Children's Research Risks: Developmental and Individual Differences*   68

Summary   70

Important Terms and Concepts   71

PART II
Foundations of Development

CHAPTER 3

Biological Foundations, Prenatal Development, and Birth   72

Genetic Foundations   73
The Genetic Code   74
The Sex Cells   75
Boy or Girl?   76

Multiple Offspring 76
Patterns of Genetic Inheritance 77
Chromosomal Abnormalities 82

Reproductive Choices 84

Genetic Counseling 84
Prenatal Diagnosis and Fetal Medicine 84

SOCIAL ISSUES: HEALTH *The Pros and Cons of Reproductive Technologies 86*

Prenatal Development 88

Conception 88
Period of the Zygote 89

MILESTONES *Prenatal Development 90*

Period of the Embryo 91
Period of the Fetus 92

Prenatal Environmental Influences 94

Teratogens 95
Other Maternal Factors 103

Childbirth 107

The Baby's Adaptation to Labor and Delivery 108
The Newborn Baby's Appearance 109
Assessing the Newborn's Physical Condition: The Apgar Scale 109

Approaches to Childbirth 109

Natural, or Prepared, Childbirth 110
Home Delivery 111
Labor and Delivery Medication 112

Birth Complications 112

Oxygen Deprivation 112
Preterm and Low-Birth-Weight Infants 113
Birth Complications, Parenting, and Resilience 117

SOCIAL ISSUES: HEALTH *A Cross-National Perspective on Health Care and Other Policies for Parents and Newborn Babies 118*

Heredity, Environment, and Behavior: A Look Ahead 118

The Question, "How Much?" 120
The Question, "How?" 121

BIOLOGY AND ENVIRONMENT *A Case of Epigenesis: Smoking During Pregnancy Alters Gene Expression 125*

Summary 126

Important Terms and Concepts 127

CHAPTER 4

Infancy: Early Learning, Motor Skills, and Perceptual Capacities 128

The Organized Infant 129

Reflexes 130
States 132

CULTURAL INFLUENCES *Cultural Variation in Infant Sleeping Arrangements 134*

SOCIAL ISSUES: HEALTH *The Mysterious Tragedy of Sudden Infant Death Syndrome 136*

Neonatal Behavioral Assessment 138
Learning Capacities 139

Motor Development in Infancy 147

The Sequence of Motor Development 147

MILESTONES *Some Gross- and Fine-Motor Attainments of the First Two Years 148*

Motor Skills as Dynamic Systems 148
Fine-Motor Development: Reaching and Grasping 150

Perceptual Development in Infancy 152

Touch 153
Taste and Smell 154
Hearing 155

BIOLOGY AND ENVIRONMENT *"Tuning In" to Familiar Speech, Faces, and Music: A Sensitive Period for Culture-Specific Learning 156*

MILESTONES *Development of Touch, Taste, Smell, and Hearing 158*

Vision 158

SOCIAL ISSUES: EDUCATION *Development of Infants with Severe Visual Impairments 162*

Intermodal Perception 166

MILESTONES *Visual Development in Infancy 167*

Understanding Perceptual Development 168

Early Deprivation and Enrichment: Is Infancy a Sensitive Period of Development? 169

Summary 172

Important Terms and Concepts 173

CHAPTER 5

Physical Growth 174

The Course of Physical Growth 176

Changes in Body Size 176
Changes in Body Proportions 176
Changes in Muscle–Fat Makeup 177
Skeletal Growth 178
Gains in Gross-Motor Skills 178

MILESTONES *Gross-Motor Development in Early and Middle Childhood 179*

SOCIAL ISSUES: EDUCATION *Sex Differences in Gross-Motor Development 180*

Hormonal Influences on Physical Growth 181
Worldwide Variations in Body Size 183
Secular Trends 184

Brain Development 184

Development of Neurons 185
Development of the Cerebral Cortex 186

BIOLOGY AND ENVIRONMENT *Brain Plasticity: Insights from Research on Brain-Damaged Children and Adults 188*

Advances in Other Brain Structures 189
Brain Development in Adolescence 190
Sensitive Periods in Brain Development 191

Factors Affecting Physical Growth 192

Heredity 192

BIOLOGY AND ENVIRONMENT *Low-Level Lead Exposure and Children's Development* 193

    Nutrition 194

    Infectious Disease 201

    Emotional Well-Being 202

Puberty: The Physical Transition to Adulthood 203

    Sexual Maturation in Girls 203

    Sexual Maturation in Boys 203

    MILESTONES *Pubertal Development in North American Boys and Girls* 204

    Individual and Group Differences in Pubertal Growth 204

The Psychological Impact of Pubertal Events 205

    Is Puberty Inevitably a Period of Storm and Stress? 205

    Reactions to Pubertal Changes 206

    Pubertal Change, Emotion, and Social Behavior 207

    Pubertal Timing 208

Puberty and Adolescent Health 210

    Eating Disorders 210

    Sexuality 212

SOCIAL ISSUES: HEALTH *Lesbian, Gay, and Bisexual Youths: Coming Out to Oneself and Others* 216

    Sexually Transmitted Disease 217

    Adolescent Pregnancy and Parenthood 217

    A Concluding Note 221

Summary 221

Important Terms and Concepts 223

PART III
Cognitive and Language Development

CHAPTER 6

Cognitive Development: Piagetian, Core Knowledge, and Vygotskian Perspectives 224

Piaget's Cognitive-Developmental Theory 226

    Basic Characteristics of Piaget's Stages 226

    Piaget's Ideas About Cognitive Change 226

The Sensorimotor Stage: Birth to 2 Years 228

    Sensorimotor Development 228

    Follow-Up Research on Infant Cognitive Development 230

    Evaluation of the Sensorimotor Stage 236

SOCIAL ISSUES: EDUCATION *Baby Learning from TV and Video: The Video Deficit Effect* 237

MILESTONES *Some Cognitive Attainments of Infancy and Toddlerhood* 238

The Preoperational Stage: 2 to 7 Years 239

    Advances in Mental Representation 239

    Limitations of Preoperational Thought 243

    Follow-Up Research on Preoperational Thought 245

MILESTONES *Some Cognitive Attainments of Early Childhood* 248

    Evaluation of the Preoperational Stage 248

The Concrete Operational Stage: 7 to 11 Years 249

    Concrete Operational Thought 249

    Limitations of Concrete Operational Thought 252

    Follow-Up Research on Concrete Operational Thought 252

MILESTONES *Some Cognitive Attainments of Middle Childhood and Adolescence* 253

The Formal Operational Stage: 11 Years and Older 253

    Hypothetico-Deductive Reasoning 253

    Propositional Thought 254

    Consequences of Adolescent Cognitive Changes 255

    Follow-up Research on Formal Operational Thought 257

Piaget and Education 259

Overall Evaluation of Piaget's Theory 260

    Is Piaget's Account of Cognitive Change Clear and Accurate? 260

    Does Cognitive Development Take Place in Stages? 260

    Piaget's Legacy 261

The Core Knowledge Perspective 261

    Infancy: Physical and Numerical Knowledge 262

    Children as Naïve Theorists 264

    Evaluation of the Core Knowledge Perspective 265

Vygotsky's Sociocultural Theory 266

    Children's Private Speech 266

    Social Origins of Cognitive Development 267

    Vygotsky's View of Make-Believe Play 269

Vygotsky and Education 269

CULTURAL INFLUENCES *Social Origins of Make-Believe Play* 270

    Reciprocal Teaching 271

    Cooperative Learning 271

Evaluation of Vygotsky's Theory 272

CULTURAL INFLUENCES *Children in Village and Tribal Cultures Observe and Participate in Adult Work* 273

Summary 273

Important Terms and Concepts 275

CHAPTER 7

Cognitive Development: An Information-Processing Perspective 276

The Information-Processing Approach 278

A General Model of Information Processing 278

    Components of the Mental System 278

    Implications for Development 280

Developmental Theories of Information Processing 282

    Case's Neo-Piagetian Theory 283

    Siegler's Model of Strategy Choice 284

SOCIAL ISSUES: EDUCATION *Speech–Gesture Mismatches: Using the Hand to Read the Mind* 285

Attention 286

    Sustained, Selective, and Adaptable Attention 286

    Planning 289

BIOLOGY AND ENVIRONMENT *Children with Attention-Deficit Hyperactivity Disorder* 290

Memory 292

Strategies for Storing Information 292

SOCIAL ISSUES: EDUCATION *Media Multitasking Disrupts Learning* 293

Retrieving Information 294
Knowledge and Semantic Memory 296
Episodic Memory 297
Eyewitness Memory 300

BIOLOGY AND ENVIRONMENT *Infantile Amnesia* 301

Metacognition 303

Metacognitive Knowledge 303
Cognitive Self-Regulation 304

MILESTONES *Development of Information Processing* 306

Applications of Information Processing to Academic Learning 307

Reading 307
Mathematics 310
Scientific Reasoning 313

Evaluation of the Information-Processing Approach 314

Summary 316

Important Terms and Concepts 317

CHAPTER 8

Intelligence 318

Definitions of Intelligence 320

Alfred Binet: A Holistic View 320
The Factor Analysts: A Multifaceted View 321

Recent Advances in Defining Intelligence 323

Combining Psychometric and Information-Processing Approaches 323
Sternberg's Triarchic Theory 323
Gardner's Theory of Multiple Intelligences 325

Measuring Intelligence 326

SOCIAL ISSUES: EDUCATION *Emotional Intelligence* 327

Some Commonly Used Intelligence Tests 327
Aptitude and Achievement Tests 328
Tests for Infants 329
Computation and Distribution of IQ Scores 330

What Do Intelligence Tests Predict, and How Well? 330

Stability of IQ Scores 330
IQ as a Predictor of Academic Achievement 331
IQ as a Predictor of Occupational Attainment 332
IQ as a Predictor of Psychological Adjustment 333

Ethnic and Socioeconomic Variations in IQ 334

Explaining Individual and Group Differences in IQ 335

Genetic Influences 335
Adoption Studies: Joint Influence of Heredity and Environment 337

CULTURAL INFLUENCES *The Flynn Effect: Massive Generational Gains in IQ* 338

Race and Ethnicity: Genetic or Cultural Groupings? 339
Cultural Bias in Testing 339
Reducing Cultural Bias in Testing 342

SOCIAL ISSUES: EDUCATION *High-Stakes Testing* 343

Home Environment and Mental Development 344

Early Intervention and Intellectual Development 347

Benefits of Early Intervention 347
Strengthening Early Intervention 349

Giftedness: Creativity and Talent 350

The Psychometric View 350

SOCIAL ISSUES: EDUCATION *The Head Start REDI Program: Strengthening School Readiness in Economically Disadvantaged Preschoolers* 351

A Multifaceted View 352

Summary 356

Important Terms and Concepts 357

CHAPTER 9

Language Development 358

Components of Language 360

Theories of Language Development 360

The Nativist Perspective 360

BIOLOGY AND ENVIRONMENT *Deaf Children Invent Language* 362

BIOLOGY AND ENVIRONMENT *Language Development in Children with Williams Syndrome* 366

The Interactionist Perspective 366

Prelinguistic Development: Getting Ready to Talk 368

Receptivity to Language 368
First Speech Sounds 370
Becoming a Communicator 370

SOCIAL ISSUES: EDUCATION *Parent–Child Interaction: Impact on Language and Cognitive Development of Deaf Children* 372

Phonological Development 373

The Early Phase 373
Phonological Strategies 374
Later Phonological Development 375

Semantic Development 376

The Early Phase 376
Later Semantic Development 380
Ideas About How Semantic Development Takes Place 381

Grammatical Development 384

First Word Combinations 384
From Simple Sentences to Complex Grammar 385
Development of Complex Grammatical Forms 387
Later Grammatical Development 388
Ideas About How Grammatical Development Takes Place 388

Pragmatic Development 390

Acquiring Conversational Skills 390
Communicating Clearly 391
Narratives 392
Sociolinguistic Understanding 393

Development of Metalinguistic Awareness 394

Bilingualism: Learning Two Languages in Childhood 394

MILESTONES Language Development 395

SOCIAL ISSUES: EDUCATION Two Approaches to Bilingual Education: Canada and the United States 397

Summary 398

Important Terms and Concepts 399

PART IV
Personality and Social Development

CHAPTER 10
Emotional Development 400

Functions of Emotions 401

Emotions and Cognitive Processing 402
Emotions and Social Behavior 402
Emotions and Health 403

BIOLOGY AND ENVIRONMENT Parental Depression and Child Development 404

Other Features of the Functionalist Approach 405

Development of Emotional Expression 405

Basic Emotions 406
Self-Conscious Emotions 408
Emotional Self-Regulation 409
Acquiring Emotional Display Rules 412

Understanding and Responding to the Emotions of Others 414

Social Referencing 414
Emotional Understanding in Childhood 415
Empathy and Sympathy 416

MILESTONES Emotional Development 417

Temperament and Development 418

The Structure of Temperament 420
Measuring Temperament 421

BIOLOGY AND ENVIRONMENT Development of Shyness and Sociability 422

Stability of Temperament 423
Genetic and Environmental Influences 423
Temperament as a Predictor of Children's Behavior 425
Temperament and Child Rearing: The Goodness-of-Fit Model 426

Development of Attachment 428

Bowlby's Ethological Theory 428
Measuring the Security of Attachment 430
Stability of Attachment 432
Cultural Variations 432
Factors Affecting Attachment Security 433
Multiple Attachments 437

CULTURAL INFLUENCES The Powerful Role of Paternal Warmth in Development 439

Attachment and Later Development 439

Attachment, Parental Employment, and Child Care 441

SOCIAL ISSUES: HEALTH Does Child Care Threaten Infant Attachment Security and Later Adjustment? 442

Summary 444

Important Terms and Concepts 445

CHAPTER 11
Self and Social Understanding 446

Emergence of Self and Development of Self-Concept 448

Self-Awareness 448
The Categorical, Remembered, and Enduring Selves 450

CULTURAL INFLUENCES Cultural Variations in Personal Storytelling: Implications for Early Self-Concept 451

The Inner Self: Young Children's Theory of Mind 451
Self-Concept 456

BIOLOGY AND ENVIRONMENT "Mindblindness" and Autism 457

Cognitive, Social, and Cultural Influences on Self-Concept 459

MILESTONES Emergence of Self and Development of Self-Concept 460

Self-Esteem: The Evaluative Side of Self-Concept 461

The Structure of Self-Esteem 461
Changes in Level of Self-Esteem: The Role of Social Comparisons 462
Influences on Self-Esteem 463
Achievement-Related Attributions 464

Constructing an Identity: Who Should I Become? 468

MILESTONES Development of Self-Esteem 469

Paths to Identity 470
Identity Status and Psychological Well-Being 471

SOCIAL ISSUES: HEALTH Adolescent Suicide: Annihilation of the Self 472

Factors Affecting Identity Development 472

CULTURAL INFLUENCES Identity Development Among Ethnic Minority Adolescents 475

Thinking About Other People 476

Understanding People as Personalities 476
Understanding Social Groups: Race and Ethnicity 476

Understanding Conflict: Social Problem Solving 480

The Social Problem-Solving Process 480
Enhancing Social Problem Solving 481

Summary 482

Important Terms and Concepts 483

CHAPTER 12
Moral Development 484

Morality as Rooted in Human Nature 486

Morality as the Adoption of Societal Norms 488

Psychoanalytic Theory and the Role of Guilt 488
Social Learning Theory 490

CULTURAL INFLUENCES *Ethnic Differences in the Consequences of Physical Punishment* 493

Limitations of "Morality as the Adoption of Societal Norms" Perspective 494

Morality as Social Understanding 496

Piaget's Theory of Moral Development 496
Evaluation of Piaget's Theory 497
Kohlberg's Extension of Piaget's Theory 499
Research on Kohlberg's Stages 502
Are There Sex Differences in Moral Reasoning? 503
Influences on Moral Reasoning 504
Moral Reasoning and Behavior 506
Religious Involvement and Moral Development 507

SOCIAL ISSUES: EDUCATION *Development of Civic Responsibility* 508

Further Challenges to Kohlberg's Theory 509
The Domain Approach to Moral Understanding 510

MILESTONES *Internalization of Moral Norms and Development of Moral Understanding* 513

Development of Morally Relevant Self-Control 514

Toddlerhood 514
Childhood and Adolescence 515
Individual Differences 516

The Other Side of Self-Control: Development of Aggression 516

MILESTONES *Development of Morally Relevant Self-Control and Aggression* 517

Emergence of Aggression 517
Aggression in Early and Middle Childhood 518
Aggression and Delinquency in Adolescence 518
Stability of Aggression 519

BIOLOGY AND ENVIRONMENT *Two Routes to Adolescent Delinquency* 520

The Family as Training Ground for Aggressive Behavior 520
Social-Cognitive Deficits and Distortions 522
Community and Cultural Influences 523
Helping Children and Parents Control Aggression 523

CULTURAL INFLUENCES *Impact of Ethnic and Political Violence on Children* 524

Summary 526

Important Terms and Concepts 527

CHAPTER 13

Development of Sex Differences and Gender Roles 528

Gender Stereotypes and Gender Roles 530

Gender Stereotyping in Early Childhood 531
Gender Stereotyping in Middle Childhood and Adolescence 532
Individual and Group Differences in Gender Stereotyping 533
Gender Stereotyping and Gender-Role Adoption 534

Influences on Gender Stereotyping and Gender-Role Adoption 535

Biological Influences 535

CULTURAL INFLUENCES *Sweden's Commitment to Gender Equality* 536

Environmental Influences 538

SOCIAL ISSUES: EDUCATION *Children Learn About Gender Through Mother–Child Conversations* 540

SOCIAL ISSUES: EDUCATION *Teaching Children to Challenge Peers' Sexist Remarks* 545

Gender Identity 547

Emergence of Gender Identity 548
Gender Identity in Middle Childhood 549
Gender Identity in Adolescence 550
Gender Schema Theory 551

MILESTONES *Gender Typing* 553

To What Extent Do Boys and Girls *Really* Differ in Gender-Stereotyped Attributes? 553

Mental Abilities 554

BIOLOGY AND ENVIRONMENT *Sex Differences in Spatial Abilities* 556

Personality Traits 558

Developing Non-Gender-Stereotyped Children 562

Summary 564

Important Terms and Concepts 565

PART V

Contexts for Development

CHAPTER 14

The Family 566

Origins and Functions of the Family 568

The Family as a Social System 569

Direct Influences 569
Indirect Influences 569

SOCIAL ISSUES: HEALTH *The Transition to Parenthood* 570

Adapting to Change 571
The Family System in Context 571

Socialization Within the Family 573

Styles of Child Rearing 573
What Makes the Authoritative Style Effective? 575
Adapting Child Rearing to Children's Development 577

BIOLOGY AND ENVIRONMENT *Does Parenting Really Matter?* 578

Socioeconomic and Ethnic Variations in Child Rearing 580

CULTURAL INFLUENCES *The African-American Extended Family* 583

Family Lifestyles and Transitions 584

From Large to Small Families 584
One-Child Families 587
Adoptive Families 588
Gay and Lesbian Families 589
Never-Married Single-Parent Families 590
Divorce 590
Blended Families 594

Maternal Employment and Dual-Earner Families   595
Child Care   596
Self-Care   597

Vulnerable Families: Child Maltreatment   599

Incidence and Definitions   599
Origins of Child Maltreatment   600

SOCIAL ISSUES: HEALTH *Child Sexual Abuse   601*

Consequences of Child Maltreatment   602
Preventing Child Maltreatment   603

Summary   604

Important Terms and Concepts   605

CHAPTER 15

Peers, Media, and Schooling   606

Peer Relations   607

Development of Peer Sociability   608
Influences on Peer Sociability   611
Friendship   613
Peer Acceptance   618

BIOLOGY AND ENVIRONMENT *Bullies and Their Victims   621*

Peer Groups   622
Dating   624
Peer Pressure and Conformity   625

SOCIAL ISSUES: HEALTH *Adolescent Substance Use and Abuse   626*

MILESTONES *Development of Peer Relations   628*

Media   629

Television   629
Computers, Cell Phones, and the Internet   632
Regulating Media Use   635

Schooling   637

Class and Student Body Size   637
Educational Philosophies   638

SOCIAL ISSUES: EDUCATION *School Recess—A Time to Play,
a Time to Learn   639*

School Transitions   640
Teacher–Student Interaction   643
Grouping Practices   643

SOCIAL ISSUES: EDUCATION *Magnet Schools: Equal Access to
High-Quality Education   645*

Teaching Students with Special Needs   646
Parent–School Partnerships   647
How Well-Educated Are American Young People?   647

Summary   650

Important Terms and Concepts   652

Glossary   G-1

References   R-1

Name Index   NI-1

Subject Index   SI-1

A Personal Note to Students

My more than 30 years of teaching child development have brought me in contact with thousands of students like you—students with diverse majors, future goals, interests, and needs. Some are affiliated with my own field, psychology, but many come from other related fields—education, sociology, anthropology, family studies, social service, nursing, and biology, to name just a few. Each semester, my students' aspirations have proven to be as varied as their fields of study. Many look toward careers in applied work with children—teaching, caregiving, nursing, counseling, social service, school psychology, and program administration. Some plan to teach child development, and a few want to do research. Most hope someday to become parents, whereas others are already parents who come with a desire to better understand and rear their children. And almost all arrive with a deep curiosity about how they themselves developed from tiny infants into the complex human beings they are today.

My goal in preparing this ninth edition of *Child Development* is to provide a textbook that meets the instructional goals of your course as well as your personal interests and needs. To achieve these objectives, I have grounded this book in a carefully selected body of classic and current theory and research brought to life with stories and vignettes about children and families, most of whom I have known personally. In addition, the text highlights the joint contributions of biology and environment to the developing child, explains how the research process helps solve real-world problems, illustrates commonalities and differences between ethnic groups and cultures, discusses the broader social contexts in which children develop, and pays special attention to policy issues that are crucial for safeguarding children's well-being in today's world. Woven throughout the text is a unique pedagogical program that will assist you in mastering information, integrating the various aspects of development, critically examining controversial issues, applying what you have learned, and relating the information to real life.

I hope that learning about child development will be as rewarding for you as I have found it over the years. I would like to know what you think about both the field of child development and this book. I welcome your comments; please feel free to send them to me at Department of Psychology, Box 4620, Illinois State University, Normal, IL 61790, or in care of the publisher, who will forward them to me.

Laura E. Berk

Preface for Instructors

My decision to write *Child Development* was inspired by a wealth of professional and personal experiences. First and foremost were the interests and needs of thousands of students of child development in my classes in more than three decades of college teaching. I aimed for a text that is intellectually stimulating, that provides depth as well as breadth of coverage, that portrays the complexities of child development with clarity and excitement, and that is relevant and useful in building a bridge from theory and research to children's everyday lives.

Today, *Child Development* reaches around the globe, with editions published in six languages: English, Chinese, Georgian, Japanese, Russian, and Spanish. Instructor and student enthusiasm for the book not only has been among my greatest sources of pride and satisfaction but also has inspired me to rethink and improve each edition. I am honored and humbled to have entrusted to me the awesome responsibility of introducing the field of child development to so many students.

The 23 years since *Child Development* first appeared have been a period of unprecedented expansion and change in theory and research. This ninth edition represents these rapid transformations, with a wealth of new content and teaching tools:

■ *Diverse pathways of change are highlighted.* Investigators have reached broad consensus that variations in biological makeup, everyday tasks, and the people who support children in mastery of those tasks lead to wide individual differences in children's paths of change and resulting competencies. This edition pays more attention to variability in development and to recent theories—including ecological, sociocultural, and dynamic systems—that attempt to explain it. Multicultural and cross-cultural findings, including international comparisons, are enhanced throughout the text and in revised and expanded Cultural Influences boxes.

■ *The complex, bidirectional relationship between biology and environment is given greater attention.* Accumulating evidence on development of the brain, motor skills, cognitive and language competencies, temperament, emotional and social understanding, and developmental problems underscores the way biological factors emerge in, are modified by, and share power with experience. The interconnection between biology and environment is revisited throughout the text narrative and in the Biology and Environment boxes with new and updated topics.

■ *Inclusion of interdisciplinary research is expanded.* The move toward viewing thoughts, feelings, and behavior as an integrated whole, affected by a wide array of influences in biology, social context, and culture, has motivated developmental researchers to strengthen their ties with other fields of psychology and with other disciplines. Topics and findings included in this edition increasingly reflect the contributions of educational psychology, social psychology, health psychology, clinical psychology, neurobiology, pediatrics, sociology, anthropology, social service, and other fields.

■ *The links among theory, research, and applications—a theme of this book since its inception—are strengthened.* As researchers intensify their efforts to generate findings relevant to real-life situations, I have placed even greater weight on social policy issues and sound theory- and research-based practices. Further applications are provided in the Applying What We Know tables, which give students concrete ways of building bridges between their learning and the real world.

■ *Both health and education are granted increased attention.* The home, school, community, and larger culture are featured as contexts that powerfully influence children's health and education, with lifelong consequences for their well-being. Research on effective health- and education-related policies and practices appears throughout the text narrative and in new and revised Social Issues: Health and Social Issues: Education boxes.

■ *The role of active student learning is made more explicit.* TAKE A MOMENT..., a feature built into the chapter narrative, asks students to think deeply and critically as they read. Ask Yourself questions at the end of each major section have been thoroughly revised and expanded to promote four approaches to engaging actively with the subject matter: *Review, Connect, Apply,* and *Reflect.* This feature assists students in reflecting on what they have learned from multiple vantage points. A new Look and Listen feature, appearing periodically in the margins, presents students with opportunities to observe what real children say and do and attend to influences on children in their everyday environments.

Text Philosophy

The basic approach of this book has been shaped by my own professional and personal history as a teacher, researcher, and parent. It consists of seven philosophical ingredients that I regard as essential for students to emerge from a course with a thorough understanding of child development:

1. An understanding of major theories and the strengths and shortcomings of each. The first chapter begins by emphasizing that only knowledge of multiple theories can do justice to the richness of child development. In each topical domain, I present a variety of theoretical perspectives, indicate how each highlights previously overlooked facets of development, and discuss research that evaluates it. If one or two theories have emerged as especially prominent in a particular area, I indicate why, in terms of the theory's broad explanatory power. Consideration of contrasting theories also serves as the basis for an evenhanded analysis of many controversial issues throughout the text.

2. An appreciation of research strategies for investigating child development. To evaluate theories, students need a firm grounding in research methods and designs. I devote an entire chapter to a description and critique of research strategies. Throughout the book, numerous studies are discussed in sufficient detail for students to use what they have learned to critically assess the findings, conclusions, and implications of research.

3. *Knowledge of both the sequence of child development and the processes that underlie it.* Students are provided with a description of the organized sequence of development along with processes of change. An understanding of process—how complex combinations of biological and environmental events produce development—has been the focus of most recent research. Accordingly, the text reflects this emphasis. But new information about the timetable of change has also emerged. In many ways, children have proved to be far more competent than they were believed to be in the past. Current evidence on the sequence and timing of development, along with its implications for process, is presented throughout the book.

4. *An appreciation of the impact of context and culture on child development.* A wealth of research indicates that children live in rich physical and social contexts that affect all aspects of development. In each chapter, the student travels to distant parts of the world as I review a growing body of cross-cultural evidence. The text narrative also discusses many findings on socioeconomically and ethnically diverse children within the United States and on children with varying abilities and disabilities. Besides highlighting the role of immediate settings, such as family, neighborhood, and school, I underscore the impact of larger social structures—societal values, laws, and government programs—on children's well-being.

5. *An understanding of the joint contributions of biology and environment to development.* The field recognizes more powerfully than ever before the joint impact of hereditary/constitutional and environmental factors—that these contributions to development combine in complex ways and cannot be separated in a simple manner. Numerous examples of how biological dispositions can be maintained as well as transformed by social contexts are presented throughout the book.

6. *A sense of the interdependency of all aspects of development—physical, cognitive, emotional, and social.* Every chapter takes an integrated approach to understanding children. I show how physical, cognitive, emotional, and social development are interwoven. Within the text narrative and in a special series of Ask Yourself *Connect* questions at the end of major sections, students are referred to other parts of the book to deepen their grasp of relationships among various aspects of change.

7. *An appreciation of the interrelatedness of theory, research, and applications.* Throughout this book, I emphasize that theories of child development and the research stimulated by them provide the foundation for sound, effective practices with children. The links among theory, research, and applications are reinforced by an organizational format in which theory and research are presented first, followed by practical implications. In addition, a current focus in the field—harnessing child development knowledge to shape social policies that support children's

needs—is reflected in every chapter. The text addresses the current condition of children in the United States and around the world and shows how theory and research have sparked successful interventions.

New Coverage in the Ninth Edition

Child development is a fascinating and ever-changing field of study, with constantly emerging new discoveries and refinements in existing knowledge. The ninth edition represents this burgeoning contemporary literature, with more than 1,400 new citations. Cutting-edge topics throughout the text underscore the book's major themes. Here is a sampling:

■ **CHAPTER 1** ■ Introduction to the concept of plasticity within the section on basic issues of development • Revised and updated section on developmental cognitive neuroscience as a new area of investigation • New Social Issues: Health box on how family chaos undermines children's well-being, illustrating the power of the exosystem to affect development • Expanded and updated section on child development and social policy • Updated Social Issues: Health box on the impact of welfare reform on children's development, with U.S. welfare reform policies compared to those of other Western nations

■ **CHAPTER 2** ■ Attention throughout to the advantages of combining research methods and designs • New examples of research using systematic observation, structured interviews, correlational design, field experimentation, and microgenetic design • Expanded and updated section on neurobiological methods, including salivary cortisol as a measure of stress reactivity and new approaches to assessing brain functioning, including the geodesic sensor net (GSN) and near-infrared spectroscopy (NIRS) • Updated Biology and Environment box on prenatal iron deficiency and memory impairments in infants of diabetic mothers, illustrating research using event-related potentials (ERPs) • Updated Cultural Influences box on immigrant youths

■ **CHAPTER 3** ■ Updated Social Issues: Health box on the pros and cons of reproductive technologies • Enhanced attention to fetal brain development and behavior • Updated consideration of a wide range of teratogens • New evidence on the long-term consequences of emotional stress during pregnancy • New findings on older maternal age and prenatal and birth complications • Updated Social Issues: Health box on health care and other policies for parents and newborn babies, including the importance of generous parental leave • Introduction to the concept of gene–environment interaction, with illustrative research findings • Expanded section on epigenesis, including new examples of environmental influences on gene expression

■ **CHAPTER 4** ■ Enhanced attention to cultural influences—including infant sleep, gross- and fine-motor development, and perceptual development • New evidence on the impact of "proximal care"—extensive holding of young babies—on reducing infant crying • Updated findings on how environmental factors, including caregiving practices and the baby's physical surroundings, contribute to motor development • New evidence on the perceptual narrowing effect in speech, music, and species-related face perception and in gender- and race-related face perception • New research on development of object perception, including the role of object manipulation • Expanded and updated research on intermodal perception and its contributions to all aspects of psychological development • New findings on children adopted from Romanian orphanages bearing on the question of whether infancy is a sensitive period of development

■ **CHAPTER 5** ■ Updated Social Issues: Education box on sex differences in gross motor development, including the role of physical education • Updated consideration of advances in brain development, with special attention to the prefrontal cortex and the amygdala • New section on adolescent brain development • Updated Biology and Environment box on low-level lead exposure and children's development • Expanded attention to the impact of adult mealtime practices on children's eating behaviors • Revised and updated section on overweight and obesity, including current U.S. prevalence rates, international comparisons, and coverage of contributing factors and health and psychological consequences • New research on infants with growth faltering, highlighting the joint contributions of feeding difficulties and a disturbed parent–infant relationship • New findings on media exposure to sexual content and teenage sexual activity • New evidence on key elements of effective sex education programs • Updated research on adolescent parenthood, including long-term adjustment of adolescent parents and their children and effective interventions

■ **CHAPTER 6** ■ Updated section on infant and toddler imitation, revealing toddlers' ability to infer others' intentions • New section on symbolic understanding, including toddlers' developing grasp of words and pictures as symbolic tools • New Social Issues: Education box on baby learning from TV and video, including discussion of the video deficit effect and the negative impact of extensive early TV viewing • Updated Cultural Influences box on social origins of make-believe play • New evidence on preschoolers' magical beliefs • Enhanced discussion of school-age children's spatial reasoning, with special attention to map skills • Expanded consideration of infants' numerical knowledge, including capacity to discriminate ratios and to represent approximate large-number values • Expanded and updated research on adolescent decision making • New evidence on cultural variations in parental scaffolding of young children's mastery of challenging tasks • New findings on benefits of cooperative learning

■ **CHAPTER 7** ■ Enhanced and updated consideration of working memory, its assessment, and its implications for learning and academic achievement • New section on executive function and its component processes • Expanded section on inhibition and its contribution to many information-processing

skills • Updated Biology and Environment box on children with attention-deficit hyperactivity disorder (ADHD) • New Social Issues: Education box on the impact of "media multitasking" on learning • Revised and enhanced attention to development of episodic memory, including the relationship between semantic and episodic memory • New research on children's eyewitness memory • Enhanced discussion of differences between preschoolers from middle-income and low-income families in emergent literacy and math knowledge, including interventions that reduce the gap

■ **CHAPTER 8** ■ Updated Social Issues: Education box on emotional intelligence • Updated evidence on neurobiological correlates of mental test performance • New findings on IQ as a predictor of psychological adjustment • New evidence on how culturally acquired knowledge affects reasoning on mental test items • Enhanced Social Issues: Education box on high-stakes testing, including the impact of the U.S. No Child Left Behind Act on quality of American education • Enhanced consideration of the potential for supplementary programs to strengthen the impact of Head Start and other preschool programs serving low-income children

■ **CHAPTER 9** ■ Updated research on categorical speech perception in humans and other animals • New evidence on the contributions of joint attention and preverbal gestures to early language development • Updated findings on toddlers' earliest spoken words, including cultural variations • New findings on how phonological features of the child's native language influence early vocabulary growth • Enhanced consideration of research on young children's grammatical knowledge, including the influence of native-language syntactic forms • Updated research on consequences of bilingualism for cognitive and language development • Enhanced attention to the impact of bilingual education on academic achievement and long-term educational and occupational attainment

■ **CHAPTER 10** ■ Updated consideration of the dynamic systems perspective on development of emotional expression • Updated evidence on contributions of language development and parenting to preschoolers' emotional self-regulation • New research on consequences of effortful control for cognitive, emotional, and social development • New findings on goodness of fit, with special attention to the interacting roles of genotype and parenting on child difficultness • Updated section on consequences of early availability of a consistent caregiver for attachment security, emotion processing, and adjustment, highlighting studies of children adopted from Eastern European orphanages • New findings on the joint contributions of infant genotype, temperament, and parenting to disorganized/disoriented attachment • New evidence on contributions of fathers' play to attachment security and emotional and social adjustment • Revised and updated Social Issues: Health box on child care, attachment, and later adjustment • New section on grandparents as primary caregivers

■ **CHAPTER 11** ■ New findings on development of explicit body self-awareness in the second year, including scale errors •

New evidence on cognitive attainments and social experiences that contribute to preschoolers' mastery of false belief • Updated research on the school-age child's theory of mind, including development of recursive thought • Expanded section on implications of theory-of-mind development for social skills • Updated Biology and Environment box on "mind-blindness" and autism • New evidence on preschoolers' self-concepts, including their emerging grasp of personality traits • New findings on the contribution of parent–child conversations about the past to early self-concept • Enhanced attention to cultural variations in self-concept • New research on personal and social factors contributing to identity development in adolescence • Updated Social Issues: Health box on adolescent suicide • Enhanced section on children's understanding of social groups, racial and ethnic prejudice, and strategies for reducing prejudice • New evidence on the Promoting Alternative Thinking Strategies (PATHS) curriculum, a widely applied intervention for enhancing preschoolers' social problem solving

■ **CHAPTER 12** ■ New evidence on the relationship of early corporal punishment to later behavior problems, including cross-cultural findings • Enhanced consideration of factors that promote moral identity, along with its relationship to moral commitment • Updated Social Issues: Education box on development of civic responsibility • New findings on social-cognitive deficits and distortions of aggressive children • Updated Cultural Influences box on the impact of ethnic and political violence on children, with expanded attention to the September 11, 2001, terrorist attacks • New section on parent training programs to reduce child conduct problems, with special attention to Incredible Years

■ **CHAPTER 13** ■ New evidence on parents' differential expectations for boys' and girls' academic achievement • Revised Cultural Influences box on Sweden's commitment to gender equality, with coverage of Swedish "daddy-months" aimed at encouraging fathers' involvement in child rearing • Updated findings on teachers' differential treatment of boys and girls • New research on the power of observed sex differences in adults' occupations to affect children's occupational interests • New Social Issues: Education box on teaching children to challenge peers' sexist remarks • Updated evidence on gender intensification in adolescence • Updated consideration of factors contributing to sex differences in verbal, mathematical, and spatial abilities • New findings on sex differences in adolescent depression

■ **CHAPTER 14** ■ Updated evidence on the impact of neighborhood poverty on family functioning, including community-wide prevention efforts of the Better Beginnings, Better Futures Project • New research on long-term, favorable consequences of authoritative child rearing • Updated section on parenting and adolescent autonomy, including research on immigrant families • New evidence on socioeconomic variations in parenting • Updated research on family size and parenting quality • New findings on sibling relationships, including cultural influences and interventions to reduce sibling animosity

• Updated discussion of the one-child policy in China • New research on gay and lesbian families, including children's adjustment and gender identity • Expanded attention to the role of fathers in children's development, with special attention to the transition to parenthood, blended families, and dual-career families • Updated consideration of the consequences of child maltreatment

■ **CHAPTER 15** ■ Updated research on parental influences on peer sociability • New findings on the role of positive peer relations in school readiness • New research on characteristics of adolescent friendships, including implications of other-sex friends for adjustment • Updated findings on Internet friendships, with special attention to teenagers' use of social networking sites • Updated Biology and Environment box on bullies and their victims • Expanded consideration of the impact of biased teacher judgments on ethnic minority children's academic achievement • New statistics on U.S. children and adolescents' use of diverse media forms, including TV, computers, and cell phones • Updated evidence on the influence of various media activities, including TV, video games, texting, and social networking sites, on development and adjustment • New research on the educational consequences of widespread SES and ethnic segregation in American schools • New Social Issues: Education box on magnet schools as a means of attaining equal access to high-quality education • Revised and updated section on U.S. academic achievement in international perspective, including education in the high-performing nations of Finland, Korea, Japan, and Taiwan

Acknowledgments

The dedicated contributions of many individuals helped make this book a reality and contributed to refinements and improvements in each edition. An impressive cast of reviewers provided many helpful suggestions, constructive criticisms, and encouragement and enthusiasm for the organization and content of the book. I am grateful to each one of them.

Reviewers for the First Through Eighth Editions

Martha W. Alibali, University of Wisconsin, Madison
Ellen Altermatt, Hanover College
Daniel Ashmead, Vanderbilt University
Margarita Azmitia, University of California, Santa Cruz
Catherine L. Bagwell, University of Richmond
Lorraine Bahrick, Florida International University
Lynne Baker-Ward, North Carolina State University
David Baskind, Delta College
Carole R. Beal, University of Massachusetts
Rebecca S. Bigler, University of Texas, Austin
Dana W. Birnbaum, University of Maine at Orono
Kathryn N. Black, Purdue University
Paul Bloom, Yale University
James H. Bodle, College of Mount Saint Joseph

Cathryn L. Booth, University of Washington
J. Paul Boudreau, University of Prince Edward Island
Sam Boyd, University of Central Arkansas
Darlene A. Brodeur, Acadia University
Celia A. Brownell, University of Pittsburgh
M. Michele Burnette, Community College of Allegheny County
Lori Camparo, Whittier College
Toni A. Campbell, San Jose State University
M. Beth Casey, Boston College
Robert Cohen, University of Memphis
John Condry, Cornell University
Robert Coplan, Carleton University
Rhoda Cummings, University of Nevada, Reno
James L. Dannemiller, University of Wisconsin, Madison
Zoe Ann Davidson, Alabama A & M University
Teddi Deka, Missouri Western State University
Laura DeRose, Adelphi University
Darlene DeSantis, West Chester University
Nancy Digdon, Grant MacEwan College
Rebecca Eder, Bryn Mawr College
Richard Ely, Boston University
Claire Etaugh, Bradley University
Bill Fabricius, Arizona State University
Beverly Fagot, University of Oregon
Francine Favretto, University of Maryland
Larry Fenson, San Diego State University
Jayne Gackenbach, Grant MacEwan College
James Garbarino, Cornell University
Jane F. Gaultney, University of North Carolina, Charlotte
John C. Gibbs, Ohio State University
Peter Gordon, University of Pittsburgh
Katherine Green, Millersville University
Suzanne Gurland, Middlebury College
Craig H. Hart, Brigham Young University
Joyce A. Hemphill, University of Wisconsin, Madison
Kenneth Hill, Saint Mary's University, Halifax
Alice S. Honig, Syracuse University
Nina Howe, Concordia University
Carla L. Hudson Kam, University of California, Berkeley
Janis Jacobs, Pennsylvania State University
Scott P. Johnson, New York University
Patricia K. Kerig, Miami University of Ohio
Katherine Kipp, University of Georgia
Paul Klaczynski, Pennsylvania State University
Mareile Koenig, George Washington University Hospital
Claire Kopp, Claremont Graduate School
Beth Kurtz-Costes, University of North Carolina, Chapel Hill
Gary W. Ladd, Arizona State University
Daniel Lapsley, Ball State University
Frank Laycock, Oberlin College
Elise Lehman, George Mason University
Mary D. Leinbach, University of Oregon
Richard Lerner, Tufts University
Marc Lewis, Ontario Institute for Studies in Education, University of Toronto
Wilma M. Marshall, Douglas College
Robert S. Marvin, University of Virginia
Catherine Massey, Slippery Rock University
Ashley E. Maynard, University of Hawaii
Tom McBride, Princeton University

Carolyn J. Mebert, University of New Hampshire
Gary B. Melton, University of Nebraska, Lincoln
Mary Evelyn Moore, Illinois State University
Brad Morris, Grand Valley State University
Lois Muir, University of Wisconsin, La Crosse
John P. Murray, Kansas State University
Bonnie K. Nastasi, State University of New York at Albany
Geoff Navara, Trent University
David A. Nelson, Brigham Young University
Simone Nguyen, University of North Carolina, Wilmington
Larry Nucci, University of Illinois at Chicago
Peter Ornstein, University of North Carolina
Randall Osbourne, Indiana University East
Carol Pandey, Pierce College, Los Angeles
Thomas S. Parish, Kansas State University
B. Kay Pasley, Colorado State University
Kathy Pezdek, Claremont Graduate School
Ellen F. Potter, University of South Carolina at Columbia
Kimberly K. Powlishta, Northern Illinois University
Kathleen Preston, Humboldt State University
Bud Protinsky, Virginia Polytechnic Institute and State University
Daniel Reschly, Iowa State University
Stephen Reznick, University of North Carolina, Chapel Hill
Rosemary Rosser, University of Arizona
Alan Russell, Flinders University
Jane Ann Rysberg, California State University, Chico
Phil Schoggen, Cornell University
Maria E. Sera, University of Iowa
Beth Shapiro, Emory University
Susan Siaw, California State Polytechnic University
Linda Siegel, University of British Columbia
Robert Siegler, Carnegie Mellon University
Barbara B. Simon, Midlands Technical College
Leher Singh, Boston University
Gregory J. Smith, Dickinson College
Robert J. Sternberg, Yale University
Harold Stevenson, University of Michigan
Daniel Swingley, University of Pennsylvania
Doug Symons, Acadia University
Lorraine Taylor, University of North Carolina, Chapel Hill
Ross A. Thompson, University of California, Davis
Barbara A. Tinsley, University of Illinois at Urbana–Champaign
Kim F. Townley, University of Kentucky
Tracy Vaillancourt, McMaster University
Janet Valadez, Pan American University
Cecilia Wainryb, University of Utah
Susan K. Walker, University of Maryland
Amye R. Warren, University of Tennessee at Chattanooga
Wenfan Yan, Indiana University of Pennsylvania
Yiyuan Xu, University of Hawaii
Laura Zimmermann, Shenandoah University

Reviewers for the Ninth Edition

Rebecca Bigler, University of Texas, Austin
Natasha Cabrera, University of Maryland
Beth Casey, Boston College
John Gibbs, Ohio State University
Sara Harkness, University of Connecticut
Maria Hernandez-Reif, University of Alabama, Tuscaloosa

Scott P. Johnson, University of California, Los Angeles
Michelle L. Kelley, Old Dominion University
Karen LaParo, University of North Carolina, Greensboro
Angela F. Lukowski, University of California, Irvine
Michael Morales, State University of New York College at Plattsburgh
David A. Nelson, Brigham Young University
Larry Nelson, Brigham Young University
Anna Shusterman, Wesleyan University
Doug Symons, Acadia University
Tracy Vaillancourt, McMaster University
Cecilia Wainryb, University of Utah
Corinne Zimmerman, Illinois State University

An outstanding editorial staff in my home community contributed immeasurably to the entire project. Sara Harris, Supplements Editor and visiting assistant professor of psychology, Bradley University, coordinated the preparation of the teaching ancillaries and wrote major sections of the Instructor's Resource Manual, bringing to these tasks great depth of knowledge, impressive writing skill, enthusiasm, and imagination. Amelia Benner and Rachel Trapp, Editorial Assistants, spent countless hours searching, gathering, and organizing scholarly literature. Rachel also assisted with specifications for several highly creative MyDevelopmentLab simulations, contributed to the Explorations in Child Development video guide, designed the text's back cover, and expertly handled many additional tasks as they arose.

I have been fortunate to work with a highly capable editorial team at Pearson Education. It has been a great pleasure to work once again with Tom Pauken, Managing Editor, who oversaw the preparation of the sixth edition of *Child Development* and who returned to edit its ninth edition. His careful review of manuscript, keen organizational skills, responsive day-to-day communication, insightful suggestions, astute problem solving, interest in the subject matter, and thoughtfulness have greatly enhanced the quality of the text and made its preparation especially enjoyable and rewarding. Judy Ashkenaz and Lisa McLellan, Development Editors, carefully reviewed and commented on each chapter, helping to ensure that every thought and concept would be clearly expressed and well-developed.

My appreciation, also, to Jessica Mosher, Editor in Chief of Psychology, for reorganizing the management of my projects to enable the focused work that is vital for precise, inspired writing. The supplements package benefited from the talents and diligence of several other individuals. Leah Shiro carefully revised the chapter summaries and outlines in the Instructor's Resource Manual. Kimberly Michaud and Cheryl Wilms prepared the superb Test Bank and MyDevelopmentLab assessments. Diana Murphy designed and wrote a highly attractive PowerPoint presentation. Maria Henneberry and Phil Vandiver of Contemporary Visuals in Bloomington, IL, prepared an extraordinarily artistic and inspiring set of new video segments covering diverse topics in child development.

Donna Simons, Senior Production Project Manager, coordinated the complex production tasks that resulted in an exquisitely beautiful ninth edition. I am grateful for her keen aesthetic sense, attention to detail, flexibility, efficiency, and thoughtfulness. I thank Sarah Evertson for obtaining the exceptional photographs that so aptly illustrate the text narrative. I am also grateful for Judy Ashkenaz's fine contributions to the photo specifications and captions. Margaret Pinette, Bill Heckman, and Julie Hotchkiss provided outstanding copyediting and proofreading.

Wendy Albert, Executive Marketing Manager, prepared the beautiful print ads and informative e-mails to the field about *Child Development,* Ninth Edition. She has also ensured that accurate and clear information reached Pearson Education's sales force and that the needs of prospective and current adopters were met.

A final word of gratitude goes to my family, whose love, patience, and understanding have enabled me to be wife, mother, teacher, researcher, and text author at the same time. My sons, David and Peter, grew up with my texts, passing from childhood to adolescence and then to adulthood as successive editions were written. David has a special connection with the books' subject matter as an elementary school teacher, and Peter is now an experienced attorney and married to his vivacious, talented, and caring Melissa. All three continue to enrich my understanding through reflections on events and progress in their own lives. My husband, Ken, willingly made room for yet another time-consuming endeavor in our life together and communicated his belief in its importance in a great many unspoken, caring ways.

About the Cover and Chapter-Opening Art

I would like to extend grateful acknowledgments to the International Museum of Children's Art, Oslo, Norway, and to the International Child Art Foundation, Washington, D.C.; to the World Awareness Children's Museum, Glens Falls, New York; and to the International Collection of Child Art, Milner Library, Illinois State University, for the exceptional cover image and chapter-opening art, which depict the talents, concerns, and viewpoints of child and adolescent artists from around the world. The awe-inspiring collection of children's art gracing this text expresses family, school, and community themes; good times and personal triumphs; profound appreciation for beauty; and great depth of emotion. I am pleased to share with readers this window into children's creativity, insightfulness, sensitivity, and compassion.

CHAPTER 1

"Untitled"

Patrick, 15 years, New Mexico

This artist represents his Taos Pueblo culture with intricate patterns and rainbows of color. As the theories reviewed in this chapter reveal, a similarly complex blend of genetic, family, community, and societal forces influences child development.

Reprinted with permission from the International Collection of Child Art, Milner Library, Illinois State University, Normal, Illinois

History, Theory, and Applied Directions

N
ot long ago, I left my Midwestern home to live for a year near the small city in northern California where I spent my childhood. One morning, I visited the neighborhood where I grew up—a place I had not seen since I was 12 years old.

I stood at the entrance to my old schoolyard. Buildings and grounds that had looked large to me as a child now seemed strangely small. I peered through the window of my first-grade classroom. The desks were no longer arranged in rows but grouped in intimate clusters. Computers rested against the far wall, near where I once sat. I walked my old route home from school, the distance shrunken by my longer stride. I stopped in front of my best friend Kathryn's house, where we once drew sidewalk pictures, crossed the street to play kickball, and produced plays in the garage. In place of the small shop where I had purchased penny candy stood a child-care center, filled with the voices and vigorous activity of toddlers and preschoolers.

As I walked, I reflected on early experiences that contributed to who I am and what I am like today—weekends helping my father in his downtown clothing shop, the year my mother studied to become a high school teacher, moments of companionship and rivalry with my sister and brother, Sunday outings to museums and the seashore, and visits to my grandmother's house, where I became someone extra special.

As I passed the homes of my childhood friends, I thought of what I knew about the course of their lives. Kathryn, star pupil and president of our sixth-grade class—today a successful corporate lawyer and mother of two. Shy, withdrawn Phil, cruelly teased because of his cleft lip—now owner of a thriving chain of hardware stores and member of the city council. Julio, immigrant from Mexico who joined our class in third grade—today director of an elementary school bilingual education program and single parent of an adopted Mexican boy. And finally, my next-door neighbor Rick, who picked fights at recess, struggled with reading, repeated fourth grade, dropped out of high school, and (so I heard) moved from one job to another over the following 10 years.

As you begin this course in child development, perhaps you, too, are wondering about some of the same questions that crossed my mind during that nostalgic neighborhood walk:

- In what ways are children's home, school, and neighborhood experiences the same today as they were in generations past, and in what ways are they different?
- How are the infant's and young child's perceptions of the world the same as the adult's, and how are they different?
- What determines the features that humans have in common and those that make each of us unique—physically, mentally, and behaviorally?
- How did Julio, transplanted at age 8 to a new culture, master its language and customs and succeed in its society, yet remain strongly identified with his ethnic community?
- Why do some of us, like Kathryn and Rick, retain the same styles of responding that characterized us as children, whereas others, like Phil, change in essential ways?
- How do cultural changes—employed mothers, child care, divorce, smaller families, and new technologies—affect children's characteristics?

The Field of Child Development
Domains of Development • Periods of Development

Basic Issues
Continuous or Discontinuous Development? • One Course of Development or Many? • Relative Influence of Nature and Nurture? • A Balanced Point of View

■ **BIOLOGY AND ENVIRONMENT:** *Resilient Children*

Historical Foundations
Medieval Times • The Reformation • Philosophies of the Enlightenment • Scientific Beginnings

Mid-Twentieth-Century Theories
The Psychoanalytic Perspective • Behaviorism and Social Learning Theory • Piaget's Cognitive-Developmental Theory

Recent Theoretical Perspectives
Information Processing • Developmental Cognitive Neuroscience • Ethology and Evolutionary Developmental Psychology • Vygotsky's Sociocultural Theory • Ecological Systems Theory • New Directions: Development as a Dynamic System

■ **CULTURAL INFLUENCES:** *!Kung Infancy: Acquiring Culture*

■ **SOCIAL ISSUES: HEALTH:** *Family Chaos Undermines Children's Well-Being*

Comparing Child Development Theories

Applied Directions: Child Development and Social Policy
Culture and Public Policies • Contributions of Child Development Research • Looking Toward the Future

■ **SOCIAL ISSUES: HEALTH:** *Welfare Reform, Poverty, and Child Development*

These are central questions addressed by **child development,** an area of study devoted to understanding constancy and change from conception through adolescence. Child development is part of a larger, interdisciplinary field known as **developmental science,** which includes all changes we experience throughout the lifespan (Lerner, 2006). Great diversity characterizes the interests and concerns of the thousands of investigators who study child development. But all have a common goal: to describe and identify those factors that influence the consistencies and changes in young people during the first two decades of life. ■

▶ What is the field of child development, and what factors stimulated its expansion?

▶ How is child development typically divided into domains and periods?

The Field of Child Development

The questions just listed are not just of scientific interest. Each has *applied,* or practical, importance as well. In fact, scientific curiosity is just one factor that led child development to become the exciting field of study it is today. Research about development has also been stimulated by social pressures to improve the lives of children. For example, the beginning of public education in the early twentieth century led to a demand for knowledge about what and how to teach children of different ages. Pediatricians' interest in improving children's health required an understanding of physical growth and nutrition. The social service profession's desire to treat children's anxieties and behavior problems required information about personality and social development. And parents have continually sought advice about child-rearing practices and experiences that would promote their children's development and well-being.

Our large storehouse of information about child development is *interdisciplinary*. It has grown through the combined efforts of people from many fields. Because of the need to solve everyday problems concerning children, researchers from psychology, sociology, anthropology, biology, and neuroscience have joined forces with professionals from education, family studies, medicine, public health, and social service—to name just a few. The field of child development, as it exists today, is a monument to the contributions of these many disciplines. Its body of knowledge is not just scientifically important but also relevant and useful.

Domains of Development

To make the vast, interdisciplinary study of human constancy and change more orderly and convenient, development is often divided into three broad domains: *physical, cognitive,* and *emotional and social.* Refer to Figure 1.1 for a description and illustration of each. In this book, we will largely consider the domains of development in the order just mentioned. Yet the domains are not really distinct. Rather, they combine in an integrated, holistic fashion to yield the living, growing child. Furthermore, each domain influences and is influenced by the others. For example, in Chapter 4, you will see that new motor capacities, such as reaching, sitting, crawling, and walking (physical), contribute greatly to infants' understanding of their surroundings (cognitive). When babies think and act more competently, adults stimulate them more with games, language, and expressions of delight at their new achievements (emotional and social). These enriched experiences, in turn, promote all aspects of development.

You will encounter instances of the interwoven nature of all domains on almost every page of this book. In the margins of the text, you will find occasional *Look and Listen* activities—opportunities for you to see everyday illustrations of development by observing what real children say and do or by attending to everyday influences on children. Through these experiences, I hope to make your study of development more authentic and meaningful.

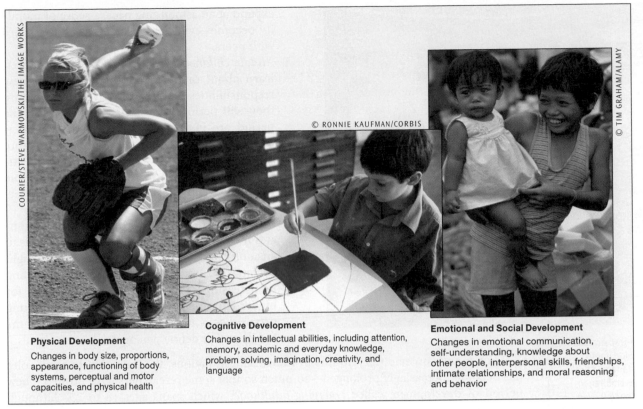

Physical Development

Changes in body size, proportions, appearance, functioning of body systems, perceptual and motor capacities, and physical health

Cognitive Development

Changes in intellectual abilities, including attention, memory, academic and everyday knowledge, problem solving, imagination, creativity, and language

Emotional and Social Development

Changes in emotional communication, self-understanding, knowledge about other people, interpersonal skills, friendships, intimate relationships, and moral reasoning and behavior

FIGURE 1.1   Major domains of development. The three domains are not really distinct. Rather, they overlap and interact.

Also, look for the *Ask Yourself* feature at the end of major sections, designed to deepen your understanding. Within it, I have included *Review* questions, which help you recall and think about information you have just read; *Connect* questions, which help you form a coherent, unified picture of child development; *Apply* questions, which encourage you to apply your knowledge to controversial issues and problems faced by parents, teachers, and children; and *Reflect* questions, which invite you to reflect on your own development and that of people you know well.

Periods of Development

Besides distinguishing and integrating the three domains, another dilemma arises in discussing development: how to divide the flow of time into sensible, manageable parts. Researchers usually use the following age periods, as each brings new capacities and social expectations that serve as important transitions in major theories:

1. *The prenatal period: from conception to birth.* In this nine-month period, the most rapid time of change, a one-celled organism is transformed into a human baby with remarkable capacities for adjusting to life in the surrounding world.
2. *Infancy and toddlerhood: from birth to 2 years.* This period brings dramatic changes in the body and brain that support the emergence of a wide array of motor, perceptual, and intellectual capacities; the beginnings of language; and first intimate ties to others. Infancy spans the first year; toddlerhood spans the second, during which children take their first independent steps, marking a shift to greater autonomy.
3. *Early childhood: from 2 to 6 years.* The body becomes longer and leaner, motor skills are refined, and children become more self-controlled and self-sufficient. Make-believe play blossoms, supporting every aspect of psychological development. Thought and language

© UWE OMMER, *1,000 FAMILIES*, TASCHEN ED

Child development is so dramatic that researchers divide it into periods. This large family of the Ivory Coast includes children in infancy, early childhood (boy in front row, girl seated in second row), middle childhood (girl in front row, girl standing in second row), and adolescence (girl standing in center).

expand at an astounding pace, a sense of morality becomes evident, and children establish ties with peers.

4. *Middle childhood: from 6 to 11 years.* Children learn about the wider world and master new responsibilities that increasingly resemble those they will perform as adults. Hallmarks of this period are improved athletic abilities; participation in organized games with rules; more logical thought processes; mastery of fundamental reading, writing, math, and other academic knowledge and skills; and advances in understanding the self, morality, and friendship.

5. *Adolescence: from 11 to 18 years.* This period initiates the transition to adulthood. Puberty leads to an adult-sized body and sexual maturity. Thought becomes abstract and idealistic, and schooling is increasingly directed toward preparation for higher education and the world of work. Young people begin to establish autonomy from the family and to define personal values and goals.

For many contemporary youths in industrialized nations, the transition to adult roles has become increasingly prolonged—so much so that some researchers have posited a new period of development called *emerging adulthood,* which spans ages 18 to 25. Although emerging adults have moved beyond adolescence, they have not yet fully assumed adult roles. Rather, during higher education and sometimes beyond, these young people intensify their exploration of options in love, career, and personal values before making enduring commitments. Because emerging adulthood first became apparent during the past few decades, researchers have just begun to study it (Arnett, 2007; Arnett & Tanner, 2006). Perhaps it is *your* period of development. In later chapters, we will touch on milestones of emerging adulthood, which build on adolescent attainments. To find out more about this period, consult the mini-chapter entitled "Emerging Adulthood," available as an online supplement to this text.

With this introduction in mind, let's turn to some basic issues that have captivated, puzzled, and sparked debate among child development theorists. Then our discussion will trace the emergence of the field and survey major theories.

▶ Identify three basic issues on which child development theories take a stand.

Basic Issues

Research on child development did not begin until the late nineteenth and early twentieth centuries. But ideas about how children grow and change have a much longer history. As these speculations combined with research, they inspired the construction of *theories* of development. A **theory** is an orderly, integrated set of statements that describes, explains, and predicts behavior. For example, a good theory of infant–caregiver attachment would (1) *describe* the behaviors of babies around 6 to 8 months of age as they seek the affection and comfort of a familiar adult, (2) *explain* how and why infants develop this strong desire to bond with a caregiver, and (3) *predict* the consequences of this emotional bond for future relationships.

Theories are vital tools for two reasons. First, they provide organizing frameworks for our observations of children. In other words, they *guide and give meaning* to what we see. Second, theories that are verified by research often serve as a sound basis for practical action. Once a theory helps us *understand* development, we are in a much better position *to know how to improve* the welfare and treatment of children.

As we will see later, theories are influenced by cultural values and belief systems of their times. But theories differ in one important way from mere opinion and belief: A theory's continued existence depends on *scientific verification*. This means that the theory must be tested using a fair set of research procedures agreed on by the scientific community, and its findings must endure, or be replicated over time. (We will consider research strategies in Chapter 2.)

Within the field of child development, many theories offer very different ideas about what children are like and how they change. The study of child development provides no ultimate truth because investigators do not always agree on the meaning of what they see. Also, children are complex beings; they change physically, cognitively, emotionally, and socially. No single theory has explained all these aspects. But the existence of many theories helps advance knowledge as researchers continually try to support, contradict, and integrate these different points of view.

Although there are many theories, we can easily organize them by looking at the stand they take on three basic issues: (1) Is the course of development continuous or discontinuous? (2) Does one course of development characterize all children, or are there many possible courses? (3) What are the roles of genetic and environmental factors—nature and nurture—in development? Let's look closely at each of these issues.

Continuous or Discontinuous Development?

Recently, the mother of 20-month-old Angelo reported to me with amazement that her young son had pushed a toy car across the living room floor while making a motorlike sound, "Brmmmm, brmmmm," for the first time. When he hit a nearby wall with a bang, Angelo let go of the car, exclaimed, "C'ash," and laughed heartily.

"How come Angelo can pretend, but he couldn't a few months ago?" his mother asked. "And I wonder what 'Brrmmmm, brmmmm' and 'Crash!' mean to Angelo? Does he understand motorlike sounds and collision the same way I do?"

Angelo's mother has raised a puzzling issue about development: How can we best describe the differences in capacities and behavior among small infants, young children, adolescents, and adults? As Figure 1.2 illustrates, major theories recognize two possibilities.

One view holds that infants and preschoolers respond to the world in much the same way as adults do. The difference between the immature and the mature being is simply one of *amount or complexity*. For example, little Angelo's thinking might be just as logical and well-organized as our own. Perhaps (as his mother reports) he can sort objects into simple categories, recognize whether he has more of one kind than another, and remember where he left his favorite toy at child care the week before. Angelo's only limitation may be that he cannot perform these skills with as much information and precision as we can. If this is so, then Angelo's development is **continuous**—a process of gradually adding more of the same types of skills that were there to begin with.

According to a second view, Angelo's thoughts, emotions, and behavior differ considerably from those of adults. His development is **discontinuous**—a process in which new ways of understanding and responding to the world emerge at specific times. From this perspective, Angelo is not yet able to

FIGURE 1.2 Is development continuous or discontinuous?
(a) Some theorists believe that development is a smooth, continuous process. Children gradually add more of the same types of skills.
(b) Other theorists think that development takes place in discontinuous stages. Children change rapidly as they step up to a new level of development and then change very little for a while. With each step, the child interprets and responds to the world in a qualitatively different way.

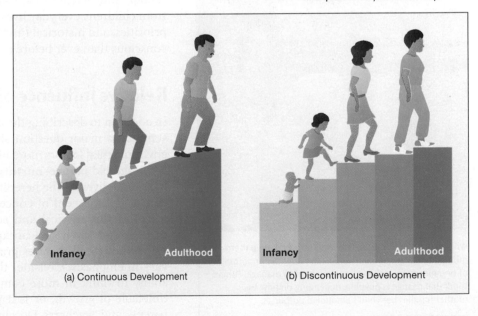

(a) Continuous Development   (b) Discontinuous Development organize objects or remember and interpret experiences as we do. Instead, he will move through a series of developmental steps, each with unique features, until he reaches the highest level of functioning.

Theories that accept the discontinuous perspective regard development as taking place in **stages**—*qualitative* changes in thinking, feeling, and behaving that characterize specific periods of development. In stage theories, development is much like climbing a staircase, with each step corresponding to a more mature, reorganized way of functioning. The stage concept also assumes that children undergo periods of rapid transformation as they step up from one stage to the next, alternating with plateaus during which they stand solidly within a stage. In other words, change is fairly sudden rather than gradual and ongoing.

Does development actually occur in a neat, orderly sequence of stages? This ambitious assumption has faced significant challenges. Later in this chapter, we will review some influential stage theories.

One Course of Development or Many?

Stage theorists assume that people everywhere follow the same sequence of development. For example, in the domain of cognition, a stage theorist might try to identify the common influences that lead children to represent their world through language and make-believe play in early childhood, to think more logically in middle childhood, and to reason more systematically and abstractly in adolescence.

At the same time, the field of child development is becoming increasingly aware that children grow up in distinct **contexts**—unique combinations of personal and environmental circumstances that can result in different paths of change. For example, a shy child who fears social encounters develops in very different contexts from those of a sociable agemate who readily seeks out other people (Kagan, 2003, 2008). Children in non-Western village societies encounter experiences in their families and communities that differ sharply from those of children in large Western cities. These different circumstances foster different cognitive capacities, social skills, and feelings about the self and others (Shweder et al., 2006).

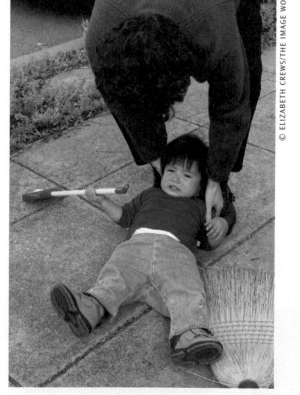

© ELIZABETH CREWS/THE IMAGE WORKS

As you will see, contemporary theorists regard the contexts that mold development as many-layered and complex. On the personal side, these include heredity and biological makeup. On the environmental side, they include both immediate settings—home, child-care center, school, and neighborhood—and circumstances that are more remote from children's everyday lives: community resources, societal values and priorities, and historical time period. Finally, researchers today are more conscious than ever before of cultural diversity in development.

Relative Influence of Nature and Nurture?

In addition to describing the course of development, each theory takes a stand on a major question about its underlying causes: Are genetic or environmental factors more important in influencing development? This is the age-old **nature–nurture controversy.** By *nature,* we mean inborn biological givens—the hereditary information we receive from our parents at the moment of conception. By *nurture,* we mean the complex forces of the physical and social world that influence our biological makeup and psychological experiences before and after birth.

Although all theories grant roles to both nature and nurture, they vary in emphasis. Consider the following questions: Is the older child's ability to think in more complex ways largely the result of an inborn timetable of growth, or is it primarily influenced by stimulation from parents and teachers? Do children acquire language because they are

Will this toddler's tantrums extend into a lifelong pattern of difficult behavior? Some theorists, stressing the importance of heredity, believe she will remain hard to manage. Others think that change is possible, depending on how the mother handles her child's emotional outbursts.

genetically predisposed to do so or because parents intensively teach them from an early age? And what accounts for the vast individual differences among children—in height, weight, physical coordination, intelligence, personality, and social skills? Is nature or nurture more responsible?

A theory's position on the roles of nature and nurture affects how it explains individual differences. Some theorists emphasize *stability*—that children who are high or low in a characteristic (such as verbal ability, anxiety, or sociability) will remain so at later ages. These theorists typically stress the importance of *heredity*. If they regard environment as important, they usually point to *early experiences* as establishing a lifelong pattern of behavior. Powerful negative events in the first few years, they argue, cannot be fully overcome by later, more positive ones (Bowlby, 1980; Johnson, 2000; Sroufe, 2005). Other theorists, taking a more optimistic view, see development as having substantial **plasticity** throughout life—as open to change in response to influential experiences (Baltes, Lindenberger, & Staudinger, 2006; Lerner & Overton, 2008; Lester, Masten, & McEwen, 2006).

Throughout this book, you will see that investigators disagree, often sharply, on the question of *stability versus plasticity*. Their answers have great applied significance. If you believe that development is largely due to nature, then providing experiences aimed at promoting change would seem to be of little value. If, on the other hand, you are convinced of the supreme importance of early experience, then you would intervene as soon as possible, offering high-quality stimulation and support to ensure that children develop at their best. Finally, if you think that environment is profoundly influential throughout development, you would provide assistance any time children or adolescents face difficulties, in the belief that, with the help of favorable life circumstances, they can recover from early negative events.

A Balanced Point of View

So far, we have discussed the basic issues of child development in terms of extremes—solutions favoring one side or the other. But as we trace the unfolding of the field in the rest of this chapter, you will see that the positions of many theorists have softened. Today, some theorists believe that both continuous and discontinuous changes occur. Many acknowledge that development has both universal features and features unique to each individual and his or her contexts. And a growing number regard heredity and environment as inseparably interwoven, each affecting the potential of the other to modify the child's traits and capacities (Cole, 2006; Gottlieb, Wahlsten, & Lickliter, 2006; Lerner, 2006; Rutter, 2007). We will discuss these new ideas about nature and nurture in Chapter 3.

Finally, as you will see later in this book, the relative impact of early and later experiences varies greatly from one domain of development to another and even—as the Biology and Environment box on pages 10–11 indicates—across individuals! Because of the complex network of factors contributing to human change and the challenge of isolating the effects of each, many theoretical viewpoints have gathered research support. Although debate continues, this circumstance has also sparked more balanced visions of child development.

ASK YOURSELF

Review ■ What is meant by a *stage* of development? Provide your own example of stagewise change. What stand do stage theorists take on the issue of continuous versus discontinuous development?

Connect ■ Provide an example of how one domain of development (physical, cognitive, or emotional/social) can affect development in another domain.

Apply ■ Anna, a high school counselor, has devised a program that integrates classroom learning with vocational training to help adolescents at risk for school dropout stay in school and transition smoothly to work life. What is Anna's position on *stability versus plasticity* in development? Explain.

Reflect ■ Cite an aspect of your development that differs from a parent's or grandparent's when he or she was your age. How might *contexts* explain this difference?

BIOLOGY and ENVIRONMENT

Resilient Children

John and his best friend, Gary, grew up in a run-down, crime-ridden inner-city neighborhood. By age 10, each had experienced years of family conflict followed by parental divorce. Reared for the rest of childhood and adolescence in mother-headed households, John and Gary rarely saw their fathers. Both dropped out of high school and were in and out of trouble with the police.

Then their paths diverged. By age 30, John had fathered two children with women he never married, had spent time in prison, was unemployed, and drank alcohol heavily. In contrast, Gary had returned to finish high school, had studied auto mechanics at a community college, and became manager of a gas station and repair shop. Married with two children, he had saved his earnings and bought a home. He was happy, healthy, and well-adapted to life. A wealth of evidence shows that environmental risks—poverty, negative family interactions and parental divorce, job loss, mental illness, and drug abuse—predispose children to future problems (Masten & Gewirtz, 2006; Sameroff, 2006; Wadsworth & Santiago, 2008). Why did Gary "beat the odds" and come through unscathed? Research on **resilience**—the ability to adapt effectively in the face of threats to development—is receiving increasing attention as

investigators look for ways to protect young people from the damaging effects of stressful life conditions. This interest has been inspired by several long-term studies on the relationship of life stressors in childhood to competence and adjustment in adolescence and adulthood (Fergusson & Horwood, 2003; Masten et al., 1995; Werner & Smith, 2001). In each study, some individuals were shielded from negative outcomes, whereas others had lasting problems. Four broad factors seemed to offer protection from the damaging effects of stressful life events.

Personal Characteristics

A child's biologically endowed characteristics can reduce exposure to risk or lead to experiences that compensate for early stressful events. High intelligence and socially valued talents (in music or athletics, for example) increase the chances that a child will have rewarding experiences in school and in the community that offset the impact of a stressful home life. Temperament is particularly powerful.

This boy's close, affectionate relationship with his father promotes resilience. A strong bond with at least one parent who combines warmth with appropriate expectations for maturity can shield children from the damaging effects of stressful life conditions.

▶ Describe major historical influences on theories of child development.

Historical Foundations

Contemporary theories of child development are the result of centuries of change in Western cultural values, philosophical thinking about children, and scientific progress. To understand the field as it exists today, we must return to its early beginnings—to ideas about children that long preceded scientific child study but that linger as important forces in current theory and research.

Medieval Times

Childhood was regarded as a separate period of life as early as medieval Europe—the sixth through the fifteenth centuries. Medieval painters often depicted children wearing loose, comfortable gowns, playing games, and looking up to adults. Written texts contained terms that distinguished children under age 7 or 8 from other people and that recognized even young teenagers as not fully mature. By the fourteenth century, manuals offering advice on many aspects of child care, including health, feeding, clothing, and games, were common

Children who have easygoing, sociable dispositions and who can readily inhibit negative emotions and impulses tend to have an optimistic outlook on life and a special capacity to adapt to change—qualities that elicit positive responses from others. In contrast, emotionally reactive and irritable children often tax the patience of people around them (Mathiesen & Prior, 2006; Vanderbilt-Adriance & Shaw, 2008; Wong et al., 2006). For example, both John and Gary moved several times during their childhoods. Each time, John became anxious and angry. Gary looked forward to making new friends and exploring a new neighborhood.

A Warm Parental Relationship

A close relationship with at least one parent who provides warmth, appropriately high expectations, monitoring of the child's activities, and an organized home environment fosters resilience (Masten & Shaffer, 2006; Taylor, 2010). But this factor (as well as the next one) is not independent of children's personal characteristics. Children who are relaxed, socially responsive, and able to deal with change are easier to rear and more likely to enjoy positive relationships with parents and other people. At the same time, some children may develop more attractive dispositions as a result of parental warmth and attention (Conger & Conger, 2002; Gulotta, 2008).

Social Support Outside the Immediate Family

The most consistent asset of resilient children is a strong bond with a competent, caring adult. For children who do not have a close bond with either parent, a grandparent, aunt, uncle, or teacher who forms a special relationship with the child can promote resilience (Masten & Reed, 2002). Gary received support from his grandfather, who listened to Gary's concerns and helped him solve problems. Gary's grandfather had a stable marriage and work life and handled stressors skillfully. Consequently, he served as a model of effective coping.

Associations with rule-abiding peers who value school achievement are also linked to resilience (Tiet, Huizinga, & Byrnes, 2010). But children who have positive relationships with adults are far more likely to establish these supportive peer ties.

Community Resources and Opportunities

Community supports—good schools, convenient and affordable health care and social services, libraries, and recreation centers—foster both parents' and children's well-being. In addition, opportunities to participate in community life help older children and adolescents overcome

adversity. Extracurricular activities at school, religious youth groups, scouting, and other organizations teach important social skills, such as cooperation, leadership, and contributing to others' welfare. As participants acquire these competencies, they gain in self-reliance, self-esteem, and community commitment (Benson et al., 2006). As a college student, Gary volunteered for Habitat for Humanity, joining a team building affordable housing in low-income neighborhoods. Community involvement offered Gary additional opportunities to form meaningful relationships, which further strengthened his resilience.

Research on resilience highlights the complex connections between heredity and environment. Armed with positive characteristics stemming from innate endowment, favorable rearing experiences, or both, children and adolescents can act to reduce stressful situations.

But when many risks pile up, they are increasingly difficult to overcome (Obradović et al., 2009). To inoculate children against the negative effects of risk, interventions must not only reduce risks but also enhance children's protective relationships at home, in school, and in the community. This means attending to both the person and the environment—strengthening children's capacities while also reducing hazardous experiences.

(Alexandre-Bidon & Lett, 1997; Lett, 1997). Laws recognized that children needed protection from people who might mistreat them, and courts exercised leniency with lawbreaking youths because of their tender years (Hanawalt, 1993).

In sum, in medieval times, if not before, clear awareness existed of children as vulnerable beings. Religious writings, however, contained contradictory depictions of children's basic nature, sometimes portraying them as possessed by the devil and in need of purification, at other times as innocent and close to angels (Hanawalt, 2003). Both ideas foreshadowed later views of childhood.

The Reformation

In the sixteenth century, the Puritan belief in original sin gave rise to the view that children were born evil and stubborn and had to be civilized (Shahar, 1990). Harsh, restrictive child-rearing practices were recommended to tame the depraved child. Children were dressed in stiff, uncomfortable clothing that held them in adultlike postures, and disobedient students were routinely beaten by their schoolmasters. Nevertheless, love and affection for their children prevented most Puritan parents from using extremely repressive measures (Moran & Vinovskis, 1986).

KUNSTHISTORISCHES MUSEUM, VIENNA, AUSTRIA/ALI MEYER/ THE BRIDGEMAN ART LIBRARY INTERNATIONAL

As early as medieval times, adults viewed childhood as a distinct developmental period. In this sixteenth-century painting, *Children's Games*, by Pieter Bruegel the Elder, boys and girls wearing loose, comfortable clothing play lively outdoor games. *[Children's Games (Kinderspiele): Detail of top right-hand corner, 1560 (oil on panel) (detail of 68945), Bruegel, Pieter the Elder (c. 1525–69).]*

As the Puritans emigrated from England to the New World, they brought the belief that child rearing was one of their most important obligations. Although they continued to regard the child's soul as tainted by original sin, they tried to teach their sons and daughters to use reason to tell right from wrong (Clarke-Stewart, 1998). As they trained their children in self-reliance and self-control, Puritan parents gradually adopted a moderate balance between severity and permissiveness.

Philosophies of the Enlightenment

The seventeenth-century Enlightenment brought new philosophies that emphasized ideals of human dignity and respect. Conceptions of childhood were more humane than those of the past.

John Locke   The writings of British philosopher John Locke (1632–1704) served as the forerunner of a twentieth-century perspective that we will discuss shortly: behaviorism. Locke viewed the child as a *tabula rasa*—Latin for "blank slate." According to this idea, children begin as nothing at all; their characters are shaped entirely by experience. Locke (1690/1892) saw parents as rational tutors who can mold the child in any way they wish through careful instruction, effective example, and rewards for good behavior. He was ahead of his time in recommending child-rearing practices that present-day research supports—for example, the use of praise and approval as rewards, rather than money or sweets. He also opposed physical punishment: "The child repeatedly beaten in school cannot look upon books and teachers without experiencing fear and anger." Locke's philosophy led to a change from harshness toward children to kindness and compassion.

Look carefully at Locke's ideas, and you will see that he regarded development as *continuous*: Adultlike behaviors are gradually built up through the warm, consistent teachings of parents. His view of the child as a tabula rasa led him to champion *nurture*—the power of the environment to shape the child. And his faith in nurture suggests the possibility of *many courses of development* and of *high plasticity at later ages* due to new experiences. Finally, Locke's philosophy characterizes children as doing little to influence their own destiny; rather, the child is the "blank slate" on which others write. This vision of a passive child has been discarded. All contemporary theories view children as active, purposeful beings who contribute substantially to their own development.

Jean-Jacques Rousseau   In the eighteenth century, French philosopher Jean-Jacques Rousseau (1712–1778) introduced a new view of childhood. Children, Rousseau claimed, are not blank slates or empty containers to be filled by adult instruction. Instead, they are *noble savages*, naturally endowed with a sense of right and wrong and an innate plan for orderly, healthy growth. Unlike Locke, Rousseau believed that children's built-in moral sense and unique ways of thinking and feeling would only be harmed by adult training. His was a child-centered philosophy in which the adult should be receptive to the child's needs at each of four stages: infancy, childhood, late childhood, and adolescence.

Rousseau's philosophy includes two influential concepts. The first is the concept of *stage*, which we discussed earlier. The second is the concept of **maturation**, which refers to a genetically determined, naturally unfolding course of growth. In contrast to Locke, Rousseau saw children as determining their own destinies. And he viewed development as a *discontinuous, stagewise* process that follows a *single, unified course* mapped out by *nature*.

Scientific Beginnings

The study of child development evolved quickly in the late nineteenth and early twentieth centuries. Early observations of children were soon followed by improved methods and theories. Each advance contributed to the firm foundation on which the field rests today.

Darwin: Forefather of Scientific Child Study A century after Rousseau, British naturalist Charles Darwin (1809–1882) joined an expedition to distant parts of the world, where he observed infinite variation among plant and animal species. He also saw that within a species, no two individuals are exactly alike. From these observations, he constructed his famous *theory of evolution.*

The theory emphasized two related principles: *natural selection* and *survival of the fittest.* Darwin explained that certain species survive in particular parts of the world because they have characteristics that fit with, or are adapted to, their surroundings. Other species die off because they are not as well-suited to their environments. Individuals within a species who best meet the environment's survival requirements live long enough to reproduce and pass on their more beneficial characteristics to future generations. Darwin's emphasis on the adaptive value of physical characteristics and behavior eventually found its way into important twentieth-century theories.

During his explorations, Darwin discovered that early prenatal growth is strikingly similar in many species. Other scientists concluded from Darwin's observation that the development of the human child follows the same general plan as the evolution of the human species. Although this belief eventually proved inaccurate, efforts to chart parallels between child growth and human evolution prompted researchers to make careful observations of all aspects of children's behavior. Out of these first attempts to document an idea about development, scientific child study was born.

The Normative Period G. Stanley Hall (1844–1924), one of the most influential American psychologists of the early twentieth century, is generally regarded as the founder of the child-study movement (Cairns & Cairns, 2006). Inspired by Darwin's work, Hall and his well-known student Arnold Gesell (1880–1961) developed theories based on evolutionary ideas. These early leaders regarded development as a *maturational process*—a genetically determined series of events that unfold automatically, much like a flower (Gesell, 1933; Hall, 1904).

Hall and Gesell are remembered less for their one-sided theories than for their intensive efforts to describe all aspects of child development. They launched the **normative approach,** in which measures of behavior are taken on large numbers of individuals and age-related averages are computed to represent typical development. Using this procedure, Hall constructed elaborate questionnaires asking children of different ages almost everything they could tell about themselves—interests, fears, imaginary playmates, dreams, friendships, everyday knowledge, and more. Similarly, through observations and parental interviews, Gesell collected detailed normative information on the motor achievements, social behaviors, and personality characteristics of infants and children.

Gesell was also among the first to make knowledge about child development meaningful to parents by informing them of what to expect at each age. If, as he believed, the timetable of development is the product of millions of years of evolution, then children are naturally knowledgeable about their needs. His child-rearing advice, in the tradition of Rousseau, recommended sensitivity to children's cues (Thelen & Adolph, 1992). Along with Benjamin Spock's *Baby and Child Care,* Gesell's books became a central part of a rapidly expanding child development literature for parents.

The Mental Testing Movement While Hall and Gesell were developing their theories and methods in the United States, French psychologist Alfred Binet (1857–1911) was also taking a normative approach to child development, but for a different reason. In the early 1900s, Binet and his colleague Theodore Simon were asked by Paris school officials to find a way to identify children with learning problems who needed to be placed in special classes.

LOOK and LISTEN

Examine several parenting-advice books in your local bookstore or library, and identify the stand each takes on the three basic issues about child development.

To address these practical educational concerns, Binet and Simon constructed the first successful intelligence test.

Binet began with a well-developed theory of intelligence. Capturing the complexity of children's thinking, he defined intelligence as good judgment, planning, and critical reflection (Sternberg & Jarvin, 2003). Then he created age-graded test items that directly measured these abilities.

In 1916, at Stanford University, Binet's test was adapted for use with English-speaking children. Since then, the English version has been known as the *Stanford-Binet Intelligence Scale*. Besides providing a score that could successfully predict school achievement, the Binet test sparked tremendous interest in individual differences in development. Comparisons of the scores of children who vary in gender, ethnicity, birth order, family background, and other characteristics became a major focus of research. And intelligence tests rose quickly to the forefront of the nature–nurture controversy.

James Mark Baldwin: Early Developmental Theorist A final important figure, long overlooked in the history of child development, is American psychologist James Mark Baldwin (1861–1934). A theorist and keen observer of children's behavior, Baldwin's (1897) rich interpretations of development are experiencing a revival today. He believed that children's understanding of their physical and social worlds develops through a sequence of stages, beginning with the simplest behavior patterns of the newborn infant and concluding with the adult's capacity to think abstractly and reflectively (Cairns & Cairns, 2006).

Yet in Baldwin's view, neither the child nor the environment controlled development. Instead, he granted nature and nurture equal importance. Children, he argued, actively revise their ways of thinking about the world, but they also learn through habit, or by copying others' behaviors. As development proceeds, the child and her social surroundings influence each other, forming an inseparable, interwoven network.

Consider these ideas, and you will see why Baldwin (1895) argued that heredity and environment should not be viewed as distinct, opposing forces. Instead, he claimed, most human characteristics are "due to both causes working together" (p. 77). As we turn now to an overview of modern theories of child development, you will find Baldwin's ideas represented in several, especially the more recent ones.

ASK YOURSELF

Review ■ Imagine a debate between John Locke and Jean-Jacques Rousseau on the nature–nurture controversy. Summarize the argument that each historical figure is likely to present.

Connect ■ What do the ideas of Rousseau, Darwin, and Hall have in common?

Reflect ■ Find out whether your parents read any child-rearing advice books when you were growing up. What questions most concerned them? Do you think the concerns of today's parents differ from those of your parents' generation? Explain.

▶ What theories influenced child development research in the mid-twentieth century?

Mid-Twentieth-Century Theories

In the mid-twentieth century, the field of child development expanded into a legitimate discipline. Specialized research centers and professional societies devoted to the scientific study of children were founded. A leader among these is the Society for Research in Child Development (SRCD), established in 1933 to promote interdisciplinary research, dissemination of information, and applications of research findings. The society's inaugural membership of 425 grew rapidly. Today, approximately 5,500 researchers, applied professionals, and students from more than 50 countries are members.

As child development attracted increasing interest, a variety of theories emerged, each of which continues to have followers today. In these theories, the European concern with the child's inner thoughts and feelings contrasts sharply with the North American academic focus on scientific precision and concrete, observable behavior.

The Psychoanalytic Perspective

By the 1930s and 1940s, parents were increasingly seeking professional help in dealing with children's emotional difficulties. The earlier normative movement had answered the question, What are children like? Now another question had to be addressed: How and why do children become the way they are? To treat psychological problems, psychiatrists and social workers turned to an emerging approach to personality development that emphasized the unique history of each child.

According to the **psychoanalytic perspective,** children move through a series of stages in which they confront conflicts between biological drives and social expectations. How these conflicts are resolved determines the person's ability to learn, to get along with others, and to cope with anxiety. Among the many individuals who contributed to the psychoanalytic perspective, two were especially influential: Sigmund Freud, founder of the psychoanalytic movement, and Erik Erikson.

Freud's Theory Freud (1856–1939), a Viennese physician, sought a cure for emotionally troubled adults by having them talk freely about painful events of their childhoods. Working with these recollections, Freud examined the unconscious motivations of his patients and constructed his **psychosexual theory,** which emphasizes that how parents manage their child's sexual and aggressive drives in the first few years is crucial for healthy personality development.

In Freud's theory, three parts of the personality—id, ego, and superego—become integrated during a sequence of five stages, summarized in Table 1.1 on page 16. The *id*, the largest portion of the mind, is the source of basic biological needs and desires. The *ego*, the conscious, rational part of personality, emerges in early infancy to redirect the id's impulses so they are discharged in acceptable ways. Between 3 and 6 years of age, the *superego*, or conscience, develops through interactions with parents, who insist that children conform to the values of society. Now the ego faces the increasingly complex task of reconciling the demands of the id, the external world, and conscience (Freud, 1923/1974). For example, when the id impulse to grab an attractive toy from a playmate confronts the superego's warning that such behavior is wrong, the ego must mediate between these two forces, deciding which will win the inner struggle or, alternatively, working out a compromise, such as asking for a turn with the toy. According to Freud, the relations established among id, ego, and superego during the preschool years determine the individual's basic personality.

Freud (1938/1973) believed that during childhood, sexual impulses shift their focus from the oral to the anal to the genital regions of the body. In each stage, parents walk a fine line between permitting too much or too little gratification of their child's basic needs. If parents strike an appropriate balance, then children grow into well-adjusted adults with the capacity for mature sexual behavior and investment in family life.

Freud's theory was the first to stress the influence of the early parent–child relationship on development—an emphasis that continues to play a role in many contemporary theories. But his perspective was eventually criticized. First, it overemphasized the influence of sexual feelings in development. Second, because it was based on the problems of sexually repressed, well-to-do adults in nineteenth-century Victorian society, it did not apply in other cultures. Finally, Freud had not studied children directly.

Erikson's Theory Several of Freud's followers took what was useful from his theory and improved on his vision. The most important of these neo-Freudians is Erik Erikson (1902–1994), who expanded the picture of development at each stage. In his **psychosocial theory,** Erikson emphasized that in addition to mediating between id impulses and superego

TABLE 1.1 | **Freud's Psychosexual Stages and Erikson's Psychosocial Stages Compared**

APPROXIMATE AGE	FREUD'S PSYCHOSEXUAL STAGE	ERIKSON'S PSYCHOSOCIAL STAGE
Birth–1 year	*Oral:* If oral needs are not met through sucking from breast or bottle, the individual may develop such habits as thumb sucking, fingernail biting, overeating, or smoking.	*Basic trust versus mistrust:* From warm, responsive care, infants gain a sense of trust, or confidence, that the world is good. Mistrust occurs if infants are neglected or handled harshly.
1–3 years	*Anal:* Toddlers and preschoolers enjoy holding and releasing urine and feces. If parents toilet train before children are ready or make too few demands, conflicts about anal control may appear in the form of extreme orderliness or disorder.	*Autonomy versus shame and doubt:* Using new mental and motor skills, children want to decide for themselves. Parents can foster autonomy by permitting reasonable free choice and not forcing or shaming the child.
3–6 years	*Phallic:* As preschoolers take pleasure in genital stimulation, Freud's Oedipus conflict for boys and Electra conflict for girls arise: Children feel a sexual desire for the other-sex parent. To avoid punishment, they give up this desire and adopt the same-sex parent's characteristics and values. As a result, the superego is formed, and children feel guilty when they violate its standards.	*Initiative versus guilt:* Through make-believe play, children gain insight into the person they can become. Initiative—a sense of ambition and responsibility—develops when parents support their child's sense of purpose. But if parents demand too much self-control, children experience excessive guilt.
6–11 years	*Latency:* Sexual instincts die down, and the superego strengthens as the child acquires new social values from adults and same-sex peers.	*Industry versus inferiority:* At school, children learn to work and cooperate with others. Inferiority develops when negative experiences at home, at school, or with peers lead to feelings of incompetence.
Adolescence	*Genital:* With puberty, sexual impulses reappear. Successful development during earlier stages leads to marriage, mature sexuality, and child rearing.	*Identity versus role confusion:* By exploring values and vocational goals, the young person forms a personal identity. The negative outcome is confusion about future adult roles.
Young adulthood		*Intimacy versus isolation:* Young adults establish intimate relationships. Because of earlier disappointments, some individuals cannot form close bonds and remain isolated.
Middle adulthood		*Generativity versus stagnation:* Generativity means giving to the next generation through child rearing, caring for others, or productive work. The person who fails in these ways feels an absence of meaningful accomplishment.
Old age		*Integrity versus despair:* Integrity results from feeling that life was worth living as it happened. Older people who are dissatisfied with their lives fear death.

© OLIVE PIERCE/BLACK STAR

Erik Erikson

demands, the ego makes a positive contribution to development, acquiring attitudes and skills that make the individual an active, contributing member of society. A basic psychosocial conflict, which is resolved along a continuum from positive to negative, determines healthy or maladaptive outcomes at each stage. As Table 1.1 shows, Erikson's first five stages parallel Freud's stages, but Erikson added three adult stages. He was one of the first to recognize the lifespan nature of development.

Unlike Freud, Erikson pointed out that normal development must be understood in relation to each culture's life situation. For example, in the 1940s, he observed that Yurok Indians of the U.S. northwest coast deprived babies of breastfeeding for the first 10 days after birth and instead fed them a thin soup. At age 6 months, infants were abruptly weaned—if necessary, by having the mother leave for a few days. From our cultural vantage point, these practices may seem cruel. But Erikson explained that because the Yurok depended on salmon, which fill the river just once a year, the development of considerable self-restraint was essential for survival. In this way, he showed that child rearing is responsive to the competencies valued and needed by the child's society.

Contributions and Limitations of the Psychoanalytic Perspective

A special strength of the psychoanalytic perspective is its emphasis on the individual's unique life history as worthy of study and understanding. Consistent with this view, psychoanalytic theorists accept the *clinical, or case study, method,* which synthesizes information from a variety of sources into a detailed picture of the personality of a single child. (We will discuss this method further in Chapter 2.) Psychoanalytic theory has also inspired a wealth of research on many aspects of emotional and social development, including infant–caregiver attachment, aggression, sibling relationships, child-rearing practices, morality, gender roles, and adolescent identity.

Despite its extensive contributions, the psychoanalytic perspective is no longer in the mainstream of child development research. Psychoanalytic theorists may have become isolated from the rest of the field because they were so strongly committed to in-depth study of individual children that they failed to consider other methods. In addition, many psychoanalytic ideas, such as psychosexual stages and ego functioning, are too vague to be tested empirically (Crain, 2005; Thomas, 2005). Nevertheless, Erikson's broad outline of psychosocial change captures the essence of psychosocial attainments at each age period. Consequently, we will return to it in later chapters.

Children of the Lacandon Mayan people of southern Mexico learn from their father how to make arrows like those of their hunter-gatherer ancestors. As Erikson recognized, this parenting practice is best understood in relation to the competencies valued and needed in Lacandon culture.

Behaviorism and Social Learning Theory

As the psychoanalytic perspective gained in prominence, child study was also influenced by a very different perspective. According to **behaviorism,** directly observable events—stimuli and responses—are the appropriate focus of study. North American behaviorism began in the early twentieth century with the work of psychologist John Watson (1878–1958), who wanted to create an objective science of psychology.

Traditional Behaviorism Watson was inspired by Russian physiologist Ivan Pavlov's studies of animal learning. Pavlov knew that dogs release saliva as an innate reflex when they are given food. But he noticed that his dogs started salivating before they tasted any food—when they saw the trainer who usually fed them. The dogs, Pavlov reasoned, must have learned to associate a neutral stimulus (the trainer) with another stimulus (food) that produces a reflexive response (salivation). Because of this association, the neutral stimulus alone could bring about a response resembling the reflex. Eager to test this idea, Pavlov successfully taught dogs to salivate at the sound of a bell by pairing it with the presentation of food. He had discovered *classical conditioning.*

Watson wanted to find out if classical conditioning could be applied to children's behavior. In a historic experiment, he taught Albert, an 11-month-old infant, to fear a neutral stimulus—a soft white rat—by presenting it several times with a sharp, loud sound, which naturally scared the baby. Little Albert, who at first had reached out eagerly to touch the furry rat, began to cry and turn his head away at the sight of it (Watson & Raynor, 1920). In fact, Albert's fear was so intense that researchers eventually challenged the ethics of studies like this one. Consistent with Locke's tabula rasa, Watson concluded that environment is the supreme force in development and that adults can mold children's behavior by carefully controlling stimulus–response associations. He viewed development as a continuous process—a gradual increase with age in the number and strength of these associations.

Another form of behaviorism was B. F. Skinner's (1904–1990) *operant conditioning theory.* According to Skinner, the frequency of a behavior can be increased by following it with a wide variety of *reinforcers*—food, drink, praise, a friendly smile, or a new toy—or decreased through *punishment,* such as disapproval or withdrawal of privileges. As a result of Skinner's work, operant conditioning became a broadly applied learning principle, which we will consider further when we explore the infant's learning capacities in Chapter 4.

Social Learning Theory Psychologists wondered whether behaviorism might offer a more direct and effective explanation of the development of children's social behavior than the less precise concepts of psychoanalytic theory. This sparked approaches that built on the principles of conditioning, offering expanded views of how children and adults acquire new responses.

Several kinds of **social learning theory** emerged. The most influential, devised by Albert Bandura (1977), emphasized *modeling*, otherwise known as *imitation* or *observational learning*, as a powerful source of development. The baby who claps her hands after her mother does so, the child who angrily hits a playmate in the same way that he has been punished at home, and the teenager who wears the same clothes and hairstyle as her friends at school are all displaying observational learning. In his early work, Bandura found that diverse factors influence children's motivation to imitate—their own history of reinforcement or punishment for the behavior, the promise of future reinforcement or punishment, and even vicarious reinforcement or punishment (observing the model being reinforced or punished).

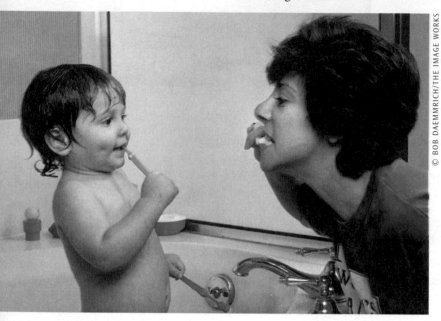

© BOB DAEMMRICH/THE IMAGE WORKS

Social learning theory recognizes that children acquire many skills through modeling. By observing and imitating her mother's behavior, this 19-month-old learns an important skill.

Bandura's work continues to influence much research on children's social development. But today, like the field of child development as a whole, his theory stresses the importance of *cognition,* or thinking. Bandura has shown that children's ability to listen, remember, and abstract general rules from complex sets of observed behaviors affects their imitation and learning. In fact, the most recent revision of Bandura's (1992, 2001) theory places such strong emphasis on how children think about themselves and other people that he calls it a *social-cognitive* rather than a social learning approach.

In Bandura's revised view, children gradually become more selective in what they imitate. From watching others engage in self-praise and self-blame and through feedback about the worth of their own actions, children develop *personal standards* for behavior and a *sense of self-efficacy*—the belief that their own abilities and characteristics will help them succeed. These cognitions guide responses in particular situations (Bandura, 1999, 2001). For example, imagine a parent who often remarks, "I'm glad I kept working on that task, even though it was hard," who explains the value of persistence, and who encourages it by saying, "I know you can do a good job on that homework!" Soon the child starts to view herself as hardworking and high-achieving and selects people with these characteristics as models. In this way, as children acquire attitudes, values, and convictions about themselves, they control their own learning and behavior.

LOOK and LISTEN

Describe an event you observed in which feedback from a parent or teacher likely strengthened a child's self-efficacy. How might the adult's message have influenced the child's self-image and choice of models?

Contributions and Limitations of Behaviorism and Social Learning Theory

Behaviorism and social learning theory have had a major impact on practices with children. **Behavior modification** consists of procedures that combine conditioning and modeling to eliminate undesirable behaviors and increase desirable responses. It has been used to relieve a wide range of serious developmental problems, such as persistent aggression, language delays, and extreme fears (Martin & Pear, 2007).

Behavior modification is also effective in dealing with common, everyday difficulties, including poor time management; unwanted habits such as nail biting and thumb sucking; and anxiety over such recurrent events as test-taking, public speaking, and medical and dental treatments. In one study, researchers reduced 4- and 5-year-olds' unruliness in a preschool classroom by reinforcing them with tokens (which they could exchange for treats) when they behaved appropriately and punishing them by taking away tokens when they screamed, threw objects, attacked other children, or refused to comply with a teacher's request (Conyers et al., 2004). In another investigation, children with acute burn injuries played a virtual reality game while nurses engaged in the painful process of changing their bandages. Visual images and sound effects delivered through a headset made the children feel as if they were in a fantasy world. As the game reinforced children's concentration and pleasure, it distracted them from the medical procedure, causing their pain and anxiety to drop sharply compared with dressing changes in which the game was unavailable (Das et al., 2005).

Nevertheless, many theorists believe that behaviorism and social learning theory offer too narrow a view of important environmental influences. These extend beyond immediate reinforcements, punishments, and modeled behaviors to children's rich physical and social worlds. Behaviorism and social learning theory have also been criticized for underestimating children's contributions to their own development. Bandura, with his emphasis on cognition, is unique among theorists whose work grew out of the behaviorist tradition in granting children an active role in their own learning.

Piaget's Cognitive-Developmental Theory

If one individual has influenced the contemporary field of child development more than any other, it is Swiss cognitive theorist Jean Piaget (1896–1980). North American investigators had been aware of Piaget's work since 1930. But they did not grant it much attention until the 1960s, mainly because Piaget's ideas were at odds with behaviorism, which dominated North American psychology in the mid-twentieth century (Cairns & Cairns, 2006). Piaget did not believe that children's learning depends on reinforcers, such as rewards from adults. According to his **cognitive-developmental theory,** children actively construct knowledge as they manipulate and explore their world.

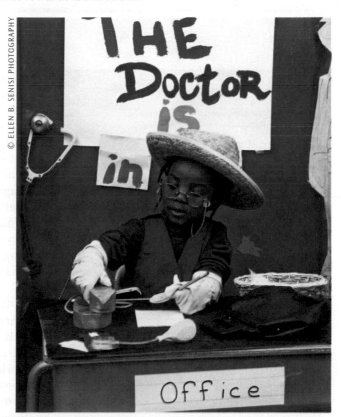

Piaget's Stages　Piaget's view of development was greatly influenced by his early training in biology. Central to his theory is the biological concept of *adaptation* (Piaget, 1971). Just as structures of the body are adapted to fit with the environment, so structures of the mind develop to better fit with, or represent, the external world. In infancy and early childhood, Piaget claimed, children's understanding is different from adults'. For example, he believed that young babies do not realize that an object hidden from view—a favorite toy or even the mother—continues to exist. He also concluded that preschoolers' thinking is full of faulty logic. For example, children younger than age 7 commonly say that the amount of liquid changes when it is poured into a different-shaped container. According to Piaget, children eventually revise these incorrect ideas in their ongoing efforts to achieve an *equilibrium,* or balance, between internal structures and information they encounter in their everyday worlds.

In Piaget's theory, as the brain develops and children's experiences expand, they move through four broad stages, each characterized by qualitatively distinct ways of thinking. Table 1.2 on page 20 provides a brief description of Piaget's stages. Cognitive development begins in the *sensorimotor stage* with the baby's use of the senses and movements to explore the world. These action patterns evolve into the symbolic but illogical thinking of the preschooler in the *preoperational stage*. Then cognition is transformed into the more organized, logical reasoning of the

In Piaget's preoperational stage, preschool children represent their earlier sensorimotor discoveries with symbols, and language and make-believe play develop rapidly. With a few props, this 5-year-old creates an imaginary doctor's office.

© ELLEN B. SENISI PHOTOGRAPHY

TABLE 1.2 | **Piaget's Stages of Cognitive Development**

STAGE	PERIOD OF DEVELOPMENT	DESCRIPTION	
Sensorimotor	Birth–2 years	Infants "think" by acting on the world with their eyes, ears, hands, and mouth. As a result, they invent ways of solving sensorimotor problems, such as pulling a lever to hear the sound of a music box, finding hidden toys, and putting objects into and taking them out of containers.	
Preoperational	2–7 years	Preschool children use symbols to represent their earlier sensori-motor discoveries. Development of language and make-believe play takes place. However, thinking lacks the logic of the two remaining stages.	
Concrete operational	7–11 years	Children's reasoning becomes logical and better organized. School-age children understand that a certain amount of lemonade or play dough remains the same even after its appearance changes. They also organize objects into hierarchies of classes and subclasses. However, thinking falls short of adult intelligence. It is not yet abstract.	**Jean Piaget**
Formal operational	11 years on	The capacity for abstract, systematic thinking enables adolescents, when faced with a problem, to start with a hypothesis, deduce testable inferences, and isolate and combine variables to see which inferences are confirmed. Adolescents can also evaluate the logic of verbal statements without referring to real-world circumstances.	

In Piaget's concrete operational stage, school-age children think in an organized, logical fashion about concrete objects. This 7-year-old understands that the quantity of pie dough remains the same after he changes its shape from a ball to a flattened circle.

school-age child in the *concrete operational stage.* Finally, in the *formal operational stage,* thought becomes the abstract, systematic reasoning system of the adolescent and adult.

Piaget devised special methods for investigating how children think. Early in his career, he carefully observed his three infant children and presented them with everyday problems, such as an attractive object that could be grasped, mouthed, kicked, or searched for. From their responses, Piaget derived his ideas about cognitive changes during the first two years. To study childhood and adolescent thought, Piaget adapted the clinical method of psychoanalysis, conducting open-ended *clinical interviews* in which a child's initial response to a task served as the basis for Piaget's next question. We will look more closely at this technique in Chapter 2.

Contributions and Limitations of Piaget's Theory Piaget convinced the field that children are active learners whose minds consist of rich structures of knowledge. Besides investigating children's understanding of the physical world, Piaget explored their reasoning about the social world. His stages have sparked a wealth of research on children's conceptions of themselves, other people, and human relationships. In practical terms, Piaget's theory encouraged the development of educational philosophies and programs that emphasize children's discovery learning and direct contact with the environment.

Despite Piaget's overwhelming contributions, his theory has been challenged. Research indicates that Piaget underestimated the competencies of infants and preschoolers. We will see in Chapter 6 that when young children are given tasks scaled down in difficulty and relevant to their everyday experiences, their understanding appears closer to that of the older child and adult than Piaget assumed. Also, adolescents generally reach their full intellectual potential only in areas of endeavor in which they have had extensive education and experience (Kuhn, 2008). These discoveries have led many researchers to conclude that the maturity of thinking depends heavily on the complexity of knowledge sampled and the individual's familiarity with the task. Furthermore, many studies show that children's performance on Piagetian problems can be improved with training—findings that call into question Piaget's assumption that discovery learning rather than adult teaching is the best way to foster development (Klahr & Nigam, 2004; Siegler & Svetina, 2006). Critics also point out that Piaget's stagewise account pays insufficient attention to social and cultural influences—and the resulting wide variation in thinking among children and adolescents of the same age.

Today, the field of child development is divided over its loyalty to Piaget's ideas (Desrochers, 2008). Those who continue to find merit in Piaget's stages often accept a modified view—one in which changes in children's thinking take place more gradually than Piaget believed (Case, 1998; Demetriou et al., 2002; Fischer & Bidell, 2006; Halford & Andrews, 2006). Among those who disagree with Piaget's stage sequence, some have embraced an approach that emphasizes continuous gains in children's cognition: information processing. And still others have been drawn to theories that highlight the role of children's social and cultural contexts. We take up these approaches in the next section.

ASK YOURSELF

Review ■ What aspect of behaviorism made it attractive to critics of the psychoanalytic perspective? How did Piaget's theory respond to a major limitation of behaviorism?

Connect ■ Although social learning theory focuses on social development and Piaget's theory on cognitive development, each has enhanced our understanding of other domains. Mention an additional domain addressed by each theory.

Apply ■ A 4-year-old becomes frightened of the dark and refuses to go to sleep at night. How would a psychoanalyst and a behaviorist differ in their views of how this problem developed?

Reflect ■ Illustrate Bandura's ideas by describing a personal experience in which you observed and received feedback from another person that strengthened your self-efficacy—belief that your abilities and characteristics will help you succeed.

Recent Theoretical Perspectives

▶ Describe recent theoretical perspectives on child development.

New ways of understanding children are constantly emerging—questioning, building on, and enhancing the discoveries of earlier theories. Today, a burst of fresh approaches and research emphases is broadening our understanding of children's development.

Information Processing

In the 1970s and 1980s, researchers turned to the field of cognitive psychology for ways to understand the development of children's thinking. The design of digital computers that use mathematically specified steps to solve problems suggested to psychologists that the human mind might also be viewed as a symbol-manipulating system through which information flows—a perspective called **information processing** (Klahr & MacWhinney, 1998; Munakata, 2006). From the time information is presented to the senses at *input* until it emerges as a behavioral response at *output,* the information is actively coded, transformed, and organized. Information-processing researchers often design flowcharts to map the precise steps individuals use to solve problems and complete tasks, much like the plans devised by programmers to get computers to perform a series of "mental operations." They seek to clarify how

FIGURE 1.3 **Information-processing flowchart showing the steps that a 5-year-old used to solve a bridge-building problem.** Her task was to use blocks varying in size, shape, and weight, some of which were planklike, to construct a bridge across a "river" (painted on a floor mat) too wide for any single block to span. The child discovered how to counterweight and balance the bridge. The arrows reveal that even after building a successful counterweight, she returned to earlier, unsuccessful strategies, which seemed to help her understand why the counterweight approach worked. (Adapted from Thornton, 1999.)

both task characteristics and cognitive limitations (for example, memory capacity or available knowledge) influence performance (Birney & Sternberg, 2011). To see the usefulness of this approach, let's look at an example.

In a study of problem solving, a researcher provided a pile of blocks varying in size, shape, and weight and asked school-age children to build a bridge across a "river" (painted on a floor mat) that was too wide for any single block to span (Thornton, 1999). Figure 1.3 shows one solution: Two planklike blocks span the water, each held in place by the counterweight of heavy blocks on the bridge's towers. Whereas older children easily built successful bridges, only one 5-year-old did. Careful tracking of her efforts revealed that she repeatedly tried unsuccessful strategies, such as pushing two planks together and pressing down on their ends to hold them in place. But eventually, her experimentation triggered the idea of using the blocks as counterweights. Her mistaken procedures helped her understand why the counterweight approach worked. Although this child had no prior understanding of counterweight and balance, she arrived at just as effective a solution as older children, who started with considerable task-relevant knowledge. Her own actions within the task facilitated problem solving.

Many information-processing models exist. Some, like the one just considered, track children's mastery of one or a few tasks. Others describe the human cognitive system as a whole (Johnson & Mareschal, 2001; Johnson-Laird, 2001; Westermann et al., 2006). These general models are used as guides for asking questions about broad age changes in children's thinking: Does a child's ability to solve problems become more organized and "planful" with age? What strategies do younger and older children use to remember new information, and how do those strategies affect children's recall?

The information-processing approach is also being used to clarify the processing of social information. For example, flowcharts exist that track the steps children use to solve social problems (such as how to enter an ongoing play group) and acquire gender-linked preferences and behaviors (Crick & Dodge, 1994; Liben & Bigler, 2002). If we can identify how social problem solving and gender stereotyping arise in childhood, then we can design interventions that promote more favorable social development.

Like Piaget's theory, the information-processing approach regards children as active, sense-making beings who modify their own thinking in response to environmental demands (Halford, 2005; Munakata, 2006). But unlike Piaget's theory, it does not divide development into stages. Rather, the thought processes studied—perception, attention, memory, categorization of information, planning, problem solving, and comprehension of written and spoken prose—usually are regarded as similar at all ages but present to a lesser or greater extent. Therefore, the view of development is one of continuous change.

A great strength of the information-processing approach is its commitment to rigorous research methods. Because it has provided precise accounts of how children of different ages engage in many aspects of thinking, its findings have led to teaching methods that help children approach academic tasks in more advanced ways (Blumenfeld, Marx, & Harris, 2006; Siegler, 2009). But information processing has fallen short in some respects. It has been better at analyzing thinking into its components than at putting them back together into a comprehensive theory. And it has had little to say about aspects of children's cognition that are not linear and logical, such as imagination and creativity (Birney & Sternberg, 2011).

Developmental Cognitive Neuroscience

Over the past three decades, as information-processing research expanded, a new area of investigation arose, called **developmental cognitive neuroscience.** It brings together researchers from psychology, biology, neuroscience, and medicine to study the relationship between changes in the brain and the developing child's cognitive processing and behavior patterns.

Improved methods for analyzing brain activity while children perform various tasks have greatly enhanced knowledge of relationships between brain functioning, cognitive capacities, and behavior (Johnson, 2005; Pennington, Snyder, & Roberts, 2007; Westermann et al., 2007). Armed with these brain-imaging techniques (which we will consider in Chapter 2), neuroscientists are tackling questions like these: How does genetic makeup combine with specific experiences at various ages to influence the growth and organization of the child's brain? How do changes in brain structures support rapid memory development in infancy and toddlerhood? What transformations in brain systems make it harder for adolescents and adults than for children to acquire a second language?

During infancy and early childhood, the brain is highly plastic—especially open to growth and reorganization as a result of experience. But a revolutionary finding of neuroscience research is that the brain retains considerable plasticity throughout life. Neuroscientists are making especially impressive progress in identifying the types of experiences that support or undermine brain development at diverse ages. They are also clarifying the brain bases of many learning and behavior disorders (Durston & Conrad, 2007; Meltzoff et al., 2009). And they are contributing to effective treatments for children with disabilities by examining the impact of various intervention techniques on both brain functioning and behavior (Luciana, 2007). Although much remains to be discovered, developmental cognitive neuroscience is already transforming our understanding of development and yielding major practical applications.

An advantage of having many theories is that they encourage researchers to attend to previously neglected dimensions of children's lives. The final four perspectives we will discuss all focus on *contexts* for development. The first of these views emphasizes that the development of many capacities is influenced by our long evolutionary history.

Ethology and Evolutionary Developmental Psychology

Ethology is concerned with the adaptive, or survival, value of behavior and its evolutionary history. Its roots can be traced to the work of Darwin. Two European zoologists, Konrad Lorenz and Niko Tinbergen, laid its modern foundations. Watching diverse animal species in their natural habitats, Lorenz and Tinbergen observed behavior patterns that promote survival. The best known of these is *imprinting*, the early following behavior of certain baby birds, such as geese, which ensures that the young will stay close to the mother and be fed and protected from danger (Lorenz, 1952). Imprinting takes place during an early, restricted period of development. If the mother goose is absent during this time but an object resembling her in important features is present, young goslings may imprint on it instead.

Observations of imprinting led to a major concept in child development: the *critical period*. It refers to a limited time during which the child is biologically prepared to acquire certain adaptive behaviors but needs the support of an appropriately stimulating environment. Many researchers have conducted studies to find out whether complex cognitive and social behaviors must be learned during certain periods. For example, if children are deprived of adequate food or physical and social stimulation during their early years, will

AP IMAGES

Ethology focuses on the adaptive, or survival, value of behavior and on similarities between human behavior and that of other species, especially our primate relatives. Observing this chimpanzee mother cuddling her 8-day-old infant helps us understand the human caregiver–infant relationship.

their intelligence be impaired? If language learning is impeded in childhood due to limited parent–child communication, is the capacity to acquire language later reduced?

In later chapters, we will discover that the term *sensitive period* applies better to human development than the strict notion of a critical period (Bornstein, 1989; Knudsen, 2004). A **sensitive period** is a time that is optimal for certain capacities to emerge because the individual is especially responsive to environmental influences. However, its boundaries are less well-defined than those of a critical period. Development can occur later, but it is harder to induce.

Inspired by observations of imprinting, British psychoanalyst John Bowlby (1969) applied ethological theory to understanding the human caregiver–infant relationship. He argued that infant smiling, babbling, grasping, and crying are built-in social signals that encourage the caregiver to approach, care for, and interact with the baby. By keeping the parent near, these behaviors help ensure that the infant will be fed, protected from danger, and provided with stimulation and affection necessary for healthy growth. The development of attachment in human infants is a complex, lengthy process that leads the baby to form a deep affectionate tie with the caregiver (Thompson, 2006). In Chapter 10, we will consider how infant, caregiver, and family context contribute to attachment and how attachment influences later development.

Observations by ethologists have shown that many aspects of children's social behavior, including emotional expressions, aggression, cooperation, and social play, resemble those of our primate relatives. Recently, researchers have extended this effort in a new area of research called **evolutionary developmental psychology.** It seeks to understand the adaptive value of species-wide cognitive, emotional, and social competencies as those competencies change with age (Geary, 2006b; King & Bjorklund, 2010). Evolutionary developmental psychologists ask questions like these: What role does the newborn's visual preference for facelike stimuli play in survival? Does it support older infants' capacity to distinguish familiar caregivers from unfamiliar people? Why do children play in gender-segregated groups? What do they learn from such play that might lead to adult gender-typed behaviors, such as male dominance and female investment in caregiving?

As these examples suggest, evolutionary psychologists are not just concerned with the genetic and biological roots of development. They recognize that humans' large brain and extended childhood resulted from the need to master the complexities of human group life, so they are also interested in learning (Bjorklund, Causey, & Periss, 2009). And they realize that today's lifestyles differ so radically from those of our evolutionary ancestors that certain evolved behaviors, such as life-threatening risk taking in adolescents and male-to-male violence, are no longer adaptive (Blasi & Bjorklund, 2003). By clarifying the origins and development of such behaviors, evolutionary developmental psychology may help spark more effective interventions.

In sum, evolutionary psychologists want to understand the entire *organism–environment system*. The next contextual perspective we will discuss, Vygotsky's sociocultural theory, serves as an excellent complement to the evolutionary viewpoint because it highlights social and cultural dimensions of children's experiences.

Vygotsky's Sociocultural Theory

The field of child development has recently seen a dramatic increase in studies addressing the cultural context of children's lives. Investigations that make comparisons across cultures, and between ethnic groups within cultures, provide insight into whether developmental pathways apply to all children or are limited to particular environmental conditions (Goodnow, 2010).

Today, much research is examining the relationship of *culturally specific beliefs and practices* to development. The contributions of Russian psychologist Lev Vygotsky (1896–1934) have played a major role in this trend. Vygotsky's (1934/1987) perspective, known as **sociocultural theory,** focuses on how *culture*—the values, beliefs, customs, and skills of a social group—is transmitted to the next generation. According to Vygotsky, *social interaction*—in particular, cooperative dialogues between children and more knowledgeable members of society—is necessary for children to acquire the ways of thinking and behaving that make up a community's culture. Vygotsky believed that as adults and more-expert peers help children master culturally meaningful activities, the communication between them becomes part of children's thinking. As children internalize the features of these dialogues, they can use the language within them to guide their own thought and actions and to acquire new skills (Berk & Harris, 2003; Winsler, Fernyhough, & Montero, 2009). The young child instructing herself while working a puzzle or setting a table for dinner has begun to produce the same kind of guiding comments that an adult previously used to help her master important tasks.

Vygotsky's theory has been especially influential in the study of children's cognition. Vygotsky agreed with Piaget that children are active, constructive beings. But whereas Piaget emphasized children's independent efforts to make sense of their world, Vygotsky viewed cognitive development as a *socially mediated process,* in which children depend on assistance from adults and more-expert peers as they tackle new challenges.

In Vygotsky's theory, children undergo certain stagewise changes. For example, when they acquire language, they gain in ability to participate in dialogues with others, and mastery of culturally valued competencies surges forward. When children enter school, they spend much time discussing language, literacy, and other academic concepts—experiences that encourage them to reflect on their own thinking (Bodrova & Leong, 2007; Kozulin, 2003). As a result, they gain dramatically in reasoning and problem solving.

At the same time, Vygotsky stressed that dialogues with experts lead to continuous changes in cognition that vary greatly from culture to culture. Consistent with this view, a major finding of cross-cultural research is that cultures select different tasks for children's learning (Rogoff, 2003). Social interaction surrounding those tasks leads to competencies essential for success in a particular culture. For example, in industrialized nations, teachers help people learn to read, drive a car, or use a computer. Among the Zinacanteco Indians of southern Mexico, adult experts guide young girls as they master complicated weaving techniques (Greenfield, 2004; Greenfield, Maynard, & Childs, 2000). In Brazil and other developing nations, child candy sellers with little or no schooling develop sophisticated mathematical abilities as the result of buying candy from wholesalers, pricing it in collaboration with adults and experienced peers, and bargaining with customers on city streets (Saxe, 1988). And as the research reported in the Cultural Influences box on page 26 indicates, adults encourage culturally valued skills in children at a remarkably early age.

Research stimulated by Vygotsky's theory reveals that children in every culture develop unique strengths. But Vygotsky's emphasis on culture and social experience led him to neglect the biological side of development. Although he recognized the importance of heredity and brain growth, he said little about their role in cognitive change. Furthermore, Vygotsky's focus on social transmission of knowledge meant that, compared with other theorists, he placed less emphasis

According to Lev Vygotsky, shown here with his daughter, many cognitive processes and skills are socially transferred from more knowledgeable members of society to children. Vygotsky's sociocultural theory helps explain the wide cultural variation in cognitive competencies.

A Cambodian girl learns traditional dance forms from her grandmother. She acquires a culturally valued skill by interacting with an older, more experienced member of her culture.

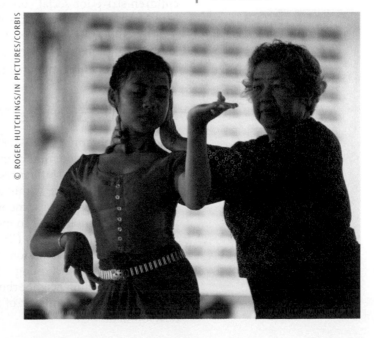

CULTURAL INFLUENCES

!Kung Infancy: Acquiring Culture

Interactions between caregivers and infants take different forms in different cultures. Through those interactions, adults start to transmit their society's values and skills to the next generation, channeling the course of future development. Focusing on a culture very different from our own, researchers studied how caregivers respond to infants' play with objects among the !Kung, a hunting-and-gathering society living in the desert regions of Botswana, Africa (Bakeman et al., 1990). Daily foraging missions take small numbers of adults several miles from the campground, but most obtain enough food to contribute to group survival by working only three out of every seven days. A mobile way of life also prevents the !Kung from collecting many possessions that require extensive care and maintenance. Adults have many free hours to relax around the campfire, and they spend this time in intense social contact with one another and with children (Draper & Cashdan, 1988; Konner, 2010).

In this culture of intimate social bonds and minimal property, objects are valued as things to be shared, not as personal possessions. This message is conveyed to !Kung children at a very early age. While carried about on their mother's hip during work hours, babies often pause to play with decorative beads worn around her neck (Konner, 2008). Between 6 and 12 months, grandmothers start to train infants in the importance of exchanging objects by guiding them in handing beads to relatives. The child's first words generally include *i* ("Here, take this") and *na* ("Give it to me"). In !Kung society, no toys are made for babies. Instead, natural objects, such as twigs, grass, stones, and nutshells, are always available, along with cooking implements. However, adults do not encourage babies to play with these objects. In fact, adults are unlikely to interact with infants while they are exploring objects independently. But when a baby offers an object to another person, adults become highly responsive, encouraging and vocalizing much more than at other times. Thus, the !Kung cultural emphasis on the interpersonal rather than physical aspects of existence is reflected in how adults interact with the very youngest members of their community.

!Kung children grow up in a hunting-and-gathering society in which possessions are a burden rather than an asset. From an early age, children experience warm social contact with adults and are taught the importance of sharing.

TAKE A MOMENT... When you next have a chance, observe the conditions under which parents in your own society respond to infants' involvement with objects. How is parental responsiveness linked to cultural values? How does it compare with findings on the !Kung?

---

on children's capacity to shape their own development. Followers of Vygotsky stress that children strive for social connection, actively participating in the conversations and social activities from which their development springs. From these joint experiences, they not only acquire culturally valued practices but also modify and transform those practices (Nelson, 2007; Rogoff, 2003). Contemporary sociocultural theorists grant the individual and society balanced, mutually influential roles.

Ecological Systems Theory

Urie Bronfenbrenner (1917–2005) is responsible for an approach to child development that has moved to the forefront of the field because it offers the most differentiated and complete account of contextual influences on children's development. **Ecological systems theory** views the child as developing within a complex *system* of relationships affected by multiple levels of the surrounding environment. Because the child's biologically influenced dispositions join with environmental forces to mold development, Bronfenbrenner characterized his perspective as a *bioecological model* (Bronfenbrenner, 2005; Bronfenbrenner & Morris, 2006).

Bronfenbrenner envisioned the environment as a series of nested structures that form a complex functioning whole, or *system*. These include but also extend beyond the home, school, and neighborhood settings in which children spend their everyday lives (see Figure 1.4). Each layer of the environment joins with the others to powerfully affect development.

The Microsystem The innermost level of the environment, the **microsystem,** consists of activities and interaction patterns in the child's immediate surroundings. Bronfenbrenner emphasizes that to understand child development at this level, we must keep in mind that all relationships are *bidirectional:* Adults affect children's behavior, but children's biologically and socially influenced characteristics—their physical attributes, personalities, and capacities—also affect adults' behavior. A friendly, attentive child is likely to evoke positive, patient reactions from parents, whereas an irritable or distractible child is more likely to receive impatience, restriction, and punishment. When these reciprocal interactions occur often over time, they have an enduring impact on development (Collins et al., 2000; Crockenberg & Leerkes, 2003b).

Third parties—other individuals in the microsystem—also affect the quality of any two-person relationship. If they are supportive, interaction is enhanced. For example, when parents encourage each other in their child-rearing roles, each engages in more effective parenting. In contrast, marital conflict is associated with inconsistent discipline and hostile reactions toward children. In response, children often react with fear and anxiety or with anger and aggression, and the well-being of both parent and child suffers (Caldera & Lindsey, 2006; Davies & Lindsay, 2004). Similarly, children can affect their parents' relationship in powerful ways. For example, as Chapter 14 will reveal, divorce is often associated with lasting adjustment problems. Yet long before the marital breakup, some children were impulsive and defiant. These behaviors may have contributed to, as well as been caused by, their parents' marital problems (Strohschein, 2005).

The Mesosystem The second level of Bronfenbrenner's model, the **mesosystem,** encompasses connections between microsystems, such as home, school, neighborhood, and child-care center. For example, a child's academic progress depends not just on activities that take place in classrooms but also on parent involvement in school life and on the extent to which academic learning is carried over into the home (Gershoff & Aber, 2006). Similarly, parent–child interaction at home is likely to affect caregiver–child interaction in the child-care setting, and vice versa. Each relationship is more likely to support development when there are links between home and child care, in the form of visits and cooperative exchanges of information.

Family–neighborhood connections are especially important for economically disadvantaged children. Affluent families are less dependent on their immediate surroundings for social support, education, and leisure pursuits. They can afford to transport their children to lessons and entertainment and even, if necessary, to better-quality schools in distant parts of the community. In low-income neighborhoods, in-school and after-school programs that substitute for lack of other resources by providing child care and art, music, sports, scouting, and other enrichment activities are associated with improved school performance and a reduction in emotional and behavior problems in middle childhood (Peters, Petrunka, & Arnold, 2003; Vandell & Posner, 1999; Vandell, Reisner, & Pierce, 2007). In adolescence, too, religious youth groups, special-interest clubs, and other neighborhood organizations contribute to favorable development, including self-confidence, school achievement,

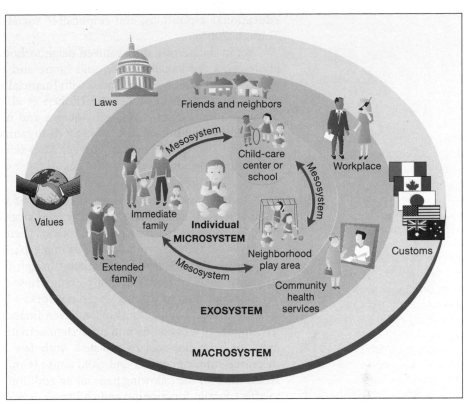

FIGURE 1.4 Structure of the environment in ecological systems theory. The *microsystem* concerns relations between the child and the immediate environment; the *mesosystem*, connections among immediate settings; the *exosystem*, social settings that affect but do not contain the child; and the *macrosystem*, the values, laws, customs, and resources of the culture that affect activities and interactions at all inner layers. The *chronosystem* (not pictured) is not a specific context. Instead, it refers to the dynamic, ever-changing nature of the person's environment.

educational aspirations, and responsible social behavior (Barnes et al., 2007; Kerestes & Youniss, 2003).

Yet in dangerous, disorganized neighborhoods, high-quality activities for children and adolescents are usually scarce, and home and neighborhood obstacles often combine to reduce involvement. Parents faced with financial and other stressors are less likely to encourage their children to participate (Kohen et al., 2008). In an investigation of elementary school students diverse in family income and neighborhood residence, those living in the least stimulating homes and the most disorganized neighborhoods were least likely to participate in after-school enrichment activities (Dearing et al., 2009). Thus, the neediest children were especially likely to miss out on these development-enhancing experiences.

The Exosystem

The **exosystem** consists of social settings that do not contain children but that nevertheless affect children's experiences in immediate settings. These can be formal organizations, such as parents' workplaces, their religious institutions, and health and welfare services in the community. For example, parents' work settings can support child rearing and, indirectly, enhance development through flexible work schedules, paid maternity and paternity leave, and sick leave for parents whose children are ill. Exosystem supports also can be informal, such as parents' social networks—friends and extended-family members who provide advice, companionship, and even financial assistance. Research confirms the negative impact of a breakdown in exosystem activities. Families who are affected by unemployment or who are socially isolated, with few personal or community-based ties, show increased rates of conflict and child abuse (Coulton et al., 2007). Refer to the Social Issues: Health box on the following page for an additional illustration of the power of the exosystem to affect family functioning and children's development.

The Macrosystem

The outermost level of Bronfenbrenner's model, the **macrosystem,** consists of cultural values, laws, customs, and resources. The priority that the macrosystem gives to children's needs affects the support they receive at inner levels of the environment. For example, in countries that require generous workplace benefits for employed parents and set high standards for child care, children are more likely to have favorable experiences in their immediate settings. As you will see later in this chapter and in other parts of this book, such programs are far less available in the United States than in other industrialized nations (Children's Defense Fund, 2009).

An Ever-Changing System

According to Bronfenbrenner, the environment is not a static force that affects children in a uniform way. Instead, it is ever-changing. Important life events, such as the birth of a sibling, the beginning of school, a move to a new neighborhood, or parents' divorce, modify existing relationships between children and their environments, producing new conditions that affect development. In addition, the timing of environmental change affects its impact. The arrival of a new sibling has very different consequences for a homebound toddler than for a school-age child with many relationships and activities beyond the family.

Bronfenbrenner called the temporal dimension of his model the **chronosystem** (the prefix *chrono-* means "time"). Life changes can be imposed on the child, as in the examples just given. Alternatively, they can arise from within the child, since as children get older they select, modify, and create many of their own settings and experiences. How they do so depends on their physical, intellectual, and personality characteristics and their environmental opportunities. Therefore, in ecological systems theory, development is neither entirely controlled by environmental circumstances nor driven solely by inner dispositions. Rather, children are both products and producers of their environments: The child and the environment form a network of interdependent effects. Notice how our discussion of resilient children on pages 10–11 illustrates this idea. You will see many more examples in this book.

LOOK and LISTEN

Ask a parent to explain his or her most worrisome child-rearing challenge. Describe one source of support at each level of Bronfenbrenner's model that might ease the parent's stress and promote favorable child development.

SOCIAL ISSUES: HEALTH

Family Chaos Undermines Children's Well-Being

Virtually all of us can recall days during our childhoods when family routines—regular mealtime, bedtime, homework time, and parent–child reading and playtimes—were disrupted, perhaps because of a change in a parent's job, a family illness, or a busy season of after-school sports. In some families, however, absence of daily structure is nearly constant, yielding a chaotic home life that interferes with healthy development (Fiese & Winter, 2010). An organized family life provides a supportive context for warm, involved parent–child interaction, which is essential to children's well-being.

Family chaos is linked to economic disadvantage—especially, single mothers with limited incomes struggling to juggle transportation challenges, inconvenient shift jobs, unstable child-care arrangements, and other daily hassles. But chaos is not limited to such families.

Survey findings reveal that considering U.S. families as a whole, mothers' time with children has remained fairly stable over the past three decades, and fathers' time has increased (Galinsky, Aumann, & Bond, 2009). But in many families, the way parents spend that time has changed. Across income levels and ethnic groups, both mothers and fathers report more multitasking while caring for children—for example, using mealtimes not just to eat but also to check homework, assign household chores, read to children, and plan family outings and celebrations (Bianchi & Raley, 2005; Serpell et al., 2002). Consequently, disruption in one family routine can disrupt others.

Possibly because of this compression of family routines, today's parents and children consistently say they have too little time together and desire more (Opinion Research Corporation, 2009; Roehlkepartain, 2004). For example, although regular mealtimes affect quality of relationships, only slightly more than half of U.S. families surveyed nationally report eating together from 3 to 5 times per week (CASA, 2006). Frequency of family meals is associated with wide-ranging positive outcomes—in childhood, enhanced language development and academic achievement, fewer behavior problems, and time spent sleeping; and in adolescence, reduced sexual risk taking, alcohol and drug use, and mental health problems. Shared mealtimes also increase the likelihood of a healthy diet and protect against obesity and

adolescent eating disorders (Adam, Snell, & Pendry, 2007; Fiese & Schwartz, 2008). As these findings suggest, regular mealtimes are a general indicator of an organized family life and positive parental involvement.

But family chaos can prevail even when families do engage in joint activities. Also vital are the conditions under which these activities occur. Unpredictable, disorganized family meals involving harsh or lax parental discipline and hostile, disrespectful communication are associated with children's adjustment difficulties (Fiese, Foley, & Spagnola, 2006). As family time becomes pressured and overwhelming, its orderly structure diminishes, and warm, relaxed parent–child engagement disintegrates.

Diverse circumstances can trigger a pileup of limited parental emotional resources, breeding family chaos. In addition to *microsystem* and *mesosystem* influences (parents with mental health problems; parental separation and divorce; single parents with few or no supportive relationships), the *exosystem* is powerful: When family time is at the mercy of external forces—

parents commuting several hours a day to and from work, child-care arrangements often failing, parents experiencing excessive workplace pressures or job loss—family routines are threatened.

Family chaos contributes to children's behavior problems, above and beyond its negative impact on parenting effectiveness (Coldwell, Pike, & Dunn, 2008). Chaotic surroundings induce in children a sense of being hassled and feelings of powerlessness, which engender anxiety and low self-esteem (Fiese & Winter, 2010).

Exosystem and macrosystem supports—including work settings with favorable family policies and high-quality child care that is affordable and reliable—can help prevent escalating demands on families that give way to chaos (Repetti & Wang, 2010). In one community, a child-care center initiated a take-home dinner program. Busy parents could special-order a healthy, reasonably priced family meal, ready to go at day's end to aid in making the family dinner a routine that enhances children's development.

A chaotic home life interferes with warm, relaxed parent–child interaction, promotes anxiety and low self-esteem in children, and contributes to behavior problems. Exosystem influences, such as excessive workplace pressures, can trigger unpredictable, disorganized family routines.

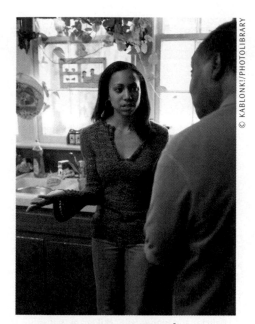

© KABLONK!/PHOTOLIBRARY

The dynamic systems perspective views the child's mind, body, and physical and social worlds as a continuously reorganizing, integrated system. In response to the physical and psychological changes of adolescence, this girl and her father must develop a new, more mature relationship.

New Directions: Development as a Dynamic System

Today, researchers recognize both consistency and variability in children's development and want to do a better job of explaining variation. Consequently, a new wave of systems theorists focuses on how children alter their behavior to attain more advanced functioning. According to this **dynamic systems perspective,** the child's mind, body, and physical and social worlds form an *integrated system* that guides mastery of new skills. The system is *dynamic,* or constantly in motion. A change in any part of it—from brain growth to physical and social surroundings—disrupts the current organism–environment relationship. When this happens, the child actively reorganizes her behavior so the components of the system work together again but in a more complex, effective way (Fischer & Bidell, 2006; Spencer & Schöner, 2003; Thelen & Smith, 2006).

Researchers adopting a dynamic systems perspective try to find out just how children attain new levels of organization by studying their behavior while they are in transition (Thelen & Corbetta, 2002). For example, when presented with an attractive toy, how does a 3-month-old baby who engages in many, varied movements discover how to reach for it? On hearing a new word, how does a 2-year-old figure out the category of objects or events to which it refers?

Dynamic systems theorists acknowledge that a common human genetic heritage and basic regularities in children's physical and social worlds yield certain universal, broad outlines of development. But biological makeup, everyday tasks, and the people who support children in mastery of those tasks vary greatly, leading to wide individual differences in specific skills. Even when children master the same skills, such as walking, talking, or adding and subtracting, they often do so in unique ways. And because children build competencies by engaging in real activities in real contexts, different skills vary in maturity within the same child. From this perspective, development cannot be characterized as a single line of change. As Figure 1.5 shows, it is more like a web of fibers branching out in many directions, each representing a different skill area that may undergo both continuous and stagewise transformations (Fischer & Bidell, 2006).

The dynamic systems view has been inspired by other scientific disciplines, especially biology and physics. It also draws on information-processing and contextual theories—evolutionary developmental psychology, sociocultural theory, and ecological systems theory.

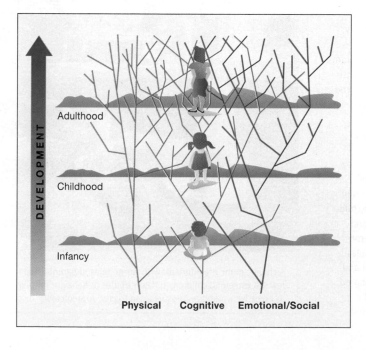

FIGURE 1.5 The dynamic systems view of development. Rather than envisioning a single line of stagewise or continuous change (refer to Figure 1.2 on page 7), dynamic systems theorists conceive of development as a web of fibers branching out in many directions. Each strand in the web represents a skill within the major domains of development—physical, cognitive, and emotional/social. The differing directions of the strands signify possible variations in paths and outcomes as the child masters skills necessary to participate in diverse contexts. The interconnections of the strands at each row of "hills" portray stagelike changes—periods of major transformation in which various skills work together as a functioning whole. As the web expands, skills become more numerous, complex, and effective. (Adapted from Fischer & Bidell, 2006.)

Dynamic systems research is still in its early stages. The perspective has largely been applied to children's motor and cognitive skills, but some investigators have drawn on it to explain emotional and social development as well (Campos, Frankel, & Camras, 2004; Fogel & Garvey, 2007; Lewis, 2000). Consider the young teenager, whose body and reasoning powers are changing massively and who also is confronting the challenges of secondary school. Researchers following parent–child interaction over time found that the transition to adolescence disrupted family communication. It became unstable and variable for several years—a mix of positive, neutral, and negative exchanges (Granic et al., 2003). Gradually, as parent and adolescent devised new, more mature ways of relating to one another, the system reorganized and stabilized. Once again, interaction became predictable and mostly positive.

As dynamic systems research illustrates, today investigators are tracking and analyzing development in all its complexity. In doing so, they hope to move closer to an all-encompassing approach to understanding change.

A S K   Y O U R S E L F

Review ■ Explain how each recent theoretical perspective regards children as active contributors to their own development.

Connect ■ Return to the Biology and Environment box on pages 10–11. How does the story of John and Gary illustrate bidirectional influences within the microsystem, as described in ecological systems theory?

Apply ■ Mario wants to find out precisely how children of different ages recall stories. Anna is interested in how adult–child communication in different cultures influences children's story-telling. Which theoretical perspective has Mario probably chosen? How about Anna? Explain.

Reflect ■ To illustrate the chronosystem in ecological systems theory, select an important event from your childhood, such as a move to a new neighborhood, a class with an inspiring teacher, or parental divorce. How did the event affect you? How might its impact have differed had you been five years younger? How about five years older?

Comparing Child Development Theories

▶ Identify the stand taken by each major theory on the basic issues of child development.

In the preceding sections, we reviewed major theoretical perspectives in child development research. They differ in many respects. First, they focus on different domains of development. Some, such as the psychoanalytic perspective and ethology, emphasize emotional and social development. Others, such as Piaget's cognitive-developmental theory, information processing, and Vygotsky's sociocultural theory, stress changes in thinking. The remaining approaches—behaviorism, social learning theory, evolutionary developmental psychology, ecological systems theory, and the dynamic systems perspective—discuss many aspects of children's functioning. Second, every theory contains a point of view about child development. **TAKE A MOMENT...** As we conclude our review of theoretical perspectives, identify the stand each theory takes on the controversial issues presented at the beginning of this chapter. Then check your analysis against Table 1.3 on page 32.

Finally, we have seen that every theory has strengths and limitations. Perhaps you find that you are attracted to some theories but have doubts about others. As you read more about child development in later chapters, you may find it useful to keep a notebook in which you test your theoretical likes and dislikes against the evidence. Don't be surprised if you revise your ideas many times, just as theorists have done since the beginning of systematic child study. By the end of this course, you will have built your own personal perspective on child development. Very likely, it will be an *eclectic position*, or blend of several theories, because every viewpoint we have considered has contributed to what we know about children.

TABLE 1.3 | **Stances of Major Theories on Basic Issues in Child Development**

THEORY	CONTINUOUS OR DISCONTINUOUS DEVELOPMENT?	ONE COURSE OF DEVELOPMENT OR MANY?	RELATIVE INFLUENCE OF NATURE AND NURTURE?
Psychoanalytic perspective	*Discontinuous:* Psychosexual and psychosocial development takes place in stages.	*One course:* Stages are assumed to be universal.	*Both nature and nurture:* Innate impulses are channeled and controlled through child-rearing experiences. *Early experiences* set the course of later development.
Behaviorism and social learning theory	*Continuous:* Development involves an increase in learned behaviors.	*Many possible courses:* Behaviors reinforced and modeled may vary from child to child.	*Emphasis on nurture:* Development results from conditioning and modeling. *Both early and later experiences* are important.
Piaget's cognitive-developmental theory	*Discontinuous:* Cognitive development takes place in stages.	*One course:* Stages are assumed to be universal.	*Both nature and nurture:* Development occurs as the brain grows and children exercise their innate drive to discover reality in a generally stimulating environment. *Both early and later experiences are important.*
Information processing	*Continuous:* Children gradually improve in perception, attention, memory, and problem-solving skills.	*One course:* Changes studied characterize most or all children.	*Both nature and nurture:* Children are active, sense-making beings who modify their thinking as the brain grows and they confront new environmental demands. *Both early and later experiences* are important.
Ethology and evolutionary developmental psychology	*Both continuous and discontinuous:* Children gradually develop a wider range of adaptive behaviors. Sensitive periods occur, in which qualitatively distinct capacities emerge fairly suddenly.	*One course:* Adaptive behaviors and sensitive periods apply to all members of a species.	*Both nature and nurture:* Evolution and heredity influence behavior, and learning lends greater flexibility and adaptiveness to it. In sensitive periods, *early experiences* set the course of later development.
Vygotsky's sociocultural theory	*Both continuous and discontinuous:* Language acquisition and schooling lead to stagewise changes. Dialogues with more expert members of society also lead to continuous changes that vary from culture to culture.	*Many possible courses:* Socially mediated changes in thought and behavior vary from culture to culture.	*Both nature and nurture:* Heredity, brain growth, and dialogues with more expert members of society jointly contribute to development. *Both early and later experiences* are important.
Ecological systems theory	*Not specified.*	*Many possible courses:* Children's characteristics join with environmental forces at multiple levels to mold development in unique ways.	*Both nature and nurture:* Children's characteristics and the reactions of others affect each other in a bidirectional fashion. Layers of the environment influence child-rearing experiences. *Both early and later experiences* are important.
Dynamic systems perspective	*Both continuous and discontinuous:* Change in the system is always ongoing. Stagelike transformations occur as children reorganize their behavior so components of the system work as a functioning whole.	*Many possible courses:* Biological makeup, everyday tasks, and social experiences vary, yielding wide individual differences in specific skills.	*Both nature and nurture:* The child's mind, body, and physical and social surroundings form an integrated system that guides mastery of new skills. *Both early and later experiences* are important.

▶ Explain the importance of social policies for safeguarding children's well-being, and cite factors that affect the policy-making process, noting the role of child development research.

Applied Directions: Child Development and Social Policy

In recent years, the field of child development has become increasingly concerned with applying its vast knowledge base to solving pressing social problems. Today, we know much more than ever before about family, school, and community contexts that foster physically healthy and cognitively and socially competent children. Yet a nation's values, policies, and programs powerfully affect children's experiences in these immediate contexts.

Social policy is any planned set of actions by a group, institution, or governing body directed at attaining a social goal. When widespread social problems arise, nations attempt to solve them through a special type of social policy called **public policy**—laws and government programs designed to improve current conditions. Return to Bronfenbrenner's ecological systems theory, and note how the concept of the macrosystem suggests that sound public policies are essential for protecting children's well-being. For example, when poverty increases and families become homeless, a country might decide to build more low-cost housing, provide economic aid to homeowners having difficulty making mortgage payments, raise the minimum wage, and increase welfare benefits. When reports indicate that many children are not achieving well in school, federal and state governments might grant more tax money to school districts, strengthen teacher preparation, and make sure that help reaches children who need it most at the earliest possible age.

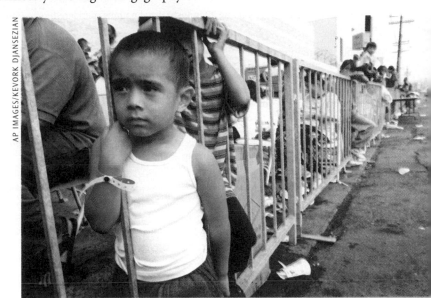

In Los Angeles, a 4-yr-old waits to receive a "back-to-school" giveaway of clothing, shoes, and school supplies. Stricken by poverty at such a young age, this boy faces a high risk of lifelong health, cognitive, and social problems.

U.S. public policies safeguarding children and youths have lagged behind policies in other developed nations. A striking indicator is that the United States outranks nearly all other economically advanced countries in child poverty (UNICEF, 2007, 2010b). Nearly 21 percent of U.S. children are poor—a rate that climbs to 33 percent for Hispanic children, 34 percent for Native-American children, and 36 percent for African-American children. Families hit hardest are parents under age 25 with young children. For single mothers with infants and preschoolers, the poverty rate in the United States is nearly 50 percent (DeNavas-Walt, Proctor, & Smith, 2009; U.S. Census Bureau, 2011b). These dire statistics are expected to worsen, due to the recent economic recession (Foundation for Child Development, 2010). Historically, a lag of several years typically occurs between the onset of a recession and its worst impact on children.

Furthermore, of all Western nations, the United States has the highest percentage of extremely poor children. Nearly 8 percent of U.S. children live in deep poverty (at less than half the poverty threshold, the income level judged necessary for a minimum living standard). In contrast, in Denmark, Finland, Norway, and Sweden, child poverty rates have remained at 5 percent or less for several decades, and deep child poverty is rare (UNICEF, 2007, 2010b). The earlier poverty begins, the deeper it is, and the longer it lasts, the more devastating are its effects. Children of poverty are more likely than other children to suffer from lifelong poor physical health, persistent deficits in cognitive development and academic achievement, high school dropout, early pregnancy, mental illness, and antisocial behavior (Aber, Jones, & Raver, 2007; Dearing, McCartney, & Taylor, 2006; Morgan et al., 2009; Ryan, Fauth, & Brooks-Gunn, 2006).

As Table 1.4 on page 34 reveals, the United States does not rank well on any key measure of children's health and well-being. And in an international assessment of children's overall well-being, in which each economically advanced country's combined material, health, and educational performance was compared with the average of 24 nations as a whole, the United States ranked at the bottom (see Figure 1.6 on page 34) (UNICEF, 2010b).

The problems of U.S. children and youths extend beyond the indicators in Table 1.4. Despite improved health-care provisions signed into law in 2010, the United States remains the only industrialized nation without a universal, publicly funded health-care system. Approximately 10 percent of U.S. children—most in low-income families—have no health insurance (Kenney, Lynch, & Cook, 2010). Furthermore, the United States has been slow to move toward national standards and funding for child care. Affordable child care is in short supply, and much of it is substandard in quality (Lamb & Ahnert, 2006; Muenchow & Marsland, 2007). In families affected by divorce, weak enforcement of child support payments heightens poverty in mother-headed households. When non-college-bound young

TABLE 1.4 | **How Does the United States Compare to Other Nations on Indicators of Children's Health and Well-Being?**

INDICATOR	U.S. RANK[a]	SOME COUNTRIES THE UNITED STATES TRAILS
Childhood poverty (among 24 industrialized nations considered)	24th	Canada, Czech Republic, Germany, United Kingdom, Norway, Sweden, Poland, Spain[b]
Infant deaths in the first year of life (worldwide)	28th	Canada, Hong Kong, Ireland, Singapore, Spain
Teenage pregnancy rate (among 28 industrialized nations considered)	28th	Australia, Canada, Czech Republic, Denmark, Hungary, Iceland, Poland, Slovakia
Public expenditure on education as a percentage of gross domestic product[c] (among 22 industrialized nations considered)	12th	Belgium, France, Iceland, New Zealand, Portugal, Spain, Sweden
Public expenditure on early childhood education and child care as a percentage of gross domestic product (among 14 industrialized nations considered)	9th	Austria, Germany, Italy, Netherlands, France, Sweden
Public expenditure on health as a percentage of total health expenditure, public plus private (among 27 industrialized nations considered)	26th	Austria, Australia, Canada, France, Hungary, Iceland, Switzerland, New Zealand

[a]1 = highest, or best, rank.

[b]U.S. childhood poverty and, especially, deep poverty rates greatly exceed poverty in these nations. For example, the poverty rate is 12 percent in United Kingdom, 9.5 percent in Canada, 6 percent in the Czech Republic, 4 percent in Norway, and 2.5 percent in Sweden. Deep poverty affects just 2.5 percent of children in Canada, and a fraction of 1 percent in the other countries just listed.

[c]Gross domestic product is the value of all goods and services produced by a nation during a specified time period. It provides an overall measure of a nation's wealth.

Sources: Canada Campaign 2000, 2009; OECD, 2010a, 2010b; U.S. Census Bureau, 2011b; U.S. Department of Education, 2011b.

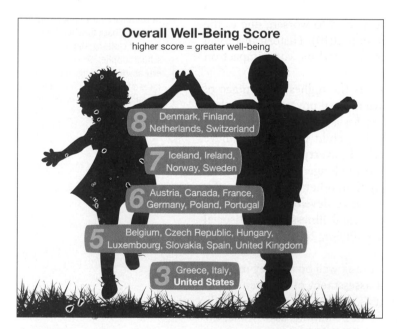

FIGURE 1.6 Children's overall well-being in 24 economically advanced nations. Researchers determined the percentage of children in each country who fell below the average for all nations combined on three dimensions of inequality: (1) *material well-being* (prevalence of deep poverty; living space and educational resources in the home); (2) *educational well-being* (high school students' literacy, math, and science achievement); and (3) *health well-being* (adolescents' self-reported healthy eating, physical activity, and health complaints). Then, for each dimension, 3 points were assigned for a better-than-average performance, 2 points for a close-to-average performance, and 1 point for a below-average performance. Thus, the highest score a country could attain was 9, the lowest score 3. (Adapted from UNICEF, 2010, *The Children Left Behind: A League Table of Inequality in the World's Richest Countries, Innocenti Report Card 9,* p. 2, Florence, Italy: Innocenti Research Centre.)

people finish high school, many lack the vocational preparation they need to contribute fully to society. And 8 percent of 16- to 24-year-olds who dropped out of high school have not returned to earn a diploma (U.S. Department of Education, 2011b).

Why have attempts to help children and youths been so difficult to realize in the United States? A complex set of cultural, political, and economic forces is involved.

Culture and Public Policies

TAKE A MOMENT... Consider the question, Who should be responsible for rearing young children? How would you answer it? Here are some typical responses from my students: "If parents decide to have a baby, then they should be ready to care for it." "Most people are not happy about others intruding into family life." "If parents work hard, then they won't need government assistance." These statements reflect a widely held opinion in the United States—that the care and rearing of young children, and paying for that care, are the duty of parents, and only parents. This view has a long history—one in which independence, self-reliance, and the privacy of family life emerged as central American values (Halfon & McLearn, 2002). It is one reason, among others, that the public has been slow to endorse government-supported benefits for all families, such as high-quality child care and paid employment leave for meeting family needs. And it has also contributed to the large number of U.S. children who remain poor, even though their parent or parents are gainfully employed (Gruendel & Aber, 2007; Pohl, 2002; UNICEF, 2007, 2010).

Consider our discussion so far, and you will see that it reflects cultural variation in values that strongly influence public policies: the extent to which *individualism* versus *collectivism* prevails. In **individualistic societies,** people think of themselves as separate entities and are largely concerned with their own personal needs. In **collectivist societies,** people define themselves as part of a group and stress group goals over individual goals (Triandis, 1995, 2005). As these definitions suggest, the two cultural patterns are associated with two distinct views of the self. Individualistic societies value an *independent self,* which emphasizes personal achievement and individual choice. In contrast, collectivist societies value an *interdependent self,* which stresses social harmony, obligations to others, and collaboration. Both independence and interdependence are part of the makeup of every person and occur in varying mixtures (Greenfield et al., 2003; Tamis-LeMonda et al., 2008). But societies vary greatly in the extent to which they emphasize each alternative and—as later chapters will reveal—instill it in their young.

Although individualism tends to increase as cultures become more complex, cross-national differences remain. The United States is strongly individualistic, whereas most Western European countries lean toward collectivism.

Furthermore, less consensus exists among American than among European citizens on issues of child and family policy, resulting in fewer and more limited programs—ones that target the most economically disadvantaged while leaving many needy children unserved (Ripple & Zigler, 2003). And good social programs are expensive; they must compete for a fair share of a country's economic resources. Children can easily remain unrecognized because they cannot vote or speak out to protect their own interests. Instead, they must rely on the goodwill of others to make them an important government priority.

Without vigilance from child advocates, policies directed at solving a particular social problem can work at cross-purposes with children's well-being, leaving them in dire straits or even worsening their condition. Consider, for example, U.S. welfare policy aimed at returning welfare recipients to the workforce. As the Social Issues: Health box on page 36 makes clear, these policies can help or harm children, depending on whether they lift a family out of poverty.

Contributions of Child Development Research

As the evidence in the Social Issues: Health box suggests, for a policy to be effective in meeting children's needs, research must guide it at every step—during design, implementation, and evaluation of the program. Events of the 1960s and 1970s initiated the current trend toward greater involvement of child development researchers in the policy process (Phillips & Styfco, 2007).

For example, in 1965, research on the importance of early experiences for children's intellectual development played a major role in the founding of Project Head Start, the largest educational and family-services intervention program for poverty-stricken preschool children in the United States. In Chapter 8, we will see that several decades of research on early rapid brain growth and plasticity and the short- and long-term benefits of early intervention helped Head Start survive and contributed to repeated increases in government support (Guerra, Graham, & Tolan, 2011). In another instance, findings on the severe impact of malnutrition on early brain development led to the establishment of the U.S. Special Supplemental Food Program for Women, Infants, and Children (WIC). Since the 1970s, WIC has supplied poverty-stricken women and their young children with food packages, nutrition education, breastfeeding support, and referral to health and social services.

At this California resource center, families learn about healthy eating and also receive food. Programs designed to ensure adequate child nutrition are partly shaped by child development research, which recognizes the impact of public policy.

© DAVID BACON/THE IMAGE WORKS

SOCIAL ISSUES: HEALTH

Welfare Reform, Poverty, and Child Development

In 1997, the United States changed its welfare policy, instituting welfare-to-work programs that ended decades of guaranteed government financial aid to needy families. In the revised system, called Temporary Aid to Needy Families (TANF), after time-limited assistance, recipients must go to work or face reduced or terminated benefits. The goal is to encourage families to become self-sufficient. A family can be on TANF for only 24 continuous months, with a lifetime limit of 60 months, and the states can further restrict these benefits. For example, a state can prevent payments from increasing if recipients have more children, and it can deny teenage single mothers any benefits.

Until recently, most evaluations of TANF focused on declines in the number of families on the welfare rolls. By these standards, welfare-to-work seemed to be a resounding success. But as researchers looked more closely, they found that some people made successful transitions to financial independence—typically, those who had more schooling and fewer mental health problems. Others, however, had difficulty meeting work requirements, lost their benefits, and fell deeper into poverty (Lower-Basch, 2010). For example, as welfare caseloads declined, the incomes of low-skilled, less educated single mothers dropped sharply (Lindsey & Martin, 2003).

Designers of welfare-to-work assumed it would be beneficial for children. But moving off welfare without increasing family income poses serious risks to child development. In one study, mothers who left welfare and also left poverty engaged in more positive parenting and had preschoolers who showed more favorable cognitive development, compared with working mothers whose incomes remained below the poverty threshold. Among these mothers, harsh, coercive parenting remained high (Smith et al., 2001). In other research, families who moved from welfare to a combination of welfare and

work experienced a greater reduction in young children's behavior problems than families who moved to total reliance on work (Dunifon, Kalil, & Danziger, 2003; Gennetian & Morris, 2003). Why was the welfare–work combination so beneficial? Most welfare recipients must take unstable jobs with erratic work hours, low wages, and minimal or no benefits. Working while retaining some welfare support probably gave mothers an added sense of economic stability. It also sustained government-provided health insurance (Medicaid), a major source of U.S. parents' worry about leaving welfare (Slack et al., 2007). The resulting reduction of financial anxiety seemed to enhance children's adjustment.

In sum, welfare reform promotes children's development only when it results in a more adequate standard of living. Punitive aspects of welfare-to-work that reduce or cut off benefits push families deeper into poverty, with destructive consequences for children's well-being. Because of a shortage of affordable child care in the United States (care for one child can consume 50 percent or more of a minimum-wage earner's income), mothers of young children are least able to earn enough by working. Yet poverty is most harmful to development when it occurs early in life (see page 33).

Welfare policies in other Western nations do not just encourage parents to be better providers. They also protect children from the damaging effects of poverty. Great Britain, for example, reduced its child poverty rate by more than half over the past decade, continuing to do so even during the recent recession. (In contrast, U.S. child poverty is now at its highest level in 20 years.)

How did Britain do so? First, it took steps "to make work pay"—by initiating a minimum wage

A young mother applies for food stamps, health coverage, and cash assistance for her 5-year-old. A restrictive, time-limited welfare-to-work program did not lead to self-sufficiency but, instead, has left her unemployed and unable to meet her child's basic needs.

sufficient to cover a family's basic needs, by reducing taxes for low-income workers, and by providing a tax credit to employed parents with limited incomes (Waldfogel, 2010, p. 4). Second, it raised the economic well-being of families with children, regardless of whether parents were employed, by guaranteeing all a modest minimum income and providing an extra amount for families with young children. Finally, it invested in children in ways that support working parents while preventing the transfer of poverty to the next generation—instituting free universal preschool for all 3- and 4-year-olds, expanding government child-care subsidies, and raising standards for child-care quality. The British success story offers important lessons. To effectively tackle poverty, U.S. policies must help poor families rear children while they move toward financial independence.

As researchers examined the impact of child and family services, they saw how settings remote from children's daily lives affect their well-being. As a result, investigators broadened their focus to include wider social contexts, such as workplace, community, mass media, and government. They also addressed the impact of societal changes on children, including high rates of poverty, divorce, family violence, teenage parenthood, maternal employment, and nonparental child care. All these efforts have helped to refine existing policies, inspire new initiatives, and expand our understanding of child development.

Over the past 50 years, the number of policy-relevant articles in *Child Development*, one of the field's leading scientific journals, has increased fivefold (Phillips & Styfco, 2007).

The field of child development now recognizes that sound public policy is among the most powerful tools for preventing developmental problems and enhancing children's quality of life.

Looking Toward the Future

Public policies aimed at fostering children's development can be justified on two grounds. The first is that children are the future—the parents, workers, and citizens of tomorrow. Investing in children yields valuable returns to a nation's economy and quality of life (Heckman & Masterov, 2004).

Second, child-oriented policies can be defended on humanitarian grounds—children's basic rights as human beings. In 1989, the U.N. General Assembly, with the assistance of experts from many child-related fields, drew up the *Convention on the Rights of the Child,* a legal agreement among nations that commits each cooperating country to work toward guaranteeing environments that foster children's development, protect them from harm, and enhance their community participation and self-determination. Examples of rights include the highest attainable standard of health; an adequate standard of living; free and compulsory education; a happy, understanding, and loving family life; protection from all forms of abuse and neglect; and freedom of thought, conscience, and religion, subject to appropriate parental guidance and national law.

Although the United States played a key role in drawing up the Convention, it is one of only two nations in the world whose legislature has not yet ratified it. (The other is war-torn Somalia, which does not have a centralized government in full control of the country.) American individualism has stood in the way. Opponents maintain that the Convention's provisions would shift the burden of child rearing from the family to the state (Melton, 2005).

Although the worrisome condition of many children and families persists, efforts are being made to improve their condition. Throughout this book, we will discuss many successful programs that could be expanded. Also, growing awareness of the gap between what we know and what we do to better children's lives has led experts in child development to join with concerned citizens as advocates for more effective policies. As a result, several influential interest groups devoted to the well-being of children have emerged.

In the United States, one of the most vigorous is the Children's Defense Fund—a nonprofit organization founded by Marian Wright Edelman in 1973—which engages in public education, legal action, drafting of legislation, congressional testimony, and community organizing. It also publishes many reports on U.S. children's condition, government-sponsored programs that serve children and families, and research-based proposals for improving those programs. To learn more about the Children's Defense Fund, visit its website at *www.childrensdefense.org.* Another energetic advocacy organization is the National Center for Children in Poverty, dedicated to advancing the economic security, health, and welfare of U.S. children in low-income families by informing policy makers of relevant research. To explore its activities, visit *www.nccp.org.*

Finally, more researchers are partnering with community and government agencies to enhance the social relevance of their investigations. They are also doing a better job of disseminating their findings in easily understandable, compelling ways, through reports to government officials, websites aimed at increasing public understanding, and collaborations with the media to ensure accurate and effective reporting in newspaper stories, magazine articles, and radio and television documentaries (Gruendel & Aber, 2007; Shonkoff & Bales, 2011). In these ways, researchers are helping to create the sense of immediacy about the condition of children and families that is necessary to spur a society into action.

First Lady Michelle Obama's "Let's Move!" campaign gives a high public profile to the issue of childhood obesity. Such advocacy efforts help create a sense of immediacy about improving conditions for children and families.

A S K   Y O U R S E L F

Review ■ Explain why both strong advocacy and policy-relevant research are vital for designing and implementing public policies that meet children's needs.

Connect ■ Give an example of how cultural values and economic decisions affect child-oriented public policies. What level of Bronfenbrenner's ecological systems theory contains these influences?

Apply ■ Check your local newspaper or one or two national news magazines to see how often articles on the condition of children and families appear. Why is it important for researchers to communicate with the general public about children's needs?

Reflect ■ Do you agree with the widespread American sentiment that government should not become involved in family life? Explain.

S U M M A R Y

The Field of Child Development (p. 4)

What is the field of child development, and what factors stimulated its expansion?

- **Child development** is an area of study devoted to understanding constancy and change from conception through adolescence. It is part of the larger, interdisciplinary field **developmental science,** which includes changes throughout the lifespan. Research on child development has been stimulated both by scientific curiosity and social pressures to better children's lives.

How is child development typically divided into domains and periods?

- Development is often divided into physical, cognitive, and emotional and social domains. These domains are not really distinct; they combine in an integrated, holistic fashion.

- Researchers generally divide child development into the following age periods: (1) the prenatal period (conception to birth), (2) infancy and toddlerhood (birth to 2 years), (3) early childhood (2 to 6 years), (4) middle childhood (6 to 11 years), and (5) adolescence (11 to 18 years). To describe the prolonged transition to adulthood typical of contemporary young people in industrialized nations, researchers have posited a new period of development, emerging adulthood, spanning ages 18 to 25 years.

Basic Issues (p. 6)

Identify three basic issues on which child development theories take a stand.

- Each **theory** of child development takes a stand on three fundamental issues: (1) Is development a **continuous** process, or is it **discontinuous,** following a series of distinct **stages?** (2) Does one general course of development characterize all children, or are there many possible courses, influenced by

the **contexts** in which children grow up? (3) Are genetic or environmental factors more important in influencing development (the **nature–nurture controversy),** and are individual differences stable or characterized by substantial **plasticity?**

- Recent theories take a balanced stand on these issues. And contemporary researchers realize that answers may vary across domains of development and even, as research on **resilience** illustrates, across individuals.

Historical Foundations (p. 10)

Describe major historical influences on theories of child development.

- As early as medieval times, the sixth through the fifteenth centuries, childhood was regarded as a separate period of life.

- In the sixteenth and seventeenth centuries, the Puritan conception of original sin led to a harsh philosophy of child rearing. The seventeenth-century Enlightenment brought a new emphasis on human dignity and respect that led to more humane views of childhood. Locke's notion of the child as a tabula rasa ("blank slate") provided the basis for twentieth-century behaviorism, while Rousseau's view of children as noble savages foreshadowed the concepts of stage and **maturation**.

- Inspired by Darwin's theory of evolution, efforts to observe children directly began in the late nineteenth and early twentieth centuries. Soon after, Hall and Gesell introduced the **normative approach,** which produced a large body of descriptive facts about children. Binet and Simon constructed the first successful intelligence test, which sparked interest in individual differences in development and led to a heated controversy over nature versus nurture.

- Baldwin's theory was ahead of its time in granting nature and nurture equal importance and regarding children and their social surroundings as mutually influential.

Mid-Twentieth-Century Theories (p. 14)

What theories influenced child development research in the mid-twentieth century?

- In the 1930s and 1940s, psychiatrists and social workers turned to the **psychoanalytic perspective** for help in treating children's emotional and behavior problems. In Freud's **psychosexual theory,** children move through five stages, during which three parts of the personality—id, ego, and superego—become integrated.

- Erikson's **psychosocial theory** builds on Freud's theory, emphasizing the development of culturally relevant attitudes and skills, and—with the addition of three adult stages—the lifespan nature of development.

© DANITA DELMONT/ALAMY

- As the psychoanalytic perspective gained in prominence, **behaviorism** emerged, focusing on directly observable events (stimuli and responses) in an effort to create an objective science of psychology. Skinner's operant conditioning theory emphasizes the role of reinforcement and punishment in increasing or decreasing the frequency of a behavior. A related approach, Alfred Bandura's **social learning theory,** focuses on modeling as the major means through which children acquire new responses. Its most recent revision, a social-cognitive approach, stresses the role of thinking in children's imitation and learning.

- Behaviorism and social learning theory gave rise to **behavior modification** procedures to eliminate undesirable behaviors and increase desirable responses.

- Piaget's **cognitive-developmental theory** emphasizes that children actively construct knowledge as they move through four stages, beginning with the baby's sensorimotor action patterns and ending with the abstract, systematic reasoning system of the adolescent and adult. Piaget's theory has stimulated a wealth of research on children's thinking and has encouraged educational programs that emphasize discovery learning.

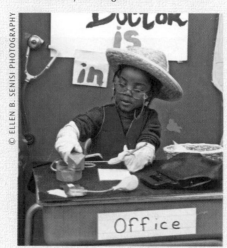

Recent Theoretical Perspectives (p. 21)

Describe recent theoretical perspectives on child development.

- **Information processing** views the mind as a complex, symbol-manipulating system, much like a computer. This approach helps investigators achieve a detailed understanding of what children of different ages do when faced with tasks and problems.

- Over the past three decades, researchers in **developmental cognitive neuroscience** have begun to study the relationship between changes in the brain and the developing child's cognitive processing and behavior patterns. They have made progress in identifying the types of experiences to which the brain is sensitive at various ages and in clarifying the brain bases of many learning and behavior disorders.

- Four contemporary perspectives emphasize contexts for development. **Ethology** stresses the adaptive value of behavior and inspired the **sensitive period** concept. In a new area of research called **evolutionary developmental psychology,** researchers have extended this emphasis, seeking to understand the adaptiveness of species-wide competencies as they change over time.

- Vygotsky's **sociocultural theory**, which views cognitive development as a socially mediated process, has enhanced our understanding of cultural variation. Through cooperative dialogues with more expert members of society, children use language to guide their own thought and actions and acquire culturally relevant knowledge and skills.

- Bronfenbrenner's **ecological systems theory** views the child as developing within a complex system of relationships affected by multiple, nested layers of the environment—**microsystem, mesosystem, exosystem,** and **macrosystem.** The **chronosystem** represents the dynamic, ever-changing nature of children and their experiences.

- A new wave of theorists has adopted a **dynamic systems perspective** to better understand how children alter their behavior to attain more advanced functioning. According to this view, the mind, body, and physical and social worlds form an integrated system that guides mastery of new skills. A change in any part of the system prompts the child to reorganize her behavior so the various components work together again, but in a more complex, effective way.

Comparing Child Development Theories (p. 31)

Identify the stand taken by each major theory on the basic issues of child development.

- Theories that are major forces in child development research vary in their focus on different domains of development, in their view of how development occurs, and in their strengths and limitations. (For a full summary, see Table 1.3 on page 32.)

Applied Directions: Child Development and Social Policy (p. 32)

Explain the importance of social policies for safeguarding children's well-being, and cite factors that affect the policy-making process, noting the role of child development research.

- The field of child development has become increasingly concerned with applying its vast knowledge base to solving pressing social problems. When widespread problems arise, nations attempt to solve them through a special type of **social policy** called **public policy**. Favorable laws and government programs are essential for safeguarding children's positive experiences in family, school, and community contexts.

- One important factor influencing public policies is the extent to which a society's values are **individualistic** (emphasizing individual well-being) or **collectivist** (emphasizing group needs and goals). Other factors are a nation's economic resources and the role of organizations and individuals that advocate for children's needs. Largely because of strongly individualistic American values, U.S. public policies favoring children and youths have lagged behind policies in other developed nations.

- Policy-relevant research helps refine existing policies, forge new policy directions, and expand our understanding of child development.

IMPORTANT TERMS AND CONCEPTS

behavior modification (p. 18)
behaviorism (p. 17)
child development (p. 4)
chronosystem (p. 28)
cognitive-developmental theory (p. 19)
collectivist society (p. 35)
contexts (p. 8)
continuous development (p. 7)
developmental cognitive neuroscience (p. 23)
developmental science (p. 4)
discontinuous development (p. 7)
dynamic systems perspective (p. 30)

ecological systems theory (p. 26)
ethology (p. 23)
evolutionary developmental psychology (p. 24)
exosystem (p. 28)
individualistic society (p. 35)
information processing (p. 21)
macrosystem (p. 28)
maturation (p. 12)
mesosystem (p. 27)
microsystem (p. 27)
nature–nurture controversy (p. 8)
normative approach (p. 13)

plasticity (p. 9)
psychoanalytic perspective (p. 15)
psychosexual theory (p. 15)
psychosocial theory (p. 15)
public policy (p. 33)
resilience (p. 10)
sensitive period (p. 24)
social learning theory (p. 18)
social policy (p. 33)
sociocultural theory (p. 25)
stage (p. 8)
theory (p. 6)

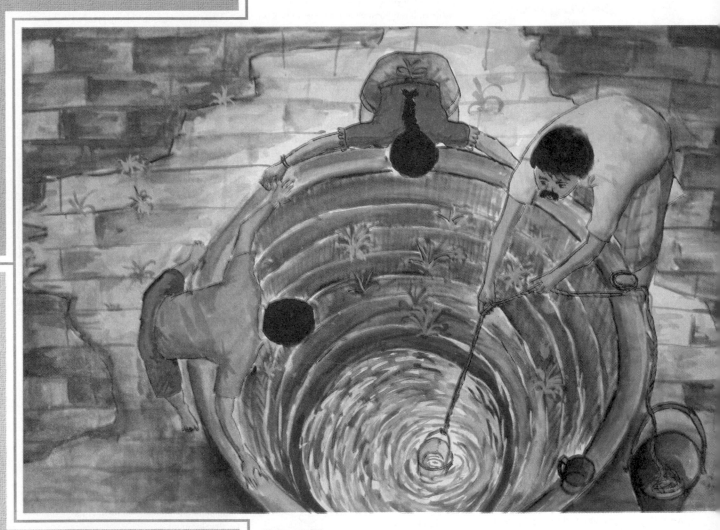

CHAPTER 2

"The Well"

Chayman Seth, 13 years, India

Two children gaze intently into a well as an adult retrieves life-sustaining water. Research strategies provide insights into how best to protect, nourish, and encourage children so they will thrive—now and in the future.

Reprinted with permission from the International Museum of Children's Art, Oslo, Norway

Research Strategies

From Theory to Hypothesis

Common Research Methods
Systematic Observation • Self-Reports: Interviews and Questionnaires • Neurobiological Methods • The Clinical, or Case Study, Method • Methods for Studying Culture

■ **BIOLOGY AND ENVIRONMENT:** *Prenatal Iron Deficiency and Memory Impairments in Infants of Diabetic Mothers: Findings of ERP Research*

■ **CULTURAL INFLUENCES:** *Immigrant Youths: Adapting to a New Land*

Reliability and Validity: Keys to Scientifically Sound Research
Reliability • Validity

General Research Designs
Correlational Design • Experimental Design • Modified Experimental Designs

■ **SOCIAL ISSUES: EDUCATION:** *Can Musical Experiences Enhance Intelligence?*

Designs for Studying Development
The Longitudinal Design • The Cross-Sectional Design • Improving Developmental Designs

Ethics in Research on Children

■ **SOCIAL ISSUES: HEALTH:** *Children's Research Risks: Developmental and Individual Differences*

A s my colleague Ron crossed the street between his academic department and our laboratory school, his face reflected apprehension. After weeks of planning, Ron was ready to launch his study on the development of children's peer relations. From his own school years, he recalled the anguish of several classmates who were taunted and shunned by peers. Ron thought his research could help rejected children, many of whom go on to lead troubled lives. So he was puzzled by a request to appear before the school's research committee.

The meeting included teachers and administrators charged with evaluating research proposals for their ethical integrity. A third-grade teacher spoke up: "Ron, I see the value of your work, but frankly, I'm concerned about your asking my students to indicate which classmates they like most and which they like least. I've got a couple of kids who are strongly disliked, and I'm doing my best to keep a lid on the situation. There's also an immigrant West Indian child who's new to my classroom, and she's being ostracized because of the way she dresses and speaks. If you come in and start sensitizing my class to whom they like and dislike, the children are going to share these opinions. Unfortunately, I think your study could promote conflict and negative interaction!"

Imagine Ron's dismay at the prospect of abandoning his research. This chapter looks at the research process—the many challenges investigators face as they plan and implement studies of children. By the time Ron arrived at the laboratory school, prepared to collect his data, he had already traveled a long and arduous path. First, he had spent many weeks developing a researchable idea, based on theory and prior knowledge of children's peer relations. Next, he had chosen an appropriate research strategy, a step that involves two main tasks: First, he selected from a variety of *research methods*—participants' specific activities, such as taking tests, answering questionnaires, responding to interviews, or being observed. Second, he decided on a *research design*—an overall plan for his study that would permit the best test of his research idea. Finally, Ron had scrutinized his procedures for any possible harm they might cause to participants.

Still, as Ron approached a committee charged with protecting the welfare of research participants, he faced an ethical dilemma. Research, whether on animals or humans, must meet certain standards that protect participants from stressful treatment. Because of children's immaturity and vulnerability, extra precautions must be taken to ensure that their rights are not violated. In the final section of this chapter, you will learn how Ron resolved the committee's challenge to the ethical integrity of his research. ■

From Theory to Hypothesis

In Chapter 1, we saw how theories structure the research process by identifying important research concerns and, occasionally, preferred methods for collecting data. We also discussed how theories guide the application of findings to real-life circumstances and practices with children. In fact, research usually begins with a prediction drawn from a theory, called a **hypothesis.** Think back to the various child development

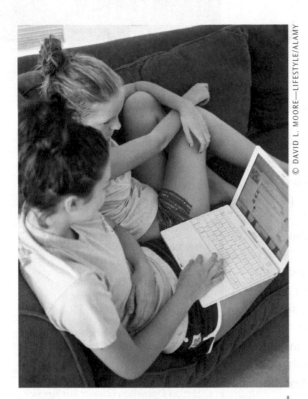

What factors influence teenagers' use of online social networking? Researchers interested in this topic may start with a research question, or they may form a hypothesis, or prediction, to test.

▶ Describe the role of theories, hypotheses, and research questions in the research process.

theories presented in Chapter 1. Many hypotheses can be drawn from any one of them that, once tested, would reflect on the accuracy of the theory.

Sometimes research pits a hypothesis taken from one theory against a hypothesis taken from another. For example, a theorist who emphasizes the role of maturation in development would predict that adult encouragement will have little effect on the age at which children utter their first words, learn to count, or tie their shoes. A sociocultural theorist, in contrast, would speculate that these skills can be promoted through adult teaching.

At other times, research tests predictions drawn from a single theory. For example, ecological systems theory suggests that providing isolated, divorced mothers with social supports will lead them to be more patient with their children. An ethologist might hypothesize that an infant's cry will stimulate strong physiological arousal in adults who hear it, motivating them to soothe and protect a suffering baby.

Occasionally, little or no theory exists on a topic of interest. In these instances, the investigator may start with a *research question,* such as, Have recent world events—for example, the U.S wars in Iraq and Afghanistan and a global rise in terrorism—heightened children's fears and anxieties? Which teenagers are the heaviest users of Internet communication—text messaging, social networking sites such as MySpace and Facebook, and chat rooms? What functions does Internet communication serve in the lives of teenagers? Hypotheses and research questions offer investigators vital guidance as they settle on research methods and research designs.

At this point, you may be wondering, Why learn about research strategies? Why not leave these matters to research specialists and concentrate on what we already know about children and how this knowledge can be applied? There are two reasons. First, each of us must be a wise and critical consumer of knowledge. Knowing the strengths and limitations of various research strategies is important in separating dependable information from misleading results. Second, individuals who work directly with children may be in a unique position to build bridges between research and practice by conducting studies, either on their own or in partnership with experienced investigators. Community agencies such as schools, mental health facilities, and parks and recreation programs are increasingly collaborating with researchers in identifying key research issues and designing, implementing, and evaluating interventions aimed at enhancing children's development (Guerra, Graham, & Tolan, 2011). To broaden these efforts, an understanding of the research process is essential.

▶ Describe research methods commonly used to study children, noting strengths and limitations of each.

Common Research Methods

How does a researcher choose a basic approach to gathering information about children? Common methods include systematic observation, self-reports (such as questionnaires and interviews), clinical or case studies of a single child, and ethnographies of the life circumstances of a specific group of children. Table 2.1 summarizes the strengths and limitations of each of these methods.

Systematic Observation

Observations of the behavior of children, and of adults who are important in their lives, can be made in different ways. One approach is to go into the field, or natural environment, and record the behavior of interest—a method called **naturalistic observation.**

TABLE 2.1 | **Strengths and Limitations of Common Information-Gathering Methods**

METHOD	DESCRIPTION	STRENGTHS	LIMITATIONS
Systematic Observation			
Naturalistic observation	Observation of behavior in natural contexts	Reflects participants' everyday behaviors.	Cannot control conditions under which participants are observed. Accuracy of observations may be reduced by observer influence and observer bias.
Structured observation	Observation of behavior in a laboratory, where conditions are the same for all participants	Grants each participant an equal opportunity to display the behavior of interest. Permits study of behaviors rarely seen in everyday life.	May not yield observations typical of participants' behavior in everyday life. Accuracy of observations may be reduced by observer influence and observer bias.
Self-Reports			
Clinical interview	Flexible interviewing procedure in which the investigator obtains a complete account of the participant's thoughts	Comes as close as possible to the way participants think in everyday life. Great breadth and depth of information can be obtained in a short time.	May not result in accurate reporting of information. Flexible procedure makes comparing individuals' responses difficult.
Structured interview, questionnaires, and tests	Self-report instruments in which each participant is asked the same questions in the same way	Permits comparisons of participants' responses and efficient data collection. Researchers can specify answer alternatives that participants might not think of in an open-ended interview.	Does not yield the same depth of information as a clinical interview. Responses are still subject to inaccurate reporting.
Neurobiological Methods	Methods that measure the relationship between nervous system processes and behavior	Reveals which central nervous system structures contribute to development and individual differences in certain competencies. Helps researchers infer the perceptions, thoughts, and emotions of infants and young children, who cannot report them clearly.	Cannot reveal with certainty the meaning of autonomic or brain activity. Many factors besides those of interest to the researcher can influence a physiological response.
Clinical, or Case Study, Method	A full picture of one individual's psychological functioning, obtained by combining interviews, observations, test scores, and sometimes neurobiological assessments	Provides rich, descriptive insights into the many factors affecting development.	May be biased by researchers' theoretical preferences. Findings cannot be applied to individuals other than the participant.
Ethnography	Participant observation of a culture or distinct social group. By making extensive field notes, the researcher tries to capture the culture's unique values and social processes.	Provides a more complete description than can be derived from a single observational visit, interview, or questionnaire.	May be biased by researchers' values and theoretical preferences. Findings cannot be applied to individuals and settings other than the ones studied.

A study of preschoolers' responses to their peers' distress provides a good example of this technique (Farver & Branstetter, 1994). Observing 3- and 4-year-olds in child-care centers, the researchers recorded each instance of crying and the reactions of nearby children—whether they ignored, watched, or commented on the child's unhappiness; scolded or teased; or shared, helped, or expressed sympathy. Caregiver behaviors—explaining why a child was crying, mediating conflict, or offering comfort—were noted to see if adult sensitivity was related to children's caring responses. A strong relationship emerged. The great strength of naturalistic observation is that investigators can see directly the everyday behaviors they hope to explain.

Naturalistic observation also has a major limitation: Not all children have the same opportunity to display a particular behavior in everyday life. In the study just mentioned,

In naturalistic observation, the researcher goes into the field and records the behavior of interest. This researcher, who is observing children at a summer camp, may be noting their playmate choices, cooperation, helpfulness, or conflicts.

some children might have witnessed a child crying more often than others or been exposed to more cues for positive social responses from caregivers. For this reason, they might have displayed more compassion.

Researchers commonly deal with this difficulty by making **structured observations,** in which the investigator sets up a laboratory situation that evokes the behavior of interest so that every participant has an equal opportunity to display the response. In one study, 2-year-olds' emotional reactions to harm that they thought they had caused were observed by asking them to take care of a rag doll that had been modified so its leg would fall off when the child picked it up. To make the child feel at fault, once the leg detached, an adult, "talking for" the doll, said, "Ow!" Researchers recorded children's facial expressions of sadness and concern for the injured doll, efforts to help the doll, and body tension—responses that indicated remorse and a desire to make amends. In addition, mothers were asked to engage in brief conversations about emotions with their children (Garner, 2003). Toddlers whose mothers more often explained the causes and consequences of emotion were more likely to express concern for the injured doll.

Structured observation permits greater control over the research situation than does naturalistic observation. In addition, the method is especially useful for studying behaviors—such as parent–child or friendship interactions—that investigators rarely have an opportunity to see in everyday life. When aggressive and nonaggressive 10-year-old boys were observed playing games with their best friend in a laboratory, the aggressive boys and their friends more often violated game rules, cheated, and encouraged each other to engage in these dishonest acts. In addition, observers rated these boys' interactions as angrier and less cooperative than the interactions of nonaggressive boys and their friends (Bagwell & Coie, 2004). The researchers concluded that rather than being warm and supportive, aggressive boys' close peer ties provide a context in which they practice hostility and other negative acts, which may contribute to their antisocial behavior.

In this study, antisocial boys' laboratory interactions were probably similar to their natural behaviors. The boys acted negatively even though they knew they were being observed. But the great disadvantage of structured observations is that most of the time, we cannot be certain that participants behave in the laboratory as they do in their natural environments.

Collecting Systematic Observations The procedures used to collect systematic observations vary, depending on the research problem posed. Some investigators choose to describe the entire behavior stream—everything said and done over a certain time period. In one study, researchers wanted to find out whether maternal sensitivity in infancy and early childhood contributes to readiness for formal schooling at ages 5 to 6 years (Hirsh-Pasek & Burchinal, 2006). Between age 6 months and 4½ years, the investigators periodically videotaped 15-minute mother–child play sessions. Then they rated each session for maternal positive emotion, support, stimulating play, and respect for the child's autonomy—ingredients of sensitivity that did predict better language and academic progress when the children reached kindergarten.

When researchers need information on only one or a few kinds of behavior, they can use more efficient procedures. In one approach, **event sampling,** the observer records all instances of a particular behavior during a specified time period. In the study of preschoolers' responses to their peers' distress reported earlier, the researchers used event sampling by recording each instance in which a child cried, followed by other children's reactions.

Another way to observe efficiently is **time sampling.** In this procedure, the researcher records whether certain behaviors occur during a sample of short intervals. First, a checklist of the target behaviors is prepared. Then the observation period is divided into a series of brief time segments. For example, a half-hour observation period might be divided into 120 fifteen-second intervals. The observer watches the target person and checks off behaviors during each interval, repeating this process until the observation period is complete. Recently, my collaborators and I used time sampling to find out how parents and children spent time while visiting a community children's museum. Our observers followed more than one hundred parent–child pairs for 10 minutes each, checking off parent and child behaviors during 20 thirty-second intervals. Findings revealed that, on average, parents and children were jointly engaged in the museum's exhibits during 45 percent of the intervals. During an additional 30 percent, parents remained nearby, closely observing their children's activities (Mann, Braswell, & Berk, 2005). Clearly, the museum afforded parents many opportunities to interact with and learn about their children.

Researchers have devised ingenious ways of observing children's difficult-to-capture behaviors. For example, to record instances of bullying, a group of investigators set up video cameras overlooking a classroom and a playground and had fourth to sixth graders wear small remote microphones and pocket-sized transmitters (Craig, Pepler, & Atlas, 2000). Results revealed that bullying occurred often—at rates of 2.4 episodes per hour in the classroom and 4.5 episodes per hour on the playground. Yet only 15 to 18 percent of the time did teachers take steps to stop the harassment. We will return to the topic of bullying in Chapter 15.

Limitations of Systematic Observation

A major problem with systematic observation is **observer influence**—the effects of the observer on the behavior studied. The presence of a watchful, unfamiliar individual may cause both children and adults to react in unnatural ways. For children under age 7 or 8, observer influence is generally limited to the first session or two. Young children cannot stop "being themselves" for long, and they quickly get used to the observer's presence. But older children and adults often engage in more socially desirable behavior when they know that they are being observed. In these instances, researchers can take participants' responses as an indication of the best behavior they can display under the circumstances.

To minimize observer influence, an adaptation period, in which observers visit the research setting so participants can get used to their presence, can be helpful. Another approach is to ask individuals who are part of the child's natural environment to do the observing. For example, in some studies, parents have been trained to record their children's behavior and, occasionally, their own. Besides reducing the impact of an unfamiliar observer, this method limits the amount of time needed to gather observations, as some information can take a long time to obtain.

In one such study, researchers wanted to know how 8- to 16-year-olds reacted to their parents' marital conflicts and whether children's responses affected the course of those conflicts. For a two-week period, parents recorded each conflict episode soon after it occurred, along with their own emotions, the tactics they used, their child's behavior, and whether the conflict was resolved (Schermerhorn, Chow, & Cummings, 2010). Findings revealed that children's negativity (expressing anger, sadness, or fear; misbehaving, yelling at the parents, or engaging in aggression) predicted increasing parental negativity and the likelihood that a conflict would remain unresolved. In contrast, when children acted assertively, in ways aimed at reducing conflict (helping out, comforting parents, taking sides, or trying to make peace), parents' emotions became more positive, and they more often worked out their differences.

Another serious danger in observational research is **observer bias.** When observers are aware of the purposes of a study, they may see and record what they expect to see rather than what participants actually do. Therefore, people who have no knowledge of the investigator's hypotheses—or, at least, have little personal investment in them—are best suited to collect the observations.

LOOK and LISTEN

Find a parent and young child to observe by visiting a home, a grocery store, a mall, or a public park. Choose an easily identifiable behavior, and ask the parent for permission to jot down each instance of its occurrence during a 15-minute period. What did you learn about the challenges of making systematic observations?

Finally, although systematic observation provides invaluable information on how children and adults behave, it tells us little about the reasoning behind their responses. For this kind of information, researchers must turn to self-report techniques.

Self-Reports: Interviews and Questionnaires

Self-reports ask research participants to provide information on their perceptions, thoughts, abilities, feelings, attitudes, beliefs, and past experiences. They range from relatively unstructured clinical interviews, the method used by Piaget to study children's thinking, to highly structured interviews, questionnaires, and tests.

Clinical Interviews   In a **clinical interview**, researchers use a flexible, conversational style to probe for the participant's point of view. In the following example, Piaget questioned a 3-year-old child about his understanding of dreams:

> *Where does the dream come from?*—I think you sleep so well that you dream.—*Does it come from us or from outside?*—From outside.—*When you are in bed and you dream, where is the dream?*—In my bed, under the blanket. I don't really know. If it was in my stomach, the bones would be in the way and I shouldn't see it.—*Is the dream there when you sleep?*—Yes, it is in the bed beside me. (Piaget, 1926/1930, pp. 97–98)

Although a researcher conducting clinical interviews with more than one child would typically ask the same first question to establish a common task, individualized prompts are used to provide a fuller picture of each child's reasoning (Ginsburg, 1997).

The clinical interview has two major strengths. First, it permits people to display their thoughts in terms that are as close as possible to the way they think in everyday life. Second, the clinical interview can provide a large amount of information in a fairly brief period. For example, in an hour-long session, we can obtain a wide range of child-rearing information from a parent—far more than we could capture by observing for the same amount of time.

© BILL ARON/PHOTOEDIT

The conversational style of the clinical interview allows children to express their thoughts as they do in everyday life. But unless questions are carefully designed, responses may not accurately reflect participants' views and experiences.

Limitations of Clinical Interviews   A major limitation of the clinical interview has to do with the accuracy with which people report their thoughts, feelings, and experiences. Some participants, wanting to please the interviewer, may make up answers that do not represent their actual thinking. When asked about past events, some may have trouble recalling exactly what happened. And because the clinical interview depends on verbal ability and expressiveness, it may underestimate the capacities of individuals who have difficulty putting their thoughts into words. To minimize these problems, skillful interviewers word questions carefully. They also watch for cues indicating that the participant may not have clearly understood a question or may need extra time to feel comfortable in the interview situation.

Interviews on certain topics are particularly vulnerable to distortion. In a few instances, researchers have been able to compare parents' and children's descriptions of past events with information gathered years earlier, at the time the events occurred. Reports of psychological states and family processes obtained on the two occasions showed little or no agreement (Henry et al., 1994). Parents often recall their child's development in glowing terms, reporting faster progress, fewer childhood problems, and child-rearing practices more in line with current expert advice than with records of behavior (Yarrow, Campbell, & Burton, 1970). Interviews that focus on current rather than past information and on specific characteristics rather than global judgments show a better match with observations and other sources of information. Even so, parents are far from perfect in describing their practices and their children's personalities, preferences, and cognitive abilities (Rothbart & Bates, 2006; Saudino, 2003; Waschbusch, Daleiden, & Drabman, 2000).

Finally, the clinical interview has been criticized because of its flexibility. When questions are phrased differently for each participant, variations in responses may reflect the manner of interviewing rather than real differences in the way individuals think about a topic. To reduce this problem, researchers can use a second self-report method, the structured interview.

Structured Interviews, Tests, and Questionnaires In a **structured interview,** each individual is asked the same set of questions in the same way. This approach eliminates the possibility that an interviewer might press and prompt some participants more than others. Structured interviews are also much more efficient than clinical interviews. Answers are briefer, and researchers can obtain written responses from an entire group at the same time. Furthermore, by listing answer alternatives, researchers can specify the activities and behaviors of interest—ones that participants might not think of in an open-ended clinical interview. For example, when parents were asked what they considered "the most important thing for children to prepare them for life," 62 percent checked "to think for themselves" when this alternative appeared on a list. Yet only 5 percent thought of it during a clinical interview (Schwarz, 1999).

Nevertheless, structured interviews can still be affected by inaccurate reporting. And they do not yield the same depth of information as a clinical interview. Currently, more researchers are combining the two approaches to see if they yield consistent findings and a clearer picture than either method can alone (Yoshikawa et al., 2008). In a study of adolescent mothers, questionnaire responses revealed that those reporting the least emotional support from their own mothers at the time of the baby's birth managed to attain higher levels of education six years later (Way & Leadbeater, 1999). Clinical interviews with the teenagers helped explain this puzzling finding: Low maternal emotional support was partly due to anger and disappointment over the early birth, more likely to be expressed by mothers who also held high educational aspirations for their daughters.

Neurobiological Methods

Researchers' desire to uncover the biological bases of perceptual, cognitive, and emotional responses has led to the use of **neurobiological methods,** which measure the relationship between nervous system processes and behavior. Investigators use these methods to find out which nervous system structures contribute to development and individual differences. Neurobiological methods also help researchers infer the perceptions, thoughts, and emotions of infants and young children, who cannot report their psychological experiences clearly.

Involuntary activities of the autonomic nervous system[1]—changes in heart rate, blood pressure, respiration, pupil dilation, electrical conductance of the skin, and stress hormone levels—are highly sensitive to psychological state. For example, heart rate can be used to infer whether an infant is staring blankly at a stimulus (heart rate is stable), processing information (heart rate slows during concentration), or experiencing distress (heart rate rises). Heart rate variations are also linked to certain emotions, such as interest, fear, anger, and sadness (Fox & Card, 1998; Hastings, Zahn-Waxler, & Usher, 2007).

Saliva concentrations of the hormone *cortisol* provide information about children's stress reactivity. Known as the "fight or flight" hormone, cortisol increases respiration rate, blood

---

[1]The autonomic nervous system, which regulates involuntary actions, is divided into two parts: (1) the *sympathetic nervous system,* which mobilizes energy to deal with threatening situations (as when your heart rate rises in response to a fear-arousing event); and (2) the *parasympathetic nervous system,* which acts to conserve energy (as when your heart rate slows as you focus on an interesting stimulus).

pressure, and blood sugar; suppresses immune system functioning; and heightens memory for emotionally charged events so they will be avoided in the future. Chronically abnormal cortisol levels, either too high or too low—evident in children exposed to severe deprivation (such as early orphanage rearing), parental neglect, or abuse—signal a disrupted stress-response system. As we will see in later chapters, negative outcomes include impaired growth, illness, and learning and behavior problems (Loman & Gunnar, 2010; Lupien et al., 2009). And as Chapter 10 will reveal, distinct patterns of autonomic activity—indicated by heart rate, cortisol level, and other physiological measures—are related to aspects of temperament, such as shyness and sociability (Kagan & Fox, 2006).

Autonomic indicators have been enriched by diverse measures of brain functioning, described in Table 2.2. Among these methods, the two most frequently used detect changes in *electrical activity* in the cerebral cortex—the brain's outer layers, which play a central role in complex mental functions, including attention, perception, memory, language, reasoning, planning, and problem solving. In an *electroencephalogram (EEG),* researchers examine brain-wave patterns for stability and organization—signs of mature functioning of the cortex. And as a child processes a particular stimulus, *event-related potentials (ERPs)* detect the general location of brain-wave activity—a technique often used to study preverbal infants' responsiveness to various stimuli, the impact of experience on development of regions of the cerebral cortex, and atypical brain functioning in children at risk for learning and emotional problems (DeBoer, Scott, & Nelson, 2007; deRegnier, 2005). For example, different wave patterns appear when 3-month-olds from English-speaking homes hear passages in English, Italian, and Dutch, suggesting that the infants can discriminate the intonation patterns of the three languages and indicating the brain regions involved (Shafer, Shucard, & Jaeger, 1999). And as the Biology and Environment box on the following page illustrates, ERP findings are clarifying the impact of deficient prenatal nutrition on early brain development and cognitive functioning.

TABLE 2.2 | Methods for Measuring Brain Functioning

METHOD	DESCRIPTION
Electroencephalogram (EEG)	Electrodes embedded in a head cap record electrical activity in the brain's outer layers—the cerebral cortex. Today, researchers use an advanced tool called a geodesic sensor net (GSN) to hold interconnected electrodes (up to 128 for infants and 256 for children and adults) in place through a cap that adjusts to each person's head shape, yielding improved brain-wave detection (see page 49).
Event-related potentials (ERPs)	Using the EEG, the frequency and amplitude of brain waves in response to particular stimuli (such as a picture, music, or speech) are recorded in multiple areas of the cerebral cortex. Enables identification of general regions of stimulus-induced activity.
Functional magnetic resonance imaging (fMRI)	While the person lies inside a tunnel-shaped apparatus that creates a magnetic field, a scanner magnetically detects increased blood flow and oxygen metabolism in precise areas of the brain as the individual processes particular stimuli. The scanner typically records images every 1 to 4 seconds; these are combined into a computerized moving picture of activity anywhere in the brain (not just its outer layers). Not appropriate for children younger than age 5 to 6, who cannot remain still during testing. Cost of equipment and testing is much higher than that of EEG and ERPs.
Positron emission tomography (PET)	After injection or inhalation of a radioactive substance, the person lies on an apparatus with a scanner that emits fine streams of X-rays, which detect increased blood flow and oxygen metabolism in areas of the brain as the person processes particular stimuli. As with fMRI, the result is a computerized moving picture of "online" activity anywhere in the brain, but not appropriate for children younger than age 5 to 6 and high in cost.
Near-infrared spectroscopy (NIRS)	Using thin, flexible optical fibers attached to the scalp, infrared (invisible) light is beamed at the brain; its absorption by areas of the cerebral cortex varies with changes in blood flow and oxygen metabolism as the individual processes particular stimuli. The result is a computerized moving picture of active areas in the cerebral cortex. Unlike fMRI and PET, NIRS is appropriate for infants and young children, who can move within limited range.

BIOLOGY and ENVIRONMENT

Prenatal Iron Deficiency and Memory Impairments in Infants of Diabetic Mothers: Findings of ERP Research

Diabetes affects nearly 11 percent of Americans age 20 and older—a rate that has risen sharply over the past quarter century as a result of widespread overweight and obesity. Although it is increasing among all sectors of the population, diabetes is at least twice as likely to affect low-income ethnic minority as white adults. Today, about 5 percent of pregnant mothers are diabetic—a rate that has more than doubled over the past decade. Most had the disease before becoming pregnant; others developed it during pregnancy (American Diabetes Association, 2011). In either case, their newborn babies are at risk for long-term problems.

In the early weeks of pregnancy, when organs are forming, a diabetic mother's out-of-control blood glucose increases the risk of birth defects. Later in pregnancy, excess blood glucose causes the fetus to be "overfed" and to grow unusually large, often causing birth complications. Furthermore, to metabolize this flood of maternal glucose, the fetus secretes abnormally high levels of insulin—a circumstance that greatly increases demand for oxygen. To extract extra oxygen from the mother's system, the fetus increases production of oxygen-carrying red blood cells. This expanding red blood-cell mass requires extra iron, which the fetus can obtain only by taxing its own iron stores in the liver, muscles, heart, and brain.

In animal research on maternal diabetes, by late pregnancy iron stores decline sharply in the brain's temporal lobes (located on each side of the brain, just above the ears), which house structures centrally involved in memory development—specifically, the *hippocampus,* which plays a crucial role in the formation of new memories. Prenatal iron depletion interferes with growth of brain cells and their connections, permanently reducing the size and altering the structure of the hippocampus and impairing memory in laboratory rats (Jorgenson et al., 2005; Schmidt et al., 2007).

In human research, diabetic mothers bear children who, at school age, tend to score lower than their agemates on intelligence tests (Rizzo et al., 1997). Is prenatal iron deficiency and resulting early damage to the brain's memory areas responsible? In a series of studies, Charles Nelson (2007) and his collaborators used ERPs to assess young infants' memory performance,

focusing on a particular slow brain wave in the temporal lobes believed to reflect memory processing.

Typically developing newborns come to recognize their mother's voice through repeated exposure during pregnancy; they suck more on a nipple to hear a recording of it than the voice of an unfamiliar woman (DeCasper & Spence, 1988). In a comparison of newborns of diabetic mothers likely to have a brain iron deficiency (based on a measure of body iron stores) with normal-iron controls, ERPs were recorded as the babies listened to sound clips of their mother's or a stranger's voice (Sidappa et al., 2004). The controls showed a distinctive ERP slow wave to each stimulus, indicating recognition of the mother's voice. The brain iron-deficient babies showed no difference in brain waves to the two stimuli, suggesting memory impairment of prenatal origin.

Do these memory deficits persist beyond the newborn period—evidence that diabetes-linked prenatal brain damage has lasting consequences? The researchers recorded ERPs while 6-month-old infants alternately viewed a videotaped image of their mother's face and that of an unfamiliar woman. Consistent with the newborn findings, control infants responded with distinct ERP slow waves in the temporal lobes to the two faces, while infants of diabetic mothers displayed no difference. Even after months of experience, they could not recognize their mother's facial image (Nelson et al., 2000).

At an 8-month follow-up, babies were given a more challenging memory task. After feeling a novel object (an unusually shaped wooden block) held beneath an apron so they could not see it, the infants were tested visually: They viewed photos of the novel object interspersed with photos of familiar objects (Nelson et al., 2003). Again, infants of diabetic mothers showed no ERP evidence of distinguishing the novel object from other stimuli. The control babies, in contrast, responded to the novel object with a stronger temporal-lobe slow wave, suggesting a ready ability to recognize the novel stimulus, even when presented in a different sensory modality.

COURTESY OF DR. CHARLES A. NELSON, HARVARD UNIVERSITY

To study the impact of prenatal diabetes on early memory development, researchers use a geodesic sensor net, consisting of optical fibers attached to a head cap, to obtain this 8-month-old's electrical brain waves during a challenging memory task.

Nelson and his colleagues followed their research participants through the preschool years, amassing additional ERP and behavioral evidence for poorer memory (especially more rapid forgetting) in children born to diabetic mothers than in controls (Riggins et al., 2009). The ERP findings highlight a previously hidden pregnancy complication: As a result of iron depletion in critical brain areas, a diabetic pregnancy places the fetus at risk for lasting memory deficits and, thus, for long-term learning and academic problems. The researchers believe that damage to the hippocampus, located deep inside the temporal lobes, is responsible—a hypothesis they hope to pursue as new methods making possible fMRIs on babies become available.

Nelson's research underscores the need for more effective ways of intervening with iron supplementation in diabetic pregnancies, as well as the importance of sufficient dietary iron for every expectant mother and her developing fetus. Diabetes prevention is also vital, through weight control, increased exercise, and improved diet beginning in childhood—topics we take up in Chapter 5.

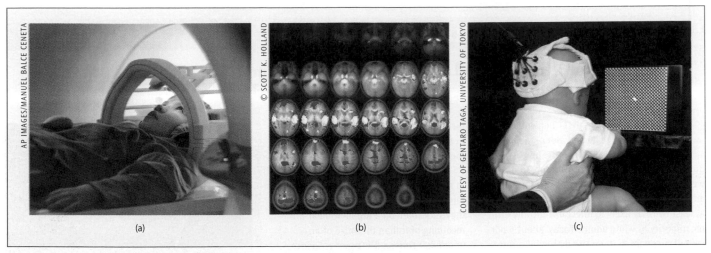

FIGURE 2.1   Functional magnetic resonance imaging (fMRI) and near infrared spectroscopy (NIRS). (a) This 6-year-old is part of a study that uses fMRI to find out how his brain processes light and motion. (b) The fMRI image shows which areas of the boy's brain are active while he views changing visual stimuli. (c) Here, NIRS is used to investigate a 2-month-old's response to a visual stimulus. During testing, the baby can move freely within a limited range. (Photo © From G. Taga, K. Asakawa, A. Maki, Y. Konishi, & H. Koisumi, 2003, "Brain Imaging in Awake Infants by Near-Infrared Optical Topography," *Proceedings of the National Academy of Sciences, 100,* p. 10723. Reprinted by permission.)

Neuroimaging techniques, which yield detailed, three-dimensional computerized pictures of the entire brain and its active areas, provide the most precise information about which brain regions are specialized for certain capacities and about abnormalities in brain functioning. In *positron emission tomography (PET),* the child must lie quietly on a scanner bed, and in *functional magnetic resonance imaging (fMRI),* inside a tunnel-like apparatus. But unlike PET, fMRI does not depend on X-ray photography, which requires injection of a radioactive substance. Rather, when a child is exposed to a stimulus, fMRI detects changes in blood flow and oxygen metabolism throughout the brain magnetically; a computer combines frequently recorded images into a colorful, moving picture of parts of the brain used to perform a given activity (see Figures 2.1a and b).

Because PET and fMRI require that the participant lie as motionless as possible for an extended time, they are not suitable for infants and young children (Nelson, Thomas, & de Haan, 2006). A neuroimaging technique that works well in infancy and early childhood is *near-infrared spectroscopy (NIRS),* in which infrared (invisible) light is beamed at regions of the cerebral cortex to measure blood flow and oxygen metabolism while the child attends to a stimulus (refer again to Table 2.2). Because the apparatus consists only of thin, flexible optical fibers attached to the scalp using a head cap, a baby can sit on the parent's lap and move during testing—as Figure 2.1c illustrates (Hespos et al., 2010). But unlike PET and fMRI, which map activity changes throughout the brain, NIRS examines only the functioning of the cerebral cortex.

Neurobiological methods are powerful tools for uncovering relationships between the brain and psychological development. But like all research methods, they have limitations. Even though a stimulus produces a consistent pattern of autonomic or brain activity, investigators cannot be certain that an individual has processed it in a certain way. And a researcher who takes a change in heart rate, respiration, or brain activity as an indicator of information processing or emotional state must make sure that the change was not due instead to hunger, boredom, fatigue, or body movements (Nicholson, 2006). Consequently, other methods—both observations and self-reports—must be combined with brain-wave and -imaging findings to clarify their meaning.

The Clinical, or Case Study, Method

An outgrowth of psychoanalytic theory, the **clinical,** or **case study, method** brings together a wide range of information on one child, including interviews, observations, test scores, and sometimes neurobiological measures. The aim is to obtain as complete a picture as possible of that child's psychological functioning and the experiences that led up to it.

The clinical method is well-suited to studying the development of certain types of individuals who are few in number but vary widely in characteristics. For example, the method has been used to find out what contributes to the accomplishments of *prodigies*—extremely gifted children who attain adult competence in a field before age 10 (Moran & Gardner, 2006). Consider Adam, a boy who read, wrote, and composed musical pieces before he was out of diapers. By age 4, Adam was deeply involved in mastering human symbol systems—French, German, Russian, Sanskrit, Greek, the computer programming language BASIC, ancient hieroglyphs, music, and mathematics. Adam's parents provided a home rich in stimulation and reared him with affection, firmness, and humor. They searched for schools in which he could both develop his abilities and form rewarding social relationships. He graduated from college at age 18 and continued to pursue musical composition. Would Adam have realized his potential without the chance combination of his special gift and nurturing, committed parents? Probably not, researchers concluded (Feldman, 2004).

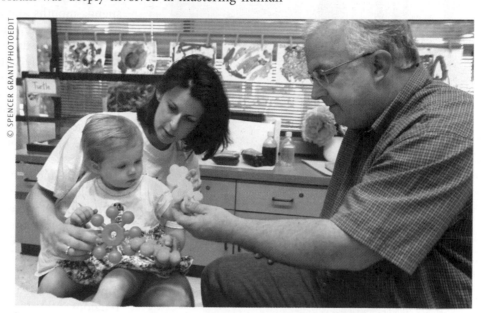

The clinical method yields richly detailed case narratives that offer valuable insights into the many factors affecting development. Nevertheless, like all other methods, it has drawbacks. Because information often is collected

Using the clinical, or case study, method, this researcher combines interviews with the mother and observations and testing of the child to construct an in-depth picture of the child's psychological functioning.

unsystematically and subjectively, researchers' theoretical preferences may bias their observations and interpretations. In addition, investigators cannot assume that their conclusions apply, or generalize, to anyone other than the child studied (Stanovich, 2007). Even when patterns emerge across several cases, it is wise to confirm them with other research strategies.

Methods for Studying Culture

To study the impact of culture, researchers adjust the methods just considered or tap procedures specially devised for cross-cultural and multicultural research (Triandis, 2007). Which approach investigators choose depends on their research goals.

Sometimes researchers are interested in characteristics that are believed to be universal but that vary in degree from one culture to the next: Are parents warmer or more directive in some cultures than in others? How strong are gender stereotypes in different nations? In each instance, several cultural groups will be compared, and all participants must be questioned or observed in the same way. Therefore, researchers draw on the observational and self-report procedures we have already considered, adapting them through translation so they can be understood in each cultural context. For example, to study cultural variation in parenting practices, the same questionnaire, asking for ratings on such items as "I often hug and kiss my child" or "I scold my child when his/her behavior does not meet my expectations," is given to all participants (Wu et al., 2002). Still, investigators must be mindful of cultural differences in familiarity with responding to self-report instruments, which may bias their findings (Van de Vijver, Hofer, & Chasiotis, 2010).

At other times, researchers want to uncover the *cultural meanings* of children's and adults' behaviors by becoming as familiar as possible with their way of life. To achieve this goal,

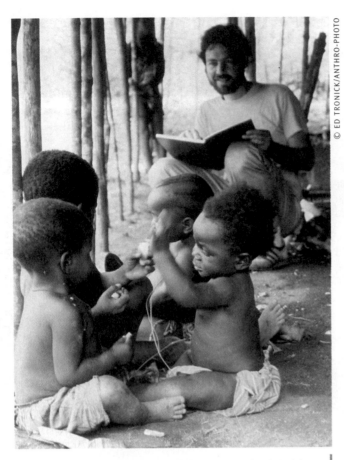

This Western ethnographer spent months living among the Efe people of the Republic of Congo. Here he observes young children sharing food. The Efe value and encourage cooperation and generosity at an early age.

investigators rely on a method borrowed from the field of anthropology—**ethnography.** Like the clinical method, ethnographic research is a descriptive, qualitative technique. But instead of aiming to understand a single individual, it is directed at understanding a culture or a distinct social group through *participant observation.* Typically, the researcher spends months and sometimes years in the cultural community, participating in its daily life. Extensive field notes are gathered, consisting of a mix of observations, self-reports from members of the culture, and careful interpretations by the investigator (Miller, Hengst, & Wang, 2003; Shweder et al., 2006). Later, these notes are put together into a description of the community that tries to capture its unique values and social processes.

The ethnographic method assumes that by entering into close contact with a social group, researchers can understand the beliefs and behaviors of its members in a way that is not possible with an observational visit, interview, or questionnaire. Some ethnographies take in many aspects of children's experience, as one researcher did in describing what it is like to grow up in a small American town. Others focus on one or a few settings, such as home, school, or neighborhood life (Higginbottom, 2006; Peshkin, 1997; Valdés, 1998). And still others are limited to a particular practice, such as uncovering cultural and religious influences on children's make-believe play. For example, ethnographic findings reveal that East Indian Hindu parents encourage preschoolers to communicate with "invisible" characters. They regard this activity as linked to *karma* (the cycle of birth and death) and believe that the child may be remembering a past life. In contrast, Christian fundamentalist parents often discourage children from pretending to be unreal characters, believing that such play promotes dangerous spiritual ideas and deceitful behavior (Taylor & Carlson, 2000). Researchers may supplement traditional self-report and observational methods with ethnography if they suspect that unique meanings underlie cultural differences, as the Cultural Influences box on the following page reveals.

Ethnographers strive to minimize their influence on the culture they are studying by becoming part of it. Nevertheless, as with clinical studies, investigators' cultural values and theoretical commitments sometimes lead them to observe selectively or misinterpret what they see. Finally, the findings of ethnographic studies cannot be assumed to generalize beyond the people and settings in which the research was conducted.

ASK YOURSELF

Review ■ Why might a researcher choose structured observation over naturalistic observation? How about the reverse? What might lead the researcher to opt for clinical interviewing over systematic observation?

Connect ■ What strengths and limitations do the clinical, or case study, method and ethnography have in common?

Apply ■ A researcher wants to study the thoughts and feelings of children who have a parent on active duty in the military. Which method should she use? Why?

CULTURAL INFLUENCES

Immigrant Youths: Adapting to a New Land

During the past quarter century, a rising tide of immigrants has come to North America, fleeing war and persecution in their homelands or seeking better life opportunities. Today, nearly one-fourth of U.S. children and adolescents have foreign-born parents, making them the fastest-growing segment of the U.S. youth population. About 20 percent of these young people are foreign-born themselves, mostly from Latin America, the Caribbean, and Asia (Hernandez, Denton, & Macartney, 2008; Suarez-Orozco, Todorova, & Qin, 2006).

How well are immigrant youths adapting to their new country? To find out, researchers use multiple research methods—academic testing, questionnaires assessing psychological adjustment, and in-depth ethnographies.

Academic Achievement and Adjustment

Although educators and laypeople often assume that the transition to a new country has a negative impact on psychological well-being, evidence reveals that many children of immigrant parents from diverse countries adapt amazingly well. Students who are first-generation (foreign-born) and second-generation (American-born, with immigrant parents) often achieve in school as well as or better than students of native-born parents (Fuligni, 2004; Hernandez, Denton, & Macartney, 2008; Saucier et al., 2002). Findings on psychological adjustment are similar. Compared with their agemates, adolescents from immigrant families are less likely to commit delinquent and violent acts, to use drugs and alcohol, or to have early sex. They are also less likely to be obese or to have missed school because of illness. And they tend to report just as high, and at times higher, self-esteem as young people with native-born parents (Fuligni, 1998; Saucier et al., 2002; Supple & Small, 2006).

These outcomes are strongest for Chinese, Filipino, Japanese, Korean, and East Indian youths (Fuligni, 2004; Louie, 2001; Portes & Rumbaut, 2005). Variation in adjustment is greater among Mexican, Central American, and Southeast Asian (Hmong, Cambodian, Laotian, Thai, and Vietnamese) young people, who show elevated rates of school failure and dropout, delinquency, teenage parenthood, and drug use. Disparities in parental economic resources, education, English-language proficiency, and support of children contribute to these trends (García Coll & Marks, 2009; Supple & Small, 2006).

Still, many first- and second-generation youths whose parents face considerable financial hardship and who speak little English are successful (Fuligni & Yoshikawa, 2003; Hernandez, Denton, & Macartney, 2008). Factors other than income are responsible—notably, family values and strong ethnic-community ties.

Family and Ethnic-Community Influences

Ethnographies reveal that immigrant parents view education as the surest way to improve life chances (García Coll & Marks, 2009; Goldenberg et al., 2001). Aware of the challenges their children face, they typically emphasize trying hard. They remind their children that, because educational opportunities were not available in their native countries, they themselves are often limited to menial jobs. And while preserving their culture's values, these parents also make certain adaptations—for example, supporting education for daughters even though their culture of origin approves of it only for sons.

Adolescents from these families internalize their parents' valuing of academic achievement, endorsing it more strongly than agemates with native-born parents (Fuligni, 2004; Su & Costigan, 2009). Because minority ethnicities usually stress allegiance to family and community over individual goals, first- and second-generation young people often feel a strong sense of obligation to their parents. They view school success as an important way of repaying their parents for the hardships they have endured (Bacallao & Smokowski, 2007; Fuligni, Yip, & Tseng, 2002). Both family relationships and school achievement protect these youths from risky behaviors (see the Biology and Environment box on resilient children on pages 10–11 in Chapter 1).

Immigrant parents of successful youths typically develop close ties to an ethnic community, which exerts additional control through a high consensus on values and constant monitoring of young people's activities. The following comments capture the power of these family and community forces:

- *Elizabeth, age 16, from Vietnam, straight-A student, like her two older sisters:* My parents

These Hmong boys perform in an ethnic festival in St. Paul, Minnesota, where many Hmong immigrants have settled. Cultural values that engender allegiance to family and community promote high achievement and protect many immigrant youths from involvement in risky behaviors.

know pretty much all the kids in the neighborhood. Everybody here knows everybody else. It's hard to get away with much. (Zhou & Bankston, 1998, pp. 93, 130)

- *Juan, teenager from Mexico:* A really big part of the Hispanic population [is] being close to family, and the family being a priority all the time. I hate people who say, "Why do you want to go to a party where your family's at? Don't you want to get away from them?" You know, I don't really get tired of them. I've always been really close to them. That connection to my parents, that trust that you can talk to them, that makes me Mexican. (Bacallao & Smokowski, 2007, p. 62)

The experiences of well-adjusted immigrant youths are not problem-free. Chinese adolescents who had arrived in the United States within the previous year described their adjustment as very difficult because they were not proficient in English and, as a result, found many everyday tasks challenging and felt socially isolated (Yeh et al., 2008). Young immigrants also encounter racial and ethnic prejudices and experience tensions between family values and the new culture—challenges we will take up in Chapter 11. In the long term, however, family and community cohesion, supervision, and high expectations promote favorable outcomes.

> ▶ Explain how reliability and validity apply to research methods and to the overall accuracy of research findings and conclusions.

Reliability and Validity: Keys to Scientifically Sound Research

Once investigators choose their research methods, they must ensure that their procedures provide trustworthy information. To be acceptable to the scientific community, self-reports, observations, and physiological measures must be both *reliable* and *valid*—two keys to scientifically sound research.

Reliability

Suppose you and a research partner go into an elementary school classroom and record how attentive and cooperative each child is. But although you are simultaneously rating the same children, you and your partner come up with very different judgments. Or perhaps you question a group of children about their interests, but a week later, when you ask them again, they give you very different answers. **Reliability** refers to the consistency, or repeatability, of measures of behavior. To be reliable, observations and evaluations of peoples' actions cannot be unique to a single observer. Instead, observers must agree on what they see. And an interview, test, or questionnaire, when given again within a short time (before participants could reasonably be expected to change their opinions or develop new responses), must yield similar results on both occasions.

Researchers determine the reliability of data in various ways. In observational research, observers are asked to evaluate the same behaviors, and agreement between them—called *inter-rater reliability*—is obtained. Reliability of self-report and neurobiological data can be

© GERRIT DE HEUS/ALAMY IMAGES

demonstrated by comparing children's responses to the same measures on separate occasions, an approach called *test–retest reliability*. In the case of self-reports, researchers can also compare children's answers on different forms of the same test or questionnaire. And if necessary, reliability can be estimated from a single testing session by comparing children's answers on different halves of the test.

Because clinical and ethnographic studies do not yield quantitative scores that can be matched with those of another observer or test form, other procedures must be used to determine the reliability of these methods. After examining the qualitative records, one or more judges can see if they agree with the researcher that the patterns and themes identified are grounded in evidence and are plausible (Silverman, 2006).

Validity

For research methods to have high **validity,** they must accurately measure characteristics that the researcher set out to measure. **TAKE A MOMENT...** After thinking about this idea, can you come up with an example that shows why reliability is essential for valid research? Methods that are implemented carelessly, unevenly, or inconsistently cannot possibly represent what an investigator originally intended to study.

But to guarantee validity, researchers must go further. They often examine the content of observations and self-reports to make sure all behaviors of interest are included. For example, a test intended to measure fifth-grade children's knowledge of mathematics would not be valid if it contained only addition problems but no subtraction, multiplication, or division problems (Miller, 2007). Another approach is to see how effective a method is in predicting behavior we would reasonably

This boy may excel on math tests, but how well does he do on real-world tasks such as counting money or making change? If a test is valid, it should predict related behaviors in everyday life.

expect it to predict. If scores on a math test are valid, they should be related to how well children do on their math assignments in school or even to how quickly and accurately they can make change in a game of Monopoly.

As we turn now to research designs, you will discover that the concept of validity can also be applied more broadly: to the overall accuracy of research findings and conclusions. In setting up an investigation, researchers must safeguard two types of validity. The first, **internal validity,** is the degree to which *conditions internal to the design of the study* permit an accurate test of the researcher's hypothesis or question. If, during any phase of the investigation—selecting participants, choosing research settings and tasks, and implementing procedures—participants' behavior is influenced by factors unrelated to the hypothesis, then the accuracy of the results is in doubt. Second, researchers must consider **external validity,** the degree to which their *findings generalize to settings and participants outside the original study.* Ensuring that samples, tasks, and contexts for conducting research represent the real-world people and situations that the investigator aims to understand is key to this type of accuracy.

LOOK and LISTEN

Ask a teacher, counselor, social worker, or nurse to describe a question about development he or she would like researchers to address. After reading this chapter, recommend research strategies best suited to answering the question.

A S K   Y O U R S E L F

Review ■ Explain why, although a research method must be reliable to be valid, reliability *does not guarantee* validity.

Connect ■ Why is it better for a researcher to use multiple methods rather than just one method to test a hypothesis or answer a research question?

Apply ■ In studying the development of attention in school-age children, a researcher wonders whether to make naturalistic observations or structured observations. Which approach is best for ensuring internal validity? How about external validity? Why?

General Research Designs

In deciding on a research design, investigators choose a way of setting up a study that permits them to test their hypotheses with the greatest certainty possible. Two main designs are used in all research on human behavior: *correlational* and *experimental.*

▶ Distinguish correlational and experimental research designs, noting strengths and limitations of each.

Correlational Design

In a **correlational design,** researchers gather information on individuals, generally in natural life circumstances, and make no effort to alter their experiences. Then they look at relationships between participants' characteristics and their behavior or development. Suppose we want to answer such questions as, Do parents' styles of interacting with their children have any bearing on children's intelligence? Does attending a child-care center promote children's friendliness with peers? How do child abuse and neglect affect children's self-esteem and relationships with peers? In these and many other instances, the conditions of interest are difficult or impossible to arrange and control and must be studied as they currently exist.

Correlational studies have one major limitation: We cannot infer cause and effect. For example, if we find that parental interaction is related to children's intelligence, we would not know whether parents' behavior actually *causes* intellectual differences among children. In fact, the opposite is possible: The behaviors of highly intelligent children may be so attractive that they cause parents to interact more favorably. Or a third variable that we did not even

Do parents who speak more to their toddlers have children who are advanced in language development? A correlational design is well-suited to answering this question, but it does not permit inferences about cause and effect.

consider, such as the amount of noise and distraction in the home, may cause changes in both parental interaction and children's intelligence.

In correlational studies, and in other types of research designs, investigators often examine relationships by using a **correlation coefficient**—a number that describes how two measures, or variables, are associated with each other. Although other statistical approaches to examining relationships also exist, we will encounter the correlation coefficient in discussing research findings throughout this book. So let's look at what it is and how it is interpreted. A correlation coefficient can range in value from +1.00 to –1.00. The *magnitude,* or *size, of the number* shows the *strength of the relationship.* A zero correlation indicates no relationship; the closer the value is to either +1.00 or –1.00, the stronger the relationship (see Figure 2.2). For instance, a correlation of –.78 is high, –.52 is moderate, and –.18 is low. Note, however, that correlations of +.52 and –.52 are equally strong. The *sign of the number* refers to the *direction of the relationship.* A positive sign (+) means that as one variable *increases,* the other also *increases.* A negative sign (–) indicates that as one variable *increases,* the other *decreases.*

Let's look at some examples of how a correlation coefficient works. One researcher reported a +.55 correlation between a measure of maternal language stimulation and the size of children's vocabularies at age 2 years (Hoff, 2003). This is a moderate correlation, which indicates that mothers who spoke more to their toddlers had children who were more advanced in language development. In two other studies, child-rearing practices were related to children's compliance in consistent ways. First, maternal warmth and sensitivity during play correlated positively (+.34) with 2-year-olds' willingness to comply with their mother's directive to clean up toys (Feldman & Klein, 2003). Second, the extent to which mothers spoke harshly, interrupted, and controlled their 4-year-olds' play correlated negatively (–.31 for boys and –.42 for girls) with children's compliance (Smith et al., 2004). The more mothers expressed affection and support, the more their children cooperated. And the more mothers restricted and coerced, the less the children cooperated (see Figure 2.3 for visual portrayals of these relationships).

All these investigations found correlations between parenting and young children's behavior. **TAKE A MOMENT...** Are you tempted to conclude that maternal behaviors influenced children's responses? Although the researchers suspected this was so, they could not be sure of cause and effect. Can you think of other possible explanations? Finding a relationship in a correlational study does suggest that tracking down its cause—with a more powerful experimental strategy, if possible—would be worthwhile.

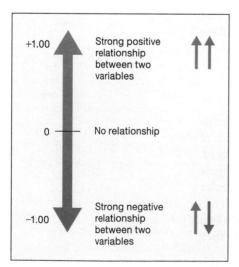

FIGURE 2.2 The meaning of correlation coefficients. The magnitude of the number indicates the *strength* of the relationship. The sign of the number (+ or –) indicates the *direction* of the relationship.

Experimental Design

An **experimental design** permits inferences about cause and effect because researchers use an evenhanded procedure to assign people to two or more treatment conditions. In an experiment, the events and behaviors of interest are divided into two types: independent and dependent variables. The **independent variable** is the one the investigator expects to cause changes in another variable. The **dependent variable** is the one the investigator expects to be influenced by the independent variable. Cause-and-effect relationships can be detected because the researcher directly *controls* or *manipulates* changes in the independent variable by exposing participants to the treatment conditions. Then the researcher compares their performance on measures of the dependent variable.

In one **laboratory experiment,** researchers explored the impact of adults' angry interactions on children's adjustment (El-Sheikh, Cummings, & Reiter, 1996).

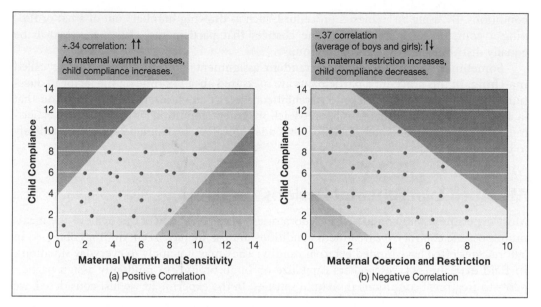

FIGURE 2.3 **A positive and a negative correlation.** A researcher reported that maternal warmth and sensitivity were positively correlated with children's willingness to comply with their mother's directive to clean up toys (a). A second researcher reported that maternal restriction and coercion were negatively correlated with children's compliance (b). Each dot represents a participant's score on the two variables—maternal behavior and child compliance. Both correlations are moderate in strength because the pattern of dots deviates from a straight line, which would be a perfect correlation. Notice how in the positive correlation, as maternal warmth *increases,* child compliance tends to *increase.* In the negative correlation, as maternal restriction *increases,* child compliance tends to *decrease.* If a pattern of dots shows no upward or downward trend, then the correlation is near zero, indicating little or no relationship between the two variables.

They hypothesized that the way angry encounters end (independent variable) affects children's emotional reactions (dependent variable). Four- and 5-year-olds were brought one at a time to a laboratory, accompanied by their mothers. One group was exposed to an *unresolved-anger treatment,* in which two adult actors entered the room and argued but did not work out their disagreements. The other group witnessed a *resolved-anger treatment,* in which the adults ended their disputes by apologizing and compromising. As Figure 2.4 shows, when they witnessed a follow-up adult conflict, more children in the resolved-anger treatment showed a decline in distress, as measured by fewer anxious facial expressions, less freezing in place, and less seeking of closeness to their mothers. The experiment revealed that anger resolution can reduce the stressful impact of adult conflict on children.

In experimental studies, investigators must take special precautions to control for participants' characteristics that could reduce the internal validity of their findings. For example, in the study just described, if more children from homes high in parental conflict ended up in the unresolved-anger treatment, we could not tell what produced the results—the independent variable or the children's backgrounds. Parental conflict and the treatment conditions would be **confounding variables**—so closely associated that their effects on an outcome cannot be distinguished. To protect against this problem, researchers engage in **random assignment** of participants to treatment

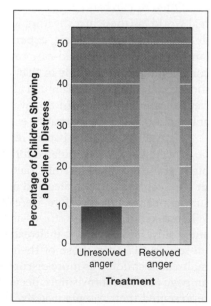

FIGURE 2.4 **Does the way adults end their angry encounters affect children's emotional reactions?** A laboratory experiment revealed that children who had previously witnessed adults resolving their disputes by apologizing and compromising were more likely to decline in distress when witnessing subsequent adult conflicts than were children who witnessed adults leaving their arguments unresolved. Notice in this graph that only 10 percent of children in the unresolved-anger treatment declined in distress (see bar on left), whereas 42 percent of children in the resolved-anger treatment did so (see bar on right). (Adapted from El-Sheikh, Cummings, & Reiter, 1996.)

conditions. By using an unbiased procedure, such as drawing numbers out of a hat or flipping a coin, investigators increase the chances that participants' characteristics will be equally distributed across treatment groups.

Sometimes researchers combine random assignment with another technique called **matching.** In this procedure, participants are measured ahead of time on the factor in question—in our example, exposure to parental conflict. Then children high and low on that factor are assigned in equal numbers to each treatment condition. In this way, the experimental groups are deliberately matched, or made equivalent, on characteristics that are likely to distort the results.

Modified Experimental Designs

Most experiments are conducted in laboratories, where researchers can achieve the maximum possible control over treatment conditions. But, as we have seen, findings obtained in laboratories often have limited external validity: They may not apply to everyday situations. In **field experiments,** researchers capitalize on opportunities to randomly assign participants to treatment conditions in natural settings. In the experiment we just considered, we can conclude that the emotional climate established by adults affects children's behavior in the laboratory. But does it have the same effect in daily life?

Another study helps answer this question. Ethnically diverse, poverty-stricken families with a 2-year-old child were scheduled for a home visit, during which researchers assessed family functioning and child problem behaviors by asking parents to respond to questionnaires and videotaping parent–child interaction. The families were then randomly assigned to either an intervention condition, called the Family Check-Up, or a no-intervention control group. The intervention consisted of three home-based sessions in which a consultant gave parents feedback about their child-rearing practices and their child's adjustment, explored parents' willingness to improve, and identified community services appropriate to each family's needs (Dishion et al., 2008). Findings showed that families assigned to the Family Check-Up (but not controls) gained in positive parenting, which predicted a reduction in child problem behaviors—sometimes still evident a year later, when participating children were reassessed at age 3. In other field experiments, adaptations of the Family Check-up were effective in improving parenting of adolescents and reducing rates of antisocial behavior and substance use (Stormshak & Dishion, 2009; Stormshak et al., 2011). See the Social Issues: Education box on the following page for another example of field research—this time with implications for how best to foster children's intelligence.

Often researchers cannot randomly assign participants and manipulate conditions in the real world, as these investigators were able to do. Sometimes they can compromise by conducting **natural,** or **quasi-, experiments.** Treatments that already exist, such as different family environments, child-care centers, or schools, are compared. These studies differ from correlational research only in that groups of participants are carefully chosen to ensure that their characteristics are as much alike as possible. Occasionally, the same participants experience both treatments. In this way, investigators do their best to avoid confounding variables and to rule out alternative explanations for treatment effects.

Natural experiments permit researchers to examine the impact of conditions that cannot be experimentally manipulated for ethical reasons—for example, the influence of premature birth, grade retention, or child maltreatment on development (Sameroff & MacKenzie, 2003). In one such study, maltreated and nonmaltreated 8- to 12-year-olds were enrolled in the same summer camp and, therefore, were observed and questioned under similar social conditions. When asked to complete stories about parenting that tapped themes of conflict, discipline, autonomy, and affection, maltreated children gave responses that were less elaborate and more negative than those of their nonmaltreated counterparts. Furthermore, peers rated maltreated children as more disruptive, more aggressive, and less cooperative (see Figure 2.6 on page 60). Not surprisingly, peers strongly disliked these youngsters. Finally, children who represented their parents negatively in stories were especially likely to display maladaptive

SOCIAL ISSUES: EDUCATION

Can Musical Experiences Enhance Intelligence?

In a 1993 experiment, researchers reported that college students who listened to a Mozart sonata for a few minutes just before taking a test of spatial reasoning abilities did better on the test than students who took the test after listening to relaxation instructions or sitting in silence (Rauscher, Shaw, & Ky, 1993). Strains of Mozart, the investigators concluded, seem to induce changes in the brain that "warm up" neural connections, thereby improving thinking. But the gain in performance, widely publicized as the "Mozart effect," was small, lasted briefly, and proved difficult to replicate (Pietschnig, Voracek, & Formann, 2010). Rather than involving a real change in ability, listening to Mozart seemed to improve arousal and mood, yielding better concentration on the test (Schellenberg et al., 2007).

Despite mounting evidence that the Mozart effect was uncertain at best, the media and politicians were enthralled with the idea that a brief exposure of the brain to classical music in infancy, when neural connections are forming rapidly, might yield lifelong intellectual benefits. For a time, the states of Georgia, Tennessee, and South Dakota provided free classical music CDs

for every newborn baby leaving the hospital. Yet no studies of the Mozart effect have ever been conducted on infants! And an experiment with school-age children failed to demonstrate any intellectual gains as a result of simply listening to music (McKelvie & Low, 2002).

Research suggests that to produce lasting gains in mental-test scores, interventions must be long-lasting and involve children's active participation. Consequently, Glenn Schellenberg (2004) wondered, Can music lessons enhance intelligence? Children who take music lessons must practice regularly, exhibit extended focused attention, read music, memorize lengthy musical passages, understand diverse musical structures, and master technical skills. These experiences might foster cognitive processing, particularly during childhood, when regions of the brain are taking on specialized functions and are highly sensitive to environmental influences.

Schellenberg recruited 132 six-year-olds—children just old enough for formal lessons. First, the children took an intelligence test and were rated on social maturity, permitting the researchers to see whether music lessons would affect some aspects of development but not others. Next, the children were randomly assigned to one of four experimental conditions. Two were music groups; one received piano lessons and the other voice lessons. The third group took drama lessons—a condition that shed light on whether intellectual gains were unique to musical experiences. The fourth group—a no-lessons control—was offered music lessons the following year. All music and drama instruction took place at the prestigious Royal Conservatory of Music in Toronto, where experienced teachers taught the children in small groups. After 36 weeks of lessons, a longitudinal follow-up was conducted: The children's intelligence and social maturity were assessed again.

All four groups gained in mental-test performance, probably because the participants had just entered grade school, which usually leads to an increase in intelligence test scores (see Chapter 8). But the two music groups consistently gained more than the drama and no-lessons control groups (see Figure 2.5). Their advantage, though just a few points, extended across many mental abilities, including verbal

© TOM GRILL/CORBIS/GLOW IMAGES

Children taking music lessons make greater gains in mental test performance than children taking drama lessons or no lessons at all. Music making involves diverse, intellectually challenging activities: reading notation, memorizing lengthy passages, analyzing musical structures, and mastering technical skills.

and spatial skills and speed of thinking. At the same time, only the drama group improved in social maturity.

In sum, active, sustained musical experiences can lead to small increases in intelligence among 6-year-olds that do not arise from comparable drama lessons. But other enrichment activities with similar properties, such as reading, science, math, and chess programs, may confer similar benefits. All demand that children invest far more time and effort than they would in listening to a Mozart sonata. Nevertheless—despite absence of evidence to support their claims—music companies persist in selling CDs with such titles as "Music for Accelerated Learning" and "The Mozart Effect: Music for Newborns—A Bright Beginning."

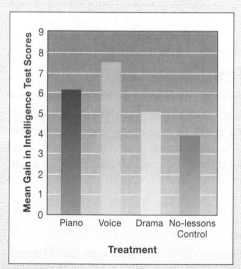

FIGURE 2.5 Music lessons promote gains in intelligence. In a field experiment comparing 36 weeks of piano and voice lessons with drama lessons and a no-lessons control, children in the two groups receiving music lessons showed slightly greater gains in intelligence test performance. (Adapted from Schellenberg, 2004.)

FIGURE 2.6 A natural, or quasi-, experiment on the relationship of child maltreatment to children's social adjustment. Researchers brought maltreated and nonmaltreated children together at a summer camp so they could be observed under similar conditions. After only a short time together, peers consistently rated maltreated children as less well-adjusted—more disruptive, more aggressive, and less cooperative. (Adapted from Shields, Ryan, & Cicchetti, 2001.)

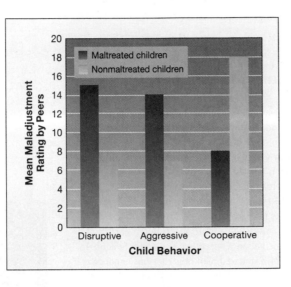

social behaviors (Shields, Ryan, & Cicchetti, 2001). The investigators concluded that maltreated children's internalized, unfavorable parenting images probably contribute to their poor social adjustment. And their poor adjustment reduces their access to the healing effects of warm, enjoyable relationships with peers. Despite intriguing findings like these, natural experiments cannot achieve the precision and rigor of true experimental research.

To help you compare correlational and experimental designs, Table 2.3 summarizes their strengths and limitations. Now let's take a close look at designs for studying development.

ASK YOURSELF

Review ■ Why are natural experiments less precise than laboratory and field experiments?

Connect ■ Reread the description of the study of aggressive boys and their friendships on page 44. What type of design did the researchers use, and why?

Apply ■ A researcher compares children who went to summer leadership camps with children who attended athletic camps. She finds that those who attended leadership camps are friendlier.

Should the investigator tell parents that sending children to leadership camps will cause them to be more sociable? Why or why not?

Reflect ■ Design a study to investigate whether time devoted to adult–child picture-book reading in the preschool years contributes to reading readiness at school entry. List steps you will take to protect the internal and external validity of your investigation.

▶ Describe designs for studying development, noting strengths and limitations of each.

Designs for Studying Development

Scientists interested in child development require information about the way research participants change over time. To answer questions about development, they must extend correlational and experimental approaches to include measurements at different ages. Longitudinal and cross-sectional designs are special *developmental research* strategies. In each, age comparisons form the basis of the research plan.

The Longitudinal Design

In a **longitudinal design,** participants are studied repeatedly at different ages, and changes are noted as they get older. The time spanned may be relatively short (a few months to several years) or very long (a decade or even a lifetime).

Advantages of the Longitudinal Design The longitudinal approach has two major strengths. First, because it tracks the performance of each person over time, researchers can identify common patterns as well as individual differences in development. Second, longitudinal studies permit investigators to examine relationships between early and later events and behaviors. Let's illustrate these ideas.

A group of researchers wondered whether children who display extreme personality styles—either angry and explosive or shy and withdrawn—retain the same dispositions

TABLE 2.3 | **Strengths and Limitations of General Research Designs**

DESIGN	DESCRIPTION	STRENGTHS	LIMITATIONS
Correlational design	The investigator obtains information on participants without altering their experiences.	Permits study of relationships between variables.	Does not permit inferences about cause-and-effect relationships.
Laboratory experiment	Under controlled laboratory conditions, the investigator manipulates an independent variable and looks at its effect on a dependent variable; requires random assignment of participants to treatment conditions.	Permits inferences about cause-and-effect relationships.	Findings may not generalize to the real world.
Field experiment	The investigator randomly assigns participants to treatment conditions in natural settings.	Permits generalization of experimental findings to the real world.	Control over the treatment is generally weaker than in a laboratory experiment.
Natural, or quasi-, experiment	The investigator compares already existing treatments in the real world, carefully selecting groups of participants to ensure that their characteristics are as much alike as possible.	Permits study of many real-world conditions that cannot be experimentally manipulated.	Findings may be due to variables other than the treatment.

when they become adults. In addition, the researchers wanted to know what kinds of experiences promote stability or change in personality and what consequences explosiveness and shyness have for long-term adjustment. To answer these questions, the researchers delved into the archives of the Guidance Study, a well-known longitudinal investigation that was initiated in 1928 at the University of California, Berkeley, and continued for several decades (Caspi, Elder, & Bem, 1987, 1988).

Results revealed that the two personality styles were moderately stable. Between ages 8 and 30, a good number of individuals remained the same, whereas others changed substantially. When stability did occur, it appeared to be due to a "snowballing effect," in which children evoked responses from adults and peers that acted to maintain their dispositions. Explosive youngsters were likely to be treated with anger, whereas shy children were apt to be ignored. As a result, the two types of children came to view their social worlds differently. Explosive children regarded others as hostile; shy children regarded them as unfriendly (Caspi & Roberts, 2001). Together, these factors led explosive children to sustain or increase their unruliness and shy children to continue to withdraw.

Persistence of extreme personality styles affected many areas of adult adjustment. For men, the results of early explosiveness were most apparent in their work lives, in the form of conflicts with supervisors, frequent job changes, and unemployment. Because few women in this sample of an earlier generation worked after marriage, their family lives were most affected. Explosive girls grew up to be hotheaded wives and mothers who were especially prone to divorce. Sex differences in the long-term consequences of shyness were even greater. Men who had been withdrawn in childhood were delayed in marrying, becoming fathers, and developing careers. However, because a withdrawn, unassertive style was socially acceptable for females in the mid-twentieth century, women who had shy personalities showed no special adjustment problems.

Problems in Conducting Longitudinal Research
Despite their strengths, longitudinal investigations pose a number of problems that can compromise both internal and external validity. A common difficulty is **biased sampling**—the failure to enlist participants who represent the population of interest. People who willingly participate in research that requires them to be observed and tested over many years are likely to have distinctive characteristics—perhaps a special appreciation for the scientific value of research, or a unique need or desire for medical, mental health, or educational services provided by the investigators.

As a result, we cannot easily generalize from them to the rest of the population. Furthermore, longitudinal samples generally become more biased as the investigation proceeds because of **selective attrition.** Participants may move away or drop out for other reasons, and those who continue are likely to differ in important ways from those who drop out.

The very experience of being repeatedly observed, interviewed, and tested can also interfere with a study's validity. As children and adults are alerted to their own thoughts, feelings, and actions, they may consciously revise them in ways that have little to do with age-related change. In addition, with repeated testing, participants may become "test-wise." Their performance may improve as a result of **practice effects**—better test-taking skills and increased familiarity with the test—not because of factors commonly associated with development.

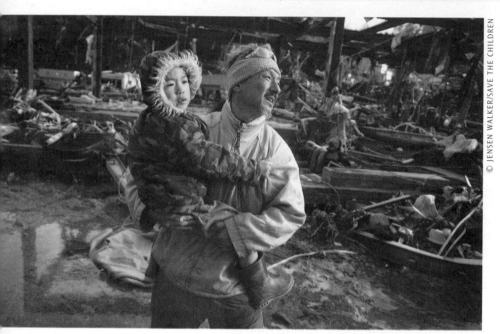

© JENSEN WALKER/SAVE THE CHILDREN

This 6-year-old and his father, who lost their home in the March 2011 tsunami in northern Japan, receive aid from Save the Children, an international organization serving vulnerable children and families. This destructive historical event will likely induce a cohort effect for many Japanese children.

The most widely discussed threat to the validity of longitudinal findings is cultural–historical change, commonly called **cohort effects.** Longitudinal studies examine the development of *cohorts*—children developing in the same time period who are influenced by particular cultural and historical conditions. Results based on one cohort may not apply to children developing at other times. For example, look back at the findings on female shyness described in the previous section, which were gathered in the 1950s. Today's shy young women tend to be poorly adjusted—a difference that may be due to changes in gender roles in Western societies. Shy adults, whether male or female, feel more depressed, have fewer social supports, and may do less well in educational and career attainment than their agemates (Caspi, 2000; Caspi et al., 2003; Mounts et al., 2006). Similarly, a longitudinal study of social development would probably result in quite different findings if it were carried out in the first decade of the twenty-first century, around the time of World War II, or during the Great Depression of the 1930s.

Cohort effects don't just operate broadly on an entire generation. They also occur when specific experiences influence some children but not others in the same generation. For example, children who witnessed the terrorist attacks of September 11, 2001 (either because they were near Ground Zero or because they saw injury and death on TV) or who had a parent, other relative, or family member directly exposed were far more likely than other children to display persistent emotional problems, including intense fear, anxiety, and depression (Mullett-Hume et al., 2008; Pfeffer et al., 2007; Rosen & Cohen, 2010). A study of one New York City sample suggested that as many as one-fourth of the city's children were affected (Hoven et al., 2005).

Finally, changes occurring within the field of child development may create problems for longitudinal research covering an extended time period. Theories and methods that first inspired a longitudinal study may become outdated. For this reason, as well as the others just mentioned, many recent longitudinal studies span only a few months or years. Although short-term longitudinal research does not yield the same breadth of information as long-term studies, it does spare researchers some formidable obstacles.

The Cross-Sectional Design

The length of time it takes for many behaviors to change, even in limited longitudinal studies, has led researchers to turn to a more convenient strategy for studying development. In the **cross-sectional design,** groups of people differing in age are studied at the same point in time.

Advantages of the Cross-Sectional Design The cross-sectional design is an efficient strategy for describing age-related trends. And because participants are measured only once, researchers need not be concerned about such difficulties as selective attrition, practice effects, or changes in the field that might make the findings obsolete by the time the study is complete.

An investigation in which students in grades 3, 6, 9, and 12 filled out a questionnaire asking about their sibling relationships provides a good illustration (Buhrmester & Furman, 1990). Findings revealed that sibling interaction was characterized by greater equality and less power assertion with age. Also, feelings of sibling companionship declined during adolescence. The researchers thought that several factors contributed to these age differences. As later-born children become more competent and independent, they no longer need, and are probably less willing to accept, direction from older siblings. And as adolescents move from psychological dependence on the family to greater involvement with peers, they may have less time and emotional need to invest in siblings. As you will see in Chapter 14, subsequent research has confirmed these intriguing ideas about the development of sibling relationships.

Problems in Conducting Cross-Sectional Research Despite its convenience, cross-sectional research does not provide evidence about development at the level at which it actually occurs: the individual. For example, in the cross-sectional study of sibling relationships just discussed, comparisons are limited to age-group averages. We cannot tell if important individual differences exist. Indeed, longitudinal findings reveal that adolescents vary considerably in the changing quality of their sibling relationships. Although many become more distant, others become more supportive and intimate, still others more rivalrous and antagonistic (Branje et al., 2004; Kim et al., 2006; Whiteman & Loken, 2006).

Cross-sectional studies—especially those that cover a wide age span—have another problem. Like longitudinal research, they can be threatened by cohort effects. For example, comparisons of 5-year-old cohorts and 15-year-old cohorts—groups born and reared in different years—may not really represent age-related changes. Instead, they may reflect unique experiences associated with the time period in which the age groups were growing up.

Improving Developmental Designs

Researchers have devised ways of building on the strengths and minimizing the weaknesses of longitudinal and cross-sectional approaches. Several modified developmental designs have resulted.

Sequential Designs To overcome some of the limitations of traditional developmental designs, investigators sometimes use **sequential designs,** in which they conduct several cross-sectional or longitudinal investigations (called *sequences*). The sequences might study participants over the same ages but in different years, or they might study participants over different ages but during the same years. Figure 2.7 illustrates the second of these options. As it also reveals,

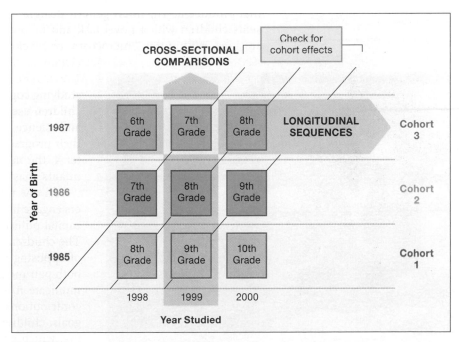

FIGURE 2.7 Example of a sequential design. Three cohorts, born in 1985 (blue), 1986 (orange), and 1987 (pink), respectively, are followed longitudinally for three years. Testing the cohorts in overlapping grades enables researchers to check for cohort effects by comparing participants born in different years when they reach the same grade (see diagonals). In a study using this design, same-grade adolescents who were members of different cohorts scored similarly on a questionnaire assessing family harmony, indicating no cohort effects. By following each cohort for just three years, the investigator could infer a developmental trend across five years, from sixth to tenth grade.

some sequential designs combine longitudinal and cross-sectional strategies, an approach that has three advantages:

- We can find out whether cohort effects are operating by comparing participants of the same age who were born in different years. In Figure 2.7, for example, we can compare the longitudinal samples at seventh, eighth, and ninth grades. If they do not differ, we can rule out cohort effects.
- We can make both longitudinal and cross-sectional comparisons. If outcomes are similar, we can be especially confident about the findings.
- The design is efficient. In our example, we can find out about change over a five-year period by following each cohort for three years.

In a study that used the design in Figure 2.7, researchers wanted to find out if family harmony changed as young people experienced the dramatic physical and psychological changes of adolescence (Baer, 2002). A questionnaire assessing emotional bonding among family members was given to three adolescent cohorts, each born a year apart. In longitudinal follow-ups, each cohort again responded to the questionnaire during the following two years.

Findings for the three cohorts converged: All reported (1) a slight decline in family harmony with grade and (2) similar levels of family harmony as they reached the same grade, confirming that there were no cohort effects. Therefore, the researchers concluded that family closeness diminishes steadily from sixth to tenth grade, noting, however, that the change is mild—not enough to threaten supportive family ties. **TAKE A MOMENT...** Turn back to our discussion of parent–adolescent communication as a dynamic system on page 31 in Chapter 1 and our consideration of adolescent sibling relationships on page 63. How are those results helpful in interpreting the outcomes of the sequential study just described?

Examining Microcosms of Development In the examples of developmental research we have discussed, observations of children are fairly widely spaced. When we observe once a year or every few years, we can describe change, but we cannot easily capture the processes that produce it. The **microgenetic design,** an adaptation of the longitudinal approach, presents children with a novel task and follows their mastery over a series of closely spaced sessions. Within this "microcosm" of development, researchers observe how change occurs (Flynn & Siegler, 2007; Kuhn, 1995; Siegler & Crowley, 1991). The microgenetic design is especially useful for studying cognitive development—for example, the strategies children use to acquire knowledge in reading, mathematics, and science, along with teaching interventions that facilitate their progress (Siegler, 2002, 2006). As you will see in Chapter 4, the microgenetic design has also been used to trace infants' mastery of motor skills.

In one microgenetic study, researchers had sixth graders engage in frequent debate of controversial issues (such as capital punishment) over a school year (Kuhn et al., 2008). The children worked in pairs, collaborating against a series of opposing pairs, who took the opposite side. Only when both pair members agreed on an argument could they communicate it—a rule aimed at promoting more thoughtful contributions along with critical reflection. To further these goals, children conducted dialogues using instant messaging, which preserved a record that enabled them to reflect on their arguments and discuss possible improvements. Findings revealed that over time, most children made an increasing number of statements indicating awareness of argument quality, especially to the opposition ("Give us some reasons." "You haven't answered."). The more such

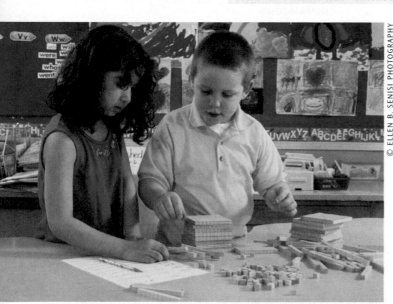

© ELLEN B. SENISI PHOTOGRAPHY

How do these first graders make use of manipulatives to master place value in arithmetic? A microgenetic design, which permits researchers to follow children's mastery of a challenging task, is uniquely suited to answering this question.

statements children made, the more they improved in debate skill, especially in counterargument and rebuttal—the most challenging debate activities.

Microgenetic studies, however, are difficult to carry out. Researchers must pore over hours of recorded information, analyzing each participant's behavior many times. In addition, the time required for children to change is hard to anticipate. It depends on a careful match between the child's capabilities and the demands of the task. Finally, as in other longitudinal research, practice effects can distort microgenetic findings. As a check, researchers can compare microgenetic with cross-sectional observations. If new behaviors that emerge microgenetically reflect typical development, they should match the behaviors displayed by more advanced participants in cross-sectional studies, who are observed only once (Kuhn, 1995). When researchers overcome the challenges of microgenetic research, they reap the benefits of seeing development as it takes place.

Combining Experimental and Developmental Designs Perhaps you noticed that all the examples of longitudinal and cross-sectional research we have considered permit only correlational, not causal, inferences. Yet causal information is also desirable, both for testing theories and for finding ways to enhance development. Sometimes researchers can explore the causal link between experiences and development by experimentally manipulating the experiences. If, as a result, development is enhanced, then we have strong evidence for a causal association. Today, research that combines an experimental strategy with either a longitudinal or a cross-sectional approach is becoming increasingly common. For a summary of the strengths and limitations of developmental research designs, refer to Table 2.4.

LOOK and LISTEN

Find a recent news article reporting a research study on children. Obtain the original research report from its scientific journal, and identify the research method(s) and design(s) used, listing strengths and limitations. Did the news article describe the findings accurately?

TABLE 2.4 | **Strengths and Limitations of Developmental Research Designs**

DESIGN	DESCRIPTION	STRENGTHS	LIMITATIONS
Longitudinal	The investigator studies the same group of participants repeatedly at different ages.	Permits study of common patterns and individual differences in development and relationships between early and later events and behaviors.	Age-related changes may be distorted because of biased sampling, selective attrition, practice effects, and cohort effects. Theoretical and methodological changes in the field can make findings obsolete.
Cross-sectional	The investigator studies groups of participants differing in age at the same time.	More efficient than the longitudinal design. Avoids problems of selective attrition, practice effects, and theoretical and methodological changes in the field.	Does not permit study of individual developmental trends. Age differences may be distorted because of cohort effects.
Sequential	The investigator conducts several cross-sectional or longitudinal investigations (called sequences). These might study participants over the same ages but in different years, or they might study participants over different ages but during the same years.	When the design includes longitudinal sequences, permits both longitudinal and cross-sectional comparisons. Also reveals cohort effects. Enables tracking of age-related changes more efficiently than the longitudinal design.	May have the same problems as longitudinal and cross-sectional strategies, but the design itself helps identify difficulties.
Microgenetic	The investigator presents children with a novel task and follows their mastery over a series of closely spaced sessions.	Offers insights into how change occurs.	Requires intensive study of participants' moment-by-moment behaviors; the time required for participants to change is difficult to anticipate. Practice effects may distort developmental trends.

A S K   Y O U R S E L F

Review ■ Explain how cohort effects can distort the findings of both longitudinal and cross-sectional studies. How does the sequential design reveal cohort effects?

Connect ■ Review the study on music lessons and intelligence reported in the Social Issues: Education box on page 59. Explain how it combines an experimental with a developmental design. What advantage does this approach offer?

Apply ■ A researcher wants to know whether children enrolled in child-care centers in the first few years of life do as well in school as those who are not in child care. Which developmental design is appropriate for answering this question? Explain.

Reflect ■ Suppose a researcher asks you to enroll your baby in a 10-year longitudinal study. What factors would lead you to agree and to stay involved? Do your answers shed light on why longitudinal studies often have biased samples? Explain.

▶ What special ethical issues arise in doing research on children?

Ethics in Research on Children

Research into human behavior creates ethical issues because, unfortunately, the quest for scientific knowledge can sometimes exploit people. When children take part in research, the ethical concerns are especially complex. Children are more vulnerable than adults to physical and psychological harm. In addition, immaturity makes it difficult or impossible for children to evaluate for themselves what participation in research will mean. For these reasons, special ethical guidelines for research on children have been developed by the federal government, by funding agencies, and by research-oriented associations such as the American Psychological Association (2002) and the Society for Research in Child Development (2007).

Table 2.5 presents a summary of children's basic research rights. **TAKE A MOMENT...** After examining them, think back to the ethical controversy faced by my colleague Ron, described at the beginning of this chapter. Then read about the following research situations,

TABLE 2.5 | Children's Research Rights

RESEARCH RIGHT	DESCRIPTION
Protection from harm	Children have the right to be protected from physical or psychological harm in research. If in doubt about the harmful effects of research, investigators should seek the opinion of others. When harm seems possible, investigators should find other means for obtaining the desired information or abandon the research.
Informed consent	All research participants, including children, have the right to have explained to them, in language appropriate to their level of understanding, all aspects of the research that may affect their willingness to participate. When children are participants, informed consent of parents as well as others who act on the child's behalf (such as school officials) should be obtained, preferably in writing. Children, and the adults responsible for them, have the right to discontinue participation in the research at any time.
Privacy	Children have the right to concealment of their identity on all information collected in the course of research. They also have this right with respect to written reports and any informal discussions about the research.
Knowledge of results	Children have the right to be informed of the results of research in language that is appropriate to their level of understanding.
Beneficial treatments	If experimental treatments believed to be beneficial are under investigation, children in control groups have the right to alternative beneficial treatments if they are available.

Sources: American Psychological Association, 2002; Society for Research in Child Development, 2007.

each of which also poses a serious ethical dilemma. What precautions do you think should be taken in each instance? Is either so threatening to children's well-being that it should not be carried out?

- In a study of moral development, a researcher wants to assess children's ability to resist temptation by videotaping their behavior without their knowledge. She promises 7-year-olds a prize for solving difficult puzzles but tells them not to look at a classmate's correct solutions, which are deliberately placed at the back of the room. Informing children ahead of time that cheating is being studied or that their behavior is being monitored will destroy the purpose of the study.
- A researcher is interviewing fifth graders about their experiences with bullying. A girl describes frequent name-calling and derogatory comments by her older sister. Although the girl is unhappy, she wants to handle the problem on her own. If the researcher alerts the girl's parents to provide protection and help, he will violate his promise to keep participants' responses private.

Did you find it difficult to evaluate these examples? Virtually every organization that has devised ethical principles for research has concluded that conflicts arising in research situations do not have simple right or wrong answers. The ultimate responsibility for the ethical integrity of research lies with the investigator. But researchers are advised—and often required—to seek advice from others. Committees for this purpose (like the one that evaluated Ron's research) exist in colleges, universities, and other institutions. These *institutional review boards (IRBs)* assess proposed studies on the basis of a **risks-versus-benefits ratio,** which involves weighing the costs to participants in terms of inconvenience and possible psychological or physical injury against the study's value for advancing knowledge and improving conditions of life.

Ron's procedures, the school's research committee claimed, might not offer children sufficient **protection from harm.** If there are any risks to the safety and welfare of participants that the research does not justify, then preference is always given to the research participants. Vulnerability to harm, as the Social Issues: Health box on page 68 reveals, varies with children's age and characteristics. Occasionally, further inquiry can help resolve perplexing ethical dilemmas. In Ron's case, he provided the research committee with findings showing that asking elementary school children to identify disliked peers does not cause them to interact less frequently or more negatively with those children (Bell-Dolan, Foster, & Sikora, 1989). At the same time, Ron agreed to take special precautions when requesting such information. He promised to ask all the children to keep their comments confidential. He also arranged to conduct the study at a time when classmates have limited opportunity to interact with one another—just before a school vacation (Bell-Dolan & Wessler, 1994). With these safeguards in place, the committee approved Ron's research.

The ethical principle of **informed consent**—people's right to have all aspects of a study explained to them that might affect their willingness to participate—requires special interpretation when participants cannot fully appreciate the research goals and activities. Parental consent is meant to protect the safety of children whose ability to decide is not yet fully mature. In addition, researchers should obtain the agreement of other individuals who act on children's behalf, such as institutional officials when research is conducted in schools, child-care centers, or hospitals. This is especially important when studies include special groups, such as abused children, whose parents may not always represent their best interests (refer again to the Social Issues: Health box).

As soon as children are old enough to appreciate the purpose of the research, and certainly by 7 years of age, their own informed consent should be obtained in addition to parental consent. Around age 7, changes in children's thinking permit them to better understand basic scientific principles and the needs of others. Researchers should respect and enhance these new capacities by giving school-age children a full explanation of research activities in language they can understand (Fisher, 1993). Careful attention to informed consent helps resolve dilemmas about revealing children's responses to parents, teachers, or other authorities when those responses suggest that the child's welfare is in

SOCIAL ISSUES: HEALTH

Children's Research Risks: Developmental and Individual Differences

Researchers interested in children face formidable challenges in defining their ethical responsibilities. Compared with adults, children are less capable of benefiting from research experiences. Furthermore, most risks children encounter are psychological rather than physical (as in medical research) and therefore difficult to anticipate or even detect (Thompson, 1992). Consider, for example, 7-year-old Henry, who did not want to answer a researcher's questions about how he feels about his younger brother, who has physical disabilities. Because Henry's parents told him they had given permission for his participation, he did not feel free to say no. Or take 11-year-old Isabelle, who tried to solve a problem but failed. Despite the researcher's assurances that the task was set up to be impossible, Isabelle ended up doubting her own competence.

How can we make sure that children are subjected to the least research risk possible? One valuable resource is our expanding knowledge of age-related capacities and individual differences. Research risks vary with development in complex ways. Some risks decrease with age, others increase, and still others occur at many or all ages (Thompson, 1990). And because of their personal characteristics and life circumstances, some children are more vulnerable to harm than others.

Age Differences

Research plans for younger children typically receive the most scrutiny because their limited cognitive competencies restrict their ability to make reasoned decisions and resist violations of their rights. In addition, as Henry's predicament illustrates, young children's limited social power can make it hard to refuse participation. In research that examined children's understanding of research procedures, 9-year-olds had great difficulty identifying their research rights and recognizing violations of those rights. Even 12-year-olds struggled to grasp their rights to decline participation, be protected from harm, and be given the study's results (Bruzzese & Fisher, 2003). And regardless of age, most children and adolescents thought that withdrawing from a study would have negative consequences and felt external pressure to continue. For example, they believed the researcher would be unhappy if they stopped (Ondrusek et al.,

1998). But if researchers briefly name and explain each research right, comprehension improves, especially among adolescents.

Whereas young children often fail to comprehend the research process, older children are more susceptible to procedures that threaten the way they view themselves. As middle childhood brings greater sensitivity to others' evaluations, giving false negative feedback or inducing failure (as happened to Isabelle) becomes more stressful. In adolescence, when questioning of authority is common, young people may be better at sizing up and rejecting researchers' deceptive evaluations (Thompson, 1992).

Children's Unique Characteristics

At times, children's backgrounds and experiences introduce vulnerabilities. For example, in certain ethnic minority communities, where deference to authority, maintaining pleasant relationships, and meeting the needs of a guest (the researcher) are highly valued, children and parents may be likely to consent when they would rather not do so (Fisher et al., 2002). In other

circumstances, such as child maltreatment, parents are not necessarily good advocates for their children's rights. The consent of an additional adult invested in the child's welfare—a relative, teacher, or therapist—may be necessary to protect the child. And in some cases, such as teenagers who are substance abusers or delinquents, parents may be so eager to get them into contact with professionals that they are willing to agree to almost any research, with little forethought (Drotar et al., 2000).

Finding ways to reconcile the risks-versus-benefits conflicts we have considered is vital because research on children is of great value to society. As institutional review boards evaluate each study, participants' age and unique characteristics should be central to the discussion. Children and adolescents need clear, age-appropriate explanations of their rights, reminders of those rights as the research proceeds, and invitations to ask questions about anything they do not understand (Kon & Klug, 2006). And their decision should be the final word in most investigations, even though this standard is not mandatory in current guidelines.

© LISA F. YOUNG/ALAMY

In consenting to participate in a study, this teenager may not fully understand that she has the right to withdraw without penalty. And adolescents are especially vulnerable to certain research risks, such as false negative feedback that threatens their self-concept.

danger. Children can be told in advance that if they report that someone is harming them, the researcher will tell an appropriate adult to take action to ensure the child's safety (Jennifer & Cowie, 2009).

Finally, all ethical guidelines advise that special precautions be taken in the use of deception and concealment, as occurs when researchers observe children from behind one-way mirrors, give them false feedback about their performance, or misrepresent the real purpose of the research. By their very nature, studies involving deception breach the research right to make a fully informed decision about participation. Furthermore, deception can be particularly disturbing to children, who rely on a basic faith in the honesty of adults to feel secure.

Nevertheless, when revealing the purpose of a study would compromise internal validity, deception may be necessary. Its appropriateness depends on whether a study's potential benefits to society are great enough to justify infringing on informed consent and risking other harm (Fisher, 2005). In one controversial investigation, researchers planned to study children's formation of stereotypes and prejudices against a visible minority group by having most students in summer school classes wear red T-shirts (the "majority") and several children in each class wear yellow T-shirts (the "minority"), without giving the children any reason for the groupings (Brown & Bigler, 2002). At the end of the summer session, the children would be asked to rate the likability of each of their classmates, and to rate each group on positive and negative traits ("friendly," "smart," "dirty," "mean").

At first, teachers refused to allow the study, arguing that students assigned to the "minority" group could be psychologically harmed. But the investigators countered that millions of racial and ethnic minority children and children with disabilities are placed in a similar position every day and that it would be of great value to the mostly white participants to better understand the consequences of being a minority group member (Bigler, 2007). As a result, the teachers allowed the research to go forward.

When deception is used with adults, **debriefing,** in which the researcher provides a full account and justification of the activities, occurs after the research session is over. Debriefing should also be done with children, and in the study just described it seemed to work well. Still, young children often lack the cognitive skills to understand the reasons for deceptive procedures, and despite explanations they may leave the research situation with their belief in the honesty of adults undermined. Ethical standards permit deception in research with children if investigators satisfy IRBs that nondeceptive alternatives do not offer sufficient scientific controls to test the hypothesis under investigation. Nevertheless, because deception may have serious emotional consequences for some youngsters, many child development specialists believe that researchers should use it only if the risk of harm is minimal.

A S K   Y O U R S E L F

Review ■ Explain why researchers must consider children's age-related capacities to ensure that they are protected from harm and have freely consented to research.

Connect ■ In the experiment on music lessons and intelligence reported in the Social Issues: Education box on page 59, why was it ethically important for the researchers to offer music lessons to the no-lessons control group during the year after completion of the study?

Apply ■ As a researcher was engaged in naturalistic observation of preschoolers' play, one child said, "Stop watching me!" Referring to the research rights listed in Table 2.5, indicate how the researcher should respond, and why.

Reflect ■ Would you approve the study on stereotyping and prejudice, in which summer-school students (without an explanation) were asked to wear colored T-shirts that identified them as members of "majority" and "minority" groups? Explain. What ethical safeguards do you believe are vital in research that requires deception of children to ensure internal validity?

S U M M A R Y

From Theory to Hypothesis
(p. 41)

Describe the role of theories, hypotheses, and research questions in the research process.

- Research usually begins with a **hypothesis,** a prediction about behavior drawn from a theory, or—when little or no theory exists on a topic of interest—with a research question. On the basis of the hypothesis or question, the investigator selects research methods (specific activities of participants) and a research design (overall plan for the study).

Common Research Methods
(p. 42)

Describe research methods commonly used to study children, noting strengths and limitations of each.

- **Naturalistic observations**, gathered in children's everyday environments, permit researchers to see directly the everyday behaviors they hope to explain. In contrast, **structured observations** in laboratories give every participant an equal opportunity to display the behaviors of interest.

- Observations can preserve participants' entire stream of behavior, or they can be limited to one or a few behaviors, as in **event sampling** and **time sampling. Observer influence** and **observer bias** can reduce the accuracy of observational findings.

- Self-reports may be flexible and open-ended, like the **clinical interview**, which permits participants to express their thoughts in ways similar to their thinking in everyday life. Alternatively, **structured interviews**, tests, and questionnaires are more efficient, permitting researchers to specify activities and behaviors that participants might not think of in an open-ended interview. Both approaches depend on participants' ability and willingness to engage in accurate reporting. Currently, more researchers are combining the two approaches to see if they yield a clearer picture than either method can alone.

- **Neurobiological methods** measure the relationship between nervous system processes and behavior. Among autonomic nervous system indicators, saliva concentrations of the hormone cortisol provide information about stress reactivity. Electroencephalogram (EEG) and event-related potentials (ERPs) detect changes in electrical activity in the cerebral cortex.

- Neuroimaging techniques, such as positron emission tomography (PET) and functional magnetic resonance imaging (fMRI), yield the most precise information about brain region specialization and abnormalities in brain functioning. Near-infrared spectroscopy (NIRS) is well-suited for use with infants and young children. However, investigators cannot be sure that a child demonstrating a particular pattern of autonomic or brain activity has actually processed a stimulus in a certain way.

- The **clinical,** or **case study, method** provides an in-depth understanding of a single child. But collection of information may be unsystematic and subjective, and researchers cannot generalize beyond the child studied.

- To uncover the cultural meanings of children's and adults' behaviors, researchers rely on **ethnography,** engaging in participant observation. But investigators' cultural values and theoretical commitments may lead them to observe selectively or misinterpret what they see.

Reliability and Validity: Keys to Scientifically Sound Research (p. 54)

Explain how reliability and validity apply to research methods and to the overall accuracy of research findings and conclusions.

- **Reliability** refers to the consistency, or repeatability, of measures of behavior. In observational research, inter-rater reliability is determined by having observers evaluate the same behaviors. For self-report and neurobiological measures, test–retest reliability is determined. In clinical and ethnographic research, reliability involves assessing whether the patterns and themes identified by the researcher are grounded in evidence and are plausible.

- A research method has high **validity** if, after examining its content and relationships with other measures of behavior, the researcher finds that it reflects what it was intended to measure. The concept of validity can also be applied to the overall accuracy of research findings and conclusions. In designing a study, investigators must ensure **internal validity**—that conditions internal to the design permit an accurate test of the hypothesis or question. They must also consider **external validity**—the degree to which findings generalize to settings and participants outside the original study.

General Research Designs
(p. 55)

Distinguish correlational and experimental research designs, noting strengths and limitations of each.

- A **correlational design** examines relationships between variables without altering people's experiences. The **correlation coefficient** is often used to measure the association between variables. Correlational studies do not permit cause-and-effect inferences, but they can be helpful in identifying relationships that are worth exploring with a more powerful experimental strategy.

- An **experimental design** permits cause-and-effect inferences. Researchers manipulate an **independent variable** by exposing participants to two or more treatment conditions. Then they determine what effect this variable has on a **dependent variable**. **Random assignment** and **matching** ensure that characteristics of participants and treatment conditions do not operate as **confounding variables**, reducing the internal validity of experimental findings.

- **Laboratory experiments** usually achieve a high degree of control, but their findings may not apply to everyday life. In **field experiments**, researchers randomly assign participants to treatment conditions in the real world. Some investigators conduct **natural**, or **quasi-**, **experiments**, comparing existing treatments. However, these approaches are less rigorous than true experimental designs.

Designs for Studying Development (p. 60)

Describe designs for studying development, noting strengths and limitations of each.

- In the **longitudinal design**, participants are studied repeatedly at different ages to identify common patterns as well as individual differences in development, and the relationship between early and later events and behaviors. Problems include **biased sampling**, **selective attrition**, **practice effects**, and long-term changes in accepted theories and methods. **Cohort effects** threaten the validity of longitudinal findings because of difficulty generalizing to children growing up during other time periods.

- The **cross-sectional design**, in which groups of children differing in age are studied at the same point in time, offers an efficient approach to investigating development. However, it is limited to comparisons of age-group averages and vulnerable to cohort effects.

- By comparing participants of the same age who were born in different years, investigators use **sequential designs** to test for cohort effects, make longitudinal and cross-sectional comparisons, and gather information about development efficiently. In the **microgenetic design**, researchers track change as it occurs to gain insights into processes of development. However, the time required for children to change is hard to anticipate, and practice effects can bias findings.

Ethics in Research on Children (p. 66)

What special ethical issues arise in doing research on children?

- Because of their immaturity, children are especially vulnerable to harm and often cannot evaluate the risks and benefits of research. Ethical principles and institutional review boards (IRBs) that weigh research in terms of a **risks-versus-benefits ratio** help ensure **protection from harm**. In addition to parental consent and agreement of others acting on children's behalf, researchers should seek the **informed consent** of children age 7 and older. The use of deception, though sometimes necessary, is especially risky with children because **debriefing** can undermine their faith in the trustworthiness of adults.

IMPORTANT TERMS AND CONCEPTS

biased sampling (p. 61)
clinical interview (p. 46)
clinical, or case study, method (p. 50)
cohort effects (p. 62)
confounding variables (p. 57)
correlation coefficient (p. 56)
correlational design (p. 55)
cross-sectional design (p. 62)
debriefing (p. 69)
dependent variable (p. 56)
ethnography (p. 52)
event sampling (p. 44)
experimental design (p. 56)

external validity (p. 55)
field experiment (p. 58)
hypothesis (p. 41)
independent variable (p. 56)
informed consent (p. 67)
internal validity (p. 55)
laboratory experiment (p. 56)
longitudinal design (p. 60)
matching (p. 58)
microgenetic design (p. 64)
natural, or quasi-, experiment (p. 58)
naturalistic observation (p. 42)
neurobiological methods (p. 47)

observer bias (p. 45)
observer influence (p. 45)
practice effects (p. 62)
protection from harm (p. 67)
random assignment (p. 57)
reliability (p. 54)
risks-versus-benefits ratio (p. 67)
selective attrition (p. 62)
sequential designs (p. 63)
structured interview (p. 47)
structured observation (p. 44)
time sampling (p. 45)
validity (p. 54)

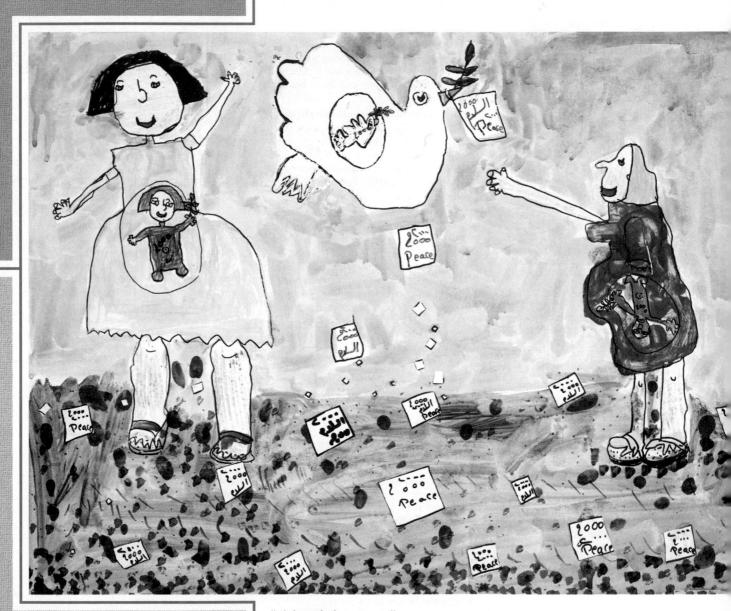

CHAPTER 3

"Giving Birth to Peace"

Lotfeh Mohamed El Masri, 11 years, Lebanon

This painting captures expectant parents' hopes for a compassionate world in which to rear their children. How is the one-celled organism gradually transformed into a baby with the human capacity to play, dream, and create? What factors support or undermine this earliest period of development? Chapter 3 provides answers to these questions.

Reprinted with permission from the International Child Art Foundation, Washington, DC

Biological Foundations, Prenatal Development, and Birth

"It's a girl," announces the doctor, holding up the squalling newborn baby as her new parents gaze with amazement at their miraculous creation.

"A girl! We've named her Sarah!" exclaims the proud father to eager relatives waiting for news of their new family member.

As we join these parents in thinking about how this wondrous being came into existence and imagining her future, we are struck by many questions. How could this baby, equipped with everything necessary for life outside the womb, have developed from the union of two tiny cells? What ensures that Sarah will, in due time, roll over, reach for objects, walk, talk, make friends, learn, imagine, and create—just like other typical children born before her? Why is she a girl and not a boy, dark-haired rather than blond, calm and cuddly instead of wiry and energetic? What difference will it make that Sarah is given a name and place in one family, community, nation, and culture rather than another?

To answer these questions, we begin by considering genetic foundations. Because nature has prepared us for survival, all humans have features in common. Yet each of us is also unique. **TAKE A MOMENT...** Think about several children you know well, and jot down the most obvious physical and behavioral similarities between them and their parents. Did you find that one child shows combined features of both parents, another resembles just one parent, whereas a third is not like either parent? These directly observable characteristics are called **phenotypes.** They depend in part on the individual's **genotype**—the complex blend of genetic information that determines our species and influences all our unique characteristics. Yet phenotypes, as our discussion will show, are also affected by environmental influences—ones that begin even before conception.

Next, we trace prenatal development, the most rapid period of growth, during which complex transactions between heredity and environment profoundly affect children's health and well-being. Then we turn to the drama of birth and to the problems of infants who are born underweight or too early.

As our discussion proceeds, some findings about the influence of nature and nurture may surprise you. For example, many people believe that when children inherit unfavorable characteristics, not much can be done to help them. Others are convinced that the damage done to a child by a harmful environment can easily be corrected. We will see that neither of these assumptions is true. In the final section of this chapter, we take up the question of how nature and nurture work together to shape the course of development.

Genetic Foundations

Each of us is made up of trillions of units called *cells*. Within every cell is a control center, or *nucleus*, that contains rodlike structures called **chromosomes,** which store and transmit genetic information. Human chromosomes come in 23 matching pairs (an exception is the XY pair in males, which we will discuss shortly). Each member of a pair corresponds to the other in size, shape, and genetic functions. One is inherited from the mother and one from the father (see Figure 3.1 on page 74).

Genetic Foundations
The Genetic Code • The Sex Cells • Boy or Girl? • Multiple Offspring • Patterns of Genetic Inheritance • Chromosomal Abnormalities

Reproductive Choices
Genetic Counseling • Prenatal Diagnosis and Fetal Medicine

■ **SOCIAL ISSUES: HEALTH:** *The Pros and Cons of Reproductive Technologies*

Prenatal Development
Conception • Period of the Zygote • Period of the Embryo • Period of the Fetus

Prenatal Environmental Influences
Teratogens • Other Maternal Factors

Childbirth
The Baby's Adaptation to Labor and Delivery • The Newborn Baby's Appearance • Assessing the Newborn's Physical Condition: The Apgar Scale

Approaches to Childbirth
Natural, or Prepared, Childbirth • Home Delivery • Labor and Delivery Medication

Birth Complications
Oxygen Deprivation • Preterm and Low-Birth-Weight Infants • Birth Complications, Parenting, and Resilience

■ **SOCIAL ISSUES: HEALTH:** *A Cross-National Perspective on Health Care and Other Policies for Parents and Newborn Babies*

Heredity, Environment, and Behavior: A Look Ahead
The Question, "How Much?" • The Question, "How?"

■ **BIOLOGY AND ENVIRONMENT:** *A Case of Epigenesis: Smoking During Pregnancy Alters Gene Expression*

▶ What are genes, and how are they transmitted from one generation to the next?

▶ Describe various patterns of genetic inheritance.

▶ Describe major chromosomal abnormalities, and explain how they occur.

The Genetic Code

Chromosomes are made up of **deoxyribonucleic acid,** or **DNA.** As Figure 3.2 shows, DNA is a long double-stranded molecule that looks like a twisted ladder. Each rung of the ladder consists of a pair of chemical substances called *bases.* Although the bases always pair up in the same way across the ladder rungs—A with T, C with G—they can occur in any order along its sides. It is this sequence of base pairs that provides genetic instructions. A **gene** is a segment of DNA along the length of the chromosome. Genes can be of different lengths—perhaps 100 to several thousand ladder rungs long. An estimated 20,000 to 25,000 genes lie along the human chromosomes (Human Genome Program, 2008).

We share some of our genetic makeup with even the simplest organisms, such as bacteria and molds, and most of it with other mammals, especially primates. Between 98 and 99 percent of chimpanzee and human DNA is identical. This means that only a small portion of our heredity is responsible for the traits that make us human, from our upright gait to our extraordinary language and cognitive capacities. And the genetic variation from one human to the next is even less! Individuals around the world are about 99.1 percent genetically identical (Gibbons, 1998; Gibbons et al., 2004). But it takes a change in only a single base pair to influence human traits. And such tiny changes can combine in unique ways across multiple genes, thereby amplifying variability within the human species.

A unique feature of DNA is that it can duplicate itself through a process called **mitosis.** This special ability permits a single cell, formed at conception, to develop into a complex human being composed of a great many cells. Refer again to Figure 3.2, and you will see that during mitosis, the chromosomes copy themselves. As a result, each new body cell contains the same number of chromosomes and the identical genetic information.

FIGURE 3.2 **DNA's ladderlike structure.** This figure shows that the pairings of bases across the rungs of the ladder are very specific: Adenine (A) always appears with thymine (T), and cytosine (C) always appears with guanine (G). Here, the DNA ladder duplicates by splitting down the middle of its ladder rungs. Each free base picks up a new complementary partner from the area surrounding the cell nucleus.

Genes accomplish their task by sending instructions for making a rich assortment of proteins to the *cytoplasm*, the area surrounding the cell nucleus. Proteins, which trigger chemical reactions throughout the body, are the biological foundation on which our characteristics are built. How do humans, with far fewer genes than scientists once thought (only twice as many as the worm or fly), manage to develop into such complex beings? The answer lies in the proteins our genes make, which break up and reassemble in staggering variety—about 10 to 20 million altogether. Simpler species have far fewer proteins. Furthermore, the communication system between the cell nucleus and cytoplasm, which fine-tunes gene activity, is more intricate in humans than in simpler organisms. Within the cell, a wide range of environmental factors modify gene expression (Lashley, 2007). So even at this microscopic level, biological events are the result of *both* genetic and nongenetic forces.

The Sex Cells

New individuals are created when two special cells called **gametes,** or sex cells—the sperm and ovum—combine. A gamete contains only 23 chromosomes, half as many as a regular body cell. Gametes are formed through a cell division process called **meiosis,** which halves the number of chromosomes normally present in body cells. When sperm and ovum unite at fertilization, the resulting cell, called a **zygote,** will again have 46 chromosomes.

The steps involved in meiosis are shown in Figure 3.3. First, the chromosomes pair up, and each one copies itself. Then a special event called **crossing over** occurs, in which

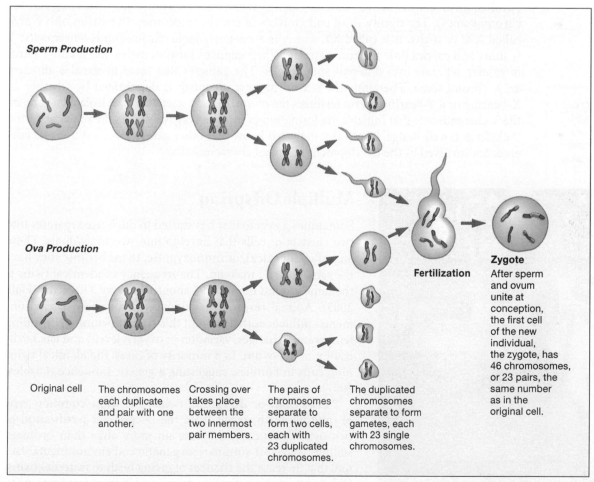

Sperm Production

Ova Production

Fertilization

Zygote
After sperm and ovum unite at conception, the first cell of the new individual, the zygote, has 46 chromosomes, or 23 pairs, the same number as in the original cell.

Original cell

The chromosomes each duplicate and pair with one another.

Crossing over takes place between the two innermost pair members.

The pairs of chromosomes separate to form two cells, each with 23 duplicated chromosomes.

The duplicated chromosomes separate to form gametes, each with 23 single chromosomes.

FIGURE 3.3   The cell division process of meiosis, leading to gamete formation. (Here, original cells are depicted with 2 rather than the full complement of 23 pairs.) Meiosis creates gametes with only half the usual number of chromosomes. When sperm and ovum unite at conception, the first cell of the new individual (the zygote) has the correct, full number of chromosomes.

chromosomes next to each other break at one or more points along their length and exchange segments, so that genes from one are replaced by genes from another. This shuffling of genes creates new hereditary combinations. Next, the chromosome pairs separate into different cells, but chance determines which member of each pair will gather with others and end up in the same gamete. Finally, each chromosome leaves its partner and becomes part of a gamete containing only 23 chromosomes instead of the usual 46.

These events make the likelihood extremely low—about 1 in 700 trillion—that nontwin siblings will be genetically identical (Gould & Keeton, 1996). The genetic variability produced by meiosis is adaptive: Because it generates offspring that vary in phenotype, it increases the chances that at least some members of a species will cope with ever-changing environments and will survive.

In the male, four sperm are produced when meiosis is complete. Also, the cells from which sperm arise are produced continuously throughout life. For this reason, a healthy man can father a child at any age after sexual maturity. In the female, meiosis results in just one ovum; the remaining genetic material degenerates. In addition, the female is born with all her ova already present in her ovaries, and she can bear children for only three to four decades. Still, there are plenty of female sex cells. About 1 to 2 million are present at birth, 40,000 remain at adolescence, and approximately 350 to 450 will mature during a woman's childbearing years (Moore & Persaud, 2008).

Boy or Girl?

Return to Figure 3.1, and note the 22 matching pairs of chromosomes, which geneticists number from longest (1) to shortest (22). These are called **autosomes** (meaning *not* sex chromosomes). The twenty-third pair consists of **sex chromosomes.** In females, this pair is called XX; in males, it is called XY. The X is a relatively large chromosome, whereas the Y is short and carries little genetic material. When gametes form in males, the X and Y chromosomes separate into different sperm cells. The gametes that form in females all carry an X chromosome. Therefore, the sex of the new organism is determined by whether an X-bearing or a Y-bearing sperm fertilizes the ovum. In fact, scientists have isolated a gene on the Y chromosome that initiates the formation of male sex organs during the prenatal period (Sekido & Lovell-Badge, 2009). But they also know that other genes, some yet to be discovered, are involved in the development of sexual characteristics.

These identical, or monozygotic, twins were created when a duplicating zygote separated into two clusters of cells, which developed into two individuals with the same genetic makeup.

© F4FOTO/ALAMY

Multiple Offspring

Sometimes a zygote that has started to duplicate separates into two clusters of cells that develop into two individuals. These are called **identical,** or **monozygotic, twins** because they have the same genetic makeup. The frequency of identical twins is the same around the world—about 1 in every 330 births (Hall, 2003). Animal research has uncovered a variety of environmental influences that prompt this type of twinning, including temperature changes, variation in oxygen levels, and late fertilization of the ovum. In a minority of cases, the identical twinning runs in families, suggesting a genetic influence (Lashley, 2007).

Fraternal, or **dizygotic, twins,** the most common type of multiple birth, result from the release and fertilization of two ova. Genetically, they are no more alike than ordinary siblings. Table 3.1 summarizes genetic and environmental factors that increase the chances of giving birth to fraternal twins. Older maternal age, fertility drugs, and in vitro fertilization (to be discussed shortly) are major causes of the dramatic rise in fraternal twinning and other multiple births in industrialized

TABLE 3.1 | **Maternal Factors Linked to Fraternal Twinning**

FACTOR	DESCRIPTION
Ethnicity	Occurs in 4 per 1,000 births among Asians, 8 per 1,000 births among whites, 12 to 16 per 1,000 births among blacks[a]
Family history of twinning	Occurs more often among women whose mothers and sisters gave birth to fraternal twins
Age	Rises with maternal age, peaking between 35 and 39 years, and then rapidly falls
Nutrition	Occurs less often among women with poor diets; occurs more often among women who are tall and overweight or of normal weight as opposed to slight body build
Number of births	Is more likely with each additional birth
Fertility drugs and in vitro fertilization	Is more likely with fertility hormones and in vitro fertilization (see page 86), which also increase the chances of bearing triplets, quadruplets, or quintuplets

[a]Worldwide rates, not including multiple births resulting from use of fertility drugs.

Sources: Hall, 2003; Hoekstra et al., 2008; Lashley, 2007.

nations over the past several decades (Machin, 2005; Russell et al., 2003). Currently, fraternal twins account for 1 in about every 60 births in the United States (U.S. Department of Health and Human Services, 2010a).

Patterns of Genetic Inheritance

Two forms of each gene occur at the same place on the chromosomes, one inherited from the mother and one from the father. Each form of a gene is called an **allele.** If the alleles from both parents are alike, the child is **homozygous** and will display the inherited trait. If the alleles differ, then the child is **heterozygous,** and relationships between the alleles determine the phenotype.

Dominant–Recessive Relationships In many heterozygous pairings, **dominant–recessive inheritance** occurs: Only one allele affects the child's characteristics. It is called *dominant*; the second allele, which has no effect, is called *recessive*. Hair color is an example. The allele for dark hair is dominant (we can represent it with a capital *D*), whereas the one for blond hair is recessive (symbolized by a lowercase *b*). A child who inherits a homozygous pair of dominant alleles *(DD)* and a child who inherits a heterozygous pair *(Db)* will both be dark-haired, even though their genotypes differ. Blond hair can result only from having two recessive alleles *(bb)*. Still, heterozygous individuals with just one recessive allele *(Db)* can pass that trait to their children. Therefore, they are called **carriers** of the trait.

Some human characteristics and disorders that follow the rules of dominant–recessive inheritance are listed in Table 3.2 and Table 3.3 on page 78, respectively. As you can see, many disabilities and diseases are the product of recessive alleles. One of the most frequently occurring recessive disorders is *phenylketonuria*, or *PKU*, which affects the way the body breaks down proteins contained in many foods. Infants born with two recessive alleles lack an enzyme that converts one of the basic amino acids that make up proteins (phenylalanine) into a byproduct essential for body functioning

TABLE 3.2 | **Examples of Dominant and Recessive Characteristics**

DOMINANT	RECESSIVE
Dark hair	Blond hair
Normal hair	Pattern baldness
Curly hair	Straight hair
Nonred hair	Red hair
Facial dimples	No dimples
Normal hearing	Some forms of deafness
Normal vision	Nearsightedness
Farsightedness	Normal vision
Normal vision	Congenital eye cataracts
Normally pigmented skin	Albinism
Double-jointedness	Normal joints
Type A blood	Type O blood
Type B blood	Type O blood
Rh-positive blood	Rh-negative blood

Note: Many normal characteristics that were previously thought to be due to dominant–recessive inheritance, such as eye color, are now regarded as due to multiple genes. For the characteristics listed here, there still seems to be general agreement that the simple dominant–recessive relationship holds.

Source: McKusick, 2011.

TABLE 3.3 | **Examples of Dominant and Recessive Diseases**

DISEASE	DESCRIPTION	MODE OF INHERITANCE	INCIDENCE	TREATMENT
Autosomal Diseases				
Cooley's anemia	Pale appearance, retarded physical growth, and lethargic behavior begin in infancy.	Recessive	1 in 500 births to parents of Mediterranean descent	Frequent blood transfusion; death from complications usually occurs by adolescence.
Cystic fibrosis	Lungs, liver, and pancreas secrete large amounts of thick mucus, leading to breathing and digestive difficulties.	Recessive	1 in 2,000 to 2,500 Caucasian births; 1 in 16,000 births to North Americans of African descent	Bronchial drainage, prompt treatment of respiratory infection, dietary management. Advances in medical care allow survival with good life quality into adulthood.
Phenylketonuria (PKU)	Inability to metabolize the amino acid phenylalanine, contained in many proteins, causes severe central nervous system damage in the first year of life.	Recessive	1 in 8,000 births	Placing the child on a special diet results in average intelligence and normal lifespan. Subtle deficits in memory, planning, decision making, and problem solving are often present.
Sickle cell anemia	Abnormal sickling of red blood cells causes oxygen deprivation, pain, swelling, and tissue damage. Anemia and susceptibility to infections, especially pneumonia, occur.	Recessive	1 in 500 births to North Americans of African descent	Blood transfusions, painkillers, prompt treatment of infection. No known cure; 50 percent die by age 55.
Tay-Sachs disease	Central nervous system degeneration, with onset at about 6 months, leads to poor muscle tone, blindness, deafness, and convulsions.	Recessive	1 in 3,600 births to Jews of European descent and to French Canadians	None. Death occurs by 3 to 4 years of age.
Huntington disease	Central nervous system degeneration leads to muscular coordination difficulties, mental deterioration, and personality changes. Symptoms usually do not appear until age 35 or later.	Dominant	1 in 18,000 to 25,000 births to North Americans	None. Death occurs 10 to 20 years after symptom onset.
Marfan syndrome	Tall, slender build; thin, elongated arms and legs; and heart defects and eye abnormalities, especially of the lens. Excessive lengthening of the body results in a variety of skeletal defects.	Dominant	1 in 5,000 to 10,000 births	Correction of heart and eye defects is sometimes possible. Death from heart failure in early adulthood is common.
X-Linked Diseases				
Duchenne muscular dystrophy	Degenerative muscle disease. Abnormal gait, loss of ability to walk between 7 and 13 years of age.	Recessive	1 in 3,000 to 5,000 male births	None. Death from respiratory infection or weakening of the heart muscle usually occurs in adolescence.
Hemophilia	Blood fails to clot normally; can lead to severe internal bleeding and tissue damage.	Recessive	1 in 4,000 to 7,000 male births	Blood transfusions. Safety precautions to prevent injury.
Diabetes insipidus	Insufficient production of the hormone vasopressin results in excessive thirst and urination. Dehydration can cause central nervous system damage.	Recessive	1 in 2,500 male births	Hormone replacement.

Note: For recessive disorders, carrier status can be detected in prospective parents through a blood test or genetic analyses. For all disorders listed, prenatal diagnosis is available (see Table 3.5 on p. 85).

Sources: Kliegman et al., 2008; Lashley, 2007; McKusick, 2011.

(tyrosine). Without this enzyme, phenylalanine quickly builds to toxic levels that damage the central nervous system. By 1 year, infants with untreated PKU suffer from permanent intellectual disability.

Despite its potentially damaging effects, PKU provides an excellent illustration of the fact that inheriting unfavorable genes does not always lead to an untreatable condition. All U.S. states require that each newborn be given a blood test for PKU. If the disease is found, doctors place the baby on a diet low in phenylalanine. Children who receive this treatment nevertheless show mild deficits in certain cognitive skills, such as memory, planning, decision making, and problem solving, because even small amounts of phenylalanine interfere with brain functioning (DeRoche & Welsh, 2008). But as long as dietary treatment begins early and continues, children with PKU usually attain an average level of intelligence and have a normal lifespan.

In dominant–recessive inheritance, if we know the genetic makeup of the parents, we can predict the percentage of children in a family who are likely to display or carry a trait. Figure 3.4 illustrates this for PKU. For a child to inherit the condition, each parent must have a recessive allele *(p)*. As the figure also illustrates, a single gene can affect more than one trait. Because of their inability to convert phenylalanine into tyrosine (which is responsible for pigmentation), children with PKU usually have light hair and blue eyes. Furthermore, children vary in the degree to which phenylalanine accumulates in their tissues and in the extent to which they respond to treatment. This is due to the action of **modifier genes,** which enhance or dilute the effects of other genes.

Only rarely are serious diseases due to dominant alleles. Think about why this is so. Children who inherit the dominant allele always develop the disorder. They seldom live long enough to reproduce, so the harmful dominant allele is eliminated from the family's heredity in a single generation. Some dominant disorders, however, do persist. One is *Huntington disease*, a condition in which the central nervous system degenerates. Why has this disorder endured? Its symptoms usually do not appear until age 35 or later, after the person has passed the dominant allele to his or her children.

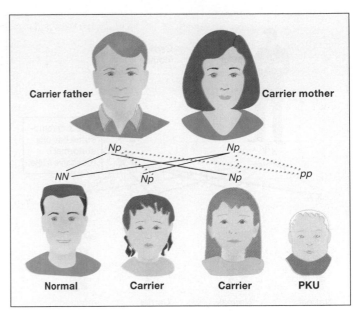

FIGURE 3.4 Dominant–recessive mode of inheritance, as illustrated by PKU. When both parents are heterozygous carriers of the recessive gene *(p)*, we can predict that 25 percent of their offspring are likely to be normal *(NN)*, 50 percent are likely to be carriers *(Np)*, and 25 percent are likely to inherit the disorder *(pp)*. Notice that the PKU-affected child, in contrast to his siblings, has light hair. The recessive gene for PKU affects more than one trait. It also leads to fair coloring.

Incomplete Dominance In some heterozygous circumstances, the dominant–recessive relationship does not hold completely. Instead, we see **incomplete dominance,** a pattern of inheritance in which both alleles are expressed in the phenotype, resulting in a combined trait, or one that is intermediate between the two.

The *sickle cell trait*, a heterozygous condition present in many black Africans, provides an example. *Sickle cell anemia* (see Table 3.3) occurs in full form when a child inherits two recessive alleles. They cause the usually round red blood cells to become sickle (crescent-moon) shaped, especially under low-oxygen conditions. The sickled cells clog the blood vessels and block the flow of blood, causing intense pain, swelling, and tissue damage. Despite medical advances that today allow 85 percent of affected children to survive to adulthood, North Americans with sickle cell anemia have an average life expectancy of only 55 years (Driscoll, 2007). Heterozygous individuals are protected from the disease under most circumstances. However, when they experience oxygen deprivation—for example, at high altitudes or after intense physical exercise—the single recessive allele asserts itself, and a temporary, mild form of the illness occurs.

The sickle cell allele is common among black Africans for a special reason. Carriers of it are more resistant to malaria than are individuals with two alleles for normal red blood cells. In Africa, where malaria is common, these carriers survived and reproduced more frequently than others, leading the gene to be maintained in the black population. But in regions of the world where the risk of malaria is low, the frequency of the gene is declining. For example, only 8 percent of African Americans are carriers, compared with 20 percent of black Africans (National Center for Biotechnology Information, 2007).

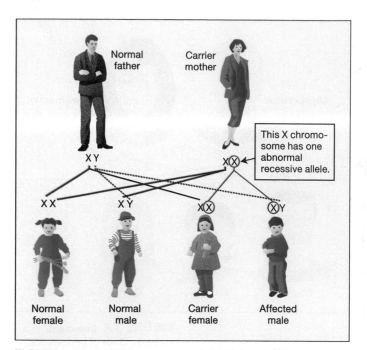

FIGURE 3.5 **X-linked inheritance.** In the example shown here, the allele on the father's X chromosome is normal. The mother has one normal and one abnormal recessive allele on her X chromosomes. By looking at the possible combinations of the parents' alleles, we can predict that 50 percent of these parents' male children are likely to have the disorder, and 50 percent of their female children are likely to be carriers of it.

X-Linked Inheritance Males and females have an equal chance of inheriting recessive disorders carried on the autosomes, such as PKU and sickle cell anemia. But when a harmful allele is carried on the X chromosome, **X-linked inheritance** applies. Males are more likely to be affected because their sex chromosomes do not match. In females, any recessive allele on one X chromosome has a good chance of being suppressed by a dominant allele on the other X. But the Y chromosome is only about one-third as long and therefore lacks many corresponding alleles to override those on the X. A well-known example is *hemophilia*, a disorder in which the blood fails to clot normally. Figure 3.5 shows its greater likelihood of inheritance by male children whose mothers carry the abnormal allele.

Besides X-linked disorders, many other sex differences reveal the male to be at a disadvantage. Rates of miscarriage, infant and childhood deaths, birth defects, learning disabilities, behavior disorders, and broad intellectual disability all are greater for boys (Butler & Meaney, 2005). It is possible that these sex differences can be traced to the genetic code. The female, with two X chromosomes, benefits from a greater variety of genes. Nature, however, seems to have adjusted for the male's disadvantage. Worldwide, about 107 boys are born for every 100 girls, and judging from miscarriage and abortion statistics, an even greater number of boys are conceived (United Nations, 2010).

Nevertheless, in recent decades, the proportion of male births has declined in many industrialized countries, including the United States, Canada, and European nations (Jongbloet et al., 2001). Some researchers attribute the trend to a rise in stressful living conditions, which heighten spontaneous abortions, especially of male fetuses (Catalano et al., 2010). In a test of this hypothesis, male-to-female birth ratios in East Germany were examined over the 54-year period between 1946 and 1999. The ratio was lowest in 1991, the year that the country's economy collapsed (Catalano, 2003). Similarly, in a California study spanning the decade of the 1990s, the percentage of male fetal deaths increased in months in which unemployment (a major stressor) also rose above its typical level (Catalano et al., 2009).

Genomic Imprinting More than 1,000 human characteristics follow the rules of dominant–recessive and incomplete-dominance inheritance (McKusick, 2011). In these cases, whichever parent contributes a gene to the new individual, the gene responds in the same way. Geneticists, however, have identified some exceptions. In **genomic imprinting,** alleles are *imprinted,* or chemically marked, so that one pair member (either the mother's or the father's) is activated, regardless of its makeup (Hirasawa & Feil, 2010). The imprint is often temporary; it may be erased in the next generation, and it may not occur in all individuals.

Imprinting helps us understand certain puzzling genetic patterns. For example, children are more likely to develop diabetes if their father, rather than their mother, suffers from it. And people with asthma or hay fever tend to have mothers, not fathers, with the illness. Imprinting is involved in several childhood cancers and in *Prader-Willi syndrome*, a disorder with symptoms of broad intellectual disability and severe obesity (Butler, 2009). It may also explain why Huntington disease, when inherited from the father, tends to emerge at an earlier age and to progress more rapidly (Gropman & Adams, 2007).

Genomic imprinting can also operate on the sex chromosomes, as *fragile X syndrome*—the most common inherited cause of intellectual disability—reveals. In this disorder, which affects about 1 in 4,000 males and 1 in 6,000 females, an abnormal repetition of a sequence of DNA bases occurs in a special spot on the X chromosome, damaging a particular gene. The defective gene at the fragile site is expressed only when it is passed from mother to child. Because the disorder is X-linked, males are more severely affected (Hagerman et al., 2009).

Females usually have a normally functioning gene on their other X chromosome (inherited from the father) that partially compensates for the abnormal gene.

EEG and fMRI research on children with fragile X syndrome reveals reduced size, structural abnormalities, and atypical activity in many areas of the cerebral cortex (Schneider, Hagerman, & Hessl, 2009). Deficits range from mild learning disabilities to severe intellectual disability. Certain physical features, such as enlarged ears, a long face with a prominent chin, and (in males) enlarged testicles are common. About 30 percent of individuals with fragile X syndrome also have symptoms of *autism*, a serious disorder usually diagnosed in early childhood that involves impaired social interaction, delayed or absent language and communication, and repetitive motor behavior (Schwarte, 2008).

A 9-year-old who has fragile X syndrome participates in an art class with typical students. This X-linked disorder, which causes intellectual disabilities, is expressed only when an abnormal gene is passed from mother to child.

Mutation Although less than 3 percent of pregnancies result in the birth of a baby with a hereditary abnormality, these children account for about 20 percent of infant deaths and contribute substantially to lifelong impaired physical and mental functioning (U.S. Department of Health and Human Services, 2010f). How are harmful genes created in the first place? The answer is **mutation,** a sudden but permanent change in a segment of DNA. A mutation may affect only one or two genes, or it may involve many genes, as in the chromosomal disorders we will discuss shortly. Some mutations occur spontaneously, simply by chance. Others are caused by hazardous environmental agents.

Although nonionizing forms of radiation—electromagnetic waves and microwaves—have no demonstrated impact on DNA, ionizing (high-energy) radiation is an established cause of mutation. Women who receive repeated doses before conception are more likely to miscarry or give birth to children with hereditary defects. The incidence of genetic abnormalities, such as physical malformations and childhood cancer, is also higher in children whose fathers are exposed to radiation in their occupation. However, infrequent and mild exposure to radiation does not cause genetic damage (Jacquet, 2004). Rather, high doses over a long period impair DNA.

The examples just given illustrate *germline mutation*, which takes place in the cells that give rise to gametes. When the affected individual mates, the defective DNA is passed on to the next generation. In a second type, called *somatic mutation*, normal body cells mutate, an event that can occur at any time of life. The DNA defect appears in every cell derived from the affected body cell, eventually becoming widespread enough to cause disease (such as cancer) or disability.

It is easy to see how disorders that run in families can result from germline mutation. But somatic mutation may be involved in these disorders as well. Some people harbor a genetic susceptibility that causes certain body cells to mutate easily in the presence of triggering events (Weiss, 2005). This helps explain why some individuals develop serious illnesses (such as cancer) as a result of smoking, exposure to pollutants, or psychological stress, while others do not.

Polygenic Inheritance So far, we have discussed patterns of inheritance in which people either display a particular trait or do not. These cut-and-dried individual differences are much easier to trace to their genetic origins than are characteristics that vary on a continuum among people, such as height, weight, intelligence, and personality. These traits are due to **polygenic inheritance,** in which many genes determine the characteristic in question. Polygenic inheritance is complex, and much about it is still unknown. In the final section of this chapter, we will discuss how researchers infer the influence of heredity on human attributes when they do not know the precise patterns of inheritance.

Chromosomal Abnormalities

Besides harmful recessive alleles, abnormalities of the chromosomes are a major cause of serious developmental problems. Most chromosomal defects result from mistakes occurring during meiosis, when the ovum and sperm are formed. A chromosome pair does not separate properly, or part of a chromosome breaks off. Because these errors involve far more DNA than problems due to single genes, they usually produce many physical and mental symptoms.

© ROBIN NELSON/PHOTOEDIT

Despite impaired development, this toddler with Down syndrome profits from growing up in a stimulating, caring environment. As his physical therapist engages him in water play, he benefits intellectually, physically, and emotionally.

Down Syndrome The most common chromosomal disorder, occurring in 1 out of every 770 live births, is *Down syndrome*. In 95 percent of cases, it results from a failure of the twenty-first pair of chromosomes to separate during meiosis, so the new individual inherits three of these chromosomes rather than the normal two. For this reason, Down syndrome is sometimes called *trisomy 21*. In other, less frequent forms, an extra twenty-first chromosome is attached to part of another chromosome (called *translocation* pattern). Or an error occurs during the early stages of mitosis, causing some but not all body cells to have the defective chromosomal makeup (called *mosaic* pattern) (U.S. Department of Health and Human Services, 2011a). Because the mosaic type involves less genetic material, symptoms may be less extreme.

The consequences of Down syndrome include intellectual disability, memory and speech problems, limited vocabulary, and slow motor development. Brain-imaging studies reveal a reduction in size of the brain, which is more pronounced in certain regions of the cerebral cortex (Pinter et al., 2001). Affected individuals also have distinct physical features—a short, stocky build, a flattened face, a protruding tongue, almond-shaped eyes, and (in 50 percent of cases) an unusual crease running across the palm of the hand. In addition, infants with Down syndrome are often born with eye cataracts, hearing loss, and heart and intestinal defects (U.S. Department of Health and Human Services 2011a). Because of medical advances, fewer individuals with Down syndrome die early than was the case in the past. Many survive into their fifties and a few into their sixties to eighties. However, more than half of affected individuals who live past age 40 show symptoms of *Alzheimer's disease*, the most common form of dementia (Wiseman et al., 2009). Genes on chromosome 21 are linked to this disorder.

Infants with Down syndrome smile less readily, show poor eye-to-eye contact, have weak muscle tone, and explore objects less persistently (Slonims & McConachie, 2006). But when parents encourage them to engage with their surroundings, children with Down syndrome develop more favorably. They also benefit from infant and preschool intervention programs, although emotional, social, and motor skills improve more than intellectual performance (Carr, 2002). Clearly, environmental factors affect how well children with Down syndrome fare.

As Figure 3.6 shows, the risk of bearing a baby with Down syndrome rises dramatically with maternal age. But exactly why older mothers are more likely to release ova with meiotic errors is not yet known (Martin, 2008). In about 5 to 10 percent of cases, the extra genetic material originates with the father. Some studies suggest a role for advanced paternal age, while others show no age effects (De Souza, Alberman, & Morris, 2009; Dzurova & Pikhart, 2005; Sherman et al., 2005).

FIGURE 3.6   Risk of Down Syndrome and all chromosomal abnormalities by maternal age. Risk rises sharply after age 35. (From R. L. Schonberg & C. J. Tifft, 2007, "Birth Defects and Prenatal Diagnosis," from *Children with Disabilities*, 6/e, M. L. Matshaw, L. Pellegrino, & N. J. Roizen, editors, p. 85. Baltimore: Paul H. Brookes Publishing Co., Inc. Adapted by permission.)

TABLE 3.4 | Sex Chromosomal Disorders

DISORDER	DESCRIPTION	INCIDENCE	TREATMENT
XYY syndrome	Extra Y chromosome. Above-average height, large teeth, and sometimes severe acne. Normal to mildly impaired intelligence. Male sexual development and fertility are normal.	1 in 1,000 male births	No special treatment necessary.
Triple X syndrome (XXX)	Extra X chromosome. Tallness and impaired verbal intelligence. Female sexual development and fertility are normal.	1 in 500 to 1,250 female births	Special education to treat verbal ability problems.
Klinefelter syndrome (XXY)	Extra X chromosome. Tallness, body fat distribution resembling that of females, incomplete development of sex characteristics at puberty, sterility, and impaired verbal intelligence.	1 in 900 male births	Hormone therapy at puberty to stimulate development of sex characteristics; special education to treat verbal ability problems.
Turner syndrome (XO)	Missing X chromosome. Short stature, webbed neck, incomplete development of sex characteristics at puberty, sterility, and impaired spatial intelligence.	1 in 2,500 to 8,000 female births	Hormone therapy in childhood to stimulate physical growth and at puberty to promote development of sex characteristics; special education to treat spatial ability problems.

Sources: Geerts, Steyaert, & Fryns, 2003; Kesler, 2007; Saitta & Zackai, 2005; Simpson et al., 2003.

Abnormalities of the Sex Chromosomes Disorders of the autosomes other than Down syndrome usually disrupt development so severely that miscarriage occurs. When such babies are born, they rarely survive beyond early childhood. In contrast, sex chromosome disorders often are not recognized until adolescence when, in some deviations, puberty is delayed. The most common problems involve the presence of an extra chromosome (either X or Y) or the absence of one X in females (see Table 3.4).

Research has discredited a variety of myths about individuals with sex chromosome disorders. For example, as Table 3.4 reveals, males with *XYY syndrome* are not necessarily more aggressive and antisocial than XY males. And most children with sex chromosome disorders do not suffer from broad intellectual disability. Rather, their intellectual problems are usually very specific. Verbal difficulties—for example, with reading and vocabulary—are common among girls with *triple X syndrome* and boys with *Klinefelter syndrome*, both of whom inherit an extra X chromosome. In contrast, girls with *Turner syndrome*, who are missing an X, have trouble with spatial relationships—for example, drawing pictures, telling right from left, following travel directions, and noticing changes in facial expressions (Kesler, 2007; Lawrence et al., 2003; Simpson et al., 2003). Brain-imaging research confirms that adding to or subtracting from the usual number of X chromosomes alters development of certain brain structures, yielding particular intellectual deficits (Cutter et al., 2006; Itti et al., 2006).

A S K   Y O U R S E L F

Review ■ Cite evidence indicating that both heredity and environment contribute to the development of children with PKU and Down syndrome.

Review ■ Using your knowledge of X-linked inheritance, explain why males are more vulnerable than females to miscarriage, infant death, genetic disorders, and other problems.

Connect ■ Referring to ecological systems theory (Chapter 1, pages 26–28), explain why parents of children with genetic disorders often experience increased stress. What factors, within and beyond the family, can help these parents support their children's development?

Apply ■ Gilbert's genetic makeup is homozygous for dark hair. Jan's is homozygous for blond hair. What color is Gilbert's hair? How about Jan's? What proportion of their children are likely to be dark-haired? Explain.

▶ What procedures can assist prospective parents in having healthy children?

Reproductive Choices

In the past, many couples with genetic disorders in their families chose not to bear a child at all rather than risk the birth of a baby with abnormalities. Today, genetic counseling and prenatal diagnosis help people make informed decisions about conceiving, carrying a pregnancy to term, or adopting a child.

Genetic Counseling

Genetic counseling is a communication process designed to help couples assess their chances of giving birth to a baby with a hereditary disorder and choose the best course of action in view of risks and family goals (Resta et al., 2006). Individuals likely to seek counseling are those who have had difficulties bearing children—for example, repeated miscarriages—or who know that genetic problems exist in their families. In addition, women who delay childbearing past age 35 are often candidates for genetic counseling. After this time, the overall rate of chromosomal abnormalities rises sharply (refer again to Figure 3.6). But because younger mothers give birth in far greater numbers than older mothers, they still bear the majority of babies with genetic defects. Therefore, some experts argue that maternal needs, not age, should determine referral for genetic counseling (Berkowitz, Roberts, & Minkoff, 2006).

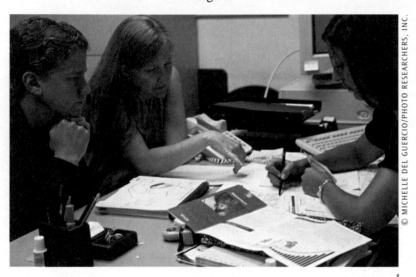

Working with a genetic counselor, a couple assess their risk of bearing a child with inherited abnormalities. Using this information, they can decide whether to try to conceive, use reproductive technologies, or adopt.

If a family history of intellectual disability, psychological disorders, physical defects, or inherited diseases exists, the genetic counselor interviews the couple and prepares a *pedigree*, a picture of the family tree in which affected relatives are identified. The pedigree is used to estimate the likelihood that parents will have an abnormal child, using the genetic principles discussed earlier in this chapter. For many disorders, molecular genetic analyses (in which DNA is examined) can reveal whether the parent is a carrier of the harmful gene. Carrier detection is possible for all the recessive diseases listed in Table 3.3, as well as others, and for fragile X syndrome.

When all the relevant information is in, the genetic counselor helps people consider appropriate options. These include taking a chance and conceiving, choosing from among a variety of reproductive technologies (see the Social Issues: Health box on pages 86–87), or adopting a child.

Prenatal Diagnosis and Fetal Medicine

If couples who might bear a child with abnormalities decide to conceive, several **prenatal diagnostic methods**—medical procedures that permit detection of developmental problems before birth—are available (see Table 3.5). Women of advanced maternal age are prime candidates for *amniocentesis* or *chorionic villus sampling*. Except for *maternal blood analysis*, however, prenatal diagnosis should not be used routinely because of injury risks to the developing organism.

Prenatal diagnosis has led to advances in fetal medicine. For example, by inserting a needle into the uterus, doctors can administer drugs to the fetus. Surgery has been performed to repair such problems as heart, lung, and diaphragm malformations, urinary tract

TABLE 3.5 | Prenatal Diagnostic Methods

METHOD	DESCRIPTION
Amniocentesis	The most widely used technique. A hollow needle is inserted through the abdominal wall to obtain a sample of fluid in the uterus. Cells are examined for genetic defects. Can be performed by the 14th week after conception; 1 to 2 more weeks are required for test results. Small risk of miscarriage.
Chorionic villus sampling	A procedure that can be used if results are desired or needed very early in pregnancy. A thin tube is inserted into the uterus through the vagina, or a hollow needle is inserted through the abdominal wall. A small plug of tissue is removed from the end of one or more chorionic villi, the hairlike projections on the membrane surrounding the developing organism. Cells are examined for genetic defects. Can be performed at 9 weeks after conception; results are available within 24 hours. Entails a slightly greater risk of miscarriage than amniocentesis. Also associated with a small risk of limb deformities, which increases the earlier the procedure is performed.
Fetoscopy	A small tube with a light source at one end is inserted into the uterus to inspect the fetus for defects of the limbs and face. Also allows a sample of fetal blood to be obtained, permitting diagnosis of such disorders as hemophilia and sickle cell anemia, as well as neural defects (see below). Usually performed between 15 and 18 weeks after conception but can be done as early as 5 weeks. Entails some risk of miscarriage.
Ultrasound	High-frequency sound waves are beamed at the uterus; their reflection is translated into a picture on a video screen that reveals the size, shape, and placement of the fetus. Permits assessment of fetal age, detection of multiple pregnancies, and identification of gross physical defects; also used to guide amniocentesis, chorionic villus sampling, and fetoscopy. When used five or more times, may increase the chances of low birth weight.
Ultrafast MRI	Sometimes used as a supplement to ultrasound, where brain or other abnormalities are detected and MRI can provide greater diagnostic accuracy. The ultrafast technique overcomes image blurring due to fetal movements. No evidence of adverse effects.
Maternal blood analysis	By the second month of pregnancy, some of the developing organism's cells enter the maternal bloodstream. An elevated level of alpha-fetoprotein may indicate kidney disease, abnormal closure of the esophagus, or neural tube defects, such as anencephaly (absence of most of the brain) and spina bifida (bulging of the spinal cord from the spinal column). Isolated cells can be examined for genetic defects.
Preimplantation genetic diagnosis	After in vitro fertilization and duplication of the zygote into a cluster of about 8 to 10 cells, 1 or 2 cells are removed and examined for hereditary defects. Only if that sample is free of detectable genetic disorders is the fertilized ovum implanted in the woman's uterus.

Sources: Hahn & Chitty, 2008; Jokhi & Whitby, 2011; Kumar & O'Brien, 2004; Moore & Persaud, 2008; Sermon, Van Steirteghem, & Liebaers, 2004.

obstructions, and neural defects. Fetuses with blood disorders have been given blood transfusions. And those with immune deficiencies have received bone marrow transplants that succeeded in creating a normally functioning immune system (Deprest et al., 2010).

These techniques frequently result in complications, the most common being premature labor and miscarriage (Schonberg & Tifft, 2007). Yet parents may be willing to try almost any option, even one with only a slim chance of success. Currently, the medical profession is struggling with how to help parents make informed decisions about fetal surgery.

Advances in *genetic engineering* also offer new hope for correcting hereditary defects. As part of the Human Genome Project—an ambitious international research program aimed at deciphering the chemical makeup of human genetic material (genome)—researchers have mapped the sequence of all human DNA base pairs. Using that information, they are "annotating" the genome—identifying all its genes and their functions, including their protein products and what these products do. A major goal is to understand the estimated 4,000 human disorders, both those due to single genes and those resulting from a complex interplay of multiple genes and environmental factors.

Already, thousands of genes have been identified, including those involved in hundreds of diseases, such as cystic fibrosis; Duchenne muscular dystrophy; Huntington disease; Marfan syndrome; heart, digestive, blood, eye, and nervous system abnormalities; and many forms of cancer (National Institutes of Health, 2011). As a result, new treatments are being explored, such as *gene therapy*—correcting genetic abnormalities by delivering DNA carrying a functional gene to the cells. In recent experiments, gene therapy relieved symptoms

SOCIAL ISSUES: HEALTH

The Pros and Cons of Reproductive Technologies

Some couples decide not to risk pregnancy because of a family history of genetic disease. Many others—in fact, one-sixth of all couples who try to conceive—discover that they are sterile. And some never-married adults and gay and lesbian partners want to bear children. Today, increasing numbers of individuals are turning to alternative methods of conception to fulfill the wish of parenthood. These technologies have become the subject of heated debate.

Donor Insemination and In Vitro Fertilization

For several decades, *donor insemination*—injection of sperm from an anonymous man into a woman—has been used to overcome male reproductive difficulties. In recent years, it has also enabled women without a male partner to become pregnant. Donor insemination is 70 to 80 percent successful, resulting in about 40,000 deliveries and 52,000 newborn babies in the United States each year (Wright et al., 2008).

In vitro fertilization is another reproductive technology that has become increasingly common. Since the first "test tube" baby was born in England in 1978, 1 percent of all children in developed countries—about 40,000 babies in the United States—have been conceived through this technique annually (Jackson, Gibson, & Wu, 2004). With in vitro fertilization, a woman is given hormones that stimulate the ripening of several ova. These are removed surgically and placed in a dish of nutrients, to which sperm are added. Once an ovum is fertilized and begins to duplicate into several cells, it is injected into the mother's uterus.

By mixing and matching gametes, pregnancies can be brought about when either or both partners have a reproductive problem. Usually, in vitro fertilization is used to treat women whose fallopian tubes are permanently damaged. But a modified technique permits a single sperm to be injected directly into an ovum, thereby overcoming most male fertility problems. And a "sex sorter" method helps ensure that couples who carry X-linked diseases (which usually affect males) have a daughter. Fertilized ova and sperm can even be frozen and stored in embryo banks for future use, thereby guaranteeing healthy zygotes should age or illness lead to fertility problems.

The overall success rate of assisted reproductive techniques is about 35 percent. However, success declines steadily with age, from 40 percent in women younger than age 35 to 8 percent in women age 43 and older (Pauli et al., 2009).

Children conceived through these methods may be genetically unrelated to one or both of their parents. In addition, most parents who used in vitro fertilization do not tell their children about their origins. Does lack of genetic ties or secrecy surrounding these techniques interfere with parent–child relationships? Perhaps because of a strong desire for parenthood, caregiving is actually somewhat warmer for young children conceived through donor insemination or in vitro fertilization. Also, in vitro infants are as securely attached to their parents, and in vitro children and adolescents as well-adjusted, as their counterparts who were naturally conceived (Golombok et al., 2004; Punamaki, 2006; Wagenaar et al., 2008).

Although reproductive technologies have many benefits, serious questions have arisen about their use. In many countries, including the United States, doctors are not required to keep records of donor characteristics, though information about the child's genetic background might be critical in the case of serious disease (Adamson, 2005). Another concern is that the in vitro "sex sorter" method will lead to parental sex selection, thereby eroding the moral value that boys and girls are equally precious.

Furthermore, about 50 percent of in vitro procedures result in multiple births. Most are twins, but 9 percent are triplets and higher-order multiples. Consequently, among in vitro babies, the rate of low birth weight is 2.6 times as high as in the general population (Wright et al., 2008). Risk of major birth defects also doubles because of many factors, including drugs used to induce ripening of ova and delays in fertilizing ova outside the womb (Neri, Takeuchi, & Palermo, 2008). In sum, in vitro fertilization poses greater risks than natural conception to infant survival and healthy development.

Surrogate Motherhood

An even more controversial form of medically assisted conception is *surrogate motherhood*. In this procedure, in vitro fertilization may be used to impregnate a woman (called a surrogate) with a couple's fertilized ovum. Alternatively, sperm from a man whose partner is infertile may be used to inseminate the surrogate, who agrees to turn the baby over to the natural father. The child is then adopted by his partner. In both cases, the surrogate is paid a fee for her childbearing services.

Although most of these arrangements proceed smoothly, those that end up in court highlight serious risks for all concerned. In one case, both parties rejected the infant with severe disabilities that resulted from the pregnancy. In several others, the surrogate mother wanted to keep the baby, or the couple changed their

---

in hemophilia patients and in patients with severe immune system dysfunction. A few, however, experienced serious side effects (Gillet et al., 2009). In another approach, called *proteomics*, scientists modify gene-specified proteins involved in disease (Van Eyk & Dunn, 2008).

Genetic treatments seem some distance in the future for most single-gene defects, however, and even further off for diseases involving multiple genes that combine in complex ways with one another and the environment. Fortunately, 95 percent of fetuses examined through prenatal diagnosis are normal (Moore & Persaud, 2008). The availability of such tests allows many individuals whose family history would have caused them to avoid pregnancy to bear healthy children.

minds during the pregnancy. These children came into the world in the midst of conflict that threatened to last for years.

Because surrogacy usually involves the wealthy as contractors for infants and the less economically advantaged as surrogates, it may promote exploitation of financially needy women. In addition, most surrogates already have children of their own, and knowledge that their mother would give away a baby may cause these children to worry about the security of their own family circumstances.

New Reproductive Frontiers

Reproductive technologies are evolving faster than societies can weigh the ethics of these procedures. Doctors have used donor ova from younger women in combination with in vitro fertilization to help postmenopausal women become pregnant. Most recipients are in their forties, but some in their fifties and sixties, and a few at age 70, have given birth. These cases raise questions about bringing children into the world whose parents may not live to see them reach adulthood. Based on U.S. life expectancy data, 1 in 3 mothers and 1 in 2 fathers having a baby at age 55 will die before their child enters college (U.S. Census Bureau, 2011b).

Currently, experts are debating other reproductive options. At donor banks, customers can select ova or sperm on the basis of physical characteristics and even IQ. And scientists are devising ways to alter the DNA of human ova, sperm, and embryos to protect against hereditary disorders—techniques that could be used to engineer other desired characteristics. Many worry that these practices are dangerous steps toward selective breeding through "designer babies"—controlling offspring traits by manipulating genetic makeup.

Although new reproductive technologies permit many barren couples to rear healthy newborn babies, laws are needed to regulate such practices. In Australia, New Zealand, Sweden, and Switzerland, individuals conceived with donor gametes have a right to information about their genetic origins (Frith, 2001). Pressure from those working in the field of assisted reproduction may soon lead to similar policies in the United States. Australia, Canada, and the Netherlands prohibit any genetic alteration of human gametes, with other nations following suit (Isasi, Nguyen, & Knoppers, 2006). But some scientists argue that this total ban is too restrictive because it interferes with serving therapeutic needs.

In the case of surrogate motherhood, the ethical problems are so complex that 11 U.S. states and the District of Columbia have sharply restricted the practice (Human Rights Campaign, 2008). Australia, Canada, and many European nations have banned it, arguing that the status of a baby should not be a matter of commercial arrangement. Denmark, France, and Italy have prohibited in vitro fertilization for women past menopause. At present, nothing is known about the psychological consequences of being a product of these procedures. Research on how such children grow up, including what they know and how they feel about their origins, is important for weighing the pros and cons of these techniques.

Fertility drugs and in vitro fertilization often result in multiple fetuses. These quadruplets are healthy, but babies born with the aid of reproductive technologies are at high risk for low birth weight and major birth defects.

ASK YOURSELF

Review ■ Why is genetic counseling called a *communication process?* Who should seek it?

Review ■ Describe the ethical pros and cons of fetal surgery, surrogate motherhood, and postmenopausal-assisted childbearing.

Apply ■ Imagine that you must counsel a couple considering in vitro fertilization using donor ova to overcome infertility. What medical and ethical risks would you raise?

Reflect ■ Imagine you are a carrier of fragile X syndrome and want to have children. Would you choose pregnancy, adoption, or surrogacy? If you became pregnant, would you opt for prenatal diagnosis? Explain.

▶ List the three periods of prenatal development, and describe the major milestones of each.

Prenatal Development

The sperm and ovum that unite to form the new individual are uniquely suited for the task of reproduction. The ovum is a tiny sphere, measuring 1/175 inch in diameter, that is barely visible to the naked eye as a dot the size of the period at the end of this sentence. But in its microscopic world, it is a giant—the largest cell in the human body. The ovum's size makes it a perfect target for the much smaller sperm, which measure only 1/500 inch.

Conception

About once every 28 days, in the middle of a woman's menstrual cycle, an ovum bursts from one of her *ovaries*, two walnut-sized organs located deep inside her abdomen, and is drawn into one of two *fallopian tubes*—long, thin structures that lead to the hollow, soft-lined uterus (see Figure 3.7). While the ovum is traveling, the spot on the ovary from which it was released, now called the *corpus luteum*, secretes hormones that prepare the lining of the uterus to receive a fertilized ovum. If pregnancy does not occur, the corpus luteum shrinks, and the lining of the uterus is discarded two weeks later with menstruation.

The male produces sperm in vast numbers—an average of 300 million a day. In the final process of maturation, each sperm develops a tail that permits it to swim long distances, upstream in the female reproductive tract, through the *cervix* (opening of the uterus), and into the fallopian tube, where fertilization usually takes place. The journey is difficult, and many sperm die. Only 300 to 500 reach the ovum, if one happens to be present. Sperm

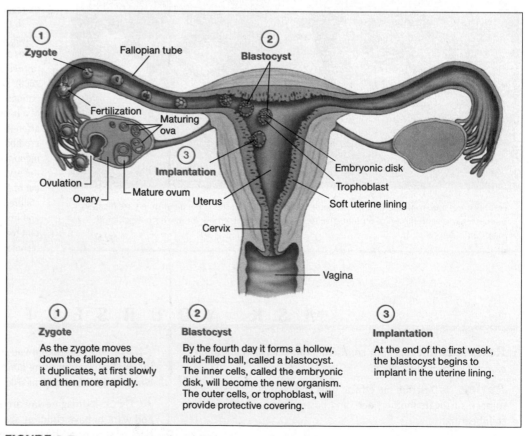

FIGURE 3.7 **Female reproductive organs, showing fertilization, early cell duplication, and implantation.** (From *Before We Are Born*, 6th ed., by K. L. Moore & T. V. N. Persaud, p. 87. Copyright © 2003, reprinted with permission from Elsevier, Inc.)

live for up to 6 days and can lie in wait for the ovum, which survives for only 1 day after being released into the fallopian tube. However, most conceptions result from intercourse during a 3-day period—on the day of ovulation or during the 2 days preceding it (Wilcox, Weinberg, & Baird, 1995).

With conception, the story of prenatal development begins to unfold. The vast changes that take place during the 38 weeks of pregnancy are usually divided into three periods: (1) the period of the zygote, (2) the period of the embryo, and (3) the period of the fetus. As we look at what happens in each, you may find it useful to refer to the Milestones table on page 90.

Conception. In this photo taken with the aid of a powerful microscope, two sperm penetrate the surface of the ovum, the largest cell in the human body. When one sperm succeeds in fertilizing the ovum, the resulting zygote begins to duplicate.

Period of the Zygote

The period of the zygote lasts about two weeks, from fertilization until the tiny mass of cells drifts down and out of the fallopian tube and attaches itself to the wall of the uterus. The zygote's first cell duplication is long and drawn out; it is not complete until about 30 hours after conception. Gradually, new cells are added at a faster rate. By the fourth day, 60 to 70 cells exist that form a hollow, fluid-filled ball called a *blastocyst* (refer again to Figure 3.7). The cells on the inside of the blastocyst, called the *embryonic disk*, will become the new organism; the thin outer ring of cells, termed the *trophoblast*, will become the structures that provide protective covering and nourishment.

Implantation Between the seventh and ninth days, implantation occurs: The blastocyst burrows deep into the uterine lining where, surrounded by the woman's nourishing blood, it starts to grow in earnest. At first, the trophoblast (protective outer layer) multiplies fastest. It forms a membrane, called the **amnion,** that encloses the developing organism in *amniotic fluid*, which helps keep the temperature of the prenatal world constant and provides a cushion against any jolts caused by the woman's movement. A *yolk sac* emerges that produces blood cells until the developing liver, spleen, and bone marrow are mature enough to take over this function (Moore & Persaud, 2008).

The events of these first two weeks are delicate and uncertain. As many as 30 percent of zygotes do not survive this period. In some, the sperm and ovum do not join properly. In others, for some unknown reason, cell duplication never begins. By preventing implantation in these cases, nature eliminates most prenatal abnormalities (Sadler, 2009).

The Placenta and Umbilical Cord By the end of the second week, cells of the trophoblast form another protective membrane—the **chorion,** which surrounds the amnion. From the chorion, tiny fingerlike *villi,* or blood vessels, emerge.[1] As these villi burrow into the uterine wall, a special organ called the *placenta* starts to develop. By bringing the mother's and the embryo's blood close together, the **placenta** permits food and oxygen to reach the developing organism and waste products to be carried away. A membrane forms that allows these substances to be exchanged but prevents the mother's and the embryo's blood from mixing directly.

The placenta is connected to the developing organism by the **umbilical cord,** which first appears as a primitive body stalk and, during the course of pregnancy, grows to a length of 1 to 3 feet. The umbilical cord contains

Period of the zygote: seventh to ninth day. The fertilized ovum duplicates at an increasingly rapid rate, forming a hollow ball of cells, or blastocyst, by the fourth day after fertilization. Between the seventh and ninth day, as shown here, the blastocyst burrows into the uterine lining.

---

[1]Recall from Table 3.5 on page 85 that *chorionic villus sampling* is a prenatal diagnostic method that can be performed very early, at nine weeks after conception. In this procedure, tissues from the ends of the villi are removed and examined for genetic abnormalities.

Milestones

Prenatal Development

TRIMESTER	PERIOD	WEEKS	LENGTH AND WEIGHT	MAJOR EVENTS
First	Zygote	1		The one-celled zygote multiplies and forms a blastocyst.
		2		The blastocyst burrows into the uterine lining. Structures that feed and protect the developing organism begin to form—*amnion, chorion, yolk sac, placenta,* and *umbilical cord.*
	Embryo	3–4	¼ inch (6 mm)	A primitive brain and spinal cord appear. Heart, muscles, ribs, backbone, and digestive tract begin to develop.
		5–8	1 inch (2.5 cm); ½ ounce (4 g)	Many external body structures (face, arms, legs, toes, fingers) and internal organs form. Production of neurons begins, occurring at an astounding pace. The sense of touch emerges, and the embryo can move.
	Fetus	9–12	3 inches (7.6 cm); less than 1 ounce (28 g)	Rapid increase in size begins. Nervous system, organs, and muscles become organized and connected, and new behavioral capacities (kicking, thumb sucking, mouth opening, and rehearsal of breathing) appear. External genitals are well-formed, and the fetus's sex is evident.
Second		13–24	12 inches (30 cm); 1.8 pounds (820 g)	The fetus continues to enlarge rapidly. In the middle of this period, the mother can feel fetal movements. Vernix and lanugo keep the fetus's skin from chapping in the amniotic fluid. Most of the brain's neurons are in place by 24 weeks. Eyes are sensitive to light, and the fetus reacts to sound.
Third		25–38	20 inches (50 cm); 7.5 pounds (3,400 g)	The fetus has a good chance of survival if born during this time. Size increases. Lungs mature. Rapid brain development causes sensory and behavioral capacities to expand. In the middle of this period, a layer of fat is added under the skin. Antibodies are transmitted from mother to fetus to protect against disease. Most fetuses rotate into an upside-down position in preparation for birth.

Sources: Moore & Persaud, 2008.

Photos: (from top to bottom): © Claude Cortier/Photo Researchers, Inc.; © G. Moscoso/Photo Researchers, Inc.; © John Watney/Photo Researchers, Inc.; © James Stevenson/Photo Researchers, Inc.; © Lennart Nilsson, *A Child Is Born*/Scanpix

one large vein that delivers blood loaded with nutrients and two arteries that remove waste products. The force of blood flowing through the cord keeps it firm, much like a garden hose, so it seldom tangles while the embryo, like a space-walking astronaut, floats freely in its fluid-filled chamber (Moore & Persaud, 2008).

By the end of the period of the zygote, the developing organism has found food and shelter in the uterus. Already, it is a very complex being. These dramatic beginnings take place before most mothers know they are pregnant.

Period of the Embryo

The period of the **embryo** lasts from implantation through the eighth week of pregnancy. During these brief six weeks, the most rapid prenatal changes take place, as the groundwork is laid for all body structures and internal organs. Because all parts of the body are forming, the embryo is especially vulnerable to interference with healthy development. But the short time span of embryonic growth helps limit opportunities for serious harm.

Last Half of the First Month
In the first week of this period, the embryonic disk forms three layers of cells: (1) the *ectoderm*, which will become the nervous system and skin; (2) the *mesoderm*, from which will develop the muscles, skeleton, circulatory system, and other internal organs; and (3) the *endoderm*, which will become the digestive system, lungs, urinary tract, and glands. These three layers give rise to all parts of the body.

At first, the nervous system develops fastest. The ectoderm folds over to form the *neural tube*, or primitive spinal cord. At 3½ weeks, the top swells to form the brain. While the nervous system is developing, the heart begins to pump blood, and muscles, backbone, ribs, and digestive tract appear. At the end of the first month, the curled embryo—only ¼ inch long—consists of millions of organized groups of cells with specific functions.

The Second Month
In the second month, growth continues rapidly. The eyes, ears, nose, jaw, and neck form. Tiny buds become arms, legs, fingers, and toes. Internal organs are more distinct: The intestines grow, the heart develops separate chambers, and the liver and spleen take over production of blood cells so that the yolk sac is no longer needed. Changing body proportions cause the embryo's posture to become more upright.

At 7 weeks, production of *neurons* (nerve cells that store and transmit information) begins deep inside the neural tube at the astounding pace of more than 250,000 per minute (Nelson, 2011). Once formed, neurons begin traveling along tiny threads to their permanent locations, where they will form the major parts of the brain.

At the end of this period, the embryo—about 1 inch long and ¹⁄₇ ounce in weight—can already sense its world. It responds to touch, particularly in the mouth area and on the soles of the feet. And it can move, although its tiny flutters are still too light to be felt by the mother (Moore & Persaud, 2008).

© LENNART NILSSON, A CHILD IS BORN/SCANPIX

- Beginning of ears
- Brain
- Will become eyes
- Will become the jaw
- Heart
- Lower limb buds will become legs
- Upper limb buds will become arms
- Beginning of muscles and backbone

Period of the embryo: fourth week. This 4-week-old embryo is only ¼ inch long, but many body structures have begun to form.

© LENNART NILSSON, A CHILD IS BORN/SCANPIX

Period of the embryo: seventh week. The embryo's posture is more upright. Body structures—eyes, nose, arms, legs, and internal organs—are more distinct. The embryo responds to touch but is still too tiny to be felt by the mother.

Period of the Fetus

The period of the **fetus,** from the ninth week to the end of pregnancy, is the longest prenatal period. During this "growth and finishing" phase, the organism increases rapidly in size, especially from the ninth to the twentieth week.

Period of the fetus: eleventh week. The brain and muscles are better connected. The fetus can kick, bend its arms, and open and close its hands and mouth. The yolk sac shrinks as the internal organs assume blood cell production.

© LENNART NILSSON, A CHILD IS BORN/SCANPIX

The Third Month In the third month, the organs, muscles, and nervous system start to become organized and connected. When the brain signals, the fetus kicks, bends its arms, forms a fist, curls its toes, turns its head, opens its mouth, and even sucks its thumb, stretches, and yawns. Body position changes occur as often as 25 times per hour (Einspieler, Marschik, & Prechtl, 2008). The tiny lungs begin to expand and contract in an early rehearsal of breathing movements. By the twelfth week, the external genitals are well-formed, and the sex of the fetus can be detected with ultrasound (Sadler, 2009). Other finishing touches appear, such as fingernails, toenails, tooth buds, and eyelids. The heartbeat can now be heard through a stethoscope.

Prenatal development is sometimes divided into *trimesters*, or three equal time periods. At the end of the third month, the first trimester is complete.

The Second Trimester By the middle of the second trimester, between 17 and 20 weeks, the new being has grown large enough that the mother can feel its movements. A white, cheeselike substance called **vernix** covers the skin, protecting it from chapping during the long months spent in the amniotic fluid. White, downy hair called **lanugo** also covers the entire body, helping the vernix stick to the skin.

At the end of the second trimester, many organs are well-developed. Also, most of the brain's billions of neurons are in place; few will be produced after this time. However, *glial cells*, which support and feed the neurons, continue to increase rapidly throughout the remaining months of pregnancy, as well as after birth. Consequently, brain weight increases tenfold from the twentieth week until birth (Roelfsema et al., 2004). At the same time, neurons begin forming *synapses*, or connections, at a rapid pace.

Brain growth means new behavioral capacities. The 20-week-old fetus can be stimulated as well as irritated by sounds. Slow eye movements appear, with rapid eye movements following at 22 weeks. And if a doctor looks inside the uterus using fetoscopy (refer again to Table 3.5), fetuses try to shield their eyes from the light with their hands, indicating that sight has begun to emerge (Moore & Persaud, 2008). Still, a fetus born at this time cannot survive. Its lungs are too immature, and the brain cannot yet control breathing movements or body temperature.

The Third Trimester During the final trimester, a fetus born early has a chance of survival. The point at which the baby can first survive, called the **age of viability,** occurs sometime between 22 and 26 weeks (Moore & Persaud, 2008). A baby born between the seventh and eighth months, however, usually needs oxygen assistance to breathe. Although the brain's respiratory center is now mature, tiny air sacs in the lungs are not yet ready to inflate and exchange carbon dioxide for oxygen.

The brain continues to make great strides. The *cerebral cortex*, the seat of human intelligence, enlarges. Convolutions and grooves in its surface appear, permitting a dramatic increase in surface area that allows for maximum prenatal brain growth without the full-term baby's head becoming too large to pass through the birth canal. As neural connectivity and organization improve, the fetus spends more time awake. At 20 weeks, fetal heart rate reveals no periods of alertness. But by 28 weeks, fetuses are awake about 11 percent of the time, a figure that rises to 16 percent just before birth (DiPietro et al., 1996). Between 30 and 34 weeks, fetuses show rhythmic alternations between sleep and wakefulness that gradually increase in organization (Rivkees, 2003). Around this time, synchrony between fetal heart rate and motor activity peaks: A rise in heart rate is usually followed within 5 seconds by a burst of motor activity (DiPietro et al., 2006). These are clear signs that coordinated neural networks are beginning to form in the brain.

By the end of pregnancy, the fetus takes on the beginnings of a personality. Higher fetal activity in the last weeks of pregnancy predicts a more active infant in the first month of life—a relationship that, for boys, persists into early childhood (Groome et al., 1999). Fetal activity is linked in other ways to infant temperament. In one study, more active fetuses during the third trimester became 1-year-olds who could better handle frustration and 2-year-olds who were less fearful, in that they more readily interacted with toys and with an unfamiliar adult in a laboratory (DiPietro et al., 2002). Perhaps fetal activity level is an indicator of healthy neurological development, which fosters adaptability in childhood. The relationships just described, however, are only modest. As we will see in Chapter 10, sensitive caregiving can modify the temperaments of children who have difficulty adapting to new experiences.

The third trimester also brings greater responsiveness to external stimulation. Between 23 and 30 weeks, connections form between the cerebral cortex and brain regions involved in pain sensitivity. By this time, painkillers should be used in any surgical procedures (Lee et al., 2005). Around 28 weeks, fetuses blink their eyes in reaction to nearby sounds (Kisilevsky & Low, 1998; Saffran, Werker, & Werner, 2006). And at 30 weeks, fetuses presented with a repeated auditory stimulus against the mother's abdomen initially react with a rise in heart rate and body movements. But over the next 5 to 6 minutes, responsiveness gradually

Period of the fetus: twenty-second week. This fetus is almost 1 foot long and weighs around 1 pound. Its movements can be felt by touching the mother's abdomen. If born now, the fetus has a slim chance of surviving.

Period of the fetus: thirty-sixth week. This fetus fills the uterus. To nourish it, the umbilical cord and placenta have grown large. Vernix (cheeselike substance) protects the skin from chapping. The fetus has accumulated fat to aid temperature regulation after birth. In two more weeks, it will be full term.

declines, indicating *habituation* (adaptation) to the sound. If the stimulus is reintroduced after a 10-minute delay, heart rate falls off far more quickly (Dirix et al., 2009). This suggests that fetuses can remember for at least a brief period.

Within the next six weeks, fetuses distinguish the tone and rhythm of different voices and sounds: They show systematic heart rate changes in response to a male versus a female speaker, to the mother's voice versus a stranger's, to a stranger speaking their native language (English) versus a foreign language (Mandarin Chinese), and to a simple familiar melody (descending tones) versus an unfamiliar melody (ascending tones) (Granier-Deferre et al., 2003; Huotilainen et al., 2005; Kisilevsky et al., 2003, 2009; Lecanuet et al., 1993). And in one clever study, mothers read aloud Dr. Seuss's lively book *The Cat in the Hat* each day during the last six weeks of pregnancy. After birth, their infants learned to turn on recordings of the mother's voice by sucking on nipples. They sucked hardest to hear *The Cat in the Hat*—the sound they had come to know while still in the womb (DeCasper & Spence, 1988).

TAKE A MOMENT... On the basis of these findings, would you recommend that expectant mothers provide fetuses with stimulation specially designed to enhance later mental development? Notice how risky it is to draw such conclusions. First, specific forms of fetal stimulation, such as reading aloud or playing classical music, are unlikely to have a long-lasting impact on cognitive development because of the developing child's constantly changing capacities and experiences, which can override the impact of fetal stimulation (Lecanuet, Granier-Deferre, & DeCasper, 2005). Second, although ordinary stimulation contributes to the functioning of sensory systems, excessive input can be dangerous. For example, animal studies indicate that a sensitive period (see page 24 in Chapter 1) exists in which the fetal ear is highly susceptible to injury. During that time, prolonged exposure to sounds that are harmless to the mature ear can permanently damage fetal inner-ear structures (Pierson, 1996).

In the final three months, the fetus gains more than 5 pounds and grows 7 inches. As it fills the uterus, it gradually moves less often. In addition, brain development, which enables the organism to inhibit behavior, contributes to this decline in physical activity (DiPietro et al., 1996). In the eighth month, a layer of fat is added to assist with temperature regulation. The fetus also receives antibodies from the mother's blood to protect against illnesses, since the newborn's own immune system will not work well until several months after birth. In the last weeks, most fetuses assume an upside-down position, partly because of the shape of the uterus and also because the head is heavier than the feet. Growth slows, and birth is about to take place.

ASK YOURSELF

Review ■ Why is the period of the embryo regarded as the most dramatic prenatal period? Why is the period of the fetus called the "growth and finishing" phase?

Connect ■ How is brain development related to fetal capacities and behavior? What implications do individual differences in fetal behavior have for the baby's temperament after birth?

Apply ■ Amy, two months pregnant, wonders how the developing organism is being fed and what parts of the body have formed. "I don't look pregnant yet, so does that mean not much development has taken place?" she asks. How would you respond to Amy?

▶ Cite factors that influence the impact of teratogens, noting agents that are known teratogens.

▶ Describe the impact of additional maternal factors on prenatal development.

Prenatal Environmental Influences

Although the prenatal environment is far more constant than the world outside the womb, many factors can affect the embryo and fetus. In the following sections, you will see that there is much that parents—and society as a whole—can do to create a safe environment for development before birth.

Teratogens

The term **teratogen** refers to any environmental agent that causes damage during the prenatal period. Scientists chose this label (from the Greek word *teras*, meaning "malformation" or "monstrosity") because they first learned about harmful prenatal influences from cases in which babies had been profoundly damaged. But the harm done by teratogens is not always simple and straightforward. It depends on the following factors:

- *Dose*. As we discuss particular teratogens, you will see that larger doses over longer time periods usually have more negative effects.
- *Heredity*. The genetic makeup of the mother and the developing organism plays an important role. Some individuals are better able than others to withstand harmful environments.
- *Other negative influences*. The presence of several negative factors at once, such as additional teratogens, poor nutrition, and lack of medical care, can worsen the impact of a single harmful agent.
- *Age*. The effects of teratogens vary with the age of the organism at time of exposure. To understand this last idea, think of the *sensitive period* concept. Recall that a sensitive period is a limited time span in which a part of the body or a behavior is biologically prepared to develop rapidly. During that time, it is especially sensitive to its surroundings. If the environment is harmful, then damage occurs, and recovery is difficult and sometimes impossible.

Figure 3.8 summarizes prenatal sensitive periods. Look at it carefully, and you will see that some parts of the body, such as the brain and eye, have sensitive periods that extend

FIGURE 3.8 Sensitive periods in prenatal development. Each organ or structure has a sensitive period, during which its development may be disturbed. Blue horizontal bars indicate highly sensitive periods. Green horizontal bars indicate periods that are somewhat less sensitive to teratogens, although damage can occur. (Adapted from *Before We Are Born*, 7th ed., by K. L. Moore and T. V. N. Persaud, p. 313. Copyright © 2008, reprinted with permission from Elsevier, Inc.)

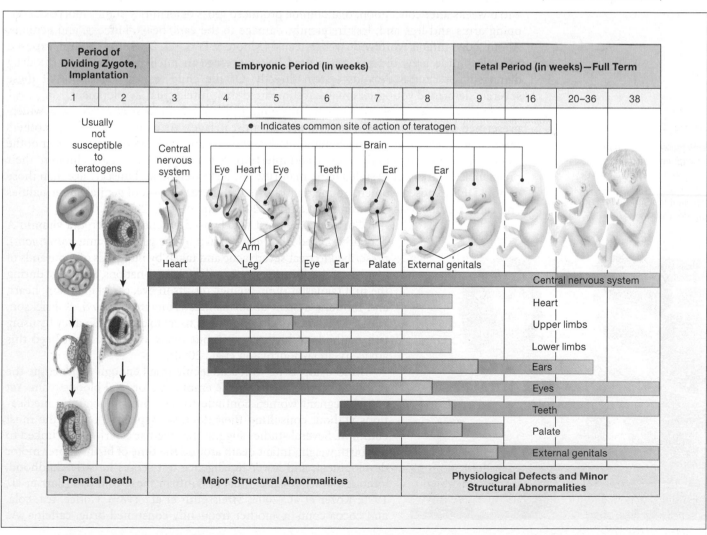

throughout prenatal development. Other sensitive periods, such as those for the limbs and palate, are much shorter. Figure 3.8 also indicates that we can make some general statements about the timing of harmful influences: In the *period of the zygote*, before implantation, teratogens rarely have any impact. If they do, the tiny mass of cells is usually so damaged that it dies. The *embryonic period* is the time when serious defects are most likely to occur because the foundations for all body parts are being laid down. During the *fetal period*, teratogenic damage is usually minor. However, organs such as the brain, ears, eyes, teeth, and genitals can still be strongly affected.

The effects of teratogens go beyond immediate physical damage. Some health outcomes are delayed and may not show up for decades. Furthermore, psychological consequences may occur indirectly, as a result of physical damage. For example, a defect resulting from drugs the mother took during pregnancy can affect others' reactions to the child as well as the child's ability to explore the environment. Over time, parent–child interaction, peer relations, and opportunities to explore may suffer. Furthermore, prenatally exposed children may be less resilient in the face of environmental risks, such as single parenthood, parental emotional disturbance, or maladaptive parenting (Yumoto, Jacobson, & Jacobson, 2008). As a result, their long-term adjustment may be compromised.

Notice how an important idea about development discussed in Chapter 1 is at work here: *bidirectional influences* between child and environment. Now let's look at what scientists have discovered about a variety of teratogens.

Prescription and Nonprescription Drugs In the early 1960s, the world learned a tragic lesson about drugs and prenatal development. At that time, a sedative called *thalidomide* was widely available in Canada, Europe, and South America. When taken by mothers 4 to 6 weeks after conception, thalidomide produced gross deformities of the embryo's developing arms and legs and, less frequently, damage to the ears, heart, kidneys, and genitals. About 7,000 infants worldwide were affected (Moore & Persaud, 2008). As children exposed to thalidomide grew older, many scored below average in intelligence. Perhaps the drug damaged the central nervous system directly. Or the child-rearing conditions of these severely deformed youngsters may have impaired their intellectual development.

Another medication, a synthetic hormone called *diethylstilbestrol (DES)*, was widely prescribed between 1945 and 1970 to prevent miscarriages. As daughters of these mothers reached adolescence and young adulthood, they showed unusually high rates of cancer of the vagina, malformations of the uterus, and infertility. When they tried to have children, their pregnancies more often resulted in prematurity, low birth weight, and miscarriage than those of non-DES-exposed women. Young men showed an increased risk of genital abnormalities and cancer of the testes (Hammes & Laitman, 2003; Palmer et al., 2001).

Many prescription and non-prescription medications can impair embryonic and fetal development. Before taking any drug, expectant mothers must seriously consider its risks.

© BLEND IMAGES/ALAMY

Currently, the most widely used potent teratogen is a vitamin A derivative called *Accutane* (known by the generic name *isotretinoin*), prescribed to treat severe acne and taken by hundreds of thousands of women of childbearing age in industrialized nations. Exposure during the first trimester of pregnancy results in eye, ear, skull, brain, heart, and immune system abnormalities (Honein, Paulozzi, & Erickson, 2001). Accutane's packaging warns users to avoid pregnancy by using two methods of birth control, but many women do not heed this advice (Garcia-Bournissen et al., 2008).

Indeed, any drug with a molecule small enough to penetrate the placental barrier can enter the embryonic or fetal bloodstream. Yet many pregnant women continue to take over-the-counter medications without consulting their doctors. Aspirin is one of the most common. Several studies suggest that regular aspirin use is linked to low birth weight, infant death around the time of birth, poorer motor development, and lower intelligence test scores in early childhood, although other research fails to confirm these findings (Barr et al., 1990; Kozer et al., 2003; Streissguth et al., 1987). Coffee, tea, cola, and cocoa contain another frequently consumed drug, caffeine. As amounts exceed 100 milligrams per day (equivalent to one cup of coffee), low birth weight and miscarriage increase (CARE Study Group, 2008; Weng, Odouli, & Li, 2008). And anti-depressant medications are linked to increased risk of premature delivery and birth complications, including respiratory distress and persistent high blood pressure in infancy (Alwan & Friedman, 2009; Lund, Pedersen, & Henriksen, 2009; Udechuku et al., 2010).

Because children's lives are involved, we must take findings like these seriously. At the same time, we cannot be sure that these frequently used drugs actually cause the problems mentioned. Often mothers take more than one drug. If the embryo or fetus is injured, it is hard to tell which drug might be responsible or whether other factors correlated with drug taking are really at fault. Until we have more information, the safest course for pregnant women is to avoid such drugs entirely. Unfortunately, many women do not know that they are pregnant during the early weeks of the embryonic period, when exposure to medications (and other teratogens) can be of greatest threat.

Illegal Drugs The use of highly addictive mood-altering drugs, such as cocaine and heroin, has become more widespread, especially in poverty-stricken inner-city areas, where these drugs provide a temporary escape from a daily life of hopelessness. About 4 percent of U.S. pregnant women take these substances (Substance Abuse and Mental Health Services Administration, 2010).

Babies born to users of cocaine, heroin, or methadone (a less addictive drug used to wean people away from heroin) are at risk for a wide variety of problems, including prematurity, low birth weight, physical defects, breathing difficulties, and death at or around the time of birth (Bandstra et al., 2010; Howell, Coles, & Kable, 2008; Schuetze & Eiden, 2006). In addition, these infants are born drug-addicted. They are often feverish and irritable and have trouble sleeping, and their cries are abnormally shrill and piercing—a common symptom among stressed newborns (Bauer et al., 2005). When mothers with many problems of their own must care for these babies, who are difficult to calm, cuddle, and feed, behavior problems are likely to persist.

Throughout the first year, heroin- and methadone-exposed infants are less attentive to the environment than nonexposed babies, and their motor development is slow. After infancy, some children get better, whereas others remain jittery and inattentive. The kind of parenting they receive may explain why difficulties continue for some but not for others (Hans & Jeremy, 2001).

Evidence on cocaine suggests that some prenatally exposed babies develop lasting problems. Cocaine constricts the blood vessels, causing oxygen delivery to the developing organism to fall for 15 minutes following a high dose. It also can alter the production and functioning of neurons and the chemical balance in the fetus's brain. These effects may contribute to an array of cocaine-associated physical defects, including eye, bone, genital, urinary tract, kidney, and heart deformities; brain hemorrhages and seizures; and severe growth retardation (Covington et al., 2002; Feng, 2005; Salisbury et al., 2009).

Several studies report perceptual, motor, attention, memory, language, and impulse-control problems that persist into the preschool and school years (Dennis et al., 2006; Lester & Lagasse, 2010; Linares et al., 2006; Singer et al., 2004). And compared to nonexposed infants, cocaine-exposed babies show greater stress reactivity, as indicated by a more rapid rise in saliva concentrations of cortisol to emotionally arousing events (Eiden, Veira, & Granger, 2009). By school age, children with a history of prenatal cocaine exposure display a reduced cortisol response during stressful mental activity (Lester et al., 2010). Recall from Chapter 2 that cortisol levels that are either too high or too low signal a disrupted stress response system—a risk factor for illness and learning and behavior problems.

Other investigations, however, report no major negative effects of prenatal cocaine exposure (Behnke et al., 2006; Frank et al., 2005; Hurt et al., 2009). These contradictory findings indicate how difficult it is to isolate the precise damage caused by illegal drugs. Cocaine users vary greatly in the amount, potency, and purity of the cocaine they ingest. Also, they often take several drugs, display other high-risk behaviors, suffer from poverty and other stressors, and engage in insensitive caregiving—factors that worsen outcomes for children (Jones, 2006). But researchers have yet to determine exactly what accounts for findings of cocaine-related damage in some studies but not in others.

LOOK and LISTEN

On a trip to your grocery or drugstore, examine the fine print on nonprescription medication labels, such as pain relievers, and on energy drinks containing high levels of caffeine. Are the prenatal risks of these products clearly conveyed?

This 3-day-old infant, born many weeks before his due date, breathes with the aid of a respirator. Prematurity and low birth weight can result from a variety of environmental influences, including maternal drug and tobacco use.

Another illegal drug, marijuana, is used more widely than heroin or cocaine. Researchers have linked prenatal marijuana exposure to smaller head size (a measure of brain growth); to attention, memory, and academic achievement difficulties; to impulsivity and overactivity; and to depression as well as anger and aggression in childhood and adolescence (Goldschmidt et al., 2004; Gray et al., 2005; Huizink & Mulder, 2006; Jutras-Aswad et al., 2009). As with cocaine, however, lasting consequences are not well-established. Overall, the effects of illegal drugs are far less consistent than the impact of two legal substances to which we now turn: tobacco and alcohol.

Tobacco   Although smoking has declined in Western nations, an estimated 14 percent of U.S. women smoke during their pregnancies (Tong et al., 2009). The best-known effect of smoking during the prenatal period is low birth weight. But the likelihood of other serious consequences, such as miscarriage, prematurity, cleft lip and palate, impaired heart rate and breathing during sleep, infant death, and asthma and cancer later in childhood, also increases (Howell, Coles, & Kable, 2008; Jaakkola & Gissler, 2004; Mossey et al., 2009). The more cigarettes a mother smokes, the greater the chances that her baby will be affected. And if a pregnant woman stops smoking at any time, even during the third trimester, she reduces the likelihood that her infant will be born underweight and suffer from future problems (Klesges et al., 2001).

Even when a baby of a smoking mother appears to be born in good physical condition, slight behavioral abnormalities may threaten the child's development. Newborns of smoking mothers are less attentive to sounds, display more muscle tension, are more excitable when touched and visually stimulated, and more often have colic (persistent crying)—findings that suggest subtle negative effects on brain development (Law et al., 2003; Sondergaard et al., 2002). Consistent with this view, prenatally exposed youngsters tend to have shorter attention spans, difficulties with impulsivity and overactivity, poorer memories, lower mental test scores, and higher levels of disruptive, aggressive behavior (Fryer, Crocker, & Mattson, 2008; Lindblad & Hjern, 2010; Nigg & Breslau, 2007).

Exactly how can smoking harm the fetus? Nicotine, the addictive substance in tobacco, constricts blood vessels, lessens blood flow to the uterus, and causes the placenta to grow abnormally. This reduces the transfer of nutrients, so the fetus gains weight poorly. Also, nicotine raises the concentration of carbon monoxide in the bloodstreams of both mother and fetus. Carbon monoxide displaces oxygen from red blood cells, damaging the central nervous system and slowing body growth in the fetuses of laboratory animals (Friedman, 1996). Similar effects may occur in humans.

From one-third to one-half of nonsmoking pregnant women are "passive smokers" because their husbands, relatives, or co-workers use cigarettes. Passive smoking is also related to low birth weight, infant death, childhood respiratory illnesses, and possible long-term attention, learning, and behavior problems (Best, 2009; Pattenden et al., 2006). Clearly, expectant mothers should avoid smoke-filled environments.

Alcohol   In his moving book *The Broken Cord*, Michael Dorris (1989), a Dartmouth University anthropology professor, described what it was like to rear his adopted son Abel (called Adam in the book), whose biological mother died of alcohol poisoning shortly after his birth. A Sioux Indian, Abel was born with **fetal alcohol spectrum disorder (FASD),** a term that encompasses a range of physical, mental, and behavioral outcomes caused by prenatal alcohol exposure. As Table 3.6 shows, children with FASD are given one of three diagnoses, which vary in severity:

1. **Fetal alcohol syndrome (FAS),** distinguished by (a) slow physical growth, (b) a pattern of three facial abnormalities (short eyelid openings; a thin upper lip; a smooth or flattened philtrum, or indentation running from the bottom of the nose to the center of the

TABLE 3.6	Fetal Alcohol Spectrum Disorder: Criteria for Diagnosis		
	DIAGNOSTIC CATEGORY		
Criteria	*FAS*	*p-FAS*	*ARND*
Slow physical growth	Yes	No	No
Facial abnormalities: • Short eyelid openings • Thin upper lip • Smooth or flattened philtrum	All three are present	Two of the three are present	None are present
Brain injury	Impairment in a minimum of three areas of functioning	Impairment in a minimum of three areas of functioning	Impairment in a minimum of three areas of functioning

Source: Loock et al., 2005.

upper lip), and (c) brain injury, evident in a small head and impairment in at least three areas of functioning—for example, memory, language and communication, attention span and activity level (overactivity), planning and reasoning, motor coordination, or social skills. Other defects—of the eyes, ears, nose, throat, heart, genitals, urinary tract, or immune system—may also be present. Abel was diagnosed as having FAS. As is typical for this disorder, his mother drank heavily throughout pregnancy.

2. **Partial fetal alcohol syndrome (p-FAS),** characterized by (a) two of the three facial abnormalities just mentioned and (b) brain injury, again evident in at least three areas of impaired functioning. Mothers of children with p-FAS generally drank alcohol in smaller quantities, and children's defects vary with the timing and length of alcohol exposure. Furthermore, recent evidence suggests that paternal alcohol use around the time of conception can induce genetic alterations, thereby contributing to symptoms (Ouko et al., 2009).

3. **Alcohol-related neurodevelopmental disorder (ARND),** in which at least three areas of mental functioning are impaired, despite typical physical growth and absence of facial abnormalities. Again, prenatal alcohol exposure, though confirmed, is less pervasive than in FAS (Chudley et al., 2005; Loock et al., 2005).

Even when provided with enriched diets, FAS babies fail to catch up in physical size during infancy or childhood. Mental impairment associated with all three FASD diagnoses is also permanent: In his teens and twenties, Abel Dorris had trouble concentrating and keeping a routine job, and he suffered from poor judgment. For example, he would buy something and not wait for change or would wander off in the middle of a task. He died in 1991, at age 23, after being hit by a car.

The more alcohol a woman consumes during pregnancy, the poorer the child's motor coordination, speed of information processing, attention, memory, reasoning, and intelligence and achievement test scores during the preschool and school years (Burden, Jacobson, & Jacobson, 2005; Korkman, Kettunen, & Autti-Raemoe, 2003; Mattson, Calarco, & Lang, 2006). In adolescence and early adulthood, FASD is associated with persisting attention and motor-coordination deficits, poor school performance, trouble with the law, inappropriate social and sexual behaviors, alcohol and drug abuse, and lasting mental health problems, including high stress reactivity and depression (Barr et al., 2006; Fryer, Crocker, & Mattson, 2008; Hellemans et al., 2010; Howell et al., 2006; Streissguth et al., 2004).

How does alcohol produce its devastating effects? First, it interferes with production and migration of neurons in the primitive neural tube. EEG and fMRI research reveals reduced brain size, damage to many brain structures, and abnormalities in brain functioning, including the electrical and chemical activity involved in transferring messages from one part of the brain to another (Haycock, 2009; Spadoni et al., 2007). Second, the body uses large quantities of oxygen to metabolize alcohol. A pregnant woman's heavy drinking draws away oxygen that the developing organism needs for cell growth.

Left photo: This toddler's mother drank heavily during pregnancy. Her widely spaced eyes, thin upper lip, and short eyelid openings are typical of fetal alcohol syndrome (FAS). Right photo: This 12-year-old has the mental impairments, small head, and facial abnormalities of FAS. She also shows the slow physical growth that accompanies the disorder.

About 25 percent of U.S. mothers report drinking at some time during their pregnancies. As with heroin and cocaine, alcohol abuse is higher in poverty-stricken women. On some Native-American reservations, the incidence of FAS is as high as 10 to 20 percent (Szlemko, Wood, & Thurman, 2006; Tong et al., 2009). Unfortunately, when affected girls later become pregnant, the poor judgment caused by the syndrome often prevents them from understanding why they themselves should avoid alcohol. Thus, the tragic cycle is likely to be repeated in the next generation.

How much alcohol is safe during pregnancy? Even mild drinking, less than one drink per day, is associated with reduced head size and body growth among children followed into adolescence (Jacobson et al., 2004; Martinez-Frias et al., 2004). Recall that other factors, both genetic and environmental, can make some fetuses more vulnerable to teratogens. Therefore, no amount of alcohol is safe. Couples planning a pregnancy and expectant mothers should avoid alcohol entirely.

Radiation Earlier we saw that ionizing radiation can cause mutation, damaging DNA in ova and sperm. When mothers are exposed to radiation during pregnancy, the embryo or fetus can suffer additional harm. Defects due to radiation were tragically apparent in the children born to pregnant women who survived the atomic bombing of Hiroshima and Nagasaki during World War II. Similar abnormalities surfaced in the nine months following the 1986 Chernobyl, Ukraine, nuclear power plant accident. After each disaster, the incidence of miscarriage and of babies born with underdeveloped brains, physical deformities, and slow physical growth rose dramatically (Hoffmann, 2001; Schull, 2003). Evacuation of residents in areas near the Japanese nuclear facility damaged by the March 2011 earthquake and tsunami was intended to prevent these devastating outcomes.

Even when a radiation-exposed baby seems normal, problems may appear later. For example, even low-level radiation, as the result of industrial leakage or medical X-rays, can increase the risk of childhood cancer (Fattibene et al., 1999). In middle childhood, prenatally exposed Chernobyl children showed abnormal EEG brain-wave activity, lower intelligence test scores, and rates of language and emotional disorders two to three times greater

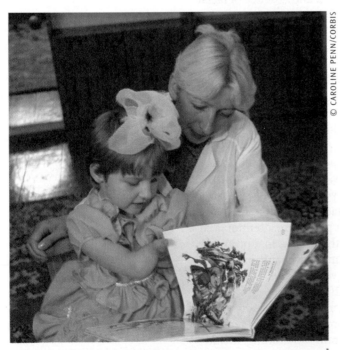

This child's deformities are linked to radiation exposure early in pregnancy, caused by the Chernobyl nuclear power plant disaster in 1986. Prenatal radiation exposure also increases the risk of low intelligence and language and emotional disorders.

than those of nonexposed Russian children. Furthermore, the more tension parents reported, due to forced evacuation from their homes and worries about living in irradiated areas, the poorer their children's emotional functioning (Loganovskaja & Loganovsky, 1999; Loganovsky et al., 2008). Stressful rearing conditions seemed to combine with the damaging effects of prenatal radiation to impair children's development.

Women should do their best to avoid medical X-rays during pregnancy. If dental, thyroid, chest, or other X-rays are necessary, insisting on the use of an abdominal X-ray shield is a key protective measure.

Environmental Pollution In industrialized nations, an astounding number of potentially dangerous chemicals are released into the environment. More than 75,000 are in common use in the United States, and many new pollutants are introduced each year. When 10 newborns were randomly selected from U.S. hospitals for analysis of umbilical cord blood, researchers uncovered a startling array of industrial contaminants—287 in all! They concluded that many babies are "born polluted" by chemicals that not only impair prenatal development but also increase the chances of health problems and life-threatening diseases later on (Houlihan et al., 2005). Prenatal exposure to traffic-related air pollution due to residence near roadways, for example, is linked to lower birth weight, with complicated pregnancies at greater risk (Rich et al., 2009; Seo et al., 2010).

Certain pollutants cause severe prenatal damage. In the 1950s, an industrial plant released waste containing high levels of *mercury* into a bay providing seafood and water for the town of Minamata, Japan. Many children born at the time displayed physical deformities, intellectual disability, abnormal speech, difficulty in chewing and swallowing, and uncoordinated movements. High levels of prenatal mercury exposure disrupt production and migration of neurons, causing widespread brain damage (Clarkson, Magos, & Myers, 2003; Hubbs-Tait et al., 2005). Prenatal mercury exposure from maternal seafood diets, assessed by measuring mercury concentration in umbilical-cord blood and tissue, predicts deficits in speed of cognitive processing and motor, attention, and verbal test performance during the school years (Boucher et al., 2010; Debes et al., 2006). Pregnant women are wise to avoid eating long-lived predatory fish, including swordfish, albacore tuna, and shark, which are heavily contaminated with mercury.

For many years, *polychlorinated biphenyls (PCBs)* were used to insulate electrical equipment, until research showed that, like mercury, they found their way into waterways and entered the food supply. In Taiwan, prenatal exposure to very high levels of PCBs in rice oil resulted in low birth weight, discolored skin, deformities of the gums and nails, EEG brainwave abnormalities, and delayed cognitive development (Chen & Hsu, 1994; Chen et al., 1994). Steady, low-level PCB exposure is also harmful. Women who frequently ate PCB-contaminated fish, compared with those who ate little or no fish, had infants with lower birth weights, smaller heads, greater stress reactivity, persisting attention and memory difficulties, and lower intelligence test scores in childhood (Boucher, Muckle, & Bastien, 2009; Jacobson & Jacobson, 2003; Stewart et al., 2008).

Another teratogen, *lead*, is present in paint flaking off the walls of old buildings and in certain materials used in industrial occupations. High levels of prenatal lead exposure are consistently related to prematurity, low birth weight, brain damage, and a wide variety of physical defects. Even at low levels, affected infants and children show slightly poorer mental and motor development (Bellinger, 2005; Jedrychowski et al., 2009). The greater the prenatal lead exposure, the lower children's test scores.

Finally, prenatal exposure to *dioxins*—toxic compounds resulting from incineration—is linked to brain, immune system, and thyroid damage in babies and to an increased incidence of breast and uterine cancers in women, perhaps through altering hormone levels (ten Tusscher & Koppe, 2004). Furthermore, even tiny amounts of dioxin in the paternal blood stream cause a dramatic change in the sex ratio of offspring: Affected men father nearly twice as many girls as boys (Ishihara et al., 2007; Mocarelli et al., 2000). Dioxin seems to impair the fertility of Y-bearing sperm prior to conception.

Maternal Disease Five percent of women catch an infectious disease while pregnant. Most of these illnesses, such as the common cold, seem to have no impact on the embryo or fetus. However, as Table 3.7 on page 102 indicates, certain diseases can cause extensive damage.

LOOK and LISTEN

Ask several adults who hope someday to be parents to explain what they know about several teratogens. How great is their need for prenatal education?

TABLE 3.7 | **Effects of Some Infectious Diseases During Pregnancy**

DISEASE	MISCARRIAGE	PHYSICAL MALFORMATIONS	INTELLECTUAL DISABILITY	LOW BIRTH WEIGHT AND PREMATURITY
Viral				
Acquired immune deficiency syndrome (AIDS)	✗	?	✔	?
Chickenpox	✗	✔	✔	✔
Cytomegalovirus	✔	✔	✔	✔
Herpes simplex 2 (genital herpes)	✔	✔	✔	✔
Mumps	✔	?	✗	✗
Rubella (German measles)	✔	✔	✔	✔
Bacterial				
Chlamydia	✔	?	✗	✔
Syphilis	✔	✔	✔	?
Tuberculosis	✔	?	✔	✔
Parasitic				
Malaria	✔	✗	✗	✔
Toxoplasmosis	✔	✔	✔	✔

✔ = established finding, ✗ = no present evidence, ? = possible effect that is not clearly established.

Sources: Jones, Lopez, & Wilson, 2003; Kliegman et al., 2008; Mardh, 2002; O'Rahilly & Müller, 2001.

Viruses. In the mid-1960s, a worldwide epidemic of *rubella* (three-day, or German, measles) led to the birth of more than 20,000 American babies with serious defects and to 13,000 fetal and newborn deaths. Consistent with the sensitive-period concept, the greatest damage occurs when rubella strikes during the embryonic period. More than 50 percent of infants whose mothers become ill during that time show deafness; eye deformities, including cataracts; heart, genital, urinary, intestinal, bone, and dental defects; and intellectual disability. Infection during the fetal period is less harmful, but low birth weight, hearing loss, and bone defects may still occur. The organ damage inflicted by prenatal rubella often leads to lifelong health problems, including severe mental illness (especially schizophrenia), diabetes, cardiovascular disease, and thyroid and immune-system dysfunction in adulthood (Brown, 2006; Duszak, 2009). Routine vaccination in infancy and childhood has made new rubella outbreaks unlikely in industrialized nations. But an estimated 100,000 cases of prenatal infection continue to occur each year, primarily in developing countries in Africa and Asia with weak or absent immunization programs (Bale, 2009).

The *human immunodeficiency virus (HIV)*, which can lead to *acquired immune deficiency syndrome (AIDS)*, a disease that destroys the immune system, has infected increasing numbers of women over the past two decades. Currently, women account for one-fourth of cases in North America, Western Europe, and East Asia. Although the incidence of AIDS has declined in industrialized nations, the disease is rampant in developing countries, where 95 percent of new infections occur, more than half of which affect women. In South Africa, for example, nearly 30 percent of all pregnant women are HIV-positive (Quinn & Overbaugh, 2005; South African Department of Health, 2009). HIV-infected expectant mothers pass the deadly virus to the fetus 20 to 30 percent of the time.

AIDS progresses rapidly in infants. By 6 months, weight loss, diarrhea, and repeated respiratory illnesses are common. The virus also causes brain damage, as indicated by seizures, gradual loss in brain weight, and delayed mental and motor development. Nearly half of prenatal AIDS babies die by 1 year of age and 90 percent by age 3 (Devi et al., 2009). Antiretroviral drug treatment reduces prenatal AIDS transmission by as much as 95 percent, with no harmful consequences of drug therapy for children. These medications have led to a dramatic decline in prenatally acquired AIDS in Western nations. Although distribution is increasing, antiretroviral drugs are still not widely available in impoverished regions of the world (UNICEF, 2010a).

As Table 3.7 reveals, the developing organism is especially sensitive to the family of herpes viruses, for which no vaccine or treatment exists. Among these, *cytomegalovirus* (the most frequent prenatal infection, transmitted through respiratory or sexual contact) and *herpes simplex 2* (which is sexually transmitted) are especially dangerous. In both, the virus invades the mother's genital tract, infecting babies either during pregnancy or at birth. Both diseases often have no symptoms, very mild symptoms, or symptoms with which people are unfamiliar, thereby increasing the likelihood of contagion. Pregnant women who are not in a mutually monogamous relationship are at greatest risk.

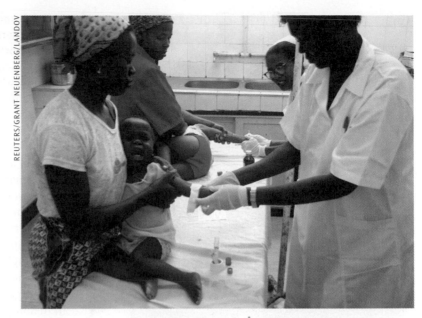

Babies are tested for the HIV virus in a clinic in Mozambique, Africa. Prenatal treatment with antiretroviral drugs reduces transmission of AIDS from mother to child by as much as 95 percent.

Bacterial and Parasitic Diseases. Table 3.7 also includes several bacterial and parasitic diseases. Among the most common is *toxoplasmosis*, caused by a parasite found in many animals. Pregnant women may become infected from eating raw or undercooked meat or from contact with the feces of infected cats. About 40 percent of women who have the disease transmit it to the developing organism. If it strikes during the first trimester, it is likely to cause eye and brain damage. Later infection is linked to mild visual and cognitive impairments. And about 80 percent of affected newborns with no obvious signs of damage develop learning or visual disabilities in later life (Jones, Lopez, & Wilson, 2003). Expectant mothers can avoid toxoplasmosis by making sure that the meat they eat is well-cooked, having pet cats checked for the disease, and turning over care of litter boxes to other family members.

Other Maternal Factors

Besides exposure to teratogens, maternal exercise, nutrition, and emotional well-being affect the embryo and fetus. In addition, many expectant parents wonder how a mother's age affects the course of pregnancy. We examine each of these factors in the following sections.

Exercise In healthy, physically fit women, regular moderate exercise, such as walking, swimming, biking, or an aerobic workout, is related to increased birth weight and a reduction in risk for certain complications, such as pregnancy-induced maternal diabetes and high blood pressure (Kalisiak & Spitznagle, 2009; Olson et al., 2009). However, frequent, vigorous, extended exercise—working up a sweat for more than 30 minutes, four or five days a week, especially late in pregnancy—results in lower birth weight than in healthy, nonexercising controls (Clapp et al., 2002; Leet & Flick, 2003). Hospital-sponsored childbirth education programs frequently offer exercise classes and suggest appropriate routines that help women prepare for labor and delivery.

During the last trimester, when the abdomen grows very large, mothers have difficulty moving freely and often must cut back on exercise. Most women, however, do not engage in sufficient moderate exercise during pregnancy to promote their own and their baby's health (Poudevigne & O'Connor, 2006). An expectant mother who remains fit experiences fewer physical discomforts, such as back pain, upward pressure on the chest, or difficulty breathing in the final weeks.

Nutrition During the prenatal period, when children are growing more rapidly than at any other time, they depend totally on the mother for nutrients. A healthy diet that results in a maternal weight gain of 25 to 30 pounds (10 to 13.5 kilograms) helps ensure the health of mother and baby.

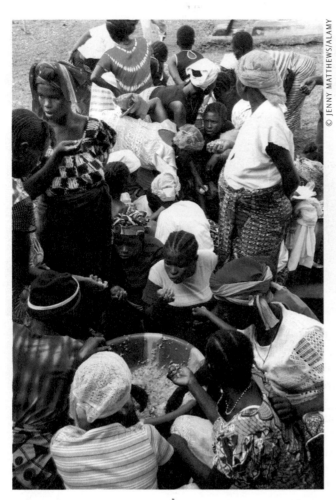

Pregnant women of Sierra Leone share a healthy meal they prepared together. They belong to a support group that seeks to improve maternal and infant health by preventing prenatal malnutrition.

Consequences of Prenatal Malnutrition. During World War II, a severe famine occurred in the Netherlands, giving scientists a rare opportunity to study the impact of nutrition on prenatal development. Findings revealed that the sensitive-period concept operates with nutrition, just as it does with teratogens. Women affected by the famine during the first trimester were more likely to have miscarriages or give birth to babies with physical defects. When women were past the first trimester, fetuses usually survived, but many were born underweight and had small heads (Stein et al., 1975).

Prenatal malnutrition can cause serious damage to the central nervous system. The poorer the mother's diet, the greater the loss in brain weight, especially if malnutrition occurred during the last trimester. During that time, the brain is increasing rapidly in size, and for it to reach its full potential, the mother must have a diet high in all the basic nutrients (Morgane et al., 1993). An inadequate diet during pregnancy can also distort the structure of other organs, including the liver, kidneys, and pancreas, resulting in lifelong health problems, including cardiovascular disease and diabetes in adulthood (Barker, 2008; Whincup et al., 2008).

Because poor nutrition suppresses development of the immune system, prenatally malnourished babies frequently catch respiratory illnesses (Chandra, 1991). In addition, they often are irritable and unresponsive to stimulation. Like drug-addicted newborns, they have a high-pitched cry that is particularly distressing to their caregivers. In poverty-stricken families, these effects quickly combine with a stressful home life. With age, low intelligence test scores and serious learning problems become more apparent (Pollitt, 1996).

Prevention and Treatment. Many studies show that providing pregnant women with adequate food has a substantial impact on the health of their newborn babies. Yet the growth demands of the prenatal period require more than just increased quantity of food. Vitamin–mineral enrichment is also crucial.

For example, taking a folic acid supplement around the time of conception reduces by more than 70 percent abnormalities of the neural tube, such as *anencephaly* and *spina bifida* (see Table 3.5 on page 85). Folic acid supplementation early in pregnancy also reduces the risk of other physical defects, including cleft lip and palate, urinary tract abnormalities, and limb deformities. Furthermore, adequate folic acid intake during the last 10 weeks of pregnancy cuts in half the risk of premature delivery and low birth weight (Goh & Koren, 2008; MCR Vitamin Study Research Group, 1991; Scholl, Hediger, & Belsky, 1996).

Because of these findings, U.S. government guidelines recommend that all women of childbearing age consume 0.4 milligrams of folic acid per day. For women who have previously had a pregnancy affected by neural tube defect, the recommended amount is 4 or 5 milligrams (dosage must be carefully monitored, as excessive intake can be harmful) (American Academy of Pediatrics, 2006). About half of U.S. pregnancies are unplanned, so government regulations mandate that bread, flour, rice, pasta, and other grain products be fortified with folic acid. As Figure 3.9 shows, mandatory grain fortification has resulted in substantial reductions in neural tube defects in the United States and other nations (Berry, 2010).

Other vitamins and minerals also have established benefits. Enriching women's diets with calcium helps prevent maternal high blood pressure and premature births. Adequate magnesium and zinc reduce the risk of many prenatal and birth complications (Durlach, 2004; Kontic-Vucinic, Sulovic, & Radunovic, 2006). Fortifying table salt with iodine virtually eradicates *infantile hypothyroidism*, a condition of stunted growth and cognitive impairment, caused by prenatal iodine deficiency—a common cause of intellectual disability in many parts of the developing world (Williams, 2008). Sufficient vitamin C and iron beginning early in pregnancy promote growth of the placenta and healthy birth weight (Christian, 2003). And in Chapter 2, we saw that prenatal iron depletion as a result of maternal diabetes interferes with development of brain structures involved in memory, thereby impairing children's learning (see page 45). Nevertheless, a supplement program should complement, not replace, efforts to improve maternal diets during pregnancy. For women who do not get enough food or an adequate variety of foods, multivitamin tablets are a necessary, but not a sufficient, intervention.

When poor nutrition continues throughout pregnancy, infants usually require more than dietary improvement. In response to their tired, restless behavior, parents tend to be less sensitive and stimulating. The babies, in turn, become even more passive and withdrawn. Successful interventions must break this cycle of apathetic caregiver–baby interaction. Some do so by teaching parents how to interact effectively with their infants; others focus on stimulating infants to promote active engagement with their physical and social surroundings (Grantham-McGregor et al., 1994; Grantham-McGregor, Schofield, & Powell, 1987).

Although prenatal malnutrition is highest in poverty-stricken regions of the world, it is not limited to developing countries. The U.S. Special Supplemental Food Program for Women, Infants, and Children (WIC), which provides food packages and nutrition education to low-income pregnant women, reaches about 90 percent of those who qualify because of their extremely low incomes (U.S. Department of Agriculture, 2009). But many U.S. women who need nutrition intervention are not eligible for WIC.

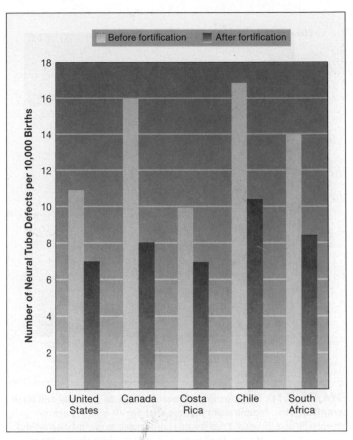

FIGURE 3.9 Decline in rates of neural tube defects in five countries after introduction of grain fortification with folic acid. (From J. Berry, 2010, "Fortification of Flour with Folic Acid," *Food and Nutrition Bulletin, 31*, p. S27. Reprinted by permission.)

Emotional Stress When women experience severe emotional stress during pregnancy, their babies are at risk for a wide variety of difficulties. Intense anxiety—especially during the first two trimesters—is associated with higher rates of miscarriage, prematurity, low birth weight, infant respiratory and digestive illnesses, colic (persistent infant crying), sleep disturbances, and irritability during the child's first three years (Field, 2011; Lazinski, Shea, & Steiner, 2008; van der Wal, van Eijsden, & Bonsel, 2007).

How can maternal stress affect the developing organism? **TAKE A MOMENT...** To understand this process, list the changes you sensed in your own body the last time you were under stress. When we experience fear and anxiety, stimulant hormones released into our bloodstream cause us to be "poised for action." Large amounts of blood are sent to parts of the body involved in the defensive response—the brain, the heart, and muscles in the arms, legs, and trunk. Blood flow to other organs, including the uterus, is reduced. As a result, the fetus is deprived of a full supply of oxygen and nutrients.

Maternal stress hormones also cross the placenta, causing a dramatic rise in fetal stress hormones (evident in the amniotic fluid) and in fetal heart rate, blood pressure, blood glucose, and activity level (Kinsella & Monk, 2009; Weinstock, 2008). These processes are believed to increase the lifelong risk of serious illnesses, such as cardiovascular disease and diabetes (Stocker, Arch, & Cawthorne, 2005).

Excessive fetal stress may permanently alter neurological functioning as well, thereby heightening stress reactivity in later life. In several studies, infants and children of mothers who experienced severe prenatal anxiety displayed cortisol levels that were either abnormally high or abnormally low, both of which signal reduced physiological capacity to manage stress. Consistent with these findings, such children are more upset than their agemates when faced with novel or challenging experiences (Brand et al., 2006; Huizink et al., 2008; Yehuda et al., 2005). In other research, adolescents and young adults who had been exposed to stress prenatally continued to display elevated stress reactivity (Entringer et al., 2009;

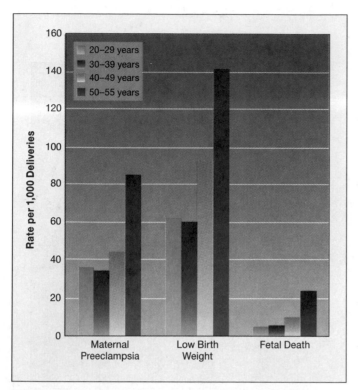

FIGURE 3.10 Relationship of maternal age to prenatal and birth complications. Complications increase after age 40, with a sharp rise between 50 and 55 years. Preeclampsia (also known as toxemia) is a serious disorder of the second and third trimesters involving high blood pressure, sudden weight gains, headaches, and swelling of the face, hands, and feet. Without immediate treatment, the condition progresses rapidly and is a leading cause of maternal and infant illness and death. Similarly, low birth weight greatly increases the risk of infant death and health problems. (Adapted from Salihu et al., 2003.)

Van den Bergh et al., 2008). Furthermore, maternal emotional stress during pregnancy predicts childhood anxiety, short attention span, anger, aggression, overactivity, and lower mental test scores, above and beyond the impact of other risks, such as maternal smoking during pregnancy, low birth weight, postnatal maternal anxiety, and low family income (de Weerth & Buitelaar, 2005; Gutteling et al., 2006; Lazinski, Shea, & Steiner, 2008; Van den Bergh, 2004).

But stress-related prenatal complications are greatly reduced when mothers have partners, other family members, and friends who offer social support (Glover, Bergman, & O'Connor, 2008). The relationship of social support to positive pregnancy outcomes and subsequent child development is particularly strong for low-income women, who often lead highly stressful lives (Olds et al., 2002, 2004). Enhancing supportive social networks for pregnant mothers can help prevent prenatal complications.

Maternal Age Over the past thirty years, first births to women in their thirties have increased more than fourfold, and those to women in their early forties have doubled. Many more couples are putting off childbearing until their careers are well-established and they know they can support a child. Recall that women who delay having children until their thirties or forties face increased risk of infertility, miscarriage, and babies born with chromosomal defects. Are other pregnancy complications also more common for older mothers? Research consistently indicates that healthy women in their thirties have about the same rates as those in their twenties (Bianco et al., 1996; Dildy et al., 1996; Prysak, Lorenz, & Kisly, 1995). Thereafter, as Figure 3.10 shows, complication rates increase, with a sharp rise among women age 50 to 55—an age at which, because of menopause and aging reproductive organs, few women can conceive naturally (Salihu et al., 2003; Usta & Nassar, 2008).

In the case of teenage mothers, does physical immaturity cause prenatal problems? As we will see in Chapter 5, nature tries to ensure that once a girl can conceive, she is physically ready to carry and give birth to a baby. Infants born to teenagers have a higher rate of problems, but not directly because of maternal age. Most pregnant teenagers come from low-income backgrounds, where stress, poor nutrition, and health problems are common. Also, many are afraid to seek medical care or, in the United States, do not have access to care because they lack health insurance (U.S. Department of Health and Human Services, 2010a).

As we conclude our discussion of the prenatal environment, refer to Applying What We Know on the following page, which lists "do's and don'ts" for a healthy pregnancy. Public education about these vital precautions can greatly reduce prenatal health problems and their long-term negative consequences.

ASK YOURSELF

Review ■ Why is it difficult to determine the prenatal effects of many environmental agents, such as drugs and pollution?

Connect ■ List teratogens and other maternal factors that affect brain development during the prenatal period. Using Figure 3.9 on page 95, explain why the central nervous system is often affected when the prenatal environment is compromised.

Apply ■ Nora, pregnant for the first time, believes that a few cigarettes and a glass of wine a day won't be harmful. Provide Nora with research-based reasons for not smoking or drinking.

Reflect ■ If you had to choose five environmental influences to publicize in a campaign aimed at promoting healthy prenatal development, which ones would you choose, and why?

APPLYING WHAT WE KNOW

Do's and Don'ts for a Healthy Pregnancy

DO	DON'T
Do make sure that you have been vaccinated against infectious diseases that are dangerous to the embryo and fetus, such as rubella, before you get pregnant. Most vaccinations are not safe during pregnancy.	Don't take any drugs without consulting your doctor.
Do see a doctor as soon as you suspect that you are pregnant, and continue to get regular medical checkups throughout pregnancy.	Don't smoke. If you have already smoked during part of your pregnancy, cut down or, better yet, quit. If other members of your family smoke, ask them to quit or to smoke outside.
Do eat a well-balanced diet and take vitamin–mineral supplements, as prescribed by your doctor, both prior to and during pregnancy. Gain 25 to 30 pounds gradually.	Don't drink alcohol from the time you decide to get pregnant.
Do obtain literature from your doctor, local library, and bookstore about prenatal development and care, and ask questions about anything that concerns you.	Don't engage in activities that might expose your embryo or fetus to environmental hazards, such as radiation or chemical pollutants. If you work in an occupation that involves these agents, ask for a safer assignment or a leave of absence.
Do keep physically fit through moderate exercise. If possible, join a special exercise class for expectant mothers.	Don't engage in activities that might expose your embryo or fetus to harmful infectious diseases, such as toxoplasmosis.
Do avoid emotional stress. If you are a single parent, find a relative or friend you can count on for emotional support.	Don't choose pregnancy as a time to go on a diet.
Do get plenty of rest. An overtired mother is at risk for pregnancy complications.	Don't gain too much weight during pregnancy. A very large weight gain is associated with complications.
Do enroll in a prenatal and childbirth education class with your partner or other companion. When parents know what to expect, the nine months before birth can be one of the most joyful times of life.	

Childbirth

▶ Describe the three stages of childbirth, the baby's adaptation to labor and delivery, and the newborn baby's appearance.

It is not surprising that childbirth is often referred to as labor. It is the hardest physical work that a woman may ever do. A complex series of hormonal exchanges between mother and fetus initiates the process, which divides naturally into three stages (see Figure 3.11 on page 108):

1. *Dilation and effacement of the cervix.* This is the longest stage of labor, lasting an average of 12 to 14 hours with a first birth and 4 to 6 hours with later births. Contractions of the uterus gradually become more frequent and powerful, causing the cervix, or uterine opening, to widen and thin to nothing, forming a clear channel from the uterus into the birth canal, or vagina.
2. *Delivery of the baby.* This second stage is much shorter than the first, lasting about 50 minutes for a first baby and 20 minutes in later births. Strong contractions of the uterus continue, but the mother also feels a natural urge to squeeze and push with her abdominal muscles. As she does so with each contraction, she forces the baby down and out.
3. *Birth of the placenta.* Labor comes to an end with a few final contractions and pushes. These cause the placenta to separate from the wall of the uterus and be delivered in about 5 to 10 minutes.

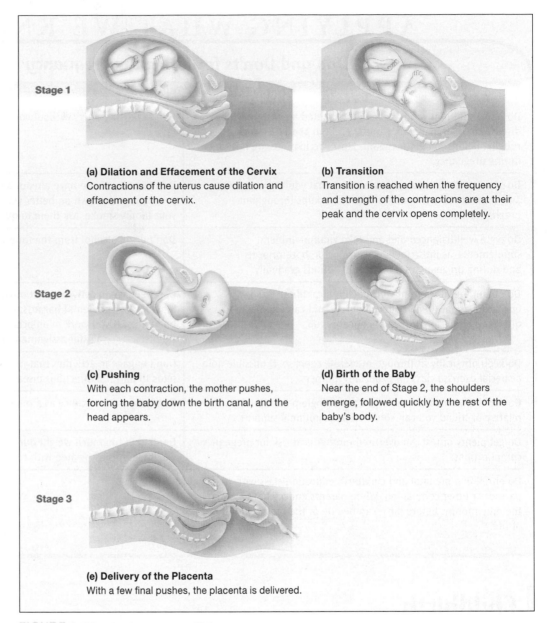

Stage 1

(a) Dilation and Effacement of the Cervix
Contractions of the uterus cause dilation and effacement of the cervix.

(b) Transition
Transition is reached when the frequency and strength of the contractions are at their peak and the cervix opens completely.

Stage 2

(c) Pushing
With each contraction, the mother pushes, forcing the baby down the birth canal, and the head appears.

(d) Birth of the Baby
Near the end of Stage 2, the shoulders emerge, followed quickly by the rest of the baby's body.

Stage 3

(e) Delivery of the Placenta
With a few final pushes, the placenta is delivered.

FIGURE 3.11   The three stages of labor.

The Baby's Adaptation to Labor and Delivery

At first glance, labor and delivery seem like a dangerous ordeal for the baby. The strong uterine contractions expose the head to a great deal of pressure, and they squeeze the placenta and the umbilical cord repeatedly. Each time, the baby's supply of oxygen is temporarily reduced.

Fortunately, healthy babies are equipped to withstand these traumas. The force of the contractions intensifies the baby's production of stress hormones. Unlike during pregnancy, during childbirth high levels of infant cortisol and other stress hormones are adaptive. They help the baby withstand oxygen deprivation by sending a rich supply of blood to the brain and heart (Gluckman, Sizonenko, & Bassett, 1999). In addition, stress hormones prepare the baby to breathe by causing the lungs to absorb any remaining fluid and by expanding the bronchial tubes (passages leading to the lungs). Finally, stress hormones arouse infants into alertness so they are born wide awake, ready to interact with their world (Lagercrantz & Slotkin, 1986).

The Newborn Baby's Appearance

Parents are often surprised at the odd-looking newborn—a far cry from the storybook image many had in their minds. The average newborn is 20 inches long and weighs 7½ pounds; boys tend to be slightly longer and heavier than girls. The head is large in relation to the trunk and legs, which are short and bowed. This combination of a large head (with its well-developed brain) and a small body means that human infants learn quickly in the first few months of life. But unlike most other mammals, they cannot get around on their own until much later.

Even though newborn babies may not match parents' idealized image, some features do make them attractive. Their round faces, chubby cheeks, large foreheads, and big eyes make adults feel like picking them up and cuddling them (Berman, 1980).

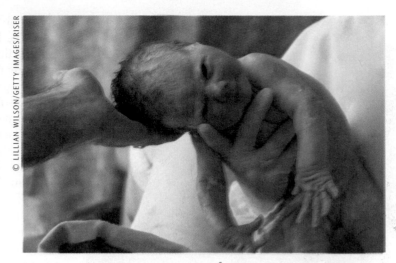

To accommodate the well-developed brain, a newborn's head is large in relation to the trunk and legs. The round face, chubby cheeks, and big eyes are attractive to adults, inducing them to pick up and cuddle the newborn.

Assessing the Newborn's Physical Condition: The Apgar Scale

Infants who have difficulty making the transition to life outside the uterus need special help at once. To assess the baby's physical condition, doctors and nurses use the **Apgar Scale.** As Table 3.8 shows, a rating of 0, 1, or 2 on each of five characteristics is made at 1 minute and again at 5 minutes after birth. A combined Apgar score of 7 or better indicates that the infant is in good physical condition. If the score is between 4 and 6, the baby requires assistance in establishing breathing and other vital signs. If the score is 3 or below, the infant is in serious danger and requires emergency medical attention. Two Apgar ratings are given because some babies have trouble adjusting at first but do quite well after a few minutes (Apgar, 1953).

TABLE 3.8 | **The Apgar Scale**

	SCORE		
SIGN[a]	**0**	**1**	**2**
Heart rate	No heartbeat	Under 100 beats per minute	100 to 140 beats per minute
Respiratory effort	No breathing for 60 seconds	Irregular, shallow breathing	Strong breathing and crying
Reflex irritability (sneezing, coughing, and grimacing)	No response	Weak reflexive response	Strong reflexive response
Muscle tone	Completely limp	Weak movements of arms and legs	Strong movements of arms and legs
Color[b]	Blue body, arms, and legs	Body pink with blue arms and legs	Body, arms, and legs completely pink

[a]To remember these signs, you may find it helpful to use a technique in which the original labels are reordered and renamed as follows: color = **A**ppearance, heart rate = **P**ulse, reflex irritability = **G**rimace, muscle tone = **A**ctivity, and respiratory effort = **R**espiration. Together, the first letters of the new labels spell **Apgar**.
[b]The skin tone of nonwhite babies makes it difficult to apply the "pink" color criterion. However, newborns of all races can be rated for pinkish glow resulting from the flow of oxygen through body tissues..

Source: Apgar, 1953.

Approaches to Childbirth

Childbirth practices, like other aspects of family life, are molded by the society of which mother and baby are a part. In many village and tribal cultures, expectant mothers are well-acquainted with the childbirth process. For example, the Jarara of South America and the Pukapukans of the Pacific Islands treat birth as a vital part of daily life. The Jarara mother

▶ Describe natural childbirth and home delivery, and explain the risks of using pain-relieving drugs during labor and delivery.

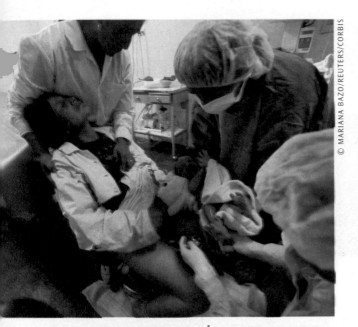

In this Peruvian health clinic, families are encouraged to incorporate traditional village practices into the birth experience. Here, a familiar attendant supports and soothes a new mother as her baby is delivered.

gives birth in full view of the entire community, including small children. The Pukapukan girl is so familiar with the events of labor and delivery that she frequently can be seen playing at it. Using a coconut to represent the baby, she stuffs it inside her dress, imitates the mother's pushing, and lets the nut fall at the proper moment. In most nonindustrialized cultures, women are assisted—though often not by medical personnel—during labor and delivery. Among the Mayans of the Yucatán, the mother leans against a woman called the "head helper," who supports her weight and breathes with her during each contraction. And in Bolivia, a Siriono mother delivers her own baby in a hammock with a crowd of women close by, who keep her company. The father cuts the umbilical cord and joins the mother in tending to the newborn for the first few days (Jordan, 1993; Mead & Newton, 1967; Reed, 2005).

In Western nations, childbirth has changed dramatically over the centuries. Before the late 1800s, birth usually took place at home and was a family-centered event. The industrial revolution brought greater crowding to cities, along with new health problems. As a result, childbirth moved from home to hospital, where the health of mothers and babies could be protected. Once doctors assumed responsibility for childbirth, women's knowledge of it declined, and relatives and friends no longer participated (Borst, 1995).

By the 1950s and 1960s, women had begun to question the medical procedures that had come to be used routinely during labor and delivery. Many felt that use of strong drugs and delivery instruments had robbed them of a precious experience and was often neither necessary nor safe for the baby. Gradually, a natural childbirth movement arose in Europe and spread to North America. Its purpose was to make hospital birth as comfortable and rewarding for mothers as possible. Today, most hospitals offer birth centers that are family-centered and homelike. *Freestanding birth centers*, which permit greater maternal control over labor and delivery, including choice of delivery positions, presence of family members and friends, and early contact between parents and baby, also exist. And a small number of North American women reject institutional birth entirely and choose to have their babies at home.

Natural, or Prepared, Childbirth

Natural, or **prepared, childbirth** consists of a group of techniques aimed at reducing pain and medical intervention and making childbirth as rewarding an experience as possible. Most natural childbirth programs draw on methods developed by Grantly Dick-Read (1959) in England and Ferdinand Lamaze (1958) in France. These physicians recognized that cultural attitudes had taught women to fear the birth experience. An anxious, frightened woman in labor tenses muscles, heightening the pain that usually accompanies strong contractions.

In a typical natural childbirth program, the expectant mother and a companion (a partner, relative, or friend) participate in three activities:

In a hospital birth center, a mother gives birth, assisted by the father. A companion's support is a vital part of natural childbirth, which is associated with shorter labors, fewer complications, and a more rewarding birth experience.

* *Classes.* The expectant mother and her companion attend a series of classes in which they learn about the anatomy and physiology of labor and delivery. Knowledge about the birth process reduces a mother's fear.
* *Relaxation and breathing techniques.* Expectant mothers are taught relaxation and breathing exercises aimed at counteracting the pain of uterine contractions.
* *Labor coach.* The companion learns how to help during childbirth by reminding the mother to relax and breathe, massaging her back, supporting her body, and offering encouragement and affection.

Social Support and Natural Childbirth Social support is important to the success of natural childbirth techniques. In Guatemalan and American hospitals that routinely isolated patients during childbirth, some mothers were randomly assigned a doula—a Greek word referring to a trained lay attendant—who stayed with them throughout labor and delivery, talking to them, holding their hands, and rubbing their backs to promote relaxation. These mothers had fewer birth complications, and their labors were several hours shorter than those of women who did not have supportive companionship. Guatemalan mothers who received doula support also interacted more positively with their babies after delivery, talking, smiling, and gently stroking (Kennell et al., 1991; Sosa et al., 1980).

Other studies indicate that mothers who are supported during labor and delivery—either by a lay birth attendant or by a relative or friend with doula training—less often have instrument-assisted or cesarean (surgical) deliveries or need medication to control pain. Also, their babies' Apgar scores are higher, and they are more likely to be breastfeeding at a two-month follow-up (Campbell et al., 2006, 2007; Hodnett et al., 2003; McGrath & Kennell, 2008). The continuous rather than intermittent support of a doula during labor and delivery strengthens these outcomes. It is particularly helpful during a first childbirth, when mothers are more anxious (Scott, Berkowitz, & Klaus, 1999). And this aspect of natural childbirth makes Western hospital-birth customs more acceptable to women from parts of the world where assistance from family and community members is the norm (Dundek, 2006).

LOOK and LISTEN

Talk to several mothers about social supports available to them during labor and delivery. From the mothers' perspectives, how did those supports (or lack of support) affect the birth experience?

Positions for Delivery When natural childbirth is combined with delivery in a birth center or at home, mothers often give birth in an upright, sitting position rather than lying flat on their backs with their feet in stirrups (the traditional hospital delivery room practice). Use of special seats to enable an upright birth has become more common. When mothers are upright, labor is shortened because contractions are stronger and pushing is more effective. The baby benefits from a richer supply of oxygen because blood flow to the placenta is increased (Lawrence et al., 2009). Because the mother can see the delivery, she can work with the doctor or midwife, adjusting her pushing to ensure that the baby's head and shoulders emerge slowly, which reduces the chances of tearing the mother's tissues. Compared with those who give birth lying on their backs, women who choose an upright position are less likely to use pain-relieving medication (Romano & Lothian, 2008).

In another increasingly popular method, water birth, the mother sits in a warm tub of water, which supports her weight, relaxes her, and provides her with the freedom to move into any position she finds most comfortable. Water birth is associated with reduced maternal stress, shorter labor, and greater likelihood of medication-free delivery than both back-lying and seated positions (Cluett & Burns, 2009). As long as water birth is carefully managed by health professionals, it poses no additional risk of infection or safety to mothers or babies (Zanetti-Daellenbach et al., 2007).

© FRANCE KEYSER/IN VISU/CORBIS

An increasingly popular childbirth option is water birth. Sitting in a warm tub of water relaxes this mother, supports her weight, and gives her the freedom to move into a comfortable position.

Home Delivery

Home birth has always been popular in certain industrialized nations, such as England, the Netherlands, and Sweden. The number of American women choosing to have their babies at home rose during the 1970s and 1980s but remains small, at less than 1 percent (U.S. Department of Health and Human Services, 2010a). These mothers want birth to be an important part of family life, to avoid unnecessary medical procedures, and to have greater control over their own care and that of their babies than hospitals permit. Although some home births are attended by doctors, many more are handled by *certified nurse–midwives*, who have degrees in nursing and additional training in childbirth management.

Is it just as safe to give birth at home as in a hospital? For healthy women who are assisted by a well-trained doctor or midwife, it seems so because complications rarely occur (Fullerton, Navarro, & Young, 2007; Wax, Pinette, & Cartin, 2010). However, if attendants are not carefully trained and prepared to handle emergencies, the rate of infant death is high (Mehlmadrona & Madrona, 1997). When mothers are at risk for any kind of complication, the appropriate place for labor and delivery is the hospital, where life-saving treatment is available.

Labor and Delivery Medication

Although natural childbirth techniques lessen or eliminate the need for pain-relieving drugs, some form of medication is used in more than 80 percent of U.S. births (Althaus & Wax, 2005). *Analgesics*, drugs used to relieve pain, may be given in mild doses during labor to help a mother relax. *Anesthetics* are a stronger type of painkiller that blocks sensation. Currently, the most common approach to controlling pain during labor is *epidural analgesia*, in which a regional pain-relieving drug is delivered continuously through a catheter into a small space in the lower spine. Unlike older spinal block procedures, which numb the entire lower half of the body, epidural analgesia limits pain reduction to the pelvic region. Because the mother retains the capacity to feel the pressure of contractions and to move her trunk and legs, she is able to push during the second stage of labor.

Although pain-relieving drugs help women cope with childbirth and enable doctors to perform essential medical interventions, they also cause problems. Epidural analgesia, for example, weakens uterine contractions. As a result, labor is prolonged, and the chances of cesarean (surgical) delivery increase (Nguyen et al., 2010). And because drugs rapidly cross the placenta, exposed newborns tend to have lower Apgar scores, to be sleepy and withdrawn, to suck poorly during feedings, and to be irritable when awake (Caton et al., 2002; Eltzschig, Lieberman, & Camann, 2003; Emory, Schlackman, & Fiano, 1996). Although no confirmed long-term consequences for development exist, the negative impact of these drugs on the newborn's adjustment supports the current trend to limit their use.

A S K   Y O U R S E L F

Review ■ Describe the features and benefits of natural childbirth. What aspect contributes greatly to favorable outcomes, and why?

Connect ■ Contrast the positive impact of the baby's production of stress hormones during childbirth with the negative impact of maternal stress on the fetus, discussed on pages 105–106.

Apply ■ On seeing her newborn baby for the first time, Caroline exclaimed, "Why is she so out of proportion?" What observations prompted Caroline to ask this question? Explain why her baby's appearance is adaptive.

Reflect ■ If you were an expectant parent, would you choose home birth? Why or why not?

▶ What risks are associated with oxygen deprivation and with preterm and low-birth-weight infants, and what factors can help infants who survive a traumatic birth?

Birth Complications

We have seen that some babies—in particular, those whose mothers are in poor health, do not receive good medical care, or have a history of prenatal problems—are especially likely to experience birth complications. Inadequate oxygen, a pregnancy that ends too early, and low birth weight pose serious risks to development that we have touched on many times. Let's look at the impact of each complication on later development.

Oxygen Deprivation

A small number of infants experience *anoxia*, or inadequate oxygen supply, during the birth process. Sometimes the problem results from a failure to start breathing within a few minutes. Healthy newborns can survive periods of little or no oxygen longer than adults can; they reduce their metabolic rate, thereby conserving the limited oxygen available. Nevertheless, brain damage is likely if regular breathing is delayed more than 10 minutes (Kendall & Peebles, 2005).

At other times, anoxia occurs during labor. A common cause is squeezing of the umbilical cord, a condition that is especially likely when infants are in **breech position**—turned in such a way that the buttocks or feet would be delivered first (1 in every 25 births). Because of this danger, breech babies often experience a cesarean (surgical) delivery. An additional cause of oxygen deprivation is *placenta abruptio*, or premature separation of the placenta (complicating about 1 percent of pregnancies), a life-threatening event that requires immediate delivery. Factors related to it include multiple fetuses, advanced maternal age (40 and older), and teratogens that cause abnormal development of the placenta, such as tobacco and cocaine (Oyelese & Ananth, 2006).

Still another condition that can lead to anoxia is **Rh factor incompatibility** between the mother's and baby's blood types. When the mother is Rh negative (lacks the Rh protein) and the father is Rh positive (has the Rh protein), the baby may inherit the father's Rh-positive blood type. If even a little of a fetus's Rh-positive blood crosses the placenta into the Rh-negative mother's bloodstream, she begins to form antibodies to the foreign protein. If these enter the fetus's system, they destroy red blood cells, reducing the supply of oxygen. Intellectual disability, miscarriage, heart damage, and infant death can occur. It takes time for the mother to produce antibodies, so firstborn children are rarely affected. The danger increases with each pregnancy. Fortunately, Rh incompatibility can be prevented in most cases. After the birth of each Rh-positive baby, Rh-negative mothers are given a vaccine to prevent the buildup of antibodies.

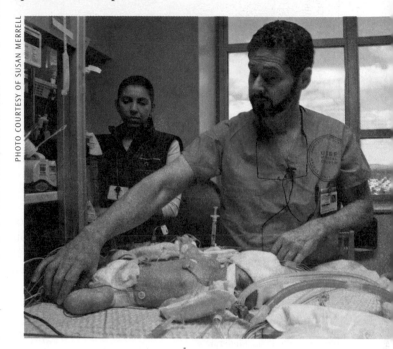

Treatment for this newborn, who experienced oxygen deprivation, combines a cooling head cap with a cooling water blanket to lower body temperature, which helps prevent brain damage.

After initial brain injury from anoxia, another phase of cell death can occur several hours later. Placing anoxic newborns in a head-cooling device shortly after birth for 72 hours substantially reduces this secondary brain damage (detected through MRI brain scans) and increases scores on a newborn behavioral assessment (Hoehn et al., 2008; Lin et al., 2006). Another alternative—whole-body cooling by having anoxic newborns lie on a precooled water blanket—leads to an impressive reduction in death and disability rates during the first two years (Shankaran et al., 2005).

How do children who experience anoxia during labor and delivery fare as they get older? Research suggests that the greater the oxygen deprivation, the poorer children's cognitive and language skills in early and middle childhood (Hopkins-Golightly, Raz, & Sander, 2003). Although effects of even mild to moderate anoxia often persist, many children improve over time (Bass et al., 2004; Raz, Shah, & Sander, 1996).

When development is severely impaired, the anoxia was probably extreme. Perhaps it was caused by prenatal insult to the baby's respiratory system, or it may have happened because the infant's lungs were not yet mature enough to breathe. For example, babies born more than six weeks early commonly have *respiratory distress syndrome* (otherwise known as *hyaline membrane disease*). Their tiny lungs are so poorly developed that the air sacs collapse, causing serious breathing difficulties. Today, mechanical respirators keep many such infants alive. In spite of these measures, some babies suffer permanent brain damage from lack of oxygen, and in other cases their delicate lungs are harmed by the treatment itself. Respiratory distress syndrome is only one of many risks for babies born too soon, as we will see in the following section.

Preterm and Low-Birth-Weight Infants

Babies born three weeks or more before the end of a full 38-week pregnancy or who weigh less than 5½ pounds (2,500 grams) have for many years been referred to as "premature." A wealth of research indicates that premature babies are at risk for many problems. Birth weight is the best available predictor of infant survival and healthy development. Although outcomes have improved over the past several decades, many newborns who weigh less than 3½ pounds (1,500 grams) experience difficulties that are not overcome—an effect that

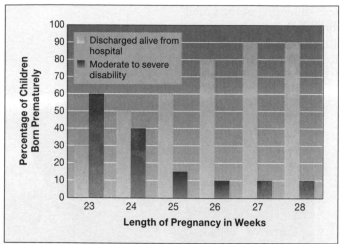

FIGURE 3.12 Rates of infant survival and child disabilities by length of pregnancy. In a follow-up of more than 2,300 babies born between 23 and 28 weeks gestation, the percentage who displayed moderate to severe disabilities (assessed during the preschool years) increased with reduced length of pregnancy. Severe disabilities included cerebral palsy (unlikely to ever walk), severely delayed mental development, deafness, and blindness. Moderate disabilities included cerebral palsy (able to walk with assistance), moderately delayed mental development, and hearing impairments partially correctable with a hearing aid. (Adapted from Bolisetty et al., 2006.)

strengthens as length of pregnancy and birth weight decrease (see Figure 3.12) (Baron & Rey-Casserly, 2010; Bolisetty et al., 2006; Dombrowski, Noonan, & Martin, 2007). Brain abnormalities, frequent illness, inattention, overactivity, sensory impairments, poor motor coordination, language delays, low intelligence test scores, deficits in school learning, and emotional and behavior problems are some of the difficulties that persist through childhood and adolescence and into adulthood (Aarnoudse-Moens, Weisglas-Kuperus, & van Goudoever, 2009; Clark et al., 2008; Delobel-Ayoub et al., 2009; Nosarti et al., 2011).

About 1 in 13 American infants is born underweight. The problem can strike unexpectedly, but it is highest among poverty-stricken women (U.S. Department of Health and Human Services, 2010f). These mothers, as indicated earlier, are more likely to be undernourished, under stress, and exposed to other harmful environmental influences—factors strongly linked to low birth weight. In addition, they often do not receive the prenatal care necessary to protect their vulnerable babies.

Prematurity is also common in multiple births. About 60 percent of twins and more than 90 percent of triplets are born early and low birth weight (U.S. Department of Health and Human Services, 2010f). Because space inside the uterus is restricted, twins gain less weight than singletons in the second half of pregnancy.

Preterm versus Small-for-Date Infants Although low-birth-weight infants face many obstacles to healthy development, most go on to lead normal lives; about half of those born at 23 to 24 weeks gestation and weighing only a couple of pounds at birth have no disability (refer again to Figure 3.12). To better understand why some babies do better than others, researchers divide them into two groups. **Preterm infants** are those born several weeks or more before their due date. Although they are small, their weight may still be appropriate, based on time spent in the uterus. **Small-for-date infants** are below their expected weight considering length of the pregnancy. Some small-for-date infants are actually full-term. Others are preterm babies who are especially underweight.

Of the two types of babies, small-for-date infants usually have more serious problems. During the first year, they are more likely to die, catch infections, and show evidence of brain damage. By middle childhood, they are smaller in stature, have lower intelligence test scores, are less attentive, achieve more poorly in school, and are socially immature (Hediger et al., 2002; O'Keefe et al., 2003; Sullivan et al., 2008). Small-for-date infants probably experienced inadequate nutrition before birth. Perhaps their mothers did not eat properly, the placenta did not function normally, or the babies themselves had defects that prevented them from growing as they should. In some of these babies, an abnormally functioning placenta permitted ready transfer of stress hormones from mother to fetus. Consequently, small-for-date infants are especially likely to suffer from neurological impairments that permanently weaken their capacity to manage stress (Wust et al., 2005).

Even among preterm newborns whose weight is appropriate for length of pregnancy, just seven more days—from 34 to 35 weeks—greatly reduces rates of illness, costly medical procedures, and lengthy hospital stays (although they need greater medical intervention than full-term babies) (Gladstone & Katz, 2004). And despite being relatively low-risk for disabilities, a substantial number of 34-week preterms are below average in physical growth and mildly to moderately delayed in cognitive development in early and middle childhood (Morse et al., 2009; Pietz et al., 2004; Stephens & Vohr, 2009). Yet doctors often induce births several weeks preterm, under the misconception that these babies are developmentally "mature."

Consequences for Caregiving Imagine a scrawny, thin-skinned infant whose body is only a little larger than the size of your hand. You try to play with the baby by stroking and talking softly, but he is sleepy and unresponsive. When you feed him, he sucks poorly. During the short, unpredictable periods in which he is awake, he is usually irritable.

The appearance and behavior of preterm babies can lead parents to be less sensitive and responsive in caring for them. Compared to full-term infants, preterm babies—especially those who are very ill at birth—are less often held close, touched, and talked to gently. At times, mothers of these infants resort to interfering pokes and verbal commands, in an effort to obtain a higher level of response from the baby (Barratt, Roach, & Leavitt, 1996; Feldman, 2007c). This may explain why preterm babies as a group are at risk for child abuse.

Research reveals that distressed, emotionally reactive preterm infants are especially susceptible to the effects of parenting quality: Among a sample of preterm 9-month-olds, the combination of infant negativity and angry or intrusive parenting yielded the highest rates of behavior problems at 2 years of age. But with warm, sensitive parenting, distressed preterm babies' rates of behavior problems were the lowest (Poehlmann et al., 2011). When preterm infants are born to isolated, poverty-stricken mothers who cannot provide good nutrition, health care, and parenting, the likelihood of unfavorable outcomes escalates. In contrast, parents with stable life circumstances and social supports usually can overcome the stresses of caring for a preterm infant. In these cases, even sick preterm babies have a good chance of catching up in development by middle childhood (Ment et al., 2003).

These findings indicate that how well preterm infants fare has a great deal to do with the parent–child relationship. Consequently, interventions directed at supporting both sides of this tie are more likely to help these infants recover.

Interventions for Preterm Infants

A preterm baby is cared for in a special Plexiglas-enclosed bed called an *isolette*. Temperature is carefully controlled because these infants cannot yet regulate their own body temperature effectively. To help protect the baby from infection, air is filtered before it enters the isolette. When a preterm infant is fed through a stomach tube, breathes with the aid of a respirator, and receives medication through an intravenous needle, the isolette can be very isolating indeed! Physical needs that otherwise would lead to close contact and other human stimulation are met mechanically.

Special Infant Stimulation. In proper doses, certain kinds of stimulation can help preterm infants develop. In some intensive care nurseries, preterm babies can be seen rocking in suspended hammocks or lying on waterbeds designed to replace the gentle motion they would have received while still in the mother's uterus. Other forms of stimulation have also been used—an attractive mobile or a tape recording of a heartbeat, soft music, or the mother's voice. These experiences promote faster weight gain, more predictable sleep patterns, and greater alertness (Arnon et al., 2006; Marshall-Baker, Lickliter, & Cooper, 1998; Standley, 1998).

Touch is an especially important form of stimulation. In baby animals, touching the skin releases certain brain chemicals that support physical growth—effects believed to occur in humans as well. When preterm infants were massaged several times each day in the hospital, they gained weight faster and, at the end of the first year, were more advanced in mental and motor development than preterm infants not given this stimulation (Field, 2001; Field, Hernandez-Reif, & Freedman, 2004).

In developing countries where hospitalization is not always possible, skin-to-skin "kangaroo care" is the most readily available intervention for promoting the survival and recovery of preterm babies. It involves placing the infant in a vertical position between the mother's breasts or next to the father's chest (under the parent's clothing) so the parent's body functions as a human incubator. Kangaroo care offers fathers a unique opportunity to increase their involvement in caring for the preterm newborn. Because of its many physical and psychological benefits, the technique is often used in Western nations as a supplement to hospital intensive care.

Kangaroo skin-to-skin contact fosters improved oxygenation of the baby's body, temperature regulation, sleep, breastfeeding, alertness, and infant survival (Feldman, 2007b; Lawn et al., 2010). In addition, the kangaroo position provides the baby with gentle stimulation of all sensory modalities: hearing (through the parent's voice), smell (through proximity to the parent's body), touch (through skin-to-skin contact), and visual (through the upright position). Mothers and fathers practicing kangaroo care feel more confident about caring for

Top photo: New mothers in a hospital ward in the Philippines practice skin-to-skin "kangaroo care," widely used in developing countries to promote the survival and recovery of preterm babies. In Western nations, kangaroo care is used as a supplement to hospital intensive care. *Bottom photo:* A U.S. mother engages in the technique with her fragile newborn.

their fragile babies, interact more sensitively and affectionately, and feel more attached to them (Dodd, 2005; Feldman et al., 2002, 2003).

Together, these factors may explain why preterm babies given many hours of kangaroo care in their early weeks, compared to those given little or no such care, are more likely to explore novel toys and also score higher on measures of mental and motor development during the first year (Charpak, Ruiz-Peláez, & Figueroa, 2005; Feldman, 2007b; Tessier et al., 2003). Because of its diverse benefits, more than 80 percent of U.S. hospital nurseries now offer kangaroo care to preterm newborns (Field et al., 2006).

Training Parents in Infant Caregiving Skills. Interventions that support parents of preterm infants generally teach them about the infant's characteristics and promote caregiving skills. For parents with adequate economic and personal resources to care for a preterm infant, just a few sessions of coaching in recognizing and responding to the baby's needs are linked to enhanced parent–infant interaction, reduced infant crying and improved sleep, more rapid language development in the second year, and steady gains in mental test scores that equal those of full-term children by middle childhood (Achenbach, Howell, & Aoki, 1993; Newnham, Milgrom, & Skouteris, 2009).

When preterm infants live in stressed, low-income households, long-term intensive intervention is necessary. In the Infant Health and Development Project, preterm babies born into poverty received a comprehensive intervention that combined medical follow-up, weekly parent training sessions, and cognitively stimulating child care from 1 to 3 years of age. More than four times as many intervention children as no-intervention controls (39 versus 9 percent) were within normal range at age 3 in intelligence, psychological adjustment, and physical growth (Bradley et al., 1994). In addition, mothers in the intervention group were more affectionate and more often encouraged play and cognitive mastery in their children—one reason their 3-year-olds may have been developing so favorably (McCarton, 1998).

At ages 5 and 8, children who had attended the child-care program regularly—for more than 350 days over the three-year period—continued to show better intellectual functioning. The more they attended, the higher they scored, with greater gains among those whose birth weights were higher (see Figure 3.13). In contrast, children who attended only sporadically gained little or even lost ground (Hill, Brooks-Gunn, & Waldfogel, 2003). In a follow-up at age 18, the higher-birth-weight participants remained advantaged over controls in academic achievement. They also engaged in fewer risky behaviors, such as unprotected sexual activity and alcohol and drug use (McCormick et al., 2006).

These findings confirm that babies who are both preterm and economically disadvantaged require *intensive* intervention. And special strategies, such as extra adult–child interaction, may be necessary to achieve lasting changes in children with the lowest birth weights.

Very Low Birth Weight, Environmental Advantages, and Long-Term Outcomes
Although very-low-birth-weight babies often have lasting problems, in a Canadian study, young adults who had weighed between 1 and 2.2 pounds (500 to 1,000 grams) at birth were doing well in overall quality of life (Saigal et al., 2006). At 22 to 25 years of age, they resembled normal-birth-weight individuals in educational attainment, rates of marriage and parenthood, and (for those who had no neurological or sensory impairments) employment status. Researchers believe that home, school, and societal advantages combine to explain these excellent outcomes (Hack & Klein, 2006). Most participants in this study were reared in two-parent middle-class homes, attended good schools where they received special services, and benefited from Canada's universal health-care system.

But even the best environments cannot "fix" the enormous biological risks associated with very low birth weight. A better course of action would be to prevent this serious threat to infant survival and development. The high rate of underweight babies in the United States—one of the worst in the industrialized world—could be greatly reduced by improving the health and social conditions described in the Social Issues: Health box on pages 118–119.

Birth Complications, Parenting, and Resilience

In the preceding sections, we considered a variety of birth complications. Now let's try to put the evidence together. Can any general principles help us understand how infants who survive a traumatic birth are likely to develop? A landmark study carried out in Hawaii provides some answers.

In 1955, Emmy Werner began to follow the development of nearly 700 infants on the island of Kauai who had experienced mild, moderate, or severe birth complications. Each was matched, on the basis of family economic status and ethnicity, with a healthy newborn (Werner & Smith, 1982). Findings showed that the likelihood of long-term difficulties increased if birth trauma was severe. But among mildly to moderately stressed children, those growing up in stable families did almost as well on measures of intelligence and psychological adjustment as those with no birth problems. Those exposed to poverty, family disorganization, and mentally ill parents often developed serious learning difficulties, behavior problems, and emotional disturbance.

The Kauai study tells us that as long as birth injuries are not overwhelming, a supportive home environment can restore children's growth. But the most intriguing cases in this study were the handful of exceptions. A few children with fairly serious birth complications and troubled family environments grew into competent adults who fared as well as controls in career attainment and psychological adjustment. Werner found that these children relied on factors outside the family and within themselves to overcome stress. Some had attractive personalities that drew positive responses from relatives, neighbors, and peers. In other instances, a grandparent, aunt, uncle, or babysitter provided the needed emotional support (Werner, 1989; Werner & Smith, 1992, 2001).

Do these outcomes remind you of the characteristics of resilient children, discussed in Chapter 1? The Kauai study and other similar investigations reveal that the impact of early biological risks often wanes as children's personal characteristics and social experiences contribute increasingly to their functioning (Laucht, Esser, & Schmidt, 1997; Resnick et al., 1999). In sum, when the overall balance of life events tips toward the favorable side, children with serious birth problems can develop successfully. And when negative factors outweigh positive ones, even a sturdy newborn can become a lifelong casualty.

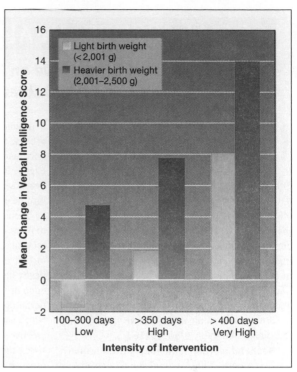

FIGURE 3.13 Influence of intensity of early intervention for low-income, preterm babies on intellectual functioning at age 8. Infants born preterm received cognitively stimulating child care from 1 through 3 years of age. Those who attended the program sporadically gained little in intellectual functioning (heavier-weight babies) or lost ground (lighter-weight babies). The more often children attended, the greater their intellectual gains. Heavier babies consistently gained more than lighter babies. But boosting the intensity of intervention above 400 days led to a dramatic increase in the performance of the light-weight group. (Adapted from Hill, Brooks-Gunn, & Waldfogel, 2003.)

ASK YOURSELF

Review ■ Sensitive care can help preterm infants recover, but they are less likely than full-term newborns to receive such care. Explain why.

Connect ■ List factors discussed in this chapter that increase the chances that an infant will be born underweight. How many of these factors could be prevented by better health care for expectant mothers and babies?

Apply ■ Cecilia and Adena each gave birth to a 3-pound baby seven weeks preterm. Cecilia is single and poverty-stricken. Adena and her partner are happily married and earn a good income. Plan an intervention appropriate for helping each baby develop.

Reflect ■ Many people object to the use of extraordinary medical measures to save extremely low-birth-weight babies because of their high risk of developing serious physical, cognitive, and emotional problems. Do you agree or disagree? Explain.

SOCIAL ISSUES: HEALTH

A Cross-National Perspective on Health Care and Other Policies for Parents and Newborn Babies

nfant mortality—the number of deaths in the first year of life per 1,000 live births—is an index used around the world to assess the overall health of a nation's children. Although the United States has the most up-to-date health-care technology in the world, it has made less progress in reducing infant deaths than many other countries. Over the past three decades, it has slipped in the international rankings, from seventh in the 1950s to twenty-eighth in 2011. Members of America's poor ethnic minorities are at greatest risk. African-American and Native-American babies are twice as likely as white infants to die in the first year of life (U.S. Census Bureau, 2011a, 2011b).

Neonatal mortality, the rate of death within the first month of life, accounts for 67 percent of the infant death rate in the United States. Two factors are largely responsible for neonatal mortality. The first is serious physical defects, most of which cannot be prevented. The percentage of babies born with physical defects is about the same in all ethnic and income groups. The second leading cause of neonatal mortality is low birth weight, which is largely preventable. African-American and Native-American babies are more than twice as likely as white infants to be born early and underweight (U.S. Census Bureau, 2011b).

Widespread poverty and weak health-care programs for mothers and young children are largely responsible for these trends. Unfortunately, 8 percent of pregnant women in the United States wait until after the first trimester to seek prenatal care or receive none at all. More than 10 percent of low-income minority mothers, and nearly 30 percent of adolescent mothers, receive inadequate prenatal care (Hueston, Geesey, & Diaz, 2008; U.S. Department of Health

and Human Services, 2010a). Many of these mothers lack health insurance, and although the poorest are eligible for government-sponsored health services, many other low-income women do not qualify.

Besides financial hardship, some mothers have other reasons for not seeking early prenatal care. These include both *situational barriers* (difficulty finding a doctor, getting an appointment, and arranging transportation, and insensitive or unsatisfying experiences with clinic staff) and *personal barriers* (psychological stress, the demands of caring for other young children, family crises, lack of knowledge about signs of pregnancy and benefits of prenatal care, and ambivalence about the pregnancy). Many also engage in high-risk behaviors, such as smoking and drug abuse, which they do not want to reveal to health professionals (Maupin et al., 2004).

Each country listed in Figure 3.14 that outranks the United States in infant survival provides all its citizens with government-sponsored health-care benefits. And each takes extra steps to make sure that pregnant mothers and babies have access to good nutrition, high-quality medical care, and social and economic supports that promote effective parenting.

For example, all Western European nations guarantee women a certain number of prenatal visits at very low or no cost. After a baby is born, a health professional routinely visits the home to provide counseling about infant care and to arrange continuing medical services. Home assis-

This doctor in Memphis, Tennessee, works with high-risk pregnancies, delivering babies whose poverty-stricken mothers have had little or no prenatal care. Nations that provide government-sponsored health-care benefits for all citizens outrank the United States in infant survival.

tance is especially extensive in the Netherlands. For a token fee, each mother is granted a specially trained maternity helper, who assists with infant care, shopping, housekeeping, meal preparation, and the care of other children during the days after delivery (Zwart, 2007).

Paid, job-protected employment leave is another vital societal intervention for new parents. Canadian mothers are eligible for 15 weeks' maternity leave at 55 percent of prior earnings (up to a maximum of $413 per week), and Canadian mothers or fathers can take an additional 35 weeks of parental leave at the same rate. Paid leave is widely available in other industrial-

▶ Explain the various ways heredity and environment may combine to influence complex traits.

Heredity, Environment, and Behavior: A Look Ahead

Throughout this chapter, we have discussed a wide variety of genetic and early environmental influences, each of which has the power to alter the course of development. When we consider them together, it may seem surprising that any newborn babies arrive intact. Yet the vast majority—over 90 percent in North America—do. These developing members of the human species, even those born into the same family—and who therefore share both genes ized nations as well. Sweden has the most generous parental leave program in the world. Mothers can begin maternity leave 60 days prior to expected delivery, extending it to six weeks after birth; fathers are granted two weeks of birth leave. In addition, either parent can take full leave for 16 months at 80 percent of prior earnings, followed by an additional three months at a modest flat rate. Each parent is also entitled to another 18 months of unpaid leave. Furthermore, many countries supplement basic paid leave. In Germany, for example, after a fully paid three-month leave, a parent may take one more year at a flat rate and three additional years at no pay (OECD, 2006; Waldfogel, 2001).

Yet in the United States, the federal government mandates *only 12 weeks of unpaid leave* for employees in companies with at least 50 workers. Most women, however, work in smaller businesses, and many of those who work in large enough companies cannot afford to take this much unpaid leave (Hewlett, 2003). Similarly, though paternal leave predicts fathers' increased involvement in infant care at the end of the first year, many fathers take little or none at all (Nepomnyaschy & Waldfogel, 2007; OECD, 2006). In 2002, California became the first state to guarantee a mother or father paid leave—up to six weeks at half salary, regardless of the size of the company. Since then, Hawaii, New Jersey, New York, Rhode Island, and the territory of Puerto Rico have passed similar legislation.

Nevertheless, six weeks of childbirth leave (the norm in the United States) is not enough. When a family is stressed by a baby's arrival, leaves of six weeks or less are linked to increased maternal anxiety, depression, conflict between work and family responsibilities, and negative interactions with the baby. A longer leave (12 weeks or more) predicts favorable maternal mental health, supportive marital interaction, and sensitive caregiving (Feldman, Sussman, & Zigler, 2004; Hyde et al., 2001). Single women and their babies are most hurt by the absence of a generous national paid-leave policy. These mothers, who are usually the sole source of support for their families, can least afford to take time from their jobs.

In countries with low infant mortality rates, expectant mothers need not wonder how or where they will get health care and other resources to support their baby's development. The powerful impact of universal, high-quality health care, generous parental leave, and other social services on maternal and infant well-being provides strong justification for these policies.

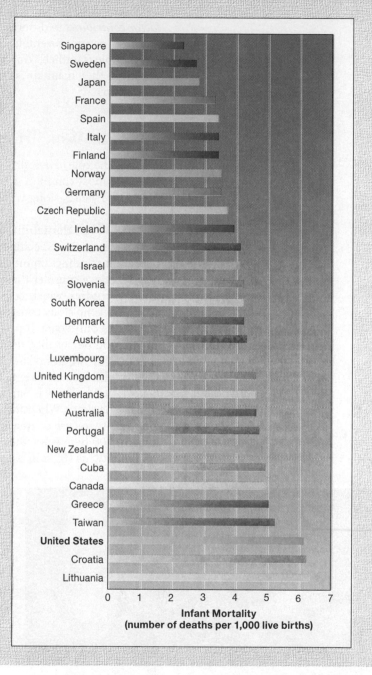

FIGURE 3.14 **Infant mortality in 30 nations.** Despite its advanced health-care technology, the United States ranks poorly. It is twenty-eighth in the world, with a death rate of 6.1 infants per 1,000 births. (Adapted from U.S. Census Bureau, 2011a.)

and environment—vary greatly in characteristics. We also know that some are affected more than others by their homes, neighborhoods, and communities. How do scientists explain the impact of heredity and environment when they seem to work in so many different ways?

Behavioral genetics is a field devoted to uncovering the contributions of nature and nurture to this diversity in human traits and abilities. All contemporary researchers agree that both heredity and environment are involved in every aspect of development. But for polygenic traits (those due to many genes) such as intelligence and personality, scientists are a long way from knowing the precise hereditary influences involved. Although they are making progress in identifying variations in DNA sequences associated with complex traits, so far these genetic markers explain only a small amount of variation in human behavior, and a minority of cases of most psychological disorders (Plomin, 2005; Plomin & Davis, 2009). For the most part, scientists are still limited to investigating the impact of genes on complex characteristics indirectly.

Some believe that it is useful and possible to answer the question of *how much each factor contributes* to differences among children. A growing consensus, however, regards that question as unanswerable. These investigators believe that heredity and environment are inseparable (Gottlieb, Wahlsten, & Lickliter, 2006; Lerner & Overton, 2008). The important question, they maintain, is *how nature and nurture work together.* Let's consider each position in turn.

The Question, "How Much?"

To infer the role of heredity in complex human characteristics, researchers use special methods. The most common is the *heritability estimate.* Let's look closely at the information this procedure yields, along with its limitations.

Heritability   **Heritability estimates** measure the extent to which individual differences in complex traits in a specific population are due to genetic factors. We will take a brief look at heritability findings on intelligence and personality here and will return to them in later chapters, when we consider these topics in greater detail. Heritability estimates are obtained from **kinship studies,** which compare the characteristics of family members. The most common type of kinship study compares identical twins, who share all their genes, with fraternal twins, who share only some. If people who are genetically more alike are also more similar in intelligence and personality, then the researcher assumes that heredity plays an important role.

Kinship studies of intelligence provide some of the most controversial findings in the field of child development. Some experts claim a strong genetic influence, whereas others believe that heredity is barely involved. Currently, most kinship findings support a moderate role for heredity. When many twin studies are examined, correlations between the scores of identical twins are consistently higher than those of fraternal twins. In a summary of more than 10,000 twin pairs, the correlation for intelligence was .86 for identical twins and .60 for fraternal twins (Plomin & Spinath, 2004).

Adriana and Tamara, identical twins separated at birth by adoption, were unaware of each other's existence. When they met at age 20, they discovered many similarities—academic achievement, love of dancing, and even taste in clothing. Clearly, heredity contributes to psychological characteristics. Nevertheless, generalizing from twin evidence to the population is controversial.

© JACQUIE HEMMERDINGER/THE NEW YORK TIMES/REDUX

Researchers use a complex statistical procedure to compare these correlations, arriving at a heritability estimate ranging from 0 to 1.00. The value for intelligence is about .50 for child and adolescent twin samples in Western industrialized nations. This suggests that differences in genetic makeup explain half the variation in intelligence. Adopted children's mental test scores are more strongly related to their biological parents' scores than to those of their adoptive parents, offering further support for the role of heredity (Petrill & Deater-Deckard, 2004).

Heritability research also reveals that genetic factors are important in personality. For frequently studied traits, such as sociability, anxiety, agreeableness, and activity level, heritability estimates obtained on child, adolescent, and young adult twins are moderate, in the .40s and .50s (Caspi & Shiner, 2006; Rothbart & Bates, 2006; Wright et al., 2008).

Twin studies of schizophrenia—a psychological disorder involving delusions and hallucinations, difficulty distinguishing fantasy from reality, and irrational and inappropriate behaviors—consistently yield high heritabilities, around .80. The role of heredity in antisocial behavior and major depression, though still apparent, is less strong, with heritabilities in the .30s and .40s (Faraone, 2008). Again, adoption studies support these results. Biological relatives of schizophrenic and depressed adoptees are more likely than adoptive relatives to share the same disorder (Plomin et al., 2001; Ridenour, 2000; Tienari et al., 2003).

Limitations of Heritability The accuracy of heritability estimates depends on the extent to which the twin pairs studied reflect genetic and environmental variation in the population. Within a population in which all people have very similar home, school, and community experiences, individual differences in intelligence and personality would be largely genetic, and heritability estimates would be close to 1.00. Conversely, the more environments vary, the more likely they are to account for individual differences, yielding lower heritability estimates. In twin studies, most twin pairs are reared together under highly similar conditions. Even when separated twins are available for study, social service agencies have often placed them in advantaged homes that are alike in many ways (Rutter et al., 2001). Because the environments of most twin pairs are less diverse than those of the general population, heritability estimates are likely to exaggerate the role of heredity.

Heritability estimates are controversial measures because they can easily be misapplied. For example, high heritabilities have been used to suggest that ethnic differences in intelligence, such as the poorer performance of black children compared to white children, have a genetic basis (Jensen, 1969, 1985, 1998; Rushton & Jensen, 2005, 2006). Yet this line of reasoning is widely regarded as incorrect. Heritabilities computed on mostly white twin samples do not tell us what causes test score differences between ethnic groups. We have already seen that large economic and cultural differences are involved. In Chapter 8, we will discuss research indicating that when black children are adopted into economically advantaged homes at an early age, their mental test scores are well above average and substantially higher than those of children growing up in impoverished families.

Perhaps the most serious criticism of heritability estimates has to do with their limited usefulness. They give us no precise information on how intelligence and personality develop or how children might respond to environments designed to help them develop as far as possible (Baltes, Lindenberger, & Staudinger, 2006). Indeed, the heritability of children's intelligence increases as parental education and income increase—that is, as children grow up in conditions that allow them to make the most of their genetic endowment. In impoverished environments, children are prevented from realizing their potential. Consequently, enhancing their experiences through interventions, such as increasing parent education and income and providing high-quality preschool or child care, has a greater impact on the development of economically disadvantaged than advantaged children (Bronfenbrenner & Morris, 2006; Turkheimer et al., 2003).

In sum, although heritability estimates confirm that heredity contributes to a broad array of complex traits, they tell us nothing about how environment can modify genetic influences. Still, scientists often rely on positive heritabilities before initiating more costly molecular analyses in search of specific genes that contribute to personality traits and disorders.

The Question, "How?"

Today, most researchers view development as the result of a dynamic interplay between heredity and environment. How do nature and nurture work together? Several concepts shed light on this question.

Gene–Environment Interaction The first of these ideas is **gene–environment interaction,** which means that because of their genetic makeup, individuals differ in their responsiveness to qualities of the environment (Rutter, 2011). In other words, children have unique, genetically influenced reactions to particular experiences. Let's explore this idea in Figure 3.15. Gene–environment interaction can apply to any characteristic; here it is illustrated for intelligence. Notice that when environments vary from extremely unstimulating to highly enriched, Ben's intelligence test score increases steadily, Linda's rises sharply and then falls off, and Ron responds only after the environment becomes modestly stimulating.

FIGURE 3.15 Gene–environment interaction, illustrated for intelligence by three children who differ in responsiveness to quality of the environment. As environments vary from extremely unstimulating to highly enriched, Ben's intelligence test score increases steadily, Linda's rises sharply and then falls off, and Ron's begins to increase only after the environment becomes modestly stimulating.

Gene–environment interaction highlights two important points. First, it shows that because each of us has a unique genetic makeup, we respond differently to the same environment. Notice in Figure 3.16 how a poor environment results in similarly low scores for all three individuals. But when the environment provides a moderate level of stimulation, Linda is by far the best-performing child. And in a highly enriched environment, Ben does best, followed by Ron, both of whom now outperform Linda. Second, sometimes different gene–environment combinations can make two children look the same! For example, if Linda is reared in a minimally stimulating environment, her score will be about 100—average for children in general. Ben and Ron can also obtain this score, but to do so, they must grow up in a fairly enriched home (Gottlieb, Wahlsten, & Lickliter, 2006).

Recently, researchers have made strides in identifying gene–environment interactions in personality development. Recall the finding reported on page 115—that distressed, emotionally negative preterm infants are more responsive than other babies to both inept and good parenting. Similarly, in Chapter 10 we will see that young children with a gene that increases their risk of an emotionally reactive temperament respond especially strongly to variations in parenting quality (Pluess & Belsky, 2011). When parenting is favorable, they gain control over their emotions and adjust as well or better than other children. But when parenting is unfavorable, they become increasingly irritable, difficult, and poorly adjusted, more so than children not at genetic risk.

Canalization Another way of understanding how heredity and environment combine comes from the concept of **canalization**—the tendency of heredity to restrict the development of some characteristics to just one or a few outcomes. A behavior that is strongly canalized develops similarly in a wide range of environments; only strong environmental forces can change it (Waddington, 1957). For example, infant perceptual and motor development seems to be strongly canalized because all normal human babies eventually roll over, reach for objects, sit up, crawl, and walk. It takes extreme conditions to modify these behaviors or cause them not to appear. In contrast, intelligence and personality are less strongly canalized; they vary much more with changes in the environment.

When we look at behaviors constrained by heredity, we can see that canalization is highly adaptive. Through it, nature ensures that children will develop certain species-typical skills under a wide range of rearing conditions, thereby promoting survival.

Gene–Environment Correlation A major problem in trying to separate heredity and environment is that they are often correlated (Rutter, 2011; Scarr & McCartney, 1983). According to the concept of **gene–environment correlation,** our genes influence the environments to which we are exposed. The way this happens changes with age.

Passive and Evocative Correlation. At younger ages, two types of gene–environmental correlation are common. The first is called passive correlation because the child has no control over it. Early on, parents provide environments influenced by their own heredity. For example, parents who are good athletes emphasize outdoor activities and enroll their children in swimming and gymnastics. Besides being exposed to an "athletic environment," the children may have inherited their parents' athletic ability. As a result, they are likely to become good athletes for both genetic and environmental reasons.

The second type of gene–environment correlation is *evocative*. The responses children evoke from others are influenced by the child's heredity, and these responses strengthen the child's original style. For example, an active, friendly baby is likely to receive more social stimulation than a passive, quiet infant. And a cooperative, attentive child probably receives more patient and sensitive interactions from parents than an inattentive, distractible child. In support of this idea, the less genetically alike siblings are, the more their parents treat them

© LOU CYPHER/CORBIS

This mother shares her love of the piano with her daughter, who also may have inherited her mother's musical talent. When heredity and environment are correlated, the influence of one cannot be separated from the influence of the other.

differently, in both warmth and negativity. Thus, parents' treatment of identical twins is highly similar, whereas their treatment of fraternal twins and nontwin biological siblings is only moderately so. And little resemblance exists in parents' warm and negative interactions with unrelated stepsiblings (see Figure 3.16) (Reiss, 2003).

Active Correlation. In older children, *active* gene–environment correlation becomes common. As children extend their experiences beyond the immediate family and are given the freedom to make more choices, they actively seek environments that fit with their genetic tendencies. The well-coordinated, muscular child spends more time at after-school sports, the musically talented youngster joins the school orchestra and practices his violin, and the intellectually curious child is a familiar patron at her local library.

This tendency to actively choose environments that complement our heredity is called **niche-picking** (Scarr & McCartney, 1983). Infants and young children cannot do much niche-picking because adults select environments for them. In contrast, older children and adolescents are much more in charge of their environments.

Niche-picking explains why pairs of identical twins reared apart during childhood and later reunited may find, to their surprise, that they have similar hobbies, food preferences, and vocations—a trend that is especially marked when twins' environmental opportunities are similar (Plomin, 1994). Niche-picking also helps us understand why identical twins become somewhat more alike, and fraternal twins and adopted siblings less alike, in intelligence with age (Bouchard, 2004; Loehlin, Horn, & Willerman, 1997). And niche-picking sheds light on why adolescent identical twin pairs—far more often than same-sex fraternal pairs, ordinary siblings, or adopted siblings—report similar stressful life events influenced by personal decisions and actions, such as failing a course, quitting a job, or getting in trouble for drug-taking (Bemmels et al., 2008).

The influence of heredity and environment is not constant but changes over time. With age, genetic factors may become more important in influencing the environments we experience and choose for ourselves.

FIGURE 3.16 Similarity in mothers' interactions for pairs of siblings differing in genetic relatedness. The correlations shown are for maternal negativity. The pattern illustrates evocative genetic–environmental correlation. Identical twins evoke similar maternal treatment because of their identical heredity. As genetic resemblance between siblings declines, the strength of the correlation drops. Mothers vary their interactions as they respond to each child's unique genetic makeup. (Adapted from Reiss, 2003.)

Environmental Influences on Gene Expression

Notice how, in the concepts just considered, heredity is granted priority. In gene–environment interaction, it affects responsiveness to particular environments. In canalization, it *restricts* the development of certain behaviors. Similarly, gene–environmental correlation is viewed as *driven* by genetics, in that children's genetic makeup causes them to receive, evoke, or seek experiences that actualize their hereditary tendencies (Plomin, 2009; Rutter, 2011).

A growing number of researchers take issue with the supremacy of heredity, arguing that it does not dictate children's experiences or development in a rigid way. In one study, boys with a genetic tendency toward antisocial behavior (based on the presence of a gene on the X chromosome known to predispose both animals and humans to aggression) were no more aggressive than boys without this gene, *unless* they also had a history of severe child abuse (Caspi et al., 2002). Boys with and without the gene did not differ in their experience of abuse, indicating that the "aggressive genotype" did not increase exposure to abuse. And in a large Finnish adoption study, children of schizophrenic mothers reared by healthy adoptive parents showed little mental illness—no more than a control group with healthy biological and adoptive parents. In contrast, schizophrenia and other psychological impairments piled up in adoptees whose biological and adoptive parents were both disturbed (Tienari et al., 2003; Tienari, Wahlberg, & Wynne, 2006).

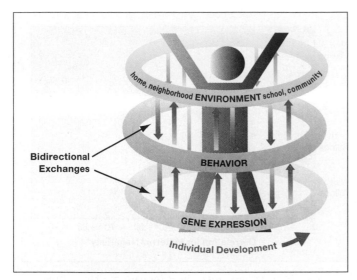

FIGURE 3.17 The epigenetic framework. Development takes place through ongoing, bidirectional exchanges between heredity and all levels of the environment. Genes affect behavior and experiences. Experiences and behavior also affect gene expression. (Adapted from Gottlieb, 2007.)

Furthermore, parents and other caring adults can uncouple adverse gene–environment correlations. They often provide children with positive experiences that modify the expression of heredity, yielding favorable outcomes. For example, in a study that tracked the development of 5-year-old identical twins, pair members resembled each other in aggression. And the more aggression they displayed, the more maternal anger and criticism they received (a gene–environment correlation). Nevertheless, some mothers treated their twins differently. When followed up at age 7, twins who had been targets of more maternal negativity engaged in even more antisocial behavior. In contrast, their better-treated, genetically identical counterparts showed a reduction in disruptive acts (Caspi et al., 2004). Good parenting protected them from a spiraling, antisocial course of development.

Accumulating evidence reveals that the relationship between heredity and environment is not a one-way street, from genes to environment to behavior. Rather, like other system influences considered in this and the previous chapter, it is *bidirectional:* Genes affect children's behavior and experiences, but their experiences and behavior also affect gene expression (Diamond, 2009; Gottlieb, 2003; Rutter, 2007). Stimulation—both *internal* to the child (activity within the cytoplasm of the cell, release of hormones into the bloodstream) and *external* to the child (home, neighborhood, school, and society)—modifies gene activity.

Researchers call this view of the relationship between heredity and environment the *epigenetic framework* (Gottlieb, 1998, 2007). It is depicted in Figure 3.17. **Epigenesis** means development resulting from ongoing, bidirectional exchanges between heredity and all levels of the environment. To illustrate, providing a baby with a healthy diet increases brain growth, which translates into new connections between nerve cells, which transform gene expression. This opens the door to new gene–environment exchanges—for example, advanced exploration of objects and interaction with caregivers, which further enhance brain growth and gene expression. These ongoing, bidirectional influences foster cognitive and social development. In contrast, harmful environments can negatively affect gene expression (see the Biology and Environment box on the following page for an example). And at times, the impact is so profound that later experiences can do little to change characteristics (such as intelligence and personality) that originally were flexible.

A major reason that researchers are interested in the nature–nurture issue is that they want to improve environments so that children can develop as far as possible. The concept of epigenesis reminds us that development is best understood as a series of complex exchanges between nature and nurture. Although children cannot be changed in any way we might desire, environments can modify genetic influences. The success of any attempt to improve development depends on the characteristics we want to change, the genetic makeup of the child, and the type and timing of our intervention.

ASK YOURSELF

Review ■ What is epigenesis, and how does it differ from gene–environment interaction and gene–environment correlation? Provide an example of each.

Connect ■ Explain how each of the following concepts supports the conclusion that genetic influences on human characteristics are not constant but change over time: somatic mutation (page 81), niche-picking (page 123), and epigenesis (page 124).

Apply ■ Bianca's parents are accomplished musicians. At age 4, Bianca began taking piano lessons. By age 10, she was accompanying the school choir. At age 14, she asked if she could attend a special music high school. Explain how gene–environment correlation promoted Bianca's talent.

Reflect ■ What aspects of your own development—for example, interests, hobbies, college major, or vocational choice—are probably due to niche-picking? Explain.

BIOLOGY and ENVIRONMENT

A Case of Epigenesis: Smoking During Pregnancy Alters Gene Expression

A wealth of experimental research with animals confirms that environment can modify the genome in ways that have no impact on a gene's sequence of base pairs but nevertheless affect the operation of that gene (Zhang & Meaney, 2010). This epigenetic interplay, in which a gene's impact on the individual's phenotype depends on the gene's context, is now being vigorously investigated in humans.

Maternal smoking during pregnancy is among the risk factors for *attention-deficit hyperactivity disorder (ADHD)*—one of the most common disorders of childhood, which we will take up in greater detail in Chapter 7. ADHD symptoms—inattention, impulsivity, and overactivity—typically result in serious academic and social problems. Some studies report that individuals who are homozygous for a chromosome-5 gene (DD) containing a special repeat of base pairs are at increased risk for ADHD, though other research has not confirmed any role for this gene (Fisher et al., 2002; Gill et al., 1997; Waldman et al., 1998).

Animal evidence suggests that one reason for this inconsistency may be that environmental influences associated with ADHD—such as prenatal exposure to toxins—modify the gene's activity. To test this possibility, researchers recruited several hundred mothers and their 6-month-old babies, obtaining infant blood samples for molecular genetic analysis and asking mothers whether they smoked regularly during pregnancy (Kahn et al., 2003). At a 5-year follow-up, parents responded to a widely used behavior rating scale that assesses children for ADHD symptoms.

Findings revealed that by itself, the DD genotype was unrelated to impulsivity, overactivity, or oppositional behavior. But children whose mothers had smoked during pregnancy scored higher in these behaviors than children of nonsmoking mothers. Furthermore, as Figure 3.19 shows, 5-year-olds with both prenatal nicotine exposure and the DD genotype obtained substantially higher impulsivity, overactivity, and oppositional scores than all other groups—outcomes that persisted even after a variety of other factors (quality of the home environment and maternal ethnicity, marital status, and post-birth smoking) had been controlled.

Another investigation following participants into adolescence obtained similar findings, suggesting that the epigenetic effect persists (Becker et al., 2008). What processes might account for it? In animal research, tobacco smoke stimulates the DD genotype to release chemicals in the brain that that promote impulsivity and overactivity (Ernst, Moolchan, & Robinson, 2001). These behaviors, in turn, often evoke harsh, punitive parenting, which can trigger defiance in children.

The DD genotype is widespread, present in more than 50 percent of people. Thus, the majority of children prenatally exposed to nicotine are at high risk for learning and behavior problems (refer to page 98). Growing evidence indicates that other genes, in epigenetic interplay with as yet unknown environmental factors, also contribute to ADHD symptoms (Hudziak & Rettew, 2009).

© IMAGE SOURCE/GETTY IMAGES

Because his mother smoked during pregnancy, this baby may be at risk for attention-deficit hyperactivity disorder (ADHD). Prenatal nicotine exposure seems to alter expression of a chromosome-5 gene in ways that greatly heighten impulsivity, overactivity, and oppositional behavior.

FIGURE 3.18 Combined influence of maternal prenatal smoking and genotype on impulsivity and overactivity at age 5. In the absence of prenatal smoking, 5-year-olds who were homozygous for a chromosome-5 gene (DD) showed no elevation in impulsivity and overactivity (orange bar) compared with children of other genotypes (Dd or dd) (red bar). Among children of all genotypes, prenatal smoking was associated with an increase in these behaviors (green and purple bars). And the combination of prenatal smoking and DD genotype greatly magnified impulsivity and overactivity (purple bar). Children's oppositional behavior followed a similar epigenetic pattern. (Adapted from Kahn et al., 2003.)

SUMMARY

Genetic Foundations (p. 73)

What are genes, and how are they transmitted from one generation to the next?

- Each individual's **phenotype,** or directly observable characteristics, is a product of both **genotype** and environment. **Chromosomes,** rodlike structures within the cell nucleus, contain our hereditary endowment. Along their length are **genes,** segments of **deoxyribonucleic acid (DNA)** that send instructions for making a rich assortment of proteins to the cell's cytoplasm.

- **Gametes,** or sex cells, are produced through a cell division process called **meiosis. Crossing over** and chance assortment of chromosomes into gametes ensure that each gamete receives a unique set of genes from each parent. Once sperm and ovum unite, the resulting **zygote** starts to develop into a complex human being through cell duplication, or **mitosis.**

- If the fertilizing sperm carries an X chromosome, the child will be a girl; if it contains a Y chromosome, a boy.

Describe various patterns of genetic inheritance.

- **Homozygous** individuals have two identical **alleles.** If the alleles differ, the individual is **heterozygous,** and relationships between the alleles determine the phenotype. In **dominant–recessive inheritance,** only the dominant allele affects the child's phenotype; a child must inherit two recessive alleles to display the recessive trait. Heterozygous individuals become **carriers** of the recessive trait. In **incomplete dominance,** both alleles are expressed in the phenotype. **Modifier genes** enhance or dilute the effects of other genes.

- In **X-linked inheritance,** a harmful allele is carried on the X chromosome. Males are more likely than females to be affected. In **genomic imprinting,** one parent's allele is activated, regardless of its makeup.

- Harmful genes arise from **mutation,** which can occur spontaneously or be caused by hazardous environmental agents. Human traits that vary on a continuum, such as intelligence and personality, result from **polygenic inheritance**—the effects of many genes.

Describe major chromosomal abnormalities, and explain how they occur.

- Most chromosomal abnormalities are due to errors during meiosis. The most common is Down syndrome, which results in physical defects and broad intellectual disability. **Sex chromosome** abnormalities, such as XYY, triple X, Klinefelter, and Turner syndromes, are milder than defects of the **autosomes.**

Reproductive Choices (p. 84)

What procedures can assist prospective parents in having healthy children?

- **Genetic counseling** helps couples at risk for giving birth to children with genetic abnormalities consider appropriate options. **Prenatal diagnostic methods** allow early detection of genetic problems.

© MICHELLE DEL GUERCIO/ PHOTO RESEARCHERS, INC.

- Reproductive technologies, such as donor insemination, in vitro fertilization, surrogate motherhood, and postmenopausal-assisted childbirth, enable individuals to become parents who otherwise would not, but they raise serious legal and ethical concerns.

Prenatal Development (p. 88)

List the three periods of prenatal development, and describe the major milestones of each.

- The period of the zygote lasts about two weeks, from fertilization until the blastocyst becomes deeply implanted in the uterine lining. During this time, structures that will support prenatal growth begin to form, including the **placenta** and the **umbilical cord.**

- During the period of the **embryo,** from weeks 2 to 8, the foundations for all body structures are laid down. The nervous system develops fastest, as the neural tube forms. Other organs follow rapidly. By the end of this period, production of neurons occurs at an astounding pace, and the embryo responds to touch and can move.

- The period of the **fetus,** lasting until the end of pregnancy, involves a dramatic increase in body size and completion of physical structures. At the end of the second trimester, most of the brain's neurons are in place.

- The fetus reaches the **age of viability** at the beginning of the final trimester, between 22 and 26 weeks. The brain continues to develop rapidly, and new sensory and behavioral capacities emerge. Gradually, the lungs mature, the fetus fills the uterus, and birth is near.

Prenatal Environmental Influences (p. 94)

Cite factors that influence the impact of teratogens, noting agents that are known teratogens.

- The impact of **teratogens** varies with the amount and length of exposure, genetic makeup of mother and fetus, presence or absence of other harmful agents, and age of the organism at time of exposure. Drugs, tobacco, alcohol, radiation, environmental pollution, and maternal diseases are teratogens that can endanger the developing organism.

- Babies born to users of heroin, methadone, or cocaine are at risk for prematurity, low birth weight, and physical defects and are born drug-addicted. Evidence on long-term effects, however, is mixed.

- Infants whose parents use tobacco are often born underweight, may have physical defects, and are at risk for attention, learning, and behavior problems in childhood.

- Maternal alcohol consumption can lead to **fetal alcohol spectrum disorder (FASD). Fetal alcohol syndrome (FAS)** involves slow physical growth, facial abnormalities, and mental impairments. Milder forms—**partial fetal alcohol syndrome (p-FAS)** and **alcohol-related neurodevelopmental disorder (ARND)**—affect children whose mothers consumed smaller quantities of alcohol.

- Prenatal exposure to high levels of radiation, mercury, lead, dioxins, and PCBs leads to physical malformations and severe brain damage. Low-level exposure has been linked to cognitive deficits and emotional and behavior disorders.

- Among infectious diseases, rubella causes wide-ranging abnormalities. Babies with prenatally transmitted HIV rapidly develop AIDS, leading to brain damage and early death. Cytomegalovirus, herpes simplex 2, and toxoplasmosis can also be devastating to the embryo and fetus.

Describe the impact of additional maternal factors on prenatal development.

- Prenatal malnutrition can lead to low birth weight, damage to the brain and other organs, and suppression of immune system development. Maternal vitamin–mineral supplementation, including folic acid, can prevent prenatal and birth complications.

- Severe emotional stress is associated with many pregnancy complications and may permanently alter fetal neurological functioning. Its impact can be reduced by providing mothers with social support.

■ Aside from the risk of chromosomal abnormalities in older women, maternal age through the thirties is not a major cause of prenatal problems. Poor health and environmental risks associated with poverty are the strongest predictors of pregnancy complications in both teenagers and older women.

Childbirth (p. 107)

Describe the three stages of childbirth, the baby's adaptation to labor and delivery, and the newborn baby's appearance.

■ In the first stage of childbirth, contractions widen and thin the cervix. In the second stage, the mother feels an urge to push the baby through the birth canal. In the final stage, the placenta is delivered. During labor, infants produce high levels of stress hormones, which help them withstand oxygen deprivation, clear the lungs for breathing, and arouse them into alertness at birth.

■ Newborn babies have large heads and small bodies. The **Apgar Scale** is used to assess their physical condition at birth.

Approaches to Childbirth (p. 109)

Describe natural childbirth and home delivery, and explain the risks of using pain-relieving drugs during labor and delivery.

■ In **natural,** or **prepared, childbirth,** the expectant mother and a companion attend classes about labor and delivery, master relaxation and breathing techniques to counteract pain, and prepare for coaching during childbirth. Social support from a partner, relative, or doula reduces the length of labor and the incidence of birth complications.

■ Home birth is as safe as hospital birth for healthy mothers who are assisted by a well-trained doctor or midwife.

■ The use of analgesics and anesthetics during childbirth can prolong labor and cause newborns to be withdrawn and irritable and to feed poorly.

Birth Complications (p. 112)

What risks are associated with oxygen deprivation and with preterm and low-birth-weight infants, and what factors can help infants who survive a traumatic birth?

■ Inadequate oxygen supply during labor and delivery can damage the brain and other organs. Effects of even mild to moderate anoxia often persist, although many children improve over time.

■ Low birth weight, a major cause of **neonatal** and **infant mortality** and wide-ranging developmental problems, is most common in infants born to poverty-stricken women and in multiple births. Compared with **preterm infants,** whose weight is appropriate for time spent in the uterus, **small-for-date infants** usually have longer-lasting difficulties.

■ Interventions include providing special stimulation in the intensive care nursery and teaching parents how to care for and interact with their babies. Preterm infants in stressed, low-income households need long-term, intensive intervention.

■ When infants experience birth trauma, a supportive family environment or relationships with other caring adults can help restore their growth. Even infants with serious birth complications can recover with the help of positive life events.

Heredity, Environment, and Behavior: A Look Ahead (p. 118)

Explain the various ways heredity and environment may combine to influence complex traits.

■ **Behavioral genetics** looks at the contributions of nature and nurture to complex traits. Researchers use **kinship studies** to compute **heritability estimates,** which show that genetic factors contribute to such traits as intelligence and personality. However, the accuracy and usefulness of these estimates have been challenged, and they tell us nothing about how environment can modify genetic influences.

■ According to the concepts of **gene–environment interaction** and **canalization,** heredity influences children's responsiveness to varying environments. **Gene–environment correlation** and **niche-picking** describe how children's genes affect the environments to which they are exposed. **Epigenesis** reminds us that development is best understood as a series of complex exchanges between nature and nurture.

IMPORTANT TERMS AND CONCEPTS

age of viability (p. 92)
alcohol-related neurodevelopmental disorder (ARND) (p. 99)
allele (p. 77)
amnion (p. 89)
Apgar Scale (p. 109)
autosomes (p. 76)
behavioral genetics (p. 119)
breech position (p. 113)
canalization (p. 122)
carrier (p. 77)
chorion (p. 89)
chromosomes (p. 73)
crossing over (p. 75)
deoxyribonucleic acid (DNA) (p. 74)
dominant–recessive inheritance (p. 77)
embryo (p. 91)
epigenesis (p. 124)
fetal alcohol spectrum disorder (FASD) (p. 98)
fetal alcohol syndrome (FAS) (p. 98)

fetus (p. 92)
fraternal, or dizygotic, twins (p. 76)
gametes (p. 75)
gene (p. 74)
genetic counseling (p. 84)
gene–environment correlation (p. 122)
gene–environment interaction (p. 121)
genomic imprinting (p. 80)
genotype (p. 73)
heritability estimate (p. 120)
heterozygous (p. 77)
homozygous (p. 77)
identical, or monozygotic, twins (p. 76)
incomplete dominance (p. 79)
infant mortality (p. 118)
kinship studies (p. 120)
lanugo (p. 92)
meiosis (p. 75)
mitosis (p. 74)
modifier genes (p. 79)

mutation (p. 81)
natural, or prepared, childbirth (p. 110)
neonatal mortality (p. 118)
niche-picking (p. 123)
partial fetal alcohol syndrome (p-FAS) (p. 99)
phenotype (p. 73)
placenta (p. 89)
polygenic inheritance (p. 81)
prenatal diagnostic methods (p. 84)
preterm infants (p. 114)
Rh factor incompatibility (p. 113)
sex chromosomes (p. 76)
small-for-date infants (p. 114)
teratogen (p. 95)
umbilical cord (p. 89)
vernix (p. 92)
X-linked inheritance (p. 80)
zygote (p. 75)

CHAPTER 4

"Playing by Tops"

Takashi Hariya, 5 years, Japan

With wide-eyed eagerness and curiosity, these young children explore a fascinating pair of spinning tops. Research confirms that infants are remarkably capable beings who rapidly make sense of constantly changing sounds, shapes, patterns, and surfaces in their surroundings.

Reprinted with permission from the International Museum of Children's Art, Oslo, Norway

Infancy: Early Learning, Motor Skills, and Perceptual Capacities

The Organized Infant
Reflexes • States • Neonatal Behavioral Assessment • Learning Capacities

■ **CULTURAL INFLUENCES:** *Cultural Variation in Infant Sleeping Arrangements*

■ **SOCIAL ISSUES: HEALTH:** *The Mysterious Tragedy of Sudden Infant Death Syndrome*

Motor Development in Infancy
The Sequence of Motor Development • Motor Skills as Dynamic Systems • Fine-Motor Development: Reaching and Grasping

Perceptual Development in Infancy
Touch • Taste and Smell • Hearing • Vision • Intermodal Perception • Understanding Perceptual Development

■ **BIOLOGY AND ENVIRONMENT:** *"Tuning In" to Familiar Speech, Faces, and Music: A Sensitive Period for Culture-Specific Learning*

■ **SOCIAL ISSUES: EDUCATION:** *Development of Infants with Severe Visual Impairments*

Early Deprivation and Enrichment: Is Infancy a Sensitive Period of Development?

Enthralled with their new baby, Yolanda and Jay came to my child development class when Joshua was 4 weeks old to share their reactions to new parenthood. Holding little Joshua over his shoulder while patting him gently, Jay remarked, "When we first saw him—a tiny bundle with his arms and legs all scrunched up, so helpless looking—we couldn't imagine how we would ever figure out how to meet his needs. But you know, almost from the start, Joshua has been able to help us!"

Yolanda demonstrated by speaking softly to Joshua. "Look how he perks up and turns toward the sound of our voices!" she said. As she touched Joshua's palm, he grasped at her fingers and the edge of her sleeve. "And look!" Yolanda continued. "See how he grasps at whatever comes near his hand, and how tightly he holds on."

As Joshua snuggled against Jay's chest, Jay noted, "When he's unhappy, we hold him so he can feel our heartbeats." Joshua whimpered, so Jay began walking around the room. "When he's bored, we carry him to a new place and sing to him. Usually, that's enough to quiet him. His cry is becoming a language we can understand."

Jay placed Joshua on his tummy on a blanket-covered table. "See," he announced proudly, "he can lift his head and do little half push-ups." When Jay turned Joshua on his back, Joshua stared at Yolanda's bright pink blouse, his face utterly absorbed. Lifting Joshua and giving him a kiss, Jay exclaimed, "He's just determined to master his world!"

As Yolanda's and Jay's observations confirm, our view of infancy—the period of development that spans the first year of life—has changed drastically over the past century. At one time, the newborn, or *neonate,* was considered a passive, incompetent being whose world was, in the words of turn-of-the-twentieth-century psychologist William James, "a blooming, buzzing confusion." Careful observations of infants' behavior and more refined methods enabling researchers to test babies' capacities confirm that, from the outset, infants display many complex abilities.

Infant development proceeds at an astonishing pace. Excited relatives who visit just after birth and then return a few months later often remark that the baby does not seem like the same individual! Although researchers agree that infants are competent, fervent debates continue over questions like these: What capacities are present from the beginning? Which mature with the passage of time? And which result from the baby's constant interaction with her physical and social worlds? In this chapter, we explore the infant's early reflexes, ability to learn, motor skills, and perceptual capacities—along with the debates that surround these remarkable competencies.

The Organized Infant

The newborn baby, as we saw in Chapter 3, is homely looking, with a head that appears too large in relation to the potbellied trunk and bowlegged lower body. Yet a few hours spent with a neonate reveal a wide variety of capacities that are crucial for survival and for evoking care and attention from adults. In relating to their physical and social worlds, babies are active from the very start.

▶ Explain the functions of
newborn reflexes, and
describe changing states of
arousal during infancy,
emphasizing sleep and crying.

▶ Why is neonatal behavioral
assessment useful?

▶ Describe infant learning
capacities, the conditions
under which they occur, and
the unique value of each.

Reflexes

A **reflex** is an inborn, automatic response to a particular form of stimulation. Reflexes are the neonate's most obvious organized patterns of behavior. When a father, changing his newborn baby's diaper, bumps the side of the table, the infant flings her arms wide, then brings them back toward her body. As a mother softly strokes her infant's cheek, the baby turns his head in her direction. **TAKE A MOMENT...** Look at Table 4.1, and see if you can identify the newborn reflexes described here and the ones Joshua displayed in the introduction to this chapter. Then let's consider the meaning and purpose of these curious behaviors.

Adaptive Value of Reflexes Some reflexes have survival value. The rooting reflex helps a breastfed baby find the mother's nipple. Babies display it only when hungry and touched by another person, not when they touch themselves (Rochat & Hespos, 1997). At birth, babies adjust their sucking pressure to how easily milk flows from the nipple (Craig & Lee, 1999). And if sucking were not automatic, our species would be unlikely to survive for a single generation! The swimming reflex helps a baby who is accidentally dropped into water stay afloat, increasing the chances of retrieval by the caregiver.

Other reflexes probably helped babies survive during our evolutionary past. For example, the Moro, or "embracing," reflex is believed to have helped infants cling to their mothers when they were carried about all day. If the baby happened to lose support, the reflex caused the infant to embrace and, along with the palmar grasp reflex (so strong during the first

TABLE 4.1 | **Some Newborn Reflexes**

REFLEX	STIMULATION	RESPONSE	AGE OF DISAPPEARANCE	FUNCTION
Eye blink	Shine bright light at eyes or clap hand near head.	Infant quickly closes eyelids.	Permanent	Protects infant from strong stimulation
Rooting	Stroke cheek near corner of mouth.	Head turns toward source of stimulation.	3 weeks (becomes voluntary head turning at this time)	Helps infant find the nipple
Sucking	Place finger in infant's mouth.	Infant sucks finger rhythmically.	Replaced by voluntary sucking after 4 months	Permits feeding
Swimming[a]	Occurs when infant is face down in pool of water.	Baby paddles and kicks in swimming motion.	4–6 months	Helps infant survive if dropped into water
Moro	Hold infant horizontally on back and let head drop slightly, or produce a sudden loud sound against surface supporting infant.	Infant makes an "embracing" motion by arching back, extending legs, throwing arms outward, and then bringing arms in toward the body.	6 months	In human evolutionary past, may have helped infant cling to mother
Palmar grasp	Place finger in infant's hand, and press against palm.	Infant spontaneously grasps finger.	3–4 months	Prepares infant for voluntary grasping
Tonic neck	Turn baby's head to one side while infant is lying awake on back.	Infant lies in a "fencing position." One arm is extended in front of eyes on side to which head is turned, other arm is flexed.	4 months	May prepare infant for voluntary reaching
Stepping	Hold infant under arms, and permit bare feet to touch a flat surface.	Infant lifts one foot after another in stepping response.	2 months in infants who gain weight quickly; sustained in lighter infants	Prepares infant for voluntary walking
Babinski	Stroke sole of foot from toe toward heel.	Toes fan out and curl as foot twists in.	8–12 months	Unknown

[a]Placing infants in a pool of water is dangerous. See discussion on page 131.

Sources: Knobloch & Pasamanick, 1974; Prechtl & Beintema, 1965; Thelen, Fisher, & Ridley-Johnson, 1984 week that it can support the baby's entire weight), regain her hold on the mother's body (Kessen, 1967; Prechtl, 1958).

Several reflexes help parents and infants establish gratifying interaction. A baby who searches for and successfully finds the nipple, sucks easily during feedings, and grasps when her hand is touched encourages parents to respond lovingly and feel competent as caregivers. Reflexes can also help parents comfort the baby because they permit infants to control distress and amount of stimulation. As any new parent who makes sure to bring along a pacifier on an outing with a young baby knows, sucking helps quiet a fussy infant.

In the Moro reflex, loss of support or a sudden loud sound causes the baby to extend the legs and throw the arms outward in an "embracing" motion.

Reflexes and the Development of Motor Skills A few reflexes form the basis for complex motor skills that will develop later. For example, the tonic neck reflex may prepare the baby for voluntary reaching. When infants lie on their backs in this "fencing position," they naturally gaze at the hand in front of their eyes. The reflex may encourage them to combine vision with arm movements and, eventually, reach for objects (Knobloch & Pasamanick, 1974).

Certain reflexes—such as the palmar grasp, swimming, and stepping—drop out early, but the motor functions involved are renewed later. The stepping reflex, for example, looks like a primitive walking response. Unlike other reflexes, it appears in a wide range of situations—with the newborn's body in a sideways or upside-down position, with feet touching walls or ceilings, and even with legs dangling in the air (Adolph & Berger, 2006). One reason that babies frequently engage in the alternating leg movements of stepping is their ease compared with other movement patterns; repetitive movement of one leg or of both legs at once requires more effort.

In infants who gain weight quickly in the weeks after birth, the stepping reflex drops out because thigh and calf muscles are not strong enough to lift the baby's chubby legs. But if the lower part of the infant's body is dipped in water, the reflex reappears because the buoyancy of the water lightens the load on the baby's muscles (Thelen, Fisher, & Ridley-Johnson, 1984). When stepping is exercised regularly, babies display more spontaneous stepping movements and gain muscle strength. Consequently, they tend to walk several weeks earlier than if stepping is not practiced (Zelazo et al., 1993). However, there is no special need for infants to practice the stepping reflex—all normal babies walk in due time.

In the case of the swimming reflex, trying to build on it is risky. Although young babies placed in a swimming pool will paddle and kick, they swallow large amounts of water. This lowers the concentration of salt in the baby's blood, which can cause brain swelling and seizures. Despite this remarkable reflex, swimming lessons are best postponed until at least 3 years of age.

The Importance of Assessing Reflexes Look at Table 4.1 again, and you will see that most newborn reflexes disappear during the first six months. Researchers believe that this is due to a gradual increase in voluntary control over behavior as the cerebral cortex develops. Pediatricians test reflexes carefully, especially if a newborn has experienced birth trauma, because reflexes can reveal the health of the baby's nervous system. Weak or absent reflexes, overly rigid or exaggerated reflexes, and

When held upright under the arms, newborns show a reflexive stepping response, which forms the basis for later walking.

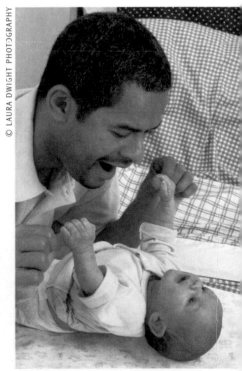

The palmar grasp reflex is so strong during the first week after birth that many infants can use it to support their entire weight.

reflexes that persist beyond the point in development when they should normally disappear can signal brain damage (Schott & Rossor, 2003; Zafeiriou, 2000). However, individual differences in reflexive responses exist that are not cause for concern. An observer must assess newborn reflexes along with other characteristics to distinguish normal from abnormal central nervous system functioning (Touwen, 1984).

States

Throughout the day and night, newborn infants move in and out of five **states of arousal,** or degrees of sleep and wakefulness, described in Table 4.2. During the first month, these states alternate frequently. The most fleeting is quiet alertness, which usually moves quickly toward fussing and crying. Much to the relief of their fatigued parents, newborns spend the greatest amount of time asleep—about 16 to 18 hours a day. Because the fetus tends to synchronize periods of rest and activity with those of the mother, newborns—even those who are 4 to 6 weeks preterm—sleep more at night than during the day (Heraghty et al., 2008; Rivkees, 2003). Nevertheless, young babies' sleep–wake cycles are affected more by fullness–hunger than by darkness–light (Davis, Parker, & Montgomery, 2004; Goodlin-Jones, Burnham, & Anders, 2000).

Between birth and 2 years, the organization of sleep and wakefulness changes substantially. Total sleep time declines slowly; the average 2-year-old still needs 12 to 13 hours per day. But periods of sleep and wakefulness become fewer but longer, and the sleep–wake pattern increasingly conforms to a *circadian rhythm,* or 24-hour schedule. By 2 to 3 months, infants respond more to darkness–light. Babies of this age who are exposed to more bright sunlight—for example, through regular early-afternoon stroller rides—sleep better at night (Harrison, 2004). Most 6- to 9-month-olds take two daytime naps; by about 18 months, children generally need only one nap. Finally, between 3 and 5 years, napping subsides (Iglowstein et al., 2003).

These changing arousal patterns are due to brain development, but they are also affected by culturally influenced beliefs and practices and individual parents' needs (Super & Harkness, 2002). In interviews of Dutch and U.S. middle-class parents that focused on their babies' sleep, the Dutch parents viewed sleep regularity as far more important than the U.S. parents

TABLE 4.2 | Infant States of Arousal

STATE	DESCRIPTION	DAILY DURATION IN NEWBORN
Regular, or NREM, sleep	The infant is at full rest and shows little or no body activity. The eyelids are closed, no eye movements occur, the face is relaxed, and breathing is slow and regular.	8–9 hours
Irregular, or REM, sleep	Gentle limb movements, occasional stirring, and facial grimacing occur. Although the eyelids are closed, occasional rapid eye movements can be seen beneath them. Breathing is irregular.	8–9 hours
Drowsiness	The infant is either falling asleep or waking up. Body is less active than in irregular sleep but more active than in regular sleep. The eyes open and close; when open, they have a glazed look. Breathing is even but somewhat faster than in regular sleep.	Varies
Quiet alertness	The infant's body is relatively inactive, with eyes open and attentive. Breathing is even.	2–3 hours
Waking activity and crying	The infant shows frequent bursts of uncoordinated body activity. Breathing is very irregular; face may be relaxed or tense and wrinkled. Crying may occur.	1–4 hours

Source: Wolff, 1966.

did. And whereas the U.S. parents regarded a predictable sleep schedule as emerging naturally from within the child, the Dutch parents were convinced—on the basis of Dutch infant-care traditions—that a schedule had to be imposed, or the baby's development might suffer (Super et al., 1996; Super & Harkness, 2010). At age 6 months, the Dutch babies were put to bed earlier and slept, on average, 2 hours more per day than their U.S. counterparts.

Motivated by demanding work schedules and other needs, many Western parents try to get their babies to sleep through the night as early as age 3 to 4 months by offering an evening feeding before putting them down in a separate, quiet room. In this way, they push young infants to the limits of their neurological capacities. Not until the middle of the first year is the secretion of *melatonin,* a hormone within the brain that promotes drowsiness, much greater at night than during the day (Sadeh, 1997).

Furthermore, as the Cultural Influences box on page 134 reveals, isolating infants to promote sleep is rare elsewhere in the world. When babies sleep with their parents, their average sleep period remains constant at three hours from 1 to 8 months of age. Only at the end of the first year, as REM sleep (the state that usually prompts waking) declines, do infants move in the direction of an adultlike sleep–waking schedule (Ficca et al., 1999).

Even after infants sleep through the night, they continue to wake occasionally. In sleep observations and in surveys of parents in Australia, Israel, and the United States, night wakings increased around 6 months and again between 1½ and 2 years and then declined (Armstrong, Quinn, & Dadds, 1994; Scher, Epstein, & Tirosh, 2004; Scher et al., 1995). As Chapter 10 will reveal, around the middle of the first year, infants are forming a clear-cut attachment to their familiar caregiver and begin protesting when he or she leaves. And the challenges of toddlerhood—the ability to range farther from the caregiver and increased awareness of the self as separate from others—often prompt anxiety, evident in disturbed sleep and clinginess. When parents offer comfort, these behaviors subside.

Although arousal states become more organized with age, striking individual differences in daily rhythms exist that affect parents' attitudes toward and interactions with the baby. A few newborns sleep for long periods, increasing the energy their well-rested parents have for sensitive, responsive care. Other babies wake frequently and cry often, and their parents must exert great effort to soothe them. If these parents do not succeed, they may feel less competent and positive toward their infant—responses that pose serious risks to parent and family well-being (Sadeh et al., 2007; Smart & Hiscock, 2007).

Arousal patterns also have implications for early cognitive progress. Babies who spend more time quietly alert probably receive more social stimulation and opportunities to explore and, therefore, may be slightly ahead in mental development (Gertner et al., 2002). And as with adults, sleep enhances babies' learning and memory. Because newborns spend so much time sleeping, the capacity to learn about external stimuli during sleep may be essential for infants' adaptation to their surroundings. In one study, eye movements and ERP brain-wave recordings confirmed that sleeping newborns readily learned that a tone would be followed by a puff of air to the eye (Fifer et al., 2010). And 15-month-olds who took hour-long naps after listening to short, similarly structured "sentences" of nonsense words were better than their non-napping agemates at recognizing the common structure in new sentences and remembering it after a 24-hour delay (Gómez, Bootzin, & Nadel, 2006; Hupbach et al., 2009). Napping facilitated retention of higher-order word patterns—a skill essential for language development.

Of the states listed in Table 4.2, the two extremes—sleep and crying—have been of greatest interest to researchers. Each tells us something about normal and abnormal early development.

Sleep Sleep is made up of at least two states. During irregular, or **rapid-eye-movement (REM) sleep,** brain-wave activity, measured with the EEG, is remarkably similar to that of the waking state. The eyes dart beneath the lids; heart rate, blood pressure, and breathing are uneven, and slight body movements occur. The expression "sleeping like a baby" was probably not meant to describe this state! In contrast, during regular, or **non rapid eye-movement (NREM) sleep,** the body is almost motionless, and heart rate, breathing, and brain-wave activity are slow and even.

LOOK and LISTEN

Interview a parent of a baby about sleep challenges. What strategies has the parent tried to ease these difficulties? Are the techniques likely to be effective, in view of evidence on infant sleep development?

CULTURAL INFLUENCES

Cultural Variation in Infant Sleeping Arrangements

While awaiting the birth of a new baby, North American parents typically furnish a room as the infant's sleeping quarters. For decades, child-rearing advice from experts strongly encouraged nighttime separation of baby from parent. For example, the most recent edition of Benjamin Spock's *Baby and Child Care* recommends that babies sleep in their own room by 3 months of age, explaining, "By 6 months, a child who regularly sleeps in her parents' room may become dependent on this arrangement" (Spock & Needlman, 2004, p. 60). And the American Academy of Pediatrics (2005) has issued a controversial warning that parent–infant bedsharing may increase the risk of sudden infant death syndrome (SIDS).

Yet parent–infant "cosleeping" is the norm for approximately 90 percent of the world's population, in cultures as diverse as the Japanese, the rural Guatemalan Maya, the Inuit of northwestern Canada, and the !Kung of Botswana. Japanese and Korean children usually lie next to their mothers in infancy and early childhood, and many continue to sleep with a parent or other family member until adolescence (Takahashi, 1990; Yang & Hahn, 2002). Among the Maya, mother–infant cosleeping is interrupted only by the birth of a new baby, at which time the older child is moved next to the father or to another bed in the same room (Morelli et al., 1992). Cosleeping is also common in U.S. ethnic minority families (McKenna & Volpe, 2007). African-American children, for example, frequently fall asleep with their parents and remain with them for part or all of the night (Buswell & Spatz, 2007).

Cultural values strongly influence infant sleeping arrangements. In one study, researchers interviewed Guatemalan Mayan mothers and American middle-class mothers about their sleeping practices. Mayan mothers stressed the importance of promoting an *interdependent self* (see page 35 in Chapter 1), explaining that cosleeping builds a close parent–child bond, which is necessary for children to learn the ways of people around them. In contrast, American mothers emphasized an *independent self*, mentioning their desire to instill early autonomy, prevent bad habits, and protect their own privacy (Morelli et al., 1992).

Over the past two decades, cosleeping has increased in Western nations. In the United States, an estimated 13 percent of infants routinely bedshare, and an additional 30 to 35 percent sometimes do so (Buswell & Spatz, 2007; Willinger et al., 2003). Proponents of the practice say that it helps infants sleep, makes breastfeeding more convenient, and provides valuable bonding time—especially for employed parents who have limited contact with their baby during the day (McKenna & Volpe, 2007).

During the night, cosleeping babies breastfeed three times longer than infants who sleep alone. Because infants arouse to nurse more often when sleeping next to their mothers, some researchers believe that cosleeping may actually help safeguard babies at risk for sudden infant death syndrome (SIDS) (see the Social Issues: Health box on page 136). Consistent with this view, SIDS is rare in Asian cultures where cosleeping is widespread, including Cambodia, China, Japan, Korea, Thailand, and Vietnam (McKenna, 2002; McKenna & McDade, 2005). And contrary to popular belief, cosleeping does not decrease mothers' total sleep time, although they experience more brief awakenings, which permit them to check on their baby (Mao et al., 2004).

Infant sleeping practices affect other aspects of family life. For example, Mayan babies doze off in the midst of ongoing family activities and are carried to bed by their mothers. In contrast, for many American parents, bedtime often involves a lengthy, elaborate ritual. Perhaps bedtime struggles, so common in Western homes but rare elsewhere in the world, are related to the stress young children feel when they must fall asleep without assistance (Latz, Wolf, & Lozoff, 1999).

Critics of bedsharing warn that cosleeping children will develop emotional problems, especially excessive dependency. Yet a longitudinal study following children from the end of pregnancy through age 18 showed that young people who had bedshared in the early years were no different from others in any aspect of adjustment (Okami, Weisner, & Olmstead, 2002). Another concern is that infants might become trapped under the parent's body or in soft covers and suffocate. Parents who are obese or who use alcohol, tobacco, or illegal drugs do pose a serious risk to their sleeping babies, as does the use of quilts and comforters or an overly soft mattress (Willinger et al., 2003).

But with appropriate precautions, parents and infants can cosleep safely (McKenna & Volpe, 2007). In cultures where cosleeping is widespread, parents and infants usually sleep with light covering on hard surfaces, such as firm mattresses, floor mats, and wooden planks, or infants sleep in a cradle or hammock next to the parents' bed (McKenna, 2001, 2002). And when sharing the same bed, infants typically lie on their back or side facing the mother—positions that promote frequent, easy communication between parent and baby and arousal if breathing is threatened.

Finally, breastfeeding mothers usually assume a distinctive sleeping posture: They face the infant, with knees drawn up under the baby's feet and arm above the baby's head. Besides facilitating feeding, the position prevents the infant from sliding down under covers or up under pillows (Ball, 2006). Because this posture is also seen in female great apes while sharing sleeping nests with their infants, researchers believe it may have evolved to enhance infant safety.

© STEPHEN L. RAYMER/NATIONAL GEOGRAPHIC IMAGE COLLECTION

This Cambodian father and child sleep together, a practice common in diverse cultures. Many parents believe that cosleeping promotes a close parent–child bond.

Like children and adults, newborns alternate between REM and NREM sleep. However, as Figure 4.1 shows, they spend far more time in the REM state than they ever will again. REM sleep accounts for 50 percent of the newborn baby's sleep time. By 3 to 5 years, it has declined to an adultlike level of 20 percent (Louis et al., 1997).

Why do young infants spend so much time in REM sleep? In older children and adults, the REM state is associated with dreaming. Babies probably do not dream, at least not in the same way we do. But researchers believe that the stimulation of REM sleep is vital for growth of the central nervous system. Young infants seem to have a special need for this stimulation because they spend little time in an alert state, when they can get input from the environment. In support of this idea, the percentage of REM sleep is especially great in the fetus and in preterm babies, who are even less able than full-term newborns to take advantage of external stimulation (de Weerd & van den Bossche, 2003; Peirano, Algarin, & Uauy, 2003).

While the brain-wave activity of REM sleep safeguards the central nervous system, the rapid eye movements protect the health of the eye. Eye movements cause the vitreous (gelatin-like substance within the eye) to circulate, thereby delivering oxygen to parts of the eye that do not have their own blood supply (Blumberg & Lucas, 1996). During sleep, when the eye and the vitreous are still, visual structures are at risk for anoxia. As the brain cycles through REM-sleep periods, rapid eye movements stir up the vitreous, ensuring that the eye is fully oxygenated.

Because newborn babies' normal sleep behavior is organized and patterned, observations of sleep states can help identify central nervous system abnormalities. In infants who are brain-damaged or who have experienced birth trauma, disturbed REM–NREM sleep cycles are often present. Babies with poor sleep organization are likely to be behaviorally disorganized and, therefore, to have difficulty learning and eliciting caregiver interactions that enhance their development. In follow-ups during the preschool years, they show delayed motor, cognitive, and language development (de Weerd & van den Bossche, 2003; Feldman, 2006; Holditch-Davis, Belyea, & Edwards, 2005). And the brain-functioning problems that underlie newborn sleep irregularities may culminate in sudden infant death syndrome, a major cause of infant mortality (see the Social Issues: Health box on page 136).

Crying Crying is the first way that babies communicate, letting parents know that they need food, comfort, and stimulation. During the weeks after birth, all babies have some fussy periods when they are difficult to console. But most of the time, the nature of the cry, combined with the experiences that led up to it, helps guide parents toward its cause. The baby's cry is a complex auditory stimulus that varies in intensity, from a whimper to a message of all-out distress (Gustafson, Wood, & Green, 2000; Wood, 2009). As early as the first few weeks, infants can be identified by the unique vocal "signature" of their cries, which helps parents locate their baby from a distance (Gustafson, Green, & Cleland, 1994).

Young infants usually cry because of physical needs. Hunger is the most common cause, but babies may also cry in response to temperature change when undressed, a sudden noise, or a painful stimulus. An infant's state also affects proneness to cry. A baby who, when quietly alert, regards a colorful or noise-making object with interest may burst into tears when confronted with the same object while in a state of mild discomfort. And newborns (as well as older infants) often cry at the sound of another crying baby (Dondi, Simion, & Caltran, 1999; Geangu et al., 2010). Some researchers believe that this response reflects an inborn

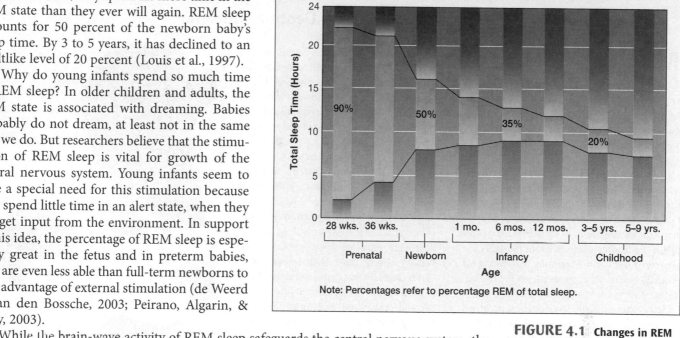

FIGURE 4.1 Changes in REM sleep, NREM sleep, and the waking state from the prenatal period to middle childhood. REM sleep declines steadily over the prenatal period and the first few years of life. Between 3 and 5 years, it accounts for about the same percentage of sleep time as it does in adulthood. (Adapted from de Weerd & van den Bossche, 2003; Roffwarg, Muzio, & Dement, 1996.)

SOCIAL ISSUES: HEALTH

The Mysterious Tragedy of Sudden Infant Death Syndrome

Millie awoke with a start one morning and looked at the clock. It was 7:30, and Sasha had missed both her night waking and her early morning feeding. Wondering if she was all right, Millie and her husband, Stuart, tiptoed into the room. Sasha lay still, curled up under her blanket. She had died silently during her sleep.

Sasha was a victim of **sudden infant death syndrome (SIDS),** the unexpected death, usually during the night, of an infant younger than 1 year of age that remains unexplained after thorough investigation. In industrialized nations, SIDS is the leading cause of infant mortality between 1 week and 12 months, accounting for about 20 percent of these deaths in the United States (Mathews & MacDorman, 2008).

SIDS victims usually show physical problems from the beginning. Early medical records of SIDS babies reveal higher rates of prematurity and low birth weight, poor Apgar scores, and limp muscle tone. Abnormal heart rate and respiration and disturbances in sleep–wake activity and in REM–NREM cycles while asleep are also involved (Cornwell & Feigenbaum, 2006; Kato et al., 2003). At the time of death, many SIDS babies have a mild respiratory infection (Blood-Siegfried, 2009). This seems to increase the chances of respiratory failure in an already vulnerable baby.

Mounting evidence suggests that impaired brain functioning is a major contributor to SIDS. Between 2 and 4 months, when SIDS is most likely to occur, reflexes decline and are replaced by voluntary, learned responses. Neurological weaknesses may prevent SIDS babies from acquiring behaviors that replace defensive reflexes (Lipsitt, 2003). As a result, when breathing difficulties occur during sleep, the infants do not wake up, shift their position, or cry out for help. Instead, they simply give in to oxygen deprivation and death. In support of this

interpretation, autopsies reveal that the brains of SIDS babies contain unusually low levels of serotonin (a brain chemical that assists with arousal when survival is threatened) as well as other abnormalities in centers that control breathing and arousal (Duncan et al., 2010).

Several environmental factors are linked to SIDS. Maternal cigarette smoking, both during and after pregnancy, as well as smoking by other caregivers, doubles risk of the disorder. Babies exposed to cigarette smoke arouse less easily from sleep and have more respiratory infections (Richardson, Walker, & Horne, 2009; Shah, Sullivan, & Carter, 2006). Prenatal abuse of drugs that depress central nervous system functioning (alcohol, opiates, and barbiturates) increases the risk of SIDS as much as fifteenfold (Hunt & Hauck, 2006). Babies of drug-abusing mothers are especially likely to display SIDS-related brain abnormalities (Kinney, 2009).

SIDS babies are also more likely to sleep on their stomachs than on their backs and often are wrapped very warmly in clothing and blankets. Infants who sleep on their stomachs less often wake when their breathing is disturbed (Richardson, Walker, & Horne, 2008). In other cases, healthy babies sleeping face down on soft bedding may die from continually breathing their own exhaled breath.

Quitting smoking and drug taking, changing an infant's sleeping position, and removing a few bedclothes can reduce the incidence of SIDS. For example, if women refrained from smoking while pregnant, an estimated 30 percent of SIDS cases would be prevented. Public education campaigns that encourage parents to put babies down on their backs have cut the incidence of SIDS in half in many Western nations (Moon, Horne, & Hauck, 2007). Another protective measure is pacifier use: Sleeping babies who suck arouse more easily in

© BANANASTOCK/JUPITERIMAGES

Public education campaigns encouraging parents to place infants on their backs to sleep have cut the incidence of SIDS in half in many Western nations.

response to breathing and heart-rate irregularities (Li et al., 2006). Nevertheless, compared with white infants, SIDS rates are two to six times higher in poverty-stricken minority groups, where parental stress, substance abuse, reduced access to health care, and lack of knowledge about safe sleep practices are widespread (Colson et al., 2009; Pickett, Luo, & Lauderdale, 2005).

When SIDS does occur, surviving family members require a great deal of help to overcome a sudden and unexpected death. As Millie commented six months after Sasha's death, "It's the worst crisis we've ever been through. What's helped us most are the comforting words of others who've experienced the same tragedy."

capacity to react to the suffering of others. Furthermore, crying typically increases during the early weeks, peaks at about 6 weeks, and then declines (Barr, 2001). Because this trend appears in many cultures with vastly different infant care practices, researchers believe that normal readjustments of the central nervous system underlie it.

Adult Responsiveness to Infant Cries. **TAKE A MOMENT...** The next time you hear a baby cry, notice your own reaction. The sound stimulates strong feelings of arousal and discomfort in men and women, parents and nonparents alike (Murray, 1985). This powerful response is probably innately programmed to help ensure that babies receive the care and protection they need to survive.

APPLYING WHAT WE KNOW

Soothing a Crying Baby

TECHNIQUE	EXPLANATION
Talk softly or play rhythmic sounds.	Continuous, monotonous, rhythmic sounds (such as a clock ticking, a fan whirring, or peaceful music) are more effective than intermittent sounds.
Offer a pacifier.	Sucking helps babies control their own level of arousal.
Massage the baby's body.	Stroking the baby's torso and limbs with continuous, gentle motions relaxes the baby's muscles.
Swaddle the baby.	Restricting movement and increasing warmth often soothe a young infant.
Lift the baby to the shoulder and rock or walk.	This combination of physical contact, upright posture, and motion is an effective soothing technique, causing young infants to become quietly alert.
Take the baby for a short car ride or a walk in a baby carriage; swing the baby in a cradle.	Gentle, rhythmic motion of any kind helps lull the baby to sleep.
Combine several of the methods just listed.	Stimulating several of the baby's senses at once is often more effective than stimulating only one.
If these methods do not work, let the baby cry for a short period.	Occasionally, a baby responds well to just being put down and will, after a few minutes, fall asleep.

Sources: Campos, 1989; Evanoo, 2007; Lester, 1985; Reisman, 1987.

Although parents do not always interpret their baby's cry correctly, their accuracy improves with experience. As babies get older, parents react to more subtle cues in the cry—not just intensity but also whimpering and calling sounds (Thompson & Leger, 1999). These cues, together with the context of the cry, help them figure out what is wrong. If the baby has not eaten for several hours, she is likely to be hungry. If a period of wakefulness and stimulation preceded the cry, the infant may be tired. A sharp, piercing, sustained cry usually means the baby is in pain and prompts caregivers to rush to the infant. Very intense cries are rated as more unpleasant and produce greater physiological arousal in adults (Crowe & Zeskind, 1992). These adaptive reactions help ensure that an infant in danger will quickly get help.

At the same time, parents vary widely in responsiveness. Parents who are high in empathy (ability to take the perspective of others in distress) and who hold "child-centered" attitudes toward infant care (for example, believe that babies cannot be spoiled by being picked up) are more likely to respond quickly and sensitively to a crying baby (Leerkes, 2010; Zeifman, 2003). And in one study, mothers who believed that they could easily control the crying of an artificial baby (whose quieting was unrelated to the mother's behavior) had difficulty detecting changes in cry sounds, engaged in less sensitive infant care, and had infants who developed into uncooperative toddlers (Donovan, Leavitt, & Walsh, 1997, 2000). The internal state of these mothers—who reacted defensively when they couldn't calm the artificial baby—seemed to interfere with their ability to cope effectively with infant crying.

Soothing a Crying Infant. Fortunately, there are many ways to soothe a crying baby when feeding and diaper changing do not work (see Applying What We Know above). The technique that Western parents usually try first, lifting the infant to the shoulder and rocking or walking, is highly effective. Another common soothing method is swaddling—wrapping the baby snugly in a blanket. The Quechua, who live in the cold, high-altitude desert regions of Peru, dress young babies in several layers of clothing and blankets that cover the head and body, a technique that reduces crying and promotes sleep (Tronick, Thomas, & Daltabuit, 1994). It also allows the baby to conserve energy for early growth in the harsh Peruvian highlands.

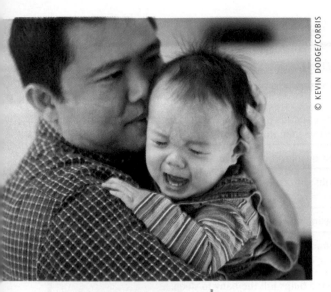

To soothe his crying infant, this father holds the baby upright against his gently moving body. The combination of physical contact, upright posture, and motion causes babies to stop crying and become quietly alert.

Will reacting promptly and consistently to infant cries give babies a sense of confidence that their needs will be met and, over time, reduce fussing and complaining? Or will it strengthen crying behavior and produce a miniature tyrant? Answers are contradictory.

According to *ethological theory,* parental responsiveness is adaptive in that it ensures that the infant's basic needs will be met (see Chapter 1, page 24). At the same time, it brings the baby into close contact with the caregiver, who encourages the infant to communicate through means other than crying. In support of this view, two studies showed that mothers who were slow or failed to respond to their young baby's cries had infants who cried more at the end of the first year (Bell & Ainsworth, 1972; Hubbard & van IJzendoorn, 1991). Furthermore, in many tribal and village societies and in non-Western developed nations (such as Japan), where babies are in physical contact with their caregivers nearly continuously, infants show shorter bouts of crying than their American counterparts (Barr, 2001). When Western parents choose to practice "proximal care" by holding their babies extensively, amount of crying in the early months is reduced by about one-third (St James-Roberts et al., 2006).

But not all research indicates that rapid parental responsiveness reduces infant crying (van IJzendoorn & Hubbard, 2000). The conditions that prompt crying are complex, and parents must make reasoned choices about what to do on the basis of culturally accepted practices, the suspected reason for the cry, and the context in which it occurs—for example, in the privacy of their own home or while having dinner at a restaurant. Fortunately, with age, crying declines and occurs more often for psychological (demands for attention, expressions of frustration) than physical reasons. Virtually all researchers agree that parents can lessen older babies' need to cry by encouraging more mature ways of expressing their desires, such as gestures and vocalizations.

Abnormal Crying. Like reflexes and sleep patterns, the infant's cry offers a clue to central nervous system distress. The cries of brain-damaged babies and those who have experienced prenatal and birth complications are often shrill, piercing, and shorter in duration than those of healthy infants (Boukydis & Lester, 1998; Green, Irwin, & Gustafson, 2000). Even neonates with a fairly common problem—*colic,* or persistent crying—tend to have high-pitched, harsh-sounding cries (Zeskind & Barr, 1997). Although the cause of colic is unknown, certain newborns, who react especially strongly to unpleasant stimuli, are susceptible. Because their crying is intense, they find it harder to calm down than other babies. Colic generally subsides between 3 and 6 months (Barr et al., 2005; St James-Roberts, 2007).

In an intervention aimed at reducing colic, nurses made periodic home visits, providing parents with help in identifying their baby's early warning signs of becoming overly aroused, in using effective soothing techniques, and in modifying light, noise, and activity in the home to promote predictable sleep–wake cycles (Keefe et al., 2005). Colicky infants who received the intervention spent far less time crying than no-intervention controls—1.3 versus 3 hours per day.

Most parents try to respond to a crying baby's call for help with extra care and attention, but sometimes the cry is so unpleasant and the infant so difficult to soothe that parents become frustrated, resentful, and angry. Preterm and ill babies are more likely to be abused by highly stressed parents, who sometimes mention a high-pitched, grating cry as one factor that caused them to lose control and harm the baby (St James-Roberts, 2007; Zeskind & Lester, 2001). We will discuss a host of additional influences on child abuse in Chapter 14.

LOOK and LISTEN

In a public setting, watch several parents soothe their crying babies. What techniques did the parents use, and how successful were they?

Neonatal Behavioral Assessment

A variety of instruments enable doctors, nurses, and researchers to assess the organized functioning of newborn babies. The most widely used of these tests, T. Berry Brazelton's **Neonatal Behavioral Assessment Scale (NBAS),** evaluates the baby's reflexes, muscle tone, state changes, responsiveness to physical and social stimuli, and other reactions (Brazelton

& Nugent, 1995). A recently developed instrument consisting of similar items, the *Neonatal Intensive Care Unit Network Neurobehavioral Scale (NNNS)*, is specially designed for use with newborns at risk for developmental problems because of low birth weight, preterm delivery, prenatal substance exposure, or other conditions (Lester & Tronick, 2004). Scores are used to recommend appropriate interventions and to guide parents in meeting their baby's unique needs.

The NBAS has been given to many infants around the world. As a result, researchers have learned about individual and cultural differences in newborn behavior and how child-rearing practices can maintain or change a baby's reactions. For example, NBAS scores of Asian and Native-American babies reveal that they are less irritable than Caucasian infants. Mothers in these cultures encourage their babies' calm dispositions through swaddling, close physical contact, and nursing at the first signs of discomfort (Murett-Wagstaff & Moore, 1989; Small, 1998). The Kipsigis of rural Kenya, who highly value infant motor maturity, massage babies regularly and begin exercising the stepping reflex shortly after birth. These customs contribute to Kipsigis babies' strong but flexible muscle tone at 5 days of age (Super & Harkness, 2009). In Zambia, Africa, maternal care can quickly change the poor NBAS scores of undernourished infants. The Zambian mother carries her baby about on her hip all day, pro-

This mother of the El Molo people of northern Kenya carries her baby in a sling all day. This practice, also adopted by many Western parents, provides rich sensory stimulation and promotes an alert, calm disposition.

viding a rich variety of sensory stimulation. As a result, an unresponsive newborn often becomes an alert, contented 1-week-old (Brazelton, Koslowski, & Tronick, 1976).

TAKE A MOMENT... Using these examples, can you explain why a single neonatal assessment score is not a good predictor of later development? Because newborn behavior and parenting combine to influence development, *changes in scores* over the first week or two of life (rather than a single score) provide the best estimate of the baby's ability to recover from the stress of birth. NBAS "recovery curves" predict normal brain functioning (as assessed by EEG and fMRI), intelligence, and absence of emotional and behavior problems with moderate success well into the preschool years (Brazelton, Nugent, & Lester, 1987; Ohgi et al., 2003a, 2003b).

In some hospitals, health professionals use the NBAS or the NNNS to help parents get to know their newborns through discussion or demonstration of the capacities these instruments assess. Parents who participate in these programs, compared with no-intervention controls, interact more effectively with their babies—more often establishing eye contact, smiling, vocalizing, and soothing in response to infant signals (Browne & Talmi, 2005; Bruschweiler-Stern, 2004). Although lasting effects on development have not been demonstrated, neonatal behavioral assessment interventions are useful in helping the parent–infant relationship get off to a good start.

Learning Capacities

Learning refers to changes in behavior as the result of experience. Babies come into the world with built-in learning capacities that permit them to profit from experience immediately. Infants are capable of two basic forms of learning, which were introduced in Chapter 1: classical and operant conditioning. They also learn through their natural preference for novel stimulation. Finally, shortly after birth, babies learn by observing others; they can imitate the facial expressions and gestures of adults.

Classical Conditioning   Newborn reflexes make **classical conditioning** possible in the young infant. In this form of learning, a neutral stimulus is paired with a stimulus that leads to a reflexive response. Once the baby's nervous system makes the connection between the two stimuli, the new stimulus produces the behavior by itself. Classical conditioning helps infants recognize which events usually occur together in the everyday world, so they can anticipate what is about to happen next. As a result, the environment becomes more orderly and predictable. Let's take a closer look at the steps of classical conditioning.

Imagine a mother who gently strokes her infant's forehead each time she settles down to nurse the baby. Soon the mother notices that each time the baby's forehead is stroked, he makes active sucking movements. The infant has been classically conditioned. Here is how it happened (see Figure 4.2):

- Before learning takes place, an **unconditioned stimulus (UCS)** must consistently produce a reflexive, or **unconditioned, response (UCR).** In our example, the stimulus of sweet breast milk (UCS) resulted in sucking (UCR).
- To produce learning, a *neutral stimulus* that does not lead to the reflex is presented just before, or at about the same time as, the UCS. The mother stroked the baby's forehead as each nursing period began. The stroking (neutral stimulus) was paired with the taste of milk (UCS).
- If learning has occurred, the neutral stimulus alone produces a response similar to the reflexive response. The neutral stimulus is then called a **conditioned stimulus (CS),** and the response it elicits is called a **conditioned response (CR).** We know that the baby has been classically conditioned because stroking his forehead outside the feeding situation (CS) results in sucking (CR).

If the CS is presented alone enough times, without being paired with the UCS, the CR will no longer occur, an outcome called **extinction.** In other words, if the mother repeatedly strokes the infant's forehead without feeding him, the baby will gradually stop sucking in response to stroking.

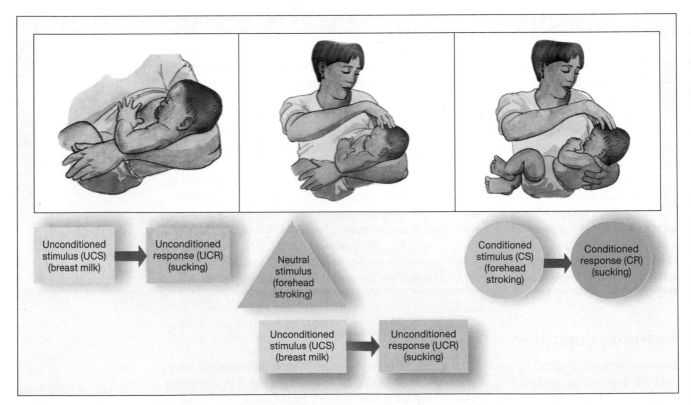

FIGURE 4.2 The steps of classical conditioning. The example here shows how a mother classically conditioned her baby to make sucking movements by stroking his forehead at the beginning of feedings.

Young infants can be classically conditioned most easily when the association between two stimuli has survival value. Learning which stimuli regularly accompany feeding improves the infant's ability to get food and survive (Blass, Ganchrow, & Steiner, 1984). In contrast, some responses, such as fear, are very difficult to classically condition in young babies. Until infants have the motor skills to escape unpleasant events, they have no biological need to form these associations. After age 6 months, however, fear is easy to condition. **TAKE A MOMENT...** Return to Chapter 1, page 17, to review John Watson's famous experiment in which he conditioned Little Albert to withdraw and cry at the sight of a furry white rat. Then test your knowledge of classical conditioning by identifying the UCS, UCR, CS, and CR in Watson's study. In Chapter 10, we will discuss the development of fear, as well as other emotional reactions.

Operant Conditioning   In classical conditioning, babies build expectations about stimulus events in the environment, but their behavior does not influence the stimuli that occur. In **operant conditioning,** infants act, or *operate*, on the environment, and stimuli that follow their behavior change the probability that the behavior will occur again. A stimulus that increases the occurrence of a response is called a **reinforcer.** For example, sweet liquid *reinforces* the sucking response in newborns. Removing a desirable stimulus or presenting an unpleasant one to decrease the occurrence of a response is called **punishment.** A sour-tasting fluid *punishes* newborns' sucking response. It causes them to purse their lips and stop sucking entirely.

Many stimuli besides food can serve as reinforcers of infant behavior. For example, newborns will suck faster on a nipple when doing so produces interesting sights and sounds, including visual designs, music, or human voices (Floccia, Christophe, & Bertoncini, 1997). Even preterm babies will seek reinforcing stimulation. In one study, they increased their contact with a soft teddy bear that "breathed" at a rate reflecting the infant's respiration, whereas they decreased their contact with a nonbreathing bear (Thoman & Ingersoll, 1993). As these findings suggest, operant conditioning is a powerful tool for finding out what stimuli babies can perceive and which ones they prefer.

As infants get older, operant conditioning includes a wider range of responses and stimuli. For example, researchers have hung special mobiles over the cribs of 2- to 6-month-olds. When the baby's foot is attached to the mobile with a long cord, the infant can, by kicking, make the mobile turn. Under these conditions, it takes only a few minutes for infants to start kicking vigorously. This technique has yielded important information about infant memory. Two-month-olds remember how to activate the mobile for 1 to 2 days after training, and 3-month-olds for one week. By 6 months, memory increases to two weeks (Rovee-Collier, 1999; Rovee-Collier & Bhatt, 1993). Around the middle of the first year, babies can manipulate switches or buttons to control stimulation. When 6- to 18-month-olds pressed a lever to make a toy train move around a track, duration of memory continued to increase with age; 13 weeks after training, 18-month-olds still remembered how to press the lever (Hartshorn et al., 1998b). Figure 4.3 shows this dramatic rise in retention of operant responses over the first year and a half.

Even after 2- to 6-month-olds forget an operant response, they need only a brief prompt—an adult who shakes the mobile—to reinstate the memory (Hildreth & Rovee-Collier, 2002). And when 6-month-olds are given a chance to reactivate the response themselves for just a couple of minutes—jiggling the mobile by kicking or moving the train by

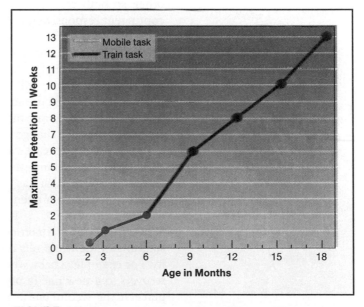

FIGURE 4.3 Increase in retention of operant responses in two tasks from 2 to 18 months. Two- to 6-month-olds were trained to make a kicking response that turned a mobile. Six- to 18-month-olds were trained to press a lever that made a toy train move around a track. Six-month-olds learned both responses and retained them for an identical length of time, indicating that the tasks are comparable. Consequently, researchers could plot a single line tracking gains in retention of operant responses from 2 to 18 months of age. The line shows that memory improves dramatically. (From C. Rovee-Collier & R. Barr, 2001, "Infant Learning and Memory," in G. Bremner & A. Fogel, eds., *Blackwell Handbook of Infant Development,* Oxford, U.K.: Blackwell, p. 150. Reprinted by permission of Blackwell Publishing Ltd.)

COURTESY OF CAROLYN ROVEE-COLLIER

This 12-month-old has learned to press a lever to make a toy train move around a track—a response she is likely to remember when re-exposed to the task after increasingly long intervals.

lever-pressing—their memory not only returns but extends dramatically, to about 17 weeks (Hildreth, Sweeney, & Rovee-Collier, 2003). Furthermore, with just five widely spaced adult-provided reminders of the train task scheduled over 1½ years, babies trained at age 6 months still remembered the response after reaching their second birthday (Hartshorn, 2003).

At first, infants' memory for operant responses is highly *context dependent.* If 2- to 6-month-olds are not tested in the same situation in which they were trained—with the same mobile and crib bumper and in the same room—they remember poorly (Hayne, 2004; Hayne & Rovee-Collier, 1995). This specificity of infant memory also applies to imitation; young babies will imitate adult-modeled actions on a toy only when given a toy identical in color and features to the one the adult used. After 9 months, the importance of context declines. Older infants and toddlers remember how to push a button to make a toy train move or how to make a toy animal emit a sound even when the toy's features are altered and testing takes place in a different room (Hartshorn et al., 1998a; Hayne, Boniface, & Barr, 2000; Learmonth, Lamberth, & Rovee-Collier, 2004). Crawling is strongly associated with 9-month-olds' formation of an increasingly context-free memory (Herbert, Gross, & Hayne, 2007). As babies move on their own and experience frequent changes in context, they apply learned responses more flexibly, generalizing them to relevant new situations.

As Chapter 6 will make clear, operant conditioning has also been used to study babies' ability to group similar stimuli into categories. It plays a vital role in the formation of social relationships as well. As the baby gazes into the adult's eyes, the adult looks and smiles back, and then the infant looks and smiles again. The behavior of each partner reinforces the other, so both continue their pleasurable interaction. In Chapter 10, we will see that this contingent responsiveness contributes to the development of infant–caregiver attachment.

Habituation   At birth, the human brain is set up to be attracted to novelty. Infants tend to respond more strongly to a new element that has entered their environment, an inclination that ensures that they will continually add to their knowledge base. **Habituation** refers to a gradual reduction in the strength of a response due to repetitive stimulation. Looking, heart rate, and respiration rate may all decline, indicating a loss of interest. Once this has occurred, a new stimulus—a change in the environment—causes the habituated response to return to a high level, an increase called **recovery.** For example, when you walk through a familiar space, you notice things that are new or different—a recently hung picture on the wall or a piece of furniture that has been moved. Habituation and recovery make learning more efficient by focusing our attention on those aspects of the environment we know least about.

Window into Early Attention, Memory, and Knowledge.   Researchers studying infants' understanding of the world rely on habituation and recovery more than any other learning capacity. For example, a baby who first *habituates* to a visual pattern (a photo of a baby) and then *recovers* to a new one (a photo of a bald man) appears to remember the first stimulus and perceive the second one as new and different from it. This method of studying infant attention, perception, and memory, illustrated in Figure 4.4a, can be used with newborns, including preterm infants (Kavsek & Bornstein, 2010). It has even been used to study the fetus's sensitivity to external stimuli—for example, by measuring changes in fetal heart rate when various repeated sounds are presented (Dirix et al., 2009). Habituation to an auditory stimulus is evident in the third trimester of pregnancy.

Preterm and newborn babies require a long time—about three or four minutes—to habituate and recover to novel visual stimuli. By 4 or 5 months, however, they need as little as 5 to 10 seconds to take in a complex visual stimulus and recognize it as different from a previous one. Yet a fascinating exception to this trend exists: Two-month-olds actually take

FIGURE 4.4   Using habituation to study infant perception and memory. In the habituation phase, infants view a photo of a baby until their looking declines. In the test phase, infants are again shown the baby photo, but this time it appears alongside a photo of a bald-headed man. (a) When the test phase occurs soon after the habituation phase (within minutes, hours, or days, depending on the age of the infants), participants who remember the baby face and distinguish it from the man's face show a *novelty preference;* they recover to the new stimulus. (b) When the test phase is delayed for weeks or months, infants who continue to remember the baby face shift to a *familiarity preference;* they recover to the familiar baby face rather than to the novel man's face.

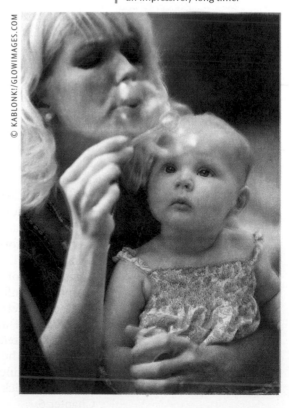

(a) **Novelty Preference**
(Recovery to a new stimulus)
Assesses Recent Memory

(b) **Familiarity Preference**
(Recovery to the familiar stimulus)
Assesses Remote Memory

longer to habituate to novel visual forms than do newborns and older infants (Colombo, 2002). Later we will see that 2 months is also a time of dramatic gains in visual perception. Perhaps when young babies are first able to perceive certain information, they require more time to take it in. Another factor contributing to the long habituation times of young babies is their difficulty disengaging attention from a stimulus. By 4 months, attention becomes more flexible—a change believed to be due to development of structures in the cerebral cortex controlling eye movements (Blaga & Colombo, 2006; Posner & Rothbart, 2007a). (Nevertheless, as will be apparent shortly, a few babies continue to have trouble shifting attention.)

Recovery to a new stimulus, or *novelty preference,* assesses infants' *recent memory.* **TAKE A MOMENT...** Think about what happens when you return to a place you have not seen for a long time. Instead of attending to novelty, you are likely to focus on aspects that are familiar: "I recognize that. I've been here before!" Like adults, infants shift from a novelty preference to a familiarity preference as more time intervenes between the habituation and test phases in research. That is, babies recover to the familiar stimulus rather than to a novel stimulus (see Figure 4.4b) (Bahrick & Pickens, 1995; Courage & Howe, 1998; Flom & Bahrick, 2010; Richmond, Colombo, & Hayne, 2007). By focusing on that shift, researchers can also use habituation to assess *remote memory,* or memory for stimuli to which infants were exposed weeks or months earlier.

With age, infants detect and remember an extraordinarily wide range of stimuli from the constantly changing flow of objects, actions, and events in their surroundings. They are especially attentive to the movements of objects and people, and they retain such information over many weeks. In one study, 5½-month-old babies habituated to a video in which they saw the face of a woman performing an action (either brushing teeth, blowing bubbles, or brushing hair) (Bahrick, Gogate, & Ruiz, 2002). In a test phase one minute later and again after a seven-week delay, infants watched the familiar video next to a novel video, in which the action changed while the woman's face remained the same. As Figure 4.5 on page 144 indicates, infants clearly remembered the action. At one minute, most showed a *novelty preference,* looking longer at the new action than the old action. But at seven weeks, most showed a *familiarity preference,* looking longer at the familiar action than the new action. In fact, the babies were so attentive to the woman's action that they ignored her face! In an additional test phase assessing face recognition in a novel video (the woman's face changed while her original action remained the same), infants showed no facial preference.

These findings, and others in this chapter, confirm that infants find motion so captivating that they attend to and remember an action far better than the features of the person engaging in it! Later we also will see that

A 5-month-old watches intently as his mother blows bubbles. Infants are captivated by people's actions and remember them for an impressively long time.

© KABLONK!/GLOWIMAGES.COM

FIGURE 4.5 Infants' recent and remote memory for human actions. Infants 5½ months old habituated to a video that showed the face of a woman while she performed an action, such as brushing teeth. In two test phases, they saw the familiar video next to a novel video, in which the action changed—for example, to brushing hair—while the woman's face remained the same. In the *immediate test phase* (one minute later), which assessed *recent memory,* infants displayed a novelty preference; they looked longer at the novel action than the familiar action. In the delayed test phase (seven weeks later), which assessed *remote memory,* infants showed a *familiarity preference;* they looked longer at the familiar action than the novel action. These findings reveal that young infants remember human actions for an impressively long time. (Adapted from Bahrick, Gogate, & Ruiz, 2002.)

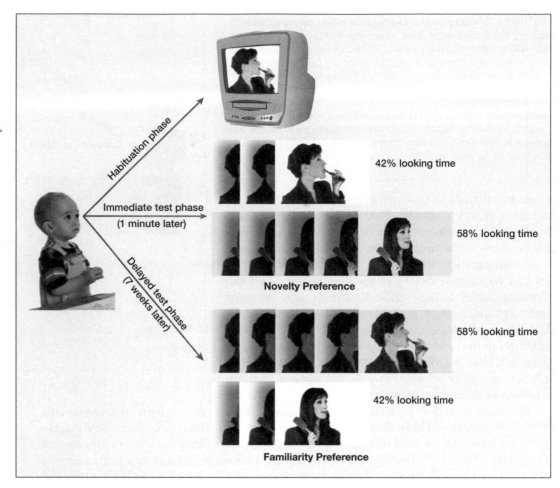

babies are excellent at discriminating faces in static displays (such as the ones in Figure 4.4). However, infants' memory for the faces of unfamiliar people and for other static patterns is short-lived—at 3 months, only about 24 hours, and at the end of the first year, several days to a few weeks (Fagan, 1973; Pascalis, de Haan, & Nelson, 1998). In comparison, 3-month-olds' memory for the unusual movements of objects (such as a metal nut tied to the end of a string, swinging back and forth) persists for at least three months (Bahrick, Hernandez-Reif, & Pickens, 1997).

Note that in habituation research, infants retain certain information over much longer time spans than they do in operant conditioning studies (refer again to Figure 4.3 on page 141). Clearly, infants learn and remember a great deal just by watching objects and events around them. They need not be physically active to acquire new information (although, as will become clear later, motor activity facilitates certain aspects of perception and cognition).

Habituation and recovery have been used to assess a wide range of infant perceptual and cognitive capacities—speech perception, musical and visual pattern perception, object perception, categorization, and knowledge of the social world. These studies reveal yet another disparity with operant conditioning research: When assessed through habituation, infant learning is not as *context dependent.* In this and subsequent chapters, we will see many examples of infants' *detection of relationships*—for example, speech sounds that often occur together, objects that belong to the same category, and the match between an object's rhythm and tempo of movement and its sounds. As early as 3 months, infants use their current awareness of relationships to make sense of new information (Bahrick, 2010).

Despite the strengths of habituation research, its findings are not clear-cut. When looking, sucking, or heart rate declines and recovers, what babies actually know about the stimuli to which they responded is sometimes uncertain. We will return to this difficulty in Chapter 6.

Habituation and Later Mental Development. Habituation and recovery to visual stimuli are among the earliest available predictors of intelligence in childhood, adolescence, and young adulthood. Correlations between the speed of these responses in infancy and the mental test scores of 3- to 21-year-olds consistently range from the .30s to the .60s (Fagan, Holland, & Wheeler, 2007; Kavsek, 2004; McCall & Carriger, 1993). In one study, the speed with which fetal startle reactions in the third trimester of pregnancy declined to a repeatedly presented loud sound was modestly associated with cognitive performance (assessed through recovery to novel photos of human faces) at 6 and 9 months of age (Gaultney & Gingras, 2005).

Habituation and recovery seem to be an especially effective early index of intelligence because they assess memory as well as quickness and flexibility of thinking, which underlie intelligent behavior at all ages. Compared with infants who habituate and recover quickly, infants who are "long lookers" on these tasks have difficulty redirecting their attention from one spot to another. Instead of taking in the overall arrangement of a stimulus followed by its finer details, they get stuck on certain small features and, consequently, process much less information (Colombo, 2002; Colombo et al., 2004). When researchers used a red spotlight to induce 5-month-old long lookers to attend to all parts of a complex design, the babies changed their approach and scanned visual stimuli just as "short lookers" do. As a result, they improved in discrimination and memory for visual stimuli (Jankowski, Rose, & Feldman, 2001). Investigators have yet to explore the impact of such early intervention on intellectual development.

So far, we have considered only one type of memory—*recognition.* It is the simplest form of memory: All the baby has to do is indicate (by looking, kicking, or pressing a lever) whether a new stimulus is identical or similar to a previous one. A second, more challenging form of memory is *recall*—remembering something not present. Can infants engage in recall? By the middle of the first year, they can, as indicated by their ability to find hidden objects and imitate the actions of others hours or days after they observed the behavior. We will take up recall in Chapter 7.

Newborn Imitation Babies come into the world with a primitive ability to learn through **imitation**—by copying the behavior of another person. For example, Figure 4.6 shows a human newborn imitating two adult facial expressions (Meltzoff & Moore, 1977). The newborn's capacity to imitate extends to certain gestures, such as head and index-finger movements, and has been demonstrated in many ethnic groups and cultures (Meltzoff & Kuhl, 1994; Nagy et al., 2005). As the figure reveals, even newborn chimpanzees, our closest evolutionary ancestors, imitate some behaviors (Myowa-Yamakoshi et al., 2004).

Although newborns' capacity to imitate is widely accepted, a few studies have failed to reproduce the human findings (see Anisfeld, 2005). And because newborn mouth and tongue movements occur with increased frequency to almost any arousing change in stimulation (such as lively music or flashing lights), some researchers argue that certain newborn "imitative" responses are actually mouthing—a common early exploratory response to interesting stimuli (Jones, 2009). Furthermore, imitation is harder to induce in babies 2 to 3 months old than just after birth. Therefore, skeptics believe that the newborn imitative capacity is little more than an automatic response that declines with age, much like a reflex (Heyes, 2005).

FIGURE 4.6 Imitation by human and chimpanzee newborns. The human infants in the middle row imitating (left) tongue protrusion and (right) mouth opening are 2 to 3 weeks old. The chimpanzee imitating both facial expressions is 2 weeks old. (From A. N. Meltzoff & M. K. Moore, 1977, "Imitation of Facial and Manual Gestures by Human Neonates," *Science, 198,* p. 75. Reprinted by permission of the publisher and A. N. Meltzoff. And from M. Myowa-Yamakoshi et al., 2004, "Imitation in Neonatal Chimpanzees [Pan Troglodytes]." *Developmental Science, 7,* p. 440. Copyright © 1977 by AAAS, copyright 2004 by Blackwell Publishing. Reprinted by permission.)

Others claim that newborns imitate a variety of facial expressions and head movements with effort and determination, even after short delays—when the adult is no longer demonstrating the behavior (Hayne, 2002; Meltzoff & Moore, 1999). Furthermore, these investigators argue that imitation—unlike reflexes—does not decline. Human babies several months old often do not imitate an adult's behavior right away because they first try to play familiar social games—mutual gazing, cooing, smiling, and waving their arms. But when an adult models a gesture repeatedly, older human infants soon get down to business and imitate (Meltzoff & Moore, 1994). Similarly, imitation declines in baby chimps around 9 weeks of age, when mother–baby mutual gazing and other face-to-face exchanges increase.

According to Andrew Meltzoff, newborns imitate much as older children and adults do—by actively trying to match body movements they *see* with ones they *feel* themselves make (Meltzoff, 2007). Later we will encounter evidence that young infants are remarkably adept at coordinating information across sensory systems.

Indeed, scientists have identified specialized cells in many areas of the cerebral cortex of primates—called **mirror neurons**—that underlie these capacities. Mirror neurons fire identically when a primate hears or sees an action and when it carries out that action on its own (Rizzolatti & Craighero, 2004). Brain-imaging studies confirm that human adults have especially elaborate systems of mirror neurons, which enable us to observe another person's behavior (such as smiling or throwing a ball) while simulating the behavior in our own brain. Mirror neurons are believed to be the biological basis of a variety of interrelated, complex social abilities, including imitation, empathic sharing of emotions, and understanding others' intentions (Iacoboni, 2009; Schulte-Ruther et al., 2007).

Brain-imaging findings support a functioning mirror-neuron system as early as 6 months of age. Using NIRS, researchers found that the same motor areas of the cerebral cortex were activated in 6-month-olds and in adults when they observed a model engage in a behavior that could be imitated (tapping a box to make a toy pop out) as when they themselves engaged in a motor action (Shimada & Hiraki, 2006). In contrast, when infants and adults observed an object that appeared to move on its own, without human intervention (a ball hanging from the ceiling on a string, swinging like a pendulum), motor areas were not activated.

Still, Meltzoff's view of newborn imitation as a flexible, voluntary capacity remains controversial. Mirror neurons, though possibly functional at birth, undergo an extended period of development (Bertenthal & Longo, 2007; Lepage & Théoret, 2007). Similarly, as we will see in Chapter 6, the capacity to imitate expands greatly over the first two years. But however limited it is at birth, imitation is a powerful means of learning—far faster than individual trial-and-error and discovery (Meltzoff et al., 2009). Using imitation, young infants explore their social world, not only learning from other people but getting to know them by matching their behavioral states. As babies notice similarities between their own and others' actions, they experience other people as "like me" and, thus, learn about themselves (Meltzoff, 2007). In this way, infant imitation may serve as the foundation for understanding others' thoughts and feelings, which we will take up in Chapters 10 and 11. Finally, caregivers take great pleasure in a baby who imitates their facial gestures and actions, which helps get the infant's relationship with parents off to a good start.

ASK YOURSELF

Review ■ Provide an example of classical conditioning, of operant conditioning, and of habituation/recovery in young infants. Why is each type of learning useful? Cite differences between operant conditioning and habituation findings on infant memory.

Connect ■ How do the diverse capacities of newborn babies contribute to their first social relationships? List as many examples as you can.

Apply ■ After a difficult birth, 2-day-old Kelly scores poorly on the NBAS. How would you address her mother's concern that Kelly might not develop normally?

Reflect ■ What is your attitude toward parent–infant cosleeping? Is it influenced by your cultural background?

Motor Development in Infancy

Virtually all parents eagerly await mastery of new motor skills, recording with pride when their infants first hold up their heads, reach for objects, sit by themselves, and walk alone. Parents' are understandably excited about these achievements, which allow babies to master their bodies and the environment in new ways. For example, sitting upright gives infants a new perspective on the world. Reaching permits babies to find out about objects by acting on them. And when infants can move on their own, their opportunities for exploration multiply.

Babies' motor achievements have a powerful effect on their social relationships. Once infants can crawl, parents start to restrict their activities by saying "no" and expressing mild impatience. Walking often brings the first "testing of wills" (Biringen et al., 1995). Despite her parents' warnings, one newly walking 12-month-old continued to pull items from shelves that were off limits. "I said, 'Don't do that!'" her mother would repeat firmly, taking her toddler's hand and redirecting her attention.

At the same time, newly walking babies more actively attend to and initiate social interaction—seeking out parents for greetings, hugs, or a gleeful game of hide-and-seek, and reaching for, pointing at, and carrying objects of interest to adults (Clearfield, Osborne, & Mullen, 2008; Karasik et al., 2011). Parents, in turn, increase their use of language, playful activities, and expressions of affection. Certain motor skills, such as reaching and pointing, enable infants to communicate more effectively. And when babies encounter risky situations, such as sloping walkways or dangerous objects, parents intervene, combining emotional warnings with rich verbal and gestural information that help infants notice critical features of their surroundings, regulate motor actions, and acquire language (Campos et al., 2000; Karasik et al., 2008). Finally, babies' delight—laughing, smiling, and babbling—as they work on new motor skills triggers pleasurable reactions in others, which encourage infants' efforts further (Mayes & Zigler, 1992). Motor, social, cognitive, and language competencies develop together and support one another.

The Sequence of Motor Development

Gross-motor development refers to control over actions that help infants get around in the environment, such as crawling, standing, and walking. *Fine-motor development* has to do with smaller movements, such as reaching and grasping. The Milestones table on page 148 shows the average age at which U.S. infants and toddlers achieve a variety of gross- and fine-motor skills. It also presents the age range during which most babies accomplish each skill, indicating large individual differences in *rate* of motor progress. Also, a baby who is a late reacher will not necessarily be a late crawler or walker. We would be concerned about a child's development only if many motor skills were seriously delayed.

Historically, researchers assumed that motor skills were separate, innate abilities that emerged in a fixed sequence governed by a built-in maturational timetable. This view has long been discredited. Rather, motor skills are interrelated. Each is a product of earlier motor attainments and a contributor to new ones. And children acquire motor skills in highly individual ways. For example, most Western babies crawl before they pull to a stand and walk. Yet one infant I know, who disliked being placed on her tummy but enjoyed sitting and being held upright, pulled to a stand and walked before she crawled! Babies display such skills as rolling, sitting, crawling, and walking in diverse orders rather than in the sequence implied by motor norms (Adolph, Karasik, & Tamis-LeMonda, 2010).

Many influences—both internal and external to the child—join together to influence the vast transformations in motor competencies of the first two years. The *dynamic systems perspective,* introduced in Chapter 1 (see page 30), helps us understand how motor development takes place.

▶ How does the dynamic systems perspective explain motor development?

▶ Identify factors that influence gross- and fine-motor development during the first two years.

Milestones

Some Gross- and Fine-Motor Attainments of the First Two Years

MOTOR SKILL	AVERAGE AGE ACHIEVED	AGE RANGE IN WHICH 90 PERCENT OF INFANTS ACHIEVE THE SKILL
When held upright, holds head erect and steady	6 weeks	3 weeks–4 months
When prone, lifts self by arms	2 months	3 weeks–4 months
Rolls from side to back	2 months	3 weeks–5 months
Grasps cube	3 months, 3 weeks	2–7 months
Rolls from back to side	4½ months	2–7 months
Sits alone	7 months	5–9 months
Crawls	7 months	5–11 months
Pulls to stand	8 months	5–12 months
Plays pat-a-cake	9 months, 3 weeks	7–15 months
Stands alone	11 months	9–16 months
Walks alone	11 months, 3 weeks	9–17 months
Builds tower of two cubes	11 months, 3 weeks	10–19 months
Scribbles vigorously	14 months	10–21 months
Walks up stairs with help	16 months	12–23 months
Jumps in place	23 months, 2 weeks	17–30 months
Walks on tiptoe	25 months	16–30 months

Note: These milestones represent overall age trends. Individual differences exist in the precise age at which each milestone is attained.

Sources: Bayley, 1969, 1993, 2005.

Photos: (top) © Laura Dwight Photography; (middle) © Laura Dwight Photography; (bottom) © David Young-Wolff/PhotoEdit

Motor Skills as Dynamic Systems

According to **dynamic systems theory of motor development,** mastery of motor skills involves acquiring increasingly complex *systems of action.* When motor skills work as a system, separate abilities blend together, each cooperating with others to produce more effective ways of exploring and controlling the environment. For example, control of the head and upper chest combine into sitting with support. Kicking, rocking on all fours, and reaching combine to become crawling. Then crawling, standing, and stepping are united into walking (Adolph & Berger, 2006; Thelen, 1989).

Each new skill is a joint product of the following factors: (1) central nervous system development, (2) the body's movement capacities, (3) the goals the child has in mind, and (4) environmental supports for the skill. Change in any element makes the system less stable, and the child starts to explore and select new, more effective motor patterns. The factors that induce change vary with age. In the early weeks of life, brain and body growth are especially important as infants achieve control over the head, shoulders, and upper torso. Later, the baby's goals (getting a toy or crossing the room) and environmental supports (parental encouragement, objects in the infant's everyday setting) play a greater role.

The broader physical environment also profoundly influences motor skills. Infants with stairs in their home learn to crawl up stairs at an earlier age and also more readily master a back-descent strategy—the safest but also the most challenging position because the baby must turn around at the top, give up visual guidance of her goal, and crawl backward (Berger, Theuring, & Adolph, 2007). And if children were reared on the moon, with its reduced gravity, they would prefer jumping to walking or running!

When a skill is first acquired, infants must refine it. For example, one baby, just starting to crawl, often collapsed on her tummy and moved backward instead of forward. Soon she figured out how to propel herself forward by alternately pulling with her arms and pushing with her feet, "belly-crawling" in various ways for several weeks (Vereijken & Adolph, 1999). As they attempt a new skill, most babies move back and forth between its presence and absence: An infant might roll over, sit, crawl, or take a few steps on Monday but not do so again until Friday, and then not again until the following week. And related, previously mastered skills often become less secure. As the novice walker experiments with balancing the body vertically over two small moving feet, balance during sitting may become temporarily less stable (Adolph & Berger, 2006; Chen et al., 2007). This variability is evidence of loss of stability in the system—in dynamic systems theory, a necessary transition between a less mature and a more mature, stable state.

Furthermore, motor mastery involves intense practice. In learning to walk, toddlers practice six or more hours a day, traveling the length of 29 football fields! Gradually their small, unsteady steps change to a longer stride, their feet move closer together, their toes point to the front, and their legs become symmetrically coordinated (Adolph, Vereijken, & Shrout, 2003). As movements are repeated thousands of times, they promote new connections in the brain that govern motor patterns.

Dynamic systems theory shows us why motor development cannot be genetically determined. Because it is motivated by exploration and the desire to master new tasks, heredity can map it out only at a general level. Rather than being *hardwired* into the nervous system, behaviors are *softly assembled,* allowing for different paths to the same motor skill (Adolph, 2008; Thelen & Smith, 2006).

Dynamic Motor Systems in Action To find out how infants acquire motor capacities, researchers conduct *microgenetic studies* (see Chapter 2, page 64), following babies from their first attempts at a skill until it becomes smooth and effortless. Using this research strategy, James Galloway and Esther Thelen (2004) held sounding toys alternately in front of infants' hands and feet, from the time they first showed interest until they engaged in well-coordinated reaching and grasping. As Figure 4.7 shows, the infants violated the normative sequence of arm and hand control preceding leg and foot control, shown in the Milestones table on page 148. They first explored the toys with their feet—as early as 8 weeks of age, at least a month before reaching with their hands!

Why did babies reach "feet first"? Because the hip joint constrains the legs to move less freely than the shoulder constrains the arms, infants could more easily control their leg movements. Consequently, foot reaching required far less practice than hand reaching. As these findings confirm, rather than following a strict, predetermined cephalocaudal pattern, the order in which motor skills develop depends on the anatomy of the body part being used, the surrounding environment, and the baby's efforts.

This baby scales a staircase purposefully, determined to reach the top. Still a novice stair climber, she is likely to repeat the ascent many times, experimenting with the skill until her speed and coordination improve.

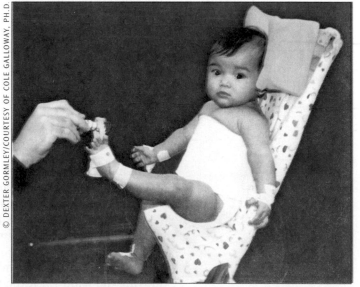

FIGURE 4.7 Reaching "feet first." When sounding toys were held in front of babies' hands and feet, they reached with their feet as early as 8 weeks of age, a month or more before they reached with their hands— a clear violation of the cephalocaudal pattern. Reduced freedom of movement in the hip joint makes leg movements easier to control than arm movements. This 2½-month-old skillfully explores an object with her foot.

LOOK and LISTEN

Spend an hour observing a newly crawling or walking baby. Note the goals that motivate the baby to move, along with the baby's effort and motor experimentation. Describe parenting behaviors and features of the environment that promote mastery of the skill.

Cultural Variations in Motor Development Cross-cultural research further illustrates how early movement opportunities and a stimulating environment contribute to motor development. Half a century ago, Wayne Dennis (1960) observed infants in Iranian orphanages who were deprived of the tantalizing surroundings that induce infants to acquire motor skills. These babies spent their days lying on their backs in cribs, without toys to play with. As a result, most did not move on their own until after 2 years of age. When they finally did move, the constant experience of lying on their backs led them to scoot in a sitting position rather than crawl on their hands and knees. Because babies who scoot come up against objects such as furniture with their feet, not their hands, they are far less likely to pull themselves to a standing position in preparation for walking. Indeed, by 3 to 4 years of age, only 15 percent of the Iranian orphans were walking alone.

Cultural variations in infant-rearing practices affect motor development. **TAKE A MOMENT...** Take a quick survey of several parents you know, asking this question: Should sitting, crawling, and walking be deliberately encouraged? Answers vary widely from culture to culture. Japanese mothers, for example, believe such efforts are unnecessary because children "just learn" (Seymour, 1999). Among the Zinacanteco Indians of southern Mexico and Gusii of Kenya, rapid motor progress is actively discouraged. Babies who walk before they know enough to keep away from cooking fires and weaving looms are viewed as dangerous to themselves and disruptive to others (Greenfield, 1992).

In contrast, among the Kipsigis of Kenya and the West Indians of Jamaica, babies hold their heads up, sit alone, and walk considerably earlier than North American infants. In both societies, parents emphasize early motor maturity, practicing formal exercises to stimulate particular skills (Adolph, Karasik, & Tamis-LeMonda, 2010). In the first few months, babies are seated in holes dug in the ground, with rolled blankets to keep them upright. Walking is promoted by frequently standing babies in adults' laps, bouncing them on their feet, and exercising the stepping reflex (see page 130) (Hopkins & Westra, 1988; Super, 1981). As parents in these cultures support babies in upright postures and rarely put them down on the floor, their infants usually skip crawling—a motor skill regarded as crucial in Western nations!

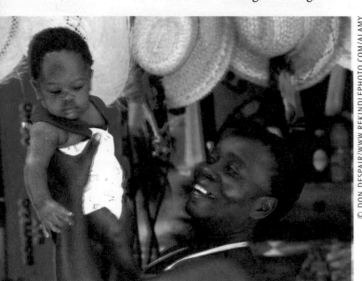

This West Indian mother of Jamaica "walks" her baby up her body in a deliberate effort to promote early mastery of walking.

© DON DESPAIR/WWW.REKINDLEPHOTO.COM/ALAMY

Finally, because it decreases exposure to "tummy time," the current Western practice of having babies sleep on their backs to protect them from SIDS (see page 136) delays gross-motor milestones of rolling, sitting, and crawling (Majnemer & Barr, 2005; Scrutton, 2005). To prevent these delays, caregivers can regularly expose babies to the tummy-lying position during waking hours.

Fine-Motor Development: Reaching and Grasping

Of all motor skills, reaching may play the greatest role in infant cognitive development. By grasping things, turning them over, and seeing what happens when they are released, infants learn a great deal about the sights, sounds, and feel of objects.

Reaching and grasping, like many other motor skills, start out as gross, diffuse activity and move toward mastery of fine movements. Figure 4.8 illustrates some milestones of reaching over the first nine months. Newborns will actively work to bring their hands into their field of vision: In a dimly lit room, they keep their hand within a narrow beam of light, moving the hand when the light beam moves (van der Meer, 1997). Newborns also make poorly coordinated swipes, called **prereaching,** toward an object in front of them, but because of poor arm and hand control they rarely contact the object. Like newborn reflexes, prereaching drops out around 7 weeks of age, when babies improve in eye movements involved in tracking and fixating on objects, which are essential for accurate reaching. Yet these early behaviors suggest that infants are biologically prepared to coordinate hand with eye in the act of exploring (Rosander & von Hofsten, 2002; von Hofsten, 2004).

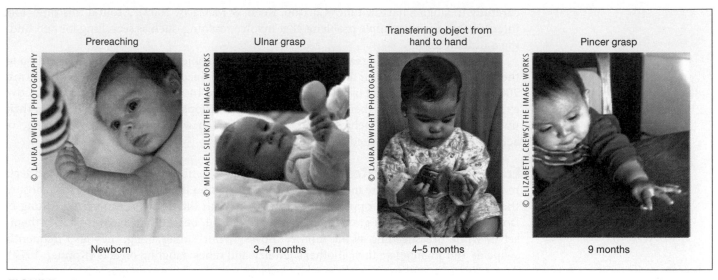

FIGURE 4.8 **Some milestones of reaching and grasping.** The average age at which each skill is attained is given. (Ages from Bayley, 1969; Rochat, 1989.)

Development of Reaching and Grasping At about 3 to 4 months, as infants develop the necessary eye, head, and shoulder control, reaching reappears as purposeful, forward arm movements in the presence of a nearby toy and gradually improves in accuracy (Bhat, Heathcock, & Galloway, 2005; Spencer et al., 2000). By 5 to 6 months, infants reach for an object in a room that has been darkened during the reach by switching off the lights—a skill that improves over the next few months (Clifton et al., 1994; McCarty & Ashmead, 1999). This indicates that the baby does not need to use vision to guide the arms and hands in reaching. Rather, reaching is largely controlled by *proprioception*—our sense of movement and location in space, arising from stimuli within the body. When vision is freed from the basic act of reaching, it can focus on more complex adjustments, such as fine-tuning actions to fit the distance and shape of objects.

Reaching improves as depth perception advances and as infants gain greater control of body posture and arm and hand movements. Four-month-olds aim their reaches ahead of a moving object so they can catch it (von Hofsten, 1993). Around 5 months, babies reduce their efforts when an object is moved beyond their reach (Robin, Berthier, & Clifton, 1996). By 7 months, the arms become more independent: Infants reach for an object by extending one arm, rather than both (Fagard & Pezé, 1997). During the next few months, infants become more efficient at reaching for moving objects—ones that spin, change direction, and move sideways, closer, or farther away (Fagard, Spelke, & von Hofsten, 2009; Wentworth, Benson, & Haith, 2000).

Once infants can reach, they modify their grasp. The newborn's grasp reflex is replaced by the **ulnar grasp,** a clumsy motion in which the baby's fingers close against the palm. Still, even 4-month-olds adjust their grasp to the size and shape of an object—a capacity that improves over the first year as infants orient the hand more precisely and do so in advance of contacting the object (Barrett, Traupman, & Needham, 2008; Witherington, 2005). Around 4 to 5 months, when infants begin to sit up, both hands become coordinated in exploring objects. Babies of this age can hold an object in one hand while the other scans it with the tips of the fingers, and they frequently transfer objects from hand to hand (Rochat & Goubet, 1995). By the end of the first year, infants use the thumb and index finger in a well-coordinated **pincer grasp.** Then the ability to manipulate objects greatly expands. The 1-year-old can pick up raisins and blades of grass, turn knobs, and open and close small boxes.

Between 8 and 11 months, reaching and grasping are well-practiced. As a result, attention is released from the motor skill to events that occur before and after obtaining the object. For example, 10-month-olds easily modify their reach to anticipate their next action. They reach for a ball faster when they intend to throw it than when they intend to drop it carefully through a narrow tube (Claxton, Keen, & McCarty, 2003). Around this time, too, infants begin to solve simple problems that involve reaching, such as searching for and finding a hidden toy.

Finally, the capacity to reach for and manipulate an object increases infants' attention to the way an adult reaches for and plays with that same object (Hauf, Aschersleben, & Prinz, 2007). Perhaps with the aid of mirror neurons (see page 146), babies match their own active experience of reaching to their perception of others' actions. As a result, they broaden their understanding of others' behaviors and—as they watch what others do—of the range of actions that can be performed on various objects.

Early Experience and Reaching   Like other motor milestones, early experience affects reaching. In cultures where mothers carry their infants on their hips or in slings for most of the day, babies have rich opportunities to explore with their hands. Among the !Kung of Botswana, Africa, infants grasp their mothers' colorful, beaded necklaces to steady themselves while breastfeeding as the mother moves. While riding along, they also frequently swipe at and manipulate their mother's jewelry and other dangling objects (Konner, 1977). As a result, !Kung infants are advanced in development of reaching and grasping. And because babies of Mali and Uganda spend half or more of their day held in sitting or standing positions, which facilitate reaching, they, too, develop manual skills earlier than Western infants, who spend much of their day lying down (Adolph, Karasik, & Tamis-LeMonda, 2010).

Babies' visual surroundings are also influential. In a well-known study, institutionalized infants given a moderate amount of visual stimulation—at first, simple designs and, later, a mobile hung over their crib—reached for objects six weeks earlier than infants given nothing to look at. A third group given massive stimulation—patterned crib bumpers and mobiles at an early age—also reached sooner than unstimulated babies. But this heavy enrichment took a toll: These infants looked away and cried a great deal, and they were less advanced in reaching than the moderately stimulated group (White & Held, 1966). These findings remind us that more stimulation is not necessarily better. Trying to push infants beyond their current readiness to handle stimulation can undermine the development of important motor skills. We will return to this theme at the end of this chapter, and in Chapter 5, where we consider brain development.

ASK YOURSELF

Review ■ Cite evidence that motor development is a joint product of biological, psychological, and environmental factors.

Connect ■ Provide several examples of how motor development supports infants' attainment of cognitive and social competencies.

Apply ■ List everyday experiences that promote infants' mastery of reaching, grasping, sitting, and crawling. Why should caregivers place young infants in a variety of waking-time body positions?

Reflect ■ Do you favor early, systematic training of infants in motor skills such as crawling, walking, and stair climbing? Why or why not?

▶ Describe the newborn baby's sensitivity to touch, taste, smell, and sound, noting changes during infancy.

▶ Describe the development of vision in infancy, with special emphasis on depth, pattern, face, and object perception.

Perceptual Development in Infancy

TAKE A MOMENT... List research findings in previous sections that illustrate the close link between perception and action in babies' discovery of new skills. To reach for and manipulate objects, maintain balance, or move across various surfaces, infants must continually coordinate their motor behavior with perceptual information. Acting and perceiving are not separate aspects of experience. Instead, motor activity is a vital means for exploring and learning about the world, and improved perception brings about more effective motor activity. The union of perceptual and motor information is basic to our nervous systems, and each domain supports development of the other (Adolph & Berger, 2006; von Hofsten, 2004).

What can young infants perceive with their senses, and how does perception change with age? Researchers have sought answers to these questions for two reasons. First, studies of infant perception reveal in what ways babies are biologically prepared to perceive their world, and how brain development and experience expand their capacities. Second, infant perception sheds light on other aspects of development. For example, because touch, vision, and hearing enable us to interact with others, they are basic to emotional and social development. Through hearing, language is learned. And because knowledge of the world is first gathered through the senses, perception provides the foundation for cognitive development.

Studying infant perception is especially challenging because babies cannot describe their experiences. Fortunately, investigators can make use of a variety of nonverbal responses that vary with stimulation, such as looking, sucking, head turning, facial expressions, and reaching. As noted earlier, researchers also rely on operant conditioning and habituation to find out whether infants can make certain discriminations. And eye-movement tracking, in which researchers examine infants' inspection of stimuli, attention to particular features, and gaze-shifting as stimuli move along various trajectories, has revealed much about infant visual capacities. Neurobiological measures—such as stimulus-induced changes in respiration, heart rate, and brain activity (using ERPs and NIRS)—are also used. We will see examples of these methods as we explore the baby's sensitivity to touch, taste, smell, sound, and visual stimulation.

▶ Describe how intermodal perception develops during infancy.

▶ How does differentiation theory explain perceptual development?

Touch

Touch is a fundamental means of interaction between parents and babies. Within the first few days, mothers can recognize their own newborn by stroking the infant's cheek or hand (Kaitz et al., 1993). Touch helps stimulate early physical growth (see Chapter 3), and it is vital for emotional development. Therefore, it is not surprising that sensitivity to touch is well-developed at birth.

The reflexes listed in Table 4.1 on page 130 reveal that the newborn baby responds to touch, especially around the mouth, on the palms, and on the soles of the feet. During the prenatal period, these areas, along with the genitals, are the first to become sensitive to touch (Humphrey, 1978; Streri, 2005).

At birth, infants are quite sensitive to pain. If male newborns are circumcised, anesthetic is sometimes not used because of the risk of giving drugs to a very young infant. Babies often respond to pain with a high-pitched, stressful cry and a dramatic rise in heart rate, blood pressure, palm sweating, pupil dilation, and muscle tension (Lehr et al., 2007; Warnock & Sandrin, 2004). Measures of brain activity during painful medical procedures, using ERP and NIRS, reveal that preterm and male babies show intense activation of sensorimotor areas in the cerebral cortex (Bartocci et al., 2006; Slater et al., 2010). Because of central nervous system immaturity, these infants seem to feel pain especially intensely.

Recent research establishing the safety of certain local anesthetics for newborns promises to ease the pain of medical procedures. Offering a nipple that delivers a sugar solution is also helpful; it quickly reduces crying and discomfort in young babies, preterm and full-term alike. Breast milk may be especially effective: Even the smell of the milk of the baby's mother reduces infant distress to a routine blood-test heelstick more effectively than the odor of another mother's milk or of formula (Nishitani et al., 2009). And combining sweet liquid with gentle holding by the parent lessens pain even more. Research on infant mammals indicates that physical touch releases *endorphins*—painkilling chemicals in the brain (Axelin, Salanterä, & Lehtonen, 2006; Gormally et al., 2001).

Allowing a baby to endure severe pain overwhelms the nervous system with stress hormones, which can disrupt the child's developing capacity to handle common, everyday stressors. The result is heightened pain sensitivity, sleep disturbances, feeding problems, and difficulty calming down when upset (Mitchell & Boss, 2002).

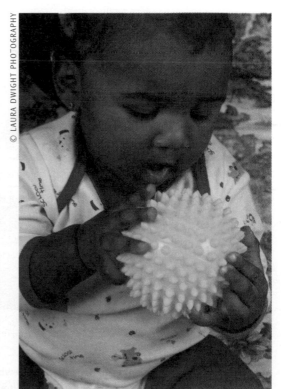

© LAURA DWIGHT PHOTOGRAPHY

This 6-month-old uses touch to investigate an object, turning the ball between her palms and examining its unusual texture with her fingertips while staring at it intently.

Gentle touching, in contrast, enhances babies' positive responsiveness to their physical and social surroundings. An adult's soft caresses induce infants to smile and become more attentive to the adult's face (Stack & Muir, 1992). And parents vary their style of touching, depending on whether the goal of their interaction is to comfort, convey affection, or induce smiling, attention, or play in their baby (Jean & Stack, 2009; Stack 2010).

Even newborns use touch to investigate their world. Using their palms, they can distinguish the shapes (prism versus cylinder) and textures (smooth versus rough) of small objects, as indicated by their tendency to hold on longer to an object with an unfamiliar shape or texture than to a familiar object (Sann & Streri, 2008; Streri, Lhote, & Dutilleul, 2000). As reaching develops, babies frequently run their lips and tongue over the surface of novel objects, then remove the object to look at it. This exploratory mouthing peaks in the middle of the first year as hand–mouth contact becomes more accurate (Lew & Butterworth, 1997). Then it declines in favor of more elaborate touching with the hands, in which infants turn, poke, and feel the surface of things while looking at them intently (Ruff et al., 1992).

Taste and Smell

Facial expressions reveal that newborns can distinguish several basic tastes. Like adults, they relax their facial muscles in response to sweetness, purse their lips when the taste is sour, and show a distinct archlike mouth opening when it is bitter (Steiner, 1979; Steiner et al., 2001). These reactions are important for survival: The food that best supports the infant's early growth is the sweet-tasting milk of the mother's breast. Not until 4 months do babies prefer a salty taste to plain water, a change that may prepare them to accept solid foods (Mennella & Beauchamp, 1998).

Nevertheless, newborns can readily learn to like a taste that at first evoked either a neutral or a negative response. For example, babies allergic to cow's-milk formula who are given a soy- or other vegetable-based substitute (typically very strong and bitter-tasting) soon prefer it to regular formula. A taste previously disliked can come to be preferred when it is paired with relief of hunger (Harris, 1997).

As with taste, certain odor preferences are present at birth. For example, the smell of bananas or chocolate causes a relaxed, pleasant facial expression, whereas the odor of rotten eggs makes the infant frown (Steiner, 1979). During pregnancy, the amniotic fluid is rich in tastes and smells that vary with the mother's diet—early experiences that influence newborns' preferences. In a study carried out in the Alsatian region of France, where anise is frequently used to flavor foods, researchers tested newborns for their reaction to the anise odor (Schaal, Marlier, & Soussignan, 2000). The mothers of some babies had regularly consumed anise during the last two weeks of pregnancy; the other mothers had never consumed it. When presented with the anise odor on the day of birth, the babies of the anise-consuming mothers spent more time turning toward the odor. In contrast, infants of non-anise-consuming mothers were far more likely to turn away with a negative facial expression (see Figure 4.9). These different reactions were still apparent four days later, even though all mothers had refrained from consuming anise during this time.

In many mammals, the sense of smell plays an important role in protecting the young from predators by helping mothers and babies identify each other. Although smell is less well-developed in humans, traces of its survival value remain.

Immediately after birth, infants placed face down between their mother's breasts spontaneously latch on to a nipple and begin sucking within an hour. If one breast is washed to remove its natural scent, most newborns move toward the

(a) Responses by newborns of anise-consuming mothers

(b) Responses by newborns of non-anise-consuming mothers

FIGURE 4.9 Examples of facial expressions of newborns exposed to the odor of anise whose mothers' diets differed in anise-flavored foods during late pregnancy. (a) Babies of anise-consuming mothers spent more time turning toward the odor and sucking, licking, and chewing. (b) Babies of non-anise-consuming mothers more often turned away with a negative facial expression. (From B. Schaal, L. Marlier, & R. Soussignan, 2000, "Human Foetuses Learn Odours from Their Pregnant Mother's Diet," *Chemical Senses, 25,* p. 731. © Oxford University Press 2000. Reprinted by permission of Oxford University Press.)

unwashed breast, indicating that they are guided by smell (Varendi & Porter, 2001). At 4 days of age, breastfed babies prefer the smell of their own mother's breast to that of an unfamiliar lactating woman (Cernoch & Porter, 1985). And both breast- and bottle-fed 3- to 4-day-olds orient more and display more mouthing to the smell of unfamiliar human milk than to formula milk, indicating that (even without postnatal exposure) the odor of human milk is more attractive to newborns (Marlier & Schaal, 2005). Newborns' dual attraction to the odors of their mother and of breast milk helps them locate an appropriate food source and, in the process, distinguish their caregiver from other people.

Hearing

Although conduction of sound through structures of the ear and transmission of auditory information to the brain are inefficient at birth, newborn infants can hear a wide variety of sounds—sensitivity that improves greatly over the first few months (Saffran, Werker, & Werner, 2006; Tharpe & Ashmead, 2001). Responsiveness to sound provides support for the young baby's exploration of the environment. Infants as young as 3 days old turn their eyes and head in the general direction of a sound. The ability to identify the precise location of a sound improves greatly over the first six months and shows further gains through the preschool years (Litovsky & Ashmead, 1997).

At birth, infants prefer complex sounds, such as noises and voices, to pure tones. And babies only a few days old can tell the difference between a variety of sound patterns: a series of tones arranged in ascending versus descending order; tone sequences with a rhythmic downbeat (as in music) versus those without; utterances with two versus three syllables; the stress patterns of words, such as "*ma*-ma" versus "ma-*ma*"; and even two languages spoken by the same bilingual speaker, as long as those languages differ in their rhythmic features—for example, French versus Russian (Mastropieri & Turkewitz, 1999; Ramus, 2002; Sansavini, Bertoncini, & Giovanelli, 1997; Trehub, 2001; Winkler et al., 2009).

Over the first year, infants organize sounds into increasingly elaborate patterns. Around 2 to 4 months, they can distinguish changes in tempo—the same tone sequence played slightly faster (Baruch & Drake, 1997). Between 4 and 7 months, they show a sense of musical phrasing. They prefer Mozart minuets with pauses between phrases to those with awkward breaks (Krumhansl & Jusczyk, 1990). Around 6 to 7 months, they can distinguish musical tunes on the basis of variations in rhythmic patterns, including beat structure (duple or triple) and accent structure (emphasis on the first note of every beat unit or at other positions) (Hannon & Johnson, 2004). And by the end of the first year, infants recognize the same melody when it is played in different keys (Trehub, 2001). As we will see shortly, 6- to 12-month-olds make comparable discriminations in human speech: They readily detect sound regularities that will facilitate later language learning.

Speech Perception Young infants listen longer to human speech than to structurally similar nonspeech sounds (Vouloumanos, 2010). And they can detect the sounds of any human language. Newborns make fine-grained distinctions among many speech sounds. For example, when given a nipple that turns on the "*ba*" sound, babies suck vigorously for a while and then habituate. When the sound switches to "*ga*," sucking picks up, indicating that infants detect this subtle difference. Using this method, researchers have found only a few speech sounds that newborns cannot discriminate. Their ability to perceive sounds not found in their own language is more precise than an adult's (Aldridge, Stillman, & Bower, 2001; Jusczyk & Luce, 2002).

TAKE A MOMENT... Listen carefully to yourself the next time you talk to a young baby. You will probably speak in ways that highlight important parts of the speech stream—use a slow, clear, high-pitched, expressive voice with a rising tone at the end of phrases and sentences and a pause before continuing. Adults probably communicate this way because they notice that infants are more attentive when they do so. Indeed, newborns prefer speech with these characteristics, in part because it eases their perceptual learning (Saffran, Werker, & Werner, 2006). In addition, they will suck more on a nipple to hear a recording of their own mother's voice than that of an unfamiliar woman and to hear their native language as opposed

BIOLOGY and ENVIRONMENT

"Tuning In" to Familiar Speech, Faces, and Music: A Sensitive Period for Culture-Specific Learning

To share experiences with members of their family and community, babies must become skilled at making perceptual discriminations that are meaningful in their culture. As we have seen, at first babies are sensitive to virtually all speech sounds, but around 6 months, they narrow their focus, limiting the distinctions they make to the language they hear and will soon learn to speak.

The ability to perceive faces shows a similar **perceptual narrowing effect**—perceptual sensitivity that becomes increasingly attuned with age to information most often encountered. After habituating to one member of each pair of faces in Figure 4.10, 6-month-olds were shown the familiar and novel faces side by side. For both pairs, they recovered to (looked longer

at) the novel face, indicating that they could discriminate individual faces of both humans and monkeys equally well (Pascalis, de Haan, & Nelson, 2002). But at 9 months, infants no longer showed a novelty preference when viewing the monkey pair. Like adults, they could distinguish only the human faces.

The perceptual narrowing effect appears again in musical rhythm perception. Western adults are accustomed to the even-beat pattern of Western music—repetition of the same rhythmic structure in every measure of a tune—and easily notice rhythmic changes that disrupt this familiar beat. But present them with music that does not follow this typical Western rhythmic form—Baltic folk tunes, for example—and they fail to pick up on rhythmic-pattern deviations. Six-month-olds, however, can detect such disruptions in both Western and non-Western melodies. But by 12 months, after added exposure to Western music, babies are no longer aware of deviations in foreign musical rhythms, although their sensitivity to Western rhythmic structure remains unchanged (Hannon & Trehub, 2005b).

Several weeks of regular interaction with a foreign-language speaker and of daily opportunities to listen to non-Western music fully restore 12-month-olds' sensitivity to wide-ranging speech sounds and music rhythms (Hannon & Trehub, 2005a; Kuhl, Tsao, & Liu, 2003). Similarly, 6-month-olds given three months of training in discriminating individual monkey faces, in which each image is labeled with a distinct name ("Carlos," "Iona") instead of the generic label "monkey," retain their ability to discriminate monkey faces at 9 months (Scott & Monesson, 2009). Adults given similar extensive experiences, by contrast, show little improvement in perceptual sensitivity.

Taken together, these findings suggest a heightened capacity—or sensitive period—in the second half of the first year, when babies are biologically prepared to "zero in" on socially meaningful perceptual distinctions. Notice how, between 6 and 12 months, learning is especially rapid across several domains (speech, faces, and music) and is easily modified by experience. This suggests a broad neurological change—perhaps a special time of brain development in which babies analyze everyday stimulation of all kinds similarly, in ways that prepare them to participate in their cultural community.

FIGURE 4.10 Discrimination of human and monkey faces. Which of these pairs is easiest for you to tell apart? After habituating to one of the photos in each pair, infants were shown the familiar and the novel face side-by-side. For both pairs, 6-month-olds recovered to (looked longer at) the novel face, indicating that they could discriminate human and monkey faces equally well. By 12 months, babies lost their ability to distinguish the monkey faces. Like adults, they showed a novelty preference only to human stimuli. (From O. Pascalis et al., 2002, "Is Face Processing Species-Specific During the First Year of Life?" *Science, 296,* p. 1322. Copyright © 2002 by AAAS. Reprinted with permission from AAAS.)

to a foreign language (Moon, Cooper, & Fifer, 1993; Spence & DeCasper, 1987). These preferences may have developed from hearing the muffled sounds of the mother's voice before birth.

Over the first year, infants learn much about the organization of sounds in their native language. As they listen to people talking, they learn to focus on meaningful sound variations. ERP brain-wave recordings reveal that around 5 months, babies become sensitive to syllable stress patterns in their own language (Weber et al., 2004). Between 6 and 8 months, they start to "screen out" sounds not used in their native tongue (Anderson, Morgan, & White, 2003; Polka & Werker, 1994). As the Biology and Environment box above explains, this increased responsiveness to native-language sounds is part of a general "tuning" process in the second half of the first year—a possible sensitive period in which babies acquire a range of perceptual skills for picking up socially important information.

Soon after, infants focus on larger speech units that are critical to figuring out meaning. They recognize familiar words in spoken passages and listen longer to speech with clear clause and phrase boundaries (Johnson & Seidl, 2008; Jusczyk & Hohne, 1997; Soderstrom et al., 2003). Around 7 to 9 months, infants extend this sensitivity to speech structure to individual words. They begin to divide the speech stream into wordlike units (Jusczyk, 2002; Saffran, Werker, & Werner, 2006).

Analyzing the Speech Stream   How do infants make such rapid progress in perceiving the structure of language? Research shows that they have an impressive **statistical learning capacity.** By analyzing the speech stream for patterns—repeatedly occurring sequences of sounds—they acquire a stock of speech structures for which they will later learn meanings, long before they start to talk around age 12 months.

In one set of studies, researchers had 8- and 9-month-olds listen to a continuous sequence of nonsense syllables. Then they gave the babies brief, new syllable sequences; some conformed to the syllable patterns in the original sequence, while others did not. The babies quickly inferred syllable structure: They preferred to listen to new speech that preserved the original syllable patterns. In other words, they listened for statistical regularities, discriminating syllables that often occur together (indicating that they belong to the same word) from syllables that seldom occur together (indicating a word boundary). To cite an English example, consider the word sequence *pretty#baby*. After listening to the speech stream for just one minute (about 60 words), babies can distinguish a word-internal syllable pair *(pretty)* from a word-external syllable pair *(ty#ba)* (Saffran, Aslin, & Newport, 1996; Saffran & Thiessen, 2003).

Once infants locate words, they focus on the words and (as we will see in Chapter 9) detect syllable-stress regularities—for example, in English and Dutch, that the onset of a strong syllable (*hap*-py, *rab*-bit) often signals a new word (Swingley, 2005; Thiessen & Saffran, 2007). By 10 months, infants can detect words that start with weak syllables, such as "sur*prise*," by listening for sound regularities before and after the words (Jusczyk, 2001; Kooijman, Hagoort, & Cutler, 2009).

Infants also attend to regularities in word sequences. In a study using nonsense words, 7-month-olds distinguished the ABA structure of "*ga ti ga*" and "*li na li*" from the ABB structure of "*wo fe fe*" and "*ta la la*" (Marcus et al., 1999). They seemed to detect simple word order rules—a capacity that may help them figure out basic grammar. After extracting these rules, babies generalize them to nonspeech sounds. Seven-month-olds who were exposed to regularities in sequences of nonsense words could identify similar patterns in strings of musical tones and animal sounds. But when presented alone, these stimuli yielded no rule learning (Marcus, Fernandes, & Johnson, 2007). Analyzing speech seems to help babies structure other aspects of their auditory world.

Clearly, babies have a powerful ability to extract regularities from complex, continuous speech. Some researchers believe infants are innately equipped with a general statistical learning capacity for detecting structure in the environment, which they also apply to visual stimulation (Kirkham, Slemmer, & Johnson, 2002). Indeed, because communication is often multisensory (simultaneously verbal, visual, and tactile), infants receive much support from other senses in analyzing speech. When mothers speak to 5- to 8-month-olds, they often provide temporal synchrony between words, object motions, and touch—for example, saying "doll" while moving a doll and, sometimes, having the doll touch the infant (Gogate, Bahrick, & Watson, 2000). In doing so, they create a supportive learning environment: In two studies, 7-month-olds remembered associations between sounds and objects only when they heard the sound and saw the object move simultaneously (Gogate & Bahrick, 1998, 2001).

Finally, infants' special responsiveness to speech encourages parents to talk to their baby. Doing so strengthens infants' language

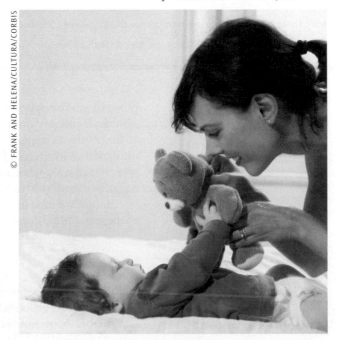

Parents often name a toy or other object—for example, saying "bear"—while moving the toy and, sometimes, having it touch the infant. This multisensory communication helps babies associate words with objects.

© FRANK AND HELENA/CULTURA/CORBIS

Milestones

Development of Touch, Taste, Smell, and Hearing

AGE	TOUCH	TASTE AND SMELL	HEARING
Birth	• Responds to touch and pain. • Distinguishes shape of object placed in palm.	• Distinguishes sweet, sour, and bitter tastes; prefers sweetness. • Distinguishes odors; prefers those of sweet-tasting foods. • Prefers smell of own mother's amniotic fluid and the lactating breast.	• Prefers complex sounds to pure tones. • Distinguishes some sound patterns. • Prefers listening to own mother's voice over unfamiliar woman's voice, and to native language as opposed to foreign language. • Makes subtle distinctions between almost all speech sounds, including sounds not found in own language. • Turns eyes and head in the general direction of a sound.
1–6 months	• Frequently engages in exploratory mouthing of objects.	• Prefers a salty taste to plain water. • Readily changes taste preferences through experience.	• Prefers listening to human speech over structurally similar nonspeech sounds. • Organizes sounds into increasingly elaborate patterns, such as musical phrases. • Identifies location of a sound more precisely. • By the end of this period, becomes sensitive to syllable stress patterns in own language.
7–12 months			• Recognizes the same melody played in different keys. • "Screens out" sounds not used in native language. • Detects speech units crucial to understanding meaning, including familiar words and regularities in sound and word sequences.

Note: These milestones represent overall age trends. Individual differences exist in the precise age at which each milestone is attained.

Photos: (top) © Blend Images/Alamy; (middle) © Michael Newman/PhotoEdit; (bottom) © Laura Dwight Photography

processing. The opportunity to view an adult's face while she says two similar native-language sounds facilitates 6-month-olds' sound discrimination (Teinonen et al., 2008). Similarly, at first, infants depend on the union of auditory and visual stimuli to pick up emotional information in speech. Three- and 4-month-olds can distinguish happy- from sad-sounding speech, but only while looking at people's faces. Later, babies can discriminate positive from negative emotion in each sensory modality—first voices, then faces (Walker-Andrews, 1997).

Before we turn to visual development, consult the Milestones table above for a summary of the perceptual capacities we have just considered.

Vision

For exploring the environment, humans depend on vision more than any other sense. At birth, however, vision is the least developed of the senses. Visual structures in both the eye and the brain are not yet fully formed. For example, cells in the *retina*, the membrane lining

FIGURE 4.11 View of the human face by the newborn and the adult. The newborn baby's limited focusing ability and poor visual acuity lead the mother's face, even when viewed from close up, to look more like the fuzzy image in (a) than the clear image in (b). Also, newborn infants have some color vision, although they have difficulty discriminating colors. Researchers speculate that colors probably appear similar, but less intense, to newborns than they do to older infants and adults. (From Kellman & Arterberry, 2006; Slater et al., 2010.)

© MICHAEL NEWMAN/PHOTOEDIT

(a) Newborn View   (b) Adult View

the inside of the eye that captures light and transforms it into messages that are sent to the brain, are not as mature or densely packed as they will be in several months. The optic nerve that relays these messages, and visual centers in the brain that receive them, will not be adultlike for several years. And the muscles of the *lens,* which permit us to adjust our focus to varying distances, are weak (Kellman & Arterberry, 2006).

As a result, newborns cannot focus their eyes well, and their **visual acuity,** or fineness of discrimination, is limited. At birth, infants perceive objects at a distance of 20 feet about as clearly as adults do at 600 feet (Slater et al., 2010). In addition, unlike adults (who see nearby objects most clearly), newborn babies see unclearly across a wide range of distances (Banks, 1980; Hainline, 1998). As a result, images such as the parent's face, even close up, look like the blurry image in Figure 4.11. And despite their preference for colored over gray stimuli, newborn babies are not yet good at discriminating colors (Kellman & Arterberry, 2006).

The visual system develops rapidly over the first few months. Around 2 months, infants can focus on objects about as well as adults; by 4 months, color discrimination is adultlike (Kellman & Arterberry, 2006). Visual acuity improves rapidly, reaching 20/80 by 6 months and an adult level of about 20/20 by 4 years (Slater et al., 2010).

Although they cannot yet see well, newborns actively explore their environment by scanning it for interesting sights and tracking moving objects. However, their eye movements are slow and inaccurate. Scanning and tracking improve over the first half-year as infants see more clearly and better control their eye movements. In addition, as young infants build an organized perceptual world, they scan more thoroughly and systematically, strategically picking up important information and anticipating with their eye movements what they expect to happen next in a series of events (Haith, 1994; Johnson, Slemmer, & Amso, 2004; von Hofsten et al., 1998). Consequently, scanning enhances perception, and—in bidirectional fashion—perception also enhances scanning.

As infants explore their visual field, they figure out the characteristics of objects and how they are arranged in space. To understand how they do so, let's examine the development of three aspects of vision: depth, pattern, and object perception.

Depth Perception   *Depth perception* is the ability to judge the distance of objects from one another and from ourselves. It is important for understanding the layout of the environment and for guiding motor activity.

Figure 4.12 shows the well-known **visual cliff,** designed by Eleanor Gibson and Richard Walk (1960) and used in the earliest studies of depth perception. It consists of a Plexiglas covered table with a platform at the center, a "shallow" side with a checkerboard pattern just under the glass, and a "deep" side with a checkerboard several feet below the glass. The researchers found that crawling babies readily crossed the shallow side, but

FIGURE 4.12 The visual cliff. Plexiglas covers the deep and shallow sides. By refusing to cross the deep side and showing a preference for the shallow side, this infant demonstrates the ability to perceive depth.

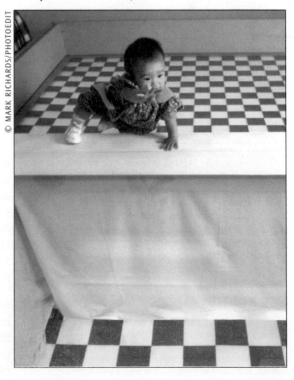

© MARK RICHARDS/PHOTOEDIT

most avoided the deep side. They concluded that around the time that infants crawl, most distinguish deep from shallow surfaces and avoid drop-offs.

The visual cliff shows that crawling and avoidance of drop-offs are linked, but not how they are related or when depth perception first appears. Recent research has looked at babies' ability to detect specific depth cues, using methods that do not require that they crawl.

Emergence of Depth Perception.   How do we know when an object is near rather than far away? **TAKE A MOMENT...** Try these exercises to find out: Pick up a small object (such as your cup), and move it toward and then away from your face. Did its image grow larger as it approached and smaller as it receded? Next time you take a bike or car ride, notice that nearby objects move past your field of vision more quickly than those far away.

Motion is the first depth cue to which infants are sensitive. Babies 3 to 4 weeks old blink their eyes defensively when an object moves toward their face as if it is going to hit (Nánez & Yonas, 1994). As they are carried about and as people and things turn and move before their eyes, infants learn more about depth. By the time they are 3 months old, motion has helped babies figure out that objects are not flat but three-dimensional (Arterberry, Craton, & Yonas, 1993).

Binocular depth cues arise because our two eyes have slightly different views of the visual field. In a process called *stereopsis,* the brain blends these two images, resulting in perception of depth. Research in which two overlapping images are projected before the baby, who wears special goggles to ensure that each eye receives only one image, reveals that sensitivity to binocular cues emerges between 2 and 3 months and improves rapidly over the first year (Birch, 1993; Brown & Miracle, 2003). Infants soon make use of binocular cues in their reaching, adjusting arm and hand movements to match the distance of objects from the eyes.

Last to develop are *pictorial depth cues,* the ones artists use to make a painting look three-dimensional. Examples include receding and overlapping lines and line junctions (as in the drawing of a cube) that create the illusion of perspective, changes in texture (nearby textures are more detailed than faraway ones), overlapping objects (an object partially hidden by another object is perceived to be more distant), height-in-the-picture-plane (objects closer to the horizon appear farther away), and shadows cast on surfaces (indicating a separation in space between the object and the surface). Habituation research indicates that 3- to 4-month-olds are sensitive to cues of overlapping lines and line junctions. For example, 4-month-olds discriminate between the structurally "possible" and "impossible" drawings of a cube in Figure 4.13; they look much longer at the impossible alternative, as if puzzled by it (Bertin & Bhatt, 2006; Shuwairi, Albert, & Johnson, 2007). Studies in which researchers observe whether babies reach toward closer-appearing parts of images containing pictorial cues reveal that pictorial sensitivity improves considerably between 5 and 7 months (Arterberry, 2008; Kavsek, Granrud, & Yonas, 2009).

Why does perception of depth cues emerge in the order just described? Researchers speculate that motor development is involved. For example, control of the head during the early weeks of life may help babies notice motion and binocular cues. Around the middle of the first year, the ability to turn, poke, and feel the surface of objects promotes sensitivity to pictorial cues as infants pick up information about size, texture, and three-dimensional shape (Bushnell & Boudreau, 1993; Soska, Adolph, & Johnson, 2010). And as we will see next, research shows that another aspect of motor progress—independent movement—plays a vital role in refinement of depth perception.

Independent Movement and Depth Perception.   A mother I know described her newly crawling 9-month-old as a "fearless daredevil." "If I put April down in the middle of our bed, she crawls right over the edge," the mother exclaimed. "The same thing's happened by the stairs." Will April become wary of the side of the bed and the staircase as she becomes a more experienced

Habituation Phase

(a) Habituation

Test Phase

(b) Possible Cube

(c) Impossible Cube

FIGURE 4.13 Testing infants' responsiveness to pictorial depth cues—overlapping lines and line junctions. (a) Infants were habituated to a line drawing of a cube made to look three-dimensional with over-lapping-line and line-junction cues, but with a critical section covered, so looking preference for the makeup of that section could be tested. Next, the infants were shown two test displays in alternation: (b) a structurally "possible" cube and (c) a cube made to look structurally "impossible" by altering the coherence of pictorial cues. Four-month-olds spent much more time looking at the impossible cube, as if puzzled by it—a preference suggesting pictorial-cue sensitivity. (From S. M. Shuwairi, M. K. Albert, & S. P. Johnson, 2007, "Discrimination of Possible and Impossible Objects in Infancy," *Psychological Science, Vol. 18, No. 4,* p. 304, copyright © 2007, Association of Psychological Science. Reprinted by Permission of SAGE Publications.)

crawler? Research suggests that she will. Infants with more crawling experience (regardless of when they started to crawl) are far more likely to refuse to cross the deep side of the visual cliff (Campos et al., 2000).

From extensive everyday experience, babies gradually figure out how to use depth cues to detect the danger of falling. But because the loss of postural control that leads to falling differs greatly for each body position, babies must undergo this learning separately for each posture. In one study, 9-month-olds, who were experienced sitters but novice crawlers, were placed on the edge of a shallow drop-off that could be widened (Adolph, 2002, 2008). While in the familiar sitting position, infants avoided leaning out for an attractive toy at distances likely to result in falling. But in the unfamiliar crawling posture, they headed over the edge, even when the distance was extremely wide! And newly walking babies, while avoiding sharp drop-offs, career down slopes and over uneven surfaces without making the necessary postural adjustments, even when their mothers discourage them from proceeding! Thus, they fall frequently (Adolph et al., 2008; Joh & Adolph, 2006). As infants discover how to avoid falling in various postures and situations, their understanding of depth expands.

Crawling experience promotes other aspects of three-dimensional understanding. For example, seasoned crawlers are better than their inexperienced agemates at remembering object locations and finding hidden objects (Bai & Bertenthal, 1992; Campos et al., 2000). Why does crawling make such a difference? **TAKE A MOMENT...** Compare your own experience of the environment when you are driven from one place to another with what you experience when you walk or drive yourself. When you move on your own, you are much more aware of landmarks and routes of travel, and you take more careful note of what things look like from different points of view. The same is true for infants.

In fact, crawling promotes a new level of brain organization, as indicated by more organized EEG brain-wave activity in the cerebral cortex (Bell & Fox, 1996). Perhaps crawling strengthens certain neural connections, especially those involved in vision and understanding of space. As the Social Issues: Education box on page 162 reveals, the link between independent movement and spatial knowledge is also evident in a population with very different perceptual experience: infants with severe visual impairments.

Pattern Perception Even newborns prefer to look at patterned rather than plain stimuli (Fantz, 1961). As they get older, infants prefer more complex patterns. For example, 3-week-olds look longest at black-and-white checkerboards with a few large squares, whereas 8- and 14-week-olds prefer those with many squares (Brennan, Ames, & Moore, 1966).

Contrast Sensitivity. A general principle, called **contrast sensitivity,** explains early pattern preferences (Banks & Ginsburg, 1985). *Contrast* refers to the difference in the amount of light between adjacent regions in a pattern. If babies *are sensitive to* (can detect) the contrast in two or more patterns, they prefer the one with more contrast. To understand this idea, look at the checkerboards in the top row of Figure 4.14. To us, the one with many small squares has more contrasting elements. Now look at the bottom row, which shows how these checkerboards appear to infants in the first few weeks of life. Because of their poor vision, very young babies cannot resolve the small features in more complex patterns, so they prefer to look at the large, bold checkerboard. Around 2 months, when detection of fine-grained detail has

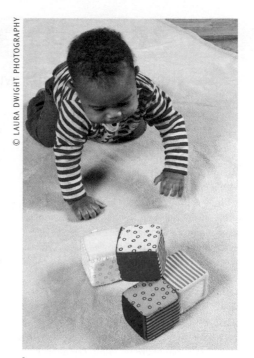

As this 8-month-old becomes adept at crawling, his experience fosters other aspects of three-dimensional understanding—for example, remembering object locations and how objects appear from different viewpoints.

Bold checkerboard   Complex checkerboard

Appearance of checkerboards to very young infants

FIGURE 4.14 The way two checkerboards differing in complexity look to infants in the first few weeks of life. Because of their poor vision, very young infants cannot resolve the fine detail in the *complex checkerboard*. It appears blurred, like a gray field. The large, *bold checkerboard* appears to have more contrast, so babies prefer to look at it. (Adapted from M. S. Banks & P. Salapatek, 1983, "Infant Visual Perception," in M. M. Haith & J. J. Campos [Eds.], *Handbook of Child Psychology: Vol. 2. Infancy and Developmental Psychobiology* [4th ed.], New York: John Wiley & Sons, p. 504. Reprinted with permission from John Wiley & Sons, Inc.)

SOCIAL ISSUES: EDUCATION

Development of Infants with Severe Visual Impairments

Research on infants who can see little or nothing at all dramatically illustrates the interdependence of vision, motor exploration, social interaction, and understanding of the world. In a longitudinal study, infants with a visual acuity of 20/800 or worse—that is, they had only dim light perception or were blind—were followed through the preschool years. Compared to agemates with less severe visual impairments, they showed serious delays in all aspects of development. Motor and cognitive functioning suffered the most; with age, performance in both domains became increasingly distant from that of other children (Hatton et al., 1997).

What explains these profound developmental delays? Minimal or absent vision can alter the child's experiences in at least two crucial, interrelated ways.

Impact on Motor Exploration and Spatial Understanding

Infants with severe visual impairments attain gross- and fine-motor milestones many months later than their sighted counterparts (Levtzion-Korach et al., 2000). For example, on average, blind infants do not reach for and manipulate objects until 12 months, crawl until 13 months, or walk until 19 months (compare these averages to the norms in the Milestones table on page 148). Why is this so?

Infants with severe visual impairments must rely on sound to identify the whereabouts of objects. But sound does not function as a precise clue to object location until much later than vision—around the middle of the first year (Litovsky & Ashmead, 1997). And because infants who cannot see have difficulty engaging their caregivers, adults may not provide them with rich early exposure to sounding objects. As a result, the baby comes to understand relatively late that there is a world of interesting objects to explore.

Until "reaching on sound" is achieved, infants with severe visual impairments are not motivated to move independently. Because of their own uncertainty coupled with their parents' protectiveness and restraint to prevent injury, blind infants are typically tentative in their movements. These factors delay motor development further.

Motor and cognitive development are closely linked, especially for infants with little or no

vision. These babies build an understanding of the location and arrangement of objects in space only after reaching and crawling (Bigelow, 1992). Inability to imitate the motor actions of others presents additional challenges as these children get older, contributing to declines in motor and cognitive progress relative to peers with better vision (Hatton et al., 1997).

Impact on the Caregiver–Infant Relationship

Infants who see poorly have great difficulty evoking stimulating caregiver interaction. They cannot make eye contact, imitate, or pick up nonverbal social cues. Their emotional expressions are muted; for example, their smile is fleeting and unpredictable. And because they cannot gaze in the same direction as a partner, they are greatly delayed in establishing a shared focus of attention on objects as the basis for play (Bigelow, 2003). Consequently, these infants may receive little adult attention and other stimulation vital for all aspects of development.

When a visually impaired child does not learn how to participate in social interaction during infancy, communication is compromised in early childhood. In an observational study of blind children enrolled in preschools with sighted agemates, the blind children seldom initiated contact with peers and teachers. When they did interact, they had trouble interpreting the meaning of others' reactions and responding appropriately (Preisler, 1991, 1993).

Interventions

Parents, teachers, and caregivers can help infants with minimal vision overcome early developmental delays through stimulating, responsive interaction. Until a close emotional bond with an adult is forged, babies with visual impairments cannot establish vital links with their environments.

Techniques that help infants become aware of their physical and social surroundings include

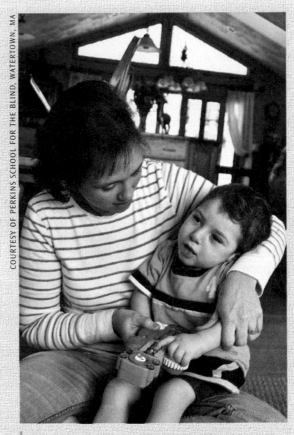

COURTESY OF PERKINS SCHOOL FOR THE BLIND, WATERTOWN, MA

This 3-year-old was born with severe visual impairment caused by brain damage. Using manipulative play that combines touch and sound, his caregiver helps him make sense of his physical and social environment.

heightened sensory input through combining sound and touch (holding, touching, or bringing the baby's hands to the adult's face while talking or singing), engaging in many repetitions, and consistently reinforcing the infant's efforts to make contact. Manipulative play with objects that make sounds is also vital.

Finally, rich language stimulation can compensate for visual loss (Conti-Ramsden & Pérez-Pereira, 1999). It gives young children a ready means of finding out about objects, events, and behaviors they cannot see. Once language emerges, many children with limited or no vision show impressive rebounds. Some acquire a unique capacity for abstract thinking, and most master social and practical skills that enable them to lead productive, independent lives.

improved, infants become sensitive to the greater contrast in complex patterns and spend more time looking at them. Contrast sensitivity continues to improve during infancy and childhood (Gwiazda & Birch, 2001).

Combining Pattern Elements. In the early weeks of life, infants respond to the separate parts of a pattern. They stare at single, high-contrast features and have difficulty shifting their gaze away toward other interesting stimuli (Hunnius & Geuze, 2004a, 2004b). In exploring drawings of human faces, for example, 1-month-olds often limit themselves to the edges of the stimulus and focus on the hairline or chin. At 2 to 3 months, when scanning ability and contrast sensitivity improve, they thoroughly explore a pattern's internal features, pausing briefly to look at each salient part (Bronson, 1994). (Recall from page 145 that some babies continue to focus on small features and, therefore, take in less information.)

Babies' scanning also varies with pattern characteristics. When exposed to dynamic stimuli, such as the mother's nodding, smiling face, 6-week-olds fixate more on internal features (the mouth and eyes) than on edges. But when stimuli are static, thorough inspection of the entire stimulus is delayed, occurring only after 4 months (Hunnius & Geuze, 2004b). And when presented with complex stimuli, such as a still frame or a video clip from the TV program *Sesame Street*, babies increase their inspection time over the second half-year as they try to make sense of the image (Courage, Reynolds, & Richards, 2006). Exploring complex patterns, especially those with moving stimuli, is more demanding than exploring simple stationary patterns—a difference we must keep in mind as we examine research on pattern perception, which is based largely on static stimuli.

Once babies take in all aspects of a pattern, they integrate the parts into a unified whole. Around 4 months, they are so good at detecting pattern organization that they perceive subjective boundaries that are not really present. For example, they perceive a square in the center of Figure 4.15a, just as you do (Ghim, 1990). Older infants carry this responsiveness to subjective form further, applying it to complex, moving stimuli. For example, 9-month-olds look much longer at an organized series of moving lights that resembles a human being walking than at upside-down or scrambled versions (Bertenthal, 1993). At 12 months, infants detect familiar objects represented by incomplete drawings, even when as much as two-thirds of the drawing is missing (see Figure 4.15b) (Rose, Jankowski, & Senior, 1997). As these findings reveal, infants' increasing knowledge of objects and actions supports pattern perception.

Face Perception
Infants' tendency to search for structure in a patterned stimulus applies to face perception. Newborns prefer to look at photos and simplified drawings of faces with features arranged naturally (upright) rather than unnaturally (upside down or sideways) (see Figure 4.16a and b on page 164) (Cassia, Turati, & Simion, 2004; Mondloch et al., 1999). They also track a facelike pattern moving across their visual field farther than they track other stimuli (Johnson, 1999). And although their ability to distinguish real faces on the basis of inner features is limited, newborns prefer photos of faces with eyes open and a direct gaze (Farroni et al., 2002; Turati et al., 2006). Yet another amazing capacity is their tendency to look longer at faces judged by adults as attractive (Slater et al., 2000). At least in early infancy, this attractiveness preference extends beyond human faces to nonhuman animal faces, such as domestic cats and wild tigers (Quinn et al., 2008). It may be the origin of the widespread social bias favoring physically attractive people.

Some researchers claim that these behaviors reflect a built-in capacity to orient toward members of one's own species, just as many newborn animals do (Johnson, 2001; Slater & Quinn, 2001). In support of this view, the upright face preference occurs only when newborns view stimuli in the periphery of their visual field—an area of the retina governed by primitive brain centers (Cassia, Simion, & Umiltá, 2001). Others assert that newborns simply prefer any stimulus in which the most salient elements are arranged horizontally in the upper part of a pattern—like the "eyes" in Figure 4.16b. Indeed, newborns do prefer nonfacial patterns with these characteristics over other nonfacial arrangements (Cassia, Turati, & Simion, 2004;

(a)

(b)

FIGURE 4.15 Subjective boundaries in visual patterns. (a) Do you perceive a square in the middle of the top figure? By 4 months of age, infants do, too. (b) What does the image on the bottom, missing two-thirds of its outline, look like to you? By 12 months, infants detect a motorcycle. After habituating to the incomplete motorcycle image, they were shown an intact motorcycle figure paired with a novel form. Twelve-month-olds recovered to (looked longer at) the novel figure, indicating that they recognized the motorcycle pattern on the basis of very little visual information. (Adapted from Ghim, 1990; Rose, Jankowski, & Senior, 1997.)

FIGURE 4.16 Early face perception. Newborns prefer to look at the photo of a face (a) and the simple pattern resembling a face (b) over the upside-down versions. (c) When the complex drawing of a face on the left and the equally complex, scrambled version on the right are moved across newborns' visual field, they follow the face longer. But if the two stimuli are stationary, infants show no preference for the face until around 2 months of age. (From Cassia, Turati, & Simion, 2004; Johnson, 1999; Mondloch et al., 1999.)

Simion et al., 2001). But a bias favoring the facial pattern possibly promotes such preferences. Still other researchers argue that newborns are exposed to faces more often than to other stimuli—early experiences that could quickly "wire" the brain to detect faces and prefer attractive ones (Nelson, 2001).

Although newborns respond to facelike structures, they cannot discriminate a complex, static image of the human face from other, equally complex configurations (see Figure 4.16c). But from repeated exposures to their mother's face, they quickly learn to prefer her face to that of an unfamiliar woman, although they are sensitive only to its broad outlines, not its fine-grained features. Babies quickly apply their tendency to search for pattern to face perception. Around 2 months, when they can scan an entire stimulus and combine pattern elements into an organized whole, they recognize and prefer their mother's detailed facial features to those of another woman (Bartrip, Morton, & de Schonen, 2001). And they prefer a complex drawing of the human face to other equally complex stimulus arrangements (Dannemiller & Stephens, 1988).

Around 3 months, infants make fine distinctions among the features of different faces—for example, between photographs of two strangers, even when the faces are moderately similar (Farroni et al., 2007). At 5 months—and strengthening over the second half-year—infants perceive emotional expressions as organized wholes. They treat positive faces (happy or surprised) as different from negative ones (sad or fearful) (Bornstein & Arterberry, 2003; Ludemann, 1991). Around this time, babies rely increasingly on relational information to process faces. When researchers slightly alter the distance among the eyes and mouth in a photo of a face, 5-month-olds detect that the face has changed (Hayden et al., 2007).

Experience influences face processing, leading babies to form group biases at a tender age. As early as 3 months, infants prefer and more easily discriminate among female faces than among male faces (Quinn et al., 2002; Ramsey-Rennels & Langlois, 2006). The greater time infants spend with female adults explains this effect, since babies with a male primary caregiver prefer male faces. Furthermore, 3- to 6-month-olds exposed mostly to members of their own race prefer to look at the faces of members of that race and more easily detect differences among those faces (Bar-Haim et al., 2006; Kelly et al., 2007a, 2007b). This own-race face preference is absent in babies who have frequent contact with members of other races, and it can be reversed through exposure to racial diversity (Sangrigoli et al., 2005). **TAKE A MOMENT...** Notice how early experience promotes *perceptual narrowing* with respect to gender and racial information in faces, as occurs for species information, discussed in the Biology and Environment box on page 156.

Clearly, extensive face-to-face interaction with caregivers contributes to infants' refinement of face perception. As we will see in Chapter 10, babies' developing sensitivity to the human face supports their earliest social relationships and helps regulate exploration of the environment in adaptive ways.

Object Perception Research on pattern perception involves only two-dimensional stimuli, but our environment is made up of stable, three-dimensional objects. Do young infants perceive a world of independently existing objects—knowledge essential for distinguishing the self, other people, and things?

Size and Shape Constancy. As we move around the environment, the images that objects cast on our retina constantly change in size and shape. To perceive objects as stable and unchanging, we must translate these varying retinal images into a single representation.

Size constancy—perception of an object's size as the same, despite changes in the size of its retinal image—is evident in the first week of life. To test for it, researchers habituated infants to a small cube at varying distances from the eye, in an effort to desensitize them to changes in the cube's retinal image size and direct their attention to the object's actual size. When the small cube was presented together with a new, large cube—but at different distances so that they cast retinal images of the same size—all babies recovered to (looked longer at) the novel large cube, indicating that they distinguished objects on the basis of actual size, not retinal image size (Slater et al., 2010).

Perception of an object's shape as stable, despite changes in the shape projected on the retina, is called **shape constancy.** Habituation research reveals that it, too, is present within the first week of life, long before babies can actively rotate objects with their hands and view them from different angles (Slater & Johnson, 1999).

In sum, both size and shape constancy seem to be built-in capacities that help babies detect a coherent world of objects. Yet they provide only a partial picture of young infants' object perception.

Perception of Object Identity. At first, infants rely heavily on motion and spatial arrangement to identify objects (Juszczyk et al., 1999; Spelke & Hermer, 1996). When two objects are touching and either move in unison or stand still, babies younger than 4 months cannot distinguish between them. Infants, as we saw earlier in this chapter, are fascinated by moving objects. While observing objects' motions, they pick up additional information about objects' boundaries, such as shape, color, and texture.

For example, as Figure 4.17 reveals, around 2 months, babies first realize that a moving rod whose center is hidden behind a box is a complete rod rather than two rod pieces. Motion, a textured background, and a small box (so most of the rod is visible) are necessary for young infants to infer object unity. They need all these cues to heighten the distinction between objects in the display because their ability to scan for salient information is still immature (Amso & Johnson, 2006; Johnson et al., 2002).

As infants become familiar with many objects and can integrate each object's diverse features into a unified whole, they rely more on shape, color, and pattern and less on motion (Slater et al., 2010). Babies as young as 4½ months can discriminate two touching objects on the basis of their features in simple, easy-to-process situations. And prior exposure to one of the test objects enhances 4½-month-olds' ability to discern the boundary between two touching objects—a finding that highlights the role of experience (Dueker, Modi, & Needham, 2003; Needham, 2001).

In everyday life, objects frequently move in and out of sight, so infants must keep track of their disappearance and reappearance to perceive their identity. Habituation research, in which a ball moves back and forth behind a screen, reveals that at age 4 months, infants first perceive the ball's path as continuous (see Figure 4.18) (Johnson et al., 2003). Between 4 and 5 months, infants can monitor increasingly intricate paths of objects. As indicated by their future-oriented eye movements (looking ahead to where they expect an object to appear from behind a barrier), 5-month-olds even keep track of an object that travels on a curvilinear course at varying speeds (Rosander & von Hofsten, 2004). Again, experience—the opportunity to track a moving object along a fully visible path of movement just before testing—enhances young infants' predictive eye tracking (Johnson & Shuwairi, 2009).

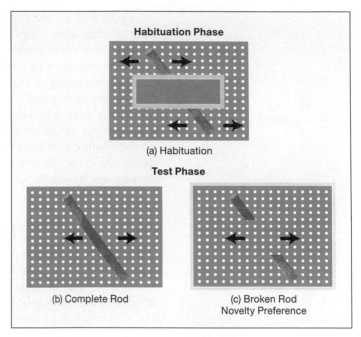

FIGURE 4.17 Testing infants' ability to perceive object unity. (a) Infants were habituated to a rod moving back and forth behind a box against a textured background. Next, they were shown two test displays in alternation: (b) a complete rod and (c) a broken rod with a gap corresponding to the location of the box. Each stimulus was moved back and forth against the textured background, in the same way as the habituation stimulus. Infants 2 months of age and older typically recovered to (looked longer at) the broken rod than the complete rod. Their novelty preference suggests that they perceive the rod behind the box in the first display as a single unit. (Adapted from Johnson, 1997.)

FIGURE 4.18 Testing infants' ability to perceive an object's path of movement. (a) Infants were habituated to a ball moving back and forth behind a screen. Next, they were shown two test displays in alternation: (b) a ball undergoing continuous back-and-forth motion, with its full trajectory visible, and (c) a ball undergoing discontinuous motion, out of and back into view just as in the habituation stimulus, but without moving behind a visible screen. As long as the ball was out of sight only briefly in the habituation display, 4-month-olds typically recovered to (looked longer at) the discontinuous motion than the continuous motion. Their novelty preference suggests that they perceive the motion of the ball behind the screen in the first display as continuous. (From S. P. Johnson et al., 2003, "Infants' Perception of Object Trajectories," *Child Development, 74,* pp. 98, 101. © 2003 The Society for Research in Child Development, Inc. Reprinted by permission of Blackwell Publishing Ltd.)

From 4 to 11 months, infants increasingly rely on featural information to detect the identity of an object traveling behind a screen—at first, form (size and shape) and later in the first year, surface features (pattern and then color) (Wilcox & Woods, 2009). And as before, experience—in particular, physically manipulating the object—boosts older infants' attention to its surface features.

In sum, perception of object identity is mastered gradually over the first year. We will consider a related attainment—infants' understanding of object permanence—awareness that an object still exists when hidden—in Chapter 6.

The Milestones table on the following page provides an overview of the vast changes in visual perception during the first year. Up to this point, we have considered the sensory systems one by one. Now let's examine their coordination.

Intermodal Perception

Our world provides rich, continuous *intermodal stimulation*—simultaneous input from more than one modality, or sensory system. In **intermodal perception,** we make sense of these running streams of light, sound, tactile, odor, and taste information, perceiving them as integrated wholes. We know, for example, that an object's shape is the same whether we see it or touch it, that lip movements are closely coordinated with the sound of a voice, and that dropping a rigid object on a hard surface will cause a sharp, banging sound.

Recall that newborns turn in the general direction of a sound and reach for objects in a primitive way. These behaviors suggest that infants expect sight, sound, and touch to go together. Research reveals that babies perceive input from different sensory systems in a unified way by detecting **amodal sensory properties**—information that is not specific to a single modality but that overlaps two or more sensory systems, such as rate, rhythm, duration, intensity, temporal synchrony (for vision and hearing), and texture and shape (for vision and touch). Consider, for example, the sight and sound of a bouncing ball or the face and voice of a speaking person. In each event, visual and auditory information are conveyed simultaneously and with the same rate, rhythm, duration, and intensity.

© DAVID YOUNG-WOLFF/PHOTOEDIT

Within the first half-year, infants master a remarkable range of intermodal relationships. This baby picks up associations between the sight, sound, and feel of his father's guitar.

Even newborns are impressive perceivers of amodal properties. After touching an object (such as a cylinder) placed in their palms, they recognize it visually, distinguishing it from a different-shaped object (Sann & Streri, 2007). And they require just one exposure to learn the association between the sight and sound of a toy, such as a rhythmically jangling rattle (Morrongiello, Fenwick, & Chance, 1998).

Within the first half-year, infants master a remarkable range of intermodal relationships. Three- to 4-month-olds can match faces with voices on the basis of lip–voice synchrony, emotional expression, and even age and gender of the speaker: On hearing a voice, they look longer at an appropriate face than at an inappropriate one (Bahrick, Netto, & Hernandez-Reif, 1998). Between 4 and 6 months, infants can perceive and remember the unique face–voice pairings of unfamiliar adults (Bahrick, Hernandez-Reif, & Flom, 2005).

How does intermodal perception develop so quickly? Young infants seem biologically primed to focus on amodal information. Their detection of amodal relations—for example, the common tempo and rhythm in sights and sounds—precedes and seems to provide the basis for detecting more specific intermodal matches, such as the relation between a particular person's face and the sound of her voice or between an object and its verbal label (Bahrick, Hernandez-Reif, & Flom, 2005).

Intermodal sensitivity is crucial for perceptual development. In the early months, infants detect amodal properties only when exposed to intermodal stimulation. For example, 3-month-olds discriminated a change in the rhythm of a toy hammer tapping from an audiovisual display but not from a purely auditory presentation (just hearing the tapping) or a purely visual presentation (just seeing the hammer move) (Bahrick, Flom, & Lickliter, 2003). Intermodal stimulation makes amodal properties (such as rhythm) stand out. As a result, inexperienced

Milestones

Visual Development in Infancy

AGE	ACUITY, COLOR PERCEPTION, FOCUSING, AND EXPLORATION	DEPTH PERCEPTION	PATTERN PERCEPTION	OBJECT PERCEPTION
Birth–1 month	• Visual acuity is 20/600. • Scans the visual field and tracks moving objects.	• Responds to motion, blinking defensively when an object moves toward the face.	• Prefers large, bold patterns. • Responds to separate parts of a pattern, focusing on single, high-contrast features. • Prefers to look at simplified drawings of facelike patterns and at photos of faces with eyes open and a direct gaze. • Shows preference for attractive faces over less attractive ones.	• Displays size and shape constancy.
2–3 months	• Has adultlike focusing ability. • Scans more thoroughly and systematically. 	• Responds to binocular depth cues.	• Prefers patterns with finer details. • Thoroughly scans internal pattern features. • Begins to perceive overall pattern structure. • Prefers complex drawings of human face to other, equally complex stimulus arrangements. • Prefers and more easily discriminates among female than male faces. • Recognizes and prefers mother's face and distinguishes among faces of strangers.	• Uses motion and spatial arrangement to identify objects.
4–5 months	• Color discrimination is adultlike.	• Sensitivity to binocular depth cues improves. • Begins to respond to pictorial depth cues.	• Perceives subjective boundaries in simple patterns. • Increasingly relies on relational information (such as distance among features) to differentiate faces. • Distinguishes emotionally positive from emotionally negative facial expressions.	• Uses shape, color, and texture to identify objects. • Perceives an object's path of movement as continuous without seeing the entire path.
6–9 months	• Visual acuity improves greatly, to 20/80. • Scans the visual field and tracks moving objects more efficiently.	• Responsiveness to pictorial depth cues improves.	• Improves at detecting subjective form in complex patterns. • Increasingly perceives facial expressions of emotion as organized wholes.	
10–12 months			• Continues to improve at detecting subjective form: Detects familiar objects represented by incomplete drawings.	

Note: These milestones represent overall age trends. Individual differences exist in the precise age at which each milestone is attained.

Photos: (top row right) © Laura Dwight Photography; (second row left) © Andrew Olney/Getty Images/Stone; (second row right) © Laura Dwight/PhotoEdit; (third row left) © Laura Dwight Photography; (bottom rows left) © Laura Dwight Photography; (bottom rows right) © Laura Dwight Photography perceivers notice a unitary event (the hammer's intricate tapping) and are not distracted by momentarily irrelevant aspects of the situation, such as the hammer's color or orientation.

In contrast, young infants notice changes in purely visual properties, such as color, orientation, and pattern, only when exposed to purely visual information (Bahrick, Lickliter, & Flom, 2004). With experience, perceptual capacities become more flexible. In the second half of the first year, infants can discriminate amodal properties in both intermodal and unimodal (sights or sounds alone) stimulation. But early on, when much input is unfamiliar and confusing, intermodal stimulation helps babies selectively attend to and make sense of their surroundings.

In addition to easing infants' perception of the physical world, intermodal perception facilitates social and language processing, as evidence reviewed earlier in this chapter illustrates. Recall that an adult's gentle touch induces infants to attend to her face (see page 154). And as infants gaze at an adult's face, they initially require both vocal and visual input to distinguish positive from negative emotional expressions. Furthermore, in their earliest efforts to make sense of language, infants profit from temporal synchrony between a speech sound and the motion of an object (see page 157). Similarly, sound–movement temporal synchrony facilitates perception of rhythm and beat in music (Trainor, 2007). When 7-month-olds were bounced while listening to an unaccented musical rhythm, some infants on every second beat (duple rhythm) and others on every third beat (triple rhythm), the babies later preferred the accented version of the music they had experienced intermodally (Phillips-Silver & Trainor, 2005).

In sum, intermodal perception is a fundamental ability that fosters all aspects of psychological development. When caregivers provide many concurrent sights, sounds, touches, and smells, babies process more information, learn faster, and show better memory (Bahrick, 2010). Intermodal perception is yet another fundamental capacity that assists infants in their active efforts to build an orderly, predictable world.

LOOK and LISTEN

While watching a parent and infant playing, list instances of parental intermodal stimulation and communication. What is the baby likely learning about people, objects, or language from each intermodal experience?

Understanding Perceptual Development

Now that we have reviewed the development of infant perceptual capacities, how can we put together this diverse array of amazing achievements? Widely accepted answers come from the work of Eleanor and James Gibson. According to the Gibsons' **differentiation theory,** infants actively search for **invariant features** of the environment—those that remain stable—in a constantly changing perceptual world. In pattern perception, for example, young babies search for features that stand out and orient toward faces. Soon they explore internal features and notice *stable relationships* among them. As a result, they detect patterns, such as complex designs and individual faces. Similarly, babies analyze the speech stream for regularities, detecting words, word-order sequences, and—within words—consistent syllable-stress patterns. The development of intermodal perception also reflects this principle. Infants seek out invariant relationships—first, amodal properties, such as common rate and rhythm, in a voice and face; later, more detailed associations, such as unique voice–face matches.

The Gibsons described their theory as *differentiation* (where *differentiate* means "analyze" or "break down") because over time the baby detects finer and finer invariant features among stimuli. In addition to pattern perception and intermodal perception, differentiation applies to depth and object perception: Recall how in each, sensitivity to motion precedes detection of fine-grained features. So one way of understanding perceptual development is to think of it as a built-in tendency to seek order and consistency—a capacity that becomes increasingly fine-tuned with age (Gibson, 1970; Gibson, 1979).

Acting on the environment is vital in perceptual differentiation. According to the Gibsons, perception is guided by the discovery of **affordances**—the action possibilities that a situation offers an organism with certain motor capabilities (Gibson, 2000, 2003). By moving about and exploring the environment, babies figure out which objects can be grasped, squeezed, bounced, or stroked and whether a surface is safe to cross or presents the possibility of falling. Sensitivity to these affordances means that we spend far less time correcting ineffective actions than we would otherwise. It makes our actions future-oriented and largely successful rather than reactive and blundering.

To illustrate, recall how infants' changing capabilities for independent movement affect their perception. When babies crawl, and again when they walk, they gradually realize that a steeply sloping surface *affords the possibility* of falling (see Figure 4.19). With added weeks of practicing each skill, they become hesitant to crawl or walk down a risky incline. Experience in trying to keep their balance on various surfaces makes crawlers and walkers more aware of the consequences of their movements. Crawlers come to detect when surface slant places so much body weight on their arms that they will fall forward, and walkers come to sense when an incline shifts body weight so

COURTESY OF KAREN ADOLPH, NEW YORK UNIVERSITY

their legs and feet can no longer hold them upright. Learning is gradual and effortful because newly crawling and walking babies traverse many types of surfaces in their homes each day (Adolph, 2008; Adolph & Joh, 2009). As they experiment with balance and postural adjustments to accommodate each, they perceive surfaces in new ways that guide their movements. As a result, they act more competently. **TAKE A MOMENT...** Can you think of other links between motor action and perceptual development described in this chapter?

Some researchers believe that babies do more than make sense of experience by searching for invariant features and discovering affordances: They also *impose meaning* on what they perceive, constructing categories of objects and events in the surrounding environment. We have seen the glimmerings of this *cognitive* point of view in this chapter. For example, older babies *interpret* a familiar face as a source of pleasure and affection and a pattern of blinking lights as a moving human being. We will save our discussion of infant cognition for later chapters, acknowledging that this cognitive perspective also offers insight into the achievements of infancy. In fact, many researchers combine these two positions, regarding infant development as proceeding from a perceptual to a cognitive emphasis over the first year of life.

FIGURE 4.19 Acting on the environment plays a major role in perceptual differentiation. Crawling and walking change the way babies perceive a sloping surface. The newly crawling infant on the left plunges headlong down the slope. He has not yet learned that it affords the possibility of falling. The toddler on the right, who has been walking for more than a month, approaches the slope cautiously. Experience in trying to remain upright but frequently tumbling over has made him more aware of the consequences of his movements. He perceives the incline differently than he did at a younger age.

A S K   Y O U R S E L F

Review ■ Using examples, explain why intermodal stimulation is vital for infants' developing understanding of their physical and social worlds.

Connect ■ According to differentiation theory, perceptual development reflects infants' active search for invariant features. Provide examples from research on hearing, pattern perception, and intermodal perception.

Apply ■ After several weeks of crawling, Ben learned to avoid going headfirst down a steep incline. Now he has started to walk. Can his mother trust him not to try walking down a steep surface? Explain, using the concept of affordances.

Reflect ■ Are young infants more competent than you thought they were before you read this chapter? List the capacities that most surprised you.

Early Deprivation and Enrichment: Is Infancy a Sensitive Period of Development?

▶ How does research on early deprivation and enrichment shed light on the question of whether infancy is a sensitive period of development?

Throughout this chapter, we have considered how a variety of early experiences affect the development of motor and perceptual skills. In view of the findings already reviewed, it is not surprising that many investigations have reported that stimulating physical surroundings and warm caregiving that is responsive to infants' self-initiated efforts promote active exploration of the environment and earlier attainment of developmental milestones (see, for example, Belsky & Fearon, 2002; Bendersky & Lewis, 1994).

The powerful effect of early experience is dramatically apparent in infants who lack the rich, varied stimulation of normal homes. Babies reared in severely deprived family situations or in institutions remain substantially below average in physical and psychological development and display emotional and behavior problems throughout childhood and adolescence (Rutter et al., 2010). These findings indicate that early experience has a profound impact, but they do not tell us whether infancy is a *sensitive period*. That is, if babies do not experience appropriate stimulation of their senses in the first year or two of life, can they fully recover? This question is controversial. Recall from Chapter 1 that some theorists argue that early experience leaves a lasting imprint on the child's competence. Others believe that most developmental delays resulting from events in the early years of life can be overcome.

Studies of animals exposed to extreme forms of sensory deprivation provide ample evidence that sensitive periods exist. For example, early, varied visual experiences must occur for the brain's visual centers to develop normally. If a 1-month-old kitten is deprived of light for just three or four days, these areas of the brain degenerate. If the kitten is kept in the dark during the fourth week of life and beyond, the damage is severe and permanent (Crair, Gillespie, & Stryker, 1998). And the general quality of the early environment affects overall brain growth. When animals reared from birth in physically and socially stimulating surroundings are compared with those reared in isolation, the brains of the stimulated animals are larger (Greenough & Black, 1992).

For ethical reasons, we cannot deliberately deprive some infants of normal rearing experiences and observe the impact on their brains and competencies. Instead, we must turn to natural experiments, in which children were victims of deprived early environments that were later rectified. Such studies have revealed some parallels with the animal evidence just described.

For example, when babies are born with cataracts (clouded lenses, preventing clear visual images) in both eyes, those who have corrective surgery within 4 to 6 months show rapid improvement in vision, except for subtle aspects of face perception, which require early visual input to the cerebral cortex to develop (Le Grand et al., 2003; Maurer, Mondloch, & Lewis, 2007). The longer cataract surgery is postponed beyond infancy, the less complete the recovery in visual skills. And if surgery is delayed until adulthood, vision is severely and permanently impaired (Lewis & Maurer, 2005).

Studies of infants placed in orphanages who were later exposed to family rearing confirm the importance of a generally stimulating physical and social environment for psychological development. In one investigation, researchers followed the progress of a large sample of children transferred between birth and 3½ years from Romanian orphanages to adoptive families in Great Britain (Beckett et al., 2006; O'Connor et al., 2000; Rutter et al., 1998, 2004, 2010). On arrival, most were impaired in all domains of development. By the preschool years, catch-up in physical size was dramatic. Cognitive catch-up was impressive for children adopted before age 6 months, who consistently attained average mental test scores in childhood and adolescence, performing as well as a comparison group of early-adopted British-born children.

But Romanian children who had been institutionalized for more than the first six months showed serious intellectual deficits (see Figure 4.20). Although they improved in mental test scores during middle childhood (perhaps as a result of added time in their adoptive homes and special services at school), they remained substantially below average. And most displayed at least three serious mental health problems, such as inattention, overactivity, unruly behavior, and autistic-like symptoms (social disinterest, stereotyped behavior) (Kreppner et al., 2007, 2010). A major correlate of both time spent in the institution and poor cognitive and emotional functioning was below-average head size, suggesting that early lack of stimulation permanently damaged the brain (Sonuga-Barke, Schlotz, & Kreppner, 2010).

Neurobiological findings indicate that early, prolonged institutionalization leads to a generalized reduction in activity in the cerebral cortex, especially the prefrontal cortex, which (as we will see in

These children in an orphanage in Romania receive little adult contact or stimulation. The longer they remain in this barren environment, the more likely they are to display profound impairment in all domains of development.

© ANDREW HOLBROOKE/CORBIS

Chapter 5) governs complex cognition and impulse control. Neural fibers connecting the prefrontal cortex with other brain structures involved in control of emotion are also reduced (Eluvathingal et al., 2006; Nelson, 2007). Consequently, as Chapter 10 will reveal, by the second half of the first year, institutionalized infants have difficulty discriminating others' emotional expressions—a persistent deficiency that contributes to their emotional and social adjustment problems.

Among institutionalized infants, abnormal development in one domain often impedes progress in others. For example, adoptive parents of children from orphanages often report visual impairments. A frequent problem is *strabismus* ("crossed eyes"), in which the eyes, because of muscle weakness, do not converge on the same point in space. Untreated infants, for whom strabismus persists longer than a few months, show abnormalities in the brain's visual structures and permanent deficits in visual acuity, depth perception, tracking of moving objects, and perception of the spatial layout of the environment (Tychsen, 2001). Also, the bland, colorless rooms where orphanage infants spend their days, rarely touched or spoken to, lead to deficits in intermodal perception (Cermak & Daunhauer, 1997). Children who have trouble integrating information across modalities tend to be overwhelmed by stimulation, reacting to it with disorganized behavior or withdrawal—a circumstance that impedes all domains of development.

Unfortunately, many infants reared in underprivileged environments—whether homes or institutions—continue to be affected by disadvantaged conditions during their childhood years. Interventions that break this pattern with warm, stimulating caregiver interaction and environmental enrichment can have lasting cognitive and social benefits. In the Bucharest Early Intervention Project, about 200 institutionalized Romanian babies were randomized into conditions of either care as usual or transfer to high-quality foster families between ages 5 and 30 months. Specially trained social workers provided foster parents with counseling and support in managing children's diverse developmental problems. Follow-ups between 2½ and 4 years revealed that the foster-care group exceeded the institutional-care group in intelligence test scores, language skills, perception of emotional expressions, emotional responsiveness, and EEG and ERP assessments of brain activity. On all measures, the earlier the foster placement, the better the outcome (Nelson et al., 2007; Smyke et al., 2009). Yet consistent with an early sensitive period, the foster-care group remained behind never-institutionalized agemates living with Bucharest families. In sum, to be maximally effective, intensive intervention must begin early.

Finally, in addition to impoverished environments, ones that overwhelm children with expectations beyond their current capacities also undermine development. In recent years, expensive early learning centers have sprung up, in which infants are trained with letter and number flash cards, and slightly older toddlers are given a full curriculum of reading, math, science, art, gym, and more. There is no evidence that these programs yield smarter, better "superbabies" (Hirsh-Pasek & Golinkoff, 2003). To the contrary, trying to prime infants with stimulation for which they are not ready can cause them to withdraw, threatening their spontaneous interest and pleasure in learning and creating conditions much like those of stimulus deprivation! We will return to this theme when we take up brain development in Chapter 5.

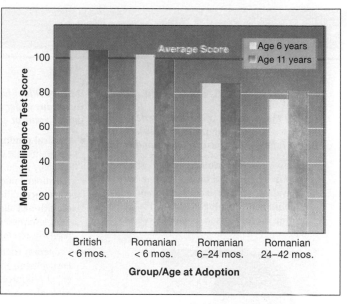

FIGURE 4.20 Relationship of age at adoption to mental test scores at ages 6 and 11 among British and Romanian adoptees. Children transferred from Romanian orphanages to British adoptive homes in the first six months of life attained average scores and fared as well as British early-adopted children, suggesting that they had fully recovered from extreme early deprivation. Romanian children adopted after 6 months of age performed well below average. And although those adopted after age 2 improved between ages 6 and 11, they continued to show serious intellectual deficits. (Adapted from Beckett et al., 2006.)

ASK YOURSELF

Review ■ Explain why either too much stimulation or too little stimulation over an extended time negatively disrupts early development.

Connect ■ What implications do findings on children from Eastern European orphanages have for the controversy over the lasting impact of early experiences on development (see Chapter 1, page 9)?

Reflect ■ Do you think infancy is a sensitive period? Explain, using research evidence.

S U M M A R Y

The Organized Infant (p. 129)

Explain the functions of newborn reflexes, and describe changing states of arousal during infancy, emphasizing sleep and crying.

■ **Reflexes** are the newborn baby's most obvious organized patterns of behavior. Some have survival value, others help parents and infants establish gratifying interaction, and still others provide the foundation for voluntary motor skills.

■ Although newborns move in and out of five **states of arousal,** they spend most of their time asleep. Sleep includes at least two states: **rapid-eye-movement (REM)** and **non-rapid-eye-movement (NREM) sleep.** Newborns spend about 50 percent of their sleep time in REM sleep, far more than they ever will again. REM sleep provides stimulation essential for central nervous system development. Individual and cultural differences in sleep–wake patterns are evident in early infancy. Disturbed REM–NREM cycles are a sign of central nervous system abnormalities, which may lead to sudden infant death syndrome (SIDS).

■ A crying baby stimulates strong feelings of discomfort in nearby adults. The intensity of the cry and experiences leading up to it help parents identify what is wrong. Once feeding and diaper changing have been tried, a highly effective soothing technique is lifting the baby to the shoulder and rocking or walking. Ethological research indicates that parental responsiveness to infant crying leads to less crying over time.

Why is neonatal behavioral assessment useful?

■ The most widely used instrument for assessing the organized functioning of newborn infants, Brazelton's **Neonatal Behavioral Assessment Scale (NBAS),** helps researchers understand individual and cultural differences in newborn behavior. Sometimes it is used to teach parents about their baby's capacities.

Describe infant learning capacities, the conditions under which they occur, and the unique value of each.

■ **Classical conditioning** helps infants to associate events that usually occur together in the everyday world. Infants can be classically conditioned most easily when the pairing of an **unconditioned stimulus (UCS)** and a **conditioned stimulus (CS)** has survival value—for example, learning which stimuli regularly accompany feeding.

■ In **operant conditioning,** infants act on their environment, and their behavior is followed by either **reinforcers,** which increase the occurrence of a preceding behavior, or **punishment,** which either removes a desirable stimulus or presents an unpleasant one to decrease the occurrence of a response. Retention of operant responses increases dramatically over the first 18 months. In young infants, interesting sights and sounds and pleasurable caregiver interaction serve as effective reinforcers.

■ **Habituation** and **recovery** reveal that at birth, babies are attracted to novelty. With age, infants habituate and recover more quickly. Novelty preference assesses infants' recent memory, whereas familiarity preference assesses their remote memory. Habituation research shows that young infants are especially attracted to motion and remember the movements of objects and people for weeks to months. Habituation and recovery are effective early predictors of intelligence because they assess memory and quickness and flexibility of thinking.

■ Newborns have a primitive ability to imitate adults' facial expressions and gestures. **Imitation** is a powerful means of learning that may serve as the foundation for understanding others' thoughts and feelings. Scientists have identified specialized cells called **mirror neurons** that underlie these capacities. However, whether newborn imitation is a voluntary capacity remains controversial.

Motor Development in Infancy (p. 147)

How does the dynamic systems perspective explain motor development?

■ According to **dynamic systems theory of motor development,** children acquire new motor skills by combining existing skills into increasingly complex systems of action. Each new skill is a joint product of central nervous system development, the body's movement possibilities, the child's goals, and environmental supports for the skill.

Identify factors that influence gross- and fine-motor development during the first two years.

■ Movement opportunities and a stimulating environment profoundly affect motor development, as shown by research on infants reared in deprived institutions. Cultural values and child-rearing customs also contribute to motor development.

■ During the first year, infants master reaching and grasping. The poorly coordinated **prereaching** of newborns drops out. Gradually, reaching becomes more flexible and accurate, and the clumsy **ulnar grasp** becomes the well-coordinated **pincer grasp.**

Perceptual Development in Infancy (p. 152)

Describe the newborn baby's sensitivity to touch, taste, smell, and sound, noting changes during infancy.

■ The senses of touch, taste, smell, and hearing are well-developed at birth. Newborns use their palms to distinguish the shapes of small objects. They are also highly sensitive to pain and prefer sweet tastes. Around 4 months, liking for the salty taste emerges and probably supports acceptance of solid foods. Newborns orient toward the odor of their own mother's amniotic fluid and that of the lactating breast—responses that help them identify their caregiver and locate an appropriate food source.

■ Newborns can distinguish a few sound patterns, as well as nearly all speech sounds. Over the first year, infants organize sounds into increasingly elaborate patterns.

■ Newborns can distinguish almost all speech sounds. They prefer listening to slow, clear, high-pitched expressive voices, to their own mother's voice, and to speech in their native language. Around the middle of the first year, they start to "screen out" sounds not used in their own language.

■ Infants' impressive **statistical learning capacity** enables them to detect speech patterns for which they will later learn meanings. In the second half-year, babies detect word boundaries and, soon after, syllable-stress regularities within words. They also detect simple word-order rules that may help them figure out the basic grammar of their language. Multisensory communication, such as mothers' tendency to label an object while demonstrating, supports infants' language learning.

Describe the development of vision in infancy, with special emphasis on depth, pattern, face, and object perception.

■ Vision is the least developed of the newborn's senses. As the eye and visual centers in the brain develop during the first few months, focusing ability, **visual acuity,** scanning, tracking, and color perception improve rapidly.

■ Research on depth perception reveals that responsiveness to motion develops first, followed by sensitivity to binocular and then to pictorial depth cues. Experience in crawling enhances depth perception and other aspects of three-dimensional understanding, but babies must learn to avoid drop-offs for each body position.

■ **Contrast sensitivity** accounts for early pattern preferences. At first, babies stare at single, high-contrast features. At 2 to 3 months, they explore a pattern's internal features and, over time, discriminate increasingly complex, meaningful patterns.

■ Newborns prefer to look at photos and simplified drawings of faces, but researchers disagree on whether they have a built-in tendency to orient toward human faces. Around 2 months, infants recognize and prefer their mother's facial features, and at 3 months, they distinguish the features of different faces. From 5 months on, they perceive emotional expressions as organized wholes. Experience promotes a **perceptual narrowing effect,** leading babies to form group biases—for example, a preference for female and own-race faces.

■ At birth, **size** and **shape constancy** help infants construct a coherent world of objects. Initially, infants depend on motion and spatial arrangement to identify objects. After 4 months, they rely increasingly on object features, such as distinct shape, color, and pattern. Around this time, they first perceive the path of a ball moving back and forth behind a screen as continuous. Soon they can monitor increasingly intricate paths of objects, as they look for featural information to detect the identity of a moving object.

Describe how intermodal perception develops during infancy.

■ Infants' remarkable capacity to engage in **intermodal perception** enables them to combine information across sensory modalities. Detection of **amodal sensory properties,** such as rate, rhythm, duration, intensity, temporal synchrony, and texture and shape, seems to provide the basis for detecting more specific intermodal relationships. Intermodal perception is a fundamental ability that fosters all aspects of psychological development, including perception of the physical world and social and language processing.

How does differentiation theory explain perceptual development?

■ According to **differentiation theory,** perceptual development is a matter of detecting increasingly fine-grained **invariant features** in a constantly changing perceptual world. Perceptual differentiation is guided by discovery of **affordances**—the action possibilities that a situation offers the individual.

Early Deprivation and Enrichment: Is Infancy a Sensitive Period of Development? (p. 169)

How does research on early deprivation and enrichment shed light on the question of whether infancy is a sensitive period of development?

■ Evidence that infancy is a sensitive period comes from natural experiments, such as babies placed in orphanages who were later adopted into families. Prolonged early deprivation can disrupt brain growth and result in persistent intellectual impairments and mental health problems. To be maximally effective, intensive intervention aimed at breaking the pattern of disadvantaged conditions must begin early. Environments that overwhelm infants with stimulation beyond their current capacities also undermine development.

IMPORTANT TERMS AND CONCEPTS

affordances (p. 168)
amodal sensory properties (p. 166)
classical conditioning (p. 140)
conditioned response (CR) (p. 140)
conditioned stimulus (CS) (p. 140)
contrast sensitivity (p. 161)
differentiation theory (p. 168)
dynamic systems theory of motor development (p. 148)
extinction (p. 140)
habituation (p. 142)
imitation (p. 145)
intermodal perception (p. 166)

invariant features (p. 168)
mirror neurons (p. 146)
Neonatal Behavioral Assessment Scale (NBAS) (p. 138)
non-rapid-eye-movement (NREM) sleep (p. 133)
operant conditioning (p. 141)
perceptual narrowing effect (p. 156)
pincer grasp (p. 151)
prereaching (p. 150)
punishment (p. 141)
rapid-eye-movement (REM) sleep (p. 133)
recovery (p. 142)

reflex (p. 130)
reinforcer (p. 141)
shape constancy (p. 165)
size constancy (p. 164)
states of arousal (p. 132)
statistical learning capacity (p. 157)
sudden infant death syndrome (SIDS) (p. 136)
ulnar grasp (p. 151)
unconditioned response (UCR) (p. 140)
unconditioned stimulus (UCS) (p. 140)
visual acuity (p. 159)
visual cliff (p. 159)

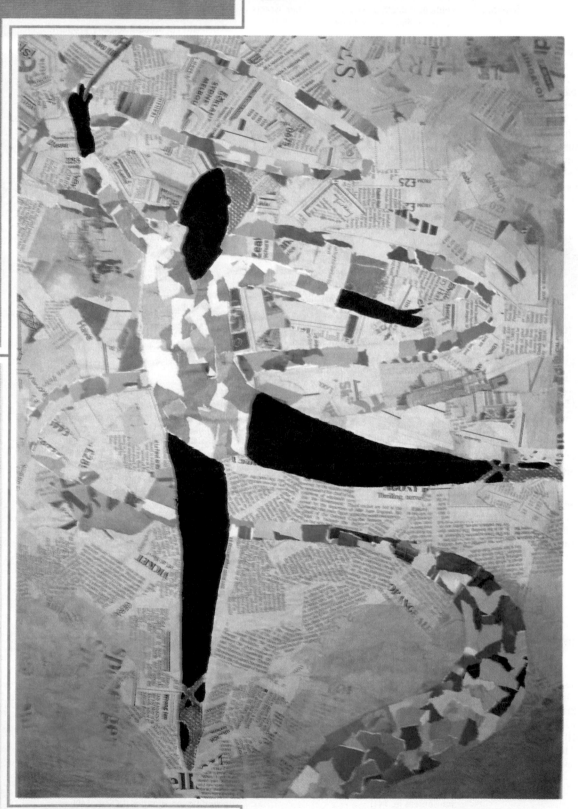

CHAPTER 5

"Rhythmic Gymnast"
Deanna Hodgson
12 years, United Kingdom

The dramatic gains in strength and coordination of adolescence are evident in this young dancer's grace and expressiveness. Her exuberant leap radiates self-confidence and pleasure in her expanding physical capacities.

Reprinted with permission from the International Child Art Foundation, Washington, DC

Physical Growth

O n Sabrina's eleventh birthday, her friend Joyce gave her a surprise party, but Sabrina seemed somber during the celebration. Although Sabrina and Joyce had been close friends since third grade, their relationship was faltering. Sabrina was a head taller and some 20 pounds heavier than most girls in her sixth-grade class. Her breasts were well-developed, her hips and thighs had broadened, and she had begun to menstruate. In contrast, Joyce still had the short, lean, flat-chested body of a school-age child.

Ducking into the bathroom while Joyce and the other girls put candles on the cake, Sabrina frowned at her image in the mirror. "I'm so big and heavy," she whispered. At church youth group on Sunday evenings, Sabrina broke away from Joyce and joined the eighth-grade girls. Around them, she didn't feel so large and awkward.

Once a month, parents gathered at Sabrina's and Joyce's school to discuss child-rearing concerns. Sabrina's parents, Franca and Antonio, attended whenever they could. "How you know they are becoming teenagers is this," volunteered Antonio. "The bedroom door is closed, and they want to be alone. Also, they contradict and disagree. Anything I say to Sabrina, she gives me an argument."

"All our children were early developers," Franca added. "But it was easier for the boys—being tall made them feel big and important. Sabrina is moody, she avoids her old friends, and she thinks about boys instead of her studies. As a little girl, she was skinny, but now she says she is too fat and needs to diet. I try to be patient with her," reflected Franca sympathetically.

During the first two decades of life, the human body changes continuously and dramatically. The average individual's height multiplies more than threefold, and weight increases as much as 15- to 20-fold. The top-heavy, chubby infant, whose head represents a quarter of the body's total length, gradually becomes the better-proportioned child and eventually the taller, broader, more muscular teenager. This chapter traces the course of human growth, along with biological and environmental factors that regulate and influence it.

As Sabrina's behavior indicates, physical and psychological development are closely linked. But just how the child's transforming body is related to cognitive, emotional, and social changes has puzzled philosophers and scientists for centuries. In particular, they have pondered this question with respect to *puberty*. **TAKE A MOMENT...** Ask several parents of young children what they expect their sons and daughters to be like as teenagers. You will probably get answers like these: "Rebellious and reckless," "Full of rages and tempers" (Buchanan & Holmbeck, 1998). This widespread view dates back to eighteenth-century philosopher Jean-Jacques Rousseau (see Chapter 1), who believed that the biological upheaval of puberty triggered heightened emotionality, conflict, and defiance of adults.

In the early twentieth century, major theorists picked up this storm-and-stress perspective. The most influential, G. Stanley Hall, described adolescence as a cascade of instinctual passions, a period so turbulent that it resembled the era in which humans evolved from savages into civilized beings.

Were Rousseau and Hall correct in seeing adolescence as a period of biologically engendered storm and stress? Or do social and cultural factors combine with biology to influence psychological development? In our discussion, we will see what contemporary research says about this issue. ∎

The Course of Physical Growth
Changes in Body Size • Changes in Body Proportions • Changes in Muscle–Fat Makeup • Skeletal Growth • Gains in Gross-Motor Skills • Hormonal Influences on Physical Growth • Worldwide Variations in Body Size • Secular Trends

■ **SOCIAL ISSUES: EDUCATION:** *Sex Differences in Gross-Motor Development*

Brain Development
Development of Neurons • Development of the Cerebral Cortex • Advances in Other Brain Structures • Brain Development in Adolescence • Sensitive Periods in Brain Development

■ **BIOLOGY AND ENVIRONMENT:** *Brain Plasticity: Insights from Research on Brain-Damaged Children and Adults*

Factors Affecting Physical Growth
Heredity • Nutrition • Infectious Disease • Emotional Well-Being

■ **BIOLOGY AND ENVIRONMENT:** *Low-Level Lead Exposure and Children's Development*

Puberty: The Physical Transition to Adulthood
Sexual Maturation in Girls • Sexual Maturation in Boys • Individual and Group Differences in Pubertal Growth

The Psychological Impact of Pubertal Events
Is Puberty Inevitably a Period of Storm and Stress? • Reactions to Pubertal Changes • Pubertal Change, Emotion, and Social Behavior • Pubertal Timing

Puberty and Adolescent Health
Eating Disorders • Sexuality • Sexually Transmitted Disease • Adolescent Pregnancy and Parenthood • A Concluding Note

■ **SOCIAL ISSUES: HEALTH:** *Lesbian, Gay, and Bisexual Youth: Coming Out to Oneself and Others*

- Describe the course of physical growth, including changes in body size, proportions, muscle–fat makeup, and skeleton, and their relationship to gains in gross-motor skills.

- Describe hormonal influences on physical growth.

- Discuss factors that contribute to worldwide variations and secular trends in physical growth.

The Course of Physical Growth

Compared with other animals, primates (including humans) experience a prolonged period of physical growth. Mice and rats develop from birth to puberty in just a few weeks—about 2 percent of the lifespan. By contrast, in chimpanzees, the species most similar to humans genetically, growth takes about seven years, or 16 percent of the lifespan. Physical immaturity is even more exaggerated in humans, who devote about 20 percent of their total years to growing. This prolonged physical immaturity is adaptive (Konner, 2010). By ensuring that children remain dependent on adults, it gives them added time to acquire the knowledge and skills essential for life in a complex social world.

Changes in Body Size

The most obvious signs of physical growth are changes in overall body size. During infancy, these changes are rapid—faster than at any other time after birth. By the end of the first year, a typical infant's height is 50 percent greater than at birth; by 2 years, it is 75 percent greater. Similarly, birth weight typically doubles by age 5 months, triples by 1 year, and quadruples by age 2. If children kept growing at this rate, by age 10 they would be 10 feet tall and weigh over 200 pounds! Fortunately, growth slows in early and middle childhood, when children add about 2 to 3 inches in height and 5 pounds in weight each year. Then, puberty brings a sharp acceleration. On average, adolescents gain 10 to 11 inches in height and about 50 to 75 pounds in weight.

Two types of growth curves are used to track overall changes in body size. The first, shown in Figure 5.1a, is a **distance curve,** which plots the average size of a sample of children at each age, indicating typical yearly progress toward maturity. The figure shows gains in height; weight gain follows a similar trend. Notice how during infancy and childhood the two sexes are similar, with the typical girl just slightly shorter (and lighter) than the typical boy. Around age 10 to 11, the typical North American and European girl becomes taller (and heavier) for a time because her pubertal growth spurt takes place two years earlier than the boy's (Archibald, Graber, & Brooks-Gunn, 2006; Bogin, 2001). At age 14, however, she is surpassed by the typical boy, whose growth spurt has now started, whereas hers is almost finished. Growth in height is complete for most North American and European girls by age 16, for boys by age 17½.

Figure 5.1b shows a second type of growth curve, the **velocity curve,** which plots the average amount of growth at each yearly interval, revealing the exact timing of growth spurts. Note the rapid but decelerating growth in infancy; a slower, constant rate during early and middle childhood; and a sharp increase in early adolescence, followed by a swift decrease as the body approaches its adult size.

Changes in Body Proportions

As the child's overall size increases, parts of the body grow at different rates. Two growth patterns describe these changes. The first is the **cephalocaudal trend**—from the Latin for "head to tail." Recall from Chapter 3 that during the prenatal period, the head develops first from the primitive embryonic disk, followed by the lower part of the body. After birth, the head and chest continue to have a growth advantage, but the trunk and legs gradually pick up speed. In the second pattern, the **proximodistal trend,** growth proceeds, literally, from "near to far"—from the center of the body

The dramatic rate of body growth in the first two years is evident when we look at a 4-month-old side by side with a 2-year-old. Height increases by 75 percent, and weight quadruples.

© BARBARA PEACOCK/CORBIS

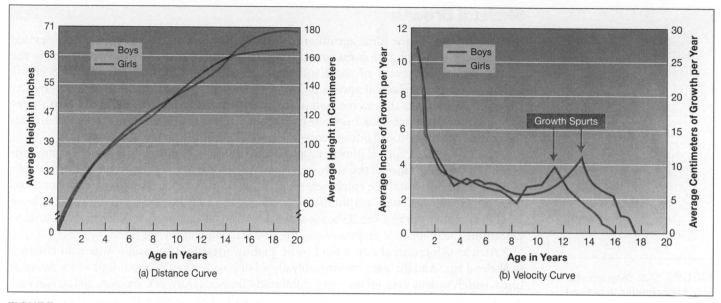

FIGURE 5.1 Distance and velocity curves for height. (a) The *distance curve* plots average size at each age and shows typical yearly progress toward maturity. (b) The *velocity curve* plots average amount of growth at each yearly interval and reveals the timing of growth spurts. The curves are based on cross-sectional height measurements taken on thousands of U.S. children. (U.S. Department of Health and Human Services, 2000.)

outward. In the prenatal period, the head, chest, and trunk grow first, then the arms and legs, finally the hands and feet. During infancy and childhood, the arms and legs continue to grow somewhat ahead of the hands and feet.

During puberty, growth proceeds in the reverse direction. The hands, legs, and feet accelerate first, followed by the torso, which accounts for most of the adolescent height gain (Sheehy et al., 1999). This pattern helps explain why young adolescents often appear awkward and out of proportion—long-legged, with giant feet and hands.

In infancy and childhood, girls and boys have similar body proportions. During adolescence, however, large differences appear, caused by the action of sex hormones on the skeleton. Boys' shoulders broaden relative to the hips, whereas girls' hips broaden relative to the shoulders and waist. Of course, boys also end up considerably larger than girls, and their legs are longer in relation to the rest of the body. The major reason is that boys have two extra years of preadolescent growth, when the legs are growing the fastest.

LOOK and LISTEN

Observe 10- to 14-year-olds on school grounds or at another gathering place, noting changes in body size and proportions, along with sex differences in timing of the growth spurt.

Changes in Muscle–Fat Makeup

Body fat (most of which lies just beneath the skin) increases in the last few weeks of prenatal life and continues to do so after birth, reaching a peak at about 9 months of age. This early rise in "baby fat" helps the infant keep a constant body temperature. Starting in the second year and continuing into middle childhood, most toddlers slim down (Fomon & Nelson, 2002). At birth, girls have slightly more body fat than boys, a difference that persists into the early school years and then magnifies. Around age 8, girls start to add more fat on their arms, legs, and trunk; they continue to do so throughout puberty, while the arm and leg fat of adolescent boys decreases (Siervogel et al., 2000).

Muscle accumulates slowly throughout infancy and childhood, with a dramatic rise at adolescence. Both sexes gain muscle at puberty, but this increase is 150 percent greater in boys, who develop larger skeletal muscles, hearts, and lung capacity (Rogol, Roemmich, & Clark, 2002). Also, the number of red blood cells—and therefore the ability to carry oxygen from the lungs to the muscles—increases in boys but not in girls. Altogether, boys gain far more muscle strength than girls, contributing to their superior athletic performance during the teenage years (Ramos et al., 1998).

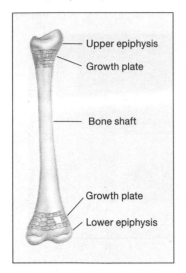

FIGURE 5.2 Diagram of a long bone showing upper and lower epiphyses. Cartilage cells are produced at the growth plates of the epiphyses and gradually harden into bone.

Skeletal Growth

Because children of the same age differ in *rate* of physical growth, researchers have devised methods for measuring progress toward physical maturity that are useful for studying the causes and consequences of these individual differences. The best estimate of a child's physical maturity is **skeletal age**—a measure of development of the bones of the body. The embryonic skeleton is first formed out of soft, pliable tissue called *cartilage*. In the sixth week of pregnancy, cartilage cells begin to harden into bone, a gradual process that continues throughout childhood and adolescence (Moore & Persaud, 2008).

Just before birth, special growth centers, called **epiphyses**, appear at the two extreme ends of each of the long bones of the body (see Figure 5.2). Cartilage cells continue to be produced at the growth plates of these epiphyses, which increase in number throughout childhood and then, as growth continues, get thinner and disappear. After that, no further growth in bone length is possible. As Figure 5.3 shows, skeletal age can be estimated by X-raying the bones to determine the number of epiphyses and the extent to which they are fused.

African-American children tend to be slightly ahead of Caucasian-American children in skeletal age. And girls are considerably ahead of boys—a gap of about four to six weeks at birth, which widens over infancy and childhood (Tanner, Healy, & Cameron, 2001). Girls are advanced in development of other organs as well. This greater physical maturity may contribute to girls' greater resistance to harmful environmental influences. As noted in Chapter 3, girls experience fewer developmental problems than boys and have lower infant and childhood mortality rates.

FIGURE 5.3 Hand X-rays showing skeletal maturity in a toddler and a teenager. In the toddler's hand (left), wide gaps exist between the wrist bones and at the ends of the finger and arm bones. In the teenager (right), who has reached adult size, the wrist and long bones are completely fused.

Gains in Gross-Motor Skills

Changes in size, proportions, and muscle strength support an explosion of new gross-motor skills. As the body becomes more streamlined and less top-heavy, the center of gravity shifts downward, toward the trunk. The resulting improvement in balance paves the way for new motor skills involving large muscles.

Advances in Early and Middle Childhood By age 2, preschoolers' gaits become smooth and rhythmic—secure enough that they soon leave the ground, first by running and jumping and then, between 3 and 6 years, by hopping, galloping, and skipping. Eventually, upper and lower body skills combine into more effective actions (Haywood & Getchell, 2005). Whereas 2- and 3-year-olds throw a ball rigidly, using only the arms, 4- and 5-year-olds use a smooth, flexible motion, involving the shoulders, torso, trunk, and legs, that makes the ball travel faster and farther.

During the school years, improved balance, strength, agility, and flexibility support refinements in running, jumping, hopping, and ball skills. Children sprint across the playground, play hopscotch in intricate patterns, kick and dribble soccer balls, and swing bats at pitched balls. The Milestones table on the following page summarizes gross-motor achievements in early and middle childhood. At adolescence, increased body size and muscle bring continued motor gains.

The same principle that governs motor development during the first two years continues to operate in childhood and adolescence. Children integrate previously acquired skills into more complex, *dynamic systems of action*. (Return to Chapter 4, page 148, to review this concept.) Then they revise each skill as their bodies grow larger and stronger, their central nervous systems become better developed, their interests and goals become clearer, and their

Milestones

Gross-Motor Development in Early and Middle Childhood

AGE	GROSS-MOTOR SKILLS
2–3 years	• Walks more rhythmically; hurried walk changes to run • Jumps, hops, throws, and catches with rigid upper body • Pushes riding toy with feet; little steering
3–4 years	• Walks up stairs, alternating feet, and down stairs, leading with one foot • Jumps and hops, flexing upper body • Throws and catches with slight involvement of upper body; still catches by trapping ball against chest • Pedals and steers tricycle
4–5 years	• Walks down stairs, alternating feet • Runs more smoothly • Gallops and skips with one foot • Throws ball with increased body rotation and transfer of weight on feet; catches ball with hands • Rides tricycle rapidly; steers smoothly
5–6 years	• Increases running speed to 12 feet per second • Gallops more smoothly; engages in true skipping and sideways stepping • Displays mature, whole-body throwing and catching pattern; increases throwing speed • Rides bicycle with training wheels
7–12 years	• Increases running speed to more than 18 feet per second • Displays continuous, fluid skipping and sideways stepping • Increases vertical jump from 4 to 12 inches and broad jump from 3 to over 5 feet; accurately jumps and hops from square to square • Increases throwing and kicking speed, distance, and accuracy • Increases ability to catch small balls thrown over greater distances • Involves the whole body in batting a ball; batting increases in speed and accuracy • Hand dribbling changes from awkward slapping of the ball to continuous, relaxed, even stroking

Note: These milestones represent overall age trends. Individual differences exist in the precise age at which each milestone is attained.

Sources: Cratty, 1986; Haywood & Getchell, 2005; Malina & Bouchard, 1991.

Photos: (top) © Lawrence Migdale/Photo Researchers, Inc.; (upper middle) © Bob Daemmrich/PhotoEdit; (lower middle) © David Madison/Getty Images/Photographer's Choice; (bottom) © Lynn Harty Photography/Alamy

environments present new challenges. Sex differences in motor skills, already present in the preschool years, illustrate these multiple influences. Size and strength contribute to boys' superior athletic performance in adolescence but cannot fully account for their childhood advantage. As the Social Issues: Education box on page 180 reveals, the social environment plays a prominent role.

Organized Youth Sports Partly because of parents' concerns about safety and the availability and attractions of TV, computer and video games, and the Internet, today's school-age children and adolescents devote less time to outdoor, informal physical play than children in

SOCIAL ISSUES: EDUCATION

Sex Differences in Gross-Motor Development

Sex differences in gross-motor development are present as early as the preschool years, increase during middle childhood, and are large at adolescence. What underlies this expanding gender gap, and how can we ensure that both boys and girls have opportunities that optimize skill and enjoyment of athletics?

Early and Middle Childhood

In early childhood, boys are advanced over girls in abilities that emphasize force and power. By age 5, they can broad-jump slightly farther, run slightly faster, and throw a ball about 5 feet farther. During middle childhood, these differences intensify. For example, on average, a 12-year-old boy can throw a ball 43 feet farther than a 12-year-old girl. Boys are also more adept at batting, kicking, dribbling, and catching. Their slightly greater muscle mass and, in the case of throwing, slightly longer forearms contribute to their skill advantages. And partly because of greater overall physical maturity, girls have an edge in fine-motor skills of handwriting and drawing and in gross-motor capacities that depend on balance and agility, such as hopping and skipping (Fischman, Moore, & Steele, 1992; Haywood & Getchell, 2005).

Sex differences in motor skills increase with age. However, differences in physical capacity remain small throughout childhood, suggesting that social pressures for boys, more than girls, to be active and physically skilled exaggerate small genetically based sex differences. In support of this view, boys can throw a ball much farther than girls only when using their dominant hand. Practice—such as fathers more often playing catch with sons than with daughters—seems to be largely responsible for this advantage. When boys use their nondominant hand, the sex difference is minimal (Williams, Haywood, & Painter, 1996).

Research confirms that parents hold higher expectations for boys' athletic performance—a social message that children absorb at an early age. From first through twelfth grade, girls are less positive than boys about the value of sports and their own sports ability—differences explained in part by parental beliefs (Fredricks & Eccles, 2002). The stronger girls' belief that females are incompetent at sports (such as hockey or soccer), the lower girls judge their own ability and the poorer their actual performance (Belcher et al., 2003; Chalabaev, Sarrazin, & Fontayne, 2009). Girls have few opportunities in school to reverse these gender-based

appraisals. To devote more time to academic instruction, U.S. schools have cut back on physical education. Currently, only 15 percent of U.S. elementary and middle schools provide a physical education class at least three days a week, and just 6 percent provide a daily class (Lee et al., 2007).

Adolescence

Not until puberty do sharp sex differences in physical size and muscle strength account for large differences in athletic ability. During adolescence, girls' gains in gross-motor performance are slow and gradual, leveling off by age 14. In contrast, boys show a dramatic spurt in strength, speed, and endurance that continues through the teenage years, widening the gender gap. By midadolescence, few girls perform as well as the average boy in running speed, broad jump, or throwing distance. And practically no boys score as low as the average girl (Haywood & Getchell, 2005; Malina & Bouchard, 1991).

In 1972, the U.S. federal government required schools receiving public funds to provide equal opportunities for males and females in all educational programs, including athletics. Since then, girls' high school extracurricular sports participation has increased, although it still falls far short of boys. In a recent survey of all 50 U.S. state high school athletic associations, 41 percent of sports participants were girls, 59 percent boys (National Federation of State High School Associations, 2009).

By high school, only 58 percent of U.S. boys and 55 percent of girls take any physical education, and daily physical education classes are offered in just 2 percent of U.S. high schools (Centers for Disease Control and Prevention, 2007; U.S. Department of Health and Human Services, 2010g). For both sexes, physical activity declines during adolescence, a trend that parallels school cutbacks (typically to conserve costs) in required physical education. The drop is sharper for girls, two-thirds of whom (compared with just half of boys) take no physical education during their senior year.

Interventions

Besides improving motor performance, sports and exercise influence cognitive and social development. Interschool and intramural athletics provide important lessons in teamwork, problem solving, assertiveness, and competition. And regular, sustained physical activity is associated

Parental encouragement of girls' involvement in sports is a vital factor in reducing the gender gap in athletic participation, skill, and enjoyment.

with healthier dietary habits, enhanced functioning of the immune and cardiovascular systems, better sleep quality, and favorable psychological well-being, as indicated by better academic performance and reduced alcohol and drug use in adolescence (Brand et al., 2010; Castelli et al., 2007; Pate et al., 2000).

Special steps must be taken to raise girls' confidence that they can do well at athletics. Educating parents about the minimal differences between school-age boys' and girls' physical capacities and sensitizing them to unfair biases against promotion of athletic ability among girls may prove helpful. Greater emphasis on skill training for girls, along with increased attention to their athletic achievements, is also likely to improve their participation and performance.

Finally, daily physical education in school, emphasizing enjoyable games and individual exercise rather than competition, is particularly motivating for girls and is associated with lasting positive consequences (Weinberg et al., 2000). In a longitudinal study, participating in team or individual sports at age 14 predicted high rates of physical activity at age 31. Endurance sports such as running and cycling—activities that can easily be performed on one's own time, without expensive equipment or special facilities—were especially likely to carry over into adulthood (Tammelin et al., 2003). The stamina these activities require fosters high *physical self-efficacy*—belief in one's ability to sustain an exercise program (Motl et al., 2002; Telama et al., 2005).

previous generations. At the same time, organized sports, such as Little League baseball and soccer and hockey leagues, have expanded tremendously, filling many hours that children used to spend gathering spontaneously for physical play on sidewalks and playgrounds. About half of U.S. youngsters—60 percent of boys and 37 percent of girls—participate in organized sports outside of school hours at some time between ages 5 and 18 (National Council of Youth Sports, 2008).

For most children, joining community athletic teams is associated with increased self-esteem and social skills (Daniels & Leaper, 2006; Fletcher, Nickerson, & Wright, 2003). Among shy children, sports participation seems to play a protective role, fostering self-confidence and a decline in social anxiety, perhaps because it provides a sense of group belonging and a basis for communicating with peers (Findlay & Coplan, 2008). And children who view themselves as good at sports are more likely to continue playing on teams in adolescence, which predicts greater participation in sports and other physical fitness activities in early adulthood (Kjonniksen, Anderssen, & Wold, 2009; Marsh et al., 2007).

In some cases, though, the arguments of critics—that youth sports overemphasize competition and substitute adult control for children's natural experimentation with rules and strategies—are valid. Children who join teams so early that the necessary skills are beyond their abilities soon lose interest. Coaches and parents who criticize rather than encourage can prompt intense anxiety in some children. Rather than promoting elite performance, high parental pressure to excel at sports and frequent, intense practice are linked to children's emotional difficulties and early athletic dropout (Tofler, Knapp, & Drell, 1998; Wall & Côté, 2007).

In most organized sports, health and safety rules help ensure that injuries are infrequent and mild. The exception is football, which has a high rate of serious injury (Radelet et al., 2002). But frequent, intense practice in any sport can lead to painful "overuse" injuries and, in extreme cases, to stress-related fractures resulting in premature closure of the epiphyses of the long bones (Frank et al., 2007).

When parents and coaches emphasize effort, improvement, participation, and teamwork, young athletes enjoy sports more, exert greater effort to improve their skills, and perceive themselves as more competent at their chosen sport (Ullrich-French & Smith, 2006). This positive emphasis helps promote physical activity, an important factor at a time when inactivity is pervasive among U.S. children and adolescents. Only 49 percent of school-age boys and 35 percent of girls are active enough for good health—that is, engage in at least moderate-intensity exercise for one hour or more per day. As children move into adolescence, these rates drop sharply, to just 25 percent of boys and 11 percent of girls (Troiano et al., 2007; U.S. Department of Health and Human Services, 2010g).

Hormonal Influences on Physical Growth

The endocrine glands control the vast physical changes of childhood and adolescence. They manufacture *hormones*, chemical substances secreted by specialized cells in one part of the body that pass to and influence cells in another.

The most important hormones for human growth are released by the **pituitary gland,** located at the base of the brain near the **hypothalamus,** a structure that initiates and regulates pituitary secretions (see Figure 5.4). Once pituitary

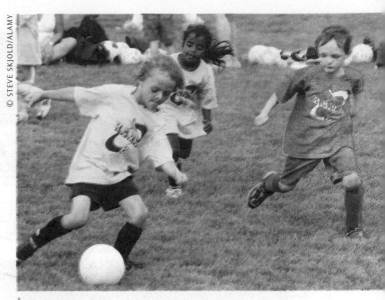

When coaches emphasize effort, teamwork, and skills over competition, school-age children benefit both physically and socially from playing team sports and are more likely to remain active in adolescence.

LOOK and **LISTEN**

Observe a youth athletic league game, such as soccer, baseball, or hockey. Do coaches and parents encourage children's effort and skill gains, or are they overly focused on winning? Cite examples of adult and child behaviors.

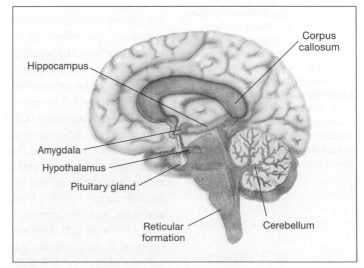

FIGURE 5.4 Cross-section of the human brain, showing the location of the hypothalamus and pituitary gland. Also shown are five additional structures—the cerebellum, the reticular formation, the amygdala, the hippocampus, and the corpus callosum—that we will discuss in a later section.

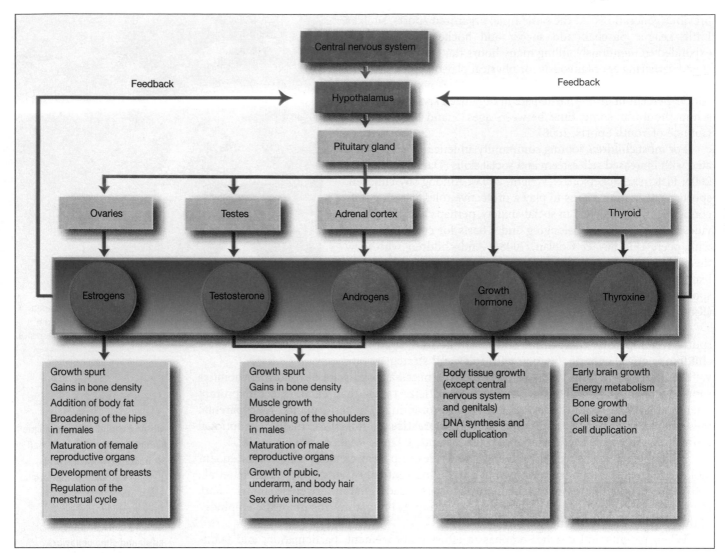

FIGURE 5.5 Hormonal influences on postnatal growth. The hypothalamus stimulates the pituitary gland to release hormones that either induce growth directly or stimulate other endocrine glands to release growth-inducing hormones (red lines). A highly sensitive feedback loop exists in which the hypothalamus detects hormone levels in the bloodstream and instructs the pituitary gland to increase or decrease the amount of each hormone accordingly (blue lines).

hormones enter the bloodstream, they act directly on body tissues to induce growth, or they stimulate the release of other hormones from endocrine glands located elsewhere in the body. The hypothalamus contains special receptors that detect hormone levels in the bloodstream. Through a highly sensitive feedback loop, it instructs the pituitary gland to increase or decrease the amount of each hormone. In this way, growth is carefully controlled. You may find it useful to refer to Figure 5.5 as we review major hormonal influences.

Growth hormone (GH), the only pituitary secretion produced continuously throughout life, affects development of all tissues except the central nervous system and the genitals. GH production doubles during puberty, contributing to tremendous gains in body size, and then decreases after final adult height is reached. GH acts directly on the body and also stimulates the liver and epiphyses of the skeleton to release another hormone, *insulin-like growth factor 1 (IGF-1),* which triggers cell duplication throughout the body, especially the skeleton, muscles, nerves, bone marrow (origin of blood cells), liver, kidney, skin, and lungs.

Although GH does not seem to affect prenatal growth, it is necessary for physical development from birth on. About 2 percent of children suffer from inherited conditions that cause either GH deficiency or IGF-1 deficiency (in which GH fails to stimulate IGF-1). Without medical intervention, such children reach an average mature height of only 4 to 4½ feet. When treated early with injections of GH or IGF-1 (depending on the disorder), these children show catch-up growth and then grow at a normal rate, becoming much taller than they would have without treatment (Bright, Mendoza, & Rosenfeld, 2009; Saenger, 2003).

A second pituitary hormone, **thyroid-stimulating hormone (TSH),** prompts the thyroid gland in the neck to release *thyroxine*, which is necessary for brain development and for GH to have its full impact on body size. Infants born with a deficiency of thyroxine must receive it at once, to prevent permanent intellectual disability. Once the most rapid period of brain development is complete, thyroxine deficiency no longer affects the central nervous system but still causes children to grow more slowly than average. With prompt treatment, however, they eventually reach normal size (Salerno et al., 2001).

Sexual maturation is controlled by pituitary secretions that stimulate the release of sex hormones. Although we think of **estrogens** as female hormones and **androgens** as male hormones, both types are present in each sex, but in different amounts. The boy's testes release large quantities of the androgen *testosterone,* which leads to muscle growth, body and facial hair, and other male sex characteristics. Androgens (especially testosterone for boys) exert a GH-enhancing effect, contributing greatly to gains in body size. The testes also secrete small amounts of estrogen—the reason that 50 percent of boys experience temporary breast enlargement. In both sexes, estrogens also increase GH secretion, adding to the growth spurt and, in combination with androgens, stimulating gains in bone density, which continue into early adulthood (Cooper, Sayer, & Dennison, 2006; Styne, 2003).

Estrogens released by girls' ovaries cause the breasts, uterus, and vagina to mature, the body to take on feminine proportions, and fat to accumulate. Estrogens also contribute to regulation of the menstrual cycle. *Adrenal androgens,* released from the adrenal glands located on top of each kidney, influence girls' height spurt and stimulate growth of underarm and pubic hair. They have little impact on boys, whose physical characteristics are influenced mainly by androgen and estrogen secretions from the testes.

Worldwide Variations in Body Size

TAKE A MOMENT... Glance into almost any school classroom, and notice the wide individual differences in body growth. Diversity in physical size is especially apparent when we travel to different nations. Worldwide, a 9-inch gap exists between the smallest and the largest 8-year-olds. The shortest children, found in South America, Asia, the Pacific Islands, and parts of Africa, include such ethnic groups as Colombian, Burmese, Thai, Vietnamese, Ethiopian, and Bantu. The tallest children—living in Australia, northern and central Europe, Canada, and the United States, come from Czech, Dutch, Latvian, Norwegian, Swiss, and African populations (Meredith, 1978; Ruff, 2002).

Ethnic variations in growth rate are also common: African-American and Asian children tend to mature faster than Caucasian-American children, who are slightly ahead of European children (Eveleth & Tanner, 1990; Komlos & Breitfelder, 2008). These findings remind us that *growth norms* (age-related averages for height and weight) must be applied cautiously, especially in countries with high immigration rates and many ethnic minorities.

Both heredity and environment contribute to these differences. Body size sometimes reflects evolutionary adaptations to a particular climate. Long, lean physiques are typical in hot, tropical regions and short, stocky ones in cold, Arctic areas (Katzmarzyk & Leonard, 1998). Also, children who grow tallest usually live in developed countries, where food is plentiful and infectious diseases are largely controlled. Physically small children tend to live in less-developed regions, where poverty, hunger, and disease are common (Bogin, 2001). When families move from poor to wealthy nations, their children not only grow taller but also change to a longer-legged body shape. (Recall that during childhood, the legs are growing fastest.) For example, U.S.-born school-age children of immigrant Guatemalan Mayan parents are, on average, 4½ inches taller, with legs nearly 3 inches longer, than their agemates in Guatemalan Mayan villages (Bogin et al., 2002; Varela-Silva et al., 2007).

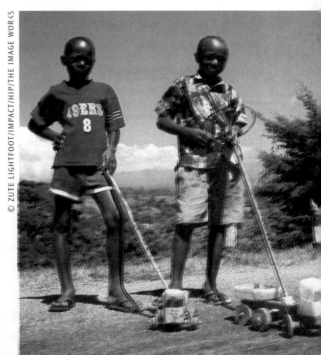

© ZUTE LIGHTFOOT/IMPACT/HIP/THE IMAGE WORKS

Body size is often the result of evolutionary adaptations to a particular climate. These boys of Tanzania, who live on the hot African plains, have long, lean physiques that permit their bodies to cool easily.

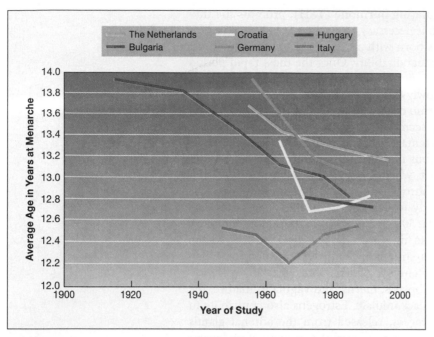

FIGURE 5.6 Secular trend in age at menarche in six industrialized nations. Age of menarche declined from 1900 to 1970. Thereafter, a few countries showed a modest, continuing decline due to rising rates of overweight and obesity. Others leveled off or underwent a slight reversal. (From S. M. P. F. de Muinck Keizer-Schrama & D. Mul, 2001, "Trends in Pubertal Development in Europe," *Human Reproduction Update*, 7, p. 289. © European Society of Human Reproduction and Embryology. Reproduced by permission of Oxford University Press/Human Reproduction and S. M. P. F. de Muinck Keizer-Schrama.)

Secular Trends

Over the past 150 years, **secular trends in physical growth**—changes in body size from one generation to the next—have occurred in industrialized nations. In Australia, Canada, Japan, New Zealand, the United States, and nearly all European countries, most children today are taller and heavier than their parents and grandparents were as children (Ong, Ahmed, & Dunger, 2006). The secular gain appears early in life, increases over childhood and early adolescence, and then declines as mature body size is reached. This pattern suggests that the larger size of today's children is mostly due to a faster rate of physical development. Consistent with this view, age of first menstruation declined steadily from 1900 to 1970, by about 3 to 4 months per decade. Although evidence on boys is sparse, they, too, show signs of having reached puberty earlier in recent decades (Euling et al., 2008).

Improved health and nutrition are largely responsible. As developing nations make socioeconomic progress, they also show secular gains (Ji & Chen, 2008). Secular trends are smaller for low-income children, who have poorer diets and are more likely to suffer from growth-stunting illnesses. And in regions with widespread poverty, famine, and disease, either no secular change or a secular decrease in body size has occurred (Barnes-Josiah & Augustin, 1995; Cole, 2000).

In most industrialized nations, the secular gain in height has slowed, and—as Figure 5.6 illustrates—the trend toward earlier first menstruation has stopped or undergone a slight reversal. But in the United States and a few European countries, soaring rates of overweight and obesity are responsible for a modest, continuing trend toward earlier menarche (Kaplowitz, 2008; Parent et al., 2003).

ASK YOURSELF

Review ■ What aspects of physical growth account for the long-legged appearance of many 8- to 12-year-olds?

Connect ■ Relate secular trends in physical growth to the concept of cohort effects, discussed on page 62 in Chapter 2.

Apply ■ Nine-year-old Allison dislikes physical education and thinks she isn't good at sports. What strategies can be used to improve her involvement and pleasure in physical activity?

Reflect ■ How does your height compare with that of your parents and grandparents when they were your age? Do your observations illustrate secular trends?

▶ Cite major milestones in brain development, at the level of individual brain cells and at the level of the cerebral cortex.

▶ Describe changes in other brain structures and in the adolescent brain, and discuss evidence on sensitive periods in brain development.

Brain Development

The human brain is the most elaborate and effective living structure on earth today. Despite its complexity, it reaches its adult size earlier than any other organ. We can best understand brain growth by looking at it from two vantage points: (1) the microscopic level of individual brain cells and (2) the larger level of the cerebral cortex, the most complex brain structure and the one responsible for the highly developed intelligence of our species.

Development of Neurons

The human brain has 100 to 200 billion **neurons,** or nerve cells, that store and transmit information, many of which have thousands of direct connections with other neurons. Unlike other body cells, neurons are not tightly packed together. Between them are tiny gaps, or **synapses,** where fibers from different neurons come close together but do not touch (see Figure 5.7). Neurons send messages to one another by releasing chemicals called **neurotransmitters,** which cross synapses.

The basic story of brain growth concerns how neurons develop and form this elaborate communication system. Figure 5.8 summarizes major milestones of brain development. In the prenatal period, neurons are produced in the embryo's primitive neural tube. From there, they migrate to form the major parts of the brain (see Chapter 3, page 91). Once neurons are in place, they differentiate, establishing their unique functions by extending their fibers to form synaptic connections with neighboring cells. During infancy and early childhood, neural fibers increase at an astounding pace (Huttenlocher, 2002; Moore & Persaud, 2008). A surprising aspect of brain growth is **programmed cell death,** which makes space for these connective structures: As synapses form, many surrounding neurons die—20 to 80 percent, depending on the brain region (de Haan & Johnson, 2003; Stiles, 2008). Fortunately, during the prenatal period, the neural tube produces far more neurons than the brain will ever need.

As neurons form connections, *stimulation* becomes vital to their survival. Neurons that are stimulated by input from the surrounding environment continue to establish synapses, forming increasingly elaborate systems of communication that support more complex abilities. At first, stimulation results in massive overabundance of synapses, many of which serve identical functions, thereby ensuring that the child will acquire the motor, cognitive, and social skills that our species needs to survive. Neurons that are seldom stimulated soon lose their synapses, in a process called **synaptic pruning** that returns neurons not needed at the moment to an uncommitted state so they can

FIGURE 5.7 **Neurons and their connective fibers.** This photograph of several neurons, taken with the aid of a powerful microscope, shows the elaborate synaptic connections that form with neighboring cells.

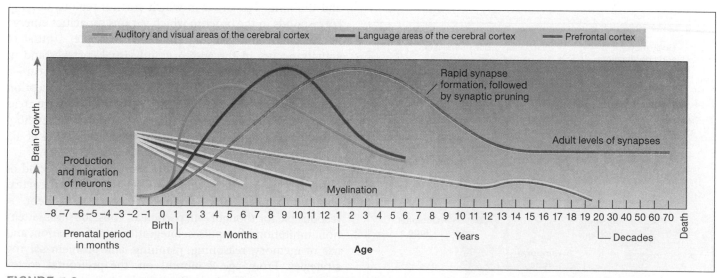

FIGURE 5.8 **Major milestones of brain development.** Formation of synapses is rapid during the first two years, especially in the auditory, visual, and language areas of the cerebral cortex. The prefrontal cortex undergoes more extended synaptic growth. In each area, overproduction of synapses is followed by synaptic pruning. The prefrontal cortex is among the last regions to attain adult levels of synaptic connections—in mid- to late adolescence. Myelination occurs at a dramatic pace during the first two years, more slowly through childhood, followed by an acceleration at adolescence. The multiple yellow lines indicate that the timing of myelination varies among different brain areas. For example, neural fibers continue to myelinate over a longer period in the language areas, and especially in the prefrontal cortex, than in the visual and auditory areas. (Adapted from Thompson & Nelson, 2001.)

support future development. In all, about 40 percent of synapses are pruned during childhood and adolescence (Webb, Monk, & Nelson, 2001). For this process to go forward, appropriate stimulation of the child's brain is vital during periods in which the formation of synapses is at its peak (Nelson, Thomas, & de Haan, 2006).

If few new neurons are produced after the prenatal period, what causes the dramatic increase in brain size during infancy and early childhood? About half the brain's volume is made up of **glial cells,** which are responsible for **myelination,** the coating of neural fibers with an insulating fatty sheath (called *myelin*) that improves the efficiency of message transfer. Glial cells multiply rapidly from the fourth month of pregnancy through the second year of life—a process that continues at a slower pace through middle childhood and accelerates again in adolescence. Gains in neural fibers and myelination are responsible for the extraordinary increase in overall size of the brain—from nearly 30 percent of its adult weight at birth to 70 percent by age 2 and 90 percent at age 6 (Johnson, 2005; Knickmeyer et al., 2008).

Brain development can be compared to molding a "living sculpture." First, neurons and synapses are overproduced; then, cell death and synaptic pruning sculpt away excess building material to form the mature brain—a process jointly influenced by genetically programmed events and the child's experiences. The resulting "sculpture" is a set of interconnected regions, each with specific functions—much like countries on a globe that communicate with one another (Johnston et al., 2001). This "geography" of the brain permits researchers to study its organization using neurobiological methods, such as EEG, ERP, fMRI, and NIRS (see page 48 in Chapter 2 to review). We will encounter these measures as we turn now to the development of the cerebral cortex.

Development of the Cerebral Cortex

The **cerebral cortex** surrounds the rest of the brain, resembling half of a shelled walnut. It is the largest brain structure—accounting for 85 percent of the brain's weight and containing the greatest number of neurons and synapses. Because the cerebral cortex is also the last brain structure to stop growing, it is sensitive to environmental influences for a much longer period than any other part of the brain.

Regions of the Cerebral Cortex Figure 5.9 shows specific functions of regions of the cerebral cortex, such as receiving information from the senses, instructing the body to move, and thinking. The order in which cortical regions develop corresponds to the order in which various capacities emerge in the infant and growing child. For example, a burst of activity occurs in the auditory and visual cortexes and in areas responsible for body movement over the first year—a period of dramatic gains in auditory and visual perception and mastery of motor skills (Johnson, 2005). Language areas are especially active from late infancy through the preschool years, when language development flourishes (Pujol et al., 2006; Thompson et al., 2000).

The cortical regions with the most extended period of development are the *frontal lobes.* The **prefrontal cortex,** lying in front of areas controlling body movement, is responsible for thought—in particular, consciousness, attention, inhibition of impulses, integration of information, and use of memory, reasoning, planning, and problem-solving strategies. From age 2 months on, the prefrontal cortex functions more effectively. But it undergoes especially rapid myelination and formation and pruning of synapses during the preschool and school years, followed by another period of accelerated growth in adolescence, when it reaches an adult level of synaptic connections (Nelson, 2002; Nelson, Thomas, & de Haan, 2006; Sowell et al., 2002).

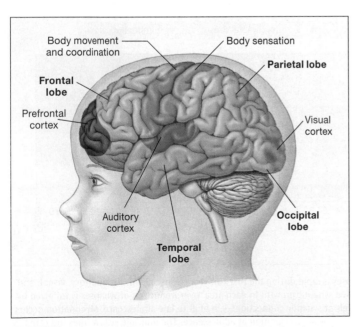

FIGURE 5.9 The left side of the human brain, showing the cerebral cortex. The cortex is divided into different lobes, each containing a variety of regions with specific functions. Some major regions are labeled here.

Lateralization and Plasticity of the Cerebral Cortex The cerebral cortex has two *hemispheres,* or sides, that differ in their functions. Some tasks are done mostly by the left hemisphere, others by the right. For example, each hemisphere receives sensory information from the side of the body opposite to it and controls only that side.[1] For most of us, the left hemisphere is largely responsible for verbal abilities (such as spoken and written language) and positive emotion (such as joy). The right hemisphere handles spatial abilities (judging distances, reading maps, and recognizing geometric shapes) and negative emotion (such as distress) (Banish & Heller, 1998; Nelson & Bosquet, 2000). In left-handed people, this pattern may be reversed or, more commonly, the cortex may be less clearly specialized than in right-handers.

Why does this specialization of the two hemispheres, called **lateralization,** occur? Studies using fMRI reveal that the left hemisphere is better at processing information in a sequential, analytic (piece-by-piece) way, a good approach for dealing with communicative information—both verbal (language) and emotional (a joyful smile). In contrast, the right hemisphere is specialized for processing information in a holistic, integrative manner, ideal for making sense of spatial information and regulating negative emotion. A lateralized brain may have evolved because it enabled humans to cope more successfully with changing environmental demands (Falk, 2005). It permits a wider array of functions to be carried out effectively than if both sides processed information exactly the same way.

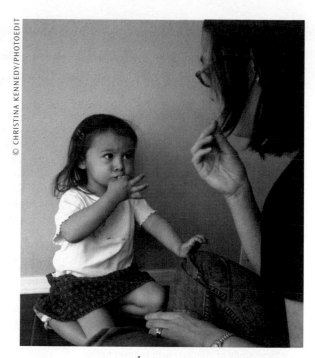

Because this deaf toddler is learning to communicate in sign language, a spatial skill, she will depend more on the right hemisphere of the cerebral cortex for language processing than her hearing agemates will.

Brain Plasticity. Researchers study when brain lateralization occurs to learn more about **brain plasticity.** A highly plastic cerebral cortex, in which many areas are not yet committed to specific functions, has a high capacity for learning. And if a part of the cortex is damaged, other parts can take over the tasks it would have handled. But once the hemispheres lateralize, damage to a specific region means that the abilities it controls cannot be recovered to the same extent or as easily as earlier.

At birth, the hemispheres have already begun to specialize. Most newborns favor the right side of the body in their head position and reflexive reactions (Grattan et al., 1992; Rönnqvist & Hopkins, 1998). Most also show greater activation (detected with either ERP or NIRS) in the left hemisphere while listening to speech sounds or displaying a positive state of arousal. In contrast, the right hemisphere reacts more strongly to nonspeech sounds and to stimuli (such as a sour-tasting fluid) that evoke negative emotion (Davidson, 1994; Fox & Davidson, 1986; Hespos et al., 2010).

Nevertheless, research on brain-damaged children and adults offers dramatic evidence for substantial plasticity in the young brain, summarized in the Biology and Environment box on page 188. Furthermore, early experience greatly influences the organization of the cerebral cortex. For example, deaf adults who, as infants and children, learned sign language (a spatial skill) depend more than hearing individuals on the right hemisphere for language processing (Neville & Bavelier, 2002). And toddlers who are advanced in language development show greater left-hemispheric specialization for language than their more slowly developing agemates (Mills et al., 2005). Similarly, while performing motor and cognitive tasks, children show diffuse fMRI activity in the cerebral cortex relative to adolescents and adults, for whom activity is concentrated in certain cortical areas (Casey et al., 2002; Luna et al., 2001). Apparently, the very process of acquiring motor, cognitive, and language skills promotes lateralization.

In sum, the brain is more plastic during the first few years than it will be ever again. An overabundance of synaptic connections supports brain plasticity, ensuring that young children will acquire certain capacities even if some areas are damaged. And although the cortex is programmed from the start for hemispheric specialization, experience greatly influences the rate and success of its advancing organization.

---

[1]The eyes are an exception. Messages from the right half of each retina go to the right hemisphere; messages from the left half of each retina go to the left hemisphere. Thus, visual information from *both* eyes is received by *both* hemispheres.

BIOLOGY and ENVIRONMENT

Brain Plasticity: Insights from Research on Brain-Damaged Children and Adults

In the first few years of life, the brain is highly plastic. It can reorganize areas committed to specific functions in ways that the mature brain cannot. Consistently, adults who suffered brain injuries in infancy and early childhood show fewer cognitive impairments than adults with later-occurring injuries (Holland, 2004; Huttenlocher, 2002). Nevertheless, the young brain is not totally plastic. When it is injured, its functioning is compromised. The extent of plasticity depends on several factors, including age at time of injury, site of damage, and skill area.

Brain Plasticity in Infancy and Early Childhood

In a large study of children with injuries to the cerebral cortex that occurred before birth or in the first six months of life, language and spatial skills were assessed repeatedly into adolescence (Akshoomoff et al., 2002; Stiles, 2001a; Stiles et al., 2005, 2008). All the children had experienced early brain seizures or hemorrhages. Brain-imaging techniques (fMRI and PET) revealed the precise site of damage.

Regardless of whether injury occurred in the left or right cerebral hemisphere, the children showed delays in language development that persisted until about 3½ years of age. That damage to either hemisphere affected early language competence indicates that at first, language functioning is broadly distributed in the brain. But by age 5, the children caught up in vocabulary and grammatical skills. Undamaged areas—in either the left or the right hemisphere—had taken over these language functions.

Compared with language, spatial skills were more impaired after early brain injury. When preschool through adolescent-age youngsters were asked to copy designs, those with early right-hemispheric damage had trouble with holistic processing—accurately representing the overall shape. In contrast, children with left-hemispheric damage captured the basic shape but omitted fine-grained details. Nevertheless, the children improved in drawing skills with age—gains that do not occur in brain-injured adults (Akshoomoff et al., 2002; Stiles et al., 2003, 2008).

Clearly, recovery after early brain injury is greater for language than for spatial skills. Why is this so? Researchers speculate that spatial processing is the older of the two capacities in

our evolutionary history and, therefore, more lateralized at birth (Stiles, 2001b; Stiles et al., 2002, 2008). But early brain injury has far less impact than later injury on *both* language and spatial skills. In sum, the young brain is remarkably plastic.

The Price of High Plasticity in the Young Brain

Despite impressive recovery of language and (to a lesser extent) spatial skills, children with early brain injuries show deficits in a wide variety of complex mental abilities during the school years. For example, their reading and math progress is slow. And in telling stories, they produce simpler narratives than agemates without early brain injuries (although many catch up in narrative skills by early adolescence) (Reilly, Bates, & Marchman, 1998; Reilly et al., 2004). Furthermore, the more brain tissue destroyed in infancy or early childhood, the poorer children score on intelligence tests (Anderson et al., 2006).

High brain plasticity, researchers explain, comes at a price. When healthy brain regions take over the functions of damaged areas, a "crowding effect" occurs: Multiple tasks must be done by a smaller than usual volume of brain tissue. Consequently, the brain processes information less quickly and accurately than it would if it were intact. Complex mental abilities of all kinds suffer into middle childhood, and often longer, because performing them well requires considerable space in the cerebral cortex (Huttenlocher, 2002).

Later Plasticity

Brain plasticity is not restricted to early childhood. Though far more limited, reorganization in the brain can occur later, even in adulthood. For example, adult stroke victims often display considerable recovery, especially in response to stimulation of language and motor skills. Brain-imaging techniques reveal that structures adjacent to the permanently damaged area or in

© JIM WEST/THE IMAGE WORKS

This preschooler, who experienced brain damage in infancy, has been spared massive impairments because of early, high brain plasticity. A teacher guides his hand in drawing shapes to strengthen spatial skills, which are more impaired than language.

the opposite cerebral hemisphere reorganize to support the impaired ability (Kalra & Ratan, 2007; Murphy & Corbett, 2009).

In infancy and childhood, the goal of brain growth is to form neural connections that ensure mastery of essential skills. Animal research reveals that plasticity is greatest while the brain is forming many new synapses; it declines during synaptic pruning (Murphy & Corbett, 2009). At older ages, specialized brain structures are in place, but after injury they can still reorganize to some degree. The adult brain can produce a small number of new neurons. And when an individual practices relevant tasks, the brain strengthens existing synapses and generates new ones (Nelson, Thomas, & de Haan, 2006).

Plasticity seems to be a basic property of the nervous system. Researchers hope to discover how experience and brain plasticity work together throughout life so they can help people of all ages—with and without brain injuries—develop at their best.

Lateralization and Handedness. Research on handedness supports the joint contribution of nature and nurture to brain lateralization. As early as the tenth prenatal week, most fetuses show a right-hand preference during thumb-sucking (Hepper, McCartney, & Shannon, 1998). And by age 6 months, infants typically reach more smoothly and efficiently with their right than their left arm. These tendencies, believed to be biologically based, may contribute to the right-handed bias of most children by the end of the first year (Hinojosa, Sheu, & Michel, 2003; Rönnqvist & Domellöf, 2006). During toddlerhood and early childhood, handedness gradually extends to a wider range of skills.

Handedness reflects the greater capacity of one side of the brain—the individual's **dominant cerebral hemisphere**—to carry out skilled motor action. Other important abilities are generally located on the dominant side as well. For right-handed people—in Western nations, 90 percent of the population—language is housed in the left hemisphere with hand control. For the left-handed 10 percent, language is occasionally located in the right hemisphere or, more often, shared between the hemispheres (Perelle & Ehrman, 2009). This indicates that the brains of left-handers tend to be less strongly lateralized than those of right-handers.

Left-handed parents show only a weak tendency to have left-handed children (Vuoksimaa et al., 2009). One genetic theory proposes that most children inherit a gene that *biases* them for right-handedness and a left-dominant cerebral hemisphere. But that bias is not strong enough to overcome experiences that might sway children toward a left-hand preference (Annett, 2002). Even prenatal events may profoundly affect handedness. Both identical and fraternal twins are more likely than ordinary siblings to differ in hand preference, probably because twins usually lie in opposite orientations in the uterus (Derom et al., 1996). The orientation of most singleton fetuses—facing toward the left—is believed to promote greater control over movements on the body's right side (Previc, 1991).

Handedness also involves practice. It is strongest for complex skills requiring extensive training, such as eating with utensils, writing, and engaging in athletic activities. And wide cultural differences exist: In Tanzania, Africa, where children are physically restrained and punished for favoring the left hand, less than 1 percent of adults are left-handed (Provins, 1997).

Although rates of left-handedness are elevated among people with intellectual disability and mental illness, atypical brain lateralization is probably not responsible for these individuals' problems. Rather, early damage to the left hemisphere may have caused their disabilities while also leading to a shift in handedness. In support of this idea, left-handedness is associated with prenatal and birth difficulties that can result in brain damage, including prolonged labor, prematurity, and Rh incompatibility (Powls et al., 1996; Rodriguez & Waldenström, 2008).

Most left-handers, however, have no developmental problems—in fact, unusual lateralization may have certain advantages. Left- and mixed-handed young people are slightly advantaged in speed and flexibility of thinking, and they are more likely than their right-handed agemates to develop outstanding verbal and mathematical talents (Flannery & Liederman, 1995; Gunstad et al., 2007). More even distribution of cognitive functions across both hemispheres may be responsible.

Advances in Other Brain Structures

Besides the cerebral cortex, several other areas of the brain make strides during childhood and adolescence. All of these changes involve establishing links among parts of the brain, increasing the coordinated functioning of the central nervous system. (To see where the structures we are about to discuss are located, turn back to Figure 5.4 on page 181.)

At the rear and base of the brain is the **cerebellum,** a structure that aids in balance and control of body movement. Fibers linking the cerebellum to the cerebral cortex grow and myelinate from birth through the preschool years, contributing to dramatic gains in motor coordination: By the time they start school, children can play hopscotch, throw and catch a ball with well-coordinated movements, and print letters of the alphabet. Connections between the cerebellum and the cerebral cortex also support thinking (Diamond, 2000). Children with damage to the cerebellum usually display both motor and cognitive deficits, including problems with memory, planning, and language (Noterdaeme et al., 2002; Riva & Giorgi, 2000).

The **reticular formation,** a structure in the brain stem that maintains alertness and consciousness, generates synapses and myelinates from early childhood into adolescence. Neurons in the reticular formation send out fibers to many other areas of the brain. Many go to the prefrontal lobes of the cerebral cortex, contributing to improvements in sustained, controlled attention.

An inner-brain structure called the **hippocampus,** which plays a vital role in memory and in images of space that help us find our way, undergoes rapid synapse formation and myelination in the second half of the first year, when recall memory and independent movement emerge. Over the preschool and elementary school years, the hippocampus and surrounding areas of the cerebral cortex continue to develop swiftly, establishing connections with one another and with the prefrontal cortex (Nelson, Thomas, & de Haan, 2006). These changes make possible dramatic gains in memory (ability to use strategies to store and retrieve information) and spatial understanding (drawing and reading of maps), which we will take up in Chapters 6 and 7.

Also located in the inner brain, adjacent to the hippocampus, is the **amygdala,** a structure that plays a central role in processing emotional information. The amygdala is sensitive to facial emotional expressions, especially fear (Whalen et al., 2009). It also enhances memory for emotionally salient events, thereby ensuring that information relevant for survival—stimuli that evoke fear or signify safety—will be retrieved on future occasions. This capacity for emotional learning seems to emerge in early childhood: Damage to the amygdala in the first few years leads to loss of ability to learn about fear and safety signals and typically results in wide-ranging socially inappropriate behaviors (Shaw, Brierley, & David, 2005). Throughout childhood and adolescence, connections between the amygdala and the prefrontal cortex, which governs regulation of emotion, form and myelinate (Tottenham, Hare, & Casey, 2009).

The **corpus callosum** is a large bundle of fibers connecting the two cerebral hemispheres. Production of synapses and myelination of the corpus callosum increase at 1 year, peak between 3 and 6 years, and then continue at a slower pace through middle childhood and adolescence (Thompson et al., 2000). The corpus callosum supports smooth coordination of movements on both sides of the body and integration of perception, attention, memory, language, and problem solving. The more complex the task, the more essential is communication between the hemispheres.

Brain Development in Adolescence

From middle childhood to adolescence, connectivity among distant regions of the cerebral cortex expands and attains rapid communication. As a result, the prefrontal cortex becomes a more effective "executive"—overseeing and managing the integrated functioning of various areas, yielding more complex, flexible, and adaptive thinking and behavior (Blakemore & Choudhury, 2006; Lenroot & Giedd, 2006). Consequently, adolescents gain in diverse cognitive skills, including speed of thinking, attention, memory, planning, capacity to integrate information, and regulation of cognition and emotion.

But these advances occur gradually over the teenage years. fMRI evidence reveals that adolescents recruit the prefrontal cortex's connections with other brain areas less effectively than adults do. Because the *prefrontal cognitive-control network* still requires fine-tuning, teenagers' performance on tasks requiring self-restraint, planning, and future orientation (rejecting a smaller immediate reward in favor of a larger delayed reward) is not yet fully mature (Luna et al., 2001; McClure et al., 2004; Steinberg et al., 2009).

Adding to these self-regulation difficulties are changes in the brain's *emotional/social network.* As humans and other mammals become sexually mature, neurons become more responsive to excitatory neurotransmitters. As a result, adolescents react more strongly to stressful events and experience pleasurable

In adolescence, changes in the brain's emotional/social network outpace development of the cognitive control network. As a result, teenagers do not yet have the capacity to control their powerful drive for new—and sometimes risky—experiences.

© STEVE SKJOLD/ALAMY

stimuli more intensely. But because the cognitive control network is not yet functioning optimally, most teenagers find it hard to manage these powerful influences (Casey, Getz, & Galvan, 2008; Spear, 2008; Steinberg et al., 2008). This imbalance contributes to adolescents' unchecked drive for novel experiences, including drug taking, reckless driving, unprotected sex, and delinquent activity, especially among those who are highly stressed and engage in reward seeking to counteract chronic emotional pain.

In addition, the surge in sex hormones (both estrogens and androgens) at puberty heightens sensitivity of the prefrontal cortex and inner brain structures (such as the amygdala) to the hormone *oxytocin,* secreted by the pituitary gland. In new mothers, oxytocin promotes caregiving behavior. In teenagers, it increases responsiveness to emotional and social stimuli, including feedback from others (Steinberg, 2008). Enhanced oxytocin sensitivity helps explain why adolescents, as we will we will see in Chapter 15, are so self-conscious and sensitive to others' opinions. It also contributes to teenagers' receptiveness to peer influence—a strong predictor of adolescent risk taking of all kinds (Gardner & Steinberg, 2005; Ranking et al., 2004).

Of course, not all teenagers display this rise in risk taking in the form of careless, dangerous acts: Temperament, parenting, and school and neighborhood resources (which are linked to opportunities to take risks) make a difference. Nevertheless, transformations in the adolescent brain enhance our understanding of both the cognitive advances and worrisome behaviors of this period, along with teenagers' need for adult patience, oversight, and guidance.

Sensitive Periods in Brain Development

We have seen that stimulation of the brain is vital when it is growing most rapidly. Both animal and human studies, as noted in Chapter 4, reveal that early, extreme sensory deprivation results in permanent brain damage and loss of functions—findings that verify the existence of sensitive periods in brain development. Recall, also, that research on children adopted from Romanian orphanages indicates that deprived institutional care extending beyond the first six months results in persistent intellectual impairments and mental health problems (see page 170).

Much evidence confirms that the brain is particularly spongelike during the first few years, enabling children to acquire new skills easily and quickly. How, then, can we characterize appropriate stimulation during this time? To answer this question, researchers distinguish between two types of brain development. The first, **experience-expectant brain growth,** refers to the young brain's rapidly developing organization, which depends on ordinary experiences— opportunities to interact with people, hear language and other sounds, see and touch objects, and move about and explore the environment. As a result of millions of years of evolution, the brains of all infants, toddlers, and young children *expect* to encounter these experiences and, if they do, grow normally. The second type of brain development, **experience-dependent brain growth,** occurs throughout our lives. It consists of additional growth and refinement of established brain structures as a result of specific learning experiences that vary widely across individuals and cultures (Greenough & Black, 1992). Reading and writing, playing computer games, weaving an intricate rug, and practicing the violin are examples. The brain of a violinist differs in certain ways from that of a poet because each has exercised different brain regions for a long time.

Experience-expectant brain development occurs early and naturally, as caregivers offer babies and preschoolers age-appropriate play materials and engage them in enjoyable daily routines—a shared meal, a game of peekaboo, a bath before bed, a picture book to talk about, or a song to sing. The resulting growth provides the foundation for later-occurring, experience-dependent development (Huttenlocher, 2002; Shonkoff & Phillips, 2001). In Chapter 4, we indicated that not just

Experience-expectant brain growth occurs naturally, through ordinary, stimulating experiences. As they explore spring flowers with magnifying glasses, these preschoolers engage in the type of informal activity that best promotes brain development in the early years.

understimulation but also overstimulation—overwhelming children with tasks and expectations for which they are not yet ready—can threaten their development. No evidence exists for a sensitive period in the first five or six years for mastering skills that depend on extensive training, such as reading, musical performance, or gymnastics (Bruer, 1999). To the contrary, rushing early learning harms the brain by overwhelming its neural circuits, thereby reducing the brain's sensitivity to the everyday experiences it needs for a healthy start in life.

A S K   Y O U R S E L F

Review ■ How does stimulation affect brain development? Cite evidence at the level of neurons and at the level of the cerebral cortex.

Connect ■ What stance on the nature–nurture issue does evidence on development of handedness support? Document your answer with research findings.

Apply ■ Lucia experienced damage to the left hemisphere of her cerebral cortex shortly after birth. As a first grader, she shows impressive recovery of language and spatial skills, but she lags behind her peers in academic progress. What accounts for her recovery of skills? How about her cognitive deficits?

Reflect ■ Which infant enrichment program would you choose: one that emphasizes social games and gentle talking and touching, or one that includes reading and number drills and classical music lessons? Explain.

▶ How do heredity, nutrition, infectious disease, and parental affection contribute to physical growth and health?

Factors Affecting Physical Growth

Physical growth, like other aspects of development, results from a complex interplay between genetic and environmental factors. Although heredity remains important, environmental factors continue to affect genetic expression. Good nutrition, relative freedom from disease, and emotional well-being are essential to children's healthy development, while environmental pollutants can be a threat. The Biology and Environment box on the following page considers the extent to which one of the most common pollutants, low-level lead, undermines children's mental and emotional functioning.

Heredity

Because identical twins are much more alike in body size than fraternal twins, we know that heredity contributes considerably to physical growth (Estourgie-van Burk et al., 2006). When diet and health are adequate, height and rate of physical growth (as measured by skeletal age and timing of first menstruation) are largely determined by heredity. In fact, as long as negative environmental influences, such as poor nutrition or illness, are not severe, children and adolescents typically show *catch-up growth*—a return to a genetically influenced growth path once conditions improve. Still, the brain, the heart, the digestive system, and many other internal organs may be permanently compromised (Hales & Ozanne, 2003). (Recall the consequences of inadequate prenatal nutrition for long-term health, discussed on page 104 in Chapter 3.)

Genes influence growth by controlling the body's production of and sensitivity to hormones. Mutations can disrupt this process, leading to deviations in physical size. Occasionally, a mutation becomes widespread in a population. Consider the Efe of the Republic of Congo, whose typical adult height is less than 5 feet. For genetic reasons, the impact of growth hormone (GH) is reduced in Efe children (Bailey, 1990). By age 5, the average Efe child is shorter than over 97 percent of North American agemates. The Efe's small size probably evolved because it reduces their caloric requirements in the face of food scarcity in the rain forests of Central Africa and enables them to move easily through the dense forest underbrush (Perry & Dominy, 2009).

BIOLOGY and ENVIRONMENT

Low-Level Lead Exposure and Children's Development

Lead is a highly toxic element that, at blood levels exceeding 60 µg/dL (micrograms per deciliter), causes brain swelling, hemorrhaging, disrupted functioning of neurons, and widespread cell death. Before 1980, exposure to lead resulted from use of lead-based paints for the interiors of residences (infants and young children often ate paint flakes) and from use of leaded gasoline (car exhaust resulted in a highly breathable form of lead). Laws limiting the lead content of paint and mandating lead-free gasoline led to a sharp decline in children's lead levels, from an average of 15 µg/dL in 1980 to 1.8 µg/dL today (Jones et al., 2009; Meyer et al., 2003).

But in areas near airports with significant burning of jet fuel, near industries using lead production processes, or where lead-based paint remains in older homes, children's blood levels are still markedly elevated. In some areas, water-pipe corrosion has caused lead to rise in drinking water. Contaminated soil and imported consumer products, such as toys made of leaded plastic, are additional sources of exposure (Cole & Winsler, 2010). About 15 percent of low-income children living in large central cities, and 19 percent of African-American children, have blood-lead levels exceeding 10 µg/dL (the U.S. government official "level of concern"), warranting immediate efforts to reduce exposure (Jones et al., 2009).

How much lead exposure is too much? Does lead contamination, even in small quantities, impair children's mental functioning? Until recently, answers were unclear. Studies reporting a negative relationship between children's current lead levels and cognitive performance had serious limitations. Researchers knew nothing about children's history of lead exposure and often failed to control for factors associated with both blood-lead levels and mental test scores (such as family income, home environmental quality, and nutrition) that might account for the findings.

Over the past two decades, a host of longitudinal studies of the developmental consequences of lead have been conducted in multiple countries, including the United States, Australia, Mexico City, and Yugoslavia. Some focused on inner-city, economically disadvantaged minority children, others on middle- and upper-middle-class suburban children, and one on children living close to a lead smelter. Each tracked children's lead exposure over an extended time and included relevant controls.

All but one site reported negative relationships between lead exposure and children's IQs (Canfield et al., 2003; Hubbs-Tait et al., 2005; Lanphear et al., 2005). Higher blood levels were also associated with deficits in verbal and visual-motor skills and with distractibility, overactivity, poor organization, weak academic performance, and behavior problems. And an array of additional findings suggested that persistent childhood lead exposure contributes to antisocial behavior in adolescence (Needleman et al., 2002; Nevin, 2006; Stretesky & Lynch, 2004).

The investigations did not agree on an age period of greatest vulnerability. In some, relationships were strongest in toddlerhood and early childhood; in others, at the most recently studied age, suggesting cumulative effects over time. Still other studies reported similar lead-related cognitive deficits from infancy through adolescence. Overall,

This girl and her family of Kosovo, displaced by war, have lived for a decade on land polluted by lead. Long-term negative effects of lead exposure include learning impairments and behavior problems.

poorer mental test scores associated with lead exposure persisted over time and seemed to be permanent. Children given drugs to induce excretion of lead (chelation) did not improve (Dietrich et al., 2004; Rogan et al., 2001). And negative cognitive consequences were evident at all levels of lead exposure—even below 10 µg/dL (Canfield et al., 2003; Lanphear et al., 2005; Wright et al., 2008).

Furthermore, in several investigations, cognitive consequences were much greater for children from low-income than middle- and high-income families (see, for example, Figure 5.10) (Bellinger, Leviton, & Sloman, 1990; Ris et al., 2004; Tong, McMichael, & Baghurst, 2000). A stressed, disorganized home life seems to heighten lead-induced damage. Dietary factors can also magnify lead's toxic effects. Iron and zinc deficiencies, especially common in economically disadvantaged children, increase lead concentration in the blood (Noonan et al., 2003; Wolf, Jimenez, & Lozoff, 2003; Wright et al., 2003).

In sum, lead impairs mental development and contributes to behavior problems. Children from low-income families are more likely both to live in lead-contaminated areas and to experience additional risks that magnify lead-induced damage. Because lead is a stable element, its release into the air and soil is difficult to reverse. Therefore, in addition to laws that control lead pollution, interventions that reduce the negative impact of lead—through involved parenting, dietary enrichment, better schools, and public education about lead hazards—are vital.

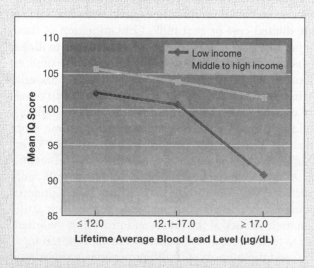

FIGURE 5.10 Relationship of lifetime average lead exposure to 11- to 13-year-olds' IQ by family economic status. In this study, conducted in the lead-smelting city of Port Pirie, Australia, blood-lead levels of 375 children were measured repeatedly from birth to age 11 to 13. The lead-exposure-related drop in IQ was much greater for children from economically disadvantaged than advantaged families. (Adapted from Tong, McMichael, & Baghurst, 2000.)

Twin studies reveal that genetic makeup also affects body weight (Kinnunen, Pietilainen, & Rissanen, 2006). At the same time, environment—in particular, nutrition and eating habits—plays an especially important role.

Nutrition

Nutrition is important at any time of development, but it is especially crucial during the first two years because the baby's brain and body are growing so rapidly. Pound for pound, an infant's energy needs are twice those of an adult. Twenty-five percent of babies' total caloric intake is devoted to growth, and infants need extra calories to keep their rapidly developing organs functioning properly (Meyer, 2009).

Breastfeeding versus Bottle-Feeding
Babies need not only enough food but also the right kind of food. In early infancy, breast milk is ideally suited to their needs, and bottled formulas try to imitate it. Applying What We Know on the following page summarizes major nutritional and health advantages of breast milk.

Midwives in India support a mother as she learns to breastfeed her infant. Breastfeeding is especially important in developing countries, where it helps protect babies against life-threatening infections and early death.

Because of these benefits, breastfed babies in poverty-stricken regions are much less likely to be malnourished and 6 to 14 times more likely to survive the first year of life. The World Health Organization recommends breastfeeding until age 2 years, with solid foods added at 6 months. These practices, if widely followed, would save the lives of more than a million infants annually (World Health Organization, 2011). Even breastfeeding for just a few weeks offers some protection against respiratory and intestinal infections, which are devastating to young children in developing countries. Also, because a nursing mother is less likely to get pregnant, breastfeeding helps increase spacing between siblings, a major factor in reducing infant and childhood deaths in nations with widespread poverty. (Note, however, that breastfeeding is not a reliable method of birth control.)

Yet many mothers in the developing world do not know about the benefits of breastfeeding. In Africa, the Middle East, and Latin America, most babies get some breastfeeding, but fewer than 40 percent are exclusively breastfed for the first 6 months, and one-fourth are fully weaned from the breast by 1 year (UNICEF, 2009). In place of breast milk, mothers give their babies commercial formula or low-grade nutrients, such as rice water or highly diluted cow or goat milk. Contamination of these foods as a result of poor sanitation is common and often leads to illness and infant death. The United Nations has encouraged all hospitals and maternity units in developing countries to promote breastfeeding as long as mothers do not have viral or bacterial infections (such as HIV or tuberculosis) that can be transmitted to the baby. Today, most developing countries have banned the practice of giving free or subsidized formula to new mothers.

Partly as a result of the natural childbirth movement, breastfeeding has become more common in industrialized nations, especially among well-educated women. Today, 75 percent of American mothers breastfeed, but more than half stop by 6 months (U.S. Centers for Disease Control and Prevention, 2010). And despite the health benefits of breast milk, only 50 percent of preterm infants are breastfed at hospital discharge. Breastfeeding a preterm baby presents special challenges, including maintaining a sufficient milk supply with artificial pumping until the baby is mature enough to suck at the breast and providing the infant with enough sucking experience to learn to feed successfully (Callen & Pinelli, 2005). Kangaroo care (see pages 115–116 in Chapter 3) and the support of health professionals are helpful.

Because breast milk is so easily digestible, a breastfed infant becomes hungry every 1½ to 2 hours, compared to every 3 or 4 hours for a bottle-fed baby. This makes breastfeeding inconvenient for many employed women. Not surprisingly, mothers who return to work sooner wean their babies from the breast earlier (Kimbro, 2006). But mothers who cannot be with their babies all the time can still combine breast- and bottle-feeding. The U.S.

APPLYING WHAT WE KNOW

Reasons to Breastfeed

NUTRITIONAL AND HEALTH ADVANTAGES	EXPLANATION
Provides the correct balance of fat and protein	Compared with the milk of other mammals, human milk is higher in fat and lower in protein. This balance, as well as the unique proteins and fats contained in human milk, is ideal for a rapidly myelinating nervous system.
Ensures nutritional completeness	A mother who breastfeeds need not add other foods to her infant's diet until the baby is 6 months old. The milks of all mammals are low in iron, but the iron contained in breast milk is much more easily absorbed by the baby's system. Consequently, bottle-fed infants need iron-fortified formula.
Helps ensure healthy physical growth	One-year-old breastfed babies are leaner (have a higher percentage of muscle to fat), a growth pattern that persists through the preschool years and that may help prevent later overweight and obesity.
Protects against many diseases	Breastfeeding transfers antibodies and other infection-fighting agents from mother to baby and enhances functioning of the immune system. Compared with bottle-fed infants, breastfed babies have far fewer allergic reactions and respiratory and intestinal illnesses. Breast milk also has anti-inflammatory effects, which reduce the severity of illness symptoms. Breastfeeding in the first four months (especially when exclusive) is linked to lower blood cholesterol levels in childhood and, thereby, may help prevent cardiovascular disease.
Protects against faulty jaw development and tooth decay	Sucking the mother's nipple instead of an artificial nipple helps avoid malocclusion, a condition in which the upper and lower jaws do not meet properly. It also protects against tooth decay due to sweet liquid remaining in the mouths of infants who fall asleep while sucking on a bottle.
Ensures digestibility	Because breastfed babies have a different kind of bacteria growing in their intestines than do bottle-fed infants, they rarely suffer from constipation or other gastrointestinal problems.
Smooths the transition to solid foods	Breastfed infants accept new solid foods more easily than do bottle-fed infants, perhaps because of their greater experience with a variety of flavors, which pass from the maternal diet into the mother's milk.

Sources: American Academy of Pediatrics, 2005a; Buescher, 2001; Michels et al., 2007; Owen et al., 2008; Rosetta & Baldi, 2008; Wayerman, Rothenbacher, & Brenner, 2006.

Department of Health and Human Services (2009a) advises exclusive breastfeeding for the first 6 months and inclusion of breast milk in the baby's diet until at least 1 year.

Women who do not breastfeed sometimes worry that they are depriving their baby of an experience essential for healthy psychological development. Yet breastfeeding mothers are not more attached to their babies, and breastfed and bottle-fed children in industrialized nations do not differ in emotional adjustment (Fergusson & Woodward, 1999; Jansen, de Weerth, & Riksen-Walraven, 2008). Some studies report a small advantage in intelligence test performance for children and adolescents who were breastfed, after controlling for many factors. Most, however, find no cognitive benefits (Der, Batty, & Deary, 2006; Holme, MacArthur, & Lancashire, 2010).

Nutrition in Childhood and Adolescence Around 1 year, infants' diets should include all the basic food groups. As children approach age 2, their appetites become unpredictable. Preschoolers eat well at one meal but barely touch their food at the next. And many become picky eaters. This decline in appetite occurs because growth has slowed. Furthermore, preschoolers' wariness of new foods is adaptive. If they stick to familiar foods, they are less likely to swallow dangerous substances when adults are not around to protect them (Birch & Fisher, 1995). Parents need not worry about variations in amount eaten from meal to meal. Over the course of a day, preschoolers compensate for eating little at one meal by eating more at a later one (Hursti, 1999).

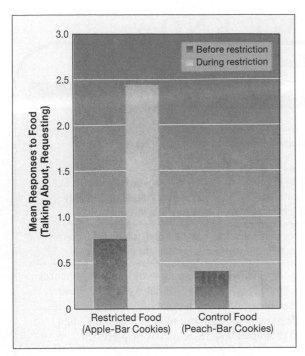

FIGURE 5.11 Children's spontaneous behavioral responses to a tasty food before and during restriction at snack times. Three- to 6-year-olds talked about, requested, and otherwise attempted to obtain a tasty food (apple-bar cookies) three times more often after they were restricted from eating it. They rarely responded this way to an equally tasty control food (peach-bar cookies) that remained unrestricted throughout the study. (Adapted from Fisher & Birch, 1999.)

LOOK and LISTEN

Arrange to join a family with at least one preschooler for a meal, and closely observe parental mealtime practices. Are they likely to promote healthy eating habits? Explain.

Children tend to imitate the food choices and eating practices of people they admire, both adults and peers. For example, mothers who drink milk or soft drinks tend to have 5-year-old daughters with a similar beverage preference (Fisher et al., 2001). In Mexico, where children see family members delighting in the taste of peppery foods, preschoolers enthusiastically eat chili peppers, whereas most U.S. children reject them (Birch, Zimmerman, & Hind, 1980).

Repeated, unpressured exposure to a new food also increases acceptance (Fuller et al., 2005). Serving broccoli or tofu increases children's liking for these healthy foods. In contrast, offering sweet fruit or soft drinks promotes "milk avoidance" (Black et al., 2002).

Although children's healthy eating depends on a wholesome food environment, too much parental control over eating limits children's opportunities to develop self-control. When parents offer bribes ("Finish your vegetables, and you can have an extra cookie"), children tend to like the healthy food less and the treat more (Birch, Fisher, & Davison, 2003). Similarly, restricting access to tasty foods focuses children's attention on those foods and increases their desire to eat them. After caregivers in a child-care center prevented 3- to 6-year-olds from selecting apple-bar cookies at snack time by enclosing them in a transparent jar but gave them free access to peach-bar cookies (which they liked just as well), the children more often talked about and asked for the apple-bar cookies and otherwise tried to obtain them (see Figure 5.11) (Fisher & Birch, 1999). And when given access, they ate more apple-bar cookies than they had during previous, unrestricted snack times.

During puberty, rapid body growth leads to a dramatic rise in food intake. This increase in nutritional requirements comes at a time when eating habits are the poorest. Of all age groups, adolescents are the most likely to skip breakfast (a practice linked to obesity), eat on the run, and consume empty calories rather than nutrient-rich fruits and vegetables (Ritchie et al., 2007; Striegel-Moore & Franko, 2006). Fast-food restaurants, where teenagers often gather, have begun to offer some healthy menu options, but adolescents need guidance in choosing these alternatives. Eating fast food and school purchases from snack bars and vending machines is strongly associated with consumption of high-fat foods and soft drinks (Bowman et al., 2004; Kubik et al., 2003).

Frequency of family meals is a powerful predictor of healthy eating—greater intake of fruits, vegetables, grains, and milk products and reduced soft drink and fast-food consumption (Burgess-Champoux et al., 2009; Fiese & Schwartz, 2008). But compared to families with children, those with adolescents eat fewer meals together. Finding ways to arrange family meals, despite busy schedules, can greatly improve teenagers' diets.

Malnutrition In developing countries and war-torn areas where food resources are limited, malnutrition is widespread. Recent evidence indicates that about 27 percent of the world's children suffer from malnutrition before age 5 (World Health Organization, 2010b). The 10 percent who are severely affected suffer from two dietary diseases.

Marasmus is a wasted condition of the body caused by a diet low in all essential nutrients. It usually appears in the first year of life when a baby's mother is too malnourished to produce enough breast milk and bottle-feeding is also inadequate. Her starving baby becomes painfully thin and is in danger of dying.

Kwashiorkor is caused by an unbalanced diet very low in protein. The disease usually strikes after weaning, between 1 and 3 years of age. It is common in regions where children get just enough calories from starchy foods but little protein. The child's body responds by breaking down its own protein reserves. Soon the belly enlarges, the feet swell, the hair falls out, and a skin rash appears. A once bright-eyed, curious youngster becomes irritable and listless.

The baby on the left, of Niger, Africa, has marasmus, a wasted condition caused by a diet low in all essential nutrients. The swollen abdomen of the toddler on the right, also of Niger, is a symptom of kwashiorkor, which results from a diet very low in protein. If these children survive, they are likely to be growth stunted and to suffer from lasting organ damage and serious cognitive and emotional impairments.

Children who survive these extreme forms of malnutrition often grow to be smaller in all body dimensions and suffer from lasting damage to the brain, heart, liver, or other organs (Müller & Krawinkel, 2005). When their diets do improve, they tend to gain excessive weight (Uauy et al., 2008). A malnourished body protects itself by establishing a low basal metabolism rate, which may endure after nutrition improves. Also, malnutrition may disrupt appetite-control centers in the brain, causing the child to overeat when food becomes plentiful.

Learning and behavior are also seriously affected. In one long-term study of marasmic children, an improved diet led to some catch-up growth in height, but not in head size (Stoch et al., 1982). The malnutrition probably interfered with growth of neural fibers and myelination, causing a permanent loss in brain weight. And animal evidence reveals that a deficient diet alters the production of neurotransmitters in the brain—an effect that can disrupt all aspects of development (Haller, 2005). These children score low on intelligence tests, show poor fine-motor coordination, and have difficulty paying attention (Bryce et al., 2008; Liu et al., 2003). They also display a more intense stress response to fear-arousing situations, perhaps caused by the constant, gnawing pain of hunger (Fernald & Grantham-McGregor, 1998).

Recall from our discussion of prenatal malnutrition in Chapter 3 that the passivity and irritability of malnourished children worsen the impact of poor diet. These behaviors may appear even when protein-calorie deprivation is only mild to moderate. They also accompany *iron-deficiency anemia,* a condition affecting about 25 percent of infants and children worldwide that interferes with many central nervous system processes. Withdrawal, listlessness, and inability to be soothed when upset reduce the iron-deficient baby's capacity to pay attention, explore, and evoke sensitive caregiving from parents (Lozoff, 2007; Lozoff et al., 2008). These infants score lower than their nonanemic counterparts in motor and mental development, with iron supplementation alone failing to correct the difference. In one follow-up, young adults who had been profoundly iron-deficient as babies but iron-sufficient thereafter nevertheless performed poorly on diverse cognitive tasks (Lukowski et al., 2010). Consequently, in addition to improving early iron status, interventions must foster development by supporting the parent–child relationship.

Inadequate nutrition is not confined to developing countries. Because government-sponsored supplementary food programs do not reach all families in need, an estimated 21 percent of U.S. children suffer from *food insecurity*—uncertain access to enough food for a healthy, active life. Food insecurity is especially high among single-parent families (35 percent) and low-income ethnic minority families—for example, African Americans and

Hispanics (25 and 27 percent, respectively) (U.S. Department of Agriculture, 2011b). Although few of these children have marasmus or kwashiorkor, their physical growth and ability to learn are still affected.

Obesity Today, 32 percent of U.S. children and adolescents are overweight, more than half of them extremely so: 17 percent suffer from **obesity,** a greater-than-20-percent increase over healthy weight, based on *body mass index (BMI)*—a ratio of weight to height associated with body fat. (A BMI above the 85th percentile for the child's age and sex is considered overweight, a BMI above the 95th percentile obese.) During the past several decades, a rise in overweight and obesity has occurred in many Western nations, with large increases in Canada, Germany, Israel, Greece, Ireland, New Zealand, the United Kingdom, and the United States (Ogden et al., 2010; World Health Organization, 2009, 2010a). Smaller increases have occurred in other industrialized nations, including Australia, Finland, the Netherlands, Norway, and Sweden.

Obesity rates are also increasing rapidly in developing countries as urbanization shifts the population toward sedentary lifestyles and diets high in meats and energy-dense refined

IMAGINECHINA VIA AP IMAGES

foods (World Health Organization, 2010a, 2010b). In China, for example, where obesity was nearly nonexistent a generation ago, today 20 percent of children are overweight, with 7 percent obese—a nearly fivefold increase over the past twenty-five years, with boys affected more than girls (Ding, 2008). Childhood obesity in China is especially high in cities, where it has reached 10 percent (Ji & Chen, 2008). In addition to lifestyle changes, a prevailing belief in Chinese culture that excess body fat represents prosperity and health—carried over from a half-century ago, when famine caused millions of deaths—has contributed to this alarming upsurge. High valuing of sons may induce Chinese parents to offer boys especially generous portions of meat, dairy products, and other energy-dense foods that were once scarce but now are widely available.

Overweight rises with age, from 21 percent among U.S. preschoolers to 35 percent among school-age children and adolescents (Ogden et al., 2010). In a longitudinal study of more than 1,000 U.S. children, overweight preschoolers were five times more likely than their normal-weight peers to be overweight at age 12 (Nader et al., 2006). And an estimated 70 percent of affected teenagers

Chinese boys attending a weight-loss camp prepare for a swim. Such camps are a response to China's rapid increase in overweight and obesity—the result of lifestyle changes in a culture that equates excess body fat with prosperity.

become overweight adults (U.S. Department of Health and Human Services, 2011b).

Besides serious emotional and social difficulties, obese children are at risk for lifelong health problems. Symptoms that begin to appear in the early school years—high blood pressure, high cholesterol levels, respiratory abnormalities, and insulin resistance—are powerful predictors of heart disease and other circulatory difficulties, type 2 diabetes, gallbladder disease, sleep and digestive disorders, many forms of cancer, and early death (Krishnamoorthy, Hart, & Jelalian, 2006; World Cancer Research Fund, 2007). Indeed, type 2 diabetes—formerly also known as "adult-onset" diabetes because it was rarely seen in childhood—is rising rapidly among overweight children, sometimes leading to early, severe complications, including stroke, kidney failure, and circulatory problems that heighten the risk of eventual blindness and leg amputation (Hannon, Rao, & Arslanian, 2005).

Causes of Obesity. Not all children are equally at risk for excessive weight gain. Overweight children tend to have overweight parents, and identical twins are more likely to share the disorder than fraternal twins. But heredity accounts for only a *tendency* to gain weight (Kral & Faith, 2009).

The importance of environment is seen in the consistent relationship of low education and income to overweight and obesity in industrialized nations, especially among ethnic minorities—in the United States, African-American, Hispanic, and Native-American children and adults (Anand et al., 2001; Ogden et al., 2010). Factors responsible include lack of knowledge about healthy diet; a tendency to buy high-fat, low-cost foods; neighborhoods that lack convenient access to affordable, healthy foods in grocery stores and restaurants; and family stress, which can prompt overeating.

Furthermore, as noted on page 197, children who were undernourished in their early years are at risk for later excessive weight gain. In industrialized nations, many studies confirm that infants whose mothers smoked during pregnancy and who therefore are often born underweight (see Chapter 3) are more likely to suffer from childhood overweight and obesity (Rogers, 2009). Nevertheless, in the developing world (unlike in industrialized countries), obesity risk is greatest for individuals living in economically well-off households, probably because of greater food availability and reduced activity levels (Subramanian et al., 2011).

Parental feeding practices also contribute to childhood obesity. Overweight children are more likely to eat larger quantities of high-calorie sugary and fatty foods, perhaps because these foods are prominent in the diets offered by their parents, who also tend to be overweight. Interviews with more than 3,000 U.S. parents revealed that many served their 4- to 24-month-olds French fries, pizza, candy, sugary fruit drinks, and soda on a daily basis. On average, infants consumed 20 percent and toddlers 30 percent more calories than they needed (Briefel et al., 2004). Recent research confirms a strengthening relationship between rapid weight gain in infancy and later obesity (Botton et al., 2008; Chomtho et al., 2008).

Some parents anxiously overfeed, interpreting almost all their child's discomforts as a desire for food. Others pressure their children to eat, a practice common among immigrant parents and grandparents who, as children themselves, survived periods of food deprivation. Still other parents are overly controlling, restricting when, what, and how much their child eats and worrying that the child will gain too much weight (Moens, Braet, & Soetens, 2007). In each case, parents fail to help children learn to regulate their own food intake. Also, parents of overweight children often use high-fat, sugary foods to reinforce other behaviors, leading children to attach great value to treats (Sherry et al., 2004).

Because of these experiences, obese children soon develop maladaptive eating habits. They are more responsive than normal-weight individuals to external stimuli associated with food—taste, sight, smell, time of day, and food-related words—and less responsive to internal hunger cues (Jansen et al., 2003; Temple et al., 2007). They also eat faster and chew their food less thoroughly, a behavior pattern that appears as early as 18 months of age (Drabman et al., 1979).

Another factor consistently associated with weight gain is insufficient sleep (Nielsen, Danielsen, & Sørensen, 2011). Reduced sleep may increase time available for eating, leave children too fatigued for physical activity, or disrupt the brain's regulation of hunger and metabolism.

Overweight children are less physically active than their normal-weight peers. Inactivity is both cause and consequence of excessive weight gain. Research reveals that the rise in childhood obesity is due in part to the many hours U.S. children spend watching television. In a study that tracked children's TV viewing from ages 4 to 11, the more TV children watched, the more body fat they added. Children who devoted more than 3 hours per day to TV accumulated 40 percent more fat than those devoting less than 1¾ hours (see Figure 5.12) (Proctor et al., 2003). Watching TV reduces time devoted to physical exercise, and TV ads encourage children to eat fattening, unhealthy snacks. Children permitted to have a TV in their bedroom—a practice linked to especially high TV viewing—are at even greater risk for overweight (Adachi-Mejia et al., 2007).

Finally, the broader food environment affects the incidence of obesity. The Pima Indians of Arizona, who two decades ago changed from a traditional diet of plant foods to a high-fat, typically American diet, have one of the world's highest obesity rates. Compared with descendants of their

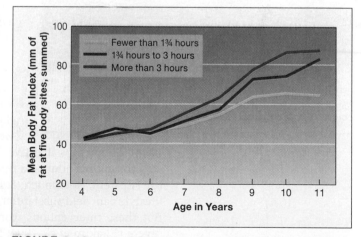

FIGURE 5.12 Relationship of television viewing to gains in body fat from ages 4 to 11. Researchers followed more than 100 children from ages 4 to 11, collecting information on hours per day of television viewing and on body fat, measured in millimeters of skinfold thickness at five body sites (upper arms, shoulders, abdomen, trunk, and thighs). The more TV children watched, the greater the gain in body fat. At ages 10 to 11, the difference between children watching fewer than 1¾ hours and those watching more than 3 hours had become large. (Adapted from M. H. Proctor et al., 2003, "Television Viewing and Change in Body Fat from Preschool to Early Adolescence: The Framingham Children's Study," *International Journal of Obesity*, 27, p. 831. Reprinted by permission from Macmillan Publishers Ltd.)

ancestors living in the remote Sierra Madre region of Mexico, the Arizona Pima have body weights 50 percent greater. Half the population has diabetes (eight times the national average), with many in their twenties and thirties already disabled by the disease—blind, in wheelchairs, and on kidney dialysis. The Pima have a genetic susceptibility to overweight, but it emerges only under Western dietary conditions (Gladwell, 1998; Traurig et al., 2009). Other ethnic groups with a hereditary tendency to gain weight are the Pacific Islanders, including native Hawaiians and Samoans (Furusawa et al., 2010). Many now eat an Americanized diet of high-calorie processed and fast foods, and over 80 percent are overweight.

Consequences of Obesity. Unfortunately, physical attractiveness is a powerful predictor of social acceptance. In Western societies, both children and adults rate obese youngsters as unlikable, stereotyping them as lazy, sloppy, dirty, ugly, stupid, and deceitful (Kilpatrick & Sanders, 1978; Penny & Haddock, 2007; Tiggemann & Anesbury, 2000). In school, obese children and adolescents are often socially isolated. They report more emotional, social, and school difficulties, including peer teasing and consequent low self-esteem, depression, and (among obese teenagers) suicidal thoughts and suicide attempts. Because unhappiness and overeating contribute to each other, the child remains overweight (Puhl & Latner, 2007; Zeller & Modi, 2006). Persistent obesity from childhood into adolescence predicts serious disorders, including defiance, aggression, and severe depression (Schwimmer, Burwinkle, & Varni, 2003; Young-Hyman et al., 2006).

Students enjoy school lunches prepared from healthy, fresh ingredients, thanks to a program instituted by a former chef who transformed their school food service, eliminating processed foods high in fat and sugar.

The psychological consequences of obesity combine with continuing discrimination to result in reduced life chances. Overweight individuals are less likely than their normal-weight agemates to receive financial aid for college, be rented apartments, find mates, and be offered jobs. And they report frequent mistreatment by family members, peers, co-workers, and health-care professionals, which contributes further to physical and psychological health problems (Carr & Friedman, 2005; Puhl, Heuer, & Brownell, 2010).

Treating Obesity. Childhood obesity is difficult to treat because it is a family disorder. In one study, only one-fourth of overweight parents judged their overweight children to have a weight problem (Jeffrey, 2004). Consistent with these findings, most obese children do not get any treatment.

The most effective interventions are family-based and focus on changing behaviors (Oude et al., 2009). In one program, both parent and child revised their eating patterns, exercised daily, and reinforced each other with praise and points for progress, which they exchanged for special activities and times together. The more weight parents lost, the more their children lost (Wrotniak et al., 2004). Follow-ups after five and ten years showed that children maintained weight loss more effectively than adults—a finding that underscores the importance of intervening at an early age (Epstein, Roemmich, & Raynor, 2001). Treatment programs that focus on both diet and lifestyle can yield substantial, long-lasting weight reduction among children and adolescents. But these interventions work best when parents' and children's weight problems are not severe (Eliakim et al., 2004; Nemet et al., 2005).

Children consume one-third of their daily energy intake at school. Therefore, schools can help reduce obesity by serving healthier meals and ensuring regular physical activity. Because obesity is expected to rise further without broad prevention strategies, many U.S. states and cities have passed obesity-reduction legislation (Levi et al., 2009). Among measures taken are weight-related school screenings for all children, improved nutrition standards and limited vending machine access in schools, additional recess time in the elementary grades and increased physical education time in all grades, obesity awareness and weight-reduction programs as part of school curricula, and menu nutrition labeling (including calories counts) in chain and fast-food restaurants.

LOOK and LISTEN

Contact your state and city governments to find out about their childhood obesity prevention legislation. Can policies be improved?

Infectious Disease

In well-nourished children, ordinary childhood illnesses have no effect on physical growth. But when children are poorly fed, disease interacts with malnutrition in a vicious spiral, with potentially severe consequences.

Infectious Disease and Malnutrition   In developing nations where a large proportion of the population lives in poverty, children do not receive routine immunizations. As a result, illnesses such as measles and chicken pox, which typically do not appear until after age 3 in industrialized nations, occur much earlier. Poor diet depresses the body's immune system, making children far more susceptible to disease. Of the 9 million annual deaths of children under age 5 worldwide, 98 percent are in developing countries and 70 percent are due to infectious diseases (World Health Organization, 2010b).

Disease, in turn, is a major contributor to malnutrition, hindering both physical growth and cognitive development. Illness reduces appetite and limits the body's ability to absorb foods, especially in children with intestinal infections. In developing countries, widespread diarrhea, resulting from unsafe water and contaminated foods, leads to growth stunting and nearly 3 million childhood deaths each year (World Health Organization, 2010b). Studies carried out in the slums and shantytowns of Brazil and Peru reveal that the more persistent diarrhea is in early childhood, the shorter children are in height and the lower they score on mental tests during the school years (Checkley et al., 2003; Niehaus et al., 2002).

Most developmental impairments and deaths due to diarrhea can be prevented with nearly cost-free *oral rehydration therapy (ORT),* in which sick children are given a glucose, salt, and water solution that quickly replaces fluids the body loses. Since 1990, public health workers have taught nearly half the families in the developing world how to administer ORT. Also, supplements of zinc (essential for immune system functioning), which cost only 30 cents for a month's supply, substantially reduce the incidence of severe and prolonged diarrhea (Aggarwal, Sentz, & Miller, 2007). Through these interventions, the lives of millions of children are saved each year. Still, only a minority of children with diarrhea in the world's poorest countries—such as Chad, Morocco, Somalia, and Togo—receive ORT (World Health Organization, 2010b).

Immunization   In industrialized nations, childhood diseases have declined dramatically during the past half-century, largely as a result of widespread immunization of infants and young children. Nevertheless, about 20 percent of U.S. infants and toddlers are not fully immunized. Of the 80 percent who receive a complete schedule of vaccinations in the first two years, some do not receive the immunizations they need later, in early childhood. Overall, 30 percent of U.S. preschoolers lack essential immunizations. The rate rises to 32 percent for poverty-stricken children, many of whom do not receive full protection until age 5 or 6, when it is required for school entry (U.S. Department of Health and Human Services, 2010g). In contrast, fewer than 10 percent of preschoolers lack immunizations in Denmark and Norway, and fewer than 7 percent in Canada, the Netherlands, Sweden, and the United Kingdom (World Health Organization, 2010b).

Why does the United States lag behind these other countries in immunization? As noted in earlier chapters, many U.S. children do not have access to the health care they need. In 1994, all medically uninsured children in the United States were guaranteed free immunizations, a program that has led to gains in immunization rates. Still, the cost of the doctor's visit to obtain the immunization may not be covered.

AP IMAGES/CORPUS CHRISTI CALLER-TIMES, RACHEL DENNY CLOW

A 4-year-old receives several immunizations at a public health clinic. Such clinics are often the only option for families who lack private health insurance. About 30 percent of U.S. preschoolers lack essential immunizations.

Inability to pay for vaccines is only one cause of inadequate immunization. Parents with little education and with stressful daily lives often fail to schedule vaccination appointments, and those without a primary-care physician do not want to endure long waits in crowded U.S. public health clinics (Falagas & Zarkadoulia, 2008). Some parents have been influenced by media reports suggesting a link between a mercury-based preservative used for decades in vaccines and a rise in the number of children diagnosed with autism. But large-scale studies show no association with autism and no consistent effects on cognitive performance (Dales, Hammer, & Smith, 2001; Richler et al., 2006; Stehr-Green et al., 2003; Thompson et al., 2007). Still, as a precautionary measure, mercury-free versions of childhood vaccinations are now available.

In areas where many parents have refused to immunize their children, outbreaks of whooping cough and rubella have occurred, with life-threatening consequences (Kennedy & Gust, 2008; Tuyen & Bisgard, 2003). Public education programs directed at increasing parental knowledge about the importance and safety of timely immunizations are badly needed.

Emotional Well-Being

We may not think of affection as necessary for healthy physical growth, but it is as vital as food. **Growth faltering** is a term applied to infants whose weight, height, and head circumference are substantially below age-related growth norms and who are withdrawn and apathetic (Black, 2005). In as many as half such cases, a disturbed parent–infant relationship contributes to the failure to grow normally. These infants often keep their eyes on nearby adults, anxiously watching their every move, and they rarely smile at their caregiver (Steward, 2001).

Family circumstances surrounding growth faltering help explain these reactions. During feeding, diaper changing, and play, mothers of these infants seem cold and distant, at other times impatient and hostile (Hagekull, Bohlin, & Rydell, 1997). In response, babies try to protect themselves by keeping track of the threatening adult's whereabouts and, when she approaches, avoiding her gaze. Often an unhappy marriage or parental psychological disturbance contributes to these serious caregiving problems. And most of the time, the baby is irritable and displays abnormal feeding behaviors, such as poor sucking or vomiting, that both disrupt growth and lead parents to feel anxious and helpless, which stress the parent–infant relationship further (Batchelor, 2008; Linscheid, Budd, & Rasnake, 2005).

When treated early, by intervening in infant feeding problems, helping parents with their own life challenges, and encouraging sensitive caregiving, these babies show quick catch-up growth. But if the disorder is not corrected in infancy, most children remain small and show lasting cognitive and emotional difficulties (Black et al., 2007; Drewett, Corbett, & Wright, 2006).

Extreme emotional deprivation can interfere with the production of GH and lead to **psychosocial dwarfism,** a growth disorder that appears between 2 and 15 years of age. Typical characteristics include decreased GH secretion, very short stature, immature skeletal age, and serious adjustment problems, which help distinguish psychosocial dwarfism from normal shortness (Tarren-Sweeney, 2006). When such children are removed from their emotionally inadequate environments, their GH levels quickly return to normal, and they grow rapidly. But if treatment is delayed, the dwarfism can be permanent.

A S K   Y O U R S E L F

Review ■ Explain why breastfeeding can have lifelong consequences for the development of babies born in poverty-stricken regions of the world.

Connect ■ How are bidirectional influences between parent and child involved in the impact of malnutrition on psychological development?

Apply ■ Ten-month-old Shaun is below average in height and painfully thin. He has a serious growth disorder. List possibilities, and indicate what clues you would look for to tell which one Shaun has.

Reflect ■ In rearing a child, which feeding and other child-rearing practices would you use, and which would you avoid, to prevent overweight and obesity?

Puberty: The Physical Transition to Adulthood

▶ Describe sexual maturation in girls and boys, noting genetic and environmental influences on pubertal timing.

During **puberty,** young people attain an adult-sized body and become capable of producing offspring. Accompanying rapid body growth are changes in physical features related to sexual functioning. Some, called **primary sexual characteristics,** involve the reproductive organs directly (ovaries, uterus, and vagina in females; penis, scrotum, and testes in males). Others, called **secondary sexual characteristics,** are visible on the outside of the body and serve as additional signs of sexual maturity (for example, breast development in females and the appearance of underarm and pubic hair in both sexes). As the Milestones table on page 204 shows, these characteristics develop in a fairly standard sequence, although the ages at which each begins and is completed vary greatly. Typically, pubertal development takes about four years, but some adolescents complete it in two years, whereas others take five to six years.

Sexual Maturation in Girls

Female puberty usually begins with the budding of the breasts and the growth spurt. **Menarche,** or first menstruation (from the Greek word *arche,* meaning "beginning"), typically occurs relatively late in the sequence of pubertal events—around age 12½ for North American girls, 13 for Western Europeans. But the age range is wide, from 10½ to 15½ years. Following menarche, breast and pubic hair growth are completed, and underarm hair appears.

Notice in the Milestones table that nature delays sexual maturity until the girl's body is large enough for childbearing; menarche takes place after the peak of the height spurt. As an extra measure of security, for 12 to 18 months following menarche, the menstrual cycle often occurs without the release of an ovum from the ovaries (Archibald, Graber, & Brooks-Gunn, 2006; Bogin, 2001). But this temporary period of sterility does not occur in all girls, and it cannot be counted on for protection against pregnancy.

Sexual Maturation in Boys

The first sign of puberty in boys is the enlargement of the testes (glands that manufacture sperm), accompanied by changes in the texture and color of the scrotum. Pubic hair emerges soon after, about the same time the penis begins to enlarge (Rogol, Roemmich, & Clark, 2002).

Refer again to the Milestones table, and you will see that the growth spurt occurs much later in the sequence of pubertal events for boys than for girls. Also, boys'

Sex differences in pubertal growth are obvious in these middle school students. Although all are about the same age, the girl is much taller and more mature-looking than the boys.

height gain is more intense and longer lasting. When it reaches its peak around age 14, enlargement of the testes and penis is nearly complete, and underarm hair appears. Facial and body hair also emerge just after the peak in body growth and increase gradually for several years. Another landmark of male physical maturity is the deepening of the voice as the larynx enlarges and the vocal cords lengthen. (Girls' voices also deepen slightly.) Voice change usually takes place at the peak of the male growth spurt and often is not complete until puberty is over (Archibald, Graber, & Brooks-Gunn, 2006).

Milestones

Pubertal Development in North American Girls and Boys

GIRLS	AVERAGE AGE ATTAINED	AGE RANGE
Breasts begin to "bud"	10	8–13
Height spurt begins	10	8–13
Pubic hair appears	10.5	8–14
Peak strength spurt	11.6	9.5–14
Peak height spurt	11.7	10–13.5
Menarche (first menstruation) occurs	12.5	10.5–14
Peak weight spurt	12.7	10–14
Adult stature reached	13	10–16
Pubic hair growth completed	14.5	14–15
Breast growth completed	15	10–17

BOYS	AVERAGE AGE ATTAINED	AGE RANGE
Testes begin to enlarge	11.5	9.5–13.5
Pubic hair appears	12	10–15
Penis begins to enlarge	12	10.5–14.5
Height spurt begins	12.5	10.5–16
Spermarche (first ejaculation) occurs	13.5	12–16
Peak height spurt	14	12.5–15.5
Peak weight spurt	14	12.5–15.5
Facial hair begins to grow	14	12.5–15.5
Voice begins to deepen	14	12.5–15.5
Penis and testes growth completed	14.5	12.5–16
Peak strength spurt	15.3	13–17
Adult stature reached	15.5	13.5–17.5
Pubic hair growth completed	15.5	14–17

Sources: Chumlea et al., 2003; Herman-Giddens, 2006; Rogol, Roemmich, & Clark, 2002; Rubin et al., 2009; Wu, Mendola, & Buck, 2002.

Photos: (left) © David Young-Wolff/PhotoEdit; (right) © Bill Aron/PhotoEdit

While the penis is growing, the prostate gland and seminal vesicles (which together produce semen, the fluid containing sperm) enlarge. Then, around age 13½, **spermarche,** or first ejaculation, occurs (Rogol, Roemmich, & Clark, 2002). For a while, the semen contains few living sperm. So, like girls, boys have an initial period of reduced fertility.

Individual and Group Differences in Pubertal Growth

Heredity contributes substantially to the timing of pubertal changes. Identical twins are more similar than fraternal twins in attainment of most pubertal milestones, including growth spurt, menarche, breast development, body hair, and voice change (Eaves et al., 2004; Mustanski et al., 2004). Nutrition and exercise also make a difference. In females, a sharp rise in body weight and fat may trigger sexual maturation. Fat cells release a protein called *leptin*, which is believed to signal the brain that girls' energy stores are sufficient for puberty—a likely reason that breast and pubic hair growth and menarche occur earlier for heavier and, especially, obese girls. In contrast, girls who begin rigorous athletic training at an early age or who eat very little (both of which reduce the percentage of body fat) usually experience later puberty (Kaplowitz, 2008; Lee et al., 2007; Rubin et al., 2009). Few studies, however, report a link between body fat and puberty in boys.

Variations in pubertal growth also exist between regions of the world and between income and ethnic groups. Physical health plays a major role. In poverty-stricken regions where malnutrition and infectious disease are common, menarche is greatly delayed, occurring as late as age 14 to 16 in many parts of Africa. Within developing countries, girls from higher-income families consistently reach menarche 6 to 18 months earlier than those from economically disadvantaged homes (Parent et al., 2003).

But in industrialized nations where food is abundant, the joint roles of heredity and environment in pubertal growth are apparent. For example, breast and pubic hair growth begin, on average, around age 9 in African-American girls—a year earlier than in Caucasian-American girls. And African-American girls reach menarche about six months earlier, around age 12. Although widespread overweight and obesity in the black population contribute, a genetically influenced faster rate of physical maturation is also involved. Black girls usually reach menarche before white girls of the same age and body weight (Chumlea et al., 2003; Herman-Giddens, 2006; Hillard, 2008).

Early family experiences may also affect pubertal timing. One theory suggests that humans have evolved to be sensitive to the emotional quality of their childhood environments. When children's safety and security are at risk, it is adaptive for them to reproduce early. Research indicates that girls and (less consistently) boys with a history of family conflict, harsh parenting, or parental separation tend to reach puberty early. In contrast, those with warm, stable family ties reach puberty relatively late (Belsky et al., 2007; Bogaert, 2005; Ellis & Essex, 2007; Mustanski et al., 2004; Tremblay & Frigon, 2005). Critics offer an alternative explanation—that mothers who reached puberty early are more likely to bear children earlier, which increases the likelihood of marital conflict and separation (Mendle et al., 2006). But longitudinal evidence on a large, ethnically diverse sample of U.S. girls followed from birth through age 15 confirmed the former chain of influence: from harsh parenting in childhood to earlier menarche to increased sexual risk taking in adolescence (Belsky et al., 2010).

The Psychological Impact of Pubertal Events

▶ What factors influence adolescents' reactions to the physical changes of puberty?

▶ Describe the impact of pubertal timing on adolescent adjustment, noting sex differences.

TAKE A MOMENT... Think back to your late elementary school and junior high days. As you reached puberty, how did your feelings about yourself and your relationships with others change? Were your reactions similar to those predicted by Rousseau and Hall, described at the beginning of this chapter?

Is Puberty Inevitably a Period of Storm and Stress?

Contemporary research suggests that the notion of adolescence as a biologically determined period of storm and stress is greatly exaggerated. Certain problems, such as eating disorders, depression, suicide (see Chapter 11), and lawbreaking (see Chapter 12), occur more often than earlier (Farrington, 2009; Graber, 2004). But the overall rate of serious psychological disturbance rises only slightly (by about 3 percent) from childhood to adolescence, when it is nearly the same as in the adult population—about 15 percent (Roberts, Attkisson, & Rosenblatt, 1998). Although some teenagers encounter serious difficulties, emotional turbulence is not routine.

The first researcher to point out the wide variability in adolescent adjustment was anthropologist Margaret Mead (1928). She returned from the Pacific islands of Samoa with a startling conclusion: Because of the culture's relaxed social relationships and openness toward sexuality, adolescence "is perhaps the pleasantest time the Samoan girl (or boy) will ever know" (p. 308). In Mead's alternative view, the social environment is entirely responsible for the range of teenage experiences, from erratic and agitated to calm and stress-free.

Later researchers found that Samoan adolescence was not as untroubled as Mead had assumed (Freeman, 1983). Still, Mead's work had an enormous impact. Today we know that biological, psychological, and social forces combine to influence adolescent development (Susman & Dorn, 2009). Most tribal and village societies have a briefer transition to adulthood, but adolescence is not absent (Weisfield, 1997). In industrialized nations, where successful participation in economic life requires many years of education, young people face prolonged dependence on parents and postponement of sexual gratification. As a result, adolescence is greatly extended, and teenagers confront a wider array of psychological challenges. In the following sections, we will see many examples of how multiple factors combine to affect teenagers' adjustment.

Reactions to Pubertal Changes

Two generations ago, menarche was often traumatic. Today, girls commonly react with surprise, undoubtedly due to the sudden onset of the event. Otherwise, they typically report a mixture of positive and negative emotions (DeRose & Brooks-Gunn, 2006). Yet wide individual differences exist that depend on prior knowledge and support from family members, which in turn are influenced by cultural attitudes toward puberty and sexuality.

For girls who have no advance information, menarche can be shocking and disturbing. In the 1950s, up to 50 percent received no prior warning, and of those who did, many were given negative, "grin-and-bear-it" messages (Costos, Ackerman, & Paradis, 2002; Shainess, 1961). Today, few girls are uninformed, a shift that is probably due to parents' greater willingness to discuss sexual matters and to the spread of health education classes (Omar, McElderry, & Zakharia, 2003). Almost all girls get some information from their mothers. And some evidence suggests that compared with Caucasian-American families, African-American families may better prepare girls for menarche, treat it as an important milestone, and express less conflict over girls reaching sexual maturity—factors that lead African-American girls to react more favorably (Martin, 1996).

This 13-year-old's bat mitzvah ceremony, the culmination of extensive study and reflection, recognizes her as an adult with moral and religious responsibilities in the Jewish community. In the larger society, however, she will experience no change in status.

Like girls' reactions to menarche, boys' reactions to spermarche reflect mixed feelings. Virtually all boys know about ejaculation ahead of time, but many say that no one spoke to them before or during puberty about physical changes (Omar, McElderry, & Zakharia, 2003). Usually they get their information from reading materials or websites. Even boys who had advance information often say that their first ejaculation occurred earlier than they expected and that they were unprepared for it. As with girls, boys who feel better prepared tend to react more positively (Stein & Reiser, 1994). But whereas almost all girls tell a friend that they are menstruating, far fewer boys tell anyone about spermarche (DeRose & Brooks-Gunn, 2006; Downs & Fuller, 1991). Overall, boys get much less social support than girls for the physical changes of puberty. They might benefit, especially, from opportunities to ask questions and discuss feelings with a sympathetic parent or health professional.

Many tribal and village societies celebrate physical maturity with an *adolescent initiation ceremony,* a ritualized announcement to the community that marks an important change in privilege and responsibility. Consequently, young people know that reaching puberty is valued in their culture. In contrast, Western societies grant little formal recognition to movement from childhood to adolescence or from adolescence to adulthood. Ceremonies such as the Jewish bar or bat mitzvah and the *quinceañera* in Hispanic communities (celebrating a 15-year-old girl's sexual maturity and marriage availability) resemble initiation ceremonies, but only within the ethnic or religious subculture. They do not mark a significant change in social status in the larger society.

Instead, Western adolescents are granted partial adult status at many different ages—for example, an age for starting employment, for driving, for leaving high school, for voting, and for drinking. And in some contexts (at home and at school), they may still be regarded as children. The absence of a single widely accepted marker of physical and social maturity makes the process of becoming an adult more confusing.

Pubertal Change, Emotion, and Social Behavior

A common belief is that puberty has something to do with adolescent moodiness and the desire for greater physical and psychological separation from parents. Let's see what research says about these relationships.

Adolescent Moodiness Higher pubertal hormone levels are linked to greater moodiness, but only modestly so (Buchanan, Eccles, & Becker, 1992; Graber, Brooks-Gunn, & Warren, 2006). What other factors might contribute? In several studies, the moods of children, adolescents, and adults were monitored by having them carry electronic pagers. Over a one-week period, they were beeped at random intervals and asked to write down what they were doing, whom they were with, and how they felt.

As expected, adolescents reported less favorable moods than school-age children and adults (Larson et al., 2002; Larson & Lampman-Petraitis, 1989). But negative moods were linked to a greater number of negative life events, such as difficulties getting along with parents, disciplinary actions at school, and breaking up with a boyfriend or girlfriend. Negative events increased steadily from childhood to adolescence, and teenagers also seemed to react to them with greater emotion than children (Larson & Ham, 1993). (Recall that stress reactivity is heightened by changes in brain neurotransmitter activity during adolescence.)

Compared with the moods of older adolescents and adults, those of younger adolescents (ages 12 to 16) were less stable, often varying from cheerful to sad and back again. These mood swings were strongly related to situational changes. High points of adolescents' days were times spent with friends and in self-chosen leisure activities. Low points tended to occur in adult-structured settings—class, job, and religious services. Furthermore, emotional highs coincided with Friday and Saturday evenings, especially in high school (see Figure 5.13). Going out with friends and romantic partners increases so dramatically during adolescence that it becomes a "cultural script" for what is *supposed* to happen. Teenagers who spend weekend evenings at home often feel profoundly lonely (Larson & Richards, 1998).

Yet another contributor to adolescent moodiness is change in sleep schedules. Although teenagers need almost as much sleep as they did in middle childhood (about nine hours), they go to bed much later than they did as children, perhaps because of increased neural sensitivity to evening light. This sleep "phase delay" strengthens with pubertal development. But today's teenagers—with more evening social activities, part-time jobs, and bedrooms equipped with TVs, computers, and phones—get much less sleep than teenagers of previous generations (Carskadon, Acebo, & Jenni, 2004; Carskadon et al., 2002). Sleep-deprived adolescents are more likely to suffer from depressed mood, achieve poorly in school, and engage in high-risk behaviors, including drinking and reckless driving (Dahl & Lewin, 2002; Hansen et al., 2005). Later school start times ease but do not eliminate sleep loss.

Fortunately, frequent reports of negative mood level off in late adolescence, when teenagers' emotions also become more stable (Holsen, Kraft, & Vittersø, 2000; Natsuaki, Biehl, & Ge, 2009). And overall, teenagers with supportive family and peer relationships more often report positive and less often negative moods than their agemates with few social supports (Weinstein et al., 2006). In contrast, poorly adjusted young people—with low self-esteem, conduct difficulties, or delinquency—tend to react with stronger negative emotion to unpleasant daily experiences, perhaps compounding their adjustment problems (Schneiders et al., 2006).

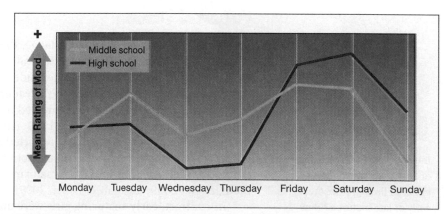

FIGURE 5.13 Younger and older adolescents' emotional experiences across the week. Adolescents' reports revealed that emotional high points are on Fridays and Saturdays. Mood drops on Sunday, before returning to school, and during the week, as students spend much time in adult-structured settings in school. (From R. Larson & M. Richards, 1998, "Waiting for the Weekend: Friday and Saturday Night as the Emotional Climax of the Week," in A. C. Crouter & R. Larson [Eds.], *Temporal Rhythms in Adolescence: Clocks, Calendars, and the Coordination of Daily Life*, San Francisco: Jossey-Bass, p. 41. Reprinted by permission of John Wiley & Sons, Inc.)

Puberty brings an increase in parent–child conflict—psychological distancing that may be a modern substitute for physical departure from the family. Unlike nonhuman primates and adolescents in many nonindustrialized cultures, teenagers in industrialized societies continue living with their parents.

Parent–Child Relationships Recall the observations of Sabrina's father in the introduction to this chapter—that as children enter adolescence, they resist spending time with the family and become more argumentative. Research in cultures as diverse as the United States and Turkey shows that puberty is related to a rise in parent–child conflict, which persists into the mid-teenage years (Gure, Ucanok, & Sayil, 2006; Laursen, Coy, & Collins, 1998; McGue et al., 2005).

Why should a youngster's more adultlike appearance trigger these disputes? From an evolutionary perspective, the association may have adaptive value. Among nonhuman primates, the young typically leave the family group around the time of puberty. The same is true in many nonindustrialized cultures (Caine, 1986; Schlegel & Barry, 1991). Departure of young people discourages sexual relations between close blood relatives. But adolescents in industrialized nations, who are still economically dependent on parents, cannot leave the family. Consequently, a modern substitute seems to have emerged: psychological distancing.

As children become physically mature, they demand to be treated in adultlike ways. And as we will see in later chapters, adolescents' new powers of reasoning may also contribute to a rise in family tensions. Parent–adolescent disagreements focus largely on everyday matters such as driving, dating partners, and curfews (Adams & Laursen, 2001). But beneath these disputes lie serious concerns: parental efforts to protect teenagers from substance use, auto accidents, and early sex. The larger the gap between parents' and adolescents' views of teenagers' readiness for new responsibilities, the more they quarrel (Deković, Noom, & Meeus, 1997).

Parent–daughter conflict tends to be more intense than conflict with sons, perhaps because girls reach puberty earlier and parents place more restrictions on girls (Allison & Schultz, 2004). But most disputes are mild, and by late adolescence, only a small minority of families experience continuing friction. Parents and teenagers display both conflict and affection, and they usually agree on important values, such as honesty and the importance of education.

Although separation from parents is adaptive, both generations benefit from warm, protective family bonds throughout the lifespan. As the teenage years conclude, parent–adolescent interactions are less hierarchical, setting the stage for mutually supportive relationships in adulthood (Laursen & Collins, 2009).

Pubertal Timing

In addition to dramatic physical change, the timing of puberty has a major impact on psychological adjustment. Findings of several studies indicate that both adults and peers viewed early-maturing boys as relaxed, independent, self-confident, and physically attractive. Popular with agemates, they tended to hold leadership positions in school and to be athletic stars. In contrast, late-maturing boys expressed more anxiety and depressed mood than their on-time counterparts (Brooks-Gunn, 1988; Huddleson & Ge, 2003). But early-maturing boys, though viewed as well-adjusted, reported slightly more psychological stress, depressed mood, and problem behaviors (sexual activity, smoking, drinking, aggression, delinquency) than both their on-time and later-maturing agemates (Ge, Conger, & Elder, 2001; Natsuaki, Biehl, & Ge, 2009; Susman & Dorn, 2009).

In contrast, early-maturing girls were unpopular, withdrawn, lacking in self-confidence, anxious, and prone to depression, and they held few leadership positions and achieved less well in school (Ge, Conger, & Elder, 1996; Graber et al., 1997; Graber, Brooks-Gunn, & Warren, 2006; Jones & Mussen, 1958). And like early-maturing boys, they were more involved in deviant behavior (smoking, drinking, early sexual activity) (Caspi et al., 1993; Dick et al., 2000; Ge et al., 2006). In contrast, their later-maturing counterparts were regarded as physically attractive, lively, sociable, and leaders at school. In one study of several hundred eighth graders, however, negative effects were not evident among early-maturing African-American

LOOK and LISTEN

Interview several classmates of both sexes about their own pubertal timing. Were they early or late maturers? How did pubertal timing affect their experiences in school and with peers?

girls, whose families—and perhaps friends as well—tend to be more unconditionally wel-coming of menarche (see page 206) (Michael & Eccles, 2003).

Two factors largely account for these trends: (1) how closely the adolescent's body matches cultural ideals of physical attractiveness and (2) how well young people fit in phys-ically with their agemates.

The Role of Physical Attractiveness TAKE A MOMENT... Flip through the pages of your favorite popular magazine. You will see evidence of our society's view of an attractive female as thin and long-legged and of a good-looking male as tall, broad-shouldered, and muscular. The female image is a girlish shape that favors the late developer. The male image fits the early-maturing boy.

Consistent with these preferences, early maturing Caucasian girls tend to report a less positive **body image**—conception of and attitude toward their physical appearance—than their on-time and late-maturing agemates. Compared with African-American and Hispanic girls, Caucasian girls are more likely to have internalized the cultural ideal of female attrac-tiveness. Most want to be thinner (Rosen, 2003; Stice, Presnell, & Bearman, 2001; Williams & Currie, 2000). Although boys are less consistent, early, rapid maturers are more likely to be satisfied with their physical characteristics (Alsaker, 1995; Sinkkonen, Anttila, & Siimes, 1998).

Body image is a strong predictor of young people's self-esteem (Harter, 2006). But the negative effects of pubertal timing on body image and—as we will see next—emotional adjustment are greatly amplified when accompanied by other stressors (Stice, 2003).

The Importance of Fitting in with Peers Physical status in relation to peers also explains differences in adjustment between early and late maturers. From this perspective, early-maturing girls and late-maturing boys have difficulty because they fall at the extremes in physical development. Recall that Sabrina felt "out of place" when with her agemates. Not surpris-ingly, adolescents feel most comfortable with peers who match their own level of biological maturity (Stattin & Magnusson, 1990).

Because few agemates of the same pubertal status are available, early-maturing adolescents of both sexes seek out older compan-ions, who often encourage them into activities they are not yet ready to handle. And hormonal influences on the brain's emotional/social network (see pages 190–191) are stronger for early maturers, further magnifying their receptiveness to sexual activity, drug and alcohol use, and minor delinquent acts (Ge et al., 2002; Steinberg, 2008). Perhaps because of such involvements, early maturers of both sexes report feeling emotionally stressed and show declines in academic performance (Mendle, Turkheimer, & Emery, 2007; Natsuaki, Biehl, & Ge, 2009).

At the same time, the young person's context greatly increases the likelihood that early pubertal timing will lead to negative out-comes. Early maturers in economically disadvantaged neighbor-hoods are especially vulnerable to establishing ties with deviant peers, which heightens their defiant, hostile behavior (Obeidallah et al., 2004). And because families in such neighbor-hoods tend to be exposed to chronic, severe stressors and to have few social supports, these early maturers are also more likely to experience harsh, inconsistent parenting, which, in turn, predicts both deviant peer associations and antisocial activity (Ge et al., 2002, 2011).

Long-Term Consequences Do the effects of pubertal timing persist? Follow-ups reveal that early-maturing girls, especially, are prone to lasting difficulties. In one study, early-maturing boys' depression subsided by age 13, but depressed early-maturing girls tended to remain depressed (Ge at al., 2003). In another study, which followed young people from ages 14 to 24, early-maturing boys again showed good adjustment. Early-maturing girls, however, reported poorer-quality relationships with family and friends, smaller social networks, and lower life satisfaction into early adulthood than their on-time counterparts (Graber et al., 2004). Similarly, in a Swedish investigation, achievement and substance use difficulties of

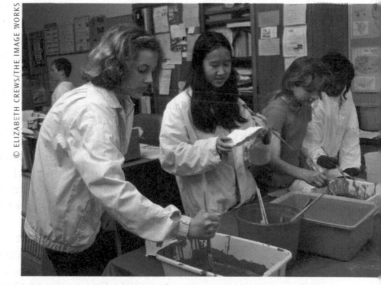

© ELIZABETH CREWS/THE IMAGE WORKS

These 11-year-olds vary greatly in pubertal timing. Outside of school, early maturers often seek out older companions, who may encourage them into deviant activities. Early-maturing girls, especially, are at risk for lasting difficulties.

early-maturing girls lingered, in the form of greater alcohol abuse and lower educational attainment than their agemates (Andersson & Magnusson, 1990; Stattin & Magnusson, 1990).

Recall that childhood family conflict and harsh parenting are linked to earlier pubertal timing, more so for girls than for boys (see page 205). Perhaps many early-maturing girls enter adolescence with emotional and social difficulties. As the stresses of puberty interfere with school performance and lead to unfavorable peer pressures, poor adjustment extends and deepens (Graber, 2003). Clearly, interventions that target at-risk early-maturing adolescents are needed. These include educating parents and teachers and providing adolescents with counseling and social supports so they will be better prepared to handle the emotional and social challenges of this transition.

ASK YOURSELF

Review ■ Summarize the impact of pubertal timing on adolescent development.

Connect ■ How might adolescent moodiness contribute to the psychological distancing between parents and children that accompanies puberty? (*Hint:* Think about bidirectional influences in parent–child relationships.)

Apply ■ As a school-age child, Chloe enjoyed leisure activities with her parents. Now, as a 14-year-old, she spends hours in her room and resists going on weekend family excursions. Explain Chloe's behavior.

Reflect ■ Recall your own reactions to the physical changes of puberty. Are they consistent with research findings? Explain.

▶ What factors contribute to eating disorders in adolescence?

▶ Discuss cultural, social, and personal influences on adolescent sexual attitudes and behavior.

▶ Cite factors involved in the development of homosexuality.

▶ Discuss factors related to sexually transmitted disease and teenage pregnancy and parenthood, noting prevention and intervention strategies.

Puberty and Adolescent Health

The arrival of puberty brings new health concerns related to the young person's efforts to meet physical and psychological needs. As adolescents attain greater autonomy, their personal decision making becomes important, in health as well as other areas. Yet none of the health concerns we are about to discuss can be traced to a single cause. Rather, biological, psychological, family, peer, and cultural factors jointly contribute.

Eating Disorders

Girls who reach puberty early, who are very dissatisfied with their body image, and who grow up in homes where concern with weight and thinness is high are at risk for eating problems. Severe dieting is the strongest predictor of an eating disorder in adolescence (Lock & Kirz, 2008). The two most serious are anorexia nervosa and bulimia nervosa.

Anorexia Nervosa **Anorexia nervosa** is a tragic eating disorder in which young people starve themselves because of a compulsive fear of getting fat. Typically appearing between ages 14 and 16, it affects about 1 percent of North American and Western European teenage girls. During the past half-century, cases have increased sharply, fueled by cultural admiration of female thinness. Anorexia nervosa is equally common in all social-class groups, but Asian-American, Caucasian-American, and Hispanic girls are at greater risk than African-American girls, who tend to be more satisfied with their size and shape (Granillo, Jones-Rodriguez, & Carvajal, 2005; Ozer & Irwin, 2009; Steinhausen, 2006). Boys account for 10 to 15 percent of anorexia cases; about half of these are gay or bisexual young people who are uncomfortable with a strong, muscular appearance (Raevuori et al., 2009; Robb & Dadson, 2002).

Individuals with anorexia have an extremely distorted body image. Even after they have become severely underweight, they see themselves as too heavy. Most go on self-imposed diets so strict that they struggle to avoid eating in response to hunger. To enhance weight loss, they exercise strenuously.

In their attempt to reach "perfect" slimness, individuals with anorexia lose between 25 and 50 percent of their body weight. Because a normal menstrual cycle requires about 15 percent body fat, either menarche does not occur or menstrual periods stop. Malnutrition causes pale skin, brittle discolored nails, fine dark hairs all over the body, and extreme sensitivity to cold. If it continues, the heart muscle can shrink, the kidneys can fail, and irreversible brain damage and loss of bone mass can occur. About 6 percent of individuals with anorexia die of the disorder, as a result of either physical complications or suicide (Katzman, 2005).

Forces within the person, the family, and the larger culture give rise to anorexia nervosa. Identical twins share the disorder more often than fraternal twins, indicating a genetic influence. Abnormalities in neurotransmitters in the brain, linked to anxiety and impulse control, may make some individuals more susceptible (Kaye, 2008; Lock & Kirz, 2008). And problem eating behavior in early childhood—persistently refusing to eat or eating very little—is linked to anorexia in adolescence (Nicholls & Viner, 2009). Many young people with anorexia have unrealistically high standards for their own behavior and performance, are emotionally inhibited, and avoid intimate ties outside the family. Consequently, they are often excellent students who are responsible and well-behaved. But as we have seen, the societal image of "thin is beautiful" contributes to the poor body image of many girls—especially early-maturing girls, who are at greatest risk for anorexia nervosa (Hogan & Strasburger, 2008).

In addition, parent–adolescent interactions reveal problems related to adolescent autonomy. Often the mothers of these girls have high expectations for physical appearance, achievement, and social acceptance and are overprotective and controlling. Fathers tend to be emotionally distant. These parental attitudes and behavior may contribute to affected girls' persistent anxiety and fierce pursuit of perfection in achievement, respectable behavior, and thinness (Kaye, 2008). Nevertheless, it remains unclear whether maladaptive parent–child relationships precede the disorder, emerge as a response to it, or both. In a longitudinal study in which 12- to 16-year-old girls were followed for four years, unhealthy eating behaviors led to conflict-ridden interactions with parents, not the reverse (Archibald et al., 2002).

Because individuals with anorexia typically deny or minimize the seriousness of their disorder, treating it is difficult (Couturier & Lock, 2006). Hospitalization is often necessary to prevent life-threatening malnutrition. The most successful treatment is family therapy plus medication to reduce anxiety and neurotransmitter imbalances (Robin & Le Grange, 2010; Treasure & Schmidt, 2005). As a supplementary approach, behavior modification—in which individuals hospitalized with anorexia are rewarded with praise, social contact, and opportunities for exercise when they eat and gain weight—is helpful.

© LAUREN GREENFIELD/INSTITUTE

Aiva, age 16, an anorexia nervosa patient, is shown at left weighing just 77 pounds on the day she entered treatment. At right, Aiva appears 10 weeks later, on her last day of treatment. Less than 50 percent of young people with anorexia fully overcome the disorder.

Still, less than 50 percent of young people with anorexia recover fully. For many, eating problems continue in less extreme form. About 10 percent show signs of a less severe, but nevertheless debilitating, disorder: bulimia nervosa. And the chronic anxiety associated with both eating disorders increases girls' risk for major depression in both adolescence and adulthood (Godart et al., 2006).

Bulimia Nervosa In **bulimia nervosa,** young people (again, mainly girls, but gay and bisexual boys are also vulnerable) engage in strict dieting and excessive exercise accompanied by binge eating, often followed by deliberate vomiting and purging with laxatives (Herzog, Eddy, & Beresin, 2006; Wichstrøm, 2006). Bulimia typically appears in late adolescence and is more common than anorexia nervosa, affecting about 2 to 4 percent of teenage girls, only 5 percent of whom previously suffered from anorexia.

Twin studies show that bulimia, like anorexia, is influenced by heredity (Klump, Kaye, & Strober, 2001). Overweight and early menarche increase the risk. Some adolescents with bulimia, like those with anorexia, are perfectionists. But most are impulsive, sensation-seeking young people who lack self-control in many areas, engaging in petty shoplifting, alcohol abuse, and other risky behaviors. And although girls with bulimia, like those with anorexia, are pathologically anxious about gaining weight, they may have experienced their parents as disengaged and emotionally unavailable rather than overcontrolling (Fairburn & Harrison, 2003).

In contrast to young people with anorexia, those with bulimia usually feel depressed and guilty about their abnormal eating habits and desperately want help. As a result, bulimia is usually easier to treat than anorexia, through support groups, nutrition education, training in changing eating habits, and anti-anxiety, antidepressant, and appetite-control medication (Hay & Bacaltchuk, 2004).

Sexuality

With the arrival of puberty, hormonal changes—in particular, the production of androgens in young people of both sexes—lead to an increase in sex drive (Halpern, Udry, & Suchindran, 1997). In response, adolescents become very concerned about managing sexuality in social relationships. New cognitive capacities involving perspective taking and self-reflection affect their efforts to do so. Yet like the eating behaviors we have just discussed, adolescent sexuality is heavily influenced by the young person's social context.

The Impact of Culture TAKE A MOMENT... When did you first learn "the facts of life"—and how? Was sex discussed openly in your family, or was it treated with secrecy? Exposure to sex, education about it, and efforts to limit the sexual curiosity of children and adolescents vary widely around the world. At one extreme are a number of Middle Eastern peoples, who murder girls if they lose their virginity before marriage. At the other extreme are several Asian and Pacific Island groups with highly permissive sexual attitudes and practices. For example, among the Trobriand Islanders of Papua New Guinea, older companions provide children with instruction in sexual practices, and adolescents are expected to engage in sexual experimentation with a variety of partners (Weiner, 1988).

Despite the prevailing image of sexually free adolescents, sexual attitudes in North America are relatively restrictive. Typically, parents provide little or no information about sex, discourage sex play, and rarely talk about sex in children's presence. When young people become interested in sex, only about half report getting information from parents about intercourse, pregnancy prevention, and sexually transmitted disease. Many parents avoid meaningful discussions about sex out of fear of embarrassment or concern that the adolescent will not take them seriously (Wilson et al., 2010). Yet warm, open give-and-take, as described in Applying What We Know on the following page, is associated with teenagers' adoption of parents' views and with reduced sexual risk taking (Jaccard, Dodge, & Dittus, 2003; Usher-Seriki, Bynum, & Callands, 2008).

Adolescents who do not get information about sex from their parents are likely to learn from friends, books, magazines, movies, TV, and the Internet (Jaccard, Dodge, & Dittus, 2002; Sutton et al., 2002). On prime-time TV shows, which adolescents watch more than other TV offerings, 80 percent of programs contain sexual content. Most depict partners as spontaneous and passionate, taking no steps to avoid pregnancy or sexually transmitted disease, and experiencing no negative consequences (Roberts, Henriksen, & Foehr, 2004). In several studies, teenagers' media exposure to sexual content positively predicted current sexual activity, intentions to be sexually active in the future, and subsequent sexual activity, pregnancies, and sexual harassment behaviors (offensive name-calling or touching, pressuring a peer for a date), even after many other relevant factors were controlled (Brown & L'Engle, 2009; Chandra et al., 2008; Roberts, Henriksen, & Foehr, 2009).

Not surprisingly, adolescents who are prone to early sexual activity choose to consume more sexualized media (Steinberg & Monahan, 2011). Still, the Internet is a hazardous "sex educator." In a survey of a large sample of U.S. 10- to 17-year-old Web users, 42 percent said they had viewed online pornographic websites (images of naked people or people having sex) while surfing the Internet in the past 12 months. Of these, 66 percent indicated they had encountered the images accidentally and did not want to view them. Youths who felt depressed, had been bullied by peers, or were involved in delinquent activities had more encounters with Internet pornography, which may have intensified their adjustment problems (Wolak, Mitchell, & Finkelhor, 2007).

Consider the contradictory messages young people receive. On one hand, adults emphasize that sex at a young age and outside marriage is wrong. On the other hand, the social

APPLYING WHAT WE KNOW

Communicating with Adolescents About Sexual Issues

STRATEGY	EXPLANATION
Foster open communication.	Let the teenager know you are a willing and trustworthy resource by stating that you are available when questions arise and will answer fully and accurately.
Use correct terms for body parts.	Correct vocabulary gives the young person a basis for future discussion and also indicates that sex is not a forbidden topic.
Use effective discussion techniques.	Listen, encourage the adolescent to participate, ask open-ended rather than yes/no questions, and give supportive responses. Avoid dominating and lecturing, which cause teenagers to withdraw.
Reflect before speaking.	When the adolescent asks questions or offers opinions about sex, remain nonjudgmental. If you differ with the teenager's views, convey your perspective in a nonthreatening manner, emphasizing that although you disagree, you are not attacking his or her character. Trying to dictate the young person's behavior generally results in alienation.
Keep conversations going.	Many parents think their job is finished once they have had the "big talk" in early adolescence. But young people are more likely to be influenced by an accumulation of smaller discussions. If open communication begins early and is sustained, the teenager is more likely to return with thoughts and questions.

Source: Berkowitz, 2004; Wilson et al., 2010.

environment extols sexual excitement, experimentation, and promiscuity. American teenagers are left bewildered, poorly informed about sexual facts, and with little sound advice on how to conduct their sex lives responsibly.

Adolescent Sexual Attitudes and Behavior Although differences between subcultural groups exist, the sexual attitudes of U.S. adolescents and adults have become more liberal over the past 40 years. Compared with a generation ago, more people approve of sexual intercourse before marriage, as long as two people are emotionally committed to each other (ABC News, 2004; Hoff, Greene, & Davis, 2003). During the past decade, adolescents have swung slightly back toward more conservative sexual beliefs, largely in response to the risk of sexually transmitted disease, especially AIDS, and to teenage sexual abstinence programs sponsored by schools and religious organizations (Akers et al., 2011; Ali & Scelfo, 2002).

Trends in adolescents' sexual behavior are consistent with their attitudes. Rates of extramarital sex among U.S. young people rose for several decades but have recently declined (U.S. Department of Health and Human Services, 2010g). Nevertheless, as Figure 5.14 reveals, a substantial percentage of young people are sexually active by ninth grade (age 14 to 15).

Overall, teenage sexual activity rates are similar in the United States and other Western countries: Nearly half of adolescents have had intercourse. But quality of sexual experiences differs. U.S. youths become sexually active earlier than their Canadian and European counterparts (Boyce et al., 2006; U.S. Department of Health and Human Services, 2010g). And about 14 percent of adolescent boys in the United States—more than in other Western nations—have had sexual relations

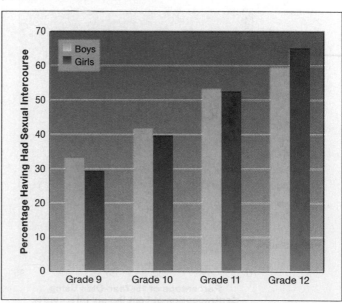

FIGURE 5.14 U.S. adolescents who report ever having had sexual intercourse. Many young U.S. adolescents are sexually active—more than in other Western nations. Boys tend to have their first intercourse earlier than girls. In tenth and eleventh grades, rates of boys and girls having had sexual intercourse are similar. In twelfth grade, girls' rate exceeds boys'. (From U.S. Department of Health and Human Services, 2010d.)

Adolescence is an especially important time for the development of sexuality. But American teenagers receive contradictory and confusing messages about the appropriateness of sex.

© RICHARD HUTCHINGS/PHOTOEDIT

with three or more partners in the past year (Alan Guttmacher Institute, 2010). Most teenagers, however, have had only one or two sexual partners by the end of high school.

Characteristics of Sexually Active Adolescents Early and frequent sexual activity is linked to personal, family, peer, and educational characteristics. These include childhood impulsivity, weak sense of personal control over life events, early pubertal timing, parental divorce, single-parent and stepfamily homes, large family size, little or no religious involvement, weak parental monitoring, disrupted parent–child communication, sexually active friends and older siblings, poor school performance, lower educational aspirations, and tendency to engage in norm-violating acts, including alcohol and drug use and delinquency (Coley, Votruba-Drzal, & Schindler, 2009; Crockett, Raffaelli, & Shen, 2006; Siebenbruner, Zimmer-Gembeck, & Egeland, 2007; Zimmer-Gembeck & Helfand, 2008).

Because many of these factors are associated with growing up in a low-income family, it is not surprising that early sexual activity is more common among young people from economically disadvantaged homes. Living in a neighborhood high in physical deterioration, crime, and violence also increases the likelihood that teenagers will be sexually active (Ge et al., 2002). In such neighborhoods, social ties are weak, adults exert little oversight or control over adolescents' activities, and negative peer influences are widespread. In fact, the high rate of sexual activity among African-American teenagers—65 percent report having had sexual intercourse, compared with 46 percent of all U.S. young people—is largely accounted for by widespread poverty in the black population (Darroch, Frost, & Singh, 2001; U.S. Department of Health and Human Services, 2010g).

Early and prolonged father absence predicts higher rates of intercourse and pregnancy among adolescent girls, after many family background and personal characteristics are controlled (Ellis et al., 2003). Perhaps father absence exposes young people to the dating and sexual behaviors of their mothers, who serve as models for their physically maturing children. An alternative, evolutionary account proposes that fathers' investment in parenting encourages daughters to delay sexual activity in favor of seeking a similarly committed male partner to ensure their offspring's well-being. Because father-absent girls view male commitment as uncertain, they may readily enter into casual sexual relationships.

Contraceptive Use Although adolescent contraceptive use has increased in recent years, about 20 percent of sexually active teenagers in the United States are at risk for unintended pregnancy because they do not use contraception consistently (see Figure 5.15) (Alan Guttmacher Institute, 2002, 2005; Fortenberry et al., 2010). Why do so many fail to take precautions? Typically, teenagers respond, "I was waiting until I had a steady boyfriend," or "I wasn't planning to have sex." As we will see in Chapter 6, although adolescents can consider multiple possibilities when faced with a theoretical problem, they often fail to apply this advanced reasoning to everyday situations.

One reason is that advances in perspective taking—the capacity to imagine what others may be thinking and feeling—lead teenagers, for a time, to be extremely concerned about what others think of them. Also, in the midst of everyday social pressures, adolescents often overlook the potential consequences of risky behaviors. And many teenagers—especially

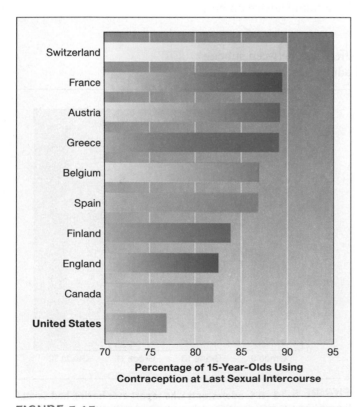

FIGURE 5.15 Contraceptive use by sexually active 15-year-olds in ten industrialized nations. Sexually active U.S. teenagers are less likely to use contraception (condom, contraceptive pill, or both) consistently than teenagers in other industrialized nations. (Adapted from Godeau et al., 2008; U.S. Department of Health and Human Services, 2010g.)

those from troubled, low-income families—do not have realistic expectations about the impact of early parenthood on their current and future lives (Stevens-Simon, Sheeder, & Harter, 2005).

As these findings suggest, the social environment also contributes to adolescents' reluctance to use contraception. Those without the rewards of meaningful education and work are especially likely to engage in irresponsible sex, sometimes within relationships characterized by exploitation. About 11 percent of U.S. girls and 5 percent of boys say they were pressured to have intercourse when they were unwilling (U.S. Department of Health and Human Services, 2010g).

In contrast, teenagers who report good relationships with parents and who talk openly with them about sex and contraception are more likely to use birth control (Henrich et al., 2006; Kirby, 2002a). But few adolescents believe their parents would be understanding and supportive. School sex education classes, as well, often leave teenagers with incomplete or incorrect knowledge. Some do not know where to get birth control counseling and devices; those who do often worry that a doctor or family planning clinic might not keep their visits confidential. About 20 percent of adolescents using health services say that if their parents were notified, they would still have sex, but without contraception (Jones et al., 2005).

Sexual Orientation So far, we have focused only on heterosexual behavior. About 4 percent of U.S. 15- to 44-year-olds identify as lesbian, gay, or bisexual (Mosher, Chandra, & Jones, 2005). An unknown number experience same-sex attraction but have not come out to friends or family (see the Social Issues: Health box on page 216). Adolescence is an equally crucial time for the sexual development of these individuals, and societal attitudes, again, loom large in how well they fare.

Heredity makes an important contribution to homosexuality: Identical twins of both sexes are more likely than fraternal twins to share a homosexual orientation; so are biological (as opposed to adoptive) relatives (Kendler et al., 2000; Kirk et al., 2000). Furthermore, male homosexuality tends to be more common on the maternal than on the paternal side of families, suggesting that it may be X-linked (see Chapter 3). Indeed, one gene-mapping study found that among 40 pairs of homosexual brothers, 33 (82 percent) had an identical segment of DNA on the X chromosome. One or several genes in that region might predispose males to become homosexual (Hamer et al., 1993).

How might heredity lead to homosexuality? According to some researchers, certain genes affect the level or impact of prenatal sex hormones, which modify brain structures in ways that induce homosexual feelings and behavior (Bailey et al., 1995; LeVay, 1993). Keep in mind, however, that both genetic and environmental factors can alter prenatal hormones. Girls exposed prenatally to very high levels of androgens or estrogens—either because of a genetic defect or from drugs given to the mother to prevent miscarriage—are more likely to become lesbian or bisexual (Meyer-Bahlburg et al., 1995). Furthermore, gay men also tend to be later in birth order and to have a higher-than-average number of older brothers (Blanchard & Bogaert, 2004). One possibility is that mothers with several male children sometimes produce antibodies to androgens, reducing the prenatal impact of male sex hormones on the brains of later-born boys.

Stereotypes and misconceptions about homosexuality and bisexuality continue to be widespread. For example, contrary to common belief, most homosexual adolescents are not "gender-deviant" in dress or behavior. Also, attraction to members of the same sex is not limited to lesbian, gay, and bisexual teenagers. About 50 to 60 percent of adolescents who report having engaged in homosexual acts identify as heterosexual (Savin-Williams & Diamond, 2004). And a study of lesbian, bisexual, and "unlabeled" young women confirmed that bisexuality is not, as often assumed, a transient state (Diamond, 2008). Over a 10-year period, few bisexuals changed to a lesbian or heterosexual orientation, and most reported stable proportions of same-sex versus other-sex attractions over time.

The evidence to date indicates that genetic and prenatal biological influences are largely responsible for homosexuality; the origins of bisexuality are not yet known. In our evolutionary past, homosexuality may have served the adaptive function of reducing aggressive competition for other-sex mates, thereby promoting the survival of group members (Rahman & Wilson, 2003).

SOCIAL ISSUES: HEALTH

Lesbian, Gay, and Bisexual Youths: Coming Out to Oneself and Others

Cultures vary as much in their acceptance of homosexuality as in their approval of extramarital sex. In the United States, homosexuals are stigmatized, as shown by the degrading language often used to describe them. This makes forming a sexual identity a much greater challenge for lesbian, gay, and bisexual youths than for their heterosexual counterparts.

Wide variations in sexual identity formation exist, depending on personal, family, and community factors. Yet interviews with gay and lesbian adolescents and adults reveal that many (though not all) move through a three-phase sequence in coming out to themselves and others.

Feeling Different

Many gay men and lesbians say they felt different from other children when they were young. Typically, this first sense of their biologically determined sexual orientation appears between ages 6 and 12, in play interests more like those of the other gender (Rahman & Wilson, 2003). Boys may find that they are less interested in sports, more drawn to quieter activities, and more emotionally sensitive than other boys; girls that they are more athletic and active than other girls.

By age 10, many of these children start to engage in *sexual questioning*—wondering why the typical heterosexual orientation does not apply to them. Often, they experience their sense of being different as deeply distressing. Compared with children who are confident of their homosexuality, sexual-questioning children report greater anxiety about peer relationships and greater dissatisfaction with their biological gender over time (Carver, Egan, & Perry, 2004).

Confusion

With the arrival of puberty, feeling different clearly encompasses feeling sexually different. In research on ethnically diverse lesbian, gay, and bisexual youths, awareness of a same-sex physical attraction occurred, on average, between ages 11 and 12 for boys and 14 and 15 for girls, perhaps because adolescent social pressures toward heterosexuality are particularly intense for girls (D'Augelli, 2006; Diamond, 1998).

Realizing that homosexuality has personal relevance generally sparks additional confusion. A few adolescents resolve their discomfort by crystallizing a lesbian, gay, or bisexual identity quickly, with a flash of insight into their sense of

being different. But most experience an inner struggle and a deep sense of isolation— outcomes intensified by lack of role models and social support (D'Augelli, 2002; Safren & Pantalone, 2006).

Some throw themselves into activities they associate with heterosexuality. Boys may go out for athletic teams; girls may drop softball and basketball in favor of dance. And many homosexual youths (more females than males) try heterosexual dating, sometimes to hide their sexual orientation and at other times to develop intimacy skills that they later apply to same-sex relationships (D'Augelli, 2006; Dubé, Savin-Williams, & Diamond, 2001). Those who are extremely troubled and guilt-ridden may escape into alcohol, drugs, and suicidal thinking. Suicide attempts are unusually high among lesbian, gay, and bisexual young people (Morrow, 2006; Teasdale & Bradley-Engen, 2010).

Self-Acceptance

By the end of adolescence, the majority of gay, lesbian, and bisexual teenagers accept their sexual identity. But they face another crossroad: whether to tell others. Powerful stigma against their sexual orientation leads some to decide that disclosure is impossible: While self-defining as gay, they otherwise "pass" as heterosexual (Savin-Williams, 2001). When homosexual youths do come out, they often face intense hostility, including verbal abuse and physical attacks because of their sexual orientation. These experiences trigger emotional distress, depression, suicidal thoughts, school truancy, and drug use in victims (Almeida et al., 2009; Birkett, Espelage, & Koenig, 2009).

Nevertheless, many young people eventually acknowledge their sexual orientation publicly, usually by telling trusted friends first. Once teenagers establish a same-sex sexual or romantic relationship, many come out to parents. Few parents respond with severe rejection; most are either positive or slightly negative and disbelieving. Still, lesbian, gay, and bisexual young people report lower levels of family support than their heterosexual agemates (Needham & Austin, 2010;

Teenagers prepare to celebrate ALLY week, which encourages students to be allies against bullying and harassment of gay, lesbian, bisexual, and transgender schoolmates. When people react positively, coming out strengthens the young person's view of homosexuality as a fulfilling identity.

Savin-Williams & Ream, 2003). Yet parental understanding is the strongest predictor of favorable adjustment—including reduced *internalized homophobia,* or societal prejudice turned against the self (D'Augelli, Grossman, & Starks, 2005, 2008).

When people react positively, coming out strengthens the young person's view of homosexuality as a valid, meaningful, and fulfilling identity. Contact with other gays and lesbians is important for reaching this phase, and changes in society permit many adolescents in urban areas to attain it earlier than their counterparts did a decade or two ago. Gay and lesbian communities exist in large cities, along with specialized interest groups, social clubs, religious groups, newspapers, and periodicals. But teenagers in small towns and rural areas may have difficulty meeting other gay and lesbian youths and finding a supportive environment. These adolescents have a special need for caring adults and peers who can help them find self- and social acceptance.

Lesbian, gay, and bisexual teenagers who succeed in coming out to themselves and others integrate their sexual orientation into a broader sense of identity, a process we will address in Chapter 11. As a result, energy is freed for other aspects of psychological growth. In sum, coming out can foster many aspects of adolescent development, including self-esteem, psychological well-being, and relationships with family and friends.

Sexually Transmitted Disease

Sexually active adolescents, both homosexual and heterosexual, are at risk for sexually transmitted diseases (STDs). Adolescents have the highest incidence of STDs of all age groups. Despite a recent decline in STDs in the United States, one out of six sexually active teenagers contracts one of these illnesses each year—a rate three or more times as high as that of Canada and Western Europe (Health Canada, 2008; U.S. Department of Health and Human Services, 2009b). Teenagers at greatest risk are the same ones most likely to engage in irresponsible sexual behavior—poverty-stricken young people who feel a sense of hopelessness (Niccolai et al., 2004). Left untreated, STDs can lead to sterility and life-threatening complications.

By far the most serious STD is AIDS. In contrast to other Western nations, where the incidence of AIDS among people under age 30 is low, one-fifth of U.S. AIDS cases occur in young people between ages 20 and 29. Because AIDS symptoms typically do not emerge until 8 to 10 years after infection with the HIV virus, nearly all these cases originated in adolescence. Drug-abusing teenagers who share needles and male adolescents who have sex with HIV-positive same-sex partners account for most cases, but heterosexual spread of the disease remains high, especially among teenagers with more than one partner in the previous 18 months. It is at least twice as easy for a male to infect a female with any STD, including AIDS, as for a female to infect a male. Currently, females account for about 25 percent of new U.S. cases among adolescents and young adults (U.S. Department of Health and Human Services, 2010c).

As a result of school courses and media campaigns, about 60 percent of U.S. middle-school students and 90 percent of high school students are aware of basic facts about AIDS. But most have limited understanding of other STDs and their consequences, underestimate their own susceptibility, and are poorly informed about how to protect themselves (Ethier et al., 2003; U.S. Centers for Disease Control and Prevention, 2007).

Furthermore, high school students report engaging in oral sex much more often than intercourse, and with more partners. But few say they are consistently using STD protection during oral sex, which is a significant mode of transmission of several STDs, including chlamydia, gonorrhea, herpes, and perhaps AIDS (Prinstein, Meade, & Cohen, 2003; U.S. Centers for Disease Control and Prevention, 2010). Concerted efforts are needed to educate young people about the full range of STDs and risky sexual behaviors.

Adolescent Pregnancy and Parenthood

About 740,000 U.S. teenage girls (15,000 of them younger than age 15)—an estimated 20 percent of those who had sexual intercourse—became pregnant in the most recently reported year. Although the U.S. adolescent pregnancy rate declined steadily over the past two decades, it remains higher than that of most other industrialized countries. Three factors heighten the incidence of adolescent pregnancy: (1) Effective sex education reaches too few teenagers; (2) convenient, low-cost contraceptive services for adolescents are scarce; and (3) many families live in poverty, which encourages young people to take risks without considering the future implications of their behavior.

Because nearly one-third of U.S. adolescent pregnancies end in abortion, the number of American teenage births is considerably lower than it was 50 years ago (Alan Guttmacher Institute, 2011). Still, it is up to nine times higher than in most other developed nations (see Figure 5.16). But teenage parenthood is a much greater problem today because adolescents are far less likely to marry before childbirth. In 1960, only 15 percent of teenage births were to unmarried females, compared

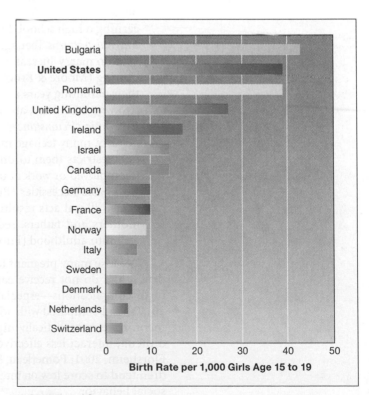

FIGURE 5.16 Birth rates among 15 to 19-year-olds in 15 industrialized nations. The U.S. adolescent birth rate greatly exceeds that of most other industrialized nations. (From U.S. Centers for Disease Control and Prevention, 2011.)

For a young couple who face limited educational and career prospects, becoming parents seems to offer a direct route to adulthood. But teenage parenthood is typically associated with poverty, low educational attainment, and marital instability.

with 87 percent today (Child Trends, 2011). Increased social acceptance of single motherhood, along with the belief of many teenage girls that a baby might fill a void in their lives, means that very few girls give up their infants for adoption.

Correlates and Consequences of Adolescent Parenthood

Becoming a parent is especially challenging for adolescents, who have not yet established a clear sense of direction for their own lives. Longitudinal research tracking girls from birth through adolescence reveals that life conditions and personal attributes jointly contribute to adolescent childbearing and also interfere with teenage mothers' capacity to parent effectively (Jaffee et al., 2001).

Teenage parents are far more likely to be poor than their agemates who postpone childbearing. Their backgrounds often include low parental warmth and involvement, domestic violence and child abuse, repeated parental divorce and remarriage, adult models of unmarried parenthood, and residence in neighborhoods where other adolescents display these risks. Girls at risk for early pregnancy do poorly in school, engage in alcohol and drug use, have a childhood history of aggressive and antisocial behavior, associate with deviant peers, and experience high rates of depression (Elfenbein & Felice, 2003; Hillis et al., 2004; Luster & Haddow, 2005). A high percentage of out-of-wedlock births are to low-income minority teenagers. Many turn to early parenthood as a way to move into adulthood when educational and career avenues are unavailable.

The lives of expectant teenagers, already troubled in many ways, tend to worsen in several respects after the baby is born:

- *Educational attainment.* Only about 70 percent of U.S. adolescent mothers graduate from high school, compared with 95 percent of girls who wait to become parents (National Women's Law Center, 2007). Lack of material resources—often due to living apart from one's own parents and not having access to child care—greatly reduces the likelihood of earning a high school diploma (Mollborn, 2007).
- *Marital patterns.* Teenage motherhood reduces the chances of marriage and, for those who do marry, increases the likelihood of divorce compared with peers who delay childbearing (Moore & Brooks-Gunn, 2002). Consequently, teenage mothers spend more of their parenting years as single parents. About 35 percent become pregnant again within two years. Of these, about half go on to deliver a second child (Child Trends, 2011).
- *Economic circumstances.* Because of low educational attainment, marital instability, and poverty, many teenage mothers are on welfare. If they are employed, their limited education restricts them to unsatisfying, low-paid jobs. Many adolescent fathers, as well, are unemployed or work at unskilled jobs, usually earning too little to provide their children with basic necessities (Bunting & McAuley, 2004). An estimated 50 percent have committed illegal acts resulting in imprisonment (Elfenbein & Felice, 2003). And for both mothers and fathers, reduced educational and occupational attainment often persists well into adulthood (Furstenberg, 2007; Taylor, 2009).

Because many pregnant teenage girls have inadequate diets, smoke, use alcohol and other drugs, and do not receive early prenatal care, their babies often experience pregnancy and birth complications—especially preterm and low birth weight (Khashan, Baker, & Kenny, 2010). And compared with adult mothers, adolescent mothers know less about child development, have unrealistically high expectations of their infants, perceive their babies as more difficult, interact less effectively with them, and more often engage in child abuse (Moore & Florsheim, 2001; Pomerleau, Scuccimarri, & Malcuit, 2003; Sieger & Renk, 2007). Their children tend to score low on intelligence tests, achieve poorly in school, and engage in disruptive social behavior.

Furthermore, adolescent parenthood frequently is repeated in the next generation (Brooks-Gunn, Schley, & Hardy, 2002). In longitudinal studies that followed mothers—some who gave birth as teenagers, others who postponed parenting—and their children for several decades, mothers' age at first childbirth strongly predicted the age at which their offspring, both daughters and sons, became parents (Barber, 2001; Campa & Eckenrode, 2006; Hardy et al., 1998; Meade, Kershaw, & Ickovics, 2008). The researchers found that adolescent parenthood was linked to a set of related, unfavorable family conditions and personal characteristics that negatively influenced development over an extended time and, therefore, often transferred to the next generation.

One important factor was quality of the home environment: Compared with children in other families, children of unmarried adolescent mothers had families that were less warm, supportive, and stimulating, even after mothers' prebirth education and income were controlled. Younger mothers' cognitive deficits and reduced educational attainment played a part, increasing the likelihood that their children would experience long-term poor-quality home environments. Another factor was father absence: Consistent with findings reported earlier for sexual activity and pregnancy (see page 214), several studies found far greater intergenerational continuity in adolescent parenthood, especially for daughters, when teenage mothers remained unmarried (Barber, 2001; Campa & Eckenrode, 2006; Meade, Kershaw, & Ickovics, 2008).

Even when children born to teenage mothers do not become early childbearers, their development is often compromised in terms of likelihood of high school graduation, financial independence in adulthood, and long-term physical and mental health (Moore, Morrison, & Greene, 1997; Pogarsky, Thornberry, & Lizotte, 2006). Still, outcomes vary widely. If a teenage mother finishes high school, secures gainful employment, avoids additional births, and finds a stable partner, long-term disruptions in her own and her child's development will be less severe.

Prevention Strategies Preventing teenage pregnancy means addressing the many factors underlying early sexual activity and lack of contraceptive use. Too often, sex education courses are given late (after sexual activity has begun), last only a few sessions, and are limited to a catalog of facts about anatomy and reproduction. Sex education that goes beyond this minimum does not encourage early sex, as some opponents claim (Kirby, 2002c). It does improve awareness of sexual facts—knowledge that is necessary for responsible sexual behavior.

Knowledge, however, is not enough. Sex education must help teenagers build a bridge between what they know and what they do. Today, the most effective sex education programs combine these key elements:

- They teach techniques for handling sexual situations—including refusal skills for avoiding risky sexual behaviors and communication skills for improving contraceptive use—through role-playing and other activities in which young people practice those behaviors.
- They deliver clear, accurate messages that are appropriate for participating adolescents' culture and sexual experiences.
- They last long enough to have an impact.
- They provide specific information about contraceptives and ready access to them.

Many studies show that sex education that includes these components can delay the initiation of sexual activity, increase contraceptive use, change attitudes (for example, strengthen future orientation), and reduce pregnancy rates (Kirby, 2002b, 2008; Thomas & Dimitrov, 2007).

Proposals to increase access to contraceptives are the most controversial aspect of U.S. adolescent pregnancy prevention efforts. Many adults argue that placing birth control pills or condoms in the hands of teenagers is equivalent to approving of early sex. Yet sex education programs focusing on abstinence have little or no impact on delaying teenage sexual activity or preventing pregnancy (Rosenbaum, 2009; Underhill, Montgomery, & Operario, 2007).

In Canada and Western Europe, where community- and school-based clinics offer adolescents contraceptives and where universal health insurance helps pay for them, teenage sexual activity is no higher than in the United States—but pregnancy, childbirth, and abortion rates are much lower (Schalet, 2007). Radio and TV campaigns promoting contraceptive use—used widely in Africa, Europe, India, and South America—are associated with a reduction in early sexual activity and with an increase in teenagers' use of birth control (Keller & Brown, 2002).

LOOK and LISTEN

Contact a nearby public school district and ask for information about its sex education curriculum. Considering research findings, do you think it is likely to be effective in delaying initiation of sexual activity and reducing adolescent pregnancy rates?

A young teenager involved in a Teen Outreach service project prepares a meal for cancer patients. Volunteer work and related class discussions aimed at skill-building promote self-respect and community connection while reducing adolescent pregnancy and school failure.

Efforts to prevent adolescent pregnancy and parenthood must go beyond improving sex education and access to contraception to build academic and social competence (Allen, Seitz, & Apfel, 2007). In one study, researchers randomly assigned at-risk high school students to either a year-long community service class, called Teen Outreach, or regular classroom experiences in health or social studies. In Teen Outreach, adolescents spent at least 20 hours per week in volunteer work tailored to their interests. They returned to school for discussions that focused on enhancing their community service skills and ability to cope with everyday challenges. At the end of the school year, pregnancy, school failure, and school suspension were substantially lower in the group enrolled in Teen Outreach, which fostered social skills, connection to the community, and self-respect (Allen et al., 1997).

Finally, school involvement is linked to delayed initiation of sexual activity and to reduced teenage pregnancy, perhaps because it increases interaction with and attachment to adults who discourage risk taking, and it strengthens belief in a promising future (Harris, 2008). We will take up factors that promote adolescents' commitment to school in Chapter 15.

Intervening with Adolescent Parents The most difficult and costly way to deal with adolescent parenthood is to wait until it happens. Young mothers need health care, encouragement to stay in school, job training, instruction in parenting and life-management skills, and high-quality, affordable child care. School programs that provide these services reduce the incidence of low-birth-weight babies, increase mothers' educational success, and prevent additional childbearing (Key et al., 2008; Seitz & Apfel, 2005).

Adolescent mothers also benefit from relationships with family members and other adults who are sensitive to their developmental needs. In one study, African-American teenage mothers who had a long-term "mentor" relationship—an aunt, neighbor, or teacher who provided emotional support and guidance—were far more likely than those without a mentor to stay in school and graduate (Klaw, Rhodes, & Fitzgerald, 2003).

Home visiting programs are also helpful. The Nurse–Family Partnership, currently implemented in hundreds of counties across 29 U.S. states, aims to reduce pregnancy and birth complications, promote competent parenting, and improve family conditions for first time, low-income expectant mothers, many of them teenagers. A registered nurse visits the home regularly during pregnancy and the baby's first two years to provide intensive social support—a sympathetic ear; assistance in accessing community services and the help of family members; and encouragement to finish high school, find work, and engage in future family planning.

To evaluate the intervention, researchers randomly assigned over 1,000 mothers to nurse-visiting or comparison conditions (just prenatal care, or prenatal care plus infant referral for developmental problems) and followed the families through the child's first three years of elementary school (Olds et al., 2004, 2007). From their baby's birth on, home visited mothers were on a more favorable life course: They had fewer subsequent births, longer intervals between births, more frequent contact with the child's father, more stable intimate partnerships, less welfare dependence, and a greater sense of control over their lives. At school age, intervention children exceeded comparison children in language development, intelligence test scores, and academic achievement, and they also displayed fewer behavior problems.

Programs focusing on fathers attempt to increase their financial and emotional commitment to the baby. Although nearly half of young fathers visit their children during the first few years, contact usually diminishes. By the time the child starts school, fewer than one-fourth have regular paternal contact. As with teenage mothers, support from family members helps fathers stay involved (Bunting & McAuley, 2004). Teenage mothers who receive financial and child-care assistance and emotional support from the child's father are less distressed and more likely to sustain a relationship with him (Cutrona et al., 1998; Gee & Rhodes, 2003). And infants with lasting ties to their teenage fathers receive warmer, more stimulating caregiving and show better long-term adjustment (Florsheim & Smith, 2005; Furstenberg & Harris, 1993).

COURTESY OF THE WYMAN CENTER

A Concluding Note

The rapid, complex physical and psychological changes of puberty make teenagers vulnerable to certain problems. Yet adolescents' unhealthy behaviors are not an irrational response to inner turmoil, as theorists once believed. Rather, every level of the ecological system affects teenagers' well-being.

Furthermore, we have seen that teenagers with one problem frequently display others—a co-occurrence that you will encounter again when we look at delinquency, depression, suicide, substance abuse, and school underachievement and failure. To design more powerful interventions, researchers must deal with simultaneous risks and the multiple factors that contribute to them. **TAKE A MOMENT...** Think back to the successful intervention efforts discussed in the preceding sections. Notice how they employ several strategies, target multiple behaviors, and involve several contexts.

Finally, adolescence is not only a time of risk but also a time of tremendous opportunity. Teenagers gain a better understanding of how the world works, greater control over their own social contexts, broader access to social support, and increased ability to avoid or alter risky behaviors. Families, schools, communities, and nations must create conditions that enable adolescents to exercise their expanding capacity for positive health practices. This is a theme we will revisit in later chapters.

ASK YOURSELF

Review ■ Compare risk factors for anorexia nervosa and bulimia nervosa. How do treatments and outcomes differ for the two disorders?

Connect ■ Explain how unfavorable life experiences and personal attributes associated with teenage parenthood increase the chances that it will be repeated in the next generation.

Apply ■ At age 17, Veronica dropped out of school, moved in with her boyfriend Todd, and gave birth to Ben. A few months later, Todd left Veronica, saying he couldn't stand being tied down with the baby. Suggest interventions likely to protect Veronica and Ben from lasting hardships.

Reflect ■ Describe sex education classes that you experienced in school. Did they help you postpone early sex and engage in more responsible sexual behavior? Explain.

SUMMARY

The Course of Physical Growth (p. 176)

Describe the course of physical growth, including changes in body size, proportions, muscle–fat makeup, and skeleton, and their relationship to gains in gross-motor skills.

■ **Distance** and **velocity curves** show the overall pattern of change in body size: Gains in height and weight are rapid during infancy, slower during early and middle childhood, and rapid again during puberty.

■ In childhood, physical growth follows **cephalocaudal** and **proximodistal trends**. During puberty, growth proceeds in the reverse direction, and sex differences in body proportions appear. Body fat increases quickly during the first nine months, then rapidly again at adolescence for girls. Muscle accumulates slowly until puberty, when it rises dramatically, especially for boys.

■ The best measure of a child's physical maturity is **skeletal age,** which is based on the number of **epiphyses** and the extent to which they are fused. Girls are ahead of boys, a gap that widens over infancy and childhood.

■ In early childhood, body growth causes the child's center of gravity to shift toward the trunk, which paves the way for new gross-motor skills. During the school years, improved balance, strength, agility, and flexibility support refinements in running, jumping, hopping, and ball skills. Increased body size and muscle strength lead to continued motor gains in adolescence. As they develop, children integrate previously acquired motor skills into more complex, dynamic systems of action.

■ In childhood, boys' advantage over girls in many gross-motor skills largely reflects parental expectations and practice. By adolescence, sex differences in size and strength play a greater role.

Describe hormonal influences on physical growth.

■ Physical growth is controlled by two vital hormones released by the **pituitary gland,** located at the base of the brain near the **hypothalamus,** which initiates and regulates pituitary secretions: **growth hormone (GH),** which affects the development of almost all body tissues; and **thyroid-stimulating hormone (TSH),** which—by prompting the thyroid gland to release thyroxine—affects brain development and body size. Sexual maturation is controlled by the sex hormones— **estrogens** and **androgens**.

Discuss factors that contribute to worldwide variations and secular trends in physical growth.

■ Worldwide variations in body size are the combined result of heredity and environment, including evolutionary adaptations to climate, availability of food, and prevalence of disease.

- **Secular trends in physical growth** have occurred in industrialized nations, where, because of improved health and nutrition, most children are taller and heavier than their ancestors and reach puberty earlier.

Brain Development (p. 184)

Cite major milestones in brain development, at the level of individual brain cells and at the level of the cerebral cortex.

- The human brain reaches its adult size earlier than any other organ. Once **neurons** are in place, they rapidly form **synapses** and release **neurotransmitters,** which cross synapses to send messages to other neurons. As the brain grows, **programmed cell death** occurs, making room for growth of neural fibers that form synaptic connections.

- Stimulation determines which neurons will continue to establish new synapses and which will undergo **synaptic pruning. Glial cells,** responsible for **myelination,** multiply rapidly through the second year and continue to do so more slowly through adolescence, contributing to large gains in brain weight.

- Regions of the **cerebral cortex** develop in the order in which various capacities emerge in the infant and child. The frontal lobes, which contain the **prefrontal cortex,** have the most extended period of development, reaching an adult level of synapses in adolescence. Although some **lateralization,** or specialization of the cerebral hemispheres, exists at birth, **brain plasticity** remains high for the first few years. Both heredity and early experience contribute to brain organization.

- Hand preference, which reflects an individual's **dominant cerebral hemisphere,** first appears in infancy and gradually extends to a wider range of skills. Research on handedness supports the joint contribution of nature and nurture to brain lateralization.

Describe changes in other brain structures and in the adolescent brain, and discuss evidence on sensitive periods in brain development.

- In childhood and adolescence, connections strengthen among parts of the brain. Fibers linking the **cerebellum** to the cerebral cortex grow and myelinate, enhancing motor coordination and cognition. The **reticular formation,** responsible for alertness and consciousness; the **hippocampus,** which plays a vital role in memory and spatial orientation; and the **amygdala,** which is centrally involved in processing emotional information, also develop and link with the cerebral cortex. The **corpus callosum,** which connects the two cerebral hemispheres, supports coordinated movement and cognitive activities.

- Pruning of unused synapses in the cerebral cortex continues during adolescence, and growth and myelination of stimulated neural fibers accelerate, supporting diverse cognitive skills. Because advances in cognitive control are gradual, teenagers tend to perform less well than adults on tasks requiring inhibition, planning, and future orientation.

- Neurons become more responsive to excitatory neurotransmitters during adolescence, contributing to teenagers' drive for novel experiences. Heightened sensitivity to oxytocin increases responsiveness to emotional and social stimuli, including peer influence. These changes in the brain's emotional/social network outpace those in the cognitive-control network, resulting in self-regulation difficulties.

- Animal and human studies reveal the existence of sensitive periods in which appropriate stimulation is necessary for optimal brain development. **Experience-expectant brain growth** depends on ordinary experiences—early opportunities to interact with people, hear language, and explore the environment. No evidence exists for a sensitive period in the first five or six years of life for **experience-dependent brain growth,** which relies on specific learning experiences. Environments that overwhelm children with inappropriately advanced expectations can harm the brain's potential.

© ELLEN B. SENISI PHOTOGRAPHY

Factors Affecting Physical Growth (p. 192)

How do heredity, nutrition, infectious disease, and parental affection contribute to physical growth and health?

- With adequate diet and health, height and rate of physical growth depend largely on heredity. Although genetic makeup also affects weight, nutrition and eating habits are powerful influences.

- Breast milk is ideally suited to infants' nutritional needs and is crucial for protecting their health in the developing world. As growth slows around age 2, appetites become unpredictable, and many children become picky eaters. Repeated, unpressured exposure to a new food increases acceptance. During puberty, food intake rises dramatically, but adolescents' eating habits are the poorest. Family mealtimes increase healthy eating.

- Many children in developing countries suffer from **marasmus** and **kwashiorkor,** two diseases caused by malnutrition that can permanently impair body growth and brain development. Food insecurity affects children even in industrialized countries.

- **Obesity** is a growing problem in both industrialized and developing nations. Although heredity contributes to obesity, parental feeding practices, maladaptive eating habits, reduced sleep, lack of exercise, and Western high-fat diets are more powerful influences. Obese children are often socially isolated and display more emotional, social, and school difficulties and behavior problems than their normal-weight peers. Effective treatments for obesity are family-based; schools can also help by serving healthier meals and ensuring physical activity.

- Malnutrition interacts with infectious disease to undermine physical growth. In developing countries, where diarrhea leads to millions of childhood deaths, oral rehydration therapy (ORT) and zinc supplements can save lives. Widespread immunization has led to a dramatic decline in childhood diseases, but rates are lower in the United States than in other industrialized nations because many economically disadvantaged children lack access to necessary health care. Parental stress and misconceptions about vaccine safety also contribute.

- **Growth faltering** illustrates the importance of parental affection for healthy infant physical growth. Extreme and prolonged emotional deprivation in childhood can lead to **psychosocial dwarfism.**

Puberty: The Physical Transition to Adulthood (p. 203)

Describe sexual maturation in girls and boys, noting genetic and environmental influences on pubertal timing.

- At **puberty,** changes in **primary** and **secondary sexual characteristics** accompany rapid body growth. **Menarche** occurs relatively late in the girl's sequence of pubertal events, after the growth spurt, breast growth, and appearance of pubic and underarm hair. In boys, the growth spurt occurs later, preceded by enlargement of the sex organs and **spermarche.** This is followed by growth of facial and body hair and deepening of the voice.

- Heredity, nutrition, overall health, and early family experiences all contribute to the timing of puberty. Menarche is delayed in regions of the world with widespread malnutrition and infectious disease. In industrialized nations, ethnic variations—for example, earlier menarche in African-American than in Caucasian-American girls—reflect both heredity and environment.

The Psychological Impact of Pubertal Events (p. 205)

What factors influence adolescents' reactions to the physical changes of puberty?

■ Puberty is not a biologically determined period of storm and stress. Adjustment varies widely and is a product of biological, psychological, and social forces.

■ Girls generally react to menarche with mixed emotions, although those who receive advance information and support from family members respond more positively. Boys, who receive less social support than girls for the physical changes of puberty, react to spermarche with mixed feelings.

■ Besides higher pubertal hormone levels, negative life events, sleep loss, and adult-structured situations are associated with adolescents' negative moods. Psychological distancing between parent and child at puberty may be a modern substitute for physical departure from the family, which typically occurs at puberty in primate species. Parent–adolescent conflict also reflects teenagers' new powers of reasoning and efforts by their parents to protect teenagers from risky situations.

Describe the impact of pubertal timing on adolescent adjustment, noting sex differences.

■ Early-maturing boys and late-maturing girls have a more positive **body image** and usually adjust well in adolescence. In contrast, early-maturing girls and late-maturing boys experience emotional and social difficulties, which—for girls—persist into young adulthood.

Puberty and Adolescent Health (p. 210)

What factors contribute to eating disorders in adolescence?

■ Girls who reach puberty early, who are dissatisfied with their body image, and who grow up in families where thinness is emphasized are at risk for eating disorders. Heredity seems to make some adolescents more susceptible.

■ **Anorexia nervosa** typically affects girls who are perfectionists and have overprotective, controlling mothers and emotionally distant fathers. **Bulimia nervosa** is often associated with lack of self-control and disengaged parenting.

Discuss cultural, social, and personal influences on adolescent sexual attitudes and behavior.

■ North American attitudes toward adolescent sex are relatively restrictive, and parents and the mass media deliver contradictory messages. Over the past 40 years, sexual attitudes and behavior of adolescents have become more liberal.

■ Early, frequent sexual activity is linked to factors associated with economic disadvantage, including weak parental monitoring and hazardous neighborhoods. Many sexually active teenagers do not practice contraception consistently. Adolescent cognitive processes and weak social supports for responsible sexual behavior, including access to birth control, underlie this failure to take precautions against pregnancy.

Cite factors involved in the development of homosexuality.

■ Biological factors, including heredity and prenatal hormone levels, play an important role in homosexuality. Lesbian, gay, and bisexual teenagers face special challenges in establishing a positive sexual identity.

Discuss factors related to sexually transmitted disease and teenage pregnancy and parenthood, noting prevention and intervention strategies.

■ Early sexual activity, combined with inconsistent contraceptive use, results in high rates of sexually transmitted diseases (STDs) among U.S. teenagers.

■ Life conditions linked to poverty, along with personal attributes, contribute to adolescent childbearing. Teenage parenthood is associated with school dropout, reduced chances of marriage, greater likelihood of divorce, and long-term economic disadvantage.

■ Effective sex education, access to contraceptives, and programs that build academic and social competence help prevent early pregnancy. Young mothers need school programs that provide job training, instruction in parenting and life-management skills, and child care. They also benefit from positive family relationships and from home visiting programs that provide intensive social support. When teenage fathers stay involved, children develop more favorably.

IMPORTANT TERMS AND CONCEPTS

amygdala (p. 190)
androgens (p. 183)
anorexia nervosa (p. 210)
body image (p. 209)
brain plasticity (p. 187)
bulimia nervosa (p. 211)
cephalocaudal trend (p. 176)
cerebellum (p. 189)
cerebral cortex (p. 186)
corpus callosum (p. 190)
distance curve (p. 176)
dominant cerebral hemisphere (p. 189)
epiphyses (p. 178)
estrogens (p. 183)
experience-dependent brain growth (p. 191)

experience-expectant brain growth (p. 191)
glial cells (p. 186)
growth faltering (p. 202)
growth hormone (GH) (p. 182)
hippocampus (p. 190)
hypothalamus (p. 181)
kwashiorkor (p. 196)
lateralization (p. 187)
marasmus (p. 196)
menarche (p. 203)
myelination (p. 186)
neurons (p. 185)
neurotransmitters (p. 185)
obesity (p. 198)
pituitary gland (p. 181)

prefrontal cortex (p. 186)
primary sexual characteristics (p. 203)
programmed cell death (p. 185)
proximodistal trend (p. 176)
psychosocial dwarfism (p. 202)
puberty (p. 203)
reticular formation (p. 190)
secondary sexual characteristics (p. 203)
secular trends in physical growth (p. 184)
skeletal age (p. 178)
spermarche (p. 203)
synapses (p. 185)
synaptic pruning (p. 185)
thyroid-stimulating hormone (TSH) (p. 183)
velocity curve (p. 176)

CHAPTER 6

"My Cousins"

Woranun Pongpechprai, 13 years, Thailand

These cousins enjoy molding clay into vibrant fruitlike forms. As Chapter 6 will reveal, children make sense of their multifaceted surroundings through their own explorations and the assistance of more expert partners.

Reprinted with permission from the International Museum of Children's Art, Oslo, Norway

Cognitive Development: Piagetian, Core Knowledge, and Vygotskian Perspectives

Piaget's Cognitive-Developmental Theory
Basic Characteristics of Piaget's Stages • Piaget's Ideas About Cognitive Change

The Sensorimotor Stage: Birth to 2 Years
Sensorimotor Development • Follow-Up Research on Infant Cognitive Development • Evaluation of the Sensorimotor Stage

■ **SOCIAL ISSUES: EDUCATION:** *Baby Learning from TV and Video: The Video Deficit Effect*

The Preoperational Stage: 2 to 7 Years
Advances in Mental Representation • Limitations of Preoperational Thought • Follow-Up Research on Preoperational Thought • Evaluation of the Preoperational Stage

The Concrete Operational Stage: 7 to 11 Years
Concrete Operational Thought • Limitations of Concrete Operational Thought • Follow-Up Research on Concrete Operational Thought

The Formal Operational Stage: 11 Years and Older
Hypothetico-Deductive Reasoning • Propositional Thought • Consequences of Adolescent Cognitive Changes • Follow-Up Research on Formal Operational Thought

Piaget and Education

Overall Evaluation of Piaget's Theory
Is Piaget's Account of Cognitive Change Clear and Accurate? • Does Cognitive Development Take Place in Stages? • Piaget's Legacy

The Core Knowledge Perspective
Infancy: Physical and Numerical Knowledge • Children as Naïve Theorists • Evaluation of the Core Knowledge Perspective

Vygotsky's Sociocultural Theory
Children's Private Speech • Social Origins of Cognitive Development • Vygotsky's View of Make-Believe Play

■ **CULTURAL INFLUENCES:** *Social Origins of Make-Believe Play*

Vygotsky and Education
Reciprocal Teaching • Cooperative Learning

Evaluation of Vygotsky's Theory

■ **CULTURAL INFLUENCES:** *Children in Village and Tribal Cultures Observe and Participate in Adult Work*

L eslie, a preschool teacher, paused to look around her class of busy 3- and 4-year-olds. "Their minds are such a curious blend of logic, fantasy, and faulty reasoning," she remarked to a visiting parent. "Every day, I'm startled by the maturity and originality of what they say and do. Yet at other times, their thinking seems limited and inflexible."

Leslie's comments sum up the puzzling contradictions of young children's thought. Hearing a loud thunderclap outside, 3-year-old Sammy exclaimed, "A magic man turned on the thunder!" Even after Leslie explained that thunder is caused by lightning, not by a person turning it on or off, Sammy persisted: "Then a magic lady did it."

In other respects, Sammy's thinking was surprisingly advanced. He could name, categorize, and identify similarities and differences among dozens of dinosaurs in his favorite picture books. "Anatosaurus and Tyrannosaurus walk on their back legs," he told the class during group time. "Then they can use their front legs to pick up food!" But at the snack table, while watching Priti pour her milk from a short, wide carton into a tall, thin glass, Sammy looked at his own identical carton and asked, "How come you got lots of milk, and I only got this little bit?" He did not realize that he had just as much—that his carton, though shorter than Priti's glass, was also wider.

Cognition refers to the inner processes and products of the mind that lead to "knowing." It includes all mental activity—attending, remembering, symbolizing, categorizing, planning, reasoning, problem solving, creating, and fantasizing. Indeed, mental processes make their way into virtually everything human beings do. To adapt to changing environmental conditions, other species benefit from camouflage, feathers or fur coats, and remarkable speed. Humans, in contrast, rely on thinking, not only adapting to their environments but also transforming them. Our extraordinary mental capacities are crucial for our survival.

This chapter and the two that follow examine cognitive development: how the intellectual capacities of infants change into the capacities of the child, adolescent, and adult. Researchers studying cognitive development address three main issues:

- They chart its *typical course,* identifying transformations that most children undergo from birth to maturity. They ask: Do all aspects of cognition develop uniformly, or do some develop at faster rates than others?
- They examine *individual differences.* At every age, some children think more or less maturely, and differently, than others. Chapters 6 and 7 focus primarily on the general course of cognitive development, Chapter 8 on individual differences. But we will encounter both concerns in all three chapters.
- They uncover the *mechanisms* of cognitive development—how genetic and environmental factors combine to yield patterns of change.

In this chapter, we address three distinct perspectives on how cognitive development occurs. Two, *Piaget's cognitive-developmental theory* and the *core knowledge perspective,* have a biological emphasis. The third, *Vygotsky's sociocultural theory,* stresses social and cultural contributions to children's thinking.

In considering each of these views, we will see that children move from simpler to more complex cognitive skills, becoming more effective thinkers with age. But children's immature capacities are not merely incomplete, less effective versions of adults'. For children, focusing on a limited amount of information may be adaptive (Bjorklund, 2012). For example, noticing only a few features of an intricate pattern probably protects against overstimulation in young babies. And comparing the amounts of milk in a short, wide carton and a tall, thin glass by attending only to height, not width, may allow preschoolers to develop a thorough grasp of height, in preparation for effectively integrating height with other dimensions.

The adaptiveness of cognitive immaturity has important implications for education. It suggests that hurrying children to higher levels may undermine their progress. Piaget was among the first theorists to stress the importance of *readiness* to learn—presenting appropriately challenging tasks while avoiding overly complex stimulation that may confuse and overwhelm children. Let's begin with Piaget's theory. ■

▶ According to Piaget, how does cognition develop?

Piaget's Cognitive-Developmental Theory

Swiss cognitive theorist Jean Piaget received his education in zoology, and his theory has a distinct biological flavor. According to Piaget, human infants do not start out as cognitive beings. Instead, out of their perceptual and motor activities, they build and refine psychological structures—organized ways of making sense of experience that permit them to adapt more effectively to the environment. Children develop these structures actively, using current structures to select and interpret experiences, and modifying those structures to take into account more subtle aspects of reality. Because Piaget viewed children as discovering, or *constructing*, virtually all knowledge about their world through their own activity, his theory is described as a **constructivist approach** to cognitive development.

Basic Characteristics of Piaget's Stages

Piaget believed that children move through four stages—sensorimotor, preoperational, concrete operational, and formal operational—during which infants' exploratory behaviors transform into the abstract, logical intelligence of adolescence and adulthood. Piaget's stage sequence has three important characteristics:

- The stages provide a *general theory* of development, in which all aspects of cognition change in an integrated fashion, following a similar course.
- The stages are *invariant;* they always occur in a fixed order, and no stage can be skipped.
- The stages are *universal;* they are assumed to characterize children everywhere. (Piaget, Inhelder, & Szeminska, 1948/1960)

Piaget regarded the order of development as rooted in the biology of the human brain. But he emphasized that individual differences in genetic and environmental factors affect the speed with which children move through the stages (Piaget, 1926/1928). Let's consider some of Piaget's central concepts.

Piaget's Ideas About Cognitive Change

According to Piaget, specific psychological structures called **schemes**—organized ways of making sense of experience—change with age. At first, schemes are sensorimotor action patterns. Watch a 6-month-old baby catch sight of, grasp, and release objects. Her "dropping scheme" is fairly rigid—she simply lets go of a rattle or teething ring. By 18 months, her dropping scheme has become deliberate and creative. Given an opportunity, she might toss all sorts of objects down the basement stairs, throwing some up in the air, bouncing others off walls, releasing some gently and others forcefully.

Soon, instead of just acting on objects, the toddler shows evidence of thinking before she acts. For Piaget, this change marks the transition from a sensorimotor approach to the world to a cognitive approach based on **mental representations**—internal depictions of information that the mind can manipulate. Our most powerful mental representations are *images*—mental pictures of objects, people, and spaces—and *concepts,* categories in which similar objects or events are grouped together. We use a mental image to retrace our steps when we've misplaced something or to imitate another's behavior long after observing it. By thinking in concepts and labeling them (for example, *ball* for all rounded, movable objects used in play), we become more efficient thinkers, organizing our diverse experiences into meaningful, manageable, and memorable units.

In Piaget's theory, two processes account for this change from sensorimotor to representational schemes and for further changes in representational schemes from childhood to adulthood: *adaptation* and *organization*.

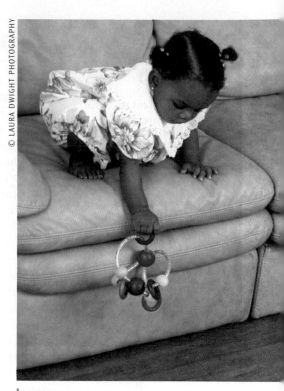

In Piaget's theory, the baby's first schemes are sensorimotor action patterns. As this 11-month-old experiments with her dropping scheme, her behavior becomes more deliberate and varied.

Adaptation

TAKE A MOMENT… The next time you have a chance, notice how young children tirelessly repeat actions that lead to interesting effects. They are illustrating a key Piagetian concept. **Adaptation** involves building schemes through direct interaction with the environment. It consists of two complementary activities: *assimilation* and *accommodation*. During **assimilation,** we use our current schemes to interpret the external world. The infant who repeatedly drops objects is assimilating them into his sensorimotor "dropping scheme." And the preschooler who, seeing a camel at the zoo, calls out, "Horse!" has sifted through her conceptual schemes until she finds one that resembles the strange-looking creature. In **accommodation,** we create new schemes or adjust old ones after noticing that our current way of thinking does not capture the environment completely. The baby who drops objects in different ways is modifying his dropping scheme to take account of the varied properties of objects. And the preschooler who calls a camel a "lumpy horse" has noticed that camels differ from horses in certain ways and has revised her scheme accordingly.

According to Piaget, the balance between assimilation and accommodation varies over time. When children are not changing much, they assimilate more than they accommodate—a steady, comfortable state that Piaget called cognitive *equilibrium.* During times of rapid cognitive change, children are in a state of *disequilibrium,* or cognitive discomfort. Realizing that new information does not match their current schemes, they shift from assimilation to accommodation. After modifying their schemes, they move back toward assimilation, exercising their newly changed structures until they are ready to be modified again.

Piaget's term for this back-and-forth movement between equilibrium and disequilibrium is **equilibration.** Each time equilibration occurs, more effective schemes are produced. Because the times of greatest accommodation are the earliest ones, the sensorimotor stage is Piaget's most complex period of development.

Organization

Schemes also change through **organization,** a process that occurs internally, apart from direct contact with the environment. Once children form new schemes, they rearrange them, linking them with other schemes to create a strongly interconnected cognitive system. For example, eventually the baby relates "dropping" to "throwing" and to his developing understanding of "nearness" and "farness." According to Piaget, schemes truly reach equilibrium when they become part of a broad network of structures that can be jointly applied to the surrounding world (Piaget, 1936/1952).

In the following sections, we begin by considering development as Piaget saw it, noting research that supports his observations. Then, for each stage, we look at more recent evidence, some inspired by Piaget's theory and some that challenges his ideas.

▶ Describe major cognitive
attainments of Piaget's
sensorimotor stage.

▶ What does follow-up research
reveal about infant cognitive
development and the
accuracy of Piaget's
sensorimotor stage?

The Sensorimotor Stage: Birth to 2 Years

The **sensorimotor stage** spans the first two years of life. Its name reflects Piaget's belief that infants and toddlers "think" with their eyes, ears, hands, and other sensorimotor equipment. They cannot yet carry out many activities mentally. Yet the advances of the sensorimotor stage are so vast that Piaget divided it into six substages, summarized in Table 6.1. Piaget based this sequence on a very small sample: his own three children. He observed his son and two daughters carefully and presented them with everyday problems (such as hidden objects) that helped reveal their understanding of the world.

According to Piaget, at birth infants know so little that they cannot explore purposefully. The **circular reaction** provides a special means of adapting their first schemes. It involves stumbling onto a new experience caused by the baby's own motor activity. The reaction is "circular" because, as the infant tries to repeat the event again and again, a sensorimotor response that originally occurred by chance strengthens into a new scheme. Imagine a 2-month-old who accidentally makes a smacking noise after a feeding. Finding the sound intriguing, the baby tries to repeat it until she becomes quite expert at smacking her lips.

The circular reaction initially centers on the infant's own body but later turns outward, toward manipulation of objects. In the second year, it becomes experimental and creative, aimed at producing novel effects in the environment. Infants' difficulty inhibiting new and interesting behaviors may underlie the circular reaction. This immaturity in inhibition seems to be adaptive, helping to ensure that new skills will not be interrupted before they strengthen (Carey & Markman, 1999). Piaget considered revisions in the circular reaction so important that, as Table 6.1 shows, he named the sensorimotor substages after them.

Sensorimotor Development

Piaget saw newborn reflexes as the building blocks of sensorimotor intelligence. In Substage 1, babies suck, grasp, and look in much the same way, no matter what experiences they encounter. In one amusing example, a mother described how her 2-week-old daughter lay on the bed next to her sleeping father, who suddenly awoke with a start. The baby had latched on and begun to suck on his back!

Repeating Chance Behaviors Around 1 month, as babies enter Substage 2, they start to gain voluntary control over their actions through the *primary circular reaction*, by repeating chance behaviors largely motivated by basic needs. This leads to some simple motor habits, such as sucking the fist or thumb. Babies in this substage also begin to vary their

TABLE 6.1 | **Summary of Piaget's Sensorimotor Stage**

SENSORIMOTOR SUBSTAGE	TYPICAL ADAPTIVE BEHAVIORS
1. Reflexive schemes (birth–1 month)	Newborn reflexes (see Chapter 4, page 130)
2. Primary circular reactions (1–4 months)	Simple motor habits centered around the infant's own body; limited anticipation of events
3. Secondary circular reactions (4–8 months)	Actions aimed at repeating interesting effects in the surrounding world; imitation of familiar behaviors
4. Coordination of secondary circular reactions (8–12 months)	Intentional, or goal-directed, behavior; ability to find a hidden object in the first location in which it is hidden (object permanence); improved anticipation of events; imitation of behaviors slightly different from those the infant usually performs
5. Tertiary circular reactions (12–18 months)	Exploration of the properties of objects by acting on them in novel ways; imitation of novel behaviors; ability to search in several locations for a hidden object (accurate A–B search)
6. Mental representation (18 months–2 years)	Internal depictions of objects and events, as indicated by sudden solutions to problems; ability to find an object that has been moved while out of sight (invisible displacement); deferred imitation; and make-believe play

behavior in response to environmental demands. For example, they open their mouths differently for a nipple than for a spoon. And they start to anticipate events: A hungry 3-month-old is likely to stop crying as soon as his mother enters the room—a signal that feeding time is near.

During Substage 3, from 4 to 8 months, infants sit up and become skilled at reaching for and manipulating objects—motor achievements that strengthen the *secondary circular reaction,* through which they try to repeat interesting events in the surrounding environment that are caused by their own actions. For example, Piaget (1936/1952) dangled several dolls in front of his 4-month-old son, Laurent. After accidentally knocking them and producing a fascinating swinging motion, Laurent gradually built the sensorimotor scheme of "hitting." Improved control over their own behavior also permits infants to imitate others' behavior more effectively. However, 4- to 8-month-olds cannot adapt flexibly and quickly enough to imitate novel behaviors (Kaye & Marcus, 1981). Although they enjoy watching an adult demonstrate a game of pat-a-cake, they are not yet able to participate.

Intentional Behavior In Substage 4, 8- to 12-month-olds combine schemes into new, more complex action sequences. Now, behaviors leading to new schemes no longer have a random, hit-or-miss quality—*accidentally* bringing the thumb to the mouth or *happening* to hit the doll. Instead, 8- to 12-month-olds can engage in **intentional,** or **goal-directed, behavior,** coordinating schemes deliberately to solve simple problems. The clearest example comes from Piaget's famous object-hiding task, in which he shows the baby an attractive toy and then hides it behind his hand or under a cover. Infants in this substage can find the object by coordinating two schemes—"pushing" aside the obstacle and "grasping" the toy. Piaget regarded these *means–end action sequences* as the foundation for all problem solving.

Retrieving hidden objects is evidence that infants have begun to master **object permanence,** the understanding that objects continue to exist when they are out of sight. But this awareness is not yet complete. Babies still make the **A-not-B search error:** If they reach several times for an object at one hiding place (A), then see it moved to another (B), they still search for it in the first hiding place (A). Piaget concluded that the babies do not yet have a clear image of the object as persisting when hidden from view.

Infants in Substage 4, who can better anticipate events, sometimes use their capacity for intentional behavior to try to change those events. A 10-month-old might crawl after his mother when she is putting on her coat, whimpering to keep her from leaving. Also, babies can imitate behaviors slightly different from those they usually perform. After watching someone else, they try to stir with a spoon, push a toy car, or drop raisins into a cup (Piaget, 1945/1951).

In Substage 5, the *tertiary circular reaction,* in which toddlers repeat behaviors with variation, emerges. Recall the example on page 227 of the child dropping objects over the basement steps in diverse ways. This deliberately exploratory approach makes 12- to 18-month-olds better problem solvers. For example, they can figure out how to fit a shape through a hole in a container by turning and twisting it, and they can use a stick to obtain a toy that is out of reach. According to Piaget, this capacity to experiment leads to a more advanced understanding of object permanence. Toddlers look for a hidden toy in more than one location, displaying an accurate A–B search. Their more flexible action patterns also permit them to imitate many more behaviors—stacking blocks, scribbling on paper, and making funny faces.

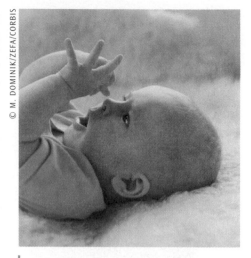

Seeing his hands touch, open, and close, a 3-month-old tries to repeat the movements. This primary circular reaction helps him gain voluntary control over his actions.

After accidentally batting the dangling fish, this 4-month-old tries to recapture the fascinating swinging motion, in a secondary circular reaction.

To find the toy hidden under the cloth, a 10-month-old engages in intentional, goal-directed behavior—the basis for all problem solving.

Using the tertiary circular reaction, this baby takes a deliberately exploratory approach to problem solving, twisting and turning a block until it fits through its matching hole.

The capacity for mental representation enables this 2-year-old to engage in make-believe play. As pretending expands in early childhood, mental symbols become major instruments of thinking.

Mental Representation In Substage 6, sensorimotor development culminates in mental representation. One sign of this capacity is that 18- to 24-month-olds arrive at solutions to problems suddenly rather than through trial-and-error behavior, apparently experimenting with actions inside their heads. Seeing her doll carriage stuck against the wall, Piaget's daughter Lucienne paused for a moment, as if to "think," then immediately turned the toy in a new direction.

Representation also enables older toddlers to solve advanced object-permanence problems involving *invisible displacement*—finding a toy moved while out of sight, such as into a small box while under a cover. Second, it permits **deferred imitation**—the ability to remember and copy the behavior of models who are not present. And it makes possible **make-believe play,** in which children act out everyday and imaginary activities. As the sensorimotor stage draws to a close, mental symbols have become major instruments of thinking.

Follow-Up Research on Infant Cognitive Development

Many studies suggest that infants display a variety of understandings earlier than Piaget believed. Recall the operant conditioning research reviewed in Chapter 4, in which newborns sucked vigorously on a nipple to gain access to interesting sights and sounds. This behavior, which closely resembles Piaget's secondary circular reaction, shows that infants explore and control their external world long before 4 to 8 months. In fact, they do so as soon as they are born.

To discover what infants know about hidden objects and other aspects of physical reality, researchers often use the **violation-of-expectation method.** They may *habituate* babies to a physical event (expose them to the event until their looking declines) to familiarize them with a situation in which their knowledge will be tested. Or they may simply show babies an *expected event* (one that follows physical laws) and an *unexpected event* (a variation of the first event that violates physical laws). Heightened attention to the unexpected event suggests that the infant is "surprised" by a deviation from physical reality—and, therefore, is aware of that aspect of the physical world.

The violation-of-expectation method is controversial. Some critics believe that it indicates limited, implicit (nonconscious) awareness of physical events—not the full-blown, conscious understanding that was Piaget's focus in requiring infants to act on their surroundings, as in searching for hidden objects (Campos et al., 2008; Munakata, 2001; Thelen & Smith, 1994). Others maintain that the method reveals only babies' perceptual preference for novelty, not their knowledge of the physical world (Bremner, 2010; Cohen, 2010; Hood, 2004; Kagan, 2008). Let's examine this debate in light of recent research on object permanence.

Object Permanence In a series of studies using the violation-of-expectation method, Renée Baillargeon and her collaborators claimed to have found evidence for object permanence in the first few months of life. Figure 6.1 illustrates one of these studies (Aguiar & Baillargeon, 2002; Baillargeon & DeVos, 1991). After habituating to a short and a tall carrot moving behind a screen, babies were given two test events: (1) an *expected event,* in which the short carrot moved behind a screen, could not be seen in its window, and reappeared on the other side, and (2) an *unexpected event,* in which the tall carrot moved behind a screen, could not be seen in its window (although it was taller than the window's lower edge), and reappeared. Infants as young as 2½ to 3½ months looked longer at the unexpected event, suggesting that they had some awareness that an object moved behind a screen would continue to exist.

Additional violation-of-expectation studies yielded similar results (Baillargeon, 2004; Wang, Baillargeon, & Paterson, 2005). But several researchers using similar procedures failed to confirm some of Baillargeon's findings (Bogartz, Shinskey, & Schilling, 2000; Cashon & Cohen, 2000; Cohen & Marks, 2002; Rivera, Wakeley, & Langer, 1999). Baillargeon and others maintain that these opposing investigations did not include crucial controls. And they emphasize that infants look longer at a wide variety of unexpected events involving hidden objects (Newcombe, Sluzenski, & Huttenlocher, 2005; Wang, Baillargeon, & Paterson, 2005). Still, critics question what babies' looking preferences tell us about what they actually know.

But recall from Chapter 4 that 4- and 5-month-olds will track a ball's path of movement as it disappears and reappears from behind a barrier, even gazing ahead to where they expect it to emerge—a behavior suggesting awareness that objects persist when out of view. As further support for such awareness, 5- to 9-month-olds more often engaged in such predictive tracking when a ball viewed on a computer screen gradually rolled behind a barrier than when it disappeared instantaneously or imploded (rapidly decreased in size) at the barrier's edge (see Figure 6.2 on page 232) (Bertenthal, Longo, & Kenny, 2007). Babies seemed to interpret a ball rolling behind a barrier as continued existence, instantaneous disappearance or implosion as disappearance (or at least a discontinuous path of movement).

In related research, 6-month-olds' ERP brain-wave activity was recorded as they watched two events on a computer screen. In one event, a black square moved until it covered an object, then moved away to reveal the object (object permanence). In the other event, as a black square began to move across an object, the object disintegrated (object disappearance) (Kaufman, Csibra, & Johnson, 2005). Only while watching the first event did the infants display a particular brain-wave pattern in the right temporal lobe—the same pattern adults exhibit when told to sustain a mental image of an object.

If young infants do have some notion of object permanence, how do we explain Piaget's finding that even infants capable of reaching do not try to search for hidden objects before 8 months of age? Violation-of-expectation tasks require only that the baby react (through looking) to whether a post-object-hiding scene accords with ordinary experience. Searching for a hidden object is far more cognitively demanding: The baby must *predict* where the hidden object is. Consistent with this idea, infants solve some object-hiding tasks before others: Eight- to 10-month-olds remove the cover from a partially hidden object before they are able to do so from a fully covered object (Moore & Meltzoff, 2008). And 10-month olds search for an object placed on a table and covered by a cloth before they search for an object that a hand deposits under a cloth (Moore & Meltzoff, 1999). In the second, more difficult task, infants seem to expect the object to reappear in the hand because that is where the object initially disappeared. When the hand emerges without the object, they conclude that there is no other place the object could be. Not until 14 months can most babies infer that the hand deposited the object under the cloth.

Around this age, toddlers also know that objects continue to exist in their hidden locations after the babies have left the location. After seeing an object hidden in a cupboard, when toddlers returned the next day, they correctly searched for the object in its original location (Moore & Meltzoff, 2004). When exposed to a similar cupboard in a new room, the toddlers behaved as adults do: They saw no reason to search.

Habituation Events
Short-carrot event   Tall-carrot event

(a)

Test Events
Expected event   Unexpected event

(b)   (c)

FIGURE 6.1 Testing young infants for understanding of object permanence using the violation-of-expectation method. (a) First, infants were habituated to two events: a short carrot and a tall carrot moving behind a yellow screen, on alternate trials. Next, the researchers presented two test events. The color of the screen was changed to help infants notice its window. (b) In the *expected event,* the carrot shorter than the window's lower edge moved behind the blue screen and reappeared on the other side. (c) In the *unexpected event,* the carrot taller than the window's lower edge moved behind the screen, did not appear in the window, but then emerged intact on the other side. Infants as young as 2½ to 3½ months looked longer at the *unexpected event,* suggesting that they had some understanding of object permanence. (Adapted from R. Baillargeon & J. DeVos, 1991, "Object Permanence in Young Infants: Further Evidence," *Child Development, 62,* p. 1230. © 1991, John Wiley and Sons. Adapted with permission of John Wiley and Sons.)

LOOK and LISTEN

Using an attractive toy and cloth, try several object-hiding tasks with 8- to 14-month-olds. Is their search behavior consistent with research findings?

(a) Ball rolls behind screen.

(b) Ball instantaneously disappears.

(c) Ball implodes.

FIGURE 6.2   Testing 5- to 9-month-olds for understanding of object permanence using predictive eye tracking. When a ball viewed on a computer screen rolled behind a barrier (a), 5- to 9-month-olds engaged in predictive tracking—gazing ahead to the edge of the screen where they expected the ball to emerge. Babies were much less likely to predictively track when (b) a ball instantaneously disappeared on reaching the location of the first white circle and abruptly reappeared at the location of the second white circle or (c) a ball imploded—rapidly decreased in size—as it approached the barrier's edge, then rapidly increased in size as it reappeared on the other side. These findings suggest that by the middle of the first year, babies interpret a ball rolling behind a barrier as continuing to exist. (Adapted from Bertenthal, Longo, & Kenny, 2007.)

Searching for Objects Hidden in More Than One Location Once 8- to 12-month-olds search for hidden objects, they make the A-not-B search error. For some years, researchers thought that infants make this mistake because they have trouble remembering an object's new location after it has been hidden in more than one place. But many studies indicate that poor memory cannot account for infants' unsuccessful performance. For example, between 6 and 12 months, infants increasingly *look* at the correct location, even while *reaching* incorrectly (Ahmed & Ruffman, 1998; Hofstadter & Reznick, 1996).

Some evidence suggests that 8- to 12-month-olds search at A (where they found the object on previous reaches) instead of B (its most recent location) because they have trouble inhibiting a previously rewarded motor response (Diamond, Cruttenden, & Neiderman, 1994). In support of this view, the more prior reaches to A, the greater the likelihood that the infant will reach again toward A when the object is hidden at B. Another possibility is that after finding the object several times at A, babies do not attend closely when it is hidden at B (Ruffman & Langman, 2002).

A more comprehensive explanation is that a complex, dynamic system of factors—having built a habit of reaching toward A, continuing to look at A, having the hiding place at B appear similar to the one at A, and maintaining a constant body posture—increases the chances that the baby will make the A-not-B search error. Disrupting any one of these factors increases accurate searching at B (Thelen et al., 2001). Adult communicative cues are an added influence—eye contact, smiling, speech ("Look here!"), and pointing after repeatedly hiding at A, which bias the baby to search A (Topál et al., 2008). When these cues are removed, the A-not-B error is reduced. Furthermore, infant expertise at the motor skills required by the search task is vital (Berger, 2010). Older infants are still perfecting reaching and grasping (see Chapter 4). If these skills are challenging, they have little attention left to focus on inhibiting their habitual reach toward A.

In sum, mastery of object permanence is a gradual achievement. Babies' understanding becomes increasingly complex with age: They must perceive an object's identity by integrating feature and movement information (see Chapter 4, page 165), distinguish the object from the barrier concealing it and the surface on which it rests, keep track of the object's whereabouts, and use this knowledge to obtain the object (Cohen & Cashon, 2006; Moore & Meltzoff, 2008). Success at simple object search and A–B search tasks coincides with rapid development of the frontal lobes of the cerebral cortex (Bell, 1998). Also crucial are a wide variety of experiences perceiving, acting on, and remembering objects.

Mental Representation In Piaget's theory, before about 18 months, infants are unable to mentally represent experience. Yet 8- to 10-month-olds' ability to recall the location of hidden objects after delays of more than a minute, and 14-month olds' recall after delays of a day or more, indicate that babies construct mental representations of objects and their whereabouts (McDonough, 1999; Moore & Meltzoff, 2004). And in studies of deferred imitation, categorization, and problem solving, representational thought is evident even earlier.

Deferred and Inferred Imitation. Piaget studied imitation by noting when his three children demonstrated it in their everyday behavior. Under these conditions, a great deal must be known about the infant's daily life to be sure that deferred imitation—which requires infants to represent a model's past behavior—has occurred.

Laboratory research suggests that deferred imitation is present at 6 weeks of age! Infants who watched an unfamiliar adult's facial expression imitated it when exposed to the same adult the next day (Meltzoff & Moore, 1994). As motor capacities improve, infants copy actions with objects. In one study, adults showed 6- and 9-month-olds a novel series of actions with a puppet: taking its glove off, shaking the glove to ring a bell inside, and replacing the glove. When tested a day later, infants who had seen the novel actions were far more likely to imitate them (see Figure 6.3). And when researchers paired a second, motionless puppet with the first puppet a day before the demonstration, 6-month-olds generalized the actions to this new, very different-looking puppet (Barr, Marrott, & Rovee-Collier, 2003). Even more impressive, after having seen Puppet A paired with B and Puppet B paired with C on successive days, infants transferred modeled actions from A to C and from C to A, though they had not directly observed this pair together (Townsend & Rovee-Collier, 2007). Already, infants can form flexible mental representations that include chains of relevant associations.

Gains in recall, expressed through deferred imitation, are accompanied by changes in brain-wave activity during memory tasks. This suggests that improvements in memory storage in the cerebral cortex contribute to these advances (Bauer et al., 2006). Between 12 and 18 months, toddlers use deferred imitation skillfully to enrich their range of schemes. They retain modeled behaviors for at least several months, copy the actions of peers as well as adults, and imitate across a change in context—for example, enact at home a behavior seen at child care (Klein & Meltzoff, 1999; Meltzoff & Williamson, 2010). The ability to recall modeled behaviors in the order they occurred—evident as early as 6 months—also strengthens over the second year (Bauer, 2006; Rovee-Collier & Cuevas, 2009). And when toddlers imitate in correct sequence, they remember more behaviors (Knopf, Kraus, & Kressley-Mba, 2006).

Toddlers even imitate rationally, by *inferring* others' intentions! They are more likely to imitate purposeful than accidental behaviors (Carpenter, Akhtar, & Tomasello, 1998a). And they adapt their imitative acts to a model's goals. If 12-month-olds see an adult perform an unusual action for fun (make a toy dog enter a miniature house by jumping through the chimney, even though its door is wide open), they copy the behavior. But if the adult engages in the odd behavior because she *must* (she makes the dog go through the chimney only after first trying to use the door and finding it locked), 12-month-olds typically imitate the more efficient action (putting the dog through the door) (Schwier et al., 2006; see also Gergely, Bekkering, & Király, 2003).

Between 14 and 18 months, toddlers become increasingly adept at imitating actions an adult *tries* to produce, even if these are not fully realized (Bellagamba, Camaioni, & Colonnesi, 2006; Meltzoff, 1995; Olineck & Poulin-Dubois, 2007). On one occasion, a mother attempted to pour some raisins into a bag but missed, spilling them onto the counter. A moment later, her 18-month-old son climbed onto a stool and began dropping the raisins into the bag, indicating that he had inferred his mother's intention and used it to guide his imitative actions (Falck-Ytter, Gredebäck, & von Hofsten, 2006). By age 2, children mimic entire social roles—Mommy, Daddy, baby—during make-believe play.

Though advanced in terms of Piaget's predictions, toddlers' ability to represent others' intentions—a cornerstone of social understanding and communication—seems to have roots in earlier sensorimotor activity. Infants' skill at engaging in goal-directed actions—reaching for objects at 3 to 4 months, pointing to objects at 9 months—predicts their awareness of an adult's similar behavior as goal-directed in a violation-of-expectation task (Gerson & Woodward, 2010; Woodward, 2009). And the better 10-month-olds are at detecting the goals of others' gazes and reaches, the more accurately they infer an adult's intention from her incomplete actions four months later (Olineck & Poulin-Dubois, 2009).

Categorization. Even young infants can *categorize*, grouping similar objects and events into a single representation—an ability that is incompatible with a strictly sensorimotor approach to the world. Categorization reduces the enormous amount of new information infants encounter every day, helping them learn and remember (Rakison, 2010).

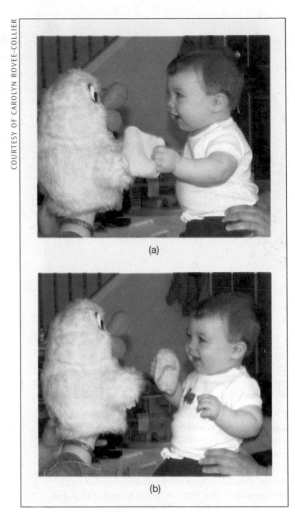

COURTESY OF CAROLYN ROVEE-COLLIER

(a)

(b)

FIGURE 6.3 Testing infants for deferred imitation. After researchers performed a novel series of actions with a puppet, this 6-month-old imitated the actions a day later—(a) removing the glove; (b) shaking the glove to ring a bell inside. With age, gains in recall are evident in deferred imitation of others' behavior over longer delays.

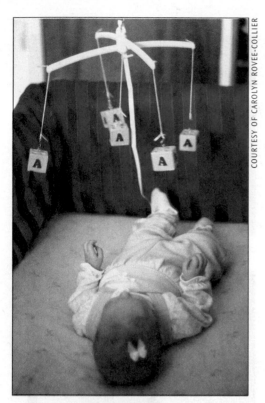

COURTESY OF CAROLYN ROVEE-COLLIER

FIGURE 6.4 Investigating infant categorization using operant conditioning. Three-month-olds were taught to kick to move a mobile made of small blocks, all with the letter A on them. After a delay, kicking returned to a high level only if the babies were shown a mobile whose elements were labeled with the same form (the letter A). If the form was changed (from As to 2s), infants no longer kicked vigorously. While making the mobile move, the babies had grouped together its features. They associated the kicking response with the category A and, at later testing, distinguished it from the category 2. (Bhatt, Rovee-Collier, & Weiner, 1994; Hayne, Rovee-Collier, & Perris, 1987.)

LOOK and LISTEN

Observe a toddler playing with a variety of small toys—some representing animals and some representing household objects. What play behaviors reveal the child's ability to categorize?

Recall the operant conditioning research in which infants kicked to move a mobile attached to their foot by a long cord (see Chapter 4, page 141). Figure 6.4 illustrates a creative variation of this task, used to investigate infant categorization. Similar studies reveal that in the first few months, babies categorize stimuli on the basis of shape, size, and other physical properties (Wasserman & Rovee-Collier, 2001). By 6 months of age, they can categorize on the basis of two correlated features—for example, the shape and color of the alphabet letter (Bhatt et al., 2004). This ability to categorize using clusters of features prepares babies for acquiring many complex everyday categories.

Habituation has also been used to study infant categorization. Researchers show babies a series of pictures belonging to one category and then see whether they recover to (look longer at) a picture that is not a member of the category (see Figure 6.5). Findings reveal that in the second half of the first year, infants group objects into an impressive array of categories—food items, furniture, birds, land animals, air animals, sea animals, plants, vehicles, kitchen utensils, and spatial location ("above" and "below," "on" and "in") (Bornstein, Arterberry, & Mash, 2010; Casasola, Cohen, & Chiarello, 2003; Oakes, Coppage, & Dingel, 1997). Besides organizing the physical world, infants of this age categorize their emotional and social worlds. They sort people and their voices by gender and age, have begun to distinguish emotional expressions, can separate people's natural actions (walking) from other motions, and expect people (but not inanimate objects) to move spontaneously (Spelke, Phillips, & Woodward, 1995; see also Chapter 4, page 163).

Babies' earliest categories are based on similar overall appearance or prominent object part: legs for animals, wheels for vehicles. By the second half of the first year, more categories appear to be based on subtle sets of features (Cohen, 2003; Mandler, 2004a; Quinn, 2008). Older infants can even make categorical distinctions when the perceptual contrast between two categories is minimal (birds versus airplanes).

As they gain experience in comparing to-be-categorized items in varied ways and as their store of verbal labels expands, toddlers start to categorize flexibly: When 14-month-olds are given four balls and four blocks, some made of soft rubber and some of rigid plastic, their sequence of object touching reveals that after classifying by shape, they can switch to classifying by material (soft versus hard) if an adult calls their attention to the new basis for grouping (Ellis & Oakes, 2006).

In addition to touching and sorting, toddlers' categorization skills are evident in their play behaviors. After watching an adult give a toy dog a drink from a cup, most 14-month-olds shown a rabbit and a motorcycle offered the drink only to the rabbit (Mandler & McDonough, 1998). They clearly understood that certain actions are appropriate for some categories of items (animals) but not others (vehicles).

By the end of the second year, toddlers' grasp of the animate–inanimate distinction expands. Nonlinear motions are typical of animates (a person or a dog jumping), linear motions of inanimates (a car or a table pushed along a surface). At 18 months, toddlers more often imitate a nonlinear motion with a toy that has animate-like parts (legs), even if it represents an inanimate (a bed). At 22 months, displaying a fuller understanding, they imitate a nonlinear motion only with toys in the animate category (a cat but not a bed) (Rakison, 2005, 2006). They seem to realize that whereas animates are self-propelled and therefore have varied paths of movement, inanimates move only when acted on, in highly restricted ways.

Researchers disagree on how babies arrive at these impressive attainments. One view holds that older infants and toddlers categorize more effectively because they become increasingly sensitive to fine-grained perceptual features and to stable relations among these features—for example, objects with flapping wings and feathers belong to one category; objects with rigid wings, windows, and a smooth surface belong to another category (Cohen & Cashon, 2006; Oakes et al., 2009; Rakison & Lupyan, 2008). An alternative view is that before the end of the first year, babies undergo a fundamental shift from a perceptual to a conceptual basis for constructing categories, increasingly grouping objects by their common function or behavior (birds versus airplanes, cars versus motorcycles, dogs versus cats) (Mandler, 2004b).

All researchers acknowledge that infants' and toddlers' exploration and expanding knowledge of objects contribute to advances in categorization, eventually enriching conceptual understanding. In addition, adult labeling of a set of objects with a consistently applied word ("Look at the car!" "Do you see the car?") calls babies' attention to commonalities among objects, fostering categorization as early as 3 to 4 months of age (Ferry, Hespos, & Waxman, 2010). Toddlers' vocabulary growth, in turn, enhances categorization by highlighting new categorical distinctions (Cohen & Brunt, 2009; Waxman, 2003).

Variations among languages lead to cultural differences in development of categories. Korean toddlers, who learn a language in which object names are often omitted from sentences, develop object-sorting skills later than their English-speaking counterparts (Gopnik & Choi, 1990). At the same time, Korean contains a common word, *kkita*, with no English equivalent, referring to a tight fit between objects in contact—a ring on a finger, a cap on a pen—and Korean toddlers are advanced in forming the spatial category "tight-fit" (Choi et al., 1999). After English-speaking 18-month-olds heard the word *tight* while observing several instances of objects fitting together tightly, they readily acquired the tight-fit category (Casasola, Bhagwat, & Burke, 2009). Those who viewed the events without the label did not form this challenging category.

FIGURE 6.5 Using habituation to study infant categorization. After habituating to a series of items belonging to one category (in this example, animals), infants are shown two novel items, one that is a member of the category (dog) and one that is not (car). If infants recover to (look longer at or spend more time manipulating) the out-of-category item (car), this indicates that they distinguish it from the set of within-category items (animals). Habituating another group of infants to a series of vehicles and seeing if, when presented with the two test items, they recover to the dog confirms that babies can distinguish animals from vehicles.

Problem Solving. As Piaget indicated, around 7 to 8 months, infants develop intentional means–end action sequences, which they use to solve simple problems, such as pulling on a cloth to obtain a toy resting on its far end (Willatts, 1999). Soon after, infants' representational skills permit more effective problem solving than Piaget's theory suggests.

By 10 to 12 months, infants can engage in **analogical problem solving**—applying a solution strategy from one problem to other relevant problems. In one study, babies of this age were given three similar problems, each requiring them to overcome a barrier, grasp a string, and pull it to get an attractive toy. The problems differed in many aspects of their superficial features—texture and color of the string, barrier, and floor mat and type of toy (horse, doll, or car). For the first problem, the parent demonstrated the solution, encouraging the infant to imitate. Babies obtained the toy more readily with each additional problem (Chen, Sanchez, & Campbell, 1997). Similarly, 12-month-olds who were repeatedly presented with a spoon in the same orientation (handle to one side) readily adapted their motor actions when the spoon was presented in the opposite orientation (handle to the other side), successfully transporting food to their mouths most of the time (McCarty & Keen, 2005).

These findings suggest that at the end of the first year, infants form flexible mental representations of how to use tools to get objects. With age, children become better at reasoning by analogy, generalizing across increasingly dissimilar situations (Goswami, 1996). But even in the first year, infants have some ability to move beyond trial-and-error experimentation, represent a solution mentally, and use it in new contexts.

Symbolic Understanding. One of the most momentous advances in early development is the realization that words can be used to cue mental images of things not physically present—a symbolic capacity called **displaced reference** that emerges around the first birthday. It greatly expands toddlers' capacity to learn about the world through communicating with others.

Observations of 12-month-olds reveal that they respond to the label of an absent toy by looking at and gesturing toward the spot where it usually rests (Saylor, 2004). And on hearing the name of a parent or sibling who has just left the room, most 13-month-olds turn toward the door (DeLoache & Ganea, 2009). The more experience toddlers have with an object and its verbal label, the more likely they are to call up a mental representation when they hear the object's name. As memory and vocabulary improve, skill at displaced reference expands.

But at first, toddlers have difficulty using language to acquire new information about an absent object—an ability that is essential to learn from symbols. In one study, an adult taught 19- and 22-month-olds a name for a stuffed animal—"Lucy" for a frog. Then, with the frog out of sight, the adult told the toddler that some water had spilled, so "Lucy's all wet!" Finally, the adult showed the toddler three stuffed animals—a wet frog, a dry frog, and a pig—and said, "Get Lucy!" (Ganea et al., 2007). Although all the children remembered that Lucy was a frog, only the 22-month-olds identified the wet frog as Lucy. Nevertheless, older toddlers' reliance on verbal information is fragile. When a verbal message about a toy's new location conflicts with a previously observed location, most 23-month-olds simply go to the initial location. At 30 months, children succeed at finding the toy (Ganea & Harris, 2010). The capacity to use language as a flexible symbolic tool—to modify an existing mental representation—improves from the end of the second into the third year.

Awareness of the symbolic function of pictures also emerges in the second year. Even newborns perceive a relation between a picture and its referent, as indicated by their preference for looking at a photo of their mother's face (see page 164 in Chapter 4). At the same time, infants do not treat pictures as symbols. Rather, they touch, rub, and pat a color photo of an object, or pick it up and manipulate it—behaviors that reveal confusion about the picture's true nature. This manual exploration increases from 4 to 9 months and then declines, becoming rare around 18 months (DeLoache et al., 1988; DeLoache & Ganea, 2009).

As long as pictures strongly resemble real objects, by the middle of the second year toddlers treat them symbolically. After hearing a novel label ("blicket") applied to a color photo of an unfamiliar object, most 15- to 24-month-olds—when presented with both the real object and its picture and asked to indicate the "blicket"—gave a symbolic response. They selected either the real object or both the object and its picture, not the picture alone, a tendency that strengthened with age (Ganea et al., 2009). Around this time, toddlers increasingly use pictures as vehicles for communicating with others and acquiring new knowledge. They point to, name, and talk about pictures, and they can apply something learned from a book with realistic-looking pictures to real objects, and vice versa (Ganea, Pickard, & DeLoache, 2008).

But even after coming to appreciate the symbolic nature of pictures, young children continue to have difficulty grasping the distinction between some pictures (such as line drawings) and their referents, as we will see shortly when address the symbolic capacities of preschoolers. How do infants and toddlers interpret another ever-present, pictorial medium—video? Turn to the Social Issues: Education box on the following page to find out.

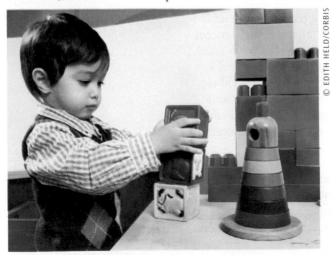

Did this toddler learn to build a block tower through repeatedly acting on objects, as Piaget assumed? Or was he born with built-in cognitive equipment that jump-starts his understanding of relationships between objects?

© EDITH HELD/CORBIS

Evaluation of the Sensorimotor Stage

The Milestones table on page 238 summarizes the remarkable cognitive attainments we have just considered, along with related milestones that we will take up later in this chapter. **TAKE A MOMENT...** Compare this table with the description of Piaget's account of sensorimotor development on pages 228–230. You will see that infants anticipate events, actively search for hidden objects, display an accurate A–B search, flexibly vary their sensorimotor schemes, engage in make-believe play, and treat pictures and video images symbolically within Piaget's time frame. Yet other capacities—including secondary circular reactions, first signs of object permanence, deferred imitation, categorization, problem solving by analogy, and displaced reference of words—emerge earlier than Piaget expected. These findings show that the cognitive attainments of infancy and toddlerhood do not develop together in the neat, stepwise fashion Piaget predicted.

SOCIAL ISSUES: EDUCATION

Baby Learning from TV and Video: The Video Deficit Effect

Children first become TV and video viewers in early infancy, as they are exposed to programs watched by parents and older siblings. Many parents also turn on TV shows or videos aimed at viewers not yet out of diapers, such as the Baby Einstein products. About 40 percent of U.S. 3-month-olds watch regularly, a figure that rises to 90 percent at age 2, a period during which average viewing time increases from just under an hour to 1½ hours per day (Zimmerman, Christakis, & Meltzoff, 2007). Although parents assume that babies learn from TV and videos, research indicates that they cannot take full advantage of them.

Initially, infants respond to videos of people as if viewing people directly—smiling, moving their arms and legs, and (by 6 months) imitating actions of a televised adult. But they confuse the images with the real thing (Barr, Muentener, & Garcia, 2007; Marian, Neisser, & Rochat, 1996). When 9- to 19-month-olds were shown videos of attractive toys, the 9-month-olds manually explored the screen, as they do with pictures. By 19 months, touching and grabbing had declined in favor of pointing at the images (Pierroutsakos & Troseth, 2003). Nevertheless, toddlers continue to have difficulty applying what they see on video to real situations.

In a series of studies, some 2-year-olds watched through a window while a live adult hid an object in an adjoining room, while others watched the same event on a video screen. Children in the direct viewing condition retrieved the toy easily; those in the video condition had trouble doing so (Troseth, 2003; Troseth & DeLoache, 1998). This **video deficit effect**—poorer performance after a video than a live demonstration—has also been found for 2-year-olds' deferred imitation, word learning, and means–end problem solving (Deocampo, 2003;

Hayne, Herbert, & Simcock, 2003; Krcmar, Grela, & Linn, 2007).

One explanation for the video deficit effect is that 2-year-olds typically do not view a video character as offering socially relevant information. After an adult on video announced where she hid a toy, few 2-year-olds searched (Schmidt, Crawley-Davis, & Anderson, 2007). In contrast, when the adult stood in front of the child and uttered the same words, 2-year-olds promptly retrieved the object.

Toddlers seem to discount information on video as relevant to their everyday experiences because people do not look at, converse, and play with them directly, as their caregivers do. In one study, researchers gave some 2-year-olds an interactive video experience (using a two-way, closed-circuit video system). An adult on video interacted with the child for five minutes—calling the child by name, talking about the child's siblings and pets, waiting for the child to respond, and playing interactive games (Troseth, Saylor, & Archer, 2006). Compared with 2-year-olds who viewed the same adult in a noninteractive video, those in the interactive condition were far more successful in using a verbal cue from a person on video to retrieve a toy.

Around age 2½, the video deficit effect declines. Before this age, the American Academy of Pediatrics (2001) recommends against mass media exposure, emphasizing that babies require rich responsive exchanges with caregivers and exploration of their physical surroundings for optimal brain growth and psychological

This baby thinks the child she sees on the TV screen is real. Not until she is about 2½ will she understand how onscreen images relate to real people and objects.

development (see Chapter 5, page 191). In support of this advice, amount of TV viewing is negatively related to 8- to 18-month-olds' language progress (Tanimura et al., 2004; Zimmerman, Christakis, & Meltzoff, 2007). And 1- to 3-year-old heavy viewers tend to have attention, memory, and reading difficulties in the early school years (Christakis et al., 2004; Zimmerman & Christakis, 2005).

Toddlers face a complex task in making sense of video. Although they no longer confuse it with reality, they do not know how to mentally represent the relationship between video images and real objects and people. Video for 2-year-olds is likely to work best as a teaching tool when it is rich in social cues—close-ups of characters who look directly at the camera, address questions to viewers, and pause to invite their response. Repetition of video programs also helps children over age 2 make sense of video content (Anderson, 2004).

Recent research raises questions about Piaget's view of how infant development takes place. Consistent with Piaget's ideas, sensorimotor action helps infants construct some forms of knowledge. For example, in Chapter 4 we saw that experience in crawling enhances depth perception and ability to find hidden objects. Yet we have also seen evidence that infants comprehend a great deal before they are capable of the motor behaviors that Piaget assumed led to those understandings. How can we account for babies' amazing cognitive accomplishments?

Unlike Piaget, who thought infants constructed all mental representations out of sensorimotor activity, most researchers now believe that young babies have some built-in cognitive equipment for making sense of experience. But intense disagreement exists over the extent of this initial understanding. As we have seen, much evidence on infant cognition rests on the violation-of-expectation method. Researchers who lack confidence in this

Milestones

Some Cognitive Attainments of Infancy and Toddlerhood

APPROXIMATE AGE	COGNITIVE ATTAINMENTS
Birth–1 month	• Secondary circular reactions using limited motor skills, such as sucking a nipple to gain access to interesting sights and sounds
1–4 months	• Awareness of many physical properties, including object permanence, object solidity, and object support, as suggested by violation-of-expectation findings (see pages 262–263) • Deferred imitation of an adult's facial expression after a short delay (one day) • Categorization of objects perceptually, on the basis of similar overall appearance or prominent object part
4–8 months	• Improved physical knowledge and basic numerical knowledge (see pages 263–264) • Deferred imitation of an adult's novel actions on objects over a short delay (one to three days) • Categorization of objects on the basis of subtle sets of features, even when the perceptual contrast between categories is minimal
8–12 months	• Ability to search for a hidden object when covered by a cloth, then when a hand deposits it under a cloth • Ability to solve simple problems by analogy to a previous problem
12–18 months	• Ability to search in several locations for a hidden object (accurate A–B search) • Awareness that objects continue to exist in their hidden locations even after the toddler has left the location • Deferred imitation of an adult's novel actions on objects after long delays (at least several months) and across a change in context, such as from child care to home • Rational imitation, inferring the model's intentions • Flexible categorization of objects, first on one basis and then on another • Displaced reference of words
18 months–2 years	• Ability to find an object moved while out of sight (invisible displacement) • Deferred imitation of actions an adult tries to produce, even if these are not fully realized, indicating a capacity to infer others' intentions • Deferred imitation of everyday behaviors in make-believe play • Beginning awareness of pictures and video as symbols of reality

Note: These milestones represent overall age trends. Individual differences exist in the precise age at which each milestone is attained.

TAKE A MOMENT... Which of the capacities listed in this table indicate that mental representation emerges earlier than Piaget believed?

Photos: © Kin Images/Getty Images/Riser; © Laura Dwight Photography; © Newmann/Corbis; © Laura Dwight Photography; © Myrleen Ferguson Cate/PhotoEdit; © Michael Newman/PhotoEdit

method argue that babies' cognitive starting point is limited. For example, some believe that newborns begin life with a set of biases for attending to certain information and with general-purpose learning procedures—such as powerful techniques for analyzing complex perceptual information. Together, these capacities enable infants to construct a wide variety of schemes (Bahrick, 2010; Huttenlocher, 2002; Quinn, 2008; Rakison, 2010). Others, convinced by violation-of-expectation findings, argue that infants start life with considerable innate knowledge, which "jump-starts" their cognitive development. This *core knowledge perspective* has gained ground in the past decade. We will discuss its strengths and limitations after considering Piaget's stages of childhood and adolescence.

A S K   Y O U R S E L F

Review ■ Using the discussion on pages 230–236, construct your own summary table of infant and toddler cognitive development. Which entries in your table are consistent with Piaget's sensorimotor stage? Which ones develop earlier than Piaget anticipated?

Connect ■ Recall from Chapter 4 (page 163) that by the middle of the first year, infants identify objects by their features and paths of movement, even when they cannot observe the entire path. How might these attainments contribute to understanding of object permanence?

Apply ■ Several times, after her father hid a teething biscuit under a red cup, 10-month-old Mimi retrieved it easily. Then Mimi's father hid the biscuit under a nearby yellow cup, but Mimi persisted in searching for it under the red cup. What factors might be contributing to Mimi's inaccurate search behavior?

Reflect ■ What advice would you give the typical U.S. parent about permitting an infant or toddler to watch as much as 1 to 1½ hours of TV or video per day? Explain.

The Preoperational Stage: 2 to 7 Years

▶ Describe advances in mental representation and cognitive limitations during the preoperational stage.

▶ What does follow-up research reveal about preschoolers' cognitive development and the accuracy of Piaget's preoperational stage?

As children move from the sensorimotor to the **preoperational stage,** which spans the years 2 to 7, the most obvious change is an extraordinary increase in representational, or symbolic, activity. Infants' and toddlers' mental representations are impressive, but in early childhood, representational capacities blossom.

Advances in Mental Representation

Piaget acknowledged that language is our most flexible means of mental representation. By detaching thought from action, it permits far more efficient thinking than was possible earlier. When we think in words, we can deal with past, present, and future at once and combine concepts in unique ways, as when we imagine a hungry caterpillar eating bananas or monsters flying through the forest at night.

But Piaget did not regard language as the primary ingredient in childhood cognitive change. Instead, he believed that sensorimotor activity leads to internal images of experience, which children then label with words (Piaget, 1936/1952). In support of Piaget's view, children's first words have a strong sensorimotor basis, usually referring to objects that move or can be acted on or to familiar actions (see Chapter 9). And as we have seen, infants acquire an impressive range of categories long before they use words to label them.

Still, Piaget underestimated the power of language to spur children's cognition. Research inspired by Vygotsky's theory, which we take up later, confirms that language is a powerful source of cognitive development, not just an indicator of it.

Make-Believe Play Make-believe is another excellent example of the development of representation in early childhood. Piaget believed that through pretending, children practice and strengthen newly acquired representational schemes. Drawing on his ideas, researchers have traced changes in make-believe play during the preschool years.

Development of Make-Believe Play. **TAKE A MOMENT…** Visit a child-care center or a family with several young children, and compare an 18-month-old's pretending with that of a 2- to 3-year-old. Jot down examples of the following three advances:

- *Play detaches from the real-life conditions associated with it.* In early pretending, toddlers use only realistic objects—a toy telephone to talk into or a cup to drink from. Their earliest pretend acts usually imitate adults' actions and are not yet flexible. Children younger than age 2, for example, will pretend to drink from a cup but refuse to pretend a cup is a hat (Rakoczy, Tomasello, & Striano, 2005). They have trouble using an object (cup) that already has an obvious use as a symbol for another object (hat).

LOOK and LISTEN

Observe the make-believe play of several 2- to 4-year-olds at home or in a preschool or child-care center. Describe pretend acts that exemplify important developmental changes.

After age 2, children pretend with less realistic toys (a block for a telephone receiver). Gradually, they can imagine objects and events, without any support from the real world (O'Reilly, 1995; Striano, Tomasello, & Rochat, 2001). And by age 3, they flexibly understand that an object (a yellow stick) may take on one fictional identity in one pretend game (a toothbrush) and another fictional identity (a carrot) in a different pretend game (Wyman, Rakoczy, & Tomasello, 2009).

- *Play becomes less self-centered.* At first, make-believe is directed toward the self; for example, children pretend to feed only themselves. Soon, children direct pretend actions toward other people or objects, pouring tea for a parent or feeding a doll. Early in the third year, they become detached participants, assigning make-believe intentions to objects—making a doll feed itself or pushing a button to launch a rocket. Make-believe becomes less self-centered as children realize that agents and recipients of pretend actions can be independent of themselves (McCune, 1993).

- *Play includes more complex combinations of schemes.* An 18-month-old can pretend to drink from a cup but does not yet combine pouring and drinking. Later, children combine pretend schemes with those of peers in **sociodramatic play,** the make-believe with others that is under way by the end of the second year and increases rapidly in complexity during early childhood (Kavanaugh, 2006a). By age 4 to 5, children build on one another's play ideas, create and coordinate several roles, and have a sophisticated understanding of story lines (Göncü, 1993).

Children as young as age 2 display awareness that make-believe is a representational activity. They distinguish make-believe from real experiences and grasp that pretending is a deliberate effort to act out imaginary ideas—an understanding that strengthens over early childhood (Lillard, 2003; Rakoczy, Tomasello, & Striano, 2004; Sobel, 2006). **TAKE A MOMENT...** Listen closely to a group of preschoolers as they assign roles and negotiate plans in sociodramatic play: "*You pretend to be* the astronaut," "Wait, *I gotta set up* the spaceship." In communicating about pretend, children think about their own and others' fanciful representations—evidence that they have begun to reason about people's mental activities.

© LAURA DWIGHT PHOTOGRAPHY

Make-believe play becomes more sophisticated over the preschool years. Children increasingly coordinate make-believe roles and pretend with less realistic toys—for example, a toy truck as an electric hair clipper.

Benefits of Make-Believe. Today, Piaget's view of make-believe as mere practice of representational schemes is regarded as too limited. Play not only reflects but also contributes to children's cognitive and social skills. Sociodramatic play has been studied most thoroughly. Compared with social nonpretend activities (such as drawing or putting puzzles together), during sociodramatic play preschoolers' interactions last longer, show more involvement, draw more children into the activity, and are more cooperative (Creasey, Jarvis, & Berk, 1998).

It is not surprising, then, that preschoolers who devote more time to sociodramatic play are seen as more socially competent by their teachers (Connolly & Doyle, 1984). And many studies reveal that make-believe strengthens a wide variety of mental abilities, including sustained attention, memory, logical reasoning, language and literacy, imagination, creativity, understanding of emotions, and the ability to reflect on one's own thinking and take another's perspective (Bergen & Mauer, 2000; Elias & Berk, 2002; Hirsh-Pasek et al., 2009; Lindsey & Colwell, 2003; Ogan & Berk, 2009; Ruff & Capozzoli, 2003).

Between 25 and 45 percent of preschoolers and young school-age children spend much time in solitary make-believe, creating *imaginary companions*—special fantasized friends endowed with humanlike qualities. For example, one preschooler created Nutsy and Nutsy, a pair of boisterous birds who lived outside her bedroom window (Gleason, Sebanc, & Hartup, 2000; Taylor et al., 2004). Imaginary companions were once viewed as a sign of maladjustment, but research challenges this assumption. Children with an invisible playmate typically treat it with kindness and affection and say it offers caring, comfort, and good company, just as their real friendships do (Gleason & Hohmann, 2006; Hoff, 2005). Such children also display more complex and imaginative pretend play, produce more elaborate narratives about their personal

APPLYING WHAT WE KNOW

Enhancing Make-Believe Play in Early Childhood

STRATEGY	DESCRIPTION
Provide sufficient space and play materials.	Generous space and materials allow for many play options and reduce conflict.
Encourage children's play without controlling it.	Model, guide, and build on young preschoolers' play themes. Provide open-ended suggestions ("Would the animals like a train ride?"), and talk with the child about the thoughts, motivations, and emotions of play characters. These forms of adult support lead to more elaborate pretending. Refrain from directing the child's play; excessive adult control destroys the creativity and pleasure of make-believe.
Offer a variety of both realistic materials and materials without clear functions.	Children use realistic materials—trucks, dolls, tea sets, dress-up clothes, and toy scenes (house, farm, garage, airport)—to act out everyday roles in their culture. Materials without clear functions (blocks, cardboard cylinders, paper bags, sand) inspire fantastic role play—"pirate" and "creature from outer space."
Ensure that children have many rich real-world experiences to inspire positive fantasy play.	Opportunities to participate in real-world activities with adults and to observe adult roles in the community provide children with rich social knowledge to integrate into make-believe. Restricting television viewing, especially programs with violent content, limits the degree to which violent themes and aggressive behavior become part of children's play (see Chapter 15).
Help children solve social conflicts constructively.	Cooperation is essential for sociodramatic play. Help children resolve disagreements constructively. For example, ask, "What could you do if you want a turn?" If the child doesn't know, suggest some options and help the child implement them.

Sources: Berk, Mann, & Ogan, 2006; Nielsen & Christie, 2008; Ogan & Berk, 2009.

experiences and about events in storybooks, are advanced in understanding others' viewpoints and emotions, and are more sociable with peers (Bouldin, 2006; Gleason, 2002; Taylor & Carlson, 1997; Trionfi & Reese, 2009).

Refer to Applying What We Know above for ways to enhance preschoolers' make-believe. Later we will return to the origins and consequences of make-believe from an alternative perspective—that of Vygotsky.

Drawings When given crayon and paper, even toddlers scribble in imitation of others. Gradually, marks on the page take on meaning. A variety of cognitive factors influence the development of children's artful representations (Golomb, 2004). These include the realization that pictures can serve as symbols, improved planning and spatial understanding, and the emphasis that the child's culture places on artistic expression.

From Scribbles to Pictures. Typically, drawing progresses through the following sequence:

1. *Scribbles.* At first, children's intended representation is contained in their gestures rather than in the resulting marks on the page. For example, one 18-month-old made her crayon hop around the page and, as it produced a series of dots, explained, "Rabbit goes hop-hop" (Winner, 1986).

   Recall from page 236 that by the middle of the second year, toddlers treat realistic-looking pictures symbolically. But they have difficulty interpreting line drawings. When an adult held up a drawing indicating which of two objects preschoolers should drop down a chute, 3-year-olds used the drawing as a symbol to guide their behavior but 2-year-olds did not (Callaghan, 1999).

2. *First representational forms.* Around age 3, children's scribbles start to become pictures, although few 3-year olds spontaneously draw so others can tell what their picture represents. Often children make a gesture with the crayon, notice that they have drawn a

FIGURE 6.6 **Examples of young children's drawings.** The universal tadpolelike shape that children use to draw their first picture of a person is shown on the left. The tadpole soon becomes an anchor for greater detail as arms, fingers, toes, and facial features sprout from the basic shape. By the end of the preschool years, children produce more complex, differentiated pictures like the one on the right, drawn by a 6-year-old. (*Left:* From H. Gardner, 1980, *Artful Scribbles: The Significance of Children's Drawings,* New York: Basic Books, p. 64. Reprinted by permission of Basic Books, a member of Perseus Book Group. *Right:* From E. Winner, August 1986, "Where Pelicans Kiss Seals," *Psychology Today, 20*[8], p. 35. Reprinted by permission from the collection of Ellen Winner.)

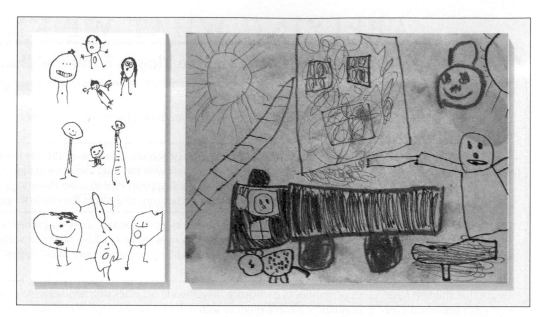

recognizable shape, and then label it—as with a child who made some random marks on a page and then, noticing that his scribbles resembled noodles, called his creation "chicken pie and noodles" (Winner, 1986).

A major milestone in drawing occurs when children use lines to represent the boundaries of objects. This enables 3- and 4-year-olds to draw their first picture of a person. Fine-motor and cognitive limitations lead the preschooler to reduce the figure to the simplest form that still looks human—the universal "tadpole" image, a circular shape with lines attached, shown on the left in Figure 6.6. Four-year-olds add features, such as eyes, nose, mouth, hair, fingers, and feet, as the tadpole drawings illustrate.

3. *More realistic drawings.* Greater realism in drawings develops gradually, as perception, language (ability to describe visual details), memory, and fine-motor capacities improve (Toomela, 2002). Five- and 6-year-olds create more complex drawings, like the one on the right in Figure 6.6, containing more conventional human and animal figures, with the head and body differentiated.

Older preschoolers' drawings still contain perceptual distortions because they have just begun to represent depth (Cox & Littlejohn, 1995). Use of depth cues, such as overlapping objects, smaller size for distant than for near objects, diagonal placement, and converging lines, increases during middle childhood (Nicholls & Kennedy, 1992). And instead of depicting objects separately (as in the drawing in Figure 6.6), older school-age children relate them in an organized spatial arrangement (Case & Okamoto, 1996).

FIGURE 6.7 **Human figure drawings produced by nonschooled 10- to 15-year-olds of the Jimi Valley of Papua New Guinea.** Many produced (a) "stick" figures or (b) "contour" figures, which resemble the tadpole form of young preschoolers. (From M. Martlew & K. J. Connolly, 1996, "Human Figure Drawings by Schooled and Unschooled Children in Papua New Guinea," *Child Development, 67,* pp. 2750–2751. © 1996, John Wiley and Sons. Adapted with permission of John Wiley and Sons.)

Cultural Variations in Development of Drawing. In cultures with rich artistic traditions, children create elaborate drawings that reflect the conventions of their culture. Adults encourage young children in drawing activities by offering suggestions, modeling ways to draw, and asking children to label their pictures. Peers, as well, discuss one another's drawings and copy from one another's artwork (Boyatzis, 2000; Braswell, 2006). All of these cultural practices enhance young children's drawing progress.

But in cultures with little interest in art, even older children and adolescents produce only simple forms. In the Jimi Valley, a remote region of Papua New Guinea with no indigenous pictorial art, many children do not attend school and therefore have little opportunity to develop drawing skills. When asked to draw a human figure for the first time, most nonschooled Jimi 10- to 15-year-olds produced nonrepresentational scribbles and shapes or simple "stick" or "contour" images (see Figure 6.7) (Martlew & Connolly, 1996). These forms seem to be a universal beginning in drawing. Once children realize that lines must evoke human features, they find solutions to figure drawing that follow the general sequence of development described earlier.

(a)   (b)

Symbol–Real-World Relations To make believe and draw—and to understand other forms of representation, such as photographs, models, and maps—preschoolers must realize that each symbol corresponds to something specific in everyday life. Grasping this correspondence grants children a powerful cognitive tool for finding out about objects and places they have not experienced directly. Earlier in this chapter, we saw that by the middle of the second year, children grasp the symbolic function of realistic-looking pictures (such as photos). When do children comprehend other more challenging symbols—for example, three-dimensional models that stand for real-world spaces?

In one study, 2½- and 3-year-olds watched an adult hide a small toy (Little Snoopy) in a scale model of a room and then were asked to retrieve it. Next, they had to find a larger toy (Big Snoopy) hidden in the room that the model represented. Not until age 3 could most children use the model as a guide to finding Big Snoopy in the real room (DeLoache, 1987). The 2½-year-olds did not realize that the model could be both *a toy room* and *a symbol of another room*. They had trouble with **dual representation**—viewing a symbolic object as both an object in its own right and a symbol.

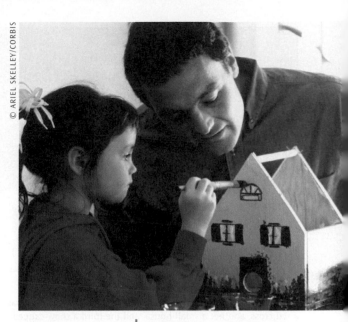

Children who experience a variety of symbols come to understand that one object—a birdhouse—can stand for another: a full-sized house that people live in.

In support of this interpretation, when researchers made the model room less prominent as an object, by placing it behind a window and preventing children from touching it, more 2½-year-olds succeeded at the search task (DeLoache, 2000, 2002). Recall, also, that in make-believe play, 1½- to 2-year-olds cannot use an object that has an obvious use (cup) to stand for another object (hat). And 2-year-olds do not yet realize that a line drawing—an object in its own right—also represents real-world objects (see page 241).

Similarly, when presented with objects disguised in various ways and asked what each "looks like" and what each "is really and truly," preschoolers have difficulty. For example, when asked whether a candle that looks like a crayon "is really and truly" a crayon or whether a stone painted to look like an egg "is really and truly" an egg, children younger than age 6 often responded "yes" (Flavell, Green, & Flavell, 1987). But simplify these *appearance–reality tasks* by permitting children to solve them nonverbally, by selecting from an array of objects the one that "really" has a particular identity, and most 3-year-olds perform well (Deák, Ray, & Brenneman, 2003). They realize that an object can be one thing (a candle) while symbolizing another (a crayon).

How do children grasp the dual representation of symbolic objects? When adults point out similarities between models and real-world spaces, 2½-year-olds perform better on the find-Snoopy task (Peralta de Mendoza & Salsa, 2003). Also, insight into one type of symbol–real-world relation helps preschoolers master others. For example, children regard realistic-looking pictures as symbols early because a picture's primary purpose is to stand for something; it is not an interesting object in its own right (Preissler & Carey, 2004; Simcock & DeLoache, 2006). And 3-year-olds who can use a model of a room to locate Big Snoopy readily transfer their understanding to a simple map (Marzolf & DeLoache, 1994).

In sum, exposing young children to diverse symbols—picture books, photos, drawings, models, make-believe, and maps—helps them appreciate that one object can stand for another. With age, children come to understand a wide range of symbols that have little physical similarity to what they represent (Liben, 2009). As a result, doors open to vast realms of knowledge.

Limitations of Preoperational Thought

Aside from gains in representation, Piaget described preschoolers in terms of what they *cannot* understand (Beilin, 1992). As the term *pre*operational suggests, he compared them to older, more competent children who have reached the concrete operational stage. According to Piaget, young children are not capable of **operations**—mental representations of actions that obey logical rules. Rather, their thinking is rigid, limited to one aspect of a situation at a time, and strongly influenced by the way things appear at the moment.

FIGURE 6.8 **Piaget's three-mountains problem.** Each mountain is distinguished by its color and by its summit. One has a red cross, another a small house, and the third a snow-capped peak. Children at the preoperational stage respond egocentrically. They cannot select a picture that shows the mountains from the doll's perspective. Instead, they simply choose the photo that reflects their own vantage point.

Egocentric and Animistic Thinking For Piaget, the most fundamental deficiency of preoperational thinking is **egocentrism**—failure to distinguish others' symbolic viewpoints from one's own. He believed that when children first mentally represent the world, they tend to focus on their own viewpoint and assume that others perceive, think, and feel the same way they do.

Piaget's most convincing demonstration of egocentrism involves his *three-mountains problem,* described in Figure 6.8. He also regarded egocentrism as responsible for preoperational children's *animistic thinking*—the belief that inanimate objects have lifelike qualities, such as thoughts, wishes, feelings, and intentions (Piaget, 1926/1930). The 3-year-old who charmingly explains that the sun is angry at the clouds and has chased them away is demonstrating this kind of reasoning. According to Piaget, because young children egocentrically assign human purposes to physical events, magical thinking is especially common during the preschool years.

Piaget argued that young children's egocentric bias prevents them from *accommodating,* or reflecting on and revising their faulty reasoning in response to their physical and social worlds. To understand this shortcoming, let's consider some additional tasks that Piaget gave to children.

Inability to Conserve Piaget's famous conservation tasks reveal several deficiencies of preoperational thinking. **Conservation** refers to the idea that certain physical characteristics of objects remain the same, even when their outward appearance changes. For example, in the conservation-of-liquid problem, the child is shown two identical tall glasses of water and asked if they contain equal amounts. Once the child agrees, the water in one glass is poured into a short, wide container, changing the water's appearance but not its amount. Then the child is asked whether the amount of water is the same or has changed. Preoperational children think the quantity has changed. They explain, "There is less now because the water is way down here" (that is, its level is so low) or, "There is more now because it is all spread out." Figure 6.9 illustrates other conservation tasks that you can try with children.

FIGURE 6.9 **Some Piagetian conservation tasks.** Children at the preoperational stage cannot yet conserve. These tasks are mastered gradually over the concrete operational stage. Children in Western nations typically acquire conservation of number, mass, and liquid sometime between 6 and 7 years and of weight between 8 and 10 years.

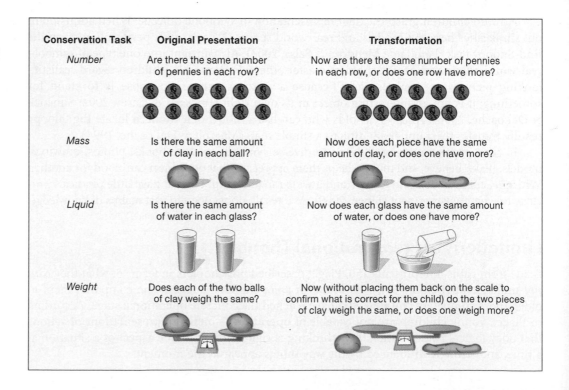

Conservation Task	Original Presentation	Transformation
Number	Are there the same number of pennies in each row?	Now are there the same number of pennies in each row, or does one row have more?
Mass	Is there the same amount of clay in each ball?	Now does each piece have the same amount of clay, or does one have more?
Liquid	Is there the same amount of water in each glass?	Now does each glass have the same amount of water, or does one have more?
Weight	Does each of the two balls of clay weigh the same?	Now (without placing them back on the scale to confirm what is correct for the child) do the two pieces of clay weigh the same, or does one weigh more?

The inability to conserve highlights several related aspects of preoperational children's thinking. First, their understanding is *centered*, or characterized by **centration.** They focus on one aspect of a situation, neglecting other important features. In conservation of liquid, the child *centers* on the height of the water, failing to realize that changes in width compensate for the changes in height. Second, children are easily distracted by the *perceptual appearance* of objects. Third, children treat the initial and final *states* of the water as unrelated events, ignoring the *dynamic transformation* (pouring of water) between them.

The most important illogical feature of preoperational thought is *irreversibility.* **Reversibility**—the ability to go through a series of steps in a problem and then mentally reverse direction, returning to the starting point—is part of every logical operation. In the case of conservation of liquid, the preoperational child cannot imagine the water being poured back into its original container and so fails to see how the amount must remain the same.

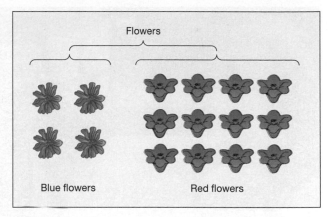

FIGURE 6.10 A Piagetian class inclusion problem. Children are shown 16 flowers, 4 of which are blue and 12 of which are red. Asked, "Are there more red flowers or flowers?" the preoperational child responds, "More red flowers," failing to realize that both red and blue flowers are included in the category "flowers."

Lack of Hierarchical Classification Preoperational children have difficulty with **hierarchical classification**—the organization of objects into classes and subclasses on the basis of similarities and differences. Piaget's famous *class inclusion problem,* illustrated in Figure 6.10, demonstrates this limitation. Preoperational children center on the overriding feature, red. They do not think reversibly, moving from the whole class (flowers) to the parts (red and blue) and back again.

Follow-Up Research on Preoperational Thought

Over the past three decades, researchers have challenged Piaget's account of preschoolers as cognitively deficient. Because many Piagetian problems contain unfamiliar elements or too many pieces of information for young children to handle at once, preschoolers' responses often do not reflect their true abilities. Piaget also missed many naturally occurring instances of effective reasoning by preschoolers. Let's look at some examples.

Egocentric, Animistic, and Magical Thinking Do young children really believe that a person standing elsewhere in a room sees exactly what they see? When researchers adapt Piaget's three-mountains problem to include familiar objects and use methods other than picture selection (which is difficult even for 10-year-olds), 4-year-olds show clear awareness of others' vantage points (Borke, 1975; Newcombe & Huttenlocher, 1992). Even 2-year-olds realize that what they see sometimes differs from what another person sees. When asked to help an adult looking for a lost object, 24-month-olds—but not 18-month-olds—handed her a toy resting behind a bucket that was within the child's line of sight but not visible to the adult (Moll & Tomasello, 2006).

Nonegocentric responses also appear in young children's conversations. For example, preschoolers adapt their speech to fit the needs of their listeners. Four-year-olds use shorter, simpler expressions when talking to 2-year-olds than to agemates or adults (Gelman & Shatz, 1978). And in describing objects, children do not use such words as "big" and "little" in a rigid, egocentric fashion. Instead, they *adjust* their descriptions to allow for context. By age 3, children judge a 2-inch shoe as little when seen by itself (because it is much smaller than most shoes) but as big for a tiny 5-inch-tall doll (Ebeling & Gelman, 1994).

Even toddlers have some appreciation of others' perspectives. In discussing deferred imitation, we saw that they have begun to infer others' intentions (see page 233). And in Chapters 10 and 11, we will encounter evidence that young children have a much greater appreciation of other people's mental states than Piaget's notion of egocentrism implies. In fairness, however, in his later writings Piaget (1945/1951) described preschoolers' egocentrism as a *tendency* rather than an inability. As we revisit the topic of perspective taking, you will see that it develops gradually throughout childhood and adolescence.

Although these preschoolers understand that a robot with life-like features is not really alive, they may believe that it has perceptual and psychological capacities, such as seeing and thinking.

Piaget also overestimated preschoolers' animistic beliefs. Even infants and toddlers have begun to distinguish animate from inanimate, as indicated by their remarkable categorical distinctions between living and nonliving things (see page 234). By age 2½, children give psychological explanations ("he likes to" or "she wants to") for people and occasionally for animals, but rarely for objects (Hickling & Wellman, 2001). And 3- to 5-year-olds asked whether a variety of animals and objects can eat, grow, talk, think, remember, see, or feel mostly attribute these capacities to animals, not objects. In addition, they rarely attribute biological properties (like eating and growing) to robots, indicating that they are well aware that even a self-moving object with lifelike features is not alive. But unlike adults, preschoolers often say that robots have perceptual and psychological capacities—for example, seeing, thinking, and remembering (Jipson & Gelman, 2007; Subrahmanyam, Gelman, & Lafosse, 2002). These responses result from incomplete knowledge about certain objects, and they decline with age.

Similarly, preschoolers think that magic accounts for events they cannot otherwise explain, as in 3-year-old Sammy's magical explanation of thunder in the opening to this chapter. Consequently, most 3- and 4-year-olds believe in the supernatural powers of fairies, goblins, and other enchanted creatures (Rosengren & Hickling, 2000). But their notions of magic are flexible and appropriate. For example, older 3-year-olds and 4-year-olds think that violations of physical laws (walking through a wall) and mental laws (turning on the TV just by thinking about it) require magic more than violations of social conventions (taking a bath with shoes on) (Browne & Woolley, 2004). And they are more likely to say that a magical process—wishing—caused an event (an object to appear in a box) when a person made the wish before the event occurred, the event was consistent with the wish (the wished-for object rather than another object appeared in the box), and no alternative causes were apparent (Woolley, Browne, & Boerger, 2006). These features of causality are the same ones preschoolers rely on in ordinary situations.

Between ages 4 and 8, as children gain familiarity with physical events and principles, their magical beliefs decline. They figure out who is really behind Santa Claus and the Tooth Fairy, and they realize that magicians' feats are due to trickery (Subbotsky, 2004). And increasingly, children say that characters and events in fantastical stories aren't real (Woolley & Cox, 2007). Still, because children entertain the possibility that something imaginary might materialize, they may react with anxiety to scary stories, TV shows, and nightmares.

Logical Thought Many studies show that when preschoolers are given tasks that are simplified and made relevant to their everyday lives, they do not display the illogical characteristics that Piaget saw in the preoperational stage. For example, when a conservation-of-number task is scaled down to include only three items instead of six or seven, 3-year-olds perform well (Gelman, 1972). And when preschoolers are asked what happens to substances (such as sugar) after they are dissolved in water, they give accurate explanations. Most 3- to 5-year-olds know that the substance is conserved—that it continues to exist, can be tasted, and makes the liquid heavier, even though it is invisible in the water (Au, Sidle, & Rollins, 1993; Rosen & Rozin, 1993).

Preschoolers' ability to reason about transformations is evident on other problems. They can engage in impressive *reasoning by analogy* about physical changes. When presented with the picture-matching problem "Play dough is to cut-up play dough as apple is to . . . ?," even 3-year-olds choose the correct answer (a cut-up apple) from a set of alternatives, several of which (a bitten apple, a cut-up loaf of bread) share physical features with the right choice (Goswami, 1996). These findings indicate that in familiar contexts, preschoolers can overcome appearances and think logically about cause and effect.

LOOK and LISTEN

Try the conservation of number and mass tasks in Figure 6.9 with a 3- or 4-year-old. Next, simplify conservation of number by reducing the number of pennies, and relate conservation of mass to the child's experience by pretending the clay is baking dough and transforming it into cupcakes. Did the child perform more competently?

Finally, even without detailed biological or mechanical knowledge, preschoolers realize that the insides of animals are responsible for certain cause–effect sequences (such as willing oneself to move) that are impossible for nonliving things, such as machines (Gelman, 2003; Keil & Lockhart, 1999). Preschoolers seem to use illogical reasoning only when they must grapple with unfamiliar topics, too much information, or contradictory facts that they cannot reconcile (Ruffman, 1999).

Categorization Despite their difficulty with Piagetian class inclusion tasks, preschoolers organize their everyday knowledge into nested categories at an early age. By the beginning of early childhood, children's categories include objects that go together because of their common function, behavior, and natural kind (animate versus inanimate), despite varying widely in perceptual features.

Indeed, 2- to 5-year-olds readily draw inferences about nonobservable characteristics shared by category members. For example, after being told that a bird has warm blood and a stegosaurus (dinosaur) has cold blood, preschoolers infer that a pterodactyl (labeled a dinosaur) has cold blood, even though it closely resembles a bird (Gopnik & Nazzi, 2003). And when shown a set of three characters—two of whom look different but share an inner trait ("outgoing") and two of whom look similar but have different inner traits (one "shy," one "outgoing")—preschoolers rely on the trait category, not physical appearance, to predict similar preferred activities (Heyman & Gelman, 2000).

During the second and third years, and perhaps earlier, children's categories differentiate. They form many *basic-level categories*—ones at an intermediate level of generality, such as "chairs," "tables," "dressers," and "beds." By the third year, preschoolers easily move back and forth between basic-level categories and *general categories,* such as "furniture." And they break down basic-level categories into *subcategories,* such as "rocking chairs" and "desk chairs."

Preschoolers' rapidly expanding vocabularies and general knowledge support their impressive skill at categorizing. As they learn more about their world, they devise theories about underlying characteristics shared by category members, which help them identify new instances (Gelman & Kalish, 2006; Gelman & Koenig, 2003). For example, they realize that animals have an inborn potential for certain physical characteristics and behaviors that determine their identity. In categorizing, they look for causal links among these features. In one study, researchers invented two categories of animals—one with horns, armor, and a spiky tail; the other with wings, large ears, long toes, and a monkeylike tail (see Figure 6.11). Four-year-olds who were given a theory that identified an inner cause for the coexistence of the animals' features—animals in the first category "like to fight"; those in the second category "like to hide in trees"—easily classified new examples of animals. But 4-year-olds for whom animal features were merely pointed out or who were given a separate function for each feature could not remember the categories (Krascum & Andrews, 1998).

As this investigation suggests, adults' explanations are a major source of young children's categorical learning (Gelman & Kalish, 2006). Picture-book reading is an especially rich context for understanding categories.

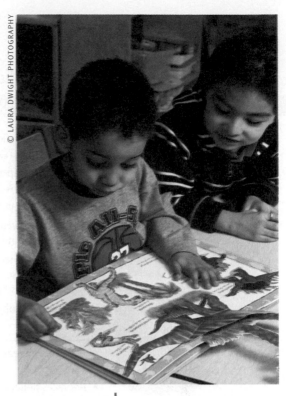

These 4-year-olds understand that a category ("dinosaurs") can be based on underlying characteristics ("cold-blooded"), not just on perceptual features such as upright posture and scaly skin.

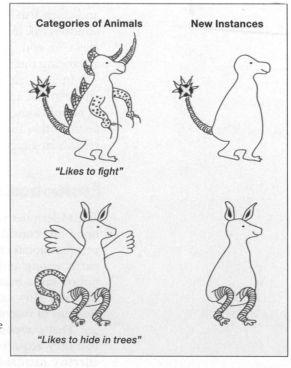

FIGURE 6.11 Categories of imaginary animals shown to preschoolers. When an adult provided a theory about the coexistence of animals' features—"likes to fight" and "likes to hide in trees"—4-year-olds easily classified new instances of animals with only one or two features. Without the theory, preschoolers could not remember the categories. Theories about underlying characteristics support the formation of many categories in early childhood. (From R. M. Krascum & S. Andrews, 1998, "The Effects of Theories on Children's Acquisition of Family-Resemblance Categories," *Child Development, 69,* p. 336. © 1998, John Wiley and Sons. Reprinted with permission of John Wiley and Sons.)

Milestones

Some Cognitive Attainments of Early Childhood

APPROXIMATE AGE	COGNITIVE ATTAINMENTS
2–4 years	• Shows a dramatic increase in representational activity, as reflected in language, make-believe play, drawing, understanding of symbol–real-world relations, and categorization • Takes the perspective of others in simplified, familiar situations and in everyday, face-to-face communication • Distinguishes animate beings from inanimate objects; denies that magic can alter everyday experiences • Grasps conservation, notices transformations, reverses thinking, and understands many cause-and-effect relationships in familiar contexts • Categorizes objects on the basis of common function, behavior, and natural kind, not just perceptual features. Devises ideas about underlying characteristics that category members share and uses inner causal features to categorize objects varying widely in external appearance. • Sorts familiar objects into hierarchically organized categories
4–7 years	• Becomes increasingly aware that make-believe (and other thought processes) are representational activities • Replaces beliefs in magical creatures and events with plausible explanations

Note: These milestones represent overall age trends. Individual differences exist in the precise age at which each milestone is attained.

Photos: (top) © Ellen B. Senisi/The Image Works; (bottom) © Ryan McVay/Getty Images/Photodisc

While looking at books with their preschoolers, parents provide information that guides children's inferences about the structure of categories: "Penguins live at the South Pole, swim, and catch fish," or "Fish breathe by taking water into their mouths." Furthermore, young children ask many questions about their world ("What do crawfish eat? Why does it have claws?") and generally get informative answers, which are particularly well-suited to advancing their conceptual understanding (Chouinard, 2007).

In sum, although preschoolers' category systems are less complex than those of older children and adults, they already have the capacity to classify hierarchically and on the basis of nonobvious properties. And they use logical, causal reasoning to identify the interrelated features that form the basis of a category and to classify new members. Finally, they often rely on language to advance their knowledge of categories.

Evaluation of the Preoperational Stage

The Milestones table above provides an overview of the cognitive attainments of early childhood just considered. **TAKE A MOMENT...** Compare them with Piaget's description of the preoperational child on pages 243–245. The evidence as a whole indicates that Piaget was partly wrong and partly right about young children's cognitive capacities. When given simplified tasks based on familiar experiences, preschoolers show the beginnings of logical thinking. How can we make sense of the contradictions between Piaget's conclusions and the findings of recent research?

That preschoolers have some logical understandings that strengthen with age indicates that they acquire operational reasoning gradually. Over time, children rely on increasingly effective mental (as opposed to perceptual) approaches to solving problems. For example, children who cannot use counting to compare two sets of items do not conserve number. Rather, they rely on perceptual cues to compare the amounts in two sets of items (Rouselle, Palmers, & Noël, 2004; Sophian, 1995). Once preschoolers can count, they apply this skill to conservation-of-number tasks involving just a few items. As counting improves, they extend the strategy to problems with more items. By age 6, they understand that number remains the same after a transformation in the length and spacing of a set of items as long as nothing is added or taken away (Halford & Andrews, 2006). Consequently, they no longer need to count to verify their answer. Thus, children pass through several steps on the way to a full understanding of relationships among variables in conservation problems, although (as Piaget indicated) they do not fully grasp conservation until the school years.

Evidence that preschool children can be trained to perform well on Piagetian problems also supports the idea that operational thought does not emerge all at once (Ping & Goldin-Meadow, 2008; Siegler & Svetina, 2006). Children who possess some understanding would naturally benefit from training, unlike those with none at all.

The gradual development of logical operations poses yet another challenge to Piaget's stage concept. Although the minds of young children still have a great deal of developing to do, research shows that they are considerably more capable than Piaget assumed.

ASK YOURSELF

Review ■ Select two of the following features of preoperational thought: egocentrism, a focus on perceptual appearances, difficulty reasoning about transformations, and lack of hierarchical classification. Present evidence indicating that preschoolers are more capable thinkers than Piaget assumed.

Connect ■ Make-believe play promotes both cognitive and social development (see page 240). Explain why this is so.

Apply ■ Three-year-old Will understands that his tricycle isn't alive and can't feel or move on its own. But watching the setting sun, Will exclaimed, "The sun is tired. It's going to sleep!" Explain this apparent contradiction in Will's reasoning.

Reflect ■ Did you have an imaginary companion as a young child? If so, what was your companion like, and why did you create it? Were your parents aware of your companion? What was their attitude toward it?

The Concrete Operational Stage: 7 to 11 Years

▶ What are the major characteristics of Piaget's concrete operational stage?

▶ Discuss follow-up research on concrete operational thought.

According to Piaget, the **concrete operational stage,** extending from about 7 to 11 years, marks a major turning point in cognitive development. Thought becomes far more logical, flexible, and organized, more closely resembling the reasoning of adults than that of younger children.

Concrete Operational Thought

Concrete operations are evident in the school-age child's performance on a wide variety of Piagetian tasks. Let's look closely at these diverse accomplishments.

Conservation The ability to pass *conservation tasks* provides clear evidence of *operations*— mental actions that obey logical rules. In conservation of liquid, for example, children state that the amount of liquid has not changed, and they are likely to offer an explanation something like this: "The water's shorter, but it's also wider. Pour it back—you'll see it's the same amount." Notice how the child is capable of *decentration*, focusing on several aspects of a problem and relating them, rather than centering on only one. This explanation also illustrates *reversibility*—the capacity to imagine the water being returned to the original container as proof of conservation.

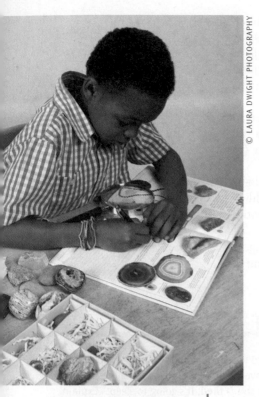

This 8-year-old carefully sorts and classifies the rocks in his collection. An improved ability to categorize underlies school-age children's interest in collecting objects.

Classification Between ages 7 and 10, children pass Piaget's *class inclusion problem.* This indicates that they are more aware of classification hierarchies and can focus on relations between a general and two specific categories at the same time—that is, on three relations at once (Hodges & French, 1988; Ni, 1998). Collections—stamps, coins, rocks, bottle caps—become common in middle childhood. At age 10, one boy I know spent hours sorting and resorting his large box of baseball cards, grouping them first by league and team membership, then by playing position and batting average. He easily separated the players into various classes and subclasses and could rearrange them.

Seriation The ability to order items along a quantitative dimension, such as length or weight, is called **seriation.** To test for it, Piaget asked children to arrange sticks of different lengths from shortest to longest. Older preschoolers can put the sticks in a row to create the series, but they do so haphazardly, making many errors. In contrast, 6- to 7-year-olds create the series efficiently, moving in an orderly sequence from the smallest stick to the next largest, and so on.

The concrete operational child can also seriate mentally, an ability called **transitive inference.** In a well-known problem, Piaget (1967) showed children pairings of sticks of different colors. From observing that stick *A* is longer than stick *B* and that stick *B* is longer than stick *C*, children must infer that *A* is longer than *C*. Like Piaget's class inclusion task, transitive inference requires children to integrate three relations at once: *A–B, B–C, A–C.* When researchers take steps to ensure that children remember the premises (*A–B* and *B–C*), 7-year-olds grasp transitive inference (Andrews & Halford, 1998; Wright, 2006).

Spatial Reasoning Piaget found that school-age children's understanding of space is more accurate than that of preschoolers. Let's consider children's **cognitive maps**—mental representations of familiar large-scale spaces, such as their neighborhood or school. Drawing a map of a large-scale space requires considerable perspective-taking skill. Because the entire space cannot be seen at once, children must infer its layout by relating its separate parts.

Preschoolers and young school-age children include *landmarks* on the maps they draw, but their arrangement is not always accurate. They do better when asked to place stickers showing the location of desks and people on a map of their classroom. But if the map is rotated to a position other than the orientation of the classroom, they have difficulty (Liben & Downs, 1993). Their use of a rotated map to find objects hidden in a room improves when the locations form a meaningful pattern, such as the outline of a dog (see Figure 6.12) (Uttal et al., 2001). Pointing out the pattern helps children *reason by analogy* from the rotated map to corresponding locations in the room.

FIGURE 6.12 Five-year-olds' use of a rotated map to find objects hidden in a room. In one condition (a), locations on the map were connected to form a meaningful pattern—the outline of a dog. In a second condition (b), the locations on the map were not connected. The map showing the dog outline resulted in more correct searches for a hidden object than the map with no outline. (Adapted from Uttal et al., 2001.)

Around age 8 to 10, children's maps become better organized, showing landmarks along an *organized route of travel.* At the same time, children are able to give clear, well-organized directions for getting from place to place by using a "mental walk" strategy—imagining a person's movements along a route (Gauvain & Rogoff, 1989). By the end of middle childhood, children combine landmarks and routes into an *overall view of a large-scale space.* And they readily draw and read maps of extended outdoor environments, even when the orientation of the map and the space it represents do not match (Liben, 2009). Ten- to 12-year-olds also comprehend *scale*—the proportional relation between a space and its representation on a map (Liben, 2006).

Map-related experiences enhance children's map skills. When teachers asked fourth graders to write down the clues they used to decide where stickers (signifying landmark locations) should go on a map of an outdoor space, children's accuracy improved greatly (Kastens & Liben, 2007). Such self-generated explanations seem to induce learners to reflect on and revise their own thinking, sparking gains in many types of problem solving among school-age children and adolescents. And a computer-based curriculum called *Where Are We,* consisting of 12 map-reading and map-making lessons, led to substantial improvements in second to fourth graders' performance on diverse mapping tasks (Liben, Kastens, & Stevenson, 2001).

Cultural frameworks influence children's map making. In many non-Western communities, people rarely use maps for way finding but rely on information from neighbors, street vendors, and shopkeepers. Also, compared to their Western agemates, non-Western children less often ride in cars and more often walk, which results in intimate neighborhood knowledge. When 12-year-olds in small cities in India and in the United States drew maps of their neighborhoods, the Indian children represented many landmarks and aspects of social life, such as people and vehicles, in a small area near their home. The U.S. children drew a more formal, extended space, highlighting main streets and key directions (north–south, east–west) but including few landmarks (see Figure 6.13) (Parameswaran, 2003). Although the U.S. children's maps scored higher in cognitive maturity, this difference reflected cultural interpretations of the task. When asked to create a map to "help people find their way," the Indian children drew spaces as far-reaching and organized as the U.S. children's.

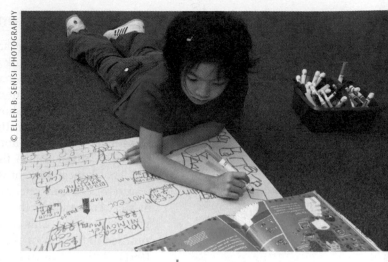

A 6-year-old's drawing of a neighborhood map depicts familiar buildings and other landmarks, but she does not yet place them accurately along a route of travel.

LOOK and LISTEN

Ask a 6- to 8-year-old and a 9- to 12-year-old to draw a neighborhood map showing important landmarks, such as the school, a friend's house, or a shopping area. In what ways do the children's maps differ?

(a) (b)

FIGURE 6.13 Maps drawn by 12-year-olds from India and the United States. (a) The Indian child depicted many landmarks and features of social life in a small area near her home. (b) The U.S. child drew a more extended space and highlighted main streets and key directions. (Reprinted from *Journal of Environmental Psychology,* Vol. 23, No. 4, G. Parameswaran, 2003, "Experimenter Instructions as a Mediator in the Effects of Culture on Mapping One's Neighborhood," pp. 415–416. Copyright 2003, with permission from Elsevier.)

Limitations of Concrete Operational Thought

As the name of this stage suggests, concrete operational thinking suffers from one important limitation: Children think in an organized, logical fashion only when dealing with concrete information they can perceive directly. Their mental operations work poorly with abstract ideas—ones not apparent in the real world. Consider children's solutions to transitive inference problems. When shown pairs of sticks of unequal length, children 7 years and older readily figure out that if stick *A* is longer than stick *B* and stick *B* is longer than stick *C*, then *A* is longer than *C*. But until age 11 or 12, they have difficulty with a hypothetical version of this task: "Susan is taller than Sally and Sally is taller than Mary. Who is the tallest?"

That logical thought is at first tied to immediate situations helps account for a special feature of concrete operational reasoning: Children master concrete operational tasks step by step. For example, they usually grasp conservation of number first, then liquid and mass, and then weight. This *continuum of acquisition* (or gradual mastery) of logical concepts is another indication of the limitations of concrete operational thinking (Fischer & Bidell, 1991). Rather than coming up with general logical principles that they apply to all relevant situations, school-age children seem to work out the logic of each problem separately.

Follow-Up Research on Concrete Operational Thought

According to Piaget, brain development combined with rich and varied experiences should lead children everywhere to reach the concrete operational stage. Yet already we have seen that specific cultural and teaching practices affect children's task performance (Rogoff, 2003).

In tribal and village societies, conservation is often delayed. Among the Hausa of Nigeria, who live in small agricultural settlements and rarely send their children to school, even basic conservation tasks—number, length, and liquid—are not understood until age 11 or later (Fahrmeier, 1978). This suggests that participating in relevant everyday activities helps children master conservation and other Piagetian problems (Light & Perret-Clermont, 1989). Many children in Western nations, for example, think of fairness in terms of equal distribution—a value emphasized in their culture. They frequently divide materials, such as crayons or treats, equally among their friends. Because they often see the same quantity arranged in different ways, they grasp conservation early.

The very experience of going to school seems to promote mastery of Piagetian tasks. When children of the same age are tested, those who have been in school longer do better on transitive inference problems (Artman & Cahan, 1993). Opportunities to seriate objects, to learn about order relations, and to remember the parts of complex problems are probably responsible.

Yet certain informal, nonschool experiences can also foster operational thought. Brazilian 6- to 9-year-old street vendors, who seldom attend school, do poorly on Piaget's class inclusion tasks. But they perform much better than economically advantaged schoolchildren on versions relevant to street vending—for example, "If you have 4 units of mint chewing gum and 2 units of grape chewing gum, is it better to sell me the mint gum or [all] the gum?" (Ceci & Roazzi, 1994). Similarly, around age 7 to 8, Zinacanteco Indian girls of southern Mexico, who learn to weave elaborately designed fabrics as an alternative to schooling, engage in mental transformations to figure out how a warp strung on a loom will turn out as woven cloth—reasoning expected at the concrete operational stage. American children of the same age, who do much better than Zinacanteco children on Piagetian tasks, have great difficulty with these weaving problems (Maynard & Greenfield, 2003).

On the basis of such findings, some investigators have concluded that the forms of logic required by Piagetian tasks do not emerge spontaneously but are heavily influenced by training, context, and cultural conditions. The Milestones table on the following page summarizes the cognitive attainments of middle childhood discussed in the preceding sections, along with those that will follow in adolescence.

© DAVID FRAZIER/THE IMAGE WORKS

This Brazilian street vendor might do poorly on Piagetian class inclusion tasks, but he is likely to understand that "all the chewing gum" represents a larger quantity than the amount of any one flavor.

Milestones

Some Cognitive Attainments of Middle Childhood and Adolescence

APPROXIMATE AGE	COGNITIVE ATTAINMENTS
Middle childhood **7–11 years**	• Thinks in a more organized, logical fashion about concrete information, as indicated by gradual mastery of Piagetian conservation, class inclusion, and seriation problems, including transitive inference • Displays more effective spatial reasoning, as indicated by ability to construct well-organized cognitive maps and give clear directions
Adolescence **11–18 years**	• Reasons abstractly in situations that offer many opportunities for hypothetico-deductive reasoning and propositional thought • Grasps the logical necessity of propositional thought, permitting reasoning about premises that contradict reality • Displays imaginary audience and personal fable, which gradually decline • Improves in decision-making strategies

Note: These milestones represent overall age trends. Individual differences exist in the precise age at which each milestone is attained.

Photos: (top) Michael Newman/PhotoEdit; (bottom) © Simon Jarratt/Corbis

---

ASK YOURSELF

Review ■ Children's performance on conservation tasks illustrates a continuum of acquisition of logical concepts. Review the preceding sections, and list additional examples of gradual development of operational reasoning.

Connect ■ Using research on cognitive maps, conservation, and class inclusion, explain how tasks not adapted to children's cultural contexts can underestimate their cognitive competencies.

Apply ■ Nine-year-old Adrienne spends many hours helping her father build furniture in his woodworking shop. How might this experience facilitate Adrienne's advanced performance on Piagetian seriation problems?

Reflect ■ Which aspects of Piaget's description of the concrete operational stage do you accept? Which do you doubt? Explain, citing research evidence.

The Formal Operational Stage: 11 Years and Older

▶ Describe major characteristics of the formal operational stage and typical consequences of adolescents' advancing cognition.

▶ What does follow-up research reveal about formal operational thought?

According to Piaget, around age 11 young people enter the **formal operational stage,** in which they develop the capacity for abstract, systematic, scientific thinking. Whereas concrete operational children can "operate on reality," formal operational adolescents can "operate on operations." They no longer require concrete things or events as objects of thought. Instead, they can come up with new, more general logical rules through internal reflection (Inhelder & Piaget, 1955/1958). Let's look at two major features of the formal operational stage.

Hypothetico-Deductive Reasoning

Piaget believed that at adolescence, young people become capable of **hypothetico-deductive reasoning.** When faced with a problem, they start with a *hypothesis,* or prediction about variables that might affect an outcome, from which they *deduce* logical, testable inferences.

FIGURE 6.14 Piaget's pendulum problem. Adolescents who engage in hypothetico-deductive reasoning think of variables that might possibly affect the speed with which a pendulum swings through its arc. Then they isolate and test each variable, as well as testing the variables in combination. Eventually they deduce that the weight of the object, the height from which it is released, and how forcefully it is pushed have no effect. Only string length makes a difference.

Then they systematically isolate and combine variables to see which of these inferences are confirmed in the real world. Notice how this form of problem solving begins with possibility and proceeds to reality. In contrast, concrete operational children start with reality—with the most obvious predictions about a situation. If these are not confirmed, they usually cannot think of alternatives and fail to solve the problem.

Adolescents' performance on Piaget's famous *pendulum problem* illustrates this new approach. Suppose we present several school-age children and adolescents with strings of different lengths, objects of different weights to attach to the strings, and a bar from which to hang the strings (see Figure 6.14). Then we ask each of them to figure out what influences the speed with which a pendulum swings through its arc.

Formal operational adolescents hypothesize that four variables might be influential: (1) the length of the string, (2) the weight of the object hung on it, (3) how high the object is raised before it is released, and (4) how forcefully the object is pushed. By varying one factor at a time while holding the other three constant, they test each variable separately and, if necessary, also in combination. Eventually they discover that only string length makes a difference.

In contrast, concrete operational children cannot separate the effects of each variable. They may test for the effect of string length without holding weight constant—comparing, for example, a short, light pendulum with a long, heavy one. Also, they typically fail to notice variables that are not immediately suggested by the concrete materials of the task—for example, how high the object is raised or how forcefully it is released.

Propositional Thought

A second important characteristic of Piaget's formal operational stage is **propositional thought**—adolescents' ability to evaluate the logic of propositions (verbal statements) without referring to real-world circumstances. In contrast, children can evaluate the logic of statements only by considering them against concrete evidence in the real world.

In a study of propositional reasoning, an adult showed children and adolescents a pile of poker chips and asked whether statements about the chips were true, false, or uncertain (Osherson & Markman, 1975). In one condition, the adult hid a chip in her hand and then presented the following propositions:

> "*Either* the chip in my hand is green *or* it is not green."
> "The chip in my hand is green *and* it is not green."

In another condition, the researcher made the same statements while holding either a red or a green chip in full view.

School-age children focused on the concrete properties of the poker chips. When the chip was hidden, they replied that they were uncertain about both statements. When it was visible, they judged both statements to be true if the chip was green and false if it was red. In contrast, adolescents analyzed the logic of the statements. They understood that the "either-or" statement is always true and the "and" statement is always false, regardless of the poker chip's color.

Although Piaget did not view language as playing a central role in cognitive development, he acknowledged its importance in adolescence. Formal operations require language-based and other symbolic systems that do not stand for real things, such as those in higher mathematics. Secondary school students use such systems in algebra and geometry. Formal operational thought also involves

In Piaget's formal operational stage, adolescents engage in propositional thought. As these students discuss problems in a social studies class, they reason logically with propositions that do not refer to real-world circumstances.

APPLYING WHAT WE KNOW

Handling Consequences of Teenagers' New Cognitive Capacities

ABSTRACT THOUGHT EXPRESSED AS . . .	SUGGESTION
Sensitivity to public criticism	Refrain from finding fault with the adolescent in front of others. If the matter is important, wait until you can speak to the teenager alone.
Exaggerated sense of personal uniqueness	Acknowledge the adolescent's unique characteristics. At opportune times, encourage a more balanced perspective by pointing out that you had similar feelings as a young teenager.
Idealism and criticism	Respond patiently to the adolescent's grand expectations and critical remarks. Point out positive features of targets, helping the teenager see that all societies and people are blends of virtues and imperfections.
Difficulty making everyday decisions	Refrain from deciding for the adolescent. Model effective decision making, and offer diplomatic suggestions about the pros and cons of alternatives, the likelihood of various outcomes, and learning from poor choices.

verbal reasoning about abstract concepts. Adolescents show that they can think in this way when they ponder the relations among time, space, and matter in physics or wonder about justice and freedom in philosophy.

Consequences of Adolescent Cognitive Changes

The development of increasingly complex, effective thinking leads to dramatic revisions in the way adolescents see themselves, others, and the world in general. But just as adolescents are occasionally awkward in using their transformed bodies, so they initially falter in their more advanced thinking. Teenagers' self-concern, idealism, criticism, and indecisiveness, though perplexing to adults, are usually beneficial in the long run. Applying What We Know above suggests ways to handle the everyday consequences of teenagers' newfound cognitive capacities.

Self-Consciousness and Self-Focusing Adolescents' ability to reflect on their own thoughts, combined with physical and psychological changes they are undergoing, leads them to think more about themselves. Piaget believed that a new form of egocentrism arises, in which adolescents again have difficulty distinguishing their own and others' perspectives (Inhelder & Piaget, 1955/1958). Piaget's followers suggest that two distorted images of the relationship between self and others appear.

The first is called the **imaginary audience,** adolescents' belief that they are the focus of everyone else's attention and concern (Elkind & Bowen, 1979). As a result, they become extremely self-conscious, often going to great lengths to avoid embarrassment. The imaginary audience helps explain the long hours adolescents spend inspecting every detail of their appearance and why they are so sensitive to public criticism. To teenagers, who believe that everyone is monitoring them, a critical remark from a parent or teacher can be mortifying.

A second cognitive distortion is the **personal fable.** Certain that others are observing and thinking about them, teenagers develop an inflated opinion of their own importance—a feeling that they are special and unique. Many adolescents view themselves as reaching great heights of omnipotence and also sinking to unusual depths of despair—experiences others cannot possibly understand (Elkind, 1994). One teenager wrote in her diary, "My parents' lives are so ordinary, so stuck in a rut. Mine will be different. I'll realize my hopes and ambitions." Another, upset when a boyfriend failed to return her affections, rebuffed her mother's comforting words: "Mom, you don't know what it's like to be in love!"

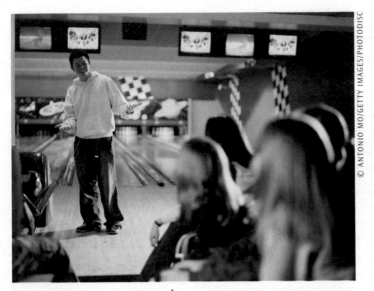

This teenager's swagger reflects self-confidence and delight that all eyes are on him. As long as the personal fable engenders a view of oneself as highly capable and influential, it may help young people cope with the challenges of adolescence.

Although imaginary-audience and personal-fable ideation is common in adolescence, these distorted visions of the self do not result from egocentrism, as Piaget suggested. Rather, they are partly an outgrowth of advances in perspective taking, which cause young teenagers to be more concerned with what others think (Vartanian & Powlishta, 1996).

In fact, certain aspects of the imaginary audience may serve positive, protective functions. In a study in which adolescents were asked why they worry about the opinions of others, they responded that they do so because others' evaluations have important *real* consequences—for self-esteem, peer acceptance, and social support (Bell & Bromnick, 2003). The idea that others care about their appearance and behavior also has emotional value, helping teenagers hold onto important relationships as they struggle to separate from parents and establish an independent sense of self (Vartanian, 1997).

With respect to the personal fable, in an investigation of sixth through tenth graders, sense of omnipotence predicted self-esteem and overall positive adjustment. Viewing the self as highly capable and influential helps young people cope with the challenges of adolescence. In contrast, sense of personal uniqueness was modestly associated with depression and suicidal thinking (Aalsma, Lapsley, & Flannery, 2006). Focusing on the distinctiveness of one's own experiences may interfere with forming close, rewarding relationships, which provide social support in stressful times. And when combined with a sensation-seeking personality, the personal fable seems to contribute to adolescent risk taking by reducing teenagers' sense of vulnerability (Alberts, Elkind, & Ginsberg, 2007). Young people with high personal-fable and sensation-seeking scores tend to take more sexual risks, more often use drugs, and commit more delinquent acts than their agemates (Greene et al., 2000).

Idealism and Criticism Because abstract thinking permits adolescents to think about possibilities, it opens up the world of the ideal. Teenagers can imagine alternative family, religious, political, and moral systems, and they want to explore them. They often construct grand visions of a world with no injustice, discrimination, or tasteless behavior. The disparity between teenagers' idealism and adults' more realistic view creates tension between parent and child. Envisioning a perfect family against which their parents and siblings fall short, adolescents become fault-finding critics.

Overall, however, teenage idealism and criticism are advantageous. Once adolescents come to see other people as having both strengths and weaknesses, they are better able to work for social change and to form positive, lasting relationships (Elkind, 1994).

Decision Making Adolescents handle many cognitive tasks more effectively than they did when younger. But recall from Chapter 5 that changes in the brain's emotional/social network outpace development of the prefrontal cortex's cognitive-control network. Consequently, teenagers perform less well than adults in planning and decision making, where they must inhibit emotion and impulses in favor of thinking rationally.

Good decision making involves: (1) identifying pros and cons of each alternative, (2) assessing the likelihood of various outcomes, (3) evaluating one's choice in terms of whether one's goals were met, and, if not, (4) learning from the mistake and making a better future decision. When researchers modified a card game to trigger strong emotion by introducing immediate feedback about gains and losses after each choice, teenagers behaved more irrationally, taking far greater risks than adults in their twenties (Figner et al., 2009). In a second condition, in which players were merely asked what they would do at each step of the game but were not given feedback, adolescents and adults did not differ in quality of decision making. Additional evidence confirms that adolescents, relative to adults, are more influenced by the possibility of immediate reward—more willing to take risks and less likely to avoid potential harm (Cauffman et al., 2010; Ernst & Spear, 2009; Steinberg et al., 2009).

Nevertheless, other research indicates that teenagers are less effective than adults at decision making even under "cool," unemotional conditions (Huizenga, Crone, & Jansen, 2007). In one study, participants were given challenging hypothetical real-world dilemmas—whether to have cosmetic surgery, which parent to live with after divorce—and asked to explain how they would decide. Adults outperformed adolescents, more often considering alternatives, weighing benefits and risks, and suggesting advice seeking, especially in areas (such as medical decisions) where they had little experience (Halpern-Felsher & Cauffman, 2001).

Furthermore, in making decisions, adolescents, more often than adults (who also have difficulty), fall back on well-learned intuitive judgments (Jacobs & Klaczynski, 2002). Consider a hypothetical problem requiring a choice, on the basis of two arguments, between taking a traditional lecture class and taking a computer-based class. One argument contains large-sample information: course evaluations from 150 students, 85 percent of whom liked the computer class. The other argument contains small-sample personal reports: complaints of two honor-roll students who both hated the computer class and enjoyed the traditional class. Many adolescents, even though they knew that selecting the large-sample argument was "more intelligent," still based their choice on the small-sample argument, which resembled the informal opinions they depend on in everyday life (Klaczynski, 2001).

In sum, the heat of the moment, when making a good decision depends on inhibiting "feel-good" behavior and the appeal of immediate rewards, the brain's emotional/social network tends to prevail, and adolescents are far more likely than adults to emphasize short-term over long-term goals. In Chapter 5, we also noted that processing skills governed by the prefrontal cognitive-control system develop gradually, into the early twenties. Like other aspects of brain development, the cognitive-control system is affected by experience (Kuhn, 2009). As "first-timers" in many situations, adolescents do not have sufficient knowledge to consider pros and cons and predict likely outcomes. After engaging in risky behavior without negative consequences, teenagers rate its benefits higher and its risks lower than peers who have not tried it (Halpern-Felsher et al., 2004).

Over time, young people learn from their successes and failures, gather information from others about factors that affect decision making, and reflect on the decision-making process (Byrnes, 2003; Reyna & Farley, 2006). But because engaging in risk taking without experiencing harm can heighten adolescents' sense of invulnerability, they need supervision and protection from high-risk experiences until their decision making improves.

Follow-Up Research on Formal Operational Thought

Research on formal operational thought poses questions similar to those we discussed with respect to Piaget's earlier stages: Does formal operational thinking appear earlier than Piaget expected? Do all individuals reach formal operations during their teenage years?

Are Children Capable of Hypothetico-Deductive and Propositional Thinking?

School-age children show the glimmerings of hypothetico-deductive reasoning. In simplified situations involving no more than two possible causal variables, 6-year-olds understand that hypotheses must be confirmed by appropriate evidence. They also realize that once a hypothesis is supported, it shapes predictions about what might happen in the future (Ruffman et al., 1993). But school-age children cannot sort out evidence that bears on three or more variables at once. And as we will see when we take up information-processing research on scientific reasoning in Chapter 7, children have difficulty explaining why a pattern of observations supports a hypothesis, even when they recognize the connection between the two.

With respect to propositional thought, when a simple set of premises defies real-world knowledge ("All cats bark. Rex is a cat. Does Rex bark?"), 4- to 6-year-olds can reason logically in make-believe play. In justifying their answer, they are likely to say, "We can pretend cats bark!" (Dias & Harris, 1988, 1990). But in an entirely verbal mode, children have great difficulty reasoning from premises that contradict reality or their own beliefs.

Consider this set of statements: "If dogs are bigger than elephants and elephants are bigger than mice, then dogs are bigger than mice." Children younger than age 10 judge this reasoning to be false because not all of the relations specified occur in real life (Moshman & Franks, 1986; Pillow, 2002). They have more trouble than adolescents inhibiting activation of well-learned knowledge ("Elephants are larger than dogs") that impedes effective reasoning (Klaczynski, Schuneman, & Daniel, 2004; Simoneau & Markovits, 2003). Partly for this reason, they fail to grasp the **logical necessity** of propositional thought—that the accuracy of conclusions drawn from premises rests on the rules of logic, not on real-world confirmation.

Furthermore, in reasoning with propositions, school-age children rarely think carefully about the major premise and, therefore, violate the most basic rules of logic (Markovits, Schleifer, & Fortier, 1989). For example, when given the following problem, they almost always draw an incorrect conclusion:

> *Major premise:* If Susan hits a tambourine, then she will make a noise.
> *Second premise:* Suppose that Susan does not hit a tambourine.
> *Question:* Did Susan make a noise?
> *Wrong conclusion:* No, Susan did not make a noise.

Notice that the major premise did *not* state that Susan makes a noise *if, and only if,* she hits a tambourine. Adolescents generally detect that Susan could make noise in other ways, partly because they are better at searching their knowledge for examples that contradict wrong conclusions (Klaczynski, 2004; Markovits & Barrouillet, 2002).

As with hypothetico-deductive reasoning, in early adolescence young people become better at analyzing the *logic* of propositions, regardless of their *content.* And as they get older, they handle problems requiring increasingly complex mental operations. In justifying their reasoning, they move from giving a concrete example ("She could have hit a drum instead of a tambourine") to explaining the logical rules on which it is based ("We can be certain that Susan did not hit a tambourine. But we cannot be certain that Susan did not make a noise; she might have done so in many other ways") (Müller, Overton, & Reese, 2001; Venet & Markovits, 2001). These capacities, however, do not appear suddenly at puberty. Rather, gains occur gradually from childhood on—findings that call into question the emergence of a new stage of cognitive development at adolescence (Kuhn, 2009; Moshman, 2005).

Do All Individuals Reach the Formal Operational Stage? TAKE A MOMENT...

Try giving one or two of the formal operational tasks just described to your friends. How well do they do? Even well-educated adults often have difficulty (Kuhn, 2009; Markovits & Vachon, 1990)!

Why are so many adults not fully formal operational? One reason is that people are most likely to think abstractly and systematically on tasks in which they have had extensive guidance and practice in using such reasoning. This conclusion is supported by evidence that taking college courses leads to improvements in formal reasoning related to course content. Math and science prompt gains in propositional thought, social science in methodological and statistical reasoning (Lehman & Nisbett, 1990). Like concrete reasoning in children, formal operations do not emerge in all contexts at once but are specific to situation and task (Keating, 2004).

Individuals in tribal and village societies rarely do well on tasks typically used to assess formal operational reasoning (Cole, 1990). For example, people in nonliterate societies often refuse requests to engage in propositional thought. Take this hypothetical proposition: "In the North, where there is snow, all bears are white. Novaya Zemlya is in the Far North, and it always has snow. What color are the bears there?" In response, a Central Asian peasant explains that he must see the event to discern its logical implications. Yet the peasant uses

These adolescents of Indonesia's highland rainforests would probably have difficulty with Piaget's formal operational tasks. But in familiar situations, they exhibit complex reasoning, coordinating multiple variables as they construct a tree house.

© ANDERS RYMAN/CORBIS

propositions to defend his point of view: "*If* a man . . . had seen a white bear and had told about it, [*then*] he could be believed, *but* I've never seen one and *hence* I can't say" (Luria, 1976, pp. 108–109). Although he rarely displays it in everyday life, the peasant is clearly capable of formal operational thought!

Piaget acknowledged that without the opportunity to solve hypothetical problems, people in some societies might not display formal operations. Still, researchers ask, Does formal operational thinking result largely from children's and adolescents' independent efforts to make sense of their world, as Piaget claimed? Or is it a culturally transmitted way of thinking that is specific to literate societies and is taught in school? In an Israeli study of seventh to ninth graders, after controlling for participants' age, researchers found that years of schooling fully accounted for early adolescent gains in propositional thought (Artman, Cahan, & Avni-Babad, 2006). School tasks, the investigators speculated, provide crucial experiences in setting aside the "if . . . then" logic of everyday conversations that is often used to convey intentions, promises, and threats ("If you don't do your chores, then you won't get your allowance") but that conflicts with the logic of academic reasoning. In school, then, adolescents encounter rich opportunities to realize their neurological potential to think more effectively.

ASK YOURSELF

Review ■ Describe research findings that challenge Piaget's notion of a new stage of cognitive development at adolescence.

Connect ■ How does evidence on adolescent decision making help us understand teenagers' risk taking in sexual activity and drug use?

Apply ■ Clarissa, age 14, is convinced that no one appreciates how hurt she feels at not being invited to the homecoming dance. Meanwhile, 15-year-old Justine, alone in her room,

pantomimes being sworn in as student body president with her awestruck parents, teachers, and peers looking on. Which aspect of the personal fable is each girl displaying? Which girl is more likely to be well-adjusted, which poorly adjusted? Explain.

Reflect ■ Cite examples of your own idealistic thinking or poor decision making as a teenager. How has your thinking changed?

Piaget and Education

▶ Describe educational implications of Piaget's theory.

Three educational principles derived from Piaget's theory continue to influence teacher training and classroom practices, especially during early childhood:

- *Discovery learning.* In a Piagetian classroom, children are encouraged to discover for themselves through spontaneous interaction with the environment. Instead of presenting ready-made knowledge verbally, teachers provide a rich variety of activities designed to promote exploration and discovery, including art, puzzles, table games, dress-up clothing, building blocks, books, measuring tools, natural science tasks, and musical instruments.

- *Sensitivity to children's readiness to learn.* In a Piagetian classroom, teachers introduce activities that build on children's current thinking, challenging their incorrect ways of viewing the world. But they do not try to speed up development by imposing new skills before children indicate they are interested and ready.

- *Acceptance of individual differences.* Piaget's theory assumes that all children go through the same sequence of development, but at different rates. Therefore, teachers must plan activities for individual children and small groups, not just for the whole class. In addition, teachers evaluate educational progress in relation to the child's previous development, rather than on the basis of normative standards, or average performance of same-age peers.

Like his stages, educational applications of Piaget's theory have met with criticism, especially his insistence that young children learn mainly through acting on the environment and his neglect of other important avenues, such as verbal teaching and corrective feedback (Brainerd, 2003). Nevertheless, Piaget's influence on education has been powerful. He gave teachers new ways to observe, understand, and enhance young children's development and offered strong theoretical justification for child-oriented approaches to teaching.

▶ Summarize contributions and shortcomings of Piaget's theory.

Overall Evaluation of Piaget's Theory

Piaget's contributions to the field of child development are greater than those of any other theorist. He awakened psychologists and educators to a view of children as curious knowledge seekers who contribute actively to their own development. And his pioneering efforts to both describe and explain development inspired the current focus on *mechanisms of cognitive change*—precise accounts of biological, psychological, and environmental factors that lead children to modify their thinking, which we will encounter in Chapter 7 (McClelland & Siegler, 2001). Finally, Piaget's theory offers a useful "road map" of development that is accurate in many respects, though incorrect in others. His cognitive milestones remain powerful aids to understanding emotional, social, and moral development.

Nevertheless, the wealth of research that Piaget's theory inspired has uncovered weaknesses in his theory. Let's consider two major challenges posed by his critics.

Is Piaget's Account of Cognitive Change Clear and Accurate?

Piaget's explanation of cognitive change focuses on broad transformations in thinking through equilibration and its attendant processes of adaptation and organization. But exactly what the child does to equilibrate is vague. Recall our description of *organization*—that the structures of each stage form a coherent whole. Piaget was not explicit about how the diverse achievements of each stage are bound together by a single, underlying form of thought—and efforts to confirm this coherence have not succeeded. On a variety of tasks, infants and young children appear more competent, and adolescents and adults less competent, than Piaget assumed. Today, researchers agree that the child's efforts to assimilate, accommodate, and reorganize structures cannot adequately explain these patterns of change.

Furthermore, Piaget's belief that infants and young children must act on the environment to revise their thinking is too narrow a notion of how learning takes place. We have seen that as early as 2 to 3 months, babies group objects into categories and have some awareness of hidden objects—findings inconsistent with manual activity as the principal means of cognitive change (Johnson, 2010). And without explicit adult teaching, including verbal explanations, children may not always notice or come to understand aspects of a situation necessary for building more effective schemes. With its overemphasis on the child's initiative, Piaget's theory has been of limited practical value in devising teaching strategies that foster children's optimum learning.

Piaget believed that young children learn mainly by acting on the environment, but adult teaching is also essential. In this hands-on science lesson, children look to their teacher for guidance.

Does Cognitive Development Take Place in Stages?

We have seen that many cognitive changes proceed slowly and gradually. Also, periods of cognitive equilibrium are rare. Instead, children are constantly modifying structures and acquiring new skills. Today, virtually all experts agree that children's cognition is less broadly stagelike than Piaget believed (Bjorklund, 2012). Furthermore, contemporary researchers disagree on how general or specific cognitive development actually is.

Some theorists agree with Piaget that development is a *general process,* following a similar course across the diverse cognitive domains of physical, numerical, and social knowledge. But they reject the existence of stages, believing instead that thought processes are alike at all ages—just present to a greater or lesser extent—and that variations in children's knowledge and experience largely account for uneven performance across domains. These assumptions form the basis of the *information-processing perspective,* discussed in Chapter 7.

Other researchers think that the stage notion is valid but that it must be modified. They point to strong evidence for certain stagelike changes, such as the flourishing of representation around age 2 and the move toward abstract, systematic thinking in adolescence. Yet they also recognize many smaller developments that lead up to these transformations. In Chapter 7, we will consider a *neo-Piagetian perspective* that combines Piaget's stage approach with information-processing ideas (Case, 1996, 1998; Halford, 2002; Halford & Andrews, 2006). In this view, Piaget's strict definition of stage is modified into a less tightly knit concept, in which related competencies develop over an extended period, depending on brain development and specific experiences.

Still others deny not only Piaget's stages but also his belief that the human mind is made up of general reasoning abilities that can be applied to any cognitive task. They argue that the remarkable competencies of infants and young children indicate that cognitive development begins with far more than sensorimotor reflexes. Rather, infants come into the world with several basic, built-in types of knowledge, each of which jump-starts vital aspects of cognition. We will take up this *core knowledge* perspective in the next section.

Piaget's Legacy

Although Piaget's description of development is no longer fully accepted, researchers are far from consensus on how to modify or replace it. Some have begun to search for points of contact among the alternative perspectives just mentioned. Others blend Piaget's emphasis on the child as an active agent with a stronger role for context—the objects, events, and people in children's lives. For example, followers of Vygotsky's theory are intensively studying social and cultural influences on children's thinking—an area Piaget neglected.

Diverse theories and lines of investigation leave research into children's thinking far more fragmented today than several decades ago, when Piaget's theory held sway. Nevertheless, researchers continue to draw inspiration from Piaget's vision of the child as an active, constructive learner and his lifelong quest to understand how children acquire new capacities. Piaget's findings have served as the starting point for virtually every major contemporary line of research on cognitive development.

A S K   Y O U R S E L F

Review ■ Cite examples of findings that have led contemporary researchers to challenge Piaget's account of cognitive change.

Connect ■ How are educational principles derived from Piaget's theory consistent with his emphasis on an active child who takes responsibility for her own learning?

Reflect ■ Which aspects of Piaget's theory do you accept? Which do you doubt? Explain, citing research evidence.

The Core Knowledge Perspective

According to the **core knowledge perspective,** infants begin life with innate, special-purpose knowledge systems referred to as *core domains of thought.* Each of these "prewired" understandings permits a ready grasp of new, related information and therefore supports early, rapid development of certain aspects of cognition. Each core domain has a long evolutionary history and is essential for survival (Carey & Markman, 1999; Leslie, 2004; Spelke,

▶ Explain the core knowledge perspective on cognitive development, noting research that supports its assumptions.

▶ What are the strengths and limitations of the core knowledge perspective?

2004; Spelke & Kinzler, 2007). Core knowledge theorists argue that infants could not make sense of the multifaceted stimulation around them without having been genetically "set up" in the course of evolution to comprehend its crucial aspects.

Two core domains have been studied extensively in infancy. The first is *physical knowledge*—in particular, understanding of objects and their effects on one another. The second is *numerical knowledge*—the capacity to keep track of multiple objects and to add and subtract small quantities. Physical and numerical knowledge enabled our ancestors to secure food and other resources from the environment.

The core knowledge perspective asserts that an inherited foundation makes possible remarkably advanced knowledge systems early in development. In Chapter 9, we will consider a nativist (or inborn) view of preschoolers' amazing language skill that regards *linguistic knowledge* as etched into the structure of the human brain. Furthermore, infants' early orientation toward people (see Chapter 4) provides the foundation for rapid development of *psychological knowledge*—in particular, understanding of people as agents who have mental states (such as emotions, intentions, desires, beliefs, and perspectives) that influence their behavior, which is vital for surviving in human groups. And young children demonstrate impressive *biological knowledge,* including ideas about inheritance of characteristics and about bodily processes, such as birth, growth, illness, and death.

Rather than regarding development as a general process, core knowledge theorists see it as *domain-specific* and uneven, with each core domain developing independently. And although initial knowledge is assumed to be innate, that knowledge becomes more elaborate as children explore, play, and interact with others (Geary & Bjorklund, 2000; Leslie, 2004; Spelke & Kinzler, 2007). Children are viewed as *naïve theorists,* building on core knowledge concepts to explain their everyday experiences in the physical, psychological, and biological realms. Let's examine a sampling of findings that shed light on the existence of core domains of thought.

Infancy: Physical and Numerical Knowledge

Do infants display impressive physical and numerical understandings so early that some knowledge must be innate? Again, the violation-of-expectation method has been used to answer this question. Besides research on early awareness of object permanence (see page 231), core knowledge theorists point to evidence indicating that young infants are aware of basic object properties and that they build on this knowledge quickly, acquiring more detailed understandings as they are exposed to relevant outcomes in their everyday experiences (Baillargeon, 2004; Baillargeon et al., 2009; Luo & Baillargeon, 2005).

For example, 2½-month-olds seem to recognize that one solid object cannot move through another solid object. In one study, some infants saw an object lowered into a container with an opening, whereas others saw an object lowered into a container with no opening (see Figure 6.15). Babies in the closed-container condition looked longer, suggesting that this impossible event violated their notions of physical reality (Hespos & Baillargeon, 2001). By 6½ months, infants look longer when an object much wider than an opening appears to pass through that opening than they do at an appropriately sized object passing through (Aguiar & Baillargeon, 2003). Around 7½ months, infants spend more time looking at an object too tall to fit inside a container that disappears into the container than they do at an object that is the right height (Hespos & Baillargeon, 2001, 2006). And at 9½ months, they expect an object placed inside a transparent container to be visible through that container (Baillargeon et al., 2009).

Furthermore, in the first half-year, infants are sensitive to basic principles of object support. Babies as young as 4½ months stare intently at a box resting in midair, with nothing to hold it in place (Needham & Baillargeon, 1993). And 6½-month-olds' attention increases and their reaching behavior decreases when an object is placed on top of another object with most of its bottom surface not in contact with the lower object—conditions that would cause the top object to fall (Baillargeon, 1994; Hespos & Baillargeon, 2008). Around 8 months, infants are sensitive to position of contact: When a large, oblong box rests horizontally on a small, square box, babies expect the large box to be centered over the small box so it is adequately supported (Huettel & Needham, 2000).

FIGURE 6.15 **Testing infants for understanding of object solidity using the violation-of-expectation method.** Infants in the *expected event: open-container condition* saw a tall object and a tall container standing a short distance apart. An adult's right hand grasped a knob attached to the top of the object, while her left hand rotated the container forward so infants could see its opening. After a few seconds, the container was returned to its original position. Then the right hand lifted the object and lowered it into the container. Finally, the hand lifted the object out of the container and set it down. Infants in the *unexpected event: closed-container condition* saw the same event, with one exception: The container's top was closed, so it should have been impossible for the object to be lowered into the container. (In fact, the container had a false, magnetic top that adhered to the bottom of the object, which could be lowered into it.) Infants as young as 2½ months looked longer at the unexpected, closed-container event, suggesting awareness of object solidity. (Adapted from S. J. Hespos & R. Baillargeon, "Reasoning About Containment Events in Very Young Infants," *Cognition, 78,* p. 213. © Elsevier. Reprinted with permission.)

Research also suggests that young infants have basic number concepts (Spelke, 2004; Spelke & Kinzler, 2007). In the best-known study, 5-month-olds saw a screen raised to hide a single toy animal, then watched a hand place a second toy behind the screen. Finally the screen was removed to reveal either one or two toys. As Figure 6.16 on page 264 reveals, infants looked longer at the impossible, one-toy display, suggesting that they kept track of the two objects, which would require them to add one object to another. In additional experiments using this task, 5-month-olds looked longer at three objects than two. These findings and those of similar investigations suggest that babies can discriminate quantities up to three and use that knowledge to perform simple arithmetic—both addition and subtraction (in which two objects are covered and one object is removed) (Kobayashi et al., 2004; Kobayashi, Hiraki, & Hasegawa, 2005; Wynn, Bloom, & Chiang, 2002).

Other research shows that 6-month-olds can distinguish among large sets of items when the difference between those sets is very great—at least a factor of two. For example, they can tell the difference between 8 and 16 dots but not between 6 and 12 (Lipton & Spelke, 2004; Xu, Spelke, & Goddard, 2005). Six-month-olds can also discriminate ratios—for example, several scenes in which the ratio of blue pellets to yellow Pac-Men is 2 to 1 from several scenes in which the ratio is 4 to 1 (McCrink & Wynn, 2007). And like the experiment in Figure 6.16, 9-month-olds can perform operations on sets of items, adding and subtracting (McCrink & Wynn, 2004). As a result, some researchers believe that infants can represent approximate large-number values, in addition to small-number discriminations.

These impressive findings suggest that some notion of quantity is present in the first year. But like other violation-of-expectation results, they are controversial (Bremner, 2010). Critics question whether other aspects of object displays, rather than numerical sensitivity, are responsible for the findings (Cohen &

If another duck is added or one is taken away, will this baby know that the quantity has changed? Research suggests that young infants can discriminate quantities up to three and use that knowledge to perform simple addition and subtraction.

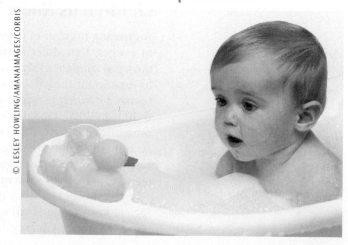

© LESLEY HOWLING/AMANAIMAGES/CORBIS

FIGURE 6.16 Testing infants for basic number concepts.
(a) First, infants saw a screen raised in front of a toy animal. Then an identical toy was added behind the screen. Next, the researchers presented two outcomes. (b) In the *expected outcome,* the screen dropped to reveal two toy animals. (c) In the *unexpected outcome,* the screen dropped to reveal one toy animal. Five-month-olds shown the unexpected outcome looked longer than 5-month-olds shown the expected outcome. The researchers concluded that infants can discriminate the quantities "one" and "two" and use that knowledge to perform simple addition: 1 + 1 = 2. A variation of this procedure suggested that 5-month-olds could also do simple subtraction: 2 − 1 = 1. (From K. Wynn, 1992, "Addition and Subtraction by Human Infants." Adapted with permission of Macmillan Publishers Ltd., *Nature, 358,* p. 749.)

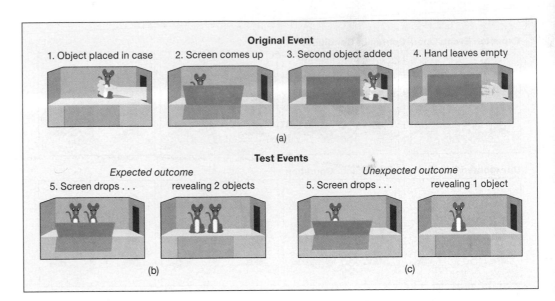

Marks, 2002; Langer, Gillette, & Arriaga, 2003; Mix, Huttenlocher, & Levine, 2002; Wakeley, Rivera, & Langer, 2000). According to these investigators, claims for infants' knowledge of number concepts are surprising, given other research indicating that before 14 to 16 months, toddlers have difficulty making less-than and greater-than comparisons between small sets. And as we will see in Chapter 7, not until the preschool years do children answer correctly when asked to add and subtract small sets of items.

Core knowledge theorists respond that infant looking behaviors may be a more reliable indicator of understanding than older children's verbal and motor behaviors, which may not always display their true competencies (Wynn, 2002). And ERP brain-wave recordings taken while babies view correct and incorrect solutions to simple arithmetic equations reveal a response pattern identical to the pattern adults show when they detect errors (Berger, Tzur, & Posner, 2006).

Finally, proponents of the core knowledge perspective point to studies of two peoples living in Brazil's remote Amazon regions, whose cultures have no verbal counting routines: the Piraha, who lack number words beyond "two" in their language; and the Munduruku, who have number words only up to "three." Despite this numerical language deprivation (which impedes learning about number through social communication), Piraha and Munduruku adults demonstrate primitive number knowledge that resembles findings on infants: They can accurately discriminate and compare numerical quantities only up to three (Gordon, 2004; Pica et al., 2004). Still, critics continue to argue that such knowledge is not built-in but, rather, constructed over an extended time period.

Children as Naïve Theorists

A growing number of researchers believe that children form naïve theories, or explanations of events, that differ among core domains. According to this **theory theory** (meaning *theory of children as theorists*), after children observe an event, they draw on innate concepts to explain, or theorize about, its cause. Then they test their naïve theory against experience, revising it when it cannot adequately account for new information (Gelman, 2003; Gelman & Kalish, 2006; Gopnik & Nazzi, 2003). These revisions often lead to stagelike changes—dramatic, qualitative shifts in the complexity of concepts and explanations. Although this account of cognitive change is similar to Piaget's, theory theorists claim that because children start with innate knowledge, their reasoning advances quickly, with sophisticated cause-and-effect explanations evident much earlier than Piaget proposed.

The most extensively investigated naïve theory is children's *theory of mind*—the psychological knowledge of self and others that forms rapidly during the first few years, which we will consider in Chapter 11. Preschoolers also have naïve physical and biological theories.

When researchers asked 3- and 4-year-olds to explain events that had either a psychological, a physical, or a biological cause, the children reasoned about each event in ways consistent with its core domain. For a child who pours orange juice instead of milk on his cereal, they offered mostly psychological explanations ("He *thought* it was milk"). But for a boy who tries to float in the air by jumping off a stool but falls, they gave mostly physical explanations ("He's too *heavy* to float"). And a girl who tries to hang from a tree branch "forever" but lets go elicited biological explanations ("Her arms got *hurting*"). In everyday conversation, too, preschoolers typically offer psychological, physical, and biological explanations that are linked appropriately to the behaviors of humans, animals, and objects (Hickling & Wellman, 2001; Wellman, Hickling, & Schultz, 1997).

Although young children are impressive theorists, their reasoning in different domains develops at different rates. Physical and psychological explanations are prevalent at age 2, probably because these understandings originate in infancy. But because grasping biological processes is difficult, young preschoolers frequently use psychological concepts to explain biological events (Carey, 1995, 1999; Inagaki & Hatano, 2002). For example, when asked whether they can tell a pain to go away or a heartbeat to stop, many 3-year-olds say yes!

In contrast, 4-year-olds know that they cannot control biological processes (Inagaki, 1997). And by age 6, children interpret biological processes, especially those of humans, in terms of a "life force" derived from food and water that enables living things to grow, energizes their activity, and prevents them from becoming ill. When asked what will happen if a child eats very little, they are likely to say, "If we don't eat food, we lose energy and die" (Inagaki & Hatano, 2004, p. 359). Nevertheless, psychological accounts of biological events persist into the early school years.

Biological knowledge emerges later in children from widely varying cultures, suggesting that unlike other core domains, it may have only a weak innate foundation. Alternatively, it may depend entirely on a lengthy process of construction based on experience. For example, when told stories about a child born to one parent and raised by another, not until ages 5 to 7 do North American and European children show knowledge of biological inheritance, consistently predicting that an adopted child will resemble her birth parents in physical characteristics (such as hair type and skin color) but resemble her adoptive parents in beliefs and skills (Gimenez & Harris, 2002; Solomon et al., 1996; Weissman & Kalish, 1999).

In some non-Western village societies, this distinction between the influence of biology and that of social learning on human traits is not attained until adolescence or adulthood (Bloch, Solomon, & Carey, 2001; Mahalingham, 1999). The Vezo of Madagascar hold certain folk beliefs that make it harder for their children to grasp biological inheritance—for example, that a pregnant mother who spends much time thinking about another person can cause her baby to look like that person! Because Vezo children do not go to school, they are not exposed to biology lessons that contradict such folk beliefs (Astuti, Solomon, & Carey, 2004). They must, instead, notice and gradually make sense of the fact that children and their biological parents resemble each other physically—a challenging task that is not mastered until ages 14 to 20.

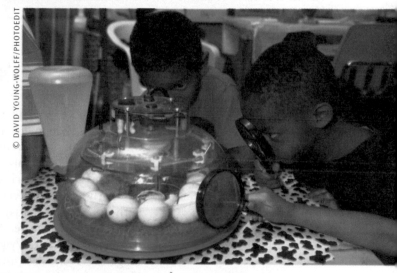

Preschoolers' biological reasoning develops slowly, suggesting no more than a weak innate foundation. But by age 6, children interpret biological processes—such as what makes these chicks hatch and grow—in terms of a "life force" energized by food and water.

Evaluation of the Core Knowledge Perspective

Core knowledge theorists offer a fascinating evolutionary account of why certain cognitive skills emerge early and develop rapidly. And more seriously than other perspectives, they have addressed the question, What allows learning to get off the ground? As a result, they have enriched our understanding of infants' and young children's thinking.

Nevertheless, critics take issue with the core knowledge assumption, based on violation-of-expectation evidence, that infants are endowed with *knowledge* (Bremner, 2010). And indisputable evidence for built-in core knowledge requires that it be demonstrated in all core domains in the absence of any relevant opportunities to learn—at birth or close to it

(Johnson, 2010). Currently, debate continues over just what babies start out with—domain-specific understandings or minimal perceptual biases that combine with powerful, general learning strategies to permit rapid discovery of various types of knowledge.

While emphasizing native endowment, the core knowledge perspective acknowledges that experience is essential for children to elaborate this initial knowledge. So far, however, it has not offered greater clarity than Piaget's theory about how heredity and environment jointly produce cognitive change. It does not tell us just what children do to revise their innate structures. And it says little about which experiences are most important in each domain and how those experiences advance children's thinking.

Finally, the core knowledge perspective, like Piaget's theory, views children as building more adequate structures largely through their own activity. It pays little attention to children's learning in interaction with others—the unique strength of Vygotsky's theory, which we take up next. Despite these limitations, the ingenious studies and provocative findings of core knowledge research have sharpened the field's focus on specifying the starting point for human cognition and carefully tracking the changes that build on it.

A S K   Y O U R S E L F

Review ■ What are core domains of thought? Cite examples of innate knowledge in the physical and numerical domains. Why do some researchers question the existence of innate knowledge?

Connect ■ Describe similarities and differences between Piaget's theory and the theory theory.

▶ Explain Vygotsky's view of cognitive development, noting the importance of social experience and language.

▶ According to Vygotsky, what is the role of make-believe play in cognitive development?

Vygotsky's Sociocultural Theory

Piaget's theory and the core knowledge perspective emphasize the biological side of cognitive development. Both identify the most important source of cognition as the child himself—a busy, self-motivated explorer who forms ideas and tests them against the world. Lev Vygotsky, while also viewing children as active seekers of knowledge, emphasized the profound effects of rich social and cultural contexts on their thinking.

Early events in Vygotsky's life contributed to his vision of human cognition as inherently social and language-based. As a university student, he was interested primarily in a verbal field—literature. After graduating, he first became a teacher and only later turned to psychology. Because Vygotsky died of tuberculosis at age 37, his theory is not as complete as Piaget's. Nevertheless, the field of child development has experienced a burst of interest in Vygotsky's sociocultural perspective. His appeal lies mainly in his rejection of an individualistic view of the developing child in favor of a socially formed mind (Bakhurst, 2007; Tudge & Scrimsher, 2003).

According to Vygotsky, infants are endowed with basic perceptual, attention, and memory capacities that they share with other animals. These develop during the first two years through direct contact with the environment. Then rapid growth of language leads to a profound change in thinking. It broadens preschoolers' participation in social dialogues with more knowledgeable individuals, who encourage them to master culturally important tasks. Soon young children start to communicate with themselves much as they converse with others. As a result, basic mental capacities are transformed into uniquely human, higher cognitive processes.

Children's Private Speech

TAKE A MOMENT... Watch preschoolers as they play and explore the environment, and you will see that they frequently talk out loud to themselves. For example, as a 4-year-old worked a puzzle at preschool one day, I heard him say, "Where's the red piece? I need the red one. Now a blue one. No, it doesn't fit. Try it here."

Piaget (1923/1926) called these utterances *egocentric speech,* reflecting his belief that young children have difficulty taking the perspectives of others. Their talk, he said, is often "talk for self" in which they express thoughts in whatever form they happen to occur, regardless of whether a listener can understand. Piaget believed that cognitive development and certain social experiences eventually bring an end to egocentric speech. Specifically, through disagreements with peers, children see that others hold viewpoints different from their own. As a result, egocentric speech declines in favor of social speech, in which children adapt what they say to their listeners.

Vygotsky (1934/1986) disagreed strongly with Piaget's conclusions. Because language helps children think about mental activities and behavior and select courses of action, Vygotsky saw it as the foundation for all higher cognitive processes, including controlled attention, deliberate memorization and recall, categorization, planning, problem solving, abstract reasoning, and self-reflection. In Vygotsky's view, children speak to themselves for self-guidance. As they get older and find tasks easier, their self-directed speech is internalized as silent, *inner speech*—the internal verbal dialogues we carry on while thinking and acting in everyday situations.

Over the past three decades, almost all studies have supported Vygotsky's perspective (Berk & Harris, 2003; Winsler, 2009). As a result, children's self-directed speech is now called **private speech** instead of egocentric speech. Children use more of it when tasks are appropriately challenging (neither too easy nor too hard), after they make errors, or when they are confused about how to proceed. Figure 6.17 shows how 5- and 6-year-olds' private speech increased as researchers made a problem-solving task moderately difficult, then decreased as the task became very difficult (Fernyhough & Fradley, 2005).

With age, as Vygotsky predicted, private speech goes underground, changing into whispers and silent lip movements. Furthermore, children who freely use self-guiding private speech during a challenging activity are more attentive and involved and show better task performance than their less talkative agemates (Al-Namlah, Fernyhough, & Meins, 2006; Lidstone, Meins, & Fernyhough, 2010; Winsler, Naglieri, & Manfra, 2006).

Finally, compared with their agemates, children with learning and behavior problems engage in higher rates of private speech over a longer period of development (Berk, 2001b; Ostad & Sorensen, 2007; Paladino, 2006; Winsler et al., 2007). They seem to use private speech to help compensate for impairments in attention and cognitive processing that make many tasks more difficult for them.

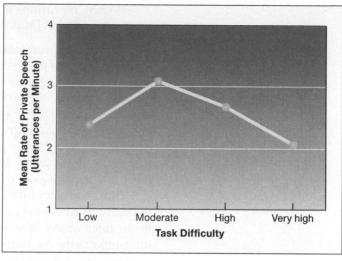

FIGURE 6.17 Relationship of private speech to task difficulty among 5- and 6-year-olds. Researchers increased the difficulty of a problem-solving task. Private speech rose as the task became moderately difficult, then declined as it became highly difficult. Children are more likely to use private speech for self-guidance when tasks are within their zone of proximal development, or range of mastery. (Adapted from Fernyhough & Fradley, 2005.)

Social Origins of Cognitive Development

Where does private speech come from? Vygotsky (1930–1935/1978) believed that children's learning takes place within the **zone of proximal development**—a range of tasks too difficult for the child to do alone but possible with the help of adults and more skilled peers. Consider the joint activity of 3-year-old Sammy and his mother as she helps him put together a difficult puzzle:

Sammy: I can't get this one in. [*Tries to insert a piece in the wrong place.*]
Mother: Which piece might go down here? [*Points to the bottom of the puzzle.*]
Sammy: His shoes. [*Looks for a piece resembling the clown's shoes but tries the wrong one.*]
Mother: Well, what piece looks like this shape? [*Points again to the bottom of the puzzle.*]
Sammy: The brown one. [*Tries it, and it fits; then attempts another piece and looks at his mother.*]

Private speech helps this preschooler explore possibilities in a handful of bubbles. As Vygotsky theorized, children use self-directed speech to guide their thinking and behavior.

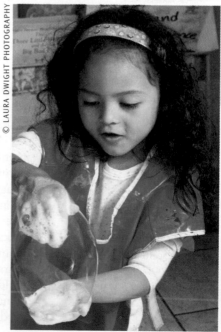

© LAURA DWIGHT PHOTOGRAPHY

Mother: Try turning it just a little. [*Gestures to show him.*]

Sammy: There! [*Puts in several more pieces while his mother watches.*]

By questioning, prompting, and suggesting strategies, Sammy's mother keeps the puzzle within his zone of proximal development, at a manageable level of difficulty.

To promote cognitive development, social interaction must have certain features. One is **intersubjectivity,** the process whereby two participants who begin a task with different understandings arrive at a shared understanding (Newson & Newson, 1975). Intersubjectivity creates a common ground for communication, as each partner adjusts to the other's perspective. Adults try to promote it when they translate their own insights in ways that are within the child's grasp. As the child stretches to understand the adult, she is drawn into a more mature approach to the situation.

The capacity for intersubjectivity is present early, in parent–infant mutual gaze, exchange of vocal and emotional signals, imitation, and joint play with objects, and in toddlers' capacity to infer others' intentions (Csibra, 2010; Feldman, 2007c). Later, language facilitates intersubjectivity. As conversational skills improve, preschoolers increasingly seek others' help and direct that assistance to ensure that it is beneficial. Between ages 3 and 5, children strive for intersubjectivity in dialogues with peers, as when they affirm a playmate's message, add new ideas, and contribute to ongoing play to sustain it. They may say, "I think [this way]. What do you think?"—evidence for a willingness to share viewpoints (Berk, 2001a). In these ways, children create zones of proximal development for one another.

A second important feature of social interaction is **scaffolding**—adjusting the support offered during a teaching session to fit the child's current level of performance. When the child has little notion of how to proceed, the adult uses direct instruction, breaking the task into manageable units, suggesting strategies, and offering rationales for using them. As the child's competence increases, effective scaffolders—like Sammy's mother—gradually and sensitively withdraw support, turning over responsibility to the child. Then children take the language of these dialogues, make it part of their private speech, and use this speech to organize their independent efforts.

Scaffolding captures the form of teaching interaction that occurs as children work on school or school-like tasks, such as puzzles, model building, picture matching, and (later) academic assignments. It may not apply to other contexts that are equally vital for cognitive development—for example, play or everyday activities, during which adults usually support children's efforts without deliberately teaching. To encompass children's diverse opportunities to learn through involvement with others, Barbara Rogoff (1998, 2003) suggests the term **guided participation,** a broader concept than scaffolding. It refers to shared endeavors between more expert and less expert participants, without specifying the precise features of communication. Consequently, it allows for variations across situations and cultures.

What evidence supports Vygotsky's ideas on the social origins of cognitive development? A wealth of research indicates that when adults promote intersubjectivity by being stimulating, responsive, and supportive, they foster many competencies—attention, language, complex play, and understanding of others' perspectives (Bornstein et al., 1992; Charman et al., 2001; Morales et al., 2000). Furthermore, children whose parents are effective scaffolders use more private speech, are more successful when attempting difficult tasks on their own, and are advanced in overall cognitive development (Berk & Spuhl, 1995; Conner & Cross, 2003; Mulvaney et al., 2006). Among Caucasian-American parent–child pairs, adult cognitive support—teaching in small steps and offering strategies—predicts children's mature thinking and academic competence (Stright et al., 2001). And adult emotional support—offering encouragement and transferring responsibility to the child—predicts children's effort (Neitzel & Stright, 2003).

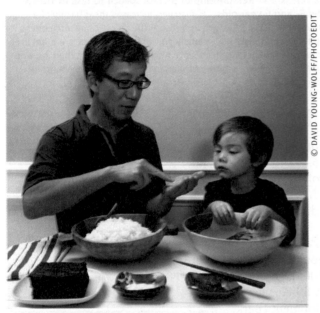

© DAVID YOUNG-WOLFF/PHOTOEDIT

A father engages in scaffolding by breaking the task of preparing rice balls into manageable units, suggesting strategies, and gradually turning over responsibility to the child.

LOOK and LISTEN

Ask a preschooler to join you in working a difficult puzzle or other challenging task. How did you scaffold the child's progress? Did the child display any self-guiding private speech?

Nevertheless, effective scaffolding can take different forms in different cultures. In an investigation of Hmong families who had emigrated from Southeast Asia to the United States, once again, parental cognitive support was associated with children's advanced reasoning skills. But unlike Caucasian-American parents, who emphasize independence by encouraging their children to think of ways to approach a task, Hmong parents—who highly value interdependence and child obedience—frequently tell their children what to do (for example, "put this block piece here, then this piece on top of it") (Stright, Herr, & Neitzel, 2009). Among Caucasian-American children, such directive scaffolding is associated with kindergartners' lack of self-control and behavior problems (Neitzel & Stright, 2003). Among the Hmong children, however, it predicted favorable kindergarten adjustment—capacity to follow rules, be organized, and finish assignments.

Vygotsky's View of Make-Believe Play

In accord with his emphasis on social experience and language as vital forces in cognitive development, Vygotsky (1933/1978) regarded make-believe play as a unique, broadly influential zone of proximal development in which *children advance themselves* as they try out a wide variety of challenging skills. In Vygotsky's theory, make-believe is the central source of development during the preschool years, leading development forward in two ways.

First, as children create imaginary situations, they learn to act in accord with internal ideas, not just in response to external stimuli. While pretending, children continually use one object to stand for another—a stick for a horse, a folded blanket for a sleeping baby—and, in doing so, change the object's usual meaning. Gradually they realize that thinking (or the meaning of words) is separate from objects and that ideas can be used to guide behavior.

Second, the rule-based nature of make-believe strengthens children's capacity to think before they act. Pretend play, Vygotsky pointed out, constantly demands that children act against their impulses because they must follow the rules of the play scene. For example, a child pretending to go to sleep obeys the rules of bedtime behavior. A child imagining himself as a father and a doll as his child conforms to the rules of parental behavior (Bodrova & Leong, 2007). Through enacting rules in make-believe, children better understand social norms and expectations and strive to follow them.

Much evidence fits with Vygotsky's conclusion that make-believe play serves as a zone of proximal development, supporting many competencies. Turn back to pages 240–241 to review evidence that make-believe enhances a diverse array of cognitive and social skills. Pretending is also rich in private speech—a finding that supports its role in helping children bring action under the control of thought (Krafft & Berk, 1998). And preschoolers who spend more time engaged in sociodramatic play are better at following classroom rules and regulating their emotions and behavior (Berk, Mann, & Ogan, 2006; Lemche et al., 2003).

Finally, Vygotsky questioned Piaget's belief that make-believe arises spontaneously in the second year of life. Vygotsky argued that, like other higher cognitive processes, the elaborate pretending of the preschool years has social origins. Research reviewed in the Cultural Influences box on page 270 supports the view that children learn to pretend under the guidance of experts.

Vygotsky and Education

▶ Describe educational implications of Vygotsky's theory.

Vygotsky's theory offers new visions of teaching and learning—ones that emphasize the importance of social context and collaboration. Like Piagetian classrooms, Vygotskian classrooms accept individual differences and provide opportunities for children's active participation. But a Vygotskian classroom goes beyond independent discovery to promote *assisted discovery*. Teachers guide children's learning with explanations, demonstrations, and verbal prompts, tailoring their interventions to each child's zone of proximal development. Assisted discovery is aided by *peer collaboration,* as children work in groups, teaching and helping one another.

CULTURAL INFLUENCES

Social Origins of Make-Believe Play

One of the activities my husband, Ken, used to do with our two sons when they were young was to bake pineapple upside-down cake, a favorite treat. One day as a cake was in the making, 21-month-old Peter stood on a chair at the kitchen sink, busily pouring water from one cup to another.

"He's in the way, Dad!" complained 4-year-old David, trying to pull Peter away from the sink.

"Maybe if we let him help, he'll give us some room," Ken suggested. As David stirred the batter, Ken poured some into a small bowl for Peter, moved his chair to the side of the sink, and handed him a spoon.

"Here's how you do it, Petey," instructed David, with a superior air. Peter watched David stir, then tried to copy his motion. When it was time to pour the batter, Ken helped Peter hold and tip the small bowl.

"Time to bake it," said Ken.

"Bake it, bake it," repeated Peter, watching Ken slip the pan into the oven.

Several hours later, we observed one of Peter's earliest instances of make-believe play. He got his pail from the sandbox and, after filling it with a handful of sand, carried it into the kitchen and set it on the floor in front of the oven. "Bake it, bake it," Peter called to Ken. Together, father and son placed the pretend cake in the oven.

Piaget and his followers concluded that toddlers discover make-believe independently, once they are capable of representational schemes. Vygotsky challenged this view, pointing out that society provides children with opportunities to represent culturally meaningful activities in play. Make-believe, like other complex mental activities, is first learned under the guidance of experts. In the example just described, Peter extended his capacity to represent daily events when Ken drew him into the baking task and helped him act it out in play.

Current evidence supports the idea that early make-believe is the combined result of children's readiness to engage in it and social experiences that promote it. In one observational study of U.S. middle-class toddlers, 75 to 80 percent of make-believe involved mother–child interaction (Haight & Miller, 1993). At 12 months, almost all play episodes were initiated by mothers. But by the end of the second year, half of pretend episodes were initiated by each.

During make-believe, mothers offer toddlers a rich array of cues that signal they are pretending—looking and smiling at the child more, making more exaggerated movements, and using more "we" talk (acknowledging that pretending is a joint endeavor) than they do during the same real-life event (Lillard, 2007). These maternal cues encourage toddlers to join in and probably facilitate their ability to distinguish pretend from real acts, which strengthens over the second and third years (Lillard & Witherington, 2004; Ma & Lillard, 2006).

Also, when adults participate, toddlers' make-believe is more elaborate (Keren et al., 2005). They are more likely to combine pretend acts into complex sequences, as Peter did when he put the sand in the bucket ("making the batter"), carried it into the kitchen, and (with Ken's help) put it in the oven ("baking the cake"). The more parents pretend with their toddlers, the more time their children devote to make-believe.

In some cultures, such as those of Indonesia and Mexico, where extended-family households and sibling caregiving are common, make-believe is more frequent and complex with older siblings than with mothers. As early as age 3 to 4, children provide rich, challenging stimulation to their younger brothers and sisters, take these teaching responsibilities seriously, and, with age, become better at them (Zukow-Goldring, 2002). In a study of Zinacanteco Indian children of southern Mexico, by age 8, sibling teachers were highly skilled at showing 2-year-olds how to play at everyday tasks, such as washing and cooking (Maynard, 2002). They often guided toddlers verbally and physically through the task and provided feedback.

A Kenyan child guides his younger brother in pretend play. In cultures where sibling caregiving is common, make-believe with older siblings is more frequent and complex than with mothers.

In Western middle-class families, older siblings less often teach deliberately but still serve as influential models of playful behavior. In a study of New Zealand families of Western European descent, when both a parent and an older sibling were available, toddlers more often imitated the actions of the sibling, especially when siblings engaged in make-believe (Barr & Hayne, 2003).

Make-believe play is a major means through which children extend their cognitive skills and learn about important activities in their culture. Vygotsky's theory, and the findings that support it, tell us that providing a stimulating environment is not enough to promote early cognitive development. In addition, toddlers must be invited and encouraged by more skilled members of their culture to participate in the social world around them. Parents and teachers can enhance early make-believe by playing often with toddlers, guiding and elaborating their make-believe themes.

Vygotsky's educational message for the preschool years is to provide socially rich, meaningful activities in children's zones of proximal development and a wealth of opportunities for make-believe play—the ultimate means of fostering the self-discipline required for later academic learning. Once formal schooling begins, Vygotsky emphasized literacy activities (Scrimsher & Tudge, 2003). As children talk about literature, mathematics, science, and social studies, their teachers inform, correct, and ask them to explain. As a result, children reflect on their own thought processes and shift to a higher level of cognitive activity in which they think about how to symbolize ideas in socially useful ways. Gradually they become proficient in manipulating and controlling the symbol systems of their culture.

Let's look at two Vygotsky-based educational innovations, each of which incorporates assisted discovery and peer collaboration.

Reciprocal Teaching

Originally designed to improve reading comprehension in poorly achieving students, this teaching method has been extended to other subjects and all schoolchildren. In **reciprocal teaching,** a teacher and two to four students form a collaborative group and take turns leading dialogues on the content of a text passage. Within the dialogues, group members apply four cognitive strategies: questioning, summarizing, clarifying, and predicting.

The dialogue leader (at first a teacher, later a student) begins by *asking questions* about the content of the text passage. Students offer answers, raise additional questions, and, in case of disagreement, reread the original text. Next, the leader *summarizes* the passage, and children discuss the summary and *clarify* unfamiliar ideas. Finally, the leader encourages students to *predict* upcoming content based on clues in the passage.

Elementary and middle school students exposed to reciprocal teaching show impressive gains in reading comprehension compared to controls taught in other ways (Rosenshine & Meister, 1994; Sporer, Brunstein, & Kieschke, 2009; Takala, 2006). Notice how reciprocal teaching creates a zone of proximal development in which children gradually learn to scaffold one another's progress and assume more responsibility for comprehending text passages. Also, by collaborating with others, children forge group expectations for high-level thinking and acquire skills vital for learning and success in everyday life.

Cooperative Learning

Although reciprocal teaching uses peer collaboration, a teacher guides it, helping to ensure its success. According to Vygotsky, more expert peers can also spur children's development, as long as they adjust the help they provide to fit the less mature child's zone of proximal development. Recall that Piaget, too, thought that peer interaction could contribute to cognitive change. He asserted that peers' clashing viewpoints—arguments jarring the child into noticing an agemate's viewpoint—were necessary for peer interaction to foster logical thought.

Today, peer collaboration is widely used, but evidence is mounting that it promotes development only under certain conditions. A crucial factor is **cooperative learning,** in which small groups of classmates work toward common goals. Conflict and disagreement seem less important than the extent to which peers achieve intersubjectivity—by resolving differences of opinion, sharing responsibilities, and providing one another with sufficient explanations to correct misunderstandings. And in line with Vygotsky's theory, children profit more when their peer partner is an "expert"—especially capable at the task. When older or more expert students assist younger or less expert students, both benefit in achievement and self-esteem, with stronger effects for low-income, minority students (Ginsburg-Block, Rohrbeck, & Fantuzzo, 2006: Renninger, 1998).

Because working in groups comes more easily to children reared in collectivist than in individualistic cultures, Western children usually require extensive guidance for cooperative learning to succeed. When teachers prompt, explain, model, and have children roleplay how to work together effectively, cooperative learning results in higher-level explanations, greater enjoyment of learning, and achievement gains across a wide range of school subjects (Gillies, 2000, 2003; Terwel et al., 2001; Webb et al., 2008). It also enhances peer relationships generally, leading students to cooperate more in future group activities within and outside the classroom (Blatchford

Children reared in individualistic cultures typically need extensive teacher guidance to engage in cooperative learning. For these first graders, teacher support promotes pleasure, higher-level explanations, and achievement gains.

et al., 2006; Tolmie et al., 2010). Teaching through cooperative learning broadens Vygotsky's concept of the zone of proximal development, from a single child in collaboration with an expert partner (adult or peer) to multiple partners with diverse forms of expertise stimulating and encouraging one another.

▶ Cite strengths and limitations of Vygotsky's theory.

Evaluation of Vygotsky's Theory

In granting social experience a fundamental role in cognitive development, Vygotsky's theory helps us understand the wide cultural variation in cognitive skills. Whereas Piaget emphasized universal cognitive change, Vygotsky's theory leads us to expect highly diverse paths of development. The reading, writing, and mathematical activities of children who attend school in literate societies generate cognitive capacities different from those in tribal and village cultures, where children receive little formal schooling. But the elaborate spatial skills of Australian Aborigines, whose food-gathering missions require that they find their way through barren desert regions, and the proportional reasoning of Brazilian fishermen, promoted by their navigational experiences, are just as advanced (Carraher, Schliemann, & Carraher, 1988; Kearins, 1981). Each is a unique form of symbolic thinking required by activities that make up that culture's way of life.

Vygotsky's (1934/1986) theory also underscores the vital role of teaching in cognitive development. According to Vygotsky, from communicating with more expert partners, children engage in "verbalized self-observation," reflecting on, revising, and controlling their own thought processes. In this way, parents' and teachers' engagement with children prompts profound advances in the complexity of children's thinking.

Vygotsky's theory has not gone unchallenged. Although he acknowledged the role of diverse symbol systems (such as pictures, maps, and mathematical expressions) in the development of higher cognitive processes, he elevated language to highest importance. But in some cultures, verbal dialogues are not the only—or even the most important—means through which children learn. When Western parents help children with challenging tasks, they assume much responsibility for children's motivation by frequently giving verbal instructions and conversing with the child. Their communication resembles the teaching that occurs in school, where their children will spend years preparing for adult life. But in cultures that place less emphasis on schooling and literacy, parents often expect children to take greater responsibility for acquiring new skills through keen observation and participation in community activities (Paradise & Rogoff, 2009; Rogoff, 2003). The Cultural Influences box on the following page illustrates this difference.

Finally, in focusing on social and cultural influences, Vygotsky said little about biological contributions to children's cognition. His theory does not address how basic motor, perceptual, memory, and problem-solving capacities spark changes in children's social experiences, from which more advanced cognition springs. Nor does it tell us just how children internalize social experiences to advance their mental functioning (Miller, 2009; Moll, 1994). Consequently, like the other perspectives addressed in this chapter, Vygotsky's theory is vague in its explanation of cognitive change. It is intriguing to imagine the broader theory that might exist today had Piaget and Vygotsky—the two twentieth-century giants of cognitive development—had a chance to weave together their extraordinary accomplishments.

A S K   Y O U R S E L F

Review ■ Describe features of social interaction that support children's cognitive development. How does such interaction create a one of proximal development?

Connect ■ Explain how Piaget's and Vygotsky's theories complement each other. How would classroom practices inspired by these theories be similar? How would they be different?

Apply ■ Tanisha sees her 5-year-old son Toby talking aloud to himself as he plays. She wonders whether she should discourage this behavior. Use Vygotsky's theory and related research to explain why Toby talks to himself. How would you advise Tanisha?

Reflect ■ When do you use private speech? Does it serve a self-guiding function for you, as it does for children? Explain.

CULTURAL INFLUENCES

Children in Village and Tribal Cultures Observe and Participate in Adult Work

In Western societies, children are largely excluded from participating in adult work, which generally takes place outside the home. The role of equipping children with the skills they need to become competent workers is assigned to school. In early childhood, middle-class parents' interactions with children emphasize child-focused activities designed to prepare children to succeed in school—especially adult–child conversations and play that enhance language, literacy, and other school-related knowledge. In village and tribal cultures, children receive little or no schooling, spend their days in contact with or participating in adult work, and start to assume mature responsibilities in early childhood (Rogoff et al., 2003). Consequently, parents have little need to rely on conversation and play to teach children.

A study comparing 2- and 3-year-olds' daily lives in four cultures—two U.S. middle-class suburbs, the Efe hunters and gatherers of the Republic of Congo, and a Mayan agricultural town in Guatemala—documented these differences (Morelli, Rogoff, & Angelillo, 2003). In the U.S. communities, young children had little access to adult work and spent much time conversing and playing with adults. In contrast, the Efe and Mayan children rarely engaged in these child-focused activities. Instead, they spent their day close to—and frequently observing—adult work, which often took place in or near the Efe campsite or the Mayan family home.

An ethnography of a remote Mayan village in Yucatán, Mexico, shows that when young children are legitimate onlookers and participants in a daily life structured around adult work, their competencies differ from those of Western preschoolers (Gaskins, 1999; Gaskins, Haight, & Lancy, 2007). Yucatec Mayan adults are subsistence farmers. Men tend cornfields, aided by sons age 8 and older. Women prepare meals, wash clothes, and care for the livestock and garden, assisted by daughters and by sons too young to work in the fields. Children join in these activities from the second year on. When not participating, they are expected to be self-sufficient. Young children make many nonwork decisions for themselves—how much to sleep and eat, what to wear, when to take their daily bath, and even when to start school. As a result, Yucatec Mayan preschoolers are highly competent at self-care. In contrast, their make-believe play is limited; when it occurs, they usually imitate adult work. Otherwise, they watch others—for hours each day.

Yucatec Mayan parents rarely converse or play with preschoolers or scaffold their learning. Rather, when children imitate adult tasks, parents conclude that they are ready for more responsibility. Then they assign chores, selecting tasks the child can do with little help so that adult work is not disturbed. If a child cannot do a task, the adult takes over and the child observes, reengaging when able to contribute.

Expected to be autonomous and helpful, Yucatec Mayan children seldom display attention-getting behaviors or ask others for something interesting to do. From an early age, they can

A Mayan 3-year-old, imitating her mother, balances a basin of water on her head. Yucatec Mayan children observe and participate in the work of their community from an early age.

sit quietly for long periods—through a lengthy religious service or a three-hour truck ride. And when an adult interrupts their activity and directs them to do a chore, they respond eagerly to the type of command that Western children frequently avoid or resent. By age 5, Yucatec Mayan children spontaneously take responsibility for tasks beyond those assigned.

SUMMARY

Piaget's Cognitive-Developmental Theory (p. 226)

According to Piaget, how does cognition develop?

- Piaget's **constructivist approach** assumes that children discover knowledge through their own activity, moving through four invariant, universal stages. According to Piaget, newborn infants have little in the way of built-in structures; only at the end of the second year are they capable of a cognitive approach to the world through **mental representations**.

- In Piaget's theory, psychological structures, or **schemes**, change with age in two ways: through **adaptation**, which consists of two complementary activities—**assimilation** and **accommodation**; and through **organization**, the internal rearrangement of schemes to form a strongly interconnected cognitive system. **Equilibration** describes the changing balance of assimilation and accommodation that gradually leads to more effective schemes.

The Sensorimotor Stage: Birth to 2 Years (p. 228)

Describe major cognitive attainments of Piaget's sensorimotor stage.

- In the **sensorimotor stage**, the **circular reaction** provides a means of adapting first schemes, and the newborn baby's reflexes transform into the older infant's more flexible action patterns. Eight- to 12-month-olds develop **intentional**, or **goal-directed, behavior** and begin to master **object permanence**.

Twelve- to 18-month-olds become better problem solvers and no longer make the **A-not-B search error**. Between 18 and 24 months, mental representation is evident in sudden solutions to problems, mastery of object permanence tasks involving invisible displacement, **deferred imitation**, and **make-believe play**.

What does follow-up research reveal about infant cognitive development and the accuracy of Piaget's sensorimotor stage?

- Many studies suggest that infants display various understandings earlier than Piaget believed. Some awareness of object permanence, as revealed by the **violation-of-expectation method**, may be evident in the first few months, although searching for hidden objects is a true cognitive advance. Young infants also display deferred imitation, categorization, and **analogical problem solving**, and toddlers imitate rationally, by inferring others' intentions—attainments that require mental representation.

- **Displaced reference**—the realization that words can be used to cue mental images of things not physically present—is a major symbolic advance that occurs around the first birthday. The capacity to use language to modify mental representations improves from the end of the second into the third year. By the middle of the second year, toddlers treat realistic-looking pictures symbolically.

- Today, most researchers believe that newborns have more built-in cognitive equipment for making sense of experience than Piaget assumed, although they disagree on how much initial understanding infants have.

The Preoperational Stage: 2 to 7 Years (p. 239)

Describe advances in mental representation and cognitive limitations during the preoperational stage.

- Rapid advances in mental representation— notably, language, make-believe play, and drawing—occur during Piaget's **preoperational stage**. With age, make-believe becomes increasingly complex, evident in **sociodramatic play**. Children's drawings increase in complexity and realism.

- **Dual representation** improves during the third year as children realize that photographs, drawings, models, and simple maps correspond to circumstances in the real world.

- Piaget described preschoolers as not yet capable of **operations**. Because **egocentrism** prevents children from accommodating, it contributes to animistic thinking, **centration**, and lack of **reversibility**—difficulties that cause preschoolers to fail **conservation** and **hierarchical classification** tasks.

What does follow-up research reveal about preschoolers' cognitive development and the accuracy of Piaget's preoperational stage?

- When preschoolers are given familiar and simplified problems, their performance is more mature than Piaget assumed. They recognize differing perspectives, appreciate that animals (but not inanimate objects) have biological properties, have flexible and appropriate notions of magic, and reason about transformations and cause-and-effect relations.

- Preschoolers also show impressive skill at categorizing on the basis of nonobservable characteristics, revealing that their thinking is not dominated by appearances. Rather than being absent in the preschool years, operational thinking develops gradually.

The Concrete Operational Stage: 7 to 11 Years (p. 249)

What are the major characteristics of Piaget's concrete operational stage?

- During the **concrete operational stage**, thought becomes more logical, flexible, and organized. Mastery of conservation requires decentration and reversibility. Children also become proficient at hierarchical classification and **seriation**, including **transitive inference**. Spatial reasoning improves, as indicated by children's **cognitive maps**.

- Concrete operational thought is limited in that children have difficulty reasoning about abstract ideas. Mastery of Piaget's concrete operational tasks takes place gradually.

Discuss follow-up research on concrete operational thought.

- Cultural practices and schooling affect children's mastery of Piagetian tasks. Concrete operations are heavily influenced by training, context, and cultural conditions.

The Formal Operational Stage: 11 Years and Older (p. 253)

Describe major characteristics of the formal operational stage and typical consequences of adolescents' advancing cognition.

- In Piaget's **formal operational stage**, adolescents become capable of **hypothetico-deductive reasoning**. When faced with a problem, they start with a hypothesis about variables that might affect an outcome; deduce logical, testable inferences; and systematically isolate and combine variables to see which inferences are confirmed.

- Adolescents also develop **propositional thought**—the ability to evaluate the logic of verbal statements without referring to real-world circumstances.

- As adolescents reflect on their own thoughts, two distorted images of the relationship between self and other appear: the **imaginary audience** and the **personal fable**. Both result from gains in perspective taking.

- Adolescents' capacity to think about possibilities prompts idealistic visions at odds with everyday reality, and they often become fault-finding critics.

- Compared with adults, adolescents are less effective at decision making. They take greater risks under emotionally charged conditions, less often weigh alternatives, and more often fall back on well-learned intuitive judgments.

What does follow-up research reveal about formal operational thought?

- On tasks requiring hypothetico-deductive reasoning, school-age children cannot evaluate evidence that bears on three or more variables at once. They also do not grasp the **logical necessity** of propositional thought.

- Adolescents and adults are most likely to think abstractly and systematically in situations in which they have had extensive guidance and practice in using such reasoning. Individuals in tribal and village societies rarely do well on tasks typically used to assess formal operational reasoning. Learning activities in school provide adolescents with rich opportunities to acquire formal operations.

Piaget and Education (p. 259)

Describe educational implications of Piaget's theory.

- A Piagetian classroom promotes discovery learning, sensitivity to children's readiness to learn, and acceptance of individual differences.

Overall Evaluation of Piaget's Theory (p. 260)

Summarize contributions and shortcomings of Piaget's theory.

- Piaget emphasized children's active contributions to their own development, inspired the contemporary focus on mechanisms of cognitive change, and provided a useful "road map" of cognitive development. However, he offered only a vague account of how cognition changes. Children's cognitive attainments are less coherent and more gradual than Piaget's stages indicate.

- Some researchers reject Piaget's stages while retaining his view of cognitive development as an active, constructive process. Others support a less tightly knit stage concept. Still others deny both Piaget's stages and his belief in the existence of general reasoning abilities.

The Core Knowledge Perspective (p. 261)

Explain the core knowledge perspective on cognitive development, noting research that supports its assumptions.

- According to the **core knowledge perspective**, infants are innately equipped with core domains of thought that support rapid cognitive development. Each core domain is essential for survival and develops independently, resulting in uneven, domain-specific changes. Violation-of-expectation research suggests that young infants have impressive physical and numerical knowledge.

- The **theory theory** regards children as naïve theorists who draw on innate concepts to explain their everyday experiences and then test their theory, revising it to account for new information. In support of this view, children reason about everyday events in ways consistent with the event's core domain. Physical and psychological explanations emerge earlier than biological explanations, suggesting that biological knowledge may have little or no innate foundation.

What are the strengths and limitations of the core knowledge perspective?

- Core knowledge researchers are testing intriguing ideas about why certain cognitive skills emerge early and develop rapidly. But critics believe that violation-of-expectation studies are not adequate to show that infants are endowed with knowledge. The core knowledge perspective has not offered clarity on how cognition changes.

Vygotsky's Sociocultural Theory (p. 266)

Explain Vygotsky's view of cognitive development, noting the importance of social experience and language.

- Vygotsky viewed human cognition as inherently social and saw language as the foundation for all higher cognitive processes. According to Vygotsky, **private speech**, or language used for self-guidance, emerges out of social communication as adults and more skilled peers help children master challenging tasks within their **zone of proximal development**. Eventually, private speech is internalized as inner, verbal thought.

- **Intersubjectivity** and **scaffolding** are two features of social interaction that promote transfer of cognitive processes to children. **Guided participation** recognizes cultural and situational variations in adult support of children's efforts.

According to Vygotsky, what is the role of make-believe play in cognitive development?

- Vygotsky viewed make-believe play as a unique, broadly influential zone of proximal development in which children learn to act in accord with internal ideas rather than on impulse.

Vygotsky and Education (p. 269)

Describe educational implications of Vygotsky's theory.

- A Vygotskian classroom emphasizes assisted discovery through teachers' guidance and peer collaboration. When formal schooling begins, literacy activities prompt children to shift to a higher level of cognitive activity, in which they proficiently manipulate and control their culture's symbol systems.

- Vygotsky-based educational innovations include **reciprocal teaching** and **cooperative learning**, in which multiple partners stimulate and encourage one another.

Evaluation of Vygotsky's Theory (p. 272)

Cite strengths and limitations of Vygotsky's theory.

- Vygotsky's theory helps us understand wide cultural variation in cognitive skills and underscores the vital role of teaching in cognitive development. But in some cultures, verbal dialogues are not the only or most important means through which children learn. Vygotsky said little about biological contributions to cognition and about how children internalize social experiences to advance their thinking.

IMPORTANT TERMS AND CONCEPTS

A-not-B search error (p. 229)
accommodation (p. 227)
adaptation (p. 227)
analogical problem solving (p. 235)
assimilation (p. 227)
centration (p. 245)
circular reaction (p. 228)
cognition (p. 225)
cognitive maps (p. 250)
concrete operational stage (p. 249)
conservation (p. 244)
constructivist approach (p. 226)
cooperative learning (p. 271)
core knowledge perspective (p. 261)
deferred imitation (p. 230)
displaced reference (p. 235)

dual representation (p. 243)
egocentrism (p. 244)
equilibration (p. 227)
formal operational stage (p. 253)
guided participation (p. 268)
hierarchical classification (p. 245)
hypothetico-deductive reasoning (p. 253)
imaginary audience (p. 255)
intentional, or goal-directed, behavior (p. 229)
intersubjectivity (p. 268)
logical necessity (p. 258)
make-believe play (p. 230)
mental representation (p. 227)
object permanence (p. 229)
operations (p. 243)
organization (p. 227)

personal fable (p. 255)
preoperational stage (p. 239)
private speech (p. 267)
propositional thought (p. 254)
reciprocal teaching (p. 271)
reversibility (p. 245)
scaffolding (p. 268)
schemes (p. 226)
sensorimotor stage (p. 228)
seriation (p. 250)
sociodramatic play (p. 240)
theory theory (p. 264)
transitive inference (p. 250)
video deficit effect (p. 237)
violation-of-expectation method (p. 230)
zone of proximal development (p. 267)

CHAPTER 7

"An Amazing Sight"

Ralph, 11 years, New York

A child takes in the amazing sight of a colossal dinosaur skeleton. During the school years, children's capacity to attend to, remember, transform, and use information to solve problems expands greatly.

Reprinted with permission from the International Collection of Child Art, Milner Library, Illinois State University, Normal, Illinois

Cognitive Development: An Information-Processing Perspective

The Information-Processing Approach

A General Model of Information Processing
Components of the Mental System • Implications for Development

Developmental Theories of Information Processing
Case's Neo-Piagetian Theory • Siegler's Model of Strategy Choice

■ **SOCIAL ISSUES: EDUCATION:** *Speech–Gesture Mismatches: Using the Hand to Read the Mind*

Attention
Sustained, Selective, and Adaptable Attention • Planning

■ **BIOLOGY AND ENVIRONMENT:** *Children with Attention-Deficit Hyperactivity Disorder*

Memory
Strategies for Storing Information • Retrieving Information • Knowledge and Semantic Memory • Episodic Memory • Eyewitness Memory

■ **SOCIAL ISSUES: EDUCATION:** *Media Multitasking Disrupts Learning*

■ **BIOLOGY AND ENVIRONMENT:** *Infantile Amnesia*

Metacognition
Metacognitive Knowledge • Cognitive Self-Regulation

Applications of Information Processing to Academic Learning
Reading • Mathematics • Scientific Reasoning

Evaluation of the Information-Processing Approach

"**F**inally!" 6-year-old Margarita explained the day she entered first grade. "Now I get to go to real school just like Victor!" Holding her 9-year-old brother's hand, Margarita walked confidently through the school doors, ready for a more disciplined approach to learning than she had experienced in early childhood.

Margarita had entered a new world of challenging mental activities. In a single morning, she and her classmates met in reading groups, worked on single-digit addition and subtraction, painted a mural depicting tropical plants and animals to complement their study of rainforests, and wrote in journals about what they liked best about a field trip to a botanical garden. Meanwhile, in Victor's fourth-grade class, Mr. Sharp reminded the children of the inverse relationship between addition and subtraction and asked them to estimate the size of solutions to three-digit subtraction problems. After recess, he drew their attention to this week's list of spelling words: "Fourth graders, why is it easy to remember these words and use them all in the essays we're going to write?" Victor's hand shot up. "They're all related to our unit on electricity," he exclaimed. "See—battery, magnetism, circuit. . . ."

Information-processing research sheds light on how children develop the attention, memory, and self-management skills and knowledge to succeed at these diverse tasks. Unlike the perspectives covered in Chapter 6, information processing is not a unified theory of cognitive development. Rather, it is an approach followed by researchers who thoroughly study specific aspects of cognition in an effort to uncover *mechanisms of change*—how children and adults operate on information, detecting, transforming, storing, accessing, and modifying it further as it makes its way through the cognitive system.

In this chapter, we review basic assumptions of the information-processing approach along with models of the human cognitive system that are major forces in child development research. As we do so, we will consider several general cognitive changes—in processing capacity, processing speed, and "executive" processing (purposeful management of cognitive activities)—that contribute vitally to children's increasingly complex, effective thinking with age. Next, we delve into two basic processes involved in all human thinking: attention and memory. We also consider how children's expanding knowledge of the world and awareness of their own mental activities enhance their cognitive processing.

As we examine these topics, we will return to a familiar theme: the impact of task demands and cultural contexts on children's thinking. We pay special attention to how schooling, with its emphasis on literacy, mathematics, scientific reasoning, and retention of discrete pieces of information, channels cognitive development in culturally specific ways. Although information-processing theorists are especially interested in internal, self-generated cognitive changes, they also want to find out how external influences—teaching techniques, the design of learning environments and tasks, and cultural values and practices—affect children's thinking. We conclude with an evaluation of information processing as a framework for understanding cognitive development. ■

The Information-Processing Approach

Most information-processing theorists view the mind as a complex symbol-manipulating system through which information from the environment flows, often using the metaphor of a computer. First, information is *encoded*—taken in by the system and retained in symbolic form. Then a variety of internal processes operate on it, *recoding* it, or revising its symbolic structure into a more effective representation, and then *decoding* it, or interpreting its meaning by comparing and combining it with other information in the system. When these cognitive operations are complete, individuals use the information to make sense of their experiences and to solve problems.

Notice the clarity and precision of the computer analogy of human mental functioning. Researchers use computer-like diagrams and flowcharts to try to map the exact series of steps children and adults follow when faced with a task or problem (Miller, 2009). Some researchers do this in such detail that the same mental operations can be programmed into a computer. Then the researcher conducts *simulations* to see if the computer responds as children and adults do on certain tasks. Other investigators intensively study children's and adults' thinking by tracking eye movements, analyzing error patterns, and examining self-reports of mental activity. Regardless of approach, all share a strong commitment to explicit models of thinking that guide the questions they raise about components of cognitive development and thorough testing of each component.

▶ Describe the store model of the human information processing system, noting implications for cognitive development and related findings.

A General Model of Information Processing

The computer-like view of the cognitive system adopted, either directly or indirectly, by most information-processing researchers emerged in the late 1960s and early 1970s. Called the *store model,* it focuses on general units of cognitive functioning, assuming that we hold, or store, information in three parts of the mental system for processing: the *sensory register;* the *short-term memory store;* and the *long-term memory store* (see Figure 7.1) (Atkinson & Shiffrin, 1968). As information flows sequentially through each, we can use *mental strategies* to operate on and transform it, increasing the chances that we will retain information, use it efficiently, and think flexibly, adapting the information to changing circumstances. To understand this more clearly, let's look at each component of the mental system.

Components of the Mental System

First, information enters the **sensory register.** Here, a broad panorama of sights and sounds are represented directly but stored only momentarily. **TAKE A MOMENT...** Look around you, and then close your eyes. An image of what you saw persists for a few seconds but then decays, or disappears, unless you use mental strategies to preserve it. For example, by *attending to* some information more carefully than to other information, you increase the chances that it will transfer to the next step of the information-processing system.

In the second part of the mind, the **short-term memory store,** we retain attended-to information briefly so we can actively "work" on it to reach our goals. One way of looking at the short-term store is in terms of its *basic capacity,* often referred to as *short-term memory:* how many pieces of information can be held at once for a few seconds. Suppose you were asked to perform an operation on the following numerals: 1, 4, 2, 3, 6. If you could not briefly hold onto the digits, you would be unable solve the problem. In line with this example, a commonly used basic short-term memory task measures *verbatim digit span*—the longest sequence of items (such as a list of randomly ordered numerical digits) a person can repeat back in exact order. Among adults, average digit span is about seven items (Cowan, 2001).

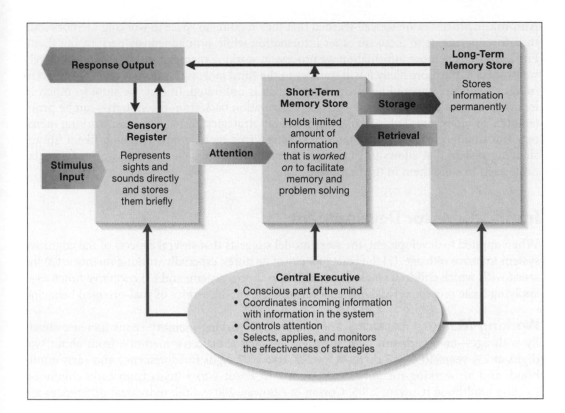

FIGURE 7.1 Model of the human information-processing system. Information flows through three parts of the mental system: the *sensory register, short-term memory store,* and *long-term memory store.* In each, mental strategies can be used to manipulate information, increasing the efficiency and flexibility of thinking and the chances that information will be retained. The *central executive* is the conscious, reflective part of the mental system. It coordinates incoming information with information already in the system, decides what to attend to, and oversees the use of strategies.

But we must almost always go beyond passively maintaining verbatim information to actively thinking about that information. Consequently, most researchers endorse a contemporary view of the short-term store, which offers a more meaningful indicator of its capacity, called **working memory**—the number of items that can be briefly held in mind while also engaging in some effort to monitor or manipulate those items. Working memory can be thought of as a "mental workspace" that we use to accomplish many activities in everyday life.

Researchers use a variety of tasks to assess working-memory capacity. A *verbal memory-span task* might ask children to repeat a sequence of numerical digits backward; memorize a list of words while also verifying the accuracy of simple math computations; or listen to a set of short sentences, remember the final word in each, and then repeat the words in correct order. In a *visual/spatial-span task,* researchers might present children with a set of distinctly colored circles in an arrangement on a screen and then ask them to point to the spot in an identical empty grid where each circle was located. Working-memory span is typically about two items fewer than short-term memory span. As we will soon see, children's performance on working-memory tasks is a good predictor of their capacity to learn.

Recall that the sensory register, though limited, can take in a wide panorama of information. The capacity of working memory is far more restricted. But by engaging in a variety of basic cognitive procedures, such as focusing attention on relevant items and repeating (rehearsing) them rapidly, we increase the chances that information will be retained and accessible to ongoing thinking (Cowan & Alloway, 2009).

To manage the cognitive system's activities, the **central executive** directs the flow of information, implementing the basic procedures just mentioned and also engaging in more sophisticated activities that enable complex, flexible thinking. For example, the central executive coordinates incoming information with information already in the system, and it selects, applies, and monitors strategies that facilitate memory storage, comprehension, reasoning, and problem solving (Baddeley, 2000; Pressley & Hilden, 2006). The central executive is the conscious, reflective part of our mental system. It ensures that we harness our cognitive processes purposefully, to attain our goals.

The more effectively the central executive joins with working memory to process information, the better learned those cognitive activities will be and the more *automatically* we can apply them. Consider the richness of your thinking while you automatically drive a car.

Automatic processes are so well-learned that they require no space in working memory and, therefore, permit us to focus on other information while simultaneously performing them. Furthermore, the more information we process in working memory and the more effectively we process it, the more likely it will transfer to the third and largest storage area—**long-term memory,** our permanent knowledge base, which is unlimited. In fact, we store so much in long-term memory that *retrieval*—getting information back from the system—can be problematic. To aid retrieval of information, we apply strategies, just as we do in working memory. Information in long-term memory is *categorized* by its contents, much like a library shelving system that allows us to retrieve items by following the same network of associations used to store them in the first place.

Implications for Development

When applied to development, the store model suggests that several aspects of the cognitive system improve with age: (1) the *basic capacity* of its stores, especially working memory; (2) the *speed* with which children work on information in the system; and (3) *executive function*— applying basic procedures and higher-level strategies in the service of goal-oriented behavior.

Working-Memory Capacity   Short-term and working-memory spans increase steadily with age—on a verbatim digit span task tapping short-term memory, from about two digits at 2½ years, to 4 or 5 digits at 7 years, to 6 or 7 digits in adolescence and early adulthood; and on working-memory tasks, from 2 to about 4 to 5 items from early childhood to early adulthood (Cowan, 2005; Cowan & Alloway, 2009). Still, individual differences are evident at all ages, and they are of particular concern because working-memory capacity predicts intelligence test scores and academic achievement in diverse subjects in middle childhood and adolescence (Colom et al., 2007; Gathercole et al., 2005; St Clair-Thompson & Gathercole, 2006).

Indeed, children with persistent learning difficulties in reading and math are often deficient in working-memory capacity. And the poorer they perform on working-memory span tasks, the more severe their achievement problems, even after controlling for individual differences in intelligence (Alloway, 2009; Gathercole et al., 2006; Geary et al., 2007). Reduced working-memory capacity creates a bottleneck for learning. In an observational study of 5- and 6-year-olds who scored very low in working-memory capacity, the children often failed at school assignments that made heavy memory demands (Gathercole, Lamont, & Alloway, 2006). They were unable to follow complex instructions, lost their place in tasks with multiple steps, and frequently abandoned work before finishing it. The children struggled because they could not hold in mind sufficient information to complete their assignments.

Compared to their economically advantaged agemates, children from poverty-stricken families are more likely to score low on working-memory span tasks—an important contributor to their generally poorer academic achievement (Farah et al., 2006; Noble, McCandiliss, & Farah, 2007). In one study, years of childhood spent in poverty predicted reduced working-memory capacity in early adulthood (Evans & Schamberg, 2009). Childhood physiological measures of stress (elevated blood pressure and stress hormone levels, including cortisol) largely explained this poverty–work-memory association. Chronic stress, as we saw in Chapter 4, can impair brain structure and function, especially the prefrontal cortex and its connections with the hippocampus, which govern working-memory capacity.

In a large British sample of over 3,000 5- to 11-year-olds, nearly 10 percent were identified as having very low working-memory scores, the majority of whom were struggling in school (Alloway et al., 2009). Clearly, interventions are needed that reduce memory loads so these children can learn. Effective approaches include communicating in short sentences with familiar vocabulary, repeating task instructions, asking children to repeat back crucial information to ensure they remember, breaking complex tasks into manageable parts, and encouraging children to use external memory aids (such as lists of useful spellings when writing, number lines when doing math) (Gathercole & Alloway, 2008). **TAKE A MOMENT...** Do these techniques remind you of *scaffolding,* a style of teaching discussed in Chapter 6 (see page 268) known to promote cognitive development?

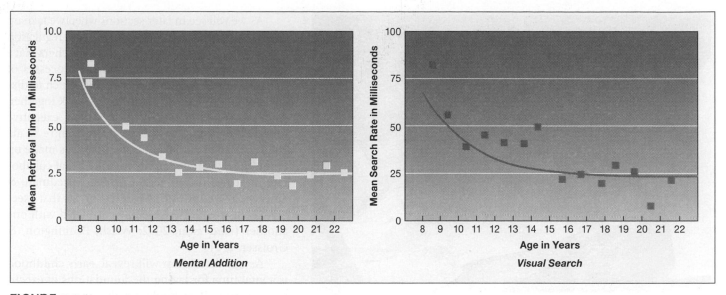

FIGURE 7.2 Age-related decline in processing time, illustrated for mental addition and visual search. Processing speed improves similarly across many tasks. This common trend implies an age-related gain in basic processing capacity. (*Left:* Reprinted from *Journal of Experimental Child Psychology,* Vol. 45, No. 3, R. Kail, "Developmental Functions for Speeds of Cognitive Processes," p. 361, copyright 1988, with permission from Elsevier. *Right:* From R. Kail, "Processing Time Declines Exponentially During Childhood and Adolescence," *Developmental Psychology, 27,* p. 265. Copyright © 1991 by the American Psychological Association. Adapted with permission of the American Psychological Association.)

Speed of Processing   Developmental increases in working-memory capacity in part reflect gains in processing speed. Efficient processing releases working-memory resources to support storage of information. The faster children can repeat to-be-learned information either out loud or silently to themselves, the larger their memory spans (Cowan & Alloway, 2009; Luna et al., 2004).

Research confirms that with age, children process information more efficiently. In a series of studies, Robert Kail (1991, 1993, 1997) gave 7- to 22-year-olds a variety of cognitive tasks in which they had to respond as quickly as possible. For example, in a name-retrieval task, they had to judge whether pairs of pictures were physically identical or had the same name (for instance, two umbrellas, one opened and one closed). In a mental addition task, they were given addition problems and answers, and they had to indicate whether the solutions were correct. And in a visual search task, they were shown a single digit and asked to signal if it was among a set of digits that appeared on a screen. On all tasks, processing time decreased with age. More important, the rate of change—a fairly rapid decline in processing time, trailing off around age 12—was similar across many activities (see Figure 7.2).

The changes in processing speed shown in Figure 7.2 have been found in Canada, Korea, and the United States (Fry & Hale, 1996; Kail & Park, 1992). Similarity in development across diverse tasks in several cultures implies a fundamental change in efficiency of the information-processing system, perhaps due to myelination or synaptic pruning in the brain (Kail, 2003). Increased processing speed enables older children and adults to scan information more quickly, to transform it more rapidly, and therefore to hold more information in working memory at once. Efficient cognitive processing influences academic achievement indirectly—by augmenting working-memory resources and, thus, supporting many complex cognitive activities (Rinderman & Neubauer, 2004).

Executive Function   The central executive, as noted earlier, is the overall supervisor of the cognitive system, managing its activities to ensure that we attain our goals. After observing that adults with damage to the prefrontal cortex were deficient in diverse executive skills, researchers became interested in studying the development of **executive function**—the set of cognitive operations and strategies necessary for self-initiated, purposeful behavior in relatively novel, challenging situations. These include controlling attention, suppressing impulses in favor of adaptive responses, coordinating information in working memory, and planning, organizing, monitoring, and flexibly redirecting thought and behavior.

While collaborating on a complex map-making project, these 4th-graders must focus their attention, inhibit inappropriate responses, think flexibly, and coordinate information in working memory. These skills are aspects of executive function, which develops rapidly in middle childhood.

As we will see in later sections when we take up children's attention, strategy use, and self-regulation in complex cognitive activities, researchers have investigated each of the component processes of executive function. But they still have much to discover about how those components work together. And whereas some investigators view executive function as a unitary capacity (Brookshire et al., 2004; Zelazo et al., 2003), others see it as made up of multiple, distinct cognitive abilities that collaborate in goal-directed action (Welsh, Friedman, & Spieker, 2008). Indeed, research suggests that executive skills are, at best, weakly correlated with one another (Anderson, 2002; Welsh, Pennington, & Groisser, 1991).

As our discussion will reveal, early childhood is a vital time for laying the foundations of executive function: Preschoolers make strides in focusing attention, inhibiting inappropriate responses, and thinking flexibly—developments that parallel rapid synapse formation followed by synaptic pruning in the prefrontal cortex (see Figure 5.9 on page 186). During the school years—a time of continued synaptic pruning and maturing of the prefrontal cortex—executive function undergoes its most energetic period of development (Welsh, 2002). Children handle increasingly difficult tasks that require the integration of working memory, inhibition, planning, flexible use of strategies, and self-monitoring and self-correction of behavior (Luciana, 2003; Welsh, Pennington, & Groisser, 1991). And executive function improves further in adolescence, when the prefrontal cortex attains an adult level of synapses.

Heritability evidence suggests substantial genetic contributions to individual differences in working-memory capacity and attentional processing, including inhibiting inappropriate responses (Hansell et al., 2001; Polderman et al., 2009; Young et al., 2009). And molecular genetic analyses are identifying specific genes related to severely deficient functioning of executive components, such as control of attention and impulses, which (as we will soon see) contributes to learning and behavior disorders, such as attention-deficit hyperactivity disorder (ADHD).

But in both typically and atypically developing children, heredity combines with environmental contexts to influence executive function. In Chapter 2, we saw how prenatal iron deficiency places children at risk for lasting memory deficits (see page 49). And in Chapter 3, we reviewed evidence indicating that prenatal teratogens can compromise executive function by impairing attention, impulse control, and memory. Finally, our discussion in this chapter will confirm that supportive parenting and educational experiences are essential for optimal development of executive components and their eventual synthesis into planning, flexible strategic thinking, and self-regulation.

▶ How do Case's neo-Piagetian theory and Siegler's model of strategy choice explain changes in children's thinking?

Developmental Theories of Information Processing

Although the store model has implications for development, it began with the aim of explaining adult information processing, not how children's thinking changes. Next, we consider two *developmental* approaches to information processing. The first, Case's *neo-Piagetian perspective*, uses Piaget's theory as a starting point, recasting his stage sequence in information-processing terms to construct an overall vision of cognitive development. The second, Siegler's *model of strategy choice*, highlights children's experimentation with and selection of mental strategies to account for the diversity and ever-changing nature of children's cognition.

Case's Neo-Piagetian Theory

Robbie Case's (1992, 1998) **neo-Piagetian theory** accepts Piaget's stages but attributes change within each stage, and movement from one stage to the next, to increases in the efficiency with which children use their limited working-memory capacity. Each stage involves a distinct type of cognitive structure: in infancy, sensory input and physical actions; in early childhood, internal representations of events and actions; in middle childhood, simple transformations of representations; and in adolescence, complex transformations of representations. As children become more efficient processors, the amount of information they can hold and combine in working memory expands, making movement to a higher stage possible. Three factors contribute to cognitive change:

- *Brain development.* Neurological changes, including myelination, synaptic growth, and synaptic pruning, improve the efficiency of thought, leading to readiness for each stage. According to Case, biology imposes a systemwide ceiling on cognitive development. At any given time, the child cannot exceed a certain upper limit of processing speed. (Refer back to age-related gains in speed of processing on page 281.)

- *Practice with schemes and automization.* In Case's theory, Piagetian schemes are the child's mental strategies. Within each stage, through repeated use, the child's schemes become automatic, freeing working-memory resources for combining existing schemes and generating new ones. Notice how Case's mechanisms of cognitive change offer a clarified view of Piaget's concepts of assimilation and accommodation. *Practicing schemes* (assimilation) leads to *automization,* which *releases working memory* for other activities, permitting *scheme combination and construction* (accommodation).

- *Formation of central conceptual structures.* Once the schemes of a Piagetian stage become automatic and brain development further increments processing speed, enough space in working memory is available to consolidate schemes into an improved representational form. As a result, children generate **central conceptual structures**—networks of concepts and relations that permit them to think about a wide range of situations in more advanced ways. Consequently, processing efficiency expands further (Case, 1996, 1998). When children form new central conceptual structures, they move to the next stage of development.

Let's take a familiar set of tasks—conservation—to illustrate Case's ideas. Imagine a 5-year-old who cannot yet conserve liquid but who has some isolated schemes: (1) After water is poured from a tall glass into a short glass, the height of the water level is reduced. (2) After water is poured from a thin into a wide glass, the width of the water increases. As the child gains experience in transferring liquids from one container to another, these schemes become automatic, and she combines them into a conserving response. A similar sequence occurs in other conservation situations—involving, for example, mass and weight. Eventually the child coordinates several task-specific conserving responses into a new, broadly applicable principle: a central conceptual structure. When this happens, cognition moves from simple to complex transformations of representations, or from concrete to formal operational thought.

Case and his colleagues have applied his theory to many tasks: solving arithmetic word problems, understanding stories, drawing pictures, sight-reading music, handling money, and interpreting social situations (Case, 1992, 1998; Case & Okamoto, 1996). In each case, children coordinate an increasing number of task dimensions with age. In understanding stories, for example, preschoolers grasp only a single story line. By the early school years, they combine two story lines into a single plot. Around age 9 to 11, central conceptual structures integrate multiple dimensions: Children tell coherent stories with a main plot and several subplots.

Case's (1998) theory offers an information-processing account of the *continuum of acquisition*—that many understandings appear in specific situations at different times rather than being mastered all at once (see page 252 in Chapter 6). First, different forms of the same logical insight, such as the various conservation tasks, vary in their processing demands; those acquired later

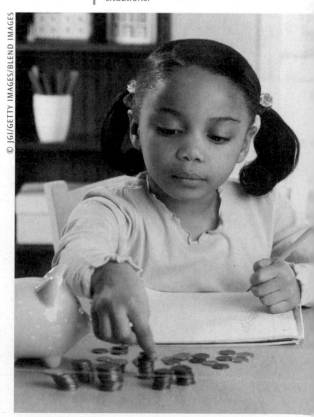

As she practices counting money, this 6-year-old becomes a more efficient processor, coordinating an increasing number of task dimensions into a central conceptual structure—a general representation that she can apply in many situations.

© JGI/GETTY IMAGES/BLEND IMAGES

require that more information be held and combined in working memory. Second, children's experiences vary widely. A child who often listens to and tells stories displays more advanced central conceptual structures in storytelling than in other activities. And children who do not show central conceptual structures expected for their age can usually be trained to attain them (Case, Griffin, & Kelly, 2001). Therefore, Case's theory is better able than Piaget's to account for unevenness in cognitive development. Although Case's ideas remain to be tested with many more tasks, his theory is unique in offering an integrated picture of how children's processing efficiency, practice with strategies, and efforts to reorganize their thinking interact to produce development.

Siegler's Model of Strategy Choice

Robert Siegler's (1996, 2006) **model of strategy choice** uses an evolutionary metaphor— "natural selection"—to help us understand cognitive change. When given challenging problems, children generate a *variety* of strategies, testing the usefulness of each. With experience, some strategies are *selected*; they become more frequent and "survive." Others become less frequent and "die off." Like the evolution of physical traits, children's mental strategies display *variation* and *selection,* yielding adaptive problem-solving techniques—ones best suited to solving the problems at hand.

To study children's strategy use, Siegler used the microgenetic research design (see Chapter 2, pages 64–65), presenting children with problems over an extended time period. He found that children experiment with diverse strategies on many types of problems—basic math facts, numerical estimation, conservation, memory for lists of items, reading first words, telling time, spelling, and even tic-tac-toe. Consider 5-year-old Darryl, who was adding marbles tucked into pairs of small bags that his kindergarten teacher had set out on a table. As Darryl dealt with each pair, his strategies varied. Sometimes he guessed, not applying any strategy. At other times, he counted from 1 on his fingers. For example, for bags containing 2 + 4 marbles, his fingers popped up one by one as he exclaimed, "1, 2, 3, 4, 5, 6!" Occasionally he started with the lower digit, 2, and "counted on" ("2, 3, 4, 5, 6"). Or he began with the higher digit, 4, and counted on ("4, 5, 6"), a strategy called *min* because it minimizes the work. Sometimes he retrieved the answer from memory.

Siegler found that strategy use for basic math facts—and many other types of problems—follows an *overlapping-waves pattern* (see Figure 7.3). Performance tends to progress from a single incorrect approach, to a highly variable state in which children try different strategies, to use of a more advanced procedure. Even 2-year-olds solving simple problems, such as how to use a tool to obtain an out-of-reach toy, display this sequence (Chen & Siegler, 2000; Siegler, 2007). While trying strategies, children observe which work best, which work less well, and which are ineffective. Gradually they select strategies on the basis of two adaptive criteria: *accuracy* and *speed*—for basic addition, the *min* strategy. As children home in on effective strategies, they learn more about the problems at hand. As a result, correct solutions become more strongly associated with problems, and children display the most efficient strategy—automatic retrieval of the answer.

How do children move from less to more effective strategies? Often they discover faster, more accurate strategies by using more time-consuming techniques. For example, by repeatedly counting on fingers, Darryl began to recognize the number of fingers he held up. And by alternating between counting from the lower digit and using *min*, Darryl directly observed *min*'s greater speed and accuracy (Siegler & Jenkins, 1989). Indeed, when given the same problems repeatedly over a short time interval, children regress from more advanced to less advanced approaches on as many as 40 percent of the trials! The more variable their strategies, the better their eventual

FIGURE 7.3 Overlapping-waves pattern of strategy use in problem solving. When given challenging problems, a child generates a variety of strategies, each represented by a wave. The waves overlap because the child tries several different strategies at the same time. Use of each strategy, depicted by the height of the wave, is constantly changing. As the child observes which strategies work best, which work less well, and which are ineffective, the one that results in the most rapid, accurate solutions wins out. (From R. S. Siegler, *Emerging Minds: The Process of Change in Children's Thinking.* Copyright © 1996 by Oxford University Press, Inc. Used by permission of Oxford University Press, Inc.)

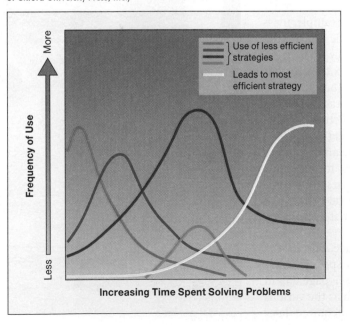

Frequency of Use — More / Less

Use of less efficient strategies

Leads to most efficient strategy

Increasing Time Spent Solving Problems

SOCIAL ISSUES: EDUCATION

Speech–Gesture Mismatches: Using the Hand to Read the Mind

Mr. Beal introduced his fourth-grade class to the concept of equivalence—that the quantity on one side of an equals sign is the same as the quantity on the other side. Then he watched as several children stepped up to the blackboard to work the following problem: $5 + 3 + 4 = \underline{\quad} + 4$.

"I added $5 + 3 + 4 + 4$ equals 16," Kerry said, pointing to each number as she mentioned it and then to the blank as she gave her answer, ignoring the placement of the equals sign. Kerry's speech and gestures were consistent: Both revealed an incorrect strategy.

Noelle, who went next, gave the same incorrect explanation. But her gestures sent a different message. As she spoke, she pointed to each number on the left, then touched the equals sign, then the 4 on the right, and finally rested her finger on the blank. Noelle showed a *speech–gesture mismatch:* Her hand movements suggested she knew more than she could say. Over the next few weeks, Noelle mastered equivalence problems more rapidly than Kerry. How can we account for Noelle's faster progress?

Children who produce speech–gesture mismatches seem to be in a transitional state. Their behavior indicates that they are considering two contradictory strategies at once, a sign of readiness to learn. In a microgenetic study, two groups of children who did not have a full understanding of addition-based equivalence problems were identified: speech–gesture matched and speech–gesture mismatched. As the children worked more problems, some in each group received feedback about the accuracy of their answers along with instruction explaining the equivalence principle; others received no intervention. Finally, the children's learning was assessed as they worked problems on their own (Goldin-Meadow, 2003a, 2006b).

Children who received instruction following a speech–gesture mismatch were more likely than others to move out of that state to a correct answer, based on a speech–gesture match. They also more often generalized their new knowledge to multiplication-based equivalence problems ($5 \times 3 \times 4 = 5 \times \underline{\quad}$). Interestingly, the few speech–gesture match children who improved with instruction generalized what they learned only if they first passed through a speech–gesture mismatch phase. Correct strategies appeared first in gesture and only later in speech.

Children on the verge of learning appear to have strategies that are accessible to gesture but not to speech (Goldin-Meadow, 2002). Perhaps expressing a strategy in gesture that differs from one in speech facilitates awareness of conflicting ideas, encouraging the child to resolve the discrepancy in favor of the more effective strategy. Children in a mismatch state are particularly open to teaching.

Parents and teachers can use children's gestures to provide instruction at the most opportune moment. Indeed, many adults are attuned to children's speech–gesture mismatches, and others can be taught to notice them (Goldin-Meadow, 2005a). In one study, adults were more likely to teach a variety of problem-solving strategies to children who displayed mismatches than to children who did not (Goldin-Meadow & Singer, 2003). In doing so, they encouraged the "mismatchers" to try out many strategies, which—as Siegler's model of strategy choice makes clear—facilitates learning.

Finally, adults who gesture while teaching encourage students to use their hands to support learning, which leads to improved performance (Goldin-Meadow, Cook, & Mitchell, 2009). How does gesturing contribute to advances in understanding? By enabling children (and adults) to represent thoughts they cannot yet express in words, it lightens demands on working memory (Ping & Goldin-Meadow, 2010). As a result, learners can allocate additional cognitive resources to grappling with the task.

This second grader's hand gesture suggests that he understands more than he can articulate. Such speech–gesture mismatches provide opportune moments for instruction.

performance (Siegler, 2007). Even on a single item, children may generate varying procedures, as indicated by occasions in which their words and gestures differ (see the Social Issues: Education box above for the significance of these mismatches for readiness to learn).

Problems with certain features help children discover a better strategy (Luwel, Siegler, & Verschaffel, 2008). When Darryl opened a pair of bags, one containing ten marbles, the other two marbles, he realized that *min* would be best. Teaching children to reason logically with concepts relevant to the problems at hand also helps (Alibali, Phillips, & Fischer, 2009; Siegler & Svetina, 2006). First graders more often use *min* after realizing that regardless of the order in which two sets are combined, they yield the same results ($2 + 4 = 6$ and $4 + 2 = 6$). Finally, when children are taught an effective strategy, they usually adopt it, abandoning less successful techniques (Siegler & Booth, 2004). Sometimes, however, children do not immediately take advantage of new, more adaptive strategies. As we will see in later

LOOK and LISTEN

Over 2 to 3 days, present a 5- to 7-year-old with a set of math problems just ahead of his or her current level of mastery, noting the child's solution strategies. (If you can't tell by observing, ask the child, "How did you do that?"). Could you see the child experimenting with diverse strategies?

sections, using a new strategy taxes working memory, and children may resist giving up a well-established, nearly automatic procedure for a new one because gains in speed of thinking are small at first.

Siegler's model reveals that no child thinks in just one way, even on a single task. A child given the same problem on two occasions often uses different approaches. Strategy variability is vital for devising new, more adaptive ways of thinking, which "evolve" through extensive experience solving problems.

The model of strategy choice offers a powerful image of development that overcomes deficiencies of the stage approach in accounting for both diversity and continuous change in children's thinking. By exploiting the microgenetic method, researchers have captured periods of high variability in children's strategy use that contribute vitally to cognitive advances. Typical cross-sectional and longitudinal studies, which easily miss such periods, make cognitive change appear more abrupt (and therefore stagelike) than it actually is.

ASK YOURSELF

Review ■ Summarize evidence indicating that speed of information processing increases with age, contributing to gains in working-memory capacity. In Case's neo-Piagetian theory, how do gains in processing efficiency contribute to development?

Connect ■ Recall the dynamic systems perspective, which assumes that periods of instability precede a reorganized, more effectively functioning, stable system (see pages 30–31 in Chapter 1 and pages 148–149 in Chapter 4). How are findings on children's strategy development consistent with this idea?

Apply ■ Five-year-old Kayla used several strategies to solve conservation-of-number problems involving rows of pennies. On one, she said, "The rows aren't the same." On the next, she said, "The rows have the same number because you didn't add any." On the third, she said, "I counted the pennies. The rows have the same number." Did she move from a more to a less mature strategy? Explain. Why is it beneficial for Kayla to experiment with strategies?

Reflect ■ Think of a challenging task that you recently completed successfully. Describe executive skills you implemented, explaining how each contributed to your success.

▶ Describe the development of attention, including sustained, selective, and adaptable strategies.

Attention

The following sections address children's processing in major parts of the cognitive system—how children encode information, hold and transform it in working memory so it will transfer to long-term memory, and retrieve it so they can think and solve problems. We begin with research on the development of attention. Attention is fundamental to human thinking because it determines which information will be considered in any task. Parents and teachers are well aware that young children spend only a short time involved in tasks, have difficulty focusing on relevant details, and find it difficult to switch mental sets (usually persist in one way of doing something). During early and middle childhood, attention improves greatly, becoming more sustained, selective, and adaptable.

Sustained, Selective, and Adaptable Attention

During the first year, infants attend to novel and eye-catching events, orienting to them more quickly and tracking their movements more effectively. They also spend more time focused on complex stimuli, such as toys and videos, and display greater slowing of heart rate while engaged—a physiological indicator of *sustained attention* (Richards, 2008). In toddlerhood, children become increasingly capable of intentional, or goal-directed, behavior (see Chapter 6, page 229). Consequently, attraction to novelty declines (but does not disappear), and sustained attention improves further, especially during play. A toddler who engages in goal-directed behavior even in a limited way, such as stacking blocks or putting them in a container, must sustain attention to reach the goal. In a study of toddlers and young preschoolers, sustained attention during play with toys increased sharply between ages 2 and 3½ years (Ruff & Capozzoli, 2003).

Rapid growth of the prefrontal cortex, the capacity to generate increasingly complex play goals (children must concentrate to attain them), and adult scaffolding of attention are jointly responsible for this gain in sustained attention (Ruff & Capozzoli, 2003). When parents help toddlers and young preschoolers maintain a focus of attention by offering suggestions, questions, and comments about the child's current interest, sustained attention improves. More attentive children are better developed, cognitively and socially (Bono & Stifter, 2003; Murphy et al., 2007; Pérez-Edgar et al., 2010). Many skills, including language, exploration, problem solving, academic learning, social interaction, cooperation, and complex play, benefit from an improved ability to concentrate.

As sustained attention increases, children become better at focusing on only those aspects of a situation that are relevant to their goals. To study this increasing selectivity of attention, researchers introduce irrelevant stimuli into a task and see how well children respond to its central elements. For example, they might present a stream of numbers on a computer screen and ask children to press a button whenever a particular sequence of two digits (such as "1" and then "9") appears. Findings show that selective attention improves sharply between ages 6 and 10, with gains continuing through adolescence (Gomez-Perez & Ostrosky-Solis, 2006; Tabibi & Pfeffer, 2007; Vakil et al., 2009). Tasks tapping everyday requirements for selective attention reveal similar trends. In one study, researchers showed 6- to 11-year-olds computer images of safe and dangerous road-crossing scenes, sometimes with and sometimes without visual and auditory distractors (Tabibi & Pfeffer, 2007). Ability to distinguish safe from dangerous sites increased with age, even in the presence of distractors (see Figure 7.4), and also correlated positively with scores on laboratory attention tasks.

Older children are also better at flexibly adapting their attention to task requirements, switching mental sets within a task. When asked to sort a deck of cards with pictures that vary in both color and shape, children age 5 and older readily switch their basis of sorting from color to shape when asked to do so. Younger children persist in sorting in just one way, even though they know the rule system relevant to the task (pre-switch: *red* goes in this box, *blue* in that box; post-switch: *circles* go in this box, *triangles* in that box) (Brooks et al., 2003; Zelazo, Carlson, & Kesek, 2008).

Furthermore, with age, children adapt their attention to changes in their own learning. When given lists of items to learn and allowed to select half for further study, first graders do not choose systematically, but third graders select those they had previously missed (Masur, McIntyre, & Flavell, 1973). In research presenting complex information, such as prose passages, the ability to allocate attention based on previous performance continues to improve into the college years (Brown, Smiley, & Lawton, 1978).

How do children acquire selective, adaptable attention? Gains in two components of executive function—inhibition and attentional strategies—play vital roles.

Inhibition Sustained, selective, and adaptable attention requires **inhibition**—the ability to control internal and external distracting stimuli. Individuals who are skilled at inhibition can prevent the mind from straying to alternative attractive thoughts and can keep stimuli unrelated to a current goal from capturing their attention (Dempster & Corkill, 1999). By controlling irrelevant stimuli, inhibition frees working-memory resources for the task at hand and, therefore, supports many information-processing skills (Bjorklund & Harnishfeger, 1995; Handley et al., 2004; Klenberg, Korkman, & Lahti-Nuuttila, 2001).

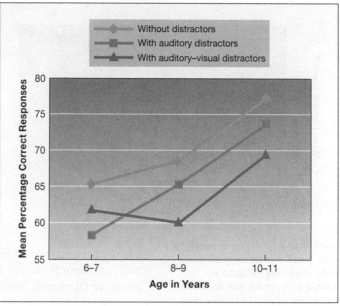

FIGURE 7.4 Gains in selective attention from age 6 to 11 years on a task requiring children to distinguish safe from dangerous road-crossing scenes. Children viewed computer images of road-crossing scenes, pushing a green key to indicate a safe scene and a red key to indicate an unsafe scene. On some sets of scenes, researchers introduced visual and auditory distractors, such as a dog barking, a train whistling, or a boy shouting. Accuracy increased with age, even under distracting conditions. (Adapted from Tabibi & Pfeffer, 2007.)

Amid the distractions of a subway car, these readers remain engrossed in their books. Gains in inhibition between ages 6 and 10 contribute to a dramatic improvement in selective attention—the capacity to focus on a task, ignoring irrelevant stimuli.

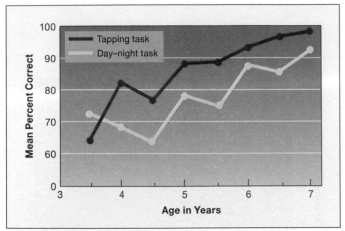

FIGURE 7.5 **Gains between ages 3 and 7 in performance on tasks requiring children to inhibit an impulse and focus on a competing goal.** In the tapping task, children had to tap once when the adult tapped twice and tap twice when the adult tapped once. In the day–night task, children had to say "night" to a picture of the sun and "day" to a picture of the moon with stars. (From A. Diamond, 2004, "Normal Development of Prefrontal Cortex from Birth to Young Adulthood: Cognitive Functions, Anatomy, and Biochemistry," as appeared in D. T. Stuss & R. T. Knight [Eds.], *Principles of Frontal Lobe Function.* New York: Oxford University Press, p. 474. Reprinted by permission of Adele Diamond.)

Besides helping children remember, reason, and solve problems, it assists them in managing their behavior in social situations. As we will see in later chapters, to get along with others, children must learn to restrain impulses and keep negative emotions in check.

The ability to inhibit thoughts and behavior improves from infancy on. Between ages 3 and 4, for example, preschoolers perform considerably better in situations in which they must follow some commands but not others, as in the game "Simon Says" (Jones, Rothbart, & Posner, 2003). On more complex tasks requiring children to inhibit distracting stimuli, marked gains occur from early to middle childhood. Consider, for example, a task in which the child must tap once after the adult taps twice and tap twice after the adult taps once, or must say "night" to a picture of the sun and "day" to a picture of the moon. As Figure 7.5 shows, 3- and 4-year-olds make many errors. But by age 6 to 7, children find such tasks easy (Johnson, Im-Bolter, & Pascual-Leone, 2003; Kirkham, Cruess, & Diamond, 2003). They can resist the "pull" of their attention toward a dominant stimulus—a skill that predicts social maturity as well as subsequent reading and math achievement, from kindergarten through high school (Blair & Razza, 2007; Duncan et al., 2007; Rhoades, Greenberg, & Domitrovich, 2009). ERP and fMRI measures reveal a steady age-related increase in activation of the prefrontal cortex while children engage in these inhibitory tasks (Bartgis, Lilly, & Thomas, 2003; Diamond, 2004; Luna et al., 2001).

High-quality preschool education can enhance inhibition and other attentional components of executive function. In *Tools of the Mind*—a preschool curriculum inspired by Vygotsky's theory—scaffolding of attention is woven into virtually all classroom activities (Bodrova & Leong, 2007). For example, teachers provide external aids to support attention: A child might hold a drawing of an ear as a reminder to listen and not interrupt a classmate who is telling a story. Teachers also lead games requiring frequent inhibition and rule-switching. And they encourage make-believe play, which helps children suppress impulses and use thought to guide behavior (see page 269 in Chapter 6). When preschoolers from low-income families, who often show deficits in attention, were randomly assigned to either Tools or comparison classrooms, the Tools children performed substantially better on end-of-year tasks assessing inhibition and other attentional capacities (Diamond et al., 2007). Nurturing attention through the Tools curriculum may prove powerful in early prevention of academic and behavior problems.

In sum, by clearing unnecessary stimuli, inhibition increases available space in working memory. This, in turn, opens the door to higher-level strategy use—working more effectively with information held in mind.

Attentional Strategies   Patricia Miller and her colleagues gave 3- to 9-year-olds a task requiring a selective attentional strategy—a large box with rows of doors that could be opened. On half the doors were pictures of cages, indicating that behind each was an animal. On the other half were pictures of houses, indicating that they contained household objects. Children were asked to remember the location of each object in one group, then given a study period in which they could open any doors they wished. Next they were shown pictures of each relevant object, one at a time, and asked to point to the object's location (DeMarie-Dreblow & Miller, 1988; Miller et al., 1986; Woody-Ramsey & Miller, 1988). The most efficient attentional strategy—opening only doors with relevant pictures on them—emerged and became refined in the following sequence:

1. **Production deficiency.** Preschoolers rarely engage in attentional strategies. In other words, they usually fail to *produce* strategies when they could be helpful. On the task just described, they simply opened all the doors.

2. **Control deficiency.** Young elementary school children sometimes produce strategies, but not consistently. They have difficulty *controlling*, or executing, strategies effectively. For example, 5-year-olds began to apply a selective attentional strategy—opening only relevant doors—but, at times, reverted to opening irrelevant doors.

3. **Utilization deficiency.** Slightly later, children execute strategies consistently, but their performance either does not improve or improves less than that of older children. For many 6- and 7-year-olds, opening only the relevant doors did not increase memory for object locations after the pictures were removed from the doors.

4. **Effective strategy use.** By the mid-elementary school years, children use strategies consistently, and performance improves (Miller, 2000).

As we will soon see, this sequence also characterizes children's use of memory strategies. Why, when children first use a strategy, does it not work well? Applying a new strategy generally requires so much effort and attention that little space in working memory remains to perform other parts of the task well (Woody-Dorning & Miller, 2001). Another reason a new strategy may not lead to performance gains is that young children are not good at monitoring their task performance (Schneider & Bjorklund, 2003). Because they fail to keep track of how well a strategy is working, they do not apply it consistently or refine it in other ways.

Planning

With age, children's attention undergoes a profound advance that contributes greatly to executive function: **Planning** involves thinking out a sequence of acts ahead of time and allocating attention accordingly to reach a goal (Scholnick, 1995). The seeds of effective planning are present in infancy. When researchers showed 2- and 3-month-olds a series of pictures that alternated in a predictable left–right sequence, the babies quickly learned to shift their focus to the location of the next stimulus before it appeared (Wentworth & Haith, 1998). And recall 4-month-olds' ability to engage in predictive tracking of objects' movements (see page 165 in Chapter 4). Even young infants' attention seems to be "future-oriented."

But on relatively simple tasks requiring children to reason about how best to implement a future action, preschoolers have great difficulty generating a plan. In one study, 3- to 5-year-olds were shown a doll named Molly, a camera, and a miniature zoo with a path, along which were three animal cages. The first and third cages had storage lockers next to them; the middle cage, with no locker, housed a kangaroo (see Figure 7.6). The children were told that Molly could follow the path only once and that she wanted to take a picture of the kangaroo, but there was no locker beside the kangaroo's cage in which to store the camera. Then they were asked, "What locker could you leave the camera in so Molly can get

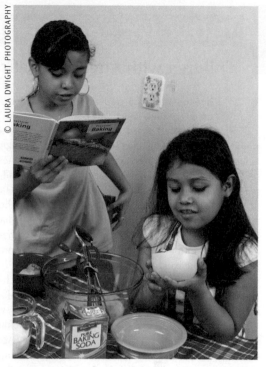
© LAURA DWIGHT PHOTOGRAPHY

While following a recipe, an 11-year-old provides her 7-year-old sister with guidance in planning, first gathering the ingredients and then combining them in correct sequence. With many everyday opportunities to practice, planning improves with age.

FIGURE 7.6 Miniature zoo used to assess preschoolers' planning. After being told that Molly wanted to take a picture of the kangaroo but could follow the path only once, preschoolers were asked to indicate which locker the camera should be left in so Molly could get it and take the photo. Not until age 5 did children plan, more often selecting the first locker; younger children chose the two lockers equally often. (Adapted from McColgan & McCormack, 2008.)

BIOLOGY and ENVIRONMENT

Children with Attention-Deficit Hyperactivity Disorder

While the other fifth graders worked quietly at their desks, Calvin squirmed, dropped his pencil, looked out the window, fiddled with his shoelaces, and talked aloud. "Hey Joey," he yelled over the heads of several classmates, "wanna play ball after school?" But the other children weren't eager to play with Calvin, who was physically awkward and failed to follow the rules of the game. He had trouble taking turns at bat. In the outfield, he tossed his mitt in the air and looked elsewhere when the ball came his way. Calvin's desk was a chaotic mess. He often lost his books, pencils, and other school materials, and he had trouble remembering assignments or deadlines.

Symptoms of ADHD

Calvin is one of 3 to 7 percent of U.S. school-age children with **attention-deficit hyperactivity disorder (ADHD),** which involves inattention, impulsivity, and excessive motor activity resulting in academic and social problems (American Psychiatric Association, 2000; Goldstein, 2011). Boys are diagnosed about four times as often as girls. However, many girls with ADHD seem to be overlooked, either because their symptoms are less flagrant or because of a gender bias: A difficult, disruptive boy is more likely to be referred for treatment (Abikoff et al., 2002; Biederman et al., 2005).

Children with ADHD cannot stay focused on a task that requires mental effort for more than a few minutes. They often act impulsively, ignoring social rules and lashing out with hostility when frustrated. Many, though not all, are *hyperactive,* exhausting parents and teachers and irritating other children with their excessive motor activity. For a child to be diagnosed with ADHD, these symptoms must have appeared before age 7 as a persistent problem.

Because of their difficulty concentrating, children with ADHD score 7 to 15 points lower than other children on intelligence tests (Barkley, 2002). Researchers agree that executive-function deficiencies underlie ADHD symptoms. According to one view, children with ADHD are impaired in capacity to inhibit action in favor of thought—a basic difficulty that results in wide-ranging inadequacies in executive processing and, therefore, in impulsive, disorganized behavior (Barkley, 2003). Another hypothesis is that ADHD is the direct result of a cluster of executive-processing problems that interfere with the ability to guide one's own actions (Brown, 2005, 2006). Research confirms that children with ADHD do poorly on tasks requiring sustained attention; find it hard to ignore irrelevant information; have difficulty with memory, planning, reasoning, and problem

solving in academic and social situations; and often fail to manage frustration and intense emotion (Barkley, 2003, 2006).

Origins of ADHD

ADHD runs in families and is highly heritable: Identical twins share it far more often than fraternal twins (Freitag et al., 2010; Rasmussen et al., 2004). Children with ADHD show abnormal brain functioning, including reduced electrical and blood-flow activity and structural abnormalities in the prefrontal cortex and in other areas involved in attention, inhibition of behavior, and additional aspects of motor control (see page 186 in Chapter 5) (Mackie et al., 2007; Sowell et al., 2003). Also, the brains of children with ADHD grow more slowly and are about 3 percent smaller in overall volume, with a thinner cerebral cortex, than the brains of unaffected agemates (Narr et al., 2009; Shaw et al., 2007). Several genes that disrupt functioning of the neurotransmitters serotonin (involved in inhibition and self-control) and dopamine (required for effective cognitive processing) have been implicated in the disorder (Bobb et al., 2006; Faraone & Mick, 2010).

At the same time, ADHD is associated with environmental factors. Prenatal teratogens, such as tobacco, alcohol, and environmental pollutants, are linked to inattention and

it and take a photo of the kangaroo?" (McColgan & McCormack, 2008). Below age 5, children were unable to plan effectively; they selected the two lockers with equal frequency. Yet in a task with the same elements that asked children to reason about the past—Molly took the kangaroo's picture, stored the camera in a locker, and after traveling the path can't find it, so at which location is she likely to recover it?—4-year-olds often succeeded.

These findings—and others—indicate marked gains in planning around 5 years of age (Hudson, Sosa, & Shapiro, 1997). Apparently, reasoning about a sequence of future events, which the child has never before experienced, is more difficult than reasoning about a sequence of past events, which the child has directly observed.

On more complex planning tasks, further improvement occurs during middle childhood. When 5- to 9-year-olds were given lists of items to obtain from a play grocery store, older children more often took time to scan the store before shopping and also paused more often to look for each item before moving to get it. Consequently, they followed shorter routes through the aisles (Gauvain & Rogoff, 1989; Szepkouski, Gauvain, & Carberry, 1994).

Planning in most everyday tasks requires children to coordinate attention skills with other cognitive processes. To solve problems involving multiple steps, children must imagine future possibilities, postpone action in favor of evaluating alternatives, organize task materials (such as items on a grocery list), and remember the steps of their plan so they can attend to each one in sequence. Along the way, they must monitor how well the plan works and revise it if necessary. Clearly, planning places heavy demands on working memory. Not

For the 7-year-old on the right, who has ADHD, a classroom offering many opportunities for active learning may combine with other interventions to help her sustain attention.

hyperactivity (see Chapter 3). Furthermore, children with ADHD are more likely to come from homes in which marriages are unhappy and family stress is high. But a stressful home life rarely causes ADHD. Rather, these children's behaviors can contribute to family problems, which intensify the child's preexisting difficulties.

Treating ADHD

Calvin's doctor eventually prescribed stimulant medication, the most common treatment for ADHD. As long as dosage is carefully regulated, these drugs reduce activity level and improve attention, academic performance, and peer relations for about 70 percent of children who take them (Greenhill, Halperin, & Abikoff, 1999). Stimulant medication seems to increase activity in the frontal lobes, thereby improving the child's capacity to sustain attention and to inhibit off-task and self-stimulating behavior.

In 2006, an advisory panel convened by the U.S. Food and Drug Administration warned that stimulants might impair heart functioning, even causing sudden death in a few individuals, and advocated warning labels describing these potential risks. Debate over the safety of medication for ADHD is likely to intensify. In any case, medication is not enough. Drugs cannot teach children to compensate for inattention and impulsivity. The most effective treatment approach combines medication with interventions that model and reinforce appropriate academic and social behavior (American Academy of Pediatrics, 2005a; Smith, Barkley, & Shapiro, 2006).

Family intervention is also important. Inattentive, overactive children strain the patience of parents, who are likely to react punitively and inconsistently—a child-rearing style that strengthens defiant, aggressive behavior. In fact, in 50 to 75 percent of adolescent cases, these two sets of behavior problems occur together (Goldstein, 2011).

Some media reports suggest that the number of U.S. children diagnosed with ADHD has increased greatly. But two large surveys yielded similar overall prevalence rates 25 years ago and today. Nevertheless, the incidence of ADHD is much higher in some communities than in others. At times, children are overdiagnosed and unnecessarily medicated because their parents and teachers are impatient with inattentive, active behavior that is within normal range (Mayes, Bagwell, & Erkulwater, 2008). In Hong Kong, where academic success is particularly prized, children are diagnosed at more than twice the rate in the United States. But in Great Britain, where doctors are hesitant to label children with ADHD or to prescribe medication, children are underdiagnosed and often do not receive the treatment they need (Taylor, 2004).

ADHD is usually a lifelong disorder. Adults with ADHD continue to need help—in structuring their environments, regulating negative emotion, selecting appropriate careers, and understanding their condition as a biological deficit rather than a character flaw.

surprisingly, even when young children do plan, they succeed only on tasks with a small number of steps.

Children learn much from cultural tools that support planning—directions for playing games, patterns for construction, recipes for cooking—especially when they collaborate with more expert planners. When 4- to 7-year-olds were observed jointly constructing a toy with their mothers, the mothers provided basic information about the usefulness of plans and how to implement specific steps: "Do you want to look at the picture and see what goes where? What piece do you need first?" After working with their mothers, younger children more often referred to the plan when building on their own (Gauvain, 2004; Gauvain, de la Ossa, & Hurtado-Ortiz, 2001).

Having many opportunities to practice planning helps children understand its components and use that knowledge. Parents can foster planning by encouraging it in everyday activities, from loading the dishwasher to planning for a vacation. In one study, parent–child discussions involving planning at ages 4 to 9 predicted planning competence in adolescence (Gauvain & Huard, 1999). The demands of academic tasks—and teachers' explanations of how to plan—also contribute to gains in planning.

The attentional strategies we have just considered are crucial for both school and life success. Unfortunately, some children have grave difficulties paying attention. See the Biology and Environment box above for a discussion of the serious learning and behavior problems of children with attention-deficit hyperactivity disorder.

Review ■ How does inhibition support development of attention and other information-processing skills?

Connect ■ What other components of executive function likely contribute to improved planning in middle childhood? What can adults do to scaffold children's planning skills?

Apply ■ At age 7, Jonah played his piano pieces from beginning to end instead of spending extra time on the hard sections. Around age 8, he devoted more time to sections he knew least well, but his performance did not improve for several months. What explains Jonah's gradual gains in strategy use and performance?

Reflect ■ Describe an instance in which you applied a strategy for the first time but experienced a utilization deficiency. Why do you think the deficiency occurred, and how did you overcome it?

▶ Describe the development of strategies for storing and retrieving information from memory.

▶ Explain the development of episodic memory and its relationship to semantic memory.

▶ How does eyewitness memory change with age, and what factors influence the accuracy of children's reports?

Memory

As attention improves, so do *memory strategies*—deliberate mental operations we use to increase the likelihood of retaining information in working memory and transferring it to our long-term knowledge base. In Chapters 4 and 6, we saw that during the first two years, memory for objects, people, and events—as assessed in operant conditioning, habituation, and deferred-imitation studies—undergoes dramatic gains. With age, babies remember more information over longer periods (see pages 141 and 233).

But relative to children and adults, infants and toddlers engage in little effortful, strategic memorizing. For the most part, they remember unintentionally, as part of their ongoing activities (Bjorklund, 2012). And when memory strategies emerge in early childhood, they are not very successful at first (Schneider, 2002). Not until middle childhood do these executive techniques take a giant leap forward.

Strategies for Storing Information

Researchers have studied the development of three strategies that enhance memory for new information: rehearsal, organization, and elaboration.

Rehearsal, Organization, and Elaboration **TAKE A MOMENT...** Next time you have a list of things to learn, such as major cities in your state or country, or items to buy at the supermarket, notice your behavior. You are likely to repeat the information to yourself, a memory strategy called **rehearsal**—a procedure mentioned earlier that holds information in working memory. And you will probably group related items (for example, all the cities in the same part of the country), a strategy called **organization.**

Why are young children not adept at rehearsal and organization? Memory strategies require extra space in working memory and time and effort to perfect. Even when school-age children use these strategies more often—around age 7 for rehearsal and age 8 for organization—many show *control* and *utilization deficiencies* (Bjorklund, Dukes, & Brown, 2009). For example, 7- to 8-year-olds often rehearse in a piecemeal fashion. When given the word *cat* in a list of items, they say, "*Cat, cat, cat.*" In contrast, older children combine previous words with each new item, saying "*Desk, man, yard, cat, cat.*" This more active rehearsal approach, in which neighboring words create contexts for one another that trigger recall, yields much better memory (Lehman & Hasselhorn, 2007, 2010). Similarly, younger children usually organize items by their everyday association: "*hat–head,*" "*carrot–rabbit.*" Older children group such items into *taxonomic categories,* based on common properties— clothing, body parts, food, animals. Placing more items in a few categories permits more efficient organization, dramatically improving memory (Bjorklund et al., 1994). Experience with materials that form clear categories and adult demonstration and prompting to organize helps children use organization and, eventually, apply the strategy to less clearly related materials (Güller et al., 2010; Schlagmüller & Schneider, 2002).

SOCIAL ISSUES: EDUCATION

Media Multitasking Disrupts Learning

"Mom, I'm going to study for my biology test now," called 16-year-old Ashley while shutting her bedroom door. Sitting down at her desk, she accessed a popular social-networking website on her laptop, donned headphones and began listening to a favorite song on her MP3 player, and placed her cell phone next to her elbow so she could hear it chime if any text messages arrived. Only then did she open her textbook and begin to read.

In a survey of a nationally representative sample of U.S. 8- to 18-year-olds, more than two-thirds reported engaging in two or more media activities at once, some or most of the time (Rideout, Foehr, & Roberts, 2010). Their most frequent type of media multitasking is listening to music while doing homework, but many also report watching TV or using the Internet while studying (Jeong & Fishbein, 2007). The presence of a television or computer in the young person's bedroom is a strong predictor of this behavior (Foehr, 2006). And it extends into classrooms, where students can be seen text-messaging under their desks or surfing the Internet on cell phones.

Research confirms that media multitasking greatly reduces learning. In one experiment, participants were given two tasks: learning to predict the weather in two different cities using colored shapes as cues and keeping a mental tally of how many high-pitched beeps they heard through headphones. Half the sample performed the tasks simultaneously, the other half separately. Both groups learned to predict the weather in the two-city situation, but the multitaskers were unable to apply their learning to new weather problems (Foerde, Knowlton, & Poldrack, 2006).

fMRI evidence revealed that the participants working only on the weather task activated the hippocampus, which plays a vital role in *explicit memory*—conscious, strategic recall, which enables new information to be used flexibly and adaptively in contexts outside the original learning situation (see page 190 in Chapter 5). In contrast, the multitaskers activated subcortical areas involved in *implicit memory*—a shallower, automatic form of learning that takes place unconsciously.

As early as 1980, studies linked heavy media use with executive-function difficulties (Nunez-Smith et al., 2008). Frequent media multitaskers, who are accustomed to continuously shifting their attention between tasks, have a harder time filtering out irrelevant stimuli when they are not multitasking (Ophir, Nass, & Wagner, 2009).

Checking phone and text messages while studying may seem harmless—and irresistible. But research suggests that the attention shifting involved in media multitasking interferes with learning.

Beyond superficial preparation for her biology test, Ashley is likely to have trouble concentrating and strategically processing new information after turning off her computer and MP3 player. Experienced teachers often complain that compared to students of a generation ago, today's teenagers are more easily distracted and learn less thoroughly. One teacher reflected, "It's the way they've grown up—working short times on many different things at one time" (Clay, 2009, p. 40).

Furthermore, older children are more likely to apply several memory strategies at once, rehearsing, organizing, and stating category names. The more strategies they use, the better they remember (Coyle & Bjorklund, 1997; Schwenck, Bjorklund, & Schneider, 2007). Although younger children's use of multiple memory strategies may have little impact on performance, their tendency to experiment is adaptive, allowing them to discover which strategies work best on different tasks and how to combine them effectively. For example, second to fourth graders know that a good way to study lists is to organize the items first, next rehearse category names, and then rehearse individual items (Hock, Park, & Bjorklund, 1998).

By the end of middle childhood, children start to use a third memory strategy, **elaboration.** It involves creating a relationship, or shared meaning, between two or more pieces of information that do not belong to the same category. For example, to learn the words *fish* and *pipe,* you might generate the verbal statement or mental image, "The fish is smoking a pipe." This highly effective memory technique becomes more common during adolescence as young people improve at holding two or more items in mind while generating complex, meaningful associations (Schneider & Pressley, 1997).

In sum, older-school-age children and adolescents have become adept at strategic memorizing. But while doing schoolwork, they frequently engage in other pursuits—most often, media activities, such as text messaging and e-mailing friends, listening to music, and watching TV or videos. To find out what happens to knowledge acquisition when students engage in this "media multitasking," consult the Social Issues: Education box above.

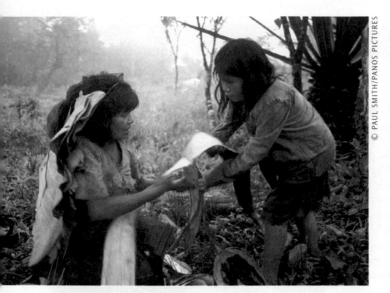

This child of the U'wa people of Colombia, who have no written tradition, would have trouble recalling isolated bits of information, as school tasks require. But she demonstrates keen memory for the steps involved in making traditional cocara leaf hats.

Culture, Schooling, and Memory Strategies People usually employ memory strategies when they need to remember information for its own sake. On many other occasions, memory occurs as a natural byproduct of participation in daily activities (Rogoff, 2003). In a study illustrating this idea, 4- and 5-year-olds were told either to *play with* a set of toys or to *remember* them. The play condition produced far better recall because the children engaged in many spontaneous organizations. These included using objects in typical ways (putting a shoe on a doll's foot) and narrating their activities: "I'm squeezing this lemon," or "Fly away in this helicopter, doggie" (Newman, 1990).

A repeated finding is that people in non-Western cultures who lack formal schooling rarely use or benefit from instruction in memory strategies because they see no practical reason to use these techniques (Rogoff & Mistry, 1985). Tasks that require children to remember isolated bits of information, which are common in school, strongly motivate use of memory strategies. In fact, Western children get so much practice with this type of learning that they do not refine techniques that rely on cues available in every life, such as spatial location and arrangement of objects (Mistry, 1997). For example, Guatemalan Mayan 9-year-olds do slightly better than their U.S. agemates when told to remember the placement of 40 familiar objects in a play scene. U.S. children often rehearse object names when it would be more effective to keep track of spatial relations (Rogoff & Waddell, 1982). The development of memory strategies, then, is not just a matter of a more competent information-processing system. It is also a product of task demands and cultural circumstances.

Retrieving Information

Once information enters our long-term knowledge base, we must *retrieve* (or recover) it to use it again. We retrieve information in three ways: through recognition, recall, and reconstruction. As we discuss these approaches to remembering, we will consider how children's expanding knowledge base affects their memory performance. We will also delve into the accuracy of a special type of memory—children's eyewitness accounts in legal proceedings—that can seriously affect their own and others' welfare.

Recognition and Recall TAKE A MOMENT... Show a young child a set of 10 pictures or toys. Then mix them up with some unfamiliar items, and ask the child to point to the ones in the original set. Noticing that a stimulus is identical or similar to one previously experienced is called **recognition.** It is the simplest form of retrieval, since the material to be remembered is fully present during testing to serve as its own retrieval cue.

As the habituation research discussed in Chapters 4 and 6 reveals, even young infants are good at recognition. The ability to recognize a larger number of stimuli over longer delays improves steadily with age, reaching a near-adult level during the preschool years. For example, after viewing a series of 80 pictures, 4-year-olds correctly discriminated 90 percent from pictures not in the original set (Brown & Campione, 1972). Because recognition appears early and develops rapidly, it is probably a fairly automatic process. Nevertheless, the ability of older children to apply strategies during storage, such as rehearsal and organization, increases the number of items recognized later (Mandler & Robinson, 1978).

TAKE A MOMENT... Now keep the items out of view, and ask the child to name the ones she saw. This more challenging task requires **recall**—generating a mental representation of an absent stimulus. The beginnings of recall appear in the second half of the first year for memories that are strongly cued. Think back to the rapid gains in deferred imitation under way after age 6 months, discussed in Chapter 6—good evidence for recall. Development of recall lags behind recognition from infancy on. In early childhood, young children's recall in tasks that require retention of pieces of information is far poorer than their recognition. At age 2, children can recall no more than one or two items, at age 4 only about three or four (Perlmutter, 1984).

Improvement in recall over the preschool years is strongly associated with language development, which greatly enhances long-lasting representations of both lists of items and past experiences (Melby-Lervag & Hulme, 2010; Ornstein, Haden, & Elischberger, 2006; Simcock & Hayne, 2003). Yet even when asked to recall an event that occurred weeks earlier, young children report only part of what could be remembered. In one longitudinal study, sixth graders were asked to tell what happened when they went to an archeological museum in kindergarten. They said less about the experience than when they had been asked the same question as kindergartners, six weeks after the museum trip. But in response to specific retrieval cues, including photos of the event, sixth graders remembered a great deal. And in some respects, their recall was more accurate (Hudson & Fivush, 1991). For example, they inferred that adults had hidden artifacts in a sandbox for them to find, whereas in kindergarten they simply recalled digging for objects.

Compared with recognition, recall shows far greater improvement because older children make use of a wider range of retrieval cues. With age, the long-term knowledge base grows larger and becomes organized into increasingly elaborate, hierarchically structured networks (Bjorklund, 2012; Schneider, 2002). When representations of items or experiences are interconnected in long-term memory, many internal retrieval cues can be used to recall them later.

Reconstruction   When we must remember complex, meaningful material, we do not merely copy material into the system at storage and faithfully reproduce it at retrieval. Instead, we select and interpret information we encounter in our everyday lives in terms of our existing knowledge. Once we have transformed the material, we often have difficulty distinguishing it from the original (Bartlett, 1932). Constructive processing can take place during any phase of information processing. It can occur during storage. In fact, the memory strategies of organization and elaboration are within the province of constructive memory because both involve generating relationships between stimuli. Constructive processing can also involve **reconstruction** of information, or recoding it while it is in the system or being retrieved.

Do children reconstruct stored information? Clearly, they do. When asked to recall and retell a story, children, like adults, condense, integrate, and add information. By age 5 or 6, children recall important features of a story while forgetting unimportant ones, combine information into more tightly knit units, reorder the sequence of events in more logical fashion, and even include new information that fits with a passage's meaning (Bischofshausen, 1985).

Furthermore, when children receive new information related to a story they previously recalled, they reconstruct the story further. In one study, before telling each of three stories, an adult gave kindergartners information about a main character that was positive ("a nice" child), negative ("not a nice" child), or neutral. Children reconstructed the main character's behaviors to fit with prior information (Greenhoot, 2000). Compared with those in the neutral condition, those in the positive condition offered a more positive account, those in the negative condition a more negative account. Seven to ten days later, a fourth story gave children additional information about the main character. In some conditions, the new information was consistent with the original information; in others, it conflicted—for example, the "nice" child was now described as a "mean" child. Children again revised their recollections of the main character's behavior accordingly.

In revising information in meaningful ways, children give themselves a wealth of helpful retrieval cues to use during recall. Over time, as originally provided information decays, children make more inferences about actors and actions, adding events and interpretations that help make sense of a story. This process

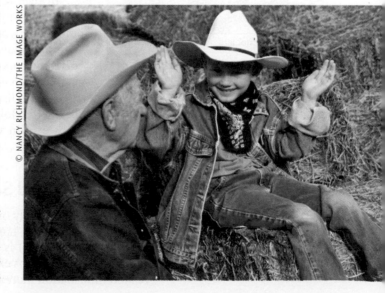

As he tells a story to his grandfather, this child growing up on a Colorado ranch engages in reconstruction, selecting, interpreting, and reordering events and details.

© NANCY RICHMOND/THE IMAGE WORKS

increases the coherence of reconstructed information and, therefore, its memorableness. Gains in working-memory capacity and language skills, which support the organization and complexity of children's recollections, predict the extent to which 9- to 11-year-olds reframe their story recall in response to new information—overriding previously acquired events and viewpoints, elaborating on and integrating old and new details into a coherent picture (Tsethlikai & Greenhoot, 2006). At the same time, as these findings reveal, much information children and adults recall can be inaccurate.

Another View of Reconstruction: Fuzzy-Trace Theory   So far, we have emphasized deliberate reconstruction of meaningful material, using new information and the long-term knowledge base to interpret it. According to C. J. Brainerd and Valerie Reyna's (1993, 2001) **fuzzy-trace theory,** when we first encode information, we reconstruct it automatically, creating a vague, fuzzy version called a **gist,** which preserves essential meaning without details and is especially useful for reasoning. Although we can also retain a literal, verbatim version, we have a bias toward gist because it requires less space in working memory, freeing attention for the steps involved in thinking. For example, a person choosing among several recipes to prepare a dish for dinner relies on gist representations, noting which recipes are easier and have low-cost ingredients. But once he has selected a recipe, he needs verbatim information to prepare it. Because he is unlikely to have remembered those details, he consults the cookbook.

Fuzzy-trace theorists take issue with the assumption that all reconstructions are transformations of verbatim memory. Instead, they believe that both verbatim and gist memories are present but are stored separately to be used for different purposes. With age, children rely less on verbatim memory and more on fuzzy, reconstructed gists. To illustrate, researchers presented children with the following problem: "Farmer Brown owns many animals. He has three dogs, five sheep, seven chickens, nine horses, and eleven cows." Then they asked two types of questions: (1) questions requiring verbatim knowledge ("How many cows does Farmer Brown own, eleven or nine?") and (2) questions requiring only gist information ("Does Farmer Brown have more cows or more horses?"). As Figure 7.7 shows, preschoolers were better at answering verbatim- than gist-dependent questions, whereas the reverse was true for second graders (Brainerd & Gordon, 1994).

Fuzzy-trace theory adds to our understanding of reconstruction by indicating that it can occur immediately, as soon as information is encoded. Fuzzy-trace research reveals that although memory is vital for reasoning, getting bogged down in details (as young children tend to do) can interfere with effective problem solving. And because fuzzy traces are less likely than verbatim memories to be forgotten, gists can serve as enduring retrieval cues, contributing to improved recall of details with age (Brainerd & Reyna, 1995).

In such recall, however, gists heighten the chances of reporting false items consistent with the fuzzy meaning of an experience. After studying a list containing the words *bed, rest, wake, tired, dream, blanket, nap,* and *snooze,* adolescents and adults—who are more skilled gist thinkers—not only recall more items correctly than children but also mention more gist-related words not in the list, such as *sleep.* Children's false reports, in contrast, are frequently unrelated to a just-studied list—for example, *candy* or *fire* following presentation of the *sleep* list (Brainerd, Holliday, & Reyna, 2004; Brainerd et al., 2006). Fuzzy-trace theory helps explain why some memory inaccuracies decrease with age, while others increase.

FIGURE 7.7 Preschoolers' and second graders' performance on verbatim and gist memory questions. Preschoolers did better on the verbatim than on the gist memory test; for second graders, the reverse was true. (Adapted from Brainerd & Gordon, 1994.)

Knowledge and Semantic Memory

Our vast, taxonomically organized and hierarchically structured general knowledge system, consisting of concepts, language meanings, facts, and rules (such as memory strategies and arithmetic procedures) is often referred to as **semantic memory.** In previous sections, we suggested that children's expanding knowledge promotes improved memory by making new, related information more meaningful so that it is easier to store and retrieve.

A landmark study testing this idea looked at how well third- through eighth-grade chess experts could remember complex chessboard arrangements (Chi, 1978). The children recalled the configurations considerably better than adults who knew how to play chess but were not especially knowledgeable—findings that cannot be explained by the selection of very bright youngsters with exceptional memories. When participants were given a digit-span task, however, the adults did better.

In Chi's study of chess-playing children, better memory was credited to a larger chess-related knowledge base. Experts also have more elaborately structured knowledge. In another investigation, researchers classified elementary school children as either experts or novices in knowledge of soccer and then gave both groups lists of soccer and nonsoccer items to learn. As in Chi's study, the experts remembered far more items on the soccer list (but not on the nonsoccer list) than the nonexperts. And during recall, the experts' listing of items was better organized, as indicated by clustering of items into categories (Schneider & Bjorklund, 1992). This greater organization at retrieval suggests that highly knowledgeable children apply memory strategies in their area of expertise with little or no effort—by rapidly associating new items with the large number they already know. Such *automatic* recall lets experts devote more working-memory resources to using recalled information to reason and solve problems (Bjorklund & Douglas, 1997).

Knowledge, though powerfully influential, is not the only important factor in children's strategic memory processing. Children who are expert in an area are usually highly motivated as well. Faced with new information, they ask themselves, "What can I do to learn this more effectively?" As a result, they not only acquire knowledge more quickly but also *actively use what they know* to add more. In contrast, academically unsuccessful children fail to ask how previously stored information can clarify new information. This, in turn, interferes with the development of a broad knowledge base (Schneider & Bjorklund, 1998). In sum, extensive knowledge and use of memory strategies support one another.

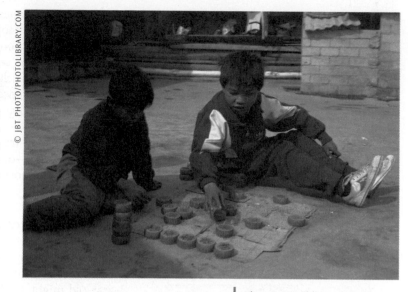

These young Chinese chess players have become experts at the game. Their extensive knowledge of chess-related information gives them an advantage over less knowledgeable adults in accurately recalling complex chessboard arrangements.

Episodic Memory

The knowledge that makes up semantic memory does not require storage of when or where the information was acquired. In this way, it differs from **episodic memory,** recollections of personally experienced events that occurred at a specific time and place—for example, what you did after you got up this morning or how you celebrated your high school graduation. In Chapters 4 and 6, we saw that children begin acquiring semantic knowledge (such as categories and word meanings) in infancy, and by early childhood, their knowledge base is considerable (Murphy, 2002). Although they have less than older individuals, the structure of their semantic knowledge and the cognitive processes that support its acquisition are similar to those of adults.

Researchers agree that semantic memory develops earlier than episodic memory. Although infants and toddlers have some ability to encode unique events, their capacity to organize those events temporally and to retrieve event details is limited. Not until 3 or 4 years of age do children seem to have a well-functioning episodic memory system (Howe & Courage, 1997).

Semantic knowledge contributes vitally to the development of episodic memory (Murphy, McKone, & Slee, 2003). Children who have acquired substantial knowledge for interpreting personally experienced events are better able to recall those events than children with less knowledge (Robertson & Köhler, 2007). In addition to rapidly expanding semantic knowledge, 3- to 6-year-olds improve in memory for relations among stimuli. For example, in a set of photos, they remember not just the animals they saw but the contexts in which they saw them—a bear emerging from a tunnel, a zebra tied to a tree on a city street (Lloyd, Doydum, & Newcombe, 2009). The capacity to bind together information supports the development of episodic memory in early childhood.

Furthermore, young children's sense of self must be sufficiently developed to support episodic memory. To recall events, children must link time- and place-specific information to the self—to their own inner sense of "mental time travel" (Wheeler, Stuss, & Tulving, 1997, p. 332). They must realize that the remembered event is actually something that they themselves previously experienced—a milestone attained early in the preschool years.

In the following sections, we trace the development of two types of episodic memory: (1) memory for recurring events—ones that children experience repeatedly in the course of their everyday lives; and (2) memory for significant one-time events that children integrate into their personal life stories.

Scripts Like adults, preschoolers remember repeated events—what you do when you go to child care or get ready for bed—in terms of **scripts, general descriptions of what occurs and when it occurs in a particular situation.** Young children's scripts begin as a structure of main acts. For example, when asked to tell what happens at a restaurant, a 3-year-old might say, "You go in, get the food, eat, and then pay." Although children's first scripts contain only a few acts, as long as events in a situation take place in causal order, they are almost always recalled in correct sequence. Still, to obtain young children's scripted reports, adults must work hard, asking questions and prompting (Bauer, 2002, 2006). With age, scripts become more spontaneous and elaborate, as in this 5-year-old's account of going to a restaurant: "You go in. You can sit in the booths or at a table. Then you tell the waitress what you want. You eat. If you want dessert, you can have some. Then you pay and go home" (Hudson, Fivush, & Kuebli, 1992).

Scripts are a special form of reconstructive memory. When we experience repeated events, we fuse them into the same script representation. Then any specific instance of a scripted experience becomes hard to recall. **TAKE A MOMENT...** Try recalling what you had for dinner two or three days ago. Unless it was out of the ordinary, you probably cannot remember. The same is true for young children. In this way, scripts help prevent long-term memory from being cluttered with unimportant information.

Scripts help children (and adults) organize and interpret everyday experiences. Once formed, they can be used to predict what will happen on similar occasions in the future. Children rely on scripts to assist recall when listening to and telling stories. They also act out scripts in make-believe play as they pretend to go on a trip or play school. And scripts support children's earliest efforts at planning as they represent sequences of actions that lead to desired goals (Hudson & Mayhew, 2009).

Some researchers believe that the general event structures of scripts provide a foundation for organizing memory for unique events—a special birthday party or weekend trip. When given general event cues ("Tell me what happened one time *when you went to a birthday party*"), children as young as 3 could retrieve specific memories (Hudson & Nelson, 1986). But when given other cues, such as an emotion ("Tell me what happened one time *when you were scared*"), preschoolers had difficulty (Hudson et al., 1992). Let's turn to the development of this second type of episodic memory.

Autobiographical Memory Each of us has a unique **autobiographical memory, made up of representations of one-time events that are long-lasting because they are imbued** with personal meaning. How does memory for autobiographical events—the day a sibling was born or the first time you took an airplane—arise and persist for a lifetime? At least two developments make this possible. First, as noted earlier, children must have a sufficiently clear self-image to serve as an anchor for personally significant events. That is, they must be able to encode events as "something that happened to me"—a milestone reached around age 2 years (see Chapter 11) (Howe, Courage, & Rooksby, 2009). Second, children must integrate their experiences into a meaningful, time-organized life story. They learn to structure personally significant memories in narrative form by conversing about them with adults—

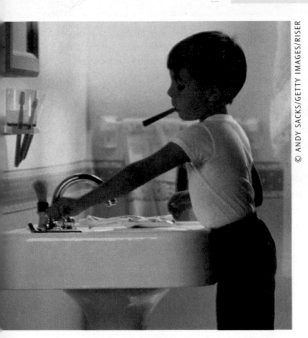

© ANDY SACKS/GETTY IMAGES/RISER

Children remember repeated events in terms of scripts, general descriptions of what happens in a particular situation. With age, scripts become more elaborate: "You squeeze out the toothpaste and brush your teeth. You rinse your mouth, then your toothbrush."

especially parents, who expand on their fragmented recollections (Nelson & Fivush, 2004).

Parents begin talking about past events with children as young as age 1½ to 2 years. As preschoolers' cognitive and language skills improve, parents' conversations about past events become more complex. Gradually, children adopt the narrative thinking of these dialogues: Their independent descriptions of special events become better organized, detailed, enriched with a personal perspective, and related to the larger context of their lives (Fivush, 2001). A young preschooler simply reports, "I went camping." Older preschoolers include specifics: when and where the event happened and who was present. With age, preschoolers add evaluative information—why, for example, an event was exciting, difficult, funny, sad, or made them feel proud or embarrassed ("I loved sleeping all night in the tent!")—that explains the event's personal significance.

Adults use two styles to elicit children's autobiographical narratives. In the *elaborative style,* they follow the child's lead, discussing topics of interest to the child, asking varied questions, adding information to the child's statements, and volunteering their own recollections and evaluations of events. For example, after visiting the zoo, one parent asked her 4-year-old, "What was the first thing we did? Why weren't the parrots in their cages? I thought the roaring lion was scary. What did you think?" In this way, the parent helped the child reestablish and reorganize his memory of the outing. In contrast, adults who use the *repetitive style* keep repeating the same questions regardless of the child's interest, providing little additional information: "Do you remember the zoo? What did we do at the zoo? What did we do there?"

Preschoolers who experience the elaborative style recall more information about past events, and they also produce more organized and detailed personal stories when followed up 1 to 2 years later (Cleveland & Reese, 2005; Farrant & Reese, 2000). Parents can be trained to use an elaborative style, and doing so enhances the richness of preschoolers' autobiographical memories (Reese & Newcombe, 2007).

As children talk with adults about the past, they not only expand their autobiographical recollections but also create a shared history that strengthens close relationships and self-understanding. In line with these ideas, parents and preschoolers with secure attachment bonds engage in more elaborate reminiscing than those with insecure bonds, who generally limit themselves to the repetitive style (Bost et al., 2006; Fivush & Reese, 2002). And children of elaborative-style parents describe themselves in clearer, more consistent ways (Bird & Reese, 2006). When, in past-event conversations, a child discovers that she finds swimming, running, climbing, getting together with friends, and going to the zoo fun, she can begin to connect these specific experiences into a general understanding of "what I enjoy." The result is a clearer image of herself.

Beginning in the preschool years, girls tend to have better organized and detailed autobiographical memories than boys (Bauer et al., 2007). And compared with Asian children, Western children produce narratives with more talk about their own thoughts, emotions, and preferences—knowledge that contributes to an appreciation of the personal meaning of events and, therefore, to better recall (Wang, 2008). These differences fit with variations in parent–child conversations. Parents reminisce in greater detail and talk more about the emotional significance of events with daughters (Bruce, Dolan, & Phillips-Grant, 2000; Fivush, 2009). And collectivist cultural valuing of interdependence leads many Asian parents to discourage children from talking about themselves. Chinese parents, for example, engage in less detailed and evaluative past-event dialogues with their preschoolers (Fivush & Wang, 2005; Wang, 2006a). Consistent with these early experiences, women report an earlier age of first memory and more vivid early memories than men. And Western adults' autobiographical memories include earlier, more detailed events that focus more on their own roles than do the memories of Asians, who tend to highlight the roles of others (Wang, 2003, 2006b).

Autobiographical memory becomes increasingly elaborate over middle childhood and adolescence. Teenagers expand greatly on the evaluative, personal meaning of autobiographical

© ROBERT BRENNER/PHOTOEDIT

As this toddler talks with his mother about past experiences, she responds in an elaborative style, asking varied questions and contributing her own recollections. Through such conversations, she enriches his autobiographical memory.

LOOK and LISTEN

Observe a parent or teacher conversing with one or more 4- to 7-year-olds about a special one-time past event, such as a vacation, birthday celebration, or school field trip. Did the adult use the elaborative style? How detailed and evaluative were the children's recollections?

events—a change that may reflect a more intense desire to make sense of past experiences in their quest for an identity (see Chapter 11) (Pasupathi & Wainryb, 2010). Nevertheless, few of us can retrieve autobiographical events that happened to us before age 3. Why do we experience this *infantile amnesia?* Refer to the Biology and Environment box on the following page for research aimed at answering this question.

Eyewitness Memory

The accuracy and completeness of children's episodic memories are central to their ability to recount relevant experiences when testifying in court cases involving child abuse and neglect, child custody, and other legal matters. Until recently, children younger than age 5 were rarely asked to testify, and not until age 10 were they assumed fully competent to do so. As a result of societal reactions to rising rates of child abuse and the difficulty of prosecuting perpetrators, legal requirements for child testimony have been relaxed in the United States (Sandler, 2006). Children as young as age 3 frequently serve as witnesses.

Compared with preschoolers, school-age children are better at giving accurate, detailed descriptions of past experiences and correctly inferring others' motives and intentions. Older children are also more resistant to misleading questions that attorneys may ask when probing for more information or trying to influence the child's response (Roebers & Schneider, 2001). What makes younger children more prone to memory errors? The following factors are involved:

- Responding to interview questions is challenging for children whose language competence is not well-developed. Preschoolers are often unaware when they do not understand, and they answer the question anyway.
- Preschoolers are especially poor at *source-monitoring*—identifying where they got their knowledge, even minutes after they acquired it. They often confuse what they heard or saw on TV with what actually occurred.
- Accurately reporting certain temporal information is difficult for younger children. Before age 8 to 10, they are far better at providing the sequence of what happened than saying how often and on which dates an event occurred.
- Younger children are less skilled at *inhibition*—ignoring irrelevant information—which contributes to their greater willingness to accept adult suggestions that are inconsistent with experienced events.
- When an adult asks a yes-or-no question ("Was he holding a screwdriver?"), younger children are more likely to agree, perhaps out of a desire to please.
- Preschoolers' bias toward verbatim representations (encoding specifics) leads them to forget more easily than older children, whose gist memories persist over time and serve as retrieval cues for details. (But, as noted on page 296, older children are prone to memory inaccuracies consistent with their gists.)
- Because younger children are less competent at using narratives to report their autobiographical memories systematically and completely, they may omit information that they actually remember (Brainerd, Reyna, & Poole, 2000; Melinder, Endestad, & Magnusson, 2006; Pipe & Salmon, 2009; Poole & Lindsay, 2001; Roberts & Powell, 2005).

Nevertheless, when properly questioned, even 3-year-olds can recall recent events accurately (Peterson & Rideout, 1998). And in the face of biased interviewing, adolescents and adults often form elaborate false memories (Ceci et al., 2007).

Suggestibility   Court testimony often involves repeated questioning—a procedure that, by itself, negatively affects children's response consistency and accuracy (Krähenbühl, Blades, & Eiser, 2009). When adults lead witnesses by suggesting incorrect "facts," interrupt their denials, reinforce them for giving desired answers, or use a confrontational questioning style, they further increase the likelihood of incorrect reporting—by children and adolescents alike (Bruck & Ceci, 2004; Owen-Kostelnik, Reppucci, & Meyer, 2006).

In one study, 4- to 7-year-olds were asked to recall details about a visitor who had come to their classroom a week earlier. Half the children received a low-pressure interview containing leading questions that implied abuse ("He took your clothes off, didn't he?"). The other half

BIOLOGY and ENVIRONMENT

Infantile Amnesia

If infants and toddlers remember many aspects of their everyday lives, how do we explain **infantile amnesia**—that most of us cannot retrieve events that happened to us before age 3? The reason we forget cannot be merely the passage of time because we can recall many events that happened long ago (Eacott, 1999). At present, several accounts of infantile amnesia exist.

One theory credits brain development, suggesting that vital changes in the hippocampus and the prefrontal cortex may pave the way for an *explicit memory* system—one in which children remember consciously rather than *implicitly*, without conscious awareness (Nelson, 1995). But mounting evidence indicates that even young infants engage in conscious recall: Their memory processing is not fundamentally different from that of children and adults. For example, as with adults, infant retention is greater with increased training and with training distributed over several sessions rather than massed into one session. And like adults, babies given memory prompts (retrieval cues) readily recover forgotten responses (see pages 141–142 in Chapter 4) (Bauer, 2006; Hayne & Simcock, 2009; Rovee-Collier & Cuevas, 2009).

Another conjecture is that older children and adults often use verbal means for storing information, whereas infants' and toddlers' memory processing is largely nonverbal—an incompatibility that may prevent long-term retention of early experiences. To test this idea, researchers sent two adults to the homes of 2- to 4-year-olds with a highly unusual toy that the children were likely to remember: the Magic Shrinking Machine, depicted in Figure 7.8. One adult showed the child how, after inserting an object in an opening on the top of the machine and turning a crank that activated flashing lights and musical sounds, the child could retrieve a smaller, identical object (discretely dropped down a chute by the second adult) from behind a door on the front of the machine.

A day later, the researchers tested the children to see how well they recalled the event. Their nonverbal memory—based on acting out the "shrinking" event and recognizing the "shrunken" objects in photos—was excellent. But even when they had the vocabulary, children younger than age 3 had trouble describing features of the "shrinking" experience. Verbal recall increased sharply between ages 3 and 4—the period during which children "scramble over the amnesia barrier" (Simcock & Hayne, 2003, p. 813). In a second study, preschoolers could not translate their nonverbal memory for the game into language six months to one year later, when their language had improved dramatically and they viewed a photo of the shrinking machine. Their verbal reports were "frozen in time," reflecting their limited language skill at the age they played the game (Simcock & Hayne, 2002).

These findings help us reconcile infants' and toddlers' remarkable memory skills with infantile amnesia. During the first few years, children rely heavily on nonverbal memory techniques, such as visual images and motor actions. But as language develops, their ability to use it to refer to preverbal memories requires strong contextual cues, such as direct exposure to the physical setting of the to-be-recalled experience (Morris & Baker-Ward, 2007). Only after age 3 do children often represent events verbally. As children encode one-time events in verbal form, they can use language-based cues to retrieve them, increasing the accessibility of these memories at later ages (Hayne, 2004).

Other findings indicate that the advent of a clear self-image contributes to the end of infantile amnesia. Without it, the child cannot construct an autobiography (Howe, Courage, & Rooksby, 2009). Toddlers who were advanced in development of a sense of self demonstrated better verbal memories a year later while conversing about past events with their mothers (Harley & Reese, 1999).

Very likely, both neurobiological change and social experience contribute to the decline of infantile amnesia. Brain development and adult–child interaction may jointly foster self-awareness, language, and improved memory, which enable children to talk with adults about personally significant past experiences (Bauer, 2007; Howe, Courage, & Rooksby, 2009). As a result, preschoolers begin to construct a long-lasting autobiographical narrative of their lives and enter into the history of their family and community.

(a)

(b)

(c)

FIGURE 7.8 The Magic Shrinking Machine, used to test young children's verbal and nonverbal memory of an unusual event. After being shown how the machine worked, the child participated in selecting objects from a polka-dot bag, dropping them into the top of the machine (a) and turning a crank, which produced a "shrunken" object (b). When tested the next day, 2- to 4-year-olds' nonverbal memory for the event was excellent. But below 36 months, verbal recall was poor, based on the number of features recalled about the game during an open-ended interview (c). Recall improved between 36 and 48 months, the period during which infantile amnesia subsides. (From G. Simcock & H. Hayne, 2003, "Age-Related Changes in Verbal and Nonverbal Memory During Early Childhood," *Developmental Psychology, 39,* pp. 807, 809. Copyright © 2003 by the American Psychological Association. Reprinted with permission of the American Psychological Association.) *Photos:* Ross Coombes/Courtesy of Harlene Hayne.

© MICHAEL NEWMAN/PHOTOEDIT

School-age eyewitnesses are better able than preschoolers to give accurate, detailed descriptions and correctly infer others' motives and intentions. This police officer can promote accurate recall by using a warm, supportive tone and avoiding leading questions.

received a high-pressure interview in which an adult told the child that her friends had said "yes" to the leading questions, praised the child for agreeing ("You're doing great"), and, if the child did not agree, repeated the question. Children were far more likely to give false information—even fabricating quite fantastic events—in the high-pressure condition (Finnilä et al., 2003). And children who have constructed a false memory often continue to give false reports when later questioned by an impartial interviewer (Garven, Wood, & Malpass, 2000).

By the time children appear in court, weeks, months, or even years have passed since the target events, and memory is likely to have decayed. When a long delay is combined with biased interviewing and with stereotyping of the accused ("He's in jail because he's been bad"), children can easily be misled into giving false information (Gilstrap & Ceci, 2005; Quas et al., 2007). The more distinctive and personally relevant an event is, the more likely children are to recall it accurately over time. For example, a year later, even when exposed to misleading information, children correctly reported details of an injury that required emergency room treatment (Peterson, Parsons, & Dean, 2004).

In many child sexual abuse cases, anatomically correct dolls are used to prompt children's recall. This method helps older children provide more detail about experienced events that otherwise might not be reported because of shame or embarrassment. However, it increases the suggestibility of preschoolers, prompting them to report physical and sexual contact that never happened (Goodman & Melinder, 2007).

Interventions Adults must prepare child witnesses so they understand the courtroom process and know what to expect. In some places, "court schools" take children through the setting and give them an opportunity to role-play court activities. Practice interviews—in which children learn to provide the most accurate, detailed information possible and to admit not knowing rather than agreeing or guessing—are helpful (Saywitz, Goodman, & Lyon, 2002). For example, when 3- and 4-year-olds are trained to monitor the source of their memories (recall whether an event occurred in real life or on TV) and to reject misleading source information, they responded more accurately to questions about new events (Thierry & Spence, 2002).

At the same time, legal professionals must use interviewing procedures that increase children's accurate reporting. Unbiased, open-ended questions or statements that prompt children to disclose details—"Tell me what happened" or "You said there was a man; tell me more about the man"—reduce the risk of suggestibility, even in young children (McAuliff, 2009). Also, a warm, supportive interview tone fosters accurate recall, perhaps by easing children's fears so they feel freer to counter an interviewer's false suggestions (Ceci, Bruck, & Battin, 2000).

If children are likely to experience emotional trauma or later punishment (as in a family dispute) for answering questions, courtroom procedures can be adapted to protect them. For example, children can testify over closed-circuit TV so they do not have to face an abuser. When it is not wise for a child to participate directly, expert witnesses can provide testimony that reports on the child's psychological condition and includes important elements of the child's story.

ASK YOURSELF

Review ■ According to fuzzy-trace theory, why do we encode information in gist form? Describe the development of gist and verbatim representations, and explain how gist contributes to improved reasoning and more detailed recall—but also to certain memory errors—with age.

Connect ■ Using what you know about development of autobiographical memory, explain why preschoolers' eyewitness testimony usually is less accurate than that of older children. What situational factors make children's reporting even more inaccurate?

Apply ■ When asked what happens at kindergarten, 5-year-old Ali replies, "First, you have center time and circle time. Sometimes you listen to a story. Next you eat your snack and go outdoors." But Ali can't remember what she did during center time two days ago. Explain Ali's memory performance. Why is this type of memory useful?

Reflect ■ Describe your earliest autobiographical memory. How old were you when the event occurred? Do your responses fit with research on infantile amnesia?

Metacognition

▶ Describe the development of metacognitive knowledge and cognitive self-regulation.

Throughout this chapter, we have mentioned many ways in which cognitive processing becomes more reflective and deliberate with age. These trends suggest that another form of knowledge may influence how well children remember and solve problems: **metacognition**—awareness and understanding of various aspects of thought.

During early and middle childhood, metacognition expands greatly as children construct a naïve **theory of mind,** a coherent understanding of people as mental beings, which they revise as they encounter new evidence. Most investigations into theory of mind address children's "mind reading"—their ability to detect their own and other people's perceptions, feelings, desires, and beliefs. We will take up this aspect when we consider emotional and social understanding in Chapters 10 and 11. A second facet of metacognitive research concerns children's knowledge of mental activity—*what it means to think.* To master increasingly complex tasks, children and adolescents must *think about their own thinking,* arriving at such realizations as "I'd better write that phone number down, or I'll forget it" and "This paragraph is complicated; I'll have to read it again to grasp the point."

For metacognitive knowledge to be helpful, children must closely monitor their cognitive activities. When they encounter difficulties, they must use what they know about thinking to redirect their efforts, systematically deploying attention, memory, reasoning, and problem-solving strategies to reach their goals. In the following sections, we consider these high-level aspects of executive function.

Metacognitive Knowledge

With age, children become increasingly conscious of their own cognitive capacities, of strategies for processing information, and of task variables that aid or impede performance.

Knowledge of Cognitive Capacities TAKE A MOMENT... Listen closely to young children's conversations, and you will find early awareness of mental activities. As their vocabularies expand, 2-year-olds' verbs include such words as *want, think, remember,* and *pretend,* which they use appropriately to refer to internal states (Wellman, 2002). By age 3, children realize that thinking takes place inside their heads and that a person can think about something without seeing, talking about, or touching it (Flavell, Green, & Flavell, 1995).

But preschoolers' understanding of the workings of the mind is limited. Three- and 4-year-olds conclude that mental activity stops while people wait, look at pictures, or read books—when no obvious cues indicate that they are thinking (Flavell, Green, & Flavell, 1993, 1995, 2000). Furthermore, children younger than age 6 pay little attention to the *process* of thinking but, instead, focus on outcomes of thought. When asked about subtle distinctions between mental states, such as *know* and *forget,* they express confusion (Lyon & Flavell, 1994). And they often insist that they have always known information they just learned (Taylor, Esbensen, & Bennett, 1994).

School-age children have a more complete grasp of cognitive processes. Six- and 7-year-olds realize, for example, that doing well on a task depends on paying attention—concentrating and exerting effort (Miller & Bigi, 1979). Their understanding of *sources of knowledge* also expands: They realize that people can extend their knowledge not just by directly observing events and talking to others but also by making *mental inferences* (Miller, Hardin, & Montgomery, 2003).

By age 10, children distinguish mental activities on the basis of *certainty of knowledge.* They are aware that if you "remember," "know," or "understand," you are more certain than if you "guess," "estimate," or "compare." They also grasp the interrelatedness of cognitive processes—for example, that remembering is crucial for understanding and that understanding strengthens memory (Schwanenflugel, Fabricius, & Noyes, 1996; Schwanenflugel, Henderson, & Fabricius, 1998).

© LEILA CUTLER/ALAMY

This 7-year-old's expression reveals that she is thinking hard. As school-age children increasingly reflect on their mental activities, they realize that they can extend their knowledge not just by directly observing events but also by making mental inferences.

How, then, should we describe the difference between younger and older children's understanding of cognitive capacities? Preschoolers view the mind as a passive container of information and have difficulty inferring what people are thinking about. In view of their limited awareness of how knowledge is acquired, it is not surprising that preschoolers rarely plan or use memory strategies. In contrast, older children regard the mind as an active, constructive agent that selects and transforms information (Flavell, 2000).

Language development (especially mental-state vocabulary) and capacity for more complex thinking contribute greatly to school-age children's more reflective, process-oriented view of the mind (Lecce et al., 2010). So do relevant experiences. In a study of rural children of Cameroon, Africa, those who attended school had a more advanced awareness of mental activities than those who did not (Vinden, 2002). In school, teachers often call attention to the workings of the mind by reminding children to pay attention, remember mental steps, share points of view with peers, and evaluate their own and others' reasoning.

Knowledge of Strategies   Consistent with their more active view of the mind, school-age children are far more conscious of mental strategies than preschoolers. When shown video clips depicting two children using different recall strategies and asked which one is likely to produce better memory, kindergarten and young elementary school children knew that rehearsing or organizing is better than looking or naming. Older children recognize more subtle differences—that organizing is better than rehearsing (Justice, 1986; Schneider, 1986).

Between third and fifth grade, children develop a much better appreciation of how and why strategies work (Alexander et al., 2003). Consequently, fifth graders are considerably better than younger school-age children at discriminating good from bad reasoning, regardless of its outcome (correctness of answer, happiness with a choice) (Amsterlaw, 2006). When given examples varying in quality, fifth graders consistently rated "good" reasoning as based on weighing of possibilities (rather than jumping to conclusions) and gathering of evidence (rather than ignoring important facts), even if such reasoning led to an unfavorable result.

Once children become conscious of the many factors that influence mental activity, they combine them into a more effective understanding. By the end of middle childhood, children start to consider how *interactions* among multiple variables—age and motivation of the learner, effective use of strategies, and nature and difficulty of the task—affect performance (Schneider, 2010; Wellman, 1990). In this way, metacognitive knowledge becomes more complex and integrated.

Cognitive Self-Regulation

LOOK and LISTEN

Observe a teacher explaining an assignment or a parent helping his or her child with homework. List adult strategies aimed at promoting self-regulation, and explain why each is helpful.

Although metacognitive knowledge expands, school-age children and adolescents often have difficulty putting what they know about thinking into action. They are not yet proficient at **cognitive self-regulation,** the process of continually monitoring and controlling progress toward a goal—planning, checking outcomes, and redirecting unsuccessful efforts. For example, most third to sixth graders know that they should group items when memorizing, reread a complicated paragraph to make sure they understand it, and relate new information to what they already know. But they do not always do so. And as we saw in Chapter 6, many teenagers, though aware of the ingredients of good reasoning, fail to engage in effective decision making.

To study cognitive self-regulation, researchers sometimes look at the impact of children's awareness of memory strategies on how well they remember. By second grade, the more children know about memory strategies, the more they recall—a relationship that strengthens over middle childhood (Pierce & Lange, 2000). And when children apply a strategy consistently, their knowledge of strategies strengthens, resulting in a bidirectional

APPLYING WHAT WE KNOW

Promoting Children's Cognitive Self-Regulation

STRATEGY	DESCRIPTION
Stress the importance of planful learning.	Encourage children to organize the learning task and to plan—by considering a variety of ways to approach the task and by setting appropriate learning goals, including how much time and practice they will need to complete it.
Suggest effective learning strategies.	Show children how to use effective learning strategies, and explain why those strategies work well, so children know when and why to use certain strategies in the future.
Emphasize monitoring of progress.	Encourage children to check progress toward their learning goals through self-monitoring, asking such questions as, "Am I staying focused?" "Am I using the strategy, as planned?" "Is the strategy working, or do I need to adjust it?"
Provide for evaluation of strategy effectiveness.	Have children evaluate their performance to improve learning, by answering such questions as, "How well did I do?" "Were my learning strategies effective?" "What strategies might work better?" "What other tasks might benefit from these strategies?"

Source: Schunk & Zimmerman, 2003.

relationship between metacognition and strategic processing that enhances self-regulation (Schlagmüller & Schneider, 2002).

Why does cognitive self-regulation develop gradually? Monitoring and controlling task outcomes is highly demanding, requiring constant evaluation of effort and progress. Throughout elementary and secondary school, better self-regulatory skills predict academic success (Valiente et al., 2008; Zimmerman & Cleary, 2009). Students who do well in school know whether or not their learning is going well. If they encounter obstacles, they take steps to address them—for example, organize the learning environment, review confusing material, or seek support from more expert adults or peers. This active, purposeful approach contrasts sharply with the passive orientation of students who achieve poorly.

Parents and teachers play vital roles in promoting children's self-regulation (Larkin, 2010). In one study, researchers observed parents helping their children with problem solving during the summer before third grade. Parents who patiently pointed out important features of the task and suggested strategies had children who, in the classroom, more often discussed ways to approach problems and monitored their own performance (Stright et al., 2001). In another investigation, first-grade teachers who provided clear organizational information about classroom rules, procedures, and assignments had students who engaged in more independent work and who were advanced in reading progress (Cameron et al., 2008). Finally, explaining the effectiveness of strategies—telling children not just what to do but why to do it—is particularly helpful because it provides a rationale for future action.

Applying What We Know above lists ways to foster children's cognitive self-regulation. Children who acquire effective self-regulatory skills develop a sense of *academic self-efficacy*—confidence in their own ability, which supports future self-regulation (Zimmerman & Moylan, 2009). As we turn now to development within academic skill areas, we will encounter the importance of self-regulation again. But first, consult the Milestones table on page 306, which summarizes the diverse changes in information processing we have considered.

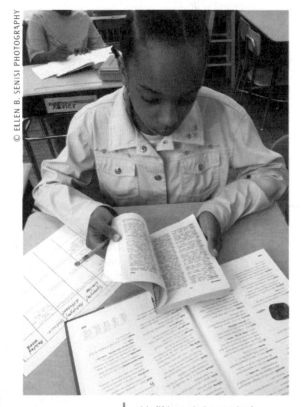

This fifth-grader's capacity for cognitive self-regulation is evident in the way she organizes materials, keeping her textbook glossary and dictionary handy. When she encounters an unfamiliar word while working on an assignment, she swiftly looks up its definition.

Milestones

Development of Information Processing

AGE	BASIC ABILITIES	STRATEGIES	KNOWLEDGE	METACOGNITION
2–5 years	• Working-memory capacity and processing speed increase. • Many processing skills are evident, including attention, recognition, recall, and reconstruction.	• Attention becomes more focused and sustained, and adaptable and planful attention emerge. • Inhibition improves. • Experimentation with and adaptive selection among strategies are evident.	• Semantic memory expands and becomes better organized. • Episodic memory emerges and becomes more elaborate. • Familiar events are remembered in scripts. • Autobiographical memory emerges and takes on narrative organization.	• Awareness of mental activities is present, but preschoolers view the mind as a passive container of information.
6–10 years	• Working-memory capacity and processing speed continue to increase.	• Attention becomes increasingly selective, adaptable, and planful. • Inhibition continues to improve. • Memory strategies of rehearsal, organization, and elaboration emerge and become more effective. • Ability to use multiple strategies at once increases. • Reliance on gist memory for reasoning increases.	• Semantic memory continues to expand and become better organized. • Autobiographical memory becomes more elaborate.	• View of the mind as an active constructive agent develops. • Knowledge of cognitive processes and their relationships increases. • Knowledge of the impact of strategies on performance increases. • Knowledge of interactions among cognitive processes, strategies, and type of task increases. • Cognitive self-regulation improves gradually.
11 years–adulthood	• Working-memory capacity and processing speed continue to increase, but at a slower pace.	• Inhibition and attention and memory strategies continue to improve.	• Semantic memory expands further and becomes more intricately organized. • Autobiographical memory becomes more focused on personal meaning.	• Metacognitive knowledge and cognitive self-regulation continue to improve.

Note: These milestones represent overall age trends. Individual differences exist in the precise age at which each milestone is attained.

Photos: (top) © Ellen B. Senisi Photography; (middle left) © Ellen B. Senisi/The Image Works; (middle right) © David Young-Wolff/PhotoEdit; (bottom) © Jeff Greenberg/PhotoEdit

A S K   Y O U R S E L F

Review ■ What evidence indicates that preschoolers view the mind as a passive container of information, whereas school-age children view it as an active, constructive agent?

Connect ■ How does research on adolescent brain development contribute to our understanding of the gradual development of cognitive self-regulation and the special self-regulatory challenges of the teenage years (see pages 190–191 in Chapter 5)?

Apply ■ Although 9-year-old Melody knows she should look over her homework, she nevertheless often turns in assignments with careless mistakes. What might account for the gap between what Melody knows and what she does?

Reflect ■ Suppose you had the opportunity to help a second grader with the following assignment: Write a five-sentence paragraph comparing and contrasting fruits and vegetables. What would you do to promote cognitive self-regulation?

Applications of Information Processing to Academic Learning

▶ Discuss the development of reading, mathematics, and scientific reasoning, noting implications of research findings for teaching.

Over the past two decades, fundamental discoveries about the development of information processing have been applied to children's mastery of academic skills. In various academic subjects, researchers are identifying the cognitive ingredients of skilled performance, tracing their development, and pinpointing differences in cognitive skills between good and poor learners. They hope, as a result, to design teaching methods that will improve children's learning. In the following sections, we discuss several of these efforts in reading, mathematics, and scientific reasoning.

Reading

Reading makes use of many skills at once, taxing all aspects of our information-processing system. We must perceive single letters and letter combinations, translate them into speech sounds, recognize the visual appearance of many common words, hold chunks of text in working memory while interpreting their meaning, and combine the meanings of various parts of a text passage into an understandable whole. Because reading is so demanding, most or all of these skills must be done automatically. If one or more are poorly developed, they will compete for space in our limited working memories, and reading performance will decline. Becoming a proficient reader is a complex process that begins in the preschool years.

Early Childhood   Preschoolers understand a great deal about written language long before they learn to read and write in conventional ways. This is not surprising: Children in industrialized nations live in a world filled with written symbols. Each day, they observe and participate in activities involving storybooks, calendars, lists, and signs and, while doing so, try to figure out how written symbols convey meaning. Children's active efforts to construct literacy knowledge through informal experiences are called **emergent literacy.**

Young preschoolers search for units of written language as they "read" memorized versions of stories and recognize familiar signs ("PIZZA"). But they do not yet understand the symbolic function of the elements of print (Bialystok & Martin, 2003). Many preschoolers think that a single letter stands for a whole word or that each letter in a person's signature represents a separate name. In fact, initially preschoolers do not distinguish between drawing and writing. Around age 4, their writing shows some distinctive features of print, such as separate forms arranged in a line. But they often include picturelike devices, such as writing "sun" by using a yellow marker or a circular shape (Levin & Bus, 2003). They use their understanding of the symbolic function of drawings to make a "drawing of print."

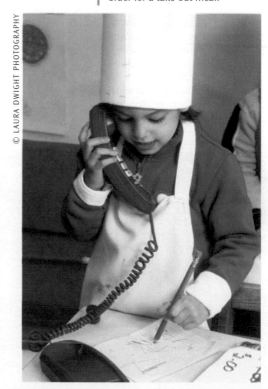

Preschoolers acquire literacy knowledge informally by participating in everyday activities involving written symbols. This young chef "jots down" a phone order for a take-out meal.

© LAURA DWIGHT PHOTOGRAPHY

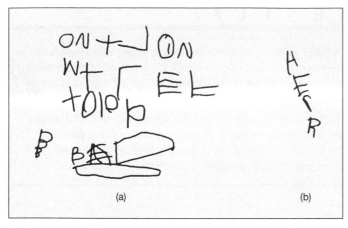

(a)   (b)

FIGURE 7.9 **A story (a) and a grocery list (b) written by a 4-year-old child.** This child's writing has many features of real print. It also reveals an awareness of different kinds of written expression. (From McGee, Lea M.; Richgels, Donald J., *Literacy's Beginnings: Supporting Young Readers and Writers*, 4th Edition, © 2004. Reprinted by permission of Pearson Education, Inc., Upper Saddle River, NJ.)

FIGURE 7.10 **Some kindergarten reading readiness skills by family income.** The gap in emergent literacy development between entering-kindergarten students from low-income and middle-income families is large. (Adapted from Lee & Burkham, 2002.)

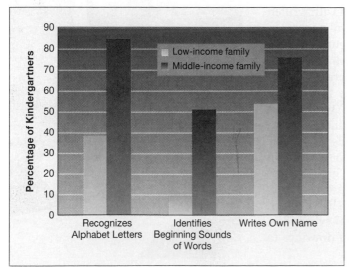

Preschoolers revise these ideas as their perceptual and cognitive capacities improve, as they encounter writing in many contexts, and as adults help them with written communication. Gradually, they notice more features of written language and depict writing that varies in function, as in the "story" and "grocery list" in Figure 7.9.

Eventually children figure out that letters are parts of words and are linked to sounds in systematic ways, as seen in the invented spellings typical between ages 5 and 7. At first, children rely on sounds in the names of letters: "ADE LAFWTS KRMD NTU A LAVATR" ("eighty elephants crammed into a[n] elevator"). Over time, they grasp sound–letter correspondences and learn that some letters have more than one common sound and that context affects their use (*a* is pronounced differently in "cat" than in "table") (McGee & Richgels, 2012).

Literacy development builds on a broad foundation of spoken language and knowledge about the world (Dickinson, Golinkoff, & Hirsh-Pasek, 2010). Over time, children's language and literacy progress facilitate each other. **Phonological awareness**—the ability to reflect on and manipulate the sound structure of spoken language, as indicated by sensitivity to changes in sounds within words, to rhyming, and to incorrect pronunciation—is a strong predictor of emergent literacy knowledge (Dickinson et al., 2003; Paris & Paris, 2006). When combined with sound–letter knowledge, it enables children to isolate speech segments and link them with their written symbols. Vocabulary and grammatical knowledge are also influential. And adult–child narrative conversations enhance diverse language skills essential for literacy progress.

The more informal literacy experiences preschoolers have, the better their language and emergent literacy development and their later reading skills (Dickinson & McCabe, 2001; Speece et al., 2004). Pointing out letter–sound correspondences and playing language–sound games enhance children's awareness of the sound structure of language and how it is represented in print (Ehri & Roberts, 2006; Foy & Mann, 2003). *Interactive reading,* in which adults discuss storybook content with preschoolers, promotes many aspects of language and literacy development. Adult-supported writing activities that focus on narrative, such as preparing a letter or a story, also have wide-ranging benefits (Purcell-Gates, 1996; Wasik & Bond, 2001). In longitudinal research, each of these literacy experiences is linked to improved reading achievement in middle childhood (Hood, Conlon, & Andrews, 2008; Senechal & LeFevre, 2002; Storch & Whitehurst, 2001).

Compared to their economically advantaged agemates, preschoolers from low-income families have fewer home and preschool language and literacy learning opportunities—a major reason that they are behind in emergent literacy skills and in reading achievement throughout the school years (Foster et al., 2005; Foster & Miller, 2007; Turnbull et al., 2009). Age-appropriate books, for example, are scarce in their environments. In one survey of four middle- and low-income communities, the middle-income neighborhoods averaged 13 books per child, the low-income neighborhoods just 1 book for every 300 children (Neuman & Celano, 2001).

On average, a preschooler from a low-income family is read to for a total of 25 hours during early childhood, a middle-income child for 1,000 hours. The gap in early literacy experiences translates into large differences in knowledge and skills vital for reading readiness at kindergarten entry (see Figure 7.10). Kindergartners who are behind in emergent literacy development tend to remain behind, performing poorly in reading in the early grades (National Early Literacy Panel, 2008). Over time, skilled readers acquire wide-ranging knowledge more efficiently, progressing more rapidly than poor readers in all achievement areas (Neuman, 2006). In this way, literacy deficiencies at the start of school contribute to

APPLYING WHAT WE KNOW

Supporting Emergent Literacy in Early Childhood

STRATEGY	EXPLANATION
Provide literacy-rich home and preschool environments.	Homes and preschools with abundant reading and writing materials—including a wide variety of children's storybooks, some relevant to children's ethnic backgrounds—open the door to a wealth of language and literacy experiences.
Engage in interactive book reading.	When adults discuss story content, ask open-ended questions about story events, explain the meaning of words, and point out features of print, they promote language development, comprehension of story content, knowledge of story structure, and awareness of units of written language.
Provide outings to libraries, museums, parks, zoos, and other community settings.	Visits to child-oriented community settings enhance children's general knowledge and offer many opportunities to see how written language is used in everyday life. They also provide personally meaningful topics for narrative conversation, which promotes many language skills essential for literacy development.
Point out letter–sound correspondences, play rhyming and other language-sound games, and read rhyming poems and stories.	Experiences that help children isolate the sounds in words foster phonological awareness—a powerful predictor of early childhood literacy knowledge and later reading and spelling achievement.
Support children's efforts at writing, especially narrative products.	Assisting children in their efforts to write—especially letters, stories, and other narratives—fosters many language and literacy skills.
Model literacy activities.	When children see adults engaged in reading and writing activities, they better understand the diverse everyday functions of literacy skills and the knowledge and pleasure that literacy brings. As a result, children's motivation to become literate is strengthened.

Sources: McGee & Richgels, 2012; Neuman, 2006.

widening achievement disparities between economically advantaged and disadvantaged children that often persist into high school.

Providing low-income parents with children's books, along with guidance in how to stimulate emergent literacy, greatly enhances literacy activities in the home (High et al., 2000; Huebner & Payne, 2010). And when preschool teachers were given a tuition-free college course on effective early childhood literacy instruction, they readily applied what they learned, offering many more literacy activities in their classrooms (Dickinson & Sprague, 2001). For ways to support early childhood literacy development, see Applying What We Know above.

Middle Childhood   As children make the transition from emergent literacy to conventional reading, phonological awareness continues to predict reading (and spelling) progress. Other information-processing skills also contribute. Gains in processing speed foster school-age children's rapid conversion of visual symbols into sounds—an ability that also distinguishes good from poor readers (McBride-Chang & Kail, 2002). Visual scanning and discrimination play important roles and improve with reading experience (Rayner, Pollatsek, & Starr, 2003). Performing all these skills efficiently releases working memory for higher-level activities involved in comprehending the text's meaning.

Until recently, researchers were involved in an intense debate over how to teach children to read. Those who took a **whole-language approach** argued that from the beginning, children should be exposed to text in its complete form—stories, poems, letters, posters, and lists—so that they can appreciate the communicative function of written language. According to this view, as long as reading is kept meaningful, children will be motivated to discover the specific skills they need (Watson, 1989). Other experts advocated a **phonics approach,** believing that children should first be coached on *phonics*—the basic rules for translating

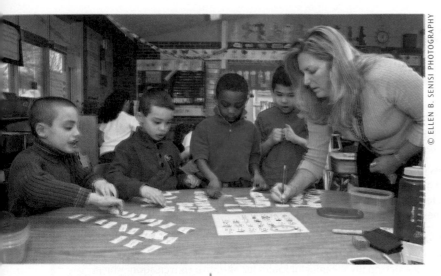

With their teacher's guidance, first graders identify words and sort them by initial consonant. Effective reading instruction balances teaching of phonics with exposure to interesting, meaningful texts.

written symbols into sounds. Only after mastering these skills should they get complex reading material (Rayner & Pollatsek, 1989).

Many studies show that children learn best with a mixture of both approaches. In kindergarten, first, and second grades, teaching that includes phonics boosts reading scores, especially for children who lag behind in reading progress (Stahl & Miller, 2006; Xue & Meisels, 2004). And when teachers combine real reading and writing with teaching of phonics and engage in other excellent teaching practices—encouraging children to tackle reading challenges and integrating reading into all school subjects—first graders show far greater literacy progress (Pressley et al., 2002).

Why might combining phonics with whole language work best? Learning relations between letters and sounds enables children to *decode,* or decipher, words they have never seen before. Children who enter school low in phonological awareness make far better reading progress when given training in phonics (Casalis & Cole, 2009). Soon they detect new letter–sound relations while reading on their own, and as their fluency in decoding words increases, they are freer to attend to text meaning. Without early phonics training, such children (many of whom come from poverty-stricken families) are substantially behind their agemates in text comprehension skills by third grade (Foster & Miller, 2007).

Yet too much emphasis on basic skills may cause children to lose sight of the goal of reading: understanding. Children who read aloud fluently without registering meaning know little about effective reading strategies—for example, that they must read more carefully if they will be tested than if they are reading for pleasure, that they must draw connections between parts of a passage to comprehend effectively, and that explaining a passage in their own words is a good way to assess comprehension. Providing instruction aimed at increasing knowledge and use of such strategies readily enhances reading performance from third grade on (McKeown & Beck, 2009; Paris & Paris, 2006).

Around age 7 to 8, children make a major shift—from "learning to read" to "reading to learn" (Melzi & Ely, 2009). As decoding and comprehension skills become efficient, adolescent readers actively engage with the text, adjusting the way they read to fit their current purpose—at times seeking new facts and ideas, at other times questioning, agreeing with, or disagreeing with the writer's viewpoint.

Mathematics

Mathematical reasoning, like reading, builds on informally acquired knowledge. Recall from Chapter 6 that violation-of-expectation evidence suggests that babies have some basic number concepts (see page 263), although the connection between these early discriminations and later quantitative development is not yet clear. Between 14 and 16 months, toddlers display a beginning grasp of **ordinality,** or order relationships between quantities—for example, that 3 is more than 2 and 2 is more than 1 (Starkey, 1992; Strauss & Curtis, 1984). And 2-year-olds often indicate without counting that certain sets of items have "lots," "many," or "little" in relation to others (Ginsburg, Lee, & Boyd, 2008). These attainments serve as the basis for more complex understandings.

Early Childhood Sometime in the third year, children begin to count. By the time children turn 3, most can count rows of about five objects, saying the correct number words, although they do not know exactly what the words mean. For example, when asked for *one,* they give one item, but when asked for *two, three, four,* or *five,* they usually give a larger, but incorrect, amount. Nevertheless, 2½- to 3½-year-olds understand that a number word refers to a unique quantity—that when a number label changes (for example, from *five* to *six*), the number of items should also change (Sarnecka & Gelman, 2004).

By age 3½ to 4, most children have mastered the meaning of numbers up to *ten*, count correctly, and grasp the vital principle of **cardinality**—that the last word in a counting sequence indicates the quantity of items in a set (Geary, 2006a). Mastery of cardinality increases the efficiency of children's counting. By age 4, children use counting to solve simple arithmetic problems. At first, their strategies are tied to the order of numbers as presented; when given 2 + 4, they count on from 2 (Bryant & Nunes, 2002). But soon they experiment with other strategies and master the *min* strategy, a more efficient approach (refer back to Siegler's model of strategy choice, pages 284–286). Around this time, children realize that subtraction cancels out addition. Knowing, for example, that 4 + 3 = 7, they infer without counting that 7 − 3 = 4 (Rasmussen, Ho, & Bisanz, 2003). Grasping basic arithmetic rules greatly facilitates rapid computation.

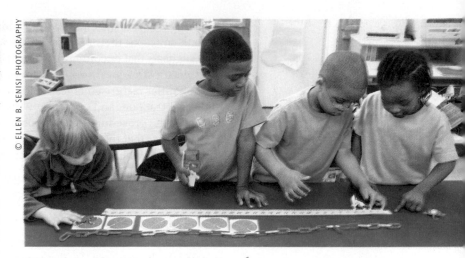

Preschoolers "hop" a toy frog along a number line, measuring the length of each jump. Through informal exploration of number concepts, they construct basic arithmetic understandings essential for learning math skills later on.

Understanding basic arithmetic computation makes possible beginning *estimation*—the ability to generate approximate answers, which can be used to evaluate the accuracy of exact answers. After watching several doughnuts being added to or removed from a plate of four to ten doughnuts, 3- and 4-year-olds make sensible predictions of how many doughnuts are on the plate (Zur & Gelman, 2004). Still, children can estimate only just beyond the limit of their calculation competence (Dowker, 2003). For example, those who can solve addition problems with sums up to 10 can estimate answers with sums up to about 20. And as with arithmetic operations, children try out diverse estimation strategies, gradually moving to more accurate, efficient techniques.

The arithmetic knowledge just described emerges in many cultures around the world. But children construct these understandings sooner when adults provide many occasions for counting, comparing quantities, and talking about number concepts (Ginsburg, Lee, & Boyd, 2008; Klibanoff et al., 2006). Math proficiency at kindergarten entry predicts math achievement years later, in elementary and secondary school (Duncan et al., 2007; Geary, 2006a).

As with emergent literacy, children from low-income families begin kindergarten with considerably less math knowledge than their economically advantaged agemates—a gap due to differences in environmental supports. For example, just a few sessions devoted to playing a number board game with an adult led to a dramatic improvement in number concepts and counting proficiency of 4-year-olds from low-income families (Siegler, 2009). And in an early childhood math curriculum called Building Blocks, materials that promote math concepts and skills enable teachers to weave math into many preschool daily activities, from block-building to art to stories (Clements & Sarama, 2008). Compared with agemates randomly assigned to other preschool programs, economically disadvantaged preschoolers experiencing Building Blocks showed substantially greater year-end gains in math concepts and skills, including counting, sequencing, and arithmetic computation.

LOOK and LISTEN

Ask several parents of preschoolers what they routinely do to help their children learn about math. Then ask what they do to support literacy. Do the parents promote math as much as literacy learning?

Middle Childhood Mathematics teaching in elementary school builds on and greatly enriches children's informal knowledge of number concepts and counting. Written notation systems and formal computational techniques enhance children's ability to represent numbers, compute, and estimate. Over the early elementary school years, children acquire basic math facts through a combination of frequent practice, reasoning about number concepts, and teaching that conveys effective strategies. (Return to pages 284–285 for research supporting the importance of both extended practice and a grasp of concepts.) Eventually, children retrieve answers automatically and apply this knowledge to more complex problems.

Arguments about how to teach math resemble those in reading, pitting drill in computing against "number sense," or understanding. Again, a blend of both approaches is most beneficial (Fuson, 2009). In learning basic math, poorly performing students use cumbersome techniques or try to retrieve answers from memory too soon. They have not sufficiently experimented with strategies to see which are most effective and to reorganize their observations in logical, efficient ways—for example, noticing that multiplication problems involving 2 (2 × 8) are equivalent to addition doubles (8 + 8). On tasks that reveal their grasp of math concepts, their performance is weak (Canobi, 2004; Canobi, Reeve, & Pattison, 2003). This suggests that encouraging students to apply strategies and making sure they understand why certain strategies work well are essential for solid mastery of basic math.

A similar picture emerges for more complex skills, such as carrying in addition, borrowing in subtraction, and operating with decimals and fractions. Children taught by rote cannot apply the procedure to new problems. Instead, they persistently make mistakes, following a "math rule" that they recall incorrectly because they do not understand it (Carpenter et al., 1999). Look at the following subtraction errors:

$$
\begin{array}{r}
427 \\
-138 \\
\hline
311
\end{array}
\qquad
\begin{array}{r}
7002 \\
-5445 \\
\hline
1447
\end{array}
$$

In the first problem, the child consistently subtracts the smaller from the larger digit, regardless of which is on top. In the second, the child skips columns with zeros in a borrowing operation and, whenever there is a zero on top, writes the bottom digit as the answer.

Children who have rich opportunities to experiment with problem solving, to appreciate the reasons behind strategies, and to evaluate solution techniques seldom make such errors. In one study, second graders who were taught in these ways not only mastered correct procedures but even invented their own successful strategies—some of them superior to standard, school-taught methods! Consider this solution:

$$
\begin{array}{cccc}
3 & 15 & 14 & 12 \\
\cancel{4} & \cancel{6} & \cancel{5} & \cancel{2} \\
-1 & 9 & 6 & 8 \\
\hline
2 & 6 & 8 & 4
\end{array}
$$

In subtracting, the child performed all trades first, flexibly moving either from right to left or from left to right, and then subtracted all four columns—a highly efficient, accurate approach (Fuson & Burghard, 2003).

In a German study, the more teachers emphasized conceptual knowledge—by having children actively construct meanings in word problems before practicing computation and memorizing math facts—the more children gained in math achievement from second to third grade (Staub & Stern, 2002). Children with these learning experiences draw on their solid knowledge of relationships between operations (for example, that the inverse of division is multiplication) to generate efficient, flexible procedures (De Brauwer & Fias, 2009). And because they have been encouraged to estimate answers, if they go down the wrong track in computation, they are usually self-correcting. Furthermore, they appreciate connections between math operations and problem contexts. They can solve a word problem ("If Jesse spent $3.45 for bananas, $2.62 for bread, and $3.55 for peanut butter, can he pay for it all with a $10 bill?") quickly through estimation instead of exact calculation (De Corte & Verschaffel, 2006).

In Asian countries, students receive a variety of supports for acquiring mathematical knowledge and often excel at both math reasoning and computation. Use of the metric system, which presents ones, tens, hundreds, and thousands values in all areas of measurement, helps Asian children grasp place value. The consistent structure of number words in Asian languages (*ten-two* for 12, *ten-three* for 13) also makes this idea clear (Miura & Okamoto, 2003). And because Asian number words are shorter and more quickly pronounced, more digits can be held in working memory at once, increasing the speed of thinking. Furthermore, Chinese parents provide their children with extensive everyday practice in counting and computation—experiences that contribute to the superiority of Chinese over U.S. children's math knowledge, even before school entry (Siegler & Mu, 2008; Zhou et al., 2006).

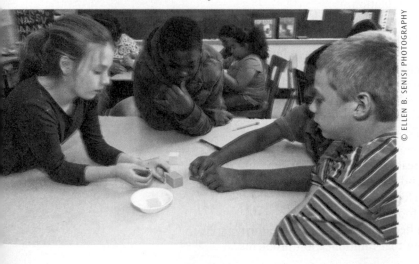

Fifth graders use manipulative materials to help them understand mathematical concepts such as "squared" and "cubed." Learning experiences that promote conceptual knowledge help children become more flexible, effective math problem solvers.

© ELLEN B. SENISI PHOTOGRAPHY

Finally, compared with the United States, math lessons in Asian classrooms devote more time to exploring math concepts and strategies and less to drill and repetition (Woodward & Ono, 2004; Zhou & Peverly, 2005). As Chapter 15 will reveal, Asian countries consistently score at or near the top in international comparisons of high school achievement in math—and in other subjects as well.

Scientific Reasoning

During a free moment in physical education class, 13-year-old Heidi wondered why more of her tennis serves and returns passed the net and dropped in her opponent's court when she used a particular brand of balls. "Is it something about their color or size?" she asked herself. "Hmm . . . or maybe it's their surface texture—that might affect their bounce."

According to Deanna Kuhn, the heart of scientific reasoning is coordinating theories with evidence. A scientist can clearly describe the theory he or she favors, knows what evidence is needed to support it and what would refute it, and can explain how pitting evidence against theories has led to the acceptance of one theory as opposed to others. What evidence would Heidi need to confirm her theory about the tennis balls?

Kuhn (2002) has conducted extensive research into the development of scientific reasoning, using problems that resemble Piaget's tasks in that several variables might affect an outcome. In one series of studies, third, sixth, and ninth graders and adults were first given evidence, sometimes consistent and sometimes conflicting with theories, then questioned about the accuracy of each theory.

For example, participants were given a problem much like Heidi's: to theorize about which of several features of sports balls—size (large or small), color (light or dark), surface texture (rough or smooth), or presence or absence of ridges on the surface—influences the quality of a player's serve. Next, they were told about the theory of Mr. (or Ms.) S, who believes that the ball's size is important, and the theory of Mr. (or Ms.) C, who thinks color matters. Finally, the interviewer presented evidence, placing balls with certain characteristics into two baskets, one labeled "good serve" and the other "bad serve" (see Figure 7.11).

FIGURE 7.11 Which features of these sports balls—size, color, surface texture, or presence or absence of ridges—influence the quality of a player's serve? This set of evidence suggests that color might be important, since light-colored balls are largely in the good-serve basket and dark-colored balls in the bad-serve basket. But the same is true for texture! The good-serve basket has mostly smooth balls, the bad-serve basket rough balls. Since all light-colored balls are smooth and all dark-colored balls are rough, we cannot tell whether color or texture makes a difference. But we can conclude that size and presence or absence of ridges are not important because these features are equally represented in the good-serve and bad-serve baskets. (Adapted from Kuhn, Amsel, & O'Loughlin, 1988.)

Age-Related Change   Kuhn found that the capacity to reason like a scientist improves with age. The youngest participants often discounted obviously causal variables, ignored evidence conflicting with their own initial judgments, and distorted evidence in ways consistent with their theory. When one third grader, who judged that size was causal (with large balls producing good serves and small balls producing bad serves), was shown incomplete evidence (a single, large, light-colored ball in the good-serve basket and no balls in the bad-serve basket), he insisted on the accuracy of Mr. S's theory (which was also his own). Asked to explain, he stated flatly, "Because this ball is big . . . the color doesn't really matter" (Kuhn, 1989, p. 677).

These findings, and others like them, suggest that on complex, multivariable tasks, children—instead of viewing evidence as separate from and bearing on a theory—often blend the two into a single representation of "the way things are." Children are especially likely to overlook evidence that does not match their prior beliefs when a causal variable is implausible (like color affecting performance of a sports ball) and when task demands (number of variables to be evaluated) are high (Zimmerman, 2005, 2007). The ability to distinguish theory from evidence and use logical rules to examine their relationship improves from childhood through adolescence, continuing into adulthood (Kuhn & Dean, 2004; Kuhn & Pearsall, 2000).

How Scientific Reasoning Develops   What factors support skill at coordinating theory with evidence? Greater working-memory resources, permitting simultaneous comparison of a theory and the effects of several variables, is vital. In addition, participants benefit from exposure to increasingly complex problems and instruction that highlights critical features of scientific reasoning—for example, why a scientist's expectations in a particular

At an engineering summer camp, high school students design a catapult for shooting water balloons. As they coordinate theory with evidence, reflecting on and revising their problem-solving strategies, they gain in scientific reasoning.

situation are inconsistent with everyday beliefs and experiences (Chinn & Malhotra, 2002). These findings explain why scientific reasoning is strongly influenced by years of schooling, whether individuals grapple with traditional scientific tasks (like the sports ball problem) or engage in informal reasoning—for example, justifying a theory about what causes children to fail in school (Amsel & Brock, 1996; Kuhn, 1993).

Researchers believe that sophisticated *metacognitive understanding* is vital for scientific reasoning (Kuhn, 2009; Kuhn & Pease, 2006). Microgenetic research (see pages 64–65 in Chapter 2) shows that when older children and adolescents regularly pit theory against evidence over many weeks, they experiment with various strategies, reflect on and revise them, and become aware of the nature of logic. Then they apply their abstract appreciation of logic to a wide variety of situations. The ability to *think about* theories, *deliberately isolate* variables, *consider all influential* variables, and *actively seek* disconfirming evidence is rarely present before adolescence (Kuhn, 2000; Kuhn et al., 2008; Moshman, 1998).

Though far more competent than children, adolescents and adults vary widely in scientific reasoning skills. Many continue to show a self-serving bias, applying logic more effectively to ideas they doubt than to those they favor (Klaczynski, 1997; Klaczynski & Narasimham, 1998). Reasoning scientifically requires the metacognitive capacity to evaluate one's objectivity—to be fair-minded rather than self-serving (Moshman, 2005). As we will see in Chapter 11, this flexible, open-minded approach is not just a cognitive attainment but a personality trait—one that assists teenagers greatly in forming an identity and developing morally.

Children and adolescents develop scientific reasoning skills in a similar step-by-step fashion on different kinds of tasks. In a series of studies, 10- to 20-year-olds were given sets of problems graded in difficulty. One set contained causal-experimental tasks like the sports ball problem in Figure 7.11, another contained quantitative-relational tasks like Piaget's pendulum problem, and still another consisted of verbal propositional tasks (see pages 257–258 in Chapter 6). In each type of task, adolescents mastered component skills in sequential order by expanding their metacognitive awareness (Demetriou et al., 1993, 1996, 2002). For example, on causal-experimental tasks, they first became aware of the many variables—separately and in combination—that could influence an outcome. This enabled them to formulate and test hypotheses. Over time, adolescents combined separate skills into a smoothly functioning system, constructing a general model that they could apply to many instances of a given type of problem.

Do the metacognitive advances just described remind you of the concept of *central conceptual structures* in Robbie Case's neo-Piagetian theory, discussed on page 283? Piaget also underscored the role of metacognition in formal operational thought when he spoke of "operating on operations" (see Chapter 6, page 253). But information-processing findings confirm that scientific reasoning does not result from an abrupt, stagewise change, as Piaget believed. Instead, it develops gradually out of many specific experiences with different types of problems, each of which requires children and adolescents to match theory against evidence and reflect on and evaluate their thinking.

▶ Summarize the strengths and limitations of the information-processing approach.

Evaluation of the Information-Processing Approach

A major strength of the information-processing approach is its explicitness and precision in breaking down complex cognitive activities into their components. Information processing has provided a wealth of detailed evidence on how younger versus older and more-skilled versus less-skilled individuals attend, remember, reason, and solve problems. It also offers precise mechanisms of cognitive development; Table 7.1 summarizes the most important of these. TAKE A MOMENT... As you review them, think back to theories and findings that illustrate the role of each. Finally, because of its precision, information-processing

TABLE 7.1	Mechanisms of Cognitive Development from the Information-Processing Perspective
MECHANISM	**DESCRIPTION**
Basic processing capacity	Capacity of the mental system increases, enabling more information to be held in working memory at once.
Processing efficiency	Speed of basic operations increases, freeing up available space in working memory for additional mental activities.
Encoding of information	Encoding, in the form of attention, becomes more thorough and better adapted to task demands.
Inhibition	Ability to prevent internal and external distracting stimuli from capturing attention improves, freeing up working memory for remembering, reasoning, and solving problems.
Strategy execution	Strategies become more effective, improving storage, retrieval, and use of information for reasoning and problem solving.
Knowledge	Amount and structure of the knowledge base increase, making new, related information more meaningful so it is easier to store and retrieve.
Metacognitive knowledge	Awareness and understanding of cognitive processes expand.
Self-regulation	Self-regulation improves, leading strategies to be applied more effectively in a wider range of situations.

research has contributed greatly to the design of teaching techniques that advance many aspects of children's thinking.

The principal limitation of the information-processing perspective stems, ironically, from its central strength: By analyzing cognition into its components, information processing has had difficulty reassembling them into a broad, comprehensive theory of development. As we have seen, the neo-Piagetian perspective is one effort to build a general theory by retaining Piaget's stages while drawing on information-processing mechanisms to explain cognitive change.

Furthermore, the computer metaphor, while bringing precision to research on the human mind, has drawbacks. Computer models of cognitive processing, though complex in their own right, do not reflect the richness of real-life learning experiences. They overlook aspects of cognition that are not linear and logical, such as imagination and creativity. Moreover, computers do not have desires, interests, and intentions, nor can they engage in interaction with others, as children do when they learn from parents, teachers, and peers. Perhaps because of the narrowness of the computer metaphor, information processing has not told us much about the links between cognition and other areas of development. In later chapters, we will look at findings of investigators who have applied information-processing assumptions to children's thinking about certain aspects of their social world. But in research on children's social and moral understanding, extensions of Piaget's theory still prevail.

Despite its shortcomings, the information-processing approach holds great promise. The near future is likely to bring new breakthroughs in understanding mechanisms of cognitive development and neurological changes that underlie various mental activities, and in identifying teaching techniques that support children's learning.

ASK YOURSELF

Review ■ Why are gains in metacognition important for the development of scientific reasoning? How can teachers promote the development of scientific reasoning?

Connect ■ Using mechanisms of cognitive development discussed in this chapter, explain why teaching both basic skills and understanding of concepts and strategies is vital for children's progress in reading and mathematics.

Apply ■ Review Heidi's reasoning about the impact of several variables on the bounce of tennis balls on page 313. What features of her thinking suggest that she is beginning to reason scientifically?

Reflect ■ Describe early, informal experiences important for literacy and math development that you experienced while growing up. How do you think those experiences contributed to your academic progress after you started school?

S U M M A R Y

The Information-Processing Approach (p. 278)

■ Information-processing theorists view the mind as a complex, symbol-manipulating system through which information flows, much like a computer. Researchers use computer-like diagrams and flowcharts to analyze thinking into its components, mapping the precise steps involved in thinking about a task or problem.

A General Model of Information Processing (p. 278)

Describe the store model of the human information processing system, noting implications for cognitive development and related findings.

■ We hold, or store, information in three parts of the mental system for processing. The **sensory register** takes in a wide panorama of information, but only momentarily. The **short-term memory store** retains attended-to information briefly so we can actively manipulate it in **working memory** to accomplish our goals. The **central executive** is the conscious, reflective part of the system, directing the flow of information and implementing basic procedures and complex strategies. The more effectively we process information, the greater the likelihood that mental activities will become **automatic processes** and that information will transfer to **long-term memory,** our limitless, permanent knowledge base.

■ The store model suggests, and research confirms, that several aspects of the cognitive system improve with age. Working-memory capacity increases, with individual differences predicting intelligence test scores and academic achievement. Gains in processing speed also occur, contributing to working-memory resources. Furthermore, children make strides in **executive function,** with preschoolers gaining in attention, suppressing impulses, and flexible thinking and school-age children and adolescents in integration of cognitive operations and strategies that enable increasingly difficult tasks.

Developmental Theories of Information Processing (p. 282)

How do Case's neo-Piagetian theory and Siegler's model of strategy choice explain changes in children's thinking?

■ Case's **neo-Piagetian theory** accepts Piaget's stages but attributes change within and between stages to greater efficiency in use of working-memory capacity. Brain development, practice with schemes and automization, and formation of **central conceptual structures** contribute to development. Case's theory provides an information-processing explanation of the continuum of acquisition—that many understandings appear in specific situations at different times—and thus is better able than Piaget's theory to account for unevenness in cognitive development.

■ Siegler's **model of strategy choice** highlights children's experimentation with and selection of mental strategies to account for the diversity and ever-changing nature of children's thinking. Strategy development follows an overlapping-waves pattern. When given challenging problems, children generate a variety of strategies, gradually selecting from them on the basis of accuracy and speed.

Attention (p. 286)

Describe the development of attention, including sustained, selective, and adaptable strategies.

■ Gains in sustained attention depend on rapid growth of the prefrontal cortex, the capacity to generate increasingly complex play goals, and adult scaffolding of attention. As sustained attention increases, children become better at focusing on relevant aspects of a task and at flexibly adapting attention to task requirements. Sustained, selective, and adaptable attention depend on **inhibition,** the ability to control distracting stimuli.

■ Development of attentional (and memory) strategies tends to occur in four phases: (1) **production deficiency** (failure to produce the strategy); (2) **control deficiency** (failure to execute the strategy effectively); (3) **utilization deficiency** (consistent use of the strategy, but with little or no performance improvement); and (4) **effective strategy use.**

■ From age 5 on, children undergo marked advances in **planning.** They learn much from cultural tools that support planning, adult guidance and encouragement, and opportunities to practice.

Memory (p. 292)

Describe the development of strategies for storing and retrieving information from memory.

■ Although the beginnings of memory strategies can be seen in early childhood, young children seldom engage in **rehearsal** or **organization.** As use of these strategies improves, school-age children combine them; the more strategies they use simultaneously, the better they remember. **Elaboration** emerges at the end of middle childhood. Task demands and cultural circumstances influence the development of memory strategies.

■ **Recognition,** the simplest form of retrieval, is a fairly automatic process that is highly accurate by the preschool years. **Recall**—generating a mental representation of an absent stimulus—is more challenging, shows much greater improvement with age, and is strongly associated with language development.

■ Even young children engage in **reconstruction** when remembering complex, meaningful material. As originally provided information decays and new information is presented, children make more inferences, and the coherence of reconstructed information and its memorableness increase. However, much recalled information can be inaccurate.

■ According to **fuzzy-trace theory,** when information is encoded, it is reconstructed automatically into a **gist**—a vague, fuzzy version that is especially useful for reasoning. With age, children rely less on verbatim memory and more on reconstructed gists, contributing to improved recall of details with age.

Explain the development of episodic memory and its relationship to semantic memory.

■ **Semantic memory**—our vast general knowledge system—contributes vitally to and develops earlier than **episodic memory.** Not until 3 or 4 years of age do children have a well-functioning memory system of personally experienced events that occurred at a specific time and place.

- Like adults, young children remember familiar experiences in terms of **scripts**—a special form of episodic memory that permits them to predict what might happen on future similar occasions. And as preschoolers talk with adults about personally significant past events, they adopt the narrative thinking generated in these dialogues, forming an **autobiographical memory.** Children whose parents use an elaborative rather than a repetitive conversational style produce more coherent and detailed personal stories.

How does eyewitness memory change with age, and what factors influence the accuracy of children's reports?

- Compared with preschoolers, school-age children are better at giving accurate and detailed eyewitness accounts and resisting adults' misleading questions. When a biased adult repeatedly asks leading questions, children are far more likely to give false information. Negative stereotyping of the accused and a long delay between the events and the child's eyewitness report further contribute to inaccurate reporting.

Metacognition (p. 303)

Describe the development of metacognitive knowledge and cognitive self-regulation.

- **Metacognition** expands greatly as children construct a naïve **theory of mind,** a coherent understanding of people as mental beings. From early to middle childhood, children become increasingly conscious of cognitive capacities and strategies. They come to view the mind as an active, constructive agent rather than a passive container of information. As older children consider interactions among variables, metacognitive knowledge becomes more complex and integrated.

- **Cognitive self-regulation**—continually monitoring and controlling progress toward a goal—develops gradually. It improves with adult instruction in effective strategy use and predicts academic success.

Applications of Information Processing to Academic Learning (p. 307)

Discuss the development of reading, mathematics, and scientific reasoning, noting the implications of research findings for teaching.

- **Emergent literacy** reveals that young children understand a great deal about written language before they read and write in conventional ways. Preschoolers gradually revise incorrect ideas about the meaning of written symbols as their cognitive capacities improve, as they encounter writing in many contexts, and as adults help them with written communication.

- **Phonological awareness** strongly predicts emergent literacy knowledge and later reading achievement. Vocabulary and grammatical knowledge, adult–child narrative conversations, and informal literacy-related experiences also foster literacy development.

- As children make the transition to conventional literacy, phonological awareness, processing speed, and visual scanning and discrimination contribute to reading progress. A combination of **whole-language** and **phonics approaches** is most effective for teaching beginning reading.

- Mathematical reasoning also builds on informally acquired knowledge. Toddlers beginning grasp of **ordinality** serves as the basis for more complex understandings. As preschoolers gain experience with counting, they understand **cardinality** and begin to solve simple addition and subtraction problems. When adults provide many occasions for counting and comparing quantities, children construct basic numerical concepts sooner.

- During the early school years, children acquire basic math facts through a combination of frequent practice, reasoning about number concepts, and teaching that conveys effective strategies. The best mathematics instruction combines practice in experimenting with strategies and conceptual understanding.

- The ability to coordinate theory with evidence—the heart of scientific reasoning—improves from childhood to adolescence. Greater working-memory resources and exposure to increasingly complex problems in school contribute to the metacognitive understanding that is vital for reasoning scientifically.

© BOB DAEMMRICH/THE IMAGE WORKS

Evaluation of the Information-Processing Approach (p. 314)

Summarize the strengths and limitations of the information-processing approach.

- A major strength of the information-processing approach is its precision in breaking down cognition into its components. Information processing research has contributed greatly to the design of teaching techniques that advance children's thinking.

- Nevertheless, computer models of cognitive processing do not reflect the richness of real-life learning experiences and have not told us much about the links between cognition and other areas of development.

IMPORTANT TERMS AND CONCEPTS

attention-deficit hyperactivity disorder (ADHD) (p. 290)
autobiographical memory (p. 298)
automatic processes (p. 280)
cardinality (p. 311)
central conceptual structures (p. 283)
central executive (p. 279)
cognitive self-regulation (p. 304)
control deficiency (p. 288)
effective strategy use (p. 289)
elaboration (p. 293)
emergent literacy (p. 307)
episodic memory (p. 297)
executive function (p. 281)

fuzzy-trace theory (p. 296)
gist (p. 296)
infantile amnesia (p. 301)
inhibition (p. 287)
long-term memory (p. 280)
metacognition (p. 303)
model of strategy choice (p. 284)
neo-Piagetian theory (p. 283)
ordinality (p. 310)
organization (p. 292)
phonics approach (p. 309)
phonological awareness (p. 308)
planning (p. 289)

production deficiency (p. 288)
recall (p. 294)
recognition (p. 294)
reconstruction (p. 295)
rehearsal (p. 292)
scripts (p. 298)
semantic memory (p. 296)
sensory register (p. 278)
short-term memory store (p. 278)
theory of mind (p. 303)
utilization deficiency (p. 289)
whole-language approach (p. 309)
working memory (p. 279)

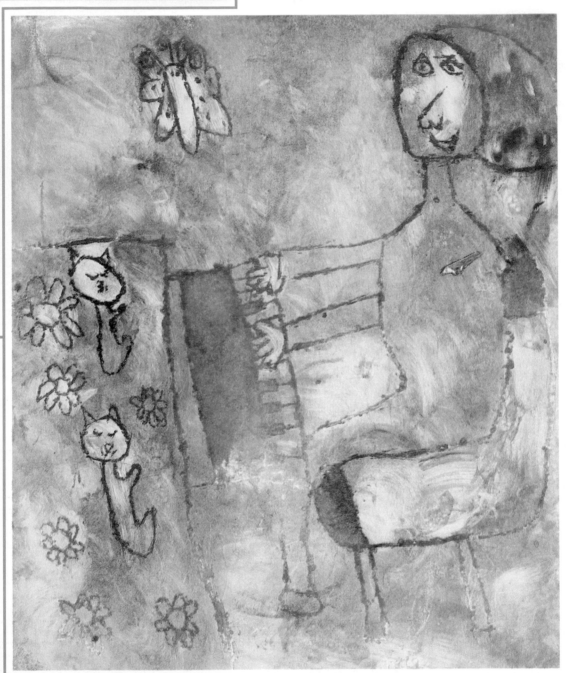

CHAPTER 8

"Playing the Piano"
Eliska Feitiova
7 years, Czech Republic

Although intelligence tests predict children's academic achievement, they are far less effective at evaluating the creativity and talent evident in this pianist's fluid playing—or in the artist's expressive image.

Reprinted with permission from the International Museum of Children's Art, Oslo, Norway

Intelligence

Definitions of Intelligence
Alfred Binet: A Holistic View • The Factor Analysts: A Multifaceted View

Recent Advances in Defining Intelligence
Combining Psychometric and Information-Processing Approaches • Sternberg's Triarchic Theory • Gardner's Theory of Multiple Intelligences

■ **SOCIAL ISSUES: EDUCATION:** *Emotional Intelligence*

Measuring Intelligence
Some Commonly Used Intelligence Tests • Aptitude and Achievement Tests • Tests for Infants • Computation and Distribution of IQ Scores

What Do Intelligence Tests Predict, and How Well?
Stability of IQ Scores • IQ as a Predictor of Academic Achievement • IQ as a Predictor of Occupational Attainment • IQ as a Predictor of Psychological Adjustment

Ethnic and Socioeconomic Variations in IQ

Explaining Individual and Group Differences in IQ
Genetic Influences • Adoption Studies: Joint Influence of Heredity and Environment • Race and Ethnicity: Genetic or Cultural Groupings? • Cultural Bias in Testing • Reducing Cultural Bias in Testing • Home Environment and Mental Development

■ **CULTURAL INFLUENCES:** *The Flynn Effect: Massive Generational Gains in IQ*

■ **SOCIAL ISSUES: EDUCATION:** *High-Stakes Testing*

Early Intervention and Intellectual Development
Benefits of Early Intervention • Strengthening Early Intervention

■ **SOCIAL ISSUES: EDUCATION:** *The Head Start REDI Program: Strengthening School Readiness in Economically Disadvantaged Preschoolers*

Giftedness: Creativity and Talent
The Psychometric View • A Multifaceted View

James Cleveland is past president of Jumpstart, a U.S. nonprofit organization that provides 3- to 5-year-olds from low-income families with several hundred hours per year of intensive, supplementary educational enrichment, aimed at increasing their readiness for kindergarten. Several times a week, Jumpstart corps members (college students and older adults) go to a preschool or child-care center, where they read to and converse with two to three designated children, engage in additional individualized learning activities, and play collaborative games in small groups. Currently, Jumpstart serves more than 9,000 preschoolers across the country.

After stepping into Jumpstart's top leadership position, James wrote to his nationwide staff, expressing his passion and resolve to help ever-increasing numbers of at-risk children start school with the literacy, self-regulation, and social skills they need to succeed. He had an inspiring personal story to tell.

James started public school as a weak, self-doubting reader—the very situation Jumpstart strives to prevent. He struggled with language arts assignments and frequently spent recess at his desk, barred from participating because he could not do—and soon refused to do—his reading work. "Pressure from my teacher and the embarrassment of being singled out added to my frustration," James recalled.

After weeks without progress, James's teacher called his parents. His father, an African American who had not had the chance to go to college, responded immediately. "He became my inspiration," said James. "He regarded his involvement as vital to my academic success—and to a life path of greater opportunity than his own."

James's father began taking him to the public library regularly. On each visit, he guided James in selecting a book, insisting that he choose a challenging one. Then father and son read together, jointly deciphering difficult passages. If James did not understand a word, they looked it up in the dictionary. "That unlocked the world of reading for me," said James, who went on to become a voracious reader, an excellent student, valedictorian of his high school class, and a graduate of Stanford University.

James summed up: "My dad's involvement taught me firsthand about the power of caring adult intervention. I began believing in myself because I knew my dad believed in me." His father's inspiration led James to devote his energies to early educational intervention—a topic we consider in depth later in this chapter.

The **psychometric approach** to cognitive development is the basis for the wide variety of intelligence tests available for assessing children's mental abilities. Unlike Piagetian, Vygotskian, and information-processing views, which focus on the *process* of thinking, the psychometric perspective is *product*-oriented, largely concerned with outcomes and results—how many and what kinds of questions children of different ages answer correctly. Psychometric researchers ask questions like these:

- What factors, or dimensions, make up intelligence, and how do they change with age?
- How can intelligence be measured so that scores predict future academic achievement, career attainment, and other aspects of intellectual success?
- Are mental test scores largely stable over childhood and adolescence, or can performance change dramatically?
- To what extent do children of the same age differ in intelligence, and what explains those differences?

© ELLEN B. SENISI PHOTOGRAPHY

To what extent do children of the same age differ in intelligence, and what explains those differences? Heredity plays a role, but so do children's home environments and the kind of schooling they experience.

▶ Describe changing definitions of intelligence on which mental tests are based.

LOOK and LISTEN

Ask several of your classmates to list three traits that characterize an intelligent toddler, an intelligent preschooler, an intelligent school-age child, and an intelligent adolescent. Did your respondents view the makeup of intelligence as changing with age? Explain.

As we examine these questions, we will quickly become immersed in the long-standing debate over the contribution of nature (heredity) and nurture (environment) to intelligence and the related controversy over whether intelligence tests are biased, or inaccurate, measures of the mental abilities of members of certain ethnic minority groups. We will see how the cognitive perspectives considered in previous chapters, as well as research on environmental contexts—home, school, societal attitudes, and public policies—have contributed to our understanding of children's test performance. We conclude with a discussion of giftedness, in the form of talent and creativity. ■

Definitions of Intelligence

TAKE A MOMENT... Jot down a list of behaviors that you regard as typical of highly intelligent people. Does your list contain just one or two items or a great many? In a study in which laypeople and experts completed a similar exercise, both groups viewed intelligence as made up of at least three broad attributes: verbal ability, practical problem solving, and social competence (Sternberg & Detterman, 1986). But respondents differed in their descriptions of these attributes. And contemporary experts showed much less agreement about the makeup of intelligence than did experts in a similar study conducted a half-century earlier!

Clearly, most people think of intelligence as a complex combination of attributes, though little consensus exists among experts on its ingredients. And whereas some people view the various abilities that make up intelligence as closely interconnected, others expect them to be relatively distinct—to correlate weakly (Siegler & Richards, 1980). This tension between intelligence as a single capacity versus a collection of loosely related skills is ever-present in historical and current theories on which mental tests are based.

Alfred Binet: A Holistic View

The social and educational climate of the late nineteenth and early twentieth centuries led to the development of the first intelligence tests. With the beginning of universal public education in Europe and North America—allowing all children, not just society's privileged, to enroll in school—educators sought methods to identify students who were unable to benefit from regular classroom instruction. The first successful intelligence test, constructed by French psychologist Alfred Binet and his colleague Theodore Simon in 1905, responded to this need.

The French Ministry of Instruction asked Binet to devise an objective method for assigning pupils to special classes—one based on mental ability, not classroom disruptiveness. Other researchers had tried to assess intelligence using simple measures of sensory responsiveness and reaction time (Cattell, 1890; Galton, 1883). In contrast, Binet believed that test items should tap complex mental activities involved in intelligent behavior, such as memory and reasoning. Consequently, Binet and Simon (1908) devised a test of general ability that included a variety of verbal and nonverbal items, each requiring thought and judgment. Their test was also the first to associate items of increasing difficulty with chronological age (Wasserman & Tulsky, 2005). This enabled Binet and Simon to estimate how much a child was behind or ahead of her agemates in intellectual development.

The Binet test was so successful in predicting school performance that it became the basis for new intelligence tests. In 1916, Lewis Terman at Stanford University adapted it for use with English-speaking schoolchildren. Since then, the English version has been known as the *Stanford-Binet Intelligence Scale.* As we will see later, the Stanford-Binet has changed greatly; it no longer provides just a single, holistic measure of intelligence.

The Factor Analysts: A Multifaceted View

To find out whether intelligence is a single trait or an assortment of abilities, researchers used a complicated correlational procedure called **factor analysis,** which identifies sets of test items that cluster together, meaning that test-takers who do well on one item in a cluster tend to do well on the others. Distinct clusters are called *factors.* For example, if vocabulary, verbal comprehension, and verbal analogy items all correlate highly, they form a factor that the investigator might label "verbal ability." Using factor analysis, many researchers tried to identify the mental abilities that contribute to successful intelligence test performance.

Early Factor Analysts
British psychologist Charles Spearman (1927) was the first influential factor analyst. He found that all test items he examined correlated with one another. As a result, he proposed that a common underlying **general intelligence,** called *g,* influenced each of them. At the same time, noticing that the test items were not perfectly correlated, Spearman concluded that they varied in the extent to which *g* contributed to them and suggested that each item, or a set of similar items, also measured a **specific intelligence** unique to the task.

Spearman downplayed the significance of specific intelligences, regarding *g* as central and supreme. Because test items that involved forming relationships and applying general principles clustered together especially strongly—and also were the best predictors of cognitive performance outside the testing situation—he inferred that *g* represents abstract reasoning capacity.

American psychologist Louis Thurstone (1938) questioned the importance of *g.* His factor analysis of college students' scores on more than 50 intelligence tests indicated that separate, unrelated factors exist. Declaring the supremacy of these factors, Thurstone called them *primary mental abilities.*

Contemporary Extensions
Spearman and Thurstone eventually resolved their differences, each acknowledging findings that supported the other's perspective (Wasserman & Tulsky, 2005). Current theorists and test designers, combining both approaches, propose *hierarchical models* of mental abilities. At the highest level is *g,* assumed to be present to some degree in all separate factors. These factors, in turn, are measured by *subtests,* groups of related items. Subtest scores provide information about a child's strengths and weaknesses. They also can be combined into a total score representing general intelligence.

Contemporary theorists have extended factor-analytic research. The two most influential are R. B. Cattell and John Carroll, each of whom offers a unique, multifaceted perspective on intelligence.

Crystallized versus Fluid Intelligence. According to Raymond B. Cattell (1971, 1987), in addition to *g,* intelligence consists of two broad factors: **Crystallized intelligence** refers to skills that depend on accumulated knowledge and experience, good judgment, and mastery of social customs—abilities acquired because they are valued by the individual's culture. On intelligence tests, vocabulary, general information, and arithmetic problems are examples of items that emphasize crystallized intelligence. In contrast, **fluid intelligence** depends more heavily on basic information-processing skills—the ability to detect relationships among stimuli, the speed with which the individual can analyze information, and the capacity of working memory. Fluid intelligence, which is assumed to be influenced more by conditions in the brain and less by culture, often works with crystallized intelligence to support effective reasoning, abstraction, and problem solving (Horn & Noll, 1997).

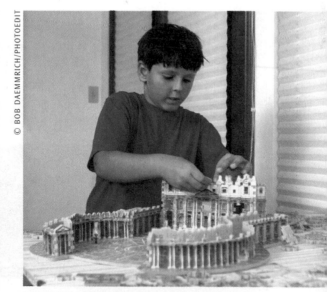

To solve a complex three-dimensional puzzle based on the design of St. Peter's Basilica in Rome, this 10-year-old, who has never seen the building, relies on fluid intelligence—the ability to analyze information efficiently and to detect relationships among stimuli.

Among children with similar cultural and educational backgrounds, crystallized and fluid intelligence are highly correlated and difficult to distinguish in factor analyses, probably because children high in fluid intelligence acquire information more easily. But in children differing greatly in cultural and educational experiences, the two abilities show little relationship; children with the same fluid capacity may perform quite differently on crystallized tasks (Horn, 1994). As these findings suggest, Cattell's theory has important implications for the issue of *cultural bias* in intelligence testing. Tests aimed at reducing culturally specific content usually emphasize fluid over crystallized items.

The Three-Stratum Theory of Intelligence. Using improved factor-analytic methods, John Carroll (1993, 2005) reanalyzed relationships among items in hundreds of studies. His findings yielded a **three-stratum theory of intelligence** that elaborates the models proposed by Spearman, Thurstone, and Cattell. Carroll represented the structure of intelligence as having three tiers. As Figure 8.1 shows, *g* presides at the top. In the second tier are an array of *broad abilities,* which Carroll considered the basic biological components of intelligence; they are arranged from left to right in terms of decreasing relationship with *g*. In the third tier are *narrow abilities*—specific behaviors through which people display the second-tier factors.

Carroll's model is the most comprehensive factor-analytic classification of mental abilities to date. As we will see in the next section, it provides a useful framework for researchers seeking to understand mental-test performance in cognitive-processing terms. It also reminds us of the great diversity of intellectual factors. Currently, no test measures all of Carroll's factors.

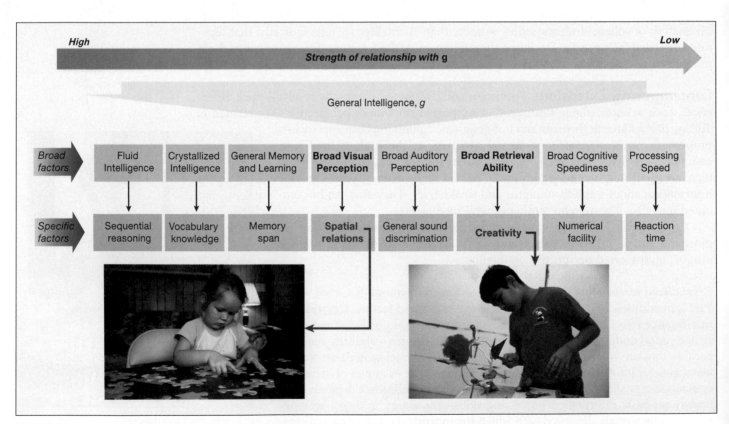

FIGURE 8.1 Carroll's hierarchical model of intelligence. At the top is general intelligence, or *g*. The second tier shows eight broad abilities, or factors, arranged from left to right in terms of decreasing strength of relationship with *g*. In the third tier are examples of narrow factors, specific behaviors through which people display the broad abilities. The child on the left is completing a spatial-relations task in which she solves a puzzle—a type of broad visual perception. The child on the right is applying his broad retrieval ability as he uses art materials creatively. Carroll's model reflects the wide array of abilities tapped by mental tests, but no single test includes all of his factors. (Adapted from Carroll, 1993, 2005.) *Photos:* (left) © J. Burleson/Alamy; (right) © Jeff Greenberg/PhotoEdit

Recent Advances in Defining Intelligence

Many researchers believe that factors on intelligence tests have limited usefulness unless we can identify the cognitive processes responsible for those factors. Once we discover exactly what separates individuals who can solve certain mental test items from those who cannot, we will know more about why a particular child does well or poorly and what skills must be strengthened to improve performance.

▶ How do contemporary researchers use and expand componential analyses of intelligence test scores to define intelligence?

Combining Psychometric and Information-Processing Approaches

To overcome the limitations of factor analysis, investigators combine psychometric and information-processing approaches. They conduct **componential analyses** of children's test scores, looking for relationships between aspects (or components) of information processing and children's intelligence test performance.

Processing speed, measured in terms of reaction time on diverse cognitive tasks, is moderately related to general intelligence and to gains in mental test performance over time (Deary, 2001; Li et al., 2004). Individuals whose central nervous systems function more efficiently, permitting them to take in and manipulate information quickly, appear to have an edge in intellectual skills. In support of this interpretation, fast, strong ERPs (EEG brain waves in response to stimulation) predict both speedy cognitive processing and higher mental test scores (Rijsdijk & Boomsma, 1997; Schmid, Tirsch, & Scherb, 2002). Also, fMRI research reveals that the metabolic rate of the cerebral cortex is lower for high-scoring individuals, suggesting that they require less mental energy for thinking (Neubauer & Fink, 2009; van den Heuvel et al., 2009).

But other factors, including flexible attention, memory, and reasoning strategies, are as important as basic processing efficiency in predicting IQ, and they explain some of the relationship between response speed and good test performance (Lohman, 2000; Miller & Vernon, 1992). Indeed, measures of working-memory capacity (see page 280 in Chapter 7) correlate well with mental test scores—especially fluid measures—in both school-age children and adults (Conway, Kane, & Engle, 2003; de Ribaupierre & Lecerf, 2006; Kane, Hambrick, & Conway, 2005). Children who apply strategies effectively acquire more knowledge and can retrieve it rapidly—advantages that carry over to test performance. Similarly, recall from Chapter 7 that working-memory resources depend in part on effective inhibition—keeping irrelevant information from intruding on the task at hand. Inhibition and sustained and selective attention are among a wide array of attentional skills that are good predictors of IQ (Schweizer, Moosbrugger, & Goldhammer, 2006).

As these findings illustrate, identifying relationships between cognitive processing and mental test scores brings us closer to isolating the cognitive skills that contribute to high intelligence. But the componential approach has one major shortcoming: It regards intelligence as entirely due to causes within the child. In previous chapters, we have seen how cultural and situational factors also affect children's thinking. Robert Sternberg has expanded the componential approach into a comprehensive theory that views intelligence as a product of inner and outer forces.

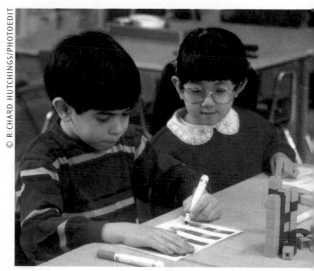

First graders solve problems using specially designed math manipulatives. Children who apply strategies effectively acquire more knowledge and can retrieve it rapidly. As a result, they score higher on intelligence tests.

Sternberg's Triarchic Theory

As Figure 8.2 on page 324 shows, Sternberg's (2001, 2005, 2008) **triarchic theory of successful intelligence** is made up of three broad, interacting intelligences: (1) *analytical intelligence,* or information-processing skills; (2) *creative intelligence,* the capacity to solve novel problems;

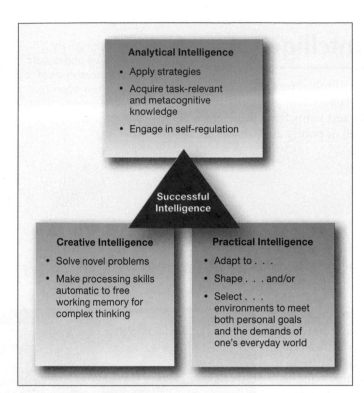

FIGURE 8.2 Sternberg's triarchic theory of successful intelligence. People who behave intelligently balance three interrelated intelligences—analytical, creative, and practical—to achieve success in life, defined by their personal goals and the requirements of their cultural communities.

and (3) *practical intelligence,* application of intellectual skills in everyday situations. Intelligent behavior involves balancing all three intelligences to achieve success in life, according to one's personal goals and the requirements of one's cultural community.

Analytical Intelligence *Analytical* intelligence consists of the information-processing components that underlie all intelligent acts: applying strategies, acquiring task-relevant and metacognitive knowledge, and engaging in self-regulation. But on mental tests, processing skills are used in only a few of their potential ways, resulting in far too narrow a view of intelligent behavior. As we have seen, children in tribal and village societies do not necessarily perform well on measures of "school" knowledge but thrive when processing information in out-of-school situations that most Westerners would find highly challenging.

Creative Intelligence In any context, success depends not only on processing familiar information but also on generating useful solutions to new problems. People who are *creative* think more skillfully than others when faced with novelty. Given a new task, they apply their information-processing skills in exceptionally effective ways, rapidly making those skills automatic so that working memory is freed for more complex aspects of the situation. Consequently, they quickly move to high-level performance. Although all of us are capable of some creativity, only a few individuals excel at generating novel solutions. We will address the ingredients of creativity in greater detail at the end of this chapter.

Practical Intelligence Finally, intelligence is a *practical,* goal-oriented activity aimed at *adapting to, shaping,* or *selecting environments.* Intelligent people skillfully *adapt* their thinking to fit with both their desires and the demands of their everyday worlds. When they cannot adapt to a situation, they try to *shape,* or change, it to meet their needs. If they cannot shape it, they *select* new contexts that better match their skills, values, or goals. Practical intelligence reminds us that intelligent behavior is never culture-free. Children with certain life histories do well at the behaviors required for success on intelligence tests and adapt easily to the testing conditions and tasks. Others, with different backgrounds, may misinterpret or reject the testing context. Yet such children often display sophisticated abilities in daily life—for example, telling stories, engaging in complex artistic activities, or interacting skillfully with other people.

To examine the validity of the triarchic theory, Sternberg and his collaborators gave thousands of children and adolescents in Finland, Spain, Russia, and the United States test items that tap analytical, creative, and practical skills. Factor analyses repeatedly indicated that the three intelligences are relatively distinct (Grigorenko & Sternberg, 2001; Sternberg, 2003a; Sternberg et al., 1999, 2001).

The triarchic theory emphasizes the complexity of intelligent behavior and the limitations of current intelligence tests in assessing that complexity. For example, out-of-school, practical forms of intelligence are vital for life success and help explain why cultures vary widely in the behaviors they regard as intelligent (Sternberg et al., 2000). When researchers asked ethnically diverse parents to describe an intelligent first grader, Caucasian Americans mentioned cognitive traits. In contrast, ethnic minorities (Cambodian, Filipino, Vietnamese, and Mexican immigrants) saw noncognitive capacities—motivation, self-management, and social skills—as particularly important (Okagaki & Sternberg, 1993). According to Sternberg, mental tests can easily underestimate, and even overlook, the intellectual strengths of some children, especially ethnic minorities.

Gardner's Theory of Multiple Intelligences

In yet another view of how information-processing skills underlie intelligent behavior, Howard Gardner's (1983, 1993, 2000) **theory of multiple intelligences** defines intelligence in terms of distinct sets of processing operations that permit individuals to solve problems, create products, and discover new knowledge in a wide range of culturally valued activities. Dismissing the idea of general intelligence, Gardner proposes at least eight independent intelligences (see Table 8.1).

Gardner believes that each intelligence has a unique biological basis, a distinct course of development, and different expert, or "end-state," performances. At the same time, he emphasizes that a lengthy process of education is required to transform any raw potential into a mature social role (Connell, Sheridan, & Gardner, 2003). Cultural values and learning opportunities affect the extent to which a child's strengths are realized and the way they are expressed.

Gardner acknowledges that if tests were available to assess all these abilities, they should show little relationship to one another. But he finds neurological support for their separateness particularly compelling. Research indicating that damage to a certain part of the adult brain influences only one ability (such as linguistic or spatial), while sparing others, suggests that the affected ability is independent. The existence of people with unusual profiles of intelligence also fits with Gardner's belief in distinct abilities. Individuals with *savant syndrome*, who display one area of outstanding strength alongside deficits in many others, provide an illustration. Children with *autism* occasionally show this pattern. Though severely impaired in language and communication, a few individuals with autism have remarkable abilities, always featuring dazzling memory. These usually involve numerical and spatial skills—such as effortless calculation, detailed drawing, or performance of long piano pieces after hearing them only once—that are primarily housed in the right hemisphere of the cerebral cortex. Savant syndrome often is associated with damage to the left cerebral hemisphere, which may have caused the right hemisphere to compensate, yielding an "island of strength" (Treffert, 2010).

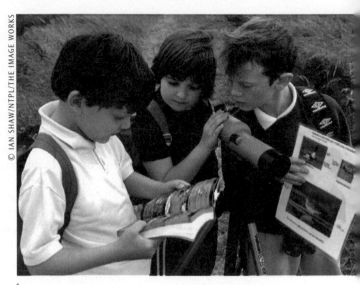

According to Gardner, children are capable of at least eight distinct intelligences. As these children distinguish among bird species, they enrich their naturalist intelligence.

TABLE 8.1 | Gardner's Multiple Intelligences

INTELLIGENCE	PROCESSING OPERATIONS	END-STATE PERFORMANCE POSSIBILITIES
Linguistic	Sensitivity to the sounds, rhythms, and meaning of words and the functions of language	Poet, journalist
Logico-mathematical	Sensitivity to, and capacity to detect, logical or numerical patterns; ability to handle long chains of logical reasoning	Mathematician
Musical	Ability to produce and appreciate pitch, rhythm (or melody), and aesthetic quality of the forms of musical expressiveness	Instrumentalist, composer
Spatial	Ability to perceive the visual-spatial world accurately, to perform transformations on those perceptions, and to re-create aspects of visual experience in the absence of relevant stimuli	Sculptor, navigator
Bodily-kinesthetic	Ability to use the body skillfully for expressive as well as goal-directed purposes; ability to handle objects skillfully	Dancer, athlete
Naturalist	Ability to recognize and classify all varieties of animals, minerals, and plants	Biologist
Interpersonal	Ability to detect and respond appropriately to the moods, temperaments, motivations, and intentions of others	Therapist, salesperson
Intrapersonal	Ability to discriminate complex inner feelings and to use them to guide one's own behavior; knowledge of one's own strengths, weaknesses, desires, and intelligences	Person with detailed, accurate self-knowledge

Sources: Gardner, 1993, 1998a, 2000.

Does Gardner's theory remind you of the *core knowledge perspective*, discussed in Chapter 6? Indeed, he accepts the existence of innately specified, core domains of thought, present at birth or emerging early in life. Then, as children respond to the demands of their culture, they transform those intelligences to fit the activities they are called on to perform. Gardner's theory has stimulated innovations in education extending from kindergarten through college in many countries (Chen, Moran, & Gardner, 2009). Applications typically provide students with many opportunities to construct knowledge through hands-on projects that foster diverse intelligences, in classroom communities that highly value individual differences in abilities. Gardner's work has been especially helpful in efforts to understand and nurture children's special talents, a topic we address at the end of this chapter.

Critics of Gardner's theory, however, question the independence of his intelligences. They point out that the unusual skills of people with savant syndrome are mechanical and inflexible because those skills are not aided by other abilities. In contrast, excellence in most fields requires a combination of intelligences. A talented musician, for example, uses logico-mathematical intelligence to interpret the score, linguistic intelligence to respond to teaching, spatial intelligence to orient to the keyboard, interpersonal intelligence to react to the audience, and intrapersonal intelligence to play expressively. Furthermore, some exceptionally gifted individuals have abilities that are broad rather than limited to a particular domain (Piirto, 2007). Finally, current mental tests do tap several of Gardner's intelligences (linguistic, logico-mathematical, and spatial), and evidence for *g* suggests that they have at least some features in common (Visser, Ashton, & Vernon, 2006).

Nevertheless, Gardner calls attention to several intelligences not tapped by intelligence tests. For example, his interpersonal and intrapersonal intelligences include a set of capacities for dealing with people and understanding oneself. As the Social Issues: Education box on the following page indicates, researchers are attempting to define and measure these vital abilities.

A S K   Y O U R S E L F

Review ■ Using Sternberg's triarchic theory, explain the limitations of current mental tests in assessing the complexity of human intelligence.

Connect ■ Describe similarities between Gardner's theory of multiple intelligences and the core knowledge perspective on cognitive development (see Chapter 6, pages 261–262). What questions raised about this view also apply to Gardner's theory?

Apply ■ Eight-year-old Charya, an immigrant from Cambodia, had difficulty responding to test items asking for word definitions and general information. But she solved puzzles easily, and she quickly figured out which number comes next in a complex series. How does Charya score in crystallized and fluid intelligence? What might explain the difference?

Reflect ■ Select one of your intellectual strengths from Gardner's multiple intelligences, listed in Table 8.1 on page 325. How do you display that intelligence? What other intelligences contribute to your strong performance?

▶ Describe commonly used intelligence tests for children, distinguish between aptitude and achievement tests, and discuss the usefulness of infant tests.

▶ How are IQ scores computed and distributed in large, representative samples?

Measuring Intelligence

Although intelligence tests sample only a narrow range of human cognitive capacities, psychologists and educators give them to school-age children because the scores, as we will see shortly, are modest to good predictors of future success—in school, on the job, and in other aspects of life. The *group-administered tests* given from time to time in classrooms permit large numbers of students to be tested at once and are useful for instructional planning and for identifying students who require more extensive evaluation with *individually administered tests*. Unlike group tests, which teachers can give with minimal training, individually administered tests demand considerable training and experience to give well. The examiner not only considers the child's answers but also carefully observes the child's behavior, noting such reactions as attention to and interest in the tasks and wariness of the adult. These observations provide insights into whether the test results accurately reflect the child's abilities.

SOCIAL ISSUES: EDUCATION

Emotional Intelligence

During recess, Emily handed a birthday party invitation to every fifth-grade girl except Claire, who looked on sadly as her classmates chattered about the party. But one of Emily's friends, Jessica, looked troubled. Pulling Emily aside, she exclaimed, "Why'd you do that? You hurt Claire's feelings—you embarrassed her! If you bring invitations to school, you've got to give everybody one!" And after school, Jessica comforted Claire, saying, "If you aren't invited, I'm not going, either!"

Jessica's IQ is only slightly above average, but she excels at *emotional intelligence*—a term that has captured public attention because of popular books suggesting that it is an overlooked set of skills that can greatly improve life success (Goleman, 1995, 1998). According to one influential definition, **emotional intelligence** is a set of emotional abilities that enable individuals to process and adapt to emotional information (Salovey & Pizarro, 2003). To measure it, researchers have devised items tapping emotional skills that enable people to manage their own emotions and interact competently with others. One test requires individuals to identify and rate the strength of emotions expressed in photographs of faces (emotional perception), to reason about emotions in social situations (emotional understanding), to identify which emotions promote certain thoughts and activities (emotional facilitation), and to evaluate the effectiveness of strategies for controlling negative emotions (emotion regulation). Factor analyses of the scores of hundreds of adolescents and young adults identified several emotional

capacities as well as a higher-order general factor (Mayer, Salovey, & Caruso, 2003).

Emotional intelligence is no more than modestly related—and sometimes unrelated—to IQ and academic achievement. Among school-age children, adolescents, and adults, it is positively associated with self-esteem, empathy, prosocial behavior, cooperation, leadership skills, and life satisfaction and negatively related to drug and alcohol use, dependency, depression, and aggressive behavior (Brackett, Mayer, & Warner, 2004; Mavroveli et al., 2007, 2009; Petrides et al., 2006). In adulthood, emotional intelligence predicts many aspects of workplace success, including managerial effectiveness, productive co-worker relationships, and job performance (Mayer, Roberts, & Barsade, 2008; Mayer, Salovey, & Caruso, 2008).

Only a few assessments of emotional intelligence are available for children. These require careful training of teachers in observing and recording children's emotional skills during everyday activities, gathering information from parents, and taking ethnic backgrounds into account (Denham, 2005; Denham & Burton, 2003). As more and better measures are devised,

These first graders display high emotional intelligence as they accurately interpret a younger child's frustration and take time to help him put on heavy winter outerwear.

they may help identify children with weak social and emotional competencies who would profit from intervention (Denham, 2006; Stewart-Brown & Edmunds, 2007).

The concept of emotional intelligence has increased teachers' awareness that providing experiences that meet students' social and emotional needs can improve their adjustment. Lessons that teach emotional understanding, respect and caring for others, strategies for regulating emotion, and resistance to unfavorable peer pressure—using active learning techniques that provide skill practice both in and out of the classroom—are becoming more common (Bowkett & Percival, 2011).

Some Commonly Used Intelligence Tests

Two individual tests—the Stanford-Binet and the Wechsler—are most often used to identify highly intelligent children and diagnose those with learning problems. Figure 8.3 on page 328 provides examples of items that typically appear on intelligence tests for children.

The Stanford-Binet Intelligence Scales The modern descendant of Alfred Binet's first successful intelligence test is the **Stanford-Binet Intelligence Scales, Fifth Edition,** for individuals from age 2 to adulthood. This latest edition measures general intelligence and five intellectual factors: fluid reasoning, quantitative reasoning, knowledge, visual-spatial processing, and working memory (Roid, 2003). Each factor includes both a verbal mode and a nonverbal mode of testing, yielding 10 subtests in all. The nonverbal subtests, which do not require spoken language, are especially useful when assessing individuals with limited English, hearing impairments, or communication disorders. The knowledge and quantitative reasoning factors emphasize crystallized intelligence (culturally loaded, fact-oriented

FIGURE 8.3 Test items like those on commonly used intelligence tests for children. The verbal items emphasize culturally loaded, fact-oriented information (crystallized intelligence). The perceptual- and spatial-reasoning, working-memory, and processing-speed items emphasize aspects of information processing and are assumed to assess more biologically based skills (fluid intelligence).

information), such as vocabulary and arithmetic problems. In contrast, the fluid reasoning, visual-spatial processing, and working-memory factors, which tap fluid intelligence, are assumed to be less culturally biased.

A special edition of the test, the *Stanford-Binet Intelligence Scales for Early Childhood,* includes fewer items and is tailored for assessing children between ages 2 years and 7 years 3 months. This makes the current Stanford-Binet more useful than its previous edition for diagnosing intellectual difficulties in early childhood.

The Wechsler Intelligence Scale for Children

The **Wechsler Intelligence Scale for Children–IV (WISC–IV)** is the fourth edition of a widely used test for 6- through 16-year-olds. A downward extension of it, the *Wechsler Preschool and Primary Scale of Intelligence–III (WPPSI–III),* is appropriate for children 2 years 6 months through 7 years 3 months (Wechsler, 2002, 2003). The Wechsler tests offered both a measure of general intelligence and a variety of factor scores long before the Stanford-Binet. As a result, many psychologists and educators came to prefer them.

The WISC–IV includes four broad intellectual factors: verbal reasoning, perceptual reasoning, working memory, and processing speed. Each factor is made up of two or three subtests, yielding 10 separate scores in all. The WISC–IV was designed to downplay crystallized, culture-dependent intelligence, which is emphasized on only one factor (verbal reasoning). The remaining three factors focus on fluid, information-processing skills. According to the test designers, the result is the most theoretically current and "culture-fair" intelligence test available (Williams, Weiss, & Rolfhus, 2003). The Wechsler tests were the first to use samples representing the total population of the United States, including ethnic minorities, to devise standards for interpreting test scores.

Aptitude and Achievement Tests

Two other types of tests are closely related to intelligence tests. **Aptitude tests** assess an individual's potential to learn a specialized activity. For example, mechanical aptitude is the capacity to acquire mechanical skills, musical aptitude is the capacity to acquire musical skills, and scholastic aptitude is the capacity to master school tasks. The well-known Scholastic Assessment Test (SAT) and American College Testing Assessment (ACT), which you may have submitted as part of your college application, yield measures of scholastic aptitude. In contrast, **achievement tests** aim to assess actual knowledge and skill attainment. When a school district assesses fourth-grade reading comprehension or a college professor gives a final exam, an achievement test has been used.

Note, however, that differences among intelligence, aptitude, and achievement tests are not clear-cut. Certain items on each, especially those assessing verbal and math skills, are similar. As this overlap suggests, most tests tap both aptitude and achievement, though in different balances. The three test types do differ in breadth of content. Intelligence tests assess the widest array of skills. Aptitude tests are narrower, focusing on particular skill areas. And achievement tests cover the narrowest range because they are aimed at measuring recent learning, usually in particular school subjects.

Tests for Infants

Accurately measuring infants' intelligence is a challenge because they cannot answer questions or follow directions. All we can do is present them with stimuli, coax them to respond, and observe their behavior. In addition, these young test-takers are not necessarily cooperative. To compensate for their unpredictable behaviors, some tests depend heavily on information supplied by parents.

Most infant measures emphasize perceptual and motor responses. But increasingly, new tests are being developed that tap early language, cognition, and social behavior, especially with older infants and toddlers. One commonly used test, the *Bayley Scales of Infant and Toddler Development,* is suitable for children between 1 month and 3½ years. The most recent edition, the *Bayley–III,* has three main subtests: (1) the Cognitive Scale, which includes such items as attention to familiar and unfamiliar objects, looking for a fallen object, and pretend play; (2) the Language Scale, which taps understanding and expression of language—for example, recognition of objects and people, following simple directions, and naming objects and pictures; and (3) the Motor Scale, which assesses gross- and fine-motor skills, such as grasping, sitting, stacking blocks, and climbing stairs (Bayley, 2005).

Two additional Bayley–III scales depend on parental report: (4) the Social-Emotional Scale, which asks caregivers about such behaviors as ease of calming, social responsiveness, and imitation in play; and (5) the Adaptive Behavior Scale, which asks about adaptation to the demands of daily life, including communication, self-control, following rules, and getting along with others.

PHOTO BY STEPHEN AUSMUS/USDA

Despite careful construction, most infant tests —including previous editions of the Bayley—predict later intelligence poorly. Infants and toddlers easily become distracted, fatigued, or bored during testing, so their scores often do not reflect their true abilities. And infant perceptual and motor items differ from the tasks given to older children, which increasingly emphasize verbal, conceptual, and problem-solving skills. In contrast, the Bayley–III Cognitive and Language Scales, which better dovetail with childhood tests, are good predictors of preschool mental test performance (Albers & Grieve, 2007). But because most infant scores do not tap the same dimensions of intelligence assessed in older children, they are conservatively labeled **developmental quotients (DQs)** rather than IQs.

A trained examiner administers a test based on the Bayley Scales of Infant Development to a 1-year-old sitting in her mother's lap. Compared with earlier editions, the Bayley-III Cognitive and Language Scales better predict preschool mental test performance.

Infant tests are somewhat better at making long-term predictions for very low-scoring babies. Today, they are largely used for *screening*—helping to identify for further observation and intervention infants whose very low scores mean that they are at risk for future developmental problems.

Recall from Chapter 4 that speed of habituation and recovery to visual stimuli is among the best infant correlates of later intelligence (see page 145). One test, the *Fagan Test of Infant Intelligence,* consists entirely of habituation/recovery items. To take it, the infant sits on the mother's lap and views a series of pictures. After exposure to each, the examiner records looking time toward a novel picture paired with the familiar one. Outside of highly controlled laboratory conditions, however, measures of babies' looking behavior are unreliable, or inconsistent from one occasion to the next. Because of its low test–retest reliability (see Chapter 2, page 54), the Fagan test is less successful than researchers' assessments of infant habituation/recovery in predicting childhood mental test scores. And contradictory findings exist concerning whether Fagan test scores are useful for identifying infants at risk for delays in mental development (Andersson, 1996; Fagan & Detterman, 1992; Tasbihsazan, Nettelbeck, & Kirby, 2003).

FIGURE 8.4 **Normal distribution of intelligence test scores.** To determine the percentage of same-age individuals in the population a person with a certain IQ outperformed, add the figures to the left of that IQ score. For example, an 8-year-old child with an IQ of 115 scored better than 84 percent of the population of 8-year-olds.

Computation and Distribution of IQ Scores

Intelligence tests for infants, children, and adults are scored in the same way—by computing an **intelligence quotient (IQ),** which indicates the extent to which the raw score (number of items passed) deviates from the typical performance of same-age individuals. To make this comparison possible, test designers engage in **standardization**—giving the test to a large, representative sample and using the results as the *standard* for interpreting scores.

Within the standardization sample, scores at each age level form a **normal distribution,** in which most scores cluster around the mean, or average, with progressively fewer falling toward each extreme (see Figure 8.4). This *bell-shaped distribution* results whenever researchers measure individual differences in large samples. When intelligence tests are standardized, the mean IQ is set at 100. An individual's IQ is higher or lower than 100 by an amount that reflects how much his or her test performance deviates from the standardization-sample mean.

Because we know the percentage of people who fall within each unit of the normal curve, we can figure out exactly what any IQ score means. For example, a child with an IQ of 100 performed better than 50 percent of same-age children. A child with an IQ of 85 did better than only 16 percent, whereas a child with an IQ of 130 outperformed 98 percent. The IQs of the great majority of people (96 percent) fall between 70 and 130; only a few achieve higher or lower scores.

ASK YOURSELF

Review ■ Why are aptitude and achievement tests closely related to intelligence tests and to each other?

Connect ■ Both the Stanford-Binet and the Wechsler tests provide a measure of general intelligence and an array of subtest scores. What evidence presented earlier in this chapter supports the use of these hierarchical models of intelligence?

Apply ■ Assia's score on the Stanford-Binet Intelligence Scales is 115; Leila's score is 145. Using Figure 8.4, explain how well each child performed in relation to other children her age.

▶ Discuss the stability of IQ and its prediction of academic achievement, occupational attainment, and psychological adjustment.

What Do Intelligence Tests Predict, and How Well?

Psychologists and educators who use test scores to make decisions about children's educational placement assume that the scores are good indicators of future intelligence and scholastic performance. How well does IQ actually fare as a predictive measure?

Stability of IQ Scores

Stability refers to how effectively IQ at one age predicts itself at the next. Do children who obtain a particular IQ score at age 3 or 4 perform about the same during elementary school and again in high school? To answer this question, researchers rely on longitudinal studies in which the same children are tested repeatedly.

Correlational Stability One way of examining the stability of IQ is to correlate scores obtained at different ages. This tells us whether children who score low or high in comparison to their agemates at one age continue to do so later. Examining these correlations, researchers have identified two generalizations about the stability of IQ:

- *The older the child at time of first testing, the better the prediction of later IQ.* Preschool IQs do not predict school-age scores well; correlations are typically no better than in the .30s. But after age 6, stability improves, with many correlations in the .70s and .80s. Relationships between two testings in adolescence are as high as the .80s and .90s (Deary et al., 2004; Kaufman & Lichtenberger, 2002).
- *The closer in time two testings are, the stronger the relationship between the scores.* In one long-term study, 4-year-old IQ correlated with 5-year-old IQ at .52, but prediction dropped to .46 by age 9 and to .42 by age 12 (Schneider et al., 1999).

Why do preschool scores predict less well than later scores? One reason is that with age, test items focus less on concrete knowledge and more on complex reasoning and problem solving, which require different skills. Another explanation is that during periods of rapid development, children frequently change places in a distribution. One child may spurt ahead and reach a plateau; a second child, progressing slowly and steadily, may eventually overtake the first. Finally, IQ may become more stable after schooling is under way because daily classroom activities and test items become increasingly similar. Then, variations among children in quality of school experiences and in mastery of those experiences may help sustain individual differences in IQ.

Stability of Absolute Scores So far, we have considered IQ stability in terms of how well children maintain their relative standing among agemates. Stability can also be viewed in *absolute* terms—by examining each child's profile of IQ scores over repeated testings. Longitudinal research reveals that the majority of children show substantial IQ fluctuations during childhood and adolescence—typically 10 to 20 points, and sometimes much more (McCall, 1993; Weinert & Hany, 2003).

Children who change the most tend to have orderly profiles, with scores either increasing or decreasing with age. Examining personality traits and life experiences associated with these profiles reveals that gainers tended to be more independent and competitive about doing well in school. Also, their parents were more likely to use warm, rational discipline and encourage them to succeed. In contrast, decliners often had parents who used either very severe or very lax discipline and who offered little intellectual stimulation (Honzik, Macfarlane, & Allen, 1948; McCall, Appelbaum, & Hogarty, 1973; Sontag, Baker, & Nelson, 1958).

When children who live in poverty are selected for special study, many show mental-test score declines. According to the **environmental cumulative deficit hypothesis,** the negative effects of underprivileged rearing conditions increase the longer children remain in those conditions. As a result, early cognitive deficits lead to more deficits, which become harder to overcome (Klineberg, 1963). In support of this idea, many studies show that children from economically disadvantaged families fall further and further behind their agemates in both IQ and achievement as they get older, and children who suffer from more stressors (such as parental divorce, job loss, illness, or deaths in the family) experience greater declines (Gutman, Sameroff, & Cole, 2003; Gutman, Sameroff, & Eccles, 2002).

In sum, many children show substantial changes in the absolute value of IQ that are the combined result of personal characteristics, child-rearing practices, and living conditions. Nevertheless, once IQ becomes reasonably stable in a correlational sense, it predicts a variety of important outcomes.

IQ as a Predictor of Academic Achievement

In thousands of studies, correlations between IQ and achievement test scores range from the .40s to the .80s, typically falling between .50 and .60 (Deary et al., 2007; Rhode & Thompson, 2007; Zhu & Weiss, 2005). Students with higher IQs also get better grades and stay in school

Research indicates that IQ predicts academic achievement. But other factors, including motivation and personality characteristics, are at least as important in accounting for children's learning in school.

longer. Beginning at age 7, IQ is moderately correlated with adult educational attainment (McCall, 1977).

Why does IQ predict scholastic performance? Some researchers believe that both IQ and achievement depend on the same abstract reasoning processes that underlie *g*. Consistent with this interpretation, IQ correlates best with achievement in the more abstract school subjects, such as English, mathematics, and science (Jensen, 1998). Other researchers disagree, arguing that both IQ and achievement tests draw on the same pool of culturally specific information. From this perspective, an intelligence test is, in fact, partly an achievement test, and a child's past experiences affect performance on both measures. Support for this view comes from evidence that crystallized intelligence (which reflects acquired knowledge) is a better predictor of academic achievement than is its fluid counterpart (Kaufman, Kamphaus, & Kaufman, 1985; Kunina et al., 2007).

As you can imagine, researchers who believe that heredity contributes strongly to individual differences in IQ prefer the first of these explanations. Those who favor the power of environment prefer the second. We will delve into this nature–nurture debate shortly, but for now let's note that although IQ predicts achievement better than any other tested measure, the correlation is far from perfect. Other factors, such as motivation and personality characteristics that lead some children to try hard in school, are at least as important as IQ in accounting for individual differences in school performance.

IQ as a Predictor of Occupational Attainment

If IQ scores were unrelated to long-term life success, psychologists and educators would probably be less concerned with them. But research indicates that childhood IQ predicts adult occupational attainment just about as well as it correlates with academic achievement. By second grade, children with the highest IQs are more likely, as adults, to enter prestigious professions, such as engineering, law, medicine, and science (McCall, 1977).

Again, the relationship between IQ and occupational attainment is far from perfect. Factors related to family background, such as parental encouragement, modeling of career success, and connections in the world of work, also predict occupational choice and attainment (Kalil, Levine, & Ziol-Guest, 2005). Furthermore, one reason that IQ is associated with occupational status is that IQ-like tests (the SAT and ACT) affect access to higher education. Educational attainment is a stronger predictor than IQ of occupational success and income (Ceci & Williams, 1997).

Another prominent factor in occupational achievement is personality. Examining seven longitudinal studies spanning one to four decades, researchers found that, after childhood IQ and parents' educational and occupational attainment were controlled, such traits as childhood emotional stability, conscientiousness, and sociability positively predicted career success, whereas belligerence and negative emotionality forecast unfavorable career outcomes, including job instability, reduced occupational prestige, and lower income (Roberts et al., 2007).

Finally, once a person enters an occupation, **practical intelligence**—mental abilities apparent in the real world but not in testing situations—predicts on-the-job performance as well as, and sometimes better than, IQ. Yet mental test performance and practical intelligence require distinctly different capacities. Whereas test items are formulated by others, provide complete information, are often detached from real life, and have only one solution, practical problems are not clearly defined, are embedded in everyday experiences, and generally have several appropriate solutions, each with strengths and limitations (Sternberg et al., 2000). Practical intelligence is evident in the assembly-line worker who discovers the fewest moves needed to complete a product or the business manager who increases productivity by making her subordinates feel valued. Unlike IQ, practical intelligence does not vary with ethnicity. And the two types of intelligence are unrelated and make independent contributions to job success (Cianciolo et al., 2006; Sternberg, 2003a).

In sum, occupational outcomes are a complex function of traditionally measured intelligence, education, family influences, motivation, and practical know-how. Current evidence indicates that IQ, though influential, is not more important than these other factors.

IQ as a Predictor of Psychological Adjustment

IQ is moderately correlated with emotional and social adjustment. For example, higher-IQ children and adolescents tend to be better-liked by their agemates. But the reasons for this association are not clear. Besides IQ, good peer relations are linked to patient but firm child-rearing practices and an even-tempered, sociable personality, both of which are positively correlated with IQ (Hogan, Harkness, & Lubinski, 2000; Scarr, 1997).

Another way of exploring the relationship of IQ to psychological adjustment is to look at the mental test performance of aggressive youths who frequently engage in lawbreaking acts. On average, juvenile delinquents score about 8 points lower in IQ than nondelinquents; persistently aggressive children and adolescents are especially deficient in verbal ability (Dodge, Coie, & Lynam, 2006). Perhaps similar genetic and environmental factors (such as proneness to impulsivity, parenting quality, and family functioning) influence both IQ and conduct problems. Alternatively, low IQ (especially verbal scores) may predispose children to conduct difficulties by affecting their ability to make mature moral judgments, evaluate future consequences of their actions, and control their emotions and behavior. Consistent with both interpretations, longitudinal research indicates that low IQ in early and middle childhood is associated with later antisocial behavior only when children also score high in emotional and behavior problems and when their poor intellectual functioning persists (Fergusson, Horwood, & Ridder, 2005; Leech et al., 2003).

Lower childhood mental test scores are also associated with other psychological disorders, including high anxiety and depression in adolescence and adulthood (Martin et al., 2007; Zammit et al., 2004). But these relationships are modest, and they are further reduced after childhood family instability and economic disadvantage are controlled (Fergusson, Horwood, & Ridder, 2005; Gale et al., 2009). In Chapter 1, we saw that children high in intelligence are more resilient in the face of stressful life experiences (see page 10).

In sum, IQ predicts diverse life success indicators, but does so imperfectly. These findings provide strong justification for not relying on IQ alone when forecasting a child's future or making important educational placement decisions.

This teenager's practical intelligence—evident in his ability to diagnose the cause of a malfunctioning computer and ably repair it—taps distinctly different capacities than those represented by IQ.

A S K   Y O U R S E L F

Review ■ Provide two competing explanations for the correlation between IQ and academic achievement.

Connect ■ Describe evidence from previous chapters that non-Western children with little or no formal schooling display considerable practical intelligence, despite poor performance on tasks commonly used to assess Western children's cognitive skills. (*Hint:* See Chapter 6, page 251, and Chapter 7, page 294.)

Apply ■ When 5-year-old Paul had difficulty adjusting to kindergarten, his teacher arranged for special testing. Paul's IQ turned out to be below average, at 95. When discussing Paul's score with his parents and teacher, what should the psychologist say about the stability of IQ?

Reflect ■ How do James's experiences, described in the opening to this chapter, fit with findings on children who show mental test score gains with age?

▶ Describe ethnic and socioeconomic variations in IQ.

Ethnic and Socioeconomic Variations in IQ

People in industrialized nations are stratified on the basis of what they do at work and how much they earn for doing it—factors that determine their social position and economic well-being. Researchers assess a family's standing on this continuum through an index called **socioeconomic status (SES),** which combines three interrelated—but not completely overlapping—variables: (1) years of education and (2) the prestige of one's job and the skill it requires, both of which measure social status; and (3) income, which measures economic status.

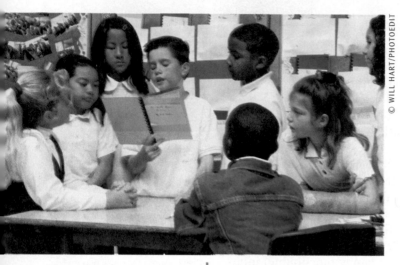

These students' IQ scores may vary with ethnicity and SES. Research designed to uncover the reasons for these associations has generated heated controversy.

In searching for the roots of socioeconomic disparities, researchers have compared the IQ scores of SES and ethnic groups because certain ethnicities (for example, African American and Hispanic) are heavily represented at lower SES levels and others (for example, Caucasian and Asian American) at middle and upper SES levels. These findings are responsible for the IQ nature–nurture debate. If group differences in IQ exist, then either heredity varies with SES and ethnicity, or certain groups have fewer opportunities to acquire the skills needed for successful test performance.

American black children and adolescents score, on average, 10 to 12 IQ points below American white children. Although the difference has been shrinking over the past several decades, a substantial gap—present by age 3—remains (Edwards & Oakland, 2006; Flynn, 2007; Nisbett, 2009; Peoples, Fagan, & Drotar, 1995). Hispanic children fall midway between black and white children, and Asian Americans score slightly higher than their white counterparts—about 3 points (Ceci, Rosenblum, & Kumpf, 1998).

The gap between middle- and low-SES children—about 9 points—accounts for some of the ethnic differences in IQ, but not all. When black children and white children are matched on parental education and income, the black–white IQ gap is reduced by a third to a half (Brooks-Gunn et al., 2003). Of course, IQ varies greatly *within* each ethnic and SES group. For example, as Figure 8.5 shows, the IQ distributions of blacks and whites overlap substantially. About 20 percent of blacks score above the white mean, and the same percentage of whites score below the black mean. In fact, ethnicity and SES account for only about one-fourth of the total variation in IQ. Nevertheless, these group differences are large enough and of serious enough consequence that they cannot be ignored.

In the 1970s, the IQ nature–nurture controversy escalated after psychologist Arthur Jensen (1969) published a controversial monograph entitled, "How Much Can We Boost IQ

FIGURE 8.5 IQ score distributions for black and for white children. The means represent approximate values obtained in studies of children reared by their biological parents.

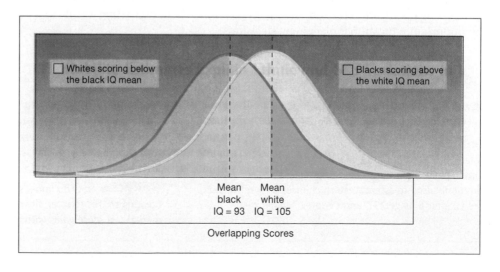

☐ Whites scoring below the black IQ mean

☐ Blacks scoring above the white IQ mean

Mean black IQ = 93   Mean white IQ = 105

Overlapping Scores

and Scholastic Achievement?" Jensen's answer was "not much." He claimed—and still maintains—that heredity is largely responsible for individual, ethnic, and SES differences in IQ (Jensen, 1998, 2001; Rushton & Jensen, 2006, 2010). Jensen's work sparked an outpouring of research studies and responses, including ethical challenges reflecting deep concern that his conclusions would fuel social prejudices. Richard Herrnstein and Charles Murray rekindled the controversy with *The Bell Curve* (1994). Like Jensen, they argued that heredity contributes substantially to individual and SES differences in IQ, and they implied that heredity plays a sizable role in the black–white IQ gap.

As with Jensen's monograph, Herrnstein and Murray's book was praised by some researchers and deplored by others, who underscored its damaging social consequences. Let's look closely at some important evidence.

Explaining Individual and Group Differences in IQ

Researchers have carried out hundreds of studies aimed at explaining individual, ethnic, and SES differences in mental abilities. The evidence is of three broad types: (1) investigations addressing the importance of heredity, (2) those that look at whether IQ scores are biased measures of the abilities of low-SES and minority children, and (3) those that examine the influence of children's home environments on their mental test performance.

Genetic Influences

Recall from Chapter 3 that behavioral geneticists examine the relative contributions of heredity and environment to complex traits by conducting *kinship studies,* which compare the characteristics of family members. Let's look closely at what they have discovered about IQ.

Heritability of Intelligence In Chapter 3, we introduced the *heritability estimate.* To review briefly, researchers correlate the IQs of family members who vary in the extent to which they share genes. Then, using a complicated statistical procedure to compare the correlations, they arrive at an index of heritability, ranging from 0 to 1, which indicates the proportion of variation in a specific population due to genetic factors.

Figure 8.6 summarizes findings on IQ correlations from more than 100 studies on approximately 50,000 pairs of twins and other relatives (Bouchard & McGue, 1981; Scarr,

▶ Discuss the contributions of heredity and environment to individual and group differences in IQ.

▶ Evaluate evidence on whether ethnic differences in IQ result from test bias, and discuss efforts to reduce cultural bias in testing.

▶ Summarize the impact of shared and nonshared environmental influences on IQ.

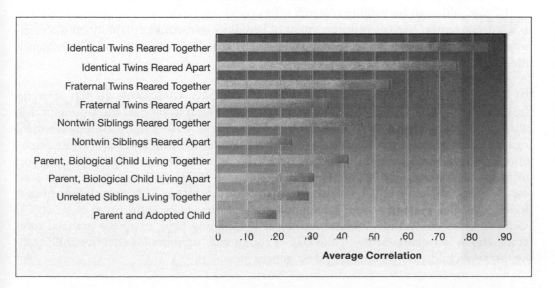

FIGURE 8.6 Worldwide summary of IQ correlations between twins and other relatives. The correlations show that the greater the genetic similarity between family members, the more similar their IQ scores. But the same correlations also show that greater environmental similarity yields more similar IQ scores. (Adapted from Bouchard & McGue, 1981; Scarr, 1997.)

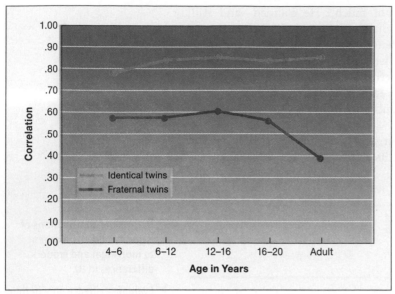

FIGURE 8.7 **Cross-sectional age-related changes in IQ correlations for identical and fraternal twins.** Correlations for identical twins increase modestly into adulthood, whereas those for fraternal twins drop sharply at adolescence. Similar trends appear when twins are followed longitudinally. The findings are derived from studies including thousands of twin pairs. (From M. McGue, T. J. Bouchard, Jr., W. G. Iacono, & D. T. Lykken, 1993, "Behavioral Genetics of Cognitive Ability: A Life-Span Perspective," in R. Plomin & G. E. McCleam [Eds.], *Nature, Nurture, and Psychology,* 1993, p. 63. Copyright © 1993 by the American Psychological Association. Adapted by permission of the American Psychological Association and M. McGue.)

1997). The greater the genetic similarity between family members, the more they resemble one another in IQ. In fact, two correlations reveal that heredity is, without question, partially responsible for individual differences in mental test performance. The correlation for identical twins reared apart (.76) is much higher than for fraternal twins reared together (.55).

Age-related changes in these twin correlations provide additional support for the contribution of heredity. As Figure 8.7 shows, correlations for identical twins increase modestly into adulthood, whereas those for fraternal twins drop sharply at adolescence. Do these trends remind you of the *niche-picking* idea, discussed in Chapter 3? Common rearing experiences support the similarity of fraternal twins during childhood. But as they get older and experience more influences outside their families, each fraternal twin follows a path of development, or finds a niche, that fits with his or her unique genetic makeup. As a result, their IQ scores diverge. In contrast, the genetic likeness of identical twins causes them to seek out similar niches in adolescence and adulthood. Consequently, their IQ resemblance strengthens (Loehlin, Horn, & Willerman, 1997; McGue et al., 1993).

Although kinship research underscores the importance of heredity, the correlations in Figure 8.6 reveal that environment is clearly involved. Correlations for twin, nontwin sibling, and parent–child pairs living together are stronger than for those living apart. And parents and adopted children, as well as unrelated siblings living together, show low positive correlations, again supporting the influence of environment.

As indicated in Chapter 3, heritability estimates usually are derived from comparisons of identical and fraternal twins. In Western industrialized nations, the typical value is about .50, meaning that half the variation in IQ is due to individual differences in heredity. But the values vary greatly between studies, ranging from the .40s to the .80s (Jacobs et al., 2007; Plomin, 2003).

Furthermore, recall from Chapter 3 that this moderate heritability estimate may be too high because twins reared together often experience very similar overall environments. Even twins reared apart generally are placed in homes that are advantaged and similar in many ways. When the range of environments to which twins are exposed is restricted, heritabilities underestimate the role of environment and overestimate the role of heredity.

In sum, although heritability research offers convincing evidence that genes contribute to IQ, disagreement persists over the extent of heredity's role. And heritability estimates do not reveal the complex processes through which genetic and environmental factors influence intelligence as children develop.

Do Heritability Estimates Explain Ethnic and SES Variations in IQ? Despite the limitations of the heritability estimate, Jensen relied on it to support the argument that ethnic and SES differences in IQ have a strong genetic basis. This line of reasoning is widely regarded as inappropriate. Heritability estimates computed *within* black and white populations, though similar, provide no direct evidence on what accounts for between-group differences (Plomin et al., 2001; Sternberg, Grigorenko, & Kidd, 2005). Also, in Chapter 3 we saw that the heritability of IQ is *higher* under advantaged (higher-SES) than disadvantaged (lower-SES) rearing conditions (Bronfenbrenner & Morris, 2006; Turkheimer et al., 2003). Factors associated with low income and poverty, including weak or absent prenatal care, family stress, low-quality schools, and lack of community supports for effective child rearing, prevent children from attaining their genetic potential.

According to geneticist Richard Lewontin (1976, 1995), using within-group heritabilities to account for between-group differences is like comparing different seeds in different soil. Imagine planting a handful of flower seeds in a pot of soil generously enriched with fertilizer and another handful in a pot with very little fertilizer. The plants in each pot vary in height, but those in the first pot grow much taller than those in the second. *Within each group,* individual differences in plant height are largely due to heredity because the growth environments of all plants were about the same. But the average difference in height *between the two groups* is probably environmental because the second group got far less fertilizer.

To verify this conclusion, we could design a study in which we expose the second group of seeds to a full supply of fertilizer and see if they reach an average height that equals that of the first group. Then we would have powerful evidence that environment is responsible for the group difference. As we turn now to adoption research, we will see that researchers have conducted natural experiments of this kind.

Adoption Studies: Joint Influence of Heredity and Environment

In adoption studies, researchers gather two types of information: (1) correlations of the IQs of adopted children with those of their biological and adoptive parents, for insight into genetic and environmental influences; and (2) changes in the absolute value of IQ as a result of growing up in an advantaged adoptive family, for evidence on the power of the environment.

Findings consistently reveal that when young children are adopted into caring, stimulating homes, their IQs rise substantially compared with the IQs of nonadopted children who remain in economically deprived families (van IJzendoorn, Juffer, & Poelhuis, 2005). But adopted children benefit to varying degrees. In one investigation, called the Texas Adoption Project, children of two extreme groups of biological mothers—those with IQs below 95 and those with IQs above 120—were adopted at birth by parents who were well above average in income and education. During the school years, the children of the low-IQ biological mothers scored above average in IQ but did less well than the children of high-IQ biological mothers placed in similar adoptive families (see Figure 8.8). Furthermore, parent–child correlations revealed that as the children grew older, they became more similar in IQ to their biological mothers and less similar to their adoptive parents (Loehlin, Horn, & Willerman, 1997).

The Texas Adoption Project and other similar investigations confirm that *both* environment and heredity contribute to IQ. In fact, children adopted in the early years attain IQs that, on average, match the scores of their adoptive parents' biological children and the scores of nonadopted peers in their schools and communities (van IJzendoorn, Juffer, & Poelhuis, 2005). These outcomes suggest a sizable role for environment in explaining SES variations in mental test scores. At the same time, adoption studies repeatedly reveal stronger correlations between the IQ scores of biological relatives than between those of adoptive relatives—clear evidence for a genetic contribution (Bouchard, 1997; Plomin et al., 2001; Scarr, 1997).

Adoption research also sheds light on the black–white IQ gap. In two studies, African-American children adopted into economically well-off white homes during the first year of life scored high on intelligence tests, attaining mean IQs of 110 and 117 by middle childhood—20 to 30 points higher than the typical scores of children growing up in low-income black communities (Moore, 1986; Scarr & Weinberg, 1983). In one investigation, the IQs of black adoptees declined in adolescence, perhaps because of the challenges faced by minority teenagers in forming an ethnic identity that blends birth and adoptive backgrounds (DeBerry, Scarr, &

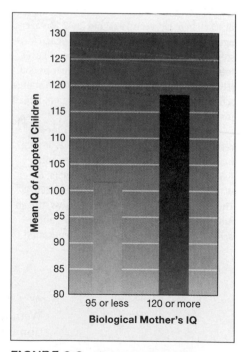

FIGURE 8.8 IQs of adopted children as a function of biological mothers' IQ in the Texas Adoption Project. Children of both low-IQ and high-IQ biological mothers scored above average in IQ, but those of the high-IQ mothers did better. (Adapted from Loehlin, Horn, & Willerman, 1997.)

CULTURAL INFLUENCES

The Flynn Effect: Massive Generational Gains in IQ

After gathering IQ scores from 20 industrialized nations that had either military mental testing or frequent testing of other large, representative samples, James Flynn (1994, 1999, 2007) reported a finding so consistent and intriguing that it became known as the **Flynn effect:** IQs have increased steadily from one generation to the next. The largest increases have occurred on fluid-ability tests of spatial reasoning—tasks often assumed to be "culture-fair" and, therefore, largely genetically based. Figure 8.9 shows these gains for one such test, administered to military samples consisting of almost all young men in Belgium, Israel, the Netherlands, and Norway. IQ rose, on average, 18 points per generation (30 years).

Consistent with this *secular trend* (see page 184 in Chapter 5 to review this concept), when intelligence tests are revised, the new standardization sample almost always performs better than the previous one. After locating every study in which the same individuals had taken two or more versions of Stanford-Binet or Wechsler tests (a total of 81 samples, with nearly 10,000 participants), Flynn used the data to estimate the rate of IQ change between 1932 and 2002. On average, IQ increased about ⅓ point per year, steadily over time and similarly across all ages, for a total of 22 points over the 46-year period (Flynn, 2007; Flynn & Weiss, 2007). When subtest scores were examined, gains were (again) largest for fluid-ability tasks.

The Flynn effect has been reconfirmed in research spanning the years 1986 to 2004 that included over 27,000 nationally representative U.S. 5- to 13-year-olds (Ang, Rodgers, & Wänström, 2010; Rodgers & Wänström, 2007). The effect held for both genders; across African Americans, Hispanics, and Caucasians; and across families varying in maternal education

and household income. And it was accelerated among children who had college-educated mothers and who were growing up in financially well-off homes.

Clearly, the Flynn effect is environmental. Improved education, health, technological innovations (including TV and computers), more time devoted to cognitively demanding leisure activities (from chess to video games), a generally more stimulating world, and greater test-taking motivation may have contributed to the better reasoning ability of each successive generation (Flynn, 2003; Rodgers & Wänström, 2007; Steen, 2009).

Recently, the Flynn effect has slowed or stopped in certain developed nations with especially favorable health, social, and economic conditions (Scandinavia, for example) (Schneider, 2006; Sundet, Barlaug, & Torjussen, 2004). At the same time, it has spread to the developing world. The IQs of rural schoolchildren in Kenya underwent a large increase from 1984 to 1998 (Daley et al., 2003). During this period, TV sets appeared in some households, parental education and literacy increased, and family size declined,

permitting parents to devote more time and resources to each child.

Notice that the generational gain in intelligence (18 points) is larger than the black–white IQ gap (about 12 to 13 points), indicating that environmental explanations for ethnic differences in IQ are highly plausible. Flynn argues that large, environmentally induced IQ increases over time present a major challenge to the assumption that black–white and other ethnic variations in IQ are genetic (Dickens & Flynn, 2001; Flynn, 2007; Nisbett, 2009).

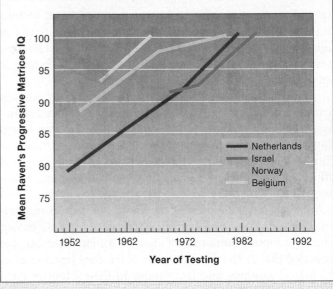

FIGURE 8.9 The Flynn effect: Generational gains in performance on a test of spatial reasoning in four nations. Findings are based on military testing that includes nearly all young adults in each country. (From J. R. Flynn, 1999, "Searching for Justice: The Discovery of IQ Gains over Time," *American Psychologist, 54,* p. 7. Copyright © 1999 by the American Psychological Association. Adapted with permission from the American Psychological Association and James Flynn.)

Weinberg, 1996). When this process is filled with emotional turmoil, it can dampen motivation on tests and in school.

Still, the black adoptees remained above the IQ average for low-SES African Americans. The IQ gains of black children "reared in the culture of the tests and schools" are consistent with a wealth of evidence that poverty severely depresses the scores of many ethnic minority children (Nisbett, 2009). Dramatic gains in IQ from one generation to the next further support the conclusion that, given new experiences and opportunities, members of oppressed groups can move far beyond their current test performance. See the Cultural Influences box above to learn about the *Flynn effect.*

Race and Ethnicity: Genetic or Cultural Groupings?

DNA analyses reveal wide genetic variation *within* races (identified by physical features, such as skin color) and minimal genetic variation *between* them (Lewontin, 2003; Sternberg, Grigorenko, & Kidd, 2005; Templeton, 2002). Members of ethnic groups that have been the focus of the IQ nature–nurture controversy are far more similar in cultural values, experiences, and opportunities than in genetic makeup.

Nevertheless, many people incorrectly assume that genetic, racial differences underlie ethnic group differences in psychological traits. Yet racial labels themselves are often arbitrary. In the United States, "black" designates people with dark skin. In Brazil and Peru, where "black" refers to hair texture, eye color, and stature, many African Americans would be called "white." Asians and the !Kung of Botswana, Africa, could be regarded as one race because they have similarly shaped eyes. Alternatively, Asians, Native Americans, and Swedes might be grouped together because of their similarly shaped teeth (Fish, 2002; Renzetti & Curran, 1998).

Differences in racial designations over time and across nations underscore their unclear boundaries. On the U.S. Census form, ten racial categories appeared in 1930, only five in 1990, and six in 2000, with respondents permitted to check more than one race—all six, if they chose! On the 2010 form, racial categories expanded to 15, and once again respondents were allowed to mark as many as appropriate, and they also could write in specific races not listed.

Many racial designations encompass enormous cultural, linguistic, and biological diversity: "Black" includes, for example, people from Africa, Haiti, and Jamaica; "Hispanic" includes people from Argentina, Costa Rica, Cuba, Guatemala, and Spain. In research as in census surveys, people self-identify, expressing their cultural heritage and sense of group belonging. Finally, in countries as culturally diverse as the United States, ethnic mixing is extensive. Consider this Hawaiian native's description of his ethnicity: "I'm Asian on my birth certificate and the census form, but I'm really multiracial. My mother's parents were Japanese, my father's mother was Filipino, and my father's father was Irish."

As one scholar of race relations summed up, "Classification of human beings into races is in the end a futile exercise" (Payne, 1998, p. 32). And perpetuating the belief that some ethnic groups are genetically inferior in IQ promotes an ever-present danger: unfair allocation of resources, making an unfounded assumption seem true.

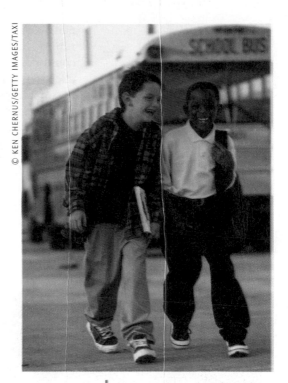

These children, brothers by adoption, are growing up in the same stimulating, advantaged home. Adoption research supports the view that experiences and opportunities explain racial and ethnic differences in IQ.

Cultural Bias in Testing

A controversial question raised about ethnic differences in IQ has to do with whether they result from *test bias.* If a test samples knowledge and skills that not all groups of children have had equal opportunity to learn, or if the testing situation impairs the performance of some groups but not others, then the resulting score is a biased, or unfair, measure.

Some experts reject the idea that intelligence tests are biased, claiming that they are intended to represent success in the common culture. According to this view, because IQ predicts academic achievement equally well for majority and minority children, IQ tests are fair to both groups (Edwards & Oakland, 2006; Jensen, 2002). Others believe that lack of exposure to certain communication styles and knowledge, along with negative stereotypes about the test-taker's ethnic group, can undermine children's performance (Ceci & Williams, 1997; Sternberg, 2005). Let's look at the evidence.

Communication Styles Ethnic minority families often foster unique language skills that do not match the expectations of most classrooms and testing situations. Shirley Brice Heath (1990), an anthropologist who spent many hours observing in low-SES black homes in a southeastern U.S. city, found that African-American adults rarely asked their children the types of knowledge-training questions typical of middle-SES white families ("What color is it?" "What's this story about?"), which resemble the questioning style of tests and classrooms. Instead, the black parents asked only "real" questions, ones that they themselves could not answer. Often these were analogy questions ("What's that like?") or story-starter questions ("Did you hear Sally this morning?") that called for elaborate responses about personal experiences and had no "right answer."

These experiences led the black children to develop complex verbal skills at home, such as storytelling and exchanging quick-witted remarks. But their language emphasized emotional and social concerns rather than facts about the world. Not surprisingly, when the black children started school, many were unfamiliar with and confused by the "objective" questions they encountered on tests and in classrooms.

Also, African-American children often take a unique approach to storytelling that reflects a culturally specific form of narrative. Instead of the *topic-focused* style of most school-age children, who describe an experience from beginning to end, they use a *topic-associating* style, in which they blend several similar experiences. One 9-year-old, for example, related having a tooth pulled, then described seeing her sister's tooth being pulled, next told how she had removed one of her baby teeth, and concluded, "I'm a pullin' teeth expert . . . call me, and I'll be over'" (McCabe, 1997, p. 164). Despite its complexity, many teachers criticize this culturally distinctive narrative form as "disorganized," and it is not included in verbal test items (Beck, 2008). Rather, mental tests typically ask children to rearrange events in consecutive order.

© EASTCOTT-MOMATIUK/THE IMAGE WORKS

This Canadian Inuit grandmother and granddaughter communicate collaboratively, smoothly coordinating actions in cleaning freshly caught fish. Many children from ethnic minority families are unfamiliar with the hierarchical communication style typical of classrooms—a reason they may do poorly on tests and assignments.

Furthermore, many ethnic minority parents without extensive schooling prefer a *collaborative style of communication* when completing tasks with children. They work together in a coordinated, fluid way, each focused on the same aspect of the problem. This pattern of adult–child engagement has been observed in Native American, Canadian Inuit, Hispanic, and Guatemalan Mayan cultures (Chavajay & Rogoff, 2002; Crago, Annahatak, & Ningiuruvik, 1993; Delgado-Gaitan, 1994; Paradise & Rogoff, 2009). With increasing education, parents establish a *hierarchical style of communication,* like that of classrooms and tests. The parent directs each child to carry out an aspect of the task, and children work independently (Greenfield, Suzuki, & Rothstein-Fish, 2006). This sharp discontinuity between home and school communication practices may contribute to low-SES minority children's lower IQ and school performance.

Indeed, intelligence testing is an extreme of this directive approach. Tasks are presented in only one way, and test-takers get no feedback. When an adult refuses to reveal whether the child is on the right track, minority children may react with "disruptive apprehension"—giving any answer that comes to mind and rejecting the testing situation as personally irrelevant (Ferguson, 1998). In one study, Australian Aboriginal 7- to 14-year-olds—who scored far below their Australian European agemates on a typical, paper-and-pencil math skills test—showed dramatic performance gains when given a computerized, interactive version. The computerized test provided immediate feedback about the accuracy of answers and, after an incorrect response, allowed the child to invoke a brief, narrated lesson on how to solve the item (Hippisley, Douglas, & Houghton, 2005). Providing feedback and prompting children to look at missed problems in new ways resulted in a more "culture-fair" assessment of their math competencies.

LOOK and LISTEN

Review the perceptual- and spatial-reasoning, working-memory, and processing-speed items in Figure 8.3 on page 328, which emphasize fluid intelligence. For each, describe one home and one school experience likely to facilitate children's performance.

Knowledge Many researchers argue that IQ scores are affected by specific information acquired as part of majority-culture upbringing. Consistent with this view, low-SES African-American preschoolers often miss vocabulary words on mental tests that have alternative meanings in their cultural community—for example, interpreting the word *frame* to mean "physique" or *wrapping* as "rapping," referring to the style of music (Champion, 2003a).

Knowledge affects ability to reason effectively. When researchers assessed black and white community college students' familiarity with vocabulary taken from items on an intelligence test, the whites had considerably more knowledge (Fagan & Holland, 2007). But the black students were just as capable as the white students at learning new words, either from dictionary definitions or from their use in sentences. When verbal comprehension, similarities, and analogies test items depended on words and concepts that the white students knew better, the whites scored higher than the blacks. But when the same types of items involved words and concepts that the two groups knew equally well, the two groups did not differ. Prior knowledge, not reasoning ability, fully explained ethnic differences in performance.

Even nonverbal test items, such as spatial reasoning, depend on learning opportunities. For example, using small blocks to duplicate designs and playing video games requiring fast responding and mental rotation of visual images increase success on spatial test items (Dirks, 1982; Maynard, Subrahmanyam, & Greenfield, 2005). Low-income minority children, who often grow up in more "people-oriented" than "object-oriented" homes, may lack opportunities to use games and objects that promote certain intellectual skills.

Furthermore, the sheer amount of time a child spends in school predicts IQ. When children of the same age who are in different grades are compared, those who have been in school longer score higher on intelligence tests. Similarly, the earlier young people leave school, the greater their loss of IQ points (Ceci, 1991, 1999). Taken together, these findings indicate that children's exposure to the knowledge and ways of thinking valued in classrooms has a sizable impact on their intelligence test performance.

When same-age children are compared, those who have spent more time in school have higher IQs—evidence that exposure to the knowledge and ways of thinking valued in classrooms improves mental test performance.

Stereotypes

TAKE A MOMENT... Imagine trying to succeed at an activity when the prevailing attitude is that members of your group are incompetent. What might you be feeling and saying to yourself? **Stereotype threat**—the fear of being judged on the basis of a negative stereotype—can trigger anxiety that interferes with performance. Mounting evidence confirms that stereotype threat undermines test taking in children and adults (McKown & Strambler, 2009; Steele, 1997). For example, researchers gave African-American, Hispanic-American, and Caucasian-American 6- to 10-year-olds verbal tasks. Some children were told that the tasks were "not a test." Others were told that they were "a test of how good children are at school problems"—a statement designed to induce stereotype threat in the ethnic minority children. Among children who were aware of ethnic stereotypes (such as "black people aren't smart"), African Americans and Hispanics performed far worse in the "test" condition than in the "not a test" condition. Caucasian children, in contrast, performed similarly in both conditions (see Figure 8.10) (McKown & Weinstein, 2003). The researchers concluded that only under the "not a test" instructions did the minority children do as well as would have been expected on the basis of a prior measure of their verbal ability.

Over middle childhood, children become increasingly conscious of ethnic stereotypes, and those from stigmatized groups are especially mindful of them. By early adolescence, many low-SES, minority students start to devalue doing well in school, saying it is not important to them (Cooper & Huh, 2008; Major et al., 1998). Self-protective disengagement, sparked by stereotype threat, may be responsible. This weakening of motivation can have serious long-term consequences. Research shows that self-discipline—effort and delay of gratification—predicts school performance at least as well as IQ does—and sometimes better (Duckworth & Seligman, 2005).

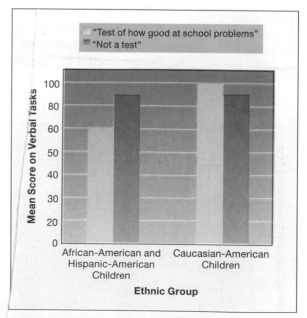

FIGURE 8.10 Effect of stereotype threat on performance. Among African-American and Hispanic-American children who were aware of ethnic stereotypes, being told that verbal tasks were a "test of how good children are at school problems" led to far worse performance than being told that tasks "were not a test." These statements had little impact on the performance of Caucasian-American children. (Adapted from McKown & Weinstein, 2003.)

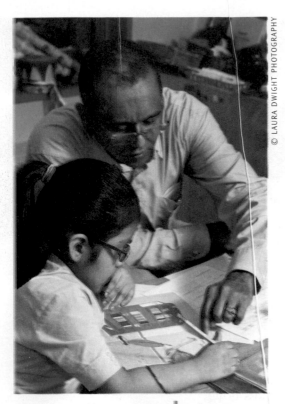

By tailoring teaching to students' individual needs, dynamic assessment reveals what a child can learn with social support.

Reducing Cultural Bias in Testing

Although not all experts agree, many acknowledge that IQ scores can underestimate the intelligence of children from ethnic minority groups. A special concern exists about incorrectly labeling minority children as slow learners and assigning them to remedial classes, which are far less stimulating than regular school experiences. Because of this danger, test scores need to be combined with assessments of children's adaptive behavior—their ability to cope with the demands of their everyday environments. The child who does poorly on an IQ test yet plays a complex game on the playground or figures out how to rewire a broken TV is unlikely to be mentally deficient.

In addition, culturally relevant testing procedures enhance minority children's performance. In an approach called **dynamic assessment,** an innovation consistent with Vygotsky's *zone of proximal development,* the adult introduces purposeful teaching into the testing situation to find out what the child can attain with social support (Lidz, 2001; Sternberg & Grigorenko, 2002). Dynamic assessment often follows a pretest–intervene–retest procedure. While intervening, the adult seeks the teaching style best suited to the child and communicates strategies that the child can apply in new situations.

Research shows that "static" assessments, such as IQ scores, frequently underestimate how well children do on test items after receiving adult assistance. Children's receptivity to teaching and their capacity to transfer what they have learned to novel problems add considerably to the prediction of future performance (Haywood & Lidz, 2007; Sternberg & Grigorenko, 2002; Tzuriel, 2001). In one study, Ethiopian 6- and 7-year-olds who had recently immigrated to Israel scored well below their Israeli-born agemates on spatial reasoning tasks. The Ethiopian children had little experience with this type of thinking. After several dynamic assessment sessions in which the adult suggested effective strategies, the Ethiopian children's scores rose sharply, nearly equaling those of Israeli-born children (see Figure 8.11). They also transferred their learning to new test items (Tzuriel & Kaufman, 1999).

Dynamic assessment is time-consuming and requires extensive knowledge of minority children's cultural values and practices. As yet the approach has not been more effective than traditional tests in predicting academic achievement (Grigorenko & Sternberg, 1998). Better correspondence may emerge in classrooms where teaching interactions resemble the dynamic testing approach—namely, individualized assistance on tasks carefully selected to help the child move beyond her current level of development.

But rather than adapting testing to support high-quality classroom learning experiences, U.S. education is placing greater emphasis on traditional test scores. To upgrade the academic achievement of poorly performing students, a *high-stakes testing* movement has arisen, making progress through the school system contingent on test performance. As the Social Issues: Education box on the following page indicates, this stepped-up emphasis on passing standardized tests has narrowed the focus of instruction in many classrooms to test preparation, and it may widen SES and ethnic group differences in educational attainment.

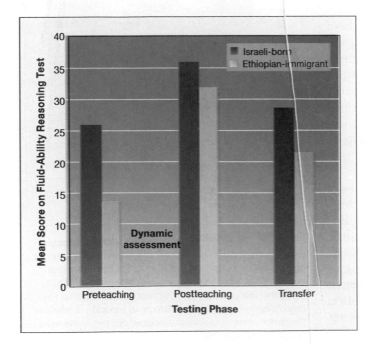

FIGURE 8.11 Influence of dynamic assessment on mental test scores of Ethiopian-immigrant and Israeli-born 6- and 7-year-olds. Each child completed test items in a preteaching phase, a postteaching phase, and a transfer phase, in which they had to generalize their learning to new problems. After dynamic assessment, Ethiopian and Israeli children's scores were nearly equal. Ethiopian children also transferred their learning to new test items, performing much better in the transfer phase than in the preteaching phase. (Adapted from Tzuriel & Kaufman, 1999.)

SOCIAL ISSUES: EDUCATION

High-Stakes Testing

To better hold schools accountable for educating students, during the past two decades many U.S. states have mandated that students pass exams for high school graduation. Currently, about two-thirds of public high school students take exit exams (Center on Education Policy, 2009). As these high-stakes achievement tests spread, schools stepped up their testing programs, extending them downward to elementary school. Some states and school districts also made grade promotion (in New York City, as early as the third grade) and secondary-school academic course credits contingent on test scores.

The U.S. No Child Left Behind Act broadens high-stakes testing to the identification of "passing" and "failing" schools. The law mandates that each state evaluate every public school's performance through annual achievement testing and publicize the results. Schools that consistently perform poorly (have a high percentage of failing students) must give parents options for upgrading their children's education, such as transfers to nearby higher-performing schools or enrollment in remedial classes. When they lose students, such schools also lose state and federal funds. Some states offer schoolwide rewards for high scores, including official praise and financial bonuses to school staff. Penalties imposed for low scores include staff firing, withdrawal of accreditation, state takeover, closure, or other restructuring.

Proponents of high-stakes testing believe that it introduces greater rigor into classroom teaching, improves student motivation and achievement, and either turns around poor-performing schools or protects students from being trapped in them. But accumulating evidence indicates that high-stakes testing often undermines, rather than upgrades, the quality of education.

Research shows that high-stakes tests cause teachers to spend large amounts of time on activities that closely resemble test items—typically, drill-based exercises. Classroom experiences and assignments that require high-level reasoning, including extended writing and research projects, are de-emphasized, as are subjects not covered on the tests (Jones & Egley, 2004; Ravitch, 2010). In a national survey of U.S. teachers, those in states with high-stakes tests reported that to "cover" the material likely to be tested, they felt pressured to move through the curriculum too quickly, yielding surface knowledge rather than in-depth understanding (Center on Education Policy, 2007).

Because the main goal of high-stakes testing is to upgrade the performance of poorly achieving students, low-income and ethnic minority children are especially likely to be exposed to narrowly focused, regimented teaching (Darling-Hammond, 2010). Simultaneously, the educational needs of gifted and talented students are neglected (Scot, Callahan, & Urquhart, 2009).

An additional concern is that high-stakes testing promotes fear—a poor motivator for upgrading teaching and learning. Principals and teachers worry about losing funding and their jobs if students do poorly—punishments that have sparked unprecedented levels of adult cheating and other educationally detrimental behaviors. These range from giving students answers, changing students' scores, and offering students rewards (including money and expensive toys) for earning high scores to suspending or expelling students likely to perform poorly just before test administration (Nichols & Berliner, 2007).

Furthermore, many students who get passing school grades, even high grades, fail high-stakes exams because a time-limited test can tap only a small sampling of the skills covered in the classroom (Hursh, 2007). Students most likely to score poorly are minority youths living in poverty. When they are punished with course failure and grade retention, their self-esteem and motivation drop sharply. Research confirms that high-stakes testing requirements have contributed to the high dropout rates among U.S. inner-city minority youths (Balfanz et al., 2007).

The trend toward teaching to tests induced by high-stakes testing contrasts sharply with the emphasis on teaching for deeper understanding in countries that rank at the top in cross-cultural comparisons of academic achievement (see Chapter 15). Even after hundreds of hours of class time devoted to test preparation, thousands of U.S. students fail school-exit exams and do not graduate. Although most retake these exams, some fail repeatedly, with potentially dire consequences for the course of their lives.

Clearly, serious issues remain for lawmakers and educators to resolve about the use of high-stakes tests. These include their questionable power to spark school reforms that make students better learners.

Classroom teaching narrowly focused on preparation for high-stakes tests leads to superficial learning and loss of interest. When low-income minority youths test poorly and are punished with course failure and grade retention, they are likely to drop out.

In view of its many problems, should intelligence testing in schools be suspended? Most experts reject this solution. Without testing, important educational decisions would be based only on subjective impressions, perhaps increasing discriminatory placement of minority children. Intelligence tests are useful when interpreted carefully by psychologists and educators who are sensitive to cultural influences on test performance. And despite their limitations, IQ scores continue to be valid measures of school learning potential for the majority of Western children.

APPLYING WHAT WE KNOW

Features of a High-Quality Home Life in Infancy and Toddlerhood, Early Childhood, and Middle Childhood: The HOME Subscales

INFANCY AND TODDLERHOOD	EARLY CHILDHOOD	MIDDLE CHILDHOOD
Emotional and verbal responsiveness of the parent	Cognitive stimulation through toys, games, and reading material	Parental emotional and verbal responsiveness
Parental acceptance of the child	Language stimulation	Emotionally positive parent–child relationship
Organization of the physical environment	Organization of the physical environment	Parental encouragement of social maturity
Provision of appropriate play materials	Emotional support: parental pride, affection, and warmth	Provision for active stimulation
Parental involvement with the child	Stimulation of academic behavior	Growth-fostering materials and experiences
Opportunities for variety in daily stimulation	Parental modeling and encouragement of social maturity	Family participation in developmentally stimulating experiences
	Opportunities for variety in daily stimulation	Parental involvement in child rearing
	Avoidance of physical punishment	Physical environment: safe, clean, and conducive to development

Sources: Bradley, 1994; Bradley et al., 2001.

Home Environment and Mental Development

As noted earlier, children of the *same* ethnic and SES background vary greatly in mental test scores. Many studies support the conclusion that factors in the home environment contribute to these differences.

Researchers divide home influences into two broad types: **Shared environmental influences** pervade the general atmosphere of the home and, therefore, *similarly* affect siblings living in it. Examples include the availability of stimulating toys and books and parental modeling of cognitively challenging activities. **Nonshared environmental influences** make siblings *different* from one another. Unique treatment by parents, birth order and spacing, and special events that affect one sibling more than the other (such as moving to a new neighborhood) are examples.

Shared Environmental Influences Two types of research shed light on the role of shared environmental influences: (1) studies in which researchers observe home environmental qualities and relate them to IQ; and (2) studies examining the impact of family beliefs about intellectual success on student performance.

Observations of Home Environmental Qualities. The **Home Observation for Measurement of the Environment (HOME)** is a checklist for gathering information about the quality of children's home lives through observation and parental interview (Caldwell & Bradley, 1994). Refer to Applying What We Know above for factors that HOME measures in infancy and toddlerhood, early childhood, and middle childhood.

Evidence on HOME confirms the findings of decades of research—that stimulation provided by parents is moderately linked to mental development. Regardless of SES and ethnicity, an organized, stimulating physical setting and parental encouragement, involvement, and affection repeatedly predict better language and IQ scores in toddlerhood and early childhood (Berger, Paxson, & Waldfogel, 2009; Foster et al., 2005; Fuligni, Han, & Brooks-Gunn, 2004; Klebanov et al., 1998; Linver, Martin, & Brooks-Gunn, 2004; Mistry et al., 2008). In a study in which researchers controlled for both SES and home environmental quality, the black–white disparity in preschoolers' IQ diminished to just a few points (Smith, Duncan, & Lee, 2003).

The extent to which parents talk to infants and toddlers contributes strongly to early language progress, which, in turn, predicts intelligence and academic achievement in elementary school (Hart & Risley, 1995). Recall from Chapter 7 that knowledge of the sound structure of language (phonological awareness), vocabulary and grammatical development, and wide-ranging general knowledge are vital for learning to read.

The HOME–IQ relationship declines in middle childhood, perhaps because older children spend increasing amounts of time in school and other out-of-home settings (Luster & Dubow, 1992). Nevertheless, two middle-childhood HOME scales are especially strong predictors of academic achievement: provision for active stimulation (for example, encouraging hobbies and organizational memberships) and family participation in developmentally stimulating experiences (visiting friends, attending theater performances) (Bradley, Caldwell, & Rock, 1988).

Yet we must interpret these correlational findings cautiously. In all the studies, children were reared by their biological parents, with whom they share not just a common environment but also a common heredity. Parents who are genetically more intelligent may provide better experiences as well as give birth to genetically brighter children, who evoke more stimulation from their parents. Research supports this hypothesis, which refers to *genetic–environmental correlation* (see Chapter 3, page 122). The HOME–IQ correlation is stronger for biological than for adopted children, suggesting that parent–child genetic similarity elevates the relationship (Saudino & Plomin, 1997).

But heredity does not account for the entire association between home environment and mental test scores. Family living conditions—both HOME scores and resources in the surrounding neighborhood—continue to predict children's IQ beyond the contribution of parental IQ and education (Chase-Lansdale et al., 1997; Klebanov et al., 1998). These findings highlight the vital importance of environmental quality.

Family Beliefs About Intellectual Success. Regardless of SES, newly arrived immigrant parents from Asia and Latin America emphasize the importance of intellectual success, and their children do remarkably well in school. (Return to the Cultural Influences box on page 53 in Chapter 2 to review these findings.) Parental support for achievement is greater in higher-SES families in which both parent and child IQs are higher, making it difficult to isolate the impact of family beliefs on children's performance. Is IQ responsible for immigrant families' high valuing of intellectual endeavors and their children's superior academic performance? Probably not; recent arrivals are unlikely to be more intelligent than American–born children whose parents arrived a decade or two earlier. Rather, immigrant parents' belief that education is the surest way to improve life chances seems to play a profound role (Cooper, Dominguez, & Rosas, 2005; Fuligni & Yoshikawa, 2003).

Parental beliefs are also linked to academic performance among nonimmigrant children. In a study of more than 1,300 U.S. Caucasian- and African-American families with school-age children, parental expectations for educational attainment predicted parents' involvement

A Mexican-American mother looks over examples of her third grader's assignments at a parent–teacher conference. Parents who highly value education are more involved in their children's school life, which is associated with higher achievement.

in their children's school activities, supervision of homework, and—two years later—children's reading and math achievement (Zhan, 2005). Similarly, an investigation of Asian-American, Hispanic, and Caucasian-American families revealed that within each group, the more education parents expected their fourth and fifth graders to attain, the higher the children's school grades (Okagaki & Frensch, 1998). Parental expectations were not merely responsive to their child's prior achievements. Rather, regardless of children's grades the previous year, parental beliefs predicted school performance.

Think back to James's father's conviction that academic success could transform James's life path, described in the opening to this chapter. Warm, appropriately demanding child rearing, cognitively stimulating parent–child activities, and parents' school involvement seem to be the major means through which parents convey such beliefs to their children (Davis-Kean, 2005; Okagaki, 2001). We will consider parenting and achievement further in Chapters 11 and 14.

Nonshared Environmental Influences The experiences of children growing up in the same family, while similar in some ways, differ in others. Parents may favor one child or assign children special roles—for example, one expected to achieve in school, a second to get along with others. Each child also experiences sibling relationships differently.

Kinship research suggests that nonshared environmental factors are more powerful than shared influences on IQ. Turn back to Figure 8.6 on page 335. Notice the relatively low IQ correlations between unrelated siblings living together—a direct estimate of the effect of shared environment. Recall, also, that in adolescence the IQ resemblance between fraternal twins declines (see page 336). This trend, which also characterizes nontwin siblings, is particularly marked for unrelated siblings, whose IQs at adolescence are no longer correlated. These findings indicate that the impact of the shared environment on IQ is greatest in childhood (Finkel & Pedersen, 2001; Loehlin, Horn, & Willerman, 1997). Thereafter, it gives way to nonshared influences, as young people spend more time outside the home, encounter experiences unlike those of their siblings, and seek environments consistent with their genetic makeup.

Nevertheless, few studies have examined nonshared environmental influences on IQ. The most extensively studied factors are sibling birth order and spacing. For years, researchers thought that earlier birth order and wider spacing might grant children more parental attention and stimulation and, therefore, result in higher IQs. But recent evidence indicates that birth order and spacing are unrelated to IQ (Rodgers, 2001; Rodgers et al., 2000; Wichman, Rodgers, & MacCallum, 2006). Why is this so? Parents' differential treatment of siblings appears to be far more responsive to children's personalities, interests, and behaviors than to these family-structure variables.

Finally, some researchers believe that the most potent nonshared environmental influences are unpredictable, unique events—an inspiring English teacher, a summer at a special camp, or perhaps a period of intense sibling rivalry (McCall, 1993). To understand the role of these nonshared factors in mental development, we need intensive case studies of children growing up in the same family.

LOOK and LISTEN

Ask several parents to describe a unique event, such as an inspiring teacher or a special experience, that seemed to boost their child's school performance. Then ask the children for their views of these nonshared influences.

A S K   Y O U R S E L F

Review ■ Why can't heritability estimates explain ethnic differences in IQ? Using research findings, describe environmental factors that contribute to these differences.

Connect ■ Explain how dynamic assessment is consistent with Vygotsky's zone of proximal development and with scaffolding (see Chapter 6, pages 267–268).

Apply ■ Josefina, a Hispanic fourth grader, does well on homework assignments. But when her teacher announces, "It's time for a test to see how much you've learned," Josefina usually does poorly. How might stereotype threat explain this inconsistency?

Reflect ■ Do you think that intelligence tests are culturally biased? What evidence and observations influenced your conclusions?

Early Intervention and Intellectual Development

▶ Discuss the impact of early intervention on intellectual development.

In the 1960s, as part of the "War on Poverty" in the United States, many intervention programs for economically disadvantaged preschoolers were initiated. Their goal was to offset the declines in IQ and achievement common among low-SES schoolchildren by addressing learning problems early, before formal schooling begins. The most extensive of these federal programs, **Project Head Start,** began in 1965. A typical Head Start center provides children with a year or two of preschool, along with nutritional and health services. Parent involvement is central to the Head Start philosophy. Parents serve on policy councils, contribute to program planning, work directly with children in classrooms, attend special programs on parenting and child development, and receive services directed at their own emotional, social, and vocational needs. Currently, Head Start serves about 904,000 children and their families across the nation (Head Start, 2010).

Benefits of Early Intervention

More than two decades of research have established the long-term benefits of early intervention. The most extensive of these studies combined data from seven interventions implemented by universities or research foundations. Results showed that poverty-stricken children who attended programs scored higher in IQ and achievement than controls during the first two to three years of elementary school. After that, differences declined (Lazar & Darlington, 1982). But on real-life measures of school adjustment, children and adolescents who had received intervention remained ahead. They were less likely to be placed in special education or retained in grade, and a greater number graduated from high school. They also showed lasting benefits in attitudes and motivation: They were more likely to give achievement-related reasons (such as school or job accomplishments) for being proud of themselves.

A separate report on one program, the High/Scope Perry Preschool Project, revealed benefits lasting well into adulthood. More than 100 African-American 3- and 4-year-olds were randomly assigned either to a cognitively enriching two-year preschool program or to no intervention. During weekly visits to the homes of the intervention group, teachers showed parents how to teach and read to their children. Besides improved school adjustment, preschool intervention was associated with increased employment and reduced pregnancy and delinquency rates in adolescence. At age 27, those who had attended preschool were more likely to have graduated from high school, to have enrolled in college, to have higher earnings, be married, and own their own home—and less likely to have ever been diagnosed as mentally impaired or to be on welfare or involved with the criminal justice system (see Figure 8.12 on page 348). The most recent follow-up, at age 40, revealed that the intervention group sustained its advantage on all measures of life success, including education, income, family life, and law-abiding behavior (Schweinhart, 2010; Schweinhart et al., 2005).

Do the effects on school adjustment of these well-designed and well-delivered interventions generalize to Head Start and other community-based preschool interventions? Gains are similar, though not as strong. Head Start preschoolers, who are more economically disadvantaged than children in other programs, have more severe learning and behavior problems. And quality of services in

For these preschoolers, the benefits of early intervention are likely to include lasting advantages on real-life measures of school adjustment, including attitudes and motivation.

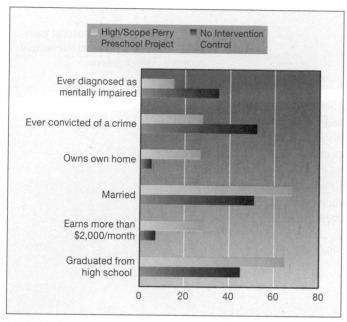

FIGURE 8.12 **Some outcomes of the High/Scope Perry Preschool Project on follow-up at age 27.** Although two years of a cognitively enriching preschool program did not eradicate the effects of growing up in poverty, children who received intervention were advantaged over no-intervention controls on all measures of life success when they reached adulthood. (Adapted from Schweinhart, 2010; Schweinhart et al., 2005.)

Head Start—though better than in most preschool education programs serving low-SES children—often does not equal that of model university-based programs (Resnick, 2010; U.S. Department of Health and Human Services, 2010e). But interventions of documented high quality are associated with diverse, long-lasting favorable outcomes, including higher rates of high school graduation and college enrollment and lower rates of adolescent drug use and delinquency (Garces, Thomas, & Currie, 2002; Love et al., 2006; Mashburn, 2008).

A consistent finding is that gains in IQ and achievement test scores from attending Head Start and other interventions quickly dissolve. In the Head Start Impact Study, a nationally representative sample of 5,000 Head Start–eligible 3- and 4-year-olds was randomly assigned to one year of Head Start or to a control group that could attend other types of pre-school programs (U.S. Department of Health and Human Services, 2010e). By year's end, Head Start 3-year-olds had gained relative to controls in vocabulary, emergent literacy, and math skills; 4-year-olds in vocabulary, emergent literacy, and color identification. Head Start 3-year-olds also benefitted socially, displaying declines in overactivity and withdrawn behavior. But except for language skills, academic test-score advantages were no longer evident by end of first grade.

What explains these disappointing outcomes? Head Start children typically enter inferior public schools in poverty-stricken neighborhoods, which undermine the benefits of preschool education (Brooks-Gunn, 2003; Ramey, Ramey, & Lanzi, 2006). But in the Chicago Child–Parent Centers—a program emphasizing literacy intervention and parent involvement that began at age 3 and continued through third grade—gains in academic achievement were still evident in junior high school (Reynolds & Temple, 1998).

Furthermore, when high-quality intervention starts in infancy and extends through early childhood, children display cognitive and academic achievement advantages throughout childhood and adolescence (Brooks-Gunn, 2004; Ramey, Ramey, & Lanzi, 2006). The Carolina Abecedarian Project illustrates these positive outcomes. In the 1970s, more than 100 infants from poverty-stricken families, ranging in age from 3 weeks to 3 months, were randomly assigned to either a treatment group or a control group. Treatment infants were enrolled in full-time, year-round child care through the preschool years. There they received stimulation aimed at promoting motor, cognitive, language, and social skills and, after age 3, literacy and math concepts. All children received nutrition and health services; the primary difference between treatment and controls was the intensive child-care experience.

As Figure 8.13 shows, by 12 months of age, the IQs of the two groups diverged. Treatment children sustained their lead until last tested—at age 21. In addition, throughout their years of schooling, treatment youths achieved considerably higher scores than controls in reading and math. These gains translated into more years of schooling completed, higher rates of college enrollment and employment in skilled jobs, and lower rates of drug use and adolescent parenthood (Campbell et al., 2001, 2002; Campbell & Ramey, 2010).

Recognition of the greater power of intervening as early as possible led the U.S. Congress to provide limited funding for services directed at infants and toddlers who already

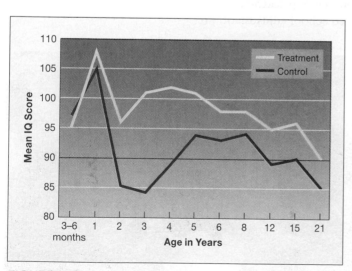

FIGURE 8.13 **IQ scores of treatment and control children from infancy to 21 years in the Carolina Abecedarian Project.** At 1 year, treatment children outperformed controls, an advantage consistently maintained through age 21. The IQ scores of both groups declined gradually during childhood and adolescence—a trend probably due to the damaging impact of poverty on mental development. (Adapted from Campbell et al., 2001.)

have serious developmental problems or who are at risk for problems because of poverty. **Early Head Start,** begun in 1995, currently has 700 sites serving 63,000 low-income families. It offers an array of coordinated services—child care, educational experiences for infants and toddlers, parenting education, family social support, and health care—delivered through a center-based, home-based, or mixed approach, depending on community needs. A recent evaluation, conducted when children reached age 3, showed that intervention led to warmer, more stimulating parenting, a reduction in harsh discipline, gains in cognitive and language development, and lessening of child aggression (Love et al., 2005; Love, Chazan-Cohen, & Raikes, 2007; Raikes et al., 2010). The strongest effects occurred at sites mixing center and home-visiting services—a combination that may intensify educational and family services.

Even when intervention is delayed until age 3 or 4, the improved school adjustment that results from attending a one- or two-year Head Start program is impressive. The comprehensiveness of Head Start—provision of health, nutrition, education, and family social services—along with its emphasis on parent involvement may be responsible. The more involved parents are in Head Start, the better their child-rearing practices and the more stimulating their home learning environments. These factors are positively related to preschoolers' independence and task persistence in the classroom and to their year-end academic, language, and social skills (Marcon, 1999b; McLoyd, Aikens, & Burton, 2006; Parker et al., 1999).

Strengthening Early Intervention

Excellent early intervention is highly cost effective when compared with the cost of providing special education, treating criminal behavior, and supporting unemployed adults. Economists estimate a lifetime return to society of $300,000 to $500,000 on an investment of about $17,000 per preschool child—a potential total savings of many billions of dollars if every poverty-stricken preschooler in the United States were enrolled (Heckman et al., 2010).

What factors contributed to the enduring impact of such outstanding programs as the High/Scope Perry Preschool Project, the Chicago Child–Parent Centers, and the Carolina Abecedarian Project? According to one analysis, they shared the following critical features:

- *Starting early.* The Abecedarian Program began in the first months of life, the High/ Scope Perry Preschool Project and the Chicago Child–Parent Centers as early as age 3.
- *Employing well-educated, well-compensated teachers.* Most teachers in the three programs had at least a bachelor's degree in education, and they were paid competitively with public school teachers—factors resulting in low staff turnover and stability in teacher–child relationships.
- *Maintaining generous teacher–child ratios and small class sizes.* In the Abecedarian Program, the teacher–infant ratio was 1 to 3, the teacher–toddler ratio 1 to 4. Preschool ratios in the three programs ranged from 1 to 5 to 1 to 8.
- *Offering intensive intervention.* Each program included many hours of classroom contact with children in the early years—in the High/Scope Perry Preschool Project and Chicago Child–Parent Centers, full days for up to two school years; in the Abecedarian Project, full days, year-round, for five years.
- *Emphasizing parent involvement, education, and support.* The High/Scope Perry Preschool Project and the Chicago Child–Parent Centers made concerted efforts to involve parents in their children's learning.
- *Focusing on the whole child.* The three programs promoted all aspects of children's development—not just academic skills. They recognized that a child who is ill, hungry, weak in social skills, or suffering from emotional or behavior problems is unable to learn at his or her best.

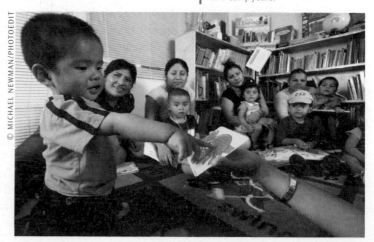

In an Early Head Start classroom, mothers and toddlers gather for a picture-book reading session. The effects of intervention are more likely to endure when programs begin at very young ages and are intensive, involving many hours of child contact that extend through the early years.

To achieve lasting favorable results, designers of today's early intervention programs must include these key ingredients (Galinsky, 2006). Also, the number of children served must be greatly expanded. Unfortunately, because of limited funding, only 60 percent of poverty-stricken 3- and 4-year-olds attend some type of preschool program, with Head Start serving just half of these children (Magnuson & Shager, 2010). And many preschoolers whose parents' income just surpasses the Head Start income eligibility requirements also receive no intervention.

A few supplementary programs—such as Jumpstart, described at the beginning of this chapter—have responded to this shortage by delivering educational intervention to children in child-care centers, as well as strengthening intervention in Head Start and other preschool classrooms. Evaluations indicate that 3- to 5-year-olds who experience Jumpstart show greater year-end gains in language, literacy, task persistence, and social skills than non-Jumpstart children in the same Head Start or other early childhood settings (Harris & Berk, 2011; Jumpstart Evaluation Team, 2008). To find out about another highly successful supplementary intervention, see the Social Issues: Education box on the following page.

▶ Evaluate theories of creativity, and discuss ways to nurture creativity and talent.

Giftedness: Creativity and Talent

Throughout this chapter, we have seen that intelligence includes much more than mental abilities that predict success in school. Today, educators recognize that **gifted** children—those who display exceptional intellectual strengths—have diverse characteristics. Some have IQ scores above 130, the standard definition of giftedness based on intelligence test performance (Gardner, 1998b). High-IQ children, as we have seen, have keen memories and an exceptional capacity to solve challenging academic problems. Yet recognition that intelligence tests do not sample the entire range of human mental skills has led to an expanded conception of giftedness, which includes creativity.

Creativity is the ability to produce work that is *original* yet *appropriate*—something that others have not thought of but that is useful in some way (Kaufman & Sternberg, 2007; Sternberg, 2003b). Judgments of creativity reflect not only the uniqueness and quality of the product but also the process of arriving at it. Rather than following established rules, a creative work pulls together previously disparate ideas. Typically, it also involves hard work and the need to overcome obstacles on the way to the final product.

In addition to its value on the job and in daily life, creativity is vital for societal progress. Without it, there would be no new inventions, scientific findings, movements in art, or social programs. Therefore, understanding its ingredients and nurturing them from childhood are of paramount importance. As we will see in the following sections, ideas about creativity have changed radically during the past two decades.

The Psychometric View

Until recently, a purely cognitive perspective dominated research on creativity. Commonly used tests tapped **divergent thinking**—the generation of multiple and unusual possibilities when faced with a task or problem. Divergent thinking contrasts with **convergent thinking,** which involves arriving at a single correct answer and is emphasized on intelligence tests (Guilford, 1985).

Because highly creative children (like high-IQ children) are often better at some types of tasks than others, a variety of tests of divergent thinking are available (Runco, 1992a, 1993; Torrance, 1988). A verbal measure might ask children to name uses for common objects (such as a newspaper). A figural measure might ask them to come up with drawings based on a circular motif (see Figure 8.15 on page 352). A "real-world problem" measure requires students to suggest solutions to everyday problems. Responses to all these tests can be scored for the number of ideas generated and their originality. For example, on a verbal test, saying that a newspaper can be used "as handgrips for a bicycle" would be more original than saying it can be used "to clean things."

SOCIAL ISSUES: EDUCATION

The Head Start REDI Program: Strengthening School Readiness in Economically Disadvantaged Preschoolers

Preschoolers attending Head Start reap cognitive and social benefits, but gains are limited and dissipate over time. Most children from economically disadvantaged families enter kindergarten behind national norms in knowledge and skills essential for school success. Head Start programs typically have far fewer classroom resources than the model programs that have yielded stronger outcomes. And Head Start lead teachers—nearly 20 percent of whom have neither an associate's nor a bachelor's degree and only 40 percent of whom have state teaching certificates—are often not prepared to handle the developmental delays and problems of children in their classrooms (Hulsey et al., 2010).

Responding to these quality concerns, the Head Start REDI (Research-based Developmentally Informed) program is an enrichment curriculum designed to be integrated into existing Head Start classroom learning activities. Before school begins, Head Start teachers participate in workshops where they learn research-based strategies for enhancing language, literacy, and social skills known to predict school success. Then, throughout the school year, they receive several hours per week of one-to-one mentoring from master teachers, who model, coach, and provide ongoing feedback to ensure that they implement REDI effectively.

To foster language and emergent literacy, REDI emphasizes interactive reading. Teachers discuss two books per week with children, reinforcing new vocabulary words with pictures and other props and scaffolding children's conversation to increase the complexity of their oral language. Language sound games promote phonological awareness, and alphabet-letter learning is encouraged through specially designed materials in learning centers. (Return to Chapter 7, page 308, for evidence on the effectiveness of these techniques for advancing young children's emergent literacy skills.)

In the social domain, REDI focuses on skills that enable children to participate fully in classroom social life: helping, sharing, taking turns, and resolving conflicts, which build rewarding teacher and peer relationships. REDI also includes experiences that help children focus attention, inhibit impulsive behavior, and organize their goal-directed activities—skills that predict academic achievement throughout elementary and high school (Blair & Razza, 2007; Duncan et al., 2007). For lessons in social skills, teachers use puppet characters and role-play demonstrations, and they provide children with opportunities to practice social skills in cooperative projects and games.

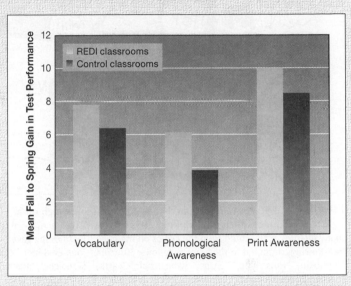

FIGURE 8.14 Fall to spring gains in language and emergent literacy skills in Head Start REDI and control classrooms. Head Start children receiving the REDI supplementary intervention exceeded children in typical Head Start classrooms in vocabulary, phonological awareness, and print awareness. Phonological awareness gains consist of two skills: combining parts of words, such as "b" and "air" (bear); and dividing compound words—for example, saying "snowshoe" without "snow." Print awareness gains involved identifying written letters of the alphabet. (Adapted from Bierman et al., 2008.)

A teacher trained in Head Start REDI strategies engages in interactive reading with a preschooler. The REDI program has succeeded in strengthening the impact of Head Start on children's school readiness.

REDI is remarkably successful at strengthening Head Start children's school readiness. In a field experiment in which 44 Head Start classrooms were randomly assigned to either REDI or usual classroom practice, the REDI children made greater year-end gains in language and emergent literacy skills (see Figure 8.14) (Bierman et al., 2008). REDI children were also advantaged in social skills, including accurately recognizing other's emotions, resolving peer conflicts, inhibiting aggressive behavior, and actively engaging in learning activities.

In sum, REDI strengthens the immediate impact of Head Start—positive effects that are likely due to REDI's impact on teaching quality. End-of-year observations revealed that in Head Start REDI classrooms, compared with typical Head Start classrooms, teachers talked with children more often and in more cognitively complex ways, established a more positive classroom climate, and more often used management strategies that prevented disruptive behavior (Domitrovich et al., 2009).

FIGURE 8.15 Responses of an 8-year-old who scored high on a figural measure of divergent thinking. This child was asked to make as many pictures as she could from the circles on the page. The titles she gave her drawings, from left to right, are as follows: "Dracula," "one-eyed monster," "pumpkin," "Hula-Hoop," "poster," "wheelchair," "earth," "stop-light," "moon," "planet," "movie camera," "sad face," "picture," "beach ball," "the letter *O*," "car," "glasses." Tests of divergent thinking tap only one of the complex cognitive contributions to creativity. (Reprinted by permission of Laura E. Berk.)

Tests of divergent thinking are known as the *psychometric approach to creativity* because they permit scores to be compared to the performance of standardization samples. Yet critics note that these measures are poor predictors of creative accomplishment in everyday life because they tap only one of the complex cognitive contributions to creativity (Plucker & Makel, 2010). And they say nothing about personality traits, motivation, and environmental circumstances that foster creative potential. Still, divergent-thinking tests do tap relevant skills, have been the major focus of research on creativity in children, and (as we will see shortly) have enhanced our understanding of the development of creativity.

A Multifaceted View

Recent theories agree that many elements must converge for creativity to occur (Kozbelt, Beghetto, & Runco, 2010; Renzulli, 2006). One influential multifaceted approach is Robert Sternberg and Todd Lubart's (1991, 1996) **investment theory of creativity.** According to Sternberg and Lubart, pursuing a novel project (one not being tackled by others) increases the chances of arriving at a creative, highly valued product. But whether a person invests in novelty—initiates an original project and brings it to fruition—depends on that person's cognitive, personality, motivational, and environmental resources, summarized in Table 8.2. Each must be present to catalyze creativity, although strength in one (such as perseverance) can compensate for weakness in another (an environment that is lukewarm toward novel ideas).

Contrary to popular belief, creativity is neither determined at birth nor the prized possession of an elite few. Many people can develop it to varying degrees, and it is likely to reach greater heights when nurtured from an early age. Let's look at the components of creativity and how to strengthen them in children.

Cognitive Resources Creative work brings together a variety of high-level cognitive skills. It requires *problem finding*—detecting a gap in current knowledge, a need for a new product, or a deficiency in existing procedures. Once a problem is found, *the ability to define it*—to move it from a vague to a clearly specified state—becomes important. In both children and adults, the more effort devoted to defining the problem, the more original the final product (Runco & Okuda, 1988; Sternberg, 2003b).

TABLE 8.2 | Resources Necessary for Creativity

COGNITIVE	PERSONALITY	MOTIVATIONAL AND ENVIRONMENTAL
Problem finding	Innovative style of thinking	Settings rich in stimulation
Divergent thinking	Curiosity	Emphasis on intellectual curiosity
Convergent thinking: evaluating competing ideas	Willingness to take intellectual risks	Systematic teaching that builds talent
Insight	Tolerance of ambiguity	Availability of time to reflect on ideas
Knowledge	Courage of one's convictions	Encouragement of original ideas and evaluation of those ideas
		Emphasis on intrinsic motivation

Divergent thinking is essential for generating novel solutions to problems. But the successful creator must also choose the best responses, setting aside fruitless options. Therefore, creativity involves *alternating between divergent and convergent thinking* (Guignard & Lubart, 2006). In narrowing the range of possibilities, creative individuals rely on *insight processes*—combining and restructuring elements in sudden but useful ways. For example, the use of analogies and metaphors to identify unique connections is common among people who have made outstanding creative contributions (Barron, 1988). At an early age, children engage in this kind of thinking (see Chapter 6, page 246, and Chapter 9, page 380). Furthermore, *evaluating competing ideas* to select the most promising is vital. School-age children's evaluative ability can be enhanced by instructions to critically assess the originality of ideas (Runco, 1992b).

Finally, extensive *knowledge* is necessary to make a creative contribution to any field (Lubart, Georgsdottir, & Besançon, 2009). Without it, people cannot recognize or understand new ideas. Consider this cognitive ingredient, and you will see why high creativity is usually manifested as **talent**—outstanding performance in one or a few related fields. Case studies reveal that excellence in such endeavors as creative writing, mathematics, science, music, visual arts, athletics, and leadership have roots in specialized interests and skills that appear in childhood (Moran & Gardner, 2006). And research supports the *10-year-rule* in development of master-level creativity—a decade between initial exposure to a field and sufficient expertise to produce a creative work (Simonton, 2000). Furthermore, IQ and creativity correlate only modestly, typically around .20 to .40 (Lubart, 2003). Beyond an above-average general intelligence, other factors are necessary for creative giftedness.

As sixth graders rehearse a play that they have written, they gain experience with diverse cognitive resources that contribute to creativity, including problem finding, insight processes, and evaluating competing ideas.

Personality Resources Certain personality characteristics foster the cognitive components of creativity, ensuring that they are applied to best advantage:

- *Innovative style of thinking.* Creative individuals not only see things in new ways but also enjoy doing so. They prefer loosely structured activities involving innovative problem finding rather than already defined tasks.
- *Perseverance and tolerance of ambiguity.* Working toward creative goals brings periods when pieces of the problem do not fit together—prompting many children and adults to give up or pursue the first (but not the best) solution. Creativity requires patience and persistence in the face of obstacles.
- *Willingness to take risks.* Creativity requires a willingness to deviate from the crowd, to undertake challenges when outcomes are uncertain.
- *The courage of one's convictions.* Because their ideas are novel, creators may at times doubt them, especially when criticized by skeptical teachers or peers. People who think creatively often encounter resistance, ranging from puzzlement to hostility. Creative endeavors require independence of judgment and high self-esteem (Sternberg & Lubart, 1996).

Motivational Resources Motivation for creativity must be *task-focused* rather than *goal-focused.* Task-focusing motivators, such as the desire to meet a high standard, energize work and keep attention on the problem. Goal-focusing motivators, in contrast, often impair performance by diverting attention from the task to extrinsic rewards such as grades and prizes. In one study, 7- to 11-year-old girls worked on collages, some competing for prizes and others expecting that the prizes would be raffled off. The products of those in the first group were much less creative (Amabile, 1982).

Extrinsic rewards are not always detrimental to creativity. Teaching children how to engage in divergent thinking on a task and rewarding them for original responses increases the frequency of those responses (Collins & Amabile, 1999). And an occasional reward for a

This 14-year-old attends a middle school with specialized courses in the performing arts. She benefits from opportunities to work with master teachers and to interact with peers who share her passion for dance.

creative product can underscore the social value of creativity and encourage children to embark on innovative projects. But when rewards are overemphasized, children focus only on these goals, and creativity suffers.

Environmental Resources Studies of the backgrounds of talented children and highly accomplished adults often reveal a family life focused on the child's needs—warm, sensitive parents who provide a stimulating home life, are devoted to developing their child's abilities, and provide models of hard work and high achievement. These parents are reasonably demanding but not driving or overambitious (Winner, 2000, 2003). They arrange for caring teachers while the child is young and for more rigorous master teachers as the child's talent develops.

Many gifted children and adolescents are socially isolated, partly because their highly driven, nonconforming, and independent styles leave them out of step with peers and partly because they enjoy solitude, which is necessary to develop their talents. Still, gifted children desire gratifying peer relationships, and some—more often girls than boys—try to become better-liked by hiding their abilities. Compared with their ordinary agemates, gifted youths, especially girls, report more emotional and social difficulties, including low self-esteem and depression (Reis, 2004).

Classrooms in which gifted youths can interact with like-minded peers, choose topics for extended projects, take intellectual risks, and reflect on ideas without being rushed to the next assignment foster creativity (Besançon & Lubart, 2008). In classrooms where knowledge acquisition is stressed over using knowledge originally, children's thinking tends to become *entrenched*—limited to commonplace associations that produce correct answers. Talented students, when not sufficiently challenged, sometimes lose their drive to excel. But when pushed too hard by parents or teachers, by adolescence these students are likely to ask, "Why am I doing this?" If the answer is not "Because it interests me," they may decide not to pursue their gift (Winner, 2000, p. 166).

Refer to Applying What We Know on the following page for ways that parents and teachers can promote children's creativity. Although many schools offer programs for the gifted, debate about their effectiveness typically focuses on factors irrelevant to creativity—whether to offer enrichment in regular classrooms, pull children out for special instruction (the most common practice), or advance brighter pupils to a higher grade. Overall, gifted children fare well within each of these models, as long as the special activities foster the ingredients of creative thought (Guignard & Lubart, 2007).

Some societies focus so narrowly on high academic achievement as an index of success that they dampen the development of creativity. The collectivism characteristic of Asian cultures often leads teachers to emphasize mastery of knowledge and analytical skills over generating new ideas, which requires students to stand out from the crowd. In one study, Chinese college students' artwork was judged less creative than that of U.S. students by experts from both countries (Niu & Sternberg, 2001). In interventions aimed at promoting creative expression in high school art classes in Beijing, students were asked to make collages. One group received a general instruction to be creative, a second group specific instructions in *how* to be creative ("fold or tear materials so their shapes and sizes do not limit creative expression"), and a control group no creativity instructions. Students in the two creative conditions generated products that were more creative than those produced by students in the control group, with the specific-instruction group performing best (Niu & Sternberg, 2003). A brief prompt—especially, guidance in how to take a creative approach—readily enhanced artistic originality.

Gardner's theory of multiple intelligences has inspired several model school programs that provide enrichment to all students in diverse disciplines, so any child capable of high-level, creative performance can manifest it. Meaningful activities, each tapping a specific intelligence or set of intelligences, serve as contexts for assessing strengths and weaknesses

LOOK and LISTEN

Interview an elementary school teacher about his or her teaching practices aimed at fostering children's creativity. In the teacher's view, what contemporary societal and school policies promote and/or impede educational efforts to enhance children's creativity?

APPLYING WHAT WE KNOW

Promoting Children's Creativity

SUGGESTION	DESCRIPTION
Encourage idea generation and evaluation.	Offer opportunities for divergent thinking and praise it, even when some ideas are silly or irrelevant. Then engage children in constructive criticism: When an idea has little value, suggest new approaches that include aspects of the child's idea, thereby demonstrating that most ideas must be refined to be useful.
Encourage sensible risk taking.	Provide assignments and activities that include choices and that have more than one acceptable answer. Avoid praising children mainly for high test scores or papers based on one right answer, which may lead them to avoid new ways of thinking.
Encourage tolerance of ambiguity.	Point out that creative individuals often feel unsure of whether they are on the right track. Encourage children to accept these feelings and to spend time working through uncertainty. Emphasize that doing so will result in better ideas.
Help children believe in their ability to be creative.	Remind children that the value of a creative idea does not depend on teachers' or classmates' approval but, rather, on the idea's originality and usefulness.
Help children find what they love to do.	Encourage children to explore new fields rather than just accepting interests that you value. To help them uncover their true interests, ask each child to demonstrate an ability or talent for the class, and point out the diversity of worthwhile interests.
Model creative thinking.	Balance teaching knowledge with teaching how to think about that knowledge. Help children reason across subjects, pointing out that creative insights often result from integrating material across fields, not from memorizing information.

Source: Sternberg, 2003b.

and, on that basis, teaching new knowledge and original thinking (Gardner, 2000; Hoerr, 2004). For example, linguistic intelligence might be fostered through storytelling or play-writing; spatial intelligence through drawing, sculpting, or taking apart and reassembling objects; and kinesthetic intelligence through dance or pantomime.

Evidence is still needed on how well these programs nurture children's talents and creativity. But they have already succeeded in one way—by highlighting the strengths of some students who previously had been considered unexceptional or even at risk for school failure (Kornhaber, 2004). Consequently, they may be especially useful in identifying talented low-SES, ethnic minority children, who are often underrepresented in school programs for the gifted (McBee, 2006). How best to maximize the creative resources of the coming generation—the future poet and scientist as well as the everyday citizen—is a challenge for future research.

ASK YOURSELF

Review ■ Summarize the benefits of early intervention programs, such as Head Start, for poverty-stricken children. What program characteristics might contribute to and strengthen those benefits?

Connect ■ Using what you learned about brain development in Chapter 5 (see pages 186–192), explain why intensive intervention for poverty-stricken children starting in infancy and continuing through early childhood has a greater impact on IQ than intervention starting later.

Connect ■ How is high-stakes testing likely to affect encouragement of creativity in classrooms? Explain.

Reflect ■ Describe several childhood experiences that you believe enhanced your creativity, along with ones that might have discouraged it. In the latter instances, what would you do differently to foster children's creative potential? Use research to justify your recommendations.

S U M M A R Y

Definitions of Intelligence
(p. 320)

Describe changing definitions of intelligence on which mental tests are based.

■ The **psychometric approach** to cognitive development is the basis for intelligence tests that assess individual differences in children's mental abilities. The first successful test, developed by Binet in 1905, provided a single, holistic measure of intelligence.

■ Researchers used **factor analysis** to determine whether intelligence is a single trait or an assortment of abilities. Spearman proposed an underlying **general intelligence,** or *g*, though he acknowledged various types of **specific intelligence.** Thurstone, in contrast, viewed intelligence as a set of distinct primary mental abilities.

■ Contemporary theorists propose hierarchical models of mental abilities. Cattell's identification of **crystallized** and **fluid intelligence** has influenced attempts to reduce cultural bias in intelligence testing. Carroll's **three-stratum theory of intelligence** is the most comprehensive factor-analytic classification of mental abilities.

Recent Advances in Defining Intelligence (p. 323)

How do contemporary researchers use and expand componential analyses of intelligence test scores to define intelligence?

■ **Componential analyses** of children's test scores have revealed relationships between aspects of information processing—processing speed, working-memory capacity, and flexible attention, memory, and reasoning strategies—and intelligence test performance. Extending these efforts, Sternberg's **triarchic theory of successful intelligence** views intelligence as an interaction of analytical intelligence (information-processing skills), creative intelligence (capacity to solve novel problems), and practical intelligence (application of intellectual skills in everyday situations).

■ Gardner's **theory of multiple intelligences** identifies at least eight distinct intelligences, each with a unique biological basis and course of development. It has stimulated educational innovations, helped in understanding and nurturing children's special talents, and calls attention to abilities not measured by intelligence tests, such as **emotional intelligence.**

Measuring Intelligence (p. 326)

Describe commonly used intelligence tests for children, distinguish between aptitude and achievement tests, and discuss the usefulness of infant tests.

■ The **Stanford-Binet Intelligence Scales, Fifth Edition,** and the **Wechsler Intelligence Scale for Children–IV (WISC–IV)** are most often used to identify highly intelligent children and diagnose those with learning problems. Each provides a measure of general intelligence and a profile of subtest scores; each has a downward extension, tailored for assessing the intelligence of preschoolers.

■ Two related types of tests are **aptitude tests,** which assess potential to learn a specialized activity, and **achievement tests,** which assess actual knowledge and skill attainment. Both types of tests include items similar to those found on intelligence tests.

■ Most infant tests, which consist largely of perceptual and motor responses, predict later intelligence poorly and are largely used for screening—helping to identify infants who are at risk for future problems. As a result, infant scores are called **developmental quotients (DQs)** rather than IQs.

How are IQ scores computed and distributed in large, representative samples?

■ Intelligence tests are scored by computing an **intelligence quotient (IQ).** It compares the test-taker's raw score to the scores of a **standardization** sample of same-age individuals, whose performances form a **normal distribution,** with mean IQ set at 100. IQ reflects the extent to which test performance deviates from the standardization-sample mean.

What Do Intelligence Tests Predict, and How Well?
(p. 330)

Discuss the stability of IQ and its prediction of academic achievement, occupational attainment, and psychological adjustment.

■ After age 6, IQ scores show substantial correlational stability. The older the child at time of first testing and the closer in time two testings are, the stronger the relationship between the scores. However, most children show substantial fluctuations in the absolute value of IQ as a result of personality traits, child-rearing practices, and living conditions.

■ IQ is moderately correlated with adult academic achievement, occupational attainment, and emotional and social adjustment, but the underlying causes of these findings are complex. Other traits, including education, family influences, motivation, and **practical intelligence,** also contribute substantially to life success.

Ethnic and Socioeconomic Variations in IQ (p. 334)

Describe ethnic and socioeconomic variations in IQ.

■ Black children and children of low **socioeconomic status (SES)** score lower on intelligence tests than white and middle-SES children, respectively. These findings that have kindled the IQ nature–nurture debate.

Explaining Individual and Group Differences in IQ (p. 335)

Discuss the contributions of heredity and environment to individual and group differences in IQ.

- Heritability estimates support a moderate role for heredity in IQ individual differences. Kinship studies indicate that the greater the genetic similarity between family members, the more similar their IQ scores. However, heritabilities cannot be used to explain between-group ethnic and SES differences in test scores.

- Adoption studies indicate that advantaged rearing conditions can substantially raise IQ. But stronger correlations of the IQs of adopted children with biological relatives than with adoptive relatives provide evidence for a genetic contribution.

- African-American children reared in economically well-off white homes attain above-average IQs by middle childhood. A dramatic generational increase in IQ – known as the **Flynn effect**—also supports the role of environmental factors and challenges the assumption that racial and ethnic variations in IQ are mostly genetic.

Evaluate evidence on whether ethnic differences in IQ result from test bias, and discuss efforts to reduce cultural bias in testing.

- Experts disagree on whether ethnic differences in IQ result from test bias. Although IQ predicts academic achievement equally well for majority and minority children, culturally specific communication styles, knowledge, and **stereotype threat** can lead to test scores that underestimate minority children's intelligence.

- Combining test scores with assessments of children's adaptive behavior helps safeguard against test bias. **Dynamic assessment,** which introduces purposeful teaching into the testing situation to measure what the child can attain with social support, enhances minority children's performance.

Summarize the impact of shared and nonshared environmental influences on IQ.

- Research using the **Home Observation for Measurement of the Environment (HOME)** indicates that overall quality of the home— a **shared environmental influence**—consistently predicts language progress and IQ. Although parent–child genetic similarity plays a part in the HOME–IQ relationship, a warm, stimulating family environment promotes mental ability. Parental belief in the importance of intellectual endeavors also has a powerful impact on academic performance.

- Kinship research suggests that **nonshared environmental influences** are more powerful than shared influences and strengthen in adolescence and adulthood. The most potent nonshared factors may be unpredictable, one-time events.

Early Intervention and Intellectual Development (p. 347)

Discuss the impact of early intervention on intellectual development.

- **Project Head Start** is the most extensive federally funded preschool program for low-income children in the United States.

- Research on high-quality early interventions shows that immediate IQ and achievement score gains decline within a few years, while benefits in school adjustment persist. And one program yielded advantages for preschool intervention children on adulthood indicators of life success, including education, income, and law-abiding behavior.

- The earlier intervention starts, the longer it lasts, and the more intensive the program, the broader and more enduring the benefits. **Early Head Start** offers coordinated services for infants and toddlers and their families, with positive effects on parenting, cognitive and language development, and lessening of aggression.

Giftedness: Creativity and Talent (p. 350)

Evaluate theories of creativity, and discuss ways to nurture creativity and talent.

- Recognition that intelligence includes more than mental abilities that predict school success has expanded conceptions of **giftedness** to include **creativity.** The psychometric approach, emphasizing the distinction between **divergent** and **convergent thinking,** is too narrow to predict real-world creative accomplishment. New, multifaceted approaches, such as the **investment theory of creativity,** look at a wide variety of intellectual, personality, motivational, and environmental resources that are necessary to initiate creative projects and bring them to fruition.

- High creativity is usually manifested as **talent,** and talented children typically have parents and teachers who nurture their exceptional abilities. However, many gifted children, especially girls, report emotional and social difficulties. They are best served by educational programs in which they can interact with like-minded peers, take intellectual risks, reflect on ideas, and acquire skills relevant to their talents.

IMPORTANT TERMS AND CONCEPTS

achievement test (p. 328)
aptitude test (p. 328)
componential analysis (p. 323)
convergent thinking (p. 350)
creativity (p. 350)
crystallized intelligence (p. 321)
developmental quotient (DQ) (p. 329)
divergent thinking (p. 350)
dynamic assessment (p. 342)
Early Head Start (p. 349)
emotional intelligence (p. 327)
environmental cumulative deficit hypothesis (p. 331)
factor analysis (p. 321)

fluid intelligence (p. 321)
Flynn effect (p. 338)
general intelligence, or *g* (p. 321)
gifted (p. 350)
Home Observation for Measurement of the Environment (HOME) (p. 344)
intelligence quotient (IQ) (p. 330)
investment theory of creativity (p. 352)
nonshared environmental influences (p. 344)
normal distribution (p. 330)
practical intelligence (p. 332)
Project Head Start (p. 347)
psychometric approach (p. 319)
shared environmental influences (p. 344)

socioeconomic status (SES) (p. 334)
specific intelligence (p. 321)
standardization (p. 330)
Stanford-Binet Intelligence Scales, Fifth Edition (p. 327)
stereotype threat (p. 341)
talent (p. 353)
theory of multiple intelligences (p. 325)
three-stratum theory of intelligence (p. 322)
triarchic theory of successful intelligence (p. 323)
Wechsler Intelligence Scale for Children–IV (WISC–IV) (p. 328)

CHAPTER 9

"Gabonese Market Stalls"
Fabric Dossa
10 years, Gabon

A lively chorus of voices permeates this open-air market. Language is an astounding, distinctly human achievement. How does it develop so rapidly and easily in childhood?

Reprinted with permission from the World Awareness Children's Museum, Glens Falls, New York. Catalog #94569. www.worldchildrens museum.org

Language Development

"**D**one!" 1-year-old Erin said emphatically, wriggling in her highchair. Oscar and Marilyn looked at each other and exclaimed in unison, "Did she say, 'Done'?" Lifting Erin down, Marilyn responded, "Yes! You're done," to her daughter's first clear word. In the next few weeks, more words appeared—among them "Mama," "Dada," "please," "thanks," and "sure."

Marilyn spoke to Erin and her 11-year-old brother, Amos, in English. But Oscar, determined that his second child would become bilingual, used only Spanish, his native tongue. As Erin reached the 18-month mark, her vocabulary grew rapidly, and she mixed words from the two languages. "Book!" she called out, thrusting her favorite picture book toward Oscar in a gesture that meant, "Read this!" As father and daughter "read" together, Erin labeled: "*Nariz*" ("nose"). "*Boca*" ("mouth"). "Head." "*Ojos*" ("eyes"). "Hippo." "*Grande!*" (referring to the size of the hippo). On reaching the last page, she exclaimed, "*Gracias!*" and slipped off Oscar's lap.

By her second birthday, Erin had a vocabulary of several hundred words and often combined them: "So big!" "*Muy grande*" ("very big"), "More cracker," "*Dame galleta*" ("Give me cracker"), and "*No quiero*" ("I don't want to"). Amused by Erin's willingness to imitate almost anything, Amos taught her a bit of slang. During mealtime conversations, Erin would interject, "Geta picture" ("Get the picture"). And when asked a question, she sometimes casually answered, "Whatever."

At age 2½, Erin conversed easily. After a family excursion to the aquarium, Marilyn asked, "What did you see?"

"A big turtle put his head in the shell," Erin replied.

"Why did he do that?"

"He goed away. He's sleepy."

Language—the most awesome of universal human achievements—develops with extraordinary speed in early childhood. At age 1, Erin used single words to name familiar objects and convey her desires. Only a year and a half later, she had a diverse vocabulary and combined words into grammatically correct sentences. Even her mistakes ("goed") revealed an active, rule-oriented approach to language. Before reaching her third birthday, Erin used language creatively to satisfy her desires, converse with others, and experiment with social roles. And she moved easily between her two native tongues, speaking English with her mother and brother and Spanish with her father.

Children's amazing linguistic accomplishments raise puzzling issues about development. How do children acquire a vast vocabulary and intricate grammatical system in such a short time? Is language a separate capacity, with its own prewired, special-purpose neural system in the brain? Or is it governed by powerful general cognitive abilities that humans also apply to other aspects of their physical and social worlds? Do all children acquire language in the same way, or do individual and cultural differences exist?

Our discussion opens with prominent theories of language development that differ sharply in answers to these questions. Next we turn to infant preparatory skills that set the stage for the child's first words. Then, to appreciate the diverse linguistic skills children master, we follow the common practice of dividing language into four components. For each, we consider, first, *what* develops, and then a more controversial question: *How* do children acquire so much in so little time? We conclude with a discussion of the challenges and benefits of bilingualism—mastering two languages—in childhood. ■

Components of Language

Theories of Language Development
The Nativist Perspective • The Interactionist Perspective

■ **BIOLOGY AND ENVIRONMENT:** *Deaf Children Invent Language*

■ **BIOLOGY AND ENVIRONMENT:** *Language Development in Children with Williams Syndrome*

Prelinguistic Development: Getting Ready to Talk
Receptivity to Language • First Speech Sounds • Becoming a Communicator

■ **SOCIAL ISSUES: EDUCATION:** *Parent–Child Interaction: Impact on Language and Cognitive Development of Deaf Children*

Phonological Development
The Early Phase • Phonological Strategies • Later Phonological Development

Semantic Development
The Early Phase • Later Semantic Development • Ideas About How Semantic Development Takes Place

Grammatical Development
First Word Combinations • From Simple Sentences to Complex Grammar • Development of Complex Grammatical Forms • Later Grammatical Development • Ideas About How Grammatical Development Takes Place

Pragmatic Development
Acquiring Conversational Skills • Communicating Clearly • Narratives • Sociolinguistic Understanding

Development of Metalinguistic Awareness

Bilingualism: Learning Two Languages in Childhood

■ **SOCIAL ISSUES: EDUCATION:** *Two Approaches to Bilingual Education: Canada and the United States*

▶ What are the four components of language?

Components of Language

Language consists of several subsystems that have to do with sound, meaning, overall structure, and everyday use. Language development entails mastering each of these aspects and combining them into a flexible communication system.

The first component, **phonology,** refers to the rules governing the structure and sequence of speech sounds. If you have ever visited a foreign country where you did not know the language, you probably wondered how anyone could analyze the rapid flow of speech into organized strings of words. Yet in English, you easily apply an intricate set of rules to comprehend and produce complicated sound patterns. How you acquired this ability is the story of phonological development.

Semantics, the second component, involves vocabulary—the way underlying concepts are expressed in words and word combinations. When young children first use a word, it often does not mean the same thing as it does to adults. To build a versatile vocabulary, children must refine the meanings of thousands of words and connect them into elaborate networks of related terms.

Once mastery of vocabulary is under way, children combine words and modify them in meaningful ways. **Grammar,** the third component of language, consists of two main parts: **syntax,** the rules by which words are arranged into sentences, and **morphology,** the use of grammatical markers indicating number, tense, case, person, gender, active or passive voice, and other meanings (the endings -s and -ed are examples in English).

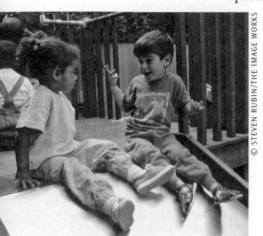

© STEVEN RUBIN/THE IMAGE WORKS

To communicate effectively, these preschoolers must combine language subsystems of sound, meaning, structure, and everyday use. How they accomplish this feat raises puzzling—and fascinating— questions about development.

Finally, **pragmatics** refers to the rules for engaging in appropriate and effective communication. To converse successfully, children must take turns, stay on the same topic as their conversational partner, and state their meaning clearly. They also must figure out how gestures, tone of voice, and context clarify meaning. Furthermore, because society dictates how language should be spoken, pragmatics involves *sociolinguistic knowledge.* Children must acquire certain interaction rituals, such as verbal greetings and leave-takings. They must adjust their speech to mark important social relationships, such as differences in age and status. And they must master their culture's narrative mode of sharing personally meaningful experiences with others.

As we take up the four components of language, you will see that they are interdependent. Acquisition of each facilitates mastery of the others.

▶ Describe and evaluate major theories of language development.

Theories of Language Development

During the first half of the twentieth century, researchers identified language milestones that applied to children around the globe: All babbled around 6 months, said their first words at about 1 year, combined words at the end of the second year, and had mastered a vast vocabulary and most grammatical constructions by 4 to 5 years. The regularity and rapidity of these achievements suggested a process largely governed by maturation, inspiring the nativist perspective on language development. In recent years, new evidence has spawned the interactionist perspective, which emphasizes the joint roles of children's predispositions and communicative experiences in language acquisition.

The Nativist Perspective

Linguist Noam Chomsky (1957) proposed a *nativist* theory that regards language as a uniquely human accomplishment, etched into the structure of the brain. Focusing on grammar, Chomsky reasoned that the rules for sentence organization are too complex to be directly taught to or discovered by even a cognitively sophisticated young child. Rather, Chomsky proposed that all children have a **language acquisition device (LAD)**—an innate system that permits them, once they have acquired sufficient vocabulary, to combine words into grammatically consistent, novel utterances and to understand the meaning of sentences they hear.

How can a single LAD account for children's mastery of the world's diverse languages? According to Chomsky (1976, 1997), within the LAD is a **universal grammar,** a built-in storehouse of rules common to all human languages. Young children use this knowledge to decipher grammatical categories and relationships in any language to which they are exposed. Because the LAD is specifically suited for language processing, children master the structure of language spontaneously, with only limited language exposure (Pinker, 1999). In this way, the LAD ensures that language, despite its complexity, will be acquired early and swiftly.

Evidence Relevant to the Nativist Perspective Are children innately primed to acquire language? Research reviewed in the Biology and Environment box on page 362, suggesting that children have a remarkable ability to invent new language systems, provides some of the most powerful support for this perspective. Three additional sets of evidence— efforts to teach language to animals, localization of language functions in the human brain, and investigations into whether a sensitive period for language development exists—are consistent with Chomsky's view. Let's look at each in turn.

Can Animals Acquire Language? Is the ability to master a grammatically complex language system unique to humans? To find out, many attempts have been made to teach language to animals, including dolphins, parrots, gorillas, orangutans, and chimpanzees. With extensive training, members of each of these species can acquire a vocabulary ranging from several dozen to several hundred symbols and can produce and respond to short, novel sentences, although they do so less consistently than a preschool child (Herman & Uyeyama, 1999; Pepperberg, 2000; Savage-Rumbaugh, Shanker, & Taylor, 1998).

Chimpanzees are closest to humans in the evolutionary hierarchy. Common chimps, the species studied most often, have been taught artificial languages (in which a computer keyboard generates visual symbols) and American Sign Language. Yet even after years of training, common chimps are unable to produce strings of three or more symbols that conform to a rule-based structure. Their language limitations may, in part, reflect a narrow understanding of others' mental states. Common chimps can accurately predict others' goals if those goals are readily apparent in behavior—for example, whether or not someone is willing to share food with them. But they may not recognize less obvious intentions, including ones that motivate use of language—for example, that others want to exchange knowledge and ideas (Tomasello, Call, & Hare, 2003).

Bonobo chimps are more intelligent and social than common chimps. The linguistic attainments of a bonobo named Kanzi are especially impressive (Savage-Rumbaugh, Shanker, & Taylor, 1998). While young, Kanzi picked up his mother's artificial language by observing trainers interact with her. To encourage his language development, Kanzi's caregivers communicated both in the artificial language and in English. Kanzi rarely combined words, preferring to join a word to a gesture—for example, "*carry* + [gesture to person]," meaning "you carry Kanzi." But through listening to fluent speech, he acquired remarkable comprehension of English, including the ability to discriminate hundreds of English words and to act out unusual sentences he had not heard before, such as "Put the money in the mushroom." And Kanzi could usually detect the difference between novel, reversed sentences—"Take the potato outdoors" and "Go outdoors and get the potato" (Savage-Rumbaugh et al., 1993; Shanker, Savage-Rumbaugh, & Taylor, 1999).

Still, researchers disagree on Kanzi's linguistic achievements. Some argue that he is a remarkable conversationalist (Greenspan & Shanker, 2004). Others claim that he uses language only to get what he wants (a strawberry to eat), not to share information (talk about strawberries) (Seidenberg & Petitto, 1987). And Kanzi's mastery of grammar does not exceed that of a human 2-year-old, who (as we will see) is not far along in grammatical development. Overall, the findings support Chomsky's assumption of a uniquely human capacity for an elaborate grammar. No evidence exists that even the brightest animals can comprehend and produce sentences that are both complex *and* novel.

A bonobo chimp points to visual symbols to communicate with researcher Sue Savage-Rumbaugh, who is tracking his language development.

© FRANZ LANTING STUDIO/ALAMY

BIOLOGY and ENVIRONMENT

Deaf Children Invent Language

Can children develop complex, rule-based language systems with only minimal language input, or with input so inconsistent that the rules of grammar are not readily apparent? If so, this evidence would support for Chomsky's idea that the human brain is prewired for language development (Goldin-Meadow, 2005b, 2006a). Research reveals that deaf children can generate an intricate natural language, even when reared in linguistically deficient environments.

Minimal Language Input

In a series of studies, Susan Goldin-Meadow (2009) and her colleagues followed deaf toddlers and preschoolers whose parents discouraged manual signing and addressed them verbally. None of the children made progress in acquiring spoken language or used even the most common gestures of their nation's sign language. Nevertheless, they spontaneously produced a gestural communication system, called *home-sign*, strikingly similar in basic structure to hearing children's verbal language.

The deaf children developed gestural vocabularies with distinct forms for nouns and verbs, each of which stood for a class of objects or a class of actions (for example, a *twist* gesture to request that someone open a jar and to convey that a door knob will not open), similar to the meanings of spoken words. Furthermore, the children combined gestures into novel sentences conforming to basic grammatical rules

that were not necessarily those of their parents' spoken language (Goldin-Meadow, Gelman, & Mylander, 2005; Goldin-Meadow et al., 1994). For example, to describe a large bubble he had just blown, one child first pointed at a bubble jar and then used two open palms with fingers spread to denote the act of "blowing up big."

The children did not pick up their gesture systems from parents, whose gestures were limited—no different from the gestures that hearing speakers produce while talking (Goldin-Meadow, 2003a). Rather, the children created homesign, and they used it for the same diverse purposes as any language—to comment on objects and events, to ask questions, to influence others' actions, to tell stories, to talk about their own and others' signs, and to talk to themselves (Goldin-Meadow, 2009).

Language becomes a flexible means of communicating when it is used to talk about non-present objects and events. In referring to the nonpresent, the deaf children followed the same sequence of development as hearing children—first denoting objects and events in the recent past or anticipated but immediate future, next the more remote past and future, and finally hypothetical and fantasized events (Morford & Goldin-Meadow, 1997). One homesigning child pointed over his shoulder to signify the past,

then pointed to a picture of a poodle, and finally pointed to the floor in front of him, saying, "I used to have a poodle!"

Hearing children reach language milestones earlier and acquire a far more complex grammar than children inventing homesign. These findings indicate that a rich language environment with partners who "speak" the same language fosters the attainments just mentioned. But without access to conventional language, deaf children generate their own language

In Nicaragua, educators brought deaf children and adolescents together to form a community. Within two decades, they devised a new language—Nicaraguan Sign Language.

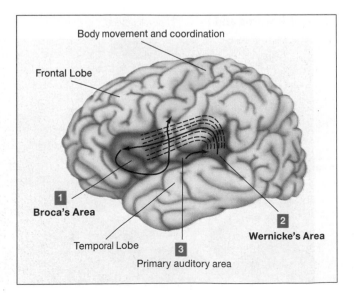

Language Areas in the Brain. Recall from Chapter 5 that for most individuals, language is housed largely in the left hemisphere of the cerebral cortex. Within it are two important language-related structures (see Figure 9.1). To clarify their functions, researchers have, for several decades, studied adults who experienced damage to these structures and display *aphasias*, or communication disorders. The patients' linguistic deficits suggested

FIGURE 9.1 Broca's and Wernicke's areas, in the left hemisphere of the cerebral cortex. (1) Broca's area, located in the frontal lobe, supports grammatical processing and language production. (2) Wernicke's area, located in the temporal lobe, is involved in comprehending word meaning. Contrary to what was once believed, however, neither area is solely or even mainly responsible for these functions. Instead, each cooperates with many other regions of the left hemisphere. Wernicke's area and Broca's area communicate through a bundle of nerve fibers represented by dashed lines. Among the regions from which Wernicke's area receives impulses is (3) the primary auditory area, where sensations from the ears are sent. Broca's area communicates with motor areas involved in speaking.

system. In Nicaragua, educators brought deaf children and adolescents, each with a unique homesign, together to form a community. Although they had no shared language, in less than two decades they developed an elaborate one—Nicaraguan Sign Language—that matched other human languages in structural complexity (Senghas & Coppola, 2001).

Inconsistent Language Input

An unusual study of a rare child whose language environment was not the typical rich form also illustrates children's remarkable capacity to invent language. Simon, a deaf child, was born to deaf parents who did not start to learn American Sign Language (ASL) (which is as elaborate as any spoken language) until they were adolescents. As with the deaf children just described, Simon's parents were exposed only to oral language in childhood. They communicated with Simon in ASL from infancy, but because they were late ASL learners, they had not attained the grammatical complexity of native signers, and they used many ASL structures inconsistently. (See the section on a sensitive period for language development on page 364.) Simon has a hearing younger sibling and went to a school with hearing teachers and

children; his only ASL input came from his parents.

When Simon was 7, researchers gave him a challenging ASL grammar task, which assessed his knowledge of the verb *to move* (Singleton and Newport, 2004). In ASL, accurately expressing motion requires up to seven grammatical markers, which indicate (1) the object's path, (2) the object's orientation, (3) the manner in which the object moves (for example, bouncing or rolling), (4) the object's location relative to a secondary object, (5) the position of the secondary object with respect to the path, (6) the features of the moving object (category, size, or shape), and (7) the features of the secondary object. The researchers compared Simon's performance with that of several reference groups: his parents, deaf school-age children of deaf native-signing parents, and deaf native-signing adults.

Findings confirmed that Simon's parents' ASL grammar was much weaker than that of native-signing adults. Yet Simon's language

did not mirror his parents' error-ridden input. Instead, he introduced a level of regularity into his language that surpassed his parents' usage. As Figure 9.2 shows, his score on the "to move" task exceeded the average score of native-signing deaf children and approached the performance of native-signing deaf adults. Simon managed to extract the regularities from his parents' imperfect language and magnify them, arriving at a highly systematic grammar.

Deaf children's remarkable capacity to invent language, despite minimal or inconsistent input, is compatible with the existence of an innate LAD. As we will see, however, other theorists claim that nonlinguistic cognitive capacities, applied to the task of communicating, are responsible.

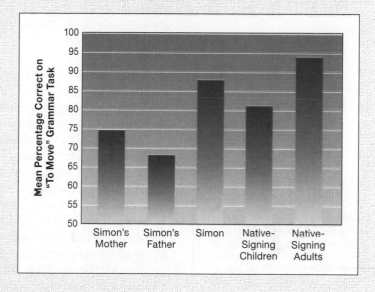

FIGURE 9.2 Simon's performance on a challenging ASL grammar task, compared with the performance of his parents and native-signing children and adults. Despite inconsistent input from his parents, 7-year-old Simon showed excellent mastery of ASL grammar, exceeding the average performance of native-signing deaf children and approaching of native-signing deaf adults. (Adapted from Singleton & Newport, 2004.)

that **Broca's area,** located in the left frontal lobe, supports grammatical processing and language production, while **Wernicke's area,** located in the left temporal lobe, plays a role in comprehending word meaning.

But recent brain-imaging research suggests more complicated relationships between language functions and brain structures. The impaired pronunciation and grammar of patients with Broca's aphasia and the meaningless speech streams of patients with Wernicke's aphasia involve the spread of injury to nearby cortical areas and widespread abnormal activity in the left cerebral hemisphere, triggered by the brain damage (Bates et al., 2003; Keller et al., 2009). Contrary to long-held belief, Broca's and Wernicke's areas are not solely or even mainly responsible for specific language functions. Nevertheless, depending on the site of injury to the adult left hemisphere, language deficits do vary predictably. Damage to frontal-lobe areas usually yields language production problems, damage to the areas in the temporal lobes comprehension problems—patterns that are highly consistent across individuals (Dick et al., 2004).

The broad association of language functions with left-hemispheric regions is consistent with Chomsky's notion of a brain prepared to process language. But recall from Chapter 5 that at birth, the brain is not fully lateralized; it is highly plastic. Language areas in the cerebral cortex *develop* as children acquire language (Mills & Conboy, 2005; Mareschal et al.,

2007). Although the left hemisphere is biased for language processing, if it is injured in the first few years, other regions take over language functions, and most such children eventually attain normal language competence (see page 188 in Chapter 5). Thus, left-hemispheric localization is not necessary for effective language processing. For example, recall from Chapter 5 that deaf adults who as children learned sign language depend more on the right hemisphere. Additional research reveals that many parts of the brain participate in language activities to differing degrees, depending on the language skill and the individual's mastery of that skill (Shafer & Garrido-Nag, 2007).

Grammatical competence, however, may depend more on specific brain structures than the other components of language. When 2- to 2½-year-old children and adults listened to short sentences—some syntactically correct, others with phrase-structure violations—both groups showed similarly distinct ERP brain-wave patterns for each sentence type in the left frontal and temporal lobes (Oberecker & Friederici, 2006; Oberecker, Friedrich, & Friederici, 2005). This suggests that 2½-year-olds process sentence structures with the same neural system as adults do. Furthermore, in older children and adults with left-hemispheric brain damage, grammatical abilities are more impaired than semantic or pragmatic abilities, which seem to draw more on right-hemispheric regions (Baynes & Gazzaniga, 1988; Stromswold, 2000).

Finally, when the young brain allocates language to the right hemisphere after injury—as a result of left-hemispheric damage or learning of sign language—it localizes it in roughly the same regions that typically support language in the left hemisphere (Newman et al., 2002; Rosenberger et al., 2009). This suggests that those regions are uniquely disposed for language processing.

A Sensitive Period for Language Development. Must language be acquired early in life, during an age span in which the brain is particularly responsive to language stimulation? Evidence for a sensitive period coinciding with brain lateralization would support the nativist position that language development has unique biological properties.

To test this idea, researchers have examined the language competence of deaf adults who acquired their first language—American Sign Language (ASL)—at different ages. The later learners, whose parents chose to educate them through the oral method, which relies on speech and lip-reading and discourages signing, did not acquire spoken language because of their profound deafness. And consistent with the sensitive period notion, those who learned ASL in adolescence or adulthood never became as proficient at any aspect of language as those who learned in childhood (recall Simon's parents, in Figure 9.2, who scored lower on a test of complex grammar than he did because they had not acquired ASL until adolescence) (Mayberry, 2010; Newport, 1991; Singleton & Newport, 2004). Furthermore, the typical right-hemispheric localization of ASL functions, which require visual–spatial processing of hand, arm, and facial movements, is greatly reduced in individuals who learned ASL beyond childhood (Newman et al., 2002). However, a precise age cutoff for a decline in first-language competence has not been established.

Is acquiring a second language also harder after a sensitive period has passed? In one study, researchers examined U.S. census data, selecting immigrants from Spanish- and Chinese-speaking countries who had resided in the United States for at least 10 years. The census form had asked the immigrants to rate how competently they spoke English, from "not at all" to "very well"—self-reports that correlate strongly with objective language measures. As age of immigration increased from infancy and early childhood into adulthood, English proficiency declined, regardless of respondents' level of education (see Figure 9.3) (Hakuta, Bialystok, & Wiley, 2003). Other research confirms an age-related decline beginning around age 5 to 6 in capacity to acquire a second language with a native accent

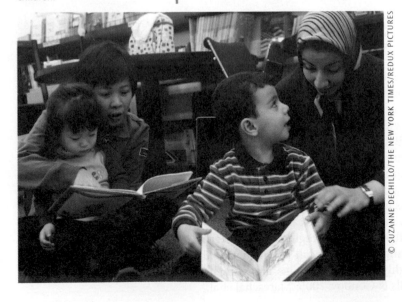

Immigrant mothers read English with their children as part of a library literacy program. Because childhood is a sensitive period for optimum language development, these mothers may never become as proficient in English as their children.

© SUZANNE DECHILLO/THE NEW YORK TIMES/REDUX PICTURES

(Flege, Yeni-Komshian, & Liu, 1999; Flege et al., 2006). Furthermore, ERP and fMRI measures of brain activity indicate that second-language processing is less lateralized, and also overlaps less with brain areas devoted to first-language processing, in older than in younger learners (Neville & Bruer, 2001). But second-language competence does not drop sharply at a certain age. Rather, a continuous, age-related decrease occurs.

What factors underlie the younger-age language-learning advantage? Some researchers assign a key role to the narrowing of speech perception during the second half of the first year—from discrimination among nearly all language sounds to heightened sensitivity to sound distinctions in the language (or languages) the baby hears (see Chapter 4, page 156). As a result, neural networks become dedicated to processing native-language sounds, strengthening native-language learning while weakening capacity to acquire unfamiliar languages. As preliminary evidence for this view, 7-month-olds' skill at perceiving native-language sounds, along with their insensitivity to sound variations in languages they do not hear, predicts rapid vocabulary and grammatical development in the second and third years (Kuhl et al., 2005; Kuhl, 2009).

In sum, the more "committed" the brain is to native-language patterns, the better children's mastery of their native language and the less effectively they acquire foreign languages (Kuhl, 2006). This neural commitment increases with mastery of language and, thus, with age.

Limitations of the Nativist Perspective

Chomsky's theory has had a major impact on current views of language development. But despite wide acceptance of Chomsky's belief in humans' unique, biologically based capacity to acquire language, his account of development has been challenged on several grounds.

First, researchers have had great difficulty specifying Chomsky's universal grammar. A persistent problem is the absence of a complete description of these abstract grammatical structures or even an agreed-on list of how many exist or the best examples of them. According to Chomsky's critics, one set of rules cannot account for the multiplicity of grammatical forms—indeed, variation in every structural way possible—among the world's 5,000 to 8,000 languages (Christiansen & Chater, 2008; Evans & Levinson, 2009; Tomasello, 2003, 2005). How children manage to link such rules with the extraordinary diversity in strings of words they hear is also unclear.

Second, Chomsky's assumption that grammatical knowledge is innately determined does not fit with certain observations of language development. Once children begin to use an innate grammatical structure, we would expect them to apply it to all relevant instances in their language. But later we will encounter evidence that children refine and generalize many grammatical forms gradually, engaging in much piecemeal learning and making errors along the way (Tomasello, 2000, 2003, 2006). Complete mastery of some forms (such as the passive voice) is not achieved until well into middle childhood (Tager-Flusberg & Zukowski, 2009). This suggests that more experimentation and learning are involved than Chomsky assumed.

Chomsky's theory also lacks comprehensiveness. For example, it cannot explain how children weave statements together into connected discourse and sustain meaningful conversations. Perhaps because Chomsky did not dwell on the pragmatic side of language, his theory grants little attention to the quality of language input or to social experience in supporting language progress. Furthermore, the nativist perspective does not regard children's cognitive capacities as important. Yet in Chapter 6, we saw that cognitive development is involved in children's early vocabulary growth. And studies of children with broad intellectual disability (see the Biology and Environment box on page 366) show that cognitive competence also influences children's grammatical mastery.

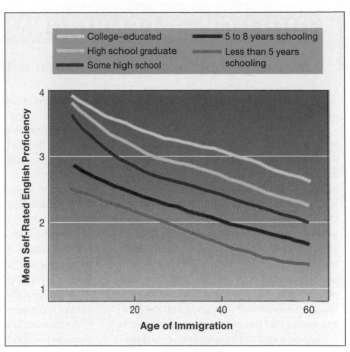

FIGURE 9.3 Relationship between age of immigration to the United States and self-rated English proficiency, illustrated for native Spanish speakers. As age of immigration increased, English proficiency decreased for individuals at all levels of education, from a few years of elementary school to a college education. Findings for native Chinese speakers were similar. (From K. Hakuta, E. Bialystok, & E. Wiley, 2003, "Critical Evidence: A Test of the Critical Period Hypothesis for Second-Language Acquisition," *Psychological Science*, Vol. 14, No. 1, p. 37, copyright © 2003, Association for Psychological Science. Reprinted by permission of SAGE Publications.)

BIOLOGY and ENVIRONMENT

Language Development in Children with Williams Syndrome

Williams syndrome, a rare disorder occurring in only one in 7,500 births, results from deletion of genetic material on the seventh chromosome. Affected individuals have facial, heart, and kidney abnormalities and mild to serious intellectual disability. With IQ scores typically ranging from 50 to 70, they are just as mentally impaired as individuals with Down syndrome—yet they are far more advanced in language skills (Bellugi et al., 2000; Tager-Flusberg, 2007). For many years, researchers took this apparent "decoupling" of cognition and language as evidence that language is controlled by an innate LAD. But new evidence on language attainments associated with the disorder reveals that this conclusion is not warranted.

Infants with Williams syndrome are strongly oriented toward the social world—extremely gregarious and fascinated by faces and voices (Zitzer-Comfort et al., 2010). Their language development, though delayed, is impressive. During the preschool years, children with Williams syndrome have larger vocabularies and produce grammatically more complex sentences than children with Down syndrome (Mervis & Robinson, 2000). For example, the longest sentence of one 3-year-old with Williams syndrome was "Please have some grapes in my cup right now." Her counterpart with Down syndrome said, "Here-ya-go" and "Hold me" (Jarrold, Baddeley, & Hewes, 1998, p. 361). By adolescence, the vocabularies of young people with Williams syndrome contain many unusual words. When asked to name as many animals as possible, one teenager said, "weasel, newt, salamander, Chihuahua, ibex, yak" (Bellugi et al., 1992, p. 11).

Yet affected individuals have trouble with highly challenging grammatical rules. For example, French-speaking adolescents with Williams syndrome do poorly on grammatical gender assignment—matching masculine and feminine articles (such as *un* versus *une*) with nouns by attending to word endings and noting exceptions. Normally developing French children master this gender system by age 4 (Karmiloff-Smith et al., 1997). And a study of English-speaking adults revealed difficulties with subtle verb forms ("He struggle the dog" rather than "He struggled with the dog") (Karmiloff-Smith et al., 1998).

Why does Williams syndrome lead to an uneven language profile—areas of both strength and weakness? Growing evidence indicates that the cognitive deficits of Williams syndrome profoundly alter the course of language development. Children with the disorder are relatively good at memorizing but poor at rule learning (Karmiloff-Smith et al., 2003; Rowe & Mervis, 2006). To compensate, they capitalize on their social strengths, attending closely to faces and voices and acquiring as much language by rote as they can.

In support of this explanation, toddlers with Williams syndrome do not build their early vocabularies on intentional gestures (such as pointing) and advances in categorization, as typically developing children do (Laing et al., 2002). Instead, they more often mimic others, so much so that they frequently speak without comprehending what they are saying. Preschool and school-age children with Williams syndrome have pragmatic deficits: They make many irrelevant remarks during conversations and are poor at adapting what they say to

Despite intellectual disability, this child with Williams syndrome is likely to display impressive language skills. But his cognitive deficits will limit his ability to master complex language rules.

others' needs (Asada et al., 2010a, 2010b). Furthermore, working-memory capacity is more strongly correlated with grammatical development in children with Williams syndrome than in typically developing children (Robinson, Mervis, & Robinson, 2003). All of these findings are consistent with a heavy reliance on memory to learn language.

In sum, although the language of individuals with Williams syndrome is impressive in view of their cognitive limitations, it is impaired in significant ways. The evidence indicates that language is not as separate from other human mental abilities as Chomsky's LAD assumes.

The Interactionist Perspective

Recent ideas about language development emphasize *interactions* between inner capacities and environmental influences. One type of interactionist theory applies the information-processing perspective to language development. A second type emphasizes social interaction.

Information-Processing Theories The most influential information-processing accounts are derived from research with *connectionist*, or *artificial neural network, models*. Connectionist researchers design computer systems to simulate the multilayered networks of neural connections in the brain and program them with basic learning procedures—for example, to respond to regularities in the speech stream. Then the artificial network is exposed to various types of language input and given feedback about the accuracy of its responses. When a response is correct, the connections that produced it strengthen; when incorrect, they weaken. If the network's overall pattern of responses resembles that of children of different ages, researchers conclude that the network is a good model of human learning and development.

Tests with certain language sounds, words, and basic grammatical forms show that these networks capture children's early errors and gradually detect adult linguistic patterns. In acquiring the past tense, for example, a network first constructed some simple rules—for example, "Retrieve the past-tense form from memory." "Add *-ed* to any verb"—which at times resulted in mistakes. With further experience, the network modified and combined rules to arrive at adult usage: "For frequently used verbs (such as *go*), retrieve the unique past-tense form from memory *(went)*." "For novel or infrequently used verbs, form the past tense by adding *–ed*" (Taatgen & Anderson, 2002). Notice that neural networks are not biased to learn language. Instead, their designers assume that children make sense of their complex language environments by applying powerful, analytic cognitive capacities of a general kind rather than capacities especially tuned to language (Bates, 1999; Elman, 2001; Munakata, 2006).

Other theorists blend Chomsky's nativist perspective with the information-processing proposal that the human brain is extraordinarily skilled at detecting patterns. Recall the research presented in Chapter 4 (see page 157), which showed that infants are amazing statistical analyzers of the sound stream, capable of detecting which adjacent sounds often occur together and which do not—a skill that helps them discriminate words in fluent speech. Using this *statistical learning capacity,* infants identify basic language patterns by applying the same strategies they use to make sense of their nonlinguistic experiences. At the same time, researchers recognize that such statistical computations are not sufficient to account for mastery of higher-level aspects of language—for example, intricate grammatical structures that require a grasp of distant relationships between words and phrases (Aslin & Newport, 2009). Currently, statistical learning theorists are investigating how sensitivity to statistical regularities might combine with other general-cognitive and language-specific processing abilities to explain children's acquisition of increasingly complex language structures (Saffran, 2009).

Proponents of information-processing approaches draw on biological evidence, pointing out that regions of the brain housing language also govern other similar perceptual, motor, and cognitive abilities. For example, ERP and fMRI studies reveal that damage to the left hemisphere, including Wernicke's area, results in difficulty comprehending both language and other patterned stimuli, such as music and series of moving lights that depict familiar shapes (Bates et al., 2003; Saygin et al., 2004; Saygin, Leech, & Dick, 2010). Indeed, Wernicke's area—once thought to be language-specific—is actually more strongly associated with comprehension of nonverbal than of verbal sound (Dick et al., 2004).

Information-processing theorists have tested their ideas mostly with simplified language stimuli, presented to artificial neural networks and to children in laboratories. In many instances, they cannot be certain that the learning strategies identified generalize to children's language acquisition in everyday social contexts. Other interactionist theorists believe that children's social skills and language experiences are centrally involved in language development.

Social Interactionist Theories According to the social interactionist perspective, native capacity, a strong desire to understand others and to be understood by them, and a rich language environment combine to help children discover the functions and regularities of language. An active child, well-endowed for making sense of language, strives to communicate. In doing so, she cues her caregivers to provide appropriate language experiences, which in turn help her relate the content and structure of language to its social meanings (Bohannon & Bonvillian, 2009; Chapman, 2006).

Among social interactionists, disagreement continues over whether children make sense of their complex language environments by applying general cognitive capacities or capacities specially tuned to language (Lidz, 2007; Shatz, 2007; Tomasello, 2003, 2006). Nevertheless, as we chart the course of language development, we will encounter much support for their central premise—that children's social competencies and language experiences greatly affect language development. In reality, native endowment, cognitive-processing strategies, and social experience may operate in different balances with respect to each component of language. Today, we still know much more about the course of language development than about precisely how it takes place.

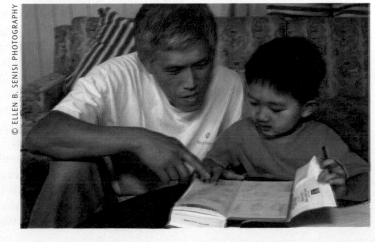

According to the social interactionist perspective, native capacity, a strong desire to communicate, and exposure to a rich language environment combine to help this preschooler discover the functions and regularities of language.

© ELLEN B. SENISI PHOTOGRAPHY

A S K   Y O U R S E L F

Review ■ Summarize outcomes of attempts to teach language to animals. Are results consistent with the nativist assumption that human children are uniquely endowed with an LAD? Explain.

Review ■ How do the two types of interactionist theories of language development differ from nativist views and from each other?

Connect ■ Cite research in this chapter and in Chapter 5 indicating that with age, areas of the cortex become increasingly specialized for language. Relate these findings to the concept of brain plasticity.

Apply ■ Describe evidence for the existence of a sensitive period for language learning. What are the practical implications of these findings for teaching children a second language?

▶ Discuss receptivity to language, development of speech sounds, and conversational skills during infancy.

Prelinguistic Development: Getting Ready to Talk

From the very beginning, infants are prepared to acquire language. During the first year, sensitivity to language, cognitive and social skills, and environmental supports pave the way for the onset of verbal communication.

Receptivity to Language

Recall from Chapter 4 that newborns are especially sensitive to the pitch range of the human voice and prefer speech—especially their mother's voice and their native tongue—to other sounds, perhaps because of repeated exposure to their mother speaking during pregnancy. We have also seen that newborns make fine-grained distinctions between virtually any human-language sounds. Because this skill may help them crack the phonological code of their native tongue, let's look at it more closely.

Learning Native-Language Sound Categories and Patterns As adults, we analyze the speech stream into **phonemes,** the smallest sound units that signal a change in meaning, such as the difference between the consonant sounds in "pa" and "ba." Phonemes are not the same across all languages. For example, "ra" and "la" are distinct sounds to English speakers but sound the same to speakers of Japanese. Similarly, English speakers have trouble perceiving the difference between two "p" sounds—a soft "p" and a sharp "p" with a burst of air—used to distinguish meaning in the Thai language. This tendency to perceive as identical a range of sounds that belong to the same phonemic class is called **categorical speech perception.** Newborns, like adults, are capable of it. And humans—as well as other primates and chinchillas—categorize not only speech but also nonspeech sounds (Burnham & Mattock, 2010). These findings indicate that categorical perception is not unique to linguistic input. Rather, it is a property of the auditory system, and human languages take advantage of it.

Young infants are sensitive to a much wider range of speech categories than exists in their own language. As they listen actively to the talk of people around them, they focus on meaningful sound variations. Between 6 and 8 months, they start to organize speech into the phonemic categories of their own language—that is, they stop attending to sounds that will not be useful in mastering their native tongue or, in the case of bilingual exposure, sounds not part of both languages they are about to learn (Burns et al., 2007; Kuhl et al., 1992; Mattock et al., 2008; Polka & Werker, 1994).

Interestingly, visual language discrimination—by monitoring a speaker's face and lip movements—changes similarly. At 4 to 6 months, infants can distinguish their native language (English) from an unfamiliar language (French) merely by watching silent video clips of adults saying sentences in each language. At 8 months, however, English-learning infants no longer make this visual distinction. But 8-month-olds from French–English bilingual homes continue to separate the two languages visually—a discrimination that helps them learn two languages at once (Weikum et al., 2007).

As older infants focus intently on language regularities, they soon recognize familiar words in spoken passages, listen longer to speech with clear clause and phrase boundaries, and divide the speech stream into wordlike units (see Chapter 4, page 157, to review). They also extend their sensitivity to speech structure to individual words. Using phoneme sequences and stress patterns, 7-month-olds can distinguish sounds that typically begin words from those that do not (Swingly, 2005; Thiessen & Saffran, 2007). For example, English and Dutch infant learners often rely on the onset of a strong syllable to indicate a new word, as in "*ani*mal" and "*pud*ding." By 10 months, they can detect words that start with weak syllables, such as "sur*prise*" (Jusczyk, 2001; Kooijman, Hagoort, & Cutler, 2009). The reverse pattern—earlier detection of words starting with weak syllables—characterizes infants acquiring Canadian French, which includes more words with a weak–strong stress pattern (Polka & Sundara, 2003).

This mother speaks to her 8-month-old using infant-directed speech—short, clearly pronounced sentences with high-pitched, exaggerated expression. This form of communication eases the task of understanding language.

Taken together, these findings reveal that in the second half of the first year, infants have begun to detect the internal structure of sentences and words—information that will be vital for linking speech units with their meanings. How do babies accomplish these feats? We have seen that they are vigilant *statistical analyzers* of sound patterns; in the second half of the first year, they can distinguish adjacent syllables that frequently occur together (signaling that they belong to the same word) from those that seldom occur together (signaling a word boundary). Research suggests that infants first use these statistical learning abilities to locate words in speech. Then they focus on the words, detecting regular patterns of syllable stress (Saffran & Thiessen, 2007). Furthermore, babies of this age are budding *rule learners*. At 7 months, they can distinguish an ABA from an ABB pattern in the structure of short, non-sense-word sequences—a capacity that may eventually help them grasp basic syntax (Marcus et al., 1999) (see page 157 in Chapter 4).

Clearly, infants acquire a great deal of language-specific knowledge before they start to talk around 12 months of age. As we will see, certain features of adult speech greatly assist them in detecting meaningful speech units.

Adult Speech to Young Language Learners Adults in many countries speak to babies in **infant-directed speech (IDS),** a form of communication made up of short sentences with high-pitched, exaggerated expression, clear pronunciation, distinct pauses between speech segments, clear gestures to support verbal meaning, and repetition of new words in a variety of contexts ("See the *ball*." "The *ball* bounced!") (Fernald et al., 1989; O'Neill et al., 2005). Deaf parents use a similar style of communicating when signing to their babies (Masataka, 1996).

Parents do not seem to be deliberately trying to teach infants to talk when they use IDS; many of the same speech qualities appear when adults communicate with nonnative speakers. Rather, IDS probably arises from adults' desire to hold babies' attention and ease their task of understanding, and it works effectively in these ways. From birth on, infants prefer IDS over other kinds of adult talk (Aslin, Jusczyk, & Pisoni, 1998). By 5 months, they are more emotionally responsive to it and can discriminate the tone quality of IDS with different meanings—for example, approving versus soothing utterances (Moore, Spence, & Katz, 1997; Werker, Pegg, & McLeod, 1994). Mothers' exaggerated pronunciation in IDS is strongly associated with 6- to 12-month-olds' increasing sensitivity to the phonemic categories of their native language and with detection of words in the speech stream (Liu, Kuhl, & Tsao, 2003; Thiessen, Hill, & Saffran, 2005). And in the second year, the short, simple phrases leading up to a noun ("*Where's the* kitty?" "*See the* kitty."), common in IDS, facilitate detection of word meanings (Fernald & Hurtado, 2006). Perhaps these phrases enable toddlers to anticipate that an important word is coming and, thus, listen closely for it.

Parents fine-tune IDS, adjusting the length and content of their utterances to fit babies' changing needs—adjustments that enable toddlers to join in and that foster language progress in the second and third years (Murray, Johnson, & Peters, 1990; Rowe, 2008). In addition, toddlers' first words and phrases are usually ones they hear often in their caregivers' IDS (Cameron-Faulkner, Lieven, & Tomasello, 2003).

LOOK and LISTEN

While observing a parent and baby playing, describe how the parent adapts his or her language to the child's needs. Did the parent use IDS?

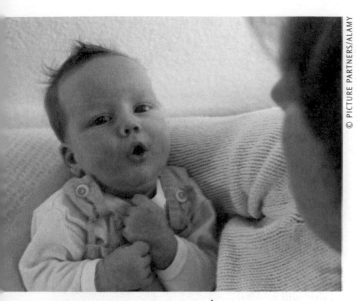

© PICTURE PARTNERS/ALAMY

This 3-month-old's pleasant, vowel-like "oo" noises are known as cooing. Soon she will add consonants, and around 6 months, like babies everywhere, begin to babble.

First Speech Sounds

Around 2 months, babies begin to make vowel-like noises, called **cooing** because of their pleasant "oo" quality. Gradually, consonants are added, and around 6 months **babbling** appears, in which infants repeat consonant–vowel combinations, often in long strings such as "babababab" and "nanananana."

Babies everywhere (even those who are deaf) start babbling at about the same age and produce a similar range of early sounds. But for babbling to develop further, infants must hear human speech. In hearing-impaired babies, these speechlike sounds are delayed and limited in diversity of sounds produced over time (Bass-Ringdahl, 2010; Moeller et al., 2007). And a deaf infant not exposed to sign language will stop babbling entirely (Oller, 2000).

In one case, a deaf-born 5-month-old received a *cochlear implant*—an electronic device inserted into the ear that converts external sounds into a signal to stimulate the auditory nerve. She showed typical babbling in infancy and resembled her hearing age-mates in language development at 3 to 4 years (Schauwers et al., 2004). But if auditory input is not restored until after age 2 (the usual time for cochlear implant surgery), children remain behind in language development. And if implantation occurs after age 4, language delays are severe and persistent (Govaerts et al., 2002; Svirsky, Teoh, & Neuburger, 2004). These outcomes suggest an early sensitive period in which exposure to speech is essential for the brain to develop the necessary organization for normal speech processing.

Babies initially produce a limited number of sounds and then expand to a much broader range (Oller et al., 1997). Around 7 months, babbling includes consonant–vowel syllables common in spoken languages. And as caregivers respond contingently to infant babbles, infants modify their babbling to include sound patterns like those in the adult's speech (Goldstein & Schwade, 2008). By 8 to 10 months, babbling reflects the sounds and intonation of children's language community, some of which are transferred to their first words ("Mama," "Dada") (Boysson-Bardies & Vihman, 1991).

TAKE A MOMENT... The next time you hear an older baby babbling, notice how certain sounds appear in particular contexts—for example, when exploring objects, looking at books, or walking upright (Blake & Boysson-Bardies, 1992). Infants seem to be experimenting with the sound system and meaning of language before they speak in conventional ways. Toddlers continue babbling for four or five months after they say their first words.

Deaf infants exposed to sign language from birth babble with their hands much as hearing infants do through speech (Petitto & Marentette, 1991). Furthermore, hearing babies of deaf, signing parents produce babblelike hand motions with the rhythmic patterns of natural sign languages (Petitto et al., 2001, 2004). This sensitivity to language rhythm, evident not just in perception of speech but also in babbling, whether spoken or signed, supports both discovery and production of meaningful language units.

Becoming a Communicator

At birth, infants are prepared for some aspects of conversational behavior. For example, newborns initiate interaction through eye contact and terminate it by looking away. By 3 to 4 months, infants start to gaze in the same general direction adults are looking—a skill that becomes more accurate at 10 to 11 months. Around this time, babies become sensitive to adults' precise direction of gaze, suggesting that they realize that others' focus provides information about their communicative intentions (to talk about an object) or other goals (to obtain an object) (Brooks & Meltzoff, 2005; Senju, Csibra, & Johnson, 2008). Indeed, 12-month-olds look where an adult is looking only when the adult's eyes are open. And 12- to 14-month-olds are more likely to engage in gaze following when no obstacles block an adult's line of sight to an object (Brooks & Meltzoff, 2002; Dunphy-Lelii & Wellman, 2004). Around their first birthday, babies realize that a person's visual gaze signals a vital connection between the viewer and his or her surroundings, and they want to participate.

This **joint attention,** in which the child attends to the same object or event as the caregiver, who often labels it, contributes greatly to early language development. Infants and toddlers who frequently experience it sustain attention longer, comprehend more language, produce meaningful gestures and words earlier, and show faster vocabulary development through 2 years of age (Brooks & Meltzoff, 2008; Carpenter, Nagell, & Tomasello, 1998; Flom & Pick, 2003; Silvén, 2001). Gains in joint attention at the end of the first year enable babies to establish a "common ground" with the adult, through which they can figure out the meaning of the adult's verbal labels.

Between 4 and 6 months, interactions between caregivers and babies begin to include *give-and-take,* as in pat-a-cake and peekaboo games. At first, the parent starts the game and the baby is an amused observer. But even 4-month-olds are sensitive to the structure and timing of these interactions, smiling more at an organized than a disorganized peekaboo exchange (Rochat, Querido, & Striano, 1999). By 12 months, babies participate actively, trading roles with the caregiver. As they do so, they practice the turn-taking pattern of human conversation, a vital context for acquiring language and communication skills. Infants' play maturity and vocalizations during games predict advanced language progress in the second year (Rome-Flanders & Cronk, 1995).

Around the first birthday, babies extend their joint attention and social interaction skills: They *point* toward an object or location while looking back toward the caregiver, in an effort to direct the adult's attention and influence their behavior. One-year-olds also grasp the communicative function of others' pointing. They interpret pointing to indicate the location of a hidden toy only when the adult also makes eye contact, not when the adult looks down at his finger (Liszkowski, Carpenter, & Tomasello, 2007; Tomasello, Carpenter, & Liszkowski, 2007).

Infant pointing leads to two communicative gestures. The first is the **protodeclarative,** in which the baby points to, touches, or holds up an object while looking at others to make sure they notice. In the second, the **protoimperative,** the baby gets another person to do something by reaching, pointing, and often making sounds at the same time (Carpenter, Nagell, & Tomasello, 1998a). Over time, some of these gestures become explicitly symbolic—much like those in children's early make-believe play (see Chapter 6). For example, a 1- to 2-year-old might flap her arms to indicate "butterfly" or raise her palms to signal "all gone" (Goldin-Meadow, 1999).

Besides using communicative gestures to serve their own goals, 12-month-olds adapt these gestures to the needs of others. In one study, they pointed more often to an object whose location a searching adult did not know than to an object whose location the adult did know (Liszkowski, Carpenter, & Tomasello, 2008). Already, the cooperative processes essential for effective communication—modifying messages to suit others' intentions and knowledge—are under way. Soon toddlers integrate words with gestures, using the gesture to expand their verbal message, as in pointing to a toy while saying "give" (Capirci et al., 2005). Gradually, gestures recede, and words become dominant.

Toddlers' use of preverbal gestures predicts faster early vocabulary growth in the second and third years (Brooks & Meltzoff, 2008; Rowe, Özçalişkan, & Goldin-Meadow, 2008). And the earlier toddlers form word–gesture combinations and the greater number they use, the sooner they produce two-word utterances at the end of the second year and the more complex their sentences at age 3½ (Özçalişkan & Goldin-Meadow, 2005; Rowe & Goldin-Meadow, 2009). Clearly gesture is at the cutting edge of early language development, serving as a steppingstone to more advanced constructions.

We have seen that caregivers who respond sensitively and involve infants in dialogue-like exchanges encourage early language progress. Yet in some cultures, such as the Kaluli of Papua New Guinea, the people of Western Samoa, and the Maya of southern Mexico, adults rarely communicate with young children and never play social games with them. Not until infants crawl and walk do siblings take charge, talk to toddlers, and respond to their vocalizations.

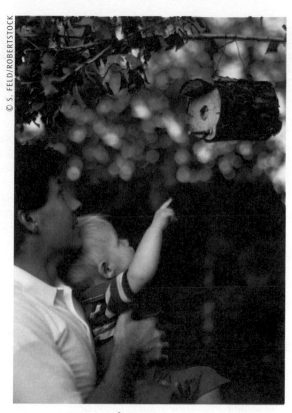

© S. FELD/ROBERTSTOCK

This baby uses a preverbal gesture to draw his father's attention to the birdhouse. A verbal response from his father promotes the transition to spoken language.

LOOK and LISTEN

Observe a 12- to 18-month-old for 30 to 60 minutes at home or child care, jotting down descriptions of preverbal gestures and word–gesture combinations. Does the toddler's use of gestures fit with research findings?

SOCIAL ISSUES: EDUCATION

Parent–Child Interaction: Impact on Language and Cognitive Development of Deaf Children

About 2 to 3 out of every 1,000 American infants is born profoundly or fully deaf (ASHA, 2011). When a deaf child cannot participate fully in communication with care-givers, development is severely compromised. Yet the consequences of deafness for children's language and cognition vary with social context, as revealed by comparing deaf children of hearing parents with deaf children of deaf parents.

Over 90 percent of deaf children have hearing parents who are not fluent in sign language. In toddlerhood and early childhood, these children often are delayed in development of language and make-believe play. In middle childhood, many achieve poorly in school, are deficient in social skills, and display impulse-control problems (Arnold, 1999; Edmondson, 2006). Yet deaf children of deaf parents escape these difficulties! Their language (use of sign), play maturity, and impulse control are on a par with hearing children's. After school entry, deaf children of deaf parents learn easily and get along well with adults and peers (Bornstein et al., 1999; Spencer & Lederberg, 1997).

These differences can be traced to early par-ent–child communication. Children with limited and less sensitive parental communication lag behind their agemates in achieving control over their behavior—in thinking before they act. Beginning in infancy, hearing parents of deaf children are less positive, less responsive to the child's efforts to communicate, less effective at achieving joint attention and turn-taking, less involved in play, and more directive and intrusive

(Spencer, 2000; Spencer & Meadow-Orlans, 1996). In contrast, the quality of interaction between deaf children and deaf parents resembles that of hearing children and hear-ing parents.

Hearing parents are not to blame for their deaf child's problems. Rather, they lack experience with visual communication, which enables deaf parents to respond readily to a deaf child's needs. Deaf parents know they must wait for the child to turn toward them before interacting (Loots & Devise, 2003). Hearing parents tend to speak or gesture while the child's attention is directed else-where—a strategy that works with a hearing but not with a deaf partner. When the child is confused or unresponsive, hearing parents often feel overwhelmed and become overly controlling (Jamieson, 1995).

The impact of deafness on language and cognitive development can best be under-stood by considering how it affects parents and other significant people in the child's life. Deaf children need access to language models—deaf adults and peers—to experi-ence natural language learning. And their hearing parents benefit from social support along with training in how to interact sensi-tively with a nonhearing partner.

Screening techniques can identify deaf babies at birth. Many U.S. states and an increas-ing number of Western nations require that every newborn be tested, enabling immediate enrollment in programs aimed at fostering

Unlike many hearing parents of deaf children, this mother is fluent in sign language. Using visual com-munication, she responds readily to her 3-year-old's efforts to communicate. Consequently, the child displays language progress typical for her age.

effective parent–child interaction. When chil-dren with profound hearing loss start to receive intervention within the first year of life, they show much better language, cognitive, and social development (Vohr et al., 2008; Yoshinaga-Itano, 2003).

Yet Kaluli, Samoan, and Mayan children acquire language within the normal time frame (de León, 2000; Ochs, 1988).

These findings suggest that adult molding of communication during the first year is not essential. But by the second year, caregiver–child interaction contributes greatly to the transition to language. In observations of mother–child play at 9 and 13 months, the frequency with which mothers joined in the child's activity, offered verbal prompts, and imitated and expanded on the child's vocalizations predicted how early children attained major language milestones, including first words, a 50-word vocabulary, two-word combinations, and use of language to talk about the past. The relationship of maternal responsiveness to language progress was particularly strong at 13 months (Tamis-LeMonda, Bornstein, & Baumwell, 2001).

As the Social Issues: Education box above illustrates, when a child's disability makes it difficult for parents to engage in responsive communication, children show profound delays in both language and cognitive development. For ways that caregivers can support early language learning, see Applying What We Know on the following page.

APPLYING WHAT WE KNOW

Supporting Early Language Learning

STRATEGY	CONSEQUENCE
Respond to infants' coos and babbles with speech sounds and words.	Encourages experimentation with sounds that can later be blended into first words. Provides experience with the turn-taking pattern of human conversation.
Establish joint attention and comment on what the child sees.	Predicts earlier onset of language and faster vocabulary development.
Play social games, such as pat-a-cake and peekaboo, with infants and toddlers.	Provides experience with the turn-taking pattern of human conversation.
Engage children in frequent conversations.	Predicts faster early language development and later academic success.
Expand slightly on what the child just said, adding new information.	Saying something like, "You want juice? I have some juice. It's apple juice!" to a toddler models use of language just ahead of the child's current level, thereby promoting language progress.
Read to children often, engaging them in dialogues about picture books.	Provides exposure to many aspects of language, including vocabulary, grammar, communication skills, and information about written symbols and story structures important for literacy progress.

ASK YOURSELF

Review ■ Cite findings indicating that both infant capacities and caregiver communication contribute to prelinguistic development.

Connect ■ Explain how parents' use of infant-directed speech illustrates Vygotsky's zone of proximal development (see Chapter 6, pages 267–268).

Apply ■ Fran frequently corrects her 17-month-old son Jeremy's attempts to talk and—fearing that he won't use words—refuses to respond to his gestures. How might Fran be contributing to Jeremy's slow language progress?

Reflect ■ Find an opportunity to speak to an infant or toddler. How did your manner of speaking differ from the way you typically speak to an adult? What features of your speech are likely to promote early language development, and why?

Phonological Development

▶ Describe the course of phonological development.

TAKE A MOMENT... Listen in on a 1- to 2-year-old trying out her first handful of words. You will probably hear an assortment of interesting pronunciations ("nana" for "banana," "oap" for "soap," "weddy" for "ready"), as well as some wordlike utterances that do not resemble adult forms—for "translations," you must ask the toddler's parent. Phonological development is a complex process that depends on the child's ability to attend to sound sequences, produce sounds, and combine them into understandable words and phrases. Between 1 and 4 years, children make great progress at this task. In trying to talk like people around them, they draw on their impressive capacity to distinguish the phonemic categories of their native language, which is well developed by the end of the first year. They also adopt temporary strategies for producing sounds that bring adult words within their current range of physical and cognitive capabilities (Menn & Stoel-Gammon, 2009). Let's see how they do so.

The Early Phase

Children's first words are influenced in part by the small number of sounds they can pronounce (Stoel-Gammon, 2011; Stoel-Gammon & Sosa, 2007). The easiest sound sequences start with consonants, end with vowels, and include repeated syllables, as in "Mama," "Dada,"

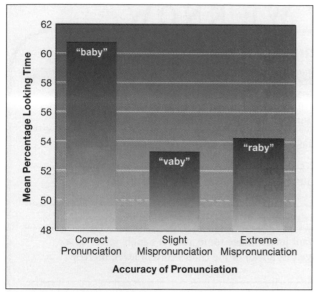

FIGURE 9.4 One-year-olds know the correct pronunciation of familiar words. Babies viewed pairs of familiar objects (such as a baby and a dog) accompanied by a voice speaking the word for one of the objects with either correct pronunciation ("baby"), slight mispronunciation ("vaby"), or considerable mispronunciation ("raby"). They looked longest at the appropriate object when a word was pronounced correctly. In each condition, time spent looking at the correct object exceeded 50 percent, indicating that babies recognized the words whether or not they were pronounced correctly. (Adapted from Swingley & Aslin, 2002.)

"bye-bye," and "nigh-nigh" (for "night-night"). Sometimes young speakers use the same sound to represent a variety of words, making their speech hard to understand (Ingram, 1999). For example, one toddler substituted "bat" for as many as 12 different words, including "bad," "bark," "bent," and "bite."

Research confirms that toddlers and young preschoolers with more words in their spoken vocabularies can pronounce more speech sounds and syllable structures (Smith, McGregor, & Demille, 2006; Stoel-Gammon, 2011). Fortunately, languages cater to young children's phonological limitations. Throughout the world, sounds resembling "Mama," "Dada," and "Papa" refer to parents, so it is not surprising that these are among the first words produced by children everywhere. Also, in infant-directed speech, adults often use simplified words to talk about things of interest to toddlers—"bunny" for rabbit, "choo-choo" for train. These word forms support the child's first attempts to talk.

One-year-olds first learning to talk know how familiar words—such as *dog, baby,* and *ball*—are supposed to sound, even when they mispronounce them. Researchers showed 14-month-olds pairs of objects (such as a baby and a dog), accompanied by a voice speaking the word for one of the objects, with either correct pronunciation ("baby"), slight mispronunciation ("vaby"), or considerable mispronunciation ("raby") (Swingley & Aslin, 2002). The toddlers easily detected the correct pronunciation: They looked longer at the appropriate object when a word was pronounced correctly than when it was either mildly or extremely mispronounced (see Figure 9.4). And they respond this way to mispronunciations of either beginning or ending consonants (Swingley, 2009).

Nevertheless, when learning a new word, toddlers often do not pick up the fine details of its sounds, which contributes to their pronunciation errors. In several studies, 14-month-olds were unable to associate two similar-sounding nonsense words ("bih" and "dih") with different objects, despite easily detecting the "b"–"d" contrast in sound discrimination tasks (Fennell & Werker, 2003; Stager & Werker, 1997). Why don't toddlers apply their impressive sensitivity to speech sounds when acquiring new words? Associating words with their referents places extra demands on toddlers' limited working memories. Intent on communicating, they focus on the word–referent pairing while sacrificing the word's sounds, which they encode imprecisely.

As toddlers' vocabularies increase, they become better at using their perceptual abilities to distinguish similar-sounding new words. Once they acquire several sets of words that sound alike, they may be motivated to attend more closely to fine-grained distinctions between others.

Phonological Strategies

By the middle of the second year, children move from trying to pronounce whole syllables and words to trying to pronounce each individual sound within a word. As a result, they can be heard experimenting with phoneme patterns. One 21-month-old pronounced "juice" as "du," "ju," "dus," "jus," "sus," "zus," "fus," "tfus," "jusi," and "tfusi" within a single hour (Fee, 1997). This marks an intermediate phase of development in which pronunciation is partly right and partly wrong. Because young children get more practice perceiving and producing phoneme patterns that occur frequently in their language, they pronounce words containing those patterns more accurately and rapidly (Majorano & D'Odorico, 2011; Zamuner, Gerken, & Hammond, 2004). Unique-sounding words are generally difficult to pronounce. A close look reveals that children apply systematic strategies to challenging words so that these words fit with their pronunciation capacities yet resemble adult utterances. Although individual differences exist in the precise strategies that children adopt (see Table 9.1 for examples), they follow a general developmental pattern (Vihman, 1996).

At first, children produce *minimal words,* focusing on the stressed syllable and trying to pronounce its consonant–vowel combination ("du" or "ju" for "juice"). Soon they add ending consonants ("jus"), adjust vowel length ("beee" for "please"), and add unstressed syllables ("mae-do" for "tomato"). Finally, they produce the full word with a correct stress pattern, although they may still need to refine its sounds ("timemba" for "remember," "pagetti" for "spaghetti") (Demuth, 1996; Salidis & Johnson, 1997).

Children's errors are similar across a range of languages, including Cantonese, Czech, English, French, Italian, Quiché (a Guatemalan Mayan language), Spanish, and Swedish. But rate of phonological progress depends on the complexity of a language's sound system and the importance of certain sounds for conveying meaning. Cantonese-speaking children, for example, develop more quickly than English-speaking children. Many Cantonese words are single syllables, but a change in a syllable's tone can change its meaning. Chinese children master this tone system by age 2 (So & Dodd, 1995). Among children acquiring English, "v" is a late-appearing sound, whereas Swedish children master it early. In English, "v" is relatively infrequent; in Swedish, it is common and vital for distinguishing words (Ingram, 1999).

	Common Phonological Strategies Used by Young Children to Simplify Pronunciation of Adult Words
TABLE 9.1	

STRATEGY	EXAMPLE
Repeating the first consonant-vowel in a multisyllable word	"TV" becomes "didi," "cookie" becomes "gege."
Deleting unstressed syllables in a multisyllable word	"Banana" becomes "nana," "giraffe" becomes "raffe."
Replacing fricatives (hissing sounds) with stop consonant sounds	"Sea" becomes "tea," "say" becomes "tay."
Replacing consonant sounds produced in the rear and palate area of the vocal tract with ones produced in the frontal area	"Kid" becomes "tid," "goose" becomes "doose."
Replacing liquid sounds ("l" or "r") with glides ("y" or "w")	"Lap" becomes "yap," "ready" becomes "weddy."
Deleting the final consonant of a word	"Bike" becomes "bai," "more" becomes "muh," "bottom" becomes "bada."
Reducing a consonant cluster to a single consonant	"Clown" becomes "cown," "play" becomes "pay."

Source: Ingram, 1986.

Over the preschool years, children's pronunciation improves greatly. Maturation of the vocal tract and the child's active problem-solving efforts are largely responsible, since children's phonological errors are resistant to adult correction. One father tried repeatedly to get his 2½-year-old daughter to pronounce the word "music," but she persisted with "ju-jic." When her father made one last effort, she replied, "Wait 'til I big. Then I say 'ju-jic,' Daddy!"

Later Phonological Development

Although phonological development is largely complete by age 5, a few syllable stress patterns signaling subtle differences in meaning are not acquired until middle childhood or adolescence. For example, when shown pairs of pictures and asked to distinguish the "greenhouse" from the "green house," most children recognized the correct label by third grade and produced it between fourth and sixth grade (Atkinson-King, 1973). Changes in syllabic stress when certain abstract words take on endings ("humid" to "humidity," "method" to "methodical") are not mastered until adolescence (Camarata & Leonard, 1986).

These late attainments are probably affected by the semantic complexity of the words, in that hard-to-understand words are also more difficult to pronounce. Even at later ages, working simultaneously on the sounds and meaning of a new word may overload the cognitive system, causing children to sacrifice pronunciation temporarily until they better grasp the word's meaning.

ASK YOURSELF

Review ■ Why do young toddlers often fail to pick up the fine details of a new word's sounds, even though they can perceive those sounds?

Apply ■ As his father placed a bowl of pasta on the dinner table, 2-year-old Luke exclaimed, "So 'licious!" Explain Luke's phonological strategy.

Reflect ■ For one week, keep a log of words you mispronounce or do not pronounce fluently (you slow down to say them). Are they words that convey complex concepts or words with sounds that are relatively infrequent in English or in your native tongue? Research indicates that these factors, which affect children's pronunciation, also affect the pronunciation of adults.

▶ Summarize the course of semantic development, noting individual differences.

▶ Discuss ideas about how semantic development takes place, including the influence of memory and strategies for word learning.

Semantic Development

Word comprehension begins in the middle of the first year. When 6-month-olds listened to the words "Mommy" and "Daddy" while looking at side-by-side videos of their parents, they looked longer at the video of the named parent (Tincoff & Jusczyk, 1999). At 9 months, after hearing a word paired with an object, babies looked longer at other objects in the same category than at those in a different category (Balaban & Waxman, 1997). On average, children say their first word around 12 months. By age 6, they understand the meaning of about 10,000 words (Bloom, 1998). To accomplish this feat, children learn about five new words each day.

As these achievements reveal, children's **comprehension,** the language they understand, develops ahead of **production,** the language they use. For example, toddlers follow many simple directions ("Bring me your book," "Don't touch the lamp") even though they cannot yet express all these words in their own speech. A five-month lag exists between the time English-speaking toddlers comprehend 50 words (around 13 months) and the time they produce that many (around 18 months) (Menyuk, Liebergott, & Schultz, 1995).

Think back to the distinction made in Chapter 7 between two types of memory—recognition and recall. Comprehension requires only that children *recognize* the meaning of a word. But for production, children must *recall,* or actively retrieve from their memories, not only the word but also the concept for which it stands. Still, the two capacities are related. The speed and accuracy of toddlers' comprehension of spoken language increase dramatically over the second year. And toddlers who are faster and more accurate in comprehension tend to show more rapid growth in words understood and produced as they approach age 2 (Fernald, Perfors, & Marchman, 2006). Quick comprehension frees space in working memory for picking up new words and for the more demanding task of using them to communicate.

The Early Phase

To learn words, children must identify which concept each label picks out in their language community. **TAKE A MOMENT...** Ask several parents to list their toddlers' first spoken words. Notice how these words build on the sensorimotor foundations Piaget described and on categories infants have formed (see Chapter 6). In a study tracking the first 10 words used by several hundred U.S. and Chinese (both Mandarin- and Cantonese-speaking) babies, important people ("Mama," "Dada"), common objects ("ball," "bread"), and sound effects ("woof-woof," "vroom") were mentioned most often. And as Table 9.2 shows, action words ("hit," "grab," "hug") and social routines ("hi," "bye"), though also appearing frequently in all three groups, were more often produced by Chinese than U.S. babies, who also named more important people—cultural differences we will consider shortly (Tardif et al., 2008). Other investigations concur that earliest words usually include people, objects that move, foods, animals (in families with pets), familiar actions ("hug"), outcomes of such actions ("hot," "ouch"), and social terms (Hart, 2004; Nelson, 1973). In their first 50 words, toddlers rarely name things that just sit there, like "table" or "vase."

Young toddlers add to their vocabularies slowly, at a pace of one to three words per week. Gradually, the number of

TABLE 9.2	Rank-Ordered Top 20 Earliest Words Produced by U.S. and Chinese (Mandarin- and Cantonese-Speaking) Toddlers		
	ENGLISH (UNITED STATES)	**MANDARIN (HONG KONG)**	**CANTONESE (BEIJING)**
	Daddy	**Daddy**	Mommy
	Mommy	Aah	**Daddy**
	BaaBaa	**Mommy**	*Grandma (paternal)*
	Bye	*YumYum*	*Grandpa (paternal)*
	Hi	Sister (older)	**Hello**
	UhOh	**UhOh**	*Hit*
	Grr	Hit	Uncle (paternal)
	Bottle	**Hello**	Grab/Grasp
	YumYum	Milk	*Auntie (maternal)*
	Dog	Naughty	**Bye**
	No	*Brother (older)*	**UhOh**
	WoofWoof	*Grandma (maternal)*	Ya/Wow
	Vroom	*Grandma (paternal)*	*Sister (older)*
	Kitty	**Bye**	**WoofWoof**
	Ball	Bread	*Brother (older)*
	Baby	*Auntie (maternal)*	Hug/Hold
	Duck	Ball	Light
	Cat	*Grandpa (paternal)*	*Grandma (maternal)*
	Ouch	Car	Egg
	Banana	**WoofWoof**	*Vroom*

Note. All words translated into English equivalents. Boldface words are common across all three languages. Italicized words are common across two languages.

Source: T. Tardif, P. Fletcher, W. Liang, Z. Zhang, N. Kaciroti, & V. A. Marchman, 2008, "Baby's First 10 Words," *Developmental Psychology, 44,* p. 932, Copyright © 2008 by the American Psychological Assoication. Reprinted with permission of the American Psychological Association.

words learned accelerates. The increase is much more rapid in comprehension than in production, as illustrated by English and Italian learners' vocabulary growth between 8 and 16 months, shown in Figure 9.5 (Caselli et al., 1995). Because rate of word learning between 18 and 24 months is so impressive (one or two words per day), many researchers concluded that toddlers undergo a *spurt in vocabulary*—a transition between a slow and a faster learning phase once the number of words produced reaches 50 to 100. But recent evidence indicates that most children do not experience a vocabulary spurt (Ganger & Brent, 2004). Rather, they show a steady, continuous increase in rate of word learning that persists through the preschool years, when children add as many as nine new words per day.

How do young children build their vocabularies so quickly? An improved ability to categorize experience (see Chapter 6), recall words, and pronounce new words is involved (Dapretto & Bjork, 2000; Stoel-Gammon, 2011). In addition, a better grasp of others' intentions, evident in toddlers' imitation around 18 months (see page 233), supports rapid vocabulary growth because it helps toddlers figure out what others are talking about (Golinkoff & Hirsh-Pasek, 2006; Tomasello, 2003). Furthermore, as toddlers' experiences broaden, they have a wider range of interesting objects and events to label. For example, children approaching age 2 more often mention places to go ("park," "store"). And as they construct a clearer self-image, they add more words that refer to themselves ("me," "mine," "Katy"), to their own and others' bodies and clothing ("eyes," "mouth," "jacket"), and to their attitudes, desires, and emotions ("like," "want," "happy," "mad,") (Hart, 2004).

Researchers have discovered that children can connect a new word with an underlying concept after only a brief encounter, a process called **fast-mapping.** Even 15- to 18-month-olds comprehend new labels remarkably quickly, but they need more repetitions of the word's use across several situations than preschoolers, who process speech-based information faster and are better able to categorize and recall it (Akhtar & Montague, 1999; Fernald, Perfors, & Marchman, 2006).

Toddlers' understanding of a fast-mapped word is incomplete at first, deepening with repeated exposure (Swingley, 2010). They start to form networks of related concepts and words, which help them fast-map new words, contributing to the age-related increase in rate of word learning. In one study, researchers gave 18-month-olds extended training on a set of novel words in 12 weekly sessions by showing the child pictures and talking about word meanings ("See the *crab*. The *crab* lives in the ocean"). Compared with no-practice controls, trained toddlers acquired a second set of novel words far more rapidly (Gershkoff-Stowe & Hahn, 2007). And preschoolers become adept at fast-mapping two or more new words encountered in the same situation (Wilkinson, Ross, & Diamond, 2003).

Individual and Cultural Differences Although children typically produce their first word around their first birthday, the range is large, from 8 to 18 months—variation due to a complex blend of genetic and environmental influences. Many studies show that girls are slightly ahead of boys in early vocabulary growth (Fenson et al., 1994; Van Hulle, Goldsmith, & Lemery, 2004). The most common biological explanation is girls' faster rate of physical maturation, which is believed to promote earlier development of the left cerebral hemisphere.

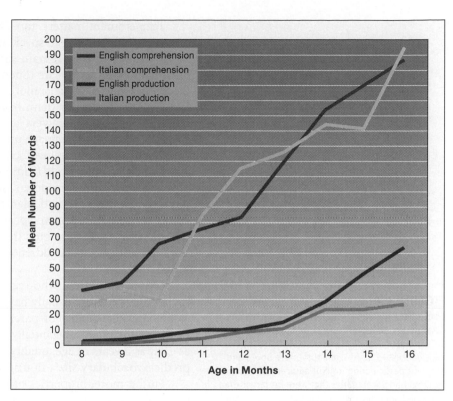

FIGURE 9.5 English and Italian learners' vocabulary growth between 8 and 16 months. Rate of word learning gradually accelerates. The increase in vocabulary size is far more rapid in comprehension than in production. (Reprinted from *Cognitive Development*, Vol. 10, No. 2, M. C. Caselli, et al., "A Cross-Linguistic Study of Early Lexical Development," p. 172, copyright 1995, with permission from Elsevier.)

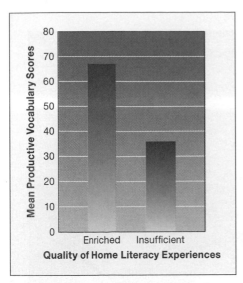

FIGURE 9.6 **Relationship of quality of home literacy experiences to productive vocabulary scores at age 2.** In families diverse in SES, 2-year-olds with rich home literacy experiences (access to many age-appropriate books and frequent participation in joint adult–child book-reading) had vocabularies that were far larger than those of 2-year-olds with insufficient literacy experiences. (Adapted from Tamis-LeMonda et al., 2006.)

This Chinese toddler probably's communication with her routines. As a result, communication with her an expressive style of early many words for social focused on building social relationship is likely to display learning,

Temperament matters, too. Shy toddlers often wait until they understand a great deal before trying to speak. Once they do speak, their vocabularies increase rapidly, although they remain slightly behind their agemates in language skills during the preschool years (Spere et al., 2004). Temperamentally negative toddlers also acquire language more slowly (Salley & Dixon, 2007). Their high emotional reactivity diverts them from processing linguistic information, and their relationships with caregivers are often conflict-ridden and, therefore, poorly suited to promoting language progress.

The quantity of caregiver–child conversation and richness of adults' vocabulary also play a strong role (Zimmerman et al., 2009). Commonly used words for objects appear early in toddlers' speech (refer again to Table 9.2), and the more often caregivers use a particular noun, the earlier that noun will become part of young children's productive vocabularies (Goodman, Dale, & Li, 2008). Mothers talk more to toddler-age girls than to boys, and parents converse less often with shy than with sociable children (Leaper, Anderson, & Sanders, 1998; Patterson & Fisher, 2002).

Low-SES children, who receive less verbal stimulation in their homes than higher-SES children, usually have smaller vocabularies (Hoff, 2006). In addition to amount and quality of parent–child interaction, limited parent–child book reading contributes substantially (see page 308 in Chapter 7). As Figure 9.6 shows, as early as 2 years of age, quality of children's home literacy experiences strongly predicts vocabulary size (Tamis-LeMonda et al., 2006).

Furthermore, properties of the child's native language are influential. Two-year-olds' spoken vocabularies vary substantially across languages—for example, about 180 to 200 words for children acquiring Swedish, 250 to 300 words for children acquiring English, and 500 words for children acquiring Mandarin Chinese (Bleses et al., 2008; Tardif et al., 2009). In Swedish, a complicated phonology makes syllable and word boundaries challenging to discriminate and pronounce. In contrast, Mandarin Chinese presents children with many short words that have easy-to-pronounce initial consonants. Within Mandarin words, each syllable is given one of four distinct tones, aiding discrimination.

Young children also have unique styles of early language learning, which affect early vocabulary development. Most toddlers use a **referential style;** their vocabularies consist mainly of words that refer to objects. A smaller number of toddlers use an **expressive style;** compared with referential children, they initially produce many more social formulas and pronouns ("thank you," "done," "I want it"), uttered as compressed phrases that sound like single words ("Iwannit"). Recall, from the opening to this chapter, Erin's early use of largely expressive-style words. These language styles reflect early ideas about the functions of language. Referential-style toddlers think words are for naming things, whereas expressive-style toddlers believe words are for talking about people's feelings and needs. The vocabularies of referential-style children grow faster because all languages contain many more nouns than social terms (Bates et al., 1994).

What accounts for a toddler's language style? Rapidly developing referential-style children often have an especially active interest in exploring objects. They also eagerly imitate their parents' frequent naming of objects, and their parents imitate back—a strategy that supports swift vocabulary growth by helping children remember new labels (Masur & Rodemaker, 1999). Expressive-style toddlers tend to be highly sociable, and their parents more often use verbal routines ("How are you?" "It's no trouble") that support social relationships (Goldfield, 1987).

The two language styles are also linked to culture. Nouns are particularly common in the vocabularies of English-speaking toddlers, but Chinese, Japanese, and Korean toddlers have more words for social routines. Mothers' speech in each culture reflects this difference (Choi & Gopnik, 1995; Fernald & Morikawa, 1993; Tardif, Gelman, & Xu, 1999). American mothers frequently label objects when interacting with their babies. Asian mothers, perhaps because of a cultural emphasis on the importance of group membership, teach social routines as soon as their children begin to speak.

Notice how these findings support the social interactionist perspective: Children's inner dispositions and their linguistic and social worlds combine to influence both rate and makeup of early language progress.

Types of Words Three types of words—object, action, and state—are most common in young children's vocabularies. Each provides important information about the course of semantic development.

Object and Action Words. Young language learners in many cultures have more object than action words in their beginning vocabularies (Bornstein & Cote, 2004; Kern, 2007). If actions are an especially important means through which infants learn about their world, why this early emphasis on naming objects?

One reason is that nouns refer to concepts (such as *table, bird,* or *dog*) that are easy to perceive (Gentner & Namy, 2004). When adults point to, label, and talk about an object, they help the child discern the word's meaning. In contrast, verbs require more complex understandings—of relationships between objects and actions. And when adults use a verb, the selected action usually is not taking place (Poulin-Dubois & Forbes, 2006). A parent who says the word *move* is probably referring to a past event ("Someone *moved* the bowl") or a future event ("Let's *move* the bowl"). Because learning verbs is more cognitively challenging, preschoolers speaking quite different languages take longer to extend a new verb ("*push* the bike") to other instances of the same action ("*push* the box") than they do to extend a novel noun to other objects in the same category (Imai et al., 2008). In mastering verb meanings, they benefit from many examples of the same verb used in different contexts.

Nevertheless, young children learning Chinese, Japanese, and Korean—languages in which nouns are often omitted from adults' sentences, while verbs are stressed—acquire verbs more readily than their English-speaking agemates (Kim, McGregor, & Thompson, 2000; Tardif, 2006). Besides increased exposure to verbs, Chinese-speaking children hear a greater variety of verbs denoting physical actions, which are easiest to master—for example, several verbs for *carry,* each referring to a different way of carrying, such as on one's back, in one's arms, or with one's hands (Ma et al., 2009).

State Words. Between 2 and 2½ years, children's use of *state* (or modifier) words expands to include labels for attributes of objects, such as size and color ("big," "red") and possession ("my toy," "Mommy purse"). Words referring to the functions of objects ("dump truck," "pickup truck") appear soon after (Nelson, 1976).

When state words are related in meaning, general distinctions (which are easier) appear before more specific ones. Thus, among words referring to the size of objects, children first acquire *big–small,* then *tall–short, high–low,* and *long–short,* and finally *wide–narrow* and *deep–shallow.* The same is true for temporal terms. Between ages 3 and 5, children first master *now–then* and *before–after,* followed by *today–yesterday* and *today–tomorrow* (Stevenson & Pollitt, 1987).

State words referring to object location provide additional examples of how cognition influences vocabulary development. Before age 2, children can easily imitate an adult's action in putting an object *in* or *on* another object, but they have trouble imitating the placement of one object *under* another. These terms appear in children's vocabularies in just this order, with all three achieved around age 2½ (Clark, 1983).

Because state words refer to qualities of objects and actions, children can use them to express a wide variety of concepts. As preschoolers master these words, their language becomes increasingly flexible.

Underextensions and Overextensions When young children first learn words, they often do not use them just as adults do. They may apply words too narrowly, an error called **underextension.** At 16 months, my younger son used the word "bear" to refer only to a

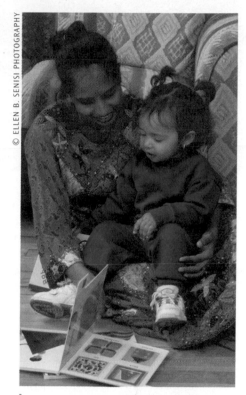

As this mother labels objects, her daughter adds those words to her growing vocabulary. In young language learners, acquisition of nouns often precedes verbs because nouns refer to easy-to-perceive concepts.

LOOK and LISTEN

Ask several parents of 15- to 20-month-olds to list all the words their child uses. Are the relative numbers of object, action, and state words consistent with research evidence? Ask the parents for examples of underextensions and overextensions.

When asked to name items their teacher removes from the can, these toddlers are likely to make the error of overextension—for example, call all the vehicles "cars." But they identify the objects accurately when the teacher names them.

special teddy bear to which he had become attached. A more common error between 1 and 2½ years is **overextension**—applying a word to a wider collection of objects and events than is appropriate. For example, a toddler might use the word "car" for buses, trains, trucks, and fire engines.

Toddlers' overextensions reflect their remarkable sensitivity to categorical relations. They apply a new word to a group of similar experiences, such as "dog" for any furry, four-legged animal or "open" to mean opening a door, peeling fruit, and untying shoe laces. Furthermore, the toddler who refers to trucks, trains, and bikes as "cars" is likely to point to these objects correctly when given their names in comprehension tasks (Naigles & Gelman, 1995). This suggests that children often overextend deliberately because they have difficulty recalling or have not acquired a suitable word. And when a word is hard to pronounce, toddlers frequently substitute a related one they can say (Bloom, 2000). As vocabulary and pronunciation improve, overextensions disappear.

Word Coinages and Metaphors Children as young as age 2 fill in for words they have not yet learned by coining new words based on ones they know—for example, "plant-man" for a gardener, or "crayoner" for a child using crayons. These early expressions reveal a remarkable, rule-governed approach to language.

Preschoolers also extend language meanings through metaphor—like the 3-year-old who described a stomachache as a "fire engine in my tummy" (Winner, 1988). Young preschoolers' metaphors involve concrete, sensory comparisons: "Clouds are pillows," "Leaves are dancers." As their vocabulary and knowledge of the world expand, children appreciate nonsensory comparisons: "Friends are like magnets," "Time flies by" (Keil, 1986; Özçalişkan, 2005). Metaphors permit children to communicate in especially vivid and memorable ways.

Later Semantic Development

During the elementary school years, vocabulary increases fourfold, eventually exceeding comprehension of 40,000 words (Anglin, 1993). On average, children learn about 20 new words each day, a rate of growth greater than in early childhood (see Figure 9.7). In addition to fast-mapping, older school-age children, especially those with excellent reading comprehension, enlarge their vocabularies by analyzing the structure of complex words. From *happy* and *decide,* they can derive the meanings of *happiness* and *decision* (Larsen & Nippold, 2007). They also figure out many more word meanings from context (Nagy & Scott, 2000).

As at earlier ages, children benefit from engaging in conversation with more expert speakers, especially when their partners use and explain complex words (Weizman & Snow, 2001). But because written language contains a far more diverse and complex vocabulary than spoken language, reading contributes enormously to vocabulary growth. Children who engage in as little as 21 minutes of independent reading per day are exposed to nearly 2 million words per year (Cunningham & Stanovich, 1998).

As their knowledge expands and becomes better organized (see Chapter 7), older school-age children think about and use words more precisely: In addition to the verb *fall,* for example, they also use *topple, tumble,* and *plummet* (Berman, 2007). Word definitions also illustrate this change. Five- and 6-year-olds offer concrete descriptions referring to functions or appearance—*knife:* "when you're cutting carrots"; *bicycle:* "it's got wheels, a chain, and handlebars." By the end of elementary school, synonyms and explanations of categorical relationships appear—*knife:* "Something you could cut with. A saw is like a knife. It could also be a weapon" (Wehren, De Lisi, & Arnold, 1981). This advance reflects older children's ability to deal with word meanings on an entirely verbal plane. They can add new words to their vocabulary simply by being given a definition.

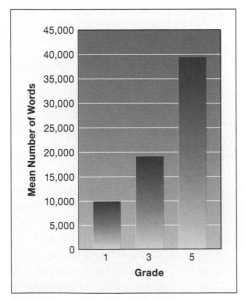

FIGURE 9.7 Estimated increase in vocabulary during the school years. Increase in word comprehension from grades 1 to 5 exceeds that of early childhood. (Adapted from Anglin, 1993.)

School-age children's more reflective and analytical approach to language permits them to appreciate the multiple meanings of words—to recognize, for example, that many words, such as *cool* or *neat,* have psychological as well as physical meanings: "What a cool shirt!" or "That movie was really neat!" This grasp of double meanings permits 8- to 10-year-olds to comprehend subtle metaphors, such as "sharp as a tack" and "spilling the beans" (Nippold, Taylor, & Baker, 1996; Wellman & Hickling, 1994). It also leads to a change in children's humor. Riddles and puns that alternate between different meanings of a key word are common: "Hey, did you take a bath?" "Why, is one missing?"

As they transition to adolescence, young people add a variety of abstract words—*counterintuitive, revolutionized, philosophy*—to their vocabularies. They also master sarcasm and irony and appreciate the difference between the two—that sarcasm is a critical comment directed at a specific target, whereas irony expresses unmet expectations that are not the fault of anyone in particular (Glenwright & Pexman, 2010; Winner, 1988). After his mother prepares a dish for dinner that he dislikes, an 11-year-old might quip sarcastically, "Oh boy, my favorite!" School-age children sometimes realize that a sarcastic remark is insincere if it is said in an exaggerated, mocking tone of voice. But adolescents need only notice the discrepancy between a statement and its context to grasp the intended meaning (Capelli, Nakagawa, & Madden, 1990).

Similarly, grasp of figurative language improves greatly in adolescence. Proverbs—especially those that express subtle attitudes—are especially challenging. They can be used to comment ("Blood is thicker than water"), interpret ("His bark is worse than his bite"), advise ("Humility often gains more than pride"), warn ("Of idleness comes no goodness"), and encourage ("Every cloud has a silver lining"). As with other aspects of semantic development, reading proficiency fosters understanding of proverbs (Nippold, Allen, & Kirsch, 2001). And a better grasp of figurative language enables teenagers to appreciate adult literary works.

Ideas About How Semantic Development Takes Place

Research shows that adult feedback facilitates semantic development. When adults go beyond correcting and explain ("That's not a car. It's a truck. See, it has a place to put things in"), toddlers are more likely to move toward conventional word meanings (Chapman, Leonard, & Mervis, 1986). Still, adults cannot tell children exactly what concept each new word picks out. If an adult points to a dog and says, "doggie," the word may refer to any four-legged animal, the dog's shaggy ears, or its barking sound. Therefore, the child's cognitive processing must play a major role.

The Influence of Memory Young children's fast-mapping is supported by a special part of short-term memory, a **phonological store** that permits us to retain speech-based information. The faster preschoolers can recall a just-presented sequence of nonsense words (a measure of phonological memory skill), the larger their current vocabulary and the greater their vocabulary growth over the following year (Gathercole et al., 1999; Parra, Hoff, & Core, 2010). This suggests that a child with good phonological memory has a better chance of transferring new words to long-term memory and linking them with relevant concepts.

By the end of the second year, phonological memory is so good that toddlers can recognize familiar words on the basis of their initial sounds. When given only the first two or three phonemes of a word they know ("ba" for "baby," "daw" for "doggie"), 18- to 24-month-olds looked at the correct object, responding as accurately and quickly as they did to the whole word. Furthermore, toddlers with better verbal recognition scores had larger productive vocabularies (Fernald, Swingley, & Pinto, 2001). Early in development, phonological memory is linked to advanced vocabulary development. Being able to identify a word rapidly on the basis of initial sounds has clear advantages: It frees working memory for other language tasks, such as comprehending longer and more complex strings of words.

But phonological memory does not provide a full account of word learning. After age 5, semantic knowledge influences the speed with which children form phonological traces, and both factors affect vocabulary growth (Gathercole et al., 1997). Even at younger ages (as we will see next), children rely heavily on words they know to detect the meanings of new ones.

LOOK and LISTEN

Record examples of 8- to 10-year-olds' humor, or examine storybooks for humor aimed at second through fourth graders. Does it require a grasp of the multiple meanings of words?

Strategies for Word Learning Young children figure out the meanings of words by contrasting them with words they already know and assigning the new label to a gap in their vocabulary. On hearing a new word in conversation, 2-year-olds repeat the word or acknowledge it with "yeah" or "uh-huh" in their next verbalization more than 60 percent of the time (Clark, 2007). These findings suggest that they assign the word a preliminary meaning and start to use it right away. Over time, they refine the word's meaning, striving to match its conventional use in their language community.

When learning a new noun, toddlers and preschoolers acquiring diverse languages tend to assume it refers to an object category at the basic level—an intermediate level of generality (see page 247 in Chapter 6). This preference helps young children narrow the range of possible meanings. Once they acquire a basic-level name *(dog)*, they add names at other hierarchical levels, both more general *(animal)* and more specific *(beagle, greyhound)* (Imai & Haryu, 2004; Waxman & Lidz, 2006).

How do children discover which concept each word picks out? This process is not yet fully understood. One speculation is that early in vocabulary growth, children adopt a **mutual exclusivity bias**—the assumption that words refer to entirely separate (nonoverlapping) categories (Markman, 1992). Two-year-olds seem to rely on mutual exclusivity when the objects named are perceptually distinct—for example, differ clearly in shape. After hearing the names for two distinct novel objects (a clip and a horn), they assign each word correctly, to the whole object and not to a part of it (Waxman & Senghas, 1992).

Indeed, children's first several hundred nouns refer mostly to objects well-organized by shape. Once toddlers have acquired about 75 words, a **shape bias** is clearly evident: Previous learning of nouns based on shape heightens attention to the shape properties of additional objects. In research in which toddlers repeatedly played with and heard names for novel objects of different shapes ("That's a *wif*") over a nine-week period, they soon formed the generalization that only similarly shaped objects have the same name (Smith et al., 2002; Yoshida & Smith, 2003). Toddlers with this training added more than three times as many object names to their vocabularies outside the laboratory as did untrained controls. Because shape is a perceptual property relevant to most object categories for which young preschoolers have already learned names, the shape bias helps them master additional names of objects, and vocabulary accelerates.

Once the name of a whole object is familiar, on hearing a new name for the object, 2- and 3-year-olds set aside the mutual exclusivity assumption. For example, if the object *(bottle)* has a part that stands out *(spout)*, children readily apply the new label to it (Hansen & Markman, 2009). In these instances, mutual exclusivity helps limit the possibilities the child must consider. Still, mutual exclusivity and object shape cannot account for preschoolers' remarkably flexible responses when objects have more than one name.

By age 3, preschoolers' memory, categorization, and language skills have expanded, and they readily assign multiple labels to many objects (Deák, Yen, & Pettit, 2001). For example, they refer to a sticker of a gray goose as "sticker," "goose," and "gray." Children often call on other components of language for help in these instances. According to one proposal, preschoolers discover many word meanings by observing how words are used in syntax, or the structure of sentences—a hypothesis called **syntactic bootstrapping** (Gleitman et al., 2005; Naigles & Swenson, 2007). Consider an adult who says, "This is a *citron* one," while showing a child a yellow car. Two- and 3-year-olds conclude that a new word used as an adjective for a familiar object (car) refers to a property of that object (Hall & Graham, 1999; Imai & Haryu, 2004). As preschoolers hear the word in various sentence structures ("That lemon is bright *citron*"), they use syntactic information to refine the word's meaning and generalize it to other categories.

Young children also take advantage of the rich social information that adults frequently provide when they introduce new words. For example, they often draw on their expanding ability to infer others' intentions and perspectives (Akhtar & Tomasello, 2000). In one study, an adult performed an action on an object and then used a new label while looking back

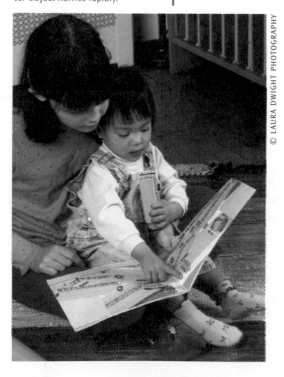

As her sister says, "It's a bus!," this 17-month-old points at a picture of a school bus while holding a toy bus in her hand. Heightened attention to object shape helps toddlers master object names rapidly.

© LAURA DWIGHT PHOTOGRAPHY

and forth between the child and the object, as if to invite the child to play. Two-year-olds concluded that the label referred to the action, not the object (Tomasello & Akhtar, 1995). Toddlers can even accurately interpret an adult's ambiguous request for an object ("Where's the ball?") by referring to their recent experience with that adult. They retrieve the particular object the adult had just played with (ball in a red bucket), not an identical object that another adult played with (ball in a blue bucket) (Saylor & Ganea, 2007). And 3-year-olds use information about a speaker's recently expressed desires (recalling which of two novel objects an adult said she liked) to figure out a word referent ("I really want to play with the *riff*") (Saylor & Troseth, 2006).

Adults also inform children directly about word meanings. Parents commonly highlight the meaning of adjectives by using the new label with several objects (a "red car," a "red truck")—information that helps children infer that the word refers to an object property (Hall, Burns, & Pawluski, 2003). And adults often explain which of two or more words to use, saying, for example: "You can call it a sea creature, but it's better to say *dolphin*." Parents who provide such clarifying information have preschoolers whose vocabularies grow more quickly (Callanan & Sabbagh, 2004; Deák, 2000).

Explaining Vocabulary Development Children acquire vocabulary so efficiently and accurately that some theorists believe that they are innately biased to induce word meanings using certain principles, such as mutual exclusivity and syntactic bootstrapping (Lidz, Gleitman, & Gleitman, 2004; Woodward & Markman, 1998). But critics observe that a small set of built-in, fixed principles is not sufficient to account for the varied, flexible manner in which children master vocabulary (Deák, 2000). And many word-learning strategies cannot be innate because children acquiring different languages use different approaches to mastering the same meanings. For example, English-speaking children rely on syntactic bootstrapping to tell the difference between one object ("This is *a dax*"), multiple objects of the same category ("Those are *daxes*"), and a proper name ("This is *Dax*") (Hall, Lee, & Belanger, 2001). In Japanese, all nouns are treated the same syntactically ("This is *dax*"). But Japanese preschoolers find ways to compensate for the missing syntactic cues, learning just as quickly as their English-speaking agemates (Imai & Haryu, 2001).

An alternative perspective is that vocabulary growth is governed by the same cognitive strategies that children apply to nonlinguistic stimuli. A recent account, called the **emergentist coalition model,** proposes that word-learning strategies *emerge* out of children's efforts to decipher language. Children draw on a *coalition* of cues—perceptual, social, and linguistic—that shift in importance with age (see Figure 9.8) (Golinkoff & Hirsh-Pasek, 2006). Infants rely solely on perceptual cues—for example, a parent shaking a toy while naming it. Toddlers, while still sensitive to perceptual features (such as object shape and physical action), increasingly attend to social cues—the speaker's direction of gaze and gestures (Hollich, Hirsh-Pasek, & Golinkoff, 2000; Pruden et al., 2006). And as language develops further, linguistic cues—syntax and intonation (stress, pitch, and loudness)—play larger roles.

Preschoolers are most successful at figuring out new word meanings when several kinds of information are available (Saylor, Baldwin, & Sabbagh, 2005). Researchers have just begun to study the multiple cues they use for different types of words and how their combined strategies change with development. We still have much to discover about how children's inner capacities join with patterns of information in the environment to yield the phenomenal pace of semantic development.

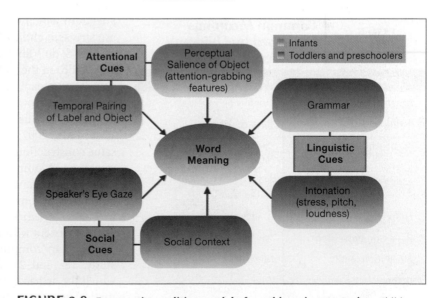

FIGURE 9.8 Emergentist coalition model of word-learning strategies. Children draw on a coalition of cues—perceptual, social, and linguistic—to infer word meanings. With age, these cues shift in importance. Infants rely solely on perceptual cues. While remaining sensitive to perceptual features, toddlers increasingly attend to social cues. As language develops further, preschoolers add linguistic cues. (From R. M. Golinkoff & K. Hirsh-Pasek, 2006, "Baby Wordsmith: From Associationist to Social Sophisticate," *Current Directions in Psychological Science*, Vol. 15, No. 1, p. 31, copyright © 2006, Association for Psychological Science. Reprinted by permission of SAGE Publications.)

ASK YOURSELF

Review ■ Using your knowledge of phonological and semantic development, explain why "Mama" and "Dada" are usually among children's first words.

Connect ■ Explain how children's strategies for word learning support an interactionist perspective on language development.

Apply ■ Katy's first words included "see," "give," and "thank you," and her vocabulary grew slowly during the second year. What style of language learning did she display, and what factors might have contributed to it?

Apply ■ At age 20 months, Nathan says "candy" when he sees buttons, pebbles, marbles, cough drops, and chocolate kisses. Are Nathan's naming errors random or systematic? Why are they an adaptive way of communicating?

▶ Describe the course of grammatical development.

▶ Discuss ideas about how grammatical development takes place, including strategies and communicative support for mastering new structures.

Grammatical Development

Studying children's grammar requires that they use more than one word in an utterance. Researchers have puzzled over the following questions about grammatical development: Do children build a consistent grammar resembling that of adults relatively easily and quickly, or do they acquire complex forms little by little? Are language-specific strategies, general cognitive strategies, or both involved in children's progress? What is the role of adult teaching—in particular, corrective feedback for grammatical errors? As we chart the course of grammatical development, we will consider evidence on these issues.

First Word Combinations

Sometime between 1½ and 2½ years, as productive vocabulary reaches 200 to 250 words, children transition from word–gesture combinations to joining two words: "Mommy shoe," "go car," "more cookie." These two-word utterances are called **telegraphic speech** because, like a telegram, they focus on high-content words and omit smaller, less important ones, such as *can, the,* and *to.* For children learning languages that emphasize word order, such as English and French, endings like *-s* and *-ed* are not yet present. In languages in which word order is flexible and small grammatical markers are stressed, children's first sentences include them from the start (de Villiers & de Villiers, 1999).

Children the world over use two-word utterances to express a wide variety of meanings (see Table 9.3). Are they applying a consistent grammar? According to one view, a more complete, and perhaps adult-like, grammar lies behind these two-word sentences (Gleitman et al., 1988; Lidz, 2007; Valian, 1991, 2005). Indeed, children often use the same construction to express different propositions. For example, a child might say, "Mommy cookie" when he sees his mother eating a cookie and also when he wants her to give him a cookie. Perhaps the more elaborate structures are present in the child's mind, but because of limited space in working memory, he cannot yet produce the longer word string.

Consistent with this idea, children seem more knowledgeable about grammar in comprehension than in production (Lidz, 2007). In one study, 18- and 24-month-olds listened to grammatical sentences in which the article *the* preceded a noun, as well as three types of ungrammatical sentences: *the* was dropped, replaced by a nonsense word (*el*), or replaced by an alternate English word (*and*), as follows: "*Can you see the/and/el ball?*" (Kedar, Casasola, & Lust, 2006). When presented with video images of objects, toddlers of both ages oriented more quickly and more accurately toward the correct object following grammatical sentences. Similarly, when shown two videos—one in which a duck acts on a bunny, the other in which a bunny acts on a duck—2-year-olds looked

TABLE 9.3	Common Meanings Expressed by Children's Two-Word Utterances
MEANING	**EXAMPLE**
Agent–action	"Tommy hit"
Action–object	"Give cookie"
Agent–object	"Mommy truck" (meaning "Mommy, push the truck")
Action–location	"Put table" (meaning "Put X on the table")
Entity–location	"Daddy outside"
Possessor–possession	"My truck"
Attribution–entity	"Big ball"
Demonstrative–entity	"That doggie"
Notice–noticed object	"Hi mommy"; "Hi truck"
Recurrence	"More milk"
Nonexistence–nonexistent or disappeared object	"No shirt"; "No more milk"

Source: Brown, 1973.

longer at the video event that correctly matched a sentence containing a novel verb ("The duck *is gorping* the bunny") (see Figure 9.9) (Gertner, Fisher, & Eisengart, 2006). This suggests that 2-year-olds have some awareness of subject-verb-object word order, which they generalize to comprehension of new verbs.

But other researchers point out that the study depicted in Figure 9.9 had a training phase, in which the same characters and nouns (*duck* and *bunny*) were presented with familiar verbs in subject-verb-object constructions. This may have primed 2-year-olds to look in the correct direction when tested with a novel verb (Dittmar et al., 2008). In subsequent research that eliminated any syntactic cues during training, 2-year-olds showed no preference for either video during testing (Chan et al., 2010). Not until close to age 3 did children show some evidence of looking more often at the correct illustration of the novel-verb sentence.

Additional findings confirm that toddlers do not yet have a consistent, flexible grammar. Rather, their two-word sentences are largely made up of simple formulas, such as "more + X" and "eat + X," with many different words inserted in the X position. Toddlers rarely make gross word-order errors, such as saying "chair my" instead of "my chair." But their word-order regularities are usually copies of adult word pairings: "How about *more sandwich*?" or "Let's see if you can *eat the berries*?" (Tomasello & Brandt, 2009). When children entering the two-word phase were taught several noun and verb nonsense words (for example, *meek* for a doll and *gop* for a snapping action), they easily combined the new nouns with words they knew well, as in "more meek." But they seldom produced word combinations with the new verbs (Tomasello, 2000; Tomasello et al., 1997).

Much evidence shows that children younger than age 3 do poorly when asked to use newly learned verbs in constructions in which they have not heard the verbs used before (Tomasello, 2003). Their inability to use verbs flexibly implies that they do not yet grasp subject–verb and verb–object relations—the foundation of English grammar. According to this alternative view, young children first acquire "concrete pieces of language" from frequent word pairings that they hear. Only gradually do they generalize from those pieces to construct the word-order and other grammatical rules of their native tongue (Bannard, Lieven, & Tomasello, 2009; Tomasello, 2006).

(a)   "The duck is gorping the bunny!"   (b)

FIGURE 9.9 Are English-learning 2-year-olds aware of subject–verb–object word order? Two-year-olds viewed two side-by-side videos accompanied by a sentence with a novel verb—for example, "The duck is *gorping* the bunny." They spent more time looking at the event that matched the sentence—in this case, the duck acting on the bunny rather than the bunny acting on the duck. But this conclusion is controversial; practice during the training phase of the study may have primed 2-year-olds to look in the correct direction. (From Y. Gertner, C. Fisher, & J. Eisengart, 2006, "Learning Words and Rules: Abstract Knowledge of Word Order in Early Sentence Comprehension," *Psychological Science, 17,* p. 686. Reprinted by permission.)

From Simple Sentences to Complex Grammar

In the third year, three-word sentences appear in which English-speaking children clearly follow a subject–verb–object word order. Children learning other languages adopt the word order of the adult speech they hear. For "It is broken," a German child says, "*Kaputt ist der*" (literally, "Broken is it"). Between ages 2½ and 3, children create sentences in which adjectives, articles, nouns, verbs, and prepositional phrases start to conform to an adult structure, indicating that they have begun to master the grammatical categories of their language.

Gradual Mastery of Grammatical Structures Nevertheless, studies of children acquiring diverse languages, including Dutch, English, Hebrew, Inuktitut (spoken by the Inuit of Arctic Canada), Italian, Portuguese, and Russian, reveal that their first use of grammatical rules is piecemeal—applied to only one or a few verbs, not across the board. As children listen for familiar verbs in adult discourse, they expand their own utterances containing those verbs, drawing on adult usage as their model (Allen, 1996; Gathercole, Sebastián, & Soto, 1999; Lieven, Pine, & Baldwin, 1997; Stoll, 1998). One child, for example, added the preposition *with* to the verb *open* ("You open with scissors") but not to the word *hit* ("He hit me stick").

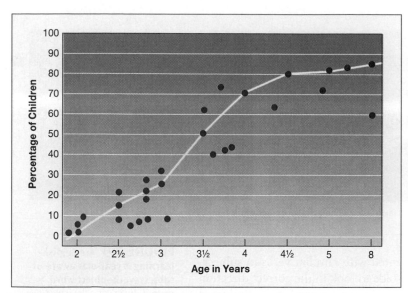

FIGURE 9.10 Percentage of children in different studies who could use a new verb in the subject–verb–object form after hearing it in another construction. Each dot in the graph represents the findings of one study. Ability to use the new verb—an indicator of the child's capacity to apply the subject–verb–object structure broadly—rose steadily with age. Children master this fundamental grammatical construction gradually. (Reprinted from *Cognition*, Vol. 74, No. 3, M. Tomasello, "Do Young Children Have Adult Syntactic Competence?" p. 223, copyright 2000, with permission from Elsevier.)

Only gradually do preschoolers refine and generalize their early grammatical forms. In a number of investigations, English-learning children were tested for their ability to produce novel sentences that conformed to basic English syntax. They had to use a new verb in the subject–verb–object form after hearing it in a different construction, such as passive ("Ernie is getting *gorped* by the dog"). The percentage of children who performed well (when asked what the dog was doing, they responded, "He's *gorping* Ernie") rose steadily with age. But as Figure 9.10 shows, not until 3½ to 4 could the majority of children apply the fundamental subject–verb–object structure broadly, to newly acquired verbs (Chan et al., 2010; Tomasello, 2003, 2006).

Because English relies on word order to express basic meanings, English-speaking preschoolers grasp unusual subject–verb–object expressions—an inanimate subject acting on an animate object, as in "The cup *meeks* the chicken," where *meek* means push—between ages 3 and 4. In languages where word order often deviates from the subject–verb–object construction, such as German and Cantonese Chinese, many 3½-year-olds prefer the reverse interpretation; they assume the animate noun (chicken) to be the agent (the chicken *meeks* the cup) (Chan, Lieven, & Tomasello, 2009). As these findings indicate, the age at which children flexibly grasp subject–verb–object word order depends on how available and consistent the form is in the child's language environment.

Development of Grammatical Morphemes Once children form three-word sentences, they add **grammatical morphemes**[1]—small markers that change the meaning of sentences, as in "John's dog" and "he *is* eating." English-speaking 2- and 3-year-olds acquire these morphemes in a regular sequence, shown in Table 9.4 (Brown, 1973; de Villiers & de Villiers, 1973). Given the difficulty of the task, however, their errors are surprisingly few (Maratsos, 1998).

What explains this sequence of development? Two characteristics of morphemes play important roles. The first is *structural complexity*. For example, adding the ending *-ing* or *-s* is structurally less complex than using forms of the verb *to be*. In the latter, the child must express correct tense and also make the subject and verb agree ("I *am* coming" versus "They *are* coming"). Second, grammatical morphemes differ in *semantic complexity*, or the number and difficulty of the meanings they express. Adding *-s* to a word requires only one semantic distinction—the difference between one and more than one. In contrast, using *to be* involves many more, including an understanding of person, number, and time of occurrence (Slobin, 1982).

Look again at Table 9.4, and you will see that some morphemes with irregular forms are acquired before those with regular forms. For example, children use past-tense irregular verbs, such as *ran* and *broke*, before they acquire the regular *-ed* ending. But once children apply a regular morphological rule, they extend it to words that are exceptions, a type of error called **overregularization.** Expressions like "My toy car *breaked*" and "We each have two *foots*" appear between 2 and 3 years of age and persist into middle childhood (Marcus et al., 1992). Children less often make this error on frequently used irregular verbs, such as the past tense of *go (went)* and *say (said).* For rarely used verbs such as *grow* and *sing,* the error rate can be higher than 50 percent (Maratsos, 2000).

---

[1]A *morpheme* is the smallest unit of meaning in speech; any further division violates the meaning or produces meaningless units. Both "dog" and "-s" are morphemes; "-s" is a *grammatical morpheme.*

Why do children show this inconsistent pattern? Because they hear frequently used irregular forms often in adult speech, they probably learn those by rote memory. For less common irregulars, children alternate between correct and overregularized forms for months or even several years. According to one view, as children hear more instances in others' speech, the irregular form eventually wins out (Elman, 2003; Maratsos, 2000). At times, however, preschoolers do overregularize frequently used exceptions, as when they say "ated," "felled," or "feets." In these instances, perhaps their memory for the irregular morpheme fails, so they call on the –*ed* or –*s* rule, and overregularization results.

Development of Complex Grammatical Forms

Once children master the auxiliary verb *to be,* the door is open to a variety of new expressions. Negatives and questions are examples.

Negatives Three types of negation appear in the following order in 2½- to 3-year-olds learning languages as different as Cantonese, English, and Tamil (spoken in India): (1) *nonexistence,* in which the child remarks on the absence of something ("No cookie," "All gone crackers"); (2) *rejection,* in which the child expresses opposition to something ("No take bath"); and (3) *denial,* in which the child denies the truthfulness of something ("That not my kitty") (Clancy, 1985; Tam & Stokes, 2001; Vaidyanathan, 1991).

These early constructions probably result from imitating parental speech. When parents express nonexistence or rejection, they often put *no* at the beginning of the sentence: "No more cookies" or "No, you can't have another cracker." Around 3 to 3½ years, as children add auxiliary verbs and become sensitive to the way they combine with negatives, correct negative forms appear: "There aren't any more cookies" (nonexistence), "I don't want a bath" (rejection), and "That isn't my kitty" (denial) (Tager-Flusberg & Zukowski, 2009).

Questions Like negatives, questions first appear during the early preschool years and develop in an orderly sequence. English-speaking children, as well as those who speak many other languages, can use rising intonation to convert an utterance into a yes/no question: "Mommy baking cookies?" As a result, they produce such expressions quite early.

Correct question form in English requires that children invert the subject and auxiliary verb. In *wh-* questions—ones that begin with *what, where, which, who, when, why,* and *how*—the *wh-* word must also be placed at the beginning of the sentence. When first creating questions, 2-year-olds use many formulas: "Where's *X*?" "What's *X*?" "Can I *X*?" (Dabrowska, 2000; Tomasello, 1992, 2003). Preschoolers' question asking remains variable for a couple of years. A common error is to omit the auxiliary verb ("What he doing?"). Another is to fail to invert the subject and auxiliary verb when asking certain questions ("What she will do?" "Why he can go?") but not others ("How do you like it?" "What do you want?") (Rowland et al., 2005; Rowland & Pine, 2000). The correct expressions tend to be those that occur most often in caregivers' speech. And sometimes children produce errors in subject–auxiliary verb agreement ("Where does the dogs play?") and

| TABLE 9.4 | Order of Acquisition of English Grammatical Morphemes |

MORPHEME	EXAMPLE
1. Verb present progressive ending ("-ing")	"He singing."
2. Preposition "on"	"On horsie."
3. Preposition "in"	"In wagon."
4. Noun plural ("-s")	"Cats."
5. Verb irregular past tense	"He ran." "It broke."
6. Noun possessive	"Daddy's hat."
7. Verb uncontractible "be" form used with adjective, preposition, or noun phrase	"Are kitties sleepy?"
8. Articles "a and "the"	"A cookie." "The bunny."
9. Verb regular past tense ending ("-ed")	"He kicked it."
10. Verb present tense, third person singular regular ending	"He likes it."
11. Verb present tense, third person singular irregular ending	"She has [from *have*] a cookie." "He does [from *do*] a good job."
12. Auxiliary verb uncontractible "be" forms	"Are you eating?"
13. Verb contractible "be" forms used with adjective, preposition, or noun phrase	"He's inside." "They're sleepy."
14. Auxiliary verb contractible "be" forms	"He's coming." "Doggie's eating."

Source: Brown, 1973.

As she sorts berries with her mother, this 3-year-old is acquiring Bhoti, the language of her community in India. Like English-speaking preschoolers, she is likely to master yes/no questions before *wh-* questions, which are semantically and structurally more difficult.

in subject case ("Where can me sit?"). These diverse errors are difficult to reconcile with the existence of a built-in universal grammar (Rowland, 2007). As with other grammatical constructions, children seem to produce accurate questions piecemeal and gradually.

Among English-, Korean-, and Tamil-speaking preschoolers, correct question form appears first for yes/no and later for *wh-* constructions (Clancy, 1989; Vaidyanathan, 1988). Among *wh-* questions, which are semantically and structurally more difficult, *what, where,* and *who* tend to precede *how, why,* and *when,* which are harder to understand and answer (de Villiers, 2000).

Other Complex Constructions Between ages 3½ and 6, children produce more intricate constructions. First, connectives appear, joining whole sentences ("Mom picked me up, *and* we went to the park") and verb phrases ("I got up *and* ate breakfast"). The most general connective, *and,* is used first, followed by connectives expressing more specific meanings: *then* and *when* for temporal relations, *because* and *so* for causal relations, *or* for exclusion, *if* for conditionals, and *but* for opposition (Bloom et al., 1980). As with other grammatical forms, first use of connectives is piecemeal, largely limited to imitations of parental use (Morris, 2008). Over time, preschoolers' use increasingly conforms to the rules of their language.

Later, children produce embedded sentences ("I think *he will come*"), tag questions ("Dad's going to be home soon, *isn't he?*"), indirect object–direct object structures ("He showed *his friend* the present"), and passive sentences ("The dog *was patted by* the girl"). As the preschool years draw to a close, children use most grammatical structures of their native language competently (Tager-Flusberg & Zukowski, 2009).

Later Grammatical Development

During the school years, mastery of complex constructions improves. For example, English-speaking children use the passive voice more frequently, and they more often extend it from an abbreviated structure ("It got broken") into full statements ("The glass was broken by Mary") (Israel, Johnson, & Brooks, 2000; Tomasello, 2006). Older children also apply the passive voice to a wider range of nouns and verbs. Preschoolers comprehend the passive best when the subject of the sentence is an animate being and the verb is an action word ("The *boy is kissed* by the girl"). Over the school years, children extend the passive form to inanimate subjects ("The *hat* was worn by the man") and experiential verbs ("The dog *was seen* by the cat") (Lempert, 1990; Pinker, Lebeaux, & Frost, 1987).

Although the passive form is challenging, once again language input makes a difference. English-speaking adults rarely use full and experiential passives in everyday conversation. In languages in which adults use these forms often, such as Inuktitut (spoken by the Inuit people), children produce them earlier (Allen & Crago, 1996). And exposure to adult speech containing a variety of passive-sentence types (as opposed to just one type) prompts 4- and 5-year-olds to produce more passive utterances (Savage et al., 2006). Varied input seems to foster a general representation of the passive construction.

Another later grammatical achievement is advanced understanding of infinitive phrases—the difference between "John is eager to please" and "John is easy to please" (Berman, 2007; Chomsky, 1969). Like gains in vocabulary, appreciation of these subtle grammatical distinctions in middle childhood and adolescence is supported by an improved capacity to analyze and reflect on language and to attend to multiple linguistic and situational cues.

Ideas About How Grammatical Development Takes Place

Preschoolers' mastery of most of the grammar of their language is an astounding feat. How to explain it is perhaps the most disputed issue in the study of language development.

Strategies for Acquiring Grammar Evidence that grammatical development is an extended, learned process, beginning with knowledge of specific instances and building toward general categories and rules, has raised questions about Chomsky's nativist account. Some experts have concluded that grammar is a product of general cognitive development—children's tendency to search for consistencies and patterns of all sorts (Bloom, 1999; MacWhinney, 2005; Maratsos, 1998; Tomasello, 2003, 2006). Yet among these theorists, debate continues over just how children master grammar.

According to one view, young children rely on other properties of language to detect basic grammatical regularities. In **semantic bootstrapping,** for example, they use word meanings to figure out sentence structure. Children might begin by grouping together words with "agent qualities" (things that cause actions) as *subjects* and words with "action qualities" as *verbs*. Then they merge these categories with observations of how words are used in sentences (Bates & MacWhinney, 1987; Braine, 1994). In this way, children lay down a basic grammatical framework, which they modify over time to account for exceptions. In some languages, however, semantic categories (such as "agent") and basic grammatical structures (such as "subject") do not match up—a major problem for semantic bootstrapping. In Tagalog, a language spoken in the Philippines, certain agents can be subjects, but others cannot. Yet Tagalog-speaking children acquire the main grammar of their language within a typical time frame (Maratsos, 1998).

Other theorists believe that children master grammar through direct observation of the structure of language: They notice which words appear in the same positions in sentences, take the same morphological endings, and are similarly combined with other words. Over time, from exposure to many instances, they group words into grammatical categories and use them appropriately in sentences (Bannard, Lieven, & Tomasello, 2009; Bloom, 1999; Chang, Dell, & Bock, 2006; Tomasello, 2003, 2011).

Still other theorists agree with the essence of Chomsky's position. One idea accepts semantic bootstrapping but proposes that the grammatical categories into which children group word meanings are innate—present at the outset (Pinker, 1989, 1999). Another theory holds that children do not start with innate knowledge but have a special *language-making capacity*—a set of procedures for analyzing the language they hear that supports the discovery of grammatical regularities. Research on children learning more than 40 different languages reveals common patterns, consistent with a basic set of strategies (Slobin, 1985, 1997). Yet controversy persists over whether a universal language-processing device exists or whether children who hear different languages devise unique strategies (Lidz, 2007; Marchman & Thal, 2005).

Communicative Support for Grammatical Development Besides investigating the child's capacities, researchers have examined features of adult–child communication that might ease the task of mastering grammar. Previous research reported that although adults frequently correct children's mistaken inferences about word meaning ("That's not a bird, it's a butterfly"), they rarely provide direct feedback about grammar (Brown & Hanlon, 1970). Yet parents often correct their child's grammatical errors *indirectly*—in ways that inform the child about conventional usage while keeping the conversation going.

Responding to these 2-year-olds, a preschool teacher expands their brief sentences and recasts them into grammatically correct form—techniques that inform children about correct grammar.

In a study in which three English-learning and two French-learning children were followed from ages 2 to 4, researchers coded thousands of utterances for errors in pronunciation, word choice, and grammar, along with parents' immediate responses and children's reactions to those responses (Chouinard & Clark, 2003). Findings revealed that parents reformulated as many as two-thirds of children's erroneous expressions—a rate that was similar across the error types and the five children.

Many adult reformulations inform children about grammar through two techniques, often used in combination: **recasts**—restructuring inaccurate speech into correct form; and **expansions**—elaborating on children's speech, increasing its complexity (Bohannon & Stanowicz, 1988). For example, if a child says, "I gotted new red shoes," the parent might respond, "Yes, you got a pair of new red shoes," *recasting* the incorrect features of the child's statement while also *expanding* its complexity. After such corrective input, 2- to 4-year-olds often shift to correct forms—improvements still evident several months later (Saxton, Backley, & Gallaway, 2005).

Other grammatical prompts ask children to clarify what they mean so interaction can continue. For example, when a 2½-year-old said, "I want hugging Ava," his mother queried, "What do you want?" In one study, such error-contingent clarifying questions led 2½-year-olds to shift from an incorrect to a correct form 16 percent of the time, and 4-year-olds 34 percent of the time (Saxton, Houston-Price, & Dawson, 2005). Clarifying questions may encourage children to reflect on their utterances and apply what they know about correct grammar more consistently.

Nevertheless, the impact of such feedback has been challenged. The techniques are not used in all cultures and, in a few investigations, did not affect children's grammar (Strapp & Federico, 2000; Valian, 1999). But in some societies, older siblings may take over the task of providing young children with feedback, and parents may do so in other culturally pre-scribed ways. For example, on certain occasions, New Guinean Kaluli and Western Samoan adults tell children what to say by facing the child toward her listener, speaking for the child, and commanding, *"Elema,"* which means, "Say like that" (Ochs, 1988). Low-SES Western parents engage in similar practices (Hart & Risley, 1995).

In sum, virtually all investigators agree that young children are amazing processors of linguistic structure. But the extent to which adult communication helps children correct errors and take the next grammatical step forward remains a contested issue in child language research.

A S K   Y O U R S E L F

Review ■ To what extent do children use a consistent grammar in their early two- and three-word utterances? Explain, using research evidence.

Connect ■ Provide several examples of how children's cognitive development influences their mastery of grammar.

Apply ■ Three-year-old Jason's mother told him that the family would take a vacation in Miami. The next morning, Jason announced, "I gotted my bags packed. When are we going to Your-ami?" How do language researchers explain Jason's errors?

Reflect ■ Do you favor a nativist, an information-processing, or a social interactionist account of grammatical development, or some combination? Use research evidence to support your position.

▶ Describe the course of pragmatic development.

Pragmatic Development

Besides mastering phonology, vocabulary, and grammar, children must learn to use language effectively in social contexts—by taking turns, staying on the same topic, stating their messages clearly, and conforming to cultural rules for interaction. During the preschool years, children make considerable headway in mastering the pragmatics of language.

Acquiring Conversational Skills

Young children are already skilled conversationalists. In face-to-face interaction, they make eye contact, respond appropriately to their partner's remarks, and take turns (Pan & Snow, 1999). With age, the number of turns over which children can sustain interaction and their ability to maintain a topic over time increase, but even 2-year-olds converse effectively (Snow et al., 1996).

In early childhood, additional conversational strategies are added. In the **turnabout,** the speaker not only comments on what has just been said but also adds a request to get the partner to respond again. Because 2-year-olds cannot generate many words in each turn, they seldom use turnabouts, but children do so increasingly over the next few years (Goelman, 1986). Between ages 5 and 9, more advanced conversational strategies appear, such as **shading,** in which a speaker initiates a change of topic gradually by modifying the focus of discussion (Wanska & Bedrosian, 1985).

Effective conversation also depends on understanding **illocutionary intent**—what a speaker means to say, even if the form of the utterance is not perfectly consistent with it. By age 3, children comprehend a variety of requests for action not directly expressed as requests:

"I need a pencil" or "Why don't you tickle me?" (Garvey, 1974). During middle childhood, illocutionary knowledge develops further. For example, an 8-year-old who has forgotten to do his chores understands that when his mother says, "The garbage is beginning to smell," she really means, "Take that garbage out!" (Ackerman, 1978). Appreciating form–intention pairings like this one requires children to make subtle inferences that are beyond preschoolers' cognitive capacities.

Still, surprisingly advanced conversational abilities are present early, and adults' patient, sensitive interactions with young children encourage and sustain them. Throughout this chapter, we have seen examples of how adult–child conversation fosters language development. Whether observed at home or in preschool, it is consistently related to general measures of language progress (Hart & Risley, 1995; NICHD Early Child Care Research Network, 2006). Dialogues with caregivers about storybooks are particularly effective (Hoff, 2010). They expose children to great breadth of language knowledge, including how to communicate in a clear, coherent narrative style—a skill that undoubtedly contributes to the association between joint storybook reading and literacy development (see Chapter 7, page 308).

Finally, the presence of a sibling enhances young children's conversational skills. Toddlers closely monitor conversations between their twin or older siblings and parents, and they often try to join in. When they do, these verbal exchanges last longer, with each participant taking more turns (Barton & Strosberg, 1997; Barton & Tomasello, 1991). As they listen to these conversations, younger siblings pick up important skills, such as use of personal pronouns ("I" versus "you"), which are more common in the early vocabularies of later-born than of first-born siblings (Pine, 1995). Furthermore, older siblings' remarks to a younger brother or sister often focus on regulating interaction: "Do you like Kermit?" "OK, your turn" (Oshima-Takane & Robbins, 2003). This emphasis probably contributes to younger siblings' conversational skills.

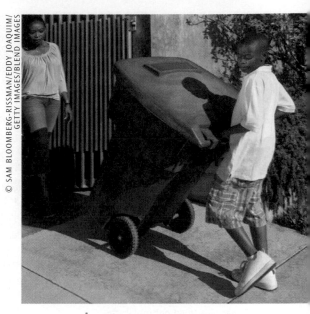

When his mother exclaims, "It's trash pickup day!" this 10-year-old comprehends her statement as an indirect request to wheel the trash can out to the curb. Understanding of illocutionary intent improves in middle childhood.

Communicating Clearly

To communicate effectively, we must produce clear verbal messages and recognize when messages we receive are unclear so we can ask for more information. These aspects of language are called **referential communication skills.**

Typically, laboratory tasks designed to assess children's ability to communicate clearly present them with challenging situations in which they must describe to a listener one object among a group of similar objects. For example, in one study, 3- to 10-year-olds were shown several eight-object arrays. In each, the objects were similar in size, shape, and color. Most 3-year-olds gave ambiguous descriptions. When asked for clarification, they relied heavily on gestures, such as pointing (Deutsch & Pechmann, 1982). The ability to send clear messages improved steadily with age.

When preschoolers are given simpler tasks or engage in face-to-face interaction with familiar people, they adjust their speech to their listener's perspective quite well. **TAKE A MOMENT...** But try engaging a preschooler in conversation on the telephone, jotting down what you and the child say. Here is an excerpt of one 4-year-old's phone conversation with his grandfather:

> *Grandfather:* How old will you be?
> *John:* Dis many. *[Holding up four fingers.]*
> *Grandfather:* Huh?
> *John:* Dis many. *[Again holding up four fingers.]* (Warren & Tate, 1992, pp. 259–260)

Young children's conversations appear less mature in highly demanding situations in which they cannot see their listeners' reactions or rely on typical conversational aids, such as gestures and objects to talk about. But when asked to tell a listener how to solve a simple puzzle, 3- to 6-year-olds give more specific directions over the phone than in person, indicating that they realize the need for more verbal description on the phone (Cameron & Lee, 1997). Between ages 4 and 8, both conversing and giving directions over the phone improve

FIGURE 9.11 **Testing for referential communication skills.** When an adult instructed, "Put the frog on the book in the box," 4- and 5-year-olds could not resolve the ambiguity between the phrases "on the book" and "in the box." They stuck to their first inference and put one of the frogs on the empty book. Not until middle childhood can children integrate the two competing representations by selecting the frog on the book and placing it in the box. (Adapted from Hurewitz et al., 2000.)

greatly. Telephone talk provides an excellent example of how preschoolers' communication skills depend on the demands of the situation.

Children's ability to evaluate the adequacy of messages they receive also improves with age. Around age 3, preschoolers start to ask others to clarify ambiguous messages. At first, children recognize when a message provides a poor description of a concrete object (Ackerman, 1993). Only later can they tell when a message contains inconsistencies. For example, when researchers showed 4- and 5-year-olds the scene in Figure 9.11 and instructed, "Put the frog on the book in the box," preschoolers could not resolve the ambiguity. Most put a frog on the empty book rather than in the box, even though they used similar embedded phrases in their own speech ("The frog *on the book* went to Mrs. Squid's house") (Hurewitz et al., 2000).

Notice how this task requires children to *inhibit* attention from being drawn to the empty book in the scene, which increases the salience of the first part of the directive, "Put the frog *on the book*." When asked to listen to the instruction with their back to the display, which temporarily blocked the scene's distracting features, almost all 4- and 5-year-olds processed the entire message and responded correctly (Meroni & Crain, 2003).

Narratives

Conversations with adults about past experiences contribute to dramatic gains in children's ability to produce well-organized, detailed, expressive narratives (see page 299 in Chapter 7). When asked to relate a personally important event, 4-year-olds typically produce brief renditions called *leapfrog narratives,* jumping from one event to another in a disorganized fashion. Between 4½ and 5, children start to produce *chronological narratives,* placing events in temporal sequence and building to a high point: "We went to the lake. We fished and waited. Paul waited, and he got a huge catfish." Around age 6, chronological narratives extend into *classic narratives,* in which children add a resolution: "After Dad cleaned the catfish, we cooked it and ate it all up!" (McCabe & Bliss, 2003).

Preschoolers' limited working memories are partly responsible for their restricted narratives. In addition, young children often presume more shared knowledge than their listener has, so they offer little orienting information about events, such as time, place, and participants. Preschoolers' narratives also contain few *evaluations*—comments about how and why events took place or about their own and others' thoughts, feelings, and intentions. During middle childhood, orienting information, detailed descriptions, and connectives that lend coherence to the story ("next," "then," "so," "finally") increase. And evaluative comments rise steadily in middle childhood and adolescence (Melzi & Ely, 2009). When parents use the elaborative strategy discussed in Chapter 7 to help young children construct narratives, preschoolers produce more organized, detailed, and evaluative personal stories (see page 299).

Like narrative, make-believe play requires children to organize events around a plot, constructing a connected, meaningful story line. Pretend-play and narrative competence support each other (Nicolopoulou, 2006). When 4-year-olds created narratives in a make-believe context ("Tell me a story using these toys"), they generated more complex, coherent stories than agemates who were directly prompted (Ilgaz & Aksu-Koç, 2005). The pretend props and actions served as powerful cues for narrative events, reducing memory demands during storytelling. And in a school program, 5- to 7-year-olds who participated in 14 weeks of joint adult–child dramatization of a work of children's literature showed greater gains in narrative development than agemates who merely listened to an adult read the story over 14 sessions, with no playacting (Baumer, Ferholt, & Lecusay, 2005).

Because children pick up the narrative styles of parents and other significant adults in their lives, their narrative forms vary widely across cultures. As noted in Chapter 8, instead of relating a

A class of preschoolers reenacts the first Thanksgiving as Pilgrims and Indians. Make-believe experiences with props that cue story events reduce memory demands, enabling young children to generate more complex, coherent narratives.

single experience from beginning to end, African-American children often use a *topic-associating style*, blending several similar anecdotes. As a result, their narratives are usually longer and more complex than those of American white children (Champion, 2003b). Japanese children also connect events with a common theme, using a structure that resembles *haiku*, a culturally valued poetic form (Minami, 1996).

The ability to generate clear oral narratives contributes to literacy development, enhancing reading comprehension and preparing children for producing longer, more explicit written narratives. In families who regularly eat meals together, children are advanced in language and literacy development, perhaps because mealtimes offer many opportunities to listen to and relate personal stories (Snow & Beals, 2006).

Sociolinguistic Understanding

As early as the preschool years, children are sensitive to language adaptations to social expectations, known as **speech registers.** In one study, 4- to 7-year-olds were asked to act out roles with hand puppets. Even the youngest children showed that they understood the stereotypic features of different social positions. They used more commands when playing socially dominant and male roles, such as teacher, doctor, and father. When playing less dominant and feminine roles, such as student, patient, and mother, they spoke more politely and used more indirect requests (Andersen, 1992, 2000).

The importance of register adjustments is evident in how often parents teach social routines, such as politeness. Before infants can grasp the gesture's meaning, parents encourage them to wave "bye-bye." By age 2, when children fail to say "please" and "thank you," or "hi" and "good-bye," parents often model and demand an appropriate response.

Some cultures have elaborate systems of polite language. In Japan, for example, politeness affects many aspects of verbal and nonverbal communication, which vary with gender, age, social status, and familiarity of speaker and listener. Japanese mothers and preschool teachers constantly model and teach these expressions as a means of promoting in children a kind, considerate attitude toward others. As a result, preschoolers acquire a large repertoire of polite forms (Burdelski, 2010; Nakamura, 2001). When greeting customers in a make-believe store, even 1-year-olds use the greeting *"Irasshaimase!"* ("Welcome!"). Two- and 3-year-olds use more complicated polite speech, such as *"Mata oide-kudasai"* ("Please come again"). And 3- and 4-year-olds make considerable headway in acquiring the complex honorific/humble language of Japanese society, which is fully mastered in middle childhood.

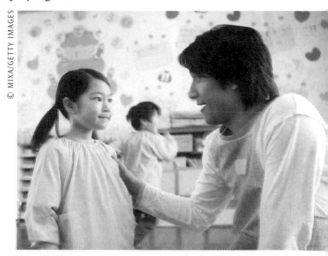

This Japanese kindergartner uses the correct expression of respect when addressing her teacher, thereby acknowledging his high social status. She is well on her way to mastering her culture's elaborate system of polite forms.

Adolescence brings dramatic gains in capacity to adapt language style to social context, in part because teenagers enter many more situations than they did at younger ages. To succeed on the debate team, they must speak in a persuasive, well-organized, rapid-fire fashion. At work, they must respond to customers cheerfully and courteously. On a date, they must communicate with heightened sensitivity and intimacy. Greater skill at reflecting on the features of language and engaging in cognitive self-regulation also supports effective use of speech registers (Obler, 2008). Teenagers are far more likely than school-age children to practice what they want to say in an expected situation, review what they did say, and figure out how they could say it better.

ASK YOURSELF

Review ■ Summarize findings indicating that adult–child conversations promote preschoolers' pragmatic skills.

Connect ■ What cognitive advances contribute to the development of referential communication?

Apply ■ What pragmatic skills are evident in Erin's utterances, presented in the introduction to this chapter? How did Erin's parents and brother encourage her pragmatic development?

Reflect ■ List examples of speech registers you use in daily life. What childhood experiences might have influenced your mastery of these registers?

▶ Describe the development of metalinguistic awareness and its role in language-related attainments.

Development of Metalinguistic Awareness

Consider the following exchange between a mother and her 5-year-old child:

Child: What's that?
Mother: It's a food processer.
Child: [*frowning*] No, you're the food processer, that's a food process.

This preschooler, conscious of word endings, expected *-er* to signify an animate agent, like *baker* or *dancer*. The child shows the beginnings of **metalinguistic awareness**—the ability to think about language as a system. Researchers have been especially interested in when metalinguistic awareness emerges and the role it plays in a variety of language-related accomplishments.

Around age 4, children know that word labels are arbitrary and not part of the objects to which they refer. When asked if an object could be called by a different name in a new language, they say "yes." They can also make some basic syntactic judgments—for example, that a puppet who says, "Nose your touch" or "Dog the pat," is saying his sentences backwards (Chaney, 1992). And by age 5, children have a good sense of the concept of "word." When an adult reading a story stops to ask, "What was the last word I said?" they almost always answer correctly for all parts of speech—they do not say "on-the-floor" instead of "floor" or "is-a" instead of "a" (Karmiloff-Smith et al., 1996). These early metalinguistic understandings are good predictors of vocabulary and grammatical development (Smith & Tager-Flusberg, 1982).

Nevertheless, full flowering of metalinguistic skills does not occur until middle childhood, as cognition advances and teachers point out features of language in reading and writing activities. Between ages 4 and 8, children make great strides in *phonological awareness* (Homer, 2009). Whereas preschoolers are sensitive to rhyme and other changes in word sounds, third graders can identify all the phonemes in a word. Recall from Chapter 7 that phonological awareness strongly predicts reading progress. Then literacy promotes further metalinguistic development by enabling language to become an object of thought that can be analyzed and dissected.

Consistent with this view, school-age children also make strides in morphological awareness, including the ability to manipulate word endings and generalize them to novel contexts (as in the example at the beginning of this section) (Duncan, Casalis, & Cole, 2009). And around age 8, children can judge the grammatical correctness of a sentence even if its meaning is false or senseless (Bialystok, 1986). Furthermore, metalinguistic knowledge is evident in elementary school children's improved ability to define words and appreciate their multiple meanings in puns, riddles, and metaphors—skills that continue to improve in adolescence (Berman, 2007).

As we will see next, bilingual children are advanced in metalinguistic awareness, as well as other cognitive skills. But before we conclude with this topic, refer to the Milestones table on the following page, which provides an overview of language development.

▶ How do children become bilingual, and what are the advantages of bilingualism?

Bilingualism: Learning Two Languages in Childhood

Throughout the world, many children grow up *bilingual,* learning two languages and sometimes more than two. Recall from Chapter 2 that both the United States and Canada have large immigrant populations. An estimated 20 percent of U.S. children—10 million in all—speak a language other than English at home (U.S. Census Bureau, 2011b).

Children can become bilingual in two ways: (1) by acquiring both languages at the same time in early childhood, as Erin did, or (2) by learning a second language after mastering the first. Children of bilingual parents who teach them both languages in infancy and early childhood separate the language systems from the start (see page 368), distinguishing

Milestones

Language Development

AGE	PHONOLOGY	SEMANTICS	GRAMMAR	PRAGMATICS
Birth–1 year	• Coos, then babbles • Organizes speech sounds into phonemic categories of native language • Babbles using sound and intonation patterns of native language	• Prefers to listen to mother's voice and to native language • Analyzes speech stream for words and syllable stress patterns • Begins to comprehend words, and recognizes familiar words • Uses communicative gestures	• Notices the structure of word sequences, distinguishing ABA from ABB patterns • Develops sensitivity to clause and phrase boundaries	• Establishes joint attention • Engages in vocal exchanges and turn-taking games
1–2 years	• Recognizes correct pronunciation of familiar words • Uses systematic strategies to simplify word pronunciation	 • Says first words • Vocabulary grows to several hundred words	• Combines two words in telegraphic speech • As three-word sentences appear, gradually adds grammatical morphemes	• Engages in conversational turn taking and topic maintenance
3–5 years	• Improves in phonological awareness • Improves in word pronunciation 	• Coins words to fill in for words not yet mastered • Understands metaphors based on concrete, sensory comparisons	• Gradually generalizes grammatical forms • Continues to add grammatical morphemes in a regular order	• Masters additional conversational strategies, such as the turnabout • Begins to grasp illocutionary intent • Adjusts speech to listener's perspective and to social expectations • Asks for clarification of ambiguous messages • Produces chronological narratives
6–10 years	• Extends phonological awareness to all phonemes in words • Masters syllable stress patterns signaling subtle differences in meaning	• At school entry, understands the meaning of about 10,000 words • Acquires meanings of new words from context and from definitions • Appreciates the multiple meanings of words, as indicated by metaphors and humor	 • Refines complex grammatical structures, such as the passive voice and infinitive phrases	• Uses advanced conversational strategies, such as shading • Refines understanding of illocutionary intent • Communicates clearly in demanding situations, such as on the telephone • Produces classic narratives rich in orienting information and evaluations
11 years– adulthood	 • Masters syllable stress patterns of abstract words	• Comprehends over 40,000 words, including many abstract terms • Understands subtle, nonliteral word meanings, as in sarcasm, irony, and proverbs	• Continues to refine complex grammatical structures	• Ability to communicate clearly and in accord with social expectations in diverse situations improves

Note: These milestones represent overall age trends. Individual differences exist in the precise age at which each milestone is attained.

Photos: (top left) © Ellen B. Senisi Photography; (top right) © Visions of America, LLC/Alamy; (middle left) © Gulf Images/Photolibrary; (middle right) © Laura Dwight Photography; (bottom left) © Kablonk/Photolibrary

FIGURE 9.12 Monolingual and bilingual 6-year-olds' English vocabulary comprehension scores for "school" words and "home" words. Although bilingual school-children's English vocabularies were smaller than those of their monolingual agemates, the difference applied only to words often used at home, where bilinguals' native language is spoken. The two groups were equivalent in comprehension of words often used at school, which bilingual children had ample opportunity to learn. (Adapted from Bialystok et al., 2009.)

If these children become fluent in both of their parents' native languages, they are likely to be advanced in many aspects of cognitive development and in metalinguistic awareness.

© LAURA DWIGHT PHOTOGRAPHY

their sounds, saying their first word, producing 50 words across the two languages (around age 1½), and attaining other early language milestones according to a typical timetable (Bialystok et al., 2009a; Conboy & Thal, 2006; Genesee & Nicoladis, 2007). Preschoolers acquire normal native ability in the language of their surrounding community and good-to-native ability in the second language, depending on their exposure to it (Genesee, 2001). When school-age children acquire a second language, they generally take five to seven years to attain speaking and writing skills on a par with those of native-speaking agemates (Paradis, 2007).

Like many bilingual adults, bilingual children sometimes engage in **code switching**—producing an utterance in one language that contains one or more "guest" words from the other—without violating the grammar of either language. Children may engage in code switching because they lack the vocabulary to convey a particular thought in one language, so they use the other. But children who code-switch the most are those whose parents often do so. Bilingual adults frequently code-switch to express cultural identity, and children may follow suit—as when a Korean child speaking English switches to Korean on mentioning her piano teacher, a sign of respect for authority (Chung, 2006). Opportunities to listen to code switching may facilitate bilingual development (Gawlitzek-Maiwald & Tracy, 1996). For example, a child accustomed to hearing French sentences with English guest words may rely on sentence-level cues to figure out English word meanings.

Compared to their monolingual agemates, bilingual children have somewhat smaller vocabularies in each language. But the difference seems largely due to opportunity to acquire certain words. For example, a close look at bilingual 6-year-olds who spoke a minority language at home but attended English-speaking schools revealed that they did not differ from monolinguals in comprehension of English words often used at school (such as animals, plants, and shapes) (see Figure 9.12) (Bialystok et al., 2009a). The bilingual children scored lower only in English words likely to be used at home (foods, household items), where they heard and spoke their other language.

A large body of research shows that children who become fluent in two languages are advanced in cognitive development. Brain-imaging research reveals that individuals who acquire two languages earlier and to greater proficiency develop denser neuronal connections in language areas of the left hemisphere (Mechelli et al., 2004). Bilingual children outperform others on tests of selective attention, inhibition of irrelevant information, analytical reasoning, concept formation, and cognitive flexibility (Bialystok, 2001; Bialystok & Martin, 2004; Carlson & Meltzoff, 2008). They are also advanced in certain aspects of metalinguistic awareness, such as detection of errors in grammar, meaning, and conventions of conversation (responding politely, relevantly, and informatively). And children transfer their phonological awareness skills in one language to the other, especially if the two languages share phonological features and letter–sound correspondences, as Spanish and English do (Bialystok, McBride-Chang, & Luk, 2005; Siegal, Iozzi, & Surian, 2009; Snow & Kang, 2006). These capacities, as noted earlier, enhance reading achievement.

The advantages of bilingualism provide strong justification for bilingual education programs in schools. The Social Issues: Education box on the following page describes the vastly differing approaches to bilingual education in the United States and Canada. In both countries, however, many immigrant children do not receive support for their native language in classrooms. Currently, some schools are trying a new approach—*two-way bilingual programs,* in which children with limited proficiency in English who speak a common native language and children who are fluent in English are assigned in equal numbers to the same classroom. Teaching is aimed at helping all children become fluent in both languages and at increasing cross-cultural understanding (Padilla, 2006). The goal is to foster the linguistic, cognitive, and cultural enrichment of the entire nation.

SOCIAL ISSUES: EDUCATION

Two Approaches to Bilingual Education: Canada and the United States

Canadian national education policies actively promote bilingual education. Children with an official minority-language background (French in the English-speaking provinces, English in French-speaking Quebec) have the right to elementary and secondary education in their respective languages. In addition, schools are encouraged to provide programs that maintain the languages and cultures of immigrants to Canada and also to promote First Nations languages. Although such programs are in short supply, funding for them is increasing. Overall, Canada places a high value on bilingual education that enhances minority children's native-language competence.

Nationally, French–English bilingualism has increased by 12 percent since the mid-1990s (Statistics Canada, 2007f). A major reason is Canada's *language immersion programs,* in which English-speaking elementary school children are taught entirely in French for several years. Currently, about 7 percent of Canadian elementary school students are enrolled. The immersion strategy succeeds in developing children who are proficient in both languages, and who, by grade 6, achieve as well in reading, writing, and math as their counterparts in the regular English program (Harley & Jean, 1999; Holobow, Genesee, & Lambert, 1991; Turnbull, Hart, & Lapkin, 2003). The Canadian government is taking steps to expand language immersion opportunities, in hopes of increasing the percentage of 15- to 19-year-olds who speak both English and French (Government of Canada, 2009).

In the United States, fierce disagreement exists over how to educate minority children with limited English proficiency. Some believe that time spent communicating in the child's native tongue detracts from English-language achievement, which is crucial for success in the worlds of school and work. Other educators, committed to developing minority children's native language while fostering mastery of English, note that providing instruction in the native tongue lets minority children know that their heritage is respected. It also prevents inadequate proficiency in both languages. Minority children who gradually lose their first language as a result of being taught the second end up limited in both languages for a time (Ovando & Collier, 1998). This circumstance leads to serious academic difficulties and is believed to contribute to the high rates of school failure and dropout among low-SES Hispanic young people, who make up nearly 50 percent of the U.S. language-minority population.

At present, public opinion and educational practice favor English-only instruction. Many U.S. states have passed laws declaring English to be their official language, creating conditions in which schools have no obligation to teach minority students in languages other than English. Yet in classrooms where both Spanish and English are integrated into the curriculum, U.S. minority students are more involved in learning, participate more actively in class discussions, and acquire speaking and reading skills in the second language more easily—gains that predict better academic achievement, increased likelihood of college attendance and graduation, and greater occupational attainment (Guglielmi, 2008). In contrast, when teachers speak only in a language that children can barely understand, minority children display frustration, boredom, withdrawal, and escalating academic difficulties (Kieffer, 2008). This downward spiral in achievement is greatest in high-poverty schools, where

In this English–Spanish bilingual classroom, children are more involved in learning, participate more actively in class discussions, and acquire the second language more easily than they would in an English-only classroom.

resources to support the needs of language-minority children are especially scarce.

Supporters of U.S. English-only education often point to the success of Canadian language immersion programs, in which classroom lessons are conducted in the second language. But Canadian parents enroll their children in immersion classrooms voluntarily, and both French and English are majority languages that are equally valued in Canada. Furthermore, teaching in the child's native language is merely delayed, not ruled out. For U.S. non–English-speaking minority children, whose native languages are not valued by the larger society, a different strategy seems necessary: one that promotes children's native-language skills while they learn English.

ASK YOURSELF

Review ■ Explain why metalinguistic awareness expands greatly in middle childhood. What might account for bilingual children's advanced metalinguistic skills?

Connect ■ How can bilingual education promote ethnic minority children's cognitive and academic development?

Apply ■ Reread the examples of Erin's language at the beginning of this chapter. Were Marilyn and Oscar wise to teach Erin both English and Spanish? Does Erin's mixing of the two languages indicate confusion? Justify your answers with research findings.

Reflect ■ Did you acquire a second language at home or study one in school? If so, when did you begin, and how proficient are you in the second language? Considering research on bilingualism, what changes would you make in your second-language learning, and why?

SUMMARY

Components of Language
(p. 360)

What are the four components of language?

■ Language consists of four subsystems:
(1) **phonology,** the rules governing the structure and sequence of speech sounds; (2) **semantics,** the way underlying concepts are expressed in words; (3) **grammar,** consisting of **syntax,** the rules by which words are arranged in sentences, and **morphology,** markers that vary word meaning; and (4) **pragmatics,** the rules for engaging in appropriate and effective conversation.

Theories of Language Development (p. 360)

Describe and evaluate major theories of language development.

■ Chomsky's nativist theory proposes a **language acquisition device (LAD)** containing a **universal grammar,** or storehouse of rules common to all languages. The LAD permits children, once they have sufficient vocabulary, to speak grammatically and comprehend sentences in any language to which they are exposed. Animal research is consistent with this perspective, revealing that a complex language system is unique to humans.

■ The broad association of language functions, especially grammatical competence, with left-hemispheric regions of the cerebral cortex is in accord with Chomsky's notion of a brain prepared to process language. Evidence for a sensitive period of language development also supports the nativist view.

■ Researchers have challenged the nativist perspective on several grounds, including the difficulty of specifying a universal grammar. Also, children's continuous, gradual mastery of many constructions is inconsistent with the nativist assumption of innately determined grammatical knowledge.

■ According to the interactionist perspective, language development results from exchanges between inner capacities and environmental influences. The most influential information-processing accounts are connectionist, or artificial neural network, models, which show that powerful, general cognitive capacities are sufficient to detect certain linguistic patterns. Other evidence confirms that babies identify basic language patterns with the same strategies they use to understand nonlinguistic experiences.

■ Social interactionists believe that children's social skills and language experiences combine with native capacity to profoundly affect language development. But debate continues over whether children make sense of their complex language environments by applying general cognitive capacities or capacities specially tuned to language.

Prelinguistic Development: Getting Ready to Talk (p. 368)

Discuss receptivity to language, development of speech sounds, and conversational skills during infancy.

■ Newborns are capable of **categorical speech perception** and are sensitive to a wider range of speech categories than exists in their own language. Between 6 and 8 months, infants start to organize speech into the phonemic categories of their native tongue. In the second half of the first year, they have begun to analyze the internal structure of sentences and words. Adults' use of **infant-directed speech (IDS)** eases language learning for babies.

© LAURA DWIGHT PHOTOGRAPHY

■ Infants begin **cooing** around 2 months, **babbling** around 6 months. Over the first year, the range of babbled sounds expands. Then, as infants get ready to talk, sound and intonation patterns start to resemble those of the child's native language.

■ At 10 to 11 months, babies' skill at establishing **joint attention** improves, and by the end of the first year they actively engage in turn-taking games and use two communicative gestures, the **protodeclarative** and the **protoimperative,** to influence others' behavior. By the second year, caregiver–child interaction contributes greatly to language progress.

Phonological Development
(p. 373)

Describe the course of phonological development.

■ First words are influenced partly by the sounds children can pronounce. Because associating new words with their referents taxes toddlers'

working memories, they tend to miss the fine details of a new word's sounds, which contributes to early pronunciation errors.

■ Young children apply systematic phonological strategies to simplify challenging pronunciations. Gradually, they refine minimal words into full words with correct stress patterns. As the vocal tract matures and preschoolers engage in active problem solving, pronunciation improves greatly. But syllable stress patterns signaling subtle differences in meaning are not mastered until middle childhood or adolescence.

Semantic Development
(p. 376)

Summarize the course of semantic development, noting individual differences.

■ Language **comprehension** develops ahead of **production.** For most children, rate of word learning increases steadily and continuously from toddlerhood through the preschool years. To build vocabulary quickly, children engage in **fast-mapping.**

■ Girls show faster early vocabulary growth than boys, and temperamentally shy or negative toddlers acquire language more slowly. Low-SES children, who experience less verbal stimulation, usually have smaller vocabularies. Most toddlers use a **referential style** of language learning; their early words mainly refer to objects. Some use an **expressive style,** producing more social formulas and pronouns.

■ Early vocabularies typically emphasize object words; action and state words appear soon after. When first learning words, children make errors of **underextension** and **overextension.** Their word coinages and metaphors expand the range of meanings they can express.

■ Reading contributes enormously to vocabulary growth in middle childhood. School-age children can grasp word meanings from definitions, and comprehension of metaphor and humor expands. Adolescents' ability to reason abstractly leads to an appreciation of irony, sarcasm, and figurative language.

Discuss ideas about how semantic development takes place, including the influence of memory and strategies for word learning.

■ A special part of short-term memory, a **phonological store** that permits retention of speech-based information, supports young children's vocabulary growth. After age 5, semantic knowledge also influences how quickly children form phonological traces, and both factors affect word learning.

- Children figure out the meanings of words by contrasting them with words they already know and assigning new words to gaps in their vocabulary. According to one view, children are innately biased to induce word meanings using certain principles, such as a **mutual exclusivity bias** and **syntactic bootstrapping.**

- An alternate perspective is that children build their vocabularies with the same cognitive strategies that they apply to nonlinguistic stimuli. According to the **emergentist coalition model,** children figure out word meanings from a coalition of cues—perceptual, social, and linguistic—which shift in importance with age.

Grammatical Development
(p. 384)

Describe the course of grammatical development.

- Between 1½ and 2½ years, vocabulary reaches 200 to 250 words and two word utterances called **telegraphic speech** appear. These early word combinations do not reflect a consistent, flexible grammar. As children generate three-word sentences, they use grammatical rules in a piecemeal fashion, gradually refining and generalizing structures.

- English-speaking children add **grammatical morphemes** in a consistent order that reflects both structural and semantic complexity. Once children acquire a regular morphological rule, they **overregularize,** extending it to words that are exceptions. Over time, children master expressions based on auxiliary verbs, such as negatives and questions. Between ages 3½ and 6, they add a variety of intricate constructions. Certain forms, such as the passive voice and infinitive phrases, continue to be refined in middle childhood.

Discuss ideas about how grammatical development takes place, including strategies and communicative support for mastering new structures.

- Some experts believe grammar is a product of general cognitive development. According to one view, children engage in **semantic bootstrapping,** relying on word meanings to figure out sentence structure. Others believe that children master grammar through direct observation of the structure of language. Still others agree with the essence of Chomsky's theory. One idea accepts semantic bootstrapping but proposes that grammatical categories are innate. Another speculation is that children have a built-in set of procedures for analyzing language, which supports the discovery of grammatical regularities.

- Adults provide children with indirect feedback about grammatical errors by asking for clarification or by restructuring their speech using **recasts** and **expansions.** However, the impact of such feedback on grammatical development has been challenged.

© ELLEN B. SENISI PHOTOGRAPHY

Pragmatic Development (p. 390)

Describe the course of pragmatic development.

- Even 2-year-olds are effective conversationalists. Strategies that help sustain interaction, such as **turnabout** and **shading,** are added in early and middle childhood. Children's understanding of **illocutionary intent** also improves, and they also acquire more effective **referential communication skills.**

- From the preschool to school years, children produce more organized, detailed, and evaluative narratives, which vary widely in form across cultures. The ability to generate clear oral narratives contributes to literacy development. Preschoolers are already sensitive to **speech registers.** Parents tutor young children in politeness routines, emphasizing the importance of adapting language to social expectations.

Development of Metalinguistic Awareness
(p. 394)

Describe the development of metalinguistic awareness and its role in language-related attainments.

- Preschoolers show the beginnings of **metalinguistic awareness.** Their understandings are good predictors of vocabulary and grammatical development and, in the case of phonological awareness, literacy development. Major advances in metalinguistic skills take place in middle childhood.

Bilingualism: Learning Two Languages in Childhood
(p. 394)

How do children become bilingual, and what are the advantages of bilingualism?

- Children who learn two languages in early childhood acquire each according to a typical timetable. When school-age children acquire a second language after mastering the first, they take five to seven years to attain the competence of native-speaking agemates. Bilingual children sometimes engage in **code switching** between the two languages.

- Bilingual children are advanced in cognitive development and metalinguistic awareness—advantages that provide strong justification for bilingual education programs in schools.

IMPORTANT TERMS AND CONCEPTS

babbling (p. 370)
Broca's area (p. 363)
categorical speech perception (p. 368)
code switching (p. 396)
comprehension (p. 376)
cooing (p. 370)
emergentist coalition model (p. 383)
expansions (p. 389)
expressive style (p. 378)
fast-mapping (p. 377)
grammar (p. 360)
grammatical morphemes (p. 386)
illocutionary intent (p. 390)
infant-directed speech (p. 369)
joint attention (p. 371)

language acquisition device (LAD) (p. 360)
metalinguistic awareness (p. 394)
morphology (p. 360)
mutual exclusivity bias (p. 382)
overextension (p. 380)
overregularization (p. 386)
phoneme (p. 368)
phonological store (p. 381)
phonology (p. 360)
pragmatics (p. 360)
production (p. 376)
protodeclarative (p. 371)
protoimperative (p. 371)
recasts (p. 389)

referential communication skills (p. 391)
referential style (p. 378)
semantic bootstrapping (p. 389)
semantics (p. 360)
shading (p. 390)
shape bias (p. 382)
speech registers (p. 393)
syntactic bootstrapping (p. 382)
syntax (p. 360)
telegraphic speech (p. 384)
turnabout (p. 390)
underextension (p. 379)
universal grammar (p. 361)
Wernicke's area (p. 363)

10

"Love of Mother"

Name Unknown, 15 years, Korea

Assertively grasping his mother's hand, a young child ventures confidently into the wider world. A secure attachment bond with a warm, sensitive caregiver provides children with vital support for exploring and mastering their environment.

Reprinted with permission from the International Collection of Child Art, Milner Library, Illinois State University, Normal, Illinois

Emotional Development

On a spring day, 4-month-old Zach, cradled in his father's arms, arrived at the door of my classroom, which had been transformed into a playroom for the morning. Behind him, led by their mothers, came 13-month-old Emily and 23-month-old Brenda. My students and I spent the next hour watching the three children closely. Especially captivating were the children's emotional reactions to people and objects. Zach grinned gleefully as his dad lifted him in the air, and he responded with an excited giggle to a tickle followed by a lively kiss on the tummy. When I offered Zach a rattle, his brows knit, his face sobered, and he eyed the rattle intently as he mobilized all his energies to reach for it.

Transferred to my arms and then to the laps of several students, Zach remained at ease (although he reserved a particularly broad smile for his father). In contrast, Emily and Brenda were wary. When I offered a toy and coaxed Emily toward it, she pulled back and glanced at her mother, as if to check whether the new adult and tantalizing object were safe to explore. With her mother's encouragement, Emily approached cautiously and accepted the toy. A greater capacity to understand the situation, along with her mother's explanations, helped Brenda adjust, and soon she was engrossed in play. During the hour, Brenda displayed a wide range of emotions, including embarrassment at seeing chocolate on her chin in a mirror and pride as I remarked on the tall block tower she had built.

Emotional development—formerly overshadowed by cognition—is an exciting, rapidly expanding area of research. Our discussion opens with the functions of emotions in all aspects of human activity. Next, we chart age-related gains in children's emotional expression and understanding. We will account for Zach, Emily, and Brenda's expanding emotional capacities as they engage in increasingly complex interactions with their changing physical and social worlds. Our attention then turns to individual differences in temperament and personality. We will examine biological and environmental contributions to these differences and their consequences for future development. Finally, we look at attachment to the caregiver—the infant's first affectionate tie. We will see how the feelings of security that grow out of this bond support the child's exploration, sense of independence, and expanding social relationships. ■

Functions of Emotions

TAKE A MOMENT... Think back over the past day or so. Do you recall feeling happy, sad, fearful, or angry in response to a grade on a test or a conversation with a friend? These events trigger emotion because you care about their outcomes. Your **emotion** is a rapid appraisal of the personal significance of the situation, which prepares you for action. For example, happiness leads you to approach, sadness to passively withdraw, fear to actively move away, and anger to overcome obstacles. An emotion, then, expresses your readiness to establish, maintain, or change your relation to the environment on a matter of importance to you (Campos, Frankel, & Camras, 2004; Saarni et al., 2006).

A number of theorists take a **functionalist approach to emotion,** emphasizing that the broad function of emotions is to energize behavior aimed at attaining personal goals (Barrett & Campos, 1987; Campos, Frankel, & Camras, 2004; Frijda, 2000; Saarni et al.,

Functions of Emotions
Emotions and Cognitive Processing • Emotions and Social Behavior • Emotions and Health • Other Features of the Functionalist Approach

■ **BIOLOGY AND ENVIRONMENT:** *Parental Depression and Child Development*

Development of Emotional Expression
Basic Emotions • Self-Conscious Emotions • Emotional Self-Regulation • Acquiring Emotional Display Rules

Understanding and Responding to the Emotions of Others
Social Referencing • Emotional Understanding in Childhood • Empathy and Sympathy

Temperament and Development
The Structure of Temperament • Measuring Temperament • Stability of Temperament • Genetic and Environmental Influences • Temperament as a Predictor of Children's Behavior • Temperament and Child Rearing: The Goodness-of-Fit Model

■ **BIOLOGY AND ENVIRONMENT:** *Development of Shyness and Sociability*

Development of Attachment
Bowlby's Ethological Theory • Measuring the Security of Attachment • Stability of Attachment • Cultural Variations • Factors That Affect Attachment Security • Multiple Attachments • Attachment and Later Development

■ **CULTURAL INFLUENCES:** *The Powerful Role of Paternal Warmth in Development*

Attachment, Parental Employment, and Child Care

■ **SOCIAL ISSUES: HEALTH:** *Does Child Care Threaten Infant Attachment Security and Later Adjustment?*

▶ Describe the functionalist approach to emotional development.

2006). Events can become personally relevant in several ways. First, you may already have a goal in mind, such as doing well on a test, so the testing situation prompts strong emotion. Second, others' social behavior may alter a situation's significance for you, as when a friend visits and you respond warmly to her friendly greeting. Third, any sensation or state of mind—a sight, sound, taste, smell, touch, memory, or imagining—can become personally relevant and evoke emotion, positive or negative. Your emotional reaction, in turn, affects your desire to repeat the experience.

In each case, emotions arise from ongoing exchanges between the person and the environment, flexibly serving different functions as the individual's circumstances change (Thompson, Winer, & Goodvin, 2011). Functionalist theorists believe that emotions are central in all our endeavors—cognitive processing, social behavior, and even physical health. Let's see how emotions organize and regulate experiences in each domain.

This 17-year-old, an experienced guitarist, is well-prepared for performance. Nevertheless, he reports that high anxiety sometimes interferes, diverting his attention from the cognitive demands of guitar playing.

© ELLEN B. SENISI PHOTOGRAPHY

Emotions and Cognitive Processing

Emotional reactions can lead to learning that is essential for survival. For example, a caregiver's highly charged "No!" is sufficient to keep most newly walking toddlers from touching an electric outlet or careening down a staircase. The toddler need not experience a shock or a fall to avoid these dangers.

The emotion–cognition relationship is evident in the impact of anxiety on performance. Among children and adults, high anxiety impairs thinking, especially on complex tasks, by diverting attention from cognitive processing to task-irrelevant threatening stimuli and worrisome thoughts (Derakshan & Eysenck, 2009). Emotions can also powerfully affect memory. For example, compared to their less stressed agemates, preschool and school-age children who were highly upset by an inoculation at the doctor's office tended to remember the event better, probably because they focused more attention on the threatening experience (Alexander et al., 2002; Goodman et al., 1991).

The relationship between emotion and cognition is bidirectional—a dynamic interplay already under way in early infancy (Lewis, 1999). In one study, researchers taught 2- to 8-month-olds to pull a string to activate pleasurable sights and sounds. As the infants learned the task, they responded with interest, happiness, and surprise. Then, for a short period, pulling the string no longer turned on the attractive stimuli. The babies' emotional reactions quickly changed—mostly to anger but occasionally to sadness. Once the contingency was restored, the infants who had reacted angrily showed renewed interest and enjoyment, whereas the sad babies turned away (Lewis, Sullivan, & Ramsay, 1992). Emotions were interwoven with cognitive processing, serving as outcomes of mastery and as the energizing force for continued involvement and learning.

Emotions and Social Behavior

Children's emotional signals, such as smiling, crying, and attentive interest, powerfully affect the behavior of others. Similarly, the emotional reactions of others regulate children's social behavior.

Careful analyses of caregiver–infant interaction reveal that by 3 months, a complex communication system is in place in which each partner responds in an appropriate and carefully timed fashion to the other's cues (Weinberg et al., 1999). In several studies, researchers disrupted this exchange of emotional signals by having the parent assume either a still-faced, unreactive pose or a depressed emotional state. Two- to 7-month-olds tried facial expressions, vocalizations, and body movements to get the parent to respond again. When these efforts failed, they turned away, frowned, and cried (Moore, Cohn, & Campbell, 2001; Papousek, 2007). This *still-face reaction* occurs only when natural human communication is disrupted (not to a still-faced doll or to the mother wearing a still-faced mask) and is identical in American, Canadian, and Chinese babies, suggesting that it is a built-in withdrawal response to caregivers' lack of communication (Kisilevsky et al., 1998; Legerstee & Markova,

2007). Clearly, when engaged in face-to-face interaction, even young infants expect their partners to be emotionally responsive. To learn more about the impact of parental depression on children's emotional and social adjustment, consult the Biology and Environment box on page 404.

With age, emotional expressions become deliberate means through which infants communicate, and babies monitor the emotional expressions of others to assess their intentions and perspectives. For example, caregivers initiate nearly all positive emotional exchanges with young babies. But by 9 months, infants become initiators, smiling before the caregiver smiles (Cohn & Tronick, 1987). Furthermore, recall from Chapter 9 that by the end of the first year, babies become increasingly skilled at *joint attention*—following the caregiver's line of regard. In these joint attentional episodes, infants and toddlers pick up not only verbal information but also emotional information. Later in this chapter, we will see that when faced with unfamiliar people, objects, or events, older infants pay close attention to their caregiver's affect, using it as a guide for how to respond. Through this checking of others' emotions, called *social referencing*, young children learn how to behave in a great many everyday situations. One 18-month-old, on first witnessing his newborn sister cry, monitored his mother's reaction. On subsequent occasions, he patted the baby and comforted, "No, no, Peach [her nickname], no tears."

Emotions and Health

Much research indicates that emotions influence children's physical well-being. In Chapter 5, we discussed two childhood growth disorders—*growth faltering* and *psychosocial dwarfism*—that involve emotional deprivation. Many other studies indicate that persistent psychological stress, manifested in anxiety, depressed mood, anger, and irritability, is associated with a variety of health difficulties from infancy to adulthood. For example, stress elevates heart rate and blood pressure and depresses the immune response—reactions that may explain its relationship with cardiovascular disease, infectious illness, and several forms of cancer. Stress also reduces digestive activity as blood flows to the brain, heart, and extremities to mobilize the body for action. Consequently, it can lead to gastrointestinal difficulties, including constipation, diarrhea, colitis, and ulcers (Antoni & Lutgendorf, 2007; Ray, 2004). And stress not only induces illness but results from it—a feedback loop that can cause both to worsen over time.

In a dramatic demonstration of the emotion–health relationship, researchers followed children adopted into Canadian homes who had been exposed to chronic stress as a result of at least 8 months of early rearing in extremely depleted Romanian orphanages, where they lacked adult attention and stimulation and suffered from infectious and dietary diseases—most commonly, intestinal parasites, hepatitis, and anemia. Compared with healthy agemates who had been adopted shortly after birth, these physically ill, emotionally deprived children showed extreme reactivity to stress, as indicated by high concentrations of the stress hormone *cortisol* in their saliva—a physiological response linked to persistent illness and learning and behavior problems, including deficits in concentration and control of anger and other impulses. The longer the children spent in orphanage care, the higher their cortisol levels, even six and a half years after adoption (Gunnar et al., 2001; Gunnar & Cheatham, 2003). In other investigations, orphanage children displayed abnormally low cortisol—a blunted physiological stress response that may be the central nervous system's adaptation to earlier, frequent cortisol elevations (Loman & Gunnar, 2010). Extremely low cortisol interferes with release of growth hormone (GH) and, thus, can stunt children's physical growth.

Fortunately, sensitive adult care helps normalize cortisol production in both typically developing and emotionally traumatized infants and young children. Good parenting seems to protect the young brain from the potentially damaging effects of both excessive and inadequate stress-hormone exposure (Gunnar & Quevedo, 2007; Tarullo & Gunnar, 2006). After adoption into caring families, orphanage children's cortisol production moves toward typical levels, and growth and behavior problems lessen (Gunnar & Vasquez, 2001). Nevertheless, as we saw in Chapter 4 and will see again in this chapter, many institutionalized children adopted after spending much of their first year in deprived institutions suffer from serious, lasting adjustment difficulties.

BIOLOGY and ENVIRONMENT

Parental Depression and Child Development

About 8 to 10 percent of women experience chronic depression—mild to severe feelings of sadness, distress, and withdrawal that continue for months or years. Often, the beginnings of this emotional state cannot be pinpointed. In other instances, depression emerges or strengthens after childbirth but fails to subside as the new mother adjusts to hormonal changes in her body and gains confidence in caring for her baby. This is called *postpartum depression*.

Although it is less recognized and studied, fathers, too, experience chronic depression. About 3 to 5 percent of fathers report symptoms after the birth of a child (Madsen & Juhl, 2007; Thombs, Roseman, & Arthurs, 2010). Parental depression can interfere with effective parenting and seriously impair children's development. Genetic makeup increases the risk of depressive illness, but social and cultural factors are also involved.

Maternal Depression

During Julia's pregnancy, her husband, Kyle, showed so little interest in the baby that Julia worried that having a child might be a mistake. Then, shortly after Lucy was born, Julia's mood plunged. She felt anxious and weepy, overwhelmed by Lucy's needs, and angry at loss of control over her own schedule. When Julia approached Kyle about her own fatigue and his unwillingness to help with the baby, he snapped that she was overreacting. Julia's childless friends stopped by just once to see Lucy but did not call again.

Julia's depressed mood quickly affected her baby. In the weeks after birth, infants of depressed mothers sleep poorly, are less attentive to their surroundings, and have elevated levels of the stress hormone cortisol (Field, 1998). The more extreme the depression and the greater the number of stressors in a mother's life (such as marital discord, little or no social support, and poverty), the more the parent–child relationship suffers (Simpson et al., 2003). Julia rarely smiled at, comforted, or talked to Lucy, who responded to her mother's sad, vacant gaze by turning away, crying, and often looking sad or angry herself (Feldman et al., 2009; Field, 2011). Julia, in turn, felt guilty and inadequate, and her depression deepened. By age 6 months, Lucy showed symptoms common in babies of depressed mothers—delays in motor and mental development, an irritable mood, and attachment difficulties (Cornish et al., 2005; McMahon et al., 2006).

When maternal depression persists, the parent–child relationship worsens. Depressed mothers view their infants and children more negatively than independent observers do (Forman et al., 2007). And they use inconsistent discipline—sometimes lax, at other times too forceful. As we will see in later chapters, children who experience these maladaptive parenting practices often have serious adjustment problems. Some withdraw into a depressed mood themselves; others become impulsive and aggressive (Hay et al., 2003). In one study, infants born to mothers who were depressed during pregnancy were four times as likely as babies of nondepressed mothers to have engaged in violent antisocial behavior (such as fighting, bullying, assault with a weapon, and extreme bodily harm) by age 16, after other stressors in the mother's life that could contribute to youth antisocial conduct had been controlled (Hay et al., 2010).

Paternal Depression

Paternal depression is also linked to dissatisfaction with marriage and family life after childbirth and to other life stressors, including job loss and divorce (Bielawska-Batorowicz & Kossakowska-Petrycka, 2006). In a study of a large representative sample of British parents and babies, researchers assessed depressive symptoms of fathers shortly after birth and again the following year. Then they tracked the children's development into the preschool years. Persistent paternal depression was, like maternal depression, a strong predictor of child behavior problems—especially overactivity, defiance, and aggression in boys (Ramchandani et al., 2008).

Paternal depression is linked to frequent father–child conflict as children grow older (Kane & Garber, 2004). Over time, children subjected to parental negativity develop a

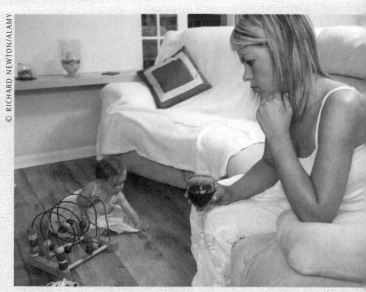

This depressed mother appears completely disengaged from her infant. In response, the baby is likely to become negative and irritable, to eventually withdraw, and to develop serious emotional and behavior problems.

© RICHARD NEWTON/ALAMY

pessimistic worldview—one in which they lack self-confidence and perceive their parents and other people as threatening. Children who constantly feel in danger are especially likely to become overly aroused in stressful situations, easily losing control in the face of cognitive and social challenges (Sturge-Apple et al., 2008). Although children of depressed parents may inherit a tendency to develop emotional and behavior problems, quality of parenting is a major factor in their adjustment.

Interventions

Early treatment is vital to prevent parental depression from interfering with the parent–child relationship. Julia's doctor referred her to a therapist, who helped Julia and Kyle with their marital problems. At times, antidepressant medication is prescribed.

In addition to alleviating parental depression, therapy that encourages depressed mothers to revise their negative views of their babies and to engage in emotionally positive, responsive caregiving is vital for reducing young children's attachment and other developmental problems (Forman et al., 2007). When a depressed parent does not respond easily to treatment, a warm relationship with the other parent or another caregiver can safeguard children's development (Mezulis, Hyde, & Clark, 2004).

Other Features of the Functionalist Approach

In addition to the vital role of emotions in cognitive, social, and physical development, functionalist theorists point out that emotions contribute to the emergence of self-awareness. For example, the interest and excitement that babies display when acting on novel objects help them forge a *sense of self-efficacy*—confidence in their own ability to control events in their surroundings (Harter, 2006). By the middle of the second year, when self-awareness is sufficiently developed, children begin to experience a new array of emotions with distinct functions. Recall Brenda's expressions of pride and embarrassment—two *self-conscious emotions* that have to do with evaluating the self's goodness or badness in relation to standards for morality, social behavior, and task mastery (Saarni et al., 2006).

Finally, the functionalist approach emphasizes that to adapt to their physical and social worlds, children must gain control over their emotions, just as they do their motor, cognitive, and social behavior. As part of this increasing *emotional self-regulation*, children must master their culture's rules for when and how to convey emotion. As a result, by late childhood, few emotions are expressed as openly and freely as they were in the early years of life. With these ideas in mind, let's chart the course of emotional development.

ASK YOURSELF

Review ■ Using research findings, provide an example of the impact of emotions on children's (1) cognitive processing, (2) social behavior, and (3) physical health.

Connect ■ Does the still-face reaction help us understand infants' responses to parental depressed mood, reviewed in the Biology and Environment box on page 404? Explain.

Apply ■ Recently divorced, Jeannine—mother of 3-month-old Jacob—feels lonely, depressed, and anxious about finances. How might Jeannine's emotional state affect Jacob's emotional and social adjustment? What can be done to help Jeannine and Jacob?

Reflect ■ Using one of your own experiences, illustrate the bidirectional relationship between emotion and cognition.

Development of Emotional Expression

▶ How does the expression of basic emotions change during infancy?

▶ Describe the development of self-conscious emotions, emotional self-regulation, and conformity to emotional display rules.

Because infants cannot describe their feelings, determining exactly which emotions they are experiencing is a challenge. Although vocalizations and body movements provide some information, researchers have relied most on facial expressions. Cross-cultural evidence reveals that people around the world associate photographs of different facial expressions with emotions in the same way (Ekman, 2003; Ekman & Friesen, 1972). These findings inspired researchers to analyze infants' facial patterns carefully to determine the range of emotions they display at different ages.

Nevertheless, assuming a close correspondence between a pattern of behavior and an underlying emotional state can lead to error. Infants, children, and adults use diverse responses to express a particular emotion. For example, babies on the visual cliff (see page 159 in Chapter 4) generally do not display a fearful facial expression, though they do show other signs of fear—drawing back and refusing to crawl over the deep side. Recall, also, from Chapter 4 that the emotional expressions of blind babies, who cannot make eye contact, are muted, prompting parents to withdraw (see page 162). When therapists show parents how blind infants express emotions through finger movements, parents become more interactive (Fraiberg, 1971; Saarni et al., 2006). Furthermore, the same general response can express several emotions. Depending on the situation, a smile might convey joy, embarrassment, contempt, or a social greeting.

In line with the *dynamic systems perspective* (see page 30 in Chapter 1), emotional expressions vary with the person's developing capacities, goals, and context (Lewis, 2000, 2008). To infer babies' emotions more accurately, researchers must attend to multiple interacting expressive cues—vocal, facial, and gestural—and see how they differ across situations believed to elicit different emotions.

Basic Emotions

Basic emotions—happiness, interest, surprise, fear, anger, sadness, disgust—are universal in humans and other primates and have a long evolutionary history of promoting survival. Do infants come into the world with the ability to express basic emotions? Although signs of some emotions are present, babies' earliest emotional life consists of little more than two global arousal states: attraction to pleasant stimulation and withdrawal from unpleasant stimulation (Camras et al., 2003; Fox, 1991). Only gradually do emotions become clear, well-organized signals.

The dynamic systems perspective helps us understand how this happens: Children coordinate separate skills into more effective, emotionally expressive systems as the central nervous system develops and the child's goals and experiences change (Camras & Shutter, 2010). Videotaping the facial expressions of her daughter from 6 to 14 weeks, Linda Camras (1992) found that in the early weeks, the baby displayed a fleeting angry face as she was about to cry and a sad face as her crying waned. These expressions first appeared on the way to or away from full-blown distress and were not clearly linked to the baby's experiences and desires. With age, she was better able to sustain an angry signal when she encountered a blocked goal and a sad signal when she could not overcome an obstacle.

According to one view, sensitive, contingent caregiver communication, in which parents selectively mirror aspects of the baby's diffuse emotional behavior, helps infants construct emotional expressions that more closely resemble those of adults (Gergely & Watson, 1999). With age, face, gaze, voice, and posture start to form organized patterns that vary meaningfully with environmental events. For example, by the middle of the first year, babies typically respond to the parent's playful interaction with a joyful face, pleasant babbling, and a relaxed posture, as if to say, "This is fun!" In contrast, an unresponsive parent often evokes a sad face, fussy sounds, and a drooping body (sending the message, "I'm despondent") or an angry face, crying, and "pick me up" gestures (as if to say, "Change this unpleasant event!") (Weinberg & Tronick, 1994; Yale et al., 1999). Gradually, emotional expressions become well-organized and specific—and therefore provide more precise information about the baby's internal state.

Four basic emotions—happiness, anger, sadness, and fear—have received the most research attention. Let's see how they develop.

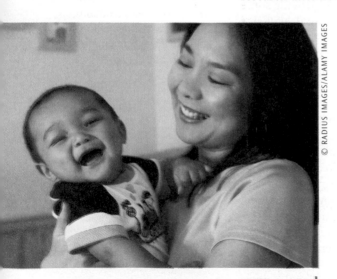

A baby's joyous laughter encourages his mother to respond in kind, binding them together in a warm, affectionate relationship that promotes all aspects of development.

Happiness Happiness—expressed first in blissful smiles, later through exuberant laughter—contributes to many aspects of development. When infants achieve new skills, they smile and laugh, displaying delight in motor and cognitive mastery. As the smile encourages caregivers to be affectionate and stimulating, the baby smiles even more (Aksan & Kochanska, 2004). Happiness binds parent and child into a warm, supportive relationship that fosters the infant's developing competencies.

During the early weeks, newborn babies smile when full, during REM sleep, and in response to gentle touches and sounds, such as stroking of the skin, rocking, and the mother's soft, high-pitched voice. By the end of the first month, infants smile at dynamic, eye-catching sights, such as a bright object jumping suddenly across their field of vision. And as infants attend to the parent's face, and the parent talks and smiles, babies knit their brows, open their mouths to coo, and move their arms and legs excitedly, gradually becoming more emotionally positive until, between 6 and 10 weeks, the parent's communication evokes a broad grin called the **social smile** (Lavelli & Fogel, 2005; Sroufe & Waters, 1976). These changes parallel the development of infant perceptual capacities—in particular, babies' sensitivity to visual patterns, including the human face (see Chapter 4). And social smiling becomes better organized and stable as babies learn to use it to evoke and sustain pleasurable face-to-face interaction.

Laughter, which appears around 3 to 4 months, reflects faster processing of information than smiling. But as with smiling, the first laughs occur in response to very active stimuli, such as the parent saying playfully, "I'm gonna get you!" and kissing the baby's tummy. As infants understand more about their world, they laugh at events with subtler elements of surprise, such as a silent game of peekaboo (Sroufe & Wunsch, 1972).

Around the middle of the first year, infants smile and laugh more when interacting with familiar people, a preference that strengthens the parent–child bond. Between 8 and 10 months, infants more often interrupt their play with an interesting toy to relay their delight to an attentive adult (Venezia et al., 2004). And like adults, 10- to 12-month-olds have several smiles, which vary with context— a broad, "cheek-raised" smile in response to a parent's greeting; a reserved, muted smile for a friendly stranger; and a "mouth-open" smile during stimulating play (Bolzani et al., 2002; Messinger & Fogel, 2007). By the end of the first year, the smile has become a deliberate social signal.

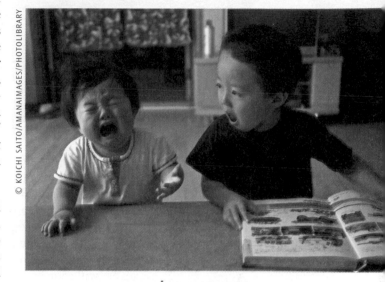

This 8-month-old knows just what object she wants and who is keeping it from her. Angry reactions increase as babies become capable of intentional behavior and better able to identify obstacles to reaching their goals.

Anger and Sadness Newborn babies respond with generalized distress to a variety of unpleasant experiences, including hunger, painful medical procedures, changes in body temperature, and too much or too little stimulation (see Chapter 4). From 4 to 6 months into the second year, angry expressions increase in frequency and intensity (Braungart-Rieker, Hill-Soderlund, & Karrass, 2010). Older infants also react with anger in a wider range of situations—when an interesting object or event is removed, an expected pleasant event does not occur, their arms are restrained, the caregiver leaves for a brief time, or they are put down for a nap (Camras et al., 1992; Stenberg & Campos, 1990; Sullivan & Lewis, 2003).

Why do angry reactions increase with age? As infants become capable of intentional behavior (see Chapter 6), they want to control their own actions and the effects they produce and will purposefully try to change an undesirable situation (Alessandri, Sullivan, & Lewis, 1990). They are also more persistent about obtaining desired objects and less easily distracted from those goals (Mascolo & Fischer, 2007). Furthermore, older infants are better at identifying who caused them pain or removed a toy. Their anger is particularly intense when a caregiver from whom they have come to expect warm behavior causes discomfort. The rise in anger is also adaptive. New motor capacities enable angry infants to defend themselves or overcome obstacles (Izard & Ackerman, 2000). Finally, anger motivates caregivers to relieve a baby's distress and, in the case of separation, may discourage them from leaving again soon.

Although expressions of sadness also occur in response to pain, removal of an object, and brief separations, they are less common than anger (Alessandri, Sullivan, & Lewis, 1990). In contrast, sadness occurs often when infants are deprived of a familiar, loving caregiver or when caregiver–infant communication is seriously disrupted (refer again to the Biology and Environment box on page 404).

Fear Like anger, fear rises during the second half of the first year into the second year (Braungart-Rieker, Hill-Soderland, & Karrass, 2010). Older infants hesitate before playing with a new toy, and newly crawling infants soon back away from heights (see Chapter 4). But the most frequent expression of fear is to unfamiliar adults, a response called **stranger anxiety**. Many infants and toddlers are quite wary of strangers, although the reaction does not always occur. It depends on several factors: temperament (some babies are generally more fearful), past experiences with strangers, and the current situation. When an unfamiliar adult picks up the infant in a new setting, stranger anxiety is likely. But if the adult sits still while the baby moves around and a parent remains nearby, infants often show positive and curious behavior (Horner, 1980). The stranger's style of interaction—expressing warmth, holding out an attractive toy, playing a familiar game, and approaching slowly rather than abruptly—reduces the baby's fear.

LOOK and LISTEN

While observing an 8- to 18-month-old with his or her parent, gently approach the baby, offering a toy. Does the baby respond with stranger anxiety? To better understand the baby's behavior, ask the parent to describe his or her temperament and past experiences with strangers.

Stranger anxiety appears in many infants after 6 months. But this baby, safe in his father's arms, also expresses curiosity, reaching out warily toward an unfamiliar adult who eases his fear by smiling and approaching slowly.

Cross-cultural research reveals that infant-rearing practices can modify stranger anxiety. Among the Efe hunters and gatherers of the Republic of Congo, where the maternal death rate is high, infant survival is safeguarded by a collective caregiving system in which, starting at birth, Efe babies are passed from one adult to another. Consequently, Efe infants show little stranger anxiety (Tronick, Morelli, & Ivey, 1992). In contrast, among infants in Israeli kibbutzim (cooperative agricultural settlements), who live in isolated communities vulnerable to terrorist attacks, wariness of strangers is widespread. By the end of the first year, when infants look to others for cues about how to respond emotionally, kibbutz babies display far greater stranger anxiety than their city-reared counterparts (Saarni et al., 2006).

The rise in fear after age 6 months keeps newly mobile babies' enthusiasm for exploration in check. Once wariness develops, infants use the familiar caregiver as a **secure base,** or point from which to explore, venturing into the environment and then returning for emotional support. As part of this adaptive system, encounters with strangers lead to two conflicting tendencies: approach (indicated by interest and friendliness) and avoidance (indicated by fear). The infant's behavior is a balance between the two.

Eventually, as cognitive development permits toddlers to discriminate more effectively between threatening and nonthreatening people and situations, stranger anxiety and other fears of the first two years decline. This change is adaptive because adults other than caregivers will soon be important in children's development. Fear also wanes as children acquire a wider array of strategies for coping with it, as you will see when we discuss emotional self-regulation.

Self-Conscious Emotions

Besides basic emotions, humans are capable of a second, higher-order set of feelings, including guilt, shame, embarrassment, envy, and pride. These are called **self-conscious emotions** because each involves injury to or enhancement of our sense of self. We feel guilt when we know that we have harmed someone and we want to correct the wrongdoing. When we are ashamed or embarrassed, we have negative feelings about our behavior, and we want to retreat so others will no longer notice our failings. In contrast, pride reflects delight in the self's achievements, and we are inclined to tell others what we have accomplished and to take on further challenges (Saarni et al., 2006).

Self-conscious emotions appear in the middle of the second year, as 18- to 24-month-olds become firmly aware of the self as a separate, unique individual. Toddlers show shame and embarrassment by lowering their eyes, hanging their heads, and hiding their faces with their hands. They show guiltlike reactions, too, like the 22-month-old who returned a toy she had grabbed and patted her upset playmate. Pride also emerges around this time, and envy by age 3 (Barrett, 2005; Garner, 2003; Lewis et al., 1989).

Besides self-awareness, self-conscious emotions require an additional ingredient: adult instruction in *when* to feel proud, ashamed, or guilty. The situations in which adults encourage self-conscious emotions vary from culture to culture. In Western individualistic nations, most children are taught to feel pride over personal achievement—throwing a ball the farthest, winning a game, and (later on) getting good grades. In collectivist cultures such as China and Japan, calling attention to purely personal success evokes embarrassment and self-effacement. And violating cultural standards by failing to show concern for others—a parent, a teacher, or an employer—sparks intense shame (Akimoto & Sanbonmatsu, 1999; Lewis, 1992).

As their self-concepts develop, children become increasingly sensitive to praise and blame or to the possibility of such feedback from parents, teachers, and other adults who matter to them, often viewing their expectations as obligatory rules ("Dad said you're 'posed to take turns"). By age 3, self-conscious emotions are clearly linked to self-evaluation (Lewis,

1995; Thompson, Meyer, & McGinley, 2006). Preschoolers show much more pride when they succeed in difficult rather than easy tasks and much more shame when they fail simple rather than hard tasks (Lewis, Alessandri, & Sullivan, 1992).

Quality of adult feedback influences these early self-evaluative reactions. When parents repeatedly comment on the worth of the child and her performance ("That's a bad job!" "I thought you were a good girl"), children experience self-conscious emotions intensely—more shame after failure, more pride after success. In contrast, when parents focus on how to improve performance ("You did it this way; now try doing it that way"), they induce moderate, more adaptive levels of shame and pride and greater persistence on difficult tasks (Kelley, Brownell, & Campbell, 2000; Lewis, 1998).

Among Western children, intense shame is associated with feelings of personal inadequacy ("I'm stupid"; "I'm a terrible person") and with maladjustment—withdrawal and depression as well as intense anger and aggression toward those who participated in the shame-evoking situation (Lindsay-Hartz, de Rivera, & Mascolo, 1995; Mills, 2005). In contrast, guilt—when it occurs in appropriate circumstances and is neither excessive nor accompanied by shame—is related to good adjustment. Guilt helps children resist harmful impulses, and it motivates a misbehaving child to repair the damage and behave more considerately (Mascolo & Fischer, 2007; Tangney, Stuewig, & Mashek, 2007). But overwhelming guilt—involving such high emotional distress that the child cannot make amends—is linked to depressive symptoms as early as age 3 (Luby et al., 2009).

The consequences of shame for children's adjustment, however, may vary across cultures. In Asian collectivist societies, where people define themselves in relation to their social group, shame is viewed as an adaptive reminder of the importance of others' judgments (Bedford, 2004). Chinese parents, for example, believe that it is important for a misbehaving child to feel ashamed. As early as age 2½, they frequently use shame to teach right from wrong, while mindful that excessive shaming could harm the child's self-esteem (Fung, 1999). Not surprisingly, Chinese children add the word *shame* to their vocabularies by age 3, much earlier than their American counterparts do (Shaver, Wu, & Schwartz, 1992).

A teacher's praise reinforces this 6-year-old's pride in completing a sheet of challenging math problems. But even when no adult is present, school-age children experience pride, guilt, and other self-conscious emotions.

As children develop inner standards of excellence and good behavior and a sense of personal responsibility, the circumstances under which they experience self-conscious emotions change. Unlike preschoolers, school-age children experience pride in a new accomplishment and guilt over a transgression even when no adult is present (Harter & Whitesell, 1989). Also, school-age children no longer report guilt for any mishap, as they did earlier, but only for intentional wrongdoing, such as ignoring responsibilities, cheating, or lying (Ferguson, Stegge, & Damhuis, 1991). These changes reflect the older child's more mature sense of morality, a topic we will take up in Chapter 12.

Emotional Self-Regulation

Besides expressing a wider range of emotions, children learn to manage their emotional experiences. **Emotional self-regulation** refers to the strategies we use to adjust our emotional state to a comfortable level of intensity so we can accomplish our goals. It requires several cognitive capacities that we discussed in Chapter 7—attention focusing and shifting, the ability to inhibit thoughts and behavior, and planning, or actively taking steps to relieve a stressful situation (Eisenberg & Spinrad, 2004; Thompson & Goodvin, 2007). When you remind yourself that an anxiety-provoking event will be over soon, suppress your anger at a friend's behavior, or decide not to see a scary horror film, you are engaging in emotional self-regulation.

Emotional self-regulation requires voluntary, effortful management of emotions. This capacity for *effortful control* improves gradually, as the result of development of the prefrontal cortex and the assistance of caregivers, who help children manage intense emotion and teach them strategies for doing so (Fox & Calkins, 2003; Rothbart, Posner, & Kieras, 2006). Individual differences in control of emotion are evident in infancy and, by early childhood, play such a vital role in children's adjustment that—as we will see later—effortful control is considered a major dimension of temperament. Let's turn now to changes in emotional self-regulation from infancy to adolescence.

Infancy In the early months, infants have only a limited capacity to regulate their emotional states. When their feelings get too intense, they are easily overwhelmed. They depend on the soothing interventions of caregivers—being lifted to the shoulder, rocked, gently stroked, and talked to softly—for distraction and reorienting of attention.

More effective functioning of the prefrontal cortex increases the baby's tolerance for stimulation. Between 2 and 4 months, caregivers build on this capacity by initiating face-to-face play and attention to objects. In these interactions, parents arouse pleasure in the baby while adjusting the pace of their own behavior so the infant does not become overwhelmed and distressed. As a result, the baby's tolerance for stimulation increases further (Kopp & Neufeld, 2003).

By 4 to 6 months, the ability to shift attention and engage in self-soothing helps infants control emotion. Babies who more readily turn away from highly stimulating novel events (a toy fire truck with siren blaring and lights flashing) or engage in self-soothing are less prone to distress (Crockenberg & Leerkes, 2003a). At the end of the first year, crawling and walking enable infants to regulate emotion more effectively by approaching or retreating from various situations. And further gains in attention permit toddlers to sustain interest in their surroundings and in play activities for a longer time (Rothbart & Bates, 2006).

Infants whose parents "read" and respond contingently and sympathetically to their emotional cues tend to be less fussy and fearful, to express more pleasurable emotion, to be more interested in exploration, and to be easier to soothe (Braungart-Rieker, Hill-Soderlund, & Karrass, 2010; Crockenberg & Leerkes, 2004; Volling et al., 2002). In contrast, parents who respond impatiently or angrily or who wait to intervene until the infant has become extremely agitated reinforce the baby's rapid rise to intense distress. This makes it harder for parents to soothe the baby in the future—and for the baby to learn to calm herself. When caregivers fail to regulate stressful experiences for infants who cannot yet regulate them for themselves, brain structures that buffer stress may fail to develop properly, resulting in an anxious, emotionally reactive child who has a reduced capacity for managing emotional problems (Feldman, 2007; Little & Carter, 2005).

In the second year, gains in representation and language lead to new ways of regulating emotion. A vocabulary for talking about feelings—"happy," "love," "surprised," "scary," "yucky," "mad"—develops rapidly after 18 months, but toddlers are not yet good at using language to manage their emotions. Temper tantrums tend to occur because toddlers cannot control the intense anger that often arises when an adult rejects their demands, particularly when they are fatigued or hungry (Mascolo & Fischer, 2007). Toddlers whose parents are emotionally sympathetic but set limits (by not giving in to tantrums), who distract the child by offering acceptable alternatives to the prohibited activity, and who later suggest better ways to handle adult refusals display more effective anger-regulation strategies and social skills during the preschool years (Lecuyer & Houck, 2006).

Patient, sensitive parents also encourage toddlers to describe their internal states. Then, when 2-year-olds feel distressed, they can guide caregivers in helping them. For example, while listening to a story about monsters, one 22-month-old whimpered, "Mommy, scary." Her mother put down the book and gave her a consoling hug.

Early Childhood After age 2, children frequently talk about feelings, and language becomes a major means of actively trying to control them (Cole, Armstrong, & Pemberton, 2010). By age 3 to 4, preschoolers verbalize a variety of emotional self-regulation strategies. For example, they know they can

Through adult–child conversations that prepare children for difficult experiences, preschoolers learn techniques for regulating emotions. With her mother's reassurance, a 3-year-old is ready for the daily transition to preschool.

© ELLEN B. SENISI PHOTOGRAPHY

APPLYING WHAT WE KNOW

Helping Children Manage Common Fears of Early Childhood

FEAR	SUGGESTION
Monsters, ghosts, and darkness	Reduce exposure to frightening stories in books and on TV until the child is better able to distinguish between appearance and reality. Make a thorough "search" of the child's room for monsters, showing him that none are there. Leave a night-light burning, sit by the child's bed until he falls asleep, and tuck in a favorite toy for protection.
Preschool or child care	If the child resists going to preschool but seems content once there, the fear is probably separation. Provide a sense of warmth and caring while gently encouraging independence. If the child fears being at preschool, find out what is frightening—the teacher, the children, or a crowded, noisy environment. Provide extra support by accompanying the child and gradually lessening the amount of time you are present.
Animals	Do not force the child to approach a dog, cat, or other animal that arouses fear. Let the child move at her own pace. Demonstrate how to hold and pet the animal, showing the child that when treated gently, the animal is friendly. If the child is larger than the animal, emphasize this: "You're so big. That kitty is probably afraid of *you!*"
Intense fears	If a child's fear is intense, persists for a long time, interferes with daily activities, and cannot be reduced in any of the ways just suggested, it has reached the level of a *phobia*. Sometimes phobias are linked to family problems, and counseling is needed to reduce them. At other times, phobias diminish without treatment as the child's capacity for emotional self-regulation improves.

blunt emotions by restricting sensory input (covering their eyes or ears to block out an unpleasant sight or sound), talking to themselves ("Mommy said she'll be back soon"), or changing their goals (deciding that they don't want to play anyway after being excluded from a game). Children's use of these strategies means fewer emotional outbursts over the preschool years (Thompson & Goodvin, 2007). As the examples suggest, shifting attention away from sources of frustration continues to be an effective approach to managing emotion. Three-year-olds who can distract themselves when frustrated tend to become cooperative school-age children with few problem behaviors (Gilliom et al., 2002).

By watching adults handle their own feelings and respond to those of others, preschoolers pick up strategies for regulating emotion. Warm, patient parents who use verbal guidance, including suggesting and explaining strategies and prompting children to generate their own, strengthen children's capacity to handle stress (Colman et al., 2006; Morris et al., 2011). Such children are more likely to use private speech (verbal self-guidance) to regulate emotion (Atencio & Montero, 2009). In contrast, when parents rarely express positive emotion, dismiss children's feelings as unimportant, and have difficulty controlling their own anger, children have continuing problems in managing emotion that seriously interfere with psychological adjustment (Hill et al., 2006; Katz & Windecker-Nelson, 2004; Thompson & Meyer, 2007).

As with infants and toddlers, preschoolers who experience negative emotion intensely have greater difficulty shifting their attention away from disturbing events and inhibiting their feelings. They are more likely to be anxious and fearful, respond with irritation to others' distress, react angrily or aggressively when frustrated, and get along poorly with teachers and peers (Chang et al., 2003; Eisenberg et al., 2005a; Raikes et al., 2007). Because these emotionally reactive children become increasingly difficult to rear, they are often targets of ineffective parenting, which compounds their poor self-regulation.

Adult–child conversations that prepare children for difficult experiences also foster emotional self-regulation (Thompson & Goodman, 2010). Parents who discuss what to expect and ways to handle anxiety offer techniques that children can apply. Nevertheless, preschoolers' vivid imaginations and incomplete grasp of the distinction between appearance and reality make fears common in early childhood. Consult Applying What We Know above for ways adults can help young children manage fears.

Middle Childhood and Adolescence Rapid gains in emotional self-regulation occur after school entry, as emotion regulation strategies become more varied, sophisticated, and flexible (Raffaelli, Crockett, & Shen, 2005). Between ages 6 and 8—as they become aware of the difference between feeling an emotion and expressing it—children increasingly reserve the full performance of emotional expressions for communicating with others. When alone—although they report experiencing emotions just as intensely—they abbreviate their emotional expressions, representing them internally, just as they internalize their private speech (see Chapter 6) (Holodynski, 2004). This emergence of a *mental level* of emotional self-communication helps children reflect on their emotions and, therefore, manage them.

At the same time, school-age children face new challenges in regulating negative emotion, prompted by their developing sense of self-worth and expanding knowledge of the wider world. Common fears of the school years include poor academic performance, rejection by classmates, the possibility of personal harm (being robbed or shot), threats to parental health, and media events (wars and disasters) (Gullone, 2000; Weems & Costa, 2005). School-age children's fears are shaped in part by their culture. For example, in China, where self-restraint and compliance with social standards are highly valued, more children mention failure and adult criticism as salient fears than in Australia or the United States. Chinese children, however, are not more fearful overall (Ollendick et al., 1996). The number and intensity of fears they report resemble those of Western children.

By age 10, most children shift adaptively between two general strategies for managing emotion. In **problem-centered coping,** they appraise the situation as changeable, identify the difficulty, and decide what to do about it. If problem solving does not work, they engage in **emotion-centered coping,** which is internal, private, and aimed at controlling distress when little can be done about an outcome (Kliewer, Fearnow, & Miller, 1996; Lazarus & Lazarus, 1994). For example, when faced with an anxiety-provoking test or a friend who is angry at them, older school-age children view problem solving and seeking social support as the best strategies. But when outcomes are beyond their control—for example, after receiving a bad grade—they opt for distraction or try to redefine the situation in ways that help them accept it: "Things could be worse. There'll be another test." School-age children's improved ability to appraise situations and reflect on thoughts and feelings means that, compared with preschoolers, they more often use these internal strategies to manage emotion (Brenner & Salovey, 1997).

Cognitive development, including gains in planning and inhibition, and a wider range of social experiences contribute to flexible, effective coping strategies. When emotional self-regulation has developed well, young people acquire a sense of *emotional self-efficacy*—a feeling of being in control of their emotional experience (Saarni, 2000; Thompson & Goodman, 2010). This fosters a favorable self-image and an optimistic outlook, which help them face further emotional challenges.

Acquiring Emotional Display Rules

In addition to regulating internal emotional states, children must learn to control what they communicate to others. Young preschoolers have some ability to modify their expressive behavior. For example, when denied a cookie before dinnertime, one 2-year-old paused, picked up her blanket, and walked from the hard kitchen floor to the soft family-room carpet where she could comfortably throw herself down and howl loudly!

At first, children modify emotional expressions to serve personal needs, and they exaggerate their true feelings (as this child did to get attention and a cookie). Soon, they learn to restrain their expressive behavior and substitute other reactions, such as smiling when feeling anxious or disappointed. All societies have **emotional display rules** that specify when, where, and how it is appropriate to express emotions.

As early as the first few months, parents encourage infants to suppress negative emotion by often imitating their expressions of interest, happiness, and surprise and rarely imitating their expressions of anger and sadness. Baby boys get more of this training than girls, in part because boys have a harder time regulating negative emotion (Else-Quest et al., 2006;

LOOK and LISTEN

Ask several school-age children and adolescents how they would manage their emotions in the following situations: (1) a friend is angry with them, and (2) they receive a bad grade on an important test. Do their responses reflect flexible, adaptive coping?

Malatesta et al., 1986). As a result, the well-known sex difference—females as emotionally expressive and males as emotionally controlled—is promoted at a tender age. Perhaps because of greater social pressure to suppress emotion, school-age boys are less accurate than girls in describing their emotions. In a Canadian study, after watching an emotionally arousing video, boys were less likely than girls to report feelings that matched their facial expressions (Strayer & Roberts, 1997). This disconnect between boys' public messages (facial expressions) and verbal acknowledgment of feelings probably contributes to the gender difference in intimacy of close relationships, which we examine in Chapter 13.

Although caregiver shaping of emotional behavior begins early, children only gradually gain the ability to conform to display rules. By age 3, capacity for self-regulation predicts children's skill at portraying an emotion they do not feel—for example, reacting cheerfully after receiving an undesirable gift (Kieras et al., 2005). These emotional "masks" are largely limited to positive feelings of happiness and surprise. Children of all ages (like adults) find it harder to act angry, sad, or disgusted than pleased (Lewis, Sullivan, & Vasen, 1987). These trends reflect social pressures: To foster harmonious relationships, most cultures teach children to communicate positive feelings and inhibit unpleasant emotional displays.

Through interacting with parents, teachers, and peers, children learn how to express negative emotion in ways likely to evoke a desired response from others. School-age children increasingly prefer verbal strategies to crying, sulking, or aggression (Shipman et al., 2003). As these findings suggest, children gradually become consciously aware of display rules. Kindergartners typically say they obey the rules to avoid punishment and gain approval from others. By third grade, children understand the value of display rules in ensuring social harmony (Jones, Abbey, & Cumberland, 1998). School-age children who justify emotional display rules by referring to concern for others' feelings are rated as especially helpful, cooperative, and socially responsive by teachers and as better liked by peers (Garner, 1996; McDowell & Parke, 2000).

Collectivist cultures place particular emphasis on emotional display rules, although they vary in how they teach children to inhibit negative displays. In a striking illustration, researchers studied children in two collectivist subcultures in rural Nepal. In response to stories about emotionally charged situations (such as peer aggression or an unjust parental punishment), Hindu children more often said they would feel angry but would try to mask their feelings. Buddhist children, in contrast, interpreted the situation so that they felt "just OK" rather than angry. "Why be angry?" they explained. "The event already happened" (see Figure 10.1). In line with this difference, Hindu mothers reported that they often teach their children how to control their emotional behavior, whereas Buddhist mothers pointed to the value their religion places on a calm, peaceful disposition (Cole & Tamang, 1998; Cole, Tamang, & Shrestha, 2006). Compared to both Nepalese groups, U.S. children preferred conveying their anger verbally in these situations; for example, to an unjust punishment, they answered, "If I say I'm angry, he'll stop hurting me!" (Cole, Bruschi, & Tamang, 2002). Notice how this response fits with the Western individualistic emphasis on personal rights and self-expression.

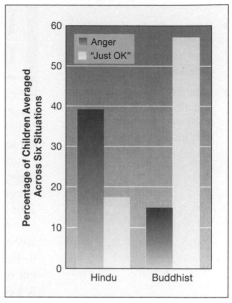

FIGURE 10.1 Hindu and Buddhist children's reports of feeling anger and "just OK" in response to emotionally charged situations. Hindu children reported that they would feel more anger. Buddhist children, whose religion values a calm, peaceful disposition, more often stated that they would feel "just OK." The children sometimes selected other emotions, such as "happy," "sad," or "scared," but these did not differ between the two subcultures and are not shown. (Adapted from Cole & Tamang, 1998.)

ASK YOURSELF

Review ■ Why do many infants show stranger anxiety in the second half of the first year? What factors can increase or decrease wariness of strangers?

Connect ■ Why do children of depressed parents have difficulty regulating emotion (see page 402)? What implications do their weak self-regulatory skills have for their response to cognitive and social challenges?

Apply ■ At age 14 months, Reggie built a block tower and gleefully knocked it down. But at age 2, he called to his mother and pointed proudly to his tall block tower. What explains this change in Reggie's emotional behavior?

Reflect ■ How do you typically manage negative emotion? Describe several recent examples. How might your early experiences, gender, and cultural background have influenced your style of emotional self-regulation?

▶ Describe the development of emotional understanding from infancy through middle childhood.

▶ Describe the development of empathy from infancy into adolescence, noting individual differences.

Understanding and Responding to the Emotions of Others

Children's emotional expressiveness is intimately tied to their ability to interpret the emotional cues of others. We have seen that in the first few months, infants match the feeling tone of the caregiver in face-to-face communication. Some researchers claim that young babies respond in kind to others' emotions through a built-in, automatic process of *emotional contagion* (Stern, 1985). Others, however, believe that infants acquire these emotional contingencies through operant conditioning—for example, learning that a smile generally triggers pleasurable feedback and that distress prompts a comforting response (Saarni et al., 2006).

Around 3 to 4 months, infants can match the emotion in a voice with the appropriate face of a speaking person, and they become sensitive to the structure and timing of face-to-face interactions. When they gaze, smile, or vocalize, they now expect their social partner to respond in kind, and they reply with positive vocal and emotional reactions (Markova & Legerstee, 2006; Rochat, Striano, & Blatt, 2002). Within these exchanges, babies become increasingly aware of the range of emotional expressions (Montague & Walker-Andrews, 2001). Recall from Chapter 4 (see page 146) that out of this early imitative communication, infants start to view others as "like me"—an awareness believed to lay the foundation for understanding others' thoughts and feelings (Meltzoff, 2007).

From 5 months on, infants perceive facial expressions as organized patterns (see Chapter 4). Responding to emotional expressions as organized wholes suggests that these signals are becoming meaningful to babies. Between 7 and 12 months, ERPs recorded while infants attend to facial expressions reveal reorganized brain-wave patterns resembling those of adults, suggesting enhanced processing of emotional cues (Grossmann, Striano, & Friederici, 2007).

As skill at establishing joint attention improves, infants realize that an emotional expression not only has meaning but is also a meaningful reaction to a specific object or event (Moses et al., 2001; Tomasello, 1999). Once these understandings are in place, infants actively seek emotional information from trusted caregivers.

Social Referencing

Beginning at 8 to 10 months, when infants start to evaluate unfamiliar people, objects, and events in terms of their own safety and security, they often engage in **social referencing**—relying on another person's emotional reaction to appraise an uncertain situation (Mumme et al., 2007). Many studies show that a caregiver's emotional expression (happy, angry, or fearful) influences whether a 1-year-old will be wary of strangers, play with an unfamiliar toy, or cross the deep side of the visual cliff (de Rosnay et al., 2006; Stenberg, 2003; Striano & Rochat, 2000). The caregiver's voice—either alone or combined with a facial expression—is more effective than a facial expression alone (Kim, Walden, & Knieps, 2010; Vaish & Striano, 2004). The voice conveys both emotional and verbal information, and the baby need not turn toward the adult but, instead, can focus on evaluating the novel event.

As recall memory and language skills improve, and as parents' warnings to their newly walking youngsters become more frequent and intense, babies retain these emotional messages over longer time intervals. At 11 months, they respond appropriately after a delay of a few minutes, at 14 months after a delay of an hour or more (Hertenstein & Campos, 2004). By the middle of the second year, social referencing expands to include indirect emotional signals. After observing an adult react angrily to a second adult's play with a toy, 18-month-olds increased their monitoring of the angry adult's facial expression and reduced their touching of the object (Repacholi & Meltzoff, 2007).

As toddlers begin to appreciate that others' emotional reactions may differ from their own, social referencing allows them to compare their own and others' assessments of events. In one study, an adult showed 14- and 18-month-olds broccoli and crackers. In one condition, she acted delighted with the taste of broccoli but disgusted with the taste of crackers. In the other

LOOK and LISTEN

Observe a toddler and parent at a playground, park, or shopping mall, noting circumstances that trigger social referencing. How does the parent convey emotional information? How does the toddler respond?

condition, she showed the reverse preference. When asked to share the food, 14-month-olds offered only the type of food they themselves preferred—usually crackers. In contrast, 18-month-olds gave the adult whichever food she appeared to like, regardless of their own preferences (Repacholi & Gopnik, 1997).

In sum, in social referencing, toddlers move beyond simply reacting to others' emotional messages. They use those signals to evaluate the safety and security of their surroundings, to guide their own actions, and to gather information about others' intentions and preferences. These experiences, along with cognitive and language development, probably help toddlers refine the meanings of emotions of the same valence—for example, happiness versus surprise, anger versus fear—during the second year (Gendler, Witherington, & Edwards, 2008; Saarni et al., 2006).

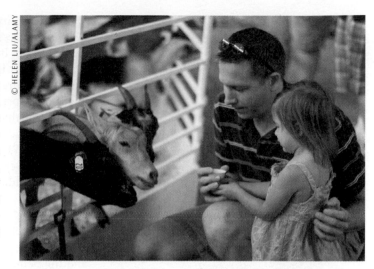

A toddler engages in social referencing, concluding from her father's calm, confident manner that it is safe to approach these unfamiliar animals.

Emotional Understanding in Childhood

During the preschool years, children's emotional understanding expands rapidly, as their everyday talk about emotions reveals:

Two-year-old: [After father shouted at child, she became angry, shouting back] I'm mad at you, Daddy. I'm going away. Goodbye.

Two-year-old: [Commenting on another child who refused to take a nap and cried] Mom, Annie cry. Annie sad.

Six-year-old: [In response to mother's comment, "It's hard to hear the baby crying"] Well, it's not as hard for me as it is for you. *[When mother asked why]* Well, you like Johnny better than I do! I like him a little, and you like him a lot, so I think it's harder for you to hear him cry.

Six-year-old: [Comforting a small boy in church whose mother had gone up to communion] She'll be right back. Don't be afraid. I'm here. (Bretherton et al., 1986, pp. 536, 540, 541)

Cognitive Development and Emotional Understanding
As these examples show, early in the preschool years, children refer to causes, consequences, and behavioral signs of emotion, and over time their understanding becomes more accurate and complex (Stein & Levine, 1999). By age 4 to 5, they correctly judge the causes of many basic emotions ("He's happy because he's swinging very high"; "He's sad because he misses his mother"). Preschoolers' explanations tend to emphasize external factors over internal states, a balance that changes with age (Levine, 1995). In Chapter 11, we will see that after age 4, children appreciate that both desires and beliefs motivate behavior. Once these understandings are secure, children's grasp of how internal factors can trigger emotion expands.

Preschoolers can also predict what a playmate expressing a certain emotion might do next. Four-year-olds know that an angry child might hit someone and that a happy child is more likely to share (Russell, 1990). And they realize that thinking and feeling are interconnected—that a person reminded of a previous sad experience is likely to feel sad (Lagattuta, Wellman, & Flavell, 1997). Furthermore, they come up with effective ways to relieve others' negative feelings, such as hugging to reduce sadness (Fabes et al., 1988).

In middle childhood, ability to consider conflicting cues when explaining others' emotions improves. When asked what might be happening in a picture showing a happy-faced child with a broken bicycle, 4- and 5-year-olds tended to rely only on the emotional expression: "He's happy because he likes to ride his bike." By age 8 to 9, children more often reconciled the two cues: "He's happy because his father promised to help fix his broken bike" (Gnepp, 1983; Hoffner & Badzinski, 1989). Similarly, older children are more aware of circumstances likely to spark mixed emotions, each of which may be positive or negative and may differ in intensity (Larsen, To, & Fireman, 2007; Pons et al., 2003). Preschoolers, by contrast, staunchly deny that two emotions can occur at once, much as they do not integrate two variables (height and width) in a Piagetian conservation-of-liquid task (see Chapter 6).

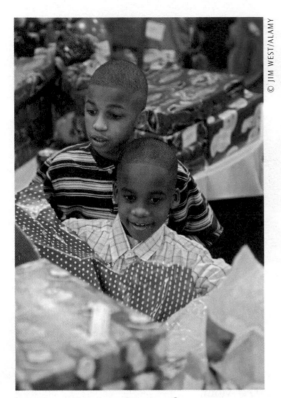

© JIM WEST/ALAMY

The older of these siblings clearly realizes—even if his younger brother doesn't—that it is possible to experience two emotions at once: happiness at getting a Christmas gift but disappointment with the gift itself.

Appreciating mixed emotions helps school-age children realize that people's expressions may not reflect their true feelings (Misailidi, 2006; Saarni, 1999). It also fosters awareness of self-conscious emotions, which are more complex in expression than basic emotions. For example, between ages 6 and 7, children improve sharply in ability to distinguish pride from happiness and surprise (Tracy, Robins, & Lagattuta, 2005). And 8- and 9-year-olds understand that pride combines two sources of happiness—joy in accomplishment and joy that a significant person recognized that accomplishment (Harter, 1999). As with the development of *metacognition* (thinking about thought), discussed in Chapter 7, striking gains in thinking about emotion occur in middle childhood.

Social Experience and Emotional Understanding The more mothers label emotions, explain them, and express warmth and enthusiasm when conversing with preschoolers, the more "emotion words" children use and the better developed their emotional understanding (Fivush & Haden, 2005; Laible & Song, 2006). Maternal prompting of emotional thoughts ("What makes him afraid?") is a good predictor of 2-year-olds' emotion language. For older preschoolers, explanations ("He's sad because his dog ran away") are more important (Cervantes & Callanan, 1998). Does this remind you of the concept of *scaffolding*, discussed in Chapter 6—that to be effective, adult teaching must adjust to children's increasing competence?

Preschoolers whose parents frequently acknowledge their emotional reactions and explicitly teach them about diverse emotions are better able to judge others' emotions when tested at later ages (Denham & Kochanoff, 2002). Discussions in which family members disagree are particularly helpful. In one study, when mothers explained feelings and negotiated and compromised during conflicts with their 2½-year-olds, their children, at age 3, were advanced in understanding emotion and used similar strategies to resolve disagreements (Laible & Thompson, 2002). Such dialogues seem to help children reflect on the causes and consequences of emotion while modeling mature communication skills. Furthermore, 3- to 5-year-olds who have a warm, relaxed relationship with their mothers (a secure attachment bond) better understand emotion. Attachment security is related to warmer and more elaborative parent–child narratives, including discussions of feelings that highlight the emotional significance of events (Laible, 2004; Laible & Song, 2006; Raikes & Thompson, 2006).

As preschoolers learn more about emotion from interacting with adults, they engage in more emotion talk with siblings and friends, especially during make-believe play (Hughes & Dunn, 1998). Make-believe, in turn, contributes to emotional understanding, especially when children play with siblings (Youngblade & Dunn, 1995). The intense nature of the sibling relationship, combined with frequent acting out of feelings, makes pretending an excellent context for early learning about emotions. And when parents intervene in sibling disputes by reasoning and negotiating, preschoolers gain in sensitivity to their siblings' feelings (Perlman & Ross, 1997). They more often refer to their siblings' emotional perspective ("You get mad when I don't share") and engage in less fighting.

Knowledge about emotions helps children greatly in their efforts to get along with others. As early as 3 to 5 years of age, it is related to friendly, considerate behavior; willingness to make amends after harming another; and constructive responses to disputes with agemates (Dunn, Brown, & Maguire, 1995; Garner & Estep, 2001; Hughes & Ensor, 2010). Also, the more preschoolers refer to feelings when interacting with playmates, the better liked they are by their peers (Fabes et al., 2001). Children seem to recognize that acknowledging others' emotions and explaining their own enhance the quality of relationships.

Empathy and Sympathy

In empathy, understanding and expression of emotions are interwoven, since both awareness of the emotions of another and the vicarious experience of those emotions are required for an empathic response. Current theorists agree that **empathy** involves a complex interaction of cognition and affect: the ability to detect different emotions, to take another's emotional perspective, and to feel with that person, or respond emotionally in a similar way. Beginning in the preschool years, empathy is an important motivator of **prosocial,** or **altruistic, behavior**—actions that benefit another person without any expected reward for the self (Eisenberg, Fabes, & Spinrad, 2006; Spinrad & Eisenberg, 2009). Yet in some children, empathizing with an upset adult or peer does not yield acts of kindness and helpfulness but instead escalates into *personal distress*. In trying to reduce these feelings, the child focuses on his own anxiety rather than on the person in need. As a result, empathy does not lead to **sympathy**—feelings of concern or sorrow for another's plight.

Development of Empathy Empathy has roots early in development. Newborn babies tend to cry in response to the cry of another baby (see pages 135–136 in Chapter 4). And earlier we noted young infants' matching of others' emotional expressions. In sensitive, face-to-face communication, infants "connect" emotionally with their caregivers—experiences believed to be the foundation for empathy and concern for others (Zahn-Waxler, 1991).

Like self-conscious emotions, true empathy requires children to understand that the self is distinct from other people. As self-awareness strengthens at the end of the second year, toddlers begin to empathize. With age, they not only sense another's unhappiness but become better at inferring from the situation what might help relieve it (Svetlova, Nichols, & Brownell, 2010). For example, 2- to 2½-year-olds will readily hand a blanket to an adult who is rubbing her arms, shivering, and saying, "Brrrr." And they are likely to respond to their mother's simulated sadness by offering a hug or comforting words, or trying to distract her with a toy (Zahn-Waxler & Radke-Yarrow, 1990). Children of this age even react with concern and consoling behavior to an adult who experiences harm (someone destroys her treasured possession) but who shows no overt emotion (Vaish, Carpenter, & Tomasello, 2009). Older toddlers seem to be able to engage in basic *affective perspective-taking*—inferring how another feels by imagining themselves in that person's place.

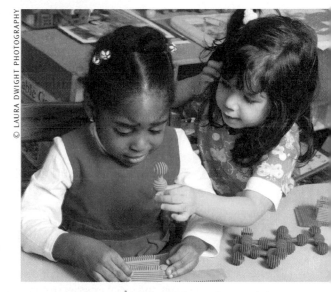

As language develops, children rely more on words to console others, indicating a more reflective level of empathy (Bretherton et al., 1986). When a 4-year-old received a Christmas gift that she hadn't included on her list for Santa, she assumed it belonged to another little girl and pleaded with her parents, "We've got to give it back—Santa's made a big mistake. I think the girl's crying 'cause she didn't get her present!"

Empathy increases over the elementary school years as children understand a wider range of emotions and take multiple cues into account in assessing others' feelings (Ricard & Kamberk-Kilicci, 1995). During late childhood and adolescence, advances in perspective taking permit an empathic response not just to people's immediate distress but also to their general life condition (Hoffman, 2000). The ability to empathize with the poor, oppressed, and sick requires an advanced form of perspective taking in which the young person understands that people lead continuous emotional lives beyond the current situation.

A preschooler comforts a sad classmate. As children's language and perspective-taking skills expand, empathy increases and, in children who are good at regulating emotion, leads to sympathetic concern and prosocial behavior.

Individual Differences Temperament plays a role in whether empathy occurs and whether it prompts sympathetic, prosocial behavior or a personally distressed, self-focused response. Twin studies reveal that empathy is moderately heritable (Knafo et al., 2009). Children who are sociable, assertive, and good at regulating emotion are more likely than poor emotion regulators to empathize with others' distress, display sympathetic concern, and engage in prosocial behavior, helping, sharing, and comforting others in distress (Bengtsson, 2005; Eisenberg et al., 1998; Valiente et al., 2004). Such children are also more likely to empathize with others' positive emotions of joy and happiness (Sallquist et al., 2009).

In contrast, aggressive children's high hostility, weakened capacity to take another's perspective, and impulsive acting out of negative feelings blunt their capacity for empathy and sympathy. Many show a decline—rather than the typical rise—in concern for others during middle childhood (Hastings et al., 2000; Strayer & Roberts, 2004b). And shy children may not display sympathetic concern because they are easily overwhelmed by anxiety when others are distressed (Eisenberg et al., 1996).

Individual differences in empathy and sympathy are evident in children's facial and neurobiological responses. In a series of studies, children watched videotapes of people in need, such as two children lying on the ground crying. Children who reacted with facial or physiological markers of concern—an interested, caring expression or a decrease in heart rate, suggesting orienting and attention—usually behaved prosocially when offered a chance to help. Those who showed facial and physiological evidence of distress—frowning, lip biting, and a rise in heart rate—were less prosocial (Fabes et al., 1994; Miller et al., 1996). Similarly, empathy is related to EEG brain-wave activity—a mild increase in the left hemisphere (which houses positive emotion) among children showing facial signs of empathy. In contrast, children who do not show these empathic signs often display a sharp EEG increase in the right hemisphere (which houses negative emotion)—an indication that they are overwhelmed by negative emotion (Jones, Field, & Davalos, 2000; Pickens, Field, & Nawrocki, 2001).

Parenting profoundly influences empathy and sympathy. When parents are warm, encourage emotional expressiveness, and show sensitive, empathic concern for their youngsters' feelings, their children are likely to react in a concerned way to the distress of others—relationships that persist into adolescence and early adulthood (Koestner, Franz, & Weinberger, 1990; Michalik et al., 2007; Strayer & Roberts, 2004a). Besides modeling sympathy, parents can help children learn to regulate angry feelings, which disrupt empathy and sympathy. They can also teach children the importance of kindness and can intervene when they display inappropriate emotion—strategies that predict high levels of sympathetic responding (Eisenberg, 2003). And parents can provide opportunities for children to show sympathetic concern through charitable giving and community service activities.

In contrast, angry, punitive parenting disrupts empathy and sympathy at an early age—particularly among children who are poor emotion regulators and, therefore, respond to parental hostility with especially high levels of personal distress (Valiente et al., 2004). In one study, physically abused toddlers at a child-care center rarely expressed concern at a peer's unhappiness but, rather, reacted with fear, anger, and physical attacks (Klimes-Dougan & Kistner, 1990). The children's reactions resembled their parents' insensitive responses to others' suffering.

These findings, like others discussed so far, reveal wide variations in children's emotional dispositions. As we turn now to the topic of temperament, we will encounter additional evidence for the joint contributions of heredity and environment to these differences. But first, consult the Milestones table on the following page for an overview of the emotional attainments just considered.

ASK YOURSELF

Review ■ What do preschoolers understand about emotion, and how do cognition and social experience contribute to their understanding?

Connect ■ Why is good emotional self-regulation vital for empathy to result in sympathy and prosocial behavior?

Connect ■ Cite ways that parenting contributes to emotional understanding, self-conscious emotions, empathy, and sympathy. Do you see any patterns? Explain.

Apply ■ When 15-month-old Ellen fell down while running, she looked at her mother, who smiled and exclaimed, "Oh, wasn't that a funny tumble!" How is Ellen likely to respond emotionally, and why?

▶ What is temperament, and how is it measured?

▶ Discuss the roles of heredity and environment in the stability of temperament, the relationship of temperament to cognitive and social functioning, and the goodness-of-fit model.

Temperament and Development

When we describe one person as cheerful and upbeat, another as active and energetic, and still others as calm, cautious, persistent, or prone to angry outbursts, we are referring to **temperament**—early-appearing, stable individual differences in reactivity and self-regulation. *Reactivity* refers to quickness and intensity of emotional arousal, attention, and motor action. *Self-regulation*, as we have seen, refers to strategies that modify

Milestones

Emotional Development

AGE	EMOTIONAL EXPRESSIVENESS	EMOTIONAL UNDERSTANDING
Birth–6 months	• Social smile emerges • Laughter appears • Expressions of happiness increase when interacting with familiar people • Emotional expressions gradually become organized signals that are meaningfully related to environmental events	• Detects emotions by matching the caregiver's feeling tone in face-to-face communication
7–12 months	• Anger and fear increase in frequency and intensity • Uses caregiver as a secure base • Regulates emotion by approaching and retreating from stimulation	• Detects the meaning of others' emotional signals • Engages in social referencing
1–2 years	• Self-conscious emotions emerge but depend on monitoring and encouragement of adults • Begins to use language to assist with emotional self-regulation	• Begins to appreciate that others' emotional reactions may differ from one's own • Acquires a vocabulary of emotional terms • Displays empathy
3–6 years	• Self-conscious emotions are clearly linked to self-evaluation • As representation and language improve, uses active strategies for regulating emotion • Begins to conform to emotional display rules; can pose a positive emotion he or she does not feel	• Understanding of causes, consequences, and behavioral signs of emotion improves in accuracy and complexity • As language develops, empathy becomes more reflective
7–11 years	• Self-conscious emotions are integrated with inner standards of excellence and good behavior • Uses internal strategies for engaging in emotional self-regulation; shifts adaptively between problem-centered and emotion-centered coping • Conformity to and conscious awareness of emotional display rules improve	• Can reconcile conflicting cues when explaining others' emotions • Is aware that people can have mixed feelings and that their expressions may not reflect their true feelings • Empathy increases as emotional understanding and perspective taking improve

Note: These milestones represent overall age trends. Individual differences exist in the precise age at which each milestone is attained.

Photos: (left) © Robert Dant/Alamy; (top right) © Laura Dwight Photography; (bottom right) © Ellen B. Senisi Photography

that reactivity (Rothbart & Bates, 2006). The psychological traits that make up temperament are believed to form the cornerstone of the adult personality.

In 1956, Alexander Thomas and Stella Chess initiated the New York Longitudinal Study, a groundbreaking investigation of the development of temperament that followed 141 children from early infancy well into adulthood. Results showed that temperament can increase a child's chances of experiencing psychological problems or, alternatively, protect a child from the negative effects of a stressful home life. At the same time, Thomas and Chess (1977) discovered that parenting practices can modify children's temperaments considerably.

These findings stimulated a growing body of research on temperament, including its stability, biological roots, and interaction with child-rearing experiences. Let's begin to explore these issues by looking at the structure, or makeup, of temperament and how it is measured.

The Structure of Temperament

Thomas and Chess's model of temperament, consisting of nine dimensions listed in Table 10.1, inspired all others that followed. When detailed descriptions of infants' and children's behavior obtained from parent interviews were rated on these dimensions, certain characteristics clustered together, yielding three types of children:

- The **easy child** (40 percent of the sample) quickly establishes regular routines in infancy, is generally cheerful, and adapts easily to new experiences.
- The **difficult child** (10 percent of the sample) has irregular daily routines, is slow to accept new experiences, and tends to react negatively and intensely.
- The **slow-to-warm-up child** (15 percent of the sample) is inactive, shows mild, low-key reactions to environmental stimuli, is negative in mood, and adjusts slowly to new experiences.

Note that 35 percent of the children did not fit any of these categories. Instead, they showed unique blends of temperamental characteristics.

The difficult pattern has sparked the most interest because it places children at high risk for adjustment problems—both anxious withdrawal and aggressive behavior in early and middle childhood (Bates, Wachs, & Emde, 1994; Ramos et al., 2005; Thomas, Chess, & Birch, 1968). Compared with difficult children, slow-to-warm-up children present fewer problems in the early years. However, they tend to show excessive fearfulness and slow, constricted behavior in the late preschool and school years, when they are expected to respond

TABLE 10.1 | Two Models of Temperament

THOMAS AND CHESS		ROTHBART	
Dimension	*Description*	*Dimension*	*Description*
Activity level	Ratio of active periods to inactive ones	*Reactivity*	
Rhythmicity	Regularity of body functions, such as sleep, wakefulness, hunger, and excretion	Activity level	Level of gross-motor activity
Distractibility	Degree to which stimulation from the environment alters behavior—for example, whether crying stops when a toy is offered	Attention span/ persistence	Duration of orienting or interest
		Fearful distress	Wariness and distress in response to intense or novel stimuli, including time to adjust to new situations
Approach/ withdrawal	Response to a new object, food, or person		
Adaptability	Ease with which child adapts to changes in the environment, such as sleeping or eating in a new place	Irritable distress	Extent of fussing, crying, and distress when desires are frustrated
		Positive affect	Frequency of expression of happiness and pleasure
Attention span and persistence	Amount of time devoted to an activity, such as watching a mobile or playing with a toy	*Self-Regulation*	
Intensity of reaction	Energy level of response, such as laughing, crying, talking, or gross-motor activity	Effortful control	Capacity to voluntarily suppress a dominant, reactive response in order to plan and execute a more adaptive response
Threshold of responsiveness	Intensity of stimulation required to evoke a response		
Quality of mood	Amount of friendly, joyful behavior as opposed to unpleasant, unfriendly behavior		

actively and quickly in classrooms and peer groups (Chess & Thomas, 1984; Schmitz et al., 1999).

Today, the most influential model of temperament is Mary Rothbart's (refer again to Table 10.1). It combines related traits proposed by Thomas and Chess and other researchers, yielding a concise list of just six dimensions. For example, "distractibility" and "attention span and persistence" are considered opposite ends of the same dimension, which is labeled "attention span/persistence." A unique feature of Rothbart's model is inclusion of both "fearful distress" and "irritable distress," which distinguish between reactivity triggered by fear and reactivity due to frustration. And the model deletes overly broad dimensions, such as "rhythmicity," "intensity of reaction," and "threshold of responsiveness" (Rothbart, Ahadi, & Evans, 2000; Rothbart & Mauro, 1990). A child who is rhythmic in sleeping is not necessarily rhythmic in eating or bowel habits. And a child who smiles and laughs intensely is not necessarily intense in fear, irritability, or motor activity.

Rothbart's dimensions are supported by factor analyses of many measures of children's temperament (see page 321 in Chapter 8 to review the concept of factor analysis). Notice how her dimensions represent the three underlying components included in the definition of temperament: (1) *emotion* ("fearful distress," "irritable distress," "positive affect," and "soothability"), (2) *attention* ("attention span/persistence"), and (3) *action* ("activity level"). According to Rothbart, individuals differ not only in their reactivity on each dimension but also in the self-regulatory dimension of temperament, **effortful control**—the capacity to voluntarily suppress a dominant response in order to plan and execute a more adaptive response (Rothbart, 2003; Rothbart & Bates, 2006). Variations in effortful control are evident in how effectively a child can focus and shift attention, inhibit impulses, and manage negative emotion.

TAKE A MOMENT... Turn back to page 287 in Chapter 7 to review the concept of *inhibition*, and note its strong resemblance to *effortful control*. As we will see later, researchers assess these capacities in similar ways. Their converging concepts, measures, and findings reveal that the same mental activities lead to effective regulation in both the cognitive and emotional/social domains.

Measuring Temperament

Temperament is often assessed through interviews or questionnaires given to parents. Behavior ratings by pediatricians, teachers, and others familiar with the child and laboratory observations by researchers have also been used. Parental reports are convenient and take advantage of parents' depth of knowledge of the child across many situations (Gartstein & Rothbart, 2003). Although information from parents has been criticized as being biased, parental reports are moderately related to researchers' observations of children's behavior (Majdandžić & van den Boom, 2007; Mangelsdorf, Schoppe, & Buur, 2000). And parent perceptions are vital for understanding how parents view and respond to their child.

Observations by researchers in the home or laboratory avoid the subjectivity of parental reports but can lead to other inaccuracies. In homes, observers find it hard to capture all relevant information, especially events that are rare but important, such as infants' response to frustration. And in the unfamiliar lab setting, fearful children who calmly avoid certain experiences at home may become too upset to complete the session if the lab does not permit avoidance (Wachs & Bates, 2001). Still, researchers can better control children's experiences in the lab. And they can conveniently combine observations of behavior with neurobiological measures to gain insight into the biological bases of temperament.

Most neurobiological research has focused on children who fall at opposite extremes of the positive-affect and fearful-distress dimensions of temperament: **inhibited, or shy, children,** who react negatively to and withdraw from novel stimuli; and **uninhibited, or sociable, children,** who display positive emotion to and approach novel stimuli. As the Biology and Environment box on page 422 reveals, biologically based reactivity—evident in heart rate, hormone levels, and EEG brain waves in the frontal region of the cerebral cortex—differentiates children with inhibited and uninhibited temperaments.

BIOLOGY and ENVIRONMENT

Development of Shyness and Sociability

Two 4-month-old babies, Larry and Mitch, visited the laboratory of Jerome Kagan, who observed their reactions to a variety of unfamiliar experiences. When exposed to new sights and sounds, such as a moving mobile decorated with colorful toys, Larry tensed his muscles, moved his arms and legs with agitation, and began to cry. In contrast, Mitch remained relaxed and quiet, smiling and cooing at the excitement around him.

As toddlers, Larry and Mitch returned to the laboratory, where they experienced several procedures designed to induce uncertainty. Electrodes were placed on their bodies and blood pressure cuffs on their arms to measure heart rate; toy robots, animals, and puppets moved before their eyes; and unfamiliar people entered and behaved in unexpected ways or wore novel costumes. While Larry whimpered and quickly withdrew, Mitch watched with interest, laughed at the strange sights, and approached the toys and strangers.

On a third visit, at age 4½, Larry barely talked or smiled during an interview with an unfamiliar adult. In contrast, Mitch asked questions and communicated his pleasure at each new activity. In a playroom with two unfamiliar peers, Larry pulled back and watched, while Mitch made friends quickly.

In longitudinal research on several hundred Caucasian infants followed into adolescence, Kagan found that about 20 percent of 4-month-old babies were, like Larry, easily upset by novelty; 40 percent, like Mitch, were comfortable, even delighted, with new experiences. About 20 to 30 percent of these extreme groups retained their temperamental styles as they grew older (Kagan, 2003; Kagan & Saudino, 2001; Kagan et al., 2007). But most children's dispositions became less extreme over time. Genetic makeup and child-rearing experiences jointly influenced stability and change in temperament.

Neurobiological Correlates of Shyness and Sociability

Individual differences in arousal of the *amygdala*, an inner brain structure that controls avoidance reactions, contribute to these contrasting temperaments. In shy, inhibited children, novel stimuli easily excite the amygdala and its connections to the cerebral cortex and sympathetic nervous system, which prepares the body to act in the face of threat. In sociable, uninhibited children, the same level of stimulation evokes minimal neural excitation (Kagan

& Fox, 2006). In support of this theory, while viewing photos of unfamiliar faces, adults who had been classified as inhibited in the second year of life showed greater fMRI activity in the amygdala than adults who had been uninhibited as toddlers (Schwartz et al., 2003). And additional neurobiological responses known to be mediated by the amygdala distinguish these two emotional styles:

• *Heart rate.* From the first few weeks of life, the heart rates of shy children are consistently higher than those of sociable children, and they speed up further in response to unfamiliar events (Schmidt et al., 2007; Snidman et al., 1995).

• *Cortisol.* Saliva concentrations of the stress hormone cortisol tend to be higher, and to rise more in response to a stressful event, in shy than in sociable children (Schmidt et al., 1997, 1999; Zimmermann & Stansbury, 2004).

• *Pupil dilation, blood pressure, and skin surface temperature.* Compared with sociable children, shy children tend to show greater pupil dilation, rise in blood pressure, and cooling of the fingertips when faced with novelty (Kagan et al., 1999, 2007).

Another physiological correlate of approach–withdrawal to people and objects is the pattern of EEG brain waves in the frontal lobes of the cerebral cortex. Shy infants and preschoolers show greater EEG activity in the right frontal lobe, which is associated with negative emotional reactivity; sociable children show the opposite pattern (Fox et al., 2008; Kagan et al., 2007). Neural activity in the amygdala, which is transmitted to the frontal lobes, probably contributes to these differences. Inhibited children also show greater generalized activation of the cerebral cortex, an indicator of high emotional arousal and monitoring of new situations for potential threats (Henderson et al., 2004).

Child-Rearing Practices

According to Kagan, extremely shy or sociable children inherit a physiology that biases them toward a particular temperamental style. Yet heritability research indicates that genes contribute only modestly to shyness and sociability (Kagan & Fox, 2006). Experience has a powerful impact.

Child-rearing practices affect the chances that an emotionally reactive baby will become a fearful child. Warm, supportive parenting reduces shy infants' and preschoolers' intense

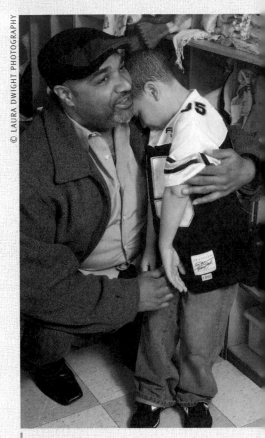

A strong physiological response to novel stimuli prompts this child to cling to his father. With patient, insistent encouragement, parents can help shy children overcome the urge to retreat from unfamiliar events.

physiological reaction to novelty, whereas cold, intrusive parenting heightens anxiety (Coplan, Arbeau, & Armer, 2008; Hane et al., 2008). And if parents overprotect infants and young children who dislike novelty, they make it harder for the child to overcome an urge to retreat. Parents who make appropriate demands for their child to approach new experiences help shy youngsters develop strategies for regulating fear (Rubin & Burgess, 2002).

When inhibition persists, it leads to excessive cautiousness, low self-esteem, and loneliness (Fordham & Stevenson-Hinde, 1999; Rubin, Stewart, & Coplan, 1995). In adolescence, persistent shyness increases the risk of severe anxiety, especially social phobia—intense fear of being humiliated in social situations (Kagan & Fox, 2006). For inhibited children to acquire effective social skills, parenting must be tailored to their temperaments—a theme we will encounter again in this and later chapters.

Stability of Temperament

Young children who score low or high on attention span, irritability, sociability, shyness, or effortful control tend to respond similarly when assessed again several months to a few years later and, occasionally, even into the adult years (Caspi et al., 2003; Kochanska & Knaack, 2003; Majdandžić & van den Boom, 2007; Rothbart, Ahadi, & Evans, 2000; van den Akker et al., 2010). However, the overall stability of temperament is low in infancy and toddlerhood and only moderate from the preschool years on (Putnam, Samson, & Rothbart, 2000). Some children remain the same, but many others change.

Why isn't temperament more stable? A major reason is that temperament itself develops with age. To illustrate, let's look at irritability and activity level. Recall from Chapter 4 that most babies fuss and cry in the early months. As infants better regulate their attention and emotions, many who initially seemed irritable become calm and content. In the case of activity level, the meaning of the behavior changes. At first, an active, wriggling infant tends to be highly aroused and uncomfortable, whereas an inactive baby is often alert and attentive. Once infants move on their own, the reverse is so! An active crawler is usually alert and interested in exploration, whereas a very inactive baby may be fearful and withdrawn.

These discrepancies help us understand why long-term prediction from early temperament is best achieved after age 3, when children's styles of responding are better established (Roberts & DelVecchio, 2000). In line with this idea, between ages 2½ and 3, children improve substantially and also perform more consistently across a wide variety of tasks requiring effortful control, such as waiting for a reward, lowering their voice to a whisper, succeeding at games like "Simon Says," and selectively attending to one stimulus while ignoring competing stimuli (Kochanska, Murray, & Harlan, 2000; Li-Grining, 2007). Researchers believe that around this time, areas in the prefrontal cortex involved in suppressing impulses develop rapidly (Gerardi-Caulton, 2000; Rothbart & Bates, 2006).

Nevertheless, the ease with which children manage their reactivity in early childhood depends on the type and strength of the reactive emotion involved. Preschoolers who were highly fearful as 2-year-olds score slightly better than their agemates in effortful control as 4-year-olds. In contrast, angry, irritable 2-year-olds tend to be less effective at effortful control at later ages (Bridgett et al., 2009; Kochanska & Knaack, 2003; Kochanska, Murray, & Harlan, 2000).

In sum, many factors affect the extent to which a child's temperament remains stable, including development of the biological systems on which temperament is based, the child's capacity for effortful control, and the success of her efforts, which depend on the quality and intensity of her emotional reactivity. When we consider the evidence as a whole, the low to moderate stability of temperament makes sense. It also confirms that experience can modify biologically based temperamental traits considerably, although children rarely change from one extreme to another—that is, a shy preschooler practically never becomes highly sociable, and irritable children seldom become easygoing. With these ideas in mind, let's turn to genetic and environmental contributions to temperament and personality.

Genetic and Environmental Influences

The word *temperament* implies a genetic foundation for individual differences in personality. Research indicates that identical twins are more similar than fraternal twins across a wide range of temperamental traits (activity level, attention span, shyness/sociability, irritability, and effortful control) and personality measures (introversion/extroversion, anxiety, agreeableness, curiosity and imaginativeness, and impulsivity) (Bouchard, 2004; Bouchard & Loehlin, 2001; Caspi & Shiner, 2006; Roisman & Fraley, 2006; Saudino & Cherny, 2001). In Chapter 3, we noted that heritability estimates derived from twin studies suggest a moderate role for genetic factors in temperament and personality: About half of individual differences have been attributed to differences in genetic makeup.

Nevertheless, genetic influences vary with the temperamental trait and the age of the individual being studied. For example, heritability estimates are higher for expressions of negative emotion than for positive emotion. And the role of heredity is considerably less in infancy than in childhood and later years, when temperament becomes more stable (Wachs & Bates, 2001).

Although genetic influences on temperament are clear, environment is also powerful. For example, persistent nutritional and emotional deprivation profoundly alters temperament, resulting in maladaptive emotional reactivity. Recall from Chapter 5 that even after dietary improvement, children exposed to severe malnutrition in infancy remain more distractible and fearful than their agemates. Also, higher levels of home noise and crowding are linked to withdrawal and irritability in the second year (Matheny & Phillips, 2001; Wachs, 2006). And earlier in this chapter, we noted that children who spent their infancy in deprived orphanages are easily overwhelmed by stressful events. Their poor regulation of emotion results in inattention and weak impulse control, including frequent expressions of anger (see page 197).

Other research shows that child rearing has much to do with whether infants and young children maintain their temperamental traits. In fact, heredity and environment often jointly contribute to temperament, since a child's approach to the world affects the experiences to which she is exposed. To illustrate how this works, let's look closely at ethnic differences in temperament.

This Japanese grandmother holds her grandchild close while interacting gently and soothingly. These caregiving behaviors contribute to Japanese babies' calm, emotionally restrained temperamental style.

Cultural Variations Compared with North American Caucasian infants, Chinese and Japanese babies tend to be less active, irritable, and vocal; more easily soothed when upset; and better at quieting themselves (Kagan et al., 1994; Lewis, Ramsay, & Kawakami, 1993). Chinese and Japanese babies are also more fearful and inhibited, remaining closer to their mothers in an unfamiliar playroom and displaying more anxiety when interacting with a stranger (Chen, Wang, & DeSouza, 2006). And they are more emotionally restrained, smiling, laughing, and crying less than Caucasian-American babies (Camras et al., 1998; Gartstein et al., 2010).

These variations may have genetic roots, but they are supported by cultural beliefs and practices. Japanese mothers usually say that babies come into the world as independent beings who must learn to rely on their parents through close physical contact. American mothers typically believe just the opposite—that they must wean the baby away from dependency toward autonomy. Consistent with these beliefs, Asian mothers interact gently, soothingly, and gesturally with their babies, whereas Caucasian mothers use a more active, stimulating, verbal approach (Rothbaum et al., 2000b). Also, recall from our discussion of emotional self-regulation that Chinese and Japanese adults discourage babies from expressing strong emotion, which contributes further to their infants' tranquility.

Nonshared Environment In families with several children, an additional influence on temperament is at work. Recall from Chapter 8 that *nonshared environmental influences*— those that make siblings different from one another—play an important role in intelligence. They are also influential in personality development. **TAKE A MOMENT...** Ask several parents to describe each of their children's personalities. You will see that they often emphasize differences between siblings: "She's a lot more active." "He's more sociable." "She's far more persistent." As a result, parents often regard siblings as more distinct than other observers do. In a large study of 1- to 3-year-old twin pairs, parents rated identical twins as resembling each other less in temperament than researchers' ratings indicated. And whereas researchers rated fraternal twins as moderately similar, parents viewed them as somewhat opposite in temperamental style (see Figure 10.2) (Saudino, 2003).

Parents' tendency to emphasize each child's unique qualities affects their child-rearing practices. In a study of 3-year-old identical twins, mothers' differential treatment of each twin predicted differences between twins in psychological adjustment. The pair member who received more warmth and less harshness was more positive in mood and prosocial behavior and less likely to have behavior problems (Deater-Deckard et al., 2001). Each child, in turn, evokes responses from caregivers that are consistent with parental beliefs and the child's developing temperament.

Besides different experiences within the family, siblings have distinct experiences with teachers, peers, and others in their community that affect personality development. And as they get older, siblings often seek ways to differ from one another. For all these reasons, both identical and fraternal twins tend to become increasingly dissimilar in personality with age (Loehlin & Martin, 2001; McCartney, Harris, & Bernieri, 1990). The less contact twins have with each other, the stronger this effect.

Are nonshared factors more important in personality development than *shared environmental influences*—those that affect all siblings similarly? In Chapter 14, we will see that shared factors, such as family stress and child-rearing styles, also affect children's personalities. In sum, we must think of temperament and personality as affected by a complex mix of environmental conditions, some child-specific and others stemming from shared family conditions.

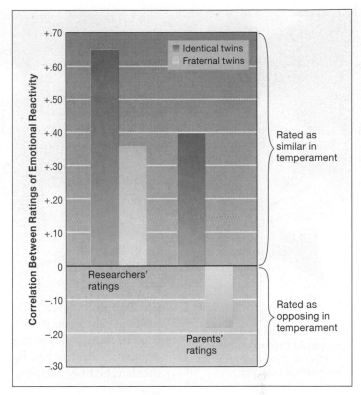

FIGURE 10.2 Temperament correlations for identical and fraternal twin pairs, as rated by researchers and parents. Parents rated 1- to 3-year-old identical twins as resembling each other less in temperament than researchers did. And whereas researchers rated fraternal twins as moderately similar, parents rated them as somewhat opposing in temperament. The correlations depicted here are for emotional reactivity. Activity level, shyness, and attention span/persistence yielded similar findings. (Adapted from Saudino, 2003.)

Temperament as a Predictor of Children's Behavior

Research on temperament provides a powerful illustration of the child's contribution to his or her own development. Children's temperamental traits consistently predict their cognitive and social functioning.

Almost as soon as it can be measured, children's attention span forecasts their learning and cognitive development. For example, persistence during the first year correlates with infant mental test scores and preschool IQ (Matheny, 1989). During early and middle childhood, persistence continues to predict IQ, along with literacy and mathematical progress and grades in school. In contrast, distractibility, high activity level, and difficult temperament are linked to poor school performance (Coplan, Barber, & Lagacé-Séguin, 1999; Martin, Olejnik, & Gaddis, 1994; Strelau, Zawadzki, & Piotrowska, 2001).

Temperament is also related to social behavior. Highly active preschoolers tend to be sociable with peers, but they also become involved in more conflict than their less active agemates. Shy, inhibited children often watch classmates and engage in anxious behaviors that discourage interaction, such as hovering around play activities and rarely speaking (Chen, Wang, & DeSouza, 2006; Henderson et al., 2004). And as we will see in Chapter 12, inhibited children's high anxiety leads to more discomfort after wrongdoing and a greater sense of responsibility to others. As a result, early fearfulness protects children against becoming aggressive. In contrast, irritable, impulsive children are at risk for aggressive and antisocial conduct (Sanson, Hemphill, & Smart, 2004; Vitaro et al., 2006).

In some cases, as with shy children, social behavior seems to be a direct result of temperament. In other instances, it reflects the way people respond to the child's emotional style.

These fifth graders collaborating on a science project exhibit a high capacity for effortful control—a dimension of temperament that predicts academic achievement and many other favorable outcomes.

For example, active, impulsive and irritable, anger-prone children often elicit negative interaction, which leads to conflict (Bridgett et al., 2009; van den Akker et al., 2010). As Chapter 12 will make clear, the relationship of early impulsivity and emotional negativity with later aggression and lawbreaking acts has much to do with the inept parenting often evoked by distractible, headstrong children.

Finally, beginning in the preschool years, children's capacity for effortful control is linked to favorable development and adjustment in cultures as diverse as China and the United States (Zhou, Lengua, & Wang, 2009). Positive outcomes include persistence, task mastery, academic achievement, cooperation, moral maturity (such as concern about wrongdoing and willingness to apologize), empathy, sympathy, and prosocial behaviors of sharing and helpfulness (Eisenberg, 2010; Kochanska & Aksan, 2006; Posner & Rothbart, 2007; Valiente, Lemery-Chalfant, & Swanson, 2010). Effortful control is also positively related to children's resistance to stress. For example, it buffers them against the negative impact of parental conflict, perhaps because children high in effortful control can shift attention away from their parents' negative behaviors and their own anxiety to more positive features of their social environments (David & Murphy, 2007). At the same, time, as we will see next, parenting practices can impede or promote children's effortful control, thereby profoundly altering the link between early temperament and development.

Temperament and Child Rearing: The Goodness-of-Fit Model

If a child's disposition interferes with learning or getting along with others, adults must gently but consistently counteract the child's maladaptive style. Thomas and Chess (1977) proposed a **goodness-of-fit model** to explain how temperament and environment together can produce favorable outcomes. Goodness of fit involves creating child-rearing environments that recognize each child's temperament while encouraging more adaptive functioning.

Goodness of fit helps explain why difficult children (who withdraw from new experiences and react negatively and intensely) are at high risk for later adjustment problems. These children frequently experience parenting that fits poorly with their dispositions. As infants, they are less likely to receive sensitive caregiving (van den Boom & Hoeksma, 1994). By the second year, their parents—especially in low-SES families—tend to use angry, punitive discipline, which undermines the development of effortful control. As the child reacts with defiance and disobedience, parents become increasingly stressed (Bridgett et al., 2009; Paulussen-Hoogeboom et al., 2007). As a result, they continue their coercive tactics and also discipline inconsistently, sometimes rewarding the child's noncompliance by giving in to it (Calkins, 2002). These practices sustain and even increase the child's irritable, conflict-ridden style (van Aken et al., 2007; Pesonen et al., 2008).

In contrast, when parents are positive and sensitive, which helps babies regulate emotion, difficultness declines by age 2 to 3 (Feldman, Greenbaum, & Yirmiya, 1999; Raikes et al., 2007). In toddlerhood and childhood, parental sensitivity, support, clear expectations, and limits foster effortful control, reducing the likelihood that difficultness will persist and lead to emotional and social difficulties (Cipriano & Stifter, 2010; Jaffari-Bimmel et al., 2006).

Recent evidence indicates that temperamentally difficult children function much worse than other children when exposed to inept parenting, yet benefit most from good parenting (Pluess & Belsky, 2011). Using molecular genetic analyses, researchers are investigating gene–environment interactions (see page 121 in Chapter 3) that explain this finding. In one study, 2-year-olds with a chromosome 17 gene containing a certain repetition of DNA base pairs (called short 5-HTTLPR), which interferes with functioning of the inhibitory neurotransmitter serotonin (and, thus, greatly increases the risk of negative mood and self-regulation difficulties), became increasingly irritable as their mothers' anxiety about parenting increased (Ivorra et al., 2010). Maternal anxiety had little impact on children without this genetic marker. In another investigation, preschoolers with the short 5-HTTLPR gene benefited, especially, from positive parenting. With parental affection and support, their capacity for self-regulation equaled that of agemates with a low-risk genotype (Kochanska, Philibert, & Barry, 2009).

Effective parenting of challenging children, however, also depends on life conditions—good parental mental health, marital harmony, and favorable economic conditions (Schoppe-Sullivan et al., 2007). In a comparison of the temperaments of Russian and U.S. babies, Russian infants were more emotionally negative, fearful, and upset when frustrated (Gartstein, Slobodskaya, & Kinsht, 2003). At the time of the study, Russia's national economy was severely depressed. Because of financial worries and longer work hours, Russian parents may have lacked time and energy for the patient parenting that protects against difficultness.

Cultural values also affect the fit between parenting and child temperament, as research in China illustrates. In the past, collectivist values, which discourage self-assertion, led Chinese adults to evaluate shy children positively. Several studies showed that shy Chinese children of a decade or two ago appeared well-adjusted, both academically and socially (Chen, Rubin, & Li, 1995; Chen et al., 1998). But rapid expansion of a market economy in China, which requires assertiveness and sociability for success, may be responsible for a recent change in Chinese parents' and teachers' attitudes toward childhood shyness (Chen, Wang, & DeSouza, 2006; Yu, 2002). Among Shanghai fourth graders, the association between shyness and adjustment also changed over time. Whereas shyness was positively correlated with teacher-rated competence, peer acceptance, leadership, and academic achievement in 1990, these relationships weakened in 1998 and reversed in 2002, when they mirrored findings of Western research (see Figure 10.3) (Chen et al., 2005). Cultural context makes a difference in whether shy children receive support or disapproval and whether they adjust well or poorly.

An effective match between rearing conditions and child temperament is best accomplished early, before unfavorable temperament–environment relationships produce maladjustment. Both difficult and shy children benefit from warm, accepting parenting that makes firm but reasonable demands for mastering new experiences. With reserved, inactive toddlers, highly stimulating parenting—questioning, instructing, and pointing out objects—fosters exploration. Yet for highly active toddlers, these same parental behaviors are too directive, dampening their play and curiosity (Miceli et al., 1998).

The goodness-of-fit model reminds us that babies have unique dispositions that adults must accept. Parents can neither take full credit for their children's virtues nor be blamed for all their faults. But parents can turn an environment that exaggerates a child's problems into one that builds on the child's strengths. In the following sections, we will see that goodness of fit is also at the heart of infant–caregiver attachment. This first intimate relationship grows out of interaction between parent and baby, to which the emotional styles of both partners contribute.

A parent's firm but affectionate approach to child rearing can help temperamentally difficult children gain in self-regulatory capacity.

FIGURE 10.3 **Changes over time in correlations between shyness and adjustment among Chinese fourth graders.** In 1990, shy Chinese children appeared well-adjusted. But as China's market economy expanded and valuing of self-assertion and sociability increased, the direction of the correlations shifted. In 2002, shyness was negatively associated with adjustment. These findings are for teacher-rated competence and peer acceptance. Those for leadership (holding offices in student organizations) and academic achievement changed similarly. (Adapted from Chen et al., 2005.)

▶ What are the unique features of ethological theory of attachment?

▶ Describe how researchers measure the security of attachment, and discuss the stability of attachment patterns.

▶ Discuss infants' formation of multiple attachments and the role of early attachment quality in later development.

Development of Attachment

Attachment is the strong, affectionate tie we have with special people in our lives that leads us to experience pleasure and joy when we interact with them and to be comforted by their nearness in times of stress. By the second half of the first year, infants have become attached to familiar people who have responded to their needs.

TAKE A MOMENT... Watch how babies of this age single out their parents for special attention. When the parent enters the room, the baby breaks into a broad, friendly smile. When she picks him up, he pats her face, explores her hair, and snuggles against her. When he feels anxious or afraid, he crawls into her lap and clings closely.

Freud first suggested that the infant's emotional tie to the mother is the foundation for all later relationships. Contemporary research indicates that—although the parent–infant bond is vitally important—later development is influenced not just by early attachment experiences but also by the continuing quality of the parent–child relationship.

Attachment has also been the subject of intense theoretical debate. Recall from Chapter 1 how the *psychoanalytic perspective* regards feeding as the central context in which caregivers and babies build this close emotional bond. *Behaviorism*, too, emphasizes the importance of feeding, but for different reasons. According to a well-known behaviorist explanation, infants learn to prefer the mother's soft caresses, warm smiles, and tender words because these events are paired with tension relief as she satisfies the baby's hunger.

Although feeding is an important context for building a close relationship, attachment does not depend on hunger satisfaction. In the 1950s, a famous experiment showed that rhesus monkeys reared with terry-cloth and wire-mesh "surrogate mothers" clung to the soft terry-cloth substitute, even though the wire-mesh "mother" held the bottle and infants had to climb on it to be fed (Harlow & Zimmerman, 1959). Human infants, too, become attached to family members who seldom feed them, including fathers, siblings, and grandparents. And toddlers in Western cultures who sleep alone and experience frequent daytime separations from their parents sometimes develop strong emotional ties to cuddly objects, such as blankets or teddy bears, that play no role in infant feeding!

Both psychoanalytic and behaviorist accounts of attachment have another problem: They emphasize the caregiver's contribution to the attachment relationship but pay little attention to the importance of the infant's characteristics.

Baby monkeys reared with "surrogate mothers" preferred to cling to a soft terry-cloth "mother" over a wire-mesh "mother" holding a bottle—evidence that parent–infant attachment is based on more than satisfaction of hunger.

Bowlby's Ethological Theory

Today, **ethological theory of attachment,** which recognizes the infant's emotional tie to the caregiver as an evolved response that promotes survival, is the most widely accepted view. John Bowlby (1969), who first applied this idea to the infant–caregiver bond, retained the psychoanalytic idea that quality of attachment to the caregiver has profound implications for the child's feelings of security and capacity to form trusting relationships.

At the same time, Bowlby was inspired by Konrad Lorenz's studies of imprinting (see Chapter 1). Bowlby believed that the human infant, like the young of other animal species, is endowed with a set of built-in behaviors that keep the parent nearby to protect the infant from danger and to provide support for exploring and mastering the environment (Waters & Cummings, 2000). Contact with the parent also ensures that the baby will be fed, but Bowlby pointed out that feeding is not the basis for attachment. Rather, attachment can best be understood in an evolutionary context in which survival of the species—through ensuring both safety and competence—is of utmost importance.

According to Bowlby, the infant's relationship with the parent begins as a set of innate signals that call the adult to the baby's side. Over time, a true affectionate bond forms, supported by new emotional and cognitive capacities as well as by a history of warm, sensitive care. Attachment develops in four phases:

1. *Preattachment phase* (birth to 6 weeks). Built-in signals—grasping, smiling, crying, and gazing into the adult's eyes—help bring newborn babies into close contact with other humans. Babies of this age recognize their own mother's smell, voice, and face (see Chapter 4). But they are not yet attached to her, since they do not mind being left with an unfamiliar adult.

2. *"Attachment-in-the-making" phase* (6 weeks to 6 to 8 months). During this phase, infants respond differently to a familiar caregiver than to a stranger. For example, the baby smiles, laughs, and babbles more freely with the mother and quiets more quickly when she picks him up. As infants learn that their own actions affect the behavior of those around them, they begin to develop a *sense of trust*—the expectation that the caregiver will respond when signaled—but they still do not protest when separated from her.

3. *"Clear-cut" attachment phase* (6 to 8 months to 18 months to 2 years). Now attachment to the familiar caregiver is evident. Babies display **separation anxiety,** becoming upset when their trusted caregiver leaves. Like stranger anxiety (see page 405), separation anxiety does not always occur; it depends on infant temperament and the current situation. But in many cultures, separation anxiety increases between 6 and 15 months, suggesting that infants have developed a clear understanding that the caregiver continues to exist when not in view. Consistent with this idea, babies who have not yet mastered Piagetian object permanence usually do not become anxious when separated from the parent (Lester et al., 1974).

   Besides protesting the parent's departure, older infants and toddlers try hard to maintain her presence. They approach, follow, and climb on her in preference to others. And they use the familiar caregiver as a secure base from which to explore.

4. *Formation of a reciprocal relationship* (18 months to 2 years and on). By the end of the second year, rapid growth in representation and language enables toddlers to understand some of the factors that influence the parent's coming and going and to predict her return. As a result, separation protest declines. Now children negotiate with the caregiver, using requests and persuasion to alter her goals. For example, one 2-year-old asked her parents to read a story before leaving her with a babysitter. The extra time with her parents, along with a better understanding of where they were going ("to have dinner with Uncle Charlie") and when they would be back ("right after you go to sleep"), helped this child withstand her parents' absence.

LOOK and LISTEN

Watch an 8- to 18-month-old at play for 20 to 30 minutes. Describe the baby's use of the parent or other familiar caregiver as a secure base from which to explore.

© ELLEN B. SENISI PHOTOGRAPHY

Because this 2-year-old has the language and representational skills to predict his mother's return, separation anxiety declines. He accepts his mother's departure.

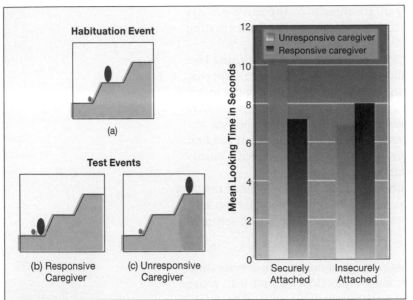

Habituation Event

(a)

Test Events

(b) Responsive Caregiver

(c) Unresponsive Caregiver

FIGURE 10.4 **Testing toddlers for internal working models of attachment.** (a) First, 12- to 16-month-olds were habituated to a video of two animated shapes, one large (the "caregiver") and one small (the "child"). The caregiver traveled halfway up an incline to a plateau, and the child began to "cry," depicted by pulsing and bouncing accompanied by an infant cry. Next the researchers presented two test events: (b) In the *responsive-caregiver outcome*, the caregiver returned to the child. (c) In the *unresponsive-caregiver outcome*, the caregiver continued up the slope away from the child. Securely attached toddlers looked longer at the unresponsive outcome, depicting caregiver behavior inconsistent with their attachment-related expectations. Insecurely attached toddlers did not differentiate between the two test events. (Adapted from Johnson, Dweck, & Chen, 2007.)

According to Bowlby (1980), out of their experiences during these four phases, children construct an enduring affectionate tie that they can use as a secure base in the parents' absence. This image serves as an **internal working model,** or set of expectations about the availability of attachment figures, their likelihood of providing support during times of stress, and the self's interaction with those figures. The internal working model becomes a vital part of personality, serving as a guide for all future close relationships (Bretherton & Munholland, 2008).

Consistent with these ideas, as early as the second year, toddlers form attachment-related expectations about parental comfort and support. In two studies, securely attached 12- to 16-month-olds looked longer at a video of an unresponsive caregiver (inconsistent with their expectations) than a video of a responsive caregiver. Insecurely attached toddlers, in contrast, did not distinguish between the two (see Figure 10.4) (Johnson, Dweck, & Chen, 2007; Johnson et al., 2010). With age, children continually revise and expand their internal working model as their cognitive, emotional, and social capacities increase and as they interact with parents and form other close bonds with adults, siblings, and friends.

Measuring the Security of Attachment

Although all family-reared babies become attached to a familiar caregiver by the second year, the quality of this relationship differs from child to child. Some infants appear relaxed and secure in the presence of the caregiver; they know they can count on her for protection and support. Others seem anxious and uncertain.

A widely used laboratory technique for assessing the quality of attachment between 1 and 2 years of age is the **Strange Situation**. In designing it, Mary Ainsworth and her colleagues (1978) reasoned that securely attached infants and toddlers should use the parent as a secure base from which to explore in an unfamiliar playroom. In addition, when the parent leaves, an unfamiliar adult should be less comforting than the parent. The Strange Situation takes the baby through eight short episodes in which brief separations from and reunions with the caregiver occur (see Table 10.2).

Observing infants' responses to these episodes, researchers identified a secure attachment pattern and three patterns of insecurity; a few babies cannot be classified (Ainsworth et al., 1978; Barnett & Vondra, 1999; Main & Solomon, 1990; Thompson, 2006). Although separation anxiety varies among the groups, the baby's reunion responses define attachment quality.

- **Secure attachment.** These infants use the parent as a secure base. When separated, they may or may not cry, but if they do, it is because the parent is absent and they prefer her to the stranger. When the parent returns, they actively seek contact, and their crying is reduced immediately. About 60 percent of North American infants in middle-SES families show this pattern. (In low-SES families, a smaller proportion of babies show the secure pattern, with higher proportions falling into the insecure patterns.)

- **Avoidant attachment.** These infants seem unresponsive to the parent when she is present. When she leaves, they usually are not distressed, and they react to the stranger in much the same way as to the parent. During reunion, they avoid or are slow to greet the parent, and when picked up, they often fail to cling. About 15 percent of North American infants in middle-SES families show this pattern.

TABLE 10.2 | Episodes in the Strange Situation

EPISODE	EVENTS	ATTACHMENT BEHAVIOR OBSERVED
1	Researcher introduces parent and baby to playroom and then leaves.	
2	Parent is seated while baby plays with toys.	Parent as a secure base
3	Stranger enters, is seated, and talks to parent.	Reaction to unfamiliar adult
4	Parent leaves room. Stranger responds to baby and offers comfort if baby is upset.	Separation anxiety
5	Parent returns, greets baby, and offers comfort if necessary. Stranger leaves room.	Reaction to reunion
6	Parent leaves room.	Separation anxiety
7	Stranger enters room and offers comfort.	Ability to be soothed by stranger
8	Parent returns, greets baby, offers comfort if necessary, and tries to reinterest baby in toys.	Reaction to reunion

Note: Episode 1 lasts about 30 seconds; each of the remaining episodes lasts about 3 minutes. Separation episodes are cut short if the baby becomes very upset. Reunion episodes are extended if the baby needs more time to calm down and return to play.

Source: Ainsworth et al., 1978.

- **Resistant attachment.** Before separation, these infants seek closeness to the parent and often fail to explore. When the parent leaves, they are usually distressed, and on her return they combine clinginess with angry, resistive behavior, struggling when held and sometimes hitting and pushing. Many continue to cry and cling after being picked up and cannot be comforted easily. About 10 percent of North American infants in middle-SES families show this pattern.
- **Disorganized/disoriented attachment.** This pattern reflects the greatest insecurity. At reunion, these infants show confused, contradictory behaviors—for example, looking away while the parent is holding them or approaching the parent with flat, depressed emotion. Most display a dazed facial expression, and a few cry out unexpectedly after having calmed down or display odd, frozen postures. About 15 percent of North American infants in middle-SES families show this pattern.

Researchers have modified Strange Situation procedures to make them appropriate for preschoolers, looking closely at the child's seeking of physical closeness, eye contact, expressions of emotion, and content and style of parent-directed speech—especially during reunion episodes. The resulting preschool attachment classifications are modestly associated with previously obtained infant assessments (Crittenden, 2000; Main & Cassidy, 1988; Moss et al., 2005b).

An alternative method, the **Attachment Q-Sort,** suitable for children between 1 and 4 years, depends on home observations (Waters et al., 1995). Either the parent or a highly trained observer sorts 90 behaviors—such as "Child greets mother with a big smile when she enters the room," "If mother moves very far, child follows along," and "Child uses mother's facial expressions as a good source of information when something looks risky or threatening"—into nine categories, ranging from "highly descriptive" to "not at all descriptive" of the child. Then a score, ranging from high to low in security, is computed.

Because the Q-Sort taps a wider array of attachment-related behaviors than the Strange Situation, it may better reflect the parent–child relationship in everyday life. However, the Q-sort method is time-consuming, requiring a nonparent informant to spend several hours observing the child before sorting the descriptors, and it does not differentiate between types of insecurity. The Q-Sort responses of expert observers correspond well with babies' secure-base behavior in the

This securely attached 1-year-old actively seeks contact and is calmed by his father's return. An avoidantly attached toddler would be slow to greet the parent; a resistantly attached child would be both clingy and angry.

© ELIZABETH CREWS

Strange Situation; more research is needed to verify a correspondence for preschoolers (Posada, 2006). Parents' Q-Sorts, however, show little relationship with Strange Situation assessments (van IJzendoorn et al., 2004). Parents of insecure children, especially, may have difficulty accurately reporting their child's attachment behaviors.

Stability of Attachment

Research on the stability of attachment patterns between 1 and 2 years of age yields a wide range of findings. In some studies, as many as 70 to 90 percent of babies remain the same in their reactions to parents; in others, only 30 to 40 percent do (Thompson, 2000, 2006). A close look at which babies stay the same and which ones change yields a more consistent picture. Quality of attachment is usually secure and stable for middle-SES babies experiencing favorable life conditions. And infants who move from insecurity to security typically have well-adjusted mothers with positive family and friendship ties. Perhaps many became parents before they were psychologically ready but, with social support, grew into the role.

In contrast, in low-SES families with many daily stresses and little social support, attachment generally moves away from security or changes from one insecure pattern to another (Belsky et al., 1996; Fish, 2004; Vondra, Hommerding, & Shaw, 1999; Vondra et al., 2001). In one long-term follow-up of a poverty-stricken sample, many securely attached infants ended up insecure when reassessed in early adulthood. Child maltreatment, maternal depression, and poor family functioning in adolescence distinguished these young people from the few who stayed securely attached (Weinfield, Sroufe, & Egeland, 2000; Weinfield, Whaley, & Egeland, 2004).

These findings indicate that securely attached babies more often maintain their attachment status than insecure babies, whose relationship with the caregiver is, by definition, fragile and uncertain. The exception is disorganized/disoriented attachment—an insecure pattern that is as stable as attachment security: Nearly 70 percent retain this classification over the second year, and the majority remain highly insecure over the long term, continuing to express confused, ambivalent feelings toward parents in early adulthood (Hesse & Main, 2000; Sroufe et al., 2005; Weinfield, Whaley, & Egeland, 2004). As you will soon see, many disorganized/disoriented infants experience extremely negative caregiving, which may disrupt emotional self-regulation so severely that attachment disorganization persists.

Cultural Variations

Cross-cultural evidence indicates that attachment patterns may have to be interpreted differently in certain cultures. For example, as Figure 10.5 reveals, German infants show considerably more avoidant attachment than American babies do. But German parents value independence and encourage their infants to be non-clingy, so the baby's behavior may be an intended outcome of cultural beliefs and practices (Grossmann et al., 1985). In contrast, a study of infants of the Dogon people of Mali, Africa, revealed that none showed avoidant attachment to their mothers (True, Pisani, & Oumar, 2001). Even when grandmothers are primary caregivers (as they are with firstborn sons), Dogon mothers remain available to their babies, holding them close and nursing them promptly in response to hunger and distress.

Japanese infants, as well, rarely show avoidant attachment (refer again to Figure 10.5). Rather, many are resistantly attached, but this reaction may not represent true insecurity. Japanese mothers spend much

FIGURE 10.5 A cross-cultural comparison of infants' reactions in the Strange Situation. A high percentage of German babies seem avoidantly attached, whereas a substantial number of Japanese and Israeli kibbutz infants appear resistantly attached. Note that these responses may not reflect true insecurity. Instead, they are probably due to cultural differences in child-rearing practices. (Adapted from Sagi et al., 1995; van IJzendoorn & Kroonenberg, 1988; van IJzendoorn & Sagi-Schwartz, 2008.)

time in close physical contact with their babies and rarely leave them in others' care, so the Strange Situation probably induces greater stress in them than in infants who experience frequent maternal separations (Takahashi, 1990). Also, Japanese parents expect their babies to be quite upset during reunion in the Strange Situation. They view the attention-seeking that is part of resistant attachment as a normal indicator of infants' efforts to satisfy dependency and security needs (Rothbaum et al., 2000a, 2007). Likewise, infants in Israeli kibbutzim frequently show resistant attachment. For these babies, who can sense the fear of unfamiliar people that is pervasive in their communities (see page 406), the Strange Situation probably induces unusual distress (van IJzendoorn & Sagi, 1999). Despite these and other cultural variations, the secure pattern is still the most common attachment quality in all societies studied to date (van IJzendoorn & Sagi-Schwartz, 2008).

Factors That Affect Attachment Security

What factors might influence attachment security? Researchers have looked closely at four important influences: (1) early availability of a consistent caregiver, (2) quality of caregiving, (3) the baby's characteristics, and (4) family context, including parents' internal working models.

Early Availability of a Consistent Caregiver   What happens when a baby does not have the opportunity to establish a close tie to a caregiver? In a series of studies, René Spitz (1946) observed institutionalized infants whose mothers had given them up between 3 and 12 months of age. After being placed in a large ward where each shared a nurse with at least seven others, the babies lost weight, wept, withdrew from their surroundings, and had difficulty sleeping. If a consistent caregiver did not replace the mother, the depression deepened rapidly. These institutionalized babies had emotional problems because they were prevented from forming a bond with one or a few adults (Rutter, 1996).

Another study supports this conclusion. Researchers followed the development of infants in an institution with a good caregiver–child ratio and a rich selection of books and toys. However, staff turnover was so rapid that the average child had 50 different caregivers by age 4½! Many of these children became "late adoptees" who were placed in homes after age 4. Most developed deep ties with their adoptive parents, indicating that a first attachment bond can develop as late as 4 to 6 years of age (Hodges & Tizard, 1989; Tizard & Rees, 1975). But these children were also more likely to display attachment difficulties, including an excessive desire for adult attention, "overfriendliness" to unfamiliar adults and peers, failure to check back with the parent in anxiety-arousing situations, and few friendships.

Children who spent their first year or more in deprived Eastern European orphanages—though also able to bond with their adoptive or foster parents—show elevated rates of attachment insecurity (van den Dries et al., 2009; Smyke et al., 2010). And they, too, are at high risk for emotional and social difficulties. Whereas many are indiscriminately friendly, others are sad, anxious, and withdrawn (Chisholm, 1998; Fisher et al., 1997; O'Connor et al., 2003). These symptoms typically persist and are associated with wide-ranging mental health problems in middle childhood and adolescence, including cognitive impairments, inattention and hyperactivity, depression, and either social avoidance or aggressive behavior (Kreppner et al., 2007, 2010; O'Connor et al., 2003; Rutter et al., 2007, 2010; Zeanah, 2000).

Furthermore, as early as 7 months, institutionalized children show reduced ERP brain waves in response to facial expressions of emotion and have trouble discriminating such expressions—outcomes that suggest disrupted formation of neural structures involved in "reading" emotions (Parker et al., 2005). These problems are still evident in preschoolers adopted during the second year, who find it hard to match appropriate facial expressions with situations in stories (Fries & Pollak, 2004). Consistent with these findings, MRI evidence reveals that in adopted children with longer institutional stays, the volume of the *amygdala*—a brain region devoted to processing emotional information (see page 190 in Chapter 5)—is atypically large (Tottenham et al., 2011). The larger the amygdala, the worse adopted children perform on emotion-processing tasks and the poorer their emotion

Dogon mothers of Mali, West Africa, stay close to their babies and respond promptly and gently to infant hunger and distress. With their mothers consistently available, none of the Dogon babies show avoidant attachment.

A father and baby engage in a sensitively tuned form of communication called interactional synchrony, in which they match emotional states, especially positive ones. Among Western infants, this style of communication predicts secure attachment.

regulation—deficits that contribute to their social-relationship and adjustment problems. Overall, the evidence on orphanage children indicates that fully normal emotional development depends on establishing a close tie with a caregiver early in life.

Quality of Caregiving Dozens of studies report that **sensitive caregiving**—responding promptly, consistently, and appropriately to infants and holding them tenderly and carefully—is moderately related to attachment security in both biological and adoptive mother–infant pairs and in diverse cultures and SES groups (Belsky & Fearon, 2008; DeWolff & van IJzendoorn, 1997; van IJzendoorn et al., 2004). In contrast, insecurely attached infants tend to have mothers who engage in less physical contact, handle them awkwardly or in a "routine" manner, and are sometimes resentful and rejecting, particularly in response to infant distress (Ainsworth et al., 1978; Isabella, 1993; McElwain & Booth-LaForce, 2006; Pederson & Moran, 1996).

Also, in studies of Western babies, a special form of communication called **interactional synchrony** separates the experiences of secure from insecure babies. It is best described as a sensitively tuned "emotional dance," in which the caregiver responds to infant signals in a well-timed, rhythmic, appropriate fashion. In addition, both partners match emotional states, especially the positive ones (Bigelow et al., 2010; Isabella & Belsky, 1991; Nievar & Becker, 2008). Earlier we saw that sensitive face-to-face play, in which interactional synchrony occurs, increases babies' sensitivity to others' emotional messages and helps them regulate emotion. But moderate adult–infant coordination is a better predictor of attachment security than "tight" coordination, in which the adult responds to most infant cues (Jaffee et al., 2001). Perhaps warm, sensitive caregivers use a relaxed, flexible style of communication in which they comfortably accept and repair emotional mismatches, returning to a synchronous state.

Cultures vary in their view of sensitivity toward infants. Among the Gusii people of Kenya, for example, mothers rarely cuddle, hug, or interact playfully with their babies, although they are very responsive to their infants' needs. Yet most Gusii infants appear securely attached (LeVine et al., 1994). This suggests that security depends on attentive caregiving, not necessarily on moment-by-moment contingent interaction. Puerto Rican mothers, who highly value obedience and socially appropriate behavior, often physically direct and limit their babies' actions—a style of caregiving linked to attachment security in Puerto Rican culture (Carlson & Harwood, 2003). But in many Western cultures, such physical control and restriction of exploration are viewed as intrusive and predict insecurity (Belsky & Fearon, 2008; Whipple, Bernier, & Mageau, 2011).

Compared with securely attached infants, avoidant babies tend to receive overstimulating care. Their mothers might, for example, talk energetically to them while they are looking away or falling asleep. By avoiding the mother, these infants try to escape from overwhelming interaction. Resistant infants often experience inconsistent care: Their mothers are unresponsive to infant signals. Yet when the baby begins to explore, these mothers interfere, shifting the infant's attention back to themselves. As a result, the baby is overly dependent as well as angry at the mother's lack of involvement (Cassidy & Berlin, 1994; Isabella & Belsky, 1991).

Highly inadequate caregiving is a powerful predictor of disruptions in attachment. Child abuse and neglect (topics we will consider in Chapter 14) are associated with all three forms of attachment insecurity. Among maltreated infants, disorganized/disoriented attachment is especially high (van IJzendoorn, Schuengel, & Bakermans-Kranenburg, 1999). Persistently depressed mothers, mothers with very low marital satisfaction, and parents suffering from a traumatic event, such as serious illness or loss of a loved one, also tend to promote the uncertain behaviors of this pattern (Campbell et al., 2004; Madigan et al., 2006; Moss et al., 2005b). And some mothers of disorganized/disoriented infants engage in frightening, contradictory, and unpleasant behaviors, such as looking scared, teasing the baby, holding the baby stiffly at a distance, roughly pulling the baby by the arm, or seeking reassurance from the upset child (Abrams, Rifkin, & Hesse, 2006; Lyons-Ruth, Bronfman, & Parsons, 1999; Moran et al., 2008). Perhaps the baby's disorganized behavior reflects a conflicted reaction to the parent, who sometimes comforts but at other times arouses fear.

Infant Characteristics Because attachment is the result of a *relationship* that builds between two partners, infant characteristics should affect how easily it is established. In Chapter 3, we saw that prematurity, birth complications, and newborn illness make caregiving more taxing. In families under stress, these difficulties are linked to attachment insecurity. In one study, the *combination* of preterm birth and maternal depression—but not preterm birth alone—increased the likelihood of insecure attachment at 12 months (Poehlmann & Fiese, 2001). Infants with special needs probably require greater sensitivity, which stressed parents often cannot provide. But at-risk newborns whose parents have the time and patience to care for them fare quite well in attachment security (Brisch et al., 2005; Cox, Hopkins, & Hans, 2000).

The role of infant temperament in attachment security has been intensely debated. Some researchers believe that infants who are irritable and fearful may simply react to brief separations with intense anxiety, regardless of the parent's sensitivity to the baby (Kagan, 1998; Kagan & Fox, 2006). Consistent with this view, emotionally reactive, difficult babies are more likely to develop later insecure attachments (van IJzendoorn et al., 2004; Vaughn, Bost, & van IJzendoorn, 2008).

Again, however, other evidence suggests that parental mental health and caregiving are involved. In a study extending from birth to age 2, difficult infants more often had highly anxious mothers—a combination that, by the second year, often resulted in a "disharmonious relationship" characterized by both maternal insensitivity and attachment insecurity (Symons, 2001). Infant difficultness and maternal anxiety seemed to perpetuate each other, impairing caregiving and the security of the parent–infant bond.

Other research focusing on disorganized/disoriented attachment has uncovered gene–environment interactions (Gervai, 2009). In one of these investigations, mothers' experience of unresolved loss of a loved one or other trauma was associated with attachment disorganization only in infants with a chromosome-11 gene having a certain repetition of DNA base pairs (called DRD4 7-repeat), which is linked to deficient self-regulation (see Figure 10.6) (van IJzendoorn & Bakermans-Kranenburg, 2006). Babies with this genetic marker, who face special challenges in managing intense emotion, were more vulnerable to the negative impact of maternal adjustment problems.

If children's temperaments alone determined attachment security, we would expect attachment, like temperament, to be at least moderately heritable. Yet twin comparisons reveal that the heritability of attachment is virtually nil (O'Connor & Croft, 2001; Roisman & Fraley, 2008). In fact, about two-thirds of siblings—whether identical twins, fraternal twins, nontwin siblings, unrelated siblings, or foster infants—establish similar attachment patterns with their parent, although the siblings often differ in temperament (Cole, 2006; Dozier et al., 2001). This suggests that the strongest parental influences on attachment security are *nonshared* experiences, reflecting most parents' efforts to adjust their caregiving to each child's individual needs.

A major reason that children's characteristics do not show strong relationships with attachment quality is that their influence depends on goodness of fit. From this perspective, *many* child attributes can lead to secure attachment as long as caregivers sensitively adjust their behavior to fit the baby's needs (Seifer & Schiller, 1995; Sroufe, 1985).

Interventions that teach parents to interact sensitively with difficult-to-care-for infants are highly successful in enhancing both quality of caregiving and attachment security (Velderman et al., 2006). One program that focused on both maternal sensitivity and effective discipline was particularly effective in reducing stress reactivity (as indicated by lower cortisol levels) and disruptive behavior among toddlers with the DRD4 7-repeat gene, who are at risk for later attention-deficit hyperactivity disorder and externalizing behavior problems (Bakermans-Kranenburg et al., 2008a, 2008b; Bakermans-Kranenburg & van IJzendoorn, 2011). These findings suggest that the DRD4 7-repeat gene makes children more susceptible to the effects of both negative and positive parenting!

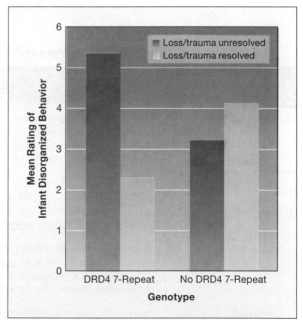

FIGURE 10.6 **The combination of maternal unresolved loss/trauma and infant DRD4 7-repeat gene predicts disorganized/disoriented attachment.** Mothers' experience of unresolved loss or other trauma was associated with disorganized/disoriented attachment only in 1-year-olds with the DRD4 7-repeat gene. (A rating of disorganized behavior in the Strange Situation higher than 5 leads to the attachment classification of disorganized/disoriented.) (Adapted from van IJzendoorn & Bakermans-Kranenburg, 2006.)

© IMAGEBROKER/ALAMY

Family circumstances are linked to attachment quality. Observing her parents' heated quarrels may undermine this child's sense of emotional security.

Family Circumstances As we have indicated in this and previous chapters, quality of caregiving can be fully understood only in terms of the larger context of the parent–child relationship. Job loss, a failing marriage, financial strain, and other stressors can undermine attachment indirectly, by interfering with the sensitivity of parental care. These stressors can also affect babies' sense of security directly by altering the emotional climate of the family (for example, exposing them to angry adult interactions) or by disrupting familiar daily routines (Finger et al., 2009; Raikes & Thompson, 2005).

The arrival of a new sibling illustrates how family circumstances can affect attachment quality. In one study, firstborn preschoolers who declined in attachment security after the birth of a baby had mothers who were depressed, anxious, or hostile before the birth. These symptoms were associated with marital friction (which the firstborns probably sensed) as well as with unfavorable mother–firstborn interaction. When mothers had cooperative marriages, coped well with the second birth, and stayed involved with their older child, preschoolers maintained a secure attachment bond (Teti et al., 1996). The availability of social supports, especially parents with a good relationship who assist each other with caregiving, reduces family stress and predicts greater attachment security (Belsky, 2006; Owen & Cox, 1997).

Parents' Internal Working Models Parents bring to the family context their own history of attachment experiences, from which they construct internal working models that they apply to the bonds they establish with their babies. To assess parents' "state of mind" with respect to attachment, Mary Main and her colleagues devised the *Adult Attachment Interview*, which asks adults to evaluate childhood memories of attachment experiences (Main & Goldwyn, 1998).

As Table 10.3 shows, quality of parents' working models is clearly related to children's attachment security in infancy and early childhood—results replicated in Canada, Germany, Great Britain, Japan, the Netherlands, and the United States. Parents who discuss their childhoods with objectivity and balance tend to have securely attached children. In contrast, parents who dismiss the importance of early relationships or describe them in angry, confused

TABLE 10.3 | **Relationship of Parents' Internal Working Models to Infant Attachment Security**

TYPE OF INTERNAL WORKING MODEL	DESCRIPTION	INFANT ATTACHMENT CLASSIFICATION[a]
Autonomous/secure	These parents show objectivity and balance in discussing their childhood experiences, whether these were positive or negative. They neither idealize their parents nor feel angry about the past. Their explanations are coherent and believable. About 58 percent of North American mothers and fathers without psychological disturbance are autonomous/secure.	Secure
Dismissing	These parents devalue the importance of their attachment relationships. They tend to idealize their parents without being able to recall specific experiences. What they do recall is discussed intellectually, with little emotion. About 23 percent of North American mothers and 28 percent of fathers without psychological disturbance are dismissing.	Avoidant
Preoccupied	These parents talk about their childhood experiences with highly charged emotion, sometimes expressing anger toward their parents. They appear overwhelmed and confused about their early attachments and cannot discuss them coherently. About 19 percent of North American mothers and 15 percent of fathers without psychological disturbance are preoccupied.	Resistant
Unresolved	These parents show characteristics of any of the three other patterns. At the same time, they reason in a disorganized and confused way when loss of a loved one or experiences of physical or sexual abuse are discussed. Besides displaying one of the other patterns, about 18 percent of North American mothers and 15 percent of fathers without psychological disturbance are unresolved.	Disorganized/disoriented

[a] Correspondences between type of maternal working model and infant attachment classification hold for 60 to 70 percent of mother–infant pairs.

Source: Bakermans-Kranenburg & van IJzendoorn, 2009; Bretherton & Munholland, 2008.

ways usually have insecurely attached children (Behrens, Hesse, & Main, 2007; Steele, Steele, & Fonagy, 1996; van IJzendoorn, 1995). Caregiving behavior helps explain these associations. Parents with autonomous/secure representations are warmer and more sensitive with their babies. They are also more likely to be supportive and to encourage learning and mastery in their preschoolers, who, in turn, are more affectionate and comfortably interactive with them (Coyl, Newland, & Freeman, 2010; Pederson et al., 1998; Slade et al., 1999).

But we must not assume any direct transfer of parents' childhood experiences to quality of attachment with their own children. Internal working models are *reconstructed memories* affected by many factors, including relationship experiences over the life course, personality, and current life satisfaction. Longitudinal research reveals that negative life events can weaken the link between an individual's own attachment security in infancy and a secure internal working model in adulthood. And insecurely attached babies who become adults with insecure internal working models often have lives that, based on adulthood self-reports, are filled with family crises (Waters et al., 2000; Weinfield, Sroufe, & Egeland, 2000).

In sum, our early rearing experiences do not destine us to become either sensitive or insensitive parents. Rather, the way we *view* our childhoods—our ability to come to terms with negative events, to integrate new information into our working models, and to look back on our own parents in an understanding, forgiving way—appears to be much more influential in how we rear our children than the actual history of care we received (Bretherton & Munholland, 2008).

Multiple Attachments

As we have indicated, babies develop attachments to a variety of familiar people—not just mothers but also fathers, grandparents, siblings, and professional caregivers. Although Bowlby (1969) believed that infants are predisposed to direct their attachment behaviors to a single special person, especially when they are distressed, his theory allowed for these multiple attachments.

Fathers An anxious, unhappy 1-year-old who is permitted to choose between the mother and the father as a source of comfort and security will usually choose the mother. But this preference typically declines over the second year. And when babies are not distressed, they approach, vocalize to, and smile equally often at both parents, who in turn are equally responsive to their infant's social bids (Bornstein, 2006; Parke, 2002).

Fathers' sensitive caregiving and interactional synchrony with infants, like mothers', predict attachment security (Lundy, 2003; van IJzendoorn et al., 2004). But as infancy progresses, mothers and fathers in many cultures, including Australia, Canada, Germany, India, Israel, Italy, Japan, and the United States, tend to interact differently with their babies: Mothers devote more time to physical care and expressing affection, fathers to playful interaction (Freeman & Newland, 2010; Roopnarine et al., 1990).

Mothers and fathers also play differently. Mothers more often provide toys, talk to infants, and gently play conventional games like pat-a-cake and peekaboo. In contrast, fathers—especially with their infant sons—tend to engage in highly arousing physical play with bursts of excitement and surprise that increase as play progresses (Feldman, 2003). As long as fathers are also sensitive, this stimulating, startling play style helps babies regulate emotion in intensely arousing situations and may prepare them to venture confidently into active, unpredictable contexts, including novel physical environments and play with peers (Cabrera et al., 2007; Hazen et al., 2010; Paquette, 2004). In a German study, fathers' sensitive, challenging play with preschoolers predicted favorable emotional and social adjustment from kindergarten to early adulthood (Grossmann et al., 2008).

Play is a vital context in which fathers build secure attachments (Newland, Coyl, & Freeman, 2008). It may be especially influential in cultures where long work hours prevent most fathers from sharing in infant caregiving, such as Japan (Hewlett, 2004; Shwalb et al., 2004). In many Western nations, however, a strict division of parental roles—mother as caregiver, father as playmate—has changed over the past several decades in response to women's workforce participation and to cultural valuing of gender equality.

LOOK and LISTEN

Observe parents at play with infants at home or a family gathering. Describe both similarities and differences in mothers' and fathers' behaviors. Are your observations consistent with research findings?

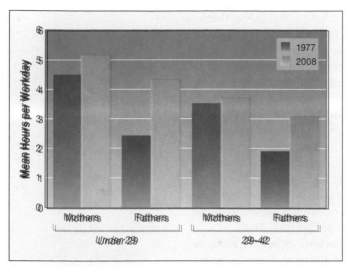

FIGURE 10.7 **Average amount of time per workday U.S. employed mothers and fathers reported spending with their children (age 12 and younger) in 1977 and 2008.** In national surveys of several thousand employed parents, mothers' time with children remained fairly stable from 1977 to 2008; fathers' time increased substantially. (Adapted from Galinsky, Aumann, & Bond, 2009.)

A recent U.S. national survey of several thousand employed workers indicated that U.S. fathers under age 29 devote about 85 percent as much time to children as mothers do—on average, just over 4 hours per workday, nearly double the hours young fathers reported three decades ago. Although fathers age 29 to 42 spend somewhat less time with children, their involvement has also increased substantially (see Figure 10.7). Today, nearly one-third of U.S. employed women say that their spouse or partner shares equally in or takes most responsibility for child-care tasks (Galinsky, Aumann, & Bond, 2009). Paternal availability to children is fairly similar across SES and ethnic groups, with one exception: Hispanic fathers spend more time engaged, probably because of the particularly high value that Hispanic cultures place on family involvement (Cabrera & García-Coll, 2004; Parke et al., 2004a).

Mothers in dual-earner families tend to engage in more playful stimulation of their babies than mothers who are at home full-time (Cox et al., 1992). But fathers who are primary caregivers retain their arousing play style (Lamb & Oppenheim, 1989). These highly involved fathers are less gender-stereotyped in their beliefs; have sympathetic, friendly personalities; often had fathers who were more involved in rearing them; and regard parenthood as an especially enriching experience (Cabrera et al., 2000; Levy-Shiff & Israelashvili, 1988).

Fathers' involvement with babies occurs within a complex system of family attitudes and relationships. When both parents believe that men are capable of nurturing infants, fathers devote more time to caregiving (Beitel & Parke, 1998). A warm marital bond promotes both parents' sensitivity and involvement with babies, but it is particularly important for fathers (Lamb & Lewis, 2004). See the Cultural Influences box on the following page for cross-cultural evidence documenting this conclusion—and also highlighting the powerful role of paternal warmth in children's development.

Grandparent Primary Caregivers Nearly 2.4 million U.S. children—4 to 5 percent of the child population—live with their grandparents but apart from parents, in so-called *skipped-generation families* (U.S. Census Bureau, 2011b). The number of grandparents rearing grandchildren has increased over the past two decades. The arrangement occurs in all ethnic groups, though more often in African-American, Hispanic, and Native-American families than in Caucasian families. Although grandparent caregivers are more likely to be women than men, many grandfathers participate. Grandparents generally step in when parents' troubled lives—as a result of substance abuse, child abuse and neglect, domestic violence, mental illness, imprisonment, or adolescent parenthood—threaten children's well-being (Fuller-Thomson & Minkler, 2005, 2007; Minkler & Fuller-Thomson, 2005). Often these families take in two or more children.

As a result, grandparents tend to assume the parenting role under highly stressful life circumstances. Unfavorable child-rearing experiences have left their mark on children, who show high rates of learning difficulties, depression, and antisocial behavior. Absent parents' adjustment difficulties strain family relationships. Parents may interfere by violating the grandparents' behavioral limits, taking grandchildren away without permission, or making promises to children that they do not keep. These youngsters also introduce financial burdens into households that often are already low-income (Mills, Gomez-Smith, & De Leon, 2005; Williamson, Softas-Nall, & Miller, 2003). And grandparent caregivers, at a time when they anticipated having more time for spouses, friends, and leisure, instead have less. Many report feeling emotionally drained, depressed, and worried about what will happen to the children if their own health fails (Hayslip et al., 2002; Kolomer & McCallion, 2005).

© ELLEN B. SENISI PHOTOGRAPHY

Despite stressful family conditions, grandparents who provide long-term physical and emotional care form deep attachments with their grandchildren.

CULTURAL INFLUENCES

The Powerful Role of Paternal Warmth in Development

Research in diverse cultures demonstrates that fathers' warmth contributes to children's long-term favorable development. In studies of many societies and ethnic groups around the world, researchers coded paternal expressions of love and nurturance—evident in such behaviors as cuddling, hugging, comforting, playing, verbally expressing love, and praising the child's behavior. Fathers' sustained affectionate involvement predicted later cognitive, emotional, and social competence as strongly as did mothers' warmth—and occasionally more strongly (Rohner & Veneziano, 2001; Veneziano, 2003). And in Western cultures, paternal warmth and secure attachment are associated with children's mature social behavior and a reduction in a wide range of difficulties, including childhood emotional and behavior problems and adolescent substance abuse and delinquency (Grant et al., 2000; Michiels et al., 2010; Nelson & Coyne, 2009; Tacon & Caldera, 2001).

Fathers who devote little time to physical caregiving express warmth through play. In a German study, fathers' play sensitivity—accepting toddlers' play initiatives, adapting play behaviors to toddlers' capacities, and responding appropriately to toddlers' expressions of emotion—predicted children's secure internal working models of attachment during middle childhood and adolescence (Grossmann et al., 2002). Through

play, fathers seemed to transfer to young children a sense of confidence about parental support, which may strengthen their capacity to master many later challenges.

What factors promote paternal warmth? Cross-cultural research reveals a consistent relationship between the amount of time fathers spend near infants and toddlers and their expressions of caring and affection (Rohner & Veneziano, 2001). Consider the Aka hunters and gatherers of Central Africa, where fathers spend more time in physical proximity to their babies than in any other known society. Observations reveal that Aka fathers are within arm's reach of infants more than half the day. They pick up, cuddle, and play with their babies at least five times as often as fathers in other hunting-and-gathering societies. Why are Aka fathers so involved? The bond between Aka husband and wife is unusually cooperative and intimate. Throughout the day, couples share hunting, food preparation, and social and leisure activities. The more time Aka parents are together, the greater the father's loving interaction with his baby (Hewlett, 1992).

In Western cultures as well, happily married fathers whose partners cooperate with them in parenting spend more time with and interact more effectively with infants. In contrast, marital dissatisfaction is associated with insensitive

In diverse cultures, fathers' warmth predicts long-term favorable cognitive, emotional, and social development.

paternal care (Brown et al., 2010; Lundy, 2002; Sevigny & Loutzenhiser, 2010). Clearly, fathers' warm relationships with their partners and their babies are closely linked. Evidence for the power of fathers' affection, reported in virtually every culture and ethnic group studied, is reason to encourage more men to engage in nurturing care of young children.

Nevertheless, because they provide physical and emotional care for an extended time and are invested in the child's well-being, grandparent caregivers forge significant attachment relationships with their grandchildren (Poehlmann, 2003). Warm grandparent–grandchild bonds help protect children from worsening adjustment problems, even under conditions of great hardship. Interviews reveal that children often feel loved, cared for, and optimistic about their futures (Hicks & Goedereis, 2009; Sands, Goldberg-Glen, & Shin, 2009). Still, grandparent caregivers have a tremendous need for social and financial support and intervention services for their at-risk grandchildren.

Attachment and Later Development

According to psychoanalytic and ethological theories, the inner feelings of affection and security that result from a healthy attachment relationship support all aspects of psychological development. Consistent with this view, an extended longitudinal study by Alan Sroufe and his collaborators found that preschoolers who were securely attached as babies were rated by their teachers as higher in self-esteem, social skills, and empathy than were their insecurely attached counterparts, who displayed more behavior problems. When studied again at age 11 in summer camp, children who had been secure infants had more favorable relationships with peers, closer friendships, and better social skills, as judged by camp counselors. And as these well-functioning school-age children became adolescents and young adults, they continued to benefit from more supportive social networks, formed more stable and gratifying romantic relationships, and attained higher levels of education (Elicker, Englund, & Sroufe, 1992; Sroufe, 2002; Sroufe et al., 2005).

For some researchers, these findings seem to indicate that secure attachment in infancy causes improved cognitive, emotional, and social competence in later years. Yet contrary evidence exists. In other longitudinal studies, secure infants generally fared better than insecure infants, but not always (Fearon et al., 2010; McCartney et al., 2004; Schneider, Atkinson, & Tardif, 2001; Stams, Juffer, & van IJzendoorn, 2002). Disorganized/disoriented attachment, however, is an exception: It is consistently related to internalizing problems (fear and anxiety) and externalizing problems (anger and aggression) during the preschool and school years. Disorganized children also show inappropriate role reversals: In an apparent effort to compensate for their parent's confused communication, they use either exaggerated comforting or hostility to try to control the parent's behavior (Lyons-Ruth, 1996; Lyons-Ruth, Easterbrooks, & Cibelli, 1997; Moss et al., 2004, 2006; Moss, Cyr, & Dubois-Comtois, 2004).

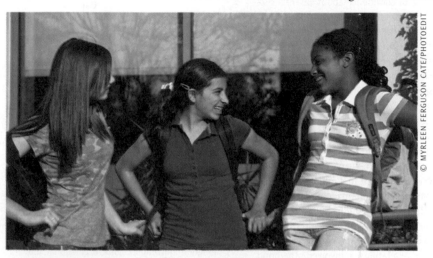

Parental sensitivity—not just in infancy but throughout childhood—likely contributed to these teenagers' social confidence and capacity for friendship.

What accounts for the inconsistency in research findings on the consequences of early attachment quality? Mounting evidence indicates that *continuity of caregiving* determines whether attachment security is linked to later development (Lamb et al., 1985; Thompson, 2006). Children whose parents respond sensitively not just in infancy but also in later years are likely to develop favorably. In contrast, children whose parents react insensitively or who, over a long period, are exposed to a negative family climate tend to establish lasting patterns of avoidant, resistant, or disorganized behavior and are at greater risk for developmental difficulties.

A close look at the relationship between parenting and children's adjustment in the first few years supports this interpretation. Recall that parents of disorganized/disoriented infants tend to have serious psychological problems or engage in highly maladaptive caregiving—conditions that usually persist and that are strongly linked to poor adjustment in children (Lyons-Ruth, Bronfman, & Parsons, 1999). And when more than 1,000 children were tracked from age 1 to 3 years, those with histories of secure attachment followed by sensitive parenting scored highest in cognitive, emotional, and social outcomes. Those with histories of insecure attachment followed by insensitive parenting scored lowest, while those with mixed histories of attachment and maternal sensitivity scored in between (Belsky & Fearon, 2002). Specifically, insecurely attached infants whose mothers became more positive and supportive in early childhood showed signs of developmental recovery.

Does this trend remind you of our discussion of *resilience* in Chapter 1? A child whose parental caregiving improves or who has other compensating affectionate ties outside the immediate family can bounce back from adversity. In contrast, a child who experiences tender care in infancy but lacks sympathetic ties later on is at risk for problems.

Turn back to the evidence on page 428, which indicates that as early as the second year, toddlers have formed attachment-related expectations about parental comfort and support. With cognitive development and continuing experiences with caregivers, this rudimentary internal working model expands into a broader, more complex representation. Recall from page 414 that parents of securely attached preschoolers converse with them in more elaborative ways, especially about emotion. Some researchers believe that these narratives facilitate children's construction of a coherent image of the self in relation to attachment figures (Fivush, 2006; Thompson 2008). Then, as children encounter new attachment-related experiences, they refine and "update" their internal working model.

Although a secure attachment in infancy does not guarantee continued good parenting, it does launch the parent–child relationship on a positive path that is likely to continue.

Much research shows that an early warm, positive parent–child tie, sustained over time, promotes many aspects of children's development: a more confident and complex self-concept, more advanced emotional understanding, stronger emotional self-regulation, more favorable relationships with teachers and peers, more effective social skills, a stronger sense of moral responsibility, and higher motivation to achieve in school (Thompson, 2006, 2008). But the effects of early attachment security are *conditional*—dependent on the quality of the child's future relationships. Finally, as our discussion has already revealed and as you will see again in future chapters, attachment is just one of the complex influences on children's psychological development.

A S K   Y O U R S E L F

Review ■ What factors explain stability in attachment pattern for some children and change for others? Are these factors also involved in the link between attachment in infancy and later development? Explain.

Connect ■ Review research on emotional self-regulation on page 408. How do the caregiving experiences of securely attached infants promote the development of emotional self-regulation?

Apply ■ In evaluating her childhood attachment experiences, Monica recalls her mother as tense and distant. Is Monica's newborn daughter likely to develop an insecure attachment? Explain, using research on adults' internal working models.

Reflect ■ How would you characterize your internal working model? What factors, in addition to your early relationship with your parents, might have influenced it?

Attachment, Parental Employment, and Child Care

▶ Discuss the implications of parental employment and child care for attachment security and early psychological development.

Over the past three decades, women have entered the labor force in record numbers. Today, more than 60 percent of U.S. mothers with a child under age 2 are employed (U.S. Census Bureau, 2011b). In response to this trend, researchers and laypeople alike have raised questions about the impact on the attachment bond of child care and daily separations of infant from parent.

The Social Issues: Health box on page 442 reviews the current controversy over whether child care threatens young children's development. As you will see, the weight of evidence suggests that *quality of care* is crucially important. Infants and young children exposed to long hours of mediocre to poor nonparental care, regardless of whether they come from middle- or low-SES homes, score lower on measures of cognitive and social skills (Belsky et al., 2007; Hausfather et al., 1997; NICHD Early Child Care Research Network, 2000b, 2001a, 2003b, 2006). In contrast, good child care can reduce the negative impact of a stressed, poverty-stricken home life, and it sustains the benefits of growing up in an economically advantaged family (Lamb & Ahnert, 2006; McCartney et al., 2007; NICHD Early Child Care Research Network, 2003b).

TAKE A MOMENT... Visit several child-care settings, and take notes on what you see. In contrast to most European countries and to Australia and New Zealand, where child care is nationally regulated and funded to ensure its quality, reports on U.S. child care raise serious concerns. Standards are set by the individual states and vary widely. In studies of quality, only 20 to 25 percent of child-care centers and family child-care settings (in which a caregiver cares for children in her home) provided infants and toddlers with sufficiently positive, stimulating experiences to promote healthy psychological development. Most settings offered substandard care (NICHD Early Child Care Research Network, 2000a, 2004b).

Unfortunately, many U.S. children from low-income families experience inadequate child care (Brooks-Gunn, 2004). But U.S. settings providing the very worst care tend to serve middle-SES families. These parents are especially likely to place their children in for-profit centers, where quality tends to be lowest. Low-SES children more often attend publicly subsidized, nonprofit centers, which have smaller group sizes and better teacher–child ratios (Lamb & Ahnert, 2006). Still, child-care quality for low-SES children varies widely.

SOCIAL ISSUES: HEALTH

Does Child Care Threaten Infant Attachment Security and Later Adjustment?

Are infants who experience daily separations from their employed parents and early placement in child care at risk for attachment insecurity and developmental problems? Some researchers think so, but others disagree. Let's look closely at the evidence.

Attachment Quality

Some studies suggest that babies placed in full-time child care before 12 months of age are more likely to display insecure attachment in the Strange Situation (Belsky, 2001, 2005). But the best current evidence—from the U.S. National Institute of Child Health and Development (NICHD) Study of Early Child Care, the largest longitudinal investigation to date, including more than 1,300 infants and their families—confirms that use of nonparental care by itself does not affect attachment quality (NICHD Early Child Care Research Network, 1997, 2001b). Rather, the relationship between child care and emotional well-being depends on both family and child-care experiences.

Family Circumstances

We have seen that family conditions affect children's attachment security and later adjustment. Findings of the NICHD Study confirmed that parenting quality, assessed using a combination of maternal sensitivity and HOME scores (see page 344 in Chapter 8), exerted a more powerful impact on children's adjustment than did exposure to child care (NICHD Early Childhood Research Network, 1998: Watamura et al., 2011).

For employed parents, balancing work and caregiving can be stressful. Mothers who are fatigued and anxious because they feel overloaded by work and family pressures may respond less sensitively to their babies, thereby risking the infant's security. And as paternal involvement in caregiving has risen (see page 436), many more U.S. fathers in dual-earner families also report work–family-life conflict (Galinsky, Aumann, & Bond, 2009).

Quality and Extent of Child Care

Nevertheless, poor-quality child care may contribute to a higher rate of insecure attachment. In the NICHD Study, when babies were exposed to combined home and child-care risk factors—insensitive caregiving at home along with insensitive caregiving in child care, long hours in child care, or more than one child-care arrangement—the rate of attachment insecurity increased. Overall, mother–child interaction was more favorable when children attended higher-quality child care and also spent fewer hours in

child care (NICHD Early Child Care Research Network, 1997, 1999).

Furthermore, when children reached age 3, a history of higher-quality child care predicted better social skills (NICHD Early Child Care Research Network, 2002b). However, at age 4½ to 5, children averaging more than 30 child-care hours per week displayed more behavior problems, especially defiance, disobedience, and aggression. For those who had been in child-care centers as opposed to family child-care homes, this outcome persisted through elementary school (Belsky et al., 2007; NICHD Early Child Care Research Network, 2003a, 2006).

But these findings do not necessarily mean that child care causes behavior problems. Rather, heavy exposure to substandard care, which is widespread in the United States, may promote these difficulties, especially when combined with family risk factors. A closer look at NICHD participants during the preschool years revealed that those in both poor-quality home and child-care environments fared worst in social skills and problem behaviors, whereas those in both high-quality home and child care environments fared best. In between were preschoolers in high-quality child care but poor-quality homes (Watamura et al., 2011). These children benefited from the *protective influence* of high-quality child care.

Evidence from other industrialized nations confirms that full-time child care need not harm children's development. In Australia, for example, infants who spend full days in government-funded, high-quality child-care centers have a higher rate of secure attachment than infants informally cared for by relatives, friends, or babysitters. And amount of time in child care is unrelated to Australian preschoolers' behavior problems (Love et al., 2003).

Still, some children may be particularly stressed by long child-care hours. Many infants, toddlers, and preschoolers attending child-care centers for full days show a mild increase in saliva concentrations of cortisol across the day—a pattern that does not occur on days they spend at home. In one study, children rated as highly fearful by their caregivers experienced an especially sharp increase in cortisol levels (Watamura et al., 2003). Inhibited children may find the constant company of large numbers of peers particularly stressful.

Conclusions

Taken together, research suggests that some infants may be at risk for attachment insecurity and later adjustment problems due to inadequate

High-quality child care, with generous caregiver–child ratios, small group sizes, and knowledgeable caregivers, can be part of a system that promotes all aspects of child development, including attachment security.

child care, long hours in such care, and the joint pressures their parents experience from full-time employment and parenthood. But it is inappropriate to use these findings to justify a reduction in child-care services. When family incomes are limited or mothers who want to work are forced to stay at home, children's emotional security is not promoted.

Instead, it makes sense to increase the availability of high-quality child care and to relieve work–family-life conflict by providing parents with paid employment leave (see page 119 in Chapter 3) and opportunities for part-time work. In the NICHD study, part-time (as opposed to full-time) employment during the baby's first year was associated with greater maternal sensitivity and a higher-quality home environment, which yielded more favorable development in early childhood (Brooks-Gunn, Han, & Waldfogel, 2010).

Finally, for child care to foster attachment security, the professional caregiver's relationship with the baby is vital. When caregiver–child ratios are generous, group sizes are small, and caregivers are educated about child development and child rearing, caregivers' interactions are more positive and children develop more favorably—cognitively, emotionally, and socially (McCartney et al., 2007; NICHD Early Child Care Research Network, 2000a, 2002a, 2006). Child care with these characteristics can become part of an ecological system that relieves parental and child stress, thereby promoting healthy attachment and development.

APPLYING WHAT WE KNOW

Signs of Developmentally Appropriate Infant and Toddler Child Care

PROGRAM CHARACTERISTIC	SIGNS OF QUALITY
Physical setting	Indoor environment is clean, in good repair, well-lighted, and well-ventilated. Fenced outdoor play space is available. Setting does not appear overcrowded when children are present.
Toys and equipment	Play materials are appropriate for infants and toddlers and are stored on low shelves within easy reach. Cribs, highchairs, infant seats, and child-sized tables and chairs are available. Outdoor equipment includes small riding toys, swings, slide, and sandbox.
Caregiver–child ratio	In child-care centers, caregiver–child ratio is no greater than 1 to 3 for infants and 1 to 6 for toddlers. Group size (number of children in one room) is no greater than 6 infants with 2 caregivers and 12 toddlers with 2 caregivers. In family child care, caregiver is responsible for no more than 6 children; within this group, no more than 2 are infants and toddlers. Staffing is consistent, so infants and toddlers can form relationships with particular caregivers.
Daily activities	Daily schedule includes times for active play, quiet play, naps, snacks, and meals. It is flexible rather than rigid, to meet the needs of individual children. Atmosphere is warm and supportive, and children are never left unsupervised.
Interactions among adults and children	Caregivers respond promptly to infants' and toddlers' distress; hold, talk to, sing to, and read to them; and interact with them in a manner that respects the individual child's interests and tolerance for stimulation.
Caregiver qualifications	Caregiver has some training in child development, first aid, and safety.
Relationships with parents	Parents are welcome anytime. Caregivers talk frequently with parents about children's behavior and development.
Licensing and accreditation	Child-care setting, whether a center or a home, is licensed by the state. Voluntary accreditation by the National Academy of Early Childhood Programs *(www.naeyc.org/accreditation)*, or the National Association for Family Child Care *(www.nafcc.org)* is evidence of an especially high-quality program.

Source: Copple & Bredekamp, 2009.

See Applying What We Know above for signs of high-quality child care for infants and toddlers, based on standards for **developmentally appropriate practice.** These standards, devised by the U.S. National Association for the Education of Young Children, specify program characteristics that meet the developmental and individual needs of young children, based on both current research and consensus among experts. When child care meets standards for developmentally appropriate practice, children's learning opportunities and the warmth, sensitivity, and stability of their caregivers are especially high.

Child care in the United States is affected by a macrosystem of individualistic values and weak government regulation and funding. Furthermore, many parents think that their children's child-care experiences are higher in quality than they really are. Unable to identify good care, they do not demand it (Helburn, 1995). In recent years, recognizing that child care is in a state of crisis, the U.S. federal government and some states have allocated additional funds to subsidize its cost, primarily for low-income families. Though far from meeting the need, this increase in resources has had a positive impact on child-care quality and accessibility (Children's Defense Fund, 2009).

Good child care is a cost-effective means of supporting the development of all children. For children whose development is at risk, it can serve as effective early intervention, much like the programs we discussed in Chapter 8. We will revisit the topics of parental employment and child care in Chapter 14, when we focus on their consequences for development during childhood and adolescence.

Review ■ Cite evidence that high-quality infant and toddler child care supports development, whereas poor-quality care undermines it.

Apply ■ Randi and Mike are worried that placing their 6-month-old baby, Lucinda, in child care may disrupt Lucinda's sense of security. List steps that Randi and Mike can take to ensure that Lucinda's experiences—at home and in child care—support her emotional and social development.

S U M M A R Y

Functions of Emotions (p. 401)

Describe the functionalist approach to emotional development.

- The **functionalist approach** emphasizes that the broad function of **emotions** is to energize behavior aimed at attaining personal goals. Emotions are central in cognitive processing, social behavior, and physical health. Emotions also contribute to the emergence of self-awareness, which makes possible new, self-evaluative emotions. Gradually, children gain voluntary control over their emotions.

Development of Emotional Expression (p. 405)

How does the expression of basic emotions change during infancy?

- During the first six months, **basic emotions** gradually become clear, well-organized signals. The **social smile** appears between 6 and 10 weeks, laughter around 3 to 4 months. Happiness strengthens the parent–child bond and reflects and promotes motor and cognitive mastery.

© RADIUS IMAGES/ALAMY IMAGES

- Anger and fear (especially in the form of **stranger anxiety**) increase from the second half of the first year into the second year, as infants' cognitive and motor capacities improve. Newly mobile babies use the familiar caregiver as a **secure base** from which to explore.

Describe the development of self-conscious emotions, emotional self-regulation, and conformity to emotional display rules.

- During toddlerhood, self-awareness and adult instruction provide the foundation for **self-conscious emotions:** guilt, shame, embarrassment, envy, and pride. With age, these emotions become more internally governed.

- **Emotional self-regulation** emerges as the prefrontal cortex develops and as caregivers sensitively assist infants in adjusting their emotional reactions. With motor, cognitive, and language development and warm parental guidance, children acquire more effective self-regulatory strategies. Children who experience negative emotion intensely find it harder to inhibit feelings and shift attention away from disturbing events.

- By age 10, most children can shift adaptively between **problem-centered** and **emotion-centered coping** in regulating emotion. Emotionally well-regulated children are optimistic and cooperative and have positive relationships with teachers and peers.

- Young preschoolers start to conform to their culture's **emotional display rules.** From infancy on, parents encourage children—especially boys—to suppress negative emotion. In middle childhood, children understand the value of display rules in ensuring social harmony.

Understanding and Responding to the Emotions of Others (p. 414)

Describe the development of emotional understanding from infancy through middle childhood.

- Around the middle of the first year, infants respond to emotional expressions as organized, meaningful wholes. Beginning at 8 to 10 months, they engage in **social referencing,** seeking emotional information from caregivers in uncertain situations. By the middle of the second year, toddlers realize that others' emotional reactions may differ from their own.

- Preschoolers understand many causes, consequences, and behavioral signs of emotion. The capacity to consider conflicting cues when explaining others' feelings improves in middle childhood, along with an appreciation of mixed emotions. Warm parental conversations about emotions and interactions with siblings and friends, especially make-believe play, are excellent contexts for learning about emotions.

Describe the development of empathy from infancy into adolescence, noting individual differences.

- As toddlers develop self-awareness, they begin to empathize. During childhood and adolescence, gains in language, emotional understanding, and perspective taking support an increase in **empathy,** which motivates **prosocial,** or **altruistic, behavior.**

- Children who are sociable, assertive, and good at regulating emotion are more likely than poor emotion regulators to move from empathy to sympathetic, prosocial behavior. Warm parents who encourage emotional expressiveness, show empathic concern, and help their child regulate angry feelings promote development of empathy and sympathy. Angry, punitive parenting disrupts these capacities.

Temperament and Development (p. 418)

What is temperament, and how is it measured?

- Children vary widely in **temperament**—early-appearing, stable individual differences in reactivity and self-regulation. The New York Longitudinal Study identified three patterns: the **easy child,** the **difficult child,** and the **slow-to-warm-up child.** The most influential model of temperament, devised by Rothbart, includes dimensions representing emotion, attention, and action, along with **effortful control,** the ability to regulate one's reactivity.

- Temperament is assessed through parental reports, behavior ratings by others familiar with the child, and laboratory observations. Most neurobiological research has focused on distinguishing **inhibited, or shy, children** from **uninhibited, or sociable, children.**

Discuss the roles of heredity and environment in the stability of temperament, the relationship of temperament to cognitive and social functioning, and the goodness-of-fit model.

■ Long-term prediction from early temperament is best achieved after age 3, when styles of responding are better established. Although temperament is moderately heritable, both shared environmental influences and non-shared influences—evident in parents' tendency to emphasize each child's unique qualities—contribute.

■ Children's temperamental traits consistently predict their cognitive and social functioning. Effortful control is linked to generally favorable development and adjustment.

■ The **goodness-of-fit model** describes how a child's temperament and environment work together to affect later development. Parenting practices that fit well with the child's temperament help children achieve more adaptive functioning.

Development of Attachment (p. 428)

What are the unique features of ethological theory of attachment?

■ The most widely accepted perspective on development of **attachment**—our strong affectionate tie with special people in our lives—is **ethological theory,** which recognizes the infant's emotional tie to the caregiver as an evolved response that promotes survival.

■ Around 6 to 8 months, **separation anxiety** and use of the parent as a secure base indicate the existence of a true attachment bond. Separation anxiety declines as representation and language develop, enabling preschoolers to better understand the parent's coming and going. From early caregiving experiences, children construct an **internal working model** that serves as a guide for all future close relationships.

Describe how researchers measure the security of attachment, and discuss the stability of attachment patterns.

■ Researchers using the **Strange Situation** to measure the quality of attachment between ages 1 and 2 have identified four attachment patterns: **secure, avoidant, resistant,** and **disorganized/disoriented.** The **Attachment Q-Sort**, based on home observations of children between ages 1 and 4 years, yields a score ranging from high to low in security.

■ Securely attached babies in middle-SES families with favorable life conditions more often maintain their attachment pattern than insecure babies. However, the disorganized/disoriented pattern is highly stable. Cultural conditions must be considered in interpreting the meaning of attachment patterns.

■ Attachment security is influenced by early availability of a consistent caregiver, quality of caregiving, the fit between the baby's temperament and parenting practices, and family circumstances. **Sensitive caregiving** is moderately related to secure attachment. In Western cultures, **interactional synchrony** characterizes the experiences of securely attached babies.

© AFRIPICS.COM/ALAMY

■ Parents' internal working models are good predictors of children's attachment security, but parents' childhood experiences do not transfer directly to quality of attachment with their own children.

Discuss infants' formation of multiple attachments and the role of early attachment quality in later development.

■ Infants develop strong affectionate ties to fathers, who tend to engage in more exciting, physical play with babies than do mothers. Sensitive, stimulating play is a vital context in which fathers and babies build secure attachments, predicting favorable emotional and social adjustment.

■ Grandparents who serve as primary caregivers for grandchildren in skipped-generation families forge significant attachment ties that help protect children with troubled family lives from adjustment problems.

■ Secure attachment in infancy launches the parent–child relationship on a positive path. But continuity of caregiving determines whether attachment security is linked to later development. If caregiving improves, children can recover from an insecure attachment history.

Attachment, Parental Employment, and Child Care (p. 441)

Discuss the implications of parental employment and child care for attachment security and early psychological development.

■ Research indicates that quality of care is crucially important. Spending many hours in mediocre to poor-quality child care, especially when combined with family risk factors, predicts insecure attachment and less favorable cognitive, emotional, and social development.

■ When child-care settings meet professionally accepted standards for **developmentally appropriate practice,** children's learning opportunities and the warmth, sensitivity, and stability of their caregivers are especially high. Good child care can also serve as effective early intervention for children whose development is at risk.

IMPORTANT TERMS AND CONCEPTS

attachment (p. 428)
Attachment Q-Sort (p. 431)
avoidant attachment (p. 430)
basic emotions (p. 406)
developmentally appropriate practice (p. 443)
difficult child (p. 420)
disorganized/disoriented attachment (p. 431)
easy child (p. 420)
effortful control (p. 421)
emotion (p. 401)
emotion-centered coping (p. 412)
emotional display rules (p. 412)

emotional self-regulation (p. 409)
empathy (p. 416)
ethological theory of attachment (p. 428)
functionalist approach to emotion (p. 401)
goodness-of-fit model (p. 426)
inhibited, or shy, child (p. 421)
interactional synchrony (p. 434)
internal working model (p. 430)
problem-centered coping (p. 412)
prosocial, or altruistic, behavior (p. 417)
resistant attachment (p. 431)
secure attachment (p. 430)

secure base (p. 408)
self-conscious emotions (p. 408)
sensitive caregiving (p. 434)
separation anxiety (p. 429)
slow-to-warm-up child (p. 420)
social referencing (p. 414)
social smile (p. 406)
Strange Situation (p. 430)
stranger anxiety (p. 407)
sympathy (p. 417)
temperament (p. 418)
uninhibited, or sociable, child (p. 421)

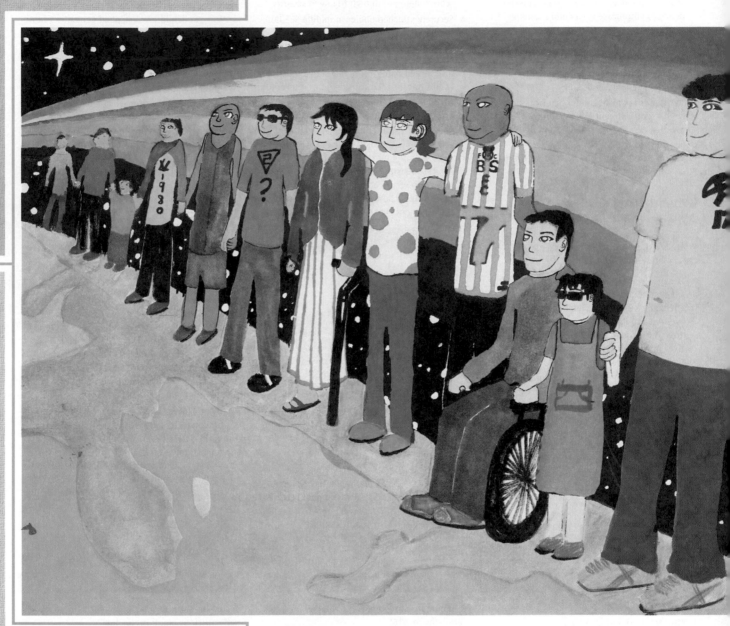

CHAPTER 11

"Hand in Hand"

Shing Nok Man, 11 years, Hong Kong

As young people construct a self-concept, they see themselves as distinct individuals with unique abilities, accomplishments, and aspirations but also as vitally connected to others.

Reprinted with permission from the International Museum of Children's Art, Oslo, Norway

Self and Social Understanding

"**G**randpa, look at my new shirt!" exclaimed 4-year-old Ellen at her family's annual reunion. "See, it's got a ladybug on it, and a yellow flower, and . . ."

Ellen's voice trailed off as she realized that all eyes were on her 1-year-old cousin, who was about to take his first steps. As little David tottered forward, the grownups laughed and cheered. No one—not even Grandpa, who was usually so attentive and playful—took note of Ellen and her new shirt.

Ellen retreated to the bedroom, where she threw a blanket over her head. Arms outstretched, she peered through the blanket's loose weave and made her way back to the living room. "Here I come, the scary ghost," announced Ellen, deliberately bumping into David, who toppled over and burst into tears.

Pulling off the blanket, Ellen caught her mother's disapproving glance and protested, "I couldn't see him, Mom!"

Ellen's mother insisted that Ellen apologize and help David up. But she couldn't help marveling at Ellen's skillful capacity for trickery.

This chapter addresses the development of **social cognition**, or how children come to understand their multifaceted social world. Like our discussion of cognitive development in Chapters 6 and 7, this chapter is concerned with how children think about and interpret experience. The experience of interest, however, is no longer the child's physical surroundings but the self and other people.

Researchers interested in social cognition seek answers to questions like these: When do infants discover that they are separate beings, distinct from other people and objects? How does children's understanding of their own and others' mental lives change with age? (For example, what new realizations underlie Ellen's creative act of deception?) When children and adolescents are asked to describe their own and others' characteristics, what do they say?

As we answer these and other questions, you will see that the trends identified for cognitive development also apply to children's social understanding:

- Social-cognitive development proceeds *from concrete to abstract*. Children start by noticing observable characteristics—their own and others' appearance and behavior. Soon after, they become aware of internal processes—the existence of desires, beliefs, intentions, abilities, and attitudes.
- Social cognition becomes *better organized* with age as children integrate separate behaviors into an appreciation of their own and others' personalities and identities.
- Children revise their ideas about the causes of behavior—from *simple, one-sided explanations* to *complex, interacting relationships* between person and situation.
- Social cognition moves toward *metacognitive understanding*. With age, children's thinking extends beyond social reality to reflections on their own and other's social thoughts.

Although nonsocial and social cognition share many features, social cognition is more complex. Movements of things—for example, a rolling ball—can be fully explained by the physical forces that act on objects. In contrast, a person's behavior is affected not only by others' actions but also by inner states that we cannot observe directly.

In view of this complexity, we might expect social cognition to develop more slowly than nonsocial cognition. Surprisingly, it does not. Unique features of social experience

Emergence of Self and Development of Self-Concept
Self-Awareness • The Categorical, Remembered, and Enduring Selves • The Inner Self: Children's Theory of Mind • Self-Concept • Cognitive, Social, and Cultural Influences on Self-Concept

■ **CULTURAL INFLUENCES:** *Cultural Variations in Personal Storytelling: Implications for Early Self-Concept*

■ **BIOLOGY AND ENVIRONMENT:** *"Mindblindness" and Autism*

Self-Esteem: The Evaluative Side of Self-Concept
The Structure of Self-Esteem • Changes in Level of Self-Esteem: The Role of Social Comparisons • Influences on Self-Esteem • Achievement-Related Attributions

Constructing an Identity: Who Should I Become?
Paths to Identity • Identity Status and Psychological Well-Being • Factors Affecting Identity Development

■ **SOCIAL ISSUES: HEALTH:** *Adolescent Suicide: Annihilation of the Self*

■ **CULTURAL INFLUENCES:** *Identity Development Among Ethnic Minority Adolescents*

Thinking About Other People
Understanding People as Personalities • Understanding Social Groups: Race and Ethnicity

Understanding Conflict: Social Problem Solving
The Social Problem-Solving Process • Enhancing Social Problem Solving

are probably responsible. First, because people are animated beings and objects of deep emotional investment, they are especially interesting to think about. Second, social experience constantly prompts children to revise their social cognitions by presenting them with discrepancies between the behaviors they expect and those that occur. Finally, because we are all human beings, with the same basic nervous system and a background of similar experiences, interpreting behavior from the self's viewpoint often helps us understand others' actions. When it does not, humans are equipped with a powerful capacity—*perspective taking*—that enables us to infer others' thoughts and feelings.

Our discussion is organized around three broad aspects of development: thinking about the self, thinking about other people, and understanding conflict, including how to solve social problems. We have already considered some social–cognitive topics—for example, referential communication skills in Chapter 9 and emotional understanding in Chapter 10. Research on moral reasoning and on understanding of gender, also social–cognitive topics, is so extensive that each merits a chapter of its own. We will consider them in Chapters 12 and 13. ■

▶ Describe the development of self-awareness in infancy and toddlerhood, along with the emotional and social capacities it supports.

▶ Describe the development of the categorical, remembered, and enduring selves.

▶ Discuss theory-of-mind development from early to middle childhood, citing social consequences and contributing factors.

▶ Discuss the development of self-concept from early childhood through adolescence, noting cognitive, social, and cultural influences.

Emergence of Self and Development of Self-Concept

Infancy is a rich formative period for development of both physical and social understanding. In Chapter 6, you learned that infants develop an appreciation of the permanence of objects. And in Chapter 10, we saw that over the first year, infants recognize and respond appropriately to others' emotions and distinguish familiar from unfamiliar people. That both objects and people achieve an independent, stable existence for infants implies that knowledge of the self as a separate, permanent entity is also emerging. Self-development begins with the dawning of self-awareness in infancy and gradually evolves into a rich, multifaceted, organized view of the self's characteristics and capacities during childhood and adolescence.

Self-Awareness

As early as the first few months of life, infants smile and return friendly behaviors to their reflection in a mirror. When do they realize that the baby smiling back at them is the self?

Beginnings of Self-Awareness At birth, infants sense that they are physically distinct from their surroundings. For example, newborns display a stronger rooting reflex in response to external stimulation (an adult's finger touching their cheek) than to self-stimulation (their own hand contacting their cheek) (Rochat & Hespos, 1997). Newborns' remarkable capacity for *intermodal perception* (see page 166 in Chapter 4) supports the beginnings of self-awareness (Rochat, 2003). As they feel their own touch, feel and watch their limbs move, and feel and hear themselves cry, babies experience intermodal matches that differentiate their own body from surrounding bodies and objects.

Over the first few months, infants distinguish their own visual image from other stimuli, but their self-awareness is limited—expressed only in perception and action. When shown two side-by-side video images of their kicking legs, one from their own perspective (camera behind the baby) and one from an observer's perspective (camera in front of the baby), 3-month-olds looked longer at the observer's view (see Figure 11.1a). In another video-image comparison, they looked longer at a reversal of their leg positions than at a normal view (see Figure 11.1b) (Rochat, 1998). By 4 months, infants look and smile

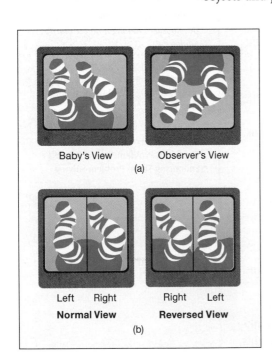

Baby's View   Observer's View
(a)

Left   Right   Right   Left
Normal View   **Reversed View**
(b)

FIGURE 11.1 Three-month-olds' emerging self-awareness, as indicated by reactions to video images. (a) When shown two side-by-side views of their kicking legs, babies looked longer at the novel, observer's view than at their own view. (b) When shown a normal view of their leg positions alongside a reversed view, infants looked longer at the novel, reversed view. (Adapted from Rochat, 1998.)

more at video images of others than at video images of themselves, indicating that they view another person (as opposed to the self) as a potential social partner (Rochat & Striano, 2002).

This discrimination of one's own limb and facial movements from those of others in real-time video presentations reflects an *implicit sense of self–world differentiation*. It serves as the foundation for *explicit self-awareness:* an objective understanding that the self is a unique object in a world of objects, which includes representations of one's own physical features and body dimensions.

Explicit Self-Awareness During the second year, toddlers become consciously aware of the self's physical features. In several studies, 9- to 28-month-olds were placed in front of a mirror. Then, under the pretext of wiping the baby's face, each mother rubbed red dye on her child's nose or forehead. Younger babies touched the mirror as if the red mark had nothing to do with them. But those older than 20 months rubbed their noses or foreheads, indicating awareness of their unique facial appearance (Bard et al., 2006; Lewis & Brooks-Gunn, 1979). And some toddlers act silly or coy in front of the mirror, playfully experimenting with the way the self looks (Bullock & Lutkenhaus, 1990).

Around age 2, **self-recognition**—identification of the self as a physically unique being—is well under way. Children point to themselves in photos and refer to themselves by name. In fact, mirror self-recognition predicts other milestones that reflect representation of the self, including use of personal pronouns ("me," "my," "mine") and emergence of make-believe play (Lewis & Ramsay, 2004). Soon children identify themselves in images with less detail and fidelity than mirrors. Around age 2½, most reach for a sticker surreptitiously placed on top of their heads when shown themselves in a live video, and around age 3, most recognize their own shadow (Cameron & Gallup, 1988; Suddendorf, Simcock, & Nielsen, 2007).

As self-recognition takes shape, older toddlers also construct an explicit body self-awareness. They realize that their own body can serve as an obstacle. When asked to push a shopping cart while standing on a mat attached to its rear axle, most 18- to 21-month-olds (but not younger children) figured out how to remove themselves from the mat so the cart would move—an ability that improved with age (Moore et al., 2007).

Nevertheless, toddlers lack an objective understanding of their own body dimensions. They make **scale errors,** attempting to do things that their body size makes impossible. For example, they will try to put on dolls' clothes, fit themselves into a doll-sized chair, or walk through a doorway too narrow for them to pass through (Brownell, Zerwas, & Ramani, 2007; DeLoache, Uttal, & Rosengren, 2004). Scale errors decline around age 2, but many 2½-year-olds still make them. Young preschoolers are still learning to process physical information about their own bodies in they same way they do for other objects.

Influences on Self-Awareness What experiences contribute to gains in self-awareness? During the first year, as infants act on the environment, they probably notice effects that help them sort out self, other people, and objects (Nadel, Prepin, & Okanda, 2005; Rochat, 2001). For example, batting a mobile and seeing it swing in a pattern different from the infant's own actions informs the baby about the relation between self and physical world. Smiling and vocalizing at a caregiver who smiles and vocalizes back help clarify the relation between self and social world. And watching the movements of one's own hands and feet provides still another kind of feedback—one under much more direct control than the movements of other people or objects. The contrast between these experiences helps infants sense that they are separate from external reality.

Researchers do not yet know exactly how toddlers acquire the various aspects of explicit self-awareness. But sensitive caregiving seems to play a role. Compared to their insecurely attached agemates, securely attached toddlers display more complex self-related actions during play, such as making a doll labeled as the self take a drink or kiss a teddy bear. They also show greater knowledge of their own and their parents' physical features—for example, in labeling of body parts (Pipp, Easterbrooks, & Brown, 1993; Pipp, Easterbrooks, & Harmon,

This 20-month-old's response indicates that she recognizes her unique physical features and is aware of herself as a separate being, distinct from other people and objects.

LOOK and LISTEN

Ask several parents of 1½- to 2-year-olds if they have observed any instances of scale errors. Have the parent hand the toddler doll-sized clothing (hat, jacket, or shoe) or furniture (table, chair, or slide) and watch for scale errors.

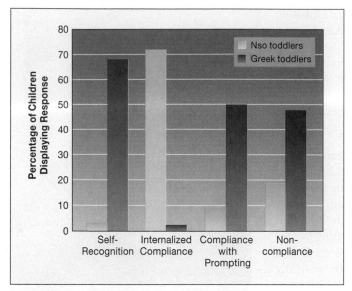

FIGURE 11.2 Self-recognition and compliance among Nso and Greek toddlers. At 18 to 20 months, toddlers were tested for mirror self-recognition and for compliance (they were told not to open a transparent container with an attractive food). Among Greek toddlers, whose culture values independence, many more had attained self-recognition. But Nso toddlers, reared in an interdependent culture, were greatly advanced in compliance (following directions without prompting), whereas Greek toddlers either needed reminders or did not comply. (Adapted from Keller et al., 2004.)

1992). And 18-month-olds who often establish joint attention with their caregivers are advanced in mirror self-recognition (Nichols, Fox, & Mundy, 2005). Joint attention offers toddlers many opportunities to compare their own and others' reactions to objects and events, which may enhance toddlers' awareness of their own physical uniqueness.

Cultural variations exist in early self-development. Urban German and Greek toddlers attain mirror self-recognition earlier than toddlers of the Nso people of Cameroon, a collectivist rural farming society that highly values social harmony and responsibility to others (Keller et al., 2004, 2005). Compared to their German and Greek counterparts, Nso mothers engage in less face-to-face communication and object stimulation and more body contact and physical stimulation of their babies. German and Greek practices reflect a *distal parenting style* common in cultures that value *independence;* the Nso practices a *proximal parenting style* typical in cultures that value *interdependence.* In line with these differences, Nso proximal parenting is associated with later attainment of self-recognition but earlier emergence of toddlers' compliance with adult requests (see Figure 11.2).

Self-Awareness and Early Emotional and Social Development Self-awareness quickly becomes a central part of children's emotional and social lives. In the final months of the first year, as infants start to behave intentionally, they learn that their own goals (touching a breakable object, grabbing a peer's toy) frequently conflict with the goals of others. Soon, they realize that the self can be the focus of others' intentions and emotional reactions. As a result, they become increasingly sensitive to variations in caregivers' emotional messages (Thompson, 2006). This sets the stage for social referencing and, in the middle of the second year, emergence of self-conscious emotions (see pages 414 and 408 in Chapter 10).

Self-awareness also leads to first efforts to understand another's perspective. We have seen in previous chapters that toddlers increasingly appreciate others' intentions, feelings, and desires. They also begin to empathize (see page 415). Furthermore, mirror self-awareness precedes sustained, mutual peer imitation—a partner banging an object, the toddler copying the behavior, the partner imitating back, and the toddler copying again (Asendorpf, Warkentin, & Baudonniere, 1996). These exchanges indicate that the toddler not only is interested in the playmate but also realizes that the playmate is interested in him or her.

Two-year-olds' self-recognition leads to a sense of ownership. The stronger their self-definitions, the more possessive 2-year-olds tend to be, claiming objects as "Mine!" (Fasig, 2000; Levine, 1983). A firmer sense of self also enables children to cooperate in resolving disputes over objects, playing games, and solving simple problems (Brownell & Carriger, 1990; Caplan et al., 1991). Accordingly, when trying to promote friendly peer interaction, parents and teachers can accept young children's possessiveness as a sign of self-assertion ("Yes, that's your toy") and then encourage compromise ("but in a little while, would you give someone else a turn?"), rather than insisting on sharing.

The Categorical, Remembered, and Enduring Selves

By the end of the second year, language becomes a powerful tool in self-development. Because it permits children to represent and express the self more clearly, it greatly enhances self-awareness. Between 18 and 30 months, children construct a **categorical self** as they classify themselves and others on the basis of perceptually distinct attributes and behaviors—age ("baby," "boy," or "man"), gender ("boy" or "girl"), and physical characteristics ("big," "strong"). They also start to refer to the self's goodness and badness ("I good girl." "Tommy mean!") and competencies ("Did it!" "I can't") (Stipek, Gralinski, & Kopp, 1990).

Recall from Chapter 7 that adult–child conversations about the past lead to an autobiographical memory. This life-story narrative grants the child a **remembered self**—a more

CULTURAL INFLUENCES

Cultural Variations in Personal Storytelling: Implications for Early Self-Concept

Preschoolers of many cultural backgrounds participate in personal storytelling with their parents. Striking cultural differences exist in parents' selection and interpretation of events in these early narratives, affecting the way children view themselves.

In one study, researchers spent hundreds of hours over a two-year period studying the storytelling practices of six middle-SES Irish-American families in Chicago and six middle-SES Chinese families in Taiwan. From extensive videotapes of adults' conversations with 2½-year-olds, the investigators identified personal stories and coded them for content, quality of their endings, and evaluation of the child (Miller, Fung, & Mintz, 1996; Miller et al., 1997).

Parents in both cultures discussed pleasurable holidays and family excursions in similar ways and with similar frequency. But Chinese parents more often told long stories about the child's misdeeds—using impolite language, writing on the wall, or playing in an overly rowdy way. These narratives were conveyed with warmth and caring, stressed the impact of misbehavior on others ("You made Mama lose face"), and often ended with direct teaching of proper behavior ("Saying dirty words is not good"). By contrast, in the few instances in which Irish-American stories referred to transgressions, parents downplayed their seriousness,

attributing them to the child's spunk and assertiveness.

Early narratives about the child seem to launch preschoolers' self-concepts on culturally distinct paths (Miller, Fung, & Koven, 2007). Influenced by Confucian traditions of strict discipline and social obligations, Chinese parents integrated these values into their stories, affirming the importance of not disgracing the family and explicitly conveying expectations in the story's conclusion. Although Irish-American parents disciplined their children, they rarely dwelt on misdeeds in storytelling. Rather, they cast the child's shortcomings in a positive light, perhaps to promote self-esteem.

Whereas most Americans believe that favorable self-esteem is crucial for healthy development, Chinese adults generally see it as unimportant or even negative—as impeding the child's willingness to listen and to be corrected (Miller et al., 2002). Consistent with this view, the Chinese parents did little to cultivate their child's individuality. Instead, they used storytelling to guide the child toward socially

A Chinese mother speaks gently to her children about proper behavior. By pointing out how children's misdeeds affect others, Chinese parents promote a self-concept that emphasizes social obligations.

responsible behavior. Hence, the Chinese child's self-image emphasizes membership in the collective and obligations to others, whereas the North American child's is more autonomous (Wang, 2006b).

coherent portrait than is offered by the isolated, episodic memories of the first few years. By participating in personal storytelling, children come to view the self as a unique, continuously existing individual embedded in a world of others. As early as age 2, parents use these discussions to impart rules, standards, and evaluative information about the child, as when they say, "You added the milk when we made mashed potatoes. That's a very important job!" (Nelson, 2003). As the Cultural Influences box above reveals, these narratives are a major means through which caregivers imbue the young child's sense of self with cultural values.

As they talk about personally significant events and as their cognitive skills advance, preschoolers gradually develop an **enduring self**—a view of themselves as persisting over time. Not until age 4 are children certain that a video image of themselves replayed a few minutes after it was filmed is still "me" (Povinelli, 2001). Similarly, when researchers asked 3- to 5-year-olds to imagine a future event (walking next to a waterfall) and to envision a future personal state by choosing from three items (a raincoat, money, a blanket) the one they would need to bring with them, performance—along with future-state justifications ("I'm gonna get wet")—increased sharply between ages 3 and 4 (Atance & Meltzoff, 2005).

The Inner Self: Children's Theory of Mind

As children think more about themselves and others, they form a naïve *theory of mind*—a coherent understanding of their own and others' rich mental lives. Recall from our discussion of metacognition in Chapter 7 that after age 2, preschoolers refer to mental states frequently and appropriately in everyday language. Although they confuse certain mental terms (see page 303), they are clearly aware of an **inner self** of private thoughts and imaginings.

How does the young child view this inner self, and how does this view change with age? Investigators are interested in this question because ideas about the mind are powerful tools in explaining and predicting both our own and others' everyday behaviors. Children's developing theory of mind contributes vitally to **perspective taking**—the capacity to imagine what others may be thinking and feeling and to distinguish those viewpoints from one's own. Perspective taking, in turn, is crucial for a wide variety of social–cognitive achievements, including understanding others' emotions (Chapter 10), referential communication skills (Chapter 9), and (as we will see shortly) self-concept and self-esteem.

Early Understandings of Mental States Over the first year of life, infants build an implicit appreciation of people as animate beings whose behavior is governed by intentions, desires, and feelings. This sets the stage for the verbalized mental understandings that blossom in early childhood.

In Chapter 10, we saw that 3-month-olds smile more at people than at objects and become upset when a person poses a still face and fails to communicate. By 6 months, when infants see people talk, they expect the talk to be directed at other people, not at inanimate objects (Legerstee, Barna, & DiAdamo, 2000). At the end of the first year, babies view people as intentional beings who can share and influence one another's mental states, a milestone that opens the door to new forms of communication—joint attention, social referencing, preverbal gestures, and language. These early milestones serve as the foundation for later mental understandings. In longitudinal research, 10-month-olds' ability to discern others' intentions predicted theory-of-mind competence at age 4 (Wellman et al., 2008).

At the end of the second and continuing over the third year, children display a clearer grasp of people's emotions and desires, evident in their increasing mental-state vocabulary, capacity to empathize, and realization that people often differ from one another and from themselves in likes, dislikes, wants, needs, and wishes ("Mommy likes green beans. Daddy doesn't. He likes carrots. I like carrots, too!") (Cassidy et al., 2005; Rakoczy, Warneken, & Tomasello, 2007). Still, appreciating the distinction between others' desires and one's own develops gradually. Whereas 18-month-olds can take into account differences in food preferences using another's emotional expression (see page 415 in Chapter 10), 2- and 3-year-olds continue to have difficulty with more challenging tasks—such as selecting a gift for someone based on that person's desires (Atance, Bélanger, & Meltzoff, 2010). As children gain experience in observing what others like and dislike, their performance improves.

These findings confirm that toddlers and young preschoolers comprehend mental states that can be readily inferred from their own and others' actions. But their understanding is limited to a simplistic **desire theory of mind:** They think that people always act in ways consistent with their desires and do not realize that less obvious, more interpretive mental states, such as beliefs, also affect behavior (Bartsch & Wellman, 1995).

Development of Belief–Desire Reasoning Between ages 3 and 4, children increasingly refer to their own and others' thoughts and beliefs (Wellman, 2011). And from age 4 on, they exhibit a **belief–desire theory of mind,** a more advanced view in which both beliefs and desires determine actions, and they understand the relationship between these inner states (Gopnik & Wellman, 1994; Ziv & Frye, 2003). Turn back to the beginning of this chapter, and notice how 4-year-old Ellen deliberately tries to alter her mother's *belief* about the motive behind her pretending, in hopes of warding off any *desire* on her mother's part to punish her. From early to middle childhood, efforts to alter others' beliefs increase, suggesting that children more firmly realize the power of belief to influence action.

Dramatic evidence for preschoolers' belief–desire reasoning comes from games that test whether they realize that *false beliefs*—ones that do not represent reality accurately—can guide people's behavior. **TAKE A MOMENT...** Show a child two small closed boxes, one a familiar Band-Aid box and the other a plain, unmarked box (see Figure 11.3). Then say, "Pick the box you think has the Band-Aids in it." Children usually pick the marked container. Next, open the boxes and show the child that, contrary to her own belief, the marked one is empty and the unmarked one contains the Band-Aids. Finally, introduce the child to a hand puppet and explain, "Here's Pam. She has a cut, see? Where do you think she'll look for Band-Aids? Why would she look in there? Before you looked inside, did you think that the plain box contained Band-Aids? Why?" (Bartsch & Wellman, 1995; Gopnik & Wellman, 1994). Only a handful of 3-year-olds can explain Pam's—and their own—false beliefs, but many 4-year-olds can.

Some researchers claim that the procedures just described, which require verbal explanations, grossly underestimate younger children's ability to attribute false beliefs to others. Relying on the violation-of-expectation method (which depends on looking behavior), these investigators assert that children comprehend others' false beliefs by age 15 months (Baillargeon, Scott, & He, 2010). But like other violation-of-expectation evidence, this conclusion is controversial (see Chapter 6) (Ruffman & Perner, 2005; Sirios & Jackson, 2007). In another study relying on active behavior (helping), most 18-month-olds—after witnessing an object moved from one box to another while an adult was not looking—helped the adult, when he tried to open the original box, locate the object in the new box (Buttelmann, Carpenter, & Tomasello, 2009). Still, much more evidence is needed to confirm that toddlers implicitly grasp mental states as complex as false belief (Poulin-Dubois, Brooker, & Chow, 2009). Indeed, their performance may be based on a far simpler rule: *lack of perceptual access leads to not knowing*—that a person who hasn't seen the contents of a particular container can't know what's in it and, therefore, will be mistaken (Fabricius & Khalil, 2003).

Among children of diverse cultural and SES backgrounds, false-belief understanding strengthens gradually after age 3½, becoming more secure between ages 4 and 6 (Amsterlaw & Wellman, 2006; Callaghan et al., 2005; Flynn, 2006). Mastery of false belief signals a change in representation—the ability to view beliefs as *interpretations,* not just reflections, of reality. Does this remind you of school-age children's more active view of the mind, discussed in Chapter 7? Belief–desire reasoning may mark the beginnings of this overall change.

FIGURE 11.3 Example of a false-belief task. (a) An adult shows a child the contents of a Band-Aid box and an unmarked box. The Band-Aids are in the unmarked container. (b) The adult introduces the child to a hand puppet named Pam and asks the child to predict where Pam would look for the Band-Aids and to explain Pam's behavior. The task reveals whether children understand that without having seen that the Band-Aids are in the unmarked container, Pam will hold a false belief.

Reasoning About Beliefs in Middle Childhood With the realization that people can increase their knowledge by making *mental inferences* (see Chapter 7), school-age children extend false-belief understanding further. In several studies, researchers told children complex stories involving one character's belief about a second character's belief. Then the children answered questions about what the first character thought the second character would do (see Figure 11.4 on page 454). By age 6 to 7, children were aware that people form beliefs about other people's beliefs and that these *second-order beliefs* can also be wrong!

Appreciation of *second-order false belief* enables children to pinpoint the reasons that another person arrived at a certain belief (Astington, Pelletier, & Homer, 2002; Harris, 2006; Miller, 2009; Naito & Seki, 2009). Notice how it requires the ability to view a situation from at least two perspectives—that is, to reason simultaneously about what two or more people are thinking, a form of perspective taking called **recursive thought.** We think recursively when we make such statements as, "*Lisa believes* that *Jason believes* the letter is under his pillow, but that's *not what Jason really believes; he knows* the letter is in the desk."

On other complex tasks requiring recursive thought, performance also improves over middle childhood. Consider a study addressing children's appreciation of the role of people's *preexisting beliefs* in interpreting a new, ambiguous situation. School-age children listened to a story in which Cathy and Sarah see their classmate, Joan, holding a doll in front of a donation box full of toys for poor children. Cathy likes Joan. Sarah, however, dislikes Joan, believing she's a troublemaker. Children were asked how Cathy and Sarah might interpret Joan's behavior. Would they, for example, appreciate that Cathy would likely think Joan was donating the doll out of kindness, whereas Sarah would probably think she was stealing the doll? Results revealed that not until age 7 to 8 could children clearly explain how

(a)

Jason has a letter from a friend. Lisa wants to read the letter, but Jason doesn't want her to. Jason puts the letter under his pillow.

(b)

Jason leaves the room to help his mother.

(c)

While Jason is gone, Lisa takes the letter and reads it. Jason returns and watches Lisa, but Lisa doesn't see Jason. Then Lisa puts the letter in Jason's desk.

FIGURE 11.4 Example of a second-order false-belief task. After relating the story in the sequence of pictures, the researcher asks a second-order false-belief question: "Where does Lisa think Jason will look for the letter? Why?" Around age 7, children answer correctly—that Lisa thinks Jason will look under his pillow because Lisa doesn't know that Jason saw her put the letter in the desk. (Adapted from Astington, Pelletier, & Homer, 2002.)

people's prior beliefs might affect their viewpoints (Pillow, 1991). Around this age, children also grasp that two people are likely to interpret the same event—such as an ambiguous fragment removed from a larger drawing they have never seen—differently, no matter what beliefs or other biases they bring to the situation (Lalonde & Chandler, 2002). They recognize that that the same reality can be construed in many ways.

In sum, compared to younger children, school-age children have a far more sophisticated view of the mind: They regard it as an active interpreter of experience. (Return to page 303 in Chapter 7 to review a similar advance in metacognitive knowledge at about the same time.)

Social Consequences Preschoolers' capacity to use both beliefs and desires to predict people's behavior becomes a powerful tool for reflecting on thoughts and emotions and a good predictor of social skills (Harwood & Farrar, 2006; Watson et al., 1999). False-belief understanding is linked to gains in young children's capacity to discuss thoughts and feelings in conversations with friends (Hughes, Ensor, & Marks, 2010). And it predicts quality of sociodramatic play—specifically, the capacity to engage in joint planning, to negotiate pretend roles, and to imagine verbally, without the support of real objects (Jenkins & Astington, 2000). It is also associated with early reading ability, probably because it helps children comprehend story narratives (Astington & Pelletier, 2005). To follow a story line, children generally must link plot actions with characters' motives and beliefs.

Once children grasp the relation between beliefs and behavior, they apply their understanding to a wider range of situations. For example, children who pass false-belief tasks have more accurate eyewitness memories (see Chapter 7, page 300) (Templeton & Wilcox, 2000). They realize that one person can present misinformation to another, which can affect the second individual's beliefs. Consequently, in reporting observed events, such children are more likely to resist attempts to mislead them.

The ability to engage in recursive thought enables these children to understand that conflicts often arise out of multiple, yet legitimate, interpretations of the same reality. This capacity leads to dramatic gains in social skills.

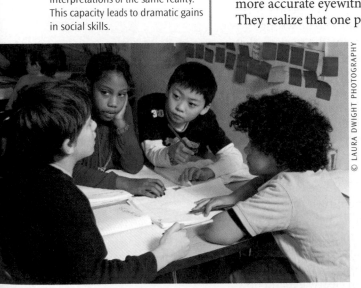

School-age children's capacity for recursive thought leads to further, dramatic gains in social skills. They now understand that conflicts often arise because of multiple yet legitimate interpretations of the same reality (Carpendale & Lewis, 2006). Consequently, they often call on their recursive capacity to clear up misunderstandings: "I thought you would think I was just kidding when I said that." They also rely on it to decide when to disguise their real thoughts and feelings: "He'll think I'm jealous if I tell him I don't like his new video game, so I'll act like I do."

As these findings illustrate, theory-of-mind development from early to middle childhood strengthens children's appreciation of the relation between their own and others' beliefs and promotes their reasoned attempts to change others' beliefs. As a result, it contributes to many social competencies.

Factors Contributing to Children's Theory of Mind
How do children develop a theory of mind beginning at such a young age? Research suggests that language, executive function, make-believe play, and social experiences all contribute.

Language and Verbal Reasoning. The prefrontal cortex seems to play a crucial role in theory-of-mind development. ERP brain-wave recordings obtained while 4- to 6-year-olds reasoned about others' beliefs revealed that children who pass false-belief tasks (as opposed to those who fail) display a pattern of activity in the left prefrontal cortex similar to that of adults engaged in the same tasks (Liu et al., 2009). This left-prefrontal ERP pattern typically appears when adults reason verbally about mental concepts.

Understanding the mind requires the ability to reflect on thoughts, which language makes possible. Many studies indicate that language ability strongly predicts preschoolers' grasp of false belief (Milligan, Astington, & Dack, 2007). Children who spontaneously use, or are trained to use, complex sentences with mental-state words are especially likely to pass false-belief tasks (de Villiers & de Villiers, 2000; Hale & Tager-Flusberg, 2003). The Quechua village people of the Peruvian highlands refer to mental states such as "think" and "believe" indirectly, because their language lacks mental-state terms. Quechua children have difficulty with false-belief tasks for years after children in industrialized nations have mastered them (Vinden, 1996). In contrast, Chinese languages have verb markers that can label the word "believe" as decidedly false. When adults use those markers within false-belief tasks, Chinese preschoolers perform better (Tardif, Wellman, & Cheung, 2004).

Executive Function. Several aspects of preschoolers' executive function—ability to inhibit inappropriate responses, think flexibly, and plan—predict current performance on false-belief tasks as well as improvements over time (Hughes, 1998; Hughes & Ensor, 2007; Sabbagh et al., 2006). Like language, these cognitive skills enhance children's capacity to reflect on their experiences and mental states. Gains in inhibition, considered in Chapter 7, predict false-belief understanding particularly strongly, perhaps because false-belief tasks require suppression of an irrelevant response—the tendency to assume that others' knowledge and beliefs are the same as one's own (Birch & Bloom, 2003; Carlson, Moses, & Claxton, 2004).

Security of Attachment and Maternal "Mind-Mindedness." In longitudinal research, mothers of securely attached babies were more likely to comment appropriately on their infants' mental states: "Do you *remember* Grandma?" "You really *like* that swing." These mothers continued to describe their children, when they reached preschool age, in terms of mental characteristics: "She's got a mind of her own!" This maternal "mind-mindedness" was positively associated with early mental-state attainments, such as understanding that others may have desires discrepant from one's own, as well as later performance on false-belief and other theory-of-mind tasks (Laranjo et al., 2010; Meins et al., 1998, 2003; Ruffman et al., 2006).

Parental commentary about mental states—initially, "desire" talk ("want," "like," "wish") and, later, more advanced "think," "believe," "know" remarks—exposes infants and young children to concepts and language that help them think about their own and others' mental lives (Taumoepeau & Ruffman, 2006). Some researchers suggest that children's reflections on inner states are among the representations that make up their internal working models of close relationships (see page 430 in Chapter 10) (Reese, Newcombe, & Bird, 2006; Symons, 2004). This mental-state knowledge emerges earlier—and seems to be more objective and richer—among securely attached children, whose parents frequently refer to desires, intentions, beliefs, and emotions.

Make-Believe Play. Earlier we noted that theory of mind fosters children's sociodramatic play. But make-believe also offers a rich context for thinking about the mind. As children act out roles, they imagine and express the thoughts and emotions of the characters they portray and their implications (Kavanaugh, 2006b). These experiences may increase children's awareness that belief influences behavior. In support of this idea, preschoolers who engage in extensive fantasy role play or who have imaginary companions—and, thus, are deeply absorbed in creating make-believe characters—are advanced in understanding of false belief and other aspects of the mind (Astington & Jenkins, 1995; Lalonde & Chandler, 1995).

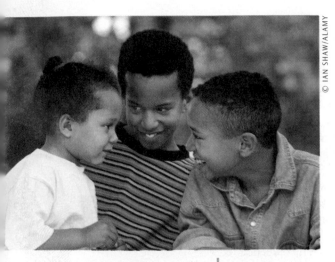

Because this preschooler has two older siblings, she participates in more family talk about thoughts, beliefs, and emotions. Sibling interactions contribute to false-belief and other mental-state understandings.

LOOK and LISTEN

While observing a parent or teacher conversing with a preschool child, record features of interaction that promote false-belief and other mental-state understandings.

Social Interaction. Preschoolers with siblings who are also children (but not infants)—and especially those with older siblings or with two or more siblings—tend to be more aware of false belief. Children with older siblings close in age, and those with more siblings, are exposed to—and participate in—more family talk about thoughts, beliefs, and emotions (Hughes et al., 2010; McAlister & Peterson, 2006, 2007; Symons, 2004). Similarly, preschool friends who often engage in mental-state talk are advanced in false-belief and other mental-state understandings (de Rosnay & Hughes, 2006; Hughes & Dunn, 1998).

Style of adult–child interaction also contributes. Rich conversations between parents and 2-year-olds—especially, discourse with many explanations of people's actions and with well-connected exchanges in which each speaker's remark is related to the other's previous remark—predict subsequent mastery of false belief (Ensor & Hughes, 2008; Lohmann & Tomasello, 2003). And at age 4, elaborative, well-connected parent–child conversations continue to be associated with children's theory-of-mind progress (Ontai & Thompson, 2010). References to mental states occur especially often in well-connected dialogue, which may provoke deeper insights than other forms of talk. In line with Vygotsky's theory, these interactive experiences offer children opportunities to talk about inner states, receive feedback, observe different viewpoints, and become increasingly aware of their own and others' mental activities.

Core knowledge theorists (see Chapter 6, page 261) believe that to profit from the social experiences just described, children must be biologically prepared to develop a theory of mind. They claim that children with *autism,* for whom mastery of false belief is either greatly delayed or absent, are deficient in the brain mechanism that enables humans to detect mental states. See the Biology and Environment box on the following page to find out more about the biological basis of reasoning about the mind.

Self-Concept

As children develop an appreciation of their inner mental world, they think more intently about themselves. During early childhood, knowledge and evaluation of the self's characteristics expands (Harter, 2003, 2006). Children begin to construct a **self-concept,** the set of attributes, abilities, attitudes, and values that an individual believes defines who he or she is.

Early Childhood Ask a 3- to 5-year-old to tell you about himself, and you are likely to hear something like this: "I'm Tommy. I'm 4 years old. I can wash my hair all by myself. I have a new Tinkertoy set, and I made this big, big tower." Preschoolers' self-concepts largely consist of observable characteristics, such as their name, physical appearance, possessions, and everyday behaviors (Harter, 2006; Watson, 1990).

By age 3½, children also describe themselves in terms of typical emotions and attitudes ("I'm happy when I play with my friends"; "I don't like scary TV programs;" "I usually do what Mommy says"), suggesting a beginning understanding of their unique psychological characteristics (Eder & Mangelsdorf, 1997). And by age 5, children's degree of agreement with a battery of such statements coincides with maternal reports of their personality traits, indicating that older preschoolers have a sense of their own timidity, agreeableness, and positive or negative affect (Brown et al., 2008). As further support for this emerging grasp of personality, when given a trait label ("shy," "mean"), 4-year-olds infer appropriate motives and feelings. For example, they know that a shy person doesn't like to be with unfamiliar people (Heyman & Gelman, 1999). But preschoolers do not yet say, "I'm helpful" or "I'm shy." Direct references to personality traits must wait for greater cognitive maturity.

Preschoolers' self-concepts emphasize observable characteristics and typical emotions and attitudes. If asked to describe herself, this child might say, "I like to pour my own milk!"

BIOLOGY and ENVIRONMENT

"Mindblindness" and Autism

Michael stood at the water table in Leslie's classroom, repeatedly filling a plastic cup and dumping out its contents—dip-splash, dip-splash—until Leslie came over and redirected his actions. Without looking at Leslie's face, Michael moved to a new repetitive pursuit: pouring water from one cup into another and back again. As other children entered the play space and conversed, Michael hardly noticed.

Michael has *autism* (a term that means "absorbed in the self"), the most severe behavior disorder of childhood. Like other children with autism, by age 3 he displayed deficits in three core areas of functioning. First, he had only limited ability to engage in nonverbal behaviors required for successful social interaction, such as eye gaze, facial expressions, gestures, imitation, and give-and-take. Second, his language was delayed and stereotyped. He used words to echo what others said and to get things he wanted, not to connect socially or exchange ideas. Third, he engaged in much less make-believe play than other children (Frith, 2003; Walenski, Tager-Flusberg, & Ullman, 2006). And Michael showed another typical feature of autism: His interests were narrow and overly intense. For example, one day he sat for more than an hour spinning a toy Ferris wheel.

Researchers agree that autism stems from abnormal brain functioning, usually due to genetic or prenatal environmental causes. Beginning in the first year, children with the disorder have larger-than-average brains, perhaps due to massive overgrowth of synapses and lack of synaptic pruning, which accompanies normal development of cognitive, language, and communication skills (Courchesne, Carper, & Akshoomoff, 2003).

The amygdala, especially, grows abnormally large in childhood, followed by a greater than average reduction in size in adolescence and adulthood. This deviant growth pattern is believed to contribute to deficits in emotional responsiveness and social interaction involved in the disorder (Schumann et al., 2009; Schumann & Amaral, 2010). The larger the amygdala compared with typically developing children, the more severe the child's social and communicative impairments. Furthermore, fMRI studies reveal that autism is associated with reduced activity in areas of the cerebral cortex involved in processing emotional and social information,

and with weaker connections between the amygdala and the temporal lobes (important for processing facial expressions) (Monk et al., 2010; Théoret et al., 2005).

Mounting evidence reveals that children with autism have a deficient theory of mind. Long after they reach the intellectual level of an average 4-year-old, they have great difficulty with false belief. Most find it hard to attribute mental states to themselves or others (Steele, Joseph, & Tager-Flusberg, 2003). They rarely use mental-state words, such as *believe, think, know, feel,* and *pretend.*

As early as the second year, children with autism show deficits in emotional and social capacities believed to contribute to an understanding of mental life. Compared with other children, they have difficulty distinguishing facial expressions and less often establish joint attention, point to share interest in an object or event, engage in social referencing, or imitate an adult's novel behaviors (Chawarska & Shic, 2009; Mundy & Stella, 2000; Vivanti et al., 2008). And because children with autism are relatively insensitive to eye gaze as a cue to what a speaker is talking about, they often assume that another person's language refers to what they themselves are looking at—a possible reason for their frequent nonsensical expressions (Baron-Cohen, Baldwin, & Crowson, 1997).

Do these findings indicate that autism is due to an impairment in an innate, core brain function, which leaves the child "mindblind" and therefore unable to engage in human sociability? Some researchers think so (Baron-Cohen & Belmonte, 2005; Scholl & Leslie, 2000). But others point out that individuals with broad intellectual disability but not autism also do poorly on tasks assessing mental understanding (Yirmiya et al., 1998). This suggests that some kind of general intellectual impairment is involved.

One conjecture is that children with autism are impaired in executive function. This leaves

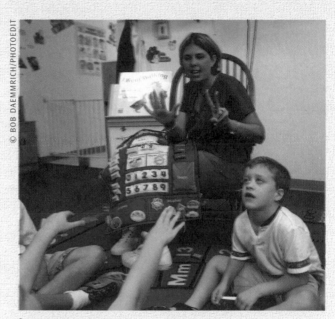

This child, who has autism, is barely aware of his teacher and classmates. His "mindblindness" might be due to a basic deficit in social awareness, a general impairment in executive function, or a deficit in holistic processing.

them deficient in skills involved in flexible, goal-oriented thinking, including shifting attention to address relevant aspects of a situation, inhibiting irrelevant responses, applying strategies to hold information in working memory, and generating plans (Joseph & Tager-Flusberg, 2004; Robinson et al., 2009).

Another possibility is that children with autism display a peculiar style of information processing, preferring to process the parts of stimuli over patterns and coherent wholes (Happé & Frith, 2006). Deficits in thinking flexibly and in holistic processing of stimuli would each interfere with understanding the social world because social interaction requires quick integration of information from various sources and evaluation of alternative possibilities.

It is not clear which of these hypotheses is correct. Some research suggests that impairments in social awareness, flexible thinking, processing coherent wholes, and verbal ability contribute independently to autism (Morgan, Maybery, & Durkin, 2003; Pellicano et al., 2006). Perhaps several biologically based deficits underlie the tragic social isolation of children like Michael.

Middle Childhood Over time, children organize their observations of typical behaviors and internal states into general dispositions. A major change occurs between ages 8 and 11, as the following self-description by an 11-year-old illustrates:

> My name is A. I'm a human being. I'm a girl. I'm a truthful person. I'm not pretty. I do so-so in my studies. I'm a very good cellist. I'm a very good pianist. I'm a little bit tall for my age. I like several boys. I like several girls. I'm old-fashioned. I play tennis. I am a very good swimmer. I try to be helpful. I'm always ready to be friends with anybody. Mostly I'm good, but I lose my temper. I'm not well liked by some girls and boys. I don't know if I'm liked by boys or not. (Montemayor & Eisen, 1977, pp. 317–318).

Instead of specific behaviors, this child emphasizes competencies: "a very good cellist," "so-so in my studies" (Damon & Hart, 1988). She also describes her personality, mentioning both positive and negative traits: "truthful" but "short-tempered." Older school-age children are far less likely than younger children to describe themselves in extreme, all-or-none ways.

These evaluative self-descriptions result from school-age children's frequent **social comparisons**—judgments of their own appearance, abilities, and behavior in relation to those of others. Whereas 4- to 6-year-olds can compare their own performance to that of a single peer, older children can compare multiple individuals, including themselves (Butler, 1998; Harter, 2003, 2006). Consequently, they conclude that they are "very good" at some things, "so-so" at others, and "not good" at still others.

Adolescence In early adolescence, the self differentiates further. Teenagers mention a wider array of traits, which vary with social context—for example, self with mother, father, close friends, and romantic partner, and as student, athlete, and employee. As one young teenager commented:

> I'm an extrovert with my friends: I'm talkative, pretty rowdy, and funny.... With my parents, I'm more likely to be depressed. I feel sad as well as mad and also hopeless about ever pleasing them.... At school, I'm pretty intelligent. I know that because I'm smart when it comes to how I do in classes. I'm curious about learning new things, and I'm also creative when it comes to solving problems.... I can be a real introvert around people I don't know well.... I worry a lot about what others my age who are not my closest friends must think of me, probably that I'm a total dork. (Harter, 2006, p. 531)

Notice, also, that young adolescents unify separate traits ("smart" and "curious") into more abstract descriptors ("intelligent"). But these generalizations about the self are not interconnected and are often contradictory. For example, 12- to 14-year-olds might mention opposing traits—"intelligent" and "clueless," "extrovert" and "introvert." These disparities result from expansion of the adolescent's social world, which creates pressure to display different selves in different relationships. As adolescents' awareness of these inconsistencies grows, they frequently agonize over "which is the real me" (Harter, 1999, 2003, 2006).

From middle to late adolescence, cognitive changes enable teenagers to combine their traits into an organized system. Their use of qualifiers ("I have a *fairly* quick temper," "I'm not *thoroughly* honest") reveals their increased acceptance of situational variations in psychological qualities. Older adolescents also add integrating principles, which make sense of formerly troublesome contradictions. "I'm very adaptable," said one young person. "When I'm around my friends, who think that what I say is important, I'm talkative, but around my family I'm quiet because they're never interested enough to really listen to me" (Damon, 1990, p. 88).

LOOK and LISTEN

Pose the following question to a 12- to 14-year-old and a 16- to 18-year-old: "What are you like as a person?" Do differences in their self-descriptions match research findings on development of self-concept?

Compared with school-age children, teenagers place more emphasis on social virtues, such as being friendly, considerate, kind, and cooperative—traits that reflect adolescents' increasing concern with being viewed positively by others. Among older adolescents, personal and moral values also emerge as key themes. Here is how one 17-year-old described herself:

> I'm a pretty conscientious person.... Eventually I want to go to law school, so developing good study habits and getting top grades are both essential.... I'd like to be an ethical person who treats other people fairly.... I don't always live up to that standard; that is, sometimes I do something that doesn't feel ethical. When that happens, I get a little depressed because I don't like myself as a person. But I tell myself that it's natural to make mistakes, so I don't really question the fact that deep down inside, the real me is a moral person. (Harter, 2006, pp. 545–546)

This well-integrated account differs from the fragmented, listlike self-descriptions typical of children. As adolescents revise their views of themselves to include enduring beliefs and plans, they move toward the kind of unity of self that is central to identity development.

Cognitive, Social, and Cultural Influences on Self-Concept

What factors account for these revisions in self-concept? Cognitive development certainly affects the changing *structure* of the self. School-age children, as we saw in Chapter 6, can better coordinate several aspects of a situation in reasoning about their physical world. Similarly, in the social realm, they combine typical experiences and behaviors into stable psychological dispositions, blend positive and negative characteristics, and compare their own characteristics with those of many peers (Harter, 2006). And formal operational thought transforms the adolescent's vision of the self into a complex, well-organized, internally consistent picture (Harter, 1999, 2003).

The changing *content* of the self is a product of both cognitive capacities and feedback from others. Sociologist George Herbert Mead (1934) described the self as a **generalized other**—a blend of what we imagine important people in our lives think of us. He proposed that a psychological self emerges when children adopt a view of the self that resembles others' attitudes toward the child. Mead's ideas indicate that perspective-taking skills—in particular, an improved ability to infer what other people are thinking—are crucial for developing a self-concept based on personality traits. During middle childhood and adolescence, young people become better at "reading" messages they receive from others. And as school-age children internalize others' expectations, they form an *ideal self* that they use to evaluate their real self. As we will see shortly, a large discrepancy between the two can greatly undermine self-esteem, leading to sadness, hopelessness, and depression.

Parental support contributes vitally to the clarity and optimism of children's self-concepts. In one study, the richness of mothers' emotional communication in narratives about the past—evaluations of positive events and explanations of children's negative feelings and their resolution ("Talking about your teacher moving away helped you feel better")—predicted greater consistency in 5- and 6-year-olds' reports of their personal characteristics (Bird & Reese, 2006). And school-age children with a history of elaborative parent–child conversations construct more positive, detailed personal narratives and thus have more complex, favorable, and coherent self-images (Harter, 2006).

In middle childhood, children also look to more people beyond the family for information about themselves as they enter a wider range of settings in school and community. And self-descriptions now include frequent references to social groups: "I'm a Boy Scout, a paper boy, and a Prairie City soccer player," remarked one 10-year-old. Gradually, as children move into adolescence, their sources of self-definition become more selective. Although parents and teachers remain influential, self-concept becomes increasingly vested in feedback from close friends (Oosterwegel & Oppenheimer, 1993).

Keep in mind, however, that the content of self-concept varies from culture to culture. In earlier chapters, we noted that Asian parents stress harmonious interdependence, Western parents separateness and self-assertion (Markus & Kitayama, 1991). Turn back to the Cultural Influences box on page 451, and notice this difference in parents' personal storytelling with their young children. These contrasting values are apparent in school-age children's self-concepts. When asked to recall personally significant past experiences (their last birthday, a time their parent scolded them), U.S. children gave longer accounts including more personal preferences, skills, and opinions. Chinese children, in contrast, more often referred to social interactions and to others. Similarly, in their self-descriptions, U.S. children listed more personal attributes ("I'm smart," "I like hockey"), Chinese children more attributes involving group membership and relationships ("I belong to the Lee family," "I'm in second grade," "I like to help my mom wash dishes") (Wang, 2004, 2006b).

As school-age children spend more time away from home, their self-descriptions increasingly refer to social groups—for example, "I'm a member of our school's cooking club!"

Milestones

Emergence of Self and Development of Self-Concept

AGE	MILESTONES
1–2 years	• Awareness of self as physically distinct from surroundings increases. • Recognizes image of self and, by end of this period, uses own name or personal pronoun to refer to self. • Constructs explicit body self-awareness, and scale errors decline.
3–5 years	• Forms a categorical self by classifying the self and others on the basis of perceptually distinct attributes (age, gender, physical characteristics), goodness and badness, and competencies. • Constructs a remembered self, in the form of a life-story narrative. • Desire theory of mind expands into a belief–desire theory, as indicated by understanding of false belief. • Forms a self-concept consisting of observable characteristics and typical emotions and attitudes.
6–10 years	• Appreciates second-order false beliefs and the role of preexisting beliefs in interpreting a new, ambiguous situation—attainments reflecting capacity to engage in recursive thought. • Emphasizes personality traits and both positive and negative attributes in self-concept. • Makes social comparisons among multiple individuals.
11 years and older	• Unifies separate traits, such as "smart" and "talented," into more abstract descriptors, such as "intelligent," in self-concept. • Combines traits making up self-concept into an organized system.

Note: These milestones represent overall age trends. Individual differences exist in the precise age at which each milestone is attained.

Photos: (top) © Laura Dwight Photography; (middle) © blue jean images/Getty Images; (bottom) © Laura Dwight Photography

Finally, although school-age children from diverse cultures view themselves as more knowledgeable about their own inner attributes than significant adults, Japanese children attribute considerably greater knowledge to parents and teachers than American children do (Mitchell et al., 2010). Perhaps because of their more interdependent self, Japanese children are more likely to assume that people share common understandings and that, therefore, their inner states are more transparent to others.

In sum, in characterizing themselves, children from individualistic cultures seem to be more egoistic and competitive, those from collectivist cultures more concerned with connections to others—a finding that underscores the powerful impact of the social environment on self-concept. The Milestones table above summarizes the vast changes in the self from infancy through adolescence.

ASK YOURSELF

Review ■ How does cognitive development affect changes in self-concept from early childhood to adolescence?

Connect ■ Recall from Chapter 6 (page 246) that between ages 4 and 8, children figure out who is really behind the activities of Santa Claus and the Tooth Fairy, and they realize that magicians use trickery. How might these understandings be related to their developing theory of mind?

Apply ■ Suggest ways that parents can promote a sturdy sense of self in infants and toddlers.

Self-Esteem: The Evaluative Side of Self-Concept

So far, we have focused on how the general structure and content of self-concept change with age. Another component of self-concept is **self-esteem,** the judgments we make about our own worth and the feelings associated with those judgments. High self-esteem implies a realistic evaluation of the self's characteristics and competencies, coupled with an attitude of self-acceptance and self-respect.

Self-esteem ranks among the most important aspects of self-development because evaluations of our own competencies affect emotional experiences, future behavior, and long-term psychological adjustment. As soon as a categorical self with features that can be judged positively or negatively is in place, children become self-evaluative beings. Around age 2, they call a parent's attention to an achievement, such as completing a puzzle, by pointing and saying something like "Look, Mom!" In addition, 2-year-olds are likely to smile when they succeed at a task an adult set for them and to look away or frown when they fail (Stipek, Recchia, & McClintic, 1992). Self-esteem originates early, and its structure becomes increasingly elaborate with age.

▶ Discuss development of and influences on self-esteem from early childhood through adolescence.

▶ Discuss achievement-related attributions, and suggest ways to foster a mastery-oriented approach in children.

The Structure of Self-Esteem

TAKE A MOMENT... Think about your own self-esteem. Besides a global appraisal of your worth as a person, do you have an array of separate self-judgments concerning how well you perform at different activities?

Researchers have studied the multifaceted nature of self-esteem by applying *factor analysis* (see page 321 in Chapter 8) to children's ratings of the extent to which statements like these are true: "I am good at homework." "I'm usually the one chosen for games." "Most kids like me." By age 4, preschoolers have several self-judgments—for example, about learning things in school, making friends, getting along with parents, and feeling physically attractive (Marsh, Ellis, & Craven, 2002). Compared with that of older children, however, their understanding is limited.

The structure of self-esteem depends on evaluative information available to children and their ability to process that information. Around age 6 to 7, children in diverse Western cultures have formed at least four broad self-evaluations: academic competence, social competence, physical/athletic competence, and physical appearance. Within these are more refined categories that become increasingly distinct with age (Marsh, 1990; Marsh & Ayotte, 2003; Van den Bergh & De Rycke, 2003). Furthermore, the capacity to view the self in terms of stable dispositions enables school-age children to combine their separate self-evaluations into a general psychological image of themselves—an overall sense of self-esteem (Harter, 2003, 2006). Consequently, self-esteem takes on the hierarchical structure shown in Figure 11.5 on page 462.

Children attach greater importance to certain self-judgments, giving them more weight in the total picture. Although individual differences exist, during childhood and adolescence perceived physical appearance correlates more strongly with global self-esteem than any other self-esteem factor (Klomsten, Skaalvik, & Espnes, 2004; Shapka & Keating, 2005). Emphasis on appearance—in the media, among peers, and in society—has major implications for overall satisfaction with the self.

The arrival of adolescence adds several new dimensions of self-esteem—close friendship, romantic appeal, and job competence—that reflect important concerns of this period (Harter, 1999, 2003, 2006). Furthermore, adolescents become more discriminating in the people to whom they look for validation of their self-esteem. Some rely more on parents, others more on teachers, and still others more on peers—differences that reflect the extent to which teenagers believe that people in each context are interested in and respect them as individuals (Harter, Waters, & Whitesell, 1998).

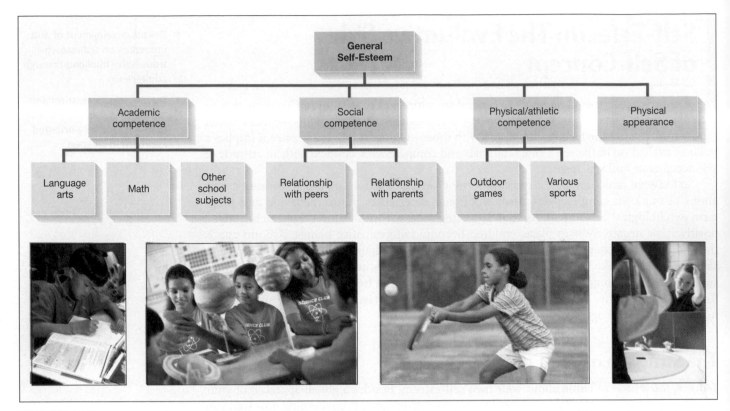

FIGURE 11.5 **Hierarchical structure of self-esteem in the mid-elementary school years.** From their experiences in different settings, school-age children form at least four separate self-esteems: academic competence, social competence, physical/athletic competence, and physical appearance. These differentiate into additional self-evaluations and combine to form a general sense of self-esteem. *Photos:* (far left) © Mary Kate Denny/PhotoEdit; (middle left) © Tim Pannell/CORBIS; (middle right) © Mitch Wojnarowicz/The Image Works; (far right) Radius Images/Photolibrary

Changes in Level of Self-Esteem: The Role of Social Comparisons

Because preschoolers have trouble distinguishing between their desired and their actual competence, they usually rate their own ability as extremely high and underestimate task difficulty (Harter, 2003, 2006). In early childhood, high self-esteem is adaptive, contributing greatly to preschoolers' initiative during a period in which they must master many new skills.

Self-esteem declines over the first few years of elementary school as children evaluate themselves in various areas (Marsh, Craven, & Debus, 1998; Wigfield et al., 1997). This decline occurs as children receive more competence-related feedback, as their performances are increasingly judged in relation to those of others, and as they become cognitively capable of social comparison.

To protect their self-esteem, most children eventually balance social comparisons with personal achievement goals (Ruble & Flett, 1988). Perhaps for this reason, the drop in self-esteem in the early school years is seldom harmful. Then, from fourth grade on, self-esteem rises and remains high for the majority of young people, who feel especially good about their peer relationships and athletic capabilities (Cole et al., 2001; Impett et al., 2008; Twenge & Campbell, 2001). The main exception is a decline in self-worth for some adolescents after transition to middle and high school. Entry into a new school, accompanied by new teacher and peer expectations, may temporarily interfere with the ability to make realistic judgments about behavior and performance. In Chapter 15, we will examine these school transition effects. For most young people, however, becoming an adolescent leads to feelings of pride and self-confidence.

Influences on Self-Esteem

From middle childhood to adolescence, individual differences in self-esteem become increasingly stable (Trzesniewski, Donnellan, & Robins, 2003). And positive relationships among self-esteem, valuing of various activities, and success at those activities emerge and strengthen with age. For example, academic self-esteem is a powerful predictor of young people's judgments of the importance and usefulness of school subjects, willingness to exert effort, achievement, and eventual career choice (Denissen, Zarrett, & Eccles, 2007; Valentine, DuBois, & Cooper, 2004; Whitesell et al., 2009). Children and adolescents with high social self-esteem are consistently better-liked by their peers (Jacobs et al., 2002). And as we saw in Chapter 5, sense of athletic competence is positively associated with investment in and performance at sports.

Furthermore, across age, sex, SES, and ethnic groups, individuals with mostly favorable self-esteem profiles tend to be well-adjusted, sociable, and conscientious. In contrast, low self-esteem in all areas is linked to a wide array of adjustment difficulties (DuBois et al., 1999; Kim & Cicchetti, 2006; Robins et al., 2001). But certain self-esteem factors are more strongly related to adjustment. Adolescents who feel highly dissatisfied with parental relationships often are aggressive and antisocial. Those with poor academic self-esteem tend to be anxious and unfocused. And those who view their peer relationships negatively are likely to be anxious and depressed (Marsh, Parada, & Ayotte, 2004; Rudolph, Caldwell, & Conley, 2005). And although virtually all teenagers become increasingly concerned about others' opinions, those who are overly dependent on social approval place their self-esteem continually "on the line." As a result, they report frequent self-esteem shifts—on average, about once a week (Harter & Whitesell, 2003). Let's take a closer look at factors that affect self-esteem—both its level and its stability.

During adolescence, self-esteem typically rises, fostered by pride in new competencies and growing self-confidence. This teenager beams as she displays the blue ribbon she won at an agricultural fair.

Culture As with self-concept, cultural forces profoundly affect self-esteem. An especially strong emphasis on social comparison in school may underlie the finding that despite their higher academic achievement, Chinese and Japanese children score lower than U.S. children in self-esteem—a difference that widens with age (Harter, 2006; Hawkins, 1994; Twenge & Crocker, 2002). In Asian classrooms, competition is tough, and achievement pressure is high. At the same time, because their culture values modesty and social harmony, Asian children rely less on social comparisons to promote their own self-esteem. Rather, they tend to be reserved about judging themselves positively but generous in their praise of others (Falbo et al., 1997).

Gender-stereotyped expectations also affect self-esteem. In one study, the more 5- to 8-year-old girls talked with friends about the way people look, watched TV shows focusing on physical appearance, and perceived their friends as valuing thinness, the greater their dissatisfaction with their physical self and the lower their overall self-esteem a year later (Dohnt & Tiggemann, 2006). By adolescence, girls feel less confident than boys about their physical appearance and athletic abilities. With respect to academic self-esteem, boys, again, are somewhat advantaged: Whereas girls score higher in language arts self-esteem, boys have higher math, science, and physical/athletic self-esteem—even when children of equal skill levels are compared (Fredericks & Eccles, 2002; Jacobs et al., 2002; Kurtz-Costes et al., 2008). At the same time, girls exceed boys in self-esteem dimensions of close friendship and social acceptance.

Although only a slight difference exists between boys and girls in overall self-esteem, a widely held assumption is that boys' overall sense of self-worth is much higher than girls' (Marsh & Ayotte, 2003; Young & Mroczek, 2003). Girls may think less well of themselves because they internalize this negative cultural message.

An 11-year-old performs a traditional African dance at a community Kwanzaa celebration. A stronger sense of ethnic pride may contribute to African-American children's higher self-esteem relative to their Caucasian agemates.

Compared with their Caucasian agemates, African-American children tend to have slightly higher self-esteem, perhaps because of warm extended families and a stronger sense of ethnic pride (Gray-Little & Hafdahl, 2000). Finally, children and adolescents who attend schools or live in neighborhoods where their SES and ethnic groups are well-represented feel a stronger sense of belonging and have fewer self-esteem problems (Gray-Little & Carels, 1997).

Child-Rearing Practices Children and adolescents whose parents are warm and accepting, provide reasonable expectations for mature behavior, and engage in positive problem solving (resolve conflicts by collaborating with the child on a solution) feel especially good about themselves (Lindsey et al., 2008; McKinney, Donnelly, & Renk, 2008; Wilkinson, 2004). Warm, positive parenting lets young people know that they are accepted as competent and worthwhile. And firm but appropriate expectations, backed up with explanations, help them make sensible choices and evaluate themselves against reasonable standards.

Parental warmth and acceptance combined with firm but appropriate expectations help children develop a positive, realistic sense of self-esteem.

Controlling parents—those who too often help or make decisions for their child—communicate a sense of inadequacy to children. Having parents who are repeatedly disapproving and insulting is also linked to low self-esteem (Kernis, 2002; Pomerantz & Eaton, 2000). Children subjected to such parenting need constant reassurance, and many rely heavily on peers to affirm their self-worth—a risk factor for adjustment difficulties, including aggression, antisocial behavior, and delinquency (Donnellan et al., 2005).

In contrast, overly tolerant, indulgent parenting is linked to unrealistically high self-esteem, which also undermines development. These children—whom researchers label *narcissistic* because they combine an inflated sense of superiority with obsessive worry about what others think of them—are vulnerable to temporary, sharp drops in self-esteem when their overblown self-images are challenged (Thomaes et al., 2010). They tend to lash out at peers who express disapproval and display adjustment problems, including meanness and aggression (Hughes, Cavell, & Grossman, 1997; Thomaes et al., 2008).

American cultural values have increasingly emphasized a focus on the self that may lead parents to indulge children and boost their self-esteem too much. The self-esteem of U.S. youths rose sharply from the 1970s to the 1990s—a period in which much popular parenting literature advised promoting children's self-esteem (Twenge & Campbell, 2001). Yet compared with previous generations, U.S. youths are achieving less well and displaying more antisocial behavior and other adjustment problems (Berk, 2005). Research confirms that children do not benefit from compliments ("You're terrific") that have no basis in real attainment (Damon, 1995). Rather, the best way to foster a positive, secure self-image is to encourage children to strive for worthwhile goals. Over time, a bidirectional relationship emerges: Achievement fosters self-esteem, which contributes to further effort and gains in performance (Gest, Domitrovich, & Welsh, 2005; Marsh et al., 2005).

What can adults do to promote, and to avoid undermining, this mutually supportive relationship between motivation and self-esteem? Some answers come from research on the precise content of adults' messages to children in achievement situations.

Achievement-Related Attributions

Attributions are our common, everyday explanations for the causes of behavior—our answers to the question "Why did I or another person do that?" We group the causes of our own and others' behavior into two broad categories: external, environmental causes and internal, psychological causes. Then we further divide psychological causes into two types: *ability* and *effort*. In assigning a cause, we use certain rules: If a behavior occurs for many people but only in a single situation (for example, the whole class gets A's on Mrs. Apple's French test), we conclude that it is externally caused (the test was easy). In contrast, if an individual displays a behavior in many situations (Sally always gets A's on French tests), we judge the behavior to be internally caused—by ability, effort, or both (Sally is smart and works hard).

In Chapter 8, we showed that although intelligence predicts school achievement, the relationship is far from perfect. Individual differences in **achievement motivation**—the tendency to persist at challenging tasks—are just as important. Today, researchers regard achievement-related attributions as the main reason some children display initiative when faced with obstacles to success, whereas others give up easily.

Emergence of Achievement-Related Attributions Around age 3, children begin making attributions about their successes and failures. These attributions affect their *expectancies of success,* which influence their willingness to try hard in the future.

Many studies show that preschoolers are "learning optimists" who rate their own ability very high, often underestimate task difficulty, and hold positive expectancies of success. When asked to react to a situation in which one person does worse on a task than another, young children indicate that the lower-scoring person can still succeed if she keeps on trying (Schuster, Ruble, & Weinert, 1998). Cognitively, preschoolers cannot yet distinguish the precise causes of their successes and failures. Instead, they view all good things as going together: A person who tries hard is also a smart person who is going to succeed.

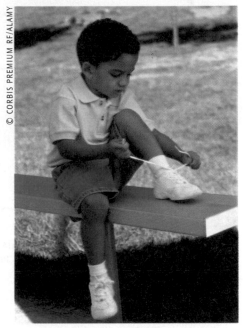

Nevertheless, by age 3, some children give up easily when faced with a challenge, expressing shame and despondency after failing. These nonpersisters have a history of parental criticism of their worth and performance and of excessive control—frequent parental commands and intrusive attempts to take over when the child attempts a challenging task (Kelley, Brownell, & Campbell, 2000; Moorman & Pomerantz, 2008). In contrast, their enthusiastic, highly motivated agemates have parents who patiently support the child's initiative ("Why don't you try the next one on your own?") while offering information about how to succeed.

Furthermore, when preschool nonpersisters use dolls to act out an adult's reaction to failure, they anticipate disapproval—saying, for example, "He's punished because he can't do the puzzle." Persisters say, "He worked hard but just couldn't finish. He wants to try again" (Burhans & Dweck, 1995). Preschoolers readily internalize adult evaluations. Whereas persisters view themselves as "good," nonpersisters see themselves as "bad" (Heyman, Dweck, & Cain, 1992). Already, nonpersisters seem to base their self-esteem entirely on others' judgments, not on inner standards. Consequently, they show early signs of maladaptive achievement behaviors that become more common during middle childhood.

Most preschoolers are "learning optimists" who believe they can succeed if they keep trying. Their attributions support initiative in the face of challenging tasks.

Mastery-Oriented versus Learned-Helpless Children As a result of improved reasoning skills and frequent evaluative feedback, school-age children gradually become able to distinguish ability, effort, and external factors in explaining their performance (Dweck, 2002). Those who are high in achievement motivation make **mastery-oriented attributions,** crediting their successes to ability—a characteristic they can improve through trying hard and can count on when faced with new challenges. This **incremental view of ability**—that it can increase through effort—influences the way mastery-oriented children interpret negative events. They attribute failure to factors that can be changed or controlled, such as insufficient effort or a difficult task (Heyman & Dweck, 1998). Whether these children succeed or fail, they take an industrious, persistent approach to learning.

Mastery-oriented children credit their successes to ability, and they seek information on how to increase their ability through effort. As a result, they approach challenging tasks with determination and persistence.

In contrast, children who develop **learned helplessness** attribute their failures, not their successes, to ability. When they succeed, they are likely to conclude that external events, such as luck, are responsible. Unlike their mastery-oriented counterparts, they hold an **entity view of ability**—that it cannot be improved by trying hard (Cain & Dweck, 1995). When a task is difficult, these children experience an anxious loss of control. They give up without really trying.

Children's attributions affect their goals. Mastery-oriented children focus on *learning goals*—seeking information on how best to increase their ability through effort.

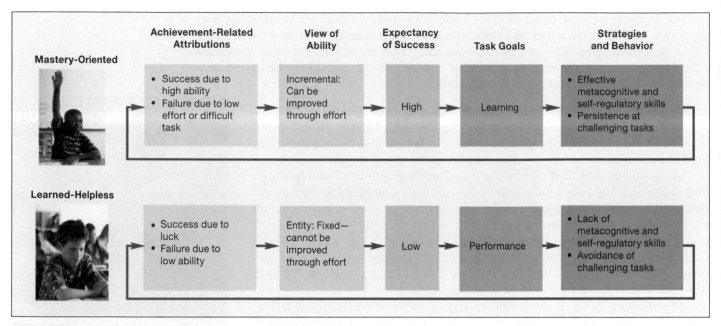

FIGURE 11.6 **Consequences of mastery-oriented and learned-helpless attributional styles.**
Photos: (top) © Michael Newman/PhotoEdit; (bottom) © Image Source Black/Alamy Images

Hence, their performance increases over time (Blackwell, Trzesniewski, & Dweck, 2007). In contrast, learned-helpless children focus on *performance goals*—obtaining positive and avoiding negative evaluations of their fragile sense of ability. Over time, learned-helpless children's ability no longer predicts how well they do. In one study, the more fourth to sixth graders held self-critical attributions, the lower they rated their competence, the less they knew about effective study strategies, the more they avoided challenge, and the poorer their academic performance. These outcomes strengthened their entity view of ability (Pomerantz & Saxon, 2001). Because learned-helpless children fail to connect effort with success, they do not develop the metacognitive and self-regulatory skills necessary for high achievement (see Chapter 7). Lack of effective learning strategies, reduced persistence, low performance, and a sense of loss of control sustain one another in a vicious cycle (Chan & Moore, 2006).

In adolescence, young people attain a fully differentiated understanding of the relationship between ability and effort. They realize that people who vary in ability can achieve the same outcome with different degrees of effort (Butler, 1999). When adolescents view their own ability as fixed and low, they conclude that mastering a challenging task is not worth the cost—extremely high effort. To protect themselves from painful feelings of failure, these learned-helpless young people select less demanding courses and careers. As Figure 11.6 shows, learned helplessness prevents children from realizing their potential.

Influences on Achievement-Related Attributions What accounts for the different attributions of mastery-oriented and learned-helpless children? As with preschoolers, adult communication plays a key role. When parents hold an entity view of ability, their children's self-evaluations and school grades conform more closely to parental ability judgments than do those of children whose parents deny that ability is fixed (Pomerantz & Dong, 2006). Parents who believe that little can be done to improve ability may ignore information that is inconsistent with their perceptions, giving their child little opportunity to counteract a negative parental evaluation.

Indeed, children with a learned-helpless style often have parents who believe that their child is not very capable and must work much harder than others to succeed. When the child fails, the adult might say, "You can't do that, can you? It's OK if you quit" (Hokoda & Fincham, 1995). After the child succeeds, the parent might offer feedback evaluating the child's traits ("You're so smart"). Trait statements—even when positive—encourage children

LOOK and LISTEN

Observe a school-age child working on a challenging homework assignment under the guidance of a parent or other adult. What features of the adult's communication likely foster mastery-oriented attributions? How about learned helplessness?

to adopt an entity view of ability, leading them to question their competence in the face of setbacks and to retreat from challenge (Mueller & Dweck, 1998).

Teachers' messages also affect children's attributions. Teachers who attribute children's failures to effort, who are caring and helpful, and who emphasize learning goals tend to have mastery-oriented students (Anderman et al., 2001; Daniels, Kalkman, & McCombs, 2001; Natale et al., 2009). In a study of 1,600 third to eighth graders, students who viewed their teachers as providing positive, supportive learning conditions worked harder and participated more in class—factors that predicted high achievement, which sustained children's belief in the value of effort. In contrast, students with unsupportive teachers regarded their performance as externally controlled (by their teachers or by luck). This attitude predicted withdrawal from learning activities and declining achievement—outcomes that led children to doubt their ability (Skinner, Zimmer-Gembeck, & Connell, 1998).

For some children, performance is especially likely to be undermined by adult feedback. Despite their higher achievement, girls more often than boys attribute poor performance to lack of ability. Girls tend to receive messages from teachers and parents that their ability is at fault when they do not do well, and negative stereotypes (for example, that girls are weak at math) reduce their interest and effort (Bleeker & Jacobs, 2004; Cole et al., 1999). And low-SES, ethnic-minority children often receive less favorable feedback from teachers, especially when assigned to homogeneous groups of poorly achieving students in school—conditions that result in a drop in academic self-esteem and achievement (Harris & Graham, 2007; Ogbu, 1997).

Finally, cultural values affect the likelihood that children will develop learned helplessness. Asian parents and teachers are more likely than their American counterparts to hold an incremental view of ability and to view trying hard as a moral responsibility—messages they transmit to children (Mok, Kennedy & Moore, 2011; Pomerantz, Ng, & Wang, 2008). Furthermore, because of the high value their culture places on self-improvement, Asians attend more to failure than to success because failure indicates where corrective action is needed. Americans, in contrast, focus more on success because it enhances self-esteem. Observations of U.S. and Chinese mothers' responses to their fourth- and fifth-graders' puzzle solutions revealed that the U.S. mothers offered more praise after success, whereas the Chinese mothers more often pointed out the child's inadequate performance. And regardless of success or failure, Chinese mothers made more task-relevant statements aimed at ensuring that children exerted sufficient effort to do well ("You concentrated on it"; "You only got 6 out of 12") (see Figure 11.7). When children continued with the task after mothers left the room, the Chinese children showed greater gains in performance (Ng, Pomerantz, & Lam, 2007).

Fostering a Mastery-Oriented Approach Attribution research suggests that well-intended messages from adults sometimes undermine children's competence. An intervention called **attribution retraining** encourages learned-helpless children to believe that they can overcome failure by exerting more effort. Children are given tasks difficult enough that they will experience some failure, followed by repeated feedback that helps them revise their attributions: "You can do it if you try harder." After they succeed, children receive additional feedback—"You're really good at this"; "You really tried hard on that one"—so that they attribute their success to both ability and effort, not chance. Another approach is to encourage low-effort students to focus less on grades, more on mastering a task for its own sake, and more on individual performance improvement than on comparisons with classmates (Hilt, 2004; Horner & Gaither, 2004; Yeh, 2010). Instruction in effective strategies and cognitive self-regulation is also vital, to compensate for development lost in this area and to ensure that renewed effort pays off (Borkowski & Muthukrisna, 1995; Wigfield et al., 2006).

Attribution retraining is most effective when begun early, before children's views of themselves become hard to change. School-age children with low academic self-esteem whose parents regularly used mastery-oriented practices while helping with homework had gained in sense of academic competence,

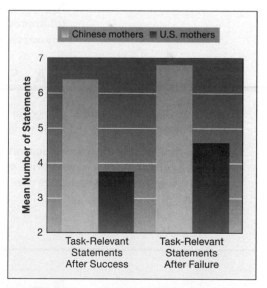

FIGURE 11.7 Chinese and U.S. mothers' task-relevant statements in response to their fourth-grade child's success or failure on puzzle tasks. Observations revealed that regardless of whether their child had just succeeded or failed, Chinese mothers were more likely than U.S. mothers to make task-relevant statements aimed at ensuring that the child exerted high effort. (Adapted from Ng, Pomerantz, & Lam, 2007.)

APPLYING WHAT WE KNOW

Fostering a Mastery-Oriented Approach to Learning

CONTEXT	STRATEGIES
Provision of tasks	Select tasks that are meaningful, responsive to a diversity of pupil interests, and appropriately matched to current competence so the child is challenged but not overwhelmed.
Parent and teacher encouragement	Communicate warmth, confidence in the child's abilities, the value of achievement, and the importance of effort in success.
	Model high effort in overcoming failure.
	(For teachers) Communicate often with parents, suggesting ways to foster children's effort and progress.
	(For parents) Monitor schoolwork; provide scaffolded assistance that promotes knowledge of effective strategies and cognitive self-regulation.
Performance evaluations	Make evaluations private; avoid publicizing success or failure through wall posters, stars, privileges to "smart" children, and prizes for "best" performance.
	Emphasize individual progress and self-improvement.
School environment	Offer small classes, which permit teachers to provide individualized support for mastery.
	Provide for cooperative learning and peer tutoring, in which children assist one another; avoid ability grouping, which makes evaluations of children's progress public.
	Accommodate individual and cultural differences in styles of learning.
	Create an atmosphere that values academics and sends a clear message that all students can learn.

Sources: Hilt, 2004; Wigfield et al., 2006.

willingness to try hard on difficult tasks, and positive emotion six months later (Pomerantz, Ng, & Wang, 2006). The strategies summarized in Applying What We Know above are helpful in preventing learned helplessness. Consult the Milestones table on the following page for an overview of development of self-esteem.

ASK YOURSELF

Review ■ Describe and explain changes in the structure and level of self-esteem from early childhood to adolescence.

Connect ■ What cognitive changes support the transition to a self-concept emphasizing competencies, personality traits, and social comparisons? (*Hint:* See page 283 in Chapter 7.)

Apply ■ Should parents try to promote children's self-esteem by telling them they're "smart" or "wonderful"? Are children harmed if they do not feel good about everything they do? Why or why not?

Reflect ■ Recall your own attributions for academic successes and failures when you were in elementary school. What are those attributions like now? What messages from others may have contributed to your attributions?

▶ Describe the four identity statuses, along with factors affecting identity development.

Constructing an Identity: Who Should I Become?

Adolescents' well-organized self-descriptions and differentiated sense of self-esteem provide the cognitive foundation for forming an **identity,** first recognized by psychoanalyst Erik Erikson (1950, 1968) as a major personality achievement and a crucial step toward becoming

Milestones

Development of Self-Esteem

AGE	MILESTONES
1–2 years	• Expressions of pleasure in mastery are evident. • Sensitivity to adults' evaluations appears.
3–5 years	• Self-esteem is typically high and consists of several separate self-evaluations. • Achievement-related attributions appear but are undifferentiated; for example, a person who tries hard is smart and will succeed.
6–10 years	• Self-esteem becomes hierarchically organized; separate self-evaluations (academic, social, and physical/athletic competence, physical appearance) are integrated into an overall sense of self-esteem. • As children receive competence-related feedback and make social comparisons, self-esteem declines but then rises. • Achievement-related attributions differentiate into ability, effort, and external factors.
11 years–adulthood	• New dimensions of self-esteem are added (close friendship, romantic appeal, job competence). • Self-esteem continues to rise. • Achievement-related attributions reflect full differentiation of ability and effort.

Note: These milestones represent overall age trends. Individual differences exist in the precise age at which each milestone is attained.

Photos: (top) © Nancy Richmond/The Image Works; (middle) © Robin Sachs/PhotoEdit; (bottom) © David Young-Wolff/PhotoEdit

a productive, content adult. Constructing an identity involves defining who you are, what you value, and the directions you choose to pursue in life. One expert described it as an explicit theory of oneself as a rational agent—one who acts on the basis of reason, takes responsibility for those actions, and can explain them (Moshman, 2005). This search for what is true and real about the self drives many choices—vocation, interpersonal relationships, community involvement, ethnic-group membership, and expression of one's sexual orientation, as well as moral, political, and religious ideals.

Erikson believed that successful psychosocial outcomes of infancy and childhood pave the way toward a coherent, positive identity. (Return to Chapter 1, page 16, to review Erikson's stages.) Although the seeds of identity formation are planted early, not until late adolescence and emerging adulthood do young people become absorbed in this task. According to Erikson, in complex societies teenagers experience an *identity crisis*—a temporary period of distress as they experiment with alternatives before settling on values and goals. They go through a process of inner soul-searching, sifting through characteristics that defined the self in childhood and combining them with emerging traits, capacities, and commitments. Then they mold these into a solid inner core that provides a sense of sameness as they move through different roles in daily life. Once formed, identity continues to be refined throughout life as people reevaluate earlier commitments and choices.

Current theorists agree with Erikson that questioning of values, plans, and priorities is necessary for a mature identity, but they no longer describe this process as a "crisis" (Kroger, 2005). In fact, Erikson himself did not believe that adolescents' inner struggle need be severe to arrive at a clear, unified identity (Côté, 2009). For most young people, identity development is not traumatic or disturbing but, rather, a process of *exploration* followed by *commitment*. As young people try out life possibilities, they gather important information about themselves and their environment and gradually move toward making enduring decisions. In the process, they forge an organized self-structure (Arnett, 2000, 2006; Moshman, 2005).

Erikson described the negative outcome of adolescence as *identity confusion*. If young people's earlier conflicts were resolved negatively or if society limits their choices to ones that do not match their abilities and desires, they may appear shallow, directionless, and unprepared for the psychological challenges of adulthood. In the following sections, we will see that young people go about the task of defining the self in ways that closely match Erikson's description.

Paths to Identity

Using a clinical interviewing procedure devised by James Marcia (1980) or briefer questionnaire measures, researchers evaluate progress in identity development on two key criteria derived from Erikson's theory: *exploration* and *commitment*. Their various combinations yield four *identity statuses,* summarized in Table 11.1: **identity achievement,** commitment to values, beliefs, and goals following a period of exploration; **identity moratorium,** exploration without having reached commitment; **identity foreclosure,** commitment in the absence of exploration; and **identity diffusion,** an apathetic state characterized by lack of both exploration and commitment.

Identity development follows many paths. Some young people remain in one status, whereas others experience many status transitions. And the pattern often varies across *identity domains,* such as sexual orientation, vocation, and religious, political, and other worldviews. Many young people change from "lower" statuses (foreclosure or diffusion) to "higher" statuses (moratorium or achievement) between their mid-teens and mid-twenties, but about as many remain stable, and some move in the reverse direction (Kroger, 2005, 2007; Kroger, Martinussen, & Marcia, 2010). The number of domains explored and the intensity with which they are examined vary widely. Almost all young people grapple with work, close relationships, and family. Others add political, religious, community, and leisure-time commitments, some of which are more central to their identity than others.

TABLE 11.1 | **The Four Identity Statuses**

IDENTITY STATUS	DESCRIPTION	EXAMPLE
Identity achievement	Having already explored alternatives, identity-achieved individuals are committed to a clearly formulated set of self-chosen values and goals. They feel a sense of psychological well-being, of sameness through time, and of knowing where they are going.	When asked how willing she would be to give up going into her chosen occupation if something better came along, Lauren responded, "Well, I might, but I doubt it. I've thought long and hard about law as a career. I'm pretty certain it's for me."
Identity moratorium	*Moratorium* means "delay or holding pattern." These individuals have not yet made definite commitments. They are in the process of exploring—gathering information and trying out activities, with the desire to find values and goals to guide their lives.	When asked whether he had ever had doubts about his religious beliefs, Ramón said, "Yes, I guess I'm going through that right now. I just don't see how there can be a God and yet so much evil in the world."
Identity foreclosure	Identity-foreclosed individuals have committed themselves to values and goals without exploring alternatives. They accept a ready-made identity chosen for them by authority figures—usually parents but sometimes teachers, religious leaders, or romantic partners.	When asked if she had ever reconsidered her political beliefs, Emily answered, "No, not really, our family is pretty much in agreement on these things."
Identity diffusion	Identity-diffused individuals lack clear direction. They are not committed to values and goals, nor are they actively trying to reach them. They may never have explored alternatives or may have found the task too threatening and overwhelming.	When asked about his attitude toward nontraditional gender roles, Justin responded, "Oh, I don't know. It doesn't make much difference to me. I can take it or leave it."

Because attending college provides opportunities to explore educational and career options as well as lifestyles, college students make more identity progress, increasingly engaging in focused, in-depth consideration and reconsideration of potential commitments (Klimstra et al., 2010; Luyckx et al., 2006; Montgomery & Côté, 2003). After college, young people often sample various life experiences through travel or short-term volunteer jobs in such programs as the U.S. Peace Corps. Those who go to work immediately after high school graduation often settle on a self-definition earlier. But if they encounter obstacles to realizing their occupational goals because of lack of training or vocational choices, they are at risk for long-term identity foreclosure or diffusion (Cohen et al., 2003; Eccles et al., 2003).

At one time, researchers thought that adolescent girls postponed establishing an identity, focusing instead on Erikson's next stage, intimacy development. Some girls do show more sophisticated reasoning in intimacy-related domains, such as sexuality and family versus career priorities. Otherwise, adolescents of both sexes typically make progress on identity concerns before experiencing genuine intimacy in relationships (Berman et al., 2006; Kroger, 2007).

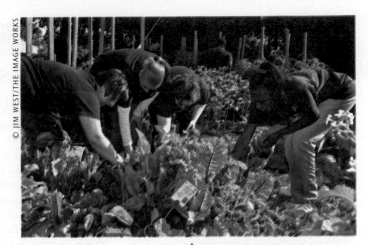

Harvesting produce for a food bank provides these adolescents with an opportunity to explore community values and goals, potentially contributing to their identity development.

Identity Status and Psychological Well-Being

According to identity theorists, individuals who move away from foreclosure and diffusion toward moratorium and achievement build a well-structured identity that integrates various domains. As a result, they experience a gratifying sense of personal continuity, competence, and social connection—of being the same person across time and contexts and of becoming a capable, respected, member of the adult community (Luyckx et al., 2009; Snarey & Bell, 2003). A wealth of research supports the conclusion that identity achievement and moratorium are psychologically healthy routes to a mature self-definition, whereas long-term foreclosure and diffusion are maladaptive.

Although adolescents in moratorium are often anxious about the challenges they face, they resemble identity-achieved individuals in using an *active, information-gathering cognitive style* to make personal decisions and solve problems: They seek out relevant information, evaluate it carefully, and critically reflect on and revise their views (Berzonsky, 2003, 2011; Berzonsky & Kuk, 2000). Young people who are identity-achieved or exploring have higher self-esteem, are more open to alternative ideas and values, feel more in control of their own lives, are more likely to view school and work as feasible avenues for realizing their aspirations, and are more advanced in moral reasoning (Berzonsky et al., 2011; Kroger, 2007; Serafini & Adams, 2002). When asked for a "turning point" narrative (an account of a past event that they view as important in understanding themselves), identity-achieved individuals tell stories containing more sophisticated personal insights and portraying negative life events as followed by good outcomes—personal renewal, improvement, and enlightenment (McLean & Pratt, 2006).

Adolescents stuck in either foreclosure or diffusion are passive in the face of identity concerns and have adjustment difficulties. Foreclosed individuals display a *dogmatic, inflexible cognitive style,* internalizing the values and beliefs of parents and others without deliberate evaluation and resisting information that threatens their position (Berzonsky & Kuk, 2000; Berzonsky et al., 2011). Most fear rejection by people on whom they depend for affection and self-esteem. A few foreclosed teenagers who are alienated from their families and society may join cults or other extremist groups, uncritically adopting a way of life that is different from their past.

Long-term diffused teenagers are the least mature in identity development. They typically use a *diffuse-avoidant cognitive style* in which they avoid dealing with personal decisions and problems and, instead, allow current situational pressures to dictate their reactions (Berzonsky & Kuk, 2000; Krettenauer, 2005). Taking an "I don't care" attitude, they entrust themselves to luck or fate, tend to go along with the crowd, and are focused on short-term personal pleasure. As a result, they often experience time management and academic difficulties and, of

SOCIAL ISSUES: HEALTH

Adolescent Suicide: Annihilation of the Self

The suicide rate increases from childhood to old age, but it jumps sharply at adolescence. Currently, suicide is the third-leading cause of death among American youths, after motor vehicle collisions and homicides. Perhaps because U.S. teenagers experience more stresses and fewer supports than in the past, the adolescent suicide rate tripled between the mid-1960s and the mid-1990s, followed by a slight decline (Spirito & Esposito-Smythers, 2006; U.S. Census Bureau, 2011b). At the same time, rates of adolescent suicide vary widely among industrialized nations—low in Greece, Italy, the Netherlands, and Spain; intermediate in Australia, Canada, Japan, and the United States; and high in Finland, New Zealand, and Singapore (Bridge, Goldstein, & Brent, 2006). These international differences remain unexplained.

Factors Related to Adolescent Suicide

Striking sex differences in suicidal behavior exist. The number of boys who kill themselves exceeds the number of girls by a ratio of 3 or 4 to 1. Girls make more unsuccessful suicide attempts and use methods from which they are more likely to be revived, such as a sleeping pill overdose. In contrast, boys tend to choose techniques that lead to instant death, such as firearms or hanging (Langhinrichsen-Rohling, Friend, & Powell, 2009). Gender-role expec-

tations may contribute; less tolerance exists for feelings of helplessness and failed efforts in males than in females.

Possibly due to higher levels of support from extended families, African Americans, Asian Americans, and Hispanics have lower suicide rates than Caucasian Americans. Recently, however, suicide has risen among African-American adolescent males; the current rate approaches that of Caucasian-American males. And Native-American youths commit suicide at rates two to six times national averages (Balis & Postolache, 2008; U.S. Census Bureau, 2011b). High rates of profound family poverty, school failure, alcohol and drug abuse, and depression probably underlie these trends.

Gay, lesbian, and bisexual youths also are at high risk, attempting suicide three times as often as other adolescents. Those who have tried to kill themselves report more family conflict over their gender-atypical behavior, inner turmoil about their sexuality, problems in romantic relationships, and peer rejection due to their sexual orientation (D'Augelli et al., 2005).

Suicide tends to occur in two types of young people. The first group includes adolescents who are highly intelligent but solitary, withdrawn, and unable to meet their own standards or those of important people in their lives. Members of a

second, larger group show antisocial tendencies and express their despondency through bullying, fighting, stealing, increased risk taking, and drug abuse (Evans, Hawton, & Rodham, 2004). Besides being hostile and destructive, they turn their anger and disappointment inward.

Suicidal adolescents often have a family history of emotional and antisocial disorders and suicide. In addition, they are likely to have experienced multiple stressful life events, including economic disadvantage, parental separation and divorce, absence of family warmth, frequent parent–child conflict, and abuse and neglect. Stressors typically increase during the period preceding a suicide attempt or completion (Beautrais, 2003; Kaminski et al., 2010). Triggering events include parental blaming of the teenager for family problems, the breakup of an important peer relationship, or the humiliation of having been caught engaging in irresponsible, antisocial acts.

Public policies resulting in cultural disintegration have amplified suicide rates among Native-American youths. From the late 1800s to the 1960s or 1970s, Native families were forced to enroll their children in government-run residential boarding schools designed to erase tribal affiliations. In these repressive institutions, children were not allowed to "be

all young people, are the most likely to commit antisocial acts and to use and abuse drugs (Archer & Waterman, 1990; Berzonsky et al., 2011; Schwartz et al., 2005). Often at the heart of their apathy and impulsiveness is a sense of hopelessness about the future that puts many at risk for serious depression and suicide (see the Social Issues: Health box above).

Factors Affecting Identity Development

Adolescent identity formation begins a lifelong, dynamic process in which a change in either the individual or the context opens up the possibility of reformulating identity (Kunnen & Bosma, 2003). A wide variety of factors influence identity development.

Personality Identity status, as we have just seen, is both cause and consequence of personality characteristics. Adolescents who are conformist and obedient and who assume that absolute truth is always attainable tend to be foreclosed, whereas those who are self-indulgent and doubt they will ever feel certain about anything are more often identity-diffused. Young people who are curious and open-minded and who appreciate that they can use rational criteria to choose among alternatives are more likely to be in a state of moratorium or identity achievement (Berzonsky & Kuk, 2000; Berzonsky et al., 2011; Boyes & Chandler, 1992). This flexible, self-reflective approach helps them greatly in pursuing educational, vocational, and other life goals.

Indian" in any way—culturally, linguistically, artistically, or spiritually (Goldston et al., 2008). The experience left many young people academically unprepared and emotionally scarred, contributing to family and community disorganization in current and succeeding generations. Consequently, alcohol abuse, youth crime, and suicide rates escalated (Barnes, Josefowitz, & Cole, 2006; Howell & Yuille, 2004). Today, perceived discrimination and weak identification with one's tribal culture remain powerful predictors of suicidal thoughts among Native-American youths (Yoder et al., 2006).

Why does suicide increase in adolescence? One factor seems to be teenagers' improved ability to plan ahead. Although some act impulsively, many young people at risk take purposeful steps toward killing themselves. Other cognitive changes also contribute. Belief in the personal fable (see Chapter 6) leads many depressed young people to conclude that no one could possibly understand their intense pain. As a result, despair, hopelessness, and isolation deepen.

Prevention and Treatment

Picking up on signals from a troubled teenager is a crucial first step in suicide prevention. Parents and teachers must be trained to recognize warning signs. Schools and community settings, such as recreational and religious organizations, can help by strengthening adolescents' connec-

tions with their cultural heritage and providing knowledgeable, approachable, and sympathetic adults, peer support groups, and information about telephone hot lines (Goldston et al., 2008; Spirito et al., 2003). Once a teenager takes steps toward suicide, staying with the young person, listening, and expressing compassion and concern until professional help can be obtained are essential.

Treatments for depressed and suicidal adolescents range from antidepressant medication to individual, family, and group therapy. Sometimes hospitalization is necessary to ensure the teenager's safety. Until the adolescent improves, removing weapons, knives, razors, scissors, and drugs from the home is vital. Strengthening social supports and training young people in effective strategies for coping with stress and depressed mood promote resilience and can prevent repeated suicide attempts (Asarnow et al., 2005; Kalafat, 2005). On a broader scale, gun-control legislation that limits adolescents' access to the most frequent and deadly suicide method in the United States would greatly reduce both the number of suicides and the high teenage homicide rate (Commission on Adolescent Suicide Prevention, 2005).

After a suicide, family and peer survivors need support to help them cope with grief, anger, and guilt over not having been able to

Individual, family, and group therapy can help adolescents develop effective strategies for coping with stress and depressed mood, promoting resilience and preventing repeated suicide attempts.

help the victim. Teenage suicides often occur in clusters: One such death increases the likelihood of other suicides among depressed peers who knew the young person or heard about the death through the media (Bearman & Moody, 2004; Feigelman & Gorman, 2008). In view of this trend, an especially watchful eye must be kept on vulnerable adolescents after a suicide happens. Restraint by journalists in publicizing teenage suicides also aids prevention.

Family Teenagers' identity development is enhanced when their families serve as a "secure base" from which they can confidently move out into the wider world. In families of diverse ethnicities, adolescents who feel attached to their parents and say they provide effective guidance, but who also feel free to voice their own opinions, tend to be in a state of moratorium or identity achievement (Berzonsky, 2004; Luyckx et al., 2006; Schwartz et al., 2005). Foreclosed teenagers usually have close bonds with parents but lack opportunities for healthy separation. And diffused young people report the lowest levels of parental support and warm, open communication (Reis & Youniss, 2004; Zimmerman & Becker-Stoll, 2002).

Recall that parents who engage in positive problem solving—who resolve conflicts by seeking their child's input and collaborating on a solution—foster high self-esteem. Notice, also, how this approach promotes the balance between family relatedness and autonomy that supports identity development (Deci & Ryan, 2002).

Peers Interaction with diverse peers through school and community activities encourages adolescents to explore values and role possibilities (Barber et al., 2005). And close friends, like parents, can act as a secure base, providing emotional support, assistance, and models of identity development. In one study, 15-year-olds with warm, trusting peer ties were more involved in exploring relationship issues—for example, thinking about what they valued in a life partner (Meeus, Oosterwegel, & Vollebergh, 2002.) In another study, college students' attachment to friends predicted progress in choosing a career (Felsman & Blustein, 1999).

APPLYING WHAT WE KNOW

Supporting Healthy Identity Development

STRATEGY	EXPLANATION
Engage in warm, open communication.	Provides both emotional support and freedom to explore values and goals.
Initiate discussions that promote high-level thinking at home and at school.	Encourages rational, deliberate selection among competing beliefs and values.
Provide opportunities to participate in extracurricular activities and vocational training programs.	Permits young people to explore the real world of adult work.
Provide opportunities to talk with adults and peers who have worked through identity questions.	Offers models of identity achievement and advice on how to resolve identity concerns.
Provide opportunities to explore ethnic heritage and learn about other cultures in an atmosphere of respect.	Fosters identity achievement in all areas and ethnic tolerance, which supports the identity explorations of others.

School, Community, and Culture Identity development also depends on schools and communities that offer rich and varied opportunities for exploration. Supportive experiences include classrooms that promote high-level thinking, teachers and counselors who encourage low-SES and ethnic minority students to go to college, extracurricular and community activities that offer teenagers responsible roles consistent with their interests and talents, and vocational training that immerses adolescents in the real world of adult work (Coatsworth et al., 2005; Cooper, 1998).

Culture strongly influences an aspect of mature identity not captured by the identity-status approach: constructing a sense of self-continuity despite major personal changes. In one study, researchers asked Native Canadian and cultural-majority 12- to 20-year-olds to describe themselves in the past and in the present and then to justify why they were the same continuous person (Lalonde & Chandler, 2005). Both groups gave increasingly complex responses with age, but their strategies differed. Most cultural-majority adolescents used an individualistic approach: They described an *enduring personal essence,* a core self that remained the same despite change. In contrast, Native Canadian youths took an interdependent approach that emphasized a *constantly transforming self,* resulting from new roles and relationships. They typically constructed a *coherent narrative* in which they linked together various time slices of their life with a thread explaining how they had changed in meaningful ways.

Finally, societal forces are also responsible for the special challenges faced by gay, lesbian, and bisexual youths (see Chapter 5) and by ethnic minority adolescents in forming a secure identity (see the Cultural Influences box on the following page). Applying What We Know above summarizes ways that adults can support adolescents in their quest for identity.

A S K   Y O U R S E L F

Review ■ List personal and contextual factors that promote identity development.

Connect ■ Explain the close link between adolescent identity development and cognitive processes.

Apply ■ Eighteen-year-old Brad's parents worry that he will waste time at college because he is unsure about his major and career goals. Explain why Brad's uncertainty might be advantageous for his identity development.

Reflect ■ Does your identity status vary across the domains of sexuality, close relationships, vocation, religious beliefs, and political values? Describe factors that may have influenced your identity development in an important domain.

CULTURAL INFLUENCES

Identity Development Among Ethnic Minority Adolescents

Most adolescents are aware of their cultural ancestry but relatively unconcerned about it. However, for teenagers who are members of minority groups, **ethnic identity**—a sense of ethnic group membership and attitudes and feelings associated with that membership—is central to the quest for identity. As they develop cognitively and become more sensitive to feedback from the social environment, minority youths become painfully aware that they are targets of prejudice and discrimination. This discovery complicates their efforts to develop a sense of cultural belonging and a set of personally meaningful goals.

Minority youths often feel caught between the standards of the larger society and the traditions of their culture of origin. In many immigrant families from collectivist cultures, adolescents' commitment to obeying their parents and fulfilling family obligations lessens the longer the family has been in the immigrant-receiving country—a circumstance that induces **acculturative stress**, psychological distress resulting from conflict between the minority and the host culture (Phinney, Ong, & Madden, 2000). When immigrant parents tightly restrict their teenagers through fear that assimilation into the larger society will undermine their cultural traditions, their youngsters often rebel, rejecting aspects of their ethnic background.

At the same time, discrimination can interfere with the formation of a positive ethnic identity. In one study, Mexican-American youths who had experienced more discrimination were less likely to explore their ethnicity and to report feeling good about it (Romero & Roberts, 2003). Those with low ethnic pride showed a sharp drop in self-esteem in the face of discrimination.

With age, some ethnic minority young people progress from ethnic-identity diffusion or foreclosure through moratorium to ethnic-identity achievement. But because the process of forging an ethnic identity can be painful and confusing, others show no change, and still others regress (Seaton, Scottham, & Sellers, 2006). Young people with parents of different ethnicities face extra challenges. In a large survey of high school students, part-black biracial teenagers reported as much discrimination as their monoracial black counterparts, yet they felt less positively about their ethnicity. And compared with monoracial minorities, many biracials—including black–white, black–Asian, white–Asian, black–Hispanic, and white–Hispanic—regarded ethnicity as less central to their identities (Herman, 2004). Perhaps these adolescents encountered fewer opportunities in their homes and communities to forge a strong sense of belonging to either culture.

Adolescents whose family members encourage them to disprove ethnic stereotypes of low achievement or antisocial behavior typically surmount the threat that discrimination poses to a favorable ethnic identity. These young people manage experiences of unfair treatment effectively, by seeking social support and engaging in direct problem solving (Phinney & Chavira, 1995; Scott, 2003). Also, adolescents whose families taught them the history, traditions, values, and language of their ethnic group and who frequently interact with same-ethnicity peers are more likely to forge a favorable ethnic identity (Hughes et al., 2006; McHale et al., 2006).

How can society help minority adolescents resolve identity conflicts constructively? Here are some relevant approaches:

- Promote effective parenting, in which children and adolescents benefit from family ethnic pride yet are encouraged to explore the meaning of ethnicity in their own lives.
- Ensure that schools respect minority youths' native languages, unique learning styles, and right to a high-quality education.
- Foster contact with peers of the same ethnicity, along with respect between ethnic groups (García Coll & Magnuson, 1997).

A strong, secure ethnic identity is associated with higher self-esteem, optimism, a sense of mastery over the environment, and more positive attitudes toward one's ethnicity (St. Louis & Liem, 2005; Umaña-Taylor & Updegraff, 2007; Worrell & Gardner-Kitt, 2006). For these reasons,

Stilt walkers celebrate their heritage at a Caribbean youth festival. Minority youths whose cultural heritage is respected in their communities are more likely to incorporate ethnic values and customs into their identity.

adolescents with a positive connection to their ethnic group are better-adjusted. They cope more effectively with stress, report higher levels of psychological well-being, show better achievement in school, and have fewer emotional and behavior problems than agemates who identify only weakly with their ethnicity (Ghavami et al., 2011; Greene, Way, & Pahl, 2006; Seaton, Scottham, & Sellers, 2006; Umaña-Taylor & Alfaro, 2006). For teenagers faced with potential or actual adversity, ethnic identity is a powerful source of resilience.

Forming a **bicultural identity**—by exploring and adopting values from both the adolescent's subculture and the dominant culture—offers added benefits. Biculturally identified adolescents tend to be achieved in other areas of identity as well and to have especially favorable relations with members of other ethnic groups (Phinney, 2007; Phinney et al., 2001). In sum, achievement of ethnic identity enhances many aspects of emotional and social development.

▶ Discuss changes in children's appreciation of others' attributes and understanding of social groups, including factors that contribute to prejudice and ways to reduce it.

Thinking About Other People

Children's understanding of other people—the inferences they make about their attributes, both as individuals and as members of particular social groups—has much in common with their developing understanding of themselves. As we will see, these facets of social cognition also become increasingly differentiated and well organized with age.

Understanding People as Personalities

Person perception refers to the way we size up the qualities of people with whom we are familiar. Researchers study person perception by asking children to describe people they know, using methods similar to those that focus on children's self-concepts. For example, the researcher might ask, "Can you tell me what kind of person _____ is?"

Like their self-descriptions, young children's descriptions of others focus on concrete activities, behaviors, and commonly experienced emotions and attitudes. As noted in our discussion of self-concept, older preschoolers have begun to notice consistencies in the actions and internal states of people they know (see page 456). Around age 8, they mention personality traits. At first, these references are closely tied to behavior and consist of implied dispositions: "He's always fighting with people" or "She steals and lies" (Rholes, Newman, & Ruble, 1990). Later, children mention traits directly, but they use vague, stereotyped language, such as "good," "nice," or "acts smart." Gradually, sharper trait descriptions appear— "honest," "trustworthy," "generous," "polite," "selfish"—and children become more convinced of the stability of such dispositions (Droege & Stipek, 1993; Ruble & Dweck, 1995).

During adolescence, as abstract thinking becomes better established, inferences about others' personalities are drawn together into organized character sketches (O'Mahoney, 1989). As a result, between ages 14 and 16, teenagers present rich accounts of people they know that integrate physical traits, typical behaviors, and inner dispositions.

Understanding Social Groups: Race and Ethnicity

Children's person perception, like that of adults, is strongly influenced by social-group membership. As we will see, at an early age, children begin to acquire stereotypes about social groups, and those stereotypes can easily overwhelm their capacity to size up people as individuals.

As with their categorical self (see page 450), young children classify people into social groups on the basis of perceptually distinct attributes, such as age, gender, and race. Children's understanding of gender has been so extensively investigated that we will address it in detail in Chapter 13. Here we focus on a rapidly growing literature on children's developing conceptions of race and ethnicity.

Most 3- and 4-year-olds have formed basic concepts of race and ethnicity, in that they can apply the labels "black" and "white" to pictures, dolls, and people (Aboud, 2003). Although indicators of social class—education and occupational prestige—are not accessible to young children, they can distinguish rich from poor on the basis of physical characteristics, such as clothing, residence, and possessions (Ramsey, 1991).

By the early school years, children absorb prevailing societal attitudes, associating power and privilege with white people and poverty and inferior status with people of color. They do not necessarily acquire these views directly from parents or friends. In one study, although white school-age children assumed that parents' and friends' racial attitudes would resemble their own, no similarities in attitudes emerged (Aboud & Doyle, 1996). Perhaps white parents are reluctant to discuss their racial and ethnic views with children, and friends also say little. Given limited or ambiguous information, children seem to fill in the gaps with information they encounter in their environments and then infer others' attitudes on the basis of their own.

Consistent with this idea, research indicates that children pick up much information about group status from messages in their surroundings. These include (1) social contexts that present a world sorted into groups, such as racial and ethnic segregation in schools and communities; and (2) experiences involving explicit labeling of groups, even when the group distinctions presented are neutral rather than stereotypic (Bigler & Liben, 2007).

In one experiment, 7- to 12-year-olds attending a summer school program were randomly assigned to social groups, denoted by colored T-shirts (yellow or blue) that the children wore. The researchers hung posters in the classroom that depicted unfamiliar yellow-group members as having higher status—for example, as having won more athletic and spelling competitions. When teachers recognized the social groups by using them as the basis for seating arrangements, task assignments, and bulletin-board displays, children in the high-status group evaluated their own group more favorably than the other group, and children in the low-status group viewed their own group less favorably (Bigler, Brown, & Markell, 2001). But when teachers ignored the social groupings, no prejudice emerged.

These findings indicate that children do not necessarily form stereotypes even when some basis for them exists—in this instance, information on wall posters. But when an authority figure validates a status hierarchy by labeling, sorting, or treating groups differently, children do form biased attitudes.

In-Group and Out-Group Biases: Development of Prejudice Studies in diverse Western nations confirm that by age 5 to 6, white children generally evaluate their own racial group favorably and other racial groups less favorably or negatively—biases that also characterize many adults. *In-group favoritism* emerges first; children simply prefer their own group, generalizing from self to similar others (Bennett et al., 2004; Cameron et al., 2001). And the ease with which a trivial group label supplied by an adult can induce in-group favoritism is striking. In one study, Caucasian-American 5-year-olds were told that they were members of a group based on T-shirt color, but this time, no information was provided about group status, and the children never met any group members. Still they displayed vigorous in-group favoritism (Dunham, Baron, & Carey, 2011). When shown photos of unfamiliar agemates wearing either an in-group or an out-group shirt, the children claimed to like members of their own group better, gave them more resources, expected more generous behavior from them, and engaged in biased recall of individuals' behavior that favored the in-group.

Out-group prejudice requires a more challenging social comparison between in-group and out-group. But it does not take long for white children to acquire negative attitudes toward ethnic minority out-groups, especially when such attitudes are encouraged by circumstances in their environments. When white Canadian 4- to 7-year-olds living in a white community and attending nearly all-white schools sorted positive and negative adjectives into boxes labeled as belonging to a white child and a black child, out-group prejudice emerged at age 5 (see Figure 11.8) (Aboud, 2003).

Unfortunately, many ethnic minority children show a reverse pattern: *out-group favoritism*, in which they assign positive characteristics to the privileged ethnic majority and negative characteristics to their own group. In one study, researchers asked African-American 5- to 7-year-olds to recall information in stories either consistent or inconsistent with stereotypes of blacks. The children recalled more stereotypic traits, especially if they agreed with negative cultural views of African Americans or rated their own skin tone as lighter and, therefore, may have identified themselves with the white majority (Averhart & Bigler, 1997). In a similar investigation, Native Canadian second to fourth graders recalled more positive attributes about white Canadians and more negative attributes about Native Canadians (Corenblum, 2003). A societal context that devalues people of color makes minority children vulnerable to internalizing those beliefs.

But recall that with age, children pay more attention to inner traits. The capacity to classify the social world in multiple ways enables school-age children to understand that people can be both "the same" and "different"—those who look different need not think, feel, or act differently (Aboud, 2008). Consequently, voicing of negative attitudes toward minorities declines. After age 7 to 8, both majority and minority

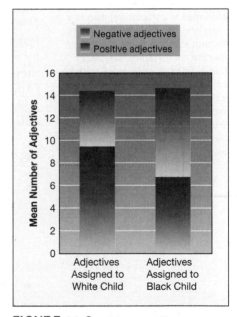

FIGURE 11.8 White Canadian 5-year-olds' expressions of in-group favoritism and out-group prejudice. When asked to sort positive and negative adjectives into boxes labeled as belonging to a white child and a black child, white Canadian 5-year-olds assigned a greater number of positive adjectives (such as *clean, nice, smart*) to the white child than to the black child—evidence for in-group favoritism. In addition to viewing the black child less positively, the white Canadian 5-year-olds also assigned a greater number of negative adjectives (such as *dirty, naughty, cruel*) to the black child— evidence for *out-group prejudice*. (Adapted from Aboud, 2003.)

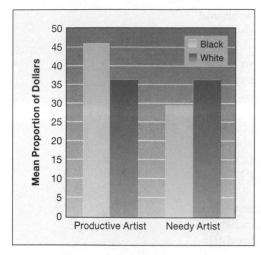

FIGURE 11.9 White fourth graders' racially biased distribution of money to child artists. When dividing money earned from selling children's art among three child artists—two white and one black—the fourth graders gave more money to a productive black artist (who countered a stereotype) than to a productive white artist and less money to a needy black artist (who conformed to a stereotype) than to a needy white artist. In both instances, the fourth graders seemed to engage in subtle, unintentional prejudice. (From A. V. McGillicuddy-De Lisi, M. Daly, & A. Neal, 2006, "Children's Distributive Justice Judgments: Aversive Racism in Euro-American Children?" *Child Development, 77,* p. 1072. Copyright © 2006, John Wiley and Sons. Adapted by permission of John Wiley and Sons.)

children express *in-group favoritism,* and white children's prejudice against *out-group* members often weakens (Nesdale et al., 2005; Ruble et al., 2004). Most school-age children and adolescents are also quick to verbalize that it is wrong to exclude others from peer-group and learning activities on the basis of skin color—discrimination they evaluate as unfair (Killen et al., 2002).

Yet even in children and adolescents who are aware of the injustice of discrimination, prejudice can operate subtly, unintentionally, and without awareness—as it does in many white adults (Dovidio et al., 2004; Dunham, Baron, & Banaji, 2006). Consider a study in which white second and fourth graders were asked to divide fairly among three child artists—two white and one black—money that had been earned from selling the children's art. In each version of the task, one artist was labeled as "productive" (making more art works), one as "the oldest," and one as "poor and needing money for lunch." By age 8 to 9, most children recognize that special consideration is appropriate for children who perform exceptionally or are at a disadvantage. But racial stereotypes interfered with fourth graders' even-handed application of these principles. They gave more money to a productive black artist (who countered the racial stereotype of "low achiever") than to a productive white artist and less money to a needy black artist (who conformed to the racial stereotype of "poor") than to a needy white artist (see Figure 11.9) (McGillicuddy-De Lisi, Daly, & Neal, 2006).

Findings like these raise the question of whether the decline in overt racial bias during middle childhood is a true decrease or whether it reflects older children's growing awareness of widely held standards that deem prejudice to be inappropriate—or (more likely) both. Around age 10, most children have internalized social norms and become increasingly concerned that their attitudes and behaviors are seen as consistent with them (Selman, 1980). Simultaneously, white children start to avoid talking about race to appear unbiased, just as many adults do. In a matching game in which willingness to label photos of people by race aided performance, 10- and 11-year-olds were so reluctant to mention race that they performed more poorly than 8- and 9-year-olds, who freely used racial descriptors (Apfelbaum et al., 2008). At least to some degree, then, older school-age children's desire to present themselves in a socially acceptable light may contribute to reduced expressions of out-group prejudice.

Nevertheless, the extent to which children hold racial and ethnic biases varies, depending on the following personal and situational factors:

- *A fixed view of personality traits.* Children who believe that people's personality traits are fixed rather than changeable often judge others as either "good" or "bad." Ignoring motives and circumstances, they readily form extreme impressions on the basis of limited information. For example, they might infer that "a new child at school who tells a lie to try to get other kids to like her" is a simply bad kid (Heyman & Dweck, 1998; Levy & Dweck, 1999).

- *Overly high self-esteem.* Children (and adults) with very high self-esteem are more likely to hold racial and ethnic prejudices (Baumeister et al., 2003; Bigler, Brown, & Markell, 2001). These narcissistic individuals seem to belittle disadvantaged individuals or groups to justify and protect their own extremely favorable, yet insecure, self-evaluations. Furthermore, children of diverse backgrounds who say their own ethnicity makes them feel especially "good"—and thus perhaps socially superior—are more likely to display in-group favoritism and out-group prejudice (Pfeifer et al., 2007).

- *A social world in which people are sorted into groups.* The more adults highlight group distinctions and the less interracial contact that is available in families, schools, and communities, the more likely white children and adolescents will express in-group favoritism and out-group prejudice (Killen et al., 2010). For example, white children with little other-group contact are highly vulnerable to expressions of subtle prejudice, such as interpreting an African-American agemate in an ambiguous situation as engaged in bad behavior (cheating, stealing, or otherwise harming others) (McGlothlin & Killen, 2006).

Reducing Prejudice Research confirms that an effective way to reduce prejudice—in children and adults alike—is through intergroup contact, in which racially and ethnically different individuals have equal status, work toward common goals, and become personally acquainted, and in which authority figures (such as parents and teachers) expect them to engage in such interaction. Children assigned to cooperative learning groups with peers of diverse backgrounds show low levels of prejudice in their expressions of likability and in their behavior. For example, they form more cross-race friendships (Pettigrew & Tropp, 2006). Sharing of thoughts and feelings with close cross-race friends, in turn, reduces even subtle, unintentional prejudices, which are highly resistant to change (Turner, Hewstone, & Voci, 2007). But the positive effects of cooperative learning seem not to generalize to out-group members who are not part of these learning teams.

Long-term contact and collaboration among neighborhood, school, and community groups may be the best way to reduce prejudice (Rutland, Killen, & Abrams, 2010). Consistent with this view, white 5- and 6-year-olds attending an ethnically mixed school relied on their everyday experiences to construct generally positive out-group attitudes (Aboud, 2003). Classrooms that expose children to broad ethnic diversity, teach them to understand and value those differences, directly address the damage caused by prejudice and discrimination, emphasize moral values of justice and fairness, and encourage perspective taking and empathy both prevent children from forming negative biases and reduce already acquired biases (Pfeifer, Brown, & Juvonen, 2007).

In addition, inducing children to view others' traits as malleable is helpful. The more school-age children and adolescents believe that people can change their personalities, the more they report liking, wanting to spend time with, and perceiving themselves as similar to members of disadvantaged out-groups. Furthermore, young people who believe in the malleability of human attributes spend more time volunteering to help the needy—for example, by serving meals to the homeless or reading to poverty-stricken preschoolers (Karafantis & Levy, 2004). Volunteering may, in turn, promote a malleable view of others by inducing young people to imagine themselves in the place of the underprivileged and thus helping them appreciate the social conditions that lead to disadvantage.

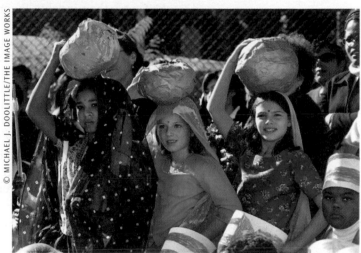

Fourth graders prepare to perform a Hindu dance for International Day at their culturally diverse school. Long-term contact and collaboration with members of other ethnic groups reduce prejudice.

Regrettably, despite the 1954 U.S. Supreme Court *Brown v. Board of Education* decision ordering schools to desegregate, school integration in the United States—which increased steadily until the late 1980s—has receded dramatically as courts terminated their desegregation orders and returned this authority to states and cities. Most U.S. white, black, and Hispanic students now attend schools where the majority of their fellow students are of their own race. White students are the most isolated group—typically in schools that are 80 percent white. And when African-American and Hispanic students attend mixed-race schools, they usually do so with other minorities (Frankenberg, Lee, & Orfield, 2003). Consequently, today's U.S. schools seldom offer exposure to the diversity necessary for countering negative racial and ethnic biases but, instead, largely perpetuate prejudices. Ideals and policies promoting interethnic contact and respect yield far more extensive school integration in Canada. Still, in both nations, 30 to 40 percent of Native children (Native American and Native Canadian) live on reservation lands, where they attend segregated schools (Statistics Canada, 2008; U.S. Census Bureau, 2011b).

Many studies indicate that attending integrated classrooms leads to higher achievement, educational attainment, and occupational aspirations among ethnic minority students—especially when integration begins in the early grades (Hanushek, Kain, & Rivkin, 2002). School integration also greatly increases the likelihood that young people will lead integrated lives as adults (Schofield, 1995). Environments in which students of diverse ethnicities learn together offer a common, inclusive social identity that reduces intergroup bias (Cameron et al., 2006; Dweck, 2009). Furthermore, integrated schools provide many opportunities to grapple with multiple perspectives, which challenge students to think about their social world in more complex ways. As we saw earlier in this chapter, school-age children's developing capacity to take the perspective of others—especially, their ability to engage in recursive thought—contributes greatly to interpersonal understanding and positive social behavior.

▶ Discuss the development of social problem-solving skills, noting ways to enhance social problem solving in children.

Understanding Conflict: Social Problem Solving

Children, including those who are good friends, sometimes come into conflict. With age, they apply their insights about themselves and others to an understanding of how to resolve situations in which their goals and the goals of agemates are at odds. Even preschoolers seem to handle most quarrels constructively; only rarely do their disagreements result in hostile encounters. Overall, conflicts are not very frequent when compared with children's friendly, cooperative interactions.

TAKE A MOMENT... At your next opportunity, observe young children's play, noting their disputes over objects ("That's mine!" "I had it first!"), entry into and control over play activities ("I'm on your team, Jerry." "No, you're not!"), and disagreements over facts, ideas, and beliefs ("I'm taller than he is." "No, you aren't!"). Children take these matters quite seriously. From the preschool to the school years, conflicts shift from material concerns to psychological and social issues (Chen et al., 2001). In Chapter 6, we noted that resolution of conflict, rather than conflict per se, promotes development. Social conflicts provide repeated occasions for **social problem solving**—generating and applying strategies that prevent or resolve disagreements, resulting in outcomes that are both acceptable to others and beneficial to the self. To engage in social problem solving, children must bring together diverse social understandings.

The Social Problem-Solving Process

Nicki Crick and Kenneth Dodge (1994) organize the steps of social problem solving into the circular model shown in Figure 11.10. Notice how this flowchart takes an *information-processing approach,* clarifying exactly what a child must do to grapple with and solve a social problem. It enables identification of processing deficits, so intervention can be tailored to meet individual needs.

Social problem solving profoundly affects peer relations. Children who get along well with agemates interpret social cues accurately, formulate goals (being helpful to peers) that enhance relationships, and have a repertoire of effective problem-solving strategies—for example, politely asking to play and requesting an explanation when they do not understand a peer's behavior. In contrast, children with peer difficulties often hold biased social expectations. Consequently, they attend selectively to social cues (such

FIGURE 11.10 An information-processing model of social problem solving. The model is circular because children often engage in several information-processing activities at once—for example, interpreting information as they notice it and continuing to consider the meaning of another's behavior while they generate and evaluate problem-solving strategies. The model also takes into account the impact of mental state on social information processing—in particular, children's knowledge of social rules, their representations of past social experiences, and their expectations for future experiences. Peer evaluations and responses to enacted strategies are also important factors in social problem solving. (Adapted from N. R. Crick and K. A. Dodge, 1994, "A Review and Reformulation of Social Information-Processing Mechanisms in Children's Social Adjustment," *Psychological Bulletin, 115,* 74–101, Figure 2 [adapted], pg. 76. Copyright © 1994 by the American Psychological Association. Reprinted with permission of the American Psychological Association.)

as hostile acts) and misinterpret others' behavior (view an unintentional jostle as hostile). Their social goals (satisfying an impulse, getting even with or avoiding a peer) often lead to strategies that damage relationships (Dodge, Coie, & Lynam, 2006; Youngstrom et al., 2000). They might barge into a play group without asking, use threats and physical force, or fearfully hover around peers' activities.

Children improve greatly in social problem solving over the preschool and early school years, largely as a result of gains in perspective-taking capacity—in particular, recursive thought (Carpendale & Lewis, 2006). Instead of grabbing, hitting, or insisting that another child obey, 5- to 7-year-olds tend to rely on friendly persuasion and compromise, to think of alternative strategies when an initial one does not work, and to resolve disagreements without adult intervention (Chen et al., 2001; Mayeux & Cillessen, 2003). Sometimes they suggest creating new, mutual goals, reflecting awareness that how they solve current problems will influence the future of the relationship (Yeates, Schultz, & Selman, 1991). By kindergarten, the accuracy and effectiveness of each component of social problem solving are related to socially competent behavior (Dodge et al., 1986).

Enhancing Social Problem Solving

Intervening with children who have weak social problem-solving skills can enhance development in several ways. Besides improving peer relations, effective social problem solving gives children a sense of mastery in the face of stressful life events. It reduces the risk of adjustment difficulties in children from low-SES and troubled families (Goodman, Gravitt, & Kaslow, 1995).

In one intervention—the *Promoting Alternative Thinking Strategies (PATHS)* curriculum for preschool children—teachers provide children with weekly lessons in the ingredients of social problem solving. Using stories, puppet characters, discussion, and role-play demonstrations, they teach such skills as detecting others' thoughts and feelings, planning sequences of action, generating effective strategies, and anticipating probable outcomes. In evaluations of PATHS, preschoolers who had completed 30 lessons in their Head Start classrooms scored higher than no-intervention controls in accurately "reading" others' thoughts and emotions, selecting competent solutions to social conflicts, and cooperating and communicating verbally with peers (Bierman et al., 2008; Domitrovich, Cortes, & Greenberg, 2007).

Generating and evaluating strategies, however, are only part of the social problem-solving process. In a comprehensive year-long intervention called *Making Choices,* third graders diverse in SES received multiple lessons on each social problem-solving component depicted in Figure 11.10 as a supplement to their routine health curriculum. And those in a Making Choices–Plus condition received the intervention plus teacher and family enhancements: Teachers were given guidance in positive classroom discipline and in implementing activities aimed at strengthening emotion regulation, and parents received newsletters offering suggestions for follow-up exercises at home (Fraser et al., 2005, 2011). Regardless of SES, intervention children—compared with children in regular health classes—gained in teacher-rated social competence and declined in aggression over the school year, with reduced aggression still evident at a six-month follow up. Children in the Making Choices–Plus condition performed especially well on story-based assessments of knowledge of the various social problem-solving steps.

Practice in enacting responses may strengthen intervention outcomes. Sometimes children know how to solve a social problem effectively but do not apply their knowledge (Rudolph & Heller, 1997). And children who have repeatedly enacted maladaptive responses may need to rehearse alternatives to overcome their habitual behaviors and to spark more adaptive social information processing.

On a final note, programs aimed at augmenting perspective taking and social problem solving are not the only approaches to helping children with social difficulties. Because their parents often model poor social skills and use ineffective child-rearing practices, intensive family intervention may be necessary—a topic we will return to several times in later chapters.

LOOK and LISTEN

At a playground, beach, or other public setting, watch for an hour or so as young children play, noting how they resolve conflicts. Do nearby adults guide them in social problem solving? How effective are adult interventions?

© CINDY CHARLES/PHOTOEDIT

In role-playing a conflict, these elementary school students learn to resolve social problems by considering others' perspectives and also practice effective solution strategies.

ASK YOURSELF

Review ■ Explain how improved perspective taking contributes to gains in social problem solving from early to middle childhood.

Connect ■ How might school integration contribute to social–cognitive capacities that reduce prejudice, including perspective taking and empathy?

Apply ■ Ten-year-old Marla believes her classmate Becky will never get good grades because she's lazy. Jane believes that Becky tries but can't concentrate because her parents are divorcing. Why is Marla more likely than Jane to develop prejudices?

Reflect ■ Describe several efforts by schools, religious institutions, and youth organizations in your community to combat racial and ethnic prejudices in children.

SUMMARY

Emergence of Self and Development of Self-Concept (p. 448)

Describe the development of self-awareness in infancy and toddlerhood, along with the emotional and social capacities it supports.

■ Self-awareness begins at birth, supported by newborns' capacity for intermodal perception. Three- to 4-month-olds' reactions to their own visual image suggest an implicit awareness of being physically distinct from their surroundings.

■ Around age 2, **self-recognition** is well under way. Toddlers become explicitly aware of the self's physical features, as indicated by responses to their own image in mirrors and photos and use of personal pronouns. However, toddlers lack an objective understanding of their own body size, as indicated by their **scale errors**.

■ Sensitive caregiving promotes early self-development. Toddlers in collectivist cultures with a proximal parenting style attain self-recognition later.

■ Increasing self-awareness sets the stage for social referencing, self-conscious emotions, perspective taking, empathy, sustained imitative play, peer competition for objects, and cooperation.

Describe the development of the categorical, remembered, and enduring selves.

■ Language development permits young preschoolers to construct a **categorical self** as they classify themselves and others on the basis of age, perceptually distinct attributes and behaviors, and goodness and badness. Adult–child conversations about the past lead to an autobiographical memory that grants the child a **remembered self** and an **enduring self.**

Discuss theory-of-mind development from early to middle childhood, citing social consequences and contributing factors.

■ Young preschoolers develop an **inner self** of private thoughts and imaginings, which contributes vitally to **perspective taking.** As toddlers and young preschoolers comprehend mental states that can be readily inferred from their own and others' actions, they form a **desire theory of mind,** thinking that people's actions are always consistent with their desires.

■ Between ages 3 and 4, children develop a **belief–desire theory of mind,** as mastery of false belief reveals. As school-age children realize that people can increase their knowledge by making mental inferences, they grasp second-order false belief. Performance on other complex tasks requiring **recursive thought** also improves over middle childhood.

© LAURA DWIGHT PHOTOGRAPHY

■ False-belief understanding is associated with gains in sociodramatic play, with early reading ability, with more accurate eyewitness memory, and with social skills. School-age children use their capacity for recursive thought to clear up misunderstandings and to persuade others.

■ Factors contributing to the development of theory of mind include language and verbal reasoning; executive function; parent–child conversations about mental states; make-believe play; and social interaction with siblings, friends, and adults.

Discuss the development of self-concept from early childhood through adolescence, noting cognitive, social, and cultural influences.

■ As children think more intently about themselves, they construct a **self-concept.** In middle childhood, self-concept shifts from a focus on observable characteristics and typical emotions and attitudes to competencies, personality traits, and **social comparisons.** Adolescents unify separate traits into more abstract descriptors, forming an organized system that emphasizes social virtues and personal and moral values.

■ Changes in self-concept are supported by cognitive development, perspective-taking skills (as suggested by Mead's concept of the **generalized other**), and feedback from others. Self-concept varies across cultures: Children in individualistic cultures focus on personal characteristics, those in collectivist cultures on group membership and relationships.

Self-Esteem: The Evaluative Side of Self-Concept (p. 461)

Discuss development of and influences on self-esteem from early childhood through adolescence.

■ **Self-esteem** becomes hierarchically organized and declines over the first few years of elementary school as children start to make social comparisons. Except for a temporary drop associated with school transition, self-esteem rises from fourth grade on, with new dimensions added in adolescence.

■ From middle childhood to adolescence, individual differences in self-esteem become increasingly stable. Favorable self-esteem profiles are associated with positive adjustment; low self-esteem in all areas is linked to adjustment difficulties. Cultural forces, including relative emphasis on social comparison and gender-stereotyped expectations, affect self-esteem.

- Children whose parents are warm and accepting and who provide reasonable expectations for mature behavior have higher self-esteem. Excessive parental control is linked to low self-esteem and indulgent parenting to unrealistically high self-esteem.

Discuss achievement-related attributions, and suggest ways to foster a mastery-oriented approach in children.

- School-age children begin to distinguish ability, effort, and external factors in their **attributions** for success and failure. Children with **mastery-oriented attributions** credit their successes to high ability and their failures to insufficient effort and hold an **incremental view of ability.** Children with **learned helplessness** attribute successes to external factors, such as luck, and failures to low ability and hold an **entity view of ability.**

- Children who experience negative feedback about their ability, messages that evaluate their traits, and pressure to focus on performance goals are likely to develop learned helplessness. Caring, helpful parents and teachers who emphasize learning goals foster a mastery orientation. **Attribution retraining** encourages learned-helpless children to believe they can overcome failure through effort.

Constructing an Identity: Who Should I Become? (p. 468)

Describe the four identity statuses, along with factors affecting identity development.

- Erikson first recognized formation of an **identity** as the major personality achievement of adolescence. **Identity achievement** (exploration followed by commitment) and **identity moratorium** (exploration without having reached commitment) are psychologically healthy identity statuses. Long-term **identity foreclosure** (commitment without exploration) and **identity diffusion** (lack of both exploration and commitment) are related to adjustment difficulties.

- An information-gathering cognitive style, parental attachment along with freedom to explore, interaction with diverse peers, close friendships, and schools and communities that provide rich and varied opportunities promote healthy identity development. Similarly, supportive parents, peers, and schools can foster a secure **ethnic identity** among minority adolescents. A **bicultural identity** offers additional emotional and social benefits.

Thinking About Other People (p. 476)

Discuss changes in children's appreciation of others' attributes and understanding of social groups, including factors that contribute to prejudice and ways to reduce it.

- **Person perception** refers to how we size up the qualities of familiar people. Like their self-descriptions, children's descriptions of others increasingly emphasize personality traits and become more organized with age.

- Basic concepts of race, ethnicity, and social class emerge in the preschool years. By the early school years, children absorb prevailing attitudes toward social groups from messages in their environments.

- White children show in-group favoritism and out-group prejudice by age 5 to 6. Ethnic minority children often absorb their culture's ethnic stereotypes and, as a result, show out-group favoritism. The capacity to classify the social world in multiple ways, along with growing awareness of the inappropriateness of prejudice, leads to a decline in overt prejudice in middle childhood. However, subtle prejudice often persists. Children who view personality as fixed, have overly high self-esteem, and experience a social world in which people are sorted into groups are more likely to harbor ethnic prejudices.

- Long-term intergroup contact and collaboration are highly effective in reducing prejudice, and inducing children to view others' traits as malleable is also helpful. School integration—a powerful basis for combating negative ethnic and racial biases—has receded dramatically in the United States.

Understanding Conflict: Social Problem Solving (p. 480)

Discuss the development of social problem-solving skills, noting ways to enhance social problem solving in children.

- **Social problem-solving** skills—noticing and interpreting social cues, clarifying social goals, generating and evaluating strategies, and enacting responses—improve over early and middle childhood and predict socially competent behavior. Interventions that teach effective social problem-solving skills improve peer relations and reduce the risk of adjustment difficulties.

IMPORTANT TERMS AND CONCEPTS

acculturative stress (p. 475)
achievement motivation (p. 465)
attribution retraining (p. 467)
attributions (p. 464)
belief–desire theory of mind (p. 452)
bicultural identity (p. 475)
categorical self (p. 450)
desire theory of mind (p. 452)
enduring self (p. 451)
entity view of ability (p. 465)
ethnic identity (p. 475)

generalized other (p. 459)
identity (p. 468)
identity achievement (p. 470)
identity diffusion (p. 470)
identity foreclosure (p. 470)
identity moratorium (p. 470)
incremental view of ability (p. 465)
inner self (p. 452)
learned helplessness (p. 465)
mastery-oriented attributions (p. 465)
person perception (p. 476)

perspective taking (p. 452)
recursive thought (p. 453)
remembered self (p. 450)
scale errors (p. 449)
self-concept (p. 456)
self-esteem (p. 461)
self-recognition (p. 449)
social cognition (p. 447)
social comparisons (p. 458)
social problem solving (p. 480)

CHAPTER 12

"Peace Will Come One Day"
Nelma Sahinovic
12 years, Bosnia

This portrayal of a benevolent world expresses the artist's keen moral sensibilities. Human nature, family, peers, school, and culture all contribute to the cognitive, emotional, and behavioral ingredients of morality.

Reprinted with permission from the International Child Art Foundation, Washington, DC

Moral Development

Morality as Rooted in Human Nature

Morality as the Adoption of Societal Norms
Psychoanalytic Theory and the Role of Guilt • Social Learning Theory • Limitations of "Morality as the Adoption of Societal Norms" Perspective

■ **CULTURAL INFLUENCES:** *Ethnic Differences in the Consequences of Physical Punishment*

Morality as Social Understanding
Piaget's Theory of Moral Development • Evaluation of Piaget's Theory • Kohlberg's Extension of Piaget's Theory • Research on Kohlberg's Stages • Are There Sex Differences in Moral Reasoning? • Influences on Moral Reasoning • Moral Reasoning and Behavior • Religious Involvement and Moral Development • Further Challenges to Kohlberg's Theory • The Domain Approach to Moral Understanding

■ **SOCIAL ISSUES: EDUCATION:** *Development of Civic Responsibility*

Development of Morally Relevant Self-Control
Toddlerhood • Childhood and Adolescence • Individual Differences

The Other Side of Self-Control: Development of Aggression
Emergence of Aggression • Aggression in Early and Middle Childhood • Aggression and Delinquency in Adolescence • Stability of Aggression • The Family as Training Ground for Aggressive Behavior • Social-Cognitive Deficits and Distortions • Community and Cultural Influences • Helping Children and Parents Control Aggression

■ **BIOLOGY AND ENVIRONMENT:** *Two Routes to Adolescent Delinquency*

■ **CULTURAL INFLUENCES:** *Impact of Ethnic and Political Violence on Children*

T hree-year-old Leisl grabbed a toy from Ava, a neighbor child who had come to play. "Give it back!" Ava cried. "It's mine!"

Leisl's mother bent down. "Look!" she explained. "Ava's about to cry. She was playing with the teddy bear, and when you took it, you made her sad. Let's give the bear back to Ava." Gently, she freed the toy from Leisl's hands and returned it to Ava. For a moment, Leisl looked hurt, but she soon busied herself with her blocks. A few moments later, Leisl turned to Ava. "Want some of these?" she offered generously, making a pile of blocks for Ava. "We can share!"

Now consider Leisl at age 11, reacting to a newspaper article about an elderly woman, soon to be evicted from her crumbling home because city inspectors judged it a fire and health hazard. "Look at what they're trying to do!" exclaimed Leisl. "They're going to throw this poor lady out of her house. You don't just knock someone's home down! Where're her friends and neighbors? Why aren't they over there fixing up that house?"

Eleven-year-old Leisl has come a long way from the preschool child just beginning to appreciate others' rights and feelings. That beginning, however, is an important one. Preschooler Leisl's prosocial invitation to her visiting playmate is part of an emerging picture. Accompanying gains in self-awareness and representational capacities at the end of the second year is another crowning achievement: The child becomes a moral being. Recall that around this time, empathy and sympathetic concern emerge (Chapter 10), and children soon begin to evaluate their own and others' behavior as "good" or "bad" (Chapter 11). As children's cognition and language develop and their social experiences broaden, they express increasingly elaborate moral thoughts accompanied by intense emotion that—as with 11-year-old Leisl—sometimes escalates to moral outrage.

In all cultures, morality is promoted by an overarching social organization that specifies rules for good conduct. At the same time, morality has roots in each major aspect of our psychological makeup:

● Morality has an *emotional component*. Powerful feelings cause us to empathize with another's distress or to feel guilty when we are the cause of that distress.
● Morality also has an important *cognitive component*. Children's developing social understanding enables them to make increasingly profound judgments about actions they believe to be right or wrong.
● Morality has a vital *behavioral component*. Experiencing morally relevant thoughts and feelings increases the likelihood, but does not guarantee, that people will act in accord with them.

Traditionally, these three aspects of morality have been studied separately: Biological and psychoanalytic theories focus on emotions, cognitive-developmental theory on moral thought, and social learning theory on moral behavior. Today, a growing body of research reveals that all three facets are interrelated. Still, major theories disagree on which is primary. And as we will see, the aspect a theory emphasizes has major implications for how it conceptualizes the basic trend of moral development: the shift from superficial, or externally controlled, responses to behavior based on inner standards, or moral under-standing. Truly moral individuals do not merely do the right thing for the sake of social conformity or to meet the expectations of authority figures. Rather, they have developed compassionate concerns and ideals of good conduct, which they follow in a wide variety of situations.

Our discussion of moral development begins by highlighting the strengths and limitations of the theories just mentioned in light of recent research. Next we consider the important related topic of self-control. The development of a personal resolve to keep the self from doing anything it feels like doing is crucial for translating moral commitments into action. We conclude with a discussion of the other side of self-control—the development of aggression. ■

▶ Describe and evaluate the biological perspective on morality.

Morality as Rooted in Human Nature

In the 1970s, biological theories of human social behavior suggested that many morally relevant behaviors and emotions have roots in our evolutionary history (Wilson, 1975). This view was supported by the work of ethologists, who observed animals aiding other members of their species, often at great personal risk (Lorenz, 1983). For example, ants, bees, and termites show extremes of self-sacrifice. Large numbers will sting or bite an animal that threatens the hive, a warlike response that often results in their own death. Dogs who breach a master's prohibition by damaging furniture or defecating indoors sometimes display intense regret, expressed as distress and submission.

Among primates, chimpanzees (who are genetically closest to humans) conform to moral-like rules, which group members enforce in one another. For example, when males attack females, they avoid using their sharp canine teeth. If a male does harm a female, the entire colony responds with a chorus of indignant barks, sometimes followed by a band of females chasing off the aggressor (de Waal, 1996). Chimps also reciprocate favors, generously grooming and sharing food with those who have done the same for them. And they engage in kind and comforting acts. Juveniles sometimes soothe frightened or injured peers, and adult females will adopt a baby that has lost its mother (Goodall, 1990). Furthermore, shortly after a physical fight, former combatants may embrace, hold hands, and groom, intensifying friendly behaviors in an apparent effort to restore their long-term relationship (de Waal, 2001, 2006). On the basis of this evidence, researchers reasoned that evolution must have made similar biologically based provisions for moral acts in humans.

Although a variety of built-in bases for morality have been posited, empathy or caring and self-sacrifice (as the above examples suggest) are of prime importance (Haidt & Kesebir, 2010). In other species, most of these acts occur within family groups, whose members have common reproductive interests. Humans, too, are biased to aid family members—helping that strengthens as genetic relatedness increases and that is particularly strong in life-and-death situations, such as entering a burning building to save a life or donating a kidney for a transplant (Neyer & Lang, 2003). But humans also have an unmatched capacity to make sacrifices for nonrelatives—by investing time and effort in helping the needy in their communities, donating generously to charities, aiding others in emergencies, and giving their lives for their country in wartime (Becker & Eagly, 2004; Van Lange et al., 2007).

Evolutionary theorists speculate that our unique capacity to act prosocially toward genetic strangers originated several million years ago, in the small hunting-and-gathering bands—including both kin and nonkin—in which we spent 95 percent of our evolutionary history. To limit selfishness (which can quickly undermine group functioning), humans developed informal systems of social exchange, in which they acted benevolently toward others with the expectation that others might do the same for them in the future. These reciprocal exchanges (as noted earlier) occur in other species, especially primates, but they are far more common, varied, and highly developed in humans (Van Vugt & Van Lange, 2006). The willingness of many members of a group to aid others and engage in self-sacrifice ensures that the majority will survive and

Chimpanzees conform to moral-like rules, such as sharing food, and enforce those rules in one another. Researchers speculate that moral acts in humans have a similar biological basis.

© STEVE BLOOM IMAGES/ALAMY

reproduce. Under these conditions, traits that foster altruism undergo natural selection, becoming increasingly prominent in succeeding generations.

How might genes encourage prosocial acts and, thereby, promote survival of the species? Many researchers believe that prewired emotional reactions are involved (de Waal, 2006; Haidt, 2001, 2003; Hoffman, 2000; Trivers, 1971). In Chapter 10, we noted that newborns cry when they hear another baby cry, a possible precursor of empathy. As Figure 12.1 illustrates, 6-month-olds' reaching behaviors convey a preference for an individual who helps over one who hinders others—an attitude present so early that the investigators speculated it is built in (Hamlin, Wynn, & Bloom, 2007). As toddlers approach age 2, they show clear empathic concern, and they begin experiencing self-conscious emotions, which greatly enhance their responsiveness to social expectations.

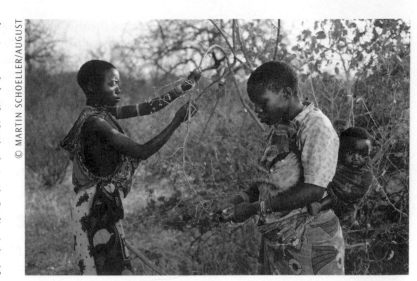

© MARTIN SCHOELLER/AUGUST

The unique human capacity to act prosocially toward nonrelatives is believed to have originated several million years ago in small hunting-and-gathering bands. Here, gatherers of the Hadza people of Tanzania pick berries to share among families at their camp.

Researchers have identified areas within the prefrontal cortex (the ventromedial area, located just behind the bridge of the nose, and the orbitofrontal area, resting above the orbits of the eyes) that are vital for emotional responsiveness to the suffering of others and to one's own misdeeds. Functioning of the prefrontal cortex improves over the first two years, preceding children's increased empathic concern (see Chapter 5). Furthermore, adults with damage to these areas rarely react with empathy to others' distress, do poorly on tests of social reasoning, and are relatively unconcerned about conforming to social norms (Damasio, 1994; Eslinger et al., 2007; Moll, de Oliveira-Souza, & Zahn, 2009). Early-occurring ventromedial and orbitofrontal damage severely disrupts social learning, resulting in extreme antisocial behavior (Anderson et al., 1999; Eslinger, 1998). And EEG and fMRI research reveals that psychopaths, who inflict harm on others without any trace of empathy or guilt, show reduced activity in these areas (Raine, 1997).

Humans' elaborate mirror neuron systems are also believed to support empathic responding (see Chapter 4, page 146). fMRI evidence indicates that self-experienced pain and observations of another's facial reactions to pain activate corresponding areas in the cerebral cortex (Botvinick et al., 2005). Even the intensity of pain experienced by another is reflected in heightened cortical activity– a response that correlates positively with observers' self-reported empathy (Budell, Jackson, & Rainville, 2010; Saarela et al., 2007).

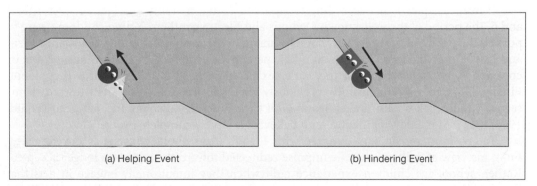

(a) Helping Event   (b) Hindering Event

FIGURE 12.1 **Infants prefer an individual who helps to one who hinders others.** Researchers exposed 6- and 10-month-olds to a scene in which a climber (red circle) repeatedly tried to climb a hill. After the third attempt, the infants saw alternating instances of helping and hindering events: (a) A helper (yellow triangle) aided the climber by pushing it from behind, or (b) a hinderer (blue square) pushed the climber down the hill. Then the infants were presented with the helper and the hinderer and encouraged to choose between the two. The overwhelming majority—100 percent of 6-month-olds and 88 percent of 10-month-olds—reached for the helper. The researchers concluded that babies have a built-in preference for individuals who aid others. Others, however, claim that social experiences during the first six months offer many relevant learning opportunities. (From J. K. Hamlin, K. Wynn, & P. Bloom, 2007, "Social Evaluation by Preverbal Infants," *Nature, 450,* p. 557. Copyright © 2007, Rights Managed by Nature Publishing Group. Reprinted by permission from Macmillan Publishers Ltd.)

But biological theories of morality as simply a matter of feelings rooted in human nature have limitations. Recall from Chapter 10 that empathy, sympathy, pride, guilt, and other self-conscious emotions require strong caregiving supports to develop, and their mature expression depends on cognitive development. Furthermore, although emotion is one basis for moral action, it is not a complete account. For example, most of us would question the behavior of a parent who decides not to take a sick child to the doctor out of empathy with the child's fear and anxiety.

Still, the biological perspective reminds us of morality's adaptive value. Because of the necessity for group living, humans have evolved an elaborate brain-based moral substrate that counteracts self-centered motives and promotes concern for others.

▶ Describe and evaluate the psychoanalytic perspective on moral development.

▶ Describe and evaluate the social learning perspective on moral development.

▶ Cite central features of the cognitive-developmental approach to moral development.

Morality as the Adoption of Societal Norms

The two perspectives we are about to discuss—psychoanalytic theory and social learning theory—offer different accounts of how children become moral beings. Yet both regard moral development as a matter of **internalization**: adopting societal standards for right action as one's own. In other words, both focus on how morality moves from society to individual—how children acquire norms, or prescriptions for good conduct, widely held by members of their social group.

Our consideration of these theories will reveal that several factors jointly affect the child's willingness to adopt societal standards:

- Parental style of discipline, which varies with the type of misdeed
- The child's characteristics, including age and temperament
- The parent's characteristics
- The child's view of both the misdeed and the reasonableness of parental demands

As this list indicates, internalization results from a combination of influences within the child and the rearing environment. When the process goes well, external forces foster the child's positive inclinations and counteract the child's negative inclinations (Turiel, 2006). In the following sections, we will see many examples of this idea.

Psychoanalytic Theory and the Role of Guilt

Recall from Chapter 1 that according to Sigmund Freud, morality emerges between ages 3 and 6, the period of the well-known Oedipus and Electra conflicts. Young children desire to possess the parent of the other sex, but they abandon this wish because they fear punishment and loss of parental love. To maintain their parents' affection, children form a *superego*, or conscience, by *identifying* with the same-sex parent, whose moral standards they adopt. Finally, children turn the hostility previously aimed at the same-sex parent toward themselves, which evokes painful feelings of guilt each time they disobey the superego (Freud, 1925/1961). Moral development, Freud believed, is largely complete by age 5 to 6.

Today, most researchers disagree with Freud's ideas about conscience development. First, his view of guilt as a hostile impulse redirected toward the self is no longer accepted. Rather, school-age children experience guilt when they intentionally engage in acts that harm others and feel personally responsible for the outcome (see Chapter 10). Second, Freud assumed that fear of punishment and loss of parental love motivate conscience formation. Yet children whose parents frequently use threats, commands, or physical force tend to violate standards often and feel little guilt, whereas parental warmth and responsiveness predict greater guilt following transgressions (Kochanska et al., 2002, 2005, 2008). And if a parent withdraws love after misbehavior—for example, refuses to speak to or states a dislike for the child—children often respond with high levels of self-blame, thinking "I'm no good" or "Nobody loves me." Eventually, to protect themselves from overwhelming guilt, these children may deny the emotion and, as a result, also develop a weak conscience (Kochanska, 1991; Zahn-Waxler et al., 1990).

Inductive Discipline In contrast, conscience formation is promoted by a type of discipline called **induction,** in which an adult helps the child notice others' feelings by pointing out the effects of the child's misbehavior on others, especially noting their distress and making clear that the child caused it. For example, to a young preschool child, the parent might say, "She's crying because you won't give back her teddy bear," as Leisl's mother did in the introduction to this chapter. To older preschoolers, parents can explain why the child's action was harmful, perhaps by referring to the other person's intentions: "Don't yell at him. That makes him feel sad. He was trying to help you!" And with further cognitive advances, more subtle psychological explanations are possible: "He felt proud of his tower, and you hurt his feelings by knocking it down" (Hoffman, 2000).

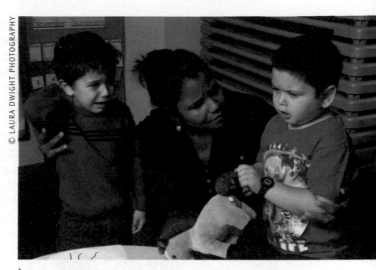

A teacher explains to a child how his misbehavior affects others, calling attention to his classmate's distress. Inductive discipline encourages empathy and sympathetic concern, which motivate prosocial behavior.

When generally warm parents provide explanations that match the child's capacity to understand, while firmly insisting that the child listen and comply, induction is effective as early as age 2. Preschoolers whose parents use this approach are more likely to refrain from wrongdoing, confess and repair damages after misdeeds (as Leisl did when she invited Ava to play with her blocks), and display prosocial behavior (Kerr et al., 2004; Volling, Mahoney, & Rauer, 2009; Zahn-Waxler, Radke-Yarrow, & King, 1979).

Induction remains powerfully effective at older ages. In one study, the more adolescents reported that their mothers used induction (as opposed to power assertion and love withdrawal), the stronger their **moral identity**—endorsement of moral values (such as fairness, kindness, and generosity) as central to their self-concept (Patrick & Gibbs, 2011). Adolescents also reacted to induction with greater guilt and emotional acceptance, and they more often viewed it as a fair and appropriate parental response. Maternal expressions of disappointed expectations (emphasizing that the teenager is capable of a higher moral standard) tended to co-occur with induction and contributed to its prediction of moral identity.

The success of induction may lie in its power to motivate active commitment to moral norms, in the following ways:

- Induction gives children information about how to behave that they can use in future situations.
- By emphasizing the impact of the child's actions on others, induction encourages empathy and sympathetic concern, which motivate prosocial behavior (Krevans & Gibbs, 1996).
- Giving children reasons for changing their behavior encourages them to adopt moral standards because those standards make sense.
- Children who consistently experience induction may form a *script* for the negative emotional consequences of harming others: Child causes harm, inductive message points out harm, child feels empathy for victim, child makes amends (Hoffman, 2000). The script deters future transgressions.
- Children and adolescents who view discipline as fair are more likely to listen to, accept, and internalize the parent's message (Bugental & Grusec, 2006). And as teenagers increasingly mention moral qualities in their self-descriptions (see page 459 in Chapter 11), parental expressions of disappointed expectations may strengthen the impact of induction by highlighting the discrepancy between the young person's actions and self-definition.

In contrast, discipline that relies too heavily on threats of punishment or withdrawal of love makes children and adolescents so angry or anxious and frightened that they cannot think clearly enough to figure out what they should do. As a result, these practices do not get children to internalize moral norms, and—as noted earlier—also interfere with empathy and prosocial responding (Eisenberg, Fabes, & Spinrad, 2006; Padilla-Walker, 2008). Nevertheless, warnings, disapproval, and commands are sometimes necessary to get an unruly child to listen to an inductive message (Grusec, 2006).

LOOK and LISTEN

Provide several older school-age children and adolescents with three different examples of parental responses to a child's transgression against another: induction, power assertion, and love withdrawal. Ask the participants to judge the fairness of each form of discipline and to describe how they would feel after experiencing it.

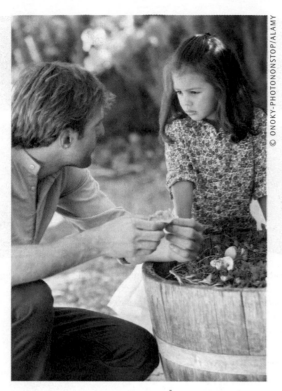

When children are impulsive and low in anxiety, a secure attachment relationship motivates conscience development. This preschooler wants to follow parental rules to preserve an affectionate, supportive relationship with her father.

The Child's Contribution Although good discipline is crucial for conscience development, children's characteristics affect the success of parenting techniques. For example, in Chapter 10 we noted that empathy is moderately heritable. More empathic children require less power assertion and are more responsive to induction.

Temperament is also influential. Mild, patient tactics—requests, suggestions, and explanations—are sufficient to prompt guilt reactions and conscience development in anxious, fearful preschoolers (Kochanska et al., 2002). But with fearless, impulsive children, gentle discipline has little impact. Power assertion also works poorly: It undermines the child's capacity for effortful control, which strongly predicts moral internalization, empathy, sympathy, and prosocial behavior (Kochanska & Aksan, 2006; Kochanska & Knaack, 2003). Parents of impulsive children can foster conscience development by building a warm, affectionate relationship that promotes secure attachment and by combining firm correction of misbehavior with induction (Kochanska, Aksan, & Joy, 2007). When children are so low in anxiety that parental interventions cause them little discomfort, a close parent–child bond provides an alternative foundation for morality. It motivates children to listen to parents' inductions and follow their rules as a means of preserving an affectionate, supportive relationship.

In sum, to foster early moral development, parents must tailor their disciplinary strategies to their child's personality. Does this remind you of goodness of fit, discussed in Chapter 10? Return to page 426 to review this idea.

The Role of Guilt Although little support exists for Freudian ideas about conscience development, Freud was correct that guilt is an important motivator of moral action. By the end of toddlerhood, guilt reactions are evident, and preschoolers' assertions to others reveal that they have internalized the parent's moral voice: "Didn't you hear my mommy? We'd better not play with these toys" (Thompson, 2009).

Inducing *empathy-based guilt* (expressions of personal responsibility and regret, such as "I'm sorry I hurt him") by explaining that the child's behavior is causing someone distress is a means of influencing children without using coercion. Empathy-based guilt reactions are associated with stopping harmful actions, repairing damage caused by misdeeds, and engaging in future prosocial behavior (Baumeister, 1998; Eisenberg, Eggum, & Edwards, 2010). At the same time, parents must help children deal with guilt feelings constructively—by guiding them to make up for immoral behavior rather than minimizing or excusing it (Bybee, Merisca, & Velasco, 1998).

But contrary to what Freud believed, guilt is not the only force that compels us to act morally. Nor is moral development complete by the end of early childhood. Rather, it is a gradual process, beginning in the preschool years and extending into adulthood.

Social Learning Theory

The social learning perspective does not regard morality as a special human activity with a unique course of development. Rather, moral behavior is acquired just like any other set of responses: through reinforcement and modeling.

Importance of Modeling Operant conditioning—reinforcement for good behavior with approval, affection, and other rewards—is not enough for children to acquire moral responses. For a behavior to be reinforced, it must first occur spontaneously. Yet many prosocial acts, such as sharing, helping, or comforting an unhappy playmate, occur so rarely at first that reinforcement cannot explain their rapid development in early childhood. Rather, social learning theorists believe that children learn to behave morally largely through *modeling*—observing and imitating adults who demonstrate appropriate behavior (Bandura, 1977; Grusec, 1988). Once children acquire a moral response, such as sharing or telling the truth, reinforcement in the form of praising the act ("That was a very nice thing to do") or the child's character ("You're a very kind and considerate boy") increases its frequency (Mills & Grusec, 1989).

Many studies show that having helpful or generous models increases young children's prosocial responses. And certain characteristics of the model affect children's willingness to imitate:

- *Warmth and responsiveness.* Preschoolers are more likely to copy the prosocial actions of an adult who is warm and responsive than those of a cold, distant adult (Yarrow, Scott, & Waxler, 1973). Warmth seems to make children more attentive and receptive to the model and is itself an example of a prosocial response.
- *Competence and power.* Children admire and therefore tend to imitate competent, powerful models—especially older peers and adults (Bandura, 1977).
- *Consistency between assertions and behavior.* When models say one thing and do another—for example, announce that "it's important to help others" but rarely engage in helpful acts—children generally choose the most lenient standard of behavior that adults demonstrate (Mischel & Liebert, 1966).

Modeling helpful behavior is especially influential in the early years. This 3-year-old watches attentively as his father demonstrates how to fold laundry.

Models are most influential in the early years. In one study, toddlers' eager, willing imitation of their mothers' behavior predicted moral conduct (not cheating in a game) and guilt following transgressions at age 3 (Forman, Aksan, & Kochanska, 2004). At the end of early childhood, children who have had consistent exposure to caring adults tend to behave prosocially whether or not a model is present: They have internalized prosocial rules from repeated observations and encouragement by others (Mussen & Eisenberg-Berg, 1977).

Effects of Punishment Many parents are aware that angrily yelling at, slapping, and spanking children are ineffective disciplinary tactics. A sharp reprimand or physical force to restrain or move a child is justified when immediate obedience is necessary—for example, when a 3-year-old is about to run into the street. In fact, parents are most likely to use forceful methods under these conditions. But to foster long-term goals, such as acting kindly toward others, they tend to rely on warmth and reasoning (Kuczynski, 1984). And in response to very serious transgressions, such as lying or stealing, they often combine power assertion with reasoning (Grusec, 2006; Grusec & Goodnow, 1994).

Frequent punishment, however, promotes only immediate compliance, not lasting changes in behavior. Children who are repeatedly criticized, shouted at, or hit are likely to display the unacceptable response again as soon as adults are out of sight. The more harsh threats, angry physical control (yanking an object from the child, handling the child roughly), and physical punishment children experience, the more likely they are to develop serious, lasting mental health problems. These include weak internalization of moral rules; depression, aggression, antisocial behavior, and poor academic performance in childhood and adolescence; and depression, alcohol abuse, criminality, and partner and child abuse in adulthood (Afifi et al., 2006; Bender et al., 2007; Gershoff, 2002a; Kochanska, Aksan, & Nichols, 2003; Lynch et al., 2006).

Harsh punishment has several undesirable side effects:

- Parents often spank in response to children's aggression (Holden, Coleman, & Schmidt, 1995). Yet the punishment itself models aggression!
- Harshly treated children react with anger, resentment, and a chronic sense of being personally threatened, which prompts a focus on the self's distress rather than a sympathetic orientation to others' needs (see Chapter 10, page 417).
- Children who are frequently punished develop a more conflict-ridden and less supportive parent–child relationship and also learn to avoid the punitive parent (McLoyd &

Smith, 2002; Shaw, Lacourse, & Nagin, 2005). Consequently, the parent has little opportunity to teach desirable behaviors.

● By stopping children's misbehavior temporarily, harsh punishment gives adults immediate relief, reinforcing them for using coercive discipline. For this reason, a punitive adult is likely to punish with greater frequency over time, a course of action that can spiral into serious abuse.

● Children, adolescents, and adults whose parents used *corporal punishment*—the use of physical force to inflict pain but not injury—are more accepting of such discipline (Deater-Deckard et al., 2003; Vitrup & Holden, 2010). In this way, use of physical punishment may transfer to the next generation.

Although corporal punishment spans the SES spectrum, its frequency and harshness are elevated among less educated, economically disadvantaged parents (Giles-Sims, Straus, & Sugarman, 1995; Lansford et al., 2004, 2009). And consistently, parents with conflict-ridden marriages and with mental health problems (who are emotionally reactive, depressed, or aggressive) are more likely to be punitive and also to have hard-to-manage children, whose disobedience evokes more parental harshness (Berlin et al., 2009; Erath et al., 2006; Knafo & Plomin, 2006; Taylor et al., 2010). These parent–child similarities suggest that heredity contributes to the link between punitive discipline and children's adjustment difficulties. But heredity is not a complete explanation. **TAKE A MOMENT...** Return to page 124 in Chapter 3 to review findings indicating that good parenting can shield children who are genetically at risk for aggression and antisocial activity from developing those behaviors.

Furthermore, in a longitudinal study extending from 15 months to 3 years, early corporal punishment predicted emotional and behavior problems in children of diverse temperaments (Mulvaney & Mebert, 2007). Negative outcomes were simply more pronounced among temperamentally difficult children. Other longitudinal findings reveal a similar link between physical punishment and later child and adolescent aggression, even after child, parenting, and family characteristics that might otherwise account for the relationship were controlled (Berlin et al., 2009; Lansford et al., 2009, 2011; Taylor et al., 2010).

Ethnographic evidence indicates that corporal punishment increases in societies with autocratic political decision making and cultures of violence (Ember & Ember, 2005). Yet among countries differing widely in characteristics—including economic well-being, educational attainment of the population, and individualistic versus collectivist orientations—increased use of yelling, scolding, and corporal punishment is positively associated with child anxiety and aggression (Gershoff et al., 2010; Lansford et al., 2005). The corporal punishment–child anxiety/aggression associations are slightly less strong in countries where the practice is widely accepted, perhaps because parents in those nations apply it in a milder, less impulsive manner. But negative child outcomes nevertheless persist.

In view of these findings, the widespread use of corporal punishment by American parents is cause for concern. A survey of a nationally representative sample of U.S. households revealed that although corporal punishment increases from infancy to age 5 and then declines, the percentage of parents who use it is high at all ages (see Figure 12.2). Most parents report physically punishing their children only occasionally—on average, once or twice per month. Still, an alarming 35 to 50 percent of U.S. infants—who are not yet capable of complying with adult directives—get spanked or hit (Oldershaw, 2002). And more than one-fourth of physically punishing U.S. parents report having used a hard object, such as a brush or a belt (Gershoff, 2002b).

FIGURE 12.2 Prevalence of corporal punishment by child's age. Estimates are based on the percentage of parents in a nationally representative U.S. sample of nearly 1,000 who reported one or more instances of spanking, slapping, pinching, shaking, or hitting with a hard object in the past year. Physical punishment increases sharply during early childhood and then declines, but it is high at all ages. (From M. A. Straus & J. H. Stewart, 1999, "Corporal Punishment by American Parents: National Data on Prevalence, Chronicity, Severity, and Duration in Relation to Child and Family Characteristics," *Clinical Child and Family Psychology Review, 2,* p. 59. Adapted with kind permission from Springer Science and Business Media and Murray A. Straus.)

CULTURAL INFLUENCES

Ethnic Differences in the Consequences of Physical Punishment

In an African-American community, six elders, all of whom had volunteered to serve as mentors for parents facing child-rearing challenges, met to discuss parenting issues at a social service agency. Their attitudes toward discipline were strikingly different from those of the white social workers who had brought them together. Each elder argued that successful child rearing required appropriate physical tactics. At the same time, they voiced strong disapproval of screaming or cursing at children, calling such out-of-control parental behavior "abusive." Ruth, the oldest and most respected member of the group, characterized good parenting as a complex combination of warmth, teaching, talking nicely, and disciplining physically. She related how an older neighbor advised her to handle her own children when she was a young parent:

> She said to me, says don't scream . . . talk to them real nice and sweet and when they do something ugly and you don't like it . . . she say you get a nice little switch and you won't have any trouble with them and from that day . . . that's the way I raised 'em. (Mosby et al., 1999, pp. 511–512)

The others chimed in, emphasizing *mild* punishment: "Just tap 'em a little bit." "When you do things like [get too harsh] you're wronging yourself" (Mosby et al., 1999, pp. 511–512).

Although corporal punishment is linked to a wide array of negative child outcomes, exceptions do exist. In one longitudinal study, researchers followed several hundred families for 12 years, collecting information from mothers on disciplinary strategies in early and middle childhood and from both mothers and their children on problem behaviors in

adolescence. Even after many child and family characteristics were controlled, the findings were striking: In Caucasian-American families, physical punishment was positively associated with adolescent aggression and antisocial behavior. In African-American families, by contrast, the more mothers had disciplined physically in childhood, the less their teenagers displayed angry, acting-out behavior and got in trouble at school and with the police (Lansford et al., 2004).

African-American and Caucasian-American parents seem to mete out physical punishment differently. In black families, such discipline is typically culturally approved, mild, delivered in a context of parental

African-American parents' disciplinary tactics often include mild physical punishment. Because the practice is culturally approved and delivered in a context of parental warmth, children may view it as an effort to encourage maturity.

warmth, and aimed at helping children become responsible adults. White parents, in contrast, usually consider physical punishment to be wrong, so when they resort to it, they are often highly agitated and rejecting of the child (Dodge, McLoyd, & Lansford, 2006). As a result, most black children may view spanking as a practice carried out with their best interests in mind, whereas white children may regard it as an "act of personal aggression" (Gunnoe & Mariner, 1997, p. 768).

In support of this view, when several thousand ethnically diverse children were followed from preschool through the early school years, spanking was associated with a rise in behavior problems if parents were cold and rejecting

but not if they were warm and supportive (McLoyd & Smith, 2002). In another study, spanking predicted depressive symptoms only among a minority of African-American children whose mothers disapproved of the practice and, as a result, tended to use it when they were highly angry and frustrated (McLoyd et al., 2007).

These findings are not an endorsement of physical punishment. Other forms of discipline, including time out, withdrawal of privileges, and the positive strategies listed on page 495, are far more effective. But it is noteworthy that the meaning and impact of physical discipline vary sharply with its intensity level, context of warmth and support, and cultural approval.

A prevailing American belief is that corporal punishment, if implemented by caring parents, is harmless, perhaps even beneficial. But as the Cultural Influences box above reveals, this assumption is valid only under conditions of limited use in certain social contexts.

Alternatives to Harsh Punishment Alternatives to criticism, slaps, and spankings can help parents avoid the undesirable effects of punishment. A technique called **time out** involves removing children from the immediate setting—for example, by sending them to their rooms—until they are ready to act appropriately. When a child is out of control, a few minutes in time out can be enough to change behavior while also giving angry parents time to cool off (Morawska & Sanders, 2011). Another approach is *withdrawal of privileges*, such as playing outside or watching a favorite TV program. Like time out, removing privileges allows parents to avoid using harsh techniques that can easily intensify into violence.

Although its usefulness is limited, punishment can play a valuable role in moral development. Earlier we noted that mild warnings and disapproval are occasionally necessary to get the child to attend to the parent's inductive message. When parents do decide to use punishment, they can increase its effectiveness in three ways:

- *Consistency.* Permitting children to act inappropriately on some occasions but scolding them on others confuses them, and the unacceptable act persists (Acker & O'Leary, 1996).
- A *warm parent–child relationship.* Children of involved, caring parents find the interruption in parental affection that accompanies punishment especially unpleasant. They want to regain parental warmth and approval as quickly as possible.
- *Explanations.* Providing reasons for mild punishment helps children relate the misdeed to expectations for future behavior. This approach leads to a far greater reduction in misbehavior than using punishment alone (Larzelere et al., 1996).

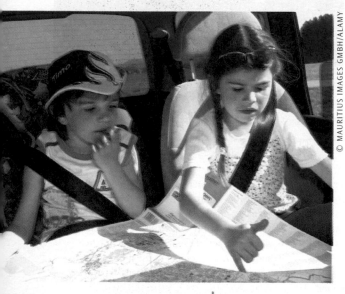

With parental guidance and encouragement, these sisters follow their route on a map during a long car trip. This positive parenting strategy keeps them constructively involved and reduces the likelihood of misbehavior.

Positive Relationships, Positive Parenting The most effective forms of discipline encourage good conduct—by building a mutually respectful bond with the child, letting the child know ahead of time how to act, and praising mature behavior (Zahn-Waxler & Robinson, 1995). When sensitivity, cooperation, and shared positive emotion are evident in joint activities between parents and their toddlers or preschoolers, children show firmer conscience development—expressing empathy after transgressions, behaving responsibly, playing fairly in games, and considering others' welfare (Kochanska et al., 2005, 2008). An early, mutually responsive, pleasurable parent–child tie continues to predict a firmer conscience into the early school years (Kochanska & Murray, 2000). Parent–child closeness leads children to heed parental demands because the child feels a sense of commitment to the relationship.

Consult Applying What We Know on the following page for ways to parent positively. Parents who use these strategies focus on long-term social and life skills—cooperation, problem solving, and consideration for others. As a result, they greatly reduce the need for punishment.

Limitations of "Morality as the Adoption of Societal Norms" Perspective

As previously noted, both psychoanalytic and social learning theories view moral development as a process of adopting societal norms. Personal commitment to societal standards of good conduct is an essential aspect of moral development. Without an internalized, shared moral code and the cultivation of empathy through parental warmth and inductive discipline, people would disregard one another's rights whenever their desires conflicted and would transgress whenever they were unobserved.

But theories that regard morality as entirely a matter of internalizing norms have been criticized because prevailing standards may be at odds with important ethical principles and humanitarian goals. Under these conditions, deliberate violation of norms is not immoral but justifiable and courageous (Appiah, 2010). **TAKE A MOMENT...** Think about historical figures who rose to greatness because they refused to accept certain societal norms. Abraham Lincoln's opposition to slavery, Susan B. Anthony's leadership in the crusade for women's suffrage, and Martin Luther King Jr.'s campaign to end racial prejudice are examples. Can you name others?

With respect to children, parental concern about internalization of societal norms is often accompanied by other goals. At times, parents may accept noncompliance if the child provides a reasonable justification (Kuczynski & Hildebrandt, 1997). Consider a boy who violates a

APPLYING WHAT WE KNOW

Positive Parenting

PRACTICE	EXPLANATION
Use transgressions as opportunities to teach.	When a child engages in harmful or unsafe behavior, intervene firmly, and then use induction, which motivates children to make amends and behave prosocially.
Reduce opportunities for misbehavior.	On long car trips, bring back-seat activities that relieve children's restlessness. At the supermarket, converse with children and let them help with shopping. As a result, children learn to occupy themselves constructively when options are limited.
Provide reasons for rules.	When children appreciate that rules are rational, not arbitrary, they are more likely to strive to follow the rules.
Arrange for children to participate in family routines and duties.	By joining with adults in preparing a meal, washing dishes, or raking leaves, children develop a sense of responsible participation in family and community life and acquire many practical skills.
When children are obstinate, try compromising and problem solving.	When a child refuses to obey, express understanding of the child's feelings ("I know it's not fun to clean up"), suggest a compromise ("You put those away, I'll take care of these"), and help the child think of ways to avoid the problem in the future. Responding firmly but kindly and respectfully increases the likelihood of willing cooperation.
Encourage mature behavior.	Express confidence in children's capacity to learn and appreciation for effort and cooperation: "You gave that your best!" "Thanks for helping!" Adult encouragement fosters pride and satisfaction in succeeding, thereby inspiring children to improve further.
Be sensitive to children's physical and emotional resources.	When children are tired, ill, or bored, they are likely to engage in attention-getting, disorganized, or otherwise improper behavior as a reaction to discomfort. In these instances, meeting the child's needs makes more sense than disciplining.

Sources: Berk, 2001a; Grusec, 2006; Nelson, 1996.

parental prohibition by cutting a cake reserved for a family celebration and giving a piece to a hungry playmate. As the parent begins to reprimand, the boy explains that the playmate had not eaten all day and that the refrigerator was nearly empty, leaving no alternative. In this instance, many parents would value the morality of the boy's claims.

Cognitive-developmental theorists believe that neither identification with parents nor teaching, modeling, and reinforcement are the major means through which children become moral. The cognitive-developmental approach assumes that individuals, rather than internalizing existing rules and expectations, develop morally through **construction**—actively attending to and interrelating multiple perspectives on situations in which social conflicts arise and thereby attaining new moral understandings. In other words, children make moral evaluations and decisions on the basis of concepts they construct about justice and fairness. As these concepts become increasingly adequate with age, children arrive at a deeper understanding of morality—as something that *must be true* in the social world, just as conservation *must be true* in the physical world (Gibbs, 1991, 2010).

In sum, the cognitive-developmental position on morality is unique in its view of the child as a thinking moral being who wonders about right and wrong and searches for moral truth. These theorists regard changes in children's reasoning as the heart of moral development.

© DANITA DELIMONT/ALAMY

Sharing a fruit, these playmates of the Shuar people of Ecuador also reflect on when, with whom, and why they ought to share. According to the cognitive-development perspective, children actively construct concepts of justice and fairness, which become increasingly adequate with age.

ASK YOURSELF

Review ■ Describe evidence indicating that many morally relevant behaviors have roots in our evolutionary history.

Connect ■ Summarize the main features of the psychoanalytic and social learning perspectives on moral development. What shortcomings do these two views share?

Apply ■ Alice and Wayne want their two young children to develop a strong, internalized conscience and to become generous, caring individuals. List some parenting practices that would foster these goals, and explain why each is effective.

Reflect ■ Did you display a strong, internalized conscience as a child? How do you think temperament, parenting practices, family living conditions, and cultural background affected your childhood moral maturity?

▶ Describe and evaluate Piaget's theory of moral development.

▶ Describe Kohlberg's theory of moral development, and discuss research on his stages.

▶ Describe influences on moral reasoning and its relationship to moral behavior.

▶ Discuss challenges to Kohlberg's theory.

▶ How do children distinguish moral imperatives from social conventions and matters of personal choice?

Morality as Social Understanding

According to the cognitive-developmental perspective, cognitive maturity and social experience lead to advances in moral understanding, from a superficial orientation to physical power and external consequences toward a more profound appreciation of interpersonal relationships, societal institutions, and law-making systems (Carpendale, 2009; Gibbs, 1995, 2010). As their grasp of social cooperation expands, children's ideas about what ought to be done when the needs and desires of people conflict also change, toward increasingly just, fair, and balanced solutions to moral problems.

Piaget's Theory of Moral Development

Piaget's (1932/1965) early work on children's moral judgments originally inspired the cognitive-developmental perspective. Using clinical interviews, Piaget questioned 5- to 13-year-old Swiss children about their understanding of rules in the game of marbles. He also told children stories in which characters' intentions to engage in right or wrong action differed from the consequences of their behavior. In the best known of these stories, children were asked which of two boys is naughtier, and why—well-intentioned John, who accidentally breaks 15 cups while on his way to dinner, or ill-intentioned Henry, who breaks a single cup while stealing some jam. From children's responses, Piaget identified two broad stages of moral understanding.

Heteronomous Morality (about 5 to 8 Years) *Heteronomous* means under the authority of another. As the term **heteronomous morality** suggests, children in this first stage view rules as handed down by authorities (God, parents, and teachers), as having a permanent existence, as unchangeable, and as requiring strict obedience. For example, younger children state that the rules of the game of marbles cannot be changed, explaining that "God didn't teach [the new rules]," "you couldn't play any other way," or "it would be cheating. . . . A fair rule is one that is in the game" (Piaget, 1932/1965, pp. 58, 59, 63).

According to Piaget, two factors limit children's moral understanding: (1) cognitive immaturity, especially a limited capacity to imagine other perspectives and **realism**—the tendency to view mental phenomena, including rules, as fixed external features of reality; and (2) the power of adults to insist that children comply, which promotes unquestioning respect for rules and those who enforce them. Together, egocentrism, realism, and adult power result in superficial moral understandings. Younger children think that all people view rules in the same way and that rules are absolutes rather than cooperative principles that can be modified at will. In judging an act's wrongness, they focus on impressive consequences rather than on intent to do harm. For example, in the story about John and Henry mentioned earlier, they regard John as naughtier, despite his innocent intentions, because he broke many more cups.

Morality of Cooperation (about 9 to 10 Years and Older)

Cognitive development, gradual release from adult control, and peer interaction lead children to make the transition to the second stage, **morality of cooperation,** in which they no longer view rules as fixed but see them as flexible, socially agreed-on principles that can be revised to suit the will of the majority. Piaget regarded peer disagreements as especially facilitating. Through them, children realize that people's perspectives on moral action can differ and that intentions, not concrete consequences, should serve as the basis for judging behavior.

Furthermore, as children interact as equals with peers, they learn to settle conflicts in mutually beneficial ways. Gradually, they start to use a standard of fairness called *reciprocity,* in which they express the same concern for the welfare of others as they do for themselves. Piaget found that children start with a crude, tit-for-tat understanding of reciprocity: "You scratch my back, and I'll scratch yours." This defines the beginning of the morality of cooperation. Older children and adolescents move beyond this payback morality to a grasp of the importance of mutuality of expectations, called **ideal reciprocity**—the idea expressed in the Golden Rule: "Do unto others as you would have them do unto you." Ideal reciprocity helps young people realize that rules can be reinterpreted and revised to take individual motives and circumstances into account, thereby ensuring just outcomes for all.

In Piaget's view, peer disagreements facilitate children's transition from heteronomous morality— the belief that rules are absolute and unchangeable—to a morality of cooperation: the understanding that rules are flexible, socially agreed-on principles.

Evaluation of Piaget's Theory

Follow-up research indicates that Piaget's theory accurately describes the general direction of change in moral judgment. With age, outer features, such as physical damage or getting punished, give way to subtler considerations, such as the actor's intentions or the needs and desires of others. Also, much evidence confirms Piaget's conclusion that moral understanding is supported by cognitive maturity, gradual release from adult control, and peer interaction—findings we will consider when we turn to extensions of Piaget's work by Lawrence Kohlberg and his followers. Nevertheless, several aspects of Piaget's theory have been questioned because they underestimate the moral capacities of young children.

Intentions and Moral Judgments

Look back at the story about John and Henry on the previous page. Because bad intentions are paired with little damage and good intentions with a great deal of damage, Piaget's method yields a conservative picture of young children's ability to appreciate intentions. When questioned about moral issues in a way that makes a person's intention as obvious as the harm done, preschool and early school-age children are capable of judging ill-intentioned people as naughtier and more deserving of punishment than well-intentioned ones (Helwig, Zelazo, & Wilson, 2001; Jones & Thomson, 2001).

As further evidence, by age 4, children clearly recognize the difference between two morally relevant intentional behaviors: truthfulness and lying. They approve of telling the truth and disapprove of lying, even when a lie remains undetected (Bussey, 1992). And by age 7 to 8—earlier than suggested by Piaget's findings—children integrate their judgments of lying and truth telling with prosocial and antisocial intentions. They evaluate very negatively certain types of truthfulness—for example, blunt statements, particularly when made in public contexts where they are especially likely to have negative social consequences (telling a friend that you don't like her drawing) (Bussey, 1999; Ma et al., 2011).

Although both Chinese and Canadian schoolchildren consider lying about antisocial acts "very naughty," Chinese children—influenced by collectivist values—more often rate lying favorably when the intention is modesty, as when a student who has thoughtfully picked up litter from the playground says, "I didn't do it" (Lee et al., 1997, 2001). Similarly,

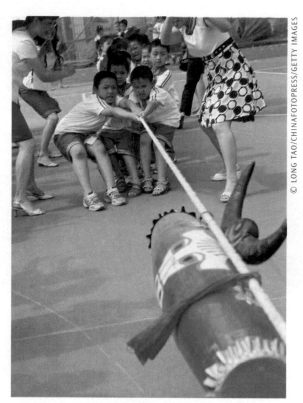

Influenced by collectivist values, Chinese schoolchildren often condone lying when the intention is modesty. These children are likely to say they won a drum-pulling competition because of group effort, even when they know that one or two children deserve most of the credit.

Chinese children are more likely than Canadian children to favor lying to support the group at the expense of the individual (saying you're sick so, as a poor singer, you won't harm your class's chances of winning a singing competition). In contrast, Canadian children more often favor lying to support the individual at the expense of the group (claiming that a friend who is a poor speller is actually a good speller because he wants to represent the class in a spelling competition) (Fu et al., 2007).

Nevertheless, an advanced understanding of the morality of intentions does await the morality of cooperation. Younger children are more likely to *center*, or focus on, salient features and consequences in their judgments, while neglecting and hence failing to integrate other important information. For example, preschoolers more often than older children evaluate lies as always wrong (Peterson, Peterson, & Seeto, 1983). They also judge lies that lead to punishment more negatively than lies that do not (Bussey, 1992). And preschoolers tend to focus on the here-and-now, ignoring a guilt-relevant prior event. Shown a series of pictures depicting one child pushing another off a playground swing and then swinging on it himself, many young children simply declare the perpetrator to be "happy, he's swinging on the swing" (Arsenio, Gold, & Adams, 2006).

Furthermore, through the early school years, children generally interpret statements of intention in a rigid, heteronomous fashion. They believe that once you say you will do something, you are obligated to follow through, even if uncontrollable circumstances (such as an accident) make it difficult or impossible to do so. By age 9 or 10, children realize that not keeping your word is much worse in some situations than in others—namely, when you are able to do so and have permitted another person to count on your actions (Mant & Perner, 1988). In sum, Piaget was partly right and partly wrong about this aspect of moral reasoning.

Reasoning About Authority Research on young children's understanding of authority reveals that they do not regard adults with the unquestioning respect Piaget assumed. Even preschoolers judge certain acts, such as hitting and stealing, to be wrong regardless of the opinions of authorities. When asked to explain, 3- and 4-year-olds express concerns about harming other people rather than obeying adult dictates (Smetana, 1981, 1985).

By age 4, children have differentiated notions about the legitimacy of authority figures, which they refine during the school years. In several studies, children in kindergarten through sixth grade were asked questions designed to assess their view of how broad an adult's authority should be. Almost all denied that adults have general authority (Laupa, 1995). For example, they rejected a principal's right to set rules and issue directives in settings other than his own school.

With respect to nonmoral concerns, such as the rules of a game, children usually base the legitimacy of authority on a person's knowledge, not on social position. And when a directive is fair and caring (for example, telling children to stop fighting or to share candy), children view it as right, regardless of who states it—a principal, a teacher, a class president, or another child. Even among Korean children, whose culture places a high value on respect for and deference to adults, 7- to 11-year-olds evaluate negatively a teacher's or principal's order to keep fighting, to steal, or to refuse to share—a response that strengthens with age (Kim, 1998; Kim & Turiel, 1996).

As these findings reveal, adult status is not required for preschool and school-age children to view someone as an authority. Knowledgeable peers or those who act to protect others' rights are regarded as just as legitimate. But in reasoning about authority, preschool and young elementary school children do tend to place greater weight than older children on power, status, and consequences for disobedience.

Stagewise Progression Many children display both heteronomous and cooperative moral reasoning, raising doubts about whether each Piagetian stage represents a general, unifying organization of moral judgment responses. But to be fair, Piaget (1932/1965) also observed this mixture in children and, therefore, regarded the two moralities as fluid, over-lapping phases rather than tightly knit stages.

Finally, moral development is currently viewed as a more extended process than Piaget believed. Kohlberg's six-stage sequence, to which we turn next, identifies three stages beyond the first appearance of the morality of cooperation. Nevertheless, Kohlberg's theory is a continuation of the research begun by Piaget.

Kohlberg's Extension of Piaget's Theory

Like Piaget, Kohlberg was interested in moral reasoning and used a clinical interviewing procedure to study its development. But whereas Piaget asked children to judge and explain which of two children in a pair of stories was naughtier, Kohlberg used a more open-ended approach: He presented people with hypothetical moral dilemmas and asked what the main actor should do and why.

The Clinical Interview In Kohlberg's *Moral Judgment Interview,* individuals resolve dilemmas that present conflicts between two moral values and justify their decisions. The best-known of these, the "Heinz dilemma," pits the value of obeying the law (not stealing) against the value of human life (saving a dying person):

> In Europe, a woman was near death from cancer. There was one drug that the doctors thought might save her. A druggist in the same town had discovered it, but he was charging ten times what the drug cost him to make. The sick woman's husband, Heinz, went to everyone he knew to borrow the money, but he could only get together half of what it cost. The druggist refused to sell the drug for less or let Heinz pay later. So Heinz got desperate and broke into the man's store to steal the drug for his wife. Should Heinz have done that? Why or why not? (paraphrased from Colby et al., 1983, p. 77)

In addition to explaining their answer, participants are asked to evaluate the conflicting moral values on which the dilemma is based. Scoring of responses is highly intricate and demanding (Gibbs, Basinger, & Grime, 2003; Miller, 2007).

Kohlberg emphasized that it is *the way an individual reasons about the dilemma,* not *the content of the response* (whether or not to steal) that determines moral judgment maturity. Individuals who believe that Heinz should steal the drug and those who think he should not can be found at each of Kohlberg's first four stages. Only at the highest two stages do moral reasoning and content come together in a coherent ethical system, in which individuals agree not only on *why* certain actions are justified but also on *what* people ought to do when facing a moral dilemma (Kohlberg, Levine, & Hewer, 1983). Given a choice between obeying the law and preserving individual rights, the most advanced moral thinkers support individual rights—in the Heinz dilemma, stealing the drug to save a life.

A Questionnaire Approach For more efficient gathering and scoring of moral reasoning, researchers have devised short-answer questionnaires. The most recent, the *Sociomoral Reflection Measure–Short Form (SRM–SF),* poses 11 questions that (like Kohlberg's clinical interview) ask individuals to evaluate the importance of moral values and to reason about them. Here are four of the 11 questions:

- Let's say a friend of yours needs help and may even die, and you're the only person who can save him or her. How important is it for a person (without losing his or her own life) to save the life of a friend?
- What about saving the life of anyone? How important is it for a person (without losing his or her own life) to save the life of a stranger?
- How important is it for people not to take things that belong to other people?
- How important is it for people to obey the law? (Gibbs, Basinger, & Fuller, 1992, pp. 151–152)

After reading each question, participants rate the importance of the value it addresses (as "very important," "important," or "not important") and write a brief explanation of their rating. The explanations are coded according to a revised rendition of Kohlberg's stages. Scores on the SRM–SF correlate well with those obtained from the Moral Judgment Interview and show similar age trends, but they are far less time-consuming to obtain (Basinger, Gibbs, & Fuller, 1995; Gibbs, Basinger, & Grime, 2003; Gibbs et al., 2007).

Kohlberg's Stages of Moral Understanding

In his initial investigation, Kohlberg (1958) extended the age range Piaget studied, including participants who were well into adolescence (10-, 13-, and 16-year-old boys). Then he followed the participants longitudinally, reinterviewing them at three- to four-year intervals over the next 20 years (Colby et al., 1983). Analyzing age-related changes in the boys' moral judgments, Kohlberg generated his six-stage sequence.

As with Piaget's progression of development, Kohlberg's first three stages characterize children as moving from a morality focused on outcomes to one based on ideal reciprocity. Inclusion of older adolescents yielded the fourth stage, in which young people expand their notion of ideal reciprocity to encompass societal rules and laws as vital for ensuring that people treat one another justly. Relying on moral judgment responses of a small minority of adolescents, Kohlberg extended his sequence further, positing a fifth and sixth stage. As we will see, these stages have remained infrequent in subsequent research.

Kohlberg organized his six stages into three general levels and made stronger claims than Piaget about a fixed order of moral change. In doing so, however, Kohlberg drew on characteristics that Piaget used to describe his cognitive stage sequence:

- Kohlberg regarded his moral stages as universal and invariant—a sequence of steps through which people everywhere move in a fixed order.
- He viewed each new stage as building on reasoning of the preceding stage, resulting in a more logically consistent and morally adequate concept of justice.
- He saw each stage as an organized whole—a qualitatively distinct structure of moral thought that a person applies across a wide range of situations (Colby & Kohlberg, 1987).

Furthermore, Kohlberg believed that moral understanding is promoted by the same factors Piaget thought were important for cognitive development: (1) disequilibrium, or actively grappling with moral issues and noticing weaknesses in one's current thinking; and (2) gains in perspective taking, which permit individuals to resolve moral conflicts in increasingly complex and effective ways. **TAKE A MOMENT...** As we examine Kohlberg's developmental sequence and illustrate it with responses to the Heinz dilemma, look for changes in cognition and perspective taking that each stage assumes.

The Preconventional Level. At the **preconventional level,** morality is externally controlled. Children accept the rules of authority figures and judge actions by their consequences. Behaviors that result in punishment are viewed as bad, those that lead to rewards as good.

- *Stage 1: The punishment and obedience orientation.* Children at this stage, while recognizing that others may have different thoughts and feelings, still find it difficult to consider two points of view in a moral dilemma. As a result, they overlook people's intentions. Instead, they focus on fear of authority and avoidance of punishment as reasons for behaving morally.

  Prostealing: "If you let your wife die, you will . . . be blamed for not spending the money to help her, and there'll be an investigation of you and the druggist for your wife's death" (Kohlberg, 1969, p. 381).

  Antistealing: "You shouldn't steal the drug because you'll be caught and sent to jail if you do. If you do get away, [you'd be scared that] the police would catch up with you any minute" (Kohlberg, 1969, p. 381).

- *Stage 2: The instrumental purpose orientation.* Children realize that people can have different perspectives in a moral dilemma, but at first this understanding is concrete. They view right action as flowing from self-interest and understand reciprocity as equal exchange of favors: "You do this for me, and I'll do that for you."

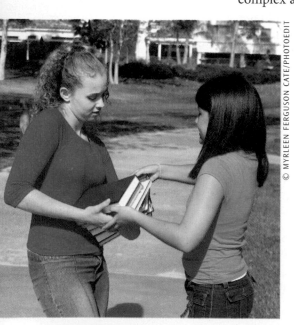

If the child on the right expects a favor in return for helping her friend, she is at Kohlberg's pre-conventional level. If she is motivated by ideal reciprocity, as in the Golden Rule, she has advanced to the conventional level.

© MYRLEEN FERGUSON CATE/PHOTOEDIT

Prostealing: "[I]f Heinz decides to risk jail to save his wife, it's his life he's risking; he can do what he wants with it. And the same goes for the druggist; it's up to him to decide what he wants to do" (Rest, 1979, p. 26).

Antistealing: "[Heinz] is running more risk than it's worth [to save a wife who is near death]" (Rest, 1979, p. 27).

The Conventional Level At the **conventional level,** individuals continue to regard conformity to social rules as important, but not for reasons of self-interest. Rather, they believe that actively maintaining the current social system ensures positive human relationships and societal order.

- *Stage 3: The "good boy–good girl" orientation, or the morality of interpersonal cooperation.* The desire to obey rules because they promote social harmony first appears in the context of close personal ties. Stage 3 individuals want to maintain the affection and approval of friends and relatives by being a "good person"—trustworthy, loyal, respectful, helpful, and nice. The capacity to view a two-person relationship from the vantage point of an impartial, outside observer supports this new approach to morality. At this stage, the individual understands *ideal reciprocity,* as expressed in the Golden Rule.

    Prostealing: "No one will think you're bad if you steal the drug, but your family will think you're an inhuman husband if you don't. If you let your wife die, you'll never be able to look anyone in the face again" (Kohlberg, 1969, p. 381).

    Antistealing: "It isn't just the druggist who will think you're a criminal, everyone else will too. . . . [Y]ou'll feel bad thinking how you brought dishonor on your family and yourself" (Kohlberg, 1969, p. 381).

- *Stage 4: The social-order-maintaining orientation.* At this stage, the individual takes into account a larger perspective—that of societal laws. Moral choices no longer depend on close ties to others. Instead, rules must be enforced in the same evenhanded fashion for everyone, and each member of society has a personal duty to uphold them. The Stage 4 individual believes that laws should be obeyed because they are vital for ensuring societal order and cooperation between people.

    Prostealing: "Heinz has a duty to protect his wife's life; it's a vow he took in marriage. But it's wrong to steal, so he would have to take the drug with the idea of paying the druggist for it and accepting the penalty for breaking the law later."

    Antistealing: "It's a natural thing for Heinz to want to save his wife but . . . Even if his wife is dying, it's still his duty as a citizen to obey the law. . . . If everyone starts breaking the law in a jam, there'd be no civilization, just crime and violence" (Rest, 1979, p. 30).

The Postconventional or Principled Level Individuals at the **postconventional level** move beyond unquestioning support for the laws and rules of their own society. They define morality in terms of abstract principles and values that apply to all situations and societies.

- *Stage 5: The social-contract orientation.* At Stage 5, individuals regard laws and rules as flexible instruments for furthering human purposes. They can imagine alternatives to their own social order, and they emphasize fair procedures for interpreting and changing the law. When laws are consistent with individual rights and the interests of the majority, each person follows them because of a *social-contract orientation*—free and willing participation in the system because it brings about more good for people than if it did not exist.

    Prostealing: "Although there is a law against stealing, the law wasn't meant to violate a person's right to life. . . . If Heinz is prosecuted for stealing, the law needs to be reinterpreted to take into account situations in which it goes against people's natural right to keep on living."

    Antistealing: At this stage, there are no antistealing responses.

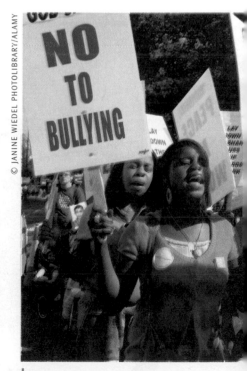

© JANINE WIEDEL PHOTOLIBRARY/ALAMY

Protestors in London march with families of teenage victims of bullying. In imagining an end to social ills, these young people convey a principled level of maturity.

- *Stage 6: The universal ethical principle orientation.* At this highest stage, right action is defined by self-chosen ethical principles of conscience that are valid for all humanity, regardless of law and social agreement. Stage 6 individuals typically mention such abstract principles as equal consideration of the claims of all human beings and respect for the worth and dignity of each person.

> *Prostealing:* "It doesn't make sense to put respect for property above respect for life itself. [People] could live together without private property at all. Respect for human life and personality is absolute, and accordingly [people] have a mutual duty to save one another from dying" (Rest, 1979, p. 37).

> *Antistealing:* At this stage, there are no antistealing responses.

Research on Kohlberg's Stages

Kohlberg's original research and other longitudinal studies using hypothetical dilemmas provide the most convincing evidence for his stage sequence. With few exceptions, individuals move through the first four stages in the predicted order (Boom, Wouters, & Keller, 2007; Colby et al., 1983; Dawson, 2002; Walker, 1989; Walker & Taylor, 1991b).

A striking finding is that development of moral reasoning, whether assessed longitudinally or cross-sectionally, with the Moral Judgment Interview or the SRM–SF, and in diverse Western industrialized or non-Western village cultures, is slow and gradual (Colby et al., 1983; Gibbs et al., 2007; Snarey, 1985). Reasoning at Stages 1 and 2 decreases from late childhood to early adolescence, while Stage 3 reasoning increases through mid-adolescence and then declines. Stage 4 reasoning rises over the teenage years until, among college-educated young adults, it is the typical response. Few people move beyond Stage 4. As noted earlier, postconventional morality is so rare that no clear evidence exists that Kohlberg's Stage 6 actually follows Stage 5.

Are Kohlberg's Stages Organized Wholes? TAKE A MOMENT... Think of an actual moral dilemma you faced recently. How did you solve it? Did your reasoning fall at the same stage as your thinking about the Heinz dilemma? If each of Kohlberg's stages forms an organized whole, then individuals should use the same level of moral reasoning across many tasks and situations—for everyday moral problems as well as for hypothetical dilemmas. In fact, real-life conflicts, such as whether to continue helping a friend who is taking advantage of you, often elicit moral reasoning below a person's actual capacity because they involve practical considerations and mix cognition with intense emotion (Carpendale, 2000). Although adolescents and adults still mention reasoning as their most frequent strategy for resolving these dilemmas, they also refer to other strategies—talking through issues with others, relying on intuition, and calling on religious and spiritual ideas. And they report feeling drained, confused, and torn by temptation—an emotional side of moral judgment not tapped by hypothetical situations, which evoke the upper limits of moral thought because they allow reflection without the interference of personal risk (Walker, 2004).

The influence of situational factors on moral reasoning indicates that, like Piaget's cognitive and moral stages, Kohlberg's moral stages are loosely organized and overlapping. Rather than developing in a neat, stepwise fashion, people draw on a range of moral responses that vary with context. With age, this range shifts upward as less mature moral reasoning is gradually replaced by more advanced moral thought.

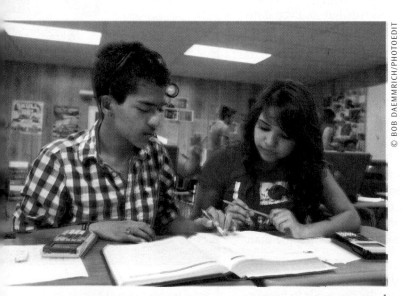

© BOB DAEMMRICH/PHOTOEDIT

Should the student on the left continue to collaborate on an assignment with his classmate after realizing that he is doing nearly all the work? Such real-life moral dilemmas mix cognition with intense emotion.

Cognitive Influences on Moral Reasoning As Kohlberg anticipated, moral maturity is positively correlated with IQ, performance on Piagetian cognitive tasks, and per-

spective-taking skill (Krebs & Gilmore, 1982; Lickona, 1976; Selman, 1976; Walker & Hennig, 1997). Kohlberg's stage sequence also makes sense to adolescents and adults who have not studied his theory—findings that support the vital contribution of cognitive development to moral maturity. When Russian high school and Dutch university students were asked to sort statements typical of Kohlberg's stages, they tended to rank reasoning at each consecutive stage as more sophisticated. But beyond their own current stage, they had difficulty ordering statements; the higher the stage, the more participants disagreed in their rankings (Boom, Brugman, & van der Heijden, 2001).

At the same time, Kohlberg argued that cognitive and perspective-taking attainments are not sufficient to ensure moral advances, which also require reorganization of thought unique to the moral domain. But so far, the domain in which the cognitive ingredients required for more mature moral judgment first emerges—cognitive, social, or moral—remains unclear. In Chapters 6 and 7, we encountered a wealth of evidence indicating that children display more advanced reasoning on tasks with which they have more extensive experience. Young people who frequently grapple with social and moral issues may actually construct the cognitive supports for moral development directly—while reasoning about social or moral concerns (Carpendale, 2009; Gibbs, 2010).

Are There Sex Differences in Moral Reasoning?

As we have seen, real-life moral dilemmas highlight the role of emotion in moral judgment. Return to Leisl's moral reasoning in the opening to this chapter and notice how her argument focuses on caring and commitment to others. Carol Gilligan (1982) is the best-known of those who have argued that Kohlberg's theory—originally formulated on the basis of interviews with males—does not adequately represent the morality of girls and women. Gilligan believes that feminine morality emphasizes an "ethic of care" that Kohlberg's system devalues. Leisl's reasoning falls at Kohlberg's Stage 3 because it is based on mutual trust and affection. In contrast, Stages 4 to 6 emphasize justice—an abstract, rational commitment to moral ideals. According to Gilligan, a concern for others is a *different* but no less valid basis for moral judgment than a focus on impersonal rights.

Many studies have tested Gilligan's claim that Kohlberg's approach underestimates the moral maturity of females, and most do not support it (Turiel, 2006; Walker, 2006). On hypothetical dilemmas, everyday moral problems, and the SMR–SF, adolescent and adult females display reasoning at the same stage as their male counterparts and often at a higher stage. Themes of justice and caring appear in the responses of both sexes, and when girls do raise interpersonal concerns, they are not downgraded in Kohlberg's system (Jaffee & Hyde, 2000; Walker, 1995). Rather, many studies report that girls shift from Stage 2 to Stage 3 reasoning earlier than boys (Gibbs et al., 2007). These findings suggest that although Kohlberg emphasized justice rather than caring as the highest of moral ideals, his theory taps both sets of values.

This teenager takes pleasure in helping her grandmother with everyday tasks. Adolescents of both sexes express themes of justice and caring in their moral responses, but females appear to emphasize care, especially when reasoning about real-life dilemmas.

Nevertheless, some evidence indicates that although the morality of males and females includes both orientations, females tend to stress care, or empathic perspective taking, whereas males either stress justice or focus equally on justice and care (Jaffee & Hyde, 2000; Wark & Krebs, 1996; Weisz & Black, 2002). This difference in emphasis, which appears more often in real life than in hypothetical dilemmas, may reflect women's greater involvement in daily activities involving care and concern for others.

Indeed, both cultural and situational contexts profoundly affect use of a care orientation. In one study, U.S. and Canadian 17- to 26-year-old females showed more complex reasoning about care issues than their male counterparts. But Norwegian males were just as advanced

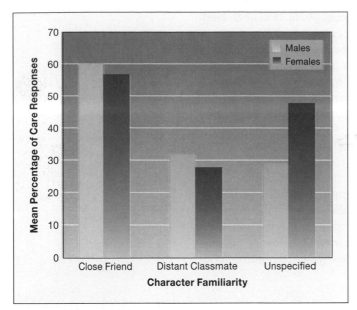

FIGURE 12.3 Relationship of familiarity of the main character in a moral dilemma to care responses. Both male and female university students gave more care responses when considering a close friend than a distant classmate. Sex differences appeared only in the unspecified condition, where females may have assumed greater familiarity. (From M. K. Ryan, B. David, & K. J. Reynolds, 2004, "Who Cares? The Effect of Gender and Context on the Self and Moral Reasoning," *Psychology of Women Quarterly, 28,* 246–255. Copyright © 2004 by the American Psychological Association. Reprinted by permission of the American Psychological Association.)

as Norwegian females in care-based understanding (Skoe, 1998). Perhaps Norwegian culture, which explicitly endorses gender equality, induces boys and men to think deeply about interpersonal obligations. And in an Australian investigation, researchers presented university students with one of three versions of a moral dilemma, in which the main character varied in familiarity: (1) a close friend in class, (2) a person "known only vaguely" from class, or (3) a classmate whose relationship was unspecified (Ryan, David, & Reynolds, 2004). When asked whether they would permit the character who was in danger of failing the course to borrow a copy of their recently completed assignment despite risk of cheating, both male and female participants gave more care responses when considering a close friend than a socially distant classmate. As Figure 12.3 shows, gender differences emerged only in the unspecified condition, where women—who tend to forge closer relationships—may have assumed greater familiarity.

In sum, current evidence indicates that justice and caring are not gender-specific moralities. Perhaps Piaget (1932/1965) himself said it best: "Between the more refined forms of justice . . . and love properly so called, there is no longer any real conflict" (p. 324).

Influences on Moral Reasoning

Many factors affect maturity of moral reasoning, including the young person's personality and a wide range of social experiences—child-rearing practices, peer interaction, schooling, and aspects of culture. Growing evidence suggests that, as Kohlberg believed, these experiences work in two ways: They encourage young people to take the perspective of others, and they present cognitive challenges, which stimulate young people to think about moral problems in more complex ways.

Personality A flexible, open-minded approach to new information and experiences is linked to gains in moral reasoning, just as it is to identity development (Hart et al., 1998; Matsuba & Walker, 1998). Because open-minded young people are more socially skilled, they have more opportunities for social participation. A richer social life enhances exposure to others' perspectives, and open-mindedness helps adolescents derive moral insights from that exposure. In contrast, adolescents who have difficulty adapting to new experiences are less likely to be interested in others' moral ideas and justifications.

Child-Rearing Practices Child-rearing practices associated with mature moral reasoning combine warmth, exchange of ideas, and appropriate demands for maturity. Children and adolescents who gain most in moral understanding have parents who engage in moral discussions, encourage prosocial behavior, insist that others be treated respectfully and fairly, and create a supportive atmosphere by listening sensitively, asking clarifying questions, and presenting higher-level reasoning (Carlo et al., 2011; Pratt, Skoe, & Arnold, 2004; Wyatt & Carlo, 2002). In one study, 11-year-olds were asked what they thought an adult would say to justify a moral rule, such as not lying, stealing, or breaking a promise. Those with warm, demanding, communicative parents were far more likely than their agemates to point to the importance of ideal reciprocity: "I trusted you," "You wouldn't like it if I did it to you" (Leman, 2005). In contrast, when parents lecture, use threats, or make sarcastic remarks, children show little or no change in moral reasoning over time (Walker & Taylor, 1991a).

In sum, parents who facilitate moral understanding are affectionate, verbal, and rational and promote a cooperative style of family life. Notice that these are the very characteristics, discussed earlier in this chapter, that foster moral internalization in young children.

Schooling For the most part, moral reasoning advances in late adolescence and early adulthood only as long as a person remains in school (Dawson et al., 2003; Gibbs et al., 2007). Higher education introduces young people to social issues that extend beyond personal relationships to entire political and cultural groups. Consistent with this idea, college students who report more perspective-taking opportunities (for example, classes that emphasize open discussion of opinions, friendships with others of different cultural backgrounds) and who indicate that they have become more aware of social diversity tend to be advanced in moral reasoning (Comunian & Gielen, 2006; Mason & Gibbs, 1993a, 1993b).

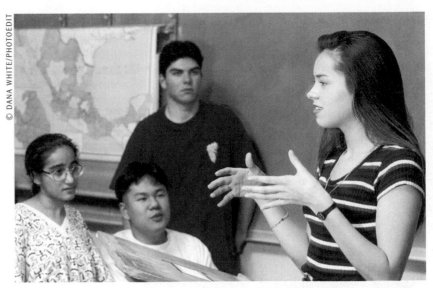

Through opportunities to discuss ideas with culturally diverse peers, these high school students gain in perspective taking and moral understanding.

Peer Interaction Research supports Piaget's belief that interaction among peers who present differing viewpoints promotes moral understanding. When young people negotiate and compromise, they realize that social life can be based on cooperation between equals rather than on authority relations (Killen & Nucci, 1995). Adolescents who report more close friendships and who more often participate in conversations with their friends are advanced in moral reasoning (Schonert-Reichl, 1999). The mutuality and intimacy of friendship, which foster decisions based on consensual agreement, may be particularly important for moral development. Furthermore, recall from Chapter 11 that intergroup contact—cross-race friendships and interactions in schools and communities—reduces racial and ethnic prejudice. It also affects young people morally, strengthening their conviction that race-based and other forms of peer exclusion are wrong (Crystal, Killen, & Ruck, 2008).

Peer discussions and role-playing of moral problems have provided the basis for interventions aimed at improving high school and college students' moral understanding. For these interventions to be effective, young people must be highly engaged—confronting, critiquing, and attempting to clarify one another's viewpoints (Berkowitz & Gibbs, 1983; Comunian & Gielen, 2006). And because moral development occurs gradually, many peer interaction sessions over weeks or months typically are needed to produce moral change.

Culture Individuals in industrialized nations move through Kohlberg's stages more rapidly and advance to a higher level than individuals in village societies, who rarely move beyond Stage 3. One explanation of these cultural differences is that in village societies, moral cooperation is based on direct relations between people and does not allow for the development of advanced moral understanding (Stages 4 to 6), which depends on appreciating the role of larger social structures, such as laws and government institutions, in resolving moral conflict (Gibbs et al., 2007).

In support of this view, in cultures where young people participate in the institutions of their society at early ages, moral reasoning is advanced. For example, on *kibbutzim,* small but technologically complex agricultural settlements in Israel, children receive training in the governance of their community in middle childhood. By third grade, they mention more concerns about societal laws and rules when discussing moral conflicts than do Israeli city-reared or U.S. children (Fuchs et al., 1986). During adolescence and adulthood, a greater percentage of kibbutz than American individuals reach Kohlberg's Stages 4 and 5 (Snarey, Reimer, & Kohlberg, 1985).

A second possible reason for cultural variation is that responses to moral dilemmas in collectivist cultures (including village societies) are often more other-directed than in Western Europe and North America (Miller, 2007). In both village and industrialized societies that highly value interdependency, statements portraying the individual as vitally connected to the social group are common. In one study, both male and female Japanese adolescents, who

© EARL & NAZIMA KOWALL/CORBIS

These adolescents living in a village in China's Pamir Mountains view moral cooperation as based on direct relations between people. Their moral reasoning is likely to emphasize a close connection between individual and group responsibility.

almost always integrate care- and justice-based reasoning, placed greater weight on caring, which they regarded as a communal responsibility. As one boy remarked, *yasashii* (kindness/gentleness) and *omoiyari* (empathy) are "something 'normal' that everyone shows" (Shimizu, 2001). Similarly, in research conducted in India, even highly educated people (expected to have attained Kohlberg's Stages 4 and 5) viewed solutions to moral dilemmas as the responsibility of the entire society, not of a single person (Miller & Bersoff, 1995).

These findings raise the question of whether Kohlberg's highest level represents a culturally specific way of thinking—one limited to Western societies that emphasize individual rights and an appeal to an inner, private conscience. At the same time, a review of over 100 studies confirmed an age-related trend consistent with Kohlberg's Stages 1 to 4 in more than 40 societies (Gibbs et al., 2007; Snarey, 1985). A common morality of justice and care is clearly evident in the responses of people from vastly different cultures.

Moral Reasoning and Behavior

A central assumption of the cognitive-developmental perspective is that moral understanding should affect moral motivation. As young people grasp the moral "logic" of human social cooperation, they are upset when this logic is violated. As a result, they realize that behaving in line with one's thinking is vital for creating and maintaining a just social world (Blasi, 1994; Gibbs, 2010). Consistent with this idea, higher-stage adolescents more often act prosocially by helping, sharing, and defending victims of injustice and by volunteering in their communities (Carlo et al., 1996, 2011; Comunian & Gielen, 2000, 2006). Also, they less often engage in cheating, aggression, and other antisocial or delinquent behaviors (Raaijmakers, Engels, & Van Hoof, 2005; Stams et al., 2006).

Yet the connection between more mature moral reasoning and action is only modest. As we have seen, moral behavior is influenced by many factors besides cognition, including the emotions of empathy, sympathy, and guilt; individual differences in temperament; and a long history of cultural experiences and intuitions that affect moral choice and decision making (Haidt & Kesebir, 2010). *Moral identity* (refer back to page 489) also affects moral behavior (Hardy & Carlo, 2011). When moral goals are personally important, individuals are more likely to feel obligated to act on their moral judgments. In a study of low-SES African-American and Hispanic teenagers, those who emphasized moral traits and goals in their self-descriptions displayed exceptional levels of community service, but they did not differ from their agemates in moral reasoning (Hart & Fegley, 1995). That a synthesis of moral concern with sense of self can motivate moral action is also supported by a study of moral exemplars who have made outstanding contributions to such causes as civil rights, medical ethics, and religious freedom. Interview responses revealed that their most distinguishing characteristic is "seamless integration" of moral vision with personal identity (Colby & Damon, 1992, p. 309).

Researchers have begun to identify the origins of moral identity in hopes of capitalizing on it to promote moral commitment. As we saw earlier in this chapter, child-rearing practices—inductive discipline and clearly conveyed moral expectations—augment adolescents' moral identity. Strengthening moral self-perceptions at an early age may be a powerful way to increase the chances that moral cognitions are realized in behavior. In longitudinal research, firm conscience development (as measured by internalization of parents' rules) and empathic concern to mother's distress (a hurt finger) during the preschool years predicted strong moral self-perceptions at age 5, which—in turn—positively predicted children's competent, prosocial, rule-abiding behavior at age 6½ (Kochanska et al., 2010). Parenting strategies that launch conscience development and empathy on an early, favorable path may contribute vitally, in the long term, to moral identity and action.

Another possibility is that *just educational environments*—in which teachers guide students in democratic decision making and rule setting, resolving disputes civilly, and taking responsibility for others' welfare—enhance moral commitment (Atkins, Hart, & Donnelly, 2004). In one study, tenth graders who reported fair teacher treatment were more likely than those who had experienced unjust treatment (an unfair detention or a lower grade than they deserved) to regard excluding a peer on the basis of race as a moral transgression (Crystal, Killen, & Ruck, 2010). A compassionate and just school climate may be particularly important for poverty-stricken ethnic minority children and adolescents. For many such students, meaningful participation in their school community may be the crucial factor that prevents them from pessimistically concluding that prejudice and diminished opportunity are pervasive in society and, therefore, insurmountable (Hart & Atkins, 2002).

Schools can also expand students' opportunities to experience and explore moral emotions, thoughts, and actions by promoting civic engagement. As the Social Issues: Education box on page 508 reveals, encouraging civic responsibility in young people can help them see the connection between their personal interests and the public interest—an insight that may foster all aspects of morality.

LOOK and LISTEN

Would you characterize your high school as a *just educational environment?* Cite specific features and experiences that may have contributed to students' moral development and civic engagement.

Religious Involvement and Moral Development

Recall that in resolving real-life moral dilemmas, many people express notions of religion and spirituality. For these individuals, morality and spirituality are inseparable; their moral values, judgments, and behaviors are deeply embedded in their faith.

Religion is especially important in U.S. family life. In recent national polls, nearly two-thirds of Americans reported actively practicing religion, compared with one-half of those in Canada, one-third of those in Great Britain and Italy, and even fewer elsewhere in Europe (CIA, 2009; Gallup News Service, 2006; Jones, 2003). People who are affiliated with a church, synagogue, or mosque and who regularly attend religious services include many parents with children. By middle childhood, children have begun to formulate religious and spiritual ideas that are remarkably complex and that serve as moral forces in their lives.

National survey findings reveal that 81 percent of U.S. teenagers identify with one religion, and an additional 3 percent with two religions (Smith & Denton, 2005). During adolescence, formal religious involvement declines—among U.S. youths, from 55 percent at ages 13 to 15 to 40 percent at ages 17 to 18 (Donahue & Benson, 1995; Kerestes & Youniss, 2003). The drop coincides with increased autonomy and efforts to construct a personally meaningful religious identity—a task usually not complete until the late teens or twenties (Hunsberger, Pratt, & Pancer, 2001).

These young choir members, who are part of a religious community, are likely to be advantaged in moral values and behavior compared with nonaffiliated peers.

But adolescents who remain part of a religious community are advantaged in moral values and behavior. Compared with nonaffiliated youths, they are more involved in community service activities aimed at helping the less fortunate (Kerestes, Youniss, & Metz, 2004). And religious involvement promotes responsible academic and social behavior and discourages misconduct (Dowling et al., 2004). It is associated with lower levels of drug and alcohol use, early sexual activity, and delinquency (Regnerus, Smith, & Fritsch, 2003).

A variety of factors probably contribute to these favorable outcomes. In a study of inner-city high school students, religiously involved adolescents were more likely to report trusting relationships with parents, adults, and friends who hold similar worldviews. The more activities they shared with this network, the higher they scored in empathic concern and prosocial behavior (King & Furrow, 2004). Furthermore, religious education and youth activities directly teach concern for others and provide opportunities for moral discussions and civic engagement. And adolescents who feel connected to a higher being may develop

SOCIAL ISSUES: EDUCATION

Development of Civic Responsibility

On Thanksgiving Day, Jill, Todd, and Brett joined their parents at a soup kitchen to serve a holiday dinner to poverty-stricken people. Throughout the year, Jill and Brett volunteered on Saturday mornings at a nursing home, conversing with bedridden elders. During a congressional election campaign, the three teenagers raised questions about issues at special youth meetings with candidates. At school, Todd and his girlfriend formed an organization devoted to promoting ethnic and racial tolerance.

These young people show a strong sense of *civic responsibility*—a complex combination of cognition, emotion, and behavior. Civic responsibility involves knowledge of political issues, a desire to make a difference in the community, and skills for achieving civic goals, such as how to resolve differing views fairly and conduct meetings so that all participants have a voice (Flanagan & Faison, 2001).

When young people engage in community service that exposes them to people in need or to public issues, they are especially likely to express a commitment to future service. And youth volunteers—who tend to be advanced in moral reasoning—gain further in moral maturity as a result of participating (Gibbs et al., 2007; Hart, Atkins, & Donnelly, 2006). Family, school, and community experiences contribute to adolescents' civic responsibility.

Family Influences

Teenagers whose parents encourage them to form opinions about controversial issues are more knowledgeable about civic issues and better able to see them from more than one perspective (Santoloupo & Pratt, 1994). Also, adolescents whose parents engage in community service and stress compassion tend to hold socially responsible values. When asked what causes unemployment or poverty, they more often mention situational and societal factors (lack of education, government policies, or the state of the economy) than individual factors (low intelligence or personal problems). Youths who endorse situational and societal causes, in turn, have more altruistic life goals, such as working to eradicate poverty or to preserve the earth for future generations (Flanagan & Tucker, 1999). And they engage in more civic activities into early adulthood (Zaff, Malanchuk, & Eccles, 2008).

School and Community Influences

A democratic climate at school, in which teachers promote discussion of controversial issues while insisting that students listen to and respect one another, fosters knowledge and critical analysis of political concerns and commitment to social causes (Torney-Purta, Barber, & Wilkenfeld, 2007). Furthermore, high school students who view their community as one in which adults care about youths and work to make the community better report higher levels of civic participation (Kahne & Sporte, 2008). Participation in nonsport extracurricular activities at school and in youth organizations is also associated with civic commitment persisting into adulthood (Obradović & Masten, 2007).

Two aspects of these involvements seem to account for their lasting impact. First, they introduce adolescents to the vision and skills required for mature civic engagement. Within student government, special-interest organizations, and other groups, young people see how their actions affect the wider school and community. They realize that collectively they can achieve results greater than any one person can achieve alone. And they learn to work together, balancing strong convictions with compromise (Atkins, Hart, & Donnelly, 2004; Kirshner, 2009). Second, while producing a weekly newspaper, participating in a dramatic production, or implementing a service project, young people explore political and moral ideals. Often they redefine their identities to include a responsibility to combat others' misfortunes (Wheeler, 2002).

The power of family, school, and community to promote civic responsibility may lie in discussions, educational practices, and activities that jointly foster moral thought, emotion, and behavior. In a comparison of nationally representative samples of 14-year-olds in 28 nations, U.S. young people excelled at community

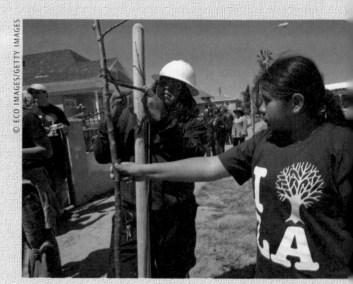

For this young teenager in Los Angeles, planting a tree during an Earth Day celebration promotes a sense of civic responsibility—an effect that may persist into adulthood.

service, with 50 percent reporting membership in organizations devoted to volunteering (Torney-Purta, 2002).

Currently, 66 percent of U.S. public schools provide students with community service opportunities. Nearly half of these schools have *service-learning programs*, which integrate service activities into the academic curriculum, and about one-third of students enroll. High school students who are required to serve their communities express as strong a desire to remain engaged as do students who volunteer. And when they reach early adulthood, they are equally likely to vote and to participate in community organizations (Hart et al., 2007; Metz & Youniss, 2005).

Still, most U.S. schools offering service learning do not have policies encouraging or mandating such programs (Scales & Roehlkepartain, 2004). Furthermore, low-SES, inner-city youths—although they express high interest in social justice and contributing to society—score substantially lower than higher-SES youths in civic knowledge and participation (Balsano, 2005). A broad societal commitment to fostering civic character must pay special attention to supportive school and community experiences for these young people, so their eagerness to make a difference can be realized.

certain inner strengths, including prosocial values and a strong moral identity, that help them resolve real-life moral dilemmas maturely and translate their thinking into action (Hardy & Carlo, 2005; Sherrod & Spiewak, 2008).

Because most teenagers, regardless of formal affiliation, identify with a religious denomination and say they believe in a higher being, religious institutions may be uniquely suited to foster moral and prosocial commitments and discourage risky behaviors (Bridges & Moore, 2002). For youths in inner-city neighborhoods with few alternative sources of social support, outreach by religious institutions can lead to life-altering involvement (Jang & Johnson, 2001). An exception arises in religious cults, where rigid indoctrination into the group's beliefs, suppression of individuality, and estrangement from society all work against moral maturity (Richmond, 2004).

Further Challenges to Kohlberg's Theory

Although much support exists for Kohlberg's theory, it continues to face challenges. The most important of these concern Kohlberg's conception of moral maturity, the applicability of his stage model to moral reasoning and behavior in everyday life, and the appropriateness of his stages for characterizing children's moral reasoning.

A key controversy has to do with Kohlberg's belief that moral maturity is not achieved until the postconventional level. Yet if people had to reach Stages 5 and 6 to be truly morally mature, few individuals anywhere would measure up! John Gibbs (1991, 2010) argues that "postconventional morality" should not be viewed as the standard of maturity against which other levels are judged. Gibbs finds maturity in a revised understanding of Stages 3 and 4 that emphasizes ideal reciprocity. These stages are not "conventional," or based on social conformity, as Kohlberg assumed. Instead, they require profound moral constructions—an understanding of ideal reciprocity as the basis for relationships between people (Stage 3) and for widely accepted moral standards, set forth in rules and laws (Stage 4).

According to Gibbs (2010), "postconventional" moral reasoning is part of a highly reflective, metacognitive endeavor in which people grapple with existential issues: What is the meaning of life? Why be moral? Most people who contemplate such questions have attained advanced education, usually in philosophy—which sheds light on why Stages 5 and 6 are so rare. Occasionally, however, as a result of soul-searching life crises, life-threatening events, or spiritual awakenings, adolescents and adults without formal training in philosophy generate ethical insights into the meaning of existence—transformations that may heighten their resolve to lead a moral life. As a result, Gibbs notes, "postconventional" moral judgment is sometimes seen as early as adolescence, when young people first become capable of the formal operational and perspective-taking capacities needed to engage in it.

A more radical challenge comes from Dennis Krebs and Kathy Denton (2005), who claim that Kohlberg's theory inadequately accounts for morality in everyday life. Pointing to wide variability in maturity of moral reasoning across situations, these researchers favor abandoning Kohlberg's stages for a *pragmatic approach to morality*. They assert that each person makes moral judgments at varying levels of maturity, depending on the individual's current context and motivations: Conflict over a business deal is likely to evoke Stage 2 (instrumental purpose) reasoning, a friendship or marital dispute Stage 3 (ideal reciprocity) reasoning, and a breach of contract Stage 4 (social-order-maintaining) reasoning (Krebs et al., 1991). According to Krebs and Denton, everyday moral judgments—rather than being efforts to arrive at just solutions—are practical tools that people use to achieve their goals. To benefit personally, they often must advocate cooperation with others. But many people act first and then invoke moral judgments to rationalize their actions, regardless of whether the behavior is self-centered or altruistic (Haidt, 2001; Haidt & Kesebir, 2010). And sometimes people use moral judgments for immoral purposes—for example, to excuse their transgressions, blame others, or attract unmerited admiration. This pragmatism of moral reasoning, Krebs and Denton argue, is responsible for the lack of a strong association between moral judgment maturity and behavior.

Do people strive to resolve moral dilemmas in the fairest way possible, using the most advanced reasoning of which they are capable, only when presented with hypothetical dilemmas or real-life conflicts in which they are not personally involved? Gibbs (2006) points out that despite their mixed motives in everyday situations, people often rise above self-gratification to support others' rights. For example, moral exemplars in business—rather than yielding to Stage 2 reasoning—endorse the importance of trust, integrity, good faith, and just laws and codes of conduct (Damon, 2004). Furthermore, the pragmatic approach fails to recognize people's awareness of the greater adequacy of higher-stage moral judgments, which some individuals act on despite highly corrupt environments. And people who engage in sudden altruistic action may have previously considered the relevant moral issues so thoroughly that their cognitive structures activate automatically, inducing an immediate response (Gibbs et al., 2009a; Pizarro & Bloom, 2003). In these instances, individuals who appear to be engaging in after-the-fact rationalization are actually behaving with great forethought.

Finally, Kohlberg's stages tell us much more about moral understanding in adolescence and adulthood than in early and middle childhood. Nancy Eisenberg created dilemmas relevant to children's everyday lives that pit satisfying one's own desires against acting prosocially—for example, going to a birthday party versus taking time to help an injured peer and missing the party as a result (Eisenberg, 1986; Eisenberg et al., 1991, 1995). She found that children's *prosocial moral reasoning* is more advanced than Kohlberg's stages suggest. Furthermore, empathic perspective taking strengthens prosocial moral thought and its realization in everyday behavior (Eisenberg, Fabes, & Spinrad, 2006; Eisenberg, Zhoe, & Koller, 2001).

In sum, because Kohlberg focused on young children's tendency to center on prominent external features in their social world, he underestimated their potential for deeper moral understanding. In the following sections, we consider additional evidence on both child and adolescent moral reasoning.

The Domain Approach to Moral Understanding

Researchers taking a *domain approach to moral understanding* focus on children's developing capacity to distinguish and coordinate **moral imperatives,** which protect people's rights and welfare, from two other types of social rules and expectations: **social conventions,** customs determined solely by consensus, such as table manners and rituals of social interaction (saying "hello," "please," "thank you"); and **matters of personal choice,** such as friends, hairstyle, and leisure activities, which do not violate rights and are up to the individual (Killen, Margie, & Sinno, 2006; Nucci, 1996; Smetana, 2006). According to domain theorists, children construct these systems of social knowledge out of their experiences with three types of regularities in their social world (Turiel, 2006). And research reveals that children arrive at these distinctions early, displaying more advanced moral reasoning than assumed by the externally controlled vision of Kohlberg's preconventional morality.

Moral versus Social-Conventional Distinctions Interviews with 3- and 4-year-olds reveal that they judge moral violations (unprovoked hitting, stealing an apple) as more wrong than violations of social conventions (eating ice cream with your fingers). They also say that moral violations would be wrong regardless of the setting—for example, in another country or school. And they indicate that moral (but not social-conventional) transgressions would be wrong even if an authority figure did not see them and no rules existed to prohibit them (Smetana, 2006; Yan & Smetana, 2003).

How do young children arrive at these distinctions? According to Elliott Turiel (2006), they do so by reflecting on their everyday social relations. They observe that after a moral offense, peers respond with strong negative emotion, describe their own injury or loss, tell another child to stop, or retaliate (Arsenio & Fleiss, 1996). And an adult who intervenes is likely to call attention to the victim's rights and feelings. Violations of social convention elicit less intense peer reactions. And in these situations, adults usually demand obedience without explanation or point to the importance of keeping order.

But while realizing that moral transgressions are worse than social-conventional violations, preschool and young school-age children (as Piaget pointed out) tend to reason rigidly and superficially *within* the moral domain, making judgments based on salient features and consequences while neglecting other important information. They claim that stealing and lying are always wrong, even when a person has a morally sound reason for doing so (Lourenco, 2003). Their explanations for why hitting others is wrong, even in the absence of rules against hitting, are simplistic and centered on physical harm—for example, "When you get hit, it hurts, and you start to cry" (Nucci, 2008). And their focus on outcomes means that they fail to realize that a promise is still a promise, even if it is unfulfilled (Maas, 2008; Maas & Abbeduto, 2001).

As they construct a flexible appreciation of moral rules, children clarify and link moral imperatives and social conventions. Gradually their understanding becomes more complex, taking into account an increasing number of variables, including the purpose of the rule; people's intentions, knowledge, and beliefs; and the context of people's behavior. School-age children, for example, distinguish social conventions with a clear *purpose* (not running in school hallways to prevent injuries) from ones with no obvious justification (crossing a "forbidden" line on the playground). They regard violations of purposeful conventions as closer to moral transgressions (Buchanan-Barrow & Barrett, 1998).

With age, children also realize that people's *intentions* and the *context* of their actions affect the moral implications of violating a social convention. In a Canadian study, many 6-year-olds

Wearing a short, tight dress is a matter of personal choice to this teenager. But as her mother may point out, wearing the dress to a religious service would violate social conventions and potentially offend other congregants, yielding moral implications.

always disapproved of flag burning, citing its physical consequences. But 8- to 10-year-olds made subtle distinctions, stating that because of a flag's symbolic value, burning it to express disapproval of a country or to start a cooking fire is worse than burning it accidentally. They also stated that public flag burning is worse than private flag burning because it inflicts emotional harm on others. But they recognized that burning a flag is a form of freedom of expression, and most agreed that it would be acceptable in a country that treated its citizens unfairly (Helwig & Prencipe, 1999).

In addition, school-age children appreciate that people whose *knowledge* differs may not be equally responsible for moral transgressions. Many 7-year-olds tolerate a teacher's decision to give more snacks to girls than to boys because she thinks (incorrectly) that girls need more food. But when a teacher gives girls more snacks because she holds an *immoral belief* ("It's all right to be nicer to girls than boys"), almost all children judge her actions negatively (Wainryb & Ford, 1998).

Relation of Personal and Moral Domains

Preschoolers display a budding awareness of the personal domain, conveyed through such statements as, "I'm gonna wear *this* shirt." As children's grasp of moral imperatives and social conventions strengthens, so does their conviction that certain choices are up to the individual. Early on, children learn that parents and teachers are willing to compromise on personal issues and, at times, on social-conventional matters but not on moral concerns.

Likewise, when children and adolescents challenge adult authority, they typically do so within the personal domain (Nucci, 2001, 2005). In diverse Western and non-Western cultures, concern with matters of personal choice intensifies during the teenage years—a reflection of adolescents' quest for identity and increasing independence (Neff & Helwig, 2002; Nucci, 2002). As, young people increasingly insist that parents not encroach on the personal arena (dress, hairstyle, diary records, friendships), disputes over these issues occur more often. Teenagers whose parents frequently intrude into their personal affairs report greater psychological stress (Hasebe, Nucci, & Nucci, 2004). In contrast, adolescents typically say that parents have a right to tell them what to do in moral and social-conventional situations. And when these issues spark disagreements, teenagers seldom challenge parental authority (Smetana & Daddis, 2002).

Notions of personal choice, in turn, enhance children's moral understanding. As early as age 6, children view freedom of speech and religion as individual rights, even if laws exist that deny those rights (Helwig, 2006). And they regard laws that discriminate against individuals—for example, laws that deny certain people access to medical care or education—as wrong and worthy of violating (Helwig & Jasiobedzka, 2001). In justifying their responses, children appeal to personal privileges and, by the end of middle childhood, to democratic ideals, such as the importance of individual rights for maintaining a fair society.

At the same time, older school-age children place limits on individual choice, depending on circumstances. While they believe that nonacademic matters (such as where to go on field trips) are best decided democratically, they regard the academic curriculum as the province of teachers, based on teachers' superior ability to make such choices (Helwig & Kim, 1999).

As they enlarge the range of issues they regard as personal, adolescents think more intently about conflicts between personal choice and community obligation—whether, and under what conditions, it is permissible to restrict speech, religion, marriage, childbearing, group membership, and other individual rights (Helwig, 1995; Wainryb, 1997). Teenagers display more subtle thinking than school-age children on such issues. For example, when asked if it is OK to exclude a child from a friendship or peer group on the basis of race or gender, fourth graders usually say exclusion is always unfair. But by tenth grade, young people, though increasingly mindful of fairness, indicate that under certain conditions—in intimate relationships (friendship) and private contexts (at home or in a small club), and on the basis of gender more often than race—exclusion is OK (Killen et al., 2002, 2007; Rutland, Killen, & Abrams, 2010). In explaining, they mention the right to personal choice as well as concerns about effective group functioning. Justifying her belief that members of an all-boys music club need not let a girl in, one tenth grader said, "It's not nice . . . but it's their club." Another commented, "[The girls and the boys] probably wouldn't relate on very many things" (Killen et al., 2002, p. 62).

As adolescents integrate personal rights with ideal reciprocity, they demand that the protections they want for themselves extend to others. For example, with age, they are more likely to defend the government's right to limit individual freedom to engage in risky health behaviors, such as smoking and drinking, in the interest of the larger public good (Flanagan, Stout, & Gallay, 2008). Similarly, they are increasingly mindful of the overlap among moral imperatives, social conventions, and personal choice. Eventually they realize that violating strongly held conventions in favor of asserting personal choices—showing up at a wedding in a T-shirt, talking out of turn at a student council meeting—can harm others, either by inducing distress or by undermining fair treatment. Over time, as their grasp of fairness deepens, young people realize that many social conventions have moral implications: They are vital for maintaining a just and peaceful society (Nucci, 2001). Notice how this understanding is central to Kohlberg's Stage 4, which is typically attained as adolescence draws to a close.

Culture and Moral, Social-Conventional, and Personal Distinctions

Children and adolescents in diverse Western and non-Western cultures use similar criteria to reason about moral, social-conventional, and personal concerns (Neff & Helwig, 2002; Nucci, 2002, 2005). For example, Chinese and Japanese young people, whose cultures place a high value on respect for authority, nevertheless say that adults have no right to interfere in their personal matters, such as how they spend their free time (Hasebe, Nucci, & Nucci, 2004; Helwig et al., 2003). A Colombian child illustrated this vehement defense of the right to personal control when asked if a teacher had the right to tell a student where to sit during circle time. In the absence of a moral reason from the teacher, the child emphatically declared, "She should be able to sit wherever she wants" (Ardila-Rey & Killen, 2001, p. 249).

Still, certain behaviors are classified differently across cultures. For example, East Indian Hindu children believe it is morally wrong to eat chicken the day after a father's death because, according to Hindu religious teachings, this will prevent the father's soul from reaching salvation. To American children, in contrast, this practice is an arbitrary convention

Milestones

Internalization of Moral Norms and Development of Moral Understanding

AGE	INTERNALIZATION OF MORAL NORMS	MORAL UNDERSTANDING
2–5 years	• Models many morally relevant behaviors • Responds with empathy-based guilt to transgressions	• Tends to focus on salient features and consequences in moral judgment, such as physical damage, getting punished, or an adult's power or status • Begins to show sensitivity to others' intentions in moral judgment • At the end of this period, has a differentiated understanding of authority figures' legitimacy • Distinguishes moral imperatives, social conventions, and matters of personal choice
6–11 years	• Internalizes many norms of good conduct, including prosocial standards 	• Continues to emphasize superficial factors, including physical consequences and self-interest, in responses to moral dilemmas (Piaget's "heteronomous" and Kohlberg's preconventional Stages 1 and 2 morality) • Gradually understands ideal reciprocity and increasingly emphasizes people's intentions and expectations in moral judgment (Piaget's morality of cooperation and Kohlberg's "conventional" Stage 3 morality) • Clarifies and coordinates moral imperatives, social conventions, and matters of personal choice and, in judging violations, considers more variables—purpose of the rule, people's intentions, and context
12 years– adulthood		• Increasingly emphasizes ideal reciprocity as the basis for interpersonal relationships and societal laws (Kohlberg's "conventional" Stages 3 and 4 morality) • Becomes increasingly aware of the moral implications of social conventions and matters of personal choice • Highly reflective moral judgments that grapple with existential issues appear among a few individuals, usually with advanced education (Kohlberg's "postconventional" Stages 5 and 6) • Relationship between moral reasoning and behavior strengthens

Note: These milestones represent overall age trends. Individual differences exist in the precise age at which each milestone is attained.

Photos: (top) © Bob Ebbesen/Alamy; (middle) © Rachel Epstein/PhotoEdit; (bottom) © Steve Skjold/Alamy Images

(Shweder, Mahapatra, & Miller, 1990). But when children are asked about acts that obviously lead to harm or violate rights—breaking promises, destroying another's property, or kicking harmless animals—cross-cultural similarity prevails (Turiel, 2006). We are reminded, once again, that justice considerations are a universal feature of moral thought.

The research reviewed in the preceding sections reveals the richness and diversity of children's moral understanding. To fully represent the development of moral thought, researchers must examine children's responses to a wide range of problems. Consult the Milestones table above to review changes in moral internalization and construction during childhood and adolescence.

Review ■ How do recursive thought and understanding of ideal reciprocity contribute to moral development? Why are Kohlberg's Stages 3 and 4 morally mature constructions?

Connect ■ Do adolescents' efforts to resolve conflicts between personal choice and moral imperatives reflect their increasingly profound grasp of justice? Explain, citing examples.

Apply ■ Tam grew up in a small village culture, Lydia in a large industrial city. At age 15, Tam reasons at Kohlberg's Stage 3, Lydia at Stage 4. What factors probably account for the difference?

Reflect ■ Do you favor a cognitive-developmental or a pragmatic approach to morality, or both? What research evidence and personal experiences influenced your viewpoint?

▶ Discuss the development of morally relevant self-control, noting implications of individual differences for cognitive and social competencies.

Development of Morally Relevant Self-Control

The study of moral judgment tells us what people think they should do, and why, when faced with a moral problem. But people's good intentions often fall short. Whether children and adults act in accord with their beliefs depends in part on characteristics we call will-power, firm resolve, or, more simply, self-control. In Chapter 10, we considered individual differences in the broad temperamental dimension of *effortful control*—the extent to which children can manage their reactivity. Here we focus specifically on self-control in the moral domain: inhibiting urges to act in ways that violate moral standards, sometimes called *resistance to temptation*. Earlier in this book we noted that parental warmth, reasonable expectations and limit-setting, verbal guidance in managing emotion, inductive discipline, and modeling promote self-controlled behavior. But these practices become more effective when children acquire the ability to resist temptation. When and how does this capacity develop?

Toddlerhood

The beginnings of self-control are supported by achievements of the second year, discussed in earlier chapters. To behave in a self-controlled fashion, children must have some ability to think of themselves as separate, autonomous beings who can direct their own actions. And they must have the representational, memory, and inhibitory skills to recall a caregiver's directive and apply it to their own behavior (Rothbart & Bates, 2006).

As these capacities emerge between 12 and 18 months, the first glimmerings of self-control appear in the form of **compliance.** Toddlers show clear awareness of caregivers' wishes and expectations and can obey simple requests and commands. But at first, self-control depends heavily on caregiver support. According to Vygotsky (1934/1986), children cannot guide their own behavior until they have integrated standards represented in adult–child dialogues into their own self-directed speech (see Chapter 6). Compliance quickly leads to toddlers' first consciencelike verbalizations—for example, correcting the self by saying "No, can't" before touching a delicate object or jumping on the sofa.

Researchers often study self-control by giving children tasks that, like the situations just mentioned, require **delay of gratification**—waiting for an appropriate time and place to engage in a tempting act. Between ages 1½ and 3, children show an increasing capacity to wait before eating a treat, opening a present, or playing with a toy (Vaughn, Kopp, & Krakow, 1984). Children who are advanced in development of attention and language tend to be better at delaying gratification—findings that help explain why girls are typically more self-controlled than boys (Else-Quest et al., 2006).

Like effortful control in general, young children's capacity to delay gratification is influenced by both biologically based temperament and quality of caregiving (Kochanska & Aksan, 2006; Kochanska & Knaack, 2003). Inhibited children find it easier to wait than angry, irritable children do. But toddlers who experience parental warmth and simple (as opposed to lengthy, detailed) statements that patiently redirect their behavior are more likely to be cooperative and resist temptation (Blandon & Volling, 2008; Hakman & Sullivan, 2009). Such parenting—which encourages and models patient, nonimpulsive behavior—is particularly important for temperamentally reactive children (refer to pages 426–427 in Chapter 10 to review these findings). As self-control improves, parents gradually increase the range of rules they expect toddlers to follow, from safety and respect for property and people to family routines, manners, and simple chores (Gralinski & Kopp, 1993).

Childhood and Adolescence

Although the capacity for self-control is in place by the third year, it is not complete. Cognitive development—in particular, gains in attention and mental representation—enables children to use a variety of effective self-instructional strategies. As a result, resistance to temptation improves.

Strategies for Resisting Temptation Walter Mischel has studied what children think and say to themselves that promotes resistance to temptation. In several studies, preschoolers were shown two rewards: a highly desirable one (10 mini-marshmallows) that they would have to wait for and a less desirable one (2 mini-marshmallows) that they could have right away (Mischel, 1996; Mischel & Ayduck, 2004). With age, performance improved (Atance & Jackson, 2009; Mischel, Shoda, & Rodriguez, 1989). At the same time, wide individual differences emerged: The most self-controlled preschoolers used any technique they could to divert their attention from the desired objects: covering their eyes, singing, even trying to sleep!

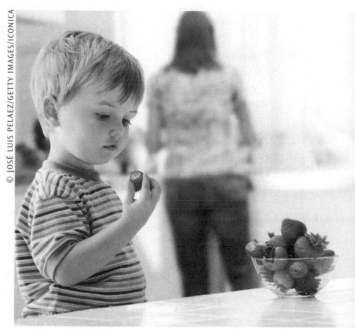

How will this 4-year-old resist temptation? If he diverts his attention by engaging in another activity or by imagining the strawberries to be inedible objects, he will be able to wait longer.

In everyday situations, preschoolers find it difficult to keep their minds off tempting activities and objects for long. When their thoughts turn to a prohibited goal, the way they mentally represent it has much to do with their success at self-control. Teaching preschoolers to transform the stimulus in ways that de-emphasize its arousing qualities—an approach that helps children shift attention and inhibit emotional reactivity—promotes delay of gratification. In one study, preschoolers who were told to think about marshmallows as "white and puffy clouds" waited much longer before eating a marshmallow reward than those who focused on marshmallows' "sweet and chewy properties" (Mischel & Baker, 1975).

Having something interesting to do while waiting also helps preschoolers divert attention from rewards and resist temptation (see earlier suggestions for reducing opportunities for misbehavior on page 495). In a modified delay-of-gratification task in which 3- to 5-year-olds could engage in enjoyable work (feeding marbles to a colorfully decorated, "hungry" Baby Bird), the amount of time children waited for a nearby, attractive reward more than doubled over simply waiting passively. But when the work was unappealing (sorting marbles), preschoolers were less successful (Peake, Hebl, & Mischel, 2002). They often looked up from the boring task, which increased the likelihood that the enticing reward would capture their attention.

During the school years, children become better at devising their own strategies for resisting temptation. By this time, self-control has become a flexible capacity for **moral self-regulation**—the ability to monitor one's own conduct, constantly adjusting it as circumstances present opportunities to violate inner standards (Kopp & Wyer, 1994; Thompson, Meyer, & McGinley, 2006).

Knowledge of Strategies Recall from Chapter 7 that metacognitive knowledge, or awareness of strategies, contributes to self-regulation. When asked about situational conditions and self-instructions likely to help delay gratification, school-age children suggested a broader array of arousal-reducing strategies with age. But not until the late elementary school years did they mention techniques involving transformations of rewards or their own

LOOK and LISTEN

Propose a situation involving waiting for a larger, delayed reward in lieu of taking an immediate, lesser reward to two or three school-age children. Ask what each child would do to delay gratification. Are the strategies children generate consistent with research findings?

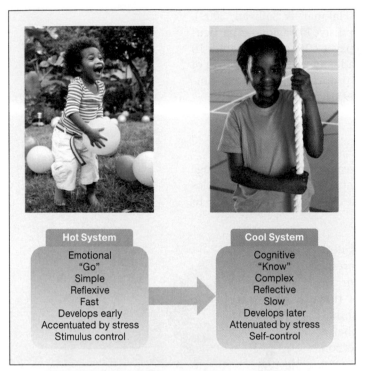

FIGURE 12.4 Characteristics of "hot" and "cool" processing systems in the development of self-control. With age, the cognitive, reflective cool system gains control over emotional, reactive hot system. **TAKE A MOMENT...** Return to Table 10.1 on page 420 in Chapter 10 to review Rothbart's reactive and self-regulatory dimensions of temperament. How are they similar to the hot and cool processing systems depicted here? (Adapted from Kross & Mischel, 2010.)

arousal states. For example, one 11-year-old proposed saying, "The marshmallows are filled with an evil spell." Another said he would tell himself, "I hate marshmallows; I can't stand them. But when the grown-up gets back, I'll tell myself 'I love marshmallows' and eat it" (Mischel & Mischel, 1983, p. 609). Once this transforming ideation appears, it greatly facilitates moral self-regulation (Rodriguez, Mischel, & Shoda, 1989).

Individual Differences

In a series of studies, 4-year-olds who were better at delaying gratification were especially adept as adolescents in applying metacognitive skills to their behavior and in inhibiting impulsive responding. In addition, their parents saw them as more responsive to reason, as better at concentrating and planning ahead, and as coping with stress more maturely. When applying to college, those who had been self-controlled preschoolers scored higher on the Scholastic Assessment Test (SAT), although they were no more intelligent than other individuals (Eigsti et al. 2006; Mischel, Shoda, & Peake, 1988; Shoda, Mischel, & Peake, 1990). Furthermore, children who are better at delaying gratification can wait long enough to interpret social cues accurately, which supports effective social problem solving and positive peer relations (Gronau & Waas, 1997).

Mischel proposes that the interaction of two processing systems—*hot* and *cool*—governs the development of self-control and accounts for individual differences (Kross & Mischel, 2010; Mischel & Ayduk, 2004). Figure 12.4 depicts the characteristics of each. With age, the emotional, reactive hot system is increasingly subordinated to the cognitive, reflective cool system, as a result of improved functioning of the prefrontal cortex, which is centrally involved in executive function (see page 281 in Chapter 7).

Throughout childhood and adolescence, temperament and parenting jointly influence the extent to which cool-system representations gain control over hot-system reactivity. **TAKE A MOMENT...** Describe evidence from this and previous chapters indicating that power-assertive, inconsistent discipline—especially with temperamentally vulnerable children—results in a poorly functioning cool system, enabling the hot system to prevail. Such children display hostile, unruly behavior and serious deficits in moral conduct. Refer to the Milestones table on the following page for a summary of changes in self-control as well as in aggression—our next topic.

▶ Discuss the development of aggression, noting various influences, and describe successful interventions.

The Other Side of Self-Control: Development of Aggression

Beginning in late infancy, all children display aggression from time to time. As opportunities to interact with siblings and peers increase, aggressive outbursts occur more often (Dodge, Coie, & Lynam, 2006; Tremblay, 2004). Although at times aggression serves prosocial ends (for example, stopping a victimizer from harming others), most human aggressive acts are clearly antisocial.

As early as the preschool years, some children show abnormally high rates of hostility, assaulting others verbally and physically with little or no provocation. If allowed to continue,

Milestones

Development of Morally Relevant Self-Control and Aggression

AGE	SELF-CONTROL	AGGRESSION
1½–5 years	• Compliance and delay of gratification emerge and improve. • Benefits from adult-provided strategies for delaying gratification.	• Proactive, or instrumental, aggression declines, while reactive (hostile aggression) increases. • Physical aggression declines, while verbal aggression increases. • Relational aggression appears.
6–11 years	• Generates an increasing variety of strategies for delaying gratification. • Displays a flexible capacity for moral self-regulation.	• Reactive, or hostile, aggression (largely verbal and relational) continues to increase. • Girls' relational aggression becomes increasingly indirect.
12–20 years	• Continues to gain in moral self-regulation.	• Teacher- and peer-reported aggression declines. • Delinquency rises, then declines.

Note: These milestones represent overall age trends. Individual differences exist in the precise age at which each milestone is attained.

Photos: (left) © David L. Moore-Lifestyle/Alamy; (right) © Stock Image/Pixland/Alamy

their belligerent behavior can lead to lasting delays in moral development, deficits in self-control, and ultimately an antisocial lifestyle. To understand this process, let's see how aggression develops during childhood and adolescence.

Emergence of Aggression

In the second half of the first year, infants develop the cognitive capacity to identify sources of anger and frustration and the motor skills to lash out at them (see Chapter 10). By the second year, aggressive acts with two distinct purposes emerge. Initially, the most common is **proactive** (or *instrumental*) **aggression,** in which children act to fulfill a need or desire—obtain an object, privilege, space, or social reward, such as adult attention or (in older children) peer admiration—and unemotionally attack a person to achieve their goal. The other type, **reactive** (or *hostile*) **aggression,** is an angry, defensive response to a provocation or a blocked goal and is meant to hurt another person (Dodge, Coie, & Lynam, 2006; Little et al., 2003).

Naturalistic observations of children in classrooms or at play reveal low positive correlations between proactive and reactive aggression (Polman et al., 2007). But when aggression is assessed using parent or teacher reports, proactive and reactive aggression are strongly correlated (Vitaro, Brendgen, & Tremblay, 2002). Thus, the extent to which the two types of aggression represent distinct styles is unclear. At least some, and perhaps many, aggressive children engage in both, and most studies do not distinguish between them.

Proactive and reactive aggression come in three forms, which are the focus of the majority of research:

- **Physical aggression** harms others through physical injury—pushing, hitting, kicking, or punching others, or destroying another's property.

Although physical aggression largely gives way to verbal aggression during early and middle childhood, gender differences remain. Boys are more physically aggressive than girls.

- **Verbal aggression** harms others through threats of physical aggression, name-calling, or hostile teasing.
- **Relational aggression** damages another's peer relationships through social exclusion, malicious gossip, or friendship manipulation.

Although verbal aggression is always direct, physical and relational aggression can be either *direct* or *indirect*. For example, hitting injures a person directly, whereas destroying property indirectly inflicts physical harm. Similarly, saying, "Do what I say, or I won't be your friend," conveys relational aggression directly, while spreading rumors, refusing to talk to a peer, or manipulating friendships by saying behind someone's back, "Don't play with her; she's a nerd," does so indirectly.

Aggression in Early and Middle Childhood

Between ages 3 and 6, physical aggression decreases, whereas verbal aggression increases (Alink et al., 2006; Tremblay et al., 1999). Rapid language development contributes to this change, but it is also due to adults' and peers' strong negative reactions to physical attacks. Furthermore, proactive aggression declines as preschoolers' improved capacity to delay gratification enables them to resist grabbing others' possessions. But reactive aggression in verbal and relational forms tends to rise over early and middle childhood (Côté et al., 2007; Tremblay, 2000). Older children are better able to detect malicious intentions and, as a result, more often respond in hostile ways.

By age 17 months, boys are considerably more physically aggressive than girls—a difference found throughout childhood in many cultures (Baillargeon et al., 2007; Card et al., 2008; Dodge, Coie, & Lynam, 2006). As we will see in Chapter 13, when we consider sex differences in aggression in greater detail, biological factors—in particular, the effects of male sex hormones (androgens) and temperamental traits on which boys and girls differ—contribute to the early greater prevalence of physical attacks by boys. Gender-role conformity is also a factor. As soon as 2-year-olds become dimly aware of gender stereotypes—that males and females are expected to behave differently—physical aggression drops off more sharply for girls than for boys (Fagot & Leinbach, 1989).

Although girls have a reputation for being verbally and relationally more aggressive than boys, Chapter 13 will reveal that the sex difference is small (Crick et al., 2004, 2006; Crick, Ostrov, & Werner, 2006). Beginning in the preschool years, girls concentrate most of their aggressive acts in the relational category. Boys inflict harm in more variable ways and, therefore, display overall rates of aggression that are much higher than girls'.

At the same time, girls more often use indirect relational tactics that—in disrupting intimate bonds especially important to girls—can be particularly mean. Whereas physical attacks are usually brief, acts of indirect relational aggression may extend for hours, weeks, or even months (Nelson, Robinson, & Hart, 2005; Underwood, 2003). In one instance, a second-grade girl formed a "pretty-girls club" at school and—for nearly an entire school year—convinced its members to exclude several classmates by saying they were "ugly and smelly." At least in childhood, then, it may not be meaningful to describe one sex as more aggressive than the other.

Aggression and Delinquency in Adolescence

Although most young people decline in teacher- and peer-reported aggression in adolescence, the teenage years are accompanied by a rise in delinquent acts. Although U.S. youth crime has declined since the mid-1990s, 12- to 17-year-olds account for a substantial proportion of police arrests—14, although they constitute only 8 percent of the population (U.S. Department of Justice, 2010). When asked directly and confidentially about lawbreaking, almost all teenagers admit to having committed some sort of offense—usually a minor crime, such as petty stealing or disorderly conduct (Flannery et al., 2003).

Both police arrests and self-reports show that delinquency rises over early and middle adolescence and then declines (Farrington, 2009; U.S. Department of Justice, 2010). Recall from Chapter 5 that changes in the brain's emotional/social network at puberty contribute to an increase in antisocial behavior among teenagers (see pages 190–191). Over time, decision making, emotional self-regulation, and moral reasoning improve; peers become less influential; and young people enter social contexts (such as higher education, work, career, and marriage) that are less conducive to lawbreaking.

For most adolescents, a brush with the law does not forecast long-term antisocial behavior. But repeated arrests are cause for concern. Teenagers are responsible for 15 percent of violent crimes in the United States (U.S. Department of Justice, 2010). A small percentage become recurrent offenders, who commit most of these crimes, and some enter a life of crime.

In adolescence, the gender gap in physical aggression widens (Chesney-Lind, 2001). Although girls account for about one in five adolescent arrests for violence, their offenses are largely limited to simple assault (such as pushing and spitting), the least serious category. Once labeled status offenses (noncriminal behavior), today these acts are more likely to lead to arrests, especially in physical exchanges with parents, who may report the youth's behavior to the police (Chesney-Lind & Belknap, 2004). Serious violent crime, however, continues to be mostly the domain of boys (Dahlberg & Simon, 2006).

SES and ethnicity are strong predictors of arrests but only mildly related to teenagers' self-reports of antisocial acts. The difference is due to the tendency to arrest, charge, and punish low-SES ethnic minority youths more often than their higher-SES white and Asian counterparts (Farrington, 2009; U.S. Department of Justice, 2010). In isolation from other life circumstances, ethnicity tells us little about youths' propensity to engage in violence and other lawbreaking acts.

Delinquency—usually petty stealing and disorderly conduct—rises in early adolescence and then declines. But a small percentage of young people engage in repeated, serious offenses and are at risk for a life of crime.

Stability of Aggression

Children high in either physical or relational aggression relative to their agemates tend to remain so over time (Côté et al., 2007; Vaillancourt et al., 2003). Following more than 1,000 Canadian, New Zealand, and U.S. boys from ages 6 to 15, researchers identified four main patterns of change. Kindergarten boys high in physical aggression (4 percent of the sample) were especially likely to move to high-level adolescent aggression, becoming involved in violent delinquency. In contrast, kindergarten boys who were moderately physically aggressive usually declined in physical aggression over time. And boys who rarely physically aggressed in early childhood typically remained nonaggressive. However, a small number of boys high in oppositional behavior (such as disobedience and inconsiderateness) but not in physical aggression were prone to less violent forms of adolescent delinquency (such as theft) (Brame, Nagin, & Tremblay, 2001; Nagin & Tremblay, 1999).

In other longitudinal evidence, high physical aggression that diminished over the school years was often replaced with indirect relational aggression. Although the trend applied to both genders, girls displayed it more often than boys (Vaillancourt, Miller, & Boyle, 2009). These children seem to deploy their improved perspective-taking capacities antisocially—to perpetrate behind-the-scenes relational attacks. Their aggressiveness actually remains stable—just expressed in a different form. For both boys and girls, persistently high physical or relational aggression predicts later internalizing and externalizing

BIOLOGY and ENVIRONMENT

Two Routes to Adolescent Delinquency

Persistent adolescent delinquency follows two paths of development, one involving a small number of youths with an onset of conduct problems in childhood, the second a larger number with an onset in adolescence. The early-onset type is far more likely to lead to a life-course pattern of aggression and criminality (Moffitt, 2006b). The late-onset type usually does not persist beyond the transition to early adulthood.

Both childhood-onset and adolescent-onset youths engage in serious offenses; associate with deviant peers; participate in substance abuse, unsafe sex, and dangerous driving; and spend time in correctional facilities. Why does antisocial activity more often continue and escalate into violence in the first group? Longitudinal studies yield similar answers to this question. Most research has focused on boys, but several investigations report that girls who were physically aggressive in childhood are also at risk for later problems—occasionally violent delinquency but more often other norm-violating behaviors and psychological disorders (Broidy et al., 2003; Chamberlain, 2003). Early relational aggression is linked to adolescent conduct problems as well.

Early-Onset Type

Early-onset youngsters seem to inherit traits that predispose them to aggressiveness (Pettit, 2004). For example, violence-prone boys are emotionally negative, restless, willful, and physically aggressive as early as age 2. They also show subtle deficits in cognitive functioning that seem to contribute to disruptions in the development of language, memory, and cognitive and emotional self-regulation (Moffitt, 2006a; Shaw et al., 2003). Some have attention-deficit hyperactivity disorder (ADHD), which compounds their learning and self-control problems (see Chapter 7, pages 290–291).

Yet these biological risks are not sufficient to sustain antisocial behavior: Most early-onset boys decline in aggression over time. Among those who follow the life-course path, inept parenting transforms their undercontrolled style into defiance and persistent aggression—strong predictors of violent delinquency in adolescence (Brame, Nagin, & Tremblay, 2001; Broidy et al., 2003). As they fail academically and are rejected by peers, they befriend other deviant youths, who facilitate one another's violent behavior while relieving loneliness (see Figure 12.5) (Hughes, 2010; Lacourse et al., 2003). Limited

cognitive and social skills result in high rates of school dropout and unemployment, contributing further to antisocial involvements. Often these boys experience their first arrest before age 14—a good indicator that they will be chronic offenders by age 18 (Patterson & Yoerger, 2002).

Preschoolers high in relational aggression also tend to be hyperactive and frequently in conflict with peers and adults (Willoughby, Kupersmidt, & Bryant, 2001). As these behaviors trigger peer rejection, relationally aggressive girls befriend other girls high in relational hostility, and their relational aggression rises (Werner & Crick, 2004). Adolescents high in relational aggression are often angry, vengeful, and defiant of adult rules. Among teenagers who combine physical and relational hostility, these oppositional reactions intensify, increasing the likelihood of serious antisocial activity (Harachi et al., 2006; Prinstein, Boergers, & Vernberg, 2001).

Late-Onset Type

Other youths first display antisocial behavior around the time of puberty, gradually increasing their involvement. Their conduct problems

difficulties and social skills deficits, including loneliness, anxiety, depression, poor-quality friendships, and antisocial activity (Campbell et al., 2006; Côté et al., 2007; Crick, Ostrov, & Werner, 2006).

As the Biology and Environment box above confirms, aggressive behavior that emerges in childhood and endures is far more likely to translate into long-term adjustment difficulties than aggression that first appears in adolescence. Although some children—especially those who are irritable, fearless, impulsive, and overactive—are at risk for aggression, whether or not they become aggressive largely depends on child-rearing conditions. Strife-ridden families, poor parenting practices, aggressive peers, and televised violence strongly predict both antisocial activity and reduced sensitivity to others' suffering. In this chapter, we focus on family and peer influences, reserving TV influences for Chapter 15. We will also see that community and cultural influences can heighten or reduce children's risk of sustaining a hostile interpersonal style.

The Family as Training Ground for Aggressive Behavior

The same parenting behaviors that undermine moral internalization and self-control—love withdrawal, power assertion, critical remarks, physical punishment, and inconsistent discipline—are linked to aggression from early childhood through adolescence in diverse cultures, with most of these practices predicting both physical and relational forms (Bradford et al., 2003; Casas et al., 2006; Côté et al., 2007; Gershoff et al., 2010; Kuppens et al., 2009; Nelson et al., 2006).

arise from typical adolescent novelty seeking and receptiveness to peer influence. For some, quality of parenting may decline for a time, perhaps as a result of family stresses or the challenges of disciplining an unruly teenager (Moffitt, 2006a). When age brings gratifying adult privileges, these youths draw on prosocial skills mastered before adolescence and abandon their antisocial ways.

A few late-onset youths do continue to engage in antisocial acts. The seriousness of their adolescent offenses seems to trap them in situations that close off opportunities for responsible behavior. Being employed or in school and forming positive, close relationships predict an end to criminal offending by age 20 to 25 (Farrington, Ttofi, & Coid, 2009; Stouthamer-Loeber et al., 2004). In contrast,

the longer antisocial young people spend in prison, the more likely they are to sustain a life of crime.

These findings suggest a need for a fresh look at policies aimed at stopping youth crime. Keeping youth offenders locked up for many years disrupts their vocational lives and access to social support during a crucial period of development, condemning them to a bleak future.

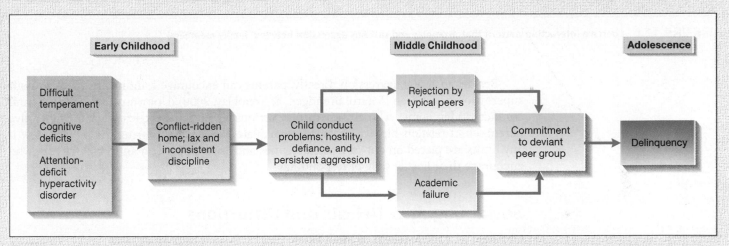

FIGURE 12.5 **Path to chronic delinquency for adolescents with childhood-onset antisocial behavior.** Difficult temperament and cognitive deficits characterize many of these youths in early childhood; some have attention-deficit hyperactivity disorder. Inept parenting transforms biologically based self-control difficulties into hostility and defiance.

Home observations of aggressive children reveal that anger and punitiveness quickly create a conflict-ridden family atmosphere and an "out-of-control" child. As Figure 12.6 on page 522 shows, the pattern begins with forceful discipline, which occurs more often with stressful life experiences (such as economic hardship or marital conflict), a parent with an unstable personality, or a temperamentally difficult child (Dodge, Coie, & Lynam, 2006). Typically, the parent threatens, criticizes, and punishes, and the child angrily resists until the parent gives in. At the end of each exchange, both parent and child get relief from stopping the other's unpleasant behavior, so the behaviors repeat and escalate.

As these cycles become more frequent, they generate anxiety and irritability among other family members, who soon join in the hostile interactions. Compared with siblings in typical families, preschool siblings who have critical, punitive parents are more aggressive toward one another. Physically, verbally, and relationally destructive sibling conflict, in turn, quickly spreads to peer relationships, contributing to poor impulse control and antisocial behavior by the early school years (Garcia et al., 2000; Ostrov, Crick, & Stauffacher, 2006).

Boys are more likely than girls to be targets of harsh, inconsistent discipline because they are more active and impulsive and therefore harder to control. When children who are extreme in these characteristics are exposed to emotionally negative, inept parenting, their capacity for emotional self-regulation, empathic responding, and guilt after transgressions is severely disrupted (Eisenberg, Eggum, & Edwards, 2010). Consequently, they lash out when disappointed, frustrated, or faced with a sad or fearful victim, and aggression persists (refer again to the Biology and Environment box).

FIGURE 12.6 Coercive interaction pattern that promotes and sustains aggression between family members.

Besides fostering aggression directly, parents can encourage it indirectly, through poor supervision of children (Vitaro, Brendgen, & Tremblay, 2000). Unfortunately, children from conflict-ridden homes who already display serious antisocial tendencies lack a cooperative parent–child relationship, which enables adequate parental monitoring. As a result, few if any limits are placed on out-of-home activities and association with antisocial friends, who encourage their hostile style of responding.

Social-Cognitive Deficits and Distortions

Children who are products of these family processes soon acquire a violent and callous view of the social world. Those who are high in reactive aggression often see hostile intent where it does not exist—in situations where peers' intentions are unclear, where harm is accidental, and even where peers are trying to be helpful (Lochman & Dodge, 1998; Orobio de Castro et al., 2002). When such children feel threatened (for example, a researcher tells them that a peer they will work with is in a bad mood and might pick a fight), they are especially likely to interpret accidental mishaps as hostile (Williams et al., 2003). As a result, they make many unprovoked attacks, which trigger aggressive retaliations.

Children high in proactive aggression have different social-cognitive deficits. Compared with their nonaggressive agemates, they believe there are more benefits and fewer costs for engaging in destructive acts (Arsenio, 2010; Dodge et al., 1997). And they are more likely to think that aggression "works," producing material rewards and reducing others' unpleasant behaviors (Arsenio & Lemerise, 2001; Goldstein & Tisak, 2004). Thus, they callously use aggression to advance their own goals and are relatively unconcerned about causing suffering in others—an aggressive style associated with later, more severe conduct problems, violent behavior, and delinquency (Marsee & Frick, 2010).

Another biased social-cognitive attribute of proactively aggressive children and youths is overly high self-esteem, even in the face of academic and social failings. When their arrogant, cocky behavior prompts others to challenge their inflated but vulnerable self-image, they lash out angrily (Costello & Dunaway, 2003; Orobio de Castro et al., 2007). Their narcissism is also associated with a sense of personal entitlement, lack of empathy, and sophisticated, highly manipulative relationally aggressive tactics aimed at gaining power over others (Barry, Frick, & Killian, 2003; Kerig & Stellwagen, 2010).

Furthermore, aggressive young people may neutralize their basic biological capacity for empathy by using such cognitive distortion techniques as blaming their victims. As a result, they retain a positive self-evaluation after behaving aggressively (Liau, Barriga, & Gibbs, 1998; McCrady et al., 2008). Looking back on his burglaries, one delinquent reflected, "If I started feeling bad, I'd say to myself, 'Tough rocks for him. He should have had his house locked better and the alarm on'" (Samenow, 1984, p. 115).

Antisocial adolescents are delayed in maturity of moral judgment, and they tend to view aggression as within the social conventional and personal domains rather than the moral domain (Harvey, Fletcher, & French, 2001; Tisak, Tisak, & Goldstein, 2006). In this way, they minimize the harmful impact of their antisocial acts, rationalizing their behavior as acceptable or even admirable. These youths also score low in moral identity. In a study of 16- to 19-year-olds, those whose moral reasoning was immature and who also judged moral values as personally unimportant were prone to self-serving cognitive distortions (such as blaming the victim or minimizing the harm done), which predicted high levels of aggressive behavior (Barriga et al., 2001). Compared with boys, girls scored higher in moral identity and lower cognitive distortions—likely contributors to their lower overall aggressiveness.

Community and Cultural Influences

In poverty-stricken neighborhoods with a wide range of stressors, including poor-quality schools, limited recreational and employment opportunities, and high adult criminality, youth antisocial behavior is more likely (Leventhal, Dupere, & Brooks-Gunn, 2009). Children and adolescents have easy access to deviant peers, drugs, and (in the United States) firearms, all of which are linked to violence. And teenagers are especially likely to be recruited into antisocial gangs, whose members commit the vast majority of violent delinquent acts (Thornberry & Krohn, 2001). Furthermore, schools in these locales typically fail to meet students' developmental needs (Chung, Mulvey, & Steinberg, 2011; Flannery et al., 2003). Large classes, weak instruction, rigid rules, and reduced academic expectations and opportunities are associated with higher rates of lawbreaking, even after other influences are controlled.

Furthermore, the community conditions just described heighten in young people a hostile view of people and relationships, a preference for immediate rewards, and a cynical attitude toward social conventions and moral norms (Simons & Burt, 2011). These social-cognitive biases, in addition to others noted in the previous section, increase the chances that adolescents will interpret situations in ways that legitimize antisocial behavior.

Ethnic and political prejudices further magnify the risk of angry, combative responses. In inner-city ghettos and in war-torn areas of the world, large numbers of children live in the midst of constant danger, chaos, and deprivation. As the Cultural Influences box on page 524 reveals, these youngsters are at risk for severe emotional stress, deficits in moral reasoning, and behavior problems.

Helping Children and Parents Control Aggression

Treatment for aggressive children must break the cycle of hostilities between family members and promote effective ways of relating to others. Interventions with preschool and school-age children have been most successful. Once antisocial patterns persist into adolescence, so many factors act to sustain them that treatment is far more difficult.

Parent Training Parent training programs based on social learning theory have been devised to improve the parenting of preschool and school-age children with conduct problems. In one highly effective approach called *Incredible Years,* parents complete 18 weekly group sessions facilitated by two professionals, who teach parenting techniques for promoting children's academic, emotional, and social skills and for managing disruptive behaviors. Sessions include coaching, modeling, and practicing effective parenting behaviors—experiences aimed at interrupting parent–child destructive interaction while promoting positive relationships and competencies (Webster-Stratton & Reid, 2010b). A special focus is positive parenting (see page 495), including giving children positive attention, encouragement, and praise for prosocial behaviors. The coercive cycles of parents and aggressive children are so pervasive that these children often are punished even when they do behave appropriately.

Incredible Years also offers a complementary six-day training program for teachers, directed at improving classroom management strategies and strengthening students' social

CULTURAL INFLUENCES

Impact of Ethnic and Political Violence on Children

Around the world, many children live with armed conflict, terrorism, and other acts of violence stemming from ethnic and political tensions. Some children may participate in fighting, either because they are forced or because they want to please adults. Others are kidnapped, assaulted, and tortured. Those who are bystanders often come under direct fire and may be killed or physically maimed. And many watch in horror as family members, friends, and neighbors flee, are wounded, or die. In the past decade, wars have left 6 million children physically disabled, 20 million homeless, and more than 1 million separated from parents (UNICEF, 2011).

When war and social crises are temporary, most children can be comforted and do not show long-term emotional difficulties. But chronic danger requires children to make substantial adjustments that can seriously impair their psychological functioning. Many children of war lose their sense of safety, become desensitized to violence, are haunted by terrifying intrusive memories, display immature moral reasoning, and build a pessimistic view of the future. Anxiety and depression increase, as do aggression and antisocial behavior (Eisenberg & Silver, 2011; Klingman, 2006). These outcomes appear to be culturally universal, appearing among children from every war zone studied—from Bosnia, Angola, Rwanda, and the Sudan to the West Bank, Gaza, Afghanistan, and Iraq (Barenbaum, Ruchkin, & Schwab-Stone, 2004).

Parental affection and reassurance are the best protection against lasting problems. When parents offer security, discuss traumatic experiences sympathetically, and serve as role models of calm emotional strength, most children can

withstand even extreme war-related violence (Gewirtz, Forgatch, & Wieling, 2008). Children who are separated from parents must rely on help from their communities. Orphans in Eritrea who were placed in residential settings where they could form close emotional ties with an adult showed less emotional stress five years later than orphans placed in impersonal settings (Wolff & Fesseha, 1999). Education and recreation programs are powerful safeguards, too, providing children with consistency in their lives along with teacher and peer supports.

With the September 11, 2001, terrorist attacks on the World Trade Center and the Pentagon, some U.S. children experienced extreme wartime violence firsthand, watching through classroom windows as the planes struck and as the towers were engulfed in flames and crumbled. Most children, however, learned about the attacks indirectly—from the media or from caregivers or peers. Although both direct and indirect exposure triggered child and adolescent distress, extended exposure—having a family member affected or repeatedly witnessing the attacks on TV—resulted in more severe symptoms (Agronick et al., 2007; Otto et al., 2007; Rosen & Cohen, 2010). During the following months, distress reactions declined, though more slowly for children with conflict-ridden parent–child relationships or preexisting adjustment problems.

A trauma counselor comforts a child amid the rubble of her neighborhood in the Gaza Strip. Many children of war lose their sense of safety. They need special support from caring adults to prevent lasting emotional problems.

Unlike many war-traumatized children in the developing world, students in New York's Public School 31, who watched from their classrooms as the towers collapsed, received immediate intervention—a "trauma curriculum" in which they expressed their emotions through writing, drawing, and discussion and participated in experiences aimed at restoring trust and tolerance (Lagnado, 2001). Older students learned about the feelings of their Muslim classmates, the dire condition of children in Afghanistan, and ways to help victims as a means of overcoming a sense of helplessness.

When wartime drains families and communities of resources, international organizations must step in and help children. Efforts to preserve children's physical, psychological, and educational well-being may be the best way to stop transmission of violence to the next generation.

skills, friendships, and emotional self-regulation. And a complementary, 22-week program intervenes directly with children teaching appropriate classroom behavior, self-control, and social skills.

Evaluations in which families with aggressive children were randomly assigned to either Incredible Years or control groups reveal that the program is highly effective at improving parenting and reducing child behavior problems. Combining parent training with teacher and/or child intervention strengthens child outcomes (Webster-Stratton & Herman, 2010). And effects of parent training endure. In one 8- to 12-year-follow-up, 75 percent of young children with serious conduct problems whose parents participated in Incredible Years were well-adjusted as teenagers (Webster-Stratton & Reid, 2010a; Webster-Stratton, Rinaldi, & Reid, 2011). These favorable effects contrast sharply with the profound adjustment problems typically displayed by youths with early-onset conduct difficulties.

Social-Cognitive Interventions The social-cognitive deficits and distortions of aggressive children prevent them from empathizing with another person's pain and suffering. And because most aggressive children have few opportunities to witness family members acting in sensitive, caring ways, they miss early experiences that are vital for promoting empathy and sympathy (see Chapter 10). In such children, these responses may have to be directly taught.

School-based social-cognitive treatments focus on teaching children and adolescents to attend to relevant, nonhostile social cues, seek additional information before acting, generate effective social problem-solving strategies, and evaluate the likely effectiveness of potential responses. These interventions increase skill in solving social problems, decrease endorsement of beliefs supporting aggression, reduce hostile behaviors, and improve relationships with peers (see page 482 in Chapter 11). Training in perspective taking also helps by promoting more accurate interpretation of social cues, empathy, and sympathetic concern for others.

Lacking resources to support such programs, many U.S. schools have implemented *zero tolerance policies,* which severely punish all disruptive and threatening behavior, major and minor, usually with suspension or expulsion. Yet often these policies are applied inconsistently: Low-SES minority students are two to three times as likely to be punished, especially for minor misbehaviors (Goode & Goode, 2007; Skiba & Rausch, 2006). No evidence exists that zero tolerance achieves its objective of reducing youth aggression and other forms of misconduct (Stinchcomb, Bazemore, & Riestenberg, 2006). To the contrary, some studies find that by excluding students from school, zero tolerance heightens high school dropout and antisocial behavior.

Comprehensive Approaches According to many researchers, effective treatment for serious, violent juvenile offenders must be multifaceted, encompassing parent training, social understanding, relating to others, and self-control. A program called EQUIP uses positive peer culture—an adult-guided but adolescent-conducted small group approach aimed at creating a prosocial climate. By themselves, peer-culture groups do not reduce antisocial behavior. Rather, they sometimes perpetuate deviant peer influences (Dodge, Dishion, & Lansford, 2006). But in EQUIP, the approach is supplemented with training in social skills, anger management, correction of cognitive distortions, and moral reasoning (DiBiase et al., 2011; Gibbs et al., 2009b). Delinquents who participated in EQUIP displayed improved social skills and conduct during the following year compared with controls receiving no intervention. Also, the more advanced moral reasoning that emerged during group meetings seemed to have a long-term impact on antisocial youths' ability to inhibit lawbreaking behavior (Leeman, Gibbs, & Fuller, 1993).

Yet even multidimensional treatments can fall short if young people remain embedded in hostile home lives, poor-quality schools, antisocial peer groups, and violent neighborhoods. In another program, called *multisystemic therapy,* counselors trained parents in communication, monitoring, and discipline skills; integrated violent youths into positive school, work, and leisure activities; and disengaged them from deviant peers. Compared with individual therapy, random assignment to the intervention led to improved parent–adolescent relationships and school performance and to a dramatic drop in number of arrests that persisted for two decades after treatment and—when participants did commit crimes—to a reduction in their severity (see Figure 12.7). Multisystemic therapy also helped limit family instability in adulthood, as measured by involvement in civil suits over divorce, paternity, or child support (Borduin, 2007; Henggeler et al., 2009; Sawyer & Borduin, 2011). Efforts to create non-aggressive environments—at the family, community, and cultural levels—are needed to help antisocial youths and to foster healthy development of all young people.

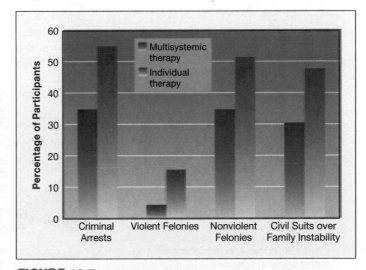

FIGURE 12.7 Impact of multisystemic therapy on arrests and family-related civil suits 22 years after treatment. A follow-up of violent youths two decades after treatment revealed that compared with participants who had been randomly assigned to individual therapy, those assigned to multisystemic therapy had fewer criminal arrests overall and—when they did commit crimes—were far less likely to perpetrate violent offenses. In addition multisystemic therapy recipients displayed reduced family instability, as measured by civil suits over divorce, paternity, or child support—evidence of more favorable adult adjustment. (Adapted from Sawyer & Borduin, 2011.)

ASK YOURSELF

Review ■ Cite factors that contribute to an improved ability to delay gratification from early to middle childhood.

Connect ■ Reread the section on adolescent parenthood in Chapter 5 (pages 217–219) and the section on adolescent suicide in Chapter 11 (pages 472–473). What factors do these problems have in common with chronic antisocial behavior?

Apply ■ Zeke had been well behaved in elementary school, but around age 13 he started spending time with the "wrong crowd." At 16, he was arrested for property damage. Is Zeke likely to become a long-term offender? Why or why not?

Reflect ■ Describe a recent instance in which your cool processing system dominated your hot-system reactivity, enabling you to resist temptation. What did your cool processing system do to gain control?

SUMMARY

Morality as Rooted in Human Nature (p. 486)

Describe and evaluate the biological perspective on morality.

■ Morality is grounded in our genetic heritage, perhaps through prewired emotional reactions. We share many morally relevant behaviors with other species, and areas within the prefrontal cortex are vital for emotional responsiveness to others' suffering. However, mature expression of moral emotions requires strong caregiving supports and cognitive attainments.

Morality as the Adoption of Societal Norms (p. 488)

Describe and evaluate the psychoanalytic perspective on moral development.

■ Both psychoanalytic and social learning theories regard moral development as a process of **internalization** of societal standards. According to Freud, morality emerges between ages 3 and 6, when the Oedipus and Electra conflicts are resolved with formation of the superego. The child adopts the moral standards of the same-sex parent and redirects hostile impulses toward the self in the form of guilt.

■ Although guilt is an important motivator of moral action, contrary to Freud's view, discipline promoting fear of punishment and loss of parental love does not foster conscience development. **Induction** is far more effective and also fosters a strong **moral identity.**

■ Contrary to Freud's belief, moral development is not complete by the end of early childhood. Rather, it proceeds gradually, extending into adulthood.

Describe and evaluate the social learning perspective on moral development.

■ Social learning theory focuses on how moral behavior is learned through reinforcement and modeling. Effective models are warm, responsive, competent, powerful, and consistent in words and deeds. By middle childhood, children have internalized prosocial rules.

■ Frequent harsh punishment results in weak moral internalization and wide-ranging adjustment problems, models aggressive behavior, and can spiral into serious abuse. Alternatives such as **time out** and withdrawal of privileges can help parents avoid these undesirable effects, as long as parents apply the techniques consistently, maintain a warm relationship with the child, and offer explanations for punishment.

■ The most effective discipline relies on positive parenting, which encourages good conduct by building a mutually respectful bond with the child.

© MAURITIUS IMAGES GMBH/ALAMY

Cite central features of the cognitive-developmental approach to moral development.

■ The cognitive-developmental approach assumes that individuals, rather than internalizing existing rules and expectations, develop morally through **construction**—actively thinking about situations in which social conflicts arise and attaining new moral understandings.

Morality as Social Understanding (p. 496)

Describe and evaluate Piaget's theory of moral development.

■ Piaget, whose work inspired the cognitive-developmental perspective on morality, identified two stages: **heteronomous morality,** in which children view moral rules in terms of **realism,** and the **morality of cooperation,** in which children regard rules as flexible, socially agreed-on principles and base fairness on **ideal reciprocity.**

■ Piaget's theory accurately describes the general direction of moral development but underestimates young children's moral capacities. Preschool and early school-age children consider intentions when making moral judgments, although they interpret intentions rigidly. They also have differentiated notions about the legitimacy of authority figures. For nonmoral concerns, they base authority on knowledge, not social position.

Describe Kohlberg's theory of moral development, and discuss research on his stages.

■ Kohlberg viewed moral development as a gradual process extending into adolescence and adulthood. Using clinical interviewing, he constructed a sequence of moral reasoning based on responses to hypothetical dilemmas.

■ Kohlberg concluded that moral reasoning gradually advances through three levels, each containing two stages: At the **preconventional level,** morality is viewed as externally controlled and actions are judged by their consequences; at the **conventional level,** conformity to laws and rules is regarded as necessary for societal order; and at the **postconventional level,** morality is defined by abstract, universal principles and values.

■ While most individuals move through Kohlberg's first four stages in the predicted order, his hypothetical moral dilemmas do not address the whole range of strategies people use to resolve real-life moral problems. Because situational factors affect moral reasoning, Kohlberg's stages are best viewed as loosely organized and overlapping.

■ Kohlberg argued that cognitive and perspective-taking attainments, though vital for moral advances, are not sufficient to ensure them. At present, the domain in which the cognitive prerequisites for mature moral reasoning first emerges—cognitive, social, or moral—remains unclear.

■ Contrary to Gilligan's claim, Kohlberg's theory does not underestimate the moral maturity of females but instead taps both justice and caring moralities.

Describe influences on moral reasoning and its relationship to moral behavior.

■ Factors contributing to moral maturity include a flexible, open-minded personality; warm, rational parenting; education level; and peer discussions of moral issues.

■ In village societies, where moral cooperation is based on direct relations between people, moral reasoning rarely moves beyond Kohlberg's Stage 3. In collectivist cultures, moral dilemma responses are more other-directed than in Western societies.

■ Maturity of moral reasoning is only modestly related to moral behavior. Moral action is also influenced by the individual's emotions, temperament, history of morally relevant experiences and intuitions, and moral identity.

■ Despite declines in formal religious involvement in adolescence, most religiously affiliated teenagers are advantaged in moral values and behavior.

Discuss challenges to Kohlberg's theory.

■ In a revised conception of moral development, moral maturity is achieved at Kohlberg's Stages 3 and 4, when young people grasp ideal reciprocity—attainments that require profound moral constructions. Some critics favor a pragmatic approach in which moral judgments are viewed as practical tools that people use to achieve their goals.

How do children distinguish moral imperatives from social conventions and matters of personal choice?

■ Even preschoolers show a basic grasp of justice, distinguishing **moral imperatives** from **social conventions** and **matters of personal choice.** Through actively making sense of people's everyday social experiences and emotional reactions, young children conclude that moral (but not social conventional) transgressions are wrong in any context.

■ School-age children gradually clarify and link moral imperatives and social conventions, taking into account the purpose of the rule; people's intentions, knowledge, and beliefs; and the context of people's behavior. The conviction that certain matters are up to the individual strengthens with age, especially in adolescence. Notions of personal choice foster moral understanding of individual rights.

Development of Morally Relevant Self-Control (p. 514)

Discuss the development of morally relevant self-control, noting implications of individual differences for cognitive and social competencies.

■ Self-control emerges in the second year in the form of **compliance.** The capacity for **delay of gratification** increases steadily between ages 1½ and 3 years and is influenced by temperament and quality of caregiving.

■ School-age children become better at devising their own strategies for resisting temptation, leading to a flexible capacity for **moral self-regulation.** Individual differences in delay of gratification predict diverse cognitive and social competencies, including effective social problem solving and positive peer relations.

The Other Side of Self-Control: Development of Aggression (p. 516)

Discuss the development of aggression, noting various influences, and describe successful interventions.

■ Aggression first appears by the second year. Over early and middle childhood, **proactive aggression** declines, while **reactive aggression** increases. Proactive and reactive aggression come in at least three forms: **physical aggression, verbal aggression,** and **relational aggression.**

■ During early childhood, physical aggression decreases, while verbal aggression increases. By age 17 months, boys are more physically aggressive than girls. Teacher-and peer-reported aggression declines in adolescence, but delinquent acts increase, especially for boys.

■ Children high in physical or relational aggression tend to remain so over time. Irritable, fearless, impulsive, and overactive children are at risk for aggression, but whether or not they become so depends on child-rearing conditions.

■ Children who are products of strife-ridden families and harsh, inconsistent discipline develop social-cognitive deficits and distortions that contribute to long-term maintenance of aggression. Widespread poverty, harsh living conditions, and inadequate schools increase antisocial acts among children and adolescents.

■ Training parents in effective child-rearing techniques and teaching children alternative ways of resolving conflict help reduce aggression. Social-cognitive interventions aimed at improving social information processing and perspective taking are also beneficial. The most effective interventions address the multiple factors that sustain antisocial behavior.

IMPORTANT TERMS AND CONCEPTS

compliance (p. 514)
construction (p. 495)
conventional level (p. 501)
delay of gratification (p. 514)
heteronomous morality (p. 496)
ideal reciprocity (p. 497)
induction (p. 489)
internalization (p. 488)

matters of personal choice (p. 510)
moral identity (p. 489)
moral imperatives (p. 510)
moral self-regulation (p. 515)
morality of cooperation (p. 497)
physical aggression (p. 517)
postconventional level (p. 501)
preconventional level (p. 500)

proactive aggression (p. 517)
reactive aggression (p. 517)
realism (p. 496)
relational aggression (p. 518)
social conventions (p. 510)
time out (p. 493)
verbal aggression (p. 518)

"Friends"
Diduli Sathsava
14 years, Sri Lanka

In a distinctly gender-typed image of friendship, this painter illustrates the high value girls place on emotional sensitivity and intimacy in close relationships.

Reprinted with permission from the International Museum of Children's Art, Oslo, Norway

Development of Sex Differences and Gender Roles

Gender Stereotypes and Gender Roles
Gender Stereotyping in Early Childhood • Gender Stereotyping in Middle Childhood and Adolescence • Individual and Group Differences in Gender Stereotyping • Gender Stereotyping and Gender-Role Adoption

Influences on Gender Stereotyping and Gender-Role Adoption
Biological Influences • Environmental Influences

■ **CULTURAL INFLUENCES:** *Sweden's Commitment to Gender Equality*

■ **SOCIAL ISSUES: EDUCATION:** *Children Learn About Gender Through Mother–Child Conversations*

■ **SOCIAL ISSUES: EDUCATION:** *Teaching Children to Challenge Peers' Sexist Remarks*

Gender Identity
Emergence of Gender Identity • Gender Identity in Middle Childhood • Gender Identity in Adolescence • Gender Schema Theory

To What Extent Do Boys and Girls *Really* Differ in Gender-Stereotyped Attributes?
Mental Abilities • Personality Traits

■ **BIOLOGY AND ENVIRONMENT:** *Sex Differences in Spatial Abilities*

Developing Non-Gender-Stereotyped Children

O n a typical morning in our university laboratory preschool, 4-year-old Jenny eagerly entered the housekeeping corner and put on a frilly long dress. Karen, setting the table nearby, produced whimpering sound effects for the baby doll in the crib. Jenny lifted the doll, sat down in the rocking chair, and whispered, "You're hungry, aren't you?" A moment later, Jenny announced, "This baby won't eat. I think she's sick. Ask Rachel if she'll be the nurse." Karen ran to find Rachel, who was coloring at the art table.

Meanwhile, Nathan called to Tommy, "Wanna play traffic?" Both boys dashed energetically toward the cars and trucks in the block corner. Soon David joined them. "I'll be policeman first!" announced Nathan, climbing onto a chair. "Green light, go!" shouted the young police officer. With this signal, Tommy and David scurried on all fours around the chair, each pushing a large wooden truck. "Red light!" exclaimed Nathan, and the trucks screeched to a halt.

"My truck beat yours," Tommy informed David.

"Only 'cause I need gas," David responded.

"Let's build a runway for the trucks," suggested Nathan. The three construction engineers began gathering large blocks for the task.

At an early age, children adopt many gender-linked standards of their culture. Jenny, Karen, and Rachel use dresses, dolls, and household props to act out a stereotypically feminine scene of nurturance. In contrast, Nathan, Tommy, and David's play is active, competitive, and masculine in theme. And both boys and girls interact more with agemates of their own sex.

Why are young children's play and social preferences so strongly gender-typed, and how do these attitudes and behaviors change with age? Do societal expectations affect children's views of themselves as masculine or feminine beings, thereby limiting their potential? To what extent do widely held beliefs about the characteristics of males and females reflect reality? Is it true that the average boy is aggressive and competitive, with good spatial and mathematical skills, whereas the average girl is passive and nurturant, with superior verbal skills? How large are differences between the sexes, and in what ways do heredity and environment contribute to them? These are the central questions asked by researchers studying gender typing. In this chapter, we will answer each of them.

Perhaps more than any other area of child development, the study of gender typing has responded to societal change. Until the early 1970s, psychologists regarded the adoption of gender-typed beliefs and behaviors as essential for healthy adjustment. Since then, this view has changed, largely because of progress in women's rights. Today, many people recognize that some gender-typed characteristics, such as extreme aggressiveness and competitiveness on the part of males and passivity and conformity on the part of females, are serious threats to mental health.

Consistent with this realization, the study of gender typing has undergone theoretical revision. Major current approaches are social learning theory, with its emphasis on modeling and reinforcement, and cognitive-developmental theory, with its focus on children as active thinkers about their social world. But neither is sufficient by itself. An information-processing view, *gender schema theory,* combines elements of both theories to explain how children acquire gender-typed knowledge.

Central to our discussion is a set of special terms. Two involve the public face of gender in society. **Gender stereotypes** are widely held beliefs about characteristics deemed appropriate for males and females. **Gender roles** are the reflection of these stereotypes in everyday behavior. A third, **gender identity,** is the private face of gender—perception of the self as relatively masculine or feminine in characteristics. Finally, **gender typing** refers broadly to any association of objects, activities, roles, or traits with biological sex in ways that conform to cultural stereotypes of gender and, therefore, encompasses all the gender-linked responses just mentioned (Liben & Bigler, 2002). As we explore each facet of gender typing in children and adolescents, you will see that biological, cognitive, and social factors are involved.

▶ Explain how the study of gender typing has responded to societal change.

▶ Describe the development of gender stereotyping from early childhood into adolescence.

▶ Cite individual and group differences in gender stereotyping, and discuss the relationship between gender stereotyping and gender-role adoption.

Gender Stereotypes and Gender Roles

Gender stereotypes have appeared in religious, philosophical, and literary works for centuries. Consider the following excerpts, from ancient times to the present:

- "Woman is more compassionate than man and has a greater propensity to tears. . . . But the male . . . is more disposed to give assistance in danger, and is more courageous than the female." (Aristotle, cited in Miles, 1935)
- "A man will say what he knows, a woman says what will please." (Jean-Jacques Rousseau, *Emile,* 1762/1955)
- "Man with the head and woman with the heart; Man to command and woman to obey; All else confusion." (Alfred, Lord Tennyson, *Home They Brought Her Warrior,* 1842)
- "Love is a mood—no more—to a man, And love to a woman is life or death." (Ella Wheeler Wilcox, *Blind,* 1882)
- "Men do not confront a relationship problem unless absolutely necessary because the risk is that they'll make things much worse. . . . Women seek out even small problems to prevent them from becoming more serious." (Lewis, *Why Don't You Understand? A Gender Relationship Dictionary,* 2009)

Although the past four decades have brought a new level of awareness about the wide range of roles possible for each gender, strong beliefs about sex differences remain. In the 1960s, researchers began asking people what personality characteristics they consider typical of men and women. Widespread agreement emerged in many studies. As Table 13.1 illustrates, **instrumental traits,** reflecting competence, rationality, and assertiveness, were regarded as masculine; **expressive traits,** emphasizing warmth, caring, and sensitivity, were viewed as feminine. Despite intense political activism promoting gender equality in the 1970s and 1980s, these stereotypes remain essentially unchanged (Lueptow, Garovich, & Lueptow, 2001; Ruble, Martin, & Berenbaum, 2006; Vonk & Ashmore, 2003). Furthermore, cross-cultural research conducted in 30 nations reveals that the instrumental–expressive dichotomy is a widely held stereotype around the world (Williams & Best, 1990).

Besides personality traits, other gender stereotypes exist. These include physical characteristics (tall, strong, and sturdy for men; soft, dainty, and graceful for women), occupations (truck driver, insurance agent, and chemist for men; elementary school teacher, secretary, and nurse for women), and activities or behaviors (good

TABLE 13.1 | **Personality Traits Regarded as Stereotypically Masculine or Feminine**

MASCULINE TRAITS	FEMININE TRAITS
Active	Aware of others' feelings
Acts as a leader	Considerate
Adventurous	Cries easily
Aggressive	Devotes self to others
Ambitious	Emotional
Competitive	Excitable in a major crisis
Doesn't give up easily	Feelings hurt easily
Dominant	Gentle
Feels superior	Home-oriented
Holds up well under pressure	Kind
Independent	Likes children
Makes decisions easily	Neat
Not easily influenced	Needs approval
Outspoken	Passive
Rough	Tactful
Self-confident	Understanding of others
Takes a stand	Warm in relations with others

at fixing things and at leading groups for men; good at child care and decorating the home for women) (Biernat, 1991; Powlishta et al., 2001).

The variety of attributes consistently identified as masculine or feminine, their broad acceptance, and their stability over time suggest that gender stereotypes are deeply ingrained patterns of thinking. What's more, they cast men in a generally positive light and women in a generally negative light. The traits, activities, and roles associated with the male gender are more numerous, diverse, and desirable than those associated with the female gender. For example, in Western cultures, stereotypically masculine occupations are far more numerous than feminine occupations (Liben & Bigler, 2002). And only a few masculine attributes, such as "aggressive" and "criminal," are negative; the overwhelming majority are advantageous and high-status. Feminine attributes, in contrast, are mostly unfavorable and low-status.

Adults apply gender stereotypes to children with a special intensity. In a study in which 20- to 40-year-olds were shown photos of children and adults and asked to rate each on "masculine," "feminine," and "neutral" personality traits, adults differentiated boys from girls more sharply than they did men from women (see Figure 13.1) (Powlishta, 2000). Given that many adults view children through a gender-biased lens, perhaps it is not surprising that by the second year, children have begun to absorb these messages.

Gender Stereotyping in Early Childhood

Recall from Chapter 11 that between 18 months and 3 years, children label their own and others' sex, using such words as *boy* and *girl* and *lady* and *man*. As children sort out what these categories mean in terms of activities and behaviors, gender stereotypes appear and expand rapidly. Before age 2, children have begun to acquire subtle associations with gender that most of us hold—men as rough and sharp, women as soft and round. In one study, 18-month-olds linked such items as fir trees and hammers with males, although they had not yet learned comparable feminine associations (Eichstedt et al., 2002). Preschoolers associate toys, articles of clothing, tools, household items, games, occupations, colors (pink and blue), and behaviors (relational and physical aggression) with one sex or the other (Banse et al., 2010; Giles & Heyman, 2005; Poulin-Dubois et al., 2002). They have even acquired gender-stereotyped metaphors—"bears are for boys"; "butterflies are for girls" (Leinbach, Hort, & Fagot, 1997).

During early childhood, gender-stereotyped beliefs strengthen—so much so that many children apply them as blanket rules rather than flexible guidelines. When children were asked whether gender stereotypes could be violated, half or more of 3- and 4-year-olds answered "no" to clothing, hairstyle, and play with certain toys (Barbie dolls and G.I. Joes) (Blakemore, 2003). Furthermore, most 3- to 6-year-olds are firm about not wanting to be friends with a child who violates a gender stereotype (a boy who wears nail polish, a girl who plays with trucks) or to attend a school where such violations are allowed (Ruble et al., 2007).

Striking evidence that young children view their world in strongly gender-stereotyped terms also comes from studies in which researchers labeled a target child as a boy or a girl and then provided either gender-typical or gender-atypical information about the target's characteristics. Then they asked children to rate the target on additional gender-stereotypic attributes. Preschoolers usually relied only on the gender label in making judgments, ignoring the specific information (Biernat, 1991; Martin, 1989). For example, when told "Tommy is a boy. Tommy's best friend is a girl, and Tommy likes to play house," children under age 6 nevertheless said that Tommy would much rather play with cars and train engines than with sewing machines and dolls.

The rigidity of preschoolers' gender stereotypes helps us understand some commonly observed everyday behaviors. Shown a picture of a Scottish bagpiper wearing a kilt, 4-year-olds are likely to insist, "Men don't wear skirts!" During free play, they exclaim that girls can't

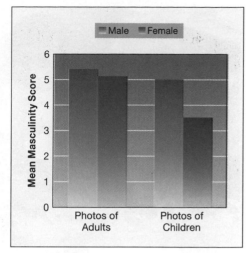

FIGURE 13.1 Adults' ratings of photos of adults and children on "masculine" personality traits. Adults perceived little difference in the adult photos but a sharp difference in the child photos, rating boys as far more "masculine" in personality traits than girls. Ratings for "feminine" personality traits were similar: Adults reported far greater difference between boys and girls than between men and women. (Adapted from Powlishta, 2000.)

Gender-stereotyped beliefs strengthen during early childhood. These pre-schoolers would probably say "no" to the suggestion that a boy be allowed to join their tea party.

be police officers and boys can't take care of babies. These one-sided judgments are a joint product of gender stereotyping in the environment and young children's cognitive limitations—in particular, their difficulty coordinating conflicting sources of information. Most preschoolers do not yet realize that characteristics *associated with* being male or female—activities, toys, occupations, hairstyle, and clothing—do not *determine* a person's sex. They have trouble understanding that males and females can be different in terms of their bodies but similar in many other ways.

Gender Stereotyping in Middle Childhood and Adolescence

By age 5, gender stereotyping of activities and occupations is well-established. During middle childhood and adolescence, knowledge of stereotypes increases in the less obvious areas of personality traits and achievement (Serbin, Powlishta, & Gulko, 1993; Signorella, Bigler, & Liben, 1993). At the same time, because older children realize that gender-stereotypic attributes are associated—but not defining—features of gender, their beliefs about possible male and female characteristics and capacities become more flexible (Banse et al., 2010; Martin, Ruble, & Szkrybalo, 2002).

Personality Traits To assess stereotyping of personality traits, researchers ask children to assign "masculine" adjectives ("tough," "rational," "cruel") and "feminine" adjectives ("gentle," "affectionate," "dependent") to either a male or a female stimulus figure. Recall from Chapter 11 that not until middle childhood are children good at sizing up people's dispositions. This same finding carries over to awareness of gender stereotypes.

Research in many countries reveals that stereotyping of personality traits increases steadily in middle childhood, becoming adultlike around age 11 (Best, 2001; Heyman & Legare, 2004). A large Canadian study examined the pattern of children's trait learning and found that the stereotypes acquired first reflected *in-group favoritism*. Kindergartners through second graders had greatest knowledge of trait stereotypes that portrayed their own gender in a positive light (Serbin, Powlishta, & Gulko, 1993). Once trait stereotyping is well under way, children characterize the in-group and the out-group as having both positive and negative qualities. Though both boys and girls view each gender as having more positive than negative traits, this effect is stronger for the in-group—evidence that in-group favoritism persists. And girls express greater in-group favoritism and out-group negativity than boys (Powlishta et al., 1994; Susskind & Hodges, 2009). Perhaps girls more readily pick up the widely held general impression of girls as "sugar and spice and everything nice" and of boys as "snakes and snails and puppy dog tails."

Achievement Areas Shortly after entering elementary school, children figure out which academic subjects and skill areas are "masculine" and which are "feminine." They often regard reading, spelling, art, and music as more for girls and mathematics, athletics, and mechanical skills as more for boys (Cvencek, Meltzoff, & Greenwald, 2011; Eccles, Jacobs, & Harold, 1990; Jacobs & Weisz, 1994). These stereotypes influence children's preferences for and sense of competence at certain subjects. For example, in both Asian and Western nations, boys tend to feel more competent than girls at math, science, and athletics, whereas girls feel more competent than boys at language arts—even when children of equal skill level are compared (Bhanot & Jovanovic, 2005; Hong, Veach, & Lawrenz, 2003; Kurtz-Costes et al., 2008).

An encouraging sign is that some gender-stereotyped beliefs about achievement may be changing. In several recent investigations carried out in Canada, France, and the United

States, a majority of elementary and secondary school students disagreed with the idea that math is a "masculine" subject (Martinot & Désert, 2007; Plante, Théoret, & Favreau, 2009; Rowley et al., 2007). And when Canadian students were given the option of rating math as a "feminine" subject (not offered in previous studies), an impressive number—though more girls than boys—expressed the view that it is predominantly feminine. The overwhelming majority of these young people, however, continued to view language arts traditionally—as largely "feminine." And they still perceived girls to do better in language arts than in math.

Toward Greater Flexibility Although school-age children are knowledgeable about a wide variety of gender stereotypes, they also develop a more open-minded view of what males and females *can do,* a trend that continues into adolescence.

In studying gender stereotyping, researchers usually ask children whether or not both genders can display a personality trait or activity—a response that measures **gender-stereotype flexibility,** or overlap in the characteristics of males and females. In a German study that followed children from ages 5 to 10, regardless of the degree of early gender-stereotype rigidity, flexibility increased dramatically from age 7 on (see Figure 13.2) (Trautner et al., 2005). As they develop the capacity to integrate conflicting social cues, children realize that a person's sex is not a certain predictor of his or her personality traits, activities, and behavior. Similarly, by the end of the school years, most children no longer view gender-typed behavior (especially that of girls) as inborn and fixed. Rather, they see it as socially influenced—affected by home rearing environments (Taylor, 1996; Taylor, Rhodes, & Gelman, 2009).

But acknowledging that boys and girls *can* cross gender lines does not mean that children always *approve* of doing so. In one longitudinal study, between ages 7 and 13, children of both genders became more open-minded about girls being offered the same opportunities as boys. This change, however, was less pronounced for boys (Crouter et al., 2007). Moreover, school-age children seem well aware of the power of such male in-group favoritism to limit girls' access to high-status opportunities. When 5- to 10-year-olds were asked why only men had been elected to the U.S. presidency, their most frequent explanation was that men would not vote for a woman candidate (Bigler et al., 2008).

Furthermore, many school-age children take a harsh view of certain violations, such as boys playing with dolls and wearing girls' clothing and girls acting noisily or roughly. They are especially intolerant when boys engage in these "cross-gender" acts, which children regard as nearly as bad as moral transgressions (Blakemore, 2003; Levy, Taylor, & Gelman, 1995). When asked for open-ended descriptions of boys and girls, children most often mention girls' physical appearance ("is pretty," "wears dresses") and boys' activities and personality traits ("likes trucks," "is rough") (Miller et al., 2009). The salience of these stereotypes helps explain why, when children of the other sex display the behaviors just mentioned, they are likely to experience severe peer disapproval.

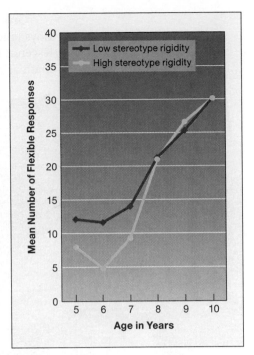

FIGURE 13.2 Changes in gender-stereotype flexibility between ages 5 and 10. In a longitudinal study, German schoolchildren responded annually to a questionnaire assessing the flexibility of their gender-stereotyped beliefs (whether they thought both genders could display a personality trait or activity). Children differing in degree of gender-stereotype rigidity at age 5 eventually became equally flexible. Findings support the powerful role of cognitive changes in inducing flexibility, since early individual differences in rigidity were not sustained. (From H. M. Trautner et al., 2005, "Rigidity and Flexibility of Gender Stereotypes in Childhood: Developmental or Differential?," *Infant and Child Development,* 14, p. 371. Copyright © 2005 John Wiley & Sons Limited. Reprinted with permission.)

Individual and Group Differences in Gender Stereotyping

By middle childhood, almost all children have acquired extensive knowledge of gender stereotypes. But they vary widely in the makeup of their understanding. The various components of gender stereotyping—activities, behaviors, occupations, and personality traits—do not correlate highly: A child may be highly knowledgeable in one area without being knowledgeable in the others (Serbin, Powlishta, & Gulko, 1993). This suggests that gender typing is like "an intricate puzzle that the child pieces together in a rather idiosyncratic way" (Hort, Leinbach, & Fagot, 1991, p. 196). To build a coherent notion of gender, children must assemble many elements. The precise pattern in which they acquire the pieces, the rate at which they do so, and the flexibility of their beliefs vary greatly from child to child.

Group differences in gender stereotyping also exist. The strongest of these is sex-related: Boys tend to hold more gender-stereotyped views than girls throughout childhood and adolescence (Steele, 2003; Turner, Gervai, & Hinde, 1993). But as we have seen, stereotyping of math as masculine seems to have declined, even among boys. And in one study, adolescents of both sexes, responding to vignettes about hypothetical high-achieving peers, expressed greater liking for the high-achieving girls (Quatman, Sokolik, & Smith, 2000). A heartening possibility is that boys are beginning to view gender roles as encompassing more varied possibilities.

The limited evidence available on ethnic minorities suggests that African-American children hold less stereotyped views of activities and achievement areas than do Caucasian-American children (Bardwell, Cochran, & Walker, 1986; Rowley et al., 2007). Perhaps this is partly a response to the less traditional gender roles seen in African-American families—for example, more employed mothers and mother-headed households (U.S. Census Bureau, 2011b). In adolescence and adulthood, higher-SES individuals tend to hold more flexible gender-stereotyped views than their lower-SES counterparts (Lackey, 1989; Serbin, Powlishta, & Gulko, 1993). Years of schooling and a wider array of life options may contribute to this difference.

Even children who are well-versed in gender-related expectations are not necessarily highly gender-typed in their everyday activities. This boy appears to view playing with dolls as appropriate for boys as well as girls.

Gender Stereotyping and Gender-Role Adoption

Does gender-stereotyped thinking influence children's gender-role adoption, thereby restricting their experiences and potential? The evidence is mixed. Gender-typed preferences and behaviors increase sharply over the preschool years—the same period in which children rapidly acquire stereotypes. And boys—the more stereotyped of the two sexes—show greater conformity to their gender role (Bussey & Bandura, 1992; Ruble, Martin, & Berenbaum, 2006).

But these parallel patterns do not tell us whether gender stereotyping shapes children's behavior. In some cases, a reverse direction of influence may operate because certain gender-role preferences are acquired long before children know much about stereotypes. For example, by the middle of the second year, boys and girls favor different toys. When researchers showed 18-month-olds paired photos of vehicles and dolls, boys looked longer than girls at the vehicles, whereas girls looked longer than boys at the dolls (see Figure 13.3) (Serbin et al., 2001).

Furthermore, children who are well-versed in gender-related expectations are sometimes highly gender-typed, and sometimes not, in their everyday activities (Downs & Langlois, 1988; Serbin, Powlishta, & Gulko, 1993; Weinraub et al., 1984). Why might this be so? First, we have seen that children master the components of gender-stereotyped knowledge in diverse ways, each of which may have different implications for their behavior. Second, by middle childhood, virtually all children know a great deal about gender stereotypes—knowledge so universal that it cannot predict variations in their behavior.

Rather than stereotype knowledge, stereotype flexibility is a good predictor of children's gender-role adoption in middle childhood. Children who believe that many stereotyped characteristics are appropriate for both sexes (for example, that it is OK for girls to play with trucks) are more likely to cross gender lines in choosing activities, playmates, and occupational roles (Liben, Bigler, & Krogh, 2002; Serbin, Powlishta, & Gulko, 1993; Signorella, Bigler, & Liben, 1993). This suggests that gender stereotypes affect behavior only when children incorporate those beliefs into their gender identities—self-perceptions of what they can and should do at play, in school, and as future participants in society. Now let's turn to various influences that promote children's gender-typed beliefs and behaviors.

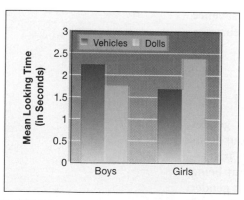

FIGURE 13.3 Eighteen-month-old girls' and boys' looking times at vehicles and dolls. Already, gender-role preferences are evident: Boys looked longer at the vehicles, whereas girls looked longer at the dolls. (Adapted from Serbin et al., 2001.)

© LAURA DWIGHT PHOTOGRAPHY

ASK YOURSELF

Review ■ Explain how young children's cognitive limitations combine with the social environment to contribute to rigid gender stereotyping in early childhood.

Review ■ What factors allow for flexibility in gender stereotyping in middle childhood and adolescence? How is gender-stereotype flexibility related to gender-typed preferences and behavior?

Connect ■ Describe parallels between the development of gender and ethnic attitudes (see Chapter 11, pages 477–478).

Apply ■ After 9-year-old Dennis enrolled in an after-school cooking class, his friends Tom and Bill began teaing him relentlessly. Cite evidence that explains this negative reaction to Dennis's "cross-gender" behavior.

Influences on Gender Stereotyping and Gender-Role Adoption

► Discuss biological influences on gender stereotyping and gender-role adoption.

► Discuss environmental influences on gender stereotyping and gender-role adoption.

According to social learning theorists, gender-stereotyped knowledge and behaviors are transmitted to children through direct teaching. As we will see shortly, much research is consistent with this view. Others argue, however, that biological makeup leads each sex to be uniquely suited to particular roles and that most societies do little more than encourage gender differences that are genetically based. Is there evidence to support this idea?

Biological Influences

Although practically no contemporary theorist would argue that "biology is destiny," serious questions about biological influences on gender typing remain. According to an evolutionary perspective, the adult life of our male ancestors was largely oriented toward competing for mates, that of our female ancestors toward rearing children. Therefore, males became genetically primed for dominance and females for intimacy, responsiveness, and cooperativeness. These sex differences in behavior exist in 97 percent of mammalian species, including chimpanzees, our closest evolutionary relative (de Waal, 1993, 2001). Evolutionary theorists claim that family and cultural forces can influence the intensity of biologically based sex differences, leading some individuals to be more gender-typed than others. But experience cannot eradicate aspects of gender typing that served adaptive functions in human history (Geary, 1999; Maccoby, 2002).

Two sources of evidence have been used to support the role of biology: (1) cross-cultural similarities in gender stereotypes and gender-role adoption and (2) the influence of hormones on gender-role behavior. Let's examine each in turn.

How Much Cross-Cultural Similarity Exists in Gender Typing?

Earlier in this chapter, we noted that the instrumental–expressive dichotomy is reflected in the gender stereotyping of many national groups. Although this finding fits with the idea that social influences simply build on genetic differences between the sexes, we must be cautious in drawing this conclusion.

A close look at cross-cultural findings reveals that most societies promote instrumental traits in males and expressive traits in females, although great diversity exists in the magnitude of this difference (Konner, 2010; Munroe & Romney, 2006; Whiting & Edwards, 1988b). For example, in Nyansongo, a small agricultural settlement in Kenya, mothers work four to five hours a day in the gardens, while older siblings care for young children, tend the cooking fire, and wash dishes. Because these duties are assigned to children of both sexes, girls do not have total responsibility for "feminine" tasks and have more time to interact with agemates. Their greater freedom and independence lead them to score higher than girls of

In the wake of devastating floods, a Bangladeshi girl breaks bricks with her mother. Although most societies promote instrumental traits in males and expressive traits in females, current conditions may alter the extent of this difference.

© RAFIQUR RAHMAN/REUTERS/CORBIS

CULTURAL INFLUENCES

Sweden's Commitment to Gender Equality

Among all nations in the world, Sweden is unique in the value it places on gender equality. More than a century ago, Sweden's ruling political party adopted equality as a central goal. One social class was not to exploit another, nor one gender another. In the 1960s, Sweden's expanding economy attracted women into the labor force in large numbers, raising the question of who would help sustain family life. Calling on the principle of equality, the Swedish people responded: fathers, just like mothers (Plantin, Mansson, & Kearney, 2003).

The Swedish "equal roles family model" maintains that husband and wife should have the same opportunity to pursue a career and should be equally responsible for housework and child care. To support this goal, Swedish fathers have had the right to paid parental employment leave longer than fathers in any other nation—since 1974. Today, in addition to two weeks of postbirth leave, Swedish fathers and mothers may share a total of 16 months of full leave at 80 percent of prior income, which can be taken any time before the child reaches 8 years of age (Swedish Social Insurance Agency, 2011a). In addition, Sweden made child-care centers available, so toddlers and preschoolers could be cared for outside the home. Otherwise, a class of less privileged women might be exploited for caregiving and domestic work—an outcome that would contradict the principle of equality.

According to several indicators, Sweden's family model is very successful. Child-care centers are numerous, of high quality, and heavily subsidized by the government. Over 80 percent of mothers of infants and preschoolers are

employed, and although Swedish fathers do not yet share housework and child care equally with mothers, they are more involved than fathers in the United States and other Western European nations (Dribe & Stanfors, 2009). Today, 90 percent of Swedish fathers take at least some parental employment leave—more than in any other nation in the world. And more than half make work adjustments—reducing work hours, turning down promotions, and refusing overtime—so they can spend additional time with children (Haas, 2003; Haas, Chronholm, & Hwang, 2006). Furthermore, Sweden has instituted "daddy-months," allocating two of the 16 months leave to fathers, which if not used are lost—a reform aimed at encouraging fathers to take more responsibility for child rearing. Consequently, over the past decade, fathers' leave use nearly doubled, from 12 to 23 percent of total leave time available (Swedish Social Insurance Agency, 2011b).

Has Sweden's progressive family policy affected the gender beliefs and behaviors of its population? A study of Swedish and American adolescents found that valuing of the "masculine" over the "feminine" role was less pronounced in Sweden than in the United States. Swedish young people regarded each gender as a blend of instrumental and expressive traits, and they more often viewed gender roles as a matter of learned tasks and domains of expertise than as inborn traits or rights and duties (Intons-Peterson, 1988). Similarly, large nationally representative surveys in Western European countries reveal that Swedish adults hold more favorable attitudes toward maternal

In Sweden, which highly values gender equality, fathers are more involved in child care than in other Western nations. Parents share 16 months of paid leave, with two "daddy-months" specifically allotted to fathers.

employment. For example, more Swedish than British and Norwegian respondents agreed that "a working mother could establish just as warm and secure a relationship with her children as a mother who does not work" (Knudsen & Waerness, 2003).

Traditional gender typing has not been eradicated in Sweden. But great progress has been made as a result of steadfastly pursuing a program of gender equality.

other tribal and village cultures in dominance, assertiveness, and playful roughhousing. In contrast, boys' caregiving responsibilities mean that they often display help-giving and emotional support (Whiting & Edwards, 1988a). Among industrialized nations, Sweden is widely recognized as a society in which traditional gender-linked beliefs and behaviors are considerably reduced (see the Cultural Influences box above).

These examples indicate that experience can profoundly influence gender typing. Nevertheless, reversals of traditional gender roles are rare. Because cross-cultural findings are inconclusive, scientists have turned to a more direct test of the importance of biology: the impact of sex hormones on gender typing.

Sex Hormones and Gender Typing

In Chapters 3 and 5, we discussed how genetic makeup, mediated by hormones, regulates sexual development and body growth. Sex hormones also affect brain development and neural activity in many animal species, and they do so in humans as well (Hines & Green, 1991). Are hormones, which so pervasively affect body structures, also important in gender-role adoption?

Play Styles and Preference for Same-Sex Peers. Experiments with animals reveal that pre-natally administered androgens (male sex hormones) increase active play in both male and female mammals. Androgens also promote male-typical sexual behavior and aggression and suppress maternal caregiving in a wide variety of species (Lephart et al., 2001; Sato et al., 2004).

Eleanor Maccoby (1998) argues that at least some of these hormonal effects extend to humans. Recall from the introduction to this chapter that as early as the preschool years, children seek out playmates of their own sex—a preference observed in many mammalian species and cultures (Beatty, 1992; Munroe & Romney, 2006). At age 4, children spend three times as much time with same-sex as with other-sex playmates. By age 6, this ratio has climbed to 11 to 1 (Martin & Fabes, 2001). Throughout the school years, children continue to show a strong preference for same-sex peers.

Why is gender segregation so widespread and persistent? According to Maccoby, early on, hormones affect play styles, leading to rough, noisy movements among boys and to calm, gentle actions among girls. Then, as children interact with peers, they choose partners whose interests and behaviors are compatible with their own. By age 2, girls appear overwhelmed by boys' rambunctious behavior and retreat from it (Benenson, Apostoleris, & Parnass, 1997). Nonhuman primates react similarly (Beatty, 1992). When a male juvenile initiates rough, physical play, male peers join in, whereas females withdraw.

During the preschool years, girls increasingly seek out other girls and like to play in pairs because of a common preference for quieter activities involving cooperative roles. Boys come to prefer larger-group play with other boys, who share a desire to run, climb, play-fight, compete, and build up and knock down (Fabes, Martin, & Hanish, 2003). Social pressures for "gender-appropriate" play and cognitive factors—in particular, gender stereotyping, the tendency to evaluate members of one's own sex more positively, and expectations of negative reactions from others for play with other-sex children—also contribute to gender segregation (Ruble, Martin, & Berenbaum, 2006).

Nevertheless, sex hormones are involved. In one study, prenatal levels of the androgen hormone testosterone (measured in amniotic fluid samples collected during amniocentesis) positively predicted "masculine"-style play in both boys and girls when they were followed up during middle childhood (Auyeung et al., 2009). Studies of exceptional sexual development are consistent with these findings.

Exceptional Sexual Development. *Congenital adrenal hyperplasia (CAH)* is a disorder in which a genetic defect causes the adrenal system to produce unusually high levels of androgens from the prenatal period onward. Although the physical development of boys remains unaffected, girls with CAH are usually born with masculinized external genitals. Most undergo surgical correction in infancy, followed by continuous drug therapy to overcome the hormone imbalance.

Interview and observational studies support the conclusion that prenatal androgen exposure influences certain aspects of "masculine" gender-role behavior. Compared with

Sex hormones are believed to influence preschoolers' tendency to choose same-sex partners who share their play style—cooperative play in pairs among girls, noisy roughhousing in groups among boys. But social pressures also promote gender segregation.

other girls, girls with CAH tend to be higher in activity level; to like cars, trucks, and blocks better than dolls; to prefer boys as playmates; and to be more interested in "masculine" careers, such as truck driver, soldier, or pilot (Beltz, Swanson, & Berenbaum, 2011; Cohen-Bendahan, van de Beek, & Berenbaum, 2005; Pasterski et al., 2011). The greater CAH girls' exposure to prenatal androgens, the more "masculine" their play and career interests (Hall et al., 2004; Servin et al., 2003). Furthermore, although girls with CAH receive more parental encouragement to play with girls' toys than do their unaffected sisters, they nevertheless prefer boys' toys—whether playing alone or in the presence of their mother or father (Pasterski et al., 2005).

Fewer studies are available on genetic males with abnormally low early androgen exposure. In *androgen insensitivity syndrome,* the testes produce normal levels of androgens, but androgen receptors in body cells are partially or completely impaired. In other conditions, androgen production by the testes is reduced. Depending on the extent of impairment, physical outcomes range from predominantly male to typically female urogenital tract and external genitals. In one study of such children, degree of reduction in prenatal androgen exposure predicted feminine gender-typed behavior, including toy choices, play behaviors, and preference for girl playmates (Jürgensen et al., 2007). Nevertheless, all children with complete androgen insensitivity syndrome were reared as girls. And children with partial androgen effects reared as girls displayed more feminine behavior than those reared as boys—findings suggesting a role for child rearing.

Other research on individuals reared from infancy as members of the other sex because they had ambiguous genitals indicates that most accepted their assigned sexual identity, though a substantial minority of CAH girls with masculinized genitals expressed considerable discomfort with being reared female (Slijper et al., 1998). Investigators attributed this outcome to both biological and social factors, including hormonal influences on the brain and parents' struggles over sex assignment, which in some cases resulted in negative attitudes toward their daughters. (Some parents, because of their baby's masculinized genitals, had initially assigned the male sex but, after determination of genetic sex, reassigned the infant to the female sex.).

Taken together, research indicates that sex hormones influence gender typing, with the most consistent findings involving activity level and associated preferences for "gender-appropriate" play, toys, and careers. But as we will see next, we must be careful not to minimize the role of experience.

Environmental Influences

In a study following almost 14,000 British children from ages 2½ to 8, gender-typed behavior was remarkably stable: The most gender-typed young preschoolers developed into the most gender-typed school-age children (Golombok et al., 2008). Although prenatal hormone exposure may predispose certain children to be more gender-typed, a wealth of evidence reveals that environmental forces provide powerful support for gender-role adoption. Adults view boys and girls differently and treat them differently. In addition, children's social contexts—home, school, and community—offer many opportunities to observe males and females behaving in gender-stereotyped ways. And beginning in early childhood, peers vigorously promote gender typing.

Perceptions and Expectations of Adults When adults are asked to observe neutrally dressed infants who are labeled as either boy or girl, they "see" qualities that fit with the baby's artificially assigned sex. In research of this kind, adults tend to rate infants' physical features and (to a lesser extent) their personality traits in a gender-stereotyped fashion (Stern & Karraker, 1989; Vogel et al., 1991). Boys, for example, are viewed as firmer, larger, better coordinated, and hardier; girls as softer, finer featured, more delicate, and less alert.

During childhood and adolescence, parents continue to hold different perceptions and expectations of their sons and daughters. They want their preschoolers to play with "gender-appropriate" toys and, with respect to child-rearing values, describe achievement, competition, and control of emotion as important for sons and warmth, "ladylike" behavior, and closely supervised activities as important for daughters (Brody, 1999; Turner & Gervai, 1995). Furthermore, when asked about attitudes toward "cross-gender" behavior, parents of preschoolers responded more negatively to the idea of boys than of girls crossing gender lines (Sandnabba & Ahlberg, 1999).

Treatment by Parents Do adults actually treat children in accord with stereotypical beliefs? A combined analysis of many studies reported that on the whole, differences in the way parents socialize boys and girls are small (Lytton & Romney, 1991). This does not mean that parental treatment is unimportant. It simply indicates that if we generalize across age periods, contexts, and behaviors, we find only a few clear trends. When the evidence is examined closely, however, consistent effects emerge. Younger children receive more direct training in gender roles than older children—a finding that is not surprising, given that gender typing occurs especially rapidly during early childhood (Golombok et al., 2008). And wide variation from study to study suggests that some parents practice differential treatment far more intensely than others.

As his clothing, bedroom décor, and toys attest, this toddler's parents have already begun to promote gender-typed preferences and behaviors.

Infancy and Early Childhood. In infancy and early childhood, parents encourage a diverse array of gender-specific play activities and behaviors. As early as the first few months—before children can express their own preferences—parents create different environments for boys and girls. Bedrooms are decorated with distinct colors and themes. Parents give sons toys that stress action and competition (guns, cars, tools, and footballs) and daughters toys that emphasize nurturance, cooperation, and physical attractiveness (dolls, tea sets, jump ropes, and jewelry) (Leaper, 1994; Leaper & Friedman, 2007).

Parents also actively reinforce independence in boys and closeness and dependency in girls. For example, parents react more positively when a son plays with cars and trucks, demands attention, runs and climbs, or tries to take toys from others. When interacting with daughters, they more often direct play activities, provide help, encourage participation in household tasks, engage in conversation, make supportive statements (approval, praise, and agreement), and refer to emotions (Clearfield & Nelson, 2006; Fagot & Hagan, 1991; Kuebli, Butler, & Fivush, 1995). Gender-typed play contexts amplify these communication differences. For example, when playing housekeeping, mothers engage in high rates of supportive emotional talk with girls (Leaper, 2000).

As these findings suggest, language is a powerful *indirect* means for teaching children about gender stereotypes and gender roles. Earlier in this chapter, we saw that most young children hold rigid beliefs about gender. Although their strict views are due in part to cognitive limitations, they also draw on relevant social experiences to construct these views. Like ethnic biases discussed in Chapter 11 (see page 476), young children's gender biases often bear little resemblance to those of their parents (Tenenbaum & Leaper, 2002). But even parents who believe strongly in gender equality unconsciously use language that highlights gender distinctions and informs children about traditional gender roles (see the Social Issues: Education box on pages 540–541).

Early in development, then, parents provide many experiences—through play materials and social interaction—that promote assertiveness, exploration, engagement with the physical world, and emotional restraint in boys and imitation, reliance on others, and emotional sensitivity in girls. These experiences, in turn, give young children a rich array of cues for constructing a view of the world that emphasizes stereotypical gender distinctions.

Middle Childhood and Adolescence. As children's skills expand during the school years, issues of achievement become more salient to parents. Observations of mothers and fathers interacting with their youngsters in teaching situations reveal that parents continue to demand greater independence from boys. When a child requests help, parents are more likely to ignore or refuse to respond to a son but to help a daughter right away. In helping a

SOCIAL ISSUES: EDUCATION

Children Learn About Gender Through Mother–Child Conversations

In an investigation of the power of language to shape children's beliefs and expectations about gender, mothers were asked to converse with their 2- to 6-year-olds about picture books containing images of male and female children and adults engaged in various activities, half consistent and half inconsistent with gender stereotypes. Each picture was accompanied by the question, "Who can X?" where X was the activity on the page.

One mother, who believed in gender equality, turned to a picture of a boy driving a boat and asked, "Who's driving the boat?"

Her 4-year-old son replied, "A sail-man."

The mother affirmed, "A sail-man. Yup, a sailor." Then she asked, "Who can be a sailor? Boys and girls?"

"Boys," the child replied.

"Boys . . . OK," the mother again affirmed. The child stated more decisively, "Only boys."

Again the mother agreed, "Only boys," and turned the page (Gelman, Taylor, & Nguyen, 2004, p. 104).

A detailed analysis of picture-book conversations revealed that mothers' directly expressed attitudes about gender stereotypes were neutral, largely because, like this mother, they typically posed questions to their children. But by age 4, children often voiced stereotypes, and—nearly one-third of the time—mothers affirmed them! Some mothers either moved on with the conversation or repeated the question, as in the conversation above, but rarely—just 2 percent of the time—did they explicitly counter a child's stereotype, and usually only when the book itself included stereotype-inconsistent pictures.

Although the researchers did not ask mothers to discuss gender, the mothers called attention to it even when they did not need to do so. In the English language, many nouns referring to people convey age-related information *(kid, baby, 2-year-old, preschooler, teenager, grownup, senior)*, whereas only a few encode gender *(male, female, sister, brother, aunt, uncle)*. Yet when using a noun to refer to a person, mothers explicitly called attention to gender more than half the time, even though the people shown in the books varied as much in age (children versus adults) as in gender. Mothers labeled gender, with either nouns or pronouns, especially often when conversing with 2-year-olds: "Is that a he or a she?" "That's a boy." "There's a girl." Such statements encourage toddlers to sort their social world into gender categories, even when the statements themselves do not explicitly convey stereotypes.

Furthermore, both mothers and children frequently expressed *generic utterances*—ones

While reading, this mother may unconsciously teach her child to see the world in gender-linked terms—by referring to gender unnecessarily or by making generic gender statements ("Most girls prefer X"; "Boys usually don't like X").

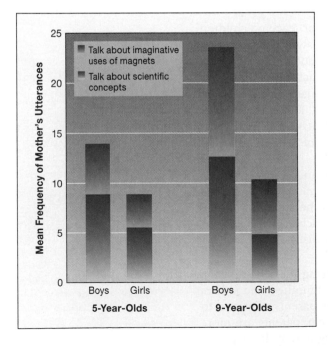

child with a task, parents behave in a more mastery-oriented fashion with sons, pointing out important features of tasks and setting higher standards—particularly during gender-typed pursuits, such as science activities (Crowley et al., 2001; Tenenbaum & Leaper, 2003). For example, when asked to play with magnets with their 5- and 9-year-olds, mothers engaged in more talk about scientific concepts and principles and more often suggested how to use the magnets imaginatively (for construction and in make-believe play) with sons than with daughters (see Figure 13.4) (Tenenbaum et al., 2005). Mothers' scientific talk at age 9 predicted children's science reading comprehension two years later, in sixth grade.

Consistent with their interaction patterns, parents hold gender-differentiated perceptions of and expectations for children's

FIGURE 13.4 Mothers' science-related talk while playing with magnets with their 5- and 9-year-old children. Mothers and children were given a powerful magnet and some small metal and plastic objects and asked to play with them. At both ages, mothers engaged in more talk about scientific concepts and imaginative uses of magnets with boys than with girls—a difference especially large at age 9. (Adapted from Tenenbaum et al., 2005.)

that were broad in scope, referring to many, or nearly all, males and females: "Boys can be sailors." "Most girls don't like trucks." Even generics that were gender-neutral ("Lots of girls in this book") or denied a stereotype ("Boys can be ballet dancers, too.") prompted children to view individuals of the same gender as alike and to ignore exceptions. As we will see later in this chapter, generics promote gender-role conformity: Statements such as "This toy is for girls" induce children to prefer the toy labeled for their own sex and to avoid the toy labeled for the other sex.

Mothers' and children's use of generics increased sharply between ages 2 and 6, a period in which gender stereotyping and gender-role conformity rise dramatically (see Figure 13.5). Initially, mothers led the way in generic talk; at age 2, they introduced these category-wide generalizations nearly three times as often as children. By age 6, however, children were producing generics more often than mothers. In addition, mother–child pairs produced more generics about males than about females, and generics were especially common in speech to and from boys, who are the more gender typed of the two sexes.

Even though these mothers overwhelmingly believed in gender equality, they did little to instill those ideas in their children. To the contrary, their most common response to children's stereotypical comments was to affirm them!

In this way, even without directly teaching stereotypes, parents—through language—provide a wealth of implicit cues that enable children to readily construct them.

Adults can combat stereotypical thinking in children through concerted efforts to avoid gendered language. Here are some suggestions:

- Refrain from labeling gender when it is unnecessary, substituting *child, friend, adult,* or *person* for *boy, girl, man,* or *woman*.
- Substitute references to individuals ("That person wants to be a firefighter") for generic expressions, or use qualifiers ("Some boys and some girls want to be firefighters").
- Monitor your own inclination to affirm children's stereotypical claims, countering these as often as possible.

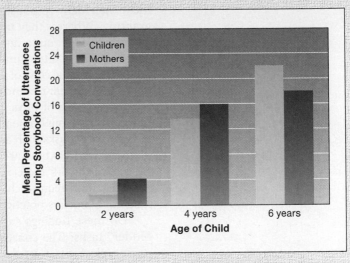

FIGURE 13.5 Mothers' and children's use of generic references to gender during storybook conversations. Mothers' and children's use of generics increased dramatically between ages 2 and 6. At age 2, mothers produced more generics than children. By age 6, children produced more generics than mothers. (From S. A. Gelman, M. G. Taylor, & S. P. Nguyen, "Mother–Child Conversations About Gender," *Monographs of the Society for Research in Child Development, 69* [1, Serial No. 275], p. 46. Copyright © 2004, John Wiley and Sons. Reprinted by permission of John Wiley and Sons.)

- Discuss gender biases in language with children, pointing out how words can shape inappropriate beliefs and expectations and asking children to avoid using gender labels and generics.

competencies in various school subjects. Mothers rate girls as better at English than boys who earn similar English grades (Frome & Eccles, 1998). And in longitudinal research, mothers rated first-grade sons as more competent than daughters at math, regardless of their child's actual performance. Maternal gender-typed judgments, in turn, influenced children's self-perceptions of math ability, the effort they devoted to math, and later math achievement, with lasting consequences (Eccles et al., 2000; Jacobs & Eccles, 1992). When the participants were followed up two years after high school graduation and again at age 24 to 25, mothers' early perceptions no longer predicted sons' outcomes. But they continued to predict daughters' self-perceptions and also their career choices. Young women whose mothers had regarded them as highly capable at math were far more likely to choose a physical science career (Bleeker & Jacobs, 2004). Yet mothers rarely made such optimistic judgments about girls.

In related research, investigators had 10- and 13-year-olds and their mothers and fathers choose courses for the children to take when they reached secondary school. Afterward, the children and parents discussed their decisions. Parents selected more language arts courses for daughters and more science courses for sons—trends also evident in children's choices. Especially striking were parents' gender-biased comments during the discussions, with daughters receiving twice as many discouraging remarks as sons across all types of courses—language arts, math, and science ("math is really hard," "that's not where your skills lie") (Tenenbaum, 2009).

LOOK and LISTEN

Watch several parents conversing with their preschoolers about picture books. How many times did the parent make generic statements about gender? How about the child? Did the parent accept or correct the child's generic utterances?

Parents' differential treatment extends to the freedom granted children in their everyday lives. Parents tend to use more directive speech (imperatives and specific suggestions) with girls than with boys (Leaper, Anderson, & Sanders, 1998). And when insisting that children meet their daily responsibilities, mothers of sons more often pair control with autonomy granting. Whereas they usually ask boys to make decisions ("When do you think would be a good time for you to do your music practice?"), parents tend to decide for girls ("Do your practicing right after dinner") (Pomerantz & Ruble, 1998b). Although school-age children interpret parental control without autonomy granting as well-intentioned guidance, they also say it makes them feel incompetent (Pomerantz & Ruble, 1998a).

Other signs of boys' greater freedom are evident in parental willingness to let them range farther from home without supervision and in assignment of chores. In many cultures, girls are given tasks such as food preparation, cleaning, and baby-sitting that keep them close to home, whereas boys are given responsibilities that take them into the surrounding world, such as yard work and errands (Whiting & Edwards, 1988a). As noted earlier, when cultural circumstances require children to perform "cross-gender" chores (as in Nyansongo), the range of behaviors practiced expands.

Do these findings suggest that children in Western cultures be assigned more "cross-gender" tasks? The consequences of doing so are not straightforward. When fathers hold stereotypical views yet their sons engage in "feminine" housework, boys experience strain in the father–child relationship, feel stressed by their responsibilities, and judge themselves as less competent (McHale et al., 1990). In contrast, a match between parental values and nontraditional child-rearing practices leads to a reduction in children's gender stereotyping and gender-role behavior and to an increase in girls' nontraditional career aspirations (Tenenbaum & Leaper, 2002; Turner & Gervai, 1995; Weisner & Wilson-Mitchell, 1990). Furthermore, in homes where fathers devote as much or more time to child care as mothers, children tend to be less gender-typed in emotional expression—sons more emotionally sensitive, daughters more self-confident (Brody, 1997).

Mothers versus Fathers. In most aspects of differential treatment of boys and girls, fathers discriminate the most. For example, in Chapter 10 we saw that fathers tend to engage in more physically stimulating play with their infant sons than daughters, whereas mothers tend to play more quietly with babies of both sexes. In childhood, fathers more than mothers encourage "gender-appropriate" behavior, and they place more pressure to achieve on sons than on daughters (Gervai, Turner, & Hinde, 1995; Wood, Desmarais, & Gugula, 2002).

Parents also seem especially committed to ensuring the gender typing of children of their own sex. While mothers go on shopping trips and bake cookies with their daughters, fathers play catch, help coach Saturday morning soccer games, and take their sons fishing. In addition to spending more time with children of their own sex, parents are more vigilant about monitoring the activities of same-sex children while the children are away from home (Leaper, 2002; Tucker, McHale, & Crouter, 2003). This pattern of greater involvement with same-sex children is another aspect of gender-role training that tends to be more pronounced for fathers (Parke, 1996).

Treatment by Teachers

In some ways, preschool and elementary school teachers reinforce children of both sexes for "feminine" rather than "masculine" behavior. In classrooms, men and women teachers alike usually value obedience and discourage assertiveness (Fagot, 1985a). This "feminine bias" is believed to promote discomfort for boys in school, but it may be as harmful—or even more so—for girls, who willingly conform, with possible long-term negative consequences for their sense of independence and self-esteem.

Teachers also act in ways that maintain and even extend gender roles taught at home. Like parents, preschool teachers give girls more encouragement to participate in adult-structured

By encouraging girls into adult-structured activities, preschool teachers provide them with extra practice in "feminine" gender-role behaviors—compliance, help-seeking, and patient waiting.

© ELLEN B. SENISI PHOTOGRAPHY

activities. Girls frequently cluster around the teacher following directions, whereas boys are attracted to play areas where adults are minimally involved (Campbell, Shirley, & Candy, 2004; Powlishta, Serbin, & Moller, 1993). As a result, boys and girls practice different social behaviors. Compliance and bids for help occur more often in adult-structured contexts; assertiveness, leadership, and creative use of materials in unstructured pursuits.

In addition, teachers often emphasize gender distinctions, as when they say, "Will the girls line up on one side and the boys on the other?" or "Boys, I wish you'd quiet down like the girls!"—labeling that promotes gender stereotyping, in-group favoritism, and out-group prejudice in children (Bigler, 1995). At the same time, teachers interrupt girls more than boys during conversation, thereby promoting boys' social dominance and girls' passivity. By age 4, children respond in kind: Boys interrupt their female teachers more than girls do (Hendrick & Stange, 1991).

As early as kindergarten, teachers give more overall attention (both positive and negative) to boys than to girls—a difference evident in diverse countries, including China, England, and the United States. They tend to praise boys more for their academic knowledge, perhaps as a means of motivating them because boys' grades are lower than girls'. And although teachers discourage unruliness in all children, they do so more frequently and forcefully with boys (Chen & Rao, 2011; Davies, 2008; Swinson & Harrop, 2009). When girls misbehave, teachers are more likely to negotiate, coming up with a joint plan to improve their conduct (Erden & Wolfgang, 2004). Teachers' more frequent use of disapproval and controlling discipline with boys seems to result from an expectation that boys will misbehave more often than girls—a belief based partly on boys' actual behavior and partly on gender stereotypes.

Observational Learning In addition to direct pressures from adults, numerous gender-typed models are available in children's environments. Despite societal changes, children continue to encounter many people in their schools and communities who conform to traditional gender roles— women as elementary school teachers, nurses, and librarians; men as school principals, computer experts, and airline pilots. In one study, researchers presented school-age children, adolescents, and college students with visual and verbal descriptions of novel occupations, in which they varied the sex of the worker and the personal value the job fulfills (money, power, altruism, time for family). At all ages, participants expressed greater interest in occupations held by workers of their own sex than identical jobs held by workers of the other sex—results confirming that merely observing sex differences in occupations affects interest in those fields (Weisgram, Bigler, & Liben, 2010). In addition, males of all ages were especially attracted to jobs depicted as highly paid, females to jobs high in altruism—values that likely contribute to the gender sorting typically seen in the workforce.

Media portrayals are also gender typed. As we will see in Chapter 15, gender roles in television programs have changed little in recent years. And gender stereotypes are especially prevalent in cartoons, music television (MTV), TV commercials, and video games (Calvert et al., 2003; Dietz, 1998; Kahlenberg & Hein, 2010). In addition, despite an increase in gender-equitable storybooks and textbooks, many children read older books in which males are main characters, take center stage in exciting plot activities, and display assertiveness and creativity, while females are submissive, dependent, and passive (Tepper & Cassidy, 1999; Turner-Bowker, 1996). And in a study of award-winning picture books for young children, fathers were represented only half as often as mothers and, when they were included, rarely expressed affection or participated in caregiving but, instead, seemed disengaged from the parenting role (Anderson & Hamilton, 2005).

When children are exposed to nonstereotyped models, they are less traditional in their beliefs and behaviors. Children who often see their parents cross traditional gender lines— mothers who are employed or who do "masculine" household tasks (repairing appliances, washing the car), fathers who do "feminine" household tasks (ironing, cooking, child care)— less often endorse gender stereotypes (Turner & Gervai, 1995; Updegraff, McHale, & Crouter,

© MICHAEL NEWMAN/PHOTOEDIT

The opportunity to assist a female veterinarian prompts this adolescent to picture herself doing similar work, rather than viewing veterinary medicine traditionally, as a male occupation.

LOOK and LISTEN

Keep a list of instances of gender typing that you notice for an entire day—in peoples' jobs, gender-role behaviors, media portrayals, and other. How prevalent are gender-typed models in your environment?

1996). Girls with career-oriented mothers show special benefits. They are more likely to engage in typically masculine activities (such as physically active play), have higher educational aspirations, and hold nontraditional career goals (Hoffman, 2000).

Furthermore, among children of divorced parents, boys in father-absent homes and girls in mother-absent homes are less gender-typed, perhaps because they have fewer opportunities to observe traditional gender roles than in a two-parent household (Brenes, Eisenberg, & Helmstadter, 1985; Williams, Radin, & Allegro, 1992). And compared with agemates in two-parent families, children from single-parent homes are more likely to have at least one other-sex friend (Kovacs, Parker, & Hoffman, 1996).

Peers Because most children associate almost exclusively with peers of their own sex, the peer context is an especially potent source of gender-role learning. In a study in which researchers followed preschoolers and kindergartners over the school year, children who spent more time playing with same-sex partners in the fall showed greater gains in gender typing—in terms of toy choices, activity level, aggression, and extent of play near adults—in the spring (Martin & Fabes, 2001).

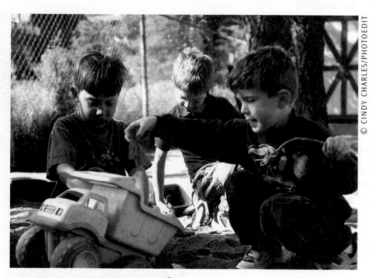

These boys positively reinforce one another's gender-typed play. Preschoolers, especially boys, tend to be intolerant of peers who play with "cross-gender" toys, criticizing and pressuring them to change their behavior.

Gender-Role Learning in Gender-Segregated Peer Groups. By age 3, same-sex peers positively reinforce one another for gender-typed play by praising, imitating, or joining in. In contrast, when children engage in "cross-gender" activities—for example, when boys play with dolls or girls with cars and trucks—peers criticize, pressure them to change their behavior, and in extreme cases harass and physically attack them. Boys are especially intolerant of "cross-gender" play in other boys (Fagot, 1984; Langlois & Downs, 1980; Thorne, 1993). A boy who frequently crosses gender lines is likely to be ostracized by other boys, even when he does engage in "masculine" activities!

Children also develop different styles of social influence in gender-segregated peer groups. To get their way in large-group play, boys often rely on commands, threats, and physical force. Girls' preference for playing in pairs leads to greater concern with a partner's needs, evident in girls' use of polite requests, persuasion, and acceptance. Girls soon find that these gentle tactics succeed with other girls but not with boys, who ignore their courteous overtures (Leaper, 1994; Leaper, Tenenbaum, & Shaffer, 1999). Boys' unresponsiveness gives girls another reason to stop interacting with them.

Over time, children come to believe in the "correctness" of gender-segregated play, which further strengthens gender segregation and stereotyped activities. In one study, 3- to 6-year-olds believed that peers would be more likely to approve of their behavior if they played with same-sex agemates—a conviction that predicted children's association with same-sex peers (Martin et al., 1999). As boys and girls separate, in-group favoritism becomes another factor that sustains the separate social worlds of boys and girls, resulting in "two distinct subcultures" of shared knowledge, beliefs, interests, and behaviors (Maccoby, 2002; Ruble, Martin, & Berenbaum, 2006).

Some educators believe that forming mixed-sex activity groups in classroom and recreational settings is a vital means of reducing gender stereotyping and broadening developmental possibilities for both sexes. To be successful, however, interventions may have to modify the styles of social influence typically learned in same-sex peer relations. Otherwise, boys are likely to dominate and girls to react passively, thereby strengthening traditional gender roles and the stereotypes each sex holds of the other.

In addition, modifying children's direct pressures on peers to conform to traditional gender roles is vital. To explore one successful intervention, in which children themselves learn to challenge peers' sexist remarks, turn to the Social Issues: Education box on the following page.

LOOK and LISTEN

While observing 3- to 5-year-olds during a free-play period in a preschool or child-care program, note the extent of gender segregation and gender-typed play. Did styles of social influence differ in boys' and girls' gender-segregated groups? Jot down examples.

SOCIAL ISSUES: EDUCATION

Teaching Children to Challenge Peers' Sexist Remarks

Rose approached Tony and Aaron, who were swinging on a tire in the schoolyard, and asked, "Can I get on, too?" "No! This is a boys' game," Tony responded. Jerry, who overheard Tony's refusal, called out, "Hey, Tony! You can't say that girls can't play!"

Peers, as we have seen, play a prominent role in encouraging children to adopt traditional gender-role attitudes and behavior. Hence, challenges like Jerry's are extremely rare in children's interactions with agemates. Can children be taught to confront peers' sexist remarks, which endorse biological sex as a legitimate basis for limiting individual roles and behaviors? If so, the impact could be powerful. Because children's sexist statements often occur out of adults' earshot, gender stereotyping within the peer group is difficult for adults to modify. Inducing peers to confront such remarks might be far more effective in getting children to be more accepting of peers who cross gender lines.

In an elementary school with an explicit curricular goal of creating a gender-equitable climate where all children—both gender-typical and gender-atypical—feel respected and included, kindergarten through third-grade classes were randomly assigned to one of two interventions aimed at reducing peers' gender-typed remarks (Lamb et al., 2009):

- *Active intervention.* On the basis of evidence that children learn more when they practice new skills and receive feedback on their performance, this condition involved active rehearsal. Children were explicitly taught six rhyming retorts (one per day, in 20-minute sessions) to peers' sexist remarks—for example, for exclusion: "You can't say that boys [girls] can't play!"; for gender-role biases: "Not true, gender doesn't limit you!" After mastering each retort, the children formed small groups in which they practiced the response in short skits they created. This enabled them to apply the retort in familiar situations and also exposed them to peer models doing the same.
- *Narrative intervention.* Children in this condition heard the same six retorts to sexist remarks, embedded in six age-appropriate stories (one per day). However, no opportunity for active rehearsal was offered. Rather, children drew a picture of their favorite part of the story, after which they listened to an additional story depicting a bullying situation and participated in a discussion of the importance of addressing (not ignoring) bullying behaviors.

Compared to children in the narrative intervention, those in the active intervention showed dramatic gains in willingness to challenge peers' sexist remarks in hypothetical scenarios (see Figure 13.6). To see whether this outcome extended to real life, researchers

© LAURA DWIGHT PHOTOGRAPHY

Children who are explicitly taught to confront peers' sexist remarks are more likely than others to counter those remarks, creating a climate of respect for boys and girls as individuals.

arranged to have participants confronted with a peer's sexist remark in the school hallway. Teachers asked each child to carry an "other-gender" item (such as a purse for boys, a tool belt for girls) to the school office. On the way, a same-sex classmate with acting ability stopped the child and made a sexist comment. Again, active-intervention children more often countered these remarks—an impressive outcome, given that children almost never engage in real-world challenges to gender-typed peer pressure.

At a six-month follow-up, a majority of children in both interventions responded to hypothetical scenarios with retorts to one or more peer sexist remarks. Perhaps active-intervention children, who were willing to confront sexist statements in everyday life, served as effective models for their narrative-intervention classmates, teaching them to challenge peer sexist comments. For girls, long-term active-intervention effects extended beyond behavior to attitudes: They gained in gender-stereotype flexibility.

In sum, a short-term active intervention is successful at getting children to counter peers' sexist statements. The spread of these retorts to other classmates suggests that active training in combating sexism can contribute to a school climate that respects and protects individual differences in children's gender typing.

FIGURE 13.6 Challenges to peers' sexist remarks by active-intervention and narrative-intervention children. Prior to intervention, only a handful of children in both conditions challenged peers' sexist remarks. Following intervention, the majority in the active-intervention group responded with one or more challenges in hypothetical scenarios. Real-life challenges, though infrequent, also occurred far more often among active-intervention children. (Adapted from Lamb et al., 2009.)

Graph: Percentage of Children Who Challenged Sexist Remarks (y-axis, 0–90) vs. Hypothetical Scenarios and Real Life (x-axis). Legend: Active intervention, Narrative intervention.

Cultural Variations. Although gender segregation is pervasive, cultures and subcultures differ in the extent of gender-typed communication within those groups. African-American and Hispanic-American lower-SES girls, for example, are generally more assertive and independent in their interactions with one another and with boys than are Caucasian-American girls (Goodwin, 1998). A comparison of Chinese and U.S. preschoolers' play revealed similar differences. Chinese 5-year-old girls used more direct commands, complaints, and critical statements when interacting with both same- and other-sex peers than their American counterparts. And Chinese boys frequently combined commands with warning, appeasing, and justifying statements, which reduced expressions of dominance in boys' playgroups: "Better not open that. You'll spill it." "I'll do it. I'm here to help you!" (Kyratzis & Guo, 2001).

In collectivist societies where group cohesion is highly valued, children may not feel a need to work as hard at maintaining same-sex peer relations through traditional interaction patterns. In addition to reducing children's ethnic prejudices (see Chapter 11), ethnically integrated classrooms might reduce gender-typed peer communication as the cross-gender influence attempts of some children rub off on others.

Siblings Growing up with siblings of the same or the other sex also affects gender typing. But sibling effects are more complex than peer influences because they depend on birth order and family size (McHale, Crouter, & Whiteman, 2003). Whereas younger siblings have little impact on older siblings' gender typing, older siblings serve as powerful models for younger siblings. In a British study, more than 5,000 mothers provided information on play and other behaviors of their 3-year-olds, each of whom had either one older sibling or no siblings. As Figure 13.7 shows, children with same-sex siblings were more gender-typed than children with no siblings, who in turn were more gender-typed than children with other-sex older siblings (Rust et al., 2000). During the school years, older siblings' influence expands, affecting younger siblings' sex-stereotyped attitudes, personality traits, and leisure pursuits (McHale et al., 2001).

Curiously, however, other research contradicts these findings, indicating that children with same-sex siblings are less stereotyped in their interests and personality traits than those from mixed-sex families (Grotevant, 1978; Tauber, 1979). How can we explain these conflicting results? Recall from Chapter 10 that siblings often strive to be different from one another. This effect is strongest when children are of the same sex and come from large

FIGURE 13.7 "Masculine" behavior scores for preschool boys and girls with same-sex older siblings, other-sex older siblings, and no siblings. In this British study, 3-year-olds with same-sex older siblings were more gender-typed than children with no siblings, who were more gender-typed than children with other-sex older siblings. Notice how boys with the lowest masculine behavior scores have older sisters, whereas girls with the highest masculine behavior scores have older brothers. (Adapted from Rust et al., 2000.)

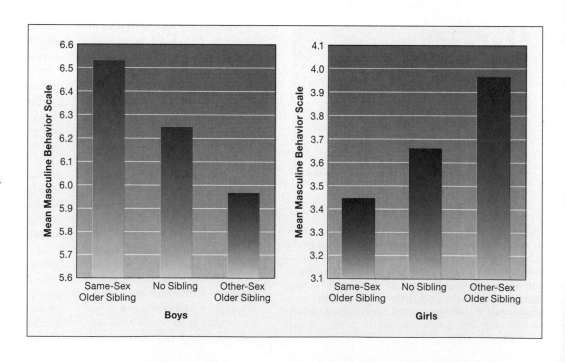

families, in which they may feel a greater need to stand out. A close look reveals that studies reporting a *modeling and reinforcement effect* (an increase in gender typing among same-sex siblings) focus on children from two-child families. In contrast, those reporting a *differentiation effect* often include children from larger families.

In addition, parents whose children are all of the same sex sometimes relax pressures toward gender typing. For example, mothers were more willing to give their child a gender-atypical toy as a gift when the child had an older, same-sex sibling (Stoneman, Brody, & MacKinnon, 1986). Also, in all-girl and all-boy families, children are more likely to be assigned "cross-gender" chores because no "gender-appropriate" child is available to do the job. Therefore, families with all same-sex siblings may provide some special opportunities to step out of traditional gender roles.

In sum, older siblings are influential models in young children's gender typing. But aspects of the family context, including family size and parental pressures, can alter this modeling effect.

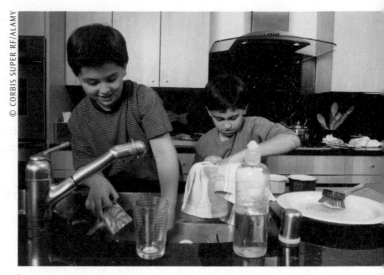

These brothers share a typically "feminine" task. When siblings are the same sex, they are more likely to be assigned "cross-gender" chores.

ASK YOURSELF

Review ■ Summarize parent, peer, and sibling influences on gender-role adoption. Why are sibling influences more complex than parent and peer influences?

Connect ■ Using research in this chapter and in Chapter 11 (see page 467), explain why girls are more susceptible than boys to learned helplessness in achievement situations.

Apply ■ List findings indicating that language and communication—between parents and children, between teachers and children, and between peers—powerfully affect children's gender stereotyping and gender-role behavior. What recommendations would you make to counteract these influences?

Reflect ■ In early and middle childhood, did you play mostly with peers of your own sex? What gender-linked attitudes and behaviors were emphasized in your peer associations? How did you view members of the other sex?

Gender Identity

▶ Discuss androgyny as well as social learning and cognitive-developmental views of the development of gender identity in early childhood.

▶ What changes in gender identity occur in middle childhood and adolescence?

▶ Explain gender schema theory.

Besides biological and environmental influences, another factor eventually affects gender stereotyping and gender-role behavior: *gender identity*, a person's perception of the self as relatively masculine or feminine in characteristics. In middle childhood, as self-concepts emphasize psychological dispositions over concrete behaviors (see Chapter 11), researchers can measure gender identity by asking children to rate themselves on personality traits. A child or adult with a "masculine" identity scores high on traditionally masculine items (*ambitious, competitive, self-sufficient*) and low on traditionally feminine items (*affectionate, cheerful, soft-spoken*). Someone with a "feminine" identity does the reverse. Although most people view themselves in gender-typed terms, a substantial minority (especially females) have a gender identity called **androgyny,** scoring high on *both* masculine and feminine personality characteristics.

Gender identity is a good predictor of psychological adjustment. "Masculine" and androgynous children and adults have higher self-esteem than "feminine" individuals (Boldizar, 1991; DiDonato & Berenbaum, 2011; Harter, 2006). In line with their flexible self-definitions, androgynous individuals are more adaptable—able to show masculine independence or feminine sensitivity, depending on the situation (Huyck, 1996; Taylor & Hall, 1982).

A close look at these findings, however, reveals that the masculine component of androgyny is largely responsible for the superior psychological health of androgynous women over those with traditional identities. Feminine women seem to have adjustment difficulties because many of their attributes are not valued highly by society (Bronstein, 2006). Nevertheless, the existence of an androgynous identity demonstrates that children can acquire a mixture of positive qualities traditionally associated with each gender—an orientation that may best help them realize their potential. In a future society in which feminine traits are socially rewarded to the same extent as masculine traits, androgyny may very well represent the ideal personality.

Emergence of Gender Identity

How do children develop a gender identity? According to *social learning theory*, behavior comes before self-perceptions. Preschoolers first acquire gender-typed responses through modeling and reinforcement and only later organize these behaviors into gender-linked ideas about themselves. In contrast, *cognitive-developmental theory* maintains that self-perceptions come before behavior. Over the preschool years, children acquire a cognitive appreciation of the permanence of their sex. They develop **gender constancy**—a full understanding of the biologically based permanence of their gender, which combines three understandings: *gender labeling, gender stability,* and *gender consistency.* Then children use this knowledge to guide their behavior. Let's trace the development of gender constancy during the preschool years.

If this 4-year-old saw her doll dressed in boys' clothing, she likely would claim it had become a boy. She has not yet attained gender consistency—the understanding that sex is biologically based and permanent.

Development of Gender Constancy Lawrence Kohlberg (1966) proposed that before age 6 or 7, children cannot maintain the constancy of their gender, just as they cannot pass Piagetian conservation problems. They attain this understanding only gradually, by moving through the following stages:

1. **Gender labeling.** By the early preschool years, children can label their own sex and that of others correctly. But when asked such questions as "When you [a girl] grow up, could you ever be a daddy?" or "Could you be a boy if you wanted to?" young children freely answer yes (Slaby & Frey, 1975). And when shown a doll whose hairstyle and clothing are transformed before their eyes, children indicate that the doll's sex has changed (Chauhan, Shastri, & Mohite, 2005; Fagot, 1985b).
2. **Gender stability.** Slightly older preschoolers have a partial understanding of the permanence of sex, in that they grasp its stability over time. But even though they know that male and female babies will eventually become boys and girls and men and women, they continue to insist that changing hairstyle, clothing, or "gender-appropriate" activities will also change a person's sex (Fagot, 1985b; Slaby & Frey, 1975).
3. **Gender consistency.** During the late preschool and early school years, children understand that sex is biologically based and remains the same even if a person dresses in "cross-gender" clothes or engages in nontraditional activities (Emmerich, 1981; Ruble et al., 2007).

Many studies confirm that the development of gender constancy follows this sequence. As Kohlberg assumed, mastery of gender constancy is associated with attainment of conservation (De Lisi & Gallagher, 1991). It is also strongly related to the ability to pass verbal appearance–reality tasks (see page 243 in Chapter 6) (Trautner, Gervai, & Nemeth, 2003). Indeed, gender-consistency tasks can be considered a type of appearance–reality problem, in that children must distinguish what a person looks like from who he or she really is.

In many cultures, young children do not have access to basic biological knowledge about gender because they rarely see members of the other sex naked. But giving children information about genital differences does not result in gender constancy. Preschoolers who have such knowledge usually say that changing a doll's clothing or hairstyle will not change their sex, but when asked to justify their response, they do not refer to sex as an innate, unchanging quality of people (Szkrybalo & Ruble, 1999). This suggests that cognitive immaturity, not social experience, is largely responsible for young children's difficulty grasping the permanence of sex.

How Well Does Gender Constancy Predict Gender-Role Adoption? Is cognitive-developmental theory correct that gender constancy is responsible for children's gender-typed behavior? Evidence for this assumption is weak. "Gender-appropriate" behavior appears so early in the preschool years that its initial appearance must result from modeling and reinforcement, as social learning theory suggests.

Although gender constancy does not initiate gender-role conformity, the cognitive changes that lead up to it do seem to facilitate gender typing. Young children who reach the stage of gender labeling early show more rapid development of "gender-appropriate" play preferences and knowledge of gender stereotypes than their late-labeling peers (Fagot, Leinbach, & O'Boyle, 1992; Zosuls et al., 2009). Similarly, understanding of gender stability prompts increased gender stereotyping, preference for same-sex playmates, choice of "gender-appropriate" toys, and identification with one's gender group (Martin & Little, 1990; Ruble et al., 2007). These findings suggest that as soon as children form basic gender categories, they use them to acquire gender-relevant information about their social world and about themselves.

The stage of gender consistency, in contrast, functions differently. Although outcomes are not entirely consistent, the realization that sex does not change despite superficial transformations in clothing or behavior seems to contribute to increasing gender-stereotype flexibility in the early school years (Ruble et al., 2007). But overall, the impact of gender constancy on gender typing is not great. As we will see next, gender-role adoption is more powerfully affected by children's beliefs about how close the connection must be between their own gender and their behavior.

Gender Identity in Middle Childhood

During middle childhood, boys' and girls' gender identities follow different paths. Self-ratings on personality traits reveal that from third to sixth grade, boys strengthen their identification with the "masculine" role, while girls' identification with "feminine" characteristics declines. While still leaning toward the "feminine" side, girls are more androgynous than boys—more likely to describe themselves as having "other-gender" characteristics (Serbin, Powlishta, & Gulko, 1993). This difference is also evident in children's activities. Whereas boys usually stick to "masculine" pursuits, girls experiment with a wider range of options. Besides cooking, sewing, and baby-sitting, they join organized sports teams and work on science projects. And girls are more likely than boys to consider future work roles stereotyped for the other gender, such as firefighter or astronomer (Liben & Bigler, 2002).

These changes are due to a mixture of cognitive and social forces. School-age children of both sexes are aware that society attaches greater prestige to "masculine" characteristics. For example, they rate "masculine" occupations as having higher status than "feminine" occupations. And they more often regard a novel job (such as *clipster,* "a person who tests batteries") as higher in status and as appropriate "for both men and women" when it is portrayed with a male worker than with a female worker (see Figure 13.8) (Liben, Bigler, & Krogh, 2001; Weisgram, Bigler, & Liben, 2010). In view of the strong association of males' activities with high status, it is not surprising that girls start to identify with "masculine" traits and are attracted to some typically masculine activities.

As school-age children make social comparisons and characterize themselves in terms of stable dispositions, their gender identity expands to include the following self-evaluations, which greatly affect their adjustment:

FIGURE 13.8 Eleven-year-olds' status ratings of novel jobs portrayed with male and female workers. Although children had no prior knowledge of these jobs and therefore had not previously stereotyped them as "masculine" or "feminine," simply portraying the job with a male worker resulted in higher status ratings. (Adapted from Liben, Bigler, & Krogh, 2001.)

This 9-year-old girl enjoys karate lessons. Whereas school-age boys usually stick to "masculine" pursuits, girls experiment with a wider range of options.

- *Gender typicality*—the degree to which the child feels similar to others of the same gender. Although children need not be highly gender-typed to judge themselves as gender-typical, their psychological well-being depends on feeling, at least to some degree, that they "fit in" with their same-sex peers (Egan & Perry, 2001).
- *Gender contentedness*—the degree to which the child feels comfortable with his or her gender assignment, which also promotes happiness and satisfaction with oneself.
- *Felt pressure to conform to gender roles*—the degree to which the child feels parents and peers disapprove of his or her gender-related traits. Because such pressure reduces the likelihood that children will explore options related to their interests and talents, children who feel strong gender-typed pressure are likely to be distressed and dissatisfied.

In a longitudinal study of third through seventh graders, *gender-typical* and *gender-contented* children gained in self-esteem over the following year. In contrast, children who were *gender-atypical* and *gender-discontented* declined in self-worth. Furthermore, gender-atypical children who reported *intense pressure to conform to gender roles* experienced serious difficulties, in the form of withdrawal, sadness, disappointment, and anxiety (Yunger, Carver, & Perry, 2004).

Clearly, how children feel about themselves in relation to their gender group becomes vitally important in middle childhood, and those who experience rejection because of their gender-atypical traits suffer profoundly. Researchers and therapists are engaged in a heated debate over how best to help children who feel gender-atypical. Some advocate making them more gender-typical, through therapy that reinforces such children for engaging in traditional gender-role activities so they will feel more compatible with same-sex peers (see, for example, Zucker, 2006). Others oppose this approach on grounds that it promotes a pathological view of gender atypicality, is likely to heighten felt pressure to conform (which predicts maladjustment), and—for children who fail to change—may result in parental rejection. These experts advocate modifying parents' and peers' attitudes, through interventions that help them become more accepting of children's gender-atypical interests and behaviors (Bigler, 2007; Conway, 2007; Crawford, 2003). **TAKE A MOMENT…** In view of what you have learned in this chapter, which approach do you think would be more successful, and why?

Gender Identity in Adolescence

According to one hypothesis, the arrival of adolescence is typically accompanied by **gender intensification**—increased gender stereotyping of attitudes and behavior, and movement toward a more traditional gender identity (Hill & Lynch, 1983). Research on gender intensification, however, is mixed, with some studies finding evidence for it and others reporting few instances (Basow & Rubin, 1999; Galambos, Almeida, & Petersen, 1990; Huston & Alvarez, 1990; Priess, Lindberg, & Hyde, 2009). When gender intensification is evident, it seems to be stronger for adolescent girls. Although girls continue to be less gender-typed than boys, some may feel less free to experiment with "other-gender" activities and behaviors than they did in middle childhood.

In young people who do exhibit gender intensification, biological, social, and cognitive factors likely are involved. As puberty magnifies sex differences in appearance, teenagers may spend more time thinking about themselves in gender-linked ways.

For some young people, early adolescence is a time of gender intensification. Pubertal changes in appearance, traditional gender-role expectations of parents, and increased concern with what others think can prompt teenagers to move toward a more traditional gender identity.

Pubertal changes might also prompt gender-typed pressures from others. Parents with traditional gender-role beliefs may encourage "gender-appropriate" activities and behavior more than they did earlier (Crouter et al., 2007; Shanahan et al., 2007). And when adolescents start to date, they may become more gender-typed as a way of increasing their attractiveness (Maccoby, 1998). Finally, cognitive changes—in particular, greater concern with what others think—might make young teenagers more responsive to gender-role expectations.

Gender intensification typically declines by late adolescence, but not all affected young people move beyond it to the same degree. Some girls struggle with gender-typed social pressures to act in ways inconsistent with their actual beliefs, avoiding conflict by suppressing their honest thoughts and feelings (Tolman, 2002). In one study, eighth-grade girls who compromised their authenticity—by withholding their true opinions and emotions to avoid parental or peer disapproval—were less likely than their more authentic agemates to display the typical adolescent rise in self-esteem (see Chapter 11, page 462) (Impett et al., 2008).

Teenagers who are encouraged to explore non-gender-typed options and to question the value of gender stereotypes for themselves and their society are more likely to build an androgynous identity. Thus, the social environment is a major force in promoting gender-role flexibility in adolescence, just as it was at earlier ages.

Gender Schema Theory

Gender schema theory is an information-processing approach that explains how environmental pressures and children's cognitions work together to shape gender typing (Martin & Halverson, 1987; Martin, Ruble, & Szkrybalo, 2002). It also integrates the various elements of gender typing—gender stereotyping, gender identity, and gender-role adoption—into a unified picture of how masculine and feminine orientations emerge and are often strongly maintained.

At an early age, children pick up gender-stereotyped preferences and behaviors from others. At the same time, they organize their experiences into *gender schemas,* or masculine and feminine categories, that they use to interpret their world. As soon as preschoolers can label and appreciate the stability of their own gender, they select gender schemas consistent with it ("Only boys can be doctors" or "Cooking is a girl's job") and apply those categories to themselves. Their self-perceptions then become gender-typed and serve as additional schemas that children use to process information and guide their own behavior.

We have seen that individual differences exist in the extent to which children endorse gender-typed views. Figure 13.9 shows different cognitive pathways for children who often apply gender schemas to their experiences and those who rarely do (Liben & Bigler, 2002).

FIGURE 13.9 Cognitive pathways for gender-schematic and gender-aschematic children. In *gender-schematic children,* the gender-salience filter immediately makes gender highly relevant: Billy sees a doll and thinks, "I'm a boy. Should boys play with dolls?" Drawing on his experiences, he answers "yes" or "no." If he answers "yes" and the doll interests him, he plays with the doll. If he answers "no," he avoids the "gender-inappropriate" toy. *Gender-aschematic children* rarely view the world in gender-linked terms: Billy simply asks, "Do I like this toy?" and responds on the basis of his interests. (Reprinted by permission of Rebecca Bigler, University of Texas, Austin.)

If working with clay were labeled "a girls' activity," would these third-grade boys continue modeling? If children believe a toy or game is for the other gender, powerful gender schemas lead them to like it less.

Consider Billy, who encounters a doll. If Billy is a *gender-schematic child,* his *gender-salience filter* immediately makes gender highly relevant. Drawing on his prior learning, he asks himself, "Should boys play with dolls?" If he answers "yes" and the toy interests him, he will approach it, explore it, and learn more about it. If he answers "no," he will respond by avoiding the "gender-inappropriate" toy. But if Billy is a *gender-aschematic child*—one who seldom views the world in gender-linked terms—he simply asks himself, "Do I like this toy?" and responds on the basis of his interests.

To examine the consequences of gender-schematic processing, researchers showed 4- and 5-year-olds "gender-neutral" toys that varied in attractiveness. An adult labeled some as boys' toys and others as girls' toys, leaving a third group unlabeled. Most children engaged in gender-schematic reasoning, preferring toys labeled for their gender and predicting that same-sex peers would also like those toys. Highly attractive toys, especially, lost their appeal when they were labeled as for the other gender (Martin, Eisenbud, & Rose, 1995). And because gender-schematic preschoolers typically conclude, "What I like, children of my own sex will also like," they often use their own preferences to add to their gender biases! For example, a girl who dislikes oysters may declare, "Only boys like oysters!" even though she has never actually been given information supporting such a stereotype (Liben & Bigler, 2002).

Gender-schematic thinking is so powerful that when children see others behaving in "gender-inconsistent" ways, they often cannot remember the behavior or distort their memory to make it "gender-consistent"—for example, when shown a picture of a male nurse, remembering him as a doctor (Liben & Signorella, 1993; Martin & Ruble, 2004). Over time, children learn much more about people, objects, and events that fit with their gender schemas than they do about "cross-gender" activities and behaviors.

Training school-age children in cognitive skills that counteract gender-biased social messages reduces their tendency to view the world in gender-schematic terms. When researchers taught 5- to 10-year-olds that ability and interest, not gender, determine whether a person can perform an activity well, children gained in stereotype flexibility and memory for "gender-inconsistent" information (story characters engaged in "cross-gender" tasks). Interestingly, classification training with gender-neutral stimuli that required children to sort objects into two categories at once (by shape and color) had the same effect (Bigler & Liben, 1992). As these findings reveal, interventions that promote multidimensional thinking about gender and other aspects of the world induce children to construct more gender-equitable beliefs. Nevertheless, gender-schematic thinking could not operate so forcefully to restrict knowledge and learning opportunities if society did not teach children a wide variety of gender-linked associations.

The Milestones table on the following page provides an overview of the changes in gender stereotyping, gender identity, and gender-role adoption we have considered.

ASK YOURSELF

Review ■ Describe the general path of gender identity development, from early childhood through adolescence, noting differences between boys and girls.

Connect ■ How might factors that affect identity development in general (see pages 472–474 in Chapter 11) influence gender identity in adolescence? Which influences would likely protect against gender intensification?

Apply ■ While looking at a book, 4-year-old Roger saw a picture of a boy cooking at a stove. Later, he recalled the person in the picture as a girl. Using gender schema theory, explain Roger's memory error.

Reflect ■ In early adolescence, did you and your friends display gender intensification? Describe examples. When did this concern with gender appropriateness decline?

Milestones

Gender Typing

AGE	GENDER STEREOTYPING AND GENDER-ROLE ADOPTION	GENDER IDENTITY
1–5 years	• Gender-stereotyped toy preferences emerge and strengthen. • Gender stereotyping of activities, occupations, and behaviors expands. • Gender segregation in peer interaction emerges and strengthens. • Girls' preference for play in pairs, boys' for play in larger groups, appears.	• Gender constancy develops in a three-stage sequence: gender labeling, gender stability, and gender consistency.
6–11 years	• Gender-stereotyped knowledge expands, especially for personality traits and achievement areas. • Gender stereotyping becomes more flexible.	• Among boys, "masculine" gender identity typically strengthens; girls' gender identity becomes more androgynous.
12–18 years	• Gender-role conformity may increase, followed by a decline. • Gender segregation becomes less pronounced.	• Gender identity may become more traditional, followed by a decline in stereotypical self-perceptions.

Note: These milestones represent overall age trends. Individual differences exist in the precise age at which each milestone is attained and in the extent of gender typing.

Photos: (top) © David Young-Wolff/PhotoEdit; (middle) © Syracuse Newspapers/L. Long/The Image Works; (bottom) © Echo/Getty Images/Cultura

To What Extent Do Boys and Girls *Really* Differ in Gender-Stereotyped Attributes?

▶ Describe sex differences in mental abilities and personality traits, noting factors that contribute to those differences.

So far, we have examined the relationship of biological, social, and cognitive factors to children's gender-typed preferences and behavior. But we have said little about the extent to which boys and girls actually differ in mental abilities and personality traits. Over the past several decades, thousands of studies have measured sex differences in these characteristics. Researchers have looked for stable differences between males and females and, from there, have searched for biological and environmental contributions to each variation.

To avoid basing conclusions on single studies and small, potentially biased samples, researchers often use a technique called *meta-analysis,* in which they reanalyze the data of many investigations together. Besides telling us whether a sex difference exists, this method provides an estimate of its size. Table 13.2 on page 554 summarizes differences between boys and girls in mental abilities and personality traits, based on current evidence. The majority of findings listed in the table are small to moderate. Furthermore, the distributions for males and females usually overlap greatly. Sex differences typically account for no more than 5 to 10 percent of individual differences, leaving most to be explained by other factors. Consequently, males and females are actually more alike than different in developmental potential. Nevertheless, as we will see shortly, a few sex differences are considerable.

TABLE 13.2 | **Sex Differences in Mental Abilities and Personality Traits**

CHARACTERISTIC	SEX DIFFERENCE
Verbal abilities	Girls are advantaged in early language development and in reading and writing achievement throughout the school years. On tests of verbal ability, girls outperform boys, more so when tests are heavily weighted with writing.
Spatial abilities	As early as infancy and persisting throughout the lifespan, boys outperform girls in certain spatial skills, with the largest differences appearing on tasks requiring mental rotation.
Mathematical abilities	In early childhood and the primary grades, girls are slightly advantaged in counting, arithmetic computation, and mastery of basic concepts. By late childhood and early adolescence, boys outperform girls on complex problems involving abstract reasoning and geometry and on math achievement tests. The difference is greatest among high-achieving students.
School performance	Girls get better grades than boys in all academic subjects throughout elementary and secondary school, including math and science. (Girls' advantage, however, does not extend to secondary school math and science achievement tests, which present complex problems not directly taught in school. See Mathematical abilities, above.)
Achievement motivation	Sex differences in achievement motivation are linked to type of task. Boys perceive themselves as more competent at and have higher expectancies for success in mathematics, science, sports, and mechanical skills. Girls have higher expectancies and set higher standards for themselves in reading, writing, literature, and art.
Emotional sensitivity	Girls score higher than boys in emotional understanding and on self-report measures of empathy and sympathy. Girls' advantage in prosocial behavior is greatest for kindness and considerateness, less apparent for helping behavior.
Fear, timidity, and anxiety	Girls are more fearful and timid than boys, a difference that is present in the first year of life. In school, girls are more anxious about failure and try harder to avoid it. Boys are greater risk takers, a difference reflected in their higher injury rates throughout childhood and adolescence.
Effortful control	Compared with boys, girls display greater effortful control, including capacity to inhibit impulses and shift attention away from irrelevant or emotionally arousing stimuli—traits that contribute to girls' better school performance and reduced incidence of behavior problems.
Compliance and dependency	Girls comply more readily with directives from adults and peers, in part because of their greater effortful control. They also seek help from adults more often and score higher in dependency on personality tests.
Activity level	Boys are more active than girls.
Depression	Adolescent girls are more likely than boys to report depressive symptoms.
Aggression	Boys are more physically aggressive than girls and, in adolescence, are far more likely to become involved in antisocial behavior and violent crime. The sex difference favoring girls in relational aggression is small.
Developmental problems	Problems more common among boys than girls include speech and language disorders, reading disabilities, and behavior problems such as hyperactivity, hostile acting-out behavior, and emotional and social immaturity. More boys are born with genetic disorders, physical disabilities, and broad intellectual disability.

Mental Abilities

Sex differences in mental abilities have sparked almost as much controversy as the ethnic and SES differences in IQ considered in Chapter 8. Although boys and girls do not differ in general intelligence, they do vary in specific mental abilities. Many researchers, believing that heredity is involved in these disparities, have attempted to identify the biological processes responsible. But no biological factor operates in a social and cultural vacuum. For each ability we will consider, experience plays a considerable role.

Verbal Abilities Early in development, girls are slightly ahead of boys in language progress (see Chapter 9). Throughout the school years, girls attain higher scores in reading achievement and account for a lower percentage of children referred for remedial reading instruction. Girls continue to score slightly higher on tests of verbal ability in middle childhood and adolescence in every country in which assessments have been conducted (Bussiére, Knighton, & Pennock, 2007; Mullis et al., 2007; Wai et al., 2010). And when verbal tests are heavily weighted with writing, girls' advantage is large (Halpern et al., 2007).

A special concern is that girls' advantage in reading and writing achievement increases in adolescence, with boys doing especially poorly in writing—trends evident in the United States and other industrialized nations (see Figure 13.10) (OECD, 2010a; U.S. Department of Education, 2007, 2010). These differences in literacy skills are believed to be major contributors to a widening gender gap in college enrollments. Whereas 40 years ago, males accounted for 60 percent of U.S. undergraduate students, today they are in the minority, at 43 percent (U.S. Department of Education, 2011b).

Recall from Chapter 9 that girls have a biological advantage in earlier development of the left hemisphere of the cerebral cortex, where language is usually localized. And fMRI research indicates that in tackling language tasks (such as deciding whether two spoken or written words rhyme), 9- to 15-year-old girls show concentrated activity in language-specific brain areas. Boys, in contrast, display more widespread activation—in addition to language areas, considerable activity in auditory and visual areas, depending on how words are presented (Burman, Bitan, & Booth, 2007). This suggests that girls are more efficient language processors than boys, who rely heavily on sensory brain regions and process spoken and written words differently.

But girls also receive more verbal stimulation from the preschool years through adolescence, which may contribute to their more efficient processing (Peterson & Roberts, 2003). Furthermore, we have seen that children view language arts as a "feminine" subject. And, as noted in Chapter 8, as a result of the high-stakes testing movement, students today spend much time at their desks being taught in a regimented way—an approach particularly at odds with boys' higher activity level, assertiveness, and incidence of learning problems.

Finally, high rates of divorce and out-of-wedlock births mean that more children today grow up without the continuous presence of a father who models and encourages good work habits and skill at reading and writing. Both maternal and paternal involvement contributes to the achievement and educational attainment of young people of both sexes (Flouri & Buchanan, 2004). But some research suggests that high-achieving African American boys are particularly likely to come from homes where fathers are warm, verbally communicative, and demanding of achievement (Grief, Hrabowski, & Maton, 1998). Clearly, reversing boys' weakening literacy skills is a high priority, requiring a concerted effort by families, schools, and supportive communities.

Mathematical Abilities Studies of sex differences in mathematical abilities in early childhood and the primary grades are inconsistent. Some find no disparities, others slight differences depending on the math skill assessed (Lachance & Mazzocco, 2006). Girls tend to be advantaged in counting, arithmetic computation, and mastery of basic concepts, perhaps because of their better verbal skills and more methodical approach to problem solving. But by late childhood and early adolescence, when math concepts and problems become more abstract and spatial, boys outperform girls, with the difference especially evident on tests requiring complex reasoning and geometry (Bielinski & Davison, 1998; Gibbs, 2010; Lindberg et al., 2010). In science achievement, too, high school boys' advantage increases as problems become more difficult (Penner, 2003).

The male advantage is evident in most countries where males and females have equal access to secondary education. But the gap is typically small, varies considerably across nations, and has diminished over the past 30 years (Aud et al., 2011; Bussiére, Knighton, & Pennock, 2007; Halpern, Wai, & Saw, 2005; Lindberg et al., 2010; U.S. Department of Education, 2009). Among the most capable, however, the gender gap is greater. In widely publicized research on more than 100,000 bright seventh and eighth graders invited to take the Scholastic Assessment Test (SAT), boys outscored girls on

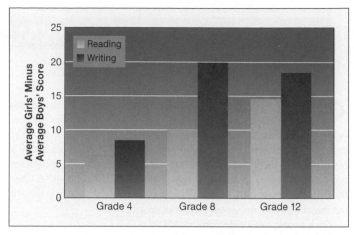

FIGURE 13.10 Reading and writing achievement gaps favoring girls at grades 4, 8, and 12. Findings are based on the U.S. National Assessment of Educational Progress. The bars represent the average girls' score minus the average boys' score. Thus, the height of the bar indicates the extent to which girls outperform boys, a difference that increases in adolescence. By grades 8 and 12, girls have an especially large advantage in writing skill. Similar trends are evident in other industrialized nations. (Adapted from U.S. Department of Education, 2007, 2010.)

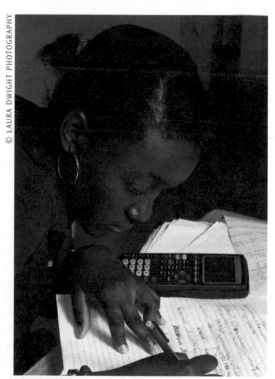

As math problems become more abstract and spatial, boys outperform girls, especially among the most capable students. The gender gap is small, however, and has declined over the past generation.

BIOLOGY and ENVIRONMENT

Sex Differences in Spatial Abilities

Spatial skills are a key focus of researchers' efforts to explain sex differences in complex mathematical reasoning. The gender gap favoring males is large for *mental rotation tasks*, in which individuals must rotate a three-dimensional figure rapidly and accurately inside their heads (see Figure 13.11). Males also do considerably better on *spatial perception tasks*, in which people must determine spatial relationships by considering the orientation of the surrounding environment. Sex differences on *spatial visualization tasks*, involving analysis of complex visual forms, are weak or nonexistent. Because many different strategies can be used to solve these tasks, both sexes may come up with effective procedures (Collaer & Hill, 2006; Voyer, Voyer, & Bryden, 1995).

Sex differences in spatial skills emerge as early as the first few months of life, in male infants' superior ability to recognize a familiar object from a new perspective—a capacity requiring mental rotation (Moore & Johnson, 2008; Quinn & Liben, 2008). The male spatial advantage is present throughout childhood, adolescence, and adulthood in many cultures (Levine et al., 1999; Silverman, Choi, & Peters, 2007). The pattern is consistent enough to suggest a biological explanation. One hypothesis is that heredity, perhaps through prenatal exposure to androgen hormones, enhances right-hemispheric functioning, giving males a spatial

FIGURE 13.11 Types of spatial tasks. Large sex differences favoring males appear on mental rotation, and males do considerably better than females on spatial perception. In contrast, sex differences on spatial visualization are weak or nonexistent. (From M. C. Linn & A. C. Petersen, 1985, "Emergence and Characterization of Sex Differences in Spatial Ability: A Meta-Analysis," *Child Development*, 56, pp. 1482, 1483, 1485. © The Society for Research in Child Development. Reproduced with permission of Blackwell Publishing Ltd.)

the mathematics subtest year after year. Yet even this disparity has been shrinking. Thirty years ago, 13 times as many boys as girls scored over 700 (out of a possible 800) on the math portion of the SAT; today, the ratio is about 4 to 1 for seventh graders and 2 to 1 for high school students (Benbow & Stanley, 1983; Wai et al., 2010).

Some researchers believe that heredity contributes substantially to the gender gap in math, especially to the tendency for more boys to be extremely talented. Accumulating evidence indicates that boys' advantage originates in two skill areas: (1) their more rapid numerical memory, which permits them to devote more energy to complex mental operations; and (2) their superior spatial reasoning, which enhances their mathematical problem solving (Geary et al., 2000; Halpern et al., 2007). Indeed, 50 years of longitudinal evidence on nationally representative samples of U.S. high school students tracked for a decade or more reveals that consistently, high spatial ability in adolescence predicts subsequent advanced educational attainment in math-intensive fields and entry into science, technology, engineering, and math (STEM) careers, beyond the contribution of verbal and math ability (Wai, Lubinski, & Benbow, 2009). See the Biology and Environment box above for further consideration of this issue.

Social pressures are also influential. We have seen that many children view math as a "masculine" subject. Also, parents typically think boys are better at it—an attitude that encourages girls to view themselves as having to work harder at math to do well, to blame their errors on lack of ability, and to regard math as less useful for their future lives. These advantage. (Recall that for most people, spatial skills are housed in the right hemisphere of the cerebral cortex.) In support of this idea, girls and women whose prenatal androgen levels were abnormally high show superior performance on spatial rotation tasks (Berenbaum, 2001; Halpern & Collaer, 2005). Women with a male twin brother, who are exposed to slightly higher levels of prenatal androgens, outperform women with a female twin sister in spatial rotation (Heil et al., 2011; Vuoksimaa et al., 2010). In some studies, spatial performance varies with daily and annual androgen levels in both men and women (Temple & Carney, 1995; Van Goozen et al., 1995).

Why might a biologically based sex difference in spatial abilities exist? Evolutionary theorists point out that mental rotation skill predicts rapid, accurate map drawing and interpretation, areas in which boys and men do better than girls and women. Over the course of human evolution, the cognitive abilities of males became adapted for hunting, which required generating mental representations of large-scale spaces to find one's way (Jones, Braithwaite, & Healy, 2003). But this explanation is controversial. Critics point out that female gatherers also needed to travel long distances to find fruits and vegetables that ripened in different seasons (Newcombe, 2007).

Experience also contributes to males' superior spatial performance. Children who engage in manipulative activities, such as block play, model building, and carpentry, do better on spatial tasks (Baenninger & Newcombe, 1995). Furthermore, playing action video games enhances many cognitive processes important for spatial skills, including visual discrimination, speed of thinking, attention shifting, tracking of multiple objects, mental rotation, and wayfinding—gains that persist and generalize to diverse situations (Spence & Feng, 2010). Boys spend far more time than girls at these pursuits.

In studies of middle and high school students, *both* spatial ability and self-efficacy at doing math were related to performance on complex math problems, with spatial skills being the stronger predictor (Casey, Nuttall, & Pezaris, 1997, 2001). Boys are advantaged in both spatial abilities and math self-confidence. Still, spatial skills respond readily to training, with improvements often larger than the sex differences themselves. But because boys and girls show similar training effects, sex differences typically persist (Liu et al., 2008; Newcombe & Huttenlocher, 2006). In one study of first graders, however, training in mental rotation strategies over several months—a more intense approach than previously tried—led girls to reach the same performance level as boys (Tzuriel & Egozi,

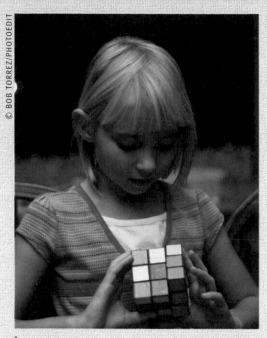

A gender gap favoring males exists for mental rotation tasks. But with intense training in mental rotation strategies, girls' performance improves markedly.

2010). These findings suggest that the right kind of early intervention can override biologically based sex differences in spatial skills.

beliefs reduce girls' self-efficacy at doing math, which undermines their performance on math achievement tests and their willingness to consider STEM careers in college (Bhanot & Jovanovic, 2005; Bleeker & Jacobs, 2004; Kenney-Benson et al., 2006). In addition, *stereotype threat*—the fear of being judged on the basis of a negative stereotype (see page 341 in Chapter 8)—causes girls to do worse than their abilities allow on difficult math problems (Ben-Zeev et al., 2005; Muzzatti & Agnoli, 2007). As a result of all these influences, girls—even those who are highly talented—are less likely to develop effective math reasoning skills.

A positive sign is that today, American boys and girls reach advanced levels of high school math and science study in equal proportions—a crucial factor in reducing sex differences in knowledge and skill (Gallagher & Kaufman, 2005). Still, extra steps must be taken to promote girls' interest in and confidence at math and science. As Figure 13.12 on page 558 shows, in cultures that value gender equality, sex differences in secondary school students' math achievement are much smaller and, in one nation, reversed! Icelandic high school girls exceed boys in math scores (Guiso et al., 2008). Similarly, in countries where few individuals view science as "masculine," secondary school girls equal or exceed boys in science achievement (Nosek et al., 2009).

Furthermore, a math curriculum beginning in kindergarten that teaches children how to apply effective spatial strategies—drawing diagrams, mentally manipulating visual images, searching for numerical patterns, and graphing—is vital (Nuttall, Casey, & Pezaris, 2005). Because girls are biased toward verbal processing and perform less well than boys in spatial

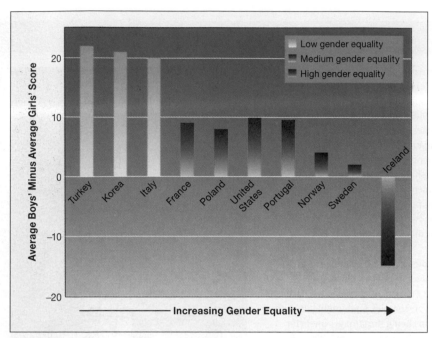

FIGURE 13.12 **Math achievement gender gaps in 10 industrialized nations, arranged in order of increasing gender equality.** Math achievement scores are based on 15-year-olds' performance on an identical test in each nation. Country gender equality is a composite measure that includes cultural attitudes toward women, women's participation in the labor force and in politics and government, and women's educational attainment and economic opportunities. As country gender equality increases, boys' advantage in math achievement declines; in Iceland, girls' math scores exceed boys'. (Adapted from Guiso et al., 2008.)

skills, they may not realize their math and science potential unless they are specifically taught how to think spatially.

Finally, role models of successful women are likely to add further to girls' interest and expectancies for success in advanced math and science courses and in STEM careers. The vastly greater presence of men in STEM fields—90 percent of engineers, 75 percent of math and computer occupations, 90 percent of physicists—is noticeable (U.S. Census Bureau, 2011b). In one study, female college science majors who viewed a video of a science conference depicting mostly males expressed a reduced sense of belonging, less desire to participate in the conference, and more neurobiological markers linked to stereotype threat (such as elevated heart rate and skin surface temperature) than their counterparts who watched a gender-balanced video (Murphy, Steele, & Gross, 2007). Exposure to women mathematicians, physical and computer scientists, and engineers might also help to convey how altruistic values, which are particularly important to girls and women (see page 543), can be fulfilled within STEM occupations.

Personality Traits

Sex differences in personality are in line with gender stereotypes. Traits most often studied include emotional sensitivity, depression, and aggression.

Emotional Sensitivity Females are more emotionally sensitive than males, a difference that appears early. Beginning in the preschool years, girls perform slightly better when asked to infer others' emotional states and the causes of those states. Relative to boys, girls are especially adept at understanding the more complex, self-conscious emotions—an advantage that extends into adulthood (Bosacki & Moore, 2004; Brown & Dunn, 1996; Bybee, 1998). Except for anger, girls also express their feelings more freely and intensely in everyday interaction (Chaplin, Cole, & Zahn-Waxler, 2005; Geary, 1998). And girls are better at identifying their feelings. When researchers observed children's facial expressions of emotion as they watched emotionally arousing videotapes and then asked them how they felt, girls' verbal reports matched their expressed emotion far more often than boys' (Strayer & Roberts, 1997).

It would be reasonable to expect these differences in emotional sensitivity to extend to empathy, sympathy, and prosocial behavior, but the evidence is mixed. On self-report measures, girls and women score higher than boys and men. When they are observed for behavioral signs, however, the gender difference is less consistent. Girls show a slight advantage in prosocial responding that is mostly evident in kindness and considerateness, less apparent in helping behavior (Eisenberg & Fabes, 1998; Eisenberg, Fabes, & Spinrad, 2006). When asked to describe the prosocial acts of their peers, adolescents reported many as-yet-unstudied examples that require self-confidence and assertiveness and, therefore, might be especially common among boys (Bergin, Talley, & Hamer, 2003). These include helping others develop skills (giving tips on how to play basketball), providing physical assistance (volunteering to mow a neighbor's lawn), and confronting others for harmful or otherwise inappropriate behavior.

As with other attributes, both biological and environmental explanations for sex differences in emotional sensitivity exist. According to one evolutionary account, females are genetically primed to be more emotionally sensitive as a way of ensuring their effectiveness as caregivers. Yet research suggests that girls are not naturally more nurturant. Before age 5, boys and girls spend equal amounts of time talking to and playing with babies (Fogel et al., 1987). In middle childhood, Caucasian boys' willingness to relate to infants declines. Yet African-American school-age boys, who endorse fewer gender stereotypes, smile, touch, and look at babies just as much as girls do (Reid & Trotter, 1993). Also, sex differences in emotional sensitivity are not evident in mothers' and fathers' interactions with their babies. In Chapter 10, we saw that fathers are just as affectionate and competent at caregiving as mothers. And in Chapter 4, we noted that men and women react similarly to the sound of a crying baby.

Cultural expectations that girls be warm and expressive and boys be distant and self-controlled seem largely responsible for the gender gap in emotional sensitivity. In infancy, mothers respond more often to a girl's happiness and distress than to a boy's (Malatesta et al., 1986). Similarly, during the preschool years, both fathers and mothers attend more to girls' than boys' sadness and anxiety, and this parental attentiveness predicts greater expression of these emotions by children two years later (Chaplin, Cole, & Zahn-Waxler, 2005). Also, parents are more likely to use inductive discipline (which promotes sympathetic concern) with girls and to pressure girls to be thoughtful and caring (Zahn-Waxler, Cole, & Barrett, 1991). Finally, recall that parents spend more time talking about emotions when conversing with daughters. Taken together, these findings suggest that girls receive far more encouragement than boys to express and reflect on feelings.

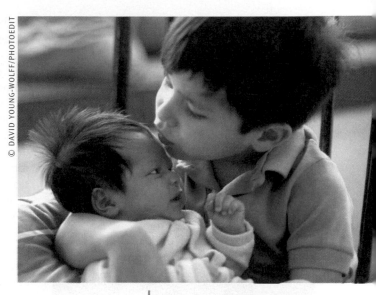

As this affectionate big brother illustrates, young boys are not naturally less nurturant toward infants than girls. Gender differences in this aspect of emotional sensitivity develop in middle childhood, largely because of cultural expectations.

Depression   Depression—feeling sad, frustrated, and hopeless about life, accompanied by loss of pleasure in most activities and disturbances in sleep, appetite, concentration, and energy—is the most common psychological problem of adolescence. Among U.S. teenagers, 20 to 50 percent experience mild to moderate feelings of depression, bouncing back after a short time. More worrisome are the 15 to 20 percent who have had one or more major depressive episodes, a rate comparable to that of adults. From 2 to 8 percent are chronically depressed—gloomy and self-critical for many months and sometimes years (Graber & Sontag, 2009; Rushton, Forcier, & Schectman, 2002).

Serious depression affects only 1 to 2 percent of children, many of whom (especially girls) remain depressed in adolescence. In addition, depression increases sharply from ages 12 to 16 in industrialized nations, with many more girls than boys displaying adolescent onset of symptoms. Teenage girls are twice as likely as boys to report persistent depressed mood—a sex difference sustained throughout the lifespan (Dekker et al., 2007; Hankin & Abela, 2005; Nolen-Hoeksema, 2002). If allowed to continue, depression seriously impairs social, academic, and vocational functioning.

The precise combination of biological and environmental factors leading to depression varies from one individual to the next. Kinship studies reveal that heredity plays an important role (Glowinski et al., 2003). Genes can induce depression by affecting the balance of neurotransmitters in the brain, the development of brain regions involved in inhibiting negative emotion, or the body's hormonal response to stress (Kaufman & Charney, 2003).

But experience can also activate depression, promoting any of these biological changes. Parents of depressed children and adolescents show a high incidence of depression and other psychological disorders. Although a genetic risk may be passed from parent to child, in earlier chapters we saw that depressed or otherwise stressed parents often form insecure attachments with their children and engage in maladaptive parenting. As a result, their child's emotional self-regulation, attachment, and self-esteem may be impaired, with serious consequences for many cognitive and social skills (Abela et al., 2005; Yap, Allen, & Ladouceur, 2008). Depressed youths usually display a learned-helpless attributional style, viewing positive

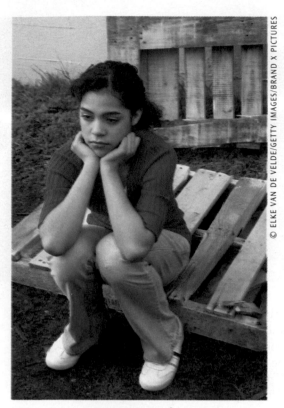

In industrialized nations, stressful life events and gender-typed coping styles—passivity, dependency, and rumination—make adolescent girls more prone to depression than boys.

academic and social outcomes as beyond their control (Graber, 2004). In a vulnerable young person, numerous negative life events can spark depression—for example, failing at something important, parental divorce, the end of a close friendship or romantic partnership, or the challenges of school transition.

Why are girls more prone to depression than boys? Biological changes associated with puberty cannot be a major factor because the gender difference is limited to industrialized nations. In developing countries, rates of depression are similar for males and females and occasionally higher in males (Culbertson, 1997). Even when females do exceed males in depression, the size of the difference varies. For example, it is smaller in China than in the United States, perhaps because of decades of efforts by the Chinese government to eliminate gender inequalities (Greenberger et al., 2000).

Instead, stressful life events and gender-typed coping styles seem to be responsible. Early-maturing girls are especially prone to depression, particularly when they also face other stressful life events (see Chapter 5). And adolescent gender intensification may strengthen girls' passivity, dependency, and tendency to ruminate on (repetitively mull over) their anxieties and problems—maladaptive approaches to tasks expected of teenagers in complex cultures. Consistent with this explanation, adolescents who identify strongly with "feminine" traits ruminate more and tend to be more depressed, regardless of their sex (Lopez, Driscoll, & Kistner, 2009; Papadakis et al., 2006). Girls who repeatedly feel overwhelmed develop an overly reactive physiological stress response and cope more poorly with challenges in the future (Hyde, Mezulis, & Abramson, 2008; Nolen-Hoeksema, 2006). In this way, stressful experiences and stress reactivity feed on one another, sustaining depression. In contrast, girls with either an androgynous or a "masculine" gender identity show low rates of depressive symptoms (Priess, Lindberg, & Hyde, 2009; Wilson & Cairns, 1988).

Unfortunately, the stereotypical view of adolescence as a period of "storm and stress" leads many adults to minimize the seriousness of adolescents' depression, misinterpreting it as just a passing phase. As a result, the overwhelming majority of depressed teenagers do not receive treatment (Asarnow et al., 2005). Yet without intervention that improves coping strategies and reduces high reactivity to stress, adolescent depression is likely to evolve into a lifelong pattern.

Aggression Aggression has attracted more research attention than any other sex difference. In Chapter 12, we noted that by the second year, boys are more *physically aggressive* than girls. But sex differences in *verbal aggression* (threats of physical harm, name-calling, and hostile teasing) and *relational aggression* (aimed at damaging another's social relationships) are minimal. A common but inaccurate assumption is that the rumor spreading, social exclusion, and other types of relationship manipulation that make up relational aggression are considerably more common in girls. But girls exceed boys only slightly (Crick et al., 2004, 2006; Crick, Ostrov, & Werner, 2006). Girls often *appear* much more relationally aggressive than boys because many girls use relational tactics nearly exclusively. Boys, by contrast, draw on a diversity of means to inflict harm—whatever works at the moment.

Although children of both sexes find relational aggression to be very hurtful, girls find it especially so, reporting more distress and judging it to be more unjust than boys do (Galen & Underwood, 1997; Murray-Close, Crick, & Galotti, 2006). Because girls place a high value on close relationships, harming a friendship is a powerful way to hurt a peer. There are other reasons, too, that relational aggression accounts for the large majority of girls' hostile acts. First, girls spend more time in close proximity to adults and are more sensitive to adult approval. They may emphasize relational aggression because it is hard for adults to detect and, therefore, to punish. Second, as Chapter 15 will make clear, dominance relations are less clear in girls' than in boys' peer groups. As a result, girls may jockey for social position frequently, engaging in relationship manipulation to protect their own status (Underwood, 2003).

Our discussion of the origins of sex differences in aggression focuses on physical aggression. At present, much less is known about factors that contribute to relational aggression.

Biological Influences. Because males' greater physical aggression is evident early in life, generalizes across cultures, and is found in many animal species, most researchers believe that biology is involved. Androgen hormones are related to aggression in animals and are also believed to play a role in humans. But children with CAH, who were exposed prenatally to abnormally high androgen levels, are not consistently more aggressive (Berenbaum & Resnick, 1997; Mathews et al., 2009). Perhaps androgens promote certain behaviors that, in some circumstances, increase the likelihood of aggressive outcomes.

The sex difference favoring girls in relational aggression is small. But because girls place a high value on close relationships, they find relational tactics especially hurtful.

One possibility is that prenatal androgens promote physical activity and competitiveness—behaviors likely to change into aggression in certain situations (Dodge, Coie, & Lynam, 2006). For example, an active, competitive child who often participates in large-group activities might become more aggressive than a child who prefers small-group pursuits. To explore this idea, researchers brought kindergartners and first graders to a laboratory where they played a game, some in same-sex pairs and others in same-sex tetrads (groups of four). In the game, children rolled a die, which indicated how many beads they could take from either a common pile (a noncompetitive move) or another player (a competitive move). Group size had no impact on girls' competitive moves, but boys displayed nearly twice as many competitive moves in tetrads as in dyads (Benenson et al., 2001). Recall that compared with girls, boys spend more time playing in large groups—an attraction, according to evolutionary theorists, adapted to preparing them for the competitive adult life of their male ancestors. Large groups, in turn, serve as contexts in which competition and striving for social dominance may promote aggression.

Another hypothesis is that sex hormones influence brain functioning in ways that affect emotional reactions. According to this view, hormone levels induce more frequent displays of excitement, anger, or anxiety, which make aggression more likely under certain conditions. Consistent with this prediction, adolescent boys with high androgen levels are more dominant and, therefore, more likely to respond with aggression when provoked by peers (Olweus et al., 1988; Tremblay et al., 1997). In one study, higher estrogen and androgen levels were related to adolescent girls' expressions of anger in a discussion session with their parents (Inoff-Germain et al., 1988).

Although more research is needed, current evidence indicates that multiple pathways exist between sex hormones and physical aggression. Clearly, too, environmental conditions have much to do with whether or not hormonally induced emotions and behaviors are channeled into aggressive acts.

Environmental Influences. In Chapter 12, we showed how coercive child-rearing practices promote aggressive behavior. Boys are more likely than girls to be affected because parents more often use physical punishment with boys, which encourages them to adopt the same tactics in their own relationships (Hester, He, & Tian, 2009; Sobring, Rodholm-Funnemark, & Palmerus, 2003).

At the same time, parents and teachers respond differently to boys' and girls' physical aggression. They often give boys positive attention or relax rules, coaxing, begging, or ignoring rather than using clear, firm prohibitions. In contrast, they usually respond negatively to girls' assertive and aggressive acts (Arnold, McWilliams, & Harvey-Arnold, 1998; Kerig, Cowan, & Cowan, 1993; Radke-Yarrow & Kochanska, 1990). The stereotypical view that "boys will be boys" may lead many adults to overlook or tolerate boys' hostility unless it is extreme, so that boys receive tacit approval for physical aggression, whereas girls suppress it.

LOOK and LISTEN

Ask several adolescents to describe instances they witnessed in which boys and girls engaged in relational aggression ("were mean to a peer"). Then ask why these behaviors occur and their likely emotional impact. Are participants' responses consistent with evidence on sex differences in relational aggression?

In gender-segregated peer groups, boys and girls express aggression in different ways. Boys more often engage in bossy, rough aggressive acts.

▶ Cite ways to reduce gender stereotyping in children.

It is not surprising, then, that school-age boys expect less parental disapproval and report feeling less guilty for aggression than girls (Perry, Perry, & Weiss, 1989).

Gender-segregated peer groups extend adults' lessons about expressing aggression, with boys often engaging in high rates of bossy, rough, aggressive acts while girls encourage one another to refrain from physical fighting. In one study, emotionally reactive preschool and kindergarten boys who mostly played with other boys showed an increase in teacher-reported problem behaviors ("starts fights," "is defiant to adults") over the school year. Among emotionally reactive girls who often played with other girls, problem behaviors decreased (Fabes et al., 1997). Perhaps these girls begin to vent their anger indirectly. By middle childhood, girls' relational aggression is more malicious than boys' and more likely to be directed at close friends (Pronk & Zimmer-Gembeck, 2010; Rose & Rudolph, 2006). Boys, in contrast, more often use relational aggression to exclude peers from large groups because of poor athletic skill, perceived "feminine" identity, or physical weakness.

In sum, early experiences tend to promote physical aggression in boys but to dampen it in girls, encouraging them to find covert, relational outlets for their hostility. Overall, biological predispositions and social encouragement jointly contribute to sex differences in aggression.

Developing Non-Gender-Stereotyped Children

We have seen that children's developmental possibilities can be seriously limited by persistent gender stereotypes in their culture. Despite wide recognition of the importance of rearing children who feel free to express their human qualities without fear of violating gender-role expectations, no easy recipe exists for accomplishing this difficult task. It must be tackled on many fronts—at home, at school, and in the wider society.

Biology clearly affects children's gender typing, channeling boys toward active, competitive play and girls toward quieter, more intimate interaction—a difference that leads each sex, on average, to seek out activities and social experiences consistent with those predispositions. But substantial revisions in gender roles and in relationships between males and females—along with wide individual, family, and cultural variations—reveal that most aspects of gender typing are not built into human nature (Maccoby, 2000b). Furthermore, a long human childhood ensures that experiences can greatly influence biologically based sex differences (Ruble, Martin, & Berenbaum, 2006).

Throughout our discussion, we have mentioned strategies for reducing gender stereotyping and gender-role conformity. These are summarized in Applying What We Know on the following page. But even children fortunate enough to grow up in homes and schools that minimize stereotyping will eventually encounter it in the media and in the typical roles of men and women in their communities. Consequently, children need early experiences that repeatedly counteract their readiness to absorb our culture's extensive network of gender-linked associations.

Because preschoolers' cognitive limitations lead them to assume that cultural practices determine gender, Sandra Bem (1993, 1998) suggests that parents and teachers make a concerted effort to delay young children's learning of gender-stereotyped messages. Adults can begin by eliminating traditional gender roles from their own behavior and from the alternatives they provide for children. For example, mothers and fathers can take turns making dinner, bathing children, and driving the family car and can provide sons and daughters with both trucks and dolls, both pink and blue clothing. Teachers can make sure that all

APPLYING WHAT WE KNOW

Reducing Children's Gender Stereotyping and Gender-Role Conformity

STRATEGY	EXPLANATION
Permit children to choose among diverse toys and activities.	Encouraging children to select toys and activities on the basis of their interests, not "gender appropriateness," counters gender stereotypes and gives children a broader array of experiences.
Avoid transmitting gender stereotypes of achievement areas; point out that high effort improves competence in all areas.	Avoiding gender stereotypes about what boys and girls are "good at" encourages children's sense of competence at, interest in, and motivation to achieve in areas stereotyped for the other gender, thereby enabling them to realize their academic potential.
Teach children to appreciate differences among individuals.	Emphasizing individual differences (for example, one woman saying about another, "She's so interesting because she's different from me!") reduces the pressure children feel to adopt stereotypical attitudes and behaviors associated with their own gender.
Avoid unnecessary references to gender and gender stereotypes in your language.	Avoiding gender labels and generic utterances ("The boys aren't paying attention." "Most girls like art.") by referring, instead, to individuals ("Mark, Sam, and Jenny aren't paying attention." "Susie likes art.") prevents children from viewing same-sex individuals as alike and from accepting gender stereotypes.
Provide non-gender-stereotyped models.	Exposure to adults engaged in nonstereotyped activities and occupations promotes children's awareness that multiple choices are available to them.
Stress the complexity of gender groups.	Comments like "Some boys are good at math, and some girls are good at math," or "Some boys like sports, and some boys don't like sports," teach children that ability and interest, not gender, determine individual performance.
Arrange for mixed-sex interaction.	Children who have opportunities to engage in joint endeavors with other-sex peers are less likely to form gender stereotypes.
Discuss gender biases with children.	Discussing why certain social roles (such as president) are typically linked to one gender helps children to appreciate environmental causes of bias and to reject explanations based on innate sex differences.

children spend some time each day in both adult-structured and unstructured activities. Adults can also avoid using language that conveys gender stereotypes and can shield children from media presentations that do the same.

Once children notice the wide array of gender stereotypes in their society, parents and teachers can point out exceptions. For example, they can arrange for children to see men and women pursuing nontraditional careers and can explain that interests and skills, not sex, should determine a person's occupation. With older children, adults can discuss the historical roots and current consequences of gender inequalities—why, for example, there has not yet been a female U.S. president, why fathers rarely stay home with young children, and why stereotyped views of men and women are hard to change. In addition, Bem (1983) suggests providing children with a "sexism schema"—a knowledge framework for processing gender stereotypes and prejudice that triggers moral indignation. In this way, children can participate in promoting positive social change. (For an illustration, return to the Social Issues: Education box on page 545, in which children were taught to recognize and confront peers' sexist remarks.)

Research shows that school-age children who hold flexible beliefs about what boys and girls can do are more likely to notice instances of gender discrimination (Brown & Bigler, 2004). As children build concepts of themselves and their social world that are not limited by a masculine–feminine dichotomy, they contribute to the transformation of societal values, bringing us closer to a time when people will be released from the constraints of traditional gender roles.

ASK YOURSELF

Review ■ Cite evidence that both biological and environmental factors contribute to girls' advantage in verbal abilities and to boys' advantage in mathematical reasoning.

Review ■ Explain possible *indirect* links between androgen hormones and boys' greater physical aggression, noting the influence of both family and peer-group experiences.

Connect ■ Using Bronfenbrenner's ecological systems theory (see Chapter 1, page 26), describe steps that can be taken at each level of the environment to reduce gender stereotyping in children.

Apply ■ Thirteen-year-old Donna, who has a "feminine" gender identity, reached puberty early, is dissatisfied with her physical appearance, and often ruminates about how well her peers like her. Explain why Donna is at risk for depression.

SUMMARY

Explain how the study of gender typing has responded to societal change.

■ Largely because of progress in women's rights, **gender typing** is no longer regarded as essential for healthy adjustment. Current research focuses on how biological, cognitive, and social factors influence development of **gender stereotypes**, **gender roles,** and **gender identity,** and on how to free children from gender-based societal expectations.

Gender Stereotypes and Gender Roles (p. 530)

Describe the development of gender stereotyping from early childhood into adolescence.

■ Children begin acquiring gender stereotypes early in the preschool years. By middle childhood, they are aware of stereotypes for activities, behaviors, occupations, achievement areas, and—for personality—**instrumental** and **expressive traits.** Gains in **gender-stereotype flexibility** occur in middle childhood and adolescence, but children still may disapprove of violations of gender-role expectations, especially by males.

Cite individual and group differences in gender stereotyping, and discuss the relationship between gender stereotyping and gender-role adoption.

■ Children acquire gender stereotypes in idiosyncratic ways, yielding wide individual differences. Boys hold more rigid gender-stereotyped views than girls, white children more than black children. Higher-SES adolescents and adults hold more flexible views than their lower-SES counterparts.

■ Awareness of gender stereotypes is only weakly related to gender-role adoption. Stereotype flexibility, however, is a good predictor of school-age children's willingness to cross gender lines.

Influences on Gender Stereotyping and Gender-Role Adoption (p. 535)

Discuss biological influences on gender stereotyping and gender-role adoption.

■ According to an evolutionary perspective, males are genetically primed for dominance and females for intimacy, responsiveness, and cooperation. Cross-cultural similarities in gender typing have been found, but cultures vary widely in the extent to which they promote gender-role conformity.

© RAFIQUR RAHMAN/REUTERS/CORBIS

■ Prenatal androgen levels contribute to sex differences in play styles and to preference for same-sex peers. Research on children with congenital adrenal hyperplasia (CAH) and androgen insensitivity syndrome supports the role of androgens in "masculine" gender-role adoption.

Discuss environmental influences on gender stereotyping and gender-role adoption.

■ Beginning in infancy, adults hold gender-stereotyped perceptions and expectations of children. Early on, parents reinforce "gender-appropriate" play activities and behaviors and often use language that highlights gender distinctions.

■ In middle childhood, parents demand higher achievement from boys and hold gender-stereotyped beliefs about children's academic abilities, with consequences for achievement and career choices. Fathers tend to differentiate between boys and girls more than mothers.

■ Teachers reinforce children of both sexes for "feminine" behavior while also promoting traditional gender roles. Children also learn through observation of gender-typed models in the surrounding environment.

■ Interaction with same-sex peers further reinforces children's "gender-appropriate" activity choices and promotes gender-typed styles of social influence.

■ The impact of siblings on gender typing varies with birth order and family size. In larger families, same-sex siblings often strive to be different from one another and are likely to be less stereotyped.

Gender Identity (p. 547)

Discuss androgyny as well as social learning and cognitive-developmental views of the development of gender identity in early childhood.

■ Although most people have a traditional gender identity, a substantial minority are **androgynous,** combing both masculine and feminine characteristics. Masculine and androgynous identities are linked to better psychological adjustment.

■ According to social learning theory, pre-schoolers first acquire gender-typed responses through modeling and reinforcement and then organize these into gender-linked ideas about themselves. Cognitive-developmental theory suggests that **gender constancy** must precede gender-typed behavior.

■ Children master gender constancy in three stages: **gender labeling**, **gender stability**, and **gender consistency.** Contrary to cognitive-developmental predictions, "gender-appropriate" behavior is acquired long before gender constancy. Whereas gender labeling and gender stability strengthen early gender-role adoption, gender consistency seems to contribute to gender-stereotype flexibility.

What changes in gender identity occur in middle childhood and adolescence?

■ In middle childhood, boys strengthen their identification with the "masculine" role, while girls become more androgynous. Gender identity includes self-evaluations of gender typicality, contentedness, and felt pressure to conform to gender roles—each of which affects adjustment.

■ Some research suggests that early adolescence is a period of **gender intensification,** in which gender stereotyping of attitudes and behavior increases, though evidence is mixed.

Explain gender schema theory.

■ **Gender schema theory** is an information-processing approach that explains how environmental pressures and children's cognitions jointly shape gender typing. As children learn gender-stereotyped preferences and behaviors, they form masculine and feminine gender schemas that they apply to themselves and their worlds. Highly gender-schematic children view themselves and their surroundings in gender-linked terms and, as a result, learn more about "gender-appropriate" than "gender-inappropriate" activities and behaviors.

To What Extent Do Boys and Girls *Really* Differ in Gender-Stereotyped Attributes? (p. 553)

Describe sex differences in mental abilities and personality traits, noting factors that contribute to those differences.

■ Most sex differences in mental abilities and personality traits are small to moderate. Girls tend to be advantaged in language development, reading and writing, counting, arithmetic computation, mastery of basic math concepts, and emotional understanding. Boys are better at certain spatial skills and at complex mathematical reasoning.

■ Biological factors, adult encouragement, and learning opportunities contribute to sex differences in language, spatial, and math skills. Girls' greater emotional sensitivity is largely due to gender-stereotyped expectations and child-rearing practices.

■ The higher rate of depression in adolescent girls in industrialized nations largely results from stressful life events and gender-typed coping styles. Gender intensification in early adolescence may strengthen girls' passivity and dependency, which interfere with their ability to cope with challenges.

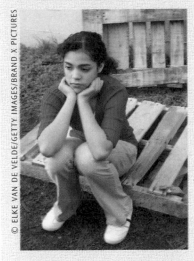

■ Androgen hormones contribute to greater physical aggression in males but may exert their effects indirectly by influencing activity level, emotional reactions, or dominance. Parents and teachers are more likely to encourage physical aggression in boys while suppressing it in girls—lessons reinforced by gender-segregated peer groups.

Developing Non-Gender-Stereotyped Children (p. 562)

Cite ways to reduce gender stereotyping in children.

■ Parents and teachers can counteract young children's readiness to absorb gender-linked associations by eliminating traditional gender roles from their own behavior. Once children notice gender stereotypes, adults can point out exceptions and discuss the arbitrariness of many gender inequalities.

IMPORTANT TERMS AND CONCEPTS

androgyny (p. 547)
expressive traits (p. 530)
gender consistency (p. 548)
gender constancy (p. 548)
gender identity (p. 530)

gender intensification (p. 550)
gender labeling (p. 548)
gender roles (p. 530)
gender schema theory (p. 551)
gender stability (p. 548)

gender-stereotype flexibility (p. 533)
gender stereotypes (p. 530)
gender typing (p. 530)
instrumental traits (p. 530)

CHAPTER 14

"Untitled"

Anagha, 12 years, Kuwait

Of all contexts influencing children's development, the family is the most powerful. This depiction of parents and child strolling in a tranquil wintry landscape evokes the sense of safety and security that the family provides.

Reprinted with permission from the International Museum of Children's Art, Oslo, Norway

The Family

"I don't remember much family togetherness when I was a kid," 19-year-old Hannah reflected over dinner with Aunt Eva and Uncle Charlie. "Our parents couldn't talk things out with each other, and they weren't very open with us. We almost never sat down to a meal or went anywhere together. I joined Girl Scouts and went to summer camp. I liked the activities and made good friends, but they couldn't make up for the absence of warm family time."

When Hannah was 9, her parents divorced, and she moved across the country with her mother. At first, her father arranged visits every few months, taking Hannah out to eat and to the movies and buying her whatever she asked for. Back home, when Hannah objected to her mother's rules and demands, her mother would rail at her father, calling him a "Disneyland Dad" who took no serious responsibility for Hannah's upbringing. As these arguments flared repeatedly, visits from Hannah's father trailed off.

To make ends meet, Hannah's mother extended her work hours to evenings and weekends. Hannah would make a box of macaroni and cheese for dinner, eat by herself, and then—neglecting her homework—spend hours watching TV, texting her friends, or just daydreaming. She found it hard to concentrate, and her grades suffered. In high school, stormy relationships with boyfriends left Hannah feeling depressed and rejected. Aimless and "at sea," she was convinced she couldn't do anything.

At 17, Hannah got her driver's license. Longing for a sense of family togetherness, she began making repeated visits to her Aunt Eva and Uncle Charlie, who lived in a neighboring city. They listened to Hannah, encouraged her, and helped her with time management, academic, and relationship problems. Two years later, when Hannah graduated from high school with plans to enter a university, she attributed her turnabout in motivation and self-confidence to her aunt and uncle's warmth, involvement, and guidance.

The family is the child's first, and longest-lasting, context for development. Compared with other species, human children develop slowly, requiring years of protection, support, and teaching before they are ready to be independent. This gradual journey to maturity has left an imprint on human social organization everywhere: Families are pervasive, and parenting is universally important in children's lives. Children who lack a satisfying, supportive family life are likely to crave it. Some, like Hannah, find what they seek in extended family or another special adult.

Of course, other contexts also mold children's development, but none equals the family in power and breadth of influence. The attachments children form with parents and siblings usually last a lifetime and serve as models for relationships in the wider world of neighborhood and school. Within the family, children experience their first social conflicts. Discipline by parents and arguments with siblings provide important lessons in compliance and cooperation and opportunities to learn how to influence others. Finally, within the family, children learn the language, skills, and social and moral values of their culture.

We begin our discussion by examining why this social unit came into being and has survived for thousands of years. Then we describe the current view of the family as a *social system* with many interacting influences on the child. Next, we look closely at the family as the core socializing agency of society by considering child-rearing styles, factors that influence them, and their consequences for children's development. We also address recent social changes that have led to great diversity in family lifestyles. Finally, recognizing that the contemporary family is especially vulnerable to a breakdown in protective, emotionally supportive parent–child relationships, we consider the origins and consequences of child maltreatment. ■

Origins and Functions of the Family

The Family as a Social System
Direct Influences • Indirect Influences • Adapting to Change • The Family System in Context

■ **SOCIAL ISSUES: HEALTH:** *The Transition to Parenthood*

Socialization Within the Family
Styles of Child Rearing • What Makes the Authoritative Style Effective? • Adapting Child Rearing to Children's Development • Socioeconomic and Ethnic Variations in Child Rearing

■ **BIOLOGY AND ENVIRONMENT:** *Does Parenting Really Matter?*

■ **CULTURAL INFLUENCES:** *The African-American Extended Family*

Family Lifestyles and Transitions
From Large to Small Families • One-Child Families • Adoptive Families • Gay and Lesbian Families • Never-Married Single-Parent Families • Divorce • Blended Families • Maternal Employment and Dual-Earner Families • Child Care • Self-Care

Vulnerable Families: Child Maltreatment
Incidence and Definitions • Origins of Child Maltreatment • Consequences of Child Maltreatment • Preventing Child Maltreatment

■ **SOCIAL ISSUES: HEALTH:** *Child Sexual Abuse*

▶ Discuss evolutionary origins of the family, and cite functions contemporary families perform for society.

Origins and Functions of the Family

The family in its most common form—an enduring commitment between a man and a woman who feed, shelter, and nurture their children until they reach maturity—arose tens of thousands of years ago among our hunting-and-gathering ancestors. From an evolutionary perspective, the human family enhanced survival by ensuring a relatively even balance of male hunters and female gatherers within a social group, thereby providing protection against starvation at times when game was scarce (Lancaster & Whitten, 1980).

An extended relationship between a man and a woman also increased male certainty that a newborn baby was actually *his* offspring, motivating him to care and provide for mother and child and to invest in child rearing in order to increase the odds of child survival (Bjorklund, Yunger, & Pellegrini, 2002; Geary, 2000). Larger kin networks that included grandparents, aunts, uncles, and cousins formed, increasing the chances of successful competition with other humans for vital resources and providing assistance with child rearing.

Besides promoting survival of its members, the family unit of our evolutionary ancestors performed the following vital services for society:

- *Reproduction.* Replacing dying members.
- *Economic services.* Producing and distributing goods and services.
- *Social order.* Devising procedures for reducing conflict and maintaining order.
- *Socialization.* Training the young to become competent, participating members of society.
- *Emotional support.* Helping others surmount emotional crises and fostering in each person a sense of commitment and purpose.

As societies became more complex, the demands placed on the family became too much for it to sustain alone. Other institutions developed to assist with some of these functions, and families became linked to larger social structures (Parke & Kellam, 1994). For example, political and legal institutions assumed responsibility for ensuring societal order, and schools and religious institutions extended the family's socialization function. And although some family members still carry out economic tasks together (as in family-run farms and businesses), this function has largely been taken over by institutions that make up the world of work.

Despite sharing some functions with other institutions, the family continues to assume primary responsibility for three important ones especially concerned with children: reproduction, socialization, and emotional support. Researchers interested in finding out how families fulfill these functions take a **social systems perspective,** viewing the family as a complex set of interacting relationships influenced by the larger social context.

The most common family structure—the nuclear family—arose tens of thousands of years ago because it enhanced survival. *Left photo:* A Mexican family cooks a meal at a market that provides individual barbecue grills. *Right photo:* A Chinese-American family celebrates Chinese New Year in New York.

© CHARLES O. CECIL/THE IMAGE WORKS

© DAVID M. GROSSMAN/THE IMAGE WORKS

The Family as a Social System

▶ Describe the social systems perspective on family functioning.

The social systems perspective on family functioning grew out of researchers' efforts to describe and explain the complex patterns of interaction between family members. As you will see, it has much in common with Bronfenbrenner's *ecological systems theory,* discussed in Chapter 1. Family systems theorists recognize that parents do not mechanically shape their children. Rather, as you already know from earlier chapters, *bidirectional influences* exist, whereby family members mutually influence one another. The very term *family system* implies a network of interdependent relationships (Bornstein & Sawyer, 2006; Bronfenbrenner & Morris, 2006; Parke & Buriel, 2006). These system influences operate both directly and indirectly.

Direct Influences

Recently, as I passed through the checkout counter at the supermarket, I witnessed two episodes, each an example of how parents and children directly influence each other:

- Four-year-old Danny looked longingly at the tempting rows of candy as his mother lifted groceries from her cart onto the counter. "Pleeeease, can I have it, Mom?" Danny begged, holding up a package of bubble gum. "Do you have a dollar? Just one?"

  "No, not today," his mother answered. "Remember, we picked out your special cereal. That's what I need the dollar for." Gently taking the bubble gum from his hand, Danny's mother handed him the box of cereal. "Here, let's pay," she said, lifting Danny so he could see the checkout counter.
- Three-year-old Meg sat in the shopping cart while her mother transferred groceries to the counter. Suddenly Meg turned around, grabbed a bunch of bananas, and started pulling them apart.

  "Stop it, Meg!" shouted her mother, snatching the bananas from Meg's hand. But as she turned her attention to swiping her debit card, Meg reached for a chocolate bar from a nearby display. "Meg, how many times have I told you, *don't touch!*" Prying the candy from Meg's tight little fist, Meg's mother slapped her hand. Meg's face turned red with anger as she began to wail.

These observations fit with a wealth of research on the family system. Studies of families of diverse ethnicities show that when parents are firm but warm (like Danny's mother), children tend to comply with their requests. And when children cooperate, their parents are likely to be warm and gentle in the future. In contrast, parents who discipline with harshness and impatience (like Meg's mother) tend to have children who resist and rebel. Because children's misbehavior is stressful for parents, they may increase their use of punishment, leading to more unruliness by the child (Stormshak et al., 2000; Whiteside-Mansell et al., 2003). In each case, the behavior of one family member helps sustain a form of interaction in another that either promotes or undermines children's well-being.

Indirect Influences

The impact of family relationships on child development becomes even more complicated when we consider that interaction between any two family members is affected by others present in the setting. Recall from Chapter 1 that Bronfenbrenner called these indirect influences the effect of *third parties.* Researchers have become intensely interested in how a range of relationships—mother with father, parent with sibling, grandparent with parent—modify the child's direct experiences in the family. In fact, as the Social Issues: Health box on page 570 reveals, a child's birth can have a third-party impact on parents' interaction that may affect the child's development and well-being.

Third parties can serve as supports for development, or they can undermine it. For example, when parents' marital relationship is warm and considerate, mothers and fathers are more likely to engage in effective **coparenting,** mutually supporting each other's parenting behaviors. Such parents have more secure attachment relationships with their babies,

SOCIAL ISSUES: HEALTH

The Transition to Parenthood

The early weeks after a baby enters the family are full of profound changes— constant caregiving, added financial responsibilities, and less time for couples to devote to each other. In response, gender roles of husband and wife usually become more traditional, even for couples strongly committed to gender equality (Cowan & Cowan, 2000; Katz-Wise, Priess, & Hyde, 2010). Mothers change more than fathers as they spend more time at home with the baby; fathers focus more on their provider role.

For most new parents, the arrival of a baby— though often associated with mild declines in relationship satisfaction and communication quality—does not cause significant marital strain. Marriages that are gratifying and supportive tend to remain so (Doss et al., 2009; Feeney et al., 2001; Miller, 2000). But troubled marriages usually become more distressed after a baby is born. In a study of newlyweds who were interviewed annually for six years, the husband's affection, expression of "we-ness" (values and goals similar to his wife's), and awareness of his wife's daily life predicted mothers' stable or increasing marital satisfaction after childbirth. In contrast, the husband's negativity and the couple's out-of-control conflict predicted a drop in mothers' satisfaction (Shapiro, Gottman, & Carrere, 2000).

Violated expectations about division of labor in the home powerfully affect new parents' well-being. In dual-earner marriages, the larger the difference between men's and women's caregiving responsibilities, the greater the decline in marital satisfaction after childbirth, especially for women—with negative consequences for parent–infant interaction. In contrast, sharing caregiving tasks predicts greater parental happiness and sensitivity to the baby (McHale et al., 2004; Moller, Hwang, & Wickberg, 2008). An exception exists, however, for employed lower-SES women who endorse traditional gender roles. When their husbands help extensively with child care, these mothers tend to report more distress, perhaps because they feel disappointed at being unable to fulfill their desire to do most of the caregiving (Goldberg & Perry-Jenkins, 2003).

Postponing parenthood until the late twenties or thirties, as more couples do today, eases the transition to parenthood. Waiting permits couples to pursue occupational goals, gain life experience, and strengthen their relationship. Under these circumstances, men are more enthusiastic about becoming fathers and therefore

more willing to participate. And women whose careers are well under way are more likely to encourage their husbands to share housework and child care, which fosters fathers' involvement (Lee & Doherty, 2007; Schoppe-Sullivan et al., 2008).

In a study of well-educated mothers, those who had recently given birth to their second child reported just as much stress as first-time mothers (Krieg, 2007). A second birth typically requires that fathers take an even more active role in parenting—by caring for the firstborn while the mother is recuperating and by sharing in the high demands of tending to both a baby and a young child. Consequently, well-functioning families typically pull back from the traditional division of responsibilities that occurred after the first birth. Fathers' willingness to place greater emphasis on the parenting role is strongly linked to mothers' adjustment after the arrival of a second baby (Stewart, 1990). And the support and encouragement of family, friends, and partner are crucial for fathers' well-being.

Special interventions exist to ease the transition to parenthood. For those who are not at high risk for problems, counselor-led parenting groups are highly effective (Glade, Bean, & Vira, 2005; Petch & Halford, 2008). In one program, first-time expectant couples gathered once a week for six months to discuss their dreams for the family and changes in relationships sparked by the baby's arrival. Eighteen months after the program ended, participating fathers described themselves as more involved with their child than did fathers in a no-intervention condition. Perhaps because of fathers' caregiving assistance, participating mothers maintained their prebirth satisfaction with family and work roles. Three years after the birth, the marriages of all participating couples were still intact and just as happy as they had been before parenthood. In contrast, 15 percent of couples receiving no intervention had divorced (Cowan & Cowan, 1997; Schulz, Cowan, & Cowan, 2006).

High-risk parents struggling with poverty, single parenthood, or the birth of a child with disabilities usually need more intensive intervention. Programs in which a professional intervener visits the home and focuses on enhancing

First-time parents delight in their newborn. In a warm, gratifying marriage, sharing caregiving tasks is related to greater sensitivity toward the baby.

social support and parenting skills have resulted in improved parent–infant interaction and benefits for children's cognitive and social development into middle childhood (Petch & Halford, 2008). For low-income unmarried couples, the father's involvement in the pregnancy (providing the expectant mother with financial and social support, being present at the birth) enhances paternal engagement with the child in the first few years, in part because it increases his commitment to the mother and the chances that the couple will cohabit or marry (Cabrera, Fagan, & Farrie, 2008). Consequently, interventions that encourage unmarried men to be prenatally involved are a promising approach to strengthening family bonds and parenting.

Generous paid employment leave—widely available in industrialized nations but not in the United States—is crucial for easing the transition to parenthood (see page 119 in Chapter 3). Flexible work hours are also helpful. When favorable workplace policies exist and couples try to support each other's needs, the stress caused by the birth of a baby remains manageable.

and they praise and stimulate their children more and nag and scold them less. Effective coparenting, in turn, fosters a positive marital relationship (Morrill et al., 2010). In contrast, parents whose marriage is tense and hostile often interfere with one another's child-rearing efforts, are less responsive to children's needs, less consistent in discipline practices, and more likely to criticize, express anger, and punish (Caldera & Lindsey, 2006; Krishnakumar & Buehler, 2000; McHale et al., 2002). Clearly, communication and emotions generated in the marital relationship "spill over" into the parent–child relationship.

Children who are chronically exposed to angry, unresolved parental conflict have myriad problems related to disrupted emotional security and emotional self-regulation (Cummings & Merrilees, 2010; Schacht, Cummings, & Davies, 2009). These include both internalizing difficulties (especially among girls), such as blaming themselves, feeling worried and fearful, and trying to repair their parents' relationship; and externalizing difficulties (especially among boys), including anger and aggression (Cummings, Goeke-Morey, & Papp, 2004; Davies & Lindsay, 2004). Furthermore, in research carried out in nations as diverse as Bangladesh, China, Bosnia, and the United States, parental conflict consistently undermined good parenting by increasing criticism and belittling of adolescents and decreasing monitoring of their whereabouts and activities (Bradford et al., 2003). These parenting practices, in turn, heightened youth behavior problems.

Yet even when parental arguments strain children's adjustment, other family members may help restore effective interaction. Grandparents, for example, can promote children's development both directly, by responding warmly to the child and helping with caregiving (see page 438 in Chapter 10), and indirectly, by providing parents with child-rearing advice, models of child-rearing skill, and sometimes financial assistance. Of course, as with any indirect influence, grandparents can sometimes be harmful. When quarrelsome relations exist between grandparents and parents, parent–child communication and children's adjustment may suffer.

Adapting to Change

Think back to the *chronosystem* in Bronfenbrenner's theory (see page 28 in Chapter 1). The interplay of forces within the family is dynamic and ever-changing, as each member adapts to the development of other members.

For example, as children acquire new skills, parents adjust the way they treat their more competent youngsters. To cite just one example, turn back to Chapter 4, page 147, and review how babies' mastery of crawling leads parents to engage in more game playing and expressions of affection, as well as restriction of the child's activities. These changes in child rearing pave the way for new achievements and further revisions in family relationships. **TAKE A MOMENT…** Can you think of other illustrations of this idea, discussed in earlier chapters?

Parents' development affects children as well. As we will see later, the mild increase in parent–child conflict that often occurs in early adolescence is not solely due to teenagers' striving for independence. This is a time when most parents have reached middle age and—conscious that their children will soon leave home and establish their own lives—are reconsidering their own commitments (Steinberg & Silk, 2002). While the adolescent presses for greater autonomy, the parent presses for more togetherness. This imbalance promotes friction, which parent and teenager gradually resolve by accommodating to changes in each other. Indeed, no social unit other than the family is required to adjust to such vast changes in its members.

The Family System in Context

The social systems perspective, as we noted earlier, views the family as affected by surrounding social contexts. As the *mesosystem* and *exosystem* in Bronfenbrenner's model make clear, connections to the neighborhood and the larger community—both *formal organizations,* such as school, workplace, recreation center, child-care center, and religious institution, and *informal social networks* of relatives, friends, and neighbors—influence parent–child relationships.

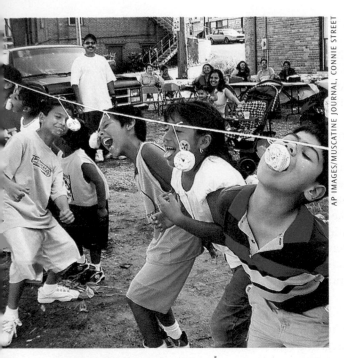

At an inner-city block party, children participate in a doughnut-eating contest while their parents look on. According to the social systems perspective, community ties are essential for families to function at their best.

In several studies, low-SES families were randomly assigned vouchers to move out of public housing into neighborhoods varying widely in affluence. Compared with their peers who remained in poverty-stricken areas, children and youths who moved into low-poverty neighborhoods showed substantially better physical and mental health and school achievement (Goering, 2003; Leventhal & Brooks-Gunn, 2003).

Unstable inner-city neighborhoods with dilapidated housing; schools, parks, and playgrounds in disarray; and lack of community centers introduce stressors that undermine parental warmth, involvement, and monitoring and increase parental harshness and inconsistency. In such neighborhoods, family violence, child abuse and neglect, children's problem behavior, youth antisocial activity, and adult criminality are especially high (Brody et al., 2003; Dunn, Schaefer-McDaniel, & Ramsay, 2010). In contrast, strong family ties to the surrounding social context—as indicated by contact with friends and relatives, organized youth activities, and regular church, synagogue, or mosque attendance—reduce family stress and adjustment problems (Boardman, 2004; Leventhal & Brooks-Gunn, 2003).

How do links between family and community reduce stress and promote child development? One answer lies in their provision of *social support*, which leads to the following benefits:

● *Parental self-worth.* A neighbor or relative who listens and tries to relieve a parent's concern enhances her self-esteem. The parent, in turn, is likely to interact in a more sensitive and involved manner with her children.
● *Parental access to valuable information and services.* A friend who suggests where a parent might find a job, housing, or affordable child care helps make the multiple roles of spouse, provider, and caregiver easier to fulfill.
● *Child-rearing controls and role models.* Friends, relatives, and other community members may encourage and demonstrate effective parenting practices and discourage ineffective ones.
● *Direct assistance with child rearing.* As children and adolescents participate in their parents' social networks and in youth-oriented community activities, other adults can influence children directly through warmth, stimulation, and exposure to a wider array of competent models. In this way, family–neighborhood ties can reduce the impact of ineffective parenting (Silk et al., 2004). Nearby adults can also intervene when they see young people skipping school or behaving antisocially.

The Better Beginnings, Better Futures Project of Ontario, Canada, is a government-sponsored set of programs aimed at preventing the dire consequences of neighborhood poverty. The most successful of these efforts, using a local elementary school as its base, provided 4- to 8-year-olds with in-class, before- and after-school, and summer enrichment activities. Workers also visited each child's parents regularly, informed them about community resources, and encouraged their involvement in the child's school and neighborhood life. And a community-wide component focused on improving the quality of the neighborhood as a place to live, by offering leadership training and adult education programs and organizing neighborhood safety initiatives and special events and celebrations (Peters, 2005; Peters, Petrunka, & Arnold, 2003). Evaluations as children reached grades 3, 6, and 9 revealed wide-ranging benefits compared with children and families living in other poverty neighborhoods without this set of programs (Peters et al., 2010). Among these were parents' sense of improved marital satisfaction, family functioning, effective child rearing, and community involvement; and gains in children's academic achievement and social adjustment, including positive relationships with peers and adults, prosocial behavior, self-regulation, and a reduction in emotional and behavior problems.

No researcher could possibly study all aspects of the social systems perspective on the family at once. But throughout this chapter, we will continually see examples of how its interlocking parts combine to influence development.

A S K   Y O U R S E L F

Review ■ Links between family and community are essential for children's well-being. Provide examples and research findings that support this idea.

Connect ■ How does the goodness-of-fit model, discussed in Chapter 10 (see page 426), illustrate central features of the social systems perspective on family functioning?

Apply ■ At the mall, you see a father getting angry with his young son. Using the social systems perspective, list as many factors as you can that might account for the father's behavior.

Reflect ■ Did any third parties—grandparents, aunts or uncles, or others—influence your relationship with your parents when you were a child? Describe how they affected interactions within your family.

Socialization Within the Family

Among the family's functions, socialization centers on children's development. Parents start to socialize their children in earnest during the second year, when toddlers are first able to comply with their directives (see Chapter 12). As children get older, parents gradually step up socialization pressures, but they vary greatly in how they go about the task. In previous chapters, we have seen how parents can foster children's competence—by building a parent–child relationship based on affection and cooperation, by serving as models and reinforcers of mature behavior, by using reasoning and inductive discipline, and by guiding and encouraging children's mastery of new skills. Now let's put these practices together into an overall view of effective parenting.

▶ Discuss child-rearing styles, and explain how effective parents adapt child rearing to children's growing competence.

▶ Describe socioeconomic and ethnic variations in child rearing, including the impact of affluence and poverty.

Styles of Child Rearing

Child-rearing styles are combinations of parenting behaviors that occur over a wide range of situations, creating an enduring child-rearing climate. In a landmark series of studies, Diana Baumrind gathered information on child rearing by watching parents interact with their preschoolers (Baumrind, 1971; Baumrind & Black, 1967). Her findings, and those of others who have extended her work, reveal three features that consistently differentiate an effective style from less effective ones: (1) *acceptance* of the child and *involvement* in the child's life, which establishes an emotional connection with the child; (2) *behavioral control* of the child through expectations, rules, and supervision, which promotes more mature behavior; and (3) *autonomy granting*, which encourages self-reliance (Barber & Olsen, 1997; Gray & Steinberg, 1999; Hart, Newell, & Olsen, 2003; Maccoby & Martin, 1983). Table 14.1 on page 574 shows how child-rearing styles differ in these features. Let's discuss each style in turn.

Authoritative Child Rearing The **authoritative child-rearing style**—the most successful approach—involves high acceptance and involvement, adaptive control techniques, and appropriate autonomy granting. Authoritative parents are warm, attentive, and sensitive to their child's needs. They establish an enjoyable, emotionally fulfilling parent–child relationship that draws the child into close connection. At the same time, authoritative parents exercise firm, reasonable behavioral control: They insist on appropriate maturity, give reasons for their expectations, use disciplinary encounters as "teaching moments" to promote the child's self-regulation, and monitor their child's whereabouts and activities. Furthermore, authoritative parents engage in gradual, appropriate *autonomy granting*, allowing the child to make decisions in areas where he is ready to make choices. They also place a premium on communication, encouraging the child to express her thoughts, feelings, and desires. And when parent and child disagree, authoritative parents engage in joint decision making when

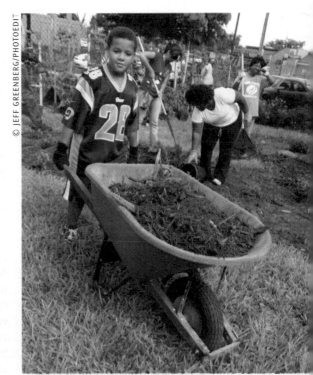

By granting children autonomy appropriate to their age and abilities, authoritative parents promote competence and maturity. This 9-year-old takes responsibility for helping to create a public garden in the Little Haiti neighborhood of Miami, Florida.

© JEFF GREENBERG/PHOTOEDIT

TABLE 14.1 | **Features of Child-Rearing Styles**

CHILD-REARING STYLE	ACCEPTANCE AND INVOLVEMENT	CONTROL	AUTONOMY GRANTING
Authoritative	Is warm, responsive, attentive, patient, and sensitive to the child's needs	Engages in adaptive behavioral control: Makes reasonable demands for mature behavior and consistently enforces and explains them	Permits the child to make decisions in accord with readiness Encourages the child to express thoughts, feelings, and desires When parent and child disagree, engages in joint decision making when possible
Authoritarian	Is cold and rejecting	Engages in coercive behavioral control: Makes excessive demands for mature behavior, using force and punishment Often uses psychological control, manipulating and intruding on the child's individuality and parental attachments	Makes decisions for the child Rarely listens to the child's point of view
Permissive	Is warm but overindulgent or inattentive	Is lax in behavioral control: Makes few or no demands for mature behavior	Permits the child to make many decisions before the child is ready
Uninvolved	Is emotionally detached and withdrawn	Is lax in behavioral control: Makes few or no demands for mature behavior	Is indifferent to the child's decision making and point of view

possible. Their willingness to accommodate to the child's perspective increases the likelihood that the child will listen to their perspective in situations where compliance is vital (Kuczynski & Lollis, 2002; Russell, Mize, & Bissaker, 2004).

Throughout childhood and adolescence, authoritative parenting is linked to many aspects of competence—an upbeat mood, self-control, task persistence, academic achievement, cooperativeness, high self-esteem, responsiveness to parents' views, and social and moral maturity (Amato & Fowler, 2002; Aunola, Stattin, & Nurmi, 2000; Gonzalez & Wolters, 2006; Mackey, Arnold, & Pratt, 2001; Milevsky et al., 2007; Steinberg, Darling, & Fletcher, 1995).

Authoritarian parents often engage in psychological control, belittling their child and using withdrawal of love as a punishment. In response, children become either anxious and withdrawn or defiant and aggressive.

Authoritarian Child Rearing The **authoritarian child-rearing style** is low in acceptance and involvement, high in coercive behavioral control, and low in autonomy granting. Authoritarian parents appear cold and rejecting. To exert control, they yell, command, criticize, and threaten. "Do it because I said so!" is their attitude. They make decisions for their child and expect the child to accept their word unquestioningly. If the child does not, authoritarian parents resort to force and punishment. They also hold excessively high expectations that do not fit the child's developing capacities.

Children of authoritarian parents are more likely to be anxious, unhappy, and low in self-esteem and self-reliance. When frustrated, they tend to react with hostility and, like their parents, resort to force when they do not get their way. Boys, especially, show high rates of anger and defiance. Although girls also engage in acting-out behavior, they are more likely to be dependent, lacking interest in exploration, and overwhelmed by challenging tasks (Hart et al., 2003; Kakihara et al., 2010; Thompson, Hollis, & Richards, 2003). Children and adolescents exposed to the authoritarian style typically achieve poorly in school. However, because of their parents' concern with controlling their behavior, they tend to achieve better and to commit fewer antisocial acts than peers with undemanding parents—that is, those whose parents use one of the two styles we will consider next (Steinberg, Blatt-Eisengart, & Cauffman, 2006).

Notice how the authoritarian style suppresses children's self-expression and independence. In addition to unwarranted behavioral control ("Do what I say!"), authoritarian parents often engage in **psychological control,** in which they attempt to take advantage of children's psychological needs by intruding on and manipulating their verbal expressions, individuality, and attachments to parents. In an attempt to decide virtually everything for the child, these parents frequently interrupt or put down the child's ideas, decisions, and choice of friends. When they are dissatisfied, they withdraw love, making their affection or attention contingent on the child's compliance. Children and adolescents subjected to psychological control exhibit adjustment problems involving both anxious, withdrawn and defiant, aggressive behaviors. Once again, boys are more likely than girls to respond with rebellious and antisocial acts (Barber & Harmon, 2002; Kakihara et al., 2010; Silk et al., 2003). And having had few opportunities for exploration, they are impaired in identity development once they reach early adulthood (Luyckx et al., 2007).

Permissive Child Rearing The **permissive child-rearing style** is warm and accepting but uninvolved. Permissive parents are either overindulgent or inattentive and, thus, engage in little behavioral control. Instead of gradually granting autonomy, they allow children to make many decisions for themselves at an age when they are not yet capable of doing so. Their children can eat meals and go to bed whenever they wish and can watch as much television as they want. They do not have to learn good manners or do household chores. Although some permissive parents truly believe in this approach, many others simply lack confidence in their ability to influence their child's behavior (Oyserman et al., 2005).

Children of permissive parents tend to be impulsive, disobedient, and rebellious. Compared with children whose parents exert more behavioral control, they are also overly demanding and dependent on adults, and they show reduced task persistence, poorer academic achievement, and more antisocial behavior. The link between permissive parenting and dependent, nonachieving, rebellious behavior is especially strong for boys (Barber & Olsen, 1997; Baumrind, 1971; Steinberg, Blatt-Eisengart, & Cauffman, 2006).

Uninvolved Child Rearing The **uninvolved child-rearing style** combines low acceptance and involvement with little behavioral control and general indifference to issues of autonomy. Often these parents are emotionally detached and depressed, so overwhelmed by life stress that they have little time or energy for children. They may respond to the child's immediate demands for easily accessible objects while failing to engage in strategies to promote long-term goals, such as establishing and enforcing rules about homework and social behavior, listening to the child's point of view, providing guidance about appropriate choices, and monitoring the child's whereabouts and activities.

At its extreme, uninvolved parenting is a form of child maltreatment called *neglect*. Especially when it begins early, it disrupts virtually all aspects of development (see Chapter 10, page 422). Even with less extreme parental disengagement, children and adolescents display many problems, including school achievement difficulties, depression, anger, and antisocial behavior (Aunola, Stattin, & Nurmi, 2000; Kurdek & Fine, 1994; Schroeder et al., 2010).

What Makes the Authoritative Style Effective?

Table 14.2 on page 576 summarizes outcomes associated with each child-rearing style just considered. As with other correlational findings, the relationship between the authoritative style and children's competence is open to interpretation. Perhaps parents of well-adjusted children are authoritative because their youngsters have especially cooperative dispositions. Children's characteristics do contribute to the ease with which parents can apply the authoritative style. Recall from earlier chapters that temperamentally fearless, impulsive children and emotionally negative, difficult children are more likely to evoke coercive, inconsistent discipline. At the same time, extra warmth and firm control succeed in modifying these children's maladaptive styles (Cipriano & Stifter, 2010; Kochanska, Philibert, & Barry, 2009; Pettit et al., 2007). And with fearful, inhibited children, parents must suppress their tendency to overprotect and take over solving the child's social problems—practices that, as we saw in Chapter 10, worsen the shy child's difficulties. Instead, inhibited children benefit from extra encouragement to be assertive and to express their autonomy (Nelson et al., 2006; Rubin & Burgess, 2002).

TABLE 14.2	Relationship of Child-Rearing Styles to Development and Adjustment Outcomes	
CHILD-REARING STYLE	**CHILDHOOD**	**ADOLESCENCE**
Authoritative	Upbeat mood; high self-esteem, self-control, task persistence, academic achievement, and cooperativeness	High self-esteem, academic achievement, and social and moral maturity
Authoritarian	Anxious, withdrawn and defiant, aggressive behavior; unhappy mood; hostile when frustrated; academic achievement difficulties	Less well-adjusted than agemates reared with the authoritative style, but somewhat better academic achievement and less antisocial behavior than agemates reared with permissive or uninvolved styles
Permissive	Impulsive, disobedient, and rebellious; overly demanding and dependent on adults; poor task persistence and academic achievement	Poor academic achievement; defiance and antisocial behavior
Uninvolved	Deficits in attachment, cognition, play, and emotional and social skills	Poor academic achievement, depression, anger, and antisocial behavior

LOOK and LISTEN

Ask several parents to explain their style of child rearing and why they use it, inquiring about acceptance and involvement, control, and autonomy granting. Look for variations in authoritativeness—more or less behavioral control—and parents' reasons for them.

Longitudinal evidence indicates that among children of diverse temperaments, authoritative child rearing in the preschool years predicts maturity and adjustment a decade later in adolescence, whereas authoritarian or permissive child rearing predicts adolescent immaturity and adjustment difficulties. And a variant of authoritativeness in which parents exert strong behavioral control—becoming directive but not coercive—yields just as favorable long-term outcomes as a more democratic approach (Baumrind, Larzelere, & Owens, 2010). Parental directiveness may stem from parents' personalities, child-rearing beliefs, or children's needs. Indeed, as the findings on temperament and parenting just mentioned illustrate, some children, because of their dispositions, require "heavier doses" of certain authoritative features.

Over time, the relationship between parenting and children's attributes becomes increasingly bidirectional as each participant modifies the actions of the other and, on the basis of past interactions, forms expectancies for the other's behavior (Kuczynski, 2003). Consider, for example, an investigation of the consequences of parental monitoring that followed adolescents from ages 14 to 18. The more parents knew about their child's whereabouts and activities, the greater the decline in delinquent acts over time. And the greater the decline in delinquency, the more parents increased in knowledge of their teenager's daily life (Laird et al., 2003).

What explains these bidirectional associations, in which parental monitoring promotes responsible youth behavior, which in turn leads to gains in parental knowledge? Parents who exert appropriate oversight are likely to parent effectively in other ways as well, giving adolescents both less opportunity and less reason to engage in delinquency. And parents who take proactive steps to intervene in their teenager's antisocial acts set the stage for a more positive parent–child relationship, in which teenagers are more willing to provide them with information. In contrast, when monitoring is lax and delinquency rises, parent–adolescent interaction may become increasingly negative. As a result, parents may further disengage from parenting, both to avoid these unpleasant exchanges and to reduce contact with a child whom they have come to dislike.

Most children and adolescents seem to view the affection, appropriate control, and respect for self-determination that make up authoritative child rearing as a well-intentioned parental effort to increase their competence. As a result, even hard-to-rear youngsters gradually respond to authoritativeness with cooperation and maturity, which promote parents' pleasure and approval of the child, sense of self-efficacy at child rearing, and likelihood of continuing to be authoritative. In sum, authoritative child rearing seems to create a *positive emotional context* for parental influence in the following ways:

● Warm, involved parents who are secure in the standards they hold for their children provide models of caring concern as well as confident, self-controlled behavior.
● Children are far more likely to comply with and internalize behavioral control that appears fair and reasonable, not arbitrary and excessive (see Chapter 12).
● Parents who combine warmth with rational and reasonable behavioral control are likely to be more effective reinforcing agents, praising children for striving to meet their expectations and making good use of disapproval, which works best when applied by an adult who has been warm and caring (see Chapter 12).

- By making demands and engaging in autonomy granting that fit with children's ability to take responsibility for their own behavior, authoritative parents let children know that they are competent individuals who can do things successfully for themselves. In this way, parents foster favorable self-esteem and cognitive and social maturity (see Chapter 11).
- Supportive features of the authoritative style are a powerful source of resilience, protecting children from the negative effects of family stress and poverty (Beyers et al., 2003).

Still, a few theorists remain convinced that parenting has little impact on child development. They claim that because parents and children share genes, parents provide children with genetically influenced child rearing that does little more than enhance children's built-in propensities. But as the Biology and Environment box on page 578 confirms, a host of findings demonstrate that parenting does contribute vitally to children's competence.

Adapting Child Rearing to Children's Development

Because authoritative parents continually adapt to children's increasing competence, their practices change with children's age. A gradual lessening of control and increase in autonomy granting promote favorable development.

Parenting in Middle Childhood: Coregulation In middle childhood, the amount of time children spend with parents declines dramatically. Children's growing independence means that parents must deal with new issues. As one mother described it, "I've struggled with how many chores to assign, how much allowance to give, whether their friends are good influences, and what to do about problems at school. And then there's the challenge of keeping track of them when they're out—or even when they're home and I'm not there to see what's going on."

Despite these new concerns, child rearing becomes easier for parents who established an authoritative style during the early years. Reasoning is more effective with school-age children because of their greater capacity for logical thinking and their increased respect for parents' expert knowledge (Collins, Madsen, & Susman-Stillman, 2002). And children of parents who communicate openly and engage in joint decision making when possible are more likely to listen to parents' perspectives in situations where compliance is vital (Russell, Mize, & Bissaker, 2004).

As children demonstrate that they can manage daily activities and responsibilities, effective parents gradually shift control from adult to child. They do not let go entirely but, rather, engage in **coregulation,** a form of supervision in which parents exercise general oversight while letting children take charge of moment-by-moment decision making. Coregulation grows out of a warm, cooperative relationship between parent and child based on give-and-take. Parents must guide and monitor from a distance and effectively communicate expectations when they are with their children. And children must inform parents of their whereabouts, activities, and problems so parents can intervene when necessary (Maccoby, 1984). Coregulation supports and protects children while preparing them for adolescence, when they will make many important decisions themselves.

Although school-age children often press for greater independence, they also know how much they need their parents' support. In one study, fifth and sixth graders described parents as the most influential people in their lives, often turning to them for affection, advice, enhancement of self-worth, and assistance with everyday problems (Furman & Buhrmester, 1992).

An 11-year-old phones home during an outing with friends. By engaging in coregulation—letting her take charge of daily activities while exercising general oversight—her parents prepare her for greater independence in adolescence.

Parenting in Adolescence: Fostering Autonomy During adolescence, striving for **autonomy**—a sense of oneself as a separate, self-governing individual—becomes a salient task. Autonomy has two vital aspects: (1) an *emotional component*—relying more on oneself and less on parents for support and guidance—and (2) a *behavioral component*—making

BIOLOGY and ENVIRONMENT

Does Parenting Really Matter?

Several highly publicized reviews of research claim that parents are only minor players in children's development—that their impact is overshadowed by the effects of children's genetic makeup and the peer culture (Harris, 1998, 2002). These conclusions are largely based on evidence that siblings reared in the same family show little resemblance in parent-rated temperament (see Chapter 10, page 425, to review), a finding interpreted to mean that parenting is merely a reaction to children's genetic dispositions and does not change children in any appreciable way. No wonder, say proponents of this position, that many studies report only a weak to moderate parenting effect on children's development. A related contention is that children and adolescents resemble their friends more strongly than their siblings. Therefore, peers must be more powerful than parents in influencing children's behavior.

A host of researchers have refuted these assertions, offering evidence that parents—though not the sole influence—exert a profound impact (Berk, 2005; Collins et al., 2000; Hart, 2007; Hart, Newell, & Olsen, 2003; Maccoby, 2000a; Steinberg, 2001). Let's look at their findings:

- *Well-designed research reveals that the relation between parenting and children's development is sometimes substantial.* For example, in one large-scale study, the correlation between authoritative parenting and adolescents' social responsibility was .76 for mothers, .49 for fathers (Hetherington et al., 1999). Similarly, when parents engage in joint problem solving with their adolescent youngsters; establish firm, consistent control; and monitor the adolescent's whereabouts, research shows strong negative relationships with antisocial behavior (Patterson & Forgatch, 1995).
- *Parenting often has different effects on different children.* When weak associations between parenting and children's development are found, they do not necessarily reflect the feeble impact of parenting.

Rather, some child-rearing practices affect different children in different ways. And although parents respond differently to children with different temperaments, the relationship is not just a reactive one. **TAKE A MOMENT...** Cite ways, considered in this and in previous chapters, that parents can modify the maladaptive styles of impulsive, difficult, and shy children.

- *Longitudinal research suggests that parenting affects children's development.* Many longitudinal studies indicate that the influence of parenting on diverse aspects of children's development holds even after controlling for children's earlier characteristics (see, for example, Baumrind, Larzelere, & Owens, 2010; Carlson, 1998; D'Onofrio et al., 2006; Laird et al., 2003). These findings suggest that parents' influence is profound and lasting.
- *Parenting interventions show that when child rearing improves, children's development changes accordingly.* The most powerful evidence that parents matter comes from intervention experiments. In one study, recently divorced single mothers of school-age sons were randomly assigned to 14 weekly sessions of parent training and support. Compared to no-intervention controls, the mothers reduced their use of coercive discipline in the year following intervention, and their sons showed fewer behavior problems and deviant peer associations. In a nine-year follow-up, these changes translated into a reduction in adolescent delinquency (DeGarmo & Forgatch, 2005; Forgatch & DeGarmo, 1999; Forgatch et al., 2009). Furthermore, recall from Chapter 12 that training programs targeting parenting skills can break cycles of parent–child hostility, thereby lessening children's aggressive behavior (see page 523).

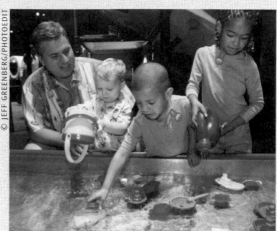

Research confirms that parents profoundly influence children's development. When warm parents provide rich, varied experiences, they foster children's positive capacities.

- *Parents influence children's peer relations.* Children and adolescents resemble their friends because young people choose friends who are similar to themselves. But beginning in the preschool years, parents propel children toward certain peers by managing their social activities. And as we will see in Chapter 15, authoritative child rearing affects the values and inclinations children and adolescents bring to the peer situation and, therefore, their choice of friends and their peer interactions and activities (Furman et al., 2002; Laird et al., 2003; Zhou et al., 2002).
- *Some parenting influences cannot be measured easily.* Many people report memorable moments with parents that made a lasting impression. In contrast, a parent's broken promise or discovered deception can destroy parent–child trust and change the impact of future parenting.

In sum, parenting effects combine in complex ways with many other factors, including heredity and peers. Although the contribution of each factor cannot always be partitioned neatly from the others, parents emerge as vigorously influential in wide-ranging research.

decisions independently by carefully weighing one's own judgment and the suggestions of others to arrive at a well-reasoned course of action (Collins & Laursen, 2004; Steinberg & Silk, 2002). Autonomy is closely related to adolescents' quest for identity. Young people who successfully construct personally meaningful values and life goals are autonomous. They have given up childish dependency on parents for a more mature, responsible relationship.

A variety of changes within the adolescent support autonomy. In Chapter 5, we saw that puberty triggers psychological distancing from parents. In addition, as young people look more mature, parents give them more freedom to think and decide for themselves, more opportunities to regulate their own activities, and more responsibility (McElhaney et al., 2009). Cognitive development also paves the way for autonomy: Gradually, adolescents solve problems and make decisions more effectively. And an improved ability to reason about social relationships leads adolescents to *deidealize* their parents, viewing them as "just people." Consequently, they no longer bend as easily to parental authority as they did when younger.

TAKE A MOMENT... Think back to what we said in earlier chapters about the type of parenting that fosters achievement motivation, identity formation, and moral maturity. You will find a common theme: Effective parenting of adolescents strikes a balance between *connection* and *separation*. In diverse ethnic groups, SES levels, nationalities, and family structures (including single-parent, two-parent, and stepparent), warm, supportive parent–adolescent ties that make appropriate demands for maturity while permitting young people to explore ideas and social roles foster autonomy—predicting high self-reliance, effortful control, academic achievement, work orientation, favorable self-esteem, social competence, and ease of separating in the transition to college (Bean, Barber, & Crane, 2007; Eisenberg et al., 2005b; Supple et al., 2009; Vazsonyi, Hibbert, & Snider, 2003; Wang, Pomerantz, & Chen, 2007).

Conversely, parents who are coercive or psychologically controlling interfere with the development of autonomy. These tactics are linked to low self-esteem, depression, drug and alcohol use, and antisocial behavior—outcomes that often persist into adulthood (Barber, Stolz, & Olsen, 2005; Bronte-Tinkew, Moore, & Carrano, 2006; Wissink, Deković, & Meijer, 2006).

Nevertheless, parents often report that living with teenagers is stressful. Earlier we described the family as a *system* that must adapt to changes in its members. The rapid physical and psychological changes of adolescence trigger conflicting expectations in parent–child relationships. In Chapter 12, we noted that interest in making choices about personal matters strengthens in adolescence. Yet parents and teenagers—especially young teenagers—differ sharply on the appropriate age for granting certain privileges, such as control over clothing, school courses, going out with friends, and dating (Smetana, 2002). Parents typically say that the young person is not yet ready for these signs of independence at a point when the teenager thinks they should have been granted long ago! Consistent parental monitoring of the young person's daily activities, through a cooperative relationship in which the adolescent willingly discloses information, is linked to a variety of positive outcomes— prevention of delinquency, reduction in sexual activity, improved school performance, and positive psychological well-being (Crouter & Head, 2002; Jacobson & Crockett, 2000).

Parents' own development can also lead to conflict with teenagers. While their children face a boundless future and a wide array of choices, middle-aged parents must come to terms with the fact that their own possibilities are narrowing (Holmbeck, 1996). Often parents can't understand why the adolescent wants to skip family activities to be with peers. And teenagers fail to appreciate that parents want the family to be together as often as possible because an important period in their adult life—child rearing—will soon end.

At times, adolescents assert their autonomy by resisting parental authority. But most maintain close parental ties, especially when parents give them the freedom to explore ideas and social roles.

Immigrant parents from cultures that place a high value on family closeness and obedience to authority have greater difficulty adapting to their teenagers' push for autonomy, often reacting more strongly to adolescent disagreement (Phinney & Ong, 2001). And as adolescents acquire the host culture's language and are increasingly exposed to its individualistic values, immigrant parents may become even more critical, prompting teenagers to rely less on the family network for social support. The resulting *acculturative stress* (see page 475 in Chapter 11) is associated with a decline in self-esteem and a rise in anxiety, depressive symptoms, and deviant behavior, including alcohol use and delinquency (Crane et al., 2005; Park, 2009; Suarez-Morales & Lopez, 2009; Warner et al., 2006).

Throughout adolescence, the quality of the parent–child relationship is the single most consistent predictor of mental health. In well-functioning families, young people remain attached to parents and seek their advice, but they do so in a context of greater freedom (Collins & Steinberg, 2006; Steinberg, 2001). The mild conflict that typically arises facilitates adolescent identity and autonomy by helping family members learn to express and tolerate disagreement. Conflicts also inform parents of adolescents' changing needs and expectations, signaling a need for adjustments in the parent–child relationship.

By middle to late adolescence, most parents and children achieve this mature, mutual relationship, and harmonious interaction is on the rise. The reduced time that Western teenagers spend with their families—for U.S. youths, a drop from 33 percent of waking hours in fifth grade to 14 percent in twelfth grade—has little to do with conflict (Larson et al., 1996). Rather, it results from the large amount of unstructured time available to teenagers in North America and Western Europe—on average, nearly half their waking hours (Larson, 2001). Young people tend to fill these free hours with activities that take them away from home— part-time jobs, a growing array of leisure and volunteer pursuits, and time with friends.

But this drop in family time is not universal. In one study, urban low- and middle-SES African-American youths showed no decline from childhood to adolescence in hours spent at home with family—a typical pattern in cultures with collectivist values (Larson et al., 2001). Furthermore, teenagers living in risky neighborhoods tend to have more trusting relationships with parents and adjust more favorably when their parents maintain tighter control and pressure them not to engage in worrisome behaviors (McElhaney & Allen, 2001). In harsh surroundings, young people seem to interpret more measured granting of autonomy as a sign of parental caring.

Socioeconomic and Ethnic Variations in Child Rearing

Study after study confirms that the authoritative style predicts favorable development in children and adolescents varying widely in SES and culture (Crouter & Head, 2002; Slicker & Thornberry, 2002; Vazonyi, Hibbert, & Snider, 2003). At the same time, SES and ethnic differences in parenting do exist.

Socioeconomic Status As SES rises and falls, parents and children face changing circumstances that affect family functioning, with each component of SES (educational attainment, occupational prestige and skill, and income) contributing. Researchers have yet to unravel these specific influences. Education and earnings are powerfully influential, with occupation playing a lesser but nevertheless important role (Duncan & Magnusson, 2003).

SES is linked to timing of parenthood and to family size. People who work in skilled and semiskilled manual occupations (for example, construction workers, truck drivers, and custodians) tend to marry and have children earlier, as well as give birth to more children, than people in professional and technical occupations. The two groups also differ in child-rearing values and expectations. When asked about personal qualities they desire for their children, lower-SES parents tend to emphasize external characteristics, such as obedience, politeness, neatness, and cleanliness. In contrast, higher-SES parents emphasize psychological traits, such as curiosity, happiness, self-direction, and cognitive and social maturity (Duncan & Magnusson, 2003; Hoff, Laursen, & Tardif, 2002; Lareau, 2003).

These differences are reflected in family interaction. Parents higher in SES talk to, read to, and otherwise stimulate their babies and preschoolers more (see Chapter 9, page 378). With older children and adolescents, they use more warmth, explanations, inductive discipline, and verbal praise; set higher academic and other developmental goals; and allow their children to make more decisions. Commands ("Do that because I told you to"), criticism, and physical punishment all occur more often in low-SES households (Bush & Peterson, 2008; Mandara et al., 2009).

Education contributes substantially to these differences. Higher-SES parents' interest in providing verbal stimulation and nurturing inner traits is supported by years of schooling, during which they learned to think about abstract, subjective ideas and, thus, to invest in their children's cognitive and social development (Mistry et al., 2008; Vernon-Feagans et al., 2008). At the same time, greater economic security enables parents to devote more time, energy, and material resources to nurturing their children's psychological characteristics

(Cheadle & Amato, 2011; Votruba-Drzal, 2003). In contrast, high levels of stress sparked by economic insecurity contribute to low-SES parents' reduced provision of stimulating interaction and activities as well as greater use of coercive discipline (Brooks-Gunn, Klebanov, & Duncan, 1996; Chin & Phillips, 2004; Conger & Donnellan, 2007).

Because of limited education and low social status, many low-SES parents feel powerless in their relationships beyond the home. At work, for example, they must obey the rules of others in positions of authority. When they get home, their parent–child interaction seems to duplicate these experiences—but now they are in authority. Higher-SES parents, in contrast, typically have more control over their own lives. At work, they are used to making independent decisions and convincing others of their point of view. At home, they are more likely to teach these skills to their children (Greenberger, O'Neil, & Nagel, 1994).

Poverty When families slip into poverty, effective parenting and children's development are profoundly threatened. Consider Zinnia Mae, who grew up in a close-knit black community located in a small southeastern American city (Heath, 1990). As unemployment struck the community and citizens moved away, 16-year-old Zinnia Mae caught a ride to Atlanta. Two years later, she was the mother of a daughter and twin boys, and she had moved into high-rise public housing.

Zinnia Mae worried constantly about scraping together enough money to put food on the table, finding baby-sitters so she could go to the laundry or grocery, freeing herself from rising debt, and locating the twins' father, who had stopped sending money. Her most frequent words were, "I'm so tired." The children had only one set meal—breakfast; otherwise, they ate whenever they were hungry or bored. Their play space was limited to the living-room sofa and a mattress on the floor. Toys consisted of scraps of a blanket, spoons and food cartons, a small rubber ball, a few plastic cars, and a roller skate abandoned in the building. At a researcher's request, Zinnia Mae agreed to tape-record her interactions with her children. Cut off from family and community ties and overwhelmed by financial strain and feelings of helplessness, she found herself unable to join in activities with her children. In 500 hours of tape, she started a conversation with them only 18 times.

The constant stressors that accompany poverty gradually weaken the family system. Poor families have many daily hassles—bills to pay, the car breaking down, loss of welfare and unemployment payments, something stolen from the house, to name just a few. When daily crises arise, parents become depressed, irritable, and distracted; hostile interactions increase; and children's development suffers (Conger & Donnellan, 2007; Evans, 2006). Negative outcomes are especially severe in single-parent families, in families who must live in poor housing and dangerous neighborhoods, and in homeless families—conditions that make everyday existence even more difficult, while reducing social supports that assist in coping with economic hardship (Hart, Atkins, & Matsuba, 2008; Leventhal & Brooks-Gunn, 2003).

Besides stress and conflict, reduced parental involvement and depleted home learning environments (like that of Zinnia Mae) profoundly affect poor children's cognitive and emotional well-being. As noted in earlier chapters, poverty that begins early and persists has devastating effects on children's physical and mental health, intelligence, and school achievement.

This family, already struggling financially, became homeless after a trailer park fire. The persistent stressors that accompany poverty weaken the family system, with profoundly negative consequences for children's well-being.

Affluence Despite their advanced education and greater material wealth, affluent parents—those in prestigious occupations with six-figure annual incomes—too often fail to engage in family interaction and parenting that promote favorable development. In several studies, researchers tracked youths growing up in high-SES suburbs (Luthar & Latendresse, 2005a). By seventh grade, many showed serious problems that worsened in high school. Their school grades were poor, and they were more likely than low-SES youths to engage in alcohol and drug use and to report high levels of anxiety and depression (Luthar & Becker, 2002; Luthar & Goldstein, 2008). Furthermore, among affluent (but not low-SES) teenagers, substance use was correlated with anxiety and depression, suggesting that wealthy youths

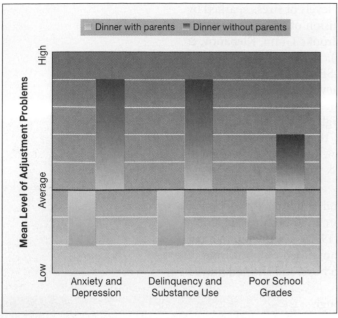

FIGURE 14.1 **Relationship of regularly eating dinner with parents to affluent youths' adjustment problems.** Compared with sixth graders who often ate dinner with their parents, those who rarely did so were far more likely to display anxiety and depression, delinquency and substance use, and poor school grades, even after many other aspects of parenting were controlled. In this study, frequent family mealtimes also protected inner-city youths from delinquency and substance use and from classroom learning problems. (Adapted from Luthar & Latendresse, 2005b.)

took drugs to self-medicate—a practice that predicts persistent abuse (Luthar & Sexton, 2004).

Why are so many affluent youths troubled? Compared to their better-adjusted counterparts, poorly adjusted affluent young people report less emotional closeness and supervision from their parents, who lead professionally and socially demanding lives. As a group, wealthy parents are nearly as physically and emotionally unavailable to their youngsters as parents coping with serious financial strain. At the same time, these parents often make excessive demands for achievement (Luthar & Becker, 2002). Adolescents whose parents value their accomplishments more than their character and emotional well-being are more likely to have academic and emotional problems.

For both affluent and low-SES youths, a simple routine—eating dinner with parents—is associated with a reduction in adjustment difficulties, even after many other aspects of parenting are controlled (see Figure 14.1) (Luthar & Latendresse, 2005b). Interventions that make wealthy parents aware of the high costs of a competitive lifestyle and minimal family time are badly needed.

Ethnicity Although authoritative parenting is broadly advantageous, ethnic minority parents often have distinct child-rearing beliefs and practices that reflect cultural values and family context. Let's take some examples.

Compared with Western parents, Chinese parents describe their parenting as less warm and more controlling. They are more directive in teaching and scheduling their children's time, as a way of fostering self-control and high achievement. Chinese parents may appear less warm than Western parents because they withhold praise, which they believe results in self-satisfied and poorly motivated children (Chao, 1994; Chen, 2001). High control reflects the Confucian belief in strict discipline, respect for elders, and socially desirable behavior, taught by deeply involved parents. Chinese parents report expressing affection and concern and using induction and other reasoning-oriented discipline as much as American parents do, but they more often shame a misbehaving child (see Chapter 10), withdraw love, and use physical punishment (Cheah et al., 2009; Shwalb et al., 2004; Wu et al., 2002). When these practices become excessive, resulting in an authoritarian style high in psychological or coercive control, Chinese children display the same negative outcomes as Western children: poor academic achievement, anxiety, depression, and aggressive behavior (Chan, 2010; Nelson et al., 2005, 2006; Pong, Johnston, & Chen, 2010; Wang, Pomerantz, & Chen, 2007).

In Hispanic families, Asian Pacific Island families, and Caribbean families of African and East Indian origin, firm insistence on respect for parental authority is paired with high parental warmth—a combination suited to promoting competence and strong feelings of family loyalty (Harrison et al., 1994; Roopnarine & Evans, 2007). In one study, Mexican-American mothers living in poverty who adhered strongly to their cultural traditions tended to combine warmth with strict, even somewhat harsh, control—a style that served a protective function, in that it was associated with reduced child and adolescent conduct problems (Hill, Bush, & Roosa, 2003). Although at one time viewed as coercive, contemporary Hispanic-American fathers typically spend much time with their children and are warm and sensitive (Cabrera & García Coll, 2004; Jambunathan, Burts, & Pierce, 2000). In Caribbean families that have immigrated to the United States, fathers' authoritativeness—but not mothers'—predicted preschoolers' literacy and math skills, probably because Caribbean fathers take a larger role in guiding their children's academic progress (Roopnarine et al., 2006).

© BRAND X PICTURES/ALAMY

In Hispanic families, respect for parental authority is often paired with high parental warmth—a combination that promotes competence and strong family loyalty.

CULTURAL INFLUENCES

The African-American Extended Family

The African-American extended family can be traced to the African heritage of most black Americans. In many African societies, newly married couples do not start their own households. Instead, they live with a large extended family, which assists its members with all aspects of daily life. This tradition of maintaining a broad network of kinship ties traveled to North America during the period of slavery. Since then, it has served as a protective shield against the destructive impact of poverty and racial prejudice on African-American family life. Today, more black than white adults have relatives other than their own children living in the same household. African-American parents also live closer to kin, often establish family-like relationships with friends and neighbors, see more relatives during the week, and perceive relatives as more important in their lives (Boyd-Franklin, 2006; McAdoo & Younge, 2009).

By providing emotional support and sharing income and essential resources, the African-American extended family helps reduce the stress of poverty, single parenthood, and inner-city neighborhood disorganization (Jarrett, Jefferson, & Kelly, 2010). Extended-family members often help with child rearing, and adolescent mothers living in extended families are more likely to complete high school, get a job, and avoid dependence on welfare than mothers living on their own—factors that in turn benefit children's well-being (Gordon, Chase-Lansdale, & Brooks-Gunn, 2004; Trent & Harlan, 1994).

For single mothers who were very young at the time of their child's birth, extended-family living continues to be associated with more positive mother–child interaction during the preschool years. Otherwise, establishing an independent household with the help of nearby relatives is related to improved child rearing. Perhaps this arrangement permits the more mature teenage mother who has developed effective parenting skills to implement them (Chase-Lansdale, Brooks-Gunn, & Zamsky, 1994). In families rearing adolescents, kinship support increases the likelihood of effective parenting, which is related to adolescents' self-reliance, emotional well-being, and reduced antisocial behavior (Simons et al., 2006; Taylor, 2010).

Finally, the extended family plays an important role in transmitting African-American culture. Compared with nuclear family households, extended-family arrangements place more emphasis on cooperation and moral and religious values. And older black adults, such as grandparents and great-grandparents, regard educating children about their African

Three generations come together at a neighborhood festival. Strong bonds with extended family members have helped protect many African-American children against the destructive impact of poverty and racial prejudice.

heritage as especially important (Mosley-Howard & Evans, 2000; Taylor, 2000). Family reunions—sometimes held in grandparents' and great-grandparents' hometowns in the South—are especially common among African Americans, giving young people a strong sense of their roots (Boyd-Franklin, 2006). These influences strengthen family bonds, protect children's development, and increase the chances that the extended-family lifestyle will carry over to the next generation.

Although wide variation exists, low-SES African-American parents tend to expect immediate obedience. But like findings just reported for Mexican Americans, when African-American families live in depleted, crime-ridden neighborhoods and have few social supports, strict control may have a positive effect, preventing antisocial involvements. Other research suggests that black parents use firm control for broader reasons—to promote self-reliance, self-regulation, and a watchful attitude in risky surroundings, which protects children from becoming victims of crime. Consistent with this view, low-SES African-American parents who use more controlling strategies tend to have more cognitively and socially competent children (Brody & Flor, 1998). Recall, also, that a history of physical punishment is associated with a reduction in antisocial behavior among African-American adolescents but with an increase among Caucasian-American adolescents (see page 493 in Chapter 12). Most African-American parents who use strict, "no-nonsense" discipline use physical punishment sparingly and combine it with warmth and reasoning.

The family structure and child-rearing customs of many minorities buffer the stress and disorganization caused by poverty. As the Cultural Influences box above illustrates, the **extended-family household,** in which one or more adult relatives live with the parent–child nuclear family unit, is a vital feature of ethnic minority family life that has enabled many families to rear children successfully, despite severe economic deprivation and prejudice. Extended family ties provide yet another example of the remarkable capacity of families to mobilize their cultural traditions to safeguard children's development under conditions of high life stress.

A S K   Y O U R S E L F

Review ■ Explain why authoritative parenting is linked to favorable academic and social outcomes among children and adolescents. Is the concept of authoritative parenting useful for understanding effective parenting across cultures? Explain.

Connect ■ How do factors that promote autonomy in adolescence also foster identity development? (To review the influence of parenting on identity, see page 473 in Chapter 11.)

Apply ■ Prepare a short talk for a parent–teacher organization, maintaining that parents matter greatly in children's lives. Support each of your points with research evidence.

Reflect ■ How would you classify your parents' child-rearing styles? What factors might have influenced their approach to child rearing?

- Describe the influence of family size on child rearing, and explain how sibling relationships affect development.

- How do children fare in adoptive, gay and lesbian, and never-married single-parent families?

- What factors influence children's adjustment to divorce and blended-family arrangements?

- How do maternal employment and life in dual-earner families affect children's development?

- Discuss the influence of child-care quality on preschoolers' development and the impact of self-care on school-age children's adjustment.

Family Lifestyles and Transitions

Families in industrialized nations have become more diverse. Today, there are fewer births per family unit, more adults who want to adopt, more lesbian and gay parents who are open about their sexual orientation, and more never-married parents. Further, high rates of divorce, remarriage, and maternal employment have reshaped the family system.

In the following sections, we discuss these changes in the family, emphasizing how each affects family relationships and children's development. **TAKE A MOMENT...** As you consider this array of family forms, think back to the social systems perspective. Note how children's well-being, in each instance, depends on the quality of family interaction, which is sustained by supportive ties to kin and community and by favorable public policies.

From Large to Small Families

In 1960, the average number of children per American woman of childbearing age was 3.1. Currently, it is 2.1 in the United States, 1.9 in the United Kingdom, 1.8 in Australia, 1.7 in Sweden, 1.6 in Canada, 1.4 in Germany, and 1.3 in Italy and Japan (U.S. Census Bureau, 2011a, 2011b).

In addition to more effective birth control, a major reason for this decline is that a family size of one or two children is more compatible with a woman's decision to divide her energies between family and work. The tendency of many couples to delay having children until they are well-established professionally and secure economically (see Chapter 3) also contributes to smaller family size. Furthermore, marital instability plays a role: More couples today get divorced before their childbearing plans are complete. Finally, caring for children and providing them with opportunities is expensive—yet another contributing factor to a smaller family size. According to a conservative estimate, today's new parents in the United States will spend about $280,000 to rear a child from birth to age 18, and many will incur substantial additional expense for higher education (U.S. Department of Agriculture, 2011a).

Family Size and Child Development Popular advice to prospective parents often recommends limiting family size in the interests of "child-rearing quality"—more parental affection, attention, and material resources per child, which enhance children's intellectual development. Do large families really make less intelligent children, as prevailing attitudes suggest? To find out, researchers turned to a large, two-generation longitudinal study.

Starting in 1972, the U.S. National Longitudinal Survey of Youth (NLSY) followed a representative sample of several thousand U.S. 14- to 22-year-olds; in 1986 the children of the original participants were added to the investigation. Because both cohorts took intelligence tests, the researchers could examine the relationship of sibling birth order within families to IQ, to find out whether having additional children depresses children's intellectual functioning.

As the horizontal lines in Figure 14.2 reveal, children's mental test performance did not decline with later birth order—a finding that contradicts the belief that having more children depresses their intellectual ability. At the same time, the differences among the lines show that the larger the family, the lower the scores of all siblings. The researchers also found that the link between family size and children's IQ can be explained by a strong trend for mothers who score lower in intelligence to give birth to more children (Rodgers et al., 2000). In other NLSY research, among children of bright, economically advantaged mothers, the family size–IQ correlation disappeared (Guo & VanWey, 1999). This suggests that low SES contributes powerfully to the lower IQs of both mothers and children in large families.

Other evidence confirms that rather than parenting quality declining as new children are born, parents reallocate their energies. In a longitudinal study of a nationally representative sample of Canadian two-parent families, new births led to a decrease in maternal affection toward older siblings, though most mothers probably remained generally warm. At the same time, the consistency of parenting—the extent to which mothers insisted that older children meet their expectations for mature behavior, such as completing chores, doing homework, and treating other respectfully—rose over time (Strohschein et al., 2008). After a new baby joined the family, mothers seemed to reorganize their parenting practices to best meet all their children's needs.

In sum, although many good reasons exist for limiting family size, the concern that additional births will reduce child-rearing effectiveness and, thus, children's intelligence and life chances is not warranted. Rather, young people with lower mental test scores—many of whom dropped out of school, live in poverty, lack hope for their future, and fail to engage in family planning—are most likely to have large families (Amato et al., 2008). For adolescents with these risk factors, educational and family planning interventions are crucial (see Chapter 5, page 220).

Growing Up with Siblings

Despite declines in family size, 80 percent of North American and European children grow up with at least one sibling (Dunn, 2004b). Siblings influence development both directly, through relationships with one another, and indirectly, through the impact of an additional child on parents' behavior. In previous chapters, we examined some consequences of having brothers and sisters, including effects on early language development, personality, self- and social understanding, and gender typing. Now let's look closely at the quality of the sibling relationship.

Emergence of Sibling Relationships. The arrival of a baby brother or sister is a difficult experience for most preschoolers, who—realizing that they must now share their parents' attention and affection—often become demanding, clingy, and deliberately naughty for a time. Attachment security also typically declines, especially for children over age 2 (old enough to feel threatened and displaced) and for those with mothers under stress (Baydar, Greek, & Brooks-Gunn, 1997; Teti et al., 1996).

Yet resentment is only one feature of a rich emotional relationship that soon develops between siblings. Older children also show affection and sympathetic concern—kissing and patting the baby and calling out, "Mom, he needs you," when the infant cries. By the end of the first year, babies usually spend much time with older siblings and are comforted by their presence during short parental absences. Throughout childhood, children continue to treat older siblings as attachment figures, turning to them for comfort in stressful situations when parents are unavailable (Seibert & Kerns, 2009).

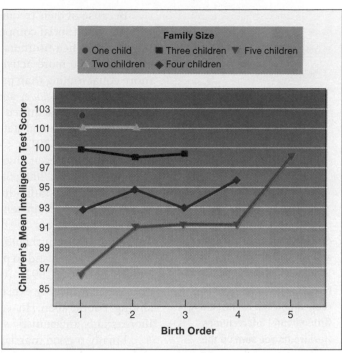

FIGURE 14.2 Relationship of birth order and family size to intelligence. In the U.S. National Longitudinal Survey of Youth, children's IQs did not decline with later birth order, as would be predicted if large families diluted the quality of children's experiences. To the contrary, in the largest families, the youngest children tended to score higher than their siblings. But note the differences among the lines, which indicate that the larger the family, the lower the scores of all siblings. (From J. L. Rodgers, H. H. Cleveland, E. van den Oord, & D. C. Rowe, 2000, "Resolving the Debate over Birth Order, Family Size, and Intelligence," *American Psychologist, 55,* p. 607. Copyright © 2000 by the American Psychological Association. Reprinted by permission of the American Psychological Association.)

Because of their frequency and emotional intensity, sibling interactions are unique contexts in which social competence expands. In the second year, toddlers often imitate and join in play with their brothers and sisters, and between their second and fourth birthdays, they gradually take more active roles. Siblings who are close in age relate to one another on a more equal footing than parents and children. They often engage in joint pretend, talk about feelings, tease, deceive, and—when conflicts arise—call attention to their own wants and needs. The skills acquired through these experiences contribute to understanding of emotions and other mental states, perspective taking, moral maturity, and competence in relating to peers (Kramer, 2011). Consistent with these outcomes, positive sibling ties predict favorable adjustment, even among hostile children at risk for social difficulties (Modry-Mandell, Gamble, & Taylor, 2007; Stormshak et al., 1996).

Nevertheless, individual differences in sibling relationships emerge soon after the new baby's arrival. Certain temperamental traits—high emotional reactivity or activity level—increase the chances of sibling conflict (Brody, Stoneman, & McCoy, 1994; Dunn, 1994). Parenting is also influential: Maternal warmth toward both children is related to positive sibling interaction and to preschoolers' support of a distressed younger sibling (Volling, 2001; Volling & Belsky, 1992). And mothers who frequently play with their children and head off potential conflicts by explaining the toddler's wants and needs to the preschool sibling foster sibling cooperation. In contrast, maternal harshness and lack of involvement result in increasingly antagonistic sibling relationships (Howe, Aquan-Assee, & Bukowski, 2001).

Finally, a good marriage is linked to preschool siblings' capacity to cope adaptively with jealousy and conflict (Volling, McElwain, & Miller, 2002). Perhaps good communication between parents serves as a model of effective problem solving. It may also foster a generally happy family environment, giving children less reason to feel jealous.

Sibling Relationships in Middle Childhood. Sibling rivalry tends to increase in middle childhood. As children participate in a wider range of activities, parents often compare siblings' traits and accomplishments. The child who gets less parental affection, more disapproval, or fewer material resources is likely to be resentful and show poorer adjustment over time (Dunn, 2004b; Tamrouti-Makkink et al., 2004).

For same-sex siblings who are close in age, parental comparisons are more frequent, resulting in more quarreling and antagonism. This effect is particularly strong when parents are under stress as a result of financial worries, marital conflict, single parenthood, or child negativity (Jenkins, Rasbash, & O'Connor, 2003). Parents whose energies are drained become less careful about being fair. Perhaps because fathers, overall, spend less time with children than mothers do, children react especially intensely when fathers prefer one child (Brody, Stoneman, & McCoy, 1992).

Although conflict rises, most school-age siblings continue to rely on one another for companionship, assistance, and emotional support (Siebert & Kerns, 2009). When researchers asked siblings about shared daily activities, children mentioned that older siblings often helped younger siblings with academic and peer challenges. And both offered each other help with family issues (Tucker, McHale, & Crouter, 2001). But for siblings to reap these benefits, parental encouragement of warm, considerate sibling ties is vital. The more positive their relationship, the more siblings resolve disagreements constructively, turn to one another for emotional support and concrete forms of assistance, and contribute to resilience in the face of major stressors, such as parental separation and divorce (Conger, Stocker, & McGuire, 2009; Soli, McHale, & Feinberg, 2009).

When siblings get along well, the older sibling's academic and social competence tends to "rub off on" the younger sibling, fostering higher achievement and more positive peer relations (Brody & Murry, 2001; Lamarche et al., 2006). But destructive sibling conflict in middle childhood is associated with detrimental outcomes, including conflict-ridden peer relationships, anxiety, depressed mood, and later substance use and delinquency, even after other family relationship factors are controlled (Criss & Shaw, 2005; Kim et al., 2007; Stocker, Burwell, & Briggs, 2002).

LOOK and LISTEN

Arrange to observe a toddler and preschooler sibling pair at home for about an hour, recording instances of sibling cooperation and conflict along with parental interventions. How would you sum up the quality of this sibling relationship?

Although sibling rivalry tends to increase in middle childhood, siblings also provide each other with emotional support and, sometimes, patient help with difficult tasks.

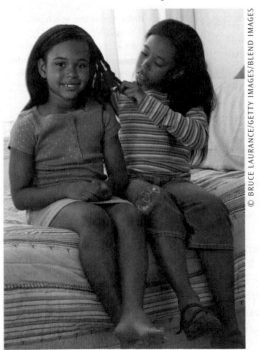

© BRUCE LAURANCE/GETTY IMAGES/BLEND IMAGES

Providing parents with training in mediation—how to get siblings to lay down ground rules, clarify points of agreement and disagreement, and discuss possible solutions—increases siblings' awareness of one another's perspectives and reduces animosity (Smith & Ross, 2007). And direct intervention with sibling pairs, in sessions that teach emotional understanding, perspective taking, emotional self-regulation, and conflict management, enhances positive interaction and reduces the need for parents to intervene in siblings' negative emotional exchanges (Kennedy & Kramer, 2008).

Sibling Relationships in Adolescence. Like parent–child relationships, sibling interactions adapt to development at adolescence. As younger siblings become more self-sufficient, they accept less direction from their older brothers and sisters, and sibling influence declines. Also, as teenagers become more involved in friendships and romantic relationships, they invest less time and energy in their siblings, who are part of the family from which they are trying to establish autonomy. As a result, sibling relationships often become less intense, in both positive and negative feelings (Hetherington, Henderson, & Reiss, 1999; Kim et al., 2006).

Despite a drop in companionship, attachment between siblings, like closeness to parents, remains strong for most young people. Overall, siblings who established a positive bond in childhood continue to display greater affection and caring, which contribute to more favorable adolescent adjustment (Kim et al., 2007; Samek & Rueter, 2011). Older siblings frequently offer useful advice as their younger teenage brothers and sisters face challenges in romantic relationships, schoolwork, and decisions about the future. Consistent with the high value girls place on emotional closeness, sisters report greater intimacy with their siblings than brothers do, and sister–sister pairings tend to be the closest (Kim et al., 2006). Culture also influences quality of sibling relationships. In one study, Mexican-American adolescents who expressed a strong Mexican cultural orientation resolved sibling conflicts more cooperatively—compromising rather than controlling or confronting—than did those more oriented toward U.S. individualistic values (Killoren, Thayer, & Updegraff, 2008).

Sibling interaction at adolescence continues to be affected by other relationships, and vice versa. Teenagers whose parents are warm and supportive and who have a history of caring friendships have more positive sibling ties (Bussell et al., 1999; Kramer & Kowal, 2005). And in bidirectional fashion, warm adolescent sibling relationships contribute to more gratifying friendships (Yeh & Lempers, 2004). Finally, mild sibling differences in perceived parental affection no longer trigger jealousy but, instead, predict greater sibling warmth (Feinberg et al., 2003). Perhaps adolescents interpret a unique relationship with parents, as long as it is generally accepting, as a gratifying sign of their own individuality.

One-Child Families

Although sibling relationships bring many benefits, they are not essential for healthy development. Contrary to popular belief, only children are not spoiled, and in some respects, they are advantaged. U.S. children growing up in one-child and multichild families do not differ in self-rated personality traits (Mottus, Indus, & Allik, 2008). And compared to children with siblings, only children are higher in self-esteem and achievement motivation, do better in school, and attain higher levels of education. One reason may be that only children have somewhat closer relationships with parents, who may exert more pressure for mastery and accomplishment (Falbo, 1992). Furthermore, only children have just as many close, high-quality friendships as children with siblings. However, they tend to be less well-accepted in the peer group, perhaps because they have not had opportunities to learn effective conflict-resolution strategies through sibling interactions (Kitzmann, Cohen, & Lockwood, 2002).

Favorable development also characterizes only children in China, where a one-child family policy has been strictly enforced in urban areas for more than three decades to control population growth (Yang, 2008). Compared with agemates who have siblings, Chinese only children are advanced in cognitive development and academic achievement. They also

Limiting family size has been a national policy in the People's Republic of China for more than three decades. In urban areas, the majority of couples have no more than one child.

© PHOTOALTO/JAMES HARDY/GETTY IMAGES

feel more emotionally secure, perhaps because government disapproval promotes tension in families with more than one child (Falbo & Poston, 1993; Jiao, Ji, & Jing, 1996; Yang et al., 1995). Chinese mothers usually ensure that their children have regular contact with first cousins (who are considered siblings). Perhaps as a result, Chinese only children do not differ from agemates with siblings in social skills and peer acceptance (Hart, Newell, & Olsen, 2003). The next generation of Chinese only children, however, will have no first cousins.

China's birth rate, at 1.5 per woman overall and .7 in its largest cities, is now lower than that of many developed nations. As a result, its elderly population is rapidly increasing while its working-age population has leveled off—an imbalance that threatens the country's economic progress. And because sons are more highly valued than daughters, the policy has resulted in an epidemic of abortions of female fetuses and abandonment of girl babies, yielding a vastly skewed population sex ratio (130 male births for every 100 female births) that jeopardizes social stability (Zhu & Hesketh, 2009). Consequently, China is considering relaxing the one-child policy, but it is now so culturally ingrained that couples say they would not have a second child, even if offered the opportunity (LaFraniere, 2011).

Adoptive Families

Adults who are infertile, who are likely to pass along a genetic disorder, or who are older and single but want a family are turning to adoption in increasing numbers. Those who have children by birth, too, sometimes choose to expand their families through adoption. Adoption agencies try to ensure a good fit by seeking parents of the same ethnic and religious background as the child and, where possible, choosing parents who are the same age as typical biological parents. Because the availability of healthy babies has declined (fewer young unwed mothers give up their babies than in the past), more people in North America and Western Europe are adopting from other countries or accepting children who are past infancy or who have known developmental problems (Schweiger & O'Brien, 2005).

Adopted children and adolescents—whether or not they were born in their adoptive parents' country—tend to have more learning and emotional difficulties than other children, a difference that increases with the child's age at time of adoption (Nickman et al., 2005; van IJzendoorn, Juffer, & Poelhuis, 2005; Verhulst, 2008). And whereas children adopted prior to their first birthday are as securely attached to their parents as nonadopted children are, those adopted later show higher rates of attachment insecurity (van den Dries et al., 2009).

Various explanations exist for adoptees' more problematic childhoods. The biological mother may have been unable to care for the child because of problems believed to be partly genetic, such as alcoholism or severe depression, and may have passed this tendency to her offspring. Or perhaps she experienced stress, poor diet, or inadequate medical care during pregnancy. Furthermore, children adopted after infancy are more likely than their nonadopted peers to have a preadoptive history of conflict-ridden family relationships, lack of parental affection, neglect and abuse, or deprived institutional rearing. Finally, adoptive parents and children, who are genetically unrelated, are less alike in intelligence and personality than are biological relatives—differences that may threaten family harmony.

Despite these risks, most adopted children fare well, and those with preexisting problems usually make rapid progress (Arcus & Chambers, 2008; Bimmel et al., 2003). In a study of internationally adopted children in the Netherlands, sensitive maternal care and secure attachment in infancy predicted cognitive and social competence at age 7 (Stams, Juffer, & van IJzendoorn, 2002). And children with troubled family histories who are adopted at older ages generally improve in feelings of trust and affection for their adoptive parents, as they come to feel loved and supported (Veríssimo & Salvaterra, 2006).

By adolescence, adoptees' lives are often complicated by unresolved curiosity about their roots. Some have difficulty accepting the possibility that they may never know their birth

Through family involvement in events like this Chinese Culture Day celebration, these parents increase the likelihood that their adopted children will develop identities that are a healthy blend of their birth and rearing backgrounds.

XINHUA/LANDOV

parents. Others worry about what they would do if their birth parents suddenly reappeared. Adopted teenagers also face a more challenging process of defining themselves as they try to integrate aspects of their birth family and their adoptive family into their emerging identity.

Nevertheless, most adoptees appear well-adjusted as adults. When parents have been warm, open, and supportive in their communication about adoption, their children typically forge a positive sense of self (Brodzinsky, 2011). And as long as their parents took steps to help them learn about their heritage, young adults who were adopted into a different ethnic group or culture usually develop identities that are healthy blends of their birth and rearing backgrounds (Nickman et al., 2005; Thomas & Tessler, 2007).

Clearly, adoption is a satisfying family alternative for most parents and children who experience it. Good outcomes can be promoted by careful pairing of children with parents and provision of guidance to adoptive families by well-trained social service professionals.

Gay and Lesbian Families

According to recent estimates, about 20 to 35 percent of lesbian couples and 5 to 15 percent of gay couples are parents, most through previous heterosexual marriages, some through adoption, and a growing number through reproductive technologies (Gates et al., 2007; Goldberg, 2010; Patterson & Riskind, 2010). These figures underreport actual numbers, as many gay and lesbian parents are reluctant to disclose their identities. In the past, because of laws assuming that homosexuals could not be adequate parents, those who divorced a heterosexual partner lost custody of their children. Today, some U.S. states hold that sexual orientation in itself is irrelevant to custody. A few U.S. states, however, ban gay and lesbian couples from adopting children. Among other countries, gay and lesbian adoptions are legal in Argentina, Belgium, Brazil, Canada, Iceland, Mexico, the Netherlands, Norway, South Africa, Spain, Sweden, the United Kingdom, and Uruguay.

Most research on homosexual families is limited to volunteer samples. Findings indicate that gay and lesbian parents are as committed to and effective at child rearing as heterosexual parents and sometimes more so (Bos, van Balen, & van den Boom, 2007; Tasker, 2005). Also, whether born to or adopted by their parents or conceived through donor insemination, the children of homosexuals did not differ from the children of heterosexuals in mental health, peer relations, or gender-role behavior (Allen & Burrell, 1996; Bos & Sandfort, 2010; Farr, Forssell, & Patterson, 2010; Goldberg, 2010). Two additional studies, which surmounted the potential bias associated with a volunteer sample by including all lesbian-mother families who had conceived children at a fertility clinic, also reported that children were developing favorably (Brewaeys et al., 1997; Chan, Raboy, & Patterson, 1998). Likewise, among participants drawn from a representative sample of British mothers and their 7-year-olds, children reared in lesbian-mother families did not differ from children reared in heterosexual families in adjustment and gender-role preferences (Golombok et al., 2003).

Gay and lesbian parents are as committed to and effective at child rearing as heterosexual parents. Their children are well-adjusted, and the large majority develop a heterosexual orientation.

Furthermore, children of gay and lesbian parents are similar to other children in sexual orientation: The large majority are heterosexual (Tasker, 2005). But some evidence suggests that more adolescents from homosexual families experiment for a time with partners of both sexes, perhaps as a result of being reared in families and communities especially tolerant of nonconformity and difference (Bos, van Balen, & van den Boom, 2004; Golombok & Tasker, 1996; Stacey & Biblarz, 2001). In support of this view, a Dutch investigation found that 8- to 12-year-old children of lesbian parents felt slightly less parental pressure to conform to gender roles than did children of heterosexual parents. The two groups were similar in other aspects of gender identity (gender typicality and gender contentedness, see page 550 in Chapter 13). At the same time, the children of lesbian parents reported greater sexual questioning—less certainty about future heterosexual attractions and relationships, though the group difference was mild (see Figure 14.3 on page 590) (Bos & Sandfort, 2010).

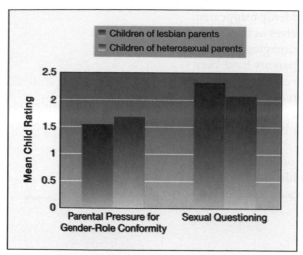

FIGURE 14.3 **Reports of parental pressure for gender-role conformity and of sexual questioning by 8- to 12-year-olds of lesbian and heterosexual parents.** Compared with children of heterosexual parents, children of lesbian parents rated parental pressure slightly lower and sexual questioning higher. Neither group expressed strong parental pressure or sexual questioning (participants rated each on a 4-point scale, and mean ratings ranged from 1.5 to 2.3). (Adapted from Bos & Sandfort, 2010.)

A major concern of gay and lesbian parents is that their children will be stigmatized by their parents' sexual orientation. Most studies indicate that incidents of teasing and bullying are rare because parents and children carefully manage the information they reveal to others (Tasker, 2005). But in an Australian study, even though most third to tenth graders were guarded about discussing their parents' relationship with peers, nearly half reported harassment (Ray & Gregory, 2001). Overall, children of gay and lesbian parents can be distinguished from other children mainly by issues related to living in a nonsupportive society.

Never-Married Single-Parent Families

Over the past several decades, births to unmarried mothers in industrialized nations have increased dramatically. Today, about 40 percent of U.S. births are to single mothers, more than double the percentage in 1980. Whereas teenage parenthood has recently declined (see page 217 in Chapter 5), unwed motherhood among women in their twenties and older has risen, especially among those in their thirties and forties in high-status occupations (U.S. Census Bureau, 2011b). But these higher-SES, older single mothers are still few in number, and little is known about their children's development.

In the United States, African-American young women make up the largest group of never-married parents. About 64 percent of births to black mothers in their twenties are to women without a partner, compared with 28 percent of births to white women (U.S. Census Bureau, 2011b). African-American women postpone marriage more and childbirth less than women in other U.S. ethnic groups. Job loss, persistent unemployment, and consequent inability of many black men to support a family have contributed to the number of African-American never-married, single-mother families.

Never-married African-American mothers tap the extended family, especially their own mothers and sometimes male relatives, for help in rearing their children (Gasden, 1999; Jayakody & Kalil, 2002). For about one-third, marriage—not necessarily to the child's biological father—occurs within nine years after birth of the first child (Wu, Bumpass, & Musick, 2001). These couples function much like other first-marriage parents. Their children are often unaware that the father is a stepfather, and parents do not report the child-rearing difficulties usually associated with remarriage that we will discuss shortly (Ganong & Coleman, 1994).

Still, for low-SES women, never-married parenthood generally increases financial hardship. Nearly 50 percent of white mothers and 60 percent of black mothers have a second child while unmarried. And they are far less likely than divorced mothers to receive paternal child support payments. Consequently, many children in single-mother homes display adjustment problems associated with economic adversity (Kotchick, Dorsey, & Heller, 2005). Furthermore, children of never-married mothers who lack a father's consistent warmth and involvement show less favorable cognitive development and engage in more antisocial behavior than children in low-SES, first-marriage families (Waldfogel, Craigie, & Brooks-Gunn, 2010). But marriage to the child's biological father benefits children only when the father is a reliable source of economic and emotional support. For example, when a mother pairs up with an antisocial father, her child is at far greater risk for conduct problems than if she had reared the child alone (Jaffee et al., 2003).

Over time, most unwed fathers—who usually have no more than a modest education and are doing poorly financially—spend less and less time with their children (Lerman, 2010). Strengthening social support, education, and employment opportunities for low-SES parents would greatly enhance the well-being of unmarried mothers and their children.

Divorce

Between 1960 and 1985, divorce rates in Western nations rose dramatically before stabilizing in most countries. The United States has experienced a decline in divorces over the past decade, largely due to a rise in age at first marriage (Amato & Dorius, 2010). Nevertheless, the United States continues to have the highest divorce rate in the world (see Figure 14.4). Of the 45 percent of American marriages that end in divorce, half involve children. At any given time, one-fourth of U.S. children live in single-parent households. Although most reside with their mothers, the percentage in father-headed households has increased steadily, to about 12 percent (Federal Interagency Forum on Child and Family Statistics, 2011).

Children of divorce spend an average of five years in a single-parent home—almost a third of childhood. For many, divorce leads to new family relationships. About two-thirds of divorced parents marry again. Half of their children eventually experience a third major change—the end of their parents' second marriage (Hetherington & Kelly, 2002).

These figures reveal that divorce is not a single event in the lives of parents and children. Instead, it is a transition that leads to a variety of new living arrangements, accompanied by changes in housing, income, and family roles and responsibilities. Since the 1960s, many studies have reported that marital breakup is stressful for children. But research also reveals great individual differences (Hetherington, 2003). How well children fare depends on many factors: the custodial parent's psychological health, the child's characteristics, and social supports within the family and surrounding community.

Immediate Consequences Family conflict often rises around the time of divorce as parents try to settle disputes over children and possessions. Once one parent moves out, additional events threaten supportive interactions between parents and children. Mother-headed households typically experience a sharp drop in income. In the United States, 27 percent of divorced mothers with young children live in poverty and many more are low-income, getting less than the full amount of child support from the absent father or none at all (Grall, 2009). They often have to move to lower-cost housing, reducing supportive ties to neighbors and friends.

The transition from marriage to divorce typically leads to high maternal stress, depression, and anxiety and to a disorganized family situation. Declines in well-being are greatest for mothers of young children (Williams & Dunne-Bryant, 2006). Predictable events and routines—meals and bedtimes, household chores, and joint parent–child activities—usually disintegrate. As children react with distress and anger to their less secure home lives, discipline may become harsh and inconsistent. Contact with noncustodial fathers decreases over time (Hetherington & Kelly, 2002). Fathers who see their children only occasionally are inclined to be permissive and indulgent, making the mother's task of managing the child even more difficult.

The more parents argue and fail to provide children with warmth, involvement, and consistent guidance, the poorer children's adjustment. About 20 to 25 percent of children in divorced families display severe problems, compared with about 10 percent in nondivorced families (Lansford, 2009; Noller et al., 2008). At the same time, reactions vary with children's age, temperament, and sex.

Children's Age. Preschool and early school-age children often blame themselves for a marital breakup and fear that both parents may abandon them (Lansford et al., 2006a). Hence, they are more likely to display both anxious, fearful and angry, defiant reactions than older children and adolescents with the cognitive maturity to understand that they are not responsible for their parents' divorce.

Still, many school-age and adolescent youngsters also react strongly, experiencing depressed mood, declining in school performance, becoming unruly, and escaping into undesirable peer activities, such as running away, truancy, and early sexual activity, particularly

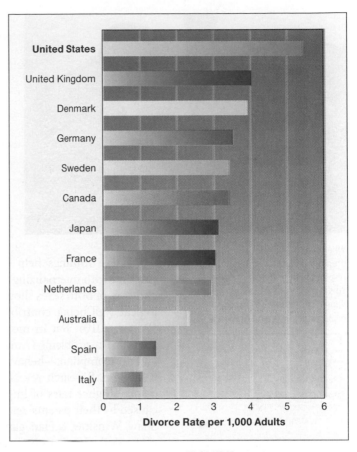

FIGURE 14.4 **Divorce rates in 12 industrialized nations.** The U.S. divorce rate is the highest in the industrialized world, far exceeding divorce rates in other countries. (Adapted from U.S. Census Bureau, 2011b.)

When parents divorce, young children often blame themselves and respond with both fear and anger. This father's soothing words help his daughter understand that she is not responsible for the marital breakup.

when family conflict is high and parental supervision is low (D'Onofrio et al., 2006; Lansford et al., 2006a). Some older children—especially the oldest child in the family—display more mature behavior, willingly taking on family and household tasks, care of younger siblings, and emotional support of a depressed, anxious mother. But if these demands are too great, these children may eventually become resentful, withdraw from the family, and engage in angry, acting-out behavior (Hetherington, 1999).

Children's Temperament and Sex. Exposure to stressful life events and inadequate parenting magnifies the problems of temperamentally difficult children (Lengua et al., 2000). Easy children, who are less often targets of parental anger, also cope better with adversity.

These findings help explain sex differences in response to divorce. Girls sometimes respond with internalizing reactions such as crying, self-criticism, and withdrawal. More often, children of both sexes show demanding, attention-getting behavior. These declines in psychological well-being contribute to the poorer academic achievement of children of divorce (Potter, 2010). But in mother-custody families, boys are at slightly greater risk for serious adjustment problems (Amato, 2001, 2010). Recall from Chapter 13 that boys are more active and noncompliant—behaviors that increase with exposure to parental conflict and inconsistent discipline. Research reveals that long before the marital breakup, sons of divorcing couples display higher rates of impulsivity, defiance, and aggression—behaviors that may have been caused by their parents' marital problems while also contributing to them (Hetherington, 1999; Shaw, Winslow, & Flanagan, 1999; Strohschein, 2005). As a result, more boys enter the period of turmoil surrounding divorce with reduced capacity to cope with family stress.

Perhaps because their behavior is more unruly, boys of divorcing parents tend to receive less emotional support from mothers, teachers, and peers. Furthermore, the cycles of coercive interaction between angry, defiant sons and their divorced mothers soon spread to sibling relations, compounding adjustment difficulties (Hetherington & Kelly, 2002; Sheehan et al., 2004). After divorce, children who are challenging to rear generally get worse.

Long-Term Consequences Most children show improved adjustment by two years after divorce. Yet overall, children and adolescents of divorced parents continue to score slightly lower than children of continuously married parents in academic achievement, self-esteem, social competence, and emotional and behavior problems (Amato, 2001; Lansford, 2009). Children with difficult temperaments who were entrenched in family conflict are more likely to drop out of school, to be depressed, and to engage in antisocial behavior in adolescence. And divorce is linked to problems with adolescent sexuality and development of intimate ties. Young people who experienced parental divorce—especially more than once—display higher rates of early sexual activity and adolescent parenthood (Wolfinger, 2000). Some experience other lasting difficulties—reduced educational attainment, troubled romantic relationships and marriages, divorce in adulthood, and unsatisfying parent–child relationships (Amato, 2006, 2010; Lansford, 2009). Thus, divorce can have consequences for subsequent generations.

The overriding factor in positive adjustment following divorce is effective parenting—how well the custodial parent handles stress and shields the child from family conflict, and the extent to which each parent uses authoritative child rearing (Leon, 2003; Wolchik et al., 2000). Where the custodial parent is the mother, contact with fathers is also important. In the United States, paternal contact has risen over the past three decades, with about one-third of children today experiencing at least weekly visits (Amato & Dorius, 2010).

The more paternal contact and the warmer the father–child relationship, the less children of divorce react with defiance and aggression (Dunn et al., 2004). For girls, a good father–child relationship protects against early sexual activity and unhappy romantic involvements (Clarke-Stewart & Hayward, 1996; McLanahan, 1999). High father–child contact, however, occurs more often in families where the mother–child relationship is positive and divorced parents are courteous and cooperative (Dunn, 2004a).

LOOK and LISTEN

Discuss with a few of your contemporaries who experienced parental divorce in childhood their view of its long-term impact. Ask them to address factors they see as having fostered or impeded their adjustment to the divorce.

Several studies report that outcomes for sons are better when the father is the custodial parent (Clarke-Stewart & Hayward, 1996; McLanahan, 1999). Fathers' greater economic security and image of authority seem to help them engage in effective parenting with sons. And boys in father-custody families may benefit from greater involvement of both parents because noncustodial mothers participate more in their children's lives than do noncustodial fathers.

Although divorce is painful for children, remaining in an intact but high-conflict family is worse than making the transition to a low-conflict single-parent household (Greene et al., 2003; Strohschein, 2005). However, more parents today are divorcing because they are moderately (rather than extremely) dissatisfied with their relationship. Research suggests that children in these low-discord homes are especially puzzled and upset. Perhaps these youngsters' inability to understand the marital breakup and grieve over the loss of a seemingly happy home life explain why the adjustment problems of children of divorce have intensified over time (Amato, 2001; Lansford, 2009).

Regardless of the extent of their friction, parents who set aside their disagreements and engage in effective coparenting greatly improve their children's chances of growing up competent, stable, and happy. As Figure 14.5 shows, in a study of 8- to 15-year-olds, young people who experienced both high parental acceptance and high consistency of discipline had the lowest levels of adjustment problems (Wolchik et al., 2000). Caring extended-family members, teachers, siblings, and friends also reduce the likelihood that divorce will result in long-term difficulties (Hetherington, 2003; Lussier et al., 2002).

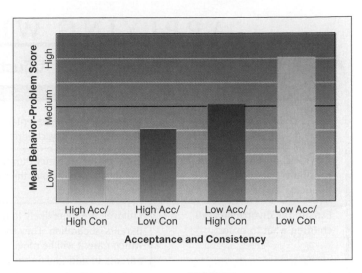

FIGURE 14.5 Relationship of child-rearing styles to children's adjustment following divorce. High parental acceptance and consistency in discipline are associated with a low level of behavior problems. As child rearing diminished in quality, behavior problems increased. When both parental acceptance and consistency in discipline were low, behavior problems were severe. All 8- to 15-year-olds in this study had experienced a highly stressful divorce. (Adapted from Wolchik et al., 2000.)

Divorce Mediation, Joint Custody, and Child Support Awareness that divorce is highly stressful for parents and children has led to community-based services aimed at helping them through this difficult time. One such service is *divorce mediation,* a series of meetings between divorcing couples and a trained professional aimed at reducing family conflict, including legal battles over property division and child custody. Research reveals that mediation increases out-of-court settlements, effective coparenting, sustained involvement of both parents in their children's lives, and parents' and children's feelings of well-being (Douglas, 2006; Emery, Sbarra, & Grover, 2005). In one study, parents who had resolved disputes through mediation, as opposed to an adversarial legal process, were still more involved in their children's lives 12 years later (Emery, Sbarra, & Grover, 2005).

To further encourage parents to resolve their disputes, parent education programs are becoming common. During several sessions, professionals teach parents about the positive impact of constructive conflict resolution and of respectful, cooperative coparenting on children's well-being (Braver et al., 2005; Cookston et al., 2006; Wolchik et al., 2002). Because of the demonstrated impact of parent education on parental cooperation, courts in many U.S. states may require parents to attend a program.

Joint custody, which grants each parent an equal say in important decisions about the child's upbringing, is becoming increasingly common. Children usually reside with one parent and see the other on a fixed schedule, similar to the typical sole-custody situation. In other cases, parents share physical custody, and children move between homes and sometimes between schools and peer groups. These transitions can be especially hard on some children. Joint-custody parents report little conflict—fortunately so, since the success of the arrangement depends on coparenting. And their children, regardless of living arrangements, tend to be better-adjusted than their counterparts in sole maternal-custody homes (Bauserman, 2002).

Finally, many single-parent families depend on child support from the absent parent to relieve financial strain. All U.S. states have procedures for withholding wages from parents who fail to make these payments. Although child support is usually not enough to lift a single-parent family out of poverty, it can ease its burdens substantially. Noncustodial fathers who have generous visitation schedules and see their children often are more likely to pay child support regularly (Amato & Sobolewski, 2004). And increases in contact with the child

APPLYING WHAT WE KNOW

Helping Children Adjust to Their Parents' Divorce

SUGGESTION	EXPLANATION
Shield children from conflict.	Witnessing intense parental conflict is very damaging to children. If one parent insists on expressing hostility, children fare better if the other parent does not respond in kind.
Provide children with as much continuity, familiarity, and predictability as possible.	Children adjust better during the period surrounding divorce when their lives have some stability—for example, the same school, bedroom, babysitter, playmates, and daily schedule.
Explain the divorce and tell children what to expect.	Children are more likely to develop fears of abandonment if they are not prepared for their parents' separation. They should be told that their parents will not be living together anymore, which parent will be moving out, and when they will be able to see that parent. If possible, parents should explain the divorce together, providing a reason that each child can understand and assuring children that they are not to blame.
Emphasize the permanence of the divorce.	Fantasies of parents getting back together can prevent children from accepting the reality of their current life. Children should be told that the divorce is final and that they cannot change this fact.
Respond sympathetically to children's feelings.	Children need a supportive and understanding response to their feelings of sadness, fear, and anger. For children to adjust well, their painful emotions must be acknowledged, not denied or avoided.
Engage in authoritative parenting.	Parents who engage in authoritative parenting—providing affection and acceptance, reasonable demands for mature behavior, and consistent, rational discipline—greatly reduce their children's risk of maladjustment following divorce.
Promote a continuing relationship with both parents.	When parents disentangle their lingering hostility toward the former spouse from the child's need for a continuing relationship with the other parent, children adjust well. Grandparents and other extended-family members can help by not taking sides.

Source: Teyber, 2001.

and in child support over time predict better coparenting relationships (Hofferth, Forry, & Peters, 2010). Applying What We Know above summarizes ways to help children adjust to their parents' divorce.

Blended Families

Life in a single-parent family often is temporary. About 60 percent of divorced parents remarry within a few years. Others *cohabit,* or share a sexual relationship and a residence with a partner outside of marriage. Parent, stepparent, and children form a new family structure called the **blended,** or **reconstituted, family.** For some children, this expanded family network is positive, bringing greater adult attention. But most have more adjustment problems than children in stable, first-marriage families (Jeynes, 2007; Nicholson et al., 2008). Switching to stepparents' new rules and expectations can be stressful, and children often regard steprelatives as intruders. How well they adapt is, again, related to the overall quality of family functioning (Hetherington & Kelly, 2002). This depends on which parent forms a new relationship, the child's age and sex, and the complexity of blended-family relationships. As we will see, older children and girls seem to have the hardest time.

Mother–Stepfather Families Because mothers generally retain custody of children, the most common form of blended family is a mother–stepfather arrangement. Boys tend to adjust quickly, welcoming a stepfather who is warm, who refrains from exerting his authority too quickly, and who offers relief from coercive cycles of mother–son interaction. Mothers' friction with sons also declines as a result of greater economic security, another adult to share household tasks, and an end to loneliness (Visher, Visher, & Pasley, 2003).

Stepfathers who marry rather than cohabit are more involved in parenting, perhaps because men who choose to marry a mother with children are more interested in and skilled at child rearing (Hofferth & Anderson, 2003). Girls, however, often have difficulty with their custodial mother's remarriage. Stepfathers disrupt the close ties many girls have established with their mothers, and girls often react with sulky, resistant behavior (Bray, 1999).

But age affects these findings. Older school-age children and adolescents of both sexes display more irresponsible, acting-out behavior than their peers not in stepfamilies (Hetherington & Stanley-Hagan, 2000; Robertson, 2008). If parents are warmer and more involved with their biological children than with their stepchildren, older children are more likely to notice and challenge unfair treatment. And adolescents often view the new stepparent as a threat to their freedom, especially if they experienced little parental monitoring in the single-parent family. When teenagers have affectionate, cooperative relationships with their mothers, many develop good relationships with stepfathers following remarriage—a circumstance linked to more favorable adolescent well-being (King, 2009; Yuan & Hamilton, 2006).

Father–Stepmother Families

Remarriage of noncustodial fathers often leads to reduced contact with their biological children, especially when fathers remarry quickly, before they have established postdivorce parent–child routines (Dunn, 2002; Juby et al., 2007). When fathers have custody, children typically react negatively to remarriage. One reason is that children living with fathers often start out with more problems. Perhaps the biological mother could no longer handle the difficult child (usually a boy), so the father and his new partner are faced with a youngster who has behavior problems. In other instances, the father has custody because of a very close relationship with the child, and his remarriage disrupts this bond (Buchanan, Maccoby, & Dornbusch, 1996).

Girls, especially, have a hard time getting along with their stepmothers, either because the remarriage threatens the girl's bond with her father or because she becomes entangled in loyalty conflicts between the two mother figures. But the longer children live in father–stepmother households, the closer they feel to their stepmothers and the more positive their interaction with them becomes (King, 2007). With time and patience, children of both genders benefit from the support of a second mother figure.

Support for Blended Families

Parenting education and couples counseling can help parents and children adapt to the complexities of blended families. Effective approaches encourage stepparents to move into their new roles gradually by first building a warm relationship with the child, which makes more active parenting possible (Nicholson et al., 2008). Counselors can offer couples guidance in coparenting to limit loyalty conflicts and provide consistency in child rearing. And tempering parents' unrealistic expectations for children's rapid adjustment—by pointing out that building a unified blended family often takes years—makes it easier for families to endure the transition and succeed.

Unfortunately, the divorce rate for second marriages is even higher than that for first marriages. Parents with antisocial tendencies and poor child-rearing skills are particularly likely to have several divorces and remarriages. The more marital transitions children experience, the greater their adjustment difficulties (Amato, 2010). These families usually require prolonged, intensive therapy.

When stepparents build warm relationships with stepchildren before moving into their parenting role, they ease children's adjustment to life in a blended family.

Maternal Employment and Dual-Earner Families

Today, U.S. single and married mothers are in the labor market in nearly equal proportions, and more than three-fourths of those with school-age children are employed (U.S. Census Bureau, 2011b). In Chapter 10, we saw that the impact of maternal employment on early development depends on the quality of child care during parents' working hours, the continuing parent–child relationship, and fathers' participation in caregiving. The same is true in later years. In addition, the mother's work satisfaction has a bearing on how children fare.

© SIMON JARRATT/CORBIS

Employed mothers who enjoy their work while also valuing the parenting role tend to have children who show higher self-esteem, more positive family and peer relations, less gender-stereotyped beliefs, and better school performance.

Maternal Employment and Child Development When mothers enjoy their work and remain committed to parenting, children show favorable adjustment—higher self-esteem, more positive family and peer relations, less gender-stereotyped beliefs, and better grades in school. Girls, especially, profit from the image of female competence. Regardless of SES, daughters of employed mothers perceive women's roles as involving more freedom of choice and satisfaction and are more achievement- and career-oriented (Hoffman, 2000).

Parenting practices contribute to these benefits. Employed mothers who value their parenting role are more likely to use authoritative child rearing and coregulation (see page 577). Also, children in dual-earner households devote more daily hours to doing homework under parental guidance and participate more in household chores. And maternal employment often leads fathers—especially those who believe in the importance of the paternal role and who feel successful at rearing children—to take on greater child-care responsibilities (Jacobs & Kelley, 2006). Paternal involvement is associated with higher intelligence and achievement, more mature social behavior, greater gender-stereotype flexibility in childhood and adolescence, and generally better mental health in adulthood (Coltrane, 1996; Pleck & Masciadrelli, 2004).

But when employment places heavy demands on a mother's or a father's schedule or is stressful for other reasons, children are at risk for ineffective parenting. Working many hours or experiencing a negative workplace atmosphere is associated with reduced parental sensitivity, fewer joint parent–child activities, and poorer cognitive development throughout childhood and adolescence (Brooks-Gunn, Han, & Waldfogel, 2002; Bumpus, Crouter, & McHale, 2006; Strazdins et al., 2006). Negative consequences are magnified when low-SES mothers spend long days at low-paying, menial, or physically taxing jobs—conditions linked to maternal depression and harsh, inconsistent discipline (Raver, 2003). In contrast, part-time employment and flexible work schedules are associated with parents' enhanced satisfaction with family life and good adjustment in children and adolescents (Frederiksen-Goldsen & Sharlach, 2000; Hill et al., 2006). By preventing work–family life conflict, these arrangements help parents meet children's needs.

Support for Employed Parents and Their Families In dual-earner families, the father's willingness to share child-care responsibilities is a crucial factor. If he helps little or not at all, the mother carries a double load, at home and at work, leading to fatigue, distress, and little time and energy for children. Fortunately, compared to three decades ago, today's U.S. fathers are far more involved in child care (see page 483 in Chapter 10). But their increased participation has resulted in a growing number of fathers who also report work–family life conflict (Galinsky, Aumann, & Bond, 2009).

Employed parents need assistance from work settings and communities in their child-rearing roles. Part-time employment, flexible schedules, job sharing, and paid leave when children are ill help parents juggle the demands of work and child rearing. Equal pay and equal employment opportunities for women also are important. Because these policies enhance financial status and morale, they improve the way mothers feel and behave when they return home at the end of the working day.

Child Care

Over the past several decades, the number of young children in child care in the United States has steadily increased to more than 60 percent (U.S. Census Bureau, 2011b). Over half of 3- to 6-year-olds not yet in kindergarten are cared for in child-care centers, with the remainder in family child-care homes or looked after informally by a relative or their fathers. But nearly one-fourth of preschoolers, most from low-income families, experience several types of care at once, transitioning between two—and sometimes more than two—settings each day. In addition to a changing cast of caregivers, children in multiple care settings must cope with longer hours in child care (Federal Interagency Forum on Child and Family Statistics, 2011; NICHD Early Child Care Research Network, 2006).

With age, children typically shift from home-based to center care. Children of higher-income parents and children of very low-income parents are especially likely to be in center care. Many lower-income working parents rely on care by relatives because they are not eligible for public preschool or government-subsidized center child care (Bainbridge et al., 2005; Meyers et al., 2004).

Recall from Chapter 8 that early intervention can enhance the development of economically disadvantaged children. As noted in Chapters 1 and 10, however, much U.S. child care is of poor quality. Refer to Chapter 10, pages 441–442, for a discussion of the negative consequences of exposing infants and toddlers to substandard child care and to many weekly hours of child care. Preschoolers, as well, suffer when placed in poor-quality child care, especially for long hours, scoring lower in cognitive and social skills and higher in behavior problems (Belsky, 2006b; Lamb & Ahnert, 2006; NICHD Early Childhood Research Network, 2003b, 2006). Externalizing difficulties are especially likely to endure through middle childhood and into adolescence after extensive exposure to mediocre care (Belsky et al., 2007; Vandell et al., 2010). And when children experience the instability of several child-care settings, the emotional problems of temperamentally difficult preschoolers worsen considerably (De Schipper, van IJzendoorn, & Tavecchio, 2004; De Schipper et al., 2004).

In contrast, good child care enhances cognitive, language, and social development, especially for low-SES children—effects that persist into elementary school and, for academic achievement, into adolescence (Belsky et al., 2007; Burchinal, Vandergrift, & Pianta, 2010; NICHD Early Child Care Research Network, 2006; Vandell et al., 2010). In a study that followed 400 very low-income children over the preschool years, center-based care was more strongly associated with cognitive gains than were other child-care arrangements, probably because good-quality child-care centers are more likely to provide a systematic educational program. At the same time, better-quality experiences in all types of child care predicted modest improvements in cognitive, emotional, and social development (Loeb et al., 2004).

What are the ingredients of high-quality child care for preschoolers? Large-scale studies identify several important factors: group size (number of children in a single space), caregiver–child ratio, caregivers' educational preparation, and caregivers' personal commitment to learning about and caring for children. When these characteristics are favorable, adults are more verbally stimulating and sensitive to children's needs (Lamb & Ahnert, 2006).

Applying What We Know on page 598 summarizes characteristics of high-quality early childhood programs, based on standards devised by the U.S. National Association for the Education of Young Children. Unfortunately, much U.S. child care is substandard: too often staffed by underpaid adults without specialized educational preparation, overcrowded with children, and (in the case of family child care) unlicensed and therefore not monitored for quality. And child care is expensive: For U.S. families with just one preschooler, it consumes, on average, 29 percent of the typical earnings of a single mother and 10 percent of the earnings of a two-parent family (NACCRRA, 2010).

In contrast, in Australia and Western Europe, government-subsidized child care that meets rigorous standards is widely available, and caregivers are paid on the same salary scale as elementary school teachers (Waldfogel, 2001). Because the United States does not have national child-care policies, it lags behind other industrialized nations in supply, quality, and affordability of child care.

Self-Care

High-quality child care is vital for parents' peace of mind and children's well-being, even during middle childhood. An estimated 5 million 5- to 14-year-olds in the United States are **self-care children,** who regularly look after themselves for some period of time during after-school hours (Afterschool Alliance, 2009). As Figure 14.6 shows, self-care rises dramatically with age. It also increases with SES, perhaps because of the greater safety of higher-income neighborhoods. But when

FIGURE 14.6 Prevalence of self-care and participation in after-care programs by U.S. elementary and middle-school students. A survey of a large, nationally representative sample of U.S. parents confirms that self-care rises sharply in middle school. Many parents say that if after-care programs were available in their neighborhoods, they would enroll their children. (From Afterschool Alliance, 2009.)

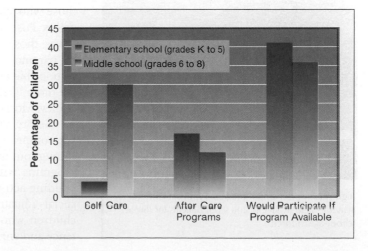

APPLYING WHAT WE KNOW

Signs of Developmentally Appropriate Early Childhood Programs

PROGRAM CHARACTERISTIC	SIGNS OF QUALITY
Physical setting	Indoor environment is clean, in good repair, and well-ventilated. Classroom space is divided into richly equipped activity areas, including make-believe play, blocks, science, math, games and puzzles, books, art, and music. Fenced outdoor play space is equipped with swings, climbing equipment, tricycles, and sandbox.
Group size	In preschools and child-care centers, group size is no greater than 18 to 20 children with two teachers.
Caregiver–child ratio	In preschools and child-care centers, teacher is responsible for no more than 8 to 10 children. In family child-care homes, caregiver is responsible for no more than 6 children.
Daily activities	Children select many of their own activities and learn through experiences relevant to their own lives, mainly in small groups or individually. Teachers facilitate children's involvement, accept individual differences, and adjust expectations to children's developing capacities.
Interactions between adults and children	Teachers move among groups and individuals, asking questions, offering suggestions, and adding more complex ideas. Teachers use positive guidance techniques, such as modeling and encouraging expected behavior and redirecting children to more acceptable activities.
Teacher qualifications	Teachers have college-level specialized preparation in early childhood development, early childhood education, or a related field.
Relationships with parents	Parents are encouraged to observe and participate. Teachers talk frequently with parents about children's behavior and development.
Licensing and accreditation	Child-care setting, whether a center or a home, is licensed by the state. Voluntary accreditation by the NAEYC Academy for Early Childhood Program Accreditation *(www.naeyc.org/accreditation)* or the National Association for Family Child Care *(www.nafcc.org)* is evidence of an especially high-quality program.

Sources: Copple & Bredekamp, 2009.

High-quality after-school programs with enrichment activities yield academic and social benefits for low-SES school-age children.

lower-SES parents lack alternatives to self-care, their children spend more hours on their own (Casper & Smith, 2002).

Some studies report that self-care children suffer from low self-esteem, antisocial behavior, poor academic achievement, and fearfulness. Others show no such effects. Children's maturity and the way they spend their time seem to explain these contradictions. Among younger school-age children, those who spend more hours alone have more adjustment difficulties (Vandell & Posner, 1999). As children become old enough to look after themselves, those who have a history of authoritative child rearing, are monitored by parental telephone calls, and have regular after-school chores appear responsible and well-adjusted. In contrast, children left to their own devices are more likely to bend to peer pressures and engage in antisocial behavior (Coley, Morris, & Hernandez, 2004; Vandell et al., 2006).

Before age 8 or 9, most children need supervision because they are not yet competent to handle emergencies (Galambos & Maggs, 1991). Also, throughout middle childhood and early adolescence, attending after-school programs with well-trained staffs, generous adult–child ratios, and skill-building activities is linked to good school performance and emotional and social adjustment (Durlak & Weissberg, 2007; Granger, 2008). Low-SES children who participate in "after-care" programs offering academic assistance and enrichment activities (scouting, music and art lessons, clubs) show special benefits. They exceed their self-care counterparts in classroom work habits, academic achievement, and prosocial behavior and display fewer behavior problems (Lauer et al., 2006; Vandell et al., 2006).

Unfortunately, good after-care is in especially short supply in low-income neighborhoods, and children from the poorest families are least likely to participate in enrichment activities (Afterschool Alliance, 2009; Dearing et al., 2009). A survey of a large, nationally representative sample of U.S. parents revealed if programs were available in their neighborhoods, many would enroll their children (refer again to Figure 14.6). A special need exists for well-planned programs in poverty-stricken areas—ones that provide safe environments, warm relationships with adults, and enjoyable, goal-oriented activities.

LOOK and LISTEN

In your community, what school-based after-care programs are available, and how plentiful are they in low-income neighborhoods? If possible, visit a program, observing for supportive adult involvement, academic assistance, and enrichment activities.

A S K   Y O U R S E L F

Review ■ Describe and explain changes in sibling relationships from early childhood to adolescence. What can parents do to promote positive sibling ties?

Connect ■ Review research on resilience in Chapter 1 (see pages 10–11). Are factors that foster resilience similar to those that promote favorable adjustment to parental divorce and blended families? Explain.

Apply ■ Steve and Marissa are in the midst of an acrimonious divorce. Their 9-year-old son, Dennis, has become hostile and defiant. How can Steve and Marissa help Dennis adjust?

Reflect ■ What after-school child-care arrangements did you experience in elementary school? How do you think they influenced your development?

Vulnerable Families: Child Maltreatment

▶ Discuss the origins of child maltreatment, its consequences for development, and prevention strategies.

Throughout our discussion of family transitions, we have considered many factors, both within and outside the family, that contribute to parents' capacity to be warm, consistent, and appropriately demanding. As we turn to the topic of child maltreatment, we will see that when these vital supports for effective child rearing break down, children—and their parents—can suffer terribly.

Incidence and Definitions

Child maltreatment is as old as human history, but only recently has the problem been widely acknowledged and research aimed at understanding it. Perhaps public concern has increased because child maltreatment is especially common in large industrialized nations. In the most recently reported year, about 700,000 U.S. children (10 out of every 1,000) were identified as victims (U.S. Department of Health and Human Services, 2010b). Because most cases go unreported, the true figures are much higher.

Child maltreatment takes the following forms:

- *Physical abuse.* Assaults, such as kicking, biting, shaking, punching, or stabbing, that inflict physical injury
- *Sexual abuse.* Fondling, intercourse, exhibitionism, commercial exploitation through prostitution or production of pornography, and other forms of sexual exploitation
- *Neglect.* Failure to meet a child's basic needs for food, clothing, medical attention, education, or supervision
- *Emotional abuse.* Acts that could cause serious mental or behavioral disorders, including social isolation, repeated unreasonable demands, ridicule, humiliation, intimidation, or terrorizing

Neglect accounts for 78 percent of reported cases, physical abuse for 18 percent, emotional abuse for 9 percent, and sexual abuse for 10 percent (U.S. Department of Health and Human

Services, 2010b). These figures sum to more than 100 percent because a single case report can include more than one form. Child welfare authority investigations suggest that from 45 to 90 percent of cases involve multiple types of maltreatment—on average, three kinds (Finkelhor et al., 2005).

Parents commit more than 80 percent of abusive incidents. Other relatives account for about 5 percent. The remainder are perpetrated by parents' unmarried partners, school officials, camp counselors, and other adults. Mothers engage in neglect more often than fathers, whereas fathers engage in sexual abuse more often than mothers. Maternal and paternal rates of physical and emotional abuse are fairly similar. And in an especially heartrending 18 percent of cases, parents jointly commit the abusive acts. Infants and young preschoolers are at greatest risk for neglect, preschool and school-age children for physical, emotional, and sexual abuse. But each type occurs at every age (Trocomé & Wolfe, 2002; U.S. Department of Health and Human Services, 2010b).

Origins of Child Maltreatment

Early findings suggested that child maltreatment was rooted in adult psychological disturbance (Kempe et al., 1962). But although child maltreatment is more common among disturbed parents, it soon became clear that a single "abusive personality type" does not exist. Parents who were abused as children do not necessarily become abusers (Buchanan, 1996; Simons et al., 1991). And sometimes even "normal" parents harm their children!

For help in understanding child maltreatment, researchers turned to the social systems perspective on family functioning. They discovered that many interacting variables—at the family, community, and cultural levels—contribute. Table 14.3 summarizes factors associated with physical and emotional abuse and neglect. For a discussion of child sexual abuse, see the Social Issues: Health box on the following page.

The Family Within the family, children whose characteristics make them more challenging to rear are more likely to become targets of abuse. These include premature or very sick babies and children who are temperamentally difficult, are inattentive or overactive, or have other developmental problems. Child factors, however, only slightly increase the risk (Jaudes & Mackey-Bilaver, 2008; Sidebotham et al., 2003). Whether such children are maltreated largely depends on parents' characteristics.

Maltreating parents are less skillful than other parents in handling discipline confrontations and getting children to cooperate in working toward common goals. They also suffer from biased thinking about their child. For example, they often evaluate transgressions as worse than they are, attribute their baby's crying or their child's misdeeds to a stubborn or bad disposition, and feel powerless in parenting—perspectives that lead them to move quickly toward physical force (Bugental & Happaney, 2004; Crouch et al., 2008).

Once abuse begins, it quickly becomes part of a self-sustaining relationship. The small irritations to which abusive parents react—a fussy baby, a preschooler who knocks over her milk, or a child who will not mind immediately—soon become bigger ones. Then the harshness increases. By the preschool years, abusive and neglectful parents seldom interact with their children. When they do, they rarely express pleasure and affection; the communication is almost always negative (Wolfe, 2005).

Most parents have enough self-control not to respond with abuse to their children's misbehavior or developmental problems. Other factors combine with these conditions to prompt an extreme response. Unmanageable parental stress is strongly associated with maltreatment. Abusive parents respond to stressful

TABLE 14.3	Factors Related to Child Maltreatment
FACTOR	**DESCRIPTION**
Parent characteristics	Psychological disturbance; alcohol and drug abuse; history of abuse as a child; belief in harsh physical discipline; desire to satisfy unmet emotional needs through the child; unreasonable expectations for child behavior; young age (most under 30); low educational level
Child characteristics	Premature or very sick baby; difficult temperament; inattentiveness and overactivity; other developmental problems
Family characteristics	Low income or poverty; homelessness; marital instability; social isolation; partner abuse; frequent moves; large family with closely spaced children; overcrowded living conditions; disorganized household; lack of steady employment; other signs of high life stress
Community	Characterized by violence and social isolation; few parks, child-care centers, preschool programs, recreation centers, or religious institutions to serve as family supports
Culture	Approval of physical force and violence as ways to solve problems

Sources: U.S. Department of Health and Human Services, 2010; Wekerle & Wolfe, 2003; Whipple, 2006.

SOCIAL ISSUES: HEALTH

Child Sexual Abuse

Until recently, child sexual abuse was considered rare, and adults often dismissed children's claims of abuse. In the 1970s, efforts by professionals and media attention led to recognition of child sexual abuse as a serious and widespread problem. About 66,000 cases in the United States were confirmed in the most recently reported year (U.S. Department of Health and Human Services, 2010b). But this figure greatly underestimates the extent of sexual abuse, since most victims either delay disclosure for a long time or remain silent (London et al., 2005).

Characteristics of Abusers and Victims

Sexual abuse is committed against children of both sexes, but more often against girls. Most cases are reported in middle childhood, but sexual abuse also occurs at younger and older ages. For some victims, abuse begins early in life and continues for many years (Hoch-Espada, Ryan, & Deblinger, 2006; Trickett & Putnam, 1998).

Typically, the abuser is a male, either a parent or someone the parent knows well—a father, stepfather, or live-in boyfriend or, somewhat less often, an uncle or older brother. But in about 25 percent of cases, mothers are the offenders, more often with sons (Boroughs, 2004). If the abuser is a nonrelative, the person is usually someone the child has come to know and trust. However, the Internet and mobile phones have become avenues through which other adults commit sexual abuse—for example, by exposing children and adolescents to pornography and online sexual advances as a way of "grooming" them for sexual acts offline (Wolak et al., 2008).

Abusers make the child comply in a variety of distasteful ways, including deception, bribery, verbal intimidation, and physical force. You may wonder how any adult—especially a parent or close relative—could violate a child sexually. Many offenders deny their own responsibility, blaming the abuse on the willing participation of a seductive youngster. Yet children are not capable of making a deliberate, informed decision to enter into a sexual relationship! Even older children and adolescents are not free to say yes or no. Rather, the responsibility lies with abusers, who tend to have characteristics that predispose them toward sexual exploitation of children. They have great difficulty controlling their impulses and may suffer from psychological disorders, including alcohol and drug abuse. Often they pick out children who are unlikely to

defend themselves or to be believed—those who are physically weak, emotionally deprived, socially isolated, or affected by disabilities (Bolen, 2001).

Reported cases of child sexual abuse are linked to poverty, marital instability, and resulting weakening of family ties. Children who live in homes with a constantly changing cast of characters—repeated marriages, separations, and new partners—are especially vulnerable. But children in economically advantaged, stable families are also victims, although their abuse is more likely to escape detection (Putnam, 2003).

Consequences of Sexual Abuse

The adjustment problems of child sexual abuse victims—including anxiety, depression, low self-esteem, mistrust of adults, and anger and hostility—are often severe and can persist for years after the abusive episodes. Younger children frequently react with sleep difficulties, loss of appetite, and generalized fearfulness. Adolescents may run away and show suicidal reactions, substance abuse, and delinquency. At all ages, persistent abuse accompanied by force, violence, and a close relationship to the perpetrator (incest) has a more severe impact (Trickett et al., 2001; Wolfe, 2006). And repeated sexual abuse, like physical abuse, is associated with central nervous system damage (Cicchetti, 2007).

Sexually abused children frequently display precocious sexual knowledge and behavior. In adolescence, abused young people often become promiscuous, and as adults, they show increased arrest rates for sex crimes (mostly against children) and prostitution (Salter et al., 2003; Whipple, 2006). Furthermore, women who were sexually abused are likely to choose partners who abuse them and their children. As mothers, they often engage in irresponsible and coercive parenting, including child abuse and neglect (Pianta, Egeland, & Erickson, 1989). In these

Children in Hyderabad, India, participate in a "Stay Safe" campaign against child abuse and sexual exploitation—part of a global effort to prevent all forms of abuse.

ways, the harmful impact of sexual abuse is transmitted to the next generation.

Prevention and Treatment

Treating child sexual abuse is difficult. The reactions of family members—anxiety about harm to the child, anger toward the abuser, and sometimes hostility toward the victim for telling—can increase children's distress. Because sexual abuse typically appears in the midst of other serious family problems, long-term therapy with children and parents is usually needed (Olafson & Boat, 2000). The best way to reduce the suffering of victims is to prevent sexual abuse from continuing. Today, courts are prosecuting abusers more vigorously and taking children's testimony more seriously (see Chapter 7).

Educational programs that teach children to recognize inappropriate sexual advances and whom to turn to for help reduce the risk of abuse (Finkelhor, 2009). Yet because of controversies over educating children about sexual abuse, few schools offer these interventions. New Zealand is the only country with a national, school-based prevention program targeting sexual abuse. In Keeping Ourselves Safe, children and adolescents learn that abusers are rarely strangers. Parent involvement ensures that home and school collaborate in teaching children self-protection skills. Evaluations reveal that virtually all New Zealand parents and children support the program and that it has helped many children avoid or report abuse (Sanders, 2006).

situations with high emotional arousal. And low income, low education (less than a high-school diploma), unemployment, alcohol and drug use, marital conflict, domestic violence, overcrowded living conditions, frequent moves, and extreme household disorganization are common in abusive homes (Wekerle et al., 2007; Wulczyn, 2009). These conditions increase the chances that parents will be too overwhelmed to meet basic child-rearing responsibilities or will vent their frustrations by lashing out at their children.

The Community The majority of abusive and neglectful parents are isolated from both formal and informal social supports. Because of their life histories, many have learned to mistrust and avoid others and are poorly skilled at establishing and maintaining positive relationships. Also, maltreating parents are more likely to live in unstable, crime-ridden neighborhoods with few links between family and community, such as parks, recreation centers, and religious institutions—living conditions that heighten parenting stress and, thus, the likelihood of physical abuse (Coulton et al., 2007; Guterman et al., 2009). These families lack "lifelines" to others and have no one to turn to for help during stressful times.

The Larger Culture Cultural values, laws, and customs profoundly affect the chances that child maltreatment will occur when parents feel overburdened. Societies that view violence as an appropriate way to solve problems set the stage for child abuse.

Although the United States has laws to protect children from maltreatment, widespread support exists for use of physical force with children, as we saw in Chapter 12. Many countries—including Austria, Croatia, Cyprus, Denmark, Finland, Germany, Israel, Latvia, Norway, Spain, Sweden, and Uruguay—have outlawed corporal punishment, a measure that dampens both physical discipline and abuse (Zolotor & Puzia, 2010). Furthermore, all industrialized nations except the United States and France now prohibit corporal punishment in schools (Center for Effective Discipline, 2005). The U.S. Supreme Court has twice upheld the right of school officials to use corporal punishment. Fortunately, 20 U.S. states have passed laws that ban it.

Consequences of Child Maltreatment

The family circumstances of maltreated children impair the development of attachment (see Chapter 10), emotional self-regulation, empathy and sympathy, self-concept, social skills, and academic motivation. Over time, these youngsters show serious adjustment problems, including school failure, severe depression, aggressive behavior, peer difficulties, substance abuse, and violent crime (Cicchetti & Toth, 2006; Sanchez & Pollak, 2009; Wolfe et al., 2001). Emotional and behavior problems often persist into adulthood (Kaplow & Widom, 2007).

How do these damaging consequences occur? Recall our discussion in Chapter 12 of hostile cycles of parent–child interaction. For abused children, these are especially severe. Also, a family characteristic strongly associated with child abuse is partner abuse (Gewirtz & Edleson, 2004; Kitzmann et al., 2003). Clearly, the home lives of abused children overflow with adult conduct that leads to profound distress, including emotional insecurity (see page 571), and to aggression as a way of solving problems.

Furthermore, demeaning parental messages, in which children are ridiculed, humiliated, rejected, or terrorized, result in low self-esteem, high anxiety, self-blame, depression, and efforts to escape from extreme psychological pain—at times severe enough to lead to attempted suicide in adolescence (Wolfe, 2005). At school, maltreated children present serious discipline problems. Their noncompliance, poor motivation, and cognitive immaturity interfere with academic achievement, further undermining their chances for life success (Wekerle & Wolfe, 2003).

Finally, repeated abuse is associated with central nervous system damage, including abnormal EEG brain-wave activity, fMRI-detected reduced size and impaired functioning of the cerebral cortex and corpus callosum, and atypical production of the stress hormone cortisol—initially too high but, after months of abuse, often too low. Over time, the massive trauma of persistent abuse seems to blunt children's normal physiological response to stress (Cicchetti, 2007; Teicher et al., 2004; Watts-English et al., 2006). These effects increase the chances that abused children's cognitive and emotional problems will endure.

Preventing Child Maltreatment

Because child maltreatment is embedded in families, communities, and society as a whole, efforts to prevent it must be directed at each of these levels. Many approaches have been suggested, from teaching high-risk parents effective child-rearing strategies to developing broad social programs aimed at improving economic conditions and community services.

We have seen that providing social supports to families is effective in easing parental stress. This approach sharply reduces child maltreatment as well (Azar & Wolfe, 1998). A trusting relationship with another person is the most important factor in preventing mothers with childhood histories of abuse from repeating the cycle with their own youngsters (Egeland, Jacobvitz, & Sroufe, 1988). Parents Anonymous, a U.S. organization with affiliate programs around the world, helps child-abusing parents learn constructive parenting practices, largely through social supports. Its local chapters offer self-help group meetings, daily phone calls, and regular home visits to relieve social isolation and teach responsible child-rearing skills.

Early intervention aimed at strengthening both child and parent competencies can improve parenting practices, thereby preventing child maltreatment (Howard & Brooks-Gunn, 2009). Healthy Families America, a program that began in Hawaii and has spread to 430 sites across the United States and Canada, identifies families at risk for maltreatment during pregnancy or at birth. Each receives three years of home visitation, in which a trained worker helps parents manage crises, encourages effective child rearing, and puts parents in touch with community services to meet their own and their children's needs (Healthy Families America, 2011). In an evaluation in which over 600 families were randomly assigned to either intervention or control groups, Healthy Families home visitation alone reduced only neglect, not abuse (Duggan et al., 2004). But adding a *cognitive component* dramatically increased its impact. When home visitors helped parents change negative appraisals of their children—by countering inaccurate interpretations (for example, that the baby is behaving with malicious intent), and by working on solving child-rearing problems—physical punishment and abuse dropped sharply by the end of one year of intervention (see Figure 14.7) (Bugental et al., 2002). Another home-visiting program shown to reduce child abuse and neglect is the Nurse–Family Partnership, discussed on page 220 in Chapter 5 (Olds et al., 2009).

Still, many experts believe that child maltreatment cannot be eliminated as long as violence is widespread and harsh physical punishment is regarded as acceptable. In addition, combating poverty and its diverse correlates—family stress and disorganization, inadequate food and medical care, teenage parenthood, low-birth-weight babies, and parental hopelessness—would protect many children.

Although more cases reach the courts than in decades past, child maltreatment remains a crime that is difficult to prove. Usually, the only witnesses are the child victims or other loyal family members. And even when the evidence is strong, judges hesitate to impose the ultimate safeguard against further harm: permanently removing the child from the family. There are several reasons for their reluctance. First, in the United States, government intervention into family life is viewed as a last resort. Second, despite destructive family relationships, maltreated children and their parents usually are attached to one another. Most of the time, neither desires separation. Finally, the U.S. legal system tends to regard children as parental property rather than as human beings in their own right, and this also has stood in the way of court-ordered protection.

This poster by a sixth grader, expressing her wish for "a safe and nurturing environment," won an award from the Inter-Agency Council on Child Abuse and Neglect. (Courtesy ICAN Associates, Los Angeles County Inter-Agency Council on Child Abuse & Neglect, ican4kids.org.)

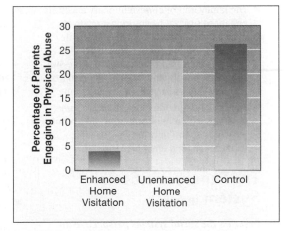

FIGURE 14.7 Impact of a home visitation program with a cognitive component on preventing physical abuse of young children. In an enhanced home visitation condition, home visitors not only provided social support, encouraged effective child rearing, and connected families with community resources but also helped at-risk parents change their negative appraisals of their babies and solve child-rearing problems. After one year of intervention, this cognitive component sharply reduced physical abuse of babies (hitting, shaking, beating, kicking, biting) compared with an unenhanced home visitation condition and a no-intervention control. (Adapted from Bugental et al., 2002.)

Even with intensive treatment, some adults persist in their abusive acts. An estimated 1,700 U.S. children, most of them infants and preschoolers, die from maltreatment each year (U.S. Department of Health and Human Services, 2010b). When parents are unlikely to change their behavior, the drastic step of separating parent from child and legally terminating parental rights is the only justifiable course of action.

Child maltreatment is a distressing and horrifying topic. When we consider how often it occurs in nations that claim to place a high value on the dignity and worth of the individual, it is even more appalling. But there is reason to be optimistic. Great strides have been made over the past several decades in understanding and preventing child maltreatment.

A S K   Y O U R S E L F

Review ■ Explain how personal and situational factors that contribute to child maltreatment illustrate the social systems perspective on family functioning.

Connect ■ After reviewing factors linked to adolescent parenthood (Chapter 5, pages 218–219), explain why it places children at risk for abuse and neglect.

Apply ■ Claire told her 6-year-old daughter to be careful never to talk to or take candy from strangers. Why is Claire's directive not adequate to protect her daughter from sexual abuse?

Reflect ■ Describe a challenging time for your family during your childhood. What aspects of the experience increased stress? What factors helped you and your parents cope with adversity?

S U M M A R Y

Origins and Functions of the Family (p. 568)

Discuss evolutionary origins of the family, and cite functions contemporary families perform for society.

■ The family unit of our evolutionary ancestors enhanced survival by ensuring a relatively even balance of male hunters and female gatherers within a social group. Larger kin networks increased the chances of successful competition with other humans for resources and provided assistance with child rearing.

■ Though contemporary families share some functions with other institutions, they retain primary responsibility for reproduction, socialization, and emotional support.

The Family as a Social System (p. 569)

Describe the social systems perspective on family functioning.

■ Contemporary researchers view the family from a **social systems perspective**—as a complex set of interacting relationships influenced by the larger social context. Family members mutually influence one another, both directly and indirectly. Effective **coparenting** depends on cooperation between parents. Connections to the community, through both formal organizations and informal social networks, provide social support that promotes effective family interaction and children's development.

Socialization Within the Family (p. 573)

Discuss child-rearing styles, and explain how effective parents adapt child rearing to children's growing competence.

■ Three features differentiate major **child-rearing styles:** (1) acceptance and involvement; (2) behavioral control; and (3) autonomy granting. The **authoritative child-rearing style** involves high acceptance and involvement, adaptive control techniques, and appropriate autonomy granting. It promotes cognitive, emotional, and social competence from early childhood into adolescence in children of diverse temperaments. Over time, the authoritative style creates a positive emotional context for parental influence as the relationship between parenting and children's attributes becomes increasingly bidirectional.

■ The **authoritarian child-rearing style** is low in acceptance and involvement, high in coercive behavioral and **psychological control,** and low in autonomy granting. It is associated with anxious, withdrawn, dependent child behavior and with high rates of anger, defiance, and aggression. The **permissive child-rearing style** is high in acceptance, low in behavioral control, and lax in autonomy granting. Children reared permissively are typically impulsive, disobedient, rebellious, demanding, and dependent. The **uninvolved child-rearing style** combines low acceptance and involve-

ment with little behavioral control and indifference to autonomy issues. At its extreme, it constitutes neglect, disrupting virtually all aspects of development.

■ In middle childhood, effective parents engage in **coregulation,** exerting general oversight over children, who increasingly make their own decisions. During adolescence, mature **autonomy** is fostered by parenting that strikes a balance between connection and separation.

Describe socioeconomic and ethnic variations in child rearing, including the impact of affluence and poverty.

■ Although the authoritative style predicts favorable development in children varying widely in SES and culture, SES and ethnic differences in parenting exist. Higher-SES parents are more verbal and stimulating, relying more on warmth and explanations; low-SES parents use more commands, criticism, and coercive discipline.

- The constant stressors linked to poverty result in less involved child rearing. Daily hassles, hostile family interactions, and depleted home learning environments negatively affect children's cognitive and emotional well-being.

- By adolescence, children of affluent parents often have academic, emotional, and substance abuse problems. Excessive achievement pressures and emotional isolation from parents underlie their difficulties.

- Chinese, Hispanic, Asian Pacific Island, and low-SES African-American parents tend to be controlling, which can be adaptive when combined with warmth. But excessive control impairs children's adjustment.

- Extended-family households are common among ethnic minorities and help protect children from the stress and disorganization of poverty.

Family Lifestyles and Transitions (p. 584)

Describe the influence of family size on child rearing, and explain how sibling relationships affect development.

- Contrary to a widespread assumption, larger family size does not reduce life chances or intelligence. Rather, the link between family size and children's IQ reflects the fact that mothers with low IQs tend to bear more children.

- Despite declining family size, most children grow up with at least one sibling. Because of their frequency and emotional intensity, sibling interactions are unique contexts for expanding social competence. Sibling rivalry tends to increase in middle childhood, when parental comparisons become more frequent. In adolescence, sibling relationships often become less intense as teenagers strive for autonomy, but attachment to siblings typically remains strong.

- Only children are as well-adjusted as children with siblings, and they are advantaged in self-esteem, academic achievement, and educational attainment.

How do children fare in adoptive, gay and lesbian, and never-married single-parent families?

- Adopted children tend to have more learning and emotional difficulties than other children, and by adolescence, their lives are often complicated by unresolved curiosity about their roots. By adulthood, however, most adoptees are well-adjusted.

- Gay and lesbian parents are as committed to and effective at child rearing as heterosexual parents. Their children are similar to other children in mental health, peer relations, gender-role behavior, and sexual orientation. During adolescence, more youths from homosexual families experiment with partners of both sexes.

- Never-married parenthood generally increases economic hardship for low-SES women. Children of never-married mothers who lack a father's warmth and involvement show less favorable cognitive development and engage in more antisocial behavior than children in low-SES, first-marriage families.

What factors influence children's adjustment to divorce and blended-family arrangements?

- Although all children experience painful emotional reactions during the period surrounding divorce, children with difficult temperaments and boys are at greater risk for adjustment problems. While children of divorce show improved functioning over time, divorce is linked to early sexual activity, adolescent parenthood, and long-term relationship difficulties.

- The overriding factor in positive adjustment following divorce is effective parenting. Positive father–child relationships foster favorable outcomes, as do caring extended family members, teachers, siblings, and friends. Divorce mediation and parent education programs can help promote parental cooperation.

- When divorced parents enter new relationships and form **blended**, or **reconstituted, families**, girls, older children, and children in father–stepmother families tend to have more adjustment problems. Stepparents who are warm and who move into their new roles gradually help children adjust.

How do maternal employment and life in dual-earner families affect children's development?

- When employed mothers enjoy their work and remain committed to parenting, their children show favorable adjustment. But when employment is stressful because of time demands or other reasons, children are at risk for ineffective parenting and adjustment difficulties.

- In dual-earner families, the father's willingness to share child-care responsibilities is linked to many positive child outcomes. Workplace supports, such as part-time employment, flexible schedules, and paid leave, help parents meet the demands of work and child rearing.

Discuss the influence of child-care quality on preschoolers' development and the impact of self-care on school-age children's adjustment.

- Preschoolers exposed to poor-quality care, especially for long hours, score lower in cognitive and social skills and higher in behavior problems.

- Key ingredients of high-quality child care include small group size, generous caregiver–child ratio, and caregivers' educational preparation and commitment to learning about and caring for children. High-quality care enhances cognitive, language, and social development, especially for low-SES children.

© JIM WEST/ALAMY

- Authoritative child rearing, parental monitoring, and regular after-school chores lead **self-care children** to be responsible and well-adjusted. Good "after-care" programs also aid school performance and emotional and social adjustment, with low-SES children showing special benefits.

Vulnerable Families: Child Maltreatment (p. 599)

Discuss the origins of child maltreatment, its consequences for development, and prevention strategies.

- Maltreating parents use ineffective discipline and hold negative biases toward their child. Unmanageable parental stress and social isolation increase the chances that abuse and neglect will occur. Societies that approve of the use of force and violence to solve problems promote child abuse.

- Maltreated children are impaired in development of attachment, emotional self-regulation, empathy and sympathy, self-concept, social skills, and academic motivation. They are also more likely to suffer central nervous system damage. Successful prevention of child maltreatment requires efforts at the family, community, and societal levels.

IMPORTANT TERMS AND CONCEPTS

authoritarian child-rearing style (p. 574)
authoritative child-rearing style (p. 573)
autonomy (p. 577)
blended, or reconstituted, family (p. 594)
child-rearing styles (p. 573)

coparenting (p. 569)
coregulation (p. 577)
extended-family household (p. 583)
permissive child-rearing style (p. 575)
psychological control (p. 574)

self-care children (p. 597)
social systems perspective (p. 568)
uninvolved child-rearing style (p. 575)

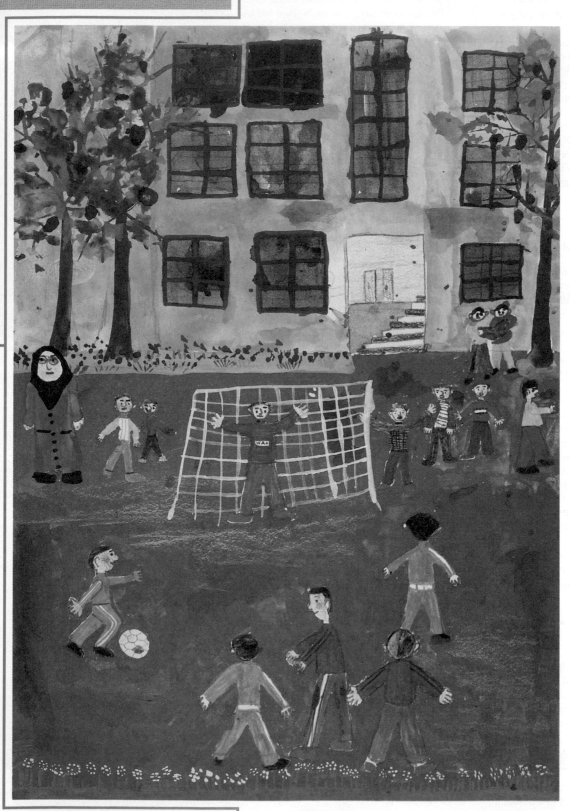

"Sports Time at School"

Mojtaba Khashei
10 years, Iran

Young friends play an energetic game of soccer in their schoolyard. Peer relationships are vital sources of support, contributing greatly to all aspects of children's development.

Reprinted with permission from the International Museum of Children's Art, Oslo, Norway

Peers, Media, and Schooling

Stu and Pete became friends in their school's Connections program, which smoothes the transition to middle school by assigning small groups of sixth graders to the same classes and lunch hour, so they feel "connected" in their new, large-school environment. During an end-of-year discussion in health class, Ms. Stevens asked what their new-school experiences had been like.

"Well," Stu began, "at the beginning of the year, it wasn't easy. People were bouncing around, trying to find friends they felt comfortable with. I wasn't sure I was going to fit in. In the past few weeks, though, Pete and I just sort of clicked."

"Same with Katy and me," Jessamyn chimed in. "I used to have another group of friends in fifth grade, but I lost interest. I mean, when they got here, they were trying too hard to be popular."

"Can you explain that a little?" Ms. Stevens asked.

"Well, every time they talked to someone, they acted like a different person—kinda two-faced. It was annoying."

"How do you know someone's going to be a good friend?" asked Ms. Stevens.

"You've gotta have the same interests, and Stu and me, we've kinda got the same personality," replied Pete. "We both like computer stuff like playing games and instant messaging. Also, a friend has to be somebody who makes you feel good about yourself. I wouldn't be friends with someone who's always making me feel bad."

"Yeah," Katy agreed. "I know kids who'll say they're a friend but they're real nasty. They don't show any kindness or understanding. Mostly, everyone dislikes them."

Beyond the family, which contexts strongly influence children and adolescents? The answer is clear: peers, with whom they share countless play, classroom, and extracurricular activities; media—especially television, computers, cell phones, and the Internet, which consume large amounts of their free time; and school, which helps the family transmit culturally valued knowledge to the next generation.

In the first part of this chapter, we look closely at the development of peer sociability, friendship, peer acceptance, and peer groups, along with their profound significance for children's social competence and adjustment. Next we consider the impact of various media on cognitive and social development. Finally, we turn to the school—how class and school size, educational philosophy, teacher–student interaction, and grouping of students affect educational experiences and learning. We conclude with a look at schooling and achievement in international perspective, with special attention to how well American schools prepare young people for productive work lives. ∎

Peer Relations
Development of Peer Sociability • Influences on Peer Sociability • Friendship • Peer Acceptance • Peer Groups • Dating • Peer Pressure and Conformity

■ **BIOLOGY AND ENVIRONMENT:** *Bullies and Their Victims*

■ **SOCIAL ISSUES: HEALTH:** *Adolescent Substance Use and Abuse*

Media
Television • Computers, Cell Phones, and the Internet • Regulating Media Use

Schooling
Class and Student Body Size • Educational Philosophies • School Transitions • Teacher–Student Interaction • Grouping Practices • Teaching Students with Special Needs • Parent–School Partnerships • How Well-Educated Are American Young People?

■ **SOCIAL ISSUES: EDUCATION:** *School Recess—A Time to Play, a Time to Learn*

■ **SOCIAL ISSUES: EDUCATION:** *Magnet Schools: Equal Access to High-Quality Education*

Peer Relations

Are peer relations crucial for development, and how do they add to children's experiences with caring adults? In previous chapters, we saw that parent and peer relations complement one another. A secure attachment bond and authoritative parenting grant children the confidence, social-cognitive understandings, and social skills they need to

▶ Trace the development of peer sociability from infancy into adolescence, and discuss various influences on peer sociability.

▶ Describe developing concepts and characteristics of friendships in childhood and adolescence, as well as implications of friendship for psychological adjustment.

▶ Describe categories of peer acceptance, the relationship of social behavior to likability, and ways to help rejected children.

▶ Discuss peer group formation and dating relationships, including their consequences for development.

▶ What factors influence conformity to peer pressure in adolescence?

enter the world of peers and form gratifying peer relationships (see Chapters 10 and 14). Peer interaction, in turn, enables children to expand their social-cognitive knowledge and social skills (see Chapters 11, 12, and 13). And in circumstances where children face profound stressors, such as parental divorce, gratifying friendships with peers can stand in, to some extent, for a supportive parent–child relationship (see Chapter 14).

In sum, peers contribute greatly to development and serve as vital sources of support in threatening situations. But as our discussion will reveal once again, they do so more effectively when children have a history of warm, supportive ties to parents.

Development of Peer Sociability

In cultures where agemates have regular contact during the first year of life, peer sociability begins early, gradually evolving into the complex, well-coordinated exchanges of childhood and adolescence. Peer sociability is supported by and contributes greatly to cognitive, emotional, and social milestones discussed in previous chapters.

Infant and Toddler Beginnings When pairs of infants are brought together in a laboratory, looking accompanied by touching is present at 3 to 4 months, peer-directed smiles and babbles by 6 months. These isolated social acts increase until, by the end of the first year, an occasional reciprocal exchange occurs in which babies grin, gesture, or otherwise imitate a playmate's behavior (Vandell & Mueller, 1995). Between 1 and 2 years, as toddlers appreciate that others have intentions, desires, and emotions distinct from their own, they increasingly view one another as playmates (Brownell & Kopp, 2007). As a result, coordinated interaction occurs more often, largely in the form of offering each other objects, sharing positive emotions, and mutual imitation involving jumping, chasing, or banging a toy (Vandell et al., 2006; Williams, Mastergeorge, & Ontai, 2010). These exchanges promote peer engagement and create joint understandings that aid verbal communication.

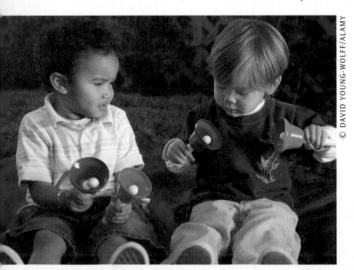

Around age 2, toddlers use words to share meanings and establish play goals, as when they say, "Let's play chase," and, after the game gets going, "Hey, good running!" (Eckerman & Peterman, 2001). Reciprocal play and positive emotion are especially frequent in toddlers' interactions with familiar agemates, suggesting that they are building true peer relationships (Ross et al., 1992).

Though limited, peer sociability is present in the first two years and is promoted by the early caregiver–child bond. From interacting with sensitive adults, babies learn how to send and interpret emotional signals in their first peer associations (Trevarthen, 2003). Toddlers who have a warm parental relationship or who attend high-quality child care with a small group size and a generous caregiver–child ratio—features that promote warm, stimulating caregiving and gentle support for engaging with peers—display more positive and extended peer exchanges. These children, in turn, show more socially competent behavior as preschoolers (Deynoot-Schaub & Riksen-Walraven, 2006a, 2006b; Howes & Matheson, 1992; Williams, Mastergeorge, & Ontai, 2010).

Babies express peer sociability in touches, smiles, and babbles that gradually develop into coordinated interaction—mostly in the form of mutual imitation—during the second year.

The Preschool Years As children become increasingly self-aware and better at communicating and at understanding others' thoughts and feelings, their skill at interacting with peers improves rapidly. Mildred Parten (1932), one of the first to study peer sociability among 2- to 5-year-olds, noticed a dramatic increase with age in joint, interactive play. She concluded that social development proceeds in a three-step sequence. It begins with **nonsocial activity**— unoccupied, onlooker behavior and solitary play. Then it shifts to **parallel play,** a limited form of social participation in which a child plays near other children with similar materials but does not try to influence their behavior. At the highest level are two forms of true social interaction. In **associative play,** children engage in separate activities but exchange toys and comment on one another's behavior. Finally, in **cooperative play,** a more advanced type of interaction, children orient toward a common goal, such as acting out a make-believe theme.

© DAVID YOUNG-WOLFF/ALAMY

Longitudinal evidence indicates that these play forms emerge in the order Parten suggested but that later-appearing forms do not replace earlier ones in a developmental sequence (Rubin, Bukowski, & Parker, 2006). Rather, all types coexist during the preschool years. **TAKE A MOMENT...** Watch children move from one play type to another in a playgroup or preschool classroom, and you will see that they often transition from onlooker to parallel to cooperative play and back again (Robinson et al., 2003). Preschoolers seem to use parallel play as a way station—a respite from the high demands of complex social interaction and a crossroad to new activities. And although nonsocial activity declines with age, it is still the most frequent form among 3- to 4-year-olds. Even among kindergartners it continues to occupy about one-third of children's free-play time. Also, both solitary and parallel play remain fairly stable from 3 to 6 years, accounting for as much of the young child's play as highly social, cooperative interaction (Rubin, Fein, & Vandenberg, 1983).

These 4-year-olds engage in parallel play, which seems to serve as a respite from the demands of complex social interaction and as a crossroad to new activities.

We now understand that it is the *type*, not the amount, of solitary and parallel play that changes during early childhood. In studies of preschoolers' play in Taiwan and the United States, researchers rated the *cognitive maturity* of nonsocial, parallel, and cooperative play by applying the categories shown in Table 15.1. Within each of Parten's play types, older children engaged in more cognitively mature behavior than younger children (Pan, 1994; Rubin, Watson, & Jambor, 1978).

Often parents wonder whether a preschooler who spends large amounts of time playing alone is developing normally. But only *certain types* of nonsocial activity—aimless wandering, hovering near peers, and functional play involving immature, repetitive motor action— are cause for concern. Children who behave reticently, by watching peers without playing, are usually temperamentally inhibited—high in social fearfulness (Coplan et al., 2004; Rubin, Bukowski, & Parker, 2006; Rubin, Burgess, & Hastings, 2002). And children who engage in solitary, repetitive behavior (banging blocks, making a doll jump up and down) tend to be immature, impulsive youngsters who find it difficult to regulate anger and aggression (Coplan et al., 2001). In the classroom, both reticent and impulsive children experience peer ostracism, with boys at greater risk for rejection than girls (Coplan & Arbeau, 2008).

But other preschoolers with low rates of peer interaction are not socially anxious or impulsive. They simply prefer to play alone, and their solitary activities are positive and constructive. Teachers encourage such play by setting out art materials, books, puzzles, and building toys. Children who spend much time at these activities are usually well-adjusted youngsters who, when they do play with peers, show socially skilled behavior (Coplan & Armer, 2007). Still, a few preschoolers who engage in such age-appropriate solitary play—again, more often boys—are rebuffed by peers. Perhaps because quiet play is inconsistent with the "masculine" gender role, boys who engage in it are at risk for negative reactions from both parents and peers and, eventually, for adjustment problems (Coplan et al., 2001, 2004).

As noted in Chapter 6, *sociodramatic play*—an advanced form of cooperative play—becomes especially common during the preschool years and supports cognitive, emotional, and social development (Göncü, Patt, & Kouba, 2004). In joint make-believe, preschoolers act out and respond to one another's pretend feelings. They also explore and gain control of fear-arousing experiences when they play doctor or pretend to search for monsters in a magical forest. As a result, they can better understand others' feelings and regulate their own

LOOK and LISTEN

Observe several 3- to 5-year-olds during a free-play period in a preschool or child-care program. How much time does each child devote to nonsocial activity, parallel play, and socially interactive play? Do children seem to use parallel play as a way station between activities?

TABLE 15.1	**Developmental Sequence of Cognitive Play Categories**	
PLAY CATEGORY	**DESCRIPTION**	**EXAMPLES**
Functional play	Simple, repetitive motor movements with or without objects; especially common during the first two years	Running around a room, rolling a car back and forth, kneading clay with no intent to make something
Constructive play	Creating or constructing something; especially common between 3 and 6 years	Making a house out of toy blocks, drawing a picture, putting together a puzzle
Make-believe play	Acting out everyday and imaginary roles; especially common between 2 and 6 years	Playing house, school, or police officer; acting out storybook or television characters
Games with rules	Understanding and following rules in play activities	Playing board games, cards, hopscotch, baseball

Source: Rubin, Fein, & Vandenberg, 1983.

(Smith, 2003). Finally, to create and manage complex plots, preschoolers must resolve their disputes through negotiation and compromise. With age, preschoolers' disagreements center less on toys and other resources and more on differences of opinion—an indication of their expanding capacity to consider others' attitudes and ideas (Chen et al., 2001; Hay, Payne, & Chadwick, 2004).

Middle Childhood and Adolescence When formal schooling begins, children are exposed to agemates who vary in many ways, including achievement, ethnicity, religion, interests, and personality. Contact with a diversity of peers strengthens school-age children's awareness of a multiplicity of viewpoints (see Chapter 11). Peer communication, in turn, profits from improved perspective taking. Children of this age can better interpret others' emotions and intentions and take them into account in peer dialogues. They are also aware of the value of emotional display rules in facilitating social interaction (see Chapter 10) (Denham et al., 2004). And school-age children's ability to understand the complementary roles of several players in relation to a set of rules permits the transition to rule-oriented games (refer again to Table 15.1).

School-age children apply their emotional and social knowledge to peer communication. Recall from Chapter 12 that sharing, helping, and other prosocial acts increase in middle childhood. In addition, younger and older children differ in how they help agemates. Kindergartners move right in and give assistance, regardless of whether it is desired. In contrast, school-age children offer to help and wait for a peer to accept before behaving prosocially. In adolescence, agemates work on tasks more cooperatively—staying on task, freely exchanging ideas, asking for opinions, and acknowledging one another's contributions (Azmitia, 1996).

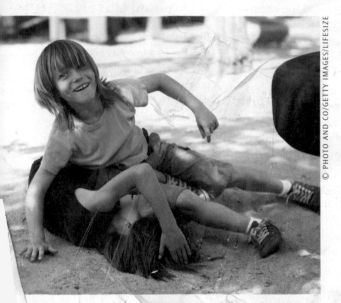

The good-natured quality of children's rough-and-tumble play distinguishes it from aggression. In our evolutionary past, rough-and-tumble may have been important for developing fighting skill and dominance relations.

Another form of peer interaction emerges in the preschool years and peaks during middle childhood, when it accounts for 10 percent of free-play behavior. **TAKE A MOMENT...** While watching children at play in a city park or a schoolyard, notice how they occasionally wrestle, roll, hit, and run after one another, alternating roles while smiling and laughing. This friendly chasing and play-fighting is called **rough-and-tumble play**. Children in many cultures engage in it with peers whom they like especially well (Pellegrini, 2004). After a rough-and-tumble episode, they continue interacting rather than separating, as they do after an aggressive encounter.

Children's rough-and-tumble play resembles the social behavior of many other young mammals. It seems to originate in parents' physical play with babies, especially fathers' play with sons (see Chapter 10). And it is more common among boys, probably because prenatal exposure to androgens predisposes boys toward active play (see Chapter 13). Boys' rough-and-tumble largely consists of playful wrestling, restraining, and hitting, whereas girls tend to engage in running and chasing, with only brief physical contact (Boulton, 1996).

In our evolutionary past, rough-and-tumble play may have been important for the development of fighting skill (Power, 2000). It also may help children establish a **dominance hierarchy**—a stable ordering of group members that predicts who will win when conflict arises. Observations of arguments, threats, and physical attacks between children reveal a consistent lineup of winners and losers that becomes increasingly stable in middle childhood and adolescence, especially among boys. Once school-age children establish a dominance hierarchy, hostility is rare (Pellegrini & Smith, 1998; Roseth et al., 2007). Children seem to use play-fighting as a safe context to assess the strength of a peer before challenging that peer's dominance.

As adolescents reach physical maturity, individual differences in strength become apparent, and rough-and-tumble play declines. When it does occur, its meaning changes: Adolescent boys' rough-and-tumble is linked to aggression (Pellegrini, 2003). After becoming embroiled in a bout, players "cheat" and hurt their opponent. In explanation, boys often say that they are retaliating, apparently to reestablish dominance. And boy–girl rough-and-tumble, though infrequent, rises slightly at adolescence, perhaps serving as a means through which teenagers playfully initiate heterosexual interaction (Pellegrini, 2006, 2009).

© PHOTO AND CO/GETTY IMAGES/LIFESIZE

Over middle childhood, children interact increasingly often with peers until, by mid-adolescence, they spend more time with peers than with any other social partners (Brown & Larson, 2009). Common interests, novel play activities, and opportunities to interact on an equal footing make peer interaction highly enjoyable. As adolescence draws to a close, most young people are proficient at many complex social behaviors.

Influences on Peer Sociability

Children first acquire skills for interacting with peers within the family. Parents influence children's peer sociability both *directly,* through attempts to influence children's peer relations, and *indirectly,* through their child-rearing practices and play behaviors (Ladd & Pettit, 2002; Rubin et al., 2005). Situational factors that adults can influence, such as the age mix of children, also make a difference, as do cultural values.

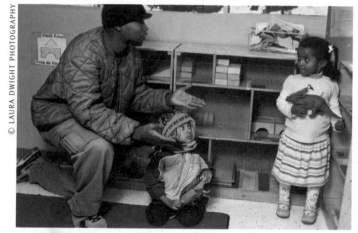

Direct Parental Influences Outside preschool, child care, and kindergarten, young children depend on parents to help them establish rewarding peer associations. Preschoolers whose parents frequently arrange informal peer play activities tend to have larger peer networks and to be more socially skilled (Ladd, LeSieur, & Profilet, 1993). In providing play opportunities, parents show children how to initiate peer contacts and encourage them to be good "hosts" who consider their playmates' needs.

Parents also influence children's peer interaction skills by offering guidance on how to act toward others. Their skillful suggestions for managing conflict, discouraging teasing, and entering a play group are associated with preschoolers' social competence and peer acceptance (Mize & Pettit, 2010; Parke et al., 2004b). As children get older and acquire effective social skills, they need less parental advice. In middle childhood and adolescence, heavy provision of parental guidance is usually aimed at children with peer-relationship problems (McDowell & Parke, 2009; Mounts, 2011).

A father gives his child a gentle lesson in getting along with others. Parents influence children's peer interaction skills by offering advice, guidance, and examples of how to behave.

Recall from Chapter 14 that during middle childhood and adolescence, parental monitoring of their child's activities protects school-age children and adolescents from antisocial involvements. Young people's disclosure of information is vital for successful monitoring. The extent to which adolescents tell parents about their whereabouts and companions is an especially strong predictor of adjustment (Brown & Bakken, 2011; Stattin & Kerr, 2000). Such disclosure, however, depends on a history of consistent monitoring and a well-functioning parent–child relationship, which (as we will see) also promotes positive peer relations.

Indirect Parental Influences Many parenting behaviors not directly aimed at promoting peer sociability nevertheless influence it. For example, inductive discipline and authoritative parenting offer a firm foundation for competence in relating to agemates. In contrast, coercive behavioral control, including harsh physical punishment, and psychological control engender poor social skills and aggressive behavior (see Chapters 12 and 14).

Furthermore, secure attachments to parents are linked to more responsive, harmonious peer interactions, larger peer networks, and warmer, more supportive friendships throughout childhood and adolescence (Laible, 2007; Lucas-Thompson & Clarke-Stewart, 2007; Wood, Emmerson, & Cowan, 2004). The sensitive, emotionally expressive parental communication that contributes to attachment security may be responsible. In one study, researchers observed parent–child conversations and rated them for the strength of the mother–child bond, as indicated by exchanges of positive emotion and parental sensitivity to the child's statements and feelings. Kindergartners who were more emotionally "connected" to their mothers displayed more empathy and prosocial behavior toward their classmates. This empathic orientation, in turn, was linked to more positive peer ties (Clark & Ladd, 2000).

Parent–child play seems particularly effective for promoting peer interaction skills. During play, parents interact with their child on a "level playing field," much as peers do (Russell, Pettit, & Mize, 1998). Highly involved, emotionally positive, and cooperative play between parents and preschoolers is associated with more positive peer relations. And perhaps because parents play more with children of their own sex, mothers' play is more strongly linked to daughters' competence, fathers' play to sons' competence (Lindsey & Mize, 2000; Pettit et al., 1998).

Finally, the quality of parents' social networks is associated with children's social competence. In one study, parents who reported high-quality friendships had school-age children who interacted more favorably with friends. This relationship was stronger for girls, perhaps because girls spend more time near parents and have more opportunity to observe their parents' friends (Simpkins & Parke, 2001). Furthermore, overlap between parents' and adolescents' social networks—frequent contact among teenagers' friends, their parents, and their friends' parents—is related to better school achievement and low levels of antisocial behavior (Parke et al., 2004b). Under these conditions, other adults in parents' networks may promote parents' values and goals and monitor teenagers in their parents' absence.

Age Mix of Children When observed in age-graded settings, such as child-care centers, schools, and summer camps, children typically interact with others close in age. Yet in cultures where children are not segregated by age for schooling and recreation, cross-age interaction is common.

The theories of Piaget and Vygotsky, discussed in Chapter 6, suggest different benefits from same- versus mixed-age interaction. Piaget emphasized experiences with children equal in status who challenge one another's viewpoints, thereby promoting cognitive, social, and moral development. In contrast, Vygotsky believed that children profit from interacting with older, more capable peers, who model and encourage more advanced skills.

Among preschoolers, younger children's play is more cognitively and socially mature in mixed-age classrooms than in single-age classrooms. Furthermore, as early as age 3 or 4, children can modify their behavior to fit the needs of a less advanced child, simplifying their communication and assuming more responsibility for a joint activity (Brody, Graziano, & Musser, 1983; Howes & Farver, 1987). Nevertheless, the oldest school-age children in mixed-age settings prefer same-age companions, perhaps because they have more compatible interests and experience more cooperative interaction. Younger children's interaction with same-age partners is also more intense and harmonious, but they often turn to older peers because of their superior knowledge and exciting play ideas.

Children clearly profit from both same-age and mixed-age relationships. From interacting with equals, they learn to cooperate and resolve conflicts, and they develop vital moral understandings of reciprocity and justice (see Chapters 11 and 12). In mixed-age settings, younger children acquire new competencies from their older companions. And when more mature youngsters help their less mature counterparts, they practice nurturance, guidance, and other prosocial behaviors.

Village children in India play a "circle tapping" game requiring high levels of cooperation. The child in the center recites a poem, the alphabet, or numbers, then circles the others, saying, "Whomever I tap, it will be their turn." The tapped child recites next.

© DORANNE JACOBSON

Cultural Values Peer sociability in collectivist societies, which stress group harmony, takes different forms than in individualistic cultures (Chen & French, 2008). For example, children in India generally play in large groups, which requires high levels of cooperation. Much of their behavior is imitative, occurs in unison, and involves close physical contact. In a game called Bhatto Bhatto, children act out a script about a trip to the market, touching one another's elbows and hands as they pretend to cut and share a tasty vegetable (Roopnarine et al., 1994).

As another example, Chinese preschoolers—unlike American preschoolers, who tend to reject reticent classmates—are typically willing to include a quiet, reserved child in play (Chen et al., 2006). In Chapter 10, we saw that until recently, collectivist values, which discourage self-assertion, led to positive evaluations of shyness in China (see page 427). Apparently, this benevolent attitude is still evident in the play behaviors of young Chinese children.

Cultural beliefs about the importance of play also affect early peer associations. Caregivers who view play as mere entertainment are less likely to provide props or to encourage pretend than those who value its cognitive and social benefits (Farver & Wimbarti, 1995a, 1995b). Preschool children of Korean-American parents, who emphasize task persistence as crucial for learning, spend less time than Caucasian-American children in joint make-believe and more time unoccupied and in parallel play (Farver, Kim, & Lee, 1995).

Return to the description of children's daily lives in a Mayan village culture on page 273 in Chapter 6. Mayan parents do not promote children's play—yet Mayan children are socially competent (Gaskins, 2000). Perhaps Western-style sociodramatic play, with its elaborate materials and wide-ranging themes, is particularly important for social development in societies where the worlds of adults and children are distinct than in village cultures where children participate in adult activities from an early age. In support of this view, observations of 2- to 6-year-olds in a Senagalese fishing village revealed that make-believe with peers was just as prevalent as in a comparison group of U.S. middle-SES age-mates (Bloch, 1989). Because sea fishing is too risky an activity for young children, the Senegalese preschoolers spent much time in their homes and yards apart from working adults. Their families also had sufficient resources to provide them with a rich array of play materials that fostered pretending.

In all societies, peer contact rises in adolescence, a trend that is strongest in industrialized nations, where young people spend most of each weekday with agemates in school. Teenagers also spend much out-of-class time together, more in some cultures than in others. For example, U.S. young people have about 50 hours of free time per week, Europeans about 45 hours, and East Asians about 33 hours (Larson, 2001). A shorter school year and less demanding academic standards, which lead American youths to devote much less time to schoolwork, account for this difference (see Figure 15.1).

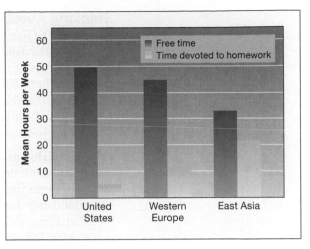

FIGURE 15.1 Weekly free time and time devoted to homework by adolescents in the United States, Europe, and East Asia. Figures are averages of those reported in many studies. American teenagers have more free time available to spend with peers than their European and, especially, Asian counterparts, largely because American adolescents spend far less time doing homework. (Adapted from Larson, 2001.)

ASK YOURSELF

Review ■ Among children who spend much time playing alone, what factors distinguish those who are likely to have adjustment difficulties from those who are well-adjusted and socially skilled?

Connect ■ What aspects of parent–child interaction probably account for the relationship between attachment security and children's peer sociability? (*Hint:* See Chapter 10, pages 434 and 437.)

Apply ■ Three-year-old Ben lives in the country, with no other preschoolers nearby. His parents wonder whether it is worth driving Ben into town once a week to participate in a peer play group. What advice would you give Ben's parents, and why?

Reflect ■ What did your parents do, directly and indirectly, that might have influenced your peer relationships in childhood and adolescence?

Friendship

Children have encounters and relationships with many peers, but they prefer some over others. Beginning in early childhood, they form **friendships**—close relationships involving companionship in which each partner wants to be with the other. Observations of 1- and 2-year-olds reveal that they initiate play, exchange expressions of positive emotion, and engage in more complex interactions with selected, familiar peers (Howes, 2009). These early mutual relationships may lay the groundwork for deeper, more meaningful friendships in childhood and adolescence.

To study friendship, researchers ask the child or a knowledgeable adult to name friends and then check whether nominated friends return the choice. They also observe friendship interactions, comparing them with other peer relationships. And they interview children about what friendship means. Findings reveal that with age, children's ideas about friendship change, as do certain features of friendships (Hartup, 2006). From the preschool years on, friendship contributes uniquely to children's emotional and social development.

Thinking About Friendship TAKE A MOMENT... Jot down a description of what *friend-ship* means to you. You probably pictured a consensual relationship involving companionship, sharing, understanding each other's thoughts and feelings, and caring for and comforting each other in times of need. In addition, mature friendships endure over time and survive occasional conflicts. But to a child, friendship begins far more concretely, as pleasurable activity. With age, friendship evolves into a relationship based on mutual consideration and emotional satisfaction (Hartup & Abecassis, 2004). Children's changing ideas about friendship follow a three-stage sequence, confirmed by both longitudinal and cross-sectional research:

1. **Friendship as a Handy Playmate (About 4 to 7 Years)** Preschoolers understand something about the uniqueness of friendship. They say that a friend is someone "who likes you," with whom you spend a lot of time playing, and with whom you share toys. But friendship does not yet have a long-term, enduring quality. Children at this stage say that a friendship can dissolve when one partner refuses to share, hits, or is not available to play. "Mark's my best friend," one 5-year-old would declare on days when the boys got along well (Damon, 1988; Hartup, 2006). But when a dispute arose, he would reverse himself: "Mark, you're not my friend!"

2. **Friendship as Mutual Trust and Assistance (About 8 to 10 Years)** In middle childhood, friendship becomes more complex and psychologically based. Consider the following 8-year-old's ideas:

   > *Why is Shelly your best friend?* Because she helps me when I'm sad, and she shares. . . . *What makes Shelly so special?* I've known her longer, I sit next to her and got to know her better. . . . *How come you like Shelly better than anyone else?* She's done the most for me. She never disagrees, she never eats in front of me, she never walks away when I'm crying, and she helps me on my homework. . . . *How do you get someone to like you?* . . . If you're nice to [your friends], they'll be nice to you. (Damon, 1988, pp. 80–81)

   As these responses show, friendship has become a mutually agreed-on relationship in which children like each other's personal qualities and respond to each other's needs and desires. And once a friendship forms, *trust* becomes its defining feature. School-age children state that a good friendship is based on acts of kindness signifying that each person can be counted on to support the other (Hartup & Abecassis, 2004). Consequently, older children regard violations of trust, such as not helping a friend who needs help, breaking promises, and gossiping behind a friend's back, as serious breaches of friendship—as Katy did in the chapter introduction. And rifts cannot be patched up simply by playing nicely after a conflict, as preschoolers and young school-age children do. Instead, apologies and explanations are necessary.

3. **Friendship as Intimacy, Mutual Understanding, and Loyalty (11 to 15 Years and Older)** When asked about the meaning of friendship, teenagers stress three characteristics. The most important is *intimacy,* or psychological closeness, which is supported by *mutual understanding* of each other's values, beliefs, and feelings. In addition, more than younger children, teenagers want their friends to be *loyal*—to stick up for them and not to leave them for somebody else (Collins & Madsen, 2006).

   As friendship takes on these deeper features, adolescents regard it as formed over time by "getting to know someone." In addition, they view friends as important in relieving psychological distress, such as loneliness, sadness, and fear. Because true mutual understanding implies forgiveness, only an extreme falling out can terminate a friendship. Here is how one teenager described his best friendship:

   > Well, you need someone you can tell anything to, all kinds of things that you don't want to spread around. That's why you're someone's friend. *Is that why Jimmy is your friend? Because he can keep a secret?* Yes, and we like the same kinds of things. We speak the same language. My mother says we're two peas in a pod. . . . *Do you ever get mad at Jimmy?* Not really. *What if he did something that got you really mad?* He'd still be my best friend. I'd tell him what he did wrong and maybe he'd understand. I could be wrong too, it depends. (Damon, 1977, p. 163)

© GEORGE DISARIO/CORBIS

During middle childhood, concepts of friendship become more psychologically based. These boys share an interest in cooking, but they want to spend time together because they like each other's personal qualities.

LOOK and LISTEN

Ask an 8- to 11-year-old to tell you what he or she looks for in a best friend. Is trust centrally important? Does the child mention personality traits, just as school-age children do in describing themselves (see Chapter 11, page 458).

Characteristics of Friendships

Changes in children's thinking about friendships are linked to characteristics of their real friendships. Let's look closely at friendship stability, interaction, and resemblance.

Friendship Selectivity and Stability. As mutual trust and loyalty increase in importance, school-age children's friendships become more selective. Preschoolers say they have lots of friends—sometimes, everyone in their class! But by age 8 or 9, children name only a handful of good friends. As teenagers focus on friendship quality, this narrowing continues. Number of best friends declines from four to six in early adolescence to only one or two in early adulthood (Hartup & Stevens, 1999).

Friendships are remarkably stable at all ages, but for younger children, stability

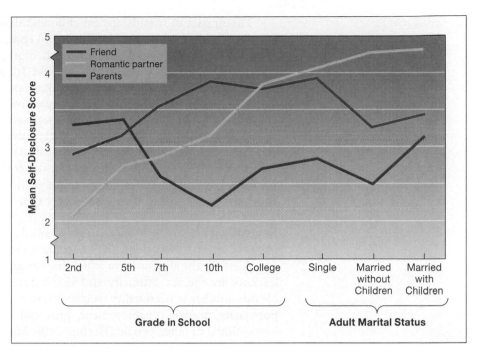

FIGURE 15.2 Age changes in reported self-disclosure to parents and peers, based on data from several studies. Self-disclosure to friends increases steadily during adolescence, reflecting intimacy as a major basis of friendship. Self-disclosure to romantic partners also rises, but it does not surpass intimacy with friends until the college years. Self-disclosure to parents declines in early adolescence, a time of mild parent–child conflict. As family relationships readjust to the young person's increasing autonomy, self-disclosure to parents rises. (From D. Buhrmester, 1996, "Need Fulfillment, Interpersonal Competence, and the Developmental Contexts of Early Adolescent Friendship," in W. M. Bukowski, A. F. Newcomb, & W. W. Hartup, Eds., *The Company They Keep: Friendship in Childhood and Adolescence,* New York: Cambridge University Press, p. 168. Reprinted with permission of Cambridge University Press.)

is largely a function of the constancy of social environments, such as school and neighborhood. Context continues to be influential at older ages, with friendships spanning several situations—such as school, religious institution, and children of parents' friends—more likely to persist (Troutman & Fletcher, 2010). At the same time, stability increases with age as friendships become psychologically based and, therefore, higher in such positive features as intimacy, self-disclosure, support, and prosocial behavior. From fourth grade through high school, about 50 to 70 percent endure over the course of a school year, and some for several years, although they often undergo temporary shifts in the strength of each partner's commitment (Berndt, 2004; Degirmencioglu et al., 1998). In middle or junior high school, varying rates of pubertal development, encounters with new peers, and romantic interests often lead to a temporary period of greater change in choice of friends (Poulin & Chan, 2010).

Interaction Between Friends. At all ages, friends have special ways of interacting. Preschoolers, for example, give twice as much reinforcement—greetings, praise, and compliance—to children they identify as friends, and they also receive more from them. Friends are more emotionally expressive, talking, laughing, and looking at one another more often than nonfriends do (Hartup, 1996, 2006; Vaughn et al., 2001). Spontaneity, intimacy, and sensitivity characterize rewarding friendships very early, although children are not able to express these ideas until much later.

A more mature understanding of friendship seems to spark greater prosocial behavior between friends. When working on a task together, school-age friends help, share, refer to each other's comments, and spend more time focused than preschool friends do (Hartup, 1996; Newcomb & Bagwell, 1995). Cooperation, generosity, mutual affirmation, and self-disclosure (see Figure 15.2) continue to rise into adolescence—trends that may reflect greater effort and skill at preserving the relationship and increased sensitivity to a friend's needs and desires (De Goede, Branje, & Meeus, 2009; Phillipsen, 1999). Adolescents also are less possessive of their friends than they were in childhood (Parker et al., 2005). Desiring a certain degree of autonomy for themselves, they recognize that friends need this, too.

Friends not only behave more prosocially but also disagree and compete with each other more than nonfriends. Because children regard friendship as based on equality, they seem especially concerned about losing a contest to a friend. Also, when children hold differing opinions, friends are more likely to voice them. At the same time, school-age and adolescent friends use negotiation to resolve conflicts more often than nonfriends do. Friends seem to realize that close relationships can survive disagreements if both parties are secure in their liking for each other (Fonzi et al., 1997; Hartup, 2006; Rose & Asher, 1999). Clearly, friendship provides an important context in which children learn to tolerate criticism and resolve disputes.

The impact of friendships on children's development depends on the nature of those friends. Children who bring kindness and compassion to their friendships strengthen one another's prosocial tendencies and form more lasting ties (Vitaro, Boivin, & Bukowski, 2009). But when aggressive children make friends, the relationship is often riddled with hostile interaction and is at risk for breakup, especially when just one member of the pair is aggressive (Ellis & Zarbatany, 2007). Aggressive girls' friendships are high in self-disclosure but full of relational hostility, including jealousy, conflict, and betrayal—techniques used to manipulate associations with others. Aggressive boys' friendships involve frequent expressions of anger, coercive statements, physical attacks, and enticements to rule-breaking behavior, as well as relational aggression (Bagwell & Coie, 2004; Crick & Nelson, 2002; Dishion, Andrews, & Crosby, 1995). These findings indicate that the social problems of aggressive children operate within their closest peer ties.

Resemblance Between Friends. The value adolescents attach to feeling "in sync" with their friends suggests that friends will become increasingly similar in attitudes and values with age. Actually, the attributes on which friends are most alike throughout childhood and adolescence are age, sex, ethnicity, and SES. But from middle childhood on, friends also resemble one another in personality (sociability, inattention/hyperactivity, aggression, depression), popularity, academic achievement, prosocial behavior, and judgments (including biased perceptions) of other people (Hartup, 2006; Mariano & Harton, 2005). And in adolescence, friends tend to be alike in identity status, educational aspirations, political beliefs, and willingness to try drugs and engage in lawbreaking acts. Over time, they become more similar in these ways (Berndt & Murphy, 2002; Selfhout, Branje, & Meeus, 2008).

Children and adolescents probably choose companions like themselves in age, sex, and ethnicity to increase the supportiveness of friendship. In-group favoritism and out-group prejudice may also influence these choices (see Chapters 11 and 13). How do children identify peers who are similar to themselves in other ways? According to some researchers, they go on "shopping expeditions" in their social networks, trying out relationships and sustaining those that "feel right" (Hartup & Abecassis, 2004). As friends spend more time together, they socialize one another, becoming increasingly alike in attitudes, values, school grades, and social behavior (Berndt & Keefe, 1995).

Nevertheless, as young people enter a wider range of school and community settings, they choose some friends who differ from themselves. For a time, young teenagers sacrifice similarity in favor of admiration for superficial features—whether a potential friend is popular, physically attractive, or athletically skilled. And early adolescents of both sexes are attracted to high-status, aggressive boys as friends, a trend that contributes to a rise in antisocial behavior and, for girls, can lead to negative experiences in their first dating relationships (Bukowski, Sippola, & Newcomb, 2000). In other instances, a friend's favorable traits are influential. In one study, low-achieving 9- to 11-year-olds who befriended a high-achieving classmate declined in academic self-esteem (because of social comparison) but nevertheless improved in academic performance (Altermatt & Pomerantz, 2005).

The task of forging a personal identity may also lead adolescents to seek friends with differing attitudes and values, as a means of exploring new perspectives within the security of a compatible relationship. Furthermore, teenagers often judge commonality in certain attributes as more important than in others. For example, compared with Caucasian-American friends, African-American and Hispanic friends place greater emphasis on shared ethnicity and less on similarity in academic achievement (Azmitia, Ittel, & Brenk, 2006; Hamm, 2000). Nevertheless, Hispanic frequently view higher-achieving friends as a source of pride (Azmitia & Cooper, 2001). Such friends play key roles in spurring improved school performance and higher educational aspirations.

Finally, children and adolescents are more likely to form friendships with agemates of other ethnicities when they attend ethnically diverse schools and live in integrated neighborhoods (Quillian & Campbell, 2003).

© ANGELA HAMPTON PICTURE LIBRARY/ALAMY

Teenagers typically choose friends whose attitudes and values resemble their own. Early adolescents are also attracted to high-status aggressive boys—a trend that contributes to a rise in antisocial behavior.

As young people form comfortable, lasting close relationships, they come to view ethnically different peers as individuals instead of through the lens of stereotypes (see Chapter 11).

Sex Differences in Friendships In middle childhood, children start to report a consistent sex difference in friendships: Emotional closeness is more common between girls than between boys (Markovits, Benenson, & Dolenszky, 2001). Girls, who are more exclusive in their friendships, frequently get together to "just talk," and their exchanges contain more self-disclosure (sharing of innermost thoughts and feelings) and mutually supportive statements. In contrast, boys more often gather for an activity—usually sports or other competitive games. Boys' discussions usually focus on recognition and mastery issues, such as achievements in sports and school, and involve more competition and conflict (Brendgen et al., 2001; Rubin, Bukowski, & Parker, 2006).

In adolescence, intimacy and loyalty become defining features of friendship. Compared to boys, girls place a higher value on emotional closeness, engaging in more self-disclosure and mutually supportive statements with friends.

Because of gender-role expectations, girls' friendships typically focus on communal concerns, boys' on achievement and status. Boys do form close friendship ties, but the quality of their friendships is more variable. Gender identity plays a role: Androgynous boys are as likely as girls to form intimate same-sex ties, whereas highly "masculine" boys are less likely to do so (Jones & Dembo, 1989).

Friendship closeness has costs as well as benefits. When friends focus on their deeper thoughts and feelings, they tend to *coruminate*, or repeatedly mull over problems and negative emotions. Corumination, while contributing to high friendship quality, also triggers anxiety and depression—symptoms more common among girls than among boys (Hankin, Stone, & Wright, 2010; Rose, Carlson, & Waller, 2007). And when conflict arises between intimate friends, more potential exists for one party to harm the other through relational aggression—for example, by divulging sensitive personal information to outsiders.

Partly for this reason, girls' closest same-sex friendships tend to be of shorter duration than boys' (Benenson & Christakos, 2003). Also, whereas boys often resolve conflicts by minimizing their importance ("It's no big deal"), this strategy tends to result in friendship break-up among girls (Bowker, 2004). When friendships are emotionally intense, minimizing rather than being "up front" about tensions in the relationship may restore superficial harmony while the underlying discontent lingers, making the friendship less stable.

In early adolescence, young people who are either very popular or very unpopular are more likely to have other-sex friends. Teenagers who are not accepted by their own sex sometimes look to the other sex for friendships. Girls have more other-sex friends than boys, a difference that widens with age as teenage girls form friendships with boys who are somewhat older (Poulin & Pedersen, 2007). Among boys without same-sex friends, having an other-sex friend is associated with feelings of competence. But among girls who lack same-sex friends, other-sex friendships are linked to less positive well-being (Bukowski, Sippola, & Hoza, 1999). Perhaps these girls are especially likely to befriend boys with negative traits, such as aggression.

Friendship and Adjustment Warm childhood and adolescent friendships that are high in trust, intimate sharing, and support contribute to many aspects of psychological health and competence into early adulthood (Bukowski, 2001; Waldrip, 2008), for several reasons:

- *Close friendships provide opportunities to explore the self and develop a deep understanding of another.* Through open, honest communication, friends become sensitive to each other's strengths and weaknesses, needs and desires—a process that supports the development of self-concept, perspective taking, and identity.
- *Close friendships provide a foundation for future intimate relationships.* Look again at Figure 15.2, and you will see that self-disclosure to friends precedes disclosure to romantic partners. Conversations with teenage friends about sexuality and romance, along with the intimacy of friendship itself, may help adolescents establish and work out problems in romantic partnerships (Connolly & Goldberg, 1999; Sullivan, 1953).

- *Close friendships help young people deal with the stresses of everyday life.* By enhancing sensitivity to and concern for another, supportive, prosocial friendships promote empathy, sympathy, and prosocial behavior. As a result, they contribute to involvement in constructive youth activities, avoidance of antisocial acts, and psychological well-being (Lansford et al., 2003; Wentzel, Barry, & Caldwell, 2004). A rewarding friendship helps protect shy children from developing emotional and behavior problems (Laursen et al., 2007). And adolescents experiencing family stress who have close friends show as high a level of well-being as children from better-functioning families (Gauze et al., 1996).
- *Close friendships can improve attitudes toward and involvement in school.* Close friendships promote good school adjustment, academically and socially, in both middle- and low-SES students (Berndt & Murphy, 2002; Wentzel, Barry, & Caldwell, 2004). Children and adolescents who enjoy interacting with friends at school may begin to view all aspects of school life more positively.

Some friendships, however, interfere with well-being. Beginning in the preschool years, the conflict-ridden interactions that occur between physically, verbally, and relationally aggressive friends are associated with poor adjustment (Sebanc, 2003). Longitudinal research reveals that children with aggressive friends increase in antisocial behavior over time (Snyder et al., 2005; Vitaro, Pedersen, & Brendgen, 2007).

Finally, children who have no friends usually have undesirable personalities: They may be easily angered, shy and anxious, or self-centered (less caring and honest) (Bowker et al., 2006; Laursen et al., 2007). Without supportive friendship as a context for acquiring more adaptive social behaviors, the maladaptive behaviors of these children tend to persist.

ASK YOURSELF

Review ■ Describe unique qualities of interaction between close friends, and explain how they contribute to development.

Review ■ Why are aggressive children's friendships likely to magnify their antisocial behavior?

Connect ■ Cite similarities in development of self-concept, described in Chapter 11 (pages 456, 458), and ideas about friendship. Explain how the discussion among Stu, Pete, Jessamyn, and Katy in the introduction to this chapter reflects friendship expectations that typically emerge at adolescence.

Apply ■ Ralph, a high school junior of Irish Catholic background, befriended Jonathan, a Chinese-American of Buddhist faith. Both boys are from middle-SES homes and are good students. Why might Ralph seek out a friend both similar to and different from himself?

Peer Acceptance

Peer acceptance refers to likability—the extent to which a child is viewed by a group of agemates, such as classmates, as a worthy social partner. Unlike friendship, peer acceptance is not a mutual relationship but a one-sided perspective, involving the group's view of an individual. Nevertheless, certain social skills that contribute to friendship also enhance peer acceptance. Better-accepted children tend to have more friends and more positive relationships with them (Lansford et al., 2006b; Pedersen et al., 2007). Like friendship, peer acceptance contributes uniquely to children's adjustment.

To assess peer acceptance, researchers usually use self-reports that measure *social preferences*—for example, asking children and adolescents to identify classmates whom they "like very much" or "like very little" (Hymel et al., 2004). Another approach assesses *social prominence*—young people's judgments of the peers most of their classmates admire. Only moderate correspondence exists between the classmates school-age children and adolescents identify as prominent (looked up to by many others) and those they say they personally prefer (Prinstein & Cillessen, 2003).

Children's self-reports yield four general categories of peer acceptance:

- **Popular children,** who get many positive votes (are well-liked)
- **Rejected children,** who get many negative votes (are disliked)

- **Controversial children,** who receive many votes, both positive and negative (are both liked and disliked)
- **Neglected children,** who are seldom mentioned, either positively or negatively

About two-thirds of students in a typical elementary school classroom fit one of these categories (Coie, Dodge, & Coppotelli, 1982). The remaining one-third, who do not receive extreme scores, are *average* in peer acceptance.

Peer acceptance is a powerful predictor of current and later psychological adjustment. Rejected children, especially, are anxious, unhappy, disruptive, poorly achieving children with low self-esteem. Both teachers and parents view them as having a wide range of emotional and social problems. Peer rejection in middle childhood is also strongly associated with poor school performance, absenteeism, dropping out, substance use, depression, antisocial behavior, and delinquency in adolescence and with criminality in early adulthood (Ladd, 2005; Laird et al., 2001; Parker et al., 1995; Rubin, Bukowski, & Parker, 2006).

However, prior influences—children's characteristics combined with parenting practices—may largely explain the link between peer acceptance and psychological adjustment. School-age children with peer-relationship problems are more likely to have preexisting, weak emotional self-regulation skills and to have experienced family stress due to low income, insensitive child rearing, and coercive discipline (Cowan & Cowan, 2004; Trentacosta & Shaw, 2009). Nevertheless, as we will see, rejected children evoke reactions from peers that contribute to their unfavorable development. Peer rejection, in turn, adds to the risk of maladjustment, beyond rejected children's maladaptive behavioral styles (Sturaro et al., 2011).

Determinants of Peer Acceptance Why is one child liked while another is rejected? A wealth of research reveals that social behavior plays a powerful role.

Popular Children. Although many popular children are kind and considerate, others are admired for their socially sophisticated yet belligerent behavior. Two subtypes of popular children exist.

Most are **popular-prosocial children,** who combine academic and social competence. They perform well in school, communicate with peers in friendly and cooperative ways, and solve social problems constructively (Cillessen & Bellmore, 2004; Newcomb, Bukowski, & Pattee, 1993).

A smaller subtype, **popular-antisocial children,** which emerges in late childhood and early adolescence, includes "tough" boys—athletically skilled but poor students who cause trouble and defy adult authority—and relationally aggressive boys and girls who enhance their own status by ignoring, excluding, and spreading rumors about other children (Rodkin et al., 2000; Rose, Swenson, & Waller, 2004; Vaillancourt & Hymel, 2006). Despite their aggressiveness, peers often view these youths as "cool," perhaps because of their athletic abilities and sophisticated but devious social skills.

Although peer admiration gives popular-antisocial children some protection against lasting adjustment difficulties, their antisocial acts require intervention (Prinstein & La Greca, 2004; Rodkin et al., 2006). With age, peers like these high-status, aggressive youths less and less, a trend that is stronger for relationally aggressive girls. The more socially prominent and controlling these girls become, the more they engage in relational aggression (Cillessen & Mayeux, 2004). Eventually peers may condemn their nasty tactics and reject them.

Rejected Children. Rejected children display a wide range of negative social behaviors. But as with popular children, not all of these disliked children look the same.

Rejected-aggressive children, the largest subtype, show high rates of conflict, physical and relational aggression, and hyperactive, inattentive, and impulsive behavior.

They are usually deficient perspective takers, misinterpreting the innocent behaviors of peers as hostile, blaming others for their social difficulties, and acting on their angry feelings (Crick, Casas, & Nelson, 2002; Hoza et al., 2005; Rubin, Bukowski, & Parker, 2006). Compared with popular-aggressive children, rejected-aggressive children are more extremely antagonistic (Prinstein & Cillessen, 2003). Rather than using aggression skillfully to attain status, rejected-aggressive children display blatantly hostile, acting-out behavior, which triggers scorn and avoidance in their peers.

In contrast, **rejected-withdrawn children** are passive and socially awkward. These timid children are overwhelmed by social anxiety, hold negative expectations for treatment by peers, and fear being scorned and attacked. Like their aggressive counterparts, they typically feel like retaliating rather than compromising in peer conflicts, although they less often act on those feelings (Hart et al., 2000; Rubin, Bowker, & Gazelle, 2010; Troop-Gordon & Asher, 2005).

Rejected children are excluded by peers as early as kindergarten. Rejection, in turn, further impairs these children's biased social information processing, heightening their hostility (Lansford et al., 2010). Soon their classroom participation declines, their feelings of loneliness and depression rise, their academic achievement falters, and they want to avoid school (Buhs, Ladd, & Herald-Brown, 2010; Gooren et al., 2011). Most have few friends, and their closest friendship bonds tend to be low in mutual support and effective conflict resolution (Rubin, Bukowski, & Parker, 2006). Some have no friends—a circumstance linked to low self-esteem, mistrust of peers, and severe adjustment difficulties (Ladd et al., 2011; Pedersen et al., 2007).

Both types of rejected children are at risk for peer harassment. But as the Biology and Environment box on the following page reveals, rejected-withdrawn children are especially likely to be victimized (Putallaz et al., 2007).

LOOK and LISTEN

Contact a nearby elementary school or a school district office to find out what practices are in place to prevent bullying. Inquire about a written antibullying policy, and request a copy.

Controversial and Neglected Children. Consistent with the mixed peer opinion they engender, controversial children display a blend of positive and negative social behaviors. They are hostile and disruptive, but they also engage in positive, prosocial acts. Even though some peers dislike them, they have qualities that protect them from exclusion. They are usually assertive and dominant, have as many friends as popular children, and are happy with their peer relationships (de Bruyn & Cillessen, 2006; Newcomb, Bukowski, & Pattee, 1993). But like their popular-antisocial and rejected-aggressive counterparts, they often bully agemates to get their way and engage in calculated relational aggression to sustain their dominance (DeRosier & Thomas, 2003; Putallaz et al., 2007). The social status of controversial children often changes over time as agemates react to their mixed behavior.

Perhaps the most surprising finding on peer acceptance is that neglected children, once thought to be in need of treatment, are usually well-adjusted. Although they engage in low rates of interaction and are considered shy by their classmates, most are just as socially skilled as average children. They do not report feeling unhappy about their social life. And when they want to, they can break away from their usual, preferred pattern of playing alone, cooperating well with peers and forming positive, stable friendships (Ladd & Burgess, 1999; Ladd et al., 2011). Consequently, neglected status (like controversial status) is often temporary. Neglected, socially competent children remind us that an outgoing, gregarious personality style is not the only path to emotional well-being. Nevertheless, a few neglected children are socially anxious and poorly skilled and, thus, at risk for peer rejection.

Helping Rejected Children A variety of interventions exist to improve the peer relations and psychological adjustment of rejected children. Most involve coaching, modeling, and reinforcing positive social skills, such as how to initiate interaction with a peer, cooperate in play, and respond to another child with friendly emotion and approval. Several of these programs have produced gains in social competence and peer acceptance still present from several weeks to a year later (Asher & Rose, 1997; DeRosier, 2007). Combining social-skills training with other treatments increases their effectiveness. Rejected children often are poor students, and their low academic self-esteem magnifies their negative reactions to teachers and classmates. Intensive academic tutoring improves both school achievement and social acceptance (O'Neil et al., 1997).

Still another approach focuses on training in perspective taking and social problem solving (see Chapter 11). But many rejected-aggressive children are unaware of their poor social skills and do not take responsibility for their social failures (Mrug, Hoza, & Gerdes, 2001). Rejected-withdrawn children, in contrast, are likely to develop a *learned-helpless* approach to peer acceptance—concluding, after repeated rebuffs, that they will never be liked (Wichmann, Coplan, & Daniels, 2004). Both types of rejected children need help attributing their peer difficulties to internal, changeable causes.

BIOLOGY and ENVIRONMENT

Bullies and Their Victims

Follow the activities of aggressive children over a school day, and you will see that they reserve their hostilities for certain peers. A particularly destructive form of interaction is **peer victimization,** in which certain children become targets of verbal and physical attacks or other forms of abuse. What sustains these repeated assault–retreat cycles between pairs of children?

About 20 percent of children are bullies, while 25 percent are repeatedly victimized. Most bullies are boys who use physically, verbally, and relationally aggressive tactics, but a considerable number of girls have bombarded vulnerable classmates with verbal and relational hostility (Cook et al., 2010). In addition to other forms of bullying, gender harassment increases in early adolescence—powerful youths (more often boys) delivering insults of a sexual nature against weaker agemates, heterosexual youths targeting sexual minority peers (Pepler et al., 2006). As bullies move into adolescence, many amplify their attacks through electronic means (Twyman et al., 2010). About 20 to 40 percent of youths have experienced "cyberbullying" through text messages, e-mail, chat rooms, or other electronic tools (Tokunaga, 2010). They often do not report it to parents or adults at school.

Many bullies are disliked, or become so, because of their cruelty. But a substantial number are socially prominent, powerful youngsters, who are broadly admired for their physical attractiveness, leadership, or athletic abilities (Vaillancourt et al., 2010c). In an effort to preserve their high social status, bullies often target already peer-rejected children, whom classmates are unlikely to defend (Veenstra et al., 2010). This helps explain why peers rarely intervene to help victims, and why about 20 to 30 percent of onlookers encourage bullies, even joining in (Salmivalli & Voeten, 2004). Bullying occurs more often in schools where teachers are viewed as unfair and uncaring and where many students judge bullying behaviors to be "OK" (Guerra, Williams, & Sadek, 2011). Indeed, bullies, and the peers who assist them, typically display social-cognitive deficits, including overly high self-esteem, pride in their acts, and indifference to harm done to their victims (Hymel et al., 2010). In a Swedish longitudinal study, early adolescent bullies continued on their antisocial paths: Over half committed crimes (often violent ones) between ages 16 and 24 (Olweus, 2011).

Chronic victims tend to be passive when active behavior is expected. On the playground, they hang around chatting or wander on their own. When bullied, they give in, cry, and assume defensive postures (Boulton, 1999). Biologically based traits—an inhibited temperament and a frail physical appearance—contribute to victimization. But victims also have histories of resistant attachment, overly controlling child rearing, and maternal overprotection—parenting that prompts anxiety, low self-esteem, and dependency, resulting in a fearful demeanor that marks these children as vulnerable (Snyder et al., 2003). Persistent bullying, in turn, engenders social-cognitive deficits (poor perspective taking, viewing peers as generally hostile), further impairing victims' emotional self-regulation and social skills—outcomes that heighten victimization (Hoglund & Leadbeater, 2007; Rosen, Milich, & Harris, 2007). As early as kindergarten, victims display adjustment difficulties that may include depression, loneliness, poor school performance, unruly behavior, and school avoidance (Paul & Cillessen, 2003). And like persistent child abuse, victimization is linked to impaired production of cortisol, suggesting a chronically disrupted physiological response to stress (Vaillancourt et al., 2010b).

Aggression and victimization are not polar opposites. One-third to one-half of victims are also aggressive. Occasionally, they retaliate against powerful bullies, who respond by abusing them again—a cycle that sustains their victim status (Kochenderfer-Ladd, 2003). Among rejected children, these bully/victims are the most despised. They often have histories of extremely maladaptive parenting, including child abuse. This combination of highly negative home and peer experiences places them at severe risk for maladjustment (Kowalski, Limber, & Agatston, 2008; Schwartz, Proctor, & Chien, 2001).

Interventions that change victimized children's negative opinions of themselves and that teach them to respond in nonreinforcing ways to their attackers are helpful. Another way to assist victimized children is to help them acquire the social skills needed to form and maintain a gratifying friendship. When children have a close friend to whom they can turn for help, bullying episodes typically end quickly.

Many bullies are disliked, or become so, because of their cruelty, but a substantial number are prominent, powerful youngsters, whom peers admire. And chronic victims are often easy targets—physically frail, passive, and rejected by peers.

Anxious, withdrawn children with a close friend have fewer adjustment problems than those with no friends (Fox & Boulton, 2006; Laursen et al., 2007).

Although modifying victimized children's behavior can help, this does not mean that they are to blame. The best way to reduce bullying is to change youth environments (including school, sports programs, recreation centers, and neighborhoods), promoting prosocial attitudes and behaviors. Effective approaches include developing school and community codes against both "traditional" and "cyber" bullying; teaching peer bystanders to intervene and to join forces with other classmates to publicly condemn bullying; enlisting parents' assistance in changing bullies' behaviors; strengthening adult supervision of high-bullying areas in schools such as hallways, lunchroom, schoolyard; and (if necessary) moving socially prominent bullies to another class or school (Kiriakidis & Kavoura, 2010; Leadbeater & Hoglund, 2006; Vaillancourt et al., 2010a).

The U.S. Department of Health and Human Services has launched a media campaign, Stop Bullying Now, www.stopbullyingnow.hrsa.gov, which raises awareness of the harmfulness of bullying through TV and radio public service announcements. It also provides parents, teachers, and students with information on prevention.

As rejected children gain in social skills, teachers must encourage peers to alter their negative opinions. Accepted children often interpret the ambiguous behaviors of disliked agemates negatively, and they selectively recall their negative acts while overlooking their positive ones (Mikami, Lerner, & Lun, 2010; Peets et al., 2007). Consequently, even in the face of contrary evidence, rejected children's negative reputations often persist. Teachers' praise and expressions of liking can modify peer judgments. And building a positive classroom climate through whole-class meetings in which children share in creating classroom rules—including prohibiting exclusion—is also helpful.

Finally, because rejected children's socially incompetent behaviors often originate in a poor fit between the child's temperament and parenting practices, interventions focusing on the child alone may not be sufficient (Bierman & Powers, 2009). As early as the preschool years, rejected children engage in similarly inept communication with parents and with peers (Black & Logan, 1995; Guralnick et al., 2007). Without interventions directed at improving the quality of parent–child interaction, rejected children will continue to practice poor interpersonal skills at home and, as a result, may soon return to their old behavior patterns.

ASK YOURSELF

Review ■ Why are rejected children at risk for maladjustment? What experiences with peers probably contribute to their serious, long-term adjustment problems?

Connect ■ Cite parenting influences on children's social skills, and explain why interventions that focus only on the rejected child are unlikely to produce lasting changes in peer acceptance (see page 619). What changes in parent–child relationships are probably necessary?

Apply ■ Each day on the school bus and during recess, Jodee—a quiet, sensitive fifth grader—was pushed, pelted with gravel, and showered with insults by her classmates. Following the advice of her well-meaning parents, she tried to ignore her tormentors. What factors made Jodee susceptible to peer victimization? How can it be prevented?

Reflect ■ Name several classmates from your high school days who were high in *social prominence*—admired by many peers. Describe these classmates' attributes. Were they also *socially preferred*—that is, peers whom you and your friends liked personally? Explain.

Peer Groups

TAKE A MOMENT... Watch children in the schoolyard or neighborhood, and notice how they often gather in groups of three to a dozen or more. In what ways are members of the same group noticeably alike?

By the end of middle childhood, children display a strong desire for group belonging. They form **peer groups,** collectives that generate unique values and standards for behavior and a social structure of leaders and followers. Whereas friendships contribute to the development of trust, sensitivity, and intimacy, peer groups provide practice in cooperation, leadership, followership, and loyalty to collective goals. Through these experiences, children experiment with and learn about the functioning of social organizations.

First Peer Groups Peer groups organize on the basis of proximity (being in the same classroom) and similarity in sex, ethnicity, academic achievement, popularity, and aggression (Rubin, Bukowski, & Parker, 2006). When groups are tracked for three to six weeks, membership changes very little. When they are followed for a year or longer, substantial change can occur, depending on whether children are reshuffled into different classrooms. When children remain together, 50 to 70 percent of groups consist mostly of the same children from year to year (Cairns, Xie, & Leung, 1998).

The practices of these informal groups lead to a "peer culture" that typically involves a specialized vocabulary, dress code, and place to "hang out." As children develop these exclusive associations, the codes of dress and behavior that grow out of them become more broadly influential. Schoolmates who deviate—by "kissing up" to teachers, wearing the wrong kind of shoes, or tattling on classmates—are often rebuffed, becoming targets of critical glances and comments. These customs bind peers together, creating a sense of group identity.

School-age children evaluate a group's decision to exclude a peer in complex ways. Most view exclusion as wrong, even when they see themselves as different from the excluded child. And with age, children are less likely to endorse excluding someone because of unconventional appearance or behavior. Girls, especially, regard exclusion as unjust, perhaps because they experience it more often than boys (Killen, Crystal, & Watanabe, 2002). But when a peer threatens group functioning, by acting disruptively or by lacking skills to participate in a valued group activity (such as sports), both boys and girls say that exclusion is justified—a perspective that strengthens with age (Killen & Stangor, 2001).

Despite these sophisticated understandings, as we have seen in this and previous chapters, children do exclude unjustly, often using relationally aggressive tactics. Peer groups—at the instigation of socially prominent leaders, who show off their power through skillfully aggressive acts—frequently oust no-longer-"respected" children. Some of these cast-outs, whose own previous hostility toward outsiders reduces their chances of being included elsewhere, turn to other low-status peers with poor social skills (Farmer et al., 2010; Werner & Crick, 2004). Socially anxious children, when ousted, often become increasingly peer-avoidant and thus more isolated (Gazelle & Rudolph, 2004). In either case, opportunities to acquire socially competent behavior diminish.

As excluded children's class participation declines, their academic achievement suffers (Buhs, Ladd, & Herald, 2006). And some aggressive children—especially popular boys—link up with popular, nonaggressive agemates (Bagwell et al., 2000; Farmer et al., 2002). In these groups, mild-mannered children may accept and even support the antisocial acts of their dominant, antisocial associates, who pick fights with other groups or bully weaker children. Consequently, teachers and counselors must target both antisocial and mixed peer groups to reduce peer aggression.

School-age children's desire for group belonging also can be satisfied through formal group ties such as scouting, 4-H, and religious youth groups, where adult involvement holds in check the negative behaviors associated with children's informal peer groups. And through working on joint projects and helping in their communities, children gain in social and moral maturity (Vandell & Shumow, 1999).

Peer groups first form in middle childhood. These boys' relaxed body language and similar way of dressing suggest a strong sense of group belonging.

Cliques and Crowds In early adolescence, peer groups become increasingly common and more tightly structured. They are organized into **cliques,** groups of about five to eight members who are friends and, therefore, usually resemble one another in family background, attitudes, values, and interests (Brown & Dietz, 2009). At first, cliques are limited to same-sex members. Among girls but not boys, being in a clique predicts academic and social competence. Clique membership is more important to girls, who use it as a context for expressing emotional closeness (Henrich et al., 2000). By mid-adolescence, mixed-sex cliques become common.

Among Western adolescents attending high schools with complex social structures, often several cliques with similar values form a larger, more loosely organized group called a **crowd.** Unlike the more intimate clique, membership in a crowd is based on reputation and stereotype, granting the adolescent an identity within the larger social structure of the school. Crowds in a typical high school might include "brains" (nonathletes who enjoy academics), "jocks" (who are very involved in sports), "populars" (class leaders who are highly social and involved in activities), "partyers" (who value socializing but care little about schoolwork), "nonconformists" (who like unconventional clothing and music), "burnouts" (who cut school and get into trouble), and "normals" (average to good students who get along with most other peers) (Kinney, 1999; Stone & Brown, 1999).

These high school drama club members form a crowd, establishing relationships on the basis of shared interests and abilities. Crowd membership grants them an identity within the larger social structure of the school.

What influences the sorting of teenagers into cliques and crowds? Crowd affiliations are linked to strengths in adolescents' self-concepts, which reflect their abilities and interests (Prinstein & La Greca, 2004). Ethnicity also plays a role. Minority teenagers who associate with an ethnically defined crowd, as opposed to a crowd reflecting their abilities and interests, may be motivated by discrimination in their school or neighborhood. Alternatively, they may have joined the crowd as an expression of a strong ethnic identity (Brown et al., 2008). Family factors are important, too. In a study of 8,000 ninth to twelfth graders, adolescents who described their parents as authoritative tended to be members of "brain," "jock," and "popular" groups that accepted both adult and peer reward systems. In contrast, boys with permissive parents aligned themselves with "partyers" and "burnouts," suggesting lack of identification with adult reward systems (Durbin et al., 1993).

These findings indicate that many peer-group values are extensions of values acquired at home. Once adolescents join a clique or crowd, it can modify their beliefs and behaviors. In research on crowd affiliation and health-risk behaviors, brains were the lowest risk takers, populars and jocks were intermediate, and nonconformists and burnouts were the highest, often engaging in unhealthy eating, substance use, and unprotected sex and agreeing that they would "do anything on a dare" (La Greca, Prinstein, & Fetter, 2001; Mackey & La Greca, 2007). But the positive impact of having academically and socially skilled peers is greatest for teenagers whose own parents are authoritative. And the negative impact of associating with antisocial, drug-using agemates is strongest for teenagers whose parents use less effective child-rearing styles (Mounts & Steinberg, 1995). In sum, family experiences affect the extent to which adolescents become like other group members over time.

As interest in dating increases, boys' and girls' cliques come together. Mixed-sex cliques provide boys and girls with models for how to interact with the other sex and a chance to do so without having to be intimate (Connolly et al., 2004). Gradually, the larger group divides into couples, several of whom spend time going out together. By late adolescence, when boys and girls feel comfortable enough about approaching each other directly, the mixed-sex clique disappears (Connolly & Goldberg, 1999).

Crowds also decline in importance. As adolescents settle on personal values and goals, they no longer feel a need to broadcast, through dress, language, and preferred activities, who they are. From tenth to twelfth grade, about half of young people switch crowds, mostly in favorable directions (Strouse, 1999). "Brains" and "normal" crowds grow and deviant crowds lose members as teenagers focus more on their future.

Dating

The hormonal changes of puberty increase sexual interest (see Chapter 5), but cultural expectations determine when and how dating begins. Asian youths start dating later and have fewer dating partners than young people in Western societies, which tolerate and even encourage early romantic involvements from middle school on (see Figure 15.3). At age 12 to 14, these relationships are usually casual, lasting only five months on average. By age 16, they have become steady relationships, typically continuing for about two years (Carver, Joyner, & Udry, 2003). This change reflects transformations in teenagers' dating goals: Early adolescents tend to mention recreation and achieving peer status as reasons for dating. By late adolescence, as young people are ready for greater intimacy, they seek dating partners who offer personal compatibility, companionship, affection, and social support (Collins & Van Dulmen, 2006a; Meier & Allen, 2009).

The achievement of intimacy between dating partners typically lags behind that between friends. And positive relationships with parents and friends contribute to the development of warm romantic ties, whereas conflict-ridden parent–adolescent and peer relationships forecast hostile dating interactions (Furman & Collins, 2009; Linder & Collins,

FIGURE 15.3 Increase in romantic relationships during adolescence. More than 16,000 U.S. youths responded to an interview in which they indicated whether they had been involved in a romantic relationship during the past 18 months. At age 12, about one-fourth of young people reported romantic involvement, a figure that rose to about three-fourths at age 18. (Adapted from Carver, Joyner, & Udry, 2003.)

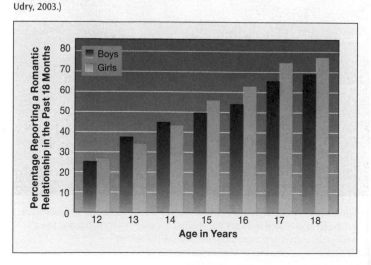

2005). Recall from Chapter 10 that according to ethological theory, early attachment bonds lead to an *internal working model,* or set of expectations about attachment figures, that guides later close relationships. Consistent with this idea, secure attachment to parents in infancy and childhood— together with recollections of that security in adolescence—predicts quality of teenagers' and young adults' friendships and romantic ties (Collins & Van Dulmen, 2006b; Collins, Welsh, & Furman, 2009). In a study of high school seniors, secure models of attachment and supportive interactions with parents predicted secure models of friendship, which, in turn, were related to the security of romantic relationships (Furman et al., 2002).

Perhaps because early adolescent dating relationships are shallow and stereotyped, early, frequent dating is related to drug use, delinquency, and poor academic achievement (Eaton et al., 2007; Miller et al., 2009). These factors, along with a history of uninvolved parenting and aggression in family and peer relationships, increase the likelihood of dating violence. About 10 to 20 percent of adolescents are physically or sexually abused by dating partners, with boys and girls equally likely to report being victims, and violence by one partner is often returned by the other (Cyr, McDuff, & Wright, 2006; Williams et al., 2008). Mental health consequences are severe, including increased anxiety, depression, suicide attempts, risky sexual behavior, and—in girls—unhealthy weight control (vomiting and use of laxatives) (Carver, Joyner, & Udry, 2003; Silverman et al., 2001; Wekerle & Avgoustis, 2003). Furthermore, whereas early-adolescent boys who date gain in status among same-sex peers, girls often experience conflict due to competition and jealousy of other girls. For all these reasons, sticking with group activities, such as parties and dances, before becoming involved with a steady boyfriend or girlfriend is best for young teenagers.

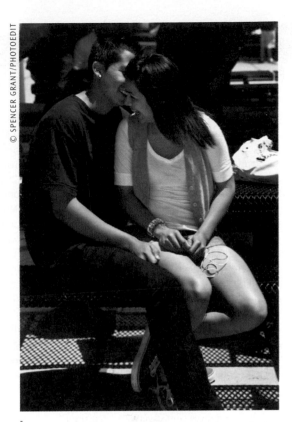

As long as dating does not begin too soon, it extends the benefits of adolescent friendships, promoting sensitivity, empathy, self-esteem, and identity development.

Gay and lesbian youths face special challenges in initiating and maintaining visible romances. Their first dating relationships seem to be short-lived and to involve little emotional commitment, but for reasons that differ from those of heterosexuals: They fear peer harassment and rejection (Diamond & Lucas, 2004). Recall from Chapter 5 that because of intense prejudice, homosexual adolescents often retreat into heterosexual dating. In addition, many have difficulty finding a same-sex partner because their gay and lesbian peers have not yet come out. Often their first contacts with other sexual-minority youths occur in support groups, where they are free to date publicly and can discuss concerns about coming out (Diamond, 2003).

As long as it does not begin too soon, dating provides lessons in cooperation, etiquette, and dealing with people in a wide range of situations. Among older teenagers, close romantic ties promote sensitivity, empathy, self-esteem, social support, and identity development. In addition, teenagers' increasing capacity for interdependence and compromise within dating probably enhances the quality of other peer relationships (Collins, Welsh, & Furman, 2009).

Still, about half of first heterosexual romances do not survive graduation, and those that do usually become less satisfying (Shaver, Furman, & Buhrmester, 1985). Because young people are still forming their identities, high school couples often find that they have little in common later. Nevertheless, warm, caring romantic ties in adolescence can have long-term implications. They are positively related to gratifying, committed relationships in early adulthood (Meier & Allen, 2009).

Peer Pressure and Conformity

Conformity to peer pressure is greater during adolescence than in childhood or early adulthood—a finding that is not surprising when we consider how much time teenagers spend together. But contrary to popular belief, adolescence is not a period in which young people blindly do what their peers ask. Peer conformity is a complex process that varies with the adolescent's age, current situation, need for social approval, and culture.

SOCIAL ISSUES: HEALTH

Adolescent Substance Use and Abuse

Teenage alcohol and drug use is pervasive in industrialized nations. According to the most recent nationally representative survey of U.S. high school students, by tenth grade, 33 percent of U.S. young people have tried smoking, 59 percent drinking, and 38 percent at least one illegal drug (usually marijuana). At the end of high school, 15 percent smoke cigarettes regularly and 16 percent have engaged in heavy drinking during the past month. About 24 percent have tried at least one highly addictive and toxic substance, such as amphetamines, cocaine, phencyclidine (PCP), Ecstasy (MDMA), inhalants, heroin, sedatives (including barbiturates), or OxyContin (a narcotic painkiller) (Johnston et al., 2010).

These figures represent a substantial decline since the mid-1990s, probably resulting from greater societal focus on the hazards of drug taking. But use of some substances—marijuana, inhalants, sedatives, and OxyContin—has risen slightly in recent years (Johnston et al., 2010). Other drugs, such as LSD, PCP, and Ecstasy, have made a comeback as adolescents' knowledge of their risks faded.

In part, drug taking reflects the sensation seeking of the teenage years. But adolescents also live in drug-dependent cultural contexts. They see adults relying on caffeine to stay alert, alcohol and cigarettes to cope with daily hassles, and other remedies to relieve stress, depression, and physical discomfort. And compared to a decade or two ago, today doctors more often prescribe—and parents frequently seek—medication to treat children's problems (Olfman & Robbins, 2012). In adolescence, these young people may readily "self-medicate" when stressed.

Most teenagers who dabble in alcohol, tobacco, and marijuana are not headed for a life of addiction. These *minimal experimenters* are usually psychologically healthy, sociable, curious young people (Shedler & Block, 1990). As Figure 15.4 shows, tobacco and alcohol use is somewhat greater among European than among U.S. adolescents, perhaps because European adults more often smoke and drink. But illegal drug use is far more prevalent among U.S. teenagers. A greater percentage of American young people live in poverty, which is linked to family and peer contexts that promote illegal drug use. At the same time, use of diverse drugs is lower among African Americans than among Hispanic and Caucasian Americans; Native-American youths rank highest in drug taking (Johnston et al., 2010; Wallace et al., 2003). Researchers have yet to explain these variations.

Adolescent experimentation with any drug should not be taken lightly. Because most drugs impair perception and thought processes, a single heavy dose can lead to permanent injury or death. And a worrisome minority of teenagers move from substance *use* to *abuse*—taking drugs regularly, requiring increasing amounts to achieve the same effect, moving to harder substances, and using enough to impair their ability to meet school, work, or other responsibilities. Three percent of high school seniors are daily drinkers, and 5 percent have taken illegal drugs on a daily basis over the past month (Johnston et al., 2010).

Correlates and Consequences of Adolescent Substance Abuse

Unlike experimenters, drug abusers are seriously troubled young people. Longitudinal evidence reveals that their impulsive, disruptive, hostile

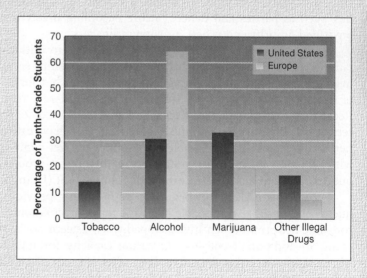

FIGURE 15.4 Tenth-grade students in the United States and Europe who have used various substances. Rates for tobacco and alcohol are based on any use in the past 30 days. Rates for marijuana and other illegal drugs are based on any lifetime use. Tobacco use and alcohol use are greater for European adolescents, whereas illegal drug use is greater for U.S. adolescents. (Adapted from CAN, 2007; Johnston et al., 2010.)

A study of several hundred U.S. middle and high school students revealed that adolescents felt greatest pressure to conform to the most obvious aspects of the peer culture—dress, grooming, and participation in social activities. Peer pressure to engage in proadult behavior, such as cooperating with parents and getting good grades, was also strong (Brown, Lohr, & McClenahan, 1986). Many teenagers said that their friends actively discouraged antisocial acts. In similar research conducted in Singapore, a culture that emphasizes family loyalty, outcomes were much the same, except that peer pressure to meet family and school obligations exceeded pressure to join in peer-culture pursuits (Sim & Koh, 2003). As these findings reveal, adults and peers often act in concert, toward desirable ends!

Resistance to peer pressure strengthens with age, though wide individual differences exist (Steinberg & Monahan, 2007; Sumter et al., 2009). Personal characteristics make a difference: Young people who feel competent and worthwhile, who score low in sensation seeking and in need for peer approval, and who are more effective decision makers are less likely style is often evident in early childhood, and they engage in other high-risk behaviors and are inclined to express their unhappiness through antisocial acts. Compared with other young people, their drug taking starts earlier and may have genetic roots (Dick, Prescott, & McGue, 2008; Tarter, Vanyukov, & Kirisci, 2008). But environmental factors also contribute. These include low SES, family mental health problems, parental and older sibling drug and alcohol abuse, lack of parental warmth and involvement, physical and sexual abuse, and poor school performance. Especially among teenagers with family difficulties, encouragement from friends who use and provide drugs increases substance abuse (Goldstein, Davis-Kean, & Eccles, 2005; Ohannessian & Hesselbrock, 2008; Prinstein, Boergers, & Spirito, 2001).

Teenagers who depend on alcohol and hard drugs to deal with daily stresses fail to learn responsible decision-making skills and alternative coping techniques. They show serious adjustment problems, including chronic anxiety, depression, and antisocial behavior, that are both cause and consequence of heavy drug taking (Kassel et al., 2005; Simons-Morton & Haynie, 2003). And they often enter into marriage, childbearing, and the work world prematurely and fail at these challenges—painful outcomes that further promote addictive behavior.

Prevention and Treatment

School and community programs that reduce drug experimentation typically combine several features:

- They promote effective parenting, including monitoring of teenagers' activities.
- They teach skills for resisting peer pressure.

- They reduce the social acceptability of drug taking by emphasizing health and safety risks (Cuijpers, 2002; Stephens et al., 2009).

But given that adolescent drug taking is widespread, interventions that prevent teenagers from harming themselves and others when they do experiment are essential. Many communities offer weekend on-call transportation services that any young person can contact for a safe ride home, with no questions asked. Providing appealing substitute activities, such as drug-free dances and sports activities, is also helpful.

Because drug abuse has different roots than occasional use, different prevention strategies are required. One approach is to work with parents early, reducing family adversity and improving parenting skills, before children are old enough for drug involvement (Velleman, Templeton, & Copello, 2005). Programs that teach at-risk teenagers effective strategies for handling life stressors and that build competence through community service reduce alcohol and drug abuse, just as they reduce teenage pregnancy (see Chapter 5).

When an adolescent becomes a drug abuser, family and individual therapy are generally needed to treat maladaptive parent–child

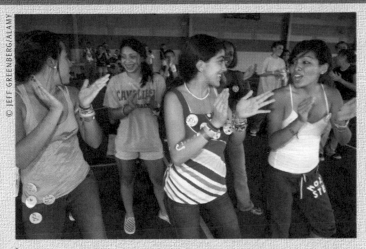

Teenagers enjoy a party sponsored by Drug Free Youth in Town (DFYIT), a substance abuse prevention program. DFYIT trains high school students as peer educators, who teach middle school students strategies for resisting peer pressure.

relationships, impulsivity, low-self-esteem, anxiety, and depression. Academic and vocational training to improve life success also helps. But even comprehensive programs have alarmingly high relapse rates—from 35 to 85 percent (Brown & Ramo, 2005; Sussman, Skara, & Ames, 2008). One recommendation is to start treatment gradually, through support-group sessions that focus on reducing drug taking. Within the group, interveners can address teenagers' low motivation to change and resistance to adult referral, which they often view as an infringement on their personal freedom. Such brief interventions lessen drug taking in the short term (Myers et al., 2001). Modest improvement may boost the young person's sense of self-efficacy for behavior change and, as a result, increase motivation to make longer-lasting changes through intensive treatment.

to fall in line with peers who engage in early sex, delinquency, and frequent drug use (Crockett, Raffaelli, & Shen, 2006; McIntyre & Platania, 2009) (see the Social Issues: Health box above).

Authoritative parenting is also influential. When parents are supportive and exert appropriate oversight, teenagers respect them—an attitude that acts as an antidote to unfavorable peer pressure (Dorius et al., 2004). In contrast, adolescents whose parents exert either too much or too little control tend to be highly peer-oriented. Youths who bend easily to peer influence display wide-ranging problems, including unstable friendships, aggression, delinquency, and declining peer popularity and increasing depressive symptoms over time (Allen, Porter, & McFarland, 2006).

Before we turn to the impact of media on children and adolescents, you may find it helpful to examine the Milestones table on page 628, which summarizes the development of peer relations.

Milestones

Development of Peer Relations

AGE	PEER SOCIABILITY	FRIENDSHIP	PEER GROUPS
Birth–2 years	• Isolated social acts increase and are gradually replaced by coordinated interaction.	• Mutual relationships with familiar peers emerge.	
2½–6 years	• Parallel play appears, remains stable, and becomes more cognitively mature. • Cooperative play, especially sociodramatic play, increases. • Rough-and-tumble play emerges.	• Friendship is viewed concretely, in terms of play and sharing toys.	
7–11 years	• Peer communication skills improve as a result of improved perspective taking and awareness of emotional display rules. • Ability to understand the complementary roles of several players improves, permitting the transition to rule-oriented games. • Peer interaction becomes more prosocial. • Rough-and-tumble play increases.	• Friendship is based on mutual trust and assistance. • Interaction between friends becomes more prosocial. • Number of close friends declines. • Friends increasingly resemble one another in personality, popularity, academic achievement, prosocial behavior, and judgments of other people.	• Peer groups emerge. • Dominance hierarchies become increasingly stable.
12–18 years	• Peer interaction becomes more cooperative. • Rough-and-tumble play declines. • Time spent with peers increases, exceeding that with any other social partners.	• Friendship is based on intimacy, mutual understanding, and loyalty. • Friends tend to be alike in identity status, educational aspirations, political beliefs, and deviant behavior. • Young people choose some friends who differ from themselves. • Number of close friends declines further. • Romantic relationships emerge and gradually last longer.	• Peer groups become more tightly structured, organized around cliques. • Cliques with similar values form crowds. • As interest in dating increases, mixed-sex cliques form. • Mixed-sex cliques and crowds gradually diminish. • Resistance to peer pressure gradually strengthens.

Note: These milestones represent overall age trends. Individual differences exist in the precise age at which each milestone is attained.

Photos: (left) © Brand X Pictures/Getty Images; (middle) © Stock Connection Distribution/Alamy; (top right) © Laura Dwight Photography; (bottom right) © Ellen B. Senisi/The Image Works

A S K   Y O U R S E L F

Review ■ Describe the distinct positive functions of friendships, cliques, and crowds. What factors lead some friendships and peer-group ties to be harmful?

Connect ■ How might gender intensification, discussed on page 550 in Chapter 13, contribute to the shallow quality of early adolescent dating relationships?

Apply ■ Thirteen-year-old Mattie's parents are warm, firm in their expectations, and consistent in monitoring her activities. Is Mattie likely to succumb to unfavorable peer pressure? Explain.

Reflect ■ How did family experiences influence your crowd membership in high school? How did your crowd membership influence your behavior?

Media

During the past half-century, the role of media in the lives of children and adolescents has undergone "revolutionary change" (Comstock & Scharrer, 2006). Although television remains the dominant form of youth media, computers now exist in most American homes and in virtually all school classrooms (Rideout, Foehr, & Roberts 2010). Among older school-age children and adolescents, time consumed by cell-phone use may eventually catch up with TV: The cell phone has become the favored channel of communication between teenagers and their friends, and young people also use it for diverse entertainment purposes, including listening to music, playing games, and accessing TV programs.

Today, U.S. 8- to 18-year-olds devote an average of 7½ hours a day (a dramatic 53 hours a week) to entertainment media of all kinds. And because many youths engage in extensive media multitasking (see page 293 in Chapter 7), they actually pack in a total of 10¾ hours of daily media content. Overall media use rises from middle childhood into early adolescence, largely due to increased TV watching and time spent listening to music on cell phones or MP3 players (see Figure 15.5). Heavy users of one medium tend to be heavy users of others (Rideout, Foehr, & Roberts, 2010). A burgeoning research literature addresses the wide-ranging impact of media on development.

Television

Exposure to television is almost universal in the industrialized world. Nearly all homes have at least one television set, and most have two or more. Average time spent watching is remarkably similar across developed nations, and young people in the developing world are not far behind (International Telecommunications Union, 2010; Scharrer & Comstock, 2003).

Widespread concern about television's impact on children's development is certainly warranted. In an unusual investigation, residents of a small Canadian town were studied just before TV reception became available in their community and again two years later. Striking changes occurred: in school-age children, a decline in reading ability and creative thinking, a rise in gender-stereotyped beliefs, and an increase in verbal and physical aggression during play; in adolescents, a sharp drop in community participation (Williams, 1986).

But television has equal potential for good. If the content of TV programming were improved and adults capitalized on it to enhance children's interest in their everyday worlds, television could be a powerful, cost-effective means of strengthening cognitive, emotional, and social development.

How Much Television Do Children View? Large surveys reveal that American children first become viewers in early infancy. About 40 percent of U.S. 3-month-olds regularly watch either TV or videos. This figure rises to 90 percent by age 2—a period in which toddlers have difficulty applying what they see on the screen to their everyday experiences (return to page 237 in Chapter 6 to review the *video deficit effect*). Between 2 and 6 years, the typical U.S. preschooler watches from 1½ to 2⅔ hours a day, depending on the survey (Rideout & Hamel, 2006; Scharrer & Comstock, 2003; Zimmerman, Christakis, & Meltzoff, 2007). Viewing time increases to an average of 3½ hours a day in middle childhood. In early adolescence, it rises further to more than 5 hours a day, as teenagers increasingly acquire MP3 players and cell phones with Internet connections that enable easy access to TV programs (Rideout, Foehr, & Roberts, 2010). In mid- to late adolescence, time devoted to TV diminishes to 3 to 4 hours a day.

▶ Discuss the influence of television on children's development.

▶ Discuss computer, cell phone, and Internet use by children and adolescents, noting benefits and concerns.

FIGURE 15.5 Time spent by U.S. 8- to 10-year-olds with various media by age. A survey of a large, nationally representative sample of U.S. young people revealed that watching TV and listening to music largely accounted for the overall rise in media use from middle childhood into early adolescence. Print media (magazines and newspapers) consumed the least media time. (From "Generation M2: Media in the Lives of 8- to 18-Year-Olds," (#8010), The Henry J. Kaiser Family Foundation, January 2010. This information was reprinted with permission from the Henry J. Kaiser Family Foundation, www.kff.org.)

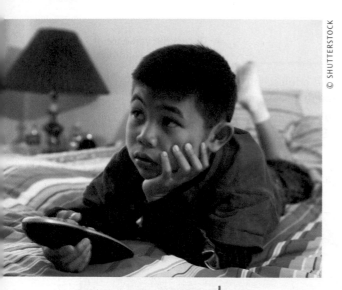

© SHUTTERSTOCK

A television placed in a child's bedroom greatly magnifies time spent watching TV. Extensive TV viewing is linked to family, peer, and health difficulties.

These figures reveal that each week, U.S. preschoolers spend about 10 to 18 hours, school-age children about 24 hours, and adolescents about 32 hours watching TV. When we consider these figures, children and adolescents devote more time to TV than to most other waking activities, including parent and peer interaction, physical activity, computer use, homework, and reading. And when quantity of viewing during school holidays and summer vacations is factored in, the typical child's annual TV viewing comes close to, and the adolescent's exceeds, amount of time spent in school.

Children vary in their attraction to television. From early childhood on, boys watch slightly more than girls. Low-SES, African-American, and Hispanic children also are more frequent viewers, and they are more likely to live in homes where the TV is left on most of the time, even if no one is watching (Rideout, Foehr, & Roberts, 2010). For many such families, perhaps few alternative, affordable forms of entertainment are available in their neighborhoods. Also, parents with limited education are more likely to engage in practices that heighten TV viewing, including eating family meals in front of the set and failing to limit children's TV access (Hesketh et al., 2007).

About one-third of U.S. preschoolers and 70 percent of school-age children and adolescents have a TV set in their bedroom; these children spend from 40 to 90 more minutes per day watching than agemates without one. And if parents watch a lot of TV, their children usually do, too (Rideout & Hamel, 2006; Rideout, Foehr, & Roberts, 2010). Extensive TV viewing is associated with family, peer, and health difficulties, perhaps because highly stressed parents and children use it as an escape (Anderson et al., 1996).

Television and Social Learning   Since the 1950s, researchers and public citizens have been concerned about television's influence on the attitudes and behaviors of young viewers. Most studies address the impact of TV violence. Others focus on the power of TV to teach undesirable gender and ethnic stereotypes and consumerism. At the same time, research confirms TV's potential for enhancing children's prosocial behavior.

Aggression.   In the United States, 57 percent of TV programs between 6 A.M. and 11 P.M. contain violent scenes, often portraying repeated physically aggressive acts that go unpunished. Victims of TV violence are rarely shown experiencing serious harm, and few programs condemn violence or depict other ways of solving problems (Center for Communication and Social Policy, 1998). In reality TV shows, verbally and relationally aggressive acts are particularly frequent (Coyne, Robinson, & Nelson, 2010). And violent content is 9 percent above average in children's programming, with cartoons being the most violent.

Reviewers of thousands of studies—using a wide variety of research designs, methods, and participants from diverse cultures—have concluded that TV violence increases the likelihood of hostile thoughts and emotions and of verbally, physically, and relationally aggressive behavior (Comstock & Scharrer, 2006; Ostrov, Gentile, & Crick, 2006). Even a brief dose has immediate effects: In laboratory research, 15 minutes of mildly violent programming heightened aggression in at least one-fourth of viewers (Anderson & Bushman, 2002). Although young people of all ages are susceptible, preschool and young school-age children are especially likely to imitate TV violence because they believe that much TV fiction is real and accept what they see uncritically.

Violent programming not only creates short-term difficulties in parent and peer relations but also has lasting negative consequences. In several longitudinal studies, time spent watching TV in childhood and early adolescence predicted aggressive behavior (including seriously violent acts) in late adolescence and early adulthood, after other factors linked to TV viewing (such as prior child and parent aggression, IQ, parent education, family income, and neighborhood crime) were controlled (see Figure 15.6) (Graber et al., 2006; Huesmann, 1986; Huesmann et al., 2003; Johnson et al., 2002). Aggressive children and adolescents have a greater appetite for TV and other media violence. And boys devote more time to violent media than girls, in part because of male-oriented themes of conquest and adventure and use of males as lead characters. Even in nonaggressive children, violent TV sparks hostile

LOOK and LISTEN

Watch a half-hour of Saturday morning cartoons and a prime-time movie on TV, and tally the number of violent acts, including those that go unpunished. How often did violence occur in each type of program? What do young viewers learn about the consequences of violence?

thoughts and behavior; its impact is simply less intense (Bushman & Huesmann, 2001).

Furthermore, television violence "hardens" children to aggression, making them more willing to tolerate it in others (Anderson et al., 2003). Heavy viewers believe that there is much more violence in society than there actually is—an effect that is especially strong for children who perceive televised aggression to be relevant to their own lives (Donnerstein, Slaby, & Eron, 1994). As these responses indicate, exposure to violent TV modifies children's attitudes toward social reality so that they increasingly match TV images.

Ethnic and Gender Stereotypes. Although educational programming for children is sensitive to issues of equity and diversity, commercial entertainment TV conveys ethnic and gender stereotypes. African Americans, Hispanics, and other ethnic minorities are underrepresented. When minorities do appear, they are more likely than whites to be depicted in secondary or lower-status roles, such as domestic workers or unskilled laborers, and as lawbreakers (Dixon & Azocar, 2006; Scharrer & Comstock, 2003).

Similarly, women appear less often than men, especially as main characters. Compared with two decades ago, today's female characters are more often involved in careers. But they continue to be portrayed as young, attractive, caring, emotional, victimized, and in subordinate family and nonprofessional roles. Furthermore, women are often sexualized, shown in scanty or provocative clothing (Collins, 2011; Signorielli, 2001). In contrast, men are depicted as dominant and powerful. Gender stereotypes are especially prevalent in cartoons, music television (MTV), and other entertainment programs for children and youths.

TV viewing is linked to gender-stereotyped attitudes and behaviors in children and adolescents, including reduced self-esteem and career aspirations, negative body image, and disordered eating in girls (American Psychological Association, 2010; Cole & Daniel, 2005; Rivadeneyra & Ward, 2005). In contrast, positive TV portrayals of women and ethnic minorities lead to more favorable views and greater willingness to form ethnically diverse friendships (Calvert et al., 2003; Graves, 1993).

Consumerism. The marketing industry aimed at selling products to youths—toys, games, foods, clothing, and a host of other items—has exploded, exposing U.S. children and adolescents to tens of thousands of TV commercials each year (American Academy of Pediatrics, 2009). TV ads are rife with gender stereotypes—depicting toys and other products as gender-specific, boys as active and competitive, girls as calm and quiet, and men and women in stereotypical roles (Kahlenberg & Hein, 2010; Paek, Nelson, & Vilela, 2010).

By age 3, children can distinguish an obvious TV ad from regular programming by its loudness, fast-paced action, and sound effects. But because many children's shows contain characters and props that are themselves products (dolls, puppets, action figures, and their accessories), the boundary between programs and commercials is blurred. Furthermore, preschoolers and young elementary school children seldom grasp the selling purpose of TV ads; they think that commercials are meant to help viewers. Around age 8 or 9, most children understand that commercials aim to sell, and by age 11, they realize that advertisers will resort to clever techniques to achieve their goals (Kunkel, 2001). Nevertheless, even older children and adolescents find many commercials alluring. And parents often underestimate the influence of TV advertising on their children (Baiocco, D'Alessio, & Laghi, 2009).

Research suggests that heavy bombardment of children with advertising contributes to a variety of child and youth problems, including family stress, overweight and obesity, materialism, and substance use. In recent surveys of adults that included many parents, over 90 percent reported that youth-directed ads greatly increase children's nagging of parents to buy items, giving rise to family conflict (Linn, 2005). Furthermore, the greater adolescents' exposure to cigarette and alcohol ads—often designed to appeal to them through youthful characters, upbeat music, and party scenes—the more likely they are to smoke and drink (Austin, Chen, & Grube, 2006; Smith & Atkin, 2003).

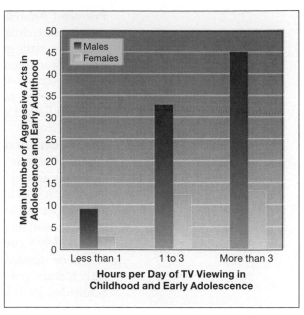

FIGURE 15.6 **Relationship of television viewing in childhood and early adolescence to aggressive acts in adolescence and early adulthood.** Interviews with more than 700 parents and youths revealed that the more TV watched in childhood and early adolescence, the greater the annual number of aggressive acts committed by the young person, as reported in follow-up interviews at ages 16 and 22. (Adapted from Johnson et al., 2002.)

Prosocial Behavior. Television that includes acts of cooperating, helping, and comforting can increase children's prosocial behavior. In one study, researchers asked more than 500 second to sixth graders to name their favorite educational TV shows and say what they learned from them. The children not only named many prosocial programs but also accurately described the lessons the programs conveyed (Calvert & Kotler, 2003). Much TV, however, mixes prosocial and antisocial messages. Prosocial programs promote children's kind and helpful acts only when they are free of violent content (Hearold, 1986).

Television, Academic Learning, and Imagination

Since the early days of television, educators have been interested in its potential for strengthening academic skills, especially among low-SES children. *Sesame Street,* especially, was created to foster children's learning. It uses lively visual and sound effects to stress basic literacy and number concepts and puppet and human characters to teach general knowledge, emotional and social understanding, and social skills. Today, *Sesame Street* is broadcast in 140 countries, making it the most widely viewed children's program in the world (Sesame Workshop, 2009).

Time devoted to watching children's educational programs is associated with gains in early literacy and math skills and to academic progress in elementary school (Ennemoser & Schneider, 2007; Linebarger et al., 2004; Wright et al., 2001). Consistent with these findings, one study reported a link between preschool viewing of *Sesame Street* and other similar educational programs and getting higher grades, reading more books, and placing more value on achievement in high school (Anderson et al., 2001).

Sesame Street has modified its previous format of presenting quick, disconnected bits of information in favor of more leisurely episodes with a clear story line (Truglio, 2000). Children's programs with slow-paced action and easy-to-follow narratives, such as *Arthur & Friends, The Magic School Bus,* and *Wishbone,* lead to more elaborate make-believe play in early childhood and to greater recall of program content and gains in vocabulary and reading skills in the early elementary school grades than programs that simply provide information (Linebarger & Piotrowski, 2010; Singer & Singer, 2005). Narratively structured educational TV eases processing demands, freeing up children's working-memory resources for applying program content to real-life situations.

Does extensive TV exposure take children away from worthwhile activities? Persistent background TV distracts infants and preschoolers from their play, diminishing time spent in focused attention and involvement with a set of toys (Courage & Howe, 2010; Schmidt et al., 2008). Educational programs, as previously noted, are beneficial, but watching entertainment TV—especially heavy viewing—detracts from children's and adolescents' reading time, school success, and social experiences (Ennemoser & Schneider, 2007; Huston et al., 1999; Wright et al., 2001). In a survey of U.S. parents of over 48,000 6- to 17-year-olds, children and adolescents with a TV in their bedroom (a sign of especially high viewing time) were less likely to experience regular family meals, care about doing well in school, participate in extracurricular activities and community service, and get enough nightly sleep (Sisson et al., 2011). They also more often displayed problematic social behaviors, including frequent arguing, disobedience, meanness to others, and sullenness or irritability.

Computers, Cell Phones, and the Internet

Unlike TV, computers and cell phones offer *interactive* media forms, through a wide range of learning, entertainment, and communication tools (Greenfield & Yan, 2007). More than 90 percent of U.S. children and adolescents live in homes with one or more computers, 80 percent of which have an Internet connection, usually a high-speed link. And virtually all U.S. public schools have integrated computers into their instructional programs and can access the Internet—trends also evident in other industrialized nations. Although higher-SES homes are more likely to have computers, over 85 percent of U.S. lower-SES families with school-age children and adolescents now have them, often with Internet access (Rideout, Foehr, & Roberts, 2010; U.S. Census Bureau, 2011b). Still, only a minority of poverty-stricken families have a home computer.

Recent survey evidence reveals that U.S. children and adolescents, on average, use the computer a half-hour a day for schoolwork and 1½ hours for pleasure—visiting social networking sites, surfing the Web, communicating by instant-messaging or e-mail, and accessing music and video games. Computer time increases with age (Rideout, Foehr, & Roberts, 2010; Roberts, Foehr, & Rideout, 2005). Most parents say they purchased a computer to enrich their child's education; more than one-third of American school-age children and adolescents have a computer in their bedroom. At the same time, parents express great concern about the influence of violent video games and of the Internet (Media Awareness Network, 2001; Rideout & Hamel, 2006).

Yet, regardless of the extent of their Internet use, not until ages 10 to 11 do children acquire an adult-level understanding of the technical complexity of the Internet as a networklike system linking a computing center with many computers (see Figure 15.7). This technical grasp is important, as it precedes and probably contributes to sophisticated knowledge of social risks of the Internet (exposure to pornography, theft of personal information, attacks by hackers) and of protection strategies (firewalls, filtering programs, password protection), which is attained around age 12 to 13 (Yan, 2006). Let's see how computers affect academic and social development.

Computers and Academic Learning Computers can have rich educational benefits. Children as young as age 3 enjoy computer activities and are able to use the mouse and type simple keyboard commands. In classrooms, small groups often gather around computers, and children more often collaborate in computer activities than in other pursuits (Svensson, 2000).

In childhood and adolescence, nongame computer use is associated with literacy progress (Calvert et al., 2005; OECD, 2005). Using the computer for word processing enables children to write freely, experimenting with letters and words without having to struggle with handwriting. Because they can revise their text's meaning and style and also check their spelling, they worry less about making mistakes. As a result, their written products tend to be longer and of higher quality. Often children jointly plan, compose, and revise text, learning from one another (Clements & Sarama, 2003).

As children get older, they increasingly use the computer for schoolwork, mostly to search the Web for information needed for school projects and to prepare written assignments—activities linked to improved academic achievement (Attewell, 2001; Judge, Puckett, & Bell, 2006). The more low-SES middle-school students use home computers to access the Internet for information gathering (either for school or for personal interests), the better their subsequent reading achievement and school grades (Jackson et al., 2006, 2011a). Perhaps those who use the Web to find information also devote more time to reading, given that many Web pages are heavily text-based.

The learning advantages of computers raise concerns about a "digital divide" between SES and gender groups. Poverty-stricken children are least likely to have home computers and Internet access. And low-SES children who do have computer Internet access devote less time to it than their higher-SES counterparts, although they compensate to some degree by going online more often on their cell phones (Lenhart et al., 2010). By the end of elementary school, boys spend more time with computers than girls and use computers somewhat differently. Boys, for example, more often connect to the Internet to download games and music, trade and sell things, and create Web pages. Girls emphasize information gathering and social networking (Jackson et al., 2008; Rideout, Foehr, & Roberts, 2010). Furthermore, in a survey of a large, nationally representative sample of Canadian 15- and 16-year-olds, boys more often than girls engaged in writing computer programs, analyzing data, and using spreadsheets and graphics programs. And many more boys than girls rated their computer skills as "excellent" (Looker & Thiessen, 2003). Schools need to ensure that girls and economically disadvantaged students have many opportunities to benefit from the diverse, cognitively enriching aspects of computer technology.

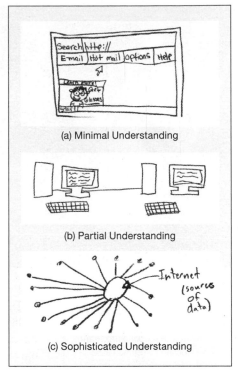

(a) Minimal Understanding

(b) Partial Understanding

(c) Sophisticated Understanding

FIGURE 15.7 Three children's drawings of the Internet, reflecting increased technical understanding with age. When elementary school children were asked to describe and draw a picture of the Internet, most children younger than age 10 revealed either a minimal understanding (viewed the Internet as one computer) or a partial understanding (viewed the Internet as a few connected computers). Most 10- and 11-year-olds had a sophisticated understanding of the Internet as a networklike system in which computing centers link with multiple computers. (From Z. Yan, 2006, "What Influences Children's and Adolescents' Understanding of the Complexity of the Internet?" *Developmental Psychology, 42*, p. 421. Copyright © 2006 by the American Psychological Association. Reprinted with permission of the American Psychological Association.)

Playing speed-and-action video games may improve these children's selective attention and spatial skills. But extensive game playing is negatively related to school performance and is associated with increased hostility and aggression, especially in boys.

Video Games Children and adolescents make extensive use of home computers for entertainment purposes, including video games. On average, U.S. school-age and adolescent boys spend nearly one-third of their computer time playing games—three times as much as girls (Rideout, Foehr, & Roberts, 2010). Most video games emphasize speed and action in violent plots in which children advance by shooting at and evading enemies. Young people also play complex exploratory and adventure games, generally with themes of conquest and aggression, and sports games, such as football and soccer. And they enjoy simulation games in which players role-play characters in a virtual reality.

Speed-and-action video games foster selective attention and spatial skills in boys and girls alike. Extensive game playing, however, is negatively related to school performance (Hastings et al., 2009; Jackson et al., 2011b; Subrahmanyam & Greenfield, 1996). And an increasing number of studies show that playing violent games, like watching violent TV, increases hostility and aggression—especially in boys, who are more avid players than girls (Anderson, 2004; Hofferth, 2010). Furthermore, video games are full of ethnic and gender stereotypes (Dietz, 1998). Much less is known about the consequences of children's experiences in computerized virtual realities. Depending on their content, some virtual-reality games may foster complex narrative skills, imagination, and prosocial behavior, whereas others may promote uncooperativeness and antisocial acts (Singer & Singer, 2005). In research conducted in Japan and the United States, young people who more often played games high in modeling of helpfulness subsequently behaved more prosocially (Gentile et al., 2009).

Compared with infrequent users, "passionate" game players tend to be anxious, withdrawn young people who use games to escape from unpleasant family and school experiences. A few become addicted: They spend several hours a day playing, constantly think about playing when they are not, and believe they play too much but cannot cut back or stop (Salguero & Morán, 2002). Excessive playing of fantasy games can blur the distinction between virtual and real life (Turkle, 1995). When such games are violent, they may contribute—along with disengaged parents, antisocial peers, and alienation from school—to commission of heinous acts by at-risk young people. Columbine High School teenage murderers Eric Harris and Dylan Klebold were obsessed with a game called *Doom,* in which players try to rack up the most kills (Subrahmanyam et al., 2001).

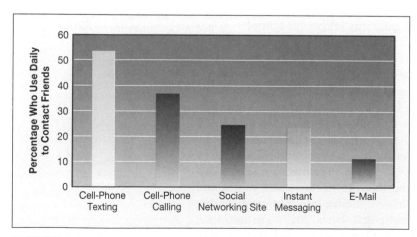

FIGURE 15.8 **Percentage of U.S. 12- to 17-year-olds who use various communication channels daily to contact friends** A nationally representative sample of 800 U.S. 12- to 17-year-olds responded to a survey about their communication strategies with friends. Cell-phone texting emerged as the preferred means of electronic communication, with over half of teenagers reporting that they used it daily. (Adapted from Lenhart et al., 2010.)

Cell Phones, the Internet, and Communication Teenagers frequently use cell phones and the Internet to communicate with friends. About 75 percent of U.S. 12- to 17-year-olds own a cell phone, a rate that has nearly doubled during the past decade. Cell-phone texting has become the preferred means of electronic interaction between teenage friends, with cell calling second, followed by social networking sites and instant messaging (see Figure 15.8). Girls use cell phones to text and call their friends considerably more often than boys (Lenhart et al., 2010). These forms of online interaction seem to support friendship closeness. In several studies, as amount of online messaging between preexisting friends increased, so did young people's perceptions of intimacy in the relationship and sense of well-being. The effect is largely due to friends' online disclosure of personal information, such as worries, secrets, and romantic feelings (Hu et al., 2004; Valkenburg & Peter, 2007a, 2007b, 2009). But about one-third of U.S. teenagers send more than 100 texts per day, half of whom send more than 200 (amounting to over 6,000 per month). The social consequences of such heavy, non–face-to-face interaction are unknown.

Although mostly communicating with friends they know, adolescents are also drawn to meeting new people over the Internet. Social networking sites such as MySpace and Facebook, which are now used by nearly three-fourths of U.S. teenagers, along with blogs, message boards, and chat rooms, open up vast alternatives beyond their families, schools, and communities (Lenhart et al., 2010). Through these online ties, young people explore central adolescent issues—sexuality, challenges in parent and peer relationships, and identity issues, including attitudes and values—in contexts that grant anonymity and, therefore, may feel less threatening than similar conversations in the real world (Subrahmanyam, Smahel, & Greenfield, 2006; Valkenburg & Peter, 2011). Online interactions with strangers also offer some teenagers vital sources of support. Socially anxious youths, for example, may engage in Internet communication to relieve loneliness while practicing and improving their social skills. And teenagers suffering from depression, eating disorders, and other problems can access message boards where participants provide mutual assistance, including a sense of group belonging and acceptance (Whitlock, Powers, & Eckenrode, 2006).

But online communication also poses dangers. In unmonitored chat rooms, teenagers are likely to encounter degrading racial and ethnic slurs and sexually obscene and harassing remarks (Subrahmanyam & Greenfield, 2008). Furthermore, in a survey of a nationally representative sample of U.S. 10- to 17-year-old Internet users, 14 percent reported having formed online friendships or romances. Although some of these youths were well-adjusted, many reported high levels of conflict with parents, peer victimization, depression, and delinquency and spent extensive time on the Internet (see Figure 15.9). They also more often had been asked by online friends for face-to-face meetings and had attended those meetings—without telling their parents (Wolak, Mitchell, & Finkelhor, 2003).

As these findings illustrate, troubled youths who use Internet communication to relieve feelings of isolation and rejection are especially vulnerable to exploitation. Adolescents who lack protective networks—family and friends with whom to discuss online encounters and appropriate and inappropriate online behaviors—may be overly trusting and may also find deceptions and harassment in Internet relationships particularly painful. Under these circumstances, Internet relationships may worsen their problems.

Regulating Media Use

The potential for TV and computer media to manipulate children's beliefs and behavior has led to strong public pressure to improve media content. In the United States, the First Amendment right to free speech has hampered efforts to regulate TV broadcasting. Instead, all programs must be rated for violent and sexual content, and all new TV sets are required to contain the V-chip (violence chip), which allows parents to block undesired material. In general, parents bear most

Cell-phone texting and social networking promote feelings of closeness and well-being in teenagers' relationships with friends. But for heavy users of electronic communication, social consequences are unknown.

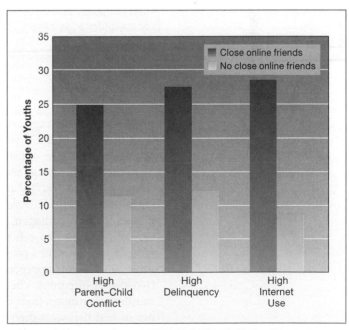

FIGURE 15.9 Association of close online friendships with parent–child conflict, delinquency, and high Internet use In this survey of a nationally representative sample of 1,500 U.S. Internet-using 10- to 17-year-olds, those who reported that they had formed close online friendships or romances were more likely to be troubled youths who spent much time on the Internet. (Adapted from Wolak, Mitchell, & Finkelhor, 2003.)

APPLYING WHAT WE KNOW

Regulating TV, Computer, and Cell Phone Use

STRATEGY	EXPLANATION
Limit TV viewing and computer use.	Parents should provide clear rules limiting TV and computer use by children and adolescents, and stick to them. The TV or computer should not be used as a babysitter for young children. Placing a TV or a computer in a child's bedroom substantially increases use and makes the child's activity hard to monitor.
Avoid using TV or computer time as a reward.	When TV or computer access is used as a reward or withheld as a punishment, children become increasingly attracted to it.
Encourage child-appropriate media experiences.	When children engage in TV and computer activities that are educational, prosocial, and age-appropriate, they gain in cognitive and social skills.
When possible, watch TV with children.	By raising questions about realism in TV depictions, expressing disapproval of on-screen behavior, and encouraging discussion, adults help children understand and evaluate TV content.
Link TV content to everyday learning experiences.	Parents can extend TV learning in ways that encourage children to engage actively with their surroundings. For example, a program on animals might spark a trip to the zoo, a visit to the library for books about animals, or new ways of observing and caring for the family pet.
Model good TV and computer practices.	Parents' media behavior—avoiding excessive TV and computer use and limiting exposure to harmful content—influences their children's media behavior.
Explain Internet technology and safety practices.	Children and adolescents who view the Internet as a networklike system are more likely to understand its social risks. They also benefit from instruction in appropriate online behavior and in the dangers of revealing personal information or getting together with people they have "met" online.
Monitor and limit cell phone use.	Parents should establish clear rules for cell phone use, including limits on number of call minutes and text messages and insistence that the car be a no-phone-use zone. To ensure teenagers' safety, parents should arrange with the young person for periodic checks of cell-phone contents.
Use an authoritative approach to child rearing.	Children of warm, involved parents who make reasonable demands for mature behavior are more likely to prefer media experiences with educational and prosocial content, less likely to use the TV or computer as an escape, and more likely to follow parental media rules.

responsibility for regulating their children's exposure to inappropriate media content. As with the V-chip for TV, parents can control children's Internet access by using filters or programs that monitor website visits. Yet surveys of U.S. parents and youths indicate that 20 to 30 percent of preschoolers and about half of school-age children and early adolescents experience no limits on TV or computer use at home. Some children begin visiting websites without parental supervision as early as age 4 (Rideout, Foehr, & Roberts, 2010; Rideout & Hamel, 2006; Varnhagen, 2007).

With respect to cell phone use, the overwhelming majority of U.S. parents who provide their child with a phone do so to be in touch wherever the teenager happens to be. And most adolescents appreciate the increased safety that a cell phone offers. Whereas about two-thirds of parents check the contents of their child's cell phone, less then half limit the number of minutes their child may use the phone, and less than one-third restrict the number of text messages their child may send or receive. Yet when parents limit amount of texting, adolescents less often report regretting a text message they sent and sending messages with sexual content, including images ("sexting") (Lenhart et al., 2010). Also, teenagers whose parents place limits on cell phone use are less likely to use cell phones in risky ways while driving (Madden & Lenhart, 2009). Applying What We Know above lists strategies parents can use to protect their children from undesirable TV and computer fare and cell phone use.

A S K   Y O U R S E L F

Review ■ Describe research findings on the academic and social benefits of television and computer use.

Apply ■ Thirteen-year-old Tommy spends hours each afternoon surfing the Web, instant messaging with online friends he has never met, and playing computer games. Explain why his parents should intervene.

Connect ■ Which subtypes of popular and rejected children, described on page 619, are most likely to be attracted to violent media? Explain.

Reflect ■ How much and what kinds of television viewing and computer use did you engage in as a child and adolescent? Did your parents have rules about TV and computer time, and did they enforce those rules? How do you think your home media environment influenced your development?

Schooling

Unlike the informal world of peer relations, the school is a formal institution designed to transmit the knowledge and skills children need to become productive members of society. By high school graduation, children in the developed world have spent, on average, about 14,000 hours in school. As noted in earlier chapters, schools are vital forces in children's development, affecting their motivation to learn and modes of remembering, reasoning, problem solving, and social and moral understanding. How do schools exert such a powerful impact? Research looking at schools as complex social systems—class and student body size, educational philosophies, transitions from one school level to the next, teacher–student relationships, and grouping practices—provides important insights.

Class and Student Body Size

The physical plants of all schools tend to be similar: Each has classrooms, hallways, a playground, and a lunchroom. But they vary widely in number of students in each class and in the school as a whole.

Is there an optimal class size? In a large field experiment, more than 6,000 Tennessee kindergartners were randomly assigned to three class types: "small" (13 to 17 students), "regular" (22 to 25 students) with only a teacher, and regular with a teacher plus a full-time teacher's aide. These arrangements continued into third grade. Small-class students—especially ethnic minority children—scored higher in reading and math achievement each year (Mosteller, 1995). Placing teachers' aides in regular-size classes had no impact. Rather, experiencing small classes from kindergarten through third grade predicted substantially higher achievement from fourth through ninth grades, after children had returned to regular-size classes. It also predicted greater likelihood of graduating from high school, particularly for low-SES students (Finn, Gerber, & Boyd-Zaharias, 2005; Nye, Hedges, & Konstantopoulos, 2001). Many school administrators, however, argue that teacher quality is far more important than class size. In one study, small class size predicted elementary students' academic progress, even after diverse measures of teacher quality were controlled (Brühwiler & Blatchford, 2011). Once again, classes of fewer than 17 students had a particularly powerful impact.

Why is small class size beneficial? With fewer children, teachers spend less time disciplining and more time teaching and giving individual attention. Also, children who learn in smaller groups show better concentration, higher-quality class participation, and more favorable attitudes toward school (Blatchford et al., 2003, 2007). The impact of small class size on children's social behavior, however, is inconsistent and may depend on the extent to which teachers include social goals in their daily plans (NICHD Early Child Care Research Network, 2004a).

Once students reach secondary school, where they move from class to class and have access to many activities outside classroom instruction, the relevant physical context is the

▶ How do class and student body size and educational philosophies affect academic and social development?

▶ Cite factors that influence adjustment following school transitions in early childhood and in adolescence.

▶ Discuss the role of teacher–student interaction and grouping practices in academic achievement.

▶ Under what conditions is placement of students with special needs in regular classrooms successful, and how can schools increase parent involvement in education?

▶ How well are American young people achieving compared with their counterparts in other industrialized nations, and what problems do non-college-bound youths face in preparing for a vocation?

school as a whole. Student body size profoundly affects school life. Members of smaller schools report more social support and caring as well as greater school engagement, as indicated by student attendance, academic preparedness, and satisfaction with classes and other school experiences (Lee, 2000; Weiss, Carolan, & Baker-Smith, 2010). Furthermore, schools with 500 to 700 students or less have fewer people to ensure that clubs, sports events, and social activities will function. As a result, young people enter a greater number and variety of activities and hold more positions of responsibility and leadership. In large schools, where plenty of students are available to fill activity slots, a smaller percentage—typically an elite who compete successfully for positions—are genuinely active (Barker & Gump, 1964; Feldman & Matjasko, 2007).

Extracurricular participation focusing on the arts, community service, and vocational development promotes diverse aspects of adjustment, including improved academic performance, reduced antisocial behavior, more favorable self-esteem and initiative, and greater peer acceptance and concern for others (Fredricks & Eccles, 2005, 2006; Mahoney, 2000). Benefits extend into adult life (see also research on youth civic responsibility, Chapter 12, page 508). Young adults who were more involved in high school clubs and organizations achieved more in their occupations and engaged in more community service, after other possibly explanatory factors (including SES, IQ, and academic performance) were controlled (Obradović & Masten, 2007).

Adolescents with academic, emotional, and social problems are especially likely to profit from extracurricular pursuits that require them to take on meaningful roles and responsibilities (Mahoney & Cairns, 1997; Marsh & Kleitman, 2002). A special advantage of small schools is that potential dropouts are far more likely to join in activities, gain recognition, and remain until graduation. In large schools, reorganizations that create smaller "schools within schools" can have the same effect.

Educational Philosophies

Each teacher brings to the classroom an educational philosophy that plays a major role in children's learning. Two philosophical approaches have received most research attention. They differ in what children are taught, in the way they are believed to learn, and in how their progress is evaluated.

Traditional versus Constructivist Classrooms In a **traditional classroom,** the teacher is the sole authority for knowledge, rules, and decision making and does most of the talking. Students are relatively passive—listening, responding when called on, and completing teacher-assigned tasks. Their progress is evaluated by how well they keep pace with a uniform set of standards for their grade.

A **constructivist classroom,** in contrast, encourages students to construct their own knowledge. Although constructivist approaches vary, many are grounded in Piaget's view of children as active agents who reflect on and coordinate their own thoughts, rather than absorbing those of others. A glance inside a constructivist classroom reveals richly equipped learning centers, small groups and individuals solving self-chosen problems, and a teacher who guides and supports in response to children's needs. Students are evaluated by considering their progress in relation to their own prior development.

In the United States, the pendulum has swung back and forth between these two views. In the 1960s and early 1970s, constructivist classrooms gained in popularity. Then, as concern arose over the academic progress of children and youths, a "back to basics" movement arose, and classrooms returned to traditional instruction. This style, still prevalent today, has become increasingly pronounced as a result of the U.S. No Child Left Behind Act, signed into law in 2001 (Darling-Hammond, 2010; Ravitch, 2010). Because it places heavy pressure on teachers and school administrators to improve achievement test scores, it has narrowed the curricular focus in many schools to preparing students to take such tests (see page 343 in Chapter 8). And to devote even more time to academic instruction, many schools have cut back on recess, despite its contribution to all domains of development (refer to the Social Issues: Education box on the following page.

SOCIAL ISSUES: EDUCATION

School Recess—A Time to Play, a Time to Learn

When 7-year-old Whitney's family moved to a new city, she left a school with three daily recess periods for one with just a single 15-minute break per day, which her second-grade teacher cancelled if any child misbehaved. Whitney, who had previously enjoyed school, complained daily of headaches and an upset stomach. Her mother, Jill, thought, "My child is stressing out because she can't move all day!" After Jill and other parents successfully appealed to the school board to add a second recess period, Whitney's symptoms vanished (Rauber, 2006).

In recent years, recess—along with its rich opportunities for child-organized play and peer interaction—has diminished or disappeared in many U.S. elementary schools (Ginsburg, 2007; Pellegrini & Holmes, 2006). Under the assumption that extra time for academics will translate into achievement gains, 7 percent of U.S. schools no longer provide recess to students as young as second grade. And over half of schools that do have recess now schedule it just once a day (U.S. Department of Education, 2011b).

Yet rather than subtracting from classroom learning, recess periods boost it! Research dating back more than 100 years confirms that distributing cognitively demanding tasks over a longer time by introducing regular breaks, rather than consolidating intensive effort within one period, enhances attention and performance at all ages. Such breaks are particularly important for children. In a series of studies, school-age children were more attentive in the classroom after recess than before it—an effect that was greater for second than fourth graders (Pellegrini, Huberty, & Jones, 1995). Teacher ratings of disruptive classroom behavior also decline for children who have more than 15 minutes of recess a day (Barros, Silver, & Stein, 2009).

In other research, kindergartners' and first graders' engagement in peer conversation and games during recess predicted gains in academic achievement, even after other factors that might explain the relationship (such as previous achievement) were controlled (Pellegrini, 1992; Pellegrini et al., 2002). Recall that children's social maturity contributes substantially to early academic competence. Recess is one of the few

School recess offers rich opportunities for child-organized games and peer interaction that promote both academic achievement and social competence.

remaining contexts devoted to child-organized games that provide practice in vital social skills—cooperation, leadership, followership, and inhibition of aggression—under adult supervision rather than adult direction. As children transfer these skills to the classroom, they may participate in discussions, collaborate, follow rules, and enjoy academic pursuits more—factors that enhance motivation and achievement.

Although older elementary school children in traditional classrooms have a slight edge in achievement test scores, constructivist settings are associated with many other benefits— gains in critical thinking, greater social and moral maturity, and more positive attitudes toward school (DeVries, 2001; Rathunde & Csikszentmihalyi, 2005; Walberg, 1986). Yet despite grave concerns about its appropriateness, even preschool and kindergarten teachers have felt increased pressure to stress teacher-directed, academic training. Young children who spend much time passively sitting and doing worksheets, as opposed to being actively engaged in learning centers, display more stress behaviors (such as wiggling and rocking), have less confidence in their abilities, prefer less challenging tasks, and are less advanced in motor, academic, language, and social skills at the end of the school year (Marcon, 1999a; Stipek, 1995). Follow-ups reveal lasting effects through elementary school in poorer study habits and achievement (Burts et al., 1992; Hart et al., 1998, 2003). These outcomes are strongest for low-SES children, with whom teachers more often use an academic approach— a disturbing trend in view of its negative impact on motivation and emotional well-being (Stipek, 2004; Stipek & Byler, 1997).

In contrast, low-SES children experiencing *Montessori education*—a constructivist method devised a century ago by Italian physician Maria Montessori—reap many benefits. Features of Montessori schooling include multiage classrooms, teaching materials specially designed to promote exploration and discovery, long time periods for individual and small-group learning in child-chosen activities, and equal emphasis on academic and social development (Lillard, 2007). In an evaluation of Montessori public preschools serving mostly urban minority children in Milwaukee, researchers compared students randomly assigned to either Montessori or other classrooms (Lillard & Else-Quest, 2006). Five-year-olds who had completed two years of Montessori education outperformed controls in literacy and math skills, cognitive flexibility, false-belief understanding, concern with fairness in solving problems with peers, and cooperative play with agemates.

New Philosophical Directions   New approaches to education, grounded in Vygotsky's sociocultural theory, capitalize on the rich social context of the classroom to spur children's learning. In these **social-constructivist classrooms,** children participate in a wide range of challenging activities with teachers and peers, with whom they jointly construct understandings. As children *appropriate* (take for themselves) the knowledge and strategies generated from working together, they become competent, contributing members of their classroom community and advance in cognitive and social development (Bodrova & Leong, 2007; Palincsar, 2003). Vygotsky's emphasis on the social origins of higher cognitive processes has inspired the following educational themes:

- *Teachers and children as partners in learning.* A classroom rich in both teacher–child and child–child collaboration transfers culturally valued ways of thinking to children.
- *Experience with many types of symbolic communication in meaningful activities.* As children master reading, writing, and mathematics, they become aware of their culture's communication systems, reflect on their own thinking, and bring it under voluntary control.
- *Teaching adapted to each child's zone of proximal development.* Assistance that both responds to current understandings and encourages children to take the next step helps ensure that each student will make the best progress possible.

In Chapter 6, we considered two Vygotsky-inspired collaborative practices: reciprocal teaching and cooperative learning (see pages 271–272). Recognizing that collaboration requires a supportive context to be most effective, another Vygotsky-based innovation makes it a schoolwide value. Classrooms become **communities of learners** where teachers guide the overall process of learning but no other distinction is made between adult and child contributors: All participate in joint endeavors and have the authority to define and resolve problems. This approach is based on the assumption that different people have different expertises that can benefit the community and that students, too, may become experts (Sullivan & Glanz, 2006). Classroom activities are often long-term projects addressing complex, real-world problems. In working toward project goals, children and teachers draw on one another's expertises and those of others within and outside the school.

In one classroom, students studied animal–habitat relationships in order to design an animal of the future, suited to environmental changes. The class formed small research groups, each of which selected a subtopic—for example, defense against predators, protection from the elements, reproduction, or food getting. Each group member assumed responsibility for part of the subtopic, consulting diverse experts and preparing teaching materials. Then group members taught one another, assembled their contributions, and brought them to the community as a whole so the knowledge gathered could be used to solve the problem (Brown, 1997; Stone, 2005). The result was a multifaceted understanding of the topic that would have been too difficult and time-consuming for any learner to accomplish alone.

A teacher and students form a community of learners to plan, plant, and track the growth of a vegetable garden. During this complex, long-term project, participating adults and children may all become experts, sharing knowledge with one another.

© ALISTAIR BERG/GETTY IMAGES/DIGITAL VISION

School Transitions

Besides size and educational philosophy, an additional structural feature of schooling contributes to student achievement and adjustment: the timing of transitions from one school level to the next. Entering kindergarten is a major milestone. Children must accommodate to new physical settings, adult authorities, daily schedules, peer companions, and academic challenges.

Early Adjustment to School In longitudinal research extending over the school year, the ease with which kindergartners made new friends, were accepted by their classmates, and related to their teachers predicted cooperative participation in classroom activities and self-directed completion of learning tasks. These behaviors, in turn, were related to gains in achievement during kindergarten (Ladd, Birch, & Buhs, 1999; Ladd, Buhs, & Seid, 2000). Furthermore, children with friendly, prosocial styles more easily made new friends, gained peer acceptance, and formed a warm bond with their teacher. In contrast, those with weak emotional self-regulation skills and argumentative, aggressive, or peer-avoidant styles established poor-quality relationships and made few friends (Birch & Ladd, 1998).

The capacity to form positive peer and teacher relationships enables kindergartners to integrate themselves into classroom environments in ways that foster both academic and social competence. In a follow-up of more than 900 4-year-olds, children of average intelligence but with above-average social skills fared better in academic achievement in first grade than children of equal mental ability who were socially below average (Konold & Pianta, 2005). Because social maturity in early childhood contributes to later academic performance, a growing number of experts propose that readiness for kindergarten be assessed in terms of not just academic skills but also social skills, including capacity to form supportive bonds with teachers and peers, to participate actively and positively in interactions with classmates, and to behave prosocially (Ladd, Herald, & Kochel, 2006; Thompson & Raikes, 2007).

Preschool interventions, too, should attend to these vital social prerequisites. Warm, responsive teacher–child interaction is vital, especially for temperamentally shy, impulsive, and emotionally negative children, who are at high risk for social difficulties (McClelland et al., 2007). In studies involving several thousand 4-year-olds in public preschools in six states, teacher sensitivity and emotional support were especially potent predictors of children's social competence during preschool and in a follow-up after kindergarten entry (Curby et al., 2009; Mashburn et al., 2008).

School Transitions in Adolescence Early adolescence is another important period of school transition: Students typically move from an intimate, self-contained elementary school classroom to a much larger, impersonal secondary school where they must shift between classes. With each school change—from elementary to middle or junior high and then to high school—adolescents' grades decline. The drop is partly due to tighter academic standards. At the same time, the transition to secondary school often brings less personal attention, more whole-class instruction, and less chance to participate in classroom decision making (Seidman, Aber, & French, 2004).

In view of these changes, it is not surprising that students rate their middle or junior-high school learning experiences less favorably than their elementary school experiences (Wigfield & Eccles, 1994). They also report that their teachers care less about them, are less friendly, grade less fairly, and stress competition more. Consequently, many young people feel less academically competent, and their liking for school and motivation decline (Barber & Olsen, 2004; Gutman & Midgley, 2000; Otis, Grouzet, & Pelletier, 2005).

Inevitably, students must readjust their feelings of self-confidence and self-worth as they encounter revised academic expectations and a more complex social world. In several studies that followed students across the middle- and high-school transitions, grade point average declined and feelings of anonymity increased after each school change. Girls fared less well than boys. On entering middle school, girls' self-esteem dropped sharply, perhaps because the transition tended to coincide with other life changes: the onset of puberty and dating (Simmons & Blythe, 1987). And after starting high school, girls felt lonelier and more anxious than boys, and—although they were doing better academically—their grades declined more rapidly (Benner & Graham, 2009; Russell, Elder, & Conger, 1997).

Adolescents facing added strains at either transition—family disruption, poverty, low parental involvement, high parental conflict, or learned helplessness on academic tasks—are at greatest risk for self-esteem and academic difficulties

© DWIGHT CENDROWSKI, WWW.CENDROWSKI.COM

This seventh grader hurries at his locker so he won't be late for class at his new middle school. Moving from a small, self-contained elementary school classroom to a large, impersonal secondary school is stressful for adolescents.

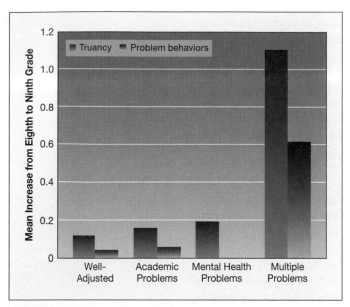

FIGURE 15.10 **Increase in truancy and out-of-school problem behaviors across the transition to high school in four groups of students** Well-adjusted students, students with only academic problems, and students with only mental health problems showed little change. (Good students with mental health problems actually declined in problem behaviors, so no purple bar is shown for them.) In contrast, multiple-problem students—with both academic and mental health difficulties—increased sharply in truancy and problem behaviors after changing schools from eighth to ninth grade. (Adapted from Roeser, Eccles, & Freedman-Doan, 1999.)

(de Bruyn, 2005; Rudolph et al., 2001; Seidman et al., 2003). Furthermore, the high school transition is particularly challenging for African-American and Hispanic students who move to a new school with substantially fewer same-ethnicity peers (Benner & Graham, 2009). Under these conditions, minority adolescents report decreased feelings of belonging and school liking, and they show steeper declines in grades.

Distressed youths whose school performance either remains low or drops sharply after school transition often show a persisting pattern of poor self-esteem, motivation, and achievement. In another study, researchers compared "multiple-problem" youths (those with both academic and mental health problems), youths with difficulties in just one area (either academic or mental health), and well-adjusted youths (those doing well in both areas) across the transition to high school. Although all groups declined in grade point average, well-adjusted students continued to get high marks and multiple-problem youths low marks, with the others falling in between. And as Figure 15.10 shows, the multiple-problem youths showed a far greater rise in truancy and out-of-school problem behaviors, such as doing something dangerous for the thrill of it, damaging public property, or getting drunk (Roeser, Eccles, & Freedman-Doan, 1999). For some, school transition initiates a downward spiral in academic performance and school involvement that leads to dropping out.

Helping Adolescents Adjust to School Transitions As these findings reveal, school transitions often lead to environmental changes that fit poorly with adolescents' developmental needs (Eccles & Roeser, 2009). They disrupt close relationships with teachers at a time when adolescents need adult support. They emphasize competition during a period of heightened self-focusing. They reduce decision making and choice as the desire for autonomy is increasing. And they interfere with peer networks as young people become more concerned with peer acceptance.

Support from parents, teachers, and peers can ease these strains. Parental involvement, monitoring, autonomy granting, and emphasis on mastery rather than merely good grades are associated with better adjustment (Grolnick et al., 2000; Gutman, 2006). Adolescents with close friends are more likely to sustain these friendships across the transition, which increases social integration and academic motivation in the new school (Aikens, Bierman, & Parker, 2005). Forming smaller units within large schools promotes closer relations with both teachers and peers and greater extracurricular involvement (Seidman, Aber, & French, 2004). And a "critical mass" of same-ethnicity peers—according to one suggestion, at least 15 percent of the student body—helps teenagers feel socially accepted and reduces fear of out-group hostility (National Research Council, 2007).

Other, less extensive changes are also effective. In the first year after a school transition, homerooms can be provided in which teachers offer academic and personal counseling and work closely with parents to promote favorable adjustment. Assigning students to classes with several familiar peers or a constant group of new peers strengthens emotional security and social support. In schools that took these steps, students were less likely to decline in academic performance or display other adjustment problems (Felner et al., 2002).

Finally, teenagers' perceptions of the sensitivity and flexibility of their school learning environments contribute substantially to successful school transitions. When schools minimize competition and differential treatment based on ability, middle school students are less likely to feel angry and depressed, to be truant, or to show declines in academic values, self-esteem, and achievement (Roeser, Eccles, & Sameroff, 2000). School rules that strike young people as fair rather than punitive also foster satisfaction with school life.

LOOK and LISTEN

Ask several secondary school students to describe their experiences after school transition. What supports for easing the stress of transition did their teachers and school provide?

Teacher–Student Interaction

The classroom is a complex social system in which teachers engage in as many as 1,000 exchanges with students each day (Jackson, 1968). Extensive research exists on teacher–student interaction, most focusing on its significance for academic achievement.

Elementary and secondary school students describe good teachers as caring, helpful, and stimulating—behaviors associated with gains in motivation, achievement, and favorable peer relations (Hughes & Kwok, 2006, 2007; Hughes, Zhang, & Hill, 2006; O'Connor & McCartney, 2007). But too many U.S. teachers emphasize repetitive drill over higher-level thinking, such as grappling with ideas and applying knowledge to new situations (Sacks, 2005). In a longitudinal investigation of a large sample of middle school students, those in more stimulating, academically demanding classrooms showed better attendance and larger gains in math achievement over the following two years (Phillips, 1997).

As we have seen, teachers do not interact in the same way with all children. Well-behaved, high-achieving students typically get more encouragement and praise, whereas unruly students have more conflicts with teachers and receive more criticism from them (Henricsson & Rydell, 2004). Caring teacher–student relationships have an especially strong impact on the achievement and social behavior of low-SES minority students and other children at risk for learning difficulties (Baker, 2006; Crosno, Kirkpatrick, & Elder, 2004). But overall, higher-SES students—who tend to be higher achieving and to have fewer learning and behavior problems—have more sensitive and supportive relationships with teachers (Jerome, Hamre, & Pianta, 2009; Pianta, Hamre, & Stuhlman, 2003).

Unfortunately, once teachers' attitudes toward students are established, they can become more extreme than is warranted by students' behavior. Of special concern are **educational self-fulfilling prophecies:** Children may adopt teachers' positive or negative views and start to live up to them.[1] As early as first grade, teachers' beliefs in children's ability to learn predict students' year-end achievement progress after controlling for students' beginning-of-year performance. This effect is particularly strong when teachers emphasize competition and publicly compare children, regularly favoring the best students (Kuklinski & Weinstein, 2001; Weinstein, 2002).

Teacher expectations have a greater impact on low-achieving than high-achieving students (Madon, Jussim, & Eccles, 1997). When a teacher is critical, high achievers can fall back on their history of success. Low-achieving students' sensitivity to self-fulfilling prophecies can be beneficial when teachers believe in them. But biased teacher judgments are usually slanted in a negative direction. In one study, African-American and Hispanic elementary school students taught by high-bias teachers (who expected them to do poorly) showed substantially lower end-of-year achievement than their counterparts taught by low-bias teachers (McKown & Weinstein, 2008). And in a Dutch investigation, teachers' subtle prejudices against Turks and Moroccans were associated with a larger achievement gap between Dutch-origin and ethnic minority first through sixth graders (van den Bergh et al., 2010). Recall our discussion of *stereotype threat* in Chapter 8. A child in the position of confirming a negative stereotype may respond with anxiety and reduced motivation, amplifying a negative self-fulfilling prophecy.

Grouping Practices

Many schools group students by ability or track them into classes in which students of similar achievement levels are taught together. The goal is to reduce the need for individual teachers to meet a wide range of academic needs.

Grouping in Elementary School *Homogeneous* groups or classes can be a potent source of self-fulfilling prophecies. Low-group students—who as early as first grade are disproportionately low-SES, minority, and male—get more drill on basic facts and skills, engage

---

[1]Most research on self-fulfilling prophecies focuses on teacher–student relationships, but the effect can occur in other social contexts, such as parent–child and peer relationships.

These first through third graders collaborate on a variety of tasks. Compared to children in single-grade classrooms, those in multigrade classrooms are usually advantaged in academic achievement, self-esteem, and attitudes toward school.

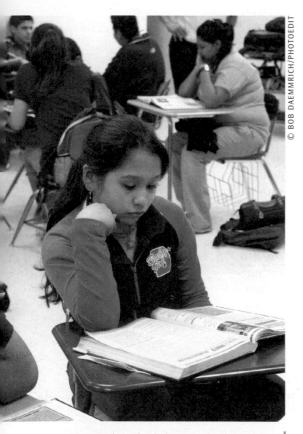

In U.S. secondary schools, low-SES minority students tend to be placed in lower-level courses with less stimulating teaching. The resulting boredom and disengagement are associated with slower academic progress and increased risk of dropping out.

in less discussion, and progress at a slower pace. Gradually, they decline in academic self-esteem and motivation and fall further behind in achievement (Lleras & Rangel, 2009; Trautwein et al., 2006; Worthy, Hungerford-Kresser, & Hampton, 2009). Unfortunately, widespread SES and ethnic segregation in U.S. schools consigns large numbers of low-SES minority students to a form of schoolwide, deleterious homogeneous grouping. Refer to the Social Issues: Education box on the following page to find out how magnet schools foster heterogeneous learning contexts, thereby reducing achievement disparities between SES and ethnic minority groups.

Another way schools can increase the *heterogeneity* of student groups is to combine two or three adjacent grades. In *multigrade classrooms,* academic achievement, self-esteem, and attitudes toward school are usually more favorable than in the single-grade arrangement, perhaps because multigrade classrooms often decrease competition and increase harmony (Lloyd, 1999; Ong, Allison, & Haladyna, 2000). The opportunity that mixed-grade grouping affords for peer tutoring may also contribute to its favorable outcomes. When older or more expert students teach younger or less expert students, both tutors and tutees benefit in achievement and self-esteem, with stronger effects for low-SES minority students and students in the early elementary school grades (Ginsburg-Block, Rohrbeck, & Fantuzzo, 2006; Renninger, 1998).

However, small, heterogeneous groups of students working together often engage in poorer-quality interaction (less accurate explanations and answers) than homogeneous groups of above-average students (Webb, Nemer, & Chizhik, 1998). In Chapter 6, we noted that for collaboration between heterogeneous peers to succeed, children often need extensive guidance (see page 271). When teachers provide this assistance, heterogeneous classrooms are desirable into middle or junior high school, resulting in clearer explanations, greater enjoyment of learning, and achievement gains across a wide range of school subjects (Gillies, 2003; Terwel et al., 2001; Webb et al., 2008).

Grouping in High School By high school, some homogeneous grouping is unavoidable because certain aspects of education must dovetail with the young person's educational and vocational plans. In the United States, high school students are counseled into college preparatory, vocational, or general education tracks. Unfortunately, low-SES minority students are assigned in large numbers to noncollege tracks, perpetuating educational inequalities of earlier years.

Longitudinal research following thousands of U.S. students from eighth to twelfth grade reveals that assignment to a college track accelerates academic progress, whereas assignment to a vocational or general education track decelerates it (Hallinan & Kubitschek, 1999). Even in secondary schools without an overarching tracking program, low-SES minority students tend to be assigned to lower course levels in most or all academic subjects, resulting in *de facto* (unofficial) *tracking* (Lucas & Behrends, 2002).

Breaking out of a low academic track is difficult. Track or course enrollment is generally based on past performance, which is limited by placement history. Interviews with African-American students revealed that many thought their previous performance did not reflect their ability. Yet teachers and counselors, overburdened with other responsibilities, had little time to reconsider individual cases (Ogbu, 2003). And compared to students in higher tracks, students in low tracks exert substantially less effort—a difference due in part to less stimulating classroom experiences (Worthy, Hungerford-Kresser, & Hampton, 2009).

SOCIAL ISSUES: EDUCATION

Magnet Schools: Equal Access to High-Quality Education

Each school-day morning, Emma leaves her affluent suburban neighborhood, riding a school bus 20 miles to a magnet school in an impoverished, mostly Hispanic inner-city community. In her sixth-grade class, she settles into a science project with her friend, Maricela, who lives in the local neighborhood. For the first hour of the day, the girls use a thermometer, ice water, and a stopwatch to determine which of several materials is the best insulator, recording and graphing their data. Throughout the school, which specializes in innovative math and science teaching, students diverse in SES and ethnicity learn side-by-side.

Despite the 1954 U.S. Supreme Court *Brown v. Board of Education* decision ordering schools to desegregate, school integration has receded since the late 1980s, as federal courts canceled their integration orders and returned this authority to states and cities. Today, the racial divide in American education is deepening. African-American children are just as likely to attend a school that serves a mostly black population as they were in the 1960s; Hispanic children are even more segregated. And when minority students attend ethnically mixed schools, they typically do so with other minorities (Frankenburg & Orfield, 2007).

U.S. schools in inner-city, low-income neighborhoods are vastly disadvantaged in funding and therefore in educational opportunities, largely because public education is primarily supported by local property taxes. Federal and state grants-in-aid are not sufficient to close this funding gap between rich and poor districts (Darling-Hammond, 2010). Consequently, in inner-city segregated neighborhoods, dilapidated school buildings; inexperienced teachers; outdated, poor-quality educational resources; and school cultures that fail to encourage strong teaching are widespread (Kozol, 2005). The negative impact on student achievement is severe.

A promising solution is the establishment of magnet schools. In addition to the usual curriculum, they emphasize a specific area of interest—such as performing arts, math and science, or technology. Families outside the school neighborhood are attracted to magnet schools (hence the name) by their rich academic offerings. Often magnets are located in low-income, minority areas, where they serve the neighborhood student population. Other students, who apply and are admitted by lottery, are bussed in—many from well-to-do city and suburban neighborhoods. In another model, all students—including those in the surrounding neighborhood—must apply. In either case, magnet schools are voluntarily desegregated.

Research confirms that less segregated education enhances minority student achievement (Linn & Welner, 2007). Is this so for magnet schools? A Connecticut study comparing seventh to tenth graders enrolled in magnet schools with those whose lottery numbers were not drawn and who therefore attended other city schools confirmed that the magnets served a far more diverse student population. Although magnet-school enrollees and nonadmitted applicants were similar in ethnicity, SES, and prior academic achievement, magnet students showed greater gains in reading and math achievement over a two-year period—outcomes especially pronounced for low-SES, ethnic minority students (Bifulco, Cobb, & Bell, 2009).

By high school, the higher-achieving peer environments of ethnically diverse schools encourage more students to pursue higher education (Frankenburg & Orfield, 2007). And as we saw in Chapter 11, a diverse student body also provides opportunities for social learning that can combat racial prejudice. In sum, magnet schools are a promising approach to overcoming the negative forces of SES and ethnic isolation in American schools.

© ELLEN B. SENISI/THE IMAGE WORKS

Third graders at a fine arts magnet school jointly create a painting. The ethnically diverse learning environments of many magnet schools enhance academic achievement, especially among low-SES minority students.

High school students are separated into academic and vocational tracks in virtually all industrialized nations. In China, Japan, and most Western European countries, high school track placement is determined by a national exam, which usually establishes the young person's future possibilities. In the United States, students who are not assigned to a college preparatory track or who do poorly in high school can still attend college. Ultimately, however, many young people do not benefit from the more open U.S. system. By adolescence, SES differences in quality of education and academic achievement are greater in the United States than in most other industrialized countries (Marks, Cresswell, & Ainley, 2006). And the United States has a higher percentage of young people—about 8 percent—who view themselves as educational failures, drop out of school, and by their mid-twenties still have not completed a high school program (U.S. Department of Education, 2011b).

Teaching Students with Special Needs

We have seen that effective teachers flexibly adjust their teaching strategies to accommodate students with a wide range of characteristics. But these adjustments are especially challenging when children have learning difficulties.

Children with Learning Difficulties U.S. legislation mandates that schools place children who require special supports for learning in the "least restrictive" (as close to normal as possible) environments that meet their educational needs. In **inclusive classrooms,** students with learning difficulties learn alongside typical students in the regular educational setting

In an inclusive second-grade classroom, a special-needs child listens to his classmate read a story. The child is likely to do well if he receives support from a special education teacher and if his classroom teacher minimizes comparisons and promotes cooperative learning.

for part or all of the school day—a practice designed to prepare them for participation in society and to combat prejudices against individuals with disabilities that lead to social exclusion (Kugelmass & Ainscow, 2004). Largely as the result of parental pressures, an increasing number of students experience *full inclusion*—full-time placement in regular classrooms.

Some students in inclusive classrooms display *mild intellectual disability:* Their IQs fall between 55 and 70, and they also show problems in adaptive behavior, or skills of everyday living (American Psychiatric Association, 2000). But the largest number—5 to 10 percent of school-age children—have **learning disabilities,** great difficulty with one or more aspects of learning, usually reading. As a result, their achievement is considerably behind what would be expected on the basis of their IQ. Sometimes, deficits express themselves in other ways—for example, as severe inattention, which depresses both IQ and achievement test scores (see page 290 in Chapter 7). The problems of students with learning disabilities cannot be traced to any obvious physical or emotional difficulty or to environmental disadvantage. Instead, deficits in brain functioning are involved (Waber, 2010). Some learning disabilities run in families, and in certain cases, specific genes have been identified that contribute to the problem (Miller, Sanchez, & Hynd, 2003; Raskind et al., 2005). In many instances, the cause is unknown.

How Effective Are Inclusive Classrooms? Although some students benefit academically from inclusion, many do not. Achievement gains depend on both the severity of the disability and the support services available (Downing, 2010). Furthermore, children with disabilities are often rejected by regular-classroom peers. Students with intellectual disabilities are overwhelmed by the social skills of their classmates; they cannot interact adeptly in a conversation or game. And the processing deficits of some students with learning disabilities lead to problems in social awareness and responsiveness (Kelly & Norwich, 2004; Lohrmann & Bambara, 2006).

Does this mean that children with special needs cannot be served in regular classrooms? Not necessarily. Often these children do best when they receive instruction in a resource room for part of the day and in the regular classroom for the remainder—an arrangement that the majority of school-age children with learning disabilities say they prefer (Vaughn & Klingner, 1998; Weiner & Tardif, 2004). In the resource room, a special education teacher works with students on an individual and small-group basis. Then, depending on their progress, children join regular classmates for different subjects and amounts of time.

Special steps must be taken to promote positive peer relations in inclusive classrooms. Cooperative learning and peer-tutoring experiences in which teachers guide children with learning difficulties and their classmates in working together lead to friendly interaction, improved peer acceptance, and achievement gains (Fuchs et al., 2002a, 2002b). Teachers can also prepare their class for the arrival of a student with special needs. Under these conditions, inclusion may foster emotional sensitivity and prosocial behavior among regular classmates.

Parent–School Partnerships

Regardless of students' age, abilities, gender, SES, or ethnicity, parent involvement in education—keeping tabs on the child's progress, communicating often with teachers, and ensuring that the child is enrolled in challenging, well-taught classes—promotes academic motivation and achievement (Hill & Taylor, 2004; Hill & Tyson, 2009; Jeynes, 2005). Parents who are in frequent contact with the school send a message to their child about the value of education, model constructive solutions to academic problems, and (as children get older) promote wise educational decisions. Involved parents also learn from other parents about which classes and teachers are the best and how to handle difficult situations. And teachers and parents are more likely to give students consistent messages about academic and behavioral expectations.

Families living in low-income, high-risk neighborhoods often feel disconnected from their children's schools, and they face daily stresses that reduce their energy for school involvement (Walker, Shenker, & Hoover-Dempsey, 2010; Warren et al., 2009). Yet stronger home–school links can relieve some of this stress. Schools can build parent–school partnerships by strengthening personal relationships between teachers and parents, showing parents how to support their child's education at home, building bridges between minority home cultures and the culture of the school, enlisting the help of neighborhood organizations with deep roots in the lives of families, and including parents in school governance so they remain invested in school goals.

How Well-Educated Are American Young People?

Our discussion has focused largely on how teachers can support the education of children and adolescents. Yet we have also seen in this and previous chapters that many factors—both within and outside schools—affect children's learning. Societal values, school resources, quality of teaching, and parental encouragement all play important roles. These multiple influences are especially apparent when schooling is examined in cross-cultural perspective.

Cross-National Research on Academic Achievement

In international studies of reading, mathematics, and science achievement, young people in China, Korea, and Japan are consistently top performers. Among Western nations, Australia, Canada, Finland, the Netherlands, and Switzerland are also in the top tier. But U.S. students typically perform at or below the international averages (see Figure 15.11) (Programme for International Student Assessment, 2009).

Why do U.S. students fall behind in academic accomplishments? According to international comparisons, instruction in the United States is less challenging, more focused on absorbing facts, and less focused on high-level reasoning and critical thinking than in other countries. A growing number of experts believe that the U.S. No Child Left Behind Act has contributed to these trends because it mandates severe sanctions for schools whose students do not meet targeted goals on achievement tests—initially, student transfers to higher-performing schools, and ultimately, staff firing, closure, state takeover, or other restructuring (Darling-Hammond, 2010;

	Country	Average Math Achievement Score
High-Performing Nations	China (Shanghai)	600
	Singapore	562
	China (Hong Kong)	555
	Korea	546
	Taiwan	543
	Finland	541
	Switzerland	534
	Japan	529
	Canada	527
	Netherlands	526
	China (Macao)	525
	New Zealand	519
	Belgium	515
	Australia	514
	Germany	513
Intermediate-Performing Nations	Iceland	507
	Denmark	503
	Norway	498
	France	497
International Average = 496	Austria	496
	Poland	495
	Sweden	494
	Czech Republic	493
	United Kingdom	492
	Hungary	490
	Luxembourg	489
	United States	**487**
	Ireland	487
	Portugal	487
	Italy	483
	Spain	483
Low-Performing Nations	Russian Federation	468
	Greece	466
	Turkey	445
	Bulgaria	428

FIGURE 15.11 Average mathematics scores of 15-year-olds by country. The Programme for International Student Assessment assesses achievement in many nations around the world. In its most recent comparison of countries' performance, the United States performed below the international average in math; in reading and science, its performance was about average. (Adapted from Programme for International Student Assessment, 2009.)

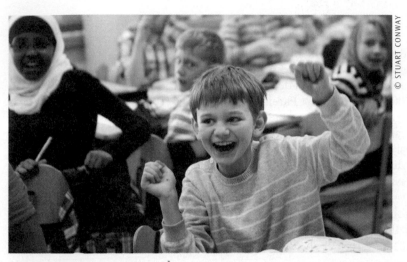

© STUART CONWAY

These Finnish students benefit from a national education system designed to cultivate initiative, problem solving, and creativity. Grounded in equal opportunity for all, Finnish education has nearly eliminated SES variations in achievement.

Noguera, 2010; Ravitch, 2010). Furthermore, compared with top-achieving nations, the United States is far less equitable in the quality of education it provides to its low-income and ethnic minority students. And U.S. teachers vary much more in training, salaries, and teaching conditions.

Finland is a case in point. In the 1980s, it abandoned a national testing system used to ability-group students and replaced it with curricula, teaching practices, and assessments aimed at cultivating initiative, problem solving, and creativity—vital abilities needed for success in the twenty-first century. Finnish teachers are highly trained: They must complete several years of graduate-level education at government expense (Sahlberg, 2010). And the Finnish education is grounded in equal opportunity for all—a policy that has nearly eliminated SES variations in achievement, despite an influx of immigrant students from low-income families into Finnish schools over the past decade.

In-depth research on learning environments in Asian nations, such as Japan, Korea, and Taiwan, also highlights social forces that foster strong student learning. Among these is cultural valuing of effort. Whereas American parents and teachers tend to regard native ability as the key to academic success, Japanese, Korean, and Taiwanese parents and teachers believe that all children can succeed academically as long as they try hard. Asian parents devote many more hours to helping their children with homework (Stevenson, Lee, & Mu, 2000). And Asian children, influenced by collectivist values, typically view striving to do well in school as a moral obligation—part of their responsibility to family and community (Hau & Ho, 2010).

As in Finland, students in Japan, Korea, and Taiwan receive the same nationally mandated, high-quality curriculum, delivered by teachers who are well-prepared, highly respected in their society, and far better paid than U.S. teachers (Kang & Hong, 2008; U.S. Department of Education, 2011a). Academic lessons are particularly well-organized and presented in ways that capture children's attention and encourage high-level thinking (Grow-Maienza, Hahn, & Joo, 2001). And Japanese teachers are three times as likely as U.S. teachers to work outside class with students who need extra help (Woodward & Ono, 2004).

The Finnish and Asian examples underscore the need for American families, schools, and the larger society to work together to upgrade education. Over the past decade, U.S. international rankings in reading, math, and science achievement have declined. And following several decades of gains, from 1999 on the U.S. National Assessment of Educational Progress—in which challenging achievement tests are given to nationally representative samples of 9-, 13-, and 17-year-olds—showed only slight gains in reading and no improvement in math (U.S. Department of Education, 2008). These disappointing achievement outcomes underscore the need for a "broader, bolder approach to U.S. education." Recommended strategies, verified by research, include:

- providing intellectually challenging, relevant instruction with real-world applications
- strengthening teacher education
- supporting parents in creating stimulating home learning environments, monitoring their children's academic progress, and communicating often with teachers
- investing in high-quality preschool education, so every child arrives at school ready to learn
- vigorously pursuing school improvements that reduce the large inequities in quality of education between SES and ethnic groups (Economic Policy Institute, 2010).

Effective educational change must take into account students' life backgrounds and future goals. As we will see next, besides improving academic instruction, special efforts are needed in vocational education to help non-college-bound youths prepare for productive work roles.

Vocational Preparation of Non-College-Bound Adolescents

Approximately one-third of U.S. young people graduate from high school without plans to go to college. Although they are more likely to find employment than those who drop out, changes in the labor market over the past several decades—labor-saving technologies, outsourcing of U.S. jobs to other countries, and a minimum wage that has not kept up with inflation—have drastically reduced viable work opportunities for high school graduates (Danziger & Ratner, 2010). About 20 percent of recent U.S. high school graduates who do not continue their education are unemployed (U.S. Department of Education, 2011b). When they do find work, most hold low-paid, unskilled jobs. In addition, they have few alternatives for vocational counseling and job placement as they transition from school to work.

American employers regard recent high school graduates as poorly prepared for skilled business and industrial occupations and manual trades. And there is some truth to this impression. In high school, about one-fourth of U.S. adolescents are employed—a greater percentage than in other developed countries. But most are middle-SES students in pursuit of spending money rather than vocational exploration and training. Low-income teenagers who need to contribute to family income or to support themselves find it much harder to get jobs (U.S. Census Bureau, 2011b).

Adolescents typically hold jobs that involve low-level, repetitive tasks and provide little contact with adult supervisors. A heavy commitment to such jobs is harmful. The more hours students work, the poorer their school attendance, the lower their grades, the less likely they are to participate in extracurricular activities, and the more likely they are to drop out (Marsh & Kleitman, 2005). Students who spend many hours at such jobs also tend to feel more distant from their parents and report more drug and alcohol use and delinquent acts (Kouvonen & Kivivuori, 2001; Staff & Uggen, 2003).

In contrast, participation in work–study programs or other jobs that provide academic and vocational learning opportunities is related to positive school and work attitudes, achievement, and reduced delinquency (Hamilton & Hamilton, 2000; Staff & Uggen, 2003). Yet high-quality vocational preparation for non-college-bound U.S. adolescents is scarce. Unlike some European nations, the United States has no widespread training systems to prepare youths for skilled business and industrial occupations and manual trades. Although U.S. federal and state governments support some job-training programs, most are too brief to make a difference and serve only a small minority of young people who need assistance.

In Germany, adolescents who do not go to a Gymnasium (college-preparatory high school) have access to one of the world's most successful work–study apprenticeship systems for entering business and industry. About two-thirds of German youths participate. After completing full-time schooling at age 15 or 16, they spend the remaining two years of compulsory education in the Berufsschule, combining part-time vocational courses with an apprenticeship that is jointly planned by educators and employers. Students train in work settings for more than 350 blue- and white-collar occupations (Deissinger, 2007). Apprentices who complete the program and pass a qualifying examination are certified as skilled workers and earn union-set wages. Businesses provide financial support because they know that the program guarantees a competent, dedicated work force (Heinz, 1999; Kerckhoff, 2002). Many apprentices are hired into well-paid jobs by the firms that train them.

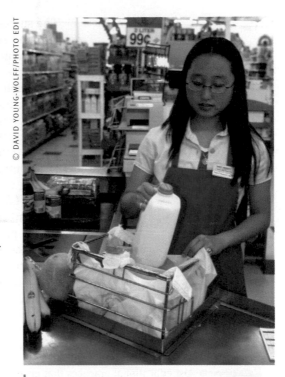

© DAVID YOUNG-WOLFF/PHOTO EDIT

Teenagers' employment opportunities are generally limited to menial, repetitive tasks. Students with a heavy time commitment to such jobs are less likely to participate in extracurricular activities and more likely to drop out of school.

AP IMAGES/CAROLYN KASTER

At a technical high school in Pennsylvania, a baking and pastry student puts the finishing touches on a cake. High-quality vocational education, integrated with academic instruction, motivates students at risk for dropping out to stay in school.

The success of the German system—and of similar systems in Austria, Denmark, Switzerland, and several Eastern European countries—suggests that a national apprenticeship program would improve the transition from high school to work for U.S. non-college-bound young people. The many benefits of bringing together the worlds of schooling and work include helping non-college-bound young people establish productive lives right after graduation, motivating at-risk youths to stay in school, and contributing to the nation's economic growth. Nevertheless, implementing an apprenticeship system poses major challenges: overcoming the reluctance of employers to assume part of the responsibility for vocational training, ensuring cooperation between schools and businesses, and preventing low-SES youths from being concentrated in the lowest-skilled apprenticeship placements or from being unable to find any placement, an obstacle that Germany itself has not yet fully overcome (Lang, 2010).

Currently, small-scale school-to-work projects in the United States are attempting to solve these problems and build bridges between learning and working. Young people who are well-prepared for an economically and personally satisfying work life are much more likely to become productive citizens, devoted family members, and contented adults. The support of families, schools, businesses, communities, and society as a whole can contribute greatly to a positive outcome.

ASK YOURSELF

Review ■ List educational practices that promote positive attitudes toward school, academic motivation, and achievement, and explain why each is effective.

Connect ■ What common factors contribute to the high academic achievement of students in Asian nations and to the academic success of immigrant youths, discussed on page 53 in Chapter 2?

Apply ■ Ray is convinced that his 5-year-old son Trip would learn more in school if only Trip's kindergarten would provide more teacher-directed lessons and worksheets and reduce the time devoted to learning-center activities. Is Ray correct? Explain.

Reflect ■ Describe your experiences in making the transition to middle or junior high school and then to high school. What made these transitions stressful? What helped you adjust?

SUMMARY

Peer Relations (p. 607)

Trace the development of peer sociability from infancy into adolescence, and discuss various influences on peer sociability.

■ Peer sociability begins in infancy with isolated social acts, followed by coordinated exchanges in the second year. During the preschool years, play moves from **nonsocial activity** to **parallel play** and then to **associative** and **cooperative play**. Sociodramatic play becomes especially frequent, supporting cognitive, emotional, and social development.

■ In middle childhood, improved perspective taking permits peer interaction to become more prosocial and cooperative and to transition to rule-oriented games. **Rough-and-tumble play**—important in our evolutionary past for developing fighting skill and establishing **dominance hierarchies**—also becomes common, especially among boys.

■ Parents influence children's social competence both directly, by providing guidance and opportunities for peer contact, and indirectly, through their child-rearing practices.

■ Same-age peers engage in more intense and harmonious exchanges, but mixed-age interaction allows children to acquire new competencies from older companions.

■ In collectivist societies, large-group, imitative play is common. Western-style sociodramatic play is particularly important for social development in societies where child and adult worlds are distinct.

Describe developing concepts and characteristics of friendships in childhood and adolescence, as well as implications of friendship for psychological adjustment.

■ For preschool and young school-age children, **friendship** is a concrete relationship based on shared activities. During middle childhood, children form friendships based on mutual trust. Teenagers' friendships are based on intimacy, mutual understanding, and loyalty.

■ With age, friendships become more selective, stable, and prosocial, providing contexts in which children learn to tolerate criticism and resolve disputes.

- Friends tend to be alike in age, sex, ethnicity, and SES—and, from middle childhood on, in personality, popularity, achievement, and prosocial behavior. Adolescent friends resemble one another in identity status, educational aspirations, political beliefs, and deviance. But to explore new perspectives, they also befriend agemates with differing attitudes and values.

- Girls form closer, more exclusive friendships than boys. Very popular and very unpopular early adolescents are more likely to have other-sex friends.

- Gratifying friendships foster self-concept, perspective taking, and identity development; provide a foundation for intimate relationships; offer support in dealing with everyday stresses; and promote good school adjustment. Aggressive friendships seriously undermine development.

Describe categories of peer acceptance, the relationship of social behavior to likability, and ways to help rejected children.

- Self-report measures of **peer acceptance** yield four main categories: **popular children, rejected children, controversial children,** and **neglected children**. Rejected children often experience lasting adjustment problems.

- **Popular-prosocial children** are academically and socially competent; **popular-antisocial children** are aggressive but admired by peers for their sophisticated social skills. **Rejected-aggressive children** display severe conduct problems, in contrast to **rejected-withdrawn children,** who are passive, socially awkward, and at high risk for **peer victimization.** Controversial children blend positive and negative behaviors. Neglected children, though often choosing to play alone, are usually socially competent and well-adjusted.

- Interventions for rejected children include coaching in social skills, intensive academic tutoring, and training in perspective taking and social problem solving. Treatments must also address maladaptive parent–child interaction.

Discuss peer group formation and dating relationships, including their consequences for development.

- By the end of middle childhood, **peer groups** emerge. Within them, children practice cooperation, leadership, followership, and loyalty to collective goals.

- Early-adolescent peer groups are organized into more intimate **cliques**, several of which may form a **crowd** that grants adolescents an identity within the larger social structure of Western schools. Peer group values extend those acquired at home. Mixed-sex cliques provide a supportive context for learning to interact with the other sex.

- Intimacy in dating lags behind that in friendships; early, frequent dating is linked to adjustment problems. Positive relationships with parents and friends contribute to warm romantic ties, which provide practice for more mature bonds.

What factors influence conformity to peer pressure in adolescence?

- Most peer pressure focuses on obvious aspects of peer culture, such as dress and participation in social activities. Resistance to unfavorable peer pressure strengthens with age and is related to adolescent personal characteristics and to authoritative parenting.

Media (p. 629)

Discuss the influence of television on children's development.

- Television is the dominant form of youth media. Boys and low-SES, African-American, and Hispanic children tend to be more frequent viewers. Extensive TV watching is associated with family, peer, and health difficulties.

- Televised violence promotes hostile thoughts and emotions, aggression, and a violent worldview. TV also conveys ethnic and gender stereotypes. Heavy bombardment of children with advertising contributes to many problems, including family stress, overweight and obesity, materialism, and substance use.

- Educational television can promote children's cognitive and academic skills, emotional and social understanding, and prosocial behavior. But heavy viewing of entertainment TV detracts from reading time, school success, and social experiences.

Discuss computer, cell phone, and Internet use by children and adolescents, noting benefits and concerns.

- Computers' educational benefits include word processing for writing and online information-gathering—activities that promote literacy progress and reading achievement. However, girls and low-SES students are disadvantaged in computer opportunities and skills.

- Speed-and-action video games foster selective attention and spatial skills, but violent games promote hostility and aggression. "Passionate" players tend to use games to escape from family and school problems.

- Teenagers' online communication with pre-existing friends, through such means as texting and instant messaging, promotes friendship closeness. Using the Internet to interact with strangers can offer vital sources of social support, but teenagers who form online friendships or romances tend to be troubled young people who are at risk for exploitation.

Schooling (p. 637)

How do class and student body size and educational philosophies affect academic and social development?

- Smaller classes in the early elementary grades promote lasting gains in academic achievement. Smaller high schools foster social support and greater school engagement.

- Older students in **traditional classrooms** have a slight edge in academic achievement over those in **constructivist classrooms**, who are advantaged in critical thinking, social and moral maturity, and positive attitudes toward school. But young children in traditional classrooms display poorer study habits and achievement through elementary school.

- Students in **social-constructivist classrooms** benefit both cognitively and socially from collaboration with teachers and peers. In classrooms organized as **communities of learners**, teachers and students draw on one another's expertises to work on complex projects with real-world meaning.

Cite factors that influence adjustment following school transitions in early childhood and in adolescence.

- The capacity to form positive peer and teacher relationships predicts favorable adjustment to kindergarten. Children with weak emotional self-regulation skills and argumentative, aggressive, or peer-avoidant styles tend to establish poor-quality relationships with teachers and peers.

- School transitions in adolescence bring larger, more impersonal school environments, in which both grades and feelings of competence decline. Girls experience more adjustment difficulties after the transition to middle school, which coincides with other life changes (puberty and the beginning of dating). Distressed young people with poor school performance are at risk for continuing academic difficulties and eventual dropout.

Discuss the role of teacher–student interaction and grouping practices in academic achievement.

■ Caring, helpful, and stimulating teaching fosters children's motivation and achievement. **Educational self-fulfilling prophecies** are particularly strong in classrooms emphasizing competition and public evaluation, and they have a greater impact on low achievers.

■ Homogeneous grouping in elementary school is linked to poorer-quality instruction and declines in self-esteem and achievement for children in low-ability groups. Multigrade classrooms promote favorable school attitudes, achievement, and self-esteem.

■ By high school, some homogeneous grouping is educationally necessary, but in the United States, high school tracking extends earlier educational inequalities. Low-SES students are at risk for unfair placement in non-college tracks.

Under what conditions is placement of students with special needs in regular classrooms successful, and how can schools increase parent involvement in education?

■ Effective placement of students with mild intellectual disability and specific **learning disabilities** in **inclusive classrooms** depends on learning experiences tailored to children's academic needs and promotion of positive peer relations.

© ELLEN B. SENISI PHOTOGRAPHY

■ Schools can increase parent involvement by fostering parent–teacher relationships, building bridges between minority home cultures and the school culture, and involving parents in school governance.

How well are American young people achieving compared with their counterparts in other industrialized nations, and what problems do non-college-bound youths face in preparing for a vocation?

■ In international studies, U.S. students typically display average or below-average performance. Compared with education in top-achieving countries, U.S. instruction is less focused on high-level reasoning and critical thinking. Whereas high-achieving nations emphasize equal opportunity for all, U.S. low-income and ethnic minority students typically attend inferior-quality schools.

■ Unlike some European nations, the United States has no widespread vocational training system to help non-college-bound adolescents prepare for skilled business and industrial occupations and manual trades.

IMPORTANT TERMS AND CONCEPTS

associative play (p. 608)
clique (p. 623)
community of learners (p. 640)
constructivist classroom (p. 638)
controversial children (p. 619)
cooperative play (p. 608)
crowd (p. 623)
dominance hierarchy (p. 610)
educational self-fulfilling prophecy (p. 643)

friendship (p. 613)
inclusive classroom (p. 646)
learning disability (p. 646)
neglected children (p. 619)
nonsocial activity (p. 608)
parallel play (p. 608)
peer acceptance (p. 618)
peer group (p. 622)
peer victimization (p. 621)

popular children (p. 618)
popular-antisocial children (p. 619)
popular-prosocial children (p. 619)
rejected children (p. 618)
rejected-aggressive children (p. 619)
rejected-withdrawn children (p. 620)
rough-and-tumble play (p. 610)
social-constructivist classroom (p. 640)
traditional classroom (p. 638)

Glossary

A

accommodation In Piaget's theory, that part of adaptation in which new schemes are created or old ones adjusted to produce a better fit with the environment. Distinguished from *assimilation*. (p. 227)

acculturative stress Psychological distress resulting from conflict between an individual's minority culture and the host culture. (p. 475)

achievement motivation The tendency to persist at challenging tasks. (p. 465)

achievement test A test that assesses actual knowledge and skill attainment. Distinguished from *aptitude test*. (p. 328)

adaptation In Piaget's theory, the process of building schemes through direct interaction with the environment. Consists of two complementary activities: *assimilation* and *accommodation*. (p. 227)

affordances The action possibilities that a situation offers an organism with certain motor capabilities. Discovery of affordances plays a vital role in perceptual differentiation. (p. 168)

age of viability The age at which a fetus born early first has a chance of survival, occurring sometime between 22 and 26 weeks. (p. 92)

alcohol-related neurodevelopmental disorder (ARND) The least severe form of fetal alcohol spectrum disorder, involving brain injury but with typical physical growth and absence of facial abnormalities. Distinguished from *fetal alcohol syndrome (FAS)* and *partial fetal alcohol syndrome (p-FAS)*. (p. 99)

allele Each of two or more forms of a gene located at the same place on the chromosomes. (p. 77)

amnion The inner membrane that encloses the prenatal organism in amniotic fluid, which helps keep temperature constant and provides a cushion against jolts caused by the mother's movement. (p. 89)

amodal sensory properties Information that is not specific to a single modality but that overlaps two or more sensory systems, such as rate, rhythm, duration, intensity, temporal synchrony (for vision and hearing), and texture and shape (for vision and touch). (p. 166)

amygdala An inner-brain structure that plays a central role in processing emotional information. (p. 190)

analogical problem solving Applying a solution strategy from one problem to other relevant problems. (p. 235)

androgens Hormones released chiefly by boys' testes, and in smaller amounts by the adrenal glands, that influence the pubertal growth spurt and stimulate muscle growth, body and facial hair, and male sex characteristics. (p. 183)

androgyny The gender identity held by individuals who score high on both traditionally masculine and traditionally feminine personality characteristics. (p. 547)

anorexia nervosa An eating disorder in which young people, mainly females, starve themselves because of a compulsive fear of getting fat and an extremely distorted body image. (p. 210)

A-not-B search error The error made by 8- to 12-month-olds who, after an object is moved from one hiding place (A) to another hiding place (B), search for it incorrectly in the first hiding place (A). (p. 229)

Apgar Scale A rating system used to assess a newborn baby's physical condition immediately after birth on the basis of five characteristics: heart rate, respiratory effort, reflex irritability, muscle tone, and color. (p. 109)

aptitude test A test that assesses an individual's potential to learn a specialized activity. Distinguished from *achievement test*. (p. 328)

assimilation In Piaget's theory, that part of adaptation in which the external world is interpreted in terms of current schemes. Distinguished from *accommodation*. (p. 227)

associative play A form of social interaction in which children engage in separate activities but interact by exchanging toys and commenting on one another's behavior. Distinguished from *nonsocial activity, parallel play,* and *cooperative play*. (p. 608)

attachment The strong, affectionate tie that humans have with special people in their lives, which leads them to feel pleasure when interacting with those people and to be comforted by their nearness in times of stress. (p. 428)

Attachment Q-Sort A method for assessing the quality of attachment between ages 1 and 4 years through home observations of a variety of attachment-related behaviors. (p. 431)

attention-deficit hyperactivity disorder (ADHD) A childhood disorder involving inattention, impulsivity, and excessive motor activity, often leading to academic and social problems. (p. 290)

attribution retraining An intervention that uses adult feedback to encourage learned-helpless children to believe that they can overcome failure through effort. (p. 467)

attributions Common, everyday explanations for the causes of behavior. (p. 464)

authoritarian child-rearing style A child-rearing style that is low in acceptance and involvement, high in coercive behavioral control, and low in autonomy granting. Distinguished from *authoritative, permissive,* and *uninvolved child-rearing styles*. (p. 574)

authoritative child-rearing style A child-rearing style that is high in acceptance and involvement, emphasizes adaptive control techniques, and includes gradual, appropriate autonomy granting. Distinguished from *authoritarian, permissive,* and *uninvolved child-rearing styles*. (p. 573)

autobiographical memory Representations of one-time events that are long-lasting because they are imbued with personal meaning. (p. 298)

automatic processes In information processing, processes that are so well-learned that they require no space in working memory and, therefore, permit the individual to focus on other information while simultaneously performing them. (p. 280)

autonomy In adolescence, a sense of oneself as a separate, self-governing individual. Involves relying more on oneself and less on parents for support and guidance and engaging in careful, well-reasoned decision making. (p. 577)

autosomes The 22 matching chromosome pairs in each human cell. (p. 76)

avoidant attachment The attachment pattern characterizing infants who seem unresponsive to the parent when she is present, are usually not distressed when she leaves, and avoid the parent when she returns. Distinguished from *secure, resistant,* and *disorganized/disoriented attachment*. (p. 430)

B

babbling Babies' repetition of consonant–vowel combinations, often in long strings, beginning around 6 months of age. (p. 370)

basic emotions Emotions such as happiness, interest, surprise, fear, anger, sadness, and disgust that are universal in humans and other primates and have a long evolutionary history of promoting survival. (p. 406)

behavioral genetics A field devoted to uncovering the contributions of nature and nurture to the diversity of human traits and abilities. (p. 119)

behaviorism An approach that regards directly observable events—stimuli and responses—as the appropriate focus of study and that views the development of behavior as taking place through classical and operant conditioning. (p. 17)

behavior modification Procedures that combine conditioning and modeling to eliminate undesirable behaviors and increase desirable responses. (p. 18)

belief–desire theory of mind The more sophisticated theory of mind that emerges around age 4, in which children understand that both beliefs and desires determine behavior. (p. 452)

biased sampling Failure to select participants who are representative of the population of interest in a study. (p. 61)

bicultural identity The identity constructed by individuals who explore and adopt values from both their family's subculture and the dominant culture. (p. 475)

blended, or **reconstituted, family** A family structure formed through cohabitation or remarriage that includes parent, child, and steprelatives. (p. 594)

body image Conception of and attitude toward one's physical appearance. (p. 209)

brain plasticity The capacity of various parts of the cerebral cortex to take over functions of damaged regions. Declines as hemispheres of the cerebral cortex lateralize. (p. 187)

breech position A position of the baby in the uterus that would cause the buttocks or feet to be delivered first. (p. 113)

Broca's area A structure located in the left frontal lobe of the cerebral cortex that supports grammatical processing and language production. (p. 363)

bulimia nervosa An eating disorder in which individuals, mainly girls but also including some gay and bisexual boys, engage in strict dieting and excessive exercise accompanied by binge eating, often followed by deliberate vomiting and purging with laxatives. (p. 211)

C

canalization The tendency of heredity to restrict the development of some characteristics to just one or a few outcomes. (p. 122)

cardinality The mathematical principle stating that the last word in a counting sequence indicates the quantity of items in the set. (p. 311)

carrier A heterozygous individual who can pass a recessive trait to his or her offspring. (p. 77)

categorical self Classification of the self on the basis of perceptually distinct attributes and behaviors, such as age, sex, physical characteristics, and goodness and badness. Develops between 18 and 30 months. Distinguished from *remembered self, enduring self,* and *inner self.* (p. 450)

categorical speech perception The tendency to perceive as identical a range of sounds that belong to the same phonemic class. (p. 368)

central conceptual structures In Case's neo-Piagetian theory, networks of concepts and relations that permit children to think about a wide range of situations in more advanced ways. Generated once the schemes of a Piagetian stage become sufficiently automatic and brain development further increments processing speed, freeing enough space in working memory to consolidate schemes into an improved representational form. (p. 283)

central executive In information processing, the conscious, reflective part of the mental system, which directs the flow of information by deciding what to attend to; coordinating incoming information with information already in the system; and selecting, applying, and monitoring strategies that facilitate memory storage, comprehension, reasoning, and problem solving. (p. 279)

centration In Piaget's theory, the tendency to focus on one aspect of a situation, neglecting other important features. (p. 245)

cephalocaudal trend An organized pattern of physical growth and motor control in which the head develops ahead of the lower part of the body ("head to tail"). Distinguished from *proximodistal trend.* (p. 176)

cerebellum A structure at the rear and base of the brain that aids in balance and control of body movement. (p. 189)

cerebral cortex The largest, most complex structure of the human brain, containing the greatest number of neurons and synapses, which accounts for the highly developed intelligence of the human species. (p. 186)

child development An area of study devoted to understanding constancy and change from conception through adolescence. (p. 4)

child-rearing styles Combinations of parenting behaviors that occur over a wide range of situations, creating an enduring child-rearing climate. (p. 573)

chorion The outer membrane that forms a protective covering around the prenatal organism. It sends out tiny hairlike villi, from which the placenta begins to develop. (p. 89)

chromosomes Rodlike structures in the cell nucleus that store and transmit genetic information. (p. 73)

chronosystem In ecological systems theory, temporal changes in children's environments, either externally imposed or arising from within the child, that produce new conditions affecting development. Distinguished from *microsystem, mesosystem, exosystem,* and *macrosystem.* (p. 28)

circular reaction In Piaget's theory, a means of adapting schemes in which babies try to repeat a chance event originally caused by their own motor activity. (p. 228)

classical conditioning A form of learning that involves associating a neutral stimulus with a stimulus that leads to a reflexive response. Once the nervous system makes the connection between the two stimuli, the new stimulus will produce the behavior by itself. (p. 140)

clinical interview An interview method in which the researcher uses a flexible, conversational style to probe for the participant's point of view. (p. 46)

clinical, or case study, method A research method in which the aim is to obtain as complete a picture as possible of one child's psychological functioning by bringing together a wide range of information, including interviews, observations, test scores, and sometimes neurobiological measures. (p. 50)

clique A group of about five to eight members who are friends and, therefore, tend to resemble one another in family background, attitudes, values, and interests. (p. 623)

code switching A strategy in which bilingual individuals produce an utterance in one language that contains one or more "guest" words from the other, without violating the grammar of either language. (p. 396)

cognition The inner processes and products of the mind that lead to "knowing," including all mental activity—attending, remembering, symbolizing, categorizing, planning, reasoning, problem solving, creating, and fantasizing. (p. 225)

cognitive-developmental theory Piaget's theory of development, which views children as actively constructing knowledge as they manipulate and explore their world and regards cognitive development as taking place in stages. (p. 19)

cognitive maps Mental representations of familiar large-scale spaces, such as school or neighborhood. (p. 250)

cognitive self-regulation The process of continuously monitoring and controlling progress toward a goal—planning, checking outcomes, and redirecting unsuccessful efforts. (p. 304)

cohort effects The effects of cultural–historical change on the accuracy of longitudinal and cross-sectional research findings. Results based on one cohort—children developing in the same time period who are influenced by particular cultural and historical conditions—may not apply to other cohorts. (p. 62)

collectivist societies Societies in which people define themselves as part of a group and stress group goals over individual goals. Distinguished from *individualistic societies.* (p. 35)

community of learners A classroom in which both teachers and students have the authority to define and resolve problems, drawing on one another's expertise and that of others as they work toward project goals, which often address complex real-world issues. (p. 640)

compliance Voluntary obedience to requests and commands. (p. 514)

componential analysis Research that combines the psychometric and information-processing approaches in an effort to identify relationships between aspects (or components) of information processing and children's intelligence test performance. (p. 323)

comprehension In language development, the words children understand. Distinguished from *production.* (p. 376)

concrete operational stage Piaget's third stage, extending from about 7 to 11 years, during which thought becomes logical, flexible, and organized in its application to concrete information. (p. 249)

conditioned response (CR) In classical conditioning, a new response produced by a conditioned stimulus (CS) that is similar to the unconditioned, or reflexive, response (UCR). (p. 140)

conditioned stimulus (CS) In classical conditioning, a neutral stimulus that, through pairing with an unconditioned stimulus (UCS), leads to a new, conditioned response (CR). (p. 140)

confounding variables Variables so closely associated that their effects on an outcome cannot be distinguished. (p. 57)

conservation The understanding that certain physical characteristics of objects remain the same, even when their outward appearance changes. (p. 244)

construction In moral development, the process of actively attending to and interrelating multiple perspectives on situations in which social conflicts arise and thereby attaining new moral understandings. (p. 495)

constructivist approach Piaget's view of cognitive development, in which children discover, or construct, virtually all knowledge about their world through their own activity. (p. 226)

constructivist classroom A classroom grounded in Piaget's view of children as active learners who construct their own knowledge. Characterized by richly equipped learning centers, small groups and individuals solving self-chosen problems, a teacher who guides and supports in response to children's needs, and evaluation that considers students' progress in relation to their own prior development. Distinguished from *traditional classroom* and *social constructivist classroom*. (p. 638)

contexts Unique combinations of personal and environmental circumstances that can result in different paths of development. (p. 8)

continuous development The view that development is a process of gradually adding more of the same types of skills that were there to begin with. Distinguished from *discontinuous development*. (p. 7)

contrast sensitivity A general principle accounting for early pattern preferences, which states that if babies can detect a difference in contrast between two or more patterns, they will prefer the one with more contrast. (p. 161)

control deficiency Inability to control, or execute, a mental strategy effectively. Distinguished from *production deficiency, utilization deficiency,* and *effective strategy use*. (p. 288)

controversial children Children who get many votes, both positive and negative, on self-report measures of peer acceptance, indicating that they are both liked and disliked. Distinguished from *popular, rejected,* and *neglected children*. (p. 618)

conventional level Kohlberg's second level of moral development, in which moral understanding is based on conforming to social rules to ensure positive human relationships and maintain societal order. (p. 501)

convergent thinking Thinking that involves arriving at a single correct answer to a problem; the type of thinking emphasized on intelligence tests. Distinguished from *divergent thinking*. (p. 350)

cooing Pleasant vowel-like noises made by infants, beginning around 2 months of age. (p. 370)

cooperative learning Collaboration on a task by a small group of peers who work toward common goals by resolving differences of opinion, sharing responsibilities, and providing one another with sufficient explanations to correct misunderstandings. (p. 271)

cooperative play A form of social interaction in which children orient toward a common goal, such as acting out a make-believe theme. Distinguished from *nonsocial activity, parallel play,* and *associative play*. (p. 608)

coparenting Parents' mutual support of each other's parenting behaviors. (p. 569)

core knowledge perspective A perspective that states that infants begin life with innate, special-purpose knowledge systems, or core domains of thought, each of which permits a ready grasp of new, related information and therefore supports early, rapid development of certain aspects of cognition. (p. 261)

coregulation A form of supervision in which parents exercise general oversight while permitting children to take charge of moment-by-moment decision making. (p. 577)

corpus callosum The large bundle of fibers connecting the two cerebral hemispheres. (p. 190)

correlation coefficient A number, ranging from +1.00 to –1.00, that describes the strength and direction of the relationship between two variables. (p. 56)

correlational design A research design in which the investigator gathers information on individuals without altering their experiences and then examines relationships between participants' characteristics and their behavior or development. Does not permit inferences about cause and effect. (p. 55)

creativity The ability to produce work that is original yet appropriate—something that others have not thought of but that is useful in some way. (p. 350)

crossing over During meiosis, the exchange of genes between chromosomes next to each other. (p. 75)

cross-sectional design A research design in which groups of participants differing in age are studied at the same point in time. Distinguished from *longitudinal design*. (p. 62)

crowd A large, loosely organized social group consisting of several cliques, with membership based on reputation and stereotype. (p. 623)

crystallized intelligence In Cattell's theory, a form of intelligence involving skills that depend on accumulated knowledge and experience, good judgment, and mastery of social customs. Distinguished from *fluid intelligence*. (p. 321)

D

debriefing Providing a full account and justification of research activities to participants after the conclusion of a study in which deception was used. (p. 69)

deferred imitation The ability to remember and copy the behavior of models who are not present. (p. 230)

delay of gratification Ability to wait for an appropriate time and place to engage in a tempting act. (p. 514)

deoxyribonucleic acid (DNA) Long, double-stranded molecules that make up chromosomes. (p. 74)

dependent variable The variable the researcher expects to be influenced by the independent variable in an experiment. (p. 56)

desire theory of mind The theory of mind of 2- to 3-year-olds, who assume that people always act in ways consistent with their desires but who do not understand the influence on behavior of interpretive mental states, such as beliefs. (p. 452)

developmental cognitive neuroscience An area of investigation that brings together researchers from psychology, biology, neuroscience, and medicine to study the relationship between changes in the brain and the developing child's cognitive processing and behavior patterns. (p. 23)

developmental quotient (DQ) A score on an infant intelligence test, computed in the same manner as an IQ but labeled more conservatively because it does not tap the same dimensions of intelligence measured in older children. (p. 329)

developmental science An interdisciplinary field devoted to the study of all changes humans experience throughout the lifespan. (p. 4)

developmentally appropriate practice Research-based standards devised by the National Association for the Education of Young Children that specify program characteristics that meet the developmental and individual needs of young children of varying ages. (p. 443)

differentiation theory The view that perceptual development involves the detection of increasingly fine-grained, invariant features of the environment. (p. 168)

difficult child A child whose temperament is characterized by irregular daily routines, slow acceptance of new experiences, and a tendency to react negatively and intensely. Distinguished from *easy child* and *slow-to-warm-up child*. (p. 420)

discontinuous development The view that development is a process in which new ways of understanding and responding to the world emerge at specific times. Distinguished from *continuous development*. (p. 7)

disorganized/disoriented attachment The attachment pattern reflecting the greatest insecurity, characterizing infants who show confused, contradictory behaviors when reunited with the parent after a separation. Distinguished from *secure, avoidant,* and *resistant attachment*. (p. 431)

displaced reference The realization that words can be used to cue mental images of things that are not physically present. (p. 235)

distance curve A growth curve that plots the average size of a sample of children at each age, indicating typical yearly progress toward maturity. Distinguished from *velocity curve*. (p. 176)

divergent thinking Thinking that involves generating multiple and unusual possibilities when faced with a task or problem; associated with creativity. Distinguished from *convergent thinking*. (p. 350)

dominance hierarchy A stable ordering of group members that predicts who will win when conflict arises. (p. 610)

dominant cerebral hemisphere The hemisphere of the cerebral cortex with greater capacity to carry out skilled motor action and where other important abilities (language) generally are located. In right-handed individuals, the left hemisphere is dominant; in left-handed individuals, language is often shared between the hemispheres. (p. 189)

dominant–recessive inheritance A pattern of inheritance in which, under heterozygous conditions, the influence of only one allele is apparent. (p. 77)

dual representation The ability to view a symbolic object as both an object in its own right and a symbol. (p. 243)

dynamic assessment An approach to testing consistent with Vygotsky's zone of proximal development in which an adult introduces purposeful teaching into the testing situation to find out what the child can attain with social support. (p. 342)

dynamic systems perspective A view that regards the child's mind, body, and physical and social worlds as an integrated system that guides mastery of new skills. A change in any part of the system disrupts the current organism–environment relationship, leading the child to reorganize his or her behavior so the components of the system work together again but in a more complex, effective way. (p. 30)

dynamic systems theory of motor development A theory that views new motor skills as reorganizations of previously mastered skills, which lead to more effective ways of exploring and controlling the environment. Each new skill is a joint product of central nervous system development, the body's movement possibilities, the child's goals, and environmental supports for the skill. (p. 148)

E

Early Head Start A U.S. federal program that provides infants and toddlers who have serious developmental problems or are at risk for problems because of poverty with coordinated early intervention services, including child care, educational experiences, parenting education, family social support, and health care. (p. 349)

easy child A child whose temperament is characterized by establishment of regular routines in infancy, general cheerfulness, and easy adaptation to new experiences. Distinguished from *difficult child* and *slow-to-warm-up child.* (p. 420)

ecological systems theory Bronfenbrenner's theory, which views the child as developing within a complex system of relationships affected by multiple levels of the surrounding environment, from immediate settings of family and school to broad cultural values, laws, customs, and resources. (p. 26)

educational self-fulfilling prophecies Teachers' positive or negative views of individual children, who tend to adopt and start to live up to those views. (p. 643)

effective strategy use Consistent use of a mental strategy, with corresponding improvement in performance. Distinguished from *production deficiency, control deficiency,* and *utilization deficiency.* (p. 289)

effortful control The self-regulatory dimension of temperament, involving voluntary suppression of a dominant response in order to plan and execute a more adaptive response. (p. 421)

egocentrism Failure to distinguish others' symbolic viewpoints from one's own. (p. 244)

elaboration A memory strategy that involves creating a relationship, or shared meaning, between two or more pieces of information that do not belong to the same category. (p. 293)

embryo The prenatal organism from 2 to 8 weeks after conception—the period when the groundwork is laid for all body structures and internal organs. (p. 91)

emergent literacy Children's active efforts to construct literacy knowledge through informal experiences. (p. 307)

emergentist coalition model The view that word-learning strategies emerge out of children's efforts to decipher language, during which they draw on a coalition of perceptual, social, and linguistic cues that shift in importance with age. (p. 383)

emotion A rapid appraisal of the personal significance of a situation, which prepares the individual for action. (p. 401)

emotional display rules A society's rules specifying when, where, and how it is appropriate to express emotions. (p. 412)

emotional intelligence A set of emotional abilities that enable individuals to process and adapt to emotional information, measured by tapping emotional skills that enable people to manage their own emotions and interact competently with others. (p. 327)

emotional self-regulation Strategies for adjusting our emotional state to a comfortable level of intensity so we can accomplish our goals. (p. 409)

emotion-centered coping A general strategy for managing emotion that is internal, private, and aimed at controlling distress when little can be done to change an outcome. Distinguished from *problem-centered coping.* (p. 412)

empathy The ability to take another individual's emotional perspective and to feel with that person, or respond emotionally in a similar way. (p. 416)

enduring self A view of the self as persisting over time. Distinguished from *categorical self, remembered self,* and *inner self.* (p. 451)

entity view of ability The view that ability is a fixed characteristic that cannot be improved through effort; associated with learned helplessness. Distinguished from *incremental view of ability.* (p. 465)

environmental cumulative deficit hypothesis The view that the negative effects of underprivileged rearing conditions increase the longer children remain in those conditions, making early cognitive deficits harder to overcome. (p. 331)

epigenesis Development resulting from ongoing, bidirectional exchanges between heredity and all levels of the environment. (p. 124)

epiphyses Growth centers at the ends of each of the long bones of the body, where new cartilage cells are produced and gradually harden. (p. 178)

episodic memory Recollections of specific personally experienced events. (p. 297)

equilibration In Piaget's theory, the back-and-forth movement between equilibrium and disequilibrium that produces more effective schemes. (p. 227)

estrogens Hormones released by girls' ovaries that cause the breasts, uterus, and vagina to mature, the body to take on feminine proportions, and fat to accumulate. Estrogens also contribute to regulation of the menstrual cycle. (p. 183)

ethnic identity A sense of ethnic group membership, and attitudes and feelings associated with that membership, as an enduring aspect of the self. (p. 475)

ethnography A descriptive, qualitative research method directed at understanding a culture or a distinct social group through participant observation—living with group members and taking field notes for an extended period. (p. 52)

ethological theory of attachment A theory formulated by Bowlby that recognizes the infant's emotional tie to the caregiver as an evolved response that promotes survival. (p. 428)

ethology An approach concerned with the adaptive, or survival, value of behavior and its evolutionary history. (p. 23)

event sampling A form of systematic observation in which the researcher records all instances of a particular behavior during a specified time period. (p. 44)

evolutionary developmental psychology An approach that seeks to understand the adaptive value of species-wide cognitive, emotional, and social competencies as those competencies change with age. (p. 24)

executive function In information processing, the set of cognitive operations and strategies necessary for self-initiated, purposeful behavior in relatively novel, challenging situations. (p. 281)

exosystem In ecological systems theory, social settings that do not contain children but that affect children's experiences in immediate settings—for example, parents' workplace, health and welfare services in the community, and parents' social networks. Distinguished from *microsystem, mesosystem, macrosystem,* and *chronosystem.* (p. 28)

expansions Adult responses that elaborate on children's speech, increasing its complexity. (p. 389)

experience-dependent brain growth Growth and refinement of established brain structures as a result of specific learning experiences that vary widely across individuals and cultures. Distinguished from *experience-expectant brain growth.* (p. 191)

experience-expectant brain growth The young brain's rapidly developing organization, which depends on ordinary experiences—opportunities to interact with people, hear language and other sounds, see and touch objects, and move about and explore the environment. Distinguished from *experience-dependent brain growth*. (p. 191)

experimental design A research design in which the investigator randomly assigns participants to two or more treatment conditions and studies the effect that manipulating an independent variable has on a dependent variable. Permits inferences about cause and effect. (p. 56)

expressive style A style of early language learning in which toddlers use language mainly to talk about their own and others' feelings and needs, with an initial vocabulary emphasizing social formulas and pronouns. Distinguished from *referential style*. (p. 378)

expressive traits Personality traits emphasizing warmth, caring, and sensitivity, that are widely regarded as feminine. Distinguished from *instrumental traits*. (p. 530)

extended-family household A household in which one or more adult relatives live with the parent–child nuclear family unit. (p. 583)

external validity The degree to which research findings generalize to settings and participants outside the original study. Distinguished from *internal validity*. (p. 55)

extinction In classical conditioning, decline of the conditioned response (CR) as a result of presenting the conditioned stimulus (CS) enough times, without being paired with the unconditioned stimulus (UCS). (p. 140)

F

factor analysis A complicated correlational procedure that identifies sets of test items that cluster together, called factors. Used to investigate whether intelligence is one trait or an assortment of abilities. (p. 321)

fast-mapping Children's ability to connect a new word with an underlying concept after only a brief encounter. (p. 377)

fetal alcohol spectrum disorder (FASD) A range of physical, mental, and behavioral outcomes caused by prenatal alcohol exposure. (p. 98)

fetal alcohol syndrome (FAS) The most severe form of fetal alcohol spectrum disorder, distinguished by slow physical growth, facial abnormalities, and brain injury; usually affects children whose mothers drank heavily throughout pregnancy. Distinguished from *partial fetal alcohol syndrome (p-FAS)* and *alcohol-related neurodevelopmental disorder (ARND)*. (p. 98)

fetus The prenatal organism from the ninth week to the end of pregnancy—the period in which body structures are completed and dramatic growth in size occurs. (p. 92)

field experiment A research design in which participants are randomly assigned to treatment conditions in natural settings. (p. 58)

fluid intelligence In Cattell's theory, a form of intelligence that depends primarily on basic information-processing skills—ability to detect relationships among stimuli, speed of analyzing information, and capacity of working memory. Distinguished from *crystallized intelligence*. (p. 321)

Flynn effect An increase in IQ from one generation to the next. (p. 338)

formal operational stage Piaget's highest stage, beginning around age 11, in which adolescents develop the capacity for abstract, systematic, scientific thinking. (p. 253)

fraternal, or dizygotic, twins Twins resulting from the release and fertilization of two ova. Genetically, they are no more alike than ordinary siblings. Distinguished from *identical, or monozygotic, twins*. (p. 76)

friendship A close relationship involving companionship in which each partner wants to be with the other. (p. 613)

functionalist approach to emotion A perspective emphasizing that the broad function of emotions is to energize behavior aimed at attaining personal goals. (p. 401)

fuzzy-trace theory A theory proposing that when we first encode information, we automatically reconstruct it into a vague, fuzzy version, or gist, which preserves essential meaning without details and is especially useful for reasoning. (p. 296)

G

gametes Sex cells, or sperm and ova, which contain half as many chromosomes as regular body cells. (p. 75)

gender consistency Kohlberg's final stage of gender understanding, in which children in the late preschool and early school years understand that sex

is biologically based and remains the same even if a person dresses in "cross-gender" clothes or engages in nontraditional activities. (p. 548)

gender constancy A full understanding of the biologically based permanence of gender, which combines three understandings: *gender labeling*, *gender stability*, and *gender consistency*. (p. 548)

gender identity An image of oneself as relatively masculine or feminine in characteristics. (p. 530)

gender intensification The increased gender stereotyping of attitudes and behavior and movement toward a more traditional gender identity that sometimes occurs with the arrival of adolescence. (p. 550)

gender labeling Kohlberg's first stage of gender understanding, in which children in the early preschool years can correctly label their own sex and that of others but do not understand that sex is biologically based and permanent. (p. 548)

gender roles The reflection of gender stereotypes in everyday behavior. (p. 530)

gender schema theory An information-processing approach to gender typing that explains how environmental pressures and children's cognitions work together to shape gender-typing. (p. 551)

gender stability Kohlberg's second stage of gender understanding, in which preschoolers grasp the stability of sex over time. (p. 548)

gender-stereotype flexibility The belief that both males and females can display a gender-stereotyped personality trait or activity. (p. 533)

gender stereotypes Widely held beliefs about characteristics deemed appropriate for males and females. (p. 530)

gender typing Any association of objects, activities, roles, or traits with biological sex in ways that conform to cultural stereotypes of gender. (p. 530)

gene A segment of a DNA molecule that contains instructions for production of various proteins that contribute to body growth and functioning. (p. 74)

gene–environment correlation The idea that heredity influences the environments to which individuals are exposed. (p. 122)

gene–environment interaction The idea that individuals' genetic makeup influences their responsiveness to qualities of the environment (p. 121)

general intelligence In Spearman's theory, a common underlying factor, called *g*, believed to influence all aspects of intelligence. Distinguished from *specific intelligence*. (p. 321)

generalized other A blend of what we imagine important people in our lives think of us, crucial to developing a self-concept based on personality traits. (p. 459)

genetic counseling A communication process designed to help couples assess their chances of giving birth to a baby with a hereditary disorder and choose the best course of action in view of risks and family goals. (p. 84)

genomic imprinting A pattern of inheritance in which alleles are imprinted, or chemically marked, in such a way that one pair member is activated, regardless of its makeup. (p. 80)

genotype An individual's genetic makeup. Distinguished from *phenotype*. (p. 73)

gifted Displaying exceptional intellectual strengths, including high IQ, creativity, and talent. (p. 350)

gist In fuzzy-trace theory, a vague, fuzzy representation of information that preserves essential meaning without details and is especially useful for reasoning. (p. 296)

glial cells Cells responsible for myelination of neural fibers, which improves the efficiency of message transfer. (p. 186)

goodness-of-fit model Thomas and Chess's model, which states that an effective match, or "good fit," between a child's temperament and the child-rearing environment promotes more adaptive functioning, whereas a "poor fit" results in adjustment problems. (p. 426)

grammar The component of language concerned with *syntax*, the rules by which words are arranged into sentences, and *morphology*, the use of grammatical markers indicating number, tense, case, person, gender, active or passive voice, and other meanings. (p. 360)

grammatical morphemes In language development, small markers that change the meaning of sentences, as in "John's dog" and "he *is* eating." (p. 386)

growth faltering Failure of an infant to grow normally, characterized by weight, height, and head circumference substantially below age-related growth norms and by withdrawn, apathetic behavior. A disturbed parent–infant relationship is often a contributing factor. (p. 202)

growth hormone (GH) A pituitary hormone that affects the development of all body tissues except the central nervous system and the genitals. (p. 182)

guided participation Shared endeavors between more expert and less expert participants, regardless of the precise features of communication. A broader concept than *scaffolding*. (p. 268)

H

habituation A gradual reduction in the strength of a response due to repetitive stimulation. (p. 142)

heritability estimate A measure of the extent to which individual differences in complex traits, such as intelligence or personality in a specific population, are due to genetic factors. (p. 120)

heteronomous morality Piaget's first stage of moral development, in which children view rules as handed down by authorities, as having a permanent existence, as unchangeable, and as requiring strict obedience. (p. 496)

heterozygous Having two different alleles at the same place on a pair of chromosomes. Distinguished from *homozygous*. (p. 77)

hierarchical classification The organization of objects into classes and subclasses on the basis of similarities and differences. (p. 245)

hippocampus An inner-brain structure that plays a vital role in memory and in images of space that help us find our way. (p. 190)

Home Observation for Measurement of the Environment (HOME) A checklist for gathering information about the quality of children's home lives through observation and parental interview. (p. 344)

homozygous Having two identical alleles at the same place on a pair of chromosomes. Distinguished from *heterozygous*. (p. 77)

hypothalamus A structure located at the base of the brain that initiates and regulates pituitary secretions. (p. 181)

hypothesis A prediction drawn from a theory. (p. 41)

hypothetico-deductive reasoning A formal operational problem-solving strategy in which adolescents begin with a hypothesis, or prediction, about variables that might affect an outcome. From the hypothesis, they *deduce* logical, testable inferences. Then they systematically isolate and combine variables to see which of those inferences are confirmed in the real world. (p. 253)

I

ideal reciprocity A standard of fairness based on mutuality of expectations, as expressed in the Golden Rule: "Do unto others as you would have them do unto you." (p. 497)

identical, or monozygotic, twins Twins that result when a zygote, during early cell duplication, separates into two clusters of cells with the same genetic makeup. Distinguished from *fraternal, or dizygotic, twins*. (p. 76)

identity A well-organized conception of the self that defines who one is, what one values, and the directions one wants to pursue in life. (p. 468)

identity achievement The identity status of individuals who, after a period of exploration, have committed themselves to self-chosen values and goals. Distinguished from *identity moratorium, identity foreclosure*, and *identity diffusion*. (p. 470)

identity diffusion The identity status of individuals who do not engage in exploration and are not committed to values and goals. Distinguished from *identity achievement, identity moratorium*, and *identity foreclosure*. (p. 470)

identity foreclosure The identity status of individuals who, without engaging in exploration, commit themselves to ready-made values and goals chosen for them by authority figures. Distinguished from *identity achievement, identity moratorium*, and *identity diffusion*. (p. 470)

identity moratorium The identity status of individuals who are exploring, but not yet committed to, self-chosen values and goals. Distinguished from *identity achievement, identity foreclosure*, and *identity diffusion*. (p. 470)

illocutionary intent In conversation, what a speaker means to say, even if the form of the utterance is not perfectly consistent with it. (p. 390)

imaginary audience Adolescents' belief that they are the focus of everyone else's attention and concern. (p. 255)

imitation Learning by copying the behavior of another person. Also known as modeling or observational learning. (p. 145)

inclusive classroom A classroom in which students with learning difficulties learn alongside typical students in a regular educational setting for part or all of the school day. (p. 646)

incomplete dominance A pattern of inheritance in which both alleles are expressed in the phenotype, resulting in a combined trait, or one that is intermediate between the two. (p. 79)

incremental view of ability The view that ability can increase through effort; associated with mastery-oriented attributions. Distinguished from *entity view of ability*. (p. 465)

independent variable The variable that the researcher expects to cause changes in another variable in an experiment. Distinguished from *dependent variable*. (p. 56)

individualistic societies Societies in which people think of themselves as separate entities and are largely concerned with their own personal needs. Distinguished from *collectivist societies*. (p. 35)

induction A type of discipline in which the adult helps the child notice others' feelings by pointing out the effects of the child's misbehavior on others, especially noting their distress and making clear that the child caused it. (p. 489)

infant-directed speech (IDS) A form of communication used by adults in many countries when speaking to babies, consisting of short sentences with high-pitched, exaggerated expression, clear pronunciation, distinct pauses between speech segments, clear gestures to support verbal meaning, and repetition of new words in a variety of contexts. (p. 369)

infant mortality The number of deaths in the first year of life per 1,000 live births. (p. 118)

infantile amnesia The inability of most people to retrieve events that happened to them before age 3. (p. 301)

information processing An approach that views the human mind as a symbol-manipulating system through which information flows and that regards cognitive development as a continuous process. (p. 21)

informed consent The right of research participants, including children, to have explained to them, in language they can understand, all aspects of a study that might affect their willingness to participate. (p. 67)

inhibited, or shy, child A child who tends to react negatively to and withdraw from novel stimuli. Distinguished from *uninhibited, or sociable, child*. (p. 421)

inhibition The ability to control internal and external distracting stimuli, which helps children remember, reason, solve problems, and manage their behavior in social situations. (p. 287)

inner self Awareness of the self's private thoughts and imaginings. Distinguished from *categorical self, remembered self*, and *enduring self*. (p. 452)

instrumental traits Personality traits reflecting competence, rationality, and assertiveness, widely regarded as masculine. Distinguished from *expressive traits*. (p. 530)

intelligence quotient (IQ) A score that indicates the extent to which an individual's raw score (number of items passed) on an intelligence test deviates from the typical performance of same-age individuals. (p. 330)

intentional, or goal-directed, behavior A sequence of actions in which schemes are deliberately coordinated to solve a problem. (p. 229)

interactional synchrony A form of communication in which the caregiver responds to infant signals in a well-timed, rhythmic, appropriate fashion, and both partners match emotional states, especially positive ones. (p. 434)

intermodal perception Perception that combines simultaneous input from more than one modality, or sensory system, resulting in an integrated whole. (p. 166)

internal validity The degree to which conditions internal to the design of a research study permit an accurate test of the researcher's hypothesis or question. Distinguished from *external validity*. (p. 55)

internal working model A set of expectations about the availability of attachment figures, their likelihood of providing support during times of stress, and the self's interaction with those figures, which becomes a guide for all future close relationships. (p. 430)

internalization In moral development, the process of adopting societal standards for right action as one's own. (p. 488)

intersubjectivity The process whereby two participants who begin a task with different understandings arrive at a shared understanding. (p. 268)

invariant features Features that remain stable in a constantly changing perceptual world. (p. 168)

investment theory of creativity Sternberg and Lubart's theory, in which an individual's investment in novel projects depends on diverse cognitive, personality, motivational, and environmental resources, each of which must be present to catalyze creativity. (p. 352)

J

joint attention A state in which child and caregiver attend to the same object or event and the caregiver labels what the child sees, which contributes to language development. (p. 371)

K

kinship studies Studies comparing the characteristics of family members to estimate the importance of heredity in complex human characteristics. (p. 120)

kwashiorkor A disease caused by an unbalanced diet very low in protein, which usually strikes after weaning, between 1 and 3 years of age. Symptoms include an enlarged belly, swollen feet, hair loss, skin rash, and irritable, listless behavior. (p. 196)

L

laboratory experiment An experiment conducted in the laboratory, permitting the maximum possible control over treatment conditions. (p. 56)

language acquisition device (LAD) In Chomsky's theory, an innate system containing a universal grammar, or set of rules common to all languages, that permits children, once they have acquired sufficient vocabulary, to understand and speak in a rule-oriented fashion. (p. 360)

lanugo White, downy hair that covers the entire body of the fetus, helping the vernix stick to the skin. (p. 92)

lateralization Specialization of functions in the two hemispheres of the cerebral cortex. (p. 187)

learned helplessness The view that success is due to external factors, such as luck, while failure is due to low ability, which cannot be improved by trying hard. Distinguished from *mastery-oriented attributions*. (p. 465)

learning disability Great difficulty with one or more aspects of learning, usually reading, resulting in achievement considerably behind what would be expected on the basis of a child's IQ. (p. 646)

logical necessity A basic property of propositional thought, which specifies that the accuracy of conclusions drawn from premises rests on the rules of logic, not on real-world confirmation. (p. 258)

longitudinal design A research design in which one group of participants is studied repeatedly at different ages. Distinguished from *cross-sectional design*. (p. 60)

long-term memory In information processing, the largest storage area of the mental system, containing our permanent knowledge base. (p. 280)

M

macrosystem In ecological systems theory, cultural values, laws, customs, and resources that influence experiences and interactions at inner levels of the environment. Distinguished from *microsystem, mesosystem, exosystem,* and *chronosystem*. (p. 28)

make-believe play A type of play in which children act out everyday and imaginary activities. (p. 230)

marasmus A wasted condition of the body caused by a diet low in all essential nutrients. Usually appears in the first year of life. (p. 196)

mastery-oriented attributions Attributions that credit success to ability, which can be improved by trying hard, and that credit failure to insufficient effort. Distinguished from *learned helplessness*. (p. 465)

matching A research procedure in which participants are measured ahead of time on the factor in question, enabling investigators to assign participants with similar characteristics in equal numbers to each treatment condition in an experiment. Ensures that groups will be equivalent on factors likely to distort the results. (p. 58)

matters of personal choice Concerns that do not violate rights or others' welfare and are up to the individual. Distinguished from *moral imperatives* and *social conventions*. (p. 510)

maturation A genetically determined, naturally unfolding course of growth. (p. 12)

meiosis The process of cell division through which gametes are formed and in which the number of chromosomes in each cell is halved. (p. 75)

menarche First menstruation. (p. 203)

mental representation An internal depiction of information that the mind can manipulate, including images and concepts. (p. 227)

mesosystem In ecological systems theory, connections between children's immediate settings, or microsystems. Distinguished from *microsystem, exosystem, macrosystem,* and *chronosystem*. (p. 27)

metacognition Awareness and understanding of various aspects of thought. (p. 303)

metalinguistic awareness The ability to think about language as a system. (p. 394)

microgenetic design A research design in which investigators present children with a novel task and follow their mastery over a series of closely spaced sessions. (p. 64)

microsystem In ecological systems theory, the innermost level of the environment, consisting of activities and interaction patterns in the child's immediate surroundings. Distinguished from *mesosystem, exosystem, macrosystem,* and *chronosystem*. (p. 27)

mirror neurons Specialized cells in many areas of the cerebral cortex in primates that underlie the ability to imitate by firing identically when a primate hears or sees an action and when it carries out that action on its own. (p. 146)

mitosis The process of cell duplication, in which each new cell receives an exact copy of the original chromosomes. (p. 74)

model of strategy choice An attempt to apply an evolutionary metaphor, "natural selection," to children's mental strategies by analyzing how, when given challenging problems, children first generate and test a variety of strategies and then select the most accurate, efficient strategies, which "survive," while others become less frequent and "die off." (p. 284)

modifier genes Genes that enhance or dilute the effects of other genes. (p. 79)

moral identity An individual's endorsement of moral values, such as fairness, kindness, and generosity, as central to his or her self-concept. (p. 489)

moral imperatives Social rules and expectations that protect people's rights and welfare. Distinguished from *social conventions* and *matters of personal choice*. (p. 510)

morality of cooperation Piaget's second stage of moral development, in which children view rules as flexible, socially agreed-on principles that can be revised to suit the will of the majority. (p. 497)

moral self-regulation The ability to monitor one's own conduct, constantly adjusting it as circumstances present opportunities to violate inner standards. (p. 515)

morphology The use of grammatical markers indicating number, tense, case, person, gender, active or passive voice, and other meanings. (p. 360)

mutation A sudden but permanent change in a segment of DNA. (p. 81)

mutual exclusivity bias Children's assumption in early vocabulary growth that words refer to entirely separate, nonoverlapping categories. (p. 382)

myelination The coating of neural fibers with myelin, an insulating fatty sheath that improves the efficiency of message transfer. (p. 186)

N

natural, or prepared, childbirth A group of techniques aimed at reducing pain and medical intervention and making childbirth as rewarding an experience as possible. Typically includes classes that provide information about the birth process, relaxation and breathing techniques to counteract the pain of uterine contractions, and a labor coach who provides encouragement and affection. (p. 110)

natural, or quasi-, experiment A research design in which the investigator compares the effects of treatments that already exist in natural settings by carefully selecting groups of participants with similar characteristics. (p. 58)

naturalistic observation A research method in which the investigator goes into the natural environment and records the behavior of interest. Distinguished from *structured observation*. (p. 42)

nature–nurture controversy Disagreement among theorists over whether genetic or environmental factors are more important influences on development. (p. 8)

neglected children Children who are seldom mentioned, either positively or negatively, on self-report measures of peer acceptance. Distinguished from *popular, rejected,* and *controversial children*. (p. 618)

Neonatal Behavioral Assessment Scale (NBAS) A test developed to assess a newborn infant's behavioral status by evaluating the baby's reflexes, muscle tone, state changes, and responsiveness to physical and social stimuli. (p. 138)

neonatal mortality The number of deaths within the first month of life per 1,000 live births. (p. 118)

neo-Piagetian theory A reinterpretation of Piaget's stages within an information-processing framework. For example, Case's theory attributes change within each stage, and movement from one stage to the next, to increases in the efficiency with which children use their limited working memory capacity. (p. 283)

neurobiological methods Research methods that measure the relationship between nervous system processes and behavior to uncover the biological bases of perceptual, cognitive, and emotional responses. (p. 47)

neurons Nerve cells that store and transmit information. (p. 185)

neurotransmitters Chemicals released by neurons that cross the synapse to send messages to other neurons. (p. 185)

niche-picking A type of genetic–environmental correlation in which individuals actively choose environments that complement their heredity. (p. 123)

non-rapid-eye-movement (NREM) sleep A "regular" sleep state in which the body is almost motionless and heart rate, breathing, and brain-wave activity are slow and even. Distinguished from *rapid-eye-movement (REM) sleep*. (p. 133)

nonshared environmental influences Environmental influences that make siblings living in the same home different from one another. Distinguished from *shared environmental influences*. (p. 344)

nonsocial activity Unoccupied, onlooker behavior and solitary play. Distinguished from *parallel play, associative play,* and *cooperative play*. (p. 608)

normal distribution A bell-shaped distribution that results when individual differences are measured in large samples. Most scores cluster around the mean, or average, with progressively fewer falling toward each extreme. (p. 330)

normative approach An approach in which measures of behavior are taken on large numbers of individuals, and age-related averages are computed to represent typical development. (p. 13)

O

obesity A greater-than-20-percent increase over healthy body weight, based on body mass index, a ratio of weight to height associated with body fat. (p. 198)

object permanence The understanding that objects continue to exist when they are out of sight. (p. 229)

observer bias The tendency of observers who are aware of the purposes of a study to see and record what they expect to see rather than what participants actually do. (p. 45)

observer influence The tendency of participants in a study to behave in unnatural ways in the presence of an observer. (p. 45)

operant conditioning A form of learning in which a spontaneous behavior is followed by a stimulus that changes the probability that the behavior will occur again. (p. 141)

operations In Piaget's theory, mental representations of actions that obey logical rules. (p. 243)

ordinality Order relationships (more than and less than) between quantities. (p. 310)

organization In Piaget's theory, the internal rearrangement and linking together of schemes so that they form a strongly interconnected cognitive system. In information processing, a memory strategy that involves grouping related information to improve recall. (pp. 227, 292)

overextension An early vocabulary error in which a word is applied to a wider collection of objects and events than is appropriate. Distinguished from *underextension*. (p. 380)

overregularization Extension of regular morphological rules to words that are exceptions. (p. 386)

P

parallel play A form of limited social participation in which a child plays near other children with similar materials but does not try to influence their behavior. Distinguished from *nonsocial activity, associative play,* and *cooperative play*. (p. 608)

partial fetal alcohol syndrome (p-FAS) A form of fetal alcohol spectrum disorder characterized by facial abnormalities and brain injury but less severe than fetal alcohol syndrome; usually seen in children whose mothers drank alcohol in smaller quantities during pregnancy. Distinguished from *fetal alcohol syndrome (FAS)* and *alcohol-related neurodevelopmental disorder (ARND)*. (p. 99)

peer acceptance Likability, or the extent to which a child is viewed by a group of agemates, such as classmates, as a worthy social partner. (p. 618)

peer group A collective of peers who generate unique values and standards for behavior and a social structure of leaders and followers. (p. 622)

peer victimization A destructive form of peer interaction in which certain children become frequent targets of verbal and physical attacks or other forms of abuse. (p. 621)

perceptual narrowing effect Perceptual sensitivity that becomes increasingly attuned with age to information most often encountered. (p. 156)

permissive child-rearing style A child-rearing style that is high in acceptance but overindulging or inattentive, low in control, and lenient rather than appropriate in autonomy granting. Distinguished from *authoritative, authoritarian,* and *uninvolved child-rearing styles*. (p. 575)

person perception The way individuals size up the attributes of people with whom they are familiar. (p. 476)

personal fable Adolescents' inflated opinion of their own importance—the belief that they are special and unique and that others cannot possibly understand their thoughts and feelings. (p. 255)

perspective taking The capacity to imagine what others may be thinking and feeling. (p. 452)

phenotype An individual's directly observable physical and behavioral characteristics, which are determined by both genetic and environmental factors. Distinguished from *genotype*. (p. 73)

phonemes The smallest sound units that signal a change in meaning. (p. 368)

phonics approach An approach to beginning reading instruction that emphasizes coaching children on phonics—the basic rules for translating written symbols into sounds—before exposing them to complex reading material. Distinguished from *whole-language approach*. (p. 309)

phonological awareness The ability to reflect on and manipulate the sound structure of spoken language, as indicated by sensitivity to changes in sounds within words, to rhyming, and to incorrect pronunciation—a strong predictor of emergent literacy knowledge. (p. 308)

phonological store A special part of short-term memory that permits retention of speech-based information and, thus, supports early vocabulary development. (p. 381)

phonology The component of language consisting of the rules governing the structure and sequence of speech sounds. (p. 360)

physical aggression A form of aggression that harms others through physical injury to themselves or their property. Distinguished from *verbal aggression* and *relational aggression*. (p. 517)

pincer grasp The well-coordinated grasp that emerges at the end of the first year, involving thumb and index finger opposition. (p. 151)

pituitary gland A gland located at the base of the brain that releases hormones affecting physical growth. (p. 181)

placenta The organ that permits exchange of nutrients and waste products between the bloodstreams of the mother and the embryo, while also preventing the mother's and embryo's blood from mixing directly. (p. 89)

planning Thinking out a sequence of acts ahead of time and allocating attention accordingly to reach a goal. (p. 289)

plasticity Openness to change in response to influential experiences. (p. 9)

polygenic inheritance A pattern of inheritance in which many genes determine a characteristic that varies on a continuum among people. (p. 81)

popular-antisocial children A subtype of popular children who are admired for their socially adept yet belligerent behavior. Includes "tough" boys who are athletically skilled, aggressive, and poor students as well as relationally aggressive children who enhance their own status by ignoring, excluding, and spreading rumors about other children. Distinguished from *popular-prosocial children*. (p. 619)

popular children Children who get many positive votes on self-report measures of peer acceptance, indicating that they are well-liked. Distinguished from *rejected, controversial,* and *neglected children*. (p. 618)

popular-prosocial children A subtype of popular children who combine academic and social competence. Distinguished from *popular-antisocial children*. (p. 619)

postconventional level Kohlberg's highest level of moral development, in which individuals define morality in terms of abstract principles and values that apply to all situations and societies. (p. 501)

practical intelligence Mental abilities apparent in the real world but not in testing situations. (p. 332)

practice effects Improvement in research participants' performance with repeated testing, resulting from better test-taking skills and increased familiarity with the test. (p. 62)

pragmatics The component of language consisting of the rules for engaging in appropriate and effective communication. (p. 360)

preconventional level Kohlberg's first level of moral development, in which morality is externally controlled—based on rewards, punishments, and the power of authority figures. (p. 500)

prefrontal cortex The region of the cerebral cortex, lying in front of areas controlling body movement, that is responsible for thought—in particular, for consciousness, attention, inhibition of impulses, integration of information, and use of memory, reasoning, planning, and problem-solving strategies. (p. 186)

prenatal diagnostic methods Medical procedures that permit detection of developmental problems before birth. (p. 84)

preoperational stage Piaget's second stage, extending from about 2 to 7 years of age, in which children undergo an extraordinary increase in representational, or symbolic, activity, although thought is not yet logical. (p. 239)

prereaching The poorly coordinated, primitive reaching movements of newborn babies. (p. 150)

preterm infants Infants born several weeks or more before their due date. (p. 114)

primary sexual characteristics Physical features of the reproductive organs—ovaries, uterus, and vagina in females; penis, scrotum, and testes in males. Distinguished from *secondary sexual characteristics*. (p. 203)

private speech Self-directed speech that children use to guide their own thinking and behavior. (p. 267)

proactive aggression A type of aggression in which children act to fulfill a need or desire—obtain an object, privilege, space, or social reward—and unemotionally attack a person to achieve their goal. Also called instrumental aggression. Distinguished from *reactive aggression*. (p. 517)

problem-centered coping A general strategy for managing emotion in which the individual appraises the situation as changeable, identifies the difficulty, and decides what to do about it. Distinguished from *emotion-centered coping*. (p. 412)

production In language development, the words and word combinations that children use. Distinguished from *comprehension*. (p. 376)

production deficiency Failure to produce a mental strategy when one could be helpful. Distinguished from *control deficiency, utilization deficiency,* and *effective strategy use*. (p. 288)

programmed cell death Death of many surrounding neurons as neural fibers and their synapses increase rapidly, which makes space for these connective structures. (p. 185)

Project Head Start A U.S. federal early intervention program for economically disadvantaged preschoolers that provides children with a year or two of preschool education, along with nutritional and health services, and encourages parent involvement in program planning and children's learning and development. (p. 347)

propositional thought A type of formal operational reasoning involving the ability to evaluate the logic of propositions (verbal statements) without referring to real-world circumstances. (p. 254)

prosocial, or **altruistic, behavior** Actions that benefit another person without any expected reward for the self. (p. 417)

protection from harm The right of research participants to be protected from risks to their safety or welfare. (p. 67)

protodeclarative A preverbal communicative gesture in which the baby points to, touches, or holds up an object while looking at others to make sure they notice. Distinguished from *protoimperative*. (p. 371)

protoimperative A preverbal communicative gesture in which the baby gets another person to do something by reaching, pointing, and often making sounds at the same time. Distinguished from *protodeclarative*. (p. 371)

proximodistal trend An organized pattern of physical growth and motor control that proceeds from the center of the body outward. Distinguished from *cephalocaudal trend*. (p. 176)

psychoanalytic perspective An approach to personality development introduced by Freud, which assumes that children move through a series of stages in which they confront conflicts between biological drives and social expectations. How these conflicts are resolved determines the person's ability to learn, to get along with others, and to cope with anxiety. (p. 15)

psychological control Parental behaviors that intrude on and manipulate children's verbal expressions, individuality, and attachments to parents. (p. 574)

psychometric approach An approach to cognitive development that focuses on outcomes and results and is the basis for intelligence tests designed to assess mental abilities. (p. 319)

psychosexual theory Freud's theory of development, which emphasizes that how parents manage their child's sexual and aggressive drives in the first few years is crucial for healthy personality development. (p. 15)

psychosocial dwarfism A growth disorder, usually appearing between 2 and 15 years of age, caused by extreme emotional deprivation. Typical characteristics include decreased growth hormone secretion, very short stature, immature skeletal age, and serious adjustment problems, which help distinguish it from typical shortness. (p. 202)

psychosocial theory Erikson's theory, which emphasizes that in each Freudian stage, individuals not only develop a unique personality but also acquire attitudes and skills that help them become active, contributing members of their society. (p. 15)

puberty Biological changes at adolescence that lead to an adult-sized body and sexual maturity. (p. 203)

public policy Laws and government programs designed to improve current conditions. (p. 33)

punishment In operant conditioning, removal of a desirable stimulus or presentation of an unpleasant stimulus, either of which decreases the occurrence of a response. (p. 141)

R

random assignment Assignment of participants in an experiment to treatment conditions using an unbiased procedure, such as drawing numbers out of a hat or flipping a coin, to increase the chances that participants' characteristics will be equally distributed across treatment groups. (p. 57)

rapid-eye-movement (REM) sleep An "irregular" sleep state in which electrical brain-wave activity is similar to that of the waking state; eyes dart beneath the lids; heart rate, blood pressure, and breathing are uneven; and slight body movements occur. Distinguished from *non-rapid-eye-movement (NREM) sleep*. (p. 133)

reactive aggression An angry, defensive response to a provocation or a blocked goal; intended to hurt another person. Also called hostile aggression. Distinguished from *proactive aggression*. (p. 517)

realism In Piaget's heteronomous stage of moral development, the child's tendency to view rules, like other mental phenomena, as fixed external features of reality. (p. 487)

recall The form of memory retrieval that involves generating a mental representation of an absent stimulus. Distinguished from *recognition*. (p. 294)

recasts Adult responses that restructure children's grammatically inaccurate speech into correct form. (p. 389)

reciprocal teaching A teaching method in which a teacher and two to four students form a cooperative group and take turns leading dialogues, creating a zone of proximal development in which children scaffold one another's progress. (p. 271)

recognition The simplest form of memory retrieval, which involves noticing that a stimulus is identical or similar to one previously experienced. Distinguished from *recall*. (p. 294)

reconstruction The type of memory that involves recoding information while it is in the mental system or being retrieved. (p. 295)

recovery Following habituation, an increase in responsiveness to a new stimulus. (p. 142)

recursive thought A form of perspective taking that requires the ability to view a situation from at least two perspectives—that is, to reason simultaneously about what two or more people are thinking. (p. 453)

referential communication skills The ability to produce clear verbal messages and to recognize when the meaning of others' messages is unclear. (p. 391)

referential style A style of early language learning in which toddlers use language mainly to label objects. Distinguished from *expressive style*. (p. 378)

reflex An inborn, automatic response to a particular form of stimulation. (p. 130)

rehearsal A memory strategy that involves repeating information to oneself. (p. 292)

reinforcer In operant conditioning, a stimulus that increases the occurrence of a response. (p. 141)

rejected-aggressive children A subtype of rejected children who show high rates of conflict, physical and relational aggression, and hyperactive, inattentive, and impulsive behavior. Distinguished from *rejected-withdrawn children*. (p. 619)

rejected children Children who get many negative votes on self-report measures of peer acceptance, indicating that they are actively disliked. Distinguished from *popular, controversial,* and *neglected children*. (p. 618)

rejected-withdrawn children A subtype of rejected children who are passive, socially awkward, and overwhelmed by social anxiety. Distinguished from *rejected-aggressive children*. (p. 619)

relational aggression A form of aggression that damages a peer's relationships through social exclusion, malicious gossip, or friendship manipulation. Distinguished from *physical aggression* and *verbal aggression*. (p. 518)

reliability The consistency, or repeatability, of measures of behavior. (p. 54)

remembered self The child's life-story narrative, or autobiographical memory, constructed from conversations with adults about the past. (p. 450)

resilience The ability to adapt effectively in the face of threats to development. (p. 10)

resistant attachment The quality of insecure attachment characterizing infants who seek closeness to the parent before her departure, are usually distressed when she leaves, and combine clinginess with angry, resistive behavior when she returns. Distinguished from *secure, avoidant,* and *disorganized/disoriented attachment*. (p. 431)

reticular formation A structure in the brain stem that maintains alertness and consciousness. (p. 190)

reversibility The ability to go through a series of steps in a problem and then mentally reverse direction, returning to the starting point. In Piaget's theory, part of every logical operation. (p. 245)

Rh factor incompatibility A condition that arises when the Rh protein is present in the fetus's blood but not in the mother's, causing the mother to build up antibodies. If these enter the fetus's system, they destroy red blood cells, reducing the oxygen supply to organs and tissues. (p. 113)

risks-versus-benefits ratio A comparison of the costs of a research study to participants in terms of inconvenience and possible psychological or physical injury against the study's value for advancing knowledge and improving conditions of life. Used in assessing the ethics of research. (p. 67)

rough-and-tumble play A form of peer interaction involving friendly chasing and play-fighting that, in our evolutionary past, may have been important for the development of fighting skill. (p. 610)

S

scaffolding Adjusting the support offered during a teaching session to fit the child's current level of performance. As competence increases, the adult gradually and sensitively withdraws support, turning responsibility over to the child. (p. 268)

scale errors Toddlers' attempts to do things that their body size makes impossible because they lack an objective understanding of their own body dimensions. (p. 449)

schemes In Piaget's theory, specific psychological structures, or organized ways of making sense of experience, that change with age. (p. 226)

scripts General descriptions of what occurs and when it occurs in a particular situation, used to organize, interpret, and predict repeated events. (p. 298)

secondary sexual characteristics Features visible on the outside of the body that do not involve the reproductive organs but serve as signs of sexual maturity, including breast development in females and the appearance of underarm and pubic hair in both sexes. Distinguished from *primary sexual characteristics*. (p. 203)

secular trends in physical growth Changes in body size and rate of growth from one generation to the next. (p. 184)

secure attachment The attachment pattern characterizing infants who use the parent as a secure base from which to explore and who are easily comforted by the parent on being reunited after a separation. Distinguished from *avoidant, resistant,* and *disorganized/disoriented attachment*. (p. 430)

secure base The baby's use of the familiar caregiver as the point from which to explore, venturing into the environment and then returning for emotional support. (p. 408)

selective attrition Selective loss of participants during an investigation, resulting in a biased sample. (p. 62)

self-care children School-age children who regularly look after themselves for some period of time during after-school hours. (p. 597)

self-concept The set of attributes, abilities, attitudes, and values that an individual believes defines who he or she is. (p. 456)

self-conscious emotions Emotions—such as shame, embarrassment, guilt, envy, and pride—that involve injury to or enhancement of the sense of self. (p. 408)

self-esteem The aspect of self-concept that involves judgments about one's own worth and the feelings associated with those judgments. (p. 461)

self-recognition Identification of the self as a physically unique being, distinct from other people and objects. (p. 449)

semantic bootstrapping In language development, children's reliance on semantics, or word meanings, to figure out sentence structure. (p. 389)

semantic memory The vast, taxonomically organized and hierarchically structured general knowledge system, consisting of concepts, language meanings, facts, and rules. (p. 296)

semantics The component of language that involves vocabulary—the way underlying concepts are expressed in words and word combinations. (p. 360)

sensitive caregiving Caregiving that involves responding promptly, consistently, and appropriately to infants and holding them tenderly and carefully. (p. 434)

sensitive period A time that is optimal for certain capacities to emerge and in which the individual is especially responsive to environmental influences. (p. 24)

sensorimotor stage Piaget's first stage, spanning the first two years of life, in which infants and toddlers "think" with their eyes, ears, hands, and other sensorimotor equipment but cannot yet carry out many activities mentally. (p. 228)

sensory register The part of the information-processing system in which sights and sounds are represented directly but stored only momentarily before they either decay or are transferred to the short-term memory store. (p. 278)

separation anxiety An infant's distressed reaction to the departure of the trusted caregiver. (p. 429)

sequential designs Research designs in which several similar cross-sectional or longitudinal investigations, or sequences, are conducted at varying times. May permit both longitudinal and cross-sectional comparisons and detection of cohort effects. (p. 63)

seriation The ability to order items along a quantitative dimension, such as length or weight. (p. 250)

sex chromosomes The twenty-third pair of chromosomes, called XX in females and XY in males, which determines the sex of the child. (p. 76)

shading A conversational strategy in which a speaker initiates a change of topic gradually by modifying the focus of discussion. (p. 390)

shape bias In early language development, children's tendency to rely heavily on shape as a distinguishing property when learning names for objects. (p. 382)

shape constancy Perception of an object's shape as stable, despite changes in the shape projected on the retina. (p. 165)

shared environmental influences Influences that pervade the general atmosphere of the home and, therefore, similarly affect siblings living in it. Distinguished from *nonshared environmental influences*. (p. 344)

short-term memory store The part of the information-processing system in which attended-to information is briefly retained so we can actively "work" on it to reach our goals. (p. 278)

size constancy Perception of an object's size as stable, despite changes in the size of its retinal image. (p. 164)

skeletal age An estimate of physical maturity based on development of the bones of the body. (p. 178)

slow-to-warm-up child A child whose temperament is characterized by inactivity; mild, low-key reactions to environmental stimuli; negative mood; and slow adjustment to new experiences. Distinguished from *easy child* and *difficult child*. (p. 420)

small-for-date infants Infants whose birth weight is below their expected weight considering the length of the pregnancy. (p. 114)

social cognition Thinking about characteristics of the self and of other people. (p. 447)

social comparisons Evaluations of one's own appearance, abilities, and behavior in relation to those of others. (p. 458)

social-constructivist classroom A classroom grounded in Vygotsky's sociocultural theory, in which children participate in a wide range of challenging activities with teachers and peers, with whom they jointly construct understandings. Distinguished from *traditional classroom* and *constructivist classroom*. (p. 640)

social conventions Customs, such as table manners and rituals of social interaction, that are determined solely by consensus. Distinguished from *moral imperatives* and *matters of personal choice*. (p. 510)

social learning theory A theory that emphasizes the role of modeling, otherwise known as imitation or observational learning, in the development of behavior. (p. 18)

social policy Any planned set of actions by a group, institution, or governing body directed at attaining a social goal. (p. 33)

social problem solving Generating and applying strategies that prevent or resolve disagreements, resulting in outcomes that are both acceptable to others and beneficial to the self. (p. 480)

social referencing Actively seeking emotional information from a trusted person in an uncertain situation. (p. 414)

social smile The smile evoked by the stimulus of the human face. First appears between 6 and 10 weeks. (p. 406)

social systems perspective A view of the family as a complex set of interacting relationships influenced by the larger social context. (p. 568)

sociocultural theory Vygotsky's theory, in which children acquire the ways of thinking and behaving that make up a community's culture through social interaction—in particular, cooperative dialogues with more knowledgeable members of society. (p. 25)

sociodramatic play The make-believe play with others that is under way around age 2 and increases rapidly in complexity during early childhood. (p. 240)

socioeconomic status (SES) A measure of a family's social position and economic well-being that combines three related variables: years of education, the prestige of one's job and the skill it requires, and income. (p. 334)

specific intelligence In Spearman's theory, a mental ability that is unique to a task. Distinguished from *general intelligence*, or *"g."* (p. 321)

speech registers Language adaptations to social expectations. (p. 393)

spermarche First ejaculation of seminal fluid. (p. 204)

stage A qualitative change in thinking, feeling, and behaving that characterizes a specific period of development. (p. 8)

standardization The practice of giving a newly constructed test to a large, representative sample of individuals and using the results as the standard for interpreting individual scores. (p. 330)

Stanford-Binet Intelligence Scales, Fifth Edition An individually administered intelligence test, appropriate for individuals age 2 to adulthood, that is the modern descendant of Alfred Binet's first successful test for children. Measures general intelligence and five intellectual factors: fluid reasoning, quantitative reasoning, knowledge, visual-spatial processing, and working memory. (p. 327)

states of arousal Different degrees of sleep and wakefulness. (p. 132)

statistical learning capacity The capacity to analyze the speech stream for repeatedly occurring sound sequences, through which infants acquire a stock of speech structures for which they will later learn meanings. (p. 157)

stereotype threat The fear of being judged on the basis of a negative stereotype, which can trigger anxiety that interferes with performance. (p. 341)

Strange Situation A laboratory technique for assessing the quality of infant–caregiver attachment between 1 and 2 years of age by observing the baby's responses to eight short episodes, in which brief separations from and reunions with the caregiver occur in an unfamiliar playroom. (p. 430)

stranger anxiety Expression of fear in response to unfamiliar adults, which appears in many babies in the second half of the first year. (p. 407)

structured interview An interview method in which each participant is asked the same questions in the same way. (p. 47)

structured observation A method in which the researcher sets up a laboratory situation that evokes the behavior of interest so that every participant has an equal opportunity to display the response. Distinguished from *naturalistic observation*. (p. 44)

sudden infant death syndrome (SIDS) The unexpected death, usually during the night, of an infant under 1 year of age that remains unexplained after thorough investigation. (p. 136)

sympathy Feelings of concern or sorrow for another's plight. (p. 417)

synapses The gaps between neurons, across which chemical messages are sent. (p. 185)

synaptic pruning Loss of synapses by seldom-stimulated neurons, thereby returning them to an uncommitted state so they can support future development. (p. 185)

syntactic bootstrapping In language development, children's discovery of word meanings by observing how words are used in syntax, or the structure of sentences. (p. 382)

syntax The rules by which words are arranged into sentences. (p. 360)

T

talent Outstanding performance in one or a few related fields. (p. 353)

telegraphic speech Young children's two-word utterances that, like a telegram, focus on high-content words, omitting smaller, less important ones. (p. 384)

temperament Early-appearing, stable individual differences in reactivity (quickness and intensity of emotional arousal, attention, and motor action) and self-regulation (strategies that modify reactivity). (p. 418)

teratogen Any environmental agent that causes damage during the prenatal period. (p. 95)

theory An orderly, integrated set of statements that describes, explains, and predicts behavior. (p. 6)

theory of mind A coherent understanding of people as mental beings, which children revise as they encounter new evidence. (p. 303)

theory of multiple intelligences Gardner's theory, which proposes at least eight independent intelligences, defined in terms of distinct sets of processing operations applied in culturally valued activities: linguistic, logico-mathematical, musical, spatial, bodily-kinesthetic, naturalist, interpersonal, and intrapersonal. (p. 325)

theory theory A theory that assumes that children draw on innate concepts to form naïve theories, or explanations of events, that differ among core domains of thought. Then they test their theory against experience, revising it when it cannot adequately account for new information. (p. 264)

three-stratum theory of intelligence Carroll's factor-analytic theory, which represents the structure of intelligence in three tiers, with *g* at the top; a second tier of biologically based broad abilities; and a third tier of specific behaviors. The most comprehensive factor-analytic classification of mental abilities to date. (p. 322)

thyroid-stimulating hormone (TSH) A pituitary hormone that stimulates the thyroid gland to release thyroxine, which is necessary for brain development and for growth hormone to have its full impact on body size. (p. 183)

time out A form of mild punishment in which children are removed from the immediate setting until they are ready to act appropriately. (p. 493)

time sampling A form of systematic observation in which the researcher records whether certain behaviors occur during a sample of short intervals. (p. 45)

traditional classroom A classroom in which the teacher is the sole authority for knowledge, rules, and decision making and students are relatively passive learners who are evaluated in relation to a uniform set of standards. Distinguished from *constructivist classroom* and *social-constructivist classroom*. (p. 638)

transitive inference The ability to seriate, or arrange items along a quantitative dimension, mentally. (p. 250)

triarchic theory of successful intelligence Sternberg's theory, which states that intelligent behavior involves balancing analytical intelligence, creative intelligence, and practical intelligence to achieve success in life, according to one's personal goals and the requirements of one's cultural community. (p. 323)

turnabout A conversational strategy in which the speaker, after commenting on what has just been said, also adds a request to get the partner to respond again. (p. 390)

U

ulnar grasp The clumsy grasp of the young infant, in which the fingers close against the palm. (p. 151)

umbilical cord The long cord connecting the prenatal organism to the placenta that delivers nutrients and removes waste products. (p. 89)

unconditioned response (UCR) In classical conditioning, a reflexive response that is produced by an unconditioned stimulus (UCS). (p. 140)

unconditioned stimulus (UCS) In classical conditioning, a stimulus that consistently produces a reflexive, or unconditioned, response (UCR). (p. 140)

underextension An early vocabulary error in which a word is applied too narrowly, to a smaller number of objects or events than is appropriate. Distinguished from *overextension*. (p. 379)

uninhibited, or **sociable, child** A child who tends to display positive emotion to and approach novel stimuli. Distinguished from *inhibited,* or *shy, child*. (p. 421)

uninvolved child-rearing style A child-rearing style that combines low acceptance and involvement with little behavioral control and general indifference to issues of autonomy. Distinguished from *authoritarian, authoritative,* and *permissive child-rearing styles*. (p. 575)

universal grammar In Chomsky's theory of language development, a built-in storehouse of grammatical rules common to all human languages. (p. 361)

utilization deficiency Failure to improve performance despite executing a mental strategy consistently. Distinguished from *production deficiency, control deficiency,* and *effective strategy use*. (p. 289)

V

validity The extent to which a research method accurately measures characteristics that the investigator set out to measure. (p. 54)

velocity curve A growth curve that plots the average amount of growth at each yearly interval for a sample of children, revealing the exact timing of growth spurts. Distinguished from *distance curve*. (p. 176)

verbal aggression A form of reactive aggression that harms others through threats of physical aggression, name-calling, or hostile teasing. Distinguished from *physical aggression* and *relational aggression*. (p. 518)

vernix A white, cheeselike substance covering the fetus, preventing the skin from chapping due to constant exposure to amniotic fluid. (p. 92)

video deficit effect In toddlers, poorer performance on a task after watching a video than a live demonstration. (p. 237)

violation-of-expectation method A method in which researchers show babies an expected event (one that follows physical laws) and an unexpected event (a variation of the first event that violates physical laws). Heightened attention to the unexpected event suggests that the infant is "surprised" by a deviation from physical reality and, therefore, is aware of that aspect of the physical world. (p. 230)

visual acuity Fineness of visual discrimination. (p. 159)

visual cliff An apparatus used to study depth perception in infants, consisting of a Plexiglas-covered table with a central platform, from which babies are encouraged to crawl. Checkerboard patterns placed at different distances beneath the glass create the appearance of a shallow and a deep side. (p. 159)

W

Wechsler Intelligence Scale for Children–IV (WISC–IV) An individually administered intelligence test, appropriate for ages 6 through 16, that measures general intelligence and four broad intellectual factors: verbal reasoning, perceptual reasoning, working memory, and processing speed. (p. 328)

Wernicke's area A language structure located in the left temporal lobe of the cerebral cortex that plays a role in comprehending word meaning. (p. 363)

whole-language approach An approach to beginning reading instruction in which, from the start, children are exposed to text in its complete form, using reading materials that are whole and meaningful to promote appreciation of the communicative function of written language. Distinguished from *phonics approach*. (p. 309)

working memory The number of items that can be briefly held in mind while also engaging in some effort to monitor or manipulate those items. A contemporary view of the short-term memory store. (p. 279)

X

X-linked inheritance A pattern of inheritance in which a recessive gene is carried on the X chromosome, so that males are more likely than females to be affected. (p. 80)

Z

zone of proximal development In Vygotsky's theory, a range of tasks too difficult for the child to do alone but possible with the help of adults and more skilled peers. (p. 267)

zygote The newly fertilized cell formed by the union of sperm and ovum at conception. (p. 75)

References

Aalsma, M., Lapsley, D. K., & Flannery, D. J. (2006). Personal fables, narcissism, and adolescent adjustment. *Psychology in the Schools, 43,* 481–491.

Aarnoudse-Moens, C. S., Weisglas-Kuperus, N., & van Goudoever, J. B. (2009). Meta-analysis of neurobehavioral outcomes in very preterm and/or very low birth weight children. *Pediatrics, 124,* 717–728.

ABC News. (2004). *The American Sex Survey: A peek beneath the sheets.* Retrieved from abcnews.go.com/images/Politics/959a1AmericanSexSurvey.pdf

Abela, J. R. Z., Hankin, B. L., Haigh, E. A. P., Adams, P., Vinokuroff, T., & Trayhern, L. (2005). Interpersonal vulnerability to depression in high-risk children: The role of insecure attachment and reassurance seeking. *Journal of Clinical Child and Adolescent Psychology, 34,* 182–192.

Aber, J. L., Jones, S. M., & Raver, C. C. (2007). Poverty and child development: New perspectives on a defining issue. In J. L. Aber, S. J. Bishop-Josef, S. M. Jones, K. T. McLearn, & D. Phillips (Eds.), *Child development and social policy: Knowledge for action* (pp. 149–166). Washington, DC: American Psychological Association.

Abikoff, H. B., Jensen, P. S., Arnold, L. L. E., Hoza, B., et al. (2002). Observed classroom behavior of children with ADHD: Relationship to gender and comorbidity. *Journal of Abnormal Child Psychology, 30,* 349–359.

Aboud, F. E. (2003). The formation of in-group favoritism and out-group prejudice in young children: Are they distinct attitudes? *Developmental Psychology, 39,* 48–60.

Aboud, F. E. (2008). A social-cognitive developmental theory of prejudice. In S. M. Quintana & C. McKown (Eds.), *Handbook of race, racism, and the developing child* (pp. 55–71). Hoboken, NJ: Wiley.

Aboud, F. E., & Doyle, A. (1996). Parental and peer influences on children's racial attitudes. *International Journal of Intercultural Relations, 20,* 371–383.

Abrams, K. Y., Rifkin, A., & Hesse, E. (2006). Examining the role of parental frightened/frightening subtypes in predicting disorganized attachment within a brief observational procedure. *Development and Psychopathology, 18,* 345–361.

Achenbach, T. M., Howell C. T., & Aoki, M. F. (1993). Nine-year outcome of the Vermont Intervention Program for low-birthweight infants, *Pediatrics, 91,* 45–55.

Acker, M. M., & O'Leary, S. G. (1996). Inconsistency of mothers' feedback and toddlers' misbehavior and negative affect. *Journal of Abnormal Child Psychology, 24,* 703–714.

Ackerman, B. P. (1978). Children's understanding of speech acts in unconventional frames. *Child Development, 49,* 311–318.

Ackerman, B. P. (1993). Children's understanding of the speaker's meaning in referential communication. *Journal of Experimental Child Psychology, 55,* 56–86.

Adachi-Mejia, A. M., Longacre, M. R., Gibson, J. J., Beach, M. L., Titus-Ernstoff, L. L., & Dalton, M. A. (2007). Children with a TV in their bedroom at higher risk for being overweight. *International Journal of Obesity, 31,* 644–651.

Adam, E. K., Snell, E. K., & Pendry, P. (2007). Sleep timing and quantity in ecological and family context: A nationally representative time-diary study. *Journal of Family Psychology, 21,* 4–19.

Adams, R., & Laursen, B. (2001). The organization and dynamics of adolescent conflict with parents and friends. *Journal of Marriage and the Family, 63,* 97–110.

Adamson, D. (2005). Regulation of assisted reproductive technologies in the United States. *Family Law Quarterly, 39,* 727–744.

Adolph, K. E. (2002). Learning to keep balance. In R. V. Kail (Ed.), *Advances in child development and behavior* (Vol. 30, pp. 1–40). Boston: Academic Press.

Adolph, K. E. (2008). Learning to move. *Current Directions in Psychological Science, 17,* 213–218.

Adolph, K. E., & Berger, S. E. (2006). Motor development. In D. Kuhn & R. Siegler (Eds.), *Handbook of child psychology: Vol. 2. Cognition, perception, and language* (6th ed., pp. 161–213). Hoboken, NJ: Wiley.

Adolph, K. E., & Joh, A. S. (2009). Multiple learning mechanisms in the development of action. In A. Woodward & A. Needham (Eds.), *Learning and the infant mind* (pp. 172–207). New York: Oxford University Press.

Adolph, K. E., Karasik, L. B., & Tamis-LeMonda, C. S. (2010). Motor skill. In M. H. Bornstein (Ed.), *Handbook of cultural developmental science* (pp. 61–88). New York: Psychology Press.

Adolph, K. E., Tamis-LeMonda, C. S., Ishak, S., Karasik, L. B., & Lobo, S. A. (2008). Locomotor experience and use of social information are posture specific. *Developmental Psychology, 44,* 1705–1714.

Adolph, K. E., Vereijken, B., & Shrout, P. E. (2003). What changes in infant walking and why. *Child Development, 74,* 475–497.

Afifi, T. O., Brownridge, D. A., Cox, B. J., & Sareen, J. (2006). Physical punishment, childhood abuse and psychiatric disorders. *Child Abuse and Neglect, 30,* 1093–1103.

Afterschool Alliance. (2009). *America after 3PM.* Retrieved from www.kidsdeservebetter.org/AA3PM.cfm

Aggarwal, R., Sentz, J., & Miller, M. A. (2007). Role of zinc administration in prevention of childhood diarrhea and respiratory illnesses: A meta-analysis. *Pediatrics, 119,* 1120–1130.

Agronick, G., Stueve, A., Vargo, S., & O'Donnell, L. (2007). New York City young adults' psychological reactions to 9/11: Findings from the Reach for Health longitudinal study. *American Journal of Community Psychology, 39,* 79–90.

Aguiar, A., & Baillargeon, R. (2002). Developments in young infants' reasoning about occluded objects. *Cognitive Psychology, 45,* 267–336.

Aguiar, A., & Baillargeon, R. (2003). Perseverative responding in a violation-of-expectation task in 6.5-month-old infants. *Cognition, 88,* 277–316.

Ahmed, A., & Ruffman, T. (1998). Why do infants make A not B errors in a search task, yet show memory for the location of hidden objects in a nonsearch task? *Developmental Psychology, 34,* 441–453.

Aikens, J. W., Bierman, K. L., & Parker, J. G. (2005). Navigating the transition to junior high school: The influence of pre-transition friendship and self-system characteristics. *Social Development, 14,* 42–60.

Ainsworth, M. D. S., Blehar, M., Waters, E., & Wall, S. (1978). *Patterns of attachment.* Hillsdale, NJ: Erlbaum.

Akers, A. Y., Gold, M. A., Bost, J. E., Adimore, A. A., Orr, D. P., & Fortenberry, J. D. (2011). Variation in sexual behaviors in a cohort of adolescent females: The role of personal, perceived peer, and perceived family attitudes. *Journal of Adolescent Health, 48,* 87–93.

Akhtar, N., & Montague, L. (1999). Early lexical acquisition: The role of cross-situational learning. *First Language, 19,* 347–358.

Akhtar, N., & Tomasello, M. (2000). The social nature of words and word learning. In R. Golinkoff & K. Hirsh-Pasek (Eds.), *Becoming a word learner: A debate on lexical acquisition.* Oxford, UK: Oxford University Press.

Akimoto, S. A., & Sanbonmatsu, D. M. (1999). Differences in self-effacing behavior between European and Japanese Americans: Effect on competence evaluations. *Journal of Cross-Cultural Psychology, 30,* 159–177.

Aksan, N., & Kochanska, G. (2004). Heterogeneity of joy in infancy. *Infancy, 6,* 79–94.

Akshoomoff, N. A., Feroleto, C. C., Doyle, R. E., & Stiles, J. (2002). The impact of early unilateral brain injury on perceptual organization and visual memory. *Neuropsychologia, 40,* 539–561.

Alan Guttmacher Institute. (2002). Teen sex and pregnancy. Retrieved from www.agi-usa.org/pubs/ib_teensex.html

Alan Guttmacher Institute. (2005). *Facts in brief: Contraceptive use.* Retrieved from www.guttmacher.org/pubs/fb_contr_use.html

Alan Guttmacher Institute. (2006). *U.S. teenage pregnancy statistics: National and state trends and trends by race and ethnicity.* New York: Author. Retrieved from www.guttmacher.org/pubs/2006/09/12/USTPstats.pdf

Alan Guttmacher Institute. (2010). *Facts on American teens' sexual and reproductive health.* Retrieved from www.guttmacher.org/pubs/FB-ATSRH.html

Alan Guttmacher Institute. (2011). *Facts on American teens' sexual and reproductive health.* Retrieved from www.guttmacher.org/pubs/FB-ATSRH.html

Albers, C. A., & Grieve, A. J. (2007). Test review: Bayley, N. (2006). Bayley Scales of Infant and Toddler Development–Third Edition. San Antonio, TX: Harcourt Assessment. *Journal of Psychoeducational Assessment, 25,* 180–190.

Alberts, A., Elkind, D., & Ginsberg, S. (2007). The personal fable and risk-taking in early adolescence. *Journal of Youth and Adolescence, 36,* 71–76.

Aldridge, M. A., Stillman, R. D., & Bower, T. G. R. (2001). Newborn categorization of vowel-like sounds. *Developmental Science, 4,* 220–232.

Alessandri, S. M., Sullivan, M. W., & Lewis, M. (1990). Violation of expectancy and frustration in early infancy. *Developmental Psychology, 26,* 738–744.

Alexander, J. M., Fabricius, W. V., Fleming, V. M., Zwahr, M., & Brown, S. A. (2003). The development of metacognitive causal explanations. *Learning and Individual Differences, 13,* 227–238.

Alexander, K., Goodman, G. S., Schaaf, J. M., Edelstein, R. S., Quas, J. A., & Shaver, P. R. (2002). The role of attachment and cognitive inhibition in children's memory and suggestibility for a stressful event. *Journal of Experimental Child Psychology, 83,* 262–290.

Alexandre-Bidon, K. L., & Lett, D. (1997). *Les enfants au Moyen Age, Ve–XVe siecles.* Paris: Hachette.

Ali, L., & Scelfo, J. (2002, December 9). Choosing virginity. *Newsweek,* pp. 60–65.

Alibali, M. W., Phillips, K. M. O., & Fischer, A. D. (2009). Learning new problem-solving strategies leads to changes in problem representation. *Cognitive Development, 24,* 89–101.

Alink, L. R. A., Mesman, J., van Zeijl, J., Stolk, M. N., Juffer, F., & Koot, H. M. (2006). The early childhood aggression curve: Development of physical aggression in 10- to 50-month-old children. *Child Development, 77,* 954–966.

Allen, J. P., Philliber, S., Herrling, S., & Kuperminc, G. P. (1997). Preventing teen pregnancy and academic failure: Experimental evaluation of a developmentally based approach. *Child Development, 64,* 729–742.

Allen, J. P., Porter, M. R., & McFarland, F. C. (2006). Leaders and followers in adolescent close friendships: Susceptibility to peer influence as a predictor of risky behavior, friendship instability, and depression. *Development and Psychopathology, 18,* 155–172.

Allen, J. P., Seitz, V., & Apfel, N. H. (2007). The sexually mature teen as a whole person. In J. L. Aber, S. J. Bishop-Josef, S. M. Jones, K. T. McLearn, & D. A. Phillips (Eds.), *New directions in prevention and intervention for teen pregnancy and parenthood* (pp. 185–199). Washington, DC: American Psychological Association.

Allen, M., & Burrell, N. (1996). Comparing the impact of homosexual and heterosexual parents on children: Meta-analysis of existing research. *Journal of Homosexuality, 32,* 19–35.

Allen, S. E. M. (1996). Aspects of argument structure acquisition in Inuktitut. Amsterdam: Benjamins.

Allen, S. E. M., & Crago, M. B. (1996). Early passive acquisition in Inuktitut. *Journal of Child Language, 23,* 129–156.

Allison, B. N., & Schultz, J. B. (2004). Parent–adolescent conflict in early adolescence. *Adolescence, 39,* 101–119.

Alloway, T. P. (2009). Working memory, but not IQ, predicts subsequent learning in children with learning difficulties. *European Journal of Psychological Assessment, 25,* 92–98.

Alloway, T. P., Gathercole, S. E., Kirkwood, H., & Elliott, J. (2009). The cognitive and behavioral characteristics of children with low working memory. *Child Development, 80,* 606–621.

Almeida, J., Johnson, R. M., Corliss, H. L., Molnar, B. E., & Azrael, D. (2009). Emotional distress among LGBT youth: The influence of perceived discrimination based on sexual orientation. *Journal of Youth and Adolescence, 38,* 1001–1014

Al-Namlah, A. S., Fernyhough, C., & Meins, E. (2006). Sociocultural influences on the development of verbal mediation: Private speech and phonological recoding in Saudi Arabian and British samples. *Developmental Psychology, 42*, 117–131.

Alsaker, F. D. (1995). Timing of puberty and reactions to pubertal changes. In M. Rutter (Ed.), *Psychosocial disturbances in young people* (pp. 37–82). New York: Cambridge University Press.

Altermatt, E. R., & Pomerantz, E. M. (2005). The implications of having high-achieving versus low-achieving friends: A longitudinal analysis. *Social Development, 14*, 61–81.

Althaus, J., & Wax, J. (2005). Analgesia and anesthesia in labor. *Obstetrics and Gynecology Clinics of North America, 32*, 231–244.

Alwan, S., & Friedman, J. M. (2009). Safety of selective serotonin reuptake inhibitors in pregnancy. *CNS Drugs, 23*, 493–509.

Amabile, T. M. (1982). Children's artistic creativity: Detrimental effects of competition in a field setting. *Personality and Social Psychology Bulletin, 8*, 573–578.

Amato, P. R. (2001). Children of divorce in the 1990s: An update of the Amato and Keith (1991) meta-analysis. *Journal of Family Psychology, 15*, 355–370.

Amato, P. R. (2006). Marital discord, divorce, and children's well-being: Results from a 20-year longitudinal study of two generations. In A. Clarke-Stewart & J. Dunn (Eds.), *Families count: Effects on child and adolescent development* (pp. 179–202). New York: Cambridge University Press.

Amato, P. R. (2010). Research on divorce: Continuing trends and new developments. *Journal of Marriage and Family, 72*, 650–666.

Amato, P. R., & Dorius, C. (2010). Father, children, and divorce. In M. E. Lamb (Ed.), *The role of the father in child development* (5th ed., pp. 177–200). Hoboken, NJ: Wiley.

Amato, P. R., & Fowler, F. (2002). Parenting practices, child adjustment, and family diversity. *Journal of Marriage and the Family, 64*, 703–716.

Amato, P. R., Landale, N. S., Havasevich-Brooks, T. C., Booth, A., Eggebeen, D. J., Schoen, R., & McHale, S. M. (2008). Precursors of young women's family formation pathways. *Journal of Marriage and Family, 70*, 1271–1289.

Amato, P. R., & Sobolewski, J. M. (2004). The effects of divorce on fathers and children: Nonresidential fathers and stepfathers. In M. E. Lamb (Ed.), *The role of the father in child development* (4th ed., pp. 341–367). Hoboken, NJ: Wiley.

American Academy of Pediatrics. (2001). Committee on Public Education: Children, adolescents, and television. *Pediatrics, 104*, 341–343.

American Academy of Pediatrics. (2005). Breastfeeding and the use of human milk. *Pediatrics, 115*, 496–506.

American Academy of Pediatrics. (2006). Folic acid for the prevention of neural tube defects. *Pediatrics, 104*, 325–327.

American Academy of Pediatrics. (2009). *Television—what children see and learn.* Retrieved from http://childdocs.com/pdf/Television%203-07.pdf

American Diabetes Association. (2011). *Diabetes statistics.* Retrieved from www.diabetes.org/diabetes-basics/diabetes-statistics

American Psychiatric Association. (2000). *DSM-IV-TR: Diagnostic and statistical manual of mental disorders—Text revision* (4th ed.). Washington, DC: Author.

American Psychological Association. (2002). Ethical principles of psychologists and code of conduct. *American Psychologist, 57*, 1060–1073.

American Psychological Association. (2010). *Report of the APA Task Force on the Sexualization of Girls.* Retrieved from www.apa.org/pi/women/programs/girls/report-full.pdf

Amsel, E., & Brock, S. (1996). The development of evidence evaluation skills. *Cognitive Development, 11*, 523–550.

Amso, D., & Johnson, S. P. (2006). Learning by selection: Visual search and object perception in young infants. *Developmental Psychology, 42*, 1236–1245.

Amsterlaw, J. (2006). Children's beliefs about everyday reasoning. *Child Development, 77*, 443–464.

Amsterlaw, J., & Wellman, H. M. (2006). Theories of mind in transition: A microgenetic study of the development of false belief understanding. *Journal of Cognition and Development, 7*, 139–172.

Anand, S. S., Yusuf, S., Jacobs, R., Davis, A. D., Yi, Q., & Gerstein, H. (2001). Risk factors, arteriosclerosis, and cardiovascular disease among Aboriginal people in Canada: The study of health assessment and risk evaluation in Aboriginal peoples (SHARE-AP). *Lancet, 358*, 1147–1153.

Anderman, E. M., Eccles, J. S., Yoon, K. S., Roeser, R., Wigfield, A., & Blumenfeld, P. (2001). Learning to value mathematics and reading: Relations to mastery and performance-oriented instructional practices. *Contemporary Educational Psychology, 26*, 76–95.

Andersen, E. (1992). *Speaking with style: The sociolinguistic skills of children.* New York: Routledge.

Andersen, E. (2000). Exploring register knowledge: The value of "controlled improvisation." In L. Menn & N. B. Ratner (Eds.), *Methods for studying language production* (pp. 225–248). Mahwah, NJ: Erlbaum.

Anderson, C. A. (2004). An update on the effects of violent video games. *Journal of Adolescence, 27*, 113–122.

Anderson, C. A., Berkowitz, L., Donnerstein, E., Huesmann, R., Johnson, J. D., Linz, D., Malamuth, N. M., & Wartella, E. (2003). The influence of media violence on youth. *Psychological Science in the Public Interest, 4*(3), 81–106.

Anderson, C. A., & Bushman, B. J. (2002). The effects of media violence on society. *Science, 295*, 2377–2379.

Anderson, D. A., & Hamilton, M. (2005). Gender role stereotyping of parents in children's picture books: The invisible father. *Sex Roles, 52*, 145–151.

Anderson, D. R., Collins, P. A., Schmitt, K. L., & Jacobvitz, R. S. (1996). Stressful life events and television viewing. *Communication Research, 23*, 243–260.

Anderson, D. R., Huston, A. C., Schmitt, K. L., Linebarger, D. L., & Wright, J. C. (2001). Early childhood television viewing and adolescent behavior. *Monographs of the Society for Research in Child Development, 66*(1, Serial No. 264).

Anderson, J. L., Morgan, J. L., & White, K. S. (2003). A statistical basis for speech sound discrimination. *Language and Speech, 46*, 155–182.

Anderson, S. W., Bechara, A., Damasio, H., Tranel, D., & Damasio, A. R. (1999). Impairment of social and moral behavior related to early damage in human prefrontal cortex. *Nature Neuroscience, 2*, 1032–1037.

Anderson, V. (2002). Executive function in children: Introduction. *Child Neuropsychology, 8*, 69–70.

Anderson, V. A., Catroppa, C., Dudgeon, P., Morse, S. A., Haritou, F., & Rosenfeld, J. V. (2006). Understanding predictors of functional recovery and outcome 30 months following early childhood head injury. *Neuropsychology, 20*, 42–57.

Andersson, H. (1996). The Fagan Test of Infant Intelligence: Predictive validity in a random sample. *Psychological Reports, 78*, 1015–1026.

Andersson, T., & Magnusson, D. (1990). Biological maturation in adolescence and the development of drinking habits and alcohol abuse among young males: A prospective longitudinal study. *Journal of Youth and Adolescence, 19*, 33–41.

Andrews, G., & Halford, G. S. (1998). Children's ability to make transitive inferences: The importance of premise integration and structural complexity. *Cognitive Development, 13*, 479–513.

Ang, S., Rodgers, J. L., & Wänström, L. (2010). The Flynn effect within subgroups in the U.S.: Gender, race, income, education, and urbanization differences in the NLSY-Children data. *Intelligence, 38*, 367–384.

Anglin, J. M. (1993). Vocabulary development: A morphological analysis. *Monographs of the Society for Research in Child Development, 58*(10, Serial No. 238).

Anisfeld, M. (2005). No compelling evidence to dispute Piaget's timetable of the development of representational imitation in infancy. In S. Hurley & N. Chater (Eds.), *Perspectives on imitation: From neuroscience to social science: Vol. 2. Imitation, human development, and culture* (pp. 107–131). Cambridge, MA: MIT Press.

Annett, M. (2002). *Handedness and brain asymmetry: The right shift theory.* Hove, UK: Psychology Press.

Antoni, M. H., & Lutgendorf, S. (2007). Psychosocial factors and disease progression in cancer. *Current Directions in Psychological Science, 16*, 42–46.

Apfelbaum, E. P., Pauker, K., Ambady, N., Sommers, S. R., & Norton, M. I. (2008). Learning (not) to talk about race: When older children underperform in social categorization. *Developmental Psychology, 44*, 1513–1518.

Apgar, V. (1953). A proposal for a new method of evaluation in the newborn infant. *Current Research in Anesthesia and Analgesia, 32*, 260–267.

Appiah, K. A. (2010). *The honor code: How moral revolutions happen.* New York: Norton.

Archer, S. L., & Waterman, A. S. (1990). Varieties of identity diffusions and foreclosures: An exploration of subcategories of the identity statuses. *Journal of Adolescent Research, 5*, 96–111.

Archibald, A. B., Graber, J. A., & Brooks-Gunn, J. (2006). Pubertal processes and physiological growth in adolescence. In G. R. Adams & M. D. Berzonsky (Eds.), *Blackwell handbook of adolescence* (pp. 24–48). Malden, MA: Blackwell.

Archibald, A. B., Linver, M. R., Graber, J. A., & Brooks-Gunn, J. (2002). Parent–

adolescent relationships and girls' unhealthy eating: Testing reciprocal effects. *Journal of Research on Adolescence, 12*, 451–461.

Arcus, D., & Chambers, P. (2008). Childhood risks associated with adoption. In T. P. Gullotta & G. M Blau (Eds.), *Family influences on childhood behavior and development* (pp. 117–142). New York: Routledge.

Ardila-Rey, A., & Killen, M. (2001). Middle-class Colombian children's evaluations of personal, moral, and social-conventional interactions in the classroom. *International Journal of Behavioral Development, 25*, 246–255.

Armstrong, K. L., Quinn, R. A., & Dadds, M. R. (1994). The sleep patterns of normal children. *Medical Journal of Australia, 161*, 202–206.

Arnett, J. J. (2000). Emerging adulthood: A theory of development from the late teens through the twenties. *American Psychologist, 55*, 469–480.

Arnett, J. J. (2006). Emerging adulthood: Understanding the new way of coming of age. In J. J. Arnett & J. L. Tanner (Eds.), *Emerging adults in America: Coming of age in the 21st century* (pp. 3–19). Washington, DC: American Psychological Association.

Arnett, J. J. (2007). Emerging adulthood: What is it and what is it good for? *Child Development Perspectives, 1*, 68–73.

Arnett, J. J., & Tanner, J. L. (Eds.). (2006). *Emerging adults in America: Coming of age in the 21st century.* Washington, DC: American Psychological Association.

Arnold, D. H., McWilliams, L., & Harvey-Arnold, E. (1998). Teacher discipline and child misbehavior in daycare: Untangling causality with correlational data. *Developmental Psychology, 34*, 276–287.

Arnold, P. (1999). Emotional disorders in deaf children. In V. L. Schwean & D. H. Saklofske (Eds.), *Handbook of psychosocial characteristics of exceptional children* (pp. 493–522). New York: Kluwer.

Arnon, S., Shapsa, A., Forman, L., Regev, R., Bauer, S., & Litmanovitz, I. (2006). Live music is beneficial to preterm infants in the neonatal intensive care unit. *Birth, 33*, 131–136.

Arsenio, W. F. (2010). Integrating emotion attributions, morality, and aggression: Research and theoretical foundations. In W. F. Arsenio & E. A. Lemerise (Eds.), *Emotions, aggression, and morality in children: Bridging development and psychopathology* (pp. 75–94). Washington, DC: American Psychological Association.

Arsenio, W. F., & Fleiss, K. (1996). Typical and behaviourally disruptive children's understanding of the emotional consequences of socio-moral events. *British Journal of Developmental Psychology, 14*, 173–186.

Arsenio, W. F., Gold, J., & Adams, E. (2006). Children's conceptions and displays of moral emotions. In M. Killen & J. Smetana (Eds.), *Handbook of moral development* (pp. 581–609). London: Psychology Press.

Arsenio, W. F., & Lemerise, E. A. (2001). Varieties of childhood bullying: Values, emotion processes, and social competence. *Social Development, 10*, 59–73.

Arterberry, M. E. (2008). Infants' sensitivity to the depth cue of height-in-the-picture-plane. *Infancy, 13*, 544–555.

Arterberry, M. E., Craton, L. G., & Yonas, A. (1993). Infants' sensitivity to motion-carried information for depth and object properties. In C. E. Granrud (Ed.), *Visual perception and cognition in infancy* (pp. 215–234). Hillsdale, NJ: Erlbaum.

Artman, L., & Cahan, S. (1993). Schooling and the development of transitive inference. *Developmental Psychology, 29,* 753–759.

Artman, L., Cahan, S., & Avni-Babad, D. (2006). Age, schooling, and conditional reasoning. *Cognitive Development, 21,* 131–145.

Asada, K. , Tomiwa, K., Masako, O., & Itakura, S. (2010b). Fluent language with impaired pragmatics in children with Williams syndrome. *Journal of Neurolinguistics, 23,* 540–552.

Asada, K., Tomiwa, K., Okada, M., & Itakura, S. (2010a). Atypical verbal communication pattern according to others' attention in children with Williams syndrome. *Research in Developmental Disabilities, 31,* 452–457.

Asarnow, J. R., Jaycox, L. H., Duan, N., LaBorde, A. P., Rea, M. M., & Murray, P. (2005). Effectiveness of a quality improvement intervention for adolescent depression in primary care clinics. *Journal of the American Medical Association, 293,* 311–319.

Asendorpf, J. B., Warkentin, V., & Baudonniere, P. (1996). Self-awareness and other-awareness II: Mirror self-recognition, social contingency awareness, and synchronic imitation. *Developmental Psychology, 32,* 313–321.

ASHA (American Speech-Language-Hearing Association). (2011). *Facts about pediatric hearing loss.* Retrieved from www.asha.org/aud/Facts-about-Pediatric-Hearing-Loss.htm

Asher, S. R., & Rose, A. J. (1997). Promoting children's social-emotional adjustment with peers. In P. Salovey & D. J. Sluyter (Eds.), *Emotional development and emotional intelligence* (pp. 193–195). New York: Basic Books.

Aslin, R. N., Jusczyk, P. W., & Pisoni, D. B. (1998). Speech and auditory processing during infancy: Constraints on and precursors to language. In D. Kuhn & R. S. Siegler (Eds.), *Handbook of child psychology: Vol. 2. Cognition, perception, and language* (5th ed., pp. 147–198). New York: Wiley.

Aslin, R. N., & Newport, E. L. (2009). What statistical learning can and can't tell us about language acquisition. In J. Colombo, P. McCardle, & L. Freund (Eds.), *Infant pathways to language: Methods, models, and research directions* (pp. 15–29). New York: Psychology Press.

Astington, J. W., & Jenkins, J. M. (1995). Theory of mind development and social understanding. *Cognition and Emotion, 9,* 151–165.

Astington, J. W., & Pelletier, J. (2005). Theory of mind, language, and learning in the early years: Developmental origins of school readiness. In B. D. Homer & C. S. Tamis-LeMonda (Eds.), *The development of social cognition and communication* (pp. 205–230). Mahwah, NJ: Erlbaum.

Astington, J. W., Pelletier, J., & Homer, B. (2002). Theory of mind and epistemological development: The relation between children's second-order false belief understanding and their ability to reason about evidence. *New Ideas in Psychology, 20,* 131–144.

Astuti, R., Solomon, G. E. A., & Carey, S. (2004). Constraints on conceptual development: A case study of the acquisition of folkbiological and folksociological knowledge in Madagascar. *Monographs of the Society for Research in Child Development, 69*(3, Serial No. 277).

Atance, C. M., Bélanger, M., & Meltzoff, A. N. (2010). Preschoolers' understanding of others' desires: Fulfilling mine enhances my understanding of yours. *Developmental Psychology, 46,* 1505–1513.

Atance, C. M., & Jackson, L. K. (2009). The development and coherence of future-oriented behaviors during the preschool years. *Journal of Experimental Child Psychology, 102,* 379–391.

Atance, C. M., & Meltzoff, A. N. (2005). My future self: Young children's ability to anticipate and explain future states. *Cognitive Development, 20,* 341–361.

Atencio, D. J., & Montero, I. (2009). Private speech and motivation: The role of language in a sociocultural account of motivational processes. In A. Winsler, C. Fernyhough, & I. Montero (Eds.), *Private speech, executive functioning, and the development of verbal self-regulation* (pp. 201–223). New York: Cambridge University Press.

Atkins, R., Hart, D., & Donnelly, T. M. (2004). Moral identity development and school attachment. In D. Narvaez & D. Lapsley (Eds.), *Morality, self and identity* (pp. 65–82). Mahwah, NJ: Erlbaum.

Atkinson, R. C., & Shiffrin, R. M. (1968). Human memory: A proposed system and its control processes. In K. W. Spence & J. T. Spence (Eds.), *Advances in the psychology of learning and motivation* (Vol. 2, pp. 90–195). New York: Academic Press.

Atkinson-King, K. (1973). Children's acquisition of phonological stress contrasts. *UCLA Working Papers in Phonetics, 25.*

Attewell, P. (2001). The first and second digital divides. *Sociology of Education, 74,* 252–259.

Au, T. K., Sidle, A. L., & Rollins, K. B. (1993). Developing an intuitive understanding of conservation and contamination: Invisible particles as a plausible mechanism. *Developmental Psychology, 29,* 286–299.

Aud, S., Hussar, W., Kena, G., Bianco, K., Frohlich, L., Kemp, J., & Tahan, K. (2011). *The condition of education 2011* (NCES 2011-033). U.S. Department of Education, National Center for Education Statistics. Washington, DC: U.S. Government Printing Office.

Aunola, K., Stattin, H., & Nurmi, J.-E. (2000). Parenting styles and adolescents' achievement strategies. *Journal of Adolescence, 23,* 205–222.

Austin, E. W., Chen, M.-J., & Grube, J. W. (2006). How does alcohol advertising influence underage drinking? The role of desirability, identification and skepticism. *Journal of Adolescent Health, 38,* 376–384.

Auyeung, B., Baron-Cohen, S., Ashwin, E., Knickmeyer, R., Taylor, K., Hackett, G., et al. (2009). Fetal testosterone predicts sexually differentiated childhood behavior in girls and boys. *Psychological Science, 20,* 144–148.

Averhart, C. J., & Bigler, R. S. (1997). Shades of meaning: Skin tone, racial attitudes, and constructive memory in African-American children. *Journal of Experimental Child Psychology, 67,* 368–388.

Axelin, A., Salanterä, S., & Lehtonen, L. (2006). 'Facilitated tucking by parents' in pain management of preterm infants—a randomized crossover trial. *Early Human Development, 82,* 241–247.

Azar, S. T., & Wolfe, D. A. (1998). Child physical abuse and neglect. In E. J. Mash & R. A. Barkley (Eds.), *Treatment of childhood disorders* (2nd ed., pp. 501–504). New York: Guilford.

Azmitia, M. (1996). Peer interactive minds: Developmental, theoretical, and methodological issues. In P. B. Baltes & U. M. Staudinger (Eds.), *Interactive minds: Lifespan perspectives on the social foundations of cognition* (pp. 133–162). New York: Cambridge University Press.

Azmitia, M., & Cooper, C. R. (2001). Good or bad? Peer influences on Latino and European American adolescents' pathways through school. *Journal of Education for Students Placed at Risk, 6,* 45–71.

Azmitia, M., Ittel, A., & Brenk, C. (2006). Latino-heritage adolescents' friendships. In X. Chen, D. C. French, & B. H. Schneider (Eds.), *Peer relationships in cultural context* (pp. 426–451). New York: Cambridge University Press.

Bacallao, M. L., & Smokowski, P. R. (2007). The costs of getting ahead: Mexican family system changes after immigration. *Family Relations, 56,* 52–66.

Baddeley, A. (2000). Short-term and working memory. In E. Tulving & R. I. M. Craik (Eds.), *The Oxford handbook of memory* (pp. 77–92). New York: Oxford University Press.

Baenninger, M., & Newcombe, N. (1995). Environmental input to the development of sex-related differences in spatial and mathematical ability. *Learning and Individual Differences, 7,* 363–379.

Baer, J. (2002). Is family cohesion a risk or protective factor during adolescent development? *Journal of Marriage and Family, 64,* 668–675.

Bagwell, C. L., & Coie, J. D. (2004). The best friendships of aggressive boys: Relationship quality, conflict management, and rule-breaking behavior. *Journal of Experimental Child Psychology, 88,* 5–24.

Bagwell, C. L., Coie, J. D., Terry, R. A., & Lochman, J. E. (2000). Peer clique participation and social status in preadolescence. *Merrill-Palmer Quarterly, 46,* 280–305.

Bahrick, L. E. (2010). Intermodal perception and selective attention to intersensory redundancy: Implications for typical social development and autism. In G. Bremner & T. D. Wachs (Eds.), *Wiley-Blackwell handbook of infant development: Vol. 1. Basic research* (2nd ed., pp. 120–166). Malden, MA: Blackwell.

Bahrick, L. E., Flom, R., & Lickliter, R. (2003). Intersensory redundancy facilitates discrimination of tempo in 3-month-old infants. *Developmental Psychobiology, 41,* 352–363.

Bahrick, L. E., Gogate, L. J., & Ruiz, I. (2002). Attention and memory for faces and actions in infancy: The salience of actions over faces in dynamic events. *Child Development, 73,* 1629–1643.

Bahrick, L. E., Hernandez-Reif, M., & Flom, R. (2005). The development of infant learning about specific face–voice relations. *Developmental Psychology, 41,* 541–552.

Bahrick, L. E., Hernandez-Reif, M., & Pickens, J. N. (1997). The effect of retrieval cues on visual preferences and memory in infancy: Evidence for a four-phase attention function. *Journal of Experimental Child Psychology, 67,* 1–20.

Bahrick, L. E., Lickliter, R., & Flom, R. (2004). Intersensory redundancy guides the development of selective attention, perception, and cognition in infancy. *Current Directions in Psychological Science, 13,* 99–102.

Bahrick, L. E., Netto, D., & Hernandez-Reif, M. (1998). Intermodal perception of adult and child faces and voices by infants. *Child Development, 69,* 1263–1275.

Bahrick, L. E., & Pickens, J. N. (1995). Infant memory for object motion across a period of three months: Implications for a four-phase attention function. *Journal of Experimental Child Psychology, 59,* 343–371.

Bai, D. L., & Bertenthal, B. I. (1992). Locomotor status and the development of spatial search skills. *Child Development, 63,* 215–226.

Bailey, J. M., Bobrow, D., Wolfe, M., & Mikach, S. (1995). Sexual orientation of adult sons of gay fathers. *Developmental Psychology, 31,* 124–129.

Bailey, R. C. (1990). Growth of African pygmies in early childhood. *New England Journal of Medicine, 323,* 1146.

Baillargeon, R. (1994). Physical reasoning in infancy. In M. S. Gazzaniga (Ed.), *The cognitive neurosciences* (pp. 181–204). Cambridge, MA: MIT Press.

Baillargeon, R. (2004). Infants' reasoning about hidden objects: Evidence for event-general and event-specific expectations. *Developmental Science, 7,* 391–424.

Baillargeon, R., & DeVos, J. (1991). Object permanence in young infants: Further evidence. *Child Development, 62,* 1227–1246.

Baillargeon, R., Li, J., Ng, W., & Yuan, S. (2009). An account of infants' physical reasoning. In A. Woodward & A. Needham (Eds.), *Learning and the infant mind* (pp. 66–116). New York: Oxford University Press.

Baillargeon, R., Scott, R. M., & He, Z. (2010). False-belief understanding in infants. *Trends in Cognitive Sciences, 14,* 110–118.

Baillargeon, R. H., Zoccolillo, M., Keenan, K., Côté, S., Pérusse, D., Wu, H.-X., & Boivin, M. (2007). Gender differences in physical aggression: A prospective population-based survey of children before and after 2 years of age. *Developmental Psychology, 43,* 13–26.

Bainbridge, J., Meyers, M. K., Tanaka, S., & Waldfogel, J. (2005). Who gets an early education? Family income and the enrollment of three- to five-year-olds from 1968 to 2000. *Social Science Quarterly, 86,* 724–745.

Baiocco, R., D'Alessio, M., & Laghi, F. (2009). Discrepancies between parents' and children's attitudes toward TV advertising. *Journal of Genetic Psychology, 170,* 176–191.

Bakeman, R., Adamson, L. B., Konner, M., & Barr, R. G. (1990). !Kung infancy: The social context of object exploration. *Child Development, 61,* 794–809.

Baker, J. A. (2006). Contributions of teacher–child relationships to positive school adjustment during elementary school. *Journal of School Psychology, 44,* 211–229.

Bakermans-Kranenburg, M. J., & van IJzendoorn, M. H. (2009). The first 10,000 adult attachment interviews: Distributions of adult attachment representations in clinical and non-clinical groups. *Attachment and Human Development, 11*(3), 223–263.

Bakermans-Kranenburg, M. J., & van IJzendoorn, M. H. (2011). Differential susceptibility to rearing environment depending on dopamine-related genes: New evidence and a meta-analysis. *Development and Psychopathology, 23,* 39–52.

Bakermans-Kranenberg, M. J., van IJzendoorn, M. H., Mesman, J., Alink, L. R. A., & Juffer, F. (2008a). Effects of an attachment-based intervention on daily cortisol moderated by dopamine receptor D4: A randomized control trial on 1- to 3-year-olds screened for externalizing behavior. *Development and Psychopathology, 20,* 805–820.

Bakermans-Kranenburg, M. J., van IJzendoorn, M. H., Pijlman, F. T. A., Mesman, J., & Juffer, F. (2008b). Experimental evidence for differential sensitivity: Dopamine D4 receptor polymorphism (DRD4 VNTR) moderates intervention effects on toddlers' externalizing behavior in a randomized control trial. *Developmental Psychology, 44,* 293–300.

Bakhurst, D. (2007). Vygotsky's demons. In H. Daniels, M. Cole, & J. V. Wertsch (Eds.), *The Cambridge companion to Vygotsky* (pp. 50–74). New York: Cambridge University Press.

Balaban, M. T., & Waxman, S. R. (1997). Do words facilitate object categorization in 9-month-old infants? *Journal of Experimental Child Psychology, 64,* 3–26.

Baldwin, J. M. (1895). *Mental development in the child and the race: Methods and processes.* New York: Macmillan.

Baldwin, J. M. (1897). *Social and ethnic interpretations in mental development: A study in social psychology.* New York: Macmillan.

Bale, J. F. (2009). Fetal infections and brain development. *Clinical Perinatology, 36,* 639–653.

Balfanz, R., Legters, N., West, T. C., & Weber, L. M. (2007). Are NCLB's measures, incentives, and improvement strategies the right ones for the nation's low-performing high schools? *American Educational Research Journal, 44,* 559–593.

Balis, T., & Postolache, T. T. (2008). Ethnic differences in adolescent suicide in the United States. *International Journal of Child Health and Human Development, 1,* 282–296.

Ball, H. (2006). Parent–infant bed-sharing behavior: Effects of feeding type and presence of father. *Human Nature, 17,* 301–318.

Balsano, A. B. (2005). Youth civic engagement in the United States: Understanding and addressing the impact of social impediments on positive youth and community development. *Applied Developmental Science, 9,* 188–201.

Baltes, P. B., Lindenberger, U., & Staudinger, U. M. (2006). Life span theory in developmental psychology. In R. M. Lerner & W. Damon (Eds.), *Handbook of child psychology: Vol. 1. Theoretical models of human development* (6th ed., pp. 569–664). Hoboken, NJ: Wiley.

Bandstra, E. S., Morrow, C. E., Mansoor, E., & Accornero, V. H. (2010). Prenatal drug exposure: Infant and toddler outcomes. *Journal of Addictive Diseases, 29,* 245–258.

Bandura, A. (1977). *Social learning theory.* Englewood Cliffs, NJ: Prentice-Hall.

Bandura, A. (1992). Perceived self-efficacy in cognitive development and functioning. *Educational Psychologist, 28,* 117–148.

Bandura, A. (1999). Social cognitive theory of personality. In L. A. Pervin & O. P. John (Eds.), *Handbook of personality: Theory and research* (2nd ed., pp. 154–196). New York: Guilford.

Bandura, A. (2001). Social cognitive theory: An agentic perspective. *Annual Review of Psychology, 52,* 1–26.

Banish, M. T., & Heller, W. (1998). Evolving perspectives on lateralization of function. *Current Directions in Psychological Science, 7,* 1–2.

Banks, M. S. (1980). The development of visual accommodation during early infancy. *Child Development, 51,* 646–666.

Banks, M. S., & Ginsburg, A. P. (1985). Early visual preferences: A review and new theoretical treatment. In H. W. Reese (Ed.), *Advances in child development and behavior* (Vol. 19, pp. 207–246). New York: Academic Press.

Bannard, C., Lieven, E., & Tomasello, M. (2009). Modeling children's early grammatical knowledge. *Proceedings of the National Academy of Sciences, 106,* 17284–17289.

Banse, R., Gawronski, B., Rebetez, C., Gutt, H., & Morton, J. B. (2010). The development of spontaneous gender stereotyping in childhood: Relations to stereotype knowledge and stereotype flexibility. *Developmental Science, 13,* 298–306.

Barber, B. K., & Harmon, E. L. (2002). Violating the self: Parental psychological control of children and adolescents. In B. K. Barber (Ed.), *Intrusive parenting: How psychological control affects children and adolescents* (pp. 15–52). Washington, DC: American Psychological Association.

Barber, B. K., & Olsen, J. A. (1997). Socialization in context: Connection, regulation, and autonomy in the family, school, and neighborhood, and with peers. *Journal of Adolescent Research, 12,* 287–315.

Barber, B. K., & Olsen, J. A. (2004). Assessing the transitions to middle and high school. *Journal of Adolescent Research, 19,* 3–30.

Barber, B. K., Stolz, H. E., & Olsen, J. A. (2005). Parental support, psychological control, and behavioral control: Assessing relevance across time, culture, and method. *Monographs of the Society for Research in Child Development, 70*(4, Serial No. 282).

Barber, B. L., Stone, M. R., Hunt, J. E., & Eccles, J. S. (2005). Benefits of activity participation: The roles of identity affirmation and peer group norm sharing. In J. L. Mahoney, R. W. Larson, & J. S. Eccles (Eds.), *Organized activities as contexts of development: Extracurricular activities, after-school and community programs* (pp. 185–210). Mahwah, NJ: Erlbaum.

Barber, J. S. (2001). The intergenerational transmission of age at first birth among married and unmarried men and women. *Social Sciences Research, 30,* 219–247.

Bard, K. A., Todd, B. K., Bernier, C., Love, J., & Leavens, D. A. (2006). Self-awareness in human and chimpanzee infants: What is measured and what is meant by the mark and mirror test? *Infancy, 9,* 191–219.

Bardwell, J. R., Cochran, S. W., & Walker, S. (1986). Relationship of parental education, race, and gender to sex role stereotyping in five-year-old kindergartners. *Sex Roles, 15,* 275–281.

Barenbaum, J., Ruchkin, V., & Schwab-Stone, M. (2004). The psychosocial aspects of children exposed to war: Practice and policy initiatives. *Journal of Child Psychology and Psychiatry, 45,* 41–62.

Bar-Haim, Y., Ziv, T., Lamy, D., & Hodes, R. M. (2006). Nature and nurture in own-race face processing. *Psychological Science, 17,* 159–163.

Barker, D. J. (2008). Human growth and cardiovascular disease. *Nestlé Nutrition Workshop Series, 61,* 21–38.

Barker, R. G., & Gump, P. V. (1964). *Big school, small school: High school size and student behavior.* Stanford, CA: Stanford University Press.

Barkley, R. A. (2002). Psychosocial treatments of attention-deficit/hyperactivity disorder in children. *Journal of Clinical Psychology, 63*(Suppl. 12), 36–43.

Barkley, R. A. (2003). Issues in the diagnosis of attention-deficit hyperactivity disorder in children. *Brain and Development, 25,* 77–83.

Barkley, R. A. (2006). Attention-deficit/hyperactivity disorder. In R. A. Barkley, D. A. Wolfe, & E. J. Mash (Eds.), *Behavioral and emotional disorders in adolescents: Nature, assessment, and treatment* (pp. 91–152). New York: Guilford.

Barnes, G. M., Hoffman, J. H., Welte, J. W., Farrell, M. P., & Dintcheff, B. A. (2007). Adolescents' time use: Effects on substance use, delinquency and sexual activity. *Journal of Youth and Adolescence, 36,* 697–710.

Barnes, R., Josefowitz, N., & Cole, E. (2006). Residential schools: Impact on Aboriginal students' academic and cognitive development. *Canadian Journal of School Psychology, 21,* 18–32.

Barnes-Josiah, D., & Augustin, A. (1995). Secular trend in the age at menarche in Haiti. *American Journal of Human Biology, 7,* 357–362.

Barnett, D., & Vondra, J. I. (1999). Atypical patterns of early attachment: Theory, research, and current directions. In J. I. Vondra & D. Barnett (Eds.), *Atypical attachment in infancy and early childhood among children at developmental risk. Monographs of the Society for Research in Child Development, 64*(3, Serial No. 258), 1–24.

Baron, I. S., & Rey-Casserly, C. (2010). Extremely preterm birth outcome: A review of four decades of cognitive research. *Neuropsychology Review, 20,* 430–452.

Baron-Cohen, S., Baldwin, D. A., & Crowson, M. (1997). Do children with autism use the speaker's direction of gaze strategy to crack the code of language? *Child Development, 68,* 48–57.

Baron-Cohen, S., & Belmonte, M. K. (2005). Autism: A window onto the development of the social and the analytic brain. *Annual Review of Neuroscience, 28,* 109–126.

Barr, H. M., Bookstein, F. L., O'Malley, K. D., Connor, P. D., Huggins, J. E., & Streissguth, A. P. (2006). Binge drinking during pregnancy as a predictor of psychiatric disorders on the structured clinical interview for DSM-IV in young adult offspring. *American Journal of Psychiatry, 163,* 1061–1065.

Barr, H. M., Streissguth, A. P., Darby, B. L., & Sampson, P. D. (1990). Prenatal exposure to alcohol, caffeine, tobacco, and aspirin: Effects on fine and gross motor performance in 4-year-old children. *Developmental Psychology, 26,* 339–348.

Barr, R., & Hayne, H. (2003). It's not what you know, it's who you know: Older

siblings facilitate imitation during infancy. *International Journal of Early Years Education, 11,* 7–21.

Barr, R., Marrott, H., & Rovee-Collier, C. (2003). The role of sensory preconditioning in memory retrieval by preverbal infants. *Learning and Behavior, 31,* 111–123.

Barr, R., Muentener, P., & Garcia, A. (2007). Age-related changes in deferred imitation from television by 6- to 18-month-olds. *Developmental Science, 10,* 910–921.

Barr, R. G. (2001). "Colic" is something infants do, rather than a condition they "have": A developmental approach to crying phenomena patterns, pacification and (patho)genesis. In R. G. Barr, I. St James-Roberts, & M. R. Keefe (Eds.), *New evidence on unexplained infant crying* (pp. 87–104). St. Louis: Johnson & Johnson Pediatric Institute.

Barr, R. G., Paterson, J. A., MacMartin, L. M., & Lehtonen, L. (2005). Prolonged and unsoothable crying bouts in infants with and without colic. *Journal of Developmental and Behavioral Pediatrics, 26,* 14–23.

Barratt, M. S., Roach, M. A., & Leavitt, L. A. (1996). The impact of low-risk prematurity on maternal behaviour and toddler outcomes. *International Journal of Behavioral Development, 19,* 581–602.

Barrett, K. C. (2005). The origins of social emotions and self-regulation in toddlerhood: New evidence. *Cognition and Emotion, 19,* 953–979.

Barrett, K. C., & Campos, J. J. (1987). Perspectives on emotional development II: A functionalist approach to emotions. In J. D. Osofsky (Ed.), *Handbook of infant development* (2nd ed., pp. 555–578). New York: Wiley.

Barrett, T. M., Traupman, E., & Needham, E. (2008). Infants' visual anticipation in grasp planning. *Infant Behavior and Development, 31,* 1–9.

Barriga, A. Q., Morrison, E. M., Liau, A. K., & Gibbs, J. C. (2001). Moral cognition: Explaining the gender difference in antisocial behavior. *Merrill-Palmer Quarterly, 47,* 532–562.

Barron, F. (1988). Putting creativity to work. In R. J. Sternberg (Ed.), *The nature of creativity: Contemporary psychological perspectives* (pp. 76–98). New York: Cambridge University Press.

Barros, R. M., Silver, E. J., & Stein, R. E. K. (2009). School recess and group classroom behavior. *Pediatrics, 123,* 431–436.

Barry, C. T., Frick, P. J., & Killian, A. L. (2003). The relation of narcissism to self-esteem and conduct problems in children: A preliminary investigation. *Journal of Clinical Child and Adolescent Psychology, 32,* 139–152.

Bartgis, J., Lilly, A. R., & Thomas, D. G. (2003). Event-related potential and behavioral measures of attention in 5-, 7-, and 9-year-olds. *Journal of General Psychology, 130,* 311–335.

Bartlett, F. C. (1932). *Remembering.* Cambridge: Cambridge University Press.

Bartocci, M., Berggvist, L. L., Lagercrantz, H., & Anand, K. J. (2006). Pain activates cortical areas in the preterm newborn brain. *Pain, 122,* 109–117.

Barton, M. E., & Strosberg, R. (1997). Conversational patterns of two-year-old twins in mother–twin–twin triads. *Journal of Child Language, 24,* 257–269.

Barton, M. E., & Tomasello, M. (1991). Joint attention and conversation in mother–

infant–sibling triads. *Child Development, 62,* 517–529.

Bartrip, J., Morton, J., & de Schonen, S. (2001). Responses to mother's face in 3-week to 5-month-old infants. *British Journal of Developmental Psychology, 19,* 219–232.

Bartsch, K., & London, K. (2000). Children's use of mental state information in selecting persuasive arguments. *Developmental Psychology, 36,* 352–365.

Bartsch, K., & Wellman, H. M. (1995). *Children talk about the mind.* New York: Oxford University Press.

Baruch, C., & Drake, C. (1997). Tempo discrimination in infants. *Infant Behavior and Development, 20,* 573–577.

Basinger, K. S., Gibbs, J. C., & Fuller, D. (1995). Context and the measurement of moral judgment. *International Journal of Behavioral Development, 18,* 537–556.

Basow, S. A., & Rubin, L. R. (1999). Gender influences on adolescent development. In N. G. Johnson & M. C. Roberts (Eds.), *Beyond appearance: A new look at adolescent girls* (pp. 25–52). Washington, DC: American Psychological Association.

Bass, J. L., Corwin, M., Gozal, D., Moore, C., Nishida, H., Parker, et al. (2004). The effect of chronic or intermittent hypoxia on cognition in childhood: A review of the evidence. *Pediatrics, 114,* 805–816.

Bass-Ringdahl, S. M. (2010). The relationship of audibility and the development of canonical babbling in young children with hearing impairment. *Journal of Deaf Studies and Deaf Education, 15,* 287–310.

Batchelor, J. (2008). 'Failure to thrive' revisited. *Child Abuse Review, 17,* 147–159.

Bates, E. (1999). Plasticity, localization, and language development. In S. H. Broman & J. M. Fletcher (Eds.), *The changing nervous system: Neurobehavioral consequences of early brain disorders* (pp. 214–247). New York: Oxford University Press.

Bates, E., & MacWhinney, B. (1987). Competition, variation, and language learning. In B. MacWhinney (Ed.), *Mechanisms of language acquisition* (pp. 157–193). Hillsdale, NJ: Erlbaum.

Bates, E., Wilson, S. M., Saygin, A. P., Dick, F., Sereno, M. I., Knight, R. T., & Dronkers, N. F. (2003). Voxel-based lesion-symptom mapping. *Nature Neuroscience, 6,* 448–450.

Bates, J. E., Wachs, T. D., & Emde, R. N. (1994). Toward practical uses for biological concepts. In J. E. Bates & T. D. Wachs (Eds.), *Temperament: Individual differences at the interface of biology and behavior* (pp. 275–306). Washington, DC: American Psychological Association.

Bauer, C. R., Langer, J. C., Shakaran, S., Bada, H. S., & Lester, B. (2005). Acute neonatal effects of cocaine exposure during pregnancy. *Archives of Pediatrics and Adolescent Medicine, 159,* 824–834.

Bauer, P. J. (2002). Early memory development. In U. Goswami (Ed.), *Blackwell handbook of child cognitive development* (pp. 127–150). Malden, MA: Blackwell.

Bauer, P. J. (2006). Event memory. In D. Kuhn & R. Siegler (Eds.), *Handbook of child psychology: Vol. 2. Cognition, perception, and language* (6th ed., pp. 373–425). Hoboken, NJ: Wiley.

Bauer, P. J. (2007). Recall in infancy: A neurodevelopmental account. *Current Directions in Psychological Science, 16,* 142–146.

Bauer, P. J., Bruch, M. M., Scholin, S. E., & Gulin, O. E. (2007). Using cue words to investigate the distribution of autobiographical memories in childhood. *Psychological Science, 18,* 910–916.

Bauer, P. J., Wiebe, S. A., Carver, L. J., Lukowski, A. F., Haight, J. C., Waters, J. M., & Nelson, C. A. (2006). Electrophysiological indexes of encoding and behavioral indexes of recall: Examining relations and developmental change late in the first year of life. *Developmental Neuropsychology, 29,* 293–320.

Baumeister, R. F. (1998). Inducing guilt. In J. Bybee (Ed.), *Guilt and children* (pp. 185–213). San Diego: Academic Press.

Baumeister, R. F., Campbell, J. D., Krueger, J. I., & Vohs, K. D. (2003). Does high self-esteem cause better performance, interpersonal success, happiness, or healthier lifestyles? *Psychological Science in the Public Interest, 4*(1), 1–44.

Baumer, S., Ferholt, B., & Lecusay, R. (2005). Promoting narrative competence through adult–child joint pretense: Lessons from the Scandinavian educational practice of playworld. *Cognitive Development, 20,* 576–590.

Baumrind, D. (1971). Current patterns of parental authority. *Developmental Psychology Monograph, 4*(1, Pt. 2).

Baumrind, D., & Black, A. E. (1967). Socialization practices associated with dimensions of competence in preschool boys and girls. *Child Development, 38,* 291–327.

Baumrind, D., Lazelere, R. E., & Owens, E. B. (2010). Effects of preschool parents' power assertive patterns and practices on adolescent development. *Parenting, 10,* 157–201.

Bauserman, R. (2002). Child adjustment in joint-custody versus sole-custody arrangements: A meta-analytic review. *Journal of Family Psychology, 16,* 91–102.

Baydar, N., Greek, A., & Brooks-Gunn, J. (1997). A longitudinal study of the effects of the birth of a sibling during the first 6 years of life. *Journal of Marriage and the Family, 59,* 939–956.

Bayley, N. (1969). *Bayley Scales of Infant Development.* New York: Psychological Corporation.

Bayley, N. (1993). *Bayley Scales of Infant Development* (2nd ed.). New York: Psychological Corporation.

Bayley, N. (2005). *Bayley Scales of Infant and Toddler Development* (3rd ed.). (Bayley III). San Antonio, TX: Harcourt Assessment.

Baynes, K., & Gazzaniga, M. S. (1988). Right hemisphere language: Insights into normal language mechanisms. In F. Plum (Ed.), *Language, communication, and the brain* (pp. 117–126). New York: Raven.

Bean, R. A., Barber, B. K., & Crane, D. R. (2007). Parental support, behavioral control, and psychological control among African American youth: The relationships to academic grades, delinquency, and depression. *Journal of Family Issues, 27,* 1335–1355.

Bearman, P. S., & Moody, J. (2004). Suicide and friendships among American adolescents. *American Journal of Public Health, 94,* 89–95.

Beatty, W. W. (1992). Gonadal hormones and sex differences in nonreproductive behaviors. In A. A. Gerall, H. Moltz, & I. L. Ward (Eds.), *Handbook of behavioral neurobiology: Vol. 11. Sexual differentiation* (pp. 85–128). New York: Plenum.

Beautrais, A. L. (2003). Life course factors associated with suicidal behaviors in young people. *American Behavioral Scientist, 46,* 1137–1156.

Beck, S. W. (2008). Cultural variation in narrative competence and its implications for children's academic success. In A. McCabe, A. L. Bailey, & G. Metzi (Eds.), *Spanish-language narration and literacy: Culture, cognition, and emotion* (pp. 332–350). New York: Cambridge University Press.

Becker, K., El-Faddagh, M., Schmidt, M. H., Esser, G., & Laucht, M. (2008). Interaction of dopamine transporter genotype with prenatal smoke exposure on ADHD symptoms. *Journal of Pediatrics, 152,* 263–269.

Becker, S., & Eagly, A. H. (2004). The heroism of women and men. *American Psychologist, 59,* 163–178.

Beckett, C., Maughan, B., Rutter, M., Castle, J., Colvert, E., & Groothues, C. (2006). Do the effects of early severe deprivation on cognition persist into early adolescence? Findings from the English and Romanian adoptees study. *Child Development, 77,* 696–711.

Bedford, O. A. (2004). The individual experience of guilt and shame in Chinese culture. *Culture and Psychology, 10,* 29–52.

Behnke, M., Eyler, F. D., Warner, T. D., Garvan, C. W., Hou, W., & Wobie, K. (2006). Outcome from a prospective, longitudinal study of prenatal cocaine use: Preschool development at 3 years of age. *Journal of Pediatric Psychology, 31,* 41–49.

Behrens, K. Y., Hesse, E., & Main, M. (2007). Mothers' attachment status as determined by the Adult Attachment Interview predicts their 6-year-olds' reunion responses: A study conducted in Japan. *Developmental Psychology, 43*(6), 1553–1567.

Beilin, H. (1992). Piaget's enduring contribution to developmental psychology. *Developmental Psychology, 28,* 191–204.

Beitel, A. H., & Parke, R. D. (1998). Paternal involvement in infancy: The role of maternal and paternal attitudes. *Journal of Family Psychology, 12,* 268–288.

Belcher, D., Lee, A., Solmon, M., & Harrison, L. (2003). The influence of gender-related beliefs and conceptions of ability on women learning the hockey wrist shot. *Research Quarterly for Exercise and Sport, 74,* 183–192.

Bell, J. H., & Bromnick, R. D. (2003). The social reality of the imaginary audience: A grounded theory approach. *Adolescence, 38,* 205–219.

Bell, M. A. (1998). Frontal lobe function during infancy: Implications for the development of cognition and attention. In J. E. Richards (Ed.), *Cognitive neuroscience of attention: A developmental perspective* (pp. 327–362). Mahwah, NJ: Erlbaum.

Bell, M. A., & Fox, N. A. (1992). The relations between frontal brain electrical activity and cognitive development during infancy. *Child Development, 63,* 1142–1163.

Bell, M. A., & Fox, N. A. (1996). Crawling experience is related to changes in cortical organization during infancy: Evidence from EEG coherence. *Developmental Psychobiology, 29,* 551–561.

Bell, S. M., & Ainsworth, M. D. S. (1972). Infant crying and maternal responsiveness. *Child Development, 43,* 1171–1190.

Bellagamba, F., Camaioni, L., & Colonnesi, C. (2006). Change in children's understanding of others' intentional actions. *Developmental Science, 9,* 182–188.

Bellamy, C. (2005). *The state of the world's children 2005.* New York: UNICEF.

Bell-Dolan, D. J., & Wessler, A. E. (1994). Ethical administration of sociometric measures: Procedures in use and suggestions for impovement. *Professional Psychology—Research and Practice, 25,* 23–32.

Bell-Dolan, D. J., Foster, S. L., & Sikora, D. M. (1989). Effects of sociometric testing on children's behavior and loneliness in school. *Developmental Psychology, 25,* 306–311.

Bellinger, D. C. (2005). Teratogen update: Lead and pregnancy. Birth Defects Research: Part A, *Clinical and Molecular Teratology, 73,* 409–420.

Bellinger, D. C., Leviton, A., & Sloman, J. (1990). Antecedents and correlates of improved cognitive performance in children exposed in utero to low levels of lead. *Environmental Health Perspectives, 89,* 5–11.

Bellugi, U., Bihrle, A., Neville, H., Jernigan, T., & Doherty, S. (1992). Language, cognition, and brain organization in a neurodevelopmental disorder. In M. Gunnar & C. Nelson (Eds.), *Developmental behavioral neuroscience* (pp. 201–232). Hillsdale, NJ: Erlbaum.

Bellugi, U., Lichtenberger, L., Jones, W., Lai, Z., & St. George, M. (2000). The neurocognitive profile of Williams syndrome: A complex pattern of strengths and weaknesses. *Journal of Cognitive Neuroscience, 12,* 1–29.

Belsky, J. (2001). Emanuel Miller Lecture: Developmental risks (still) associated with early child care. *Journal of Child Psychology and Psychiatry, 42,* 845–859.

Belsky, J. (2005). Attachment theory and research in ecological perspective: Insights from the Pennsylvania Infant and Family Development Project and the NICHD Study of Early Child Care. In K. E. Grossmann, K. Grossmann, & E. Waters (Eds.), *Attachment from infancy to adulthood: The major longitudinal studies* (pp. 71–97). New York: Guilford.

Belsky, J. (2006a). Determinants and consequences of parent–infant attachment. In L. Balter & C. S. Tamis-LeMonda (Eds.), *Child psychology: A handbook of contemporary issues* (2nd ed., pp. 53–77). New York: Psychology Press.

Belsky, J. (2006b). Early child care and early child development: Major findings of the NICHD Study of Early Child Care. *European Journal of Developmental Psychology, 3,* 95–110.

Belsky, J., Campbell, S. B., Cohn, J. F., & Moore, G. (1996). Instability of infant–parent attachment security. *Developmental Psychology, 32,* 921–924.

Belsky, J., & Fearon, R. M. P. (2002). Early attachment security, subsequent maternal sensitivity, and later child development: Does continuity in development depend on caregiving? *Attachment and Human Development, 4,* 361–387.

Belsky, J., & Fearon, R. M. P. (2008). Precursors of attachment security. In J. Cassidy & P. R. Shaver (Eds.), *Handbook of attachment: Theory, research, and clinical applications* (2nd ed., pp. 295–316). New York: Guilford.

Belsky, J. Steinberg, L. D., Houts, R. M., Friedman, S. L., DeHart, G., Cauffman, E., et al. (2007). Family rearing antecedents of pubertal timing. *Child Development, 78*, 1302–1321.

Belsky, J., Steinberg, L., Houts, R. M., & Halpern-Felsher, B. L. (2010). The development of reproductive strategy in females: Early maternal harshness → earlier menarche → increased sexual risk taking. *Developmental Psychology, 46*, 120–128.

Belsky, J., Vandell, D. L., Burchinal, M., Clarke-Stewart, K. A., McCartney, K., & Owen, M. T. (2007). Are there long-term effects of early child care? *Child Development, 78*, 681–701.

Beltz, A. M., Swanson, J. L., & Berenbaum, S. A. (2011). Gendered occupational interests: Prenatal androgen effects on psychological orientation to things versus people. *Hormones and Behavior, 60*, 313–317.

Bem, S. L. (1983). Gender schema theory and its implications for child development: Raising gender-aschematic children in a gender-schematic society. *Signs, 8*, 598–616.

Bem, S. L. (1993). *The lenses of gender: Transforming the debate on sexual inequality.* New Haven, CT: Yale University Press.

Bem, S. L. (1998). *An unconventional family.* New Haven, CT: Yale University Press.

Bemmels, H. R., Burt, A., Legrand, L. N., Iacono, W. G., & McGue, M. (2008). The heritability of life events: An adolescent twin and adoption study. *Twin Research and Human Genetics, 11*, 257–265.

Benbow, C. P., & Stanley, J. C. (1983). Sex differences in mathematical reasoning: More facts. *Science, 222*, 1029–1031.

Bender, H. L., Allen, J. P., McElhaney, K. B., Antonishak, J., Moore, C. M., Kelly, H. L., & Davis, S. M. (2007). Use of harsh physical discipline and developmental outcomes in adolescence. *Development and Psychopathology, 19*, 227–242.

Bendersky, M., & Lewis, M. (1994). Environmental risk, biological risk, and developmental outcome. *Developmental Psychology, 30*, 484–494.

Benenson, J. F., Apostoleris, N. H., & Parnass, J. (1997). Age and sex differences in dyadic and group interaction. *Developmental Psychology, 33*, 538–543.

Benenson, J. F., & Christakos, A. (2003). The greater fragility of females' versus males' closest same-sex friendships. *Child Development, 74*, 1123–1129.

Benenson, J. F., Nicholson, C., Waite, A., Roy, R., & Simpson, A. (2001). The influence of group size on children's competitive behavior. *Child Development, 72*, 921–928.

Bengtson, H. (2005). Children's cognitive appraisal of others' distressful and positive experiences. *International Journal of Behavioral Development, 29*, 457–466.

Benner, A. D., & Graham, S. (2009). The transition to high school as a developmental process among multiethnic urban youth. *Child Development, 80*, 356–376.

Bennett, M., Barrett, M., Karakozov, R., Kipiani, G., Lyons, E., Pavlenko, V., & Riazanova, T. (2004). Young children's evaluations of the ingroup and outgroups: A multi-national study. *Social Development, 13*, 124–141.

Benson, P. L., Scales, P. C., Hamilton, S. F., & Sesma, A., Jr. (2006). Positive youth development: Theory, research, and applications. In R. M. Lerner (Ed.), *Handbook of child psychology: Vol. 1.*

Theoretical models of human development (6th ed., pp. 894–941). Hoboken, NJ: Wiley.

Ben-Zeev, T., Carrasquillo, C. M., Ching, A. M. L., Patton, G. E., Stewart, T. D., & Stoddard, T. (2005). "Math is hard!" (Barbie™, 1994): Responses of threat vs. challenge-mediated arousal to stereotypes alleging intellectual inferiority. In A. M. Gallagher & J. C. Kaufman (Eds.), *Gender differences in mathematics: An integrative psychological approach* (pp. 189–206). New York: Cambridge University Press.

Berenbaum, S. A. (2001). Cognitive function in congenital adrenal hyperplasia. *Endocrinology and Metabolism Clinics of North America, 30*, 173–192.

Berenbaum, S. A., & Resnick, S. M. (1997). Early androgen effects on aggression in children and adults with congenital adrenal hyperplasia. *Psychoneuroendocrinology, 22*, 505–515.

Bergen, D., & Mauer, D. (2000). Symbolic play, phonological awareness, and literacy skills at three age levels. In K. A. Roskos & J. F. Christie (Eds.), *Play and literacy in early childhood: Research from multiple perspectives* (pp. 45–62). Mahwah, NJ: Erlbaum.

Berger, A., Tzur, G., & Posner, M. I. (2006). Infant brains detect arithmetic errors. *Proceedings of the National Academy of Sciences, 103*, 12649–12653.

Berger, L. M., Paxson, C., & Waldfogel, J. (2009). Income and child development. *Children and Youth Services Review, 31*, 978–989.

Berger, S. E. (2010). Locomotor expertise predicts infants' perseverative errors. *Developmental Psychology, 46*, 326–336.

Berger, S. E., Theuring, C., & Adolph, K. E. (2007). How and when infants learn to climb stairs. *Infant Behavior and Development, 30*, 36–49.

Bergin, C., Talley, S., & Hamer, L. (2003). Prosocial behaviours of young adolescents: A focus group study. *Journal of Adolescence, 26*, 13–32.

Berk, L. E. (2001a). *Awakening children's minds: How parents and teachers can make a difference.* New York: Oxford University Press.

Berk, L. E. (2001b). Private speech and self-regulation in children with impulse-control difficulties: Implications for research and practice. *Journal of Cognitive Education and Psychology, 2*, 1–21.

Berk, L. E. (2005). Why parenting matters. In S. Olfman (Ed.), *Childhood lost: How American culture is failing its children* (pp. 19–53). New York: Praeger.

Berk, L. E., & Harris, S. (2003). Vygotsky, Lev. In L. Nadel (Ed.), *Encyclopedia of cognitive science.* London: Macmillan.

Berk, L. E., Mann, T., & Ogan, A. (2006). Make-believe play: Wellspring for development of self-regulation. In D. Singer, K. Hirsh-Pasek & R. Golinkoff (Eds.), *Play = learning* (pp. 74–100). New York: Oxford University Press.

Berk, L. E., & Spuhl, S. T. (1995). Maternal interaction, private speech, and task performance in preschool children. *Early Childhood Research Quarterly, 10*, 145–169.

Berkowitz, C. M. (2004). *Talking to your kids about sex.* Somerville, NJ: Somerset Medical Center. Retrieved from www.somersetmedicalcenter.com/1817.cfm

Berkowitz, M. W., & Gibbs, J. C. (1983). Measuring the developmental features of moral discussion. *Merrill-Palmer Quarterly, 29*, 399–410.

Berkowitz, R. L., Roberts, J., & Minkoff, H. (2006). Challenging the strategy of maternal age-based prenatal genetic counseling. *Journal of the American Medical Association, 295*, 1446–1448.

Berlin, L. J., Ipsa, J. M., Fine, M. A., Malone, P. S., Brooks-Gunn, J., Brady-Smith, C., et al. (2009). Correlates and consequences of spanking and verbal punishment for low-income white, African-American, and Mexican-American toddlers. *Child Development, 80*, 1403–1420.

Berman, P. (1980). Are women more responsive than men to the young? A review of developmental and situational variables. *Psychological Bulletin, 88*, 668–695.

Berman, R. A. (2007). Developing linguistic knowledge and language use across adolescence. In K. Hirsh-Pasek & R. M. Golinkoff (Eds.), *Action meets word: How children learn verbs* (pp. 347–367). New York: Oxford University Press.

Berman, S. L., Weems, C. F., Rodriguez, E. T., & Zamora, I. J. (2006). The relation between identity status and romantic attachment style in middle and late adolescence. *Journal of Adolescence, 29*, 737–748.

Berndt, T. J. (2004). Children's friendships: Shifts over a half-century in perspectives on their development and effects. *Merrill-Palmer Quarterly, 50*, 206–223.

Berndt, T. J., & Keefe, K. (1995). Friends' influence on adolescents' adjustment to school. *Child Development, 66*, 1312–1329.

Berndt, T. J., & Murphy, L. M. (2002). Influences of friends and friendships: Myths, truths, and research recommendations. In R. V. Kail (Ed.), *Advances in child development and behavior* (Vol. 30, pp. 275–310). San Diego, CA: Academic Press.

Berry, J. (2010). Fortification of flour with folic acid. *Food and Nutrition Bulletin, 31*, S22–S35.

Bertenthal, B. I. (1993). Infants' perception of biomechanical motions: Intrinsic image and knowledge-based constraints. In C. Granrud (Ed.), *Visual perception and cognition in infancy* (pp. 175–214). Hillsdale, NJ: Erlbaum.

Bertenthal, B. I., Longo, M. R., & Kenny, S. (2007). Phenomenal permanence and the development of predictive tracking in infancy. *Child Development, 78*, 350–363.

Bertin, E., & Bhatt, R. S. (2006). Three-month-olds' sensitivity to orientation cues in the three-dimensional depth plane. *Journal of Experimental Child Psychology, 93*, 45–62.

Berzonsky, M. D. (2003). Identity style and well-being: Does commitment matter? *Identity: An International Journal of Theory and Research, 3*, 131–142.

Berzonsky, M. D. (2004). Identity style, parental authority, and identity commitment. *Journal of Youth and Adolescence, 33*, 213–220.

Berzonsky, M. D. (2011). A social-cognitive perspective on identity construction. In S. J. Schwartz, K. Luyckx, & V. L. Vignoles (Eds.), *Handbook of identity theory and research* (pp. 55–76). New York: Springer.

Berzonsky, M. D., Cieciuch, J., Duriez, B., & Soenens, B. (2011). The how and what of identity formation: Associations between identity styles and value orientations. *Personality and Individual Differences, 50*, 295–299.

Berzonsky, M. D., & Kuk, L. S. (2000). Identity status, identity processing style,

and the transition to university. *Journal of Adolescent Research, 15*, 81–98.

Besançon, M., & Lubart, T. (2008). Differences in the development of creative competencies in children schooled in diverse learning environments. *Learning and Individual Differences, 18*, 381–389.

Best, D. (2009). From the American Academy of Pediatrics: Technical report—Secondhand and prenatal tobacco smoke exposure. *Pediatrics, 124*, e1017–e1044.

Best, D. L. (2001). Gender concepts: Convergence in cross-cultural research and methodologies. *Cross-cultural Research: The Journal of Comparative Social Science, 35*, 23–43.

Beyers, J. M., Bates, J. E., Pettit, G. S., & Dodge, K. A. (2003). Neighborhood structure, parenting processes, and the development of youths' externalizing behaviors: A multilevel analysis. *American Journal of Community Psychology, 31*, 35–53.

Bhanot, R., & Jovanovic, J. (2005). Parents' academic gender stereotypes influence whether they intrude on their children's work. *Sex Roles, 52*, 597–607.

Bhat, A., Heathcock, J., & Galloway, J. C. (2005). Toy-oriented changes in hand and joint kinematics during the emergence of purposeful reaching. *Infant Behavior and Development, 28*, 445–465.

Bhatt, R. S., Rovee-Collier, C., & Weiner, S. (1994). Developmental changes in the interface between perception and memory retrieval. *Developmental Psychology, 30*, 151–162.

Bhatt, R. S., Wilk, A., Hill, D., & Rovee-Collier, C. (2004). Correlated attributes and categorization in the first half-year of life. *Developmental Psychobiology, 44*, 103–115.

Bialystok, E. (1986). Factors in the growth of linguistic awareness. *Child Development, 57*, 498–510.

Bialystok, E. (2001). *Bilingualism in development: Language, literacy, and cognition.* New York: Cambridge University Press.

Bialystok, E., Craik, F. I. M., Green, D. W., & Gollan, T. H. (2009a). Bilingual minds. *Psychological Science in the Public Interest, 3*, 89–129.

Bialystok, E., Luk, G., Peets, K., & Yang, S. (2009b). Receptive vocabulary differences in monolingual and bilingual children. *Bilingualism: Language and Cognition, 13*, 525–531.

Bialystok, E., & Martin, M. M. (2003). Notation to symbol: Development in children's understanding of print. *Journal of Experimental Child Psychology, 86*, 223–243.

Bialystok, E., & Martin, M. M. (2004). Attention and inhibition in bilingual children: Evidence from the dimensional change card sort task. *Developmental Science, 7*, 325–339.

Bialystok, E., McBride-Chang, C., & Luk, G. (2005). Bilingualism, language proficiency, and learning to read in two writing systems. *Journal of Educational Psychology, 97*, 580–590.

Bialystok, E., & Senman, L. (2004). Executive processes in appearance–reality tasks: The role of inhibition of attention and symbolic representation. *Child Development, 75*, 562–579.

Bianchi, S. M., & Raley, S. B. (2005). Time allocation in families. In S. M. Bianchi, L. M. Casper, & R. B. King (Eds.), *Work, family, health, and well-being* (pp. 21–48). Mahwah, NJ: Erlbaum.

Bianco, A., Stone, J., Lynch, L., Lapinski, R., Berkowitz, G., & Berkowitz, R. L. (1996). Pregnancy outcome at age 40 and older. *Obstetrics and Gynecology, 87,* 917–922.

Biederman, J., Kwon, A., Aleardi, M., Chouinard, V.-A., Marino, T., & Cole, H. (2005). Absence of gender effects on attention-deficit hyperactivity disorder: Findings in nonreferred subjects. *American Journal of Psychiatry, 162,* 1083–1089.

Bielawska-Batorowicz, E., & Kossakowska-Petrycka, K. (2006). Depressive mood in men after the birth of their offspring in relation to a partner's depression, social support, fathers' personality and prenatal expectations. *Journal of Reproductive and Infant Psychology, 24,* 21–29.

Bielinski, J., & Davison, M. L. (1998). Gender differences by item difficulty interactions in multiple-choice mathematics items. *American Educational Research Journal, 35,* 455–476.

Bierman, K. L., Domitrovich, C. E., Nix, R. L., Gest, S. D., Welsh, J. A., Greenberg, M. T., et al. (2008). Promoting academic and social-emotional school readiness: The Head Start REDI program. *Child Development, 79,* 1802–1817.

Bierman, K. L., & Powers, L. M. (2009). Social skills training to improve peer relations. In K. H. Rubin, W. M. Bukowski, & B. Laursen (Eds.), *Handbook of peer interactions, relationships, and groups* (pp. 603–621). New York: Guilford Press.

Biernat, M. (1991). A multi-component, developmental analysis of sex-typing. *Sex Roles, 24,* 567–586.

Bifulco, R., Cobb, C. D., & Bell, C. (2009). Can interdistrict choice boost student achievement? The case of Connecticut's interdistrict magnet school program. *Educational Evaluation and Policy Analysis, 31,* 323–345.

Bigelow, A. E. (1992). Locomotion and search behavior in blind infants. *Infant Behavior and Development, 15,* 179–189.

Bigelow, A. E. (2003). The development of joint attention in blind infants. *Development and Psychopathology, 15,* 259–275.

Bigelow, A. E., MacLean, K., Proctor, J., Myatt, T., Gillis, R., & Power, M. (2010). Maternal sensitivity throughout infancy: Continuity and relation to attachment security. *Infant Behavior and Development, 33,* 50–60.

Bigler, R. S. (1995). The role of classification skill in moderating environmental influences on children's gender stereotyping: A study of the functional use of gender in the classroom. *Child Development, 66,* 1072–1087.

Bigler, R. S. (2007, June). Personal communication.

Bigler, R. S., Arthur, A. E., Hughes, J. M., & Patterson, M. M. (2008). The politics of race and gender: Children's perceptions of discrimination and the U.S. presidency. *Analyses of Social Issues and Public Policy, 8,* 83–112.

Bigler, R. S., Brown, C. S., & Markell, M. (2001). When groups are not created equal: Effects of group status on the formation of intergroup attitudes in children. *Child Development, 72,* 1151–1162.

Bigler, R. S., & Liben, L. S. (1992). Cognitive mechanisms in children's gender stereotyping: Theoretical and educational implications of a cognitive-based intervention. *Child Development, 63,* 1351–1363.

Bigler, R. S., & Liben, L. S. (2007). Developmental intergroup theory: Explaining and reducing children's social stereotyping and prejudice. *Current Directions in Psychological Science, 16,* 162–166.

Bimmel, N., Juffer, F., van IJzendoorn, M. H., & Bakermans-Kranenburg, M. J. (2003). Problem behavior of internationally adopted adolescents: A review and meta-analysis. *Harvard Review of Psychiatry, 11,* 64–77.

Binet, A., & Simon, T. (1908). Le development de l'intelligence chez les enfants. *L'Année Psychologique, 14,* 1–94.

Birch, E. E. (1993). Stereopsis in infants and its developmental relation to visual acuity. In K. Simons (Ed.), *Early visual development: Normal and abnormal* (pp. 224–236). New York: Oxford University Press.

Birch, L. L., & Fisher, J. A. (1995). Appetite and eating behavior in children. *Pediatric Clinics of North America, 42,* 931–953.

Birch, L. L., Fisher, J. O., & Davison, K. K. (2003). Learning to overeat: Maternal use of restrictive feeding practices promotes girls' eating in the absence of hunger. *American Journal of Clinical Nutrition, 78,* 215–220.

Birch, L. L., Zimmerman, S., & Hind, H. (1980). The influence of social-affective context on preschool children's food preferences. *Child Development, 51,* 856–861.

Birch, S. A. J., & Bloom, P. (2003). Children are cursed: An asymmetric bias in mental-state attribution. *Psychological Science, 14,* 283–285.

Birch, S. H., & Ladd, G. W. (1998). Children's interpersonal behaviors and the teacher-child relationship. *Developmental Psychology, 34,* 934–946.

Bird, A., & Reese, E. (2006). Emotional reminiscing and the development of an autobiographical self. *Developmental Psychology, 42,* 613–626.

Biringen, Z., Emde, R. N., Campos, J. J., & Appelbaum, M. I. (1995). Affective reorganization in the infant, the mother, and the dyad: The role of upright locomotion and its timing. *Child Development, 66,* 499–514.

Birkett, M., Espelage, D. L., & Koenig, B. (2009). LGB and questioning students in schools: The moderating effects of homophobic bullying and school climate on negative outcomes. *Journal of Youth and Adolescence, 38,* 989–1000.

Birney, D. P., & Sternberg, R. J. (2011). The development of cognitive abilities. In M. H. Bornstein & M. E. Lamb (Eds.), *Developmental science: An advanced textbook* (6th ed., pp. 353–388). New York: Psychology Press.

Bischofshausen, S. (1985). Developmental differences in schema dependency for temporally ordered story events. *Journal of Psycholinguistic Research, 14,* 543–556.

Bjorklund, D. F. (2011). *Children's thinking: Cognitive development and individual differences* (5th ed.). Belmont, CA: Cengage.

Bjorklund, D. F. (2012). *Children's thinking* (5th ed.). Belmont, CA: Wadsworth Cengage Learning.

Bjorklund, D. F., Causey, K., & Periss, V. (2009). The evolution and development of human social cognition. In P. Kappeler & J. Silk (Eds.), *Mind the gap: Tracing the origins of human universals* (pp. 351–371). Berlin: Springer Verlag.

Bjorklund, D. F., & Douglas, R. N. (1997). The development of memory strategies. In N. Cowan (Ed.), *The development of memory in childhood* (pp. 83–111). Hove, UK: Psychology Press.

Bjorklund, D. F., Dukes, C., & Brown, R. D. (2009). The development of memory strategies. In M. Courage & N. Cowan (Eds.), *The development of memory in infancy and childhood* (pp. 145–168). New York: Psychology Press.

Bjorklund, D. F., & Harnishfeger, K. K. (1995). The evolution of inhibition mechanisms and their role in human cognition and behavior. In M. L. Howe & R. Pasnak (Eds.), *Emerging themes in cognitive development: Vol. 1. Foundations* (pp. 141–173). New York: Springer-Verlag.

Bjorklund, D. F., Schneider, W., Cassel, W. S., & Ashley, E. (1994). Training and extension of a memory strategy: Evidence for utilization deficiencies in high- and low-IQ children. *Child Development, 65,* 951–965.

Bjorklund, D. F., Yunger, J. L., & Pellegrini, A. D. (2002). The evolution of parenting and evolutionary approaches to childrearing. In M. H. Bornstein (Ed.), *Handbook of parenting: Vol. 2. Biology and ecology of parenting* (2nd ed., pp. 3–30). Mahwah, NJ: Erlbaum.

Black, B., & Logan, A. (1995). Links between communication patterns in mother-child, father-child, and child-peer interactions and children's social status. *Child Development, 66,* 255–271.

Black, M. M. (2005). Failure to thrive. In M. C. Roberts (Ed.), *Handbook of pediatric psychology and psychiatry* (3rd ed., pp. 499–511). New York: Guilford.

Black, M. M., Dubowitz, H., Krishnakumar, A., & Starr, R. H., Jr. (2007). Early intervention and recovery among children with failure to thrive: Follow-up at age 8. *Pediatrics, 120,* 59–69.

Black, R. E., Williams, S. M., Jones, I. E., & Goulding, A. (2002). Children who avoid drinking cow milk have low dietary calcium intakes and poor bone health. *American Journal of Clinical Nutrition, 76,* 675–680.

Blackwell, L. S., Trzesniewski, K. H., & Dweck, C. S. (2007). Implicit theories of intelligence predict achievement across an adolescent transition: A longitudinal study and an intervention. *Child Development, 78,* 246–263.

Blaga, O. M., & Colombo, J. (2006). Visual processing and infant ocular latencies in the overlap paradigm. *Developmental Psychology, 42,* 1069–1076.

Blair, C., & Razza, R. P. (2007). Relating effortful control, executive function, and false belief understanding to emerging math and literacy ability in kindergarten. *Developmental Psychology, 78,* 647–663.

Blake, J., & Boysson-Bardies, B. de (1992). Patterns in babbling: A cross-linguistic study. *Journal of Child Language, 19,* 51–74.

Blakemore, J. E. O. (2003). Children's beliefs about violating gender norms: Boys shouldn't look like girls, and girls shouldn't act like boys. *Sex Roles, 48,* 411–419.

Blakemore, S.-J., & Choudhury, S. (2006). Development of the adolescent brain: Implications for executive function and social cognition. *Journal of Child Psychology and Psychiatry, 47,* 296–312.

Blanchard, R., & Bogaert, A. F. (2004). Proportion of homosexual men who owe their sexual orientation to fraternal birth order: An estimate based on two national probability samples. *American Journal of Human Biology, 16,* 151–157.

Blandon, A. Y., & Volling, B. L. (2008). Parental gentle guidance and children's compliance within the family: A replication study. *Journal of Family Psychology, 22,* 355–366.

Blasi, A. (1994). Bridging moral cognition and moral action: A critical review of the literature. In B. Puka (Ed.), *Fundamental research in moral development: A compendium* (Vol. 2, pp. 123–167). New York: Garland.

Blasi, C. H., & Bjorklund, D. F. (2003). Evolutionary developmental psychology: A new tool for better understanding human ontogeny. *Human Development, 46,* 259–281.

Blass, E. M., Ganchrow, J. R., & Steiner, J. E. (1984). Classical conditioning in newborn humans 2–48 hours of age. *Infant Behavior and Development, 7,* 223–235.

Blatchford, P., Baines, E., Rubie-Davies, C., Bassett, P., & Chowne, A. (2006). The effect of a new approach to group-work on pupil–pupil and teacher–pupil interaction. *Journal of Educational Psychology, 98,* 750–765.

Blatchford, P., Bassett, P., Goldstein, H., & Martin, C. (2003). Are class size differences related to pupils' educational progress and classroom processes? Findings from the Institute of Education Class Size Study of Children Aged 5–7 Years. *British Educational Research Journal, 29,* 709–730.

Blatchford, P., Russell, A., Bassett, P., Brown, P., & Martin, C. (2007). The effect of class size on the teaching of pupils aged 7–11 years. *School Effectiveness and School Improvement, 18,* 147–172.

Bleeker, M. M., & Jacobs, J. E. (2004). Achievement in math and science: Do mothers' beliefs matter 12 years later? *Journal of Educational Psychology, 96,* 97–109.

Bleses, D., Vach, W., Slott, M., Wehberg, S., Thomsen, P., Madsen, T., et al. (2008). Early vocabulary development in Danish and other languages: A CDI-based comparison. *Journal of Child Language, 35,* 619–650.

Bloch, M. E. F., Solomon, G. E. A., & Carey, S. (2001). An understanding of what is passed on from parents to children: A cross-cultural investigation. *Journal of Cognition and Culture, 1,* 43–68.

Bloch, M. N. (1989). Young boys' and girls' play in the home and in the community: A cultural ecological framework. In M. N. Bloch & A. D. Pellegrini (Eds.), *The ecological context of children's play* (pp. 120–154). Norwood, NJ: Ablex.

Blood-Siegfried, J. (2009). The role of infection and inflammation in sudden infant death syndrome. *Immunopharmacology and Immunotoxicology, 31,* 516–523.

Bloom, L. (1998). Language acquisition in its developmental context. In D. Kuhn & R. S. Siegler (Eds.), *Handbook of child psychology: Vol. 2. Cognition, perception, and language* (5th ed., pp. 309–370). New York: Wiley.

Bloom, L. (2000). The intentionality model of language development: How to learn a word, any word. In R. Golinkoff, K. Hirsh-Pasek, N. Akhtar, L. Bloom, G. Hollich, L. Smith, M. Tomasello, & A. Woodward (Eds.), *Becoming a word learner: A debate on lexical acquisition.* New York: Oxford University Press.

Bloom, L., Lahey, M., Liften, K., & Fiess, K. (1980). Complex sentences: Acquisition of syntactic connections and the semantic relations they encode. *Journal of Child Language, 7,* 235–256.

Bloom, P. (1999). The role of semantics in solving the bootstrapping problem. In R. Jackendoff & P. Bloom (Eds.), *Language, logic, and concepts* (pp. 285–309). Cambridge, MA: MIT Press.

Blumberg, M. S., & Lucas, D. E. (1996). A developmental and component analysis of active sleep. *Developmental Psychobiology, 29,* 1–22.

Blumenfeld, P. C., Marx, R. W., & Harris, C. J. (2006). Learning environments. In K. A. Renninger & I. E. Sigel (Eds.), *Handbook of child psychology: Vol. 4. Child psychology in practice* (6th ed., pp. 297–342). Hoboken, NJ: Wiley.

Boardman, J. D. (2004). Stress and physical health: The role of neighborhoods as mediating and moderating mechanisms. *Social Science and Medicine, 58,* 2473–2483.

Bobb, A. J., Castellanos, F. X., Addington, A. M., & Rapoport, J. L. (2006). Molecular genetic studies of ADHD: 1991 to 2004. *American Journal of Medical Genetics Part B (Neuropsychiatric Genetics), 141B,* 551–565.

Bodrova, E., & Leong, D. J. (2007). *Tools of the mind: The Vygotskian approach to early childhood education* (2nd ed.). Upper Saddle River, NJ: Merrill/Prentice Hall.

Bogaert, A. F. (2005). Age at puberty and father absence in a national probability sample. *Journal of Adolescence, 28,* 541–546.

Bogartz, R. S., Shinskey, J. L., & Schilling, T. H. (2000). Object permanence in five-and-a-half-month-old infants. *Infancy, 1,* 403–428.

Bogin, B. (2001). *The growth of humanity.* New York: Wiley-Liss.

Bogin, B., Smith, P., Orden, A. B., Varela, S., & Loucky, J. (2002). Rapid change in height and body proportions of Maya American children. *American Journal of Human Biology, 14,* 753–761.

Bohannon, J. N., III, & Bonvillian, J. D. (2009). Theoretical approaches to language acquisition. In J. B. Gleason & B. Ratner (Ed.), *The development of language* (7th ed., pp. 227–284). Boston: Allyn and Bacon.

Bohannon, J. N., III, & Stanowicz, L. (1988). The issue of negative evidence: Adult responses to children's language errors. *Developmental Psychology, 24,* 684–689.

Boldizar, J. P. (1991). Assessing sex typing and androgyny in children: The children's sex role inventory. *Developmental Psychology, 27,* 505–515.

Bolen, R. M. (2001). *Child sexual abuse.* New York: Kluwer Academic.

Bolisetty, S., Bajuk, B., Me, A.-L., Vincent, T., Sutton, L., & Lui, K. (2006). Preterm outcome tool (POT): A simple tool to aid counselling parents of very preterm infants. *Australian and New Zealand Journal of Obstetrics and Gynaecology, 46,* 189–192.

Bolzani, L. H., Messinger, D. S., Yale, M., & Dondi, M. (2002). Smiling in infancy. In M. H. Abel (Ed.), *An empirical reflection on the smile* (pp. 111–136). Lewiston, NY: Edwin Mellen Press.

Bono, M. A., & Stifter, C. A. (2003). Maternal attention-directing strategies and infant focused attention during problem solving. *Infancy, 4,* 235–250.

Boom, J., Brugman, D., & van der Heijden, P. G. M. (2001). Hierarchical structure of moral stages assessed by a sorting task. *Child Development, 72,* 535–548.

Boom, J., Wouters, H., & Keller, M. (2007). A cross-cultural validation of stage development: A Rasch re-analysis of longitudinal socio-moral reasoning data. *Cognitive Development, 22,* 213–229.

Borduin, C. M. (2007). Multisystemic treatment of violent youth and their families. In T. A. Cavell & K. T. Malcom (Eds.), *Anger, aggression and interventions for interpersonal violence* (pp. 239–265). Mahwah, NJ: Erlbaum.

Borke, H. (1975). Piaget's mountains revisited: Changes in the egocentric landscape. *Developmental Psychology, 11,* 240–243.

Borkowski, J. G., & Muthukrisna, N. (1995). Learning environments and skill generalization: How contexts facilitate regulatory processes and efficacy beliefs. In F. Weinert & W. Schneider (Eds.), *Memory performances and competence: Issues in growth and development* (pp. 283–300). Hillsdale, NJ: Erlbaum.

Bornstein, M. H. (1989). Sensitive periods in development: Structural characteristics and causal interpretations. *Psychological Bulletin, 105,* 179–197.

Bornstein, M. H. (2006). Parenting science and practice. In K. Renninger & I. E. Sigel (Eds.), *Handbook of child psychology: Vol. 4. Child psychology in practice* (6th ed., pp. 893–949). Hoboken, NJ: Wiley.

Bornstein, M. H., & Arterberry, M. E. (2003). Recognition, discrimination, and categorization of smiling by 5-month-old infants. *Developmental Science, 6,* 585–599.

Bornstein, M. H., Arterberry, M. E., & Mash, C. (2010). Infant object categorization transcends object–context relations. *Infant Behavior and Development, 33,* 7–15.

Bornstein, M. H., & Cote, L. R. (2004). Cross-linguistic analysis of vocabulary in young children: Spanish, Dutch, French, Hebrew, Italian, Korean, and American English. *Child Development, 75,* 1115–1139.

Bornstein, M. H., & Sawyer, J. (2006). Family systems. In K. McCartney & D. Phillips (Eds.), *Blackwell handbook of early childhood development* (pp. 381–398). Malden, MA: Blackwell.

Bornstein, M. H., Selmi, A. M., Haynes, O. M., Painter, K. M., & Marx, E. S. (1999). Representational abilities and the hearing status of child/mother dyads. *Child Development, 70,* 833–852.

Bornstein, M. H., Vibbert, M., Tal, J., & O'Donnell, K. (1992). Toddler language and play in the second year: Stability, covariation, and influences of parenting. *First Language, 12,* 323–338.

Boroughs, D. S. (2004). Female sexual abusers of children. *Children and Youth Services Review, 26,* 481–487.

Borst, C. G. (1995). *Catching babies: The professionalization of childbirth, 1870–1920.* Cambridge, MA: Harvard University Press.

Bos, H., & Sandfort, T. G. M. (2010). Children's gender identity in lesbian and heterosexual two-parent families. *Sex Roles, 62,* 114–126.

Bos, H. M. W., van Balen, F., & van den Boom, D. C. (2004). Experience of parenthood, couple relationship, social support, and child-rearing goals in planned lesbian mother families. *Journal of Child Psychology and Psychiatry, 25,* 755–764.

Bos, H. M. W., van Balen, F., & van den Boom, D. C. (2007). Child adjustment and parenting in planned lesbian-parent families. *American Journal of Orthopsychiatry, 77,* 38–48.

Bosacki, S. L., & Moore, C. (2004). Preschoolers' understanding of simple and complex emotions: Links with gender and language. *Sex Roles, 50,* 659–675.

Bost, K. K., Shin, N., McBride, B. A., Brown, G. L., Vaughn, B. E., & Coppola, G. (2006). Maternal secure base scripts, children's attachment security, and mother–child narrative styles. *Attachment and Human Development, 8,* 241–260.

Botton, J., Heude, B., Maccario, J., Ducimetiére, P., & Charles, M. A. (2008). Postnatal weight and height growth velocities at different ages between birth and 5y and body composition in adolescent boys and girls. *American Journal of Clinical Nutrition, 87,* 1760–1768.

Botvinick, M., Jha, A. P., Bylsma, L. M., Fabian, S. A., Solomon, P. E., & Prkachin, K. M. (2005). Viewing facial expressions of pain engages cortical areas involved in the direct experience of pain. *Neuroimage, 25,* 312–319.

Bouchard, T. J., Jr. (2004). Genetic influence on human psychological traits: A survey. *Current Directions in Psychological Science, 13,* 148–151.

Bouchard, T. J., Jr., & Loehlin, J. C. (2001). Genes, evolution, and personality. *Behavior Genetics, 31,* 243–274.

Bouchard, T. J., Jr. (1997). IQ similarity in twins reared apart: Findings and responses to critics. In R. J. Sternberg & E. L. Grigorenko (Eds.), *Intelligence, heredity, and environment* (pp. 126–160). New York: Cambridge University Press.

Bouchard, T. J., Jr., & McGue, M. (1981). Familial studies of intelligence: A review. *Science, 212,* 1055–1058.

Boucher, O., Bastien, C. H., Saint-Amour, D., Dewailly, E., Ayotte, P., Jacobson, J. L., Jacobson, et al. (2010). Prenatal exposure to methylmercury and PCBs affects distinct stages of information processing: An event-related potential study with Inuit children. *Neurotoxicology, 31,* 373–384.

Boucher, O., Muckle, G., & Bastien, C. H. (2009). Prenatal exposure to polychlorinated biphenyls: A neuropsychologic analysis. *Environmental Health Perspectives, 117,* 7–16.

Boukydis, C. F. Z., & Lester, B. M. (1998). Infant crying, risk status and social support in families of preterm and term infants. *Early Development and Parenting, 7,* 31–39.

Bouldin, P. (2006). An investigation of the fantasy predisposition and fantasy style of children with imaginary companions. *Journal of Genetic Psychology, 167,* 17–29.

Boulton, M. J. (1996). A comparison of 8- and 11-year-old girls' and boys' participation in specific types of rough-and-tumble play and aggressive fighting: Implications for functional hypotheses. *Aggressive Behavior, 22,* 271–287.

Boulton, M. J. (1999). Concurrent and longitudinal relations between children's playground behavior and social preference, victimization, and bullying. *Child Development, 70,* 944–954.

Bowker, A. (2004). Predicting friendship stability during early adolescence. *Journal of Early Adolescence, 24,* 85–112.

Bowker, J. C. W., Rubin, K. H., Burgess, K. B., Booth-LaForce, C., & Rose-Krasnor, L. (2006). Behavioral characteristics associated with stable and fluid best friendship patterns in middle childhood. *Merrill-Palmer Quarterly, 52,* 671–693.

Bowkett, S., & Percival, S. (2011). *Coaching emotional intelligence in the classroom: A guide for 7–14.* New York: Routledge.

Bowlby, J. (1969). *Attachment and loss: Vol. 1. Attachment.* New York: Basic Books.

Bowlby, J. (1980). *Attachment and loss: Vol. 3. Loss.* New York: Basic Books.

Bowlby, J. W., & McMullen, K. (2002). *At a crossroads: First results for the 18- to 20-year-old cohort of the Youth in Transition Survey.* Ottawa, Canada: Human Resources Development Canada.

Bowman, S. A., Gortmaker, S. L., Ebbeling, C. B., Pereira, M. A., & Ludwig, D. S. (2004). Effects of fast-food consumption on energy intake and diet quality among children in a national household survey. *Pediatrics, 113,* 112–118.

Boyatzis, C. J. (2000). The artistic evolution of mommy: A longitudinal case study of symbolic and social processes. In C. J. Boyatzis & M. W. Watson (Eds.), *Symbolic and social constraints on the development of children's artistic style* (pp. 5–29). San Francisco: Jossey-Bass.

Boyce, W., Doherty-Poirier, M., MacKinnon, D., Fortin, C., Saab, H., King, M., & Gallupe, O. (2006). Sexual health of Canadian youth: Findings from the Canadian Youth, Sexual Health and HIV/AIDS Study. *Canadian Journal of Human Sexuality, 15,* 59–68.

Boyd-Franklin, N. (2006). *Black families in therapy* (2nd ed.). New York: Guilford.

Boyes, M. C., & Chandler, M. (1992). Cognitive development, epistemic doubt, and identity formation in adolescence. *Journal of Youth and Adolescence, 21,* 277–304.

Boysson-Bardies, B. de, & Vihman, M. M. (1991). Adaptation to language: Evidence from babbling and first words in four languages. *Language, 67,* 297–319.

Brackett, M. A., Mayer, J. D., & Warner, R. M. (2004). Emotional intelligence and its relation to everyday behaviour. *Personality and Individual Differences, 36,* 1387–1402.

Bradford, K., Barber, B. K., Olsen, J. A., Maughan, S. L., Erickson, L. D., Ward, D., & Stolz, H. E. (2003). A multi-national study of interparental conflict, parenting, and adolescent functioning: South Africa, Bangladesh, China, India, Bosnia, Germany, Palestine, Colombia, and the United States. *Marriage and Family Review, 35,* 107–137.

Bradley, R. H. (1994). The HOME Inventory: Review and reflections. In H. W. Reese (Ed.), *Advances in child development and behavior* (Vol. 25, pp. 241–288). San Diego, CA: Academic Press.

Bradley, R. H., Caldwell, B. M., & Rock, S. L. (1988). Home environment and school performance: A ten-year follow-up and examination of three models of environmental action. *Child Development, 59,* 852–867.

Bradley, R. H., Corwyn, R. F., McAdoo, H. P., & Garcia Coll, C. (2001). The home environments of children in the United States. Part I: Variations by age, ethnicity, and poverty status. *Child Development, 72,* 1844–1867.

Bradley, R. H., Whiteside, L., Mundfrom, D. J., Casey, P. H., Kelleher, K. J., & Pope, S. K. (1994). Contribution of early intervention and early caregiving experiences to resilience in low-birthweight, premature children living in poverty. *Journal of Clinical Child Psychology, 23,* 425–434.

Braine, M. D. S. (1994). Is nativism sufficient? *Journal of Child Language, 21,* 1–23.

Brainerd, C. J. (2003). Jean Piaget, learning, research, and American education. In B. J. Zimmerman (Ed.), *Educational psychology: A century of contributions* (pp. 251–287). Mahwah, NJ: Erlbaum.

Brainerd, C. J., Forrest, T. J., Karibian, D., & Reyna, V. F. (2006). Development of the false-memory illusion. *Developmental Psychology, 42,* 962–979.

Brainerd, C. J., & Gordon, L. L. (1994). Development of verbatim and gist memory for numbers. *Developmental Psychology, 30,* 163–177.

Brainerd, C. J., Holliday, R. E., & Reyna, V. F. (2004). Behavioral measurement of remembering phenomenologies. *Child Development, 75,* 505–522.

Brainerd, C. J., & Reyna, V. F. (1993). Memory independence and memory interference in cognitive development. *Psychological Review, 100,* 42–67.

Brainerd, C. J., & Reyna, V. F. (1995). Learning rate, learning opportunities, and the development of forgetting. *Developmental Psychology, 31,* 251–262.

Brainerd, C. J., & Reyna, V. F. (2001). Fuzzy-trace theory: Dual processes in memory, reasoning, and cognitive neuroscience. In H. W. Reese (Ed.), *Advances in child development and behavior* (Vol. 28). San Diego, CA: Academic Press.

Brainerd, C. J., Reyna, V. F., & Poole, D. A. (2000). Fuzzy-trace theory and false memory: Memory theory in the courtroom. In D. F. Bjorklund (Ed.), *Research and theory in false-memory creation in children and adults* (pp. 93–127). Mahwah, NJ: Erlbaum.

Brame, B., Nagin, D. S., & Tremblay, R. E. (2001). Developmental trajectories of physical aggression from school entry to late adolescence. *Journal of Child Psychology and Psychiatry, 42,* 503–512.

Brand, S., Gerber, M., Beck, J., Hatzinger, M., Puhse, U., & Holsboer-Trachsler, E. (2010). High exercise levels are related to favorable sleep and psychological functioning in adolescence: A comparison of athletes and controls. *Journal of Adolescent Health, 46,* 133–141.

Brand, S. R., Engel, S. M., Canfield, R. L., & Yehuda, R. (2006). The effect of maternal PTSD following in utero trauma exposure on behavior and temperament in the 9-month-old infant. *Annals of the New York Academy of Sciences, 1071,* 454–458.

Branje, S. J. T., van Lieshout, C. F. M., van Aken, M. A. G., & Haselager, G. J. T. (2004). Perceived support in sibling relationships and adolescent adjustment. *Journal of Child Psychology and Psychiatry, 45,* 1385–1396.

Braswell, G. S. (2006). Sociocultural contexts for the early development of semiotic production. *Psychological Bulletin, 132,* 877–894.

Braungart-Rieker, J. M., Hill-Soderlund, A. L., & Karrass, J. (2010). Fear and anger reactivity trajectories from 4 to 16 months: The roles of temperament, regulation, and maternal sensitivity. *Developmental Psychology, 46,* 791–804.

Braver, S. L., Griffin, W. A., Cookston, J. T., Sandler, I. N., & Williams, J. (2005). Promoting better fathering among divorced non-resident fathers. In W. M.

Pinsof & J. Lebow (Eds.), *Family psychology: The art of the science* (pp. 295–325). New York: Oxford University Press.

Bray, J. H. (1999). From marriage to remarriage and beyond: Findings from the Developmental Issues in Stepfamilies Research Project. In E. M. Hetherington (Ed.), *Coping with divorce, single parenting, and remarriage: A risk and resiliency perspective* (pp. 295–319). Mahwah, NJ: Erlbaum.

Brazelton, T. B., Koslowski, B., & Tronick, E. Z. (1976). Neonatal behavior among urban Zambians and Americans. *Journal of the American Academy of Child Psychiatry, 15,* 97–107.

Brazelton, T. B., & Nugent, J. K. (1995). *Neonatal Behavioral Assessment Scale.* London: Mac Keith Press.

Brazelton, T. B., Nugent, J. K., & Lester, B. M. (1987). Neonatal Behavioral Assessment Scale. In J. D. Osofsky (Ed.), *Handbook of infant development* (2nd ed., pp. 780–817). New York: Wiley.

Bremner, J. G. (2010). Cognitive development: Knowledge of the physical world. In J. G. Bremner & T. D. Wachs (Eds.), *Wiley-Blackwell handbook of infant development: Vol. 1. Basic research* (2nd ed., pp. 204–242). Oxford, UK: Wiley.

Brendgen, M., Markiewicz, D., Doyle, A. B., & Bukowski, W. M. (2001). The relations between friendship quality, ranked-friendship preference, and adolescents' behavior with their friends. *Merrill-Palmer Quarterly, 47,* 395–415.

Brenes, M. E., Eisenberg, N., & Helmstadter, G. C. (1985). Sex role development of preschoolers from two-parent and one-parent families. *Merrill-Palmer Quarterly, 31,* 33–46.

Brennan, W. M., Ames, E. W., & Moore, R. W. (1966). Age differences in infants' attention to patterns of different complexities. *Science, 151,* 354–356.

Brenner, E., & Salovey, P. (1997). Emotion regulation during childhood: Developmental, interpersonal, and individual considerations. In P. Salovey & D. Sluyter (Eds.), *Emotional literacy and emotional development* (pp. 168–192). New York: Basic Books.

Bretherton, I., Fritz, J., Zahn-Waxler, C., & Ridgeway, D. (1986). Learning to talk about emotions: A functionalist perspective. *Child Development, 57,* 529–548.

Bretherton, I., & Munholland, K. A. (2008). Internal working models in attachment relationships. In J. Cassidy & P. R. Shaver (Eds.), *Handbook of attachment: Theory, research, and clinical applications* (2nd ed., pp. 102–127). New York: Guilford.

Brewaeys, A., Ponjaert, I., Van Hall, E. V., & Golombok, S. (1997). Donor insemination: Child development and family functioning in lesbian mother families. *Human Reproduction, 12,* 1349–1359.

Bridge, J. A., Goldstein, T. R., & Brent, D. A. (2006). Adolescent suicide and suicidal behavior. *Journal of Child Psychology and Psychiatry, 47,* 372–394.

Bridges, L. J., & Moore, K. A. (2002). Religious involvement and children's well-being: What research tells us (and what it doesn't). *Child Trends Research Brief.* Retrieved from www.childtrends.org.

Bridgett, D. J., Gartstein, M. A., Putnam, S. P., McKay, T., Iddins, R., Robertson, C., et al. (2009). Maternal and contextual influences and the effect of temperament development during infancy on parenting in toddlerhood. *Infant Behavior and Development, 32,* 103–116.

Briefel, R. R., Reidy, K., Karwe, V., & Devaney, B. (2004). Feeding Infants and Toddlers Study: Improvements needed in meeting infant feeding recommendations. *Journal of the American Dietetic Association, 104*(Suppl. 1), s31–s37.

Bright, G. M., Mendoza, J. R., & Rosenfeld, R. G. (2009). Recombinant human insulin-like growth factor-1 treatment: Ready for primetime. *Endocrinology and Metabolism Clinics of North America, 38,* 625–638.

Brisch, K. H., Bechinger, D., Betzler, S., Heineman, H., Kachele, H., Pohlandt, F., et al. (2005). Attachment quality in very low-birthweight premature infants in relation to maternal attachment representations and neurological development. *Parenting: Science and Practice, 5,* 11–32.

Brody, G. H., & Flor, D. L. (1998). Maternal resources, parenting practices, and child competence in rural, single-parent African American families. *Child Development, 69,* 803–816.

Brody, G. H., Ge, X., Kim, S. Y., Murry, V. M., Simons, R. L., & Gibbons, F. X. (2003). Neighborhood disadvantage moderates associations of parenting and older sibling problem attitudes and behavior with conduct disorders in African American children. *Journal of Consulting and Clinical Psychology, 71,* 211–222.

Brody, G. H., Graziano, W. G., & Musser, L. M. (1983). Familiarity and children's behavior in same-age and mixed-age peer groups. *Developmental Psychology, 19,* 568–576.

Brody, G. H., & Murry, V. M. (2001). Sibling socialization of competence in rural, single-parent African American families. *Journal of Marriage and Family, 63,* 996–1008.

Brody, G. H., Stoneman, Z., & McCoy, J. K. (1992). Associations of maternal and paternal direct and differential behavior with sibling relationships: Contemporaneous and logitudinal analyses. *Child Development, 63,* 82–92.

Brody, G. H., Stoneman, Z., & McCoy, J. K. (1994). Forecasting sibling relationships in early adolescence from child temperament and family processes in middle childhood. *Child Development, 65,* 771–784.

Brody, L. R. (1997). Gender and emotion: Beyond stereotypes. *Journal of Social Issues, 53,* 369–393.

Brody, L. R. (1999). *Gender, emotion, and the family.* Cambridge, MA: Harvard University Press.

Brody, M. (2006). Child psychiatry, drugs, and the corporation. In S. Olfman (Ed.), *No child left different* (pp. 89–105). Westport, CT: Praeger.

Brodzinsky, D. M. (2011). Children's understanding of adoption: Developmental and clinical implications. *Professional Psychology: Research and Practice, 42,* 200–207.

Broidy, L. M., Nagin, D. S., Tremblay, R. E., Bates, J. E., Brame, B., Dodge, K. A., et al. (2003). Developmental trajectories of childhood disruptive behaviors and adolescent delinquency: A six-site, cross-national study. *Developmental Psychology, 39,* 222–245.

Bronfenbrenner, U. (Ed.). (2005). *Making human beings human.* Thousand Oaks, CA: Sage.

Bronfenbrenner, U., & Morris, P. A. (2006). The bioecological model of human development. In R. M. Lerner (Ed.),

Handbook of child psychology: Vol. 1. Theoretical models of human development (6th ed., pp. 297–342). Hoboken, NJ: Wiley.

Bronson, G. W. (1994). Infants' transitions toward adult-like scanning. *Child Development, 65,* 1243–1261.

Bronstein, P. (2006). The family environment: Where gender role socialization begins. In J. Worell & C. D. Goodheart (Eds.), *Handbook of girls' and women's psychological health: Gender and well-being across the lifespan* (pp. 262–271). New York: Oxford University Press.

Bronte-Tinkew, J., Moore, K. A., & Carrano, J. (2006). The father–child relationship, parenting styles, and adolescent risk behaviors in intact families. *Journal of Family Issues, 27,* 850–881.

Brooks, P. J., Hanauere, J. B., Padowska, B., & Rosman, H. (2003). The role of selective attention in preschoolers' rule use in a novel dimensional card sort. *Cognitive Development, 18,* 195–215.

Brooks, R., & Meltzoff, A. N. (2002). The importance of eyes: How infants interpret looking behavior. *Developmental Psychology, 38,* 958–966.

Brooks, R., & Meltzoff, A. N. (2005). The development of gaze following and its relation to language. *Developmental Science, 8,* 535–543.

Brooks, R., & Meltzoff, A. N. (2008). Infant gaze following and pointing predict accelerated vocabulary growth through two years of age: A longitudinal, growth curve modeling study. *Journal of Child Language, 35,* 207–220.

Brooks-Gunn, J. (1988). Antecedents and consequences of variations in girls' maturational timing. *Journal of Adolescent Health Care, 9,* 365–373.

Brooks-Gunn, J. (2003). Do you believe in magic? What we can expect from early childhood intervention programs. *Social Policy Report of the Society for Research in Child Development, 27*(1).

Brooks-Gunn, J. (2004). Intervention and policy as change agents for young children. In P. L. Chase-Lansdale, K. Kiernan, & R. J. Friedman (Eds.), *Human development across lives and generations: The potential for change* (pp. 293–340). New York: Cambridge University Press.

Brooks-Gunn, J., Han, W.-J., & Waldfogel, J. (2002). Maternal employment and child cognitive outcomes in the first three years of life: The NICHD study of early child care. *Child Development, 73,* 1052–1072.

Brooks-Gunn, J., Han, W.-J., & Waldfogel, J. (2010). First-year maternal employment and child development in the first 7 years. *Monographs of the Society for Research in Child Development, 75*(No. 2, Serial No. 296).

Brooks-Gunn, J., Klebanov, P. K., & Duncan, G. J. (1996). Ethnic differences in children's intelligence test scores: Role of economic deprivation, home environment, and maternal characteristics. *Child Development, 67,* 396–408.

Brooks-Gunn, J., Klebanov, P. K., Smith, J., Duncan, G. J., & Lee, K. (2003). The black–white test score gap in young children. Contributions of test and family characteristics. *Applied Developmental Science, 7,* 239–252.

Brooks-Gunn, J., Schley, S., & Hardy, J. (2002). Marriage and the baby carriage: Historical change and intergenerational continuity in early parenthood. In L. J. Crockett & R. K. Sibereisen (Eds.),

Negotiating adolescence in times of social change (pp. 36–57). New York: Cambridge University Press.

Brookshire, B., Levin, H. S., Song, J. X., & Zhang, L. (2004). Components of executive function in typically developing and head-injured children. *Developmental Neuropsychology, 25*, 61–83.

Brown, A. L. (1997). Transforming schools into communities of thinking and learning about serious matters. *American Psychologist, 52*, 399–413.

Brown, A. L., & Campione, J. C. (1972). Recognition memory for perceptually similar pictures in preschool children. *Journal of Experimental Psychology, 95*, 55–62.

Brown, A. L., Smiley, S. S., & Lawton, S. Q. C. (1978). The effects of experience on the selection of suitable retrieval cues for studying texts. *Child Development, 49*, 829–835.

Brown, A. M., & Miracle, J. A. (2003). Early binocular vision in human infants: Limitations on the generality of the Superposition Hypothesis. *Vision Research, 43*, 1563–1574.

Brown, A. S. (2006). Prenatal infection as a risk factor for schizophrenia. *Schizophrenia Bulletin, 32*, 200–202.

Brown, B. B., & Bakken, J. P. (2011). Parenting and peer relationships: Reinvigorating research on family–peer linkages in adolescence. *Journal of Research in Adolescence, 21*, 153–165.

Brown, B. B., & Dietz, E. L. (2009). Informal peer groups in middle childhood and adolescence. In K. H. Rubin, W. M. Bukowski, & B. Laursen (Eds.), *Handbook of peer interactions, relationships, and groups* (pp. 361–376). New York: Guilford Press.

Brown, B. B., Herman, M., Hamm, J. V., & Heck, D. (2008). Ethnicity and image: Correlates of minority adolescents' affiliation with individual-based versus ethnically defined peer crowds. *Child Development, 79*, 529–546.

Brown, B. B., & Larson, J. (2009). Peer relationships in adolescence. In R. M. Lerner & L. Steinberg (Eds.), *Handbook of adolescent psychology: Vol. 2* (3rd ed., pp. 74–103). Hoboken, NJ: Wiley.

Brown, B. B., Lohr, M. J., & McClenahan, E. L. (1986). Early adolescents' perceptions of peer pressure. *Journal of Early Adolescence, 6*, 139–154.

Brown, C. S., & Bigler, R. S. (2002). Effects of minority status in the classroom on children's intergroup attitudes. *Journal of Experimental Child Psychology, 83*, 77–110.

Brown, C. S., & Bigler, R. S. (2004). Children's perceptions of gender discrimination. *Developmental Psychology, 40*, 714–726.

Brown, G. L., Schoppe-Sullivan, S. J., Mangelsdorf, S. C., & Neff, C. (2010). Observed and reported supportive coparenting as predictors of infant–mother and infant–father attachment security. *Early Child Development and Care, 180*, 121–137.

Brown, J. D., & L'Engle, K. L. (2009). X-rated: Attitudes and behaviors associated with U.S. early adolescents' exposure to sexually explicit media. *Communication Research, 36*, 129–151.

Brown, J. R., & Dunn, J. (1996). Continuities in emotion understanding from 3 to 6 years. *Child Development, 67*, 789–802.

Brown, R. (1973). *A first language: The early stages*. Cambridge, MA: Harvard University Press.

Brown, R., & Hanlon, C. (1970). Derivational complexity and order of acquisition in child speech. In J. R. Hayes (Ed.), *Cognition and the development of language* (pp. 11–53). New York: Wiley.

Brown, S. A., & Ramo, D. E. (2005). Clinical course of youth following treatment for alcohol and drug problems. In H. A. Liddle & C. L. Rowe (Eds.), *Adolescent substance abuse: Research and clinical advances* (pp. 79–103). Cambridge, UK: Cambridge University Press.

Brown, T. E. (2005). *Attention deficit disorder: The unfocused mind in children and adults*. New Haven, CT: Yale University Press.

Brown, T. E. (2006). Executive functions and attention deficit hyperactivity disorder: Implications of two conflicting views. *International Journal of Disability, Development and Education, 53*, 35–46.

Browne, C. A., & Woolley, J. D. (2004). Preschoolers' magical explanations for violations of physical, social, and mental laws. *Journal of Cognition and Development, 5*, 239–260.

Browne, J. V., & Talmi, A. (2005). Family-based intervention to enhance infant–parent relationships in the neonatal intensive care unit. *Journal of Pediatric Psychology, 30*, 667–677.

Brownell, C. A., & Carriger, M. S. (1990). Changes in cooperation and self-other differentiation during the second year. *Child Development, 61*, 1164–1174.

Brownell, C. A., & Kopp, C. B. (2007). Transitions in toddler socioemotional development: Behavior, understanding, relationships. In C. A. Brownell & C. B. Kopp (Eds.), *Socioemotional development in the toddler years: Transitions and transformations* (pp. 1–40). New York: Guilford.

Brownell, C. A., Zerwas, S., & Ramani, G. B. (2007). "So big": The development of body self-awareness in toddlers. *Child Development, 78*, 1426–1440.

Bruce, D., Dolan, A., & Phillips-Grant, K. (2000). On the transition from childhood amnesia to recall of personal memories. *Psychological Science, 11*, 360–364.

Bruch, H. (2001). *The golden cage: The enigma of anorexia nervosa*. Cambridge, MA: Harvard University Press.

Bruck, M., & Ceci, S. J. (2004). Forensic developmental psychology: Unveiling four common misconceptions. *Current Directions in Psychological Science, 13*, 229–232.

Bruer, J. T. (1999). *The myth of the first three years*. New York: Free Press.

Brühwiler, C., & Blatchford, P. (2011). Effects of class size and adaptive teaching competency on classroom processes and academic outcome. *Learning and Instruction, 21*, 95–108.

Bruschweiler-Stern, N. (2004). A multifocal neonatal intervention. In A. J. Sameroff, S. C. McDonough, & K. L. Rosenblum (Eds.), *Treating parent–infant relationship problems* (pp. 188–212). New York: Guilford.

Bruzzese, J.-M., & Fisher, C. B. (2003). Assessing and enhancing the research consent capacity of children and youth. *Applied Developmental Science, 7*, 13–26.

Bryant, P., & Nunes, T. (2002). Children's understanding of mathematics. In U. Goswami (Ed.), *Blackwell handbook of childhood cognitive development* (pp. 412–439). Malden, MA: Blackwell.

Bryce, J., Coitinho, D., Darnton-Hill, I., Pelletier, D., & Pinstrup-Andersen, P. (2008). Maternal and child undernutrition: Effective action at national level. *Lancet, 371*, 510–526.

Buchanan, A. (1996). *Cycles of child maltreatment*. Chichester, UK: Wiley.

Buchanan, C. M., Eccles, J. S., & Becker, J. B. (1992). Are adolescents the victims of raging hormones? Evidence for activational effects of hormones on moods and behavior at adolescence. *Psychological Bulletin, 111*, 62–107.

Buchanan, C. M., & Holmbeck, G. N. (1998). Measuring beliefs about adolescent personality and behavior. *Journal of Youth and Adolescence, 27*, 609–629.

Buchanan, C. M., Maccoby, E. E., & Dornbusch, S. M. (1996). *Adolescents after divorce*. Cambridge, MA: Harvard University Press.

Buchanan-Barrow, E., & Barrett, M. (1998). Children's rule discrimination within the context of the school. *British Journal of Developmental Psychology, 16*, 539–551.

Budell, L., Jackson, P., & Rainville, P. (2010). Brain responses to facial expressions of pain: Emotional or motor mirroring? *NeuroImage, 53*, 355–363.

Buescher, E. S. (2001). Anti-inflammatory characteristics of human milk: How, where, why. *Advances in Experimental Medicine and Biology, 501*, 207–222.

Bugental, D. B., Ellerson, P. C., Lin, E. K., Rainey, B., & Kokotovic, A. (2002). A cognitive approach to child abuse prevention. *Journal of Family Psychology, 16*, 243–258.

Bugental, D. B., & Grusec, J. E. (2006). Socialization processes. In N. Eisenberg (Ed.), *Handbook of child psychology: Vol. 3. Social, emotional, and personality development* (6th ed., pp. 366–428). Hoboken, NJ: Wiley.

Bugental, D. B., & Happaney, K. (2004). Predicting infant maltreatment in low-income families: The interactive effects of maternal attributions and child status at birth. *Developmental Psychology, 40*, 234–243.

Buhrmester, D., & Furman, W. (1990). Perceptions of sibling relationships during middle childhood and adolescence. *Child Development, 61*, 1387–1398.

Buhs, E. S., Ladd, G. W., & Herald, S. L. (2006). Peer exclusion and victimization: Processes that mediate the relation between peer group rejection and children's classroom engagement and achievement. *Journal of Educational Psychology, 98*, 1–13.

Buhs, E. S., Ladd, G. W., & Herald-Brown, S. L. (2010). Victimization and exclusion: Links to peer rejection, classroom engagement, and achievement. In S. R. Jimerson, S. M. Swearer, & D. L. Espelage (Eds.), *Handbook of bullying in schools: An international perspective* (pp. 163–172). New York: Routledge.

Bukowski, W. M. (2001). Friendship and the worlds of childhood. In D. W. Nangle & C. A. Erdley (Eds.), *The role of friendship in psychological adjustment* (pp. 93–105). San Francisco: Jossey-Bass.

Bukowski, W. M., Sippola, L. K., & Hoza, B. (1999). Same and other: Interdependency between participation in same- and other-sex friendships. *Journal of Youth and Adolescence, 28*, 439–459.

Bukowski, W. M., Sippola, L. K., & Newcomb, A. F. (2000). Variations in patterns of attraction of same- and other-sex peers during early adolescence. *Developmental Psychology, 36*, 147–154.

Bullock, M., & Lutkenhaus, P. (1990). Who am I? The development of self-understanding in toddlers. *Merrill-Palmer Quarterly, 36*, 217–238.

Bumpus, M. F., Crouter, A. C., & McHale, S. M. (2006). Linkages between negative work-to-family spillover and mothers' and fathers' knowledge of their young adolescents' daily lives. *Journal of Early Adolescence, 26*, 36–59.

Bunting, L., & McAuley, C. (2004). Teenage pregnancy and parenthood: The role of fathers. *Child and Family Social Work, 9*, 295–303.

Burchinal, M., Vandergrift, N., & Pianta, R. (2010). Threshold analysis of association between child care quality and child outcomes for low-income children in pre-kindergarten programs. *Early Childhood Research Quarterly, 25*, 166–176.

Burdelski, M. (2010). Socializing politeness routines: Action, other-orientation, and embodiment in a Japanese preschool. *Journal of Pragmatics, 42*, 1606–1621.

Burden, M. J., Jacobson, S. W., & Jacobson, J. L. (2005). Relation of prenatal alcohol exposure to cognitive processing speed and efficiency in childhood. *Alcoholism: Clinical and Experimental Research, 29*, 1473–1483.

Burgess-Champoux, T. L., Larson, N., Neumark-Sztainer, D., Hannan, P. J., & Story, M. (2009). Are family meal patterns associated with overall diet quality during the transition from early to middle adolescence? *Journal of Nutrition Education and Behavior, 41*, 79–86.

Burhans, K. K., & Dweck, C. S. (1995). Helplessness in early childhood: The role of contingent worth. *Child Development, 66*, 1719–1738.

Burman, D. D., Bitan, T., & Booth, J. R. (2007). Sex differences in neural processing of language among some children. *Neuropsychologia, 46*, 1349–1362.

Burnham, D., & Mattock, K. (2010). Auditory development. In J. G. Bremner & T. D. Wachs (Eds.), *Wiley-Blackwell handbook of infant development: Vol. 1. Basic research* (pp. 81–119). Malden, MA: Wiley-Blackwell.

Burns, T. C., Yoshida, K. A., Hill, K., & Werker, J. F. (2007). The development of phonetic representation in bilingual and monolingual infants. *Applied Psycholinguistics, 28*, 455–474.

Burts, D. C., Hart, C. H., Charlesworth, R., Fleege, P. O., Mosley, J., & Thomasson, R. H. (1992). Observed activities and stress behaviors of children in developmentally appropriate and inappropriate kindergarten classrooms. *Early Childhood Research Quarterly, 7*, 297–318.

Bush, K. R., & Peterson, G. W. (2008). Family influences on child development. In T. P. Gullotta & G. M. Blau (Eds.), *Handbook of child behavioral issues: Evidence-based approaches to prevention and treatment* (pp. 43–67). New York: Routledge.

Bushman, B. J., & Huesmann, L. R. (2001). Effects of televised violence on aggression. In D. G. Singer & J. L. Singer (Eds.), *Handbook of children and the media* (pp. 223–254). Thousand Oaks, CA: Sage.

Bushnell, E. W., & Boudreau, J. P. (1993). Motor development and the mind: The potential role of motor abilities as a determinant of aspects of perceptual development. *Child Development, 64*, 1005–1021.

Bussell, D. A., Neiderhiser, J. M., Pike, A., Plomin, R., Simmens, S., Howe, G. W., et al. (1999). Adolescents' relationships to siblings and mothers: A multivariate genetic analysis. *Developmental Psychology, 35,* 1248–1259.

Bussey, K. (1992). Lying and truthfulness: Children's definitions, standards, and evaluative reactions. *Child Development, 63,* 129–137.

Bussey, K. (1999). Children's categorization and evaluation of different types of lies and truths. *Child Development, 70,* 1338–1347.

Bussey, K., & Bandura, A. (1992). Self-regulatory mechanisms governing gender development. *Child Development, 63,* 1236–1250.

Bussiére, P., Knighton, T., & Pennock, D. (2007). *Measuring up: Canadian results of the OECD PISA Study: The performance of Canada's youth in science, reading, and mathematics: 2006.* First results for Canadians aged 15. Catalogue No. 81-590-XPE—No. 3. Ottawa: Human Resources and Social Development Canada, Council of Ministers of Education, Canada and Statistics Canada. Retrieved from www.statcan.ca/english/freepub/81-590-XIE/81-590-XIE2007001.htm

Buswell, S. D., & Spatz, D. L. (2007). Parent-infant co-sleeping and its relationship to breastfeeding. *Journal of Pediatric Health Care, 21,* 22–28.

Butler, M. G. (2009). Genomic imprinting disorders in humans: A mini-review. *Journal of Assisted Reproduction and Genetics, 26,* 477–486.

Butler, M.G., & Meaney, F. J. (Eds.). (2005). *Genetics of developmental disabilities.* Boca Raton, FL: Taylor & Francis.

Butler, R. (1998). Age trends in the use of social and temporal comparison for self-evaluation: Examination of a novel developmental hypothesis. *Child Development, 69,* 1054–1073.

Butler, R. (1999). Information seeking and achievement motivation in middle childhood and adolescence: The role of conceptions of ability. *Developmental Psychology, 35,* 146–163.

Buttelmann, D., Carpenter, M., & Tomasello, M. (2009). Eighteen-month-old infants show false belief understanding in an active helping paradigm. *Cognition, 112,* 337–342.

Bybee, J. (Ed.). (1998). *Guilt and children.* San Diego, CA: Academic Press.

Bybee, J., Merisca, R., & Velasco, R. (1998). The development of reactions to guilt-producing events. In J. Bybee (Ed.), *Guilt and children* (pp. 185–213). San Diego: Academic Press.

Byrnes, J. P. (2002). The development of decision-making. *Journal of Adolescent Health, 31,* 208–215.

Byrnes, J. P. (2003). Cognitive development during adolescence. In G. R. Adams & M. D. Berzonsky (Eds.), *Blackwell handbook of adolescence* (pp. 227–246). Malden, MA: Blackwell.

Cabrera, N. J., Fagan, J., & Farrie, D. (2008). Explaining the long reach of fathers' prenatal involvement on later paternal engagement. *Journal of Marriage and Family, 70,* 1094–1107.

Cabrera, N. J., Fitzgerald, H. E., Bradley, R. H., & Roggman, L. (2007). Modeling the dynamics of paternal influence on children over the life course. *Applied Developmental Science, 11,* 185–189.

Cabrera, N. J., & Garcia-Coll, C. (2004). Latino fathers: Uncharted territory in need of much exploration. In M. E. Lamb (Ed.), *The role of the father in child*

development (4th ed., pp. 98–120). Hoboken, NJ: Wiley.

Cabrera, N. J., Tamis-LeMonda, C. S., Bradley, R. H., Hoferth, S., & Lamb, M. E. (2000). Fatherhood in the twenty-first century. *Child Development, 71,* 127–136.

Cain, K. M., & Dweck, C. S. (1995). The relation between motivational patterns and achievement cognitions through the elementary school years. *Merrill-Palmer Quarterly, 41,* 25–52.

Caine, N. (1986). Behavior during puberty and adolescence. In G. Mitchell & J. Erwin (Eds.), *Comparative primate biology: Vol. 2A. Behavior, conservation, and ecology* (pp. 327–361). New York: Alan R. Liss.

Cairns, R., Xie, H., & Leung, M.-C. (1998). The popularity of friendship and the neglect of social networks: Toward a new balance. In W. M. Bukowski & A. H. Cillessen (Eds.), *Sociometry then and now: Building on six decades of measuring children's experiences with the peer group* (pp. 25–53). San Francisco: Jossey-Bass.

Cairns, R. B., & Cairns, B. D. (2006). The making of developmental psychology. In R. M. Lerner (Ed.), *Handbook of child psychology: Vol. 1. Theoretical models of human development* (6th ed., pp. 89–165). Hoboken, NJ: Wiley.

Caldera, Y. M., & Lindsey, E. W. (2006). Coparenting, mother–infant interaction, and infant–parent attachment relationships in two-parent families. *Journal of Family Psychology, 20,* 275–283.

Caldwell, B. M., & Bradley, R. H. (1994). Environmental issues in developmental follow-up research. In S. L. Friedman & H. C. Haywood (Eds.), *Developmental follow-up* (pp. 235–256). San Diego: Academic Press.

Calkins, S. D. (2002). Does aversive behavior during toddlerhood matter? The effects of difficult temperament on maternal perceptions and behavior. *Infant Mental Health Journal, 23,* 381–402.

Callaghan, T. C. (1999). Early understanding and production of graphic symbols. *Child Development, 70,* 1314–1324.

Callaghan, T., Rochat, P., Lillard, A., Claux, M. L., Odden, H., Itakura, S., Tapanya, S., & Singh, S. (2005). Synchrony in the onset of mental-state reasoning: Evidence from five cultures. *Psychological Science, 16,* 378–384.

Callanan, M. A., & Sabbagh, M. A. (2004). Multiple labels for objects in conversations with young children: Parents' language and children's developing expectations about word meanings. *Developmental Psychology, 40,* 746–763.

Callen, J., & Pinelli, J. (2005). A review of the literature examining the benefits and challenges, incidence and duration, and barriers to breastfeeding in preterm infants. *Advances in Neonatal Care, 5,* 72–88.

Calvert, S. L., & Kotler, J. A. (2003). Lessons from children's television: The impact of the Children's Television Act on children's learning. *Applied Developmental Psychology, 24,* 275–335.

Calvert, S. L., Kotler, J. A., Zehnder, S. M., & Shockey, E. M. (2003). Gender stereotyping in children's reports about educational and informational television programs. *Media Psychology, 5,* 139–162.

Calvert, S. L., Rideout, V. J., Woolard, J. L., Barr, R. F., & Strouse, G. A. (2005). Age, ethnicity, and socioeconomic patterns in early computer use: A national survey. *American Behavioral Scientist, 48,* 590–607.

Camarata, S., & Leonard, L. B. (1986). Young children pronounce object words more accurately than action words. *Journal of Child Language, 13,* 51–65.

Cameron, C. A., & Lee, K. (1997). The development of children's telephone communication. *Journal of Applied Developmental Psychology, 18,* 55–70.

Cameron, C. E., Connor, C. M., Morrison, F. J., & Jewkes, A. M. (2008). Effects of classroom organization on letter-word reading in first grade. *Journal of School Psychology, 46,* 173–192.

Cameron, J. A., Alvarez, J. M., Ruble, D. N., & Fuligni, A. J. (2001). Children's lay theories about in-groups and out-groups: Reconceptualizing research on prejudice. *Personality and Social Psychology Review, 5,* 118–128.

Cameron, L., Rutland, A., Brown, R. J., & Douch, R. (2006). Changing children's intergroup attitudes toward refugees: Testing different models of extended contact. *Child Development, 77,* 1208–1219.

Cameron, P. A., & Gallup, G. G. (1988). Shadow recognition in human infants. *Infant Behavior and Development, 11,* 465–471.

Cameron-Faulkner, T., Lieven, E., & Tomasello, M. (2003). A construction based analysis of child-directed speech. *Cognitive Science, 27,* 843–873.

Campa, M. J., & Eckenrode, J. J. (2006). Pathways to intergenerational adolescent childbearing in a high-risk sample. *Journal of Marriage and Family, 68,* 558–572.

Campbell, A., Shirley, L., & Candy, J. (2004). A longitudinal study of gender-related cognition and behaviour. *Developmental Science, 7,* 1–9.

Campbell, D. A., Lake, M. F., Falk, M., & Backstrand, J. R. (2006). A randomized control trial of continuous support in labor by a lay doula. *Journal of Obstetrics and Gynecology and Neonatal Nursing, 35,* 456–464.

Campbell, D., Scott, K. D., Klaus, M. H., & Falk, M. (2007). Female relatives or friends trained as labor doulas: Outcomes at 6 to 8 weeks postpartum. *Birth, 34,* 220–227.

Campbell, F. A., Pungello, E. P., Miller-Johnson, S., Burchinal, M., & Ramey, C. T. (2001). The development of cognitive and academic abilities: Growth curves from an early childhood educational experiment. *Developmental Psychology, 37,* 231–242.

Campbell, F. A., & Ramey, C. T. (2010). Carolina Abecedarian Project. In A. Reynolds, A. J. Rolick, M. M. Englund, & J. A. Temple (Eds.), *Childhood programs and practices in the first decade of life: A human capital integration* (pp. 76–98). New York: Cambridge University Press.

Campbell, F. A., Ramey, C. T., Pungello, E. P., Sparling, J., & Miller-Johnson, S. (2002). Early childhood education: Young adult outcomes from the Abecedarian Project. *Applied Developmental Science, 6,* 42–57.

Campbell, S. B., Brownell, C. A., Hungerford, A., Spieker, S. J., Mohan, R., & Blessing, J. S. (2004). The course of maternal depressive symptoms and maternal sensitivity as predictors of attachment security at 36 months. *Development and Psychopathology, 16,* 231–252.

Campbell, S. B., Spieker, S., Burchinal, M., Poe, M. D., & the NICHD Early Child Care Research Network. (2006). Trajectories of aggression from toddlerhood to age 9 predict academic

and social functioning through age 12. *Journal of Child Psychology and Psychiatry, 47,* 791–800.

Campos, J. J., Anderson, D. I., Barbu-Roth, M. A., Hubbard, E. M., Hertenstein, J. J., & Witherington, D. (2000). Travel broadens the mind. *Infancy, 1,* 149–219.

Campos, J. J., Frankel, C. B., & Camras, L. (2004). On the nature of emotion regulation. *Child Development, 75,* 377–394.

Campos, J. J., Witherington, D., Anderson, D. I., Frankel, C. I., Uchiyama, I., & Barbu-Roth, M. (2008). Rediscovering development in infancy. *Child Development, 79,* 1625–1632.

Campos, R. G. (1989). Soothing pain-elicited distress in infants with swaddling and pacifiers. *Child Development, 60,* 781–792.

Camras, L. A. (1992). Expressive development and basic emotions. *Cognition and Emotion, 6,* 267–283.

Camras, L. A., Oster, H., Campos, J. J., & Bakeman, R. (2003). Emotional facial expressions in European-American, Japanese, and Chinese infants. *Annals of the New York Academy of Sciences, 1000,* 1–17.

Camras, L. A., Oster, H., Campos, J., Campos, R., Ujie, T., Miyake, K., et al. (1998). Production of emotional and facial expressions in European American, Japanese, and Chinese infants. *Developmental Psychology, 34,* 616–628.

Camras, L. A., Oster, H., Campos, J. J., Miyake, K., & Bradshaw, D. (1992). Japanese and American infants' responses to arm restraint. *Developmental Psychology, 28,* 578–583.

Camras, L. A., & Shutter, J. M. (2010). Emotional facial expressions in infancy. *Emotion Review, 2,* 120–129.

CAN (Swedish Council for Information on Alcohol and Other Drugs). (2007). *The European School Survey Project on Alcohol and Other Drugs: Key result generator, 2007.* Retrieved from www.espad.org/keyresult-generator

Canada Campaign 2000. (2009). *2009 Report Card on Child and Family Poverty in Canada: 1989–2009.* Retrieved from www.campaign2000.ca/reportcards.html

Canetto, S. S., & Sakinofsky, I. (1998). The gender paradox in suicide. *Suicide and Life-Threatening Behavior, 28,* 1–23.

Canfield, R., Henderson, C., Cory-Slechta, D., Cox, C., Jusko, T., & Lanphear, B. (2003). Intellectual impairment in children with blood lead concentrations below 10 µg per deciliter. *New England Journal of Medicine, 348,* 1517–1526.

Canobi, K. H. (2004). Individual differences in children's addition and subtraction knowledge. *Cognitive Development, 19,* 81–93.

Canobi, K. H., Reeve, R. A., & Pattison, P. E. (2003). Patterns of knowledge in children's addition. *Developmental Psychology, 39,* 521–534.

Capelli, C. A., Nakagawa, N., & Madden, C. M. (1990). How children understand sarcasm: The role of context and intonation. *Child Development, 61,* 1824–1841.

Capirci, O., Contaldo, A., Caselli, M. C., & Volterra, V. (2005). From action to language through gesture. *Gesture, 5,* 155–177.

Caplan, M., Vespo, J., Pedersen, J., & Hay, D. F. (1991). Conflict and its resolution in small groups of one- and two year olds. *Child Development, 62,* 1513–1524.

Card, N. A., Stucky, B. D., Sawalani, G. M., & Little, T. D. (2008). Direct and indirect aggression during childhood and adolescence: A meta-analytic review of gender differences, intercorrelations, and relations to maladjustment. *Child Development, 79*, 1185–1229.

CARE Study Group. (2008). Maternal caffeine intake during pregnancy and risk of fetal growth restriction: A large prospective observational study. *British Medical Journal, 337*, a2337.

Carey, S. (1995). On the origins of causal understanding. In D. Sperber, D. Premack, & A. J. Premack (Eds.), *Causal cognition* (pp. 268–308). Oxford, UK: Clarendon Press.

Carey, S. (1999). Sources of conceptual change. In E. K. Scholnick, K. Nelson, S. A. Gelman, & P. H. Miller (Eds.), *Conceptual development: Piaget's legacy* (pp. 293–326). Mahwah, NJ: Erlbaum.

Carey, S., & Markman, E. M. (1999). Cognitive development. In B. M. Bly & D. E. Rumelhart (Eds.), *Cognitive science* (pp. 201–254). San Diego: Academic Press.

Carlo, G., Koller, S. H., Eisenberg, N., Da Silva, M., & Frohlich, C. (1996). A cross-national study on the relations among prosocial moral reasoning, gender-role orientations, and prosocial behaviors. *Developmental Psychology, 32*, 231–240.

Carlo, G., Mestre, M. V., Samper, P., Tur, A., & Armenta, B. E. (2011). The longitudinal relations among dimensions of parenting styles, sympathy, prosocial moral reasoning, and prosocial behaviors. *International Journal of Behavioral Development, 35*, 116–124.

Carlson, E. A. (1998). A prospective longitudinal study of attachment disorganization/disorientation. *Child Development, 4*, 1107–1128.

Carlson, S. M., & Meltzoff, A. N. (2008). Bilingual experience and executive functioning in young children. *Developmental Science, 11*, 282–298.

Carlson, S. M., Moses, L. J., & Claxton, S. J. (2004). Individual differences in executive functioning and theory of mind: An investigation of inhibitory control and planning ability. *Journal of Experimental Child Psychology, 87*, 299–319.

Carlson, V. J., & Horwood, R. L. (2003). Attachment, culture, and the caregiving system: The cultural patterning of everyday experiences among Anglo and Puerto Rican mother–infant pairs. *Infant Mental Health Journal, 24*, 53–73.

Carpendale, J. I. M. (2000). Kohlberg and Piaget on stages and moral reasoning. *Developmental Review, 20*, 181–205.

Carpendale, J. I. M. (2009). Piaget's theory of moral development. In U. Muller, J. I. M. Carpendale, & L. Smith (Eds.), *Cambridge companion to Piaget* (pp. 270–286). New York: Cambridge University Press.

Carpendale, J., & Lewis, C. (2006). *Understanding children's worlds: How children develop social understanding.* Malden, MA: Blackwell Publishing.

Carpenter, M., Akhtar, N., & Tomasello, M. (1998). Fourteen- through 18-month-old infants differentially imitate intentional and accidental actions. *Infant Behavior and Development, 21*, 315–330.

Carpenter, M., Nagell, K., & Tomasello, M. (1998). Social cognition, joint attention, and communicative competence. *Monographs of the Society for Research in Child Development, 63*(4, Serial No. 255).

Carpenter, T. P., Fennema, E., Fuson, K., Hiebert, J., Human, P., & Murray, H. (1999). Learning basic number concepts and skills as problem solving. In E. Fennema & T. A. Romberg (Eds.), *Mathematics classrooms that promote understanding: Studies in mathematical thinking and learning series* (pp. 45–61). Mahwah, NJ: Erlbaum.

Carr, D., & Friedman, M. A. (2005). Is obesity stigmatizing? Body weight, perceived discrimination, and psychological well-being in the United States. *Journal of Health and Social Behavior, 46*, 244–256.

Carr, J. (2002). Down syndrome. In P. Howlin & O. Udwin (Eds.), *Outcomes in neurodevelopmental and genetic disorders* (pp. 169–197). New York: Cambridge University Press.

Carraher, T., Schliemann, A. D., & Carraher, D. W. (1988). Mathematical concepts in everyday life. In G. B. Saxe & M. Gearhart (Eds.), *New directions for child development* (Vol. 41, pp. 71–87). San Francisco: Jossey-Bass.

Carroll, J. B. (1993). *Human cognitive abilities: A survey of factor-analytic studies.* New York: Cambridge University Press.

Carroll, J. B. (2005). The three-stratum theory of cognitive abilities. In D. P. Flanagan & P. L. Harrison (Eds.), *Contemporary intellectual assessment: Theories, tests, and issues* (2nd ed., pp. 69–76). New York: Guilford.

Carskadon, M. A., Acebo, C., & Jenni, O. G. (2004). Regulation of adolescent sleep: Implications for behavior. In R. E. Dahl & L. P. Spear (Eds.), *Adolescent brain development: Vulnerabilities and opportunities* (pp. 276–291). New York: New York Academy of Sciences.

Carskadon, M. A., Harvey, K., Duke, P., Anders, T. F., Litt, I. F., & Dement, W. C. (2002). Pubertal changes in daytime sleepiness. *Sleep, 25*, 525–605.

Carver, K., Joyner, K., & Udry, J. R. (2003). National estimates of adolescent romantic relationships. In P. Florsheim (Ed.), *Adolescent romantic relations and sexual behavior: Theory, research, and practical implications* (pp. 23–56). Mahwah, NJ: Erlbaum.

Carver, P. R., Egan, S. K., & Perry, D. G. (2004). Children who question their heterosexuality. *Developmental Psychology, 40*, 43–53.

CASA. (2006). *The importance of family dinners III.* New York: National Center on Addiction and Substance Abuse, Columbia University.

Casalis, S., & Cole, P. (2009). On the relationship between morphological and phonological awareness: Effects of training in kindergarten and in first-grade reading. *First Language, 29*, 113–142.

Casas, J. F., Weigel, S. M., Crick, N. R., Ostrov, J. M., Woods, K. E., Yeh, E. A. J., & Huddleston-Casas, C. A. (2006). Early parenting and children's relational and physical aggression in the preschool and home contexts. *Applied Developmental Psychology, 27*, 209–227.

Casasola, M., Bhagwat, J., & Burke, A. S. (2009). Learning to form a spatial category of tight-fit relations: How experience with a label can give a boost. *Developmental Psychology, 45*, 711–723.

Casasola, M., Cohen, L. B., & Chiarello, E. (2003). Six-month-old infants' categorization of containment spatial relations. *Child Development, 74*, 679–693.

Case, R. (1992). *The mind's staircase.* Hillsdale, NJ: Erlbaum.

Case, R. (1996). Introduction: Reconceptualizing the nature of children's conceptual structures and their development in middle childhood. In R. Case & Y. Okamoto (Eds.), The role of central conceptual structures in the development of children's thought. *Monographs of the Society for Research in Child Development, 61*(1–2, Serial No. 246), pp. 1–26.

Case, R. (1998). The development of central conceptual structures. In D. Kuhn & R. Siegler (Eds.), *Handbook of child psychology: Vol. 2. Cognition, perception, and language* (5th ed., pp. 745–800). New York: Wiley.

Case, R., Griffin, S., & Kelly, W. M. (2001). Socioeconomic differences in children's early cognitive development and their readiness for schooling. In S. L. Golbeck (Ed.), *Psychological perspectives on early education* (pp. 37–63). Mahwah, NJ: Erlbaum.

Case, R., & Okamoto, Y. (Eds.). (1996). The role of central conceptual structures in the development of children's thought. *Monographs of the Society for Research in Child Development, 61*(1–2, Serial No. 246).

Caselli, M. C., Bates, E., Casadio, P., Fenson, J., Fenson, L., Sanderl, L., & Weir, J. (1995). A cross-linguistic study of early lexical development. *Cognitive Development, 10*, 159–199.

Casey, B. J., Getz, S., & Galvan, A. (2008). The adolescent brain. *Developmental Review, 28*, 62–77.

Casey, B. J., Thomas, K. M., Davidson, M. C., Kunz, K., & Franzen, P. L. (2002). Dissociating striatal and hippocampal function developmentally with a stimulus-response compatibility task. *Journal of Cognitive Neuroscience, 22*, 8647–8652.

Casey, M. B., Nuttall, R. L., & Pezaris, E. (1997). Mediators of gender differences in mathematics college entrance test scores: A comparison of spatial skills with internalized beliefs and anxieties. *Developmental Psychology, 33*, 669–680.

Casey, M. B., Nuttall, R. L., & Pezaris, E. (2001). Spatial-mechanical reasoning skills versus mathematics self-confidence as mediators of gender differences on mathematics subtests using cross-national gender-based items. *Journal for Research in Mathematics Education, 32*, 28–57.

Cashon, C. H., & Cohen, L. B. (2000). Eight-month-old infants' perceptions of possible and impossible events. *Infancy, 1*, 429–446.

Casper, L. M., & Smith, K. E. (2002). Dispelling the myths: Self-care, class, and race. *Journal of Family Issues, 23*, 716–727.

Caspi, A. (2000). The child is father of the man: Personality continuities from childhood to adulthood. *Journal of Personality and Social Psychology, 78*, 158–172.

Caspi, A., Elder, G. H., Jr., & Bem, D. J. (1987). Moving against the world: Life-course patterns of explosive children. *Developmental Psychology, 23*, 308–313.

Caspi, A., Elder, G. H., Jr., & Bem, D. J. (1988). Moving away from the world: Life-course patterns of shy children. *Developmental Psychology, 24*, 824–831.

Caspi, A., Harrington, H., Milne, B., Amell, J. W., Theodore, R. F., & Moffitt, T. E. (2003). Children's behavioral styles at age 3 are linked to their adult personality traits at age 26. *Journal of Personality, 71*, 495–513.

Caspi, A., Lynam, D., Moffitt, T. E., & Silva, P. A. (1993). Unraveling girls' delinquency: Biological, dispositional, and contextual contributions to adolescent misbehavior. *Developmental Psychology, 29*, 19–30.

Caspi, A., McClay, J., Moffitt, T. E., Mill, J., Martin, J., & Craig, I. W. (2002). Role of genotype in the cycle of violence in maltreated children. *Science, 297*, 851–854.

Caspi, A., Moffitt, T. E., Morgan, J., Rutter, M., Taylor, A., Kim-Cohen, J., & Polo-Tomas, M. (2004). Maternal expressed emotion predicts children's antisocial behavior problems: Using monozygotic-twin differences to identify environmental effects on behavioral development. *Developmental Psychology, 40*, 149–161.

Caspi, A., & Roberts, B. W. (2001). Personality development across the life course: The argument for change and continuity. *Psychological Inquiry, 12*, 49–66.

Caspi, A., & Shiner, R. L. (2006). Personality development. In N. Eisenberg (Ed.), *Handbook of child psychology: Vol. 3. Social, emotional, and personality development* (6th ed., pp. 300–365). Hoboken, NJ: Wiley.

Cassia, V. M., Simion, F., & Umiltá, C. (2001). Face preference at birth: The role of an orienting mechanism. *Developmental Science, 4*, 101–108.

Cassia, V. M., Turati, C., & Simion, F. (2004). Can a nonspecific bias toward top-heavy patterns explain newborns' face preference? *Psychological Science, 15*, 379–383.

Cassidy, J., & Berlin, L. J. (1994). The insecure/ambivalent pattern of attachment: Theory and research. *Child Development, 65*, 971–991.

Cassidy, K. W, Adamek-Griggs, R., Cosetti, M., Meier, V., Kelton, E., & Richman, L. (2005). Preschool children's understanding of conflicting desires. *Journal of Cognition and Development, 6*, 427–454.

Castelli, D. M., Hillman, C. H., Buck, S. M., & Erwin, H. E. (2007). Physical fitness and academic achievement in third- and fifth-grade students. *Journal of Sport and Exercise Psychology, 29*, 239–252.

Catalano, R., Ahern, J., Bruckner, T., Anderson, E., & Saxton, K. (2009). Gender-specific selection in utero among contemporary human birth cohorts. *Paediatric and Perinatal Epidemiology, 23*, 273–278.

Catalano, R., Zilko, C. E., Saxton, K. B., & Bruckner, T. (2010). Selection in utero: A biological response to mass layoffs. *American Journal of Human Biology, 22*, 396–400.

Catalano, R. A. (2003). Sex ratios in the two Germanies: A test of the economic stress hypothesis. *Human Reproduction, 18*, 1972–1975.

Caton, D., Corry, M. P., Frigoletto, F. D., Hokins, D. P., Liberman, E., & Mayberry, L. (2002). The nature and management of labor pain: Executive summary. *American Journal of Obstetrics and Gynecology, 186*, S1–S15.

Cattell, J. M. (1890). Mental tests and measurements. *Mind, 15*, 373–381.

Cattell, R. B. (1971). *Abilities: Their structure, growth and action.* Boston: Houghton Mifflin.

Cattell, R. B. (1987). *Intelligence: Its structure, growth and action.* Amsterdam: North-Holland.

Cauffman, E., Shulman, E. P., Steinberg, L., Claus, E., Banich, M. T., & Graham, S.

(2010). Age differences in affective decision making as indexed by performance on the Iowa Gambling Task. *Developmental Psychology, 46,* 193–207.

Ceci, S. J. (1991). How much does schooling influence general intelligence and its cognitive components? A reassessment of the evidence. *Developmental Psychology, 27,* 703–722.

Ceci, S. J. (1999). Schooling and intelligence. In S. J. Ceci & W. M. Williams (Eds.), *The nature–nurture debate: The essential readings* (pp. 168–175). Oxford: Blackwell.

Ceci, S. J., Bruck, M., & Battin, D. B. (2000). The suggestibility of children's testimony. In D. F. Bjorklund (Ed.), *False-memory creation in children and adults* (pp. 169–201). Mahwah, NJ: Erlbaum.

Ceci, S. J., Kulkofsky, S., Klemfuss, J. Z., Sweeney, C. D., & Bruck, M. (2007). Unwarranted assumptions about children's testimonial accuracy. *Annual Review of Clinical Psychology, 3,* 311–328.

Ceci, S. J., Rosenblum, T. B., & Kumpf, M. (1998). The shrinking gap between high- nd low-scoring groups: Current trends and possible causes. In U. Neisser (Ed.), *The rising curve* (pp. 287–302). Washington, DC: American Psychological Association.

Ceci, S. J., & Roazzi, A. (1994). The effects of context on cognition: Postcards from Brazil. In R. J. Sternberg (Ed.), *Mind in context* (pp. 74–101). New York: Cambridge University Press.

Ceci, S. J., & Williams, W. M. (1997). Schooling, intelligence, and income. *American Psychologist, 52,* 1051–1058.

Center for Communication and Social Policy. (Ed.). (1998). *National television violence study* (Vol. 2). Newbury Park, CA: Sage.

Center for Effective Discipline. (2005). *Worldwide bans on corporal punishment.* Retrieved from www.stophitting.com/disatschool/facts.php

Center on Education Policy. (2007). *State high school exit exams: Working to raise test scores.* Washington, D.C.: Author.

Center on Education Policy. (2009). *State high school exit exams: Trends in test programs, alternate pathways, and pass rates.* Washington, DC: Author.

Cermak, S. A., & Daunhauer, L. A. (1997). Sensory processing in the post-institutionalized child. *American Journal of Occupational Therapy, 51,* 500–507.

Cernoch, J. M., & Porter, R. H. (1985). Recognition of maternal axillary odors by infants. *Child Development, 56,* 1593–1598.

Cervantes, C. A., & Callanan, M. A. (1998). Labels and explanations in mother–child emotion talk: Age and gender differentiation. *Developmental Psychology, 34,* 88–98.

Chalabaev, A., Sarrazin, P., & Fontayne, P. (2009). Stereotype endorsement and perceived ability as mediators of the girls' gender orientation–soccer performance relationship. *Psychology of Sport and Exercise, 10,* 297–299.

Chamberlain, P. (2003). Antisocial behavior and delinquency in girls. In P. Chamberlain (Ed.), *Treating chronic juvenile offenders* (pp. 109–127). Washington, DC: American Psychological Association.

Champion, T. B. (2003a). "A matter of vocabularly": Performances of low-income African-American Head Start children on the Peabody Picture Vocabulary Test. *Communication Disorders Quarterly, 24,* 121–127.

Champion, T. B. (2003b). *Understanding storytelling among African-American children: A journey from Africa to America.* Mahwah, NJ: Erlbaum.

Chan, A., Lieven, E., & Tomasello, M. (2009). Children's understanding of the agent–patient relations in the transitive construction: Cross-linguistic comparisons between Cantonese, German, and English. *Cognitive Linguistics, 20,* 267–300.

Chan, A., Meints, K., Lieven, E., & Tomasello, M. (2010). Young children's comprehension of English SVO word order revisited: Testing the same children in act-out and intermodal preferential looking tasks. *Cognitive Development, 25,* 30–45.

Chan, L. K. S., & Moore, P. J. (2006). Development of attributional beliefs and strategic knowledge in years 5–9: A longitudinal analysis. *Educational Psychology, 26,* 161–185.

Chan, R. W., Raboy, B., & Patterson, C. J. (1998). Psychosocial adjustment among children conceived via donor insemination by lesbian and heterosexual mothers. *Child Development, 69,* 443–457.

Chan, S. M. (2010). Aggressive behaviour in early elementary school children: Relations to authoritarian parenting, children's negative emotionality and coping strategies. *Early Child Development and Care, 180,* 1253–1269.

Chandra, A., Martino, S. C., Collins, R. L., Elliott, M. N., Berry, S. H., Kanouse, D. E., & Miu, A. (2008). Does watching sex on television predict teen pregnancy? Findings from a national longitudinal survey of youth. *Pediatrics, 122,* 1047–1054.

Chandra, R. K. (1991). Interactions between early nutrition and the immune system. In *Ciba Foundation Symposium* (No. 156, pp. 77–92). Chichester, UK: Wiley.

Chaney, C. (1992). Language development, metalinguistic skills, and print awareness in 3-year-old children. *Applied Psycholinguistics, 13,* 485–514.

Chang, F., Dell, G. S., & Bock, K. (2006). Becoming syntactic. *Psychological Review, 113,* 234–272.

Chang, L., Schwartz, D., Dodge, K. A., & McBride-Chang, C. (2003). Harsh parenting in relation to child emotion regulation and aggression. *Journal of Family Psychology, 17,* 598–606.

Chao, R. K. (1994). Beyond parental control and authoritarian parenting style: Understanding Chinese parenting through the cultural notion of training. *Child Development, 65,* 1111–1119.

Chaplin, T. M., Cole, P. M., & Zahn-Waxler, C. (2005). Parental socialization of emotion expression: Gender differences and relations to child adjustment. *Emotion, 5,* 80–88.

Chapman, K. L., Leonard, L. B., & Mervis, C. B. (1986). The effect of feedback on young children's inappropriate word usage. *Journal of Child Language, 13,* 101–117.

Chapman, R. S. (2006). Children's language learning: An interactionist perspective. In R. Paul (Ed.), *Language disorders from a developmental perspective* (pp. 1–53). Mahwah, NJ: Erlbaum.

Charman, T., Baron-Cohen, S., Swettenham, J., Baird, G., Cox, A., & Drew, A. (2001). Testing joint attention, imitation, and play as infancy precursors to language and theory of mind. *Cognitive Development, 15,* 481–498.

Charpak, N., Ruiz-Peláez, J. G., & Figueroa, Z. (2005). Influence of feeding patterns and other factors on early somatic growth of healthy preterm infants in home-based kangaroo mother care: A cohort study. *Journal of Pediatric Gastroenterology and Nutrition, 41,* 430–437.

Chase-Lansdale, P. L., Brooks-Gunn, J., & Zamsky, E. S. (1994). Young African-American multigenerational families in poverty: Quality of mothering and grandmothering. *Child Development, 65,* 373–393.

Chase-Lansdale, P. L., Gordon, R., Brooks-Gunn, J., & Klebanov, P. K. (1997). Neighborhood and family influences on the intellectual and behavioral competence of preschool and early school-age children. In J. Brooks-Gunn, G. Duncan, & J. L. Aber (Eds.), *Neighborhood poverty: Context and consequences for development* (pp. 79–118). New York: Russell Sage Foundation.

Chauhan, G. S., Shastri, J., & Mohite, P. (2005). Development of gender constancy in preschoolers. *Psychological Studies, 50,* 62–71.

Chavajay, P., & Rogoff, B. (2002). Schooling and traditional collaborative social organization of problem solving by Mayan mothers and children. *Developmental Psychology, 38,* 55–66.

Chawarska, K., & Shic, F. (2009). Looking but not seeing: Atypical visual scanning and recognition of faces in 2- and 4-year-old children with autism spectrum disorder. *Journal of Autism and Developmental Disorders, 39,* 1663–1672.

Cheadle, J. E., & Amato, P. R. (2011). A quantitative assessment of Lareau's qualitative conclusions about class, race, and parenting. *Journal of Family Issues, 32,* 679–706.

Cheah, C. S. L., Leung, C. Y. Y., Tahseen, M., & Schultz, D. (2009). Authoritative parenting among immigrant Chinese mothers of preschoolers. *Journal of Family Psychology, 23,* 311–320.

Checkley, W., Epstein, L. D., Gilman, R. H., Cabrera, L., & Black, R. E. (2003). Effects of acute diarrhea on linear growth in Peruvian children. *American Journal of Epidemiology, 157,* 166–175.

Chen, D. W., Fein, G. G., Killen, M., & Tam, H.-P. (2001). Peer conflicts of preschool children: Issues, resolution, incidence, and age-related patterns. *Early Education and Development, 12,* 523–544.

Chen, E. S. L., & Rao, N. (2011). Gender socialization in Chinese kindergartens: Teachers' contributions. *Sex Roles, 64,* 103–116.

Chen, J.-Q., Moran, S., & Gardner, H. (2009). *Multiple intelligences around the world.* San Francisco: Jossey-Bass.

Chen, L.-C., Metcalfe, J. S., Jeka, J. J., & Clark, J. E. (2007). Two steps forward and one back: Learning to walk affects infants' sitting posture. *Infant Behavior and Development, 30,* 16–25.

Chen, X. (2001). Growing up in a collectivistic culture: Socialization and socioemotional development in Chinese children. In A. L. Comunian & U. P. Gielen (Eds.), *Human development in cross-cultural perspective.* Padua, Italy: Cedam.

Chen, X., Cen, G., Li, D., & He, Y. (2005). Social functioning and adjustment in Chinese children: The imprint of historical time. *Child Development, 76,* 182–195.

Chen, X., DeSouza, A. T., Chen, H., & Wang, L. (2006). Reticent behavior and experiences in peer interactions in Chinese and Canadian children. *Developmental Psychology, 42,* 656–665.

Chen, X., & French, D. C. (2008). Children's social competence in cultural context. *Annual Review of Psychology, 59,* 591–616.

Chen, X., Hastings, P. D., Rubin, K. H., Chen, H., Cen, G., & Stewart, S. L. (1998). Child-rearing attitudes and behavioral inhibition in Chinese and Canadian toddlers: A cross-cultural study. *Developmental Psychology, 34,* 677–686.

Chen, X., Rubin, K. H., & Li, D. (1995). Social functioning and adjustment in Chinese children: A longitudinal study. *Developmental Psychology, 31,* 531–539.

Chen, X., Wang, L., & DeSouza, A. (2006). Temperament, socioemotional functioning, and peer relationships in Chinese and North American children. In X. Chen, D. C. French, & B. H. Schneider (Eds.), *Peer relationships in cultural context* (pp. 123–147). New York: Cambridge University Press.

Chen, X., Wu, H., Chen, H., Wang, L., & Cen, G. (2001). Parenting practices and aggressive behavior in Chinese children. *Parenting: Science and Practice, 1,* 159–184.

Chen, Y.-C., Yu, M.-L., Rogan, W., Gladen, B., & Hsu, C.-C. (1994). A 6-year follow-up of behavior and activity disorders in the Taiwan Yu-cheng children. *American Journal of Public Health, 84,* 415–421.

Chen, Y.-J., & Hsu, C.-C. (1994). Effects of prenatal exposure to PCBs on the neurological function of children: A neuropsychological and neurophysiological study. *Developmental Medicine and Child Neurology, 36,* 312–320.

Chen, Z., Sanchez, R. P., & Campbell, T. (1997). From beyond to within their grasp: The rudiments of analogical problem solving in 10- to 13-month-olds. *Developmental Psychology, 33,* 790–801.

Chen, Z., & Siegler, R. S. (2000). Across the great divide: Bridging the gap between understanding of toddlers' and older children's thinking. *Monographs of the Society for Research in Child Development, 65*(2, Serial No. 261).

Chesney-Lind, M. (2001). Girls, violence, and delinquency: Popular myths and persistent problems. In S. O. White (Ed.), *Handbook of youth and justice* (pp. 135–158). New York: Kluwer Academic.

Chesney-Lind, M., & Belknap, J. (2004). Trends in delinquent girls' aggression and violent behavior. In M. Putallaz & K. L. Bierman (Eds.), *Aggression, antisocial behavior, and violence among girls: A developmental perspective* (pp. 203–220). New York: Guilford.

Chess, S., & Thomas, A. (1984). *Origins and evolution of behavior disorders.* New York: Brunner/Mazel.

Chi, M. T. H. (1978). Knowledge structures and memory development. In R. S. Siegler (Ed.), *Children's thinking: What develops?* (pp. 73–96). Hillsdale, NJ: Erlbaum.

Child Trends. (2011). *Teen births.* Retrieved from www.childtrendsdatabank.org/?q=node/52

Children's Defense Fund. (2009). *State of America's children: 2008.* Washington, DC: Author.

Chin, T., & Phillips, M. (2004). Social reproduction and child-rearing practices: Social class, children's agency, and the summer activity gap. *Sociology of Education, 77*(3), 185–210.

Chinn, C. A., & Malhotra, B. A. (2002). Children's responses to anomalous scientific data: How is conceptual change impeded? *Journal of Educational Psychology, 94*, 327–343.

Chisholm, K. (1998). Attachment security and indiscriminately friendly behavior in children adopted from Romanian orphanages. *Development and Psychopathology, 7*, 283–294.

Choi, S., & Gopnik, A. (1995). Early acquisition of verbs in Korean: A cross-linguistic study. *Journal of Child Language, 22*, 497–529.

Choi, S., McDonough, L., Bowerman, M., & Mandler, J. M. (1999). Early sensitivity to language-specific spatial categories in English and Korean. *Cognitive Development, 14*, 241–268.

Chomsky, C. (1969). *The acquisition of syntax in children from 5 to 10.* Cambridge, MA: MIT Press.

Chomsky, N. (1957). *Syntactic structures.* The Hague: Mouton.

Chomsky, N. (1976). *Reflections on language.* London: Temple Smith.

Chomsky, N. (1997). Language and mind: Current thoughts on ancient problems (Part 1). Retrieved from http://fccl.ksu.ru/papers/chomsky1.htm

Chomtho, S., Wells, J. C., Williams, J. E., Davies, P. S., Lucas, A., & Fewtrell, M. S. (2008). Infant growth and later body composition: Evidence from the 4-component model. *American Journal of Clinical Nutrition, 87*, 1776–1784.

Chouinard, M. M. (2007). Children's questions: A mechanism for cognitive development. *Monographs of the Society for Research in Child Development, 72*(1, Serial No. 286).

Chouinard, M. M., & Clark, E. V. (2003). Adult reformulations of child errors as negative evidence. *Journal of Child Language, 30*, 637–669.

Christakis, D. A., Zimmerman, F. J., DiGiuseppe, D. L., & McCarty, C. A. (2004). Early television exposure and subsequent attentional problems in children. *Pediatrics, 113*, 708–713.

Christian, P. (2003). Micronutrients and reproductive health issues: An international perspective. *Journal of Nutrition, 133*, 1969S–1973S.

Christiansen, M. H., & Chater, N. (2008). Language as shaped by the brain. *Behaviorial and Brain Sciences, 31*, 489–558.

Chudley, A. E., Conry, J., Cook, J. L., Loock, C., Rosales, T., & LeBlanc, N. (2005). Fetal alcohol spectrum disorder: Canadian guidelines for diagnosis. *Canadian Medical Association Journal, 172*, S1–S21.

Chumlea, W. C., Schubert, C. M., Roche, A. F., Kulin, H. E., Lee, P. A., Himes, J. H., & Sun, S. S. (2003). Age at menarche and racial comparisons in U.S. girls. *Pediatrics, 111*, 110–113.

Chung, H. H. (2006). Code switching as a communicative strategy: A case study of Korean–English bilinguals. *Bilingual Research Journal, 30*, 293–307.

Chung, H. L., Mulvey, E. P., & Steinberg, L. (2011). Understanding the school outcomes of juvenile offenders: An exploration of neighborhood influences and motivational resources. *Journal of Youth and Adolescence, 40*, 1025–1038.

CIA (Central Intelligence Agency). (2009). *World fact book.* Washington, DC: Author.

Cianciolo, A. T., Matthew, C., Sternberg, R. J., & Wagner, R. K. (2006). Tacit knowledge, practical intelligence, and expertise. In K. A. Cricsson, N. Charness,

P. J. Feltovich, & R. R. Hoffman (Eds.), *The Cambridge handbook of expertise and expert performance* (pp. 613–632). New York: Cambridge University Press.

Cicchetti, D. (2007). Intervention and policy implications of research on neurobiological functioning in maltreated children. In J. L. Aber, S. J. Bishop-Josef, S. M. Jones, K. T. McLearn, & D. A. Phillips (Eds.), *Child development and social policy* (pp. 167–184). Washington, DC: American Psychological Association.

Cicchetti, D., & Toth, S. L. (2006). Developmental psychopathology and preventive intervention. In K. A. Renninger & I. E. Sigel (Eds.), *Handbook of child psychology: Vol. 4. Child psychology in practice* (6th ed., pp. 497–547). Hoboken, NJ: Wiley.

Cillessen, A. H. N., & Bellmore, A. D. (2004). Social skills and interpersonal perception in early and middle childhood. In P. K. Smith & C. H. Hart (Eds.), *Blackwell handbook of childhood social development* (pp. 355–374). Malden, MA: Blackwell.

Cillessen, A. H. N., & Mayeux, L. (2004). From censure to reinforcement: Developmental changes in the association between aggression and social status. *Child Development, 75*, 147–163.

Cipriano, E. A., & Stifter, C. A. (2010). Predicting preschool effortful control from toddler temperament and parenting behavior. *Journal of Applied Developmental Psychology, 31*, 221–230.

Clancy, P. (1985). Acquisition of Japanese. In D. I. Slobin (Ed.), *The crosslinguistic study of language acquisition: Vol. 1. The data* (pp. 323–524). Hillsdale, NJ: Erlbaum.

Clancy, P. (1989). Form and function in the acquisition of Korean wh- questions. *Journal of Child Language, 16*, 323–347.

Clapp, J. F., III, Kim, H., Burciu, B., Schmidt, S., Petry, K., & Lopez, B. (2002). Continuing regular exercise during pregnancy: Effect of exercise volume on fetoplacental growth. *American Journal of Obstetrics and Gynecology, 186*, 142–147.

Clark, C. A., Woodward, L. J., Horwood, L. J., & Moor, S. (2008). Development of emotional and behavioral regulation in children born extremely preterm and very preterm: Biological and social influences. *Child Development, 79*, 1444–1462.

Clark, E. V. (1983). Meanings and concepts. In P. H. Mussen (Ed.), *Handbook of child psychology: Vol. 3. Cognitive development* (pp. 787–840). New York: Wiley.

Clark, E. V. (2007). Young children's uptake of new words in conversation. *Language in Society, 36*, 157–182.

Clark, K. E., & Ladd, G. W. (2000). Connectedness and autonomy support in parent–child relationships: Links to children's socioemotional orientation and peer relationships. *Developmental Psychology, 36*, 485–498.

Clarke-Stewart, K. A. (1998). Historical shifts and underlying themes in ideas about rearing young children in the United States: Where have we been? Where are we going? *Early Development and Parenting, 7*, 101–117.

Clarke-Stewart, K. A., & Hayward, C. (1996). Advantages of father custody and contact for the psychological well-being of school-age children. *Journal of Applied Developmental Psychology, 17*, 239–270.

Clarkson, T. W., Magos, L., & Myers, G. J. (2003). The toxicology of mercury—current exposures and clinical manifestations. *New England Journal of Medicine, 349*, 1731–1737.

Claxton, L. J., Keen, R., & McCarty, M. E. (2003). Evidence of motor planning in infant reaching behavior. *Psychological Science, 14*, 354–356.

Clay, R. A. (2009) Mini-multi-taskers. *Monitor on Psychology, 40*(2), 38–40.

Clearfield, M. W., & Nelson, N. M. (2006). Sex differences in mothers' speech and play behavior with 6-, 9-, and 14-month-old infants. *Sex Roles, 54*, 127–137.

Clearfield, M. W., Osborn, C. N., & Mullen, M. (2008). Learning by looking: Infants' social looking behavior across the transition from crawling to walking. *Journal of Experimental Child Psychology, 100*, 297–307.

Clements, D. H., & Sarama, J. (2003). Young children and technology: What does the research say? *Young Children, 58*(6), 34–40.

Clements, D. H., & Sarama, J. (2008). Experimental evaluation of the effects of a research-based preschool mathematics curriculum. *American Educational Research Journal, 45*, 443–494.

Cleveland, E. S., & Reese, E. (2005). Maternal structure and autonomy support in conversations about the past: Contributions to children's autobiographical memory. *Developmental Psychology, 41*, 376–388.

Clifton, R. K., Rochat, P., Robin, D. J., & Berthier, N. E. (1994). Multimodal perception in the control of infant reaching. *Journal of Experimental Psychology: Human Perception and Performance, 20*, 876–886.

Cluett, E. R., & Burns, E. (2009). Immersion in water in labour and birth. *Cochrane Database of Systematic Reviews, Issue 2.* Art. No. CD000111.

Coatsworth, J. D., Sharp, E. H., Palen, L., Darling, N., Cumsille, P., & Marta, M. (2005). Exploring adolescent self-defining leisure activities and identity experiences across three countries. *International Journal of Behavioral Development, 29*, 361–370.

Cohen, L. B. (2003). Commentary on Part I: Unresolved issues in infant categorization. In D. H. Rakison & L. M. Oakes (Eds.), *Early category and concept development: Making sense of the blooming, buzzing confusion* (pp. 193–209). New York: Oxford University Press.

Cohen, L. B. (2010). A bottom-up approach to infant perception and cognition: A summary of evidence and discussion of issues. In S. P. Johnson (Ed.), *Neoconstructivism: The new science of cognitive development* (pp. 335–346). New York: Oxford University Press.

Cohen, L. B., & Brunt, J. (2009). Early word learning and categorization: Methodological issues and recent empirical evidence. In J. Colombo, P. McCardle, & L. Freund (Eds.), *Infant pathways to language: Methods, models, and research disorders* (pp. 245–266). New York: Psychology Press.

Cohen, L. B., & Cashon, C. H. (2006). Infant cognition. In D. Kuhn & R. Siegler (Eds.), *Handbook of child psychology: Vol. 2. Cognition, perception, and language* (6th ed., pp. 214–251). Hoboken, NJ: Wiley.

Cohen, L. B., & Marks, K. S. (2002). How infants process addition and subtraction events. *Developmental Science, 5*, 186–201.

Cohen, N. J., & Farnia, F. (2011). Social-emotional adjustment and attachment in children adopted from China: Processes and predictors of change. *International*

Journal of Behavioral Development, 35, 67–77.

Cohen, N. J., Lojkasek, M., Yaghoub Zadeh, Z., Pugliese, M., & Kiefer, H. (2008). Children adopted from China: A longitudinal study of their growth and development. *Journal of Child Psychology and Psychiatry, 49*, 458–468.

Cohen, P., Kasen, S., Chen, H., Harmrk, C., & Gordon, K. (2003). Variations in patterns of developmental transitions in the emerging adulthood period. *Developmental Psychology, 39*, 657–669.

Cohen-Bendahan, C. C. C., van de Beek, C., & Berenbaum, S. A. (2005). Prenatal sex hormones effects on child and adult sex-typed behavior: Methods and findings. *Neuroscience and Biobehavioral Reviews, 29*, 353–384.

Cohn, J. F., & Tronick, E. Z. (1987). Mother–infant face-to-face interaction: The sequencing of dyadic states at 3, 6, and 9 months. *Developmental Psychology, 23*, 68–77.

Coie, J. D., Dodge, K. A., & Coppotelli, H. (1982). Dimensions and types of social status: A cross-age perspective. *Developmental Psychology, 18*, 557–570.

Colby, A., & Damon, W. (1992). *Some do care: Contemporary lives of moral commitment.* New York: Free Press.

Colby, A., & Kohlberg, L. (1987). *The measurement of moral judgment: Theoretical foundations and research validation* (Vol. 1). Cambridge, UK: Cambridge University Press.

Colby, A., Kohlberg, L., Gibbs, J. C., & Lieberman, M. (1983). A longitudinal study of moral judgment. *Monographs of the Society for Research in Child Development, 48*(1–2, Serial No. 200).

Coldwell, J., Pike, A., & Dunn, J. (2008). Maternal differential treatment and child adjustment: A multi-informant approach. *Social Development, 17*, 596–612.

Cole, C., & Winsler, A. (2010). Protecting children from exposure to lead: Old problem, new data, and new policy needs. *Social Policy Report of the Society for Research in Child Development, 24*(1).

Cole, D. A., Martin, J. M., Peeke, L. A., Seroczynski, A. D., & Fier, J. (1999). Children's over- and underestimation of academic competence: A longitudinal study of gender differences, depression, and anxiety. *Child Development, 70*, 459–473.

Cole, D. A., Maxwell, S. E., Martin, J. M., Peek, L. G., Seroczynski, A. D., & Tram, J. M. (2001). The development of multiple domains of child and adolescent self-concept: A cohort sequential longitudinal design. *Child Development, 72*, 1723–1746.

Cole, E., & Daniel, J. (Ed.). (2005). *Featuring females: Feminist analyses of media.* Washington, DC: American Psychological Association.

Cole, M. (1990). Cognitive development and formal schooling: The evidence from cross-cultural research. In L. C. Moll (Ed.), *Vygotsky and education* (pp. 89–110). New York: Cambridge University Press.

Cole, M. (2006). Culture and cognitive development in phylogenetic, historical, and ontogenetic perspective. In R. M. Lerner (Ed.), *Handbook of child psychology: Vol. 1. Theoretical models of human development* (6th ed., pp. 636–685). Hoboken, NJ: Wiley.

Cole, P. M., Armstrong, L. M., & Pemberton, C. K. (2010). The role of language in the development of emotion regulation. In S. D. Calkins & M. A. Bell (Eds.), *Child development at the intersection of emotion and cognition* (pp. 59–77). Washington, DC: American Psychological Association.

Cole, P. M., Bruschi, C. J., & Tamang, B. L. (2002). Cultural differences in children's emotional reactions to difficult situations. *Child Development, 73*, 983–996.

Cole, P. M., & Tamang, B. L. (1998). Nepali children's ideas about emotional displays in hypothetical challenges. *Developmental Psychology, 34*, 640–646.

Cole, P. M., Tamang, B. L., & Shrestha, S. (2006). Cultural variations in the socialization of young children's anger and shame. *Child Development, 77*, 1237–1251.

Cole, T. J. (2000). Secular trends in growth. *Proceedings of the Nutrition Society, 59*, 317–324.

Coley, R. L., Morris, J. E., & Hernandez, D. (2004). Out-of-school care and problem behavior trajectories among low-income adolescents: Individual, family, and neighborhood characteristics as added risks. *Child Development, 75*, 948–965.

Coley, R. L., Votruba-Drzal, E., & Schindler, H. S. (2009). Fathers' and mothers' parenting predicting and responding to adolescent sexual risk behaviors. *Child Development, 80*, 808–827.

Collaer, M. L., & Hill, E. M. (2006). Large sex difference in adolescents on a timed line judgment task: Attentional contributors and task relationship to mathematics. *Perception, 35*, 561–572.

Collins, M. A., & Amabile, T. M. (1999). Motivation and creativity. In R. J. Sternberg (Ed.), *Handbook of creativity* (pp. 297–312). Cambridge, UK: Cambridge University Press.

Collins, R. L. (2011). Content analysis of gender roles in media: Where are we now and where should we go? *Sex Roles, 64*, 290–298.

Collins, W. A., & Laursen, B. (2004). Parent–adolescent relationships and influences. In R. M. Lerner & L. Steinberg (Eds.), *Handbook of adolescent psychology* (2nd ed., pp. 331–361). New York: Wiley.

Collins, W. A., Maccoby, E. E., Steinberg, L. D., Hetherington, E. M., & Bornstein, M. H. (2000). Contemporary research on parenting: The case for nature and nurture. *American Psychologist, 55*, 218–232.

Collins, W. A., & Madsen, S. D. (2006). Personal relationships in adolescence and early adulthood. In A. L. Vangelisti & D. Perlman (Eds.), *Cambridge handbook of personal relationships* (pp. 191–209). New York: Cambridge University Press.

Collins, W. A., Madsen, S. D., & Susman-Stillman, A. (2002). Parenting during middle childhood. In M. H. Bornstein (Ed.), *Handbook of parenting: Vol. 1. Children and parenting* (2nd ed., pp. 73–101). Mahwah, NJ: Erlbaum.

Collins, W. A., & Van Dulmen, M. (2006a). Friendships and romantic relationships in emerging adulthood: Continuities and discontinuities. In J. J. Arnett & J. Tanner (Eds.), *Emerging adults in America: Coming of age in the 21st century* (pp. 219–234). Washington, DC: American Psychological Association.

Collins, W. A., & Van Dulmen, M. (2006b). "The course of true love(s)...": Origins and pathways in the development of romantic relationships. In A. Booth & A. Crouter (Eds.), *Romance and sex in adolescence and emerging adulthood: Risks and opportunities* (pp. 63–86). Mahwah, NJ: Erlbaum.

Collins, W. A., Welsh, D. P., & Furman, W. (2009). Adolescent romantic relationships. *Annual Review of Psychology, 60*, 631–652.

Collins, W. K., & Steinberg, L. (2006). Adolescent development in interpersonal context. In N. Eisenberg (Ed.), *Handbook of child psychology: Vol. 3. Social, emotional, and personality development* (6th ed., pp. 1003–1067). Hoboken, NJ: Wiley.

Colman, R. A., Hardy, S. A., Albert, M., Raffaelli, M., & Crockett, L. (2006). Early predictors of self-regulation in middle childhood. *Infant and Child Development, 15*, 421–437.

Colom, R., Escorial, S., Shih, P. C., & Privado, J. (2007). Fluid intelligence, memory span, and temperament difficulties predict academic performance of young adolescents. *Personality and Individual Differences, 42*, 1503–1514.

Colombo, J. (2002). Infant attention grows up: The emergence of a developmental cognitive neuroscience perspective. *Current Directions in Psychological Science, 11*, 196–199.

Colombo, J., Shaddy, D. J., Richman, W. A., Maikranz, J. M., & Blaga, O. M. (2004). The developmental course of habituation in infancy and preschool outcome. *Infancy, 5*, 1–38.

Colson, E. R., Rybin, D. R., Smith, L. A., Colton, T., Lister, G., & Corwin, M. J. (2009). Trends and factors associated with infant sleeping position: The National Infant Sleep Position Study, 1993–2007. *Archives of Pediatric and Adolescent Medicine, 163*, 1122–1128.

Coltrane, S. (1996). *Family man.* New York: Oxford University Press.

Commission on Adolescent Suicide Prevention. (2005). Targeted youth suicide prevention programs. In D. L. Evans, E. B. Foa, R. E. Gur, H. Hending, & C. P. O'Brien (Eds.), *Treating and preventing adolescent mental health disorders: What we know and what we don't know* (pp. 463–469). New York: Oxford University Press.

Comstock, G., & Scharrer, E. (2006). Media and popular culture. In K. A. Renninger & I. E. Sigel (Eds.), *Handbook of child psychology: Vol. 4. Child psychology in practice* (6th ed., pp. 817–863). Hoboken, NJ: Wiley.

Comunian, A. L., & Gielen, U. P. (2000). Sociomoral reflection and prosocial and antisocial behavior: Two Italian studies. *Psychological Reports, 87*, 161–175.

Comunian, A. L., & Gielen, U. P. (2006). Promotion of moral judgment maturity through stimulation of social role-taking and social reflection: An Italian intervention study. *Journal of Moral Education, 35*, 51–69.

Conboy, B. T., & Thal, D. J. (2006). Ties between the lexicon and grammar: Cross-sectional and longitudinal studies of bilingual toddlers. *Child Development, 77*, 712–735.

Conger, K. J., Stocker, C., & McGuire, S. (2009). Sibling socialization: The effects of stressful life events and experiences. In L. Kramer & K. J. Conger (Eds.), *Siblings as agents of socialization: New directions for child and adolescent development* (No. 126, pp. 44–60). San Francisco: Jossey-Bass.

Conger, R. D., & Conger, K. J. (2002). Resilience in Midwestern families: Selected findings from the first decade of a prospective, longitudinal study. *Journal of Marriage and the Family, 64*, 361–373.

Conger, R. D., & Donnellan, M. B. (2007). An interactionist perspective on the socioeconomic context of human development. *Annual Review of Psychology, 58*, 175–199.

Connell, M. W., Sheridan, K., & Gardner, H. (2003). On abilities and domains. In R. J. Sternberg & E. Grigorenko (Eds.), *Perspectives on the psychology of abilities, competencies, and expertise* (pp. 126–155). New York: Cambridge University Press.

Conner, D. B., & Cross, D. R. (2003). Longitudinal analysis of the presence, efficacy, and stability of maternal scaffolding during informal problem-solving interactions. *British Journal of Developmental Psychology, 21*, 315–334.

Connolly, J., Craig, W., Goldberg, A., & Pepler, D. (2004). Mixed-gender groups, dating, and romantic relationships in early adolescence. *Journal of Research on Adolescence, 14*, 185–207.

Connolly, J. A., & Doyle, A. B. (1984). Relations of social fantasy play to social competence in preschoolers. *Developmental Psychology, 20*, 797–806.

Connolly, J. A., & Goldberg, A. (1999). Romantic relationships in adolescence: The role of friends and peers in their emergence and development. In W. Furman, B. B. Brown, & C. Feiring (Eds.), *The development of romantic relationships in adolescence* (pp. 266–290). Cambridge, UK: Cambridge University Press.

Conti-Ramsden, G., & Pérez-Pereira, M. (1999). Conversational interactions between mothers and their infants who are congenitally blind, have low vision, or are sighted. *Journal of Visual Impairment and Blindness, 93*, 691–703.

Conway, A. R. A., Kane, M. J., & Engle, R. W. (2003). Working memory capacity and its relation to general intelligence. *Trends in Cognitive Sciences, 7*, 547–552.

Conway, L. (2007, April 5). Drop the Barbie: Ken Zucker's reparatist treatment of gender-variant children. *Trans News Updates.* Retrieved from ai.eecs.umich.edu/people/conway/TS/News/Drop%20the%20Barbie.htm

Conyers, C., Miltenberger, R., Maki, A., Barenz, R., Jurgens, M., Sailer, A., et al. (2004). A comparison of response cost and differential reinforcement of other behaviors to reduce disruptive behavior in a preschool classroom. *Journal of Applied Behavior Analysis, 37*, 411–415.

Cook, C. R., Williams, K. R., Guerra, N. G., & Kim, T. E. (2010). Variability in the prevalence of bullying and victimization: A cross-national and methodological analysis. In S. R. Jimerson, S. M. Swearer, & D. L. Espelage (Eds.), *Handbook of bullying in schools: An international perspective* (pp. 347–362). New York: Routledge.

Cookston, J. T., Braver, S. L., Griffin, W. A., De Lusé, S. R., & Miles, J. C. (2006). Effects of the Dads for Life intervention on interparental conflict and coparenting in the two years after divorce. *Family Process, 46*, 123–137.

Cooper, C., Sayer, A. A., & Dennison, E. M. (2006). The developmental environment: Clinical perspectives on effects on the musculoskeletal system. In P. Gluckman & M. Hanson (Eds.), *Developmental origins of health and disease* (pp. 392–405). Cambridge, UK: Cambridge University Press.

Cooper, C. R. (1998). *The weaving of maturity: Cultural perspectives on adolescent development.* New York: Oxford University Press.

Cooper, C. R., Dominguez, E., & Rosas, S. (2005). Soledad's dream: How immigrant children bridge their multiple worlds and build pathways to college. In C. R. Cooper, C. T. Garcia Coll, W. T. Bartko, H. Davis, & C. Chatman (Eds.), *Developmental pathways through middle childhood: Rethinking contexts and diversity as resources* (pp. 235–260). Mahwah, NJ: Erlbaum.

Cooper, R., & Huh, C. R. (2008). Improving academic possibilities of students of color during the middle school to high school transition: Conceptual and strategic considerations in a U.S. context. In J. K. Asamen, M. L. Ellis, & G. L. Berry (Eds.), *Sage handbook of child development, multiculturalism, and media* (pp. 143–162). Thousand Oaks, CA: Sage.

Coplan, R. J., & Arbeau, K. A. (2008). The stresses of a "brave new world": Shyness and school adjustment in kindergarten. *Journal of Research in Childhood Education, 22*, 377–389.

Coplan, R. J., Arbeau, K. A., & Armer, M. (2008). "Don't fret, be supportive!" Maternal characteristics linking child shyness to psychosocial and school adjustment in kindergarten. *Journal of Abnormal Child Psychology, 36*, 359–371.

Coplan, R. J., & Armer, M. (2007). A "multitude" of solitude: A closer look at social withdrawal and nonsocial play in early childhood. *Child Development Perspectives, 1*, 26–32.

Coplan, R. J., Barber, A. M., & Lagacé-Séquin, D. G. (1999). The role of child temperament as a predictor of early literacy and numeracy skills in preschoolers. *Early Childhood Research Quarterly, 14*, 537–553.

Coplan, R. J., Gavinsky-Molina, M. H., Lagace-Seguin, D., & Wichmann, C. (2001). When girls versus boys play alone: Nonsocial play and adjustment in kindergarten. *Developmental Psychology, 37*, 464–474.

Coplan, R. J., Prakash, K., O'Neil, K., & Armer, M. (2004). Do we "want" to play? Distinguishing between conflicted shyness and social disinterest in early childhood. *Developmental Psychology, 40*, 244–258.

Copple, C., & Bredekamp, S. (2009). *Developmentally appropriate practice in early childhood programs* (3rd ed.). Washington, DC: National Association for the Education of Young Children.

Corenblum, B. (2003). What children remember about ingroup and outgroup peers: Effects of stereotypes on children's processing of information about group members. *Journal of Experimental Child Psychology, 86*, 32–66.

Cornish, A. M., McMahon, C. A., Ungerer, J. A., Barnett, B., Kowalenko, N., & Tennant, C. (2005). Postnatal depression and infant cognitive and motor development in the second postnatal year: The impact of depression chronicity and infant gender. *Infant Behavior and Development, 28*, 407–417.

Cornwell, A. C., & Feigenbaum, P. (2006). Sleep biological rhythms in normal infants and those at high risk for SIDS. *Chronobiology International, 23*, 935–961.

Costello, B. J., & Dunaway, R. G. (2003). Egotism and delinquent behavior. *Journal of Interpersonal Violence, 18, 572–590.*

Costos, D., Ackerman, R., & Paradis, L. (2002). Recollections of menarche: Communication between mothers and daughters regarding menstruation. *Sex Roles, 46,* 49–59.

Côté, J. E. (2009). Identity formation and self-development in adolescence. In R. M. Lerner & L. Steinberg (Eds.), *Handbook of adolescent psychology: Vol. 1. Individual bases of adolescent development* (3rd ed., pp. 266–304). Hoboken, NJ: Wiley.

Côté, S. M., Vaillancourt, T., Barker, E. D., Nagin, D., & Tremblay, R. E. (2007). The joint development of physical and indirect aggression: Predictors of continuity and change during childhood. *Development and Psychopathology, 19,* 37–55.

Coulton, C. J., Crampton, D. S., Irwin, M., Spilsbury, J. C., & Korbin, J. E. (2007). How neighborhoods influence child maltreatment: A review of the literature and alternative pathways. *Child Abuse and Neglect, 31,* 1117–1142.

Courage, M. L., & Howe, M. L. (1998). The ebb and flow of infant attentional preferences: Evidence for long-term recognition memory in 3-month-olds. *Journal of Experimental Child Psychology, 18,* 98–106.

Courage, M. L., & Howe, M. L. (2010). To watch or not to watch: Infants and toddlers in a brave new electronic world. *Developmental Review, 30,* 101–115.

Courage, M. L., Reynolds, G. D., & Richards, J. E. (2006). Infants' attention to patterned stimuli: Developmental change from 3 to 12 months of age. *Child Development, 77,* 680–695.

Courchesne, E., Carper, R., & Akshoomoff, N. (2003). Evidence of brain overgrowth in the first year of life in autism. *Journal of the American Medical Association, 290,* 337–344.

Couturier, J. L., & Lock, J. (2006). Denial and minimization in adolescents with anorexia nervosa. *International Journal of Eating Disorders, 39,* 212–216.

Covington, C. Y., Nordstrom-Klee, B., Ager, J., Sokol, R., & Delaney-Black, V. (2002). Birth to age 7 growth of children prenatally exposed to drugs: A prospective cohort study. *Neurotoxicology and Teratology, 24,* 489–496.

Cowan, C. P., & Cowan, P. A. (1997). Working with couples during stressful transitions. In S. Dreman (Ed.), *The family on the threshold of the 21st century* (pp. 17–47). Mahwah, NJ: Erlbaum.

Cowan, C. P., & Cowan, P. A. (2000). *When partners become parents.* Mahwah, NJ: Erlbaum.

Cowan, N. (2001). The magical number 4 in short-term memory: A reconsideration of mental storage capacity. *Behavioral and Brain Sciences, 24,* 87–185.

Cowan, N. (2005). *Working memory capacity.* Hove, UK: Psychology Press.

Cowan, N., & Alloway, T. (2009). Development of working memory in childhood. In M. L. Courage & N. Cowan (Eds.), *Development of memory in infancy and childhood* (pp. 303–342). Hove, UK: Psychology Press.

Cowan, P. A., & Cowan, C. P. (2004). From family relationships to peer rejection to antisocial behavior in middle childhood. In J. B. Kupersmidt & K. A. Dodge (Eds.), *Children's peer relations: From development to intervention* (pp. 159–177). Washington, DC: American Psychological Association.

Cox, M. J., Owen, M. T., Henderson, V. K., & Margand, N. A. (1992). Prediction of infant–father and infant–mother attachment. *Developmental Psychology, 28,* 474–483.

Cox, M., & Littlejohn, K. (1995). Children's use of converging obliques in their perspective drawings. *Educational Psychology, 15,* 127–139.

Cox, S. M., Hopkins, J., & Hans, S. L. (2000). Attachment in preterm infants and their mothers: Neonatal risk status and maternal representations. *Infant Mental Health Journal, 21,* 464–480.

Coyl, D. D., Newland, L. A., & Freeman, H. (2010). Predicting preschoolers' attachment security from parenting behaviours, parents' attachment relationships and their use of social support. *Early Child Development and Care, 180,* 499–512.

Coyle, T. R., & Bjorklund, D. F. (1997). Age differences in, and consequences of, multiple- and variable-strategy use on a multi-trial sort-recall task. *Developmental Psychology, 33,* 372–380.

Coyne, S. M., Robinson, S. L., & Nelson, D. A. (2010). Does reality backbite? Verbal and relational aggression in reality television programs. *Journal of Broadcasting and Electronic Media, 54,* 282–298.

Crago, M. B., Annahatak, B., & Ningiuruvik, L. (1993). Changing patterns of language socialization in Inuit homes. *Anthropology and Education Quarterly, 24,* 205–223.

Craig, C. M., & Lee, D. N. (1999). Neonatal control of sucking pressure: Evidence for an intrinsic tau-guide. *Experimental Brain Research, 124,* 371–382.

Craig, W. M., Pepler, D., & Atlas, R. (2000). Observations of bullying in the playground and in the classroom. *School Psychology International, 21,* 22–36.

Crain, W. (2005). *Theories of development* (5th ed.). Upper Saddle River, NJ: Prentice-Hall.

Crair, M. C., Gillespie, D. C., & Stryker, M. P. (1998). The role of visual experience in the development of columns in the cat visual cortex. *Science, 279,* 566–570.

Crane, D. R., Ngai, S. W., Larson, J. H., & Hafen, M., Jr. (2005). The influence of family functioning and parent–adolescent acculturation on North American Chinese adolescent outcomes. *Family Relations, 54,* 400–410.

Cratty, B. J. (1986). *Perceptual and motor development in infants and children* (3rd ed.). Englewood Cliffs, NJ: Prentice-Hall.

Crawford, N. (2003, September). Understanding children's atypical gender behavior. *APA Monitor,* p. 40.

Creasey, G. L., Jarvis, P. A., & Berk, L. E. (1998). Play and social competence. In O. N. Saracho & B. Spodek (Eds.), *Multiple perspectives on play in early childhood education* (pp. 116–143). Albany: State University of New York Press.

Crick, N. R., Casas, J. F., & Nelson, D. A. (2002). Toward a more comprehensive understanding of peer maltreatment: Studies of relational victimization. *Current Directions in Psychological Science, 11,* 98–101.

Crick, N. R., & Dodge, K. A. (1994). A review and reformulation of social information-processing mechanisms in children's social adjustment. *Psychological Bulletin, 115,* 74–101.

Crick, N. R., & Nelson, D. A. (2002). Relational and physical victimization within friendships: Nobody told me there'd be friends like these. *Journal of Abnormal Child Psychology, 30,* 599–607.

Crick, N. R., Ostrov, J. M., Appleyard, K., Jansen, E., & Casas, J. F. (2004). Relational aggression in early childhood: You can't come to my birthday party unless. . . . In M. Putallaz & K. Bierman (Eds.), *Aggression, antisocial behavior, and violence among girls: A developmental perspective* (pp. 71–89). New York: Guilford.

Crick, N. R., Ostrov, J. M., Burr, J. E., Cullerton-Sen, C., Jansen-Yeh, E., & Ralston, P. (2006). A longitudinal study of relational and physical aggression in preschool. *Journal of Applied Developmental Psychology, 27,* 254–268.

Crick, N. R., Ostrov, J. M., & Werner, N. E. (2006). A longitudinal study of relational aggression, physical aggression, and social-psychological adjustment. *Journal of Abnormal Child Psychology, 34,* 131–142.

Criss, M. M., & Shaw, D. S. (2005). Sibling relationships as contexts for delinquency training in low income families. *Journal of Family Psychology, 19,* 592–600.

Crittenden, P. (2000). A dynamic-maturational approach to continuity and change in patterns of attachment. In P. Crittenden & A. Claussen (Eds.), *The organization of attachment relationships* (pp. 343–358). New York: Cambridge University Press.

Crockenberg, S. C., & Leerkes, E. (2003a). Infant negative emotionality, caregiving, and family relationships. In A. C. Crouter & A. Booth (Eds.), *Children's influence on family dynamics* (pp. 57–78). Mahwah, NJ: Erlbaum.

Crockenberg, S. C., & Leerkes, E. M. (2003b). Parental acceptance, postpartum depression, and maternal sensitivity: Mediating and moderating processes. *Journal of Family Psychology, 17,* 80–93.

Crockenberg, S. C., & Leerkes, E. M. (2004). Infant and maternal behaviors regulate infant reactivity to novelty at 6 months. *Developmental Psychology, 40,* 1123–1132.

Crockett, L. J., Raffaelli, M., & Shen, Y.-L. (2006). Linking self-regulation and risk proneness to risky sexual behavior: Pathways through peer pressure and early substance use. *Journal of Research on Adolescence, 16,* 503–525.

Crosno, R., Kirkpatrick, M., & Elder, G. H., Jr. (2004). Intergenerational bonding in school: The behavioral and contextual correlates of student–teacher relationships. *Sociology of Education, 77,* 60–81.

Crouch, J. L., Skowronski, J. J., Milner, J. S., & Harris, B. (2008). Parental responses to infant crying: The influence of child physical abuse risk and hostile priming. *Child Abuse and Neglect, 32,* 702–710.

Crouter, A. C., & Head, M. R. (2002). Parental monitoring and knowledge of children. In M. H. Bornstein (Ed.), *Handbook of parenting: Vol. 3. Being and becoming a parent* (2nd ed., pp. 461–483). Mahwah, NJ: Erlbaum.

Crouter, A. C., Whiteman, S. D., McHale, S. M., & Osgood, D. W. (2007). Development of gender attitude traditionality across middle childhood and adolescence. *Child Development, 78,* 911–926.

Crowe, H. P., & Zeskind, P. S. (1992). Psychophysiological and perceptual responses to infant cries varying in pitch: Comparison of adults with low and high scores on the child abuse potential inventory. *Child Abuse and Neglect, 16,* 19–29.

Crowley, K., Callanan, M. A., Tenenbaum, H. R., & Allen, E. (2001). Parents explain more often to boys than to girls during shared scientific thinking. *Psychological Science, 12,* 258–261.

Crystal, D. S., Killen, M., & Ruck, M. D. (2008). It is who you know that counts: Intergroup contact and judgments about race-based exclusion. *British Journal of Developmental Psychology, 26,* 51–70.

Crystal, D. S., Killen, M., & Ruck, M. D. (2010). Fair treatment by authorities is related to children's and adolescents' evaluations of interracial exclusion. *Applied Developmental Science, 14,* 125–136.

Csibra, G. (2010). Recognizing communicative intentions in infancy. *Mind and Language, 25,* 141–168.

Cuijpers, P. (2002). Effective ingredients of school-based drug prevention programs: A systematic review. *Addictive Behaviors, 27,* 1009–1023.

Culbertson, F. M. (1997). Depression and gender: An international review. *American Psychologist, 52,* 25–51.

Cummings, E. M., Goeke-Morey, M. C., & Papp, L. M. (2004). Everyday marital conflict and child aggression. *Journal of Abnormal Child Psychology, 32,* 191–202.

Cummings, E. M., & Merrilees, C. E. (2010). Identifying the dynamic processes underlying links between marital conflict and child adjustment. In M. S. Schulz, M. K. Pruett, P. K. Kerig, & R. D. Parke (Eds.), *Strengthening couple relationships for optimal child development* (pp. 27–40). Washington, DC: American Psychological Association.

Cunningham, A. E., & Stanovich, K. E. (1998, Spring/Summer). What reading does for the mind. *American Educator,* 8–15.

Curby, T. W., LoCasale-Crouch, J., Konold, T. R., Pianta, R. C., Howes, C., Burchinal, M., et al. (2009). The relations of observed pre-K classroom quality profiles to children's achievement and social competence. *Early Education and Development, 20,* 346–372.

Cutrona, C. E., Hessling, R. M., Bacon, P. L., & Russell, D. W. (1998). Predictors and correlates of continuing involvement with the baby's father among adolescent mothers. *Journal of Family Psychology, 12,* 369–387.

Cutter, W. J., Daly, E. M., Robertson, D. M. W., Chitnis, X. A., van Amelsvoort, T. A. M. J., & Simmons, A. (2006). Influence of X chromosome and hormones on human brain development: A magnetic resonance imaging and proton magnetic resonance spectroscopy study of Turner syndrome. *Biological Psychiatry, 59,* 273–283.

Cvencek, D., Meltzoff, A. N., & Greenwald, A. G. (2011). Math–gender stereotypes in elementary school children. *Child Development, 82,* 766–779.

Cyr, M., McDuff, P., & Wright, J. (2006). Prevalence and predictors of dating violence among adolescent female victims of child sexual abuse. *Journal of Interpersonal Violence, 21,* 1000–1017.

Dabrowska, E. (2000). From formula to schema: The acquisition of English questions. *Cognitive Linguistics, 11,* 1–20.

Dahl, R. E., & Lewin, D. S. (2002). Pathways to adolescent healthy sleep regulation and behavior. *Journal of Adolescent Health, 31,* 175–184.

Dahlberg, L. L., & Simon, T. R. (2006). Predicting and preventing youth violence: Developmental pathways and risk. In L. L. Dahlberg & T. R. Simon (Eds.), *Preventing violence: Research and evidence-based intervention strategies* (pp. 97–124). Washington, DC: American Psychological Association.

Dales, L., Hammer, S. J., & Smith, N. J. (2001). Time trends in autism and MMR immunization coverage in California. *Journal of the American Medical Association, 285,* 1183–1185.

Daley, T. C., Whaley, S. E., Sigman, M. D., Espinosa, M. P., & Neumann, C. (2003). IQ on the rise: The Flynn effect in rural Kenyan children. *Psychological Science, 14,* 215–219.

Damasio, A. R. (1994). *Descartes' error: Emotion, reason, and the human brain.* New York: Putnam.

Damon, W. (1977). *The social world of the child.* San Francisco: Jossey-Bass.

Damon, W. (1988). *The moral child.* New York: Free Press.

Damon, W. (1990). Self-concept, adolescent. In R. M. Lerner, A. C. Petersen, & J. Brooks-Gunn (Eds.), *The encyclopedia of adolescence* (Vol. 2, pp. 67–91). New York: Garland.

Damon, W. (1995). *Greater expectations: Overcoming the culture of indulgence in America's homes and schools.* New York: Free Press.

Damon, W. (2004). *The moral advantage: How to succeed in business by doing the right thing.* San Francisco: Berrett-Koehler.

Damon, W., & Hart, D. (1988). *Self-understanding in childhood and adolescence.* New York: Cambridge University Press.

Daniels, D. H. (1998). Age differences in concepts of self-esteem. *Merrill-Palmer Quarterly, 44,* 234–259.

Daniels, D. H., Kalkman, D. L., & McCombs, B. L. (2001). Young children's perspectives on learning and teacher practices in different classroom contexts: Implications for motivation. *Early Education and Development, 12,* 253–273.

Daniels, E., & Leaper, C. (2006). A longitudinal investigation of sport participation, peer acceptance, and self-esteem among adolescent girls and boys. *Sex Roles, 55,* 875–880.

Dannemiller, J. L., & Stephens, B. R. (1988). A critical test of infant pattern preference models. *Child Development, 59,* 210–216.

Danziger, S., & Ratner, D. (2010). Labor market outcomes and the transition to adulthood. *Future of Children, 20,* 133–158.

Dapretto, M., & Bjork, E. L. (2000). The development of word retrieval abilities in the second year and its relation to early vocabulary growth. *Child Development, 71,* 635–648.

Darling-Hammond, L. (2010). *The flat world and education: How America's commitment to equity will determine our future.* New York: Teachers College Press.

Darroch, J. E., Frost, J. J., & Singh, S. (2001). *Teenage sexual and reproductive behavior in developed countries: Can more progress be made?* New York: Alan Guttmacher Institute.

Darwin, C. (1877). Biographical sketch of an infant. *Mind, 2,* 285–294.

Das, D. A., Grimmer, D. A., Sparnon, A. L., McRae, S. E., & Thomas, B. H. (2005). The efficacy of playing a virtual reality game in modulating pain for children with acute burn injuries: A randomized controlled trial. *BMC Pediatrics, 5*(1), 1–10.

D'Augelli, A. R. (2002). Mental health problems among lesbian, gay, and bisexual youths ages 14 to 21. *Clinical Child Psychology and Psychiatry, 7,* 433–456.

D'Augelli, A. R. (2006). Developmental and contextual factors and mental health

among lesbian, gay, and bisexual youths. In A. M. Omoto & H. S. Howard (Eds.), *Sexual orientation and mental health: Examining identity and development in lesbian, gay, and bisexual people* (pp. 37–53). Washington, DC: American Psychological Association.

D'Augelli, A. R., Grossman, A. H., Salter, N. P., Vasey, J. J., Starks, M. T., & Sinclair, K. O. (2005). Predicting the suicide attempts of lesbian, gay, and bisexual youth. *Suicide and Life-Threatening Behavior, 35,* 646–660.

D'Augelli, A. R., Grossman, A. H., & Starks, M. T. (2008). Families of gay, lesbian, and bisexual youth: What do parents and siblings know and how do they react? *Journal of GBLT Family Studies, 4,* 95–115.

David, K. M., & Murphy, B. C. (2007). Interparental conflict and preschoolers' peer relations: The moderating roles of temperament and gender. *Social Development, 16,* 1–23.

Davidson, R. J. (1994). Asymmetric brain function, affective style, and psychopathology: The role of early experience and plasticity. *Development and Psychopathology, 6,* 741–758.

Davies, J. (2008). Differential teacher positive and negative interactions with male and female pupils in the primary school setting. *Educational and Child Psychology, 25,* 17–26.

Davies, P. T., & Lindsay, L. L. (2004). Interparental conflict and adolescent adjustment: Why does gender moderate early adolescent vulnerability? *Journal of Family Psychology, 18,* 160–170.

Davis, K. F., Parker, K. P., & Montgomery, G. L. (2004). Sleep in infants and young children. Part 1: Normal sleep. *Journal of Pediatric Health Care, 18,* 65–71.

Davis-Kean, P. E. (2005). The influence of parent education and family income on child achievement: The indirect role of parental expectations and the home environment. *Journal of Family Psychology, 19,* 294–304.

Dawson, G., Ashman, S. B., Panagiotides, H., Hessl, D., Self, J., Yamada, E., & Embry, L. (2003). Preschool outcomes of children of depressed mothers: Role of maternal behavior, contextual risk, and children's brain activity. *Child Development, 74,* 1158–1175.

Dawson, T. L. (2002). New tools, new insights: Kohlberg's moral judgment stages revisited. *International Journal of Behavioral Development, 26,* 154–166.

De Brauwer, J., & Fias, W. (2009). A longitudinal study of children's performance on simple multiplication and division problems. *Developmental Psychology, 45,* 1480–1496.

de Bruyn, E. H. (2005). Role strain, engagement and academic achievement in early adolescence. *Educational Studies, 31,* 15–27.

de Bruyn, E. H., & Cillessen, A. H. N. (2006). Popularity in early adolescence: Prosocial and antisocial subtypes. *Journal of Adolescent Research, 21,* 607–627.

De Corte, E., & Verschaffel, L. (2006). Mathematical thinking and learning. In K. A. Renninger & I. E. Sigel (Eds.), *Handbook of child psychology: Vol. 4. Child psychology in practice* (6th ed., pp. 103–152). Hoboken, NJ: Wiley.

De Goede, I. H. A., Branje, S. J. T., & Meeus, W. H. J. (2009). Developmental changes and gender differences in adolescents' perceptions of friendships. *Journal of Adolescence, 32,* 1105–1123.

de Haan, M., & Johnson, M. H. (2003). Mechanisms and theories of brain development. In M. de Haan & M. H. Johnson (Eds.), *The cognitive neuroscience of development* (pp. 1–18). Hove, UK: Psychology Press.

de León, L. (2000). The emergent participant: Interactive patterns in the socialization of Tzotzil (Mayan) infants. *Journal of Linguistic Anthropology, 8,* 131–161.

De Lisi, R., & Gallagher, A. M. (1991). Understanding gender stability and constancy in Argentinean children. *Merrill-Palmer Quarterly, 37,* 483–502.

de Ribaupierre, A., & Lecerf, T. (2006). Relationships between working memory and intelligence from a developmental perspective: Convergent evidence from a neo-Piagetian and a psychometric approach. *European Journal of Cognitive Psychology, 18,* 109–137.

de Rosnay, M., Copper, P. J., Tsigaras, N., & Murray, L. (2006). Transmission of social anxiety from mother to infant: An experimental study using a social referencing paradigm. *Behavior Research and Therapy, 44,* 1165–1175.

de Rosnay, M., & Hughes, C. (2006). Conversation and theory of mind: Do children talk their way to socio-cognitive understanding? *British Journal of Developmental Psychology, 24,* 7–37.

De Schipper, J. C., Tavecchio, L. W. C., van IJzendoorn, M. H., & van Zeijl, J. (2004). Goodness-of-fit in center day care: Relations of temperament, stability, and quality of care with the child's adjustment. *Early Childhood Research Quarterly, 19,* 257–272.

De Schipper, J. C., van IJzendoorn, M. H., & Tavecchio, L. W. C. (2004). Stability in center day care: Relations with children's well-being and problem behavior in day care. *Social Development, 13,* 531–550.

De Souza, E., Alberman, E., & Morris, J. K. (2009). Down syndrome and paternal age, a new analysis of case-control data collected in the 1960s. *American Journal of Medical Genetics, 149A,* 1205–1208.

de Villiers, J. G. (2000). Language and theory of mind: What are the developmental relationships? In S. Baron-Cohen, H. Tager-Flusberg, & D. J. Cohen (Eds.), *Understanding other minds: Perspectives from developmental cognitive neuroscience* (2nd ed.). Oxford: Oxford University Press.

de Villiers, J. G., & de Villiers, P. A. (1973). A cross-sectional study of the acquisition of grammatical morphemes in child speech. *Journal of Psycholinguistic Research, 2,* 267–278.

de Villiers, J. G., & de Villiers, P. A. (1999). Language development. In M. H. Bornstein & M. E. Lamb (Eds.), *Developmental psychology: An advanced textbook* (4th ed., pp. 313–373). Mahwah, NJ: Erlbaum.

de Villiers, J. G., & de Villiers, P. A. (2000). Linguistic determinism and the understanding of false beliefs. In P. Mitchell & K. J. Riggs (Eds.), *Children's reasoning and the mind* (pp. 87–99). Hove, UK: Psychology Press.

de Waal, F. B. M. (1996). *Good natured: The origins of right and wrong in humans and other animals.* Cambridge, MA: Harvard University Press.

de Waal, F. B. M. (2006). *Primates and philosophers: How morality evolved.* Princeton, NJ: Princeton University Press.

de Waal, F. B. M. (1993). Sex differences in chimpanzee (and human) behavior: A matter of social values? In M. Hechter, L. Nadel, & R. E. Michod (Eds.), *The

origin of values* (pp. 285–303). New York: Aldine de Gruyter.

de Waal, F. B. M. (2001). *Tree of origin.* Cambridge, MA: Harvard University Press.

de Weerd, A. W., & van den Bossche, A. S. (2003). The development of sleep during the first months of life. *Sleep Medicine Reviews, 7,* 179–191.

de Weerth, C., & Buitelaar, J. K. (2005). Physiological stress reactivity in human pregnancy—a review. *Neuroscience and Biobehavioral Reviews, 29,* 295–312.

De Wolff, M. S., & van IJzendoorn, M. H. (1997). Sensitivity and attachment: A meta-analysis on parental antecedents of infant attachment. *Child Development, 68,* 571–591.

Deák, G. O. (2000). Hunting the fox of word learning: Why "constraints" fail to capture it. *Developmental Review, 20,* 29–80.

Deák, G. O., Ray, S. D., & Brenneman, K. (2003). Children's perseverative appearance–reality errors are related to emerging language skills. *Child Development, 74,* 944–964.

Deák, G. O., Yen, L., & Pettit, J. (2001). By any other name: When will preschoolers produce several labels for a reference? *Journal of Child Language, 28,* 787–804.

Dearing, E., McCartney, K., & Taylor, B. A. (2006). Within-child associations between family income and externalizing and internalizing problems. *Developmental Psychology, 42,* 237–252.

Dearing, E., Wimer, C., Simpkins, S. D., Lund, T., Bouffard, S. M., Caronongan, P., & Kreider, H. (2009). Do neighborhood and home contexts help explain why low-income children miss opportunities to participate in activities outside of school? *Developmental Psychology, 45,* 1545–1562.

Deary, I. J. (2001). *g* and cognitive elements of information processing: An agnostic view. In R. J. Sternberg & E. L. Girgorenko (Eds.), *The general factor of intelligence: How general is it?* (pp. 417–479) Mahwah, NJ: Erlbaum.

Deary, I. J., Strand, S., Smith, P., & Fernandes, C. (2007). Intelligence and educational achievement. *Intelligence, 35,* 13–21.

Deary, I. J., Whiteman, M. C., Star, J. M., Whalley, L., & Fox, H. C. (2004). The impact of childhood intelligence on later life: Following up the Scottish Mental Surveys of 1932 and 1947. *Journal of Personality and Social Psychology, 86,* 130–147.

Deater-Deckard, K., Lansford, J. E., Dodge, K. A., Pettit, G. S., & Bates, J. E. (2003). The development of attitudes about physical punishment: An 8-year longitudinal study. *Journal of Family Psychology, 17,* 351–360.

Deater-Deckard, K., Pike, A., Petrill, S. A., Cutting, A. L., Hughes, C., & O'Connor, T. G. (2001). Nonshared environmental processes in social-emotional development: An observational study of identical twin differences in the preschool period. *Developmental Science, 4,* F1–F6.

DeBerry, K. M., Scarr, S., & Weinberg, R. (1996). Family racial socialization and ecological competence: Longitudinal assessments of African-American transracial adoptees. *Child Development, 67,* 2375–2399.

Debes, F., Budtz-Jorgensen, E., Weihe, P., White, R. F., & Grandjean, P. (2006). Impact of prenatal methylmercury exposure on neurobehavioral function at age 14 years. *Neurotoxicology and Teratology, 28,* 536–547.

DeBoer, T., Scott, L. S., & Nelson, C. A. (2007). Methods for acquiring and analyzing infant event-related potentials. In M. de Haan (Ed.), *Infant EEG and event-related potentials* (pp. 5–37). New York: Psychology Press.

DeCasper, A. J., & Spence, M. J. (1986). Prenatal maternal speech influences newborns' perception of speech sounds. *Infant Behavior and Development, 9,* 133–150.

Deci, E. L., & Ryan, R. M. (2002). Self-determination research: Reflections and future directions. In E. L. Deci & R. M. Ryan (Eds.), *Handbook of self-determination research* (pp. 431–441). Rochester, NY: University of Rochester Press.

DeGarmo, D. S., & Forgatch, M. S. (2005). Early development of delinquency within divorced families: Evaluating a randomized preventive intervention trial. *Developmental Science, 8,* 229–239.

Degirmencioglu, S. M., Urberg, K. A., Tolson, J. M., & Richard, P. (1998). Adolescent friendship networks: Continuity and change over the school year. *Merrill-Palmer Quarterly, 44,* 313–337.

Deissinger, T. (2007). "Making schools practical": Practice firms and their function in the full-time vocational school system in Germany. *Education + Training, 49,* 364–378.

Dekker, M. C., Ferdinand, R. F., van Lang, D. J., Bongers, I. L., van der Ende, J., & Verhulst, F. C. (2007). Developmental trajectories of depressive symptoms from early childhood to late adolescence: Gender differences and adult outcome. *Journal of Child Psychology and Psychiatry, 48,* 657–666.

Deković, M., Noom, M. J., & Meeus, W. (1997). Expectations regarding development during adolescence: Parent and adolescent perceptions. *Journal of Youth and Adolescence, 26,* 253–271.

Delgado-Gaitan, C. (1994). Socializing young children in Mexican-American families: An intergenerational perspective. In P. Greenfield & R. Cocking (Eds.), *Cross-cultural roots of minority child development* (p. 55–86). Hillsdale, NJ: Erlbaum.

DeLoache, J. S. (1987). Rapid change in symbolic functioning of very young children. *Science, 238,* 1556–1557.

DeLoache, J. S. (2000). Dual representation and children's use of scale models. *Child Development, 71,* 329–338.

DeLoache, J. S. (2002). The symbolmindedness of young children. In W. Hartup & R. A. Weinberg (Eds.), *Minnesota Symposia on Child Psychology* (Vol. 32, pp. 73–101). Mahwah, NJ: Erlbaum.

DeLoache, J. S., & Ganea, P. A. (2009). Symbol-based learning in infancy. In A. Woodward & A. Needham (Eds.), *Learning and the infant mind* (pp. 263–285). New York: Oxford University Press.

DeLoache, J. S., Pierroutsakos, S. L., Uttal, D. H., Rosengren, K. S., & Gottlieb, A. (1998). Grasping the nature of pictures. *Psychological Science, 9,* 205–210.

DeLoache, J. S., Uttal, D. H., & Rosengren, K. S. (2004). Scale errors offer evidence for a perception–action dissociation early in life. *Science, 304,* 1027–1029.

Delobel-Ayoub, M., Arnaud, C., White-Koning, M., Casper, C., Pierrat, V., Garel, M., et al. (2009). Behavioral problems and cognitive performance at 5 years of age after very preterm birth: The EPIPAGE Study. *Pediatrics, 123,* 1485–1492.

DeMarie-Dreblow, D., & Miller, P. H. (1988). The development of children's strategies for selective attention: Evidence for a transitional period. *Child Development, 59,* 1504–1513.

Demetriou, A., Christou, C., Spanoudis, G., & Platsidou, M. (2002). The development of mental processing: Efficiency, working memory, and thinking. *Monographs of the Society for Research in Child Development, 67*(1, Serial No. 268).

Demetriou, A., Efklides, A., Papadaki, M., Papantoniou, G., & Economou, A. (1993). Structure and development of causal-experimental thought: From early adolescence to youth. *Developmental Psychology, 29,* 480–497.

Demetriou, A., Pachaury, A., Metallidou, Y., & Kazi, S. (1996). Universals and specificities in the structure and development of quantitative-relational thought: A cross-cultural study in Greece and India. *International Journal of Behavioral Development, 19,* 255–290.

Dempster, F. N., & Corkill, A. J. (1999). Interference and inhibition in cognition and behavior: Unifying themes for educational psychology. *Educational Psychology Review, 11,* 1–88.

Demuth, K. (1996). The prosodic structure of early words. In J. Morgan & K. Demuth (Eds.), *From signal to syntax* (pp. 171–184). Mahwah, NJ: Erlbaum.

DeNavas-Walt, C., Proctor, B. D., & Smith, J. C. (2009). Income, poverty, and health insurance coverage in the United States: 2008. *U.S. Census Bureau, Current Population Reports,* P60–P236. Washington, DC: U.S. Government Printing Office.

Denham, S. A. (2005). Emotional competence counts: Assessment as support for school readiness. In K. Hirsh-Pasek, A. Kochanoff, N. S. Newcombe, & J. de Villiers (Eds.), *Using scientific knowledge to inform preschool assessment. Social Policy Report of the Society for Research in Child Development, 19*(No.1), 12.

Denham, S. A. (2006). Emotional competence: Implications for social functioning. In J. L. Luby (Ed.), *Handbook of preschool mental health: Development, disorders, and treatment* (pp. 23–44). New York: Guilford.

Denham, S. A., & Burton, R. (2003). *Social and emotional prevention and intervention programming for preschoolers.* New York: Kluwer-Plenum.

Denham, S. A., & Kochanoff, A. T. (2002). Parental contributions to preschoolers' understanding of emotion. *Marriage and Family Review, 34,* 311–343.

Denham, S. A., von Salisch, M., Olthof, T., Kochanoff, A., & Caverly, S. (2004). Emotional and social development in childhood. In P. K. Smith & C. H. Hart (Eds.), *Blackwell handbook of childhood social development* (pp. 307–328). Malden, MA: Blackwell.

Denissen, J. J. A., Zarrett, N. R., & Eccles, J. S. (2007). I like to do it, I'm able, and I know I am: Longitudinal couplings between domain-specific achievement, self-concept, and interest. *Child Development, 78,* 430–447.

Dennis, T., Bendersky, M., Ramsay, D., & Lewis, M. (2006). Reactivity and regulation in children prenatally exposed to cocaine. *Developmental Psychology, 42,* 688–697.

Dennis, W. (1960). Causes of retardation among institutionalized children: Iran. *Journal of Genetic Psychology, 96,* 47–59.

Deocampo, J. A. (2003, April). *Tools on TV: A new paradigm for testing dual representational understanding.* Poster presented at the biennial meeting of the Society for Research in Child Development, Tampa, FL.

Deprest, J. A., Devlieger, R., Srisupundit, K., Beck, V., Sandaite, I., Rusconi, S., et al. (2010). Fetal surgery is a clinical reality. *Seminars in Fetal and Neonatal Medicine, 15,* 58–67.

Der, G., Batty, G. D., & Deary, I. J. (2006). Effect of breastfeeding on intelligence in children: Prospective study, sibling pairs analysis, and meta-analysis. *British Medical Journal, 333,* 945.

Derakshan, N., & Eysenck, M. W. (2009). Anxiety, processing efficiency, and cognitive performance: New developments from attentional control theory. *European Psychologist, 14,* 168–176.

deRegnier, R.-A. (2005). Neurophysiologic evaluation of early cognitive development in high-risk infants and toddlers. *Mental Retardation and Developmental Disabilities, 11,* 317–324.

DeRoche, K., & Welsh, M. (2008). Twenty-five years of research on neurocognitive outcomes in early-treated phenylketonuria: Intelligence and executive function. *Developmental Neuropsychology, 33,* 474–504.

Derom, C., Thiery, E., Vlietinck, R., Loos, R., & Derom, R. (1996). Handedness in twins according to zygosity and chorion type: A preliminary report. *Behavior Genetics, 26,* 407–408.

DeRose, L. M., & Brooks-Gunn, J. (2006). Transition into adolescence: The role of pubertal processes. In L. Balter & C. S. Tamis-LeMonda (Eds.), *Child psychology: A handbook of contemporary issues* (2nd ed., pp. 385–414). New York: Psychology Press.

DeRosier, M. E. (2007). Peer-rejected and bullied children: A safe schools initiative for elementary school students. In J. E. Zins, M. J. Elias, & C. A. Maher (Eds.), *Bullying, victimization, and peer harassment* (pp. 257–276). New York: Haworth.

DeRosier, M. E., & Thomas, J. M. (2003). Strengthening sociometric prediction: Scientific advances in the assessment of children's peer relations. *Child Development, 75,* 1379–1392.

Desrochers, S. (2008). From Piaget to specific Genevan developmental models. *Child Development Perspectives, 2,* 7–12.

Deutsch, W., & Pechmann, T. (1982). Social interaction and the development of definite descriptions. *Cognition, 11,* 159–184.

Devi, N. P. G., Shenbagvalli, R., Ramesh, K., & Rathinam, S. N. (2009). Rapid progression of HIV infection in infancy. *Indian Pediatrics, 46,* 53–56.

DeVries, R. (2001). Constructivist education in preschool and elementary school: The sociomoral atmosphere as the first educational goal. In S. L. Golbeck (Ed.), *Psychological perspectives on early childhood education* (pp. 153–180). Mahwah, NJ: Erlbaum.

Deynoot-Schaub, M. J. G., & Riksen-Walraven, J. M. (2006a). Peer contacts of 15-month-olds in childcare: Links with child temperament, parent–child interaction and quality of childcare. *Social Development 15,* 709–729.

Deynoot-Schaub, M. J. G., & Riksen-Walraven, J. M. (2006b). Peer interaction in child care centres at 15 and 23 months: Stability and links with children's socioemotional adjustment. *Infant Behavior and Development, 29,* 276–288.

Diamond, A. (2000). Close interrelation of motor development and cognitive development and of the cerebellum and pre-frontal cortex. *Child Development, 71,* 44–56.

Diamond, A. (2004). Normal development of the prefrontal cortex from birth to young adulthood: Cognitive functions, anatomy, and biochemistry. In D. T. Stuff & R. T. Knight (Eds.), *Principles of frontal lobe function* (pp. 466–503). New York: Oxford University Press.

Diamond, A. (2009). The interplay of biology and the environment broadly defined. *Developmental Psychology, 45,* 1–8.

Diamond, A., Barnett, W. S., Thomas, J., & Munro, S. (2007). Preschool program improves cognitive control. *Science, 318,* 1387–1388.

Diamond, A., Cruttenden, L., & Neiderman, D. (1994). AB with multiple wells: 1. Why are multiple wells sometimes easier than two wells? 2. Memory or memory + inhibition. *Developmental Psychology, 30,* 192–205.

Diamond, L. M. (1998). Development of sexual orientation among adolescent and young adult women. *Developmental Psychology, 34,* 1085–1095.

Diamond, L. M. (2003). Love matters: Romantic relationships among sexual-minority adolescents. In P. Florsheim (Ed.), *Adolescent romantic relations and sexual behavior* (pp. 85–108). Mahwah, NJ: Erlbaum.

Diamond, L. M. (2008). Female bisexuality from adolescence to adulthood: Results from a 10-year longitudinal study. *Developmental Psychology, 44,* 5–14.

Diamond, L. M., & Lucas, S. (2004). Sexual-minority and heterosexual youths' peer relationships: Experiences, expectations, and implications for well-being. *Journal of Research on Adolescence, 14,* 313–340.

Dias, M. G., & Harris, P. L. (1988). The effect of make-believe play on deductive reasoning. *British Journal of Developmental Psychology, 8,* 305–318.

Dias, M. G., & Harris, P. L. (1990). The influence of the imagination on reasoning by young children. *British Journal of Developmental Psychology, 8,* 305–318.

DiBiase, A.-M., Gibbs, J. C., Potter, G. B., & Blount, M. R. (2011). *Teaching adolescents to think and act responsibly: The EQUIP approach.* Champaign, IL: Research Press.

Dick, D. M., Prescott, C., & McGue, M. (2008). The genetics of substance use and substance use disorders. In Y.-K. Kim (Ed.), *Handbook of behavior genetics* (pp. 433–453). New York: Springer.

Dick, D. M., Rose, R. J., Viken, R. J., & Kaprio, J. (2000). Pubertal timing and substance use: Associations between and within families across late adolescence. *Developmental Psychology, 36,* 180–189.

Dick, F., Dronkers, N. F., Pizzamiglio, L., Saygin, A. P., Small, S. L., & Wilson, S. (2004). Language and the brain. In M. Tomasello & D. I. Slobin (Eds.), *Beyond nature-nurture: Essays in honor of Elizabeth Bates* (pp. 237–260). Mahwah, NJ: Erlbaum.

Dickens, W. T., & Flynn, J. R. (2001). Heritability estimates versus large environmental effects: The IQ paradox resolved. *Psychological Review, 108,* 346–369.

Dickinson, D. K., & McCabe, A. (2001). Bringing it all together: The multiple origins, skills, and environmental supports of early literacy. *Learning Disabilities Research and Practice, 16,* 186–202.

Dickinson, D. K., & Sprague, K. E. (2001). The nature and impact of early childhood care environments on the language and early literacy development of children from low-income families. In S. B. Neuman & D. K. Dickinson (Eds.), *Handbook of early literacy research.* New York: Guilford.

Dickinson, D. K., Golinkoff, R. M., & Hirsh-Pasek, K. (2010). Speaking out for language: Why language is central to reading development. *Educational Researcher, 39,* 305–310.

Dickinson, D. K., McCabe, A., Anastasopoulos, L., Peisner-Feinberg, E. S., & Poe, M. D. (2003). The comprehensive language approach to early literacy: The interrelationships among vocabulary, phonological sensitivity, and print knowledge among preschool-age children. *Journal of Educational Psychology, 95,* 465–481.

Dick-Read, G. (1959). *Childbirth without fear.* New York: Harper & Brothers.

DiDonato, M. D., & Berenbaum, S. A. (2011). The benefits and drawbacks of gender typing: How different dimensions are related to psychological adjustment. *Archives of Sexual Behavior, 40,* 457–463.

Dietrich, K. N., Ware, J. H., Salganik, M., Radcliffe, J., Rogan, W. J., & Rhoads, G. C. (2004). Effect of chelation therapy on the neuropsychological and behavioral development of lead-exposed children after school entry. *Pediatrics, 114,* 19–26.

Dietz, T. L. (1998). An examination of violence and gender role portrayals in video games: Implications for gender socialization and aggressive behavior. *Sex Roles, 38,* 425–442.

Dildy, G. A., Jackson, G. M., Fowers, G. K., Oshiro, B. T., Varner, M. W., & Clark, S. L. (1996). Very advanced maternal age. Pregnancy after age 45. *American Journal of Obstetrics and Gynecology, 175,* 668–674.

Ding, Z. Y. (2008). National epidemiological survey on childhood obesity, 2006. *Chinese Journal of Pediatrics, 46,* 179–184.

DiPietro, J. A., Bornstein, M. H., Costigan, K. A., Pressman, E. K., Hahn, C.-S., & Painter, K. (2002). What does fetal movement predict about behavior during the first two years of life? *Developmental Psychobiology, 40,* 358–371.

DiPietro, J. A., Caulfield, L. E., Irizarry, R. A., Chen, P., Merialdi, M., & Zavaleta, N. (2006). Prenatal development of intrafetal and maternal–fetal synchrony. *Behavioral Neuroscience, 120,* 687–701.

DiPietro, J. A., Hodgson, D. M., Costigan, K. A., & Hilton, S. C. (1996). Fetal neurobehavioral development. *Child Development, 67,* 2553–2567.

Dirix, C. E. H., Nijhuis, J. G., Jongsma, H. W., & Hornstra, G. (2009). Aspects of fetal learning and memory. *Child Development, 80,* 1251–1258.

Dirks, J. (1982). The effect of a commercial game on children's Block Design scores on the WISC-R test. *Intelligence, 6,* 109–123.

Dishion, T. J., Andrews, D. W., & Crosby, L. (1995). Antisocial boys and their friends in early adolescence: Relationship characteristics, quality, and interactional

processes. *Child Development, 66,* 139–151.

Dishion, T. J., Shaw, D., Connell, A., Gardner, F., Weaver, C., & Wilson, M. (2008). The family checkup with high-risk indigent families: Preventing problem behavior by increasing parents' positive behavior support in early childhood. *Child Development, 79,* 1395–1414.

Dittmar, M., Abbot-Smith, K., Lieven, E. V. M., & Tomasello, M. (2008). Young German children's early syntactic competence: A preferential-looking study. *Developmental Science, 11,* 575–582.

Dixon, T. L., & Azocar, C. I. (2006). The representation of juvenile offenders by race on Los Angeles area television news. *Howard Journal of Communications, 17,* 143–161.

Dodd, V. L. (2005). Implications of kangaroo care for growth and development in preterm infants. *JOGNN, 34,* 218–232.

Dodge, K. A., Coie, J. D., & Lynam, D. (2006). Aggression and antisocial behavior in youth. In N. Eisenberg (Ed.), *Handbook of child psychology: Vol. 3. Social, emotional, and personality development* (6th ed., pp. 719–788). New York: Wiley.

Dodge, K. A., Dishion, T. J., & Lansford, J. E. (2006). Deviant peer influences in intervention and public policy for youth. *Social Policy Report of the Society for Research in Child Development, 20*(1), 3–19.

Dodge, K. A., Lochman, J. E., Harnish, J. D., Bates, J. E., & Pettit, G. S. (1997). Reactive and proactive aggression in school children and psychiatrically impaired chronically assaultive youth. *Journal of Abnormal Psychology, 106,* 37–51.

Dodge, K. A., McLoyd, V. C., & Lansford, J. E. (2006). The cultural context of physically disciplining children. In V. C. McLoyd, N. E. Hill, & K. A. Dodge (Eds.), *African-American family life: Ecological and cultural diversity* (pp. 245–263). New York: Guilford.

Dodge, K. A., Pettit, G. S., McClaskey, C. L., & Brown, M. M. (1986). Social competence in children. *Monographs of the Society for Research in Child Development, 51*(2, Serial No. 213).

Dohnt, H., & Tiggemann, M. (2006). The contribution of peer and media influences to the development of body satisfaction and self-esteem in young girls: A prospective study. *Developmental Psychology, 42,* 929–936.

Dombrowski, S. C., Noonan, K., & Martin, R. P. (2007). Low birth weight and cognitive outcomes: Evidence for a gradient relationship in an urban, poor, African American birth cohort. *School Psychology Quarterly, 22,* 26–43.

Domitrovich, C. E., Cortes, R., & Greenberg, M. T. (2007). Improving young children's social and emotional competence: A randomized trial of the preschool "PATHS" curriculum. *The Journal of Primary Prevention, 28,* 67–91.

Domitrovich, C. E., Gest, S. D., Gill, S., Bierman, K. L., Welsh, J. A., & Jones, D. (2009). Fostering high-quality teaching with an enriched curriculum and professional development support: The Head Start REDI program. *American Educational Research Journal, 46,* 567–597.

Donahue, M. J., & Benson, P. L. (1995). Religion and the well-being of adolescents. *Journal of Social Issues, 51,* 145–160.

Dondi, M., Simion, F., & Caltran, G. (1999). Can newborns discriminate between their

own cry and the cry of another newborn infant? *Developmental Psychology, 35,* 418–426.

Donnellan, M. B., Trzesniewski, K. H., Robins, R. W., Moffitt, T. E., & Caspi, A. (2005). Low self-esteem is related to aggression, antisocial behavior, and delinquency. *Psychological Science, 16,* 328–335.

Donnerstein, E., Slaby, R. G., & Eron, L. D. (1994). The mass media and youth aggression. In L. D. Eron, J. H. Gentry, & P. Schlegel (Eds.), *Reason to hope: A psychosocial perspective on violence and youth* (pp. 219–250). Washington, DC: American Psychological Association.

D'Onofrio, B. M., Turkheimer, E., Emery, R. E., Slutske, W. S., Heath, A. C., Madden, P. A., & Martin, N. G. (2006). A genetically informed study of the processes underlying the association between parental marital instability and offspring adjustment. *Developmental Psychology, 42,* 486–499.

Donovan, W. L., Leavitt, L. A., & Walsh, R. O. (1997). Cognitive set and coping strategy affect mothers' sensitivity to infant cries: A signal detection approach. *Child Development, 68,* 760–772.

Donovan, W. L., Leavitt, L. A., & Walsh, R. O. (2000). Maternal illusory control predicts socialization strategies and toddler compliance. *Developmental Psychology, 36,* 402–411.

Dorius, C. J., Bahr, S. J., Hoffman, J. P., Harmon, E. L. (2004). Parenting practices as moderators of the relationship between peers and adolescent marijuana use. *Journal of Marriage and Family, 66,* 163–178.

Dorris, M. (1989). *The broken cord.* New York: Harper & Row.

Doss, B. D., Rhoades, G. K., Stanley, S. M., & Markman, H. J. (2009). The effect of the transition to parenthood on relationship quality: An 8-year prospective study. *Journal of Personality and Social Psychology, 96,* 601–619.

Douglas, E. M. (2006). *Mending broken families: Social policies for divorced families.* Lanham, MD: Rowman & Littlefield.

Dovidio, J. F., Gaertner, S. L., Nier, J. A., Kawakami, K., & Hodson, G. (2004). Contemporary racial bias: When good people do bad things. In G. A. Miller (Ed.), *The social psychology of good and evil* (pp. 141–167). New York: Guilford.

Dowker, A. (2003). Younger children's estimates for addition: The zone of partial knowledge and understanding. In A. J. Baroody & A. Dowker (Eds.), *The development of arithmetic concepts and skills: Constructing adaptive expertise* (pp. 243–265). Mahwah, NJ: Erlbaum.

Dowling, E. M., Gestsdottir, S., Anderson, P. M., von Eye, A., Almerigi, J., & Lerner, R. M. (2004). Structural relations among spirituality, religiosity, and thriving in adolescence. *Applied Developmental Psychology, 8,* 7–16.

Downing, J. E. (2010). *Academic instruction for students with moderate and severe intellectual disabilities.* Thousand Oaks, CA: Corwin.

Downs, A. C., & Fuller, M. J. (1991). Recollections of spermarche: An exploratory investigation. *Current Psychology: Research and Reviews, 10,* 93–102.

Downs, A. C., & Langlois, J. H. (1988). Sex typing: Construct and measurement issues. *Sex Roles, 18,* 87–100.

Dozier, M., Stovall, K. C., Albus, K. E., & Bates, B. (2001). Attachment for infants in foster care: The role of caregiver state of mind. *Child Development, 72,* 1467–1477.

Drabman, R. S., Cordua, G. D., Hammer, D., Jarvie, G. J., & Horton, W. (1979). Developmental trends in eating rates of normal and overweight preschool children. *Child Development, 50,* 211–216.

Draper, P., & Cashdan, E. (1988). Technological change and child behavior among the !Kung. *Ethnology, 27,* 339–365.

Drewett, R. F., Corbett, S. S., & Wright, C. M. (2006). Physical and emotional development, appetite and body image in adolescents who failed to thrive as infants. *Journal of Child Psychology and Psychiatry, 47,* 524–531.

Dribe, M., & Stanfors, M. (2009). Does parenthood strengthen a traditional household division of labor? Evidence from Sweden. *Journal of Marriage and Family, 71,* 33–45.

Driscoll, M. C. (2007). Sickle cell disease. *Pediatrics in Review, 28,* 259–268.

Droege, K. L., & Stipek, D. J. (1993). Children's use of dispositions to predict classmates' behavior. *Developmental Psychology, 29,* 646–654.

Drotar, D., Overholser, J. C., Levi, R., Walders, N., Robinson, J. R., Palermo, T. M., & Riekert, K. A. (2000). Ethical issues in conducting research with pediatric and clinical child populations in applied settings. In D. Drotar (Ed.), *Handbook of research in pediatric and clinical child psychology* (pp. 305–326). New York: Kluwer.

Dubé, E. M., Savin-Williams, R. C., & Diamond, L. M. (2001). Intimacy development, gender, and ethnicity among sexual-minority youths. In A. R. D'Augelli & C. J. Patterson (Eds.), *Lesbian, gay, and bisexual identities and youth* (pp. 129–152). New York: Oxford University Press.

DuBois, D. L., Felner, R. D., Brand, S., & George, G. R. (1999). Profiles of self-esteem in early adolescence: Identification and investigation of adaptive correlates. *American Journal of Community Psychology, 27,* 899–932.

Duckworth, A. L., & Seligman, M. E. P. (2005). Self-discipline outdoes IQ in predicting academic performance of adolescents. *Psychological Science, 12,* 939–944.

Dueker, G. L., Modi, A., & Needham, A. (2003). 4.5-month-old infants' learning, retention and use of object boundary information. *Infant Behavior and Development, 26,* 588–605.

Duggan, A., McFarlane, E., Fuddy, L., Burrell, L., Higman, S. M., Windham, A., & Sia, C. (2004). Randomized trial of a statewide home visiting program: Impact in preventing child abuse and neglect. *Child Abuse and Neglect, 28,* 597–622.

Duncan, G. J., Dowsett, C. J., Claessens, A., Magnuson, K., Huston, A. C., Keblanov, P., et al. (2007). School readiness and later achievement. *Developmental Psychology, 43,* 1428–1446.

Duncan, G. J., & Magnuson, K. A. (2003). Off with Hollingshead: Socioeconomic resources, parenting, and child development. In M. H. Bornstein & R. H. Bradley (Eds.), *Socioeconomic status, parenting, and child development* (pp. 83–106). Mahwah, NJ: Erlbaum.

Duncan, L. G., Casalis, S., & Cole, P. (2009). Early metalinguistic awareness of derivational morphology: Observations from a comparison of English and French. *Applied Psycholinguistics, 30,* 405–440.

Duncan, S. R., Paterson, D. S., Hoffman, J. M., Mokler, D. J., Borenstein, M. S., Belliveau, R. A., et al. (2010). Brainstem serotonergic deficiency in sudden infant death syndrome. *Journal of the American Medical Association, 303,* 430–437.

Dundek, L. H. (2006) Establishment of a Somali doula program at a large metropolitan hospital. *Journal of Perinatal and Neonatal Nursing, 20,* 128–137.

Dunham, Y., Baron, A. S., & Banaji, M. R. (2006). From American city to Japanese village: A cross-cultural investigation of implicit race attitudes. *Child Development, 77,* 1129–1520.

Dunham, Y., Baron, A. S., & Carey, S. (2011). Consequences of "minimal" group affiliations in children. *Child Development, 82,* 793–811.

Dunifon, R., Kalil, A., & Danziger, S. K. (2003). Maternal work behavior under welfare reform: How does the transition from welfare to work affect child development? *Children and Youth Services Review, 25,* 55–82.

Dunn, J. (1994). Temperament, siblings, and the development of relationships. In W. B. Carey & S. C. McDevitt (Eds.), *Prevention and early intervention* (pp. 50–58). New York: Brunner/Mazel.

Dunn, J. (2002). Sibling relationships. In P. K. Smith & C. H. Hart (Eds.), *Blackwell handbook of childhood social development* (pp. 223–237). Malden, MA: Blackwell.

Dunn, J. (2004a). Annotation: Children's relationships with their nonresident fathers. *Journal of Child Psychology and Psychiatry, 45,* 659–671.

Dunn, J. (2004b). Sibling relationships. In P. K. Smith & C. H. Hart (Eds.), *Handbook of childhood social development* (pp. 223–237). Malden, MA: Blackwell.

Dunn, J., Brown, J. R., & Maguire, M. (1995). The development of children's moral sensibility: Individual differences and emotion understanding. *Developmental Psychology, 31,* 649–659.

Dunn, J., Cheng, H., O'Connor, T. G., & Bridges, L. (2004). Children's perspectives on their relationships with their nonresident fathers: Influences, outcomes and implications. *Journal of Child Psychology and Psychiatry, 45,* 553–566.

Dunn, J. R., Schaefer-McDaniel, N. J., & Ramsay, J. T. (2010). Neighborhood chaos and children's development: Questions and contradictions. In G. W. Evans & T. D. Wachs (Eds.), *Chaos and its influence on children's development: An ecological perspective* (pp. 173–189). Washington, DC: American Psychological Association.

Dunphy-Lelii, S., & Wellman, H. M. (2004). Infants' understanding of occlusion of others' line of sight: Implications for an emerging theory of mind. *European Journal of Developmental Psychology, 1,* 49–66.

Durbin, D. L., Darling, N., Steinberg, L. D., & Brown, B. B. (1993). Parenting style and peer group membership among European-American adolescents. *Journal of Research on Adolescence, 3,* 87–100.

Durlach, J. (2004). New data on the importance of gestational Mg deficiency. *Journal of the American College of Nutrition, 23,* 694S–700S.

Durlak, J. A., & Weissberg, R. P. (2007). *The impact of after-school programs that promote personal and social skills.* Chicago: Collaborative for Academic, Social, and Emotional Learning.

Durston, S., & Conrad, K. (2007). Integrating genetic, psychopharmacological and neuroimaging studies: A converging methods approach to understanding the neurobiology of ADHD. *Developmental Review, 27,* 374–395.

Duszak, R. S. (2009). Congenital rubella syndrome—major review. *Optometry, 80,* 36–43.

Dweck, C. S. (2002). Messages that motivate: How praise molds students' beliefs, motivation, and performance (in surprising ways). In J. Aronson (Ed.), *Improving academic achievement: Impact of psychological factors on education* (pp. 37–60). San Diego, CA: Academic Press.

Dweck, C. S. (2009). Prejudice: How it develops and how it can be undone. *Human Development, 52,* 371–376.

Dzurova, D., & Pikhart, H. (2005). Down syndrome, paternal age and education: Comparison of California and the Czech Republic. *BMC Public Health, 5,* 69.

Eacott, M. J. (1999). Memory for the events of early childhood. *Current Directions in Psychological Science, 8,* 46–48.

Eaton, D. K., Davis, K. S., Barrios, L., Brener, N. D., & Noonan, R. K. (2007). Associations of dating violence victimization with lifetime participation, co-occurrence, and early initiation of risk behaviors among U.S. high school students. *Journal of Interpersonal Violence, 22,* 585–602.

Eaves, L., Silberg, J., Foley, D., Bulik, C., Maes, H., & Erkanli, A. (2004). Genetic and environmental influences on the relative timing of pubertal change. *Twin Research, 7,* 471–481.

Ebeling, K. S., & Gelman, S. A. (1994). Children's use of context in interpreting "big" and "little." *Child Development, 65,* 1178–1192.

Eccles, J. S., Freedman-Doan, C., Frome, P., Jacobs, J., & Yoon, K. S. (2000). Gender-role socialization in the family: A longitudinal approach. In T. Eckes & H. M. Trautner (Eds.), *The developmental social psychology of gender* (pp. 333–360). Mahwah, NJ: Erlbaum.

Eccles, J. S., Jacobs, J. E., & Harold, R. D. (1990). Gender-role stereotypes, expectancy effects, and parents' role in the socialization of gender differences in self-perceptions and skill acquisition. *Journal of Social Issues, 46,* 183–201.

Eccles, J. S., Templeton, J., Barber, B., & Stone, M. (2003). Adolescence and emerging adulthood: The critical passage ways to adulthood. In M. H. Bornstein, L. Davidson, C. L., Keyes, K. A. Moore, & the Center for Child Well-Being (Eds.), *Well-being: Positive development across the life course* (pp. 383–406). Mahwah, NJ: Erlbaum.

Eccles, J. S., & Roeser, R. W. (2009). Schools, academic motivation, and stage-environment fit. In R. M. Lerner & L. Steinberg (Eds.), *Handbook of adolescent psychology* (Vol. 1, pp. 404–434). Hoboken, NJ: Wiley.

Eckerman, C. O., & Peterman, K. (2001). Peers and infant social/communicative development. In G. Bremner & A. Fogel (Eds.), *Blackwell handbook of infant development* (pp. 326–350). Malden, MA: Blackwell.

Economic Policy Institute. (2010). *A broader, bolder approach to education.* Retrieved from www.boldapproach.org

Eder, R. A., & Mangelsdorf, S. C. (1997). The emotional basis of early personality development: Implications for the emergent self-concept. In R. Hogan, J. Johnson, & S. Briggs (Eds.), *Handbook of personality psychology* (pp. 209–240). San Diego, CA: Academic Press.

Edmondson, P. (2006). Deaf children's understanding of other people's thought processes. *Educational Psychology in Practice, 22,* 159–169.

Edwards, O. W., & Oakland, T. D. (2006). Factorial invariance of Woodcock-Johnson III scores for African Americans and Caucasian Americans. *Journal of Psychoeducational Assessment, 24,* 358–366.

Egan, S. K., & Perry, D. G. (2001). Gender identity: A multidimensional analysis with implications for psychosocial adjustment. *Developmental Psychology, 37,* 451–463.

Egeland, B., Jacobvitz, D., & Sroufe, L. A. (1988). Breaking the cycle of abuse. *Child Development, 59,* 1080–1088.

Ehri, L. C., & Roberts, T. (2006). The roots of learning to read and write: Acquisition of letters and phonemic awareness. In D. K. Dikinson & S. B. Neuman (Eds.), *Handbook of early literacy research* (Vol. 2, pp. 113–131). New York: Guildford.

Eichstedt, J. A., Serbin, L. A., Poulin-Dubois, D., & Sen, M. G. (2002). Of bears and men: Infants' knowledge of conventional and metaphorical gender stereotypes. *Infant Behavior and Development, 25,* 296–310.

Eiden, R. D., Veira, Y., & Granger, D. A. (2009). Prenatal cocaine exposure and infant cortisol reactivity. *Child Development, 80,* 528–543.

Eigsti, I.-M., Zayas, V., Mischel, W., Shoda, Y., Ayduk, O., Dadlani, M. B., et al. (2006). Predicting cognitive control from preschool to late adolescence and young adulthood. *Psychological Science, 17,* 478–484.

Einspieler, C., Marschik, P. B., & Prechtl, H. F. R. (2008). Human motor behavior: Prenatal origin and early postnatal development. *Zeitschrift für Psychologie, 216,* 147–153.

Eisenberg, N. (1986). *Altruistic emotion, cognition, and behavior.* Hillsdale, NJ: Erlbaum.

Eisenberg, N. (2003). Prosocial behavior, empathy, and sympathy. In M. H. Bornstein & L. Davidson (Eds.), *Well-being: Positive development across the life course* (pp. 253–265). Mahwah, NJ: Erlbaum.

Eisenberg, N. (2010). Empathy-related responding: Links with self-regulation, moral judgment, and moral behavior. In M. Mikulincer & P. R. Shaver (Eds.), *Prosocial motives, emotions, and behavior: The better angels of our nature* (pp. 129–148). Washington, DC: American Psychological Association.

Eisenberg, N., Carlo, G., Murphy, B., & Van Court, P. (1995). Prosocial development in late adolescence: A longitudinal study. *Child Development, 66,* 1179–1197.

Eisenberg, N., Eggum, N. D., & Edwards, A. (2010). Empathy-related responding and moral development. In W. F. Arsenio & E. A. Lemerise (Eds.), *Emotions, aggression, and morality in children* (pp. 115–135). Washington, DC: American Psychological Association.

Eisenberg, N., & Fabes, R. A. (1998). Prosocial development. In N. Eisenberg (Ed.), *Handbook of child psychology: Vol. 3. Social, emotional, and personality development* (5th ed., pp. 701–778). New York: Wiley.

Eisenberg, N., Fabes, R., Murphy, B., Karbon, M., Smith, M., & Maszk, P. (1996). The relations of children's dispositional empathy-related responding to their emotionality, regulation, and social functioning. *Developmental Psychology, 32,* 195–209.

Eisenberg, N., Fabes, R. A., Shepard, S. A., Murphy, B. C., Jones, S., & Guthrie, I. K. (1998). Contemporaneous and longitudinal prediction of children's sympathy from dispositional regulation and emotionality. *Developmental Psychology, 34,* 910–924.

Eisenberg, N., Fabes, R. A., & Spinrad, T. L. (2006). Prosocial development. In N. Eisenberg (Ed.), *Handbook of child psychology: Vol. 3. Social, emotional, and personality development* (6th ed., pp. 646–718). Hoboken, NJ: Wiley.

Eisenberg, N., Miller, P. A., Shell, R., McNalley, S., & Shea, C. (1991). Prosocial development in adolescence: A longitudinal study. *Developmental Psychology, 27,* 849–857.

Eisenberg, N., Sadovsky, A., Spinrad, T. L., Fabes, R. A., Losoya, S., & Valiente, C. (2005a). The relations of problem behavior status to children's negative emotionality, effortful control, and impulsivity: Concurrent relations and prediction of change. *Developmental Psychology, 41,* 193–211.

Eisenberg, N., & Silver, R. C. (2011). Growing up in the shadow of terrorism. *American Psychologist, 66,* 468–481.

Eisenberg, N., & Spinrad, T. L. (2004). Emotion-related regulation: Sharpening the definition. *Child Development, 75,* 334–339.

Eisenberg, N., Zhou, Q., & Koller, S. (2001). Brazilian adolescents' prosocial moral judgment and behavior: Relations to sympathy, perspective taking, gender-role orientation, and demographic characteristics. *Child Development, 72,* 518–534.

Eisenberg, N., Zhou, Q., Spinrad, T. L., Valiente, C., Fabes, R. A., & Liew, J. (2005b). Relations among positive parenting, children's effortful control, and externalizing problems: A three-wave longitudinal study. *Child Development, 76,* 1055–1071.

Ekman, P. (2003). *Emotions revealed.* New York: Times Books.

Ekman, P., & Friesen, W. (1972). Constants across culture in the face of emotion. *Journal of Personality and Social Psychology, 17,* 124–129.

Elfenbein, D. S., & Felice, M. E. (2003). Adolescent pregnancy. *Pediatric Clinics of North America, 50,* 781–800.

Eliakim, A., Friedland, O., Kowen, G., Wolach, B., & Nemet, D. (2004). Parental obesity and higher pre-intervention BMI reduce the likelihood of a multidisciplinary childhood obesity program to succeed: A clinical observation. *Journal of Pediatric Endocrinology and Metabolism, 17,* 1055–1061.

Elias, C. L., & Berk, L. E. (2002). Self-regulation in young children: Is there a role for sociodramatic play? *Early Childhood Research Quarterly, 17,* 1–17.

Elicker, J., Englund, M., & Sroufe, L. A. (1992). Predicting peer competence and peer relationships in childhood from early parent–child relationships. In R. D. Parke & G. W. Ladd (Eds.), *Family–peer relationships: Modes of linkage* (pp. 77–106). Hillsdale, NJ: Erlbaum.

Elkind, D. (1994). *A sympathetic understanding of the child: Birth to sixteen* (3rd ed.). Boston: Allyn and Bacon.

Elkind, D., & Bowen, R. (1979). Imaginary audience behavior in children and adolescence. *Developmental Psychology, 15,* 33–44.

Ellis, A. E., & Oakes, L. M. (2006). Infants flexibly use different dimensions to categorize objects. *Developmental Psychology, 42,* 1000–1011.

Ellis, B. J., Bates, J. E., Dodge, K. A., Fergusson, D. M., Horwood, L. J., Pettit, G. S., & Woodward, L. (2003). Does father absence place daughters at special risk for early sexual activity and teenage pregnancy? *Child Development, 74,* 801–821.

Ellis, B. J., & Essex, M. J. (2007). Family environments, adrenarche, and sexual maturation: A longitudinal test of a life history model. *Child Development, 78,* 1799–1817.

Ellis, W. E., & Zarbatany, L. (2007). Explaining friendship formation and friendship stability: The role of children's and friends' aggression and victimization. *Merrill-Palmer Quarterly, 53,* 79–104.

Elman, J. (2003). Development: It's about time. *Developmental Science, 6,* 430–433.

Elman, J. L. (2001). Connectionism and language acquisition. In M. Tomasello & E. Bates (Eds.). *Language development* (pp. 295–306). Oxford, UK: Blackwell.

Else-Quest, N. M., Hyde, J. S., Goldsmith, H. H., & Van Hulle, C. A. (2006). Gender differences in temperament: A meta-analysis. *Psychological Bulletin, 132,* 33–72.

El-Sheikh, M., Cummings, E. M., & Reiter, S. (1996). Preschoolers' responses to ongoing interadult conflict: The role of prior exposure to resolved versus unresolved arguments. *Journal of Abnormal Child Psychology, 24,* 665–679.

Eltzschig, H. K., Lieberman, E. S., & Camann, W. R. (2003). Regional anesthesia and analgesia for labor and delivery. *New England Journal of Medicine, 384,* 319–332.

Eluvathingal, T. J., Chugani, H. T., Behen, M. E., Juhasz, C., Muzik, O., Maqbook, M., et al. (2006). Abnormal brain connectivity in children after early severe socioemotional deprivation: A diffusion tensor imaging study. *Pediatrics, 117,* 2093–2100.

Ember, C. R., & Ember, M. (2005). Explaining corporal punishment of children. *American Anthropologist, 107,* 609–619.

Emery, R. E., Sbarra, D., & Grover, T. (2005). Divorce mediation: Research and reflections. *Family Court Review, 43,* 22–37.

Emmerich, W. (1981). Non-monotonic developmental trends in social cognition: The case of gender constancy. In S. Strauss (Ed.), *U-shaped behavioral growth* (pp. 249–269). New York: Academic Press.

Emory, E. K., Schlackman, L. J., & Fiano, K. (1996). Drug–hormone interactions on neurobehavioral responses in human neonates. *Infant Behavior and Development, 19,* 213–220.

Ennemoser, M., & Schneider, W. (2007). Relations of television viewing and reading: Findings from a 4-year longitudinal study. *Journal of Educational Psychology, 99,* 349–368.

Ensor, R., & Hughes, C. (2008). Content or connectedness? Mother–child talk and early social understanding. *Child Development, 79,* 201–216.

Entringer, S., Kumsta, R., Hellhammer, D. H., Wadhwa, P. D., & Wüst, S. (2009). Prenatal exposure to maternal psychosocial stress and HPA axis regulation in young adults. *Hormones and Behavior, 55,* 292–298.

Epstein, L. H., Roemmich, J. N., & Raynor, H. A. (2001). Behavioral therapy in the treatment of pediatric obesity. *Pediatric Clinics of North America, 48,* 981–983.

Erath, S. A., Bierman, K. L., & the Conduct Problems Prevention Research Group. (2006). Aggressive marital conflict, maternal harsh punishment, and child aggressive-disruptive behavior: Evidence for direct and mediate relations. *Journal of Family Psychology, 20,* 217–226.

Erden, F., & Wolfgang, C. H. (2004). An exploration of the differences in prekindergarten, kindergarten, and first-grade teachers' beliefs related to discipline when dealing with male and female students. *Early Child Development and Care, 174,* 3–11.

Erikson, E. H. (1950). *Childhood and society.* New York: Norton.

Erikson, E. H. (1968). *Identity, youth, and crisis.* New York: Norton.

Ernst, M., Moolchan, E. T., & Robinson, M. L. (2001). Behavioral and neural consequences of prenatal exposure to nicotine. *Journal of the American Academy of Child and Adolescent Psychiatry, 40,* 630–641.

Ernst, M., & Spear, L. P. (2009). Reward systems. In M. de Haan & M. R. Gunnar (Eds.), *Handbook of developmental social neuroscience* (pp. 324–341). New York: Guilford.

Eslinger, P. J. (1998). Neurological and neuropsychological bases of empathy. *European Neurology, 39,* 193–199.

Eslinger, P. J., Moore, P., Troiani, V., Antani, S., Cross, K., Kwok, S., & Grossman, M. (2007). Oops! Resolving social dilemmas in frontotemporal dementia. *Journal of Neurology, Neurosurgery, and Psychiatry, 78,* 457–460.

Estourgie-van Burk, G. F., Bartels, M., van Beijsterveldt, T. C., Delemarre-van de Waal, H. A., & Boomsma, D. I. (2006). Body size in five-year-old twins: Heritability and comparison to singleton standards. *Twin Research and Human Genetics, 9,* 646–655.

Ethier, K. A., Kershaw, T., Niccolai, L., Lewis, J. B., & Ickovics, J. R. (2003). Adolescent women underestimate their susceptibility to sexually transmitted infections. *Sexually Transmitted Infections, 79,* 408–411.

Euling, S. Y., Herman-Giddens, M. E., Lee, P. A., Selevan, S. G., Juul, A., Sørensen, T. I. A., et al. (2008). Examination of U.S. puberty-timing data from 1940 to 1994 for secular trends: Panel findings. *Pediatrics, 121,* S172–S191.

Evanoo, G. (2007). Infant crying: A clinical conundrum. *Journal of Pediatric Health Care, 21,* 333–338.

Evans, E., Hawton, K., & Rodham, K. (2004). Factors associated with suicidal phenomena in adolescents: A systematic review of population-based studies. *Clinical Psychology Review, 24,* 957–979.

Evans, G. W. (2006). Child development and the physical environment. *Annual Review of Psychology, 57,* 424–451.

Evans, G. W., & Schamberg, M A. (2009). Childhood poverty, chronic stress, and adult working memory. *Proceedings of the National Academy of Sciences, 106,* 6545–6549.

Evans, N., & Levinson, S. C. (2009). The myth of language universals: Language diversity and its importance for cognitive science. *Behavioral and Brain Sciences, 32,* 429–492.

Eveleth, P. B., & Tanner, J. M. (1990). *Worldwide variation in human growth* (2nd ed.). Cambridge, UK: Cambridge University Press.

Fabes, R. A., Eisenberg, N., Hanish, L. D., & Spinrad, T. L. (2001). Preschoolers' spontaneous emotion vocabulary: Relations to likability. *Early Education and Development, 12,* 11–27.

Fabes, R. A., Eisenberg, N., Karbon, M., Troyer, D., & Switzer, G. (1994). The relations of children's emotion regulation to their vicarious emotional responses and comforting behavior. *Child Development, 65,* 1678–1693.

Fabes, R. A., Eisenberg, N., McCormick, S. E., & Wilson, M. S. (1988). Preschoolers' attributions of the situational determinants of others' naturally occurring emotions. *Developmental Psychology, 24,* 376–385.

Fabes, R. A., Martin, C. L., & Hanish, L. D. (2003). Young children's play qualities in same-, other-, and mixed-sex peer groups. *Child Development, 74,* 921–932.

Fabes, R. A., Shepard, S. A., Guthrie, I. K., & Martin, C. L. (1997). Roles of temperamental arousal and gender-segregated play in young children's social adjustment. *Developmental Psychology, 33,* 693–702.

Fabricius, W. V., & Khalil, S. (2003). False beliefs or false positives? Limits on children's understanding of mental representations. *Journal of Cognition and Development, 4,* 239–262.

Fagan, J. F., & Holland, C. R. (2007). Racial equality in intelligence: Predictions from a theory of intelligence as processing. *Intelligence, 35,* 319–334.

Fagan, J. F., Holland, C. R., & Wheeler, K. (2007). The prediction, from infancy, of adult IQ and achievement. *Intelligence, 35,* 225–231.

Fagan, J. F., III. (1973). Infant's delayed recognition memory and forgetting. *Journal of Experimental Child Psychology, 16,* 424–450.

Fagan, J. F., III, & Detterman, D. K. (1992). The Fagan Test of Infant Intelligence: A technical summary. *Journal of Applied Developmental Psychology, 13,* 173–193.

Fagard, J., & Pezé, A. (1997). Age changes in interlimb coupling and the development of bimanual coordination. *Journal of Motor Behavior, 29,* 199–208.

Fagard, J., Spelke, E., & von Hofsten, C. (2009). Reaching and grasping a moving object in 6-, 8-, and 10-month-old infants: Laterality and performance. *Infant Behavior and Development, 32,* 137–146.

Fagot, B. I. (1984). The child's expectations of differences in adult male and female interactions. *Sex Roles, 11,* 593–600.

Fagot, B. I. (1985a). Beyond the reinforcement principle: Another step toward understanding sex role development. *Developmental Psychology, 21,* 1097–1104.

Fagot, B. I. (1985b). Changes in thinking about early sex role development. *Developmental Review, 5,* 83–98.

Fagot, B. I., & Hagan, R. I. (1991). Observations of parent reactions to sex-stereotyped behaviors: Age and sex effects. *Child Development, 62,* 617–628.

Fagot, B. I., & Leinbach, M. D. (1989). The young child's gender schema: Environmental input, internal organization. *Child Development, 60,* 663–672.

Fagot, B. I., Leinbach, M. D., & O'Boyle, C. (1992). Gender labeling, gender stereotyping, and parenting behaviors. *Developmental Psychology, 28,* 225–230.

Fahrmeier, E. D. (1978). The development of concrete operations among the Hausa. *Journal of Cross-Cultural Psychology, 9,* 23–44.

Fairburn, C. G., & Harrison, P. J. (2003). Eating disorders. *Lancet, 361,* 407–416.

Falagas, M. E., & Zarkadoulia, E. (2008). Factors associated with suboptimal compliance to vaccinations in children in developed countries: A systematic review. *Current Medical Research and Opinion, 24,* 1719–1741.

Falbo, T. (1992). Social norms and the one-child family: Clinical and policy implications. In F. Boer & J. Dunn (Eds.), *Children's sibling relationships* (pp. 71–82). Hillsdale, NJ: Erlbaum.

Falbo, T., & Poston, D. L., Jr. (1993). The academic, personality, and physical outcomes of only children in China. *Child Development, 64,* 18–35.

Falbo, T., Poston, D. L., Jr., Triscari, R. S., & Zhang, X. (1997). Self-enhancing illusions among Chinese schoolchildren. *Journal of Cross-Cultural Psychology, 28,* 172–191.

Falck-Ytter, T., Gredebäck, G., & von Hofsten, C. (2006). Infants predict other people's action goals. *Nature Neuroscience, 9,* 878–879.

Falk, D. (2005). Brain lateralization in primates and its evolution in hominids. *American Journal of Physical Anthropology, 30,* 107–125.

Fantz, R. L. (1961). The origin of form perception. *Scientific American, 204,* 66–72.

Farah, M. J., Shera, D. M., Savage, J. H., Betancourt, L., Giannetta, J. M., Brodsky, N. L., et al. (2006). Childhood poverty: Specific associations with neurocognitive development. *Brain Research, 110,* 166–174.

Faraone, S. V. (2008). Statistical and molecular genetic approaches to developmental psychopathology: The pathway forward. In J. J. Hudziak (Ed.), *Developmental psychology and wellness: Genetic and environmental influences* (pp. 245–265). Washington, DC: American Psychiatric Publishing.

Faraone, S. V., & Mick, E. (2010). Molecular genetics of attention deficit hyperactivity disorder. *Psychiatric Clinics of North America, 33,* 159–180.

Farmer, T. W., Irvin, M. J., Leung, M.-C., Hall, C. M., Hutchins, B. C., & McDonough, E. (2010). Social preference, social prominence, and group membership in late elementary school: Homophilic concentration and peer affiliation configurations. *Social Psychology of Education, 13,* 271–293.

Farmer, T. W., Leung, M., Pearl, R., Rodkin, P. C., Cadwallader, T. W., & Van Acker, R. (2002). Deviant or diverse peer groups? The peer affiliations of aggressive elementary students. *Journal of Educational Psychology, 94,* 611–620.

Farr, R. J., Forssell, S. L., & Patterson, C. J. (2010). Parenting and child development in adoptive families: Does parental sexual orientation matter? *Applied Developmental Science, 14,* 164–178.

Farrant, K., & Reese, E. (2000). Maternal style and children's participation in reminiscing: Stepping stones in children's autobiographical memory development. *Journal of Cognition and Development, 1,* 193–225.

Farrington, D. P. (2009). Conduct disorder, aggression and delinquency. In R. M. Lerner & L. Steinberg (Eds.), *Handbook of adolescent psychology: Vol. 1. Individual bases of adolescent development* (3rd ed., pp. 683–722). Hoboken, NJ: Wiley.

Farrington, D. P., Ttofi, M. M., & Coid, J. W. (2009) Development of adolescence-limited, late onset, and persistent offenders from age 8 to age 48. *Aggressive Behavior, 35,* 150–163.

Farroni, T., Csibra, G., Simion, F., & Johnson, M. H. (2002). Eye contact detection in humans from birth. *Proceedings of the National Academy of Sciences, 99,* 9602–9605.

Farroni, T., Massaccesi, S., Menon, E., & Johnson, M. H. (2007). Direct gaze modulates face recognition in young infants. *Cognition, 102,* 396–404.

Farver, J. A. M., & Branstetter, W. H. (1994). Preschoolers' prosocial responses to their peers' distress. *Developmental Psychology, 30,* 334–341.

Farver, J. A. M., Kim, Y. K., & Lee, Y. (1995). Cultural differences in Korean- and Anglo-American preschoolers' social interaction and play behaviors. *Child Development, 66,* 1088–1099.

Farver, J. A. M., & Wimbarti, S. (1995a). Indonesian toddlers' social play with their mothers and older siblings. *Child Development, 66,* 1493–1503.

Farver, J. A. M., & Wimbarti, S. (1995b). Paternal participation in toddlers' pretend play. *Social Development, 4,* 19–31.

Fasig, L. G. (2000). Toddlers' understanding of ownership: Implications for self-concept development. *Social Development, 9,* 370–382.

Fattibene, P., Mazzei, R., Nuccetelli, C., & Risica, S. (1999). Prenatal exposure to ionizing radiation: Sources, effects, and regulatory aspects. *Acta Paediatrica, 88,* 693–702.

Fearon, R. P., Bakermans-Kranenburg, M. J., Lapsley, A., & Roisman, G. I. (2010). The significance of insecure attachment and disorganization in the development of children's externalizing behavior: A meta-analytic study. *Child Development, 81,* 435–456.

Federal Interagency Forum on Child and Family Statistics. (2011). *America's children: Key national indicators of well-being.* Retrieved from www.childstats.gov/americaschildren/index.asp

Fee, E. J. (1997). The prosodic framework for language learning. *Topics in Language Disorders, 17,* 53–62.

Feeney, J. A., Hohaus, L., Noller, P., & Alexander, R. P. (2001). *Becoming parents: Exploring the bonds between mothers, fathers, and their infants.* New York: Cambridge University Press.

Feigelman, W., & Gorman, B. S. (2008). Assessing the effects of peer suicide on youth suicide. *Suicide and Life-Threatening Behavior, 38,* 181–194.

Feinberg, M. E., McHale, S. M., Crouter, A. C., & Cumsille, P. (2003). Sibling differentiation: Sibling and parent relationship trajectories in adolescence. *Child Development, 74,* 1261–1274.

Feldman, A. F., & Matjasko, J. L. (2007). Profiles and portfolios of adolescent school-based extracurricular activity participation. *Journal of Adolescence, 30,* 313–332.

Feldman, D. H. (2004). Child prodigies: A distinctive form of giftedness. In R. J. Sternberg (Ed.), *Definitions and conceptions of giftedness* (pp. 133–144). Thousand Oaks, CA: Corwin Press.

Feldman, R. (2002). Parents' convergence on sharing and marital satisfaction, father involvement, and parent–child relationship in the transition to parenthood. *Infant Mental Health Journal, 21,* 176–191.

Feldman, R. (2003). Infant–mother and infant–father synchrony: The coregulation of positive arousal. *Infant Mental Health Journal, 24,* 1–23.

Feldman, R. (2006). From biological rhythms to social rhythms: Physiological precursors of mother–infant synchrony. *Developmental Psychology, 42,* 175–188.

Feldman, R. (2007a). Maternal–infant contact and child development: Insights from the kangaroo intervention. In L. L'Abate (Ed.), *Low-cost approaches to promote physical and mental health: Theory, research, and practice* (pp. 323–351). New York: Springer.

Feldman, R. (2007b). Maternal versus child risk and the development of parent–child and family relationships in five high-risk populations. *Development and Psychopathology, 19,* 293–312.

Feldman, R. (2007c). Parent–infant synchrony and the construction of shared timing; Physiological precursors, developmental outcomes, and risk conditions. *Journal of Child Psychology and Psychiatry, 48,* 329–354.

Feldman, R., Granat, A., Pariente, C., Kanety, H., Kuint, J., & Gilboa-Schechtman, E. (2009). Maternal depression and anxiety across the postpartum year and infant social engagement, fear regulation, and stress reactivity. *Journal of the American Academy of Child and Adolescent Psychiatry, 48,* 919–927.

Feldman, R., Greenbaum, C. W., & Yirmiya, N. (1999). Mother–infant affect synchrony as an antecedent of the emergence of self-control. *Developmental Psychology, 35,* 223–231.

Feldman, R., & Klein, P. S. (2003). Toddlers' self-regulated compliance to mothers, caregivers, and fathers: Implications for theories of socialization. *Developmental Psychology, 39,* 680–692.

Feldman, R., Sussman, A. L., & Zigler, E. (2004). Parental leave and work adaptation at the transition to parenthood: Individual, marital, and social correlates. *Journal of Applied Developmental Psychology, 25,* 459–479.

Feldman, R., Weller, A., Sirota, L., & Eidelman, A. I. (2003). Testing a family intervention hypothesis: The contribution of mother–infant skin-to-skin contact (kangaroo care) to family interaction, proximity, and touch. *Journal of Family Psychology, 17,* 94–107.

Felner, R. D., Favazza, A., Shim, M., Brand, S., Gu, K., & Noonan, N. (2002). Whole school improvement and restructuring as prevention and promotion: Lessons from STEP and the Project on High Performance Learning Communities. *Journal of School Psychology, 39,* 177–202.

Felsman, D. E., & Blustein, D. L. (1999). The role of peer relatedness in late adolescent career development. *Journal of Vocational Behavior, 54,* 279–295.

Feng, Q. (2005). Postnatal consequences of prenatal cocaine exposure and myocardial apoptosis: Does cocaine in utero imperil the adult heart? *British Journal of Pharmacology, 144,* 887–888.

Fennell, C. T., & Werker, J. F. (2003). Early word learners' ability to access phonetic detail in well-known words. *Language and Speech, 46,* 245–264.

Fenson, L., Dale, P. S., Reznick, J. S., Bates, E., Thal, D. J., & Pethick, S. J. (1994). Variability in early communicative development. *Monographs of the Society for Research in Child Development, 59* (5, Serial No. 242).

Ferguson, R. F. (1998). Teachers' perceptions and expectations and the black–white test score gap. In C. Jencks & M. Phillips (Eds.), *The black–white test score gap* (pp. 273–317). Washington, DC: Brookings Institution.

Ferguson, T. J., Stegge, H., & Damhuis, I. (1991). Children's understanding of guilt and shame. *Child Development, 62,* 827–839.

Fergusson, D. M., & Horwood, J. (2003). Resilience to childhood adversity: Results of a 21-year study. In S. S. Luthar (Ed.), *Resilience and vulnerability* (pp. 130–155). New York: Cambridge University Press.

Fergusson, D. M., & Woodward, L. J. (1999). Breast-feeding and later psychosocial adjustment. *Paediatric and Perinatal Epidemiology, 13,* 144–157.

Fergusson, D. M., Horwood, L. J., & Ridder, E. M. (2005). Show me the child at seven II: Childhood intelligence and later outcomes in adolescence and young adulthood. *Journal of Child Psychology and Psychiatry, 46,* 850–858.

Fernald, A., & Hurtado, N. (2006). Names in frames: Infants interpret words in sentence frames faster than words in isolation. *Developmental Science, 9,* F33–F40.

Fernald, A., & Morikawa, H. (1993). Common themes and cultural variations in Japanese and American mothers' speech to infants. *Child Development, 64,* 637–656.

Fernald, A., Perfors, A., & Marchman, V. A. (2006). Picking up speed in understanding: Speech processing efficiency and vocabulary growth across the 2nd year. *Developmental Psychology, 42,* 98–116.

Fernald, A., Swingley, D., & Pinto, J. P. (2001). When half a word is enough: Infants can recognize spoken words using partial phonetic information. *Child Development, 72,* 1003–1015.

Fernald, A., Taeschner, T., Dunn, J., Papousek, M., de Boysson-Bardies, B., & Fukui, I. (1989). A cross-language study of prosodic modifications in mothers' and fathers' speech to preverbal infants. *Journal of Child Language, 16,* 477–502.

Fernald, L. C., & Grantham-McGregor, S. M. (1998). Stress response in school-age children who have been growth-retarded since early childhood. *American Journal of Clinical Nutrition, 68,* 691–698.

Fernyhough, C., & Fradley, E. (2005). Private speech on an executive task: Relations with task difficulty and task performance. *Cognitive Development, 20,* 103–120.

Ferry, A. L., Hespos, S. J., & Waxman, S. R. (2010). Categorization in 3- and 4-month-old infants: An advantage of words over tones. *Child Development, 81,* 472–479.

Ficca, G., Fagioli, I., Giganti, F., & Salzarulo, P. (1999). Spontaneous awakenings from sleep in the first year of life. *Early Human Development, 55,* 219–228.

Field, T. (1998). Massage therapy effects. *American Psychologist, 53,* 1270–1281.

Field, T. (2001). Massage therapy facilitates weight gain in preterm infants. *Current Directions in Psychological Science, 10,* 51–54.

Field, T. (2011). Prenatal depression effects on early development: A review. *Infant Behavior and Development, 34,* 1–14.

Field, T., Hernandez-Reif, M., Feijo, L., & Freedman, J. (2006). Prenatal, perinatal and neonatal stimulation: A survey of neonatal nurseries. *Infant Behavior and Development, 29,* 24–31.

Field, T., Hernandez-Reif, M., & Freedman, J. (2004). Stimulation programs for preterm infants. *Social Policy Report of the Society for Research in Child Development, 18*(1).

Fiese, B. H., Foley, K. P., & Spagnola, M. (2006). Routine and ritual elements in family mealtimes: Contexts for child well-being and family identity. *New Directions for Child and Adolescent Development, 111,* 67–90.

Fiese, B. H., & Schwartz, M. (2008). Reclaiming the family table: Mealtimes and child health and well-being. *Social Policy Report of the Society for Research in Child Development, 22*(4), 3–18.

Fiese, B. H., & Winter, M. A. (2010). The dynamics of family chaos and its relation to children's socioemotional well-being. In G. W. Evans & T. D. Wachs (Eds.), *Chaos and its influence on children's development: An ecological perspective* (pp. 49–66). Washington, DC: American Psychological Association.

Fifer, W. P., Byrd, D. L., Kaku, M., Eigsti, I.-M., Isler, J. R., Grose-Fifer, J., et al. (2010). Newborn infants learn during sleep. *Proceedings of the National Academy of Sciences, 107,* 10320–10323.

Figner, B., Mackinlay, R. J., Wilkening, F., & Weber, E. U. (2009). Affective and deliberative processes in risky choice: Age differences in risk taking in the Columbia Card Task. *Journal of Experimental Psychology: Learning, Memory, and Cognition, 35,* 709–770.

Findlay, L. C., & Coplan, R. J. (2008). Come out and play: Shyness in childhood and the benefits of organized sports participation. *Canadian Journal of Behavioural Science, 40,* 153–161.

Finger, B., Hans, S. L., Bernstein, V. J., & Cox, S. M. (2009). Parent relationship quality and infant–mother attachment. *Attachment and Human Development, 11,* 285–306.

Finkel, D., & Pedersen, N. L. (2001). Sources of environmental influence on cognitive abilities in adulthood. In E. L. Grigorenko & R. J. Sternberg (Eds.), *Family environment and intellectual functioning: A life-span perspective* (pp. 173–194). Mahwah, NJ: Erlbaum.

Finkelhor, D. (2009). The prevention of childhood sexual abuse. *Future of Children, 19,* 169–194.

Finkelhor, D., Ormrod, R., Turner, H., & Hamby, S. L. (2005). The victimization of children and youth: A comprehensive, national survey. *Child Maltreatment, 10,* 5–25.

Finn, J. D., Gerber, S. B., & Boyd-Zaharias, J. (2005). Small classes in the early grades, academic achievement, and graduating from high school. *Journal of Educational Psychology, 97,* 214–233.

Finnilä, K., Mahlberga, N., Santtilia, P., & Niemib, P. (2003). Validity of a test of children's suggestibility for predicting responses to two interview situations differing in degree of suggestiveness. *Journal of Experimental Child Psychology, 85,* 32–49.

Fischer, K. W., & Bidell, T. (1991). Constraining nativist inferences about cognitive capacities. In S. Carey & R. Gelman (Eds.), *The epigenesis of mind: Essays on biology and cognition* (pp. 199–235). Hillsdale, NJ: Erlbaum.

Fischer, K. W., & Bidell, T. R. (2006). Dynamic development of action and thought. In R. M. Lerner (Ed.), *Handbook of child psychology: Vol. 1. Theoretical models of human development* (6th ed., pp. 313–399). Hoboken, NJ: Wiley.

Fischman, M. G., Moore, J. B., & Steele, K. H. (1992). Children's one-hand catching as a function of age, gender, and ball location. *Research Quarterly for Exercise and Sport, 63,* 349–355.

Fish, J. M. (2002). *Race and intelligence: Separating science from myth.* Mahwah, NJ: Erlbaum.

Fish, M. (2004). Attachment in infancy and preschool in low socioeconomic status rural Appalachian children: Stability and change and relations to preschool and kindergarten competence. *Development and Psychopathology, 16,* 293–312.

Fisher, C. B. (1993, Winter). Integrating science and ethics in research with high-risk children and youth. *Social Policy Report of the Society for Research in Child Development, 4*(4).

Fisher, C. B. (2005). Deception research involving children: Ethical practices and paradoxes. *Ethics and Behavior, 15,* 271–287.

Fisher, J. O., & Birch, L. L. (1999). Restricting access to palatable foods affects children's behavioral response, food selection, and intake. *American Journal of Clinical Nutrition, 69,* 1264–1272.

Fisher, J. O., Mitchell, D. S., Smiciklas-Wright, H., & Birch, L. L. (2001). Maternal milk consumption predicts the tradeoff between milk and soft drinks in young girls' diets. *Journal of Nutrition, 131,* 246–250.

Fisher, L., Ames, E. W., Chisholm, K., & Savoie, L. (1997). Problems reported by parents of Romanian orphans adopted to British Columbia. *International Journal of Behavioral Development, 20,* 67–82.

Fisher, M., Barkley, R. A., Smallish, L., & Fletcher, K. (2002). Young adult follow-up of hyperactive children: Self-reported psychiatric disorders, comorbidity, and the role of childhood conduct problems and teen CD. *Journal of Abnormal Child Psychology, 39,* 463–475.

Fisher, S. E., Francks, C., McCracken, J. T., McGough, J. J., Marlow, A. J., & MacPhie, I. L. (2002). A genomewide scan for loci involved in attention-deficit/hyperactivity disorder. *American Journal of Human Genetics, 70,* 1183–1196.

Fivush, R. (2001). Owning experience: Developing subjective perspective in autobiographical narratives. In C. Moore & K. Lemmon (Eds.), *The self in time: Developmental perspectives* (pp. 35–52). Mahwah, NJ: Erlbaum.

Fivush, R. (2006). Scripting attachment: Generalized event representations and internal working models. *Attachment and Human Development, 8,* 283–289.

Fivush, R. (2009). Sociocultural perspectives on autobiographical memory. In M. L. Courage & N. Cowan (Eds.), *The development of memory in infancy and childhood* (pp. 283–301). Hove, UK: Psychology Press.

Fivush, R., & Haden, C. A. (2005). Parent-child reminiscing and the construction of a subjective self. In B. D. Homer & C. S. Tamis-LeMonda (Eds.), *The development of social cognition and communication* (pp. 315–336). Mahwah, NJ: Erlbaum.

Fivush, R., & Reese, E. (2002). Reminiscing and relating: The development of parent-child talk about the past. In J. D. Webster & B. K. Haight (Eds.), *Critical advances in reminiscence work: From theory to application* (pp. 109–122). New York: Springer.

Fivush, R., & Wang, Q. (2005). Emotion talk in mother-child conversations of the shared past: The effects of culture, gender, and event valence. *Journal of Cognition and Development, 6,* 489–506.

Flanagan, C. A., & Faison, N. (2001). Youth civic development: Implications of research for social policy and programs. *Social Policy Report of the Society for Research in Child Development, 15*(1).

Flanagan, C. A., Stout, M., & Gallay, L. S. (2008). It's my body and none of your business: Developmental changes in adolescents' perceptions of rights concerning health. *Journal of Social Issues, 64,* 815–834.

Flanagan, C. A., & Tucker, C. J. (1999). Adolescents' explanations for political issues: Concordance with their views of self and society. *Developmental Psychology, 35,* 1198–1209.

Flannery, D. J., Hussey, D. L., Biebelhausen, L., & Wester, K. L. (2003). Crime, delinquency, and youth gangs. In G. R. Adams & M. D. Berzonsky (Eds.), *Blackwell handbook of adolescence* (pp. 502–522). Malden, MA: Blackwell.

Flannery, K. A., & Liederman, J. (1995). Is there really a syndrome involving the co-occurrence of neurodevelopmental disorder, talent, non-right handedness and immune disorder among children? *Cortex, 31,* 503–515.

Flavell, J. H. (2000). Development of children's knowledge about the mental world. *International Journal of Behavioral Development, 24,* 15–23.

Flavell, J. H., Green, F. L., & Flavell, E. R. (1987). Development of knowledge about the appearance-reality distinction. *Monographs of the Society for Research in Child Development, 51*(1, Serial No. 212).

Flavell, J. H., Green, F. L., & Flavell, E. R. (1993). Children's understanding of the stream of consciousness. *Child Development, 64,* 387–398.

Flavell, J. H., Green, F. L., & Flavell, E. R. (1995). Young children's knowledge about thinking. *Monographs of the Society for Research in Child Development, 60*(1, Serial No. 243).

Flavell, J. H., Green, F. L., & Flavell, E. R. (2000). Development of children's awareness of their own thoughts. *Journal of Cognition and Development, 1,* 97–112.

Flege, J. E., Birdsong, D., Bialystok, E., Mack, M., Sung, H., & Tsukada, K. (2006). Degree of foreign accent in English sentences produced by Korean children and adults. *Journal of Phonetics, 34,* 153–175.

Flege, J. E., Yeni-Komshian, G. H., & Liu, S. (1999). Age constraints on second-language acquisition. *Journal of Memory and Language, 41,* 78–104.

Fletcher, A. C., Nickerson, P., & Wright, K. L. (2003). Structured leisure activities in middle childhood. *Journal of Community Psychology, 31,* 641–659.

Floccia, C., Christophe, A., & Bertoncini, J. (1997). High-amplitude sucking and newborns: The quest for underlying mechanisms. *Journal of Experimental Child Psychology, 64,* 175–198.

Flom, R., & Bahrick, L. E. (2010). The effects of intersensory redundancy on attention and memory: Infants' long-term memory for orientation in audiovisual events. *Developmental Psychology, 46,* 428–436.

Flom, R., & Pick, A. D. (2003). Verbal encouragement and joint attention in 18-month-old infants. *Infant Behavior and Development, 26,* 121–134.

Florsheim, P., & Smith, A. (2005). Expectant adolescent couples' relations and subsequent parenting behavior. *Infant Mental Health Journal, 26,* 533–548.

Flouri, E., & Buchanan, A. (2004). Early father's and mother's involvement and child's later educational outcomes. *British Journal of Educational Psychology, 74,* 141–153.

Flynn, E. (2006). A microgenetic investigation of stability and continuity in theory of mind development. *British Journal of Developmental Psychology, 24,* 631–654.

Flynn, E., & Siegler, R. (2007). Measuring change: Current trends and future directions in microgenetic research. *Infant and Child Development, 16,* 135–149.

Flynn, J. R. (1994). IQ gains over time. In R. J. Sternberg (Ed.), *The encyclopedia of human intelligence* (pp. 617–623). New York: Macmillan.

Flynn, J. R. (1999). Searching for justice: The discovery of IQ gains over time. *American Psychologist, 54,* 5–20.

Flynn, J. R. (2003). Movies about intelligence: The limitations of g. *Current Directions in Psychological Science, 12,* 95–99.

Flynn, J. R. (2007). *What is intelligence? Beyond the Flynn effect.* New York: Cambridge University Press.

Flynn, J. R., & Weiss, L. G. (2007). American IQ gains from 1932 to 2002: The WISC subtests and educational progress. *International Journal of Testing, 7,* 209–224.

Foehr, U. G. (2006). *Media multitasking among American youth: Prevalence, predictors, and pairings.* Menlo Park, CA: Kaiser Family Foundation.

Foerde, K., Knowlton, B. J., & Poldrack, R. A. (2006). Modulation of competing memory systems by distraction. *Proceedings of the National Academy of Sciences, 103,* 11778–11783.

Fogel, A., & Garvey, A. (2007). Alive communication. *Infant Behavior and Development, 30,* 251–257.

Fogel, A., Melson, G. F., Toda, S., & Mistry, T. (1987). Young children's responses to unfamiliar infants. *International Journal of Behavioral Development, 10,* 1071–1077.

Fomon, S. J., & Nelson, S. E. (2002). Body composition of the male and female reference infants. *Annual Review of Nutrition, 22,* 1–17.

Fonzi, A., Schneider, B. H., Tani, F., & Tomada, G. (1997). Predicting children's friendship status from their dyadic interaction in structured situations of potential conflict. *Child Development, 68,* 496–506.

Fordham, K., & Stevenson-Hinde, J. (1999). Shyness, friendship quality, and

adjustment during middle childhood. *Journal of Child Psychology and Psychiatry, 40,* 757–768.

Forgatch, M. S., & DeGarmo, D. S. (1999). Parenting through change: An effective prevention program for single mothers. *Journal of Consulting and Clinical Psychology, 67,* 711–724.

Forgatch, M. S., Patterson, G. R., Degarmo, D. S., & Beldavs, Z. G. (2009). Testing the Oregon delinquency model with 9-year follow-up of the Oregon Divorce Study. *Development and Psychopathology, 21,* 637–660.

Forman, D. R., Aksan, N., & Kochanska, G. (2004). Toddlers' responsive imitation predicts preschool-age conscience. *Psychological Science, 15,* 699–704.

Forman, D. R., O'Hara, M. W., Stuart, S., Gorman, L. L., Larsen, K. E., & Coy, K. C. (2007). Effective treatment for postpartum depression is not sufficient to improve the developing mother-child relationship. *Development and Psychopathology, 19,* 585–602.

Fortenberry, J. D. (2010). Fate, desire, and the centrality of the relationship to adolescent condom use. *Journal of Adolescent Health, 47,* 219–220.

Foster, M. A., Lambert, R., Abbott-Shim, M., McCarty, F., & Franze, S. (2005). A model of home learning environment and social risk factors in relation to children's emergent literacy and social outcomes. *Early Childhood Research Quarterly, 20,* 13–36.

Foster, W. A., & Miller, M. (2007). Development of the literacy achievement gap: A longitudinal study of kindergarten through third grade. *Language, Speech, and Hearing Services in Schools, 38,* 173–181.

Foundation for Child Development. (2010). *Child well-being index (CWI).* Retrieved from www.fcd-us.org/our-work/child-well-being-index-cwi

Fox, C. L., & Boulton, M. J. (2006). Friendship as a moderator of the relationship between social skills problems and peer victimization. *Aggressive Behavior, 32,* 110–121.

Fox, N. A. (1991). If it's not left, it's right: Electroencephalograph asymmetry and the development of emotion. *American Psychologist, 46,* 863–872.

Fox, N. A., & Calkins, S. D. (2003). The development of self-control of emotion: Intrinsic and extrinsic influences. *Motivation and Emotion, 27,* 7–26.

Fox, N. A., & Card, J. A. (1998). Psychophysiological measures in the study of attachment. In J. Cassidy & P. Shaver (Eds.), *Handbook of attachment: Theory, research, and clinical applications* (pp. 226–245). New York: Guilford.

Fox, N. A., & Davidson, R. J. (1986). Taste-elicited changes in facial signs of emotion and the asymmetry of brain electrical activity in newborn infants. *Neuropsychologia, 24,* 417–422.

Fox, N. A., Henderson, H. A., Pérez-Edgar, K., & White, L. K. (2008). The biology of temperament: An integrative approach. In C. A. Nelson & M. Luciana (Eds.), *Handbook of developmental cognitive neuroscience* (2nd ed., pp. 839–853). Cambridge, MA: MIT Press.

Foy, J. G., & Mann, V. (2003). Home literacy environment and phonological awareness in preschool children: Differential effects for rhyme and phoneme awareness. *Applied Psycholinguistics, 24,* 59–88.

Fraiberg, S. (1971). *Insights from the blind.* New York: Basic Books.

Frank, D. A., Rose-Jacobs, R., Beeghly, M., Wilbur, M., Bellinger, D., & Cabral, H. (2005). Level of prenatal cocaine exposure and 48-month IQ: Importance of preschool enrichment. *Neurotoxicology and Teratology, 27,* 15–28.

Frank, J. B., Jarit, G. J., Bravman, J. T., & Rosen, J. E. (2007). Lower extremity injuries in the skeletally immature athlete. *Journal of the American Academy of Orthopaedic Surgeons, 15,* 356–366.

Frankenberg, E., Lee, C., & Orfield, G. (2003). *A multiracial society with segregated schools: Are we losing the dream?* Cambridge, MA: The Civil Rights Project, Harvard University.

Frankenberg, E., & Orfield, G. (2007). *Lessons in integration: Realizing the promise of racial diversity in American schools.* Charlottesville, VA: University of Virginia Press.

Fraser, M. W., Galinsky, M. J., Smokowski, P. R., Day, S. H., Terzian, M. A., Rose, R. A., & Guo, S. (2005). Social information-processing skills training to promote social competence and prevent aggressive behavior in third grade. *Journal of Consulting and Clinical Psychology, 73,* 1045–1055.

Fraser, M. W., Lee, J., Kupper, L. L., & Day, S. H. (2011). A controlled trial of the Making Choices program: Six-month follow-up. *Research on Social Work Practice, 21,* 165–176.

Frederiksen-Goldsen, K. I., & Sharlach, A. E. (2000). *Families and work: New directions in the twenty-first century.* New York: Oxford University Press.

Fredricks, J. A., & Eccles, J. S. (2002). Children's competence and value beliefs from childhood through adolescence: Growth trajectories in two male-sex-typed domains. *Developmental Psychology, 38,* 519–533.

Fredricks, J. A., & Eccles, J. S. (2005). Developmental benefits of extracurricular involvement: Do peer characteristics mediate the link between activities and youth outcomes? *Journal of Youth and Adolescence, 34,* 507–520.

Fredricks, J. A., & Eccles, J. S. (2006). Is extracurricular participation associated with beneficial outcomes? Concurrent and longitudinal relations. *Developmental Psychology, 42,* 698–713.

Freeman, D. (1983). *Margaret Mead and Samoa: The making and unmaking of an anthropological myth.* Cambridge, MA: Harvard University Press.

Freeman, H., & Newland, L. A. (2010). New directions in father attachment. *Early Child Development and Care, 180,* 1–8.

Freitag, C. M., Rohde, L. A., Lempp, T., & Romanos, M. (2010). Phenotypic and measurement influences on heritability estimates in childhood ADHD. *European Child and Adolescent Psychiatry, 19,* 311–323.

Freud, S. (1961). Some psychological consequences of the anatomical distinction between the sexes. In J. Strachey (Ed.), *Standard edition of the complete psychological works of Sigmund Freud* (Vol. 19, pp. 248–258). London: Hogarth Press. (Original work published 1925)

Freud, S. (1973). *An outline of psychoanalysis.* London: Hogarth. (Original work published 1938)

Freud, S. (1974). *The ego and the id.* London: Hogarth. (Original work published 1923)

Friedman, J. M. (1996). *The effects of drugs on the fetus and nursing infant: A handbook for health care professionals.* Baltimore: Johns Hopkins University Press.

Fries, A. B. W., & Pollak, S. D. (2004). Emotion understanding in postinstitutionalized Eastern European children. *Development and Psychopathology, 16,* 355–369.

Frijda, N. (2000). The psychologist's point of view. In M. Lewis & J. M. Haviland-Jones (Eds.), *Handbook of emotions* (pp. 59–74). New York: Guilford.

Frith, L. (2001). Gamete donation and anonymity: The ethical and legal debate. *Human Reproduction, 16,* 818–824.

Frith, U. (2003). *Autism: Explaining the enigma* (2nd ed.). Malden, MA: Blackwell.

Frome, P. M., & Eccles, J. S. (1998). Parents' influence on children's achievement-related perceptions. *Journal of Personality and Social Psychology, 74,* 435–452.

Fry, A. F., & Hale, S. (1996). Processing speed, working memory, and fluid intelligence: Evidence for a developmental cascade. *Psychological Science, 7,* 237–241.

Fryer, S. L., Crocker, N. A., & Mattson, S. N. (2008). Exposure to teratogenic agents as a risk factor for psychopathology. In T. P. Beauchaine & S. P. Hinshaw (Eds.), *Child and adolescent psychopathology* (pp. 180–207). Hoboken, NJ: Wiley.

Fu, G., Xu, F., Cameron, C. A., Heyman, G., & Lee, K. (2007). Cross-cultural differences in children's choices, categorizations, and evaluations of truths and lies. *Developmental Psychology, 43,* 278–293.

Fuchs, I., Eisenberg, N., Hertz-Lazarowitz, R., & Sharabany, R. (1986). Kibbutz, Israeli city, and American children's moral reasoning about prosocial moral conflicts. *Merrill-Palmer Quarterly, 32,* 37–50.

Fuchs, L. S., Fuchs, D., Mathes, P. G., Martinez, E. A. (2002a). Preliminary evidence on the standing of students with learning disabilities in PALS and no-PALS classrooms. *Learning Disabilities Research and Practice, 17,* 205–215.

Fuchs, L. S., Fuchs, D., Yazkian, L., & Powell, S. R. (2002b). Enhancing first-grade children's mathematical development with peer-assisted learning strategies. *School Psychology Review, 31,* 569–583.

Fuligni, A. J. (1998). Authority, autonomy, and parent–adolescent conflict and cohesion: A study of adolescents from Mexican, Chinese, Filipino, and European backgrounds. *Developmental Psychology, 34,* 782–792.

Fuligni, A. J. (2004). The adaptation and acculturation of children from immigrant families. In U. P. Gielen & J. Roopnarine (Eds.), *Childhood and adolescence: Cross-cultural perspectives* (pp. 297–318). Westport, CT: Praeger.

Fuligni, A. J., Yip, T., & Tseng, V. (2002). The impact of family obligation on the daily activities and psychological well-being of Chinese-American adolescents. *Child Development, 73,* 302–314.

Fuligni, A. J., & Yoshikawa, H. (2003). Socioeconomic resources, parenting, and child development among immigrant families. In M. H. Bornstein & R. H. Bradley (Eds.), *Socioeconomic status, parenting, and child development* (pp. 107–124). Mahwah, NJ: Erlbaum.

Fuligni, A. S., Han, W.-J., & Brooks-Gunn, J. (2004). The Infant-Toddler HOME in the 2nd and 3rd years of life. *Parenting: Science and Practice, 4,* 139–159.

Fuller, C., Keller, L., Olson, J., Plymale, A., & Gottesman, M. (2005). Helping preschoolers become healthy eaters. *Journal of Pediatric Health Care, 19,* 178–182.

Fuller-Thomson, E., & Minkler, M. (2005). Native American grandparents raising grandchildren: Findings from the Census 2000 Supplementary Survey and implications for social work practice. *Social Work, 50,* 131–139.

Fuller-Thomson, E., & Minkler, M. (2007). Mexican American grandparents raising grandchildren: Findings from the Census 2000 American Community Survey. *Families in Society, 88,* 567–574.

Fullerton, J. T., Navarro, A. M., & Young, S. H. (2007). Outcomes of planned home birth: An integrative review. *Journal of Midwifery and Women's Health, 52,* 323–333.

Fung, H. (1999). Becoming a moral child: The socialization of shame among Chinese children. *Ethos, 27,* 180–209.

Furman, W., & Buhrmester, D. (1992). Age and sex differences in perceptions of networks of personal relationships. *Child Development, 63,* 103–115.

Furman, W., & Collins, W. A. (2009). Adolescent romantic relationships and experiences. In K. Rubin, W. M. Bukowski, & B. Laursen (Eds.), *Handbook of peer interactions, relationships, and groups* (pp. 341–360). New York: Guilford Press.

Furman, W., Simon, V. A., Shaffer, L., & Bouchey, H. A. (2002). Adolescents' working models and styles for relationships with parents, friends, and romantic partners. *Child Development, 73,* 241–255.

Furstenberg, F. F. (2007). *Destinies of the disadvantaged.* New York: Russell Sage Foundation.

Furstenberg, F. F., Jr., & Harris, K. M. (1993). When and why fathers matter: Impact of father involvement on children of adolescent mothers. In R. I. Lerman & T. J. Ooms (Eds.), *Young unwed fathers* (pp. 117–138). Philadelphia: Temple University Press.

Furusawa, T., Naka, I., Yamauchi, T., Natsuhara, K., Kimura, R., Nakazawa, M., et al. (2010). The Q223r polymorphism in LEPR is associated with obesity in Pacific Islanders. *Human Genetics, 127,* 287–294.

Fuson, K. C. (2009). Avoiding misinterpretations of Piaget and Vygotsky: Mathematical teaching without learning, learning without teaching, or helpful learning-path teaching? *Cognitive Development, 24,* 343–361.

Fuson, K. C., & Burghard, B. H. (2003). Multidigit addition and subtraction methods invented in small groups and teacher support of problem solving and reflection. In A. J. Baroody & A. Dowker (Eds.), *The development of arithmetic concepts and skills* (pp. 267–304). Mahwah, NJ: Erlbaum.

Galambos, N. L., & Maggs, J. L. (1991). Children in self-care: Figures, facts, and fiction. In J. V. Lerner & N. L. Galambos (Eds.), *Employed mothers and their children* (pp. 131–157). New York: Garland.

Galambos, N. L., Almeida, D. M., & Petersen, A. C. (1990). Masculinity, femininity, and sex role attitudes in early adolescence: Exploring gender intensification. *Child Development, 61,* 1904–1914.

Gale, C. R., Hatch, S., Batty, D., & Deary, I. J. (2009). Intelligence in childhood and risk of psychological distress in adulthood: The 1958 National Child Development Survey and the 1970 British Cohort Study. *Intelligence, 37,* 592–599.

Galen, B. R., & Underwood, M. K. (1997). A developmental investigation of social aggression among children. *Developmental Psychology, 33,* 589–600.

Galinsky, E. (2006). *The economic benefits of high-quality early childhood programs: What makes the difference?* Washington, DC: Committee for Economic Development.

Galinsky, E., Aumann, K., & Bond, J. T. (2009). *Times are changing: Gender and generation at work and at home.* New York: Families and Work Institute.

Gallagher, A. M., & Kaufman, J. C. (2005). Gender differences in mathematics: What we know and what we need to know. In A. M. Gallagher & J. C. Kaufman (Eds.), *Gender differences in mathematics: An integrative psychological approach* (pp. 316–331). New York: Cambridge University Press.

Galloway, J. C., & Thelen, E. (2004). Feet first: Object exploration in young infants. *Infant Behavior and Development, 27,* 107–112.

Gallup News Service. (2006). *Religion most important to blacks, women, and older Americans.* Retrieved from www.gallup.com/poll/25585/Religion-Most-Important-Black-Women-Older-Americans.aspx?version=print

Galton, F. (1883). *Inquiries into human faculty and its development.* London: Macmillan.

Ganea, P. A., Allen, M. L., Butler, L., Carey, S., & DeLoache, J. S. (2009). Toddlers' referential understanding of pictures. *Journal of Experimental Child Psychology, 104,* 283–295.

Ganea, P. A., & Harris, P. L. (2010). Not doing what you are told: Early perseverative errors in updating mental representations via language. *Child Development, 81,* 457–463.

Ganea, P. A., Pickard, M. B., & DeLoache, J. S. (2008). Transfer between picture books and the real world by very young children. *Journal of Cognition and Development, 9,* 46–66.

Ganea, P. A., Shutts, K., Spelke, E., & DeLoache, J. S. (2007). Thinking of things unseen: Infants' use of language to update object representations. *Psychological Science, 8,* 734–739.

Ganger, J., & Brent, M. R. (2004). Reexamining the vocabulary spurt. *Developmental Psychology, 40,* 621–632.

Ganong, L. H., & Coleman, M. (1994). *Remarried family relationships.* Thousand Oaks, CA: Sage.

Garces, E., Thomas, D., & Currie, J. (2002). Longer-term effects of Head Start. *American Economic Review, 92,* 999–1012.

Garcia, M. M., Shaw, D. S., Winslow, E. B., & Yaggi, K. E. (2000). Destructive sibling conflict and the development of conduct problems in young boys. *Developmental Psychology, 36,* 44–53.

Garcia-Bournissen, F., Tsur, L., Goldstein, L. H., Staroselsky, A., Avner, M., & Asrar, F. (2008). Fetal exposure to isotretinoin—an international problem. *Reproductive Toxicology, 25,* 124–128.

García-Coll, C., & Magnuson, K. (1997). The psychological experience of immigration: A developmental perspective. In A. Booth, A. C. Crouter, & N. Landale (Eds.), *Immigration and the family* (pp. 91–131). Mahwah, NJ: Erlbaum.

Garcia Coll, C., & Marks, A. K. (2009). *Immigrant stories: Ethnicity and academics in middle childhood.* New York: Oxford University Press.

Gardner, H. (1980). *Artful scribbles: The significance of children's drawings.* New York: Basic Books.

Gardner, H. (1983). *Frames of mind*. New York: Basic Books.

Gardner, H. (1993). *Multiple intelligences: The theory in practice*. New York: Basic Books.

Gardner, H. E. (1998a). Are there additional intelligences? The case of the naturalist, spiritual, and existential intelligences. In J. Kane (Ed.), *Educational information and transformation*. Upper Saddle River, NJ: Prentice-Hall.

Gardner, H. E. (1998b). Extraordinary cognitive achievements (ECA): A symbol systems approach. In W. Damon & R. M. Lerner (Eds.), *Handbook of child psychology: Vol. 1. Theoretical models of human development* (5th ed., pp. 415–466). New York: Wiley.

Gardner, H. E. (2000). *Intelligence reframed: Multiple intelligences for the twenty-first century*. New York: Basic Books.

Gardner, M., & Steinberg, L. (2005). Peer influence on risk taking, risk preference, and risky decision making in adolescence and adulthood: An experimental study. *Developmental Psychology, 41*, 625–635.

Garmezy, N. (1993). Children in poverty: Resilience despite risk. *Psychiatry, 56*, 127–136.

Garner, P. W. (1996). The relations of emotional role taking, affective/moral attributions, and emotional display rule knowledge to low-income school-age children's social competence. *Journal of Applied Developmental Psychology, 17*, 19–36.

Garner, P. W. (2003). Child and family correlates of toddlers' emotional and behavioral responses to a mishap. *Infant Mental Health Journal, 24*, 580–596.

Garner, P. W., & Estep, K. (2001). Emotional competence, emotion socialization, and young children's peer-related social competence. *Early Education and Development, 12*, 29–48.

Gartstein, M. A., & Rothbart, M. K. (2003). Studying infant temperament via the revised infant behavior questionnaire. *Infant Behavior and Development, 26*, 64–86.

Gartstein, M. A., Slobodskaya, H. R., & Kinsht, I. A. (2003). Cross-cultural differences in temperament in the first year of life: United States of America (U.S.) and Russia. *International Journal of Behavioral Development, 27*, 316–328.

Gartstein, M. A., Slobodskaya, H. R., Zylicz, P. O., Gosztyla, D., & Nakagawa, A. (2010). A cross-cultural evaluation of temperament: Japan, USA, Poland and Russia. *International Journal of Psychology and Psychological Therapy, 10*, 55–75.

Garven, S., Wood, J. M., & Malpass, R. S. (2000). Allegations of wrongdoing: The effects of reinforcement on children's mundane and fantastic claims. *Journal of Applied Psychology, 85*, 38–49.

Garvey, C. (1974). Requests and responses in children's speech. *Journal of Child Language, 2*, 41–60.

Gasden, V. (1999). Black families in intergenerational and cultural perspective. In M. E. Lamb (Ed.), *Parenting and child development in "nontraditional" families* (pp. 221–246). Mahwah, NJ: Erlbaum.

Gaskins, S. (1999). Children's daily lives in a Mayan village: A case study of culturally constructed roles and activities. In R. Göncü (Ed.), *Children's engagement in the world: Sociocultural perspectives* (pp. 25–61). Cambridge, UK: Cambridge University Press.

Gaskins, S. (2000). Children's daily activities in a Mayan village: A culturally grounded description. *Cross-Cultural Research, 34*, 375–389.

Gaskins, S., Haight, W., & Lancy, D. F. (2007). The cultural construction of play. In A. Göncü & S. Gaskins (Eds.), *Play and development: Evolutionary, sociocultural, and functional perspectives* (pp. 179–202). Mahwah, NJ: Erlbaum.

Gates, G. J., Badgett, M. V. L., Macomber, J. E., & Chambers, K. (2007). *Adoption and foster care by gay and lesbian parents in the United States*. Los Angeles, CA: Williams Institute of the UCLA School of Law.

Gathercole, S. E., Alloway, T. P., Willis, C., & Adams, A.-M. (2006). Working memory in children with reading disabilities. *Journal of Experimental Child Psychology, 93*, 265–281.

Gathercole, S. E., Hitch, G. J., Service, E., & Martin, A. J. (1997). Phonological short-term memory and new word learning in children. *Developmental Psychology, 33*, 966–979.

Gathercole, S. E., Lamont, E., & Alloway, T. P. (2006). Working memory in the classroom. In S. Pickering (Ed.), *Working memory and education* (pp. 219–240). San Diego: Elsevier.

Gathercole, S. E., Service, E., Hitch, G. J., Adams, A., & Martin, A. J. (1999). Phonological short-term memory and vocabulary development: Further evidence on the nature of the relationship. *Applied Cognitive Psychology, 13*, 65–77.

Gathercole, S. E., Tiffany, C., Briscoe, J., Thorn, A., & ALSPAC Team. (2005). Developmental consequences of poor phonological short-term memory function in childhood: A longitudinal study. *Journal of Child Psychology and Psychiatry, 46*, 598–611.

Gathercole, V., Sebastián, E., & Soto, P. (1999). The early acquisition of Spanish verbal morphology: Across-the-board or piecemeal knowledge? *International Journal of Bilingualism, 3*, 133–182.

Gaultney, J. F., & Gingras, J. L. (2005). Fetal rate of behavioral inhibition and preference for novelty during infancy. *Early Human Development, 81*, 379–386.

Gauvain, M. (2004). Bringing culture into relief: Cultural contributions to the development of children's planning skills. In R. V. Kail (Ed.), *Advances in child development and behavior* (pp. 39–71). San Diego, CA: Elsevier.

Gauvain, M., de la Ossa, J. L., & Hurtado-Ortiz, M. T. (2001). Parental guidance as children learn to use cultural tools: The case of pictorial plans. *Cognitive Development, 16*, 551–575.

Gauvain, M., & Huard, R. D. (1999). Family interaction, parenting style, and the development of planning: A longitudinal analysis using archival data. *Journal of Family Psychology, 13*, 75–92.

Gauvain, M., & Rogoff, B. (1989). Collaborative problem solving and children's planning skills. *Developmental Psychology, 25*, 139–151.

Gauze, C., Bukowski, W. M., Aquan-Assee, J., & Sippola, L. K. (1996). Interactions between family environment and friendship and associations with self-perceived well-being during early adolescence. *Child Development, 67*, 2201–2216.

Gawlitzek-Maiwald, I., & Tracy, R. (1996). Bilingual bootstrapping. *Linguistics, 34*, 901–926.

Gazelle, H., & Rudolph, K. D. (2004). Moving toward and away from the world: Social approach and avoidance trajectories in anxious and solitary youth. *Child Development, 75*, 829–849.

Ge, X., Brody, G. H., Conger, R. D., Simons, R. L., & Murry, V. (2002). Contextual amplification of the effects of pubertal transition on African American children's deviant peer affiliation and externalized behavioral problems. *Developmental Psychology, 38*, 42–54.

Ge, X., Conger, R. D., & Elder, G. H., Jr. (1996). Coming of age too early: Pubertal influences on girls' vulnerability to psychological distress. *Child Development, 67*, 3386–3400.

Ge, X., Conger, R. D., & Elder, G. H., Jr. (2001). The relation between puberty and psychological distress in adolescent boys. *Journal of Research on Adolescence, 11*, 49–70.

Ge, X., Jin, R., Natsuaki, M. N., Frederick, X., Brody, G. H., Cutrona, C. E., & Simons, R. L. (2006). Pubertal maturation and early substance use risks among African American children. *Psychology of Addictive Behaviors, 20*, 404–414.

Ge, X., Kim, I. J., Brody, G. H., Conger, R. D., & Simons, R. L. (2003). It's about timing and change: Pubertal transition effects on symptoms of major depression among African American youths. *Developmental Psychology, 39*, 430–439.

Ge, X., Natsuaki, M. N., Jin, R., & Biehl, M. C. (2011). A contextual amplification hypothesis: Pubertal timing and girls' emotional and behavior problems. In M. Kerr, H. Stattin, R. C. M. E. Engels, G. Overbeek, & A.-K. Andershed (Eds.), *Understanding girls' problem behavior* (pp. 11–28). Chichester, UK: Wiley-Blackwell.

Geangu, E., Benga, O., Stahl, D., & Striano, T. (2010). Contagious crying beyond the first days of life. *Infant Behavior and Development, 33*, 279–288.

Geary, D. C. (1998). *Male, female: The evolution of human sex differences*. Washington, DC: American Psychological Association.

Geary, D. C. (1999). Evolution and developmental sex differences. *Current Directions in Psychological Science, 8*, 115–120.

Geary, D. C. (2000). Evolution and proximate expression of human paternal investment. *Psychological Bulletin, 126*, 55–77.

Geary, D. C. (2006a). Development of mathematical understanding. In D. Kuhn & R. Siegler (Eds.), *Handbook of child psychology: Vol. 2. Cognition, perception, and language* (pp. 777–810). Hoboken, NJ: Wiley.

Geary, D. C. (2006b). Evolutionary developmental psychology: Current status and future directions. *Developmental Review, 26*, 113–119.

Geary, D. C., & Bjorklund, D. F. (2000). Evolutionary developmental psychology. *Child Development, 71*, 57–65.

Geary, D. C., Saults, J. S., Liu, F., & Hoard, M. K. (2000). Sex differences in spatial cognition, computational fluency, and arithmetic reasoning. *Journal of Experimental Child Psychology, 77*, 337–353.

Gee, C. B., & Rhodes, J. E. (2003). Adolescent mothers' relationship with their children's biological fathers: Social support, social strain, and relationship continuity. *Journal of Family Psychology, 17*, 370–383.

Geerts, M., Steyaert, J., & Fryns, J. P. (2003). The XYY syndrome: A follow-up study on 38 boys. *Genetic Counseling, 14*, 267–279.

Gellin, B. G., Maibach, E. W., & Marcuse, E. K. (2000). Do parents understand immunizations? A national telephone survey. *Pediatrics, 106*, 1097–1102.

Gelman, R. (1972). Logical capacity of very young children: Number invariance rules. *Child Development, 43*, 75–90.

Gelman, R., & Koenig, M. A. (2003). Theory-based categorization in early childhood. In D. H. Rakison & L. M. Oakes (Eds.), *Early category and concept development* (pp. 330–359). New York: Oxford University Press.

Gelman, R., & Shatz, M. (1978). Appropriate speech adjustments: The operation of conversational constraints on talk to two-year-olds. In M. Lewis & L. A. Rosenblum (Eds.), *Interaction, conversation, and the development of language* (pp. 27–61). New York: Wiley.

Gelman, S. A. (2003). *The essential child*. New York: Oxford University Press.

Gelman, S. A., & Kalish, C. W. (2006). Conceptual development. In D. Kuhn & R. Siegler (Eds.), *Handbook of child psychology: Vol. 2. Cognition, perception, and language* (6th ed., pp. 687–733). Hoboken, NJ: Wiley.

Gelman, S. A., Taylor, M. G., & Nguyen, S. P. (2004). Mother-child conversations about gender. *Monographs of the Society for Research in Child Development, 69* (1, Serial No. 275), pp. 1–127.

Gendler, M. N., Witherington, D. C., & Edwards, A. (2008). The development of affect specificity in infants' use of emotion cues. *Infancy, 13*, 456–468.

Genesee, F. (2001). Portrait of the bilingual child. In V. Cook (Ed.), *Portraits of the second language user*. Clevedon, UK: Multilingual Matters.

Genesee, F., & Nicoladis, E. (2007). Bilingual first language acquisition. In E. Hoff & M. Shatz (Eds.), *Blackwell handbook of language development* (pp. 324–342). Malden, MA: Blackwell.

Gennetian, L. A., & Morris, P. A. (2003). The effects of time limits and make-work-pay strategies on the well-being of children: Experimental evidence from two welfare reform programs. *Children and Youth Services Review, 25*, 17–54.

Gentile, D. A., Anderson, C. A., Ykawa, S., Ihori, N., Saleem, M., Ming, L. K., et al. (2009). The effects of prosocial video games on prosocial behaviors: International evidence from correlational, longitudinal, and experimental studies. *Personality and Social Psychology Bulletin, 35*, 752–763.

Gentner, D., & Namy, L. L. (2004). The role of comparison in children's early word learning. In D. G. Hall & S. R. Waxman (Eds.), *Weaving a lexicon* (pp. 533–568). Cambridge, MA: MIT Press.

Gerardi-Caulton, G. (2000). Sensitivity to spatial conflict and the development of self-regulation in children 24–36 months of age. *Developmental Science, 3*, 397–404.

Gergely, G., Bekkering, H., & Király, I. (2003). Rational imitation in preverbal infants. *Nature, 415*, 755.

Gergely, G., & Watson, J. S. (1999). Early socioemotional development: Contingency perception and the social-biofeedback model. In P. Rochat (Ed.), *Early social cognition: Understanding others in the first months of life* (pp. 101–136). Mahwah, NJ: Erlbaum.

Gershkoff-Stowe, L., & Hahn, E. R. (2007). Fast mapping skills in the developing lexicon. *Journal of Speech, Language, and Hearing Research, 50*, 682–697.

Gershoff, E. T. (2002a). Corporal punishment by parents and associated child behaviors and experiences: A meta-analytic and theoretical review. *Psychological Bulletin, 128,* 539–579.

Gershoff, E. T. (2002b). Corporal punishment, physical abuse, and the burden of proof: Reply to Baumrind, Larzelere, and Cowan (2002), Holden (2002), and Parke (2002). *Psychological Bulletin, 128,* 602–611.

Gershoff, E. T., & Aber, J. L. (2006). Neighborhoods and schools: Contexts and consequences for the mental health and risk behaviors of children and youth. In L. Balter & C. S. Tamis-LeMonda (Eds.), *Child psychology: A handbook of contemporary issues* (2nd ed., pp. 611–645). New York: Psychology Press.

Gershoff, E. T., Grogan-Kaylor, A., Lansford, J. E., Chang, L., Zelli, A., Deater-Deckard, K., et al. (2010). Parent discipline practices in an international sample: Associations with child behaviors and moderation by perceived normativeness. *Child Development, 81,* 487–502.

Gerson, S., & Woodward, A. L. (2010). Building intentional action knowledge with one's hands. In S. P. Johnson (Ed.), *Neoconstructivism: The new science of cognitive development* (pp. 295–313). New York: Oxford University Press.

Gertner, S., Greenbaum, C. W., Sadeh, A., Dolfin, Z., Sirota, L., & Ben-Nun, Y. (2002). Sleep-wake patterns in preterm infants and 6 month's home environment: Implications for early cognitive development. *Early Human Development, 68,* 93–102.

Gertner, Y., Fisher, C., & Eisengart, J. (2006). Learning words and rules: Abstract knowledge of word order in early sentence comprehension. *Psychological Science, 17,* 684–691.

Gervai, J. (2009). Environmental and genetic influences on early attachment. *Child and Adolescent Psychiatry and Mental Health, 3,* 25. Retrieved from www.capmh.com/content/3/1/25

Gervai, J., Turner, P. J., & Hinde, R. A. (1995). Gender-related behaviour, attitudes, and personality in parents of young children in England and Hungary. *International Journal of Behavioral Development, 18,* 105–126.

Gesell, A. (1933). Maturation and patterning of behavior. In C. Murchison (Ed.), *A handbook of child psychology.* Worcester, MA: Clark University Press.

Gest, S. D., Domitrovich, C. E., & Welsh, J. A. (2005). Peer academic reputation in elementary school: Associations with changes in self-concept and academic skills. *Journal of Educational Psychology, 97,* 337–346.

Gewirtz, A., & Edleson, J. L. (2004). Young children's exposure to adult domestic violence: Toward a developmental risk and resilience framework for research and intervention. In S. Schechter (Ed.), *Early childhood, domestic violence, and poverty: Helping young children and their families,* Series Paper 6. Iowa City: University of Iowa School of Social Work.

Gewirtz, A., Forgatch, M. S., & Wieling, E. (2008). Parenting practices as potential mechanisms for child adjustment following mass trauma. *Journal of Marital and Family Therapy, 34,* 177–192.

Ghavami, N., Fingerhut, A., Peplau, L. A., Grant, S. K., & Wittig, M. A. (2011). Testing a model of minority identity achievement, identity affirmation, and psychological well-being among ethnic minority and sexual minority individuals. *Cultural Diversity and Ethnic Minority Psychology, 17,* 79–88.

Ghim, H. R. (1990). Evidence for perceptual organization in infants: Perception of subjective contours by young infants. *Infant Behavior and Development, 13,* 221–248.

Gibbons, A. (1998). Which of our genes make us human? *Science, 281,* 1432–1434.

Gibbons, R., Dugaiczyk, L. J., Girke, T., Duistermars, B., Zielinski, R., & Dugaiczyk, A. (2004). Distinguishing humans from great apes with AluYb8 repeats. *Journal of Molecular Biology, 339,* 721–729.

Gibbs, B. G. (2010). Reversing fortunes or content change? Gender gaps in math-related skill throughout childhood. *Social Science Research, 39,* 540–569.

Gibbs, J. C. (1991). Toward an integration of Kohlberg's and Hoffman's theories of morality. In W. M. Kurtines & J. L. Gewirtz (Eds.), *Handbook of moral behavior and development* (Vol. 1, pp. 183–222). Hillsdale, NJ: Erlbaum.

Gibbs, J. C. (1995). The cognitive developmental perspective. In W. M. Kurtines & J. L. Gewirtz (Eds.), *Moral development: An introduction* (pp. 27–48). Boston: Allyn and Bacon.

Gibbs, J. C. (2006). Should Kohlberg's cognitive developmental approach to morality be replaced with a more pragmatic approach? Comment on Krebs and Denton (2005). *Psychological Review, 113,* 666–671.

Gibbs, J. C. (2010). *Moral development and reality: Beyond the theories of Kohlberg and Hoffman* (2nd ed.). Boston: Pearson Allyn & Bacon.

Gibbs, J. C., Basinger, K. S., & Fuller, D. (1992). *Moral maturity: Measuring the development of sociomoral reflection.* Hillsdale, NJ: Erlbaum.

Gibbs, J. C., Basinger, K. S., & Grime, R. L. (2003). Moral judgment maturity: From clinical to standard measures. In S. J. Lopez & C. R. Snyder (Eds.), *Handbook of positive psychological assessment* (pp. 361–373). Washington, DC: American Psychological Association.

Gibbs, J. C., Basinger, K. S., Grime, R. L., & Snarey, J. R. (2007). Moral judgment development across cultures: Revisiting Kohlberg's universality claims. *Developmental Review, 24,* 443–500.

Gibbs, J. C., Moshman, D., Berkowitz, M. W., Basinger, K. S., & Grime, R. L. (2009a). Taking development seriously: Critique of the 2008 JME special issue on moral functioning. *Journal of Moral Education, 38,* 271–282.

Gibbs, J. C., Potter, G. B., DiBiase, A.-M., & Devlin, R. (2009b). The EQUIP program: Social perspective-taking for responsible thought and behavior. In B. Glick (Ed.), *Cognitive behavioral interventions for at-risk youth* (2nd ed.). Kingston, NJ: Civic Research Institute.

Gibson, E. J. (1970). The development of perception as an adaptive process. *American Scientist, 58,* 98–107.

Gibson, E. J. (2000). Perceptual learning in development: Some basic concepts. *Ecological Psychology, 12,* 295–302.

Gibson, E. J. (2003). The world is so full of a number of things: On specification and perceptual learning. *Ecological Psychology, 15,* 283–287.

Gibson, E. J., & Walk, R. D. (1960). The "visual cliff." *Scientific American, 202,* 64–71.

Gibson, J. J. (1979). *The ecological approach to visual perception.* Boston: Houghton Mifflin.

Giles, J. W., & Heyman, G. D. (2005). Young children's beliefs about the relationship between gender and aggressive behavior. *Child Development, 76,* 107–121.

Giles-Sims, J., Straus, M. A., & Sugarman, D. B. (1995). Child, maternal, and family characteristics associated with spanking. *Family Relations, 44,* 170–176.

Gill, M., Daly, G., Heron, S., Hawi, Z., & Fitzgerald, M. (1997). Confirmation of association between attention deficit hyperactivity disorder and a dopamine transporter polymorphism. *Molecular Psychiatry, 2,* 311–313.

Gillet, J.-P., Macadangdang, B., Rathke, R. L., Gottesman, M. M., & Kimchi-Sarfaty, C. (2009). The development of gene therapy: From monogenic recessive disorders to complex diseases such as cancer. *Methods in Molecular Biology, 542,* 5–54.

Gillies, R. M. (2000). The maintenance of cooperative and helping behaviours in cooperative groups. *British Journal of Educational Psychology, 70,* 97–111.

Gillies, R. M. (2003). The behaviors, interactions, and perceptions of junior high school students during small-group learning. *Journal of Educational Psychology, 95,* 137–147.

Gilligan, C. F. (1982). *In a different voice.* Cambridge, MA: Harvard University Press.

Gilliom, M., Shaw, D. S., Beck, J. E., Schonberg, M. A., & Lukon, J. L. (2002). Anger regulation in disadvantaged preschool boys: Strategies, antecedents, and the development of self-control. *Developmental Psychology, 38,* 222–235.

Gilstrap, L. L., & Ceci, S. J. (2005). Reconceptualizing children's suggestibility: Bidirectional and temporal properties. *Child Development, 76,* 40–53.

Gimenez, M., & Harris, P. L. (2002). Understanding constraints on inheritance: Evidence for biological thinking in early childhood. *British Journal of Developmental Psychology, 20,* 307–324.

Ginsburg, H. P. (1997). *Entering the child's mind: The clinical interview in psychological research and practice.* New York: Cambridge University Press.

Ginsburg, H. P., Lee, J. S., & Boyd, J. S. (2008). Mathematics education for young children: What it is and how to promote it. *Social Policy Report of the Society for Research in Child Development, 22*(1).

Ginsburg, K. R. (2007). The importance of play in promoting healthy child development and maintaining strong parent–child bonds. *Pediatrics, 119,* 182–191.

Ginsburg-Block, M. D., Rohrbeck, C. A., & Fantuzzo, J. W. (2006). A meta-analytic review of social, self-concept, and behavioral outcomes of peer-assisted learning. *Journal of Educational Psychology, 98,* 732–749.

Glade, A. C., Bean, R. A., & Vira, R. (2005). A prime time for marital/relational intervention: A review of the transition to parenthood literature with treatment recommendations. *American Journal of Family Therapy, 33,* 319–336.

Gladstone, I. M., & Katz, V. L. (2004). The morbidity of the 34- to 35-week gestation: Should we reexamine the paradigm? *American Journal of Perinatology, 21,* 9–13.

Gladwell, M. (1998, February 2). The Pima paradox. *The New Yorker,* pp. 44–57.

Gleason, T. R. (2002). Social provisions of real and imaginary relationships in early childhood. *Developmental Psychology, 38,* 979–992.

Gleason, T. R., & Hohmann, L. M. (2006). Concepts of real and imaginary friendships in early childhood. *Social Development, 15,* 128–144.

Gleason, T. R., Sebanc, A. M., & Hartup, W. W. (2000). Imaginary companions of preschool children. *Developmental Psychology, 36,* 419–428.

Gleitman, L. R., Cassidy, K., Nappa, R., Papfragou, A., & Trueswell, J. C. (2005). Hard words. *Language Learning and Development, 1,* 23–64.

Gleitman, L. R., Gleitman, H., Landau, B., & Wanner, E. (1988). Where learning begins: Initial representations for language learning. In F. Newmeyer (Ed.), *Language: Psychological and biological aspects* (Vol. 3, pp. 150–193). Cambridge, UK: Cambridge University Press.

Glenwright, M., & Pexman, P. M. (2010). Development of children's ability to distinguish sarcasm and verbal irony. *Journal of Child Language, 37,* 429–451.

Glover, V., Bergman, K., & O'Connor, T. G. (2008). The effects of maternal stress, anxiety, and depression during pregnancy on the neurodevelopment of the child. In S. D. Stone & A. E. Menken (Eds.), *Perinatal and postpartum mood disorders: Perspectives and treatment guide for the health care practitioner* (pp. 3–15). New York: Springer.

Glowinski, A. L., Madden, P. A. F., Bucholz, K. K., Lynskey, M. T., & Heath, A. C. (2003). Genetic epidemiology of self-reported lifetime DSM-IV major depressive disorder in a population-based twin sample of female adolescents. *Journal of Child Psychology and Psychiatry and Allied Disciplines, 44,* 988–996.

Gluckman, P. D., Sizonenko, S. V., & Bassett, N. S. (1999). The transition from fetus to neonate—an endocrine perspective. *Acta Paediatrica Supplement, 88*(428), 7–11.

Gnepp, J. (1983). Children's social sensitivity: Inferring emotions from conflicting cues. *Developmental Psychology, 19,* 805–814.

Godart, N. T., Perdereau, F., Curt, F., Rein, Z., Lang, F., & Venisse, J. L. (2006). Is major depressive episode related to anxiety disorders in anorexics and bulimics? *Comprehensive Psychiatry, 47,* 91–98.

Godeau, E., Nic Gabhainn, S., Vignes, C., Ross, J., Boyce, W., & Todd, J. (2008). Contraceptive use by 15-year-old students at their last sexual intercourse. *Archives of Pediatric and Adolescent Medicine, 162,* 66–73.

Goelman, H. (1986). The language environments of family day care. In S. Kilmer (Ed.), *Advances in early education and day care* (Vol. 4, pp. 153–179). Greenwich, CT: JAI Press.

Goering, J. (Ed.). (2003). *Choosing a better life? How public housing tenants selected a HUD experiment to improve their lives and those of their children: The Moving to Opportunity Demonstration Program.* Washington, DC: Urban Institute Press.

Gogate, L. J., & Bahrick, L. E. (1998). Intersensory redundancy facilitates learning of arbitrary relations between vowel sounds and objects in seven-month-old infants. *Journal of Experimental Child Psychology, 69,* 133–149.

Gogate, L. J., & Bahrick, L. E. (2001). Intersensory redundancy and 7-month-old infants' memory for arbitrary syllable–object relations. *Infancy, 2,* 219–231.

Gogate, L. J., Bahrick, L. E., & Watson, J. D. (2000). A study of multimodal motherese: The role of temporal synchrony between verbal labels and gestures. *Child Development, 71,* 878–894.

Goh, Y. I., & Koren, G. (2008). Folic acid in pregnancy and fetal outcomes. *Journal of Obstetrics and Gynaecology, 28,* 3–13.

Goldberg, A. E. (2010). *Lesbian and gay parents and their children: Research on the family life cycle.* Washington, DC: American Psychological Association.

Goldberg, A. E., & Perry-Jenkins, M. (2003). Division of labor and working-class women's well-being across the transition to parenthood. *Journal of Family Psychology, 18,* 225–236.

Goldenberg, C., Gallimore, R., Reese, L., & Garnier, H. (2001). Cause or effect? Immigrant Latino parents' aspirations and expectations, and their children's school performance. *American Educational Research Journal, 38,* 547–582.

Goldfield, B. A. (1987). The contributions of child and caregiver to referential and expressive language. *Applied Psycholinguistics, 8,* 267–280.

Goldin-Meadow, S. (1999). The development of gesture with and without speech in hearing and deaf children. In L. S. Messing & R. Campbell (Eds.), *Gesture, speech, and sign* (pp. 117–132). New York: Oxford University Press.

Goldin-Meadow, S. (2002). Constructing communication by hand. *Cognitive Development, 17,* 1385–1405.

Goldin-Meadow, S. (2003a). *Hearing gesture: How our hands help us think.* Cambridge, MA: Harvard University Press.

Goldin-Meadow, S. (2003b). *The resilience of language.* New York: Psychology Press.

Goldin-Meadow, S. (2005a). Gesture in social interactions: A mechanism for cognitive change. In B. D. Homer & C. S. Tamis-LeMonda (Eds.), *The development of social cognition and communication* (pp. 259–283). Mahwah, NJ: Erlbaum.

Goldin-Meadow, S. (2005b). What language creation in the manual modality tells us about the foundations of language. *Linguistic Review, 22,* 199–225.

Goldin-Meadow, S. (2006a). Nonverbal communication: The hand's role in talking and thinking. In D. Kuhn & R. Siegler (Eds.), *Handbook of child psychology: Vol. 2. Cognition, perception, and language* (6th ed., pp. 336–369). Hoboken, NJ: Wiley.

Goldin-Meadow, S. (2006b). Talking and thinking with our hands. *Current Directions in Psychological Science, 15,* 34–39.

Goldin-Meadow, S. (2009). Using the hands to study how children learn language. In J. Colombo, P. McCardle, & L. Freund (Eds.), *Infant pathways to language: Methods, models, and research directions* (pp. 195–210). New York: Psychology Press.

Goldin-Meadow, S., Butcher, C., Mylander, C., & Dodge, M. (1994). Nouns and verbs in a self-styled gesture system: What's in a name? *Cognitive Psychology, 27,* 259–319.

Goldin-Meadow, S., Cook, S. W., & Mitchell, Z. A. (2009). Gesturing saves cognitive resources when talking about nonpresent objects. *Cognitive Science, 34,* 602–619.

Goldin-Meadow, S., Gelman, S. A., & Mylander, C. (2005). Expressing generic

concepts with and without a language model. *Cognition, 96,* 109–126.

Goldin-Meadow, S., & Singer, M. A. (2003). From children's hands to adults' ears: Gesture's role in the learning process. *Developmental Psychology, 39,* 509–520.

Goldschmidt, L., Richardson, G. A., Cornelius, M. D., & Day, N. L. (2004). Prenatal marijuana and alcohol exposure and academic achievement at age 10. *Neurotoxicology and Teratology, 26,* 521–532.

Goldstein, M. H., & Schwade, J. A. (2008). Social feedback to infants' babbling facilitates rapid phonological learning. *Psychological Science, 19,* 515–523.

Goldstein, S. (2011). Attention-deficit/ hyperactivity disorder. In S. Goldstein & C. R. Reynolds (Eds.), *Handbook of neurodevelopmental and genetic disorders in children* (2nd ed., pp. 131–150). New York: Guilford.

Goldstein, S. E., & Tisak, M. S. (2004). Adolescents' outcome expectancies about relational aggression within acquaintanceships, friendships, and dating relationships. *Journal of Adolescence, 27,* 283–302.

Goldstein, S. E., Davis-Kean, P. E., & Eccles, J. S. (2005). Parents, peers, and problem behavior: A longitudinal investigation of the impact of relationship perceptions and characteristics on the development of adolescent problem behavior. *Developmental Psychology, 41,* 401–413.

Goldston, D. B., Molock, S. D., Whitbeck, L. B., Murakami, J. L., Zayas, L. H., & Hall, G. C. N. (2008). Cultural considerations in adolescent suicide prevention and psychosocial treatment. *American Psychologist, 63,* 14–31.

Goleman, D. (1995). *Emotional intelligence.* New York: Bantam.

Goleman, D. (1998). *Working with emotional intelligence.* New York: Bantam.

Golinkoff, R. M., & Hirsh-Pasek, K. (2006). Baby wordsmith: From associationist to social sophisticate. *Current Directions in Psychological Science, 15,* 30–33.

Golomb, C. (2004). *The child's creation of a pictorial world* (2nd ed.). Mahwah, NJ: Erlbaum.

Golombok, S., Lycett, E., MacCallum, F., Jadva, V., Murray, C., Rust, J., et al. (2004). Parenting of infants conceived by gamete donation. *Journal of Family Psychology, 18,* 443–452.

Golombok, S., Perry, B., Burston, A., Murray, C., Mooney-Somers, J., Stevens, M., & Golding, J. (2003). Children with lesbian parents: A community study. *Developmental Psychology, 39,* 20–33.

Golombok, S., Rust, J., Zervoulis, K., Croudace, T., Golding, J., & Hines, M. (2008). Developmental trajectories of sex-typed behavior in boys and girls: A longitudinal general population study of children aged 2.5–8 years. *Child Development, 79,* 1583–1593.

Golombok, S., & Tasker, F. L. (1996). Do parents influence the sexual orientation of their children? Findings from a longitudinal study of lesbian families. *Developmental Psychology, 32,* 3–11.

Gómez, R. L., Bootzin, R. R., & Nadel, L. (2006). Naps promote abstraction in language-learning infants. *Psychological Science, 17,* 670–674.

Gomez-Perez, E., & Ostrosky-Solis, F. (2006). Attention and memory evaluation across the life span: Heterogeneous effects of age and education. *Journal of Clinical and*

Experimental Neuropsychology, 28, 477–949.

Göncü, A. (1993). Development of intersubjectivity in the dyadic play of preschoolers. *Early Childhood Research Quarterly, 8,* 99–116.

Göncü, A., Patt, M. B., & Kouba E. (2004). Understanding young children's pretend play in context. In P. K. Smith & C. H. Hart (Eds.), *Blackwell handbook of childhood social development* (pp. 418–437). Malden, MA: Blackwell.

Gonzalez, A.-L., & Wolters, C. A. (2006). The relation between perceived parenting practices and achievement motivation in mathematics. *Journal of Research in Childhood Education, 21,* 203–217.

Goodall, J. (1990). *Through a window: My thirty years with the chimpanzees of Gombe.* Boston: Houghton Mifflin.

Goode, V., & Goode, J. D. (2007). De facto zero tolerance: An exploratory study of race and safe school violations. In J. Kincheloe & K. Hayes (Eds.), *Teaching city kids: Understanding and appreciating them* (pp. 85–96). New York: Peter Lang.

Goodlin-Jones, B. L., Burnham, M. M., & Anders, T. F. (2000). Sleep and sleep disturbances: Regulatory processes in infancy. In A. J. Sameroff, M. Lewis, & S. M. Miller (Eds.), *Handbook of developmental psychology* (2nd ed., pp. 309–325). New York: Kluwer.

Goodman, G. S., Hirschman, J. E., Hepps, D., & Rudy, L. (1991). Children's memory for stressful events. *Merrill-Palmer Quarterly, 37,* 109–158.

Goodman, G. S., & Melinder, A. (2007). Child witness research and forensic interviews of young children: A review. *Legal and Criminological Psychology, 12,* 1–19.

Goodman, J., Dale, P., & Li, P. (2008). Does frequency count? Parental input and the acquisition of vocabulary. *Journal of Child Language, 35,* 515–531.

Goodman, S. H., Gravitt, G. W., Jr., & Kaslow, N. J. (1995). Social problem solving: A moderator of the relation between negative life stress and depression symptoms in children. *Journal of Abnormal Child Psychology, 23,* 473–485.

Goodnow, J. J. (2010). Culture. In M. H. Bornstein (Ed.), *Handbook of cultural developmental science* (pp. 3–20). New York: Psychology Press.

Goodwin, M. H. (1998). Games of stance: Conflict and footing in hopscotch. In S. Hoyle & C. T. Adger (Eds.), *Language practices of older children* (pp. 23–46). New York: Oxford University Press.

Gooren, E. M. J. C., Pol, A. C., Stegge, H., Terwogt, M. M., & Koot, H. M. (2011). The development of conduct problems and depressive symptoms in early elementary school children: The role of peer rejection. *Journal of Clinical Child and Adolescent Psychology, 40,* 245–253.

Gopnik, A., & Choi, S. (1990). Do linguistic differences lead to cognitive differences? A cross-linguistic study of semantic and cognitive development. *First Language, 11,* 199–215.

Gopnik, A., & Nazzi, T. (2003). Words, kinds, and causal powers: A theory theory perspective on early naming and categorization. In D. H. Rakison & L. M. Oakes (Eds.), *Early category and concept development: Making sense of the blooming, buzzing confusion* (pp. 303–329). New York: Oxford University Press.

Gopnik, A., & Wellman, H. M. (1994). The 'theory' theory. In L. A. Hirschfeld & S. A. Gelman (Eds.), *Mapping the mind: Domain specificity in cognition and culture* (pp. 257–293). Cambridge, UK: Cambridge University Press.

Gordon, P. (2004). Numerical cognition without words: Evidence from Amazonia. *Science, 306,* 496–499.

Gordon, R. A., Chase-Lansdale, P. L., & Brooks-Gunn, J. (2004). Extended households and the life course of young mothers: Understanding the associations using a sample of mothers with premature, low-birth-weight babies. *Child Development, 75,* 1013–1038.

Gormally, S., Barr, R. G., Wertheim, L., Alkawaf, R., Calinoui, N., & Young, S. N. (2001). Contact and nutrient caregiving effects on newborn infant pain responses. *Developmental Medicine and Child Neurology, 43,* 28–38.

Goswami, U. (1996). Analogical reasoning and cognitive development. In H. Reese (Ed.), *Advances in child development and behavior* (Vol. 26, pp. 91–138). New York: Academic Press.

Gottlieb, G. (1998). Normally occurring environmental and behavioral influences on gene activity: From central dogma to probabilistic epigenesis. *Psychological Review, 105,* 792–802.

Gottlieb, G. (2003). On making behavioral genetics truly developmental. *Human Development, 46,* 337–355.

Gottlieb, G. (2007). Probabilistic epigenesis. *Developmental Science, 10,* 1–11.

Gottlieb, G., Wahlsten, D., & Lickliter, R. (2006). The significance of biology for human development: A developmental psychobiological systems view. In R. M. Lerner (Ed.), *Handbook of child psychology: Vol. 1. Theoretical models of human development* (6th ed., pp. 210–257). Hoboken, NJ: Wiley.

Gould, J. L., & Keeton, W. T. (1996). *Biological science* (6th ed.). New York: Norton.

Govaerts, P. J., De Beukelaer, C., Daemers, K., De Ceulaer, G., Yperman, M., Somers, T., et al. (2002). Outcome of cochlear implantation at different ages from 0 to 6 years. *Otology and Neurotology, 23,* 885–890.

Government of Canada. (2009). *The action plan for official languages 2007–2008. The next act: New momentum for Canada's linguistic duality.* Retrieved from www.pch.gc.ca/pgm/lo-ol/pubs/plan/2007-2008/index-eng.cfm

Graber, J. A. (2003). Puberty in context. In C. Hayward (Ed.), *Gender differences at puberty* (pp. 307–325). New York: Cambridge University Press.

Graber, J. A. (2004). Internalizing problems during adolescence. In R. M. Lerner & L. Steinberg (Eds.), *Handbook of adolescent psychology* (2nd ed., pp. 587–626). Hoboken, NJ: Wiley.

Graber, J. A., Brooks-Gunn, J., & Warren, M. P. (2006). Pubertal effects on adjustment in girls: Moving from demonstrating effects to identifying pathways. *Journal of Youth and Adolescence, 35,* 413–423.

Graber, J. A., Lewinsohn, P. M., Seeley, J. R., & Brooks-Gunn, J. (1997). Is psychopathology associated with the timing of pubertal development? *Journal of the American Academy of Child and Adolescent Psychiatry, 36,* 1768–1776.

Graber, J. A., Nichols, T., Lynne, S. D., Brooks-Gunn, J., & Botwin, G. J. (2006).

A longitudinal examination of family, friend, and media influences on competent versus problem behaviors among urban minority youth. *Applied Developmental Science, 10*, 75–85.

Graber, J. A., Seeley, J. R., Brooks-Gunn, J., & Lewinsohn, P. M. (2004). Is pubertal timing associated with psychopathology in young adulthood? *Journal of the American Academy of Child and Adolescent Psychiatry, 43*, 718–726.

Graber, J. A., & Sontag, L. M. (2009). Internalizing problems during adolescence. In R. M. Lerner & L. Steinberg (Eds.), *Handbook of adolescent psychology: Vol. 1. Individual bases of adolescent development* (3rd ed., pp. 642–682). Hoboken, NJ: Wiley.

Gralinski, J. H., & Kopp, C. B. (1993). Everyday rules for behavior: Mothers' requests to young children. *Developmental Psychology, 29*, 573–584.

Grall, T. S. (2009, November). *Custodial mothers and fathers and their child support: 2007. Current Population Reports*, P60–237. Washington, DC: U.S. Department of Commerce.

Granger, R. C. (2008). After-school programs and academics: Implications for policy, practice, and research. *Social Policy Report of the Society for Research in Child Development, 22*(2), 3–11.

Granic, I., Hollenstein, T., Dishion, T. J., & Patterson, G. R. (2003). Longitudinal analysis of flexibility and reorganization in early adolescence: A dynamic systems study of family interactions. *Developmental Psychology, 39*, 606–617.

Granier-Deferre, C., Bassereau, S., Ribeiro, A., Jacquet, A.-Y., & Lecanuet, J.-P. (2003). *Cardiac "orienting" response in fetuses and babies following in utero melody-learning.* Paper presented at the 11th European Conference on Developmental Psychology, Milan, Italy.

Granillo, T., Jones-Rodriguez, G., & Carvajal, S. C. (2005). Prevalence of eating disorders in Latina adolescents: Associations with substance use and other correlates. *Journal of Adolescent Health, 36*, 214–220.

Grant, K., O'Koon, J., Davis, T., Roache, N., Poindexter, L., & Armstrong, M. (2000). Protective factors affecting low-income urban African American youth exposed to stress. *Journal of Early Adolescence, 20*, 388–418.

Grantham-McGregor, S., Powell, C., Walker, S., Chang, S., & Fletcher, P. (1994). The long-term follow-up of severely malnourished children who participated in an intervention program. *Child Development, 65*, 428–439.

Grantham-McGregor, S., Schofield, W., & Powell, C. (1987). Development of severely malnourished children who received psychosocial stimulation: Six-year follow-up. *Pediatrics, 79*, 247–254.

Grattan, M. P., De Vos, E., Levy, J., & McClintock, M. K. (1992). Asymmetric action in the human newborn: Sex differences in patterns of organization. *Child Development, 63*, 273–289.

Graves, S. B. (1993). Television, the portrayal of African Americans, and the development of children's attitudes. In G. L. Berry & J. K. Asamen (Eds.), *Children and television* (pp. 179–190). Newbury Park, CA: Sage.

Gray, K. A., Day, N. L., Leech, S., & Richardson, G. A. (2005). Prenatal marijuana exposure: Effect on child depressive symptoms at ten years of age.

Neurotoxicology and Teratology, 27, 439–448.

Gray, M. R., & Steinberg, L. D. (1999). Unpacking authoritative parenting: Reassessing a multidimensional construct. *Journal of Marriage and the Family, 61*, 574–587.

Gray-Little, B., & Carels, R. (1997). The effects of racial and socioeconomic consonance on self-esteem and achievement in elementary, junior high, and high school students. *Journal of Research on Adolescence, 7*, 109–131.

Gray-Little, B., & Hafdahl, A. R. (2000). Factors influencing racial comparisons of self-esteem: A quantitative review. *Psychological Bulletin, 126*, 26–54.

Green, G. E., Irwin, J. R., & Gustafson, G. E. (2000). Acoustic cry analysis, neonatal status and long-term developmental outcomes. In R. G. Barr, B. Hopkins, & J. A. Green (Eds.), *Crying as a sign, a symptom, and a signal* (pp. 137–156). Cambridge, UK: Cambridge University Press.

Greenberger, E., Chen, C., Tallym, S. R., & Dong, Q. (2000). Family, peer, and individual correlates of depressive symptomology among U. S. and Chinese adolescents. *Journal of Consulting and Clinical Psychology, 68*, 209–219.

Greenberger, E., O'Neil, R., & Nagel, S. K. (1994). Linking workplace and homeplace: Relations between the nature of adults' work and their parenting behaviors. *Developmental Psychology, 30*, 990–1002.

Greene, K., Krcmar, M., Walters, L. H., Rubin, D. L., Hale, J., & Hale, L. (2000). Targeting adolescent risk-taking behaviors: The contributions of egocentrism and sensation-seeking. *Journal of Adolescence, 23*, 439–461.

Greene, M. L., Way, N., & Pahl, K. (2006). Trajectories of perceived adult and peer discrimination among Black, Latino, and Asian American adolescents: Patterns and psychological correlates. *Developmental Psychology, 42*, 218–238.

Greene, S. M., Anderson, E., Hetherington, E. M., Forgath, M. S., & DeGarmo, D. S. (2003). Risk and resilience after divorce. In R. Walsh (Ed.), *Normal family processes* (pp. 96–120). New York: Guilford.

Greenfield, P. (1992, June). *Notes and references for developmental psychology.* Conference on Making Basic Texts in Psychology More Culture-Inclusive and Culture-Sensitive, Western Washington University, Bellingham, WA.

Greenfield, P. M. (2004). *Weaving generations together: Evolving creativity in the Maya of Chiapas.* Santa Fe, NM: School of American Research.

Greenfield, P. M., Keller, H., Fuligni, A., & Maynard, A. (2003). Cultural pathways through universal development. *Annual Review of Psychology, 54*, 461–490.

Greenfield, P. M., Maynard, A. E., & Childs, C. P. (2000). History, culture, learning, and development. *Cross-Cultural Research, 34*, 351–374.

Greenfield, P. M., Suzuki, L. K., & Rothstein-Fish, C. (2006). Cultural pathways through human development. In K. A. Renninger & I. E. Sigel (Eds.), *Handbook of child psychology: Vol. 4. Child psychology in practice* (6th ed., pp. 655–699). Hoboken, NJ: Wiley.

Greenfield, P., & Yan, Z. (2007). Children, adolescents, and the Internet: A new field of inquiry in developmental psychology. *Developmental Psychology, 42*, 391–394.

Greenhill, L. L., Halperin, J. M., & Abikoff, H. (1999). Stimulant medications. *Journal of the American Academy of Child and Adolescent Psychiatry, 38*, 503–512.

Greenhoot, A. F. (2000). Remembering and understanding: The effects of changes in underlying knowledge on children's recollections. *Child Development, 71*, 1309–1328.

Greenough, W. T., & Black, J. E. (1992). Induction of brain structure by experience: Substrates for cognitive development. In M. R. Gunnar & C. A. Nelson (Eds.), *Minnesota Symposia on Child Psychology* (pp. 155–200). Hillsdale, NJ: Erlbaum.

Greenspan, S. I., & Shanker, S. G. (2004). *The first idea: How symbols, language, and intelligence evolved from our primate ancestors to modern humans.* Cambridge, MA: Da Capo Press.

Grief, G. L., Hrabowski, F. A., Maton, K. I. (1998). African-American fathers of high-achieving sons: Using outstanding members of an at-risk population to guide intervention. *Families in Society, 79*, 45–52.

Grigorenko, E. L., & Sternberg, R. J. (1998). Dynamic testing. *Psychological Bulletin, 124*, 75–111.

Grigorenko, E. L., & Sternberg, R. J. (2001). Analytical, creative, and practical intelligence as predictors of self-reported adaptive functioning: A case study in Russia. *Intelligence, 29*, 57–73.

Grolnick, W. S., Kurowski, C. O., Dunlap, K. G., & Hevey, C. (2000). Parental resources and the transition to junior high. *Journal of Research on Adolescence, 10*, 465–488.

Gronau, R. C., & Waas, G. A. (1997). Delay of gratification and cue utilization: An examination of children's social information processing. *Merrill-Palmer Quarterly, 43*, 305–322.

Groome, L. J., Swiber, M. J., Holland, S. B., Bentz, L. S., Atterbury, J. L., & Trimm, R. F., III. (1999). Spontaneous motor activity in the perinatal infant before and after birth: Stability in individual differences. *Developmental Psychobiology, 35*, 15–24.

Gropman, A. L., & Adams, D. R. (2007). Atypical patterns of inheritance. *Seminars in Pediatric Neurology, 14*, 34–45.

Grossmann, K., Grossmann, K. E., Fremmer-Bombik, E., Kindler, H., Scheuerer-Englisch, H., & Zimmermann, P. (2002). The uniqueness of the child–father attachment relationship: Fathers' sensitive and challenging play as a pivotal variable in a 16-year longitudinal study. *Social Development, 11*, 307–331.

Grossmann, K., Grossmann, K. E., Kindler, H., & Zimmermann, P. (2008). A wider view of attachment and exploration: The influence of mothers and fathers on the development of psychological security from infancy to young adulthood. In J. Cassidy & P. R. Shaver (Eds.), *Handbook of attachment: Theory, research, and clinical applications* (2nd ed., pp. 880–905). New York: Guilford.

Grossmann, K., Grossmann, K. E., Spangler, G., Suess, G., & Unzner, L. (1985). Maternal sensitivity and newborns' orientation responses as related to quality of attachment in Northern Germany. In I. Bretherton & E. Waters (Eds.), Growing points of attachment theory and research. *Monographs of the Society for Research in Child Development, 50* (1–2, Serial No. 209).

Grossmann, T., Striano, T., & Friederici, A. D. (2007). Developmental changes in

infants' processing of happy and angry facial expressions: A neurobehavioral study. *Brain and Cognition, 64*, 30–41.

Grotevant, H. D. (1978). Sibling constellations and sex-typing of interests in adolescence. *Child Development, 49*, 540–542.

Grow-Maienza, J., Hahn, D.-D., & Joo, C.-A. (2001). Mathematics instruction in Korean primary schools: Structures, processes, and a linguistic analysis of questioning. *Journal of Educational Psychology, 93*, 363–376.

Gruendel J., & Aber, J. L. (2007). Bridging the gap between research and child policy change: The role of strategic communications in policy advocacy. In J. L. Aber, S. J. Bishop-Josef, S. M. Jones, K. T. McLearn, & D. Phillips (Eds.), *Child development and social policy: Knowledge for action* (pp. 43–58). Washington, DC: American Psychological Association.

Grusec, J. E. (1988). *Social development: History, theory, and research.* New York: Springer-Verlag.

Grusec, J. E. (2006). The development of moral behavior and conscience from a socialization perspective. In M. Killen & J. Smetana (Eds.), *Handbook of moral development* (pp. 243–265). Philadelphia: Erlbaum.

Grusec, J. E., & Goodnow, J. J. (1994). Impact of parental discipline methods on the child's internalization of values: A reconceptualization of current points of view. *Developmental Psychology, 30*, 4–19.

Guerra, N. G., Graham, S., & Tolan, P. H. (2011). Raising healthy children: Translating child development research into practice. *Child Development, 82*, 7–16.

Guerra, N. G., Williams, K. R., & Sadek, S. (2011). Understanding bullying and victimization during childhood and adolescence: A mixed methods study. *Child Development, 82*, 295–310.

Guglielmi, R. S. (2008). Native language proficiency, English literacy, academic achievement, and occupational attainment in limited-English-proficient students: A latent growth modeling perspective. *Journal of Educational Psychology, 100*, 322–342.

Guignard, J.-H., & Lubart, T. (2006). Is it reasonable to be creative? In J. C. Kaufman & J. Baer (Eds.), *Creativity and reason in cognitive development* (pp. 269–281). New York: Cambridge University Press.

Guignard, J.-H., & Lubart, T. I. (2007). A comparative study of convergent and divergent thinking in intellectually gifted children. *Gifted and Talented International, 22*(1), 9–15.

Guilford, J. P. (1985). The structure-of-intellect model. In B. B. Wolman (Ed.), *Handbook of intelligence* (pp. 225–266). New York: Wiley.

Guiso, L., Mont, F., Sapienza, P., & Zingales, L. (2008). Culture, gender, and math. *Science, 320*, 1164–1165.

Güller, O. E., Larkina, M., Kleinknecht, E., & Bauer, P. J. (2010). Memory strategies and retrieval success in preschool children: Relations to maternal behavior over time. *Journal of Cognition and Development, 11*, 159–184.

Gullone, E. (2000). The development of normal fear: A century of research. *Clinical Psychology Review, 20*, 429–451.

Gulotta, T. P. (2008). How theory influences treatment and prevention practice within the family. In T. P. Gulotta (Ed.), *Family* influences on child behavior and development: Evidence-based prevention and treatment approaches (pp. 1–20). New York: Routledge.

Gunnar, M., & Quevedo, K. (2007). The neurobiology of stress and development. *Annual Review of Psychology, 58,* 145–173.

Gunnar, M. R., & Cheatham, C. L. (2003). Brain and behavior interfaces: Stress and the developing brain. *Infant Mental Health Journal, 24,* 195–211.

Gunnar, M. R., & Vasquez, D. M. (2001). Low cortisol and a flattening of expected daytime rhythm: Potential indices of risk in human development. *Development and Psychopathology, 13,* 515–538.

Gunnar, M. R., Morison, S. J., Chisholm, K., & Schuder, M. (2001). Salivary cortisol levels in children adopted from Romanian orphanages. *Development and Psychopathology, 13,* 611–628.

Gunnoe, M. L., & Mariner, C. L. (1997). Toward a developmental-contextual model of the effects of parental spanking on children's aggression. *Archives of Pediatrics and Adolescent Medicine, 151,* 768–775.

Gunstad, J., Spitznagel, M. B., Luyster, F., Cohen, R. A., & Paul, R. H. (2007). Handedness and cognition across the healthy lifespan. *International Journal of Neuroscience, 117,* 477–485.

Guo, G., & VanWey, L. K. (1999). Sibship size and intellectual development: Is the relationship causal? *American Sociological Review, 64,* 169–187.

Guralnick, M. J., Neville, B., Hammond, M. A., & Connor, R. T. (2007). Linkages between delayed children's social interactions with mothers and peers. *Child Development, 78,* 459–473.

Gure, A., Ucanok, Z., & Sayil, M. (2006). The associations among perceived pubertal timing, parental relations and self-perception in Turkish adolescents. *Journal of Youth and Adolescence, 35,* 541–550.

Gustafson, G. E., Green, J. A., & Cleland, J. W. (1994). Robustness of individual identity in the cries of human infants. *Developmental Psychobiology, 27,* 1–9.

Gustafson, G. E., Wood, R. M., & Green, J. A. (2000). Can we hear the causes of infants' crying? In R. G. Barr, B. Hopkins, & J. A. Green (Eds.), *Crying as a sign, a symptom, and a signal* (pp. 8–22). New York: Cambridge University Press.

Guterman, N. B., Lee, S. J., Taylor, C. A., & Rathouz, P. J. (2009). Parental perceptions of neighborhood processes, stress, personal control, and risk for physical child abuse and neglect. *Child Abuse and Neglect, 33,* 897–906.

Gutman, L. M. (2006). How student and parent goal orientations and classroom goal structures influence the math achievement of African Americans during the high school transition. *Contemporary Educational Psychology, 31,* 44–63.

Gutman, L. M., & Midgley, C. (2000). The role of protective factors in supporting the academic achievement of poor African-American students during the middle school transition. *Journal of Youth and Adolescence, 29,* 223–248.

Gutman, L. M., Sameroff, A. J., & Cole, R. (2003). Academic growth curve trajectories from 1st grade to 12th grade: Effects of multiple social risk factors and preschool child factors. *Developmental Psychology, 39,* 777–790.

Gutman, L. M., Sameroff, A. J., & Eccles, J. S. (2002). The academic achievement of African-American students during early adolescence: An examination of multiple risk, promotive, and protective factors. *American Journal of Community Psychology, 39,* 367–399.

Gutteling, B. M., de Weerth, C., Zandbelt, N., Mulder, E. J. H., Visser, G. H. A., & Buitelaar, J. K. (2006). Does maternal prenatal stress adversely affect the child's learning and memory at age six? *Journal of Abnormal Child Psychology, 34,* 789–798.

Gwiazda, J., & Birch, E. E. (2001). Perceptual development: Vision. In E. B. Goldstein (Ed.), *Blackwell handbook of perception* (pp. 636–668). Oxford: Blackwell.

Haas, L. (2003). Women in Sweden. In L. Walter (Ed.), *The Greenwood encyclopedia of women's issues worldwide: Europe.* Westport, CT: Greenwood Press.

Haas, L., Chronholm, A., & Hwang, P. (2006). Sweden. In P. Moss & M. O'Brien (Eds.), *International review of leave policies and related research, 2006* (pp. 205–216). London: Department of Trade and Industry.

Hack, M., & Klein, N. (2006). Young adult attainments of preterm infants. *Journal of the American Medical Association, 295,* 695–696.

Hagekull, B., Bohlin, G., & Rydell, A. (1997). Maternal sensitivity, infant temperament, and the development of early feeding problems. *Infant Mental Health Journal, 18,* 92–106.

Hagerman, R. J., Berry-Kravis, E., Kaufmann, W. E., Ono, M. Y., Tartaglia, N., & Lachiewicz, A. (2009). Advances in the treatment of fragile X syndrome. *Pediatrics, 123,* 378–390.

Hahn, S., & Chitty, L. S. (2008). Noninvasive prenatal diagnosis: Current practice and future perspectives. *Current Opinion in Obstetrics and Gynecology, 20,* 146–151.

Haidt, J. (2001). The emotional dog and its rational tail: A social intuitionist approach to moral judgment. *Psychological Review, 108,* 814–834.

Haidt, J. (2003). The moral emotions. In R. J. Davidson, K. R. Scherer, & H. H. Goldsmith (Eds.), *Handbook of affective sciences* (pp. 852–870). New York: Oxford University Press.

Haidt, J., & Kesebir, S. (2010). Morality. In S. T. Fiske & D. Gilbert (Eds.), *Handbook of social psychology* (5th ed., pp. 797–832). Hoboken, NJ: Wiley.

Haight, W. L., & Miller, P. J. (1993). *Pretending at home: Early development in a sociocultural context.* Albany, NY: SUNY Press.

Hainline, L. (1998). The development of basic visual abilities. In A. Slater (Ed.), *Perceptual development: Visual, auditory, and speech perception in infancy* (pp. 37–44). Hove, UK: Psychology Press.

Haith, M. M. (1994). Visual expectation as the first step toward the development of future-oriented processes. In M. M. Haith, J. B. Benson, R. J. Roberts, Jr., & B. Pennington (Eds.), *The development of future-oriented processes* (pp. 11–38). Chicago: University of Chicago Press.

Hakman, M., & Sullivan, M. (2009). The effect of task and maternal verbosity on compliance in toddlers. *Infant and Child Development, 18,* 195–205.

Hakuta, K., Bialystok, E., & Wiley, E. (2003). Critical evidence: A test of the critical period hypothesis for second-language acquisition. *Psychological Science, 14,* 31–38.

Hale, C. M., & Tager-Flusberg, H. (2003). The influence of language on theory of mind: A training study. *Developmental Science, 6,* 346–359.

Hales, C. N., & Ozanne, S. E. (2003). The dangerous road of catch-up growth. *Journal of Physiology, 547,* 5–10.

Halfon, N., & McLearn, K. T. (2002). Families with children under 3: What we know and implications for results and policy. In N. Halfon & K. T. McLearn (Eds.), *Child rearing in America: Challenges facing parents with young children* (pp. 367–412). New York: Cambridge University Press.

Halford, G. S. (2002). Information-processing models of cognitive development. In U. Goswami (Ed.), *Blackwell handbook of childhood cognitive development* (pp. 555–574). Malden, MA: Blackwell.

Halford, G. S. (2005). Development of thinking. In K. J. Holyoak & R. G. Morrison (Eds.), *The Cambridge handbook of thinking and reasoning* (pp. 529–558). New York: Cambridge University Press.

Halford, G. S., & Andrews, G. (2006). Reasoning and problem solving. In D. Kuhn & R. Siegler (Eds.), *Handbook of child psychology: Vol. 2. Cognition, perception, and language* (6th ed., pp. 557–608). Hoboken, NJ: Wiley.

Hall, C. M., Jones, J. A., Meyer-Bahlburg, H. F. L., Dolezal, C., Coleman, M., & Foster, P. (2004). Behavioral and physical masculinization are related to genotype in girls with congenital adrenal hyperplasia. *Journal of Clinical Endocrinology and Metabolism, 89,* 419–424.

Hall, D. G., Burns, T. S., & Pawluski, J. (2003). Input and word learning: Caregivers' sensitivity to lexical category distinctions. *Journal of Child Language, 30,* 711–729.

Hall, D. G., & Graham, S. A. (1999). Lexical form class information guides word-to-object mapping in preschoolers. *Child Development, 70,* 78–91.

Hall, D. G., Lee, S. C., & Belanger, J. (2001). Young children's use of syntactic cues to learn proper names and count nouns. *Developmental Psychology, 37,* 298–307.

Hall, G. S. (1904). *Adolescence* (Vols. 1–2). New York: Appleton-Century-Crofts.

Hall, J. G. (2003). Twinning. *Lancet, 362,* 735–743.

Haller, J. (2005). Vitamins and brain function. In H. R. Lieberman, R. B. Kanarek, & C. Prasad (2005). *Nutritional neuroscience* (pp. 207–233). Philadelphia: Taylor & Francis.

Hallinan, M. T., & Kubitschek, W. N. (1999). Curriculum differentiation and high school achievement. *Social Psychology of Education, 3,* 41–62.

Halpern, C. T., Udry, J. R., & Suchindran, C. (1997). Testosterone predicts initiation of coitus in adolescent females. *Psychosomatic Medicine, 59,* 161–171.

Halpern, D. F., Benbow, C. P., Geary, D. C., Gur, R. C., Hyde, J. S., & Gernsbacher, M. A. (2007). The science of sex differences in science and mathematics. *Psychological Science in the Public Interest, 8,* 1–51.

Halpern, D. F., & Collaer, M. L. (2005). Sex differences in visuospatial abilities: More than meets the eye. In P. Shah & A. Miyake (Eds.), *Handbook of visuospatial thinking* (pp. 170–212). New York: Cambridge University Press.

Halpern, D. F., Wai, J., & Saw, A. (2005). A psychobiosocial model: Why females are sometimes greater than and sometimes less than males in math achievement. In D. F. Halpern, J. Wai, & A. Saw (Eds.), *Gender differences in mathematics: An integrative psychological approach* (pp. 48–72). New York: Cambridge University Press.

Halpern-Felsher, B. L., Biehl, M., Kropp, R. Y., & Rubinstein, M. L. (2004). Perceived risks and benefits of smoking: Differences among adolescents with different smoking experiences and intentions. *Preventive Medicine, 39,* 559–567.

Halpern-Felsher, B. L., & Cauffman, E. (2001). Costs and benefits of a decision: Decision-making competence in adolescents and adults. *Journal of Applied Developmental Psychology, 22,* 257–273.

Hamer, D. H., Hu, S., Magnuson, V. L., Hu, N., & Pattatucci, A. M. L. (1993). A linkage between DNA markers on the X chromosome and male sexual orientation. *Science, 261,* 321–327.

Hamilton, S. F., & Hamilton, M. A. (2000). Research, intervention, and social change: Improving adolescents' career opportunities. In L. J. Crockett & R. K. Silbereisen (Eds.), *Negotiating adolescence in times of social change* (pp. 267–283). New York: Cambridge University Press.

Hamlin, J. K., Wynn, K., & Bloom, P. (2007). Social evaluation by preverbal infants. *Nature, 450,* 557–559.

Hamm, J. V. (2000). Do birds of a feather flock together? The variable bases for African American, Asian American, and European American adolescents' selection of similar friends. *Developmental Psychology, 36,* 209–219.

Hammes, B., & Laitman, C. J. (2003). Diethylstilbestrol (DES) update: Recommendations for the identification and management of DES-exposed individuals. *Journal of Midwifery and Women's Health, 48,* 19–29.

Hanawalt, B. A. (1993). *Growing up in medieval London: The experience of childhood in history.* New York: Oxford University Press.

Hanawalt, B. A. (2003). The child in the Middle Ages and the Renaissance. In W. Koops & M. Zuckerman (Eds.), *Beyond the century of childhood: Cultural history and developmental psychology.* Philadelphia: University of Pennsylvania Press.

Handley, S. J., Capon, A., Beveridge, M., Dennis, I., & Evans, J. St. B. T. (2004). Working memory, inhibitory control and the development of children's reasoning. *Thinking and Reasoning, 10,* 175–195.

Hane, A. A., Cheah, C., Rubin, K. H., & Fox, N. A. (2008). The role of maternal behavior in the relation between shyness and social reticence in early childhood and social withdrawal in middle childhood. *Social Development, 17,* 795–811.

Hankin, B. L., & Abela, J. R. Z. (2005). Depression from childhood through adolescence and adulthood: A developmental vulnerability and stress perspective. In B. L. Hankin & J. R. Z. Abela (Eds.), *Development of psychopathology: A vulnerability-stress perspective* (pp. 245–288). Thousand Oaks, CA: Sage.

Hankin, B. L., Stone, L., & Wright, P. A. (2010). Co-rumination, interpersonal stress generation, and internalizing symptoms: Accumulating effects and transactional influences in a multiwave study of adolescents. *Development and Psychopathology, 22,* 217–235.

Hannon, E. E., & Johnson, S. P. (2004). Infants use meter to categorize rhythms and melodies: Implications for musical structure learning. *Cognitive Psychology, 50,* 354–377.

Hannon, E. E., & Trehub, S. E. (2005a). Metrical categories in infancy and adulthood. *Psychological Science, 16,* 48–55.

Hannon, E. E., & Trehub, S. E. (2005b). Tuning in to musical rhythms: Infants learn more readily than adults. *Proceedings of the National Academy of Sciences, 102,* 12639–12643.

Hannon, T. S., Rao, G., & Arslanian, S. A. (2005). Childhood obesity and type 2 diabetes mellitus. *Pediatrics, 116,* 473–480.

Hans, S. L., & Jeremy, R. J. (2001). Postneonatal mental and motor development of infants exposed in utero to opiate drugs. *Infant Mental Health Journal, 22,* 300–315.

Hansell, N. K., Wright, M. J., Geffen, G. M., Geffen, L. B., Smith, G. A., & Martin, N. G. (2001). Genetic influence on ERP slow wave measures of working memory. *Behavioral Genetics, 31,* 603–614.

Hansen, M. B., & Markman, E. M. (2009). Children's use of mutual exclusivity to learn labels for parts of objects. *Developmental Psychology, 45,* 592–596.

Hansen, M., Janssen, I., Schiff, A., Zee, P. C., & Dubocovich, M. L. (2005). The impact of school daily schedule on adolescent sleep. *Pediatrics, 115,* 1555–1561.

Hanushek, E., Kain, J., & Rivkin, S. (2002). *New evidence about Brown v. Board of Education: The complex effects of school racial composition on achievement.* Working Paper 8741. Cambridge, MA: National Bureau of Economic Research.

Happé, F., & Frith, U. (2006). The weak coherence account: Detail-focused cognitive style in autism spectrum disorders. *Journal of Autism and Developmental Disorders, 1,* 1–21.

Harachi, T. W., Fleming, C. B., White, H. R., Ensminger, M. E., Abbott, R. D., Catalano, R. F., & Haggerty, K. P. (2006). Aggressive behavior among girls and boys during middle childhood: Predictors and sequelae of trajectory group membership. *Aggressive Behavior, 32,* 279–293.

Hardy, J. B., Astone, N. M., Brooks-Gunn, J., Shapiro, S., & Miller, T. L. (1998). Like mother, like child: Intergenerational patterns of age at first birth and associations with childhood and adolescent characteristics and adult outcomes in the second generation. *Developmental Psychology, 34,* 1220–1232.

Hardy, S. A., & Carlo, G. (2005). Religiosity and prosocial behaviours in adolescence: The mediating role of prosocial values. *Journal of Moral Education, 34,* 231–249.

Hardy, S. A., & Carlo, G. (2011). Moral identity: What is it, how does it develop, and is it linked to moral action? *Child Development Perspectives, 5,* 212–218.

Harley, B., & Jean, G. (1999). Vocabulary skills of French immersion students in their second language. *Zeitschrift für Interkulterellen Fremdsprachenunterricht, 4*(2). Retrieved from www.ualberta.ca

Harley, K., & Reese, E. (1999). Origins of autobiographical memory. *Developmental Psychology, 35,* 1338–1348.

Harlow, H. F., & Zimmerman, R. (1959). Affectional responses in the infant monkey. *Science, 130,* 421–432.

Harris, G. (1997). Development of taste perception and appetite regulation. In G. Bremner, A. Slater, & G. Butterworth (Eds.), *Infant development: Recent advances* (pp. 9–30). East Sussex, UK: Erlbaum.

Harris, J. R. (1998). *The nurture assumption: Why children turn out the way they do.* New York: Free Press.

Harris, J. R. (2002). Beyond the nurture assumption: Testing hypotheses about the child's environment. In J. G. Borkowski & S. L. Ramey (Eds.), *Parenting and the child's world* (pp. 3–20). Mahwah, NJ: Erlbaum.

Harris, M. B. (2008). Primary prevention of pregnancy: Effective school-based programs. In C. Franklin, M. B. Harris, & P. Allen-Meares (Eds.), *The school practitioner's concise companion to preventing dropout and attendance problems* (pp. 89–100). New York: Oxford University Press.

Harris, P. L. (2006). Social cognition. In D. Kuhn & R. S. Siegler (Eds.), *Handbook of child psychology: Vol. 2: Cognition, perception, and language* (6th ed., pp. 811–858). Hoboken, NJ: Wiley.

Harris, S., & Berk, L. E. (March, 2011). *Impact of individualized, supplementary preschool intervention on literacy, school readiness, and socioemotional skills.* Poster presented at the biennial meeting of the Society for Research in Child Development, Montreal, Canada.

Harris, Y. R., & Graham, J. A. (2007). *The African American child: Development and challenges.* New York: Springer.

Harrison, A. O., Wilson, M. N., Pine, C. J., Chan, S. Q., & Buriel, R. (1994). Family ecologies of ethnic minority children. In G. Handel & G. G. Whitchurch (Eds.), *The psychosocial interior of the family* (pp. 187–210). New York: Aldine De Gruyter.

Harrison, Y. (2004). The relationship between daytime exposure to light and night-time sleep in 6–12-week-old infants. *Journal of Sleep Research, 13,* 345–352.

Hart, B. (2004). What toddlers talk about. *First Language, 24,* 91–106.

Hart, B., & Risley, T. R. (1995). *Meaningful differences in the everyday experience of young American children.* Baltimore: Paul H. Brookes.

Hart, C. H. (2007). Why are parents important? Linking parenting to childhood social skills in Australia, China, Japan, Russia, and the United States. In A. S. Loveless & T. B. Holman (Eds.), *The family in the new millennium: World voices supporting the "natural" clan: Vol. 1. The place of family in human society* (pp. 227–247). Westport, CT: Praeger.

Hart, C. H., Burts, D. C., Durland, M. A., Charlesworth, R., DeWolf, M., & Fleege, P. O. (1998). Stress behaviors and activity type participation of preschoolers in more and less developmentally appropriate classrooms: SES and sex differences. *Journal of Research in Childhood Education, 13,* 176–196.

Hart, C. H., Newell, L. D., & Olsen, S. F. (2003). Parenting skills and social–communicative competence in childhood. In J. O. Greene & B. R. Burleson (Eds.), *Handbook of communication and social interaction skills* (pp. 753–797). Mahwah, NJ: Erlbaum.

Hart, C. H., Yang, C., Charlesworth, R., & Burts, D. C. (2003, April). *Kindergarten teaching practices: Associations with later child academic and social/emotional adjustment to school.* Paper presented at the biennial meeting of the Society for Research in Child Development, Tampa, FL.

Hart, C. H., Yang, C., Nelson, L. J., Robinson, C. C., Olsen, J. A., & Nelson, D. A. (2000). Peer acceptance in early childhood and subtypes of socially withdrawn behavior in China, Russia, and the United States. *International Journal of Behavioral Development, 24,* 73–81.

Hart, D., & Atkins, R. (2002). Civic competence in urban youth. *Applied Developmental Science, 6,* 227–236.

Hart, D., Atkins, R., & Donnelly, T. M. (2006). Community service and moral development. In M. Killen & J. G. Smetana (Eds.), *Handbook of moral development* (pp. 633–656). Philadelphia: Erlbaum.

Hart, D., Atkins, R., & Matsuba, M. K. (2008). The association of neighborhood poverty with personality change in childhood. *Journal of Personality and Social Psychology, 44,* 1048–1061.

Hart, D., Donnelly, T. M., Youniss, J., & Atkins, R. (2007). High school community service as a predictor of adult voting and volunteering. *American Educational Research Journal, 44,* 197–219.

Hart, D., & Fegley, S. (1995). Prosocial behavior and caring in adolescence: Relations to self-understanding and social judgment. *Child Development, 66,* 1346–1359.

Harter, S. (1999). *The construction of self: A developmental perspective.* New York: Guilford.

Harter, S. (2003). The development of self-representations during childhood and adolescence. In M. R. Leary & J. P. Tangney (Eds.), *Handbook of self and identity* (pp. 610–642). New York: Guilford.

Harter, S. (2006). The self. In N. Eisenberg (Ed.), *Handbook of child psychology: Vol. 3. Social, emotional, and personality development* (6th ed., pp. 505–570). Hoboken, NJ: Wiley.

Harter, S., Waters, P., & Whitesell, N. R. (1998). Relational self-worth: Differences in perceived worth as a person across interpersonal contexts among adolescents. *Child Development, 69,* 756–766.

Harter, S., & Whitesell, N. R. (1989). Developmental changes in children's understanding of simple, multiple, and blended emotion concepts. In C. Saarni & P. Harris (Eds.), *Children's understanding of emotion* (pp. 81–116). Cambridge, UK: Cambridge University Press.

Harter, S., & Whitesell, N. R. (2003). Beyond the debate: Why some adolescents report stable self-worth over time and situation, whereas others report changes in self-worth. *Journal of Personality, 71,* 1027–1058.

Hartshorn, K. (2003). Reinstatement maintains a memory in human infants for 1½ years. *Developmental Psychobiology, 42,* 269–282.

Hartshorn, K., Rovee-Collier, C., Gerhardstein, P., Bhatt, R. S., Klein, P. J., Aaron, F., et al. (1998a). Developmental changes in the specificity of memory over the first year of life. *Developmental Psychobiology, 33,* 61–68.

Hartshorn, K., Rovee-Collier, C., Gerhardstein, P., Bhatt, R. S., Wondoloski, T. L., Klein, P., et al. (1998b). The ontogeny of long-term memory over the first year-and-a-half of life. *Developmental Psychobiology, 32,* 69–89.

Hartup, W. W. (1996). The company they keep: Friendships and their developmental significance. *Child Development, 67,* 1–13.

Hartup, W. W. (2006). Relationships in early and middle childhood. In A. L. Vangelisti & D. Perlman (Eds.), *Cambridge handbook of personal relationships* (pp. 177–190). New York: Cambridge University Press.

Hartup, W. W., & Abecassis, M. (2004). Friends and enemies. In P. K. Smith & C. H. Hart (Eds.), *Blackwell handbook of childhood social development* (pp. 285–306). Malden, MA: Blackwell.

Hartup, W. W., & Stevens, N. (1999). Friendships and adaptation across the life span. *Current Directions in Psychological Science, 8,* 76–79.

Harvey, R. J., Fletcher, J., & French, D. J. (2001). Social reasoning: A source of influence on aggression. *Clinical Psychology, Review, 21,* 447–469.

Harwood, M. D., & Farrar, M. J. (2006). Conflicting emotions: The connection between affective perspective taking and theory of mind. *British Journal of Developmental Psychology, 24,* 401–418.

Hasebe, Y., Nucci, L., & Nucci, M. S. (2004). Parental control of the personal domain and adolescent symptoms of psychopathology: A cross-national study in the United States and Japan. *Child Development, 75,* 815–828.

Hastings, E. C., Karas, T. L., Winsler, A., Way, E., Madigan, A., & Tyler, S. (2009). Young children's video/computer game use: Relations with school performance and behaviour. *Issues in Mental Health Nursing, 30,* 638–649.

Hastings, P. D., Zahn-Waxler, C. R., Robinson, J., Usher, B., & Bridges, D. (2000). The development of concern for others in children with behavior problems. *Developmental Psychology, 36,* 531–546.

Hastings, P. D., Zahn-Waxler, C., & Usher, B. A. (2007). Cardiovascular and affective responses to social stress in adolescents with internalizing and externalizing problems. *International Journal of Behavioral Development, 31,* 77–87.

Hatton, D. D., Bailey, D. B., Jr., Burchinal, M. R., & Ferrell, K. A. (1997). Developmental growth curves of preschool children with vision impairments. *Child Development, 68,* 788–806.

Hau, K.-T., & Ho, I. T. (2010). Chinese students' motivation and achievement. In M. H. Bond (Ed.), *Oxford handbook of Chinese psychology* (pp. 187–204). New York: Oxford University Press.

Hauf, P., Aschersleben, G., & Prinz, W. (2007). Baby do–baby see! How action production influences action perception in infants. *Cognitive Development, 22,* 16–32.

Hausfather, A., Toharia, A., LaRoche, C., & Engelsmann, F. (1997). Effects of age of entry, day-care quality, and family characteristics on preschool behavior. *Journal of Child Psychology and Psychiatry, 38,* 441–448.

Hawkins, J. N. (1994). Issues of motivation in Asian education. In H. F. O'Neil, Jr., & M. Drillings (Eds.), *Motivation: Theory and research* (pp. 101–115). Hillsdale, NJ: Erlbaum.

Hay, D. F., Pawlby, S., Angold, A., Harold, G. T., & Sharp, D. (2003). Pathways to violence in the children of mothers who were depressed postpartum. *Developmental Psychology, 39,* 1983–1994.

Hay, D. F., Pawlby, S., Waters, C. S., Perra, O., & Sharp, D. (2010). Mothers' antenatal depression and their children's antisocial outcomes. *Child Development, 81,* 149–165.

Hay, D. F., Payne, A., & Chadwick, A. (2004). Peer relations in childhood. *Journal of Child Psychology and Psychiatry, 45,* 84–108.

Hay, P., & Bacaltchuk, J. (2004). Bulimia nervosa. *Clinical Evidence, 12,* 1326–1347.

Haycock, P. C. (2009). Fetal alcohol spectrum disorders: The epigenetic perspective. *Biology of Reproduction, 81,* 607–617.

Hayden, A., Bhatt, R. S., Reed, A., Corbly, C. R., & Joseph, J. E. (2007). The development of expert face processing: Are infants sensitive to normal differences in second-order relational information? *Journal of Experimental Child Psychology, 97,* 85–98.

Hayne, H. (2002). Thoughts from the crib: Meltzoff and Moore (1994) alter our views of mental representation during infancy. *Infant Behavior and Development, 25,* 62–64.

Hayne, H. (2004). Infant memory development: Implications for childhood amnesia. *Developmental Review, 24,* 33–73.

Hayne, H., Boniface, J., & Barr, R. (2000). The development of declarative memory in human infants: Age-related changes in deferred imitation. *Behavioral Neuroscience, 114,* 77–83.

Hayne, H., Herbert, J., & Simcock, G. (2003). Imitation from television by 24- and 30-month-olds. *Developmental Science, 6,* 254–261.

Hayne, H., & Rovee-Collier, C. K. (1995). The organization of reactivated memory in infancy. *Child Development, 66,* 893–906.

Hayne, H., Rovee-Collier, C. K., & Perris, E. E. (1987). Categorization and memory retrieval by three-month-olds. *Child Development, 58,* 750–767.

Hayne, H., & Simcock, G. (2009). Memory development in toddlers. In M. L. Courage & N. Cowan (Eds.), *The development of memory in infancy and childhood* (pp. 43–68). Hove, UK: Psychology Press.

Hayslip, B., Emick, M. A., Henderson, C. E., & Elias, K. (2002). Temporal variations in the experiences of custodial grandparenting: A short-term longitudinal study. *Journal of Applied Gerontology, 21,* 139–156.

Haywood, H. C., & Lidz, C. S. (2007). *Dynamic assessment in practice.* New York: Cambridge University Press.

Haywood, K. M., & Getchell, N. (2005). *Life span motor development* (4th ed.). Champaign, IL: Human Kinetics.

Hazen, N. L., McFarland, L., Jacobvitz, D., & Boyd-Soisson, E. (2010). Fathers' frightening behaviours and sensitivity with infants: Relations with fathers' attachment representations, father–infant attachment, and children's later outcomes. *Early Child Development and Care, 180,* 51–69.

Head Start. (2010). *Head Start Program fact sheet.* Retrieved from www.acf.hhs.gov/programs/ohs/about/fy2010.html

Health Canada. (2008). *Report on sexually transmitted infections in Canada.* Retrieved from www.phac-aspc.gc.ca/std-mts/report/sti-its2008/index-eng.php

Healthy Families America. (2011). *Healthy Families America FAQ.* Retrieved from www.healthyfamiliesamerica.org/about_us/faq.shtml

Hearold, S. (1986). A synthesis of 1,043 effects of television on social behavior. In G. Comstock (Ed.), *Public communications and behavior* (Vol. 1, pp. 65–133). New York: Academic Press.

Heath, S. B. (1990). The children of Trackton's children: Spoken and written language and social change. In J. Stigler, G. Herdt, & R. A. Shweder (Eds.), *Cultural psychology: Essays on comparative human development* (pp. 496–519). New York: Cambridge University Press.

Heckman, J. J., & Masterov, D. V. (2004). *The productivity argument for investing in young children.* Working Paper 5, Invest in Kids Working Group, Committee for Economic Development. Retrieved from jenni.uchicago.edu/Invest

Heckman, J. J., Seong, H. M., Pinto, R., Savelyev, P., & Yavitz, A. (2010). A new cost-benefit and rate of return for the Perry Preschool Program: A summary. In A. J. Reynolds, A. J. Rolnick, M. M. Englund, & J. Temple (Eds.), *Childhood programs and practices in the first decade of life: A human capital integration* (pp. 199–213). New York: Cambridge University Press.

Hediger, M. L., Overpeck, M. D., Ruan, W. J., & Troendle, J. F. (2002). Birthweight and gestational age effects on motor and social development. *Paediatric and Perinatal Epidemiology, 16,* 33–46.

Heil, M., Kavsek, Rolke, B., Best, C., & Jansen, P. (2011). Mental rotation in female fraternal twins: Evidence for intrauterine hormone transfer? *Biological Psychology, 86,* 90–93.

Heinz, W. R. (1999). Job-entry patterns in a life-course perspective. In W. R. Heinz (Ed.), *From education to work: Cross-national perspectives* (pp. 214–231). New York: Cambridge University Press.

Helburn, S. W. (Ed.). (1995). *Cost, quality and child outcomes in child care centers.* Denver: University of Colorado.

Hellemans, K. G., Sliwowska, J. H., Verma, P., & Weinberg, J. (2010). Prenatal alcohol exposure: Fetal programming and later life vulnerability to stress, depression and anxiety disorders. *Neuroscience and Biobehavioral Reviews, 34,* 791–807.

Helms-Lorenz, M., Van de Vijver, F. J. R., & Poortinga, Y. H. (2003). Cross-cultural differences in cognitive performance and Spearman's hypothesis: g or c? *Intelligence, 31,* 9–29.

Helwig, C. C. (1995). Adolescents' and young adults' conceptions of civil liberties: Freedom of speech and religion. *Child Development, 66,* 152–166.

Helwig, C. C. (2006). Rights, civil liberties, and democracy across cultures. In M. Killen & J. G. Smetana (Eds.), *Handbook of moral development* (pp. 185–210). Philadelphia: Erlbaum.

Helwig, C. C., & Jasiobedzka, U. (2001). The relation between law and morality: Children's reasoning about socially beneficial and unjust laws. *Child Development, 72,* 1382–1393.

Helwig, C. C., & Kim, S. (1999). Children's evaluations of decision-making procedures in peer, family, and school contexts. *Child Development, 70,* 502–512.

Helwig, C. C., & Prencipe, A. (1999). Children's judgments of flags and flag-burning. *Child Development, 70,* 132–143.

Helwig, C. C., Arnold, M. L., Tan, D., & Boyd, D. (2003). Chinese adolescents' reasoning about democratic and authority-based decision making in peer, family, and school contexts. *Child Development, 74,* 783–800.

Helwig, C. C., Zelazo, P. D., & Wilson, M. (2001). Children's judgments of psychological harm in normal and noncanonical situations. *Child Development, 72,* 66–81.

Henderson, H. A., Marshall, P. J., Fox, N. A., & Rubin, K. H. (2004). Psychophysiological and behavioral evidence for varying forms and functions of nonsocial behavior in preschoolers. *Child Development, 75,* 251–263.

Hendrick, J., & Stange, T. (1991). Do actions speak louder than words? An effect of the functional use of language on dominant sex role behavior in boys and girls. *Early Childhood Research Quarterly, 6,* 565–576.

Henggeler, S. W., Schoenwald, S. K., Bourduin, C. M., Rowland, M. D., & Cunningham, P. B. (2009). *Multisystemic therapy for antisocial behavior in children and adolescents* (2nd ed.). New York: Guilford.

Henrich, C. C., Brookmeyer, K. A., Shrier, L. A., & Shahar, G. (2006). Supportive relationships and sexual risk behavior in adolescence: An ecological–transactional approach. *Journal of Pediatric Psychology, 31,* 286–297.

Henrich, C. C., Kuperminc, G. P., Sack, A., Blatt, S. J., & Leadbeater, B. J. (2000). Characteristics and homogeneity of early adolescent friendship groups: A comparison of male and female clique and non-clique members. *Applied Developmental Science, 4,* 15–26.

Henricsson, L., & Rydell, A.-M. (2004). Elementary school children with behavior problems: Teacher–child relations and self perception. A prospective study. *Merrill-Palmer Quarterly, 50,* 111–138.

Henry, B., Moffitt, T. E., Caspi, A., Langley, J., & Silva, P. A. (1994). On the "remembrance of things past": A longitudinal evaluation of the retrospective method. *Psychological Assessment, 6,* 92–101.

Hepper, P. G., McCartney, G. R., & Shannon, E. A. (1998). Lateralised behaviour in first trimester human foetuses. *Neuropsychologia, 43,* 313–315.

Heraghty, J. L., Hilliard, T. N., Henderson, A. J., & Fleming, P. J. (2008). The physiology of sleep in infants. *Archives of Disease in Childhood, 93,* 982–985.

Herbert, J., Gross, J., & Hayne, H. (2007). Crawling is associated with more flexible memory retrieval by 9-month-old infants. *Developmental Science, 10,* 183–189.

Herman, L. M., & Uyeyama, R. K. (1999). The dolphin's grammatical competency: Comments on Kako. *Animal Learning and Behavior, 27,* 18–23.

Herman, M. R. (2004). Forced to choose: Some determinants of racial identification in multiracial adolescents. *Child Development, 75,* 730–748.

Herman-Giddens, M. E. (2006). Recent data on pubertal milestones in United States children: The secular trend toward earlier development. *International Journal of Andrology, 29,* 241–246.

Hernandez, D. J., Denton, N. A., & Macartney, S. E. (2008). Children in immigrant families: Looking to America's future. *Social Policy Report of the Society for Research in Child Development, 12*(11).

Herrnstein, R. J., & Murray, C. (1994). *The bell curve: Intelligence and class structure in American life.* New York: Free Press.

Hertenstein, M. J., & Campos, J. J. (2004). The retention effects of an adult's emotional displays on infant behavior. *Child Development, 75,* 595–613.

Herzog, D. B., Eddy, K. T., & Beresin, E. V. (2006). Anorexia and bulimia nervosa. In M. K. Dulcan & J. M. Wiener (Eds.), *Essentials of child and adolescent psychiatry* (pp. 527–560). Washington, DC: American Psychiatric Publishing.

Hesketh, K., Ball, K., Crawford, D., Campbell, K., & Salmon, J. (2007). Mediators of the relationship between maternal education and children's TV viewing. *American Journal of Preventive Medicine, 33,* 41–47.

Hespos, S. J., & Baillargeon, R. (2001). Reasoning about containment events in very young infants. *Cognition, 78,* 207–245.

Hespos, S. J., & Baillargeon, R. (2006). Décalage in infants' knowledge about occlusion and containment events: Converging evidence from action tasks. *Cognition, 99,* B31–B41.

Hespos, S. J., & Baillargeon, R. (2008). Young infants' actions reveal their developing knowledge of support variables: Converging evidence for violation-of-expectation findings. *Cognition, 107,* 304–316.

Hespos, S. J., Ferry, A. L., Cannistraci, C. J., Gore, J., & Park, S. (2010). Using optical imaging to investigate functional cortical activity in human infants. In A. W. Roe (Ed.), *Imaging the brain with optical methods* (pp. 159–176). New York: Springer Science + Business Media.

Hesse, E., & Main, M. (2000). Disorganized infant, child, and adult attachment: Collapse in behavioral and attentional strategies. *Journal of the American Psychoanalytic Association, 48,* 1097–1127.

Hester, M., He, J., & Tian, L. (2009). Girls' and boys' experiences and perceptions of parental discipline and punishment while growing up in China and England. *Child Abuse Review, 18,* 401–413.

Hetherington, E. M. (1999). Social capital and the development of youth from non-divorced, divorced, and remarried families. In A. Collins (Ed.), *Minnesota Symposia on Child Psychology* (Vol. 29, pp. 177–209). Mahwah, NJ: Erlbaum.

Hetherington, E. M. (2003). Social support and the adjustment of children in divorced and remarried families. *Childhood, 10,* 237–254.

Hetherington, E. M., Henderson, S. H., & Reiss, D. (1999). Adolescent siblings in stepfamilies: Family functioning and adolescent adjustment. *Monographs of the Society for Research in Child Development, 64*(4, Serial No. 259).

Hetherington, E. M., & Kelly, J. H. (2002). *For better or worse: Divorce reconsidered.* New York: Norton.

Hetherington, E. M., & Stanley-Hagan, M. (1999). The adjustment of children with divorced parents: A risk and resiliency perspective. *Journal of Child Psychology and Psychiatry, 40,* 129–140.

Hewlett, B. S. (1992). Husband–wife reciprocity and the father–infant relationship among Aka pygmies. In B. S. Hewlett (Ed.), *Father–child relations: Cultural and biosocial contexts* (pp. 153–176). New York: Aldine De Gruyter.

Hewlett, B. S. (2004). Fathers in forager, farmer, and pastoral cultures. In M. E.

Lamb (Ed.), *The role of the father in child development* (4th ed., pp. 182–195). Hoboken, NJ: Wiley.

Hewlett, S. (2003). *Creating a life.* New York: Miramax.

Heyes, C. (2005). Imitation by association. In S. Hurley & N. Chater (Eds.), *From neuroscience to social science: Vol. 1. Mechanisms of imitation and imitation in animals* (pp. 157–177). Cambridge, MA: MIT Press.

Heyman, G. D., & Dweck, C. S. (1998). Children's thinking about traits: Implications for judgments of the self and others. *Child Development, 69,* 391–403.

Heyman, G. D., Dweck, C. S., & Cain, K. M. (1992). Young children's vulnerability to self-blame and helplessness: Relationship to beliefs about goodness. *Child Development, 63,* 401–415.

Heyman, G. D., & Gelman, S. A. (1999). The use of trait labels in making psychological inferences. *Child Development, 70,* 604–619.

Heyman, G. D., & Gelman, S. A. (2000). Preschool children's use of trait labels to make inductive inferences. *Journal of Experimental Child Psychology, 77,* 1–19.

Heyman, G. D., & Legare, C. H. (2004). Children's beliefs about gender differences in the academic and social domains. *Sex Roles, 50,* 227–239.

Hickling, A. K., & Wellman, H. M. (2001). The emergence of children's causal explanations and theories: Evidence from everyday conversation. *Developmental Psychology, 37,* 668–683.

Hicks, J. H., & Goedereis, E. A. (2009). The importance of context and the gain-loss dynamic for understanding grandparent caregivers. In K. Shifren (Ed.), *How caregiving affects development: Psychological implications for child, adolescent, and adult caregivers* (pp. 169–190). Washington, DC: American Psychological Association.

Higginbottom, G. M. A. (2006). 'Pressure of life': Ethnicity as a mediating factor in mid-life and older peoples' experience of high blood pressure. *Sociology of Health and Illness, 28,* 583–610.

High, P. C., LaGasse, L., Becker, S., Ahlgren, I., & Gardner, A. (2000). Literacy promotion in primary care pediatrics: Can we make a difference? *Pediatrics, 105,* 927–934.

Hildreth, K., & Rovee-Collier, C. (2002). Forgetting functions of reactivated memories over the first year of life. *Developmental Psychobiology, 41,* 277–288.

Hildreth, K., Sweeney, B., & Rovee-Collier, C. (2003). Differential memory-preserving effects of reminders at 6 months. *Journal of Experimental Child Psychology, 84,* 41–62.

Hill, A. L., Degnan, K. A., Calkins, S. D., & Keane, S. P. (2006). Profiles of externalizing behavior problems for boys and girls across preschool: The roles of emotion regulation and inattention. *Developmental Psychology, 42,* 913–928.

Hill, E. J., Mead, N. T., Dean, L. R., Hafen, D. M., Gadd, R., Palmer, A. A., & Ferris, M. S. (2006). Researching the 60-hour dual-earner workweek: An alternative to the "opt-out revolution." *American Behavioral Scientist, 49,* 1184–1203.

Hill, J. L., Brooks-Gunn, J., & Waldfogel, J. (2003). Sustained effects of high participation in an early intervention for low-birthweight premature infants. *Developmental Psychology, 39,* 730–744.

Hill, J. P., & Lynch, M. E. (1983). The intensification of gender-related role expectations during early adolescence. In J. Brooks-Gunn & A. Petersen (Eds.), *Girls at puberty: Biological and psychosocial perspectives* (pp. 201–228). New York: Plenum.

Hill, N. E., Bush, K. R., & Roosa, M. W. (2003). Parenting and family socialization strategies and children's mental health: Low-income Mexican-American and Euro-American mothers and children. *Child Development, 74,* 189–204.

Hill, N. E., & Taylor, L. C. (2004). Parental school involvement and children's academic achievement: Pragmatics and issues. *Current Directions in Psychological Science, 13,* 161–164.

Hill, N. E., & Tyson, D. F. (2009). Parental involvement in middle school: A meta-analytic assessment of the strategies that promote achievement. *Developmental Psychology, 45,* 740–763.

Hillard, P. J. A. (2008). Menstruation in adolescents: What's normal, what's not. *Annals of the New York Academy of Sciences, 1135,* 29–35.

Hillis, S. D., Anda, R. F., Dube, S. R., Felitti, V. J., Marchbanks, P. A., & Marks, J. S. (2004). The association between adverse childhood experiences and adolescent pregnancy, long-term psychosocial consequences, and fetal death. *Pediatrics, 113,* 320–327.

Hilt, L. M. (2004). Attribution retaining for therapeutic change: Theory, practice, and future directions. *Imagination, Cognition, and Personality, 23,* 289–307.

Hines, M., & Green, R. (1991). Human hormonal and neural correlates of sex-typed behaviors. *Review of Psychiatry, 10,* 536–555.

Hinojosa, T., Sheu, C.-F., & Michel, G. F. (2003). Infant hand-use preference for grasping objects contributes to the development of a hand-use preference for manipulating objects. *Developmental Psychobiology, 43,* 328–334.

Hippisley, J., Douglas, G., & Houghton, S. (2005). A cross-cultural comparison of numeracy skills using a written and an interactive arithmetic text. *Educational Research, 47,* 205–215.

Hirasawa, R., & Feil, R. (2010). Genomic imprinting and human disease. *Essays in Biochemistry, 48,* 187–200.

Hirschfeld, L. A. (1996). *Race in the making: Cognition, culture, and the child's construction of human kinds.* Cambridge, MA: MIT Press.

Hirsh-Pasek, K., & Burchinal, M. (2006). Mother and caregiver sensitivity over time: Predicting language and academic outcomes with variable- and person-centered approaches. *Merrill-Palmer Quarterly, 52,* 449–485.

Hirsh-Pasek, K., & Golinkoff, R. M. (2003). *Einstein never used flash cards.* New York: Rodale.

Hirsh-Pasek, K., Golinkoff, R. M., Berk, L. E., & Singer, D. G. (2009). *A mandate for playful learning in preschool: Presenting the evidence.* New York: Oxford University Press.

Hoch-Espada, A., Ryan, E., & Deblinger, E. (2006). Child sexual abuse. In J. E. Fisher & W. T. O'Donohue (Eds.), *Practitioner's guide to evidence-based psychotherapy* (pp. 177–188). New York: Springer.

Hock, H. S., Park, C. L., & Bjorklund, D. F. (1998). Temporal organization in children's strategy formation. *Journal of Experimental Child Psychology, 70,* 187–206.

Hodges, J., & Tizard, B. (1989). Social and family relationships of ex-institutional adolescents. *Journal of Child Psychology and Psychiatry, 30,* 77–97.

Hodges, R. M., & French, L. A. (1988). The effect of class and collection labels on cardinality, class-inclusion, and number conservation tasks. *Child Development, 59,* 1387–1396.

Hodnett, E. D., Gates, S., Hofmeyr, G. J., & Sakala, C. (2003). Continuous support for women during childbirth. *Cochrane Database of Systematic Reviews, 3,* CD003766.

Hoehn, T., Hansmann, G., Bührer, C., Simbruner, G., Gunn, A. J., Yager, J., et al. (2008). Therapeutic hypothermia in neonates: Review of current clinical data, ILCOR recommendations and suggestions for implementation in neonatal intensive care units. *Resuscitation, 78,* 7–12.

Hoekstra, R. A., Bartels, M., Hudziak, J. J., Van Beijsterveldt, T. C., & Boomsma, D. I. (2008). Genetic and environmental influences on the stability of withdrawn behavior in children: A longitudinal, multi-informant twin study. *Behavior Genetics, 38,* 447–461.

Hoerr, T. (2004). How MI informs teaching at New City School. *Teachers College Record, 106,* 40–48.

Hoff, E. (2003). The specificity of environmental influence: Socioeconomic status affects early vocabulary development via maternal speech. *Child Development, 74,* 1368–1378.

Hoff, E. (2006). How social contexts support and shape language development. *Developmental Review, 26,* 55–88.

Hoff, E. (2010). Context effects on young children's language use: The influence of conversational setting and partner. *First Language, 30,* 461–472.

Hoff, E., Laursen, B., & Tardif, T. (2002). Socioeconomic status and parenting. In M. H. Bornstein (Ed.), *Handbook of parenting: Vol. 2. Biology and ecology of parenting* (2nd ed., 231–252). Mahwah, NJ: Erlbaum.

Hoff, E. V. (2005). A friend living inside me: The forms and functions of imaginary companions. *Imagination, Cognition and Personality, 24,* 151–189.

Hoff, T., Greene, L., & Davis, J. (2003). *National survey of adolescents and young adults: Sexual health knowledge, attitudes and experiences.* Menlo Park, CA: Henry J. Kaiser Family Foundation.

Hofferth, S. L. (2010). Home media and children's achievement and behavior. *Child Development, 81,* 1598–1619.

Hofferth, S. L., & Anderson, K. G. (2003). Are all dads equal? Biology versus marriage as a basis for paternal investment. *Journal of Marriage and the Family, 65,* 213–232.

Hofferth, S. L., Forry, N. D., & Peters, H. E. (2010). Child support, father–child contact, and preteens' involvement with nonresidential fathers: Racial/ethnic differences. *Journal of Family Economic Issues, 31,* 14–32.

Hoffman, L. W. (2000). Maternal employment: Effects of social context. In R. D. Taylor & M. C. Wang (Eds.), *Resilience across contexts: Family, work, culture, and community* (pp. 147–176). Mahwah, NJ: Erlbaum.

Hoffman, M. L. (2000). *Empathy and moral development.* New York: Cambridge University Press.

Hoffmann, W. (2001). Fallout from the Chernobyl nuclear disaster and congenital malformations in Europe. *Archives of Environmental Health, 56,* 478–483.

Hoffner, C., & Badzinski, D. M. (1989). Children's integration of facial and situational cues to emotion. *Child Development, 60,* 411–422.

Hofstadter, M., & Reznick, J. S. (1996). Response modality affects human infant delayed-response performance. *Child Development, 67,* 646–658.

Hogan, M. J., & Strasburger, V. C. (2008). Body image, eating disorders, and the media. *Adolescent Medicine, 19,* 521–546.

Hogan, R. T., Harkness, A. R., & Lubinski, D. (2000). Personality and individual differences. In K. Pawlik & M. R. Rosensweig (Eds.), *International handbook of psychology* (pp. 283–304). London: Sage.

Hoglund, W. L., & Leadbeater, B. J. (2007). Managing threat: Do social-cognitive processes mediate the link between peer victimization and adjustment problems in early adolescence? *Journal of Research on Adolescence, 17,* 525–540.

Hokoda, A., & Fincham, F. D. (1995). Origins of children's helpless and mastery achievement patterns in the family. *Journal of Educational Psychology, 87,* 375–385.

Holden, G. W., Coleman, S. M., & Schmidt, K. L. (1995). Why 3-year-old children get spanked: Determinants as reported by college-educated mothers. *Merrill-Palmer Quarterly, 41,* 431–452.

Holditch-Davis, D., Belyea, M., & Edwards, L. J. (2005). Prediction of 3-year developmental outcomes from sleep development over the preterm period. *Infant Behavior and Development, 79,* 49–58.

Holland, A. L. (2004). Plasticity and development. *Brain and Language, 88,* 254–255.

Hollich, G. J., Hirsh-Pasek, K., & Golinkoff, R. M. (2000). Breaking the language barrier: An emergentist coalition model for the origins of word learning. *Monographs of the Society for Research in Child Development, 65*(3, Serial No. 262).

Holmbeck, G. N. (1996). A model of family relational transformations during the transition to adolescence: Parent–adolescent conflict and adaptation. In J. A. Graber, J. Brooks-Gunn, & A. C. Petersen (Eds.), *Transitions through adolescence* (pp. 167–199). Mahwah, NJ: Erlbaum.

Holme, A., MacArthur, C., & Lancashire, R. (2010). The effects of breastfeeding on cognitive and neurological development of children at 9 years. *Child: Care, Health and Development, 36,* 583–590.

Holobow, N., Genesee, F., & Lambert, W. (1991). The effectiveness of a foreign language immersion program for children from different ethnic and social class backgrounds: Report 2. *Applied Psycholinguistics, 12,* 179–198.

Holodynski, M. (2004). The miniaturization of expression in the development of emotional self-regulation. *Developmental Psychology, 40,* 16–28.

Holsen, I., Kraft, P., & Vittersø, J. (2000). Stability in depressed mood in adolescence: Results from a 6-year longitudinal study. *Journal of Youth and Adolescence, 29,* 61–78.

Homer, B. D. (2009). Literacy and metalinguistic development. In D. R. Olson & N. Torrance (Eds.), *Cambridge handbook of literacy* (pp. 487–500). New York: Cambridge University Press.

Honein, M. A., Paulozzi, L. J., & Erickson, J. D. (2001). Continued occurrence of Accutane-exposed pregnancies. *Teratology, 64,* 142–147.

Hong, Z.-R., Veach, P. M., & Lawrenz, F. (2003). An investigation of the gender stereotyped thinking of Taiwanese secondary school boys and girls. *Sex Roles, 48,* 495–504.

Honzik, M. P., Macfarlane, J. W., & Allen, L. (1948). The stability of mental test performance between two and eighteen years. *Journal of Experimental Education, 17,* 309–329.

Hood, B. M. (2004). Is looking good enough or does it beggar belief? *Developmental Science, 7,* 415–417.

Hood, M., Conlon, E., & Andrews, G. (2008). Preschool home literacy practices and children's literacy development: A longitudinal analysis. *Journal of Educational Psychology, 100,* 252–271.

Hopkins, B., & Westra, T. (1988). Maternal handling and motor development: An intracultural study. *Genetic, Social and General Psychology Monographs, 14,* 377–420.

Hopkins-Golightly, T., Raz, S., & Sander, C. J. (2003). Influence of slight to moderate risk for birth hypoxia on acquisition of cognitive and language function in the preterm infant: A cross-sectional comparison with preterm-birth controls. *Neuropsychology, 17,* 3–13.

Horn, J. L. (1994). Theory of fluid and crystallized intelligence. In R. J. Sternberg (Ed.), *Encyclopedia of intelligence* (pp. 443–451). New York: Macmillan.

Horn, J. L., & Noll, J. (1997). Human cognitive capabilities: Gf-Gc theory. In D. P. Flanagan & J. L. Genshaft (Eds.), *Contemporary intellectual assessment: Theories, tests, and issues* (pp. 53–91). New York: Guilford.

Horner, S. L., & Gaither, S. M. (2004). Attribution retraining instruction with a second-grade class. *Early Childhood Education Journal, 31,* 165–170.

Horner, T. M. (1980). Two methods of studying stranger reactivity in infants: A review. *Journal of Child Psychology and Psychiatry, 21,* 203–219.

Hort, B. E., Leinbach, M. D., & Fagot, B. I. (1991). Is there coherence among the cognitive components of gender acquisition? *Sex Roles, 24,* 195–207.

Houlihan, J., Kropp, T., Wiles, R., Gray, S., & Campbell, C. (2005). *Body burden: The pollution in newborns.* Washington, DC: Environmental Working Group.

Hoven, C. W., Duarte, C. S., Lucas, C. P., Wu, P., Mandell, D. J., & Goodwin, R. D. (2005). Psychopathology among New York City school children 6 months after September 11. *Archives of General Psychiatry, 62,* 545–552.

Howard, K. S., & Brooks-Gunn, J. (2009). The role of home-visiting programs in preventing child abuse and neglect. *Future of Children, 19,* 119–146.

Howe, M. L., & Courage, M. L. (1997). The emergence and early development of autobiographical memory. *Psychological Review, 104,* 499–523.

Howe, M. L., Courage, M. L., & Rooksby, M. (2009). The genesis and development of autobiographical memory. In M. L. Courage & N. Cowan (Eds.), *The development of memory in infancy and childhood* (pp. 177–196). Hove, UK: Psychology Press.

Howe, N., Aquan-Assee, J., & Bukowski, W. M. (2001). Predicting sibling relations over time: Synchrony between maternal management styles and sibling relationship quality. *Merrill-Palmer Quarterly, 47,* 121–141.

Howell, K. K., Coles, C. D., & Kable, J. A. (2008). The medical and developmental consequences of prenatal drug exposure. In J. Brick (Ed.), *Handbook of the medical consequences of alcohol and drug abuse* (2nd ed., pp. 219–249). New York: Haworth Press.

Howell, K. K., Lynch, M. E., Platzman, K. A., Smith, G. H., & Coles, C. D. (2006). Prenatal alcohol exposure and ability, academic achievement, and school functioning in adolescence: A longitudinal follow-up. *Journal of Pediatric Psychology, 31,* 116–126.

Howell, T. M., & Yuille, J. C. (2004). Healing and treatment of Aboriginal offenders: A Canadian example. *American Journal of Forensic Psychology, 22,* 53–76.

Howes, C. (2009). Friendship in early childhood. In K. H. Rubin, W. M. Bukowski, & B. Laursen (Eds.), *Handbook of peer interactions, relationships, and groups* (pp. 180–194). New York: Guilford.

Howes, C., & Farver, J. (1987). Social pretend play in 2-year-olds: Effects of age of partner. *Early Childhood Research Quarterly, 2,* 305–314.

Howes, C., & Matheson, C. C. (1992). Sequences in the development of competent play with peers: Social and social pretend play. *Developmental Psychology, 28,* 961–974.

Hoza, B., Gerdes, A. C., Hinshaw, S. P., Bukowski, W. M., Gold, J. A., Kraemer, H. C., et al. (2005). What aspects of peer relationships are impaired in children with attention-deficit/hyperactivity disorder? *Journal of Consulting and Clinical Psychology, 73,* 411–423.

Hu, Y., Wood, J. F., Smith, V., & Westbrook, N. (2004). Friendships through IM: Examining the relationship between instant messaging and intimacy. *Journal of Computer-Mediated Communication, 10*(1). Retrieved from jcmc.indiana.edu/vol10/issue1

Hubbard, F. O. A., & van IJzendoorn, M. H. (1991). Maternal unresponsiveness and infant crying across the first 9 months: A naturalistic longitudinal study. *Infant Behavior and Development, 14,* 299–312.

Hubbs-Tait, L., Nation, J. R., Krebs, N. F., & Bellinger, D. C. (2005). Nuerotoxicants, micronurtrients, and social environments: Individual and combined effects on children's development. *Psychological Science in the Public Interest, 6,* 57–121.

Huddleston, J., & Ge, X. (2003). Boys at puberty: Psychosocial implications. In C. Hayward (Ed.), *Gender differences at puberty* (pp. 113–134). New York: Cambridge University Press.

Hudson, J., & Nelson, K. (1986). Repeated encounters of a similar kind: Effects of familiarity on children's autobiographical memory. *Cognitive Development, 1,* 253–271.

Hudson, J. A., & Fivush, R. (1991). As time goes by: Sixth graders remember a kindergarten experience. *Applied Cognitive Psychology, 5,* 347–360.

Hudson, J. A., Fivush, R., & Kuebli, J. (1992). Scripts and episodes: The development of event memory. *Applied Cognitive Psychology, 6,* 483–505.

Hudson, J. A., Gebelt, J., Haviland, J., & Bentivegna, C. (1992). Emotional and narrative structure in young children's personal accounts. *Journal of Narrative and Life History, 2,* 129–150.

Hudson, J. A., & Mayhew, E. M. Y. (2009). The development of memory for recurring events. In M. L. Courage & N. Cowan (Eds.), *The development of memory in infancy and childhood* (pp. 69–91). Hove, UK: Psychology Press.

Hudson, J. A., Sosa, B. B., & Shapiro, L. R. (1997). Scripts and plans: The development of preschool children's event knowledge and event planning. In S. L. Friedman & E. K. Scholnick (Eds.), *The developmental psychology of planning: Why, how, and when do we plan?* (pp. 77–102). Mahwah, NJ: Erlbaum.

Hudziak, J. J., & Rettew, D. C. (2009). Genetics of ADHD. In T. E. Brown (Ed.), *ADHD comorbidties: Handbook for ADHD complications in children and adults* (pp. 23–36). Arlington, VA: American Psychiatric Publishing.

Huebner, C. E., & Payne, K. (2010). Home support for emergent literacy: Follow-up of a community-based implementation of dialogic reading. *Journal of Applied Developmental Psychology, 31,* 195–201.

Huesmann, L. R. (1986). Psychological processes promoting the relation between exposure to media violence and aggressive behavior by the viewer. *Journal of Social Issues, 42,* 125–139.

Huesmann, L. R., Moise-Titus, J., Podolski, C., & Eron, L. D. (2003). Longitudinal relations between children's exposure to TV violence and their aggressive and violent behavior in young adulthood: 1977–1992. *Developmental Psychology, 39,* 201–221.

Hueston, W. J., Geesey, M. E., & Diaz, V. (2008). Prenatal care initiation among pregnant teens in the United States: An analysis over 25 years. *Journal of Adolescent Health, 42,* 243–248.

Huettel, S. A., & Needham, A. (2000). Effects of balance relations between objects on infants' object segregation. *Developmental Science, 3,* 415–427.

Hughes, C. (2010). Conduct disorder and antisocial behavior in the under-5s. In C. L. Cooper, J. Field, U. Goswami, R. Jenkins, & B. J. Sahakian (Eds.), *Mental capital and wellbeing* (pp. 821–827). Malden, MA: Wiley-Blackwell.

Hughes, C., & Dunn, J. (1998). Understanding mind and emotion: Longitudinal associations with mental-state talk between young friends. *Developmental Psychology, 34,* 1026–1037.

Hughes, C., & Ensor, R. (2007). Executive function and theory of mind: Predictive relations from ages 2 to 4. *Developmental Psychology, 43,* 1447–1459.

Hughes, C., & Ensor, R. (2010). Do early social cognition and executive function predict individual differences in preschoolers' prosocial and antisocial behavior? In B. W. Sokol, U. Müller, J. I. M. Carpendale, A. R. Young, & G. Iarocci (Eds.), *Social interaction and the development of social understanding and executive functions* (pp. 418–441). New York: Oxford University Press.

Hughes, C., Ensor, R., & Marks, A. (2010). Individual differences in false belief understanding are stable from 3 to 6 years of age and predict children's mental state talk with school friends. *Journal of Experimental Child Psychology, 108,* 96–112.

Hughes, C., Marks, A., Ensor, R., & Lecce, S. (2010). A longitudinal study of conflict and inner state talk in children's conversations with mothers and younger siblings. *Social Development, 19,* 822–837.

Hughes, D., Rodriguez, J., Smith, E. P., Johnson, D. J., Stevenson, H. C., & Spicer, P. (2006). Parents' ethnic-racial socialization practices: A review of research and directions for future study. *Developmental Psychology, 42,* 747–770.

Hughes, F. P. (1998). Play in special populations. In O. N. Saracho & B. Spodek (Eds.), *Multiple perspectives on play in early childhood education* (pp. 171–193). Albany: State University of New York Press.

Hughes, J. N., Cavell, T. A., & Grossman, P. B. (1997). A positive view of self: Risk or protection for aggressive children? *Development and Psychopathology, 9,* 75–94.

Hughes, J. N., & Kwok, O. (2006). Classroom engagement mediates the effect of teacher–student support on elementary students' peer acceptance. *Journal of School Psychology, 43,* 465–480.

Hughes, J. N., & Kwok, O. (2007). Influence of student–teacher and parent–teacher relationships on lower achieving readers' engagement and achievement in the primary grades. *Journal of Educational Psychology, 99,* 39–51.

Hughes, J. N., Zhang, D., & Hill, C. R. (2006). Peer assessments of normative and individual teacher–student support predict social acceptance and engagement among low-achieving children. *Journal of School Psychology, 43,* 447–463.

Huizenga, H., Crone, E. A., & Jansen, B. (2007). Decision making in healthy children, adolescents and adults explained by the use of increasingly complex proportional reasoning rules. *Developmental Science, 10,* 814–825.

Huizink, A. C., Bartels, M., Rose, R. J., Pulkkinen, L., Eriksson, C. J., & Kaprio, J. (2008). Chernobyl exposure as a stressor during pregnancy and hormone levels in adolescent offspring. *Journal of Epidemiology and Community Health, 62,* e5.

Huizink, A. C., & Mulder, E. J. (2006). Maternal smoking, drinking or cannabis use during pregnancy and neurobehavioral and cognitive functioning in human offspring. *Neuroscience and Biobehavioral Reviews, 30,* 24–41.

Hulsey, L., Aikens, N., Xue, Y., Tarullo, L., & West, J. (2010). *ACF–OPRE Report: Data tables for FACES 2006, A year in Head Start report.* Washington, DC: U.S. Department of Health and Human Services.

Human Genome Program. (2008). *How many genes are in the human genome?* Retrieved from www.ornl.gov/sci/techresources/Human_Genome/faq/genenumber.shtml

Human Rights Campaign. (2008). *Surrogacy laws: State by state.* Retrieved from www.hrc.org/issues/2486.htm

Humphrey, T. (1978). Function of the nervous system during prenatal life. In U. Stave (Ed.), *Perinatal physiology* (pp. 651–683). New York: Plenum.

Hunnius, S., & Geuze, R. H. (2004a). Developmental changes in visual scanning of dynamic faces and abstract stimuli in infants: A longitudinal study. *Infancy, 6,* 231–255.

Hunnius, S., & Geuze, R. H. (2004b). Gaze shifting in infancy: A longitudinal study using dynamic faces and abstract stimuli. *Infant Behavior and Development, 27,* 397–416.

Hunsberger, B., Pratt, M., & Pancer, S. M. (2001). Adolescent identity formation: Religious exploration and commitment. *Identity, 1,* 365–386.

Hunt, C. E., & Hauck, F. R. (2006). Sudden infant death syndrome. *Canadian Medical Association Journal, 174,* 1861–1869.

Huotilainen, M., Kujala, A., Hotakainen, M., Parkkonen, L., Taulu, S., & Simola, J. (2005). Short-term memory functions of the human fetus recorded with magnetoencephalography. *Neuroreport, 16,* 81–84.

Hupbach, A., Gomez, R. L., Bootzin, R. R., & Nadel, L. (2009). Nap-dependent learning in infants. *Developmental Science, 12,* 1007–1012.

Hurewitz, F., Brown-Schmidt, S., Thorpe, K., Gleitman, L. R., & Trueswell, J. C. (2000). One frog, two frog, red frog, blue frog: Factors affecting children's syntactic choices in production and comprehension. *Journal of Psycholinguistic Research, 29,* 597–626.

Hursh, D. (2007). Assessing No Child Left Behind and the rise of neoliberal education policies. *American Educational Research Journal, 44,* 493–518.

Hursti, U. K. (1999). Factors influencing children's food choice. *Annals of Medicine, 31,* 26–32.

Hurt, H., Betancourt, L. M., Malmud, E. K., Shera, D. M., Giannetta, J. M., Brodsky, N. L., et al. (2009). Children with and without gestational cocaine exposure: A neurocognitive systems analysis. *Neurotoxicology and Teratology, 31,* 334–341.

Huston, A. C., & Alvarez, M. M. (1990). The socialization context of gender role development in early adolescence. In R. Montemayor, G. R. Adams, & T. P. Gullotta (Eds.), *From childhood to adolescence: A transitional period?* (pp. 156–179). Newbury Park, CA: Sage.

Huston, A. C., Wright, J. C., Marquis, J., & Green, S. B. (1999). How young children spend their time: Television and other activities. *Developmental Psychology, 35,* 912–925.

Huttenlocher, P. R. (2002). *Neural plasticity: The effects of environment on the development of the cerebral cortex.* Cambridge, MA: Harvard University Press.

Huyck, M. H. (1996). Continuities and discontinuities in gender identity in midlife. In V. L. Bengtson (Ed.), *Adulthood and aging* (pp. 98–121). New York: Springer-Verlag.

Hyde, J. S., Essex, M. J., Clark, R., & Klein, M. H. (2001). Maternity leave, women's employment, and marital incompatibility. *Journal of Family Psychology, 15,* 476–491.

Hyde, J. S., Mezulis, A. H., & Abramson, L. Y. (2008). The ABCs of depression: Integrating affective, biological, and cognitive models to explain the emergence of the gender difference in depression. *Psychological Review, 115,* 291–313.

Hymel, S., Schonert-Reichl, K. A., Bonanno, R. A., Vaillancourt, T., & Henderson, N. R. (2010). Bullying and morality: Understanding how good kids can behave badly. In S. Jimerson, S. M. Searer, & D. L. Espelage (Eds.), *Handbook of bullying in schools: An international perspective* (pp. 101–118). New York: Routledge.

Hymel, S., Vaillancourt, T., McDougall, P., & Renshaw, P. D. (2004). Peer acceptance

and rejection in childhood. In P. K. Smith & C. H. Hart (Eds.), *Blackwell handbook of childhood social development* (pp. 265–284). Malden, MA: Blackwell.

Iacoboni, M. (2009). Imitation, empathy, and mirror neurons. *Annual Review of Psychology, 60,* 653–670.

Iglowstein, I., Jenni, O. G., Molinari, L., & Largo, R. H. (2003). Sleep duration from infancy to adolescence: Reference values and generational trends. *Pediatrics, 111,* 302–307.

Ilgaz, H., & Aksu-Koç, A. (2005). Episodic development in preschool children's play-prompted and direct-elicited narratives. *Cognitive Development, 20,* 526–544.

Imai, M., & Haryu, E. (2001). Learning proper nouns and common nouns without clues from syntax. *Child Development, 72,* 787–802.

Imai, M., & Haryu, E. (2004). The nature of word-learning biases and their roles for lexical development: From a cross-linguistic perspective. In D. G. Hall & S. R. Waxman (Eds.), *Weaving a lexicon* (pp. 411–444). Cambridge, MA: MIT Press.

Imai, M., Li, L., Haryu, E., Okada, H., Hirsh-Pasek, K., Golinkoff, R. M., & Sigematsu, J. (2008). Novel noun and verb learning in Chinese-, English-, and Japanese-speaking children. *Child Development, 79,* 979–1000.

Impett, E. A., Sorsoli, L., Schooler, D., Henson, J. M., & Tolman, D. L. (2008). Girls' relationship authenticity and self-esteem across adolescence. *Developmental Psychology, 44,* 722–733.

Inagaki, K. (1997). Emerging distinctions between naïve biology and naïve psychology. In H. M. Wellman & K. Inagaki (Eds.), *The emergence of core domains of thought: New directions for child development #75,* (pp. 27–44). San Francisco: Jossey-Bass.

Inagaki, K., & Hatano, G. (2002). *Young children's naïve thinking about the biological world.* New York: Psychology Press.

Inagaki, K., & Hatano, G. (2004). Vitalistic causality in young children's naïve biology. *Trends in Cognitive Sciences, 8,* 356–362.

Ingram, D. (1986). Phonological development: Production. In P. Fletcher & M. Garman (Eds.), *Language acquisition* (2nd ed., pp. 223–239). Cambridge, UK: Cambridge University Press.

Ingram, D. (1999). Phonological acquisition. In M. Barrett (Ed.), *The development of language* (pp. 73–97). Philadelphia: Psychology Press/Taylor & Francis.

Inhelder, B., & Piaget, J. (1958). *The growth of logical thinking from childhood to adolescence: An essay on the construction of formal operational structures.* New York: Basic Books. (Original work published 1955)

Inoff-Germain, G., Arnold, G. S., Nottelman, E. D., Susman, E. J., Cutler, G. B., Jr., & Crousos, G. P. (1988). Relations between hormone levels and observational measures of aggressive behavior of young adolescents in family interactions. *Developmental Psychology, 24,* 129–139.

International Telecommunications Union. (2010). *The world in 2010: Facts and figures.* Retrieved from www.itu.int/net/itunews/issues/2010/10/04.aspx

Intons-Peterson, M. J. (1988). *Gender concepts of Swedish and American youth.* Hillsdale, NJ: Erlbaum.

Isabella, R. A. (1993). Origins of attachment: Maternal interactive behavior across the

first year. *Child Development, 64,* 605–621.

Isabella, R. A., & Belsky, J. (1991). Interactional synchrony and the origins of infant–mother attachment: A replication study. *Child Development, 62,* 373–384.

Isasi, R. M., Nguyen, T. M., & Knoppers, B. M. (2006) *National regulatory frameworks regarding human genetic modification technologies (somatic and germline modification).* Montréal, Québec: Centre de Recherche en Droit Public (CRDP), Université de Montréal.

Ishihara, K., Warita, K., Tanida, T., Sugawara, T., Kitagawa, H., & Hoshi, N. (2007). Does paternal exposure to 2,3,7,8-tetrachlorodibenzo-p-dioxin (TCDD) affect the sex ratio of offspring? *Journal of Veterinary Medical Science, 69,* 347–352.

Israel, M., Johnson, C., & Brooks, P. J. (2000). From states to events: The acquisition of English passive participles. *Cognitive Linguistics, 11,* 103–129.

Itti, E., Gaw, G. I. T., Pawlikowska-Haddal, A., Boone, K. B., Mlikotic, A., & Itti, L. (2006). The structural brain correlates of cognitive deficits in adults with Klinefelter's syndrome. *Journal of Clinical Endocrinology and Metabolism, 91,* 1423–1427.

Ivorra, J. L., Sanjuan, J., Jover, M., Carot, J. M., de Frutos, R., & Molto, M. D. (2010). Gene-environment interaction of child temperament. *Journal of Developmental and Behavioral Pediatrics, 31,* 545–554.

Izard, C. E., & Ackerman, B. P. (2000). Motivational, organizational, and regulatory functions of discrete emotions. In M. Lewis & J. M. Haviland-Jones (Eds.), *Handbook of emotions* (2nd ed., pp. 253–264). New York: Guilford.

Jaakkola, J. J., & Gissler, M. (2004). Maternal smoking in pregnancy, fetal development, and childhood asthma. *American Journal of Public Health, 94,* 136–140.

Jaccard, J., Dodge, T., & Dittus, P. (2002). Parent–adolescent communication about sex and birth control: A conceptual framework. In S. S. Feldman & D. A. Rosenthal (Eds.), *Talking sexuality: Parent–adolescent communication* (pp. 9–41). San Francisco: Jossey-Bass.

Jaccard, J., Dodge, T., & Dittus, P. (2003). Maternal discussions about pregnancy and adolescents' attitudes toward pregnancy. *Journal of Adolescent Health, 33,* 84–87.

Jackson, L. A., von Eye, A., Biocca, F. A., Barbatsis, G., Zhao, Y., & Fitzgerald, H. E. (2006). Does home Internet use influence the academic performance of low-income children? *Developmental Psychology, 42,* 429–435.

Jackson, L. A., von Eye, A., Fitzgerald, H. E., Witt, E. A., & Zhao, Y. (2011a). Internet use, videogame playing and cell phone use as predictors of children's body mass index (BMI), body weight, academic performance, and social and overall self-esteem. *Computers in Human Behavior, 27,* 599–604.

Jackson, L. A., von Eye, A., Witt, E. A., Zhao, Y., & Fitzgerald, H. E. (2011b). A longitudinal study of the effects of Internet use and videogame playing on academic performance and the roles of gender, race and income in these relationships. *Computers in Human Behavior, 27,* 228–239.

Jackson, L. A., von Eye, A., Zhao, Y., Kolenic, A., III, Fitzgerald, H. E., Harold, R., & von Eye, A. (2008). Race, gender, and information

technology use: The new digital divide. *Cyber Psychology and Behavior, 11,* 437–442.

Jackson, P. W. (1968). *Life in classrooms.* New York: Holt, Rinehart & Winston.

Jackson, R. A., Gibson, K. A., & Wu, Y. W. (2004). Perinatal outcomes in singletons following in vitro fertilization: A meta-analysis. *Obstetrics and Gynecology, 103,* 551–563.

Jacobs, J. E., & Eccles, J. S. (1992). The impact of mothers' gender-role stereotypic beliefs on mothers' and children's ability perceptions. *Journal of Personality and Social Psychology, 63,* 932–944.

Jacobs, J. E., & Klaczynski, P. A. (2002). The development of judgment and decision making during childhood and adolescence. *Current Directions in Psychological Science, 11,* 145–149.

Jacobs, J. E., Lanza, S., Osgood, D. W., Eccles, J. S., & Wigfield, A. (2002). Changes in children's self-competence and values: Gender and domain differences across grades one through twelve. *Child Development, 73,* 509–527.

Jacobs, J. E., & Weisz, V. (1994). Gender stereotypes: Implications for gifted education. *Roeper Review, 16,* 152–155.

Jacobs, J. N., & Kelley, M. L. (2006). Predictors of paternal involvement in childcare in dual-earner families with young children. *Fathering, 4,* 23–47.

Jacobs, N., van Os, J., Derom, C., & Thiery, E. (2007). Heritability of intelligence. *Twin Research in Human Genetics, 10,* 11–14.

Jacobson, J. L., & Jacobson, S. W. (2003). Prenatal exposure to polychlorinated biphenyls and attention at school age. *Journal of Pediatrics, 143,* 780–788.

Jacobson, K. C., & Crockett, L. J. (2000). Parental monitoring and adolescent adjustment: An ecological perspective. *Journal of Research on Adolescence, 10,* 65–97.

Jacobson, S. W., Jacobson, J. L., Sokol, R. J., Chiodo, L. M., & Corobana, R. (2004). Maternal age, alcohol abuse history, and quality of parenting as moderators of the effects of prenatal alcohol exposure on 7.5-year intellectual function. *Alcoholism: Clinical and Experimental Research, 28,* 1732–1745.

Jacquet, P. (2004). Sensitivity of germ cells and embryos to ionizing radiation. *Journal of Biological Regulators and Homeostatic Agents, 18,* 106–114.

Jaffari-Bimmel, N., Juffer, F., van IJzendoorn, M. H., Bakermans-Kranenburg, M. J., & Mooijaart, A. (2006). Social development from infancy to adolescence: Longitudinal and concurrent factors in an adoption sample. *Developmental Psychology, 42,* 1143–1153.

Jaffee, S. R., Caspi, A., Moffitt, T. E., Belsky, J., & Silva, P. (2001). Why are children born to teen mothers at risk for adverse outcomes in young adulthood? Results of a 20-year longitudinal study. *Development and Psychopathology, 13,* 377–397.

Jaffee, S. R., & Hyde, J. S. (2000). Gender differences in moral orientation: A meta-analysis. *Psychological Bulletin, 126,* 703–706.

Jaffee, S. R., Moffitt, T. E., Caspi, A., & Taylor, A. (2003). Life with (or without) father: The benefits of living with two biological parents depend on the father's antisocial behavior. *Child Development, 74,* 109–126.

Jambunathan, S., Burts, D. C., & Pierce, S. (2000). Comparisons of parenting attitudes among five ethnic groups in the United States. *Journal of Comparative Family Studies, 31*, 395–406.

Jamieson, J. R. (1995). Interactions between mothers and children who are deaf. *Journal of Early Intervention, 19*, 108–117.

Jang, S. J., & Johnson, B. R. (2001). Neighborhood disorder, individual religiosity, and adolescent use of illicit drugs: A test of multilevel hypotheses. *Criminology, 39*, 109–143.

Jankowski, J. J., Rose, S. A., & Feldman, J. F. (2001). Modifying the distribution of attention in infants. *Child Development, 72*, 339–351.

Jansen, A., Theunissen, N., Slechten, K., Nederkoorn, C., Boon, B., Mulkens, S., & Roefs, A. (2003). Overweight children overeat after exposure to food cues. *Eating Behaviors, 4*, 197–209.

Jansen, J., de Weerth, C., & Riksen-Walraven, J. M. (2008). Breastfeeding and the mother–infant relationship. *Developmental Review, 28*, 503–521.

Jarrett, R. L., Jefferson, S. R., & Kelly, J. N. (2010). Finding community in family: Neighborhood effects and African American kin networks. *Journal of Comparative Family Studies, 41*, 299–328.

Jarrold, C., Baddeley, A. D., & Hewes, A. K. (1998). Verbal and nonverbal abilities in the Williams syndrome phenotype: Evidence for diverging developmental trajectories. *Journal of Child Psychology and Psychiatry, 39*, 511–523.

Jaudes, P. K., & Mackey-Bilaver, L. (2008). Do chronic conditions increase young children's risk of being maltreated? *Child Abuse and Neglect, 32*, 671–681.

Jayakody, R., & Kalil, A. (2002). Social fathering in low-income, African-American families with preschool children. *Journal of Marriage and the Family, 64*, 504–516.

Jean, A. D. L., & Stack, D. M. (2009). Functions of maternal touch and infants' affect during face-to-face interactions: New directions for the still-face. *Infant Behavior and Development, 32*, 123–128.

Jedrychowski, W., Perera, F. P., Jankowski, J., Mrozek-Budzyn, D., Mroz, E., Flak, E., et al. (2009). Very low prenatal exposure to lead and mental development of children in infancy and early childhood. *Neuroepidemiology, 32*, 270–278.

Jeffrey, J. (2004, November). Parents often blind to their kids' weight. *British Medical Journal Online, 1*. Retrieved from http://content.health.msn.com/content/article/97/104292.htm

Jenkins, J. M., & Astington, J. W. (2000). Theory of mind and social behavior: Causal models tested in a longitudinal study. *Merrill-Palmer Quarterly, 46*, 203–220.

Jenkins, J. M., Rasbash, J., & O'Connor, T. G. (2003). The role of the shared family context in differential parenting. *Developmental Psychology, 39*, 99–113.

Jennifer, D., & Cowie, H. (2009). Engaging children and young people actively in research. In K. Bryan (Ed.), *Communication in healthcare* (pp. 135–163). New York: Peter Lang.

Jensen, A. R. (1969). How much can we boost IQ and scholastic achievement? *Harvard Educational Review, 39*, 1–123.

Jensen, A. R. (1985). The nature of the black–white difference on various psychometric tests: Spearman's hypothesis. *Behavioral and Brain Sciences, 8*, 193–219.

Jensen, A. R. (1998). *The g factor: The science of mental ability.* New York: Praeger.

Jensen, A. R. (2001). Spearman's hypothesis. In J. M. Collis & S. Messick (Eds.), *Intelligence and personality: Bridging the gap in theory and measurement* (pp. 3–24). Mahwah, NJ: Erlbaum.

Jensen, A. R. (2002). Galton's legacy to research on intelligence. *Journal of Biosocial Science, 34*, 145–172.

Jeong, S.-H., & Fishbein, M. (2007). Predictors of multitasking with media: Media factors and audience factors. *Media Psychology, 10*, 364–384.

Jerome, E. M., Hamre, B. K., & Pianta, R. C. (2009). Teacher–child relationships from kindergarten to sixth grade: Early childhood predictors of teacher-perceived conflict and closeness. *Social Development, 18*, 915–945.

Jeynes, W. H. (2005). A meta-analysis of the relation of parental involvement to urban elementary school student academic achievement. *Urban Education, 40*, 237–269.

Jeynes, W. H. (2007). The impact of parental remarriage on children: A meta-analysis. *Marriage and Family Review, 40*, 75–102.

Ji, C. Y., & Chen, T. J. (2008). Secular changes in stature and body mass index for Chinese youth in sixteen major cities, 1950s–2005. *American Journal of Human Biology, 20*, 530–537.

Jiao, S., Ji, G., & Jing, Q. (1996). Cognitive development of Chinese urban only children and children with siblings. *Child Development, 67*, 387–395.

Jipson, J. L., & Gelman, S. A. (2007). Robots and rodents: Children's inferences about living and nonliving kinds. *Child Development, 78*, 1675–1688.

Joh, A. S., & Adolph, K. E. (2006). Learning from falling. *Child Development, 77*, 89–102.

Johnson, D. E. (2000). Medical and developmental sequelae of early childhood institutionalization in Eastern European adoptees. In C. A. Nelson (Ed.), *Minnesota Symposia on Child Psychology* (Vol. 31, pp. 113–162). Mahwah, NJ: Erlbaum.

Johnson, E. K., & Seidl, A. (2008). Clause segmentation by 6-month-old infants: A crosslinguistic perspective. *Infancy, 13*, 440–455.

Johnson, J., Im-Bolter, N., & Pascual-Leone, J. (2003). Development of mental attention in gifted and mainstream children: The role of mental capacity, inhibition, and speed of processing. *Child Development, 74*, 1594–1614.

Johnson, J. G., Cohen, P., Smailes, E. M., Kasen, S., & Brook, J. S. (2002). Television viewing and aggressive behavior during adolescence and adulthood. *Science, 295*, 2468–2471.

Johnson, M. H. (1999). Ontogenetic constraints on neural and behavioral plasticity: Evidence from imprinting and face processing. *Canadian Journal of Experimental Psychology, 55*, 77–90.

Johnson, M. H. (2001). The development and neural basis of face recognition: Comment and speculation. *Infant and Child Development, 10*, 31–33.

Johnson, M. H. (2005). Developmental neuroscience, psychophysiology, and genetics. In M. H. Bornstein & M. E. Lamb (Eds.), *Developmental science: An advanced textbook* (5th ed., pp. 187–222). Mahwah, NJ: Erlbaum.

Johnson, M. H., & Mareschal, D. (2001). Cognitive and perceptual development during infancy. *Current Opinion in Neurobiology, 11*, 213–218.

Johnson, S. C., Dweck, C. S., & Chen, F. S. (2007). Evidence for infants' internal working models of attachment. *Psychological Science, 18*, 501–502.

Johnson, S. C., Dweck, C. S., Chen, F. S., Stern, H. L., Ok, S.-J., & Barth, M. (2010). At the intersection of social and cognitive development: Internal working models of attachment in infancy. *Cognitive Science, 34*, 807–825.

Johnson, S. P. (1997). Young infants' perception of object unity: Implications for development of attentional and cognitive skills. *Current Directions in Psychological Science, 6*, 5–11.

Johnson, S. P. (2010). How infants learn about the visual world. *Cognitive Science, 34*, 1158–1184.

Johnson, S. P., Amso, D., & Slemmer, J. A. (2003). Development of object concepts in infancy: Evidence for early learning in an eye-tracking paradigm. *Proceedings of the National Academy of Sciences, 100*, 10568–10753.

Johnson, S. P., Bremner, J. G., Slater, A. M., Mason, U. C., & Foster, K. (2002). Young infants' perception of unity and form in occlusion displays. *Journal of Experimental Child Psychology, 81*, 358–374.

Johnson, S. P., Bremner, J. G., Slater, A. M., Mason, U. C., Foster, K., & Cheshire, A. (2003). Infants' perception of object trajectories. *Child Development, 74*, 94–108.

Johnson, S. P., & Shuwairi, S. M. (2009). Learning and memory facilitate predictive tracking in 4-month-olds. *Journal of Experimental Child Psychology, 102*, 122–130.

Johnson, S. P., Slemmer, J. A., & Amso, D. (2004). Where infants look determines how they see: Eye movements and object perception performance in 3-month-olds. *Infancy, 6*, 185–201.

Johnson-Laird, P. N. (2001). Mental models and deduction. *Trends in Cognitive Sciences, 5*, 434–442.

Johnston, L. D., O'Malley, P. M., Bachman, J. G., & Schulenberg, J. E. (2010). *Monitoring the future: National results on adolescent drug use: Overview of key findings, 2009* (NIH Publication No. 10-7583). Bethesda, MD: National Institute on Drug Abuse.

Johnston, M. V., Nishimura, A., Harum, K., Pekar, J., & Blue, M. E. (2001). Sculpting the developing brain. *Advances in Pediatrics, 48*, 1–38.

Jokhi, R. P., & Whitby, E. H. (2011). Magnetic resonance imaging of the fetus. *Developmental Medicine and Child Neurology, 53*, 18–28.

Jones, B. D., & Egley, R. J. (2004). Voices from the frontlines: Teachers' perceptions of high-stakes testing. *Education Policy Analysis Archives, 12*(39).

Jones, C. M., Braithwaite, V. A., & Healy, S. D. (2003). The evolution of sex differences in spatial ability. *Behavioral Neuroscience, 117*, 403–411.

Jones, D. C., Abbey, B. B., & Cumberland, A. (1998). The development of display rule knowledge: Linkages with family expressiveness and social competence. *Child Development, 69*, 1209–1222.

Jones, E. F., & Thomson, N. R. (2001). Action perception and outcome valence: Effects on children's inferences of intentionality and moral and liking judgments. *Journal of Genetic Psychology, 162*, 154–166.

Jones, F. (2003). Religious commitment in Canada, 1997 and 2000. *Religious Commitment Monograph No. 3.* Ottawa, Canada: Christian Commitment Research Institute.

Jones, G. P., & Dembo, M. H. (1989). Age and sex role differences in intimate friendships during childhood and adolescence. *Merrill-Palmer Quarterly, 35*, 445–462.

Jones, H. E. (2006). Drug addiction during pregnancy: Advances in maternal treatment and understanding child outcomes. *Current Directions in Psychological Science, 15*, 126–130.

Jones, J., Lopez, A., & Wilson, M. (2003). Congenital toxoplasmosis. *American Family Physician, 67*, 2131–2137.

Jones, L. B., Rothbart, M. K., & Posner, M. I. (2003). Development of executive attention in preschool children. *Developmental Science, 6*, 498–504.

Jones, M. C., & Mussen, P. H. (1958). Self-conceptions, motivations, and interpersonal attitudes of early- and late-maturing girls. *Child Development, 29*, 491–501.

Jones, N. A., Field, T., & Davalos, M. (2000). Right frontal EEG asymmetry and lack of empathy in preschool children of depressed mothers. *Child Psychiatry and Human Development, 30*, 189–204.

Jones, R. K., Purcell, A., Singh, S., & Finer, L. B. (2005). Adolescents' reports of parental knowledge of adolescents' use of sexual health services and their reactions to mandated parental notification for prescription contraceptives. *Journal of the American Medical Association, 293*, 340–348.

Jones, R. L., Homa, D. M., Meyer, P. A., Brody, D. J., Caldwell, K. L., Pirkle J. L., et al. (2009). Trends in blood lead levels and blood lead testing among U.S. children aged 1 to 5 years: 1998–2004. *Pediatrics, 123*, e376–385.

Jones, S. (2009). The development of imitation in infancy. *Philosophical Transactions of the Royal Society B, 364*, 2325–2335.

Jongbloet, P. H., Zielhuis, G. A., Groenewoud, H. M., & Paster-De Jong, P. C. (2001). The secular trends in male:female ratio at birth in postwar industrialized countries. *Environmental Health Perspectives, 109*, 749–752.

Jordan, B. (1993). *Birth in four cultures.* Prospect Heights, IL: Waveland.

Jorgenson, L. A., Sun, M., O'Connor, M., & Georgieff, M. K. (2005). Fetal iron deficiency disrupts the maturation of synaptic function and efficacy in area CA1 of the developing rat hippocampus. *Hippocampus, 15*, 1094–1102.

Joseph, R. M., & Tager-Flusberg, H. (2004). The relationship of theory of mind and executive functions to symptom type and severity in children with autism. *Development and Psychopathology, 16*, 137–155.

Juby, H., Billette, J.-M., Laplante, B., & Le Bourdais, C. (2007). Nonresident fathers and children: Parents' new unions and frequency of contact. *Journal of Family Issues, 28*, 1220–1245.

Judge, S., Puckett, K., & Bell, S. M. (2006). Closing the digital divide: Update from the Early Childhood Longitudinal Study. *Journal of Educational Research, 100*, 52–60.

Jumpstart Evaluation Team. (2008, April). *Influence of Jumpstart implementation quality on child outcomes.* Paper presented at the annual meeting of the American Educational Research Association, New York.

Jürgensen, M., Hiort, O., Holterhus, P.-M., & Thyen, U. (2007). Gender role behavior in children with XY karyotype and disorders of sex development. *Hormones and Behavior, 51,* 443–453.

Jusczyk, P. W. (2001). In the beginning, was the word…In F. Lacerda & C. von Hofsten (Eds.), *Emerging cognitive abilities in early infancy* (pp. 173–192). Mahwah, NJ: Erlbaum.

Jusczyk, P. W. (2002). Some critical developments in acquiring native language sound organization. *Annals of Otology, Rhinology and Laryngology, 189,* 11–15.

Jusczyk, P. W., & Hohne, E. A. (1997). Infants' memory for spoken words. *Science, 277,* 1984–1986.

Jusczyk, P. W., Houston, D. M., & Newsome, M. (1999). The beginnings of word segmentation in English-learning infants. *Cognitive Psychology, 39,* 159–207.

Jusczyk, P. W., & Luce, P. A. (2002). Speech perception. In H. Pashler & S. Yantis (Eds.), *Steven's handbook of experimental psychology: Vol. 1. Sensation and perception* (3rd ed., pp. 493–536). New York: Wiley.

Justice, E. M. (1986). Developmental changes in judgments of relative strategy effectiveness. *British Journal of Developmental Psychology, 4,* 75–81.

Jutras-Aswad, D., DiNieri, J. A., Harkany, T., & Hurd, Y. L. (2009). Neurobiological consequences of maternal cannabis on human fetal development and its neuropsychiatric outcome. *European Archives of Psychiatry and Clinical Neuroscience, 259,* 395–412.

Kagan, J. (1998). Biology and the child. In N. Eisenberg (Ed.), *Handbook of child psychology: Vol. 3. Social, emotional, and personality development* (5th ed., pp. 177–236). New York: Wiley.

Kagan, J. (2003). Behavioral inhibition as a temperamental category. In R. J. Davidson, K. R. Scherer, & H. H. Goldsmith (Eds.), *Handbook of affective science* (pp. 320–331). New York: Oxford University Press.

Kagan, J. (2008). Behavioral inhibition as a risk factor for psychopathology. In T. P. Beauchaine & S. P. Hinshaw (Eds.), *Child and adolescent psychopathology* (pp. 157–179). Hoboken, NJ: Wiley.

Kagan, J., Arcus, D., Snidman, N., Feng, W. Y., Hendler, J., & Greene, S. (1994). Reactivity in infants: A cross-national comparison. *Developmental Psychology, 30,* 342–345.

Kagan, J., & Fox, N. A. (2006). Biology, culture, and temperamental biases. In N. Eisenberg (Ed.), *Handbook of child psychology: Vol. 3. Social, emotional, and personality development* (6th ed., pp. 167–225). Hoboken, NJ: Wiley.

Kagan, J., & Saudino, K. J. (2001). Behavioral inhibition and related temperaments. In R. N. Emde & J. K. Hewitt (Eds.), *Infancy to early childhood: Genetic and environmental influences on developmental change* (pp. 111–119). New York: Oxford University Press.

Kagan, J., Snidman, N., Kahn, V., & Towsley, S. (2007). The preservation of two infant temperaments into adolescence. *Monographs of the Society for Research in Child Development, 72* (2, Serial No. 287).

Kagan, J., Snidman, N., Zentner, M., & Peterson, E. (1999). Infant temperament and anxious symptoms in school-age children. *Development and Psychopathology, 11,* 209–224.

Kahlenberg, S. G., & Hein, M. M. (2010). Progression on Nickelodeon? Gender-role stereotypes in toy commercials. *Sex Roles, 62,* 830–847.

Kahn, R. S., Khoury, J., Nichols, W. C., & Lanphear, B. M. (2003). Role of dopamine transporter genotype and maternal prenatal smoking in childhood hyperactive–impulsive, inattentive, and oppositional behaviors. *Journal of Pediatrics, 143,* 104–110.

Kahne, J. E., & Sporte, S. E. (2008). Developing citizens: The impact of civic learning opportunities on students' commitments to civic participation. *American Educational Research Journal, 45,* 738–766.

Kail, R. (1991). Processing time declines exponentially during childhood and adolescence. *Developmental Psychology, 27,* 259–266.

Kail, R. (1993). The role of a global mechanism in developmental change in speed of processing. In M. L. Howe & R. Pasnak (Eds.), *Emerging themes in cognitive development: Vol. 1. Foundations.* New York: Springer-Verlag.

Kail, R. (1997). Processing time, imagery, and spatial memory. *Journal of Experimental Child Psychology, 64,* 67–78.

Kail, R. V. (2003). Information processing and memory. In M. H. Bornstein, L. Davidson, C. L. M. Keyes, K. A. Moore, and the Center for Child Well-Being (Eds.), *Well-being: Positive development across the life course* (pp. 269–280). Mahwah, NJ: Erlbaum.

Kail, R., & Park, Y. (1992). Global developmental change in processing time. *Merrill-Palmer Quarterly, 38,* 525–541.

Kaitz, M., Meirov, H., Landman, I., & Eidelman, A. I. (1993). Infant recognition by tactile cues. *Infant Behavior and Development, 16,* 333–341.

Kakihara, F., Tilton-Weaver, L., Kerr, M., & Stattin, H. (2010). The relationship of parental control to youth adjustment: Do youths' feelings about their parents play a role? *Journal of Youth and Adolescence, 39,* 1442–1456.

Kalafat, J. (2005). Suicide. In T. P. Gullotta & G. R. Adams (Eds.), *Handbook of adolescent behavioral problems: Evidence-based approaches to prevention and treatment* (pp. 231–254). New York: Springer.

Kalil, A., Levine, J. A., & Ziol-Guest, K. M. (2005). Following in their parents' footsteps: How characteristics of parental work predict adolescents' interest in parents' jobs. In B. Schneider & L. J. Waite (Eds.), *Being together, working apart: Dual-career families and the work–life balance* (pp. 422–442). New York: Cambridge University Press.

Kalisiak, B., & Sptiznagle, T. (2009). What effect does an exercise program for healthy pregnant women have on the mother, fetus, and child? *Physical Medicine and Rehabilitation, 1,* 261–267.

Kalra, L., & Ratan, R. (2007). Recent advances in stroke rehabilitation. *Stroke, 38,* 235–237.

Kaminski, J. W., Puddy, R. W., Hall, D. M., Cashman, S. Y., Crosby, A. E., & Ortega, L. G. (2010). The relative influence of different domains of social connectedness on self-directed violence in adolescence.

Kagan, J., Snidman, N., Zentner, M., & Peterson, E. *Journal of Youth and Adolescence, 39,* 460–473.

Kane, M. J., Hambrick, D. Z., & Conway, A. R. A. (2005). Working memory capacity and fluid intelligence are strongly related constructs: Comment on Ackerman, Beier, and Boyle (2005). *Psychological Bulletin, 131,* 66–71.

Kane, P., & Garber, J. (2004). The relations among depression in fathers, children's psychopathology, and father–child conflict: A meta-analysis. *Clinical Psychology Review, 24,* 339–360.

Kang, N. H., & Hong, M. (2008). Achieving excellence in teacher workforce and equity in learning opportunities in South Korea. *Educational Researcher, 37,* 200–207.

Kaplow, J. B., & Widom, C. S. (2007). Age of onset of child maltreatment predicts long-term mental health outcomes. *Journal of Abnormal Psychology, 116,* 176–187.

Kaplowitz, P. B. (2008). Link between body fat and timing of puberty. *Pediatrics, 121,* S208–S217.

Karafantis, D. M., & Levy, S. R. (2004). The role of children's lay theories about the malleability of human attributes in beliefs about volunteering for disadvantaged groups. *Child Development, 75,* 236–250.

Karasik, L. B., Tamis-LeMonda, C. S., & Adolph, K. E. (2011). Transition from crawling to walking affects infants' social actions with objects. *Child Development, 82,* 1199–1209.

Karasik, L. B., Tamis-LeMonda, C. S., Adolph, K. E., & Dimitroupoulou, K. A. (2008). How mothers encourage and discourage infants' motor actions. *Infancy, 13,* 366–392.

Karmiloff-Smith, A., Brown, J. H., Grice, S., & Paterson, S. (2003). Dethroning the myth: Cognitive dissociations and innate modularity in Williams syndrome. *Developmental Neuropsychology, 23,* 227–242.

Karmiloff-Smith, A., Grant, J., Berthoud, I., Davies, M., Howlin, P., & Udwin, O. (1997). Language and Williams syndrome: How intact is "intact"? *Child Development, 68,* 246–262.

Karmiloff-Smith, A., Grant, J., Sims, K., Jones, M., & Cuckle, P. (1996). Rethinking metalinguistic awareness: Representing and accessing knowledge about what counts as a word. *Cognition, 58,* 197–219.

Karmiloff-Smith, A., Tyler, L. K., Voice, K., Sims, K., Udwin, O., Howlin, P., & Davies, M. (1998). Linguistic dissociations in Williams syndrome: Evaluating receptive syntax in on-line and off-line tasks. *Neuropsychologia, 36,* 343–351.

Kassel, J. D., Weinstein, S., Skitch, S. A., Veilleux, J., & Mermelstein, R. (2005). The development of substance abuse in adolescence: Correlates, causes, and consequences. In J. D. Kassel, S. Weinstein, S. A. Skitch, J. Veilleux, & R. Mermelstein (Eds.), *Development of psychopathology: A vulnerability-stress perspective* (pp. 355–384). Thousand Oaks, CA: Sage.

Kastens, K. A., & Liben, L. S. (2007). Eliciting self-explanations improves children's performance on a field-based map skills task. *Cognition and Instruction, 25,* 45–74.

Kato, I., Franco, P., Groswasser, J., Scaillet, S., Kelmanson, I., Togari, H., & Kahn, A. (2003). Incomplete arousal processes in infants who were victims of sudden death. *American Journal of Respiratory and Critical Care, 168,* 1298–1303.

Katz, L. F., & Windecker-Nelson, B. (2004). Parental meta-emotion philosophy in families with conduct-problem children: Links with peer relations. *Journal of Abnormal Child Psychology, 32,* 385–398.

Katzman, D. K. (2005). Medical complications in adolescents with anorexia nervosa: A review of the literature. *International Journal of Eating Disorders, 37,* S52–S59.

Katzmarzyk, P. T., & Leonard, W. R. (1998). Climatic influences on human body size and proportions: Ecological adaptations and secular trends. *American Journal of Physical Anthropology, 106,* 483–503.

Katz-Wise, S. L., Priess, H. A., & Hyde, J. S. (2010). Gender-role attitudes and behavior across the transition to parenthood. *Developmental Psychology, 46,* 18–28.

Kaufman, A. S., Kamphaus, R. W., & Kaufman, N. L. (1985). New directions in intelligence testing: The Kaufman Assessment Battery for Children (K-ABC). In B. B. Wolman (Ed.), *Handbook of intelligence* (pp. 663–698). New York: Wiley.

Kaufman, A. S., & Lichtenberger, E. O. (2002). *Assessing adolescent and adult intelligence* (2nd ed.). Boston: Allyn and Bacon.

Kaufman, J., & Charney, D. (2003). The neurobiology of child and adolescent depression: Current knowledge and future directions. In D. Cicchetti & E. Walker (Eds.), *Neurodevelopmental mechanisms in psychopathology* (pp. 461–490). New York: Cambridge University Press.

Kaufman, J., Csibra, G., & Johnson, M. H. (2005). Oscillatory activity in the infant brain reflects object maintenance. *Proceedings of the National Academy of Sciences, 102,* 15271–15274.

Kaufman, J. C., & Sternberg, R. J. (2007, July/August). Resource review: Creativity. *Change, 39,* 55–58.

Kavanaugh, R. D. (2006a). Pretend play. In B. Spodek & O. N. Saracho (Eds.), *Handbook of research on the education of young children* (2nd ed., pp. 269–278). Mahwah, NJ: Erlbaum.

Kavanaugh, R. D. (2006b). Pretend play and theory of mind. In L. Balter & C. S. Tamis-LeMonda (Eds.), *Child psychology: A handbook of contemporary issues* (2nd ed., pp. 153–166). New York: Psychology Press.

Kavsek, M. (2004). Predicting later IQ from infant visual habituation and dishabituation: A meta-analysis. *Journal of Applied Developmental Psychology, 25,* 369–393.

Kavsek, M., & Bornstein, M. H. (2010). Visual habituation and dishabituation in preterm infants: A review and meta-analysis. *Research in Developmental Disabilities, 31,* 951–975.

Kavsek, M., Granrud, C. E., & Yonas, A. (2009). Infants' responsiveness to pictorial depth cues in preferential-reaching studies: A meta-analysis. *Infant Behavior and Development, 32,* 245–253.

Kaye, K., & Marcus, J. (1981). Infant imitation: The sensory-motor agenda. *Developmental Psychology, 17,* 258–265.

Kaye, W. (2008). Neurobiology of anorexia and bulimia nervosa. *Physiology and Behavior, 94,* 121–135.

Kearins, J. M. (1981). Visual spatial memory in Australian aboriginal children of desert regions. *Cognitive Psychology, 13,* 434–460.

Keating, D. P. (2004). Cognitive and brain development. In R. M. Lerner & L. Steinberg (Eds.), *Handbook of adolescent psychology* (2nd ed., pp. 45–84). Hoboken, NJ: Wiley.

Kedar, Y., Casasola, M., & Lust, B. (2006). Getting there faster: 18- and 24-month-old infants' use of function words to determine reference. *Child Development, 77,* 325–338.

Keefe, M. R., Barbosa, G. A., Froese-Fretz, A., Kotzer, A. M., & Lobo, M. (2005). An intervention program for families with irritable infants. *American Journal of Maternal/Child Nursing, 30,* 230–236.

Keil, F. C. (1986). Conceptual domains and the acquisition of metaphor. *Cognitive Development, 1,* 72–96.

Keil, F. C., & Lockhart, K. L. (1999). Explanatory understanding in conceptual development. In E. K. Scholnick, K. Nelson, S. A. Gelman, & P. H. Miller (Eds.), *Conceptual development: Piaget's legacy* (pp. 103–130). Mahwah, NJ: Erlbaum.

Keller, H., Borke, Y. J., Kärtner, J., Jensen, H., & Papaligoura, Z. (2004). Developmental consequences of early parenting experiences: Self-recognition and self-regulation in three cultural communities. *Child Development, 75,* 1745–1760.

Keller, H., Kärtner, J., Borke, J., Yovsi, R., & Kleis, A. (2005). Parenting styles and the development of the categorical self: A longitudinal study on mirror self-recognition in Cameroonian Nso and German families. *International Journal of Behavioral Development, 29,* 496–504.

Keller, S. N., & Brown, J. D. (2002). Media interventions to promote responsible sexual behavior. *Journal of Sex Research, 39,* 67–72.

Keller, S. S., Crow, T., Foundas, A., Amunts, K., & Roberts, N. (2009). Broca's area: Nomenclature, anatomy, typology and symmetry. *Brain and Language, 109,* 29–48.

Kelley, S. A., Brownell, C. A., & Campbell, S. B. (2000). Mastery motivation and self-evaluative affect in toddlers: Longitudinal relations with maternal behavior. *Child Development, 71,* 1061–1071.

Kellman, P. J., & Arterberry, M. E. (2006). Infant visual perception. In D. Kuhn & R. Siegler (Eds.), *Handbook of child psychology: Vol. 2. Cognition, perception, and language* (6th ed., pp. 109–160). Hoboken, NJ: Wiley.

Kelly, D. J., Liu, S., Ge, L., Quinn, P. C., Slater, A. M., Lee, K., et al. (2007a). Cross-race preferences for same-race faces extend beyond the African versus Caucasian contrast in 3-month-old infants. *Infancy, 11,* 87–95.

Kelly, D. J., Quinn, P. C., Slater, A. M., Lee, K., Ge, L., & Pascalis, O. (2007b). The other-race effect develops during infancy: Evidence of perceptual narrowing. *Psychological Science, 18,* 1084–1089.

Kelly, N., & Norwich, B. (2004). Pupils' perceptions of self and labels: Moderate learning difficulties in mainstream and special schools. *British Journal of Educational Psychology, 74,* 411–435.

Kempe, C. H., Silverman, F. N., Steele, B. F., Droegemueller, W., & Silver, H. K. (1962). The battered-child syndrome. *Journal of the American Medical Association, 181,* 17–24.

Kendall, G., & Peebles, D. (2005). Acute fetal hypoxia. The modulating effect of infection. *Early Human Development, 81,* 27–34.

Kendler, K. S., Thornton, L. M., Gilman, S. E., & Kessler, R. C. (2000). Sexual orientation in a U.S. national sample of

twin and non-twin sibling pairs. *American Journal of Psychiatry, 157,* 1843–1846.

Kennedy, A. M., & Gust, D. A. (2008). Measles outbreak associated with a church congregation: A study of immunization attitudes of congregation members. *Public Health Reports, 123,* 126–134.

Kennedy, D. E., & Kramer, L. (2008). Improving emotion regulation and sibling relationship quality: The More Fun with Sisters and Brothers Program. *Family Relations, 57,* 568–579.

Kennell, J., Klaus, M., McGrath, S., Robertson, S., & Hinkley, C. (1991). Continuous emotional support during labor in a U.S. hospital. *Journal of the American Medical Association, 265,* 2197–2201.

Kenney, G. M., Lynch, V., Cook, A., & Phong, S. (2010). Who and where are the children yet to enroll in Medicaid and the Children's Health Insurance Program? *Health Affairs, 29,* 1920–1929.

Kenney-Benson, G. A., Pomerantz, E. M., Ryan, A. M., & Patrick, H. (2006). Sex differences in math performance: The role of children's approach to schoolwork. *Developmental Psychology, 42,* 11–26.

Kerckhoff, A. C. (2002). The transition from school to work. In J. T. Mortimer & R. Larson (Eds.), *The changing adolescent experience* (pp. 52–87). New York: Cambridge University Press.

Keren, M., Feldman, R., Namdari-Weinbaum, I., Spitzer, S., & Tyano, S. (2005). Relations between parents' interactive style in dyadic and triadic play and toddlers' symbolic capacity. *American Journal of Orthopsychiatry, 75,* 599–607.

Kerestes, M., & Youniss, J. E. (2003). Rediscovering the importance of religion in adolescent development. In R. M. Lerner, F. Jacobs, & D. Wertlieb (Eds.), *Handbook of applied developmental science* (Vol. 1, pp. 165–184). Thousand Oaks, CA: Sage.

Kerestes, M., Youniss, J., & Metz, E. (2004). Longitudinal patterns of religious perspective and civic integration. *Applied Developmental Science, 8,* 39–46.

Kerig, P. K., Cowan, P. A., & Cowan, C. P. (1993). Marital quality and gender differences in parent–child interactions. *Developmental Psychology, 29,* 931–939.

Kerig, P. K., & Stellwagen, K. K. (2010). Roles of callous-unemotional traits, narcissism, and Machiavellianism in childhood aggression. *Journal of Psychopathological Behavior and Assessment, 32,* 343–352.

Kern, S. (2007). Lexicon development in French-speaking infants. *First Language, 27,* 227–250.

Kernis, M. H. (2002). Self-esteem as a multifaceted construct. In T. M. Brinthaupt & R. P. Lipka (Eds.), *Understanding early adolescent self and identity* (pp. 57–88). Albany, NY: State University of New York Press.

Kerr, D. C. R., Lopez, N. L., Olson, S. L., & Sameroff, A. J. (2004). Parental discipline and externalizing behavior problems in early childhood: The roles of moral regulation and child gender. *Journal of Abnormal Child Psychology, 32,* 369–383.

Kesler, S. R. (2007). Turner syndrome. *Child and Adolescent Psychiatric Clinics of North America, 16,* 709–722.

Kessen, W. (1967). Sucking and looking: Two organized congenital patterns of behavior in the human newborn. In H. W. Stevenson, E. H. Hess & H. L. Rheingold (Eds.), *Early behavior: Comparative and*

developmental approaches (pp. 147–179). New York: Wiley.

Key, J. D., Gebregziabher, M. G., Marsh, L. D., & O'Rourke, K. M. (2008). Effectiveness of an intensive, school-based intervention for teen mothers. *Journal of Adolescent Health, 42,* 394–400.

Khashan, A. S., Baker, P. N., & Kenny, L. C. (2010). Preterm birth and reduced birthweight in first and second teenage pregnancies: A register-based cohort study. *BMC Pregnancy and Childbirth, 10,* 36.

Kieffer, M. J. (2008). Catching up or falling behind? Initial English proficiency, concentrated poverty and the reading growth of language minority learners in the United States. *Journal of Educational Psychology, 100,* 851–868.

Kieras, J. E., Tobin, R. M., Graziano, W. G., & Rothbart, M. K. (2005). You can't always get what you want: Effortful control and children's responses to undesirable gifts. *Psychological Science, 16,* 391–396.

Killen, M., Crystal, D. S., & Watanabe, H. (2002). The individual and the group: Japanese and American children's evaluations of peer exclusion, tolerance of difference, and prescriptions for conformity. *Child Development, 73,* 1788–1802.

Killen, M., Henning, A., Kelly, M. C., Crystal, D., & Ruck, M. (2007). Evaluations of interracial peer encounters by majority and minority U.S. children and adolescents. *International Journal of Behavioral Development, 31,* 491–500.

Killen, M., Kelly, M. C., Richardson, C., Crystal, D., & Ruck, M. (2010). European American children's and adolescents' evaluations of interracial exclusion. *Group Processes and Intergroup Relations, 13,* 283–300.

Killen, M., Lee-Kim, J., McGlothlin, H., & Stangor, C. (2002). How children and adolescents evaluate gender and racial exclusion. *Monographs of the Society for Research in Child Development, 67*(4, Serial No. 271).

Killen, M., & Nucci, L. P. (1995). Morality, autonomy, and social conflict. In M. Killen & D. Hart (Eds.), *Morality in everyday life: Developmental perspectives* (pp. 52–86). Cambridge: Cambridge University Press.

Killen, M., Margie, N. G., & Sinno, S. (2006). Morality in the context of intergroup relationships. In M. Killen & J. G. Smetana (Eds.), *Handbook of moral development* (pp. 155–183). Mahwah, NJ: Erlbaum.

Killen, M., & Stangor, M. (2001). Children's social reasoning about inclusion and exclusion in gender and race peer group contexts. *Child Development, 72,* 174–186.

Killoren, S. E., Thayer, S. M., & Updegraff, K. A. (2008). Conflict resolution between Mexican origin adolescent siblings. *Journal of Marriage and Family, 70,* 1200–1212.

Kilpatrick, S. W., & Sanders, D. M. (1978). Body image stereotypes: A developmental comparison. *Journal of Genetic Psychology, 132,* 87–95.

Kim, G., Walden, T. A., & Knieps, L. J. (2010). Impact and characteristics of positive and fearful emotional messages during infant social referencing. *Infant Behavior and Development, 33,* 189–195.

Kim, J., & Cicchetti, D. (2006). Longitudinal trajectories of self-system processes and depressive symptoms among maltreated and nonmaltreated children. *Child Development, 77,* 624–639.

Kim, J. M. (1998). Korean children's concepts of adult and peer authority and moral reasoning. *Developmental Psychology, 34,* 947–955.

Kim, J. M., & Turiel, E. (1996). Korean children's concepts of adult and peer authority. *Social Development, 5,* 310–329.

Kim, J.-Y., McHale, S. M., Crouter, A. C., & Osgood, D. W. (2007). Longitudinal linkages between sibling relationships and adjustment from middle childhood through adolescence. *Developmental Psychology, 43,* 960–973.

Kim, J.-Y., McHale, S. M., Osgood, D. W., & Crouter, A. C. (2006). Longitudinal course and family correlates of sibling relationships from childhood through adolescence. *Child Development, 77,* 1746–1761.

Kim, M., McGregor, K. K., & Thompson, C. K. (2000). Early lexical development in English- and Korean-speaking children: Language-general and language-specific patterns. *Journal of Child Language, 27,* 225–254.

Kimbro, R. T. (2006). On-the-job moms: Work and breastfeeding initiation and duration for a sample of low-income women. *Maternal and Child Health Journal, 10,* 19–26.

King, A. C., & Bjorklund, D. F. (2010). Evolutionary developmental psychology. *Psicothema, 22,* 22–27.

King, P. E., & Furrow, J. L. (2004). Religion as a resource for positive youth development: Religion, social capital, and moral outcomes. *Developmental Psychology, 40,* 703–713.

King, V. (2007). When children have two mothers: Relationships with nonresident mothers, stepmothers, and fathers. *Journal of Marriage and Family, 69,* 1178–1193.

King, V. (2009). Stepfamily formation: Implications for adolescent ties to mothers, nonresident fathers, and stepfathers. *Journal of Marriage and Family, 71,* 954–968.

Kinney, D. (1999). From "headbangers" to "hippies": Delineating adolescents' active attempts to form an alternative peer culture. In J. A. McLellan & M. J. V. Pugh (Eds.), *The role of peer groups in adolescent social identity: Exploring the importance of stability and change* (pp. 21–35). San Francisco: Jossey-Bass.

Kinney, H. C. (2009). Brainstem mechanisms underlying the sudden infant death syndrome: Evidence from human pathologic studies. *Developmental Psychobiology, 51,* 223–233.

Kinnunen, M.-L., Pietilainen, K., & Rissanen, A. (2006). Body size and overweight from birth to adulthood. In L. Pulkkinen & J. Kaprio (Eds.), *Socioemotional development and health from adolescence to adulthood* (pp. 95–107). New York: Cambridge University Press.

Kinsella, M. T., & Monk, C. (2009). Impact of maternal stress, depression and anxiety on fetal neurobehavioral development. *Clinical Obstetrics and Gynecology, 52,* 425–440.

Kirby, D. (2002a). Antecedents of adolescent initiation of sex, contraceptive use, and pregnancy. *American Journal of Health Behavior, 26,* 473–485.

Kirby, D. (2002b). Effective approaches to reducing adolescent unprotected sex, pregnancy, and childbearing. *Journal of Sex Research, 39,* 51–57.

Kirby, D. (2002c). The impact of schools and school programs upon adolescent sexual behavior. *Journal of Sex Research, 39,* 27–33.

Kirby, D. B. (2008). The impact of abstinence and comprehensive sex and STD/HIV education programs on adolescent sexual behavior. *Sexuality Research and Social Policy, 5,* 18–27.

Kiriakidis, S. P., & Kavoura, A. (2010). Cyberbullying: A review of the literature on harassment through the Internet and other electronic means. *Family and Community Health, 33,* 82–93.

Kirk, K. M., Bailey, J. M., Dunne, M. P., & Martin, N. G. (2000). Measurement models for sexual orientation in a community twin sample. *Behavior Genetics, 30,* 345–356.

Kirkham, N. Z., Cruess, L., & Diamond, A. (2003). Helping children apply their knowledge to their behavior on a dimension-switching task. *Developmental Science, 6,* 449–476.

Kirkham, N. Z., Slemmer, J. A., & Johnson, S. P. (2002). Visual statistical learning in infancy: Evidence for a domain general learning mechanism. *Cognition, 83,* B35–B42.

Kirshner, B. (2009). "Power in numbers": Youth organizing as a context for exploring civic identity. *Journal of Research on Adolescence, 19,* 414–440.

Kisilevsky B. S., & Low, J. A. (1998). Human fetal behavior: 100 years of study. *Developmental Review, 18,* 1–29.

Kisilevsky, B. S., Hains, S. M. J., Brown, C. A., Lee, C. T., Cowperthwaite, B., & Stutzman, S. S. (2009). Fetal sensitivity to properties of maternal speech and language. *Infant Behavior and Development, 32,* 59–71.

Kisilevsky, B. S., Hains, S. M. J., Lee, K., Muir, D. W., Xu, F., Fu, G., et al. (1998). The still-face effect in Chinese and Canadian 3- to 6-month-old infants. *Developmental Psychology, 34,* 629–639.

Kisilevsky, B. S., Hains, S. M. J., Lee, K., Xie, X., Huang, H., Ye, H. H., et al. (2003). Effects of experience on fetal voice recognition. *Psychological Science, 14,* 220–224.

Kitzmann, K. M., Cohen, R., & Lockwood, R. L. (2002). Are only children missing out? Comparison of the peer-related social competence of only children and siblings. *Journal of Social and Personal Relationships, 19,* 299–316.

Kitzmann, K. M., Gaylord, N. K., Holt, A. R., & Kenny, E. D. (2003). Child witnesses to domestic violence: A meta-analytic review. *Journal of Consulting and Clinical Psychology, 71,* 339–352.

Kjonniksen, L., Anderssen, N., & Wold, B. (2009). Organized youth sport as a predictor of physical activity in adulthood. *Scandinavian Journal of Medicine and Science in Sports, 19,* 646–654.

Klaczynski, P. A. (1997). Bias in adolescents' everyday reasoning and its relationships with intellectual ability, personal theories, and self-serving motivation. *Developmental Psychology, 33,* 273–283.

Klaczynski, P. A. (2001). Analytic and heuristic processing influences on adolescent reasoning and decision-making. *Child Development, 72,* 844–861.

Klaczynski, P. A. (2004). A dual-process model of adolescent development: Implications for decision making, reasoning, and identity. In R. Kail (Ed.), *Advances in child development and behavior* (Vol. 31, pp. 73–123). San Diego, CA: Academic Press.

Klaczynski, P. A., & Narasimham, G. (1998). Development of scientific reasoning biases: Cognitive versus ego-protective explanations. *Developmental Psychology, 34,* 175–187.

Klaczynski, P. A., Schuneman, M. J., & Daniel, D. B. (2004). Theories of conditional reasoning: A developmental examination of competing hypotheses. *Developmental Psychology, 40,* 559–571.

Klahr, D., & MacWhinney, B. (1998). Information processing. In D. Kuhn & R. S. Siegler (Eds.), *Handbook of child psychology: Vol. 2. Cognition, perception, and language* (5th ed., pp. 631–678). New York: Wiley.

Klahr, D., & Nigam, M. (2004). The equivalence of learning paths in early science instruction: Effects of direct instruction and discovery learning. *Psychological Science, 15,* 661–667.

Klaw, E. L., Rhodes, J. E., & Fitzgerald, L. F. (2003). Natural mentors in the lives of African-American adolescent mothers: Tracking relationships over time. *Journal of Youth and Adolescence, 32,* 223–232.

Klebanov, P. K., Brooks-Gunn, J., McCarton, C., & McCormick, M. C. (1998). The contribution of neighborhood and family income to developmental test scores over the first three years of life. *Child Development, 69,* 1420–1436.

Klein, P. J., & Meltzoff, A. N. (1999). Long-term memory, forgetting, and deferred imitation in 12-month-old infants. *Developmental Science, 2,* 102–113.

Klenberg, L., Korkman, M., & Lahti-Nuuttila, P. (2001). Differential development of attention and executive functions in 3- to 12-year-old Finnish children. *Developmental Neuropsychology, 20,* 407–428.

Klesges, L. M., Johnson, K. C., Ward, K. D., & Barnard, M. (2001). Smoking cessation in pregnant women. *Obstetrics and Gynecology Clinics of North America, 28,* 269–282.

Klibanoff, R. S., Levine, S. C., Huttenlocher, J., Vasilyeva, M., & Hedges, L. V. (2006). Preschool children's mathematical knowledge: The effect of teacher "math talk." *Developmental Psychology, 42,* 59–69.

Kliegman, R. M., Behrman, R. E., Jenson, H. B., & Stanton, B. F. (Eds.). (2008). *Nelson textbook of pediatrics e-edition.* Philadelphia: Saunders.

Kliewer, W., Fearnow, M. D., & Miller, P. A. (1996). Coping socialization in middle childhood: Tests of maternal and paternal influences. *Child Development, 67,* 2339–2357.

Klimes-Dougan, B., & Kistner, J. (1990). Physically abused preschoolers' responses to peers' distress. *Developmental Psychology, 26,* 599–602.

Klimstra, T. A., Hale, W. W., III, Raaijmakers, Q. A. W., Branje, S. J. T., & Meeus, W. H. J. (2010). Identity formation in adolescence: Change or stability? *Journal of Youth and Adolescence, 39,* 150–162.

Klineberg, O. (1963). Negro–white differences in intelligence test performance: A new look at an old problem. *American Psychologist, 18,* 198–203.

Klingman, A. (2006). Children and war trauma. In K. A. Renninger & I. E. Sigel (Eds.), *Handbook of child psychology: Vol. 4. Child psychology in practice* (6th ed., pp. 619–652). Hoboken, NJ: Wiley.

Klomsten, A. T., Skaalvik, E. M., & Espnes, G. A. (2004). Physical self-concept and sports: Do gender differences exist? *Sex Roles, 50,* 119–127.

Klump, K. L., Kaye, W. H., & Strober, M. (2001). The evolving genetic foundations of eating disorders. *Psychiatric Clinics of North America, 24,* 215–225.

Knafo, A., & Plomin, R. (2006). Parental discipline and affection and children's prosocial behavior: Genetic and environmental links. *Journal of Personality and Social Psychology, 90,* 147–164.

Knafo, A., Zahn-Waxler, C., Davidov, M., Hulle, C. V., Robinson, J. L., & Rhee, S. H. (2009). Empathy in early childhood: Genetic, environmental, and affective contributions. In O. Vilarroya, S. Altran, A. Navarro, K. Ochsner, & A. Tobena (Eds.), *Values, empathy, and fairness across social barriers* (pp. 103–114). New York: New York Academy of Sciences.

Knickmeyer, R. C., Gouttard, S., Kang, C., Evans, D., Wilber, K., Smith, J. K., et al. (2008). A structural MRI study of human brain development from birth to 2 years. *Journal of Neuroscience, 28,* 12176–12182.

Knobloch, H., & Pasamanick, B. (Eds.). (1974). *Gesell and Amatruda's developmental diagnosis.* Hagerstown, MD: Harper & Row.

Knopf, M., Kraus, U., & Kressley-Mba, R. A. (2006). Relational information processing of novel unrelated actions by infants. *Infant Behavior and Development, 29,* 44–53.

Knudsen, E. I. (2004). Sensitive periods in the development of the brain and behavior. *Journal of Cognitive Neuroscience, 16,* 1412–1425.

Knudsen, K., & Waerness, K. (2003). National context, individual characteristics, and attitudes on mothers' employment: A comparative analysis of Great Britain, Sweden, and Norway. *Acta Sociologica, 44,* 67–97.

Kobayashi, T., Hiraki, K., & Hasegawa, T. (2005). Auditory-visual intermodal matching of small numerosities in 6-month-old infants. *Developmental Science, 8,* 409–419.

Kobayashi, T., Kazuo, H., Ryoko, M., & Hasegawa, T. (2004). Baby arithmetic: One object plus one tone. *Cognition, 91,* B23–B34.

Kochanska, G. (1991). Socialization and temperament in the development of guilt and conscience. *Child Development, 62,* 1379–1392.

Kochanska, G., & Aksan, N. (2006). Children's conscience and self-regulation. *Journal of Personality, 74,* 1587–1617.

Kochanska, G., Aksan, N., & Joy, M. E. (2007). Children's fearfulness as a moderator of parenting in early socialization: Two longitudinal studies. *Developmental Psychology, 43,* 222–237.

Kochanska, G., Aksan, N., & Nichols, K. E. (2003). Maternal power assertion in discipline and moral discourse contexts: Commonalities, differences, and implications for children's moral conduct and cognition. *Developmental Psychology, 39,* 949–963.

Kochanska, G., Aksan, N., Prisco, T. R., & Adams, E. E. (2008). Mother–child and father–child mutually responsive orientation in the first 2 years and children's outcomes at preschool age: Mechanisms of influence. *Child Development, 79,* 30–44.

Kochanska, G., Forman, D. R., Aksan, N., & Dunbar, S. B. (2005). Pathways to conscience: Early mother–child mutually responsive orientation and children's moral emotion, conduct, and cognition. *Journal of Child Psychology and Psychiatry, 46,* 19–34.

Kochanska, G., Gross, J. N., Lin, M.-H., & Nichols, K. E. (2002). Guilt in young children: Development, determinants, and relations with broader system standards. *Child Development, 73,* 461–482.

Kochanska, G., & Knaack, A. (2003). Effortful control as a personality characteristic of young children: Antecedents, correlates, and consequences. *Journal of Personality, 71,* 1087–1112.

Kochanska, G., Koenig, J. L., Barry, R. A., Kim, S., & Yoon, J. E. (2010). Children's conscience during toddler and preschool years, moral self, and adaptive developmental trajectory. *Developmental Psychology, 46,* 1320–1332.

Kochanska, G., & Murray, K. T. (2000). Mother–child mutually responsive orientation and conscience development: From toddler to early school age. *Child Development, 71,* 417–431.

Kochanska, G., Murray, K. T., & Harlan, E. T. (2000). Effortful control in early childhood: Continuity and change, antecedents, and implications for social development. *Developmental Psychology, 36,* 220–232.

Kochanska, G., Philibert, R. A., & Barry, R. A. (2009). Interplay of genes and early mother–child relationship in the development of self-regulation from toddler to preschool age. *Journal of Child Psychology and Psychiatry, 50,* 1331–1338.

Kochenderfer-Ladd, B. (2003). Identification of aggressive and asocial victims and the stability of their peer victimization. *Merrill-Palmer Quarterly, 49,* 401–425.

Koestner, R., Franz, C., & Weinberger, J. (1990). The family origins of empathic concern: A 26-year longitudinal study. *Journal of Personality and Social Psychology, 58,* 709–717.

Kohen, D. E., Leventhal, T., Dahinten, V. S., & McIntosh, C. N. (2008). Neighborhood disadvantage: Pathways of effects for young children. *Child Development, 79,* 156–169.

Kohlberg, L. (1958). *The development of modes of moral thinking and choice in the years ten to sixteen.* Unpublished doctoral dissertation, University of Chicago.

Kohlberg, L. (1966). A cognitive-developmental analysis of children's sex-role concepts and attitudes. In E. E. Maccoby (Ed.), *The development of sex differences* (pp. 82–173). Stanford, CA: Stanford University Press.

Kohlberg, L. (1969). Stage and sequence: The cognitive-developmental approach to socialization. In D. A. Goslin (Ed.), *Handbook of socialization theory and research* (pp. 347–480). Chicago: Rand McNally.

Kohlberg, L., Levine, C., & Hewer, A. (1983). *Moral stages: A current formulation and a response to critics.* Basel: Karger.

Kolomer, S. R., & McCallion, P. (2005). Depression and caregiver mastery in grandfathers caring for their grandchildren. *International Journal of Aging and Human Development, 60,* 283–294.

Komlos, J., & Breitfelder, A. (2008). Differences in the physical growth of U.S.-born black and white children and adolescents ages 2–19, born 1942–2002. *Annals of Human Biology, 35,* 11–21.

Kon, A. A., & Klug, M. (2006). Methods and practices of investigators for determining participants' decisional capacity and comprehension of protocols. *Journal of Empirical Research on Human Research Ethics, 1,* 61–68.

Konner, M. (2010). *The evolution of childhood: Relationships, emotion, mind.* Cambridge, MA: Harvard University Press.

Konner, M. J. (1977). Infancy among the Kalahari Desert San. In P. H. Leiderman, S. R. Tulkin, & A. Rosenfield (Eds.), *Culture and infancy: Variations in the human experience* (pp. 287–328). New York: Academic Press.

Konner, M. J. (2008). Infant care in the Kalahari desert. In R. A. LeVine (Ed.), *Anthropology and child development* (pp. 66–72). Malden, MA: Blackwell.

Konold, T. R., & Pianta, R. C. (2005). Empirically-derived, person-oriented patterns of school readiness in typically developing children: Description and prediction to first-grade achievement. *Applied Developmental Science, 9,* 174–187.

Kontic-Vucinic, O., Sulovic, N., & Radunovic, N. (2006). Micronutrients in women's reproductive health: II. Minerals and trace elements. *International Journal of Fertility and Women's Medicine, 51,* 116–124.

Kooijman, V., Hagoort, P., & Cutler, A. (2009). Prosodic structure in early word segmentation: ERP evidence from Dutch ten-month-olds. *Infancy, 14,* 591–612.

Kopp, C. B., & Neufeld, S. J. (2003). Emotional development during infancy. In R. Davidson, K. R. Scherer, & H. H. Goldsmith (Eds.), *Handbook of affective sciences* (pp. 347–374). Oxford, UK: Oxford University Press.

Kopp, C. B., & Wyer, N, (1994). Self-regulation in normal and atypical development. In D. Cicchetti & S. L. Toth (Eds.), *Disorders and dysfunctions of the self. Rochester Symposium on Developmental Psychopathology* (Vol. 5, pp. 31–56). Rochester, NY: University of Rochester Press.

Korkman, M., Kettunen, S., & Autti-Raemoe, I. (2003). Neurocognitive impairment in early adolescence following prenatal alcohol exposure of varying duration. *Child Neurology, 9,* 117–128.

Kornhaber, M. L. (2004). Using multiple intelligences to overcome cultural barriers to identification for gifted education. In D. Boothe & J. C. Stanley (Eds.), *In the eyes of the beholder: Critical issues for diversity in gifted education* (pp. 215–225). Waco, TX: Prufrock Press.

Kotchick, B. A., Dorsey, S., & Heller, L. (2005). Predictors of parenting among African-American single mothers: Personal and contextual factors. *Journal of Marriage and Family, 67,* 448–460.

Kouvonen, A., & Kivivuori, J. (2001). Part-time jobs, delinquency, and victimization among Finnish adolescents. *Journal of Scandinavian Studies in Criminology and Crime Prevention, 2,* 191–212.

Kovacs, D. M., Parker, J. G., & Hoffman, L. W. (1996). Behavioral, affective, and social correlates of involvement in cross-sex friendship in elementary school. *Child Development, 67,* 2269–2286.

Kowalski, R. M., Limber, S. P., & Agatston, P. W. (2008). *Cyber bullying: Bullying in the digital age.* Malden, MA: Blackwell.

Kozbelt, A., Beghetto, R. A., & Runco, M. A. (2010). Theories of creativity. In J. C.

Kaufman & R. J. Sternberg (Eds.), *Cambridge handbook of creativity* (pp. 20–47). New York: Cambridge University Press.

Kozer, E., Costei, A. M., Boskovic, R., Nulman, I., Nikfar, S., & Koren, G. (2003). Effects of aspirin consumption during pregnancy on pregnancy outcomes: Meta-analysis. *Birth Defects Research, Part B, Developmental and Reproductive Toxicology, 68,* 70–84.

Kozol, J. (2005). *The shame of the nation: The restoration of apartheid schooling in America.* New York: Three Rivers Press.

Kozulin, A. (Ed.). (2003). *Vygotsky's educational theory in cultural context.* Cambridge, U.K.: Cambridge University Press.

Krafft, K., & Berk, L. E. (1998). Private speech in two preschools: Significance of open-ended activities and make-believe play for verbal self-regulation. *Early Childhood Research Quarterly, 13,* 637–658.

Krähenbühl, S., Blades, M., & Eiser, C. (2009). The effect of repeated questioning on children's accuracy and consistency in eyewitness testimony. *Legal and Criminological Psychology, 14,* 263–278.

Kral, T. V. E., & Faith, M. S. (2009). Influences on child eating and weight development from a behavioral genetics perspective. *Journal of Pediatric Psychology, 34,* 596–605.

Kramer, L. (2011). Supportive sibling relationships. In J. Caspi (Ed.), *Sibling development: Implications for mental health practitioners* (pp. 41–58). New York: Springer.

Kramer, L., & Kowal, A. K. (2005). Sibling relationship quality from birth to adolescence: The enduring contributions of friends. *Journal of Family Psychology, 19,* 503–511.

Krascum, R. M., & Andrews, S. (1998). The effects of theories on children's acquisition of family-resemblance categories. *Child Development, 69,* 333–346.

Krcmar, M., Grela, B., & Linn, K. (2007). Can toddlers learn vocabulary from television? An experimental approach. *Media Psychology, 10,* 41–63.

Krebs, D. L., Vermeulen, S. C., Carpendale, J. I. M., & Denton, K. (1991). Structural and situational influences on moral judgment: The interaction between stage and dilemma. In W. Kurtines & J. Gewirtz (Eds.), *Handbook of moral behavior and development: Theory, research, and application* (pp. 139–169). Hillsdale, NJ: Erlbaum.

Krebs, D., & Gillmore, J. (1982). The relationship among the first stages of cognitive development, role-taking abilities, and moral development. *Child Development, 53,* 877–886.

Krebs, D. L., & Denton, K. (2005). Toward a more pragmatic approach to morality: A critical evaluation of Kohlberg's model. *Psychological Review, 112,* 629–649.

Kreppner, J., Kumsta, R., Rutter, M., Beckett, C., Castle, J., Stevens, S., et al. (2010). Developmental course of deprivation-specific psychological patterns: Early manifestations, persistence to age 15, and clinical features. *Monographs of the Society for Research in Child Development, 75*(1, Serial No. 295), 79–101.

Kreppner, J., Rutter, M., Beckett, C., Castle, J., Colvert, E., Groothues, C., et al. (2007). Normality and impairment following profound early institutional deprivation: A longitudinal follow-up into early

adolescence. *Developmental Psychology, 43,* 931–946.

Krettenauer, T. (2005). The role of epistemic cognition in adolescent identity formation: Further evidence. *Journal of Youth and Adolescence, 34,* 185–198.

Krevans, J., & Gibbs, J. C. (1996). Parents' use of inductive discipline: Relations to children's empathy and prosocial behavior. *Child Development, 67,* 3263–3277.

Krieg, D. B. (2007). Does motherhood get easier the second time around? Examining parenting stress and marital quality among mothers having their first or second child. *Parenting: Science and Practice, 7,* 149–175.

Krishnakumar, A., & Buehler, C. (2000). Interparental conflict and parenting behaviors: A meta-analytic review. *Family Relations, 49,* 25–44.

Krishnamoorthy, J. S., Hart, C., & Jelalian, E. (2006). The epidemic of childhood obesity: Review of research and implications for public policy. *Social Policy Report of the Society for Research in Child Development, 9*(2).

Kroger, J. (2005). *Identity in adolescence: The balance between self and other.* New York: Routledge.

Kroger, J. (2007). *Identity development: Adolescence through adulthood* (2nd ed.). Thousand Oaks, CA: Sage.

Kroger, J., Martinussen, M., & Marcia, J. E. (2010). Identity status change during adolescence and young adulthood: A meta-analysis. *Journal of Adolescence, 33,* 683–698.

Kross, E., & Mischel, W. (2010). From stimulus control to self-control: Toward an integrative understanding of the processes underlying willpower. In R. R. Hassin, K. N. Ochsner, & Y. Trope (Eds.), *Self-control in society, mind, and brain* (pp. 428–446). New York: Oxford University Press.

Krumhansl, C. L., & Jusczyk, P. W. (1990). Infants' perception of phrase structure in music. *Psychological Science, 1,* 70–73.

Kubik, M. Y., Lytle, L. A., Hannan, P. J., Perry, C. L., & Story, M. (2003). The association of the school food environment with dietary behaviors of young adolescents. *American Journal of Public Health, 93,* 1168–1173.

Kuczynski, L. (1984). Socialization goals and mother–child interaction: Strategies for long-term and short-term compliance. *Developmental Psychology, 20,* 1061–1073.

Kuczynski, L. (2003). Beyond bidirectionality. In L. Kuczynski (Ed.), *Handbook of dynamics in parent–child relations* (pp. 3–24). Thousand Oaks, CA: Sage.

Kuczynski, L., & Hildebrandt, N. (1997). Models of conformity and resistance in socialization theory. In J. E. Grusec & L. Kuczynski (Eds.), *Parenting and children's internalization of values* (pp. 227–256). New York: Wiley.

Kuczynski, L., & Lollis, S. (2002). Four foundations for a dynamic model of parenting. In J. R. M. Gerris (Eds.), *Dynamics of parenting.* Hillsdale, NJ: Erlbaum.

Kuebli, J., Butler, S., & Fivush, R. (1995). Mother–child talk about past emotions: relations of maternal language and child gender over time. *Cognition and Emotion, 9,* 265–283.

Kugelmass, J., & Ainscow, M. (2004). Leadership for inclusion: A comparison of international practices. *Journal of Research in Special Educational Needs, 4,* 133–141.

Kuhl, P. K. (2006). A new view of language acquisition. In H. Luria, D. M. Seymour, & T. Smoke (2006), *Language and linguistics in context: Readings and applications for teachers* (pp. 29–42). Mahwah, NJ: Erlbaum.

Kuhl, P. K. (2009). Linking infant speech perception to language acquisition: Phonetic learning predicts language growth. In J. Colombo, P. McCardle, & L. Freund (Eds.), *Infant pathways to language: Methods, models, and research directions* (pp. 213–244). New York: Psychology Press.

Kuhl, P. K., Conboy, B. T., Padden, D., Nelson, T., & Pruitt, J. (2005). Early speech perception and later language development: Implications for the "critical period." *Language Learning and Development, 1,* 237–264.

Kuhl, P. K., Tsao, F.-M., & Liu, H.-M. (2003). Foreign-language experience in infancy: Effects of short-term exposure and social interaction on phonetic learning. *Proceedings of the National Academy of Sciences, 100,* 9096–9101.

Kuhl, P. K., Williams, K. A., Lacerda, F., Stevens, K. N., & Lindblom, B. (1992). Linguistic experience alters phonetic perception in infants by 6 months of age. *Science, 255,* 606–608.

Kuhn, D. (1989). Children and adults as intuitive scientists. *Psychological Review, 96,* 674–689.

Kuhn, D. (1993). Connecting scientific and informal reasoning. *Merrill-Palmer Quarterly, 39,* 74–103.

Kuhn, D. (1995). Microgenetic study of change: What has it told us? *Psychological Science, 6,* 133–139.

Kuhn, D. (2000). Why development does (and does not) occur: Evidence from the domain of inductive reasoning. In R. Siegler & J. McClelland (Eds.), *Mechanisms of cognitive development* (pp. 221–249). Mahwah, NJ: Erlbaum.

Kuhn, D. (2002). What is scientific thinking, and how does it develop? In U. Goswami (Ed.), *Blackwell handbook of childhood cognitive development* (pp. 371–393). Malden, MA: Blackwell.

Kuhn, D. (2008). Formal operations from a twenty-first century perspective. *Human Development, 51,* 48–55.

Kuhn, D. (2009). Adolescent thinking. In R. M. Lerner & L. Steinberg (Eds.), *Handbook of adolescent psychology, Vol. 1: Individual bases of adolescent development* (3rd ed., pp. 152–186). Hoboken, NJ: Wiley.

Kuhn, D., Amsel, E., & O'Loughlin, M. (1988). *The development of scientific thinking skills.* Orlando, FL: Academic Press.

Kuhn, D., & Dean, D., Jr. (2004). Connecting scientific reasoning and causal inference. *Journal of Cognition and Development, 5,* 261–288.

Kuhn, D., Iordanou, K., Pease, M., & Wirkala, C. (2008). Beyond control of variables: What needs to develop to achieve skilled scientific thinking? *Cognitive Development, 23,* 435–451.

Kuhn, D., & Pearsall, S. (2000). Developmental origins of scientific thinking. *Journal of Cognition and Development, 1,* 113–129.

Kuhn, D., & Pease, M. (2006). Do children and adults learn differently? *Journal of Cognition and Development, 7,* 279–293.

Kuklinski, M. R., & Weinstein, R. S. (2001). Classroom and developmental differences in a path model of teacher expectancy effects. *Child Development, 72,* 1554–1578.

Kumar, S., & O'Brien, A. (2004). Recent developments in fetal medicine. *British Medical Journal, 328,* 1002–1006.

Kunina, O., Wilhelm, O., Formazin, M., Jonkmann, K., & Schroeders, U. (2007). Extended criteria and predictors in college admission: Exploring the structure of study success and investigating the validity of domain knowledge. *Psychology Science, 49,* 88–114.

Kunkel, D. (2001). Children and television advertising. In D. G. Singer & J. L. Singer (Eds.), *Handbook of children and the media* (pp. 375–393). Thousand Oaks, CA: Sage.

Kunnen, E. S., & Bosma, H. A. (2003). Fischer's skill theory applied to identity development: A response to Kroger. *Identity, 3,* 247–270.

Kuppens, S., Grietens, H., Onghena, P., & Michiels, D. (2009). Associations between parental control and children's overt and relational aggression. *British Journal of Developmental Psychology, 27,* 607–623.

Kurdek, L. A., & Fine, M. A. (1994). Family acceptance and family control as predictors of adjustment in young adolescents: Linear, curvilinear, or interactive effects? *Child Development, 65,* 1137–1146.

Kurtz-Costes, B., Rowley, S. J., Harris-Britt, A., & Woods, T. A. (2008). Gender stereotypes about mathematics and science and self-perceptions of ability in late childhood and early adolescence. *Merrill-Palmer Quarterly, 54,* 386–409.

Kyratzis, A., & Guo, J. (2001). Preschool girls' and boys' verbal conflict strategies in the United States and China. *Research on Language and Social Interaction, 34,* 45–74.

La Greca, A. M., Prinstein, M. J., & Fetter, M. D. (2001). Adolescent peer crowd affiliation: Linkages with health-risk behaviors and close friendships. *Journal of Pediatric Psychology, 26,* 131–143.

Lachance, J. A., & Mazzocco, M. M. M. (2006). A longitudinal analysis of sex differences in math and spatial skills in primary school age children. *Learning and Individual Differences, 16,* 195–216.

Lackey, P. N. (1989). Adults' attitudes about assignments of household chores to male and female children. *Sex Roles, 20,* 271–281.

Lacourse, E., Nagin, D., Tremblay, R. E., Vitaro, F., & Claes, M. (2003). Developmental trajectories of boys' delinquent group membership and facilitation of violent behaviors during adolescence. *Development and Psychopathology, 15,* 183–197.

Ladd, G. W. (2005). *Children's peer relationships and social competence: A century of progress.* New Haven, CT: Yale University Press.

Ladd, G. W., Birch, S. H., & Buhs, E. S. (1999). Children's social and scholastic lives in kindergarten: Related spheres of influence? *Child Development, 70,* 1373–1400.

Ladd, G. W., Buhs, E. S., & Seid, M. (2000). Children's initial sentiments about kindergarten: Is school liking an antecedent of early classroom participation and achievement? *Merrill-Palmer Quarterly, 46,* 255–279.

Ladd, G. W., & Burgess, K. B. (1999). Charting the relationship trajectories of aggressive, withdrawn, and aggressive/ withdrawn children during early grade school. *Child Development, 70,* 910–929.

Ladd, G. W., Herald, S. L., & Kochel, K. P. (2006). School readiness: Are there social prerequisites? *Early Education and Development, 17,* 115–150.

Ladd, G. W., Kochenderfer-Ladd, B., Eggum, N. D., Kochel, K. P., & McConnell, E. M. (2011). Characterizing and comparing the friendships of anxious-solitary and unsociable preadolescents. *Child Development, 82,* 1434–1453.

Ladd, G. W., & Pettit, G. S. (2002). Parenting and the development of children's peer relationships. In M. Bornstein (Ed.), *Handbook of parenting* (2nd ed.). Mahwah, NJ: Erlbaum.

Ladd, G. W., LeSieur, K., & Profilet, S. M. (1993). Direct parental influences on young children's peer relations. In S. Duck (Ed.), *Learning about relationships* (Vol. 2, pp. 152–183). London: Sage.

LaFraniere, S. (2011, April 6). As China ages, birthrate policy may prove difficult to reverse. *New York Times.* Retrieved from www.nytimes.com/2011/04/07/world/ asia/07population.html?pagewanted=all

Lagattuta, K. H., Wellman, H. M., & Flavell, J. H. (1997). Preschoolers' understanding of the link between thinking and feeling: Cognitive cuing and emotional change. *Child Development, 68,* 1081–1104.

Lagercrantz, H., & Slotkin, T. A. (1986). The "stress" of being born. *Scientific American, 254,* 100–107.

Lagnado, L. (2001, November 2). Kids confront Trade Center trauma. *The Wall Street Journal,* pp. B1, B6.

Laible, D. (2004). Mother–child discourse in two contexts: Links with child temperament, attachment security, and socioemotional competence. *Developmental Psychology, 40,* 979–992.

Laible, D. (2007). Attachment with parents and peers in late adolescence: Links with emotional competence and social behavior. *Personality and Individual Differences, 43,* 1185–1197.

Laible, D., & Song, J. (2006). Constructing emotional and relational understanding: The role of affect and mother–child discourse. *Merrill-Palmer Quarterly, 52,* 44–69.

Laible, D. J., & Thompson, R. A. (2002). Mother–child conflict in the toddler years: Lessons in emotion, morality, and relationships. *Child Development, 73,* 1187–1203.

Laing, E., Butterworth, G., Ansari, D., Gsödl, M., Longhi, E., Panagiotaki, G., et al. (2002). Atypical development of language and social communication in toddlers with Williams syndrome. *Developmental Science, 5,* 233–246.

Laird, R. D., Jordan, K. Y., Dodge, K. A., Pettit, G. S., & Bates, J. E. (2001). Peer rejection in childhood, involvement with antisocial peers in early adolescence, and the development of externalizing behavior problems. *Development and Psychopathology, 13,* 337–354.

Laird, R. D., Pettit, G. S., Bates, J. E., & Dodge, K. A. (2003). Parents' monitoring-relevant knowledge and adolescents' delinquent behavior: Evidence of correlated developmental changes and reciprocal influences. *Child Development, 74,* 752–768.

Lalonde, C. E., & Chandler, M. J. (1995). False-belief understanding goes to school: On the social-emotional consequences of coming early or late to a first theory of mind. *Cognition and Emotion, 9,* 167–185.

Lalonde, C. E., & Chandler, M. J. (2002). Children's understanding of interpretation. *New Ideas in Psychology, 20,* 163–198.

Lalonde, C. E., & Chandler, M. J. (2005). Culture, selves, and time: Theories of personal persistence in native and non-native youth. In C. Lightfoot, C. Lalonde, & M. Chandler (Eds.), *Changing conceptions of psychological life* (pp. 207–229). Mahwah, NJ: Erlbaum.

Lamarche, V., Brendgen, M., Boivin, M., Vitaro, F., Perusse, D., & Dionne, G. (2006). Do friendships and sibling relationships provide protection against peer victimization in a similar way? *Social Development, 15,* 373–393.

Lamaze, F. (1958). *Painless childbirth.* London: Burke.

Lamb, L. M., Bigler, R. S., Liben, L. S., & Green, V. A. (2009). Teaching children to confront peers' sexist remarks: Implications for theories of gender development and educational practice. *Sex Roles, 61,* 361–382.

Lamb, M. E., & Ahnert, L. (2006). Nonparental child care: Context, concepts, correlates, and consequences. In K. A. Renninger & I. E. Sigel (Eds.), *Handbook of child psychology: Vol. 4. Child psychology in practice* (6th ed., pp. 700–778). Hoboken, NJ: Wiley.

Lamb, M. E., & Lewis, C. (2004). The development and significance of father–child relationships in two-parent families. In M. E. Lamb (Ed.), *The role of the father in child development* (4th ed., pp. 272–306). Hoboken, NJ: Wiley.

Lamb, M. E., & Oppenheim, D. (1989). Fatherhood and father–child relationships: Five years of research. In S. H. Cath, A. Gurwitt, & L. Gunsberg (Eds.), *Fathers and their families* (pp. 11–26). Hillsdale, NJ: Erlbaum.

Lamb, M. E., Thompson, R. A., Gardner, W., Charnov, E. L., & Connell, J. P. (1985). *Infant–mother attachment: The origins and developmental significance of individual differences in Strange Situation behavior.* Hillsdale, NJ: Erlbaum.

Lancaster, J. B., & Whitten, P. (1980). Family matters. *The Sciences, 20,* 10–15.

Landry, S. H., Smith, K. E., Swank, P. R., & Miller-Loncar, C. L. (2000). Early maternal and child influences on children's later independent cognitive and social functioning. *Child Development, 71,* 358–375.

Lang, M. (2010). Can mentoring assist in the school-to-work transition? *Education + Training, 52,* 359–367.

Langer, J., Gillette, P., & Arriaga, R. I. (2003). Toddlers' cognition of adding and subtracting objects in action and in perception. *Cognitive Development, 18,* 233–246.

Langhinrichsen-Rohling, J., Friend, J., & Powell, A. (2009). Adolescent suicide, gender, and culture: A rate and risk factor analysis. *Aggression and Violent Behavior, 14,* 402–414.

Langlois, J. H., & Downs, A. C. (1980). Mothers, fathers, and peers as socialization agents of sex-typed play behaviors in young children. *Child Development, 51,* 1237–1247.

Lanphear, B., Hornung, R., Khoury, J., Yolton, K., Baghurst, P., Bellinger, D., et al. (2005). Low-level environmental lead exposure and children's intellectual function: An international pooled analysis. *Environmental Health Perspectives, 113,* 894–899.

Lansford, J. E. (2009). Parental divorce and children's adjustment. *Perspectives on Psychological Science, 4,* 140–152.

Lansford, J. E., Chang, L., Dodge, K. A., Malone, P. S., Oburu, P., & Palmerus, K. (2005). Physical discipline and children's adjustment: Cultural normativeness as a moderator. *Child Development, 76,* 1234–1246.

Lansford, J. E., Criss, M. M., Dodge, K. A., Shaw, D. S., Pettit, G. S., & Bates, J. E. (2009). Trajectories of physical discipline: Early childhood antecedents and developmental outcomes. *Child Development, 80,* 1385–1402.

Lansford, J. E., Criss, M. M., Laird, R. D., Shaw, D. S., Pettit, G. S., Bates, J. E., et al. (2011). Reciprocal relations between parents' physical discipline and children's externalizing behavior during middle childhood and adolescence. *Development and Psychopathology, 23,* 225–238.

Lansford, J. E., Criss, M. M., Pettit, G. S., Dodge, K. A., & Bates, J. E. (2003). Friendship quality, peer group affiliation, and peer antisocial behavior as moderators of the link between negative parenting and adolescent externalizing behavior. *Journal of Research on Adolescence, 13,* 161–184.

Lansford, J. E., Deater-Deckard, K., Dodge, K. A., Bates, J. E., & Pettit, G. S. (2004). Ethnic differences in the link between physical punishment by parents: An updated literature review. *Clinical Child and Family Psychology Review, 3,* 199–221.

Lansford, J. E., Malone, P. S., Castellino, D. R., Dodge, K. A., Pettit, G. S., & Bates, J. E. (2006a). Trajectories of internalizing, externalizing, and grades for children who have and have not experienced their parents' divorce or separation. *Journal of Family Psychology, 20,* 292–301.

Lansford, J. E., Malone, P. S., Dodge, K. A., Pettit, G. S., & Bates, J. E. (2010). Developmental cascades of peer rejection, social information processing biases, and aggression during middle childhood. *Development and Psychopathology, 22,* 593–602.

Lansford, J. E., Putallaz, M., Grimes, C. L., Schiro-Osman, K. A., Kupersmidt, J. B., & Coie, J. D. (2006b). Perceptions of friendship quality and observed behaviors with friends: How do sociometrically rejected, average, and popular girls differ? *Merrill-Palmer Quarterly, 52,* 694–720.

Laranjo, J., Bernier, A., Meins, E., & Carlson, S. M. (2010). Early manifestations of children's theory of mind: The roles of maternal mind-mindedness and infant security of attachment. *Infancy, 15,* 300–323.

Lareau, A. (2003). *Unequal childhoods: Class, race, and family life.* Berkeley, CA: University of California Press.

Larkin, S. (2010). *Metacognition in young children.* London: Routledge.

Larsen, J. A., & Nippold, M. A. (2007). Morphological analysis in school-age children: Dynamic assessment of a word learning strategy. *Language, Speech, and Hearing Services in Schools, 38,* 201–212.

Larsen, J. T., To, Y. M., & Fireman, G. (2007). Childen's understanding and experience of mixed emotions. *Psychological Science, 18,* 186–191.

Larson, R. W. (2001). How U.S. children and adolescents spend time: What it does (and doesn't) tell us about their development. *Current Directions in Psychological Science, 10,* 160–164.

Larson, R. W., & Ham, M. (1993). Stress and "storm and stress" in early adolescence: The relationship of negative events with dysphoric affect. *Developmental Psychology, 29,* 130–140.

Larson, R. W., & Lampman-Petraitis, C. (1989). Daily emotional states as reported by children and adolescents. *Child Development, 60,* 1250–1260.

Larson, R. W., Moneta, G., Richards, M. H., & Wilson, S. (2002). Continuity, stability, and change in daily emotional experience across adolescence. *Child Development, 73,* 1151–1165.

Larson, R. W., & Richards, M. (1998). Waiting for the weekend: Friday and Saturday night as the emotional climax of the week. In A. C. Crouter & R. Larson (Eds.), *Temporal rhythms in adolescence: Clocks, calendars, and the coordination of daily life* (pp. 37–51). San Francisco: Jossey-Bass.

Larson, R. W., Richards, M. H., Moneta, G., Holmbeck, G., & Duckett, E. (1996). Changes in adolescents' daily interactions with their families from ages 10 to 18: Disengagement and transformation. *Developmental Psychology, 32,* 744–754.

Larson, R. W., Richards, M. H., Sims, B., & Dworkin, J. (2001). How urban African-American young adolescents spend their time: Time budgets for locations, activities, and companionship. *American Journal of Community Psychology, 29,* 565–597.

Larzelere, R. E., Schneider, W. N., Larson, D. B., & Pike, P. L. (1996). The effects of discipline responses in delaying toddler misbehavior recurrences. *Child and Family Behavior Therapy, 18,* 35–57.

Lashley, F. R. (2007). Essentials of clinical genetics in nursing practice. New York: Springer.

Latz, S., Wolf, A. W., & Lozoff, B. (1999). Sleep practices and problems in young children in Japan and the United States. *Archives of Pediatric and Adolescent Medicine, 153,* 339–346.

Laucht, M., Esser, G., & Schmidt, M. H. (1997). Developmental outcome of infants born with biological and psychosocial risks. *Journal of Child Psychology and Psychiatry, 38,* 843–853.

Lauer, P. A., Akiba, M., Wilkerson, S. B., Apthorp, H. S., Snow, D., & Martin-Glenn, M. (2006). Out-of-school time programs: A meta-analysis of effects for at-risk students. *Review of Educational Research, 76,* 275–313.

Laupa, M. (1995). "Who's in charge?" Preschool children's concepts of authority. *Early Childhood Research Quarterly, 9,* 1–7.

Laursen, B., Bukowski, W. M., Aunola, K., & Nurmi, J.-E. (2007). Friendship moderates prospective associations between social isolation and adjustment problems in young children. *Child Development, 78,* 1395–1404.

Laursen, B., Bukowski, W. M., Aunola, K., & Nurmi, J.-E. (2007). Friendship moderates prospective associations between social isolation and adjustment problems in young children. *Child Development, 78,* 1395–1404.

Laursen, B., & Collins, W. A. (2009). Parent–child relationships during adolescence. In R. M. Lerner (Ed.), *Handbook of adolescent psychology: Vol. 2. Contextual influences on adolescent development* (3rd ed., pp. 3–42). Hoboken, NJ: Wiley.

Laursen, B., Coy, K. C., & Collins, W. A. (1998). Reconsidering changes in parent–child conflict across adolescence: A meta-analysis. *Child Development, 69,* 817–832.

Lavelli, M., & Fogel, A. (2005). Developmental changes in the relationship between the infant's attention and emotion during early face-to-face communication: The 2-month transition. *Developmental Psychology, 41,* 265–280.

Law, K. L., Stroud, L. R., Niaura, R., LaGasse, L. L., Liu, J., & Lester, B. M. (2003). Smoking during pregnancy and newborn neurobehavior. *Pediatrics, 111,* 1318–1323.

Lawn, J. E., Mwansa-Kambafwile, J., Horta, B. L., Barros, F. C., & Cousens, S. (2010). 'Kangaroo mother care' to prevent neonatal deaths due to preterm birth complications. *International Journal of Epidemiology, 39,* i144–i154.

Lawrence, A., Lewis, L., Hofmeyr, G. J., Dowswell, T., & Styles, C. (2009). Maternal positions and mobility during the first stage labour. *Cochrane Database of Systematic Reviews,* Issue 2. Art. No. CD003934.

Lawrence, K., Kuntsi, J., Coleman, M., Campbell, R., & Skuse, D. (2003). Face and emotion recognition deficits in Turner syndrome: A possible role for X-linked genes in amygdala development. *Neuropsychology, 17,* 39–49.

Lazar, I., & Darlington, R. (1982). Lasting effects of early education: A report from the Consortium for Longitudinal Studies. *Monographs of the Society for Research in Child Development, 47*(2–3, Serial No. 195).

Lazarus, R. S., & Lazarus, B. N. (1994). *Passion and reason.* New York: Oxford University Press.

Lazinski, M. J., Shea, A. K., & Steiner, M. (2008). Effects of maternal prenatal stress on offspring development: A commentary. *Archives of Women's Mental Health, 11,* 363–375.

Le Grand, R., Mondloch, C. J., Maurer, D., & Brent, H. P. (2003). Expert face processing requires input to the right hemisphere during infancy. *Nature Neuroscience, 6,* 1108–1112.

Leadbeater, B., & Hoglund, W. (2006). Changing the social contexts of peer victimization. *Journal of the Canadian Academy of Child and Adolescent Psychiatry, 15,* 21–26.

Leaper, C. (1994). Exploring the correlates and consequences of gender segregation: Social relationships in childhood, adolescence, and adulthood. In C. Leaper (Ed.), *New directions for child development* (No. 65, pp. 67–86). San Francisco: Jossey-Bass.

Leaper, C. (2000). Gender, affiliation, assertion, and the interactive context of parent–child play. *Developmental Psychology, 36,* 381–393.

Leaper, C. (2002). Parenting girls and boys. In M. H. Bornstein (Ed.), *Handbook of parenting: Vol. 1. Children and parenting* (pp. 127–152). Mahwah, NJ: Erlbaum.

Leaper, C., Anderson, K. J., & Sanders, P. (1998). Moderators of gender effects on parents' talk to their children: A meta-analysis. *Developmental Psychology, 34,* 3–27.

Leaper, C., & Friedman, C. K. (2007). The socialization of gender. In J. E. Grusec & P. D. Hastings (Eds.), *Handbook of socialization: Theory and research* (pp. 561–587). New York: Guilford.

Leaper, C., & Tenenbaum, H. R., & Shaffer, T. G. (1999). Communication patterns of African-American girls and boys from low-income, urban backgrounds. *Child Development, 70,* 1489–1503.

Learmonth, A. E., Lamberth, R., & Rovee-Collier, C. (2004). Generalization of deferred imitation during the first year of life. *Journal of Experimental Child Psychology, 88,* 297–318.

Lecanuet, J.-P., Granier-Deferre, C., & DeCasper, A. (2005). Are we expecting too much from prenatal sensory experiences? In B. Hopkins & S. P. Johnson (Eds.), *Prenatal development of postnatal functions* (pp. 31–49). Westport, CT: Praeger.

Lecanuet, J.-P., Granier-Deferre, C., Jacquet, A.-Y., Capponi, I., & Ledru, L. (1993). Prenatal discrimination of a male and female voice uttering the same sentence. *Early Development and Parenting, 2,* 217–228.

Lecce, S., Zocchi, S., Pagnin, A., Palladino, P., & Taumoepeau, M. (2010). Reading minds: The relation between children's mental state knowledge and their metaknowledge about reading. *Child Development, 81,* 1876–1893.

Lecuyer, E., & Houck, G. M. (2006). Maternal limit-setting in toddlerhood: Socialization strategies for the development of self-regulation. *Infant Mental Health Journal, 27,* 344–370.

Lee, C.-Y. S., & Doherty, W. J. (2007). Marital satisfaction and father involvement during the transition to parenthood. *Fathering, 5,* 75–96.

Lee, J. M., Appulgiese, D., Kaciroti, N., Corwyn, R. F., Bradley, R. H., & Lumeng, J. C. (2007). Weight status in young girls and the onset of puberty. *Pediatrics, 119,* e624–e630.

Lee, K., Cameron, C. A., Xu, F., Fu, G., & Board, J. (1997). Chinese and Canadian children's evaluations of lying and truth telling: Similarities and differences in the context of pro- and antisocial behaviors. *Child Development, 68,* 924–934.

Lee, K., Xu, F., Fu, G., Cameron, C. A., & Chen, S. (2001). Taiwan and Mainland Chinese and Canadian children's categorization and evaluation of lie- and truth-telling: A modesty effect. *British Journal of Developmental Psychology, 19,* 525–542.

Lee, S. J., Ralston, H. J., Partridge, J. C., & Rosen, M. A. (2005). Fetal pain: A systematic multidisciplinary review of the evidence. *Journal of the American Medical Association, 294,* 947–954.

Lee, V. E. (2000). School size and the organization of secondary school. In M. T. Hallinan (Ed.), *Handbook of the sociology of education* (pp. 327–344). New York: Kluwer Academic.

Lee, V. E., & Burkam, D. T. (2002). *Inequality at the starting gate.* Washington, DC: Economic Policy Institute.

Leech, S. L., Day, N. L., Richardson, G. A., & Goldschmidt, L. (2003). Predictors of self-reported delinquent behavior in a sample of young adolescents. *Journal of Early Adolescence, 23,* 78–106.

Leeman, L. W., Gibbs, J. C., & Fuller, D. (1993). Evaluation of a multicomponent group treatment program for juvenile delinquents. *Aggressive Behavior, 19,* 281–292.

Leerkes, E. M. (2010). Predictors of maternal sensitivity to infant distress. *Parenting: Science and Practice, 10,* 219–239.

Leet, T., & Flick, L. (2003). Effect of exercise on birth weight. *Clinical Obstetrics and Gynecology, 46,* 423–431.

Legerstee, M., Barna, J., & DiAdamo, C. (2000). Precursors to the development of intention at 6 months: Understanding people and their actions. *Developmental Psychology, 36,* 627–634.

Legerstee, M., & Markova, G. (2007). Intentions make a difference: Infant responses to still-face and modified still-face conditions. *Infant Behavior and Development, 30,* 232–250.

Lehman, D. R., & Nisbett, R. E. (1990). A longitudinal study of the effects of undergraduate training on reasoning. *Developmental Psychology, 26,* 952–960.

Lehman, M., & Hasselhorn, M. (2007). Variable memory strategy use in children's adaptive intratask learning behavior: Developmental changes and working memory influences in free recall. *Child Development, 78,* 1068–1082.

Lehman, M., & Hasselhorn, M. (2010). The dynamics of free recall and their relation to rehearsal between 8 and 10 years of age. *Child Development, 81,* 1006–1020.

Lehr, V. T., Zeskind, P. S., Ofenstein, J. P., Cepeda, E., Warrier, I., & Aranda, J. V. (2007). Neonatal facial coding system scores and spectral characteristics of infant crying during newborn circumcision. *Clinical Journal of Pain, 23,* 417–424.

Leinbach, M. D., Hort, B. E., & Fagot, B. I. (1997). Bears are for boys: Metaphorical associations in young children's gender stereotypes. *Cognitive Development, 12,* 107–130.

Leman, P. J. (2005). Authority and moral reasons: Parenting style and children's perceptions of adult rule justifications. *International Journal of Behavioral Development, 29,* 265–270.

Lemche, E., Lennertz, I., Orthmann, C., Ari, A., Grote, K., Hafker, J., & Klann-Delius, G. (2003). Emotion-regulatory process in evoked play narratives: Their relation with mental representations and family interactions. *Praxis der Kinderpsychologie und Kinderpsychiatrie, 52,* 156–171.

Lempert, H. (1990). Acquisition of passives: The role of patient animacy, salience, and lexical accessibility. *Journal of Child Language, 17,* 677–696.

Lengua, L. J., Wolchik, S., Sandler, I. N., & West, S. G. (2000). The additive and interactive effects of parenting and temperament in predicting problems of children of divorce. *Journal of Clinical Psychology, 29,* 232–244.

Lenhart, A., Ling, R., Campbell, S., & Purcell, K. (2010). *Teens and mobile phones.* Washington, DC: Pew Internet & American Life Project.

Lenroot, R. K., & Giedd, J. N. (2006). Brain development in children and adolescents: Insights from anatomical magnetic resonance imaging. *Neuroscience and Biobehavioral Reviews, 30,* 718–729.

Leon, K. (2003). Risk and protective factors in young children's adjustment to parental divorce: A review of the research. *Family Relations, 52,* 258–270.

Lepage, J.-F., & Théoret, H. (2007). The mirror neuron system: Grasping others' actions from birth? *Developmental Science, 10,* 513–523.

Lephart, E. D., Call, S. B., Rhees, R. W., Jacobson, N. A., Weber, K. S., Bledsoe, J., & Teuscher, C. (2001). Neuroendocrine regulation of sexually dimorphic brain structure and associated sexual behavior in male rats is genetically controlled. *Biological Reproduction, 64,* 571–578.

Lerman, R. I. (2010). Capabilities and contributions of unwed fathers. *Future of Children, 20*, 63–85.

Lerner, R. M. (2006). Developmental science, developmental systems, and contemporary theories of human development. In R. M. Lerner (Ed.), *Handbook of child psychology: Vol. 1. Theoretical models of human development* (6th ed., pp. 1–17). Hoboken, NJ: Wiley.

Lerner, R. M., & Overton, W. F. (2008). Exemplifying the integrations of the relational developmental system. *Journal of Adolescent Research, 23*, 245–255.

Leslie, A. M. (2004). Who's for learning? *Developmental Science, 7*, 417–419.

Lester, B. M. (1985). Introduction: There's more to crying than meets the ear. In B. M. Lester & C. F. Z. Boukydis (Eds.), *Infant crying* (pp. 1–27). New York: Plenum.

Lester, B. M., & Lagasse, L. L. (2010). Children of addicted women. *Journal of Addictive Diseases, 29*, 259–276.

Lester, B. M., Kotelchuck, M., Spelke, E., Sellers, M. J., & Klein, R. E. (1974). Separation protest in Guatemalan infants: Cross-cultural and cognitive findings. *Developmental Psychology, 10*, 79–85.

Lester, B. M., LaGasse, L. L., Shankaran, S., Bada, H. S., Bauer, C. R., Lin, R., et al. (2010). Prenatal cocaine exposure related to cortisol stress reactivity in 11-year-old children. *Journal of Pediatrics, 157*, 288–295.

Lester, B. M., Masten, A. S., & McEwen, B. (Eds.). (2006). *Resilience in children.* New York: Annals of the New York Academy of Sciences.

Lester, B. M., & Tronick, E. Z. (2004). *NICU Network Neurobehavioral Scale (NNNS).* Baltimore, MD: Brookes.

Lett, D. (1997). *L'enfant des miracles: Enfance et société au Moyen Age, XIIe–XIIIe siecles.* Paris: Aubier.

LeVay, S. (1993). *The sexual brain.* Cambridge, MA: MIT Press.

Leventhal, T., & Brooks-Gunn, J. (2003). Children and youth in neighborhood contexts. *Current Directions in Psychological Science, 12*, 27–31.

Leventhal, T., Dupere, V., & Brooks-Gunn, J. (2009). Neighborhood influences on adolescent development. In R. M. Lerner & L. Steinberg (Eds.), *Handbook of adolescent psychology: Vol. 2* (3rd ed., pp. 411–443). Hoboken, NJ: Wiley.

Levi, J., Vinter, S., Richardson, L., St. Laurent, R., & Segal, L. M. (2009). *F as in fat: How obesity policies are failing in America.* Washington, DC: Trust for America's Health.

Levin, I., & Bus, A. G. (2003). How is emergent writing based on drawing? Analyses of children's products and their sorting by children and mothers. *Developmental Psychology, 39*, 891–905.

Levine, L. E. (1983). Mine: Self-definition in 2-year-old boys. *Developmental Psychology, 19*, 544–549.

Levine, L. J. (1995). Young children's understanding of the causes of anger and sadness. *Child Development, 66*, 697–709.

LeVine, R. A., Dixon, S., LeVine, S., Richman, A., Leiderman, P. H., Keefer, C. H., & Brazelton, T. B. (1994). *Child care and culture: Lessons from Africa.* New York: Cambridge University Press.

Levine, S. C., Huttenlocher, J., Taylor, A., & Langrock, A. (1999). Early sex differences in spatial skill. *Developmental Psychology, 35*, 940–949.

Levtzion-Korach, O., Tennenbaum, A., Schnitzer, R., & Ornoy, A. (2000). Early motor development of blind children. *Journal of Paediatric and Child Health, 36*, 226–229.

Levy, G. D., Taylor, M. G., & Gelman, S. A. (1995). Traditional and evaluative aspects of flexibility in gender roles, social conventions, moral rules, and physical laws. *Child Development, 66*, 515–531.

Levy, S. R., & Dweck, C. S. (1999). The impact of children's static vs. dynamic conceptions of people on stereotype formation. *Child Development, 70*, 1163–1180.

Levy-Shiff, R., & Israelashvili, R. (1988). Antecedents of fathering: Some further exploration. *Developmental Psychology, 24*, 434–440.

Lew, A. R., & Butterworth, G. (1997). The development of hand–mouth coordination in 2- to 5-month-old infants: Similarities with reaching and grasping. *Infant Behavior and Development, 20*, 59–69.

Lewis, K. G. (2009). *Why don't you understand? A gender relationship dictionary.* Indianapolis: Dog Ear Publishing.

Lewis, M. (1992). *Shame: The exposed self.* New York: Free Press.

Lewis, M. (1995). Embarrassment: The emotion of self-exposure and evaluation. In J. P. Tangney & K. W. Fischer (Eds.), *Self-conscious emotions* (pp. 198–218). New York: Guilford.

Lewis, M. (1998). Emotional competence and development. In D. Pushkar, W. M. Bukowski, A. E. Schwartzman, E. M. Stack, & D. R. White (Eds.), *Improving competence across the lifespan* (pp. 27–36). New York: Plenum.

Lewis, M. (1999). The role of the self in cognition and emotion. In T. Dalgleish & M. J. Power (Eds.), *Handbook of cognition and emotion* (pp. 125–142). Chichester, UK: Wiley.

Lewis, M., Alessandri, S. M., & Sullivan, M. W. (1992). Differences in shame and pride as a function of children's gender and task difficulty. *Child Development, 63*, 630–638.

Lewis, M., & Brooks-Gunn, J. (1979). *Social cognition and the acquisition of self.* New York: Plenum.

Lewis, M., & Ramsay, D. (2004). Development of self-recognition, personal pronoun use, and pretend play during the 2nd year. *Child Development, 75*, 1821–1831.

Lewis, M., Ramsay, D. S., & Kawakami, K. (1993). Differences between Japanese infants and Caucasian American infants in behavioral and cortisol response to inoculation. *Child Development, 64*, 1722–1731.

Lewis, M., Sullivan, M. W., & Ramsay, D. S. (1992). Individual differences in anger and sad expressions during extinction: Antecedents and consequences. *Infant Behavior and Development, 15*, 443–452.

Lewis, M., Sullivan, M. W., Stanger, C., & Weiss, M. (1989). Self development and self-conscious emotions. *Child Development, 60*, 146–156.

Lewis, M., Sullivan, M. W., & Vasen, A. (1987). Making faces: Age and emotion differences in the posing of emotional expressions. *Developmental Psychology, 23*, 690–697.

Lewis, M. D. (2000). The promise of dynamic systems approaches for an integrated account of human development. *Child Development, 71*, 36–43.

Lewis, M. D. (2008). Emotional habits in brain and behavior: A window on personality development. In A. Fogel, B. J. King, & S. G. Shanker (Eds.), *Human development in the twenty-first century* (pp. 72–80). New York: Cambridge University Press.

Lewis, T. L., & Maurer, D. (2005). Multiple sensitive periods in human visual development: Evidence from visually deprived children. *Developmental Psychobiology, 46*, 163–183.

Lewontin, R. (1976). Race and intelligence. In N. J. Block & G. Dworkin (Eds.), *The IQ controversy* (pp. 78–92). New York: Pantheon Books.

Lewontin, R. (1995). *Human diversity.* New York: Freeman.

Lewontin, R. (2003). *Race: The power of an illusion.* Alexandria, VA: Public Broadcasting System. Retrieved from www.pbs.org/race

Li, D.-K., Willinger, M., Petitti, D. B., Odouli, R., Liu, L., & Hoffman, H. J. (2006). Use of a dummy (pacifier) during sleep and risk of sudden infant death syndrome (SIDS): Population based case-control study. *British Medical Journal, 332*, 18–21.

Li, S.-C., Lindenberger, U., Hommel, B., Aschersleben, G., Prinz, W., & Baltes, P. B. (2004). Transformation in the couplings among intellectual abilities and constituent cognitive processes across the life span. *Psychological Science, 15*, 155–163.

Liau, A. K., Barriga, A. Q., & Gibbs, J. C. (1998). Relations between self-serving cognitive distortion and overt vs. covert antisocial behavior in adolescents. *Aggressive Behavior, 24*, 335–346.

Liben, L. S.(2006). Education for spatial thinking. In K. A. Renninger & I. E. Sigel (Eds.), *Handbook of child psychology: Vol. 4. Child psychology in practice* (6th ed., pp. 197–247). Hoboken, NJ: Wiley.

Liben, L. S. (2009). The road to understanding maps. *Current Directions in Psychological Science, 18*, 310–315.

Liben, L. S., & Bigler, R. S. (2002). The developmental course of gender differentiation: Conceptualizing, measuring, and evaluating constructs and pathways. *Monographs of the Society for Research in Child Development, 67*(2, Serial No. 269).

Liben, L. S., Bigler, R. S., & Krogh, H. R. (2001). Pink and blue collar jobs: Children's judgments of job status and job aspirations in relation to sex of worker. *Journal of Experimental Child Psychology, 79*, 346–363.

Liben, L. S., Bigler, R. S., & Krogh, H. R. (2002). Language at work: Children's gendered interpretations of occupational titles. *Child Development, 73*, 810–828.

Liben, L. S., & Downs, R. M. (1993). Understanding person-space-map relations: Cartographic and developmental perspectives. *Developmental Psychology, 29*, 739–752.

Liben, L. S., Kastens, K. A., & Stevenson, L. M. (2002). Real-world knowledge through real-world maps: A developmental guide for navigating the educational terrain. *Developmental Review, 22*, 267–322.

Liben, L. S., & Signorella, M. L. (1993). Gender-schematic processing in children: The role of initial interpretations of stimuli. *Developmental Psychology, 29*, 141–149.

Lickona, T. (1976). Research on Piaget's theory of moral development. In T. Lickona (Ed.), *Moral development and behavior* (pp. 219–240). New York: Holt, Rinehart & Winston.

Lidstone, J. S. M., Meins, E., & Fernyhough, C. (2010). The roles of private speech and inner speech in planning during middle childhood: Evidence from a dual task paradigm. *Journal of Experimental Child Psychology, 107*, 438–451.

Lidz, C. S. (2001). Multicultural issues and dynamic assessment. In L. A. Suzuki & J. G. Ponterotto (Eds.), *Handbook of multicultural assessment: Clinical, psychological, and educational applications* (2nd ed., pp. 523–539). San Francisco: Jossey-Bass.

Lidz, J. (2007). The abstract nature of syntactic representations. In E. Hoff & M. Shatz (Eds.), *Blackwell handbook of language development* (pp. 277–303). Malden, MA: Blackwell.

Lidz, J., Gleitman, H., & Gleitman, L. (2004). Kidz in the 'hood: Syntactic bootstrapping and the mental lexicon. In D. G. Hall & S. R. Waxman (Eds.), *Weaving a lexicon* (pp. 603–636). Cambridge, MA: MIT Press.

Lieven, E., Pine, J., & Baldwin, G. (1997). Lexically based learning and early grammatical development. *Journal of Child Language, 24*, 187–220.

Light, P., & Perrett-Clermont, A. (1989). Social context effects in learning and testing. In A. R. H. Gellatly, D. Rogers, & J. Sloboda (Eds.), *Cognition and social worlds* (pp. 99–112). Oxford: Clarendon Press.

Li-Grining, C. P. (2007). Effortful control among low-income preschoolers in three cities: Stability, change, and individual differences. *Developmental Psychology, 43*, 208–221.

Lillard, A. (2003). Pretend play and cognitive development. In U. Goswami (Ed.), *Blackwell handbook of childhood cognitive development* (pp. 189–205). Malden, MA: Blackwell.

Lillard, A. (2007). *Montessori: The science behind the genius.* New York: Oxford University Press.

Lillard, A., & Else-Quest, N. (2006). Evaluating Montessori education. *Science, 313*, 1893–1894.

Lillard, A. S., & Witherington, D. (2004). Mothers' behavior modifications during pretense snacks and their possible signal value for toddlers. *Developmental Psychology, 40*, 95–113.

Lin, Z. L., Yu, H. M., Chen, S. Q., Liang, Z. Q., & Zhang, Z. Y. (2006). Mild hypothermia via selective head cooling as neuroprotective therapy in term neonates with perinatal asphyxia: An experience from a single neonatal intensive care unit. *Journal of Perinatology, 26*, 180–184.

Linares, T. J., Singer, L. T., Kirchner, H., Lester, H., Short, E. J., & Min, M. O. (2006). Mental health outcomes of cocaine-exposed children at 6 years of age. *Journal of Pediatric Psychology, 31*, 85–97.

Lindberg, S. M., Hyde, J. S., Linn, M. C., & Petersen, J. L. (2010). New trends in gender and mathematics performance: A meta-analysis. *Psychological Bulletin, 136*, 1123–1135.

Lindblad, F., & Hjern, A. (2010). ADHD after fetal exposure to maternal smoking. *Nicotine and Tobacco Research, 12*, 408–415.

Linder, J. R., & Collins, W. A. (2005). Parent and peer predictors of physical aggression and conflict management in romantic relationships in early adulthood. *Journal of Family Psychology, 19,* 252–262.

Lindsay-Hartz, J., de Rivera, J., & Mascolo, M. F. (1995). Differentiating guilt and shame and their effects on motivation. In J. P. Tangney & K. W. Fischer (Eds.), *Self-conscious emotions* (pp. 274–300). New York: Guilford.

Lindsey, D., & Martin, S. K. (2003). Deepening child poverty: The not so good news about welfare reform. *Children and Youth Services Review, 25,* 165–173.

Lindsey, E. W., & Colwell, M. J. (2003). Preschoolers' emotional competence: Links to pretend and physical play. *Child Study Journal, 33,* 39–52.

Lindsey, E. W., Colwell, M. J., Frabutt, J. M., Chambers, J. C., & MacKinnon-Lewis, C. (2008). Mother–child dyadic synchrony in European-American families during early adolescence: Relations with self-esteem and prosocial behavior. *Merrill-Palmer Quarterly, 54,* 289–315.

Lindsey, E. W., & Mize, J. (2000). Parent-child physical and pretense play: Links to children's social competence. *Merrill-Palmer Quarterly, 46,* 565–591.

Linebarger, D. L., Kosanic, A. Z., Greenwood, C. R., & Doku, N. S. (2004). Effects of viewing the television program *Between the Lions* on the emergent literacy skills of young children. *Journal of Educational Psychology, 96,* 297–308.

Linebarger, D. L., & Piotrowski, J. T. (2010). Structure and strategies in children's educational television: The roles of program type and learning strategies in children's learning. *Child Development, 81,* 1582–1597.

Linn, M. C., & Petersen, A. C. (1985). Emergence and characterization of sex differences in spatial ability: A meta-analysis. *Child Development, 56,* 1479–1498.

Linn, R. L., & Welner, K. G. (2007). *Race-conscious policies for assigning students to schools: Social science research and the Supreme Court cases.* Washington, DC: National Academy Press.

Linn, S. (2005). The commercialization of childhood. In S. Olfman (Ed.), *Childhood lost: How American culture is failing our kids* (pp. 107–122). Westport, CT: Praeger.

Linscheid, T. R., Budd, K. S., & Rasnake, L. K. (2005). Pediatric feeding problems. In M. C. Roberts (Ed.), *Handbook of pediatric psychology and psychiatry* (3rd ed., pp. 481–488). New York: Guilford.

Linver, M. R., Martin, A., & Brooks-Gunn, J. (2004). Measuring infants' home environment: The IT-HOME for infants between birth and 12 months in four national data sets. *Parenting: Science and Practice, 4,* 115–137.

Lipsitt, L. P. (2003). Crib death: A biobehavioral phenomenon? *Psychological Science, 12,* 164–170.

Lipton, J., & Spelke, E. (2004). Discrimination of large and small numerosities by human infants. *Infancy, 5,* 271–290.

Liszkowski, U., Carpenter, M., & Tomasello, M. (2008). Twelve-month-olds communicate helpfully and appropriately for knowledgeable and ignorant partners. *Cognition, 108,* 732–739.

Litovsky, R. Y., & Ashmead, D. H. (1997). Development of binaural and spatial hearing in infants and children. In R. H. Gilkey & T. R. Anderson (Eds.), *Binaural and spatial hearing in real and virtual environments* (pp. 571–592). Mahwah, NJ: Erlbaum.

Little, C., & Carter, A. S. (2005). Negative emotional reactivity and regulation in 12-month-olds following emotional challenge: Contributions of maternal-infant emotional availability in a low-income sample, *Infant Mental Health Journal, 26,* 354–368.

Little, T. D., Jones, S. M., Henrich, C. C., & Hawley, P. H. (2003). Disentangling the "whys" from the "whats" of aggressive behavior. *International Journal of Behavioral Development, 27,* 122–133.

Liu, D., Sabbagh, M. A., Gehring, W. J., & Wellman, H. M. (2009). Neural correlates of children's theory of mind development. *Child Development, 80,* 318–326.

Liu, H.-M., Kuhl, P. K., & Tsao, F.-M. (2003). An association between mothers' speech clarity and infants' speech discrimination skills. *Developmental Science, 6,* F1–F10.

Liu, J., Raine, A., Venables, P. H., Dalais, C., & Mednick, S. A. (2003). Malnutrition at age 3 years and lower cognitive ability at age 11 years. *Archives of Paediatric and Adolescent Medicine, 157,* 593–600.

Liu, L. L., Uttal, D. H., Marulis, L. M., & Newcombe, N. S. (2008). Training spatial skills: What works for whom, why and for how long? Poster presented at the annual meeting of the Association for Psychological Science, Chicago.

Lleras, C., & Rangel, C. (2009). Ability grouping practices in elementary school and African American/Hispanic achievement. *American Journal of Education, 115,* 279–304.

Lloyd, L. (1999). Multi-age classes and high ability students. *Review of Educational Research, 69,* 187–212.

Lloyd, M. E., Doydum, A. O., & Newcombe, N. S. (2009). Memory binding in early childhood: Evidence for a retrieval deficit. *Child Development, 80,* 1321–1328.

Lochman, J. E., & Dodge K. A. (1998). Distorted perceptions in dyadic interactions of aggressive and nonaggressive boys: Effects of prior expectations, context, and boys' age. *Development and Psychopathology, 10,* 495–512.

Lock, J., & Kirz, N. (2008). Eating disorders: Anorexia nervosa. In W. E. Craighead, D. J. Miklowitz, & L. W. Craighead (Eds.), *Psychopathology: History, diagnosis, and empirical foundations* (pp. 467–494). Hoboken, NJ: Wiley.

Locke, J. (1892). Some thoughts concerning education. In R. H. Quick (Ed.), *Locke on education* (pp. 1–236). Cambridge, UK: Cambridge University Press. (Original work published 1690)

Loeb, S., Fuller, B., Kagan, S. L., & Carrol, B. (2004). Child care in poor communities: Early learning effects of type, quality, and stability. *Child Development, 75,* 47–65.

Loehlin, J. C., Horn, J. M., & Willerman, L. (1997). Heredity, environment, and IQ in the Texas Adoption Project. In R. J. Sternberg & E. L. Grigorenko (Eds.), *Intelligence, heredity, and environment* (pp. 105–125). New York: Cambridge University Press.

Loehlin, J. C., & Martin, N. G. (2001). Age changes in personality traits and their heritabilities during the adult years: Evidence from Australian twin registry samples. *Personality and Individual Differences, 30,* 1147–1160.

Loganovskaja, T. K., & Loganovsky, K. N. (1999). EEG, cognitive and psychopathological abnormalities in children irradiated in utero. *International Journal of Psychophysiology, 34,* 211–224.

Loganovsky, K. N., Loganovskaja, T. K., Nechayev, S. Y., Antipchuk, Y. Y., & Bomko, M. A. (2008). Disrupted development of the dominant hemisphere following prenatal irradiation. *The Journal of Neuropsychiatry and Clinical Neurosciences, 20,* 274–291.

Lohman, D. F. (2000). Measures of intelligence: Cognitive theories. In A. E. Kazdin (Ed.), *Encyclopedia of psychology: Vol. 5* (pp. 147–150). Washington, DC: American Psychological Association.

Lohmann, H., & Tomasello, M. (2003). The role of language in the development of false belief understanding: A training study. *Child Development, 74,* 1130–1144.

Lohrmann, S., & Bambara, L. M. (2006). Elementary education teachers' beliefs about essential supports needed to successfully include students with developmental disabilities who engage in challenging behaviors. *Research and Practice for Persons with Severe Disabilities, 31,* 157–173.

Loman, M. M., & Gunnar, M. R. (2010). Early experience and the development of stress reactivity and regulation in children. *Neuroscience and Biobehavioral Reviews, 34,* 867–876.

London, K., Bruck, M., Ceci, S. J., & Shuman, D. (2005). Disclosure of child sexual abuse: What does the research tell us about the ways that children tell? *Psychology and Public Policy Law, 11,* 194–226.

Loock, C., Conry, J., Cook, J. L., Chudley, A. E., & Rosales, T. (2005). Identifying fetal alcohol spectrum disorder in primary care. *Canadian Medical Association Journal, 172,* 628–630.

Looker, D., & Thiessen, V. (2003). *The digital divide in Canadian schools: Factors affecting student access to and use of information technology.* Ottawa: Statistics Canada, Catalogue no. 81-597-XIE. Retrieved from www.statcan.ca/bsolc/english/bsolc?catno=81-597-X

Loots, G., & Devise, I. (2003). The use of visual–tactile communication strategies by deaf and hearing fathers and mothers of deaf infants. *Journal of Deaf Studies and Deaf Education, 8,* 31–42.

Lopez, C. M., Driscoll, K. A., & Kistner, J. A. (2009). Sex differences and response styles: Subtypes of rumination and associations with depressive symptoms. *Journal of Clinical Child and Adolescent Psychology, 38,* 27–35.

Lorenz, K. Z. (1952). *King Solomon's ring.* New York: Crowell.

Lorenz, K. Z. (1983). *So Kam der Mensch auf den Hund.* Munich: DTV.

Louie, V. (2001). Parents' aspirations and investment: The role of social class in the educational experiences of 1.5- and second generation Chinese Americans. *Harvard Educational Review, 71,* 438–474.

Louis, J., Cannard, C., Bastuji, H., & Challamel, M.-J. (1997). Sleep ontogenesis revisited: A longitudinal 24-hour home polygraphic study on 15 normal infants during the first two years of life. *Sleep, 20,* 323–333.

Lourenco, O. (2003). Making sense of Turiel's dispute with Kohlberg: The case of the child's moral competence. *New Ideas in Psychology, 21,* 43–68.

Love, J. M., Chazan-Cohen, R., & Raikes, H. (2007). Forty years of research knowledge and use: From Head Start to Early Head Start and beyond. In J. L. Aber, S. J. Bishop-Josef, S. M. Jones, K. T. McLearn, & D. Phillips (Eds.), *Child development*

and social policy: Knowledge for action (pp. 79–95). Washington, DC: American Psychological Association.

Love, J. M., Harrison, L., Sagi-Schwartz, A., van IJzendoorn, M. H., Ross, C., & Ungerer, J. A. (2003). Child care quality matters: How conclusions may vary with context. *Child Development, 74,* 1021–1033.

Love, J. M., Kisker, E. E., Ross, C., Raikes, H., Constantine, J., Boller, K., & Brooks-Gunn, J. (2005). The effectiveness of Early Head Start for 3-year-old children and their parents: Lessons for policy and programs. *Developmental Psychology, 41,* 885–901.

Love, J. M., Tarullo, L. B., Raikes, H., & Chazan-Cohen, R. (2006). Head Start: What do we know about its effectiveness? What do we need to know? In K. McCartney & D. Phillips (2006). *Blackwell handbook of early childhood development* (pp. 550–575). Malden, MA: Blackwell.

Lower-Basch, E. (2010). *TANF in the recession and beyond.* Washington, DC: CLASP.

Lozoff, B. (2007). Iron deficiency and child development. *Food and Nutrition Bulletin, 28,* S560–S571.

Lozoff, B., Clark, K. M., Jing, Y., Armony-Sivan, R., Angelilli, M. L., & Jacobson, S. W. (2008). Dose-response relationships between iron deficiency with or without anemia and infant social-emotional behavior. *Journal of Pediatrics, 152,* 696–702.

Lubart, T. I. (2003). In search of creative intelligence. In R. J. Sternberg, J. Lautrey, & T. I. Lubart (Eds.), *Models of intelligence: International perspectives* (pp. 279–292). Washington, DC: American Psychological Association.

Lubart, T. I., Georgsdottir, A., & Besançon, M. (2009). The nature of creative giftedness and talent. In T. Balchin, B. Hymer, & D. J. Matthews (Eds.), *The Routledge international companion to gifted education* (pp. 42–49). New York: Routledge.

Luby, J., Belden, A., Sullivan, J., Hayen, R., McCadney, A., & Spitznagel, E. (2009). Shame and guilt in preschool depression: Evidence for elevations in self-conscious emotions in depression as early as age 3. *Journal of Child Psychology and Psychiatry, 50,* 1156–1166.

Lucas, S. R., & Behrends, M. (2002). Sociodemographic diversity, correlated achievement, and de facto tracking. *Sociology of Education, 75,* 328–348.

Lucas-Thompson, R., & Clarke-Stewart, K. A. (2007). Forecasting friendship: How marital quality, maternal mood, and attachment security are linked to children's peer relationships. *Journal of Applied Developmental Psychology, 28,* 499–514.

Luciana, M. (2003). The neural and functional development of the human prefrontal cortex. In M. de Haan & M. H. Johnson (Eds.), *The cognitive neuroscience of development* (pp. 157–180). New York: Psychology Press.

Luciana, M. (2007). Special issue: Developmental cognitive neuroscience. *Developmental Review, 27,* 277–282.

Ludemann, P. M. (1991). Generalized discrimination of positive facial expressions by seven- and ten-month-old infants. *Child Development, 62,* 55–67.

Lueptow, L. B., Garovich, L., & Lueptow, M. B. (2001). Social change and the persistnce of sex typing: 1974–1997. *Social Forces, 80,* 1–36.

Lukowski, A. F., Koss, M., Burden, M. J., Jonides, J., Nelson, C. A., Kaciroti, N., et al. (2010). Iron deficiency in infancy and neurocognitive functioning at 19 years: Evidence of long-term deficits in executive function and recognition memory. *Nutritional Neuroscience, 13,* 54–70.

Luna, B., Garvger, K. E., Urban, T. A., Lazar, N. A., & Sweeney, J. A. (2004). Maturation of cognitive processes from late childhood to adulthood. *Child Development, 75,* 1357–1372.

Luna, B., Thulborn, K. R., Monoz, D. P., Merriam, E. P., Garver, K. E., Minshew, N. J., et al. (2001). Maturation of widely distributed brain function subserves cognitive development. *Neuroimage, 13,* 786–793.

Lund, N., Pedersen, L. H., & Henriksen, T. B. (2009). Selective serotonin reuptake inhibitor exposure in utero and pregnancy outcomes. *Archives of Pediatrics and Adolescent Medicine, 163,* 949–954.

Lundy, B. L. (2002). Paternal sociopsychological factors and infant attachment: The mediating role of synchrony in father–infant interactions. *Infant Behavior and Development, 25,* 221–236.

Lundy, B. L. (2003). Father- and mother-infant face-to-face interactions: Differences in mind-related comments and infant attachment? *Infant Behavior and Development, 26,* 200–212.

Luo, Y., & Baillargeon, R. (2005). When the ordinary seems unexpected: Evidence for incremental physical knowledge in young infants. *Cognition, 95,* 297–328.

Lupien, S. J., McEwen, B. S., Gunnar, M. R., & Heim, C. (2009). Effects of stress throughout the lifespan on the brain, behaviour and cognition. *Nature Reviews Neuroscience, 10,* 434–445.

Luria, A. R. (1976). *Cognitive development: Its cultural and social foundations.* Cambridge, MA: Harvard University Press.

Lussier, G., Deater-Deckard, K., Dunn, J., & Davies, L. (2002). Support across two generations: Children's closeness to grandparents following parental divorce and remarriage. *Journal of Family Psychology, 16,* 363–376.

Luster, T., & Dubow, E. (1992). Home environment and maternal intelligence as predictors of verbal intelligence: A comparison of preschool and school-age children. *Merrill-Palmer Quarterly, 38,* 151–175.

Luster, T., & Haddow, J. L. (2005). Adolescent mothers and their children: An ecological perspective. In T. Luster & J. L. Haddow (Eds.), *Parenting: An ecological perspective* (2nd ed., pp. 73–101). Mahwah, NJ: Erlbaum.

Luthar, S. S., & Becker, B. E. (2002). Privileged but pressured: A study of affluent youth. *Child Development, 73,* 1593–1610.

Luthar, S. S., & Goldstein, A. S. (2008). Substance use and related behaviors among suburban late adolescents: The importance of perceived parent containment. *Development and Psychopathology, 20,* 591–614.

Luthar, S. S., & Latendresse, S. J. (2005a). Children of the affluent: Challenges to well-being. *Current Directions in Psychological Science, 14,* 49–53.

Luthar, S. S., & Latendresse, S. J. (2005b). Comparable "risks" at the socioeconomic status extremes: Preadolescents' perceptions of parenting. *Development and Psychopathology, 17,* 207–230.

Luthar, S. S., & Sexton, C. (2004). The high price of affluence. In R. V. Kail (Ed.), *Advances in child development* (Vol. 32, pp. 126–162). San Diego, CA: Academic Press.

Luwel, K., Siegler, R. S., & Verschaffel, L. (2008). A microgenetic study of insightful problem solving. *Journal of Experimental Child Psychology, 99,* 210–232.

Luyckx, K., Goossens, L., Soenens, B., & Beyers, W. (2006). Unpacking commitment and exploration: Preliminary validation of an integrative model of late adolescent identity formation. *Journal of Adolescence, 29,* 361–378.

Luyckz, K., Soenens, B., Vansteenkiste, M., Goossens, L., & Berzonsky, M. D. (2007). Parental psychological control and dimensions of identity formation in emerging adulthood. *Journal of Family Psychology, 21,* 546–550.

Luyckx, K., Vansteenkiste, M., Goossens, L., & Duriez, B. (2009). Basic need satisfaction and identity formation: Bridging self-determination theory and process-oriented identity research. *Journal of Counseling Psychology, 56,* 276–288.

Lynch, S. K., Turkheimer, E., D'Onofrio, B. M., Mendle, J., Emery, R. E., Slutske, W. S., & Martin, N. G. (2006). A genetically informed study of the association between harsh punishment and offspring behavioral problems. *Journal of Family Psychology, 20,* 190–198.

Lyon, T. D., & Flavell, J. H. (1994). Young children's understanding of "remember" and "forget." *Child Development, 65,* 1357–1371.

Lyons-Ruth, K. (1996). Attachment relationships among children with aggressive behavior problems: The role of disorganized early attachment patterns. *Journal of Consulting and Clinical Psychology, 64,* 64–73.

Lyons-Ruth, K., Bronfman, E., & Parsons, E. (1999). Maternal frightened, frightening, or atypical behavior and disorganized infant attachment patterns. *Monographs of the Society for Research in Child Development, 64*(3, Serial No. 258), 67–96.

Lyons-Ruth, K., Easterbrooks, A., & Cibelli, C. (1997). Infant attachment strategies, infant mental lag, and maternal depressive symptoms: Predictors of internalizing and externalizing problems at age 7. *Developmental Psychology, 33,* 681–692.

Lytton, H., & Romney, D. M. (1991). Parents' sex-related differential socialization of boys and girls: A meta-analysis. *Psychological Bulletin, 109,* 267–296.

Ma, F., Xu, F., Heyman, G. D., & Lee, K. (2011). Chinese children's evaluations of white lies: Weighing the consequences for recipients. *Journal of Experimental Child Psychology, 108,* 308–321.

Ma, L., & Lillard, A. S. (2006). Where is the real cheese? Young children's ability to discriminate between real and pretend acts. *Child Development, 77,* 1762–1777.

Ma, W., Golinkoff, R. M., Hisch-Pasek, K., McDonough, C., & Tardif, T. (2009). Imageability predicts the age of acquisition of verbs in Chinese children. *Journal of Child Language, 36,* 405–423.

Maas, F. K. (2008). Children's understanding of promising, lying, and false belief. *Journal of General Psychology, 13,* 301–321.

Maas, F. K., & Abbeduto L. J. (2001). Children's judgments about intentionally and unintentionally broken promises. *Journal of Child Language, 28,* 517–529.

Maccoby, E. E. (1984). Socialization and developmental change. *Child Development, 55,* 317–328.

Maccoby, E. E. (1998). *The two sexes: Growing up apart, coming together.* Cambridge, MA: Belknap/Harvard University Press.

Maccoby, E. E. (2000a). Parenting and its effects on children: On reading and misreading behavior genetics. *Annual Review of Psychology, 51,* 1–27.

Maccoby, E. E. (2000b). Perspectives on gender development. *International Journal of Behavioral Development, 24,* 398–406.

Maccoby, E. E. (2002). Gender and group process: A developmental perspective. *Current Directions in Psychological Science, 11,* 54–58.

Maccoby, E. E., & Martin, J. A. (1983). Socialization in the context of the family. In E. M. Hetherington (Ed.), *Handbook of child psychology: Vol. 4. Socialization, personality, and social development* (4th ed., pp. 1–101). New York: Wiley.

Machin, G. A. (2005). Multiple birth. In H. W. Taeusch, R. A. Ballard, & C. A. Gleason (Eds.), *Avery's disease of the newborn* (8th ed., pp. 57–62). Philadelphia: Saunders.

Mackey, E. R., & La Greca, A. M. (2007). Adolescents' eating, exercise, and weight control behaviors: Does peer crowd affiliation play a role? *Journal of Pediatric Psychology, 32,* 13–23.

Mackey, K., Arnold, M. L., & Pratt, M. W. (2001). Adolescents' stories of decision making in more and less authoritative families: Representing the voices of parents in narrative. *Journal of Adolescent Research, 16,* 243–268.

Mackie, S., Show, P., Lenroot, R., Pierson, R., Greenstein, D. K., & Nugent, T. F., III. (2007). Cerebellar development and clinical outcome in attention deficit hyperactivity disorder. *American Journal of Psychiatry, 164,* 647–655.

MacWhinney, B. (2005). Language development. In M. H. Bornstein & M. E. Lamb (Eds.), *Developmental science: An advanced textbook* (5th ed., pp. 359–387). Mahwah, NJ: Erlbaum.

Madden, M., & Lenhart, A. (2009). *Teens and distracted driving: Texting, talking and other uses of the cell phone behind the wheel.* Washington, DC: Pew Internet & American Life Project.

Madigan, S., Bakermans-Kranenburg, M. J., van IJzendoorn, M. H., Moran, G., Pederson, D. R., & Benoit, D. (2006). Unresolved states of mind, anomalous parental behavior, and disorganized attachment: A review and meta-analysis of a transmission gap. *Attachment and Human Development, 8,* 89–111.

Madon, S., Jussim, L., & Eccles, J. (1997). In search of the powerful self-fulfilling prophecy. *Journal of Personality and Social Psychology, 72,* 791–809.

Madsen, S. A., & Juhl, T. (2007). Paternal depression in the postnatal period assessed with traditional and male depression scales. *Journal of Men's Health and Gender, 4,* 26–31.

Magnuson, K., & Shager H. (2010). Early education: Progress and promise for children from low-income families. *Children and Youth Services Review, 32,* 1186–1198.

Mahalingham, R. (1999). Essentialism, power, and representation of caste: A developmental study. *Dissertation Abstracts International, 60*(2–B), 856.

Mahoney, J. L. (2000). Participation in school extracurricular activities as a moderator in the development of antisocial patterns. *Child Development, 71,* 502–516.

Mahoney, J. L., & Cairns, R. B. (1997). Do extracurricular activities protect against early school dropout? *Developmental Psychology, 33,* 241–253.

Main, M., & Cassidy, J. (1988). Categories of response to reunion with the parent at age 6: Predictable from infant attachment classifications and stable over a 1-month period. *Developmental Psychology, 24,* 415–426.

Main, M., & Goldwyn, R. (1994). *Interview-based adult attachment classifications: Related to infant–mother and infant–father attachment.* Unpublished manuscript, University of California, Berkeley.

Main, M., & Solomon, J. (1990). Procedures for identifying infants as disorganized/ disoriented during the Ainsworth Strange Situation. In M. Greenberg, D. Cicchetti, & M. Cummings (Eds.), *Attachment in the preschool years: Theory, research, and intervention* (pp. 121–160). Chicago: University of Chicago Press.

Majdanžić, M., & van den Boom, D. C. (2007). Multimethod longitudinal assessment of temperament in early childhood. *Journal of Personality, 75,* 121–167.

Majnemer, A., & Barr, R. G. (2005). Influence of supine sleep positioning on early motor milestone acquisition. *Developmental Medicine and Child Neurology, 47,* 370–376.

Major, B., Spencer, S., Schmader, T., Wolfe, C., & Crocker, J. (1998). Coping with negative stereotypes about intellectual performance: The role of psychological disengagement. *Personality and Social Psychology Bulletin, 24,* 34–50.

Majorano, M., & D'Odorico, L. (2011). The transition into ambient language: A longitudinal study of babbling and first word production of Italian children. *First Language, 31,* 47–66.

Malatesta, C. Z., Grigoryev, P., Lamb, C., Albin, M., & Culver, C. (1986). Emotion socialization and expressive development in preterm and full-term infants. *Child Development, 57,* 316–330.

Malina, R. M., & Bouchard, C. (1991). *Growth, maturation, and physical activity.* Champaign, IL: Human Kinetics.

Mandara, J., Varner, F., Greene, N., & Richman, S. (2009). Intergenerational family predictors of the black–white achievement gap. *Journal of Educational Psychology, 101,* 867–878.

Mandler, J. M. (2004a). *The foundations of mind: Origins of conceptual thought.* New York: Oxford University Press.

Mandler, J. M. (2004b). Thought before language. *Trends in Cognitive Sciences, 8,* 508–513.

Mandler, J. M., & McDonough, L. (1998). On developing a knowledge base in infancy. *Developmental Psychology, 34,* 1274–1288.

Mandler, J. M., & Robinson, C. A. (1978). Developmental changes in picture recognition. *Journal of Experimental Child Psychology, 26,* 122–136.

Mangelsdorf, S. C., Schoppe, S. J., & Buur, H. (2000). The meaning of parental reports: A contextual approach to the study of temperament and behavior problems.

In V. J. Molfese & D. L. Molfese (Eds.), *Temperament and personality across the life span* (pp. 121–140). Mahwah, NJ: Erlbaum.

Mann, T., Braswell, G., & Berk, L. E. (2005, April). *A community children's museum as a context for parent–child engagement.* Poster presented at the biennial meeting of the Society for Research in Child Development, Atlanta, GA.

Mant, C. M., & Perner, J. (1988). The child's understanding of commitment. *Developmental Psychology, 24,* 343–351.

Mao, A., Burnham, M. M., Goodlin-Jones, B. L., Gaylor, E. E., & Anders, T. F. (2004). A comparison of the sleep–wake patterns of cosleeping and solitary-sleeping infants. *Child Psychiatry and Human Development, 35,* 95–105.

Maratsos, M. (1998). The acquisition of grammar. In D. Kuhn & R. S. Siegler (Eds.), *Handbook of child psychology: Vol. 2. Cognition, perception and language* (5th ed., pp. 421–466). New York: Wiley.

Maratsos, M. (2000). More overregularizations after all: New data and discussion on Marcus, Pinker, Ullman, Hollander, Rosen, & Xu. *Journal of Child Language, 27,* 183–212.

Marchman, V. A., & Thal, D. J. (2005). Words and grammar. In M. Tomasello & D. I. Slobin (Eds.), *Beyond nature–nurture: Essays in honor of Elizabeth Bates* (pp. 141–164). Mahwah, NJ: Erlbaum.

Marcia, J. E. (1980). Identity in adolescence. In J. Adelson (Ed.), *Handbook of adolescent psychology* (pp. 159–187). New York: Wiley.

Marcon, R. A. (1999a). Differential impact of preschool models on development and early learning of inner-city children: A three-cohort study. *Developmental Psychology, 35,* 358–375.

Marcon, R. A. (1999b). Positive relationships between parent–school involvement and public school inner-city preschoolers' development and academic performance. *School Psychology Review, 28,* 395–412.

Marcus, G. F., Fernandes, K. J., & Johnson, S. P. (2007). Infant rule learning facilitated by speech. *Psychological Science, 18,* 387–391.

Marcus, G. F., Pinker, S., Ullman, M., Hollander, M., Rosen, T. J., & Xu, F. (1992). Overregularization in language acquisition. *Monographs of the Society for Research in Child Development, 57*(4, Serial No. 228).

Marcus, G. F., Vijayan, S., Rao, S. B., & Vishton, P. M. (1999). Rule learning by seven-month-old infants. *Science, 283,* 77–80.

Mardh, P. A. (2002). Influence of infection with *Chlamydia trachomatis* on pregnancy outcome, infant health and lifelong sequelae in infected offspring. *Best Practices in Clinical Obstetrics and Gynecology, 16,* 847–964.

Mareschal, D., Sirois, S., Westermann, G., & Johnson, M. (Eds.). (2007). *Neuroconstructivism: How the brain constructs cognition.* Oxford, UK: Oxford University Press.

Marian, V., Neisser, U., & Rochat, P. (1996). *Can 2-month-old infants distinguish live from videotaped interactions with their mothers* (Emory Cognition Project, Report #33). Atlanta, GA: Emory University.

Mariano, K. A., & Harton, H. C. (2005). Similarities in aggression, inattention/hyperactivity, depression, and anxiety in middle childhood friendships. *Journal of Social and Clinical Psychology, 24,* 471–496.

Markman, E. M. (1992). Constraints on word learning: Speculations about their nature, origins, and domain specificity. In M. R. Gunnar & M. P. Maratsos (Eds.), *Minnesota Symposia on Child Psychology* (Vol. 25, pp. 59–101). Hillsdale, NJ: Erlbaum.

Markova, G., & Legerstee, M. (2006). Contingency, imitation, and affect sharing: Foundations of infants' social awareness. *Developmental Psychology, 42,* 132–141.

Markovits, H., & Barrouillet, P. (2002). The development of conditional reasoning: A Piagetian reformulation of mental models theory. *Merrill-Palmer Quarterly, 39,* 131–158.

Markovits, H., Benenson, J., & Dolensky, E. (2001). Evidence that children and adolescents have internal models of peer interactions that are gender differentiated. *Child Development, 72,* 879–886.

Markovits, H., Schleifer, M., & Fortier, L. (1989). Development of elementary deductive reasoning in young children. *Developmental Psychology, 25,* 787–793.

Markovits, H., & Vachon, R. (1990). Conditional reasoning, representation, and level of abstraction. *Developmental Psychology, 26,* 942–951.

Marks, G. N., Cresswell, J., & Ainley, J. (2006). Explaining socioeconomic inequalities in student achievement: The role of home and school factors. *Educational Research and Evaluation, 12,* 105–128.

Markus, H. R., & Kitayama, S. (1991). Culture and the self: Implications for cognition, emotion, and motivation. *Psychological Review, 98,* 224–253.

Marlier, L., & Schaal, B. (2005). Human newborns prefer human milk: Conspecific milk odor is attractive without postnatal exposure. *Child Development, 76,* 155–168.

Marsee, M. A., & Frick, P. J. (2010). Callous-unemotional traits and aggression youth. In W. F. Arsenio & E. A. Lemerise (Eds.), *Emotions, aggression, and morality in children: Bridging development and psychopathology* (pp. 137–156). Washington, DC: American Psychological Association.

Marsh, H. W. (1990). The structure of academic self-concept: The Marsh/Shavelson model. *Journal of Educational Psychology, 82,* 623–636.

Marsh, H. W., & Ayotte, V. (2003). Do multiple dimensions of self-concept become more differentiated with age? The differential distinctiveness hypothesis. *Journal of Educational Psychology, 95,* 687–706.

Marsh, H. W., Craven, R., & Debus, R. (1998). Structure, stability, and development of young children's self-concepts: A multicohort-multioccasion study. *Child Development, 69,* 1030–1053.

Marsh, H. W., Ellis, L. A., & Craven, R. G. (2002). How do preschool children feel about themselves? Unraveling measurement and multidimensional self-concept structure. *Developmental Psychology, 38,* 376–393.

Marsh, H. W., Gerlach, E., Trautwein, U., Lüdtke, O., & Brettschneider, W.-D. (2007). Longitudinal study of preadolescent sport self-concept and performance: Reciprocal effects and causal ordering. *Child Development, 78,* 1640–1656.

Marsh, H. W., & Kleitman, S. (2002). Extracurricular school activities: The good, the bad, and the non-linear. *Harvard Educational Review, 72,* 464–514.

Marsh, H. W., & Kleitman, S. (2005). Consequences of employment during high school: Character building, subversion of academic goals, or a threshold? *American Educational Research Journal, 42,* 331–369.

Marsh, H. W., Parada, R. H., & Ayotte, V. (2004). A multidimensional perspective of relations between self-concept (Self Description Questionnaire II) and adolescent mental health (Youth Self Report). *Psychological Assessment, 16,* 27–41.

Marsh, H. W., Trautwein, U., Lüdtke, O., Koller, O., & Baumert, J. (2005). Academic self-concept, interest, grades, and standardized test scores: Reciprocal effects models of causal ordering. *Child Development, 76,* 397–416.

Marshall-Baker, A., Lickliter, R., & Cooper, R. P. (1998). Prolonged exposure to a visual pattern may promote behavioral organization in preterm infants. *Journal of Perinatal and Neonatal Nursing, 12,* 50–62.

Martin, C. L. (1989). Children's use of gender-related information in making social judgments. *Developmental Psychology, 25,* 80–88.

Martin, C. L., Eisenbud, L., & Rose, H. (1995). Children's gender-based reasoning about toys. *Child Development, 66,* 1453–1471.

Martin, C. L., & Fabes, C. A. (2001). The stability and consequences of young children's same-sex peer interactions. *Developmental Psychology, 37,* 431–446.

Martin, C. L., Fabes, R. A., Evans, S. M., & Wyman, H. (1999). Social cognition on the playground: Children's beliefs about playing with girls versus boys and their relations to sex segregated play. *Journal of Social and Personal Relationships, 16,* 751–771.

Martin, C. L., & Halverson, C. F., Jr. (1987). The role of cognition in sex role acquisition. In D. B. Carter (Ed.), *Current conceptions of sex roles and sex typing: Theory and research* (pp. 123–137). New York: Praeger.

Martin, C. L., & Little, J. K. (1990). The relation of gender understanding to children's sex-typed preferences and gender stereotypes. *Child Development, 61,* 1427–1439.

Martin, C. L., & Ruble, D. (2004). Children's search for gender cues: Cognitive perspectives on gender development. *Current Directions in Psychological Science, 13,* 67–70.

Martin, C. L., Ruble, D. N., & Szkrybalo, J. (2002). Cognitive theories of early gender development. *Psychological Bulletin, 128,* 903–933.

Martin, G. L., & Pear, J. (2007). *Behavior modification: What it is and how to do it* (8th ed.). Upper Saddle River, NJ: Prentice-Hall.

Martin, K. A. (1996). *Puberty, sexuality and the self: Girls and boys at adolescence.* New York: Routledge.

Martin, L. T., Kubzansky, L. D., Lewinn, K. Z., Lipsitt, L. P., Satz, P., & Buka, S. L. (2007). Childhood cognitive performance and risk of generalized anxiety disorder. *International Journal of Epidemiology, 36,* 769–775.

Martin, R. (2008). Meiotic errors in human oogenesis and spermatogenesis. *Reproductive Biomedicine Online, 16,* 523–531.

Martin, R. P., Olejnik, S., & Gaddis, L. (1994). Is temperament an important contributor to schooling outcomes in elementary school? Modeling effects of temperament and scholastic ability on academic achievement. In W. B. Carey & S. C. McDevitt (Eds.), *Prevention and early intervention* (pp. 59–68). New York: Brunner/Mazel.

Martinez-Frias, M. L., Bermejo, E., Rodríguez-Pinilla, E., & Frías, J. L. (2004). Risk for congenital anomalies associated with different sporadic and daily doses of alcohol consumption during pregnancy: A case-control study. *Birth Defects Research, Part A, Clinical and Molecular Teratology, 70,* 194–200.

Martinot, D., & Désert, M. (2007). Awareness of a gender stereotype, personal beliefs, and self-perceptions regarding math ability: When boys do not surpass girls. *Social Psychology of Education, 10,* 455–471.

Martlew, M., & Connolly, K. J. (1996). Human figure drawings by schooled and unschooled children in Papua New Guinea. *Child Development, 67,* 2743–2762.

Marzolf, D. P., & DeLoache, J. S. (1994). Transfer in young children's understanding of spatial representations. *Child Development, 65,* 1–15.

Masataka, N. (1996). Perception of motherese in a signed language by 6-month-old deaf infants. *Developmental Psychology, 32,* 874–879.

Mascolo, M. F., & Fischer, K. W. (2007). The codevelopment of self and sociomoral emotions during the toddler years. In C. A. Brownell & C. B. Kopp (Eds.), *Socioemotional development in the toddler years: Transitions and transformations* (pp. 66–99). New York: Guilford.

Mashburn, A. J. (2008). Quality of social and physical environments in preschools and children's development of academic, language, and literacy skills. *Applied Developmental Science, 12,* 113–127.

Mashburn, A. J., Pianta, R. C., Mamre, B. K., Downer, J. T., Barbarin, O. A., Bryant, D., et al. (2008). Measures of classroom quality in prekindergarten and children's development of academic, language, and social skills. *Child Development, 79,* 732–749.

Mason, M. G., & Gibbs, J. C. (1993a). Role-taking opportunities and the transition to advanced moral judgment. *Moral Education Forum, 18,* 1–12.

Mason, M. G., & Gibbs, J. C. (1993b). Social perspective taking and moral judgment among college students. *Journal of Adolescent Research, 8,* 109–123.

Masten, A. S., Coatsworth, J. D., Neemann, J., Gest, S. D., Tellegen, A., & Garmezy, N. (1995). The structure and coherence of competence from childhood through adolescence. *Child Development, 66,* 1635–1659.

Masten, A. S., & Gewirtz, A. H. (2006). Vulnerability and resilience in early child development. In K. McCartney & D. Phillips (Eds.), *Blackwell handbook of early childhood development* (pp. 22–43). Malden, MA: Blackwell.

Masten, A. S., & Reed, M. J. (2002). Resilience in development. In C. R. Snyder & S. J. Lopez (Eds.), *Handbook of positive psychology* (pp. 74–88). New York: Oxford University Press.

Masten, A. S., & Shaffer, A. (2006). How families matter in child development: Reflections from research on risk and resilience. In A. S. Masten & A. Shaffer (Eds.), *Families count: Effects on child and adolescent development* (pp. 5–25). New York: Cambridge University Press.

Mastropieri, D., & Turkewitz, G. (1999). Prenatal experience and neonatal responsiveness to vocal expressions of emotion. *Developmental Psychobiology, 35,* 204–214.

Masur, E. F., McIntyre, C. W., & Flavell, J. H. (1973). Developmental changes in apportionment of study time among items in a multi-trial free recall task. *Journal of Experimental Child Psychology, 15,* 237–246.

Masur, E. F., & Rodemaker, J. E. (1999). Mothers' and infants' spontaneous vocal, verbal, and action imitation during the second year. *Merrill-Palmer Quarterly, 45,* 392–412.

Matheny, A. P., Jr. (1989). Temperament and cognition: Relations between temperament and mental test scores. In G. A. Kohnstamm, J. E. Bates, & M. K. Rothbart (Eds.), *Temperament in childhood* (pp. 263–282). New York: Wiley.

Matheny, A. P., Jr.,& Phillips, K. (2001). Temperament and context: Correlates of home environment with temperament continuity and change. In T. D. Wachs & G. Kohnstamm (Eds.), *Temperament in context* (pp. 81–102). Mahwah, NJ: Erlbaum.

Mathews, G. A., Fane, B. A., Conway, G. S., Brook, C. G. D., & Hines, M. (2009). Personality and congenital adrenal hyperplasia: Possible effects of prenatal androgen exposure. *Hormones and Behavior, 55,* 285–291.

Mathews, T. J., & MacDorman, M. F. (2008). Infant mortality statistics from the 2005 period linked birth/infant death data set. *National Vital Statistics Reports from the Centers for Disease Control and Prevention, 57,* 1–32.

Mathiesen, K. S., & Prior, M. (2006). The impact of temperament factors and family functioning on resilience processes from infancy to school age. *European Journal of Developmental Psychology, 3,* 357–387.

Matsuba, M. K., & Walker, L. J. (1998). Moral reasoning in the context of ego functioning. *Merrill-Palmer Quarterly, 44,* 464–483.

Mattock, M., Molnar, M., Polka, L., & Burnham, D. (2008). The developmental course of lexical tone perception in the first year of life. *Cognition, 106,* 1367–1381.

Mattson, S. N., Calarco, K. E., & Lang, A. R. (2006). Focused and shifting attention in children with heavy prenatal alcohol exposure. *Neuropsychology, 20,* 361–369.

Maupin, R., Lyman, R., Fatsis, J., Prystowiski, E., Nguyen, A., & Wright, C. (2004). Characteristics of women who deliver with no prenatal care. *Journal of Maternal-Fetal and Neonatal Medicine, 16,* 45–50.

Maurer, D., Mondloch, C. J., & Lewis, T. L. (2007). Sleeper effects. *Developmental Science, 10,* 40–47.

Mavroveli, S., Petrides, K. V., Rieffe, C., & Bakker, F. (2007). Trait emotional intelligence, psychological well-being and peer-rated social competence in adolescence. *British Journal of Developmental Psychology, 25,* 263–275.

Mavroveli, S., Petrides, K. V., Sangareau, Y., & Furnham, A. (2009). Exploring the relationships between trait emotional intelligence and objective socio-emotional outcomes in childhood. *British Journal of Educational Psychology, 79,* 259–272.

Mayberry, R. I. (2010). Early language acquisition and adult language ability: What sign language reveals about the critical period for language. In M. Marshark & P. E. Spencer (Eds.), *Oxford handbook of deaf studies, language, and education* (Vol. 2, pp. 281–291). New York: Oxford University Press.

Mayer, J. D., Roberts, R. D., & Barsade, S. G. (2008). Human abilities: Emotional intelligence. *Annual Review of Psychology, 59,* 507–536.

Mayer, J. D., Salovey, P., & Caruso, D. R. (2003). *Mayer-Salovey-Caruso Emotional Intelligence Test (MSCEIT): User's manual.* Toronto, Canada: Multi-Health Systems.

Mayer, J. D., Salovey, P., & Caruso, D. R. (2008). Emotional intelligence: New ability or eclectic traits? *American Psychologist, 63,* 503–517.

Mayes, L. C., & Zigler, E. (1992). An observational study of the affective concomitants of mastery in infants. *Journal of Child Psychology and Psychiatry, 33,* 659–667.

Mayes, R., Bagwell, C., & Erkulwater, J. (2008). ADHD and the rise in stimulant use among children. *Harvard Review of Psychiatry, 16,* 151–166.

Mayeux, L., & Cillessen, A. H. N. (2003). Development of social problem solving in early childhood: Stability, change, and associations with social competence. *Journal of Genetic Psychology, 164,* 153–173.

Maynard, A. E. (2002). Cultural teaching: The development of teaching skills in Maya sibling interactions. *Child Development, 73,* 969–982.

Maynard, A. E., & Greenfield, P. M. (2003). Implicit cognitive development in cultural tools and children: Lessons from Maya Mexico. *Cognitive Development, 18,* 489–510.

Maynard, A. E., Subrahmanyam, K., & Greenfield, P. M. (2005). Technology and the development of intelligence: From the loom to the computer. In R. J. Sternberg & D. D. Preiss (Eds.), *Intelligence and technology: The impact of tools in the nature and development of human abilities* (pp. 29–53). Mahwah, NJ: Erlbaum.

McAdoo, H. P., & Younge, S. N. (2009). Black families. In H. A. Neville, B. M. Tynes, & S. O. Utsey (Eds.), *Handbook of African American psychology* (pp. 103–115). Thousand Oaks, CA: Sage.

McAlister, A., & Peterson, C. C. (2006). Mental playmates: Siblings, executive functioning and theory of mind. *British Journal of Developmental Psychology, 24,* 733–751.

McAlister, A., & Peterson, C. C. (2007). A longitudinal study of child siblings and theory of mind development. *Cognitive Development, 22,* 258–270.

McAuliff, B. D. (2009). Child victim and witness research comes of age: Implications for social scientists, practitioners, and the law. In B. L. Bottoms, C. J. Najdowski, & G. S. Goodman (Eds.), *Children as victims, witnesses, and offenders* (pp. 233–252). New York: Guilford.

McBee, M. T. (2006). A descriptive analysis of referral sources for gifted identification screening by race and socioeconomic status. *Journal of Secondary Gifted Education, 17,* 103–111.

McBride-Chang, C., & Kail, R. V. (2002). Cross-cultural similarities in the predictors of reading acquisition. *Child Development, 73,* 1392–1407.

McCabe, A. (1997). Developmental and cross-cultural aspects of children's narration. In M. Bamberg (Ed.), *Narrative development: Six approaches* (pp. 137–174). Mahwah, NJ: Erlbaum.

McCabe, A., & Bliss, L. S. (2003). *Patterns of narrative discourse: A multicultural lifespan approach.* Boston: Allyn and Bacon.

McCall, R. B. (1977). Childhood IQs as predictors of adult educational and occupational status. *Science, 197,* 482–483.

McCall, R. B. (1993). Developmental functions for general mental performance. In D. K. Detterman (Ed.), *Current topics in human intelligence* (Vol. 3, pp. 3–29). Norwood, NJ: Ablex.

McCall, R. B., Appelbaum, M. I., & Hogarty, P. S. (1973). Developmental changes in mental performance. *Monographs of the Society for Research in Child Development, 38*(3, Serial No. 150).

McCall, R. B., & Carriger, M. S. (1993). A meta-analysis of infant habituation and recognition memory performance as predictors of later IQ. *Child Development, 64,* 57–79.

McCartney, K., Dearing, E., Taylor, B., & Bub, K. (2007). Quality child care supports the achievement of low-income children: Direct and indirect pathways through caregiving and the home environment. *Journal of Applied Developmental Psychology, 28,* 411–426.

McCartney, K., Harris, M. J., & Bernieri, F. (1990). Growing up and growing apart: A developmental meta-analysis of twin studies. *Psychological Bulletin, 107,* 226–237.

McCartney, K., Owen, M., Booth, C., Clarke-Stewart, A., & Vandell, D. (2004). Testing a maternal attachment model of behavior problems in early childhood. *Journal of Child Psychology and Psychiatry, 45,* 765–778.

McCarton, C. (1998). Behavioral outcomes in low birth weight infants. *Pediatrics, 102,* 1293–1297.

McCarty, M. E., & Ashmead, D. H. (1999). Visual control of reaching and grasping in infants. *Developmental Psychology, 35,* 620–631.

McCarty, M. E., & Keen, R. (2005). Facilitating problem-solving performance among 9- and 12-month-old infants. *Journal of Cognition and Development, 6,* 209–228.

McClelland, J. L., & Siegler, R. S. (Eds.). (2001). *Mechanisms of cognitive development: Behavioral and neural perspectives.* Mahwah, NJ: Erlbaum.

McClelland, M. M., Cameron, C. E., Wanless, S. B., & Murray, A. (2007). Executive function, behavioral self-regulation, and social emotional competence: Links to school readiness. In O. Saracho & B. Spodek (Eds.), *Contemporary perspectives on social learning in early childhood education* (pp. 83–107). Charlotte, NC: Information Age Publishing.

McClure, S., Laibson, D., Loewenstein, G., & Cohen, J. (2004). Separate neural systems value immediate and delayed monetary rewards. *Science, 306,* 503–507.

McColgan, K. L., & McCormack, T. (2008). Searching and planning: Children's reasoning about past and future event sequences. *Child Development, 79,* 1477–1497.

McCormick, M. C., Brooks-Gunn, J., Buka, S. L., Goldman, J., Yu, J., Salganik, M., et al. (2006). Early intervention in low birth weight premature infants: Results at 18 years of age for the Infant Health and Development Program. *Pediatrics, 117,* 771–780.

McCrady, F., Kaufman, K., Vasey, M. W., Barriga, A. Q., Devlin, R. S., & Gibbs, J. C. (2008). It's all about me: A brief report of adolescent sex offenders' generic and sex-specific cognitive distortions. *Sexual Abuse, 20.*

McCrink, K., & Wynn, K. (2004). Large-number addition and subtraction by 9-month-old infants. *Psychological Science, 15,* 776–781.

McCrink, K., & Wynn, K. (2007). Ratio abstraction by 6-month-old infants. *Psychological Science, 18,* 740–745.

McCune, L. (1993). The development of play as the development of consciousness. In M. H. Bornstein & A. O'Reilly (Eds.), *New directions for child development* (No. 59, pp. 67–79). San Francisco: Jossey-Bass.

McDonough, L. (1999). Early declarative memory for location. *British Journal of Developmental Psychology, 17,* 381–402.

McDowell, D. J., & Parke, R. D. (2000). Differential knowledge of display rules for positive and negative emotions: Influences from parents, influences on peers. *Social Development, 9,* 415–432.

McDowell, D. J., & Parke, R. D. (2009). Parental correlates of children's peer relations: An empirical test of a tripartite model. *Developmental Psychology, 45,* 224–235.

McElhaney, K. B., & Allen, J. (2001). Autonomy and adolescent social functioning: The moderating effect of risk. *Child Development, 72,* 220–235.

McElhaney, K. B., Allen, J. P., Stephenson, J. C., & Hare, A. L. (2009). Attachment and autonomy during adolescence. In R. M. Lerner & L. Steiberg (Eds.), *Handbook of adolescent psychology: Vol. 1. Individual bases of adolescent development* (3rd ed., pp. 358–403). Hoboken, NJ: Wiley.

McElwain, N. L., & Booth-LaForce, C. (2006). Maternal sensitivity to infant distress and nondistress as predictors of infant–mother attachment security. *Journal of Family Psychology, 20,* 247–255.

McGee, L. M., & Richgels, D. J. (2012). *Literacy's beginnings: Supporting young readers and writers* (6th ed.). Boston: Allyn and Bacon.

McGillicuddy-De Lisi, A. V., Daly, M., & Neal, A. (2006). Children's distributive justice judgments: Aversive racism in Euro-American children? *Child Development, 77,* 1063–1080.

McGlothlin, H., & Killen, M. (2006). Intergroup attitudes of European American children attending ethnically homogeneous schools. *Child Development, 77,* 1375–1386.

McGrath, S. K., & Kennell, J. H. (2008). A randomized controlled trial of continuous labor support for middle-class couples: Effect on cesarean delivery rates. *Birth: Issues in Perinatal Care, 35,* 9–97.

McGue, M., Bouchard, T. J., Jr., Iacono, W. G., & Lykken, D. T. (1993). Behavioral genetics of cognitive ability: A life-span perspective. In R. Plomin & G. E. McClearn (Eds.), *Nature, nurture, and psychology* (pp. 59–76). Washington, DC: American Psychological Association.

McGue, M., Elkins, I., Walden, B., & Iacono, W. G. (2005). Perceptions of the parent–adolescent relationship: A longitudinal investigation. *Developmental Psychology, 41,* 971–984.

McHale, J. P., Kazali, C., Rotman, T., Talbot, J., Carleton, M., & Lieberson, R. (2004).

The transition to coparenthood: Parents' prebirth expectations and early coparental adjustment at 3 months postpartum. *Development and Psychopathology, 16,* 711–733.

McHale, J. P., Lauretti, A., Talbot, J., & Pouquette, C. (2002). Retrospect and prospect in the psychological study of coparenting and family group process. In J. P. McHale & W. S. Grolnick (Eds.), *Retrospect and prospect in the psychological study of families* (pp. 127–165). Mahwah, NJ: Erlbaum.

McHale, S. M., Bartko, W. T., Crouter, A. C., & Perry-Jenkins, M. (1990). Children's housework and psychosocial functioning: The mediating effects of parents' sex-role behaviors and attitudes. *Child Development, 61,* 68–81.

McHale, S. M., Crouter, A. C., Kim, J.-Y., Burton, L. M., Davis, K. D., Dotterer, A. M., & Swanson, D. P. (2006). Mothers' and fathers' racial socialization in African-American families: Implications for youth. *Child Development, 77,* 1387–1402.

McHale, S. M., Crouter, A. C., & Whiteman, S. D. (2003). The family contexts of gender development in childhood and adolescence. *Social Development, 12,* 125–148.

McHale, S. M., Updegraff, K. A., Helms-Erikson, H., & Crouter, A. C. (2001). Sibling influences on gender development in middle childhood and early adolescence: A longitudinal study. *Developmental Psychology, 37,* 115–125.

McIntyre, K. A., & Platania, J. (2009). Giving in to group pressure: The impact of socialization risk on perceived outcomes. *Current Research in Social Psychology, 15*(1). Retrieved from www.uiowa.edu/~grpproc/crisp/crisp.html

McKelvie, P., & Low, J. (2002). Listening to Mozart does not improve children's spatial ability. Final curtains for the Mozart effect. *British Journal of Developmental Psychology, 20,* 241–258.

McKenna, J. J. (2001). Why we never ask "Is it safe for infants to sleep alone?" *Academy of Breast Feeding Medicine News and Views, 7*(4), 32, 38.

McKenna, J. J. (2002, September/October). Breastfeeding and bedsharing still useful (and important) after all these years. *Mothering, 114.* Retrieved from www.mothering.com/articles/new_baby/sleep/mckenna.html

McKenna, J. J., & McDade, T. (2005). Why babies should never sleep alone: A review of the co-sleeping controversy in relation to SIDS, bedsharing, and breastfeeding. *Paediatric Respiratory Reviews, 6,* 134–152.

McKenna, J. J., & Volpe, L. E. (2007). Sleeping with baby: An Internet-based sampling of parental experiences, choices, perceptions, and interpretations in a Western industrialized context. *Infant and Child Development, 16,* 359–385.

McKeown, M. G., & Beck, I. L. (2009). The role of metacognition in understanding and supporting reading comprehension. In D. J. Hacker, J. Dunlosky, & A. C. Graesser (Eds.), *Handbook of metacognition in education* (pp. 7–25). New York: Routledge.

McKinney, C., Donnelly, R., & Renk, K. (2008). Perceived parenting, positive and negative perceptions of parents, and late adolescent emotional adjustment. *Child and Adolescent Mental Health, 13,* 66–73.

McKown, C., & Strambler, M. J. (2009). Developmental antecedents and social

and academic consequences of stereotype-consciousness in middle childhood. *Child Development, 80,* 1643–1659.

McKown, C., & Weinstein, R. S. (2003). The development and consequences of stereotype consciousness in middle childhood. *Child Development, 74,* 498–515.

McKown, C., & Weinstein, R. S. (2008). Teacher expectations, classroom context, and the achievement gap. *Journal of School Psychology, 46,* 235–261.

McKusick, V. A. (2011). *Online Mendelian inheritance in man.* Retrieved from www.nslij-genetics.org/search_omim.html

McLanahan, S. (1999). Father absence and the welfare of children. In E. M. Hetherington (Ed.), *Coping with divorce, single parenting, and remarriage: A risk and resiliency perspective* (pp. 117–145). Mahwah, NJ: Erlbaum.

McLean, K. C., & Pratt, M. W. (2006). Life's little (and big) lessons: identity statuses and meaning-making in the turning point narratives of emerging adults. *Developmental Psychology, 42,* 714–722.

McLoyd, V. C., Aikens, N. L., & Burton, L. M. (2006). Child poverty, policy, and practice. In K. A. Renninger & I. E. Sigel (Eds.), *Handbook of child psychology: Vol. 4. Child psychology in practice* (6th ed., pp. 700–778). Hoboken, NJ: Wiley.

McLoyd, V. C., Kaplan, R., Hardaway, C. R., & Wood, D. (2007). Does endorsement of physical discipline matter? Assessing moderating influences on the maternal and child psychological correlates of physical discipline in African-American families. *Journal of Family Psychology, 21,* 165–175.

McLoyd, V. C., & Smith, J. (2002). Physical discipline and behavior problems in African-American, European-American, and Hispanic children: Emotional support as a moderator. *Journal of Marriage and the Family, 64,* 40–53.

McMahon, C. A., Barnett, B., Kowalenko, N. M., & Tennant, C. C. (2006). Maternal attachment state of mind moderates the impact of postnatal depression on infant attachment. *Journal of Child Psychology and Psychiatry, 47,* 660–669.

MCR Vitamin Study Research Group. (1991). Prevention of neural tube defects: Results of the Medical Research Council Vitamin Study. *Lancet, 338,* 131–137.

Mead, G. H. (1934). *Mind, self, and society.* Chicago: University of Chicago Press.

Mead, M. (1928). *Coming of age in Samoa.* Ann Arbor, MI: Morrow.

Mead, M., & Newton, N. (1967). Cultural patterning of perinatal behavior. In S. Richardson & A. Guttmacher (Eds.), *Childbearing: Its social and psychological aspects* (pp. 142–244). Baltimore: Williams & Wilkins.

Meade, C. S., Kershaw, T. S., & Ickovics, J. R. (2008). The intergenerational cycle of teenage motherhood: An ecological approach. *Health Psychology, 27,* 419–429.

Mechelli, A., Crinion, J. T., Noppeney, U., O'Doherty, J., Ashburner, J., Frackowiak, R. S., & Price, C. J. (2004). Structural plasticity in the bilingual brain: Proficiency in a second language and age at acquisition affect grey-matter density. *Nature, 431,* 757.

Media Awareness Network. (2001). Parental awareness of Canadian children's Internet use. Retrieved from www.media-awareness.ca

Meeus, W., Oosterwegel, A., & Vollebergh, W. (2002). Parental and peer attachment

and identity development in adolescence. *Journal of Adolescence, 25,* 93–106.

Mehlmadrona, L., & Madrona, M. M. (1997). Physician- and midwife-attended home births—effects of breech, twin, and postdates outcome data on mortality rates. *Journal of Nurse-Midwifery, 42,* 91–98.

Meier, A., & Allen, G. (2009). Romantic relationships from adolescence to young adulthood: Evidence from the National Longitudinal Study of Adolescent Health. *Sociological Quarterly, 50,* 308–335.

Meins, E., Fernyhough, C., Russell, J., & Clark-Carter, D. (1998). Security of attachment as a predictor of symbolic and mentalizing abilities: A longitudinal study. *Social Development, 7,* 1–24.

Meins, E., Fernyhough, C., Wainwright, R., Clark-Carter, D., Gupta, M. D., Fradley, E., & Tucker, M. (2003). Pathways to understanding mind: Construct validity and predictive validity of maternal mindmindedness. *Child Development, 74,* 1194–1211.

Melby-Lervag, M., & Hulme, C. (2010). Serial and free recall in children can be improved by training: Evidence for the importance of phonological and semantic representations in immediate memory tasks. *Psychological Science, 21,* 1694–1700.

Melinder, A., Endestad, T., & Magnusson, S. (2006). Relations between episodic memory, suggestibility, theory of mind, and cognitive inhibition in the preschool child. *Scandinavian Journal of Psychology, 47,* 485–495.

Melton, G. B. (2005). Treating children like people: A framework for research and advocacy. *Journal of Clinical Child and Adolescent Psychology, 34,* 646–657.

Meltzoff, A. N. (1995). Understanding the intentions of others: Re-enactment of intended acts by 18-month-old children. *Developmental Psychology, 31,* 838–850.

Meltzoff, A. N. (2007). 'Like me': A foundation for social cognition. *Developmental Science, 10,* 126–134.

Meltzoff, A. N., & Kuhl, P. K. (1994). Faces and speech: Intermodal processing of biologically relevant signals in infants and adults. In D. J. Lewkowicz & R. Lickliter (Eds.), *The development of intersensory perception: Comparative perspectives* (pp. 335–369). Hillsdale, NJ: Erlbaum.

Meltzoff, A. N., Kuhl, P. K., Movellan, J., & Sejnowski, T. J. (2009). Foundations for a new science of learning. *Science, 325,* 284–288.

Meltzoff, A. N., & Moore, M. K. (1977). Imitation of facial and manual gestures by human neonates. *Science, 198,* 75–78.

Meltzoff, A. N., & Moore, M. K. (1994). Imitation, memory, and the representation of persons. *Infant Behavior and Development, 17,* 83–99.

Meltzoff, A. N., & Moore, M. K. (1999). Persons and representations: Why infant imitation is important for theories of human development. In J. Nadel & G. Butterworth (Eds.), *Imitation in infancy* (pp. 9–35). Cambridge, UK: Cambridge University Press.

Meltzoff, A. N., & Williamson, R. A. (2010). The importance of imitation for theories of social-cognitive development. In J. G. Bremner & T. D. Wachs (Eds.), *Wiley-Blackwell handbook of infant development* (2nd ed., pp. 345–364). Oxford, UK: Wiley.

Melzi, G., & Ely, R. (2009). Language development in the school years. In J. B. Gleason & N. B. Ratner (Eds.), *The*

development of language (7th ed., pp. 391–435). Boston: Allyn and Bacon.

Mendle, J., Turkheimer, E., D'Onofrio, B. M., Lynch, S., Emery, R. E., & Slutske, W. S. (2006). Family structure and age at menarche: A children-of-twins approach. *Developmental Psychology, 42,* 533–542.

Mendle, J., Turkheimer, E., & Emery, R. E. (2007). Detrimental psychological outcomes associated with early pubertal timing in adolescent girls. *Developmental Review, 27,* 151–171.

Menn, L., & Stoel-Gammon, C. (2009). Phonological development: Learning sounds and sound patterns. In J. B. Gleason & B. Ratner (Eds.), *The development of language* (7th ed., pp. 58–103). Boston: Allyn and Bacon.

Mennella, J. A., & Beauchamp, G. K. (1998). Early flavor experiences: Research update. *Nutrition Reviews, 56,* 205–211.

Ment, L. R., Vohr, B., Allan, W., Katz, K. H., Schneider, K. C., Westerveld, M., et al. (2003). Change in cognitive function over time in very low-birth-weight infants. *Journal of the American Medical Association, 289,* 705–711.

Menyuk, P., Liebergott, J. W., & Schultz, M. C. (1995). *Early language development in full-term and premature infants.* Hillsdale, NJ: Erlbaum.

Meredith, N. V. (1978). *Human body growth in the first ten years of life.* Columbia, SC: State Printing.

Meroni, L., & Crain, S. (2003). On not being led down the kindergarten path. *Proceedings of the 25th annual Boston University Conference on Language Development.* Somerville, MA: Cascadilla Press.

Mervis, C. B., Pani, J. R., & Pani, A. M. (2003). Transaction of child cognitive-linguistic abilities and adult input in the acquisition of lexical categories at the basic and subordinate levels. In D. H. Rakison & L. M. Oakes (Ed.), *Early category and concept development* (pp. 242–274). New York: Oxford University Press.

Mervis, C. B., & Robinson, B. F. (2000). Expressive vocabulary ability of toddlers with Williams syndrome or Down syndrome: A comparison. *Developmental Neuropsychology, 17,* 111–126.

Messinger, D. S., & Fogel, A. (2007). The interactive development of social smiling. In R. Kail (Ed.), *Advances in child development and behavior* (Vol. 35, pp. 327–366). Oxford, UK: Elsevier.

Metz, E. C., & Youniss, J. (2005). Longitudinal gains in civic development through school-based required service. *Political Psychology, 26,* 413–437.

Meyer, P. A., Pivetz, T., Dignam, T. A., Hma, D. M., Schoonover, J., & Brody, D. (2003). Surveillance for elevated blood lead levels among children—United States, 1997–2001. *Morbidity and Mortality Weekly Report, 52*(No. SS-10), 1–21.

Meyer, R. (2009). Infant feeding in the first year. 1: Feeding practices in the first six months of life. *Journal of Family Health Care, 19,* 13–16.

Meyer-Bahlburg, H. F. L., Ehrhardt, A. A., Rosen, L. R., Gruen, R. S., Veridiano, N. P., Vann, F. H., & Neuwalder, H. F. (1995). Prenatal estrogens and the development of homosexual orientation. *Developmental Psychology, 31,* 12–21.

Meyers, M. K., Rosenbaum, D., Ruhm, C., & Waldfogel, J. (2004). Inequality in early childhood education and care: What do we know? In K. Neckerman (Ed.), *Social inequality.* New York: Russell Sage Foundation.

Mezulis, A. H., Hyde, J. S., & Clark, R. (2004). Father involvement moderates the effect of maternal depression during a child's infancy on child behavior problems in kindergarten. *Journal of Family Psychology, 18,* 575–588.

Miceli, P. J., Whitman, T. L., Borkowski, J. G., Braungart-Riekder, J., & Mitchell, D. W. (1998). Individual differences in infant information processing: The role of temperamental and maternal factors. *Infant Behavior and Development, 21,* 119–136.

Michael, A., & Eccles, J. S. (2003). When coming of age means coming undone: Links between puberty and psychosocial adjustment among European American and African American girls. In C. Hayward (Ed.), *Gender differences at puberty* (pp. 277–303). New York: Cambridge University Press.

Michalik, N. M., Eisenberg, N., Spinrad, T. L., Ladd, B., Thompson, M., & Valiente, C. (2007). Longitudinal relations among parental emotional expressivity and sympathy and prosocial behavior in adolescence. *Social Development, 16,* 286–309.

Michels, K. B., Willett, W. C., Graubard, B. I., Vaidya, R. L., Cantwell, M. M., Sansbury, L. B., & Forman, M. R. (2007). A longitudinal study of infant feeding and obesity throughout the life course. *International Journal of Obesity, 31,* 1078–1085.

Michiels, D., Grietens, H., Onghena, P., & Kuppens, S. (2010). Perceptions of maternal and paternal attachment security in middle childhood: Links with positive parental affection and psychological adjustment. *Early Child Development and Care, 180,* 211–225.

Mikami, A. Y., Lerner, M. D., & Lun, J. (2010). Social context influences on children's rejection by their peers. *Child Development Perspectives, 4,* 123–130.

Miles, C. (1935). Sex in social psychology. In C. Murchison (Ed.), *Handbook of social psychology* (pp. 699–704). Worcester, MA: Clark University Press.

Milevsky, A., Schlechter, M., Netter, S., & Keehn, D. (2007). Maternal and paternal parenting styles in adolescents: Associations with self-esteem, depression, and life satisfaction. *Journal of Child and Family Studies, 16,* 39–47.

Miller, C. F., Lurye, L. E., Zosuls, K. M., & Ruble, D. N. (2009). Accessibility of gender stereotype domains: Developmental and gender differences in children. *Sex Roles, 60,* 870–881.

Miller, C. J., Sanchez, J., & Hynd, G. W. (2003). Neurological correlates of reading disabilities. In H. L. Swanson, K. R. Harris, & S. Graham (Eds.), *Handbook of learning disabilities* (pp. 242–255). New York: Guilford.

Miller, J. G., & Bersoff, D. M. (1995). Development in the context of everyday family relationships: Culture, interpersonal morality, and adaptation. In M. Killen & D. Hart (Eds.), *Morality in everyday life: Developmental perspectives* (pp. 259–282). Cambridge, UK: Cambridge University Press.

Miller, L. T., & Vernon, P. A. (1992). The general factor in short-term memory, intelligence, and reaction time. *Intelligence, 16,* 5–29.

Miller, P. A., Eisenberg, N., Fabes, R. A., & Shell, R. (1996). Relations of moral reasoning and vicarious emotion to young children's prosocial behavior toward peers and adults. *Developmental Psychology, 32,* 210–219.

Miller, P. H. (2000). How best to utilize a deficiency. *Child Development, 71,* 1013–1017.

Miller, P. H. (2009). *Theories of developmental psychology* (5th ed.). New York: Worth.

Miller, P. H., & Bigi, L. (1979). The development of children's understanding of attention. *Merrill-Palmer Quarterly, 25,* 235–250.

Miller, P. J., Fung, H., & Koven, M. (2007). Narrative reverberations: How participation in narrative practices co-creates persons and cultures. In S. Kitayama & D. Cohen (Eds.), *Handbook of cultural psychology* (pp. 595–614). New York: Guilford.

Miller, P. J., Fung, H., & Mintz, J. (1996). Self-construction through narrative practices: A Chinese and American comparison of early socialization. *Ethos, 24,* 1–44.

Miller, P. H., Haynes, V. F., DeMarie-Dreblow, D., & Woody-Ramsey, J. (1986). Children's strategies for gathering information in three tasks. *Child Development, 57,* 1429–1439.

Miller, P. J., Hengst, J. A., & Wang, S. (2003). Ethnographic methods: Applications from developmental cultural psychology. In P. M. Camic & J. E. Rhodes (Eds.), *Qualitative research in psychology* (pp. 219–242). Washington, DC: American Psychological Association.

Miller, P. J., Wiley, A. R., Fung, H., & Liang, C.-H. (1997). Personal storytelling as a medium of socialization in Chinese and American families. *Child Development, 68,* 557–568.

Miller, R. B. (2000). Do children make a marriage unhappy? *Family Science Review, 13,* 60–73.

Miller, S., Lansford, J. E., Costanzo, P., Malone, P. S., Golonka, M., & Killeya-Jones, L. A. (2009). Early adolescent romantic partner status, peer standing, and problem behaviors. *Journal of Early Adolescence, 29,* 839–861.

Miller, S. A. (2007). *Developmental research methods* (3rd ed.). Thousand Oaks, CA: Sage.

Miller, S. A. (2009). Children's understanding of second order mental states. *Psychological Bulletin, 135,* 749–773.

Miller, S. A., Hardin, C. A., & Montgomery, D. E. (2003). Young children's understanding of the conditions for knowledge acquisition. *Journal of Cognition and Development, 4,* 325–356.

Miller, P. J., Wang, S., Sandel, T., & Cho, G. E. (2002). Self-esteem as folk theory: A comparison of European American and Taiwanese mothers' beliefs. *Parenting: Science and Practice, 2,* 209–239.

Milligan, K., Astington, J. W., & Dack, L. A. (2007). Language and theory of mind: Meta-analysis of the relation between language ability and false-belief understanding. *Child Development, 78,* 622–646.

Mills, D., & Conboy, B. T. (2005). Do changes in brain organization reflect shifts in symbolic functioning? In L. Namy (Ed.), *Symbol use and symbolic representation* (pp. 123–153). Mahwah, NJ: Erlbaum.

Mills, D., Plunkett, K., Prat, C., & Schafer, G. (2005). Watching the infant brain learn words: Effects of language and experience. *Cognitive Development, 20,* 19–31.

Mills, R. S. L. (2005). Taking stock of the developmental literature on shame. *Developmental Review, 25,* 26–63.

Mills, R., & Grusec, J. E. (1989). Cognitive, affective, and behavioral consequences of praising altruism. *Merrill-Palmer Quarterly, 35,* 299–326.

Mills, T. L., Gomez-Smith, Z., & De Leon, J. M. (2005). Skipped generation families: Sources of psychological distress among grandmothers of grandchildren who live in homes where neither parent is present. *Marriage and Family Review, 37,* 191–212.

Minami, M. (1996). Japanese preschool children's narrative development. *First Language, 16,* 339–363.

Minkler, M., & Fuller-Thomson, E. (2005). African American grandparents raising grandchildren: A national study using the Census 2000 American Community Survey. *Journal of Gerontology, 60B,* S82–S92.

Misailidi, P. (2006). Young children's display rule knowledge: Understanding the distinction between apparent and real emotions and the motives underlying the use of display rules. *Social Behavior and Personality, 34,* 1285–1296.

Mischel, H. N., & Liebert, R. M. (1966). Effects of discrepancies between observed and imposed reward criteria on their acquisition and transmission. *Journal of Personality and Social Psychology, 3,* 45–53.

Mischel, H. N., & Mischel, W. (1983). The development of children's knowledge of self-control strategies. *Child Development, 54,* 603–619.

Mischel, W. (1996). From good intentions to willpower. In P. M. Gollwitzer & J. A. Bargh (Eds.), *The psychology of action* (pp. 197–218). New York: Guilford.

Mischel, W., & Ayduk, O. (2004). Willpower in a cognitive–affective processing system: The dynamics of delay of gratification. In R. F. Baumeister & K. D. Vohs (Eds.), *Handbook of self-regulation* (pp. 99–129). New York: Guilford.

Mischel, W., & Baker, N. (1975). Cognitive appraisals and transformations in delay behavior. *Journal of Personality and Social Psychology, 31,* 254–261.

Mischel, W., Shoda, Y., & Peake, P. K. (1988). The nature of adolescent competencies predicted by preschool delay of gratification. *Journal of Personality and Social Psychology, 54,* 687–696.

Mischel, W., Shoda, Y., & Rodriguez, M. L. (1989). Delay of gratification in children. *Science, 244,* 933–938.

Mistry, J. (1997). The development of remembering in cultural context. In N. Cowan (Ed.), *The development of memory in childhood* (pp. 343–368). Hove, UK: Psychology Press.

Mistry, R. S., Biesanz, J. C., Chien, N., Howes, C., & Benner, A. D. (2008). Socioeconomic status, parental investments, and the cognitive and behavioral outcomes of low-income children from immigrant and native households. *Early Childhood Research Quarterly, 23,* 193–212.

Mitchell, A., & Boss, B. J. (2002). Adverse effects of pain on the nervous systems of newborns and young children: A review of the literature. *Journal of Neuroscience Nursing, 34,* 228–235.

Mitchell, P., Teucher, U., Kikuno, H., & Bennett, M. (2010). Cultural variations in developing a sense of knowing your own mind: A comparison between British and Japanese children. *International Journal of Behavioral Development, 34,* 248–258.

Miura, I. T., & Okamoto, Y. (2003). Language supports for mathematics understanding and performance. In A. J. Baroody & A. Dowker (Eds.), *The development of arithmetic concepts and skills* (pp. 229–242). Mahwah, NJ: Erlbaum.

Mix, K. S., Huttenlocher, J., & Levine, S. C. (2002). Multiple cues for quantification in infancy: Is number one of them? *Psychological Bulletin, 128,* 278–294.

Mize, J., & Pettit, G. S. (2010). The mother–child playgroup as socialisation context: A short-term longitudinal study of mother–child–peer relationship dynamics. *Early Child Development and Care, 180,* 1271–1284.

Mocarelli, P., Gerthoux, P., Ferrari, E., Patterson, D. G., Jr., Kieszak, S. M., & Brambilla, P. (2000). Paternal concentrations of dioxin and sex ratio of offspring. *Lancet, 355,* 1858–1862.

Modry-Mandell, K. L., Gamble, W. C., & Taylor, A. R. (2007). Family emotional climate and sibling relationship quality: Influences on behavioral problems and adaptation in preschool-aged children. *Journal of Child and Family Studies, 16,* 61–73.

Moeller, M. P., Hoover, B., Putman, C., Arbataitis, K., Bohnenkamp, G., Peterson, B., et al. (2007). Vocalizations of infants with hearing loss compared with infants with normal hearing: Part I—Phonetic development. *Ear and Hearing, 28,* 605–627.

Moens, E., Braet, C., & Soetens, B. (2007). Observation of family functioning at mealtime: A comparison between families of children with and without overweight. *Journal of Pediatric Psychology, 32,* 52–63.

Moffitt, T. E. (2006a). Life-course-persistent versus adolescence-limited antisocial behavior. In D. Cicchetti & D. J. Cohen (Eds.), *Developmental psychopathology: Vol. 3. Risk, disorder, and adaptation.* (2nd ed., pp. 570–598). Hoboken, NJ: Wiley.

Moffitt, T. E. (2006b). A review of research on the taxonomy of life-course persistent versus adolescent-limited antisocial behavior. In F. T. Cullen, J. P. Wright, & K. Blevins (Eds.), *Taking stock: The status of criminological theory* (pp. 277–311). New Brunswick, NJ: Transaction Publishers.

Mok, M. M. C., Kennedy, K. J., & Moore, P. J. (2011). Academic attribution of secondary students: Gender, year level and achievement level. *Educational Psychology, 31,* 87–104.

Moll, H., & Tomasello, M. (2006). Level I perspective-taking at 24 months of age. *British Journal of Developmental Psychology, 24,* 603–613.

Moll, I. (1994). Reclaiming the natural line in Vygotsky's theory of cognitive development. *Human Development, 37,* 333–342.

Moll, J., de Oliveira-Souza, R., & Zahn, R. (2009). Neuroscience and morality: Moral judgments, sentiments, and values. In D. Narvaez & D. K. Lapsley (Eds.), *Personality, identity, and character: Explorations in moral psychology* (pp. 106–135). Cambridge, UK: Cambridge University Press.

Mollborn, S. (2007). Making the best of a bad situation: Material resources and teenage parenthood. *Journal of Marriage and Family, 69,* 92–104.

Moller, K., Hwang, C. P., & Wickberg, B. (2008). Couple relationship and transition to parenthood: Does workload at home matter? *Journal of Reproductive and Infant Psychology, 26,* 57–68.

Mondloch, C. J., Lewis, T., Budreau, D. R., Maurer, D., Dannemiller, J. L., Stephens, B. R., & Kleiner-Gathercoal, K. A. (1999). Face perception during early infancy. *Psychological Science, 10,* 419–422.

Monk, C., Sloan, R., Myers, M. M., Ellman, L., Werner, E., Jeon, J., et al. (2010). Neural circuitry of emotional face processing in autism spectrum disorders. *Journal of Psychiatry and Neuroscience, 35,* 105–114.

Montague, D. P. F., & Walker-Andrews, A. S. (2001). Peekaboo: A new look at infants' perception of emotion expressions. *Developmental Psychology, 37,* 826–838.

Montemayor, R., & Eisen, M. (1977). The development of self-conceptions from childhood to adolescence. *Developmental Psychology, 13,* 314–319.

Montgomery, M. J., & Côté, J. E. (2003). The transition to college: Adjustment, development, and outcomes. In G. R. Adams & M. D. Berzonsky (Eds.), *Blackwell handbook of adolescence* (pp. 179–194). Malden, MA: Blackwell.

Moon, C., Cooper, R. P., & Fifer, W. P. (1993). Two-day-old infants prefer their native language. *Infant Behavior and Development, 16,* 495–500.

Moon, R. Y., Horne, R. S. C., & Hauck, F. R. (2007). Sudden infant death syndrome. *Lancet, 370,* 1578–1587.

Moore, C., Mealiea, J., Garon, N., & Povinelli, D. (2007). The development of body self-awareness. *Infancy, 11,* 157–174.

Moore, D. R., & Florsheim, P. (2001). Interpersonal processes and psychopathology among expectant and nonexpectant adolescent couples. *Journal of Consulting and Clinical Psychology, 69,* 101–113.

Moore, D. S., & Johnson, S. P. (2008). Mental rotation in human infants: A sex difference. *Psychological Science, 19,* 1063–1066.

Moore, D. S., Spence, M. J., & Katz, G. S. (1997). Six-month-olds' categorization of natural infant-directed utterances. *Developmental Psychology, 33,* 980–989.

Moore, E. G. J. (1986). Family socialization and the IQ test performance of traditionally and transracially adopted black children. *Developmental Psychology, 22,* 317–326.

Moore, G. A., Cohn, J. F., & Campbell, S. B. (2001). Infant affective responses to mother's still face at 6 months differentially predict externalizing and internalizing behaviors at 18 months. *Developmental Psychology, 37,* 706–714.

Moore, K. A., Morrison, D. R., & Greene, A. D. (1997). Effects on the children born to adolescent mothers. In R. A. Maynard (Ed.), *Kids having kids* (pp. 145–180). Washington, DC: Urban Institute.

Moore, K. L., & Persaud, T. V. N. (2008). *Before we are born* (7th ed.). Philadelphia: Saunders.

Moore, M. K., & Meltzoff, A. N. (1999). New findings on object permanence: A developmental difference between two types of occlusion. *British Journal of Developmental Psychology, 17,* 563–584.

Moore, M. K., & Meltzoff, A. N. (2004). Object permanence after a 24-hr delay and leaving the locale of disappearance: The role of memory, space, and identity. *Developmental Psychology, 40,* 606–620.

Moore, M. K., & Meltzoff, A. N. (2008). Factors affecting infants' manual search for occluded objects and the genesis of object permanence. *Infant Behavior and Development, 31,* 168–180.

Moore, M. R., & Brooks-Gunn, J. (2002). Adolescent parenthood. In M. H. Bornstein (Ed.), *Handbook of parenting: Vol. 3* (2nd ed., pp. 173–214). Mahwah, NJ: Erlbaum.

Moorman, E. A., & Pomerantz, E. M (2008). The role of mothers' control in children's mastery orientation: A time frame analysis. *Journal of Family Psychology, 22,* 734–741.

Morales, M., Mundy, P., Delgado, C. E. F., Yale, M., Messinger, D., Neal, R., & Schwartz, H. K. (2000). Responding to joint attention across the 6- through 24-month age period and early language acquisition. *Journal of Applied Developmental Psychology, 21,* 283–298.

Moran, G., Forbes, L., Evans, E., Tarabulsy, G. M., & Madigan, S. (2008). Both maternal sensitivity and atypical maternal behavior independently predict attachment security and disorganization in adolescent mother–infant relationships. *Infant Behavior and Development, 31,* 321–325.

Moran, G. F., & Vinovskis, M. A. (1986). The great care of godly parents: Early childhood in Puritan New England. In A. B. Smuts & J. W. Hagen (Eds.), History and research in child development. *Monographs of the Society for Research in Child Development, 50*(4–5, Serial No. 211), pp. 24–37.

Moran, S., & Gardner, H. (2006). Extraordinary achievements: A developmental and systems analysis. In D. Kuhn & R. Siegler (Eds.), *Handbook of child psychology: Vol. 2. Cognition, perception, and language* (6th ed., pp. 905–949). Hoboken, NJ: Wiley.

Morawska, A., & Sanders, M. (2011). Parental use of time out revisited: A useful or harmful parenting strategy? *Journal of Child and Family Studies, 20,* 1–8.

Morelli, G. A., Rogoff, B., & Angelillo, C. (2003). Cultural variation in young children's access to work or involvement in specialized child-focused activities. *International Journal of Behavioral Development, 27,* 264–274.

Morelli, G. A., Rogoff, B., Oppenheim, D., & Goldsmith, D. (1992). Cultural variation in infants' sleeping arrangements: Questions of independence. *Developmental Psychology, 28,* 604–613.

Morford, J. P., & Goldin-Meadow, S. (1997). From here and now to there and then: The development of displaced reference in homesign and English. *Child Development, 68,* 420–435.

Morgan, B., Maybery, M., & Durkin, K. (2003). Weak central coherence, poor joint attention, and low verbal ability: Independent deficits in early autism. *Developmental Psychology, 28,* 604–613.

Morgan, P. L., Farkas, G., Hillemeier, M. M., & Maczuga, S. (2009). Risk factors for learning-related behavior problems at 24 months of age: Population-based estimates. *Journal of Abnormal Child Psychology, 37,* 401–413.

Morgane, P. J., Austin-LaFrance, R., Bronzino, J., Tonkiss, J., Diaz-Cintra, S., Cintra, L., et al. (1993). Prenatal malnutrition and development of the brain. *Neuroscience and Biobehavioral Reviews, 17,* 91–178.

Morrill, M. I., Hines, D. A., Mahmood, S., & Córdova, J. V. (2010). Pathways between marriage and parenting for wives and husbands: The role of coparenting. *Family Process, 49,* 59–73.

Morris, A. S., Silk, J. S., Morris, M. D. S., & Steinberg, L. (2011). The influence of mother–child emotion regulation strategies on children's expression of anger and sadness. *Developmental Psychology, 47,* 213–225.

Morris, B. J. (2008). Logically speaking: Evidence for item-based acquisition of the connectives AND & OR. *Journal of Cognition and Development, 9,* 67–88.

Morris, G., & Baker-Ward, L. (2007). Fragile but real: Children's capacity to use newly acquired words to convey preverbal memories. *Child Development, 78,* 448–458.

Morrongiello, B. A., Fenwick, K. D., & Chance, G. (1998). Crossmodal learning in newborn infants: Inferences about properties of auditory-visual events. *Infant Behavior and Development, 21,* 543–554.

Morrow, D. F. (2006). Gay, lesbian, and transgender adolescents. In D. F. Morrow & L. Messinger (Eds.), *Sexual orientation and gender expression in social work practice* (pp. 177–195). New York: Columbia University Press.

Morse, S. B., Zheng, H., Tang, Y., & Roth, J., (2009). Early school-age outcomes of late preterm infants. *Pediatrics, 123,* e622–e629.

Mosby, L., Rawls, A. W., Meehan, A. J., Mays, E., & Pettinari, C. J. (1999). Troubles in interracial talk about discipline: An examination of African American child rearing narratives. *Journal of Comparative Family Studies, 30,* 489–521.

Mosely-Howard, G. S., & Evans, C. B. (2000). Relationships and contemporary experiences of the African-American family: An ethnographic case study. *Journal of Black Studies, 30,* 428–451.

Moses, L. J., Baldwin, D. A., Rosicky, J. G., & Tidball, G. (2001). Evidence for referential understanding in the emotions domain at twelve and eighteen months. *Child Development, 72,* 718–735.

Mosher, W. D., Chandra, A., & Jones, J. (2005). *Sexual behavior and selected health measures: Men and women 15–44 years of age, United States, 2002.* (Advance data from Vital and Health Statistics, No. 362). Hyattsville, MD: National Center for Health Statistics.

Moshman, D. (1998). Cognitive development beyond childhood. In D. Kuhn & R. S. Siegler (Eds.), *Handbook of child psychology: Vol. 2. Cognition, perception, and language* (5th ed., pp. 947–978). New York: Wiley.

Moshman, D. (2005). *Adolescent psychological development: Rationality, morality, and identity* (2nd ed.). Mahwah, NJ: Erlbaum.

Moshman, D., & Franks, B. A. (1986). Development of the concept of inferential validity. *Child Development, 57,* 153–165.

Moss, E., Cyr, C., Bureau, J.-F., Tarabulsy, G. M., & Dubois-Comtois, K. (2005b). Stability of attachment during the preschool period. *Developmental Psychology, 41,* 773–783.

Moss, E., Cyr, C., & Dubois-Comtois, K. (2004). Attachment at early school age and developmental risk: Examining family contexts and behavior problems of controlling-caregiving, controlling-punitive, and behaviorally disorganized children. *Developmental Psychology, 40,* 519–532.

Moss, E., Smolla, N., Guerra, I., Mazzarello, T., Chayer, D., & Berthiaume, C. (2006). Attachment and self-reported internalizing and externalizing behavior problems in a school period. *Canadian Journal of Behavioural Science, 38,* 142–157.

Mossey, P. A., Little, J., Munger, R. G., Dixon, M. J., & Shaw, W. C. (2009). Cleft lip and palate. *Lancet, 374,* 1773–1785.

Mosteller, F. (1995). The Tennessee Study of Class Size in the Early School Grades. *Future of Children, 5*(2), 113–127.

Motl, R. W., Dishman, R. K., Saunders, R. P., Dowda, M., Felton, G., Ward, D. S., & Pate, R. R. (2002). Examining social-cognitive determinants of intention and physical activity among black and white adolescent girls using structural equation modeling. *Health Psychology, 21,* 459–467.

Mottus, R., Indus, K., & Allik, J. (2008). Accuracy of only children stereotype. *Journal of Research in Personality, 42,* 1042–1052.

Mounts, N. S. (2011). Parental management of peer relationships and early adolescents' social skills. *Journal of Youth and Adolescence, 40,* 416–427.

Mounts, N. S., & Steinberg, L. D. (1995). An ecological analysis of peer influence on adolescent grade point average and drug use. *Developmental Psychology, 31,* 915–922.

Mounts, N. S., Valentiner, D. P., Anderson, K. L., & Boswell, M. K. (2006). Shyness, sociability, and parental support for the college transition: Relation to adolescents' adjustment. *Journal of Youth and Adolescence, 35,* 71–80.

Mrug, S., Hoza, B., & Gerdes, A. C. (2001). Children with attention-deficit/hyperactivity disorder: Peer relationships and peer-oriented interventions. In D. W. Nangle & C. A. Erdley (Eds.), *The role of friendship in psychological adjustment* (pp. 51–77). San Francisco: Jossey-Bass.

Mueller, C. M., & Dweck, C. S. (1998). Intelligence praise can undermine motivation and performance. *Journal of Personality and Social Psychology, 75,* 33–52.

Muenchow, S., & Marsland, K. W. (2007). Beyond baby steps: Promoting the growth and development of U.S. child-care policy. In J. L. Aber, S. J. Bishop-Josef, S. M. Jones, K. T. McLearn, & D. Phillips (Eds.), *Child development and social policy: Knowledge for action* (pp. 97–112). Washington, DC: American Psychological Association.

Müller, O., & Krawinkel, M. (2005). Malnutrition and health in developing countries. *Canadian Medical Association Journal, 173,* 279–286.

Müller, U., Overton, W. F., & Reese, K. (2001). Development of conditional reasoning: A longitudinal study. *Journal of Cognition and Development, 2,* 27–49.

Mullett-Hume, E., Anshel, D., Guevara, V., & Cloitre, M. (2008). Cumulative trauma and posttraumatic stress disorder among children exposed to the 9/11 World Trade Center attack. *American Journal of Orthopsychiatry, 78,* 103–108.

Mullis, I. V. S., Martin, M. O., Kennedy, A. M., & Foy, P. (2007). *PIRLS 2006 international report: IEA's Progress in International Reading Literacy Study.* Boston: TIMSS & PIRLS International Study Center.

Mulvaney, M. K., McCartney, K., Bub, K. L., & Marshall, N. L. (2006). Determinants of dyadic scaffolding and cognitive outcomes in first graders. *Parenting: Science and Practice, 6,* 297–310.

Mulvaney, M. K., & Mebert, C. J. (2007). Parental corporal punishment predicts behavior problems in early childhood. *Journal of Family Psychology, 21,* 389–397.

Mumme, D. L., Bushnell, E. W., DiCorcia, J. A., & Lariviere, L. A. (2007). Infants' use of gaze cues to interpret others' actions and emotional reactions. In R. Flom, K. Lee, & D. Muir (Eds.), *Gaze-following: Its development and significance* (pp. 143–170). Mahwah, NJ: Erlbaum.

Munakata, Y. (2001). Task-dependency in infant behavior: Toward an understanding of the processes underlying cognitive development. In F. Lacerda, C. von Hofsten, & M. Heimann (Eds.), *Emerging cognitive abilities in early infancy* (pp. 29–52). Mahwah, NJ: Erlbaum.

Munakata, Y. (2006). Information processing approaches to development. In D. Kuhn & R. S. Siegler (Eds.), *Handbook of child psychology: Vol. 3. Cognition, perception, and language* (6th ed., pp. 426–463). Hoboken, NJ: Wiley.

Munakata, Y., & Stedron, J. M. (2002). Modeling infants' perception of object unity: What have we learned? *Developmental Science, 5,* 176.

Mundy, P., & Stella, J. (2000). Joint attention, social orienting, and nonverbal communication in autism. In A. M. Wetherby & B. M. Prizant (Eds.), *Autism spectrum disorders* (Vol. 9, pp. 55–77). Baltimore, MD: Paul H. Brookes.

Munroe, R. L., & Romney, A. K. (2006). Gender and age differences in same-sex aggregation and social behavior. *Journal of Cross-Cultural Psychology, 37,* 3–19.

Murett-Wagstaff, S., & Moore, S. G. (1989). The Hmong in America: Infant behavior and rearing practices. In J. K. Nugent, B. M. Lester, & T. B. Brazelton (Eds.), *Biology, culture, and development* (Vol. 1, pp. 319–339). Norwood, NJ: Ablex.

Murphy, G. L. (2002). *The big book of concepts.* Cambridge, MA: MIT Press.

Murphy, K., McKone, E., & Slee, J. (2003). Dissociations between implicit and explicit memory in children: The role of strategic processing and the knowledge base. *Journal of Experimental Child Psychology, 84,* 124–165.

Murphy, L. M. B., Laurie-Rose, C., Brinkman, T. M., & McNamara, K. A. (2007). Sustained attention and social competence in typically developing preschool-aged children. *Early Child Development and Care, 177,* 133–149.

Murphy, M. C., Steele, C. M., & Gross, J. J. (2007). Signaling threat: How situational cues affect women in math, science, and engineering settings. *Psychological Science, 18*(10), 879–885.

Murphy, T. H., & Corbett, D. (2009). Plasticity during recovery: From synapse to behaviour. *Nature Reviews Neuroscience, 10,* 861–872.

Murray, A. D. (1985). Aversiveness is in the mind of the beholder. In B. M. Lester & C. F. Z. Boukydis (Eds.), *Infant crying* (pp. 217–239). New York: Plenum.

Murray, A. D., Johnson, J., & Peters, J. (1990). Fine-tuning of utterance length to preverbal infants: Effects on later language development. *Journal of Child Language, 17,* 511–525.

Murray-Close, D., Crick, N. R., & Galotti, K. M. (2006). Children's moral reasoning regarding physical and relational aggression. *Social Development, 15,* 345–372.

Mussen, P. H., & Eisenberg-Berg, N. (1977). *Roots of caring, sharing, and helping.* San Francisco: Freeman.

Mustanski, B. S., Viken, R. J., Kaprio, J., Pulkkinen, L., & Rose, R. J. (2004). Genetic and environmental influences on pubertal development: Longitudinal data from Finnish twins at ages 11 and 14. *Developmental Psychology, 40,* 1188–1198.

Muzzatti, B., & Agnoli, F. (2007). Gender and mathematics: Attitudes and stereotype threat susceptibility in Italian children. *Developmental Psychology, 43,* 747–759.

Myers, M. G., Brown, S. A., Tate, S., Abrantes, A., & Tomlinson, K. (2001). *Adolescents, alcohol, and substance abuse* (pp. 275–296). New York: Guilford.

Myowa-Yamakoshi, M., Tomonaga, M., Tanaka, M., & Matsuzawa, T. (2004). Imitation in neonatal chimpanzees *(Pan troglodytes). Developmental Science, 7,* 437–442.

NACCRRA (National Association of Child Care Resource and Referral Agencies). (2010). Parents and the high cost of child care: 2010 update. Retrieved from http://www.naccrra.org/publications/ naccrra-publications/parents-and-the-high-cost-of-child-care.php

Nadel, J., Prepin, K., & Okanda, M. (2005). Experiencing contingency and agency: First step toward self-understanding in making a mind? *Interaction Studies, 6,* 447–462.

Nader, P. R., O'Brien, M., Houts, R., Bradley, R., Belsky, J., Crosnoe, R., et al. (2006). Identifying risk for obesity in early childhood. *Pediatrics, 118,* e594–e601.

Nagin, D., & Tremblay, R. E. (1999). Trajectories of boys' physical aggression, opposition, and hyperactivity on the path to physically violent and nonviolent juvenile delinquency. *Child Development, 70,* 1181–1196.

Nagy, E., Compagne, H., Orvos, H., Pal, A., Molnar, P., & Janszky, I. (2005). Index finger movement imitation by human neonates: Motivation, learning, and left-hand preference. *Pediatric Research, 58,* 749–753.

Nagy, W. E., & Scott, J. A. (2000). Vocabulary processes. In M. L. Kamil & P. B. Mosenthal (Eds.), *Handbook of reading research* (Vol. 3, pp. 269–284). Mahwah, NJ: Erlbaum.

Naigles, L. G., & Gelman, S. A. (1995). Overextensions in comprehension and production revisited: Preferential-looking in a study of dog, cat, and cow. *Journal of Child Language, 22,* 19–46.

Naigles, L. R., & Swenson, L. D. (2007). Syntactic supports for word learning. In E. Hoff & M. Shatz (Eds.), *Blackwell handbook of language development* (pp. 212–231). Malden, MA: Blackwell.

Naito, M., & Seki, Y. (2009). The relationship between second-order false belief and display rules reasoning: Integration of cognitive and affective social understanding. *Developmental Science, 12,* 150–164.

Nakamura, K. (2001). The acquisition of polite language by Japanese children. In K. E. Nelson, A. Aksu-Koc, & C. E. Johnson (Eds.), *Children's language: Vol. 10. Developing narrative and discourse competence* (pp. 93–112). Mahwah, NJ: Erlbaum.

Nánez, J., Sr., & Yonas, A. (1994). Effects of luminance and texture motion on infant defensive reactions to optical collision. *Infant Behavior and Development, 17,* 165–174.

Narr, K. L., Woods, R. P., Lin J., Kim, J., Phillips, O. R., Del'Homme, M., et al.

(2009). Widespread cortical thinning is a robust anatomical marker for attention-deficit/hyperactivity disorder. *Journal of the American Academy of Child and Adolescent Psychiatry, 48,* 1014–1022.

Natale, K., Viljaranta, J., Lerkkanen, M.-K., Poikkeus, A.-M., & Nurmi, J.-E. (2009). Cross-lagged associations between kindergarten teachers' causal attributions and children's task motivation and performance in reading. *Educational Psychology, 29,* 603–619.

National Center for Biotechnology Information, National Institutes of Health. (2007). *Genes and disease: Sickle cell anemia.* Retrieved from www.ncbi .nlm.nih.gov/bookshelf/br.fcgi?book= gnd&part=anemiasicklecell

National Council of Youth Sports. (2008). *Report on trends and participation in organized youth sports.* Stuart, FL: Author.

National Early Literacy Panel. (2008). *Developing early literacy: A scientific synthesis of early literacy development and implications for intervention.* Jessup, MD: National Institute for Literacy.

National Federation of State High School Associations. (2009). *2007–08 High School Athletics Participation Survey.* Retrieved from www.nfhs.org/Participation/ HistoricalSearch.aspx

National Institutes of Health. (2011). *Genes and disease.* Retrieved from www.ncbi .nlm.nih.gov/books/NBK22183

National Research Council. (2007). *Race conscious policies for assigning students to schools: Social science research and the Supreme Court cases.* Washington, DC: National Academy Press.

National Women's Law Center. (2007). *When girls don't graduate we all fail.* Washington, DC: Author.

Natsuaki, M. N., Biehl, M. C., & Ge, X. (2009). Trajectories of depressed mood from early adolescence to young adulthood: The effects of pubertal timing and adolescent dating. *Journal of Research on Adolescence, 19,* 47–74.

Needham, A. (2001). Object recognition and object segregation in 4.5-month-old infants. *Journal of Experimental Child Psychology, 78,* 3–24.

Needham, A., & Baillargeon, R. (1993). Intuitions about support in 4.5-month-old infants. *Cognition, 47,* 121–148.

Needham, B. L., & Austin, E. L. (2010). Sexual orientation, parental support, and health during the transition to young adulthood. *Journal of Youth and Adolescence, 39,* 1189–1198.

Needleman, H. L., MacFarland, C., Ness, R. B., Reinberg, S., & Tobin, M. J. (2002). Bone lead levels in adjudicated delinquents: A case control study. *Neurotoxicology and Teratology, 24,* 711–717.

Neff, K. D., & Helwig, C. C. (2002). A constructivist approach to understanding the development of reasoning about rights and authority within cultural contexts. *Cognitive Development, 17,* 1429–1450.

Neitzel, C., & Stright, A. D. (2003). Mothers' scaffolding of children's problem solving: Establishing a foundation of academic self-regulatory competence. *Journal of Family Psychology, 17,* 147–159.

Nelson, C. A. (1995). The ontogeny of human memory: A cognitive neuroscience perspective. *Developmental Psychology, 31,* 723–738.

Nelson, C. A. (2001). The development and neural bases of face recognition. *Infant and Child Development, 10,* 3–18.

Nelson, C. A. (2002). Neural development and lifelong plasticity. In R. M. Lerner, F. Jacobs, & D. Wertlieb (Eds.), *Handbook of applied developmental science* (Vol. 1, pp. 31–60). Thousand Oaks, CA: Sage.

Nelson, C. A. (2007). A developmental cognitive neuroscience approach to the study of atypical development: A model system involving infants of diabetic mothers. In D. Coch, G. Dawson, & K. W. Fischer (Eds.), *Human behavior, learning, and the developing brain: Atypical development* (pp. 1–27). New York: Guilford.

Nelson, C. A., III. (2011). Neural development and lifelong plasticity. In D. P. Keating (Ed.), *Nature and nurture in early child development* (pp. 45–69). New York: Cambridge University Press.

Nelson, C. A., & Bosquet, M. (2000). Neurobiology of fetal and infant development: Implications for infant mental health. In C. H. Zeanah, Jr. (Ed.), *Handbook of infant mental health* (2nd ed., pp. 37–59). New York: Guilford.

Nelson, C. A., Thomas, K. M., & de Haan, M. (2006). Neural bases of cognitive development. In D. Kuhn & R. Siegler (Eds.), *Handbook of child psychology: Vol. 2. Cognition, perception, and language* (6th ed., pp. 3–57). Hoboken, NJ: Wiley.

Nelson, C. A., Wewerka, S., Borscheid, A. J., deRegnier, R., & Georgieff, M. K. (2003). Electrophysiologic evidence of impaired cross-modal recognition memory in 8-month-old infants of diabetic mothers. *Journal of Pediatrics, 142,* 575–582.

Nelson, C. A., Wewerka, S., Thomas, K. M., Tribby-Walbridge, S., deRegnier, R., & Georgieff, M. K. (2000). Neurocognitive sequelae of infants of diabetic mothers. *Behavioral Neuroscience, 114,* 950–956.

Nelson, C. A., III, Zeanah, C. H., Fox, N. A., Marshall, P. J., Smyke, A. T., & Guthrie, D. (2007). Cognitive recovery in socially deprived young children: The Bucharest Early Intervention Project. *Science, 318,* 1937–1940.

Nelson, D. A., & Coyne, S. M. (2009). Children's intent attributions and feelings of distress: Associations with maternal and paternal parenting practices. *Journal of Abnormal Child Psychology, 37,* 223–237.

Nelson, D. A., Hart, C. H., Yang, C., Olsen, J. A., & Jin, S. (2006). Aversive parenting in China: Associations with child physical and relational aggression. *Child Development, 77,* 554–572.

Nelson, D. A., Nelson, L. J., Hart, C. H., Yang, C., & Jin, S. (2005). Parenting and peer-group behavior in cultural context. In X. Chen, B. Schneider, & D. French (Eds.), *Peer relations in cultural context.* New York Cambridge University Press.

Nelson, D. A., Robinson, C. C., & Hart, C. H. (2005). Relational and physical aggression of preschool-age children: Peer status linkages across informants. *Early Education and Development, 16,* 115–139.

Nelson, K. (1973). Structure and strategy in learning to talk. *Monographs of the Society for Research in Child Development, 38*(1–2, Serial No. 149).

Nelson, K. (1976). Some attributes of adjectives used by young children. *Cognition, 4,* 13–30.

Nelson, K. (2003). Narrative and the emergence of a consciousness of self. In G. D. Fireman & T. E. McVay, Jr. (2003). *Narrative and consciousness: Literature, psychology, and the brain* (pp. 17–36). London: Oxford University Press.

Nelson, K. (2007). *Young minds in social worlds: Experience, meaning, and memory*. Cambridge, MA: Harvard University Press.

Nelson, K., & Fivush, R. (2004). The emergence of autobiographical memory: A social cultural developmental theory. *Developmental Review, 111*, 486–511.

Nelson, W. E. (Ed.). (1996). *Nelson textbook of pediatrics*. Philadelphia: Saunders.

Nemet, D., Barkan, S., Epstein, Y., Friedland, O., Kowen, G., & Eliakim, A. (2005). Short- and long-term beneficial effects of a combined dietary–behavioral–physical activity intervention for the treatment of childhood obesity. *Pediatrics, 115*, e443–e449.

Nepomnyaschy, L., & Waldfogel, J. (2007). Paternity leave and fathers' involvement with their young children. *Community, Work and Family, 10*, 427–453.

Neri, Q., Takeuchi, T., & Palermo, G. D. (2008). An update of assisted reproductive technologies in the United States. *Annals of the New York Academy of Sciences, 1127*, 41–48.

Nesdale, D., Durkin, K., Maas, A., & Griffiths, J. (2005). Threat, group identification, and children's ethnic prejudice. *Social Development, 14*, 189–205.

Neubauer, A. C., & Fink, A. (2009). Intelligence and neural efficiency. *Neuroscience and Biobehavioral Reviews, 33*, 1004–1023.

Neuman, S. B. (2006). The knowledge gap: Implications for early education. In D. K. Dickinson & S. B. Neuman (Eds.) *Handbook of early literacy research* (Vol. 2, pp. 29–40). New York: Guilford.

Neuman, S. B., & Celano, D. (2001). Access to print in middle- and low-income communities: An ecological study of four neighborhoods. *Reading Research Quarterly, 36*, 8–26.

Neville, H. J., & Bavelier, D. (2002). Human brain plasticity: Evidence from sensory deprivation and altered language experience. In M. A. Hofman, G. J. Boer, A. J. G. D. Holtmaat, E. J. W. van Someren, J. Berhaagen, & D. F. Swaab (Eds.), *Plasticity in the adult brain: From genes to neurotherapy* (pp. 177–188). Amsterdam: Elsevier Science.

Neville, H. J., & Bruer, J. T. (2001). Language processing: How experience affects brain organization. In D. B. Bailey, Jr., J. T. Bruer, F. J. Symons, & J. W. Lichtman (Eds.), *Critical thinking about critical periods* (pp. 151–172). Baltimore: Paul H. Brookes.

Nevin, R. (2006). Understanding international crime trends: The legacy of preschool lead exposure. *Environmental Research, 104*, 315–316.

Newcomb, A. F., & Bagwell, C. (1995). Children's friendship relations: A meta-analytic review. *Psychological Bulletin, 117*, 306–347.

Newcomb, A. F., Bukowski, W. M., & Pattee, L. (1993). Children's peer relations: A meta-analytic review of popular, rejected, neglected, controversial, and average sociometric status. *Psychological Bulletin, 113*, 99–128.

Newcombe, N. S. (2007). Taking science seriously: Straight thinking about spatial sex differences. In S. J. Ceci & W. M. Williams (Eds.), *Why aren't more women in science?* (pp. 69–77). Washington, DC: American Psychological Association.

Newcombe, N., & Huttenlocher, J. (1992). Children's early ability to solve perspective-taking problems. *Developmental Psychology, 28*, 635–643.

Newcombe, N. S., & Huttenlocher, J. (2006). Development of spatial cognition. In

D. Kuhn & R. Siegler (Eds.), *Handbook of child psychology: Vol. 2. Cognition, perception, and language* (6th ed., pp. 734–776). Hoboken, NJ: Wiley.

Newcombe, N. S., Sluzenski, J., & Huttenlocher, J. (2005). Preexisting knowledge versus on-line learning: What do young infants really know about spatial location? *Psychological Science, 16*, 222–227.

Newland, L. A., Coyl, D. D., & Freeman, H. (2008). Predicting preschoolers' attachment security from fathers' involvement, internal working models, and use of social support. *Early Child Development and Care, 178*, 785–801.

Newman, A. J., Bavelier, D., Corina, D., Jezzard, P., & Neville, H. J. (2002). A critical period for right hemisphere recruitment in American sign language processing. *Nature Neuroscience, 5*, 76–80.

Newman, L. S. (1990). Intentional and unintentional memory in young children: Remembering vs. playing. *Journal of Experimental Child Psychology, 50*, 243–258.

Newnham, C. A., Milgrom, J., & Skouteris, H. (2009). Effectiveness of a modified mother–infant transaction program on outcomes for preterm infants from 3 to 24 months of age. *Infant Behavior and Development, 32*, 17–26.

Newport, E. L. (1991). Contrasting conceptions of the critical period for language. In S. Carey & R. Gelman (Eds.), *The epigenesis of mind: Essays on biology and cognition* (pp. 111–130). Hillsdale, NJ: Erlbaum.

Newson, J., & Newson, E. (1975). Intersubjectivity and the transmission of culture: On the social origins of symbolic functioning. *Bulletin of the British Psychological Society, 28*, 437–446.

Neyer, F. J., & Lang, F. R. (2003). Blood is thicker than water: Kinship orientation across adulthood. *Journal of Personality and Social Psychology, 84*, 310–321.

Ng, F. F., Pomerantz, E. M., & Lam, S. (2007). European American and Chinese parents' responses to children's success and failure: Implications for children's responses. *Developmental Psychology, 43*, 1239–1255.

Nguyen, U.-S. D. T., Rothman, K. J., Demissie, S., Jackson, D., Liang, J. M., & Ecker, J. L. (2010). Epidural analgesia and risks of cesarean and operative vaginal deliveries in nulliparous and multiparous women. *Maternal and Child Health Journal, 14*, 705–712.

Ni, Y. (1998). Cognitive structure, content knowledge, and classificatory reasoning. *Journal of Genetic Psychology, 159*, 280–296.

Niccolai, L. M., Ethier, K. A., Kershaw, T. S., Lewis, J. B., Meade, C. S., & Ickovics, J. R. (2004). New sex partner acquisition and sexually transmitted disease risk among adolescent females. *Journal of Adolescent Health, 34*, 216–223.

NICHD (National Institute of Child Health and Human Development) Early Child Care Research Network. (1997). The effects of infant child care on infant–mother attachment security: Results of the NICHD Study of Early Child Care. *Child Development, 68*, 860–879.

NICHD (National Institute of Child Health and Human Development) Early Child Care Research Network. (1998). Relations between family predictors and child outcomes: Are they weaker for children in child care? *Developmental Psychology, 34*, 1119–1128.

NICHD (National Institute of Child Health and Human Development) Early Child Care Research Network. (1999). Child care and mother–child interaction in the first 3 years of life. *Developmental Psychology, 35*, 1399–1413.

NICHD (National Institute of Child Health and Human Development) Early Child Care Research Network. (2000a). Characteristics and quality of child care for toddlers and preschoolers. *Applied Developmental Science, 4*, 116–135.

NICHD (National Institute of Child Health and Human Development) Early Child Care Research Network. (2000b). The relation of child care to cognitive and language development. *Child Development, 71*, 960–980.

NICHD (National Institute of Child Health and Human Development) Early Child Care Research Network. (2001a, April). *Early child care and children's development prior to school entry*. Symposium presented at the biennial meeting of the Society for Research in Child Development, Minneapolis, MN.

NICHD (National Institute of Child Health and Human Development) Early Child Care Research Network. (2001b). Before Head Start: Income and ethnicity, family characteristics, child care experiences, and child development. *Early Education and Development, 12*, 545–575.

NICHD (National Institute of Child Health and Human Development) Early Child Care Research Network. (2002a). Childcare structure → process → outcome: Direct and indirect effects of child-care quality on young children's development. *Psychological Science, 13*, 199–206.

NICHD (National Institute of Child Health and Human Development) Early Child Care Research Network. (2002b). The interaction of child care and family risk in relation to child development at 24 and 36 months. *Applied Developmental Science, 6*, 144–156

NICHD (National Institute of Child Health and Human Development) Early Child Care Research Network. (2003a). Does amount of time spent in child care predict socioemotional adjustment during the transition to kindergarten? *Child Development, 74*, 976–1005.

NICHD (National Institute of Child Health and Human Development) Early Child Care Research Network. (2003b). Does quality of child care affect child outcomes at age 4 1/2? *Developmental Psychology, 39*, 451–469.

NICHD (National Institute of Child Health and Human Deveopment) Early Child Care Research Network. (2004a). Does class size in first grade relate to children's academic and social performance or observed classroom processes? *Developmental Psychology, 40*, 651–664.

NICHD (National Institute of Child Health and Human Development) Early Child Care Research Network. (2004b). Trajectories of physical aggression from toddlerhood to middle childhood. *Monographs of the Society for Research in Child Development, 69*(4, Serial No. 278).

NICHD (National Institute of Child Health and Human Development) Early Child Care Research Network. (2006). Child-care effect sizes for the NICHD Study of Early Child Care and Youth Development. *American Psychologist, 61*, 99–116.

Nicholls, A. L., & Kennedy, J. M. (1992) Drawing development: From similarity of features to direction. *Child Development, 63*, 227–241.

Nicholls, D. E., & Viner, R. M. (2009). Childhood risk factors for lifetime anorexia nervosa by age 30 in a national birth cohort. *Journal of the American Academy of Child and Adolescent Psychiatry, 48*, 791–799.

Nichols, K. E., Fox, N., & Mundy, P. (2005). Joint attention, self-recognition, and neurocognitive function in toddlers. *Infancy, 7*, 35–51.

Nichols, S. L., & Berliner, D. C. (2007). The pressure to cheat in a high-stakes testing environment. In E. M. Anderman & T. B. Murdock (Eds.), *Psychology of academic cheating* (pp. 289–311). San Francisco: Jossey-Bass.

Nicholson, C. (2006, September). Thinking it over: fMRI and psychological science. *APS Observer*, pp. 21–25.

Nicholson, J. M., Sanders, M. R., Halford, W. K., Phillips, M., & Whitton, S. W. (2008). The prevention and treatment of children's adjustment problems in stepfamilies. In J. Pryor (Ed.), *International handbook of stepfamilies: Policy and practice in legal, research, and clinical environments* (pp. 485–521). Hoboken, NJ: Wiley.

Nickman, S. L., Rosenfeld, A. A., Fine, P., MacIntyre, J. C., Pilowsky, D. J., & Howe, R.-A. (2005). Children in adoptive families: Overview and update. *Journal of the American Academy of Child and Adolescent Psychiatry, 44*, 987–995.

Nicolopoulou, A. (2006). The interplay of play and narrative in children's development: Theoretical reflections and concrete examples. In A. Göncü & S. Gaskins (Eds.), *Play and development: Evolutionary, sociocultural, and functional perspectives* (pp. 247–276). Hillsdale, NJ: Erlbaum.

Niehaus, M. D., Moore, S. R., Patrick, P. D., Derr, L. L., Lorntz, B., Lima, A. A., & Gurerrant, R. L. (2002). Early childhood diarrhea is associated with diminished cognitive function 4 to 7 years later in children in a northeast Brazilian shantytown. *American Journal of Tropical Medicine and Hygiene, 66*, 590–593.

Nielsen, L. S., Danielsen, K. V., & Sørensen, T. I. (2011). Short sleep duration as a possible cause of obesity: Critical analysis of the epidemiological evidence. *Obesity Reviews, 12*, 78–92.

Nielsen, M., & Christie, T. (2008). Adult modeling facilitates young children's generation of novel pretend acts. *Infant and Child Development, 17*, 151–162.

Nievar, M. A., & Becker, B. J. (2008). Sensitivity as a privileged predictor of attachment: A second perspective on De Wolff & van IJzendoorn's meta-analysis. *Social Development, 17*, 102–114.

Nigg, J. T., & Breslau, N. (2007). Prenatal smoking exposure, low birth weight, and disruptive behavior disorders. *Journal of the American Academy of Child and Adolescent Psychiatry, 46*, 362–369.

Nippold, M. A., Allen, M. M., & Kirsch, D. I. (2001). Proverb comprehension as a function of reading proficiency in preadolescents. *Language, Speech and Hearing Services in the Schools, 32*, 90–100.

Nippold, M. A., Taylor, C. L., & Baker, J. M. (1996). Idiom understanding in Australian youth: A cross-cultural comparison. *Journal of Speech and Hearing Research, 39*, 442–447.

Nisbett, R. E. (2009). *Intelligence and how to get it*. New York: Norton

Nishitani, S., Miyamura, T., Tagawa, M., Sumi, M., Takase, R., Doi, H., et al.

(2009). The calming effect of a maternal breast milk odor on the human newborn infant. *Neuroscience Research, 63,* 66–71.

Niu, W., & Sternberg, R. J. (2001). Cultural influences on artistic creativity and its evaluation. *International Journal of Psychology, 36,* 225–241.

Niu, W., & Sternberg, R. J. (2003). Societal and school influences on student creativity: The case of China. *Psychology in the Schools, 40,* 103–114.

Noble, K. G., McCandiliss, B. D., & Farah, M. J. (2007). Socioeconomic gradients predict individual differences in neurocognitive abilities. *Developmental Science, 10,* 464–480.

Noguera, P. (2010, June 14). A new vision for school reform. *The Nation,* pp. 11–14.

Nolen-Hoeksema, S. (2002). Gender differences in depression. In I. H. Gotlib & C. L. Hammen (Eds.), *Handbook of depression* (pp. 492–509). New York: Guilford.

Nolen-Hoeksema, S. (2006). The etiology of gender differences in depression. In C. M. Mazure & G. Puryear (Eds.), *Understanding depression in women: Applying empirical research to practice and policy* (pp. 9–43). Washington, DC: American Psychological Association.

Noller, P., Feeney, J. A., Sheehan, G., Darlington, Y., & Rogers, C. (2008). Conflict in divorcing and continuously married families: A study of marital, parent–child and sibling relationships. *Journal of Divorce and Remarriage, 49,* 1–24.

Noonan, C. W., Kathman, S. J., Sarasua, S. M., & White, M. C. (2003). Influence of environmental zinc on the association between environmental and biological measures of lead in children. *Journal of Exposure Analysis and Environmental Epidemiology, 13,* 318–323.

Nosarti, C., Walshe, M., Rushe, T. M., Rifkin, L., Wyatt, J., Murray, R. M., et al. (2011). Neonatal ultrasound results following very preterm birth predict adolescent behavioral and cognitive outcome. *Developmental Neuropsychology, 36,* 118–135.

Nosek, B. A., Smyth, F. L., Siriram, N., Lindner, N. M., Devos, T., Ayala, A., et al. (2009). National differences in gender–science stereotypes predict national sex differences in science and math achievement. *Proceedings of the National Academy of Sciences, 106,* 10593–10597.

Noterdaeme, M., Mildenberger, K., Minow, F., & Amorosa, H. (2002). Evaluation of neuromotor deficits in children with autism and children with a specific speech and language disorder. *European Child and Adolescent Psychiatry, 11,* 219–225.

Nucci, L. (2008). *Nice is not enough: Facilitating moral development.* Upper Saddle River, NJ: Prentice Hall.

Nucci, L. P. (1996). Morality and the personal sphere of action. In E. Reed, E. Turiel, & T. Brown (Eds.), *Values and knowledge* (pp. 41–60). Hillsdale, NJ: Erlbaum.

Nucci, L. P. (2001). *Education in the moral domain.* New York: Cambridge University Press.

Nucci, L. P. (2002). The development of moral reasoning. In U. Goswami (Ed.), *Blackwell handbook of childhood cognitive development* (pp. 303–325). Malden, MA: Blackwell.

Nucci, L. P. (2005). Culture, context, and the psychological sources of human rights concepts. In W. Edelstein & G. Nunner-

Winkler (Eds.), *Morality in context* (pp. 365–394). Amsterdam, Netherlands: Elsevier.

Nunez-Smith, M., Wolf, E., Huang, H. M., Chen, P. G., Lee, L., Emanuel, E. J., et al. (2008). *The impact of media on child and adolescent health.* Retrieved from www.commonsensemedia.org.

Nuttall, R. L., Casey, M. B., & Pezaris, E. (2005). Spatial ability as a mediator of gender differences on mathematics tests: A biological–environmental framework. In A. M. Gallagher & C. J. Kaufman (Eds.), *Gender differences in mathematics: An integrated psychological approach* (pp. 121–142). New York: Cambridge University Press.

Nye, B., Hedges, L. V., & Konstantopoulos, S. (2001). Are effects of small classes cumulative? Evidence from a Tennessee experiment. *Journal of Educational Research, 94,* 336–345.

Oakes, L. M., Coppage, D. J., & Dingel, A. (1997). By land or by sea: The role of perceptual similarity in infants' categorization of animals. *Developmental Psychology, 33,* 396–407.

Oakes, L. M., Horst, J. S., Kovack-Lesh, K. A., & Perone, S. (2009). How infants learn categories. In A. Woodward & A. Needham (Eds.), *Learning and the infant mind* (pp. 144–171). New York: Oxford University Press.

Obeidallah, D., Brennan, R. T., Brooks-Gunn, J., & Earls, F. (2004). Links between pubertal timing and neighborhood contexts: Implications for girls' violent behavior. *Journal of the American Academy of Child and Adolescent Psychiatry, 43,* 1460–1468.

Oberecker, R., & Friederici, A. D. (2006). Syntactic event-related potential components in 24-month-olds' sentence comprehension. *Neuroreport, 17,* 1017–1021.

Oberecker, R., Friedrich, M., & Friederici, A. D. (2005). Neural correlates of syntactic processing in two-year-olds. *Journal of Cognitive Neuroscience, 17,* 1667–1678.

Obler, L. K. (2008). Developments in the adult years. In J. B. Gleason & B. Ratner (Eds.), *The development of language* (7th ed., pp. 436–464). Boston: Allyn and Bacon.

Obradović, J., Long, J. D., Cutuli, J. J., Chan, C. K., Hinz, E., Heistad, D., & Masten, A. S. (2009). Academic achievement of homeless and highly mobile children in an urban school district: Longitudinal evidence on risk, growth, and resilience. *Development and Psychopathology, 21,* 493–518.

Obradović, J., & Masten, A. S. (2007). Developmental antecedents of young adult civic engagement. *Applied Developmental Science, 11,* 2–19.

Ochs, E. (1988). *Culture and language development: Language acquisition and language socialization in a Samoan village.* Cambridge, UK: Cambridge University Press.

O'Connor, E., & McCartney, K. (2007). Examining teacher–child relationships and achievement as part of an ecological model of development. *American Educational Research Journal, 44,* 340–369.

O'Connor, T. G., & Croft, C. M. (2001). A twin study of attachment in preschool children. *Child Development, 72,* 1501–1511.

O'Connor, T. G., Marvin, R. S., Rutter, M., Olrich, J. T., Britner, P. A., & the English

and Romanian Adoptees Study Team. (2003). Child–parent attachment following early institutional deprivation. *Development and Psychopathology, 15,* 19–38.

O'Connor, T. G., Rutter, M., Beckett, C., Keaveney, L., Dreppner, J. M., & the English and Romanian Adoptees Study Team. (2000). The effects of global severe privation on cognitive competence: Extension and longitudinal follow-up. *Child Development, 71,* 376–390.

OECD (Organisation for Economic Cooperation and Development). (2005). *Education at a glance: OECD indicators 2005.* Paris: Author.

OECD (Organisation for Economic Cooperation and Development). (2006). *Starting strong II: Early childhood education and care.* Paris: OECD Publishing. Retrieved from www .sourceoecd.org/education/9264035451

OECD (Organisation for Economic Cooperation and Development). (2010a). *Education at a glance 2010: OECD indicators.* Paris: Author. Retrieved from www.oecd.org/document/52/0,3746,en_2649_39263238_45897844_1_1_1_1,00 .html

OECD (Organisation for Economic Cooperation and Development). (2010b). *OECD Health data: 2010.* Retrieved from www.oecd.org/document/44/0,3746,en_2649_37407_2085228_1_1_1_37407,00 .html

Ogan, A., & Berk, L. E. (2009, April). *Effects of two approaches to make-believe play training on self-regulation in Head Start children.* Paper presented at the biennial meeting of the Society for Research in Child Development, Denver, CO.

Ogbu, J. U. (1997). Understanding the school performance of urban blacks: Some essential background knowledge. In H. J. Walberg, O. Reyes, & R. P. Weissberg (Eds.), *Children and youth: Interdisciplinary perspectives* (pp. 190–222). Thousand Oaks, CA: Sage.

Ogbu, J. U. (2003). *Black American students in an affluent suburb: A study of academic disengagement.* Mahwah, NJ: Erlbaum.

Ogden, C. L., Carroll, M. D., Curtin, L. R., Lamb, M. M., & Flegal, K. M. (2010). Prevalence of high body mass index in U.S. children and adolescents, 2007–2008. *Journal of the American Medical Association, 303,* 242–249.

Ohannessian, C. M., & Hesselbrock, V. M. (2008). Paternal alcoholism and youth substance abuse: The indirect effects of negative affect, conduct problems, and risk taking. *Journal of Adolescent Health, 42,* 198–200.

Ohgi, S., Arisawa, K., Takahashi, T., Kusumoto, T., Goto, Y., Akiyama, T., & Saito, H. (2003a). Neonatal Behavioral Assessment Scale as a predictor of later developmental disabilities of low-birthweight and/or premature infants. *Brain and Development, 25,* 313–321.

Ohgi, S., Takahashi, T., Nugent, J. K., Arisawa, K., & Akiyama, T. (2003b). Neonatal behavioral characteristics and later behavioral problems. *Clinical Pediatrics, 42,* 679–686.

Ohlsson, G., Buchhave, P., Leandersson, U., Nordstrom, L., Rydhstrom, H., & Sjolin, I. (2001). Warm tub bathing during labor: Maternal and neonatal effects. *Acta Obstetricia et Gynecologica Scandinavica, 80,* 311–314.

Okagaki, L. (2001). Parental beliefs, parenting style, and children's intellectual development. In E. L. Grigorenko & R. J.

Sternberg (Eds.), *Family environment and intellectual functioning: A life-span perspective* (pp. 141–172). Mahwah, NJ: Erlbaum.

Okagaki, L., & Frensch, P. A. (1998). Parenting and children's school achievement: A multi-ethnic perspective. *American Educational Research Journal, 35,* 123–144.

Okagaki, L., & Sternberg, R. J. (1993). Parental beliefs and children's school performance. *Child Development, 64,* 36–56.

Okami, P., Weisner, T., & Olmstead, R. (2002). Outcome correlates of parent–child bedsharing: An eighteen-year longitudinal study. *Developmental and Behavioral Pediatrics, 23,* 244–253.

O'Keefe, M. J., O'Callaghan, M., Williams, G. M., Najman, J. M., & Bor, W. (2003). Learning, cognitive, and attentional problems in adolescents born small for gestational age. *Pediatrics, 112,* 301–307.

Olafson, E., & Boat, B. W. (2000). Long-term management of the sexually abused child: Considerations and challenges. In R. M. Reece (Ed.), *Treatment of child abuse: Common ground for mental health, medical, and legal practitioners* (pp. 14–35). Baltimore: Johns Hopkins University Press.

Oldershaw, L. (2002). *A national survey of parents of young children.* Toronto: Invest in Kids.

Olds, D. L., Eckenrode, J., Henderson, C., Kitzman, H., Cole, R., Luckey, D., et al. (2009). Preventing child abuse and neglect with home visiting by nurses. In K. A. Dodge & D. L. Coleman (Eds.), *Preventing child maltreatment* (pp. 29–54). New York: Guilford.

Olds, D. L., Kitzman, H., Cole, R., Robinson, J., Sidora, K., Luckey, D. W., et al. (2004). Effects of nurse home-visiting on maternal life course and child development: Age 6 follow-up results of a randomized trial. *Pediatrics, 114,* 1550–1559.

Olds, D. L., Kitzman, H., Hanks, C., Cole, R., Anson, E., Sidora-Arcoleo, K., et al. (2007). Effects of nurse home visiting on maternal and child functioning: Age-9 follow-up of a randomized trial. *Pediatrics, 120,* e832–e845.

Olds, D. L., Robinson, J., O'Brien, R., Luckey, D. W., Pettitt, L. M., Henderson, C. R., Jr., et al. (2002). Home visiting by paraprofessionals and by nurses: A randomized, controlled trial. *Pediatrics, 110,* 486–496.

Olfman, S., & Robbins, B. D. (Eds.). (2012). *Drugging our children.* New York: Praeger.

Olineck, K. M., & Poulin-Dubois, D. (2007). Imitation of intentional actions and internal state language in infancy predict preschool theory of mind skills. *European Journal of Developmental Psychology, 4,* 14–30.

Olineck, K. M., & Poulin-Dubois, D. (2009). Infants' understanding of intention from 10 to 14 months: Interrelations among violation of expectancy and imitation tasks. *Infant Behavior and Development, 32,* 404–415.

Ollendick, T. H., Yang, B., King, N. J., Dong, X., & Akande, A. (1996). Fears in American, Australian, Chinese, and Nigerian children and adolescents: A cross-cultural study. *Journal of Child Psychology and Psychiatry, 37,* 213–220.

Oller, D. K. (2000). *The emergence of the speech capacity.* Mahwah, NJ: Erlbaum.

Oller, D. K., Eilers, R. E., Urbano, R., & Cobo-Lewis, A. B. (1997). Development of precursors to speech in infants exposed to two languages. *Journal of Child Language, 24,* 407–425.

Olson, D., Sikka, R. S., Hayman, J., Novak, M., & Stavig, C. (2009). Exercise in pregnancy. *Current Sports Medicine Reports, 8,* 147–153.

Olweus, D. (2011). Bullying at school and later criminality: Findings from three Swedish community samples of males. *Criminal Behaviour and Mental Health, 21,* 151–156.

Olweus, D., Mattison, A., Schalling, D., & Low, H. (1988). Circulating testosterone levels and aggression in adolescent males: A causal analysis. *Psychosomatic Medicine, 50,* 261–272.

O'Mahoney, J. F. (1989). Development of thinking about things and people: Social and nonsocial cognition during adolescence. *Journal of Genetic Psychology, 150,* 217–224.

Omar, H., McElderry, D., & Zakharia, R. (2003). Educating adolescents about puberty: What are we missing? *International Journal of Adolescent Medicine and Health, 15,* 79–83.

Ondrusek, N., Abramovitch, R., Pencharz, P., & Koren, G. (1998). Empirical examination of the ability of children to consent to clinical research. *Journal of Medical Ethics, 24,* 158–165.

O'Neil, R., Welsh, M., Parke, R. D., Wang, S., & Strand, C. (1997). A longitudinal assessment of the academic correlates of early peer acceptance and rejection. *Journal of Clinical Child Psychology, 26,* 290–303.

O'Neill, M., Bard, K. A., Kinnell, M., & Fluck, M. (2005). Maternal gestures with 20-month-old infants in two contexts. *Developmental Science, 8,* 352–359.

Ong, K. K., Ahmed, M. L., & Dunger, D. B. (2006). Lessons from large population studies on timing and tempo of puberty (secular trends and relation to body size): the European trend. *Molecular and Cellular Endocrinology, 254–255,* 8–12.

Ong, W., Allison, J., & Haladyna, T. M. (2000). Student achievement of third graders in comparable single-age and multiage classrooms. *Journal of Research in Childhood Education, 14,* 205–215.

Ontai, L. L., & Thompson, R. A. (2010). Attachment, parent–child discourse, and theory-of-mind development. *Social Development, 17,* 47–60.

Oosterwegel, A., & Oppenheimer, L. (1993). *The self-system: Developmental changes between and within self-concepts.* Hillsdale, NJ: Erlbaum.

Ophir, E., Nass, C., & Wagner, A. D. (2009). Cognitive control in media multitaskers. *Proceedings of the National Academy of Sciences, 106,* 15583–15587.

Opinion Research Corporation. (2009). American teens say they want more time with parents. Retrieved from www .napsnet.com/pdf_archive/47/68753.pdf

O'Rahilly, R., & Müller, F. (2001). *Human embryology and teratology.* New York: Wiley-Liss.

O'Reilly, A. W. (1995). Using representations: Comprehension and production of actions with imagined objects. *Child Development, 66,* 999–1010.

Ornstein, P. A., Haden, C. A., & Elischberger, H. B. (2006). Children's memory development: Remembering the past and preparing for the future. In E. Bialystok & F. I. M. Craik (Eds.), *Lifespan cognition: Mechanisms of change* (pp. 143–161). New York: Oxford University Press.

Orobio de Castro, B., Brendgen, M., Van Boxtel, H., Vitaro, F., & Schaepers, L. (2007). "Accept me, or else…": Disputed overestimation of social competence predicts increases in proactive aggression. *Journal of Abnormal Child Psychology, 35,* 165–178.

Orobio de Castro, B., Veerman, J. W., Koops, W., Bosch, J. D., & Monshouwer, H. J. (2002). Hostile attribution of intent and aggressive behavior: A meta-analysis. *Child Development, 73,* 916–934.

Osherson, D. N., & Markman, E. M. (1975). Language and the ability to evaluate contradictions and tautologies. *Cognition, 2,* 213–226.

Oshima-Takane, Y., & Robbins, M. (2003). Linguistic environment of second-born children. *First Language, 23,* 21–40.

Ostad, S. A., & Sorensen, P. M. (2007). Private speech and strategy-use patterns: Bidirectional comparisons of children with and without mathematical difficulties in a developmental perspective. *Journal of Learning Disabilities, 40,* 2–14.

Ostrov, J. M., Crick, N. R., & Stauffacher, K. (2006). Relational aggression in sibling and peer relationships during early childhood. *Applied Developmental Psychology, 27,* 241–253.

Ostrov, J. M., Gentile, D. A., & Crick, N. R. (2006). Media exposure, aggression, and prosocial behavior during early childhood: A longitudinal study. *Social Development, 15,* 612–627.

Otis, N., Grouzet, F. M. E., & Pelletier, L. G. (2005). Latent motivational change in an academic setting: A three-year longitudinal study. *Journal of Educational Psychology, 97,* 170–183.

Otto, M. W., Henin, A., Hirshfeld-Becker, D. R., Pollack, M. H., Biederman, J., & Rosenbaum, J. (2007). Posttraumatic stress disorder symptoms following media exposure to tragic events: Impact of 9/11 on children at risk for anxiety disorders. *Journal of Anxiety Disorders, 21,* 888–902.

Oude, L. H., Baur, L., Jansen, H., Shrewsbury, V. A., O'Malley, C., Stolk, R. P., & Summerbell, C. D. (2009). *Interventions for treating obesity in children.* Cochrane Database of Systematic Reviews, Issue 4. Chichester, UK: Wiley.

Ouko, L. A., Shantikumar, K., Knezovich, J., Haycock, P., Schnugh, D. J., & Ramsay, M. (2009). Effect of alcohol consumption on CpG methylation in the differentially methylated regions of H19 and IG-DMR in male gametes: Implications for fetal alcohol spectrum disorders. *Alcoholism, Clinical and Experimental Research, 33,* 1615–1627.

Ovando, C. J., & Collier, V. P. (1998). *Bilingual and ESL classrooms: Teaching in multicultural contexts.* Boston: McGraw-Hill.

Owen, C. G., Whincup, P. H., Kaye, S. J., Martin, R. M., Smith, G. D., Cook, D. G., et al. (2008). Does initial breastfeeding lead to lower blood cholesterol in adult life? A quantitative review of the evidence. *American Journal of Clinical Nutrition, 88,* 305–314.

Owen, M. T., & Cox, M. J. (1997). Marital conflict and the development of infant–parent attachment relationships. *Journal of Family Psychology, 11,* 152–164.

Owen-Kostelnik, J., Reppucci, N. D., & Meyer, J. R. (2006). Testimony and interrogation of minors: Assumptions about maturity and morality. *American Psychologist, 61,* 286–304.

Oyelese, Y., & Ananth, C. V. (2006). Placental abruption. *Obstetrics and Gynecology, 108,* 1005–1016.

Oyserman, D., Bybee, D., Mowbray, C., & Hart-Johnson, T. (2005). When mothers have serious mental health problems: Parenting as a proximal mediator. *Journal of Adolescence, 28,* 443–463.

Özçaliskan, S. (2005). On learning to draw the distinction between physical and metaphorical motion: Is metaphor an early emerging cognitive and linguistic capacity? *Journal of Child Language, 32,* 291–318.

Özçaliskan, S., & Goldin-Meadow, S. (2005). Gesture is at the cutting edge of early language development. *Cognition, 96,* B101–B113.

Ozer, E. M., & Irwin, C. E., Jr. (2009). Adolescent and young adult health: From basic health status to clinical interventions. In R. M. Lerner & L. Steinberg (Eds.), *Handbook of adolescent psychology: Vol. 1. Individual bases of adolescent development* (pp. 618–641). Hoboken, NJ: Wiley.

Padilla, A. M. (2006). Second language learning: Issues in research and teaching. In P. A. Alexander & P. H. Winne (Eds.), *Handbook of educational psychology* (pp. 571–591). Mahwah, NJ: Erlbaum.

Padilla-Walker, L. M. (2008). 'My mom makes me so angry!' Adolescent perceptions of mother–child interactions as correlates of adolescent emotions. *Social Development, 17,* 306–325.

Paek, H.-J., Nelson, M. R., & Vilela, A. M. (2011). Examination of gender-role portrayals in television advertising across seven countries. *Sex Roles, 64,* 192–207.

Paladino, J. (2006). *Private speech in children with autism: Developmental course and functional utility.* Unpublished doctoral dissertation, Illinois State University.

Palincsar, A. S. (2003). Advancing a theoretical model of learning and instruction. In B. J. Zimmerman (Ed.), *Educational psychology: A century of contributions* (pp. 459–475). Mahwah, NJ: Erlbaum.

Palmer, J. R., Hatch, E. E., Rao, R. S., Kaufman, R. H., Herbst, A. L., & Noller, K. L. (2001). Infertility among women exposed prenatally to diethylstilbestrol. *American Journal of Epidemiology, 154,* 316–321.

Pan, B. A., & Snow, C. E. (1999). The development of conversation and discourse skills. In M. Barrett (Ed.), *The development of language* (pp. 229–249). Hove, UK: Psychology Press.

Pan, H. W. (1994). Children's play in Taiwan. In J. L. Roopnarine, J. E. Johnson, & F. H. Hooper (Eds.), *Children's play in diverse cultures* (pp. 31–50). Albany, NY: SUNY Press.

Papadakis, A. A., Prince, R. P., Jones, N. P., & Strauman, T. J. (2006). Self-regulation, rumination, and vulnerability to depression in adolescent girls. *Development and Psychopathology, 18,* 815–829.

Papousek, M. (2007). Communication in early infancy: An arena of intersubjective learning. *Infant Behavior and Development, 30,* 258–266.

Paquette, D. (2004). Theorizing the father–child relationship: Mechanisms and developmental outcomes. *Human Development, 47,* 193–219.

Paradis, J. (2007). Second language acquisition in childhood. In E. Hoff & M. Shatz (Eds.), *Blackwell handbook of language development* (pp. 387–405). Malden, MA: Blackwell.

Paradise, R., & Rogoff, B. (2009). Side by side: Learning by observing and pitching in. *Ethos, 27,* 102–138.

Parameswaran, G. (2003). Experimenter instructions as a mediator in the effects of culture on mapping one's neighborhood. *Journal of Environmental Psychology, 23,* 409–417.

Parent, A., Teilmann, G., Juul, A., Skakkebaek, N. E., Toppari, J., & Bourguingnon, J. (2003). The timing of normal puberty and the age limits of sexual precocity: Variations around the world, secular trends, and changes after migration. *Endocrine Reviews, 24,* 668–693.

Paris, S. G., & Paris, A. H. (2006). Assessments of early reading. In K. A. Renninger & I. E. Sigel (Eds.), *Handbook of child psychology: Vol. 4. Child psychology in practice* (6th ed., pp. 48–74). Hoboken, NJ: Wiley.

Park, W. (2009). Acculturative stress and mental health among Korean adolescents in the United States. *Journal of Human Behavior in the Social Environment, 19,* 626–634.

Parke, R. D. (1996). *Fatherhood.* Cambridge, MA: Cambridge University Press.

Parke, R. D. (2002). Fathers and families. In M. H. Bornstein (Ed.), *Handbook of parenting: Vol. 3* (2nd ed., pp. 27–73). Mahwah, NJ: Erlbaum.

Parke, R. D., & Buriel, R. (2006). Socialization in the family: Ethnic and ecological perspectives. In N. Eisenberg (Ed.), *Handbook of child psychology: Vol. 3. Social, emotional, and personality development* (6th ed., pp. 429–504). Hoboken, NJ: Wiley.

Parke, R. D., Coltrane, S., Fabricius, W., Powers, J., & Adams, M. (2004a). Assessing father involvement in Mexican-American families. In R. Day & M. E. Lamb (Eds.), *Conceptualizing and measuring paternal involvement* (pp. 17–38). Mahwah, NJ: Erlbaum.

Parke, R. D., & Kellam, S. G. (Eds.) (1994). *Exploring family relationships with other social contexts.* Hillsdale, NJ: Erlbaum.

Parke, R. D., Simpkins, S. D., McDowell, D. J., Kim, M., Killian, C., Dennis, J., et al. (2004b). Relative contributions of families and peers to children's social development. In P. K. Smith & C. H. Hart (Eds.), *Blackwell handbook of childhood social development* (pp. 156–177). Malden, MA: Blackwell.

Parker, F. L., Boak, A. Y., Griffin, K. W., Ripple, C., & Peay, L. (1999). Parent–child relationship, home learning environment, and school readiness. *School Psychology Review, 28,* 413–425.

Parker, J. G., Rubin, K. H., Price, J., & DeRosier, M. E. (1995). Peer relationships, child development, and adjustment: A developmental psychopathology perspective. In D. Cicchetti & D. Cohen (Eds.), *Developmental psychopathology: Vol. 2. Risk, disorder, and adaptation* (pp. 96–161). New York: Wiley.

Parker, S. W., Nelson, C. A., & the Bucharest Early Intervention Project Core Group. (2005). The impact of early institutional rearing on the ability to discriminate facial expressions of emotion: An event-related potential study. *Child Development, 76,* 54–72.

Parra, M., Hoff, E., & Core, C. (2010). Relations among language exposure, phonological memory, and language development in Spanish–English bilingually developing 2-year-olds. *Journal of Experimental Child Psychology, 108,* 113–125.

Parten, M. (1932). Social participation among preschool children. *Journal of Abnormal and Social Psychology, 27,* 243–269.

Pascalis, O., de Haan, M., & Nelson, C. A. (1998). Long-term recognition memory for faces assessed by visual paired comparison in 3- and 6-month-old infants. *Journal of Experimental Psychology: Learning, Memory, and Cognition, 24,* 249–260.

Pascalis, O., de Haan, M., & Nelson, C. A. (2002). Is face processing species-specific during the first year of life? *Science, 296,* 1321–1323.

Pasterski, V. L., Geffner, M. E., Brain, C., Hindmarsh, P., & Brook, C. (2005). Prenatal hormones and postnatal socialization by parents as determinants of male-typical toy play in girls with congenital adrenal hyperplasia. *Child Development, 76,* 264–278.

Pasterski, V., Geffner, M. E., Brain, C., Hindmarsh, P., Brook, C., & Hines, M. (2011). Prenatal hormones and childhood sex segregation: Playmate and play style preferences in girls with congenital adrenal hyperplasia. *Hormones and Behavior, 59,* 549–555.

Pasupathi, M., & Wainryb, C. (2010). On telling the whole story: Facts and interpretations in autobiographical memory narratives from childhood through midadolescence. *Developmental Psychology, 46,* 735–746.

Pate, R. R., Trost, S. G., Levin, S., & Dowda, M. (2000). Sports participation and health-related behaviors among U.S. youth. *Archives of Pediatric and Adolescent Medicine, 154,* 904–911.

Patrick, R. B., & Gibbs, J. C. (2011). Inductive discipline, parental expression of disappointed expectations, and moral identity in adolescence. *Journal of Youth and Adolescence, 36.* Retrieved from www.springerlink.com/content/3756j25633363325/

Pattenden, S., Antova, T., Neuberger, M., Nikiforov, B., De Sario, M., Grize, L., & Heinrich, J. (2006). Parental smoking and children's respiratory health: Independent effects of prenatal and postnatal exposure. *Tobacco Control, 15,* 294–301.

Patterson, C. J., & Riskind, R. G. (2010). To be a parent: Issues in family formation among gay and lesbian adults. *Journal of GLBT Family Studies, 6,* 326–340.

Patterson, G. R., & Fisher, P. A. (2002). Recent developments in our understanding of parenting: Bidirectional effects, causal models, and the search for parsimony. In M. H. Bornstein (Ed.), *Handbook of parenting: Vol. 5. Practical issues in parenting* (2nd ed., pp. 59–88). Mahwah, NJ: Erlbaum.

Patterson, G. R., & Forgatch, M. S. (1995). Predicting future clinical adjustment from treatment outcome and process variables. *Psychological Assessment, 7,* 275–285.

Patterson, G. R., & Yoerger, K. (2002). A developmental model for early- and late-onset delinquency. In J. B. Reid & G. R. Patterson (Eds.), *Antisocial behavior in children and adolescents* (pp. 147–172). Washington, DC: American Psychological Association.

Paul, J. J., & Cillessen, A. H. N. (2003). Dynamics of peer victimization in early adolescence: Results from a four-year longitudinal study. *Journal of Applied School Psychology, 19,* 25–43.

Pauli, S. A., Berga, S. L., Shang, W., & Session, D. R. (2009). Current status of the approach to assisted reproduction. *Pediatric Clinics of North America, 56,* 467–488.

Paulussen-Hoogeboom, M. C., Stams, G. J. J. M., Hermanns, J. M. A., & Peetsma, T. T. D. (2007). Child negative emotionality and parenting from infancy to preschool: A meta-analytic review. *Developmental Psychology, 43,* 438–453.

Payne, R. J. (1998). *Getting beyond race: The changing American culture.* Boulder, CO: Westview.

Peake, P. K., Hebl, M., & Mischel, W. (2002). Strategic attention deployment for delay of gratification in working and waiting situations. *Developmental Psychology, 38,* 313–326.

Pedersen, S., Vitaro, F., Barker, E. D., & Anne, I. H. (2007). The timing of middle-childhood peer rejection and friendship: Linking early behavior to early adolescent adjustment. *Child Development, 78,* 1037–1051.

Pederson, D. R., Gleason, K. E., Moran, G., & Bento, S. (1998). Maternal attachment representations, maternal sensitivity, and the infant–mother attachment relationship. *Developmental Psychology, 34,* 925–933.

Pederson, D. R., & Moran, G. (1996). Expressions of the attachment relationship outside of the Strange Situation. *Child Development, 67,* 915–927.

Peets, K., Hodges, E. V. E., Kikas, E., & Salmivalli, C. (2007). Hostile attributions and behavioral strategies in children: Does relationship type matter? *Developmental Psychology, 43,* 889–900.

Peirano, P., Algarin, C., & Uauy, R. (2003). Sleep–wake states and their regulatory mechanisms throughout early human development. *Journal of Pediatrics, 143,* S70–S79.

Pellegrini, A. D. (1992). Kindergarten children's social cognitive status as a predictor of first grade success. *Early Childhood Research Quarterly, 7,* 565–577.

Pellegrini, A. D. (2003). Perceptions and functions of play and real fighting in early adolescence. *Child Development, 74,* 1522–1533.

Pellegrini, A. D. (2004). Rough-and-tumble play from childhood through adolescence: Development and possible functions. In P. K. Smith & C. H. Hart (Eds.), *Blackwell handbook of childhood social development* (pp. 438–453). Malden, MA: Blackwell.

Pellegrini, A. D. (2006). The development and function of rough-and-tumble play in childhood and adolescence: A sexual selection theory. In A. Göncü & S. Gaskins (Eds.), *Play and development: Evolutionary, sociocultural, and functional perspectives* (pp. 77–98). Mahwah, NJ: Erlbaum.

Pellegrini, A. D. (2009). *The role of play in human development.* New York: Oxford University Press.

Pellegrini, A. D., & Holmes, R. M. (2006). The role of recess in primary school. In D. G. Singer, R. M. Golinkoff, & K. Hirsh-Pasek (Eds.), *Play = learning* (pp. 36–53). New York: Oxford University Press.

Pellegrini, A. D., Huberty, P. D., & Jones, I. (1995). The effects of recess timing on children's playground and classroom behaviors. *American Educational Research Journal, 32,* 845–864.

Pellegrini, A. D., Kato, K., Blatchford, P., & Baines, E. (2002). A short-term longitudinal study of children's playground games across the first year of school: Implications for social competence and adjustment to school. *American Educational Research Journal, 39,* 991–1015.

Pellegrini, A. D., & Smith, P. K. (1998). Physical activity play: The nature and function of a neglected aspect of play. *Child Development, 69,* 577–598.

Pellicano, E., Maybery, M., Durkin, K., & Maley, A. (2006). Multiple cognitive capabilities/deficits in children with an autism spectrum disorder: "Weak" central coherence and its relationship to theory of mind and executive control. *Development and Psychopathology, 18,* 77–98.

Penner, A. M. (2003). International gender item difficulty interactions in mathematics and science achievement tests. *Journal of Educational Psychology, 95,* 650–655.

Pennington, B. F., Snyder, K. A., & Roberts, R. J., Jr. (2007). Developmental cognitive neuroscience: Origins, issues, and prospects. *Developmental Review, 27,* 428–441.

Penny, H., & Haddock, G. (2007). Anti-fat prejudice among children: The 'mere proximity' effect in 5–10 year olds. *Journal of Experimental Social Psychology, 43,* 678–683.

Peoples, C. E., Fagan, J. F., III, & Drotar, D. (1995). The influence of race on 3-year-old children's performance on the Stanford-Binet: Fourth Edition. *Intelligence, 21,* 69–82.

Pepler, D. J., Craig, W. M., Connolly, J. A., Yuile, A., McMaster, L., & Jiang, D. (2006). A developmental perspective on bullying. *Aggressive Behavior, 32,* 376–384.

Pepperberg, I. M. (2000). *The Alex studies: Cognitive and communicative abilities of grey parrots.* Cambridge, MA: Harvard University Press.

Peralta de Mendoza, O. A., & Salsa, A. M. (2003). Instruction in early comprehension and use of a symbol–referent relation. *Cognitive Development, 18,* 269–284.

Perelle, I. B., & Ehrman, L. (2009). Handedness: A behavioral laterality manifestation. In Y.-K. Kim (Ed.), *Handbook of behavior genetics* (pp. 331–342). New York: Springer Science + Business Media.

Pérez-Edgar, K., McDermott, J. N. M., Korelitz, K., Degnan, K. A., Curby, T. W., Pine, D. S., et al. (2010). Patterns of sustained attention in infancy shape the developmental trajectory of social behavior from toddlerhood through adolescence. *Developmental Psychology, 46,* 1723–1730.

Perlman, M., & Ross, H. S. (1997). The benefits of parent intervention in children's disputes: An examination of concurrent changes in children's fighting styles. *Child Development, 64,* 690–700.

Perlmutter, M. (1984). Continuities and discontinuities in early human memory: Paradigms, processes, and performances. In R. V. Kail, Jr., & N. E. Spear (Eds.), *Comparative perspectives on the development of memory* (pp. 253–287). Hillsdale, NJ: Erlbaum.

Perry, D. G., Perry, L. C., & Weiss, R. J. (1989). Sex differences in the consequences that children anticipate for aggression. *Developmental Psychology, 25,* 171–184.

Perry, G. H., & Dominy, N. J. (2009). Evolution of the human pygmy phenotype. *Trends in Ecology and Evolution, 24,* 218–225.

Peshkin, A. (1978). *Growing up American: Schooling and the survival of the community.* Chicago: University of Chicago Press.

Peshkin, A. (1997). *Places of memory: Whiteman's schools and native American communities.* Mahwah, NJ: Erlbaum.

Pesonen, A.-K., Räikkönen, K., Heinonen, K., & Komsi, N. (2008). A transactional model of temperamental development: Evidence of a relationship between child temperament and maternal stress over five years. *Social Development, 17,* 326–340.

Petch, J., & Halford, W. K. (2008). Psycho-education to enhance couples' transition to parenthood. *Clinical Psychology Review, 28,* 1125–1137.

Peters, R. D. (2005). A community-based approach to promoting resilience in young children, their families, and their neighborhoods. In R. D. Paters, B. Leadbeater, & R. J. McMahon (Eds.), *Resilience in children, families, and communities: Linking context to practice and policy* (pp. 157–176). New York: Kluwer Academic.

Peters, R. D., Bradshaw, A. J., Petrunka, K., Nelson, G., Herry, Y., Craig, W. M., et al. (2010). The Better Beginnings, Better Futures Project: Findings from grade 3 to grade 9. *Monographs of the Society for Research in Child Development, 75*(3, Serial No. 297).

Peters, R. D., Petrunka, K., & Arnold, R. (2003). The Better Beginnings, Better Futures Project: A universal, comprehensive, community-based prevention approach for primary school children and their families. *Journal of Clinical Child and Adolescent Psychology, 32,* 215–227.

Peterson, C., Parsons, T., & Dean, M. (2004). Providing misleading and reinstatement information a year after it happened: Effects on long-term memory. *Memory, 12,* 1–13.

Peterson, C., & Rideout, R. (1998). Memory for medical emergencies experienced by 1- and 2-year-olds. *Developmental Psychology, 34,* 1059–1072.

Peterson, C., & Roberts, C. (2003). Like mother, like daughter: Similarities in narrative style. *Developmental Psychology, 39,* 551–562.

Peterson, C. C., Peterson, J.L., & Seeto, D. (1983). Developmental changes in ideas about lying. *Child Development, 54,* 1529–1535.

Petitto, L. A., Holowka, S., Sergio, L. E., Levy, B., & Ostry, D. J. (2004). Baby hands that move to the rhythm of language: Hearing babies acquiring sign languages babble silently on the hands. *Cognition, 93,* 43–73.

Petitto, L. A., Holowka, S., Sergio, L. E., & Ostry, D. (2001). Language rhythms in babies' hand movements. *Nature, 413,* 35–36.

Petitto, L. A., & Marentette, P. F. (1991). Babbling in the manual mode: Evidence for the ontogeny of language. *Science, 251,* 1493–1496.

Petrides, K. V., Sangareau, Y., Furnham, A., & Fredrickson, N. (2006). Trait emotional intelligence and children's peer relations at school. *Social Development, 15,* 537–547.

Petrill, S. A., & Deater-Deckard, K. (2004). The heritability of general cognitive ability: A within-family adoption design. *Intelligence, 32,* 403–409.

Pettigrew, T. F., & Tropp, L. R. (2006). A meta-analytic test of intergroup contact theory. *Journal of Personality and Social Psychology, 90,* 751–783.

Pettit, G. S. (2004). Violent children in developmental perspective. *Current*

Directions in Psychological Science, 13, 194–197.

Pettit, G. S., Brown, E. G., Mize, J., & Lindsey, E. (1998). Mothers' and fathers' socializing behaviors in three contexts: Links with children's peer competence. *Merrill-Palmer Quarterly, 44,* 173–193.

Pettit, G. S., Keiley, M. K., Laird, R. D., Bates, J. E., & Dodge, K. A. (2007). Predicting the developmental course of mother-reported monitoring across childhood and adolescence from early proactive parenting, child temperament, and parents' worries. *Journal of Family Psychology, 21,* 206–217.

Pfeffer, C. R., Altemus, M., Heo, M., & Jiang, H. (2007). Salivary cortisol and psychopathology in children bereaved by the September 11, 2001 terror attacks. *Biological Psychiatry, 61,* 957–965.

Pfeifer, J. H., Brown, C. S., & Juvonen, J. (2007). Teaching tolerance in schools: lessons learned since *Brown v. Board of Education* about the development and reduction of children's prejudice. *Social Policy Report of the Society for Research in Child Development, 22*(2).

Pfeifer, J. H., Ruble, D. N., Bachman, M. A., Alvarez, J. M., Cameron, J. A., & Fuligni, A. J. (2007). Social identities and intergroup bias in immigrant and nonimmigrant children. *Developmental Psychology, 43,* 496–507.

Phillips, D., & Styfco, S. J. (2007). Child development research and public policy: Triumphs and setbacks on the way to maturity. In J. L. Aber, S. J. Bishop-Josef, S. M. Jones, K. T. McLearn, & D. Phillips (Eds.), *Child development and social policy: Knowledge for action* (pp. 11–27). Washington, DC: American Psychological Association.

Phillips, M. (1997). What makes schools effective? A comparison of the relationships of communitarian climate and academic climate to mathematics achievement and attendance during middle school. *American Educational Research Journal, 34,* 633–662.

Phillipsen, L. C. (1999). Associations between age, gender, and group acceptance and three components of friendship quality. *Journal of Early Adolescence, 19,* 438–464.

Phillips-Silver, J., & Trainor, L. J. (2005). Feeling the beat: Movement influences infant rhythm perception. *Science, 308,* 1430.

Phinney, J. S. (2007). Ethnic identity exploration in emerging adulthood. In J. J. Arnett & J. L. Tanner (Eds.), *Emerging adults in America: Coming of age in the 21st century* (pp. 117–134). Washington, DC: American Psychological Association.

Phinney, J. S., & Chavira, V. (1995). Parental ethnic socialization and adolescent outcomes in ethnic minority families. *Journal of Research on Adolescence, 5,* 31–53.

Phinney, J. S., Horenczyk, G., Liebkind, K., & Vedder, P. (2001). Ethnic identity, immigration, and well-being: An interactional perspective. *Journal of Social Issues, 57,* 493–510.

Phinney, J. S., & Ong, A. (2001). *Family obligations and life satisfaction among adolescents from immigrant and non-immigrant families: Direct and moderated effects.* Unpublished manuscript, California State University.

Phinney, J. S., Ong, A., & Madden, T. (2000). Cultural values and intergenerational value discrepancies in immigrant and non-immigrant families. *Child Development, 71,* 528–539.

Piaget, J. (1926). *The language and thought of the child.* New York: Harcourt, Brace & World. (Original work published 1923)

Piaget, J. (1928). *Judgment and reasoning in the child.* New York: Harcourt, Brace & World. (Original work published 1926)

Piaget, J. (1930). *The child's conception of the world.* New York: Harcourt, Brace & World. (Original work published 1926)

Piaget, J. (1951). *Play, dreams, and imitation in childhood.* New York: Norton. (Original work published 1945)

Piaget, J. (1952). *The origins of intelligence in children.* New York: International Universities Press. (Original work published 1936)

Piaget, J. (1965). *The moral judgment of the child.* New York: Free Press. (Original work published 1932)

Piaget, J. (1967). *Six psychological studies.* New York: Vintage.

Piaget, J. (1971). *Biology and knowledge.* Chicago: University of Chicago Press.

Piaget, J., Inhelder, B., & Szeminska, A. (1960). *The child's conception of geometry.* New York: Basic Books. (Original work published 1948)

Pianta, R. C., Egeland, B., & Erickson, M. F. (1989). The antecedents of maltreatment: Results of the Mother–Child Interaction Research Project. In D. Cicchetti & V. Carlson (Eds.), *Child maltreatment* (pp. 203–253). New York: Cambridge University Press.

Pianta, R. C., Hamre, B., & Stuhlman, M. (2003). Relationships between teachers and children. In W. M. Reynolds & G. E. Miller (Eds.), *Handbook of psychology: Educational psychology* (Vol. 7, pp. 199–234). New York: Wiley.

Pica, P., Lerner, C., Izard, V., & Dehaene, S. (2004). Exact and approximate arithmetic in an Amazonian indigene group. *Science, 306,* 499–503.

Pickens, J., Field, T., & Nawrocki, T. (2001). Frontal EEG asymmetry in response to emotional vignettes in preschool age children. *International Journal of Behavioral Development, 25,* 105–112.

Pickett, K. E., Luo, Y., & Lauderdale, D. S. (2005). Widening social inequalities in risk for sudden infant death syndrome. *American Journal of Public Health, 95,* 1976–1981.

Pierce, S. H., & Lange, G. (2000). Relationships among metamemory, motivation and memory performance in young school-age children. *British Journal of Developmental Psychology, 18,* 121–135.

Pierroutsakos, S. L., & Troseth, G. L. (2003). Video verité: Infants' manual investigation of objects on video. *Infant Behavior and Development, 26,* 183–199.

Pierson, L. (1996). Hazards of noise exposure on fetal hearing. *Seminars in Perinatology, 20,* 21–29.

Pietschnig, J., Voracek, M., & Formann, A. K. (2010). Mozart effect–Shmozart effect: A meta-analysis. *Intelligence, 38,* 314–323.

Pietz, J., Peter, J., Graf, R., Rauterberg, R. I., Rupp, A., & Sontheimer, D. (2004). Physical growth and neurodevelopmental outcome of nonhandicapped low-risk children born preterm. *Early Human Development, 79,* 131–143.

Piirto, J. (2007). *Talented children and adults* (3rd ed.). Waco, TX: Prufrock Press.

Pillow, B. H. (1991). Children's understanding of biased social cognition. *Developmental Psychology, 27,* 539–551.

Pillow, B. H. (2002). Children's and adults' evaluation of the certainty of deductive inferences, inductive inferences, and guesses. *Child Development, 73,* 779–792.

Pine, J. M. (1995). Variation in vocabulary development as a function of birth order. *Child Development, 66,* 272–281.

Ping, R. M., & Goldin-Meadow, S. (2008). Hands in the air: Using ungrounded iconic gestures to teach children conservation of quantity. *Developmental Psychology, 44,* 1277–1287.

Ping, R. M., & Goldin-Meadow, S. (2010). Gesturing saves cognitive resources when talking about nonpresent objects. *Cognitive Science, 34,* 602–619.

Pinker, S. (1989). *Learnability and cognition.* Cambridge, MA: MIT Press.

Pinker, S. (1999). *Words and rules: The ingredients of language.* New York: Basic Books.

Pinker, S., Lebeaux, D. S., & Frost, L. A. (1987). Productivity and constraints in the acquisition of the passive. *Cognition, 26,* 195–267.

Pinter, J. D., Eliez, S., Schmitt, J. E., Capone, G. T., & Reiss, A. L. (2001). Neuroanatomy of Down's syndrome: A high-resolution MRI study. *American Journal of Psychiatry, 158,* 1659–1665.

Pipe, M.-E., & Salmon, K. (2009). Memory development and the forensic context. In M. L. Courage & N. Cowan (Eds.), *The development of memory in infancy and childhood* (pp. 241–282). Hove, UK: Psychology Press.

Pipp, S., Easterbrooks, M. A., & Brown, S. R. (1993). Attachment status and complexity of infants' self- and other-knowledge when tested with mother and father. *Social Development, 2,* 1–14.

Pipp, S., Easterbrooks, M. A., & Harmon, R. J. (1992). The relation between attachment and knowledge of self and mother in one-year-old infants to three-year-old infants. *Child Development, 63,* 738–750.

Pizarro, D. A., & Bloom, P. (2003). The intelligence of the moral intuitions: Comment on Haidt (2001). *Psychological Review, 110,* 193–196.

Plante, I., Théoret, M., & Favreau, O. E. (2009). Student gender stereotypes: Contrasting the perceived maleness and femaleness of mathematics and language. *Educational Psychology, 29,* 385–405.

Plantin, L., Mansson, S.-A., & Kearney, J. (2003). Talking and doing fatherhood: On fatherhood and masculinity in Sweden and England. *Fathering, 1,* 3–26.

Pleck, J. H., & Masciadrelli, B. P. (2004). Paternal involvement by U.S. residential fathers: Levels, sources, and consequences. In M. E. Lamb (Ed.), *The role of the father in child development* (4th ed., pp. 222–271). Hoboken, NJ: Wiley

Plomin, R. (1994). *Genetics and experience: The interplay between nature and nurture.* Thousand Oaks, CA: Sage.

Plomin, R. (2003). General cognitive ability. In R. Plomin & J. C. DeFries (Eds.), *Behavioral genetics in the postgenomic era* (pp. 183–201). Washington, DC: American Psychological Association.

Plomin, R. (2005). Finding genes in child psychology and psychiatry: When are we going to be there? *Journal of Child Psychology and Psychiatry, 46,* 1030–1038.

Plomin, R. (2009). The nature of nurture. In K. McCartney & R. A. Weinberg (Eds.), *Experience and development: A festschrift in honor of Sandra Wood Scarr* (pp. 61–80). New York: Psychology Press.

Plomin, R., & Davis, O. S. P. (2009). The future of genetics in psychology and psychiatry: Microarrays, genome-wide association, and non-coding RNA. *Journal of Child Psychology and Psychiatry, 50,* 63–71.

Plomin, R., DeFries, J. C., McClearn, G. E., & McGuffin, P. (2001). *Behavioral genetics* (4th ed.). New York: Worth.

Plomin, R., & Spinath, F. M. (2004). Intelligence: Genetics, genes, and genomics. *Journal of Personality and Social Psychology, 86,* 112–129.

Plucker, J. A., & Makel, M. C. (2010). Assessment of creativity. In J. C. Kaufman & R. J. Sternberg (Eds.), *Cambridge handbook of creativity* (pp. 48–73). New York: Cambridge University Press.

Pluess, M., & Belsky, J. (2011). Prenatal programming of postnatal plasticity? *Development and Psychopathology, 23,* 29–38.

Poehlmann, J. (2003). An attachment perspective on grandparents raising their very young grandchildren: Implications for intervention and research. *Infant Mental Health Journal, 24,* 149–173.

Poehlmann, J., & Fiese, B. H. (2001). The interaction of maternal and infant vulnerabilities on developing attachment relationships. *Development and Psychopathology, 13,* 1–11.

Poehlmann, J., Schwichtenberg, A. J. M., Shlafer, R. J., Hahn, E., Bianchi, J.-P., & Warner, R. (2011). Emerging self-regulation in toddlers born preterm or low birth weight: Differential susceptibility to parenting. *Developmental and Psychopathology, 23,* 177–193.

Pogarsky, G., Thornberry, T. P., & Lizotte, A. J. (2006). Developmental outcomes for children of young mothers. *Journal of Marriage and Family, 68,* 332–344.

Pohl, R. (2002). *Poverty in Canada.* Ottawa: Innercity Ministries.

Polderman, T. J. C., de Geus, J. C., Hoekstra, R. A., Bartels, M., van Leeuwen, M., Verhulst, F. C., et al. (2009). Attention problems, inhibitory control, and intelligence index overlapping genetic factors: A study in 9-, 12-, and 18-year-old twins. *Neuropsychology, 23,* 381–391.

Polka, L., & Sundara, M. (2003). Word segmentation in monolingual and bilingual infant learners of English and French. In *Proceedings of the 15th International Congress of Phonetic Sciences* (Vol. 1, pp. 1021–1024). Barcelona, Spain: University Autonoma Barcelona.

Polka, L., & Werker, J. F. (1994). Developmental changes in perception of nonnative vowel contrasts. *Journal of Experimental Psychology: Human Perception and Performance, 20,* 421–435.

Pollitt, E. (1996). A reconceptualization of the effects of undernutrition on children's biological, psychosocial, and behavioral development. *Social Policy Report of the Society for Research in Child Development, 10*(5).

Polman, H., Orobio de Castro, B., Koops, W., van Boxtel, H. W., & Merk, W. W. (2007). A meta-analysis of the distinction between reactive and proactive aggression in children and adolescents. *Journal of Abnormal Child Psychology, 35,* 522–535.

Pomerantz, E. M., & Dong, W. (2006). Effects of mothers' perceptions of children's competence: The moderating role of mothers' theories of competence. *Developmental Psychology, 42,* 950–961.

Pomerantz, E. M., & Eaton, M. M. (2000). Developmental differences in children's conceptions of parental control: "They love me, but they make me feel incompetent." *Merrill-Palmer Quarterly, 46,* 140–167.

Pomerantz, E. M., Ng, F. F., & Wang, Q. (2006). Mothers' mastery-oriented involvement in children's homework: Implications for the well-being of children with negative perceptions of competence. *Journal of Educational Psychology, 98,* 99–111.

Pomerantz, E. M., Ng, F. F., & Wang, Q. (2008). Culture, parenting, and motivation: The case of East Asia and the United States. In M. L. Maehr, S. A., Karabenick, & T. C. Urdan (Eds.), *Advances in motivation and achievement: Social psychological perspectives* (Vol. 15, pp. 209–240). Bingley, UK: Emerald Group.

Pomerantz, E. M., & Ruble, D. N. (1998a). The multidimensional nature of control: Implications for the development of sex differences in self-evaluation. In J. Heckhausen & C. S. Dweck (Eds.), *Motivation and self-regulation across the life span* (pp. 159–184). New York: Cambridge University Press.

Pomerantz, E. M., & Ruble, D. N. (1998b). The role of maternal control in the development of sex differences in child self-evaluative factions. *Child Development, 69,* 458–478.

Pomerantz, E. M., & Saxon, J. L. (2001). Conceptions of ability as stable and self-evaluative processes: A longitudinal examination. *Child Development, 72,* 152–173.

Pomerleau, A., Malcuit, G., Chicoine, J. F., Séguin, R., Belhumeur, C., Germain, P., et al. (2005). Health status, cognitive and motor development of young children adopted from China, East Asia and Russia across the first 6 months after adoption. *International Journal of Behavioral Development, 29,* 445–457.

Pomerleau, A., Scuccimarri, C., & Malcuit, G. (2003). Mother–infant behavioral interactions in teenage and adult mothers during the first six months postpartum: Relations with infant development. *Infant Mental Health Journal, 24,* 495–509.

Pong, S., Johnston, J., & Chen, V. (2010). Authoritarian parenting and Asian adolescent school performance. *International Journal of Behavioral Development, 34,* 62–72.

Pons, F., Lawson, J., Harris, P. L., & de Rosnay, M. (2003). Individual differences in children's emotion understanding: Effects of age and language. *Scandinavian Journal of Psychology, 44,* 347–353.

Poole, D. A., & Lindsay, D. S. (2001). Children's eyewitness reports after exposure to misinformation from parents. *Journal of Experimental Psychology: Applied, 7,* 27–50.

Portes, A., & Rumbaut, R. G. (2005). Introduction: The second generation and the Children of Immigrants Longitudinal Study. *Ethnic and Racial Studies, 28,* 983–999.

Posada, G. (2006). Assessing attachment security at age three: Q-sort home observations and the MacArthur Strange Situation adaptation. *Social Development, 15,* 644–658.

Posner, M. I., & Rothbart, M. K. (2007a). *Educating the human brain.* Washington, DC: American Psychological Association.

Posner, M. I., & Rothbart, M. K. (2007b). Temperament and learning. In M. I. Posner & M. K. Rothbart (Eds.), *Educating the human brain* (pp. 121–146).

Washington, DC: American Psychological Association.

Potter, D. (2010). Psychosocial well-being and the relationship between divorce and children's academic achievement. *Journal of Marriage and Family, 72,* 933–946.

Poudevigne, M., & O'Connor, P. J. (2006). A review of physical activity patterns in pregnant women and their relationship to psychological health. *Sports Medicine, 36,* 19–38.

Poulin, F., & Chan, A. (2010). Friendship stability and change in childhood and adolescence. *Developmental Review, 30,* 257–272.

Poulin, F., & Pedersen, S. (2007). Developmental changes in gender composition of friendship networks in adolescent girls and boys. *Developmental Psychology, 37,* 55–104.

Poulin-Dubois, D., & Forbes, J. N. (2006). Word, intention, and action: A two-tiered model of action word learning. In K. Hirsh-Pasek & R. M. Golinkoff (Eds.), *Action meets word: How children learn verbs* (pp. 262–285). New York: Oxford University Press.

Poulin-Dubois, D., Brooker, I., & Chow, V. (2009). The developmental origins of naïve psychology in infancy. *Advances in Child Development and Behavior, 37,* 55–104.

Poulin-Dubois, D., Serbin, L. A., Kenyon, B., & Derbyshire, A. (1994). Infants' intermodal knowledge about gender. *Developmental Psychology, 30,* 436–442.

Povinelli, D. J. (2001). The self: Elevated in consciousness and extended in time. In C. Moore & K. Lemmon (Eds.), *The self in time: Developmental perspectives* (pp. 75–95). Mahwah, NJ: Erlbaum.

Powell, D., Plaut, D., & Funnell, E. (2006). Does the PMSP connectionist model of single word reading learn to read in the same way as a child? *Journal of Research in Reading, 29,* 229–250.

Power, T. G. (2000). *Play and exploration in children and animals.* Mahwah, NJ: Erlbaum.

Powlishta, K. K. (2000). The effect of target age on the activation of gender stereotypes. *Sex Roles, 42,* 271–282.

Powlishta, K. K., Sen, M. G., Serbin, L. A., Poulin-Dubois, D., & Eichstedt, J. A. (2001). From infancy through middle childhood: The role of cognitive and social factors in becoming gendered. In R. K. Unger (Ed.), *Handbook of the psychology of women and gender* (pp. 116–132). New York: Wiley.

Powlishta, K. K., Serbin, L. A., Doyle, A. B., & White, D. R. (1994). Gender, ethnic and body type biases: The generality of prejudice in childhood. *Developmental Psychology, 30,* 526–536.

Powlishta, K. K., Serbin, L. A., & Moller, L. C. (1993). The stability of individual differences in gender typing: Implications for understanding gender segregation. *Sex Roles, 29,* 723–737.

Powls, A., Botting, N., Cooke, R. W. I., & Marlow, N. (1996). Handedness in very-low-birthweight (VLBW) children at 12 years of age: Relation to perinatal and outcome variables. *Developmental Medicine and Child Neurology, 38,* 594–602.

Pratt, M. W., Skoe, E. E., & Arnold, M. L. (2004). Care reasoning development and family socialization patterns in later adolescence: A longitudinal analysis. *International Journal of Behavioral Development, 28,* 139–147.

Prechtl, H. F. R. (1958). Problems of behavioral studies in the newborn infant. In D. S. Lehrmann, R. A. Hinde, & E. Shaw (Eds.), *Advances in the study of behavior* (Vol. 1, pp. 75–98). New York: Academic Press.

Prechtl, H. F. R., & Beintema, D. (1965). *The neurological examination of the full-term newborn infant.* London: William Heinemann Medical Books.

Preisler, G. M. (1991). Early patterns of interaction between blind infants and their sighted mothers. *Child: Care, Health and Development, 17,* 65–90.

Preisler, G. M. (1993). A descriptive study of blind children in nurseries with sighted children. *Child: Care, Health and Development, 19,* 295–315.

Preissler, M. A., & Carey, S. (2004). Do both pictures and words function as symbols for 18- and 24-month-old children? *Journal of Cognition and Development, 5,* 185–212.

Pressley, M., & Hilden, D. (2006). Cognitive strategies. In D. Kuhn & R. Siegler (Eds.), *Handbook of child psychology: Vol. 2. Cognition, perception, and language* (6th ed., pp. 511–556). Hoboken, NJ: Wiley.

Pressley, M., Wharton-McDonald, R., Raphael, L. M., Bogner, K., & Roehrig, A. (2002). Exemplary first-grade teaching. In B. M. Taylor & P. D. Pearson (Eds.), *Teaching reading: Effective schools, accomplished teachers* (pp. 73–88). Mahwah, NJ: Erlbaum.

Previc, F. H. (1991). A general theory concerning the prenatal origins of cerebral lateralization. *Psychological Review, 98,* 299–334.

Priess, H. A., Lindberg, S. M., & Hyde, J. S. (2009). Adolescent gender-role identity and mental health: Gender intensification revisited. *Child Development, 80,* 1531–1544.

Prinstein, M. J., Boergers, J., & Spirito, A. (2001). Adolescents' and their friends' health-risk behavior: Factors that alter or add to peer influence. *Journal of Pediatric Psychology, 26,* 287–298.

Prinstein, M. J., Boergers, J., & Vernberg, E. M. (2001). Overt and relational aggression in adolescents: Social–psychological adjustment of aggressors and victims. *Journal of Clinical Child Psychology, 30,* 479–491.

Prinstein, M. J., & Cillessen, A. H. N. (2003). Forms and functions of adolescent peer aggression associated with high levels of peer status. *Merrill-Palmer Quarterly, 49,* 310–342.

Prinstein, M. J., & La Greca, A. M. (2004). Childhood peer rejection and aggression as predictors of adolescent girls' externalizing and health risk behaviors: A 6-year longitudinal study. *Journal of Consulting and Clinical Psychology, 72,* 103–112.

Prinstein, M. J., Meade, C. S., & Cohen, G. L. (2003). Adolescent oral sex, peer popularity, and perceptions of best friends' sexual behavior. *Journal of Pediatric Psychology, 28,* 243–249.

Proctor, M. H., Moore, L. L., Gao, D., Cupples, L. A., Bradlee, M. L., Hood, M. Y., & Ellison, R. C. (2003). Television viewing and change in body fat from preschool to early adolescence: The Framingham Children's Study. *International Journal of Obesity, 27,* 827–833.

Programme for International Student Assessment. (2009). *PISA profiles by country/economy.* Retrieved from stats.oecd.org/PISA2009Profiles

Pronk, R. E., & Zimmer-Gembeck, M. J. (2010). It's "mean," but what does it mean to adolescents? Relational aggression described by victims, aggressors, and their peers. *Journal of Adolescent Research, 25,* 175–204.

Provins, K. A. (1997). Handedness and speech: A critical reappraisal of the role of genetic and environmental factors in the cerebral lateralization of function. *Psychological Review, 104,* 554–571.

Pruden, S. M., Hirsh-Pasek, K., Golinkoff, R. M., & Hennon, E. A. (2006). The birth of words: Ten-month-olds learn words through perceptual salience. *Child Development, 77,* 266–280.

Prysak, M., Lorenz, R. P., & Kisly, A. (1995). Pregnancy outcome in nulliparous women 35 years and older. *Obstetrics and Gynecology, 85,* 65–70.

Puhl, R. M., Heuer, C. A., & Brownell, D. K. (2010). Stigma and social consequences of obesity. In P. G. Kopelman, I. D. Caterson, & W. H. Dietz (Eds.), *Clinical obesity in adults and children* (3rd ed., pp. 25–40). Hoboken, NJ: Wiley.

Puhl, R. M., & Latner, J. D. (2007). Stigma, obesity, and the health of the nation's children. *Psychological Bulletin, 133,* 557–580.

Pujol, J., Soriano-Mas, C., Ortiz, H., Sebastián-Gallés, N., Losilla, J. M., & Deus, J. (2006). Myelination of language-related areas in the developing brain. *Neurology, 66,* 339–343.

Punamaki, R.-L. (2006). Ante- and perinatal factors and child characteristics predicting parenting experience among formerly infertile couples during the child's first year: A controlled study. *Journal of Family Psychology, 20,* 670–679.

Purcell-Gates, V. (1996). Stories, coupons, and the TV Guide: Relationships between home literacy experiences and emergent literacy knowledge. *Reading Research Quarterly, 31,* 406–428.

Putallaz, M., Grimes, C. L., Foster, K. J., Kupersmidt, J. B., Coie, J. D., & Dearing, K. (2007). Overt and relational aggression and victimization: Multiple perspectives within the school setting. *Journal of School Psychology, 45,* 523–547.

Putnam, F. W. (2003). Ten-year research update review: Child sexual abuse. *Journal of the American Academy of Child and Adolescent Psychiatry, 42,* 269–278.

Putnam, S. P., Samson, A. V., & Rothbart, M. K. (2000). Child temperament and parenting. In V. J. Molfese & D. L. Molfese (Eds.), *Temperament and personality across the life span* (pp. 255–277). Mahwah, NJ: Erlbaum.

Quas, J. A., Malloy, L. C., Melinder, A., Goodman, G. S., & D'Mello, M. (2007). Developmental differences in the effects of repeated interviews and interviewer bias on young children's event memory and false reports. *Developmental Psychology, 43,* 823–837.

Quatman, T., Sokolik, E., & Smith, K. (2000). Adolescent perception of peer success: A gendered perspective over time. *Sex Roles, 43,* 61–84.

Quillian, L., & Campbell, M. E. (2003). Beyond black and white: The present and future of multiracial friendship segregation. *American Sociological Review, 68,* 540–566.

Quinn, P. C. (2008). In defense of core competencies, quantitative change, and continuity. *Child Development, 79,* 1633–1638.

Quinn, P. C., Kelly, D. J, Lee, K., Pascalis, O., & Slater, A. (2008). Preference for attractive faces extends beyond conspecifics. *Developmental Science, 11,* 76–83.

Quinn, P. C., & Liben, L. S. (2008). A sex difference in mental rotation in young infants. *Psychological Science, 19,* 1067–1070.

Quinn, P. C., Yahr, J., Kuhn, A., Slater, A. M., & Pascalis, O. (2002). Representation of the gender of human faces by infants: A preference for female. *Perception, 31,* 1109–1121.

Quinn, T. C., & Overbaugh, J. (2005). HIV/AIDS in women: An expanding epidemic. *Science, 308,* 1582–1583.

Raaijmakers, Q. A. W., Engels, R. C. M. E., & Van Hoof, A. (2005). Delinquency and moral reasoning in adolescence and young adulthood. *International Journal of Behavioral Development, 29,* 247–258.

Radelet, M. A., Lephart, S. M., Rubinstein, E. N., & Myers, J. B. (2002). Survey of the injury rate for children in community sports. *Pediatrics, 110,* e28.

Radke-Yarrow, M., & Kochanska, G. (1990). Anger in young children. In N. L. Stein, B. Leventhal, & T. Trabasso (Eds.), *Psychological and behavioral approaches to emotion* (pp. 297–310). Hillsdale, NJ: Erlbaum.

Raevuori, A., Hoek, H. W., Susser, E., Kaprio, J., Rissanen, A., & Keski-Rahkonen, A. (2009). Epidemiology of anorexia nervosa in men: A nationwide study of Finnish twins. *PLoS ONE, 4,* e4402.

Raffaelli, M., Crockett, L. J., & Shen, Y.-L. (2005). Developmental stability and change in self-regulation from childhood to adolescence. *Journal of Genetic Psychology, 166,* 54–75.

Rahman, Q., & Wilson, G. D. (2003). Born gay? The psychobiology of human sexual orientation. *Personality and Individual Differences, 34,* 1337–1382.

Raikes, H. A., & Thompson, R. A. (2005). Links between risk and attachment security: Models of influence. *Journal of Applied Developmental Psychology, 26,* 440–455.

Raikes, H. A., Robinson, J. L., Bradley, R. H., Raikes, H. H., & Ayoub, C. C. (2007). Developmental trends in self-regulation among low-income toddlers. *Social Development, 16,* 128–149.

Raikes, H. A., & Thompson, R. A. (2006). Family emotional climate, attachment security, and young children's emotion knowledge in a high-risk sample. *British Journal of Developmental Psychology, 24,* 89–104.

Raikes, H. H., Chazan-Cohen, R., Love, J. M., & Brooks-Gunn, J. (2010). Early Head Start impacts at age 3 and a description of the age 5 follow-up study. In A. J. Reynolds, A. J. Rolnick, M. M. Englund, & J. Temple (Eds.), *Childhood programs and practices in the first decade of life: A human capital integration* (pp. 99–118). New York: Cambridge University Press.

Raine, A. (1997). Antisocial behavior and psychophysiology: A biosocial perspective and a prefrontal dysfunction hypothesis. In D. M. Stoff, J. Breiling, & J. D. Maser (Eds.), *Handbook of antisocial behavior* (pp. 289–304). New York: Wiley.

Rakison, D. H. (2005). Developing knowledge of objects' motion properties in infancy. *Cognition, 96,* 183–214.

Rakison, D. H. (2006). Make the first move: How infants learn about self-propelled objects. *Developmental Psychology, 42,* 900–912.

Rakison, D. H. (2010). Perceptual categorization and concepts. In J. G. Bremner & T. D. Wachs (Eds.), *Wiley-Blackwell handbook of infant development* (2nd ed., pp. 243–270). Oxford, UK: Wiley.

Rakison, D. H., & Lupyan, G. (2008). Developing object concepts in infancy: An associative learning perspective. *Monographs of the Society for Research in Child Development, 73*(1, Serial No. 289).

Rakoczy, H., Tomasello, M., & Striano, T. (2004). Young children know that trying is not pretending: A test of the "behaving-as-if" construal of children's early concept of pretense. *Developmental Psychology, 40,* 388–399.

Rakoczy, H., Tomasello, M., & Striano, T. (2005). How children turn objects into symbols: A cultural learning account. In L. Namy (Ed.), *Symbol use and symbol representation* (pp. 67–97). New York: Erlbaum.

Rakoczy, H., Warneken, F., & Tomasello, M. (2007). "This way!" "No! That way!"—3-year-olds know that two people can have mutually incompatible desires. *Cognitive Development, 22,* 47–68.

Ramchandani, P. G., Stein, A., O'Connor, T. G., Heron, J., Murray, L., & Evans, J. (2008). Depression in men in the postnatal period and later child psychopathology: A population cohort study. *Journal of the American Academy of Child and Adolescent Psychiatry, 47,* 390–398.

Ramey, C. T., Ramey, S. L., & Lanzi, R. G. (2006). Children's health and education. In K. A. Renninger & I. E. Sigel (Eds.), *Handbook of child psychology: Vol. 4. Child psychology in practice* (6th ed., pp. 864–892). Hoboken, NJ: Wiley.

Ramey, S. L., & Ramey, C. T. (1999). Early experience and early intervention for children "at risk" for developmental delay and mental retardation. *Mental Retardation and Developmental Disabilities, 5,* 1–10.

Ramos, E., Frontera, W. R., Llorpart, A., & Feliciano, D. (1998). Muscle strength and hormonal levels in adolescents: Gender related differences. *International Journal of Sports Medicine, 19,* 526–531.

Ramos, M. C., Guerin, D. W., Gottfried, A. W., Bathurst, K., & Oliver, P. H. (2005). Family conflict and children's behavior problems: The moderating role of child temperament. *Structural Equation Modeling, 12,* 278–298.

Ramsey, P. G. (1991). Young children's awareness and understanding of social class differences. *Journal of Genetic Psychology, 152,* 71–82.

Ramsey-Rennels, J. L., & Langlois, J. H. (2006). Differential processing of female and male faces. *Current Directions in Psychological Science, 15,* 59–62.

Ramus, F. (2002). Language discrimination by newborns: Teasing apart phonotactic, rhythmic, and intonational cues. *Annual Review of Language Acquisition, 2,* 85–115.

Rangel, M. C., Gavin, L., Reed, C., Fowler, M. G., & Lee, L. M. (2006). Epidemiology of HIV and AIDS among adolescents and young adults in the United States. *Journal of Adolescent Health, 39,* 156–163.

Ranking, J., Lane, D., Gibbons, F., & Gerrard, M. (2004). Adolescent self-consciousness: Longitudinal age changes and gender differences in two cohorts. *Journal of Research on Adolescence, 14,* 1–12.

Raskauskas, J., & Stoltz, A. D. (2007). Involvement in traditional and electronic bullying among adolescents. *Developmental Psychology, 43,* 564–575.

Raskind, W. H., Igo, R. P., Jr., Chapman, N. H., Berninger, V. W., Thomson, J. B., Jatsushita, M., & Brkanac, Z. (2005). A genome scan in multigenerational families with dyslexia: Identification of a novel locus on chromosome 2q that contributions to phonological decoding efficiency. *Molecular Psychiatry, 10,* 699–711.

Rasmussen, C., Ho, E., & Bisanz, J. (2003). Use of the mathematical principle of inversion in young children. *Journal of Experimental Child Psychology, 85,* 89–102.

Rasmussen, E. R., Neuman, R. J., Heath, A. C., Levy, F., Hay, D. A., & Todd, R. D. (2004). Familial clustering of latent class and DSM-IV defined attention-deficit hyperactivity disorder (ADHD) subtypes. *Journal of Child Psychology and Psychology, 45,* 589–598.

Rast, M., & Meltzoff, A. N. (1995). Memory and representation in young children with Down syndrome: Exploring deferred imitation and object permanence. *Development and Psychopathology, 7,* 393–407.

Rathunde, K., & Csikszentmihalyi, M. (2005). The social context of middle school: Teachers, friends, and activities in Montessori and traditional school environments. *Elementary School Journal, 106,* 59–79.

Rauber, M. (2006, May 18). Parents aren't sitting still as recess disappears. *Parents in Action.* Retrieved from http://healthyschoolscampaign.org/news/media/food/2006-05_recess_disappears.php

Rauscher, F. H., Shaw, G. L., & Ky, K. N. (1993). Music and spatial task performance. *Nature, 365,* 611.

Raver, C. C. (2003). Does work pay psychologically as well as economically? The role of employment in predicting depressive symptoms and parenting among low-income families. *Child Development, 74,* 1720–1736.

Ravitch, D. (2010). *The death and life of the great American school system: How testing and choice are undermining education.* New York: Basic Books.

Ray, N., & Gregory, R. (2001). School experiences of the children of lesbian and gay parents. *Family Matters, 59,* 28–35.

Ray, O. (2004). How the mind hurts and heals the body. *American Psychologist, 59,* 29–40.

Rayner, K., & Pollatsek, A. (1989). *The psychology of reading.* Englewood Cliffs, NJ: Prentice-Hall.

Rayner, K., Pollatsek, A., & Starr, M. S. (2003). Reading. In A. F. Healy & R. W. Proctor (Eds.), *Handbook of psychology: Experimental psychology* (Vol. 4, pp. 549–574). New York: Wiley.

Raz, S., Shah, F., & Sander, C. J. (1996). Differential effects of perinatal hypoxic risk on early developmental outcome: A twin study. *Neuropsychology, 10,* 429–436.

Reed, R. K. (2005). *Birthing fathers.* New Brunswick, NJ: Rutgers University Press.

Reese, E., & Newcombe, R. (2007). Training mothers in elaborative reminiscing enhances children's autobiographical memory and narrative. *Child Development, 78,* 1153–1170.

Reese, E., Newcombe, R., & Bird, G. M. (2006). The emergence of autobiographical memory: Cognitive, social, and emotional

factors. In C. M. Flinn-Fletcher & G. M. Haberman (Eds.), *Cognition and language: Perspectives from New Zealand* (pp. 177–189). Bowen Hills, Australia: Australian Academic Press.

Regnerus, M., Smith, C., & Fritsch, M. (2003). *Religion in the lives of American adolescents: A review of the literature.* Chapel Hill, NC: National Study of Youth and Religion.

Reid, P. T., & Trotter, K. H. (1993). Children's self-presentations with infants: Gender and ethnic comparisons. *Sex Roles, 29,* 171–181.

Reilly, J. S., Bates, E. A., & Marchman, V. A. (1998). Narrative discourse in children with early focal brain injury. *Brain and Language, 61,* 335–375.

Reilly, J. S., Losh, M., Bellugi, U., & Wulfeck, B. (2004). "Frog, where are you?" Narratives in children with specific language impairment, early focal brain injury, and Williams syndrome. *Brain and Language, 88,* 229–247.

Reis, O., & Youniss, J. (2004). Patterns in identity change and development in relationships with mothers and friends. *Journal of Adolescent Research, 19,* 31–44.

Reis, S. M. (2004). We can't change what we don't recognize: Understanding the special needs of gifted females. In S. Baum (Ed.), *Twice-exceptional and special populations of gifted students* (pp. 67–80). Thousand Oaks, CA: Corwin Press.

Reisman, J. E. (1987). Touch, motion, and proprioception. In P. Salapatek & L. Cohen (Eds.), *Handbook of infant perception: Vol. 1. From sensation to perception* (pp. 265–303). Orlando, FL: Academic Press.

Reiss, D. (2003). Child effects on family systems: Behavioral genetic strategies. In A. C. Crouter & A. Booth (Eds.), *Children's influence on family dynamics: The neglected side of family relationships* (pp. 3–36). Mahwah, NJ: Erlbaum.

Renninger, K. A. (1998). Developmental psychology and instruction: Issues from and for practice. In I. Sigel & K. A. Renninger (Eds.), *Handbook of child psychology: Vol. 4. Child psychology and practice* (pp. 211–274). New York: Wiley.

Renzetti, C. M., & Curran, D. J. (1998). *Living sociology.* Boston: Allyn and Bacon.

Renzulli, J. S. (2006). Swimming upstream in a small river: Changing conceptions and practices about the development of giftedness. In M. A. Constas & R. J. Sternberg (Eds.), *Translating theory and research into educational practice* (pp. 223–254). Mahwah, NJ: Erlbaum.

Repacholi, B. M., & Gopnik, A. (1997). Early reasoning about desires: Evidence from 14- and 18-month-olds. *Developmental Psychology, 33,* 12–21.

Repacholi, B. M., & Meltzoff, A. N. (2007). Emotional eavesdropping: Infants selectively respond to indirect emotional signals. *Child Development, 78,* 503–521.

Repetti, R., & Wang, S. (2010). Parent employment and chaos in the family. In G. W. Evans & T. D. Wachs (Eds.), *Chaos and its influence on children's development: An ecological perspective* (pp. 191–208). Washington, DC: American Psychological Association.

Resnick, G. (2010). Project Head Start: Quality and links to child outcomes. In A. J. Reynolds, A. J. Rolnick, M. M. Englund, & J. Temple (Eds.), *Childhood programs and practices in the first decade of life: A human capital integration* (pp.

121–156). New York: Cambridge University Press.

Resnick, M. B., Gueorguieva, R. V., Carter, R. L., Ariet, M., Sun, Y., Roth, J., et al. (1999). The impact of low birth weight, perinatal conditions, and sociodemographic factors on educational outcome in kindergarten. *Pediatrics, 104,* e74.

Rest, J. R. (1979). *Development in judging moral issues.* Minneapolis: University of Minnesota Press.

Resta, R., Biesecker, B. B., Bennett, R. L., Blum, S., Hahn, S. E., Strecker, M. N., & Williams, J. L. (2006). A new definition of genetic counseling: National Society of Genetic Counselors' Task Force Report. *Journal of Genetic Counseling, 15,* 77–83.

Reyna, V. F., & Farley, F. (2006). Risk and rationality in adolescent decision making: Implications for theory, practice, and public policy. *Psychological Science in the Public Interest, 7,* 1–44.

Reynolds, A. J., & Temple, J. A. (1998). Extended early childhood intervention and school achievement: Age thirteen findings from the Chicago Longitudinal Study. *Child Development, 69,* 231–246.

Rhoades, B. L., Greenberg, M. T., & Domitrovich, C. E. (2009). The contribution of inhibitory control to preschoolers' social-emotional competence. *Journal of Applied Developmental Psychology, 30,* 310–320.

Rhode, T. E., & Thompson, L. A. (2007). Predicting academic achievement with cognitive ability. *Intelligence, 35,* 82–92.

Rholes, W. S., Newman, L. S., & Ruble, D. N. (1990). Understanding self and others: Developmental and motivational aspects of perceiving persons in terms of invariant dispositions. In E. Higgins & R. Sorrentino (Eds.), *Handbook of motivation and cognition: Foundations of social behavior* (Vol. 2, pp. 369–407). New York: Guilford.

Ricard, M., & Kamberk-Kilicci, M. (1995). Children's empathic responses to emotional complexity. *International Journal of Behavioral Development, 18,* 211–225.

Rich, D. Q., Demissie, K., Lu, S. E., Kamat, L., Wartenberg, D., & Rhoads, G. G. (2009). Ambient air pollutant concentrations during pregnancy and the risk of fetal growth restriction. *Journal of Epidemiology and Community Health, 63,* 488–496.

Richards, J. E. (2008). Attention in young infants: A developmental psychophysiological perspective. In C. A. Nelson & M. Luciana (Eds.), *Handbook of developmental cognitive neuroscience* (2nd ed., pp. 479–497). Cambridge, MA: MIT Press.

Richardson, H. L., Walker, A. M., & Horne, R. S. C. (2008). Sleep position alters arousal processes maximally at the high-risk age for sudden infant death syndrome. *Journal of Sleep Research, 17,* 450–457.

Richardson, H. L., Walker, A. M., & Horne, R. S. C. (2009). Maternal smoking impairs arousal patterns in sleeping infants. *Pediatric Sleep, 32,* 515–521.

Richler, J., Luyster, R., Risi, S., Hsu, W.-L., Dawson, G., & Bernier, R. (2006). Is there a 'regressive phenotype' of autism spectrum disorder associated with the measles-mumps-rubella vaccine? A CPEA study. *Journal of Autism and Developmental Disorders, 36,* 299–316.

Richmond, J., Colombo, M., & Hayne, H. (2007). Interpreting visual preferences in the visual paired-comparison task.

Journal of Experimental Psychology: Learning, Memory, and Cognition, 33, 823–831.

Richmond, L. J. (2004). When spirituality goes awry: Students in cults. *Professional School Counseling, 7,* 367–375.

Ridenour, T. A. (2000). Genetic epidemiology of antisocial behavior. In D. H. Fishbein (Ed.), *The science, treatment, and prevention of antisocial behaviors* (pp. 7.1–7.24). Kingston, NJ: Civic Research Institute.

Rideout, V., & Hamel, E. (2006). *The media family: Electronic media in the lives of infants, toddlers, preschoolers and their parents.* Menlo Park, CA: Henry J. Kaiser Family Foundation.

Rideout, V. J., Foehr, U. G., & Roberts, D. F. (2010). *Generation M²: Media in the lives of 8- to 18-year-olds.* Menlo Park. CA: Henry J. Kaiser Family Foundation.

Riggins, T., Miller, N. C., Bauer, P., Georgieff, M. K., & Nelson, C. A. (2009). Consequences of low neonatal iron status due to maternal diabetes mellitus on explicit memory performance in childhood. *Developmental Neuropsychology, 34,* 762–779.

Rijsdijk, F. V., & Boomsma, D. I. (1997). Genetic mediation of the correlation between peripheral nerve conduction velocity and IQ. *Behavior Genetics, 27,* 87–98.

Rinderman, H., & Neubauer, A. C. (2004). Processing speed, intelligence, creativity, and school performance: Testing of causal hypotheses using structural equation models. *Intelligence, 32,* 573–589.

Ripple, C. H., & Zigler, E. (2003). Research, policy, and the federal role in prevention initiatives for children. *American Psychologist, 58,* 482–490.

Ris, M. D., Dietrich, K. N., Succop, P. A., Berger, O. G., & Bornschein, R. L. (2004). Early exposure to lead and neuropsychological outcome in adolescence. *Journal of the International Neuropsychological Society, 10,* 261–270.

Ritchie, L. D., Spector, P., Stevens, M. J., Schmidt, M. M., Schreiber, G. B., Striegel-Moore, R. H., et al. (2007). Dietary patterns in adolescence are related to adiposity in young adulthood in black and white females. *Journal of Nutrition, 137,* 399–406.

Riva, D., & Giorgi, C. (2000). The cerebellum contributes to higher functions during development: Evidence from a series of children surgically treated for posterior fossa tumours. *Brain, 123,* 1051–1061.

Rivadeneyra, R., & Ward, L. M. (2005). From Ally McBeal to Sábado Gigante: Contributions of television viewing to the gender role attitudes of Latino adolescents. *Journal of Adolescent Research, 20,* 453–475.

Rivera, S. M., Wakeley, A., & Langer, J. (1999). The drawbridge phenomenon: Representational reasoning or perceptual preference? *Developmental Psychology, 35,* 427–435.

Rivkees, S. A. (2003). Developing circadian rhythmicity in infants. *Pediatrics, 112,* 373–381.

Rizzo, T. A., Metzger, B. E., Dooley, S. L., & Cho, N. H. (1997). Early malnutrition and child neurobehavioral development: Insights from the study of children of diabetic mothers. *Child Development, 68,* 26–38.

Rizzolatti, G., & Craighero, L. (2004). The mirror-neuron system. *Annual Review of Neuroscience, 27,* 169–192.

Robb, A. S., & Dadson, M. J. (2002). Eating disorders in males. *Child and Adolescent Psychiatric Clinics of North America, 11,* 399–418.

Roberts, B. W., & DelVecchio, W. F. (2000). The rank-order consistency of personality traits from childhood to old age: A quantitative review of longitudinal studies. *Psychological Bulletin, 126,* 3–25.

Roberts, B. W., Kuncel, N. R., Shiner, R., Caspi, A., & Goldberg, L. R. (2007). The power of personality: The comparative validity of personality traits, socioeconomic status, and cognitive ability for predicting important life outcomes. *Perspectives on Psychological Science, 2,* 313–345.

Roberts, D. F., Foehr, U. G., & Rideout, V. (2005). *Generation M: Media in the lives of 8–18 year olds.* Menlo Park, CA: Henry J. Kaiser Family Foundation.

Roberts, D. F., Henriksen, L., & Foehr, U. G. (2004). Adolescents and media. In R. M. Lerner & L. Steinberg (Eds.), *Handbook of adolescent psychology* (2nd ed., pp. 627–664). Hoboken, NJ: Wiley.

Roberts, D. F., Henriksen, L., & Foehr, U. G. (2009). Adolescence, adolescents, and media. In R. M. Lerner & L. Steinberg (Eds.), *Handbook of adolescent psychology: Vol. 2. Contextual influences on adolescent development* (3rd ed., pp. 314–344). Hoboken, NJ: Wiley.

Roberts, K. P., & Powell, M. B. (2005). The relation between inhibitory control and children's eyewitness memory. *Applied Cognitive Psychology, 19,* 1003–1018.

Roberts, R. E., Attkisson, C. C., & Rosenblatt, A. (1998). Prevalence of psychopathology among children and adolescents. *American Journal of Psychiatry, 155,* 715–725.

Robertson, E. K., & Köhler, S. (2007). Insights from child development on the relationship between episodic and semantic memory. *Neuropsychologia, 45,* 3178–3189.

Robertson, J. (2008). Stepfathers in families. In J. Pryor (Ed.), *International handbook of stepfamilies: Policy and practice in legal, research, and clinical environments* (pp. 125–150). Hoboken, NJ: Wiley.

Robin, A. L., & Le Grange, D. (2010). Family therapy for adolescents with anorexia nervosa. In J. R. Weisz & A. E. Kazdin (Eds.), *Evidence-based psychotherapies for children and adolescents* (2nd ed., pp. 359–374). New York: Guilford.

Robin, D. J., Berthier, N. E., & Clifton, R. K. (1996). Infants' predictive reaching for moving objects in the dark. *Developmental Psychology, 32,* 824–835.

Robins, R. W., Tracy, J. L., Trzesniewski, K., Potter, J., & Gosling, S. D. (2001). Personality correlates of self-esteem. *Journal of Research in Personality, 35,* 463–482.

Robinson, B. F., Mervis, C. B., & Robinson, B. W. (2003). The roles of verbal short-term memory in the acquisition of grammar by children with Williams syndrome. *Developmental Neuropsychology, 23,* 13–31.

Robinson, C. C., Anderson, G. T., Porter, C. L., Hart, C. H., & Wouden-Miller, M. (2003). Sequential transition patterns of preschoolers' social interactions during child-initiated play: Is parallel-aware play a bi-directional bridge to other play states? *Early Childhood Research Quarterly, 18,* 3–21.

Robinson, S., Goddard, L., Dritschel, B., Wisley, M., & Howlin, P. (2009). Executive

functions in children with autism spectrum disorders. *Brain and Cognition, 71,* 362–368.

Rochat, P. (1989). Object manipulation and exploration in 2- to 5-month-old infants. *Developmental Psychology, 25,* 871–884.

Rochat, P. (1998). Self-perception and action in infancy. *Experimental Brain Research, 123,* 102–109.

Rochat, P. (2001). *The infant's world.* Cambridge, MA: Harvard University Press.

Rochat, P. (2003). Five levels of self-awareness as they unfold early in life. *Consciousness and Cognition, 12,* 717–731.

Rochat, P., & Goubet, N. (1995). Development of sitting and reaching in 5- to 6-month-old infants. *Infant Behavior and Development, 18,* 53–68.

Rochat, P., & Hespos, S. J. (1997). Differential rooting response by neonates: Evidence for an early sense of self. *Early Development and Parenting, 6,* 105–112.

Rochat, P., Querido, J. G., & Striano, T. (1999). Emerging sensitivity to the timing and structure of protoconversation. *Developmental Psychology, 35,* 950–957.

Rochat, P., & Striano, T. (2002). Who's in the mirror? Self-other discrimination in specular images by four- and nine-month-old infants. *Infant and Child Development, 11,* 289–303.

Rochat, P., Striano, T., & Blatt, L. (2002). Differential effects of happy, neutral, and sad still-faces on 2-, 4-, and 6-month-old infants. *Infant and Child Development, 11,* 289–303.

Rodgers, J. L. (2001). The confluence model: An academic "tragedy of the commons"? In E. L. Grigorenko & R. J. Sternberg (Eds.), *Family environment and intellectual functioning: A life-span perspective* (pp. 71–95). Mahwah, NJ: Erlbaum.

Rodgers, J. L., Cleveland, H. H., van den Oord, E., & Rowe, D. C. (2000). Resolving the debate over birth order, family size, and intelligence. *American Psychologist, 55,* 599–612.

Rodgers, J. L., & Wänström, L. (2007). Identification of a Flynn effect in the NLSY: Moving from the center to the boundaries. *Intelligence, 35,* 187–196.

Rodkin, P. C., Farmer, T. W., Pearl, R., & Van Acker, R. (2000). Resolving the debate over birth order, family size, and intelligence. *American Psychologist, 55,* 599–612.

Rodkin, P. C., Farmer, T. W., Pearl, R., & Van Acker, R. (2006). They're cool: Social status and peer group supports for aggressive boys and girls. *Social Development, 15,* 175–204.

Rodriguez, A., & Waldenström, U. (2008). Fetal origins of child non-right-handedness and mental health. *Child Psychology and Psychiatry, 49,* 967–976.

Rodriguez, M. L., Mischel, W., & Shoda, Y. (1989). Cognitive and personality variables in the delay of gratification of older children at risk. *Journal of Personality and Social Psychology, 57,* 358–367.

Roebers, C. M., & Schneider, W. (2001). Individual differences in children's eyewitness recall: The influence of intelligence and shyness. *Applied Developmental Science, 5,* 9–20.

Roehlkepartain, E. C. (2004). *Building strong families.* Retrieved from sparkaction.org/node/29938

Roelfsema, N. M., Hop, W. C., Boito, S. M., & Wladimiroff, J. W. (2004). Three-dimensional sonographic measurement of normal fetal brain volume during the second half of pregnancy. *American Journal of Obstetrics and Gynecology, 190,* 275–280.

Roeser, R. W., Eccles, J. S., & Freedman-Doan, C. (1999). Academic functioning and mental health in adolescence: Patterns, progressions, and routes from childhood. *Journal of Adolescent Research, 14,* 135–174.

Roeser, R. W., Eccles, J. S., & Sameroff, A. J. (2000). School as a context of early adolescents' academic and social-emotional development: A summary of research findings. *Elementary School Journal, 100,* 443–471.

Roffwarg, H. P., Muzio, J. N., & Dement, W. C. (1966). Ontogenetic development of the human sleep-dream cycle. *Science, 152,* 604–619.

Rogan, W. J., Dietrich, K. N., Ware, J. H., Dockery, D. W., Salganik, M., & Radcliffe, J. (2001). The effect of chelation therapy with succimer on neuropsychological development in children exposed to lead. *New England Journal of Medicine, 344,* 1421–1426.

Rogers, J. M. (2009). Tobacco and pregnancy. *Reproductive Toxicology, 28,* 152–160.

Rogoff, B. (1998). Cognition as a collaborative process. In D. Kuhn & R. S. Siegler (Eds.), *Handbook of child psychology: Vol. 2. Cognition, perception, and language* (5th ed., pp. 679–744). New York: Wiley.

Rogoff, B. (2003). *The cultural nature of human development.* New York: Oxford University Press.

Rogoff, B., & Mistry, J. (1985). Memory development in cultural context. In M. Pressley & C. Brainerd (Eds.), *Cognitive learning and memory in children* (pp. 117–142). New York: Springer-Verlag.

Rogoff, B., Paradise, R., Arauz, R. M., Correa-Chávez, M., & Angelillo, C. (2003). Firsthand learning through intent participation. *Annual Review of Psychology, 54,* 175–203.

Rogoff, B., & Waddell, K. J. (1982). Memory for information organized in a scene by children from two cultures. *Child Development, 53,* 1224–1228.

Rogol, A. D., Roemmich, J. N., & Clark, P. A. (2002). Growth at puberty. *Journal of Adolescent Health, 31,* 192–200.

Rohner, R. P., & Veneziano, R. A. (2001). The importance of father love: History and contemporary evidence. *Review of General Psychology, 5,* 382–405.

Roid, G. (2003). *The Stanford-Binet Intelligence Scales, Fifth Edition, Interpretive Manual.* Itasca, IL: Riverside Publishing.

Roisman, G. I., & Fraley, R. C. (2008). Behavior-genetic study of parenting quality, infant-attachment security, and their covariation in a nationally representative sample. *Developmental Psychology, 44,* 831–839.

Roisman, R., & Fraley, C. (2006). The limits of genetic influence: A behavior-genetic analysis of infant–caregiver relationship quality and temperament. *Child Development, 77,* 1656–1667.

Romano, A. M., & Lothian, J. A. (2008). Promoting, protecting, and supporting normal birth: A look at the evidence. *Journal of Obstetric, Gynecologic, and Neonatal Nursing, 37,* 94–104.

Rome-Flanders, T., & Cronk, C. (1995). A longitudinal study of infant vocalizations during mother–infant games. *Journal of Child Language, 22,* 259–274.

Romero, A. J., & Roberts, R. E. (2003). The impact of multiple dimensions of ethnic identity on discrimination and adolescents' self-esteem. *Journal of Applied Social Psychology, 33,* 2288–2305.

Rönnqvist, L., & Domellöf, E. (2006). Quantitative assessment of right and left reaching movements in infants: A longitudinal study from 6 to 36 months. *Developmental Psychobiology, 48,* 444–459.

Rönnqvist, L., & Hopkins, B. (1998). Head position preference in the human newborn: A new look. *Child Development, 69,* 13–23.

Roopnarine, J. L., & Evans, M. E. (2007). Family structural organization, mother–child and father–child relationships and psychological outcomes in English-speaking African Caribbean and Indo Caribbean families. In M. Sutherland (Ed.), *Psychological of development in the Caribbean.* Kingston, Jamaica: Ian Randle.

Roopnarine, J. L., Hossain, Z., Gill, P., & Brophy, H. (1994). Play in the East Indian context. In J. L. Roopnarine, J. E. Johnson, & F. H. Hooper (Eds.), *Children's play in diverse cultures* (pp. 9–30). Albany, NY: SUNY Press.

Roopnarine, J. L., Krishnakumar, A., Metindogan, A., & Evans, M. (2006). Links between parenting styles, parent–child academic interaction, parent–school interaction, and early academic skills and social behaviors in young children of English-speaking Caribbean immigrants. *Early Childhood Research Quarterly, 21,* 238–252.

Roopnarine, J. L., Talukder, E., Jain, D., Joshi, P., & Srivastave, P. (1990). Characteristics of holding, patterns of play, and social behaviors between parents and infants in New Delhi, India. *Developmental Psychology, 26,* 667–673.

Rosander, K., & von Hofsten, C. (2002). Development of gaze tracking of small and large objects. *Experimental Brain Research, 146,* 257–264.

Rosander, K., & von Hofsten, C. (2004). Infants' emerging ability to represent occluded object motion. *Cognition, 91,* 1–22.

Rose, A. J., & Asher, S. R. (1999). Children's goals and strategies in response to conflicts within a friendship. *Developmental Psychology, 35,* 69–79.

Rose, A. J., Carlson, W., & Waller, E. M. (2007). Prospective associations of co-rumination with friendship and emotional adjustment: Considering the socioemotional trade-offs of co-rumination. *Developmental Psychology, 43,* 1019–1031.

Rose, A. J., & Rudolph, K. D. (2006). A review of sex differences in peer relationship processes: Potential trade-offs for the emotional and behavioral development of girls and boys. *Psychological Bulletin, 132,* 98–131.

Rose, A. J., Swenson, L. P., & Waller, E. M. (2004). Overt and relational aggression and perceived popularity: Developmental differences in concurrent and prospective relations. *Developmental Psychology, 40,* 378–387.

Rose, S. A., Jankowski, J. J., & Senior, G. J. (1997). Infants' recognition of contour-deleted figures. *Journal of Experimental Psychology: Human Perception and Performance, 23,* 1206–1216.

Rosen, A. B., & Rozin, P. (1993). Now you see it, now you don't: The preschool child's conception of invisible particles in the context of dissolving. *Developmental Psychology, 29,* 300–311.

Rosen, C. S., & Cohen, M. (2010). Subgroups of New York City children at high risk of PTSD after the September 11 attacks: A signal detection analysis. *Psychiatric Services, 61,* 64–69.

Rosen, D. (2003). Eating disorders in children and young adolescents: Etiology, classification, clinical features, and treatment. *Adolescent Medicine: State of the Art Reviews, 14,* 49–59.

Rosen, P. J., Milich, R., & Harris, M. J. (2007). Victims of their own cognitions: Implicit social cognitions, emotional distress, and peer victimization. *Journal of Applied Developmental Psychology, 28,* 211–226.

Rosenbaum, J. E. (2009). Patient teenagers? A comparison of the sexual behavior of virginity pledgers and matched nonpledgers. *Pediatrics, 123,* e110–e120.

Rosenberger, L. R., Zeck, J., Berl, M. M., Moore, E. N., Ritzl, E. K., Shamim, S., et al. (2009). Interhemispheric and intrahemispheric language reorganization in complex partial epilepsy. *Neurology, 72,* 1830–1836.

Rosengren, K. S., & Hickling, A. K. (2000). The development of children's thinking about possible events and plausible mechanisms. In K. S. Rosengren, C. N. Johnson, & P. L. Harris (Eds.), *Imagining the impossible* (pp. 75–98). Cambridge, UK: Cambridge University Press.

Rosenshine, B., & Meister, C. (1994). Reciprocal teaching: A review of nineteen experimental studies. *Review of Educational Research, 64,* 479–530.

Roseth, C. J., Pellegrini, A. D., Bohn, C. M., van Ryzin, M., & Vance, N. (2007). Preschoolers' aggression, affiliation, and social dominance relationships: An observational, longitudinal study. *Journal of School Psychology, 45,* 479–497.

Rosetta, L., & Baldi, A. (2008). On the role of breastfeeding in health promotion and the prevention of allergic diseases. *Advances in Experimental Medicine and Biology, 606,* 467–483.

Ross, H. S., Conant, C., Cheyne, J. A., & Alevizos, E. (1992). Relationships and alliances in the social interactions of kibbutz toddlers. *Social Development, 1,* 1–17.

Rothbart, M. K. (2003). Temperament and the pursuit of an integrated developmental psychology. *Merrill-Palmer Quarterly, 50,* 492–505.

Rothbart, M. K., Ahadi, S. A., & Evans, D. E. (2000). Temperament and personality: Origins and outcome. *Journal of Personality and Social Psychology, 78,* 122–135.

Rothbart, M. K., & Bates, J. E. (2006). Temperament. In N. Eisenberg (Ed.), *Handbook of child psychology: Vol. 3. Social, emotional, and personality development* (6th ed., pp. 99–166). Hoboken, NJ: Wiley.

Rothbart, M. K., & Mauro, J. A. (1990). Questionnaire approaches to the study of infant temperament. In J. W. Fagen & J. Colombo (Eds.), *Individual differences in infancy: Reliability, stability, and prediction* (pp. 411–429). Hillsdale, NJ: Erlbaum.

Rothbart, M. K., Posner, M. I., & Kieras, J. (2006). Temperament, attention, and the development of self regulation. In K. McCartney & D. Phillips (Eds.), *Blackwell handbook of early childhood development* (pp. 338–357). Malden, MA: Blackwell.

Rothbaum, F., Kakinuma, M., Nagaoka, R., & Azuma, H. (2007). Attachment and amae: Parent–child closeness in the United States and Japan. *Journal of Cross-Cultural Psychology, 38,* 465–486.

Rothbaum, F., Pott, M., Azuma, H., Miyake, K., & Weisz, J. (2000b). The development of close relationships in Japan and the United States: Paths of symbiotic harmony and generative tension. *Child Development, 71,* 1121–1142.

Rothbaum, F., Weisz, J., Pott, M., Miyake, K., & Morelli, G. A. (2000a). Attachment and culture: Security in the United States and Japan. *American Psychologist, 55,* 1093–1104.

Rouselle, L., Palmers, E., & Noël, M.-P. (2004). Magnitude comparison in preschoolers: What counts? Influence of perceptual variables. *Journal of Experimental Child Psychology, 87,* 57–84.

Rousseau, J. J. (1955). *Emile.* New York: Dutton. (Original work published 1762)

Rovee-Collier, C. K. (1999). The development of infant memory. *Current Directions in Psychological Science, 8,* 80–85.

Rovee-Collier, C. K., & Bhatt, R. S. (1993). Evidence of long-term memory in infancy. *Annals of Child Development, 9,* 1–45.

Rovee-Collier, C., & Cuevas, K. (2009). Multiple memory systems are unnecessary to account for infant memory development: An ecological model. *Developmental Psychology, 45,* 160–174.

Rowe, M. L. (2008). Child-directed speech: Relation to socioeconomic status, knowledge of child development and child vocabulary skill. *Journal of Child Language, 35,* 185–205.

Rowe, M. L., & Goldin-Meadow, S. (2009). Early gesture selectively predicts later language learning. *Developmental Science, 12,* 182–187.

Rowe, M. L., & Mervis, C. B. (2006). Working memory in Williams syndrome. In T. P. Alloway & S. E. Gathercole (Eds.), *Working memory and neurodevelopmental disorders* (pp. 267–293). New York: Psychology Press.

Rowe, M. L., Özçaliskan, S., & Goldin-Meadow, S. (2008). Learning words by hand: Gesture's role in predicting vocabulary development. *First Language, 28,* 182–199.

Rowland, C. F. (2007). Explaining errors in children's questions. *Cognition, 104,* 106–134.

Rowland, C. F., & Pine, J. M. (2000). Subject-auxiliary inversion errors and wh-question acquisition: "What children do know?" *Journal of Child Language, 27,* 157–181.

Rowland, C. F., Pine, J. M., Lieven, E. V. M., & Theakston, A. L. (2005). The incidence of error in young children's wh-questions. *Journal of Speech, Language, and Hearing Research, 48,* 384–404.

Rowley, S. J., Kurtz-Costes, B., Mistry, R., & Feagans, L. (2007). Social status as a predictor of race and gender stereotypes in late childhood and early adolescence. *Social Development, 16,* 150–168.

Rubin, C., Maisonet, M., Kieszak, S., Monteilh, C., Holmes A., Flanders, D., et al. (2009). Timing of maturation and predictors of menarche in girls enrolled in a contemporary British cohort. *Paediatric and Perinatal Epidemiology, 23,* 492–504.

Rubin, K. H., Bowker, J., & Gazelle, H. (2010). Social withdrawal in childhood and adolescence: Peer relationships and social competence. In K. H. Rubin & R. J. Coplan (Eds.), *The development of shyness and social withdrawal* (pp. 131–156). New York: Guilford.

Rubin, K. H., Bukowski, W. M., & Parker, J. G. (2006). Peer interactions, relationships, and groups. In N. Eisenberg (Ed.), *Handbook of child psychology: Vol. 3. Social, emotional, and personality development* (6th ed., pp. 571–645). Hoboken, NJ: Wiley.

Rubin, K. H., & Burgess, K. B. (2002). Parents of aggressive and withdrawn children. In M. Bornstein (Ed.), *Handbook of parenting* (2nd ed., pp. 383–418). Hillsdale, NJ: Erlbaum.

Rubin, K. H., Burgess, K. B., & Coplan, R. (2002). Social withdrawal and shyness. In P. K. Smith & C. H. Hart (Eds.), *Blackwell handbook of child social development* (pp. 329–352). Oxford, UK: Blackwell.

Rubin, K. H., Burgess, K. B., & Hastings, P. D. (2002). Stability and social-behavioral consequences of toddlers' inhibited temperament and parenting behaviors. *Child Development, 73,* 483–495.

Rubin, K. H., Coplan, R. J., Chen, X., Buskirk, A. A., & Wojslawowicz, J. C. (2005). Peer relationships in childhood. In M. H. Bornstein & M. E. Lamb (Eds.), *Developmental science: An advanced textbook* (pp. 469–512). Mahwah, NJ: Erlbaum.

Rubin, K. H., Fein, G. G., & Vandenberg, B. (1983). Play. In E. M. Hetherington (Ed.), *Handbook of child psychology: Vol. 4. Socialization, personality, and social development* (4th ed., pp. 693–744). New York: Wiley.

Rubin, K. H., Stewart, S. L., & Coplan, R. J. (1995). Social withdrawal in childhood: Conceptual and empirical perspectives. In T. H. Ollendick & R. J. Prinz (Eds.), *Advances in clinical child psychology* (Vol. 17, pp. 157–196). New York: Plenum.

Rubin, K. H., Watson, K. S., & Jambor, T. W. (1978). Free-play behaviors in preschool and kindergarten children. *Child Development, 49,* 534–536.

Ruble, D. N., Alvarez, J., Bachman, M., Cameron, J., Fuligni, A., Garcia Coll, C., & Rhee, E. (2004). The development of a sense of "we": The emergence and implications of children's collective identity. In M. Bennett & F. Sani (Eds.), *The development of the social self* (pp. 29–76). Hove, UK: Psychology Press.

Ruble, D. N., & Dweck, C. S. (1995). Self-conceptions, person conceptions, and their development. In N. Eisenberg (Ed.), *Social development* (pp. 109–139). Thousand Oaks, CA: Sage.

Ruble, D. N., & Flett, G. L. (1988). Conflicting goals in self-evaluative information seeking: Developmental and ability level analyses. *Child Development, 59,* 97–106.

Ruble, D. N., Martin, C. L., & Berenbaum, S. A. (2006). Gender development. In N. Eisenberg (Ed.), *Handbook of child psychology: Vol. 3. Social, emotional, and personality development* (6th ed., pp. 226–299). Hoboken, NJ: Wiley.

Ruble, D. N., Taylor, L. J., Cyphers, L., Greulich, F. K., Lurye, L. E., & Shrout, P. E. (2007). The role of gender constancy in early gender development. *Child Development, 78,* 1121–1136.

Rudolph, D. K., & Heller, T. L. (1997). Interpersonal problem solving, externalizing behavior, and social competence in preschoolers: A knowledge-performance discrepancy? *Journal of Applied Developmental Psychology, 18,* 107–117.

Rudolph, D. K., Lambert, S. F., Clark, A. G., & Kurlakowsky, K. D. (2001). Negotiating the transition to middle school: The role of self-regulatory processes. *Child Development, 72,* 929–946.

Rudolph, K. D., Caldwell, M. S., & Conley, C. S. (2005). Need for approval and children's well-being. *Child Development, 76,* 309–323.

Ruff, C. (2002). Variation in human body size and shape. *Annual Review of Anthropology, 31,* 211–232.

Ruff, H. A., & Capozzoli, M. C. (2003). Development of attention and distractibility in the first 4 years of life. *Developmental Psychology, 39,* 877–890.

Ruff, H. A., Saltarelli, L. M., Capozzoli, M., & Dubiner, K. (1992). The differentiation of activity in infants' exploration of objects. *Developmental Psychology, 28,* 851–861.

Ruffman, T., & Perner, T. (2005). Do infants really understand false belief? *Trends in Cognitive Sciences, 9,* 462–463.

Ruffman, T. (1999). Children's understanding of logical inconsistency. *Child Development, 70,* 872–886.

Ruffman, T., & Langman, L. (2002). Infants' reaching in a multi-well A not B task. *Infant Behavior and Development, 25,* 237–246.

Ruffman, T., Perner, J., Olson, D. R., & Doherty, M. (1993). Reflecting on scientific thinking: Children's understanding of the hypothesis–evidence relation. *Child Development, 64,* 1617–1636.

Ruffman, T., Slade, L., Devitt, K., & Crowe, E. (2006). What mothers say and what they do: The relation between parenting, theory of mind, language, and conflict/cooperation. *British Journal of Developmental Psychology, 24,* 105–124.

Runco, M. A. (1992a). Children's divergent thinking and creative ideation. *Developmental Review, 12,* 233–264.

Runco, M. A. (1992b). The evaluative, valuative, and divergent thinking of children. *Journal of Creative Behavior, 25,* 311–319.

Runco, M. A. (1993). Divergent thinking, creativity, and giftedness. *Gifted Child Quarterly, 37,* 16–22.

Runco, M. A., & Okuda, S. M. (1988). Problem, discovery, divergent thinking, and the creative process. *Journal of Youth and Adolescence, 17,* 211–220.

Rushton, J. L., Forcier, M., & Schectman, R. M. (2002). Epidemiology of depressive symptoms in the National Longitudinal Study of Adolescent Health. *Journal of the American Academy of Child and Adolescent Psychiatry, 41,* 199–205.

Rushton, J. P., & Jensen, A. R. (2005). Thirty years of research on race differences in cognitive ability. *Psychology, Public Policy, and Law, 11,* 235–294.

Rushton, J. P., & Jensen, A. R. (2006). The totality of available evidence shows the race IQ gap still remains. *Psychological Science, 17,* 921–924.

Rushton, J. P., & Jensen, A. R. (2010). The rise and fall of the Flynn effect as a reason to expect a narrowing of the black–white IQ gap. *Intelligence, 38,* 213–219.

Russell, A., Mize, J., & Bissaker, K. (2004). Parent–child relationships. In P. K. Smith & C. H. Hart (Eds.), *Blackwell handbook of childhood social development* (pp. 204–222). Malden, MA: Blackwell.

Russell, A., Pettit, G. S., & Mize, J. (1998). Horizontal qualities in parent–child relationships: Parallels with and possible consequences for children's peer relationships. *Developmental Review, 18,* 313–352.

Russell, J. A. (1990). The preschooler's understanding of the causes and consequences of emotion. *Child Development, 61,* 1872–1881.

Russell, R. B., Petrini, J. R., Damus, K., Mattison, D. R., & Schwarz, R. H. (2003). The changing epidemiology of multiple births in the United States. *Obstetrics and Gynecology, 101,* 129–135.

Russell, S. T., Elder, G. H., & Conger, R. D. (1997). *School transitions and academic achievement.* Paper presented at the annual meeting of the American Sociological Association, Toronto, Canada.

Rust, J., Golombok, S., Hines, M., Johnston, K., Golding, J., & the ALSPAC Study Team. (2000). The role of brothers and sisters in the gender development of preschool children. *Journal of Experimental Child Psychology, 77,* 292–303.

Rutland, A., Killen, M., & Abrams, D. (2010). A new social-cognitive developmental perspective on prejudice: The interplay between morality and group identity. *Perspectives on Psychological Science, 5,* 279–291.

Rutter, M. (1996). Maternal deprivation. In M. H. Bornstein (Ed.), *Handbook of parenting: Vol. 4. Applied and practical parenting* (pp. 3–31). Mahwah, NJ: Erlbaum.

Rutter, M. (2007). Gene–environment interdependence. *Developmental Science, 10,* 12–18.

Rutter, M. (2011). Biological and experiential influences on psychological development. In D. P. Keating (Ed.), *Nature and nurture in early child development* (pp. 7–44). New York: Cambridge University Press.

Rutter, M., Colvert, E., Kreppner, J., Beckett, C., Castle, J., & Groothues, C. (2007). Early adolescent outcomes for institutionally deprived and non-deprived adoptees. I: Disinhibited attachment. *Journal of Child Psychology and Psychiatry, 48,* 17–30.

Rutter, M., & the English and Romanian Adoptees Study Team. (1998). Developmental catch-up, and deficit, following adoption after severe global early privation. *Journal of Child Psychology and Psychiatry, 39,* 465–476.

Rutter, M., O'Connor, T. G., and the English and Romanian Adoptees Study Team. (2004). Are there biological programming effects for psychological development? Findings from a study of Romanian adoptees. *Developmental Psychology, 40,* 81–94.

Rutter, M., Pickles, A., Murray, R., & Eaves, L. (2001). Testing hypotheses about specific environmental causal effects on behavior. *Psychological Bulletin, 127,* 291–324.

Rutter, M., Sonuga-Barke, E. J, Beckett, C., Castle, J., Kreppner, J., Kumsta, R., et al. (2010). Deprivation-specific psychological patterns: Effects of institutional deprivation. *Monographs of the Society for Research in Child Development, 75*(1, Serial No. 295).

Ryan, M. K., David, B., & Reynolds, K. J. (2004). Who cares? The effect of gender and context on the self and moral reasoning. *Psychology of Women Quarterly, 28,* 246–255.

Ryan, R. M., Fauth, R. C., & Brooks-Gunn, J. (2006). Childhood poverty: Implications for school readiness and early childhood education In B. Spodek & O. N. Saracho (Eds.), *Handbook of research on the education of young children* (2nd ed., pp. 323–346). Mahwah, NJ: Erlbaum.

Saarela, M. V., Hlushchuk, Y., Williams, A. C. de C., Schürmann, M., Kalso, E., & Hari, R. (2007). The compassionate brain: Humans detect intensity of pain from another's face. *Cerebral Cortex, 17,* 230–237.

Saarni, C. (1999). *The development of emotional competence.* New York: Guilford.

Saarni, C. (2000). Emotional competence: A developmental perspective. In R. Bar-On & J. D. A. Parker (Eds.), *Handbook of emotional intelligence* (pp. 68–91). San Francisco: Jossey-Bass.

Saarni, C., Campos, J. J., Camras, L. A., & Witherington, D. (2006). Emotional development: Action, communication, and understanding. In N. Eisenberg (Ed.), *Handbook of child psychology: Vol. 3. Social, emotional, and personality development* (6th ed., pp. 226–299). Hoboken, NJ: Wiley.

Sabbagh, M. A., Xu, F., Carlson, S. M., Moses, L. J., & Lee, K. (2006). The development of executive functioning and theory of mind: A comparison of Chinese and U.S. preschoolers. *Psychological Science, 17,* 74–81.

Sacks, P. (2005). "No child left": What are schools for in a democratic society? In S. Olfman (Ed.), *Childhood lost: How American culture is failing our kids* (pp. 185–202). Westport, CT: Praeger.

Sadeh, A. (1997). Sleep and melatonin in infants: A preliminary study. *Sleep, 20,* 185–191.

Sadeh, A., Flint-Ofir, E., Tirosh, T., & Tikotzky, L. (2007). Infant sleep and parental sleep-related cognitions. *Journal of Family Psychology, 21,* 74–87.

Sadler, T. W. (2009). *Langman's medical embryology* (11th ed.). Baltimore: Lippincott Williams & Wilkins.

Saenger, P. (2003). Dose effects of growth hormone during puberty. *Hormone Research, 60*(Suppl. 1), 52–57.

Saffran, J. R. (2009). Acquiring grammatical patterns: Constraints on learning. In J. Colombo, P. McCardle, & L. Freund (Eds.), *Infant pathways to language: Methods, models, and research disorders* (pp. 31–47). New York: Psychology Press.

Saffran, J. R., Aslin, R. N., & Newport, E. L. (1996). Statistical learning by 8-month-old infants. *Science, 274,* 1926–1928.

Saffran, J. R., & Thiessen, E. D. (2003). Pattern induction by infant language learners. *Developmental Psychology, 39,* 484–494.

Saffran, J. R., & Thiessen, E. D. (2007). Domain-general learning capacities. In E. Hoff & M. Shatz (Eds.), *Blackwell handbook of language development* (pp. 68–86). Malden, MA: Blackwell.

Saffran, J. R., Werker, J. F., & Werner, L. A. (2006). The infant's auditory world: Hearing, speech, and the beginnings of language. In D. Kuhn & R. Siegler (Eds.), *Handbook of child psychology: Vol. 2. Cognition, perception, and language* (6th ed., pp. 58–108). Hoboken, NJ: Wiley.

Safren, S. A., & Pantalone, D. W. (2006). Social anxiety and barriers to resllience among lesbian, gay, and bisexual adolescents. In A. M. Omoto & H. S. Kurtzman (Eds.), *Sexual orientation and mental health: Examining identity and development in lesbian, gay, and bisexual young people* (pp. 55–71). Washington, DC: American Psychological Association.

Sagi, A., van IJzendoorn, M. H., Aviezer, O., Donnell, F., Koren-Karie, N., Joels, T., & Harel, Y. (1995). Attachments in a multiple-caregiver and multiple-infant environment: The case of the Israeli kibbutzim. In E. Waters, B. E. Vaughn, G. Posada, & K. Kondo-Ikemura (Eds.), Caregiving, cultural, and cognitive perspectives on secure-base behavior and working models: New growing points in attachment theory and research. *Monographs of the Society for Research in Child Development, 60* (1, Serial No. 244), 71–91.

Sahlberg, P. (2010). Educational change in Finland. In A. Hargreaves, M. Fullan, A. Lieberman, & D. Hopkins (Eds.), *Second international handbook of educational change*. New York: Springer.

Saigal, S., Stoskopf, B., Streiner, D., Boyle, M., Pinelli, J., & Paneth, N. (2006). Transition of extremely low-birth-weight infants from adolescence to young adulthood. *Journal of the American Medical Association, 295,* 667–675.

Saitta, S. C., & Zackai, E. H. (2005). Specific chromosome disorders in newborns. In H. W. Taeusch, R. A. Ballard, & C. A. Gleason (Eds.), *Avery's diseases of the newborn* (8th ed., pp. 204–215). Philadelphia: Saunders.

Salerno, M., Micillo, M., Di Maio, S., Capalbo, D., Ferri, P., & Lettiero, T. (2001). Longitudinal growth, sexual maturation and final height in patients with congenital hypothyroidism detected by neonatal screening. *European Journal of Endocrinology, 145,* 377–383.

Salguero, R. A. T., & Morán, R. M. B. (2003). Measuring problem video game playing in adolescents. *Addiction, 97,* 1601–1606.

Salidis, J., & Johnson, J. S. (1997). The production of minimal words: A longitudinal case study of phonological development. *Language Acquisition, 6,* 1–36.

Salihu, H. M., Shumpert, M. N., Slay, M., Kirby, R. S., & Alexander, G. R. (2003). Childbearing beyond maternal age 50 and fetal outcomes in the United States. *Obstetrics and Gynecology, 102,* 1006–1014.

Salisbury, A. L., Ponder, K. L., Padbury, J. F., & Lester, B. M. (2009). Fetal effects of psychoactive drugs. *Clinics in Perinatology, 36,* 595–619.

Salley, B. J., & Dixon, W. E., Jr. (2007). Temperamental and joint attentional predictors of language development. *Merrill-Palmer Quarterly, 53,* 131–154.

Sallquist, J., Eisenberg, N., Spinrad, T. L., Eggum, N. D., & Gaertner, B. M. (2009). Assessment of preschoolers' positive empathy: Concurrent and longitudinal relations with positive emotion, social competence, and sympathy. *Journal of Positive Psychology, 4,* 223–233.

Salmivalli, C., & Voeten, M. (2004). Connections between attitudes, group norms, and behaviour in bullying situations. *International Journal of Behavioral Development, 28,* 246–258.

Salovey, P., & Pizarro, D. A. (2003). The value of emotional intelligence. In R. J. Sternberg, J. Lautrey, & T. I. Lubart (Eds.), *Models of intelligence: International*

perspectives (pp. 263–278). Washington, DC: American Psychological Association.

Salter, D., McMillan, D., Richards, M., Talbot, T., Hodges, J., Bentovim, A., & Hastings, R. (2003). Development of sexually abusive behavior in sexually victimized males: A longitudinal study. *Lancet, 361,* 471–476.

Samek, D. R., & Rueter, M. A. (2011). Considerations of elder sibling closeness in predicting younger sibling substance use: Social learning versus social bonding explanations. *Journal of Family Psychology, 25,*931–941.

Samenow, S. E. (1984). *Inside the criminal mind.* New York: Random House.

Sameroff, A. (2006). Identifying risk and protective factors for healthy child development. In A. Clarke-Stewart & J. Dunn (Eds.), *Families count: Effects on child and adolescent development* (pp. 53–76). New York: Cambridge University Press.

Sameroff, A. J., & MacKenzie, M. J. (2003). Research strategies for capturing transactional models of development: The limits of the possible. *Development and Psychopathology, 15,* 613–640.

Sanchez, M. M., & Pollak, S. D. (2009). Socioemotional development following early abuse and neglect: Challenges and insight from translational research. In M. de Haan & M. R. Gunnar (Eds.), *Handbook of developmental social neuroscience* (pp. 497–520). New York: Guilford.

Sanders, O. (2006). Evaluating the Keeping Ourselves Safe Programme. Wellington, NZ: Youth Education Service, New Zealand Police.

Sandler, J. C. (2006). Alternative methods of child testimony: A review of law and research. In C. R. Bartol & A. M. Bartol (Eds.), *Current perspectives in forensic psychology and criminal justice* (pp. 203–212). Thousand Oaks, CA: Sage.

Sandnabba, N. K., & Ahlberg, C. (1999). Parents' attitudes and expectations about children's cross-gender behavior. *Sex Roles, 40,* 249–263.

Sands, R. G., Goldberg-Glen, R. S., & Shin, H. (2009). The voices of grandchildren of grandparent caregivers: A strengths-resilience perspective. *Child Welfare, 88,* 25–45.

Sangrigoli, S., Pallier, C., Argenti, A. M., Ventureyra, V. A. G., & de Schonen, S. (2005). Reversibility of the other-race effect in face recognition during childhood. *Psychological Science, 16,* 440–444.

Sann, C., & Streri, A. (2007). Perception of object shape and texture in human newborns: Evidence from cross-modal transfer tasks. *Developmental Science, 10,* 399–410.

Sann, C., & Streri, A. (2008). The limits of newborn's grasping to detect texture in a cross-modal transfer task. *Infant Behavior and Development, 31,* 523–531.

Sansavini, A., Bertoncini, J., & Giovanelli, G. (1997). Newborns discriminate the rhythm of multisyllabic stressed words. *Developmental Psychology, 33,* 3–11.

Sanson, A., Hemphill, S. A., & Smart, D. (2004). Connections between temperament and social development: A review. *Social Development, 13,* 142–170.

Santoloupo, S., & Pratt, M. W. (1994). Age, gender, and parenting style variations in mother–adolescent dialogues and adolescent reasoning about political issues. *Journal of Adolescent Research, 9,* 241–261.

Sapp, F., Lee, K., & Muir, D. (2000). Three-year-olds' difficulty with the appearance–reality distinction: Is it real or is it apparent? *Developmental Psychology, 36,* 547–560.

Sarnecka, B. W., & Gelman, S. A. (2004). Six does not just mean a lot: Preschoolers see number words as specific. *Cognition, 92,* 329–352.

Sato, T., Matsumoto, T., Kawano, H., Watanabe, T., Uematsu, Y., & Semine, K. (2004). Brain masculinization requires androgen receptor function. *Proceedings of the National Academy of Sciences, 101,* 1673–1678.

Saucier, J. F., Sylvestre, R., Doucet, H., Lambert, J., Frappier, J. Y., Charbonneau, L., & Malus, M. (2002). Cultural identity and adaptation to adolescence in Montreal. In F. J. C. Azima & N. Grizenko (Eds.), *Immigrant and refugee children and their families: Clinical, research, and training issues* (pp. 133–154). Madison, WI: International Universities Press.

Saudino, K. J. (2003). Parent ratings of infant temperament: Lessons from twin studies. *Infant Behavior and Development, 26,* 100–107.

Saudino, K. J., & Cherny, S. S. (2001). Sources of continuity and change in observed temperament. In R. N. Emde & J. K. Hewitt (Eds.), *Infancy to early childhood: Genetic and environmental influences on developmental change* (pp. 89–110). New York: Oxford University Press.

Saudino, K. J., & Plomin, R. (1997). Cognitive and temperamental mediators of genetic contributions to the home environment during infancy. *Merrill-Palmer Quarterly, 43,* 1–23.

Savage, C., Lieven, E., Theakston, A., & Tomasello, M. (2006). Structural priming as implicit learning in language acquisition: The persistence of lexical and structural priming in 4-year-olds. *Language Learning and Development, 2,* 27–49.

Savage-Rumbaugh, S., Shanker, S. G., & Taylor, T. J. (1998). *Apes, language, and the human mind.* New York: Oxford University Press.

Savage-Rumbaugh, E. S., Murphy, J., Sevcik, R. A., Brakke, K. E., Williams, S. L., & Rumbaugh, D. M. (1993). Language comprehension in ape and child. *Monographs of the Society for Research in Child Development, 58*(3–4, Serial No. 233).

Savin-Williams, R. C. (2001). A critique of research on sexual minority youths. *Journal of Adolescence, 24,* 5–13.

Savin-Williams, R. C., & Diamond, L. M. (2004). Sex. In R. M. Lerner & L. Steinberg (Eds.), *Handbook of adolescent development* (2nd ed., pp. 189–231). Hoboken, NJ: Wiley.

Savin-Williams, R. C., & Ream, G. L. (2003). Suicide attempts among sexual-minority male youth. *Journal of Clinical Child and Adolescent Psychology, 32,* 509–522.

Sawyer, A. M., & Borduin, C. M. (2011). Effects of multisystemic therapy through midlife: A 21.9-year follow-up to a randomized clinical trial with serious and violent juvenile offenders. *Journal of Consulting and Clinical Psychology, 79,* 643–652.

Saxe, G. B. (1988, August–September). Candy selling and math learning. *Educational Researcher, 17*(6), 14–21.

Saxton, M., Backley, P., & Gallaway, C. (2005). Negative input for grammatical

errors: Effects after a lag of 12 weeks. *Journal of Child Language, 32,* 643–672.

Saxton, M., Houston-Price, C., & Dawson, N. (2005). The prompt hypothesis: Clarification requests as corrective input for grammatical errors. *Applied Psycholinguistics, 26,* 393–414.

Saygin, A. P., Leech, R., & Dick, F. (2010). Nonverbal auditory agnosia with lesion to Wernicke's area. *Neuropsychologia, 48,* 107–113.

Saygin, A. P., Wilson, S. M., Dronkers, N. F., & Bates, E. (2004). Action comprehension in aphasia: Linguistic and non-linguistic deficits and their lesion correlates. *Neuropsychologia, 42,* 1788–1804.

Saylor, M. M. (2004). Twelve- and 16-month-old infants recognize properties of mentioned absent things. *Developmental Science, 7,* 599–611.

Saylor, M. M., Baldwin, D. A., & Sabbagh, M. A. (2005). Word learning: A complex product. In G. Hall & S. Waxman (Eds.), *Weaving a lexicon.* Cambridge, MA: MIT Press.

Saylor, M. M., & Ganea, P. (2007). Infants interpret ambiguous requests for absent objects. *Developmental Psychology, 43,* 696–704.

Saylor, M. M., & Troseth, G. L. (2006). Preschoolers use information about speakers' desires to learn new words. *Cognitive Development, 21,* 214–231.

Saywitz, K. J., Goodman, G. S., & Lyon, T. D. (2002). Interviewing children in and out of court: Current research and practice implications. In J. E. B. Myers & L. Berliner (Eds.), *The APSAC handbook on child maltreatment* (2nd ed., pp. 349–377). Thousand Oaks, CA: Sage.

Scales, P. C., & Roehlkepartain, E. C. (2004). *Community service and service learning in U.S. public schools, 2004. Findings from a national survey.* St. Paul, MN: National Youth Leadership Council.

Scarr, S. (1997). Behavior-genetic and socialization theories of intelligence: Truce and reconciliation. In R. J. Sternberg & E. L. Grigorenko (Eds.), *Intelligence, heredity, and environment* (pp. 3–41). New York: Cambridge University Press.

Scarr, S., & McCartney, K. (1983). How people make their own environments: A theory of genotype environment effects. *Child Development, 54,* 424–435.

Scarr, S., & Weinberg, R. A. (1983). The Minnesota Adoption Studies: Genetic differences and malleability. *Child Development, 54,* 260–267.

Schaal, B., Marlier, L., & Soussignan, R. (2000). Human foetuses learn odours from their pregnant mother's diet. *Chemical Senses, 25,* 729–737.

Schacht, P. M., Cummings, E. M., & Davies, P. T. (2009). Fathering in family context and child adjustment: A longitudinal analysis. *Journal of Family Psychology, 23,* 790–797.

Schalet, A. (2007). Adolescent sexuality viewed through two different cultural lenses. In M. S. Tepper & A. F. Owens (Eds.), *Sexual health: Vol. 3. Moral and cultural foundations* (pp. 365–387). Westport, CT: Praeger.

Scharrer, E., & Comstock, G. (2003). Entertainment televisual media: Content patterns and themes. In E. L. Palmer & B. M. Young (Eds.), *The faces of televisual media: Teaching, violence, selling to children* (pp. 161–193). Mahwah, NJ: Erlbaum.

Schauwers, K., Gillis, S., Daemers, K., De Beukelaer, C., De Ceulaer, G., Yperman, M., & Govaerts, P. J. (2004). Normal hearing and language development in a deaf-born child: Cochlear implants. *Otology and Neurotology, 25,* 924–929.

Schellenberg, E. G. (2004). Music lessons enhance IQ. *Psychological Science, 15,* 511–514.

Schellenberg, E. G., Nakata, T., Hunter, P. G., & Tamoto, S. (2007). Exposure to music and cognitive performance: Tests of children and adults. *Psychology of Music, 35,* 5–19.

Scher, A., Epstein, R., & Tirosh, E. (2004). Stability and changes in sleep regulation: A longitudinal study from 3 months to 3 years. *International Journal of Behavioral Development, 28,* 268–274.

Scher, A., Tirosh, E., Jaffe, M., Rubin, L., Sadeh, A., & Lavie, P. (1995). Sleep patterns of infants and young children in Israel. *International Journal of Behavioral Development, 18,* 701–711.

Schermerhorn, A. C., Chow, S.-M., & Cummings, E. M. (2010). Developmental family processes and interparental conflict: Patterns of microlevel influences. *Developmental Psychology, 46,* 869–885.

Schlagmüller, M., & Schneider, W. (2002). The development of organizational strategies in children: Evidence from a micro-genetic longitudinal study. *Journal of Experimental Child Psychology, 81,* 298–319.

Schlegel, A., & Barry, H., III. (1991). *Adolescence: An anthropological inquiry.* New York: Free Press.

Schmid, R. G., Tirsch, W. S., & Scherb, H. (2002). Correlation between spectral EEG parameters and intelligence test variables in school-age children. *Clinical Neurophysiology, 113,* 1647–1656.

Schmidt, A. T., Waldow, K. J., Grove, W. M., Salinas, J. A., & Georgieff, M. K. (2007). Dissociating the long-term effects of fetal/neonatal iron deficiency on three types of learning in the rat. *Behavioral Neuroscience, 121,* 475–482.

Schmidt, L. A., Fox, N. A., Rubin, K. H., Sternberg, E. M., Gold, P. W., & Smith, C. C. (1997). Behavioral and neuroendocrine responses in shy children. *Developmental Psychobiology, 35,* 119–135.

Schmidt, L. A., Fox, N. A., Schulkin, J., & Gold, P. W. (1999). Behavioral and psychophysiological correlates of self-presentation in temperamentally shy children. *Developmental Psychobiology, 30,* 127–140.

Schmidt, L. A., Santesso, D. L., Schulkin, J., & Segalowitz, S. J. (2007). Shyness is a necessary but not sufficient condition for high salivary cortisol in typically developing 10-year-old children. *Personality and Individual Differences, 43,* 1541–1551.

Schmidt, M. E., Crawley-Davis, A. M., & Anderson, D. R. (2007). Two-year-olds' object retrieval based on television: Testing a perceptual account. *Media Psychology, 9,* 389–409.

Schmidt, M. E., Pempek, T. A., Kirkorian, H. L., Lund, A. F., & Anderson, D. R. (2008). The effect of background television on the toy play behavior of very young children. *Child Development, 79,* 1137–1151.

Schmitz, S., Fulker, D. W., Plomin, R., Zahn-Waxler, C., Emde, R. N., & DeFries, J. C. (1999). Temperament and problem behaviour during early childhood. *International Journal of Behavioural Development, 23,* 333–355.

Schneider, A., Hagerman, R. J., & Hessl, D. (2009). Fragile X syndrome—from genes to cognition. *Developmental Disabilities, 15,* 333–342.

Schneider, B. H., Atkinson, L., & Tardif, C. (2001). Child–parent attachment and children's peer relations: A quantitative review. *Developmental Psychology, 37,* 86–100.

Schneider, D. (2006). Smart as we can get? *American Scientist, 94,* 311–312.

Schneider, W. (1986). The role of conceptual knowledge and metamemory in the development of organizational processes in memory. *Journal of Experimental Child Psychology, 42,* 218–236.

Schneider, W. (2002). Memory development in childhood. In U. Goswami (Ed.), *Blackwell handbook of childhood cognitive development* (pp. 236–256). Malden, MA: Blackwell.

Schneider, W. (2010). Metacognition and memory development in childhood and adolescence. In H. S. Waters & W. Schneider (Eds.), *Metacognition, strategy use, and instruction* (pp. 54–81). New York: Guilford.

Schneider, W., & Bjorklund, D. F. (1992). Expertise, aptitude, and strategic remembering. *Child Development, 63,* 461–473.

Schneider, W., & Bjorklund, D. F. (1998). Memory. In D. Kuhn & R. S. Siegler (Eds.), *Handbook of child psychology: Vol. 2. Cognition, perception, and language* (5th ed., pp. 467–521). New York: Wiley.

Schneider, W., & Bjorklund, D. F. (2003). Memory and knowledge development. In J. Valsiner & K. Connolly (Eds.), *Handbook of developmental psychology.* London: Sage.

Schneider, W., Perner, J., Bullock, M., Stefanek, J., & Ziegler, A. (1999). Development of intelligence and thinking. In F. E. Weinert & W. Schneider (Eds.), *Individual development from 3 to 12: Findings from the Munich Longitudinal Study* (pp. 9–28). Cambridge, UK: Cambridge University Press.

Schneider, W., & Pressley, M. (1997). *Memory development between two and twenty* (2nd ed.). Mahwah, NJ: Erlbaum.

Schneiders, J., Nicolson, N. A., Berkhof, J., Feron, F. J., van Os, J., & deVries, M. W. (2006). Mood reactivity to daily negative events in early adolescence: Relationship to risk for psychopathology. *Developmental Psychology, 42,* 543–554.

Schofield, J. W. (1995). Review of research on school desegregation's impact on elementary and secondary students. In J. Banks & C. M. Banks (Eds.), *Handbook of research on multicultural education* (pp. 597–617). New York: Simon & Schuster.

Scholl, B. J., & Leslie, A. M. (2000). Minds, modules, and meta-analysis. *Child Development, 72,* 696–701.

Scholl, T. O., Hediger, M. L., & Belsky, D. (1996). Prenatal care and maternal health during adolescent pregnancy: A review and meta-analysis. *Journal of Adolescent Health, 15,* 444–456.

Scholnick, E. K. (1995, Fall). Knowing and constructing plans. *SRCD Newsletter,* pp. 1–2, 17.

Schonberg, R. L., & Tifft, C. J. (2007). Birth defects and prenatal diagnosis. In M. L. Batshaw, L. Pellegrino, & N. J. Roizen (Eds.), *Children with disabilities* (6th ed., pp. 83–96). Baltimore: Paul H. Brookes.

Schonert-Reichl, K. A. (1999). Relations of peer acceptance, friendship adjustment, and social behavior to moral reasoning during early adolescence. *Journal of Early Adolescence, 19,* 249–279.

Schoppe-Sullivan, S. J., Brown, G. L., Cannon, E. A., Mangelsdorf, S. C., & Sokolowski, M. S. (2008). Maternal gatekeeping, coparenting quality, and fathering behavior in families with infants. *Journal of Family Psychology, 22,* 389–398.

Schoppe-Sullivan, S. J., Mangelsdorf, S. C., Brown, G. L., & Sokolowski, M. S. (2007). Goodness-of-fit in family context: Infant temperament, marital quality, and early coparenting behavior. *Infant Behavior and Development, 30,* 82–96.

Schott, J. M., & Rossor, M. N. (2003). The grasp and other primitive reflexes. *Journal of Neurological and Neurosurgical Psychiatry, 74,* 558–560.

Schroeder, R. D., Bulanda, R. E., Giordano, P. C., & Cernkovich, S. A. (2010). Parenting and adult criminality: An examination of direct and indirect effects by race. *Journal of Adolescent Research, 25,* 64–98.

Schuetze, P., & Eiden, R. D. (2006). The association between maternal cocaine use during pregnancy and physiological regulation in 4- to 8-week-old infants: An examination of possible mediators and moderators. *Journal of Pediatric Psychology, 31,* 15–26.

Schull, W. J. (2003). The children of atomic bomb survivors: A synopsis. *Journal of Radiological Protection, 23,* 369–384.

Schulte-Ruther, M., Markowitsch, H. J., Fink, G. R., & Piefke, M. (2007). Mirror neuron and theory of mind mechanisms involved in face-to-face interactions: A functional magnetic resonance imaging approach to empathy. *Journal of Cognitive Neuroscience, 19,* 1354–1372.

Schulz, M. S., Cowan, C. P., & Cowan, P. A. (2006). Promoting healthy beginnings: A randomized controlled trial of a preventive intervention to preserve marital quality during the transition to parenthood. *Journal of Consulting and Clinical Psychology, 74,* 20–31.

Schumann, C. M., & Amaral, D. G. (2010). The human amygdala in autism. In P. J. Whalen & E. A. Phelps (Eds.), *The human amygdala* (pp. 362–381). New York: Guilford.

Schumann, C. M., Barnes, C. C., Lord, C., & Courchesne, E. (2009). Amygdala enlargement in toddlers and autism related to severity of social and communication impairments. *Biological Psychiatry, 66,* 942–949.

Schunk, D. H., & Zimmerman, B. J. (2003). Self-regulation and learning. In W. M. Reynolds & G. E. Miller (Eds.), *Handbook of psychology* (Vol. 7, pp. 59–78). New York: Wiley.

Schuster, B., Ruble, D. N., & Weinert, F. E. (1998). Causal inferences and the positivity bias in children: The role of the covariation principle. *Child Development, 69,* 1577–1596.

Schwanenflugel, P. J., Fabricius, W. V., & Noyes, C. R. (1996). Developing organization of mental verbs: Evidence for the development of a constructivist theory of mind in middle childhood. *Cognitive Development, 11,* 265–294.

Schwanenflugel, P. J., Henderson, R. L., & Fabricius, W. V. (1998). Develping organisation of mental verbs and theory of mind in middle childhood: Evidence from extensions. *Developmental Psychology, 34,* 514–524.

Schwarte, A. R. (2008). Fragile X syndrome. *School Psychology Quarterly, 23,* 290–300.

Schwartz, C. E., Wright, C. I., Shin, L. M., Kagan, J., & Raugh, S. L. (2003). Inhibited and uninhibited infants "grown up": Adult amygdalar response to novelty. *Science, 300,* 1952–1953.

Schwartz, D., Proctor, L. J., & Chien, D. H. (2001). The aggressive victim of bullying: Emotional and behavioral dysregulation as a pathway to victimization by peers. In J. Juonen & S. Graham (Eds.), *Peer harassment in school: The plight of the vulnerable and victimized* (pp. 147–174). New York: Guilford.

Schwartz, S. J., Pantin, H., Prado, G., Sullivan, S., & Szapocznik, J. (2005). Family functioning, identity, and problem behavior: Immigrant early adolescents. *Journal of Early Adolescence, 25,* 392–420.

Schwarz, N. (1999). Self-reports: How the questions shape the answers. *American Psychologist, 54,* 93–105.

Schweiger, W. K., & O'Brien, M. (2005). Special needs adoption: An ecological systems approach. *Family Relations, 54,* 512–522.

Schweinhart, L. J. (2010). The challenge of the HighScope Perry Preschool study. In A. J. Reynolds, A. J. Rolnick, M. M. Englund, & J. Temple (Eds.), *Childhood programs and practices in the first decade of life: A human capital integration* (pp. 199–213). New York: Cambridge University Press.

Schweinhart, L. J., Montie, J., Xiang, Z., Barnett, W. S., Belfield, C. R., & Nores, M. (2005). *Lifetime effects: The High/Scope Perry Preschool Study through age 40.* Ypsilanti, MI: High/Scope Press.

Schweizer, K., Moosbrugger, H., & Goldhammer, F. (2006). The structure of the relationship between attention and intelligence. *Intelligence, 33,* 589–611.

Schwenck, C., Bjorklund, D. F., & Schneider, W. (2007). Factors influencing the incidence of utilization deficiencies and other patterns of recall/strategy-use relations in a strategic memory task. *Child Development, 22,* 197–212.

Schwier, C., van Maanen, C., Carpenter, M., & Tomasello, M. (2006). Rational imitation in 12-month-old infants. *Infancy, 10,* 303–311.

Schwimmer, J. B., Burwinkle, T. M., & Varni, J. W. (2003). Health-related quality of life of severely obese children and adolescents. *Journal of the American Medical Association, 289,* 1813–1819.

Scot, T. P., Callahan, C. M., & Urquhart, J. (2009). Paint-by-number teachers and cookie-cutter students: The unintended effects of high-stakes testing on the education of gifted students. *Roeper Review, 31,* 40–52.

Scott, K. D., Berkowitz, G., & Klaus, M. (1999). A comparison of intermittent and continuous support during labor: A meta-analysis. *American Journal of Obstetrics and Gynecology, 180,* 1054–1059.

Scott, L. D. (2003). The relation of racial identity and racial socialization to coping with discrimination among African Americans. *Journal of Black Studies, 20,* 520–538.

Scott, L. S., & Monesson, A. (2009). The origin of biases in face perception. *Psychological Science, 20,* 676–680.

Scrimsher, S., & Tudge, J. (2003). The teaching/learning relationship in the first years of school: Some revolutionary implications of Vygotsky's theory. *Early Education and Development, 14,* 293–312.

Scrutton, D. (2005). Influence of supine sleeping positioning on early motor milestone acquisition. *Developmental Medicine and Child Neurology, 47,* 364.

Seaton, E. K., Scottham, K. M., & Sellers, R. M. (2006). The status model of racial identity development in African American adolescents: Evidence of structure, trajectories, and well-being. *Child Development, 77,* 1416–1426.

Sebanc, A. M. (2003). The friendship features of preschool children: Links with prosocial behavior and aggression. *Social Development, 12,* 249–268.

Seibert, A. C., & Kerns, K. A. (2009). Attachment figures in middle childhood. *International Journal of Behavioral Development, 33,* 347–355.

Seidenberg, M. S., & Petitto, L. A. (1987). Communication, symbolic communication, and language: Comment on Savage-Rumbaugh, McDonald, Sevcik, Hopkins, and Rupert. *Journal of Experimental Psychology: General, 116,* 279–287.

Seidman, E., Aber, J. L., & French, S. E. (2004). Assessing the transitions to middle and high school. *Journal of Adolescent Research, 19,* 3–30.

Seidman, E., Lambert, L. E., Allen, L., & Aber, J. L. (2003). Urban adolescents' transition to junior high school and protective family transactions. *Journal of Early Adolescence, 23,* 166–193.

Seifer, R., & Schiller, M. (1995). The role of parenting sensitivity, infant temperament, and dyadic interaction in attachment theory and assessment. In E. Waters, B. E. Vaughn, G. Posada, & K. Kondo-Ikemura (Eds.), *Caregiving, cultural, and cognitive perspectives on secure-base behavior and working models: New growing points of attachment theory and research. Monographs of the Society for Research in Child Development, 60*(2–3, Serial No. 244).

Seitz, V., & Apfel, N. H. (2005). Creating effective school-based interventions for pregnant teenagers. In R. DeV. Peters, B. Leadbeater, & R. J. McMahon (Eds.), *Resilience in children, families, and communities: Linking context to practice and policy* (pp. 65–82). New York: Kluwer Academic.

Sekido, R., & Lovell-Badge, R. (2009). Sex determination and SRY: Down to a wink and a nudge? *Trends in Genetics, 25,* 19–29.

Selfhout, M. H. W., Branje, S. J. T., & Meeus, W. H. J. (2008). The development of delinquency and perceived friendship quality in adolescent best friendship dyads. *Journal of Abnormal Child Psychology, 36,* 471–485.

Selman, R. L. (1976). Social-cognitive understanding: A guide to educational and clinical practice. In T. Lickona (Ed.), *Moral development and behavior: Theory, research, and social issues* (pp. 299–316). New York: Holt, Rinehart & Winston.

Selman, R. L. (1980). *The growth of interpersonal understanding.* New York: Academic Press.

Senechal, M., & LeFevre, J. (2002). Parental involvement in the development of children's reading skill: A five-year longitudinal study. *Child Development, 73,* 445–460.

Senghas, A., & Coppola, M. (2001). Children creating language: How Nicaraguan sign language acquired a spatial grammar. *Psychological Science, 12,* 323–328.

Senju, A., Csibra, G., & Johnson, M. H. (2008). Understanding the referential nature of looking: Infants' preference for object-directed gaze. *Cognition, 108,* 303–319.

Seo, J. H., Leem, J. H., Ha, E. H., Kim, O. J., Kim, B. M., Lee, J. Y., et al. (2010). Population-attributable risk of low birthweight related to PM10 pollution in seven Korean cities. *Paediatric and Perinatal Epidemiology, 24,* 140–148.

Serafini, T. E., & Adams, G. R. (2002). Functions of identity: Scale construction and validation. *Identity: An International Journal of Theory and Research, 2,* 361–389.

Serbin, L. A., Poulin-Dubois, D., Colburne, K. A., Sen, M. G., & Eichstedt, J. A. (2001). Gender stereotyping in infancy: Visual preferences for and knowledge of gender-stereotyped toys in the second year. *International Journal of Behavioral Development, 25,* 7–15.

Serbin, L. A., Powlishta, K. K., & Gulko, J. (1993). The development of sex typing in middle childhood. *Monographs of the Society for Research in Child Development, 58*(2, Serial No. 232).

Sermon, K., Van Steirteghem, A., & Liebaers, I. (2004). Preimplantation genetic diagnosis. *Lancet, 363,* 1633–1641.

Serpell, R., Sonnenschein, S., Baker L., & Ganapathy, H. (2002). Intimate culture of families in the early socialization of literacy. *Journal of Family Psychology, 16,* 391–405.

Servin, A., Nordenström, A., Larssonk, A., & Bohlin, G. (2003). Prenatal androgens and gender-typed behavior: A study of girls with mild and severe forms of congenital hyperplasia. *Developmental Psychology, 39,* 440–450.

Sesame Workshop. (2009). *Sesame Workshop Annual Report 2009.* Retrieved from www.sesameworkshop.org/inside/annualreport

Sevigny, P. R., & Loutzenhiser, L. (2010). Predictors of parenting self-efficacy in mothers and fathers of toddlers. *Child Care, Health and Development, 36,* 179–189.

Seymour, S. C. (1999). *Women, family, and child care in India.* Cambridge, UK: Cambridge University Press.

Shafer, V. L., & Garrido-Nag, K. (2007). The neurodevelopmental bases of language. In E. Hoff & M. Shatz (Eds.), *Blackwell handbook of language development* (pp. 21–45). Malden, MA: Blackwell.

Shafer, V. L., Shucard, D. W., & Jaeger, J. J. (1999). Electrophysiological indices of cerebral specialization and the role of prosody in language acquisition in 3-month-old infants. *Developmental Neuropsychology, 15,* 73–109.

Shah, T., Sullivan, K., & Carter, J. (2006). Sudden infant death syndrome and reported maternal smoking during pregnancy. *American Journal of Public Health, 96,* 1757–1759.

Shahar, S. (1990). *Childhood in the Middle Ages.* London: Routledge & Kegan Paul.

Shainess, N. (1961). A re-evaluation of some aspects of femininity through a study of menstruation: A preliminary report. *Comparative Psychiatry, 2,* 20–26.

Shanahan, L., McHale, S. M., Crouter, A. C., & Osgood, D. W. (2007). Warmth with mothers and fathers from middle childhood to late adolescence: Within- and between-families comparisons. *Developmental Psychology, 4,* 551–563.

Shankaran, S., Laptook, A. R., Ehrenkranz, R. A., Tyson, J. E., McDonald, S. A., & Donovan, E. F. (2005). Whole-body hypothermia for neonates with hypoxic–ischemic encephalopathy. *New England Journal of Medicine, 353,* 1574–1584.

Shanker, S. G., Savage-Rumbaugh, S., & Taylor, T. J. (1999). Kanzi: A new beginning. *Animal Learning and Behavior, 27,* 24–25.

Shapiro, A. F., Gottman, J. M., & Carrere, S. (2000). The baby and the marriage: Identifying factors that buffer against decline in marital satisfaction after the first baby arrives. *Journal of Family Psychology, 14,* 59–70.

Shapka, J. D., & Keating, D. P. (2005). Structure and change in self-concept during adolescence. *Canadian Journal of Behavioural Science, 37,* 83–96.

Shatz, M. (2007). On the development of the field. In E. Hoff & M. Shatz (Eds.), *Blackwell handbook of language development* (pp. 1–20). Malden, MA: Blackwell.

Shaver, P., Furman, W., & Buhrmester, D. (1985). Transition to college: Network changes, social skills, and loneliness. In S. Duck & D. Perlman (Eds.), *Understanding personal relationships: An interdisciplinary approach* (pp. 193–219). London: Sage.

Shaver, P. R., Wu, S., & Schwartz, J. C. (1992). Cross-cultural similarities and differences in emotion and its representation: A prototype approach. In M. S. Clark (Ed.), *Review of personality and social psychology* (Vol. 13, pp. 175–212). Newbury Park, CA: Sage.

Shaw, D. S., Gilliom, M., Ingoldsby, E. M., & Nagin, D. S. (2003). Trajectories leading to school-age conduct problems. *Developmental Psychology, 39,* 189–200.

Shaw, D. S., Lacourse, E., & Nagin, D. S. (2005). Developmental trajectories of conduct problems and hyperactivity from ages 2 to 10. *Journal of Child Psychology and Psychiatry, 46,* 931–942.

Shaw, D. S., Winslow, E. B., & Flanagan, C. (1999). A prospective study of the effects of marital status and family relations on young children's adjustment among African-American and European-American families. *Child Development, 70,* 742–755.

Shaw, P., Brierley, B., & David, A. S. (2005). A critical period for the impact of amygdala damage on the emotional enhancement of memory? *Neurology, 65,* 326–328.

Shaw, P., Eckstrand, K., Sharp, W., Blumenthal, J., Lerch, J. P., & Greenstein, D. (2007, November 16). Attention-deficit/hyperactivity disorder is characterized by a delay in cortical maturation. *Proceedings of the National Academy of Sciences Online.* Retrieved from http://www.pnas.org/cgi/content/abstract/0707741104v1

Shedler, J., & Block, J. (1990). Adolescent drug use and psychological health: A longitudinal inquiry. *American Psychologist, 45,* 612–630.

Sheehan, G., Darlington, Y., Noller, P., & Feeney, J. (2004). Children's perceptions of their sibling relationships during parental separation and divorce. *Journal of Divorce and Remarriage 41,* 69–94.

Sheehy, A., Gasser, T., Molinari, L., & Largo, R. H. (1999). An analysis of variance of the pubertal and midgrowth spurts for length and width. *Annals of Human Biology, 26,* 309–331.

Sherman, S. L., Freeman, S. B., Allen, E. G., & Lamb, N. E. (2005). Risk factors for nondisjunction of trisomy 21. *Cytogenetic Genome Research, 111,* 273–280.

Sherrod, L. R., & Spiewak, G. S. (2008). Possible interrelationships between civic engagement, positive youth development, and spirituality/religiosity. In R. M. Lerner, R. W. Roeser, & E. Phelps (Eds.), *Positive youth development and spirituality: From theory to research* (pp. 322–338). West Conshohocken, PA: Templeton Foundation Press.

Sherry, B., McDivitt, J., Birch, L. L., Cook, F. H., Sanders, S., Prish, J. L., et al. (2004). Attitudes, practices, and concerns about child feeding and child weight status among socioeconomically diverse white, Hispanic, and African-American mothers. *Journal of the American Dietetic Association, 104,* 215–221.

Shields, A., Ryan, R. M., & Cicchetti, D. (2001). Narrative representations of caregivers and emotion dysregulation as predictors of maltreated children's rejection by peers. *Developmental Psychology, 37,* 321–337.

Shimada, S., & Hiraki, K. (2006). Infant's brain responses to live and televised action. *NeuroImage, 32,* 930–939.

Shimizu, H. (2001). Japanese adolescent boys' senses of empathy (omoiyari) and Carol Gilligan's perspectives on the morality of care: A phenomenological approach. *Culture and Psychology, 7,* 453–475.

Shipman, K. L., Zeman, J., Nesin, A. E., & Fitzgerald, M. (2003). Children's strategies for displaying anger and sadness: What works with whom? *Merrill-Palmer Quarterly, 49,* 100–122.

Shoda, Y., Mischel, W., & Peake, P. K. (1990). Predicting adolescent cognitive and self-regulatory competencies from preschool delay of gratification: Identifying diagnostic conditions. *Developmental Psychology, 26,* 978–986.

Shonkoff, J. P., & Bales, S. N. (2011). Science does not speak for itself: Translating child development research for the public and its policymakers. *Child Development, 82,* 17–32.

Shonkoff, J. P., & Phillips, D. (Eds.). (2001). *Neurons to neighborhoods: The science of early childhood development.* Washington, DC: National Academy Press.

Shuwairi, S. M., Albert, M. K., & Johnson, S. P. (2007) Discrimination of possible and impossible objects in infancy. *Psychological Science, 18,* 303–307.

Shwalb, D. W., Nakazawa, J., Yamamoto, T., & Hyun, J.-H. (2004). Fathering in Japanese, Chinese, and Korean cultures: A review of the literature. In M. E. Lamb (Ed.), *The role of the father in child development* (4th ed., pp. 146–181). Hoboken, NJ: Wiley.

Shweder, R. A., Goodnow, J. J., Hatano, G., LeVine, R. A., Markus, H. R., & Miller, P. J. (2006). The cultural psychology of development: One mind, many mentalities. In R. M. Lerner (Ed.), *Handbook of child psychology: Vol. 1. Theoretical models of human development* (6th ed., pp. 716–792). Hoboken, NJ: Wiley.

Shweder, R. A., Mahapatra, M., & Miller, J. G. (1990). Culture and moral development. In J. Stigler, R. A. Shweder, & G. Herdt (Eds.), *Cultural psychology*

Essays on comparative human development (pp. 130–204). New York: Cambridge University Press.

Sidappa, A., Georgieff, M. K., Wewerka, S., Worwa, C., Nelson, C. A., & deRegnier, R. (2004). Iron deficiency alters auditory recognition memory in newborn infants of diabetic mothers. *Pediatric Research, 55,* 1034–1041.

Sidebotham, P., Heron, J., & the ALSPAC Study Team. (2003). Child maltreatment in the "children of the nineties": The role of the child. *Child Abuse and Neglect, 27,* 337–352.

Siebenbruner, J., Zimmer-Gembeck, M. J., & Egeland, B. (2007). Sexual partners and contraceptive use: A 16-year prospective study predicting abstinence and risk behavior. *Journal of Research on Adolescence, 17,* 179–206.

Siebert, A. C., & Kerns, K. A. (2009). Attachment figures in middle childhood. *International Journal of Behavioral Development, 33,* 347–355.

Siegal, M., Iozzi, L., & Surian, L. (2009). Bilingualism and conversational understanding in young children. *Cognition, 110,* 115–122.

Sieger, K., & Renk, K. (2007). Pregnant and parenting adolescents: A study of ethnic identity, emotional and behavioral functioning, child characteristics, and social support. *Journal of Youth and Adolescence, 36,* 567–581.

Siegler, R. S. (1995). How does change occur? A microgenetic study of number conservation. *Cognitive Psychology, 28,* 225–273.

Siegler, R. S. (2002). Microgenetic studies of self-explanation. In N. Granott & J. Parziale (Eds.), *Microdevelopment: Transition processes in development and learning* (pp. 31–58). New York: Cambridge University Press.

Siegler, R. S. (2006). Microgenetic analyses of learning. In D. Kuhn & R. Siegler (Eds.), *Handbook of child psychology: Vol. 2. Cognition, perception, and language* (6th ed., pp. 464–510). Hoboken, NJ: Wiley.

Siegler, R. S. (2007). Cognitive variability. *Developmental Science, 10,* 104–109.

Siegler, R. S. (2009). Improving preschoolers' number sense using information-processing theory. In O. A. Barbarin & B. H. Wasik (Eds.), *Handbook of child development and early education* (pp. 429–454). New York: Guilford.

Siegler, R. S., & Booth, J. L. (2004). Development of numerical estimation in young children. *Child Development, 75,* 428–444.

Siegler, R. S., & Crowley, K. (1991). The microgenetic method: A direct means for studying cognitive development. *American Psychologist, 46,* 606–620.

Siegler, R. S., & Jenkins, E. (1989). *How children discover new strategies.* Hillsdale, NJ: Erlbaum.

Siegler, R. S., & Mu, Y. (2008). Chinese children excel on novel mathematics problems even before elementary school. *Psychological Science, 19,* 759–763.

Siegler, R. S., & Richards, D. D. (1980). College students' prototypes of children's intelligence. Paper presented at the annual meeting of the American Psychological Association, New York.

Siegler, R. S., & Svetina, M. (2006). What leads children to adopt new strategies? A microgenetic/cross-sectional study of class inclusion. *Child Development, 77,* 997–1015.

Siervogel, R. M., Maynard, L. M., Wisemandle, W. A., Roche, A. F., Guo, S. S., Chumlea, W. C., & Towne, B. (2000). Annual changes in total body fat and fat-free mass in children from 8 to 18 years in relation to changes in body mass index: The Fels Longitudinal Study. *Annals of the New York Academy of Sciences, 904,* 420–423.

Signorella, M. L., Bigler, R. S., & Liben, L. S. (1993). Developmental differences in children's gender schemata about others: A meta-analytic review. *Developmental Review, 13,* 147–183.

Signorielli, N. (2001). Television's gender-role images and contribution to stereotyping. In D. G. Singer & J. L. Singer (Eds.), *Handbook of children and the media* (pp. 341–358). Thousand Oaks, CA: Sage.

Silk, J. S., Morris, A. S., Kanaya, T., & Steinberg, L. D. (2003). Psychological control and autonomy granting: Opposite ends of a continuum or distinct constructs? *Journal of Research on Adolescence, 13,* 113–128.

Silk, J. S., Sessa, F. M., Morris, A. S., & Steinberg, L. D. (2004). Neighborhood cohesion as a buffer against hostile maternal parenting. *Journal of Family Psychology, 18,* 135–146.

Silvén, M. (2001). Attention in very young infants predicts learning of first words. *Infant Behavior and Development, 24,* 229–237.

Silverman, B. E., Goodine, W. M., Ladouceur, M. G., & Quinn, J. (2001). Learning needs of nurses working in Canada's First Nations communities. *Journal of Continuing Education in Nursing, 32,* 38–45.

Silverman, D. (2006). *Interpreting qualitative data: Methods for analyzing talk, text, and interaction.* Thousand Oaks, CA: Sage.

Silverman, I., Choi, J., & Peters, M. (2007). The hunter-gatherer theory of sex differences in spatial abilities. *Archives of Sexual Behavior, 36,* 261–268.

Sim, T. N., & Koh, S. F. (2003). A domain conceptualization of adolescent susceptibility to peer pressure. *Journal of Research on Adolescence, 13,* 57–80.

Simcock, G., & DeLoache, J. (2006). Get the picture? The effects of iconicity on toddlers' reenactment from picture books. *Developmental Psychology, 42,* 1352–1357.

Simcock, G., & Hayne, H. (2002). Breaking the barrier? Children fail to translate their preverbal memories into language. *Psychological Science, 13,* 225–231.

Simcock, G., & Hayne, H. (2003). Age-related changes in verbal and nonverbal memory during early childhood. *Developmental Psychology, 39,* 805–814.

Simion, F., Cassia, V. M., Turati, C., & Valenza, E. (2001). The origins of face perception: Specific versus non-specific mechanisms. *Infant and Child Development, 10,* 59–65.

Simmons, R. G., & Blyth, D. A. (1987). *Moving into adolescence.* New York: Aldine De Gruyter.

Simoneau, M., & Markovits, H. (2003). Reasoning with premises that are not empirically true: Evidence for the role of inhibition and retrieval. *Developmental Psychology, 39,* 964–975.

Simons, L. G., Chen, Y.-F., Simons, R. L., Brody, G., & Cutrona, C. (2006). Parenting practices and child adjustment in different types of households: A study of African-American families. 803–825.

Simons, R. L., & Burt, C. H. (2011). Learning to be bad: Adverse social conditions, social schemas, and crime. *Criminology, 49,* 553–597.

Simons, R. L., Whitbeck, L. B., Conger, R. D., & Chyi-In, W. (1991). Intergenerational transmission of harsh parenting. *Developmental Psychology, 27,* 159–171.

Simons-Morton, B. G., & Haynie, D. L. (2003). Growing up drug free: A developmental challenge. In M. H. Bornstein, L. Davidson, C. L. M. Keyes, K. A. Moore, & the Center for Child Well-Being (Eds.), *Well-being: Positive development across the life course* (pp. 109–122). Mahwah, NJ: Erlbaum.

Simonton, D. K. (2000). Creativity: Cognitive, personal, developmental, and social aspects. *American Psychologist, 55,* 151–158.

Simpkins, S. D., & Parke, R. D. (2001). The relations between parental friendships and children's friendships: Self-reports and observational analysis. *Child Development, 72,* 569–582.

Simpson, J. A., Rholes, W. S., Campbell, L., Tran, S., & Wilson, C. L. (2003). Adult attachment, the transition to parenthood, and depressive symptoms. *Journal of Personality and Social Psychology, 84,* 1172–1187.

Simpson, J. L., de la Cruz, F., Swerdloff, R. S., Samango-Sprouse, C., Skakkebaek, N. E., & Graham, J. M., Jr. (2003). Klinefelter syndrome: Expanding the phenotype and identifying new research directions. *Genetic Medicine, 5,* 460–468.

Singer, D. G., & Singer, J. L. (2005). *Imagination and play in the electronic age.* Cambridge, MA: Harvard University Press.

Singer, L. T., Minnes, S., Short, E., Arendt, R., Farkas, K., Lewis, B., & Klein, N. (2004). Cognitive outcomes of preschool children with prenatal cocaine exposure. *Journal of the American Medical Association, 291,* 2448–2456.

Singleton, J. L., & Newport, E. L. (2004). When learners surpass their models: The acquisition of American Sign Language from inconsistent input. *Cognitive Psychology, 49,* 370–407.

Sinkkonen, J., Anttila, R., & Siimes, M. A. (1998). Pubertal maturation and changes in self-image in early adolescent Finnish boys. *Journal of Youth and Adolescence, 27,* 209–218.

Sirios, S., & Jackson, I. (2007). Social cognition in infancy: A critical review of research on higher-order abilities. *European Journal of Developmental Psychology, 4,* 46–64.

Sisson, S. B., Broyles, S. T., Newton, R. L., Jr., Baker, B. L., & Chernausek, S. D. (2011). TVs in the bedrooms of children: Does it impact health and behavior? *Preventive Medicine, 52,* 104–108.

Skiba, R. J., & Rausch, M. K. (2006). Zero tolerance, suspension, and expulsion: Questions of equity and effectiveness. In C. M. Evertson & C. S. Weinstein (Eds.), *Handbook of classroom management: Research, practice, and contemporary issues* (pp. 1063–1089). Mahwah, NJ: Erlbaum.

Skinner, B. F. (1957). *Verbal behavior.* New York: Appleton-Century-Crofts.

Skinner, E. A., Zimmer-Gembeck, M. J., & Connell, J. P. (1998). Individual differences and the development of perceived control. *Monographs of the Society for Research in Child Development, 63*(2–3, Serial No. 254).

Skoe, E. E. A. (1998). The ethic of care: Issues in moral development. In E. E. A. Skoe & A. L. von der Lippe (Eds.), *Personality development in adolescence* (pp. 143–171). London: Routledge.

Slaby, R. G., & Frey, K. S. (1975). Development of gender constancy and selective attention to same-sex models. *Child Development, 46,* 849–856.

Slack, K. S., Holl, J. L., Yoo, J., Amsden, L. B., Collins, E., & Bolger, K. (2007). Welfare, work, and health care access predictors of low-income children's physical health outcomes. *Children and Youth Services Review, 29,* 782–801.

Slade, A., Belsky, J., Aber, J. L., & Phelps, J. L. (1999). Mothers' representations of their relationships with their toddlers: Links to adult attachment and observed mothering. *Developmental Psychology, 35,* 611–619.

Slater, A., Bremner, G., Johnson, S. P., Sherwood, P., Hayes, R., & Brown, E. (2000). Newborn infants' preference for attractive faces: The role of internal and external facial features. *Infancy, 1,* 265–274.

Slater, R., Fabrizi, L., Worley, A., Meek, J., Boyd, S., & Fitzgerald, M. (2010). Premature infants display increased noxious-evoked neuronal activity in the brain compared to healthy age-matched term-born infants. *NeuroImage, 52,* 583–589.

Slater, A., & Johnson, S. P. (1999). Visual sensory and perceptual abilities of the newborn: Beyond the blooming, buzzing confusion. In A. Slater & S. P. Johnson (Eds.), *The development of sensory, motor and cognitive capacities in early infancy* (pp. 121–141). Hove, UK: Sussex Press.

Slater, A., & Quinn, P. C. (2001). Face recognition in the newborn infant. *Infant and Child Development, 10,* 21–24.

Slater, A., Riddell, P., Quinn, P. C., Pascalis, O., Lee, K., & Kelly, D. J. (2010). Visual perception. In J. G. Bremner & T. D. Wachs (Eds.), *Wiley-Blackwell handbook of infant development: Vol. 1. Basic research* (2nd ed., pp. 40–80). Chichester, UK: Wiley-Blackwell.

Slaughter, V., & Lyons, M. (2003). Learning about life and death in early childhood. *Cognitive Psychology, 46,* 1–30.

Slicker, E. K., & Thornberry, I. (2002). Older adolescent well-being and authoritative parenting. *Adolescent and Family Health, 3,* 9–10.

Slijper, F. M. E., Drop, S. L. S., Molenaar, J. C., & de Muinck Keizer-Schrama, S. M. P. F. (1998). Long-term psychological evaluation of intersex children. *Archives of Sexual Behavior, 27,* 125–144.

Slobin, D. I. (1982). Universal and particular in the acquisition of language. In L. R. Gleitman & H. E. Wanner (Eds.), *Language acquisition: The state of the art* (pp. 128–170). Cambridge, UK: Cambridge University Press.

Slobin, D. I. (1985). Crosslinguistic evidence for the language-making capacity. In D. I. Slobin (Ed.), *The crosslinguistic study of language acquisition: Vol. 2. Theoretical issues* (pp. 1157–1256). Hillsdale, NJ: Erlbaum.

Slobin, D. I. (Ed.). (1997). *The crosslinguistic study of language acquisition: Vol. 5. Expanding the contexts* (pp. 265–324). Mahwah, NJ: Erlbaum.

Slonims, V., & McConachie, H. (2006). Analysis of mother–infant interaction in infants with Down syndrome and typically developing infants. *American Journal of Mental Retardation, 111,* 273–289.

Small, M. (1998). *Our babies, ourselves*. New York: Anchor.

Smart, J., & Hiscock, H. (2007). Early infant crying and sleeping problems: A pilot study of impact on parental well-being and parent-endorsed strategies for management. *Journal of Paediatrics and Child Health, 43*, 284–290.

Smetana, J. G. (1981). Preschool children's conceptions of moral and social rules. *Child Development, 52*, 1333–1336.

Smetana, J. G. (1985). Preschool children's conceptions of transgressions: Effects of varying moral and conventional domain-related attributes. *Developmental Psychology, 21*, 18–29.

Smetana, J. G. (2002). Culture, autonomy, and personal jurisdiction in adolescent–parent relationships. In R. V. Kail & H. W. Reese (Eds.), *Advances in child development and behavior* (Vol. 29, pp. 51–87). San Diego, CA: Academic Press.

Smetana, J. G. (2006). Social-cognitive domain theory: Consistencies and variations in children's moral and social judgments. In M. Killen & J. G. Smetana (Eds.), *Handbook of moral development* (pp. 119–154). Mahwah, NJ: Erlbaum.

Smetana, J. G., & Daddis, C. (2002). Domain-specific antecedents of parental psychological control and monitoring: The role of parenting beliefs and practices. *Child Development, 73*, 563–580.

Smith, B. H., Barkley, R. A., & Shapiro, C. J. (2006). Attention-deficit/hyperactivity disorder. In E. J. Mash & R. A. Barkley (Eds.), *Treatment of childhood disorders* (3rd ed., pp. 65–136). New York: Guilford.

Smith, B. L., McGregor, K. K., & Demille, D. (2006). Phonological development in lexically precocious 2-year-olds. *Applied Psycholinguistics, 27*, 355–375.

Smith, C., & Denton, M. L. (2005). *Soul searching: The religious and spiritual lives of American teenagers*. Oxford, UK: Oxford University Press.

Smith, C. L., Calkins, S. D., Keane, S. P., Anastopoulos, A. D., & Shelton, T. L. (2004). Predicting stability and change in toddler behavior problems: Contributions of maternal behavior and child gender. *Developmental Psychology, 40*, 29–42.

Smith, C. L., & Tager-Flusberg, H. (1982). Metalinguistic awareness and language development. *Journal of Experimental Child Psychology, 34*, 449–468.

Smith, J., Duncan, G. J., & Lee, K. (2003). The black–white test score gap in young children: Contributions of test and family characteristics. *Applied Developmental Science, 7*, 239–252.

Smith, J., & Ross, H. (2007). Training parents to mediate sibling disputes affects children's negotiation and conflict understanding. *Child Development, 78*, 790–805.

Smith, J. R., Brooks-Gunn, J., Kohen, D., & McCarton, C. (2001). Transitions on and off AFDC: Implications for parenting and children's cognitive development. *Child Development, 72*, 1512–1533.

Smith, L. B., Jones, S. S., Landau, B., Gershkoff-Stowe, L., & Samuelson, L. (2002). Object name learning provides on-the-job training for attention. *Psychological Science, 13*, 13–19.

Smith, P. K. (2003). Play and peer relations. In A. Slater & G. Bremner (Eds.), *An introduction to developmental psychology* (pp. 311–333). Malden, MA: Blackwell.

Smith, S. L., & Atkin, C. (2003). Television advertising and children: Examining the intended and unintended effects. In E. L.

Palmer & B. M. Young (Eds.), *The faces of televisual media: Teaching, violence, selling to children* (pp. 301–326). Mahwah, NJ: Erlbaum.

Smyke, A. T., Zeanah, C. H., Fox, N. A., & Nelson, C. A., III. (2009). A new model of foster care for young children: The Bucharest Early Intervention Project. *Child and Adolescent Psychiatric Clinics of North America, 18*, 721–734.

Smyke, A. T., Zeanah, C. H., Fox, N. A., Nelson, C. A., & Guthrie, D. (2010). Placement in foster care enhances quality of attachment among young institutionalized children. *Child Development, 81*, 212–223.

Snarey, J. R. (1985). The cross-cultural universality of social-moral development: A critical review of Kohlbergian research. *Psychological Bulletin, 97*, 202–232.

Snarey, J. R., & Bell, D. (2003). Distinguishing structural and functional models of human development: A response to "What transits in an identity status transition?" *Identity, 3*, 221–230.

Snarey, J. R., Reimer, J., & Kohlberg, J. (1985). The development of social-moral reasoning among kibbutz adolescents: A longitudinal cross-cultural study. *Developmental Psychology, 20*, 3–17.

Snidman, N., Kagan, J., Riordan, L., & Shannon, D. C. (1995). Cardiac function and behavioral reactivity. *Psychophysiology, 32*, 199–207.

Snow, C. E., & Beals, D. E. (2006). Mealtime talk that supports literacy development. In R. W. Larson, A. R. Wiley, & K. R. Branscomb (Eds.), *Family mealtime as a context of development and socialization* (pp. 51–66). San Francisco: Jossey-Bass.

Snow, C. E., & Kang, J. Y. (2006). Becoming bilingual, biliterate, and bicultural. In K. A. Renninger & I. E. Sigel (Eds.), *Handbook of child psychology: Vol. 4. Child psychology in practice* (6th ed., pp. 75–102). Hoboken, NJ: Wiley.

Snow, C. E., Pan, B. A., Imbens-Bailey, A., & Herman, J. (1996). Learning how to say what one means: A longitudinal study of children's speech act use. *Social Development, 5*, 56–84.

Snyder, J., Brooker, M., Patrick, M. R., Snyder, A., Schrepferman, L., & Stoolmiller, M. (2003). Observed peer victimization during early elementary school: Continuity, growth, and relation to risk for child antisocial and depressive behavior. *Child Development, 74*, 1881–1898.

Snyder, J., Schrepferman, L., Oeser, J., Patterson, G., Stoolmiller, M., Johnson, K., et al. (2005). Deviancy training and association with deviant peers in young children: Occurrence and contribution to early-onset conduct problems. *Development and Psychopathology, 17*, 397–413.

So, L. K. H., & Dodd, B. J. (1995). The acquisition of phonology by Cantonese-speaking children. *Journal of Child Language, 22*, 473–495.

Sobel, D. M. (2006). How fantasy benefits young children's understanding of pretense. *Developmental Science, 9*, 63–75.

Sobring, E., Rodholm-Funnemark, M., & Palmerus, K. (2003). Boys' and girls' perceptions of parental discipline in transgression situations. *Infant and Child Development, 12*, 53–69.

Society for Research in Child Development. (2007). *SRCD ethical standards for research with children*. Retrieved from http://

www.srcd.org/index.php?option= com_content&task=view&id= 68&Itemid=110

Soderstrom, M., Seidl, A., Nelson, D. G. K., & Jusczyk, P. W. (2003). The prosodic bootstrapping of phrases: Evidence from prelinguistic infants. *Journal of Memory and Language, 49*, 249–267.

Soli, A. R., McHale, S. M., & Feinberg, M. E. (2009). Risk and protective effects of sibling relationships among African American adolescents. *Family Relations, 58*, 578–592.

Solomon, G. E. A., Johnson, S. C., Zaitchik, D., & Carey, S. (1996). Like father, like son: Children's understanding of how and why offspring resemble their parents. *Child Development, 67*, 151–171.

Sondergaard, C., Henriksen, T. B., Obel, C., & Wisborg, K. (2002). Smoking during pregnancy and infantile colic. *Journal of the American Academy of Child and Adolescent Psychiatry, 41*, 147.

Sontag, C. W., Baker, C. T., & Nelson, V. L. (1958). Mental growth and personality development: A longitudinal study. *Monographs of the Society for Research in Child Development, 23*(2, Serial No. 68).

Sonuga-Barke, E. J, Schlotz, W., & Kreppner, J. (2010). Differentiating developmental trajectories for conduct, emotion, and peer problems following early deprivation. *Monographs of the Society for Research in Child Development, 75* (1, Serial No. 295), 102–124.

Sophian, C. (1995). Representation and reasoning in early numerical development: Counting, conservation, and comparisons between sets. *Child Development, 66*, 559–577.

Sosa, R., Kennell, J., Klaus, M., Robertson, S., & Urrutia, J. (1980). The effect of a supportive companion on perinatal problems, length of labor, and mother–infant interaction. *New England Journal of Medicine, 303*, 597–600.

Soska, K. C., Adolph, K. E., & Johnson, S. P. (2010). Systems in development: Motor skill acquisition facilitates three-dimensional object completion. *Developmental Psychology, 46*, 129–138.

South African Department of Health. (2009). *2008 National Antenatal Sentinel HIV and Syphilis Prevalence Survey*. Retrieved from http://www.doh.gov.za/docs/nassps-f.html

Sowell, E. R., Thompson, P. M., Welcome, S. E., Henkenius, A. L., Toga, A. W., & Peterson, B. S. (2003). Cortical abnormalities in children and adolescents with attention-deficit hyperactivity disorder. *Lancet, 362*, 1699–1707.

Sowell, E. R., Trauner, D. A., Camst, A., & Jernigan, T. (2002). Development of cortical and subcortical brain structures in childhood and adolescence: A structural MRI study. *Developmental Medicine and Child Neurology, 44*, 4–16.

Spadoni, A. D., McGee, C. L., Frayer, S. L., & Riley, E. P. (2007). Neuroimaging and fetal alcohol spectrum disorders. *Neuroscience and Biobehavioral Reviews, 31*, 239–245.

Spear, L. P. (2008). The psychobiology of adolescence. In K. K. Kline (Ed.), *Authoritative communities: The scientific case for nurturing the whole child* (pp. 263–280). New York: Springer Science + Business Media.

Spearman, C. (1927). *The abilities of man: Their nature and measurement*. New York: Macmillan.

Speece, D. L, Ritchey, K. D., Cooper, D. H., Roth, F. P., & Schatschneider, C. (2004). Growth in early reading skills from

kindergarten to third grade. *Contemporary Educational Psychology, 29*, 312–332.

Spelke, E. S. (2004). Core knowledge. In N. Kanwisher & J. Duncan (Eds.), *Attention and performance* (Vol. 20, pp. 29–56). Oxford, UK: Oxford University Press.

Spelke, E. S., & Hermer, L. (1996). Early cognitive development: Objects and space. In R. Gelman & T. K. Au (Eds.), *Perceptual and cognitive development* (pp. 71–114). San Diego: Academic Press.

Spelke, E. S., & Kinzler, K. D. (2007). Core knowledge. *Developmental Science, 10*, 89–96.

Spelke, E. S., Phillips, A. T., & Woodward, A. L. (1995). Infants' knowledge of object motion and human action. In A. Premack (Ed.), *Causal understanding in cognition and culture* (pp. 4–78). Oxford, UK: Clarendon Press.

Spence, I., & Feng, J. (2010). Video games and spatial cognition. *Review of General Psychology, 14*, 92–104.

Spence, M. J., & DeCasper, A. J. (1987). Prenatal experience with low-frequency maternal voice sounds influences neonatal perception of maternal voice samples. *Infant Behavior and Development, 10*, 133–142.

Spencer, J. P., & Schöner, G. (2003). Bridging the representational gap in the dynamic systems approach to development. *Developmental Science, 6*, 392–412.

Spencer, J. P., Verejiken, B., Diedrich, F. J., & Thelen, E. (2000). Posture and the emergence of manual skills. *Developmental Science, 3*, 216–233.

Spencer, P. E. (2000). Looking without listening: Is audition a prerequisite for normal development of visual attention in infancy? *Journal of Deaf Studies and Education, 5*, 291–302.

Spencer, P. E., & Lederberg, A. (1997). Different modes, different models: Communication and language of young deaf children and their mothers. In L. B. Adamson & M. Romski (Eds.), *Communication and language acquisition: Discoveries from atypical development* (pp. 203–230). Baltimore, MD: Paul H. Brookes.

Spencer, P. E., & Meadow-Orlans, K. P. (1996). Play, language, and maternal responsiveness: A longitudinal study of deaf and hearing infants. *Child Development, 67*, 3176–3191.

Spere, K. A., Schmidt, L. A., Theall-Honey, L. A., & Martin-Chang, S. (2004). Expressive and receptive language skills of temperamentally shy preschoolers. *Infant and Child Development, 13*, 123–133.

Spinrad, T. L., & Eisenberg, N. (2009). Empathy, prosocial behavior, and positive development in schools. In R. Gilman, E. S. Huebner, & M. J. Furlong (Eds.), *Handbook of positive psychology in schools* (pp. 119–129). New York: Routledge.

Spirito, A., & Esposito-Smythers, C. (2006). Attempted and completed suicide. *Annual Review of Clinical Psychology, 2*, 237–266.

Spirito, A., Valeri, S., Boergers, J., & Donaldson, D. (2003). Predictors of continued suicidal behavior in adolescents following a suicide attempt. *Journal of Clinical Child and Adolescent Psychology, 32*, 284–289.

Spitz, R. A. (1946). Anaclitic depression. *Psychoanalytic Study of the Child, 2*, 313–342.

Spock, B., & Needlman, R. (2004). *Dr. Spock's baby and child care* (8th ed.). New York: Pocket.

Sporer, N., Brunstein, J. C., & Kieschke, U. (2009). Improving students' reading comprehension skills: Effects of strategy instruction and reciprocal teaching. *Learning and Instruction, 19,* 272–286.

Sroufe, L. A. (1985). Attachment classification from the perspective of infant–caregiver relationships and infant temperament. *Child Development, 56,* 1–14.

Sroufe, L. A. (2002). From infant attachment to promotion of adolescent autonomy: Prospective, longitudinal data on the role of parents in development. In J. G. Borkowski & S. L. Ramey (Eds.), *Parenting and the child's world* (pp. 187–202). Mahwah, NJ: Erlbaum.

Sroufe, L. A. (2005). Attachment and development: A prospective, longitudinal study from birth to adulthood. *Attachment and Human Development, 7,* 349–367.

Sroufe, L. A., Egeland, B., Carlson, E., & Collins, W. (2005). *Minnesota Study of Risk and Adaptation from birth to maturity: The development of the person.* New York: Guilford.

Sroufe, L. A., & Waters, E. (1976). The ontogenesis of smiling and laughter: A perspective on the organization of development in infancy. *Psychological Review, 83,* 173–189.

Sroufe, L. A., & Wunsch, J. P. (1972). The development of laughter in the first year of life. *Child Development, 43,* 1324–1344.

St Clair-Thompson, H. L., & Gathercole, S. E. (2006). Executive functions and achievements in school: Shifting, updating, inhibition, and working memory. *Quarterly Journal of Experimental Psychology, 59,* 745–759.

St James-Roberts, I. (2007). Helping parents to manage infant crying and sleeping: A review of the evidence and its implications for services. *Child Abuse Review, 16,* 47–69.

St James-Roberts, I., Alvarez, M., Csipke, E., Abramsky, T., Goodwin, J., & Sorgenfrei, E. (2006). Infant crying and sleeping in London, Copenhagen and when parents adopt a "proximal" form of care. *Pediatrics, 117,* e1146–e1155.

St. Louis, G. R., & Liem, J. H. (2005). Ego identity, ethnic identity, and the psychosocial well-being of ethnic minority and majority college students. *Identity, 5,* 227–246.

Stacey, J., & Biblarz, T. (2001). (How) Does the sexual orientation of parents matter? *American Sociological Review, 66,* 159–183.

Stack, D. M. (2010). Touch and physical contact during infancy: Discovering the richness of the forgotten sense. In J. G. Bremner & T. D. Wachs (Eds.), *Wiley-Blackwell handbook of infant development: Vol. 1. Basic research* (2nd ed., pp. 532–567). Chichester, UK: Wiley-Blackwell.

Stack, D. M., & Muir, D. W. (1992). Adult tactile stimulation during face-to-face interactions modulates five-month-olds' affect and attention. *Child Development, 63,* 1509–1525.

Staff, J., & Uggen, C. (2003). The fruits of good work: Early work experiences and adolescent deviance. *Journal of Research in Crime and Delinquency, 40,* 263–290.

Stager, C. L., & Werker, J. F. (1997). Infants listen for more phonetic detail in speech perception than in word-learning tasks. *Nature, 388,* 381–382.

Stahl, S. A., & Miller, P. D. (2006). Whole language and language experience

approaches for beginning reading: A quantitative research synthesis. In D. A. Dougherty Stahl & M. C. McKenna (Eds.), *Reading research at work: Foundations of effective practice* (pp. 9–35). New York: Guilford.

Stams, G. J., Brugman, D., Deković, M., van Rosmalen, L., van der Laan, P., & Gibbs, J. C. (2006). The moral judgment of juvenile delinquents: A meta-analysis. *Journal of Abnormal Child Psychology, 34,* 697–713.

Stams, G.-J. J. M., Juffer, R., & van IJzendoorn, M. H. (2002). Maternal sensitivity, infant attachment, and temperament in early childhood predict adjustment in middle childhood: The case of adopted children and their biologically unrelated parents. *Developmental Psychology, 38,* 806–821.

Standley, J. M. (1998). The effect of music and multimodal stimulation on responses of premature infants in neonatal intensive care. *Pediatric Nursing, 24,* 532–538.

Stanovich, K. E. (2007). *How to think straight about psychology* (8th ed.). Boston: Allyn and Bacon.

Starkey, P. (1992). The early development of numerical reasoning. *Cognition, 43,* 93–126.

Statistics Canada. (2007). *Detailed mother tongue (103), knowledge of official languages (5), age groups (17A) and sex (3) for the population of Canada, provinces, territories, census divisions and census subdivisions, 2006 census—20% sample data.* Retrieved from www.statcan.ca/bsolc/english/bsolc?catno =97-555-XWE2006016

Statistics Canada. (2008). *Aboriginal peoples in Canada in 2006: Inuit, Métis, and First Nations, 2006 census: Findings.* Retrieved from www12.statcan.ca/english/census06/analysis/aboriginal/index.cfm

Stattin, H., & Kerr, M. (2000). Parental monitoring: A reinterpretation. *Child Development, 71,* 1072–1085.

Stattin, H., & Magnusson, D. (1990). *Pubertal maturation in female development.* Hillsdale, NJ: Erlbaum.

Staub, F. C., & Stern, E. (2002). The nature of teachers' pedagogical content beliefs matters for students' achievement gains: Quasi-experimental evidence from elementary mathematics. *Journal of Educational Psychology, 94,* 344–355.

Steele, C. M. (1997). A threat in the air: How stereotypes shape intellectual identity and performance. *American Psychologist, 52,* 613–629.

Steele, H., Steele, M., & Fonagy, P. (1996). Associations among attachment classifications of mothers, fathers, and their infants. *Child Development, 67,* 541–555.

Steele, J. (2003). Children's gender stereotypes about math: The role of stereotype stratification. *Journal of Applied Social Psychology, 33,* 2587–2606.

Steele, S., Joseph, R. M., & Tager-Flusberg, H. (2003). Developmental change in theory of mind abilities in children with autism. *Journal of Autism and Developmental Disorders, 33,* 461–467.

Steen, R. G. (2009). *Human intelligence and medical illness.* New York: Springer.

Stehr-Green, P., Tull, P., Stellfeld, M., Mortenson, P. B., & Simpson, D. (2003). Autism and thimerosal-containing vaccines: Lack of consistent evidence for an association. *American Journal of Preventive Medicine, 25,* 101–106.

Stein, J. H., & Reiser, L. W. (1994). A study of white middle-class adolescent boys' responses to "semenarche" (the first ejaculation). *Journal of Youth and Adolescence, 23,* 373–384.

Stein, N., & Levine, L. J. (1999). The early emergence of emotional understanding and appraisal: Implications for theories of development. In T. Dalgleish & M. J. Power (Eds.), *Handbook of cognition and emotion* (pp. 383–408). Chichester, UK: Wiley.

Stein, Z., Susser, M., Saenger, G., & Marolla, F. (1975). *Famine and human development: The Dutch hunger winter of 1944–1945.* New York: Oxford University Press.

Steinberg, L. (2008). A social neuroscience perspective on adolescent risk-taking. *Developmental Review, 28,* 78–106.

Steinberg, L. (2001). We know some things: Parent–adolescent relationships in retrospect and prospect. *Journal of Research on Adolescence, 11,* 1–19.

Steinberg, L., Albert, D., Cauffman, E., Banich, M., & Graham, S. (2008). Age differences in sensation seeking and impulsivity as indexed by behavior and self-report: Evidence for a dual systems model. *Developmental Psychology, 44,* 1764–1778.

Steinberg, L., Blatt-Eisengart, I., & Cauffman, E. (2006). Patterns of competence and adjustment among adolescents from authoritative, authoritarian, indulgent, and neglectful homes: A replication in a sample of serious juvenile offenders. *Journal of Research on Adolescence, 16,* 47–58.

Steinberg, L., Darling, N. E., & Fletcher, A. C. (1995). Authoritative parenting and adolescent development: An ecological journey. In P. Moen, G. H. Elder, & K. Luscher (Eds.), *Examining lives in context* (pp. 423–466). Washington, DC: American Psychological Association.

Steinberg, L., Graham, S., O'Brien, L., Woolard, J., Cauffman, E., & Banich, M. (2009). Age differences in future orientation and delay discounting. *Child Development, 80,* 28–44.

Steinberg, L., & Monahan, K. C. (2007). Age differences in resistance to peer influence. *Developmental Psychology, 43,* 1531–1543.

Steinberg, L., & Monahan, K. C. (2011). Adolescents' exposure to sexy media does not hasten the initiation of sexual intercourse. *Developmental Psychology, 47,* 562–576.

Steinberg, L., & Silk, J. S. (2002). Parenting adolescents. In M. H. Bornstein (Ed.), *Handbook of parenting: Vol. 1. Children and parenting* (2nd ed., pp. 103–134). Mahwah, NJ: Erlbaum.

Steiner, J. E. (1979). Human facial expression in response to taste and smell stimulation. In H. W. Reese & L. P. Lipsitt (Eds.), *Advances in child development and behavior* (Vol. 13, pp. 257–295). New York: Academic Press.

Steiner, J. E., Glaser, D., Hawilo, M. E., & Berridge, D. C. (2001). Comparative expression of hedonic impact: Affective reactions to taste by human infants and other primates. *Neuroscience and Biobehavioral Reviews, 25,* 53–74.

Steinhausen, C. (2006). Eating disorders: Anorexia nervosa and bulimia nervosa. In C. Gillberg, R. Harrington, & H. Steinhausen (Eds.), *A clinician's handbook of child and adolescent psychiatry* (pp. 272–303). New York: Cambridge University Press.

Stenberg, C., & Campos, J. (1990). The development of anger expressions in infancy. In N. Stein, B. Leventhal, & T. Trabasso (Eds.), *Psychological and biological approaches to emotion* (pp. 247–282). Hillsdale, NJ: Erlbaum.

Stenberg, G. (2003). Effects of maternal inattentiveness on infant social referencing. *Infant and Child Development, 12,* 399–419.

Stephens, B. E., & Vohr, B. R. (2009). Neurodevelopmental outcome of the premature infant. *Pediatric Clinics of North America, 56,* 631–646.

Stephens, P. C., Sloboda, Z., Stephens, R. C., Teasdale, B., Grey, S. F., Hawthorne, R. D., & Williams, J. (2009). Universal school-based substance abuse prevention programs: Modeling targeted mediators and outcomes for adolescent cigarette, alcohol, and marijuana use. *Drug and Alcohol Dependence, 102,* 19–29.

Stern, D. (1985). *The interpersonal world of the infant.* New York: Basic Books.

Stern, M., & Karraker, K. H. (1989). Sex stereotyping of infants: A review of gender labeling studies. *Sex Roles, 20,* 501–522.

Sternberg, R. J. (2001). Beyond g: The theory of successful intelligence. In R. J. Sternberg & E. L. Grigorenko (Eds.), *The general factor of intelligence: How general is it?* (pp. 447–479). Mahwah, NJ: Erlbaum.

Sternberg, R. J. (2003a). A broad view of intelligence: The theory of successful intelligence. *Consulting Psychology Journal: Practice and Research, 55,* 139–154.

Sternberg, R. J. (2003b). The development of creativity as a decision-making process. In R. K. Sawyer, V. John-Steiner, S. Moran, R. J. Sternberg, D. H. Feldman, J. Nakamura, & M. Csikszentmihalyi (Eds.), *Creativity and development* (pp. 91–138). New York: Oxford University Press.

Sternberg, R. J. (2005). The triarchic theory of successful intelligence. In D. P. Flanagan & P. L. Harrison (Eds.), *Contemporary intellectual assessment: Theories, tests, and issues* (pp. 103–119). New York: Guilford.

Sternberg, R. J. (2008). The triarchic theory of successful intelligence. In N. Salkind (Ed.), *Encyclopedia of educational psychology* (Vol. 2, pp. 988–994). Thousand Oaks, CA: Sage.

Sternberg, R. J., Castejaon, J. L., Prieto, M. D., Hautaméaki, J., & Grigorenko, E. L. (2001). Confirmatory factor analysis of the Sternberg Triarchic Abilities Test (multiple-choice items) in three international samples: An empirical test of the triarchic theory of intelligence. *European Journal of Psychological Assessment, 17,* 1–16.

Sternberg, R. J., & Detterman, D. K. (1986). *What is intelligence?* Norwood, NJ: Ablex.

Sternberg, R. J., Forsythe, G. B., Hedlund, J., Horvath, J. A., Wagner, R. K., Williams, W. M., Snook, S. A., & Grigorenko, E. L. (2000). *Practical intelligence in everyday life.* Cambridge, UK: Cambridge University Press.

Sternberg, R. J., & Grigorenko, E. L. (2002). *Dynamic testing.* New York: Cambridge University Press.

Sternberg, R. J., Grigorenko, E. L., Ferrari, M., & Clinkenbeard, P. (1999). A triarchic analysis of an aptitude-treatment interaction. *European Journal of Psychological Assessment, 15,* 1–11.

Sternberg, R. J., Grigorenko, E. L., & Kidd, K. K. (2005). Intelligence, race, and genetics. *American Psychologist, 60,* 46–59.

Sternberg, R. J., & Jarvin, L. (2003). Alfred Binet's contributions as a paradigm for impact in psychology. In R. J. Sternberg (Ed.), *The anatomy of impact: What makes the great works of psychology great?* (pp. 89–107). Washington, DC: American Psychological Association.

Sternberg, R. J., & Lubart, T. I. (1991). An investment theory of creativity and its development. *Human Development, 34,* 1–31.

Sternberg, R. J., & Lubart, T. I. (1996). Investing in creativity. *American Psychologist, 51,* 677–688.

Stevenson, H. W., Lee, S., & Mu, X. (2000). Successful achievement in mathematics: China and the United States. In C. F. M. van Lieshout & P. G. Heymans (Eds.), *Developing talent across the lifespan* (pp. 167–183). Philadelphia: Psychology Press.

Stevenson, R., & Pollitt, C. (1987). The acquisition of temporal terms. *Journal of Child Language, 14,* 533–545.

Stevens-Simon, C., Sheeder, J., & Harter, S. (2005). Teen contraceptive decisions: Childbearing intentions are the tip of the iceberg. *Women and Health, 42,* 55–73.

Steward, D. K. (2001). Behavioral characteristics of infants with nonorganic failure to thrive during a play interaction. *American Journal of Maternal Child Nursing, 26,* 79–85.

Stewart, P. W., Lonky, E., Reihman, J., Pagano, J., Gump, B. B., & Darvill, T. (2008). The relationship between prenatal PCB exposure and intelligence (IQ). *Environmental Health Perspectives, 116,* 1416–1422.

Stewart, R. B., Jr. (1990). *The second child: Family transition and adjustment.* Newbury Park, CA: Sage.

Stewart-Brown, S., & Edmunds, L. (2007). *Educating people to be emotionally intelligent* (pp. 241–257). Westport, CT: Praeger.

Stice, E. (2003). Puberty and body image. In C. Hayward (Ed.), *Gender differences at puberty* (pp. 61–76). New York: Cambridge University Press.

Stice, E., Presnell, K., & Bearman, S. K. (2001). Relation of early menarche to depression, eating disorders, substance abuse, and comorbid psychopathology among adolescent girls. *Developmental Psychology, 37,* 608–619.

Stiles, J. (2001a). Neural plasticity in cognitive development. *Developmental Neuropsychology, 18,* 237–272.

Stiles, J. (2001b). Spatial cognitive development. In C. A. Nelson & M. Luciana (Eds.), *Handbook of developmental cognitive neuroscience* (pp. 399–414). Cambridge, MA: MIT Press.

Stiles, J. (2008). *Fundamentals of brain development.* Cambridge, MA: Harvard University Press.

Stiles, J., Bates, E. A., Thal, D., Trauner, D. A., & Reilly, J. (2002). Linguistic and spatial cognitive development in children with pre- and perinatal focal brain injury: A ten-year overview from the San Diego longitudinal project. In M. H. Johnson & Y. Munakata (Eds.), *Brain development and cognition: A reader* (2nd ed., pp. 272–291). Malden, MA: Blackwell.

Stiles, J., Moses, P., Roe, K., Akshoomoff, N. A., Trauner, D., & Hesselink, J. (2003). Alternative brain organization after prenatal cerebral injury: Convergent fMRI and cognitive data. *Journal of the International Neuropsychological Society, 9,* 604–622.

Stiles, J., Reilly, J., Paul, B., & Moses, P. (2005). Cognitive development following early brain injury: Evidence for neural adaptation. *Trends in Cognitive Sciences, 9,* 136–143.

Stiles, J., Stern, C., Appelbaum, M., & Nass, R. (2008). Effects of early focal brain injury on memory for visuospatial patterns: Selective deficits of global–local processing. *Neuropsychology, 22,* 61–73.

Stinchcomb, J. B., Bazemore, G., & Riestenberg, N. (2006). Beyond zero tolerance: Restoring justice in secondary schools. *Youth Violence and Juvenile Justice, 4,* 123–147.

Stipek, D. (1995). The development of pride and shame in toddlers. In J. P. Tangney & K. W. Fischer (Eds.), *Self-conscious emotions* (pp. 237–252). New York: Guilford.

Stipek, D. (2004). Teaching practices in kindergarten and first grade: Different strokes for different folks. *Early Childhood Research Quarterly, 19,* 548–568.

Stipek, D. J., & Byler, P. (1997). Early childhood education teachers: Do they practice what they preach? *Early Childhood Research Quarterly, 12,* 305–326.

Stipek, D. J., Gralinski, J. H., & Kopp, C. B. (1990). Self-concept development in the toddler years. *Developmental Psychology, 26,* 972–977.

Stipek, D. J., Recchia, S., & McClintic, S. (1992). Self-evaluation in young children. *Monographs of the Society for Research in Child Development, 57*(1, Serial No. 226).

Stoch, M. B., Smythe, P. M., Moodie, A. D., & Bradshaw, D. (1982). Psychosocial outcome and CT findings after growth undernourishment during infancy: A 20-year developmental study. *Developmental Medicine and Child Neurology, 24,* 419–436.

Stocker, C. J., Arch, J. R., & Cawthorne, M. A. (2005). Fetal origins of insulin resistance and obesity. *Proceedings of the Nutrition Society, 64,* 143–151.

Stocker, C. M., Burwell, R. A., & Briggs, M. L. (2002). Sibling conflict in middle childhood predicts children's adjustment in early adolescence. *Journal of Family Psychology, 16,* 50–57.

Stoel-Gammon, C. (2011). Relationships between lexical and phonological development in young children. *Journal of Child Language, 38,* 1–34.

Stoel-Gammon, C., & Sosa, A. V. (2007). Phonological development. In E. Hoff & M. Shatz (Eds.), *Blackwell handbook of language development* (pp. 238–256). Malden, MA: Blackwell.

Stoll, S. (1998). The role of Aktionsart in the acquisition of Russian aspect. *First Language, 18,* 351–378.

Stone, M. R., & Brown, B. B. (1999). Identity claims and projections: Descriptions of self and crowds in secondary school. In J. A. McLellan & M. J. V. Pugh (Eds.), *The role of peer groups in adolescent social identity: Exploring the importance of stability and change* (pp. 7–20). San Francisco: Jossey-Bass.

Stone, R. (2005). *Best classroom management practices for reaching all learners: What award-winning classroom teachers do.* Thousand Oaks, CA: Corwin Press.

Stoneman, Z., Brody, G. H., & MacKinnon, C. E. (1986). Same-sex and cross-sex siblings: Activity choices, roles, behavior, and gender stereotypes. *Sex Roles, 15,* 495–511.

Storch, S. A., & Whitehurst, G. J. (2001). The role of family and home in the literacy development of children from low-income backgrounds. In P. R. Britto & J. Brooks-Gunn (Eds.), *New directions for child and adolescent development* (No. 92, pp. 53–71). San Francisco: Jossey-Bass.

Stormshak, E. A., Bellanti, C. J., Bierman, K. L., & the Conduct Problems Prevention Research Group. (1996). The quality of sibling relationships and the development of social competence and behavioral control in aggressive children. *Developmental Psychology, 32,* 79–89.

Stormshak, E. A., Bierman, K. L., McMahon, R. J., Lengua, L. J., and the Conduct Problems Prevention Research Group. (2000). Parenting practices and child disruptive behavior problems in early elementary school. *Journal of Clinical Child Psychology, 29,* 17–29.

Stormshak, E. A., Connell, A. M., Véronneau, M.-H., Myers, M. W., Dishion, T. J., Kavanagh, K., et al. (2011). An ecological approach to promoting early adolescent mental health and social adaptation: Family-centered intervention in public middle schools. *Child Development, 82,* 209–225.

Stormshak, E. A., & Dishion, T. J. (2009). A school-based family centered intervention to prevent substance abuse: The Family Check-Up. *American Journal of Drug and Alcohol Abuse, 35,* 227–232.

Stouthamer-Loeber, M., Wei, E., Loeber, R., & Masten, A. S. (2004). Desistance from persistent serious delinquency in the transition to adulthood. *Development and Psychopathology, 16,* 897–918.

Strapp, C. M., & Federico, A. (2000). Imitations and repetitions: What do children say following recasts? *First Language, 20,* 273–290.

Straus, M. A., & Stewart, J. H. (1999). Corporal punishment by American parents: National data on prevalence, chronicity, severity, and duration, in relation to child and family characteristics. *Clinical Child and Family Psychology Review, 2,* 55–70.

Strauss, M. S., & Curtis, L. E. (1984). Development of numerical concepts in infancy. In C. Sophian (Ed.), *The 18th annual Carnegie Symposium on Cognition: Origins of cognitive skills* (pp. 131–155). Hillsdale, NJ: Erlbaum.

Strayer, J., & Roberts, W. (1997). Facial and verbal measures of children's emotions and empathy. *International Journal of Behavioral Development, 20,* 627–649.

Strayer, J., & Roberts, W. (2004a). Children's anger, emotional expressiveness, and empathy: Relations with parents' empathy, emotional expressiveness, and parenting practices. *Social Development, 13,* 229–254.

Strayer, J., & Roberts, W. (2004b). Empathy and observed anger and aggression in five-year-olds. *Social Development, 13,* 1–13.

Strazdins, L., Clements, M. S., Korda, R. J., Broom, D. H., & D'Souza, R. M. (2006). Unsociable work? Nonstandard work schedules, family relationships, and children's well-being. *Journal of Marriage and Family, 68,* 394–410.

Streissguth, A. P., Bookstein, F. L., Barr, H. M., Sampson, P. D., O'Malley, K., & Young, J. K. (2004). Risk factors for adverse life outcomes in fetal alcohol syndrome and fetal alcohol effects. *Journal of Developmental and Behavioral Pediatrics, 25,* 228–238.

Streissguth, A. P., Treder, R., Barr, H. M., Shepard, T., Bleyer, W. A., Sampson, P. D., & Martin, D. (1987). Aspirin and acetaminophen use by pregnant women and subsequent child IQ and attention decrements. *Teratology, 35,* 211–219.

Strelau, J., Zawadzki, B., & Piotrowska, A. (2001). Temperament and intelligence: A psychometric approach to the links between both phenomena. In J. M. Collis & S. Messick (Eds.), *Intelligence and personality* (pp. 61–78). Mahwah, NJ: Erlbaum.

Streri, A. (2005). Touching for knowing in infancy: The development of manual abilities in very young infants. *European Journal of Developmental Psychology, 2,* 325–343.

Streri, A., Lhote, M., & Dutilleul, S. (2000). Haptic perception in newborns. *Developmental Science, 3,* 319–327.

Stretesky, P., & Lynch, M. (2004). The relationship between lead and crime. *Journal of Health and Social Behavior, 45,* 214–229.

Striano, T., & Rochat, P. (2000). Emergence of selective social referencing in infancy. *Infancy, 1,* 253–264.

Striano, T., Tomasello, M., & Rochat, P. (2001). Social and object support for early symbolic play. *Developmental Science, 4,* 442–455.

Striegel-Moore, R. H., & Franko, D. L. (2006). Adolescent eating disorders. In R. H. Striegel-Moore & D. L. Franko (Eds.), *Child and adolescent psychopathology: Theoretical and clinical implications* (pp. 160–183). New York: Routledge.

Striegel-Moore, R. H., Thompson, D. R., Affenito, S. G., Franko, D. L., Barton, B. A., Schreiber, et al. (2006). Fruit and vegetable intake: Few adolescent girls meet national guidelines. *Preventive Medicine, 42,* 223–228.

Stright, A. D., Herr, M. Y., & Neitzel, C. (2009). Maternal scaffolding of children's problem solving and children's adjustment in kindergarten: Hmong families in the United States. *Journal of Educational Psychology, 101,* 207–218.

Stright, A. D., Neitzel, C., Sears, K. G., & Hoke-Sinex, L. (2001). Instruction begins in the home: Relations between parental instruction and children's self-regulation in the classroom. *Journal of Educational Psychology, 93,* 456–466.

Strohschein, L. (2005). Parental divorce and child mental health trajectories. *Journal of Marriage and Family, 67,* 1286–1300.

Strohschein, L., Gauthier, A. J., Campbell, R., & Kleparchuk, C. (2008). Parenting as a dynamic process: A test of the resource dilution hypothesis. *Journal of Marriage and Family, 70,* 670–683.

Stromswold, K. (2000). The cognitive neuroscience of language acquisition. In M. S. Gazzaniga (Ed.), *The new cognitive neurosciences* (pp. 909–932). Boston: MIT Press.

Strouse, D. L. (1999). Adolescent crowd orientations: A social and temporal analysis. In J. A. McLellan & M. J. V. Pugh (Eds.), *The role of peer groups in adolescent social identity: Exploring the importance of stability and change* (pp. 37–54). San Francisco: Jossey-Bass.

Sturaro, C., van Lier, P. A. C., Cuijpers, P., & Koot, H. M. (2011). The role of peer relationships in the development of early school-age externalizing problems. *Child Development, 82,* 758–765.

Sturge-Apple, M. L., Davies, P. T., Winter, M. A., Cummings, E. M., & Schermerhorn, A. (2008). Interparental conflict and children's school adjustment: The explanatory role of children's internal representations of interparental and parent–child relationships. *Developmental Psychology, 44,* 1678–1690.

Styne, D. M. (2003). The regulation of pubertal growth. *Hormone Research, 60*(Suppl.1), 22–26.

Su, T. F., & Costigan, C. L. (2008). The development of children's ethnic identity in immigrant Chinese families in Canada: The role of parenting practices and children's perceptions of parental family obligation expectations. *Journal of Early Adolescence, 29,* 638–663.

Suarez-Morales, L., & Lopez, B. (2009). The impact of acculturative stress and daily hassles on preadolescent psychological adjustment: Examining anxiety symptoms. *Journal of Primary Prevention, 30,* 335–349.

Suárez-Orozco, C., Todorova, I., & Qin, D. B. (2006). The well-being of immigrant adolescents: A longitudinal perspective on risk and protective factors. In F. A. Villarruel & T. Luster (Eds.), *The crisis in youth mental health: Critical issues and effective programs: Vol. 2. Disorders in adolescence* (pp. 53–83). Westport, CT: Praeger.

Subbotsky, E. V. (2004). Magical thinking in judgments of causation: Can anomalous phenomena affect ontological causal beliefs in children and adults? *British Journal of Developmental Psychology, 22,* 123–152.

Subrahmanyam, K., & Greenfield, P. M. (1996). Effect of video game practice on spatial skills in girls and boys. In P. M. Greenfield & R. R. Cocking (Eds.), *Interacting with video* (pp. 95–114). Norwood, NJ: Ablex.

Subrahmanyam, K., & Greenfield, P. M. (2008). Online communication and adolescent relationships. *Future of Children, 18,* 119–146.

Subrahmanyam, K., Gelman, R., & Lafosse, A. (2002). Animate and other separably moveable things. In G. Humphreys (Ed.), *Category-specificity in brain and mind* (pp. 341–371). London: Psychology Press.

Subrahmanyam, K., Greenfield, P., Kraut, R., & Gross, E. (2001). The impact of computer use on children's and adolescents' development. *Applied Developmental Psychology, 22,* 7–30.

Subramanian, S. V., Perkins, J. M., Emre, O., & Smith, G. D. (2011). Weight of nations: A socioeconomic analysis of women in low- to middle-income countries. *American Journal of Clinial Nutrition, 93,* 232–233.

Subrahmanyam, K., Smahel, D., & Greenfield, P. (2006). Connecting developmental constructions to the Internet: Identity presentation and sexual exploration in online teen chat rooms. *Developmental Psychology, 42,* 395–406.

Substance Abuse and Mental Health Services Administration. (2010). *Results from the 2009 National Survey on Drug Use and Health: Vol. 1. Summary of national findings.* (Office of Applied Studies, NSDUH Series H-38A, HHS Publication No. SMA 10-4586 Findings). Rockville, MD: Author.

Suddendorf, T., Simcock, G., & Nielsen, M. (2007). Visual self-recognition in mirrors and live videos: Evidence for a developmental asynchrony. *Cognitive Development, 22,* 185–196.

Sullivan, H. S. (1953). *The interpersonal theory of psychiatry.* New York: Norton.

Sullivan, M. C., McGrath, M. M. Hawes, K., & Lester, B. M. (2008). Growth trajectories of preterm infants: Birth to 12 years. *Journal of Pediatric Health Care, 22,* 83–93.

Sullivan, M. W., & Lewis, M. (2003). Contextual determinants of anger and other negative expressions in young infants. *Developmental Psychology, 39,* 693–705.

Sullivan, S., & Glanz, J. (2006). *Building effective learning communities: Strategies for leadership, learning, and collaboration.* Thousand Oaks, CA: Corwin Press.

Sundet, J. M., Barlaug, D. G., & Torjussen, T. M. (2004). The end of the Flynn effect? A study of secular trends in mean intelligence test scores of Norwegian conscripts during half a century. *Intelligence, 32,* 349–362.

Sumter, S. R., Bokhorst, C. L., Steinberg, L., & Westenberg, P. M. (2009). The developmental pattern of resistance to peer influence in adolescence: Will the teenager ever be able to resist? *Journal of Adolescence, 32,* 1009–1021.

Super, C. M. (1981). Behavioral development in infancy. In R. H. Monroe, R. L. Monroe, & B. B. Whiting (Eds.), *Handbook of cross-cultural human development* (pp. 181–270). New York: Garland.

Super, C. M., & Harkness, S. (2002). Culture structures the environment for development. *Human Development 45,* 270–274.

Super, C. M., & Harkness, S. (2009). The developmental niche of the newborn in rural Kenya. In J. K. Nugent, B. J. Petrauskas, & T. B. Brazelton (Eds.), *The newborn as a person: Enabling healthy development worldwide* (pp. 85–97). Hoboken, NJ: Wiley.

Super, C. M., & Harkness, S. (2010). Culture and infancy. In J. G. Bremner & T. D. Wachs (Eds.), *Wiley-Blackwell handbook of infant development: Vol. 1. Basic research* (2nd ed., pp. 623–649). Chichester, UK: Wiley-Blackwell.

Super, C. M., Harkness, S., van Tijen, N., van der Vlugt, E., Fintelman, M., & Dijkstra, J. (1996). The three R's of Dutch childrearing and the socialization of infant arousal. In S. Harkness & C. M. Super (Eds.), *Parents' cultural belief systems* (pp. 447–466). New York: Guilford.

Supple, A. J., & Small, S. A. (2006). The influence of parental support, knowledge, and authoritative parenting on Hmong and European American adolescent development. *Journal of Family Issues, 27,* 1214–1232.

Supple, A. J., Ghazarian, S. R., Peterson, G. W., & Bush, K. R. (2009). Assessing the cross-cultural validity of a parental autonomy granting measure: Comparing adolescents in the United States, China, Mexico, and India. *Journal of Cross-Cultural Psychology, 40,* 816–833.

Susman, E. J., & Dorn, L. D. (2009). Puberty: Its role in development. In R. M. Lerner & L. Steinberg (Eds.), *Handbook of adolescent psychology: Vol. 1. Individual bases of adolescent development* (3rd ed., pp. 116–151). Hoboken, NJ: Wiley.

Susskind, J. E., & Hodges, C. (2007). Decoupling children's gender-based in-group positivity from out-group negativity. *Sex Roles, 56,* 707–716.

Sussman, S., Skara, S., & Ames, S. L. (2008). Substance abuse among adolescents. *Substance Use and Misuse, 43,* 1802–1828.

Sutton, M. J., Brown, J. D., Wilson, K. M., & Klein, J. D. (2002). Shaking the tree of forbidden fruit: Where adolescents learn about sexuality and contraception. In J. D. Brown, J. R. Steele, & K. Walsh-Childers (Eds.), *Sexual teens, sexual media* (pp. 25–55). Mahwah, NJ: Erlbaum.

Svensson, A. (2000). Computers in school: Socially isolating or a tool to promote collaboration? *Journal of Educational Computing Research, 22,* 437–453.

Svetlova, M., Nichols, S. R., & Brownell, C. A. (2010). Toddlers' prosocial behavior: From instrumental to empathic to altruistic helping. *Child Development, 81,* 1814–1827.

Svirsky, M. A., Teoh, S. W., & Neuburger, H. (2004). Development of language and speech perception in congenitally profoundly deaf children as a function of age at cochlear implantation. *Audiology and Neuro-Otology, 9,* 224–233.

Swedish Social Insurance Agency. (2011a). *Föräldrapenning* [Parental benefit]. Retrieved from www.forsakringskassan.se/irj/go/km/.../foraldrapenning_eng.pdf

Swedish Social Insurance Agency. (2011b). *Statistics Sweden: Parental insurance.* Retrieved from www.scb.se/Pages/Product_____38528.aspx

Swingley, D. (2005). Statistical clustering and the contents of the infant vocabulary. *Cognitive Psychology, 50,* 86–132.

Swingley, D. (2009). Onsets and codas in 1.5-year-old toddlers' word recognition. *Journal of Memory and Language, 60,* 252–269.

Swingley, D. (2010). Fast mapping and slow mapping in children's word learning. *Language Learning and Development, 6,* 179–183.

Swingley, D., & Aslin, R. N. (2002). Lexical neighborhoods and the word-form representations of 14-month-olds. *Psychological Science, 13,* 480–484.

Swinson, J., & Harrop, A. (2009). Teacher talk directed to boys and girls and its relationship to their behaviour. *Educational Studies, 35,* 515–524.

Symons, D. K. (2001). A dyad-oriented approach to distress and mother–child relationship outcomes in the first 24 months. *Parenting: Science and Practice, 1,* 101–122.

Symons, D. K. (2004). Mental state discourse, theory of mind, and the internalization of self–other understanding. *Developmental Review, 24,* 159–188.

Szepkouski, G. M., Gauvain, M., & Carberry, M. (1994). The development of planning skills in children with and without mental retardation. *Journal of Applied Developmental Psychology, 15,* 187–206.

Szkrybalo, J., & Ruble, D. N. (1999). "God made me a girl": Sex-category constancy judgments and explanations revisited. *Developmental Psychology, 35,* 392–402.

Szlemko, W. J., Wood, J. W., & Thurman, P. J. (2006). Native Americans and alcohol: Past, present, and future. *Journal of General Psychology, 133,* 435–451.

Taatgen, N. A., & Anderson, J. R. (2002). Why do children learn to say "broke"? A model of learning the past tense without feedback. *Cognition, 86,* 123–155.

Tabibi, Z., & Pfeffer, K. (2007). Finding a safe place to cross the road: The effect of distractors and the role of attention in children's identification of safe and dangerous road-crossing sites. *Infant and Child Development, 16,* 193–206.

Tacon, A. M., & Caldera, Y. M. (2001). Attachment and parental correlates in late adolescent Mexican American women. *Hispanic Journal of Behavioral Sciences, 23,* 71–88.

Tager-Flusberg, H. (2007). Atypical language development: Autism and other neurodevelopmental disorders. In E. Hoff & M. Shatz (Eds.), *Blackwell handbook of language development* (pp. 432–453). Malden, MA: Blackwell.

Tager-Flusberg, H., & Zukowski, A. (2009). Putting words together: Morphology and syntax in the preschool years. In J. B. Gleason & B. Ratner (Ed.), *The development of language* (7th ed., pp. 139–191). Boston: Allyn and Bacon.

Takahashi, K. (1990). Are the key assumptions of the "Strange Situation" procedure universal? A view from Japanese research. *Human Development, 33,* 23–30.

Takala, M. (2006). The effects of reciprocal teaching on reading comprehension in mainstream and special (SLI) education. *Scandinavian Journal of Educational Research, 50,* 559–576.

Tam, C. W., & Stokes, S. F. (2001). Form and function of negation in early developmental Cantonese. *Journal of Child Language, 28,* 373–391.

Tamis-LeMonda, C. S., Bornstein, M. H., & Baumwell, L. (2001). Maternal responsiveness and children's achievement of language milestones. *Child Development, 72,* 748–767.

Tamis-LeMonda, C. S., Cristofaro, T. N., Rodriguez, E. T., & Bornstein, M. H. (2006). Early language development: Social influences in the first years of life. In L. Balter & C. S. Tamis-LeMonda (Eds.), *Child psychology: A handbook of contemporary issues* (pp. 79–108). New York: Psychology Press.

Tamis-LeMonda, C. S., Way, N., Hughes, D., Yoshikawa, H., Kalman, R. K., & Niwa, E. Y. (2008). Parents' goals for children: The dynamic coexistence of individualism and collectivism in cultures and individuals. *Social Development, 17,* 183–209.

Tammelin, T., Näyhä, S., Hills, A. P., & Järvelin, M. (2003). Adolescent participation in sports and adult physical activity. *American Journal of Preventive Medicine, 24,* 22–28.

Tamrouti-Makkink, I. D., Dubas, J. S., Gerris, J. R. M., & van Aken, A. G. (2004). The relation between the absolute level of parenting and differential parental treatment with adolescent siblings' adjustment. *Journal of Child Psychology and Psychiatry, 45,* 1397–1406.

Tangney, J. P., Stuewig, J., & Mashek, D. J. (2007). Moral emotions and moral behavior. *Annual Review of Psychology, 58,* 345–372.

Tanimura, M., Takahashi, K., Kataoka, N., Tomita, K., Tanabe, I., Yasuda, M., et al. (2004). Proposal: Heavy television and video viewing poses a risk for infants and young children. *Nippon Shonika Gakkai Zasshi, 108,* 709–712 (in Japanese).

Tanner, J., M., Healy, M., & Cameron, N. (2001). *Assessment of skeletal maturity and prediction of adult height (TW3 method)* (3rd ed.). Philadelphia: Saunders.

Tardif, T. (2006). But are they really verbs? Chinese words for action. In K. Hirsh-Pasek & R. M. Golinkoff (Eds.), *Action meets word: How children learn verbs* (pp.

477–498). New York: Oxford University Press.

Tardif, T., Fletcher, P., Liang, W., & Kaciroti, N. (2009). Early vocabulary development in Mandarin (Putonghua) and Cantonese. *Journal of Child Language, 36*, 1115–1144.

Tardif, T., Fletcher, P., Liang, W., Zhang, Z., Kaciroti, N., & Marchman, V. A. (2008). Baby's first 10 words. *Developmental Psychology, 44*, 929–938.

Tardif, T., Gelman, S. A., & Xu, F. (1999). Putting the "noun bias" in context: A comparison of English and Mandarin. *Child Development, 70*, 620–635.

Tardif, T., Wellman, H. M., & Cheung, K. M. (2004). False belief understanding in Cantonese-speaking children. *Journal of Child Language, 31*, 779–800.

Tarren-Sweeney, M. (2006). Patterns of aberrant eating among preadolescent children in foster care. *Journal of Abnormal Child Psychology, 34*, 623–634.

Tarter, R. E., Vanyukov, M., & Kirisci, L. (2008). Etiology of substance use disorder: Developmental perspective. In Y. Kaminer & O. G. Bukstein (Eds.), *Adolescent substance abuse: Psychiatric comorbidity and high-risk behaviors* (pp. 5–27). New York: Routledge.

Tarullo, A. R., & Gunnar, M. R. (2006). Child maltreatment and the developing HPA axis. *Hormones and Behavior, 50*, 632–639.

Tasbihsazan, R., Nettelbeck, T., & Kirby, N. (2003). Predictive validity of the Fagan Test of Infant Intelligence. *British Journal of Developmental Psychology, 21*, 585–597.

Tasker, F. (2005). Lesbian mothers, gay fathers, and their children: A review. *Developmental and Behavioral Pediatrics, 26*, 224–240.

Tauber, M. A. (1979). Parental socialization techniques and sex differences in children's play. *Child Development, 50*, 225–234.

Taumoepeau, M., & Ruffman, T. (2006). Mother and infant talk about mental states relates to desire language and emotion understanding. *Child Development, 77*, 465–481.

Taylor, C. A., Manganello, J. A., Lee, S. J., & Rice, J. C. (2010). Mother's spanking of 3-year-old children and subsequent risk of children's aggressive behavior. *Pediatrics, 125*, e1057–e1065.

Taylor, E. (2004). ADHD is best understood as a cultural construct: Against. *British Journal of Psychiatry, 184*, 9.

Taylor, J. L. (2009). Midlife impacts of adolescent parenthood. *Journal of Family Issues, 30*, 484–510.

Taylor, M., & Carlson, S. M. (1997). The relation between individual differences in fantasy and theory of mind. *Child Development, 68*, 436–455.

Taylor, M., & Carlson, S. M. (2000). The influence of religious beliefs on parental attitudes about children's fantasy behavior. In K. S. Rosengren, C. N. Johnson, & P. L. Harris (Eds.), *Imagining the impossible* (pp. 247–268). New York: Cambridge University Press.

Taylor, M., Carlson, S. M., Maring, B. L., Gerow, L., & Charley, C. M. (2004). The characteristics and correlates of fantasy in school-age children: Imaginary companions, impersonation, and social understanding. *Developmental Psychology, 40*, 1173–1187.

Taylor, M., Esbensen, B. M., & Bennett, R. T. (1994). Children's understanding of knowledge acquisition: The tendency for children to report that they have always known what they have just learned. *Child Development, 65*, 1581–1604.

Taylor, M. C., & Hall, J. A. (1982). Psychological androgyny: Theories, methods, and conclusions. *Psychological Bulletin, 92*, 347–366.

Taylor, M. G. (1996). The development of children's beliefs about the social and biological aspects of gender differences. *Child Development, 67*, 1555–1571.

Taylor, M. G., Rhodes, M., & Gelman, S. A. (2009). Boys will be boys; cows will be cows: Children's essentialist reasoning about gender categories and animal species. *Child Development, 80*, 461–481.

Taylor, R. D. (2010). Risk and resilience in low-income African American families: Moderating effects of kinship social support. *Cultural Diversity and Ethnic Minority Psychology, 16*, 344–351.

Taylor, R. L. (2000). Diversity within African-American families. In D. H. Demo & K. R. Allen (Eds.), *Handbook of family diversity* (pp. 232–251). New York: Oxford University Press.

Teasdale, B., & Bradley-Engen, M. S. (2010). Adolescent same-sex attraction and mental health: The role of stress and support. *Journal of Homosexuality, 57*, 287–309.

Teicher, M. H., Dumont, N. L., Ito, Y., Vaituzis, C., Giedd, J., & Andersen, S. L. (2004). Childhood neglect is associated with reduced corpus callosum area. *Biological Psychiatry, 56*, 80–85.

Teinonen, T., Aslin, R. N., Alku, P., & Csibra, G. (2008). Visual speech contributes to phonetic learning in 6-month-old infants. *Cognition, 108*, 850–855.

Telama, R., Yang, X., Viikari, J., Valimaki, I., Wanne, O., & Raitakari, O. (2005). Physical activity from childhood to adulthood: A 21-year tracking study. *American Journal of Preventive Medicine, 28*, 267–273.

Temple, C. M., & Carney, R. A. (1995). Patterns of spatial functioning in Turner's syndrome. *Cortex, 31*, 109–118.

Temple, J. L., Giacomelli, A. M., Roemmich, J. N., & Epstein, L. H. (2007). Overweight children habituate slower than non-overweight children to food. *Physiology and Behavior, 9*, 250–254.

Templeton, A. R. (2002). The genetic and evolutionary significance of human races. In J. M. Fish (Ed.), *Race and intelligence* (pp. 31–56). Mahwah, NJ: Erlbaum.

Templeton, L. M., & Wilcox, S. A. (2000). A tale of two representations: The misinformation effect and children's developing theory of mind. *Child Development, 71*, 402–416.

ten Tusscher, G. W., & Koppe, J. G. (2004). Perinatal dioxin exposure and later effects—A review. *Chemosphere, 54*, 1329–1336.

Tenenbaum, H. R. (2009). 'You'd be good at that': Gender patterns in parent–child talk about courses. *Social Development, 18*, 447–463.

Tenenbaum, H. R., & Leaper, C. (2002). Are parents' gender schemas related to their children's gender-related cognitions? A meta-analysis. *Developmental Psychology, 38*, 615–630.

Tenenbaum, H. R., & Leaper, C. (2003). Parent–child conversations about science: The socialization of gender inequities? *Developmental Psychology, 39*, 34–47.

Tenenbaum, H. R., Snow, C. E., Roach, K. A., & Kurland, B. (2005). Talking and reading science: Longitudinal data on sex differences in mother–child conversations in low-income families. *Journal of Applied Developmental Psychology, 26*, 1–19.

Tepper, C. A., & Cassidy, K. W. (1999). Gender differences in emotional language in children's picture books. *Sex Roles, 40*, 265–280.

Terwel, J., Gillies, R. M., van den Eeden, P., & Hoek, D. (2001). Cooperative learning processes of students: A longitudinal multilevel perspective. *British Journal of Educational Psychology, 71*, 619–645.

Tessier, R., Cristo, M., Velez, S., Giron, M., Nadeau, L., & Figueroa, Z. (2003). Kangaroo mother care: A method of protecting high-risk premature infants against developmental delay. *Infant Behavior and Development, 26*, 384–397.

Teti, D. M., Saken, J. W., Kucera, E., & Corns, K. M. (1996). And baby makes four: Predictors of attachment security among preschool-age firstborns during the transition to siblinghood. *Child Development, 67*, 579–596.

Teyber, E. (2001). *Helping children cope with divorce* (rev. ed.). San Francisco: Jossey-Bass.

Tharpe, A. M., & Ashmead, D. H. (2001). A longitudinal investigation of infant auditory sensitivity. *American Journal of Audiology, 10*, 104–112.

Thelen, E. (1989). The (re)discovery of motor development: Learning new things from an old field. *Developmental Psychology, 25*, 916–949.

Thelen, E., & Adolph, K. E. (1992). Arnold Gesell: The paradox of nature and nurture. *Developmental Psychology, 28*, 368–380.

Thelen, E., & Corbetta, D. (2002). Microdevelopment and dynamic systems: Applications to infant motor development. In N. Granott & J. Parziale (Eds.), *Microdevelopment: Transition processes in development and learning* (pp. 59–79). New York: Cambridge University Press.

Thelen, E., Fisher, D. M., & Ridley-Johnson, R. (1984). The relationship between physical growth and a newborn reflex. *Infant Behavior and Development, 7*, 479–493.

Thelen, E., Schöner, G., Scheier, C., & Smith, L. B. (2001). The dynamics of embodiment: A field theory of infant perseverative reaching. *Behavioral and Brain Sciences, 24*, 1–34.

Thelen, E., & Smith, L. B. (1994). *A dynamic systems approach to the development of cognition and action.* Cambridge, MA: Cambridge University Press.

Thelen, E., & Smith, L. B. (2006). Dynamic systems theories. In R. M. Lerner (Ed.), *Handbook of child psychology: Vol. 1. Theoretical models of human development* (6th ed., pp. 258–312). Hoboken, NJ: Wiley.

Théoret, H., Halligan, E., Kobayashi, M., Fregni, F., Tager-Flusberg, H., & Pascual-Leone, A. (2005). Impaired motor facilitation during action observation in individuals with autism spectrum disorder. *Current Biology, 15*, R84–R85.

Thierry, K. L., & Spence, M. J. (2002). Source-monitoring training facilitates preschoolers' eyewitness memory performance. *Developmental Psychology, 38*, 428–437.

Thiessen, E. D., & Saffran, J. R. (2007). Learning to learn: Infants' acquisition of stress-based strategies for word segmentation. *Language Learning and Development, 3*, 73–100.

Thiessen, E. D., Hill, E. A., & Saffran, J. R. (2005). Infant-directed speech facilitates word segmentation. *Infancy, 7*, 53–71.

Thomaes, S., Reijntjes, A., de Castro, B. O., Bushman, B. J., Poorthuis, A., & Telch, M. J. (2010). I like me if you like me: On the interpersonal modulation and regulation of preadolescents' state self-esteem. *Child Development, 81*, 811–825.

Thomaes, S., Stegge, H., Bushman, B. J., & Olthof, T. (2008). Trumping shame by blasts of noise: Narcissism, self-esteem, shame, and aggression in young adolescents. *Child Development, 79*, 1792–1801.

Thoman, E. B., & Ingersoll, E. W. (1993). Learning in premature infants. *Developmental Psychology, 29*, 692–700.

Thomas, A., & Chess, S. (1977). *Temperament and development.* New York: Brunner/Mazel.

Thomas, A., Chess, S., & Birch, H. G. (1968). *Temperament and behavior disorders in children.* New York: New York University Press.

Thomas, C. L., & Dimitrov, D. M. (2007). Effects of a teen pregnancy prevention program on teens' attitudes toward sexuality: A latent trait modeling approach. *Developmental Psychology, 43*, 173–185.

Thomas, K. A., & Tessler, R. C. (2007). Bicultural socialization among adoptive families: Where there is a will, there is a way. *Journal of Family Issues, 28*, 1189–1219.

Thomas, R. M. (2005). *Comparing theories of child development* (6th ed.). New York: New York University Press.

Thomas, S., Stegge, H., & Olthof, T. (2007). Externalizing shame responses in children: The role of fragile-positive self-esteem. *British Journal of Developmental Psychology, 25*, 559–577.

Thombs, B. D., Roseman, M., & Arthurs, E. (2010). Prenatal and postpartum depression in fathers and mothers. *Journal of the American Medical Association, 304*, 961.

Thompson, A., Hollis, C., & Richards, D. (2003). Authoritarian parenting attitudes as a risk for conduct problems: Results of a British national cohort study. *European Child and Adolescent Psychiatry, 12*, 84–91.

Thompson, P. M., Giedd, J. N., Woods, R. P., MacDonald, D., Evans, A. C., & Toga, A. W. (2000). Growth patterns in the developing brain detected by using continuum mechanical tensor maps. *Nature, 404*, 190–192.

Thompson, R. A. (1990). Vulnerability in research: A developmental perspective on research risk. *Child Development, 61*, 1–16.

Thompson, R. A. (1992). Developmental changes in research risk and benefit: A changing calculus of concerns. In B. Stanley & J. E. Sieber (Eds.), *Social research on children and adolescents: Ethical issues* (pp. 31–64). Newbury Park, CA: Sage.

Thompson, R. A. (2000). The legacy of early attachments. *Child Development, 71*, 145–152.

Thompson, R. A. (2006). The development of the person: Social understanding, relationships, conscience, self. In N. Eisenberg (Ed.), *Handbook of child psychology: Vol. 3. Social, emotional, and personality development* (6th ed., pp. 24–98). Hoboken, NJ: Wiley.

Thompson, R. A. (2008). Early attachment and later development. In J. Cassidy & P. R. Shaver (Eds.), *Handbook of attachment: Theory, research, and clinical applications* (2nd ed., pp. 348–365). New York: Guilford.

Thompson, R. A. (2009). Early foundations: Conscience and the development of moral character. In D. Narvaez & D. K. Lapsley (Eds.), *Personality, identity, and character: Explorations in moral psychology* (pp. 159–184). New York: Cambridge University Press.

Thompson, R. A., & Goodman, M. (2010). Development of emotion regulation: More than meets the eye. In A. M. Kring & D. M. Sloan (Eds.), *Emotion regulation and psychopathology: A transdiagnostic approach to etiology and treatment* (pp. 38–58). New York: Guilford.

Thompson, R. A., & Goodvin, R. (2007). Taming the tempest in the teapot. In C. A. Brownell & C. B. Kopp (Eds.), *Socioemotional development in the toddler years: Transitions and transformations* (pp. 320–341). New York: Guilford.

Thompson, R. A., & Leger, D. W. (1999). From squalls to calls: The cry as a developing socioemotional signal. In B. Lester, J. Newman, & F. Pedersen, (Eds.), *Biological and social aspects of infant crying.* New York: Plenum.

Thompson, R. A., & Meyer, S. (2007). Socialization of emotion regulation in the family. In J. J. Gross (Ed.), *Handbook of emotion regulation* (pp. 249–268). New York: Guilford.

Thompson, R. A., Meyer, S., & McGinley, M. (2006). Understanding values in relationships: The development of conscience. In M. Killen & J. G. Smetana (Eds.), *Handbook of moral development* (pp. 267–298). Mahwah, NJ: Erlbaum.

Thompson, R. A., & Nelson, C. A. (2001). Developmental science and the media: Early brain development. *American Psychologist, 56,* 5–15.

Thompson, R. A., & Raikes, H. A. (2007). The social and emotional foundations of school readiness. In D. F. Perry, R. K. Kaufmann, & J. Knitzer (Eds.), *Social and emotional health in early childhood: Building bridges between services and systems* (pp. 13–35). Baltimore, MD: Paul H. Brookes.

Thompson, R. A., Winer, A. C., & Goovin, R. (2011). The individual child: Temperament, emotion, self, and personality. In M. H. Bornstein & M. E. Lamb (Eds.), *Developmental science: An advanced textbook* (6th ed.). New York: Psychology Press.

Thompson, W. W., Price, C., Goodson, B., Shay, D. K., Benson, P., Hinrichsen, V. L., et al. (2007). Early thimerosal exposure and neuropsychological outcomes at 7 to 10 years. *New England Journal of Medicine, 357,* 1281–1292.

Thornberry, T. P., & Krohn, M. D. (2001). The development of delinquency: An interactional perspective. In S. O. White (Ed.), *Handbook of youth and justice* (pp. 289–305). Dordrecht, Netherlands: Kluwer.

Thorne, B. (1993). *Gender play: Girls and boys in school.* New Brunswick, NJ: Rutgers University Press.

Thornton, S. (1999). Creating conditions for cognitive change: The interaction between task structures and specific strategies. *Child Development, 70,* 588–603.

Thurstone, L. L. (1938). *Primary mental abilities.* Chicago: University of Chicago Press.

Tienari, P., Wahlberg, K.-E., & Wynne, L. C. (2006). Finnish adoption study of schizophrenia: Implications for family interventions. *Families, Systems, and Health, 24,* 442–451.

Tienari, P., Wynne, L. C., Laksy, K., Moring, J., Nieminen, P., & Sorri, A. (2003). Genetic boundaries of the schizophrenia spectrum: Evidence from the Finnish adoptive family study of schizophrenia. *American Journal of Psychiatry, 160,* 1587–1594.

Tiet, Q. Q., Huizinga, D., & Byrnes, H. F. (2010). Predictors of resilience among inner city youths. *Journal of Child and Family Studies, 19,* 360–378.

Tiggemann, M., & Anesbury, T. (2000). Negative stereotyping of obesity in children: The role of controllability beliefs. *Journal of Applied Social Psychology, 30,* 1977–1993.

Tincoff, R., & Jusczyk, P. W. (1999). Some beginnings of word comprehension in 6-month-olds. *Psychological Science, 10,* 172–175.

Tisak, M. S., Tisak, J., & Goldstein, S. E. (2006). Aggression, delinquency, and morality A social-cognitive perspective. In M. Killen & J. G. Smetana (Eds.), *Handbook of moral development* (pp. 611–629). Philadelphia: Erlbaum.

Tizard, B., & Rees, J. (1975). The effect of early institutional rearing on the behaviour problems and affectional relationships of four-year-old children. *Journal of Child Psychology and Psychiatry, 16,* 61–73.

Tofler, I. R., Knapp, P. K., & Drell, M. J. (1998). The achievement by proxy spectrum in youth sports: Historical perspective and clinical approach to pressured and high-achieving children and adolescents. *Adolescent Psychiatric Clinics of North America, 7,* 803–820.

Tokunaga, R. S. (2010). Following you home from school: A critical review and synthesis of research on cyberbullying victimization. *Computers in Human behavior, 26,* 277–287.

Tolman, D. L. (2002). *Dilemmas of desire: Teenage girls talk about sexuality.* Cambridge, MA: Harvard University Press.

Tolmie, A. K., Topping, K. J., Christie, D., Donaldson, C., Howe, C., Jessiman, E., et al. (2010). Social effects of collaborative learning in primary schools. *Learning and Instruction, 20,* 177–191.

Tomasello, M. (1992). *First verbs: A case study of early grammatical development.* New York: Cambridge University Press.

Tomasello, M. (1999). Having intentions, understanding intentions, and understanding communicative intentions. In P. D. Zelazo, J. W. Astington, & J. Wilde (Eds.), *Developing theories of intention: Social understanding and self-control* (pp. 63–75). Mahwah, NJ: Erlbaum.

Tomasello, M. (2000). Do young children have adult syntactic competence? *Cognition, 74,* 209–253.

Tomasello, M. (2003). *Constructing a language: A usage-based theory of language acquisition.* Cambridge, MA: Harvard University Press.

Tomasello, M. (2005). Beyond formalities: The case of language acquisition. *Linguistic Review, 22,* 183–197.

Tomasello, M. (2006). Acquiring linguistic constructions. In D. Kuhn & R. Siegler (Eds.), *Handbook of child psychology: Vol. 2: Cognition, perception, and language* (6th ed., pp. 255–298). Hoboken, NJ: Wiley.

Tomasello, M. (2011). Language development. In U. Goswami (Ed.), *Wiley-Blackwell handbook of childhood cognitive development* (2nd ed., pp. 239–257). Malden, MA: Wiley-Blackwell.

Tomasello, M., & Akhtar, N. (1995). Two-year-olds use pragmatic cues to differentiate reference to objects and actions. *Cognitive Development, 10,* 201–224.

Tomasello, M., Akhtar, N., Dodson, K., & Rekau, L. (1997). Differential productivity in young children's use of nouns and verbs. *Journal of Child Language, 24,* 373–387.

Tomasello, M., & Brandt, S. (2009). Flexibility in the semantics and syntax of children's early verb use. *Monographs of the Society for Research in Child Development, 72*(2, Serial No. 293), 113–126.

Tomasello, M., Call, J., & Hare, B. (2003). Chimpanzees understand psychological states—the question is which ones and to what extent. *Trends in Cognitive Sciences, 7,* 153–156.

Tomasello, M., Carpenter, M., & Liszkowski, U. (2007). A new look at infant pointing. *Child Development, 78,* 705–722.

Tong, S., McMichael, A. J., & Baghurst, P. A. (2000). Interactions between environmental lead exposure and sociodemographic factors on cognitive development. *Archives of Environmental Health, 55,* 330–335.

Tong, V. T., Jones, J. R., Dietz, P. M., D'Angelo, D., & Bombard, J. M. (2009, May 29). Trends in smoking before, during, and after pregnancy—Pregnancy Risk Assessment Monitoring System (PRAMS), United States, 31 Sites, 2000–2005. *Morbidity and Mortality Weekly Report, 58* (No. SS-4).

Toomela, A. (2002). Drawing as a verbally mediated activity: A study of relationships between verbal, motor, visuospatial skills and drawing in children. *International Journal of Behavioral Development, 26,* 234–247.

Topál, J., Gergely, G., Miklósi, A., Erdöhegyi, A., & Csibra, G. (2008). Infants' perseverative search errors are induced by pragmatic misinterpretation. *Science, 321,* 1831–1834.

Torney-Purta, J. (2002). The school's role in developing civic engagement: A study of adolescents in twenty-eight countries. *Applied Developmental Science, 6,* 203–212.

Torney-Purta, J., Barber, C. H., & Wilkenfeld, B. (2007). Latino adolescents' civic development in the United States: Research results from the IEA Civic Education Study. *Journal of Youth and Adolescence, 36,* 111–125.

Torrance, E. P. (1988). The nature of creativity as manifest in its testing. In R. J. Sternberg (Ed.), *The nature of creativity: Contemporary psychological perspectives* (pp. 43–75). New York: Cambridge University Press.

Tottenham, N., Hare, T. A., & Casey, B. J. (2009). A developmental perspective on human amygdala function. In P. J. Whalen & E. A. Phelps (Eds.), *The human amygdala* (pp. 107–117). New York: Guilford Press.

Tottenham, N., Hare, T. A., Millner, A., Gilhooly, T., Zevin, J. D., & Casey, B. J. (2011). Elevated amygdala response to faces following early deprivation. *Developmental Science, 14,* 190–204.

Touwen, B. C. L. (1984). Primitive reflexes—conceptual or semantic problem? In H. F. R. Prechtl (Ed.), *Continuity of neural functions from prenatal to postnatal life* (Clinics in Developmental Medicine, No. 94, pp. 115–125). Philadelphia: Lippincott.

Townsend, D. A., & Rovee-Collier, C. (2007). *The transitivity of 6-month-old infants' preconditioned memories and deferred imitation.* Paper presented at the annual meeting of the Eastern Psychological Association, Philadelphia.

Tracy, J. L., Robins, R. W., & Lagattuta, K. H. (2005). Can children recognize pride? *Emotion, 5,* 251–257.

Trainor, L. J. (2007). Do preferred beat rate and entrainment to the beat have a common origin in movement? *Empirical Musicology Review, 2,* 17–20.

Traurig, M., Mack, J., Hanson, R. L., Ghoussaini, M., Meyre, D., Knowler, W., et al. (2009). Common variation in SIM1 is reproducibly associated with BMI in Pima Indians. *Diabetes, 58,* 1682–1689.

Trautner, H. M., Gervai, J., & Nemeth, R. (2003). Appearance–reality distinction and development of gender constancy understanding in children. *International Journal of Behavioral Development, 27,* 275–283.

Trautner, H. M., Ruble, D. N., Cyphers, L., Kirsten, B., Behrendt, R., & Hartmann, P. (2005). Rigidity and flexibility of gender stereotypes in childhood: Developmental or differential? *Infant and Child Development, 14,* 365–381.

Trautwein, U., Ludtke, O., Marsh, H. W., Koller, O., & Baumert, J. (2006). Tracking, grading, and student motivation: Using group composition and status to predict self-concept and interest in ninth-grade mathematics. *Journal of Educational Psychology, 98,* 788–806.

Treasure, J., & Schmidt, U. (2005). Anorexia nervosa. *Clinical Evidence, 13,* 1148–1157.

Treffert, D. A. (2010). *Islands of genius: The bountiful mind of the autistic, acquired, and sudden savant.* London: Jessica Kingsley.

Trehub, S. E. (2001). Musical predispositions in infancy. *Annals of the New York Academy of Sciences, 930,* 1–16.

Tremblay, L., & Frigon, J.-Y. (2005). Precocious puberty in adolescent girls: A biomarker of later psychosocial adjustment problems. *Child Psychiatry and Human Development, 36,* 73–94.

Tremblay, R. E. (2000). The development of aggressive behaviour during childhood: What have we learned in the past century? *International Journal of Behavioral Development, 24,* 129–141.

Tremblay, R. E. (2004). Decade of behavior distinguished lecture: Development of physical aggression during infancy. *Infant Mental Health Journal, 25,* 399–407.

Tremblay, R. E., Japel, C., Perusse, D., Voivin, M., Zoccolillo, M., Montplaisir, J., & McDuff, P. (1999). The search for the age of "onset" of physical aggression: Rousseau and Bandura revisited. *Criminal Behavior and Mental Health, 9,* 8–23.

Tremblay, R. E., Schaal, B., Boulerice, B., Arseneault, L., Soussignan, R., & Perusse, D. (1997). Male physical aggression, social dominance, and testosterone levels at puberty: A developmental perspective. In A. Raine & P. A. Brennan (Eds.), *Biosocial bases of violence. NATO ASI Series: Series A: Life sciences* (Vol. 292, pp. 271–291). New York: Plenum.

Trent, K., & Harlan, S. L. (1994). Teenage mothers in nuclear and extended households. *Journal of Family Issues, 15,* 309–337.

Trentacosta, C. J., & Shaw, D. S. (2009). Emotional self-regulation, peer rejection, and antisocial behavior: Developmental associations from early childhood to early adolescence. *Journal of Applied Developmental Psychology, 30,* 356–365.

Trevarthen, C. (2003). Infant psychology is an evolving culture. *Human Development, 46,* 233–246.

Triandis, H. C. (2005). Issues in individualism and collectivism research. In R. M. Sorrentino, D. Cohen, J. M. Olson, & M. P. Zanna (Eds.), *Culture and social behavior: The Ontario Symposium* (Vol. 10, pp. 207–225). Mahwah, NJ: Erlbaum.

Triandis, H. C. (2007). Culture and psychology: A history of their relationship. In S. Kitayama (Ed.), *Handbook of cultural psychology* (pp. 59–76). New York: Guilford Press.

Trickett, P. K., Noll, J., Reiffman, A., & Putnam, F. (2001). Variants of intrafamilial sexual abuse experiences: Implications for short- and long-term development. *Development and Psychopathology, 13,* 1001–1019.

Trickett, P. K., & Putnam, F. W. (1998). Developmental consequences of child sexual abuse. In P. K. Trickett & C. J. Schellenbach (Eds.), *Violence against children in the family and community* (pp. 39–56). Washington, DC: American Psychological Association.

Trionfi, G., & Reese, E. (2009). A good story: Children with imaginary companions create richer narratives. *Child Development, 80,* 1301–1313.

Trivers, R. L. (1971). The evolution of reciprocal altruism. *Quarterly Review of Biology, 46,* 35–57.

Trocomé, N., & Wolfe, D. (2002). *Child maltreatment in Canada: The Canadian Incidence Study of Reported Child Abuse and Neglect.* Retrieved from http://www.hc-sc.gc.ca/pphb-dgspsp/cm-vee

Troiano, R. P., Berrigan, D., Dodd, K. W., Mâsse, L. C., Tillert, T., & McDowell, M. (2007). Physical activity in the United States measured by accelerometer. *Medicine and Science in Sports and Exercise, 40,* 181–188.

Tronick, E. Z., Morelli, G. A., & Ivey, P. (1992). The Efe forager infant and toddler's pattern of social relationships: Multiple and simultaneous. *Developmental Psychology, 28,* 568–577.

Tronick, E. Z., Thomas, R. B., & Daltabuit, M. (1994). The Quechua manta pouch: A caretaking practice for buffering the Peruvian infant against the multiple stressors of high altitude. *Child Development, 65,* 1005–1013.

Troop-Gordon, W., & Asher, S. R. (2005). Modifications in children's goals when encountering obstacles to conflict resolution. *Child Development, 76,* 568–582.

Troseth, G. L. (2003). Getting a clear picture: Young children's understanding of a televised image. *Developmental Science, 6,* 247–253.

Troseth, G. L., & DeLoache, J. S. (1998). The medium can obscure the message: Young children's understanding of video. *Child Development, 69,* 950–965.

Troseth, G. L., Saylor, M. M., & Archer, A. H. (2006). Young children's use of video as a source of socially relevant information. *Child Development, 77,* 786–799.

Troutman, D. R., & Fletcher, A. C. (2010). Context and companionship in children's

short-term versus long-term friendships. *Journal of Social and Personal Relationships, 27,* 1060–1074.

True, M. M., Pisani, L., & Oumar, F. (2001). Infant–mother attachment among the Dogon of Mali. *Child Development, 72,* 1451–1466.

Truglio, R. (2000, April). *Research guides "Sesame Street."* Public lecture presented as part of the Consider the Children program, Illinois State University, Normal, IL.

Trzesniewski, K. H., Donnellan, M. B., & Robins, R. W. (2003). Stability of self-esteem across the life span. *Journal of Personality and Social Psychology, 84,* 205–220.

Tsethlikai, M., & Greenhoot, A. F. (2006). The influence of another's perspective on children's recall of previously misconstrued events. *Developmental Psychology, 42,* 732–745.

Tucker, C. J., McHale, S. M., & Crouter, A. C. (2001). Conditions of siblings support in adolescence. *Journal of Family Psychology, 15,* 254–271.

Tucker, C. J., McHale, S. M., & Crouter, A. C. (2003). Dimensions of mothers' and fathers' differential treatment of siblings: Links with adolescents' sex-typed personal qualities. *Family Relations, 52,* 82–89.

Tudge, J., & Scrimsher, S. (2003). Lev S. Vygotsky on education: A cultural-historical, interpersonal, and individual approach to development. In B. J. Zimmerman & D. H. Schunk (Eds.), *Educational psychology: A century of contributions* (pp. 207–228). Mahwah, NJ: Erlbaum.

Turati, C., Cassia, V. M., Simion, F., & Leo, I. (2006). Newborns' face recognition: Role of inner and outer facial features. *Child Development, 77,* 297–311.

Turiel, E. (2006). The development of morality. In N. Eisenberg (Ed.), *Handbook of child psychology: Vol. 3. Social, emotional, and personality development* (6th ed., pp. 789–857). Hoboken, NJ: Wiley.

Turkheimer, E., Haley, A., Waldron, M., D'Onofrio, B., & Gottesman, I. I. (2003). Socioeconomic status modifies heritability of IQ in young children. *Psychological Science, 14,* 623–628.

Turkle, S. (1995). *Life on the screen: Identity in the age of the Internet.* New York: Simon & Schuster.

Turnbull, K. P., Anthony, A. B., Justice, L., & Bowles, R. (2009). Preschoolers' exposure to language stimulation in classrooms serving at-risk children: The contribution of group size and activity context. *Early Education and Development, 20,* 53–79.

Turnbull, M., Hart, D., & Lapkin, S. (2003). Grade 6 French immersion students' performance on large-scale reading, writing, and mathematics tests: Building explanations. *Alberta Journal of Educational Research, 49,* 6–23.

Turner, P. J., & Gervai, J. (1995). A multidimensional study of gender typing in preschool children and their parents: Personality, attitudes, preferences, behavior, and cultural differences. *Developmental Psychology, 31,* 759–772.

Turner, P. J., Gervai, J., & Hinde, R. A. (1993). Gender typing in young children: Preferences, behaviour and cultural differences. *British Journal of Developmental Psychology, 11,* 323–342.

Turner, R. N., Hewstone, M., & Voci, A. (2007). Reducing explicit and implicit

out-group prejudice via direct and extended contact: The mediating role of self-disclosure and intergroup anxiety. *Journal of Personality and Social Psychology, 93,* 369–388.

Turner-Bowker, D. M. (1996). Gender stereotyped descriptors in children's picture books: Does "Curious Jane" exist in the literature? *Sex Roles, 35,* 461–488.

Tuyen, J. M., & Bisgard, K. (2003). Community setting: Pertussis outbreak. Atlanta, GA: U.S. Centers for Disease Control and Prevention. Retrieved from http://www.cdc.gov/nip/publications/pertussis/chapter10.pdf

Twenge, J. M., & Campbell, W. K. (2001). Age and birth cohort differences in self-esteem: A cross-temporal meta-analysis. *Personality and Social Psychology Review, 5,* 321–344.

Twenge, J. M., & Crocker, J. (2002). Race and self-esteem: Meta-analyses comparing whites, blacks, Hispanics, Asians, and America Indians and comment on Gray-Little and Hafdahl (2000). *Psychological Bulletin, 128,* 371–408.

Twyman, K., Saylor, C., Taylor, L. A., & Comeaux, D. (2010). Comparing children and adolescents engaged in cyberbullying to matched peers. *Cyberpsychology, Behavior, and Social Networking, 13,* 195–199.

Tychsen, L. (2001). Critical periods for development of visual acuity, depth perception, and eye tracking. In D. B. Bailey, Jr., J. T. Bruer, F. J. Symons, & J. W. Lichtman (Eds.), *Critical thinking about critical periods* (pp. 67–82). Baltimore: Paul H. Brookes.

Tzuriel, D. (2001). *Dynamic assessment of young children.* New York: Kluwer Academic.

Tzuriel, D., & Egozi, G. (2010). Gender differences in spatial ability of young children: The effects of training and processing strategies. *Child Development, 81,* 1417–1430.

Tzuriel, D., & Kaufman, R. (1999). Mediated learning and cognitive modifiability: Dynamic assessment of young Ethiopian immigrant children to Israel. *Journal of Cross-Cultural Psychology, 30,* 359–380.

Uauy, R., Kain, J., Mericq, V., Rojas, J., & Corvalán, C. (2008). Nutrition, child growth, and chronic disease prevention. *Annals of Medicine, 40,* 11–20.

Udechuku, A., Nguyen, T., Hill, R., & Szego, K. (2010). Antidepressants in pregnancy: A systematic review. *Australian and New Zealand Journal of Psychiatry, 44,* 978–996.

Ullrich-French, S., & Smith, A. L. (2006). Perceptions of relationships with parents and peers in youth sport: Independent and combined prediction of motivational outcomes. *Psychology of Sport and Exercise, 7,* 193–214.

Umaña-Taylor, A. J., & Alfaro, E. C. (2006). Ethnic identity among U.S. Latino adolescents: Measurement and implications for well-being. In F. A. Villarruel & T. Luster (Eds.), *The crisis in youth mental health: Critical issues and effective programs: Vol. 2. Disorders in adolescence* (pp. 195–211). Westport, CT: Praeger.

Umaña-Taylor, A. J., & Updegraff, K. A. (2007). Latino adolescents' mental health: Exploring the interrelations among discrimination, ethnic identity, cultural orientation, self-esteem, and depressive symptoms. *Journal of Adolescence, 30,* 549–567.

Underhill, K., Montgomery, P., & Operario, D. (2007). Sexual abstinence only programmes to prevent HIV infection in high-income countries: Systematic review. *British Medical Journal, 335,* 248.

Underwood, M. K. (2003). *Social aggression among girls.* New York: Guilford.

UNICEF (United Nations Children's Fund). (2007). *An overview of child well-being in rich countries, Innocenti Report Card 7.* Florence, Italy: UNICEF Innocenti Research Centre.

UNICEF (United Nations Children's Fund). (2009). *Infant and young child feeding 2000–2007.* Retrieved from www.childinfo.org/breastfeeding_countrydata.php

UNICEF (United Nations Children's Fund). (2010a). *Children and AIDS: Fifth stocktaking report.* New York: United Nations.

UNICEF (United Nations Children's Fund). (2010b). *The children left behind: A league table of inequality in the world's richest countries, Innocenti Report Card 9.* Florence, Italy: UNICEF Innocenti Research Centre.

UNICEF (United Nations Children's Fund). (2011). *Children in conflict and emergencies.* Retrieved from www.unicef.org/protection/index_armedconflict.html

United Nations. (2008). *World population prospects: The 2006 revision.* Retrieved from http://www.un.org/esa/population/publications/wpp2006/wpp2006.htm

U.S. Census Bureau. (2011a). International data base. Retrieved from http://www.census.gov/ipc/www/idb

U.S. Census Bureau. (2011b). *Statistical abstract of the United States* (130th ed.). Washington, DC: U.S. Government Printing Office.

U.S. Centers for Disease Control and Prevention. (2007). *School Health Policies and Programs Study.* Atlanta: Author.

U.S. Centers for Disease Control and Prevention. (2010). *Breastfeeding report card—United States, 2010.* Retrieved from www.cdc.gov/breastfeeding/data/reportcard.htm

U.S. Centers for Disease Control and Prevention. (2011, April). Preventing pregnancy in the U.S. *Vital Signs.* Retrieved from www.cdc.gov/VitalSigns/TeenPregnancy/index.html

U.S. Department of Agriculture. (2009). *Frequently asked questions about WIC.* Retrieved from http://www.fns.usda.gov/wic/FAQs/faq.htm

U.S. Department of Agriculture. (2011a). *Expenditures on children by families, 2010.* Retrieved from www.cnpp.usda.gov

U.S. Department of Agriculture. (2011b). *Food security in the United States: Key statistics and graphics.* Retrieved from http://www.ers.usda.gov/Briefing/FoodSecurity/stats_graphs.htm

U.S. Department of Education. (2007). *The nation's report card: Writing 2007.* Retrieved from nces.edu.gov/pubsearch/pubsinfo.asp?pubid=2008468

U.S. Department of Education. (2008). *The condition of education.* Retrieved from nces.ed.gov/programs/coe/list/i4.asp

U.S. Department of Education. (2009). *The nation's report card: Mathematics 2009.* Retrieved from nces.ed.gov/nationsreportcard/mathematics

U.S. Department of Education. (2010). *The nation's report card: Reading 2010.* Retrieved from nces.ed.gov/pubsearch/pubsinfo.asp?pubid=2010458

U.S. Department of Education. (2011a). *The condition of education, 2011*. Retrieved from http://nces.ed.gov/pubsearch/pubsinfo.asp?pubid=2011033

U.S. Department of Education. (2011b). *Digest of education statistics: 2010*. Washington, DC: U.S. Government Printing Office.

U.S. Department of Health and Human Services. (2000). 2000 CDC growth charts. Retrieved from http://www.cdc.gov/growthcharts

U.S. Department of Health and Human Services. (2009a). *Benefits of breastfeeding*. Retrieved from http://www.womenshealth.gov/breastfeeding/benefits

U.S. Department of Health and Human Services. (2009b). *Sexually transmitted disease surveillance, 2008*. Atlanta, GA: Author.

U.S. Department of Health and Human Services. (2010a). Births: Final data for 2008. *National Vital Statistics Reports, 59*(1).

U.S. Department of Health and Human Services. (2010b). *Child maltreatment 2009*. Retrieved from http://www.acf.hhs.gov/programs/cb/pubs/cm09/index.htm

U.S. Department of Health and Human Services. (2010c). Diagnoses of HIV infection and AIDS in the United States and dependent areas, 2008. *HIV Surveillance Report, Vol. 20*. Retrieved from http://www.cdc.gov/hiv/surveillance/resources/reports/2008report/index.htm

U.S. Department of Health and Human Services. (2010d). *Head Start Impact Study: Final report*. Washington, DC: U.S. Government Printing Office.

U.S. Department of Health and Human Services. (2010e). National, state, and local vaccination coverage among children aged 19–35 months—United States, 2009. *Morbidity and Mortality Weekly Report, 59*, 1171–1177.

U.S. Department of Health and Human Services. (2010f). *VitalStats—mortality*. Retrieved from http://www.cdc.gov/nchs/data_access/vitalstats/VitalStats_Mortality.htm

U.S. Department of Health and Human Services. (2010g, June 4). Youth Risk Behavior Surveillance—United States, 2009. *Morbidity and Mortality Weekly Report, 59*, No. SS-5, 1–142.

U.S. Department of Health and Human Services. (2011a). *Facts about Down syndrome*. Retrieved from www.cdc.gov/ncbddd/birthdefects/DownSyndrome.html

U.S. Department of Health and Human Services. (2011b). *The Surgeon General's call to action to prevent and decrease overweight and obesity: Overweight children and adolescents*. Retrieved from www.surgeongeneral.gov/topics/obesity/calltoaction/fact_adolescents.htm

U.S. Department of Justice. (2010). *Crime in the United States, 2009*. Retrieved from www2.fbi.gov/ucr/cius2009

Updegraff, K. A., McHale, S. M., & Crouter, A. C. (1996). Gender roles in marriage: What do they mean for girls' and boys' school achievement? *Journal of Youth and Adolescence, 25*, 73–88.

Usher-Seriki, K. K., Bynum, M. S., & Callands, T. A. (2008). Mother–daughter communication about sex and sexual intercourse among middle- to upper-class African American girls. *Journal of Family Issues, 29*, 901–917.

Usta, I. M., & Nassar, A. H. (2008). Advanced maternal age. Part I: Obstetric complications. *American Journal of Perinatology, 25*, 521–534.

Uttal, D. H., Gregg, V. H., Tan, L. S., Chamberlin, M. H., & Sines, A. (2001). Connecting the dots: Children's use of a systematic figure to facilitate mapping and search. *Developmental Psychology, 37*, 338–350.

Vaidyanathan, R. (1988). Development of forms and functions of interrogatives in children: A language study of Tamil. *Journal of Child Language, 15*, 533–549.

Vaidyanathan, R. (1991). Development of forms and functions of negation in the early stages of language acquisition: A study of Tamil. *Journal of Child Language, 18*, 51–66.

Vaillancourt, T., Brendgen, M., Boivin, M., & Tremblay, R. E. (2003). A longitudinal confirmatory factor analysis of indirect and physical aggression: Evidence of two factors over time? *Child Development, 74*, 1628–1638.

Vaillancourt, T., Brittain, H., Bennett, L., Arnocky, S., McDougall, P., Hymel, S., et al. (2010a). Places to avoid: Population-based study of student reports of unsafe and high bullying areas at school. *Canadian Journal of School Psychology, 25*, 40–54.

Vaillancourt, T., Clinton, J., McDougall, P., Schmidt, L. A., & Hymel, S. (2010b). The neurobiology of peer victimization and rejection. In S. Jimerson, S. M. Swearer, & D. L. Espelage (Eds.), *Handbook of bullying in schools: An international perspective* (pp. 293–304). New York: Routledge.

Vaillancourt, T., & Hymel, S. (2006). Aggression and social status: The moderating roles of sex and peer-valued characteristics. *Aggressive Behavior, 32*, 396–408.

Vaillancourt, T., McDougall, P., Hymel, S., & Sunderani, S. (2010c). Respect or fear? The relationship between power and bullying behavior. In Jimerson, S. M. Swearer, & D. L. Espelage (Eds.), *Handbook of bullying in schools: An international perspective* (pp. 211–222). New York: Routledge.

Vaillancourt, T., Miller, J. L., & Boyle, M. H. (2009). Examining the heterotypic continuity of aggression using teacher reports: Results from a national Canadian study. *Social Development, 18*, 164–180.

Vaish, A., Carpenter, M., & Tomasello, M. (2009). Sympathy through affective perspective taking and its relation to prosocial behavior in toddlers. *Developmental Psychology, 45*, 534–543.

Vaish, A., & Striano, T. (2004). Is visual reference necessary? Contributions of facial versus vocal cues in 12-month-olds' social referencing behavior. *Developmental Science, 7*, 261–269.

Vakil, E., Blachstein, H., Sheinman, M., & Greenstein, Y. (2009). Developmental changes in attention tests norms: Implications for the structure of attention: *Child Neuropsychology, 15*, 21–39.

Valdés, G. (1998). The world outside and inside schools: Language and immigrant children. *Educational Researcher, 27*(6), 4–18.

Valentine, J. C., DuBois, D. L., & Cooper, H. (2004). The relation between self-beliefs and academic achievement: A meta-analytic review. *Educational Psychologist, 39*, 111–133.

Valian, V. (1991). Syntactic subjects in the early speech of American and Italian children. *Cognition, 40*, 21–81.

Valian, V. (1999). Input and language acquisition. In W. C. Ritchie & T. K. Bhatia (Eds.), *Handbook of child language acquisition* (pp. 497–530). San Diego: Academic Press.

Valian, V. (2005). When opportunity knocks twice: Two-year-olds' repetition of sentence subjects. *Journal of Child Language, 32*, 617–641.

Valiente, C., Eisenberg, N., Fabes, R. A., Shepard, S. A., Cumberland, A., & Losoya, S. H. (2004). Prediction of children's empathy-related responding from their effortful control and parents' expressivity. *Developmental Psychology, 40*, 911–926.

Valiente, C., Lemery-Chalfant, K., & Swanson, J. (2010). Prediction of kindergartners' academic achievement from their effortful control and emotionality: Evidence for direct and moderated relations. *Journal of Educational Psychology, 102*, 550–560.

Valiente, C., Lemery-Chalfant, K., Swanson, J., & Reiser, M. (2008). Prediction of children's academic competence from their effortful control, relationships, and classroom participation. *Journal of Educational Psychology, 100*, 67–77.

Valkenburg, P. M., & Peter, J. (2007a). Internet communication and its relation to well-being: Identifying some underlying mechanisms. *Media Psychology, 9*, 43–58.

Valkenburg, P. M., & Peter, J. (2007b). Preadolescents' and adolescents' online communication and their closeness to friends. *Developmental Psychology, 43*, 267–277.

Valkenburg, P. M., & Peter, J. (2009). Social consequences of the Internet for adolescents: A decade of research. *Current Directions in Psychological Science, 18*, 1–5.

Valkenburg, P. M., & Peter, J. (2011). Online communication among adolescents: An integrated model of its attraction, opportunities, and risks. *Journal of Adolescent Health, 48*, 121–127.

van Aken, C., Junger, M., Verhoeven, M., van Aken, M. A. G., & Deković, M. (2007). The interactive effects of temperament and maternal parenting on toddlers' externalizing behaviours. *Infant and Child Development, 16*, 553–572.

Van de Vijver, P. J. R., Hofer, J., & Chasiotis, A. (2010). Methodology. In M. H. Bornstein (Ed.), *Handbook of cultural developmental science* (pp. 21–37). New York: Psychology Press.

van den Akker, A. L. Deković, M., Prinzie, P., & Asscher, J. J. (2010). Toddlers' temperament profiles: Stability and relations to negative and positive parenting. *Journal of Abnormal Child Psychology, 38*, 485–495.

Van den Bergh, B. R. H. (2004). High antenatal maternal anxiety is related to ADHD symptoms, externalizing problems, and anxiety in 8- and 9-year-olds. *Child Development, 75*, 1085–1097.

Van den Bergh, B. R. H., & De Rycke, L. (2003). Measuring the multidimensional self-concept and global self-worth of 6- to 8-year-olds. *Journal of Genetic Psychology, 164*, 201–225.

Van den Bergh, B. R. H., Van Calster, B., Smits, T., Van Huffel, S., & Lagae, L. (2008). Antenatal maternal anxiety is related to HPA-axis dysregulation and self-reported depressive symptoms in adolescence: A prospective study on the fetal origins of depressed mood. *Neuropsychopharmacology, 33*, 536–545.

van den Bergh, E. D., Hornstra, L., Voeten, M., & Holland, R. W. (2010). The implicit prejudiced attitudes of teachers: Relations to teacher expectations and the ethnic achievement gap. *American Educational Research Journal, 47*, 497–527.

van den Boom, D. C., & Hoeksma, J. B. (1994). The effect of infant irritability on mother–infant interaction: A growth-curve analysis. *Developmental Psychology, 30*, 581–590.

van den Dries, L., Juffer, F., van IJzendoorn, M. H., & Bakermans-Kranenburg, M. J. (2009). Fostering security? A meta-analysis of attachment in adopted children. *Children and Youth Services Review, 31*, 410–421.

van den Heuvel, M. P., Stam, C. J., Kahn, R. S., & Hulshoff Pol, H. E. (2009). Efficiency of functional brain networks and intellectual performance. *Journal of Neuroscience, 29*, 7619–7624.

van der Meer, A. L. (1997). Keeping the arm in the limelight: Advanced visual control of arm movements in neonates. *European Journal of Paediatric Neurology, 4*, 103–108.

van der Wal, M. F., van Eijsden, M., & Bonsel, G. J. (2007). Stress and emotional problems during pregnancy and excessive infant crying. *Developmental and Behavioral Pediatrics, 28*, 431–437.

Van Eyk, J., & Dunn, M. J. (Eds.). (2008). *Clinical proteomics*. Weinheim, Germany: Wiley-VCH.

Van Goozen, S. H. M., Cohen-Kettenis, P. T., Gooren, I. J. G., Frijda, N. H., & Van De Poll, N. E. (1995). Gender differences in behaviour: Activating effects of cross-sex hormones. *Psychoneuroendocrinology, 20*, 171–177.

Van Hulle, C. A., Goldsmith, H. H., & Lemery, K. S. (2004). Genetic, environmental, and gender effects on individual differences in toddler expressive language. *Journal of Speech, Language, and Hearing Research, 47*, 904–912.

van IJzendoorn, M. H. (1995). Adult attachment representations, parental responsiveness, and infant attachment: A meta-analysis on the predictive validity of the adult attachment interview. *Psychological Bulletin, 117*, 387–403.

van IJzendoorn, M. H., & Bakermans-Kranenburg, M. J. (2006). DRD4 7-repeat polymorphism moderates the association between maternal unresolved loss or trauma and infant disorganization. *Attachment and Human Development, 8*, 291–307.

van IJzendoorn, M. H., & Hubbard, F. O. A. (2000). Are infant crying and maternal responsiveness during the first year related to infant–mother attachment at 15 months? *Attachment and Human Development, 2*, 371–391.

van IJzendoorn, M. H., Juffer, F., & Poelhuis, C. W. K. (2005). Adoption and cognitive development: A meta-analytic comparison of adopted and nonadopted children's IQ and school performance. *Psychological Bulletin, 131*, 301–316.

van IJzendoorn, M. H., & Kroonenberg, P. M. (1988). Cross-cultural patterns of attachment: A meta-analysis of the Strange Situation. *Child Development, 59*, 147–156.

van IJzendoorn, M. H., & Sagi, A. (1999). Cross-cultural patterns of attachment. In J. Cassidy & P. R. Shaver (Eds.), *Handbook of attachment: Theory, research, and clinical applications* (pp. 713–734). New York: Guilford.

van IJzendoorn, M. H., & Sagi-Schwartz, A. (2008). Cross-cultural patterns of attachment: Universal and contextual dimensions. In J. Cassidy & P. R. Shaver (Eds.), *Handbook of attachment* (2nd ed., pp. 880–905). New York: Guilford.

van IJzendoorn, M. H., Schuengel, C., & Bakermans-Kranenburg, M. J. (1999). Disorganized attachment in early childhood: Meta-analysis of precursors, concomitants, and sequelae. *Development and Psychopathology, 11*, 225–249.

van IJzendoorn, M. H., Vereijken, C. M. J. L., Bakermans-Kranenburg, M. J., & Riksen-Walraven, J. M. (2004). Assessing attachment security with the Attachment Q-Sort: Meta-analytic evidence for the validity of the observer AQS. *Child Development, 75*, 1188–1213.

Van Lange, P. A. M., Bekkers, R., Schuyt, T. N. M., & Van Vugt, M. (2007). From games to giving: Social value orientation predicts donations to noble causes. *Basic and Applied Social Psychology, 29*, 375–384.

Van Vugt, M., & Van Lange, P. A. M. (2006). The altruism puzzle: Psychological adaptations for prosocial behavior. In M. Schaller, J. A. Simpson, & D. T. Kenrick (Eds.), *Evolution and social psychology* (pp. 237–261). New York: Psychology Press.

Vandell, D. L., Belsky, J., Burchinal, M., Steinberg, L., Vandergrift, N., & NICHD Early Child Care Research Network. (2010). Do effects of early child care extend to age 15 years? Results from the NICHD Study of Early Child Care and Youth Development. *Child Development, 81*, 737–756.

Vandell, D. L., & Mueller, E. C. (1995). Peer play and friendships during the first two years. In H. C. Foot, A. J. Chapman, & J. R. Smith (Eds.), *Friendship and social relations in children* (pp. 181–208). New Brunswick, NJ: Transaction.

Vandell, D. L., & Posner, J. K. (1999). Conceptualization and measurement of children's after-school environments. In S. L. Friedman & T. D. Wachs (Eds.), *Measuring environment across the life span* (pp. 167–196). Washington, DC: American Psychological Association.

Vandell, D. L., & Shumow, L. (1999). After-school child care programs. *Future of Children, 9*(2), 64–80.

Vandell, D. L., Reisner, E. R., & Pierce, K. M. (2007). *Outcomes linked to high-quality after-school programs: Longitudinal findings from the Study of Promising After-School Programs.* Retrieved from www.gse.uci.edu/childcare/pdf/afterschool/PP%20Longitudinal%20Findings%20Final%20Report.pdf

Vandell, D. L., Reisner, E. R., Pierce, K. M., Brown, B. B., Lee, D., Bolt, D., & Pechman, E. M. (2006). *The study of promising after-school programs: Examination of longer term outcomes after two years of program experiences.* Madison, WI: University of Wisconsin. Retrieved from http://childcare.wceruw.org/pdf/pp/year_3_report_final.pdf

Vanderbilt-Adriance, E., & Shaw, D. S. (2008). Protective factors and the development of resilience in the context of neighborhood disadvantage. *Journal of Abnormal Child Psychology, 36*, 887–901.

Varela-Silva, M. I., Frisancho, A. R., Bogin, B., Chatkoff, D., Smith, P. K., Dickinson, F., & Winham, D. (2007). Behavioral, environmental, metabolic, and intergenerational components of early life undernutrition leading to later obesity in developing nations and in minority groups in the U.S.A. *Collegium Antropologicum, 31*, 39–46.

Varendi, H., & Porter, R. H. (2001). Breast odour as the only maternal stimulus elicits crawling toward the odour source. *Acta Paediatrica, 90*, 372–375.

Varnhagen, C. (2007). Children and the Internet. In J. Gackenbach (Ed.), *Psychology and the Internet* (2nd ed., pp, 37–54). Amsterdam: Elsevier.

Vartanian, L. R. (1997). Separation–individuation, social support, and adolescent egocentrism: An exploratory study. *Journal of Early Adolescence, 17*, 245–270.

Vartanian, L. R., & Powlishta, K. K. (1996). A longitudinal examination of the social-cognitive foundations of adolescent egocentrism. *Journal of Early Adolescence, 16*, 157–178.

Vaughn, B. E., Bost, K. K., & van IJzendoorn, M. H. (2008). Attachment and temperament. In J. Cassidy & P. R. Shaver (Eds.), *Handbook of attachment: Theory, research, and clinical applications* (2nd ed., pp. 192–216). New York: Guilford.

Vaughn, B. E., Colvin, T. N., Azria, M. R., Caya, L., & Krzysik, L. (2001). Dyadic analyses of friendship in a sample of preschool-age children attending Head Start: Correspondence between measures and implications for social competence. *Child Development, 72*, 862–878.

Vaughn, B. E., Kopp, C. B., & Krakow, J. B. (1984). The emergence and consolidation of self-control from eighteen to thirty months of age: Normative trends and individual differences. *Child Development, 55*, 990–1004.

Vaughn, S., & Klingner, J. K. (1998). Students' perceptions of inclusion and resource room settings. *Journal of Special Education, 32*, 79–88.

Vazonyi, A. T., Hibbert, J. R., & Snider, J. B. (2003). Exotic enterprise no more? Adolescent reports of family and parenting processes from youth in four countries. *Journal of Research on Adolescence, 13*, 129–160.

Veenstra, R., Lindenberg, S., Munniksma, A., & Dijkstra, J. K. (2010). The complex relation between bullying, victimization, acceptance, and rejection: Giving special attention to status, affection, and sex differences. *Child Development, 81*, 480–486.

Velderman, M. K., Bakermans-Kranenburg, M. J., Juffer, F., & van IJzendoorn, M. H. (2006). Effects of attachment-based interventions on maternal sensitivity and infant attachment: Differential susceptibility of highly reactive infants. *Journal of Family Psychology, 20*, 266–274.

Velleman, R. D. B., Templeton, L. J., & Copello, A. G. (2005). The role of the family in preventing and intervening with substance use and misuse: A comprehensive review of family interventions, with a focus on young people. *Drug and Alcohol Review, 24*, 93–109.

Venet, M., & Markovits, H. (2001). Understanding uncertainty with abstract conditional premises. *Merrill-Palmer Quarterly, 47*, 74–99.

Venezia, M., Messinger, D. S., Thorp, D., & Mundy, P. (2004). The development of anticipatory smiling. *Infancy, 6*, 397–406.

Veneziano, R. A. (2003). The importance of paternal warmth. *Cross-Cultural Research, 37*, 265–281.

Vereijken, B., & Adolph, K. E. (1999). Transitions in the development of locomotion. In G. J. P. Savelsbergh, H. L. J. van der Maas, & P. C. L. van Geert (Eds.), *Nonlinear analyses of developmental processes* (pp. 137–149). Amsterdam: Elsevier.

Verhulst, F. C. (2008). International adoption and mental health: Long-term behavioral outcome. In M. E. Garralda & J.-P. Raynaud (Eds.), *Culture and conflict in adolescent mental health* (pp. 83–105). Lanham, MD: Jason Aronson.

Veríssimo, M., & Salvaterra, F. (2006). Maternal secure-base scripts and children's attachment security in an adopted sample. *Attachment and Human Development, 8*, 261–273.

Vernon-Feagans, L., Pancsofar, N., Willoughby, M., Odom, E., Quade, A., & Cox, M. (2008). Predictors of maternal language to infants during a picture book task in the home: Family SES, child characteristics and the parenting environment. *Journal of Applied Developmental Psychology, 29*, 213–226.

Vihman, M. M. (1996). *Phonological development.* London: Blackwell.

Vinden, P. G. (1996). Junín Quechua children's understanding of mind. *Child Development, 67*, 1707–1716.

Vinden, P. G. (2002). Understanding minds and evidence for belief: A study of Mofu children in Cameroon. *International Journal of Behavioral Development, 26*, 445–452.

Visher, E. B., Visher, J. S., & Pasley, K. (2003). Remarriage families and stepparenting. In F. Walsh (Ed.), *Normal family processes* (pp. 153–175). New York: Guilford.

Visser, B. A., Ashton, M. C., & Vernon, P. A. (2006). Beyond g: Putting multiple intelligences theory to the test. *Intelligence, 34*, 487–502.

Vitaro, F., Barker, E. D., Boivin, M., Brendgen, M., & Tremblay, R. E. (2006). Do early difficult temperament and harsh parenting differentially predict reactive and proactive aggression? *Journal of Abnormal Child Psychology, 34*, 685–695.

Vitaro, F., Boivin, M., & Bukowski, W. M. (2009). The role of friendship in child and adolescent psychosocial development. In K. H. Rubin, W. M. Bukowski, & B. Laursen (Eds.), *Handbook of peer interactions, relationships, and groups* (pp. 568–585). New York: Guilford.

Vitaro, F., Brendgen, M., & Tremblay, R. E. (2000). Influence of deviant friends on delinquency: Searching for moderator variables. *Journal of Abnormal Child Psychology, 28*, 313–325.

Vitaro, F., Brendgen, M., & Tremblay, R. E. (2002). Reactive and proactive aggression: Antecedent and subsequent correlates. *Journal of Child Psychology and Psychiatry, 43*, 495–505.

Vitaro, F., Pedersen, S., & Brendgen, M. (2007). Children's disruptiveness, peer rejection, friends' deviancy, and delinquent behaviors: A process-oriented approach. *Development and Psychopathology, 19*, 433–453.

Vitrup, B., & Holden, G. W. (2010). Children's assessments of corporal punishment and other disciplinary practices: The role of age, race, SES, and exposure to spanking. *Journal of Applied Developmental Psychology, 31*, 211–220.

Vivanti, G., Nadig, A., Oonoff, S., & Rogers, S. J. (2008). What do children with autism attend to during imitation tasks? *Journal of Experimental Psychology, 101*, 186–205.

Vogel, D. A., Lake, M. A., Evans, S., & Karraker, H. (1991). Children's and adults' sex-stereotyped perceptions of infants. *Sex Roles, 24*, 605–616.

Vohr, B., Jodoin-Krauzyk, J., Tucker, R., Johnson, M. J., Topol, D., & Ahlgren, M. (2008). Early language outcomes of early-identified infants with permanent hearing loss at 12 to 16 months of age. *Pediatrics, 122*, 535–544.

Volling, B. L. (2001). Early attachment relationships as predictors of preschool children's emotion regulation with a distressed sibling. *Early Education and Development, 12*, 185–207.

Volling, B. L., & Belsky, J. (1992). Contribution of mother–child and father–child relationships to the quality of sibling interaction: A longitudinal study. *Child Development, 63*, 1209–1222.

Volling, B. L., Mahoney, A., & Rauer, A. J. (2009). Sanctification of parenting, moral socialization, and young children's conscience development. *Psychology of Religion and Spirituality, 1*, 53–68.

Volling, B. L., McElwain, N. L., & Miller, A. L. (2002). Emotion regulation in context: The jealousy complex between young siblings and its relations with child and family characteristics. *Child Development, 73*, 581–600.

Volling, B. L., McElwain, N. L., Notaro, P. C., & Herrera, C. (2002). Parents' emotional availability and infant emotional competence: Predictors of parent–infant attachment and emerging self-regulation. *Journal of Family Psychology, 16*, 447–465.

von Hofsten, C. (1993). Prospective control: A basic aspect of action development. *Human Development, 36*, 253–270.

von Hofsten, C. (2004). An action perspective on motor development. *Trends in Cognitive Sciences, 8*, 266–272.

von Hofsten, C., Viston, P., Spelke, E. S., Feng, Q., & Rosander, K. (1998). Predictive action in infancy: Tracking and reaching for moving objects. *Cognition, 67*, 255–285.

Vondra, J. I., Hommerding, K. D., & Shaw, D. S. (1999). Stability and change in infant attachment in a low-income sample. In J. I. Vondra & D. Barnett (Eds.), *Atypical attachment in infancy and early childhood among children at developmental risk. Monographs of the Society for Research in Child Development, 64*(3, Serial No. 258), 119–144.

Vondra, J. I., Shaw, D. S., Searingen, L., Cohen, M., & Owens, E. B. (2001). Attachment stability and emotional and behavioral regulation from infancy to preschool age. *Development and Psychopathology, 13*, 13–33.

Vonk, R., & Ashmore, R. D. (2003). Thinking about gender types: Cognitive organization of female and male types. *British Journal of Social Psychology, 42*, 257–280.

Votruba-Drzal, E. (2003). Income changes and cognitive stimulation in young children's home learning environments. *Journal of Marriage and Family, 65*, 341–355.

Vouloumanos, A. (2010). Three-month-olds prefer speech to other naturally occurring signals. *Language Learning and Development, 6*, 241–257.

Voyer, D., Voyer, S., & Bryden, M. P. (1995). Magnitude of sex differences in spatial abilities: A meta-analysis and consideration of critical variables. *Psychological Bulletin, 117,* 250–270.

Vuoksimaa, E., Kaprio, J., Kremen, W. S., Hokkanen, L., Viken, R. J., Tuulio-Henriksson, A., et al. (2010). Having a male co-twin masculinizes mental rotation performance in females. *Psychological Science, 21,* 1069–1071.

Vuoksimaa, E., Koskenvuo, M., Rose, R. J., & Kaprio, J. (2009). Origins of handedness: A nationwide study of 30,1671 adults. *Neuropsychologia, 47,* 1294–1301.

Vygotsky, L. S. (1978). *Mind in society: The development of higher mental processes.* Cambridge, MA: Harvard University Press. (Original works published 1930, 1933, and 1935)

Vygotsky, L. S. (1986). *Thought and language* (A. Kozulin, Trans.). Cambridge, MA: MIT Press. (Original work published 1934)

Vygotsky, L. S. (1987). Thinking and speech. In R. W. Rieber, A. S. Carton (Eds.), & N. Minick (Trans.), *The collected works of L. S. Vygotsky: Vol. 1. Problems of general psychology* (pp. 37–285). New York: Plenum. (Original work published 1934)

Waber, D. P. (2010). *Rethinking learning disabilities.* New York: Guilford.

Wachs, T. D. (2006). The nature, etiology, and consequences of individual differences in temperament. In L. Balter & C. S. Tamis-LeMonda (Eds.), *Child psychology: A handbook of contemporary issues* (pp. 27–52). New York: Psychology Press.

Wachs, T. D., & Bates, J. E. (2001). Temperament. In G. Bremner & A. Fogel (Eds.), *Blackwell handbook of infant development* (pp. 465–501). Oxford, UK: Blackwell.

Waddington, C. H. (1957). *The strategy of the genes.* London: Allen and Unwin.

Wadsworth, M. E., & Santiago, C. D. (2008). Risk and resiliency processes in ethnically diverse families in poverty. *Journal of Family Psychology, 22,* 399–410.

Wagenaar, K., Huisman, J., Cohen-Kettenis, P. T., & Delemarre-van de Waal, H. A. (2008). An overview of studies on early development, cognition, and psychosocial well-being in children born after in vitro fertilization. *Journal of Developmental and Behavioral Pediatrics, 29,* 219–230.

Wai, J., Cacchio, M., Putallaz, M., & Makel, M. C. (2010). Sex differences in the right tail of cognitive abilities: A 30-year examination. *Intelligence, 38,* 412–423.

Wai, J., Lubinski, D., & Benbow, C. P. (2009). Spatial ability for STEM domains: Aligning over 50 years of cumulative psychological knowledge solidifies its importance. *Journal of Educational Psychology, 101,* 817–835.

Wainryb, C. (1997). The mismeasure of diversity: Reflections on the study of cross-cultural differences. In H. D. Saltzstein (Ed.), *New directions for child development* (No. 76, pp. 51–65). San Francisco: Jossey-Bass.

Wainryb, C., & Ford, S. (1998). Young children's evaluations of acts based on beliefs different from their own. *Merrill-Palmer Quarterly, 44,* 484–503.

Wakeley, A., Rivera, S., & Langer, J. (2000). Can young infants add and subtract? *Child Development, 71,* 1477–1720.

Walberg, H. J. (1986). Synthesis of research on teaching. In M. C. Wittrock (Ed.), *Handbook of research on teaching* (3rd ed., pp. 214–229). New York: Macmillan.

Waldfogel, J. (2001). International policies toward parental leave and child care. *Future of Children 11,* 52–61.

Waldman, I. D., Rowe, D. C., Abramowitz, A., Kozel, S. T., Mohr, J. H., & Sherman, S. L. (1998). Association and linkage of the dopamine transporter gene and attention-deficit hyperactivity disorder in children: Heterogeneity owing to diagnostic subtype and severity. *American Journal of Human Genetics, 63,* 1767–1776.

Waldrip, A. M. (2008). With a little help from your friends: The importance of high-quality friendships on early adolescent adjustment. *Social Development, 17,* 832–852.

Waldvogel, J. (2010). *Tackling child poverty by improving child well-being: Lessons from Britain.* Washington, DC: First Focus.

Waldvogel, J., Craigie, T.-A., & Brooks-Gunn, J. (2010). Fragile families and child wellbeing. *Future of Children, 20,* 87–112.

Walenski, M., Tager-Flusberg, H., & Ullman, M. T. (2006). Language in autism. In S. O. Moldin & J. L. R. Rubenstein (Eds.), *Understanding autism: From basic neuroscience to treatment* (pp. 175–203). Boca Raton, FL: CRC Press.

Walker, J. M. T., Shenker, S. S., Hoover-Dempsey, K. V. (2010). Why do parents become involved in their children's education? Implications for school counselors. *Professional School Counseling, 14,* 27–41.

Walker, L. J. (1989). A longitudinal study of moral reasoning. *Child Development, 60,* 157–166.

Walker, L. J. (1995). Sexism in Kohlberg's moral psychology? In W. M. Kurtines & J. L. Gewirtz (Eds.), *Moral development: An introduction* (pp. 83–107). Boston: Allyn and Bacon.

Walker, L. J. (2004). Progress and prospects in the psychology of moral development. *Merrill-Palmer Quarterly, 50,* 546–557.

Walker, L. J. (2006). Gender and morality. In M. Killen & J. G. Smetana (Eds.), *Handbook of moral development* (pp. 93–118). Philadelphia: Erlbaum.

Walker, L. J., & Hennig, K. H. (1997). Moral development in the broader context of personality. In S. Hala (Ed.), *The development of social cognition* (pp. 297–327). Hove, UK: Psychology Press.

Walker, L. J., & Taylor, J. H. (1991a). Family interactions and the development of moral reasoning. *Child Development, 62,* 264–283.

Walker, L. J., & Taylor, J. H. (1991b). Stage transitions in moral reasoning: A longitudinal study of developmental processes. *Developmental Psychology, 27,* 330–337.

Walker-Andrews, A. S. (1997). Infants' perception of expressive behaviors: Differentiation of multimodal information. *Psychological Bulletin, 121,* 437–456.

Wall, M., & Côté, J. (2007). Developmental activities that lead to dropout and investment in sport. *Physical Education and Sport Pedagogy, 12,* 77–87.

Wallace, J. M., Jr., Bachman, J. G., O'Malley, P. M., Schulenberg, J. E., Cooper, S. M., & Johnston, L. D. (2003). Gender and ethnic differences in smoking, drinking, and illicit drug use among American 8th, 10th, and 12th grade students, 1976–2000. *Addiction, 98,* 225–234.

Wang, Q. (2003). Infantile amnesia reconsidered: A cross-cultural analysis. *Memory, 11,* 65–80.

Wang, Q. (2004). The emergence of cultural self-constructs: Autobiographical memory and self-description in European American and Chinese children. *Developmental Psychology, 40,* 3–15.

Wang, Q. (2006a). Earliest recollections of self and others in European American and Taiwanese young adults. *Psychological Science, 17,* 708–714.

Wang, Q. (2006b). Relations of maternal style and child self-concept to autobiographical memories in Chinese, Chinese immigrant, and European American 3-year-olds. *Child Development, 77,* 1794–1809.

Wang, Q. (2008). Emotion knowledge and autobiographical memory across the preschool years: A cross-cultural longitudinal investigation. *Cognition, 108,* 117–135.

Wang, Q., Pomerantz, E. M., & Chen, H. (2007). The role of parents' control in early adolescents' psychological functioning: A longitudinal investigation in the United States and China. *Child Development, 78,* 1592–1610.

Wang, S., Baillargeon, R., & Paterson, S. (2005). Detecting continuity violations in infancy: A new account and new evidence from covering and tube events. *Cognition, 95,* 129–173.

Wanska, S. K., & Bedrosian, J. L. (1985). Conversational structure and topic performance in mother–child interaction. *Journal of Speech and Hearing Research, 28,* 579–584.

Wark, G. R., & Krebs, D. L. (1996). Gender and dilemma differences in real-life moral judgment. *Developmental Psychology, 32,* 220–230.

Warner, L. A., Valdez, A., Vega, W. A., de la Rosa, M., Turner, R. J., & Canino, G. (2006). Hispanic drug abuse in an evolving cultural context: An agenda for research. *Drug and Alcohol Dependence, 84* (Suppl. 1), S8–S16.

Warnock, F., & Sandrin, D. (2004). Comprehensive description of newborn distress behavior in response to acute pain (newborn male circumcision). *Pain, 107,* 242–255.

Warren, A. R., & Tate, C. S. (1992). Egocentrism in children's telephone conversations. In R. M. Diaz & L. E. Berk (Eds.), *Private speech: From social interaction to self-regulation* (pp. 245–264). Hillsdale, NJ: Erlbaum.

Warren, M. R., Hong, S., Rubin, C., & Uy, P. S. (2009). Beyond the bake sale: A community-based relational approach to parent engagement in schools. *Teachers College Record, 111,* 2209–2254.

Waschbusch, D. A., Daleiden, E., & Drabman, R. S. (2000). Are parents accurate reporters of their child's cognitive abilities? *Journal of Psychopathology and Behavioral Assessment, 22,* 61–77.

Wasik, B. A., & Bond, M. A. (2001). Beyond the pages of a book: Interactive book reading and language development in preschool classrooms. *Journal of Educational Psychology, 93,* 243–250.

Wasserman, E. A., & Rovee-Collier, C. (2001). Pick the flowers and mind your As and 2s! Categorization by pigeons and infants. In M. E. Carroll & J. B. Overmier (Eds.), *Animal research and human health: Advancing human welfare through behavioral science* (pp. 263–279). Washington, DC: American Psychological Association.

Wasserman, J. D., & Tulsky, D. S. (2005). A history of intelligence assessment. In D. P. Flanagan & P. L. Harrison (Eds.), *Contemporary intellectual assessment: Theories, tests, and issues* (2nd ed., pp. 3–22). New York: Guilford.

Watamura, S. E., Donzella, B., Alwin, J., & Gunnar, M. R. (2003). Morning-to-afternoon increases in cortisol concentrations for infants and toddlers at child care: Age differences and behavioral correlates. *Child Development, 74,* 1006–1020.

Watamura, S. E., Phillips, D., Morrissey, T. W., McCartney, K., & Bub, K. (2011). Double jeopardy: Poorer social-emotional outcomes for children in the NICHD SECCYD experiencing home and child-care environments that confer risk. *Child Development, 82,* 48–65.

Waters, E., & Cummings, E. M. (2000). A secure base from which to explore close relationships. *Child Development, 71,* 164–172.

Waters, E., Merrick, S., Treboux, D., Crowell, J., & Albersheim, L. (2000). Attachment security in infancy and early adulthood: A twenty-year longitudinal study. *Child Development, 71,* 684–689.

Waters, E., Vaughn, B. E., Posada, G., & Kondo-Ikemura K. (Eds.). (1995). Caregiving, cultural, and cognitive perspectives on secure-base behavior and working models: New growing points of attachment theory and research. *Monographs of the Society for Research in Child Development, 60*(2–3, Serial No. 244).

Watson, A. C., Nixon, C. L., Wilson, A., & Capage, L. (1999). Social interaction skills and theory of mind in young children. *Developmental Psychology, 35,* 386–391.

Watson, D. J. (1989). Defining and describing whole language. *Elementary School Journal, 90,* 129–141.

Watson, J. B., & Raynor, R. (1920). Conditioned emotional reactions. *Journal of Experimental Psychology, 3,* 1–14.

Watson, M. (1990). Aspects of self development as reflected in children's role playing. In D. Cicchetti & M. Beeghly (Eds.), *The self in transition: Infancy to childhood* (pp. 281–307). Chicago: University of Chicago Press.

Watts-English, T., Fortson, B. L., Gibler, N., Hooper, S. R., & De Bellis, M. D. (2006). The psychobiology of maltreatment in childhood. *Journal of Social Issues, 62,* 717–736.

Wax, J. R., Pinette, M. G., & Cartin, A. (2010). Home versus hospital birth—process and outcome. *Obstetric and Gynecological Survey, 65,* 132–140.

Waxman, S. R. (2003). Links between object categorization and naming: Origins and emergence in human infants. In D. H. Rakison & L. M. Oakes (Eds.), *Early category and concept development: Making sense of the blooming, buzzing confusion* (pp. 193–209). New York: Oxford University Press.

Waxman, S. R., & Lidz, J. L. (2006). Early word learning. In D. Kuhn & R. Siegler (Eds.), *Handbook of child psychology: Vol. 2. Cognition, perception, and language* (6th ed., pp. 464–510). Hoboken, NJ: Wiley.

Waxman, S. R., & Senghas, A. (1992). Relations among word meanings in early lexical development. *Developmental Psychology, 28,* 862–873.

Way, N., & Leadbeater, B. (1999). Pathways toward educational achievement among African American and Puerto Rican adolescent mothers. *Developmental Psychology, 8,* 123–139.

Wayermann, M., Rothenbacher, D., & Brenner, H. (2006). Duration of breastfeeding and risk of overweight in childhood: A prospective birth cohort study from Germany. *International Journal of Obesity, 30,* 1281–1287.

Webb, N. M., Franke, M. L., Ing, M., Chan, A., De, T., Freund, D., & Battey, D. (2008). The role of teacher instructional practices in student collaboration. *Contemporary Educational Psychology, 35,* 360–381.

Webb, N. M., Nemer, K. M., & Chizhik, A. W. (1998). Equity issues in collaborative group assessment: Group composition and performance. *American Educational Research Journal, 35,* 607–651.

Webb, S. J., Monk, C. S., & Nelson, C. A. (2001). Mechanisms of postnatal neurobiological development: Implications for human development. *Developmental Neuropsychology, 19,* 147–171.

Weber, C., Hahne, A., Friedrich, M., & Friederici, A. (2004). Discrimination of word stress in early infant perception: Electrophysiological evidence. *Cognitive Brain Research, 18,* 149–161.

Webster-Stratton, C., & Herman, K. C. (2010). Disseminating Incredible Years series early-intervention programs: Integrating and sustaining services between school and home. *Psychology in the Schools, 47,* 36–54.

Webster-Stratton, C., & Reid, M. J. (2010a). The Incredible Years Parents, Teachers, and Children Training Series: A multifaceted treatment approach for young children with conduct disorders. In J. R. Weisz & A. E. Kazdin (Eds.), *Evidence-based psychotherapies for children and adolescents* (2nd ed., pp. 194–210). New York: Guilford.

Webster-Stratton, C., & Reid, M. J. (2010b). The Incredible Years program for children from infancy to pre-adolescence: Prevention and treatment of behavior problems. In R. C. Murrihy, A. D. Kidman, & T. H. Ollendick (Eds.), *Clinical handbook of assessing and treating conduct problems in youth* (pp. 117–138). New York: Springer Science + Business Media.

Webster-Stratton, C., Rinaldi, J., & Reid, J. M. (2011). Long-term outcomes of Incredible Years parenting program: Predictors of adolescent adjustment. *Child and Adolescent Mental Health, 16,* 38–46.

Wechsler, D. (2002). *WPPSI-III: Wechsler Preschool and Primary Scale of Intelligence* (3rd ed.). San Antonio, TX: Psychological Corporation.

Wechsler, D. (2003). *WISC-IV: Wechsler Intelligence Scale for Children* (4th ed.). San Antonio, TX: Psychological Corporation.

Weems, C. F., & Costa, N. M. (2005). Developmental differences in the expression of childhood anxiety symptoms and fears. *Journal of the American Academy of Child and Adolescent Psychiatry, 44,* 656–663.

Wehren, A., De Lisi, R., & Arnold, M. (1981). The development of noun definition. *Journal of Child Language, 8,* 165–175.

Weikum, W. M., Vouloumanos, A., Navarra, J., Soto-Faraco, S., Sebastián-Gallés, N., & Werker, J. F. (2007). Visual language discrimination in infancy. *Science, 316,* 1159.

Weinberg, M. K., & Tronick, E. Z. (1994). Beyond the face: An empirical study of infant affective configurations of facial, vocal, gestural, and regulatory behaviors. *Child Development, 65,* 1503–1515.

Weinberg, M. K., Tronick, E. Z., Cohn, J. F., & Olson, K. L. (1999). Gender differences in emotional expressivity and self-regulation during early infancy. *Developmental Psychology, 35,* 175–188.

Weinberg, R., Tenenbaum, G., McKenzie, A., Jackson, S., Anshel, M., Grove, R., & Fogarty, G. (2000). Motivation for youth participation in sport and physical activity: Relationships to culture, self-reported activity levels, and gender. *International Journal of Sport Psychology, 31,* 321–346.

Weiner, A. (1988). *The Trobrianders of Papua New Guinea.* New York: Holt.

Weiner, J., & Tardif, C. (2004). Social and emotional functioning of children with learning disabilities: Does special education placement make a difference? *Learning Disabilities Research and Practice, 19,* 20–32.

Weinert, F. E., & Hany, E. A. (2003). The stability of individual differences in intellectual development: Empirical evidence, theoretical problems, and new research questions. In R. J. Sternberg, J. Lautrey, & T. I. Lubart (Eds.), *Models of intelligence: International perspectives* (pp. 169–181). Washington, DC: American Psychological Association.

Weinfield, N. S., Sroufe, L. A., & Egeland, B. (2000). Attachment from infancy to early adulthood in a high-risk sample: Continuity, discontinuity, and their correlates. *Child Development, 71,* 695–702.

Weinfield, N. S., Whaley, G. J. L., & Egeland, B. (2004). Continuity, discontinuity, and coherence in attachment from infancy to late adolescence: Sequelae of organization and disorganization. *Attachment and Human Development, 6,* 73–97.

Weinraub, M., Clemens, L. P., Sockloff, A., Ethridge, T., Gracely, E., & Myers, B. (1984). The development of sex-role stereotypes in the third year: Relationships to gender labeling, gender identity, sex-typed toy preference, and family characteristics. *Child Development, 55,* 1493–1503.

Weinstein, R. S. (2002). *Reaching higher: The power of expectations in schooling.* Cambridge, MA: Harvard University Press.

Weinstein, S. M., Mermelstein, R. J., Hedeker, D., Hankin, B. L., & Flay, B. R. (2006). The time-varying influences of peer and family support on adolescent daily positive and negative affect. *Journal of Clinical Child and Adolescent Psychology, 35,* 420–430.

Weinstock, M. (2008). The long-term behavioural consequences of prenatal stress. *Neuroscience and Biobehavioral Reviews, 32,* 1073–1086.

Weisfeld, G. E. (1997). Puberty rites as clues to the nature of human adolescence. *Cross-Cultural Research, 31,* 27–54.

Weisgram, E. S., Bigler, R. S., & Liben, L. S. (2010). Gender, values, and occupational interests among children, adolescents, and adults. *Child Development, 81,* 778–796.

Weisner, T. S., & Wilson-Mitchell, J. E. (1990). Nonconventional family life-styles and sex typing in six-year-olds. *Child Development, 61,* 1915–1933.

Weiss, C. C., Carolan, B. V., & Baker-Smith, E. C. (2010). Big school, small school: (Re)testing assumptions about high school size, school engagement and mathematics achievement. *Journal of Youth and Adolescence, 39,* 163–176.

Weiss, K. M. (2005). Cryptic causation of human disease: Reading between the germ lines. *Trends in Genetics, 21,* 82–88.

Weissman, M. D., & Kalish, C. W. (1999). The inheritance of desired characteristics: Children's view of the role of intention in parent–offspring resemblance. *Quarterly Journal of Experimental Child Psychology, 73,* 245–265.

Weisz, A. N., & Black, B. M. (2002). Gender and moral reasoning: African American youths respond to dating dilemmas. *Journal of Human Behavior in the Social Environment, 6,* 17–34.

Weizman, Z. O., & Snow, C. E. (2001). Lexical output as related to children's vocabulary acquisition: Effects of sophisticated exposure and support for meaning. *Developmental Psychology, 37,* 265–279.

Wekerle, C., & Avgoustis, E. (2003). Child maltreatment, adolescent dating, and adolescent dating violence. In P. Florsheim (Ed.), *Adolescent romantic relations and sexual behavior: Theory, research, and practical implications* (pp. 213–242). Mahwah, NJ: Erlbaum.

Wekerle, C., Wall, A.-M., Leung, E., & Trocmé, N. (2007). Cumulative stress and substantiated maltreatment: The importance of caregiver vulnerability and adult partner violence. *Child Abuse and Neglect, 31,* 427–443.

Wekerle, C., & Wolfe, D. A. (2003). Child maltreatment. In E. J. Mash & R. A. Barkley (Eds.), *Child psychopathology* (2nd ed., pp. 632–684). New York: Guilford.

Wellman, H. M. (1990). *The child's theory of mind.* Cambridge, MA: MIT Press.

Wellman, H. M. (2002). Understanding the psychological world: Developing a theory of mind. In U. Goswami (Ed.), *Blackwell handbook of child cognitive development* (pp. 167–187). Malden, MA: Blackwell.

Wellman, H. M. (2011). Developing a theory of mind. In U. Goswami (Ed.), *Wiley-Blackwell handbook of childhood cognitive development* (2nd ed., pp. 258–284). Malden, MA: Wiley-Blackwell.

Wellman, H. M., & Hickling, A. K. (1994). The mind's "I": Children's conception of the mind as an active agent. *Child Development, 65,* 1564–1580.

Wellman, H. M., Hickling, A. K., & Schultz, C. A. (1997). Young children's psychological, physical, and biological explanations. In H. M. Wellman & K. Inagaki (Eds.), *The emergence of core domains of thought: New directions for child development #75* (pp. 7–25). San Francisco: Jossey-Bass.

Wellman, H. M., Lopez-Duran, S., LaBounty, J., & Hamilton, B. (2008). Infant attention to intentional action predicts preschool theory of mind. *Developmental Psychology, 44,* 618–623.

Welsh, M. C. (2002). Developmental and clinical variations in executive functions. In U. Kirk & D. Molfese (Eds.), *Developmental variations in language and learning* (pp. 139–185). Mahwah, NJ: Erlbaum.

Welsh, M. C., Friedman, S. L., & Spieker, S. J. (2008). Executive functions in developing children: Current conceptualizations and questions for the future. In K. McCartney & D. Phillips (Eds.), *Blackwell handbook of early childhood development* (pp. 167–187). Malden: Blackwell Publishing.

Welsh, M. C., Pennington, D. F., & Groisser, D. B. (1991). A normative-developmental study of executive function: A window on prefrontal function in children, *Developmental Neuropsychology, 7,* 131–149.

Weng, X., Odouli, R., & Li, D.-K. (2008). Maternal caffeine consumption during pregnancy and the risk of miscarriage: A prospective cohort study. *American Journal of Obstetrics and Gynecology, 198,* 279e1–279e8.

Wentworth, N., Benson, J. B., & Haith, M. M. (2000). The development of infants' reaches for stationary and moving targets. *Child Development, 71,* 576–601.

Wentworth, N., & Haith, M. M. (1998). Infants' acquisition of spatiotemporal expectations. *Developmental Psychology, 24,* 247–257.

Wentzel, K. R., Barry, C. M., & Caldwell, K. A. (2004). Friendships in middle school: Influences on motivation and school adjustment. *Journal of Educational Psychology, 96,* 195–203.

Werker, J. F., Pegg, J. E., & McLeod, P. (1994). A cross-language investigation of infant preference for infant-directed communication. *Infant Behavior and Development, 17,* 323–333.

Werner, E. E. (1989). Children of the Garden Island. *Scientific American, 260*(4), 106–111.

Werner, E. E., & Smith, R. S. (1982). *Vulnerable but invincible.* New York: McGraw-Hill.

Werner, E. E., & Smith, R. S. (1992). *Overcoming the odds: High risk children from birth to adulthood.* Ithaca, NY: Cornell University Press.

Werner, E. E., & Smith, R. S. (2001). *Journeys from childhood to midlife: Risk, resilience, and recovery.* Ithaca, NY: Cornell University Press.

Werner, N. E., & Crick, N. R. (2004). Maladaptive peer relationships and the development of relational and physical aggression during middle childhood. *Social Development, 13,* 495–514.

Westermann, G., Mareschal, D., Johnson, M. H., Sirois, S., Spratling, M. W., & Thomas, M. S. C. (2007). Neuroconstructivism. *Developmental Science, 10,* 75–83.

Westermann, G., Sirois, S., Shultz, T. R., & Mareschal, D. (2006). Modeling developmental cognitive neuroscience. *Trends in Cognitive Sciences, 10,* 227–232.

Whalen, P. J., Davis, F. C., Oler, J. A., Kim, H., Kim, M. J., & Neta, M. (2009). Human amygdala responses to facial expressions of emotion. In P. J. Whalen & E. A. Phelps (Eds.), *The human amygdala* (pp. 265–288). New York: Guilford.

Wheeler, M. A., Stuss, D. T., & Tulving, E. (1997). Toward a theory of episodic memory: The frontal lobes and autonoetic consciousness. *Psychological Bulletin, 121,* 331–354.

Wheeler, W. (2002). Youth leadership for development: Civic activism as a component of youth development programming and a strategy for strengthening civil society. In R. M. Lerner, F. Jacobs, & D. Wertlieb (Eds.), *Handbook of applied developmental science: Vol. 2* (pp. 491–506). Thousand Oaks, CA: Sage.

Whincup, P. H., Kaye, S. G., Owen, C. G., Huxley, R., Cook, D. G., Anazawa, S., et al. (2008). Birth weight and risk of type 2 diabetes: A systematic review. *Journal of the American Medical Association, 24,* 2886–2897.

Whipple, E. E. (2006). Child abuse and neglect: Consequences of physical, sexual, and emotional abuse of children. In H. E. Fitzgerald, B. M. Lester, & B. Zuckerman (Eds.), *The crisis in youth mental health:*

Critical issues and effective programs: Vol. 1. Childhood disorders (pp. 205–229). Westport, CT: Praeger.

Whipple, N., Bernier, A., & Mageau, G. A. (2011). Broadening the study of infant security of attachment: Maternal autonomy-support in the context of infant exploration. *Social Development, 20,* 17–32.

White, B., & Held, R. (1966). Plasticity of sensorimotor development in the human infant. In J. F. Rosenblith & W. Allinsmith (Eds.), *The causes of behavior* (pp. 60–70). Boston: Allyn and Bacon.

Whiteman, S. D., & Loken, E. (2006). Comparing analytic techniques to classify dyadic relationships: An example using siblings. *Journal of Marriage and Family, 68,* 1370–1382.

Whitesell, N. R., Mitchell, C. M., Spicer, P., & the Voices of Indian Teens Project Team. (2009). A longitudinal study of self-esteem, cultural identity, and academic success among American Indian adolescents. *Cultural Diversity and Ethnic Minority Psychology, 15,* 38–50.

Whiteside-Mansell, L., Bradley, R. H., Owen, M. T., Randolph, S. M., & Cauce, A. M. (2003). Parenting and children's behavior at 36 months: Equivalence between African-American and European-American mother–child dyads. *Parenting: Science and Practice, 3,* 197–234.

Whiting, B., & Edwards, C. P. (1988a). *Children of different worlds.* Cambridge, MA: Harvard University Press.

Whiting, B., & Edwards, C. P. (1988b). A cross-cultural analysis of sex differences in the behavior of children aged 3 through 11. In G. Handel (Ed.), *Childhood socialization* (pp. 281–297). New York: Aldine De Gruyter.

Whitlock, J. L., Powers, J. L., & Eckenrode, J. (2006). The virtual cutting edge: The Internet and adolescent self-injury. *Developmental Psychology, 42,* 407–417.

Wichman, A. L., Rodgers, J. L., & MacCallum, R. C. (2006). A multilevel approach to the relationship between birth order and intelligence. *Personality and Social Psychology Bulletin, 32,* 117–127.

Wichmann, C., Coplan, R. J., & Daniels, T. (2004). The social cognitions of socially withdrawn children. *Social Development, 13,* 377–392.

Wichstrøm, L. (2006). Sexual orientation as a risk factor for bulimic symptoms. *International Journal of Eating Disorders, 39,* 448–453.

Wigfield, A., & Eccles, J. S. (1994). Children's competence beliefs, achievement values, and general self-esteem change across elementary and middle school. *Journal of Early Adolescence, 14,* 107–138.

Wigfield, A., Eccles, J. S., Schiefele, U., Roeser, R. W., & Davis-Kean, P. (2006). Development of achievement motivation. In N. Eisenberg (Ed.), *Handbook of child psychology: Vol. 3. Social, emotional, and personality development* (6th ed., pp. 933–1002). Hoboken, NJ: Wiley.

Wigfield, A., Eccles, J. S., Yoon, K. S., Harold, R. D., Arbreton, A. J., Freedman-Doan, C., & Blumenfeld, P. C. (1997). Changes in children's competence beliefs and subjective task values across the elementary school years: A three-year study. *Journal of Educational Psychology, 89,* 451–469.

Wilcox, A. J., Weinberg, C. R., & Baird, D. D. (1995). Timing of sexual intercourse in relation to ovulation: Effects on the probability of conception, survival of the pregnancy, and sex of the baby. *New England Journal of Medicine, 333,* 1517–1519.

Wilcox, T., & Woods, R. (2009). Experience primes infants to individuate objects. In A. Woodward & A. Needham (Eds.), *Learning and the infant mind* (pp. 117–143). New York: Oxford University Press.

Wilkinson, K., Ross, E., & Diamond, A. (2003). Fast mapping of multiple words: Insights into when "the information provided" does and does not equal "the information perceived." *Applied Developmental Psychology, 24,* 739–762.

Wilkinson, R. B. (2004). The role of parental and peer attachment in the psychological health and self-esteem of adolescents. *Journal of Youth and Adolescence, 33,* 479–493.

Willatts, P. (1999). Development of means-end behavior in young infants: Pulling a support to retrieve a distant object. *Developmental Psychology, 35,* 651–667.

Williams, E., Radin, N., & Allegro, T. (1992). Sex-role attitudes of adolescents reared primarily by their fathers: An 11-year follow-up. *Merrill-Palmer Quarterly, 38,* 457–476.

Williams, G. R. (2008). Neurodevelopmental and neurophysiological actions of thyroid hormone. *Journal of Neuroendocrinology, 20,* 784–794.

Williams, J. E., & Best, D. L. (1990). *Measuring sex stereotypes: A multination study.* Newbury Park, CA: Sage.

Williams, J. M., & Currie, C. (2000). Self-esteem and physical development in early adolescence: Pubertal timing and body image. *Journal of Early Adolescence, 20,* 129–149.

Williams, K., & Dunne-Bryant, A. (2006). Divorce and adult psychological well-being: Clarifying the role of gender and age. *Journal of Marriage and Family, 68,* 1178–1196.

Williams, K., Haywood, K. I., & Painter, M. (1996). Environmental versus biological influences on gender differences in the overarm throw for force: Dominant and nondominant arm throws. *Women in Sport and Physical Activity Journal, 5,* 29–48.

Williams, P. E., Weiss, L. G., & Rolfhus, E. (2003). *WICS-IV: Theoretical model and test blueprint.* San Antonio, TX: Psychological Corporation.

Williams, S. C., Lochman, J. E., Phillips, N. C., & Barry, T. D. (2003). Aggressive and nonaggressive boys' physiological and cognitive processes in response to peer provocations. *Journal of Clinical Child and Adolescent Psychology, 32,* 568–576.

Williams, S. T., Mastergeorge, A. M., & Ontai, L. L. (2010). Caregiver involvement in infant peer interactions: Scaffolding in a social context. *Early Childhood Research Quarterly, 25,* 251–266.

Williams, S. T., Ontai, L. L., & Mastergeorge, A. M. (2010). The development of peer interaction in infancy: Exploring the dyadic processes. *Social Development, 19,* 348–368.

Williams, T. M. (1986). *The impact of television: A natural experiment in three communities.* Orlando, FL: Academic Press.

Williams, T. S., Connolly, J., Pepler, D., Craig, W., & Loporte, L. (2008). Risk models of dating aggression across different adolescent relationships: A developmental psychopathology approach. *Journal of Consulting and Clinical Psychology, 76,* 622–632.

Williamson, J., Softas-Nall, B., & Miller, J. (2003). Grandmothers raising grandchildren: An exploration of their experiences and emotions. *Counseling and Therapy for Couples with Families, 11,* 23–32.

Willinger, M., Ko, C. W., Hoffman, H. J., Kessler, R. C., & Corwin, M. J. (2003). Trends in infant bed sharing in the United States, 1993–2000: The National Infant Sleep Position Study. *Archives of Pediatric and Adolescent Medicine, 157,* 43–49.

Willoughby, J., Kupersmidt, J. B., & Bryant, D. (2001). Overt and covert dimensions of antisocial behavior. *Journal of Abnormal Child Psychology, 29,* 177–187.

Wilson, E. K., Dalberth, B. T., Koo, H. P., & Gard, J. C. (2010). Parents' perspectives on talking to preteenage children about sex. *Perspectives on Sexual and Reproductive Health, 42,* 56–63.

Wilson, E. O. (1975). *Sociobiology: The new synthesis.* Cambridge, MA: Harvard University Press.

Wilson, R., & Cairns, E. (1988). Sex-role attributes, perceived competence, and the development of depression in adolescence. *Journal of Child Psychology and Psychiatry, 29,* 635–650.

Winkler, I., Háden, G. P., Ladinig, O., Sziller, I., & Honing, H. (2009). Newborn infants detect the beat in music. *Proceedings of the National Academy of Sciences, 106,* 2468–2471.

Winner, E. (1996). *Gifted children: Myths and realities.* New York: Basic Books.

Winner, E. (1997). Exceptionally high intelligence and schooling. *American Psychologist, 52,* 1070–1081.

Winner, E. (2000). The origins and ends of giftedness. *American Psychologist, 55,* 159–169.

Winner, E. (2003). Creativity and talent. In M. H. Bornstein, L. Davidson, C. L. M. Keyes, K. A. Moore, & the Center for Child Well-Being (Eds.), *Well-being: Positive development across the life course* (pp. 371–380). Mahwah, NJ: Erlbaum.

Winsler, A. (2009). Still talking to ourselves after all these years: A review of current research on private speech. In A. Winsler, C. Fernyhough, & I. Montero (Eds.), *Private speech, executive functioning, and the development of verbal self-regulation.* New York: Cambridge University Press.

Winsler, A., Abar, B., Feder, M. A., Rubio, D. A., & Schunn, C. D. (2007). Private speech and executive functioning among high-functioning children with autistic spectrum disorders. *Journal of Autism and Developmental Disorders, 37,* 1617–1635.

Winsler, A., Fernyhough, C., & Montero, I. (2009). *Private speech, executive functioning, and the development of verbal self-regulation.* New York: Cambridge University Press.

Winsler, A., Naglieri, J., & Manfra, L. (2006). Children's search strategies and accompanying verbal and motor strategic behavior: Developmental trends and relations with task performance among children age 5 to 17. *Cognitive Development, 21,* 232–248.

Wiseman, F. K., Alford, K. A., Tybulewicz, V. L. J., & Fisher, E. M. C. (2009). Down syndrome—recent progress and future prospects. *Human Molecular Genetics, 18,* R75–R83.

Wissink, I. B., Deković, M., & Meijer, A. M. (2006). Parenting behavior, quality of the parent–adolescent relationship, and adolescent functioning in four ethnic groups. *Journal of Early Adolescence, 26,* 133–159.

Witherington, D. C. (2005). The development of prospective grasping control between 5 and 7 months: A longitudinal study. *Infancy, 7,* 143–161.

Wolak, J., Finkelhor, D., Mitchell, K. J., & Ybarra, M. L. (2008). Online "predators" and their victims: Myths, realities, and implications for prevention and treatment. *American Psychologist, 63,* 111–128.

Wolak, J., Mitchell, K. J., & Finkelhor, D. (2003). Escaping or connecting? Characteristics of youth who form close online relationships. *Journal of Adolescence, 26,* 105–119.

Wolak, J., Mitchell, K., & Finkelhor, D. (2007). Unwanted and wanted exposure to online pornography in a national sample of youth Internet users. *Pediatrics, 119,* 247–257.

Wolchik, S. A., Sandler, I. N., Millsap, R. E., Plummer, B. A., Greene, S. M., Anderson, E. R., et al. (2002). Six-year follow-up of preventive interventions for children of divorce: A randomized controlled trial. *Journal of the American Medical Association, 288,* 1874–1881.

Wolchik, S. A., Wilcox, K. L., Tein, J.-Y., & Sandler, I. N. (2000). Maternal acceptance and consistency of discipline as buffers of divorce stressors on children's psychological adjustment problems. *Journal of Abnormal Child Psychology, 28,* 87–102.

Wolf, A. W., Jimenez, E., & Lozoff, B. (2003). Effects of iron therapy on infant blood lead levels. *Journal of Pediatrics, 143,* 789–795.

Wolfe, D. A. (2005). *Child abuse* (2nd ed.) Thousand Oaks: Sage.

Wolfe, D. A., Scott, K., Wekerle, C., & Pittman, A. (2001). Child maltreatment: Risk of adjustment problems and dating violence in adolescence. *Journal of the American Academy of Child and Adolescent Psychiatry, 40,* 282–289.

Wolfe, V. V. (2006). Child sexual abuse. In E. J. Mash & R. A. Barkley (Eds.), *Treatment of childhood disorders* (3rd ed., pp. 647–727). New York: Guilford.

Wolff, P. H. (1966). The causes, controls and organization of behavior in the neonate. *Psychological Issues, 5*(1, Serial No. 17).

Wolff, P. H., & Fesseha, G. (1999). The orphans of Eritrea: A five-year follow-up study. *Journal of Child Psychology and Psychiatry and Allied Disciplines, 40,* 1231–1237.

Wolfinger, N. H. (2000). Beyond the intergenerational transmission of divorce: Do people replicate the patterns of marital instability they grew up with? *Journal of Family Issues, 21,* 1061–1086.

Wong, M. M., Nigg, J. T., Zucker, R. A., Puttler, L. I., Fitzgerald, H. E., Jester, J. M., et al. (2006). Behavioral control and resiliency in the onset of alcohol and illicit drug use: A prospective study from preschool to adolescence. *Child Development, 77,* 1016–1033.

Wood, E., Desmarais, S., & Gugula, S. (2002). The impact of parenting experience on gender stereotyped toy play of children. *Sex Roles, 47,* 39–49.

Wood, J. J., Emmerson, N. A., & Cowan, P. A. (2004). Is early attachment security carried forward into relationships with preschool peers? *British Journal of Developmental Psychology, 22,* 245–253.

Wood, R. M. (2009). Changes in cry acoustics and distress ratings while the infant is crying. *Infant and Child Development, 18,* 163–177.

Woodward, A. L.(2009). Infants' grasp of others' intentions. *Current Directions in Psychological Science, 18,* 53–57.

Woodward, A. L., & Markman, E. M. (1998). Early word learning. In D. Kuhn & R. S. Siegler (Eds.), *Handbook of child psychology: Vol. 2. Cognition, perception, and language* (5th ed., pp. 371–420). New York: Wiley.

Woodward, J., & Ono, Y. (2004). Mathematics and academic diversity in Japan. *Journal of Learning Disabilities, 37,* 74–82.

Woody-Dorning, J., & Miller, P. H. (2001). Children's individual differences in capacity: Effects on strategy production and utilization. *British Journal of Developmental Psychology, 19,* 543–557.

Woody-Ramsey, J., & Miller, P. H. (1988). The facilitation of selective attention in preschoolers. *Child Development, 59,* 1497–1503.

Woolley, J. D. (1997). Thinking about fantasy: Are children fundamentally different thinkers and believers from adults? *Child Development, 68,* 991–1011.

Woolley, J. D. (2000). The development of beliefs about direct mental–physical causality in imagination, magic, and religion. In K. S. Rosengren, C. N. Johnson, & P. L. Harris (Eds.), *Imagining the impossible* (pp. 99–129). New York: Cambridge University Press.

Woolley, J. D., Browne, C. A., & Boerger, E. A. (2006). Constraints on children's judgments of magical causality. *Journal of Cognition and Development, 7,* 253–277.

Woolley, J. D., & Cox, V. (2007). Development of beliefs about storybook reality. *Developmental Science, 10,* 681–693.

World Cancer Research Fund/American Institute for Cancer Research. (2007). *Food, nutrition, physical activity, and the prevention of cancer: A global perspective.* Washington, DC: American Institute for Cancer Research.

World Health Organization. (2009). *Obesity and overweight.* Retrieved from http://www.who.int/dietphysicalactivity/publications/facts/obesity/en/

World Health Organization. (2010a). *Population-based prevention strategies for childhood obesity.* Geneva, Switzerland: Author.

World Health Organization. (2010b). *World health statistics 2010.* Geneva, Switzerland: Author.

World Health Organization. (2011). *The World Health Organization's infant feeding recommendation.* Retrieved from www.who.int/nutrition/topics/infantfeeding_recommendation/en/index.html

Worrell, F. C., & Gardner-Kitt, D. L. (2006). The relationship between racial and ethnic identity in black adolescents: The cross-racial identity scale and the multigroup ethnic identity measure. *Identity, 6,* 293–315.

Worthy, J., Hungerford-Kresser, H., & Hampton, A. (2009). Tracking and ability grouping. In L. Christenbury, R. Bomer, & P. Smargorinsky (Eds.), *Handbook of adolescent literacy research* (pp. 220–235). New York: Guilford.

Wright, B. C. (2006). On the emergence of the discriminative mode for transitive inference. *European Journal of Cognitive Psychology, 18,* 776–800.

Wright, J. C., Huston, A. C., Murphy, K. C., St. Peters, M., Pinon, M., Scantlin, R., & Kotler, J. (2001). The relations of early television viewing to school readiness and vocabulary of children from low-income families: The Early Window Project. *Child Development, 72,* 1347–1366.

Wright, J. C., Huston, A. C., Reitz, A. L., & Piemyat, S. (1994). Young children's perceptions of television reality: Determinants and developmental differences. *Developmental Psychology, 30,* 229–239.

Wright, J. P., Dietrich, K., Ris, M., Hornung, R., Wessel, S., Lanphear, B., et al. (2008). Association of prenatal and childhood blood lead concentrations with criminal arrests in early adulthood. *PLoS Medicine, 5,* e101.

Wright, M. J., Gillespie, N. A., Luciano, M., Zhu, G., & Martin, N. G. (2008). Genetics of personality and cognition in adolescents. In J. J. Hudziak (Eds.), *Developmental psychology and wellness: Genetic and environmental influences* (pp. 85–107). Washington, DC: American Psychiatric Publishing.

Wright, R. O., Tsaih, S. W., Schwartz, J., Wright, R. J., & Hu, H. (2003). Associations between iron deficiency and blood lead level in a longitudinal analysis of children followed in an urban primary care clinic. *Journal of Pediatrics, 142,* 9–14.

Wright, V. C., Schieve, L. A., Reynolds, M. A., Jeng, G., & Kissin, D. (2004). Assisted reproductive technology surveillance— United States 2001. *Morbidity and Mortality Weekly Report, 53,* 1–20.

Wrotniak, B. H., Epstein, L. H., Raluch, R. A., & Roemmich, J. N. (2004). Parent weight change as a predictor of child weight change in family-based behavioral obesity treatment. *Archives of Pediatric and Adolescent Medicine, 158,* 342–347.

Wu, L. L., Bumpass, L. L., & Musick, K. (2001). Historical and life course trajectories of nonmarital childbearing. In L. L. Wu & B. Wolfe (Eds.), *Out of wedlock: Causes and consequences of nonmarital fertility* (pp. 3–48). New York: Russell Sage Foundation.

Wu, P., Robinson, C. C., Yang, C., Hart, C. H., Olsen, S. F., Porter, C. L., et al. (2002). Similarities and differences in mothers' parenting of preschoolers in China and the United States. *International Journal of Behavioral Development, 26,* 481–491.

Wu, T., Mendola, P., & Buck, G. M. (2002). Ethnic differences in the presence of secondary sex characteristics and menarche among U.S. girls: The Third National Health and Nutrition Examination Survey, 1988–1994. *Pediatrics, 110,* 752–757.

Wulczyn, F. (2009). Epidemiological perspectives on maltreatment prevention. *Future of Children, 19,* 39–66.

Wust, S., Entringer, S., Federenko, I. S., Schlotz, W., Helhammer, D. H. (2005). Birth weight is associated with salivary cortisol responses to psychosocial stress in adult life. *Psychoneuroendocrinology, 30,* 591–598.

Wyatt, J. M., & Carlo, G. (2002). What will my parents think? Relations among adolescents' expected parental reactions, prosocial moral reasoning and prosocial and antisocial behaviors. *Journal of Adolescent Research, 17,* 646–666.

Wyman, E., Rakoczy, H., & Tomasello, M. (2009). Normativity and context in young children's pretend play. *Cognitive Development, 24,* 146–155.

Wynn, K. (1992). Addition and subtraction by human infants. *Nature, 358,* 749–750.

Wynn, K. (2002). Do infants have numerical expectations or just perceptual preferences? Comment. *Developmental Science, 5,* 207–209.

Wynn, K., Bloom, P., & Chiang, W.-C. (2002). Enumeration of collective entities by 5-month-old infants. *Cognition, 83,* B55–B62.

Xu, F., Spelke, E. S., & Goddard, S. (2005). Number sense in human infants. *Developmental Science, 8,* 88–101.

Xue, Y., & Meisels, S. J. (2004). Early literacy instruction and learning in kindergarten: Evidence from the early childhood longitudinal study—kindergarten class of 1998–1999. *American Educational Research Journal, 41,* 191–229.

Yale, M. E., Messinger, D. S., Cobo-Lewis, A. B., Oller, D. K., & Eilers, R. E. (1999). An event-based analysis of the coordination of early infant vocalizations and facial actions. *Developmental Psychology, 35,* 505–513.

Yan, J., & Smetana, J. G. (2003). Conceptions of moral, social-conventional, and personal events among Chinese preschoolers in Hong Kong. *Child Development, 74,* 647–658.

Yan, Z. (2006). What influences children's and adolescents' understanding of the complexity of the Internet? *Developmental Psychology, 42,* 418–428.

Yang, B., Ollendick, T. H., Dong, Q., Xia, Y., & Lin, L. (1995). Only children and children with siblings in the People's Republic of China: Levels of fear, anxiety, and depression. *Child Development, 66,* 1301–1311.

Yang, C. (2008, April). *The influence of one-child policy on child rearing, family, and society in post-Mao China.* Invited address, Illinois State University.

Yang, C.-K., & Hahn, H.-M. (2002). Cosleeping in young Korean children. *Developmental and Behavioral Pediatrics, 23,* 151–157.

Yap, M. B. H., Allen, N. B., & Ladouceur, C. D. (2008). Maternal socialization of positive affect: The impact of invalidation on adolescent emotion regulation and depressive symptomatology. *Child Development, 79,* 1415–1431.

Yarrow, M. R., Campbell, J. D., & Burton, R. V. (1970). Recollections of childhood: A study of the retrospective method. *Monographs of the Society for Research in Child Development, 35*(5, Serial No. 138).

Yarrow, M. R., Scott, P. M., & Waxler, C. Z. (1973). Learning concern for others. *Developmental Psychology, 8,* 240–260.

Yeates, K. O., Schultz, L. H., & Selman, R. L. (1991). The development of interpersonal negotiation strategies in thought and action: A social-cognitive link to behavioral adjustment and social status. *Merrill-Palmer Quarterly, 37,* 369–405.

Yeh, C. J., Kim, A. B., Pituc, S. T., & Atkins, M. (2008). Poverty, loss, and resilience: The story of Chinese immigrant youth. *Journal of Counseling Psychology, 55,* 34–48.

Yeh, H.-C., & Lempers, J. D. (2004). Perceived sibling relationships and adolescent development. *Journal of Youth and Adolescence, 33,* 133–147.

Yeh, S. S. (2010). Understanding and addressing the achievement gap through individualized instruction and formative assessment. *Assessment in Education: Principles, Policy and Practice, 17,* 169–182.

Yehuda, R., Engel, S. M., Brand, S. R., Seckl, J., Marcus, S. M., & Berkowitz, G. S. (2005). Transgenerational effects of posttraumatic stress disorder in babies of mothers exposed to the World Trade Center attacks during pregnancy. *Journal of Clinical Endocrinology and Metabolism, 90,* 4115–4118.

Yirmiya, N., Erel, O., Shaked, M., & Solomonica-Levi, D. (1998). Meta-analyses comparing theory of mind abilities of individuals with autism, individuals with mental retardation, and normally developing individuals. *Psychological Bulletin, 124,* 283–307.

Yoder, K., Whitbeck, L., Hoyt, D., & LaFromboise, T. (2006). Suicide ideation among American Indian youths. *Archives of Suicide Research, 10,* 177–190.

Yoshida, H., & Smith, L. B. (2003). Known and novel noun extensions: Attention at two levels of abstraction. *Child Development, 74,* 564–577.

Yoshikawa, H., Weisner, T. S., Kalil, A., & Way, N. (2008). Mixing qualitative and quantitative research in developmental science: Uses and methodological choices. *Developmental Psychology, 44,* 344–354.

Yoshinaga-Itano, C. (2003). Early intervention after universal neonatal hearing screening: Impact on outcomes. *Mental Retardation and Developmental Disabilities Research Reviews, 9,* 252–266.

Young, J. F., & Mroczek, D. K. (2003). Predicting intraindividual self-concept trajectories during adolescence. *Journal of Adolescence, 26,* 589–603.

Young, S. E., Friedman, N. P., Miyake, A., Willcutt, E. G., Corley, R. P., Haberstick, B. C., et al. (2009). Behavioral disinhibition: Liability for externalizing spectrum disorders and its genetic and environmental relation to response inhibition across adolescence. *Journal of Abnormal Psychology, 118,* 117–130.

Youngblade, L. M., & Dunn, J. (1995). Individual differences in young children's pretend play with mother and sibling: Links to relationships and understanding of other people's feelings and beliefs. *Child Development, 66,* 1472–1492.

Young-Hyman, D., Tanofsky-Kraff, M., Yanovski, S. Z., Keil, M., Cohen, M. L., & Peyrot, M. (2006). Psychological status and weight-related distress in overweight or at-risk-for-overweight children. *Obesity, 14,* 2249–2258.

Youngstrom, E., Wolpaw, J. M., Kogos, J. L., Schoff, K., Ackerman, B., & Izard, C. (2000). Interpersonal problem solving in preschool and first grade: Developmental change and ecological validity. *Journal of Clinical Child Psychology, 29,* 589–602.

Yu, R. (2002). On the reform of elementary school education in China. *Educational Exploration, 129,* 56–57.

Yuan, A. S. V., & Hamilton, H. A. (2006). Stepfather involvement and adolescent well-being: Do mothers and nonresidential fathers matter? *Journal of Family Issues, 27,* 1191–1213.

Yuill, N., & Pearson, A. (1998). The developmental bases for trait attribution: Children's understanding of traits as causal mechanisms based on desire. *Developmental Psychology, 34,* 574–576.

Yumoto, C., Jacobson, S. W., & Jacobson, J. L. (2008). Fetal substance exposure and cumulative environmental risk in an African-American cohort. *Child Development, 79,* 1761–1776.

Yunger, J. L., Carver, P. R., & Perry, D. G. (2004). Does gender identity influence children's psychological well-being? *Developmental Psychology, 40,* 572–582.

Zafeiriou, D. I. (2000). Plantar grasp reflex in high-risk infants during the first year of life. *Pediatric Neurology, 22,* 75–76.

Zaff, J. F., Malanchuk, O., & Eccles, J. S. (2008). Predicting positive citizenship from adolescence to young adulthood: The effects of a civic context. *Applied Developmental Science, 12,* 68–53.

Zahn-Waxler, C. (1991). The case for empathy: A developmental review. *Psychological Inquiry, 2,* 155–158.

Zahn-Waxler, C., Cole, P. M., & Barrett, K. C. (1991). Guilt and empathy: Sex differences and implications for the development of depression. In J. Garber & K. A. Dodge (Eds.), *The development of emotion regulation and dysregulation* (pp. 243–272). Cambridge, UK: Cambridge University Press.

Zahn-Waxler, C., Kochanska, G., Krupnick, J., & McKnew, D. (1990). Patterns of guilt in children of depressed and well mothers. *Developmental Psychology, 26,* 51–59.

Zahn-Waxler, C., & Radke-Yarrow, M. (1990). The origins of empathic concern. *Motivation and Emotion, 14,* 107–130.

Zahn-Waxler, C., Radke-Yarrow, M., & King, R. M. (1979). Childrearing and children's prosocial initiations toward victims of distress. *Child Development, 50,* 319–330.

Zahn-Waxler, C., & Robinson, J. (1995). Empathy and guilt: Early origins of feelings of responsibility. In J. P. Tangney & K. W. Fischer (Eds.), *Self-conscious emotions* (pp. 143–173). New York: Guilford.

Zammit, S., Allebeck, P., David, A. S., Dalman, C., Hemmingsson, T., Lundberg, I., et al. (2004). A longitudinal study of premorbid IQ score and risk of developing schizophrenia, bipolar disorder, severe depression, and other nonaffective psychoses. *Archives of General Psychiatry, 61,* 354–360.

Zamuner, T. S., Gerken, L., & Hammond, M. (2004). Phonotactic probabilities in young children's speech production. *Journal of Child Language, 31,* 515–536.

Zanetti-Daellenbach, R. A., Tschudin, S., Zhong, X. Y., Holzgreve, W., Lapaire, O., & Hösli, I. (2007). Maternal and neonatal infections and obstetrical outcome in water birth. *European Journal of Obstetrics and Gynecology and Reproductive Biology, 134,* 37–43.

Zeanah, C. H. (2000). Disturbances of attachment in young children adopted from institutions. *Journal of Developmental and Behavioral Pediatrics, 21,* 230–236.

Zeifman, D. M. (2003). Predicting adult responses to infant distress: Adult characteristics associated with perceptions, emotional reactions, and timing of intervention. *Infant Mental Health Journal, 24,* 597–612.

Zelazo, N. A., Zelazo, P. R., Cohen, K. M., & Zelazo, P. D. (1993). Specificity of practice effects on elementary neuromotor patterns. *Developmental Psychology, 29,* 686–691.

Zelazo, P. D., Carlson, S. M., & Kesek, A. (2008). The development of executive function in childhood. In C. A. Nelson & M. Luciana (Eds.), *Handbook of cognitive developmental neuroscience* (2nd ed., pp. 553–574). Cambridge, MA: MIT Press.

Zelazo, P. D., Müller, U., Frye, D., & Marcovitch, S. (2003). The development of executive function in early childhood. *Monographs of the Society for Research in Child Development, 68*(3, Serial No. 274).

Zeller, M. H., & Modi, A. C. (2006). Predictors of health-related quality of life in obese youth. *Obesity Research, 14,* 122–130.

Zeskind, P. S., & Barr, R. G. (1997). Acoustic characteristics of naturally occurring cries of infants with "colic." *Child Development, 68,* 394–403.

Zeskind, P. S., & Lester, B. M. (2001). Analysis of infant crying. In L. T. Singer & P. S. Zeskind (Eds.), *Biobehavioral assessment of the infant* (pp. 149–166). New York: Guilford.

Zhan, M. (2005). Assets, parental expectations and involvement, and children's educational performance. *Children and Youth Services Review, 28,* 961–975.

Zhang, T.-Y., & Meaney, M. J. (2010). Epigenetics and the environmental regulation of the genome and its function. *Annual Review of Psychology, 61,* 439–466.

Zhou, M., & Bankston, C. L. (1998). *Growing up American: How Vietnamese children adapt to life in the United States.* New York: Russell Sage Foundation.

Zhou, Q., Eisenberg, N., Lousoya, S. H., Fabes, R. A., Reiser, M., Guthrie, I. K., et al. (2002). The relations of parental warmth and positive expressiveness to children's empathy-related responding and social functioning: A longitudinal study. *Child Development, 73,* 893–915.

Zhou, Q., Lengua, L. J., & Wang, Y. (2009). The relations of temperament reactivity and effortful control to children's adjustment problems in China and the United States. *Developmental Psychology, 45,* 724–739.

Zhou, X., Huang, J., Wang, Z., Wang, B., Zhao, Z., Yang, L., & Zheng-Zheng, Y. (2006). Parent–child interaction and children's number learning. *Early Child Development and Care, 176,* 763–775.

Zhou, Z., & Peverly, S. T. (2005). Teaching addition and subtraction to first graders: A Chinese perspective. *Psychology in the Schools, 42,* 259–272.

Zhu, J., & Weiss, L. (2005). The Wechsler Scales. In D. P. Flanagan & P. L. Harrison (Eds.), *Contemporary intellectual assessment* (2nd ed., pp. 297–324). New York: Guilford.

Zhu, W. X., & Hesketh, T. (2009). China's excess males, sex selective abortion, and one child policy: Analysis of data from 2005 national intercensus survey. *British Medical Journal, 338,* b1211.

Zimmer-Gembeck, M., & Helfand, M. J. (2008). Ten years of longitudinal research on U.S. adolescent sexual behavior: Developmental correlates of sexual intercourse, and the importance of age, gender and ethnic background. *Developmental Review, 28,* 153–224.

Zimmerman, B. J., & Cleary, T. J. (2009). Motives to self-regulate learning: A social cognitive account. In K. R. Wenzel & A. Wigfield (Eds.), *Handbook of motivation at school* (pp. 247–264). New York: Routledge.

Zimmerman, B. J., & Moylan, A. R. (2009). Self-regulation: Where metacognition and motivation intersect. In D. J. Hacker, J. Dunlosky, & A. C. Graesser (Eds.), *Handbook of metacognition in education* (pp. 299–315). New York: Routledge.

Zimmerman, C. (2005). *The development of scientific reasoning skills: What psychologists contribute to an understanding of elementary science learning.* Report to the National Research Council, Committee on Science Learning Kindergarten through Eighth Grade. Normal, IL: Illinois State University.

Zimmerman, C. (2007). The development of scientific thinking skills in elementary and middle school. *Developmental Review, 27,* 172–223.

Zimmerman, F. J., & Christakis, D. A. (2005). Children's television viewing and cognitive outcomes. *Archives of Pediatrics and Adolescent Medicine, 159,* 619–625.

Zimmerman, F. J., Christakis, D. A., & Meltzoff, A. N. (2007). Television and DVD/video viewing in children younger than 2 years. *Archives of Pediatrics and Adolescent Medicine, 161,* 473–479.

Zimmerman, F. J., Gilkerson, J., Richards, J. A., Christakis, D. A., Xu, D., Gray, S., & Yapanel, U. (2009). Teaching by listening: The importance of adult–child conversations to language development. *Pediatrics, 124,* 342–348.

Zimmerman, L. K., & Stansbury, K. (2004). The influence of emotion regulation, level of shyness, and habituation on the neuroendocrine response of three-year-old children. *Psychoneuroendocrinology, 29,* 973–982.

Zimmerman, P., & Becker-Stoll, F. (2002). Stability of attachment representations during adolescence: The influence of ego-identity status. *Journal of Adolescence, 25,* 107–124.

Zitzer-Comfort, C., Reilly, J., Korenberg, J. R., & Bellugi, U. (2010). We are social— therefore we are: The interplay of mind, culture, and genetics in Williams syndrome. In C. M. Worthman, P. M. Plotsky, D. S. Schechter, & C. A. Cummings (Eds.), *Formative experiences: The interaction of caregiving, culture, and developmental psychobiology* (pp. 136–165). New York: Cambridge University Press.

Ziv, M., & Frye, D. (2003). The relation between desire and false belief in children's theory of mind: No satisfaction? *Developmental Psychology, 39,* 859–876.

Zolotor, A. J., & Puzia, M. E. (2010). Bans against corporal punishment: A systematic review of the laws, changes in attitudes and behaviours. *Child Abuse Review, 19,* 229–247.

Zosuls, K. M., Ruble, D. N., Bornstein, M. H., & Greulich, F. K. (2009). The acquisition of gender labels in infancy: Implications for gender-typed play. *Developmental Psychology, 45,* 688–701.

Zucker, K. J. (2006). "I'm half-boy, half-girl": Play psychotherapy and parent counseling for gender identity disorder. In R. L. Spitzer, M. B. First, J. B. W. Williams, & M. Gibbon (Eds.), *DSM-IV-TR Casebook: Vol. 2. Experts tell how they treated their own patients* (pp. 322–334). Washington, DC: American Psychiatric Publishing.

Zukow-Goldring, P. (2002). Sibling care-giving. In M. H. Bornstein (Ed.), *Handbook of parenting: Vol. 3* (2nd ed., pp. 253–286). Hillsdale, NJ: Erlbaum.

Zur, O., & Gelman, R. (2004). Young children can add and subtract by predicting and checking. *Early Childhood Research Quarterly, 19,* 121–137.

Zwart, M. (2007). The Dutch system of perinatal care. *Midwifery Today with International Midwife, 81*(Spring), 46.

Name Index

A

Aalsma, M., 256
Aarnoudse-Moens, C. S., 114
Abbeduto, L. J., 511
Abbey, B. B., 413
ABC News, 213
Abecassis, M., 614, 616
Abela, J. R. Z., 559
Aber, J. L., 27, 33, 35, 37, 641, 642
Abikoff, H. B., 290, 291
Aboud, F. E., 476, 477, 479
Abrams, D., 479, 512
Abrams, K. Y., 434
Abramson, L. Y., 560
Acebo, C., 207
Achenbach, T. M., 116
Acker, M. M., 494
Ackerman, B. P., 391, 392, 407
Ackerman, R., 206
Adachi-Mejia, A. M., 199
Adam, E. K., 29
Adams, D. R., 80
Adams, E., 498
Adams, G. R., 471
Adams, R., 208
Adamson, D., 86
Adolph, K. E., 13, 131, 147, 148, 149, 150, 152, 160, 161, 169
Afifi, T. O., 491
Afterschool Alliance, 597, 599
Agatston, P. W., 621
Aggarwal, R., 201
Agnoli, F., 557
Agronick, G., 524
Aguiar, A., 230, 262
Ahadi, S. A., 421, 423
Ahlberg, C., 539
Ahmed, A., 232
Ahmed, M. L., 184
Ahnert, L., 33, 441, 597
Aikens, J. W., 642
Aikens, N. L., 349
Ainley, J., 645
Ainscow, M., 646
Ainsworth, M. D. S., 138, 430, 431, 434
Akers, A. Y., 213
Akhtar, N., 233, 377, 382, 383
Akimoto, S. A., 408
Aksan, N., 406, 490, 491, 514
Akshoomoff, N. A., 188, 457
Aksu-Koç, A., 392
Alan Guttmacher Institute, 214, 217
Alberman, E., 82
Albers, C. A., 329
Albert, M. K., 160
Alberts, A., 256
Aldridge, M. A., 155
Alessandri, S. M., 407, 409
Alexander, J. M., 304
Alexander, K., 402

Alexandre-Bidon, K. L., 11
Alfaro, E. C., 475
Algarin, C., 135
Ali, L., 213
Alibali, M. W., 285
Alink, L. R. A., 518
Allegro, T., 544
Allen, G., 624, 625
Allen, J. P., 220, 580, 627
Allen, L., 331
Allen, M., 589
Allen, M. M., 381
Allen, N. B., 559
Allen, S. E. M., 385, 388
Allik, J., 587
Allison, B. N., 208
Allison, J., 644
Alloway, T. P., 279, 280, 281
Almeida, D. M., 550
Almeida, J., 216
Al-Namlah, A. S., 267
Alsaker, F. D., 209
Altermatt, E. R., 616
Althaus, J., 112
Alvarez, M. M., 550
Alwan, S., 97
Amabile, T. M., 353
Amaral, D. G., 457
Amato, P. R., 574, 581, 585, 590, 592, 593, 595
American Academy of Pediatrics, 104, 134, 195, 237, 291, 631
American Diabetes Association, 49
American Psychiatric Association, 290, 646
American Psychological Association, 66, 631
Ames, E. W., 161
Ames, S. L., 627
Amsel, E., 313, 314
Amso, D., 159, 165
Amsterlaw, J., 304, 453
Anand, S. S., 198
Ananth, C. V., 113
Anderman, E. M., 467
Anders, T. F., 132
Andersen, E., 393
Anderson, C. A., 237, 630, 631, 634
Anderson, D. A., 543
Anderson, D. R., 237, 630, 632
Anderson, J. L., 156
Anderson, J. R., 367
Anderson, K. G., 595
Anderson, K. J., 378, 542
Anderson, S. W., 487
Anderson, V. A., 188, 282
Anderssen, N., 181
Andersson, H., 329
Andersson, T., 210
Andrews, D. W., 616
Andrews, G., 21, 249, 250, 261, 308

Andrews, S., 247
Anesbury, T., 200
Ang, S., 338
Angelillo, C., 273
Anglin, J. M., 380
Anisfeld, M., 145
Annahatak, B., 340
Annett, M., 189
Antoni, M. H., 403
Anttila, R., 209
Aoki, M. F., 116
Apfel, N. H., 220
Apfelbaum, E. P., 478
Apgar, V., 109
Appelbaum, M. I., 331
Appiah, K. A., 494
Aquan-Assee, J., 586
Arbeau, K. A., 422, 609
Arch, J. R., 105
Archer, A. H., 237
Archer, S. L., 472
Archibald, A. B., 176, 203, 211
Arcus, D., 588
Ardila-Rey, A., 512
Armer, M., 422, 609
Armstrong, K. L., 133
Armstrong, L. M., 410
Arnett, J. J., 6, 470
Arnold, D. H., 561
Arnold, M., 380
Arnold, M. L., 504, 574
Arnold, P., 372
Arnold, R., 27, 572
Arnon, S., 115
Arriaga, R. I., 264
Arsenio, W. F., 498, 510, 522
Arslanian, S. A., 198
Arterberry, M. E., 159, 160, 164, 234
Arthurs, E., 404
Artman, L., 252, 259
Asada, K., 366
Asarnow, J. R., 473, 560
Aschersleben, G., 152
Asendorpf, J. B., 450
ASHA (American Speech-Language-Hearing Association), 372
Asher, S. R., 615, 620
Ashmead, D. H., 151, 155, 162
Ashmore, R. D., 530
Ashton, M. C., 326
Aslin, R. M., 374
Aslin, R. N., 157, 367, 369
Astington, J. W., 453, 454, 455
Astuti, R., 265
Atance, C. M., 451, 452, 515
Atencio, D. J., 411
Atkin, C., 631
Atkins, R., 507, 508, 581
Atkinson, L., 440
Atkinson, R. C., 278
Atkinson-King, K., 375

Atlas, R., 45
Attewell, P., 633
Attkisson, C. C., 205
Au, T. K., 246
Aud, S., 555
Augustin, A., 184
Aumann, K., 29, 438, 442, 596
Aunola, K., 574, 575
Austin, E. L., 216
Austin, E. W., 631
Autti-Raemoe, I., 99
Auyeung, B., 537
Averhart, C. J., 477
Avgoustis, E., 625
Avni-Babad, D., 259
Axelin, A., 153
Ayduk, O., 515, 516
Ayotte, V., 461, 463
Azar, S. T., 603
Azmitia, M., 610, 616
Azocar, C. I., 631

B

Bacallao, M. L., 53
Bacaltchuk, J., 212
Backley, P., 389
Baddeley, A. D., 279, 366
Badzinski, D. M., 415
Baenninger, M., 557
Baer, J., 64
Baghurst, P. A., 193
Bagwell, C. L., 44, 291, 615, 616, 623
Bahrick, L. E., 143, 144, 157, 166, 168, 238
Bai, D. L., 161
Bailey, J. M., 215
Bailey, R. C., 192
Baillargeon, R., 230, 231, 262, 263, 453
Baillargeon, R. H., 518
Bainbridge, J., 597
Baiocco, R., 631
Baird, D. D., 89
Bakeman, R., 26
Baker, C. T., 331
Baker, J. A., 643
Baker, J. M., 381
Baker, N., 515
Baker, P. N., 218
Bakermans-Kranenburg, M. J., 434, 435, 436
Baker-Smith, E. C., 638
Baker-Ward, L., 301
Bakhurst, D., 266
Bakken, J. P., 611
Balaban, M. T., 376
Baldi, A., 195
Baldwin, D. A., 383, 457
Baldwin, G., 385
Baldwin, J. M., 14
Bale, J. F., 102

Bales, S. N., 37
Balfanz, R., 343
Balis, T., 472
Ball, H., 134
Balsano, A. B., 508
Baltes, P. B., 9, 121
Bambara, L. M., 646
Banaji, M. R., 478
Bandstra, E. A., 97
Bandura, A., 18, 490, 491, 534
Banish, M. T., 187
Banks, M. S., 159, 161
Bankston, C. L., 53
Bannard, C., 385, 389
Banse, R., 531, 532
Barber, A. M., 425
Barber, B. K., 473, 573, 575, 579, 641
Barber, C. H., 508
Barber, J. S., 219
Bard, K. A., 449
Bardwell, J. R., 534
Barenbaum, J., 524
Barenbaum, S. A., 547
Bar-Haim, Y., 164
Barker, D. J., 104
Barker, R. G., 638
Barkley, R. A., 290, 291
Barlaug, D. G., 338
Barna, J., 452
Barnes, G. M., 28
Barnes, R., 473
Barnes-Josiah, D., 184
Barnett, D., 430
Baron, A. S., 477, 478
Baron, I. S., 114
Baron-Cohen, S., 457
Barr, H. M., 96, 99
Barr, R., 141, 142, 233, 237, 270
Barr, R. G., 136, 138, 150
Barratt, M. S., 115
Barrett, K. C., 401, 408, 559
Barrett, M., 511
Barrett, T. M., 151
Barriga, A. Q., 522, 523
Barron, F., 353
Barros, R. M., 639
Barrouillet, P., 258
Barry, C. M., 618
Barry, C. T., 522
Barry, H., III, 208
Barry, R. A., 427, 575
Barsade, S. G., 327
Bartgis, J., 288
Bartlett, F. C., 295
Bartocci, M., 153
Barton, M. E., 391
Bartrip, J., 164
Bartsch, K., 452, 453
Baruch, C., 155
Basinger, K. S., 499, 500
Basow, S. A., 550
Bass, J. L., 113
Bassett, N. S., 108
Bass-Ringdahl, S. M., 370
Bastien, C. H., 101

Batchelor, J., 202
Bates, E. A., 188, 363, 367, 389
Bates, J. E., 47, 120, 378, 410, 419, 420, 421, 423, 424, 514
Battin, D. B., 302
Batty, G. D., 195
Baudonniere, P., 450
Bauer, P. J., 97, 233, 298, 299, 301
Baumeister, R. F., 478
Baumer, S., 392
Baumrind, D., 573, 575, 576, 578
Baumwell, L., 372
Bauserman, R., 593
Bavelier, D., 187
Baydar, N., 585
Bayley, N., 148, 151, 329
Baynes, K., 364
Bazemore, G., 525
Beals, D. E., 393
Bean, R. A., 570, 579
Bearman, P. S., 473
Bearman, S. K., 209
Beatty, W. W., 537
Beauchamp, G. K., 154
Beautrais, A. L., 472
Beck, I. L., 310
Beck, S. W., 340
Becker, B. E., 581, 582
Becker, B. J., 434
Becker, J. B., 207
Becker, K., 125
Becker, S., 486
Becker-Stoll, F., 473
Beckett, C., 170, 171
Bedford, O. A., 409
Bedrosian, J. L., 390
Beghetto, R. A., 352
Behnke, M., 97
Behrends, M., 644
Behrens, K. Y., 437
Beilin, H., 243
Beintema, D., 130
Bekkering, H., 233
Bélanger, M., 452
Belcher, D., 180
Belknap, J., 519
Bell, C., 645
Bell, D., 471
Bell, J. H., 256
Bell, M. A., 161, 232
Bell, S. M., 138, 633
Bellagamba, F., 233
Bell-Dolan, D. J., 67
Bellinger, D. C., 101, 193
Bellmore, A. D., 619
Bellugi, U., 366
Belmonte, M. K., 457
Belsky, D., 104
Belsky, J., 122, 169, 205, 426, 432, 434, 436, 440, 441, 442, 586, 597
Beltz, A. M., 538
Belyea, M., 135
Bem, D. J., 61
Bem, S. L., 562, 563

Bemmels, H. R., 123
Benbow, C. P., 556
Bender, H. L., 491
Bendersky, M., 169
Benenson, J. F., 561, 617
Bengtson, H., 417
Benner, A. D., 641, 642
Bennett, M., 477
Bennett, R. T., 303
Benson, J. B., 151
Benson, P. L., 11, 507
Ben-Zeev, T., 557
Berenbaum, S. A., 530, 534, 537, 538, 544, 557, 561, 562
Beresin, E. V., 211
Bergen, D., 240
Berger, A., 264
Berger, L. M., 345
Berger, S. E., 131, 148, 149, 152, 232
Bergin, C., 558
Bergman, K., 106
Berk, L. E., 25, 45, 240, 241, 267, 268, 269, 350, 464, 495, 578
Berkowitz, C. M., 213
Berkowitz, G., 111
Berkowitz, M. W., 505
Berkowitz, R. L., 84
Berlin, L. J., 434, 492
Berliner, D. C., 343
Berman, P., 109
Berman, R. A., 380, 388, 394
Berman, S. L., 471
Berndt, T. J., 615, 616, 618
Bernier, A., 434
Bernieri, F., 425
Berry, J., 104, 105
Bersoff, D. M., 506
Bertenthal, B. I., 146, 161, 163, 231, 232
Berthier, N. E., 151
Bertin, E., 160
Bertoncini, J., 141, 155
Berzonsky, M. D., 471, 472, 473
Besançon, M., 353, 354
Best, D., 98
Best, D. L., 530, 532
Beyers, J. M., 577
Bhagwat, J., 235
Bhanot, R., 532, 557
Bhat, A., 151
Bhatt, R. S., 141, 160, 234
Bialystok, E., 364, 365, 394, 396
Bianchi, S. M., 29
Bianco, A., 106
Biblarz, T., 589
Bidell, T. R., 21, 30, 252
Biederman, J., 290
Biehl, M. C., 207, 208, 209
Bielawska-Batorowicz, E., 404
Bielinski, J., 555
Bierman, K. L., 351, 481, 622, 642
Biernat, M., 531
Bifulco, R., 645
Bigelow, A. E., 162, 434
Bigi, L., 303

Bigler, R. S., 22, 69, 477, 478, 530, 531, 532, 533, 534, 543, 549, 550, 551, 552, 563
Bimmel, N., 588
Binet, A., 13, 320
Birch, E. E., 160, 163
Birch, H. G., 420
Birch, L. L., 195, 196
Birch, S. A. J., 455
Birch, S. H., 641
Bird, A., 299, 459
Bird, G. M., 455
Biringen, Z., 147
Birkett, M., 216
Birney, D. P., 22, 23
Bisanz, J., 311
Bischofshausen, S., 295
Bisgard, K., 202
Bissaker, K., 574, 577
Bjork, E. L., 377
Bjorklund, D. F., 24, 226, 260, 262, 287, 289, 292, 293, 295, 297, 568
Black, A. E., 573
Black, B., 622
Black, B. M., 503
Black, J. E., 170, 191
Black, M. M., 202
Black, R. E., 196
Blackwell, L. S., 466
Blades, M., 300
Blaga, O. M., 143
Blair, C., 288, 351
Blake, J., 370
Blakemore, J. E. O., 531, 533
Blakemore, S.-J., 190
Blanchard, R., 215
Blandon, A. Y., 515
Blasi, A., 506
Blasi, C. H., 24
Blass, E. M., 141
Blatchford, P., 271–272, 637
Blatt, L., 414
Blatt-Eisengart, I., 574, 575
Bleeker, M. M., 467, 541, 557
Bleses, D., 378
Bliss, L. S., 392
Bloch, M. E. F., 265
Bloch, M. N., 613
Block, J., 626
Bloom, L., 376, 380, 388
Bloom, P., 263, 389, 455, 487, 510
Blumberg, M. S., 135
Blumenfeld, P. C., 23
Blustein, D. L., 473
Blythe, D. A., 641
Boardman, J. D., 572
Boat, B. W., 601
Bobb, A. J., 290
Bock, K., 389
Bodrova, E., 25, 269, 288, 640
Boerger, E. A., 246
Boergers, J., 520, 627
Bogaert, A. F., 205, 215
Bogartz, R. S., 231
Bogin, B., 176, 183, 203

Bohannon, J. N., III, 367, 389
Bohlin, G., 202
Boivin, M., 616
Boldizar, J. P., 547
Bolen, R. M., 601
Bolisetty, S., 114
Bolzani, L. H., 407
Bond, J. T., 29, 438, 442, 596
Bond, M. A., 308
Boniface, J., 142
Bono, M. A., 287
Bonsel, G. J., 105
Bonvillian, J. D., 367
Boom, J., 502, 503
Boomsma, D. I., 323
Booth, J. L., 285
Booth-LaForce, C., 434
Bootzin, R. R., 133
Borduin, C. M., 525
Borke, H., 245
Borkowski, J. G., 467
Bornstein, M. H., 24, 142, 164, 234, 268, 372, 379, 437
Bornstein, M. J., 569
Boroughs, D. S., 601
Borst, C. G., 110
Bos, H. M. W., 589, 590
Bosacki, S. L., 558
Bosma, H. A., 472
Bosquet, M., 187
Boss, B. J., 153
Bost, K. K., 299, 435
Botton, J., 199
Botvinick, M., 487
Bouchard, C., 179, 180
Bouchard, T. J., Jr., 123, 335, 336, 337, 423
Boucher, O., 101
Boudreau, J. P., 160
Boukydis, C. F. Z., 138
Bouldin, P., 241
Boulton, M. J., 610, 621
Bowen, R., 255
Bower, T. G. R., 155
Bowker, A., 617
Bowker, J., 620
Bowker, J. C. W., 618
Bowkett, S., 327
Bowlby, J., 9, 24, 428, 430, 437
Bowman, S. A., 196
Boyatzis, C. J., 242
Boyce, W., 213
Boyd, J. S., 310, 311
Boyd-Franklin, N., 583
Boyd-Zaharias, J., 637
Boyes, M. C., 472
Boyle, M. H., 519
Boysson-Bardies, B. de, 370
Brackett, M. A., 327
Bradford, K., 520, 571
Bradley, R. H., 116, 344, 345
Bradley-Engen, M. S., 216
Braet, C., 199
Braine, M. D. S., 389
Brainerd, C. J., 260, 296, 300

Braithwaite, V. A., 557
Brame, B., 519, 520
Brand, S., 180
Brand, S. R., 105
Brandt, S., 385
Branje, S. J. T., 63, 615, 616
Branstetter, W. H., 43
Braswell, G., 45
Braswell, G. S., 242
Braungart-Rieker, J. M., 407, 410
Braver, S. L., 593
Bray, J. H., 595
Brazelton, T. B., 138–139
Bredekamp, S., 443, 598
Breitfelder, A., 183
Bremner, G., 141
Bremner, J. G., 230, 263, 265
Brendgen, M., 517, 522, 617, 618
Brenes, M. E., 544
Brenk, C., 616
Brennan, W. M., 161
Brenneman, K., 243
Brenner, E., 412
Brenner, H., 195
Brent, D. A., 472
Brent, M. R., 377
Breslau, N., 98
Bretherton, I., 417, 430, 436, 437
Brewaeys, A., 589
Bridge, J. A., 472
Bridges, L. J., 509
Bridgett, D. J., 423, 426
Briefel, R. R., 199
Brierley, B., 190
Briggs, M. L., 586
Bright, G. M., 182
Brisch, K. H., 435
Brock, S., 314
Brody, G. H., 547, 572, 583, 586, 612
Brody, L. R., 539, 542
Brodzinsky, D. M., 589
Broidy, L. M., 520
Bromnick, R. D., 256
Bronfenbrenner, U., 26, 121, 336, 569
Bronfman, E., 434, 440
Bronson, G. W., 163
Bronstein, P., 548
Bronte-Tinkew, J., 579
Brooker, I., 453
Brooks, P. J., 287, 388
Brooks, R., 370, 371
Brooks-Gunn, J., 33, 116, 117, 176, 203, 206, 207, 208, 218, 334, 345, 348, 441, 442, 449, 523, 572, 581, 583, 585, 590, 596, 603
Brookshire, B., 282
Brown, A. L., 287, 294, 640
Brown, A. M., 160
Brown, B. B., 456, 611, 623, 624, 626
Brown, C. S., 69, 477, 478, 479, 563
Brown, G. I., 439
Brown, J. D., 212, 219
Brown, J. R., 416, 558

Brown, R., 384, 386, 387, 389
Brown, R. D., 292, 623
Brown, S. A., 627
Brown, S. R., 449
Brown, T. E., 102, 290
Browne, C. A., 246
Browne, J. V., 139
Brownell, C. A., 409, 417, 449, 450, 465, 608
Brownell, D. K., 200
Bruce, D., 299
Bruck, M., 300, 302
Bruer, J. T., 192, 365
Brugman, D., 503
Brühwiler, C., 637
Brunstein, J. C., 271
Brunt, J., 235
Bruschi, C. J., 413
Bruschweiler-Stern, N., 139
Bruzzese, J.-M., 68
Bryant, D., 520
Bryant, P., 311
Bryce, J., 197
Bryden, M. P., 556
Buchanan, A., 555, 600
Buchanan, C. M., 175, 207, 595
Buchanan-Barrow, E., 511
Buck, G. M., 204
Budd, K. S., 202
Budell, L., 487
Buehler, C., 571
Buescher, E. S., 195
Bugental, D. B., 489, 600, 603
Buhrmester, D., 63, 625
Buhs, E. S., 620, 623, 641
Buitelaar, J. K., 106
Bukowski, W. M., 586, 609, 615, 616, 617, 619, 620, 622
Bullock, M., 449
Bumpass, L. L., 590
Bumpus, M. F., 596
Bunting, L., 218, 220
Burchinal, M., 44, 597
Burdelski, M., 393
Burden, M. J., 99
Burgess, K. B., 422, 575, 609, 620
Burgess-Champoux, T. L., 196
Burghard, B. H., 312
Burhans, K. K., 465
Buriel, R., 569
Burke, A. S., 235
Burkham, D. T., 308
Burnham, D., 368
Burnham, M. M., 132
Burns, E., 111
Burns, T. C., 368, 383
Burrell, N., 589
Burt, C. H., 523
Burton, L. M., 349
Burton, R. V., 46, 327
Burts, D. C., 582, 639
Burwell, R. A., 586
Burwinkle, T. M., 200
Bus, A. G., 307
Bush, K. R., 580, 582

Bushman, B. J., 630, 631
Bushnell, E. W., 160
Bussell, D. A., 587
Bussey, K., 497, 498, 534
Bussiére, P., 554, 555
Buswell, S. D., 134
Butler, M. G., 80
Butler, R., 458, 466
Butler, S., 539
Buttelmann, D., 453
Butterworth, G., 154
Buur, H., 421
Bybee, J., 490, 558
Byler, P., 639
Bynum, M. S., 212
Byrnes, H. F., 11
Byrnes, J. P., 257

C

Cabrera, N. J., 437, 438, 570, 582
Cahan, S., 252, 259
Cain, K. M., 465
Caine, N., 208
Cairns, B. D., 13, 14, 19
Cairns, E., 560
Cairns, R. B., 13, 14, 19, 622, 638
Calarco, K. E., 99
Caldera, Y. M., 27, 439, 571
Caldwell, B. M., 344, 345
Caldwell, K. A., 618
Caldwell, M. S., 463
Calkins, S. D., 410, 426
Call, J., 361
Callaghan, T. C., 241, 453
Callahan, C. M., 343
Callanan, M. A., 383, 416
Callands, T. A., 212
Callen, J., 194
Caltran, G., 135
Calvert, S. L., 543, 631, 632, 633
Camaioni, L., 233
Camann, W. R., 112
Camarata, S., 375
Cameron, C. A., 391
Cameron, C. E., 305
Cameron, J. A., 477
Cameron, L., 479
Cameron, N., 178
Cameron, P. A., 449
Cameron-Faulkner, T., 369
Campa, M. J., 219
Campbell, A., 543
Campbell, D. A., 111
Campbell, F. A., 348
Campbell, J. D., 46
Campbell, M. E., 616
Campbell, S. B., 402, 409, 434, 465, 520
Campbell, T., 235
Campbell, W. K., 462, 464
Campione, J. C., 294
Campos, J. J., 31, 147, 161, 230, 401, 407, 414
Campos, R. G., 137
Camras, L. A., 31, 401, 406, 407, 424

CAN (Swedish Council for Information on Alcohol and Other Drugs), 626
Canada Campaign 2000, 34
Candy, J., 543
Canfield, R., 193
Canobi, K. H., 312
Capelli, C. A., 381
Capirci, O., 371
Caplan, M., 450
Capozzoli, M. C., 240, 286, 287
Carberry, M., 290
Card, J. A., 47
Card, N. A., 518
Carels, R., 464
CARE Study Group, 97
Carey, S., 228, 243, 261, 265, 477
Carlo, G., 504, 506, 509
Carlson, E. A., 578
Carlson, S. M., 52, 241, 287, 396, 455
Carlson, V. J., 434
Carlson, W., 617
Carney, R. A., 557
Carolan, B. V., 638
Carpendale, J. I. M., 454, 481, 496, 502, 503
Carpenter, M., 233, 371, 417, 453
Carpenter, T. P., 312
Carper, R., 457
Carr, D., 200
Carr, J., 82
Carraher, D. W., 272
Carraher, T., 272
Carrano, J., 579
Carrere, S., 570
Carriger, M. S., 145, 450
Carroll, J. B., 322
Carskadon, M. A., 207
Carter, A. S., 410
Carter, J., 136
Cartin, A., 111
Caruso, D. R., 327
Carvajal, S. C., 210
Carver, K., 624, 625
Carver, P. R., 216, 550
CASA, 29
Casalis, S., 310, 394
Casas, J. F., 520, 619
Casasola, M., 234, 235, 384
Case, R., 21, 242, 261, 283, 284
Caselli, M. C., 377
Casey, B. J., 187, 190, 191
Casey, M. B., 557
Cashdan, E., 26
Cashon, C. H., 231, 232, 234
Casper, L. M., 598
Caspi, A., 61, 62, 120, 123, 124, 208, 423
Cassia, V. M., 163, 164
Cassidy, J., 431, 434
Cassidy, K. W., 452, 543
Castelli, D. M., 180
Catalano, R. A., 80
Caton, D., 112
Cattell, J. M., 320

Cattell, R. B., 321
Cauffman, E., 256, 257, 574, 575
Causey, K., 24
Cavell, T. A., 464
Cawthorne, M. A., 105
Ceci, S. J., 252, 300, 302, 332, 334, 339, 341
Celano, D., 308
Center for Communication and Social Policy, 630
Center for Effective Discipline, 602
Center on Education Policy, 343
Cermak, S. A., 171
Cernoch, J. M., 155
Cervantes, C. A., 416
Chadwick, A., 610
Chalabaev, A., 180
Chamberlain, P., 520
Chambers, P., 588
Champion, T. B., 340, 393
Chan, A., 385, 386, 615
Chan, L. K. S., 466
Chan, R. W., 589
Chan, S. M., 582
Chance, G., 166
Chandler, M. J., 454, 455, 472, 474
Chandra, A., 212, 215
Chandra, R. K., 104
Chaney, C., 394
Chang, F., 389
Chang, L., 411
Chao, R. K., 582
Chaplin, T. M., 558, 559
Chapman, K. L., 381
Chapman, R. S., 367
Charman, T., 268
Charney, D., 559
Charpak, N., 116
Chase-Lansdale, P. L., 345, 583
Chasiotis, A., 51
Chater, N., 365
Chauhan, G. S., 548
Chavajay, P., 340
Chavira, V., 475
Chawarska, K., 457
Chazan-Cohen, R., 349
Cheadle, J. E., 581
Cheah, C. S. L., 582
Cheatham, C. L., 403
Checkley, W., 201
Chen, E. S. L., 543
Chen, F. S., 430
Chen, H., 579, 582
Chen, J.-Q., 326
Chen, L.-C., 149
Chen, M.-J., 631
Chen, T. J., 184, 198
Chen, V., 582
Chen, X., 424, 425, 427, 480, 481, 582, 610, 612
Chen, Y.-C., 101
Chen, Y.-J., 101
Chen, Z., 235, 284
Cherny, S. S., 423

Chesney-Lind, M., 519
Chess, S., 419, 420, 421, 426
Cheung, K. M., 455
Chi, M. T. H., 297
Chiang, W.-C., 263
Chiarello, E., 234
Chien, D. H., 621
Children's Defense Fund, 28, 443
Childs, C. P., 25
Child Trends, 218
Chin, T., 581
Chinn, C. A., 314
Chisholm, K., 433
Chitty, L. S., 85
Chizhik, A. W., 644
Choi, J., 556
Choi, S., 235, 378
Chomsky, N., 360, 388
Chomtho, S., 199
Choudhury, S., 190
Chouinard, M. M., 248, 389
Chow, S.-M., 45
Chow, V., 453
Christakis, D. A., 237, 629
Christakos, A., 617
Christian, P., 105
Christiansen, M. H., 365
Christie, T., 241
Christophe, A., 141
Chronholm, A., 536
Chudley, A. E., 99
Chumlea, W. C., 204, 205
Chung, H. H., 396
Chung, H. L., 523
CIA (Central Intelligence Agency), 507
Cianciolo, A. T., 333
Cibelli, C., 440
Cicchetti, D., 60, 463, 601, 602
Cillessen, A. H. N., 481, 618, 619, 620, 621
Cipriano, E. A., 426, 575
Clancy, P., 387, 388
Clapp, J. F., III, 103
Clark, C. A., 114
Clark, E. V., 379, 382, 389
Clark, K. E., 611
Clark, P. A., 177, 203, 204
Clark, R., 404
Clarke-Stewart, K. A., 12, 592, 593, 611
Clarkson, T. W., 101
Claxton, L. J., 152
Claxton, S. J., 455
Clay, R. A., 293
Clearfield, M. W., 147, 539
Cleary, T. J., 305
Cleland, J. W., 135
Clements, D. H., 311, 633
Cleveland, E. S., 299
Cleveland, H. H., 585
Clifton, R. K., 151
Cluett, E. R., 111
Coatsworth, J. D., 474
Cobb, C. D., 645

Cochran, S. W., 534
Cohen, G. L., 217
Cohen, L. B., 230, 231, 232, 234, 235, 263–264, 471
Cohen, L. L., 231
Cohen, M., 62, 524
Cohen, R., 587
Cohen-Bendahan, C. C. C., 538
Cohn, J. F., 402, 403
Coid, J. W., 521
Coie, J. D., 44, 333, 481, 516, 517, 518, 521, 561, 616, 619
Colby, A., 499, 500, 502, 506
Coldwell, J., 29
Cole, C., 193
Cole, D. A., 462, 467
Cole, E., 473, 631
Cole, M., 9, 258, 435
Cole, P., 310, 394
Cole, P. M., 410, 413, 558, 559
Cole, R., 331
Cole, T. J., 184
Coleman, M., 590
Coleman, S. M., 491
Coles, C. D., 97, 98
Coley, R. L., 214, 598
Collaer, M. L., 556, 557
Collier, V. P., 397
Collins, M. A., 353
Collins, R. L., 631
Collins, W. A., 27, 208, 577, 578, 614, 624–625
Collins, W. K., 580
Colman, R. A., 411
Colom, R., 280
Colombo, J., 143, 145
Colombo, M., 143
Colonnesi, C., 233
Colson, E. R., 136
Coltrane, S., 596
Colwell, M. J., 240
Commission on Adolescent Suicide Prevention, 473
Comstock, G., 629, 630, 631
Comunian, A. L., 505, 506
Conboy, B. T., 363, 396
Conger, K. J., 11, 586
Conger, R. D., 11, 208, 581, 641
Conley, C. S., 463
Conlon, E., 308
Connell, J. P., 467
Connell, M. W., 325
Conner, D. B., 268
Connolly, J. A., 240, 617, 624
Connolly, K. J., 242
Conrad, K., 23
Conti-Ramsden, G., 162
Conway, A. R. A., 323
Conway, L., 550
Conyers, C., 19
Cook, A., 33
Cook, C. R., 621
Cook, S. W., 285
Cookston, J. T., 593
Cooper, C., 183

Cooper, C. R., 345, 474, 616
Cooper, H., 463
Cooper, R. P., 115, 156, 341
Copello, A. G., 627
Coplan, R. J., 181, 422, 425, 609, 620
Coppage, D. J., 234
Copple, C., 443, 598
Coppola, M., 363
Coppotelli, H., 619
Corbett, D., 188
Corbett, S. S., 202
Corbetta, D., 30
Core, C., 381
Corenblum, B., 477
Corkill, A. J., 287
Cornish, A. M., 404
Cornwell, A. C., 136
Cortes, R. C., 481
Costa, N. M., 412
Costello, B. J., 522
Costigan, C. L., 53
Costos, D., 206
Côté, J., 181
Côté, J. E., 469, 471
Cote, L. R., 379
Côté, S. M., 518, 519, 520
Coulton, C. J., 28, 602
Courage, M. L., 143, 163, 297, 298, 301, 632
Courchesne, E., 457
Couturier, J. L., 211
Covington, C. Y., 97
Cowan, C. P., 561, 570, 619
Cowan, N., 278, 279, 280, 281
Cowan, P. A., 561, 570, 611, 619
Cowie, H., 69
Cox, M. J., 242, 436, 438
Cox, S. M., 435
Cox, V., 246
Coy, K. C., 208
Coyl, D. D., 437
Coyle, T. R., 293
Coyne, S. M., 439, 630
Crago, M. B., 340, 388
Craig, C. M., 130
Craig, W. M., 45
Craighero, L., 146
Craigie, T.-A., 590
Crain, S., 392
Crain, W., 17
Crair, M. C., 170
Crane, D. R., 579
Craton, L. G., 160
Cratty, B. J., 179
Craven, R. G., 461, 462
Crawford, N., 550
Crawley-Davis, A. M., 237
Creasey, G. L., 240
Cresswell, J., 645
Crick, N. R., 22, 480, 518, 520, 521, 560, 616, 619, 623, 630
Criss, M. M., 586
Crittenden, P., 431
Crockenberg, S. C., 27, 410
Crocker, J., 463

Crocker, N. A., 98, 99
Crockett, L. J., 214, 412, 579, 627
Croft, C. M., 435
Crone, E. A., 257
Cronk, C., 371
Crosby, L., 616
Crosno, R., 643
Cross, D. R., 268
Crouch, J. L., 600
Crouter, A. C., 207, 533, 542, 543–544, 546, 551, 579, 580, 586, 596
Crowe, H. P., 137
Crowley, K., 64, 540
Crowson, M., 457
Cruess, L., 288
Cruttenden, L., 232
Crystal, D. S., 505, 507, 623
Csibra, G., 231, 268, 370
Csikszentmihalyi, M., 639
Cuevas, K., 233, 301
Cuijpers, P., 627
Culbertson, F. M., 560
Cumberland, A., 413
Cummings, E. M., 45, 56, 429, 571
Cunningham, A. E., 380
Curby, T. W., 641
Curran, D. J., 339
Currie, C., 209
Currie, J., 348
Curtis, L. E., 310
Cutler, A., 157, 369
Cutrona, C. E., 220
Cutter, W. J., 83
Cvencek, D., 532
Cyr, C., 440
Cyr, M., 625

D

Dabrowska, E., 387
Dack, L. A., 455
Daddis, C., 511
Dadds, M. R., 133
Dadson, M. J., 210
Dahl, R. E., 207
Dahlberg, L. L., 519
Dale, P., 378
Daleiden, E., 47
Dales, L., 202
D'Alessio, M., 631
Daley, T. C., 338
Daltabuit, M., 137
Daly, M., 478
Damasio, A. R., 487
Damhuis, I., 409
Damon, W., 458, 464, 506, 510, 614
Daniel, D. B., 258
Daniel, J., 631
Daniels, D. H., 467
Daniels, E., 181
Daniels, T., 620
Danielsen, K. V., 199
Dannemiller, J. L., 164
Danziger, S., 649
Danziger, S. K., 36

Dapretto, M., 377
Darling, N. E., 574
Darling-Hammond, L., 343, 638, 645, 647
Darlington, R., 347
Darroch, J. E., 214
Darwin, C., 13
Das, D. A., 19
D'Augelli, A. R., 216, 472
Daunhauer, L. A., 171
Davalos, M., 418
David, A. S., 190
David, B., 504
David, K. M., 426
Davidson, R. J., 187
Davies, J., 543
Davies, P. T., 27, 571
Davis, J., 213
Davis, K. F., 132
Davis, O. S. P., 120
Davis-Kean, P. E., 346, 627
Davison, K. K., 196
Davison, M. L., 555
Dawson, G., 505
Dawson, N., 390
Dawson, T. L., 502
Deák, G. O., 243, 382, 383
Dean, D., Jr., 313
Dean, M., 302
Dearing, E., 28, 33, 599
Deary, I. J., 195, 323, 331
Deater-Deckard, K., 120, 425, 492
DeBerry, K. M., 337–338
Debes, F., 101
Deblinger, E., 601
DeBoer, T., 48
De Brauwer, J., 312
de Bruyn, E. H., 620, 642
Debus, R., 462
DeCasper, A. J., 49, 94, 156
Deci, E. L., 473
De Corte, E., 312
DeGarmo, D. S., 578
Degirmencioglu, S. M., 615
De Goede, I. H. A., 615
de Haan, M., 50, 144, 156, 185, 186, 188, 190
Deissinger, T., 649
Dekker, M. C., 559
Deković, M., 208, 579
de la Ossa, J. L., 291
De Leon, J. M., 438
de León, L., 372
Delgado-Gaitan, C., 340
De Lisi, R., 380, 548
Dell, G. S., 389
DeLoache, J. S., 236, 237, 243, 449
Delobel-Ayoub, M., 114
DelVecchio, W. F., 423
DeMarie-Dreblow, D., 288
Dembo, M. H., 617
Dement, W. C., 135
Demetriou, A., 21, 314
Demille, D., 374
Dempster, F. N., 287

de Muinck Keizer-Schrama, S. M. P. F., 184
Demuth, K., 375
DeNavas-Walt, C., 33
Denham, S. A., 327, 416, 610
Denissen, J. J. A., 463
Dennis, T., 97
Dennis, W., 150
Dennison, E. M., 183
Denton, K., 509
Denton, M. L., 507
Denton, N. A., 53
Deocampo, J. A., 237
de Oliveira-Souza, R., 487
Deprest, J. A., 85
Der, G., 195
Derakhshan, N., 402
deRegnier, R.-A., 48
de Ribaupierre, A., 323
de Rivera, J., 409
DeRoche, K., 79
Derom, C., 189
DeRose, L. M., 206
DeRosier, M. E., 620
de Rosnay, M., 414, 456
De Rycke, L., 461
De Schipper, J. C., 597
de Schonen, S., 164
Désert, M., 533
Desmarais, S., 542
DeSouza, A., 424, 425, 427
De Souza, E., 82
Desrochers, S., 21
Detterman, D. K., 320, 329
Deutsch, W., 391
Devi, N. P. G., 102
de Villiers, J. G., 384, 386, 388, 455
de Villiers, P. A., 384, 386, 455
Devise, I., 372
DeVos, J., 230, 231
DeVries, R., 639
de Waal, F. B. M., 486, 487, 535
de Weerd, A. W., 135
de Weerth, C., 106, 195
DeWolff, M. S., 434
Deynoot-Schaub, M. J. G., 608
DiAdamo, C., 452
Diamond, A., 124, 189, 232, 288, 377
Diamond, L. M., 215, 216, 625
Dias, M. G., 257
Diaz, V., 118
DiBiase, A.-M., 525
Dick, D. M., 208, 627
Dick, F., 363, 367
Dickens, W. T., 338
Dickinson, D. K., 308, 309
Dick-Read, G., 110
DiDonato, M. D., 547
Dietrich, K. N., 193
Dietz, E. L., 623
Dietz, T. L., 543, 634
Dildy, G. A., 106
Dimitrov, D. M., 219
Ding, Z. Y., 198
Dingel, A., 234

DiPietro, J. A., 93, 94
Dirix, C. E. H., 94, 142
Dirks, J., 341
Dishion, T. J., 58, 525, 616
Dittmar, M., 385
Dittus, P., 212
Dixon, T. L., 631
Dixon, W. E., Jr., 378
Dodd, B. J., 375
Dodd, V. L., 116
Dodge, K. A., 22, 333, 480, 481, 493, 516, 517, 518, 521, 522, 525, 561, 619
Dodge, T., 212
D'Odorico, L., 374
Doherty, W. J., 570
Dohnt, H., 463
Dolan, A., 299
Dolenszky, E., 617
Dombrowski, S. C., 114
Domellöf, E., 189
Dominguez, E., 345
Dominy, N. J., 192
Domitrovich, C. E., 288, 351, 464, 481
Donahue, M. J., 507
Dondi, M., 135
Dong, W., 466
Donnellan, M. B., 463, 464, 581
Donnelly, R., 464
Donnelly, T. M., 507, 508
Donnerstein, E., 631
D'Onofrio, B. M., 578, 592
Donovan, W. L., 137
Dorius, C. J., 590, 592, 627
Dorn, L. D., 206, 208
Dornbusch, S. M., 595
Dorris, M., 98
Dorsey, S., 590
Doss, B. D., 570
Douglas, E. M., 593
Douglas, G., 340
Douglas, R. N., 297
Dovidio, J. F., 478
Dowker, A., 311
Dowling, E. M., 507
Downing, J. E., 646
Downs, A. C., 534, 544
Downs, A. D., 206
Downs, R. M., 250
Doydum, A. O., 298
Doyle, A. B., 240, 476
Dozier, M., 435
Drabman, R. S., 47, 199
Drake, C., 155
Draper, P., 26
Drell, M. J., 181
Drewett, R. F., 202
Dribe, M., 536
Driscoll, K. A., 560
Driscoll, M. C., 79
Droege, K. L., 476
Drotar, D., 68, 334
Dubé, E. M., 216
DuBois, D. L., 463

Dubois-Comtois, K., 440
Dubow, E., 345
Duckworth, A. L., 341
Dueker, G. L., 165
Duggan, A., 603
Dukes, C., 292
Dunaway, R. G., 522
Duncan, G. J., 288, 311, 345, 351, 580, 581
Duncan, L. G., 394
Duncan, S. R., 136
Dundek, L. H., 111
Dunger, D. B., 184
Dunham, Y., 477, 478
Dunifon, R., 36
Dunn, J., 29, 416, 456, 558, 585, 586, 592, 595
Dunn, J. R., 572
Dunn, M. J., 86
Dunne-Bryant, A., 591
Dunphy-Lelii, S., 370
Dupere, V., 523
Durbin, D. L., 624
Durkin, K., 457
Durlach, J., 104
Durlak, J. A., 598
Durston, S., 23
Duszak, R. S., 102
Dutilleul, S., 154
Dweck, C. D., 465, 478
Dweck, C. S., 430, 465, 466, 467, 476, 478, 479
Dzurova, D., 82

E

Eacott, M. J., 301
Eagly, A. H., 486
Easterbrooks, A., 440
Easterbrooks, M. A., 449–450
Eaton, D. K., 625
Eaton, M. M., 464
Eaves, L., 204
Ebeling, K. S., 245
Eccles, J. S., 180, 207, 209, 331, 463, 471, 508, 532, 541, 627, 638, 641, 642, 643
Eckenrode, J. J., 219, 635
Eckerman, C. O., 608
Economic Policy Institute, 648
Eddy, K. T., 211
Eder, R. A., 456
Edleson, J. L., 602
Edmondson, P., 372
Edmunds, L., 327
Edwards, A., 415, 521
Edwards, C. P., 535, 536, 542
Edwards, L. J., 135
Edwards, O. W., 334, 339
Egan, S. K., 216, 550
Egeland, B., 214, 432, 437, 601, 603
Eggum, N. D., 521
Egley, R. J., 343
Egozi, G., 557
Ehri, L. C., 308
Ehrman, L., 189

Eichstedt, J. A., 531
Eiden, R. D., 97
Eigsti, I.-M., 516
Einspieler, C., 92
Eisen, M., 458
Eisenberg, N., 409, 411, 417, 418, 426, 489, 510, 521, 524, 544, 558, 579
Eisenberg-Berg, N., 491
Eisenbud, L., 552
Eisengart, J., 385
Eiser, C., 300
Ekman, P., 405
Elder, G. H., 641
Elder, G. H., Jr., 61, 208, 643
Elfenbein, D. S., 218
Eliakim, A., 200
Elias, C. L., 240
Elicker, J., 440
Elischberger, H. B., 295
Elkind, D., 255, 256
Ellis, A. E., 234
Ellis, B. J., 205, 214
Ellis, L. A., 461
Ellis, W. E., 616
Elman, J. L., 367, 387
Else-Quest, N. M., 412, 514, 640
El-Sheikh, M., 56
Eltzschig, H. K., 112
Eluvathingal, T. J., 171
Ely, R., 310, 392
Ember, C. R., 492
Ember, M., 492
Emde, R. N., 420
Emery, R. E., 209, 593
Emmerich, W., 548
Emmerson, N. A., 611
Emory, E. K., 112
Endestad, T., 300
Engels, R. C. M. E., 506
Engle, R. W., 323
Englund, M., 440
Ennemoser, M., 632
Ensor, R., 416, 454, 455, 456
Entringer, S., 105
Epstein, L. H., 200
Epstein, R., 133
Erath, S. A., 492
Erden, F., 543
Erickson, J. D., 96
Erickson, M. F., 601
Erikson, E. H., 15, 468
Erkulwater, J., 291
Ernst, M., 125, 256
Eron, L. D., 631
Esbensen, B. M., 303
Eslinger, P. J., 487
Espelage, D. L., 216
Espnes, G. A., 461
Esposito-Smythers, C., 472
Esser, G., 117
Essex, M. J., 205
Estep, K., 416
Estourgie-van Burk, G. F., 192
Ethier, K. A., 217

Euling, S. Y., 184
Evanoo, G., 137
Evans, C. B., 583
Evans, D. E., 421, 423
Evans, E., 472
Evans, G. W., 280, 581
Evans, M. E., 582
Evans, N., 365
Eveleth, P. B., 183
Eysenck, M. W., 402

F

Fabes, C. A., 537, 544
Fabes, R. A., 415, 416, 417, 418, 489, 510, 537, 558, 562
Fabricius, W. V., 303, 453
Fagan, J., 570
Fagan, J. F., III, 144, 145, 329, 334, 341
Fagard, J., 151
Fagot, B. I., 518, 531, 533, 539, 542, 544, 548, 549
Fahrmeier, E. D., 252
Fairburn, C. G., 211
Faison, N., 508
Faith, M. S., 198
Falagas, M. E., 202
Falbo, T., 463, 587, 588
Falck-Ytter, T., 233
Falk, D., 187
Fantuzzo, J. W., 271, 644
Fantz, R. L., 161
Farah, M. J., 280
Faraone, S. V., 120, 290
Farley, F., 257
Farmer, T. W., 623
Farr, R. J., 589
Farrant, K., 299
Farrar, M. J., 454
Farrie, D., 570
Farrington, D. P., 205, 519, 521
Farroni, T., 163, 164
Farver, J. A. M., 43, 612, 613
Fasig, L. G., 450
Fattibene, P., 100
Fauth, R. C., 33
Favreau, O. E., 533
Fearnow, M. D., 412
Fearon, R. M. P., 169, 434, 440
Federal Interagency Forum on Child and Family Statistics, 591, 596
Federico, A., 390
Fee, E. J., 374
Feeney, J. A., 570
Fegley, S., 506
Feigelman, W., 473
Feigenbaum, P., 136
Feil, R., 80
Fein, G. G., 609
Feinberg, M. E., 586, 587
Feldman, A. F., 638
Feldman, D. H., 51
Feldman, J. F., 145
Feldman, R., 56, 115, 116, 119, 135, 268, 404, 410, 426, 437

Felice, M. E., 218
Felner, R. D., 642
Felsman, D. E., 473
Feng, J., 557
Feng, Q., 97
Fennell, C. T., 374
Fenson, L., 377
Fenwick, K. D., 166
Ferguson, R. F., 340
Ferguson, T. J., 409
Fergusson, D. M., 10, 195, 333
Ferholt, B., 392
Fernald, A., 369, 376, 377, 378, 381
Fernald, L. C., 197
Fernandes, K. J., 157
Fernyhough, C., 25, 267
Ferry, A. L., 235
Fesseha, G., 524
Fetter, M. D., 624
Fiano, K., 112
Fias, W., 312
Ficca, G., 133
Field, T., 105, 115, 116, 404, 418
Fiese, B. H., 29, 196, 435
Fifer, W. P., 133, 156
Figner, B., 256
Figueroa, Z., 116
Fincham, F. D., 466
Findlay, L. C., 181
Fine, M. A., 575
Finger, B., 436
Fink, A., 323
Finkel, D., 346
Finkelhor, D., 212, 600, 601, 635
Finn, J. D., 637
Finnilä, K., 302
Fireman, G., 415
Fischer, A. D., 285
Fischer, K. W., 21, 30, 252, 407, 409,
    410
Fischman, M. G., 180
Fish, J. M., 339
Fish, M., 432
Fishbein, M., 293
Fisher, C., 385
Fisher, C. B., 67, 68, 69
Fisher, D. M., 130, 131
Fisher, J. A., 195
Fisher, J. O., 196
Fisher, L., 433
Fisher, M., 68, 125
Fisher, P. A., 378
Fitzgerald, L. F., 220
Fivush, R., 295, 298, 299, 416, 440,
    539
Flanagan, C., 592
Flanagan, C. A., 508, 512
Flannery, D. J., 256, 519, 523
Flannery, K. A., 189
Flavell, E. R., 243, 303
Flavell, J. H., 243, 287, 303, 304, 415
Flege, J. E., 365
Fleiss, K., 510
Fletcher, A. C., 181, 574, 615
Fletcher, J., 523

Fletcher, P., 376
Flett, G. L., 462
Flick, L., 103
Floccia, C., 141
Flom, R., 143, 166, 168, 371
Flor, D. L., 583
Florsheim, P., 218, 220
Flouri, E., 555
Flynn, E., 64, 453
Flynn, J. R., 334, 338
Foehr, U. G., 212, 293, 629, 630, 632,
    633, 634, 636
Foerde, K., 293
Fogel, A., 31, 141, 406, 407, 559
Foley, K. P., 29
Fomon, S. J., 177
Fonagy, P., 437
Fontayne, P., 180
Fonzi, A., 615
Forbes, J. N., 379
Forcier, M., 559
Ford, S., 511
Fordham, K., 422
Forgatch, M. S., 524, 578
Forman, D. R., 404, 491
Formann, A. K., 59
Forry, N. D., 594
Forssell, S. L., 589
Fortenberry, J. D., 214
Fortier, L., 258
Foster, M. A., 308, 345
Foster, S. L., 67
Foster, W. A., 308, 310
Foy, J. G., 308
Fradley, E., 267
Fraiberg, S., 405
Fraley, C., 423
Fraley, R. C., 435
Frank, D. A., 97
Frank, J. B., 181
Frankel, C. B., 31, 401
Frankenberg, E., 479, 645
Franko, D. L., 196
Franks, B. A., 258
Franz, C., 418
Fraser, M. W., 481
Fredericks, J. A., 463
Frederiksen-Goldsen, K. I., 596
Fredricks, J. A., 180, 638
Freedman, J., 115
Freedman-Doan, C., 642
Freeman, D., 205
Freeman, H., 437
Freitag, C. M., 290
French, D. C., 612
French, D. J., 523
French, L. A., 250
French, S. E., 641, 642
Frensch, P. A., 346

Freud, S., 15, 488
Frey, K. S., 548
Frick, P. J., 522
Friederici, A. D., 364, 414
Friedman, C. K., 539
Friedman, J. M., 97, 98
Friedman, M. A., 200
Friedman, S. L., 282
Friedrich, M., 364
Friend, J., 472
Fries, A. B. W., 433
Friesen, W., 405
Frigon, J.-Y., 205
Frijda, N., 401
Frith, L., 87
Frith, U., 457
Fritsch, M., 507
Frome, P. M., 541
Frost, J. J., 214
Frost, L. A., 388
Fry, A. F., 281
Frye, D., 452
Fryer, S. L., 98, 99
Fryns, J. P., 83
Fu, G., 498
Fuchs, I., 505
Fuchs, L. S., 646
Fuligni, A. J., 53, 345
Fuligni, A. S., 345
Fuller, C., 196
Fuller, D., 499, 500, 525
Fuller, M. J., 206
Fuller-Thomson, E., 438
Fullerton, J. T., 111
Fung, H., 409, 451
Furman, W., 63, 578, 624, 625
Furrow, J. L., 507
Furstenberg, F. F., Jr., 218, 220
Furusawa, T., 200
Fuson, K. C., 311, 312

G

Gaddis, L., 425
Gaither, S. M., 467
Galambos, N. L., 550, 598
Gale, C. R., 333
Galen, B. R., 560
Galinsky, E., 29, 350, 438, 442, 596
Gallagher, A. M., 548, 557
Gallaway, C., 389
Gallay, L. S., 512
Galloway, J. C., 149, 151
Gallup, G. G., 449
Gallup News Service, 507
Galotti, K. M., 560
Galton, F., 320
Galvan, A., 191
Gamble, W. C., 586
Ganchrow, J. R., 141
Ganea, P., 383
Ganea, P. A., 236
Ganger, J., 377
Ganong, L. H., 590
Garber, J., 104
Garces, E., 348

Garcia, A., 237
Garcia, M. M., 521
Garcia-Bournissen, F., 96
García Coll, C., 53, 438, 475, 582
Gardner, H. E., 51, 242, 325, 326, 350,
    353, 355
Gardner, M., 191
Gardner-Kitt, D. L., 475
Garner, P. W., 44, 408, 413, 416
Garovich, L., 530
Garrido-Nag, K., 364
Gartstein, M. A., 421, 424, 427
Garven, S., 302
Garvey, A., 31
Garvey, C., 391
Gasden, V., 590
Gaskins, S., 273, 613
Gates, G. J., 589
Gathercole, S. E., 280, 381
Gathercole, V., 385
Gaultney, J. F., 145
Gauvain, M., 251, 290, 291
Gauze, C., 618
Gawlitzek-Maiwald, I., 396
Gazelle, H., 620, 623
Gazzaniga, M. S., 364
Ge, X., 207, 208, 209, 214
Geangu, E., 135
Geary, D. C., 24, 262, 280, 311, 535,
    556, 558, 568
Gee, C. B., 220
Geerts, M., 83
Geesey, M. E., 118
Gelman, R., 245, 246, 247, 311
Gelman, S. A., 245, 246, 247, 264,
    310, 362, 378, 380, 456, 533,
    541
Gendler, M. N., 415
Genesee, F., 396, 397
Gennetian, L. A., 36
Gentile, D. A., 630, 634
Gentner, D., 379
Georgsdottir, A., 353
Gerardi-Caulton, G., 423
Gerber, S. B., 637
Gerdes, A. C., 620
Gergely, G., 233, 406
Gerken, L., 374
Gershkoff-Stowe, L., 377
Gershoff, E. T., 27, 491, 492, 520
Gerson, S., 233
Gertner, S., 133
Gertner, Y., 385
Gervai, J., 435, 534, 539, 542, 543,
    548
Gesell, A., 13
Gest, S. D., 464
Getchell, N., 178, 179, 180
Getz, S., 191
Geuze, R. H., 163
Gewirtz, A. H., 10, 524, 602
Ghavami, N., 475
Ghim, H. R., 163
Gibbons, A., 74
Gibbons, P., 74

Gibbs, J. C., 489, 495, 496, 499, 500, 502, 503, 505, 506, 508, 509, 510, 522, 525, 555
Gibson, E. J., 159, 168
Gibson, J. J., 168
Gibson, K. A., 86
Giedd, J. N., 190
Gielen, U. P., 505, 506
Giles, J. W., 531
Giles-Sims, J., 492
Gill, M., 125
Gillespie, D. D., 170
Gillet, J.-P., 86
Gillette, P., 264
Gillies, R. M., 271, 644
Gilligan, C. F., 503
Gilliom, M., 411
Gilmore, J., 503
Gilstrap, L. L., 302
Gimenez, M., 265
Gingras, J. L., 145
Ginsberg, S., 256
Ginsburg, A. P., 161
Ginsburg, H. P., 46, 310, 311
Ginsburg, K. R., 639
Ginsburg-Block, M. D., 271, 644
Giorgi, C., 190
Giovanelli, G., 155
Gissler, M., 98
Glade, A. C., 570
Gladstone, I. M., 114
Gladwell, M., 200
Glanz, J., 640
Gleason, T. R., 240, 241
Gleason, T. W., 240
Gleitman, H., 383
Gleitman, L. R., 382, 383, 384
Glenwright, M., 381
Glover, V., 106
Glowinski, A. L., 559
Gluckman, P. D., 108
Gnepp, J., 415
Godart, N. T., 211
Goddard, S., 263
Goedereis, E. A., 439
Goeke-Morey, M. C., 571
Goelman, H., 390
Goering, J., 572
Gogate, L. J., 143, 144, 157
Goh, Y. I., 104
Gold, J., 498
Goldberg, A., 617, 624
Goldberg, A. E., 570, 589
Goldberg-Glen, R. S., 439
Goldenberg, C., 53
Goldfield, B. A., 378
Goldhammer, F., 323
Goldin-Meadow, S., 249, 285, 362, 371
Goldschmidt, L., 98
Goldsmith, H. H., 377
Goldstein, A. S., 581
Goldstein, M. H., 370
Goldstein, S., 290, 291
Goldstein, S. E., 522, 523, 627

Goldstein, T. R., 472
Goldston, D. B., 473
Goldwyn, R., 436
Goleman, D., 327
Golinkoff, R. M., 171, 308, 377, 383
Golomb, C., 241
Golombok, S., 86, 538, 539, 589
Gómez, R. L., 133
Gomez-Perez, E., 287
Gomez-Smith, Z., 438
Göncü, A., 240, 609
Gonzalez, A.-L., 574
Goodall, J., 486
Goode, J. D., 525
Goode, V., 525
Goodlin-Jones, B. L., 132
Goodman, G. S., 302, 402
Goodman, J., 378
Goodman, M., 411, 412
Goodman, S. H., 481
Goodnow, J. J., 25, 491
Goodvin, R., 402, 409, 411
Goodwin, M. H., 546
Gooren, E. M. J. C., 620
Gopnik, A., 235, 247, 264, 378, 415, 452, 453
Gordon, L. L., 296
Gordon, P., 264
Gordon, R. A., 583
Gormally, S., 153
Gorman, B. S., 473
Goswami, U., 235, 246
Gottlieb, G., 9, 120, 122, 124
Gottman, J. M., 570
Goubet, N., 151
Gould, J. L., 76
Govaerts, P. J., 370
Government of Canada, 397
Graber, J. A., 176, 203, 205, 207, 208, 209, 210, 559, 560, 630
Graham, J. A., 467
Graham, S., 35, 42, 641, 642
Graham, S. A., 382
Gralinski, J. H., 450, 515
Grall, T. S., 591
Granger, D. A., 97
Granger, R. C., 598
Granic, I., 31
Granier-Deferre, C., 94
Granillo, T., 210
Granrud, C. E., 160
Grant, K., 439
Grantham-McGregor, S. M., 105, 197
Grattan, M. P., 187
Graves, S. B., 631
Gravitt, G. W., Jr., 481
Gray, K. S., 98
Gray, M. R., 573
Gray-Little, B., 464
Graziano, W. G., 612
Gredebäck, G., 233
Greek, A., 585
Green, F. L., 243, 303
Green, G. E., 138
Green, J. A., 135

Green, R., 536
Greenbaum, C. W., 426
Greenberg, M. T., 288, 481
Greenberger, E., 560, 581
Greene, A. D., 219
Greene, K., 256
Greene, L., 213
Greene, M. L., 475
Greene, S. M., 593
Greenfield, P. M., 25, 35, 150, 252, 340, 341, 632, 634, 635
Greenhill, L. L., 291
Greenhoot, A. F., 295, 296
Greenough, W. T., 170, 191
Greenspan, S. I., 361
Greenwald, A. G., 532
Gregory, R., 590
Grela, B., 237
Grief, G. L., 555
Grieve, A. J., 329
Griffin, S., 284
Grigorenko, E. L., 324, 336, 339, 342
Grime, R. L., 499, 500
Groisser, D. B., 282
Grolnick, W. S., 642
Gronau, R. C., 516
Groome, L. J., 93
Gropman, A. L., 80
Gross, J., 142
Gross, J. J., 558
Grossman, A. H., 216
Grossman, P. B., 464
Grossmann, K., 432, 437, 439
Grossmann, T., 414
Grotevant, H. D., 546
Grouzet, F. M. E., 641
Grover, T., 593
Grow-Maienza, J., 648
Grube, J. W., 631
Gruendel, J., 35, 37
Grusec, J. E., 489, 490, 491, 495
Guerra, N. G., 35, 42, 621
Guglielmi, R. S., 397
Gugula, S., 542
Guignard, J.-H., 353, 354
Guilford, J. P., 350
Guiso, L., 557, 558
Gulko, J., 532, 533, 534, 549
Güller, O. E., 292
Gullone, E., 412
Gulotta, T. P., 11
Gump, P. V., 638
Gunnar, M. R., 48, 403
Gunnoe, M. L., 493
Gunstad, J., 189
Guo, G., 585
Guo, J., 546
Guralnick, M. J., 622
Gure, A., 208
Gust, D. A., 202
Gustafson, G. E., 135, 138
Guterman, N. B., 602
Gutman, L. M., 331, 641, 642
Gutteling, B. M., 106
Gwiazda, J., 163

H
Haas, L., 536
Hack, M., 116
Haddock, G., 200
Haddow, J. L., 218
Haden, C. A., 295, 416
Hafdahl, A. F., 464
Hagan, R. I., 539
Hagekull, B., 202
Hagerman, R. J., 80, 81
Hagoort, P., 157, 369
Hahn, D.-D., 648
Hahn, E. R., 377
Hahn, H.-M., 134
Hahn, S., 85
Haidt, J., 486, 487, 506, 509
Haight, W. L., 270, 273
Hainline, L., 159
Haith, M. M., 151, 159, 161, 289
Hakman, M., 515
Hakuta, K., 364, 365
Haladyna, T. M., 644
Hale, C. M., 455
Hale, S., 281
Hales, C. N., 192
Halfon, N., 34
Halford, G. S., 21, 22, 249, 250, 261
Halford, W. K., 570
Hall, C. M., 538
Hall, D. G., 382, 383
Hall, G. S., 13
Hall, J. A., 547
Hall, J. G., 76, 77
Haller, J., 197
Hallinan, M. T., 644
Halperin, J. M., 291
Halpern, C. T., 212
Halpern, D. F., 554, 555, 556, 557
Halpern-Felsher, B. L., 257
Halverson, C. F., Jr., 551
Ham, M., 207
Hambrick, D. Z., 323
Hamel, E., 629, 630, 633, 636
Hamer, D. H., 215
Hamer, L., 558
Hamilton, H. A., 595
Hamilton, M., 543
Hamilton, M. A., 649
Hamilton, S. F., 649
Hamlin, J. K., 487
Hamm, J. C., 616
Hammer, S. J., 202
Hammes, B., 96
Hammond, M., 374
Hampton, A., 644
Hamre, B. K., 643
Han, W.-J., 345, 442, 596
Hanawalt, B. A., 11
Handley, S. J., 287
Hane, A. A., 422
Hanish, L. D., 537
Hankin, B. L., 559, 617
Hanlon, C., 389
Hannon, E. E., 155, 156
Hannon, T. S., 198

Hans, S. L., 97, 435
Hansell, N. K., 282
Hansen, M., 207
Hansen, M. B., 382
Hanushek, E., 479
Hany, E. A., 331
Happaney, K., 600
Happé, F., 457
Harachi, T. W., 520
Hardin, C. A., 303
Hardy, J. B., 218, 219
Hardy, S. A., 506, 509
Hare, B., 361
Hare, T. A., 190
Harkness, A. R., 333
Harkness, S., 132, 133, 139
Harlan, E. T., 423
Harlan, S. L., 583
Harley, B., 397
Harley, K., 301
Harlow, H. F., 428
Harmon, E. L., 575
Harmon, R. J., 449–450
Harnishfeger, K. K., 287
Harold, R. D., 532
Harris, C. J., 23
Harris, G., 154
Harris, J. R., 578
Harris, K. M., 220
Harris, M. B., 220
Harris, M. J., 425, 621
Harris, P. L., 236, 257, 265, 453
Harris, S., 25, 267, 350
Harris, Y. R., 467
Harrison, A. O., 582
Harrison, P. J., 211
Harrison, Y., 132
Harrop, A., 543
Hart, B., 345, 376, 377, 390, 391
Hart, C., 198
Hart, C. H., 504, 518, 573, 574, 578,
    588, 620, 639
Hart, D., 397, 458, 506, 507, 508, 581
Harter, S., 209, 215, 405, 409, 416,
    456, 458, 459, 461, 462, 463, 547
Harton, H. C., 616
Hartshorn, K., 141, 142
Hartup, W. W., 240, 613, 614, 615,
    616
Harvey, R. J., 523
Harvey-Arnold, E., 561
Harwood, M. D., 454
Haryu, E., 382, 383
Hasebe, Y., 511, 512
Hasegawa, T., 263
Hasselhorn, M., 292
Hastings. E. C., 634
Hastings, P. D., 47, 417, 609
Hatano, G., 265
Hatton. D. D., 162
Hau, K.-T., 648
Hauck, F. R., 136
Hauf, P., 152
Hausfather, A., 441
Hawkins, J. N., 463

Hawton, K., 472
Hay, D. F., 404, 610
Hay, P., 212
Haycock, P. C., 99
Hayden, A., 164
Hayne, H., 142, 143, 146, 234, 237,
    270, 295, 301
Haynie, D. L., 627
Hayslip, B., 438
Hayward, C., 592, 593
Haywood, H. C., 342
Haywood, K. I., 180
Haywood, K. M., 178, 179, 180
Hazen, N. L., 437
He, J., 561
He, Z., 453
Head, M. R., 579, 580
Head Start, 347
Health Canada, 217
Healthy Families America, 603
Healy, M., 178
Healy, S. D., 557
Hearold, S., 632
Heath, S. B., 339, 581
Heathcock, J., 151
Hebl, M., 515
Heckman, J. J., 37, 349
Hedges, L. V., 637
Hediger, M. L., 104, 114
Heil, M., 557
Hein, M. M., 543, 631
Heinz, W. R., 649
Helburn, S. W., 443
Held, R., 152
Helfand, M., 214
Hellemans, K, G., 99
Heller, L., 590
Heller, T. L., 481
Heller, W., 187
Helmstadter, G. C., 544
Helwig, C. C., 497, 511, 512
Hemphill, S. A., 425
Henderson, H. A., 422, 425
Henderson, R. L., 303
Henderson, S. H., 587
Hendrick, J., 543
Henggeler, S. W., 525
Hengst, J. A., 52
Hennig, K. H., 503
Henrich, C. C., 215, 623
Henricsson, L., 643
Henriksen, L., 212
Henriksen, T. B., 97
Henry, B., 46
Hepper, P. G., 189
Heraghty, J. L., 132
Herald, S. L., 623, 641
Herald-Brown, S. L., 620
Herbert, J., 142, 237
Herman, K. C., 524
Herman, L. M., 361
Herman, M. R., 475
Herman-Giddens, M. E., 204, 205
Hermer, L., 165
Hernandez, D., 598

Hernandez, D. J., 53
Hernandez-Reif, M., 115, 144, 166
Herr, M. Y., 269
Herrnstein, R., 335
Hertenstein, M. J., 414
Herzog, D. B., 211
Hesketh, K., 630
Hesketh, T., 588
Hespos, S. J., 130, 187, 235, 262, 263,
    448
Hesse, E., 432, 434, 437
Hesselbrock, V. M., 627
Hessl, D., 81
Hester, M., 561
Hetherington, E. M., 578, 587, 591,
    592, 593, 594, 595
Heuer, C. A., 200
Hewer, A., 499
Hewes, A. K., 366
Hewlett, B. S., 119, 437, 439
Hewstone, M., 479
Heyes, C., 145
Heyman, G. D., 247, 456, 465, 478,
    531, 532
Hibbert, J. R., 579, 580
Hickling, A. K., 246, 265, 381
Hicks, J. H., 439
Higginbottom, G. M. A., 52
High. P. C., 309
Hildebrandt, N., 494
Hilden, D., 279
Hildreth, K., 141, 142
Hill, A. L., 411
Hill, C. R., 643
Hill, E. A., 369
Hill, E. J., 596
Hill, E. M., 556
Hill, J. L., 116, 117
Hill, J. P., 550
Hill, N. E., 582, 647
Hillard, P. J. A., 205
Hillis, S. D., 218
Hill-Soderlund, A. L., 407, 410
Hilt, 2004, 467, 468
Hind, H., 196
Hinde, R. A., 534, 542
Hines, M., 536
Hinojosa, T., 189
Hippisley, J., 340
Hiraki, K., 146, 263
Hirasawa, R., 80
Hirsh-Pasek, K., 44, 171, 240, 308,
    377, 383
Hiscock, H., 133
Hjern, A., 98
Ho, E., 311
Ho, I. T., 648
Hoch-Espada, A., 601
Hock, H. S., 293
Hodges, C., 532
Hodges, J., 433
Hodges, R. M., 250
Hodnett, E. D., 111
Hoehn, T., 113
Hoeksma, J. B., 426

Hoekstra, R. A., 77
Hoerr, T., 355
Hofer, J., 51
Hoff, E., 56, 378, 381, 391, 580
Hoff, E. V., 240
Hoff, T., 213
Hofferth, S. L., 594, 595, 634
Hoffman, L. W., 487, 489, 544, 596
Hoffman, M. L., 417
Hoffmann, W., 100
Hoffner, C., 415
Hofstadter, M., 232
Hogan, M. J., 211
Hogan, R. T., 333
Hogarty, P. S., 331
Hoglund, W. L., 621
Hohmann, L. M., 240
Hohne, E. A., 157
Hokoda, A., 466
Holden, G. W., 491, 492
Holditch-Davis, D., 135
Holland, A. L., 188
Holland, C. R., 145, 341
Hollich, G. J., 383
Holliday, R. E., 296
Hollis, C., 574
Holmbeck, G. N., 175, 579
Holme, A., 195
Holmes, R. M., 639
Holobow, N., 397
Holodynski, M., 412
Holsen, I., 207
Homer, B. D., 394, 453, 454
Hommerding, K. D., 432
Honein, M. A., 96
Hong, M., 648
Hong, Z.-R., 532
Honzik, M. P., 331
Hood, B. M., 230
Hood, M., 308
Hoover-Dempsey, K. V., 647
Hopkins, B., 150, 187
Hopkins, J., 435
Hopkins-Golightly, T., 113
Horn, J. L., 321, 322
Horn, J. M., 123, 336, 337, 346
Horne, R. S. C., 136
Horner, S. L., 467
Horner, T. M., 407
Hort, B. E., 531, 533
Horwood, J., 10
Horwood, L. J., 333
Horwood, R. L., 434
Houck, G. M., 410
Houghton, S., 340
Houlihan, J., 101
Houston-Price, C., 390
Hoven, C. W., 62
Howard, K. S., 603
Howe, M. L., 143, 297, 298, 301, 632
Howe, N., 586
Howell, C. T., 116
Howell, K. K., 97, 98, 99
Howell, T. M., 473
Howes, C., 608, 612, 613

Hoza, B., 617, 619, 620
Hrabowski, F. A., 555
Hsu, C.-C., 101
Hu, Y., 635
Huard, R. D., 291
Hubbard, F. O. A., 138
Hubbs-Tait, L., 101, 193
Huberty, P. D., 639
Huddleson, J., 208
Hudson, J. A., 290, 295, 298
Hudziak, J. J., 125
Huebner, C. E., 309
Huesmann, L. R., 630, 631
Hueston, W. J., 118
Huettel, S. A., 262
Hughes, C., 416, 454, 455, 456, 520
Hughes, D., 475
Hughes, F. P., 455
Hughes, J. N., 464, 643
Huh, C. R., 341
Huizenga, H., 257
Huizinga, D., 11
Huizink, A. C., 98, 105
Hulme, C., 295
Hulsey, L., 351
Human Genome Program, 74
Human Rights Campaign, 87
Humphrey, T., 153
Hungerford-Kresser, H., 644
Hunnius, S., 163
Hunsberger, B., 507
Hunt, C. E., 136
Huotilainen, M., 94
Hupbach, A., 133
Hurewitz, F., 392
Hursh, D., 343
Hursti, U. K., 195
Hurt, H., 97
Hurtado, N., 369
Hurtado-Ortiz, M. T., 291
Huston, A. C., 550, 632
Huttenlocher, J., 231, 245, 264, 557
Huttenlocher, P. R., 185, 188, 191, 238
Huyck, M. H., 547
Hwang, C. P., 570
Hwang, P., 536
Hyde, J. S., 119, 404, 503, 550, 560, 570
Hymel, S., 618, 619, 621
Hynd, G. W., 646

I

Iacoboni, M., 146
Iacono, W. G., 336
Ickovics, J. R., 219
Iglowstein, I., 132
Ilgaz, H., 392
Imai, M., 379, 382, 383
Im-Bolter, N., 288
Impett, E. A., 462, 551
Inagaki, K., 265
Indus, K., 587
Ingersoll, E. W., 141
Ingram, D., 375
Inhelder, B., 226, 253, 255

Inoff-Germain, G., 561
International Telecommunications Union, 629
Intons-Peterson, M. J., 536
Iozzi, L., 396
Irwin, C. E., Jr., 210
Irwin, J. R., 138
Isabella, R. A., 434
Isasi, R. M., 87
Ishihara, K., 101
Israel, M., 388
Israelashvili, R., 438
Ittel, A., 616
Itti, E., 83
Ivey, P., 408
Ivorra, J. L., 427
Izard, C. E., 407

J

Jaakkola, J. J., 98
Jaccard, J., 212
Jackson, I., 453
Jackson, L. A., 633, 634
Jackson, L. K., 515
Jackson, P., 487
Jackson, P. W., 643
Jackson, R. A., 86
Jacobs, J. E., 257, 463, 467, 532, 541, 557
Jacobs, J. N., 596
Jacobs, N., 336
Jacobson, J. L., 96, 99, 101
Jacobson, K. C., 579
Jacobson, S. W., 96, 99, 100, 101
Jacobvitz, D., 603
Jacquet, P., 81
Jaeger, J. J., 48
Jaffari-Bimmel, N., 426
Jaffee, S. F., 218, 590
Jaffee. S. R., 434
Jaffee, S. R., 503
Jaffee. S. R., 503
Jambor, T. W., 609
Jambunathan, S., 582
Jamieson, J. R., 372
Jang, S. J., 509
Jankowski, J. J., 145, 163
Jansen, A., 199
Jansen, B., 257
Jansen, J., 195
Jarrett, R. L., 583
Jarrold, C., 366
Jarvin, L., 14
Jarvis, P. A., 240
Jasiobedzka, U., 512
Jaudes, P. K., 600
Jean, A. D. L., 154
Jean, G., 397
Jedrychowski, W., 101
Jefferson, S. R., 583
Jeffrey, J., 200
Jelalian, E., 198
Jenkins, E., 284
Jenkins, J. M., 455, 586
Jenni, O. G., 207

Jennifer, D., 69
Jensen, A. R., 121, 332, 334, 335, 339
Jeong, S.-H., 293
Jeremy, R. J., 97
Jerome, E. M., 643
Jeynes, W. H., 594, 647
Ji, C. Y., 184, 198
Ji, G., 588
Jiao, S., 588
Jimenez, E., 193
Jing, Q., 588
Jipson, J. L., 246
Joh, A. S., 161, 169
Johnson, B. R., 509
Johnson, C., 388
Johnson, D. E., 9
Johnson, E. K., 157
Johnson, J., 288, 369
Johnson, J. G., 630, 631
Johnson, J. S., 375
Johnson, M. H., 22, 23, 163, 164, 185, 186, 231, 370
Johnson, S. C., 430
Johnson, S. P., 155, 157, 159, 160, 165, 266, 556
Johnson-Laird, P. N., 22
Johnston, J., 582
Johnston, L. D., 626
Johnston, M. V., 186
Jokhi, R. P., 85
Jones, B. D., 343
Jones, C. M., 557
Jones, D. C., 413
Jones, E. F., 497
Jones, F., 507
Jones, G. P., 617
Jones, H. E., 97
Jones, I., 639
Jones, J., 102, 103, 215
Jones, L. B., 288
Jones, M. C., 208
Jones, N. A., 418
Jones, R. K., 215
Jones, R. L., 193
Jones, S., 145
Jones, S. M., 33
Jones-Rodriguez, G., 210
Jongbloet, P. H., 80
Joo, C.-A., 648
Jordan, B., 110
Jorgenson, L. A., 49
Josefowitz, N., 473
Joseph, R. M., 457
Jovanovic, J., 532, 557
Joy, M. E., 490
Joyner, K., 624, 625
Juby, H., 595
Judge, S., 633
Juffer, F., 337, 588
Juffer, R., 440, 588
Juhl, T., 404
Jumpstart Evaluation Team, 350
Jürgensen, M., 538
Jusczyk, P. W., 155, 157, 165, 369, 376

Jussim, L., 643
Justice, E. M., 304
Jutras-Aswad, D., 98
Juvonen, J., 479

K

Kable, J. A., 97, 98
Kaciroti, N., 376
Kagan, J., 8, 48, 230, 422, 424, 435
Kahlenberg, S. G., 543, 631
Kahn, R. S., 125
Kahne, J. E., 508
Kail, R. V., 281, 309
Kain, J., 479
Kaitz, M., 153
Kakihara, F., 574, 575
Kalafat, J., 473
Kalil, A., 36, 332
Kalish, C. W., 247, 264, 265
Kalisiak, B., 103
Kalkman, D. L., 467
Kalra, L., 188
Kamberk-Kilicci, M., 417
Kaminski, J. W., 472
Kamphaus, R. W., 332
Kane, M. J., 323
Kane, P., 404
Kang, J. Y., 396
Kang, N. H., 648
Kaplow, J. B., 602
Kaplowitz, P. B., 184, 204
Karafantis, D. M., 479
Karasik, L. B., 147, 150, 152
Karmiloff-Smith, A., 366, 394
Karraker, K. H., 538
Karrass, J., 407, 410
Kaslow, N. J., 481
Kassel, J. D., 627
Kastens, K. A., 251
Kato, I., 136
Katz, G. S., 369
Katz, L. F., 411
Katz, V. L., 114
Katzman, D. K., 211
Katzmarzyk, P. T., 183
Katz-Wise, S. L., 570
Kaufman, A. S., 331, 332
Kaufman, J., 231, 559
Kaufman, J. C., 350, 557
Kaufman, N. L., 332
Kaufman, R., 342
Kavanaugh, R. D., 455
Kavoura, A., 621
Kavsek, M., 142, 145, 160
Kawakami, K., 424
Kaye, K., 229
Kaye, W. H., 211
Kearins, J. M., 272
Kearney, J., 536
Keating, D. P., 258, 461
Kedar, Y., 384
Keefe, K., 616
Keefe, M. R., 138
Keen, R., 152, 235
Keeton, W. T., 76

Keil, F. C., 247, 380
Kellam, S. G., 568
Keller, H., 450
Keller, M., 502
Keller, S. N., 219
Keller, S. S., 363
Kelley, M. L., 596
Kelley, S. A., 409, 465
Kellman, P. J., 159
Kelly, D. J., 164
Kelly, J. H., 591, 592, 594
Kelly, J. N., 583
Kelly, N., 646
Kelly, W. M., 284
Kempe, C. H., 600
Kendall, G., 112
Kendler, K. S., 215
Kennedy, A. M., 202
Kennedy, D. E., 587
Kennedy, J. M., 242
Kennedy, K. J., 467
Kennell, J. H., 111
Kenney, G. M., 33
Kenney-Benson, G. A., 557
Kenny, L. C., 218
Kenny, S., 231, 232
Kerckhoff, A. C., 649
Keren, M., 270
Kerestes, M., 28, 507
Kerig, P. K., 522, 561
Kern, S., 379
Kernis, M. H., 464
Kerns, K. A., 585, 586
Kerr, D. C. R., 489
Kerr, M., 611
Kershaw, T. S., 219
Kesebir, S., 486, 506, 509
Kesek, A., 287
Kesler, S. R., 83
Kessen, W., 131
Kettunen, S., 99
Key, J. D., 220
Khalil, S., 453
Khashan, A. S., 218
Kidd, K. K., 336, 339
Kieffer, M. J., 397
Kieras, J. E., 410, 413
Kieschke, U., 271
Killen, M., 478, 479, 505, 507, 510,
    512, 623
Killian, A. L., 522
Killoren, S. E., 587
Kilpatrick, S. W., 200
Kim, G., 414
Kim, J., 463
Kim, J. M., 498
Kim, J.-Y., 63, 586, 587
Kim, M., 379
Kim, S., 512
Kim, Y. K., 613
Kimbro, R. T., 194
King, A. C., 74
King, P. E., 507
King, R. M., 489
King, V., 595

Kinney, D., 623
Kinney, H. C., 136
Kinsella, M. T., 105
Kinsht, I. A., 427
Kinzler, K. D., 262, 263
Király, I., 233
Kirby, D., 215, 219
Kirby, N., 329
Kiriakidis, S. P., 621
Kirisci, L., 627
Kirk, K. M., 215
Kirkham, N. Z., 157, 288
Kirkpatrick, M., 643
Kirsch, D. I., 381
Kirshner, B., 508
Kirz, N., 211
Kisilevsky, B. S., 93, 94, 402
Kisly, A., 106
Kistner, J. A., 418, 560
Kitayama, S., 459
Kitzmann, K. M., 587, 602
Kivivuori, J., 649
Kjonniksen, L., 181
Klaczynski, P. A., 257, 258, 314
Klahr, D., 21
Klaus, M., 111
Klaw, E. L., 220
Klebanov, P. K., 345, 581
Klein, N., 116
Klein, P. J., 233
Klein, P. S., 56
Kleitman, S., 638, 649
Klenberg, L., 287
Klesges, L. M., 98
Klibanoff, R. S., 311
Kliegman, R. M., 78, 102
Kliewer, W., 412
Klimes-Dougan, B., 418
Klimstra, T. A., 471
Klineberg, O., 331
Klingman, A., 524
Klingner, J. K., 646
Klomsten, A. T., 461
Klug, M., 68
Klump, K. L., 211
Knaack, A., 423, 490, 514
Knafo, A., 417, 492
Knapp, P. K., 181
Knickmeyer, R. C., 186
Knieps, L. J., 414
Knight. R. T., 288
Knighton, T., 554, 555
Knobloch, H., 130, 131
Knopf, M., 233
Knoppers, B. M., 87
Knowlton, B. J., 293
Knudsen, E. I., 24
Knudsen, K., 536
Kobayashi, T., 263
Kochanoff, A. T., 416
Kochanska, G., 406, 423, 427, 488,
    489, 490, 491, 494, 506, 514,
    561, 575
Kochel, K. P., 641
Kochenderfer-Ladd, B., 621

Koenig, B., 216
Koenig, M. A., 247
Koestner, R., 418
Koh, S. F., 626
Kohen, D. E., 28
Kohlberg, L., 499, 500, 501, 505, 548
Köhler, S., 297
Koller, S., 510
Kolomer, S. R., 438
Komlos, J., 183
Kon, A. A., 68
Konner, M. J., 26, 152, 176, 535
Konold, T. R., 641
Konstantopoulos, S., 637
Kontic-Vucinic, O., 104
Kooijman, V., 157, 369
Kopp, C. B., 410, 450, 514, 515, 608
Koppe, J. G., 101
Koren, G., 104
Korkman, M., 99, 287
Kornhaber, M. L., 355
Koslowski, B., 139
Kossakowska-Petrycka, K., 404
Kotchick, B. A., 590
Kotler, J. A., 632
Kotler, J. A., 632
Kouba, E., 609
Kouvonen, A., 649
Kovacs, D. M., 544
Koven, M., 451
Kowal, A. K., 587
Kowalski, R. M., 621
Kozbelt, A., 352
Kozer, E., 96
Kozol, J., 645
Kozulin, A., 25
Krafft, K., 269
Kraft, P., 207
Krähenbühl, S., 300
Krakow, J. B., 514
Kral, T. V. E., 198
Kramer, L., 586, 587
Krascum, R. M., 247
Kraus, U., 233
Krawinkel, M., 197
Krcmar, M., 237
Krebs, D. L., 503, 509
Kreppner, J. M., 170, 433
Kressley-Mba, R. A., 233
Krettenauer, T., 471
Krevans, J., 489
Krieg, D. B., 570
Krishnakumar, A., 571
Krishnamoorthy, J. S., 198
Kroger, J., 469, 470, 471
Krogh, H. R., 534, 549
Krohn, M. D., 523
Kroonenberg, P. M., 432
Kross, E., 516
Krumhansl, C. L., 155
Kubik, M. Y., 196
Kubitschek, W. N., 644
Kuczynski, L., 491, 494, 574, 576
Kuebli, J., 298, 539
Kugelmass, J., 646
Kuhl, P. K., 145, 156, 365, 368, 369

Kuhn, D., 21, 64, 65, 257, 258, 313,
    314
Kuk, L. S., 471, 472
Kuklinski, M. R., 643
Kumar, S., 85
Kumpf, M., 334
Kunina, O., 332
Kunkel, D., 631
Kunnen, E. S., 472
Kupersmidt, J. B., 520
Kuppens, S., 520
Kurdek, L. A., 575
Kurtz-Costes, B., 463, 532
Kwok, O., 643
Ky, K. N., 59
Kyratzis, A., 546

L
Lachance, J. A., 555
Lackey, P. N., 534
Lacourse, E., 492, 520
Ladd, G. W., 611, 619, 620, 623, 641
Ladouceur, C. D., 559
Lafosse, A., 246
LaFraniere, S., 588
Lagacé-Séguin, D. G., 425
LaGasse, L. L., 97
Lagattuta, K. H., 415, 416
Lagercrantz, H., 108
Laghi, F., 631
Lagnado, L., 524
La Greca, A. M., 619, 624
Lahti-Nuuttila, P., 287
Laible, D. J., 416, 611
Laing, E., 366
Laird, R. D., 576, 578, 619
Laitman, C. J., 96
Lalonde, C. E., 454, 455, 474
Lam, S., 467
Lamarche, V., 586
Lamaze, F., 110
Lamb, M. E., 33, 438, 440, 441, 545,
    597
Lambert, W., 397
Lamberth, R., 142
Lamont, E., 280
Lampman-Petraitis, C., 207
Lancashire, R., 195
Lancaster, J. B., 568
Lancy, D. F., 273
Lang, A. R., 99
Lang, F. R., 486
Lang, M., 650
Lange, G., 304
Langer, J., 231, 264
Langhinrichsen-Rohling, J., 472
Langlois, J. H., 164, 534, 544
Langman, L., 232
Lanphear, B., 193
Lansford, J. E., 492, 493, 525, 591,
    592, 593, 618, 620
Lanzi, R. G., 348
Lapkin, S., 397
Lapsley, D. K., 256
Laranjo, J., 455

Lareau, A., 580
Larkin, S., 305
Larsen, J. A., 380
Larsen, J. T., 415
Larson, J., 611
Larson, R. W., 207, 580, 613
Larzelere, R. E., 494, 576, 578
Lashley, F. R., 75, 76, 77, 78
Latendresse, S. J., 581, 582
Latner, J. D., 200
Latz, S., 134
Laucht, M., 117
Lauderdale, D. S., 136
Lauer, P. A., 599
Laupa, M., 498
Laursen, B., 208, 578, 580, 618, 621
Lavelli, M., 406
Law, K. L., 98
Lawn, J. E., 115
Lawrence, A., 111
Lawrence, K., 83
Lawrenz, F., 532
Lawton, S. Q. C., 287
Lazar, I., 347
Lazarus, B. N., 412
Lazarus, R. S., 412
Lazinski, M. J., 105, 106
Leadbeater, B. J., 47, 621
Leaper, C., 181, 378, 539, 540, 542, 544
Learmonth, A. E., 142
Leavitt, L. A., 115, 137
Lebeaux, D. S., 388
Lecanuet, J.-P., 94
Lecce, S., 304
Lecerf, T., 323
Lecusay, R., 392
Lecuyer, E., 410
Lederberg, A., 372
Lee, C., 479
Lee, C.-Y. S., 570
Lee, D. N., 130
Lee, J. M., 180, 204
Lee, J. S., 310, 311
Lee, K., 345, 391, 497
Lee, S., 648
Lee, S. J., 93
Lee, V. E., 308, 638
Lee, Y., 613
Leech, R., 367
Leech, S. L., 333
Leeman, L. W., 525
Leerkes, E. M., 27, 137, 410
Leet, T., 103
LeFevre, J., 308
Legare, C. H., 532
Leger, D. W., 137
Legerstee, M., 402–403, 414, 452
Le Grand, R., 170
Le Grange, D., 211
Lehman, D. R., 258
Lehman, M., 292
Lehr, V. T., 153
Lehtonen, L., 153
Leinbach, M. D., 518, 531, 533, 549

Leman, P. J., 504
Lemche, E., 269
Lemerise, E. A., 522
Lemery, K. S., 377
Lemery-Chalfant, K., 426
Lempers, J. D., 587
Lempert, H., 388
L'Engle, K. L., 212
Lengua, L. J., 426, 592
Lenhart, A., 633, 634, 635, 636
Lenroot, R. K., 190
Leon, K., 592
Leonard, L. B., 375, 381
Leonard, W. R., 183
Leong, D. J., 25, 269, 288, 640
Lepage, J.-F., 146
Lephart, E. D., 537
Lerman, R. I., 590
Lerner, M. D., 622
Lerner, R. M., 4, 9, 120
LeSieur, K., 611
Leslie, A. M., 261, 262, 457
Lester, B. M., 9, 97, 137, 138, 139, 429
Lett, D., 11
Leung, M.-C., 622
LeVay, S., 215
Leventhal, T., 523, 572, 581
Levi, J., 200
Levin, I., 307
Levine, C., 499
Levine, J. A., 332
Levine, L. E., 450
Levine, L. J., 415
LeVine, R. A., 434
Levine, S. C., 264, 556
Levinson, S. C., 365
Leviton, A., 193
Levtzion-Korach, O., 162
Levy, G. D., 533
Levy, S. R., 478, 479
Levy-Shiff, R., 438
Lew, A. R., 154
Lewin, D. S., 207
Lewis, C., 454, 481
Lewis, K. G., 530
Lewis, M., 169, 402, 407, 408–409, 413, 424, 449
Lewis, M. D., 31, 405
Lewis, T. L., 170
Lewontin, R., 337, 339
Lhote, M., 154
Li, D., 427
Li, D.-K., 97, 136
Li, P., 378
Li, S.-C., 323
Liang, W., 376
Liau, A. K., 522
Liben, L. S., 22, 243, 250, 251, 477, 530, 531, 532, 534, 543, 549, 551, 552, 556
Lichtenberger, E. O., 331
Lickliter, R., 9, 115, 120, 122, 166, 168
Lickona, T., 503

Lidstone, J. S. M., 267
Lidz, C. S., 342
Lidz, J. L., 367, 382, 383, 384, 389
Liebaers, I., 85
Liebergott, J. W., 376
Lieberman, E. S., 112
Liebert, R. M., 491
Liederman, J., 189
Liem, J. H., 475
Lieven, E., 369, 385, 386, 389
Light, P., 252
Li-Grining, C. P., 423
Lillard, A. S., 240, 270, 639, 640
Lilly, A. R., 288
Limber, S. P., 621
Lin, Z. L., 113
Linares, T. J., 97
Lindberg, S. M., 550, 555, 560
Lindblad, F., 98
Lindenberger, U., 9, 121
Linder, J. R., 624–625
Lindsay, D. S., 300
Lindsay, L. L., 27, 571
Lindsay-Hartz, J., 409
Lindsey, D., 36
Lindsey, E. W., 27, 240, 464, 571, 612
Linebarger, D. L., 632
Linn, K., 237
Linn, M. C., 556
Linn, R. L., 645
Linn, S., 631
Linscheid, T. R., 202
Linver, M. R., 345
Lipsitt, L. P., 136
Lipton, J., 263
Liszkowski, U., 371
Litovsky, R. Y., 155, 162
Little, C., 410
Little, J. K., 549
Little, T. D., 517
Littlejohn, K., 242
Liu, D., 455
Liu, H.-M., 156, 369
Liu, J., 197
Liu, L. L., 557
Liu, S., 365
Lizotte, A. J., 219
Lleras, C., 644
Lloyd, L., 644
Lloyd, M. E., 298
Lochman, J. E., 522
Lock, J., 211
Locke, J., 12
Lockhart, K. L., 247
Lockwood, R. L., 587
Loeb, S., 597
Loehlin, J. C., 123, 336, 337, 346, 423, 425
Logan, A., 622
Loganovskaja, T. K., 101
Loganovsky, K. N., 101
Lohman, D. F., 323
Lohmann, H., 456
Lohr, M. J., 626

Lohrmann, S., 646
Loken, E., 63
Lollis, S., 574
Loman, M. M., 48, 403
London, K., 601
Longo, M. R., 146, 231, 232
Loock, C., 99
Looker, D., 633
Loots, G., 372
Lopez, A., 102, 103
Lopez, B., 579
Lopez, C. M., 560
Lorenz, K. Z., 23, 486
Lorenz, R. P., 106
Lothian, J. A., 111
Louie, V., 53
Louis, J., 135
Lourenco, O., 511
Loutzenhiser, L., 439
Love, J. M., 348, 349, 442
Lovell-Badge, R., 76
Low, J., 59
Low, J. A., 93
Lower-Basch, E., 36
Lozoff, B., 134, 193, 197
Lubart, T. I., 352, 353, 354
Lubinski, D., 333, 556
Luby, J., 409
Lucas, D. E., 135
Lucas, S., 625
Lucas, S. R., 644
Lucas-Thompson, R., 611
Luce, P. A., 155
Luciana, M., 23, 282
Ludemann, P. M., 164
Lueptow, L. B., 530
Lueptow, M. B., 530
Luk, G., 396
Lukowski, A. F., 197
Lun, J., 622
Luna, B., 187, 190, 281, 288
Lund, N., 97
Lundy, B. L., 437, 439
Luo, Y., 136, 262
Lupien, S. J., 48
Lupyan, G., 234
Luria, A. R., 259
Lussier, G., 593
Lust, B., 384
Luster, T., 218, 345
Lutgendorf, S., 403
Luthar, S. S., 581, 582
Lutkenhaus, P., 449
Luwel, K., 285
Luyckx, K., 471, 473, 575
Lykken, D. T., 336
Lynam, D., 333, 481, 516, 517, 518, 521, 561
Lynch, M., 193
Lynch, M. E., 550
Lynch, S. K., 491
Lynch, V., 33
Lyon, T. D., 302, 303
Lyons-Ruth, K., 434, 440
Lytton, H., 539

M

Ma, F., 497
Ma, L., 270
Ma, W., 379
Maas, F. K., 511
MacArthur, C., 195
Macartney, S. E., 53
MacCallum, R. C., 346
Maccoby, E. E., 535, 537, 544, 551, 562, 573, 578, 595
MacDorman, M. F., 136
Macfarlane, J. W., 331
Machin, G. A., 77
MacKenzie, M. J., 58
Mackey, E. R., 624
Mackey, K., 574
Mackey-Bilaver, L., 600
Mackie, S., 290
MacKinnon, C. E., 547
MacWhinney, B., 21, 389
Madden, C. M., 381
Madden, M., 636
Madden, T., 475
Madigan, S., 434
Madon, S., 643
Madrona, M. M., 112
Madsen, S. A., 404
Madsen, S. D., 577, 614
Mageau, G. A., 434
Maggs, J. L., 598
Magnuson, K., 350, 475
Magnusson, D., 209, 210
Magnusson, K. A., 580
Magnusson, S., 300
Magos, L., 101
Maguire, M., 416
Mahalingham, R., 265
Mahapatra, M., 513
Mahoney, A., 489
Mahoney, J. L., 638
Main, M., 430, 431, 432, 436, 437
Majdandžić, M., 421, 423
Majnemer, A., 150
Major, B., 341
Majorano, M., 374
Makel, M. C., 352
Malanchuk, O., 508
Malatesta, C. Z., 413, 559
Malcuit, G., 218
Malhotra, B. A., 314
Malina, R. M., 179, 180
Malpass, R. S., 302
Mandara, J., 580
Mandler, J. M., 234, 235, 294
Manfra, L., 267
Mangelsdorf, S. C., 421, 456
Mann, T., 45, 241, 269
Mann, V., 308
Mansson, S.-A., 536
Mant, C. M., 498
Mao, A., 134
Maratsos, M., 386, 387, 389
Marchman, V. A., 188, 376, 377, 389
Marcia, J. E., 470

Marcon, R. A., 349, 639
Marcus, G. F., 157, 369, 386
Marcus, J., 229
Mardh, P. A., 102
Marentette, P. F., 370
Mareschal, D., 22, 363–364
Margie, N. G., 510
Marian, V., 237
Mariano, K. A., 616
Mariner, C. L., 493
Markell, M., 477, 478
Markman, E. M., 228, 254, 261, 382, 383
Markova, G., 402–403, 414
Markovits, H., 258, 617
Marks, A., 454
Marks, A. K., 53
Marks, G. N., 645
Marks, K. S., 231, 263–264
Markus, H. R., 459
Marlier, L., 154, 155
Marrott, H., 233
Marschik, P. B., 92
Marsee, M. A., 522
Marsh, H. W., 181, 461, 462, 463, 464, 638, 649
Marshall-Baker, A., 115
Marsland, K. W., 33
Martin, A., 345
Martin, C. L., 530, 531, 532, 534, 537, 544, 549, 551, 552, 562
Martin, G. I., 18
Martin, J. A., 573
Martin, K. A., 206
Martin, L. T., 333
Martin, M. M., 396
Martin, N. G., 425
Martin, R., 82
Martin, R. P., 114, 425
Martin, S. K., 36
Martinez-Frias, M. L., 100
Martinot, D., 533
Martinussen, M., 470
Martlew, M., 242
Marx, R. W., 23
Marzolf, D. P., 243
Masataka, N., 369
Masciadrelli, B. P., 596
Mascolo, M. F., 407, 409, 410
Mash, C., 234
Mashburn, A. J., 348, 641
Mashek, D. J., 409
Mason, M. G., 505
Masten, A. S., 9, 10, 11, 508, 638
Mastergeorge, A. M., 608
Masterov, D. V., 37
Mastropieri, D., 155
Masur, E. F., 287, 378
Matheny, A. P., Jr., 424, 425
Matheson, C. C., 608
Mathews, G. A., 561
Mathews, T. J., 136
Mathiesen, K. S., 11
Matjasko, J. L., 638
Maton, K. I., 555

Matsuba, M. K., 504, 581
Mattock, K., 368
Mattock, M., 368
Mattson, S. N., 98, 99
Mauer, D., 240
Maupin, R., 118
Maurer, D., 170
Mauro, J. A., 421
Mavroveli, S., 327
Mayberry, R. I., 364
Maybery, M., 457
Mayer, J. D., 327
Mayes, L. C., 147
Mayes, R., 291
Mayeux, L., 481, 619
Mayhew, E. M. Y., 298
Maynard, A. E., 25, 252, 270, 341
Mazzocco, M. M. M., 555
McAdoo, H. P., 583
McAlister, A., 456
McAuley, C., 218, 220
McAuliff, B. D., 302
McBee, M. T., 355
McBride-Chang, C., 309, 396
McCabe, A., 308, 340, 392
McCall, R. B., 145, 331, 332, 346
McCallion, P., 438
McCandliss, B. D., 280
McCartney, G. R., 189
McCartney, K., 33, 122, 123, 425, 440, 441, 442, 643
McCarton, C., 116
McCarty, M. E., 151, 152, 235
McCleam, G. E., 336
McClelland, J. L., 260
McClelland, M. M., 641
McClenahan, E. L., 626
McClintic, S., 461
McClure, S., 190
McColgan, K. L., 289, 290
McCombs, B. L., 467
McConachie, H., 82
McCormack, T., 289, 290
McCormick, M. C., 116
McCoy, J. K., 586
McCrady, F., 522
McCrink, K., 263
McCune, L., 240
McDade, T., 134
McDonough, L., 232, 234
McDowell, D. J., 413, 611
McDuff, P., 625
McElderry, D., 206
McElhaney, K. B., 579, 580
McElwain, N. L., 434, 586
McEwen, B., 9
McFarland, F. C., 627
McGee, L. M., 308, 309
McGillicuddy-De Lisi, A. V., 478
McGinley, M., 409, 515
McGlothlin, H., 478
McGrath, S. K., 111
McGregor, K. K., 374, 379
McGue, M., 208, 335, 336, 627
McGuire, S., 586

McHale, S. M., 475, 542, 543–544, 546, 570, 571, 586, 596
McIntyre, C. W., 287
McIntyre, K. A., 627
McKelvie, P., 59
McKenna, J. J., 134
McKeown, M. G., 310
McKinney, C., 464
McKone, E., 297
McKown, C., 341, 643
McKusick, V. A., 77, 78, 80
McLanahan, S., 592, 593
McLean, K. C., 471
McLearn, K. T., 34
McLeod, P., 369
McLoyd, V. C., 349, 491–492, 493
McMahon, C. A., 404
McMichael, A. J., 193
MCR Vitamin Study Research Group, 104
McWilliams, L., 561
Mead, G. H., 459
Mead, M., 110, 205
Meade, C. S., 217, 219
Meadow-Orlans, K. P., 372
Meaney, F. J., 80
Meaney, M. J., 125
Mebert, C. J., 492
Mechelli, A., 396
Media Awareness Network, 633
Meeus, W. H. J., 208, 473, 615, 616
Mehlmadrona, L., 112
Meier, A., 624, 625
Meijer, A. M., 579
Meins, E., 267, 455
Meisels, S. J., 310
Meister, C., 271
Melby-Lervag, M., 295
Melinder, A., 300, 302
Melton, G. B., 37
Meltzoff, A. N., 23, 145, 146, 231, 232, 233, 237, 370, 371, 396, 414, 451, 452, 532, 629
Melzi, G., 310, 392
Mendle, J., 205, 209
Mendola, P., 204
Mendoza, J. R., 182
Menn, L., 373
Mennella, J. A., 154
Ment, L. R., 115
Menyuk, P., 376
Meredith, N. V., 183
Merisca, R., 490
Meroni, L., 392
Merrilees, C. E., 571
Mervis, C. B., 366, 381
Messinger, D. S., 407
Metz, E. C., 507, 508
Meyer, J. R., 300
Meyer, P. A., 193
Meyer, R., 194
Meyer, S., 409, 411, 515
Meyer-Bahlburg, H. F. L., 215
Meyers, M. K., 597
Mezulis, A. H., 404, 560

Miceli, P. J., 427
Michael, A., 209
Michalik, N. M., 418
Michel, G. F., 189
Michels, K. B., 195
Michiels, D., 439
Mick, E., 290
Midgley, C., 641
Mikami, A. Y., 622
Miles, C., 530
Milevsky, A., 574
Milgrom, J., 116
Milich, R., 621
Miller, A. L., 586
Miller, C. F., 533
Miller, C. J., 646
Miller, J., 438
Miller, J. G., 506, 513
Miller, J. L., 519
Miller, L. T., 323
Miller, M., 308, 310
Miller, M. A., 201
Miller, P. A., 412, 418
Miller, P. D., 310
Miller, P. H., 288, 289, 303
Miller, P. J., 52, 270, 451
Miller, R. B., 570
Miller, S., 625
Miller, S. A., 54, 272, 278, 303, 453,
    499, 505
Milligan, K., 455
Mills, D., 187, 363
Mills, R. S. L., 409, 491
Mills, T. L., 438
Minami, M., 393
Minkler, M., 438
Minkoff, H., 84
Mintz, J., 451
Miracle, J. A., 160
Misailidi, P., 416
Mischel, H. N., 491, 516
Mischel, W., 515, 516
Mistry, J., 294, 345, 580
Mitchell, A., 153
Mitchell, K. J., 212, 635
Mitchell, P., 460
Mitchell, Z. A., 285
Miura, I. T., 312
Mix, K. S., 264
Mize, J., 574, 577, 611, 612
Mocarelli, P., 101
Modi, A. C., 165, 200
Modry-Mandell, K. L., 586
Moeller, M. P., 370
Moens, E., 199
Moffitt, T. E., 520, 521
Mohite, P., 548
Mok, M. M. C., 467
Moll, H., 245
Moll, I., 272
Moll, J., 487
Mollborn, S., 218
Moller, K., 570
Moller, L. C., 543
Monahan, K. C., 212, 626

Mondloch, C. J., 163, 164, 170
Monesson, A., 156
Monk, C., 105, 457
Monk, C. S., 186
Montague, D. P. F., 414
Montague, L., 377
Montemayor, R., 458
Montero, I., 25, 411
Montgomery, D. E., 303
Montgomery, G. L., 132
Montgomery, M. J., 471
Montgomery, P., 219
Moody, J., 473
Moolchan, E. T., 125
Moon, C., 156
Moon, R. Y., 136
Moore, C., 449, 558
Moore, D. R., 218
Moore, D. S., 369, 556
Moore, E. G. J., 337
Moore, G. A., 402
Moore, J. B., 180
Moore, K. A., 219, 509, 579
Moore, K. L., 76, 85, 86, 88, 89, 90,
    91, 92, 95, 96, 178, 185
Moore, M. K., 145, 146, 231, 232
Moore, M. R., 218
Moore, P. J., 466, 467
Moore, R. W., 161
Moore, S. G., 139
Moorman, E. A., 465
Moosbrugger, H., 323
Morales, M., 268
Moran, G., 434
Moran, G. F., 11
Morán, R. M. B., 634
Moran, S., 51, 326, 353
Morawska, A., 493
Morelli, G. A., 134, 273, 408
Morford, J. P., 362
Morgan, B., 457
Morgan, J. L., 156
Morgan, P. L., 33
Morgane, P. J., 104
Morikawa, H., 378
Morrill, M. I., 571
Morris, A. S., 411
Morris, G., 301
Morris, J. E., 598
Morris, J. K., 82
Morris, P. A., 26, 36, 121, 336, 569
Morrison, D. R., 219
Morrongiello, B. A., 166
Morrow, D. F., 216
Morse, S. B., 114
Morton, J., 164
Mosby, L., 493
Moses, L. J., 414, 455
Mosher, W. D., 215
Moshman, D., 258, 314, 469, 470
Mosley-Howard, G. S., 583
Moss, E., 431, 434, 440
Mossey, P. A., 98
Mosteller, F., 637
Motl, R. W., 180

Mottus, R., 587
Mounts, N. S., 62, 611, 624
Moylan, A. R., 305
Mroczek, D. K., 463
Mrug, S., 620
Mu, X., 648
Mu, Y., 312
Muckle, G., 101
Mueller, C. M., 467
Mueller, E. C., 608
Muenchow, S., 33
Muentener, P., 237
Muir, D. W., 154
Mul, D., 184
Mulder, E. J., 98
Mullen, M., 147
Müller, F., 102
Müller, O., 197
Müller, U., 258
Mullett-Hume, E., 62
Mullis, I. V. S., 554
Mulvaney, M. K., 268, 492
Mulvey, E. P., 523
Mumme, D. L., 414
Munakata, Y., 21, 22, 230, 367
Mundy, P., 450, 457
Munholland, K. A., 430, 436, 437
Munroe, R. L., 535, 537
Murett-Wagstaff, S., 139
Murphy, B. C., 426
Murphy, G. L., 297
Murphy, K., 297
Murphy, L. M., 616, 618
Murphy, L. M. B., 287
Murphy, M. C., 558
Murphy, T. H., 188
Murray, A. D., 136, 369
Murray, C., 335
Murray, K. T., 423, 494
Murray-Close, D., 560
Murry, V. M., 586
Musick, K., 590
Mussen, P. H., 208, 491
Musser, L. M., 612
Mustanski, B. S., 204, 205
Muthukrisna, N., 467
Muzio, J. N., 135
Muzzatti, B., 557
Myers, G. J., 101
Myers, M. G., 627
Mylander, C., 362
Myowa-Yamakoshi, M., 145

N

NACCRRA (National Association
    of Child Care Resource and
    Referral Agencies), 597
Nadel, J., 449
Nadel, L., 133
Nader, P. R., 198
Nagel, S. K, 581
Nagell, K., 371
Nagin, D. S., 492, 519, 520
Naglieri, J., 267
Nagy, E., 145

Nagy, W. E., 380
Naigles, L. G., 380
Naigles, L. R., 382
Naito, M., 453
Nakagawa, N., 381
Nakamura, K., 393
Namy, L. L., 379
Nánez, J., Sr., 160
Narasimham, G., 314
Narr, K. L., 290
Nass, C., 293
Nassar, A. H., 106
Natale, K., 467
National Center for Biotechnology
    Information, 79
National Council of Youth Sports,
    181
National Early Literacy Panel, 308
National Federation of State High
    School Associations, 180
National Institutes of Health, 85
National Research Council, 642
National Women's Law Center, 218
Natsuaki, M. N., 207, 208, 209
Navarro, A. M., 111
Nawrocki, T., 418
Nazzi, T., 247, 264
Neal, A., 478
Needham, A., 165, 262
Needham, B. L., 216
Needham, E., 151
Needleman, H. L., 193
Needlman, R., 134
Neff, K. D., 511, 512
Neiderman, D., 232
Neisser, U., 237
Neitzel, C., 268, 269
Nelson, C. A., III, 48, 49, 50, 91, 144,
    156, 164, 171, 185, 186, 187, 188,
    190, 301
Nelson, D. A., 439, 518, 520, 575, 582,
    616, 619, 630
Nelson, K., 26, 171, 299, 376, 379,
    451
Nelson, M. R., 631
Nelson, N. M., 539
Nelson, S. E., 177
Nelson, V. L., 331
Nelson, W. E., 495
Nemer, K. M., 644
Nemet, D., 200
Nemeth, R., 548
Nepomnyaschy, L., 119
Neri, Q., 86
Nesdale, D., 478
Nettelbeck, T., 329
Netto, D., 166
Neubauer, A. C., 281, 323
Neuburger, H., 370
Neufeld, S. J., 410
Neuman, S. B., 308, 309
Neville, H. J., 187, 365
Nevin, R., 193
Newcomb, A. F., 615, 616, 619, 620
Newcombe, N. S., 231, 245, 298, 557

Newcombe, R., 299, 455
Newell, L. D., 573, 578, 588
Newland, L. A., 437
Newman, A. J., 364
Newman, L. C., 476
Newman, L. S., 294
Newnham, C. A., 116
Newport, E. L., 157, 363, 364, 367
Newson, E., 268
Newson, J., 268
Newton, N., 110
Neyer, F. J., 486
Ng, F. F., 467
Nguyen, S. P., 541
Nguyen, T. M., 87
Nguyen, U.-S., 112
Ni, Y., 250
Niccolai, L. M., 217
NICHD (National Institute of Child Health and Human Development) Early Child Care Research Network, 391, 441, 442, 596, 597, 637
Nicholls, A. L., 242
Nicholls, D. E., 211
Nichols, K. E., 450, 491
Nichols, S. L., 343
Nichols, S. R., 417
Nicholson, C., 50
Nicholson, J. M., 594, 595
Nickerson, P., 181
Nickman, S. L., 588, 589
Nicoladis, E., 396
Nicolopoulou, A., 392
Niehaus, M. D., 201
Nielsen, L. S., 199
Nielsen, M., 241, 449
Nievar, M. A., 434
Nigam, M., 21
Nigg, J. T., 98
Ningiuruvik, L., 340
Nippold, M. A., 380, 381
Nisbett, R. E., 258, 334, 338
Nishitani, S., 153
Niu, W., 354
Noble, K. G., 280
Noël, M.-P., 249
Noguera, P., 648
Nolen-Hoeksema, S., 559, 560
Noll, J., 321
Noller, P., 591
Noom, M. J., 208
Noonan, C. W., 193
Noonan, K., 114
Norwich, B., 646
Nosarti, C., 114
Nosek, B. A., 557
Noterdaeme, M., 190
Noyes, C. R., 303
Nucci, L. P., 505, 510, 511, 512
Nucci, M. S., 511, 512
Nugent, J. K., 138–139
Nunes, T., 311
Nunez-Smith, M., 293
Nurmi, J.-E., 574, 575

Nuttall, R. L., 557
Nye, B., 637

O

Oakes, L. M., 234
Oakland, T. D., 334, 339
Obeidallah, D., 209
Oberecker, R., 364
Obler, L. K., 393
O'Boyle, C., 549
Obradović, J., 11, 508, 638
O'Brien, A., 85
O'Brien, M., 588
Ochs, E., 372, 390
O'Connor, E., 643
O'Connor, P. J., 103
O'Connor, T. G., 106, 170, 433, 435, 586
Odouli, R., 97
OECD (Organisation for Economic Cooperation and Development), 34, 119, 554, 633
Ogan, A., 240, 241, 269
Ogbu, J. U., 467, 644
Ogden, C. L., 198
Ohannessian, C. M., 627
Ohgi, S., 139
Okagaki, L., 324, 346
Okami, P., 134
Okamoto, Y., 242, 283, 312
Okanda, M., 449
O'Keefe, M. J., 114
Okuda, S. M., 352
Olafson, E., 601
Oldershaw, L., 492
Olds, D. L., 106, 220, 603
O'Leary, S. G., 494
Olejnik, S., 425
Olfman, S., 626
Olineck, K. M., 233
Ollendick, T. H., 412
Oller, D. K., 370
Olmstead, R., 134
O'Loughlin, M., 313
Olsen, J. A., 573, 575, 579, 641
Olsen, S. F., 573, 578, 588
Olson, D., 103
Olson, D., 103
Olweus, D., 561, 621
O'Mahoney, J. F., 476
Omar, H., 206
Ondrusek, N., 68
O'Neil, R., 581, 620
O'Neill, M., 369
Ong, A., 475, 579
Ong, K. K., 184
Ong, W., 644
Ono, Y., 313, 648
Ontai, L. L., 456, 608
Oosterwegel, A., 459, 473
Operario, D., 219
Ophir, E., 293
Opinion Research Corporation, 29
Oppenheim, D., 438
Oppenheimer, L., 459
O'Rahilly, R., 102

O'Reilly, A. E., 240
Orfield, G., 479, 645
Ornstein, P. A., 295
Orobio de Castro, B., 522
Osborne, C. N., 147
Osherson, D. N., 254
Oshima-Takane, Y., 391
Ostad, S. A., 267
Ostrosky-Solis, F., 287
Ostrov, J. M., 518, 520, 521, 560, 630
Otis, N., 641
Otto, M. W., 524
Oude, L. H., 200
Ouko, L. A., 99
Oumar, F., 432
Ovando, C. J., 397
Overbaugh, J., 102
Overton, W. F., 9, 120, 258
Owen, C. G., 195
Owen, M. T., 436
Owen-Kostelnik, J., 300
Owens, E. B., 576, 578
Owens, E. B., 576, 578
Oyelese, Y., 113
Oyserman, D., 575
Ozanne, S. E., 192
Özçaliskan, S., 371, 380
Ozer, E. M., 210

P

Padilla, A. M., 396
Padilla-Walker, L. M., 489
Paek, H.-J., 631
Pahl, K., 475
Painter, M., 180
Paladino, J., 267
Palermo, G. D., 86
Palincsar, A. S., 640
Palmer, J. R., 96
Palmers, E., 249
Palmerus, K., 561
Pan, B. A., 390
Pan, H. W., 609
Pancer, S. M., 507
Pantalone, D. W., 216
Papadakis, A. A., 560
Papousek, M., 402
Papp, L. M., 571
Paquette, D., 437
Parada, R. H., 463
Paradis, J., 396
Paradis, L., 206
Paradise, R., 272, 340
Parameswaran, G., 251
Parent, A., 184, 205
Paris, A. H., 308, 310
Paris, S. G., 308, 310
Park, C. L., 293
Park, W., 579
Park, Y., 281
Parke, R. D., 413, 437, 438, 542, 568, 569, 611, 612
Parker, F. L., 349
Parker, J. G., 544, 609, 617, 619, 620, 622, 642
Parker, K. P., 132

Parker, S. W., 433, 615
Parra, M., 381
Parsons, E., 434, 440
Parsons, T., 302
Parten, M., 608
Pasamanick, B., 130, 131
Pascalis, O., 144, 156
Pascual-Leone, J., 288
Pasley, K., 594
Pasterski, V. L., 538
Pasupathi, M., 300
Pate, R. R., 180
Paterson, S., 231
Patrick, R. B., 489
Patt, M. B., 609
Pattee, L., 619, 620
Pattenden, S., 98
Patterson, C. J., 589
Patterson, G. R., 378, 520, 578
Pattison, P. E., 312
Paul, J. J., 621
Pauli, S. A., 86
Paulozzi, L. J., 96
Paulussen-Hoogeboom, M. C., 426
Pawluski, J., 383
Paxson, C., 345
Payne, A., 610
Payne, K., 309
Payne, R. J., 339
Peake, P. K., 515, 516
Pear, J., 18
Pearsall, S., 313
Pease, M., 314
Pechmann, T., 391
Pedersen, I. H., 97
Pedersen, N. L., 346
Pedersen, S., 617, 618, 620
Pederson, D. R., 434, 437
Peebles, D., 112
Peets, K., 622
Pegg, J. E., 369
Peirano, P., 135
Pellegrini, A. D., 568, 610, 639
Pelletier, J., 453, 454
Pelletier, L. G., 641
Pellicano, E., 457
Pemberton, C. K., 410
Pendry, P., 29
Penner, A. M., 555
Pennington, B. F., 23
Pennington, D. F., 282
Pennock, D., 554, 555
Penny, H., 200
Peoples, C. E., 334
Pepler, D. J., 45, 621
Pepperberg, I. M., 361
Peralta de Mendoza, O. A., 243
Percival, S., 327
Perelle, I. B., 189
Pérez-Edgar, K., 287
Pérez-Pereira, M., 162
Perfors, A., 376, 377
Periss, V., 24
Perlman, M., 416
Perlmutter, M., 295

Perner, J., 498
Perner, T., 453
Perrett-Clermont, A., 252
Perris, E. E., 234
Perry, D. G., 216, 550, 562
Perry, G. H., 192
Perry, L. C., 562
Perry-Jenkins, M., 570
Persaud, T. V. N., 76, 85, 86, 88, 89, 90, 91, 92, 95, 96, 178, 185
Peshkin, A., 52
Pesonen, A.-K., 426
Petch, J., 570
Peter, J., 635
Peterman, K., 608
Peters, H. E., 594
Peters, J., 369
Peters, M., 556
Peters, R. D., 27, 572
Petersen, A. C., 550, 556
Peterson, C., 300, 302, 555
Peterson, C. C., 456, 498
Peterson, G. W., 580
Peterson, J. L., 498
Petitto, L. A., 361, 370
Petrides, K. V., 327
Petrill, S. A., 120
Petrunka, K., 27, 572
Pettigrew, T. F., 479
Pettit, G. S., 520, 575, 611, 612
Pettit, J., 382
Peverly, S. T., 313
Pexman, P. M., 381
Pezaris, E., 557
Pezé, A., 151
Pfeffer, C. R., 62
Pfeffer, K., 287
Pfeifer, J. H., 478, 479
Philibert, R. A., 427, 575
Phillips, A. T., 234
Phillips, D., 35, 36, 191
Phillips, K., 424
Phillips, K. M. O., 285
Phillips, M., 581, 643
Phillipsen, L. C., 615
Phillips-Grant, K., 299
Phillips-Silver, J., 168
Phinney, J. S., 475, 579
Piaget, J., 19, 46, 226, 227, 229, 239, 244, 245, 250, 253, 255, 267, 496, 498, 504
Pianta, R. C., 597, 601, 641, 643
Pica, P., 264
Pick, A. D., 371
Pickard, M. B., 236
Pickens, J., 418
Pickens, J. N., 143, 144
Pickett, K. E., 136
Pierce, K. M., 27
Pierce, S. H., 304, 582
Pierroutsakos, S. L., 237
Pierson, L., 94
Pietschnig, J., 59
Pietz, J., 114
Piirto, J., 326

Pike, A., 29
Pikhart, H., 82
Pillow, B. H., 258, 454
Pine, J. M., 385, 387, 391
Pinelli, J., 194
Pinette, M. G., 111
Ping, R. M., 249, 285
Pinker, S., 388, 389
Pinter, J. D., 82
Pinto, J. P., 381
Piotrowska, A., 425
Piotrowski, J. T., 632
Pipe, M.-E., 300
Pipp, S., 449–450
Pisani, L., 432
Pisoni, D. B., 369
Pizarro, D. A., 327, 510
Plante, I., 533
Plantin, L., 536
Platania, J., 627
Pleck, J. H., 596
Plomin, R., 120, 123, 336, 337, 345, 492
Plucker, J. A., 352
Pluess, M., 122, 426
Poehlmann, J., 115, 435, 439
Poelhuis, C. W. K., 337, 588
Pogarsky, G., 219
Pohl, R., 35
Polderman, T. J. C., 282
Poldrack, R. A., 293
Polka, L., 156, 368, 369
Pollak, S. D., 433, 602
Pollatsek, A., 309, 310
Pollitt, C., 379
Pollitt, E., 104
Polman, H., 517
Pomerantz, E. M., 464, 465, 466, 467, 542, 579, 582, 616
Pomerleau, A., 218
Pong, S., 582
Pons, F., 415
Poole, D. A., 300
Porter, M. R., 627
Porter, R. H., 155
Portes, A., 53
Posada, G., 432
Posner, J. K., 27, 598
Posner, M. I., 143, 264, 288, 410
Postolache, T. T., 472
Poston, D. L., Jr., 588
Potter, D., 592
Poudevigne, M., 103
Poulin, F., 615, 617
Poulin-Dubois, D., 233, 379, 453, 531
Povinelli, D. J., 451
Powell, A., 472
Powell, C., 105
Powell, M. B., 300
Power, T. G., 610
Powers, J. L., 635
Powers, L. M., 622
Powlishta, K. K., 256, 531, 532, 533, 534, 543, 549
Powls, A., 189

Pratt, M. W., 471, 504, 507, 508, 574
Prechtl, H. F. R., 92, 130, 131
Preisler, G. M., 162
Preissler, M. A., 243
Prencipe, A., 511
Prepin, K., 449
Prescott, C., 627
Presnell, K., 209
Pressley, M., 279, 293, 310
Previc, F. H., 189
Priess, H. A., 550, 560, 570
Prinstein, M. J., 217, 520, 618, 619, 624, 627
Prinz, W., 152
Prior, M., 11
Proctor, B. D., 33
Proctor, L. J., 621
Proctor, M. H., 199
Profilet, S. M., 611
Programme for International Student Assessment, 647
Pronk, R. E., 562
Provins, K. A., 189
Pruden, S. M., 383
Prysak, M., 106
Puckett, K., 633
Puhl, R. M., 200
Pujol, J., 186
Punamaki, R.-L., 86
Purcell-Gates, V., 308
Putallaz, M., 620
Putnam, F. W., 601
Putnam, S. P., 423
Puzia, M. E., 602

Q

Qin, D. B., 53
Quas, J. A., 302
Quatman, T., 534
Querido, J. G., 371
Quevedo, K., 403
Quillian, L., 616
Quinn, P. C., 163, 164, 234, 238, 556
Quinn, R. A., 133
Quinn, T. C., 102

R

Raaijmakers, Q. A. W., 506
Raboy, B., 589
Radelet, M. A., 181
Radin, N., 544
Radke-Yarrow, M., 417, 489, 561
Radunovic, N., 104
Raevuori, A., 210
Raffaelli, M., 214, 412, 627
Rahman, Q., 215, 216
Raikes, H. A., 411, 416, 426, 436, 641
Raikes, H. H., 349
Raine, A., 487
Rainville, P., 487
Rakison, D. H., 233, 234, 238
Rakoczy, H., 239, 240, 452
Raley, S. B., 29
Ramani, G. B., 449
Ramchandani, P. G., 404

Ramey, C. T., 348
Ramey, S. L., 348
Ramo, D. E., 627
Ramos, E., 177
Ramos, M. C., 420
Ramsay, D. S., 402, 424, 449
Ramsay, J. T., 572
Ramsey, P. G., 476
Ramsey-Rennels, J. L., 164
Ramus, F., 155
Rangel, C., 644
Ranking, J., 191
Rao, G., 198
Rao, N., 543
Rasbash, J., 586
Raskind, W. H., 646
Rasmussen, C., 311
Rasmussen, E. R., 290
Rasnake, L. K., 202
Ratan, R., 188
Rathunde, K., 639
Ratner, D., 649
Rauber, M., 639
Rauer, A. J., 489
Rausch, M. K., 525
Rauscher, F. H., 59
Raver, C. C., 33, 596
Ravitch, D., 343, 638, 648
Ray, N., 590
Ray, O., 403
Ray, S. D., 243
Rayner, K., 309, 310
Raynor, H. A., 200
Raynor, R., 17
Raz, S., 113
Razza, R. P., 288, 351
Ream, G. L., 216
Recchia, S., 461
Reed, M. J., 11
Reed, R. K., 110
Rees, J., 433
Reese, E., 241, 299, 301, 455, 459
Reese, K., 258
Reeve, R. A., 312
Regnerus, M., 507
Reid, J. M., 524
Reid, M. J., 523, 524
Reid, P. T., 559
Reilly, J. S., 188
Reimer, J., 505
Reis, O., 473
Reis, S. M., 354
Reiser, L. W., 206
Reisman, J. E., 137
Reisner, E. R., 27
Reiss, D., 123, 587
Reiter, S., 56
Renk, K., 218, 464
Renninger, K. A., 271, 644
Renzetti, C. M., 339
Renzulli, J. S., 352
Repacholi, B. M., 414, 415
Repetti, R., 29
Reppucci, N. D., 300
Resnick, G., 348

Resnick, M. B., 117
Resnick, S. M., 561
Rest, J. R., 501, 502
Resta, R., 84
Rettew, D. C., 125
Rey-Casserly, C., 114
Reyna, V. F., 257, 296, 300
Reynolds, A. J., 348
Reynolds, G. D., 163
Reynolds, K. J., 504
Reznick, J. S., 232
Rhoades, B. L., 288
Rhode, T. E., 331
Rhodes, J. E., 220
Rhodes, M., 533
Rholes, W. S., 476
Ricard, M., 417
Rich, D. Q., 101
Richards, D., 574
Richards, D. D., 320
Richards, J. E., 163, 286
Richards, M., 207
Richardson, H. L., 136
Richgels, D. J., 308, 309
Richler, J., 202
Richmond, J., 143
Richmond, L. J., 509
Ridder, E. M., 333
Ridenour, T. A., 120
Rideout, R., 300
Rideout, V. J., 293, 629, 630, 632, 633, 634, 636
Ridley-Johnson, R., 130, 131
Riestenberg, N., 525
Rifkin, A., 434
Riggins, T., 19
Rijsdijk, F. V., 323
Riksen-Walraven, J. M., 195, 608
Rinaldi, J., 524
Rinderman, H., 281
Ripple, C. H., 35
Ris, M. D., 193
Riskind, R. G., 589
Risley, T. R., 345, 390, 391
Ritchie, L. D., 196
Riva, D., 190
Rivadeneyra, R., 631
Rivera, S. M., 231, 264
Rivkees, S. A., 93, 132
Rivkin, S., 479
Rizzo, T. A., 49
Rizzolatti, G., 146
Roach, M. A., 115
Roazzi, A., 252
Robb, A. S., 210
Robbins, B. D., 626
Robbins, M., 391
Roberts, B. W., 61, 332, 423
Roberts, C., 555
Roberts, D. F., 212, 293, 629, 630, 632, 633, 634, 636
Roberts, J., 84
Roberts, K. P., 300
Roberts, R. D., 327
Roberts, R. E., 205, 475

Roberts, R. J., Jr., 23
Roberts, T., 308
Roberts, W., 413, 417, 418, 558
Robertson, E. K., 297
Robertson, J., 595
Robin, A. L., 211
Robin, D. J., 151
Robins, R. W., 416, 463
Robinson, B. F., 366
Robinson, B. W., 366
Robinson, C. A., 294
Robinson, C. C., 518, 609
Robinson, J., 494
Robinson, M. L., 125
Robinson, S., 457
Robinson, S. L., 630
Rochat, P., 130, 151, 237, 240, 371, 414, 448, 449
Rock, S. L., 345
Rodemaker, J. E., 378
Rodgers, J. L., 338, 346, 585
Rodham, K., 472
Rodholm-Funnemark, M., 561
Rodkin, P. C., 619
Rodriguez, A., 189
Rodriguez, M. L., 515, 516
Roebers, C. M., 300
Roehlkepartain, E. C., 29, 508
Roelfsema, N. M., 92
Roemmich, J. N., 177, 200, 203, 204
Roeser, R. W., 642
Roffwarg, H. P., 135
Rogan, W. J., 193
Rogers, J. M., 199
Rogoff, B., 25, 26, 251, 252, 268, 272, 273, 290, 294, 340
Rogol, A. D., 177, 203, 204
Rohner, R. P., 439
Rohrbeck, C. A., 271, 644
Roid, G., 327
Roisman, G. I., 435
Roisman, R., 423
Rolfhus, E., 328
Rollins, K. B., 246
Romano, A. M., 111
Rome-Flanders, T., 371
Romero, A. J., 475
Romney, A. K., 535, 537
Romney, D. M., 539
Rönnqvist, L., 187, 189
Rooksby, M., 298, 301
Roopnarine, J. L., 437, 582, 612
Roosa, M. W., 582
Rosander, K., 150, 165
Rosas, S., 345
Rose, A. J., 562, 615, 617, 619, 620
Rose, H., 552
Rose, S. A., 145, 163
Roseman, M., 404
Rosen, A. B., 246
Rosen, C. S., 62, 524
Rosen, D., 209
Rosen, P. J., 621
Rosenbaum, J. F., 219
Rosenberger, L. R., 364

Rosenblatt, A., 205
Rosenblum, T. B., 334
Rosenfeld, R. G., 182
Rosengren, K. S., 246, 449
Rosenshine, B., 271
Roseth, C. J., 610
Rosetta, L., 195
Ross, E., 377
Ross, H. S., 416, 587, 608
Rossor, M. N., 132
Rothbart, M. K., 47, 120, 143, 288, 410, 419, 421, 423, 514
Rothbaum, F., 424, 433
Rothenbacher, D., 195
Rothstein-Fish, C., 340
Rouselle, L., 249
Rousseau, J. J., 12, 530
Rovee-Collier, C. K., 141, 142, 233, 234, 301
Rowe, D. C., 585
Rowe, M. L., 366, 369, 371
Rowland, C. F., 387, 388
Rowley, S. J., 533, 534
Rozin, P., 246
Rubin, K. H., 204, 422, 427, 575, 609, 611, 617, 619, 620, 622
Rubin, L. R., 550
Ruble, D. N., 462, 465, 476, 478, 530, 531, 532, 534, 537, 542, 544, 548, 549, 551, 552, 562
Ruchkin, V., 524
Ruck, M. D., 505, 507
Rudolph, D. K., 481, 642
Rudolph, K. D., 463, 562, 623
Rueter, M. A., 587
Ruff, C., 183
Ruff, H. A., 154, 240, 286, 287
Ruffman, J., 453
Ruffman, T., 232, 247, 257, 455
Ruiz, I., 143, 144
Ruiz-Peláez, J. G., 116
Rumbaut, R. G., 53
Runco, M. A., 350, 352, 353
Rushton, J. L., 559
Rushton, J. P., 121, 335
Russell, A., 574, 577, 611
Russell, J. A., 415
Russell, R. B., 77
Russell, S. T., 641
Rust, J., 546
Rutland, A., 479, 512
Rutter, M., 9, 121, 122, 123, 124, 170, 433
Ryan, E., 601
Ryan, M. K., 504
Ryan, R. M., 33, 60, 473
Rydell, A.-M., 202, 643

S
Saarela, M. V., 487
Saarni, C., 401, 405, 408, 412, 414, 415, 416
Sabbagh, M. A., 383, 455
Sacks, P., 643
Sadeh, A., 133

Sadek, S., 621
Sadler, T. W., 89, 92
Saenger, P., 182
Saffran, J. R., 93, 155, 157, 367, 369
Safren, S. A., 216
Sagi, A., 432, 433
Sagi-Schwartz, A., 432, 433
Sahlberg, P., 648
St. Clair-Thompson, H. L., 280
St. James-Roberts, I., 138
St. Louis, G. R., 475
Saitta, S. C., 83
Salanterä, S., 153
Salapatek, P., 161
Salerno, M., 183
Salguero, R. A. T., 634
Salidis, J., 375
Salihu, H. M., 106
Salisbury, A. L., 97
Salley, B. J., 378
Sallquist, J., 417
Salmivalli, C., 621
Salmon, K., 300
Salovey, P., 327, 412
Salsa, A. M., 243
Salter, D., 601
Salvaterra, F., 588
Samek, D. R., 587
Samenow, S. E., 522
Sameroff, A. J., 10, 58, 331, 642
Samson, A. V., 423
Sanbonmatsu, D. M., 408
Sanchez, J., 646
Sanchez, M. M., 602
Sanchez, R. P., 235
Sander, C. J., 113
Sanders, D. M., 200
Sanders, M., 493
Sanders, O., 601
Sanders, P., 378, 542
Sandfort, T. G. M., 589, 590
Sandler, J. C., 300
Sandnabba, N. K., 539
Sandrin, D., 153
Sands, R. G., 439
Sangrigoli, S., 164
Sann, C., 154, 166
Sansavini, A., 155
Sanson, A., 425
Santiago, C. D., 10
Santoloupo, S., 508
Sarama, J., 311, 633
Sarnecka, B. W., 310
Sarrazin, P., 180
Sato, T., 537
Saucier, J. F., 53
Saudino, K. J., 47, 345, 422, 423, 425
Savage, C., 388
Savage-Rumbaugh, S., 361
Savin-Williams, R. C., 215, 216
Saw, A., 555
Sawyer, A. M., 525
Sawyer, J., 569
Saxe, G. B., 25
Saxon, J. L., 466

Saxton, M., 389, 390
Sayer, A. A., 183
Saygin, A. P., 367
Sayil, M., 208
Saylor, M. M., 236, 237, 383
Saywitz, K. J., 302
Sbarra, D., 593
Scales, P. C., 508
Scarr, S., 122, 123, 333, 335–336, 337–338
Scelfo, J., 213
Schaal, B., 154, 155
Schacht, P. M., 571
Schaefer-McDaniel, N. J., 572
Schalet, A., 219
Schamberg, M. A., 280
Scharrer, E., 629, 630, 631
Schauwers, K., 370
Schectman, R. M., 559
Schellenberg, E. G., 59
Scher, A., 133
Scherb, H., 323
Schermerhorn, A. C., 45
Schiller, M., 435
Schilling, T. H., 231
Schindler, H. S., 214
Schlackman, L. J., 112
Schlagmüller, M., 292, 305
Schlegel, A., 208
Schleifer, M., 258
Schley, S., 218
Schliemann, A. D., 272
Schlotz, W., 170
Schmid, R. G., 323
Schmidt, A. T., 49
Schmidt, K. L., 491
Schmidt, L. A., 422
Schmidt, M. E., 237, 632
Schmidt, M. H., 117
Schmidt, U., 211
Schmitz, S., 421
Schneider, A., 81
Schneider, B. H., 440
Schneider, D., 338
Schneider, W., 289, 292, 293, 295, 297, 300, 304, 305, 331, 632
Schneiders, J., 207
Schofield, J. W., 479
Schofield, W., 105
Scholl, B. J., 457
Scholl, T. O., 104
Scholnick, E. K., 289
Schonberg, R. L., 82, 85
Schöner, G., 30
Schonert-Reichl, K. A., 505
Schoppe, S. J., 421
Schoppe-Sullivan, S. J., 427, 570
Schott, J. M., 132
Schroeder, R. D., 575
Schuengel, C., 434
Schuetze, P., 97
Schull, W. J., 100
Schulte-Ruther, M., 146
Schultz, C. A., 265
Schultz, J. B., 208

Schultz, L. H., 481
Schultz, M. C., 376
Schulz, M. S., 570
Schumann, C. M., 457
Schuneman, M. J., 258
Schunk, D. H., 305
Schuster, B., 465
Schwab-Stone, M., 524
Schwade, J. A., 370
Schwanenflugel, P. J., 303
Schwarte, A. R., 81
Schwartz, C. E., 422
Schwartz, D., 621
Schwartz, J. C., 409
Schwartz, M., 29, 196
Schwartz, S. J., 472, 473
Schwarz, N., 47
Schweiger, W. K., 588
Schweinhart, L. J., 347, 348
Schweizer, K., 323
Schwenck, C., 293
Schwier, C., 233
Schwimmer, J. B., 200
Scot, T. P., 343
Scott, J. A., 380
Scott, K. D., 111
Scott, L. D., 475
Scott, L. S., 48, 156
Scott, P. M., 491
Scott, R. M., 453
Scottham, K. M., 475
Scrimsher, S., 266, 270
Scrutton, D., 150
Scuccimarri, C., 218
Seaton, E. K., 475
Sebanc, A. M., 240, 618
Sebastián, E., 385
Seeto, D., 498
Seibert, A. C., 585
Seid, M., 641
Seidenberg, M. S., 361
Seidl, A., 157
Seidman, E., 641, 642
Seifer, R., 435
Seitz, V., 220
Seki, Y., 453
Sekido, R., 76
Selfhout, M. H. W., 616
Seligman, M. E. P., 341
Sellers, R. M., 475
Selman, R. L., 481, 503
Senechal, M., 308
Senghas, A., 363, 382
Senior, G. J., 163
Senju, A., 370
Sentz, J., 201
Seo, J. H., 101
Serafini, T. E., 471
Serbin, L. A., 532, 533, 534, 543, 549
Sermon, K., 85
Serpell, R., 29
Servin, A., 538
Sesame Workshop, 632
Sevigny, P. R., 439

Sexton, C., 582
Seymour, S. C., 150
Shafer, V. L., 48, 364
Shaffer, A., 11
Shaffer, T. G., 544
Shager, H., 350
Shah, F., 113
Shah, T., 136
Shahar, S., 11
Shainess, N., 206
Shanahan, L., 551
Shankaran, S., 113
Shanker, S. G., 361
Shannon, E. A., 189
Shapiro, A. F., 570
Shapiro, C. J., 291
Shapiro, L. R., 290
Shapka, J. D., 461
Sharlach, A. E., 596
Shastri, J., 548
Shatz, M., 245, 367
Shaver, P. R., 409, 625
Shaw, D. S., 11, 432, 492, 520, 586, 592, 619
Shaw, G. L., 59
Shaw, P., 190, 290
Shea, A. K., 105, 106
Shedler, J., 626
Sheeder, J., 215
Sheehan, G., 592
Sheehy, A., 177
Shen, Y.-L., 214, 412, 627
Shenker, S. S., 647
Sheridan, K., 325
Sherman, S. L., 82
Sherrod, L. R., 509
Sherry, B., 199
Sheu, C.-F., 189
Shic, F., 457
Shields, A., 60
Shiffrin, R. M., 278
Shimada, S., 146
Shimizu, H., 506
Shin, H., 439
Shiner, R. L., 120, 423
Shinskey, J. L., 231
Shipman, K. L., 413
Shirley, L., 543
Shoda, Y., 515, 516
Shonkoff, J. P., 37, 191
Shrestha, S., 413
Shrout, P. E., 149
Shucard, D. W., 48
Shumow, L., 623
Shutter, J. M., 406
Shuwairi, S. M., 160, 165
Shwalb, D. W., 437, 582
Shweder, R. A., 8, 52, 513
Sidappa, A., 49
Sidebotham, P., 600
Sidle, A. L., 246
Siebenbruner, J., 214
Siebert, A. C., 586
Siegal, M., 396
Sieger, K., 218

Siegler, R. S., 21, 23, 64, 249, 260, 284, 285, 311, 312, 320
Siervogel, R. M., 177
Signorella, M. L., 532, 534, 552
Signorielli, N., 631
Siimes, M. A., 209
Sikora, D. M., 67
Silk, J. S., 571, 572, 575, 578
Silvén, M., 371
Silver, E. J., 639
Silver, R. C., 524
Silverman, B. E., 625
Silverman, D., 54
Silverman, I., 556
Sim, T. N., 626
Simcock, G., 237, 243, 295, 301, 449
Simion, F., 135, 163, 164
Simmons, R. G., 641
Simon, T., 320
Simon, T. R., 519
Simoneau, M., 258
Simons, L. G., 583
Simons, R. L., 523, 600
Simons-Morton, B. G., 627
Simonton, D. K., 353
Simpkins, S. D., 612
Simpson, J. A., 404
Simpson, J. L., 83
Singer, D. G., 632, 634
Singer, J. L., 632, 634
Singer, L. T., 97
Singer, M. A., 285
Singh, S., 214
Singleton, J. L., 363, 364
Sinkkonen, J., 209
Sinno, S., 510
Sippola, L. K., 616, 617
Sirios, S., 453
Sisson, S. B., 632
Sizonenko, S. V., 108
Skaalvik, E. M., 461
Skara, S., 627
Skiba, R. J., 525
Skinner, B. F., 17
Skinner, E. A., 467
Skoe, E. E. A., 504
Skouteris, H., 116
Slaby, R. G., 548, 631
Slack, K. S., 36
Slade, A., 437
Slater, A., 153, 163, 165
Slater, R., 159, 164, 165
Slee, J., 297
Slemmer, J. A., 157, 159
Slicker, K. E., 580
Slijper, F. M. E., 538
Slobin, D. I., 386, 389
Slobodskaya, H. R., 427
Sloman, J., 193
Slonims, V., 82
Slotkin, T. A., 108
Sluzenski, J., 231
Smahel, D., 635
Small, M., 139
Small, S. A., 53

Smart, D., 425
Smart, J., 133
Smetana, J. G., 498, 510, 511, 579
Smiley, S. S., 287
Smith, A., 220
Smith, A. L., 181
Smith, B. H., 291
Smith, B. L., 374
Smith, C., 507
Smith, C. L., 56, 394
Smith, J., 345, 491–492, 493
Smith, J. C., 33
Smith, J. R., 36, 587
Smith, K., 534
Smith, K. E., 598
Smith, L. B., 30, 149, 230, 382
Smith, N. J., 202
Smith, P. K., 610
Smith, R. S., 10, 117
Smith, S. L., 631
Smokowski, P. R., 53
Smyke, A. T., 171, 433
Snarey, J. R., 471, 502, 505, 506
Snell, E. K., 29
Snider, J. B., 579, 580
Snidman, N., 422
Snow, C. E., 380, 390, 393, 396
Snyder, J., 618, 621
Snyder, K. A., 23
So, L. K. H., 375
Sobel, D. M., 240
Sobolewski, J. M., 593
Sobring, E., 561
Society for Research in Child
    Development, 66
Soderstrom, M., 157
Soetens, B., 199
Softas-Nall, B., 438
Sokolik, E., 534
Soli, A. R., 586
Solomon, G. E. A., 265
Solomon, J., 430
Sondergaard, C., 98
Song, J., 416
Sontag, C. W., 331
Sontag, L. M., 559
Sonuga-Barke, E. J., 170
Sophian, C., 249
Sorensen, P. M., 267
Sørensen, T. I., 199
Sosa, A. V., 373
Sosa, B. B., 290
Sosa, R., 111
Soska, K. C., 160
Soto, P., 385
Soussignan, R., 154
South African Department of
    Health, 102
Sowell, E. R., 186, 290
Spadoni, A. D., 99
Spagnola, M., 29
Spatz, D. L., 134
Spear, L. P., 191, 256
Spearman, C., 321
Speece, D. L., 308

Spelke, E. S., 151, 165, 234, 261–262,
    263
Spence, I., 557
Spence, M. J., 49, 94, 156, 302, 369
Spencer, J. P., 30, 151
Spencer, P. E., 372
Spere, K. A., 378
Spieker, S. J., 282
Spiewak, G. S., 509
Spinrad, T. L., 409, 417, 489, 510, 558
Spirito, A., 472, 473, 627
Spitz, R. A., 433
Spitznagle, T., 103
Spock, B., 13, 134
Sporer, N., 271
Sporte, S. E., 508
Sprague, K. E., 309
Spuhl, S. T., 268
Sroufe, L. A., 9, 406, 407, 432, 435,
    437, 440, 603
Stacey, J., 589
Stack, D. M., 154
Staff, J., 649
Stager, C. L., 374
Stahl, S. A., 310
Stams, G. J. M., 440, 506, 588
Standley, J. M., 115
Stanfors, M., 536
Stange, T., 543
Stangor, M., 623
Stanley, J. C., 556
Stanley-Hagan, M., 595
Stanovich, K. E., 51, 380
Stanowicz, L., 389
Stansbury, K., 422
Starkey, P., 310
Starks, M. T., 216
Starr, M. S., 309
Statistics Canada, 397, 479
Stattin, H., 209, 210, 574, 575, 611
Staub, F. C., 312
Staudinger, U. M., 9, 121
Stauffacher, K., 521
Steele, C. M., 341, 558
Steele, H., 437
Steele, J., 534
Steele, K. H., 180
Steele, M., 437
Steele, S., 457
Steen, R. G., 338
Stegge, H., 409
Stehr-Green, P., 202
Stein, J. H., 206
Stein, N., 415
Stein, R. E. K., 639
Stein, Z., 104
Steinberg, L., 190, 191, 209, 212,
    256, 523, 571, 573, 574, 575,
    578, 580, 624, 626
Steiner, J. E., 141, 154
Steiner, M., 105, 106
Steinhausen, C., 210
Stella, J., 457
Stellwagen, K. K., 522
Stenberg, C., 407

Stenberg, G., 414
Stephens, B. E., 114
Stephens, B. R., 164
Stephens, P. C., 627
Stern, D., 414
Stern, E., 312
Stern, M., 538
Sternberg, R. J., 14, 22, 23, 320, 323,
    324, 332, 333, 336, 339, 342,
    350, 352, 353, 354, 355
Stevens, N., 615
Stevenson, H. W., 648
Stevenson, L. M., 251
Stevenson, R., 379
Stevenson-Hinde, J., 422
Stevens-Simon, C., 215
Steward, D. K., 202
Stewart, J. H., 492
Stewart, P. W., 101
Stewart, R. B., Jr., 570
Stewart, S. L., 422
Stewart-Brown, S., 327
Steyaert, J., 83
Stice, E., 209
Stifter, C. A., 287, 426, 575
Stiles, J., 185, 188
Stillman, R. D., 155
Stinchcomb, J. B., 525
Stipek, D. J., 450, 461, 476, 639
Stoch, M. B., 197
Stocker, C. J., 105
Stocker, C. M., 586
Stoel-Gammon, C., 373, 374, 377
Stokes, S. F., 387
Stoll, S., 385
Stolz, H. E., 579
Stone, L., 617
Stone, M. R., 623
Stone, R., 640
Stoneman, Z., 547, 586
Storch, S. A., 308
Stormshak, E. A., 58, 569, 586
Stout, M., 512
Stouthamer-Loeber, M., 521
Strambler, M. J., 341
Strapp, C. M., 390
Strasburger, V. C., 211
Straus, M. A., 492
Strauss, M. S., 310
Strayer, J., 413, 417, 418, 558
Strazdins, L., 596
Streissguth, A. P., 96, 99
Strelau, J., 425
Streri, A., 153, 154, 166
Stretesky, P., 193
Striano, T., 239, 240, 371, 414, 449
Striegel-Moore, R. H., 196
Stright, A. D., 268, 269, 305
Strober, M., 211
Strohschein, L., 27, 585, 592, 593
Stromswold, K., 364
Strosberg, R., 391
Strouse, D. L., 624
Stryker, M. P., 170
Stuewig, J., 409

Stuhlman, M., 643
Sturaro, C., 619
Sturge-Apple, M. L., 404
Stuss, D. T., 288, 298
Styfco, S. J., 35, 36
Styne, D. M., 183
Su, T. F., 53
Suarez-Morales, L., 579
Suarez-Orozco, C., 53
Subbotsky, E. V., 246
Subrahmanyam, K., 246, 341, 634,
    635
Subramanian, K., 199
Substance Abuse and Mental Health
    Services Administration, 97
Suchindran, C., 212
Suddendorf, T., 449
Sugarman, D. B., 492
Sullivan, H. S., 617
Sullivan, K., 136
Sullivan, M., 515
Sullivan, M. C., 114
Sullivan, M. W., 402, 407, 409, 413
Sullivan, S., 640
Sulovic, N., 104
Sumter, S. R., 626
Sundara, M., 369
Sundet, J. M., 338
Super, C. M., 132, 133, 139, 150
Supple, A. J., 53, 579
Surian, L., 396
Susman, E. J., 206, 208
Susman-Stillman, A., 577
Susskind, J. E., 532
Sussman, A. L., 119
Sussman, S., 627
Sutton, M. J., 212
Suzuki, L. K., 340
Svensson, A., 633
Svetina, M., 21, 249, 285
Svetlova, M., 417
Svirsky, M. A., 370
Swanson, J., 426
Swanson, J. L., 538
Swedish Social Insurance Agency, 536
Sweeney, B., 142
Swenson, L. D., 382
Swenson, L. P., 619
Swingley, D., 157, 369, 374, 377, 381
Swinson, J., 543
Symons, D. K., 435, 455, 456
Szeminska, A., 226
Szepkouski, G. M., 290
Szkrybalo, J., 532, 549, 551
Szlemko, W. J., 100

T

Taatgen, N. A., 367
Tabibi, Z., 287
Tacon, A., 439
Tager-Flusberg, H., 365, 366, 387,
    388, 394, 455, 457
Takahashi, K., 134, 433
Takala, M., 271
Takeuchi, T., 86

Talley, S., 558
Talmi, A., 139
Tam, C. W., 387
Tamang, B. L., 413
Tamis-LeMonda, C. S., 35, 147, 150, 152, 372, 378
Tammelin, T., 180
Tamrouti-Makkink, I. D., 586
Tangney, J. P., 409
Tanimura, M., 237
Tanner, J. L., 6
Tanner, J. M., 178, 183
Tardif, C., 440, 646
Tardif, T., 376, 378, 379, 455, 580
Tarren-Sweeney, M., 202
Tarter, R. E., 627
Tarullo, A. R., 403
Tasbihsazan, R., 329
Tasker, F., 589, 590
Tasker, F. L., 589
Tauber, M. A., 546
Taumoepeau, M., 455
Tavecchio, L. W. C., 597
Taylor, A. R., 586
Taylor, B. A., 33
Taylor, C. A., 492
Taylor, C. L., 381
Taylor, E., 291
Taylor, J. H., 502, 504
Taylor, J. L., 218
Taylor, L. C., 647
Taylor, M., 52, 240, 241, 303
Taylor, M. C., 547
Taylor, M. G., 533, 541
Taylor, R. D., 11, 583
Taylor, R. L., 583
Taylor, T. J., 361
Teasdale, B., 216
Teicher, M. H., 602
Teinonen, T., 158
Telama, R., 180
Temple, C. M., 557
Temple, J. A., 348
Temple, J. L., 199
Templeton, A. R., 339
Templeton, L. J., 627
Templeton, L. M., 454
Tenenbaum, H. R., 540, 541, 542, 544
ten Tusscher, G. W., 101
Teoh, S. W., 370
Tepper, C. A., 543
Terwel, J., 271, 644
Tessier, R., 116
Tessler, R. C., 589
Teti, D. M., 436, 585
Teyber, E., 594
Thal, D. J., 389, 396
Tharpe, A. M., 155
Thayer, S. M., 587
Thelen, E., 13, 30, 130, 131, 148, 149, 230, 232
Théoret, H., 146, 457
Théoret, M., 533
Theuring, C., 149
Thierry, K. L., 302

Thiessen, E. D., 157, 369
Thiessen, V., 633
Thomaes, S., 464
Thoman, E. B., 141
Thomas, A., 419, 420, 421, 426
Thomas, C. L., 219
Thomas, D., 348
Thomas, D. G., 288
Thomas, J. M., 620
Thomas, K. A., 589
Thomas, K. M., 50, 186, 188, 190
Thomas, R. B., 137
Thomas, R. M., 17
Thombs, B. D., 404
Thompson, A., 574
Thompson, C. K., 379
Thompson, L. A., 331
Thompson, P. M., 186, 190
Thompson, R. A., 24, 68, 137, 185, 402, 409, 411, 412, 416, 430, 432, 436, 440, 450, 456, 490, 515, 641
Thompson, W. W., 202
Thomson, N. R., 497
Thornberry, I., 580
Thornberry, T. P., 219, 523
Thorne, B., 544
Thornton, S., 22
Thurman, P. J., 100
Thurstone, L. L., 321
Tian, L., 561
Tienari, P., 120, 123
Tiet, Q. Q., 11
Tifft, C. J., 82, 85
Tiggemann, M., 200, 463
Tincoff, R., 376
Tirosh, E., 133
Tirsch, W. S., 323
Tisak, J., 523
Tisak, M. S., 522, 523
Tizard, B., 433
To, Y. M., 415
Todorova, I., 53
Tofler, I. T., 181
Tokunaga, R. S., 621
Tolan, P. H., 35, 42
Tolman, D. L., 551
Tolmie, A. K., 272
Tomasello, M., 233, 239, 240, 245, 361, 365, 367, 369, 371, 377, 382, 383, 385, 386, 387, 388, 389, 391, 414, 417, 452, 453, 456
Tong, S., 193
Tong, V. T., 98, 100
Toomela, A., 242
Topàl, J., 232
Torjussen, T. M., 338
Torney-Purta, J., 508
Torrance, E. P., 350
Toth, S. L., 602
Tottenham, N., 190, 433
Touwen, B. C. L., 132
Townsend, D. A., 233
Tracy, J. L., 416
Tracy, R., 396

Trainor, L. J., 168
Traupman, E., 151
Traurig, M., 200
Trautner, H. M., 533, 548
Trautwein, U., 644
Treasure, J., 211
Treffert, D. A., 325
Trehub, S. E., 155, 156
Tremblay, L., 205
Tremblay, R. E., 516, 517, 518, 519, 520, 522, 561
Trent, K., 583
Trentacosta, C. J., 619
Trevarthen, C., 608
Triandis, H. C., 35, 51
Trickett, P. K., 601
Trionfi, G., 241
Trivers, R. L., 487
Trocomé, N., 600
Troiano, R. P., 181
Tronick, E. Z., 137, 139, 403, 406, 408
Troop-Gordon, W., 620
Tropp, L. R., 479
Troseth, G. L., 237, 383
Trotter, K. H., 559
Troutman, D. R., 615
True, M. M., 432
Truglio, R., 632
Trzesniewski, K. H., 463, 466
Tsao, F.-M., 156, 369
Tseng, V., 53
Tsethlikai, M., 296
Ttofi, M. M., 521
Tucker, C. J., 508, 542, 586
Tudge, J., 266, 270
Tulsky, D. S., 320, 321
Tulving, E., 298
Turati, C., 163, 164
Turiel, E., 498, 503, 510, 513
Turkewitz, G., 155
Turkheimer, E., 121, 209, 336
Turkle, S., 634
Turnbull, K. P., 308
Turnbull, M., 397
Turner, P. J., 534, 539, 542, 543
Turner, R. N., 479
Turner-Bowker, D. M., 543
Tuyen, J. M., 202
Twenge, J. M., 462, 463, 464
Twyman, K., 621
Tychsen, L., 171
Tyson, D. F., 647
Tzur, G., 264
Tzuriel, D., 342, 557

U

Uauy, R., 135, 197
Ucanok, Z., 208
Udechuku, A., 97
Udry, J. R., 212, 624, 625
Uggen, C., 649
Ullman, M. T., 457
Ullrich-French, S., 181
Umaña-Taylor, A. J., 475
Umiltá, C., 163

Underhill, K., 219
Underwood, M. K., 518, 560
UNICEF (United Nations Children's Fund), 33, 35, 103, 194, 524
United Nations, 80
Updegraff, K. A., 475, 543–544, 587
Urquhart, J., 343
U.S. Census Bureau, 33, 34, 87, 118, 394, 438, 441, 472, 479, 534, 558, 584, 590, 591, 595, 596, 632, 649
U.S. Centers for Disease Control and Prevention, 180, 194, 217
U.S. Department of Agriculture, 105, 198, 584
U.S. Department of Education, 34, 554, 555, 639, 645, 648, 649
U.S. Department of Health and Human Services, 77, 81, 82, 106, 111, 114, 118, 177, 180, 181, 195, 198, 201, 213, 214, 215, 217, 348, 599–600, 601, 604
U.S. Department of Justice, 518, 519
Usher, B. A., 47
Usher-Seriki, K. K., 212
Usta, I. M., 106
Uttal, D. H., 250, 449
Uyeyama, R. K., 361

V

Vachon, R., 258
Vaidyanathan, R., 387, 388
Vaillancourt, T., 519, 619, 621
Vaish, A., 414, 417
Vakil, E., 287
Valdés, G., 52
Valentine, J. C., 463
Valian, V., 384, 390
Valiente, C., 305, 417, 418, 426
van Aken, C., 426
van Balen, F., 589
van de Beek, C., 538
Vandell, D. L., 27, 597, 598, 599, 608, 623
van den Akker, A. L., 423, 426
Vandenberg, B., 609
Van den Bergh, B. R. H., 106, 461
van den Bergh, E. D., 643
van den Boom, D. C., 421, 423, 426, 589
van den Bossche, A. S., 135
van den Dries, L., 433, 588
van den Heuvel, M. P., 323
van den Oord, E., 585
Vanderbilt-Adriance, E., 11
Vandergrift, N., 597
van der Heijden, P. G. M., 503
van der Meer, A. L., 150
van der Wal, M. F., 105
Van de Vijver, P. J. R., 51
Van Dulmen, M., 624, 625
van Eijsden, M., 105
Van Eyk, J., 86
Van Goozen, S. H. M., 557

van Goudoever, J. B., 114
Van Hoof, A., 506
Van Hulle, C. A., 377
van IJzendoorn, M. H., 138, 337, 432, 433, 434, 435, 436, 437, 440, 588, 597
Van Lange, P. A. M., 486
Van Steirteghem, A., 85
Van Vugt, M., 486
VanWey, L. K., 585
Vanyukov, M., 627
Varela-Silva, M. I., 183
Varendi, H., 155
Varnhagen, C., 636
Varni, J. W., 200
Vartanian, L. R., 256
Vasen, A., 413
Vasquez, D. M., 403
Vaughn, B. E., 435, 514, 615
Vaughn, S., 646
Vazonyi, A. T., 579, 580
Veach, P. M., 532
Veenstra, R., 621
Veira, Y., 97
Velasco, R., 490
Velderman, M. K., 435
Velleman, R. D. B., 627
Venet, M., 258
Venezia, M., 407
Veneziano, R. A., 439
Vereijken, B., 149
Verhulst, F. C., 588
Veríssimo, M., 588
Vernberg, E. M., 520
Vernon, P. A., 323, 326
Vernon-Feagans, L., 580
Verschaffel, L., 285, 312
Vihman, M. M., 370, 374
Vilela, A. M., 631
Vinden, P. G., 304, 455
Viner, R. M., 211
Vinovskis, M. A., 11
Vira, R., 570
Visher, E. B., 594
Visher, J. S., 594
Visser, B. A., 326
Vitaro, F., 425, 517, 522, 616, 618
Vitrup, B., 492
Vittersø, J., 207
Vivanti, G., 457
Voci, A., 479
Voeten, M., 621
Vogel, D. A., 538
Vohr, B. R., 114, 372
Vollebergh, W., 473
Volling, B. L., 410, 489, 515, 586
Volpe, L. E., 134
Vondra, J. I., 430, 432
von Hofsten, C., 150, 151, 152, 159, 165, 233
Vonk, R., 530
Voracek, M., 59
Votruba-Drzal, E., 214, 581
Vouloumanos, A., 155
Voyer, D., 556

Voyer, S., 556
Vuoksimaa, E., 189, 557
Vygotsky, L. S., 25, 267, 269, 272, 514

W
Waas, G. A., 516
Waber, D. P., 646
Wachs, T. D., 420, 421, 424
Waddell, K. J., 294
Waddington, C. H., 122
Wadsworth, M. E., 10
Waerness, K., 536
Wagenaar, K., 86
Wagner, A. D., 293
Wahlberg, K.-E., 123
Wahlsten, D., 9, 120, 122
Wai, J., 554, 555, 556
Wainryb, C., 300, 511, 512
Wakeley, A., 231, 264
Walberg, H. J., 639
Walden, T. A., 414
Waldenström, U., 189
Waldfogel, J., 116, 117, 119, 345, 442, 590, 596, 597
Waldman, I. D., 125
Waldrip, A. M., 617
Waldvogel, J., 36
Walenski, M., 457
Walk, R., 159
Walker, A. M., 136
Walker, J. M. T., 647
Walker, L. J., 502, 503, 504
Walker, S., 534
Walker-Andrews, A. S., 158, 414
Wall, M., 181
Wallace, J. M., Jr., 626
Waller, E. M., 617, 619
Walsh, R. O., 137
Wang, L., 424, 425, 427
Wang, Q., 299, 451, 459, 467, 579, 582
Wang, S., 29, 52, 231
Wang, Y., 426
Wanska, S. K., 390
Wänström, L., 338
Ward, L. M., 631
Wark, G. R., 503
Warkentin, V., 450
Warneken, F., 452
Warner, L. A., 579
Warner, R. M., 327
Warnock, F., 153
Warren, M. P., 207, 208
Warren, M. R., 647
Waschbusch, D. A., 47
Wasik, B. A., 308
Wasserman, E. A., 234
Wasserman, J. D., 320, 321
Watamura, S. E., 442
Watanabe, H., 623
Waterman, A. S., 472
Waters, E., 406, 429, 431, 437
Waters, P., 461
Watson, A. C., 454

Watson, D. J., 309
Watson, J. B., 17
Watson, J. D., 157
Watson, J. S., 406
Watson, K. S., 609
Watson, M., 456
Watts-English, T., 602
Wax, J., 112
Wax, J. R., 111
Waxler, C. Z., 491
Waxman, S. R., 235, 376, 382
Way, N., 47, 475
Wayerman, M., 195
Webb, N. M., 271, 644
Webb, S. J., 186
Weber, C., 156
Webster-Stratton, C., 523, 524
Wechsler, D., 328
Weems, C. F., 412
Wehren, A., 380
Weikum, W. M., 368
Weinberg, C. R., 89
Weinberg, M. K., 402, 406
Weinberg, R. A., 180, 337–338
Weinberger, J., 418
Weiner, A., 212
Weiner, J., 646
Weiner, S., 234
Weinert, F. E., 331, 465
Weinfield, N. S., 432, 437
Weinraub, M., 534
Weinstein, R. S., 341, 643
Weinstein, S. M., 207
Weinstock, M., 105
Weisfield, G. E., 206
Weisglas-Kuperus, N., 114
Weisgram, E. S., 543, 549
Weisner, T. S., 134, 542
Weiss, C. C., 638
Weiss, K. M., 81
Weiss, L. G., 328, 331, 338
Weiss, R. J., 562
Weissberg, R. P., 598
Weissman, M. D., 265
Weisz, A. N., 503
Weisz, V., 532
Weizman, Z. O., 380
Wekerle, C., 600, 602, 625
Wellman, H. M., 246, 265, 303, 304, 370, 381, 415, 452, 453, 455
Welner, K. G., 645
Welsh, D. P., 625
Welsh, J. A., 464
Welsh, M. C., 79, 282
Weng, X., 97
Wentworth, N., 151, 289
Wentzel, K. R., 618
Werker, J. F., 93, 155, 156, 157, 368, 369, 374
Werner, E. E., 10, 117
Werner, L. A., 93, 155, 157
Werner, N. E., 518, 520, 560, 623
Wessler, R. E., 67
Westermann, G., 22, 23
Westra, T., 150

Whalen, P. J., 190
Whaley, G. J. L., 432
Wheeler, K., 145
Wheeler, M. A., 298
Wheeler, W., 508
Whincup, P. H., 104
Whipple, E. E., 600, 601
Whipple, N., 434
Whitby, E. H., 85
White, B., 152
White, K. S., 156
Whitehurst, G. J., 308
Whiteman, S. D., 63, 546
Whitesell, N. R., 409, 461, 463
Whiteside-Mansell, L., 569
Whiting, B., 535, 536, 542
Whitlock, J. L., 635
Whitten, P., 568
Wichman, A. L., 346
Wichmann, C., 620
Wichstrøm, L., 211
Wickberg, B., 570
Widom, C. S., 602
Wieling, E., 524
Wigfield, A., 462, 467, 468, 641
Wilcox, A. J., 89
Wilcox, S. A., 454
Wilcox, T., 166
Wiley, E., 364, 365
Wilkenfeld, B., 508
Wilkinson, K., 377
Wilkinson, R. B., 464
Willatts, P., 235
Willerman, L., 123, 336, 337, 346
Williams, E., 544
Williams, G. R., 104
Williams, J. E., 530
Williams, J. M., 209
Williams, K., 180, 591
Williams, K. R., 621
Williams, P. E., 328
Williams, S. C., 522
Williams, S. T., 608
Williams, T. M., 629
Williams, T. S., 625
Williams, W. M., 332, 339
Williamson, J., 438
Williamson, R. A., 233
Willinger, M., 134
Willoughby, J., 520
Wilson, E. K., 212, 213
Wilson, E. O., 486
Wilson, G. D., 215, 216
Wilson, M., 102, 103, 497
Wilson, R., 560
Wilson-Mitchell, J. E., 542
Wimbarti, S., 613
Windecker-Nelson, B., 411
Winer, A. C., 402
Winkler, I., 155
Winner, E., 241, 242, 354, 380, 381
Winsler, A., 25, 193, 267
Winslow, E. B., 592
Winter, M. A., 29
Wiseman, F. K., 82

Wissink, I. B., 579
Witherington, D. C., 151, 270, 415
Wolak, J., 212, 601, 635
Wolchik, S. A., 592, 593
Wold, B., 181
Wolf, A. W., 134, 193
Wolfe, D. A., 600, 602, 603
Wolfe, V. V., 601
Wolff, P. H., 132, 524
Wolfgang, C. H., 543
Wolfinger, N. H., 592
Wolters, C. A., 574
Wong, M. M., 11
Wood, E., 542
Wood, J. J., 611
Wood, J. M., 302
Wood, J. W., 100
Wood, R. M., 135
Woods, R., 166
Woodward, A. L., 233, 234, 383
Woodward, J., 313, 648
Woodward, L. J., 195
Woody-Dorning, J., 289
Woody-Ramsey, J., 288
Woolley, J. D., 246
World Cancer Research Fund, 198
World Health Organization, 194, 196, 198, 201
Worrell, F. C., 475
Worthy, J., 644
Wouters, H., 502
Wright, B. C., 250
Wright, C. M., 202
Wright, J. C., 632
Wright, J. P., 193, 625
Wright, K. L., 181
Wright, M. J., 86, 120

Wright, P. A., 617
Wright, R. O., 193
Wrotniak, B. H., 200
Wu, L. L., 590
Wu, P., 51, 582
Wu, S., 409
Wu, T., 204
Wu, Y. W., 86
Wulczyn, F., 602
Wunsch, J. P., 407
Wust, S., 114
Wyatt, J. M., 504
Wyer, N., 515
Wyman, E., 240
Wynn, K., 263, 264, 487
Wynne, L. C., 123

X

Xie, H., 622
Xu, F., 263, 378
Xue, Y., 310

Y

Yale, M. E., 406
Yan, J., 510
Yan, Z., 632, 633
Yang, B., 588
Yang, C., 587
Yang, C.-K., 134
Yap, M. B. H., 559
Yarrow, M. R., 46, 491
Yeates, K. O., 481
Yeh, C. J., 53
Yeh, H.-C., 587
Yeh, S. S., 467
Yehuda, R., 105
Yen, L., 382
Yeni-Komshian, G. H., 365

Yip, T., 53
Yirmiya, N., 426, 457
Yoder, K., 473
Yoerger, K., 520
Yonas, A., 160
Yoshida, H., 382
Yoshikawa, H., 47, 53, 345
Yoshinaga-Itano, C., 372
Young, J. F., 463
Young, S. E., 282
Young, S. H., 111
Youngblade, L. M., 416
Younge, S. N., 583
Young-Hyman, D., 200
Youngstrom, E., 481
Youniss, J. E., 28, 473, 507, 508
Yu, R., 427
Yuan, A. S. V., 595
Yuille, J. C., 473
Yumoto, C., 96
Yunger, J. L., 550, 568

Z

Zackai, E. H., 83
Zafeiriou, D. I., 132
Zaff, J. F., 508
Zahn, R., 487
Zahn-Waxler, C., 47, 417, 489, 494, 558, 559
Zakharia, R., 206
Zammit, S., 333
Zamsky, E. S., 583
Zamuner, T. S., 374
Zanetti-Daellenbach, R. A., 111
Zarbatany, L., 616
Zarkadoulia, E., 202
Zarrett, N. R., 463
Zawadzki, B., 425

Zeanah, C. H., 433
Zeifman, D. M., 137
Zelazo, N. A., 131
Zelazo, P. D., 282, 287, 497
Zeller, M. H., 200
Zerwas, S., 449
Zeskind, P. S., 137, 138
Zhan, M., 346
Zhang, D., 643
Zhang, T.-Y., 125
Zhang, Z., 376
Zhoe, Q., 510
Zhou, M., 53
Zhou, Q., 426, 578
Zhou, X., 312
Zhou, Z., 313
Zhu, J., 331
Zhu, W. X., 588
Zigler, E., 35, 119, 147
Zimmer-Gembeck, M. J., 214, 467, 562
Zimmerman, B. J., 305
Zimmerman, C., 313
Zimmerman, F. J., 237, 378, 629
Zimmerman, P., 473
Zimmerman, R., 428
Zimmerman, S., 196
Zimmermann, L. K., 422
Ziol-Guest, K. M., 332
Zitzer-Comfort, C., 366
Ziv, M., 452
Zolotor, A. J., 602
Zosuls, K. M., 549
Zucker, K. J., 550
Zukow-Goldring, P., 270
Zukowski, A., 365, 387, 388
Zur, O., 311
Zwart, M., 118

Subject Index

Figures, tables, and footnotes are indicated by f, t, and n following page numbers.

A

A-not-B search error in sensorimotor stage, 229, 232
Abacus, 310
Ability
  and effort in achievement, 464, 465, 466
  entity view of, 465, 467
  incremental view of, 465
Aboriginals, Australian, 272, 340
Abortion
  in adolescent pregnancy, 217
  spontaneous. *See* Miscarriage
Abstinence from sexual activity, 213, 219
Abstract thinking
  in concrete operational stage, 252
  in formal operational stage, 253–259
  and intelligence, 321, 332
  and language development, 365, 375, 381
  and mathematical abilities, 555
  and moral development, 501, 502, 503
  and self-concept, 458
  and social-cognitive development, 447
Abuse
  of alcohol. *See* Alcohol use and abuse
  of child, 599–604. *See also* Child maltreatment
  of drugs. *See* Drug use and abuse
  peer victimization in, 621
Academic achievement
  attributions on, 467
  class size affecting, 637
  and cognitive self-regulation, 305
  computer use in, 633
  cross-national research on, 647f, 647–648
  early intervention programs affecting, 347, 348, 351
  family beliefs on, 345–346
  gender stereotypes on, 532–533, 540f, 540–541, 554t, 554–558
  and high-stakes testing movement, 342, 343
  home environment affecting, 345
  of immigrant youths, 53
  intelligence quotient as predictor of, 331–332
  parent expectations for, 346, 540–541, 556–557
  reading skills affecting, 308–309
  school transitions affecting, 641, 642

  and self-esteem, 462f, 463
  teacher–student interaction affecting, 643
  in teenage pregnancy, 218
  working memory capacity affecting, 280
Academic learning, 307–314. *See also* Education
Acceptance in child rearing, 573, 574t
  in authoritarian style, 574
  in authoritative style, 573
  in uninvolved style, 575
Acceptance in peer relations, 618–622
Accommodation
  and adaptation in Piaget's theory, 227
  neo-Piagetian theory of, 283
  in preoperational stage, 244
Accreditation of child-care facilities, 443, 597, 598
Acculturative stress, 475, 579
Accutane and prenatal development, 96
Achievement
  ability and effort in, 464, 465, 466
  academic. *See* Academic achievement
  and anorexia nervosa, 211
  attributions related to, 464–468
  gender stereotypes on, 467, 532–533, 534
  and learned helplessness, 465–466, 466f, 467
  motivation for, 465
  and pubertal timing, 209–210
  self-esteem in, 464–468
Achievement tests, 328, 331–332
  and high-stakes testing movement, 342, 343
Acquired immune deficiency syndrome (AIDS), 213, 217
  breastfeeding in, 194
  in pregnancy, 102t, 102–103
Action words in semantic development, 379
Active correlation, 123
Activity level, and temperament, 420t
Adaptation
  and attention, 287
  in cognitive development, 19, 227
  coping strategies in. *See* Coping strategies
  Darwin on, 13
  ethology of, 23–24
  evolutionary developmental psychology on, 24
  in family changes, 571
  of immigrant youths, 53

  of neonate in delivery, 108
  in Piaget's theory, 227
  and practical intelligence, 324
  and resilience, 10–11
  in school transitions, 640–642
  in sensorimotor development, 228t
  and temperament, 93, 420t
Addiction. *See* Alcohol use and abuse; Drug use and abuse; Smoking
ADHD. *See* Attention-deficit hyperactivity disorder
Adjustment
  child-rearing styles affecting, 575–576, 576t
  divorce of parents affecting, 592, 593
  early intervention programs affecting, 347–348, 349
  and friendships, 617–618
  and gender identity, 547–548
  and identity status, 471–472, 475
  of immigrant youths, 53
  intelligence quotient as predictor of, 333
  parental conflict affecting, 571
  peer acceptance affecting, 619
  in puberty, 205–210
  and self-esteem, 463
  sexual abuse affecting, 601
Adolescence (11 to 18 years old), 6
  in adoption, 588–589
  aggression in, 517, 518–519, 520
  alcohol use and abuse in, 218, 626–627
  antisocial behavior in, 523
  autonomy in, 6, 577–580
  body composition in, 177
  body proportions in, 177
  body size in, 176, 177f, 192
  brain development in, 190–191
  catch-up growth in, 192
  child rearing in, 576, 577–580, 578
  civic responsibility in, 508
  cognitive development in, 20, 20t, 21, 190–191, 253–259
  computer and cell phone use in, 633, 634–635
  conflicts in, 208, 571, 579, 580
  conformity to peer pressure in, 625–627
  contraception in, 214f, 214–215, 219–220
  dating in, 624–625
  decision making in, 256–257
  delinquency in, 518–519, 520
  depression in, 472–473, 559, 560
  divorce of parents during, 591–592

  drug use and abuse in, 217, 218, 626–627
  eating disorders in, 210–212
  emotional intelligence in, 327
  emotional self-regulation in, 190–191
  employment in, 649
  extracurricular activities in, 638
  formal operational stage in, 253–259
  friendships in, 614, 615, 616–617
  gender identity in, 550–551, 553
  gender roles in, 553
  gender stereotypes in, 532–533, 539–542, 553
  giftedness in, 354
  growth spurts in, 183
  hair growth in, 203
  health issues in, 210–220
  height in, 176, 177
  homework time in, 613, 613f
  homosexuality in, 215–216
  hormone changes in, 183, 191, 212
  idealism and criticism in, 256
  identity formation in, 468–475, 578
  of immigrant youths, 53
  inductive discipline in, 489
  information processing in, 306
  initiation ceremonies in, 206
  language development in, 381, 393, 395
  memory in, 293, 299–300, 306
  metacognition in, 306
  milestones of development, 253
  moodiness in, 207, 207f
  moral development in, 489, 502, 504, 505–506, 510, 511, 512, 513
  motor development in, 178–179, 180
  nutrition in, 204, 210–212
  obesity in, 198, 200
  parent relationship in, 208, 577–580. *See also* Parent–adolescent relationship
  peer relations in, 209, 610–611, 614, 619, 623–627, 628
  personal and moral domains in, 511, 512
  physical development in, 203–221
  play in, 610
  pregnancy in, 217–220. *See also* Teenage pregnancy and parenthood
  psychosexual and psychosocial development in, 16t
  puberty in, 6, 203–221. *See also* Puberty
  religion in, 507–509

Adolescence (cont.)
    risk-taking behavior in, 191, 207, 214, 256, 257, 624
    school transitions in, 641–642
    scientific reasoning in, 314
    self-concept in, 458–459, 460
    self-consciousness and self-focusing in, 255–256
    self-esteem in, 461, 462, 463, 469
    sexual abuse in, 601
    sexuality in, 212–220
    sexually transmitted diseases in, 217
    shyness in, 422
    sibling relationship in, 587
    sleep schedule in, 207
    suicide in, 472–473
    television viewing in, 629, 630–631, 631f, 632
    vocational preparation in, 649–650
    voice changes in, 203
    weight in, 176
Adoption, 588–589
    in adolescent pregnancy, 218
    attachment security in, 433–434, 588
    biological knowledge on, 265
    deprivation prior to, 170, 171, 171f, 403
    and environmental influences on gene expression, 123
    by homosexual families, 589
    intelligence and IQ research in, 335f, 337–338
    of Romanian orphans, 170, 191, 403
    in surrogate motherhood, 86–87
    of twins, heritability estimates in, 120
Adrenal gland, 183
    androgens released by, 183, 537–538
    congenital hyperplasia of, 537–538, 561
Advertisements on television, 631
Advocacy for children's causes, 37
Affordances, in differentiation theory on perceptual development, 168–169
Afghanistan, 524
Africa. See also specific countries.
    attachment patterns in, 432
    body size in, 183
    child-rearing practices and newborn behavior in, 139
    HIV infection and AIDS in, 102
    menarche in, 205
    metacognitive knowledge in, 304
    sickle cell allele and malaria resistance in, 79
African Americans
    academic achievement beliefs of, 345–346
    adolescent, 214, 220, 472, 580
    as adolescent parents, 220
    anorexia nervosa of, 210
    body image of, 209

body size of, 183
child-rearing practices of, 583
communication style of, 339–340
corporal punishment of, 493
cosleeping of parents and infants, 134
drug use of, 626
emotional sensitivity of, 559
ethnic identity of, 475
extended family relationships of, 438, 583, 590
food insecurity of, 197
friendships of, 616
gender stereotypes of, 534, 546, 559
grandparents as primary caregivers of, 438
growth rate of, 183
infant mortality rate of, 118
intelligence quotient of, 334, 334f, 336, 337–338, 340–341
lead exposure of, 193
menarche of, 205, 206
in mixed-race schools, 479
moral reasoning of, 506
narrative style of, 393
out-group favoritism, 477
poverty of, 33
puberty of, 205, 208–209
school transitions of, 642
self-esteem of, 464
sexual activity in adolescence, 214
sickle cell anemia of, 79
single-parent families of, 590
skeletal age of, 178
skeletal growth of, 178
stereotype threat affecting, 341, 341f
suicide rate of, 472
teacher–student interaction of, 643
as television characters, 631
television viewing of, 630
vocabulary development affecting IQ testing of, 340–341
After-school programs, 597f, 598–599
Age
    in adolescence (11 to 18 years old), 6. See also Adolescence
    and body composition changes, 177
    and body proportion changes, 176–177
    and body size changes, 176, 177f
    and cognitive development stages, 20t
    in dating, 624, 624f
    during divorce of parents, 591–592
    in early childhood (2 to 6 years old), 5–6. See also Early childhood
    in emerging adulthood, 6
    and emotional development, 419
    of fetal viability, 92
    in immigration, 364–365, 365f
    in infancy and toddlerhood (birth to 2 years old), 5. See also Infancy and toddlerhood

and information processing, 281, 281f, 306
    maternal. See Maternal age
    in menarche, 203
    in middle childhood (6 to 11 years old), 6. See also Middle childhood
    and milestones of development. See Milestones
    and mixed-age peer relations, 612
    and motor skills, 148, 178–179, 180
    paternal, and chromosomal abnormalities, 82
    in puberty, 204, 205, 208–210
    and research risks, 68
    and scientific reasoning, 313
    skeletal, 178
    in spermarche, 204
    and visual development, 167
Aggression, 516–525
    in adolescence, 517, 518–519
    androgens in, 561
    biological influences on, 561
    bullying in, 621
    child-rearing practices in, 520–522, 523–525, 561–562
    community influences on, 523
    cultural influences on, 523
    and delinquency, 518–519, 522–523
    in early childhood, 516–517, 518
    emergence of, 517–518
    empathy in, 417
    environmental influences on, 561–562
    family influences on, 520–522, 522f
    gender stereotypes in, 518
    and intelligence quotient, 333
    interventions in, 523–525
    in middle childhood, 517, 518
    milestones of development, 517
    in peer relations, 518, 562, 616, 617, 623
    physical, 517, 518, 519, 560, 561–562
    of popular children, 619
    proactive (instrumental), 517, 522
    and punishment, 491, 492, 493
    reactive (hostile), 517, 518, 522
    of rejected children, 619
    relational, 518, 519, 520, 560, 562
    sex differences in, 518, 519, 560–562
    social cognitive deficits and distortions in, 522–523, 525
    stability of, 519–520
    structured observations of, 44
    and television viewing, 630–631, 631f
    verbal, 518, 560
    zero tolerance policies on, 525
AIDS, 213, 217
    breastfeeding in, 194
    in pregnancy, 102t, 102–103
Air pollution, prenatal exposure to, 101

Aka of Central Africa, 439
Alcohol use and abuse
    in adolescence, 218, 626–627
    and bulimia nervosa, 211
    in early pubertal maturation, 208, 209
    of homosexual youths, 216
    in pregnancy, 98–100
    teenage pregnancy in, 218
    television commercials on, 631
Alcohol-related neurodevelopmental disorder (ARND), 99t
Alertness of infants, 132, 132t
Alleles, 77
    dominant and recessive, 77–79
    genomic imprinting of, 80
Altruistic behavior. See also Prosocial behavior
    empathy in, 417
    in moral development, 486–487
Alzheimer's disease, 82
Ambidexterity, 189
Ambiguous genitals, 538
American College Testing (ACT) Assessment, 328, 332
American Psychological Association, 66
American Sign Language (ASL), 363
    chimpanzees using, 361
    and sensitive periods in language development, 364
Amnesia, infantile, 300, 301
Amniocentesis, 84, 85t
Amnion, 89
Amniotic fluid, 89
Amodal sensory properties, 166, 168
Amphetamine use in adolescence, 626
Amygdala, 190
    in adopted children, 433
    in autism, 457
    in shyness and sociability, 422
Anal stage of psychosexual development, 15, 16t
Analgesic drugs during childbirth, 112
Analogical problem solving, 235
    in concrete operational stage, 250
    in preoperational stage, 246
Analytical intelligence, 323, 324, 324f
Androgen, 183
    in adolescence, 183
    and aggression, 561
    in congenital adrenal hyperplasia, 537–538, 561
    and gender roles, 537–538
    insensitivity syndrome, 534, 538
    and spatial abilities, 557
Androgyny, 547–548, 549, 551
Anemia
    Cooley's, 78t
    iron deficiency, 197
    sickle cell, 78t, 79
Anencephaly, 104

Anesthesia
  during childbirth, 112
  for newborns, 153
Anger
  experimental research on, 57, 57f
  in infancy and toddlerhood, 407
Animals
  attachment of, 428
  imitation by, 145, 145f, 146
  language acquisition of, 361
  monkeys and apes. See Monkeys
    and apes
  sensory deprivation studies of, 170
  social behavior of, 486
Animistic thinking in preoperational
    stage, 244, 246
Anorexia nervosa, 210–211
Anoxia of infant during childbirth,
    112–113
Antiretroviral drug therapy, 102–103
Antisocial behavior
  childhood onset of, 521f
  child-rearing practices in, 578
  community and cultural influences
    on, 523
  in corporal punishment, 493
  delinquency in, 519, 520–521, 521f,
    523
  in depression of parent, 404
  environmental influences on gene
    expression for, 123, 124
  heritability of, 120, 123
  and intelligence quotient, 333
  intervention programs in, 525, 525f
  in lead exposure, 193
  in peer groups, 623
  of popular children, 619
  structured observations of, 44
Anxiety
  and cognitive processing, 402
  in corporal punishment, 492
  in early childhood, 411
  in infancy and toddlerhood,
    407–408
  in middle childhood and
    adolescence, 412
  in pregnancy, 105–106
  in separation, 429
  socioeconomic variations in,
    581–582
  stranger anxiety, 429
Apes. See Monkeys and apes
Apgar Scale, 109, 109t
Aphasia, 362, 363
Appearance–reality tasks in
    preoperational stage, 243
Appetite, 195–196
  malnutrition affecting, 197
Applied field of child development, 4
  social policy issues in, 32–37
Apprenticeship programs, 649
Approach/withdrawal response, and
    temperament, 420t, 422
Aptitude tests, 328
Argentina, gay and lesbian families
    in, 589

Arithmetic abilities. See Mathematical
    abilities
Arousal states in infants, 132t,
    132–138, 406
Artificial neural network models, 366
Asia. See also specific countries.
  academic achievement in, 345, 647,
    648
  achievement attributions in, 467
  autobiographical memory in, 299
  body size in, 183
  creativity in, 354
  dating in, 624
  emotional self-regulation in, 412,
    424
  formal operational stage in,
    258–259
  gender stereotypes in, 532
  immigrant youths from, 53
  language development in, 378, 379
  math instruction in, 312–313
  neonatal behavioral assessment in,
    139
  self-concept in, 459–460
  self-conscious emotions in, 408,
    409
  self-esteem in, 463
  sexual attitudes and behavior in,
    212
  temperament of children in, 424,
    426, 427
Asian Americans
  academic achievement beliefs of,
    346
  anorexia nervosa of, 210
  intelligence quotient of, 334
  suicide rate in adolescence, 472
Aspirin in pregnancy, 96
Assimilation
  and adaptation in Piaget's theory,
    227
  neo-Piagetian theory of, 283
Assisted discovery learning, 269
Associative play, 608, 609
Athletic activities
  gender stereotypes in, 180
  injuries in, 181
  and menarche, 204
  and motor development, 179–181
  parental pressure in, 181
  and pubertal changes, 204
  and self-esteem, 462f, 463
  sex differences in, 180, 181
Attachment, 428–443
  in adoption, 433–434, 588
  avoidant. See Avoidant attachment
  Bowlby on, 24, 428–430
  child maltreatment affecting, 434
  continuity of caregiving affecting,
    440
  cultural differences in, 432f,
    432–433, 434, 437
  and dating, 625
  disorganized/disoriented. See
    Disorganized/disoriented
    attachment

early availability of consistent
    caregiver affecting, 433–434
  and employment of parents, 438,
    438f, 441–443
  ethological theory of, 24, 428–430,
    439
  fathers affecting, 437–438, 439
  gene–environment interaction in,
    435, 435f
  infant characteristics affecting, 435,
    435f
  internal working models of, 430,
    430f, 436t, 436–437
  and later development, 439–441,
    442
  maternal depression affecting, 435,
    436
  measurement of, 430–432
  and mental state knowledge, 455
  multiple, 437–439
  and peer relations, 611
  phases of development of, 429–430
  psychoanalytic perspective on, 428,
    439
  quality of caregiving affecting, 434
  resistant. See Resistant attachment
  secure, 430
  security of. See Security of
    attachment
  stability of, 432
  and theory of mind, 455
Attachment Q-Sort, 431–432
Attachment-in-the-making phase,
    429
Attendance to school
  school size affecting, 638
  school transitions affecting, 642
Attention, 286–291
  adaptability in, 287
  deficit of, 125, 125f, 290–291
  and emotional self-regulation, 411
  encoding of information in, 315t
  and habituation of infants,
    142–143, 145
  and inhibition, 287–288, 288f, 315t
  and intelligence quotient, 323
  joint attention of infant and
    caregiver, 371, 403, 450
  in media multitasking, 293
  and memory, 288, 289
  and pattern perception of infants,
    163
  in planning tasks, 289–291
  selective, 287, 287f
  strategies in, 288–289
  sustained, 286–287
  and temperament, 420t, 421, 425
Attention-deficit hyperactivity
    disorder (ADHD), 290–291
  delinquency in, 520
  genetic factors in, 125, 290
  maternal smoking during
    pregnancy as risk factor for, 125,
    125f, 290
  symptoms of, 290
  treatment of, 291

Attributions
  achievement-related, 464–468
  definition of, 464
  mastery-oriented, 465–466, 466f,
    467–468
  retraining of, 467–468
Australia
  academic achievement in, 647
  adolescent suicide in, 472
  body size in, 183
  child-care facilities in, 441, 442,
    597
  caregiving roles of mothers and
    fathers in, 437
  divorce rate in, 591f
  emotional self-regulation in, 412
  family size in, 584
  fears of children in, 412
  intelligence testing in, 340
  moral reasoning in, 504
  mortality rate for infants in, 119f
  physical growth trends in, 184
  reproductive technology laws in,
    87
  sleep patterns of infants in, 133
  spatial skills in, 272
Austria
  corporal punishment in, 602
  infant mortality rate in, 119f
  vocational education in, 650
Authoritarian child-rearing style,
    574t, 574–575
  development and adjustment
    outcomes of, 576, 576t
Authoritative child-rearing style,
    573–574, 574t
  development and adjustment
    outcomes of, 575–576, 576t
  in divorce, 592
  effectiveness of, 575–577
  peer relations in, 627
Authority understanding in moral
    development, 498
Autism, 202, 456, 457
  in fragile X syndrome, 81
  intelligence in, 325
  and mindblindness, 457
Autobiographical memory, 298–300
  and eyewitness testimony by
    children, 300–302
  and infantile amnesia, 300, 301
  and remembered self, 450–451
Automatic processes
  in information processing, 280
  neo-Piagetian theory of, 283
Automization, 283
Autonomic nervous system, 47n,
    47–48
Autonomy issues
  in adolescence, 6, 577–580
  in anorexia nervosa, 211
  in authoritarian child rearing, 574,
    574t
  in authoritative child rearing, 573,
    574t, 577
  behavioral component of, 577–578

Autonomy issues (cont.)
  in effective child rearing, 573
  emotional component of, 577
  gender typing in, 542
  in permissive child rearing, 574t, 575
  in psychosocial development, 16t
  in uninvolved child rearing, 574t, 575
Autosomes, 76
Avoidant attachment, 430
  cultural variations in, 432
  internal working model of parents in, 436t
  later development in, 440
  mother–infant relationship in, 434

B
Babbling, 370, 608
Babinski reflex, 130t
Baby and Child Care (Spock), 13, 134
Baby fat, 177
Back to basics movement in education, 638
Bacterial diseases
  breastfeeding in, 194
  diarrhea in, 201
  in pregnancy, 102t
Balance in motor development, 178
Baldwin, James Mark, 14
Ball skills in motor development, 178, 180
Bandura, Albert, 18, 19
Bar mitzvah, 206
Bases, in DNA, 74
Bat mitzvah, 206
Bayley Scales of Infant and Toddler Development, 329
Behavior
  antisocial. See Antisocial behavior
  conditioning of. See Conditioning
  modeling of, 490–491
  and moral development, 485, 506–507
  of newborn, assessment of, 138–139
  prosocial. See Prosocial behavior
  temperament as predictor of, 425–426
Behavior modification, 18–19
  in anorexia nervosa, 211
Behavioral control in child rearing, 573, 574t
  in authoritarian style, 574–575
  in authoritative style, 573
  development and adjustment outcomes of, 576
  in middle childhood, coregulation in, 577
  in permissive style, 575
  in uninvolved style, 575
Behavioral genetics, 119–120
Behaviorism, 17–19
  attachment in, 428
  compared to other child development theories, 32t

Belgium
  gay and lesbian families in, 589
  generational gains in IQ in, 338, 338f
Belief–desire theory of mind, 452–453
Beliefs
  on academic achievement in family, 345–346
  and desires in theory of mind, 452–453
  false, 452–453, 453f, 454, 454f, 455
  second-order false, 453, 454f
  spiritual and religious. See Spirituality and religion
The Bell Curve (Herrnstein & Murray), 335
Bell-shaped distribution of intelligence test scores, 330, 330f, 334f, 335
Bhatto Bhatto game in India, 612
Bias
  in clinical or case study research, 51
  cultural, in intelligence tests, 322, 339–343
  ethnic and racial, 476–480
  and homosexual youths, 216
  in longitudinal research, 61–62
  mutual exclusivity, in semantic development, 382
  and obese children, 200
  in observational research, 45
  self-serving, in scientific reasoning, 314
  shape, in semantic development, 382
  in social groups, 476–480, 478f
  of teachers, 643
Bicultural identity, 475
Bidirectional influences
  in ecological systems theory, 27, 569
  in epigenetic framework, 124, 124f, 125
  in family, 569
  of hereditary and environment, 124
  in parent–child relationship, 576
  in prenatal development, 96
Bilingualism, 394–397
  code switching in, 396
  in education, 396, 397
  language development in, 359, 364–365, 365f, 368, 397
  language immersion programs in, 397
  sensitive period of development in, 364–365
  visual language discrimination in, 368
Binet, Alfred, 13–14, 320–321, 327
Binge eating, 211
Binocular depth cues, 160
Bioecological model of development, 26

Biological influences
  on aggression, 561
  on gender typing, 535–538
  genetic. See Genetic factors
  on morality, 486–488
Biological knowledge, in core knowledge perspective, 265
Birth
  complications of. See Birth complications
  defects at time of. See Birth defects
  labor and delivery in, 107–112. See also Childbirth
  preterm. See Preterm infants
Birth centers, freestanding, 110
Birth complications, 112–117
  crying patterns in, 138
  in fetal medicine interventions, 85
  left-handedness in, 188
  in oxygen deprivation, 112–113
  in preterm and low-birth-weight infants, 113–117
  resilience of children with, 117
  in teenage pregnancy, 218
Birth control. See Contraception
Birth defects
  in chromosomal abnormalities, 82–83
  folic acid in prevention of, 104, 105f
  left-handedness in, 188
  in malnutrition, 104
  neonatal mortality rates in, 118
  in teratogen exposure, 95–103
Birth order
  and intelligence quotient, 346, 585, 585f
  and sexual orientation, 215
Birth weight
  low, 113–117. See also Low birth weight
  of small-for-date infants, 114
Bisexual youths, 215–216
Black Americans. See African Americans
Blank slate (tabula rasa), 12
Blastocyst, 88f, 89
Blended families, 594–595
Blindness, 162
Blood pressure in obesity, 198
Blood tests
  in phenylketonuria, 79
  in pregnancy, 85, 85t
Bodily-kinesthetic intelligence, 325t
Body composition changes, 177
  hormones affecting, 183
  in puberty, 204
Body image
  in anorexia nervosa, 210
  in puberty, 209
Body mass index, 198
Body proportion changes, 176–177
Body size, 176, 177f
  genetic factors affecting, 192
  height in. See Height
  hormones affecting, 183

scale errors in awareness of, 449
secular trends in, 184
weight in. See Weight
worldwide variations in, 183
Bolivia, childbirth practices in, 110
Bonding. See Attachment
Bones
  age-related changes in, 178
  epiphyses of, 178, 178f
Botswana, !Kung society of. See !Kung of Botswana
Bottle-feeding, 194–195
Bowlby, John, 24
  on attachment, 24, 428–430
Brain, 184–192
  in adolescence, 190–191, 257
  alcohol exposure affecting development of, 99
  in amnesia, infantile, 301
  amygdala in, 190
  anorexia nervosa affecting, 211
  in arousal states, 132t, 132–138, 406
  in attention-deficit hyperactivity disorder, 290
  cerebellum in, 189–190
  cerebral cortex of. See Cerebral cortex
  cerebral hemispheres of. See Cerebral hemispheres
  corpus callosum in, 190
  in crawling experience, 161
  crying patterns in disorders of, 138
  in developmental cognitive neuroscience, 23
  in early childhood, 185
  early deprivation affecting, 170–171
  electroencephalography of. See Electroencephalography
  in empathy, 418
  environmental pollutants affecting, 101
  experience-dependent growth of, 191
  experience-expectant growth of, 191
  in fetus, 92, 93–94, 99
  function measurement methods, 48, 48t
  in handedness, 188
  in hearing, 156
  hippocampus in, 190
  imaging of, 23, 50, 50f
  in infancy, 49, 185
  in infants of diabetic mothers, 49
  information processing speed, 281
  language areas in, 362f, 362–364, 367, 396, 555
  lateralization of, 187, 189, 363
  lead exposure affecting, 101
  malnutrition affecting, 104, 197
  maltreatment affecting, 602
  mercury exposure affecting, 101
  milestones of development, 185, 185f

and Mozart effect of classical music, 59
neo-Piagetian theory on, 283
neurobiological research on, 48*t*, 48–50, 50*f*
neurons in, 185–186
oxygen deprivation affecting, 113
plasticity of, 23, 187–188
prenatal infectious diseases affecting, 102, 103
radiation exposure affecting, 100
in response to facial expressions and emotional cues, 414, 433
reticular formation in, 190
sensitive periods in development of, 191–192
in shyness and sociability, 422
in sleep, 135
in small-for-date infants, 114
thyroxine affecting, 183
Brazil
gay and lesbian families in, 589
mathematical learning among child candy sellers in, 25, 252
numerical knowledge in, 264
proportional reasoning of fishermen in, 272
Breast development, 203
variations in, 204, 205
Breastfeeding, 194–195
in cosleeping parents and infants, 134
and rooting reflex, 130, 130*t*
and smell sense of newborn, 154–155
and sucking reflex, 130, 130*t*, 131
by Yurok Indians, 16
Breathing techniques in natural childbirth, 110
Breech position, 113
Bridge-building problem, information processing in, 22, 22*f*
Broca's area of brain, 362*f*, 363
Bronfenbrenner, Urie, ecological systems theory of, 26–28, 569, 571
Bucharest Early Intervention Project, 171
Buddhist children, emotional display rules of, 413, 413*f*
Building Blocks math curriculum, 311
Bulimia nervosa, 211–212
Bullying, 620, 621
in peer groups, 623
systematic observation of, 45
Burma, body size in, 183

C

Caffeine, and prenatal development, 96–97
Calcium, in pregnancy, 104
Cambodia
cosleeping of parents and infants in, 134

intelligence definition of immigrants from, 324
Cameroon
metacognitive knowledge in, 304
self-recognition by toddlers in, 450, 450*f*
Canada
academic achievement in, 647
attachment experience of parents in, 436
bilingualism in, 394, 396, 397
body size in, 183
caregiving roles of mothers and fathers in, 437
communication style in, 340
computer use in, 633
divorce rate in, 591*f*
emotional display rules in, 413
family size in, 584, 585
gay and lesbian families in, 589
gender stereotypes in, 532, 533
identity development in, 474
immunization rate in, 201
infant mortality rate in, 119*f*
information processing speed in, 281
in-groups and out-groups in, 477, 477*f*
low-birth-weight infants in, 116
miscarriage rates in, 80
moral development in, 497–498, 503, 511
music lessons and intelligence in, 59
natives of. *See* Native Canadians
overweight and obesity rate in, 198
parental leave in, 118
physical growth trends in, 184
pregnancy of teenagers in, 219
religion in, 507
reproductive technology laws in, 87
school segregation in, 479
sexual activity of adolescents in, 213, 217, 219
sexually transmitted diseases in, 217
still-face reaction study in, 402
suicide of adolescents in, 472
television viewing in, 629
thalidomide use in, 96
truthfulness and lying in, 497–498
Canalization, 122
Cancer
in diethylstilbestrol exposure, 96
genomic imprinting in, 80
in radiation exposure, 81
in stress, 403
Cantonese language, 375, 376, 376*t*, 386
Cardinality, 311
Cardiovascular system
Apgar Scale on, 109*t*
prenatal development of, 91, 92, 93
Rh factor incompatibility affecting, 113
stress affecting, 403

Caribbean families, child-rearing practices of, 582
Carolina Abecedarian Project, 348, 348*f*, 349
Carriers of inherited traits, 77, 79, 79*f*
genetic counseling on, 84
Cartilage development, 178
Case, Robbie, neo-Piagetian theory of information processing, 282, 283–284, 314
Case studies. *See* Clinical research method
Cataracts in infants, 170
Catch-up growth
in growth hormone therapy, 182
in marasmus, 197
Categorical self, 450, 461
Categorical speech perception, 368
Categorization abilities
basic-level categories in, 247
in concrete operational stage, 250
general categories in, 247
and memory, 292, 293
in preoperational stage, 245, 245*f*, 247*f*, 247–248
in sensorimotor stage, 233–235, 234*f*
subcategories in, 247
Caucasian Americans
academic achievement beliefs of, 345–346
anorexia nervosa of, 210
body image of, 209
body size of, 183
corporal punishment of, 493
drug use of, 626
emotional sensitivity of, 559
friendships of, 616
gender stereotypes of, 534, 546, 559
growth rate of, 183
intelligence definition of, 324
intelligence quotient of, 334, 334*f*, 336, 338
menarche of, 205, 206
neonatal and infant mortality rates of, 118
neonatal behavioral assessment of, 139
play and peer sociability of, 613
scaffolding interactions of, 268, 269
skeletal age of, 178
skeletal growth of, 178
stereotype threat affecting test performance of, 341, 341*f*
suicide rate of adolescents, 472
temperament of infants, 424
Cell phones, 293, 629, 632, 634–635
parent regulation of use, 636
Cells
glial, 186
meiosis of, 75, 75*f*
mitosis of, 74
nerve, 185–186. *See also* Neurons
programmed death of, 185
sex cells, 75*f*, 75–76

Central conceptual structures, 283, 284, 314
Central executive component of information processing system, 279, 279*f*, 281
Central nervous system, 184–192. *See also* Brain
Centration in preoperational stage, 245
Cephalocaudal trend in growth, 176
Cerebellum, 189–190
Cerebral cortex, 186–189
in autism, 457
development of, 92, 93, 186–189, 190
electrical activity in, 48
in fragile X syndrome, 81
language areas in, 362*f*, 362–364, 367, 555
lateralization of, 187, 189
mirror neurons in, 146
plasticity of, 187, 188
regions of, 186, 186*f*
Cerebral hemispheres, 187, 188, 189
dominant, 189
language functions in, 363–364, 367, 396
in savant syndrome, 325
Cervix of uterus, 88, 88*f*
dilation and effacement in childbirth, 107, 108*f*
Cesarean delivery, 111, 112, 113
Chaos in family, 29
Chernobyl nuclear power plant accident, radiation exposure in, 100–101
Chess, knowledge and memory of, 297
Chicago Child–Parent Centers, 348, 349
Chicken pox, 201
in pregnancy, 102*t*
Child abuse. *See* Child maltreatment
Childbirth, 107–112
adaptation of baby to, 108
and appearance of newborn, 109
breech position in, 113
cesarean delivery in, 111, 112, 113
complications during, 112–117. *See also* Birth complications
in freestanding birth centers, 110
at home, 111–112
maternal age in. *See* Maternal age
medications during, 112
natural or prepared, 110–111
oxygen deprivation of infant in, 112–113
parental leave from employment after, 118–119, 442, 536, 570
positions of mother during, 111
and postpartum depression, 404
of preterm and low-birth-weight infant, 113–117
stages of, 107, 108*f*

Child care, 596–597
    cost of, 597
    by first-time parents, 570
    in maternal employment, 595–596
    and self-care by children, 597f,
        597–599
    social support for, 572
    in teenage parenthood, 220
Child-care facilities, 596–597
    accreditation and licensing of, 443,
        597, 598
    and attachment, 441–443
    developmentally appropriate
        practice standards in, 443, 598
    public policies on, 33, 34, 441–443
    quality of care in, 441–443, 597,
        598
    in Sweden, 536
Child development, 6–9
    cognitive. See Cognitive
        development
    contexts of. See Contexts of
        development
    as continuous or discontinuous
        process, 7f, 7–8
    course of. See Course of
        development
    definition of, 4
    determinants of, 8–9
    domains of. See Domains of
        development
    emotional and social. See
        Emotional and social
        development
    field of, 4–6
    historical views of, 10–21
    periods of. See Periods of
        development
    physical. See Physical development
    theories on. See Theories of
        development
Child Development journal, 36
Child maltreatment, 599–604
    antisocial behavior in history of,
        123
    attachment insecurity in, 434
    attachment stability in, 432
    consequences of, 601, 602
    in dating relationships, 625
    in emotional abuse, 599, 600
    empathy in, 418
    eyewitness testimony of children
        on, 300–302
    factors contributing to, 600, 600t
    incidence of, 599, 600, 601, 604
    natural experiments on, 58–60, 60f
    in neglect, 575, 599, 600
    origins of, 600–602
    in physical abuse, 599, 600
    of preterm infants, 115, 138, 600
    prevention of, 601, 603f, 603–604
    in sexual abuse, 302, 599, 600,
        601
    terminology related to, 599
Child–parent relationship. See
    Parent–child relationship

Child support
    in divorce, 591, 593–594
    in teenage parenthood, 220
Child-rearing costs, and family size,
    584
Child-rearing practices, 573–584
    adjustment outcomes of, 575–576,
        576t
    in adolescence, 576, 577–580
    and aggression, 520–522, 523–525,
        561–562
    and attachment security of child,
        433–437
    in attention-deficit hyperactivity
        disorder, 291
    authoritarian, 574t, 574–575, 576,
        576t
    authoritative, 573–574, 575–577.
        See also Authoritative child-
        rearing style
    in blended families, 594–595
    in child care facilities, 441–443
    correlational studies on, 56, 57f
    cultural influences on, 16, 139, 427,
        434
    in depression of parent, 404
    discipline in. See Discipline
    in divorce, 591, 592–593, 593f
    early availability of consistent
        caregiver in, 433–434
    eating habits and nutrition in,
        195–196
    ecological systems theory on, 27
    effective coparenting in, 569, 571
    ethnic variations in, 582–584
    experimental research on, 58
    in extended families, 583
    and family size, 584–585
    of fathers, 437–438, 439
    field experiments on, 58
    gender equality in, 536
    gender typing in, 539–542
    and genetic influences on
        development, 577, 578
    Gesell on, 13
    goodness-of-fit model of, 426–427,
        435
    grandparents as primary caregivers
        in, 438–439
    in identity development, 475
    and intelligence quotient changes,
        331
    in !Kung society of Botswana, 26
    Locke on, 12
    maltreatment of child in, 599–604
    in maternal employment, 595–596
    in middle childhood, 577
    and moral development, 488–495,
        504
    and motor development of infants,
        150
    and newborn behavior, 139
    in one-child families, 587–588
    parent training on, 578, 587, 593
    and peer relations, 611
    permissive, 574t, 575

positive parenting in, 494, 495, 523
    in poverty, 581
    and psychosocial dwarfism, 202
    and pubertal timing, 205, 210
    of Puritans, 11–12
    quality of caregiving in, 434
    and security of attachment,
        433–434
    and self-control, 514–515
    and self-esteem, 464
    and self-recognition by toddlers,
        450
    social support in, 572
    socialization in, 573–584
    socioeconomic influences on,
        580–582
    styles of, 573–577
    and teenage parenthood, 219
    and temperament of child, 422,
        424–425, 426–427, 576, 578
    uninvolved, 574t, 575
Children's Defense Fund, 37
Chimpanzees
    imitation by, 145, 145f, 146
    language acquisition of, 361
    moral-like rules of, 486
China
    academic achievement in, 647
    academic and vocational tracks in,
        645
    achievement attributions in, 467,
        467f
    autobiographical memory in, 299
    child-rearing practices in, 582
    cosleeping of parents and infants
        in, 134
    creativity in, 354
    depression in, 560
    emotional self-regulation in, 412,
        424
    family size in, 587–588
    fears of children in, 412
    gender typing in, 543, 546
    immigrant youths from, 53
    mathematics instruction in, 312
    moral development in, 497–498,
        512
    obesity in, 198
    play and peer sociability in, 612
    self-concept in, 459
    self-conscious emotions in, 409
    self-esteem in, 463
    shyness in, 427, 427f
    still-face reaction study in, 402
    storytelling practices in, 451
    temperament of children in, 424,
        426, 427, 427f
    truthfulness and lying in, 497–498
Chinese language, 375, 376, 376t,
    378, 379, 386
    and false belief tasks, 455
Chlamydia, 217
    in pregnancy, 102t
Chomsky, Noam, language
    development theory of, 360–361,
    365

Chorion, 89
Chorionic villi, 89
    sampling of, 84, 85t
Chromosomes, 73–83
    abnormalities of, 82f, 82–83, 83t
    autosomes, 76
    crossing over, 75f, 75–76
    DNA structure in, 74, 74f
    karyotype of, 74f
    in meiosis, 75f, 75–76
    mosaic pattern of, 82
    and patterns of inheritance, 77–81
    sex, 76, 80, 80f
    translocation of, 82
Chronological narratives, 392
Chronosystem in ecological systems
    theory, 28, 571
Cigarette smoking. See Smoking
Circadian rhythm, 132
Circular reactions in sensorimotor
    development, 228t, 228–229
Civic responsibility, 508
Class inclusion problems, 245, 245f,
    250
Class size in school, 637
Classical conditioning, 17, 140f,
    140–141
Classification
    and categorization abilities. See
        Categorization abilities
    in concrete operational stage, 250
    in preoperational stage, 245, 245f
Classrooms. See Schools
Cleft lip and palate, 98, 104
Clinical interviews, 43t, 46–47
    limitations of, 46–47
    on moral judgment, 499
    of Piaget, 20, 46
    reliability of, 46–47
Clinical research method, 17, 43t,
    50–51
    in psychoanalytic approach, 17, 50
    reliability of, 51, 54
Cliques, 623–624
Cocaine use
    in adolescence, 626
    in pregnancy, 97, 98, 100
Cochlear implant in hearing loss, 370
Code switching in bilingualism, 396
Coercive interaction pattern in
    family, 522f, 523
Cognition
    definition of, 225
    development of. See Cognitive
        development
    and emotions, 402
    metacognition. See Metacognition
    social. See Social cognition
Cognitive development, 4
    and academic learning, 259–260,
        307–314
    accommodation in, 227
    adaptation in, 227
    in adolescence, 20, 20t, 21,
        190–191, 253–259
    assimilation in, 227

and attachment, 440
attention in, 286–291, 315*t*
awareness of capacities in, 303–304
in bilingualism, 396
central conceptual structures in, 283, 284
concrete operational stage in, 249–253. *See also* Concrete operational stage
constructivist approach to, 226
contexts of, 8
as continuous or discontinuous process, 7–8
continuum of acquisition in, 283
core knowledge perspective of, 225, 238, 261–266
creativity in, 350–355
of deaf children, 372
definition of, 5*f*
and delinquency, 520
disequilibrium in, 227
divergent thinking in, 350–352, 352*f*, 353
in dynamic systems approach, 30*f*
in early childhood, 5–6, 239–249, 303, 347, 415, 609
in early deprivation, 170
early interventions in, 347–350, 351
and education, 259–260
and emotional understanding, 415–416
environmental influences on, 282, 344–346
equilibration in, 227
equilibrium in, 227, 260
ethological theory of, 23–24
executive function in, 281–282
family size affecting, 585, 585*f*
in fetal alcohol spectrum disorder, 98–100
formal operational stage in, 253–259. *See also* Formal operational stage
gender identity in, 548–549, 551*f*, 551–552
as general process, 261
genetic factors in, 282
in giftedness, 350–355
and habituation of infants, 145
in Head Start programs, 35
home environment affecting, 344–346
individual differences in, 225
in infancy and toddlerhood, 19, 20*t*, 133, 150, 169, 228–239, 262–264, 348
information-processing approach to, 261, 277–317, 323
integration with other domains of development, 4
intelligence tests of, 13–14, 319
lateralization of brain functions in, 188
lead exposure affecting, 193
in low birth weight, 114

malnutrition affecting, 197
maltreatment affecting, 602
maternal employment affecting, 596
mechanisms in, 225
memory in, 280, 292–302
mental representation in, 227, 230
metacognition in, 303–305, 315*t*
microgenetic research on, 64–65
in middle childhood, 6, 249–253, 303, 304
milestones of, 238, 248, 253, 306
and moral development, 485, 495, 496–499, 502–503, 505, 506, 507
neo-Piagetian theory of, 261, 282, 283–284
neuroscience approach to, 23
object permanence in, 229, 230–231, 231*f*, 232
organization in, 227, 260
oxygen deprivation during childbirth affecting, 113
and perceptual development, 169
physical and numerical knowledge in, 262–264
Piaget on, 19–21, 225, 226–261
planning in, 289*f*, 289–291
play categories in, 609, 609*t*
prenatal drug exposure affecting, 96
prenatal iron deficiency affecting, 49, 282
preoperational stage of, 239–249. *See also* Preoperational stage
private speech in, 266–267, 267*f*
psychometric approach to, 319, 320–322, 323, 350–352
reaching by infants in, 150–152
readiness to learn in, 226, 259
reading in, 307–310
schemes in, 226–227
scientific reasoning in, 313–314
self-concept in, 459
and self-control, 515–516
and self-regulation, 304–305, 315*t*, 412
sensorimotor stage of, 228–239. *See also* Sensorimotor stage
of small-for-date infants, 114
social cognition in, 18, 447–483
social origins of, 267–269
as socially mediated process, 25
sociocultural theory on, 25, 226, 266–272
socioeconomic influences on, 580–581
spatial abilities in, 557
speed of processing in, 281, 281*f*, 315*t*
stages of, 19–20, 20*t*, 226, 228–259, 260–261
strategy choice model of, 282, 284–286
theory of mind in, 303, 455
in visual impairment, 162
in Williams syndrome, 366
zone of proximal development in, 267–268

Cognitive maps in concrete operational stage, 250–251
Cognitive-developmental theory, 19–21, 226–261
compared to other child development theories, 32*t*
educational applications of, 259–260
evaluation of, 260–261
on gender identity, 548
Cohort effects
in cross-sectional studies, 63
in longitudinal research, 62
Coinage of words in semantic development, 380
Colic, 138
Collaboration, as communication style, 340
Collectivist societies
academic achievement in, 648
autobiographical memory in, 299
cooperative learning in, 271
creativity in, 354
emotional display rules in, 413
moral development in, 497–498, 505–506
peer sociability in, 612
public policy in, 35
self-conscious emotions in, 409
temperament of children in, 427
College preparatory courses, 644–645
Colombia
body size in, 183
memory of U'wa people in, 294
moral development in, 512
Color vision, 167
Commercials on television, 631
Communication
with adolescents on sexual issues, 212–213
with cell phones, 634–635
collaborative style of, 340
conversational skills in, 390–391
cultural influences on, 339–340
of deaf children, 372
expressive, 378
facial expressions in, 402–403
hierarchical style of, 340
infant-directed speech in, 369, 374
interactional synchrony in, 434, 437
and language development. *See* Language development
in prelinguistic stage, 370–372
preverbal gestures in, 371
referential, 378, 391–392, 392*f*
speech in. *See* Speech
topic-associating style of, 340
topic-focused style of, 340
turn-taking pattern in, 371
Community influences
on aggressive, 523
on child maltreatment, 602
on civic responsibility, 508
ecological systems theory on, 27–28

on family system, 572
on identity development, 474
on immigrant youths, 53
on resilient children, 11
Community service, 508
Competency
in authoritative child rearing, 574, 576, 577
modeling of, 491
Competitiveness, sex differences in, 561
Compliance, and self-control, 514
Componential analysis of intelligence tests, 323
Comprehension
development of, 376
of reading, 310
Computer analogy of information processing, 278, 315
Computer use, 293, 632–635
daily time in, 629*f*
digital divide in, 633
learning in, 633
Conception, 88–89
maternal age at time of. *See* Maternal age
paternal age at time of, 82
Concrete operational stage, 20, 20*t*, 249–253
classification in, 250
conservation in, 249, 252
continuum of acquisition in, 252
cultural influences on, 251, 251*f*, 252
limitations of thought in, 252
milestones of development, 253
research on, 252
seriation in, 250
spatial reasoning in, 250*f*, 250–251, 251*f*
Conditioned response, 140, 140*f*
Conditioned stimulus, 140, 140*f*
Conditioning
behavior modification in, 18
classical, 17, 140*f*, 140–141
operant, 17, 141*f*, 141–142, 414, 490
social learning theory on, 18
Confidentiality in research, 67
Conflict
in adolescence, 205–206, 208, 571, 579, 580
in sibling relationships, 586
social problem-solving in, 480*f*, 480–481
Conformity to peer pressure, 625–627
Confounding variables, 57
Congenital adrenal hyperplasia, 537–538, 561
Congo, Republic of
body size in, 192
stranger anxiety of infants in, 408
Connectionist models, information processing and language development in, 366

Conscience, development of, 488
Consent to research, 66t, 67
Conservation
    in concrete operational stage, 249, 252
    neo-Piagetian theory of, 283
    in preoperational stage, 244f, 244–245
Constancy of gender identity, 548–549
Construction, in cognitive and moral development, 495
Constructive memory, 295
Constructivist approach to cognitive development, 226
    classrooms in, 638, 639–640
Consumerism, 631
Contagion, emotional, 414
Contexts of development, 8, 23–28
    cultural influences in. See Cultural influences
    ecological systems theory on, 26–28
    environmental influences in. See Environmental influences
    ethology of, 23–24
    evolutionary developmental psychology on, 24
    in family system, 571–572
    and relative influence of nature and nurture, 8–9
    sociocultural theory on, 24–26
Continuous course of development, 32t
    compared to discontinuous development, 7f, 7–8
    in information processing approach, 22
    Locke on, 12
    Watson on, 17
Contraception
    in adolescence, 214f, 214–215, 219–220
    in breastfeeding, 194
    in menstrual cycle, 203
Contractions of uterus in childbirth, 107, 108f
Contrast sensitivity, 161, 161f, 163
Control
    in child rearing. See Behavioral control in child rearing
    of self. See Self-control
Control deficiency
    in attentional strategies, 288
    in memory strategies, 292
Controversial children, 619, 620
Convention on the Rights of the Child, 37
Conventional level of moral development, 501
Convergent thinking, 350, 353
Conversation
    generic references to gender in, 540–541, 541f
    in pragmatic language development, 390–391
    turn-taking pattern in, 371, 390

Cooing, 370
Cool and hot systems in self-control, 516, 516f
Cooley's anemia, 78t
Cooperation
    in learning, 271–272, 640, 646
    morality of, 497, 498, 501
    in play, 608
Coparenting, effective, 569, 571
Coping strategies
    in divorce of parents, 592
    friendships in, 618
    in middle childhood and adolescence, 412
Core knowledge perspective, 225, 238, 261–266, 326
    domains of thought in, 261–262
    evaluation of, 265–266
    on naïve theories of children, 264–265
    on physical and numerical knowledge in infancy, 262–264, 264f
    on theory of mind, 456
Coregulation in middle childhood, 577
Corporal punishment, 492, 493
    cultural influences on, 602
    prevalence of, 492, 492f
Corpus callosum, 190
Corpus luteum, 88
Correlation coefficient, 56, 56f
Correlational research, 55–56, 57f
    compared to other research designs, 61t
    correlation coefficient in, 56, 56f
    on genetic and environmental influences, 122–123
    stability of IQ scores in, 331
Cortex, cerebral. See Cerebral corte
Cortisol
    in childbirth, 108
    in early deprivation, 403
    in shyness and sociability, 422
    in stress response, 47–48, 97, 108, 403, 404
    time in child-care center affecting, 442
Corumination, 617
Cosleeping arrangements, 134
Counseling, genetic, 84
Counting
    in early childhood, 310, 311
    min strategy in, 284, 285, 311
Course of development, 32t
    Baldwin on, 14
    context affecting, 8
    as continuous or discontinuous process, 7f, 7–8
    Hall and Gesell on, 13
    in information processing approach, 22
    Locke on, 12
    in physical growth, 176–184
    relative influence of nature and nurture in, 8–9

Rousseau on, 12
    stability and plasticity in, 9
    timetable in, 13
    Watson on, 17
Court proceedings, eyewitness testimony of children in, 300–302
Crawling
    and depth perception, 160–161
    and differentiation theory on perceptual development, 169, 169f
    and emotional self-regulation by infants, 410
    in visual impairment, 162
Creativity
    definition of, 350
    divergent thinking in, 350–352, 352f, 353
    drawing in. See Drawing
    of gifted children, 350–355
    and intelligence, 323, 324, 324f
    investment theory of, 352
    promotion of, 355
    resources necessary for, 352t, 352–355
Critical period in development, 23–24
Criticism, in formal operational stage, 256
Croatia
    corporal punishment in, 602
    infant mortality rate in, 119f
Cross-cultural research, 25, 51–53. See also Cultural influences
Crossed eyes, 171
Crossing over of chromosomes, 75f, 75–76
Cross-sectional research, 62–63
    compared to other research designs, 65t
    sequential design, 63f, 63–64
Crowds and cliques in adolescence, 623–624
Crying of newborns and infants, 132, 132t, 133, 135–138
    abnormal patterns in, 138
    adult responsiveness to, 136–137
    empathy of other infants in, 135–136, 417
    soothing techniques in, 137–138
Crystallized intelligence, 321–322, 328f, 332
Cuba, infant mortality rate in, 119f
Cults, religious, 509
Cultural bias in intelligence tests, 322, 328, 339–343
Cultural influences, 8
    on academic achievement, 53, 647f, 647–648
    on achievement attributions, 467, 467f
    adolescent initiation ceremonies in, 206
    on aggression, 523
    in anorexia nervosa, 211

on attachment patterns, 432f, 432–433, 434, 437
on biological knowledge, 265
on body size, 183
on caregiving roles of mothers and fathers, 437–438, 439
on categorization skills, 235
on child care settings, 441
on child maltreatment, 602
on childbirth practices, 109–110
on child-rearing practices, 16, 139, 427, 434
on cognitive development, 251, 258–259, 273, 281, 294
on communication styles, 339–340
on concrete operational stage, 251, 251f, 252
on corporal punishment, 602
cross-cultural research on, 25, 51–53
on drawings in early childhood, 242, 242f
ecological systems theory on, 28
on emotional development, 405
on emotional display rules, 412–413
on emotional self-regulation, 412
on emotional sensitivity, 559
on ethnic and racial groups, 339
ethnographic research on, 43t, 52–53
on extended families, 583
on fathers as caregivers, 437–438, 439
on fears of children, 412
on food preferences, 196
on formal operational stage, 258–259
on friendships, 616
on gender identity, 548
on gender stereotypes, 530, 532–533, 535–536, 542, 543, 546, 559
on grammatical development, 390
on grandparents as primary caregivers, 438
on identity development, 474–475
on immigrant youths, 53
on information processing speed, 281
on intelligence assessment, 322, 324, 339–343
on intelligence quotient, 338
on knowledge, 340–341
in !Kung society of Botswana, 26
on language development, 376, 376t, 378–379, 390, 392–393
on learning tasks, 25
on make-believe play, 52, 270, 613
on map making, 251, 251f
on mathematical abilities, 25, 264, 312–313
on memory and memory strategies, 294, 299
on moral development, 497–498, 503–504, 505–506, 512

on motor development, 150, 152
on neonatal behavior, 139
on peer relations, 612–613
on periods of development, 6
on play, 270, 273, 612–613
on public policy, 34–35
on punishment, 492, 493
on reactions to pubertal changes, 206
on research participants, 68
on scaffolding, 269
on self-concept, 459–460
on self-conscious emotions, 408, 409
on self-esteem, 463–464
on self-recognition, 450, 450f
on semantic development, 376, 376t, 378–379
on sensitivity toward infants, 434
on sexuality, 212–213
on sleep, 132–133, 134
sociocultural theory on, 24–26, 266–272
on soothing of crying infants, 137, 138
on still-face reaction, 402
on storytelling practices, 451
on stranger anxiety, 408
on temperament, 424, 426, 427
Custody of children
in blended families, 594–595
in divorce, 593
in maltreatment cases, 603
Cyberbullying, 621
Cyprus, corporal punishment in, 602
Cystic fibrosis, 78t, 85
Cytomegalovirus infection in pregnancy, 102t, 103
Cytoplasm, 75
Czech Republic
body size in, 183
infant mortality rate in, 119f

D
Darwin, Charles, 13
Dating, 624f, 624–625
age at time of, 624, 624f
Day-care facilities. See Child-care facilities
Day–night tasks, 288, 288f
Deafness. See Hearing loss
Death
in anorexia nervosa, 211
in infancy, 118. See also Infant mortality
in infectious diseases, 201
in obesity, 198
in suicide. See Suicide
Debriefing in research, 69
Decentration in concrete operational stage, 249
Deception in research, 69
Decision making
in formal operational stage, 256–257
intuitive judgments in, 257

moral judgments in, 497–498, 499, 500–501
situational factors affecting, 502
Deferred imitation in sensorimotor stage, 230, 232–233, 233f
Delay of gratification, 514–515, 516
Delinquency, 520–521
and aggression, 518–519, 520, 522–523
child rearing and, 520–521, 576
in early pubertal maturation, 208, 209
early-onset, 520
and intelligence quotient, 333
intervention programs in, 525, 525f
late-onset, 520–521
Delivery of baby, 107, 108f. See also Childbirth
Denmark
corporal punishment in, 602
divorce rate in, 591f
immunization rate in, 201
infant mortality rate in, 119f
poverty rate in, 33
reproductive technology laws in, 87
vocational education in, 650
Deoxyribonucleic acid (DNA), 74, 74f
mutations in, 81
Dependent variables in experimental research, 56, 57
Depression
in adolescence, 472–473, 559, 560
in bulimia nervosa, 212
in children with depressed parent, 404
of fathers, 404
heritability of, 120
of mothers, 404, 432, 435, 436
in obesity, 200
in puberty, 208, 209
sex differences in, 559–560
socioeconomic variations in, 581–582
suicide in, 472–473. See also Suicide
Deprivation
psychosocial dwarfism in, 202, 403
in sensitive periods of development, 169–171, 191, 370
temperament in, 424
Depth perception, 159–161, 160f
binocular cues in, 160
and drawings in early childhood, 242
milestones of development, 167
motion cues in, 160
and motor development, 160–161
pictorial cues in, 160, 160f
and reaching and grasping skills, 151
visual cliff studies of, 159f, 159–160
DES (diethylstilbestrol), 96
Desires
and belief–desire reasoning, 452–453
in theory of mind, 452

Despair in psychosocial development, 16t
Development. See Child development
Developmental cognitive neuroscience, 23
Developmental quotients (DQs), 329
Developmental science, 4
Developmental theories of information processing, 282–286
Developmentally appropriate practice standards, 443, 598
Diabetes insipidus, 78t
Diabetes mellitus
in mother, and event-related potentials in infant, 49
in obesity, 198
Diarrhea, 201
oral rehydration therapy in, 201
Diet. See Nutrition
Diethylstilbestrol (DES), 96
Differentiation theory of perceptual development, 168–169, 169f
Difficult child, as temperament type, 420
attachment security in, 435
child-rearing practices and, 426–427
Diffusion of identity, 470, 470t, 471, 473
ethnic, 475
Digestive system
prenatal development of, 91
stress affecting, 403
Dilation and effacement of cervix in childbirth, 107, 108f
Dioxins, prenatal exposure to, 101
Discipline
and aggression, 521
in authoritarian child rearing, 574
in authoritative child rearing, 573
cultural influences on, 602
in depression of parent, 404
direct influences of, 569
ethnic variations in, 583
gender differences in, 521, 543, 561
inductive, 489
and intelligence quotient, 331
and moral development, 489, 491–494
socioeconomic variations in, 580, 581
training of parents on, 578
Discontinuous course of development, 32t
compared to continuous development, 7f, 7–8
Rousseau on, 12
stages in, 8
Discovery learning, 259
assisted, 269
Discrimination
ethnic and racial, 475
gender-related, 563
in obesity, 200

Diseases
and body size variations, 183
and breastfeeding, 194
infectious. See Infectious diseases
Disequilibrium in cognitive development, 227
Disorganized/disoriented attachment
gene–environment interaction in, 435, 435f
internal working model of parents in, 436t
later development in, 440
mother–infant relationship in, 434
stability of, 432
Displaced reference, and symbolic understanding of infants, 235–236
Display rules on emotions, 412–413
Distal parenting style, 450
Distance curve of physical growth, 176, 177f
Distractibility, temperament in, 420t, 421, 425, 426
Distress in empathy, 417
Divergent thinking, 350–352, 352f, 353
Divorce, 590–594
age differences in response to, 591–592
joint custody in, 593
mediation services in, 593
remarriage in, 594–595
in second marriage, 595
sex differences in response to, 592, 593
strategies improving adjustment to, 594
temperament affecting response to, 592
Dizygotic twins, 76–77, 77t. See also Fraternal twins
DNA (deoxyribonucleic acid), 74, 74f
mutations in, 81
Dogon people of Mali, attachment patterns of, 432
Domain approach to moral development, 510–513
Domains of development, 4–5
cognitive, 4, 5f. See also Cognitive development
emotional and social, 4, 5f. See also Emotional and social development
interwoven nature of, 4
physical, 4, 5f, 175–223. See also Physical development
Dominance hierarchy in peer relations, 610
Dominant cerebral hemisphere, 189
Dominant–recessive inheritance, 77–79, 79f
characteristics related to, 77, 77t
diseases related to, 77–79, 78t
incomplete dominance in, 79
Donor insemination, 86, 589

Doubt, in psychosocial development, 16t

Doula support during childbirth, 111

Down syndrome, 82, 82f

Drawing
cultural variations in, 242, 242f
of human figures, 242, 242f
of maps, 251, 251f
in preoperational stage, 241–242, 242f

Dreaming in REM sleep, 135

Dropping out of school
academic achievement affecting, 645
school size affecting, 638
school transitions affecting, 642

Drug therapy
in attention-deficit hyperactivity disorder, 291
during childbirth, 112
in HIV infection and AIDS, 102–103
in infertility, fraternal twinning related to, 76, 77t

Drug use and abuse, 626–627
in adolescence, 217, 218, 626–627
of alcohol. See Alcohol use and abuse
in early pubertal maturation, 209
HIV infection and AIDS in, 217
of homosexual youths, 216
incidence of, 626, 626f
and pregnancy, 96–98, 136, 218
prevention and treatment of, 627
and sexual activity, 217, 218
sexually transmitted diseases in, 217
socioeconomic variations in, 581–582

Dual representation in preoperational stage, 243

Dual-earner households, 595–596

Duchenne muscular dystrophy, 78t, 85

Dwarfism, psychosocial, 202

Dynamic assessment of intelligence, 342

Dynamic systems perspective of development, 30f, 30–31
compared to other child development theories, 32t
emotional development in, 405–406
motor development in, 147–150, 178

E

Ear
embryonic development of, 95f
hearing function of. See Hearing

Early childhood (2 to 6 years old), 5–6
achievement-related attributions in, 465
adjustment to school in, 641
aggression in, 516–517, 518

belief–desire reasoning in, 452–453
body composition in, 177
body proportions in, 177
brain development in, 185, 186, 188
child-care quality in, 597
cognitive development in, 239–249, 303, 347, 415, 609
definition of, 5–6
drawings in, 241–242, 242f
early intervention programs in, 347, 348, 349
eating habits in, 195–196
emotional self-regulation in, 410–411
emotional understanding in, 416
empathy in, 417
fear in, 411
friendships in, 614, 615
gait in, 178
gender identity in, 548–549, 553
gender stereotypes in, 531–532, 539, 540, 553, 562
gender typing in, 553
home environment in, 344
information processing in, 307–309, 310–311
intelligence tests in, 328
language development in, 266–267, 375, 380, 385–388, 394, 395
mathematics in, 310–311
memory in, 294–295, 297, 299, 300, 301, 306
metacognition in, 303, 306
metalinguistic awareness in, 394
modeling in, 491
moral development in, 498, 510, 511, 513
motor development in, 178, 179, 180
naturalistic observations in, 43
nonsocial activities in, 608, 609
nutrition in, 195–196
parent relationship in. See Parent–child relationship
peer relations in, 608–610, 611, 614, 628
personal and moral domains in, 511
planning in, 289f, 289–290
play in, 239–241, 608–610, 610t
preoperational stage in, 19, 20t, 239–249. See also Preoperational stage
private speech in, 266–267
psychosexual and psychosocial development in, 16t
reading in, 307–309
self-awareness in, 449
self-concept in, 456, 460
self-control in, 515–516
self-esteem in, 462, 469
social problem solving in, 481
sociocultural theory on, 266–267
television viewing in, 630, 631, 632

Early intervention programs
benefits of, 347–349
costs and benefits of, 349
in depression of parent, 404
for institutionalized infants, 171
for intellectual development, 347–350
Project Head Start in, 35, 347–350, 351

Easy child, as temperament type, 420

Eating habits, 195–196, 210–212
in anorexia nervosa, 210–211
in bulimia nervosa, 211–212
in obesity, 199, 200

Ecological systems theory, 26–28, 27f
bidirectional relationships in, 27, 569
chronosystem in, 28, 571
compared to other child development theories, 32t
exosystem in, 27f, 28, 29, 571
on family, 27, 28, 29, 569
macrosystem in, 27f, 28, 29, 33
mesosystem in, 27f, 27–28, 29, 571
microsystem in, 27, 29
on public policy, 33
third-party influences in, 27, 569

Economic status. See Socioeconomic status

Ecstasy (MDMA), 626

Ectoderm, formation of, 91

Edelman, Marian Wright, 37

Education
academic achievement in. See Academic achievement
and adolescent pregnancy, 218
and antisocial behavior, 523
attention in, 288
back to basics movement in, 638
bilingual, 396, 397
on child-rearing practices, 578, 587, 593, 595, 603
and civic responsibility, 508
cognitive-developmental theory in, 259–260
college preparatory courses in, 644–645
gender stereotypes in, 532–533, 540f, 540–541, 542–543, 545, 554t, 554–558
grouping practices in, 643–645
high-stakes testing movement in, 342, 343
of immigrant youths, 53
in magnet schools, 644, 645
memory strategies in, 294
in Montessori approach, 639–640
and moral development, 505, 507, 508
multiple intelligences theory in, 326
parent involvement in, 647
philosophies on, 638–640
public programs. See Public education programs
in schools, 637–650. See also Schools

self-fulfilling prophecies in, 643
on sex topics. See Sex education
in sexual abuse prevention and treatment, 601
on sibling relationships, 587
sociocultural theory on, 269–272, 640
socioeconomic variations in, 580, 581
of special needs students, 646
speech–gesture mismatches in, 285
television programs in, 237, 632
vocational, 644–645, 649–650

EEG. See Electroencephalography

Efe of Republic of Congo
body size of, 192
observational learning of, 273
stranger anxiety of infants, 408

Effortful control
child-rearing practices affecting, 426
and emotional self-regulation, 409–410
and temperament, 421, 426

Ego
in psychosexual development, 15
in psychosocial development, 16

Egocentrism
in formal operational stage, 256
and moral development, 496
in preoperational stage, 244, 245
in speech, 267

Ejaculation, 204, 206

Elaboration as memory strategy, 293, 295, 299

Electroencephalography, 48, 48t
in child maltreatment victims, 602
in crawling, 161
in empathy, 418
facial expressions affecting, 418
in fetal alcohol spectrum disorder, 99
in foster care and institutional care, 171
in fragile X syndrome, 81
in information processing, 323
in neonatal assessment, 140
in PCB exposure, 101
in psychopathology, 587
in radiation exposure, 100
in shyness and sociability, 422
in sleep, 133

Elementary schools, grouping practices in, 643–644

Embarrassment, 401
as self-conscious emotion, 408

Embracing (Moro) reflex, 130, 130t

Embryonic development, 90, 91
teratogen exposure affecting, 95f, 96

Embryonic disk, 88f, 89, 91

Emergentist coalition model of semantic development, 383, 383f

Emerging adulthood, definition of, 6

Emotional abuse, 599, 600

Emotional and social development, 4, 401–445
in adolescence, 190–191, 207–210
in adoption, 588
attachment in, 428–443. *See also* Attachment
basic emotions in, 406–408
and cognitive development, 415–416
context of, 8
definition of, 5*f*
and delinquency, 520
depression of parent affecting, 402, 403
divorce of parents affecting, 592
dynamic systems perspective of, 30*f*, 405–406
early availability of consistent caregiver affecting, 433–434
in early deprivation, 170–171
emotional display rules in, 412–413
empathy and sympathy in, 416–418
family role in, 568
friendships in. *See* Friendships
growth faltering in, 403
in infancy, 405–408, 452
integration with other domains of development, 4
and intelligence quotient, 333
and interpersonal intelligence, 325*t*, 326
and intrapersonal intelligence, 325*t*, 326
maltreatment affecting, 602
marital relationship of parents affecting, 571
milestones of, 419
and moral development, 485, 503
obesity affecting, 200
parent–infant relationship affecting, 202
peer acceptance affecting, 619
peer relations in. *See* Peer relations
in psychosocial dwarfism, 202, 403
pubertal timing affecting, 208–210
self-awareness in, 408–409, 450
of self-care children, 598–599
self-conscious emotions in, 405, 408–409, 416, 450
self-regulation of emotions in, 405, 409–412
sex differences in, 558–559
in social experience, 416
social referencing in, 414–415
socioeconomic variations in, 581–582
temperament in, 418–428
teratogen exposure affecting, 96
understanding and responding to emotions of others in, 414–418
visual impairment affecting, 162, 405
Emotional expression
display rules on, 412–413
facial. *See* Facial expressions
milestones of development, 419

of others, understanding and responding to, 414–418
Emotional intelligence, 327
Emotional self-regulation, 405
acquiring emotional display rules in, 412–413
in adolescence, 412
coping strategies in, 412
in early childhood, 410–411
and emotional intelligence, 327
in infancy and toddlerhood, 410
in middle childhood, 412
and temperament, 424
Emotional sensitivity, sex differences in, 558–559
Emotional well-being
identity status and, 471–472
of immigrant youths, 53
international comparison of indicators on, 33, 34*f*, 34*t*
and physical growth, 202
Emotions, 401–445
in adolescence, 207–208
anger, 57, 57*f*, 407
and cognitive processing, 402
definition of, 401
display rules on, 412–413
fear, 407–408, 411, 412
functions of, 401–405
happiness, 406–407, 416
and health, 403
of others, understanding and responding to, 414–418
sadness, 407
self-conscious, 405, 408–409, 416
self-regulation of, 405, 409–412
and social behavior, 402–403
Empathy, 416–418
evolution of, 486–488
and guilt, 490
in infancy and toddlerhood, 135–136, 137, 417, 487, 487*f*
mirror neurons in, 146, 487
in moral development, 486, 503
and self-awareness, 450
sex differences in, 503, 558–559
social cognition in, 525
Employment
in adolescence, 649
and attachment patterns, 438, 438*f*, 441–443
child care in, 441–443
gender stereotypes in, 543, 549, 552, 558, 563
and IQ as predictor of occupational attainment, 332–333
of mothers, 595–596
observation and participation of children in, 273
parental leave from, 118–119, 442, 536, 570
and self-care children, 597–599
teenage pregnancy affecting, 218
and time spent per day with children, 438, 438*f*
vocational preparation for, 649–650

in welfare-to-work programs, 35, 36
Endocrine system. *See* Hormones
Endoderm, formation of, 91
Endorphins, 153
Enduring self, 451
England
gender typing in, 543
home births in, 111
Enlightenment philosophies, 12
Enrichment in sensitive periods of development, 171
Entity view of ability, 465, 467
Environmental influences
on aggression, 561–562
on attachment security, 433–437
on attention-deficit hyperactivity disorder, 125, 290–291
Baldwin on, 14
in behaviorism, 17
canalization concept on, 122
on child maltreatment, 602
in child care facilities, 442
on cognitive development, 282
on creativity, 354–355
cultural. *See* Cultural influences
cumulative deficit hypothesis on, 331
on disorganized/disoriented attachment, 435, 435*f*
in early deprivation, 169–171
ecological systems theory on, 26–28, 27*f*
in epigenetic framework, 124, 124*f*, 125
on family system, 572
on gender typing, 538–547
and gene correlation, 122–123, 345
on gene expression, 123–124
and gene interactions, 121*f*, 121–122, 337–338, 426–427
on genetic mutations, 81
on growth rate, 183, 184
in heritability estimates, 121
in home, 344–346. *See also* Home environment
on intelligence and IQ, 121*f*, 121–122, 331, 334–335, 335*f*, 336, 337–338, 344–346
lead exposure in, 101, 193
on motor development, 149, 150
on multiple births, 76
nonshared, 344, 346, 424–425, 435
on obesity, 198–200
on physical development, 183, 184, 192, 193
pollution exposure in, 101
on prenatal development, 81, 94–106
on pubertal development, 205
and relative influence of nature and nurture, 8–9, 118–124. *See also* Nature, and relative influence of nurture
and resilience, 10–11
on semantic development, 378, 378*f*

in sensitive periods, 24
on sexual orientation, 215
shared, 344–346, 425
on sudden infant death syndrome, 136
on temperament, 422, 424–425, 426–427
teratogens in, 95–103
Epidural analgesia during childbirth, 112
Epigenesis, 124, 125
Epigenetic framework, 124, 124*f*, 125
Epiphyses, 178, 178*f*
Episodic memory, 297–300
autobiographical, 298–300
and eyewitness testimony by children, 300–302
scripts in, 298
Equality, gender-related, 180, 536, 540, 541, 563
Equilibration in cognitive development, 227
Equilibrium in cognitive development, 19, 227, 260
EQUIP program, 525
Erikson, Erik, 15–16, 16*t*, 17
on identity development, 468–470
Eritrea, emotional stress of orphans in, 524
Estimation strategies in arithmetic computations, 311
Estrogen, 183
and sexual orientation, 215
Ethical issues
in reproductive technologies, 87
in research, 17, 41, 66*t*, 66–69
and universal principles in moral development, 502
Ethiopia
body size in, 183
dynamic assessment of immigrant children from, 342, 342*f*
Ethnic and racial differences
in academic achievement beliefs, 345–346
in anorexia nervosa, 210
bias on, 476–480
in body image, 209
in body size, 183
census data on, 339
in child-rearing practices, 582–584
in cliques and crowds, 624
in communication styles, 339–340
in corporal punishment, 493
and cultural bias in testing, 339–343
in delinquency, 519
in discipline, 583
in drug use, 626
in fraternal twinning, 77*t*
in friendships, 616–617
in gender stereotypes, 534, 546
in grandparents as primary caregivers, 438
heritability research on, 121
in high-stakes testing movement, 343

Ethnic and racial differences (*cont.*)
  in identity, 339, 475
  in intelligence definition, 324
  in intelligence quotient, 334, 334*f*, 336–337, 338, 339–343
  in neonatal and infant mortality rates, 118
  in obesity, 199–200
  in self-esteem, 464
  in single-parent families, 590
  in skeletal growth, 178, 183
  stereotypes on, 341, 341*f*, 476, 478, 631
Ethnic identity, 475
Ethnographic research, 43*t*, 52–53
  reliability of, 54
Ethology, 23–24
  attachment theory in, 24, 428–430, 439
  compared to other child development theories, 32*t*
  dating relationships in, 625
  on parent response to crying, 138
Europe. *See also specific countries.*
  academic and vocational tracks in, 645
  body size in, 183
  child care in, 597
  contraceptive availability for adolescents, 219
  drug use in, 626, 626*f*
  growth rate of children in, 183
  physical growth trends in, 184
  reproductive technology laws in, 87
  sexual activity of adolescents in, 213, 217, 219
  sexually transmitted diseases in, 217
  thalidomide use in, 96
  vocational education in, 650
Event sampling in systematic observational research, 44
Event-related potentials (ERPs), 48, 48*t*, 186
  and cognitive processing speed, 323
  in emotional responses, 412, 431
  in error detection, 264
  in foster care compared to institutional care, 171
  in infants of diabetic mothers, 49
  in inhibitory tasks, 288
  and language development, 364, 365, 367
  in object permanence studies, 231
  in reasoning on beliefs, 455
  in sensory stimulation of infants, 153, 156, 187, 231
  in sleep, 133
Evocative correlation of genetic and environmental factors, 122
Evolution, theories of
  body size variations in, 183
  of Darwin, 13
  in ethology, 23
  family in, 568

gender roles in, 535
moral development in, 486–488
play activities in, 610
spatial abilities in, 557
Evolutionary developmental psychology, 24, 32*t*
Executive function, 281–282
  and attention, 287, 288
  in attention-deficit hyperactivity disorder, 290
  in autism, 457
  media multitasking affecting, 293
  and planning, 289
  and theory of mind, 455
Exercise
  in athletic activities, 179–181. *See also* Athletic activities
  benefits of, 180, 181
  in obesity, 199, 200
  in organized youth sports, 179–181
  and physical self-efficacy, 180
  in pregnancy, 103
  and pubertal development, 204
  and sex differences in motor development, 180
Exosystem in ecological systems theory, 27*f*, 28, 29, 571
Expansion technique for grammar development, 389
Experience-dependent brain growth, 191
Experience-expectant brain growth, 191
Experimental research, 55, 56–60
  on classical conditioning, 17
  combined with developmental research, 65
  compared to other research designs, 61*t*
  ethical issues in, 17
  matching technique in, 58
  modified designs, 58
  in natural settings, 58–60, 60*f*
  random assignment in, 57–58
Exploration in infancy and toddlerhood
  bidirectional influences in, 124
  and emotional development, 401
  and motor development, 147, 149
  and perceptual development, 155
  secure base for, 408, 429, 430
  visual cliff studies of, 159*f*, 159–160
  in visual impairment, 162
Explosiveness, longitudinal study of, 61
Expressive personality traits, 530
Expressive style of communication, 378
Extended families, 583–584
  of African Americans, 583, 590
External validity, 55
Extinction in classical conditioning, 140
Extracurricular activities, student body size affecting, 638
Eye blink reflex, 130*t*

Eye movements
  and object perception of infants, 165
  in objective permanence studies, 231, 232*f*
  in rapid-eye-movement sleep, 133, 135, 135*f*
  and visual acuity of infants, 159
Eyes
  embryonic development of, 95, 95*f*
  and vision, 158–166. *See also* Vision
Eyewitness testimony by children, 454
  suggestibility affecting, 300–302

F

Face perception, 163–164, 164*f*
  gender and racial preferences in, 164
  intermodal relationships in, 166, 168
  and memory of infants, 144, 144*f*
  and sensitive period for culture-specific learning, 156
Facial expressions
  in attachment-related behaviors, 431
  brain activity in response to, 414, 433
  changes during infancy, 406
  and emotional display rules, 412–413
  emotions associated with, 405
  in empathy, 418
  imitation of, by newborn, 145*f*, 145–146
  infant perception of, 164, 414
  and still-face reaction, 402–403
Facial hair development, 203
  testosterone affecting, 183
Factor analysis, 321–322
  of self-esteem, 461
Fagan Test of Infant Intelligence, 329
Fallopian tubes, 88, 88*f*
False beliefs, 452–453, 453*f*, 454
  language and verbal reasoning in, 455
  second-order, 453, 454*f*
  social interactions affecting, 456
Familiarity preference of infants, 143, 144*f*
Family, 567–605
  adaptation to changes in, 571
  adoptive, 588–589. *See also* Adoption
  and aggression, 520–522, 522*f*, 523–524
  arrival of new sibling in, 436
  attachment quality in, 436, 442
  beliefs on intellectual success in, 345–346
  blended, 594–595
  chaos in, 29
  child maltreatment in, 599–604
  child-rearing practices in, 573–584. *See also* Child-rearing practices

and civic responsibility, 508
coercive interaction pattern in, 522*f*, 523
context of, 571–572
creativity in, 354
direct influences of, 569
ecological systems theory on, 27, 28, 29, 569
ethnic variations in, 582–584
evolutionary origin of, 568
extended, 583–584, 590
fraternal twinning in, 77*t*
functions of, 568
gender roles in, 536, 543–544, 546*f*, 546–547, 562
grandparents as primary caregivers in, 438–439
home environment of, 344–346. *See also* Home environment
homosexual, 589–590
in identity development, 473, 475
of immigrant children, 53
indirect influences of, 569–571
intelligence quotient in, 335*f*, 335–336, 336*f*
lifestyles and transitions in, 584–599
mealtimes in, 29, 196, 393, 582, 582*f*
of newborn, 570
with one child, 587–588
parents in. *See* Parent(s)
siblings in, 585–587. *See also* Siblings
single-parent, 590
size of, 580, 584–588
as social system, 567, 568, 569–573
in socialization, 568, 573–584
socioeconomic influences on, 580–582
of suicide victims, 473
Family Check-Up intervention, 58
Family size, 584–588
  and intelligence, 585, 585*f*
  in one-child families, 587–588
  socioeconomic variations in, 580
Fast-mapping in semantic development, 377
Fat, body
  age-related changes in, 177
  baby fat, 177
  fear of, 210
  hormones affecting, 183
  and menarche, 204
  in puberty, 204
Fathers
  and academic achievement, 555
  age of, and chromosomal abnormalities, 82
  and attachment, 437–438, 439
  in blended families, 594–595
  child care responsibilities of, 596
  child maltreatment by, 600
  cultural influences on role of, 437–438, 439
  depression of, 404

divorce of, 591, 592–593
in effective coparenting, 569, 571
emotional sensitivity of, 559
first child of, 570
and gender equality in Sweden, 536
gender typing of children by, 542
Hispanic, 438
homosexual, 589–590
in maternal employment, 596
of newborn, 570
play activities of, 437, 438, 439, 542, 612
sibling preferences of, 586
in single-parent families, 590
teenage, 220
warmth of, 439
Father–stepmother families, 595
Favoritism
sibling preference in, 586
toward in-groups, 477–478, 532, 533, 544, 616
toward out-groups, 477
Fear
in early childhood, 411
in infancy and toddlerhood, 407–408
in middle childhood and adolescence, 412
Feeding practices
breastfeeding and bottle-feeding in, 194–195
and obesity, 199
Female and male differences. *See* Sex differences
Fertility, 88–89
prenatal DES exposure affecting, 96
in puberty, 203, 204
and reproductive technologies, 76, 77*t*, 86–87, 589
Fertilization, 88–89
in vitro, 76, 77*t*, 86, 87
Fetal alcohol spectrum disorder (FASD), 98–100
diagnostic criteria on, 99*t*
Fetal alcohol syndrome (FAS), 98–99
diagnostic criteria on, 99*t*
partial, 99, 99*t*
Fetal development, 90, 92–94
alcohol exposure affecting, 98–100, 99*t*
diagnosis and treatment of problems in, 84–86
habituation in, 94, 142, 145
Rh factor incompatibility affecting, 113
teratogens affecting, 95*f*, 96, 98
Fetal medicine, 84–86
Fetoscopy, 85*t*, 92
Fibrosis, cystic, 78*t*, 85
Field experiments, 58
compared to other research designs, 61*t*
Filipinos, intelligence definition of, 324

Fine-motor development
in infancy and toddlerhood, 147, 150–152
sex differences in, 180
in visual impairment, 162
Finland
academic achievement in, 647, 648
adolescent suicide rate in, 472
adopted children of schizophrenic mothers in, 123
corporal punishment in, 602
factor analysis of intelligence in, 324
infant mortality rate in, 119*f*
overweight and obesity rate in, 198
poverty rate in, 33
Firstborn, arrival of new sibling affecting, 436
Flowcharts on information processing, 21–22, 22*f*
Fluid intelligence, 321–322, 328*f*, 332
Flynn effect, 338, 338*f*
Folic acid in prenatal nutrition, 104, 105*f*
Food. *See also* Eating habits; Nutrition
insecurity concerning, 197–198
mercury exposure from, 101
supplement programs, 35
and taste sense of newborn, 154
toxoplasmosis from, 103
Foot reaching and motor development in infants, 149
Football, 181
Foreclosure status in identity development, 470, 470*t*, 471, 473
ethnic, 475
Formal operational stage, 20, 20*t*, 253–259
consequences of changes in, 255–257
cultural influences on, 258–259
decision making in, 256–257
hypothetico-deductive reasoning in, 253–254, 254*f*, 257
idealism and criticism in, 256
individual differences in, 258–259
propositional thought in, 254–255, 257–258
research on, 257–259
self-consciousness and self-focusing in, 255–256
Fragile X syndrome, 80–81
France
divorce rate in, 591*f*
gender stereotypes in, 532
infant mortality rate in, 119*f*
math achievement scores in, 558*f*
reproductive technology laws in, 87
smell sense of newborn in, 154, 154*f*
Fraternal twins, 76–77, 77*t*
heritability estimates from studies on, 120
intelligence quotient in, 335*f*, 336, 336*f*

niche-picking by, 123
temperament and personality of, 423, 424–425, 425*f*
Freud, Sigmund
on attachment, 428
on moral development, 488, 490
on psychosexual stages of development, 15, 16*t*
Friendships, 613–618
and adjustment, 617–618
cell phone use in, 634–635
characteristics of, 615–617
corumination in, 617
and identity formation, 616
milestones of development, 628
and moral development, 505
online, 635, 635*f*
with other sex, 617
in school transitions, 642
selectivity of, 615
self-disclosure in, 615, 615*f*
sex differences in, 617
similarity and diversity in, 616–617
stability of, 615
Frontal lobe, 186
Broca's area in, 362*f*, 363
Full inclusion of students with learning difficulties, 646
Functional magnetic resonance imaging (fMRI), 48*t*, 50, 50*f*
in adolescence, 190
in autism, 457
in fetal alcohol spectrum disorder, 99
in language development studies, 365, 367
in motor and cognitive tasks, 187
in multitasking, 293
Functional play, 609*t*
Functionalist approach to emotions, 401–405
Fuzzy-trace theory of memory, 296

G
Games. *See also* Play
cultural influences on, 612
video, 629*f*, 633, 634
Gametes, 75*f*, 75–76
in reproductive technologies, 86
Gardner, Howard, theory of multiple intelligences, 325*t*, 325–326, 354–355
Gastrointestinal system
prenatal development of, 91
stress affecting, 403
Gay and lesbian population, 215–216
dating of, 625
as parents, 589–590
Gender consistency, 548, 549
Gender constancy, 548–549
Gender contentedness, 550
Gender differences. *See* Sex differences
Gender discrimination, 563
Gender equality, 536, 540, 541, 563
in educational programs, 180

Gender identity, 547–552
in adolescence, 550–551, 553
and adoption of gender roles, 549, 550
androgynous, 547–548, 549, 551
consistency in, 548, 549
constancy in, 548–549
contentedness with, 550
definition of, 530
and depression, 560
emergence of, 548–549
gender stereotypes affecting, 534
intensification of, 550–551
labeling of, 548, 549
in middle childhood, 549*f*, 549–550, 553
milestones of development, 553
personality traits in, 547, 549
stability of, 548
typicality in, 550
Gender intensification, 550–551
Gender labeling, 548, 549
Gender roles, 529–565
adoption of, 534–547, 550
definition of, 530
equality in, 180, 536, 540, 541, 563
of first-time parents, 570
in friendships, 617
and gender identity, 549, 550
and gender schema theory, 551*f*, 551–552
in homosexual families, 589, 590*f*
in maternal employment, 596
milestones of development, 553
observational learning of, 543–544
in play activities, 529, 531–532, 533, 534, 537, 539, 544, 609
sex hormones affecting, 536–538
stereotypes on. *See* Gender stereotypes
in television programs, 631
in transition to parenthood, 570
Gender schema theory, 530, 551*f*, 551–552
Gender stability, 548
Gender stereotypes, 529–565
in achievement, 467, 532–533, 534
and adoption of gender roles, 534–547
in aggression, 518
in athletic activities, 180
cultural influences on, 530, 532–533, 535–536, 542, 543, 546, 559
definition of, 530
in early childhood, 531–532, 539, 540
flexibility in, 533, 533*f*, 534
and gender identity, 549
and gender schema theory, 551*f*, 551–552
group differences in, 534
individual differences in, 533
information processing in, 22
in language development, 540–541
meta-analysis of, 553

Gender stereotypes (*cont.*)
  in middle childhood and
    adolescence, 532–533, 534,
    539–542
  milestones of development, 553
  of parents, 539–542
  in personality traits, 530t, 530–531,
    531f, 532, 554t, 558–562
  and self-esteem, 463
  and sexist remarks of peers, 545
  strategies reducing, 562–563
  in television programs, 631
  as threat, 557
Gender typing, 529–530
  biological influences on, 535–538
  cultural influences on, 535–536
  definition of, 530
  environmental influences on,
    538–547
  evolution of, 535
  and gender identity, 549
  milestones of development, 553
  observational learning of, 543–544
  peer relations in, 544–546
  perceptions and expectations of
    adults affecting, 538--539
  sex hormones affecting, 536–538
Gender-salience filter, 552
Gene therapy, 85–86
General intelligence (*g*), 321
  in three-stratum theory of
    intelligence, 322
Generalized other, 459
Generativity and stagnation in
  psychosocial development, 16t
Genes, 74–75
  crossing over of, 75f, 75–76
  and environment correlation,
    122–123, 345
  and environment interactions,
    121f, 121–122, 337–338, 426–427
  expression of, 123–124
  heterozygous, 77
  homozygous, 77
  Human Genome Project on, 85
  modifier, 79
  mutations of, 81
Genetic counseling, 84
Genetic engineering, 85
Genetic factors, 73–83
  in anorexia nervosa, 211
  in attention-deficit hyperactivity
    disorder, 125, 125f, 290
  Baldwin on, 14
  in behavioral genetics, 119–120
  in bulimia nervosa, 211
  counseling on, 84
  in depression, 559
  in disorganized/disoriented
    attachment, 435, 435f
  dominant and recessive genes in,
    77t, 77–79, 78t, 79f
  and environment correlation,
    122–123, 345
  and environment interactions,
    121f, 121–122, 337–338, 426–427

in epigenetic framework, 124, 124f,
  125
in executive function, 282
and genomic imprinting, 80–81
Hall and Gesell on, 13
in hand preference, 189
heritability estimates on, 120–121,
  335–337, 424
in intelligence and IQ, 120,
  121–122, 332, 334, 335f,
  335–339, 345
in meiosis, 75f, 75–76
in multiple offspring, 76–77
mutations in, 81
in obesity, 198, 200
in patterns of inheritance, 77–81
in physical growth, 183, 192–194
in prosocial behavior, 487
in pubertal changes, 204
and relative influence of nature and
  nurture, 8–9, 118–124
Rousseau on, 12
in sexual characteristics, 76
in sexual orientation, 215
in temperament, 422, 423–424,
  426–427
and teratogen impact, 95
in X-linked inheritance, 80, 80f
Genital stage of psychosexual
  development, 15, 16t
Genitals
  ambiguous, 538
  in androgen insensitivity, 538
  in congenital adrenal hyperplasia,
    537
  prenatal DES exposure affecting,
    96
  prenatal development of, 92, 95f
  in puberty, 203–204
Genome, 85
Genomic imprinting, 80–81
Genotypes, 73, 77
  in attention-deficit hyperactivity
    disorder, 125, 125f
German language, 386
German measles, 202
  in pregnancy, 102, 102t
Germany
  attachment patterns in, 432, 432f,
    436
  caregiving roles of mothers and
    fathers in, 437
  corporal punishment in, 602
  divorce rate in, 591f
  family size in, 584
  gender stereotypes in, 533
  infant mortality rate in, 119f
  male-to-female birth ratios in, 80
  parental leave in, 119
  self-recognition by toddlers in, 450
  vocational education in, 649–650
Germline mutations, 81
Gesell, Arnold, 13
Gestures
  in animal acquisition of language,
    361

in hearing loss, 362
preverbal, 371
in sign language. *See* Sign
  language
and speech mismatches, 285
Gifted children, 354–355
  clinical research on, 51
Gilligan, Carol, on feminine morality,
  503
Gist memory, 296, 296f, 300
Glial cells, 186
  prenatal development of, 92
Glucose blood levels in diabetic
  pregnancy, 49
Goal-directed behavior, 353
  executive function in, 282
  in sensorimotor stage, 229
Gonorrhea, 217
Good boy–good girl orientation in
  moral development, 501
Goodness-of-fit model of child
  rearing, 426–427, 435
Government policies. *See* Public
  policy
Grammatical development, 360,
  384–390
  adult feedback in, 389–390
  brain areas in, 364
  communicative support for,
    389–390
  complex forms in, 387–388
  first word combinations in, 384t,
    384–385, 385f
  information processing theory of,
    367
  language-making capacity in, 389
  later phase of, 388
  and metalinguistic awareness,
    394
  milestones of, 395
  morphemes in, 386–387, 387t
  morphology in, 360
  nativist theory of, 361, 364, 365
  negatives in, 387
  overregularization in, 386–387
  questions in, 387–388
  semantic bootstrapping in, 389
  semantic complexity in, 386
  strategies in, 388–389
  structural complexity in, 386
  subject–verb–object expressions in,
    386, 386f
  syntax in, 360
  two-word combinations in, 384,
    384t
  universal, 361, 365
  in Williams syndrome, 366
Grandparents as primary caregivers,
  438–439
Grasping of infants and newborns,
  151f, 151–152
  pincer grasp in, 151, 151f
  as reflex, 130t, 130–131
  ulnar grasp in, 151, 151f
Gratification, delayed, 514–515,
  516

Gravity, and center of gravity changes
  in physical growth, 178
Great Britain
  attachment experience of parents
    in, 436
  attention-deficit hyperactivity
    disorder in, 291
  child poverty rate in, 36
  depression of fathers in, 404
  home births in, 111
  overweight and obesity rate in,
    198
  religion in, 507
Greece
  adolescent suicide rate in, 472
  infant mortality rate in, 119f
  obesity in, 198
  self-recognition by toddlers in,
    450, 450f
Gross-motor development, 147,
  178–181
  milestones of, 179
Groups
  peer, 622–624, 628
  in schools, 643–645
Growth, physical. *See* Physical
  development
Growth curves, 176, 177f
Growth faltering, 202, 403
Growth hormone (GH), 182, 183,
  202, 403
Growth spurts, 183, 203
Guatemala
  body size in, 183
  childbirth practices in, 111
  communication style in, 340
  cosleeping of parents and infants
    in, 134
  memory strategies in, 294
  observational learning in, 273
Guided participation, 268
Guilt
  empathy-based, 490
  in moral development, 488, 490
  in psychosocial development, 16t,
    488
  as self-conscious emotion, 408, 409
Gun control legislation in suicide
  prevention, 473
Gusii of Kenya
  mother–infant relationship and
    attachment security in, 434
  motor development of infants, 150

H
Habituation
  in categorization studies, 234, 235f
  in infancy and toddlerhood,
    142–145, 156, 165, 165f, 234,
    235f, 329
  and internal working models of
    attachment, 430, 430f
  in object perception, 165, 165f
  in object permanence, 230–231
  in prenatal development, 94, 142,
    145

Hair
    facial and body, in adolescence,
        183, 203
    inheritance of characteristics, 77, 77t
Hall, G. Stanley, 13, 175
Hand preference, 189
    and lateralization of brain, 187, 189
Happiness
    in infancy and toddlerhood,
        406–407
    in middle childhood, 416
Hausa of Nigeria, 252
Hawaiians
    birth complications in, 117
    ethnicity of, 339
    overweight, 200
Head Start programs, 35, 347–350,
    351
    Research-based Developmentally
        Informed (REDI) program of,
        351, 351f
Health
    in adolescence, 210–220
    and body size variations, 183
    and breastfeeding, 194
    and emotions, 403
    international comparison of
        indicators on, 33, 34f, 34t
Health care
    and adolescent pregnancy, 218
    in diarrhea, 201
    drug therapy in. See Drug therapy
    fetal medicine in, 84–86
    immunizations in, 102, 113,
        201–202
    in phenylketonuria, 79
    prenatal. See Prenatal health care
    reproductive technologies in, 76,
        77t, 86–87, 589
    universal access to, 33
Health insurance, public policies on,
    33
Healthy Families America, 603
Hearing
    in infancy and toddlerhood,
        155–158
    in intermodal perception, 166–168
    loss of. See Hearing loss
    milestones of development, 158
    in prenatal development, 93–94
Hearing loss
    brain development in, 187
    cochlear implant in, 370
    cognitive development in, 372
    language development in, 362–363,
        370, 372
    parent–child interactions in, 372
    in prenatal rubella, 102
    sign language in, 187, 362–363, 364
Heart rate, 47
    fetal, 93, 94
    of newborn, Apgar Scale on, 109t
    in shyness and sociability, 422
Height, 176–177
    in adolescence, 176, 177
    in body mass index, 198

and body proportion changes,
    176–177
in early childhood, 176
gender differences in, 176, 177f
genetic factors affecting, 192
in infancy and toddlerhood, 176,
    177
in middle childhood, 176
in puberty, 203
rate of changes in, 176, 177f
secular trends in, 184
worldwide variations in, 183
Heinz dilemma, 499, 500, 501
Helpfulness. See Prosocial behavior
Helplessness, learned, 465–466, 466f,
    467
Hemispheres, cerebral. See Cerebral
    hemispheres
Hemophilia, 78t, 80
    gene therapy in, 86
Heredity. See also Genetic factors
    Baldwin on, 14
    and heritability estimates, 120–121,
        335–337, 424
    and physical growth, 183, 192–194
    and relative influence of nature and
        nurture, 8–9, 118–124
Heritability estimates, 120–121
    on intelligence, 120, 121, 335–337
    on temperament, 424
Heroin use
    in adolescence, 626
    in pregnancy, 97, 98, 100
Herpes simplex virus, 217
    in pregnancy, 102t, 103
Heterogeneous groups in schools, 644
Heteronomous morality, 496, 498
Heterozygous genes, 77
Hidden objects, searching for
    in sensorimotor stage, 232, 237
    video viewing affecting, 237
Hierarchical classification in
    preoperational stage, 245, 245f
Hierarchical models of intelligence,
    321, 322f
Hierarchical style of communication,
    340
High school
    grouping practices in, 644–645
    transition to, 641–642
High/Scope Perry Preschool Project,
    347, 348f, 349
High-stakes testing movement, 342,
    343
Hindu children
    emotional display rules of, 413,
        413f
    moral development of, 512
Hippocampus, 190
    in infants of diabetic mothers, 49
    in memory, 190, 293, 301
Hispanics
    academic achievement beliefs of,
        345, 346
    anorexia nervosa of, 210
    bilingual, 397

body image of, 209
child-rearing practices of, 582, 583
communication style of, 340
drug use of, 626
ethnic identity of, 475
family and community influences
    on, 53
father–child relationships of, 438
food insecurity of, 198
friendships of, 616
gender stereotypes of, 546
grandparents as primary caregivers
    of, 438
intelligence quotient of, 334, 338
Mexican American. See Mexican
    Americans
in mixed-race schools, 479
moral reasoning of, 506
poverty of, 33
puberty of, 206
school transitions of, 642
stereotype threat affecting test
    performance of, 341, 341f
suicide rate in adolescents, 472
teacher–student interaction of, 643
as television characters, 631
television viewing of, 630
Historical development of child
    development theories, 10–21
HIV infection and AIDS, 213, 217
    breastfeeding in, 194
    in pregnancy, 102t, 102–103
Hmong immigrants, reasoning skills
    of, 269
Home births, 111–112
Home environment
    and academic achievement, 53
    and aggression, 520–522
    and attachment security, 436
    chaos in, 29
    in child maltreatment, 603
    childbirth in, 111–112
    gender roles in, 543–544
    and intelligence, 331, 337, 338,
        344–346
    nonshared influences in, 344, 346,
        424–425, 435
    and psychosocial dwarfism, 202
    and pubertal timing, 205
    and semantic development, 378,
        378f
    shared influences in, 344–346, 425
    siblings in. See Siblings
    in teenage pregnancy and
        parenthood, 214, 219, 220
Home Observation for Measurement
    of the Environment (HOME),
    344–345
Home visitation program in child
    maltreatment prevention, 603,
    603f
Homesigning, 362
Homework, weekly time spent on,
    613, 613f
Homogeneous groups in school,
    643–644

Homophobia, 216
Homosexuality
    in adolescence, 215–216, 625
    dating in, 625
    disclosure of, 216
    identity development in, 474
    of parents, 589–590
    sexually transmitted diseases in,
        217
    suicide in, 216, 472
Homozygous genes, 77
Honesty, 497–498
Hong Kong, attention-deficit
    hyperactivity disorder in, 291
Hormones
    androgen. See Androgen
    definition of, 181
    estrogen, 183, 215
    melatonin, 133
    and physical growth, 181–183, 182f
    in puberty, 183, 191, 212
    in stress response, 47–48, 97, 108,
        403, 422
    testosterone, 183
Hostile aggression (reactive), 517,
    518, 522
Hot and cool systems in self-control,
    516, 516f
Human Genome Project, 85
Human immunodeficiency virus
    (HIV) infections, 213, 217
    breastfeeding in, 194
    in pregnancy, 102t, 102–103
Humor in semantic development,
    381
Hunger, crying of infants in, 135, 137
Huntington disease, 78t, 79, 80, 85
Hyaline membrane disease, 113
Hyperactivity, in attention-deficit
    hyperactivity disorder, 290
Hypothalamus, 181f, 181–182, 182f
Hypotheses, 41–42, 253
Hypothetico-deductive reasoning in
    formal operational stage,
    253–254, 254f, 257–258
Hypothyroidism, infantile, 104

I
Iceland
    gay and lesbian families in, 589
    mathematical abilities in, 557, 558f
Id, 15
Ideal reciprocity, 497, 501, 509, 512
Ideal self in self-concept, 459
Idealism in formal operational stage,
    256
Identical twins, 76
    heritability estimates from studies
        on, 120
    intelligence quotient in, 335f, 336,
        336f
    niche-picking by, 123
    temperament and personality of,
        423, 424–425, 425f
Identification with same-sex parent,
    488

Identity, 468–475
   achievement of, 470, 470t, 471, 473, 475
   in adolescence, 468–475, 550–551, 553, 578
   bicultural, 475
   and cognitive style, 471–472
   community influences on, 474
   confusion about, 470
   crisis in, 469
   cultural influences on, 474–475
   diffusion of, 470, 470t, 471, 473, 475
   domains of, 470
   ethnic, 475
   exploration of, 469
   family affecting, 473, 475
   foreclosure status, 470, 470t, 471, 473, 475
   and friendships, 616
   gender-related, 530, 547–552. See also Gender identity
   moral, 489, 506, 523
   moratorium status, 470, 470t, 471, 473, 475
   peer groups in, 622
   peer interactions affecting, 473, 475
   and personality, 472
   and psychological well-being, 471–472
   in psychosocial development, 16t
   school affecting, 474, 475
   sexual, 215–216
   strategies supporting development of, 474
Illocutionary intent in pragmatic language development, 390–391
Imaginary audience in formal operational stage, 255, 256
Imaginary companions in preoperational stage, 240
Imitation
   deferred, 230, 232–233, 233f
   of food preferences and eating habits, 196
   infant memory of, 142, 233
   inferred, 233
   by newborn, 145f, 145–146
   and self-awareness, 450
   social learning theory on, 18
   of televised actions, 237
Immigrants
   academic achievement beliefs of, 345
   acculturative stress of, 475, 579
   adaptation of, 53
   age of, 364–365, 365f
   bilingualism of, 364–365, 365f
   child-rearing styles of, 579
   dynamic assessment of intelligence, 342, 342f
   language development in, 364–365, 365f
Immune system, malnutrition affecting, 104, 201

Immunization, 201–202
   mercury-free, 202
   in Rh incompatibility, 113
   rubella, 102
Implantation of blastocyst, 88f, 89
Imprinting, 429
   and early following behavior of animals, 23
   genomic, 80–81
Impulsivity
   in attention-deficit hyperactivity disorder, 290, 291
   temperament in, 425, 426
In vitro fertilization, 86, 87
   and fraternal twinning, 76, 77t
Incest, 601
Inclusive classrooms, 646
Incomplete dominance in genetic inheritance, 79
Incredible Years training program, 523–524
Incremental view of ability, 465
Independent self, 134
   in individualistic societies, 35
Independent variables in experimental research, 56, 57
India
   caregiving roles of mothers and fathers in, 437
   child abuse prevention programs in, 601
   ethnographic research in, 52
   maps drawn in, 251, 251f
   moral development in, 506, 512
   play and peer sociability in, 612
Individual differences
   in gender stereotypes, 533
   in puberty, 204–205
   in self-control, 516
Individualistic societies
   cooperative learning in, 271
   moral development in, 506
   peer sociability in, 612
   public policy in, 35
   self-conscious emotions in, 409
Indonesia, make-believe play in, 270
Inductive discipline, 489
Industry and inferiority in psychosocial development, 16t
Infancy and toddlerhood (birth to 2 years old), 5, 129–173
   aggression in, 517
   anger, 407
   arousal states in, 132–138, 406
   attachment in, 428, 429
   attention in, 286–287
   behavioral assessment in, 138–139
   body composition in, 177
   body proportions in, 177
   body size in, 176, 177f
   brain development in, 185, 186, 188, 191–192
   breastfeeding and bottle-feeding in, 194–195
   child-care settings in, 441–443

cognitive development in, 19, 20t, 133, 150, 169, 228–239, 262–264, 348
corporal punishment in, 492, 492f
cosleeping arrangements in, 134
crying in, 132, 132t, 133, 135–138
definition of, 5
deprivation and enrichment in, 169–171
early intervention programs in, 348, 349
emotional development in, 405–408, 452
empathy in, 135–136, 137, 417, 487, 487f
fear, 408–409
gender typing in, 539
growth faltering in, 202
habituation and recovery in, 142–145, 156, 165, 165f, 329
hand preference in, 189
happiness in, 406–407
height in, 176, 177
home environment in, 344, 345
intelligence tests in, 329
language development in, 155–157, 301, 368–380, 384–385, 395
learning capacities in, 133, 139–146, 157
mathematics in, 310
memory in, 297, 298, 300, 301
mental representation in, 232–236
modeling in, 491
mortality in. See Infant mortality
motor development in, 147–152, 178, 179
newborn infants. See Newborns
nutrition in, 194–195
object permanence in, 231–232
parent relationship in. See Parent–infant relationship
parental leave from employment during, 118–119, 442
peer relations in, 608, 628
perceptual development in, 152–169
phonological development of, 373–375
physical and numerical knowledge in, 262–264, 264f
play in, 270, 608
prelinguistic development in, 368–372
preterm infants, 113–116
psychosexual and psychosocial development in, 16t
reflexes in, 130–132, 238
sadness in, 407
self-awareness in, 448f, 448–450, 450f
self-control in, 514–515
self-esteem in, 469
semantic development in, 376–380
as sensitive period of development, 169–171
sensitivity of care in, 434, 435, 437

sensorimotor stage in, 228–239. See also Sensorimotor stage
sleep in, 132t, 132–135
social referencing in, 414–415, 452
sociocultural theory on, 266
statistical learning capacity in, 157, 367, 369
television viewing in, 629
temperament in, 93
visual impairment in, severe, 162
Infant mortality, 118
   in cosleeping of parents and infants, 134
   in home delivery, 112
   international differences in, 119f
   in prenatal drug exposure, 96
   in Rh factor incompatibility, 113
   of small-for-date infants, 114
   in sudden infant death syndrome, 134, 135, 136
Infant–parent relationship. See Parent–infant relationship
Infantile amnesia, 300, 301
Infectious diseases
   and body size variations, 183
   and breastfeeding, 194
   HIV infection and AIDS, 102t, 102–103, 194, 213, 217
   immunization against. See Immunization
   and malnutrition, 201
   and physical development, 201–202
   in pregnancy, 101–103, 102t
   pubertal development in, 205
   sexually transmitted, 217
   in stress, 403
Inferences, 453
   transitive, in concrete operational stage, 250, 252
Inferiority, and industry in psychosocial development, 16t
Infertility
   in prenatal DES exposure, 96
   reproductive technologies in, 76, 77t, 86–87, 589
Infinitive phrases in grammatical development, 388
Information processing, 21–23, 261, 277–317
   in academic learning, 307–314
   and analytical intelligence, 324
   in autism, 457
   in automatic processes, 280
   capacity of working memory in, 279, 280, 315t
   compared to other child development theories, 32t
   components of mental system in, 278–280
   computer analogy of, 278, 315
   construction and reconstruction in, 295–296
   development theories of, 282–286
   executive function in, 279, 279f, 281–282

flowcharts on, 21–22, 22f
gender schema in, 551f, 551–552
intelligence tests of, 323
and language development, 366–367
lateralization of brain functions in, 187, 188
mental strategies in, 278
milestones of development, 306
neo-Piagetian theory on, 261, 282, 283–284, 314, 315
retrieval of information in, 294–296
scientific reasoning in, 313–314
sensory register in, 278, 279, 279f
in social problem solving, 480
speed of, 281, 281f, 315t
store model of, 278–280, 279f
strategy choice model of Siegler on, 282, 284–286
Informed consent of research participants, 66t, 67
In-groups, 477–478
favoritism toward, 477–478, 532, 533, 544, 616
in school, 543
Inhalant use in adolescence, 626
Inheritance, 77–81. See also Genetic factors
biological knowledge on, 265
of chromosomal abnormalities, 82–83
dominant–recessive, 77t, 77–79, 78t, 79f
genetic counseling on, 84
genomic imprinting in, 80–81
heritability estimates on, 120–121, 335–337, 424
incomplete dominance in, 79
of mutations, 81
polygenic, 81
and relative influence of nature and nurture, 118–124
X-linked, 80, 80f
Inhibition
and attention, 287–288, 288f, 315t
and effortful control, 421
and memory, 300
temperament in, 421, 422, 425
Initiation ceremonies in adolescence, 206
Initiative in psychosocial development, 16t
Inner self, 451–456
Inner speech, 267
Innovation in creativity, 353
Input of information, 21
Insight process in creativity, 363
Institutional review boards, 67
Institutionalization
attachment security in, 433–434
early deprivation in, 170–171, 403
stress in, 403
temperament development in, 424
Instrumental aggression (proactive), 517, 522

Instrumental personality traits, 530
Instrumental purpose orientation in moral development, 500–501, 509
Insulin-like growth factor 1 (IGF-1), 182
Insurance, health, public policies on, 33
Integration of schools, 479
Integrity in psychosocial development, 16t
Intellectual development. See Cognitive development
Intellectual disabilities
classroom inclusion in, 646
in Down syndrome, 82
in environmental pollution, 101
in fragile X syndrome, 80, 81
handedness in, 189
in iodine deficiency, 104
in phenylketonuria, 79
in Prader-Willi syndrome, 80
in prenatal infections, 102, 102t
sex differences in, 80
in thyroxine deficiency, 183
Intelligence, 319–357
analytical, 323, 324, 324f
Binet on, 14, 320–321
broad and narrow abilities in, 322
canalization concept on, 122
creative, 323, 324, 324f
crystallized, 321–322, 328f, 332
cultural differences in assessment of, 322, 324
definitions of, 320–326
dynamic assessment of, 342
emotional, 327
environmental influences on, 121f, 121–122, 331, 334–335, 335f, 337–338, 344–346
factor analysis of, 321–322
and family size, 585, 585f
fluid, 321–322, 328f, 332
gene–environment interaction in, 121f, 121–122, 345
general (g), 321, 322
genetic factors in, 120, 121–122, 332, 334, 335f, 335–339, 345
and giftedness, 350–355
and habituation of infants, 145, 329
heritability estimates on, 120, 121, 335–337
hierarchical models of, 321, 322f
holistic view of, 320–321
home environment affecting, 331, 337, 338
information-processing approach to, 323
lead exposure affecting, 193
malnutrition affecting, 197
measurement of, 13–14, 326–346
and mental testing movement, 13–14
multiple intelligences theory of Gardner, 325t, 325–326, 354–355
musical experiences affecting, 59
practical, 324, 324f, 332–333

primary mental abilities in, 321
psychometric approach to, 319, 320–322, 323
in savant syndrome, 325, 326
specific, 321
static assessment of, 342
three-stratum theory of, 322
triarchic theory of, 323–324, 324f
Intelligence quotient (IQ), 330–346
and academic achievement, 331–332
and attentional skills, 323
bell-shaped distribution of, 330, 330f, 334f, 335
and birth order, 346, 585, 585f
and creativity, 353
environmental influences on, 331, 335f, 336, 337–338, 344–346
ethnic and racial differences in, 334–335, 336–337, 338, 339
and family size, 585, 585f
Flynn effect in, 338, 338f
genetic influences on, 335f, 335–339
heritability estimates on, 335–337
home environment affecting, 344–346
in lead exposure, 193
in malnutrition, 197
normal distribution of, 330, 330f
and occupational attainment, 332–333
predictive value of, 330–333
and psychological adjustment, 333
of siblings, 346, 585, 585f
and socioeconomic status, 334–335, 336–337, 338, 347, 348
stability of, 330–331
in twins, 335f, 335–336, 336f
Intelligence tests, 319, 326–346
and achievement tests, 328
and aptitude tests, 328
componential analysis of, 323
cultural bias in, 322, 328, 339–343
dynamic assessment in, 342
factor analysis in, 321–322
group administered, 326
historical development of, 13–14, 320–321
individually administered, 326
for infants, 329
intelligence quotient derived from. See Intelligence quotient
of multiple intelligences, 325
music lessons affecting scores on, 59, 59f
predictive value of, 330–333
standardization of, 330
Stanford-Binet, 14, 321, 327–328
static assessment in, 342
stereotype threat affecting performance in, 341, 341f
subtests in, 321, 327, 328
Intensification of gender identity, 550–551

Intentions
and moral judgments, 497–498, 511
in sensorimotor stage of cognitive development, 229
Interactional synchrony, and attachment security, 434, 437
Interactionist theories of language development, 366–367
Interdependent self, 134
in collectivist societies, 35
Interdisciplinary child development studies, 4
Intergenerational patterns
in intelligence quotient, 338, 338f
in sexual abuse, 601
in teenage parenthood, 218–219
Intermodal perception, 166–168, 448
Internal validity, 55, 57
Internal working model of attachment, 430, 430f, 436t, 436–437
and dating relationships, 625
Internalization of norms in moral development, 488, 494, 513
Internet, 293, 632–635
and cyberbullying, 621
and online relationships, 635, 635f
parent regulation of access to, 635
as source of sex education, 212
technical understanding of, 633, 633f
Interpersonal behavior, in multiple intelligences theory, 325t, 326
Inter-rater reliability, 54
Intersubjectivity in sociocultural theory, 268
Interventions
in aggression, 523–525
in anorexia nervosa, 211
attribution retraining in, 467–468
in blended families, 595
in bulimia nervosa, 212
in child maltreatment, 601, 603f, 603–604
on child-rearing practices, 578
costs and benefits of, 349
in depression of parent, 404
in divorce, 594
in drug use, 627
in eyewitness testimony of children, 302
food supplement programs in, 35
in gender stereotypes, 562–563
for institutionalized infants, 171
for intellectual development, 347–350
in malnutrition, 197
in obesity, 200
in peer victimization, 621
Project Head Start in, 35, 347–350, 351
public education programs in. See Public education programs

Interventions (*cont.*)
  for rejected children, 620–622
  in sexist remarks, 545, 545*f*
  in sexual abuse, 601
  in social group prejudice,
    479–480
  for social problem solving skills,
    481
  in suicide prevention, 473
  in teenage pregnancy and
    parenthood, 220
Interviews
  clinical, 20, 43*t*, 46–47, 499
  structured, 43*t*, 47
  suggestibility of children in,
    300–302
Intimacy
  development of, 471
  in friendships, 614, 615*f*
  in psychosocial development, 16*t*
Intrapersonal intelligence, 325*t*, 326
Inuit
  communication style of, 340
  cosleeping of parents and infants,
    134
  grammatical development of, 385,
    388
Invariant features in differentiation
    theory on perceptual
    development, 168, 169
Investment theory of creativity, 352
Invisible displacement, in
    sensorimotor stage of cognitive
    development, 230
Involvement in child rearing, 573,
    574*t*
  in authoritarian style, 574
  in authoritative style, 573
  in permissive style, 575
  in uninvolved style, 574*t*, 575
Iodine deficiency, prenatal, 104
Iran, motor development of infant
    orphans in, 150
Ireland, infant mortality rate in, 119*f*
Irish Americans, storytelling
    practices of, 451
Iron deficiency, 49, 197
  in pregnancy, 105
Irreversibility, in preoperational stage,
    245
Irritability
  attachment security in, 435
  temperament in, 421, 425, 426, 427
Isolation
  of gifted and creative children, 354
  of homosexual youths, 216
  in psychosocial development, 16*t*
Isolettes for preterm infants, 115
Isotretinoin, 96
Israel
  caregiving roles of mothers and
    fathers in, 437
  corporal punishment in, 602
  infant mortality rate in, 119*f*
  intelligence quotient in, 338, 338*f*
  sleep patterns of infants in, 133

Israeli kibbutzim
  attachment patterns in, 432*f*, 433
  moral development in, 505
  stranger anxiety of infants in, 408
Italy
  adolescent suicide rate in, 472
  caregiving roles of mothers and
    fathers in, 437
  divorce rate in, 591*f*
  family size in, 584
  infant mortality rate in, 119*f*
  math achievement scores in, 558*f*
  menarche in, 184*f*
  religion in, 507

J

Jamaican West Indians, motor
    development of infants, 150
Japan
  academic achievement in, 647, 648
  academic and vocational tracks in,
    645
  adolescent suicide rate in, 472
  attachment patterns in, 432*f*,
    432–433, 436
  caregiving roles of mothers and
    fathers in, 437
  cosleeping of parents and infants
    in, 134
  divorce rate in, 591*f*
  family size in, 584
  infant mortality rate in, 119*f*
  language development in, 378, 379,
    383, 393
  moral development in, 505–506,
    512
  motor development of infants in,
    150
  narrative style in, 393
  physical growth trends in, 184
  self-concept in, 460
  self-conscious emotions in, 409
  self-esteem in, 463
  temperament of infants in, 424
  video games in, 634
Jarara of South America, childbirth
    practices of, 109–110
Jealousy
  in peer relations, 616, 625
  in sibling relationships, 586, 587
Jensen, Arthur, on heritability of
    intelligence, 334–335
Jewish adolescent rites of passage,
    206
Jimi Valley (Papua New Guinea),
    drawings of children in, 242, 242*f*
Job. *See* Employment
Job training, 644–645, 649–650
  apprenticeship programs in, 649
  work–study programs in, 649
Joint attention, 403
  in language development, 371
  and self-awareness, 450
Joint custody of children, 593
Judaism, adolescent rites of passage
    in, 206

Judgments, moral, 497–498, 499
Jumpstart program, 319, 350
Justice, and moral reasoning, 503,
    504, 506
Juvenile delinquency. *See* Delinquency

K

Kaluli of Papua New Guinea, language
    development of, 371, 372, 390
Kangaroo care for preterm infants,
    115–116, 194
Karyotype of chromosomes, 74*f*
Kauai study on birth complications,
    117
Keeping Ourselves Safe, 601
Kenya
  child-rearing practices and
    newborn behavior in, 139
  gender roles in, 535–536, 542
  intelligence quotient in, 338
  mother–infant relationship and
    attachment security in, 434
  motor development of infants in,
    139, 150
Kibbutzim
  attachment patterns in, 432*f*, 433
  moral development in, 505
  stranger anxiety of infants in, 408
Kindergarten
  adjustment to, 641
  readiness for, 641
Kinship studies
  gene–environment correlation in,
    122–123, 123*f*
  heritability estimates in, 120
  intelligence quotient in, 335*f*,
    335–336, 336*f*
  nonshared environmental
    influences in, 346
  twins in. *See* Twins
Kipsigis of Kenya, motor
    development in infancy, 139,
    150
Klinefelter syndrome, 83, 83*t*
Knowledge
  certainty of, 303
  core, 261–266, 326. *See also* Core
    knowledge perspective
  and creativity, 353
  cultural influences on, 340–341
  and episodic memory, 297–298
  metacognitive, 303–304. *See also*
    Metacognition
  milestones of development, 306
  and semantic memory, 296–297
  sociolinguistic, 360, 393
  sources of, 303
Kohlberg, Lawrence
  on gender constancy, 548
  on moral development, 497,
    499–503
Korea
  academic achievement in, 647, 648
  categorization skills in, 235
  cosleeping of parents and infants
    in, 134

infant mortality rate in, 119*f*
information processing speed in,
    281
math achievement scores in, 558*f*
moral development in, 498
Korean Americans, play and peer
    sociability of, 613
Korean language, 378, 379, 388
  and bilingualism, 396
!Kung of Botswana
  child-rearing practices of, 26
  cosleeping of parents and infants,
    134
  culture of, 26
  reaching and grasping by infants,
    152
Kwashiorkor, 196

L

Labeling, gender, 548, 549
Labor and delivery, 107–112. *See also*
    Childbirth
Laboratory experiments, 56–57
  on classical conditioning, 17
  compared to other research
    designs, 61*t*
Lamaze childbirth method, 110
Language acquisition device (LAD),
    360–361, 366
Language development, 359–399
  animal studies of, 361
  in autism, 457
  babbling in, 370, 608
  in bilingualism, 359, 394–397
  brain areas in, 186, 187, 188, 362*f*,
    362–364, 367, 555
  and categorization skills, 235
  components of language in, 360
  comprehension and production of
    words in, 376
  in computer use, 633
  conversational skills in, 390–391
  correlational study of, 56
  cultural influences on, 339–340,
    341
  in deaf children, 362–363, 372
  early intervention programs
    affecting, 348, 351
  and emotional self-regulation, 410,
    411
  and empathy, 417
  first speech sounds in, 370
  first words in, 370, 373–374, 376,
    376*t*
  gender typing in, 539, 540–541
  generic references to gender in,
    540–541, 541*f*
  grammatical, 360, 384–390. *See
    also* Grammatical development
  home environment affecting, 345
  in infancy, 155–158, 301
  infant-directed speech in, 369,
    374
  information-processing theories of,
    366–367
  interactionist theories of, 366–367

intermodal perception in, 168
joint attention in, 371
language-making capacity in, 389
learning native language sound
categories and patterns in,
368–369
and linguistic intelligence, 325t,
326
and memory, 295, 301, 301f
and metacognitive knowledge, 304
metalinguistic awareness in, 394
milestones of, 395
narratives in, 392–393
nativist theory of, 360–365
parent–child interaction in, 372,
378, 378f, 389–390
phonological, 360, 373–375. See
also Phonological development
pragmatic, 360, 390–393. See also
Pragmatic language development
prelinguistic, 368–373. See also
Prelinguistic development
private speech in, 266–267
reading in, 307–310. See also
Reading
referential communication skills in,
391–392
semantic, 360, 376–383. See also
Semantic development
sensitive period in, 364–365, 370
sex differences in, 554–555
in social interaction, 367, 371
sociolinguistic understanding in,
360, 393
speech registers in, 393
and symbolic understanding, 236
television viewing affecting, 237
theories of, 360–368
theory of mind in, 455
turn-taking pattern of conversation
in, 371
visual discrimination in, 368
in visual impairment, 162
in Williams syndrome, 366
Language immersion programs in
bilingualism, 397
Lanugo, 92
Latency stage of psychosexual
development, 16t
Lateralization of brain, 187, 189
and handedness, 187, 189
and language development, 363
Latin America, academic
achievement beliefs of
immigrants from, 345
Latvia
body size in, 183
corporal punishment in, 602
Laughter in infancy and toddlerhood,
406–407
Lead exposure, 193, 193f
prenatal, 101
Leapfrog narratives, 392
Learned helplessness, 465–466, 466f,
467
attribution retraining in, 467

Learning
attention in, 287
class size affecting, 637
in classical conditioning, 140f,
140–141
cognitive-developmental theory
on, 259–260
and cognitive self-regulation, 305
cooperative, 271–272, 640, 646
culture-specific, sensitive period
for, 156
by discovery, 259, 269
of gender roles, 543–544
in guided participation, 268
in habituation, 142–145
in imitation, 145f, 145–146
individual differences in, 259
in infancy and toddlerhood, 133,
139–146, 157
information processing in,
307–314
in least restrictive environment,
646
in mastery-oriented attributions,
465
mathematics in, 310–313
media multitasking affecting, 293
and memory, 280, 293, 297
of native language sound categories
and patterns, 368–369
observational, 543–544
in operant conditioning, 141f,
141–142
peer collaboration in, 269
planning in, 291
readiness for, 226, 259, 308, 308f,
351
reading in, 307–310
recess time affecting, 639
in reciprocal teaching, 271
in scaffolding, 268
scientific reasoning in, 313–314
of second language, 364–365, 365f
in semantic development, 382–383
in service-learning programs, 508
social, 18–19. See also Social
learning
sociocultural theory on, 25
speech–gesture mismatches in,
285
statistical learning capacity in
infants, 157, 367, 369
symbolic understanding in,
235–236
from television and videos, 237,
632
Learning disabilities, 646
Learning goals in mastery-oriented
attributions, 465
Left-handedness, 187, 189
Legal issues and proceedings
in child maltreatment, 602
in divorce mediation, 593–594
eyewitness testimony by children
in, 300–302
in gay and lesbian families, 589

No Child Left Behind Act in, 343,
638, 647
in reproductive technologies,
86–87
Lens of eye, 159
Leptin, 204
Lesbian and gay population, 215–216
dating of adolescents, 625
as parents, 589–590
Licensing of child-care facilities, 443,
597, 598
Linguistic development. See
Language development
Linguistic intelligence, 325t, 326
Linguistic knowledge
in core-knowledge perspective, 262
in theory of multiple intelligences,
325t, 326
Literacy. See also Reading
emergent, 307–309
and semantic development, 378,
378f
sex differences in, 554–555, 555f
Lithuania, infant mortality rate in,
119f
Locke, John, 12
Logical necessity in propositional
thought, 258
Logical thought
in concrete operational stage, 252
in formal operational stage, 258
in preoperational stage, 246–247
Logico-mathematical intelligence,
325t, 326
Longitudinal research, 60–62
on adolescent pregnancy, 218–219
biased sampling in, 61–62
cohort effects in, 62
compared to other research
designs, 65t
on lead exposure, 193
on overweight children, 198
practice effects in, 62
on pubertal timing, 205
selective attrition in, 62
sequential design, 63f, 63–64
on temperament, 417–418
Long-term memory, 278, 279f, 280
retrieval of information from, 280,
295
Lorenz, Konrad, 23, 429
Low birth weight, 113–117
behavioral assessment in, 139
drugs associated with, 97
in environmental pollution, 101
and exercise during pregnancy,
103
infectious diseases associated with,
102t
long term outcomes in, 116–117
mortality rate in, 118
of small-for-date infants, 114
and smoking during pregnancy, 98
and stress during pregnancy, 105
in teenage pregnancies, 218
very low, 116–117

Low-income households
mathematics skills in, 311
reading readiness in, 308, 308f
Loyalty in friendships, 614, 615
Luxembourg, infant mortality rate in,
119f
Lying, 497–498

M

Macrosystem in ecological systems
theory, 27f, 28, 29
public policy in, 33
Madagascar, biological knowledge of
children in, 265
Magical thinking in preoperational
stage, 246
Magnesium in pregnancy, 104
Magnet schools, 644, 645
Magnetic resonance imaging
functional. See Functional
magnetic resonance imaging
ultrafast, in pregnancy, 85t
Make-believe play, 455
benefits of, 240–241
cognitive-developmental theory,
239–240
cultural influences on, 52, 270,
613
development of, 239–240
in early childhood, 5, 239–240,
609–610, 609t
emotional understanding in, 416
imaginary companions in, 240
narratives in, 392
in preoperational stage, 239–240
in sensorimotor stage, 230, 233
social origins of, 270
sociocultural theory on, 269, 270
strategies enhancing, 241
Making Choices program, 481
Malaria
in pregnancy, 102t
sickle cell allele and resistance to, 79
Male and female differences. See Sex
differences
Mali
attachment patterns in, 432
reaching and grasping by infants
in, 152
Malnutrition, 196–198
in anorexia nervosa, 210–211
and infectious diseases, 201
prenatal, 104–105, 114, 197
pubertal development in, 205
temperament development in, 197,
424
Maltreatment of children, 599–604.
See also Child maltreatment
Mandarin-speaking children, 376,
376t, 378
Map skills, 250f, 250–251, 251f
Marasmus, 196, 197
Marfan syndrome, 78t, 85
Marijuana use
in adolescence, 626, 626f
in pregnancy, 98

Marital relationship
and adolescent pregnancy, 218
and divorce, 590–594
ecological systems theory on, 27
in effective coparenting, 569, 571
observational research on, 45
and sibling relationships, 586
in transition to parenthood, 570
Mastery-oriented attributions,
465–466, 466f, 467–468
Matching technique in experimental
research, 58
Maternal age
in Down syndrome, 82, 82t
in fraternal twinning, 76, 77t
and genetic counseling, 84
and prenatal development, 106, 106f
and prenatal diagnostic methods, 84
in reproductive technologies, 86, 87
in teenage pregnancy, 106, 217–220
Maternal factors. See Mothers
Mathematical abilities, 310–313
in Asia, 312–313
cardinality in, 311
cross-national research on, 647f, 648
in early childhood, 310–311
estimations in, 311
gender stereotypes on, 532, 533,
541, 555–558, 558f
in infancy and toddlerhood,
262–264, 264f, 310
information processing in, 310–313
and logico-mathematical
intelligence, 325t, 326
in middle childhood, 252, 311–313
min strategy in, 284, 285, 311
in multiple intelligences theory,
325t
ordinality in, 310
sex differences in, 555–558, 558f
sociocultural theory on, 25
and spatial skills, 556–557, 558
Matters of personal choice, 510,
511–512
Maturation
of brain, 184–192
cognitive. See Cognitive
development
emotional and social. See Emotional
and social development
Hall and Gesell on, 13
moral. See Moral development
motor development in. See Motor
development
physical. See Physical development
Rousseau on, 12
sexual, 183, 203–204, 208–210
Maturational timing, pubertal,
208–210
Mayans
body size of, 183
childbirth practices of, 110
communication style of, 340
cosleeping of parents and infants,
134
growth rate of, 183

language development of, 371, 372
memory strategies of, 294
observational learning of, 273
play of, 613
MDMA (Ecstasy), 626
Mead, Margaret, 205
Mealtimes in family, 29, 196, 393,
582, 582f
Means–end action sequences, in
sensorimotor stage of cognitive
development, 229
Measles, 201
Media, 629–637
cell phones, 293, 629, 632,
634–635, 636
computers, 293, 629f, 632–635
and multitasking, impact on
learning, 293
regulating use of, 635–636
television, 629–632. See also
Television
Mediation services in divorce, 593
Medicaid, 36
Medical insurance, public policies on,
33
Medieval view of childhood, 10–11
Meiosis, 75, 75f
chromosomal abnormalities
occurring in, 82
Melatonin, 133
Memory, 292–302
accuracy of, 296, 300, 302
and attention, 288, 289
autobiographical, 298–300, 450–451.
See also Autobiographical
memory
and cognitive self-regulation, 304
constructive, 295
context-dependent, 144
cultural influences on, 294, 299
and deferred imitation, 233
elaboration strategy for, 293, 295,
299
emotions affecting, 402
episodic, 297–300
explicit, 293, 301
and eyewitness testimony by
children, 300–302, 454
fuzzy-trace theory of, 296
gist, 296, 296f, 300
in habituation, 142–145, 143f, 144f
hippocampus in, 190, 293, 301
implicit, 293, 301
and infantile amnesia, 300, 301
in infants of diabetic mothers, 49
inhibition affecting, 288, 300
language development affecting,
295, 301, 301f
and learning, 280, 293, 297
long-term, 278, 279f, 280, 295
in media multitasking, 293
nonverbal, 301, 301f
in operant conditioning, 141f,
141–142
organization strategy for, 292, 293,
295, 298, 304

phonological, 381
in planning, 290
prenatal iron deficiency affecting,
49, 282
recall, 145, 295–296, 376. See also
Recall memory
recent, of infants, 143, 144t
recognition, 145, 294, 295, 376
reconstructed, 295–296, 298, 437
rehearsal strategy for, 292, 293, 304
and remembered self, 450–451
remote, of infants, 143, 144t
retrieval of information from, 280,
281, 281f, 294–296
schooling affecting, 294
scripts in, 298
semantic, 296–297
and semantic development, 376,
381
short-term, 278–279, 279f. See also
Short-term memory
store model of, 278–279, 279f
strategies for, 292–294
television viewing affecting, 237
verbatim, 296, 296f
working. See Working memory
Menarche, 203
individual and group differences
in, 204, 205
reactions to, 206
secular trends in, 184, 184f
Menopause, reproductive
technologies in, 87
Menstrual cycle, 88, 203
estrogen in, 183
first. See Menarche
Mental development. See Cognitive
development
Mental representation, 227
and categorization skills, 233–235,
234f
in concrete operational stage, 250
dual, 243
in preoperational stage, 239–243
and problem-solving skills, 235
in sensorimotor stage, 228t, 230,
232–236
and symbolic understanding,
235–236
Mental rotation tasks, sex differences
in, 556, 556f, 557
Mental strategies in information
processing, 278, 315t
attentional, 288–289
and cognitive self-regulation, 304
control deficiency in, 288, 292
effective use of, 289
for memory, 292–294
and metacognitive knowledge, 304
min strategy in, 284, 285, 311
neo-Piagetian theory of, 283
production deficiency in, 288
strategy choice model of, 284–286
utilization deficiency in, 289, 292
Mental testing movement, 13–14. See
also Intelligence tests

Mercury, 202
prenatal exposure to, 101
Mesoderm, formation of, 91
Mesosystem in ecological systems
theory, 27f, 27–28, 29, 571
Meta-analysis of gender stereotypes,
553
Metacognition, 303–305, 315t, 452
awareness of cognitive capacities
in, 303–304
and cognitive self-regulation,
304–305
and emotional understanding, 416
and mental strategies, 304
milestones of development, 306
and moral development, 509
and scientific reasoning, 314
and self-control, 515–516
and social cognition, 447
and theory of mind, 303
Metalinguistic awareness, 394
Metaphors in semantic development,
380, 381
Methadone in pregnancy, 97
Mexican Americans
child-rearing practices of, 582, 583
ethnic identity of, 475
intelligence definition of, 324
sibling relationships of, 587
Mexico
childbirth practices in, 110
concrete operational stage in, 252
diet of children in, 196
gay and lesbian families in, 589
language development in, 371
make-believe play in, 270
motor development of infants in,
150
observational learning in, 273
social interaction and learning in,
25
Zinacanteco Indians in. See
Zinacanteco Indians
Microcosms of development, 64–65
Microgenetic research, 64–65, 65t
compared to other research
designs, 65t
on motor development in infants,
149
on speech–gesture mismatches,
285
on strategy-choice model, 286
Microsystem in ecological systems
theory, 27, 29
Middle childhood (6 to 11 years
old), 6
aggression in, 517, 518
body composition in, 177
body proportions in, 177
body size in, 176, 177f
child-rearing practices in, 577
cognitive development in, 249–253,
303, 304
concrete operational stage in, 20,
20t, 249–253. See also Concrete
operational stage

coregulation in, 577
divorce of parents during, 591–592
empathy in, 417
friendships in, 614, 615, 617
gender identity in, 549f, 549–550, 553
gender stereotypes in, 532–533, 534, 539–542, 553
gender typing in, 553
height in, 176
home environment in, 344, 345
information processing in, 306, 309–310, 311–313
language development in, 380–381, 388, 395
mathematics in, 311–313
memory in, 292, 293, 299, 306
metacognition in, 303, 304, 306
metalinguistic awareness in, 394
milestones of development, 253
moral development in, 498, 511, 512, 513
motor development in, 178–179, 180
peer relations in, 610–611, 614, 619, 628
planning in, 290
play in, 610
psychosexual and psychosocial development in, 16t
reading in, 309–310
reasoning about beliefs in, 453–454
self-concept in, 458, 459, 460
self-conscious emotions in, 409, 416
self-esteem in, 462, 463, 469
sibling relationships in, 586–587
television viewing in, 631
Middle East, sexual attitudes and behavior in, 212
Milestones
in aggression, 517
in brain development, 185, 185f
in cognitive development, 238, 248, 253, 306
in concrete operational stage, 253
in emotional development, 419
in gender typing, 553
in information processing, 306
in language development, 395
in moral development, 513
in motor development, 147, 148, 162, 179
in peer relations, 628
in perceptual development, 158
in prenatal development, 90
in preoperational stage, 248
in puberty, 204
in self-concept, 460
in self-control, 517
in self-esteem development, 469
in sensorimotor stage, 238
in visual development, 167
Min strategy, 284, 285, 311
Mindblindness, and autism, 457
Mirror neurons, 146

Mirror self-recognition of infants, 449, 450
Miscarriage
in caffeine use, 97
diethylstilbestrol prescribed for prevention of, 96
in fetal surgery, 85
gender of fetus in, 80
in infectious diseases, 102t
in malnutrition, 104
in radiation exposure, 81, 100
in stress, 105
in tobacco use, 98
Mistrust in psychosocial development, 16t
Mitosis, 74
chromosomal abnormalities occurring in, 82
Modeling
behavior modification in, 18
and deferred imitation, 233
gender typing in, 547
moral development in, 490–491
social learning theory on, 18
of sympathy, 418
Modifier genes, 79
Monkeys and apes
attachment of, 428
imitation by, 145, 145f, 146
infant discrimination of human and monkey faces, 156
language acquisition of, 361
moral-like rules of, 486
Monozygotic twins, 76. See also Identical twins
Montessori schools, 639–640
Mood quality and temperament, 420t
Moodiness in adolescence, 207, 207f
Moral development, 485–527
and aggression, 516–525
authority figures in, 498, 500, 511
and behavior, 485, 506–507
biological theories of, 486–488
and civic responsibility, 508
and cognitive development, 485, 495, 496–499, 502–503, 505, 506, 507
conventional level of, 501
cooperation in, 497, 501
cultural influences on, 497–498, 503–504, 505–506, 512
domain approach to, 510–513
education affecting, 505, 507, 508
and emotional development, 485, 503
evolution of, 486–488
good boy–good girl orientation in, 501
instrumental purpose orientation in, 500–501, 509
internalization in, 488, 494, 513
Kohlberg on, 497, 499–503
milestones of, 513
peer interaction affecting, 505
Piaget on, 496–499

postconventional or principled level of, 501–502, 509
preconventional level of, 500–501
psychoanalytic theory of, 488–490
religion in, 507–509
Rousseau on, 12
self-control in, 514–516
sex differences in, 503–504, 504f
social contract orientation in, 501
social conventions in, 510–511, 512
social learning theory on, 490–494
social norms in, 488–496
social-order-maintaining orientation in, 501, 509
social understanding in, 496–514
stages of, 500–503
universal ethical principle orientation in, 502
Moral imperatives, 510, 511
Moral Judgment Interview, 499, 500, 502
Morality, 485, 486–514
of cooperation, 497, 498, 501
heteronomous, 496, 498
pragmatic approach to, 509, 510
Moratorium in identity development, 470, 470t, 471, 473
ethnic, 475
Moro reflex, 130, 130t
Morphemes, grammatical, 386–387
order of acquisition, 387t
Morphology in grammatical development, 360, 394
Mortality. See Death
Mosaic pattern of chromosomes, 82
Mothers
adolescent, 106, 217–220
age of. See Maternal age
and attachment security of infant, 434, 435, 435f
in blended families, 594–595
blood analysis during pregnancy, 85, 85t
child maltreatment by, 600
depression of, 404, 432, 435, 436
divorce of, 591, 592
in effective coparenting, 569, 571
emotional sensitivity of, 559
employment of, 595–596
extended family relationships of, 583
first child of, 570
and gender equality in Sweden, 536
gender typing of children by, 542
homosexual, 589–590
of newborn, 570
play activities of, 270, 612
pregnancy of. See Pregnancy
of preterm infants, 115
sibling preferences of, 586
in single-parent families, 590
Mother–stepfather families, 594–595
Motion, infant perception of, 160
object identity in, 165f, 165–166
Motivation
for achievement, 465

for creativity, 353–354
moral, 506
Motor development
and bodily-kinesthetic intelligence, 325t
canalization concept on, 122
cerebellum in, 189
cerebral cortex in, 186
cultural variations in, 150, 152
and depth perception, 160–161
and differentiation theory on perceptual development, 169, 169f
in Down syndrome, 82
dynamic systems perspective of, 147–150, 178
in fetal alcohol spectrum disorder, 99
fine-motor skills in, 147, 150–152, 162, 180
gross-motor skills in, 147, 178–181, 179
in infancy, 147–152
in low birth weight, 114
microgenetic studies of, 149
milestones of, 147, 148, 162, 179
prenatal drug exposure affecting, 96, 97
reaching in. See Reaching
reflexes in, 131
in sensorimotor stage. See Sensorimotor stage
sequence of, 147
sex differences in, 179, 180
and sports activities, 179–181
in visual impairment, 162
Movement, infant perception of, 160
object identity in, 165f, 165–166
Mozart effect, 59
Multicultural research, 51–53. See also Cultural influences
Multigrade classrooms, 644
Multiple attachments, 437–439
Multiple births, 76–77
low birth weight in, 114
twin. See Twins
Multiple intelligences theory of Gardner, 325t, 325–326, 354–355
Multiplication problems in mathematics, 311–312
Multisystemic therapy in antisocial behavior, 525, 525f
Multitasking in media use, impact on learning, 293
Mumps in pregnancy, 102t
Munduruku people of Brazil, numerical knowledge of, 264
Muscle development, 177
of newborn, Apgar Scale on, 109t
Muscular dystrophy, Duchenne, 78t, 85
Music
infant recognition of, 155, 156
and intelligence test scores after music lessons, 59, 59f
intermodal perception of, 168

Music (*cont.*)
  and Mozart effect, 59
  in multiple intelligences theory, 325*t*
  and sensitive period for culture-specific learning, 156
Mutations, 81
  germline, 81
  somatic, 81
Mutual exclusivity bias in semantic development, 382
Myelination of nerves, 186

N

Naïve theories, 264–265
Naps, and learning capacity of infants, 133
Narcissism, 464
  and aggression, 522
Narratives
  and autobiographical memory, 450–451
  chronological, 392
  coherent, 474
  cultural variations in, 451
  leapfrog, 392
  in pragmatic language development, 392–393
  and remembered self, 450–451
National Assessment of Educational Progress, 648
National Association for Family Child Care, 441, 598
National Association for the Education of Young Children, 441, 597, 598
National Center for Children in Poverty, 37
National Longitudinal Survey of Youth (NLSY), 584–585, 585*f*
Native Americans
  communication style of, 340
  drug use of, 626
  fetal alcohol syndrome in, 100
  grandparents as primary caregivers of, 438
  infant mortality rate of, 118
  neonatal behavioral assessment of, 139
  obesity of, 199–200
  poverty of, 33
  in segregated schools, 479
  suicide rate in adolescence, 472–473
Native Canadians
  communication style of, 340
  cosleeping of parents and infants, 134
  grammatical development of, 385, 388
  identity development of, 474
  out-group favoritism, 477
  in segregated schools, 479
Nativist theory of language development, 360–365
  limitations of, 365

Natural childbirth, 110–111
  social support during, 111
Natural experiments, 58–60, 60*f*
  compared to other research designs, 61*t*
Natural selection
  Darwin on, 13
  in strategy choice model of information processing, 284
Naturalist intelligence, 325*t*
Naturalistic observation research method, 42–44, 43*t*
Nature, and relative influence of nurture, 8–9, 32*t*, 118–124
  in adolescence, 205
  Baldwin on, 14
  in behavioral genetics, 119–120
  bidirectional influences in, 124
  in canalization concept, 122
  in child-rearing practices, 577, 578
  in disorganized/disoriented attachment, 435, 435*f*
  and environmental influences on gene expression, 123–124
  in epigenetic framework, 124, 124*f*, 125
  in executive function, 282
  gene–environment correlation in, 122–123
  gene–environment interaction in, 121*f*, 121–122
  heritability estimates on, 120–121
  in home environment, 345
  in homosexuality, 215
  in intelligence, 120, 121, 334–335
  Locke on, 12
  Rousseau on, 12
  in temperament, 426–427
Near-infrared spectroscopy (NIRS), 48*t*, 50, 50*f*
Negatives in grammatical development, 387
Neglect, 599, 600
  by peers, 619, 620
  in uninvolved child rearing, 575
Neighborhood influences. *See* Community influences
Neonatal Behavioral Assessment Scale (NBAS), 138–139
Neonatal Intensive Care Unit Network Neurobehavioral Scale (NNNS), 139
Neonates. *See* Newborns
Neo-Piagetian theory, 261, 282, 283–284, 314, 315
Nepal, emotional display rules in, 413
Nervous system
  autonomic, 47*n*, 47–48
  brain in, 184–192. *See also* Brain
  neurons in, 185–186. *See also* Neurons
  prenatal development of, 91, 92–93, 104
Netherlands
  academic achievement in, 647
  adolescent suicide rate in, 472

adoption in, 588
attachment experience of parents in, 436
divorce rate in, 591*f*
gay and lesbian families in, 589
generational gains in IQ in, 338, 338*f*
home births in, 111
immunization rate in, 201
infant mortality rate in, 119*f*
maternity helpers in, 118
menarche in, 184*f*
prenatal malnutrition in, 104
reproductive technology laws in, 87
Neural tube formation, 91, 185
  in fetal alcohol spectrum disorder, 99
  folic acid affecting, 104, 105*f*
Neurobiological research, 43*t*, 47–50
  on development of institutionalized infants, 170–171
  reliability of, 54
  on temperament, 421, 422
Neurodevelopmental disorder, alcohol-related, 99, 99*t*
Neuroimaging techniques, 50, 50*f*
Neurons
  development of, 91, 92, 185–186
  in fetal alcohol spectrum disorder, 99
  mirror, 146
Neuroscience, developmental cognitive, 23
Neurotransmitters, 185
Neutral stimulus, 140, 140*f*
Never-married single-parent families, 590
Newborns
  adaptation to labor and delivery, 108
  anesthesia during birth affecting, 112
  Apgar Scale on, 109, 109*t*
  appearance of, 109, 129
  arousal states of, 132*t*, 132–138
  behavioral assessment of, 138–139
  breastfeeding of. *See* Breastfeeding
  crying of, 132, 132*t*, 133, 135–138, 417
  empathy of, 135–136, 417
  family adjustment to, 570
  and first-time parents, 570
  habituation and recovery of, 142
  hand movements and prereaching of, 150, 151*f*
  imitation by, 145*f*, 145–146
  with low birth weight. *See* Low birth weight
  mortality rate for, 118. *See also* Infant mortality
  oxygen deprivation during birth, 112–113
  perceptual development of, 152–169

preterm, 113–116. *See also* Preterm infants
  reflexes of, 109*t*, 130*t*, 130–132
  sleep patterns of, 132*t*, 132–135
  small for date, 114
New York Longitudinal Study, 417–418
New Zealand
  adolescent suicide rate in, 472
  child-care facilities in, 441
  infant mortality rate in, 119*f*
  make-believe play in, 270
  overweight and obesity rate in, 198
  physical growth trends in, 184
  reproductive technology laws in, 87
  sexual abuse prevention programs in, 601
Nicaragua, sign language in, 362–363
Niche-picking, 123, 336
Nicotine. *See* Smoking
Nigeria, conservation tasks in, 252
No Child Left Behind Act, 343, 638, 647
Noble savages, Rousseau view of children as, 12
Non-rapid-eye-movement (NREM) sleep, 133, 135, 135*f*
Nonshared environmental influences, 344, 346
  on attachment patterns, 435
  on intelligence, 346
  on temperament development, 424–425
Nonverbal memory, 301, 301*f*
Normal distribution of intelligence test scores, 330, 330*f*
Normative approach, 13
Norms, societal, 488–496
  internalization of, 488, 494, 513
Norway
  body size in, 183
  corporal punishment in, 602
  gay and lesbian families in, 589
  generational gains in IQ in, 338, 338*f*
  immunization in, 201
  infant mortality rate in, 119*f*
  math achievement scores in, 558*f*
  moral reasoning in, 503–504
  poverty in, 33
Novelty
  preference for, 143, 144*f*, 156
  temperament affecting reaction to, 422
Nso people of Cameroon, self-recognition by toddlers, 450, 450*f*
Nuclear power plant accidents, radiation exposure in, 100–101
Nucleus of cells, 73, 75
  chromosomes in, 73
Numerical knowledge. *See also* Mathematical abilities
  in infancy, 262–264, 264*f*
Nurse–Family Partnership, 220, 603

Nurse-midwives, certified, 111
Nurture
    Locke on, 12
    and relative influence of nature,
        8–9, 32t. See also Nature, and
        relative influence of nurture
Nutrition, 195–196
    in adolescence, 196, 204, 210–212
    and body size variations
        worldwide, 183
    in breastfeeding and bottle-feeding,
        194–195
    in early intervention programs,
        348, 349
    and eating habits. See Eating
        habits
    and fraternal twinning, 77t
    and infectious diseases, 201
    and lead exposure impact, 193
    and malnutrition, 196–198. See
        also Malnutrition
    mercury exposure from seafood in,
        101
    and obesity, 198–200
    in phenylketonuria, 77–79
    and physical growth, 183, 184, 192,
        194–200
    in pregnancy, 77t, 101, 103–105,
        114, 197
    in puberty, 196
    toxoplasmosis from food in, 103
    WIC program for, 35
Nyansongo of Kenya, gender roles in,
    535–536, 542

O

Obedience
    and gender typing, 542
    and heteronomous morality, 496
    in preconventional level of moral
        development, 500
Obesity, 198–200
    causes of, 198–200
    consequences of, 200
    menarche in, 184, 205
    in Prader-Willi syndrome, 80
    treatment of, 200
Object perception, 164–166, 165f
    eye tracking in, 165, 231, 232f
    habituation in, 165, 165f
    milestones of development, 167
    in movement, 165f, 165–166
    shape constancy in, 165
    size constancy in, 164
Object permanence
    and predictive eye tracking, 231,
        232f
    and searching for hidden objects,
        232
    in sensorimotor stage, 229,
        230–231, 231f, 232
    and separation anxiety, 429
    violation-of-expectation studies on,
        230–231, 231f
Object words in semantic
    development, 379

Objects
    categorization of. See
        Categorization abilities
    in conservation tasks. See
        Conservation
    hidden. See Hidden objects,
        searching for
    manipulation in severe visual
        impairment, 162
    physical knowledge of, in infancy,
        262, 263f
    seriation of, 250
    solidity of, 262, 263f
    sorting tasks, 287
    support of, infant awareness of,
        262
Observational learning, 18
    gender typing in, 543–544
Observational research, 42–46
    bias in, 45
    on culture, 51, 52
    event sampling in, 44
    influence of observer in, 45
    limitations of, 45–46
    naturalistic, 42–44, 43t
    participant observations in, 52
    reliability of, 54
    structured, 43t, 44
    on temperament, 421
    time sampling in, 45
    validity of, 54
Observer bias and influence, 45
Occupation. See Employment
Odor perception
    milestones of development, 158
    of newborn, 153, 154f, 154–155
One-child families, 587–588
Operant conditioning, 17, 141f,
    141–142
    and emotional expressions, 414
    and moral development, 490
Operations, 243, 249
    and concrete operational stage,
        249–253
    and formal operational stage,
        253–259
    and preoperational stage, 239–249
Oppositional behavior, and
    aggression, 519
Oral rehydration therapy (ORT), 201
Oral stage of psychosexual
    development, 15, 16t
Ordinality, 310
Organization
    in cognitive development, 227, 260
    as memory strategy, 292, 293, 295,
        298, 304
Orphanages. See Institutionalization
Out-groups, 477–478, 612
    favoritism toward, 477
    negativity toward, 532
    prejudice against, 477, 543, 616
Output, behavioral response as, 21
Ovaries, 88, 88f
Overactivity, in attention-deficit
    hyperactivity disorder, 290

Overextensions in semantic
    development, 380
Overlapping-waves pattern in
    strategy-choice model, 284, 284f
Overregularization in grammatical
    development, 386–387
Overweight, 198–200. See also
    Obesity
Ovulation, 88, 89
Ovum, 75f, 75–76
    aging of, 76
    and conception, 88–89
    in menstrual cycle, 88
    in reproductive technologies, 86,
        87
Oxygen deprivation
    in fetal alcohol syndrome, 99
    of infant during childbirth,
        112–113
    in sickle cell anemia, 79
Oxytocin, 191

P

Pacific Islanders
    adolescence of, 205
    birth complications of, 117
    body size of, 183
    childbirth practices of, 109–110
    child-rearing practices of, 582
    obesity of, 200
    sexual attitudes and behavior of,
        212
Pain
    in childbirth, medications for, 112
    newborn sensitivity to, 153
Palate
    cleft lip and palate, 98, 104
    embryonic development of, 95f, 96
Palmar grasp reflex, 130t, 130–131
Papua New Guinea
    drawings of children in, 242, 242f
    language development in, 371, 372,
        390
    sexual attitudes and behavior in,
        212
Parallel play, 608, 609
Parasitic diseases in pregnancy, 102t,
    103
Parasympathetic nervous system, 47n
Parent(s)
    academic achievement beliefs of,
        345–346, 556–557
    access to information and services,
        572
    and adolescent relationship. See
        Parent–adolescent relationship
    adolescents as, 106, 217–220
    adoption by, 588–589. See also
        Adoption
    attachment experiences of, 436t,
        436–437
    in blended families, 594–595
    child maltreatment by, 599–604,
        600t
    and child relationship. See Parent–
        child relationship

child-rearing practices of, 573–584.
        See also Child-rearing practices
    deaf, 372
    depression of, 402, 403, 559
    divorce of, 590–594
    in early intervention programs,
        348, 349
    emotional sensitivity of, 559
    employment of, 595–596
    gender stereotypes of, 539–542
    and home environment, 344–346
    homosexual, 589–590
    and infant relationship. See Parent–
        infant relationship
    infants sleeping with, 133, 134
    leave time from employment,
        34–35, 118–119, 536, 570
    of newborn, 570
    in observational research, 45
    school involvement of, 647
    self-worth of, 572
    sibling preferences of, 586
    in single-parent families. See
        Single-parent families
    training programs for, 220,
        523–524, 578, 587, 593, 595, 603
Parent–adolescent relationship, 576,
    577–580
    in anorexia nervosa, 211
    bidirectional influences in, 576
    conflict in, 208, 571, 579, 580
    and contraceptive use, 215
    and peer relations, 611
    in school transitions, 642
    separation in, 208
    and sexual activity of adolescent,
        214
    in teenage pregnancy, 214, 219
Parent–child relationship
    and achievement attributions,
        466–467, 468
    and aggression, 520–522, 561–562
    and autobiographical memory,
        299
    bidirectional influences in, 576
    in blended families, 594–595
    caregiving roles of mothers and
        fathers in, 437–438
    and cognitive self-regulation, 305
    compared to peer influence, 578
    continuity of caregiving in, 440
    correlational studies on, 56, 57f
    of deaf children, 372
    depression of parent affecting, 404
    direct influences of, 569
    and eating habits, 196, 199
    in effective coparenting, 569, 571
    and emotional self-regulation of
        child, 411
    and empathy development, 418
    experimental research on, 58
    family chaos affecting, 29
    gender typing in, 539–542
    and identity development, 475
    and intelligence quotient changes,
        331

Parent–child relationship (*cont.*)
  and language development, 372, 378, 378*f*, 389–390
  in maternal employment, 595–596
  in middle childhood, 577
  and moral development, 488–495, 504
  in one-child families, 587–588
  and peer relations, 611–612
  play in, 437, 438, 439, 611–612
  in psychosexual theory of development, 15
  and pubertal timing, 205, 210
  reading in, 319
  and resilience in child, 11
  scaffolding in, 268–269
  and self-esteem, 464
  socialization in, 573–584
  and temperament development, 422
  visual impairment of child affecting, 162
Parent–infant relationship
  attachment in, 24, 428, 429, 437–438
  caregiving roles of mothers and fathers in, 437–438
  classical conditioning in, 140, 140*f*
  depression of parent affecting, 404
  and emotional self-regulation by infant, 410
  facial expressions in, 402–403, 406
  in growth faltering, 202
  imitation in, 146
  infant characteristics affecting, 435
  interactional synchrony in, 434, 437
  intermodal stimulation in, 168
  in !Kung society of Botswana, 26
  and language development, 157–158
  make-believe play in, 270
  malnutrition affecting, 105
  and motor development of infants, 147
  operant conditioning in, 142
  in preterm infants, 114–115, 116
  in sensitive caregiving, 434, 435, 437
  and sleeping arrangements, 133, 134
  touch in, 154
  visual impairment of infant affecting, 162, 405
Parents Anonymous, 603
Parent–school partnership, 647
Partial fetal alcohol syndrome, 99, 99*t*
Participant observation in ethnography, 52
Passive correlation of genetic and environmental factors, 122
Passive smoking, 98
Passive voice in grammatical development, 388
Paternal factors. *See* Fathers

Pattern perception, 161*f*, 161–163, 163*f*
  contrast sensitivity in, 161, 161*f*, 163
  and face perception, 163–164, 164*f*. *See also* Face perception
  milestones of development, 167
Pavlov, Ivan, 17
PCBs (polychlorinated biphenyls), 101
PCP (phencyclidine) use in adolescence, 626
Pedigree, in genetic counseling, 84
Peer acceptance, 618–622
  intervention programs, 620–622
  learning disabilities and, 646
  in obesity, 200
  of only children, 587
  pubertal timing affecting, 209
Peer collaboration in education, 269
  in cooperative learning, 271–272
Peer conformity, 625–627
Peer culture, 622
  conformity to, 625–627
Peer groups, 622–624
  milestones of development, 628
Peer pressure, 625–627
Peer relations, 607–628
  acceptance in, 200, 209, 618–622
  in adolescence, 209, 610–611, 614, 619, 624–627, 628
  age mix affecting, 612
  aggression in, 518, 562, 616, 617, 623
  bullying in, 620, 621
  cell phone use in, 634–635
  in cliques, 623–624
  conformity in, 625–627
  cultural influences on, 612–613
  dating in, 624–625
  development of, 608–611
  dominance hierarchy in, 610
  in early childhood, 608–610, 611, 614, 628
  friendships in, 613–618, 628
  gender roles in, 617
  gender segregation in, 537, 544
  and gender typing, 544–546
  in groups, 622–624, 628
  in identity development, 473, 475
  in infancy and toddlerhood, 608, 628
  influence on development, 578
  and intelligence quotient, 333
  maturational timing affecting, 209
  in middle childhood, 610–611, 614, 619, 628
  milestones of development, 628
  and moral development, 505
  in obesity, 200
  observational research on, 44
  parental influences on, 611–612
  popularity in, 617, 618–622
  pressure and conformity in, 625–627
  of resilient children, 11

in school recess, 639
  in school transitions, 642
  self-awareness in, 450
  and self-concept, 459
  sex differences in, 617
  sexist remarks in, 545, 545*f*
  sociability in, 608–613
  social problem solving in, 480*f*, 480–481
  of special needs students, 646
  victimization in, 621
  in visual impairment, 162
Peer sociability, 608–613, 628
Peer victimization, 621
Pendulum problem, 254, 254*f*
Penis, 203, 204
Perceptual development, 152–171, 448
  amodal properties in, 166, 168
  deprivation affecting, 169–171
  differentiation theory of, 168–169, 169*f*
  and habituation of infants, 142–143, 143*f*, 144
  of hearing, 155–158
  intermodal, 166–168
  milestones of, 158
  perceptual narrowing effect in, 156, 164
  of smell sense, 154–155, 158
  of taste sense, 154, 158
  of touch sense, 153–154, 158
  of vision, 158–166, 167
Performance goals in learned helplessness, 466
Periods of development, 5–6
  adolescence, 6. *See also* Adolescence
  cultural influences on, 6
  early childhood, 5–6. *See also* Early childhood
  emerging adulthood, 6
  infancy and toddlerhood, 5. *See also* Infancy and toddlerhood
  middle childhood, 6. *See also* Middle childhood
  prenatal, 5. *See also* Prenatal development
Permanence, object. *See* Object permanence
Permissive child-rearing style, 574*t*, 575
  development and adjustment outcomes of, 576, 576*t*
Persistence, and temperament, 420*t*, 425
Person perception, 476
Personal choice, matters of, 510, 511–512
Personal fable, 255–256
  and risk-taking behavior, 256
Personality traits
  in anorexia nervosa, 211
  in bulimia nervosa, 211
  canalization concept on, 122
  in creativity, 353

in ethnic and racial biases, 478, 479
  expressive, 530
  and friendships, 618
  and gender identity, 547, 549
  and gender stereotypes, 530*t*, 530–531, 531*f*, 532, 554*t*, 558–562
  gene–environment interaction in, 122
  heritability research on, 120
  and identity development, 472
  instrumental, 530
  longitudinal research on, 60–61
  and moral development, 490, 504
  and occupational attainment, 332
  in person perception, 476
  in psychosexual development, 15
  of resilient children, 10–11
  in self-concept, 458
  sex differences in, 554*t*, 558–562
  stability of, 61
Perspective taking
  affective, 417
  empathy in, 417
  and moral reasoning, 502–503
  recursive thought in, 453
  in social problem solving, 481
  and theory of mind, 452
Peru
  mental state words and false-belief tasks of children in, 455
  swaddling of infants in, 137
Phallic stage of psychosexual development, 16*t*
Phencyclidine (PCP) use in adolescence, 626
Phenotypes, 73, 77
Phenylalanine, 77, 78*t*, 79
Phenylketonuria (PKU), 77, 78*t*, 79
  carriers of, 79, 79*f*
Phonemes, 368–369, 374
  memory of, 381
Phonics approach to reading, 309–310
Phonological awareness, 308, 310, 394
  early intervention programs affecting, 351
  home environment affecting, 345
Phonological development, 360, 373–375
  in bilingualism, 396
  early intervention programs affecting, 351
  early phase of, 373–374, 374*f*
  home environment affecting, 345
  later phase of, 375
  memory in, 381
  and metalinguistic awareness, 394
  milestones of, 395
  pronunciation errors in, 374, 374*f*, 375
  reading in, 308, 310, 345
  strategies in, 374–375, 375*t*
  syllable stress patterns in, 375
Phonological store, 381

Physical abuse of children, 599, 600. *See also* Child maltreatment

Physical activities. *See* Exercise

Physical aggression, 517, 518, 519, 560, 561–562

Physical development, 4, 5–6, 173–223
in adolescence, 6, 203–221
body proportion changes in, 176–177
body size changes in, 176, 183, 184
of brain, 184–192
cephalocaudal trend in, 176
course of, 176–184
definition of, 5f
emotional well-being affecting, 202
environmental influences on, 183
genetic influences on, 183, 192–194
growth curve in, 176, 177f
growth faltering in, 202
hormonal influences on, 181–183, 182f
infectious diseases affecting, 201–202
motor skills in, 178–181
muscle and fat changes in, 177
nutrition affecting, 183, 184, 192, 194–200
prenatal. *See* Prenatal development
proximodistal trend in, 176–177
secular trends in, 184, 184f
sex differences in, 177
skeletal growth in, 178
stress affecting, 403
worldwide variations in, 183

Physical education classes in school, 180

Physical knowledge in infancy, 262

Piaget, Jean, 19–21, 25, 612
clinical interviews of, 20, 46
cognitive development theory of, 19–21, 225, 226–261
legacy of, 261
on moral development, 496–499
and neo-Piagetian theory of information processing, 282, 283–284

Pictorial depth cues, 160, 160f

Pictures
and drawings in early childhood, 241–242, 242f
symbolic understanding of, in infancy, 236

Pima Indians, obesity of, 199–200

Pincer grasp, 151, 151f

Piraha people of Brazil, numerical knowledge of, 264

Pituitary gland, 181f, 181–183
hormones of, 181–183, 182f, 191

Placenta, 89
abruption of, 113
delivery of, 107, 108f

Planning
in cognitive development, 289f, 289–291
scripts in, 298

Plasticity
of brain, 23, 187–188
compared to stability in theories of development, 9
Locke on, 12

Play, 455
in adolescence, 610
associative, 608, 609
and attachment security, 437
benefits of, 240–241
categorization skills in, 234
and cognitive development, 609, 609t
cooperative, 608
cultural influences on, 273, 612–613
development of, 239–240
in early childhood, 608–610, 610t
emotional understanding in, 416
friendships in, 614
functional, 609t
gender roles in, 529, 531–532, 533, 534, 537, 539, 544, 609
gender schema theory on, 552
gender segregation in, 537, 566
imaginary companions in, 240
in infancy and toddlerhood, 608
make-believe, 455. *See also* Make-believe play
memory of, 294
in middle childhood, 610
in mixed-age groups, 612
with mothers and fathers, differences in, 437, 438, 439
narratives in, 392
parallel, 608, 609
of parent and child, 437, 438, 439, 611–612
planning in, 291
in preoperational stage, 239–241
rough-and-tumble, 610
in school recess, 639
scripts in, 298
in sensorimotor stage, 230, 233
sex differences in, 437, 438, 439, 609, 610
with siblings, 586
social origins of, 270
sociocultural theory on, 269, 270
sociodramatic, 243, 454, 455, 609–610
solitary, 608, 609
strategies enhancing, 241
video games in, 634
in visual impairment, 162

Poland, math achievement scores in, 558f

Pollution, prenatal exposure to, 101

Polychlorinated biphenyls (PCBs), 101

Polygenic inheritance, 81

Popular children, 617, 618–622
antisocial, 619
prosocial, 619

Pornography, Internet access to, 212

Portugal
infant mortality rate in, 119f
math achievement scores in, 558f

Positive discipline, 494

Positron emission tomography (PET), 48t, 50

Postconventional level of moral development, 501–502, 509

Postpartum depression, 404

Poverty, 33
attachment stability in, 432
breastfeeding in, 194
child-rearing practices in, 581
and context of family system, 572
drug use in, 626
early intervention and intellectual development in, 347–350
fetal alcohol syndrome in, 100
Head Start programs in, 35, 347–350
immunizations in, 201
infant mortality rates in, 118
infectious diseases in, 201
intelligence quotient in, 331, 336, 347, 348
international differences in, 33, 34t
low birth weight in, 114
malnutrition in, 105
memory capacity in, 280
physical development in, 183
preterm infant intervention programs in, 116
pubertal growth in, 205
public policy on, 33, 35
reading skills in, 308, 308f, 310
sexual activity of adolescents in, 214
sudden infant death syndrome in, 136
supplemental food program in, 35
welfare programs in, 35, 36

Practical intelligence, 324, 324f
and occupational attainment, 332–333

Practice effects
in longitudinal research, 62
in microgenetic studies, 65

Prader-Willi syndrome, 80

Pragmatic approach to morality, 509, 510

Pragmatic language development, 360, 390–393
conversational skills in, 390–391
narratives in, 392–393
referential communication skills in, 391–392, 392f
sociolinguistic knowledge in, 393

Preattachment phase, 429

Preconventional level of moral development, 500–501

Prefrontal cortex, 186, 190
in empathy, 487
in inhibitory tasks, 288

Pregnancy
abortion in, 217
in adolescence, 106, 217–220. *See also* Teenage pregnancy and parenthood
age at time of, 106, 106f. *See also* Maternal age
alcohol use during, 98–100
childbirth in, 107–112. *See also* Childbirth
and conception, 88–89
depression in, 404
in diabetes mellitus, 49
diagnosis and treatment of fetal problems in, 84–86
drug use during, 96–98, 136
exercise during, 103
infectious diseases during, 101–103, 102t
miscarriage in. *See* Miscarriage
nutrition during, 101, 103–105, 114
prenatal development in, 5, 88–107. *See also* Prenatal development
prenatal health care in. *See* Prenatal health care
radiation exposure during, 100–101
and reproductive technologies, 76, 77t, 86–87, 589
Rh factor incompatibility in, 113
smoking during, 98, 125, 125f, 136, 199
stress during, 105–106
teratogen exposure in, 95–103
trimesters in, 90, 92–94

Preimplantation genetic diagnosis, 85t

Prejudice
reduction of, 479–480
toward social groups, 476–480, 543, 616

Prelinguistic development, 368–373
communication in, 370–372
cooing and babbling in, 370
first speech sounds in, 370
infant-directed speech in, 369
receptivity to language in, 368–369

Premarital sex, 212–221

Premature infants. *See* Preterm infants

Prenatal development, 88–107
age of viability in, 92
body proportion changes in, 177
of brain, 185
and conception, 88–89
Darwin on, 13
definition of, 5
diabetes mellitus of mother affecting, 49
diagnosis and treatment of problems in, 84–86
embryonic, 90, 91
environmental influences on, 81, 94–106, 125

Prenatal development (*cont.*)
  fetal, 90, 92–94
  habituation in, 94, 142, 145
  and hand preference, 189
  infectious diseases affecting, 101–103, 102*t*
  maternal age affecting, 106, 106*f*
  milestones of, 90
  nutrition affecting, 103–105, 114, 197
  periods of, 88–94
  sensitive periods in, 95*f*, 95–96
  stress affecting, 105–106
  teratogens affecting, 95–103
  touch sensitivity in, 153
  trimesters in, 90, 92–94
  zygote period, 89–91
Prenatal health care
  barriers to, 118
  diagnostic tests in, 85, 85*t*
  exercise in, 103
  and infant mortality rates, 118
  nutrition in, 103–105
  recommendations on, 107
  in teenage pregnancy, 218
Preoperational stage, 19, 20*t*, 239–249
  animistic thinking in, 244, 246
  categorization in, 245, 247*f*, 247–248
  centration in, 245
  conservation in, 244*f*, 244–245
  drawings in, 241–242, 242*f*
  egocentrism in, 244, 245
  evaluation of, 248–249
  limitations of thought in, 243–245
  logical thought in, 246–247
  magical thinking in, 246
  make-believe play in, 239–241
  mental representation in, 239–243
  milestones of, 248
  problem solving in, 244, 244*f*
  research on, 245–248
Prereaching movements of newborn, 150, 151*f*
Preschool programs
  adjustment of children to, 641
  Head Start in, 35, 347–350, 351
Preschool years. *See* Early childhood
Preterm infants, 113–116
  abuse of, 115, 138
  attachment insecurity of, 435
  behavioral assessment of, 139
  breastfeeding of, 194
  caregiving for, 114–115, 116
  disabilities of, 114, 114*t*
  and drug use during pregnancy, 97
  in fetal medicine interventions, 85
  habituation and recovery of, 142
  and infectious diseases during pregnancy, 102*t*
  interventions for, 115–116, 117*f*
  maltreatment of, 115, 138, 600
  pain sensitivity of, 153
  and smoking during pregnancy, 98
  sudden infant death syndrome in, 136

Preverbal gestures, 371
Pride, 401
  in middle childhood, 416
  as self-conscious emotion, 408, 409, 416
Primary circular reactions, 228, 228*t*
Primary sexual characteristics, 203
Principled level of moral development, 501–502
Private speech, 266–267, 267*f*
Privileges withdrawn as punishment, 493–494
Proactive aggression (instrumental), 517, 522
Problem solving
  analogical, 235, 246, 250
  in bridge-building problem, 22, 22*f*
  in class inclusion problem, 245, 245*f*, 250
  creativity in, 324, 352–353
  in formal operational stage, 253–254, 254*f*
  in infancy and toddlerhood, 235
  information processing in, 22, 22*f*, 284*f*, 284–286
  in mathematics, 311–312
  in middle childhood and adolescence, 412
  in pendulum problem, 254, 254*f*
  planning in, 290
  in preoperational stage, 244, 244*f*
  scientific reasoning in, 313*f*, 313–314
  in sensorimotor stage, 235
  in social conflicts, 480*f*, 480–481
  speech–gesture mismatches in, 285
  strategy choice model of, 284*f*, 284–286
  in three-mountains problem, 244, 244*f*
Processing capacity, 279, 280, 315*t*
Processing speed, 281, 281*f*, 315*t*
  age-related changes in, 281, 281*f*
  in intelligence tests, 323
  strategy choice model on, 284
Prodigies, 354–355
  clinical method of research on, 51
Production deficiency in attentional strategies, 288
Production of words, compared to comprehension, 376
Programmed cell death in brain development, 185
Project Head Start, 35, 347–350
  Research-based Developmentally Informed (REDI) program in, 351, 351*f*
Promoting Alternative Thinking Strategies (PATHS) curriculum, 481
Pronunciation, 374. *See also* Phonological development
Propositional thought
  in formal operational stage, 254–255, 257–258
  logical necessity of, 258

Proprioception, in development of reaching and grasping, 151
Prosocial behavior
  civic responsibility in, 508
  empathy in, 86, 417, 418
  evolution of, 486–487
  modeling of, 490–491
  moral reasoning in, 506
  in peer relations, 610, 615, 616, 618
  of popular children, 619
  sex differences in, 558
  in television programs, 632
Protection from harm in research, 66*t*, 67
Protein
  and gene activity, 75, 86
  in kwashiorkor, 196
  metabolism disorder in phenylketonuria, 77, 78*t*, 79
Proteomics, 86
Protodeclarative gestures, 371
Protoimperative gestures, 371
Proverb understanding in semantic development, 381
Proximal parenting style, 450
Proximodistal trend in growth, 176–177
Psychoanalytic theories, 15–17
  attachment in, 428, 439
  clinical or case study research on, 17, 50
  compared to other child development theories, 32*t*
  contributions and limitations of, 17
  moral development in, 488–490
Psychological control in authoritarian child rearing, 574–575
Psychological disorders
  intelligence quotient in, 333
  in teratogen exposure, 96
Psychometric approach to cognitive development, 319
  combined with information-processing approach, 323
  in giftedness and creativity, 350–352
  intelligence tests in, 319, 320–322, 323. *See also* Intelligence tests
Psychosexual stages of development, 17
  compared to psychosocial stages, 16*t*
  Freud on, 15, 16*t*, 488
  morality in, 488
Psychosocial dwarfism, 202
Psychosocial stages of development
  compared to psychosexual stages, 16*t*
  Erikson on, 15–16, 16*t*, 17
Puberty, 6, 203–221
  age range in, 204
  autonomy issues in, 579
  body composition in, 177, 204
  body image in, 209
  body proportion in, 177
  body size in, 176, 203

  dating in, 624
  early versus late timing of, 208–210
  gender identity in, 551
  health issues in, 210–220
  hormone changes in, 183, 191, 212
  individual and group differences in, 204–205
  milestones of, 204
  motor development in, 180
  nutrition in, 196
  as period of storm and stress, 205–206
  physical development in, 203–205
  psychological impact of, 205–210
  reactions to changes in, 206
  secular trends in, 184, 184*f*
  sexual characteristics in, 203
  timing of, 204, 205, 208–210
Pubic hair development, 183, 203
  in hormone changes, 183
  individual and group variations in, 204, 205
Public education programs
  on HIV infection and AIDS, 217
  on immunizations, 202
  on sudden infant death syndrome, 136
Public policy, 33–37
  cultural influences on, 34–35
  definition of, 33
  ecological systems theory on, 33
  future trends in, 37
  Head Start programs in, 35, 347–350, 351
Puerto Rico, mother–infant relationship and attachment security in, 434
Pukapukans of Pacific Islands, childbirth practices of, 109–110
Punishment
  behavior modification in, 19
  consistency in, 494
  corporal, 492, 492*f*, 493, 602
  cultural influences on, 492, 493
  explanation for, 494
  Locke on, 12
  and moral development, 489, 491–494, 500
  and obedience orientation, 500
  in operant conditioning, 17, 141
  social learning theory on, 18
  time out technique in, 493
  undesirable effects of, 491–492, 493
  withdrawal of privileges in, 493–494
  in zero tolerance policies, 525
Purging, 211
Puritan beliefs on childhood, 11–12

Q

Q-Sort method in attachment assessment, 431–432
Quasi-experimental research, 58–60, 60*f*
  compared to other research designs, 61*t*

Quechua of Peru
  mental state words and false-belief tasks of, 455
  swaddling of infants, 137
Questionnaires in research, 43t, 47
  in cross-sectional studies, 63
  on moral reasoning, 499–500
  reliability of, 54
Questions
  clarifying, as grammatical prompt, 389–390
  in clinical interview, 46–47
  in grammatical development, 387–388
  in structured interview, 47
Quinceañera, 206

R
Racial differences. See Ethnic and racial differences
Radiation exposure
  genetic mutations in, 81
  in pregnancy, 100–101
Random assignment in experimental research, 57–58
Rapid-eye-movement (REM) sleep, 133, 135, 135f
Reaching
  and grasping, 151f, 151–152
  milestones of development, 151f
  and motor development in infants, 149, 150–152
  and prereaching, 150, 151f
Reactive aggression (hostile), 517, 518, 522
Reactivity, and temperament, 418–419, 420t, 421
Reading
  comprehension of, 310, 454
  decoding of words in, 310
  in early childhood, 307–309
  and emergent literacy, 307–309
  information processing in, 307–310
  interactive, 308, 319
  international differences in, 648
  in middle childhood, 309–310
  phonics approach to, 309–310
  phonological awareness in, 308, 310
  readiness for, 308, 308f
  reciprocal teaching of, 271
  and semantic development, 378, 378f, 380, 381
  sex differences in, 554–555, 555f
  whole-language approach to, 309–310
Real self, and ideal self, 459
Realism in moral development, 496
Reasoning
  abstract. See Abstract thinking
  by analogy, 246, 250
  belief–desire, 452–453
  hypothetico-deductive, 253–254, 254f, 257
  mathematical. See Mathematical abilities

in middle childhood, 453–454
  propositional thought in, 254–255, 257–258
  recursive thought in, 453, 454
  scientific, 313f, 313–314
  spatial. See Spatial reasoning and skills
  and theory of mind, 453–454, 455
Recall memory, 295–296
  automatic, 297
  episodic, 298
  in eyewitness testimony of children, 300–302
  of infants, 145
  in language development, 376
  scripts in, 298
Recast technique in grammar correction, 389
Recent memory of infants, 143, 144t
Recess time at school, 639
Recessive and dominant inheritance, 77t, 77–79, 78t, 79f
Reciprocal relationships
  in ecological systems theory, 27
  in ethological theory of attachment, 429
Reciprocal teaching, 271
Reciprocity, 497
  ideal, 497, 501, 509, 512
Recognition memory, 294, 295
  of infants, 145
  in language development, 376
Reconstituted families, 594–595
Reconstructed memory, 295–296
  internal working models as, 437
  scripts in, 298
Recovery and habituation, 142–145
Recursive thought, 453, 454
  in social problem solving, 481
Referential communication, 378, 391–392, 392f
Reflexes
  adaptive value of, 130–131
  Apgar Scale on, 109t
  classical conditioning of, 17
  of infants and newborn, 109t, 130t, 130–132, 238
  and motor development, 131
Reformation era, view of childhood in, 11–12
Rehearsal as memory strategy, 292, 293, 294, 304
Reinforcement
  behavior modification in, 18–19
  of moral development, 490–491
  in operant conditioning, 17, 141, 142, 490
  social learning theory on, 18
Reinforcers in operant conditioning, 17, 141
Rejected children, 618–622
  aggressive, 619
  bullying of, 620, 621
  interventions for, 620–622
  in peer groups, 623
  withdrawn, 620

Relational aggression, 518, 519, 520
  sex differences in, 560, 562
Relaxation techniques, in natural childbirth, 110
Reliability of research, 54
  inter-rater, 54
  test-retest, 54, 329
Religion
  adolescent rites of passage in, 206
  emotional display rules in, 413, 413f
  and moral development, 507–509
Remarriage, 594–595
Remembered self, 450–451
Remote memory, of infants, 143, 144t
Representation, mental. See Mental representation
Reproduction, as family function, 568
Reproductive choices, 84–87
  genetic counseling on, 84
  prenatal diagnosis and fetal medicine, 84–86
Reproductive system
  in conception, 88f, 88–89
  DES exposure affecting, 96
  in puberty, 203–204
Reproductive technologies, 86–87
  and fraternal twinning, 76, 77t
  for gay and lesbian families, 589
  sex sorter methods in, 86
Research, 41–71
  age of participants in, 68
  applications of, 4, 32–37
  assessed by institutional review boards, 67
  behavioral conditioning in, 17
  clinical or case study method, 17, 43t, 50–51
  confidentiality in, 67
  correlational, 55–56, 61t
  cross-sectional, 62–63, 65t
  on cultural influences, 43t, 51–53
  of Darwin, 13
  debriefing on, 69
  deception in, 69
  ethical issues in, 17, 41, 66t, 66–69
  experimental, 55, 56–60, 61t, 65
  factor analysis in, 321–322
  hypotheses in, 41–42
  informed consent of participants in, 66t, 67
  longitudinal, 60–62, 65t
  meta-analysis in, 553
  microgenetic, 64–65, 65t
  neurobiological, 43t, 47–50
  in normative approach, 13
  observational, 42–46
  protection from harm in, 66t, 67
  questions as basis of, 42
  reliability of, 54
  rights of participants in, 66t, 66–69
  risks-versus-benefits ratio in, 67, 68
  scientific verification of theories in, 7
  self-report measures in, 43t, 46–47

sequential, 63f, 63–64, 65t
  validity of, 54–55
  violation-of-expectation method in, 230–231, 231f, 262, 263, 263f, 453
Research-based Developmentally Informed (REDI) program of Head Start, 351, 351f
Resilience, 10–11
  and attachment, 440
  in birth complications, 117
Resistant attachment, 431
  internal working model of parents in, 436t
  later development in, 440
  mother–infant relationship in, 434
Resource room, 646
Respiratory distress syndrome of infants, 113
Respiratory system
  Apgar Scale on, 109t
  prenatal development of, 92, 113
  sudden infant death syndrome in disorders of, 136
Response
  in classical conditioning, 17, 140, 140f
  conditioned, 140, 140f
  in habituation, 142–145
  in operant conditioning, 141–142
  unconditioned, 140, 140f
Responsive parenting, and internal working models of attachment, 430, 430f
Responsiveness threshold, and temperament, 420t
Reticular formation, 190
Retina, 158–159
Retrieval of information, 294–296
  cues in, 295, 301
  from long-term memory, 280
  processing speed in, 281, 281f
  reconstruction in, 295–296
Reversibility
  in concrete operational stage, 249
  in preoperational stage, 245
Rh factor incompatibility, 113
Rhythmicity, and temperament, 420t, 421
Right-handedness, 187, 189
Rights of children, 37
  as research participants, 66t, 66–69
Risks-versus-benefits ratio in research, 67, 68
Risk-taking behavior
  in adolescence, 191, 207, 214, 256, 257, 624
  in creativity, 353
Rites of passage in adolescence, 206
Romanian orphans
  adoption of, 191
  early deprivation of, 170, 171, 171f, 403
  intervention project for, 171
  stress of, 403
Rooting reflex, 130, 130t, 448

Rough-and-tumble play, 610
Rousseau, Jean-Jacques, 12, 175
Rubella, 202
    in pregnancy, 102, 102t
Russia
    factor analysis of intelligence in,
        324
    temperament of children in, 427

S

Sadness in infancy and toddlerhood,
    407
Samoans
    adolescence of, 205
    language development of, 371, 372,
        390
    overweight, 200
Sampling
    event, 44
    in longitudinal research, 61–62
    time, 45
Sarcasm in semantic development,
    381
SAT, 328, 332, 516
    sex differences in scores on,
        555–556
Savant syndrome, 325, 326
Scaffolding, 280
    in early intervention programs,
        351
    and emotional understanding, 416
    in sociocultural theory, 268–269
Scale errors, 449
Schemes
    in cognitive development, 226–227
    gender-related, 551f, 551–552
    neo-Piagetian theory of, 283
Schizophrenia
    environmental influences on gene
        expression for, 123
    heritability research on, 120, 123
Scholastic Assessment Test (SAT),
    328, 332, 516
    sex differences in scores on,
        555–556
Schools, 637–650
    academic achievement in. See
        Academic achievement
    achievement attributions in, 467,
        468
    adolescent commitment to, 220
    and after-school programs, 597f,
        598–599
    AIDS education in, 217
    attendance to, 638, 642
    back to basics movement in, 638
    bilingual programs in, 396, 397
    bullying in, 621
    class size in, 637
    cliques and crowds in, 623
    cognitive-developmental theory
        applications in, 259–260
    college preparatory courses in,
        644–645
    communities of learners in, 637,
        640

community service opportunities
    in, 508
computers in, 632, 633
concrete operational thought in,
    252
constructivist classrooms in, 638,
    639–640
contraceptive services in, 219
corporal punishment in, 602
early adjustment to, 641
educational philosophies in,
    638–640
ethnic and racial prejudice in, 479
formal operational tasks in, 259
gender typing in, 542–543, 545,
    562–563
gifted children in, 354–355
grouping practices in, 643–645
heterogeneous grouping in, 644
homogeneous grouping in,
    643–644
in identity development, 474, 475
inclusive classrooms in, 646
integration of, 479
magnet, 644, 645
memory strategies in, 294
Montessori, 639–640
multigrade classes in, 644
obesity intervention programs in,
    200
parent partnership with, 647
physical education classes in, 180
readiness for, 351
recess time in, 639
resource rooms in, 646
self-fulfilling prophecies in, 643
sexist remarks of students in, 545,
    545f
sexual abuse prevention programs
    in, 601
social-cognitive interventions in,
    525
social-constructivist classrooms in,
    640
special needs students in, 646
student body size of, 638
teacher–student interaction in, 643
teacher training programs in,
    523–525
tracking in, 644–645
traditional classrooms in, 638, 639
transitions in, 640–642
vocational programs in, 644–645,
    649–650
zero tolerance policies in, 525
Schools within schools, 638
Science comprehension, gender
    stereotypes on, 532, 540, 540f,
    555–558
Scientific reasoning, 313f, 313–314
Scientific verification of theories, 7
Screening tests for infants, 329
Scripts
    memory of, 298
    in moral development, 489
Scrotum, 203

Seafood, mercury exposure from, 101
Second language, 364–365, 365f,
    394–397
Second-order beliefs, 453, 454f
Secondary circular reactions, 228t,
    229
Secondary sexual characteristics,
    203
Secular trends
    in intelligence quotient, 338
    in physical growth, 184, 184f
Secure base for infant exploration,
    408, 429, 430
Security of attachment, 416
    child care facilities affecting, 442
    and dating, 625
    and emotional understanding,
        416
    factors affecting, 433–437
    and later development, 440–441,
        442
    measurement of, 430–432
    parent experience of attachment
        affecting, 436t
    stability of, 432
Selective attrition in longitudinal
    research, 62
Self, 448–475
    annihilation of, 472
    categorical, 450, 461
    changing content of, 459
    constantly transforming, 474
    enduring, 451
    as generalized other, 459
    ideal, 459
    inner, 451–456
    remembered, 450–451
    and theory of mind, 451–456
Self-acceptance of homosexual
    youths, 216
Self-awareness, 405
    in emotional and social
        development, 408–409, 450
    and empathy, 417
    explicit, 449
    and implicit sense of self–world
        differentiation, 449
    in infancy and toddlerhood, 448f,
        448–450, 450f
    scale errors in, 449
    and self-conscious emotions,
        408–409, 450
Self-care children, 597f, 597–599
    in after-school programs, 597f,
        598–599
Self-concept, 456–460
    achievement-related attributions
        in, 464–468
    in adolescence, 458–459, 460
    cognitive development affecting,
        459
    cultural influences on, 451,
        459–460
    and development of self-conscious
        emotions, 408–409, 450
    in early childhood, 456, 460

and emotional self-regulation,
    409–412
    ethnic identity in, 475
    gender identity in. See Gender
        identity
    and memory, 298, 301
    in middle childhood, 458, 459, 460
    milestones of development, 460
    of parents, 572
    self-esteem in, 461–468. See also
        Self-esteem
    and social comparisons, 458
    storytelling practices affecting, 451
Self-confidence, maturational timing
    affecting, 208
Self-conscious emotions, 405, 450
    in middle childhood, 409, 416
Self-consciousness in adolescence,
    255–256
Self-control, 514–516
    in adolescence, 190–191, 515–516
    hot and cool systems in, 516, 516f
    individual differences in, 516
    in infancy and toddlerhood,
        514–515
    milestones of development, 517
Self-disclosure in friendships, 615f
Self-efficacy
    academic, 305
    emotional, 412
    in mathematics, 557
    physical, 180
    social learning theory on, 18
Self-esteem, 461–468
    academic, 462f, 463
    achievement-related attributions
        in, 464–468
    in adolescence, 461, 462, 463
    and aggression, 522
    in athletic or physical competence,
        462f, 463
    body image affecting, 209
    child-rearing practices affecting,
        464
    cultural influences on, 451,
        463–464
    definition of, 461
    in ethnic and racial biases, 478
    factor analysis of, 461
    in formal operational stage, 256
    gender identity affecting, 550
    milestones of development, 469
    of parents, 572
    in peer victimization, 621
    in physical appearance, 462f, 463
    school transitions affecting, 641,
        642
    of self-care children, 598
    and self-conscious emotions, 409
    in social comparisons, 462, 463
    in social competence, 462f
    structure of, 461, 462f
Self-fulfilling prophecy, educational,
    643
Self-recognition, 449, 450
    cultural variations in, 450, 450f

Self-regulation
  in adolescence, 190–191
  cognitive, 304–305, 315t
  emotional, 327, 409–412
  moral, 515
  in temperament, 418–419, 420t,
    421
Self-reports, 43t, 46–47
  in clinical interviews, 43t, 46–47
  on culture, 51, 52
  reliability of, 46–47, 54
  in structured interviews, tests, and
    questionnaires, 43t, 47
  validity of, 54
Self-sacrifice in moral development,
  486–487
Self-serving bias in scientific
  reasoning, 314
Semantic bootstrapping in
  grammatical development, 389
Semantic complexity of grammatical
  morphemes, 386
Semantic development, 360, 376–383
  in bilingualism, 396
  comprehension and production of
    words in, 376
  cultural differences in, 376, 376t,
    378–379
  emergentist coalition model of,
    383, 383f
  and false beliefs, 455
  fast-mapping in, 377
  first words in, 370, 373–374, 376,
    376t
  growth of vocabulary in, 376–377,
    377f, 380, 380f
  individual differences in,
    377–378
  learning strategies in, 382–383
  memory in, 376, 381
  syntactic bootstrapping in,
    382–383
  types of words in, 379
  underextensions and
    overextensions in, 379–380
  in Williams syndrome, 366
  word coinages and metaphors in,
    380
Semantic memory, 296–297
Semen, 204
Senegal, play and peer relations in,
  613
Sensitive caregiving, 434, 435
  continuity of, 440
  of fathers, 437, 439
Sensitive periods of development, 24
  of brain, 191–192
  for culture-specific learning, 156
  deprivation in, 169–171, 191, 370
  in language development, 364–365,
    370
  teratogen exposure in, 95f, 95–96
Sensorimotor stage, 19, 20t, 228–239
  adaptive behaviors in, 228t
  circular reactions in, 228t, 228–229
  evaluation of, 236–238

mental representation in, 232–236
milestones of development, 238
object permanence in, 229,
  230–231, 231f, 232
research on, 230–236
substages in, 228t
Sensory register in information
  processing, 278, 279, 279f
Sensory systems
  and amodal sensory properties,
    166
  development of. See Perceptual
    development
  hearing, 155–158. See also Hearing
  smell, 154–155, 158
  taste, 154, 158
  touch, 153–154, 158. See also
    Touch
  vision, 158–166. See also Vision
Sentences in grammatical
  development, 385–386
Separation
  in parent–adolescent relationship,
    208
  of parents. See Divorce
Separation anxiety, 429
September 11, 2001 terrorist attacks,
  524
Sequential research, 63f, 63–64
  compared to other research
    designs, 65t
Seriation in concrete operational
  stage, 250
Serotonin
  in sudden infant death syndrome,
    136
  and temperament, 427
Sesame Street, 632
Sex cells, 75f, 75–76
Sex chromosomes, 76
  abnormalities of, 83t, 83t
  diseases linked to, 78t, 80f, 80–81
  in fragile X syndrome, 80–81
Sex differences, 529–565
  in achievement attributions, 467
  in aggression, 518, 519, 560–562
  in athletic activities, 180, 181
  in attention-deficit hyperactivity
    disorder, 290
  in autobiographical memory, 299
  in blended families, 594–595
  in body composition of muscle and
    fat, 177
  in body proportion changes, 177
  in cliques, 623, 624
  in computer use, 633
  in delinquency, 519
  in depression, 559–560
  in discipline, 521, 543, 559, 561
  in emotional expression, 412–413
  in emotional sensitivity, 558–559
  in friendships, 617
  in height changes, 176, 177f
  in language development, 554–555
  in mathematical abilities, 555–558,
    558f

in mental abilities, 554t, 554–558
in moral development, 503–504,
  504f
in motor development, 179, 180
in muscle development, 177
in personality traits, 61, 554t,
  558–562
in physical growth, 177
in play activities, 609, 610
in puberty, 203–204, 206, 208
in response to divorce of parents,
  592, 593
in self-esteem, 463
in semantic development, 377
in sex cells, 76
in sexual abuse, 601
in sexual maturation, 203–204
in skeletal age, 178
in spatial reasoning and skills, 555,
  556f, 556–557
in suicidal behavior, 472
in television characters, 631
in X-linked inheritance, 80
Sex education
  communication strategies in, 213
  on contraception, 215, 219–220
  cultural influences on, 212
  in prevention of teenage
    pregnancy, 219–220
  on sexually transmitted diseases,
    217
  sources of information in, 212
Sex hormones, 183
  and aggression, 561
  androgen. See Androgen
  estrogen, 183, 215
  and gender typing, 536–538
  in puberty, 191
  and sexual orientation, 215
  testosterone, 183
Sex roles. See Gender roles
Sex stereotypes. See Gender
  stereotypes
Sex typing. See Gender typing
Sexism, 545, 545f, 563
Sexual abuse, 599, 601
  eyewitness memory of children
    on, 302
Sexual attitudes and behavior,
  212–220
  and contraceptive use, 214f,
    214–215
  cultural influences on, 212–213
  in psychosexual stages of
    development, 15, 16t
  sexual abuse affecting, 601
  and sexual orientation, 215–216
  and sexually transmitted diseases,
    217
  and teenage pregnancy, 217–220
  trends in, 213f, 213–214
Sexual characteristics
  genes in development of, 76
  primary and secondary, 203
Sexual identity of homosexual
  youths, 215–216

Sexual maturation, 203–204
  hormone changes in, 183
  timing of, 208–210
Sexual orientation, 215–216
  homosexuality in. See
    Homosexuality
  and identity development, 474
  of parents, 589–590
  and suicidal behavior, 472
Sexually transmitted diseases (STDs),
  217
Shading in conversational skills, 390
Shame
  in psychosocial development, 16t
  as self-conscious emotion, 408,
    409
Shape bias in semantic development,
  382
Shape constancy in object perception,
  165
Shared environmental influences,
  344–346, 425
Short-term memory, 278–279, 279f
  age-related changes in, 280
  store model of, 278–279, 279f
  in verbatim digit span task, 278,
    280
Shyness, 422
  cultural influences on, 427
  empathy in, 417
  longitudinal study of, 61
  neurobiological correlates of, 422
  sports participation in, 181
  temperament in, 421, 425, 427
Siblings, 585–587
  in adolescence, 587
  aggression of, 521
  arrival of new sibling, 436, 585–586
  attachment patterns of, 435, 436
  birth order of, 215, 346, 585, 585f
  in blended families, 594–595
  conflicts between, 586
  cross-sectional studies of, 63
  emotional understanding of, 416
  and gender typing, 546f, 546–547
  gene–environment correlation in
    studies of, 122–123, 123f
  intelligence quotient of, 346, 585,
    585f
  in middle childhood, 586–587
  nonshared environmental
    influences on, 346, 424–425, 435
  number of, 584–588
  and one-child families, 587–588
  play of, 586
  in pragmatic language
    development, 391
  rivalry between, 586
  spacing between, 346
  temperament and personality of,
    424–425, 578
  and theory of mind, 456
Sickle cell anemia, 78t, 79
Sickle cell trait, 79
SIDS (sudden infant death
  syndrome), 135, 136

Siegler, Robert, strategy choice model of information processing, 282, 284–286
Sign language
cerebral hemisphere functions in, 187, 364
chimpanzees using, 361
in hearing loss, 362–363, 364
and sensitive periods in language development, 364
Simon, Theodore, 13–14, 320
Singapore
adolescent suicide rate in, 472
infant mortality rate in, 119f
peer pressure in, 626
Single-parent families, 590
chaos in, 29
in divorce, 591, 593
extended family relationships of, 583
food insecurity in, 197
gender roles in, 544
in never-married parents, 590
poverty of, 33
in teenage pregnancy, 217–220
verbal abilities in, 555
Size constancy in object perception, 164
Size of body. See Body size
Size of family. See Family size
Skeletal age, 178
Skeletal development, 178
Skinner, B. F., operant conditioning theory of, 17
Sleep
and cosleeping arrangements, 134
cultural influences on, 132–133, 134
insufficient, weight gain in, 199
and moodiness in adolescents, 207
of newborn and infants, 132t, 132–135
non-rapid-eye-movement, 133, 135, 135f
rapid-eye-movement, 133, 135, 135f
sudden infant death in, 136
Slovenia, infant mortality rate in, 119f
Slow-to-warm-up temperament, 420–421
Small-for-date infants, 114
Smell sense
milestones of development, 158
of newborn, 153, 154f, 154–155
Smiling, in infancy, 406–407
Smoking
in adolescence, 626, 626f
and attention-deficit hyperactivity disorder, 125, 125f
passive exposure to, 98
in pregnancy, 98, 125, 125f, 199
and sudden infant death syndrome, 136
television commercials on, 631

Sociability, 422
neurobiological correlates of, 422
in peer relations, 608–613, 628
temperament in, 421, 425
Social behavior
and emotions, 402–403
and moral development, 485, 486–487
prosocial. See Prosocial behavior
Social cognition, 18, 447–483
in aggression, 522–523, 525
conflict and problem solving in, 480–481
emergence of self and self-concept in, 448–460
identity in, 468–475
person perception in, 476
self-esteem in, 461–468
social groups in, 476–480
Social comparisons
in middle childhood, 458
and self-esteem, 462, 463
Social-constructivist classrooms, 640
Social contract orientation in moral development, 501
Social conventions, 510–511, 512
Social development. See Emotional and social development
Social groups, 476–480
in-groups and out-groups, 477–478
of peers, 622–624
prejudice about, 477–480
and self-concept, 459
stereotypes on, 476, 477, 478
Social interaction
emotional intelligence in, 327
facial expressions of emotion in, 402–403
and false beliefs, 456
intersubjectivity in, 268
language development in, 367, 371
with peers. See Peer relations
prosocial behavior in. See Prosocial behavior
scaffolding in, 268–269
with siblings. See Siblings
sociocultural theory of, 25, 266–272
and theory of mind, 456
Social issues and policies, 32–37
in bilingual education, 397
in child-care facilities, 441–443
in civic responsibility, 508
definition of, 33
in emotional intelligence, 327
in family chaos, 29
in Head Start programs, 35, 351
in high-stakes testing movement, 343
international comparison of indicators on, 33, 34f, 34t, 37
in musical experiences and intelligence, 59
in neonatal and infant mortality, 118
for parents and newborns, 118–119

in reproductive technologies, 86–87
in research risks, 68
in school recess, 639
in sex differences in gross-motor development, 180
in sexual abuse, 601
in speech–gesture mismatches, 285
in substance abuse, 626–627
in video deficit effect, 237
in visual impairment, 162
in welfare programs, 35, 36
Social learning, 18–19, 32t
gender identity in, 548
gender stereotypes in, 535
moral development in, 490–494
parent training based on, 523–524
in television viewing, 630–632
Social networking sites, 635
Social-order-maintaining orientation in moral development, 501, 509
Social preference measure on popularity, 618
Social problem solving, 480f, 480–481
Social prominence measure on popularity, 618
Social referencing in infancy and toddlerhood, 414–415, 452
Social skills
early intervention programs affecting, 351
in teenage pregnancy intervention program, 220
Social smile, 406, 407
Social support
in child maltreatment prevention, 603
during childbirth, 111
in community, 572
ecological systems theory on, 28
in extended families, 583
for family system, 572
for homosexual youths, 216
during pregnancy, 106
of resilient children, 11
Social system, family as, 567, 568, 569–573
Social understanding in moral development, 496–514
Socialization, family in, 568, 573–584
Societal norms, 488–496
internalization of, 488, 494, 513
Society for Research in Child Development, 14, 66
Sociocultural theory, 24–26, 226, 266–272
compared to other child development theories, 32t
on education, 269–272, 640
evaluation of, 272
intersubjectivity in, 268
on make-believe play, 269, 270
private speech in, 266–267, 267f
scaffolding in, 268–269
zone of proximal development in, 267–268, 269

Sociodramatic play, 454, 455
in early childhood, 609–610
in preoperational stage, 243
Socioeconomic status
in adolescent pregnancy, 218
and attachment security, 430, 431
and attachment stability, 432
in breastfeeding, 194
and child-care quality, 441, 597
and child-rearing practices, 580–582
and communication style, 339–340, 633
and computer use, 632
and context of family system, 572
and corporal punishment, 492
and delinquency, 519
divorce affecting, 591, 593
ecological systems theory on, 27–28, 33
and gender stereotypes, 534
and immunization rate, 201–202
and intellectual development, 347–350, 351
and intelligence quotient, 331, 334–335, 336–337, 338, 347, 348
international comparison of, 33, 34t
and knowledge development, 340–341
in lead exposure, 193
and mathematics skills, 311
and physical development, 183, 184
and pubertal growth variations, 205
public policy on, 33, 35
and reading skills, 308f, 308–309, 310
of self-care children, 597–598
and semantic development, 378
and sexual activity of adolescents, 214
and working memory capacity, 280
Sociolinguistic knowledge, 360, 393
Sociomoral Reflection Measure–Short Form, 499–500, 502
Somatic mutations, 81
Soothing of child
in crying, 137–138
and emotional self-regulation, 410
and temperament, 421
Sorting tasks, attention in, 287
South Africa, gay and lesbian families in, 589
South America
body size in, 183
childbirth practices in, 109–110
diarrhea in, 201
thalidomide use in, 96
Spain
adolescent suicide rate in, 472
corporal punishment in, 602
divorce rate in, 591f

factor analysis of intelligence in, 324

gay and lesbian families in, 589

infant mortality rate in, 119*f*

Spanish language, 396

and bilingualism, 397

Spanking, 493

Spatial reasoning and skills

in concrete operational stage, 250*f*, 250–251, 251*f*

hippocampus in, 190

in intelligence tests, 338

lateralization of brain functions in, 188

in mental rotation tasks, 556, 556*f*, 557

in multiple intelligences theory, 325*t*, 326

in perception tasks, 556, 556*f*

sex differences in, 555, 556*f*, 556–557

in visualization tasks, 556, 556*f*

Special needs students, 646

Special Supplemental Food Program for Women, Infants, and Children, U.S. (WIC), 35, 105

Specific intelligence, 321

Spectroscopy, near-infrared (NIRS), 48*t*, 50, 50*f*

Speech

categorical perception of, 368

egocentric, 267

first sounds of, 370

and gesture mismatches, 285

infant-directed, 369, 374

infant perception and analysis of, 155–158

inner, 267

phonemes in, 368–369, 374

and phonological awareness, 308

private, 266–267, 267*f*

register adjustments in, 393

sound categories and patterns in, 368–369

telegraphic, 384

Speed of information processing, 281, 281*f*, 315*t*

age-related changes in, 281, 281*f*

in intelligence tests, 323

strategy choice model on, 284

Sperm, 75*f*, 75–76, 203, 204

and conception, 88–89

in reproductive technologies, 86, 87

and spermarche, 204, 206

Spermarche, 204, 206

Spina bifida, 104

Spirituality and religion

adolescent rites of passage in, 206

emotional display rules in, 413, 413*f*

and moral development, 507–509

Spock, Benjamin, 13, 134

Sports activities, 179–181. *See also* Athletic activities

Spouses. *See* Marital relationship

Stability

of aggression, 519–520

of attachment, 432

compared to plasticity, 9

of gender identity, 548

of intelligence quotient, 330–331

longitudinal research on, 61

of temperament, 423

Stages of development, 8

Baldwin on, 14

cognitive, 19–20, 20*t*, 226, 228–259, 260–261

concrete operational. *See* Concrete operational stage

definition of, 8

formal operational. *See* Formal operational stage

preoperational. *See* Preoperational stage

psychosexual. *See* Psychosexual stages of development

psychosocial, 15–16, 16*t*, 17

Rousseau on, 12

sensorimotor. *See* Sensorimotor stage

in sociocultural theory, 25

Stagnation and generativity in psychosocial development, 16*t*

Stanford-Binet Intelligence Scale, 14, 321, 327–328

State words in semantic development, 379

States of arousal in infants, 132*t*, 132–138

Statistical analysis, correlation coefficient in, 56, 56*f*

Statistical learning capacity in infants, 157, 367, 369

Stepfamilies, 594–595

Stepping reflex, 130*t*, 131

Stereopsis, 160

Stereotypes

in aggression, 518

ethnic and racial, 341, 341*f*

gender-related. *See* Gender stereotypes

and self-fulfilling prophecies, 643

on sexual orientation, 215

on social groups, 476, 477, 478

in television programs, 631

threat of, 341, 341*f*, 557

Sternberg triarchic theory of successful intelligence, 323–324, 324*f*

Still-face reaction, 402–403

Stimulant drugs use

in adolescence, 291

in attention-deficit hyperactivity disorder, 291

Stimulation

and brain development, 185, 186, 191–192

in classical conditioning, 17, 140*f*, 140–141

familiarity preference in, 143, 144*f*

habituation to, 142–145

intermodal, 166, 168

novelty preference in, 143, 144*f*

in operant conditioning, 141

for preterm infants, 115–116

and reaching and grasping by infants, 152

in sensitive periods of development, 169–171

tolerance of infants for, 410

in visual impairment, 162

Stop Bullying Now, 621

Store model of information processing, 278–280, 279*f*

Storytelling practices

cultural variations in, 451

and remembered self, 451

Strabismus, 171

Strange Situation technique for measuring security of attachment, 430, 431*t*, 442

cultural variations in, 432*f*, 432–433

Stranger anxiety, 407–408, 429

Strategy choice model of information processing, 282, 284–286

overlapping-waves pattern in, 284, 284*f*

Stress

acculturative, 475, 579

in adolescence, 579

aggression and antisocial behavior in, 523

and attachment security in family, 436

of bullying victims, 621

in child-care facilities, 442

child maltreatment in, 600, 602, 603

of child maltreatment victims, 602

in childbirth, 108

cortisol levels in, 47–48, 97, 108, 403, 422

depression in, 560

in divorce of parents, 592

in early deprivation, 403

fight or flight response in, 47

friendships in, 618

health effects of, 403

of infant in maternal depression, 404

male-to-female birth ratios in, 80

neurobiological research on, 47–48

in poverty, 581

in pregnancy, 105–106

prenatal cocaine exposure affecting response to, 97

in puberty, 205–210

resilience in, 10–11

in school transitions, 641–642

in shyness, 422

suicidal behavior in, 472

working memory capacity in, 280

Stress hormones, 47–48, 97, 108, 403, 422

in childbirth, 108

in early deprivation, 403

in shyness and sociability, 422

in stress response, 47–48, 97, 108, 403, 404

time in child-care center affecting, 442

Structural complexity of grammatical morphemes, 386

Structured interviews, 43*t*, 47

Structured observation research method, 43*t*, 44

Student body size of school, 638

Substance abuse, 626–627

of alcohol. *See* Alcohol use and abuse

of drugs. *See* Drug use and abuse

of tobacco. *See* Smoking

Subtraction problems in mathematics, 312

Sucking reflex, 130, 130*t*, 131

Sudden infant death syndrome (SIDS), 135, 136

Suggestibility affecting eyewitness memory of children, 300–302

Suicide

in adolescence, 216, 472–473

in clusters, 473

of homosexual youths, 216, 472

of maltreatment victims, 602

prevention and treatment strategies, 473

Superego, 15, 488

Surrogate motherhood, 86–87

Survival

and ethology of behavior, 23–24

of fittest, Darwin on, 13

Swaddling of infants, 137

Sweden

bullying in, 621

corporal punishment in, 602

divorce rate in, 591*f*

family size in, 584

gay and lesbian families in, 589

gender equality in, 536

home births in, 111

immunization rate in, 201

infant mortality rate in, 119*f*

math achievement scores in, 558*f*

parental leave in, 119

poverty rate in, 33

reproductive technology laws in, 87

semantic development in, 375, 378

Swimming reflex, 130, 130*t*, 131

Switzerland

academic achievement in, 647

body size in, 183

infant mortality rate in, 119*f*

reproductive technology laws in, 87

vocational education in, 650

Syllable stress patterns, 156, 157, 369, 375

Symbolic understanding

in preoperational stage, 243

in sensorimotor stage, 235–236

Sympathetic nervous system, 47*n*

Sympathy, 416–418
  sex differences in, 558
Synapses, 185–186, 187
  prenatal development of, 92
  pruning process, 185–186, 187
Syntactic bootstrapping in semantic development, 382–383
Syntax in grammatical development, 360
Syphilis in pregnancy, 102t
Systematic observation research methods, 42–46, 43t
Systems approach
  in dynamic systems perspective, 30–31
  in ecological systems theory, 26–28

T

Tabula rasa, 12
Tagalog language, 389
Taiwan
  academic achievement in, 648
  infant mortality rate in, 119f
  PCB exposure in, 101
Talent and creativity, 353
Tamil language, 388
Tanzania, hand preference in, 189
Tapping task, 288, 288f
Task-focused motivation, 353
Taste sense, 154
  milestones of development, 158
Taxonomic categories as memory strategy, 292
Tay-Sachs disease, 78t
Teacher–student interaction, 643
  achievement attributions in, 467, 468
  class size affecting, 637
  classroom management strategies in, 523–524
  in early intervention programs, 349
  gender typing in, 542–543
  identity development in, 474
  in school transitions, 642
  self-fulfilling prophecies in, 643
  in special needs students, 646
Teaching techniques, 643
  and academic achievement, 648
  and cognitive self-regulation, 305
  in constructivist classroom, 638, 639–640
  in cooperative learning, 271–272
  in dynamic assessment of intelligence, 342
  in early intervention programs, 349, 351
  for emotional intelligence, 327
  for gifted children, 354–355
  in heterogenous classes, 644
  in high-stakes testing movement, 343
  in homogeneous classes, 643–644
  in just educational environment, 507, 508
  in magnet schools, 644, 645
  for mathematics, 311–313

  in Montessori schools, 639–640
  and moral development, 507, 508
  for multiple intelligences, 326
  for reading, 309–310
  reciprocal, 271
  in sexist remarks, 545
  in social-constructivist classrooms, 640
  for special needs students, 646
  in traditional classrooms, 638, 639
Teen Outreach, 220
Teenage pregnancy and parenthood, 106, 217–220
  and contraceptive use, 214
  incidence of, 217f, 217–218
  intergenerational continuity in, 218–219
  outcomes in, 219
  parent–adolescent relationship in, 214
  prenatal development in, 106
  prevention strategies, 219–220
  support from father in, 220
Teenage years. See Adolescence
Teeth, embryonic development of, 95f
Telegraphic speech, 384
Television, 293, 629–632
  daily viewing time, 629f, 629–630
  educational programs on, 237, 632
  ethnic stereotypes in, 631
  gender stereotypes in, 543, 631
  infant and toddler learning from, 237
  and obesity, 199
  parent responsibilities on, 635–636
  and sexual attitudes, 212
  and social learning, 630–632
  and video deficit effect, 237, 629
  withdrawal of privileges as punishment, 494
Temper tantrums, 410
Temperament, 418–428
  and attachment security, 435
  and child-rearing practices, 422, 424–425, 426–427, 576, 578
  and corporal punishment, 492
  cultural variations in, 424, 426, 427
  definition of, 418
  and effortful control, 421, 426
  and emotional self-regulation, 424
  and empathy, 417
  environmental influences on, 422, 424–425, 426–427
  and fetal activity, 93
  genetic influences on, 422, 423–424, 426–427
  malnutrition affecting, 197, 424
  and maltreatment, 600
  measurement of, 421
  models of, 420t, 420–421, 426
  and moral development, 490
  New York Longitudinal Study of, 419
  as predictive of behavior, 425–426
  of resilient children, 10–11

  and response to divorce of parents, 592
  and self-control, 514–515
  and semantic development, 378
  of siblings, 424–425, 578
  stability of, 423
Temporal lobe, Wernicke's area in, 362f, 363
Temporary Aid to Needy Families (TANF), 36
Temptation, resistance to, delay of gratification in, 514–515
Teratogens, 95–103
Terrorism
  cohort effects in, 62
  impact on children, 524
Tertiary circular reactions, 228t, 229
Testes, 203
Testimony by children, 454
  suggestibility affecting, 300–302
Testing methods, 43t, 47, 54–55
  cultural bias in, 339–343
  on intelligence. See Intelligence tests
  practice effects in, 62
  reliability of, 54, 329
  validity of, 54–55
Testosterone, 183
Texas Adoption Project, 337, 337f
Thailand
  body size in, 183
  cosleeping of parents and infants in, 134
Thalidomide, 96
Theories of development, 6–31, 32t. See also specific theories.
  behavioral, 17–19, 32t
  cognitive-developmental, 19–21, 32t, 226–261
  comparison of, 31, 32t
  components of, 6
  as continuous or discontinuous process, 7f, 7–8
  definition of, 6
  dynamic systems, 30–31, 32t
  ecological systems, 26–28, 32t
  ethology, 23–24, 32t
  evolutionary developmental psychology, 24, 32t
  historical foundations of, 10–21
  and hypotheses, 41–42
  information processing, 21–23, 32t
  psychoanalytic, 15–17, 32t
  recent perspectives, 21–31
  on relative influence of nature and nurture, 8–9
  scientific verification of, 7
  social learning, 18–19, 32t
  sociocultural, 24–26, 32t
Theory of mind, 264–265, 303, 451–456
  in autism, 457
  belief–desire reasoning in, 452–453
  desires in, 452
  factors contributing to, 455–456

Theory theory, 264
Thinking
  convergent, 350, 353
  divergent, 350–352, 352f, 353
Third-party influences in ecological systems theory, 27, 569
Three-mountains problem, 244, 244f
Three-stratum theory of intelligence, 322
Thyroid-stimulating hormone (TSH), 183
Thyroxine, 183
Time out as punishment technique, 493
Time sampling in systematic observation research, 45
Timetable of development, Gesell on, 13
Tinbergen, Niko, 23
Tobacco. See Smoking
Toddlerhood, 5. See also Infancy and toddlerhood
Tonic neck reflex, 130t, 131
Tools of the Mind curriculum, 288
Touch
  in infancy, 153–154, 158
  in intermodal perception, 166–168
  milestones of development, 158
  for stimulation of preterm infants, 115–116
Toxoplasmosis in pregnancy, 102t, 103
Tracks, academic, 644–645
Traditional classrooms, 638, 639
Training. See Education
Traits
  carriers of, 77, 79f, 84
  dominant and recessive, 77–79
  personality. See Personality traits
  polygenic inheritance of, 81
  sickle cell, 79
Transitive inferences in concrete operational stage, 250, 252
Translocation of chromosomes, 82
Triarchic theory of successful intelligence, 323–324, 324f
Tribal and village societies
  adolescent initiation ceremonies in, 206
  conservation in, 252
  formal operational stage in, 258–259
  gender roles in, 535–536
  information processing in, 324
  moral development in, 505
  observation and participation in adult work by children in, 273
  puberty in, 205–206
  sociocultural influences on cognitive development in, 272, 273
  soothing of crying infants in, 138
Trimesters in prenatal development, 90, 92–94

Triple X syndrome, 83, 83*t*

Trisomy 21 (Down syndrome), 82

Trobriand Islanders, sexual attitudes and behavior among, 212

Trophoblast, 88*f*, 89

Trust
in friendships, 614, 615
in psychosocial development, 16*t*

Truthfulness, 497–498
and deception in research, 69

Tuberculosis in pregnancy, 102*t*

Turkey, math achievement scores in, 558*f*

Turnabout in conversational skills, 390

Turner syndrome, 83, 83*t*

Tutoring
in multigrade classrooms, 644
of special needs students, 646

Twins
anorexia nervosa of, 211
attachment of, 435
attention-deficit hyperactivity disorder in, 290
bulimia nervosa of, 211
empathy of, 417
environmental influences on gene expression in, 124
fraternal or dizygotic, 76–77, 77*t*. *See also* Fraternal twins
gene–environment correlation studies of, 123
hand preference of, 189
heritability estimate studies of, 120–121
identical or monozygotic, 76. *See also* Identical twins
intelligence quotient in, 335*f*, 335–336, 336*f*, 346
in kinship studies, 120
low birth weight of, 114
menarche of, 204
niche-picking by, 123, 336
nonshared environmental influences on, 424–425
physical growth of, 192, 194
puberty of, 204
in reproductive technologies, 86
sexual orientation of, 215
temperament and personality of, 423, 424–425, 425*f*

U

Uganda, reaching and grasping by infants in, 152

Ulnar grasp, 151, 151*f*

Ultrasound in pregnancy, 85*t*

Umbilical cord, 89–90

Unconditioned response, 140, 140*f*

Unconditioned stimulus, 140, 140*f*

Underarm hair development, 183, 203
in hormone changes, 183

Underextensions in semantic development, 379–380

Uninhibited child, temperament of, 421

Uninvolved child-rearing style, 574*t*, 575
development and adjustment outcomes of, 576*t*
neglect in, 575

United Kingdom
divorce rate in, 591*f*
family size in, 584
gay and lesbian families in, 589
infant mortality rate in, 119*f*

Universal ethical principle orientation in moral development, 502

Universal grammar, 361, 365

Unresponsive caregiver, and internal working models of attachment, 430, 430*f*

Uruguay
corporal punishment in, 602
gay and lesbian families in, 589

Uterus, 88, 88*f*
contractions in childbirth, 107, 108*f*

Utilization deficiency
in attentional strategies, 289
in memory strategies, 292

U'wa people of Colombia, memory of, 294

V

Vaccination, 201–202
mercury-free, 202
in Rh incompatibility, 113
rubella, 102

Validity of research, 54–55
in experimental studies, 57, 58
external, 55
internal, 55, 57
in longitudinal studies, 62

Values
on academic achievement, 53
cultural. *See* Cultural influences
and public policies, 34

Variables
confounding, 57
correlation of, 55–56, 56*f*, 57*f*
dependent, 56, 57
in experimental research, 56–58
independent, 56, 57

Velocity curve of physical growth, 176, 177*f*

Verbal abilities, sex differences in, 554–555

Verbal aggression, 518
sex differences in, 560

Verbatim digit span task, 278, 280

Verbatim memory, 296, 296*f*

Vernix formation, 92

Vezo of Madagascar, biological knowledge of, 265

Victims
of child maltreatment, 601, 602
of peer bullying, 621

Video deficit effect, 237, 629

Video games, 634
daily time in, 629*f*
violence in, 633

Video viewing
infant and toddler learning from, 237
interactive experiences in, 237

Vietnam
body size in, 183
cosleeping of parents and infants in, 134
immigrant youths from, 53

Vietnamese Americans
academic achievement values of, 53
intelligence definition of, 324

Village societies. *See* Tribal and village societies

Violation-of-expectation research method, 230–231, 231*f*, 262, 263, 263*f*
on false beliefs, 453

Violence
in dating relationship, 625
on television, 630–631
in video games, 633, 634
war-related, impact on children, 524

Viral diseases, 201
breastfeeding in, 194
HIV infection and AIDS. *See* HIV infection and AIDS
in pregnancy, 102*t*, 102–103

Vision
cerebral cortex area in, 186
color, 167
and depth perception, 159*f*, 159–161, 160*f*, 167
and face perception, 163–164, 164*f*
in infancy and toddlerhood, 158–166, 170
in intermodal perception, 166–168
milestones of development, 167
and object perception, 164–166, 165*f*, 167
and pattern perception, 161*f*, 161–163, 163*f*, 167
sensory deprivation affecting, 170

Visual acuity
of infants, 159, 159*f*
milestones of development, 167

Visual cliff studies, 159*f*, 159–160
facial expressions in, 405

Visual impairment
emotional development in, 162, 405
severe, development of infants with, 162

Visual language discrimination, 368

Vocabulary
in bilingualism, 359
and categorization skills, 235
cultural influences on, 340–341

first words in, 373–374
growth of, 376–377, 377*f*, 380, 380*f*
home environment affecting, 345
learning strategies for, 382–383
semantic development of, 360, 376–383. *See also* Semantic development

Vocational education, 644–645, 649–650
apprenticeship programs in, 649
work–study programs in, 649

Voice changes in puberty, 203

Volunteer work
and civic responsibility, 508
in Teen Outreach program, 220

Vygotsky, Lev, 612
sociocultural theory of, 24–26, 226, 266–272, 640

W

Walking
and motor development in infancy, 147, 149
and stepping reflex, 130*t*, 131

War, and impact of violence on children, 524

Water birth, 111

Watson, John, behaviorism theory of, 17

Wechsler Intelligence Scale for Children, 328

Weight
in anorexia nervosa, 210–211
average rate of gain in, 176
at birth, low, 113–117. *See also* Low birth weight
in body mass index, 198
and body size changes, 176
in bulimia nervosa, 211
and menarche, 204
in obesity, 198–200. *See also* Obesity
in pregnancy, 103
secular trends in, 184
worldwide variations in, 183

Welfare programs, 35, 36

Well-being
emotional. *See* Emotional well-being
identity status and, 471–472
international comparison of indicators on, 33, 34*f*, 34*t*
and physical growth, 202

Wernicke's area of brain, 362*f*, 363, 367

White Americans. *See* Caucasian Americans

Whole-language approach to reading, 309–310

Whooping cough, 202

WIC (Special Supplemental Food Program for Women, Infants, and Children), 35

Williams syndrome, language development in, 366

Withdrawal of privileges as punishment technique, 493–494
Women, Infants, and Children (WIC) supplemental food program, 35, 105
Work. *See* Employment
Working memory, 279
  and attention, 288, 289
  and automatic recall, 297
  capacity of, 279, 280, 315*t*, 323
  fuzzy-trace theory of, 296
  inhibition affecting, 288
  in neo-Piagetian theory, 283
  in planning, 290
  store model of, 278–279, 279*f*
  tasks in assessment of, 279
Work–study programs, 649
World Health Organization, 194
World Trade Center attacks, 524

Writing
  and emergent literacy, 307, 308, 308*f*
  sex differences in, 554–555, 555*f*

X
X chromosome, 76
  abnormalities of, 83, 83*t*
  diseases linked to, 78*t*, 80*f*, 80–81, 86
  in fragile X syndrome, 80–81
XO (Turner) syndrome, 83, 83*t*
X-rays
  during pregnancy, 101
  skeletal age estimates by, 178
XX chromosomes, 76
XXX syndrome, 83, 83*t*
XXY (Klinefelter) syndrome, 83, 83*t*
XY chromosomes, 73, 74*f*, 76
XYY syndrome, 83, 83*t*

Y
Y chromosome, 76, 80
  abnormalities of, 83, 83*t*
Yucatec Mayans, observational learning of, 273
Yurok Indians, breastfeeding among, 16

Z
Zambia, child-rearing practices and newborn behavior in, 139
Zero tolerance policies, 525
Zinacanteco Indians
  concrete operational stage of, 252
  make-believe play of, 270
  motor development of infants, 150
  social interaction and learning of, 25

Zinc supplements, 201
  in pregnancy, 104
Zone of proximal development, 267–268
  and dynamic assessment of intelligence, 342
  in make-believe play, 269
  in reciprocal teaching, 271
  sociocultural theory on, 267–268, 269
Zygote, 88*f*, 89–91, 90
  in fraternal or dizygotic twins, 76
  in identical or monozygotic twins, 76
  and meiosis, 75, 75*f*
  in reproductive technologies, 86
  teratogen exposure affecting, 95*f*, 96